TLA FILM
VIDEO & DVD
GUIDE

THE DISCERNING
FILM LOVER'S GUIDE
2002-03

DAVID BLEILER
EDITOR

ST. MARTIN'S GRIFFIN
New York

Designed by TLA Publications®
1520 Locust Street
Suite 200
Philadelphia, PA. 19102

TLA Publications® is a registered trademark of TLA Entertainment Group, Inc.

ISBN 0–312–28209–5

First St. Martin's Griffin Edition: October 2001

10 9 8 7 6 5 4 3 2 1

TLA FILM, VIDEO & DVD GUIDE
THE DISCERNING FILM LOVER'S GUIDE
2002-03

Edited by David Bleiler

MANAGING EDITOR/DESIGNER
Eric Moore

ASSOCIATE EDITORS
David Gorgos
Ann M. Yarabinee

CONTRIBUTING EDITOR
S. Damien Segal

CONTRIBUTING ARTISTS
Robert Dieters

CONTRIBUTING WRITERS
Scott Cranin
Scott Daly
Sam Durso
Dean C. Galanis
Gary Kramer
Raymond Murray
Scott Shrake
Irv Slifkin
Keith J. Sowders
Geo. Stewart
Matthew C. Webster

CONTENTS

INTRODUCTION

There's a wonderful new trend happening in Hollywood; hopefully moviegoers and videophiles from across the country will benefit from the fallout. It's the acknowledgment and surge in popularity of independent and foreign films on the mainstream landscape. Independent gems such as *Being John Malkovich, Traffic* and *Requiem for a Dream* are being recognized by traditional institutions like the Academy Awards while finding success at the box office. The same is happening to foreign films, such as *Crouching Tiger, Hidden Dragon* and *Life Is Beautiful*, both of which set box-office records.

In the dawn of the new millennium, there await exciting, new formats in the entertainment field that will bring a greater variety of choices to the public. Theaters, TV, VHS, DVD all compete for our attention in an ever crowded and sometimes confusing market. That is why it is my hope that the *TLA Film, Video & DVD Guide* can offer a clear voice in helping to sift through the myriad of films, and help guide the viewer to the eclectic tableau of not only mainstream films, but the wide assortment of independent and foreign titles that are now enjoying such recognition.

It is our goal to offer the reader insightful, intelligent and opinionated reviews that can assist in either choosing or avoiding films to watch at home. Since we don't attempt to review every film ever released, we are able to be more comprehensive in critical analysis, thus enabling us to pay attention to the rewarding and possibly unknown films that may have bypassed your local 24-plex.

Presented in an easy-to-read A-Z listing, the *TLA Film, Video & DVD Guide* includes over 9,500 reviews, hundreds of photos, and exhaustive index and cross-reference system. Be aware that we only include in director and star bibliographies titles that are available on VHS or DVD. We should also note that our listing is quite selective. It's not our goal to include everyone, but those who we feel have made a great impact on film past, present, and – if we are intuitive at all – future.

The history of TLA is important in understanding our commitment to film. TLA Video was established in 1985 as a subsidiary of the Theater of the Living Arts, one of the country's leading repertory cinemas. With the advent of video and the unfortunate demise of rep (which hopefully will make a welcome comeback), we concentrated our energies on home video with the same vigor as we did our theater. TLA Video is now one of the most recognized and respected video businesses in the country.

This enthusiasm also went into the production of this film guide. It is my hope that our love, regard and knowledge of film can be found on every page, and that the *TLA Film, Video & DVD Guide* will help in removing some of the promotional hype and its ensuing guesswork out of your viewing decisions – without eliminating the exhilaration of the moviegoing experience.

—David Bleiler

ABOUT THE EDITOR:

David Bleiler has been involved in the film and video industry since the 1970s. He has worked in theatrical exhibition as manager and programmer for the Philadelphia art cinema Roxy Screening Rooms; in publishing as Senior Editor of *Home Viewer Magazine* and *Video Extra*, Managing Editor of the *New York Metro Herald*, Editor of "Images in the Dark," and has worked as a freelance film reviewer; and on radio (as a guest host on numerous film shows). He is currently the video columnist for the *Philadelphia Daily News*.

Explanation of Text

Alphabetization:

The guide is alphabetized in word order, not letter order, therefore *All That Jazz* would come before *Alligator*. Also, foreign titles adhere to the English rule concerning A, An and The beginning a sentence: whereas *The Godfather* would be listed under G; *La Cage aux Folles* would be listed under C, *Das Boot* under B, etc.

Foreign articles include:

French: *La, Le, Les, Un, Une*
German: *Das, Die*
Italian: *I, Il, La, Le*
Spanish: *El, La*

(American films beginning with *El* are listed under E)

With the exception of *Mrs.*, abbreviations are alphabetized under the word's full spelling:

Mr. Smith Goes to Washington is under *Mister*;
Dr. Strangelove is under *Doctor*;
The St. Valentine's Day Massacre is under *Saint*.

Pricing:

Prices listed are as of publication date. Many full price videos (in the $79.99-$99.99 range) are reduced six to nine months after their initial video release, so please call for updated information.

Certain titles are listed even though they were not available or announced as of publication date. In these instances, they were assumed to be full price.

In a case when a title has no price, that video was unavailable for sale at publication date; but it's possible it could be reissued later. Please call for updated information.

Index Listings:

There are several instances in which a film can be found in the indexes but lacks a corresponding review. This is to make the indexes more complete and therefore more useful. However, only films on video have been mentioned.

Ordering:

To order any title listed in the *TLA Film, Video & DVD Guide*, use the handy order form located in the back of the book, or call the TLA Video 800 number listed on the form. TLA offers special rates to institutions and individuals placing large orders.

Anatomy of a Review

Title

(Year, Running Time, Country, Director)

Cast

Some Like It Hot

(1959, 122 min, US, Billy Wilder) *Jack Lemmon, Tony Curtis, Marilyn Monroe, Joe E. Brown, George Raft, Pat O'Brien.* Director Wilder's masterpiece rates as one of the funniest American comedies of all time, and it only gets better with age. Lemmon and Curtis, at their comic best, star as down-and-out musicians in 1920s Chicago who, upon witnessing the St. Valentine's Day Massacre, don wig and dress and join an all-female band to escape the murderous thugs looking for them. Marilyn is Sugar Kane, the band's beautiful blonde singer who the boys are enraptured by. Curtis romances MM (out of drag, of course) and Lemmon is courted by millionaire Brown ("Well, nobody's perfect"). They just don't come any better than this. ★★★★ VHS: $9.99; DVD: $14.99

Rating

Pricing Info
(If no price is listed, the film is currently not available for sale)

À la Mode

(1994, 90 min, France, Rémy Duchemin) *Jean Yanne, Ken Higelin, François Hautesserre.* Can you say "French fluff"? In some regards, this is too soft a term for this mildly enjoyable but ultimately wispy comedy. In keeping with the genre of "Sex and the French Teenager," *À la Mode* follows the ever eventful life of young Fausto — from the bicycle accident that leaves him orphaned to his apprenticeship with a Jewish tailor in Paris. The standard stuff is on display here: the coy redhead with whom he gets his first lay, the good-hearted best friend with a talent for farting the tunes of Beethoven...beginning to get the picture? Still, the film is amiable, gooey fun and for those in search of hollow entertainment, this will be just the ticket. (aka: *Fausto*) (French with English subtitles) ★★½ VHS: $19.99

À Nos Amours (To Our Loves)

(1983, 102 min, France, Maurice Pialat) *Sandrine Bonnaire, Evelyne Ker, Dominique Besnehard, Maurice Pialat.* A beautifully rendered portrait of a sexually explosive young girl and her tumultuous home life. Sixteen-year-old Suzanne faces the wrath of a neurotic mother, a withdrawn father and an abusive brother because of her casually nubile air and promiscuous wanderings. In this fascinating study of a smoldering family climate, Bonnaire charges the role of the troubled teenager with a powerfully erotic presence. (French with English subtitles) ★★★½

À Nous la Liberté

(1931, 97 min, France, René Clair) *Henri Marchand, Raymond Corby, Rolla France.* A surreal and satirical attack on automation and industrialization, this intoxicating, brilliantly executed romp follows the exploits of a bum who becomes a millionaire only to realize that he was happier poor. The central character and many comic scenes provided the inspiration for Charlie Chaplin's *Modern Times*. (French with English subtitles) ★★★★ VHS: $19.99

Aardman Animations

(1992, 60 min, US) An anthology of short films that is a must-see for anyone interested in clay animation. In addition to the several brilliant works featured in this collection, there is also a documentary about the Aardmans' unique style of animation. Their process of "lip-synching" original situations to pre-existing soundtracks results in astonishingly rich films that are both funny and haunting. Includes Nick Parks' Academy Award-winning *Creature Comforts*. ★★★ VHS: $29.99

Aaron Loves Angela

(1975, 98 min, US, Gordon Parks, Jr.) *Kevin Hooks, Irene Cara, Ernestine Jackson, Moses Gunn, Robert Hooks.* In this pleasing, updated "Romeo and Juliet" set in Harlem, Aaron, a black youth, falls in love with a beautiful Puerto Rican girl, Angela. Surprisingly involving and thankfully devoid of clichés. Music by José Feliciano. ★★★ VHS: $14.99

Abandon Ship!

(1957, 97 min, GB, Richard Sale) *Tyrone Power, Mai Zetterling, Lloyd Nolan, Stephen Boyd.* When a luxury ocean liner hits a derelict mine in the waters of the Atlantic, the surviving passengers must cram into the only lifeboat, now commanded by second mate Power. As they fight the elements and each other, it soon becomes a struggle for survival. A sometimes rousing, tension-filled drama. (aka: *Seven Waves Away*) ★★★ VHS: $19.99

Abbott and Costello Meet Dr. Jekyll and Mr. Hyde

(1953, 77 min, US, Charles Lamont) *Bud Abbott, Lou Costello, Boris Karloff, Reginald Denny.* After much success meeting Frankenstein and Captain Kidd, Abbott and Costello set their sights on Robert Louis Stevenson's famous doc and his alter ego. In Victorian London, Bud and Lou are policemen on the trail of Jekyll, or is it Hyde? Some good laughs though the film is not as consistently funny as their earlier efforts. ★★½ VHS: $14.99

Abbott and Costello Meet Frankenstein

(1949, 83 min, US, Charles Barton) *Bud Abbott, Lou Costello, Bela Lugosi, Lon Chaney, Jr., Glenn Strange, Jane Randolph.* Bud and Lou found great success in this very funny horror spoof. The boys get involved with Frankenstein (Strange), Dracula (Lugosi) and the Wolf Man (Chaney) — even the Invisible Man makes an "appearance." There are plenty of snappy one-liners and silly shenanigans, and Bud and Lou's enjoyment is clearly infectious. ★★★½ VHS: $14.99; DVD: $29.99

Abe Lincoln in Illinois

(1940, 110 min, US, John Cromwell) *Raymond Massey, Gene Lockhart, Ruth Gordon, Mary Howard.* Featuring a career performance by Massey as our 16th president, this outstanding biography of Abraham Lincoln, based on Robert Sherwood's Pulitzer Prize—winning play, is American history on film at its finest. The story covers Lincoln's life from his young adult years (including his romances with Ann Rutledge and Mary Todd) to his election as president. The Lincoln-Douglas debate scene is a particular highlight. ★★★★ VHS: $19.99

Abigail's Party

(1977, 105 min, GB, Mike Leigh) *Alison Steadman.* Steadman stars as an overwrought hostess of a small get-together with the neighbors. Clearly adapted from the stage, the action is filmed on video and never leaves the claustrophobic confines of her living room. As she and her guests top off with gin and tonic after gin and tonic, the sparks begin to fly and her highly strung husband becomes all the more agitated. While the piece is filled with several hilarious moments, the overall tenor becomes more and more nerve-racking due to Steadman's almost fascistic insistence that her guests "drink up." ★★½ VHS: $29.99

The Abominable Dr. Phibes

(1971, 94 min, GB, Robert Fuest) *Vincent Price, Joseph Cotten, Terry-Thomas, Peter Jeffrey, Hugh Griffith.* Price camps it up in one of the few horror films which successfully marries laughs and shivers. Cotten and Terry-Thomas are just two of the victims on whom Price seeks vengeance for his disfigurement and his wife's death. The Art Deco sets give the film a stylish look. (Sequel: *Dr. Phibes Rises Again*) ★★★ VHS: $12.99; DVD: $14.99

About Last Night. . .

(1986, 113 min, US, Edward Zwick) *Rob Lowe, Demi Moore, James Belushi, Elizabeth Perkins, George DiCenzo.* David Mamet's play "Sexual Perversity in Chicago" comes to the screen in the form of this sluggish adaptation which fails to fully capture the play's hard edge. Lowe and Moore play Chicago singles who begin an affair, but their relationship suffers from Lowe's lack of commitment. Ditto the film. Belushi and Perkins costar in far more interesting roles as the leads' respective best friends. ★★ VHS: $14.99; DVD: $29.99

Above Suspicion

(1943, 90 min, US, Richard Thorpe) *Joan Crawford, Fred MacMurray, Conrad Veidt, Basil Rathbone.* Crawford takes on the Nazis in this standard but nevertheless compelling spy thriller set in 1939. Joan and Fred are newlyweds on a European honeymoon who are asked to do their part for British intelligence. Up against Crawford, who had the benefit of those shoulders, the Germans never had a chance. ★★★ VHS: $19.99

À Nous la Liberté

Above the Law

(1988, 99 min, US, Andrew Davis) *Steven Seagal, Pam Grier, Sharon Stone, Henry Silva.* The fact that martial arts macho guy Seagal was allowed to make more movies after this, his debut, must be proof of his being above the laws of common sense. Seagal's performance is robotic and difficult to watch and the story that he gets partial credit for is conventional, convoluted and, at times, preachy. On top of all that, the fight scenes here are surprisingly tame. Director Davis had previously made the half-decent Chuck Norris film *Code of Silence* and would go on to make *The Package* and *The Fugitive*, but here his talents seem to be in hibernation; there are few action sequences of note. ★★ VHS: $9.99; DVD: $19.99

Absence of Malice

(1981, 116 min, US, Sydney Pollack) *Paul Newman, Sally Field, Wilford Brimley, Melinda Dillon, Bob Balaban, Josef Sommer.* Newman and Field's first-rate performances distinguish this absorbing social drama about Newman's efforts to clear his name after reporter Field is duped into printing an article falsely implicating him in the murder of a union leader. Dillon gives a touching performance as Newman's girlfriend also affected by the story. Screenwriter Kurt Luedtke (a former reporter) has fashioned an insightful and penetrating treatise on the responsibility of the press and of the manipulation of truth and the media. ★★★ VHS: $14.99; DVD: $19.99

Absence of the Good

(1999, 99 min, US, John Flynn) *Stephen Baldwin, Rob Knepper, Shawn Huff, Tyne Daly, Allen Garfield.* In this creepy little thriller, a Salt Lake City detective, Caleb Barnes (Baldwin), returns to work following the death of his six-year-old son. Taking on a brutal case involving a serial killer, Caleb pursues clues that show the murderer was abused as a child. A pyschiatrist (Daly) assigned to the investigation helps Caleb personally and professionally, but the film passes on the chance to explore the duality of child abuse/loss of a child completely. Instead, *Absence of the Good* tries to establish a quasi-religious meaning to the murders, claiming that the killer is "pure evil." Director Flynn has made a wholly servicable B movie, with a nice twist among the predictable genre elements, but much of this low-budget film seems cheesy. Daly and Garfield (as Caleb's commander) chew the scenery nicely. ★★ VHS: $21.99

The Absent-Minded Professor

(1961, 97 min, US, Robert Stevenson) *Fred MacMurray, Nancy Olson, Keenan Wynn, Tommy Kirk, Ed Wynn, Leon Ames.* The quintessential '60s Disney comedy! MacMurray plays the title character, who invents a bouncy substance called flubber which can make cars fly and basketball players do amazing things. Problem is, no one will believe him, and the town's evil tycoon is out to steal the invention. A fun story with lively special effects and a breezy, gee-whiz attitude. (Sequel: *Son of Flubber*) (Remade in 1997 as *Flubber*) ★★★ VHS: $19.99

Absolute Beginners

(1986, 107 min, GB, Julien Temple) *Eddie O'Connell, Patsy Kensit, David Bowie, James Fox, Ray Davies, Ege Ferret, Anita Morris, Sade, Slim Gaillard.* Temple's rousing musical is a journey into the heart of the swinging teenage scene of London in the late 1950s and the brutal racism which still afflicts that city today. O'Connell stars as a young photographer drawn into the music and fashion worlds; Kensit is the designer he's in love with. Bowie makes a neat cameo as a slick associate of the nefarious Fox, and he sings the title tune, too. The music, as orchestrated by jazz giant Gil Evans, is unbeatable and includes a truly seductive number by Sade. ★★★½ VHS: $14.99

Absolute Power

(1997, 120 min, US, Clint Eastwood) *Clint Eastwood, Gene Hackman, Ed Harris, Laura Linney, Judy Davis, Scott Glenn, Dennis Haysbert, E.G. Marshall.* There's more to worry about than campaign finances in President Alan Richmond's White House; the Secret Service has just murdered his girlfriend, and hampering a cover-up is the witness who was hiding in the next room. In this sleek, competent thriller, efficiently adapted by William Goldman (based on David Baldacci's novel), Eastwood plays Luther Whitney, a thief who is now on the run after witnessing the handywork of President Richmond (played with great vigor and venom by Hackman) and his staff. All of Washington, D.C., becomes a board game of cat and mouse as Whitney tries to elude government agents and the police. That this works at all is testament to director Eastwood — the story isn't always plausible, but it's always in focus. *Absolute Power* is a wild ride up and down the Beltway all the same. (Letterboxed VHS available for $19.99) ★★★ VHS: $14.99; DVD: $19.99

Absolution

(1978, 105 min, GB, Anthony Page) *Richard Burton, Dominic Guard, Dai Bradley, Billy Connelly.* Another wicked thriller from Anthony Shaffer, the author of *Sleuth*. Burton stars as a "holier-than-thou" priest whose teaching efforts at a Catholic boarding school are mocked by his mischievous star pupil, with tragic results. Though made in 1978, the film was not released in this country until 1988, four years after Burton's death. ★★★

Abuse

(1983, 85 min, US, Arthur Bressan, Jr.) *Richard Ryder, Raphael Sbarge.* This daring, powerful yet sensitive account of a battered adolescent's coming to grips with his abusive parents and his awakening homosexuality caused quite a stir in the gay community with its positive approach to man/boy love. While filming a documentary on child abuse for his master's thesis, 35-year-old Larry (Ryder) meets 14-year-old Thomas (Sbarge), the victim of abuse from his violent mother and father. The two become close, with Thomas beginning a healing process with the help of the older filmmaker. Their nurturing relationship, spurred by the advances of Thomas, eventually turns to love. Faced with certain breakup and, for Thomas, more beatings, they flee together to San Francisco. A controversial film which isn't quite as incendiary as it may appear. ★★★ VHS: $39.99

The Abyss

(1989, 145 min, US, James Cameron) *Ed Harris, Mary Elizabeth Mastrantonio, Michael Biehn, Leo Burmester, Todd Graff.* Outstanding special effects and production design highlight this suspenseful underwater science-fiction adventure. Though Cameron combines the same excitement and tension he created in *Aliens* and *The Terminator*, he shifts the pace halfway through the film, and the result is a heart-pounding thriller which gradually becomes an under-the-sea *E.T.* Harris stars as the commander of an oil rigging outfit who makes contact with an alien being. Forget the similarly themed *Deep Star Six* and the silly *Leviathan* which came before it, for this is far superior entertainment. (DVD Director's Cut is available for $26.99) ★★★ VHS: $14.99

Accattone

(1961, 120 min, Italy, Pier Paolo Pasolini) *Franco Citti, Franca Pasut, Silvana Corsini.* Pasolini's first feature film is a harrowing, realistic and unsentimental look inside the slums of Rome, where its denizens — the prostitutes, hustlers and petty thieves — attempt to eke out an existence any way they can. Within this underworld of corruption is Accattone (Citti), a young pimp who is torn between the easy pickings on the street and his efforts, motivated by love, to go straight. A brutal slice-of-life film which documents Pasolini's lifelong obsession with the outcasts of society, an obsession which eventually led to his death in 1975 at the hands of a man not unlike Accattone. Pasolini was assisted on the film by a young Bernardo Bertolucci. (Italian with English subtitles) ★★★½ VHS: $29.99

Accident

(1967, 105 min, GB, Joseph Losey) *Dirk Bogarde, Michael York, Jacqueline Sassard, Stanley Baker, Vivien Merchant.* Harold Pinter wrote the screenplay adaptation for this penetrating and thought-provoking examination of a love affair between a professor (Bogarde) and his student (Sassard). Bogarde and York both deliver sterling performances in this complex psychological drama. ★★★½

The Accidental Tourist

(1988, 121 min, US, Lawrence Kasdan) *William Hurt, Kathleen Turner, Geena Davis, Bill Pullman, Amy Wright, David Ogden Stiers.* Hurt stars in this Oscar-nominated adaptation of Anne Tyler's whimsical best-seller as an emotionally numb travel-guide writer who must begin life anew after the death of his young son and separation from his wife (Turner). As he sets out into the world, he becomes involved, almost unwittingly, with an eccentric dog trainer (Davis) who slowly reawakens his long-dormant feelings. The film, like its hero, is leisurely and a bit distant but also enormously endearing, thanks mostly to a refreshingly open and enchanting performance by Oscar-winner Davis. ★★★ VHS: $14.99

The Accompanist

(1992, 111 min, France, Claude Miller) *Romane Bohringer, Elena Safonova, Richard Bohringer.* Sophie, a naïve, unworldly 20-year-old pianist in Nazi-occupied France, is hired as accompanist to a concert vocalist, a beautiful and talented woman who, with her industrialist husband, is viewed as a collaborator. As the young Sophie, Bohringer's subdued, controlled performance is in marked contrast to her frenzied portrayal in *Savage Nights*. Sophie is an accompanist not only in concerts and practice sessions: She views it as her life's role, and not even the devastation and upheaval of war shakes her position of observer and accomplice. The film's denouement is curiously anticlimactic, yet is an unnerving reflection of Sophie's suppressed affect and despondency. In the end, a disturbing char-

Spencer Tracy and Katharine Hepburn star in *Adam's Rib* (1949)

acter study of an isolated individual adrift in a world of turmoil. (French with English subtitles) ★★★ VHS: $19.99

The Accused

(1988, 110 min, US, Jonathan Kaplan) *Jodie Foster, Kelly McGillis, Bernie Coulson, Leo Rossi, Ann Hearn, Steve Antin.* A harrowing and hard-hitting look at the emotional and moral consequences of rape. Foster won an Oscar for her stunning and gritty portrayal of a back-room gang-rape victim who struggles to regain her self-respect while battling an insensitive legal system. McGillis is compelling as the prosecuting attorney who becomes entangled in her own moral sense of right and wrong. Based on an actual and highly publicized incident, this superbly acted and tightly focused film expertly examines the pain endured by the victims of rape long after the crime has been committed. ★★★ VHS: $14.99

Ace Ventura, Pet Detective

(1994, 85 min, US, Tom Shadyac) *Jim Carrey, Courteney Cox, Sean Young, Tone Loc, Dan Marino.* This nauseating comedy became a surprise box-office success, sending Carrey to the unlikely ranks of stardom. The story follows the exploits of Carrey's Ace Ventura, who retrieves lost or stolen pets for their heartbroken owners. Hired by the Miami Dolphins to locate their kidnapped mascot, he finds himself doing battle with Miami's police chief, played by Young, who yawns her way through the film with the excitement of a tranquilized basset hound. (Sequel: *Ace Ventura: When Nature Calls*) ★½ VHS: $9.99; DVD: $19.99

Ace Ventura: When Nature Calls

(1995, 92 min, US, Steve Oedekerk) *Jim Carrey, Simon Callow, Ian McNeice, Bob Gunton, Tommy Davidson.* Carrey returns in this annoying hit comedy sequel as the incompetent pet detective Ace Ventura. This second film starts off with a couple of funny and silly laughs with a way over-the-top Carrey shamelessly mugging and making idiotic faces. After a few good sight gags, the ridiculous and boring plot takes over — about Ace tracking down the sacred bat of an African village — and no matter how much Carrey wiggles his ears, screams or says "All righty," this is a poor excuse for comedy and enough to insult the very memory of those broadly played Jerry Lewis comedies of the 1960s — for which Carrey obviously has an affection. No one expects highbrow from Ace, but Carrey is such a talented comedian we all have a right to expect better. ★½ VHS: $9.99; DVD: $19.99

Aclá

(1992, 86 min, Italy, Aurelio Grimaldi) *Luigi Maria Burruano, Francesco Cusimano, Lucia Sardo, Tony Sperandeo.* The inordinately harsh life of Sicilian peasant miners — and one blond, 11-year-old boy in particular — in 1930s Italy is the subject of this unrelentingly grim drama. Young Aclá, a handsome youth with a streak of independence, comes of age to accompany his father and two older brothers to the underground sulfur mines where they work six days a week for little pay and food. A virtual slave, he must endure horrible conditions made worse by the casual brutality inflicted on him. Only his dreams of the sea and escape enable Aclá to struggle against the surrounding inhumanity. Using poetic (pederastic?) license, the director displays all of the workers in the excessively hot mines laboring only in loincloths. (Italian with English subtitles) ★★½ VHS: $59.99

Across 110th Street

(1972, 102 min, US, Barry Shear) *Anthony Quinn, Yaphet Kotto, Anthony Franciosa, Richard Ward, Paul Benjamin, Ed Bernard, Antonio Fargas, Norma Donaldson.* Three black men hit a Mafia cash drop in Harlem for $300,000, killing family members, associates and two policemen, precipitating an intensive manhunt — one conducted by the police, the other by the mob with their Harlem business partners. Racism is the permeating undercurrent, defining the tensions between the Mafia and their Harlem counterparts, and mirrored in the relationship between white, old-guard captain Quinn and black lieutenant Kotto, who's placed in charge of the investigation. The film is harsh, rough-hewn and uncompromising, filled with raw anger and seething violence, and bolstered by on-target performances from the entire cast. ★★★ VHS: $14.99

Across the Pacific

(1942, 97 min, US, John Huston) *Humphrey Bogart, Mary Astor, Sydney Greenstreet, Sen Yung, Richard Loo.* Director Huston and his *Maltese Falcon* stars Bogart, Astor and Greenstreet reteamed for this involving spy thriller. Bogey goes undercover and sets sail for the Orient to get the goods on agent Greenstreet. Astor is the mysterious passenger romanced by Bogart. Suspenseful action, more humor than would be expected, and solid performances by all make this a winner. ★★★ VHS: $19.99

Acting on Impulse

(1993, 93 min, US, Sam Irvin) *Linda Fiorentino, C. Thomas Howell, Nancy Allen, Dick Sargent, Paul Bartel, Adam Ant, Mary Woronov, Isaac Hayes, Patrick Bauchau, Zelda Rubinstein.* This comic thriller has its tongue planted firmly in cheek. The ravishing Fiorentino plays a "scream queen" goddess of B-horror films. After a fatal argument in which her producer is found dead, Fiorentino sets out for a little R&R, where she is stalked by "adoring" fans. Then the body count starts piling up. Featuring a little lesbian teasing between a playful Fiorentino and Allen, and a steamy Fiorentino-Howell sex scene, the film is leisurely paced, offers a few well-placed jabs at the horror film industry, and has an eclectic supporting line-up. ★★½

Action in the North Atlantic

(1943, 127 min, US, Lloyd Bacon) *Humphrey Bogart, Raymond Massey, Alan Hale, Ruth Gordon, Sam Levene.* Bogart heads a good cast in this stirring WWII actioner with Bogey and Massey as Merchant Marine officers leading their men in action against the Nazis in the North Atlantic. ★★★ VHS: $19.99

Action Jackson

(1988, 95 min, US, Craig R. Baxley) *Carl Weathers, Craig T. Nelson, Vanity, Sharon Stone, Bill Duke.* Weathers stars as the title character in this stiffly acted but ultimately satisfying panoply of car chases, explosions and fistfights. Weathers' Jackson is an ex-cop who is determined to uncover the evil doings of an unscrupulous businessman (Nelson) who had been the instrument of Jackson's fall from grace. Vanity is the token dame who accompanies Weathers on his vengeful rampage. A pyrotechnical juggernaut that is short on script and short on ideas, but so what. It's enjoyable, combustible fun nonetheless. ★★½ VHS: $9.99; DVD: $14.99

An Actor's Revenge

(1963, 113 min, Japan, Kon Ichikawa) *Kazuo Hasegawa, Fujiko Yamamoto, Ayako Wakao.* With magnificently stylized sets, vibrant color and a spectacular performance by Kabuki actor Hasegawa, this tale of revenge and murder ranks as one of Japan's greatest films. Set in the early part of the 19th century, Hasegawa, an *onnagata* (female impersonator) of the Kabuki theatre, discovers the identity of the three nobles who forced the suicide of his parents many years before. In an elaborate scheme of revenge, our hero/heroine exacts a plot that does not have him simply kill them, but rather have the men turn against themselves or die at their own hands. A complex period melodrama that concerns itself with opposites: love/hate, illusion/reality, masculinity/femininity. (Japanese with English subtitles) ★★★★ VHS: $29.99

Adam Had Four Sons

(1941, 81 min, US, Gregory Ratoff) *Ingrid Bergman, Warner Baxter, Susan Hayward, Richard Denning, Fay Wray.* Bergman is in Bette Davis/*All This and Heaven, Too* territory as a governess looking after four children after their mother dies. Baxter is the father, and a young Hayward plays the "bad" girl who pits the family against each other. Warm dramatics and a pleasing performance by Bergman more than compensate for the sometimes predictable direction of the story line. ★★★ VHS: $19.99

Adam's Rib

(1949, 101 min, US, George Cukor) *Katharine Hepburn, Spencer Tracy, Judy Holliday, David Wayne, Tom Ewell, Jean Hagen.* In their sixth film together, Hepburn and Tracy demonstrate such a magnificent rapport on-screen that they nearly make their prior film appearances together look like blind dates by comparison. Kate and Spence play lawyers on opposite sides of an attempted murder case. He's the prosecutor, she's the defense attorney. In her first major role, Holliday is the defendant accused of trying to kill her philandering husband (Ewell). Garson Kanin and Ruth Gordon's wonderfully funny screenplay is full of sublime observations on romantic expectations and the roles men and women play (or are expected to play), and director Cukor deftly brings together slapstick, sophistication and romance to create a classic battle-of-the-sexes comedy. ★★★★ VHS: $14.99; DVD: $19.99

Adam's Rib

(1992, 77 min, USSR, Vyacheslav Krishtofovich) *Inna Churikova, Yelena Bogdanova, Svetlana Ryabova.* Based on the novel "House of Young Women" by Anatole Kourtchatkine, *Adam's Rib* is a wonderfully endearing story revolving around three generations of Russian women (a grandmother, mother, and her two daughters) all sharing the same apartment. The film slips in elements of coming-of-age and parental disputes with social commentary on the new elements of capitalism in Russia. Lida, the older daughter, is having an affair with a married man while the younger daughter is a rebel and a savvy businessperson. Mother is trying to make ends meet, take care of her ailing mother and she just happens to be picked up by a farmer at her job. A poignant and quite remarkable film. (Russian with English subtitles) ★★★★

The Addams Family

(1991, 102 min, US, Barry Sonnenfeld) *Raul Julia, Anjelica Huston, Christopher Lloyd, Christina Ricci, Dan Hedaya, Elizabeth Wilson, Dana Ivey.* Sonnenfeld's hilarious revival of the cult-TV series may be thin on plot but the action flies furiously and the laughs are abundant. Julia and Huston deliver inspired, passionately macabre performances as Gomez and Morticia, the bizzare patriarch and matriarch of Charles Addams' ghoulish family (thankfully, they do justice to the characters created by John Astin and Carolyn Jones). Lloyd feasts on the role of Uncle Fester and young Ricci is devilishly coy as the younger Addams, Wednesday, with a penchant for girl scout cookies made from *real* Girl Scouts. Followed by an equally enjoyable sequel, *Addams Family Values.* ★★★ VHS: $9.99; DVD: $24.99

Addams Family Values

(1993, 87 min, US, Barry Sonnenfeld) *Raul Julia, Anjelica Huston, Christopher Lloyd, Joan Cusack, Christina Ricci, Carol Kane, David Krumholtz.* Dripping with deliciously mordant one-liners, this outlandish sequel to *The Addams Family* is a possibly funnier outing than the original. Morticia (the unearthly and serene Huston) has a baby, Pubert, much to the delight of Gomez (Julia) and most of the family. The children, Pugsly and Wednesday, however, see the little nipper as nothing more than an usurper and respond to his arrival with murderous zeal. The kids are soon dragged off to summer camp by the baby's new nanny (Cusack), a gold-digging black widow with designs on Fester (Lloyd). This broad plot outline is ripe with hilariously morbid jokes and is a sly fable on the revenge of the outcasts. ★★★ VHS: $9.99; DVD: $24.99

Addicted to Love

(1997, 100 min, US, Griffin Dunne) *Meg Ryan, Matthew Broderick, Kelly Preston, Tcheky Karyo, Maureen Stapleton.* If love is a game for fools, then in Dunne's sometimes very funny but unrealized black comedy on obsessive love, it's not how you play the game, but whether you win or lose. When his fiancée Linda leaves him for handsome Frenchman Anton, astronomer Sam (Broderick) begins spying on her. He's soon joined by Maggie (Ryan), Anton's former girlfriend, in his *Rear Window* vigil from the abandoned building across the street. Maggie and Sam then engage in a series of revenge schemes and often hilarious bits of malicious "ex"-bashings. Though nasty as it wants to be, *Addicted to Love*'s shortcoming is that it aims for the jugular but often settles for the aorta; the mean-spiritedness just isn't consistent. When *Love* loses its edge, it becomes just another dopey, insufficient romantic comedy. ★★½ VHS: $19.99; DVD: $19.99

The Addiction

(1995, 84 min, US, Abel Ferrara) *Lili Taylor, Christopher Walken, Annabella Sciorra, Kathryn Erbe, Paul Calderon.* Needlessly dense and shot so amateurishly as to sometimes look like a student film, *The Addiction* is Ferrara's take on the vampire mythos, equating vampirism with a physical drug addiction and setting it among the angst-ridden, *tres existentielle* intellectual elite of New York's graduate student culture. Taylor plays a philosophy doctoral student who is bitten by a vampire (Sciorra). She spends the rest of the film trying to come to terms with her new existence as a nocturnal predator. Light on narrative, the film's characters spend most of their time in philosophical discussions, which works completely against the purposes of the film. While the premise of the film is intriguing and a few sequences shine through as something unique to the genre, *The Addiction* is ultimately a horror film without any scares, a philosophical meditation without any good ideas, and a vampire film without any blood. ★½ VHS: $9.99

The Adjuster

(1992, 102 min, Canada, Atom Egoyan) *Elias Koteas, Maury Chaykin, Arsinee Khanjian.* Original

and bizarre, director Egoyan's twisted tale follows Noah (Koteas), a predatory insurance adjuster who shows up at house fires to comfort the victims and process their claims. He keeps all of his clients in a run-down motel, where he visits them daily, often engaging them in sex (male and female alike). Meanwhile, his wife (Khanjian) is secretly videotaping the graphic sex she watches as part of her job as a government censor. Into the picture comes Bubba (Chaykin), an off-the-wall con artist who convinces the Renders that he wants to use their house (a lonely model unit in an as-of-yet unbuilt development) to make a film. Egoyan uses this odd conglomeration of circumstances to plumb the depths of his characters' existential loneliness and to voyeuristically expose their sexual proclivities. ★★★½ DVD: $19.99

Adoption

(1975, 89 min, Hungary, Márta Mészáros) *Kati Berek, László Szabó, Gyon Gyver Vigh.* Kari wants a child, but her married lover is insensitive to her desire. So it is up to Anna, her newfound friend, to help her fulfill her dream of motherhood and learn about love and survival. A warm and intimate drama exploring a love and friendship between two women. (Hungarian with English subtitles) ★★★ VHS: $69.99

Adrenalin, Fear the Rush

(1996, 76 min, GB/US, Albert Pyun) *Christopher Lambert, Natasha Henstridge.* After the disastrous *Cyborg*, director Pyun is back with this loud, meandering and pointless futuristic sci-fi thriller. In the 21st century, plague carriers have been quarantined. The government has created among the secluded carriers a super killing machine. Lambert and Henstridge are the cops who set out to track him down. The film begins swiftly, but immediately lands itself in a prison basement where all become trapped. It then becomes one long boring chase where the superhuman appears and disappears without explanation. Pyun gives the film a good futuristic look, but knows nothing about maintaining suspense or logic. ★ VHS: $14.99

Arsinee Khanjian bootlegs the graphic sex she's paid to censor in *The Adjuster*

Adventures in Babysitting

(1987, 99 min, US, Chris Columbus) *Elisabeth Shue, Keith Coogan, Anthony Rapp, Vincent D'Onofrio, Penelope Ann Miller, Lolita Davidovitch.* There's charm to spare in this entertaining teen comedy with Shue (long before her *Leaving Las Vegas* triumph) a delight as a babysitter whose journey into Chicago with her three charges turns into a comic nightmare. ★★★ DVD: $29.99

The Adventures of Baron Munchausen

(1989, 126 min, GB, Terry Gilliam) *John Neville, Eric Idle, Sarah Polley, Oliver Reed, Jonathan Pryce, Valentina Cortese, Uma Thurman.* The third and final entry in director Gilliam's fantasy trilogy (*Time Bandits* and *Brazil* were before it) is a whimsical, outlandishly funny and visually stunning adventure film chronicling the amazing exploits of the infamous adventurer/explorer/soldier and man-about-town, Baron Munchausen. Set during the late 18th century, the film follows the odyssey taken by a now-older Baron who travels to the Moon, Heaven and numerous exotic locations in-between, to help save a small city under siege. ★★★ VHS: $14.99; DVD: $29.99

The Adventures of Buckaroo Banzai

(1984, 103 min, US, W.D. Richter) *Peter Weller, John Lithgow, Ellen Barkin, Jeff Goldblum, Christopher Lloyd.* Renowned neurosurgeon, respected physicist and charismatic rock star...he's Buckaroo Banzai — savior of the universe and star of this gonzo sci-fi fantasy. Don't even bother to follow the pretzel-like plot twists; just remember: red lectoids dislike black lectoids, Rastafarians in silver lamé sports coats are on our side, Lord John Whorfin (alias Emilio Lizardo) is a dastardly sort and no matter where you go...there you are. ★★★ VHS: $9.99

Adventures of Don Juan

(1948, 110 min, US, Vincent Sherman) *Errol Flynn, Viveca Lindfors, Alan Hale, Una O'Connor, Raymond Burr.* Flynn is in swashbuckling good form in this opulent costumer. He stars as the legendary Spanish lover who battles the evil Duke de Lorca and protects the royal crown. Much of the mood is tongue-in-cheek, and Flynn, though a decade past his great '30s epics, still cuts a fine figure. Max Steiner's score and the outstanding sets and costumes help immeasurably. ★★★ VHS: $19.99

The Adventures of Eliza Fraser

(1976, 114 min, Australia, Tim Burstall) *Susannah York.* In the mood for an Australian burlesque period romp starring British actress Susannah York? If that doesn't scare you off, read on... Reminiscent of the American West, 1830s Australia was a lawless and untamed land and definitely not a place for a beautiful, cultured woman. Eliza Fraser not only survived but flourished despite the chains of a jealous husband, being pursued and lusted after by penal colony escapees, being involved in a shipwreck, captured by aboriginal savages and even hounded by the police. This is her *Indiana Jones*-like tale of courage and rollicking adventures. ★★½

The Adventures of Ford Fairlane

(1990, 96 min, US, Renny Harlin) *Andrew Dice Clay, Wayne Newton, Priscilla Presley, Lauren Holly,* *Gilbert Gottfried, Ed O'Neill, Robert Englund.* Forget the controversy surrounding comic Clay and his treatment of women and minorities; his starring debut is just a bad film. Clay's arrogant, chauvinistic persona, here in the form of a detective, is the center of an unfunny comedy which is poorly scripted and directed, and whose rambling plot will keep one and all scratching their head in disbelief and confusion. ★ VHS: $9.99

The Adventures of Huck Finn

(1993, 106 min, US, Stephen Sommers) *Elijah Wood, Courtney B. Vance, Jason Robards, Robbie Coltrane, Ron Perlman, Dana Ivey, Anne Heche.* Disney's version of the Mark Twain classic is a highly entertaining adaptation which should more than entrance children of most ages, effortlessly transporting them to another time and place. Sparked by two engaging performances from young Wood and Vance as Huck and Jim, respectively, the film is actually better than most screen versions — though the best is probably still the 1939 film with Mickey Rooney. Robards and Coltrane, both enjoying themselves overplaying their parts as greedy con men, add to the film's level of high-spiritedness and rustic charm, as does a good evocation of 19th-century America. ★★★

The Adventures of Huckleberry Finn

(1939, 90 min, US, Richard Thorpe) *Mickey Rooney, Walter Connelly, Rex Ingram, William Frawley.* Faithful film version of Mark Twain's family classic about the misadventures of Mississippi youths Huck Finn and Tom Sawyer, and of Huck's relationship with Jim, a runaway slave. Of all the many screen versions, this may well be the best. (aka: *Huckleberry Finn*) ★★★ VHS: $19.99

The Adventures of Mark Twain

(1986, 90 min, US, Will Vinton) Outstanding claymation highlights this average children's film about Twain characters Huck Finn, Tom Sawyer and Becky Thatcher accompanying their literary creator on a balloon ride to Halley's Comet. ★★½ VHS: $14.99

The Adventures of Milo and Otis

(1986, 76 min, Japan, Masanori Hata) *Narrated by: Dudley Moore.* Sort of like "Wild Kingdom" for the pet set, this lushly photographed nature story about the friendship and adventures of a kitten and dog has shown remarkable appeal with children. It's harmless, corny and just the change of pace from old "Lassie" reruns. ★★ VHS: $14.99; DVD: $24.99

The Adventures of Pinocchio

(1996, 94 min, US, Steve Barron) *Martin Landau, Jonathan Taylor Thomas, Genevieve Bujold, Rob Schneider, Udo Kier, Bebe Neuwirth.* Although this story has been filmed several times, most notably Disney's 1940 classic, this live-action twist offers a good cast and strong production values, particularly with the special effects that animate the wooden Pinocchio. Thomas' voice adds warmth and character to the puppet who would be boy, and Landau's Giuseppe is convincingly enraptured and befuddled by his little creation. ★★★ VHS: $9.99; DVD: $14.99

The Adventures of Priscilla, Queen of the Desert

The Adventures of Priscilla, Queen of the Desert

(1994, 102 min, Australia, Stephan Elliott) *Terence Stamp, Hugo Weaving, Guy Pearce, Bill Hunter, Sarah Chadwick.* 1960s international sex symbol Stamp is a transgendered marvel as the mature, demure but tough transsexual Bernadette who teams up with two transvestites on a cross-country trip through Australia's Outback in this rousingly fun cross-dressing musical comedy. Muscular Felicia (Pearce), sad-sack Mitzi (Weaving) and the wisecracking Bernadette leave the safe confines of Sydney in a ramshackle tour bus (named Priscilla) to travel nearly a thousand miles away to play a four-week casino engagement. Along the way, the fabulously attired threesome encounter more than their fair share of problems but through it all keep their spirits high, their feathers and sequins unruffled and their gravity-defying wigs straight (so to speak). There are moments of seriousness when homophobia, potentially violent culture clashes and regret of roads not taken confront them, but they readily conquer all in this buoyant and infectiously good-natured tale. ★★★½ VHS: $14.99; DVD: $24.99

The Adventures of Robin Hood

(1938, 106 min, US, Michael Curtiz) *Errol Flynn, Olivia de Havilland, Claude Rains, Basil Rathbone, Alan Hale, Patric Knowles, Eugene Pallette.* The quintessential swashbuckler with Flynn as a devilishly dashing Robin Hood, de Havilland as Maid Marion, Rains as a particularly villainous Prince John, and the great Rathbone, master swordsman and scene stealer, as Sir Guy. The film sports great action scenes, tongue-in-cheek humor, the very best in swordplay and glorious Technicolor cinematography. ★★★★ VHS: $14.99

The Adventures of Rocky & Bullwinkle

(2000, 88 min, US, Des McAnuff) *Robert De Niro, Jason Alexander, Rene Russo, Piper Perabo; Voices of: Keith Scott, June Foray.* A misplacement of priorities by the filmmakers, so common to big-budget adaptations of TV shows, buries this live action/computer animation blend, but the charms of our heroes almost save the day. Whereas the plots of the episodes harkened to old-time cliffhangers, writer Kenneth Lonergan fashions a road movie, thrusting Moose and Squirrel out of syndication and into real life. There they are pursued by interesting but flat caricatures of Boris, Natascha and Fearless Leader (Alexander, Russo, and De Niro). Helping the intrepid duo is an annoying and cloying FBI agent (Perabo), who seems to exist solely to placate fidgety gradeschoolers with her "Sesame Street" attitude. But under this kiddie sheen is the old subversive humor, especially evident in a breathless, traditionally animated opening segment that gets the plot churning. Even the computer-animated duo get some good barbs (and wretchedly bad puns) that sustain interest and smiles throughout the brief running time. It just could have been a whole lot better by aiming a whole lot lower. ★★ VHS: $14.99; DVD: $26.99

The Adventures of Sebastian Cole

(1999, 100 min, US, Tod Williams) *Adrian Grenier, Margaret Colin, Clark Gregg, Gabriel Macht, John Shea.* This offbeat, independently produced comedy-drama set in a small New York town is a charming film undermined by trying to tackle too much. Is it a poignant coming-of-age tale about charismatic 17-year-old Sebastian? Or a probing drama into the loving but strained relationship between him and his stepfather? Or is it a story of the difficulties of a transgendered man-to-woman trying to cope with a rebellious stepson as well as a longing for love and understanding in a backwater town? Despite it going in different directions, most will be entertained by the characters, especially Grenier who brings intensity and charm to the familiar tale of a teen stifled by life in a small town. We watch as Sebastian is forced to deal with his loving stepdad Hank go to from a strapping dude to a willowy Henrietta (a change that sends his mother packing) all the while trying to deal with bad grades, first love and a need to explore life. A refreshing, and at times original spin on the coming-of-age theme. ★★★ VHS: $79.99; DVD: $29.99

The Adventures of Sherlock Holmes

(1939, 85 min, US, Alfred L. Werker) *Basil Rathbone, Nigel Bruce.* One of the definitive Sherlock Holmes pictures, this exciting and atmospheric piece stars Rathbone and Bruce as the famous sleuth and his companion Dr. Watson. Holmes' archenemy, the evil Professor Moriarty, attempts to commit the "crime of the century" right beneath the detective's nose. ★★★

Advise and Consent

(1962, 139 min, US, Otto Preminger) *Henry Fonda, Charles Laughton, Gene Tierney, Don Murray, Lew Ayres, Burgess Meredith, Franchot Tone, Peter Lawford, Inga Swenson.* A finely interwoven plot and exceptional ensemble acting highlight Preminger's treatment of the Allen Drury novel. The machinations of government, on the floor of the Senate and behind the scenes, are examined with an eye to formal procedure and individual idiosyncrasy in this story of a controversial presidential nomination. Murray is full of idealistic vigor as the

chairman of a House sub-committee investigating the Secretary of State nominee (played by Fonda). However, when he refuses to endorse Fonda, he is blackmailed for a homosexual encounter while in the service. In his final film, Laughton offers an excellent performance as a slick Southern senator. (Letterboxed) ★★★½ VHS: $19.99

The Advocate

(1994, 101 min, GB, Leslie Megahey) *Colin Firth, Ian Holm, Amina Annabi, Jim Carter, Donald Pleasence, Nicol Williamson.* Writer-director Megahey has taken what has to be a virtually unknown medieval law and with it fashioned a scintillating black comedy masquerading as a murder mystery. Firth plays a 15th-century Parisian lawyer who escapes the rigors and hardships of the city for a simpler life in the country. But a peaceful landscape and gentle countryfolk are not what he finds when he immediately becomes embroiled in the murder trial of a young boy — and his defendant is a pig! As Firth tries to uncover the facts, he comes face to face with political corruption, religious bureaucracy and a bevy of beautiful women all trying to bed him. The situation is ripe with satiric possibilities, and Megahey has wondrously exploited them with a light touch and marvelous wit. ★★★½

Aelita: Queen of Mars

(1924, 113 min, USSR, Yakov Protazanov) *Julia Solntseva, Nikolai Batalov.* Definitely not your typical silent Soviet film, *Aelita* is a big-budget science-fiction spectacle boasting enormous, Cubist-inspired futuristic sets and wildly designed costumes. A Russian engineer, a soldier and a detective all travel to Mars where they become embroiled in a Martian proletarian uprising. Their situation gets even more complicated when the engineer falls madly in love with Queen Aelita. A huge popular success in its time, the film is an interesting precursor to Fritz Lang's similarly themed *Metropolis.* (Silent with piano accompaniment) ★★★ VHS: $29.99; DVD: $24.99

An Affair of Love
(Une Liaison d'Amour)

(2000, 78 min, France, Frédéric Fonteyne) *Nathalie Baye, Sergi López.* A sensuous, intelligent and passionate film about sex and love. Baye is radiant as a middle-aged Parisian woman who meets a younger man through a personal ad. They rendezvous to fulfill a secret sexual fantasy, vowing not to fall in love. Complications arise, however, when they do just that. The simple plot gives these two great characters room to breathe, in an exploration of desire that's both romantic and sexy. A wondrous film that has a warm, intimate feel. (French wth English subtitles) ★★★ VHS: $19.99; DVD: $24.99

An Affair to Remember

(1957, 115 min, US, Leo McCarey) *Cary Grant, Deborah Kerr, Cathleen Nesbitt.* Based on the 1939 classic *Love Affair,* this sentimental soap opera features Grant and Kerr in very appealing performances as two lovers separated by fate. Artist Grant and engaged Kerr enjoy a shipboard romance. In a famous cinematic rendezvous, they vow to meet six months later at the Empire State Building. One of them doesn't make it. Though the film is awash in hokey drama, the chemistry of the two stars, Grant's expert comic

timing and a touching romance make this a semiclassic and fan fave. (The story was told again in 1994 with Warren Beatty and Annette Bening) ★★★ VHS: $14.99; DVD: $24.99

Affliction

(1998, 113 min, US, Paul Schrader) *Nick Nolte, Sissy Spacek, James Coburn, Willem Dafoe, Mary Beth Hurt.* Career performances by Nolte and Coburn (who won an Academy Award) accentuate this sobering, absorbing, rough-going psychological study of the precarious relationship between an abusive father and his two sons. Nolte is Wade Whitehouse, the middle-aged sheriff of a small New Hampshire town. He doesn't seem to command respect as either lawman or divorced dad. When his aged mother dies, he attempts a reconciliation with his alcoholic father (Coburn) by moving back home to look after him. But painful memories of the past begin to resurface, and Wade — powerless in both his professional and personal lives — finds his world crumbling around him. Adapted from the novel by Russell Banks ("The Sweet Hereafter"), the film shares the desperation and sadness which tinged Banks' other film adaptation, but Schrader's gloomy film doesn't have *Hereafter*'s storytelling agility. But what it may lack in cinematic expression is more than made up by Nolte and Coburn's brilliant portraits — this is very much an actor's vehicle. ★★★ VHS: $14.99; DVD: $29.99

Afraid of the Dark

(1992, 91 min, GB, Mark Peploe) *James Fox, Fanny Ardant, Paul McGann, Ben Keyworth.* Screenwriter Peploe (*The Last Emperor*) turns his hand to directing with this psychological thriller in which nothing is as it seems. Fox stars as the father of a precocious kid who decides to track down a psychopath preying on the blind. To say more would be detrimental to the plot's essential twist, but the patient viewer will be rewarded. ★★½ VHS: $14.99

An African Dream

(1990, 94 min, GB, John Smallcombe) *John Kani, Kitty Aldridge.* When a young schoolteacher (Aldridge) moves to colonial South Africa with her husband, she is appalled by the racial hatred which pervades her new home. She develops a relationship with an educated African (Kani) who is teaching at a small school in the black area and is involuntarily sucked into the fray. ★★★ VHS: $79.99

The African Queen

(1951, 106 min, GB/US, John Huston) *Humphrey Bogart, Katharine Hepburn, Robert Morley, Peter Bull, Theodore Bikel.* One of the all-time greats, *The African Queen* stars Bogart (in his Oscar-winning role) and Hepburn as unlikely lovebirds who encounter the dangers of the rapids, the Germans and each other. In a quintessential performance, Hepburn plays Rose Saywer, a missionary serving in the Congo. She is paired with boozy captain Charlie Alnut (Bogey in a wonderfully endearing performance) when she must flee her village from the enemy army via Bogey's dilapidated boat. Aided by two veteran performers at the peak of their talents and an excellent screenplay, director Huston has crafted a thrilling adventure both comic and exciting. ★★★★ VHS: $14.99

Cary Grant and Deborah Kerr embrace in
An Affair to Remember

After Dark, My Sweet

(1990, 114 min, US, James Foley) *Jason Patric, Rachel Ward, Bruce Dern.* 1990 was a good year for gritty adaptations of the books of Jim Thompson. In addition to *The Grifters*, this disturbing yet highly entertaining melodrama represented a miniature revival for the novelist. Patric stars as Collie, a literally punch-drunk ex-boxer who is on the run from a mental institution. Dazed, Collie wanders into the seedier side of Palm Springs and becomes tragically entangled with an alcoholic widow (Ward) and a local con man (Dern) who are hatching a scheme to pick up some quick bucks. *After Dark, My Sweet* is an excellent and claustrophobic study of three social misfits caught in a dangerous *pas de trois*. ★★★½ VHS: $12.99; DVD: $24.99

After Hours

(1985, 97 min, US, Martin Scorsese) *Griffin Dunne, Rosanna Arquette, Teri Garr, John Heard, Linda Fiorentino, Thomas Chong, Cheech Marin, Catherine O'Hara, Dick Miller, Bronson Pinchot.* Ever had one of those days? Paul Hackett (Dunne) is about to have one of those nights. What begins as an innocent date with a kooky girl he meets at a coffee shop escalates into a night befitting a "Twilight Zone" episode. This exhilarating Scorsese black comedy follows Paul's misadventures in Greenwich Village (and vicinity) where each character confronted is crazier and more unpredictable than the one before. ★★★★ VHS: $19.99

After Life

(1998, 118 min, Japan, Kore-eda Hirokazu) *Arata, Oda Erika, Terajima Susumu.* In Hirokazu's *After Life*, the recently departed are given three days to determine the most meaningful memory of their lives, which will be their only memory for eternity — thus creating their own Heaven or Hell. The process takes place in a huge, generic municipal building, which sits in an indeterminate, foggy landscape. Each soul gets a caseworker to assist in the evaluation, prodding remembrance and reflection in examining what was truly valuable in their lives. The film is deceptively simple as it presents ordinary, unexceptional people who begin the recall process with momentous events. Inevitably, these memories lead to the small, special, seemingly insignificant moments, which in the end are the real substance of life. *After Life* is profound and moving and deeply affecting as it balances compassion with wry observation, watching the dead sift through their memories until they find the one that resonates for all eternity. Question: If you died today, what memory would you take with you? (Japanese with English subtitles) ★★★½ VHS: $29.99; DVD: $29.99

After Pilkington

(1987, 100 min, GB, Christopher Morahan) *Miranda Richardson, Bob Peck.* An Oxford professor's quiet academic lifestyle becomes imperiled when a childhood sweetheart, whom he hasn't seen in years, suddenly resurfaces and begs him to help him dispose of a corpse. An offbeat tale of obsession and murder. ★★½ VHS: $19.99

After Sex

(1997, 97 min, France, Brigitte Roüan) *Brigitte Roüan, Patrick Chesnais, Boris Terral, Nils Tavernier, Jean-Louis Richard, Françoise Arnoul.* Passionate love scenes and emotional despair mark *After Sex*, an erotic-neurotic middle-age-crisis drama from France. Director Roüan stars as Diane Clovier, a forty-something publishing executive who begins an unexpected romance with Emilio (Terral), a shaggy-haired hydroelectric engineer twenty years her junior. Jeopardizing her career as well as her life with her husband and two sons, Diane becomes consumed with the intense sexual relationship. However, it ends abruptly. Roüan, who employs jump-cut editing to tell this fractured story, threatens to make *After Sex* a vanity production, but there are only a few really pretentious moments. A subplot involving Diane's husband Philippe (Chesnais) defending a neighbor of murdering her husband reinforces Diane's predicament, and nicely complements the film's feminist themes. (aka: *Post Coitum*) (French with English subtitles) ★★★ VHS: $29.99

After the Fox

(1966, 103 min, GB, Vittorio De Sica) *Peter Sellers, Victor Mature, Britt Ekland, Akim Tamiroff, Martin Balsam.* Who would imagine Vittorio De Sica directing Peter Sellers in a film scripted by Neil Simon? Well, here it is — and not an unworthy effort, at that. Sellers is an ingenious convict who produces a film in order to cover up a big caper. As the movie star Sellers convinces to star in the "movie," Mature gets the most laughs just for being himself. ★★★ VHS: $14.99

After the Rehearsal

(1984, 72 min, Sweden, Ingmar Bergman) *Erland Josephson, Lena Olin, Ingrid Thulin.* A provocative probing of the thoughts and fears of a renowned stage director (Josephson) poised between love and solitude, ambition and resignation, bitterness and longing. On the verge of a production, he is confronted by two actresses, who in distinctly different fashions, force him into a position of self-examination. Along with *Wild Strawberries*, this is one of Bergman's most personal reflections on the demands and delusions of the artist. (Swedish with English subtitles) ★★★½ VHS: $19.99

After the Thin Man

See: The Thin Man Series

Afterburn

(1992, 100 min, US, Robert Markowitz) *Laura Dern, Robert Loggia, Vincent Spano, Michael Rooker.* Dern is arresting as a fighter pilot's widow who takes on the U.S. military when her husband's crash in an F-16 in Korea is attributed to pilot error. Knowing that her husband (Spano) was one of the most highly rated pilots, her doubts and suspicions regarding the official story escalate in the face of increasing evidence of a cover-up. Loggia delivers a strong performance as Dern's lawyer. A compelling HBO treatment of a real-life incident. ★★★½ VHS: $9.99

Afterglow

(1998, 114 min, Canada/US, Alan Rudolph) *Nick Nolte, Julie Christie, Lara Flynn Boyle, Jonny Lee Miller, Jay Underwood.* Director Rudolph again casts his eye on contemporary relationships, intertwining and enmeshing two disparate couples in crisis. Lucky (Nolte), a high-ticket handyman who takes care of the plumbing in more ways than one, is married to Phyllis (Christie), a faded former film star who seeks climactic experience — even that of grave illness. Marianne and Jeffrey, a younger, upper-strata corporate couple (Boyle and Miller), bicker in their expensive but sterile condo — a perfect reflection of their life together. A slightly surreal Montreal is the backdrop for myriad expressions of selfishness and memories reflected like images in a shattered mirror. While the older twosome have the depth of character provided by life experience, it affords them no greater ability to understand or communicate. Nolte and Christie are perfect complements; Christie providing subtle yet profound emotional depth to a character that would have been easy to overplay. The film is slightly choppy, but remains an adult exploration of the magnitude of a lie's impact, and the saving grace of its forgiveness. ★★★ VHS: $24.99

Against All Odds

(1984, 128 min, US, Taylor Hackford) *Jeff Bridges, Rachel Ward, James Woods, Jane Greer, Richard Widmark, Swoosie Kurtz, Saul Rubinek.* An interesting if not totally successful updating of the noir classic *Out of the Past*. Bridges stars as a down-and-out ex-football player who is hired by an ex-teammate-turned-gangster (Woods) to locate the woman (Ward) who he says tried to kill him. Hackford's remake relies on solid performances, star chemistry and a few plot twists to puff up what could have been a rather shopworn premise, and the film also benefits from an over-the-top performance by Woods. Greer, who plays Ward's mother, starred as the missing femme fatale in the original film. ★★½ VHS: $9.99; DVD: $24.99

Against the Wall

(1993, 111 min, US, John Frankenheimer) *Kyle MacLachlan, Samuel L. Jackson, Clarence Williams III, Harry Dean Stanton, Frederic Forrest.* This made-for-HBO docudrama chronicles the events that took place during the violent uprising at the Attica State Penitentiary in the early '70s. MacLachlan stars as the rookie guard who gets stuck in the middle and becomes a hostage for the inmates. Jackson gives a fine performance as the Islamic inmate who unofficially becomes the go-between for the media and the prisoners. This exciting, heart-pounding film is one of HBO's finest productions. ★★★★ VHS: $9.99

Agatha

(1978, 98 min, GB/US, Michael Apted) *Vanessa Redgrave, Dustin Hoffman, Timothy Dalton.* Director Apted weaves this fictional account of the 1926 11-day disappearance of famed mystery writer Agatha Christie. Redgrave's sensitive portrayal lends touching insight into "the price of fame," while helping to offset Hoffman's grating turn as the American reporter who ultimately tracks her down. ★★½ VHS: $14.99

L'Âge d'Or

(1930, 60 min, France, Luis Buñuel) Following the success of their first collaboration, *Un Chien Andalou*, Buñuel and Salvador Dali further antagonized the Right, the Church and the powers that be with this wickedly funny, bizarre and scandalous masterpiece. Buñuel has said that this dreamlike tale of mad love unconsummated is "a romantic film performed in full surrealist frenzy." (French with English subtitles) ★★★½

The Age of Innocence

(1993, 133 min, US, Martin Scorsese) *Daniel Day-Lewis, Michelle Pfeiffer, Winona Ryder, Miriam Margolyes, Richard E. Grant, Alec McCowen, Geraldine Chaplin, Robert Sean Leonard.* Scorsese's period drama is a visually dazzling and sumptuously produced, but ultimately disappointing adaptation of Edith Wharton's novel. Set in 1870s New York City, the film stars Day-Lewis as Newland Archer, a young lawyer and rising member of the ruling elite. Smitten by the Countess Olenska (Pfeiffer), a former member of polite society who has returned home surrounded by gossip over her intent to divorce her husband, Archer furthers the scandal by falling in love with her despite his betrothal to Olenska's cousin (Ryder). The acting by all three principals is superbly nuanced and first-rate; special mention goes to Margolyes as a matronly aunt. While the film aptly captures the sense of social suffocation that Wharton no doubt intended, it lacks a much-needed passion. ★★½ VHS: $14.99

Agnes Browne

(1999, 92 min, Ireland, Anjelica Huston) *Anjelica Huston, Marion O'Dwyer, Niall O'Shea, Ciaran Owens, Ray Winstone.* In 1967 Dublin, a poor widow (Huston) with seven children sets out to support her family and begin a new life for herself in the wake of social change. Culminating with a quest to see Tom Jones in concert, this is about as fun as a film about a newly widowed, dirt-poor mother can be. However, the mood is consistently spoiled by lackluster line readings, surprising being directed by such a fine actress. In spite of its flaws, *Agnes Browne* is an amiable slice of Irish life. ★★½ VHS: $14.99; DVD: $19.99

Agnes of God

(1985, 98 min, US, Norman Jewison) *Jane Fonda, Anne Bancroft, Meg Tilly.* A trio of solid performances highlight this intriguing mystery based on the Broadway hit. Fonda plays a court-appointed psychiatrist who must determine the sanity of a novice accused of murdering her newborn baby. Oscar nominations went to Bancroft as the convent's worldly Mother Superior, and Tilly as the troubled young woman. ★★★ VHS: $9.99

The Agony and the Ecstasy

(1965, 140 min, US, Carol Reed) *Charlton Heston, Rex Harrison, Diane Cilento, Harry Andrews.* Not considered a Reed classic, this historical account follows Michelangelo's aesthetic battles with Pope Julius II as he toiled on the Sistine Chapel. Heston and Harrison provide worthy performances, but the film's slightly overblown production values and its considerable length overshadow their efforts. ★★½ VHS: $9.99

Aguirre, the Wrath of God

(1972, 94 min, Germany, Werner Herzog) *Klaus Kinski, Ruy Guerra, Helena Rojo.* A mesmerizing, adventurous tale of a Spanish expedition's search for El Dorado, the lost city of gold. Along the way, a power-hungry conquistador, Aguirre, takes control and leads them on an insane journey into the Amazon and the heart of darkness. Although Herzog's hyper-realistic style of direction makes for a few slow sequences, Kinski's intense performance as the traitorous title character is riveting. A compelling portrait of a mad and brilliant leader. (German with English subtitles) ★★★½ VHS: $14.99; DVD: $29.99

Ah, Wilderness!

(1935, 98 min, US, Clarence Brown) *Lionel Barrymore, Wallace Beery, Spring Byington, Eric Linden, Mickey Rooney.* A very able cast brings Eugene O'Neill's stage comedy about a 1906 New England family merrily to life. The film's success is painting a heartwarming portrait of early 20th-century Americana while avoiding the bathetic trappings of so many films of the '30s — the *Andy Hardy* series, for example. Heading a fine ensemble is Barrymore as the patriarch of the Miller clan. Barrymore is often given the film's best lines, and he makes the most of them. Beery gives a showy portrayal as an uncle prone to drink; and Byington sparkles as the family's mother. ★★★½ VHS: $19.99

Aileen Wuornos — The Selling of a Serial Killer

(1993, 87 min, GB, Nick Broomfield) *Aileen Wuornos.* A chilling crime and justice documentary that would make the events in *The Thin Blue Line* seem like a paragon of legal competence, this mesmerizing and tenacious investigative film attempts to gather the facts in the case against convicted serial killer Aileen Wuornos. Wuornos, a lesbian and prostitute, was convicted of brutally killing seven men. Director Broomfield digs beyond the seemingly open-and-shut case and uncovers an elaborate web of deception and profiteering both on the part of law enforcement officers, her "friends" and her lover. Wuornos appears to be a thoughtful and rather intelligent woman who, while probably guilty, did not receive an ounce of justice as she was railroaded to several convictions and a date with the electric chair. ★★★★

Air America

(1990, 112 min, US, Roger Spottiswoode) *Mel Gibson, Robert Downey, Jr., Nancy Travis, David Marshall Grant.* Lumbering political satire with Gibson and Downey as off-the-wall pilots working for a covert government airline in Laos during the years of the Vietnam War. The film can't decide what it wants to be — left-wing, right-wing, comic romp, antiwar — and suffers

Aguirre, the Wrath of God

as a result. The appealing chemistry of the two stars is wasted on this nonsense. (Available letterboxed and pan & scan) ★ VHS: $14.99; DVD: $14.99

Air Bud

(1997, 97 min, US, Charles Martin Smith) *Michael Jeter, Kevin Zegers, Wendy Makkena, Norm Snively.* After the death of his beloved father, 12-year-old Josh moves with his mother and sister to a new town where he has a tough time adjusting. He soon befriends a golden retriever named Buddy. Although he is too shy to try out for the school basketball team, he plays alone until he discovers that Buddy can play a mean game of basketball. While the plot development from here is fairly obvious — Josh finds the confidence to try out for and become a member of the team, while Buddy becomes the team mascot who shoots hoops at halftime — it is nonetheless heartwarming. The ending is hokier than the rest of the film but kids should appreciate good winning out. ★★½ VHS: $14.99; DVD: $29.99

Un Air de Famille

(1996, 110 min, France, Cédric Klapisch) *Jean-Pierre Bacri, Jean-Pierre Darroussin, Catherine Frot, Agnès Jaoui, Claire Maurier.* A family's dinner gathering sets the stage for hilarious confrontations in this winning character piece. The plot is familiar, but the absence of melodrama and the subtly witty dialogue make it a winner. Maurier as the domineering mother is merely the best of a terrific ensemble cast. (French with English subtitles) ★★★½ VHS: $89.99; DVD: $29.99

Air Force

(1943, 124 min, US, Howard Hawks) *John Garfield, Gig Young, Arthur Kennedy, Charles Drake, George Tobias.* After five years of solid support and second leads, Garfield takes center stage in this crisp WWII actioner about the aerial adventures of a B-17 bomber crew, both before and after Pearl Harbor. Hawks directs with his usual keen eye for adventure. Garfield is a commanding presence, and what Warner film would be complete without Tobias? ★★★ VHS: $19.99

Air Force One

(1997, 124 min, US, Wolfgang Petersen) *Harrison Ford, Gary Oldman, Glenn Close, William H. Macy, Wendy Crewson, Dean Stockwell, Diesel Matthews.* As if American presidents — on- and offscreen — haven't suffered enough in the late 1990s, along come a couple of slimy Russian terrorists to shake things up when they take over Air Force One. In Petersen's crisp thriller, action and suspense are neatly packaged to make for one exciting ride. And Ford proves that even as the commander in chief, he's ready to kick butt whenever necessary. That occurs when Oldman and his gang of revolutionaries commandeer the president's plane while he's in Moscow. Left on his own, Ford takes on the terrorists, who have threatened to start killing hostages if their leader is not released from prison. The scenario is ripe for swift action pieces, and Petersen knows how and when to push just the right buttons. The screenplay tries to make Oldman a misguided loyalist, but his ravings soon become tired and you can't wait for Ford to kick him off the damn plane. As would be expected, Ford's smart, tough performance fuels this flight; Close makes for a no-nonsense vice-president. ★★★ VHS: $9.99; DVD: $19.99

The Air Up There

(1994, 88 min, US, Paul M. Glaser) *Kevin Bacon, Charles Gitonga Maina, Yolanda Vasquez.* An easygoing Bacon stars as an assistant college basketball coach who travels all the way to Kenya to recruit a nearly seven-foot tribesman for his team. While there, he suffers culture shock, befriends the natives, and helps right the village's wrongs. The locale provides a nice travelogue backdrop, and the finale's basketball game is rather exciting despite its obvious outcome; but this formulaic sports film is only for those who think Hollywood doesn't make enough basketball flicks. ★★ VHS: $9.99

Airheads

(1994, 91 min, US, Michael Lehmann) *Brendan Fraser, Steve Buscemi, Adam Sandler, Joe Mantegna, Michael McKean, Michael Richards, Judd Nelson, Ernie Hudson.* Lehmann's self-consciously hip, one-joke comedy is about a rock band — The Lone Rangers — who hold a radio station hostage in order to get their demo played. The one joke? That a rock band holds a radio station hostage in order to get their demo played. As repetitious as it sounds, the film isn't helped by a tired script and one-dimensional performances. However, Sandler saves the day with an amusing portrayal of the band's dim-witted drummer. ★½ VHS: $9.99

Airplane!

(1980, 86 min, US, Jim Abrahams, David Zucker & Jerry Zucker) *Robert Hays, Julie Hagerty, Robert Stack, Leslie Nielsen, Lloyd Bridges, Peter Graves, Steven Stucker.* A dash of Marx Brothers, a taste of Chaplin, a whole lot of Three Stooges slapstick, and, puns, puns and more puns are the ingredients for this send-up of every airplane disaster film from *Zero Hour* to *Airport.* This non-stop laugh fest relentlessly hits us over the head with jokes. There are so many jokes, in fact, that blinking is not advised. Besides the million or so laughs, this is the film which first introduced Nielsen as a comic actor — let's give thanks for that, too. Cameos include Beaver's mom Barbara Billingsley and Ethel Merman. (Followed by a sequel in 1982) ★★★★ VHS: $14.99; DVD: $29.99

Airplane II: The Sequel

(1982, 85 min, US, Ken Finkleman) *Robert Hays, Julie Hagerty, William Shatner, Lloyd Bridges, Peter Graves, Chad Everett, Steven Stucker, Raymond Burr, Rip Torn.* This sequel to the hit *Airplane!* doesn't pack the stomach-wrenching humor as did the first. Handed over to first-time director Finkleman, the film just can't match the pace of its predecessor. This time around, retired pilot Hays becomes the only man available to fly a Space Shuttle-like craft. Although the plot is predictable, there are still enough funny moments to satisfy fans of the first. ★★½ VHS: $14.99; DVD: $29.99

Akermania Vol. 1

(1968-84, 89 min, Belgium, Chantal Akerman) *Chantal Akerman, Maria de Medeiros, Pascale Salkin.* Three short subjects from independent feminist filmmaker Akerman. *J'ai faim, J'ai froid* (*I'm Hungry, I'm Cold*) (1984): Two young girls run away to Paris from their native Brussels and learn very direct, immediate approaches to getting their needs met. *Salute ma ville* (*Blow Up My Town*) (1968): A young woman in a small flat

with too much unchanneled energy races through the mundane activities of daily life until she's caught in the vortex of their execution. This can be seen as a precursor to Akerman's *Jeanne Dielman. Hotel Monterey* (1974): Without sound, the camera wanders through the lobby, into the elevator, hallways, various rooms and out to the roof of the hotel. This process eventually creates a portrait of impersonal space, and the people captured in it seem transient, impermanent, ephemeral. An eerie and disquieting experience. ★★★ VHS: $19.99

Akira

(1989, 102 min, Japan, Katsuhiro Otomo) A sometimes grim but entertaining look into a not-too-distant future. Taking place in neo-Tokyo, complete with bike gangs, mutants and corrupt government officials, this film pushes the boundaries of animation into a truly adult realm. Visually striking, *Akira* will especially appeal to those who grew up on a diet of "8th Man," "Astro Boy" and "Speed Racer" cartoons. A groundbreaking state-of-the-art Japanese animation classic which makes some earlier efforts (like *Laputa*) look like stick-figure drawings. (Letterboxed) (Japanese with English subtitles) ★★★★ VHS: $19.99; DVD: $24.99

Akira Kurosawa's Dreams

(1990, 120 min, Japan, Akira Kurosawa) *Mitsuko Baisho, Toshihiko Nakano, Mitsunori Isaki, Martin Scorsese.* In his most personal film, Kurosawa takes time to reflect on his innermost hopes, fears and joys. Through a series of eight vignettes, or "dreams," Kurosawa takes us through his childhood terrors, his horror at the state of the environment and the use of nuclear power, his love of art and, finally, his peaceful vision of a world where people live harmoniously with nature. Filmed in vivid, sometimes explosive colors, *Dreams* represents a thoughtful summing to the impressive filmography of this cinematic giant. (Letterboxed) (Japanese with English subtitles) ★★★★ VHS: $102.99

Aladdin

(1992, 87 min, US, John Musker & Ron Clements) *Voices of: Robin Williams, Gilbert Gottfried, Scott Weinger, Linda Larkin, Lea Salonga, Brad Kane.* Consistently entertaining and a gloriously funny achievement, *Aladdin* features a nice musical score by Alan Menken, Tim Rice and Howard Ashman; delightful animation; and wonderful laugh-out-loud jokes. This alone makes the film first-class. But it also has Robin Williams. As the voice of the genie whose iconoclastic references will split any side, Williams catapults the film to unimaginable comic heights — and the Disney artists have matched his vocal escapades with inspired drawings. A marriage made in cartoon heaven, this is Williams and Disney at their best. The third and possibly strongest of the Disney-Menken-Ashman trilogy, which also includes *The Little Mermaid* and *Beauty and the Beast.* (Followed by *Return of Jafar* and *Aladdin and the King of Thieves*) ★★★★

The Alamo

(1960, 186 min, US, John Wayne) *John Wayne, Richard Widmark, Laurence Harvey, Richard Boone, Frankie Avalon, Chill Wills.* Wayne's dream project (he served as writer, producer, director and star) is an epic of Texas-sized proportions. The story, of course, has to do with the heroic last

A

9

stand made by Texas patriots in the face of the overwhelming Mexican army. Wayne stars as a larger-than-life Davy Crockett, Widmark plays Jim Bowie, and Harvey is Will Travis. The battle scenes are impressive and include great cavalry charges and hundreds of extras. The first half of the film is slow going, but Wayne creates an effective sense of impending doom throughout. The remastered, restored full-length version. ★★★ VHS: $14.99; DVD: $19.99

Alamo Bay

(1985, 98 min, US, Louis Malle) *Ed Harris, Amy Madigan, Ho Nguyen, Donald Moffat.* Harris stars as a fisherman and Vietnam vet who, like most of his small Texas community, feels a sense of resentment towards the Asian refugees who have settled in their town. Paradoxical complexity arrives when these ex-soldiers, who once fought to defend the Vietnamese, must now fight them for jobs and a way of life. Though the film retains a certain power, Malle creates little tension in this precarious moral dilemma, letting the conflict speak for itself instead of adding dimension for the camera. ★★ VHS: $79.99

Alan and Naomi

(1992, 95 min, US, Sterling VanWagenen) *Lukas Haas, Vanessa Zaoui, Michael Gross.* Young Haas' sincere, heartfelt performance dominates this slowly paced but nevertheless touching WWII drama. Haas brings unexpected depth to the role of a 14-year-old Brooklyn youth who is forced by his family to befriend a traumatized French girl, whose father was murdered by Nazis right before her eyes. At first reluctant to associate with the neighborhood "crazy," Haas slowly develops a relationship with the girl, allowing the tormented youngster to escape her protective shell, and present a glimmer of hope for recovery. Good evocation of wartime America. ★★½ VHS: $14.99

The Alarmist

(1998, 93 min, US, Evan Dunsky) *David Arquette, Stanley Tucci, Mary McCormack, Kate Capshaw, Ryan Reynolds.* An alarmingly bad comedy, this dark tale of robbery, kidnapping and murder is painfully unfunny. Based on a stage play, and adapted for the screen by director Dunsky, *The Alarmist* concerns Tommy Hudler (Arquette), a security systems salesman who begins an affair with his first paying customer, Gale Ancona (Capshaw). Meanwhile, Tommy's boss Heinrich (Tucci), breaks into clients' homes to help business, and he becomes the chief suspect when Gale and her son are murdered. Dunsky displays such a lack of focus that his film can't decide if it wants to be a deadpan black comedy or an edgy thriller. Arquette gives an energetic, eager-to-please performance, and he is fun to watch, but Tucci looks like he would rather be anywhere else. Capshaw isn't bad, she's simply an enigma. (aka: *Life During Wartime*) ★ VHS: $19.99; DVD: $29.99

Alberto Express

(1992, 90 min, Italy, Arthur Joffe) *Sergio Castellitto, Nino Manfredi.* With a wickedly farcical premise and the presence, however brief, of Italian funny man Manfredi, this frantic family comedy should be more entertaining than it is. Alberto, a frumpy 40-year-old man about to be a first-time father, is summoned to his father's attic for a meeting. Pop, observing a family tradition, calmly begins calculating every expense incurred in raising Alberto

and presents him with a bill that must be repaid before his wife delivers his child. From this, Alberto schemes and connives his way through the continent, in hopes of somehow coming up with the money. While his antics are at times quite hilarious, Castellitto as Alberto is somehow not quite right for the part — too much of a forlorn sad-sack with not enough comic inventiveness to carry a comedy of this type. (Italian with English subtitles) ★★½ VHS: $19.99

Albino Alligator

(1997, 105 min, US, Kevin Spacey) *Matt Dillon, Faye Dunaway, Gary Sinise, Viggo Mortensen, William Fichtner, Skeet Ulrich, Joe Mantegna, M. Emmet Walsh.* Demonstrating moments of great understanding of the gangster film, Spacey's directorial debut has terrific scenes but doesn't quite come together as a whole. Borrowing a little from *The Petrified Forest*, the story concerns small-time New Orleans hoods Dillon, Sinise and Fichtner who, after bungling a burglary and having the police on their trail, hole up in a seedy bar. Taking customers and employees hostage, the little remaining remnants of rational thought these men have dissipate, eventually causing a crisis of morality for all concerned. Dillon ably walks the fine line between mug and thug, and Fichtner makes a great impression as the hoodlums' loose cannon. In this promising debut, Spacey captures the mood, but the screenplay lacks some of the necessary grit. ★★½ VHS: $14.99; DVD: $29.99

Alex in Wonderland

(1970, 109 min, US, Paul Mazursky) *Donald Sutherland, Ellen Burstyn, Jeanne Moreau.* What do you do when your filmmaking debut is a huge box-office success? Mazursky's response was this meandering trifle which poses the very same question — following, as it did, on the heels of his surprise hit *Bob & Carol & Ted & Alice.* Sutherland offers a nice portrayal of Mazursky's alter ego Alex, a hippie-dippie director whose initial triumph makes him a hot property at the studio, but whose conscience bristles at the thought of becoming another Hollywood lap-dog. Mazursky's loosely scattered narrative, along with a cameo by Federico Fellini, makes it clear that he yearns for the freedoms enjoyed by European directors. The result, sadly, is a jumble (many Americans of the era tried to imitate the European style with little success), but the subject is of enough interest to film enthusiasts to be worth a look. Burstyn is excellent as Sutherland's wife. ★★½ VHS: $19.99

Alexander Nevsky

(1938, 108 min, USSR, Sergei Eisenstein) *Nikolai Cherkassov, Nikolai Okhlopkov.* Eisenstein's first sound film is a grand epic of Prince Nevsky's heroic defense of Russia against the invading Teutonic Knights in 1242. The final battle sequence on the ice of Lake Piepus is magnificent in its visual splendor and in the use of a stirring Prokofiev score instead of natural sound. (Digitally remastered) (Russian with English subtitles) ★★★★ VHS: $29.99; DVD: $24.99

Alexandria. . . Why?

(1978, 133 min, Egypt, Youssef Chahine) *Ezzat El Alaili, Naglaa Fathi, Mohsen Mohiedine, Farid Shawqi, Gerry Sundquist, Mohsena Tawfik.* Winner of the Best Director Award at the 1979

Berlin Film Festival, this accomplished autobiographical WWII drama of illicit love is set in the teeming port city of Alexandria in 1942, where life in the besieged city remains strangely undisturbed despite the fact that advancing Rommel is only 60 miles away. The story explores two taboo love affairs: one between a Muslim man and a Jewish woman, and the other between a handsome Egyptian man and a young British soldier. An entertaining, involving drama. (Arabic with English subtitles) ★★★½ VHS: $19.99; DVD: $24.99

Alfie

(1966, 114 min, GB, Lewis Gilbert) *Michael Caine, Vivien Merchant, Shirley Anne Field, Millicent Martin, Shelley Winters, Denholm Elliott, Eleanor Bron.* Caine is flawless as an unscrupulous Cockney womanizer who can't decide whether his lustful life is really worth the effort. It's a quirky film which strips bare all the lecherous qualities nurtured within the male mystique. There's an excellent supporting cast, and this was the film that catapulted Caine into the realm of international stardom. ★★★★ VHS: $14.99; DVD: $29.99

Algiers

(1938, 95 min, US, John Cromwell) *Charles Boyer, Sigrid Gurie, Hedy Lamarr, Joseph Calleia, Alan Hale, Gene Lockhart.* A svelte and darkly handsome Boyer exudes sinister charm as Pepe le Moko, the crown prince of thieves in the Casbah, a labyrinthine complex of dens and warrens in the heart of Algiers, whose inhabitants are dedicated to the procurement of ill-gotten gains. A police inspector newly arrived from France intends to capture the nefarious Pepe, much to the amusement of the local constabulary. While the pace is somewhat laborious by contemporary standards, the film evokes an enticing aura of menace. ★★★ VHS: $12.99

Ali: Fear Eats the Soul

(1973, 94 min, Germany, Rainer Werner Fassbinder) *Brigitte Mira, El Hedi Ben Salem, Barbara Valentin, Irm Hermann.* Fassbinder's bittersweet love story about the affair between a lonely 60-year-old German cleaning woman and a reticent Moroccan auto mechanic half her age is a raw, intense look at racial attitudes and unconventional relationships. Mira and Ben Salem star as the two lovers who find brief solace with each other in spite of family objections, social rejection and racial prejudice. Fassbinder's first film to play theatrically in the U.S., *Ali* is startling in its examination of xenophobia, and is an unflinching study of the passion between "societal misfits," one of the director's favorite themes. (German with English subtitles) ★★★½

Alice

(1987, 86 min, Czechoslovakia, Jan Svankmajer) Animator Svankmajer has taken Lewis Carroll's "Alice in Wonderland" and created a distinctly original and personal interpretation of the classic children's story. Utilizing live-action with his trademark stop-motion animation, Svankmajer's *Alice* owes more to the surrealist techniques of Buñuel and Dali than to Disney. While the narration of the familiar tale unfolds, the filmmaker's interest lies less with the story's odd and fanciful characters and more with the underlying cruel, erotic and amoral ideas of an innocent girl lost during a wickedly bizarre journey. Not for children, obviously, and not even for many adults, this extraordinary work will amaze, baffle and delight fans of the surreal. (Dubbed in English) ★★★★ VHS: $19.99; DVD: $29.99

Alice

(1991, 106 min, US, Woody Allen) *Mia Farrow, Joe Mantegna, Keye Luke, Alec Baldwin, Blythe Danner, Judy Davis, William Hurt, Bernadette Peters, Cybill Shepherd, Gwen Verdon.* This is Allen's delightful paean to Lewis Carrol's "Alice in Wonderland" and Federico Fellini's *Juliet of the Spirits.* Farrow stars as Alice, a woman who has been married for 16 years to highly successful businessman Hurt. Theirs is the lifestyle of $100 lunches and shopping sprees at Bergdorf Goodman's, but something is missing for Alice; she has a calling, she's just not sure what. With the help of a strange herbalist/acupuncturist, and through the fantasy of having an affair with divorcé Mantegna, she experiences a series of whimsical, supernatural and often hilarious events which help guide her toward inner happiness. Farrow is superb as she presents the perfect female embodiment of Allen's nebbish, and Mantegna delivers his usual offbeat charm. Veteran actor Luke steals the film as the beguiling and mysterious doctor. ★★★½ VHS: $14.99; DVD: $19.99

Alice Adams

(1935, 99 min, US, George Stevens) *Katharine Hepburn, Fred MacMurray, Evelyn Venable.* In one of her best roles, Hepburn is a girl of the bourgeoisie trying to compete with the swells for the attentions of extremely eligible and quite well-heeled MacMurray in Stevens' adaptation of the Booth Tarkington novel. Throw in a little corporate skullduggery and some strikingly visualized evidences of class distinctions. ★★★★ VHS: $19.99

Alice Doesn't Live Here Anymore

(1974, 113 min, US, Martin Scorsese) *Ellen Burstyn, Kris Kristofferson, Diane Ladd, Jodie Foster, Alfred Lutter, Billy Green Bush, Vic Tayback.* Burstyn won an Oscar for her bravura performance in this touching, sometimes humorous and sensitive character study of one woman's personal liberation. After her husband dies and leaves her penniless, Alice, with her young son Tommy (Lutter), moves to Phoenix, Arizona, where she attempts to survive on her own, both emotionally and financially. Wonderful supporting roles include Ladd as Flo, Foster as Tommy's young friend, and Tayback as Mel. Kristofferson is at his best as Alice's love interest. ★★★★ VHS: $14.99

Alice in the Cities

(1973, 110 min, West Germany, Wim Wenders) *Rudiger Vogler, Yella Rottlander, Lisa Kreuzer, Chuck Berry.* Wenders' German-made films usually share several recurring themes: man's alienation and his ensuing search for meaning in life, American cultural imperialism in Germany, and the exploration of personal relationships. In *Alice in the Cities,* a brooding, remarkable examination of the director's favorite themes, we follow a 31-year-old journalist who, when traveling in the United States, suddenly finds himself with a precocious nine-year-old girl abandoned by her mother. The two return to

Germany in search of the girl's grandmother. (German with English subtitles) ★★★

Alice in Wonderland

(1950, 83 min, GB, Lou Bunin) Released a year before Disney's version of the story, this mixture of animation and live action virtually disappeared in the U.S. after threats of reprisal from the Disney studio. Closer to Lewis Carroll's original work in satirical tone than Disney's, this *Alice* is equally enjoyable for both adults and children, although aimed at the latter. The story begins at Oxford, where lonely lecturer Charles Dodgson spins fantastic tales for Alice Liddel and her two sisters. It then shifts to Wonderland, where the familiar characters of the White Rabbit, Cheshire Cat, Mad Hatter and the Queen of Hearts are brought vividly to life through stop-motion animation. The animation is impressively intercut with the live Alice, creating a fantasy world of giant talking caterpillars, gryphons and mock turtles. ★★★ VHS: $24.99

Alice in Wonderland

(1951, 75 min, US, Clyde Geronimi, Hamilton Luske & Wilfred Jackson) *Voices of: Kathryn Beaumomt, Ed Wynn, Jerry Colonna, Sterling Holloway, Richard Haydn.* Disney's adaptation of Lewis Carroll's classic is a colorful, tune-filled excursion through Wonderland. More eccentric and slightly more surreal than Disney's usual fare (with the exception of *Fantasia*), the film follows the familiar journey taken by Alice as she enters a wondrous dimension populated by the White Rabbit and talking caterpillars, where she's likely to be any size from one moment to the next. Of the songs, "I'm Late" is the most well-known, though "A Very Merry Un-Birthday" is kinda cute, too. ★★★½ VHS: $22.99; DVD: $29.99

Alice to Nowhere

(1986, 212 min, Australia, John Power) *Rosey Jones, John Waters.* An exceedingly long but at times rousing adventure yarn made for Aussie television. A woman, who doesn't know that in her possession is a cache of priceless jewels, finds herself pursued by thieves and just regular bad guys. Her adventures take her and her two guides through many perilous, grueling outback regions in this *Indiana Jones*-like epic. ★★★ VHS: $59.99

Alice's Restaurant

(1969, 111 min, US, Arthur Penn) *Arlo Guthrie, Pat Quinn, James Broderick.* Penn's follow-up to *Bonnie and Clyde* was a film version of Guthrie's communal sing-along which accurately captures the cultural upheaval going on at the end of the 1960s. Quirky and entertaining, the film features a surprisingly downbeat ending proving to be more prophetic than the hyperbole of *Easy Rider.* (Contains footage not seen in the theatrical version) ★★★ VHS: $14.99; DVD: $19.99

Alien

(1979, 117 min, US, Ridley Scott) *Sigourney Weaver, Tom Skerritt, Yaphet Kotto, Harry Dean Stanton, Ian Holm, John Hurt, Veronica Cartwright.* Terror lurks in every corner in this frightening story of a completely hostile and virtually indestructible creature which sneaks aboard the spaceship *Nostromo,* via Hurt's navel, and brings an absolute nightmare to its crew. Director Scott masterfully blends pulse-pounding suspense

and some gory, amazing F/X, and the film is greatly benefitted by H.R. Giger's outstanding production design. (Sequel: *Aliens*) (Letterboxed VHS available for $19.99) ★★★½ VHS: $14.99; DVD: $29.99

Alien 3

(1992, 115 min, US, David Fincher) *Sigourney Weaver, Charles S. Dutton, Charles Dance, Pete Postlethwaite, Paul McCann, Lance Henriksen.* The third chapter in the *Alien* series from first-time director Fincher follows two classics in the horror/sci-fi genre. Fincher had his work cut out for him — and though his film delivers some of the goods, there's no comparison to the first two films. Weaver, with shaved head, returns as Lt. Ripley, and it seems she's brought an old friend along. Ripley has crash landed at a maximum security prison on some distant bleak planet. And there's not much for her to do but balance her time between the hostile inmates and one angry alien who's come a-lookin' for one final confrontation. Like the music videos Fincher cut his teeth on, *Alien 3* has a great look but very little substance. (Sequel: *Alien Resurrection*) (Letterboxed VHS available for $19.99) ★★½ VHS: $14.99; DVD: $29.99

Alien Nation

(1988, 94 min, US, Graham Baker) *James Caan, Mandy Patinkin, Terence Stamp.* Caan is well cast as a tough L.A. cop who is partnered with an alien — from outer space. It seems in the not-so-distant future, an alien race will arrive on Earth after the destruction of their own planet, though they are welcomed with not-so-opened arms. The first half of the film is an intriguing sci-fi adventure, but the story disintegrates into a routine buddy film. Patinkin is oddly affecting as Caan's man-from-outer space partner. ★★½ VHS: $9.99; DVD: $24.99

Alien Resurrection

(1997, 120 min, US, Jean-Pierre Jeunet) *Sigourney Weaver, Winona Ryder, Dominique Pinon, Ron Perlman, Michael Wincott, Brad Dourif, Dan Hedaya, Raymond Cruz.* Weaver returns in this unsatisfying mess as Ripley, who immolated herself in the previous film while "giving birth" to an alien queen. A couple of centuries later, scientists have succeeded in cloning her in order to extract the alien queen embryo from her womb for research and weapons purposes. Unfortunately for them, they also have the "meat by-product" of Ripley herself left over. Soon, the genetically enhanced Ripley is thrust once again into the center of an alien war, this time raging on a space vessel on its way back to Earth. Ryder plays a member of a group of interstellar pirates and smugglers who are accidentally caught in the fray. The opening sequence opens beautifully, showing off director Jeunet's visual talents. But aside from a few interesting scenes, the film is a repeat of the clichés of its predecessors. The *Alien* series should have died with its heroine. (Letterboxed VHS available for $19.99) ★★ VHS: $14.99; DVD: $29.99

Alien Visitor

(1995, 92 min, Australia, Rolf De Heer) *Ulli Birve, Syd Brisbane, Aletha McGrath.* A young woman from the planet Epsilon accidentally crash lands in the Australian Outback. She meets a lone surveyor and together they walk in circles trying to understand each other. They eventually fall in love in the process. Despite a few dead-on moments of clarity, *Alien Visitor* is a rather one-dimensional character study that tries to affirm its environmental and worldly messages, but winds up beating these points into the ground, culminating in a nice but predictable ending. (aka: *Epsilon*) ★★ VHS: $19.99

Aliens

(1986, 137 min, US, James Cameron) *Sigourney Weaver, Carrie Henn, Lance Henriksen, Michael Biehn, Bill Paxton, Paul Reiser, Jenette Goldstein.* The blockbuster sequel to *Alien* does the original one better; dazzling special effects and nerve-racking suspense make this definitely not for the weak of heart. Weaver reprises her role as Warrant Officer Ripley in an Oscar-nominated performance. Ripley is convinced to return to the planet where the deadly aliens were initially found when an Earth colony loses contact with its home base. Director Cameron assaults the senses in a unrelenting barrage of terror, and just when you thought it couldn't get any more suspenseful — it does! (Letterboxed VHS available for $19.99) ★★★★ VHS: $14.99; DVD: $29.99

Alive

(1993, 125 min, US, Frank Marshall) *Ethan Hawke, Vincent Spano, Josh Hamilton, Bruce Ramsay, David Kriegel, Illeana Douglas.* Despite containing some truly trite Hollywood contrivances, this high-altitude action film offers excellent thrills and a lot of food for thought. Recounting the harrowing two-month ordeal suffered by the surviving passengers of an Uruguayan airliner which crashed in the Chilean Andes, the film begins with a bang with an extremely well-staged crash sequence. Most of the passengers were members of an Uruguayan rugby team and their captain (Spano) quickly takes charge of the situation. Soon his leadership fails and falls into the hands of the firebrand, Hawke. The film bogs down a little towards the middle, occasionally straying into the haze of religious piety. Overall, however, the film is an exciting testament to the power of the human spirit to survive in absolutely untenable conditions. ★★★

Alive and Kicking

(1996, 98 min, GB, Nancy Meckler) *Jason Flemyng, Dorothy Tutin, Antony Sher, Anthony Higgens.* A gay love story about a most unlikely couple. Tonio (Flemyng) is a young ballet dancer at the height of his career working with a dance troupe whose ranks have been decimated by AIDS. Flamboyant and narcissistic, the handsome Tonio uses his tongue and his single-minded commitment to his career as a shield against others. Now sick himself with an AIDS-related illness, he continues to prepare for the ballet "Indian Summer." He also becomes attracted to Jack (Sher), a short, bald, middle-aged therapist. Despite their differences in age, they fall in love. Written for the screen by Martin Sherman ("Bent"), this moving tale of endurance, survival and the redemptive power of love is deeply affecting despite the pedestrian handling by the director. The acting by the leads (as well as by Higgens in a small role as Tonio's dying mentor) is dynamic. (aka: *Indian Summer*) ★★★ VHS: $59.99; DVD: $24.99

All about Eve

(1950, 138 min, US, Joseph L. Mankiewicz) *Bette Davis, Anne Baxter, George Sanders, Celeste Holm,* *Gary Merrill, Hugh Marlowe, Thelma Ritter, Marilyn Monroe.* The Bette Davis classic, which still remains the definitive Hollywood movie about theatre life. Bette, in what is possibly the quintessential Davis role, stars as Margo Channing, a first lady of the theatre whose professional and personal life is changed forever when a seemingly starstruck young woman (Baxter) enters her life. A brilliantly scathing, enormously witty look behind the masks of the players who strut and fret their hour upon the stage. Holm, Sanders and Ritter are all superb in supporting roles. ★★★★ VHS: $14.99; DVD: $24.99

All about My Mother

(1999, 101 min, Spain, Pedro Almodóvar) *Cecilia Roth, Marisa Paredes, Candela Peña, Antonia San Juan, Penélope Cruz.* A sweet, funny, big-hearted valentine of a film, dedicated to "actresses who have played actresses," Almodóvar's Academy Award-winning (Best Foreign Film) melodrama at once recalls the best of those '50s Douglas Sirk movies while at the same time examining — in quintessential Almodóvar style — lives of the disenfranchised. Roth is wondrous as a mother who, mourning the death of her teenaged son, journeys back to a forgotten past and searches for the boy's father — now a transvestite prostitute. Paredes brings sublime elegance to the role of a legendary stage actress whom Roth befriends. A joyous celebration of diversity, motherhood and the theatre, this is Almodóvar at his best. (Spanish with English subtitles) ★★★★ VHS: $21.99; DVD: $29.99

All Dogs Go to Heaven

(1989, 85 min, US, Don Bluth) *Voices of: Burt Reynolds, Loni Anderson, Dom DeLuise, Melba Moore, Vic Tayback, Charles Nelson Reilly, Judith Barsi.* Charming animated tale about a roguish German shepherd who becomes the unlikely guardian to an orphaned girl named Anne Marie. Beautiful visuals from Don Bluth and company (*An American Tail*). ★★★ VHS: $14.99; DVD: $14.99

All Dogs Go to Heaven 2

(1996, 82 min, US, Paul Sebella & Larry Leker) *Voices of: Charlie Sheen, Dom DeLuise, Sheena Easton, Ernest Borgnine, George Hearn, Bebe Neuwirth.* Reprieved from the original film, Charlie is bored by Heaven and longs to leave. He gets his chance when Gabriel's horn accidentally falls to Earth and must be rescued. Reunited with his old friend Itchy, the two return to Earth where a devilish cat bestows them with earthly bodies. In a rather half-hearted plot, all the elements are entwined into a resolution that provides Charlie with some sort of newfound ethics. The passable animation and questionable story line create a lackluster movie. ★★ VHS: $14.99; DVD: $14.99

All Fall Down

(1962, 110 min, US, John Frankenheimer) *Warren Beatty, Karl Malden, Angela Lansbury, Eva Marie Saint, Brandon de Wilde, Barbara Baxley.* Adapted for the screen by William Inge, *All Fall Down* centers on a dysfunctional Cleveland family headed by alcoholic father Malden and domineering mother Lansbury. Beatty, looking impossibly young and handsome, is the eldest son Berry-berry, a louse of a drifter who returns home at the insistence of his idolizing brother de Wilde. Director Frankenheimer concentrates on the dark side of the American family, exploring a bruised familial psyche with numerous open wounds. And thanks to its perceptive direction and script, the film cuts deeper than the usual Gothic drama. It's Lansbury who walks away with the acting honors, though Baxley is fine in a small but potent role as one of Beatty's pick-ups. ★★★½ VHS: $19.99

All I Wanna Do

(1999, 97 min, US, Sarah Kernochan) *Kirsten Dunst, Gaby Hoffmann, Lynn Redgrave, Heather Matarazzo, Rachael Leigh Cook, Thomas Guiry.* The most attractive cast of young women outside of the horror genre is unfortunately dumped into this confused movie about a girls' school. Godard's School for Girls is out of money and going co-ed, unless the girls can stop the merger. *All I Wanna Do* (formerly titled *Strike!*) tries to be a sweet coming-of-age film of female bonding, but any sincerity is sorely tested by a climax that involves a choir of boys vomiting on everything. Despite the eye candy of Dunst, Hoffmann and Cook, this *Strike* couldn't end any sooner. ★½ VHS: $14.99; DVD: $29.99

All Night Long

(1981, 88 min, US, Jean-Claude Tramont) *Barbra Streisand, Gene Hackman, Dennis Quaid, Diane*

All about My Mother

All Quiet on the Western Front

Ladd, William Daniels. An offbeat and marvelous comic romp with Hackman in great form as an all-night drugstore manager who begins an affair with his neighbor's sexually frustrated wife (Streisand). She, in turn, is involved with Hackman's teenage son (Quaid). A small gem, and vastly underrated. ★★★½

All of Me

(1984, 93 min, US, Carl Reiner) *Steve Martin, Lily Tomlin, Victoria Tennant, Madolyn Smith, Richard Libertini.* Reincarnation, the hereafter, gurus and modern romance are all equally spoofed in director Reiner's splendidly funny romp which offered Martin his first real chance to prove his immense comic abilities. Tomlin costars as a dying, rich invalid whose belief in returning from the dead prompts some hasty legal maneuvering. This sends lawyer Martin to her side. But in a strange turn of events, Tomlin's soul has now been transported into the body of Martin, who only wants her out. As the inspired silliness continues, Martin engages in a battle of cosmic wills with his spiritual houseguest. Though the premise and its execution are engaging, it is really Martin's virtuoso performance which distinguishes the film. Martin literally gets in touch with both his masculine and feminine sides as he fights Tomlin for control of his body, sending him on a hilarious, slapstick search for inner tranquility. ★★★½ VHS: $6.99; DVD: $24.99

All over Me

(1997, 90 min, US, Alex Sichel) *Alison Folland, Tara Subkoff, Wilson Cruz, Cole Hauser, Leisha Hailey.* This first feature film from the Sichel sisters (Alex directed, Sylvia wrote) is a painfully tender and knowing tale of one 15-year-old girl's emerging lesbian sexuality. Set in New York's Hell's Kitchen, the story follows Claude (Folland), a high schooler secretly in love with her best friend Ellen (Subkoff), a straight gal

who in turn falls for a thuggish homophobe. How Claude deals with the emotional pain of unrequited first love as well as having to deal with coming out is the involving drama's central tale. *All over Me* is told with grit and real emotion. ★★★ VHS: $19.99

All Quiet on the Western Front

(1930, 130 min, US, Lewis Milestone) *Lew Ayres, Louis Wolheim, Slim Summerville, Beryl Mercer.* Milestone won an Oscar as Best Director for this classic antiwar film based on the Erich Maria Remarque novel about the experiences of a group of young German soldiers in battle during WWI. The film won an Oscar for Best Picture, and Ayres became a star with his haunting portrayal of the young infantryman. In supporting roles, Summerville and especially Wolheim are terrific as Ayres' fellow soldiers. (A made-for-TV version was made in 1979 with Richard Thomas and Ernest Borgnine.) ★★★★ VHS: $14.99; DVD: $24.99

All Screwed Up

(1973, 105 min, Italy, Lina Wertmüller) *Luigi Diberti, Nino Bignamini.* Two young men, orphans from the countryside, come to the big city (here Milan) looking for fame and fortune. Upon their arrival, they get arrested, swindled and fall in love, eventually living in a commune with three women while all their romantic and professional aspirations experience ups and downs. Wertmüller's social comedy — made before her more well-known and accomplished works — has its appealing moments, especially when the director allows her camera to sit still and concentrate on the characters' interpersonal relationships. But much of the film is static, and in an effort to demonstrate the frenzy of city life, the story becomes victim to what it is satirizing. The video release is badly dubbed, which doesn't help the film's coherency. ★★

All That Jazz

(1979, 119 min, US, Bob Fosse) *Roy Scheider, Ann Reinking, Jessica Lange, Ben Vereen, Leland Palmer, Cliff Gorman, John Lithgow, Keith Gordon.* Fosse's dynamic and semiautobiographical tribute to the rigors and razzle-dazzle of showbiz. Scheider portrays Fosse's self-absorbed alter ego whose creativity is well matched by his destructive excesses. Lange is a most appealing Angel of Death. Film includes some brilliant, unparalleled dance sequences. ★★★½

All the King's Men

(1949, 109 min, US, Robert Rossen) *Broderick Crawford, Mercedes McCambridge, John Ireland, Joanne Dru, John Derek.* A Best Picture Oscar went to this searing adaptation of Robert Penn Warren's Pulitzer Prize-winning novel about the rise and fall of a Huey Long-like politician. Academy Award winner Crawford gives the performance of a lifetime as the power-crazed senator. McCambridge also won an Oscar for her rich portrayal of his devoted secretary. ★★★★ VHS: $19.99; DVD: $24.99

All the Mornings of the World
(Tous les Matins du Monde)

(1991, 114 min, France, Alain Corneau) *Gérard Depardieu, Guillaume Depardieu.* Elaborately costumed and acted yet filmed in an almost serene fashion, this story of creativity, passion and betrayal between two composers in 17th-century

France should prove to be of interest to serious film lovers and of greater appeal to lovers of classical music. Marin Marais (Depardieu), a successful composer at the Court of Versailles, painfully looks back into his youth and his volatile relationship with his taciturn music teacher. Told in flashbacks with Depardieu's son, Guillaume, playing the younger Marais, the story explores the contentious relationship between the prodigious student and his gifted teacher Sainte Colombe. Studied and intense, the film's greatest moments occur in the stirring chords of its passionate Baroque music. (French with English subtitles) ★★★½ VHS: $19.99

All the President's Men

(1976, 138 min, US, Alan J. Pakula) *Robert Redford, Dustin Hoffman, Jason Robards, Jack Warden, Jane Alexander, Martin Balsam, Hal Holbrook, Ned Beatty, F. Murray Abraham.* The film that successfully captures the heady paranoia of the Watergate years. Journalism departments' enrollments skyrocketed after the Woodward-Bernstein team, who broke the Watergate story in *The Washington Post*, were portrayed in this film by Redford and Hoffman. Superlative support (including Oscar-winner Robards), an Oscar-winning script by William Goldman and taut, incisive direction by Pakula are woven together to produce an intelligent, blistering account of political chicanery and investigative prowess. Yes, this is the first time you asked the question, "What did the President know and when did he know it?" ★★★★ VHS: $14.99; DVD: $19.99

All the Pretty Horses

(2000, 112 min, US, Billy Bob Thornton) *Matt Damon, Henry Thomas, Penélope Cruz, Lucas Black, Rubén Blades, Miriam Colon, Sam Shepard, Robert Patrick, Bruce Dern.* The wide-opened vistas of Texas and Mexico set the tone for a picturesque tale of a West in transition, but the majestic scenery can't compensate for a thin story of romance, friendship and the search for adventure. Based on the acclaimed novel by Cormac McCarthy, the film — set in 1949 — follows cowboy John Grady Cole (Damon) as he and best friend Lacey Rawlins (Thomas) leave their San Antonio birthplace for the unknown wilds of Mexico. Finding work as a horse wrangler at a sprawling hacienda, Cole soon begins a forbidden love affair with the beautiful daughter (Cruz) of his cattle-baron boss. Though the film features beautiful cinematography and an involving subplot of a jailed comrade, *All the Pretty Horses* offers little else for the eye or the heart. Its romantic scenes lack sizzle, mainly due to the minor chemistry between Damon and Cruz, and the pacing veers towards lethargic. Thornton has assembled a good ensemble, however; what they do may not be all that interesting, but everyone sure seems sincere doing it. ★★ VHS: $14.99; DVD: $24.99

All the Right Moves

(1983, 91 min, US, Michael Chapman) *Tom Cruise, Craig T. Nelson, Lea Thompson, Christopher Penn.* An earnest Cruise plays a Pennsylvania high school football star who sees an athletic scholarship as a way out of his small mining town. Nelson also stars as his hot-tempered coach himself looking for a ticket out. Predictable, uneventful but slickly directed and performed. ★★ VHS: $9.99

All the Vermeers in New York

(1990, 87 min, US, Jon Jost) *Stephen Lack, Emmanuelle Chaulet, Gracie Mansion, Gordon Joseph Weiss.* Radical independent filmmaker Jost presents an austere, amusing jab at wealthy New Yorkers and the commodification of art in this story of a lonely stockbroker (Lack) who becomes obsessed with a wispy, emotionally reserved French actress (Chaulet) after he meets her in the Vermeer Room of the Metropolitan Museum. With an almost cinema verité starkness, the film uncovers the hollow lives of Manhattan's power brokers and effectively unmasks their haughty pretenses. In a clear juxaposition, Jost cuts from Lack at his brokerage job to a spirited conversation between a gallery owner (Mansion) and a struggling artist (Weiss) who is begging her for a $10,000 advance — it's a marvelously subversive interplay of images. Exquisitely shot, the film features an excellent jazz score by the Bay Area Jazz Composers Orchestra. ★★★ VHS: $19.99; DVD: $29.99

All This, and Heaven Too

(1940, 143 min, US, Anatole Litvak) *Bette Davis, Charles Boyer, Jeffrey Lynn, June Lockhart.* Handsomely produced tearjerker starring Davis and Boyer with Boyer as a 19th-century Paris aristocrat who murders his wife after falling in love with his children's governess (Davis). Great performances by the two leads. ★★★ VHS: $19.99

All Through the Night

(1942, 107 min, US, Vincent Sherman) *Humphrey Bogart, William Demarest, Peter Lorre, Phil Silvers, Jackie Gleason, Frank McHugh, Judith Anderson.* Before he tangled with Nazis in *Casablanca*, Bogart took on German spies right here in the USA. Bogey plays Gloves Donahue, a hotshot Manhattan gambler whose investigation into the murder of an old family friend leads him hot on the trail of a Nazi spy ring. With its Runyonesque characters, sparkling dialogue, snappy one-liners and detestable villains, this comic espionage thriller is a supremely enjoyable lark. Bogey is in great form and is given first-rate support. ★★★½ VHS: $19.99

Allegro non Troppo

(1976, 75 min, Italy, Bruno Bozzetto) Italian animation artist Bozzetto offers his own answer to Walt Disney's *Fantasia*. This delightfully whimsical work features a variety of bizarre creatures cavorting to the music of Debussy, Dvorak, Ravel, Sibelius, Vivaldi and Stravinsky. ★★★½ VHS: $29.99

The Alley Cats

(1966, 83 min, France, Radley Metzger) The swinging '60s have never looked so sexy, fun and erotic as in Metzger's second solo feature *The Alley Cats*. When Leslie, a member of Europe's wealthy swinging set, feels ignored by her fiancée Logan (who is in the midst of a tempestuous affair with Leslie's friend Agnes), she decides to do some swinging herself. Her first lover, the suave, debonair Christian, pleases her greatly, but is soon called away on business. Frustrated, Leslie responds to the advances of Irena, a beautiful lesbian socialite. Soon she must choose between her fiancée Logan and her awakened lesbian feelings. This newly remastered video, presented in widescreen Ultrascope, features a scintillating, jazzy lounge music soundtrack. ★★★ VHS: $19.99; DVD: $24.99

Alligator

(1980, 94 min, US, Lewis Teague) *Robert Forster, Robin Riker, Henry Silva, Michael Gazzo, Dean Jagger.* John Sayles wrote the screenplay for this tongue-in-cheek, very entertaining horror film about a giant alligator terrorizing the populace of Chicago. (Those stories about gators being flushed down the toilet are obviously true.) ★★★

Alligator Eyes

(1990, 101 min, US, John Feldman) *Annabelle Larsen, Roger Cabler, Allen McCullough.* A trio of friends hit the road to try and get away from it all but wind up deep in the middle of something else when they pick up a mysterious, sexy hitchhiker. Tensions between the four well-conceived characters mount as their relationships are tested and secrets are revealed. Though the film has an intriguing premise that never fully delivers on its potential, the engaging performances by a cast of unknowns and the film's good use of settings along the Outer Banks of North Carolina make it a trip worth taking. ★★★ VHS: $79.99

The Alligator People

(1959, 74 min, US, Roy Del Ruth) *Beverly Garland, George Macready, Lon Chaney, Jr.* Cheesy horror semiclassic about a doctor who discovers a serum enabling humans to grow back amputated parts of their bodies — guess what the side effects are. ★★ VHS: $14.99

Allonsanfan

(1974, 100 min, Italy, Paolo & Vittorio Taviani) *Marcello Mastroianni, Lea Massari, Mimsy Farmer.* The year 1816 finds Europe settling into a conservative period after the upheavals of the Napoleonic era. This unusual time is the setting for the Taviani brothers' lavish yet intelligent political costume drama. Mastroianni is Giulio, a petite bourgeois who returns to the new European order after spending time in prison. Disillusioned by what he sees, he becomes torn between his comfortable upbringing and his revolutionary ideals. Mastroianni excels as the spineless aristocrat who must decide between loyalty to his old radical compatriots or betrayal of them for personal gain. (Italian with English subtitles) ★★★½

Almonds and Raisins

(1984, 85 min, US, Russ Karel) *Narrated by: Orson Welles.* A delightful account of the history of a once-flourishing segment of American moviemaking: the Yiddish cinema. From 1927 through 1939, some 300 Yiddish films — including musicals, gangster films, screwball comedies and even a Yiddish western — were produced for the teeming New York Jewish immigrants. Few of these films exist in their entirety, but through film clips and interviews with surviving actors, directors and producers, filmmaker Karel has fashioned an enthralling image of this lost industry and culture. ★★★½ VHS: $79.99

Almost Famous

(2000, 123 min, US, Cameron Crowe) *Billy Crudup, Patrick Fugit, Kate Hudson, Frances McDormand, Jason Lee, Anna Paquin, Philip Seymour Hoffman, Fairuza Balk, Noah Taylor.* On the heels of his enormously successful *Jerry Maguire*, writer-director Crowe turns to a page of his own youth with this warm and winning comic portrait of coming-of-age amid rock's golden age. Crowe's alter ego is William Miller (engagingly played by Fugit), a 15-year-old aspiring writer who — sight unseen — lands a freelance writing assignment with *Rolling Stone* to accompany the fictitious group Stillwater on tour (Crowe actually traveled with Led Zeppelin). This smalltown boy gets a big-time lesson in the ways of the world when he meets and befriends a fractured family unit of inner and outer circle members, including the sweet-natured Penny Lane (Hudson), a "band-aid" who's in love with the band's guitarist. Crowe has captured the cadence and minutiae of the early 1970s with remarkable precision; this is a special place in time for the director, and he leaves little doubt as to its appeal. The ensemble assembled is first-rate: Crudup is a picture-perfect incarnation of an arrogant but likable rocker; Hudson is nothing short of smashing as Penny, with whom William experiences his first crush; and possibly best of all is the unflinching

Almost Famous

Amateur

McDormand as William's overprotective mother. What a time to come of age, and what a splendid reminiscence this is — hail, hail rock 'n' roll. ★★★★ VHS: $19.99; DVD: $26.99

Almost You

(1984, 96 min, US, Adam Brooks) *Brooke Adams, Griffin Dunne, Karen Young, Josh Mostel.* Mostel's wonderful supporting turn nearly makes this mediocre romantic comedy worth watching. Too bad the rest of the cast can't accomplish as much. Dunne plays a New York executive who begins an affair with his injured wife's nurse. ★★ VHS: $79.99

Along Came a Spider

(2001, 104 min, US, Lee Tamahori) *Morgan Freeman, Monica Potter, Michael Wincott, Mika Boorem, Dylan Baker, Penelope Ann Miller, Michael Moriarty, Jay O. Sanders.* Based on the first book in James Patterson's Alex Cross series, this convoluted prequel to 1997's *Kiss the Girls* brings back Freeman as the noted forensics detective, and the actor absolutely shines as the sleuthing shrink Cross. Freeman endows the good doctor with such wisdom and humanity that his appearing in this tangled thriller is a crime almost worthy of an investigation by Cross himself. Cross is brought in on the case of the kidnapping of a U.S. senator's young daughter. He teams with the Secret Service agent (Potter) who was assigned to look after the youngster. As the kidnapper plays cat and mouse with Cross, the detective tries to piece together what little clues he has to locate the girl. Director Tamahori gives the film a polished look and maintains a modicum of suspense throughout. But neither competent direction nor Freeman's graceful turn can compensate for Marc Moss' screenplay adaptation that relies too heavily on coincidence and illogical plot developments. Wincott is quite good as the kidnapper, though Potter is not believable as a government agent. ★★ VHS: $102.99; DVD: $29.99

Alphaville

(1965, 100 min, France/Italy, Jean-Luc Godard) *Eddie Constantine, Anna Karina, Akim Tamiroff, Howard Vernon.* This is quintessential Godard, complete with fragmented musical score, existential reflections, jump cuts, hyperbolic expostulation, disjointed conversations and unexpected silences. Positing the notion that a fabricated legend can communicate complex realities, Godard creates Lemmy Caution (Constantine), a chiseled-face man with a gun who's not hesitant to use it. He says he's been assigned by his newspaper (*Figaro-Pravda*) to Alphaville, a sterile, joyless urban complex, where day is as dark as night and language has no meaning, where magnificent paranoia is the correct response to abject dehumanization and routinized violence. Karina is Caution's official government tour guide, a woman of ethereal beauty and mechanical compliance, who becomes both savior and saved. Remastered print. (Letterboxed) (French with English subtitles) ★★★½ VHS: $29.99; DVD: $29.99

Alpine Fire *(Höhenfeuer)*

(1985, 117 min, Switzerland, Fredi M. Murer) *Thomas Nock, Johanna Lier.* Visually stunning and scrupulously detailed, this sublime drama is about the life and traumas of a family of four who live in near isolation in a remote area of the Alps. The film focuses on the teenage son, a mildly retarded deaf-mute whose pangs of adolescent sexual and emotional turmoil are comforted by his understanding older sister — a close bind which inevitably leads to incest. (German with English subtitles) ★★★ VHS: $79.99

Alsino and the Condor

(1982, 90 min, Nicaragua, Miguel Littin) *Dean Stockwell, Alan Esquivel.* The recipient of the Best Feature awards at the L.A. Filmex and the Moscow International Film Festival, this remarkably moving drama concerns the abrupt abduction of a young boy in a battle-scarred Nicaraguan village. Chilean director Littin strikes a rueful, poetic tone and the expressive face of Esquivel (as Alsino) captures the searing pain of a stolen childhood. (Spanish with English subtitles) ★★★½

Altered States

(1980, 120 min, US, Ken Russell) *William Hurt, Blair Brown, Bob Balaban, Charles Haid, Drew Barrymore.* This fantastic assault on the senses is one of Russell's best films. In his first starring role, Hurt portrays an inquisitive scientist who experiments with powerful mind-altering drugs in a quest for his primal self. Gradually, he undergoes a series of mental and physical transformations and experiences some spine-chilling hallucinations. Paddy Chayefsky's novel is brought to life with the help of some shocking, state-of-the-art special effects. And though Chayefsky disowned the film, and had his name removed, this is nevertheless an unforgettable film experience. Haid is terrific as one of Hurt's disbelieving colleagues. ★★★★ VHS: $9.99; DVD: $14.99

Always

(1985, 105 min, US, Henry Jaglom) *Henry Jaglom, Patrice Townsend, Andre Gregory.* One of director Jaglom's most accomplished and accessible works, this funny, semiautobiographical comedy examines the interaction of three couples spending the July 4th holiday together. As usual, Jaglom unflinchingly bares his soul in front of the camera to present a discourse on the modern relationship. ★★★ VHS: $14.99

Always

(1989, 121 min, US, Steven Spielberg) *Richard Dreyfuss, Holly Hunter, John Goodman, Audrey Hepburn, Brad Johnson.* A glossy, over-produced, technically superior remake of the 1943 Spencer Tracy/Irene Dunne favorite, *A Guy Named Joe.* Dreyfuss, in the Tracy role, stars as a dedicated Montana forest firefighter who dies in the line of duty, only to return to guide (spiritually) an apprentice firefighter — who happens to be romantically involved with the woman (Hunter) he left behind. Though the story lapses into sappy sentimentality, the strength of this Spielberg film is the conviction which a mostly talented cast brings to it. (Letterboxed) ★★½ VHS: $14.99; DVD: $24.99

Amadeus

(1984, 158 min, US, Milos Forman) *Tom Hulce, F. Murray Abraham, Jeffrey Jones, Elizabeth Berridge, Simon Callow.* Forman's masterful adaptation of Peter Shaffer's Broadway smash is a literate, humorous and visually stunning examination of the rivalry (albeit a fictional one) between musical genius Wolfgang Amadeus Mozart and court composer Antonio Salieri in 18th-century Vienna. Abraham is brilliant as the tortured Salieri, and Hulce is equally commanding as the childish Mozart. Winner of eight Academy Awards including Picture, Director and Actor (Abraham). (Letterboxed VHS available for $19.99) ★★★★ VHS: $14.99; DVD: $19.99

Amarcord

(1974, 127 min, Italy, Federico Fellini) *Magali Noel, Bruno Zanin.* Fellini uses a gentle mixture of dreamlike fantasy and bittersweet cynicism in this autobiographical examination of a small Italian town. Young Zanin (the director's alter ego) hangs out with his friends, gets in trouble, obsesses over women, and attempts to figure out his life. On the surface, the film is a funny and warm coming-of-age story (Fellini's recollection of facing a father confessor as an adolescent boy is alone worth the price of rental). But the specter of Fascism that looms throughout the picture raises complex and challenging questions. One of Fellini's most accessible and compelling films. (Italian with English subtitles) ★★★★ VHS: $29.99; DVD: $39.99

Amateur

(1995, 105 min, US, Hal Hartley) *Isabelle Huppert, Martin Donovan, Elina Löwensohn, Damian Young.* Huppert stars in this black comedy of errors about a wannabe-nymphomaniacal ex-nun who discovers an amnesiac (Donovan) left for dead on the streets of New York City. She becomes determined to unlock the mystery of his identity. Along the way, the two encounter such urban denizens as a vengeance-seeking porn star (Löwensohn), a pair of corporate assassins, and an accountant on the verge of a nervous breakdown — each holding a piece of the puzzle. Hartley's deliberately kinky examination of sex, love, identity and intimacy is more plot-driven than his earlier works, but still relies too much on having the characters speak their thoughts. However, the performances are uniformly good and the story line is quirky and appealing. ★★★ VHS: $89.99

A

Amazing Grace (Hessed Mufla)

(1992, 95 min, Israel, Amos Gutman) Set in Tel
Aviv, this intense, melancholy drama focuses on
Jonathan, a gangly and romantic gay teenager
who faces an early-life crisis when he finds himself abandoned by his lover. The youth's passions are rekindled after he befriends Thomas,
the handsome, HIV-positive older son of his
upstairs neighbor. Their budding yet tentative
relationship provides the backdrop for this
ambitious, thought-provoking social and sexual
drama which touches upon such issues as AIDS,
death, drug abuse, the gay milieu of Tel Aviv
and family dysfunction. (Hebrew with English
subtitles) ★★★ VHS: $39.99

Amazing Grace and Chuck

(1987, 115 min, US, Mike Newell) *Jamie Lee
Curtis, Gregory Peck, Alex English, William L.
Petersen.* Engaging if far-reaching Capra-esque
drama about a 12-year-old little league champ
who trades the athletic field for the political
arena when he refuses to play in protest of
nuclear arms. Soon, other athletes the world
over follow his lead. ★★½

The Amazing Panda Adventure

(1995, 90 min, US, Christopher Cain) *Stephen
Lang, Ryan Slater, Yi Ding.* Set against the magnificent backdrop of the Chinese countryside,
this story of the rescue of a panda cub has sensational scenery, lots of action and plenty of
pandas (both real and animatronic), but both
the acting and the screenplay are lackluster. A
young American boy (Slater) is sent to China to
visit his father (Lang), a panda protectionist
who is consumed by his work. Upon his arrival,
they are both off in pursuit of poachers who
have kidnapped a baby panda. The boy and the
translator, a young Chinese girl, are separated
along with the cub and attempt to find their way
back to civilization. ★★ VHS: $14.99

Amazon Women on the Moon

(1986, 85 min, US, John Landis) *Rosanna
Arquette, Griffin Dunne, Paul Bartel, Michelle
Pfeiffer, Arsenio Hall, David Alan Grier.*
Inconsistent series of vignettes is meant to evoke
the feeling of channel surfing through 57 channels of TV schlock. While some sequences are
genuinely hysterical and feature interesting
cameos (Russ Meyer as a video store clerk), the
central joke of a hokey sci-fi movie drags on way
too long. You'll be reaching for the fast-forward
button. ★★ VHS: $9.99

American Beauty

(1999, 122 min, US, Sam Mendes) *Kevin Spacey,
Annette Bening, Thora Birch, Chris Cooper, Wes
Bentley, Peter Gallagher, Mena Suvari, Allison Janney,
Scott Bakula, Sam Robards.* Satirizing the dark
recesses, or at least the banal conformity, of suburbia has been a frequent target for American
comedies. Few, however, have succeeded as
potently as *American Beauty*, a scathing, acerbic,
almost deadpan bit of hilarity whose pulse is
squarely tapped in to. Like William Holden's Joe
Gillis in *Sunset Boulevard*, Spacey's Lester
Burnham narrates from the grave, a wonderful
conceit that sets the tone for this pinpoint satire.
Lester is a 42-year-old ad exec fighting a losing
battle at work and home. His brittle wife Carolyn
(Bening) is more concerned with her real estate
business, and teenaged daughter Jane (Birch) is

Kevin Spacey explores his lust for Mena Suvari in *American Beauty*

embarrassed by them both. After a midlife crisis
reawakening, Lester's new attitude paves the way
for the story's scintillating comedy, whether it be
blackmailing his boss or lusting over his daughter's young girlfriend. Debuting director Mendes
(Broadway's "Cabaret") and writer Alan Ball have
found fresh ingredients for this oft-told story of
suburban unbliss, and an exceptional ensemble
brings it to full bloom. Spacey, who won a Best
Actor Oscar for his bristling portrayal, is miraculous as a doormat who finds his voice (a gleefully
mocking one), and Bening is just right as the wife
who refuses to change. This thorny rose is one
big beautiful blossom. Winner of 5 Academy
Awards, including Picture, Director and
Screenplay. ★★★★ VHS: $19.99; DVD: $26.99

American Boyfriends

(1990, 90 min, Canada, Sandy Wilson) *Margaret
Langrick, John Wildman.* A heartwarming though
ordinary sequel to the successful *My American
Cousin.* Set in 1965, this coming-of-age film
opens with three Canadian teenyboppers
searching for American adventure, good times,
and boys boys boys! What our three young thrill-
seekers end up with is an unforgettable lesson
about the meaning of friendship, love and
understanding. Featuring an upbeat soundtrack
of classic 1960s tunes. ★★½ VHS: $79.99

American Buffalo

(1996, 88 min, US, Michael Corrente) *Dustin
Hoffman, Dennis Franz, Sean Nelson.* David
Mamet's play receives mixed results courtesy of
director Corrente (*Federal Hill*). Franz plays
Don, a pawn shop owner who enlists the aid of
a troubled teen (Nelson) to help him steal from
a scam-artist customer. Teach (Hoffman), Don's
loser friend, convinces him to let him in on the
deal. As is often the case with Mamet, loyalties
shift, tempers flare, regrets are voiced and
recriminations are answered all during the
course of events until the inevitable conclusion.
All of Mamet's stylistic trademarks are here as
well: profane, hyper-real dialogue, ugly situations and desperate characters. Franz gives a
subtle performance, and Hoffman is terrific.
More than holding his own with these two vets,

Nelson proves his excellent performance in
Fresh was no fluke. The acting more than compensates for Corrente's static direction, which
lacks imagination and can't overcome an uncin-
ematic, filmed-play feel. ★★½ VHS: $14.99;
DVD: $19.99

American Dream

(1989, 100 min, US, Barbara Kopple) In this
stunning documentary, director Kopple brilliantly chronicles the long and bitter strike at
the Hormel Meat Packing plant in Austin,
Minnesota. She is able to capture some incredibly poignant and uncensored moments in the
lives of the people affected by the strike. She
shows how the Union Local steered its members
in the wrong direction, much to the consternation of the International, in pushing their
demands beyond the breaking point. But of
course, she doesn't let industry off the hook,
either, as she documents the steady lifestyle
decline of the American worker under laissez-
faire policies which put the bottom line and
greed above people and community. ★★★★
VHS: $19.99

American Dreamer

(1984, 105 min, US, Rick Rosenthal) *JoBeth
Williams, Giancarlo Giannini, Tom Conti.* Williams
stars in this endearing action-comedy about a
bored housewife who wins a trip to Paris via a
creative writing contest — thanks to the adventures of a female superspy, "Rebecca Ryan."
Once there, she's mugged, develops amnesia
and begins to think she *is* Rebecca Ryan. Cutish
romance and intrigue follow. Call this one
Romancing the Clone. ★★½

American Flyers

(1985, 113 min, US, John Badham) *Kevin
Costner, David Grant, Rae Dawn Chong, Robert
Townsend, Jennifer Grey.* Steve Tisch (*Breaking
Away*) wrote the screenplay for this involving
story about two estranged brothers (Costner
and Grant), each coming to terms with the
death of their father, who enter a grueling
three-day bicycle race in the Colorado Rockies.
★★½ VHS: $14.99; DVD: $14.99

The American Friend

(1977, 127 min, US/France/Germany, Wim Wenders) Bruno Ganz, Dennis Hopper, Lisa Kreuzer, Sam Fuller, Nicholas Ray. Complexities abound when a mysterious American go-between (Hopper) lures a dying man (Ganz) into a cunning game of murder and revenge. Director Wenders illustrates his favorite themes of anomie, mortality and cultural infiltration. Based on a "Ripley" novel by Patricia Highsmith. (English and German with English subtitles) ★★★

American Gigolo

(1980, 117 min, US, Paul Schrader) Richard Gere, Lauren Hutton, Hector Elizondo, Bill Duke. Gere plays Julian Kaye, a shallow, narcissistic, high-priced prostitute who becomes involved with a senator's wife (Hutton). As their affair gets steamy and serious, Gere is framed for the murder of one of his clients. And the only person who could help him — Hutton — can't. Writer-director Schrader seems to enjoy wallowing in the sleaze of Los Angeles' underbelly of pimps, addicts and whores; though he unsuccessfully tries to masquerade his tale with a pretentious and artsy examination of one man's failure to find himself. Stylish and empty. Elizondo hits just the right note as a determined detective on Gere's case. ★★ VHS: $9.99; DVD: $29.99

American Graffiti

(1973, 110 min, US, George Lucas) Richard Dreyfuss, Paul LeMat, Ron Howard, Cindy Williams, Charles Martin Smith, Mackenzie Phillips, Harrison Ford. This film turns back the clock to a summer night in 1962 — wait! This film isn't like the rest; it's the first and best of its kind. In this classic comedy, we spend the evening with a couple of teens who are getting together before leaving for college in the fall. Most of the cast is famous now, not to mention the director, who went on to do this minor space movie. Great performances, a great score and a great feel to it. (VHS available letterboxed or pan & scan) ★★★★ VHS: $14.99; DVD: $29.99

American Heart

(1993, 117 min, US, Martin Bell) Jeff Bridges, Edward Furlong, Lucinda Jenny. Director Bell picks up where Streetwise, his gripping 1984 documentary about Seattle street kids, left off with this hard-edged, brutally honest depiction of an ex-convict father and his teenage son scrapping for both a living and reconciliation. In a startling performance, Bridges plays a recently paroled jewel thief who is reunited with his estranged son (Furlong). The two move into a sleazy Seattle apartment building living amongst the city's underbelly and forgotten classes. As Bridges attempts to go straight and, however improbably, act as head of this fragile family unit, Furlong takes up with a youthful street clique, slowly entangling himself in a life of petty crime. American Heart is unflinching in its realistic portrayal of life on the edge, and only misses the mark at the very end with an unsatisfactory finale. Bridges' stinging portrayal is smartly complemented by Furlong's anguished dreamer. ★★★½ VHS: $9.99

American History X

(1998, 117 min, US, Tony Kaye) Edward Norton, Edward Furlong, Beverly D'Angelo, Jennifer Lien, Fairuza Balk, Elliott Gould, Stacy Keach. An uneven but powerful drama of racism, American History X was the focus of a post-production battle between director Kaye and New Line studio (Kaye wanted a different cut of the film released). The studio won out. Norton plays a white supremacist, neo-Nazi skinhead whose charisma and strength make him a hero to his younger brother (Furlong). After finishing a prison term (for the murder of a young black man, a gruesome scene shown in flashback), Norton is a changed man, much to the chagrin of his sibling, girlfriend and fascist friends. It's difficult to tell if this studio version is improved or weakened, because it's so hot and cold. Norton's commanding, riveting performance, however, rescues potentially pretentious moments, making the stronger scenes much more powerful. While the screenplay doesn't quite convince us of Norton's transformation in prison, that segment remains engrossing. ★★★ VHS: $19.99; DVD: $24.99

An American in Paris

(1951, 102 min, US, Vincente Minnelli) Gene Kelly, Leslie Caron, Nina Foch, Oscar Levant. The glorious music of George and Ira Gershwin and the incomparable dancing/choreography of Gene Kelly combine to make this one of the most accomplished musicals of all time. Gene plays an artist living in post-WWII Paris who is torn between waif Caron and patron. Academy Award for Best Picture. ★★★★ VHS: $14.99; DVD: $19.99

American Me

(1992, 125 min, US, Edward James Olmos) Edward James Olmos, William Forsythe, Pepe Serna, Danny De La Paz. Olmos makes an impressive directorial debut with this good-looking if heavily dramatic and clichéd prison/gang drama. Olmos stars as Santana Montoya, a Mexican youth who is incarcerated, and from his lengthy stay behind bars becomes the leader of the Mexican mafia of Folsom Prison. With the aid of his two childhood buddies (Forsythe and Serna), Montoya rules with an iron fist. On his release, however, he finds it difficult to go straight, and becomes another victim to injustice as he is unable to escape his murderous past. Though anti-gang in theme, Olmos seems to relish the violence he is protesting. A brutal, dark work that, at least, has something to say. ★★½ VHS: $9.99

American Movie

(1999, 107 min, US, Chris Smith) Mark Borchardt, Mike Schank. Mark Borchardt is a 30ish man from Menominee Falls, where every T-shirt tells a story. He tells documentarian Smith that it's no longer time to drink and dream, but to create and complete. His planned tribute to his home town, Northwestern, has been in preproduction for six years, lacking a script, a cast and funding. This spiritual heir to Herschell Gordon Lewis sometimes works on the script in his car at the airport parking lot to avoid distractions (the mother of his three children, whom he doesn't want to marry; the expectations of his parents, with whom he lives; and letter after letter demanding payment now). Whatever his failings, Mark is a trooper: scrabbling against a sea of mediocrity and despair, attempting to raise money from suspicious relatives, with grandiose plans in various nascent stages of actualization. Director Smith wisely lets Borchardt do the talking, constructing his life scene after scene. It never seems to occur to him that the documentarians are making their film while he's talking about his. In fact, everyone seems to accept the cameras with the same insouciance as the Bouviers in Grey Gardens. Smith has delivered a riveting glimpse into an R. Crumb world of muddled thinking, ill-formed beliefs and thwarted endeavors. ★★★½ VHS: $21.99; DVD: $27.99

American Pie

(1999, 95 min, US, Paul Weitz) Jason Biggs, Chris Klein, Thomas Ian Nichols, Eddie Kaye Thomas, Natasha Lyonne, Shannon Elizabeth, Eugene Levy. Though it may forever be remembered for discovering new uses for apple pie, American Pie is a consistently funny, often raunchy teen comedy that manages to capture the essence of coming-of-age while offering a succession of hilariously rude sex jokes and familiar teen shenanigans. Four friends make a vow to lose their virginity by the Senior Prom. Each goes about the task in amusing sketches of seduction, impersonation, voyeurism and public relations as the final hour draws near. Director Weitz and writer Adam Herz delight in their naughty concoction, tweaking the noses of good taste and cliché with just the right balance of travesty, cleverness and hormonal longing. The story isn't always as cutting as it wants to be, but comparisons to There's Something about Mary are inevitable. And with scenes of pastry fornication, spunk beer (don't ask) and Internet spying, it comes awful close. Klein makes the best impression as a jock who infiltrates enemy territory: the choir! Unrated version. ★★★ VHS: $14.99; DVD: $24.99

American Pimp

(2000, 87 min, US, The Hughes Brothers) Noted Hollywood outsiders the Hughes Brothers have bucked the system once again with this unflinching and brutally honest "mackumentary" that examines a staple of many urban communities: the pimp. Comprised of skillfully conducted interviews with real-life pimps, and heavily peppered with film clips from blaxploitation movies from the '70s, American Pimp asserts that many stereotypes revolving around this segment of society are firmly grounded in truth. Opening with a montage of "the man" dissing pimp morality, the film jumps across several major U.S. cities to introduce some amazing characters with mesmerizing wardrobes and more gold than Fort Knox. One pimp, Bishop Don "Magic" Juan, gave up pimping for the ministry, another went into telemarketing. But all offer zero apologies for their choice of lifestyle. Sure to provoke, the film is bubbling over with nimble verbal gymnastics, whether visiting the Player's Ball (an annual pimp convention where stables of "ho's" are displayed) or allowing these self-promoting provocateurs center stage. Grab a bottle of Cristal and chill out on your favorite leopard-skin rug, for this is badder than a muhfuh. ★★★½ VHS: $9.99; DVD: $19.99

American Pop

(1981, 96 min, US, Ralph Bakshi) After the success of Fritz the Cat and the failures of Coonskin and Lord of the Rings, renegade animator Bakshi decided to tackle the entire history of popular music, starting with Tin Pan Alley and ending in the bloated rock arena of the 1970s. Surprisingly, he makes quite a good job of it, too, cataloging the amorality that fuels this art form and so often destroys it. Bakshi's rotoscoping brings to life some great vocal characterizations. And while the script, in attempting to cover so many years in a brief hour and a half, must at times wield too broad a brush to render nuance, it does manage to capture eras in bold, vivid impressions. Featuring the music of Lou Reed, Jimi Hendrix, Janis Joplin, Helen Morgan and all stops in-between. ★★★½ VHS: $14.99; DVD: $29.99

The American President

(1995, 112 min, US, Rob Reiner) *Michael Douglas, Annette Bening, Martin Sheen, Michael J. Fox, Richard Dreyfuss, David Paymer, John Mahoney.* "I'm trying to savor the Capra-esque quality," Bening's enthusiastic lobbyist says as she enters the White House. "Capra-esque" also ably describes Reiner's sweet-natured romantic comedy set against the drama of Washington, D.C.'s behind-the-scenes deals and presidential procedure. Douglas plays a Democratic president up for reelection. An idealistic widower, he meets Bening when she lashes out against his policies — and in true Capra fashion love is on the horizon. Reiner balances the film with equal parts joyful romantic comedy and bristling political observations. Douglas is at his most likable, and Bening is simply irresistible. (Letterboxed VHS available for $19.99) ★★★ VHS: $14.99; DVD: $19.99

American Psycho

(2000, 103 min, US, Mary Harron) *Christian Bale, Willem Dafoe, Jared Leto, Reese Witherspoon, Samantha Mathis, Chloe Sevigny, Justin Theroux.* The self-congratulatory avarice of the '80s elegantly fused an antiseptic minimalism with a most conspicuous consumption. Patrick Bateman, played with obsessive splendor by Bale, skims with apparent effortlessness over the crest of the Reagan years' money tsunami. He's perfectly coifed and meticulously pampered, and the concentrated effort necessary to maintain the façade is starting to take its toll. No amount of consumerism can fill the void within this exquisitely wrapped, empty box. Perhaps it's the curse of self-awareness that pushes him over the line into the ultimate release of mass murder; when he looks in the mirror, nobody is there, and nothing he can do can cure his self-loathing. But is he really that different from the

people around him? His is a world of interchangable blondes on the arms of interchangable suits with interchangable sneering, vacant faces. His insanity is barely noticed in the world he inhabits, where murder is usually accomplished through merger. He is, in fact, a perfect representative of his life and times, a chameleon, essentially vapid, quintessentially banal, existentially adrift and unfettered. Director Harron has taken a dreadful book and crafted a wry entertainment, with able assistance from a picture-perfect cast. ★★★ VHS: $14.99; DVD: $26.99

The American Soldier

(1970, 80 min, Germany, Rainer Werner Fassbinder) *Ingrid Caven, Kurt Raab, Karl Scheydt.* Fassbinder pays homage to American film noir and the milieu of Samuel Fuller, Humphrey Bogart and Lemmy Caution in this atmospheric gangster pic. The story concerns the fatalistic prowlings of Rickey, a professional killer hired to bump off a few problem crooks (and then some) for the German police. (German with English subtitles) ★★★

An American Tail

(1986, 80 min, US, Don Bluth) *Voices of: Dom DeLuise, Christopher Plummer, Madeline Kahn.* A charming animated feature produced by Steven Spielberg about a young immigrant mouse who becomes separated from his family upon arrival in America, then finds all sorts of adventures with his new friends. The cute story, which is easy for little ones to follow, draws upon some serious subjects without heavy-handedness, and the animation is well done. (Followed by 3 sequels) ★★★ VHS: $14.99

An American Werewolf in London

(1981, 98 min, US, John Landis) *David Naughton, Griffin Dunne, Jenny Agutter, John Woodvine.* Two typical American lads on holiday in Europe find more adventure than they bargained for in this chilling and entertaining mirth-filled terror fest. Director Landis combines a great rock score, excellent F/X, an erotic love story and moments of inspired humor to tell the tale of a vacationing college student, David (Naughton), who is attacked by a werewolf on the moors of the English countryside. As his friend Jack (Dunne), who died in the same attack, haunts him from the grave in a gruesome series of deteriorating visits, a hallucinating David begins to doubt his own sanity until he eventually terrorizes London under the glow of the silvery full moon. Agutter is the nurse who takes a liking to David. Rick Baker was the first recipient for the newly created Oscar category of Makeup. (Sequel: *An American Werewolf in Paris*) ★★★½ VHS: $14.99; DVD: $26.99

An American Werewolf in Paris

(1997, 98 min, US, Anthony Waller) *Tom Everett Scott, Julie Delpy, Vince Vieluf.* A terrible rehash, *An American Werewolf in Paris* is so bad it could easily make one forget how good *An American Werewolf in London* is. Andy (Scott) and his buddies are traipsing around Europe trying to get laid when Andy saves Serafine (Delpy) from an attempted dive off the Eiffel Tower. It turns out she's a werewolf, and Andy soon finds himself bitten as well. He then must save his friends, save the girl, save Paris from other werewolves, and try not to eat everyone in the process.

Director Waller attempts to re-create some trademarks of John Landis' first film (dream-within-a-dream, the witty and rotting undead), but they are awkwardly executed. It's hard to get scared when your heroes are being chased by the worst computer graphics this side of "Babylon 5." ★½ VHS: $19.99; DVD: $29.99

American Women

(2000, 92 min, Ireland, Aileen Ritchie) *Ian Hart, Sean McGinley, Niamh Cusack, Ewan Stewart, Ruth McCabe.* A handful of boys-will-be-boys, Guinness-swilling slackers in a remote Donegal coastal town in Ireland decide to spice up the lackluster local female selection by placing an ad in a Miami, Florida, newspaper calling for young, sexy women to come to their town. Dull-edged, obvious wackiness ensues. While the box art and poster present the film as a horny teens gross-out comedy (the advertising is even a direct steal from seminal '80s teen comedy *Spring Break*), *American Women* is actually a watered-down, quaintly dull (and rather pandering) *Full Monty*-like social comedy. Certainly not painful to sit through, *American Women* is still pretty thin stuff; it's the kind of comedy that hopes and prays its audience finds those Irish accents hysterically quirky. (aka: *The Closer You Get*) ★★ VHS: $9.99

The Americanization of Emily

(1964, 117 min, US, Arthur Hiller) *Julie Andrews, James Garner, James Coburn, Melvyn Douglas.* Biting military satire with Garner in top form as an American naval officer who is the unwitting dupe in an admiral's plan to turn a Normandy invasion casualty into a publicity stunt. Andrews (in her first film after *Mary Poppins*) plays a British war widow who falls in love with Garner. Exceptional script by Paddy Chayefsky (based on William Bradford Huie's novel). ★★★½ VHS: $19.99

Amistad

(1997, 155 min, US, Steven Spielberg) *Morgan Freeman, Anthony Hopkins, Djimon Hounsou, Matthew McConaughey, Nigel Hawthorne, David Paymer, Pete Postlethwaite, Stellan Skarsgård.* In the same waters as his *Schindler's List*, director Spielberg once again casts an unflinching and unsentimental eye towards prejudice and its ugly consequences with this startling glimpse into an unknown chapter in American history. Based on an actual incident in 1839, the story begins as the slave ship *Amistad* speeds towards America. Under the leadership of Cinque (an impressive Hounsou), the slaves break free and kill all but two of their captors. However, they land on the shores of America, and stand trial for mutiny. They are eventually defended by former President John Quincy Adams (a brilliant Hopkins) in the film's powerful, stirring finale. Spielberg doesn't compromise in the depiction of the horrors faced by the slaves. Whether showing them shackled together en masse in the bowels of the ship (much like the Jews on their way to the camps), recalling the chilling practice of dumping chained human beings overboard, or examining the moralistic attitudes of a fledgling nation, the film works on an artistic level as well as an emotional one. Only an inconsistent narrative structure keeps this from being a classic story of injustice, though the central theme and context of the film will linger in the mind for a very long time.

Amistad

Amores Perros

(Letterboxed VHS available for $14.99) ★★★½
VHS: $9.99; DVD: $24.99

The Amityville Horror

(1979, 117 min, US, Stuart Rosenberg) *James Brolin, Margot Kidder, Rod Steiger, Don Stroud, Michael Sacks, Murray Hamilton.* Mediocre film version of Jay Anson's popular novel detailing the supposedly true-life events which led the Lutz family to leave their Long Island dream home. The film offers little of the ghostly scares produced by the book. ★½ DVD: $19.99

Amityville II: The Possession

(1982, 104 min, US, Damiano Damiani) *Burt Young, Rutanya Alda, Moses Gunn.* An awful Freudian prequel to the 1979 haunted house shocker, this time focusing on the original tenants, an "average American family" whose run-of-the-mill existence is ripped asunder by demonic possession. Senseless and curiously lethargic. ★ VHS: $14.99

Among Giants

(1999, 92 min, GB, Sam Miller) *Rachel Griffiths, Pete Postlethwaite, James Thornton.* The sad romance between Ray (Postlethwaite), an older, down-on-his-luck foreman, and Gerry (Griffiths), a reckless younger woman who joins his crew, is only mildly diverting despite the engaging stars. Writer Simon Beaufoy, who penned the hit *The Full Monty*, allows his lovers to run around naked, and talk sincerely about their fears and dreams, but this intriguing character study falls short of being truly special. The characters practically work at being unlikable as if they have to prove how meaningful their relationship is. As a fellow climber who helps Ray attempt to complete the unenviable task of painting miles of electrical towers in Sheffield, Steve (Thornton) provides comic relief — and some sexual tension — as he tries to get into bed with Gerry. Ultimately, the film's dreariness and its clichés overwhelm its virtues. ★★ VHS: $102.99

Amongst Friends

(1993, 88 min, US, Rob Weiss) *Joseph Lindsey, Patrick McGraw, Steve Parlavecchio, Mira Sorvino, Brett Lambson.* Tightly structured, swiftly moving and surprisingly effective, this film from director Weiss begs comparison to Scorsese's gritty classics. Strong performances and a hyperkinetic script (by Weiss) highlight this story about the lives of three youths on the deceptively mean streets of Long Island. Childhood loyalties fall prey to the harsh realities of the adult world as young men with everything look for the one thing that can never be given but only earned — respect. The

director appears as the thug at the post-holdup party who explains why he had to shoot that security guard in the ass. ★★★½ VHS: $14.99

Amor Bandido

(1980, 90 min, Brazil, Bruno Barreto) *Paulo Gracindo, Cristina Ache.* Told with melodramatic gusto and imbued with loads of nudity, this torrid and violent story of doomed love is played out amidst the backdrop of seedy, and yet beautiful, Rio de Janeiro. Thrown out by her detective father, a 17-year-old girl becomes an erotic dancer and hooker at a club in the tough Copacabana. It is here that Sandra meets Tony, a baby-faced teenager and cold-blooded killer. Fueled by loneliness and lust, the two fall passionately in love — all the while unaware that the noose of retribution is tightening around their necks. (Portuguese with English subtitles) ★★★ VHS: $19.99

El Amor Brujo

(1986, 100 min, Spain, Carlos Saura) *Antonio Gades, Laura del Sol.* Manuel de Falla's electrifying and passionate gypsy ballet is brought to the screen by the incomparable team of choreographer Antonio Gades and director Saura. Exuberant flamenco dance punctuates this steamy tale of a young widow (the undeniably sensual del Sol) who is tormented by her late husband's ghost. The strikingly handsome Gades plays her suitor, who desperately seeks to break the spell. (Spanish with English subtitles) ★★★

Amore

(1948, 78 min, Italy, Roberto Rossellini) *Anna Magnani, Federico Fellini.* Two episodes, dedicated by Rossellini to "the art of Anna Magnani," comprise this indulgent drama about the illusion and pain of love. "The Miracle" stars Magnani as a slightly retarded farm girl who is seduced by a stranger (Fellini) who she believes to be St. Joseph and her newborn son the child of God. "The Human Voice," based on a Jean Cocteau play, features Magnani as a woman distraught by the recent breakup with her lover. In a painfully personal monologue to her unseen and unheard lover on the telephone, she attempts to persuade him not to leave. Interestingly, the film was banned in New York for blasphemy. (Italian with English subtitles) ★★½ VHS: $29.99

Amores Perros (Love's a Bitch)

(2000, 154 min, Mexico, Alejandro González Iñárritu) *Emilio Echevarria, Gael García Bernal, Goya Toledo, Álvaro Guerrero, Marco Peréz, Vanessa Bauche.* In a stunning feature-film debut, director Iñárritu (a veteran of Mexican television) finds himself in the realm of Tarantino and Altman, but adding his own distinctive flavor to a provocative story of crime, betrayal, murder, seduction and unlikely redemption set in the slums and high-rises of Mexico City. Using a car crash as a focal point, the director and writer Guillermo Arriaga have several stories intersect before and after the accident, making optimum use of flashbacks and other non-linear editing techniques. Among a handful of characters in need of amor are: brothers Ramiro (a churlish petty crook) and Octavio (a dogfighter aching for his brother's wife); Valeria, a beautiful, shallow model having an affair with a married man; and El Chivo, a former revolutionary-turned-hit man who wants

to reconcile with his estranged daughter. How these lives crisscross, and what the characters must endure, forms the core of this demanding, intense, often spellbinding drama that is the cinematic equivalent of a knockout punch. ★★★★
VHS: $102.99; DVD: $29.99

Amos & Andrew

(1993, 95 min, US, E. Max Frye) *Samuel L. Jackson, Nicolas Cage, Dabney Coleman, Brad Dourif, Michael Lerner, Giancarlo Esposito, Loretta Devine.* When Andrew Sterling (Jackson), Pulitzer Prize—winning playwright and wealthy black man, arrives at his new home on an island in New England, his neighbors mistake him for a burglar and call in the local police and set in motion what was surely intended to be a comical farce, poking fun at racial attitudes. Instead, the result is non-stop inanity and annoying stereotypes. Local police chief Coleman attempts to cover his tracks by setting loose petty thief Cage (who plays Amos) on the unsuspecting Jackson. Cage and Jackson seem to sleepwalk their way through the anemic screenplay. ★ VHS: $9.99; DVD: $14.99

Amsterdamned

(1988, 114 min, The Netherlands, Dick Maas) *Huub Stapel, Monique van de Ven.* The city of Amsterdam becomes an unwitting accomplice to a series of grisly murders when a sadistic killer uses the city's canals to amphibiously stalk his prey. This "Amsterdam Vice" police thriller proves that Hollywood does not have a lock on good action films. The story follows the frantic efforts of a good-looking detective with a five-day beard (shades of you-know-who) who is assigned to seek out the underwater killer. Great locales, wonderful camera work and a heart-throbbing chase scene through the canals help make this a memorable action drama. (Dutch with English subtitles) ★★★

Anaconda

(1997, 100 min, US, Luis Llosa) *Jon Voight, Jennifer Lopez, Ice Cube, Eric Stoltz, Kari Wuhrer.* Basically this story of a bunch of people lost in the jungle and chased and killed off by a giant snake (as if you couldn't guess) succeeds at being suspenseful and fun at the same time. Where it doesn't succeed is in originality and successful execution of its special effects. The computer-generated anaconda looks terrible, but fortunately is on-screen so little (until the end) and moves so quickly that its artificiality can be overlooked by an extra-generous suspension of disbelief. Lopez is appealing in her first action role, Cube's character's fate is not what one would expect, and Voight spends the movie doing a bad impression of Al Pacino in *Scarface*. It may be brainless, but *Anaconda* manages to consistently entertain. ★★½ VHS: $12.99; DVD: $19.99

Analyze This

(1999, 103 min, US, Harold Ramis) *Robert De Niro, Billy Crystal, Lisa Kudrow, Chazz Palminteri, Joe Viterelli, Pat Cooper, Leo Rossi, Max Casella.* What has to be the funniest gangster comedy since *Some Like It Hot*, *Analyze This* is non-stop hilarity and proves that De Niro can handle comedy with the skill of his great dramatic portrayals. Who knew? A well-structured and very funny screenplay by Peter Tolan, Kenneth Lonergan and director Ramis sets up the clever, high-concept scenario: Mafia kingpin Paul Vitti

Analyze This

(De Niro) is experiencing such stress as to cause him to seek out psychiatric help. And what doctor does he put the hit on? Ben Sobel, marvelously played by Crystal. Quicker than you can say "The Godfather," Sobel's professional and private lives are turned upside-down with Vitti now thinking he has his own personal, 24-hour shrink. The rapport between the two stars is priceless — that Crystal and pal Robin Williams' *Father's Day* was such a disappointment only adds to the sheer delight of Bobby and Billy's chemistry. Of course, they're working from a much better screenplay. And it's consistently funny, from start to finish, an endless parade of sharp one-liners and sticky situations. In support, Kudrow and Palminteri are both shortchanged in their parts; but not Viterelli, who is perfect as Vitti's dense but loyal henchman. ★★★½ VHS: $14.99; DVD: $19.99

Anastasia

(1956, 105 min, US, Anatole Litvak) *Ingrid Bergman, Yul Brynner, Helen Hayes, Akim Tamiroff.* In 1956, Bergman appeared in her first American production in six years since being exiled to Europe for her affair with the director Roberto Rossellini. Shot on location in Paris, *Anastasia* heralded her triumphant return, and she was justly rewarded an Oscar for her excellent performance. Bergman stars as a woman who, while in an asylum, claimed to be the youngest daughter of executed Russian Czar Nicholas. Brynner is an ex-Russian military leader searching for a look-alike of the princess to set up a swindle. Based on the hit play, the film is a captivating story of identity and remembrance, made all the more appealing by the virtuoso portrayal by Bergman. Her reunion scene with Hayes, playing the Dowager Empress, is extremely moving. ★★★½ VHS: $14.99

Anastasia

(1997, 96 min, US, Don Bluth & Gary Goldman) *Voices of: Meg Ryan, John Cusack, Kelsey Grammer, Christopher Lloyd, Hank Azaria, Bernadette Peters, Kirsten Dunst, Angela Lansbury.* A sumptuous animated epic, with all the grace, beauty and spirit of the very best Disney classics, *Anastasia* is all the more surprising because it's *not* a Disney movie.

Okay, so it's historically inaccurate, but the filmmakers aren't telling history here, they're merely using it as a springboard for their own fairy-tale plot. The music isn't quite up to par with the better, Oscar-winning tunes of recent Disney films, but the artistry and the clever vocal casting elevate *Anastasia* far above other pretenders to the Disney throne. (Letterboxed VHS and DVD available for $29.99) ★★★ VHS: $19.99; DVD: $24.99

Anatomy

(2000, 100 min, Germany, Stefan Ruzowitzky) *Franka Potente, Benno Fürmann, Anna Loos, Holger Speckhahn.* A creepy, sick but atmospheric horror film, *Anatomy* tries to create suspense using disgusting effects to simulate realism but ends up just being disgusting. Potente (*Run Lola Run*) is Paula, an ambitious medical student who is accepted into a prestigious anatomy class. What looks like a splendid opportunity soon becomes a nightmare when she uncovers a ruthless secret medical society whose prime goal is to learn more about medicine by dissecting bodies while they are still alive. The premise is a promising one, but the filmmakers are unable to sustain tension or believability, relying on horror clichés and gross-outs for its too few scares. (German with English subtitles) ★½ VHS: $102.99; DVD: $24.99

Anatomy of a Murder

(1959, 160 min, US, Otto Preminger) *James Stewart, Goerge C. Scott, Ben Gazzara, Lee Remick, Arthur O'Connell, Eve Arden, Joseph Welch.* This riveting courtroom drama, a groundbreaker when released, maintains its punch and relevance today. The tension-filled, complex plot — about small-town lawyer Stewart defending soldier Gazzara who murdered a bartender who allegedly raped his wife Remick — is sustained by tour de force ensemble acting from the star-studded cast, highlighted by Stewart's portrayal of the deceptively easy-going defense attorney. Strong direction by Preminger is punctuated by the throbbing Duke Ellington score. ★★★★ VHS: $19.99; DVD: $24.99

Anchors Aweigh

(1945, 140 min, US, George Sidney) *Gene Kelly, Frank Sinatra, Kathryn Grayson, Dean Stockwell.* Kelly and Sinatra's first musical together is a sentimental though fun romp about two sailors on leave (a theme which would recur in *On the Town* and even indirectly in *It's Always Fair Weather*) in Tinseltown. This is the one where Gene dances with Jerry the Mouse. ★★½ VHS: $14.99; DVD: $19.99

And a Nightingale Sang

(1989, 90 min, GB, Robert Knights) *Joan Plowright, Tom Watt, Phyllis Logan, John Woodvine.* Made for "Masterpiece Theatre," this delightfully charming little comedy-drama tells the tale of a working-class British family during WWII. The story revolves around Helen, the family's eldest daughter, a 31-year-old spinster who at long last finds love with a young soldier. Filled with mirth and a smattering of social commentary, the film exhibits the same kind of tenderness for the misbegotten which makes Mike Leigh's films so thoroughly enjoyable. ★★★ VHS: $19.99

And God Created Woman

(1956, 91 min, France, Roger Vadim) *Brigitte Bardot, Curt Jurgens, Jean-Louis Trintignant.* BB Mania (Brigitte Bardot that is) pulsated after the release of this sex comedy, which by today's standards is chastefully harmless. Bardot is a man-teasing 18-year-old whose lustful encounters with the irresistible opposite sex are enacted amid the sun and splendor of St. Tropez. (French with English subtitles) ★★½ VHS: $19.99; DVD: $29.99

And God Created Woman

(1987, 98 min, US, Roger Vadim) *Rebecca DeMornay, Vincent Spano, Frank Langella.* Vadim's tepid remake of his own 1956 cause célèbre stars DeMornay in the Brigitte Bardot role. The story's about a prison escapee who just wants to play rock 'n' roll. Spano plays the carpenter wrapped around her thumb, and Langella is her sexual plaything. ★½ VHS: $14.99; DVD: $24.99

And Hope to Die

(1972, 95 min, France/Canada, René Clément) *Robert Ryan, Jean-Louis Trintignant, Aldo Ray, Tisa Farrow.* From the director of such intriguing films as *Forbidden Games, Joy House* and *Rider on the Rain* comes this stylish but disappointing thriller made in Canada. Three criminals plan and execute an elaborate plot to kidnap the moll of an underworld chief and hold her for a million-dollar ransom. (Filmed in English) ★★½

And Justice for All

(1979, 117 min, US, Norman Jewison) *Al Pacino, Jack Warden, Christine Lahti, Lee Strasberg, Joe Morton, Craig T. Nelson, Jeffrey Tambor.* Pacino received an Oscar nomination for his impassioned portrayal of an idealistic lawyer defending a judge accused of rape. Though dramatically uneven in its sometimes satirical portrait of the legal system, a good cast more than compensates for the occasional heavy-handedness. ★★½ VHS: $9.99; DVD: $24.99

And Nothing But the Truth

(1982, 90 min, GB, Karl Francis) *Glenda Jackson, Jon Finch.* This earnest examination of the roles and responsibilities of the media stars Jackson and Finch as a documentary filmmaker and reporter, respectively. While covering a story, they find themselves passionately split on how to investigate the issue at hand. The film offers an intriguing look at how television news is selected, edited and finally seen by the viewer. (aka: *Giro City*) ★★★

And Now for Something Completely Different

(1972, 80 min, GB, Ian McNaughton) *Graham Chapman, John Cleese, Eric Idle, Terry Gilliam, Michael Palin, Terry Jones, Connie Booth.* Supreme silliness prevails in this, Monty Python's first movie. Essentially it's a collection of the best of their BBC television program and features dead parrots, transvestite lumberjacks, a killer joke, upper-class twits, and a lesson on how to defend yourself against a person who is armed with fresh fruit. Nod's as good as a wink to a blind bat, eh? Say no more... ★★★ VHS: $19.99; DVD: $24.99

And Now My Love

(1974, 121 min, France, Claude Lelouch) *Marthe Keller, André Dussollier.* With the theme that one must go back generations to understand the participants in a love story, director Lelouch has fashioned an intoxicating romantic fable with the twist that the lovers don't meet until the film's final seconds. The story begins during WWI, tracing the lives of three generations of Jewish women to introduce the story's young heroine, Sara, an heiress with Marxist leanings who is waiting for the right man. That man is Simon, a petty crook who, after his imprisonment, becomes a filmmaker despite his idealistic beliefs. Lelouch mixes romance, politics, religion and many of the 20th Century's most momentous occasions in his masterful blender to serve a humorous, energetic and always fascinating discourse on human emotions and the role of fate and passion in our lives. (Dubbed) ★★★½

And the Band Played On

(1993, 145 min, US, Roger Spottiswoode) *Matthew Modine, Lily Tomlin, Alan Alda, Ian McKellen, Richard Gere, Steve Martin, Anjelica Huston, Swoosie Kurtz, Glenne Headly, Bud Cort.* Based on Randy Shilts' controversial book, this star-studded film adaptation is structured as an investigative medical thriller, and as such has an almost insurmountable problem in that the villain is a virus, its discoveries bring no joy, and there is no happy ending. Historically and scientifically comprehensive, the story centers on a government virologist, Don Francis (Modine), who almost single-handedly works on solving the mystery that was (is) HIV. The film indicts nearly everyone involved; and while powerful and engrossing, it does suffer in the depiction of gay characters and in the perception that straight men and women came to the rescue of the gay community. ★★★½ VHS: $14.99; DVD: $19.99

And the Ship Sails On

(1983, 138 min, Italy, Federico Fellini) *Freddie Jones, Barbara Jefford, Janet Suzman, Victor Poletti.* Fellini presents a deliberately artificial yet graceful spectacle aboard a luxury ocean liner in 1914. In his serious moments, Fellini concerns himself with the creative force of artistic expression and also portrays a world about to lose its innocence and plunge into WWI. The film's greatest rewards lie in its sweeping images, boldly stylized scenery, impromptu operatic turns and the usual circus of Fellini oddities. (Letterboxed) (Italian with English subtitles) ★★★ VHS: $29.99; DVD: $29.99

The Anderson Platoon

(1967, 65 min, France, Pierre Schoendoerffer) With English narration by director Schoendoerffer himself, this harrowing documentary follows the very real battle conditions endured by a group of American soldiers stationed in Vietnam. Returning to a land where he himself was stationed for 13 years with the French Army, and fascinated by America's rationale for its participation but claiming to be "on the side of the soldier," the director joined for six weeks an integrated platoon headed by a black West Point graduate, Lt. Joseph B. Anderson. Their involvement in actual combat creates real danger and fear. A fascinating film that finally produces an overwhelming sadness for the embattled young men. Please note that the quality of the tape transfer is below average. Winner of the Academy Award for Best Documentary. ★★★½ VHS: $19.99

The Anderson Tapes

(1972, 98 min, US, Sidney Lumet) *Sean Connery, Dyan Cannon, Martin Balsam, Christopher Walken, Alan King.* Connery stars as the mastermind of an elaborate scheme to rob every apartment in a large complex. Little does he know that, for one reason or another, each vault is under surveillance. The tension, along with the irony, is high in this entertaining action film from director Lumet. However, Balsam's gay caricature is offensive. ★★★

Andersonville

(1995, 168 min, US, John Frankenheimer) *Jarrod Emick, Frederic Forrest, Ted Marcoux, Cliff de Young, Jan Triska.* The most notorious Confederate prisoner of war camp during the Civil War was Andersonville, located in Georgia; the commandant was the only soldier tried for crimes against humanity after that conflict. Its squalor and misery are unflinchingly presented in this compelling made-for-cable drama. *Andersonville* begins when a small group of Union soldiers are captured and imprisoned. They are greeted by disease, brutality and death. A cesspool serves as both a toilet and bathing/drinking source, and rapacious fellow inmates rule the confines and prey on new arrivals. At its best, which is much of the time, *Andersonville* conveys in a sometimes repulsive though gripping manner the hardships endured. ★★★ VHS: $49.99

Andre

(1994, 94 min, US, George Miller) *Keith Carradine, Tina Majorina, Keith Szarabajka, Chelsea Field.* A harbor master (Carradine) and his family befriend an orphaned seal and alienate many of the human inhabitants of their Maine fishing village. Although this is based on a true story, the manipulative plot and overly dramatic ending will limit its appeal to fans of animal stories or, at least, seal lovers. ★★ VHS: $9.99

Andrei Rublev

(1965, 185 min, USSR, Andrei Tarkovsky) *Anatoli Solonitzine, Ivan Lapikov.* The life, times and art of early 15th-century icon painter Andrei Rublev are explored in this brilliant and visionary work. Told in eight imaginary episodes, the film follows the painter's journeys through Russia where the artist, numbed by the horrors he sees, gradually loses his faith in God, his ability to speak and his drive to create art. A powerful, slow and dense epic that probes into the role of the artist in society. (Russian with English subtitles) ★★★★ DVD: $39.99

Androcles and the Lion

(1952, 98 min, US, Chester Erskine) *Jean Simmons, Victor Mature, Alan Young, Maurice Evans.* George Bernard Shaw's delicious satire makes a pleasant film comedy for this story about a young tailor in Imperial Rome who saves his fellow Christians from a lion he once befriended. ★★★ VHS: $29.99

Android

(1982, 80 min, US, Aaron Lipstadt) *Klaus Kinski, Don Opper.* A fun-filled futuristic adventure set on an isolated space station. Max 404 (Opper) is a capable, somewhat waifish android — with a penchant for Jimmy Stewart movies and rock 'n' roll — whose job is to assist his creator, a renegade scientist (Kinski). Unknown to Max, the good doctor is working on a female and prototype android, destined to replace him. Part *Metropolis*, part *Frankenstein* and part *2001*, *Android* is genuinely inspired and thoroughly entertaining. ★★★

The Andromeda Strain

(1971, 131 min, US, Robert Wise) *Arthur Hill, James Olson, David Wayne, Kate Reid, Paula Kelly.* The first screen adaptation of a Michael Crichton novel is a pulse-pounding, extremely intelligent sci-fi thriller expertly directed by Wise, who summons both the suspense and style of his *The Haunting* and the imagination and enterprise of his *The Day the Earth Stood Still.* Crichton, who studied to be a doctor, makes efficient use of medical vocabulary and possibility to tell the story of a group of scientists investigating a space virus which has devastated a small New Mexico town. As they race against the clock, their only clues are two survivors: a screaming baby and an alcoholic. Reid is great as a glib doc. ★★★½ VHS: $9.99; DVD: $29.99

Andy Warhol's Bad

(1976, 100 min, US, Jed Johnson) *Carroll Baker, Perry King, Susan Tyrrell.* Andy Warhol lent his name to this slick, sick and subversive *Pink Flamingos*-like black comedy of extremely bad taste by former Warhol soundman and editor Johnson. A slumming-for-dollars Baker stars as the tough, nefarious head of a female kill-for-hire organization based in Queens which specializes in especially difficult cases. All is going well for her and her immoral ingenues until a stranger (King) enters the scene. *Bad* is gross, highly offensive and disgustingly enjoyable, though the infamous "baby splatter scene" has been edited out. ★★★

Andy Warhol's Dracula

(1974, 103 min, Italy/France, Paul Morrissey) *Udo Kier, Joe Dallesandro, Roman Polanski.* Spawned by the commercial succes of *Flesh for Frankenstein*, this campy treatment of the well-worn Transylvanian tale features Kier as Dracula, the creepy vampire in search of ripe, succulent throats and virginal blood. Leaving Hungary for the purer pastures offered in Catholic Italy, the Count's toothy appetite for a fix of virgins proves elusive as the strapping Dallesandro makes sure that the Count's intended victims are no virgins — even if it means deflowering a 14-year-old. (aka: *Blood for Dracula*) ★★½ VHS: $19.99; DVD: $39.99

Andy Warhol's Frankenstein

(1974, 94 min, Italy/Germany/France, Paul Morrissey) *Joe Dallesandro, Monique Van Vooren, Udo Kier.* B-movie dialogue, over-the-top performances and buckets of gore abound in this campy retelling of the classic horror story, served up with a weird sexual twist. Kier is the mad baron who feverishly works on piecing together body parts from the recently dead to create a pair of perfect creatures — a beautiful female and a sex-crazed male. Dallesandro plays the horny stud to the baron's wife/sister. Originally shown in 3-D, and rated a tantalizing "X." As the baron says, "You don't known life until you've fucked death in the gall bladder." (aka: *Flesh for Frankenstein*) ★★ VHS: $19.99; DVD: $39.99

Andy Warhol's Heat

(1972, 100 min, US, Paul Morrissey) *Sylvia Miles, Joe Dallesandro.* Kinky and funny, this many times vulgar takeoff of *Sunset Boulevard* stars Miles as the shrillish Sally Todd, a fading movie star (actually a has-been chorus girl) who shares her dreary home with her lesbian daughter and the latter's sadistic girlfriend. Their lives are briefly stimulated when Dallesandro enters the scene. All have the hots for Little Joe — prompting Mom to complain her daughter "can't even make a good dyke." An insightful tale of unsatisfactory sex, elusive love and ever-present alienation masked as delightful camp. (aka: *Heat*) ★★★ VHS: $19.99; DVD: $24.99

Angel

(1937, 91 min, US, Ernst Lubitsch) *Marlene Dietrich, Melvyn Douglas, Herbert Marshall, Edward Everett Horton.* A minor Lubitsch melodrama that is nearly saved by three good lead performances and the director's usual sophisticated touch. Dietrich plays a neglected diplomat's wife who is tempted by an old friend of her husband's. They may not say much but they sure look good doing it. ★★ VHS: $14.99

Angel

(1982, 126 min, Greece, Yorgos Katakouzinos) *Michael Maniatis, Dionyssis Xanthos, Katerina Helmi.* A commercial and critical hit in Greece, this was that country's first film to deal with homosexuality. The uneven drama is a harrowing, tragic account of a shy young man from a dysfunctional family (dad's an alcoholic; mom's a whore) who thinks he's found love after meeting a macho sailor. Their relationship soon becomes abusive, with the handsome Angel forced to become a transvestite prostitute in Athens. His helplessness and humiliation soon end in inevitable violence. (Greek with English subtitles) ★★½ VHS: $39.99; DVD: $29.99

An Angel at My Table

(1990, 150 min, New Zealand, Jane Campion) *Kerry Fox, Alexia Keogh, Karen Fergusson.* The story of New Zealand novelist and poet Janet Frame is lovingly rendered and subtly moving without ever employing cheap sentimental devices. Frame published various successful works while hospitalized for schizophrenia, but that's only one part of this sprawling portrait of self-discovery from *Sweetie* director Campion. A remark-

Angela's Ashes

able performance by Fox as the adult Frame. ★★★ VHS: $19.99

Angel Baby

(1997, 105 min, Australia, Michael Rymer) *John Lynch, Jacqueline McKenzie, Colin Friels.* Two magnificent performances enliven this otherwise ordinary drama about two mental patients in love. For Harry (Lynch), it is love at first sight when he meets Kate (McKenzie), a young woman who receives coded messages from "Wheel of Fortune." When the couple decide to move in together, have a baby, and stop taking their medication, things sour quickly. Director Rymer does achieve some lyrical moments, but all too often the film takes a heavy-handed approach to its sensitive subject matter. Both Lynch and McKenzie handle their big breakdown scenes well, and they look good sans clothing, but ultimately the film exploits their strong performances. In support, Friels is outstanding as Harry's frustrated brother. ★★ VHS: $79.99

Angel Dust

(1994, 116 min, Japan, Sogo [Toshihiro] Ishii) *Kaho Minami, Takeshi Wakamatsu.* This ambitious effort falls short of the mark due to an unnecessarily dense script which seems to be complex but is really only substituting convolutedness for substance. Relentlessly stylish, particularly during its excellent first half hour, the story centers around Setsuko, a police psychologist who has the bizarre ability to place herself into the mind of a killer. She begins investigating a series of murders which have been occurring at 6 p.m. each Monday on a particular line of the Tokyo subway. Each of the victims is a young woman killed by an injection of poison while in the middle of a large crowd. As the investigation progresses, Setsuko finds that she is much closer to the killer than she had originally imagined. Multiple viewings are probably required to pick up all of the film's clues and red herrings, but unfortunately the story is not involving enough to support such scrutiny. (Japanese with English subtitles) ★★½ VHS: $29.99

Angel Heart

(1986, 112 min, US, Alan Parker) *Mickey Rourke, Robert De Niro, Lisa Bonet, Charlotte Rampling.* Yes, the film with the controversial nude scene with Bonet. That's all most people seem to remember from this story about a private eye (Rourke)

and a case he is given by Mr. Louis Cypher (De Niro). Parker combines film noir and his penchant for stark, brutal realism to create a creepy, atmospheric film. Not for all tastes, due to its gore. This is the uncut version. ★★★ VHS: $9.99; DVD: $14.99

Angela's Ashes

(1999, 146 min, GB/Ireland, Alan Parker) *Emily Watson, Robert Carlyle, Michael Legge, Joe Breen, Ciaran Owens.* In adapting Frank McCourt's Pulitzer Prize–winning novel for the screen, director Parker has more than one obstacle in his way; but the biggest is the loss of the author's unique narrative voice which gave the book its humor amid the despair. The story of McCourt's impoverished childhood in Limerick, Ireland, during the 1930s and '40s remains a powerful memory piece of sacrifice, poverty and hope. But having lost that voice so essential to the novel, and being unable to capture it on film, only magnifies its few limitations as to make them appear greater than they are. A superb evocation of the era, the film details in heartbreaking fashion how the McCourt family, after the death of their youngest child, moves back to Ireland, where life becomes no easier than in America. Hunger and squalor greet them as father Malachy McCourt (Carlyle) struggles with his alcoholism, mother Angela (Watson) tries to keep the family together, and young Frank (played by Breen, Owens and Legge) attempts to live as normal a childhood as possible. The performances are uniformly good, the tone is reverent, and the family's loss significant, but the spirit of the novel seems to be slightly amiss. ★★½ VHS: $14.99; DVD: $29.99

Angèle

(1934, 130 min, France, Marcel Pagnol) *Fernandel, Orane Demazis.* Acknowledged by De Sica and Rossellini as a great inspiration in their careers, this innovative neorealist melodrama about a girl's seduction, betrayal and eventual redemption is considered by many to be Pagnol's finest work. In the naturalist setting of Provence, a naive peasant girl (Demazis) has a child. Abandoned by her lover and bullied by her domineering father (Fernandel, in his first dramatic role), she runs off to Marseilles, where she is soon forced into prostitution. Her father, a simple-minded farmer, driven by love for his daughter, goes to the city to find Angèle and return her home. (French with English subtitles) ★★★★ VHS: $59.99

The Angelic Conversation

(1985, 78 min, GB, Derek Jarman) *Judi Dench.* Eschewing narrative form, with the only dialogue being Dench's offscreen reading of twelve Shakespeare sonnets, this cryptic assemblage of stop-action photography can be slow-going; but for those who persist, this allegorical mood piece can be a hypnotically beautiful film. Featuring several Bruce Weber beauties, Jarman's soul-searching mission celebrates life and captures the sensual grace of male youth as well as his feelings on premature death caused by AIDS. Original music by Coil. An affirmation of life as well as an original and daring work. ★★★

Angelo, My Love

(1983, 115 min, US, Robert Duvall) *Angelo Evans, Michael Evans.* Duvall wrote and directed this charming tale about an 11-year-old Gypsy boy in his quest to find a stolen ancestral ring. Evans plays himself in this loosely structured and somewhat improvisational film, full of wit, energy and passion. ★★★

Angels & Insects

(1995, 117 min, US/GB, Philip Haas) *Mark Rylance, Patsy Kensit, Kristin Scott Thomas, Jeremy Kemp, Douglas Henshall.* A marvelously twisted, psychosexual period piece that examines not only the class inequities but the repressed sexual mores of Victorian society — as if *Sense and Sensibility* had been interpreted by Peter Greenaway. The story (based on A. S. Byatt's novella "Morpho Eugenia") revolves around William Adamson (Rylance), a low-born entomologist who specializes in rare tropical butterflies and moths. Adamson lands a position at the manor of Sir Harold Alabaster (Kemp) where he catalogs his employer's collection of zoological specimens as well as tutors his children. He falls in love with Alabaster's emotionally reserved daughter Eugenia (Kensit) despite the obvious attraction between him and the family's outgoing and well-educated niece, Matty (an engaging Scott Thomas). Dark family secrets lurk in the background, however, giving everything in the film an overriding sense of dread. Haas sustains a visually striking and emotionally haunting narrative that effectively uses its protagonist's fascination with insects as a metaphor for human interaction. ★★★½ VHS: $14.99

Angels in the Outfield

(1951, 99 min, US, Clarence Brown) *Paul Douglas, Janet Leigh, Keenan Wynn, Spring Byington, Ellen Corby.* This funny, semiclassic baseball fantasy stars the always delightfully gruff Douglas as the manager of the Pittsburgh Pirates, whose season makes the 1994 San Diego Padres look like champions. With the help of a young orphan and some heavenly spirits, the team turns around and makes a drive towards the pennant. There's plenty of surprise cameos, and a very young Leigh looks ravishing. (Remade in 1994) ★★★½ VHS: $14.99

Angels in the Outfield

(1994, 105 min, US, William Dear) *Danny Glover, Tony Danza, Christopher Lloyd, Brenda Fricker, Dermot Mulroney, Matthew McConaughey.* Disney's remake of the wonderfully sweet 1951 baseball fantasy has been updated both in story and technically without capturing the charm and cheerfulness of the original. In this by-the-books revision, Glover plays the manager of the team, a bunch of screw-ups and has-beens. They're soon aided by angel Lloyd and some heavenly friends, whom only a foster child can see. While some of the baseball footage is genuinely amusing, it's surrounded by sappy, even depressing dramatics. ★★ VHS: $19.99

Angels over Broadway

(1940, 80 min, US, Ben Hecht) *Rita Hayworth, Douglas Fairbanks, Jr., Thomas Mitchell, John Qualen.* One of the most offbeat and original film projects of the 1940s, *Angels over Broadway*, written and directed by noted author Hecht (in his only directing job), is a puzzling though irresistible black comedy set in the theatrical confines of New York City. A suicidal embezzler (Qualen) has his final act rewritten for him by three of life's lost souls: a failing, boozy play-

wright (Mitchell in a scintillating performance), a con man determined to do good (Fairbanks) and a call girl (the beautiful Hayworth in one of her first starring roles). ★★★ VHS: $19.99

Angels with Dirty Faces

(1938, 97 min, US, Michael Curtiz) *James Cagney, Pat O'Brien, Ann Sheridan, Humphrey Bogart, Dead End Kids.* This is the classic with Cagney and O'Brien as childhood friends; the former becomes a gangster, the latter a priest. When Jimmy returns to his old neighborhood, Pat has his hands full when the street kids "doing time" at the local parish come to idolize the criminal. *Angels* is fast-paced and well-acted, and who could forget Cagney's walk to the chair? ★★★½ VHS: $19.99

Angie

(1994, 108 min, US, Martha Coolidge) *Geena Davis, Stephen Rea, James Gandolfini, Philip Bosco.* A poor woman's *Moonstruck*, *Angie*, based on Avra Wing's novel "Angie, I Says," stars Davis as a Bensonhurst secretary who reexamines her life. Engaged to a likable, macho plumber, Angie learns she is pregnant. But instead of marrying the father, she dumps him and begins an affair with an affected Manhattan artist (Rea). The film begins on a congenial level — introducing affable characters and playful moments of schtick. Halfway through, however, the story takes a distressing turn and disintegrates into a depressing, yawn-producing soap opera. ★★

Angry Harvest

(1985, 102 min, Poland, Agnieszka Holland) *Armin Mueller-Stahl, Elisabeth Trissenaar.* A powerful, sometimes brutal and always gripping view of the Holocaust. Rosa, a Viennese matron, jumps the transport to Auschwitz; Leon, a sexually repressed farmer, reluctantly shelters and then guiltily lusts after her. Mueller-Stahl brilliantly portrays Leon, a bundle of contradictions: coarse and complicated, prissy and sadistic. He becomes infatuated with Rosa's helplessness and his own sense of control. *Angry Harvest* might be called a psychological action film in which the characters are inexorably drawn together by the forces of war. (German with English subtitles) ★★★½

The Angry Red Planet

(1959, 83 min, US, Ib Melchior) *Gerald Mohr, Nora Hayden, Les Tremayne, Jack Kruschen.* It's cheesy. It's silly. It's wonderful. This is an extremely cheesy tale of an expedition to Mars (the angry red planet) where astronauts encounter giant spider-like creatures and killer plants. The acting is stiff and the dialogue is so bad it's funny. Hilarious use of bogus scientific theories to explain what is going on is the staple in these B-flicks and you get plenty of it in this one. A perfect Saturday matinee film. ★★ VHS: $12.99

Angus

(1995, 90 min, US, Patrick Read Johnson) *George C. Scott, Charlie Talbert, Kathy Bates, Chris Owen, Ariana Richards.* Overweight and overly bright, Angus is the sworn enemy of his high school's most popular student, who makes his life a living hell. The story is taken to such lengths that it is literally painful to watch. The saving grace comes at the end in a stirring and inspired

speech from Angus about being different — it should comfort many outcasts. A good cast (with Scott as the youth's grandfather) and soundtrack help distract from the very heavy-handedness of the plot. ★★ VHS: $14.99

Anima Mundi

(1992, 30 min, US, Godfrey Reggio) From the team of director Reggio and composer Philip Glass (*Koyanisqaatsi* and *Powaqaatsi*) comes this somewhat aimless yet nevertheless visually exciting paean to the diversity of life on Earth. Produced by the World Wildlife Fund, the film is a dazzling 30-minute montage of the various fauna which inhabit the globe, all set to Glass' pulsating score. The film will probably be of interest mostly to wildlife enthusiasts and possibly children, but the final seven-minute collage of several animals at full gallop in slow motion should delight just about everyone. ★★½

Animal Behavior

(1989, 88 min, US, H. Anne Riley) *Karen Allen, Armande Assante, Holly Hunter.* A good cast is wasted in this mindless romantic comedy about a music teacher (Assante) who meets a psychologist (Allen) and her "subject": a chimp named Michael. ★ VHS: $19.99

Animal Crackers

(1930, 98 min, US, Victor Heerman) *The Marx Brothers, Margaret Dumont, Lillian Roth.* The Marx Brothers' second film finds them still struggling to get a footing in their new medium. With blocking that exposes its stage origins, *Animal Crackers* finds the farcical foursome crashing a society party being held by Dumont (who else?). Groucho makes his grand entrance as the noted African explorer Jeffrey T. Spaulding ("The 'T' stands for Edgar") while Harpo follows close behind blowing chocolate smoke bubbles. Ultimately, Chico and Harpo get roped into stealing a painting, which leads to one of their classic routines. Despite its flaws, though, the film is at times a riotous skewering of the upper class that will leave one resting assured that in "Alabama the tusks are loosa'." ★★½ VHS: $14.99

Animal Factory

(2000, 94 min, US, Steve Buscemi) *Willem Dafoe, Edward Furlong, Danny Trejo, John Heard, Mickey Rourke, Tom Arnold, Seymour Cassel, Steve Buscemi.* Nicely avoiding the usual prison drama clichés, this gritty, often compelling drama is based on the novel by Edward Bunker (*Reservoir Dogs*). Furlong plays Ron Decker, a sweet-faced young man of privilege who is sentenced to jail on a drug offense. The naïve youngster is befriended by Earl Copen (Dafoe), the powerful con who controls the prison's black market. Caught in a maelstrom of violence, sexual intimidation and corruption, Decker quickly adapts to his surroundings, exchanging innocence for guile, morality for a blind eye. An effective supporting cast includes Rourke's dentally impaired drag queen, and Arnold's sexual predator. ★★★ VHS: $14.99; DVD: $29.99

Animal Farm

(1955, 75 min, GB, John Halas & Joy Batchelor) George Orwell's famous satire on totalitarianism and fascism tells the story of a group of farm animals who band together to oust their oppressive farmer only to find that their chosen leader, the pig, is a ruthless dictator. A simplistic trans-

Anna and the King

lation, *Animal Farm*'s animation is perfunctory, and though Orwell's allegory is a striking one, there's an overall haziness to the production. This is one animated feature that's not for kids. (Remade in 1999) ★★ VHS: $29.99

Anita: Dances of Vice

(1987, 82 min, Germany, Rosa von Praunheim) *Lotti Huber, Ina Blum, Mikhael Honesseau.* Huber stars as an old woman who thinks that she is the reincarnation of Anita Berber, the infamous nude dancer in Weimar Berlin who flaunted her bisexuality, acknowledged taking drugs and generally scandalized the nation with her notorious behavior. Von Praunheim's splashy, provocative film intercuts black-and-white footage of the ragged old woman spouting her outrageous claims with colorful re-creations of the old woman living the life of her alter ego. (German with English subtitles) ★★★ VHS: $39.99

Anna

(1987, 100 min, US, Yurek Bogayevicz) *Sally Kirkland, Paulina Porizkova, Robert Fields.* Kirkland's riveting Oscar-nominated performance highlights this involving, offbeat version of *All About Eve*, about a middle-aged, once-famous Czech film actress, now struggling in New York, and the young immigrant who befriends her to learn the craft. ★★★

Anna and the King

(1999, 147 min, US, Andy Tennant) *Jodie Foster, Chow Yun-Fat, Ling Bai, Tony Felton.* In its fourth film incarnation, the memoir of 19th-century schoolteacher Anna Leonowens and her momentous trip to Siam makes for a sumptuous if not totally fluid rendering of the popular story. Filmed previously in 1946 as *Anna and the King of Siam, The King and I* in 1956 and in 1999 as an animated musical, the tale is a familiar one. The widowed Anna, accompanied by her young son, travels to Siam to tutor the king's many children. The headstrong Anna and the monarch at first clash, but in time come to respect and love one another. Director Tennant has an eye for period detail, but is less successful in creating a lasting dramatic ten-

sion, giving the film the feeling of being slightly more boring than it is. Foster, looking terrific in period costume, seems a bit out of sync with Anna, though she does bring a modern sensibility to Anna that's been absent in the previous versions. As the king, Yun-Fat is commanding but isn't able to exorcise the ghost of Yul Brynner hanging about. ★★½ VHS: $14.99; DVD: $26.99

Anna and the King of Siam

(1946, 128 min, US, John Cromwell) *Irene Dunne, Rex Harrison, Linda Darnell, Lee J. Cobb, Gale Sondergaard.* The inspiration for the musical *The King and I*, this usually overlooked classic is a perfect blend of Hollywood schmaltz and heart-tugging drama. In an effervescent performance, Dunne is Anna, a mid-19th-century English schoolteacher who travels to Bangkok to instruct the children of the King (an excellent Harrison). As the strong-willed teacher comes into conflict with the equally determined ruler, they fall in love, all the while aware neither is able to act on their feelings. (Also remade in 1999 as *Anna and the King*) ★★★½ VHS: $14.99

Anna Christie

(1930, 89 min, US, Clarence Brown) *Greta Garbo, Charles Bickford, Marie Dressler.* "Gimme a whiskey, ginger ale on the side. And don't be stingy, baby." With these words, the immortal Garbo spoke her first words on film, evolving from silent star to full-fledged screen legend. Based on Eugene O'Neill's classic play, Garbo plays Anna, the disillusioned prostitute who returns home after 15 years to her sea captain father. Dressler is outstanding as Garbo's alcoholic confidant and drinking buddy, and a youthful Bickford portrays the gruff sailor who falls in love with and then rejects the embittered woman. Though the pace may be slow and the production less than technically savvy, O'Neill's earthy prose and Garbo's radiant performance contribute to make this a rewarding film experience. ★★★ VHS: $19.99

Anna Karenina

(1935, 95 min, US, Clarence Brown) *Greta Garbo, Fredric March, Freddie Bartholomew, Basil Rathbone, Maureen O'Sullivan.* Tolstoy's tragic love story is immortalized by the outstanding performance of Garbo in the title role. Her fusion with the character of the doomed heroine is so complete that one might think that Tolstoy had her in mind when he penned the tale. Rathbone is superb as Karenin. ★★★½ VHS: $19.99

Anne Frank Remembered

(1995, 123 min, GB/US, Jon Blair) *Miep Gies; Narrated by: Kenneth Branagh, Glenn Close.* With 26 million copies of her diary sold around the world, and having been the subject of an award-winning play and an award-winning film based on that play, there's not much more one could possibly think there would be to know about Anne Frank. Such is the beauty of *Anne Frank Remembered*, an illuminating documentary which not only presents heretofore unknown and fascinating information on the courageous Jewish teen killed during WWII, but also pays tribute to Miep Gies, the heroic woman who hid the Frank family in Nazi-occupied Amsterdam for two years. All of the traditional components of the documentary are here, but director Blair and the film's participants make it seem so fresh. Wisely, Blair doesn't go for the easy tear, but instead works on the mind while touching the heart. ★★★½ VHS: $19.99

Anne of Avonlea

(1987, 224 min, Canada, Kevin Sullivan) *Colleen Dewhurst, Megan Follows, Wendy Hiller.* The adventures of Anne continue in this surprisingly enjoyable and captivating sequel to *Anne of Green Gables*. Now eighteen, Anne gets a job as a schoolteacher and, being the feisty, determined redhead that she is, she believes she is ready to try her hand at romance. Dewhurst returns as her stepmother. A humorous, heartwarming tale. ★★★

Anne of Green Gables

(1985, 198 min, Canada, Kevin Sullivan) *Colleen Dewhurst, Richard Farnsworth, Megan Follows.* Based on the best-seller by L.M. Montgomery, this enchanting story of the adventures and growing maturity of a teenage girl proves to be a captivating film experience suitable for the entire family. Anne (Follows), a dreamy orphan, is sent to beautiful Prince Edward Island to live with a stern but loving woman (Dewhurst) and her kindly brother (Farnsworth). The story follows our charming heroine as she struggles with the obstacles of adolescence and young adulthood. ★★★½ VHS: $29.99

Anne of the 1,000 Days

(1969, 145 min, US, Charles Jarrott) *Richard Burton, Genevieve Bujold, Irene Papas, Anthony Quayle.* Henry VIII is at it again as he courts, weds and later beheads Anne Boleyn. Burton gives a larger-than-life performance befitting the monarch, and Bujold is excellent in her first starring role as the doomed queen. Terrific production values (art direction, costumes, cinematography, editing) and Bujold's lovely portrayal combine to make this a commendable historical epic. ★★★ VHS: $14.99

Les Années 80 (The Eighties)

(1983, 82 min, Belgium/France, Chantal Akerman) *Aurore Clement, Lio, Magali Noel.* The creative genesis of art and the filmmaking process is examined and deconstructed in this unusually fascinating and pleasurable film. Unlike director Akerman's previous somber films, this is a giddy work: a musical set in a suburban shopping mall, and nothing like the Hollywood musicals of the past. The first part of the film features a series of confusingly repetitive and jumbled scenes of a group of women singing, talking, discussing and arguing. The film changes direction completely in the second half to reveal the end result of all this confusion — a deliriously fun musical extravaganza. A witty, tongue-in-cheek film that can be frustrating but proves to be well worth the wait. (French with English subtitles) ★★★ VHS: $79.99

Annie

(1982, 128 min, US, John Huston) *Albert Finney, Carol Burnett, Aileen Quinn, Bernadette Peters, Tim Curry, Ann Reinking.* One of the most popular and admittedly annoying songs ever to come from a Broadway musical, "Tomorrow," is given the red-carpet, zillion-piece orchestra, sing-it-till-you-drop treatment in this over-produced adaptation from director Huston (of all people to direct a musical!). Quinn is Annie, who is whisked from her orphanage to spend time with Daddy Warbucks (Finney), the richest man in the world. Burnett, who gives the film's most spirited performance, is the head of the orphanage who sees a way to "Easy Street" thanks to Annie's rich new pal. The Tony Award—winning stage production had charm in abundance; this *Annie* is cloying, abrasive and frivolous. (Remade in 1999) ★★ VHS: $14.99; DVD: $24.99

Annie

(1999, 102 min, US, Rob Marshall) *Alicia Morton, Kathy Bates, Victor Garber, Audra*

Anna Christie

McDonald, Alan Cumming, Kristin Chenoweth, Andrea McArdle. Superior to the over-produced 1982 movie version, this made-for-TV adaptation of the popular Broadway musical sticks closer to its stage origins — and is better for it. Morton makes an appealing Annie, and is surrounded by a top-notch adult cast, including Bates (who knew she could sing and dance?) as the nefarious Miss Hannigan; Garber as Daddy Warbucks; and show-stopper Cumming, who helps make "Easy Street" one for the books. ★★★ VHS: $14.99; DVD: $29.99

Annie Get Your Gun

(1950, 107 min, US, George Sidney) *Betty Hutton, Howard Keel, Louis Calhern, J. Carrol Naish, Edward Arnold, Keenan Wynn.* A colorful rendition of the classic Broadway musical. Hutton (filling in for an ailing Judy Garland) plays Annie Oakley, who challenges Keel's Frank Butler as the premier sharpshooter of the Wild West and ends up falling in love. Music by Irving Berlin, and songs includes "There's No Business Like Show Business." ★★★ VHS: $19.99; DVD: $19.99

Annie Hall

(1977, 94 min, US, Woody Allen) *Woody Allen, Diane Keaton, Tony Roberts, Paul Simon, Christopher Walken, Colleen Dewhurst, Shelley Duvall, Carol Kane.* Allen's masterpiece is still perhaps his sharpest and wittiest work to date (though some would argue that belongs to *Manhattan*). In this ultimate of crowd pleasers, Allen adroitly puts his finger on the social milieu of the '70s as he explores the ups and downs of modern relationships. Oscar winner Diane Keaton is at her best as Woody's star-crossed lover. A delightful blend of uproarious one-liners, delicious comic schtick, intuitive dialogue, smart performances and penetrating observations on today's mores, *Annie Hall* is pure enchantment. ★★★★ VHS: $14.99; DVD: $19.99

Annie Oakley

(1935, 88 min, US, George Stevens) *Barbara Stanwyck, Melvyn Douglas, Preston Foster, Moroni Olsen.* Stanwyck stars as that rootin'-tootin' markswoman Annie Oakley in this episodic but amiable western which follows her rise to fame in Buffalo Bill's Wild West Show in the 1880s. Giving a rather subdued portrayal considering the flamboyant characteristics usually associated with Oakley, Stanwyck plays Annie as a naive and rather feminine romantic who gets all gooey-eyed at the sight of an egocentric sharpshooter (Foster). The film is a little rough around the edges, though certain scenes — especially the re-creations of Bill's show — are well-staged and entertaining. Olsen is a larger-than-life Buffalo Bill. ★★★

The Anniversary

(1968, 95 min, GB, Roy Ward Baker) *Bette Davis, Sheila Hancock, Jack Hedley.* Davis camps it up like a drunken drag queen (with an eye patch) in this hammy black comedy about a manipulative mother who uses the occasion of her wedding anniversary gathering to emotionally torture her three sons. ★★½ VHS: $19.99

The Annunciation

(1990, 101 min, Hungary, András Jeles) Defying placement in any simple category, *The Annunciation* is a strange, poetic and almost surre-

al feature which — with a cast composed entirely of children from ages eight through 12 — enacts nothing less than mankind's tragic and tumultuous tale of life on earth. A self-satisfied Satan, in the guise of a pretty blond cherub boy, decides to take Adam and Eve through time, to both witness and partake in the violence, sadness and struggle brought on by their disobedience to God's will. From ancient Greek mythology to the French Revolution and eventually to a plague-stricken 19th-century London, they witness firsthand man's fruitless struggle for liberty and love. A hypnotic journey through history infused with melancholic religious and existential themes. (Hungarian with English subtitles) ★★★½ VHS: $59.95

Another Country

(1984, 90 min, GB, Marek Kanievska) *Rupert Everett, Colin Firth, Cary Elwes.* This marvelously acted and elegantly photographed film version of Julien Mitchell's hit London play speculates on the public school days of real-life traitor/defector Guy Burgess. Everett is the languid "innocent," denied entry to the school's ruling elite because of an indiscreet homosexual affair. Elwes is Everett's handsome lover. ★★★½

Another Day in Paradise

(1999, 101 min, US, Larry Clark) *James Woods, Melanie Griffith, Vincent Kartheiser, Natasha Gregson Wagner, Paul Hipp.* Clark's follow-up to his vile *Kids* fares slightly better, but is fairly negligible save for two good performances from Woods and Griffith. Two junkie teens, who support their habit by looting vending machines, are taken under the wing of a middle-aged junkie couple, who support *their* habit by robbing pharmacies and pulling other jobs. Things go swimmingly for a while, with the foursome forming a bizarre, ersatz family. That is, until the inevitable "heist-gone-wrong" part of the story. The teens are uninteresting, the story is barely watchable, and the direction is unremarkable. ★★ VHS: $14.99; DVD: $24.99

Another 48 HRS.

(1990, 98 min, US, Walter Hill) *Nick Nolte, Eddie Murphy, Brion James, Bernie Casey.* A sequel — no, let's call it a Xerox — to Murphy's 1982 debut. Director Hill keeps the action moving at a brisk enough pace and the villains have been suitably modernized for the '90s; but it's all been done before and it was much better the first time. Murphy and Nolte are carbon copies of their former selves. ★★ VHS: $14.99; DVD: $24.99

Another Stakeout

(1993, 109 min, US, John Badham) *Richard Dreyfuss, Emilio Estevez, Rosie O'Donnell.* Six years after the release of the highly enjoyable *Stakeout* comes this inferior sequel, ill-timed and only sporadically entertaining. Dreyfuss and Estevez, neither looking the worse for wear, repeat their roles as Seattle surveillance cops. Their new assignment is to lay in waiting for a government witness who has flown the coop. They are joined by Assistant D.A. O'Donnell, whose lack of both training and tact causes an immediate personality clash with our laid-back jokesters. Only a mistaken identity subplot elevates the film, as the policework is virtually nonexistent and the comedy hit-and-miss. ★★ VHS: $9.99

A

A

Another Thin Man

See: The Thin Man Series

Another Time, Another Place

(1958, 98 min, US, Lewis Allen) *Lana Turner, Barry Sullivan, Sean Connery, Glynis Johns.* Turner chews the scenery in this ordinary soap opera with Turner as a correspondent based in England during WWII who suffers a nervous breakdown when her lover dies. ★★ VHS: $14.99

Another Time, Another Place

(1984, 104 min, GB/Scotland, Michael Radford) *Phyllis Logan, Giovanni Mauriello.* This poignant drama observes the effects of a group of Italian POWs on a remote Scottish village in 1944. Three of the Italians are housed next to Janie (Logan), who lives a tedious life with her taciturn husband. As they try to relieve each other's loneliness, a sexual attraction develops between Janie and one of the POWs which both frightens and entices her. An impressive debut for writer-director Radford. ★★★ VHS: $24.99

Another Way

(1982, 102 min, Hungary, Karoly Makk) *Péter Andorai, Jadwiga Jankowska-Cieślak, Jozef Króner.* This courageous and intelligent lesbian love story is set in Hungary immediately after the 1956 uprising and concerns the mutual attraction and budding relationship between two female journalists. Livia, married to an army officer, shyly begins accepting the advances of Eva, an outspoken reporter with whom she shares an office. Director Makk (*Love*) juxtaposes this tender but doomed love affair with the high hopes and bitter suppression of the Budapest Spring. An impassioned plea for tolerance in a land long bereft of it. (Hungarian with English subtitles) ★★★ VHS: $29.99

Another Woman

(1988, 81 min, US, Woody Allen) *Gena Rowlands, Mia Farrow, Gene Hackman, Blythe Danner, Ian Holm, John Houseman, Sandy Dennis.* After the disaster of *September*, Allen turns yet again to Ingmar Bergman territory with this complex examination of a woman (Rowlands) whose life-long resistance to her passions is shattered when she accidentally overhears the confessions of a therapy patient (Farrow). Though not as subtle as *Interiors*, the film is a complete success thanks to Rowlands' remarkable performance, and the efforts of a powerhouse cast. ★★★ VHS: $14.99; DVD: $19.99

Antarctica

(1985, 112 min, Japan, Koreyoshi Kurahara) *Ken Takahura, Masako Natsume.* A harrowing adventure story about survival and companionship set in the harshest climate on earth. Based on a true incident, the film features breathtaking cinematography by Akira Shizaka and a haunting score by Vangelis. ★★★

Anthony Adverse

(1936, 137 min, US, Mervyn LeRoy) *Fredric March, Gale Sondergaard, Olivia de Havilland, Claude Rains, Edmund Gwenn.* An intermittently interesting adaptation of Hervey Allen's epic novel set during the Napoleonic era. March ably plays the title character, whose life is covered from his youthful world travels to his rise to power and his marriage to an opera star from poor beginnings. ★★ VHS: $19.99

Antigone

(1962, 93 min, Greece, George Tzavellas) *Irene Papas.* Sophocles' poetic parable is successfully translated to the screen in this eloquent drama. Papas gives a magnificent performance as Antigone, daughter of Oedipus who, following the dictates of her own conscience, is condemned to death for defying King Creon and burying her two dead brothers. Director Tzavellas, aware of the difficulties of filming Greek tragedies, substitutes the traditional chorus with an unobtrusive offscreen narrator and, coupled with Papas' excellent portrayal, brings this ancient tale to life. (Greek with English subtitles) ★★★ VHS: $29.99

Antitrust

(2001, 108 min, US, Peter Howitt) *Ryan Phillippe, Tim Robbins, Claire Forlani, Rachael Leigh Cook, Yee Jee Tso, Richard Roundtree.* It's difficult to create much suspense when characters spend most of their time typing at their computer keyboards, unless the plot hinges on whether or not the hero makes a typo. Such is the case with *Antitrust*, a tame thriller that ruins a workable premise thanks to static direction and some silly plot developments along the way. Phillippe stars as a hot-shot computer whiz who is lured by software mogul Robbins (looking suspiciously like Bill Gates) to work on a highly sensitive computer program that — unbeknownst to our young genius — would give the CEO unlimited power on a global scale. Phillippe then uncovers the truth. Red herrings fly like fish, but matter little as none of this can be taken too seriously. Robbins seems to be having fun as the charming megalomaniac, but everyone else looks like they'd rather be in *Traffic*. ★½ VHS: $19.99; DVD: $26.99

Antonia and Jane

(1991, 75 min, GB, Beeban Kidron) *Imelda Staunton, Saskia Reeves, Patricia Leventon.* This delightfully funny low-budget gem, an Anglicized, feminist homage to Woody Allen, explores the loving and tempestuous relationship between two decidedly different women. Antonia, the plain-looking, insecure but adventurous one narrates the film's opening, giving details of her hilarious obsession with Jane, her pretty, married and seemingly well-balanced childhood friend whom she is about to meet for their annual lunch. Midway through the film, Jane takes over the narration duties and gives us her side of the story. Pleasantly amusing and deceptively simple, *Antonia and Jane* is highly recommended. ★★★½ VHS: $7.99

Antonia's Line

(1995, 93 min, The Netherlands, Marleen Gorris) *Willeke van Ammelrooy, Els Dottermans, Veere Van Overloop.* A celebration of the love, unity and strength of women, this wonderfully endearing and touching family chronicle/fable centering on four generations of women playfully alternates between dramatic realism and magical realism. The story, set in a small Dutch village, spans decades — from the devastation of the post-war period to the present — and follows the fiercely independent-minded Antonia (Ammelrooy), who returns to her childhood farmhouse to till the soil and raise a family; all without the aid of the misogynist townsfolk, a hypocritical church and the often violence-prone men. Antonia is aided by her lesbian daughter, a granddaughter and great-granddaughter and a group of social rejects who flock to her. This Oscar-winning Best Foreign Film is masterful storytelling that enthralls. (Dutch with English subtitles) ★★★★ VHS: $19.99; DVD: $19.99

Antonio das Mortes

(1969, 95 min, Brazil, Glauber Rocha) *Maurico Do Valle, Odete Lara.* Brazilian filmmaker Rocha, winner of the Best Director Award at Cannes in 1969, was forced into exile after the release of this impassioned protest against the oppression of workers by the landowning class. Set in the arid northeast of Brazil, the film, mixing suspenseful storytelling with the area's rich legacy of cultural mysticism and native folk art, follows the violent uprising of a group of peasants who draw strength and inspiration when the "warrior saint," Santo Antonio, aids their rebellion. A powerful drama as well as a stirring political allegory. (Portuguese with English subtitles) ★★★½

Antz

(1998, 83 min, US, Eric Darnell & Tim Johnson) *Voices of: Woody Allen, Sharon Stone, Christopher Walken, Gene Hackman, Sylvester Stallone, Danny Glover.* The all-computer-generated animated adventure comedy *Antz* is a joyous bonanza of clever sight gags and amazing three-dimensional visual effects. As with any great animated epic, the story is full of strange characters who exhibit human traits and emotions, all brought to vibrant life by one of the most prolific collections of vocal talent. The story is simple: Z (Allen) is a neurotic worker ant who questions the enforced conformity of the colony. Daring to suggest that there's a place for individuality, he strikes the ire of the stern General Mandible (Hackman), who is engaged to Princess Bala (Stone). Z is also smitten with Bala, and after a hair-brained scheme to impress her — he swaps places with his best friend, a soldier ant (Stallone) — Z becomes a colony hero. But when Z is exposed as a fraud, he accidentally kidnaps the princess. That's when the real adventure and fun begins and a colony revolution is ignited. Wonderful for children and adults alike. ★★★½ VHS: $14.99; DVD: $34.99

Any Given Sunday

(1999, 160 min, US, Oliver Stone) *Al Pacino, Cameron Diaz, Jamie Foxx, Dennis Quaid, James Woods, LL Cool J, Jim Brown, Matthew Modine, Ann-Margret, Lawrence Taylor, Aaron Eckhart, John C. McGinley, Lauren Holly, Lela Rochon, Elizabeth Berkley.* Stone is the perfect director to capture the visceral intensity of football, the game based on the strategies of armed conflict. This is one of the most successful attempts in taking the viewer inside the action on the field of battle; you can smell the sweat and get the wind knocked out of you with every tackle. The story line is tried and true: grizzled veteran (Quaid) playing through pain, rookie loose cannon (Foxx) rewriting the playbook, second-generation owner (Diaz) making moves in the luxury box, jaded doctor (Woods) basing diagnoses on the needs of management, know-it-all sportswriters and bloodsucking family and friends. And in the center of it all, the coach (Pacino), negotiating between

Antonia's Line

tradition and new blood, steering through excesses on and off the field, attempting to instill a human dimension in an arena where the credo is hit to kill or die hard. Stone's trademark hyper-action is well-served by the ensemble's most effective performances, especially Foxx's accomplished portrayal of hot shot Willie Beaman. The film is physically exhausting to watch and, while not completely successful in imparting a sense of the game's history, serves as an intelligent entertainment. (Director's cut) ★★★½ VHS: $19.99; DVD: $24.99

Any Wednesday
(1966, 109 min, US, Robert Ellis Miller) *Jane Fonda, Jason Robards, Dean Jones, Rosemary Murphy.* Fonda sparkles in this saucy bedroom farce based on the hit Broadway comedy about a married executive (Robards) who uses his mistress' apartment to entertain clients. ★★★ VHS: $19.99

Any Which Way You Can
(1980, 116 min, US, Clint Eastwood) *Clint Eastwood, Sondra Locke, Geoffrey Lewis, Ruth Gordon, William Smith, Anne Ramsey, Logan Ramsey.* Ever so slightly more appealing than the first film, this sequel to *Every Which Way But Loose* follows bare-knuckler Clint as he reluctantly takes on challenger Smith. Clyde is back, as are a slew of stupid pet tricks and low-down humor. ★★ VHS: $14.99

Anywhere but Here
(1999, 114 min, US, Wayne Wang) *Susan Sarandon, Natalie Portman, Bonnie Bedelia, Shawn Hatosy.* Two good lead performances by Sarandon and Portman can't totally save this overly familiar, alternately touching and maudlin story of a mother and daughter which plays like a low-rent *Tumbleweeds*. Based on the best-seller by Mona Simpson, the film follows Sarandon and Portman as they move from their small town in Wisconsin to Beverly Hills for a new start. Constantly at odds, each woman finds direction and, ultimately, respect for the other. The tale of coming-of-age and starting anew was better told in the refreshing *Slums of Beverly Hills*, but the acting here is strong enough to counterbalance the film's sappiness and the occasional cliché. ★★ VHS: $14.99; DVD: $34.99

Anzio
(1968, 118 min, US, Edward Dmytryk) *Robert Mitchum, Peter Falk, Robert Ryan, Earl Holliman, Arthur Kennedy.* A few distinguished battle scenes add little to this all-star WWII actioner about the Allied invasion of Anzio. ★★ VHS: $9.99

Aparajito
(1956, 113 min, India, Satyajit Ray) *Pinaki Sen Gupla, Karuna Banerjee.* Ray's second installment of the Apu Trilogy portrays Apu's life from the age of 10, when his father moves the family to the holy city of Benares, to his entrance to college years later. The family's struggles, including the father's death and Apu's efforts to win a scholarship, are vividly chronicled in this unbearably poignant, beautifully filmed cinematic treasure. (Bengali with English subtitles) ★★★★ VHS: $19.99

The Apartment
(1960, 125 min, US, Billy Wilder) *Jack Lemmon, Shirley MacLaine, Fred MacMurray, Ray Walston.* This Oscar-winning Best Picture stars Lemmon and MacLaine in what may be their best screen performances. Lemmon plays a young executive on the go who gets more than he bargains for when he allows superiors to use his apartment for extra-marital encounters and falls in love with his boss' mistress (MacLaine). Writer-director Wilder offers his customary sardonic wit and stinging commentary to lay bare the hypocrisies of the corporate world and the imperfections of love. A scintillating comedy-drama. MacMurray, Kruschen (an Oscar nominee) and Walston offer fine support. ★★★★ VHS: $14.99; DVD: $19.99

Apartment Zero
(1989, 114 min, GB, Martin Donovan) *Colin Firth, Hart Bochner, Fabrizio Bentivoglio, Liz Smith.* A multi-layered, stylish thriller, *Apartment Zero* creates an atmosphere of wicked sexual tension through the subtle use of suggestion and innuendo. In an English-speaking community in Buenos Aires, a sexually repressed cinephile (Firth) with a penchant for the classics takes in a swaggering, handsome American boarder (Bochner) with many skeletons in his "closet." Suspicions abound as gruesome political murders haunt the Argentine city upon the arrival

of the new roommate. Firth and Bochner shine in their roles, each bringing a subtle suggestion of sexual manipulation and dormant passion to an already explosive scenario. Donovan uses stylish camerawork and extreme close-ups to seduce the viewer into his world of intrigue. ★★★ VHS: $19.99

Aphrodite
(1984, 90 min, France, Robert Fuest) *Valerie Kaprisky.* The meltingly beautiful Kaprisky stars in this sensuous, though static staging of Pierre Louys' materpiece of erotic literature. Set in the Greek islands in 1914, the story is a sensual journey into a world of licentiousness, debauchery and unleashed sexual splendor. In other words, it's not *Mary Poppins*! The complete, unrated and unedited version. (Dubbed) ★★

Apocalypse Now
(1979, 150 min, US, Francis Ford Coppola) *Martin Sheen, Marlon Brando, Robert Duvall, Frederic Forrest, Dennis Hopper, Sam Bottoms, Laurence Fishburne, Scott Glenn.* A masterpiece of modern cinema, Coppola's epic reworking of Joseph Conrad's "Heart of Darkness" is a mind-blowing, semi-hallucinatory examination of not only the insanity of the Vietnam War, but of war itself. Sheen gives a career performance as a military assassin sent on a mission deep into enemy territory to hunt down a renegade colonel (Brando). Duvall, as an air cavalry commander, gets to utter the classic line, "I love the smell of napalm in the morning." Coppola, cast and crew made a real-life, two-year sojourn into the Philippine jungle to make the film. Along the way Sheen suffered a heart attack, sets were destroyed by typhoons, and the script was rewritten daily. (The making of *Apocalypse* is expertly chronicled in the documentary *Hearts of Darkness*.) If ever there was a foray into experimental improvisation on a big-budget film, this is it. The result, which could have easily been disastrous, is instead a remarkably coherent, superbly acted peek into human cruelty and frailty. (VHS available letterboxed or pan & scan) ★★★★ VHS: $24.99; DVD: $29.99

Apollo 13
(1995, 135 min, US, Ron Howard) *Tom Hanks, Kevin Bacon, Bill Paxton, Gary Sinise, Ed Harris, Kathleen Quinlan, Brent Cullen.* Though comparisons to *The Right Stuff* are inevitable, director Howard's epic is an impressive, suspenseful telling of the near-disastrous 1970 attempted lunar landing, While lacking *The Right Stuff*'s determined style and hard edge, *Apollo 13* is nevertheless a well-crafted story of heroism in the face of insurmountable odds. History tells us of the flight of *Apollo 13*, whose mission to the moon was thwarted by a tank explosion and whose uncertain return home kept Americans spellbound for nearly a week. What Howard has created in his fascinating, straightforward adventure film — aided by excellent effects and a knowing mood of the times — is a hypnotic tale which follows almost to the letter the actual events. The cast is almost secondary to the action, but led by Hanks (as Jim Lovell), the entire ensemble lends credibility and conviction to their roles. (Letterboxed VHS available for $14.99) ★★★★ VHS: $9.99; DVD: $34.99

The Apostle

(1997, 131 min, US, Robert Duvall) *Robert Duvall, Farrah Fawcett, Miranda Richardson, Billy Bob Thornton, John Beasley, June Carter Cash.* Euliss "Sonny" Dewey (Duvall) is a Texas Pentecostal minister with some damning characteristics of his own. He's powerful and charismatic, especially when preaching the word of God. But he's got a bad temper, and when wife Fawcett asks for a divorce, he goes ballistic on her new boyfriend with a baseball bat. With the police on his trail, Sonny takes to the road and lands in Louisiana, where he starts a new church, preaching with fire and brimstone to his poor congregation. At the same time, he strikes up a relationship with a radio station secretary (Richardson) and draws the attention of a racist (Thornton) who wants to destroy his church. Although Duvall's Sonny is a flamboyant character, this is not a flamboyant movie. Its best moments are quiet ones. Duvall is galvanizing in the lead, painting an indelible picture of a complicated but flawed man on a mission. Praise should be heaped on him for delivering a compelling, challenging tale, so refreshing from the evils of most Hollywood films. And to that we add, hallelujah! ★★★½ VHS: $14.99; DVD: $19.99

The Appaloosa

(1966, 99 min, US, Sidney J. Furie) *Marlon Brando, John Saxon, Anjanette Comer.* A lushly photographed though sluggish western with Brando as a horse breeder who embarks on a south-of-the-border trek to retrieve his prized stallion, stolen by a Mexican outlaw. Saxon is the ruthless bandit. ★★ VHS: $14.99

Appointment with Death

(1988, 108 min, US, Michael Winner) *Peter Ustinov, Lauren Bacall, Carrie Fisher, John Gielgud, Piper Laurie, Hayley Mills.* Ustinov returns as Agatha Christie's Belgian detective Hercule Poirot, here investigating the murder of greedy widow Bacall. Disappointing thriller will leave you caring little about who done it. ★★ VHS: $14.99

Apprentice to Murder

(1988, 94 min, US, R.L. Thomas) *Donald Sutherland, Chad Lowe.* In the late 1920s in rural Pennsylvania, a 16-year-old farm boy befriends a "powwow" doctor (a combination of a religious faith healer and an herbalist) who may or may not be crazy and a murderer. Lowe is the innocent teenager who comes under the influence of the creepy Sutherland, the two setting out to undermine a suspected demonic neighbor. Based on a true story. Note: The cover art on the box is very misleading. It is not the spooky, satanic horror film it suggests. Rather, the film is a slowly paced mystery about manipulation and religious hysteria. ★★

The Apprenticeship of Duddy Kravitz

(1974, 121 min, Canada, Ted Kotcheff) *Richard Dreyfuss, Denholm Elliott, Jack Warden, Randy Quaid, Joe Silver.* In a career-defining role, Dreyfuss stars as Duddy Kravitz, a likable young man from Montreal's Jewish ghetto who stops at nothing and for no one in his ambitious drive for success. Set in 1948, this serio-comedic film features many enjoyable scenes and characters with the highlight being Elliott's hilarious per-

formance as a drunken English film director hired by Duddy to "tastefully" film a Bar Mitzvah. ★★★½ VHS: $14.99

April Fool's Day

(1986, 88 min, US, Fred Walton) *Deborah Foreman, Griffin O'Neal, Thomas F. Wilson.* Friday the 13th horror and teen comedy don't mix in this attempted spoof about a group of teens staying at a friend's mansion, being bumped off one by one. ★½ VHS: $9.99

Apt Pupil

(1998, 111 min, US, Bryan Singer) *Ian McKellen, Brad Renfro, Bruce Davison, Elias Koteas, David Schwimmer.* The sophomore film from *Usual Suspects* director Singer, *Apt Pupil* is a disappointing adaptation of the well-crafted Stephen King novella. Singer displays little aptitude for the subject matter: the appeal and mystique of evil, and the question of whether evil is contagious. An inscrutable Renfro plays a Holocaust-obsessed high schooler who discovers his elderly German neighbor (McKellen) is actually a Nazi war criminal. The youth's fascination with the past drives him to blackmail the old man to regale him with tales of suffering and death from his concentration camp days. Full of clichés, *Apt Pupil* features none of the style or tension of Singer's great debut, and the screenplay does nothing to illuminate or give psychological insight into the central character (Renfro's one-note portrayal doesn't help, either). McKellen, however, is terrific; he isn't as frightening as he should be, but he creates a detailed, compelling portrait of dormant evil reawakened. Sadly, this is a lamentable misfire. ★★ VHS: $19.99; DVD: $26.99

Arabesque

(1966, 105 min, US, Stanley Donen) *Gregory Peck, Sophia Loren, George Coulouris.* Director Donen (*Charade*) is in familiar Hitchcock territory with this effective spy thriller about a college professor (Peck) who unwittingly becomes involved in a plot to assassinate an Arab prime minister. Though this doesn't deliver the thrills to the degree *Charade* did, Peck and costar Loren and a rather complex story compensate. ★★★ VHS: $14.99

Arabian Nights

(1974, 130 min, Italy, Pier Paolo Pasolini) *Ninetto Davoli, Franco Merli.* Pasolini's final film in his "Trilogy of Life" series — which includes *The Decameron* and *The Canterbury Tales* — is a bawdy and visually opulent fable of idyllic sexuality based on the classic Arabian tales. Told in dreamlike vignettes, the stories derive from three cultures — Persia, Egypt and India — and range from the ninth century to the Renaissance. A celebration of joyous sensuality rarely found in our present industrialized Western culture. (Italian and Arabic with English subtitles) ★★★½

Arachnophobia

(1990, 109 min, US, Frank Marshall) *Jeff Daniels, John Goodman, Julian Sands, Harley Jane Kozak, Brian McNamara.* Marshall, a product of the Spielberg farm system, made his directorial debut with this entertaining horror-laced comedy. A highly poisonous spider from the Amazon hitches a ride stateside and takes up residence in the home of a relocated big-city

doctor (Daniels); it mates with a domestic female and thereby creates a whole new breed of creepy-crawlers. Goodman steals the show as a know-it-all, G.I. Joe exterminator. But, of course, the real stars are the spiders themselves, who provide many a non-offensive scare. ★★★ DVD: $29.99

L'Argent

(1983, 90 min, France/Switzerland, Robert Bresson) *Christian Patey, Sylvie van den Elsen, Michel Briguet.* The corrupting power of money, the cancerous spread of evil resulting from its use, and man's eventual redemption from its sins are the themes in director Bresson's thoughtful Marxist fable. Based on a short story by Tolstoy, the film — shot in Bresson's unique style of ascetic narrative — follows the tragic course of Yvon, a young truck driver accused of counterfeiting. Fired from his job as a result of a set-up, he is eventually sent to prison, where he is incarcerated for years. Losing his wife and child, Yvon finally rebels and purges himself of his rage. ★★★ VHS: $29.99

Aria

(1987, 100 min, GB, Various) *Theresa Russell, Buck Henry, Beverly D'Angelo, John Hurt, Anita Morris, Bridget Fonda, Tilda Swinton.* A sensual explosion of sight and sound, *Aria* is a bold and adventurous collage of vignettes inspired by the greatest opera arias of all time. Ten of the finest and most innovative contemporary filmmakers (including Robert Altman, Bruce Beresford, Jean-Luc Godard, Derek Jarman, Nicolas Roeg, Ken Russell, and Julien Temple) were asked to choose their favorite operatic arias and create a short interpretation of the music, independent of the original libretto. The result is a series of mini-masterpieces filled with tantalizing imagery exposing the raw emotional power and deeply erotic nature of opera. ★★★ VHS: $9.99; DVD: $24.99

Ariel

(1988, 74 min, Finland, Aki Kaurismäki) *Susanna Haavisto, Turo Pajala.* Director Kaurismäki probes in his films the gritty, near-hopeless condition of his characters with a near deadpan cinematic style graced with both insight and biting satire. This black-and-white comedy-drama of forgotten hopes and resilient love follows an alienated, down-on-his-heels drifter who, in his huge Cadillac convertible, embarks on a journey from Lapland to Helsinki that soon involves him in crime, a murder, a jail-break, a marriage and eventually a chance to escape all his problems. An invigorating black comedy that will remind one of a European Jim Jarmusch or a quirkier Wim Wenders. (Finnish with English subtitles) ★★★ VHS: $79.99

The Aristocats

(1970, 78 min, US, Wolfgang Reitherman) *Voices of: Phil Harris, Eva Gabor, Sterling Holloway, Scatman Crothers.* This Disney animated feature isn't in the same league as some of their "classics," but is charming nonetheless. Duchess and her three kittens belong to a wealthy old lady who has willed their fortune to the felines to the dismay of the butler. He kidnaps them in an attempt to get the inheritance for himself and, knowing that as city cats they will be in danger in the country, leaves them to fend for themselves. Enter the charming Thomas O'Malley, Alley Cat (Harris), who rescues them and returns them to their rightful home. The usual high Disney quality in addition to some adorable songs. ★★★½ VHS: $26.99; DVD: $29.99

Arizona Dream

(1994, 119 min, US, Emir Kusturica) *Johnny Depp, Faye Dunaway, Lili Taylor, Jerry Lewis.* Director Kusturica seemlessly blends together reality, fantasy and dreams to create this emotionally complex vision of a young man's journey into adulthood. Depp stars as a lyrical NYC government employee who travels to Arizona to attend the wedding of his car salesman uncle (a somewhat schticky Lewis). Both Dunaway and Taylor give appropriately bizarre but grounded performances as a mother and daughter who take turns seducing/torturing Depp with their weird and dangerous charms. Not for everyone and somewhat psychedelic in mood. ★★★ VHS: $19.99

Arlington Road

(1999, 119 min, US, Mark Pellington) *Jeff Bridges, Tim Robbins, Joan Cusack, Hope Davis, Mason Gamble.* Reminiscent of *The Parallax View* in terms of suspense and smarts, this stylish, tense conspiracy thriller sets a taut pace for itself and rarely lets up. In a gripping performance, Bridges is Michael Farraday, a college professor who, in the film's unnerving beginning, saves the life of his neighbor's son. Befriending the couple, the Langs (Robbins and Cusack), Farraday slowly begins to suspect that this Ozzie and Harriet couple may be plotting terrorist bombings. As he digs deeper, he soon puts himself and those around him in harm's way. Director Pellington is equally adept with his action scenes and the more intimate, personal moments. He makes sure that you're never ahead of the game, and rattles you a little if you think you have it all figured out. Robbins and Cusack underplay their parts wonderfully, bringing just the right amount of civility and menace to their roles. ★★★ VHS: $9.99; DVD: $19.99

Armageddon

(1998, 150 min, US, Michael Bay) *Bruce Willis, Ben Affleck, Billy Bob Thornton, Liv Tyler, Will Patton, Steve Buscemi.* It's hard to totally dislike a film that boasts a world-ending meteor and a cast of top-drawer actors instructed to play this action sci-fi yarn to melodramatic excess. When a meteor the size of Manhattan takes aim at our lovely planet, the world powers select a tough-talkin' oilrigger (Willis) and his colorful gang of misfit employees. This group includes the handsome Affleck as Willis' sidekick who, when not trying to save the world, keeps company with Tyler, the daughter of a mightily disapproving Willis. Others include the seriously weird Buscemi, and a more serious Patton (you know what happens to the more serious actors in epics like this — they get squashed like a bug!). The scenes in which the riggers-cum-astronauts land on the meteor are rather good, though the story doesn't equal the effects. *Armageddon* can be mindless fun if not taken too seriously because it doesn't take itself too seriously. (VHS available letterboxed or pan & scan) ★★ VHS: $14.99; DVD: $29.99

Armed and Dangerous

(1986, 113 min, US, Mark L. Lester) *John Candy, Eugene Levy, Robert Loggia, Meg Ryan.* This bungling comedy stars the big guy as an ex-policeman who becomes a security guard and, through no skill of his own, exposes a crooked union official. ★½ VHS: $9.99

Army of Darkness

(1993, 85 min, US, Sam Raimi) *Bruce Campbell, Embeth Davidtz, Bridget Fonda.* This wildly stylish and deliriously imaginative sequel to the cult classics *Evil Dead* and *Evil Dead 2* continues the misadventures of the reluctant hero, Ash (Campbell), as he, along with a chainsaw, sawed-off shotgun and a 1970s Oldsmobile, are mysteriously sent back to medieval times to retrieve "The Book of the Dead," battle netherworld demons and more. Laced with director Raimi's trademark seizure-inducing camerawork, hysterically gruesome special effects and black-humored violence, the film succeeds on all levels as we follow Ash's exploits as he attempts to get back to modern times and his job at S-Mart ("Shop smart — shop S-mart"). (Letterboxed) ★★★½ VHS: $14.99

Around the World in 80 Days

(1956, 167 min, US, Michael Anderson) *David Niven, Cantiflas, Shirley MacLaine.* A mammoth and vastly entertaining version of Jules Verne's novel. Niven stars as Phineas Fogg, the globe-trotting British gentleman whose bet that he can circle the world in 80 days leads him and Cantiflas on a succession of adventures, including meeting up with princess MacLaine. The film features 44 cameos and the location shootings are remarkable. Winner of five Oscars, including Best Picture. (Remade in 1989) ★★★★ VHS: $29.99

Around the World in Eighty Ways

(1986, 90 min, Australia, Stephen MacLean) *Philip Quast, Alan Penney, Diana Davidson.* While it would help to have a Sydney audience cue an American in on the cultural humor and inside jokes, this energetically wacky Aussie comedy is still entertaining in an easy-going, nondemanding way. Quast is Wally, a resourceful and cash-poor tour guide who comes up with the zaniest of schemes: take dear old senile dad on an improvised and very fake tour around the world — staged in a neighbor's tacky suburban home — and pocket the money that would have paid for a real trip. Quickly paced and manic, the film has a sweet, gentle heart. Quast gives a fast, funny performance — impersonating everyone from Hawaiian hula dancers to Elvis to the Pope — in this infectious, spirited comedy. ★★★

Around the World with Orson Welles

(1955, 134 min, GB, Orson Welles) In 1955, long past his *enfant terrible* stage and in what arguably should have been the most productive period of his creative life, Orson Welles was making travel documentaries for the BBC. While the programs are charming and stimulating, you're left with the feeling that you've just watched Babe Ruth play bush league. There are five episodes. "St. Germain des Pres" explores the artistic life in one of Paris' oldest quarters, with an interview with expatriate American Raymond Duncan. In "Chelsea Pensioners," Welles interviews two sets of retirees in and near London. "Madrid Bullfight" enters the bloody arena and provides just enough explanation of technique and history. Two episodes on the Basque country, "Pays Basque I & II," are lyrical poems to this borderland between Spain and France. Well worth checking out, especially for Welles' aficionados. ★★★ VHS: $19.99; DVD: $29.99

The Arrival

(1996, 109 min, US, David Twohy) *Charlie Sheen, Ron Silver, Lindsay Crouse, Teri Polo.* Clearly cast against type, Sheen stars as a radio astronomer and all-around good guy who uncovers a secret government plot and intergalactic conspiracy. When he records a radio frequency spike from outer space and delivers the news to his boss (Silver), he is promptly demoted and his discovery is covered up and destroyed. Sheen soon follows a trail to Mexico where he uncovers the truth: the temperature of the Earth is increasing, making it habitable for alien life — but deadly for humans! Pleasantly surprising, this medium-budgeted sci-fi thriller, though not entirely original (it is reminiscent of *They Live*), is consistently engaging. (Letterboxed VHS available for $14.99) ★★★ VHS: $9.99; DVD: $14.99

Arrowsmith

(1931, 101 min, US, John Ford) *Ronald Colman, Helen Hayes, Myrna Loy.* Colman's stirring performance as a dedicated medical researcher highlights this sincere, classy adaptation of the Sinclair Lewis novel. ★★★★ VHS: $14.99

Arsenic and Old Lace

(1944, 118 min, US, Frank Capra) *Cary Grant, Raymond Massey, Peter Lorre, Josephine Hull, Jean Adair, Priscilla Lane, Edward Everett Horton.* This Capra gem takes place in Brooklyn on Halloween. The skeletons aren't in the closet, they're in the basement. Grant's brother thinks he's Teddy Roosevelt, and his poison-happy aunts think of themselves as sane. Cary's other brother (played with panache by Massey) bears a striking resemblance to Boris Karloff, and hangs out with Lorre. And the viewer has as much fun watching all this as the cast obviously had in making it. ★★★★ VHS: $14.99; DVD: $19.99

The Art of War

(2000, 117 min, US, Christian Duguay) *Wesley Snipes, Anne Archer, Maury Chaykin, Donald Sutherland, Michael Biehn.* In this by-the-books thriller, Snipes plays a covert agent for the United Nations, using state-of-the-art technological gadgets and good old-fashioned blackmail to accomplish his goals. When a mission goes awry, Snipes is framed for murder. His bosses can't admit he exists, so he's on his own. What begins as a passable *Mission: Impossible*/James Bond puzzler becomes a formulaic chase and shoot-'em-up actioner. Too bad, because Snipes is in good form here. Supporting characters, however, are one-dimensional. ★½ VHS: $14.99; DVD: $24.99

Artemisia

(1998, 102 min, France, Agnes Merlet) *Valentina Cervi, Michel Serrault, Miki Manojlovic, Luca Zingaretti.* Soft-core masquerading as an art film, *Artemisia* is a biopic about the first woman painter in 17th-century Italy. The film, which presents the life and times of Artemisia Gentileschi (Cervi), has some notable things going for it — a few ideas on perspective, and ample nudity — but the dramatic crux of the narrative is flimsy. Director Merlet, who cowrote the screenplay, focuses on Artemisia's relationship with her mentor, Tassi (Manojlovic), and a large segment of the film is devoted to a trial about whether or not he raped her. Most viewers, however, will prefer watching the numerous sex scenes and nude models, for they are far more interesting. *Artemisia* tries to be an intelligent examination of a female painter trying to overcome the prejudices of the time, and it ends up being artless. (French with English subtitles) ★★ VHS: $19.99

Arthur

(1981, 97 min, US, Steve Gordon) *Dudley Moore, Liza Minnelli, John Gielgud, Geraldine Fitzgerald, Barney Martin, Ted Ross.* Recalling the very best of the screwball comedies, first-time director Gordon's hilariously sweet tale is rich in both near-convulsive one-liners and high spirits. In a role which brought him an Oscar nomination and reminds us of the true star potential he once demonstrated, Moore is perfection as the title character, a drunken poor little rich man (net worth: $700 mil) who risks it all to woo the personable (but penniless) Minnelli. Moore's endearing clown is one of the screen's great comedic inebriates, but even he is upstaged by Gielgud, who won a much-deserved Academy Award as Arthur's acerbic valet and confidant. Sadly, writer-director Gordon died shortly after the release of *Arthur*, leaving only speculation as to what joys would have followed his wonderful debut. ★★★★ VHS: $9.99; DVD: $14.99

Arthur 2: On the Rocks

(1988, 110 min, US, Bud Yorkin) *Dudley Moore, Liza Minnelli, John Gielgud, Geraldine Fitzgerald, Kathy Bates, Jack Gilford.* The presence of the original's writer-director, Steve Gordon, is sorely missed in this uninspired sequel. Moore can probably do this bit in his sleep, and he manages to produce a few laughs despite the absence of a substantial script; but for the most part, this is tough going. You wanna see lovable Dudley and Liza again, rent the original. ★½ VHS: $14.99

Article 99

(1992, 99 min, US, Howard Deutch) *Ray Liotta, Kiefer Sutherland, Forest Whitaker, Lea Thompson, John Mahoney, Eli Wallach, Kathy Baker, John C. McGinley, Keith David.* A compelling if familiar comedy-drama in the *M*A*S*H* vein about a group of dedicated doctors working for the Veterans Administration. Liotta plays the chief surgeon who, along with new-cutter-on-the-block Sutherland, leads the fight against bureaucratic red tape and administrative corruption. ★★½ VHS: $6.99

Artists and Models

(1955, 109 min, US, Frank Tashlin) *Dean Martin, Jerry Lewis, Shirley MacLaine, Dorothy Malone, Eva Gabor.* A crazy Martin-Lewis romp with artist Martin and writer Lewis trying to get ahead. Dean ultimately uses Jerry's nightly dreams as inspiration for a comic book. MacLaine plays Jerry's kooky, astrology-reading girlfriend (an image she'd begin to begin living down some 25 years later). Jerry's antics are particularly funny. ★★★ VHS: $14.99

As Good as It Gets

(1997, 139 min, US, James L. Brooks) *Jack Nicholson, Helen Hunt, Greg Kinnear, Cuba*

As Good as It Gets

Gooding, Jr., Shirley Knight, Skeet Ulrich. With one of his richest characterizations in years, Nicholson soars as a misanthropic, obsessive-compulsive writer who despite himself finds romance and friendship. Melvin (Nicholson) is the neighbor from hell to all the tenants of his New York apartment building. His compulsive personality is so off-putting that there's only one waitress at his favorite restaurant who will wait on him. That's Carol (Hunt), who's looking after her sick son. When Melvin's neighbor Simon (Kinnear), a gay artist, is seriously injured in a robbery, Melvin's life is turned around when he agrees to watch Simon's dog. Brooks and Mark Andrus' story doesn't really go very far plot-wise, but it is their funny, intuitive dialogue which causes sparks, and the cast is absolutely wonderful in bringing these characters to life. Hunt gives such a full-fledged star performance that even her Emmy Award-winning TV work doesn't prepare one for her comic precision and dramatic depth. As Simon, Kinnear's gay act is suspicious at first, but he really creates a caring, funny, three-dimensional character. An extremely well-acted, sweetly endearing and offbeat romantic comedy which won Oscars for both Jack and Helen. ★★★½ VHS: $14.99; DVD: $19.99

As Is

(1986, 86 min, US, Michael Lindsay-Hogg) *Robert Carradine, Jonathan Hadary.* Based on the acclaimed Broadway production, this powerful, opened-up play stars Carradine and Hadary as ex-lovers who are brought together when the former is stricken with AIDS. Often humorous and never morose, author William Hoffman doesn't pull his punches with either his portrayal of a gay lifestyle or the emotional toll the disease takes. ★★★ VHS: $19.99

As Summers Die

(1986, 88 min, US, Jean-Claude Tramont) *Bette Davis, Scott Glenn, Jamie Lee Curtis.* A small Southern town's richest family makes an attempt to take away farmland from an elderly black woman, believing that the land is rich with oil in this tale of greed, racism and justice

circa 1950. A pleasant if slender made-for-TV drama. ★★½

As You Desire Me

(1932, 71 min, US, George Fitzmaurice) *Greta Garbo, Melvyn Douglas, Erich von Stroheim.* Garbo gives an earnest performance in this fair adaptation of Pirandello's play. Garbo stars as an amnesiac who is reunited with husband Douglas, only she doesn't remember him. Von Stroheim is appropriately slimy as an ex-lover who has other ideas about her true identity. ★★ VHS: $19.99

As You Like It

(1936, 96 min, GB, Paul Czinner) *Laurence Olivier, Elizabeth Bergner, Sophie Stewart.* Less cinematic than 1935's deliriously kitschy *A Midsummer Night's Dream*, this more earth-and-stagebound London production still manages to entertain. Fascinating performances from Olivier and Bergner almost compensate for Czinner's unsure direction and perverse penchant for shooting speakers from behind excessively large hats. Though distracting, Olivier's ardent nervous tics add unusual depth to the exiled Orlando, but top-billed Bergner's bizarre, bifurcated Rosalind/Ganymede is symptomatic of the entire enterprise: her thick Teutonic accent spitting Elizabethan iambs disallows easy listening, and her stolid Rosalind suggests a German shepherd barking through the mouth of a kewpie doll. Uneven fun, with a William Walton score as airy as his *Hamlet* was crushing, and confusing editing credited to David Lean. ★★★ DVD: $29.99

As Young as You Feel

(1951, 77 min, US, Harmon Jones) *Monty Woolley, Thelma Ritter, David Wayne, Marilyn Monroe.* Woolley gives a spirited performance in this fetching comedy (based on a Paddy Chayefsky story) which takes a playful swipe at big business. Woolley plays an employee who is retired upon turning 65. In response, he impersonates the president of his firm's parent company to reverse the retirement policy. Things get out of hand when he is forced to continue the charade. ★★★

Ashes and Diamonds

(1958, 104 min, Poland, Andrzej Wajda) *Zbigniew Cybulski, Eva Krzyzewska.* Wajda, initiator of the Polish Film Renaissance, creates a penetrating account of a young WWII Resistance fighter whose loyalty to his comrades conflicts with his internal desires. Cybulski ("the Polish Brando") is the ambivalent youth lost in the chaos of the post-war days. A serious, insightful and brilliantly structured examination of both wartime and peacetime allegiances and turmoil. Wajda's final film in his acclaimed "War Trilogy" which includes *A Generation* and *Kanal.* (Polish with English subtitles) ★★★★ VHS: $24.99

Ashes of Time

(1994, 100 min, Hong Kong, Wong Kar-Wei) *Leslie Cheung, Tony Leung Ka Fai, Maggie Cheung, Brigitte Lin Ching Hsia.* From the director of *Chungking Express* comes this lyrical, haunting samurai tale set in a small desert village in ancient China. Ou-yang Feng (Cheung) is a swordsman who is hired to track down a band of horse thieves. But as he prepares for that hunt, he becomes stuck in the middle of a romantic entanglement between a jilted woman and her lover. (Cantonese with English subtitles) ★★★ VHS: $89.99; DVD: $29.99

Ashik Kerib

(1988, 75 min, USSR, Sergei Paradjanov) *Yiur Mgoyan, Veronika Metonidze.* Dedicated to the memory of Andrei Tarkovsky, Paradjanov's final film is an exotic and ebullient Georgian folk tale based on a story by Mikhail Lermontov. Although pregnant with symbolism and oblique nationalistic references to Georgia's ancient culture, the film remains accessible and even quite enjoyable essentially because of its age-old story of love conquering all. A handsome but poor minstrel must travel through the countryside to earn enough money to marry his young love, the beautiful daughter of a rich Turkish merchant. His fantastic adventures are spectacularly filmed in poetic, almost fantastic images. There is little dialogue, with the episodic story infused with striking visuals and hypnotic traditional music and dances. Often obscure, but always riveting. (Georgian with English subtitles) ★★★ VHS: $29.99; DVD: $34.99

Ask Any Girl

(1959, 101 min, US, Charles Walters) *Shirley MacLaine, David Niven, Gig Young, Rod Taylor.* MacLaine has one of her best early-career roles in this effervescent gender-gap comedy. She plays a small-town girl who moves to the big city, thus beginning an enchanting and laugh-filled sex farce. The story follows MacLaine's romantic trials and tribulations as she searches for the perfect mate. After a few false starts, MacLaine is employed by brothers Niven and Young. Thinking Young "the one," she cajoles Niven to help her trap his brother; which they do in a most outrageous fashion. MacLaine absolutely beguiles: she's sassy, daffy and smart. Niven is as debonair as ever. And Young is a good comic foil. One of the best of that era's sex comedies. ★★★½ VHS: $19.99

The Asphalt Jungle

(1950, 112 min, US, John Huston) *Sterling Hayden, James Whitmore, Sam Jaffe, Louis Calhearn, Marilyn Monroe.* One of Huston's most memorable efforts, this taut drama is a brilliantly stylized crime story about a group of hoods plotting a major heist. Led by a curious, almost mystical German expatriate, the gang woos the local establishment for backing. An insightful tale of moral corruption, the film is a classic example of superb ensemble acting featuring flawless characterizations by the cast. Filmed in a striking and moody black and white. ★★★★ VHS: $19.99

The Asphyx

(1972, 99 min, GB, Peter Newbrook) *Robert Stephens, Robert Powell, Jane Lapotaire.* Intriguing, highly original horror film about a 19th-century British scientist (Stephens) who uncovers one of the secrets of death and uses it to become immortal. ★★★ DVD: $24.99

The Assassination Bureau

(1969, 110 min, GB, Basil Dearden) *Diana Rigg, Oliver Reed, Telly Savalas, Curt Jurgens, Clive Revill.* Fans of the old "Avengers" series won't want to miss this lustrous black pearl of a comedy. The ex-"Mrs. Peel," Rigg, stars as a turn-of-the-century journalist who goes up against a secret society of self-appointed assassins charged with ridding the world of undesirables. Based on a story by

Robert Louis Stevenson, the film recalls such cinematic treasures as *The Abominable Doctor Phibes* and *The Wrong Box.* ★★★ VHS: $9.99

The Assassination of Trotsky

(1972, 103 min, GB/France, Joseph Losey) *Richard Burton, Alain Delon, Romy Schneider.* Losey's uneven and unhistorical account of the last days of the exiled Trotsky is buoyed by an outstanding performance from Burton. Delon is effectively enigmatic as the Stalinist assassin sent to Mexico to hunt him down. ★★

Assassins

(1995, 132 min, US, Richard Donner) *Sylvester Stallone, Antonio Banderas, Julianne Moore.* Playing an aging professional killer, Stallone looks as though he can't wait to get to the phone to fire his agent. But it's too little, too late. In this brainless actioner, Sly finds himself dogged and pursued by new hit man on the block Banderas. The young upstart means to prove himself by killing Stallone, the best in his field. The inevitable chase begins, ending in a dusty Mexican town which gives way to too many clichés. Director Donner seems to be copying John Woo, down to slow-motion shots and protagonists leaping through the air, pistols blazing. What he produces, however, is a boring and confusing movie. Stallone comes off best — that should be warning enough. Written by the Wachowski Brothers, who were *Bound* for greater success. ★½ VHS: $9.99; DVD: $19.99

The Assault

(1986, 150 min, The Netherlands, Fons Rademakers) *Derek De Lint, Marc Van Uchelen, Monique Van De Ven.* The moving and emotional story of a boy's traumatic wartime experiences and its after-effects on him as an adult, won the 1986 Academy Award for Best Foreign–Language Film, yet oddly was released on video only in the dubbed version. The film is set in two time periods: a small town during World War II, where a young boy's family is killed by the Nazis, and in the adult years of the boy, as he struggles to reconcile his parents' death and to begin a new life. (Dubbed) ★★★½ VHS: $79.99

Assault at West Point

(1993, 98 min, US, Harry Moses) *Al Freeman, Jr., Samuel L. Jackson, Sam Waterston, Seth Gilliam, John Glover, Eddie Bracken.* Told in flashback by a noticeably lighter in skin tone Freeman, this real–life tale of racism focuses on a young African-American West Point cadet (Gilliam) who is accused and finally court–martialed for faking his own attack. With Waterston and Jackson as the defendant's lawyers, the film features zombie-esque performances, and this, combined with Gilliam's even less impressive thesping, help to reduce what should have been a thought–provoking, intense experience to a disappointment. ★½ VHS: $9.99

Assault of the Killer Bimbos

(1988, 85 min, US, Anita Rosenberg) *Patti Astor, Christina Whitaker, Griffin O'Neal, Nick Cassavetes, Eddie Deezen.* Sophomoric hijinks as three buxom beauties, planning their careers in the movie biz, head for Mexico. But not before they take on over-sexed surfers, jealous boyfriends and the police. ★½ DVD: $24.99

Zbignew Cybulski gets roughed up in *Ashes and Diamonds*

Assault on Precinct 13

(1976, 90 min, US, **John Carpenter**) *Austin Stoker, Darwin Joston, Nancy Loomis*. A novice Carpenter directed this intense, immensely satisfying thriller, a harbinger of things to come from the young filmmaker. A Los Angeles gang seizes control of an almost deserted police station, forcing the officers and civilians trapped inside to fight for their lives. Suggested by Howard Hawks' *Rio Bravo*. ★★★½ VHS: $14.99; DVD: $29.99

The Assignment

(1997, 115 min, US, **Christian Duguay**) *Donald Sutherland, Ben Kingsley, Aidan Quinn*. Navy officer and family man Quinn is quite content to follow orders, toe the line, and lead a nice, quiet life. Unfortunately for him, he happens to be physically identical to the notorious terrorist the Jackal (no relation to Bruce Willis), and he is forced by CIA operative Sutherland to accept an undercover mission to put an end to the Jackal's reign. The film never achieves that neat balance between probing psychodrama and slam-bang action that John Woo's *Face/Off* typifies. This is strictly comic book stuff, and as such, it's rather entertaining. The action scenes are crisp and suspenseful, if unremarkable. ★★½ VHS: $9.99; DVD: $14.99

The Associate

(1996, 114 min, US, **Donald Petrie**) *Whoopi Goldberg, Tim Daly, Dianne Wiest, Eli Wallach, Bebe Neuwirth, Austin Pendleton, Lainie Kazan, Kenny Kerr*. A genuinely enjoyable satire of Wall Street, *The Associate* is sort of a low-keyed *Jerry Maguire* meets *Tootsie*. Whoopi plays a financial analyst who is passed over for a promotion at her Wall Street firm clearly for reasons of gender. Deciding to start her own agency, she discovers not being part of the old boys' network is bad for business — that is until she invents a fictitious male partner. With the help of savvy secretary Wiest, Whoopi takes Wall Street by storm — even if it means a little male drag. *The Associate* doesn't go as far as it could have, and isn't as consistently funny as one would wish. But it does have good-natured barbs, humorous characterizations, and Whoopi in good form. Suggested by the 1979 French comedy of the same name. ★★★ VHS: $9.99

The Astronaut's Wife

(1999, 110 min, US, **Rand Ravich**) *Johnny Depp, Charlize Theron, Joe Morton, Clea DuVall*. Despite the presence of Depp, this is nearly a worthless sci-fi/horror film. Theron is the dippy wife of national hero Depp, whose latest mission is marred by a two-minute scare when communications with NASA were lost while he was floating in space. Now back on Earth, he seems. . . different somehow. This boring, predictable, choppy, uninvolving *Rosemary's Baby* ripoff features Depp and Morton's worst performances, moronic, obvious camerawork, and a crappy, would-be cynical, twist ending. Theron tries, but it's a lost cause. ★ VHS: $14.99; DVD: $19.99

Asylum

(1972, 92 min, GB, **Roy Ward Baker**) *Peter Cushing, Herbert Lom, Charlotte Rampling*. A young psychiatrist arrives at his new job and must hear the personal stories of four inmates in this horror anthology film. Written by Robert Bloch (the creator of *Psycho*), the film is very interesting and effectively scary; some characters are better than others, but most films of this type are similarly uneven. Rampling's story is the weakest, probably because it is concerned more with psychology than with the supernatural. The first story in the quartet is the most frightening, involving the bizarre form a murdered wife's revenge takes. And just when you think the whole thing is over, one final terror awaits the unwary viewer. Fun, frightening and solidly enjoyable. ★★★ VHS: $19.99; DVD: $24.99

Asylum

(1996, 92 min, US, **James Seale**) *Robert Patrick, Malcolm McDowell, Sarah Douglas, Jason Schombing, Deborah Worthing, Henry Gibson*. A sleeper in the negative sense of the term, *Asylum*, a miscalculated thriller, stars Patrick as a suicidal P.I. who goes undercover at the local asylum when a childhood friend is found dead. This weak ripoff of *Shock Corridor* (and every other asylum movie, really) is a boring, obvious mystery — if you can't guess the outcome early on, you've never seen a mystery. ★ VHS: $79.99

At Close Range

(1986, 115 min, US, **James Foley**) *Sean Penn, Christopher Walken, Mary Stuart Masterson, Chris Penn, Crispin Glover*. This intense drama examines the brittle relationship between a teenager and his estranged father, a small-time hood who introduces the youth to petty crime and murder. As the father and son, respectively, Walken and Penn offer stunning performances. Based on a true story. ★★★½ VHS: $9.99; DVD: $19.99

At First Sight

(1999, 126 min, US, **Irwin Winkler**) *Val Kilmer, Mira Sorvino, Kelly McGillis, Nathan Lane, Steven Weber, Bruce Davison*. Adapted from the story by Dr. Oliver Sacks, whose real-life experiences inspired *Awakenings*, comes another tale of a medically impaired man who temporarily beats the odds. Not as dramatically involving nor as nicely paced as *Awakenings*, the sincere though ordinary *At First Sight* stars Kilmer as Virgil, a blind masseur who works at a mountain resort in upstate New York. When Virgil undergoes an operation and has his sight restored, he has difficulty in adjusting to a sighted world. As the sensitive Virgil, Kilmer is easy-going and nice to look at, but the part offers little for the actor to grab hold to. Lane makes a nice impression as a maverick therapist who tries to help Virgil adjust to seeing for the first time. ★★ VHS: $9.99; DVD: $14.99

At Home with the Webbers

(1993, 109 min, US, **Brad Marlowe**) *Jeffrey Tambor, Jennifer Tilly, David Arquette, Robby Benson, Luke Perry*. Could you imagine having your family broadcast live on television during its most intimate moments? The Webbers are chosen to be the stars of a new 24-hour cable show. They are moved into a house equipped with video cameras in almost every corner. Tilly plays the sex-hungry daughter who is willing to do anything to get plaster casts of male body parts. ★★½ VHS: $79.99

At Play in the Fields of the Lord

(1992, 186 min, US, **Hector Babenco**) *Tom Berenger, John Lithgow, Kathy Bates, Aidan Quinn, Daryl Hannah, Tom Waits*. An ambitious and sweeping epic about a group of fundamentalist missionaries who come in conflict with a tribe of Amazonian Indians. Berenger stars as a half-breed Native American who believes he's returned to his spiritual source. Those familiar with Peter Matthiessen's richly textured parable on faith and the soul might be disappointed by the film's lack of cohesive direction. However, the finely detailed work of the ensemble cast, coupled with the beautiful cinematography of the lush South American jungle, will carry the viewer easily through the long running time. ★★★ VHS: $19.99

At the Circus

(1939, 87 min, US, **Edward Buzzell**) *The Marx Brothers, Margaret Dumont, Eve Arden*. Lydia, oh Lydia, say, have you met Lydia... Groucho walks on the ceiling with Arden; it's all in the line of duty, of course. He's after the $10,000 stolen from the disinherited nephew of Newport heiress Dumont, which is needed to keep the circus from being taken over by the nefarious scalliwag who stole the money. Got that? Chico and Harpo are there to assist. Though not among the handful of Marx Brothers classics, there are quite a few funny scenes to be had. ★★½ VHS: $19.99

L'Atalante

(1934, 89 min, France, **Jean Vigo**) *Dita Parlo, Jean Dasté, Michel Simon*. This lyrical, cinematic poem follows a honeymooning couple (Parlo and Dasté) as they blissfully float down the Seine on a barge accompanied by their first mate, the crusty Simon. Long considered one of the greatest romance stories in film history, *L'Atalante* was one of only two films made by director Vigo before his untimely death at age 29, but this classic was surrounded by controversy and innuendo from its inception. Having just recently finished *Zero for Conduct* (which had been banned in France), Vigo was a contentious choice to direct *L'Atalante* and indeed his original cut was rejected by the movie theatre owners and ultimately re-edited. Tragically, Vigo died just weeks after the film's unsuccessful run at the box office and a year later, the film was once again amended. This unhappy saga at long last came to an end in 1989 when archivists went into the vaults and resurrected Vigo's original version of the film, now available in a remastered print. (French with English subtitles) ★★★★ VHS: $29.99

Atlantic City

(1981, 104 min, Canada, **Louis Malle**) *Burt Lancaster, Susan Sarandon, Kate Reid, Robert Joy, Hollis McLaren*. In this fascinating, intelligent character study, director Malle captures the Atlantic City of the '80s, a city living with its faded past and a fragile optimism for the future. Lancaster, in what may be the performance of his career, brilliantly plays a small-time numbers runner with notions of grandeur who gets a chance at the big score when he crosses paths with casino employee Sarandon and her ex-husband and drug pusher Joy. The simplicity of the characters' lives and dreams belies the tumultuous events which follow when all are eventually tempted by the attainable usually just beyond their grasp. Reid is especially good as a former beauty contest winner living with the ghost of her gangster husband, and Sarandon, whose first great performance this was, demonstrates the eroticism of lemons in an unforgettable scene. Arguably Malle at his best. ★★★★ VHS: $14.99

Austin Powers: The Spy Who Shagged Me

The Atomic Cafe

(1982, 90 min, US, Kevin Rafferty) A nervously funny juxtaposition of atomic propaganda films. The footage includes testament to the beauty of the blast, reassurances of the minimal cause for worry and other testing examples of governmental lunacy. ★★★ VHS: $29.99

Attack Force Z

(1981, 84 min, Australia, Tim Burstall) Mel Gibson, John Phillip Law, Sam Neill. A young Gibson stars in this competent WWII adventure film about an elite group of commandos who are assigned to rescue a defecting Japanese official from an enemy-held island in the Pacific. Awaiting the men are unbearable heat, an uncharted jungle and thousands of Japanese soldiers. ★★½

Attack of the Killer Tomatoes

(1980, 87 min, US, John DeBello) David Miller, Sharon Taylor, George Wilson, Jack Riley. Unbelievably silly horror spoof about some ravenous, rampaging tomatoes ravaging San Diego and its poor, defenseless citizens. Is there no one but the San Diego chicken to help? Will the Secret Service outwit these gruesome garnishments from a chef's salad? Will Nixon end the war? ★★

Attila 74: The Rape of Cyprus

(1975, 103 min, Greece, Michael Cacoyannis) Filmmaker Cacoyannis (*Zorba the Greek*) was in London at the time of the Turkish invasion of Cyprus in 1974. Returning immediately to his besieged homeland, he began making this part-documentary, part-personal journal. A deeply passionate and devastatingly powerful film that bears witness to the horrors of the invasion and mounts strong evidence on its accusations against the Turks, the Greek puppet leaders and international indifference. (Greek with English subtitles) ★★★½ VHS: $19.99; DVD: $29.99

Au Revoir les Enfants

(1987, 103 min, France, Louis Malle) Gaspard Manesse, Raphael Fejto, Francine Racette, Irene Jacob. Director Malle's acclaimed autobiograph-ical tale of his early school days is a poignant reminiscence of childhood camaraderie, social responsibility and the human tragedy of war. Set in occupied France during WWII, the story centers on the friendship which blossoms between two young, gifted schoolboys — one Catholic and one Jewish — when the latter hides out in a private boarding school to escape the Nazis. The beauty and mastery of Malle's film lies in his precise eye for period detail, well-structured character development, and an insightful and accurate portrayal of adolescent behavior. (French with English subtitles) ★★★★

Audrey Rose

(1977, 114 min, US, Robert Wise) Anthony Hopkins, Marsha Mason, John Beck. This over-long, plodding thriller about reincarnation tries to be both scary and meaningful, but fails in both departments. Ivy is a precocious young girl living with her well-to-do parents in New York City. A mysterious stranger (Hopkins) soon begins following the family around the city while at the same time a recurring nightmare Ivy has been having increases in both intensity and frequency. The stranger eventually approaches the family with an unbelievable tale about how his daughter, Audrey Rose, killed in an auto accident, has been reincarnated as Ivy. Mason is Ivy's distraught mother, who initially refuses to believe the story. The weak script makes the film, alternately, a ghost story, a courtroom drama and a diatribe on Eastern religion. ★½ VHS: $9.99

August

(1995, 99 min, Wales, Anthony Hopkins) Anthony Hopkins, Leslie Phillips, Kate Burton, Rhian Morgan, Gawn Grainger. Hopkins' direc-torial debut is a spry adaptation of Chekhov's "Uncle Vanya" set on the sun-drenched coast of Wales. Proficient in most regards, the film has the unfortunate honor of being held up to the mirror of Louis Malle and Andre Gregory's genius collaboration *Vanya on 42nd Street*. Hopkins eschews the minute and intricate character study of *Vanya* for a more theatrical, composed variation. The result is not as powerful by any means, but not entirely without merit. Hopkins provides his ample thespian talents in front of the camera as Ieuan (Vanya's Welsh doppleganger), a ne'er-do-well whose hopes of living high on his family's country estate are dashed by the presence of his ex-brother-in-law, an undistinguished retired college professor. This slightly comic take on Chekhov's classic tale is certain to delight those who live on a diet of BBC period pieces and the like. ★★½ VHS: $79.99

Auntie Mame

(1958, 144 min, US, Morton Da Costa) Rosalind Russell, Forrest Tucker, Patric Knowles, Coral Browne, Peggy Cass. Russell shines in a career-topping performance as everybody's favorite relative: Auntie Mame. Based on the hit play by Patrick Dennis, this gloriously funny adaptation follows the comic antics of an orphaned nephew who moves in with his eccentric aunt. A classic instance in which role and performer were destined for each other. Auntie Mame's best slogan: "Life is a banquet and most poor suckers are starving to death." (VHS available letterboxed or pan & scan) ★★★★ VHS: $14.99

Austin Powers: International Man of Mystery

(1997, 95 min, US, Jay Roach) Mike Myers, Elizabeth Hurley, Mimi Rogers, Michael York, Robert Wagner. A hilariously goofy, off-the-wall and dead-on-target spoof of James Bond and other '60s spy movies. Myers sports a set of crooked dentures, thick horn-rimmed glasses, an unsightly swath of artificial chest hair and gets decked-out in velvety '60s garb as Austin Powers, a "swingin'" 1960s English superspy. Myers also plays Powers' nemesis, the nefarious but insecure Dr. Evil. Both Powers and Dr. Evil are cryogenically frozen and thawed out in 1997, and they awake to a world that has long since surpassed them. The key to the film's side-splittingly funny humor is the loving attention to detail and its no-holds-barred, un-PC naughtiness (instead of Pussy Galore, we get a luscious femme fatale named Alotta Fagina!). A few of the jokes fall flat, and some references will be lost on all but devoted 007 fans, but *Austin Powers* nevertheless is witty, inspired lunacy from start to finish. Topped off with a fab soundtrack, this is "shag-a-delic" fun. (Letterboxed VHS available for $19.99) (Sequel: *Austin Powers: The Spy Who Shagged Me*) ★★★½ VHS: $14.99; DVD: $24.99

Austin Powers: The Spy Who Shagged Me

(1999, 95 min, US, Jay Roach) Mike Myers, Heather Graham, Seth Green, Robert Wagner, Rob Lowe, Verne Troyer, Michael York, Elizabeth Hurley. Not as fresh or consistent as the original, this still very funny sequel provides many a laugh through potty jokes and expanded retreads in place of the first film's sharper wit and innocent naughtiness. Myers returns as delusionally sexy agent Austin Powers as well as his bald-headed maniacal nemesis Dr. Evil (who gets more comic mileage this go-round). Dr. Evil escapes his space exile to travel back in time to 1969, where he incapacitates Powers by stealing his "mojo." Like Samson without his hair, Powers must also travel back to get his "mojo" rising once more. The jokes are frequent (and frequently tasteless), while the multitude of espionage movie parodies have been replaced with more '90s pop culture references. Additionally, Myers' Scottish alter ego arrives here as Fat Bastard, a makeup marvel who becomes annoying after awhile. Faring much better are some great sight gags (a hilarious tent scene), and a classic montage where characters (with smart cameos) try to describe Dr. Evil's Freudian spacecraft. (VHS available letterboxed or pan & scan) ★★★ VHS: $14.99; DVD: $24.99

Author! Author!

(1982, 110 min, US, Arthur Hiller) Al Pacino, Dyan Cannon, Tuesday Weld, Andre Gregory, Alan King. Pacino stars in this heartwarming comedy as a struggling playwright who must contend with raising his children when his flaky wife leaves him. Hiller directs a fine cast who deliver endearing performances across the board. ★★★ VHS: $14.99

Autobiography of a Princess

(1975, 59 min, GB, James Ivory) James Mason, Madhur Jaffrey. Produced by Ismail Merchant with a screenplay by Ruth Prawer Jhabvala, this is a delicate character study. An imperious princess, self-exiled in London and long-divorced, invites her father's ex-tutor to a yearly tea to reminisce about a "happier" past only to find that their memories of Royal India differ. ★★★ VHS: $29.99

An Autumn Afternoon

(1962, 115 min, Japan, Yasujiro Ozu) *Chishu Ryu, Shima Iwashita.* Master Japanese filmmaker Ozu's final film is a deceptively simple, contemplative and lyrical family drama. Continuing his theme from *Late Summer*, the story follows an aging widower who, against his wishes, arranges for a marriage for his only daughter, a move that leaves him lonely, with only his old drinking cronies for company. (Japanese with English subtitles) ★★★½ VHS: $19.99

Autumn in New York

(2000, 104 min, US, Joan Chen) *Richard Gere, Winona Ryder, Anthony LaPaglia, Elaine Stritch, Sherry Stringfield, Mary Beth Hurt.* Old-fashioned and sentimental, but not necessarily in the best sense of those words, this romantic tearjerker is long on the sap but does manage to produce a few affecting moments. Gere plays a 40-ish restaurateur and womanizer (successful on both counts) who falls for the 22-year-old daughter (Ryder) of a former girlfriend. Complications arise when he learns she hasn't long to live. Gere and Ryder exhibit little chemistry together, though individually each is satisfactory. The best performance, however, comes from Stritch as Ryder's acerbic grandmother. ★★ VHS: $14.99; DVD: $19.99

Autumn Leaves

(1956, 108 min, US, Robert Aldrich) *Joan Crawford, Cliff Robertson, Vera Miles, Lorne Greene.* Crawford is in long-suffering mode as a lonely, middle-aged secretary who weds a younger man (Robertson), only to learn he's not only married but has psychological problems as well. A tense, moody drama that occasionally gives in to the broad trappings of many a 1950s melodrama, but is involving all the same thanks to Crawford's solid performance. ★★★ VHS: $19.99

Autumn Marathon

(1979, 100 min, USSR, Georgy Panelia) *Oleg Basilashvili, Natalia Gundareva.* Mid-life crisis is the theme of this poignant and at times funny drama. Georgy, a mild-mannered Leningrad professor, finds himself dissatisfied and unfulfilled by his seemingly successful life. He becomes increasingly muddled in his relationships with his loving wife, his attractive but demanding mistress, his students and colleagues and even his jogging-buddy neighbor. (Russian with English subtitles) ★★★ VHS: $59.99

Autumn Sonata

(1978, 97 min, Sweden, Ingmar Bergman) *Ingrid Bergman, Liv Ullmann.* Director Bergman's emotionally shattering drama about the frail yet indestructible bond between a mother (Ingrid) and her daughter (Liv). Bergman and Ullmann give extraordinary portrayals. (Swedish with English subtitles). ★★★★ VHS: $29.99; DVD: $39.99

Autumn Tale

(1998, 110 min, France, Eric Rohmer) *Béatrice Romand, Marie Rivière, Alain Libolt, Alexia Portal.* A delightful conclusion to Rohmer's cycle "Tales of the Four Seasons," *Autumn Tale* is not unlike many of the French director's films in that the gentle humor stems from characters saying one thing while really meaning another. Magali (Romand) is in her forties and single. Although she claims that she has no interest in a relationship — her winery and her children take up her time — Magali's friend Isabelle (Riviere) and her son's girlfriend Rosine (Portal) conspire independently to jump-start her love life. The result is a party in which two suitors vie for Magali's affections, unbeknownst to her. Rohmer's strength is his patented ability to make ordinary characters interesting even though the situations are somewhat contrived. Typical of the director's films, *Autumn Tale* is very talky, but it is beautifully photographed, and features buoyant performances from its talented ensemble cast. (French with English subtitles) ★★★ VHS: $102.99

Avalon

(1990, 127 min, US, Barry Levinson) *Armin Mueller-Stahl, Aidan Quinn, Elizabeth Perkins, Joan Plowright, Kevin Pollack, Lou Jacobi.* Director Levinson continues his acclaimed Baltimore stories (*Diner* and *Tin Men*) with this heartfelt reminiscence — spanning five decades — about three generations of a Jewish immigrant family. Mueller-Stahl gives a towering performance as the Krichinsky family's proud patriarch, whose haunting stories of emigration to "a place called Avalon" are constantly echoing from his memory. Quinn ably plays his son, a salesman with Wanamaker-sized dreams of department store splendor. A superb evocation of post-war life, *Avalon* is a remarkable achievement: an intimate memory piece rich in atmosphere and flowing with good humor. Levinson's most personal film, and one of his best. ★★★★ VHS: $9.99; DVD: $24.99

The Avengers

(1998, 90 min, GB, Jeremiah Chechik) *Ralph Fiennes, Uma Thurman, Sean Connery, Jim Broadbent, Fiona Shaw.* Fiennes and Thurman are quite good in this otherwise underwhelming update of the classic '60s TV series. All the elements are here — the stiff-upper-lip nonchalance of the heroes, the *veddy* British costumes and production design, the tongue-in-cheek attitude. But the film never comes to life, despite some nice sequences (especially a hilarious, absurd bit with a gang of criminals wearing fuzzy teddy bear suits), some of which are cribbed from the original series. Uma and Ralph are both sexy, especially in their period dress, but have no spark between them. The real surprise, however, is Connery, a huge disappointment in his first major villain role, cartoonish and embarrassing in an admittedly badly written non-role. As such, there is *zero* threat or excitement, and the story and characters go nowhere. *The Avengers* is a frustrating missed opportunity. (VHS available letterboxed or pan & scan) ★½ VHS: $9.99; DVD: $14.99

L'Avventura (The Adventure)

(1960, 145 min, Italy, Michelangelo Antonioni) *Monica Vitti, Lea Massari.* Antonioni established his international reputation with this perceptive study of the alienation, ennui and despair suffered by a group of vacationing friends when faced with the disappearance of a young woman from the party. (Italian with English subtitles) ★★★ VHS: $29.99; DVD: $39.99

Awakenings

(1990, 121 min, US, Penny Marshall) *Robert De Niro, Robin Williams, Julie Kavner, Ruth Nelson, Penelope Ann Miller, Max Von Sydow.* Based on Oliver Sachs' true story, this extremely moving and accomplished film stars Williams as a neurologist whose experiments in a 1960s Brooklyn hospital "awaken" patients who have been victims of a decades-long "sleeping sickness." De Niro gives an astonishing performance as Leonard, Williams' first patient to undergo medical treatment. The story centers on the doctor's fight to use the experimental medicine, and the recovering and orienting process facing all the patients. Williams nicely underplays his part as the introverted physician; he and De Niro make a remarkable team. ★★★½ VHS: $12.99; DVD: $29.99

The Awful Truth

(1937, 94 min, US, Leo McCarey) *Cary Grant, Irene Dunne, Ralph Bellamy.* McCarey won a well-deserved Best Director Oscar for this hilarious screwball classic. At the peak of their comic abilities, Grant and Dunne play a divorcing couple waiting out their 90-day interlocutory period (and fighting a custody battle for their pet terrier). When they begin dating other people, each goes to great lengths to disrupt the other's newfound romance, each scheme being more outrageous than the one before it. *The Awful Truth* is screwball comedy at its best and, in addition to Grant's *Bringing Up Baby*, is the epitome of the genre. ★★★★ VHS: $19.99

An Awfully Big Adventure

(1994, 113 min, GB, Mike Newell) *Hugh Grant, Alan Rickman, Peter Firth, Georgina Cates, Alan Cox.* A dingy 1947 Liverpool is the setting for this very British comedy-drama on life within a repertory theatre troupe. Fifteen-year-old orphan Stella (Cates) finds a family and many life lessons when she is hired as a starry-eyed apprentice and part-time actress. The troupe is headed by Meredith Potter (Grant), a maniacally egotistical gay director with a taste for using and abusing the younger male workers. Grant's Meredith is a wonderful creation — a pale, nervous, obviously vain chain-smoker with looks that suggest a prissy, upper-class Clark Kent. At its best, *Adventure* is an entertaining glimpse behind the curtain, but the film suffers from a disjointed story line and a menagerie of perpetually pitiful characters. ★★½ VHS: $19.99

Ay, Carmela!

(1990, 107 min, Spain, Carlos Saura) *Carmen Maura, Andres Pajares.* Maura, the perky star of so many Pedro Almodóvar films, teams with director Saura in this stirring look at the Spanish Civil War. Carmela (Maura) and Paulino (Pajares) are Republican entertainers who contribute to the war effort by putting on shows for the troops. The film follows them as they travel to various war-torn areas of Spain, always fearful of being apprehended by the Fascists. Maura, in her first major role outside of the Almodóvar camp, delivers a sparkling, heartfelt performance as the vivacious vaudevillian whose political passions and love for the troops lead her to place her own life in danger. *Ay, Carmela!*, while clearly Republican in its sentiment, offers an evenhanded and humantistic view of Spain's bloody past. (Spanish with English subtitles) ★★★ VHS: $19.99

B. Monkey

(1999, 91 min, GB, Michael Radford) *Asia Argento, Rupert Everett, Jared Harris, Jonathan Rhys Meyers, Ian Hart. B. Monkey, or La Femme Nikita Sees the Errors of Her Ways, Marries and Settles Down in a Cottage in the Country*, is bursting with flashing style, over-the-top acting and some great action sequences. This thriller is great fun to watch, but don't try to make any sense out of the mindless plot or unbelievable characters. Argento (daughter of the famed Italian horror director) is the sexy sly jewel thief B. Monkey who, after meeting a dorky jazz-loving school teacher, decides to retire from the biz. But that "one last job" done as a favor to her crime pal Meyers becomes her undoing when the heist goes awry. Everett is wonderful as a dissipated drug lord/bon vivant whose life is spiraling out of control, yet you'd never know it from his debonair attitude. Not art, but fast-paced, classy and action-packed. And if the plot doesn't work for you, the attractive cast should. ★★½ VHS: $14.99; DVD: $29.99

Babe

(1995, 91 min, Australia, Chris Noonan) *James Cromwell, Magda Szubanski; Voices of: Christine Cavanaugh, Miriam Margolyes, Hugo Weaving, Roscoe Lee Browne.* It's hard to believe, but it would take a while to find another children's film as thoroughly irresistible as this one about a talking pig. Forget Arnold and Gordy. In fact, forget Francis, Mr. Ed and the rest of their pals, for *Babe* brings home the bacon. The story follows the misadventures of Babe, a piglet who is won by the kindly farmer Hoggett (Cromwell). On this farm, Hoggett's animals are able to communicate with each other, though each must obey the social structure the animals have set for themselves. That is, until Babe works his magic and brings all the animals together. The film ingeniously interacts the animals and humans, and its clever screenplay and a splendid use of ground-level cinematography bring all the animals (some real, some Henson creations) to life. (Sequel: *Babe: Pig in the City*) ★★★★ VHS: $14.99; DVD: $24.99

The Babe

(1992, 115 min, US, Arthur Hiller) *John Goodman, Kelly McGillis, Trini Alvarado.* As old-fashioned as the period costumes its large cast wears, *The Babe* is a brash, sentimental and entertaining look at the life of baseball legend Babe Ruth. Sticking to the facts more consistently than the pretty bad 1948 biopic *The Babe Ruth Story*, the film benefits from a larger-than-life characterization from big guy Goodman. Weighed down by some heavily dramatic scenes, the story follows Ruth's meteoric rise in the 1920s where, first as a Red Sox and then as a New York Yankee, he would make baseball history. Fans of the sport should find *The Babe* endearing, though non-fans may be at a loss, as the film almost canonizes the Bambino. ★★½ VHS: $7.49

Babe: Pig in the City

(1998, 96 min, Australia, George Miller) *James Cromwell, Magda Szubanski, Mickey Rooney; Voices of: Elizabeth Daly, Steven Wright, Adam Goldberg. Babe: Pig in the City* shatters any expectations of what a kid's film should be, stranding the famous porker in a fantasy city that is nowhere and everywhere (watch for the Sydney Opera House and the Empire State Building). Mrs. Hoggett, far from the farm, misses her connection to take Babe to a big sheepherding show. They spend the rest of the movie enduring every calamity that can befall wide-eyed tourists: Mafia chimpanzees, killer pit bulls, and the dreaded animal-control officers. Naturally, their kind hearts eventually win over hardened city-folk, but what a trip they have getting there! A ravishing odyssey that — though dark in tone and therefore maybe not for the tiniest ones — never ceases to enthrall and delight. ★★★★ VHS: $14.99; DVD: $29.99

Babes in Arms

(1939, 91 min, US, Busby Berkeley) *Judy Garland, Mickey Rooney.* Trimmed-down but delightfully entertaining version of the Rodgers and Hart Broadway musical. Garland and Rooney are terrific together as the children of vaudevillians who decide to "put on a show" to help their struggling parents. Though '30s schmaltz all the way, this is probably the best of the Judy-Mickey "Let's put on a show" musicals. ★★★ VHS: $14.99

Babette's Feast

(1987, 102 min, Denmark, Gabriel Axel) *Stéphane Audran, Bibi Andersson.* Director Axel's Oscar-winning adaptation of Isak Dinesen's ("Out of Africa") poignant novella is an inspired celebration of the triumph of art over puritanical zeal. Set in a tiny and bleak 19th-century Scandinavian village, the story follows the lives of two devoutly religious sisters who have retreated into the desolate, but safe, enclave of their pious upbringings. Into their lives comes Babette (Audran) — a maid who was forced to flee her native France and unbeknownst to the two women, was once a renowned and celebrated gourmet chef. After years of service, Babette one day receives word that she has won the lottery, and decides to lavish the household — to repay the sisters' kindness — with the most extravagant dinner ever to be seen (or tasted) on the entire Jutland peninsula, a feast which kindles the fire of humanity in the deadened souls of the tiny hamlet. (Danish and French with English subtitles) ★★★★ VHS: $19.99; DVD: $19.99

Baby Boom

(1987, 103 min, US, Charles Shyer) *Diane Keaton, Harold Ramis, Sam Shepard, James Spader.* One of the more enjoyable baby comedies which proliferated in the late 1980s. Keaton gives a charming performance as a successful executive whose life is turned upside-down when she becomes guardian to a deceased relative's infant. Ramis does the aggressive yuppie thing again, and Shepard does the nice-guy thing again. ★★★ VHS: $9.99; DVD: $14.99

Baby Doll

(1956, 114 min, US, Elia Kazan) *Carroll Baker, Karl Malden, Eli Wallach, Mildred Dunnock, Rip Torn.* The first motion picture from a major American studio ever to be publicly condemned by the Legion of Decency, this twisted piece of Southern Gothic is still quite effective some four decades after its initial release. Tennessee Williams wrote and Kazan directed this tale of "Baby Doll," a child-like bride who sleeps in a crib and endures the ever-lurking (and sexual pressures) of her "adult" husband, an over-the-top Malden. The film features excellent supporting performances, but the film belongs to Baker as Baby Doll; she is the embodiment of adolescent sexuality and manipulation. A decadent delight. ★★★½

Baby Face

(1933, 70 min, US, Alfred E. Green) *Barbara Stanwyck, George Brent, Donald Cook, John Wayne.* Stanwyck is in great form in a "bad girl" role in this provocative pre-Production Code melodrama. Stanwyck literally sleeps her way to the top

B. Monkey

when she leaves her Erie speakeasy to conquer a New York banking company, using and discarding men at her whim. A must see for Stanwyck fans, students of 1930s cinema, or anyone interested in an exorbitantly good time. ★★★ VHS: $19.99

Baby Geniuses

(1999, 95 min, US, Bob Clark) Kathleen Turner, Christopher Lloyd, Kim Cattrall, Peter MacNicol, Dom DeLuise. After the whimsical holiday favorite A Christmas Story and the likable but progressively idiotic Look Who's Talking series, you'd think that director Clark could make something mildly amusing out of an interesting concept: that babies are born with the secrets of the universe, but cannot verbalize them. Lloyd and poor Turner are the twisted masterminds behind a scientific experiment that uses these wizard babies for their own dastardly purposes, but the film is a clumsy, uneven, unfunny disaster from the first frame till the last. The only element worth noting is the clever Babe-like visual effects that syncs-up the babies' mouths with their dialogue. ★ VHS: $9.99; DVD: $14.99

Baby, It's You

(1983, 105 min, US, John Sayles) Vincent Spano, Rosanna Arquette, Matthew Modine, Robert Downey, Jr. One of the most popular films ever to play at TLA, this is Sayles' endearing ode to adolescent yearning and awakening maturity. Arquette stars in a remarkably textured performance as a young woman whose horizons expand beyond the grasp of her volatile high school beau (Spano). A warm comic remembrance of faded affections, bygone youth and the golden age of rock 'n' roll. ★★★½ VHS: $9.99

Baby, the Rain Must Fall

(1965, 100 min, US, Robert Mulligan) Steve McQueen, Lee Remick, Don Murray, Paul Fix. Based on Horton Foote's play "The Traveling Lady," this involving, unsentimental drama features McQueen (in a particularly effective performance) as a rockabilly singer, just released from prison, who reunites with his estranged wife and daughter. His uncontrolled temper and restless spirit put their reunion in jeopardy. ★★★ VHS: $19.99

Baby's Day Out

(1994, 90 min, US, Patrick Read Johnson) Lara Flynn Boyle, Brian Haley, Joe Mantegna, Joe Pantoliano. This is only for those who loved Home Alone. Just add one more villain, reduce the age of the child, add a ransom note, and you have the latest variation of a theme. The baby is adorable and the bad guys (led by Mantegna) are strangely likable, but Baby Bink crawling alone across a busy Manhattan street stretches the formula pretty thin. ★★ VHS: $9.99

Babyfever

(1994, 110 min, US, Henry Jaglom) Matt Salinger, Eric Roberts, Frances Fisher, Victoria Foyt, Zach Norman. Sometimes called the "West Coast Woody Allen," director Jaglom crafts films around topics of neurotic obsession and lets his actors run with it through a loosely structured narrative. This time around, the topic of white, middle-aged angst is reproduction: As biological clocks tick away, a collection of female friends explore their options from turkey basters to men more interested in having children than they are. The various protagonists

balance the instinct to procreate with the many entanglements and obligations inherent in late 20th-century America. Often self-indulgent and sometimes unexpectedly touching, Babyfever — like the director's other films — is an acquired taste which may not be palatable for all. But if your own clock is ticking, or if you fantasize about father-son softball games, this might suit your fancy. ★★½ VHS: $19.99

The Bachelor

(1991, 105 min, GB/Italy/Hungary, Roberto Faenza) Keith Carradine, Miranda Richardson, Kristin Scott Thomas, Max von Sydow. Richardson stars in a dual role in this sumptuous though somewhat confusing period piece about a turn-of-the-century doctor (Carradine) who is unexpectedly given a second chance at life and love when his spinster sister (Richardson) commits suicide. While cut from the same cloth as Howards End and A Room with a View, the unusual tale of a man's sexual awakening lacks the skillful tailoring of either and at times works better as a travelogue than as the character study it was meant to be. ★★ VHS: $79.99

The Bachelor

(1999, 102 min, US, Gary Sinyor) Chris O'Donnell, Renee Zellweger, Artie Lange, James Cromwell, Ed Asner, Peter Ustinov. Suggested by Buster Keaton's 1925 short Seven Chances, this tired comedy casts O'Donnell as a confirmed bachelor who must marry before his 30th birthday or forfeit a fortune. His problem is that his birthday is in one day and his fiancée has just walked out on him. O'Donnell is a likable personality, and Zellweger is as sweet as sweet can be, but there's hardly a laugh or a smile to be had in this one-note joke without a punchline. Even the sight gag of hundreds of eager brides chasing our hapless hero falls flat. ★½ VHS: $14.99; DVD: $19.99

The Bachelor and the Bobbysoxer

(1947, 95 min, US, Irving Reis) Cary Grant, Myrna Loy, Shirley Temple, Rudy Vallee. The usually dapper Grant gets a chance to let down his well-ordered hair by acting like a teenager in this delightful Oscar-winning comedy, one of Grant's biggest box-office hits. When "bobbysoxer" Temple becomes infatuated with playboy/artist Grant, little Shirley's sister, judge Loy, orders the bemused bachelor to date the adolescent adulator in the hopes she soon gets over

The Bachelor and the Bobbysoxer

him. In no time, Myrna and the born-again teenager are falling in love. Academy Award for Best Original Screenplay. ★★★½ VHS: $19.99

Bachelor Mother

(1939, 81 min, US, Garson Kanin) Ginger Rogers, David Niven, Charles Coburn. A charming romantic comedy with Rogers as a single working girl who finds an abandoned baby; everyone around her presumes it's hers, including boss Niven. Directed with style by Kanin, this is one of the better screwball romances popular at the time. ★★★ VHS: $14.99

Bachelor Party

(1984, 106 min, US, Neal Israel) Tom Hanks, Tawny Kitaen, Adrian Zmed, George Grizzard, Wendie Jo Sperber, Michael Dudikoff. In his first box-office hit, Hanks demonstrates little of the comic presence which would be tapped that same year in Splash. This goonish comedy casts Hanks as a groom-to-be celebrating his upcoming wedding. Predictable shenanigans happen as the party gets out of hand. Harmless but very silly. ★★ VHS: $9.99; DVD: $22.99

Back Street

(1961, 107 min, US, David Miller) Susan Hayward, John Gavin, Vera Miles. Ross Hunter produced this third screen adaptation of Fannie Hurst's novel, giving it the same glossy treatment as his other late-1950s melodramas (Imitation of Life, Magnificent Obsession, etc.). Hayward stars as the young woman entangled in a hopeless love affair with a married man (Gavin). Though the earlier two versions are dramatically superior, this is nevertheless an effective (if campily fantastic) soaper. ★★½ VHS: $14.99

Back to Ararat

(1990, 100 min, US/Armenia, Pea Holmquist) The 1915 death march, the eventual genocide of 1.5 million Armenians and the ensuing annexation of parts of Armenia by Turkish forces are explored in this startling documentary. In addition to recounting the horrors of the genocide, the film focuses on three generations of Armenians scattered throughout the world, all of whom dream of the day when it will be possible to return to the lands surrounding the holy mountain of Ararat. ★★★ VHS: $49.99

Back to School

(1986, 96 min, US, Alan Metter) Rodney Dangerfield, Keith Gordon, Robert Downey, Jr., Sally Kellerman, Burt Young, Ned Beatty, Sam Kinison. Dangerfield had a big hit with this funny campus comedy. The Man-of-No-Respect shines as a crass but lovable millionaire who enrolls in his son's college; both get an unexpected education. Gordon plays his son, and Downey is a fellow student. Good one-liners. ★★★ DVD: $14.99

Back to the Beach

(1987, 92 min, US, Lyndall Hobbs) Frankie Avalon, Annette Funicello, Connie Stevens. Frankie and Annette are back together again in this forced piece of baby boomer nostalgia. The sweethearts of the '60s, now parents living in the Midwest, travel to California to visit their daughter, and keep running into various '60s TV stars. Stevens, looking great as ever, is there, as well as cameos by Bob Denver, Alan Hale, Jr., Jerry Mathers, Tony Dow and Don Adams. ★★ VHS: $14.99

Back to the Future

(1985, 116 min, US, Robert Zemeckis) *Michael J. Fox, Christopher Lloyd, Crispin Glover, Lea Thompson, Casey Siemaszko, Billy Zane, Huey Lewis.* Classic time-travel comedy with Fox as a teenager who travels back in time to 1955. There he interferes with the meeting of his parents, and is forced to play Cupid to his beautiful mom and nerdish dad. Lloyd is terrific as Fox's "crazy scientist" pal, and Glover and Thompson are his parents. An inventive, very funny and well-structured screenplay, nice special effects and a genuinely charismatic cast all contribute to the enjoyment level of this box-office smash. (Followed by 2 sequels) ★★★★

Back to the Future, Part II

(1989, 107 min, US, Robert Zemeckis) *Michael J. Fox, Christopher Lloyd, Thomas F. Wilson, Lea Thompson, Elisabeth Shue.* Picking up where the original left off, Doc Brown whisks Marty and girlfriend Jennifer to the year 2015. In the future, however, the time machine is stolen by Biff, who uses it to alter the past. Doc and Marty must return to the past to save the present. If it sounds a bit confusing, it is. Fox and Lloyd return, and both are in fine form, though the screenwriters don't give either actor the opportunity for a comic tour de force as in the original. There are some truly impressive split-screen special effects, but the story is rambling and only occasionally funny. The parallel future looks more like Pottersville in *It's a Wonderful Life*, making Fox an unlikely George Bailey. This *Future* is decidedly dark and inferior to its predecessor. ★★½

Back to the Future, Part III

(1990, 119 min, US, Robert Zemeckis) *Michael J. Fox, Christopher Lloyd, Mary Steenburgen, Elisabeth Shue, Thomas F. Wilson.* The exciting finale to Zemeckis' trilogy finds our hero Marty McFly (Fox) scrambling back in time to the Old West to track down his friend Dr. Emmett Brown (Lloyd). Unlike the second film, which jumped back and forth between eons and even took a hitch into an alternative dimension, the main part of the narrative here stays with the frontier setting and to great effect. Lloyd and Fox are both in their element as they get to ham up their respective roles and Steenburgen is a pleasing addition as a Victorian schoolteacher who romances Dr. Brown. ★★★

Backbeat

(1994, 100 min, GB, Iain Softley) *Stephen Dorff, Ian Hart, Sheryl Lee, Gary Bakewell, Chris O'Neill.* With the high-octane energy of a Beatles song, *Backbeat* is the exhilarating story of artist and musician Stu Sutcliffe, who flirted with fame as the "fifth Beatle." It's 1960, and the struggling Beatles have accepted a gig at a dive bar in Hamburg. The story focuses on the friendship of best mates Sutcliffe (Dorff) and John Lennon (Hart), whose close relationship is put to the test when Sutcliffe falls in love with a bohemian German woman (Lee in a captivating performance). Though the many musical sequences are thrilling, they are only a small part of the film's success, and these scenes are smartly complemented by bristling characterizations and finely tuned dramatics. Hart gives an extraordinary portrayal which goes beyond mimicry in bringing Lennon's wit, sarcasm and genius to the surface, and Dorff is equally compelling as Stu. ★★★★

Martin Lawrence (l.) and Will Smith in 1995's *Bad Boys*

Backdraft

(1991, 135 min, US, Ron Howard) *Kurt Russell, William Baldwin, Robert De Niro, Scott Glenn, Jennifer Jason Leigh, Donald Sutherland, Rebecca DeMornay.* An impressively mounted if dramatically awkward homage to the bravery of our nation's firefighters. Russell and Baldwin star as brothers and firemen, whose volatile relationship is as explosive as the fires they fight. The fine cast also includes the splendid De Niro as a fire inspector investigating a series of arsons, and Glenn as Russell's seasoned coworker. But the real stars of the film are the spectacular firefighting scenes — director Howard has captured some awe-inspiring footage of firefighting in action. ★★★ VHS: $9.99; DVD: $24.99

Backfire

(1987, 93 min, US/Canada, Gilbert Cates) *Jeff Fahey, Karen Allen, Keith Carradine, Bernie Casey.* Another duplicitous housewife (Allen) plans to drive her wealthy shell-shocked husband (Fahey) to suicide and collect his fortune. The plan backfires when he is left an invalid in her care. Some nice twists punctuate this noirish thriller, which is short on development but contains some stylish flourishes. ★★½ VHS: $29.99

Background to Danger

(1943, 80 min, US, Raoul Walsh) *George Raft, Brenda Marshall, Sydney Greenstreet, Peter Lorre.* As a poor man's Humphrey Bogart, Raft finds himself up against the Nazis in this WWII espionage thriller which, while cheesy, is not without its fair share of twists and intrigue. Raft plays an American salesman traveling through Turkey who becomes involved with German, Russian and Turkish agents when he stumbles upon a Nazi plot trying to force the hand of Turkey to rescind its neutrality. Greenstreet is the iniquitous Nazi agent behind the set-up, and Lorre is a spy who may or may not be a Russian agent, but who definitely likes his vodka. ★★★ VHS: $19.99

The Bad and the Beautiful

(1952, 118 min, US, Vincente Minnelli) *Kirk Douglas, Lana Turner, Dick Powell, Gloria Graham, Barry Sullivan.* The film Minnelli directed in between his glorious Technicolor musicals *An American in Paris* and *The Band Wagon* is black-and-white melodrama of the highest studio order. It's a quintessential Hollywood story with Douglas as an ambitious (ruthless?) producer and his effect on an actress (Turner), a writer (Powell) and a director (Sullivan). Winner of five Oscars including Best Screenplay (Charles Schnee) and Best Supporting Actress (Graham). ★★★★ VHS: $19.99

Bad Behavior

(1992, 103 min, GB, Les Blair) *Stephen Rea, Sinead Cusack, Phil Daniels, Philip Jackson.* This mostly improvised domestic comedy skillfully hits its mark. Rea and Cusack are Gerry and Ellie McAllister: middle-aged, the parents of two sons, and owners of a North London row home in need of repairs. While he trudges off to work every day to the town planning commission, she plays host to a parade of locals who stop in to share their worries over a cup of tea. In the tradition of Mike Leigh, director Blair has molded a film where not much happens, but we are nonetheless drawn into the characters' lives on a wonderfully intimate and enjoyable level. ★★★½

Bad Boys

(1983, 105 min, US, Rick Rosenthal) *Sean Penn, Esai Morales, Reni Santoni, Ally Sheedy, Clancy Brown.* Sparks fly in this intense drama as Penn and Morales square off as adversaries in a juvenile prison. Tough and violent, the film packs quite a wallop in its presentation of youthful lives behind bars. ★★★ VHS: $14.99; DVD: $9.99

Bad Boys

(1995, 118 min, US, Michael Bay) *Will Smith, Martin Lawrence, Téa Leoni, Joe Pantoliano, Tcheky Karyo.* TV stars Lawrence and Smith trade off their sitcom personalities to good effect in this otherwise formulaic buddy movie/police actioner. The story begins when a friend is killed investigating murderous drug dealers. Teaming with an eyewitness (Leoni), they try to track down the killers while protecting their charge at the same time. Balancing comedy and action, the film is much more appealing when the two stars are snapping the one-liners rather than blasting the bullets. There are only two action sequences of note, but both are well-paced and very exciting. The subplot involving Lawrence's wife wears thin rather quickly. ★★½ VHS: $14.99; DVD: $19.99

Bad Company

(1972, 93 min, US, Robert Benton) *Jeff Bridges, Barry Brown, John Savage, Jim Davis.* This lyrical, haunting western from director Benton stars Bridges and Brown as two drifters robbing their way West during the Civil War. Benton and David Newman, who worked together on *Bonnie and Clyde*, wrote the insightful and unexpectedly humorous screenplay, and the film is enhanced by beautiful cinematography (Gordon Willis). ★★★½ VHS: $9.99

Bad Company

(1995, 108 min, US, Damian Harris) *Laurence Fishburne, Ellen Barkin, Frank Langella, Michael Beach, Spalding Gray, David Ogden Stiers.* A simplistic yet thought-provoking spy thriller which gives a sardonic clue as to what some soldiers may do once the war is over. In a role not unlike his excellent turn in *Deep Cover*, Fishburne plays a blacklisted ex-CIA agent enlisted by Barkin and Langella to join a mysterious company whose stock-in-trade is translating post—Cold War tactics (blackmail, bribery, murder) to the world of big business and high finance. This intriguing premise turns stale, however, as in high order Barkin lures Fishburne first into bed and then into a deadly hostile takeover. As sincere as the two leads are, the peripheral characters carry much more depth. ★★½

Bad Day at Black Rock

(1955, 81 min, US, John Sturges) *Spencer Tracy, Robert Ryan, Lee Marvin, Ernest Borgnine, Walter Brennan, Dean Jagger.* Tracy heads a first-rate cast in this suspenseful modern-day western with Tracy in a commanding performance as a one-armed visitor to a small town who unwittingly uncovers a local secret, which puts him in imminent danger. Director Sturges maintains high tension throughout, and the story is an invigorating study of mob mentality and the bravery to stand against it. ★★★★ VHS: $19.99

Bad Girls

(1994, 100 min, US, Jonathan Kaplan) *Madeleine Stowe, Mary Stuart Masterson, Andie MacDowell, Drew Barrymore, James Russo, James LeGros, Dermot Mulroney.* MacDowell, Barrymore and Masterson save fellow honky-tonk harlot Stowe from the hangman's noose. The four newly minted outlaws hit the road, with hired Pinkerton detectives on their trail. This revisionist, feminist western, combining elements of *Young Guns* with *The Ballad of Little Jo*, is actually better than the bullets and bustiers, girls-with-guns expectations it generates. Although certainly not perfect, with an often meandering script and many hackneyed contrivances, it's hard not to appreciate women who shoot to kill when sufficiently provoked. Also appreciated is one particularly memorable line: "If your laws don't include me, then they just don't apply to me, either." Amen, sister. ★★½ VHS: $9.99

Bad Influence

(1990, 99 min, US, Curtis Hanson) *Rob Lowe, James Spader, Lisa Zane, Christian Clemenson.* This pulsating, gritty thriller stars Spader as a successful businessman who is befriended by mys-

terious ne'er-do-well Lowe. Taking the passive yuppie under his wing, Lowe introduces Spader to the seedier side of Los Angeles life. With hints of *Strangers on a Train* and writer David Koepp's own *Apartment Zero*, their seemingly innocent friendship becomes twisted and lethal, leading to blackmail and murder. Lowe gives a well-textured portrait of deceit and malevolence, and Spader again proves that he is one of the leading actors of his generation. ★★★ VHS: $14.99

Bad Lieutenant

(1992, 96 min, US, Abel Ferrara) *Harvey Keitel, Frankie Thorn, Paul Calderone, Brian McElroy.* Erupting from the bowels of Hell comes this highly original, raw and shocking slice of life. Beginning with a corrupt, money-stealing, gambling addicted cop (Keitel) snorting coke off his dashboard after dropping his two sons off at school, we soon begin a slow, painful journey into a swirling abyss of heroin shooting, crack smoking, hooker humping and countless acts of self-degradation. Looking for redemption, our bad seed of a cop takes on a brutal rape case involving a nun, sending him further into a self-destructive Hades. The vividly realistic screenplay (cowritten by *Ms. 45* starlet Zoe Tamerlis) and the gutsy, riveting performance of Keitel combine to make this one of the sleaziest films ever made. It's not for all tastes, but is nonetheless an important film. (NC-17 version) ★★★½ VHS: $14.99; DVD: $14.99

Bad Moon

(1996, 79 min, US, Eric Red) *Michael Paré, Mariel Hemingway, Mason Gamble.* It's dog versus werewolf in this poorly written attempt to teach an old genre some new tricks. Unfortunately, all *Bad Moon* can do is roll over and play dead. Paré is some sort of adventurer who is bitten by a werewolf. He survives and, of course, we all know what that means. He relocates to the Pacific Northwest (the movie includes some fantastic scenery) to stay with his sister (Hemingway) and her child; they can't understand all the animal attacks which are plaguing the region. A cliché-ridden, lame-brained child-in-peril movie. The werewolf effects, at least, are admirable, but terribly overlit. ★½ VHS: $14.99; DVD: $19.99

The Bad News Bears

(1976, 102 min, US, Michael Ritchie) *Walter Matthau, Tatum O'Neal, Vic Morrow, Joyce Van Patten, Jackie Earle Haley.* Though two pallid sequels have soured the memory of the original, this is quite a delightful and funny baseball comedy. Matthau is especially good as a beer-guzzling, slobbish coach to a team of misfit little leaguers. O'Neal is charming as the team's last hope — a pitcher with a wicked fast ball. Followed by two sequels: *The Bad News Bears in Breaking Training* and *The Bad News Bears Go to Japan.* ★★★ VHS: $14.99

The Bad Seed

(1956, 129 min, US, Mervyn LeRoy) *Patty McCormack, Nancy Kelly, Eileen Heckart, Henry Jones.* This unsettling version of the Broadway hit about a psychopathic little girl is so effective it prompted the studio upon its release to add a closing introduction to the featured players — perhaps the birth of the tagline, "Remember, it's only a movie." McCormack and Kelly re-create their stage roles as, respectively, the amoral title

character and her disbelieving mother. ★★★½ VHS: $14.99

The Bad Sleep Well

(1960, 151 min, Japan, Akira Kurosawa) *Toshiro Mifune, Takashi Shimura.* This chilling tale of corruption in the modern Japanese corporate world stars director Kurosawa's mainstay, Mifune, as an embittered, grieving son and rising executive whose father supposedly committed suicide. Not believing the official version of his death, and convinced that a large corporation and its officials were somehow involved, Mifune plots revenge. This stylish crime thriller, based on an Ed McBain story, provides a fascinating commentary on the twisted self-interests of big business. (Letterboxed) (Japanese with English subtitles) ★★★ VHS: $29.99

Bad Taste

(1987, 90 min, New Zealand, Peter Jackson) *Peter Jackson, Pete O'Herne.* This hysterical horror spoof from first-time director Jackson, who would go on to make the gorefest *Dead Alive* and the critical success *Heavenly Creatures*, is about a group of paramilitary investigators who are the first line of defense against an attempted alien invasion of the Earth. The members of the team, including Jackson himself, must thwart an attempt by these "intergalactic wankers" to harvest the latest universal fast-food sensation: human flesh. Many horror and action clichés are sent up in the meantime and the body count and amount of gore make the film live up to its title in every way. It is funny as it is gross. *Bad Taste* is essential viewing for anyone with a strong stomach and a rowdy sense of humor. ★★★

Badlands

(1973, 95 min, US, Terrence Malick) *Martin Sheen, Sissy Spacek, Warren Oates.* As legend has it, Malick just decided that he wanted to give filmmaking a whirl. That whirl yielded a classic — a haunting, touching and often humorous piece of work. Based on the story of 1950s killer Charles Starkweather, *Badlands* boasts a richly textured screenplay, exquisite cinematography, wonderful use of music and, above all else, astonishing performances by Sheen and Spacek as young lovers on the run. In a film full of moody, funny, breathtaking sequences, the all-too-brief scene where Sheen and Spacek, hiding out in the woods, dance around while their radio plays Mickey and Sylvia singing "Love Is Strange" is a standout, a priceless moment of cinematic art. (VHS available letterboxed or pan & scan) ★★★★ VHS: $14.99; DVD: $19.99

Bagdad Cafe

(1988, 91 min, West Germany/US, Percy Adlon) *Marianne Sägebrecht, CCH Pounder, Jack Palance.* This enchanting and affectionate fable unveils, in a series of wonderful vignettes, the developing friendships among several oddball characters. Sagebrecht is a corpulent Bavarian tourist who, stranded somewhere in the Mojave Desert, arrives one day at the near-comatose Bagdad Cafe, a dusty roadside cafe run by an irascible black woman (Pounder). Director Adlon takes his time in showing their differences, as well as their blossoming friendship. A wonderful comedy-drama about misfits in tune with the world which features a show-stealing performance by Palance as an eccentric but charming painter. ★★★½ VHS: $14.99; DVD: $19.99

Bail Jumper

(1989, 95 min, US, Christian Faber) *Eszter Balint, B.J. Spalding.* Unnatural natural calamities befall two Southern thieves in love in this strange, wacky comedy. Joe and Elaine, both petty criminals, decide to leave their home in Murky Springs, Missouri, for the more promising shores of Long Island. But along the way, they are visited by a swarm of locusts, hit with a tornado and, in their new home, greeted with a tidal wave. ★★½ VHS: $19.99

The Baker's Wife

(1938, 124 min, France, Marcel Pagnol) *Raimu, Ginette LeClerc.* The wonderfully enchanting comedic actor Raimu shines as a lovesick and inconsolable baker who goes on a baking strike after he discovers that his flighty wife has run off with a handsome shepherd. The breadless villagers, desperate to get life back to normal, take the situation in their own hands in an effort to get the two back together again. Infused with humor and casting a sympathetic eye towards the villagers and provincial life, Pagnol's charming tale is successful in dealing with the natural pleasures and sufferings of life. (French with English subtitles) ★★★★ VHS: $24.99

Le Bal

(1982, 110 min, Italy/France, Ettore Scola) Within the setting of a Parisian dance hall, director Scola ingeniously presents 50 years of European social and political history through a series of vignettes. With no dialogue, just the musical accompaniment of Charles Aznavour, Irving Berlin, Charele Trene and others, *Le Bal* sweeps us through the turbulent 20th century in a highly stylized yet poignant and absorbing way. ★★★ VHS: $79.99

La Balance

(1982, 102 min, France, Bob Swaim) *Nathalie Baye, Philippe Leotard, Richard Berry.* This gangster sensation swept the French César Awards and took the Best Feature, Actor and Actress honors. Baye stars as a tough, high-class hooker caught in a cat-and-mouse struggle between her boyfriend/pimp and a determined detective. A kind of Gallic *Dirty Harry*, *La Balance* is a taut and jolting journey through the Parisian underworld. (Letterboxed) (French with English subtitles) ★★★ VHS: $29.99

The Balcony

(1963, 83 min, US/GB, Joseph Strick) *Shelley Winters, Peter Falk, Lee Grant, Ruby Dee, Leonard Nimoy.* Jean Genet's allegorical play set in a brothel comes to life in this vivid and boisterous low-budget film. Winters is the beleaguered lesbian madam of the bustling bordello. This "house of illusion," where people play out their dreams, is left undisturbed despite a ravaging rebellion outside its doors. An interesting and at times surreal find. ★★★ VHS: $19.99; DVD: $29.99

Balkan Express

(1984, 102 min, Yugoslavia, Branko Baletic) This offbeat and tragic comedy follows the manic adventures of the Balkan Express Band, a troupe of roving musicians whose music is just a cover for their real work: con men and thieves. Their easy and wild living is interrupted during the Nazi occupation as this motley group discovers that it must overcome its petty self-interests and work to overcome the oppression. Outrageously madcap and full of dramatic twists set against the dark horror of war. (Dubbed) ★★★

Ball of Fire

(1941, 111 min, US, Howard Hawks) *Gary Cooper, Barbara Stanwyck, Dana Andrews, S.Z. Sakall, Henry Travers.* Cooper stars as a professor of English researching slang for an encyclopedia — he's shy but he's a real solid sender anyway. Stanwyck is Sugarpuss O'Shea, a gangster's moll on the lam — now she's definitely rockin' with a solid eight. When Coop and his seven associates unwittingly give shelter to this killer diller, she turns their lives topsy-turvy, and when Cooper and Stanwyck hit the giggles, oh boy, it's hoi toi toi: root, zoot, cute, and solid to boot. This delightful, whimsical comedy was directed by the great Howard Hawks (*His Girl Friday*), and gave Stanwyck her second Oscar nomination. (Give a ring on the Ameche if you liked it.) ★★★½ VHS: $14.99; DVD: $24.99

Ballad in Blue

(1966, 89 min, GB, Paul Henreid) *Ray Charles, Tom Bell.* Charles found the perfect showcase for his talents in this restrained melodrama about an American jazz musician who befriends a young blind boy. The story is overly maudlin and not too substantial, but the film provides ample footage of Charles at his piano belting out his favorites including "I Got a Woman," "What'd I Say?" and "Cry." A pleasure for even the mildest of fans. ★★½

Ballad of a Soldier

(1959, 89 min, USSR, Grigori Chukhrai) *Vladimir Ivashov, Shanna Prokhorenko.* A sensitive and romantic story about a 19-year-old soldier in WWII who sets out on leave to visit his mother. The trip is punctuated with scenes of the horrors of war but is highlighted by the hero falling in love with a beautiful young girl. A moving experience, this tender love story will soften even the hardest of hearts. (Russian with English subtitles) ★★★½ VHS: $29.99

The Ballad of Cable Hogue

(1970, 121 min, US, Sam Peckinpah) *Jason Robards, Stella Stevens, David Warner, Strother Martin, Slim Pickens.* Peckinpah is in a noticably lighter mood with this vigorously entertaining western. Though the Old West is still dusty and dangerous as in any of his other more volatile works, the wild in this Wild West is for unpredictable and strange antics. Robards heads a good cast as an eccentric prospector whose dream of an oasis in the middle of the desert may not be as crazy as everyone thinks. In her best screen role, Stevens is sharp as a needle as the good-hearted, feisty prostitute who takes up with Robards. As the remaining player in this quest, Warner is splendid as an unusually loony preacher. ★★★½ VHS: $14.99

The Ballad of Gregorio Cortez

(1982, 99 min, US, Robert M. Young) *Edward James Olmos, James Gammon, Barry Corbin, Rosana DeSoto, Pepe Serna.* Sincere telling of one of the most notorious manhunts in Texas history is a gritty and unsettling examination of bigotry. Olmos stars as a young Mexican who, in a miscommunication of language, kills a U.S. sheriff and becomes the object of a state-wide hunt. ★★★ VHS: $14.99

The Ballad of Little Jo

(1993, 120 min, US, Maggie Greenwald) *Suzy Amis, Ian McKellen, Bo Hopkins, Rene Auberjonois, David Chung, Carrie Snodgress, Heather Graham, Anthony Heald.* This profound little odyssey examines feminine oppression in the tale of a young woman who finds herself wandering the countryside at the end of the Civil War. Constantly in peril of being raped by marauding ex-soldiers, she decides to head west where she masquerades as a man in a shithole mining town. Based on a true story lifted from a newspaper headline of the day, Greenwald's film delivers a wonderfully satisfying, gritty look at the Old West which rivals *Unforgiven*. Amis, in the lead role, creates an excellent portrait of rugged and determined survival. McKellen gives great support as a grizzly miner, portrayed initially as a decent man but who eventually shows his true misogynist colors. ★★★★ VHS: $14.99

The Ballad of Narayama

(1983, 130 min, Japan, Shohei Imamura) *Ken Ogata, Sumiko Sakamota.* This exquisitely photographed film paints a sublime portrait of the harsh life endured in a secluded, 19th-century

The Ballad of Narayama

village high in the mountains of northern Japan. Reacting to their raw existence, the people have adopted several unusual customs, including one which dictates that the elderly, upon reaching the age of 70, are escorted to the top of Narayama Mountain to die in solitude. Director Imamura depicts a cruel and sometimes shocking world to the viewer but one which is based on simple survival. (Letterboxed) (Japanese with English subtitles) ★★★★ VHS: $29.99

The Ballad of the Sad Cafe

(1991, 108 min, US, Simon Callow) *Vanessa Redgrave, Keith Carradine, Rod Steiger, Cork Hubbert, Austin Pendleton.* The Deep South has played host to many a curious tale, but none more bewildering than this wildly uneven but nevertheless hypnotic adaptation of the Edward Albee play, itself based on the Carson McCullers novella. Redgrave gives a bold, mesmerizing performance as Miss Amelia, the masculine town tycoon whose crew-cut and gangly walk send fear into the local residents. All except Lymon (Hubbard), a hunchback dwarf who arrives one day claiming to be her cousin. Lymon convinces her to open a cafe, which becomes the pulse of the tiny town. However, things change drastically when Miss Amelia's estranged husband, Marvin (Carradine), returns from prison. The stage is set for a battle-of-the-sexes showdown which culminates in an unbelievable fistfight finale. Not for all tastes, but for the more adventurous viewer. ★★½ VHS: $19.99

Ballot Measure 9

(1995, 72 min, US, Heather MacDonald) In contrast to its dry, didactic sounding title, this documentary about the events leading up to the vote on the 1992 Colorado and Oregon antigay ballot initiatives is in fact both thought-provoking and exhilarating. Written and directed by MacDonald, the film examines the hysteria and hatred generated by those against "special rights for gays and lesbians" especially by members of the Christian Right. MacDonald uses a low-key approach to the contentious issue, and because of it, gained access to interviews with many of the measure's more virulent proponents. Engrossing and a significant document in the history of the lesbian and gay civil rights movement. ★★★ VHS: $29.99

Balto

(1995, 78 min, US, Simon Wells) *Miriam Margolyes; Voices of: Kevin Bacon, Bridget Fonda, Bob Hoskins, Phil Collins.* A charming piece of animation featuring good vocals and high production values (another example that there really are quality children's films being made outside of the land of Disney). Balto is half-wolf, half-dog, and lives in Nome, Alaska, in the mid-1920s. Spurned by dog and man alike for his mixed heritage, he steps in to save the day when a diphtheria epidemic threatens the lives of the town's children. He leads a rag-tag team through Arctic blizzards to deliver the much-needed medicine. *Balto* is an appealing package that offers an exciting story, and a few rather sophisticated innuendos should keep adults interested as well. ★★★ VHS: $14.99

La Bamba

(1986, 108 min, US, Luis Valdez) *Lou Diamond Phillips, Esai Morales, Rosana DeSoto, Elizabeth Peña, Joe Pantoliano.* An enthralling musical biopic of 1950s singing star Richie Valens. Phillips offers a strong portrayal of the teen idol, whose course is tracked from his high school days up until his fateful crash. Morales is vibrant as Richie's brother, and DeSoto is especially good as their hard-working and loving mother. ★★★½ VHS: $9.99; DVD: $24.99

Bambi

(1942, 72 min, US) One of the few films which can be said to have affected generations that have seen it, Walt Disney's classic animated feature follows the adventures of a forest deer, Bambi, and his little forest friends, including the lovable Thumper the rabbit. The animation is brilliant, and the story will captivate viewers of all ages. (Remastered in THX) ★★★½

Bamboozled

(2000, 136 min, US, Spike Lee) *Damon Wayans, Savion Glover, Jada Pinkett-Smith, Tommy Davidson, Michael Rapaport.* Extremely disappointing effort from Lee, all the more lamentable because it could have — and should have — been great. The premise is terrific: a black TV writer, deemed too "white" by his trendy boss, decides to get himself fired by writing a show that is a throwback to blackface minstrel shows. In true *Producers* fashion, the show becomes a surprise hit, and success goes to the celebrated writer's head. Sadly, this fertile ground for satire is botched, with murky (at best) character motivations, a complete lack of focus and an almost unbearable, nasal accent adopted by Wayans. The film is, shockingly, not edgy at all (save for two hysterically funny TV commercial parodies), rather monotonous, at times incoherent, and completely unconvincing, even for a broad satire. ★★ VHS: $19.99; DVD: $24.99

Bananas

(1971, 81 min, US, Woody Allen) *Woody Allen, Louise Lasser, Carlos Montalban, Howard Cosell.* After the very funny escapades of *Take the Money and Run*, Allen sharpened both his comic skills and his filmmaking techniques to tell the riotous story of Fielding Melish, a meek and mild products tester in New York who finds himself the rebel leader of a group of South American guerrillas. The film is a non-stop barrage of sight gags and one-liners, most of which hit the bull's-eye. ★★★½ VHS: $14.99; DVD: $19.99

Band of Outsiders

(1964, 97 min, France, Jean-Luc Godard) *Anna Karina, Sami Frey.* Godard's fresh approach to the gangster musical follows the antics of three highly spirited but ineffectual crooks. An interesting aspect of the film is the insertion of Godard's personal philosophical observations and his thoughts on the action in the story. One of Godard's most interesting and accessible films. (French with English subtitles) ★★★½ VHS: $59.99

The Band Wagon

(1953, 112 min, US, Vincente Minnelli) *Fred Astaire, Cyd Charisse, Nanette Fabray, Oscar Levant, Jack Buchanan.* One of Astaire's most captivating musicals, this glorious comedic look at the mak-

ing of a Broadway show has Fred as a Hollywood actor who is persuaded to star on the Great White Way with a renowned ballerina (the beautiful Charisse). A fine score, sensational dance numbers and charming performances by all combine to make this a classic of the musical genre. ★★★★ VHS: $14.99

Bandit Queen

(1994, 119 min, India/GB, Shekhar Kapur) *Seema Biswas, Nirmal Pandey, Manoj Bajpai.* This film adaptation of the harrowing yet ultimately triumphant life of Indian folkhero Phoolan Devi is a blistering attack on her culture's horrifying treatment of women and its crushing caste system. After being raped by her new husband, Phoolan escapes and returns to her home village only to be branded a whore and banished by the village elders. Kidnapped and brutally humiliated by a gang of bandits, she eventually rises within their ranks to become the leader of her own gang. Her bitter and ruthless quest for vengeance leads her to become regarded as a savior by throngs of lowborn Indians. With an unrelentingly hard-core depiction of Indian society, the film offers a fascinating peek into the intricate and complex social machinations of India's highly organized bandit armies. Well-paced and emotionally arousing as both action-adventure story and scathing social critique. ★★★½ DVD: $24.99

Bandits

(1987, 98 min, France, Claude Lelouch) *Jean Yanne, Marie-Sophie Lelouch.* Director Lelouch has fashioned a real gem (no pun intended) about the relationship between an imprisoned jewel thief and his daughter. Yanne is charming as the father who hides his young daughter in a Swiss boarding school after a jewel heist ends in his wife's murder and his arrest. This is a near-perfect film with a great script, first-rate acting and plenty of plot twists. (French with English subtitles) ★★★★

Bandits

(1999, 110 min, Germany, Katja von Garnier) *Katja Riemann, Jasmin Tabatabai, Nicolette Krebitz, Jutta Hoffmann.* A group of female convicts, all musicians, are brought together to form a rock band under a new government rehabilitation program. They are scheduled to perform at a policemen's ball, but escape, and become huge celebrities while on the lam. This German *Thelma and Louise: The Musical* lacks that film's emotional involvement and resonance, as well as any memorable tunes. The cheesy VH-1–esque music interludes stop the movie cold, and the drama is trite and clichéd. *Bandits* has one or two fun moments, but also has the prefab feel of a feature-length advert for a band that never was, and isn't nearly as fun as the very similiar, though nearly forgotten, '70s Peter Fonda-starrer, *Outlaw Blues*. (German with English subtitles) ★★ VHS: $21.99; DVD: $27.99

Bandolero

(1968, 106 min, US, Andrew V. McLaglen) *James Stewart, Dean Martin, Raquel Welch, George Kennedy.* Stewart and Martin play sibling outlaws who escape to Mexico with Welch as a hostage. Stewart and Martin are riding in familiar western territory here, though they play well together. ★★½ VHS: $19.99

Bang the Drum Slowly

(1973, 97 min, US, John Hancock) *Robert De Niro, Michael Moriarty, Vincent Gardenia, Ann Wedgeworth, Danny Aiello.* Two stand-out performances by Moriarty and De Niro highlight this stirring drama, based on a 1956 TV drama (which starred a young Paul Newman) about the relationship between two big-league ball players: a star pitcher (Moriarty) and his catcher (De Niro), dying of Hodgkin's Disease. Gardenia is priceless as their colorful manager. ★★★½ VHS: $14.99

The Bank Dick

(1940, 74 min, US, Eddie Cline) *W.C. Fields, Cora Witherspoon, Una Merkel, Franklin Pangborn, Shemp Howard.* Inept, bungling Fields gets a job as a guard in a bank, forcing him to deal with the stress of employment as well as the encumberment of wife and family. But forget the plot. This is one of the true comedy classics. The only problem is, it's too short. ★★★½ VHS: $14.99; DVD: $29.99

Bank Robber

(1993, 94 min, US, Nick Mead) *Patrick Dempsey, Lisa Bonet, Forest Whitaker, Judge Reinhold.* Writer-director Mead combines the typical heist film with a story line inspired by Ionesco's Theatre of the Absurd to produce this entertainingly bizarre and challenging film. A pumped-up Dempsey plays a nice-guy bank robber who is forced to hide out in a creepy L.A. hotel until the heat blows over. His nightmare begins, however, as he is visited by a succession of characters who know his identity and exploit him at every turn. These include the pizza delivery boy, the hotel clerk and a gay motorcycle cop into S&M. ★★★

B*A*P*S

(1997, 90 min, US, Robert Townsend) *Halle Berry, Natalie Dessalle, Martin Landau.* In Townsend's amateurish, unfunny spoof, Berry and newcomer Dessalle star as Nisi and Mickey, two blue-collar waitresses from the South who dream of opening a hair salon/soul food restaurant. However, in this homogenized *Pretty Woman* meets *Clueless* about wish fulfillment, clashing cultures and really tacky fashion choices, dreams prove fleeting as they head to El Lay for fame and fortune. Upon their arrival, they are offered exactly that if Nisi will masquerade as the granddaughter of the former sweetheart of a dying millionaire (Landau). Are they pawns in a devious scheme? By then you just won't care. Generic R&B tunes, an annoying dramatic score, and "so-what" spot-the-star cameos can't deflect the tame writing and directing. ★½ VHS: $14.99

Bar Girls

(1995, 95 min, US, Marita Giovanni) *Nancy Allison Wolfe, Lisa Parker, Camile Griggs, Paula Sorge, Justine Slater.* The mating rites and the accompanying mind games of L.A. lesbians are uncovered in this knowing romantic comedy. Lauran Hoffman's script (based on her autobiographical play) centers most of the action at the West Hollywood Girl Bar where "love" comes easy and often. Loretta (Wolfe), a writer and one of the bar's bed-hopping regulars, meets and all-too-quickly falls for the self-assured Rachel (D'Agnostino), a bewitching aspiring actress. Their union is threatened, however, when J.R. (Riggs), an attractively butch cop, enters the scene. The sex-induced theatrics of these and other characters are detailed in both a humorous and dramatic fashion and, unlike the buoyantly chipper *Go Fish*, the women in *Bar Girls* are not entirely likable. While the acting is unremarkable and the production values minimal, the film nevertheless is endowed with spunky charm. ★★★ VHS: $14.99

Baraka

(1992, 96 min, US, Ron Fricke) "Baraka" is an ancient Sufi word meaning a blessing or the breath or essence of life from which the evolutionary process unfolds. An examination of the diversity of the world's life is the subject of this film, shot in 24 countries in Todd-AO 70mm format. Like the similar *Koyaanisqatsi*, it has no dialogue or narration and combines images and music to inform, enlighten and entertain. The subjects and areas *Baraka* explores include religion, the forces of weather and nature, tribal practices, chicken factories, and the beauty of natural formations and phenomena. Always an incredibly beautiful film, *Baraka* is unfortunately confusing, feeling sometimes like a harmless travelogue and other times like a manipulative, self-conscious political treatise. But it's terrific viewing — its scope and magnificence unfortunately diminished by the home viewing screen. Additionally, its music, taken from a variety of sources, lacks the minimalist power of Philip Glass' compositions for *Koyaanisqatsi* and *Powaqqatsi*. ★★★ VHS: $29.99; DVD: $24.99

Barb Wire

(1996, 90 min, US, David Hogan) *Pamela Anderson Lee, Temuera Morrison, Victoria Rowell, Udo Kier, Steve Railsback, Xander Berkeley.* Imagine a futuristic *Casablanca*, but with a silicone-enhanced Bogart packing automatic weapons, and you have, in a C-cup, the plot of this camp showcase for TV sex symbol Lee. In this adaptation of the comic, she plays a former soldier-now-nightclub proprietess who's content to wait out the ongoing Second American Civil War. Her peace is shattered when an ex (Morrison) walks in, on the run because of his association with a freedom fighter. He enlists her aid to help them escape. As a piece of kitsch, *Barb Wire* is somewhat enjoyable, but it's all just rather flat. Adding to the camp value is Lee's nonexistent acting ability. The production values are of the "always raining because it looked cool in *Blade Runner*" variety, and the action scenes are competently done. (Available rated and unrated) ★★ VHS: $9.99; DVD: $19.99

Barbarella

(1967, 98 min, France, Roger Vadim) *Jane Fonda, John Phillip Law, Anita Pallenberg, Milo O'Shea.* There's something for everyone in this imaginative, sexually charged sci-fi camp classic. Featuring a young Fonda — before Vietnam, exercise videos, two Oscars and rich Southern media moguls — as a fetching, pre-liberated sex goddess, this wacky film shows off all of her best bodily talents. As the sexy 40th-century space traveler, Fonda, when not fighting off demonic, razor-teethed dolls or killer canaries, displays a wonderful assortment of the latest in revealing intergalactic fashion. ★★★ VHS: $14.99; DVD: $29.99

Barbarians at the Gate

(1993, 122 min, US, Glenn Jordan) *James Garner, Jonathan Pryce, Peter Riegert, Joanna Cassidy.* It's the 1980s and it's morning in America. Entire companies are bought, sold and discarded faster than pantyhose. Multimillion-dollar leveraged buyouts are routinely handled before lunch; the billion-dollar deals take a little more time. Sweeping across this frenetic landscape is one rich former Canadian who, in a fast-paced tap dance through the boardrooms of the country, concocts a plan to purchase the leading baking corporation in the land. Fantastic parody, right? The truly fantastic element is that it's all true — well, not true in the sense of This Dialogue Guaranteed Verbatim. Garner is mesmerizing as F. Ross Johnson, CEO of RJR Nabisco, whose attempts to buy out the company are set forth in this humorous and extremely entertaining HBO production. ★★★½ VHS: $9.99

Barbarosa

(1981, 90 min, Australia, Fred Schepisi) *Willie Nelson, Gary Busey, Gilbert Roland.* A thrilling western yarn that combines the charismatic acting of Nelson and the spectacular photography and sharp, tightly controlled direction of Schepisi. A farm boy (Busey) on the lam is rescued from the ravages of the desert by the outlaw Barbarosa (Nelson). A strong alliance and friendship develops as they roam the West battling thieves, the elements and angry in-laws. ★★★ VHS: $9.99

Barbary Coast

(1935, 90 min, US, Howard Hawks) *Edward G. Robinson, Miriam Hopkins, Joel McCrea.* Hawks distinguished himself as a director par excellence in two film genres: the screwball comedy and the action-flavored drama. This story of 19th-century San Francisco during the California Gold Rush days falls into the latter category, and features the director in fine form. Robinson is perfectly cast as a gangster nightclub owner, Hopkins is the club's star attraction, and McCrea is the Easterner who comes between them. ★★★ VHS: $14.99

Barcelona

(1994, 101 min, US, Whit Stillman) *Taylor Nichols, Chris Eigeman, Tushka Bergen, Mira Sorvino.* The sophomore curse strikes again as Stillman's follow-up to his acclaimed *Metropolitan* fails to totally capture the freshness and ingenuity of his first film. Set in Spain during the last days of the Cold War, the story follows the romantic exploits of two Americans living in Barcelona. Nichols, sort of a low-rent Hugh Grant, plays a dweeby salesman whose cousin (Eigeman), a Navy attaché, arrives unexpectedly. This gives way to the two aimlessly musing about life, death, romance, politics, and whatever else randomly enters their minds. A little too chatty for its own good, Stillman's script occasionally offers amusing and accurate observations on modern relationships. Though the supporting characters aren't as well-defined as the leads — especially the women's roles, which are nothing more than window dressing. ★★½ VHS: $19.99

Barefoot in the Park

(1967, 105 min, US, Gene Saks) *Robert Redford, Jane Fonda, Mildred Natwick, Charles Boyer, Herb Edelman.* Frothy Neil Simon comedy, based on his hit Broadway play, with Redford and Fonda as newlyweds living on top of a five-floor walk-up in New York City, experiencing big city life and marital woes. Though not one of Simon's classics, there's more than enough to entertain, and a good supporting cast adds sparkle. ★★★ VHS: $14.99; DVD: $29.99

Barfly

(1987, 97 min, US, Barbet Schroeder) *Mickey Rourke, Faye Dunaway, Alice Krige, Jack Nance.* Director Schroeder has perfectly captured the spirit of Charles Bukowski's autobiography about the resilience of the creative force. Rourke, in possibly his best performance, plays the alcoholic writer who begins an affair with fellow inebriate Dunaway (remarkable in a non-typecast role), the two enjoying the seedy Los Angeles bar scene in search of libation and unorthodox fulfillment. A brilliant, hilariously funny character study. ★★★★ VHS: $19.99

The Barkleys of Broadway

(1949, 109 min, US, Charles Walters) *Fred Astaire, Ginger Rogers, Oscar Levant.* The last Astaire-Rogers musical (made after a 10-year separation) is charming fluff about a theatrical couple who split when one wants to abandon the act for "serious" drama. Screenplay by Betty Comden-Adolphe Green (*Singin' in the Rain*). ★★★ VHS: $14.99

Barnum

(1986, 113 min, GB, Terry Hughes) *Michael Crawford.* The London theatrical production of the smash musical extravaganza is brought to video in this rousing musical starring a leaping, spinning and singing Crawford ("Phantom of the Opera"). With music by Cy Coleman ("Sweet Charity," "City of Angels") and lyrics by Michael Stewart, the story follows the famed showman's career from his beginnings as a sideshow promoter to his co-founding of the Barnum & Bailey Circus, "The Greatest Show on Earth!" ★★★ VHS: $29.99; DVD: $29.99

Barocco

(1976, 102 min, France, Andre Techine) *Gérard Depardieu, Isabelle Adjani.* Depardieu and Adjani star in this frustrating noir tale of blackmail and murder. Adjani plays a young woman who convinces her ex-boxer boyfriend (Depardieu) to accept a bribe to discredit a local politician. Then the boyfriend is murdered by a hit man (also played by Depardieu). Adjani, who witnesses the murder, remembers every detail about the killer with the exception that he's a look-alike of the deceased, a fact which escapes the police, as well. It's the old, annoying Superman/Clark Kent story. Eventually and predictably, the woman reinvents the hit man as her boyfriend and they escape together. If you can get past the forced plot device of identity, *Barocco* is an acceptable thriller, but Depardieu has certainly done better. (French with English subtitles) ★★ VHS: $29.99

Barry Lyndon

(1975, 184 min, GB, Stanley Kubrick) *Ryan O'Neal, Marisa Berenson, John Alcott, Patrick Magee.* Almost all of Kubrick's films are master-pieces, and this is no exception to that rule. In *Barry Lyndon*, Kubrick goes beyond the bounds of normal cinematography and uses the camera as a paintbrush and the screen as a canvas with which to tell his story through still lifes and landscapes. Adapted from Thacker v's novel, the film follows Barry Lyndon on his search for success in 18th-century England. ★★★★ VHS: $19.99; DVD: $24.99

Barry Mackenzie Holds His Own

(1974, 93 min, Australia, Bruce Beresford) *Barry Crocker, Barry Humphries, Donald Pleasence.* This zany Aussie comedy is filled with Down Under in-jokes, raunchy humor and an always unpredictable plot. Australia's Everyman (before the advent of "Crocodile" Dundee) Barry Mackenzie (Crocker), with his Aunt Edna (drag superstar Humphries), gets into all sorts of adventures, including being kidnapped to Transylvania. Fans of low-brow, off-the-wall humor will appreciate this romp. ★★★

Barton Fink

(1991, 112 min, US, Joel Coen) *John Turturro, John Goodman, Judy Davis, Michael Lerner, Steve Buscemi, John Mahoney.* The Coen brothers have manufactured a mesmerizing parable on the death of innocence and the perversion of artistic integrity in the face of gross crudity and greed. Turturro is terrific as the title character, Barton Fink, an acclaimed, socially conscious New York playwright (styled after Clifford Odets) who is lured by Hollywood's false hope. While being reduced to another cog in the studio machine, he develops a strained camaraderie with Goodman, the next-door neighbor in his steam-bath hotel — it's a relationship which comes to define his California experience. Turturro and Goodman bring total credibility to otherwise fantastical characters in an exaggerated, surreal world of peeling wallpaper and oddly threatening drainpipes. ★★★½ VHS: $19.99

BASEketball

(1998, 103 min, US, David Zucker) *Trey Parker, Matt Stone, Dian Bachar, Yasmine Bleeth, Jenny McCarthy, Robert Vaughn, Ernest Borgnine.* This silly, funny romp won't invigorate the "dumb comedy" genre in a way that stars Parker and Stone's "South Park" has restimulated TV animation, but it's nevertheless responsible for producing a high number of jokes which poke fun at sports, television, and those which make both tick. Parker and Stone play the inventors of the latest sports craze — BASEketball, a combination of basketball and Home-Run Derby. As the popularity of the sport soars, our heroes fight to keep their integrity and their friendship intact. *BASEketball* doesn't have the fluid comic style of Zucker's previous gems like *Airplane!* and *The Naked Gun*, nor are the jokes as consistent. But between the slapstick, low-brow humor and celebrity guests, there are plenty of dumb bits which — like Parker and Stone's TV show — sometimes go too far but are funny anyway. Parker seems more at home in front of the camera than his partner-in-crime Stone, though both are equally willing to do whatever it takes to get a laugh. *BASEketball* isn't a home run; there are quite a few swings and misses, but it will make you laugh. ★★½ VHS: $9.99; DVD: $24.99

Basic Instinct

(1992, 127 min, US, Paul Verhoeven) *Michael Douglas, Sharon Stone, Jeanne Tripplehorn, George Dzunda, Dorothy Malone.* When it opened at movie theatres, this ultra-chic, sexually explicit thriller was surrounded by controversy. Picketed in several cities, the film raised a red flag for gays, lesbians and feminists with its shockingly "retro" stereotypes of man-hating lesbians with a "basic instinct" for murder. Basically an adolescent sex fantasy disguised as a murder mystery, the film follows Douglas as a burned-out cop who inadvisedly falls in "lust" with the prime suspect in a series of brutal icepick murders, lasciviously portrayed by Stone. Verhoeven, as always, directs with a sense of style and atmosphere which elevates it above the average action/thriller, but at the heart of the film is Joe Eszterhas' multi-million dollar screenplay which, while particularly hateful of women, is misanthropic on the whole. Worthy of controversy? Perhaps, but basically this is just another thriller which really doesn't cover any new ground. ("Director's Cut," with 40 additional

BASEketball

Michelle Pfeiffer laps up her role like a bowl of warm milk in *Batman Returns*

seconds, is available on VHS for $24.99) ★★
VHS: $14.99; DVD: $24.99

Basil

(1998, 102 min, GB, Radha Bharadwaj) *Christian Slater, Derek Jacobi, Claire Forlani, David Ross, Jared Leto.* A weak costumer from *Closet Land* director Bharadwaj, *Basil* fails on almost every level. Leto plays the son of a well-to-do aristocrat (a slumming Jacobi) who's forced to forego friends and fun to pursue his studies and uphold the family name. After his life is saved by gentlemanly rogue Slater (sporting a hilarious British accent), Leto strikes up a friendship with him and soon his outlook changes. Flat and uninvolving from the start, the film is full of betrayals, twists and Gothic trappings, but the execution is reminiscent of a high school Merchant-Ivory production. Nobody's heart seems to be in it, which only makes it all the more frustrating. ★½ VHS: $19.99

Basileus Quartet

(1982, 118 min, Italy, Fabio Capri) *Pierre Malet, Hector Alterio.* When one of the elderly members of a staid classical quartet dies, he is replaced by a handsome young man. His effervescent approach to life and music proves to be both a tonic and a curse as he affects each member. A stylized drama of artistic expression, the film is sabotaged by an irresponsible portrayal of a gay quartet member. (Italian with English subtitles) ★★½

Basket Case

(1982, 91 min, US, Frank Henenlotter) *Kevin Van Hentenryck, Terri Susan Smith.* If John Waters ever makes a splatter movie, it won't be any better than this, one of independent horrordom's most cherished cult classics. A country bumpkin tries to make it in New York City while saddled with his mutant brother that he carries around Times Square in a wicker basket. Few serious filmmakers have captured the seamier side of the city better than this little gross-out gem. ★★★ VHS: $24.99; DVD: $24.99

Basket Case II

(1990, 90 min, US, Frank Henenlotter) *Kevin Van Hentenryck, Heather Rattray.* Belial's back and

he's sharing his basket with a babe at Aunt Ruth's private clinic. Just as outlandish as the first, with an ending that left grind house patrons cheering in disbelief. ★★★

Basket Case 3

(1991, 90 min, US, Frank Henenlotter) Director Henenlotter's *Basket Case* series continues its downward spiral in this cheap and uninspired installment. Filled with amateur acting and saddled by a script that's mostly filler, gore fans are advised to rent Henenlotter's earlier *Brain Damage* — a gripping, imaginative little splatterfest that triumphs where this one fails. ★ VHS: $19.99

The Basketball Diaries

(1995, 102 min, US, Scott Kalvert) *Leonardo DiCaprio, Mark Wahlberg, Bruno Kirby, Lorraine Bracco, Ernie Hudson, Patrick McGaw, Juliette Lewis, James Madio.* Jim Carroll's underground, autobiographical novel depicting his young adult years as a drug addict has compelling moments of anguish and alienation, but this screen adaptation falls short in its dramatic foundation. Whereas Carroll's book took place in the mid-1960s and defined a generational mindset, the story has been ill-advisedly updated to the 1990s where counterculture ritual and spirit are at odds with MTV sensibilities. The strength of the film lies in the simplicity of the intimate relationships it develops between Carroll and his mates. As one of them, Wahlberg is especially good as an abused teen who crosses the line. In examining the lives of streetwise teens living on the mean streets of New York, *The Basketball Diaries* covers little new ground, but Carroll's vivid perspective on camaraderie and his harrowing search for redemption are at the heart of a film whose voice is muted but aware. ★★½ DVD: $29.99

Basquiat

(1996, 108 min, US, Julian Schnabel) *Jeffrey Wright, David Bowie, Michael Wincott, Benicio Del Toro, Claire Forlani, Gary Oldman, Dennis Hopper, Parker Posey, Christopher Walken, Willem Dafoe.* Wright is mesmerizing as Jean-Michael Basquiat, a poor Haitian-American graffiti artist who rapidly ascends New York's rarified art world only to lose it all to heroin addiction and an

early death. While the premise of blind ambition and the price that is to be paid has been used in films many times before (was *Citizen Kane* the first?), this story is unusual in the depiction of the title character. For instead of a headstrong, "success or bust" personality, we see an innocent and emotionally fragile artist lured, seduced and used by others — to the point where self-destruction seems the only escape. The result is an indelible portrait of an artist as a doomed young man. ★★★½ VHS: $19.99

Bastard Out of Carolina

(1996, 101 min, US, Anjelica Huston) *Jena Malone, Jennifer Jason Leigh, Ron Eldard, Glenne Headly, Micheal Rooker, Dermot Mulroney, Lyle Lovett, Grace Zabriskie.* Huston delivers a solid directorial debut making optimum use of a uniformly talented cast through a story line that easily could have surrendered to bathos. Malone is a wonder as the illegitimate daughter of an illegitimate daughter growing up in 1950s South Carolina. Her fortunes rise and fall with her mother's choice of men, illustrating economic inequities and the hardships of societal condemnation. From the casual cruelty of other children and uncaring bureaucracies to physical and sexual abuse at the hands of adults, the film delineates the financial and emotional dependence of single mothers struggling to support their families. Malone's character maintains a vibrant autonomy with the aid of a strong extended family and an unyielding if sometimes tragically misguided mother's love. Huston seems to have inherited her father's facility for revealing base human weaknesses as well as those occasional moments of triumph which elevate mundane existence and daily toil. An engrossing and involving film. ★★★ VHS: $14.99; DVD: $24.99

Bat 21

(1988, 105 min, US, Peter Markle) *Gene Hackman, Danny Glover.* America's awakening to the horrors of the Vietnam War is the theme of this rather routine action film elevated to prominence by Hackman's performance. Hackman stars as a desk officer, far removed from the war, who is literally plunged into a Viet Cong–infested jungle — and forced to fend for himself. Glover costars as the copter pilot assigned to rescue him. ★★½

Batman

(1989, 126 min, US, Tim Burton) *Michael Keaton, Jack Nicholson, Kim Basinger, Robert Wuhl, Billy Dee Williams, Jack Palance.* What can we say about this megahit? That it fell short of its potential; that Keaton's understated portrayal of the Caped Crusader — while challenging and daringly offbeat — was somehow flat; that Basinger's Vicky Vale plays far too great a role; that we couldn't understand why Williams was all but written out of the picture; and finally that the film's finale appears to have been scraped together in the midst of the writers' strike. We could say all that, but you probably wouldn't believe us anyway. Nicholson's Joker is astounding: Jack, we love ya, and you deserve every penny — it's your movie, babe. (Available letterboxed or pan & scan) ★★½ VHS: $9.99; DVD: $19.99

Batman & Robin

(1997, 125 min, US, Joel Schumacher) *George Clooney, Chris O'Donnell, Arnold Schwarzenegger, Alicia Silverstone, Uma Thurman.* Clooney becomes the third actor to don the mask and cape in this star-filled, flashy, megabudget testament to Hollywood gloss. This time, Batman and his Boy Wonder Robin (O'Donnell) are up against a truly titanic villain: the blue-faced Mr. Freeze (Schwarzenegger). While more substantial dramatically than its predecessor, it nevertheless succumbs to a problem that has plagued all the sequels: it focuses too little on its hero. Clooney is relegated to under ten minutes of screen time as Bruce Wayne, and his scenes as Batman almost all involve him playing second fiddle to the villains or to Robin and their new partner Batgirl (the unimpressive Silverstone). At least the extravagant sets and shiny costumes look good. (VHS available letterboxed or pan & scan) ★★½ VHS: $9.99; DVD: $19.99

Batman Forever

(1995, 121 min, US, Joel Schumacher) *Val Kilmer, Tommy Lee Jones, Jim Carrey, Chris O'Donnell, Nicole Kidman, Drew Barrymore, Debi Mazar.* Kilmer replaces Michael Keaton in the title role and breathes some depth of character into a role made far too enigmatic by his predecessor. As in the previous two episodes, the plot is mostly incidental filler (wacko badguys have it out for Batman...again!) that sets up outrageous pyrotechnic action sequences. But hey, the name of the game here is Gothic atmosphere, special effects and action, action and more action; and in this arena *Batman Forever* does not disappoint. O'Donnell is a circus performer who, finding himself orphaned and hellbent for vengeance, transforms himself into Robin. As for the villains, Carrey offers a spectacularly rubber-faced and over-the-top interpretation of The Riddler which overshadows Jones' Two-Face. Kidman has a throwaway role as a criminal psychologist who tries to probe the depths of Bruce Wayne's psyche — as well as some parts of his anatomy. (VHS available letterboxed or pan & scan) ★★★ VHS: $9.99; DVD: $19.99

Batman Returns

(1992, 126 min, US, Tim Burton) *Michael Keaton, Michelle Pfeiffer, Danny DeVito, Christopher Walken, Michael Murphy, Michael Gough, Paul Reubens, Jan Hooks.* Burton's follow-up to 1989's box-office mega-hit is a more entertaining foray into the shadowy world of Gotham City and the Caped Crusader. As in the original film, Keaton's brooding and gloomy Batman/Bruce Wayne character takes a back seat to the story's vivacious villains — here Pfeiffer as Catwoman and DeVito as The Penguin. Pfeiffer shines as the furtive feline anti-hero, lapping up her role like a warm bowl of milk; and DeVito ably fills the shoes of Burgess Meredith with his demented Dickensian take on the grotesquely deformed Penguin. The screenplay provides a far more interesting spin than the original through its parable of urban decay and political corruption. (VHS available letterboxed or pan & scan) ★★★ VHS: $9.99; DVD: $19.99

Batman: The Movie

(1966, 105 min, US, Leslie Martinson) *Adam West, Burt Ward, Burgess Meredith, Cesar Romero, Frank Gorshin, Lee Meriwether.* Before Keaton

and Nicholson came on the scene, there was West and Ward as the crime-fighting Dynamic Duo (you only get one crime-fighter with Keaton). All-out camp. The Joker, The Penguin, Catwoman and The Riddler battle the Caped Crusader and the Boy Won·er. ★★½ VHS: $14.99

Baton Rouge

(1988, 94 min, Spain, Rafael Moleon) *Antonio Banderas, Victoria Abril, Carmen Maura.* In this smarmy psychological thriller, a late-night encounter between prowling gigolo Banderas and monied neurotic Abril leads to double cross and murder. The socialite's recurring nightmares of rape by an unknown assailant lead her to seek help from psychologist Maura. Maura's ensuing involvement with Banderas and the lure of Abril's supposed wealth are the catalysts for plot and counterplot, along with Banderas' desire to take his younger brother — mute since their mother's death — on a road trip to the States, to Baton Rouge. Hooker with a heart of gold? No wonder he gets along so well with Melanie. (Spanish with English subtitles) ★★ VHS: $79.99

Bats

(1999, 91 min, US, Louis Morneau) *Lou Diamond Phillips, Dina Meyer, Leon, Carlos Jacott, Bob Gunton.* Genetically-altered bats have been unleashed by a deranged scientist and they're attacking a small Texas town. Phillips is the town sheriff and Meyer (who is about as convincing as Saffron Burrows in *Deep Blue Sea*) is the biologist who team to combat the little pesky critters. The dialogue is right out of a bad '50s sci-fi opus, though there's enough mayhem and blood to satisfy horror geeks with low expectations. ★★ VHS: $9.99; DVD: $24.99

*batteries not included

(1987, 106 min, US, Matthew Robbins) *Jessica Tandy, Hume Cronyn, Frank McRae, Elizabeth Peña, Dennis Boutsikaris.* Sentimental sci-fi tale about tiny alien creatures who come to the aid of a group of tenants whose building is marked for demolition. Husband and wife Cronyn and Tandy give it more class than what's up on the screen. ★★½ VHS: $7.49; DVD: $24.99

Battle Angel

(1993, 70 min, Japan, Hiroshi Fukutomi) Based on the long-running *manga* (Japanese comic book) by writer/illustrator Yukito Kishiro, this animated feature is a faithful adaptation of the artist's original work. Known as *Gunnm* in Japan, *Battle Angel* is actually two short episodic films: "Gunnm — Rusty Angel" and "Gunnm — Tears Sign." Tersely directed by Fukutomi, the story line follows the exploits of a female bounty hunter cyborg, Gally, and her numerous battles with the violent denizens of the futuristic Scrap Iron City. Fluid animation, memorable character designs, and an exciting science-fiction setting make this essential viewing for anime fans. **Note:** Production was supervised by the legendary Rin Taro (director of *Harmageddon* and *The Dagger of Kamui*), and also includes a video production art portfolio segment. (Japanese with English subtitles) ★★★½ VHS: $34.99; DVD: $29.99

Travolta's dog of a pet project *Battlefield Earth*.

Battle Beyond the Stars

(1980, 102 min, US, Jimmy T. Murakami) *Richard Thomas, John Saxon, Robert Vaughn.* John Sayles wrote the script for this entertaining sci-fi quickie produced by Roger Corman about intergalactic soldiers of fortune coming to the rescue to save the planet Akira. ★★★ VHS: $14.99; DVD: $19.99

Battle for the Planet of the Apes

(1973, 89 min, US, J. Lee Thompson) *Roddy McDowall, Paul Williams, John Huston.* The fifth and final entry in the *Planet of the Apes* series finds the apes and man warring for control of the planet. The series had long lost its charm, and this last episode is for die-hard fans only. ★★ VHS: $14.99

Battle Hymn

(1957, 108 min, US, Douglas Sirk) *Rock Hudson, Martha Hyer, Anna Kashfi, Dan Duryea, Don DeFore.* Hudson offers a sensitive performance in this heartwarming true story of a minister/Air Force pilot who helps evacuate orphans during the Korean War. ★★★ VHS: $9.99

Battle of Algiers

(1965, 123 min, Algeria, Gillo Pontecorvo) *Yacef Saadi, Jean Martin.* Director Pontecorvo brilliantly re-creates the street riots and other events that led up to Algeria's independence from France in this astonishingly realistic movie masterpiece. Pontecorvo's triumph includes his sympathetic handling of both sides of the agonizing, brutal struggle for independence. The cast of superbly used non-professional actors and the director's technical ability to create newsreel-like authenticity combine to make this a legendary film. (French with English subtitles) ★★★★ VHS: $19.99

The Battle of Austerlitz

(1960, 175 min, France/Italy, Abel Gance) *Orson Welles, Jack Palance, Claudia Cardinale, Jean-Louis Trintignant.* This is a recently restored, full-length version of Gance's grand re-creation of Napoleon's most important battle. An epic, lavish production that features an international cast. Unbelievably, the film was originally shown in a 73-minute version. (French with English subtitles) ★★★½

Battle of Britain

(1969, 132 min, GB, Guy Hamilton) *Michael Caine, Laurence Olivier, Trevor Howard, Christopher Plummer, Michael Redgrave, Ralph Richardson, Robert Shaw.* One of those WWII epics that probably cost more than the actual war effort. The action follows a stalwart group of RAF pilots who battle an invading Nazi air unit. There are lots of air battles, and the film has a cast of thousands — well, hundreds and hundreds — headed up by half the known thespians in England. Despite good special effects and extremely well-staged battle sequences, the story treads on familiar war-movie ground. ★★ VHS: $14.99

Battlefield Earth

(2000, 117 min, US, Roger Christian) *John Travolta, Barry Pepper, Forest Whitaker, Kim Coates, Richard Tyson, Kelly Preston.* A putrid, steaming, galactic-sized mound of Limburger cheese, *Battlefield Earth* is one of the most embarrassing movies we've ever suffered the indignity of sitting all the way through. Travolta conceived and produced this sci-fi dud, based on the thinly veiled Scientology manifesto by L. Ron Hubbard. Travolta also takes the vanity spot, starring as the arrogant leader of an alien race that has invaded Earth with the intent to strip-mine the planet dry. He's stunningly bad. Co-star Pepper makes for a likable hero, the reluctant leader of a scraggly band of rebels living in the wasteland. Decent visual effects are undercut by a decrepit production design, arrhythmic editing and murky cinematography (and the cameraman obviously saw *The Third Man* way too many times: nearly every shot in the movie is unnecessarily tilted). This is disjointed, tedious and every bit as bad as its reputation. We saw it so you don't *have* to, but if you're up for a dare. . . ★ VHS: $14.99; DVD: $19.99

Battleship Potemkin

(1925, 74 min, USSR, Sergei Eisenstein) *Alexander Antonov, Vladimir Barsky.* This gripping account of the revolt by the crew of the *Potemkin* and their part in the Revolution of 1905 is a landmark film for its groundbreaking use of editing and montage. The rebellion, the support for it by the people of Odessa and the ensuing attack by Cossack troops still excite and overwhelm audiences today. (Silent with a musical soundtrack) ★★★★ VHS: $19.99; DVD: $24.99

Bean

The Bawdy Adventures of Tom Jones

(1976, 94 min, GB, Cliff Owen) *Trevor Howard, Joan Collins, Terry-Thomas.* Based on the London stage musical, this mildly amusing version of Henry Fielding's tale has its moments, but it can't hold a candle to Tony Richardson's classic. The cast fails to elevate the film above its mediocre status. ★★ VHS: $59.99

Baxter

(1991, 85 min, France, Jerome Boivin) *Lisa Delamare, Jean Mercure.* This maliciously dark French comedy is told primarily from the point of view of a misanthropic bull terrier who gets bounced around to a series of different masters. Starting in the kennel, he is originally given as a present to the dowdy old mother of the pound owner's wife. But fate (or is it?) intervenes and he winds up with the sex obsessed couple next door, and then a sadistic young boy. Peppered with wry narration from the twisted mind of this pesky canine, the film points to the vicious behavior of humans and pets alike in this dog-eat-dog world. (French with English subtitles) ★★★ VHS: $19.99

The Bay Boy

(1985, 107 min, Canada, Daniel Petrie) *Kiefer Sutherland, Liv Ullmann.* A well-meaning but predictable coming-of-age drama set in 1930s Nova Scotia. Sutherland plays an awkward 16-year-old who is eager to be initiated into the rites of manhood, although opportunities are limited in the dismal mining town in which he and his mother (Ullmann) live. Attractively photographed, the film falls flat when dealing with the well-trod theme of adolescent angst. ★★ VHS: $79.99

The Beach

(1999, 119 min, US, Danny Boyle) *Leonardo DiCaprio, Robert Carlyle, Tilda Swinton, Virginia Ledoyen, Guillaume Canet.* Beautiful tropical scenery and a back-to-nature theme aren't enough to sustain interest in this picturesque though waterlogged parable of one young man's search for paradise. Looking tanned and fit, DiCaprio stars as Richard, an American traveling through Asia searching for adventure. He finds it one evening in a seedy Bangkok hotel when he meets the loony Daffy (Carlyle), who tells him of a lush and very private island. Befriending the Europeans next door, he and his new cohorts set off to find the tropical paradise. And find it they do. And it's everything the nutty Daffy said it was: gorgeous beach, perfect weather, bountiful forest, and already inhabited not only by gun-toting natives, but a secretive commune as well. The moral of the evils of civilization is played with a heavy hand here, though it is conveyed under the most attractive circumstances. But white sand, blue water and red blood are an unfulfilling triumvirate. At least the cast takes this seriously, which is more than most viewers will be able to do. ★★ VHS: $14.99; DVD: $24.99

Beach Blanket Bingo

(1965, 96 min, US, William Asher) *Frankie Avalon, Annette Funicello, Paul Lynde, Don Rickles.* Though not exactly Preston Sturges or Billy Wilder, this playful '60s beach movie is probably the best of the series. Frankie Avalon and Annette Funicello and the rest of the gang get involved with mermaids and kidnappers. ★★½ DVD: $14.99

Beaches

(1988, 123 min, US, Garry Marshall) *Bette Midler, Barbara Hershey, John Heard, Spalding Gray.* An effective though familiar tearjerker which follows the friendship — and its ups and downs — of two women through the years. Midler is dynamic, giving one of her patented larger-than-life performances as a singer/actress determined to make it in show business. Hershey, new lips and all, is slightly eclipsed in Midler's shadow, but nicely essays the role of an upper-class attorney beset by personal misfortunes. Get out the hankies for this one. ★★½ VHS: $9.99

Bean

(1997, 90 min, GB, Mel Smith) *Rowan Atkinson, Peter MacNicol, Pamela Reed, Harris Yulin, Burt Reynolds, John Mills.* Atkinson's lovable mischief maker Mr. Bean makes a rather inauspicious theatrical debut. On TV, Mr. Bean performs his hilarious and crazy antics in small set pieces, vignettes not really tied together by plot. This is possibly why they work so well. In a film stretched to 90 minutes and bound somewhat by narrative structure, only occasionally is Atkinson allowed to really let loose. The story has to do with Bean being sent by the British Museum as a guest speaker for a Los Angeles art museum unveiling "Whistler's Mother." Of course the bungling Bean knows nothing of art and gradually wreaks havoc around him. For some reason, the writers are content with snot and toilet humor, and these jokes fall flat. However, when not borrowing some TV gags (including the funny turkey bit), Atkinson does provide many a laugh when aiming his sights higher than the belt line. (Available letterboxed or pan & scan) ★★½ VHS: $9.99; DVD: $19.99

The Bear

(1989, 95 min, France, Jean-Jacques Annaud) Some people steered clear of this wildlife adventure story about an orphaned bear cub on the assumption that it would be "too cute." On a certain level, they would have been right, but what a shame to miss this spectacularly photographed and brilliantly directed tale about the cruelty and the compassion of nature and man. Filmed in the dazzling peaks of the Dolomite Mountain range (a part of the Alps which stretches from Austria to northern Italy), the film tells the story of a young cub who, upon being orphaned, wanders aimlessly until one day he meets up with a massive male grizzly. Together they flee the sights of a group of tenacious hunters who have it out for the big bear. ★★★½ VHS: $14.99; DVD: $24.99

The Beast

(1988, 109 min, US, Kevin Reynolds) *Jason Patric, George Dzundza, Steven Bauer, Stephen Baldwin.* Set in Afghanistan during the Soviet Occupation, this suspenseful war adventure follows a Russian tank crew's fight for survival when a group of Afghan civilians seek vengeance for their small village's brutal destruction. As the citizens are able to demobilize the monster tank, its crew must battle their sadistic commander as well as the Afghans, while struggling with the moral dilemma of war. Patric plays an idealistic soldier, and Dzundza is very effective as the maniacal chief. ★★★½ VHS: $14.99; DVD: $29.99

B

The Beast from 20,000 Fathoms

(1953, 80 min, US, Eugene Lourie) *Paul Christian, Paula Raymond, Cecil Kellaway.* Based on a short story by Ray Bradbury, this sci-fi favorite features nifty special effects by F/X master Ray Harryhausen. One of the first films to warn of the dangers of atomic bomb testings (the '50s tell us they would unleash some horrible monster or another), a giant beast (a prehistoric rhedosaurus to be exact) goes for a swim after its atomic wake-up call and decides to munch on the Big Apple. The Coney Island roller coaster proves to be too much for it, however. ★★★ VHS: $14.99

The Beast with Five Fingers

(1947, 89 min, US, Robert Florey) *Robert Alda, Peter Lorre, J. Carrol Naish.* A heavily atmospheric chiller about the severed hand of a dead pianist which may be murdering the pianist's squabbling inheritors during their stay in his shadowy old mansion in Italy. Despite its lurid title, the film is actually a reasonably intelligent exploration of madness and superstition with smart performances. Fine special effects and a good musical score contribute to the film's success, but its real highlight is Florey's use of the camera. He is constantly surprising the viewer with inventive ways to photograph the two or three sets used throughout the entire film. Light and shadow are used very well. The only major problem with the film is a goofy coda tacked onto its end, which effectively ridicules any supernatural element it may have contained. ★★★ VHS: $19.99

The Beast Within

(1982, 90 min, US, Philippe Mora) *Ronny Cox, Meshach Taylor.* A woman is raped by a large demon-like creature with very hairy legs and gives birth to — you guessed it — a Jekyll and Hyde–like boy who transforms himself when he gets upset. This Hulk-like tale goes absolutely nowhere. Some interesting gore effects, including a spurting decapitation scene, won't satisfy even die-hard slasher film fans. ★ VHS: $14.99

Beat Girl

(1960, 90 min, GB, Edmond T. Greville) *Gillian Hills, David Farrar, Christopher Lee, Noelle Adam, Oliver Reed.* Hills plays Jennifer, a spoiled rich girl who hates her buxom French stepmother (the atrocious Adam) and spends the movie trying to get her egoistic father (Farrar) back all to herself. She escapes to be with the beatniks at the art school, and checks out the strip club to dig up some dirt on her new stepmom. There she gets sucked in by the owner (an especially perverse Lee) and maybe learns a few lessons. Jennifer's severe outlandish, and some genuine sympathy for the woman she's smearing, work against the film's campy tendencies. Plenty of fun still exists: Jennifer's sultry opening-credits dance, Reed's poor singing/guitar-synching as the plaid-shirt called "Plaid Shirt," and the seamy secrets that are revealed are a few examples. The crisp black & white cinematography and John Barry's strong score lend a hint of class to this fabulous and fresh bad-girl movie. (aka: *Wild for Kicks*) ★★★ VHS: $24.99

Beat the Devil

(1954, 92 min, US, John Huston) *Humphrey Bogart, Gina Lollabrigida, Jennifer Jones, Peter Lorre, Robert Morley.* This offbeat black comedy left audiences in a daze when first released.

Reportedly, the filming began without a finished script, forcing Huston and a young Truman Capote to collaborate daily before shooting and allowing the actors to ad-lib many scenes. The result is a zany spoof of spy thrillers dealing with a gang of international ⟨ ⟩ooks concocting a uranium swindle. Not to be missed. ★★★½ VHS: $19.99; DVD: $24.99

Beatrice

(1987, 132 min, France, Bertrand Tavernier) *Julie Delpy, Berbard Pierre Donnadieu, Nils Tavernier.* Tavernier's somber exploration of medieval life abandons many of the traditional myths and instead concentrates on the dark side of human nature: infidelity, jealousy, humiliation, hatred, incest and murder. François, as a child, killed his mother's lover. He returns from war 25 years later, tormented by his hatred of women, to be greeted at his castle by his loving and beautiful daughter, Beatrice. Having faithfully awaited her father's return, her love turns to defiance and repulsion as her increasingly demented father turns to incest. A compelling mood piece. (French with English subtitles) (aka: *The Passion of Beatrice*) ★★★

Beau Geste

(1939, 114 min, US, William Wellman) *Gary Cooper, Brian Donlevy, Susan Hayward, Robert Preston, Ray Milland.* Part of the 1939 wave of some of the greatest films in American history, this sweeping — and superlative — version of P. C. Wren's romantic novel is every bit as exciting and moving as you would think. A strong and courageous Cooper stars as the title character, with an Oscar-nominated Donlevy as the sadistic sergeant. In essence the story of a missing gem, a debt of honor and of savagery in the Foreign Legion, this beautifully shot epic still stirs the soul. Remake of the Ronald Colman 1926 silent classic; an inferior version followed in 1966. ★★★½ VHS: $14.99

Le Beau Marriage

(A Good Marriage)

(1982, 100 min, France, Eric Rohmer) *Béatrice Romand, André Dussollier, Féodor Atkine, Arielle Dombasle.* Rohmer continues his series of "Comedies and Proverbs" with this witty and engaging story of a young student's attempts to snare the perfect man and a "good marriage." An insightful comedy of logic and love in modern Paris. (French with English subtitles) ★★★ VHS: $19.99; DVD: $29.99

Le Beau Serge

(1958, 110 min, France, Claude Chabrol) *Jean-Claude Brialy, Gerard Blain.* Chabrol's first feature film is about a young man who leaves the city to go back to the village of his youth in an attempt to rehabilitate a childhood friend, now a drunkard living in squalor. A deeply felt drama that explores male friendship and commitment. (French with English subtitles) ★★★

Beaumarchais, the Scoundrel

(1997, 100 min, France, Edouard Molinaro) *Fabrice Luchini, Sandrine Kiberlain, Michel Serrault, Michel Piccoli.* An uneven historical biography, *Beaumarchais, the Scoundrel* depicts how the celebrated playwright of "The Barber of Seville" and "The Marriage of Figaro" ultimately prompted the French Revolution. The film, set in 1773 France, is lavishly mounted, but the story's

episodes — a series of dangerous political and sexual liaisons — are greater than the whole. Beaumarchais (Luchini) is a rakish hero who angers the censors with his sarcastic barbs at the rich and powerful, spies for the government, makes arms deals with the Americans, and still finds time to seduce a handful of women. A well-made and well-acted drama sprinkled with rapier wit, a bit of swashbuckling, and moments of international intrigue. (French with English subtitles) ★★★ VHS: $94.99

The Beautician and the Beast

(1997, 107 min, US, Ken Kwapis) *Fran Drescher, Timothy Dalton, Ian McNeice, Michael Lerner, Patrick Malahide.* Drescher (TV's "The Nanny") stars as Joy Miller, a Brooklyn beautician who is mistakenly hired to be the teacher and nanny for the gaggle of children of a dictator (Dalton) of a fictitious Eastern bloc country. Before you can say Maria Von Trapp, the perky Joy whips the kids into shape, and soon her abrasive charm is taming the beastly ruler as well. This highly obvious take on *The King and I* and *Beauty and the Beast* is spotty but can be quite enjoyable, with the ever-likable Drescher in snappy comic form, even though she basically plays the same sort of grating, so-irritating-she's-adorable wench she plays on TV. ★★½ VHS: $9.99

Beautiful

(2000, 112 min, US, Sally Field) *Minnie Driver, Hallie Kate Eisenberg, Joey Lauren Adams, Kathleen Turner.* Field makes an unimpressive directorial debut with this poorly written comedy about beauty pageant contestants and the lengths one of them will go to win. The foibles of backstabbing entrants and behind-the-scenes tomfoolery have already been told with humor and style in the winning *Smile*, and half-heartedly in *Drop Dead Gorgeous*, but here they're excruciating. The biggest offense is the main character, Mona (Driver), who spends what seems to be a lifetime plotting to win the Miss American Miss contest. Mona is selfish, self-serving and mean, fine traits had this been a black comedy, but as written by Jon Bernstein, it's all meant to be heartwarming. Heartburning is more like it. Add a sorry subplot about Mona looking after a soccer-loving girl (Eisenberg, who looks like she'd rather be back doing Pepsi commercials), and this is truly one huge mess of a film. ★ VHS: $102.99; DVD: $24.99

The Beautiful Blonde from Bashful Bend

(1949, 77 min, US, Preston Sturges) *Betty Grable, Rudy Vallee, Cesar Romero.* Old West dance-hall chanteuse and eagle-eye sharpshooter Grable skips town after shooting a federal judge — Twice! Accidentally! — and poses as a schoolmarm. A minor though entertaining Sturges spoof. ★★½ VHS: $19.99

Beautiful Dreamers

(1990, 108 min, Canada, John Harrison) *Rip Torn, Colm Feore, Sheila McCarthy.* Torn stars as Walt Whitman in this touching drama in which he befriends the superintendent of a Canadian insane asylum. Their friendship results in the young doctor challenging the beliefs and practices of his profession as he tries to put a more human face on the psychiatry of the late 1800s. The film portrays the conflict between the Christian-based hierarchy of the day and the

Becket

nascent humanism represented by Whitman — it's a struggle which, it could be argued, is still with us. Torn puts in another strong performance as the free-thinking poet. ★★★

Beautiful Girls

(1996, 114 min, US, Ted Demme) *Timothy Hutton, Matt Dillon, Mira Sorvino, Michael Rapaport, Natalie Portman, Rosie O'Donnell, Max Perlich, Lauren Holly, Martha Plimpton.* A good cast gives it their best shot in this rambling comedy-drama about young adults coming dangerously close to settling into the grooves that could carry them through the rest of their lives. The problem here is that, despite a rich portrayal of life in a small, blue-collar town, screenwriter Scott Rosenberg has no compelling narrative to offer. The film is a collection of subplots which feature a smattering of great moments (O'Donnell's "anatomy of a supermodel" speech) that are, for the most part, totally out of place in the movie and the characters. Rather than the *Diner*-for-the-'90s that it could have been, it settles for *St. Elmo's Fire* set in small-town America. ★★ VHS: $14.99; DVD: $29.99

Beautiful People

(2000, 100 min, GB, Jasmin Dizdar) *Rosalind Ayres, Charles Kay, Charlotte Coleman, Nicholas Farrell.* "If life works out even a tiny bit in your favor, it can be beautiful," says Dr. Mouldy (Farrell) at the end of director Dizdar's wonderful *Beautiful People*. This sentiment sums up just how moving this dark comedy about Bosnians living in London really is. Cross-cutting among a handful of characters, each dealing with various disappointments and struggles in life, Dizdar has crafted a warmhearted, tender comedy-drama about how families are redefined and the horrors of war can affect people living far away from the battle lines. As a Serb and a Croat try to kill each other in a hospital ward, the daughter (Coleman) of a wealthy family falls in love with a refugee looking for the meaning of "Life." Meanwhile, a drugged-out teen ends up a war hero by accidentally falling asleep on supplies being shipped into a war zone. The comic reversals may at times be contrived, but Didzar nevertheless manages to make them funny and touching at the same time. *Beautiful People* is a brilliant, beautiful film. ★★★★ VHS: $69.99; DVD: $24.99

Beautiful Thing

(1996, 90 min, GB, Hettie Macdonald) *Linda Henry, Glen Barry, Scott Neal, Tameka Empson.* This affectionate story of two teenagers' sexual coming out in a working-class development in London is an inspiring, tender, emotional tale that is sure to enthrall. Jamie (Berry) is a reserved 16-year-old, close to his pub manager mum (Henry), who prefers old Hollywood musicals to sports. His friendship with neighbor Ste (Neal), a fellow student who suffers through a troubled family life, soon develops into a sexual and eventually a loving relationship. How the two boys tentatively handle their nascent sexual drives is handled in both a fresh and surprisingly upbeat fashion. A wonderful comedy-drama and possibly the best gay coming-out film of the decade. ★★★½ VHS: $19.99

Beauty and the Beast

(1946, 90 min, France, Jean Cocteau) *Jean Marais, Josette Day.* This enchanting interpretation of the famous fairy tale is a sumptuous and beguiling adventure in surrealist cinema. Marais gives a moving performance as the love-stricken Beast and Day is the beautiful object of his amour. (French with English subtitles) ★★★★ VHS: $24.99; DVD: $39.99

Beauty and the Beast

(1991, 85 min, US, Gary Trousdale & Kirk Wise) *Voices of: Robby Benson, Paige O'Hara, Jerry Orbach, Angela Lansbury.* The first animated film to be nominated for an Academy Award as Best Picture. Based on the classic fairy tale, Disney animators have created a masterpiece of color and scope, complete with refreshingly good humor and a captivating text. But what makes *Beauty* soar is the outstanding musical score by *Mermaid* and *Little Shop of Horrors* team Alan Menken and Howard Ashman. Including the Oscar-winning title ballad and the exuberant "Be Our Guest," the score has the style and brilliance of a classic Broadway musical rather than, what most musicals are today, a promo for a best-selling soundtrack. Menken and Ashman's music would be equally remarkable for a live-action film. A total delight for all ages. ★★★★

Beavis and Butt-head Do America

(1996, 80 min, US, Mike Judge) *Voices of: Mike Judge, Robert Stack, Cloris Leachman, Eric Bogosian, Richard Linklater.* MTV's lame-brained bad boys Beavis and Butt-head get the Hollywood feature film treatment — and there's good news and bad news. The good news is creator Judge's nasty wit is undiluted; the bad news is Judge is unable to maintain the pace of the TV show for a feature-length film. The film begins — à la *Pee-wee's Big Adventure* — with the boys' most valuable possession (their TV, of course) being stolen. This leads them on a cross-country search, and their ever-present mission to "score." Some of the film is laugh-out-loud funny (much as you may try to stifle a giggle), but it's never quite as funny as you want it to be. It also gets a wee *too* mean-spirited. Still, any film which ends with Englebert Humperdinck singing "Lesbian Seagull" can't be all bad. ★★½ VHS: $9.99; DVD: $24.99

Bebe's Kids

(1992, 74 min, US, Bruce Smith) *Voices of: Robin Harris, Jim Carrey.* This adult-oriented, street-hip animated feature is based on popular characters created by Harris (*House Party*). His cartoon alter-ego is smitten with the beautiful Jamika. On their first date, she greets him with her soft-spoken son, Leon, and homegirl Bebe's hellraising spawn, who turn the couple's date at a theme park into a nightmare. Also included is the highly entertaining seven-minute short *Itsy Bitsy Spider*, featuring the voice of Carrey as a *Terminator*-inspired exterminator trying to rid a home of a pest problem. ★★★ VHS: $14.99

Becket

(1964, 148 min, GB, Peter Glenville) *Peter O'Toole, Richard Burton, John Gielgud.* Burton and O'Toole deliver magnificent performances in this gritty adaptation of the Jean Anouilh play. Burton is the stoic and indomitable Thomas Becket, Archbishop of Canterbury, whose long-standing friendship with King Henry II (O'Toole) becomes irrevocably frayed as they stray down opposite political paths. A gripping and powerful historical exploration of the inhuman burdens of power. ★★★★ VHS: $19.99

Becky Sharp

(1935, 67 min, US, Rouben Mamoulian) *Miriam Hopkins, Frances Dee, Cedric Hardwicke.* The first Technicolor (three-strip) film is a witty though stagey adaptation of Thackeray's "Vanity Fair" with Hopkins giving a notable Oscar-nominated performance as the social-climbing title character. (Note: This copy is in black and white, and runs 67 minutes as opposed to its original 83 minutes. It is, unfortunately, the only version available on video.) ★★★

Becoming Colette

(1992, 97 min, US/France, Danny Huston) *Klaus Maria Brandauer, Mathilda May, Virginia Madsen, Jean-Pierre Aumont.* While never quite overcoming its pedestrian handling of a potentially illuminating subject, this steamy drama, replete with female frontal nudity and "shocking" lesbian love scenes, is filmed in a lush, bombastic and romantic style. The story concerns the early years in the life of Sidone-Gabrielle Colette, one of France's greatest and most popular writers of the 20th century. Young Gabrielle (May) meets sweet-talking bon vivant Willy (Brandauer) and quickly sweeps him off his feet. They move to Paris to begin a carefree life of society living. But when Gabrielle shows him some of her writing, he publishes the work as his own and becomes the talk of the town. It's not until she begins a lesbian relationship with a friend that the increasingly sophisticated Gabrielle starts on her road to self-determination. Despite director Huston's heavy handling, the film is entertaining in telling the story of one woman's growth, accomplished on her own terms. ★★★ VHS: $19.99

Bed and Board

(1970, 100 min, France, François Truffaut) *Jean-Pierre Léaud, Claude Jade.* Antoine Doinel is all grown up and now married to Christine from *Stolen Kisses*. But his marriage, new child, and job selling dyed flowers is certainly no recipe for happiness, and his affair with a Japanese woman threatens to tear his life apart. Like the other Doinel films, *Bed and Board* takes the drama of love affairs and growing up and twists it into a bittersweet comedy; Léaud is, as always, incredibly charming and effective as Doinel. ★★★ VHS: $19.99; DVD: $29.99

B

B

Bed of Roses

(1996, 87 min, US, Michael Goldenberg) *Christian Slater, Mary Stuart Masterson, Pamela Segall, Josh Brolin.* A pleasing if uneventful romantic comedy-drama, *Bed of Roses* casts Slater in another shy-boy role and Masterson as yet another neurotic romantic. Seeing her crying through her apartment window one night, Slater anonymously sends Masterson a bouquet of flowers. She soon learns Slater's identity, and balks at establishing a relationship with such a "perfect" man. She moves in with him anyway, though unable to fully commit. She then spends the rest of the film whining about her past and inability to love. The film sets a genuinely sweet tone as the two court and fall in love, though once they've moved in together and met the folks (a distractingly sappy episode), the film has nowhere to go and idles till its inevitable climax. ★★½ VHS: $9.99; DVD: $14.99

Bedazzled

(1967, 107 min, GB, Stanley Donen) *Dudley Moore, Peter Cook, Eleanor Bron, Raquel Welch, Barry Humphries.* This hysterical adaptation of the Faust legend stars Cook as a mischievous Mephistopheles who grants the nebbishy Moore seven wishes in exchange for his soul. All of his wishes end in disaster for Moore who only wants his Whimpy Burger coworker (Bron) to love him. The humor is hurled about so unrelentingly and with such outrageous and inventive abandon that only the most mordant of viewers won't find some cause for laughter. The screenplay by Cook provides an even better vehicle for himself and Moore than *The Wrong Box.* Welch appears as "Lust." (Remade in 2000) ★★★★ VHS: $9.99

Bedazzled

(2000, 93 min, US, Harold Ramis) *Brendan Fraser, Elizabeth Hurley, Frances O'Connor.* A light-hearted, occasionally funny remake of the 1967 Peter Cook-Dudley Moore classic comedy, with Fraser in good form as a clueless office nerd who sells his soul to the Devil (an attractive Hurley) for seven wishes. Assuming various disguises, Fraser is very appealing as the nebbishy Elliott, who — foiled by Satan at every turn — seems to never quite get what he wants. Though the script doesn't offer either Fraser or Hurley the kind of material for a knock-out comedy, Fraser's several impersonations and a breezy tempo sustained by director Ramis make this genial rather than bedazzling. ★★½ VHS: $19.99; DVD: $26.99

The Bedford Incident

(1965, 102 min, US, James B. Harris) *Richard Widmark, Sidney Poitier, Martin Balsam, Donald Sutherland.* Widmark and Poitier give compelling performances in this exciting Cold War thriller. Widmark is a ship's captain and Poitier is a newspaper reporter who are at odds with each other when a Russian ship is discovered off the coast of Greenland. ★★★ VHS: $9.99

Bedknobs and Broomsticks

(1971, 139 min, US, Robert Stevenson) *Angela Lansbury, David Tomlinson, Roddy McDowall.* Charming live-action and animated musical fantasy from Disney. An apprentice witch (Lansbury), with the help of three children, repels Nazi invaders from her British country-side home. Music is by Richard and Robert Sherman (*Mary Poppins*), and an Oscar was won for Special Effects. ★★★ VHS: $22.99; DVD: $29.99

The Bedroom Window

(1987, 112 min, US, Curtis Hanson) *Steve Guttenberg, Elizabeth McGovern, Isabelle Huppert, Wallace Shawn.* Hitchcockian thriller, with more than a nod to *Rear Window,* stars Guttenberg as a young exec who admits to seeing an attempted murder to protect his mistress, who actually saw the crime. In doing so, he becomes the prime suspect. Clever plot twists and engaging performances elevate the sometimes obvious scenario. ★★½ VHS: $9.99; DVD: $24.99

Bedrooms and Hallways

(1998, 96 min, GB, Rose Troche) *Kevin McKidd, Tom Hollander, Hugo Weaving, James Purefoy, Simon Callow, Jennifer Ehle.* Troche's follow-up to *Go Fish* is an often hilarious comedy set in London about the tangled love affairs of a group of gay men. Failed romantic Leo (McKidd) is just hitting thirty. His kitschy roommate Darren (Hollander) only reminds him of what he's missing, merrily touting Darren's frequent, illicit meetings with a lusty real estate agent (Weaving). So with nothing to lose, Leo joins a men's group to bond with his fellow males and get his mind off romance. However, the latter notion didn't account for sexy straight Irishman Brendan (Purefoy). But wait... is Brendan straight? For that matter, is Leo? And life is never as black and white as it seems, especially after Leo and his group go on a drum-thumping, chest-banging camping retreat where a snarl of love triangles and jealousy explodes. Colorful production design, glossy production values, and an energetic ensemble cast contribute to the lightheartedness. ★★★ VHS: $24.99; DVD: $29.99

Bedtime for Bonzo

(1951, 83 min, US, Frederick de Cordova) *Ronald Reagan, Diana Lynn, Jesse White.* Reagan, later to be the leader of the Free World, plays daddy to a chimp in the interests of science. Is this where George Bush got the idea for a kinder, gentler nation? Did Ron think he was really once a scientist? We don't know. The film's kinda cute, though. ★★½ VHS: $12.99

Bedtime Story

(1964, 99 min, US, Ralph Levy) *Marlon Brando, David Niven, Shirley Jones.* It's a race to the finish as con men Brando and Niven are out to outdo each other in their efforts to swindle American heiress Jones. Some good laughs, though the recent remake, *Dirty Rotten Scoundrels,* is funnier. ★★½ VHS: $14.99

Beethoven

(1936, 117 min, France, Abel Gance) *Harry Baur, Jean-Louis Barrault.* One of the pioneering masters of early French cinema, Gance had an unusually long filmmaking career which stretched over almost 60 years. His epic productions (*J'Accuse, Napoleon*) featured innovative techniques of editing and montage as well as the experimental use of music. In this symphonic epic, Harry Baur portrays the towering musical genius as a successful but lonely and heartsick man. Restored to its full length, this melodramatic look at the life of one of history's

Dudley Moore takes it all in in *Bedazzled* (1967)

little understood masters has been given a facelift and had its soundtrack restored. (French with English subtitles) ★★★ VHS: $29.99; DVD: $24.99

Beethoven

(1992, 87 min, US, Brian Levant) *Charles Grodin, Bonnie Hunt, Dean Jones, Oliver Platt, Stanley Tucci.* This congenial shaggy dog comedy holds few surprises. A runaway St. Bernard takes up residence at the middle-class home of Grodin and family. It's a comedy of errors as the big-as-life mutt creates havoc for Grodin and proves to be a canine Mary Poppins for the rest of the family. An unrecognizable Jones costars as a villainous vet, who looks suspiciously like a dastardly doc from *Marathon Man.* Preadolescent children should be entertained, though non-animal lovers should probably avoid it. ★★½ VHS: $14.99; DVD: $24.99

Beethoven's 2nd

(1993, 87 min, US, Rod Daniel) *Charles Grodin, Bonnie Hunt, Debi Mazar, Christopher Penn.* An amiable sequel. Though the accent here is more on cute than slapstick, there's enough good-natured comedy to satisfy both child and parent. That monstrous St. Bernard is now a daddy, and borrowing just a touch of treachery from *101 Dalmatians,* the adorable little puppies fall prey to a nasty villainess. Grodin returns as the head of the Newton household, and, as in the original, his slow burns, tirades and pie-in-the-face humiliations make him a most wonderful foil. ★★★ VHS: $14.99; DVD: $24.99

Beethoven's Nephew

(1985, 103 min, France/Germany, Paul Morrissey) *Wolfgang Reichmann, Ditmar Prinz, Jane Birkin, Nathalie Baye.* Morrissey sheds his well-deserved reputation as a sensationalized chronicler of life on the fringe in this thoughtful and opulent story of the destructively possessive relationship between Ludwig Von Beethoven and his handsome nephew. In a rewrite of history, Morrissey shows Beethoven in his later years as a furious and demanding "superstar" who, after winning a vicious court battle for the custody of his sister's son, becomes consumed with an insanely jealous love for the boy. With surprising control in its examination of the composer's obsession, the film elicits a deep sympathy for his torment without compromising the severity of his tyrannical grip on the boy's life. (Filmed in English) ★★★

Beetlejuice

(1988, 92 min, US, Tim Burton) *Michael Keaton, Geena Davis, Alec Baldwin, Winona Ryder, Sylvia Sidney, Catherine O'Hara.* Dick Cavett's acting is just one of the lesser surprises in Burton's breakthrough comedy about a dead couple (Davis and Baldwin) learning how to haunt their house by mad ghoul Keaton. Similar in tone to his *Pee-wee's Big Adventure*, Burton's film sports a more comprehensive story, more outlandish special effects, another great score by Danny Elfman, plus a winning performance by Ryder. ★★★½ VHS: $14.99; DVD: $19.99

Before and After

(1996, 108 min, US, Barbet Schroeder) *Meryl Streep, Liam Neeson, Edward Furlong, Julia Weldon, Alfred Molina, John Heard, Ann Magnuson.* There's a fine sense of mystery to the opening moments of *Before and After*, an awkward drama which solemnly attempts to explore the boundaries of love and law. Parents Streep and Neeson are visited by police officers when their son's girlfriend is found murdered and he was the last one to be seen with her. As the father attempts to "cover up" the evidence he discovers in the garage, his mother puts her faith in her son and legal procedure. But as the story unfolds, the narrative becomes unfocused, undecided whether to be a hard-hitting exposé of community ostracism or a sappy drama of parents coming to terms with the possibility that their child has taken a life. ★★½ VHS: $14.99

Before Night Falls

(2000, 130 min, US, Julian Schnabel) *Javier Bardem, Olivier Martinez, Johnny Depp, Andrea Di Stefano, Sean Penn, Michael Wincott, Hector Babenco, Jerzy Skolimowski.* The fallout of the political oppression and institutionalized homophobia of Castro's Cuba makes for a disturbing but dazzling portrait of a writer's tragic life. Based on the posthumously released memoir by gay Cuban poet Reinaldo Arenas, *Before Night Falls* details Arenas' life in his native country before emigrating to the United States. In a grand portrayal, Bardem plays Arenas, who was born in poverty and at a young age joined Castro's revolution. In the 1960s, he attended college where he sharpened his writing skills and discovered his sexuality. Under Castro's regime, however, it became increasingly difficult for him to fully realize either, as the government began to crack down on gays and intellectuals — resulting in Arenas' imprisonment. Director Schnabel utilizes Arenas' writings through effective voiceovers to underscore the more significant times in the author's life. The director has also greatly improved upon his previous film biography *Basquiat*, demonstrating a stronger, more fluid narrative. In addition to Bardem's stunning turn, Depp is quite effective in the dual roles of a transvestite prisoner named Bon-Bon and a prison warden. (English and Spanish with English subtitles) ★★★★ VHS: $19.99; DVD: $24.99

Before Stonewall

(1985, 87 min, US, Greta Schiller) *Narrated by: Rita Mae Brown, Harry Hay, Barbara Gittings.* This extraordinary recollection/documentary traces the evolution of the gay movement in the U.S. from the 1920s to the '60s and touches on the major milestones in the development of gay-lesbian consciousness. Aided by archival footage and memorable interviews, *Before Stonewall* vividly paints a picture of what it was like to be "in the life" during this period of repression. The pioneers of the liberation recall their experiences — from the lesbian bars in 1920s Harlem to the gay soldier's experiences in WWII to what it was like for gay blacks and Native Americans. The unwritten history of the fight for gay rights comes alive in this entertaining tribute. ★★★½ VHS: $24.99

Before Sunrise

(1995, 101 min, US, Richard Linklater) *Ethan Hawke, Julie Delpy.* A pleasant surprise about a chance encounter between two students traveling through Europe. This encounter develops into that rarest of occurrences — an enchanted commingling of mind and spirit, a gift of pure happenstance. Engaging characterizations by Hawke and Delpy and an intelligent, whimsical script capture that time of young adulthood when possibilities are unlimited and time retains the fluidity of childhood. The director makes good use of silence and empty spaces to explore how people get to know one another and, through that, themselves. Linklater has managed to create a confection which is sweet but not cloying, winsome but not silly, idealized but not artificial. ★★★ VHS: $14.99; DVD: $19.99

Before the Rain

(1994, 112 min, Macedonia, Milchio Manchevski) *Rade Serbedzija, Katrin Cartlidge.* Three interwoven stories about choices, fate and the inevitability of violence form a circle which "is not round" in this Oscar nominee for Best Foreign-Language Film. The stories focus on a young monk's relationship with an Albanian refugee; an Englishwoman's decision whether to leave her husband for a Macedonian photographer; and that photographer's return to his home village after 16 years. All of the stories converge, more or less, at the film's end, and drive home the belabored lesson that all violence — ethnic or otherwise — is futile though inescapable. The final story, the best of the three, works on a deeper level because in it we watch the approaching storm of conflict in Macedonia through the eyes of an estranged native. Featuring gorgeous camerawork, *Before the Rain* is an interesting if obvious tale. (Macedonian with English subtitles) ★★½

Before the Revolution

(1964, 112 min, Italy, Bernardo Bertolucci) *Francesco Barilli, Adrianna Asti.* An absorbing polemic about European politics and Marxism. A young man flirts with Communism and incestuously lusts after his aunt. This potentially volatile mix of youthful idealism and unbridled desire leads him to a crisis of faith over his political ideals. (Italian with English subtitles) ★★★½

Begotten

(1989, 78 min, US, Edmund E. Merhige) *Brian Salzberg, Donna Dempsey.* This disgusting nightmare vision of life as a wriggling, oozing, pus-encrusted torment is without a doubt for adventurous viewers only! The film's opening scene portrays a man (later identified as God) disemboweling himself in a river of blood; out of his corpse crawls a young maiden (later identified as Mother Earth) who proceeds to stroke the still-erect penis of the eviscerated deity and impregnate herself with his posthumous cum — get the picture? Filmed in high-contrast, grainy black and white reminiscent of the German Expressionist period, and without a scintilla of dialogue. Its visceral thrills are akin to taking a peek at life in a leper colony. ★½ VHS: $24.99; DVD: $29.99

The Beguiled

(1971, 109 min, US, Don Siegel) *Clint Eastwood, Geraldine Page, Elizabeth Hartman.* Very effective and complex psychosexual Gothic chiller with Eastwood as a wounded Union soldier who is taken in by the women of a Southern girls' school, awakening the dormant sexual emotions of head mistress Page and teacher Hartman. An unusual and exceptional study of passion and jealousy, with Eastwood giving one of his best performances. ★★★½ VHS: $14.99; DVD: $24.99

Behind Locked Doors

(1948, 62 min, US, Budd Boetticher) *Richard Carlson, Lucille Bremer, Dickie Moore, Tor Johnson.* An obvious "inspiration" for Sam Fuller's *Shock Corridor*, this poverty-row gem is every bit as manic. When he is discovered for what he is, private detective Carlson comes to regret his latest undercover assignment: find the corrupt judge hiding in the mental hospital. Death lurks at the hands of *Plan Nine from Outer Space's* Johnson, a crazed ex-boxer who can't forget the ring. As hard-edged as a tabloid headline, this 62-minute programmer recalls the glory days of Warner Brothers when films darted instead of moving, and hollered instead of talking. ★★★½ VHS: $24.99; DVD: $29.99

Behind the Veil: Nuns

(1984, 130 min, Canada, Margaret Wescott) This fascinating documentary explores the secretive and widely misunderstood world of the Catholic religious orders for women. Using thoroughly researched historical information for background, the film takes an in-depth look at the many different lifestyles of nuns — from the cloistered to the teachers and activists — and includes their individual reflections. The film also brings to light the politics within the orders as well as the continual misogyny of the male-dominated Catholic Church hierarchy. ★★★ VHS: $29.99

Being at Home with Claude

(1991, 90 min, Canada, Jean Beaudin) *Roy Dupuis, Jean-François Pichette, Gaston Lepage, Hugo Dubé.* Queer criminality meets romantic love in this riveting and unconventional murder mystery. Set in Montreal, this adaptation of Rene-Daniel Dubois' taut, claustrophobic play opens up the action and heightens its original dramatic force. The film opens with an erotic, hyperkinetic sequence focusing on a steamy sex scene which ends with a brutal murder. Three days later, Yves, a sexy male prostitute, summons the police to a judge's chamber and admits to the apparently senseless crime. Yves, the lover of the deceased Claude, soon becomes embroiled in a harrowing interrogation which lays bare his tortured soul to the tough but strangely sympathetic cop. A fine drama that works both as a suspense thriller and an absorbing tale of gay passions and desperate love. (French with English subtitles) ★★★½ VHS: $19.99

Catherine Keener and John Cusack learn all about *Being John Malkovich*

Being Human

(1994, 118 min, GB, Bill Forsyth) *Robin Williams, Kelly Hunter, John Turturro, Anna Galiena.* Williams plays a series of characters set in time periods ranging from the stone age to the new age and proves that no matter what age you live in, your life can be deathly boring — at least to those watching it on the screen. As Williams struggles dryly with daily dilemmas related to being a homo sapien, the film's unbelievably slow pace and poorly constructed episodes will give any viewer a struggle to stay awake. ★ VHS: $19.99

Being John Malkovich

(1999, 112 min, US, Spike Jonze) *John Cusack, Cameron Diaz, Catherine Keener, John Malkovich, Orson Bean, Mary Kay Place, Charlie Sheen.* Wild, dark, mysterious and, at times, uproariously funny, this profane little gem is one of the most original movies ever made. Cusack is the hapless Craig Schwartz, an immensely talented but overly morose puppeteer who toils in obscurity. He lives in a shabby New York City apartment with his wife Lotte (an almost unrecognizable Diaz), a pet shop proprietor and animal enthusiast. Desperate for an escape, Cusack takes a menial job with a filing agency on the seventh-and-a-half floor (literally a half-floor!). While retrieving a lost file, he discovers a hidden doorway behind a filing cabinet which, when entered, transports people into the psyche (body?) of John Malkovich and then, after about 15 minutes, spits them out on the Jersey turnpike. Sound strange? Well, strange is just the beginning as Cusack joins forces with Keener (as the cold-hearted, manipulative operator Maxine) to market this "portal" in the off-hours. Whatever twists and turns can be imagined from this odd setup cannot possibly compare with what director Jonze has in store. It's part comic romp, part fractured fairy tale and part existential howl. The performances are all good; however, special mention to Malkovich himself for being such a good sport about being "that guy in the jewel thief movie." His "Malkovich" scene is an instant classic. ★★★★ VHS: $14.99; DVD: $19.99

Being There

(1979, 130 min, US, Hal Ashby) *Peter Sellers, Shirley MacLaine, Melvyn Douglas, Jack Warden, Richard Dysart.* A sublime satire of the TV age and American myth-making, *Being There* stars Sellers in a tour de force performance as Chance, a dim-witted gardener whose homelessness sets him on the road to the presidency. Wandering the streets of Washington, D.C., Sellers is struck by the limo of dying millionaire/power player Douglas (in a sterling Oscar-winning performance). When he's given shelter by the influential businessman, Chance's naiveté is mistaken for insight and wisdom, ultimately making him a media darling and political prospect. Jerzy Kosinski's literate and biting adaptation of his own story has been wonderfully complemented by director Ashby's marvelous pacing and his keen observations of cultural attitudes. ★★★★ VHS: $19.99; DVD: $19.99

Beirut: The Last Home Movie

(1988, 90 min, US, Jennifer Fox) This unusual documentary, set in war-torn Beirut, eschews the typical politics one would expect and instead focuses on one wealthy (and atypical) family who decide to remain in the battle-scarred city, despite their ability to leave. Residing in an opulent 200-year-old palace, the Bustros family consists of three sisters, a brother and their mother. Seemingly oblivious to the dangers and destruction all around, this Greek Orthodox Christian family continues their normal life undisturbed. Fiercely insular, their personal feelings, relationships and motivations in staying home become the focus of the film, the result being a humanistic approach to a subject all too accustomed to inhuman violence. Academy Award winner for Best Documentary. ★★★½

Believe

(1999, 97 min, US, Robert Tinnell) *Jan Rubes, Ricky Mabe, Elisha Cuthbert, Ben Gazzara, Andrea Martin.* Young Ben is carted from one private school to another, always getting in trouble. He has a knack for scaring his fellow students with elaborate stunts. He is finally sent to live with his rich grandfather, whom he has never met. It is there that Ben begins to see the ghostly spirit of a young woman. But is he crying wolf with more stunts, or is it real this time? This ghost story has a pleasant feel to it, and plays like a Hardy Boys-Nancy Drew tale from the supernatural. Sometimes clumsy, sometimes effective, this should definitely appeal to adolescents. However, the box art is misleading. ★★½ VHS: $89.99

The Believers

(1987, 114 min, US, John Schlesinger) *Martin Sheen, Helen Shaver, Robert Loggia, Richard Masur, Jimmy Smits.* Suspenseful occult thriller with Sheen as a New York therapist whose counseling of a disturbed policeman leads him into a series of bizarre and gory ritual slayings. Director Schlesinger creates a chilling atmosphere as he juxtaposes a menacing New York City with the tribal rituals of the voodoo ceremony Santeria. ★★★ VHS: $9.99

Bell, Book & Candle

(1958, 108 min, US, Richard Quine) *James Stewart, Kim Novak, Jack Lemmon, Ernie Kovacs, Hermione Gingold.* A lively cast brightens up this fun-filled adaptation of John Van Druten's Broadway comedy about an engaged publisher (Stewart) who becomes entangled with a coven of Greenwich Village witches — and lovely (and bewitching) Novak, in particular. Great support from Lemmon as a bongo-playing warlock, Gingold as a high priestess, and Kovacs as a skeptical author. ★★★ VHS: $19.99; DVD: $24.99

Belle de Jour

(1967, 100 min, France/Italy, Luis Bunuel) *Catherine Deneuve, Jean Sorel, Genevieve Page.* Buñuel's kinky skewering of bourgeois pretensions stars a luminous Deneuve as a terminally bored doctor's wife who escapes her ennui in bizarre, masochistic sexual daydreams. These fantasies turn to reality when she lands an afternoon shift at a high-class Parisian brothel where she is given the titular alias. *Belle de Jour* is a mostly cerebral but masterful and at times giddy dialectic on sexual repression, the Church and the meaningless, philistine lives of the upper classes. As usual, Buñuel mixes fantasy, reality and flashback to the point where the viewer is pressed to wonder which is real. Deneuve is hypnotic as the wistful Belle, whose desire for sexual humiliation seems to be her only avenue for rebellion against the constraints of her social position. Page is in fine form as the Belle's madam, a lesbian who fancies the icy beauty of her newest protégé. (French with English subtitles) ★★★½ VHS: $19.99

Belle Epoque

(1993, 108 min, Spain, Fernando Trueba) *Fernando Fernan Gomez, Jorge Sanz, Maribel Verdu, Ariadna Gil.* The winner of the 1993 Academy Award for Best Foreign-Language Film, *Belle Epoque* is a disarmingly gentle and comic tale of female seduction set in the civil war-ravaged Spain of 1936. AWOL soldier Fernando (Sanz), a handsome rogue-wannabe, finds brief solace, love, sex and emotional turmoil in the home of an elderly gentleman who has four beautiful and flirtatious daughters. Each woman, with a different reason for doing so, seduces the confused but eagerly accommodating young man, all under the blind eye of Papa. The sexual shenanigans continue when Mama, a traveling cabaret performer, returns with her lover in tow and, à la *Smiles of a Summer Night*, all the characters are thrown into romantic confusion. (Spanish with English subtitles) ★★★ VHS: $19.99

La Belle Noiseuse

(1991, 240 min, France, Jacques Rivette) *Emmanuelle Beart, Michel Piccoli, Jane Birkin.* A renowned painter's ten-year hiatus comes to an end after becoming inspired by a young artist, and in particular the young artist's lover (Beart), who becomes the model for his return to the canvas. It's a slow, methodical exploration into the artistic process and the ensuing obsessions it brings for both artist and model. Rivette's brilliant direction makes this four-hour film a rich and rewarding experience. (French with English subtitles) ★★★½ VHS: $29.99

The Belle of Amherst

(1976, 90 min, US, Charles S. Dubin) *Julie Harris.* In 1976, Harris won a Tony Award for Best Actress for her tour-de-force performance as writer Emily Dickinson. This one-woman play on film captures the brilliance of Harris' portrayal and the lovely prose of the 19th-century poet. Set in two acts, the story covers through both imaginary conversation and bittersweet recollections the life of Dickinson who lived in the small town of Amherst, Massachusetts, all her life. Author William Luce magically incorporates Dickinson's writings into her monologue to illustrate how her work commented on her life. Witty and touching, and Harris standing center stage and alone for 90 minutes is simply exhilarating. ★★★½ VHS: $59.99

The Belle of New York

(1952, 82 min, US, Charles Walters) *Fred Astaire, Vera-Ellen, Marjorie Main, Keenan Wynn, Alice Pearce.* Good dance sequences highlight this otherwise ordinary Astaire musical with Fred as a Gay '90s playboy who courts Salvation Army girl Vera-Ellen. ★★½ VHS: $19.99

Belle of the Nineties

(1934, 73 min, US, Leo McCarey) *Mae West, Roger Pryor, Johnny Mack Brown.* Only somewhat restricted by the Production Code, West is her usual bouncy, naughty self in this effervescent comedy. Mae, who also wrote the snappy screenplay, stars as a Gay '90s entertainer involved with an up-and-coming boxer (Pryor). There's treachery and deceit on their course of true love, and the boxer falls victim to a set-up. He leaves her, which sends her packing to New Orleans. But as luck has it, Pryor comes to town, but he's being set up again, unknown to Mae, who is out for revenge — Mae West style. West gets to sing a couple songs, and her witty one-liners still manage to titillate. The Duke Ellington Orchestra is featured, and wait till you see West dressed up as the Statue of Liberty. ★★★ VHS: $14.99

Bellissima

(1951, 108 min, Italy, Luchino Visconti) *Anna Magnani, Tina Apicella.* With the fury of a hurricane, the magnificent Magnani sweeps into the filmmaking process as a mother determined to get her seven-year-old daughter into the movies. When a casting call is announced for an unknown girl, hundreds of stage mothers storm the Cinecittá Studios in Rome. None, however, with the determination of the blustery Maddalena Cecconi (Magnani), a working-class wife from the tenements. When her daughter Maria (the wide-eyed Apicella) is chosen for a second call, Maddalena involves herself with a variety of show business hangers-on and con artists all in the hopes of getting an edge. Visconti's neorealist glimpse into the absurdities of movie making is an intoxicating blend of observational comedy and human drama which bears the hallmarks of both Sturges and Wilder. But it's all brought together by Magnani's ferocious portrayal of a mother whose unrelenting pursuit for her daughter's success is only outweighed by the love for her child. (Italian with English subtitles) ★★★½

Bellissimo

(1987, 110 min, Italy, Gianfranco Mingozzi) This ambitious documentary sets out to encapsulate the important events, movements, stars and directors of Italy's filmmaking history during the past 40 years. Interspersing footage from many of the classics of Italian cinema (*Open City, Divorce Italian Style, 8½, Seven Beauties*) with interviews from both behind and in front of the camera, the film attempts to reconstruct a detailed history of one of the world's great filmmaking centers. Some of the interviewees include directors Federico Fellini, Bernardo Bertolucci, Pier Paolo Pasolini and Lina Wertmüller, and such leading actors as Sophia Loren, Giancarlo Giannini and Monica Vitti. An invaluable aid to all students and fans of Italian filmmaking. (Italian with English subtitles) ★★★ VHS: $29.99

Bellman and True

(1988, 112 min, GB, Richard Loncraine) *Bernard Hill, Kieran O'Brien, Richard Hope.* An outstanding crime thriller which masterfully combines the exciting tale of a computer engineer caught up in an elaborate bank heist scheme and the very human drama of that man's battle for both the safety of his kidnapped son and his own personal redemption. Hill plays Hiller, who is coerced by a ruthless gang to plan and execute a daring robbery of one of England's largest banks. Director Loncraine weaves a hypnotic

and rewarding tale rich in style, atmosphere and suspense. ★★★½ VHS: $14.99

Bells Are Ringing

(1960, 127 min, US, Vincente Minnelli) *Judy Holliday, Dean Martin, Jean Stapleton, Eddie Foy, Jr.* A good-natured adaptation of Betty Comden and Adolph Green's hit Broadway musical with Holliday re-creating her acclaimed stage role as an answering service operator who falls in love with one of her clients (Martin). Judy is a delight in her final screen appearance. Songs include "The Party's Over" and "Just in Time." ★★★ VHS: $14.99

The Bells of St. Mary's

(1945, 126 min, US, Leo McCarey) *Ingrid Bergman, Bing Crosby.* Heartwarming tale of Father O'Malley (Crosby) coming to a New York parish run by a strict Mother Superior (Bergman) where they come in conflict over how to run the school and to teach the children. Crosby repeats his Academy Award–winning role from *Going My Way.* ★★★ VHS: $14.99; DVD: $24.99

Belly

(1998, 95 min, US, Hype Williams) *Nas, DMX, Taral Hicks, Tionne "T-Boz" Watkins, Method Man.* MTV award-winning video director Williams makes an impressive debut with this brutally raw portrait of urban street life. Chart-topping rappers Nas and DMX shine in their starring roles as best friends who soon begin to grow apart as they sink deeper into the dark and dangerous world of drug dealing. With the events unfolding in a dreamlike, trance-inducing style, *Belly* manages to actually allow the viewer to gain insight into the many characters. Some may be put off by the realistic violence, the negative portrayal of women, and the use of profanity, but these are necessary in making the characters believable. ★★★ VHS: $9.99; DVD: $14.99

The Belly of an Architect

(1987, 118 min, GB, Peter Greenaway) *Brian Dennehy, Chloe Webb, Lambert Wilson.* Dennehy stars as a rotund American architect who travels to Rome with wife Webb to oversee the mounting of a show honoring 18th-century French designer Boulée. As Dennehy becomes more and more obsessed with the project, his life begins to mirror that of the ill-fated Boulée, who died of a mysterious stomach ailment. For Greenaway's part, he's obsessed with Dennehy's portly midsection. The stocky actor puts in what can only be called an immense performance as Greenaway's camera explores his tummy from all angles. While visually stunning, the film is one of Greenaway's less-successful efforts. ★★½ VHS: $14.99

Beloved

(1998, 172 min, US, Jonathan Demme) *Oprah Winfrey, Danny Glover, Thandie Newton, Kimberly Elise, Beah Richards, Lisa Gay Hamilton.* Toni Morrison's Pulitzer Prize–winning novel makes for riveting drama, but isn't as wholly successful as it could have been due to director Demme's sometimes fragmented filmmaking style. In a totally believable portrayal, Winfrey is Sethe, an ex-slave raising her family in rural Ohio. However, their isolated tranquility is shattered when they are visited by the ghost of Sethe's long-dead child, Beloved. Her presence, embraced by Sethe and her daughter Denver and viewed upon

Peter Sellers in *Being There*

B

Beloved

with suspicion by Sethe's lover Paul D. (Glover), sets in motion the resurfacing of faded memories and buried secrets of the past, acts which were only performed to escape a life of slavery. Demme has true command over the scenes of the haunting, which are spellbinding and make up much of the film. But the intricacies of the characters are often overshadowed by the film's stylized storytelling. He does, however, get superb performances from his cast, especially Elise as Denver. ★★★ VHS: $102.99; DVD: $29.99

Ben Hur
(1926, 148 min, US, Fred Niblo) *Ramon Novarro, Francis X. Bushman, May McAvoy.* One of the great spectaculars of all times, with all the pluses and minuses inherent in the genre. The chariot race and the sea battle have rarely been equaled for sheer edge-of-your-seat excitement. A Brownlow & Gill reconstruction, with the original tinting and toning, plus the two-strip Technicolor sequence and another fabulous score by Carl Davis. ★★★½ VHS: $29.99

Ben-Hur
(1959, 212 min, US, William Wyler) *Charlton Heston, Stephen Boyd, Jack Hawkins, Hugh Griffiths.* A biblical epic on a scale even the Caesars could appreciate. This tale of two friends (Heston, Boyd) who become enemies during the time of Jesus is bathed in sincerity and brimming with spectacle. Director Wyler uses all his skill with actors to even bring a human element to the production. This winner of 11 Oscars is better — and less corny — than anyone would have a right to expect. The famed chariot race remains a knockout. (VHS available letterboxed and pan & scan) ★★★½ VHS: $19.99; DVD: $24.99

Bend of the River
(1952, 91 min, US, Anthony Mann) *James Stewart, Arthur Kennedy, Rock Hudson.* Robust western adventure with Stewart and Kennedy squaring off against each other during a wagon train's journey to Oregon in the mid-1800s. ★★★ VHS: $14.99

Beneath the Planet of the Apes
(1970, 95 min, US, Ted Post) *James Franciscus, Charlton Heston, Kim Hunter, Maurice Evans.* The first sequel to *Planet of the Apes* pits astronaut Franciscus against the simian inhabitants

of a futuristic Earth in his search for Heston and crew. Not as satisfying as the original, but not without its entertaining moments. ★★½ VHS: $14.99

Beneath the Valley of the Ultravixens
(1979, 93 min, US, Russ Meyer) *Francesca Natividad, Ken Kerr, Robert Pearson.* Meyer's last theatrical release once again features the hyperkinetic editing and absurdly large breasts that have been the trademarks of his singular vision. The plot, which concerns faith healing and sexual misadventures in a small California town, is really just an excuse for an endless parade of naked bodies and bad dialogue. The film is complete schlock, of course, but Meyer is in on the joke. Perverse fun. ★★½ VHS: $79.99

Benny & Joon
(1993, 98 min, US, Jeremiah Chechik) *Johnny Depp, Mary Stuart Masterson, Aidan Quinn, Julianne Moore, Oliver Platt, CCH Pounder, Dan Hedaya.* Not since *Harold and Maude* have two crazies endeared themselves so winningly as Depp and Masterson in *Benny & Joon,* a hilarious, offbeat charmer. Quinn is Benny, a thoughtful garage mechanic who gallantly looks after his mentally ill sister (Masterson). Into their lives steps Sam (Depp), a Buster Keaton clone whom Benny wins in a card game. Soon, Sam and Joon bring new definition to "crazy in love," forcing an emotional showdown for all three characters. Writer Barry Berman's script works on many levels: as comedy, romantic fable, hip character study, and even homage to the great silent clowns. As Sam, Depp is a marvel: his silent comedy schtick is uncanny, and his soulful eyes and puppy-dog face punctuate an appealing romantic idol. Masterson ably captures the right mixture of waif and firebrand. ★★★½ VHS: $9.99; DVD: $19.99

The Benny Goodman Story
(1955, 116 min, US, Valentine Davies) *Steve Allen, Donna Reed.* With the tremendous success of *The Glenn Miller Story,* this biography of another big-band great was supposed to cash in on that film's popularity. Only problem — it didn't have James Stewart. Allen does his best in the title role in this Hollywood-ized look at the rise of the legendary

Benny Goodman, and Reed plays the June Allyson role. A good score though. ★★½ VHS: $19.99

Bent
(1997, 100 min, GB, Sean Mathias) *Clive Owen, Lothaire Bluteau, Mick Jagger, Ian McKellen, Rupert Graves.* A striking adaptation of the stage play, *Bent* shifts its drama from the decadent gay German nightlife (which earned the film its NC-17 rating during its theatrical run) to the horrors of a Nazi concentration camp. And yet, playwright Martin Sherman has created a moving love story out of the characters' despair. The intense passion that develops between Max (Owen) and Horst (Bluteau) is heartfelt, especially considering their relationship is mental and emotional, rather than physical. However, in opening up the play for the screen, director Mathias (who directed the London stage version) can not escape some of its theatrical trappings. The film's plotting is occasionally clumsy in the big dramatic moments, but *Bent* remains powerful nonetheless. Owen and Bluteau give gutsy performances in the lead roles. ★★★ VHS: $14.99

The Berlin Affair
(1986, 101 min, Italy/West Germany, Liliana Cavani) *Gudrun Landgrebe, Mio Takaki.* A searing and provocative tale of sexual obsession and domination set in 1938, where the dangerously seductive charms of a beautiful Japanese woman entrap three willing victims and take them into the netherworld of blackmail, drugs and forbidden love. (Dubbed) ★★★

Berlin Alexanderplatz
(1980, 940 min, West Germany, Rainer Werner Fassbinder) *Hanna Schygulla, Barbara Sukowa, Gunter Lamprecht, Rainer Werner Fassbinder.* Fassbinder's stunning 15½-hour epic is set in post-WWI Germany and continues through the birth and growth of Nazism. Simply told, it's the story of a slow-witted Berlin transit worker who, after accidentally killing his girlfriend and serving time, unwittingly becomes involved in the Berlin underworld. Originally produced for German TV, Fassbinder's masterpiece is one of the few films in our collection that probably works better on home video rather than at a theatre. (German with English subtitles) ★★★★

Berlin Express
(1948, 86 min, US, Jacques Tourneur) *Robert Ryan, Merle Oberon, Paul Lukas.* Authentic locations (filmed in the war-torn cities of Frankfurt and Berlin) heighten the realism of this taut and suspenseful spy thriller. Four train passengers, a cross-section of the Allied forces, band together with secretary Oberon to search for a German statesman — a key figure for German unification — who has been kidnapped by a Nazi underground. ★★★½

Berserk
(1967, 96 min, GB, Jim O'Connolly) *Joan Crawford, Diana Dors, Judy Geeson, Ty Hardin.* In this twisted, plodding shocker, Crawford is the owner of a British circus which is being haunted by brutal murders. Once the public gets wind of the performers' deaths, ticket sales begin to skyrocket. The police begin to investigate the strange circumstances and Joan herself. Crawford is typically overwrought in this late role. ★★ VHS: $19.99

Bert Rigby, You're a Fool

(1989, 94 min, US, Carl Reiner) *Robert Lindsay, Anne Bancroft, Cathryn Bradshaw, Robbie Coltrane, Bruno Kirby.* For those who have ever uttered those infamous nine words, "They sure don't make 'em like they used to," comes this sweetly old-fashioned though plodding musical comedy which is a 94-minute tribute to the musicals of the '50s. Lindsay gives an effervescent performance as an English coal miner who dreams of stardom, and through a series of odd twists, arrives in Hollywood for a chance at the brass ring. Sure, the film is too sentimental, and some scenes creak along, but it's Lindsay's performance which is the attraction here. ★★½ VHS: $14.99

Beshkempir: The Adopted Son

(1999, 81 min, Kyrgyzstan, Aktan Abdykalykov) *Mirlan Abdykalykov, Albina Imasheva, Adir Abilkassimov.* In a small village in Asiatic Russia, an infant is blessed and welcomed to Mother Earth with a ritual drawn from the old religions. The inhabitants eke out a meager existence in what is essentially an agrarian, pre-industrial society; it takes a while for the viewer to realize that the setting is present-day. Beshkempir is a young boy just at the threshold of adulthood, in his early teens, no longer a child and not yet a man. . . a tough time to find out that he is a foundling, an adopted son. This small, intimate film, set in a most alien environment, speaks to the universality of life cycles and rites of passage. The natural simplicity and unforced authenticity of the film is almost enhanced by the limited production values; the film is shot primarily in black and white, with the use of color film limited yet effective. A personal glimpse into an unknown part of the world. (Kyrgyzstani with English subtitles) ★★½ VHS: $19.99; DVD: $29.99

Besieged

(1999, 95 min, Italy, Bernardo Bertolucci) *Thandie Newton, David Thewlis, Claudio Santamaria.* In a dictatorship, teachers are subversive by definition. Shandurai (Newton), a young African woman who has just left work at a hospital ward filled with unending civilian casualties suffering war wounds, watches as her husband is dragged out of his classroom and loaded into military transport. We see her next in Rome, continuing her medical education while housekeeper for Jason (Thewlis), a reclusive pianist/composer. Believing her husband gone forever, she attempts to reestablish her life, battling the harsh memories that come to her in nightmares, and the unwelcome advances of the initially creepy, stalking Jason. But Jason proves to be easily handled, perhaps preoccupied by the circumstances that force him to divest himself of the inherited possessions that fill his home. The house is gradually stripped to the bare walls, as the self-involved Jason gradually opens up to the world that surrounds him. Director Bertolucci, already an established master of the medium, seems to have added yet another wrinkle to his arsenal of cinematic tricks: a fluid camera jumps and glides; layerings of image and sound overlap, compressing and expanding time and space. A personal tale of erotic obsession, told against a backdrop of political madness. (English and Italian with English subtitles) ★★★½ VHS: $19.99; DVD: $24.99

Best Boy

(1979, 111 min, US, Ira Wohl) This Academy Award winner follows the director's 52-year-old retarded cousin Philly as he comes to grips with his father's death, his mother's failing health and subsequent efforts to better integrate him into society. Moving yet unsentimental, Wohl has captured moments of epiphany for Philly as he realizes untapped skills and new joys such as a backstage duet with Zero Mostel singing "If I Were a Rich Man." ★★★★

Best in Show

(2000, 90 min, US, Christopher Guest) *Christopher Guest, Eugene Levy, Catherine O'Hara, Parker Posey, Fred Willard, Michael McKean, Michael Hitchcock, John Michael Higgins, Jane Lynch, Bob Balaban.* After skewering local theatre (*Waiting for Guffman*), director Guest takes on dog shows with this very funny mockumentary. An eccentric group of dog owners come together for the annual Mayflower Dog Show, and Guest nary misses a beat in capturing the absurdity of it all. Sure there are some easy targets (like Posey and Hitchcock's neurotic yuppie couple or McKean and Higgins' queeny lovers fussing over their shih tzu). And like *Guffman* not every bit works. But this is fun through and through, thanks to a plethora of laughs and wonderful characterizations. Besides, how can you resist a film that includes a doggie calendar re-enacting such favorites as *Gone with the Wind*, *Casablanca* and "McMillan and Wife"? ★★★½ VHS: $19.99; DVD: $24.99

The Best Intentions

(1992, 183 min, Sweden, Bille August) *Pernilla August, Samuel Froler, Max von Sydow.* Ingmar Bergman wrote the screenplay for this moving epic about the lives of his parents. The story begins when a young Henrik Bergman, a poor seminarian, falls for Anna, a somewhat spoiled rich girl. Despite her mother's best efforts to derail their affections, the young lovers persist and eventually wed. Their class differences become apparent immediately, but in the end, their devotion is true and the film follows their life together for 20 years, right up to Ingmar's birth. A heartwarming love story, the film's charm is augmented by winning performances from Froler and August in the lead roles. (Swedish with English subtitles) ★★★ VHS: $29.99

The Best Little Whorehouse in Texas

(1982, 114 min, US, Colin Higgins) *Burt Reynolds, Dolly Parton, Charles Durning, Dom DeLuise.* Reynolds and Parton bring a degree of charm to this glossy but uneven adaptation of the hit Broadway musical about a Texas bordello — called the Chicken Ranch — run by Parton and under attack by a local televangelist. Burt is the sheriff caught in the middle. During received an Oscar nomination for his scene-stealing bit as the Governor. ★★½ VHS: $7.49

The Best Man

(1964, 102 min, US, Franklin J. Schaffner) *Henry Fonda, Cliff Robertson, Edie Adams, Margaret Leighton, Shelley Berman, Lee Tracy.* Outstanding adaptation of Gore Vidal's vitriolic play centering on two politicians campaigning for the presidential nomination, each trying to woo support of the party and the ailing ex-president. Robertson stars as a ruthless conservative nominee running against the idealistic Fonda. Through the course of their politicking, betrayal, blackmail and political chicanery will rear their ugly heads as Vidal rips open (years before it became fashionable) the sometimes corrupt facade of politics. Tracy is excellent as the former chief. ★★★½ VHS: $19.99

The Best Man

(1999, 121 min, US, Malcolm D. Lee) *Taye Diggs, Nia Long, Morris Chestnut, Harold Perrineau, Terrence Howard.* The Best Man is an effective comedy-drama that boasts good ensemble performances and a smart script. Diggs plays an about-to-be-published author of a semiautobiographical novel which his old college friends have gotten ahold of. Through some loose lips and the thinly veiled situations in the novel, many skeletons are let out of the closet during a weekend wedding/reunion. Though the end is a bit too pat, and things are never as intense or rich as they could be, *The Best Man* is nevertheless a solid, involving and entertaining film, with many universal dilemmas addressed. ★★★ VHS: $9.99; DVD: $24.99

Best Men

(1997, 89 min, US, Tamra Davis) *Dean Cain, Andy Dick, Sean Patrick Flanery, Mitchell Whitfield, Luke Wilson, Fred Ward, Drew Barrymore.* This offbeat comedy/crime drama — about an unlikely gang of bank robbers — falters a bit but nonetheless makes for an entertaining and quirky tale; think *Dog Day Afternoon* meets a small-town "Friends." The story revolves around five buddies who — while at one of the group's wedding — become involved in a bank robbery-turned-hostage stand-off-turned-media circus. It may sound unbelievable (the one true robber is nicknamed Hamlet for his penchant for quoting Shakespeare), and the general story has been seen before, but the actors and their off-center characters save the film from being just a stupid straight-to-video actioner. Cain is especially effective as a gay ex-Marine, Dick is the dorky dude who sees his macho side come out, and Ward is the frustrated sheriff. ★★½

The Best of Times

(1986, 104 min, US, Roger Spottiswoode) *Kurt Russell, Robin Williams, Pamela Reed, Holly Palance.* This disappointing comedy manages a few smiles but considering the talent involved, there should have been more. Williams is a former high school football player who dropped the winning pass in a championship game. He stages a rematch 20 years later. Russell is his former teammate. ★★ VHS: $6.99; DVD: $24.99

Best Seller

(1987, 110 min, US, John Flynn) *James Woods, Brian Dennehy, Victoria Tennant, Paul Shenar.* Woods stars as a retired hit man whose offer to collaborate with a cop-turned-author (Dennehy) on a tell-all autobiography ruffles the feathers of his wealthy ex-employer (Shenar). Powerhouse performances by Woods and Dennehy distinguish this intriguing and tightly focused thriller. ★★★ VHS: $14.99

The Best Way

(1976, 85 min, France, Claude Miller) *Patrick Dewaere, Patrick Bouchitey.* A summer camp for boys is the setting for this absorbing study of the tensions and sexual attraction of two male counselors. Marc, the overly masculine sports director, discovers Philippe, the music teacher, dressed in women's clothing. His inability to deal with his repressed feeling causes him to humiliate and persecute Philippe to the point where he must deal with the truth of his actions. A fine drama on sexual identity and male friendships. (French with English subtitles) ★★★ VHS: $49.99

The Best Years of Our Lives

(1946, 172 min, US, William Wyler) *Fredric March, Myrna Loy, Dana Andrews, Teresa Wright, Virginia Mayo, Harold Russell.* A landmark war film, and immensely popular in its day, this Oscar-winning drama is a masterful examination into the lives of three WWII veterans returning home. March won the second of his two Oscars for his rich portrayal of a family man having difficulty reorienting himself to civilian life. A great cast includes Loy as his wife, Andrews in his best screen performance as a pilot haunted by his experiences, and Russell, a real-life amputee who also won an Oscar as a young soldier adjusting to life without hands. ★★★★ VHS: $14.99; DVD: $19.99

La Bête Humaine

(1938, 99 min, France, Jean Renoir) *Jean Gabin, Simone Simon.* This atmospheric thriller follows the actions of a psychotic train engineer who falls for a married woman and plots to kill her husband. A dark, intense work from one of the masters of the French cinema. Based on the Emile Zola novel. (French with English subtitles) ★★★½ VHS: $19.99

Betrayal

(1988, 95 min, GB, David Jones) *Ben Kingsley, Jeremy Irons, Patricia Hodge.* Harold Pinter, in adapting his acclaimed stage production, has crafted a marvelous study of entwined lives, conflicting loyalties and emotional ambiguity which is both wickedly funny and endlessly intriguing. Kingsley and Irons are bound by their literary pursuits, their enduring friendship and their mutual involvement with Kingsley's wife (Hodge). Director Jones and writer Pinter effectively use the author's theatrical device of presenting the story's many acts backwards — thus beginning with the outcome of the characters' infidelity and then tracing the steps leading to that point. The three leads are uniformly good. ★★★★

Betrayed

(1988, 127 min, US, Constantin Costa-Gavras) *Debra Winger, Tom Berenger, John Mahoney, John Heard.* Director Costa-Gavras turns his eyes on racial intolerance in this powerful but ultimately contrived thriller. Winger stars as an FBI agent who goes undercover to expose a white supremacist group responsible for a series of racially motivated murders. While its scenes of racial prejudice are all too real and emotionally devastating, the film itself is betrayed by an unbelievable romantic subplot between the agent and her prime suspect, a farmer played with chilling intensity by Berenger. ★★½ VHS: $9.99; DVD: $14.99

The Betsy

(1978, 125 min, US, Daniel Petrie) *Robert Duvall, Laurence Olivier, Tommy Lee Jones, Katharine Ross, Jane Alexander, Edward Herrmann.* An all-star cast, headed by a slumming Olivier, gives varying degrees of over-the-top performances in this over-

wrought potboiler adapted from Harold Robbins' best-seller. With only occasional moments of interest, this heavy-handed melodrama charts the course of an auto manufacturing dynasty. Olivier plays the patriarch, and Duvall is the grandson now running the company. About as subtle as a...well, Harold Robbins novel, this is the usual cacophony of lurid melodramatic loves and familial treachery. ★★ VHS: $19.99; DVD: $14.99

Betsy's Wedding

(1990, 94 min, US, Alan Alda) *Alan Alda, Madeline Kahn, Molly Ringwald, Ally Sheedy, Anthony LaPaglia, Joe Pesci, Catherine O'Hara.* Alda is in *Father of the Bride* territory with this sitcomish tale of a family preparing their daughter's wedding. Ringwald is the bride-to-be, and surprise! — the wedding plans go awry. Though Alda does create some amusing scenarios for his characters, the story is remarkably familiar and the film's pacing is either too meandering or too over-the-top to achieve a comedic consistency. LaPaglia steals the show as a mobster with a touch of class. ★★

Better off Dead

(1985, 97 min, US, Savage Steve Holland) *John Cusack, Curtis Armstrong, Diane Franklin, Kim Darby, David Ogden Stiers.* This wacky and hilarious — if underrated — comedy stars Cusack as a teenager who loses the girl of his dreams and thinks himself *Better Off Dead.* Not a satire on suicide (à la *Heathers*), but rather a collection of crazy sketches, the majority of which hit the comedic bull's-eye. ★★★ VHS: $9.99

Better Than Chocolate

(1999, 98 min, Canada, Anne Wheeler) *Wendy Crewson, Karyn Dwyer, Christina Cox, Anne-Marie MacDonald, Peter Outerbridge, Marya Delver, Kevin Mundy, Tony Nappo, Jay Brazeau.* A wildly enjoyable and refreshingly sexy tale of lesbian love winning against all odds. When 19-year-old redhead Maggie's nutty mother calls and says she is moving in, Maggie — who quit law school and has been sleeping on the couch of the lesbian bookstore — must find a sublet apartment and make it liveable fast. To complicate matters, she has just met the sultry Kim, an artistic road warrior who has rolled into town. But Maggie hasn't come out to her mother yet, so it's time to hide the sex toys and "straighten up." A boisterous and entertaining romantic comedy of errors, *Better Than Chocolate* is a raucous roller coaster of campy exploits and over-the-top situations with a gorgeous cast and a playful attitude towards sex. ★★★½ VHS: $79.99; DVD: $24.99

A Better Tomorrow

(1986, 95 min, Hong Kong, John Woo) *Chow Yun Fat, Leslie Cheung, Ti Lung, Lee Tse Ho.* The breakaway film that established Woo as a masterful action director, with Woo's camerawork giving us an incredibly violent view of extreme gunplay and evincing the strong influence of Sam Peckinpah and Sergio Leone. Lung and Yun Fat play gangsters who reunite to exact bloody revenge on crimeboss Ho; Cheung plays Lung's brother, a policeman, whose respect and love Lung tries to win back. The bonds and betrayals lay the groundwork for Woo's epic, operatic action. (Letterboxed) (VHS is English dubbed only; DVD also in Cantonese with English subtitles) ★★★½ VHS: $9.99; DVD: $24.99

Betty

(1993, 103 min, France, Claude Chabrol) *Marie Trintignant, Stéphane Audran, Jean-Francois Garreau.* Director Chabrol delivers another existential look at a French woman trying to find her place in life. Told in flashbacks, the film tells the story of Betty (Trintignant), a young alcoholic woman cast aside by her husband and desperately trying to keep her emotions and sanity in check. Betty is befriended by an older woman (Audran), and as the story unfolds, the viewer learns more about these two women's lives and how they got to where they are. *Betty* is highly emotional, tragic and ultimately satisfying. (French with English subtitles) ★★★★ VHS: $29.99

Betty Blue

(1986, 110 min, France, Jean-Jacques Beineix) *Beatrice Dalle, Jean-Hugues Anglade.* Beineix, director of the trendsetting *Diva* as well as the stilted *Moon in the Gutter*, has fashioned this humorous and engrossing tale of *amour fou.* The story follows the passionate and at times tempestuous relationship between Betty (Dalle) a vulnerable young beauty, and her boyfriend Zorg (Anglade), a young man hopelessly captivated by her enigmatic but beguiling charm. Wonderfully scripted and acted, this charmer should not be missed. (French with English subtitles) ★★★½

Between Heaven and Earth

(1992, 80 min, France, Marion Hansel) *Carmen Maura, Jean-Pierre Cassel.* Truly a bizarre French twist on *Look Who's Talking,* this odd little film stars Spanish leading lady Maura as a Parisian TV reporter whose developing fetus talks to her from in utero. As an epidemic of overdue babies and stillbirths occupy the headlines, Maura's talking zygote explains that the fetuses are essentially on strike and refuse to be born into such a miserable world. It's a slight premise on which to build a feature-length film, but certainly more could have been made of it. Maura, for her part, is always a pleasure, and performs in French with what looks to be relative ease. (French with English subtitles) ★★ VHS: $79.99

Between Heaven and Hell

(1956, 93 min, US, Richard Fleischer) *Robert Wagner, Broderick Crawford, Terry Moore, Buddy Ebsen.* An interesting if talky war drama with Wagner in his semi-successful bid to become a full-fledged movie star. He plays an unscrupulous Southern landowner whose experiences in the Pacific during WWII help him recover his lost compassion and humanity. Crawford is the maniacal commanding officer at odds with the young soldier. ★★½ VHS: $14.99

Between the Lines

(1977, 101 min, US, Joan Micklin Silver) *Jeff Goldblum, John Heard, Jill Eikenberry, Lindsay Crouse, Bruno Kirby, Stephen Collins, Joe Morton, Marilu Henner, Lane Smith.* The trials and tribulations of the staff of a Boston underground newspaper during the 1960s is at the heart of director Silver's quirky and highly spirited low-budget charmer. Full of counter-culture sentiments and refreshingly original humor, the film boasts an endearing cast of eccentrics fighting the system and fulfilling their journalistic aspirations — until faced with the fateful decision to "sell out." A solid ensemble of then-unknowns

Patricia Arquette in *Beyond Rangoon*

are all first-rate in bringing the convictions and passions of a generation to life. ★★★½

The Beverly Hillbillies

(1993, 93 min, US, Penelope Spheeris) *Jim Varney, Cloris Leachman, Lily Tomlin, Dabney Coleman, Diedrich Bader, Erica Eleniak, Lea Thompson, Rob Schneider, Dolly Parton.* It's bad news for a comedy when its funniest moments stem from surprise "star" cameos and out-takes during the end credits. Such is the case for *The Beverly Hillbillies*, a sappy, big-screen rendition of the popular 1960s TV series. In an A to B plot line, Arkansas hillbilly patriarch Jed Clampett strikes it rich, moves to Beverly (Hills, that is), and becomes the target for con artists. The comedy is played even broader than the TV series, which seems subtle by comparison. ★★ VHS: $9.99

Beverly Hills Cop

(1984, 105 min, US, Martin Brest) *Eddie Murphy, Judge Reinhold, James Russo, Paul Reiser, Bronson Pinchot, Damon Wayans.* Murphy is Axel Foley, a Detroit cop who travels to Beverly Hills to avenge a friend's death...and make the biggest grossing comedy of the decade. Not nearly as memorable as *48 Hrs.*, but entertaining if you don't think about it too much. Reinhold steals the show as Rosewood, an unorthodox cop who helps the displaced detective. Good soundtrack, and a slam-bang opening scene. ★★★ VHS: $14.99

Beverly Hills Cop II

(1987, 103 min, US, Tony Scott) *Eddie Murphy, Judge Reinhold, Jurgen Prochnow, Dean Stockwell, Paul Reiser.* This extremely disappointing sequel has none of the ingredients which made the first film the popular success it was. Murphy tries his best, but how many times can we watch him con his way into ritzy Beverly Hills establishments? There's some slick, polished direction by Scott, but it can't hide the formulaic script and forced performances. For die-hard Murphy fans only. ★★ VHS: $9.99

Beverly Hills Cop III

(1994, 103 min, US, John Landis) *Eddie Murphy, Judge Reinhold, Hector Elizondo, Bronson Pinchot, Theresa Randle, John Saxon, Alan Young.* Murphy dusts off the gun and jacket of Axel Foley for this third (and probably last) installment. Featuring uninspired direction by Landis, this occasionally amusing but incredibly formulaic film has Axel returning to California to investigate a lead in a carjack ring/murder case. The trail leads to a Disneyland-type park, which serves as a cover for the bad guys. Murphy gives an earnest try, though he's been through all this before, and it shows. However, *III* does provide more pleasure than *B.H.C. II*, and Reinhold returns once more as Rosewood. ★★½ VHS: $14.99

Beverly Hills Ninja

(1997, 89 min, US, Dennis Dugan) *Chris Farley, Nicolette Sheridan, Chris Rock, Robin Shou, Nathaniel Parker.* What could have been a funny parody of martial arts movies instead turns out to be a series of "look at the fat guy fall down" jokes which fails even at the sophomoric level it sets for itself early on. Farley is Haru, a "gravity-challenged" inept white ninja who comes to the United States to help a con woman (Sheridan) he believes to be sincerely a damsel in distress. Of course, he gets himself into a series of jams and eventually saves the day. *Beverly Hills Ninja* lacks an original idea, and has only a few funny sequences which go on much too long. ★½ VHS: $9.99; DVD: $14.99

Beware, My Lovely

(1952, 77 min, US, Harry Horner) *Robert Ryan, Ida Lupino.* This thrilling study of insanity and terror stars Ryan as a deranged handyman who holds captive his widowed employer, Lupino, inside her home. Haunted by the murder of his previous employer (whom he may or may not have killed), Ryan alternates between being a gentle if slightly dazed man and an angry, potentially violent loony. ★★★ VHS: $19.99

Beware of a Holy Whore

(1970, 103 min, Germany, Rainer Werner Fassbinder) *Lou Castel, Hanna Schygulla, Eddie Constantine, Rainer Werner Fassbinder, Ulli Lommel.* An autobiographical meditation on the turbulent interactions and shifting power relationships which make up the filmmaking process, this is RFW's *8½*, *Day for Night* and *Contempt*. Based in part on Fassbinder's own experiences making *Whity*, *Beware a Holy Whore* follows a film crew and a group of actors who anxiously lounge around an opulent Spanish hotel arguing, drinking and becoming involved in destructive sex and power games as they endlessly wait for the film's star (Constantine), production money and especially the director (played by Fassbinder) to bring them to life. This was RFW's last collaboration with the collective Anti-Teater (Fassbinder's repertory company). (German with English subtitles) ★★★ VHS: $19.99

Beyond a Reasonable Doubt

(1956, 80 min, US, Fritz Lang) *Dana Andrews, Joan Fontaine.* An anti-capital punishment newspaper publisher implicates himself in a murder by using circumstantial evidence, hoping to expose the weakness of the system. However, things go wrong when he plays it too convincingly, is found guilty and then sent to prison. Lang's final American film, while far-fetched, is an undeniably grim and gripping melodrama. ★★★

Beyond Rangoon

(1995, 100 min, US, John Boorman) *Patricia Arquette, U Aung Ko, Frances McDormand, Spalding Gray.* Arquette plays an American tourist visiting Burma who becomes involved in that country's bloody struggle for democracy in this gripping and moving political drama. After the murder of her husband and son, Laura Bowman (Arquette) attempts to find solace in the peaceful landscapes of the Far East. After witnessing in Rangoon a people's demonstration, she sets out with an "unofficial" tour guide, U Aung Ko, to see the country beyond the city. However, a military crackdown forces both of them to flee for their lives in an attempt to reach the border. Suggested by an actual incident, *Beyond Rangoon* at its best recalls *The Killing Fields* as a strong narrative and taut direction combine to tell a harrowing tale of political oppression and heroism. Expatriate professor U Aung Ko plays himself. ★★★½ VHS: $19.99

Beyond Reasonable Doubt

(1980, 117 min, New Zealand, John Laing) *David Hemmings, John Hargreaves.* A jolting, true-life drama that documents the stilted investigation and legislative practices responsible for the incarceration of a mild-mannered New Zealand farmer. Hemmings gives a powerful performance as the corrupt police inspector who makes it a personal quest to seal the fate of the accused man, a baffled witness to his own demise. This Hitchcockian tale of questionable guilt and justice is a fascinating and thoroughly engrossing motion picture. ★★★

Beyond Silence

(1997, 107 min, Germany, Caroline Link) *Sylvie Testud, Tatjana Trieb, Howie Seago, Emmanuelle Labroit.* Courtesy of the New German Feel-Good Cinema, the light and bright *Beyond Silence* is pleasant and inoffensive; so what's the point? Well, mainly, it gives a window into the world of the deaf. Lara works overtime to translate between her deaf parents and the hearing world — including us, the viewers. It becomes akin to a one-sided phone conversation. To its credit, the film is less pandering and pedantic on disabilities than others of its ilk. The story focuses on Lara and her desire to become a clarinet player. Under the tutelage of her aunt (an enemy of her parents), Lara travels to Berlin to study. A series of routine plot adornments — death, love — take us comfortably to the groaner of a Mentos commercial ending. All this is accompanied by clarinet muzak meant to demonstrate what a genius player Lara is. (German with English subtitles) ★★ VHS: $19.99

Beyond the Forest

(1949, 96 min, US, King Vidor) *Bette Davis, Joseph Cotten, Ruth Roman.* Davis misses her mark as a murderous crack shot in this tepid melodrama about a woman who'll stop at nothing to rise above her life as the wife of a country doctor (Cotten). Notable for Davis' immortal line, "What a dump." ★★ VHS: $19.99

Beyond the Mat

(1999, 102 min, US, Barry Blaustein) *Vince McMahon, Mick Foley, Jake "The Snake" Roberts, Terry Funk.* Ex-SNL writer Blaustein's labor of love casts a human light on the spectacle of Pro Wrestling. Dismissing the fact that wrestling is "faked," he gets some remarkable footage by instead showing the skill, choreography and bone-jarring violence that the wrestlers endure six days a week (or more). Foley (stagename: Mankind) is moved when his children are genuinely disturbed by his performance at a pay-per-view event (getting hit in the head a dozen times with a metal chair can have that effect). Roberts wrestles with various addictions and has some painful scenes with his estranged daughter. Funk's footage is the most moving, as his trembling half-century-old arthritic knees come to life in an Extreme Wrestling arena. But the director is a victim of his good fortune; in trying to link the compelling bits together, he comes up with empty themes of corporate betrayal and humanized grapplers. ★★½ VHS: $14.99; DVD: $29.99

Beyond the Poseidon Adventure

(1979, 115 min, US, Irwin Allen) *Michael Caine, Sally Field, Telly Savalas, Peter Boyle, Jack Warden, Shirley Knight, Shirley Jones, Karl Malden.* More upside-down adventure from producer Allen, who here directs. Judging from this disaster, he should have been at the back of his desk rather than in back of the camera. Caine, who at the time was zeroing in on a Guinness record for film appearances, plays a salvager who enters the grounded *Poseidon* and finds more survivors. The original, with its good set design and silly story, was cheesy fun; this is just cheesy. ★ VHS: $9.99

Beyond the Valley of the Dolls

(1970, 109 min, US, Russ Meyer) *Edy Williams, Dolly Reed.* A classic late-nite cult title, this brilliantly raunchy, in-name-only sequel to *Valley of the Dolls* tells the torrid tale of a female rock band, The Carrie Nations, and their deliriously funny struggle to get to the top. Featuring director Meyer's trademark wit and camerawork, this ahead-of-its-time exploitation favorite remains one of the best of the genre. Coscripted by film critic Roger Ebert. ★★★ VHS: $19.99

Beyond the Walls

(1984, 103 min, Israel, Uri Barbash) *Arnon Zadok, Muhamad Bakri, Assi Dayan.* Inside the walls of an Israeli prison, Jews and Arabs are confined in a society which mirrors the pressures and tensions on the outside. Cruelty is commonplace and loyalty is fleeting. This already volatile situation is further exacerbated by the arrival of an Israeli army officer who is jailed for attempting to speak to the PLO. As the inmates struggle with ideological hatreds on the inside, they attempt to maintain contact with their families and communities on the outside, with decreasing effectiveness and increasing frustration. The cast delivers uniformly authentic portrayals, conveyed with raw intensity and unflinching emotion. A powerful experience, a film that in the midst of centuries-old animosities manages to find some common ground and a faint hope of peace. (Hebrew with English subtitles) ★★★ VHS: $79.99

Beyond Therapy

(1987, 93 min, US, Robert Altman) *Glenda Jackson, Tom Conti, Jeff Goldblum, Julie Hagerty, Christopher Guest, Cris Campion.* Christopher Durang co-adapted his own hit off-Broadway play for the screen in this Altman comedy about the frantic goings-on of a group of sex-obsessed neurotics and their equally unbalanced psychologists. Goldblum is the bisexual Bruce, who lives with semi-swishy Bob (Guest), but who takes a liking to hopelessly frazzled Prudence (Hagerty). Conti and Jackson play two crazy therapists whose advice only makes everyone more crazy. Unpredictable, loony and wildly uneven, *Beyond Therapy* can also be quite charming in-between the out-of-control shenanigans. Though set in New York, Altman filmed in Paris. ★★½ VHS: $14.99

Bhaji on the Beach

(1994, 100 min, GB, Gurinder Chadha) *Kim Vithana, Jimmi Harkishin, Sarita Khajuria, Mo Sesay.* This well-intentioned and somewhat light-hearted look at the lives of a group of Anglo-Indian/Pakistani women has its moments, but ultimately fails to captivate. The film follows three generations of women on an outing to the British seaside resort of Blackpool. Led by the self-assured feminist Simi, they land on the beach with a variety of issues at hand. The twentysomething Ginder has drawn the wrath of her entire community for having left her abusive husband, while her counterpart, Hashida, has just discovered she's pregnant — worse news for her family, her boyfriend is black. All of these threads are loosely pulled together through Asha, a middle-aged housewife who struggles between her sense of duty and dignity. Individually, all of the stories are interesting enough, but as the film wanders among its characters, it becomes diluted and ultimately comes off like a protracted episode of "EastEnders." ★★½ VHS: $79.99

The Bible

(1966, 174 min, US, John Huston) *John Huston, Richard Harris, George C. Scott, Peter O'Toole, Ava Gardner, Franco Nero.* Dino De Laurentiis produced this megalithic and completely blundering attempt to bring the "number one best-seller" to the screen. Some projects are better left alone. Why Huston agreed to helm this ill-begotten ship is a mystery. Perhaps only so he himself could portray Noah in the film's only redeeming chapter. If you're really interested, read the book. (Letterboxed VHS available for $19.99) ★½ VHS: $9.99

Bicentennial Man

(1999, 132 min, US, Chris Columbus) *Robin Williams, Sam Neill, Embeth Davidtz, Wendy Crewson, Oliver Platt.* An affluent family in the not-so-distant future purchases the latest suburban trend: a robotic family servant. They dub him Andrew, and he goes about cooking, cleaning and the other sundry tasks expected of a robot housekeeper. But it soon becomes clear that Andrew is a little special: He soon shows signs of individuality and sets out to discover what it's like to be human. Data from "Star Trek: The Next Generation" may want to get a lawyer. In fact, anyone watching this sappy, overlong family film may join Data in a class action suit. Too bad, for the costumes, makeup and art direction are effective. Williams is understated,

The Bicycle Thief

just like the rest of the cast; to such an extent that the film has no energy. Add a weird romantic twist, and *Bicentennial Man* leaves little hope for the future. ★½ VHS: $14.99; DVD: $32.99

Les Biches

(1968, 104 min, France/Italy, Claude Chabrol) *Stéphane Audran, Jean-Louis Trintignant.* Audran has never looked more elegantly decadent than in this twisted bisexual drama of sexual domination, obsession, despair and revenge, filmed in Chabrol's trademark cool, detached style. Audran is Frederique, a glamorous woman of lesbian leaning who, on a trip to Paris, meets and then seduces a poor, enigmatic young woman named Why. She soon whisks her new love off to her home in St. Tropez to continue their affair, but the balance is changed when a man (Trintignant) enters the picture and, after a brief attraction to Why, takes up permanently with Frederique. The centerpiece of this explosive love triangle is Audran's wanton sexual appeal, a power that eventually leads to bitter consequences. (Letterboxed) (French with English subtitles) ★★★½ VHS: $29.99

The Bicycle Thief

(1948, 90 min, Italy, Vittorio De Sica) *Lamberto Maggiorani, Lianella Carelli, Enzo Staiola, Elena Altieri.* One of the undisputed neorealist classics, *The Bicycle Thief* adeptly uses the postwar devastation of Italy as harsh backdrop for this poignant story of a marginal man whose simple existence depends on his bicycle, which he needs to earn his living. He is devastated by the bicycle's theft; his family's well-being is jeopardized and the police are indifferent. He is left to his own devices to scour the city with his young son, a victim without aid or support, alienated and isolated. Filmed with great caring and compassion, and yet without sympathetic gloss, by director De Sica, who can use a single human face to speak volumes about the human condition. ★★★★ VHS: $29.99; DVD: $24.99

Il Bidone (The Swindlers)

(1955, 98 min, Italy, Federico Fellini) *Broderick Crawford, Guilietta Masina, Richard Basehart, Franco Fabrizi.* Crawford is memorable as the self-ish ringleader of a trio of con men who impersonate priests in an elaborate scam that preys on the avarice of ignorant peasants. A satire that begins as a light comedy and concludes with tragedy, this pre-flamboyant Fellini forms part two of his trilogy (which includes *La Strada* and *Nights of Cabiria*) of outsiders eking out an existence on the road. (Italian with English subtitles) ★★★ VHS: $19.99; DVD: $24.99

B

Big

(1988, 102 min, US, Penny Marshall) *Tom Hanks, Elizabeth Perkins, John Heard, Robert Loggia, Jared Rushton, Jon Lovitz, Mercedes Ruehl.* Hanks gives a wonderfully complex and funny performance as the end result of a 12-year-old boy's wish to be "big." When his wish comes true, he is thrust into an adult world of big business, office politics and romance, all the while maintaining his refreshing child's-eye view of the world. Gary Ross' delightful script takes aim at corporate rivalry, consumerism and alienation while bringing a fresh perspective to the "fish out of water" scenario. Director Marshall exhibits a playful knack for comedy both physical and verbal, though she does somewhat bask in the sentimental. ★★★½ VHS: $9.99; DVD: $22.99

The Big Bang

(1989, 81 min, US, James Toback) Beginning with his theory that the creation of the universe was the result of an "orgasmic explosion of God," director Toback (*Fingers*) leaves the world of fiction to explore various other thoughts on existence in this rambling yet entertaining documentary. Interviewing a series of people from diverse backgrounds (basketball player Darryl Dawkins, filmmaker Don Simpson, violinist Eugene Fodor, Auschwitz survivor Barbara Traub), Toback elicits their divergent thoughts on life, death, creativity, sex, love and the existence of God. A funny, touching, and even enlightening film. ★★★ VHS: $19.99

The Big Blue

(1988, 119 min, France, Luc Besson) *Rosanna Arquette, Jean Reno, Jean-Marc Barr, Griffin Dunne.* Only Besson's most ardent fans, or those of you who fantasize about things aquatic, will be swayed by the stunning underwater photography in this waterlogged story about the rivalry between two deep-sea free divers (Reno and Barr). Arquette is a ditzy New York insurance salesperson who falls in love with one of them only to be rejected for a dolphin. (Filmed in English and French with subtitles) ★★ VHS: $14.99; DVD: $29.99

The Big Brass Ring

(1999, 104 min, US, George Hickenlooper) *William Hurt, Nigel Hawthorne, Miranda Richardson, Irene Jacob.* Based on an unfilmed screenplay by Orson Welles, this lackluster drama constantly begs the question "What if Welles had...?" As adapted and directed by Hickenlooper, *The Big Brass Ring* is tepid, tired hooey elevated by some good performances. It all starts off well, with independent Governor hopeful Hurt confronted with some compromising photos from his youth, given to the press by his ex-mentor Hawthorne on the eve of the election. The possibilities of the premise are squandered for a quasi-mystery, which is subsequently solved about halfway through the film. Little of interest remains, and while the story may have been controversial at the time Welles wished to film it, in the age of Monica Lewinsky and Jerry Springer, this is last week's dishwater. ★★ VHS: $14.99; DVD: $27.99

The Big Brawl

(1980, 95 min, US, Robert Clouse) *Jackie Chan, Jose Ferrer.* This gangster film set in 1930s Chicago is more or less a showcase for the incredibly talented Chan. Lots of comedy and fighting keep the film interesting, but this is far from being one of Chan's best. Not much here for non-Jackie fans. ★★½

Big Business

(1988, 97 min, US, Jim Abrahams) *Bette Midler, Lily Tomlin, Fred Ward, Edward Herrmann, Michele Placido.* Lightning doesn't strike twice as *Ruthless People* star Midler and director Abrahams reunite in this rather tame though genial comedy. Midler and Tomlin star as two sets of twins switched at birth who run across each other's paths in the Big Apple. A good premise, a nice turn from the Divine Miss M and some nifty special effects can't save this lightweight comedy; though it does manage a few laughs, it is a disappointment considering the talent involved. ★★

The Big Chill

(1983, 105 min, US, Lawrence Kasdan) *William Hurt, Kevin Kline, Glenn Close, Tom Berenger, Jeff Goldblum, Meg Tilly, Mary Kay Place, JoBeth Williams.* Borrowing liberally from John Sayles' wonderful *Return of the Secaucus Seven*, director and coauthor Kasdan has fashioned an equally entertaining and smartly written ode to the lasting power of friendship. Utilizing a talented allstar cast, Kasdan's comedy-drama focuses on the reunion of a group of college friends from the '60s who have come together in the '80s for the funeral of one of their own. Kline and Close are a married couple who play host to their clique, which includes TV star Berenger, *People* magazine writer Goldblum (in a particularly sharp portrayal), and injured Vietnam vet Hurt. What distinguishes Kasdan's story are the personable characters and the remarkable relationships between them. *The Big Chill* is as comfortable as a longtime friend. (Includes featurette on the making of the film) ★★★½ VHS: $9.99; DVD: $24.99

The Big Combo

(1954, 89 min, US, Joseph H. Lewis) *Cornel Wilde, Richard Conte, Brian Donlevy, Jean Wallace, Earl Holliman, Lee Van Cleef.* A classic, if little acknowledged, film noir crime drama. The setting is the seedy crime underworld where a good cop (Wilde) attempts to take on a sadistic crime boss (Conte) with a luscious but oh-so-dangerous blonde bombshell (Wallace) in the middle. The cop becomes obsessed with bringing the thug to justice, but Conte's ruthless clutch on power embroils Wilde in a violent and even savage struggle. ★★★½ VHS: $19.99; DVD: $24.99

The Big Country

(1958, 167 min, US, William Wyler) *Gregory Peck, Charlton Heston, Burl Ives, Jean Simmons, Carroll Baker.* Epic western adventure starring Peck as an ex-sea captain who returns home to marry and start a ranch, becoming caught in a feud over water rights. This mammoth production also features Ives in an Oscar-winning performance as the patriarch of one of the feuding families. ★★★ VHS: $24.99; DVD: $19.99

Big Daddy

(1999, 93 min, US, Dennis Dugan) *Adam Sandler, Joey Lauren Adams, Jon Stewart, Cole and Dylan Sprouse, Rob Schneider, Joe Bologna, Kristy Swanson.* This box-office hit casts Sandler as an unlikely parental guardian to a cute five-year-old when he takes over responsibility of his vacationing roommate's son, who has been literally dropped off at his doorsteps. This *One Moron and a Kid* follows the layabout's attempts to keep the kid under control. Stupid sight gags, lazy one-liners and boring toilet humor at which only a prepubescent would smirk accentuate how unfunny all this really is. ★½ VHS: $9.99; DVD: $19.99

Big Deal on Madonna Street

(1956, 91 min, Italy, Mario Monticelli) *Marcello Mastroianni, Vittorio Gassman, Claudia Cardinale.* The wild misadventures of a group of bungling would-be crooks who attempt to rob a pawn shop and who make a complete mess of it is a classic example of *commedia all'italiana*. A hilarious parody of American caper films that many think to be one of the funniest Italian films to come out of the era. Louis Malle remade the film, but with much less success, as *Crackers*. (Italian with English subtitles) ★★★½ VHS: $29.99; DVD: $29.99

The Big Dis

(1988, 88 min, US, Gordon Eriksen & John O'Brien) This charming, black-and-white low-budget comedy-drama will remind one of Spike Lee's *She's Gotta Have It* in its often hilarious theme about the sexual attitudes and posturing of young middle-class blacks. J.D., a handsome but thoroughly sexist black soldier, returns to his family's suburban home on a weekend leave; his overwhelming ambition: to get laid. But everything seems to go wrong as he comes ever so close but never grabs the ring. ★★★ VHS: $19.99

The Big Doll House

(1971, 93 min, US, Jack Hill) *Pam Grier, Judy Brown.* Valley girls and Hollywood starlets trapped in a hellhole Filipino prison! One of the earliest and most commercially succesful of the "women-in-prison" films which were so popular in the 1970s, this is almost chaste compared to its cheesier successors. Filmed in a breezy, comedic fashion, the film features the requisite S&M beating, shower and claws-out fighting sequences to tell its tale of prisoners who revolt against their ruthless warden. ★★½ VHS: $14.99; DVD: $24.99

The Big Easy

(1987, 101 min, US, Jim McBride) *Dennis Quaid, Ellen Barkin, Ned Beatty, John Goodman, Ebbe Roe Smith, Charles Ludlam.* A glorious blend of screwball comedy and detective story, this scintillating thriller stars Quaid as a New Orleans detective who becomes involved with sexy district attorney Barkin, who is investigating local police corruption. Quaid and Barkin are about the most attractive duo on the screen in years, and their love scenes are among the steamiest, also. Great supporting cast includes Ludlam in a stand-out role as a Tennessee Williams-ish lawyer. ★★★½ VHS: $9.99; DVD: $24.99

The Big Fix

(1978, 108 min, US, Jeremy Paul Kagan) *Richard Dreyfuss, Susan Anspach, Bonnie Bedelia, John Lithgow, F. Murray Abraham.* Roger L. Simon adapted his own novel about private eye Moses Wine, a former '60s campus radical, who is hired by an old college girlfriend to help locate a fugitive from their Berkeley days. An entertaining comedy-mystery with Dreyfuss in good form as Wine. ★★★ VHS: $59.99

Big Girls Don't Cry...They Get Even

(1992, 90 min, US, Joan Micklin Silver) *Hillary Wolf, Griffin Dunne, Margaret Whitton, David Strathairn, Adrienne Shelly.* Wolf stars as Lauren (a 14-year-old with a ready canister of one-liners), who runs away after she decides that her mother, stepfather and various step-siblings just don't care about her. The ensuing search to bring her home unites the various and eccentric members of her family. Shelly gives a lovely, understated performance as Lauren's real father's artsy, very young and pregnant girlfriend. Silly but kinda cute. ★★½ VHS: $9.99

The Big Grab (Melodie en sous-sol)

(1963, 118 min, France, Henri Verneuil) *Jean Gabin, Alain Delon.* A young Delon is the punk assistant to master thief Gabin in this taut cops-and-robbers flick. Their attempt to pull off "the crime of the century" is intricately detailed as their plans become more and more complicated. A good, well-told story in the tradition of *Bob le Flambeur.* (French with English subtitles) ★★★

The Big Green

(1995, 100 min, US, Holly Goldberg Sloan) *Steve Guttenberg, Olivia d'Abo, Jay O. Sanders.* While certainly not the best of this genre of films that chronicles the transformation of a team of kids from losers to winners, there's enough here to satisfy most young viewers. A young exchange teacher from England (d'Abo) decides to teach soccer to her students, a group of kids from a very small and depressed Texas town. Guttenberg is the local sheriff who, despite his dislike of kids, ends up as her assistant coach. Among the team of fairly likable kids is the inevitable ringer, a Mexican youth whose mother is reluctant to let him play because she is an illegal alien. ★★½ VHS: $19.99

A Big Hand for the Little Lady

(1966, 95 min, US, Fielder Cook) *Henry Fonda, Joanne Woodward, Jason Robards, Burgess Meredith, Kevin McCarthy, Paul Ford.* Fonda and Woodward are in fine form in this sly western comedy. Fonda plays an ex-gambler who arrives with his wife (Woodward) in the town of Laredo just as the big card tournament begins. He enters the game, and gets the hand of a lifetime. Only before he can finish the hand, he suffers a heart attack. When his wife takes his place, the now-penniless woman has some fancy talking to do to stay in the game. And ya gotta love that surprise ending. ★★★ VHS: $19.99

The Big Heat

(1953, 90 min, US, Fritz Lang) *Glenn Ford, Lee Marvin, Gloria Grahame.* Although the story of mob operations and political corruption is pale compared to today's headlines, Lang's direction and some potent performances lose none of their impact. Especially effective are Ford as the honest cop, Marvin as the psychotic hood and an amazing Grahame as the gangster's moll. Yes, this is the one with the coffee-throwing scene. ★★★½ VHS: $19.99

The Big Hit

(1998, 91 min, US, Che-Kirk Wong) *Mark Wahlberg, Lou Diamond Phillips, Christina Applegate, Avery Brooks, Bokeem Woodbine, Antonio Sabato, Jr., Lela Rochon. The Big Hit* is a genuine-

Stanley Tucci (l.) and Tony Shalhoub in *Big Night*

ly likable action-comedy offering the visceral action of director Wong's *Crime Story* and the hip dopiness of, well, someone who's infatuated with Hong Kong action epics. Wahlberg is Melvin Smiley, a hit man with romantic and financial problems, who decides to take on a freelance assignment and kidnap the daughter (Chow) of a Japanese businessman to cash in on the ransom money. Little does he know that the teenaged girl is also the goddaughter of his boss, a powerful criminal. Soon, his well-toned assassin partners turn turncoat and offer to bring Melvin in for their boss. Wong is great at staging some action sequences, and gets a lot of comic mileage from the screenplay. If you know that Jackie Chan's *Drunken Master II* is better than the original *Drunken Master,* you'll get a big laugh out of *The Big Hit.* ★★★ VHS: $9.99; DVD: $14.99

The Big Kahuna

(2000, 91 min, US, John Swanbeck) *Kevin Spacey, Danny DeVito, Peter Facinelli.* Three white guys in suits, all wearing name tags, discuss the meaning of life in a garish hotel suite which stands in for a circle of hell. In a blasphemous misuse of talent, Spacey and De Vito play Larry and Phil, jaded and fading marketing foot soldiers who shill industrial lubricant and are looking for the big kahuna, the big deal which means redemption. Naïve, fresh-faced, born-again Bob (Facinelli) thinks he's found redemption and is oblivious to his own pitch. The film is unfocused as it awkwardly attempts to deal with big issues without generating any real spark of connection. The characters are delivered in shorthand — Larry glib, Phil wounded, Bob innocent — in what feels more like a reading than an ensemble performance. There is a hint of what was probably intended evident in the film's final sequences. Perhaps this work was more compelling in its first incarnation as a stage play; something must have motivated Spacey to co-produce and star in a film version. An interesting disappointment. ★★ VHS: $14.99; DVD: $26.99

The Big Lebowski

(1998, 117 min, US, Joel Coen) *Jeff Bridges, John Goodman, Steve Buscemi, John Turturro, David Huddleston, Julianne Moore, Philip Seymour Hoffman, David Thewlis, Sam Elliott.* His name is the Dude, a stoned-out aging hippie surfer.

And as hilariously played by Bridges in the Coen brothers' ecstatic, consistently funny and loopy comedy about bowling, mistaken identity and kidnapping, the Dude can certainly lay claim to such a moniker. Sharing only the same birth name, the Dude (alias Jeff Lebowski) is mistaken by some small-time hoods for a millionaire businessman (Huddleston), whose young trophy wife has been kidnapped. Soon, the Dude becomes entangled in a series of comic misadventures and neo-noir intrigue throughout L.A. which would make Raymond Chandler re-think *The Big Sleep* as a Marx Brothers vehicle. Brimming with broad humor, high energy and lots of laughs, the film is buoyed by the strong support of the dead-on Goodman, whose tirades and philosophies could have only been penned by the Coens, and appreciated by someone known as the Dude. ★★★½ VHS: $14.99; DVD: $19.99

Big Momma's House

(2000, 98 min, US, Raja Gosnell) *Martin Lawrence, Nia Long, Paul Giamatti.* With a nod to Eddie Murphy in *The Nutty Professor,* Lawrence goes the makeup-transformation route, but without producing the kind of laughs that (first) film generated. Lawrence plays an FBI agent who goes undercover to catch an escaped prisoner — by masquerading as an overweight, overbearing Southern grandmother. Soon, he's falling for his own "granddaughter," as well as being pursued by elderly gentlemen and taking on karate class instructors. Lawrence is a likable comedian, and he manages to create some good will with Big Momma, but the screenplay is lacking any substantial humor, at least the kind worthy of Lawrence's talents. ★★ VHS: $14.99; DVD: $24.99

Big Night

(1996, 107 min, US, Stanley Tucci & Campbell Scott) *Stanley Tucci, Tony Shalhoub, Isabella Rossellini, Ian Holm, Minnie Driver, Campbell Scott, Marc Anthony.* Adding yet another chapter to the annals of grand cinematic feasts, this charming little indie feature tells the tale of two Italian immigrant brothers who make a go at the American Dream. One part comedy and two parts drama and set in the 1950s on the North Jersey shore, the story centers around Primo (Shalhoub) and Secondo's (Tucci) desperate attempt to kickstart their failing bistro. While

Primo and Secondo go out of their way to present authentic and upscale Italian fare, their competitor down the street (Holm) is clobbering them with his low-brow, "Americanized" fare. Ultimately, they gear up for one big splash as they anticipate a visit from Italo-American bandleader Louis Prima. The ensuing feast is worthy of its long list of cinematic antecedents (*Babette's Feast, Like Water for Chocolate* and *Eat Drink Man Woman*) and will send any viewer with so much as a twinge of epicureanism rushing to their local trattoria begging for timpano. ★★★½ VHS: $19.99

The Big One

(1998, 90 min, US, Michael Moore) *Michael Moore, Studs Terkel, Garrison Keillar.* Moore (*Roger & Me*) has crafted another refreshingly clear-eyed exploration of America's corporate culture. While on a promotional tour for his latest book, "Downsize This," Moore visits recently shut-down company sites, talking with the newly unemployed about their options for the future. Attempts to speak with corporate honchos result in amazing displays of double-talk and double-think — textbook examples of lies, damn lies and statistics. The CEO of Nike actually does meet with Moore, saying at one point that U.S. workers don't want shoe manufacturing jobs (no Nike footwear is manufactured in the U.S.); Moore shows him a tape of unemployed workers in Flint, Michigan, who seem more than eager to do the job. The CEO still delivers the company line, but with downcast eyes and an unsure voice. Moore handles the complex subject matter with an accessible, light touch and many humorous highlights, yet never loses focus. Remember: the word "shareholder" does not appear once in the U.S. Constitution. ★★★★ VHS: $19.99

The Big Parade

(1925, 126 min, US, King Vidor) *John Gilbert, Renee Adoree.* Vidor's stunning antiwar film is one of the classics of silent cinema. Containing realistic, remarkably staged battle sequences and moments of rare powerful dramatics, *The Big Parade* follows the enlistment of an American soldier (silent screen great Gilbert) who fights in France during WWI. Though made at the infancy of American filmmaking, Vidor has a superior command of the medium, creating scenes as achingly intimate and disturbing as they are brilliantly constructed. This epic may have influenced Stanley Kubrick's *Paths of Glory*. ★★★★ VHS: $29.99

The Big Picture

(1989, 99 min, US, Christopher Guest) *Kevin Bacon, Emily Longstreth, Martin Short, Michael McKean, Jennifer Jason Leigh.* Hollywood, and the movie industry in particular, take it on the chin in this biting and funny satire. Reminiscent of *S.O.B.* and *This Is Spinal Tap*, *The Big Picture* pokes some good-natured and wacky, on-target jabs at the Hollywood establishment in its story of a student filmmaker who tries to direct his first feature film. Bacon stars as the talented newcomer who "goes Hollywood." While a couple of jokes may be too "in" for some, most of this material is accessible to all. Short is a highly outrageous agent. ★★★ VHS: $19.99

The Big Red One

(1980, 113 min, US, Samuel Fuller) *Lee Marvin, Mark Hamill, David Carradine, Bobby DiCicco.* Marvin is the sergeant, the archetypal soldier, in

Fuller's *The Big Red One*, a war story from the foot soldiers' point of view. It opens at the end of WWI with the sergeant's creation of the First Infantry insignia: the big red one. The film jumps a quarter century to North Africa, and follows Marvin and his squad as they trek across a thousand miles fighting for their lives. Based on his own war experiences, the film was written and directed by Fuller, who is unequalled in revealing in intimate detail the individual's struggle against the panorama of monumental cataclysm. Deliberately paced, methodically structured and finely detailed — a quintessential war film, made with compassion but not sentiment, affection but not pathos. The film's closing sequences offer unassailable testimony that there are moments in history when the horrors of war must be borne in defiance of pure evil. And, at some time, the war is finally over. ★★★½ VHS: $9.99; DVD: $14.99

The Big Sleep

(1946, 114 min, US, Howard Hawks) *Humphrey Bogart, Lauren Bacall, John Ridgely, Dorothy Malone, Elisha Cook, Jr.* Bogart is Philip Marlowe, who's not very tall but tries to be. A classic film noir, slightly seedy and heavy on atmosphere. There's lots of tough guys and guys who would be tough, lots of fast women and loose talk, cigarette smoke you could cut with a knife, and guns, lots of guns. The plot, which has something to do with Bogey being hired to protect a young, wild heiress, is so convoluted that the guy who wrote the book (Raymond Chandler) didn't know who committed one of the murders. William Faulkner was one of the scriptwriters. Includes 20 minutes of footage not previously seen, including scenes from director Hawks' first cut. ★★★★ VHS: $19.99; DVD: $19.99

The Big Squeeze

(1996, 100 min, US, Marcus De Leon) *Lara Flynn Boyle, Peter Dobson, Danny Nucci, Luca Bercovici.* If Quentin Tarantino directed an "Afterschool Special," the result might be something like *The Big Squeeze*. It's an amiable, sunny noir (a contradiction that works) about an unhappy wife and a scam artist who team to sting her born-again husband out of $130,000. *The Big Squeeze* is refreshingly upbeat, so that even its double-crossing and infidelities seem good-natured. There's also an unexpected (though successful) religious miracle theme. Unfortunately, the character intros are irritatingly cutesy, and the film as a whole tends to be too sitcomish. But the appealing performances (especially Boyle and Nucci) and light pace certainly compensate. ★★½ VHS: $14.99; DVD: $24.99

The Big Steal

(1949, 71 min, US, Don Siegel) *Robert Mitchum, Jane Greer.* Siegel's third feature film is his only true film noir, an exciting and well-paced thriller of a heist gone wrong. Mitchum gives a sturdy, three-dimensional performance of a man trying to capture the real culprits of the crime of which he has been accused. The film has witty dialogue, lots of action and numerous unexpected plot twists. Watch for a great car-chase scene early on that would become the prototype for action films. ★★★★

The Big Store

(1941, 80 min, US, Charles Riesner) *The Marx Brothers, Margaret Dumont.* This Marx Brothers

romp isn't really of the same caliber of *Duck Soup* or *Horsefeathers*, but it does produce a few laughs. Detective Groucho goes undercover at Dumont's department store, and finds Chico and Harpo and crooks. ★★½ VHS: $19.99

The Big Tease

(2000, 86 min, US, Kevin Allen) *Craig Ferguson, Frances Fisher, Mary McCormack, David Rasche.* "Stranger in a strange land" mockumentary about a gay hairstylist (is there any other kind?) who proudly leaves "bonnie Scotland" to compete in the "Olympics of hairstyling" in L.A., only to find that he's been invited as a guest. What's a girl to do? Well, with funds running low and time running out, our hero (Ferguson) launches a plan to break into the competition by dropping the name "Sean Connery" all over Tinseltown. Never dull and often amusing, this bitchy swipe at the "beautiful people" is silly, good-hearted and totally lightweight. ★★½ VHS: $14.99; DVD: $19.99

Big Time

(1988, 87 min, US, Chris Blum) *Tom Waits.* This concert film, taken from a performance at L.A.'s Wiltern Theatre, allows us to get a taste of some of Waits' multiple personalities. The raspy-voiced singer goes from character to character while singing classic songs from "Frank's Wild Years," "Rain Dogs," and other early Waits albums. ★★★

Big Top Pee-wee

(1988, 90 min, US, Randal Kleiser) *Paul Reubens, Penelope Ann Miller, Kris Kristofferson, Valeria Golino, Susan Tyrell.* Pee-wee's heart takes flight when he meets the new trapeze artist whose circus is staying at his farm. Youngsters should like this second outing for Paul Reubens' alter ego almost as much as the first: it's got kids and animals and Danny Elfman's great score. ★★½ VHS: $14.99

Big Trouble

(1985, 93 min, US, John Cassavetes) *Peter Falk, Alan Arkin, Beverly D'Angelo.* Double Indemnity meets *Ruthless People* in this plot-twisted comedy about an underpaid insurance agent (Arkin) who falls in with a fickle femme fatale (D'Angelo) and her plot to kill her wealthy husband (Falk). Director Cassavetes shows little flair for the comedic moment, but zany situations and characterizations make this an enjoyable entry. ★★★ VHS: $19.99

Big Trouble in Little China

(1986, 99 min, US, John Carpenter) *Kurt Russell, Kim Cattrall, Dennis Dun, James Hong, Victor Wong.* Russell does his best John Wayne imitation in this amiable, light-hearted adventure spoof as a tough truck driver who (sort of) helps rescue his best friend's girlfriend. It seems she was kidnapped by a 2000-year-old magician who rules a secret underground society beneath San Francisco's Chinatown. Director Carpenter crams a lot of action into the 99-minute running time, and if some of the production is overblown, there are quite a few good sequences, which make it easy to like. ★★★ VHS: $9.99; DVD: $26.99

A Bigger Splash

(1974, 90 min, GB, David Hockney) *David Hockney, Peter Schlessinger.* Controversial British painter Hockney stars as himself in this penetrating, semi-fictitious portrait of his personal and artistic life. Centered around the actual breakup of Hockney and his lover/model, Schlessinger, this witty and revealing work meditates on the relationship of art to life. Vignettes of Hockney with friends, lovers and ex-lovers create an impressionistic study of the swirling influences in one artist's world. ★★★ VHS: $29.99

Bill & Ted's Bogus Journey

(1991, 98 min, US, Peter Hewitt) *Keanu Reeves, Alex Winter, William Sadler, George Carlin, Joss Ackland, Pam Grier.* That most excellent duo, Bill and Ted, are back in this bit of lunacy. With a nod to *The Terminator*, Bill and Ted are pursued by evil look-alike robots from the future who are out to kill them. The bad guys almost succeed, which causes the good guys to meet Death. In another filmic nod (this time to *The Seventh Seal*), Bill & Ted challenge Death to a game of...Twister! It's just as silly as the first film, and Reeves and Winter clearly are having fun, though some of the comic mileage is starting to wear thin. ★★½ VHS: $9.99

Bill & Ted's Excellent Adventure

(1989, 90 min, US, Stephen Herek) *Keanu Reeves, Alex Winter, George Carlin, Bernie Casey.* Feeling overwhelmed by the world today? Thank goodness there's still every American's inalienable right of — stupidity. Bill and Ted are a couple of airheads who just wanna have fun. But when they're in danger of being shipped off to military school for failing history, what do they do? They resort to the best special effects Industrial Light and Magic can drum up. Carlin, playing an equally mindless muck from the future, comes to the Valley with a time machine for our homeboys to experience history firsthand. ★★½

A Bill of Divorcement

(1932, 69 min, US, George Cukor) *Katharine Hepburn, John Barrymore, Billie Burke.* The film which both introduced the ravishing Hepburn and started her illustrious association with director Cukor. Barrymore gives a fine performance as a veteran who returns home after a long stay at a mental hospital, trying to establish a relationship with his daughter Kate. Burke superbly plays Barrymore's wife, whose plans of remarriage significantly alter her hopes of a happy homecoming. ★★★½ VHS: $14.99

Billy Bathgate

(1991, 106 min, US, Robert Benton) *Dustin Hoffman, Nicole Kidman, Loren Dean, Bruce Willis, Steven Hill, Steve Buscemi, Stanley Tucci.* A fast-paced and tense adaptation of E. L. Doctorow's novel, recounting the fall of mobster Dutch Schultz (Hoffman) as seen through the eyes of an ambitious teenager, Billy Bathgate (Dean). Though slightly miscast, Hoffman excels as the moody gangster. Nestor Almendros' eerie cinematography imbues the film with a grim and destructive mood. ★★★

Billy Budd

(1962, 112 min, GB, Peter Ustinov) *Terence Stamp, Robert Ryan, Peter Ustinov.* In 1797, under the Rights of War Act, an English warship, *Avenger*, conscripts a young, good-natured innocent (Stamp) from a merchant ship at sea. *Avenger*'s master at arms (Ryan) is particularly sadistic, even by the standards of the British

Navy at the time, whose officers had life-and-death control over their crews. Outstanding performances from the entire cast are supported by solid direction from Ustinov, who also produced and coscripted, as well as playing the ship's captain. A strong, straightforward story of morality and honor, based on the novella by Herman Melville. ★★★½

Billy Elliot

(2000, 111 min, GB, Stephen Daldry) *Jamie Bell, Julie Walters, Gary Lewis, Jamie Draven, Jean Heywood, Stuart Wells.* It's not often a child performance comes along that makes you want to cheer, but such is the case with young Bell, who is extraordinary as an eleven-year-old coal miner's son with aspirations of dance. The youngster's gallant portrayal is just one of the many pleasures to be found in a film knee-deep in them. Billy (Bell) lives with his coal mining family in Northern England. Instead of pursuing boxing lessons like all the other lads, Billy opts for ballet when he spies a class in session. Demonstrating a talent for the dance, Billy disregards his macho father's protestations and follows his heart, eventually vying for an opening at London's Royal Ballet School. From the producers of *The Full Monty*, the film shares in common a few elements from that hit comedy, including an economically depressed backdrop, a gallery of appealing characters, and an audience-pleasing quest of an underdog going against the odds. But the film stands well on its own, as not only a refreshing look at adolescence and the realization of one's dream, but a stirring musical entertainment as well. This is all brought to the fore by Bell's wondrous dancing, which is guaranteed to leave one breathless. In the end, *Billy Elliot* lifts the spirits in totally unexpected ways — not bad for a poor coal miner's son. ★★★★ VHS: $14.99; DVD: $24.99

Billy Jack

(1971, 114 min, US, T.C. Frank [Tom Laughlin]) *Tom Laughlin, Delores Taylor.* If *Rambo: First Blood Part II* was the socio-political sensation of the 1980s, then this pacifist action-adventure is the 1970s equivalent. Laughlin plays the title character, a Native American karate expert who is pushed too far by the authorities. He fights back and becomes a folk hero in the process. Immensely popular, though not in its original theatrical run, but later in 1974 in a major re-release. ★★½ VHS: $9.99; DVD: $14.99

Billy Liar

(1963, 96 min, GB, John Schlesinger) *Tom Courtenay, Julie Christie, Finlay Currie.* One of the benchmark films in the British "kitchen sink" school of filmmaking, Schlesinger's early effort is an outstanding examination of middle-class life. Courtenay is sparkling as a young day-dreamer who is stuck in the mundanity of his boorish life. In her film debut, Christie is a wonderful young mod woman who offers Courtenay an escape into a world of fantasy. (Letterboxed) ★★★½ VHS: $29.99; DVD: $39.99

Billy Madison

(1995, 89 min, US, Tamra Davis) *Adam Sandler, Darren McGavin, Chris Farley, Steve Buscemi.* Another idiotic film from a former "SNL" regular. Sandler, who was one of the lesser gifted comics on the show, plays a moronic heir to a $600 million throne. His dad (McGavin) isn't

Jamie Bell is *Billy Elliot*

sure whether to leave the business to his idiot son, so said idiot son goes back to school (grades 1–12) to prove he's not an idiot. What follows is a series of scatological and juvenile jokes and pranks that only Beavis and Butt-head would find funny ("Heh-heh. He said 'shit'"). It's unclear who this was intended for (pre-adolescents, teens, young adults), but save for one or two funny scenes (and a saving-grace cameo from Buscemi), *Billy Madison* is one big loser. ★ VHS: $14.99; DVD: $24.99

Billy's Hollywood Screen Kiss

(1998, 89 min, US, Tommy O'Haver) *Sean P. Hayes, Brad Rowe, Meredith Scott Lynn, Paul Bartel, Holly Woodlawn.* Cute, gay hip, smart and funny, this romantic comedy makes for enjoyable viewing. Narrated by Billy (Hayes of TV's "Will and Grace"), a handsome goateed photographer, the tale follows our hapless hero's quest for Mr. Right. Frustrated by a succession of hot but unfulfilling one-night stands, Billy thinks that he's found the man of his dreams in the person of local café waiter Gabriel (Rowe), an eerie Brad Pitt lookalike who may or may not be gay himself. Gaining support from his helpful best pal Georgina (Lynn), Billy tries mightily to win the heart of his dreamy object of affection. We follow Billy's often frantic attempts to figure out whether Gabriel might be interested in him romantically. The high point is a hilarious scene with the two men in bed together. A perfect gay date movie. ★★★ VHS: $14.99; DVD: $24.99

Biloxi Blues

(1988, 106 min, US, Mike Nichols) *Matthew Broderick, Christopher Walken, Corey Parker, Casey Siemaszko, Penelope Ann Miller.* The second in Neil Simon's acclaimed autobiographical trilogy (including *Brighton Beach Memoirs* and *Broadway Bound*). Broderick is the perfect reincarnation of young Simon, who here is sent to Biloxi, Mississippi, for ten weeks of boot camp. Simon's dialogue is refreshing and funny, and his work is seasoned with both poignancy and insight. Walken is at his best as the company's possibly unstable sergeant. ★★★½

The Bingo Long Traveling All-Stars & Motor Kings

(1976, 110 min, US, John Badham) *Billy Dee Williams, James Earl Jones, Richard Pryor, Stan*

Shaw. A winning screenplay, great period design, a glorious performance by Jones and terrific supporting turns by Pryor and Shaw all contribute to make this high-spirited baseball comedy one of the 1970s' most underrated and enjoyable films. Williams stars as the manager of a black barnstorming team in the late 1930s whose group of highly irregulars becomes the main attraction in the independent league circuit. ★★★½ VHS: $9.99

Bird

(1988, 162 min, US, Clint Eastwood) *Forest Whitaker, Diane Verona, Michael Zelniker, Keith David.* Though he had many credits as director to his name before this remarkable musical biography of jazz great Charlie Parker, Eastwood for the first time demonstrated a distinctive storytelling ability. In a most challenging role, Whitaker gives a sensitive though commanding performance as the jazz man who was considered to be the greatest saxophonist of his time. In a series of flashbacks (which sometimes border on the confusing), *Bird* recalls Parker's meteoric rise in the jazz world, his troublesome home life, and the drug addiction which ultimately led to his death at the early age of 34. Verona is excellent as Parker's wife. Featuring an outstanding musical soundtrack, *Bird* is most definitely a labor of love from Eastwood. ★★★½ VHS: $19.99; DVD: $19.99

Bird on a Wire

(1990, 110 min, US, John Badham) *Mel Gibson, Goldie Hawn, David Carradine, Bill Duke.* A farfetched chase film/love story. This is commercial high-concept filmmaking at its most cynical — the whole thing is a big cut-and-paste job. Mel plays an on-the-run witness protectee who teams for some not-very-exciting misadventures with ex-girlfriend Hawn. ★½ VHS: $9.99; DVD: $24.99

The Bird with the Crystal Plumage

(1970, 98 min, Italy, Dario Argento) *Tony Musante, Suzy Kendall.* Italian maestro of the macabre Argento's directorial debut, *Bird* is a stylish murder mystery with Musante as an American author who, after witnessing an attempted homicide, becomes obsessed with solving the case himself. A string of murders are linked to this latest crime, so Musante becomes a valuable asset to a major investigation. The killer soon targets Musante and the writer comes to find himself to be both hunter and hunted. This film has all the trademarks of later Argento films: the bizarre and violent setpiece murders; the red herrings; the unusual camera angles and setups; and the inquisitive outsider who holds the key to solving the mystery. One important difference, however, is Argento's use of an atmospheric Ennio Morricone score. An impressive beginning to a career which has gotten even better. ★★★ DVD: $24.99

The Birdcage

(1996, 100 min, US, Mike Nichols) *Robin Williams, Nathan Lane, Gene Hackman, Dianne Wiest, Hank Azaria, Christine Baranski, Dan Futterman.* An often very funny and successfully Americanized, upliftingly pro-gay remake of the French farce *La Cage aux Folles*. The setting is Miami Beach's hip South Beach where Armand Goldman (Williams) runs an extravagant drag revue called The Birdcage and his longtime lover Albert (Lane) is the star attraction, billed as

Starina. The two men live in an uninhibited, gloriously tacky apartment tended by Agador (Azaria), their Guatemalan houseboy (think Lucy on steroids). The story remains the same: Armand's son wants to bring his fiancée and her right-wing parents over to meet the family, forcing the men to put on a "family values" show for the unsuspecting future in-laws. Williams is subtly fey and delivers the film's best lines, and Lane steals the show as the theatrically swishy diva "mom" with an ear-piercing squeal. The comedy is meant to be "non-offensive" to all, as the most intimate the lovers get is holding hands. (VHS available letterboxed or pan & scan) ★★★ VHS: $14.99; DVD: $19.99

Birdman of Alcatraz

(1962, 143 min, US, John Frankenheimer) *Burt Lancaster, Karl Malden, Telly Savalas, Thelma Ritter.* Giving one of his most memorable performances, Lancaster assumes the real-life role of Robert "Robby" Stroud, a hard-as-nails, world-hating convict sentenced to life who becomes an authority on birds during his incarceration. Though mainly set in Stroud's prison cell, the film is devoid of claustrophobia and is compelling throughout. Deftly directed by Frankenheimer. ★★★½ VHS: $14.99; DVD: $19.99

The Birds

(1963, 120 min, US, Alfred Hitchcock) *Rod Taylor, Tippi Hedren, Jessica Tandy, Veronica Cartwright, Suzanne Pleshette.* After his great success with *Psycho*, Hitchcock further pushed the boundaries of suspense and his own cinematic techniques with this harrowing nature-gone-awry tale. Hedren made her film debut as a carefree socialite whose initiation of a practical joke leads her to the small coastal town of Bodega Bay. Taylor is the stoic object of her prank. But nature soon has a joke of its own when our fine-feathered friends begin attacking the townspeople with no apparent motive. Hitchcock takes his time in building the tension — which by film's end is overwhelming — with a series of spectacularly staged attacks (and all this without benefit of a musical score, which is so important in creating suspense). The birthday party, the classroom scene and the finale have all assumed legendary status in both the horror genre and the director's body of work. ★★★★ VHS: $14.99; DVD: $29.99

Birdy

(1984, 120 min, US, Alan Parker) *Matthew Modine, Nicolas Cage, John Harkins, Karen Young, Bruno Kirby.* Parker's adventurous adaptation of the William Wharton best-seller poses a young man's erotic avian obsession as a logical option in a bird-brained world. Filmed largely in Philadelphia, *Birdy* features Modine as the pigeon fancier who goes to seed after a wartime trauma; Cage is his buddy, trying desperately to help his friend. ★★★½ VHS: $14.99; DVD: $24.99

Birgitt Haas Must Be Killed

(1981, 105 min, France, Laurent Heynemann) *Philippe Noiret, Jean Rochefort, Lisa Kreuzer.* A former left-wing terrorist (Kreuzer) is targeted to be assassinated and it is an unscrupulous police officer (Noiret) who plots a romantic fling as bait to snare her. An engrossing and complex police thriller. ★★★

The Birth of a Nation

(1915, 190 min, US, D.W. Griffith) *Lillian Gish, Mae Marsh, Henry B. Walthall, Miriam Cooper.* Griffith was a Hollywood pioneer and his *Birth of a Nation* was Hollywood's first epic. Hailed for its groundbreaking technical advances and mounted on an unprecedented scale, this rousing saga of two families thrown into turmoil by the Civil War features an early performance by the legendary Gish. Although marred by undeniable racist sentiments (the Ku Klux Klan are depicted as the heroes!), it remains a landmark, a movie by which all others would be measured for many years. Assistant directors were Eric Von Stoheim, Jack Conway and Raoul Walsh. ★★★★ VHS: $39.99; DVD: $29.99

The Bishop's Wife

(1947, 109 min, US, Henry Koster) *Cary Grant, Loretta Young, David Niven, Monty Woolley, Gladys Cooper, Elsa Lanchester.* An enchanted comedy with an unusually reserved Grant as an angel and Niven as an overwhelmed bishop in need of some heavenly assistance. When raising money for a new church becomes too taxing for the young clergyman, emissary Grant is sent to Earth to help, but instead is caught in the middle of a romantic triangle when bishop's wife Young becomes enamored with the handsome spirit. (Remade in 1996 as *The Preacher's Wife*) ★★★½ VHS: $14.99; DVD: $19.99

Bite the Bullet

(1975, 131 min, US, Richard Brooks) *Gene Hackman, James Coburn, Candice Bergen, Ben Johnson, Jan-Michael Vincent, Ian Bannen.* A grand, epic-sized comic western with Hackman and Coburn in good form as contestants in a 600-mile horse race, set during the turn of the century. ★★★ VHS: $9.99

Bitter Moon

(1993, 135 min, GB/France, Roman Polanski) *Hugh Grant, Kristen Scott Thomas, Peter Coyote, Emmanuelle Seigner, Victor Banerjee, Stockard Channing.* This trashy but bizarrely entertaining psychosexual drama (comedy?) is about a humorously uptight British couple (Grant and Scott Thomas) who meet up with the wheelchair-bound American expatriate Oscar (Coyote) and his voluptuously sexy wife Mimi (Seigner) on a Mediterranean cruise. Much to his frustration, Grant's Nigel becomes transfixed with Oscar's near pornographic accounts of his and Mimi's tumultuous relationship — one that includes obsessive love, excessive sex, playful sadomasochism, water sports, betrayal, bitter hatred and sick revenge (it's a long cruise). The fun really begins when it's time for the obligatory sexual games and swapping. ★★ VHS: $19.99

Bitter Sugar

(1996, 104 min, Cuba, Leon Ichaso) *René Lavan, Mayte Vilán, Miguel Guitiérrez, Larry Villanueva. Bitter Sugar* is a provocative coming-of-age story that shows how young Communists, like Gustavo (Lavan), are wrongly placing their faith in socialist Cuba. Though he is smart and handsome, Gustavo is naïve — he thinks that Castro will take care of him. Gustavo's father (Guitiérrez) has learned this is not the case, and he is now trying to compensate for wasted years; his rebellious brother (Villanueva) has injected the AIDS virus into his bloodstream as a revolutionary act; and his girlfriend (Vilán) is developing relationships with foreigners in hopes of getting to Miami. As Gustavo slowly realizes that commitment to Castro may not be the answer, he becomes politicized to an extreme degree. Director Ichaso has made a compelling film that brilliantly captures the "no future" paradox facing young Cubans today. Filmed in luminous black and white, *Bitter Sugar* is filled with vibrant music as well as sexual tensions that mask the pain hidden just beneath the surface of these fragile lives. (Spanish with English subtitles) ★★★ VHS: $19.99; DVD: $29.99

The Bitter Tears of Petra Von Kant

(1972, 124 min, Germany, Rainer Werner Fassbinder) *Hanna Schygulla, Margit Carstensen.* A lurid and stylized account of the mangled web of domination, sadomasochism and jealousy among three lesbians. One of Fassbinder's most controversial (and entertaining) works, the film takes place in a single setting — fashion designer Petra's (Carstensen) opulently appointed apartment — amid the music of Verdi and The Platters. The story focuses on the increasingly destructive power games between the mistress of the house and the object of her passion, the model Karin (Schygulla). Petra's maid also becomes involved in the mental mind games, which are played out to the hilt. (German with English subtitles) ★★★

Bizarre, Bizarre

(1937, 109 min, France, Marcel Carné) *Michel Simon, Louis Jouvet, Francoise Rosay.* Carné and Prévert fashioned this exuberant farce/burlesque/mystery with an all-French staff playing a group of Victorian Englishmen, enmeshed in a web of disguises, lies, murder and romance. An acute, humorous examination of how the French thought of their channel-mates, the British. (French with English subtitles) ★★★ VHS: $29.99

Black & White

(1999, 97 min, US, Yuri Zeltser) *Gina Gershon, Rory Cochrane, Alison Eastwood, Ron Silver.* A cheap and sleazy little thriller about a cop who is a serial killer, *Black & White* benefits from Gershon's take-charge performance as Nora "Hugs" Hugosian, a sexy LAPD officer who is the prime suspect in a string of killings. When she is not breaking in her new partner, the devoted Catholic Chris O'Brien (Cochrane), on the beat and in the bedroom, Hugs may be taking justice into her own hands by shooting her perps in the eye. Although the story is far-fetched, and the number of suspects limited, there are a few red herrings to keep this otherwise routine policer interesting. Gershon is always a pleasure to watch, even if she spouts ludicrous dialogue and has little chemistry with the ineffectual Cochrane. Mildly diverting for B-movie fans only. ★★ VHS: $19.99; DVD: $27.99

Black and White

(2000, 99 min, US, James Toback) *Oli "Power" Grant, Robert Downey, Jr., Gaby Hoffmann, Allan Houston, Ben Stiller, Brooke Shields, Elijah Wood, Bijou Phillips, Claudia Schiffer, Mike Tyson, Scott Caan, Jared Leto, Method Man, Joe Pantoliano.* A difficult treatise on race relations in contemporary America, *Black and White* is the ambitious

but unremarkable tale of disparate New Yorkers coming together — not by choice but by happenstance. Beginning with a weird, interracial three-way in Central Park, the disjointed but often compelling story follows the bumpy road of Rich Bower (Grant), a black thug who tries to go straight and make a name for himself as a hip-hop impresario. Crossing his path are: a white husband-and-wife filmmaking team (Shields, Downey) who are making a documentary on white teens emulating ghetto culture; a couple of those kids; a white cop (Stiller) determined to nab the former hood, even at the cost of blackmailing Bower's best friend into betraying him; and Mike Tyson, playing himself in a bizarre but effective casting coup. Director Toback provides strong visuals to tell this mutiracial patchwork, but is let down by his own rambling screenplay which only occasionally rises above the melodramatic and sometimes clichéd situations. Among an uneven cast, Downey is baffling as an overbearing gay husband (who even gets slapped by Tyson!). ★★½ VHS: $19.99; DVD: $24.99

Black and White in Color

(1976, 90 min, Ivory Coast, Jean-Jacques Annaud) *Jean Carmet, Jacques Dufilho.* This powerful Academy Award Winner (Best Foreign Film) explores the horror and absurdity of war as French and German factions conflict in colonial West Africa before the first World War. (French with English subtitles) ★★★★ VHS: $39.99

Black Beauty

(1994, 87 min, GB, Caroline Thompson) *Sean Bean, David Thewlis, Peter Cook, Eleanor Bron, Andrew Knott.* While the equestrian acting is outstanding, the re-creation of 19th-century England is flawless and the story line is loyal to Anna Sewell's classic book, the trials and tribulations of Black Beauty will be a bit much for most small children. The retelling of what must be one of the first animal rights stories is moving and absorbing, and the horses are unbelievably human in their responses. Score by Danny Elfman. ★★★ VHS: $14.99; DVD: $14.99

The Black Bird

(1975, 98 min, US, David Giler) *George Segal, Stéphane Audran, Elisha Cook, Jr., Lee Patrick.* This spoof of *The Maltese Falcon* has Segal as Sam Spade, Jr. in search of the famous statue, once again. Though Cook and Patrick repeat their roles from John Huston's classic, this is minimally entertaining. ★★ VHS: $14.99

Black Cat

(1991, 92 min, Hong Kong, Stephen Shin) *Jade Leung, Simon Yam, Thomas Lam.* In this Hong Kong remake/ripoff of *La Femme Nikita*, Leung kills a man in self-defense, then mindlessly shoots a cop in the head. Instead of prison, she's trained to be a top-notch assassin, which doesn't sit well with her new love interest. Aside from one or two relatively exciting moments of violence, *Black Cat* is an appallingly bad, unpleasant experience. Leung is unappealing from the start, the plot makes no sense, and the movie is ugly and dull. The film is technically wretched as well: the action scenes are cartoonish and unconvincing, the American characters all speak with Australian accents, and the production values are cheap and tacky. Apparently an

influential film in HK (and followed by a much better — though mindless — sequel itself), *Black Cat* is otherwise best forgotten. (Cantonese with English subtitles) ★½ VHS: $19.99; DVD: $29.99

The Black Cat

(1934, 66 min, US, Edgar G. Ulmer) *Boris Karloff, Bela Lugosi, David Manners, Jacqueline Wells.* Karloff and Lugosi star as archenemies who use a young couple as pawns in a sinister game of chess in this atmospheric and striking suspense classic. Karloff plays a fascistic officer whose war crimes haunt Lugosi, a kindhearted doctor. One stormy night, Lugosi travels to Karloff's ultramodern home in the wilderness to have his final reckoning with the evil man. A road accident brings into the game a young engaged couple, who realize too late what is unfolding in their overnight home. Both actors are given ample opportunity to show off their talents at playing something other than monsters. With its heavily shadowed "nouveau" sets and its wonderful, emotional musical score, *The Black Cat* is one of the best Universal horror films of the 1930s. ★★★½ VHS: $14.99

Black Cat White Cat

(1998, 129 min, Serbia, Emir Kusturica) *Bajram Severdzan, Srdan Todorovic, Branka Katic.* Typically whimsical and absurdist fun from celebrated director Kusturica. A pathetic con man tries to survive in former Yugoslavia amidst an array of equally bizarre characters. Episodic and very loose, *Black Cat White Cat* is a perfect example of "carnivalesque" cinema: way over-the-top performances, goofy calliope-like music, and crazy coincidences that scream an "isn't-this-the-way-life-is?" outlook. Your appreciation of the film depends completely on your taste for this sort of filmmaking. Those who love all things "Fellinesque" will find much to like here. Either way, this apolitical follow-up to what is considered Kusturica's masterpiece (*Underground*) is still quite accomplished and original. (Serbo-Croatian and Romany with English subtitles) ★★★ VHS: $14.99

The Black Cauldron

(1985, 80 min, US, Ted Berman & Richard Rich) *Voices of: Grant Bardsley, Susan Sheridan, Freddie Jones, John Byner, John Hurt.* Darker and scarier than anything the Disney folks have done before or since, the film tells the tale of a young farmboy who dreams of adventure and glory through battle. He sets out to fight the evil Horned King, who's obsessed with finding the all-powerful black cauldron, which has the power to raise the army of the dead. (Yes, it sounds like *Legend*, and the similarities don't stop there.) Vocal contributions are good (especially Hurt as the Horned King), but the animation is rather clunky compared to today's fluid, computer-enhanced standards. There are no songs, but Elmer Bernstein's score is good, and a few cheery supporting characters do manage to add some levity. ★★½ DVD: $29.99

Black Christmas

(1975, 98 min, Canada, Bob Clark) *Margot Kidder, Kier Dullea, Olivia Hussey, John Saxon.* A truly mean-spirited holiday psycho/slasher flick with a sorority house setting, obscene phone calls and plastic dry-cleaning bags (Didn't anyone read the warning label? This is not a toy!). Director Clark would go on to direct *Porky's*. (aka: *Silent Night, Evil Night*) ★★

Brooke Shields is a filmmaker documenting hip-hop culture in *Black and White* (2000).

Black God & White Devil

(1964, 102 min, Brazil, Glauber Rocha) Set in arid northeast Brazil, Rocha's first major film deals with Manuel, a worker who, after killing his boss in self-defense, finds himself on the run from the law. Enlightened to the horrendous conditions of the peasants by the rich landowners, he becomes a bandit of honor, a self-styled black saint, preaching bloodshed and the return of the land to the people. A violent yet lyrical political drama that utilizes an intoxicating mixture of social realism, symbolism, myths and references to Brazilian history and culture. (Portuguese with English subtitles) ★★★½ VHS: $59.99

The Black Hole

(1979, 97 min, US, Gary Nelson) *Maximilian Schell, Anthony Perkins, Yvette Mimieux, Robert Forster, Ernest Borgnine.* Disney's nod to *Star Wars* is a cheesy sci-fi adventure about a space expedition which comes in conflict with a "mad" scientist about to explore a black hole. Nice special effects and a fine score by John Barry. (Letterboxed) ★★½ VHS: $14.99

Black Legion

(1936, 83 min, US, Archie Mayo) *Humphrey Bogart, Erin O'Brien, Dick Foran, Ann Sheridan.* One of Warner's better 1930s social dramas, with Bogey as a factory worker whose frustration on the job leads him to join a Ku Klux Klan-like group. ★★★ VHS: $14.99

Black Like Me

(1964, 107 min, US, Carl Lerner) *James Whitmore, Roscoe Lee Browne, Will Geer.* In the late 1950s, a white journalist took drugs which darkened his skin color enough to allow him to "pass" for black. Based on his book, this is an emotional, well-produced and empathic adaptation recounting his experiences with racial prejudice. Whitmore, who stars as the reporter, used the same drugs in preparation for the role. The story is not as dated as it should be. ★★★ VHS: $9.99

Black Lizard

(1968, 86 min, Japan, Kinji Fukasaku) *Akihiri Maruyama, Yukio Mishima.* Mix elements of *What's Up, Tiger Lily?* with *Beyond the Valley of the Dolls*, throw in lurid color schemes and weird camera angles by a seemingly drug-imbued cinematographer and you'll have some idea of the make-up of this wildly campy detective yarn. Japan's most famous female impersonator, Maruyama, stars as the villainous jewel thief, the Black Lizard — a fatally seductive temptress who'll stop at nothing to get her dainty hands on the fabulous Star of Egypt diamond. Yukio Mishima, who adapted the original novel for the stage, is featured in this entertaining curiosity as a naked human statue in the glamorous chanteuse's demented private museum. She's so evil! (Letterboxed) (Japanese with English subtitles) ★★★

Black Magic M-66

(1987, 49 min, Japan, Masamune Shirow) Cross *The Terminator* with *Blade Runner*, add a hint of comedy, and you have the basic plot for this superb anime from master *manga* artist Shirow (*Appleseed, Dominion Tank Police*). Based on a story from Shirow's comic book, this animated science-fiction thriller follows the exploits of Sybel, a video journalist investigating a failed military experiment involving android assassins. When she finds herself one step ahead of the government task force tracking down the rogue androids, Sybel goes from covering the story to becoming a player in the all-too-real drama. Shirow blends edge-of-your-seat action sequences, comedy, suspense and unforgettable characters, and the climactic confrontation with the remaining android on a rapidly collapsing skyscraper is a must-see for all anime fans. (Japanese with English subtitles) ★★★½ VHS: $34.99

Black Magic Woman

(1990, 91 min, US, Deryn Warren) *Mark Hamill, Amanda Wyss, Apollonia.* An unnecessary rehash of *Fatal Attraction*. Hamill and Wyss are business partners and lovers whose relationship takes a turn for the worse when voodoo vixen Apollonia enters the picture. A few good chills (and Santana's theme tune) can't elevate this above the made-for-cable level. ★½ VHS: $79.99

Black Mask

(1996, 89 min, Hong Kong, Daniel Lee) *Jet Li, Ching Wan Lau, Karen Mak.* Hong Kong superstar Li plays a soldier retooled by a mad scientist to have superhuman capabilities and feel no pain. When the government decides to terminate the project and all its results, Li escapes in a bravura action scene. He attempts to live a quiet life as a librarian, playing chess with a cop friend as excitement, but his past catches up with him, and mayhem ensues. This entertaining, inventive and gory actioner is harmed by Americanization: hokey dubbing and especially incongruous hip-hop music detract from the atmosphere and fun. Still, Li's charisma and amazing wirework (choreographed by *The Matrix*'s Woo-ping Yuen) make even this watered-down version more than worthwhile. ★★½ VHS: $9.99; DVD: $14.99

Black Moon Rising

(1986, 100 min, US, Harley Cokliss) *Tommy Lee Jones, Linda Hamilton, Robert Vaughn.* A government agent hides secret information in a high-powered auto. When the car is stolen, he must battle not only the gang that stole the auto, but the hoodlums who are out to get the info back. A vigorous, better-than-average action-adventure. ★★★ VHS: $9.99; DVD: $24.99

Black Narcissus

(1946, 99 min, GB, Michael Powell & Emeric Pressburger) *Deborah Kerr, Jean Simmons, David Farrar, Sabu, Flora Robson.* This visually sumptuous tale of a group of nuns who establish a mission in a remote Himalayan outpost was once considered one of the most breathtaking color films ever made. A dramatically charged saga of physical and emotional turmoil. ★★★★ VHS: $14.99; DVD: $39.99

The Black Orchid

(1959, 96 min, US, Martin Ritt) *Sophia Loren, Anthony Quinn.* The ever-glamorous Loren "dresses down" in this high-strung melodrama about a lonely businessman (Quinn) whose courtship of a gangster's widow meets with resistance from his mentally unbalanced daughter. A minor league film from a major league director. ★½ VHS: $14.99

Black Orpheus

(1958, 103 min, Brazil, Marcel Camus) *Breno Mello, Marpessa Dawn.* This extravagant explosion of colorful sights and sounds is a modern reenactment of Orpheus and Eurydice's tragic tale set against the splendid backdrop of Carnival in Rio. Virtually non-stop visual and musical excitement. Winner of the Academy Award for Best Foreign Film. Scored by Antonio Carlos Jobim. (Portuguese with English subtitles) ★★★★ VHS: $29.99; DVD: $29.99

Black Rain

(1989, 120 min, US, Ridley Scott) *Michael Douglas, Kate Capshaw, Andy Garcia, Ken Takakura.* Scott's overblown, relentlessly grim and humorless police thriller set in modern-day Tokyo is a routine action film under the guise of an examination of a Japanese and American culture clash in police techniques. Douglas stars as a tough, world-weary cop (is there any other kind?) who is assigned with partner Garcia to escort a New York-based hit man for the Japanese mob back to Japan. When the assassin escapes, Douglas tears apart the city of Tokyo looking for him, coming into conflict with the local police force and the mob. ★½ VHS: $9.99; DVD: $24.99

Black Rain

(1990, 124 min, Japan, Shohei Imamura) *Kazuo Kitamura, Yoshiko Matsuda.* August 6, 1945 — a date that has long been etched into the

Japanese psyche, for this is when the atomic bomb was dropped on Hiroshima. Having suppressed the consequences of this national tragedy, director Imamura has, in a grimly realistic, unrelenting fashion, exposed the national wounds by dealing with both the actual bombing of the city and its terrible aftereffects. In a determinedly non-sentimental and almost documentary approach, this haunting drama follows one family who was near Hiroshima at the time of the explosion. The family attempt to rebuild their shattered lives. But within five years, all grow terribly ill due to radiation. A stunningly photographed modern masterpiece. (Japanese with English subtitles) ★★★★ VHS: $19.99

Black Rainbow

(1991, 103 min, US, Dick Hodges) *Rosanna Arquette, Tom Hulce, Jason Robards.* Arquette stars as a carnival clairvoyant whose questionable abilities take a suddenly strange turn when she begins receiving psychic transmissions from people who aren't dead — yet. Robards costars as her cynical, alchoholic father, and Hulce plays a hounding reporter who's hot for her story. A well-crafted and engaging thriller. ★★★

Black Robe

(1991, 100 min, Canada, Bruce Beresford) *Lothaire Bluteau, Aden Young, Sandrine Holt, Tantoo Cardinal.* Beresford's impassioned examination of the cruelty and oppression intentionally and unintentionally imposed by the European settlers as they brought their "civilization" and Christian beliefs to the native peoples of the New World. While the story breaks little new ground, *Black Robe* is saved from familiarity by its strikingly beautiful Canadian landscapes and its absorbing and emotional drama of faith and the will to survive. Bluteau plays a 17th-century French Jesuit missionary whose religious zeal compels him to risk martyrdom in order to bring Catholicism to the Hurons of Canada. Along with a native chief, his daughter and a young French settler, he embarks on a harrowing journey up the St. Lawrence River — a symbolic canoe ride that begins in an explosively colorful autumn and ends during a torturously inhospitable winter. ★★★½ VHS: $14.99; DVD: $19.99

The Black Room

(1935, 67 min, US, Roy William Neill) *Boris Karloff, Marian Marsh.* Karloff has a field day in this Gothic tale of twin brothers (one good, one evil, both Karloff) whose destinies are overshadowed by a family curse. ★★½ VHS: $14.99

Black Sheep

(1996, 87 min, US, Penelope Spheeris) *Chris Farley, David Spade, Tim Matheson, Christine Ebersole, Gary Busey.* After the spirited hijinks of their funny *Tommy Boy*, Farley and Spade — the Laurel and Hardy for the '90s — regurgitate the same plot but with considerably less successful results. Once again, Farley is a screw-up who must be baby-sitted by sarcastic little twit Spade. Unfortunately, Farley is less likable, Spade is not so sarcastic, and most of their routines aren't that funny. The plot has to do with big brother Matheson running for governor; Farley is his younger sibling who's "Roger Clinton, Billy Carter and every Reagan family member rolled into one." If only he were that interesting. The only few laughs that do occur are courtesy of Farley and Spade's mugging. ★★ VHS: $14.99

Harrison Ford stalks renegade androids through the streets of a futuristic L.A. in *Blade Runner*

The Black Stallion

(1979, 118 min, US, Carroll Ballard) *Kelly Reno, Mickey Rooney, Teri Garr, Hoyt Axton.* A heartwarming tale of a young boy and his devoted stallion as they share both adventures on an isolated island and a quest for a racing championship. The cinematography is ravishing. (Sequel: *The Black Stallion Returns*) ★★★½ VHS: $14.99; DVD: $14.99

The Black Stallion Returns

(1983, 105 min, US, Robert Dalva) *Kelly Reno, Vincent Spano, Allen Goorwitz, Woody Strode, Ferdinand Mayne, Teri Garr.* Adequate sequel to the 1979 family favorite. Reno is back as Alec, who finds himself in the exotic Sahara in hot pursuit of his beloved horse Black, who's been kidnapped by his original owner — desert chieftain Abu Ben Ishak (Mayne). ★★½ VHS: $14.99

Black Sunday

(1960, 87 min, Italy, Mario Bava) *Barbara Steele, John Richardson, Andrea Checchi, Arturo Dominici, Ivo Garrani, Antonio Pierfederici.* This horror classic is Bava's masterpiece. Steele stars as a condemned witch who rises from the dead to seek vengeance on the descendents of those who executed her. This Gothic tale is full of atmosphere and chilling black-and-white cinematography. As with most Italian horror films, the plot is weak and sometimes silly, but the visuals are lush and creepy. A must-see for Argento fans and classic horror buffs. ★★★½ VHS: $29.99; DVD: $24.99

Black Sunday

(1977, 143 min, US, John Frankenheimer) *Bruce Dern, Robert Shaw, Marthe Keller, Fritz Weaver, William Daniels.* From the director of *The Manchurian Candidate* comes this gripping adaptation of the Thomas Harris best-seller about a terrorist plot to blow up the Super Bowl, with a little bit of help from a demented ex-POW (Dern at his maniacal best). Shaw is the government expert on the case. ★★★ VHS: $14.99

Black Tights

(1960, 131 min, France, Terence Young) *Cyd Charisse, Moira Shearer, Zizi Jeanmaire, Roland Petit; Narrated and hosted by: Maurice Chevalier.* Exquisite ballet film featuring four classic ballet performances. (Letterboxed) ★★★ VHS: $24.99; DVD: $29.99

Black Water

(1992, 105 min, US, Nicolas Gessner) *Julian Sands, Stacey Dash, Ned Beatty, Rod Steiger.* Sands is an uptight British tax attorney and Dash is the street urchin/femme fatale he plucks off the highway in this unimaginative thriller set in the Tennessee hills. After witnessing what he thinks is a murder, Sands finds he is being tailed on his way to an innocent fishing trip. Dash offers him help, but is she playing both sides of the fence? Who knows, and more importantly, who cares? ★ VHS: $79.99

Black Widow

(1987, 101 min, US, Bob Rafelson) *Debra Winger, Theresa Russell, Sami Frey, Nicol Williamson, Dennis Hopper.* Winger and Russell square off in this spine-tingling suspense story. Russell is a jet-setting sophisticate whose husbands have a habit of dying shortly after their wedding day. Winger is the FBI agent who catches on to Russell's shenanigans and sets out to uncover her deadly scheme. Instead, the two become locked in a heated tête-à-tête (or more appropriately *coeur-a-coeur*) which sizzles with underlying sexual tension. ★★★ VHS: $9.99

Blackbeard's Ghost

(1968, 107 min, US, Robert Stevenson) *Peter Ustinov, Dean Jones, Suzanne Pleshette, Elsa Lanchester.* Fluffy Disney comedy with Ustinov as the ghost of the infamous pirate Blackbeard who helps a family fight off the bad guys. ★★½

Blackboard Jungle

(1955, 101 min, US, Richard Brooks) *Sidney Poitier, Glenn Ford, Vic Morrow, Richard Kiley, Anne Francis, Paul Mazursky.* Ford stars in this harrowing adaptation of Evan Hunter's novel about a New York teacher who is schooled in the ways of the streets by his students. In comparison to the Uzi-toting, crack-addicted youth of today's Hollywood high schools, these mid-'50s punks seem relatively harmless. But the drama here is tense and excellent performances are registered by Poitier and Morrow. ★★★½ VHS: $19.99

Blackjack

(1998, 123 min, US, John Woo) *Dolph Lundgren, Kate Vernon, Phillip MacKenzie, Fred Williamson, Saul Rubinek.* Extremely disappointing bit of nonsense from usually dynamic action maestro Woo will bore even the director's most ardent fans. Lundgren plays Jack, an ex-CIA operative who is asked by an old friend to act as a bodyguard for his vulnerable young daughter. When the girl's parents die under mysterious circumstances, she is left in the care of "Uncle" Jack. An investigation — and expected retribution — never occurs, as this plot is immediately dropped and Jack is hired by a beautiful model being stalked by a nutjob. This snooze-inducing *Bodyguard* redux is punctuated by an even sillier subplot involving Dolph's fear of the color white, due to a childhood trauma. Huh? ★½ VHS: $9.99; DVD: $29.99

Blackmail

(1929, 78 min, GB, Alfred Hitchcock) *Anny Ondra, John Longden, Sara Allgood, Cyril Ritchard.* In his first talkie (which initially started as a silent), Hitchcock demonstrates some of the cunning cinematic trickery which he would later define and master. Starting unusually slow for a Hitchcock film, the story picks up considerable speed once the plot is in motion. It has to do with a flirtatious shopgirl who murders her attempted rapist and is blackmailed by a sleazy eyewitness. Though awkwardly paced, the film nevertheless maintains suspense throughout, and contains several scenes which could only be described as pure Hitchcock. This includes a terrific sequence in which the girl only hears snippets of conversation: the word "knife" over and over. ★★★ VHS: $12.99; DVD: $19.99

Blade

(1998, 120 min, US, Stephen Norrington) *Wesley Snipes, Stephen Dorff, Kris Kristofferson, N'Bushe Wright, Udo Kier.* A terrific, energetic action/horror film with Snipes as a vampire hunter who, with the help of mentor Kristofferson and doctor Wright, plans to destroy upstart punk bloodsucker Dorff's mission to turn the Earth into one big vampire dinner. This hugely entertaining adaptation of the comic book captures the look and feel of a top-drawer graphic novel, thanks to a punchy script by David S. Goyer and imaginative, super-stylish direction by Norrington. *Blade* neatly avoids the jokey tone of most action/horror/sci-fi films, and while there is humor, it's never at the expense of the story or characters. Opening with a great, gory battle in a nightclub and

The Blair Witch Project

never letting up, *Blade* duplicates the hyperkinetic excitement of Hong Kong "heroic bloodshed" films, and despite an unnecessary plot entanglement towards the end and a slight overlength, *Blade* is one of the best escapist films in a long time. (VHS available letterboxed or pan & scan) ★★★½ VHS: $14.99; DVD: $24.99

Blade Runner

(1982, 114 min, US, Ridley Scott) *Harrison Ford, Rutger Hauer, Sean Young, Edward James Olmos, William Sanderson.* Ford stars in this jagged, futuristic thriller as an authorized exterminator of androids gone awry. Hauer and Hannah are renegade robots whose physical prowess forces Ford out of the role of hunter and into the role of hunted. Scott's space-age L.A. is a smoky, neon-drenched landscape seething with danger and decay. A stunning film adaptation of Philip K. Dick's "Do Androids Dream of Electric Sheep?" (Director's cut) (Letterboxed) ★★★★ VHS: $14.99; DVD: $24.99

The Blair Witch Project

(1999, 89 min, US, Daniel Myrick & Eduardo Sánchez) *Heather Donahue, Michael C. Williams, Joshua Leonard.* Building a legend on top of a legend, *The Blair Witch Project* purports to be footage that three student filmmakers shot while researching the myth in the cursed woods. Needless to say, the three were never found, and this film linearly pieces together their footage (video and 16mm) as a documentary. The trip starts bouncily enough, but as they become lost, the film builds a gradual suspense, thanks to the audience being placed in the very same situation as the "actors." Donahue's breakdown is particularly compelling (and almost unbearable). Stylistically it's so realistic (no music, no voice-over, no omniscient footage) that the cynical camcorder generation can finally suspend disbelief at a horror movie. However, those expecting the shocks and jumps (and accompanying catharsis) of a *Halloween* or *Scream* will be disappointed. Accept this film as it is: a "documentary" that's a totally original experiment in terror. (Sequel: *Book of Shadows: Blair Witch 2*) ★★★½ VHS: $9.99; DVD: $24.99

Blame It on Rio

(1984, 100 min, US, Stanley Donen) *Michael Caine, Joseph Bologna, Valerie Harper, Demi Moore.* This Americanized version of the French sex farce *One Wild Moment* is a surprisingly entertaining, albeit TV sitcomish, comedy about the sexual philandering among a group of friends and their ensuing bed-hopping, all under the seductive rays of Rio de Janeiro. Caine is the befuddled husband who becomes the object of desire of the nymphette daughter of his best friend, Bologna. ★★½ VHS: $9.99; DVD: $14.99

Blame It on the Bellboy

(1992, 78 min, GB, Mark Herman) *Dudley Moore, Bryan Brown, Bronson Pinchot, Richard Griffiths, Patsy Kensit, Alison Steadman, Lindsay Anderson.* A bumbling bellboy mixes the schedules of three travelers and serves up a comedy of errors. Moore, Brown and Griffiths are three visitors to Venice, and they are all staying at the same hotel. It is there that bellboy Pinchot sends each man on one of the other's business. This includes assassinating a crime boss, buying a

villa, and escaping for a "pleasure" weekend. Though this comedy never hits the inspired heights of another 1992 farce, *Noises Off*, there are a few (if silly) laughs awaiting the patient viewer. ★★

Blank Check

(1994, 90 min, US, Rupert Wainwright) *Brian Bonsall, Miguel Ferrer.* This *Home Alone* clone from Disney tries to do the Macaulay Culkin hit one better: What if he's home alone — but he has a million dollars at his disposal? Such is the case when misunderstood Preston (Bonsall) has his bike run over and is given a blank check by the bad guy (Ferrer) who did it. Preston buys a neat home down the street and lives every kid's ultimate fantasy life — until the bad guy and his associates come looking for him. Processed junk food. ★★

Blankman

(1994, 96 min, US, Mike Binder) *Damon Wayans, David Alan Grier, Jason Alexander, Robin Givens.* A charming comic satire featuring "In Living Color"'s Wayans and Grier as a pair of vigilantes. With more than a few nods to the 1960s TV series "Batman," this mindlessly entertaining film follows the pair's wild adventures fighting evil while clad in bulletproof underwear and Grandma's housecoat. Spiced with crazy comic book action and fun supporting performances, this outrageous laff-fest is sure to please those who like their comedy with a superhuman dose of satire. ★★★ VHS: $9.99

Blast 'Em

(1992, 103 min, US, Joseph Blasioli) This is a highly entertaining documentary about the competition among the paparazzi which focuses on acid-tongued imp Victor Malafronte, who pursues his celebrity prey with the precision of a trained assassin. Follow Malafronte and other photographers' exploits, including the pathetic Twinkie-addicted Queerdonna, as they stalk several stars, such as Robert De Niro, Sigourney Weaver, Michael J. Fox, John F. Kennedy, Jr. and a very funny and revealing Sally Kirkland. A must-see for stargazers everywhere. ★★★ VHS: $19.99

Blast from the Past

(1999, 106 min, US, Hugh Wilson) *Brendan Fraser, Alicia Silverstone, Sissy Spacek, Christopher Walken, Dave Foley, Joey Slotnik.* Having found success in playing fishes-out-of-water in *Encino Man* (caveman) and *George of the Jungle* (ape-man), Fraser uses his considerable comic skills to bring to life another, very appealing character: '60s-man. In this charming, funny romantic comedy, Fraser plays Adam, whose scientist father (Walken) rushes his family to the fallout shelter in 1962 when the Cuban Missile Crisis looks to escalate. Thinking the bomb has hit, they stay underground for 35 years. It's up to Adam to surface and reconnaissance food and supplies (and avoid the mutants!). He then meets Eve (Silverstone), and it's love at first sight. It's all very sweet-natured, thanks in part to Spacek and Walken's expert playing of Adam's parents, but mostly to Fraser's wide-eyed innocent. The laughs are genuine, and there's a killer dance sequence (is there anything this guy can't do?). Silverstone is appealing, though outshined by Fraser, who's slowly becoming the millennium's Cary Grant. There, we said it. ★★★ VHS: $14.99; DVD: $19.99

Blaze

(1989, 108 min, US, Ron Shelton) *Paul Newman, Lolita Davidovich, Robert Wuhl.* Shelton, who wrote and directed the terrific *Bull Durham*, is in very good form with this sexy and funny story based on Blaze Starr's autobiographical novel about the famous stripper's "scandalous" affair with Louisiana Governor Earl Long. The film tells the entertaining story of how country girl Blaze moved to the big city (New Orleans) and became mistress to the powerful "Guv'nor" Long. Shelton has a keen ear for romantic repartee, and *Blaze* is at its best in these scenes between Long and Starr. Newman gives a full-blooded, larger-than-life characterization as Long, and Davidovich is well-cast physically but lacks the spark to set her rising Starr apart from other film ecdysiasts. ★★★

Blazing Saddles

(1974, 93 min, US, Mel Brooks) *Gene Wilder, Cleavon Little, Madeline Kahn, Harvey Korman, John Hillerman, Dom DeLuise.* Brooks' uproarious comedy did wonders for making racism, sexism and bodily functions laughing matters. Richard Pryor helped script this scathing spoof of the Wild West. Kahn steals the show with her on-target Marlene Dietrich impersonation. ★★★½ VHS: $14.99; DVD: $19.99

Bleak House

(1987, 391 min, GB, Ross Devenish) *Diana Rigg, Denholm Elliott.* Charles Dickens' scathing look at the Byzantine judicial process of 19th-century England is brought to the small screen with the usual aplomb associated with BBC television. Rigg and Elliott deliver fine performances in this classic tale which follows the plight of the Jarndyce family, whose legal problems have been dragged through the courts for generations and devastated the lives of many. ★★★★ VHS: $39.99

Bleak Moments

(1971, 110 min, GB, Mike Leigh) *Anne Raitt, Eric Allen, Sarah Stephenson, Mike Bradwell.* While this early Leigh film suffers from a small budget and reduced production values, it still evidences the director's uncanny ability to sketch indelible portraits with minimal brush strokes and often with no exposition. Sylvia (Raitt) copes with caring for her mentally challenged sister (Stephenson) and a mind-numbing job as secretary in a barren urban environment. Her relationship with a schoolteacher (Allen) is devoid of any true communication — they share stilted conversation but no connection. The appearance of a guitar-playing lodger in the garage offers a short-lived flash of spontaneity in the sisters' treadmill lives. The characters drift somnambulistically in shared isolation, shared oppression, shared repression. ★★½ VHS: $29.99

Bless the Child

(2000, 107 min, US, Chuck Russell) *Kim Basinger, Holliston Coleman, Jimmy Smits, Rufus Sewell, Christina Ricci, Ian Holm.* Bless the Child is an inferior occult thriller that borrows a little from *Rosemary's Baby*, *The Omen* and a host of other scare-'em-ups, but fails to make a mark of its own as either original or scary. Basinger plays a nurse who raises her drug-addicted sister's daughter. Soon the aunt and child (who seems to possess heavenly powers) are the target of a satanic sect, who are out to harvest the girl's power. Basinger and cast sleepwalk through this silly film, whose few good scenes are offset by slow pacing and loopy plot developments. ★½ VHS: $14.99; DVD: $29.99

Blessed Event

(1932, 78 min, US, Roy Del Ruth) *Lee Tracy, Mary Brian, Dick Powell.* Tracy stars as Alvin Roberts, a very ambitious Broadway gossip columnist who makes a name for himself through his scandal-mongering. Unfortunately, he makes a lot of enemies along the way. Fast-paced dialogue highlights this Depression-era film dealing with moral and ethical dilemmas. ★★½ VHS: $19.99

Blind Date

(1987, 93 min, US, Blake Edwards) *Bruce Willis, Kim Basinger, John Larroquette, William Daniels.* Though not top-notch Edwards, there are enough laughs to keep one mildly entertained. Willis is the exec who desperately needs a date for a business dinner; Basinger is the answer to his prayers — or is she? It seems that once she drinks, she's uncontrollably manic, sort of like this comedy. ★★½ VHS: $9.99

Blind Faith

(1998, 121 min, US, Ernest Dickerson) *Charles S. Dutton, Courtney B. Vance, Lonette McKee, Kadeem Hardison, Garland Whitt.* Director Dickerson delivers a shockingly powerful piece of storytelling — hammering at themes of racism, social justice and homophobia — in this intense drama about a black teenager accused of murdering a white teen in 1950s Brooklyn. Charles, Jr. (Whitt) is a seemingly happy recent high school graduate and obedient son to the stern but upstanding Charles, Sr. (Dutton), a black policeman. One evening he is accused of killing a white youth in a park. The case initially looks open-and-shut, for there are witnesses to the crime and even the youth admits to the crime. But his uncle John (Vance in a startling performance), a determined and fiery small-time lawyer, takes on the seemingly hopeless case. The acting is first rate, the story complex, and the outcome shattering. ★★★½ VHS: $9.99

Blind Fury

(1990, 85 min, US, Phillip Noyce) *Rutger Hauer, Terry O'Quinn, Lisa Blount, Meg Foster.* Noyce has liberally culled ideas from the "Zatoichi" Japanese swordsman film series and added fine comic action-adventure footage. The incomparable Hauer stars as a Vietnam vet who, after being blinded in the jungle, is befriended by local villagers and taught the sacred art of swinging the sword. Back in the U.S., our blind, blond samurai hero battles the bad guys at every turn. With its tongue-in-cheek humor, fast-paced fight sequences and the mesmerizing screen presence of Hauer, this is a film any action fan should not miss. ★★★ VHS: $14.99; DVD: $24.99

Blind Side

(1992, 90 min, US, Geoff Murphy) *Rutger Hauer, Rebecca DeMornay, Ron Silver.* DeMornay and Silver star as a couple on a business trip to Mexico who accidentally kill a policeman and then are tormented upon their return home by a menacing Hauer. This film may sound good on paper, but it doesn't play well on the screen. DeMornay and Silver consistently overact, though Hauer does provides comic relief. If you have a couple of friends who enjoy laughing at bad movies, this is the one to watch. ★ VHS: $9.99; DVD: $14.99

Blind Trust (Pouvoir Intime)

(1987, 86 min, Canada, Yves Simoneau) This riveting suspense thriller chronicles the planning, execution and bloody aftermath of a failed armed robbery attempt in Montreal. Successfully balancing its sympathy for both the criminals as well as a guard held captive in the armored truck, this taut crime caper should keep the viewer enthralled throughout. (French with English subtitles) ★★★½

Blink

(1994, 106 min, US, Michael Apted) *Madeleine Stowe, Aidan Quinn, Laurie Metcalf, James Remar.* Stowe gives a splendid performance as a gutsy but vulnerable folk musician, blind since childhood, who regains her vision just in time to witness a murderer fleeing the scene of the crime. Quinn is the hard-boiled detective who, not blind to her considerable charms, sets out to find the killer before he finds her. What might have been just another *Wait Until Dark* rip-off is redeemed through its excellent use of visual effects and an attention to detail and character usually missing in the thriller genre. Granted, the mystery's resolution is a little slapdash with its "watch me pull a killer out of my hat" routine, but nevertheless *Blink* is a refreshingly eye-opening chiller. ★★★ VHS: $9.99

Bliss

(1985, 112 min, Australia, Ray Lawrence) *Barry Otto, Lynette Curran.* This outrageous and daring film stars Otto as Harry Joy, a wistful Sydney advertising man whose near-fatal (or was it fatal?) heart attack launches him into a surrealistic, mind-expanding and satirical adventure. A nightmarish examination of life, death, and the eternal search for happiness. ★★★½

Bliss

(1997, 103 min, US, Lance Young) *Craig Sheffer, Sheryl Lee, Terence Stamp, Casey Siemaszko, Spalding Gray.* This sexually honest tale of love and commitment stars Lee as an obsessive/compulsive housewife whose confession to husband Sheffer that she's never had an orgasm (with him) leads to much soul-searching and psychoanalysis — until he finds that she's sleeping with a sex therapist (Stamp). Sheffer enlists the therapist's aid in becoming a better lover, thus beginning a journey of sexual discovery that could heal them both. What would, in lesser hands, be yet another seamy, steamy B video release is elevated to the level of a well-mounted drama thanks to the sincerity of the cast and Young's sensitive direction. ★★★ VHS: $19.99

The Bliss of Mrs. Blossom

(1968, 93 min, GB, Joe McGrath) *Shirley MacLaine, Richard Attenborough, John Cleese, Barry Humphries.* Here's a fun-filled piece of '60s oddball British kitsch. MacLaine stars as the wife of a brassiere manufacturer (Attenborough) who keeps a man in her attic for five years! While perhaps not on the level of other British comedies of the era (*The Magic Christian*, *Bedazzled*), it's still an interesting period piece with a lot of funny moments. ★★★ VHS: $14.99

Blithe Spirit

(1945, 96 min, GB, David Lean) *Rex Harrison, Constance Cummings, Kay Hammond, Margaret Rutherford.* Noël Coward's enchanting classic stage production makes for an equally captivating film comedy, adapted for the screen by Coward himself. Harrison is wonderful as a cynical author whose life turns upside-down when the ghost of his deceased first wife materializes when he remarries. Hammond is a delight as the returning spectre, and Cummings is splendid as the second wife. But it's the hilarious and spirited performance of Rutherford as the medium Madame Arcati which is most memorable. ★★★½ DVD: $24.99

The Blob

(1958, 80 min, US, Irvin S. Yeaworth) *Steve McQueen, Aneta Corsaut.* This '50s sci-fi minor classic is a camp favorite. A very young McQueen stars as a teenager who tries to warn everyone in his small town that an intergalactic goo is on a path of destruction. Foolish adults — they never listen! (Remade in 1988) ★★½ DVD: $39.99

The Blob

(1988, 92 min, US, Chuck Russell) *Kevin Dillon, Shawnee Smith, Donovan Leitch.* Entertaining and imaginative remake of the Steve McQueen cult classic — owing more to John Carpenter's *The Thing* than to the '50s original. A gelatinous goo falls from the sky to wreak havoc on an unsuspecting small town, gobbling all in its path. Dillon and Smith are two teenagers out to stop the plasmic menace. ★★★ VHS: $14.99

Blonde Venus

(1932, 97 min, US, Josef von Sternberg) *Marlene Dietrich, Herbert Marshall, Cary Grant, Dickie Moore.* The ever-radiant Dietrich is nothing less than stunning as a woman who leaves her husband when she becomes convinced that she is no good for him. The true highlight of the film comes when Dietrich sings "Hot Voodoo" in a gorilla suit. ★★★ VHS: $14.99

Blood & Concrete

(1990, 97 min, US, Jeffrey Reiner) *Billy Zane, Jennifer Beals, Darren McGavin, Harry Shearer.* Zane delivers a delicious performance in this contemporary film noir about a larcenously hip and dissolute Everyman. When he literally stumbles over a suicidal Beals, he finds himself drawn into a convoluted maze of conflicted loyalties amid an amazing assortment of L.A. lowlifes. Deftly directed by Reiner, who cowrote the nifty script with producer Richard LaBrie, the film pays homage to its roots with acknowledgements to Samuel Fuller, John Boorman, Richard Widmark and Lee Marvin in the closing credits. ★★★ VHS: $19.99

Blood and Roses

(1961, 74 min, Italy, Roger Vadim) *Mel Ferrer, Elsa Martinelli, Annette Vadim.* Annette Vadim stars as the sexy Carmilla in this lush and provocative vampire tale. Seduced by her lesbian vampire ancestor who takes over her body, the lusty Carmilla first jumps a young maid and then her beautiful cousin. Although the cousin is engaged to be married, the women make eyes at each other throughout the film (in that Euro-soft-porn sort of way), and director Vadim plays up every lesbionic inch of it. Based on Sheridan

le Fanu's "Carmilla" and later remade as *The Vampire Lovers.* ★★½ VHS: $9.99

Blood and Sand

(1922, 80 min, US, Fred Niblo) *Rudolph Valentino, Nita Naldi.* Matador Valentino can't decide between the good girl or the vamp, so he takes it out on the bull. While the acting style in this hyperbolic classic is humorously bug-eyed and stilted when viewed today, this proved to be one of Valentino's most popular films. ★★★ VHS: $24.99

Blood and Sand

(1941, 123 min, US, Rouben Mamoulian) *Tyrone Power, Linda Darnell, Rita Hayworth, Nazimova, Anthony Quinn.* A gorgeous-looking and exciting remake of the Rudolph Valentino 1922 silent classic. Power plays a naïve bullfighter who gets led astray by the sultry Hayworth. Darnell is the woman who loves him from afar. ★★★ VHS: $19.99

Blood & Wine

(1997, 101 min, US, Bob Rafelson) *Jack Nicholson, Michael Caine, Stephen Dorff, Judy Davis, Jennifer Lopez, Harold Perrineau, Jr.* Treacherous waters run deep in this moody thriller. Though not completely successful in its storytelling, *Blood & Wine* moves at a fast clip, and its characters are always up to something — part of its noir appeal is figuring out what. Nicholson is a Miami wine merchant whose position with the city's wealthier clientele gives him access to their property — which helps when he and slimy associate Caine decide to empty their safes. When Nicholson's wife Davis decides to leave her husband and unknowingly walks off with a stolen necklace, she and son Dorff become targets of the maniacal Caine with Nicholson stuck in the middle. Rafelson gives the film a good look, but there's also nothing new to the genre here, and Dorff's romantic involvement and devotion to his stepfather's mistress (Lopez) is flimsy at best. ★★½ VHS: $14.99

Blood Feast

(1963, 70 min, US, Hershell Gordon Lewis) *Tom Wood, Connie Mason.* The first of the "Sue" films from the "master of splatter" Lewis. *Blood Feast* is the gruesome tale of Fuad Ramses, Egyptian caterer and limping psychopath. With notably bad performances. Music, photography and gore-F/X (filmed in "Blood Color") by HGL. ★ VHS: $19.99; DVD: $24.99

Blood Feud

(1979, 112 min, Italy, Lina Wertmüller) *Sophia Loren, Marcello Mastroianni, Giancarlo Giannini.* A pleasant, although not exceptional, sex comedy about a Sicilian widow in the 1920s (Loren) who receives the lustful advances of both a lawyer (Mastroianni) and a shady gangster (Giannini). Not on the same artistic level as *Swept Away* or *Seven Beauties*, it is still an enjoyable little movie filled with many of the Wertmüller touches. ★★½

Blood for Dracula

See: Andy Warhol's Dracula

Blood Guts Bullets & Octane

(1999, 87 min, US, Joe Carnahan) *Dan Leis, Ken Rudulph, Dan Harlan, Hugh McChord, Michael Saumure.* An ultra low-budget independent

crime drama, this is fairly negligible but at least sustains a degree of interest. Two down-on-their-luck used car lot owners have a get-rich-quick scheme fall onto their laps: if they keep a vintage car (with mysterious contents in the trunk) on their lot for two days, they get $250,000. Things go predictably awry. Way too derivative of Tarantino, Stone and even Mamet, the film begins like a *Pulp Fiction* student-film homage. Once the story is in motion, it becomes more interesting, with enough violence, twists and occasional smart dialogue. However, the acting is uneven, and the filmmaking style mixing film stocks and black and white and color seems to be more of a smoke screen to hide the low budget than an artistic expression. Not bad, though, for warmed-up, three-week-old leftovers. ★★ VHS: $19.99; DVD: $24.99

Blood In, Blood Out

(1993, 180 min, US, Taylor Hackford) *Damian Chapa, Jesse Borrego, Benjamin Bratt, Enrique Castillo, Victor Rivers, Delroy Lindo, Billy Bob Thornton, Ving Rhames.* An epic (at least in the realm of time) drama about the lives of three friends born and raised on the mean *calles* of East L.A. One becomes a successful artist only to succumb to drugs; another goes from a teen thug to respected cop; and the third — a blond, blue-eyed Anglo-Chicano (Chapa) — becomes a macho-posturing gang member who enters into a life of crime. There's plenty of prison action, gun-shooting and tired attempts at making the characters come alive. Watchable yes; absorbing, no. (aka: *Bound by Honor*) ★★ VHS: $9.99; DVD: $29.99

Blood in the Face

(1991, 78 min, US, Anne Bohlen, Kevin Rafferty & James Ridgeway) Directors Bohlen, Rafferty and Ridgeway, with Michael Moore, interview participants at a Nazi rally in Michigan. We enter a world where "Ronald Reagan works for the Jews," the Holocaust is a hoax and only whites have a conscience because they can blush (show blood in the face). Interspersed is footage of George Lincoln Rockwell likening Hitler to the second coming of Christ and (pre-plastic surgery) David Duke in Klan garb and Nazi uniform. It's tempting to chuckle as if this were a right-wing *Reefer Madness*, but pay attention to the soft-spoken housewife. When you find out who her husband is, you won't be laughing. ★★★ VHS: $19.99

Blood of a Poet

(1930, 58 min, France, Jean Cocteau) Considered one of the most influential avant-garde films of all time, *Blood of a Poet* explores the plight of the artist and the forces of creative thought. Constructed as a collage of dreamlike situations, autobiographical revelations and enigmatic images, the film is an odyssey into the poet's imagination. Freud described the film as being "like looking through a keyhole at a man undressing." (French with English subtitles) ★★★★ VHS: $29.99; DVD: $79.99

Blood of Beasts (Le Sang des Bêtes)

(1949, 22 min, France, Georges Franju) This landmark documentary, and first film by Franju, begins by lulling the viewer with scenes of a tranquil Parisian suburb. But tranquility is far from the theme of this film, for the camera soon enters an abattoir and begins to unflinchingly chronicle a day in the life of a slaughterhouse.

Disturbing in its methodical violence, we witness the actual slaughtering of cows, sheep, calves and even horses — all done by placid workers who systematically kill. Not for the faint of heart. Please note that the subtitles for this film are quite poor. (French with English subtitles) ★★★ VHS: $29.99

The Blood of Heroes

(1990, 97 min, US, David Peoples) *Rutger Hauer, Joan Chen, Vincent D'Onofrio).* Set in a post-apocalyptic future, this intelligent, suspenseful action film stars Hauer as the leader of sort of a minor league nomadic sports team which travels from village to village to compete against locals in a torturous, savage game called jugging, which is part football, part hockey and part bloodbath. Chen also stars as a woman so adept at the game that she joins the team in hopes of making it to "the majors" — where coveted players enjoy the good life in the confines of an underground city. ★★★

The Blood of Others

(1984, 130 min, France/Canada, Claude Chabrol) *Jodie Foster, Michael Ontkean, Sam Neill, Stéphane Audran, Lambert Wilson.* A great international cast cannot save this made-for-cable romance ineptly adapted from Simone de Beauvoir's 1946 novel. Set in Paris during the Second World War, the film stars Foster as a fashion designer who falls in love with an imprisoned French resistance fighter. In a successful attempt to get him released, she begins an affair with an influential German commander, only to be accused of collusion by her fellow countrymen. With 40 minutes missing from the original broadcast running time, this misfire from Chabrol is a sadly convoluted and uninvolving mess. (Filmed in English) ★

Blood on the Moon

(1948, 88 min, US, Robert Wise) *Robert Mitchum, Barbara Bel Geddes, Robert Preston.* This solid western tale boasts a good cast to tell the story of drifter Mitchum involved in shady goings-on out West. Preston is memorable as the villain. ★★★

The Blood Oranges

(1997, 105 min, GB, Philip Haas) *Charles Dance, Sheryl Lee, Colin Lane, Laila Robbins.* Comfortably expatriated Cyril and Fiona (Dance, Lee) live in unrooted self-obsession in an ancient, impoverished Italian village. It's 1970, and their marriage reflects the moral ambiguities of the time. They meet by literal accident another displaced couple. Catherine and Hugh (Robbins, Lane) have been on the road for a year, traveling with their three daughters as Hugh photographs. These two English couples, slumming in the Third World, exploiting without purpose, indulging without satisfaction, become enmeshed as Cyril and Fiona seek Catherine and Hugh's participation in their open relationship. The story unfolds over itself, non-linear and episodic, revealing the incredible conceit of the self-proclaimed guru. A lushly photographed, laconically paced adaptation of the John Hawkes novel. ★★½ VHS: $69.99; DVD: $24.99

Blood Relatives

(1977, 107 min, France/Canada, Claude Chabrol) *Donald Sutherland, Donald Pleasence,*

Stéphane Audran, David Hemmings. Adapted from an Ed McBain novel, this pedestrian police thriller features Sutherland as a Montreal detective assigned to a particularly savage murder case. A young girl is gruesomely killed in a back alley and the only witness, her 15-year-old cousin, implicates her brother in the case. Told in a straightforward way, Sutherland investigates, attempting to piece together the puzzle of this potentially passion-driven murder. The film starts off promisingly, but it's too one-dimensional and concludes with a decidedly anticlimactic denouement. (English language) ★★ VHS: $79.99

Blood Simple

(1984, 97 min, US, Joel Coen) *John Getz, Frances McDormand, Dan Hedaya, M. Emmet Walsh.* This extremely well-crafted first feature from the Coen Brothers pays tribute to classic film noir. The story revolves around a crazy, jealous husband who hires a shady hit man to take out his wife. Although the film was done on a shoestring budget, the Coen Brothers manage to create a technically dazzling film which boasts a gleefully ghoulish sense of humor, dazzling camera acrobatics and a plot with more loops than the L.A. Freeway. Corruption and distrust ooze from every frame of this torrid tale of tangled passions in a dusty Texas town. ★★★★ VHS: $9.99; DVD: $24.99

The Blood Spattered Bride

(La Novia Ensangrentada)

(1972, 101 min, Spain, Vincente Aranda) *Alexandra Bastedo, Simón Andreu, Maribel Martin, Dean Selmier.* Sexy lesbian vampires are on the prowl once again in this erotic, bloody and creepy Spanish production. A young bride is haunted by visions of knife-wielding beauties and castrated husbands. Her life is "saved" when Carmilla, a mysterious and elegant stranger, arrives. Carmilla, a centuries-old vampiress, and the innocent bride are immediately attracted to each other and plot the death of the bride's hated hubby who "Pierced my flesh to humiliate me. Spat inside me to enslave me." A shocking and violently bloody finale will keep the viewer engrossed as this kinky horror film brings new meaning (and warning) to the problems of marital life. Take that, Mr. Man! Based on Sheridan le Fanu's "Carmilla." (Letterboxed) (Spanish with English subtitles) ★★½ VHS: $14.99; DVD: $29.99

Blood Wedding

(1981, 72 min, Spain, Carlos Saura) *Antonio Gades, Christina Hoyos.* The first of three collaborations between director Saura and dancer/choreographer Antonio Gades (the other two are *Carmen* and *El Amor Brujo*), this stunning flamenco adaptation of Federico Garcia Lorca's tragic play, "La Boda de Sangre," is an exquisitely realized study of the theatrical process. The camera follows Gades and his cast through the process of putting on makeup, warming up and finally a full-dress run through of Gades' interpretation of the Lorca classic. Saura's camera lovingly examines the rehearsal in precise detail, giving the viewer an intimate and exciting peek into this exquisite art form. ★★★½

Bloodhounds of Broadway

(1989, 101 min, US, Howard Brookner) *Jennifer Grey, Matt Dillon, Madonna, Rutger Hauer, Randy Quaid, Julie Hagerty.* An impressive, though rather restrained, cast is the highlight of Brookner's alternately charming and forced comic mystery based on four Damon Runyon short stories. Set on New Year's Eve on Broadway in 1928, the story revolves around a group of gamblers, showgirls and aristocrats whose lives intersect after a local gangster is nearly slain. The colorful cast of characters includes Dillon as the worst gambler in New York, Grey and Madonna as showgirls, and Quaid (who best captures the spirit of Runyon) as a dim-witted high roller in love with Madonna (that's a twosome!). ★★½

Bloodline

(1979, 116 min, US, Terence Young) *Audrey Hepburn, Ben Gazzara, James Mason, Michelle Phillips, Omar Sharif.* Embarrassing screen version of Sidney Sheldon's best-seller with Audrey Hepburn as the heiress to a pharmaceutical company who takes over the business when her father dies under mysterious circumstances. ★ VHS: $14.99

Bloodsucking Freaks

(1978, 89 min, US, Joel M. Reed) Universally reviled blood-and-guts show, with the high point (or low point, depending on your tastes) being the scene in which a woman's brain is sucked out with a straw by one of the thirsty lunatics. ★ VHS: $19.99; DVD: $24.99

Bloody Mama

(1970, 90 min, US, Roger Corman) *Shelley Winters, Don Stroud, Pat Hingle, Robert De Niro, Bruce Dern.* Winters is the infamous Ma Barker, the matriarch of mayhem during the Depression. Unlike *Bonnie and Clyde*, whose characters were remotely sympathetic, this film has criminals who are totally unlikable. The film's primary assets are its players (particularly a young De Niro as one of her sons, a junkie) and its action scenes. A curiosity piece. ★★½

Johnny Depp in *Blow*

Blossoms in the Dust

(1941, 100 min, US, Mervyn LeRoy) *Greer Garson, Walter Pidgeon.* Garson and Pidgeon's first film together is a touching, familiar soap opera about a woman who loses her husband and child in an accident, inspiring her to found an orphanage. Features a good performance by Garson. ★★½ VHS: $19.99

Blow

(2001, 120 min, US, Ted Demme) *Johnny Depp, Penelope Cruz, Franka Potente, Ray Liotta, Rachel Griffiths, Paul Reubens.* It's amazing how mundane the life of George Jung was, considering he was one of the biggest marijuana and cocaine importers in U.S. history. Worse, *Blow* doesn't seem to notice, and the lack of thrills is especially evident in the wake of *Fear and Loathing, Boogie Nights* and *Traffic.* As Jung, Depp immerses himself once again into character, but there's not much there to inhabit. The story follows Jung from the early 1970s, where he starts in petty drug dealing, to his rise as a dealer working alongside Colombian drug lord Pablo Escobar. Jealousy, greed and betrayal soon bring Jung's world crashing down. Due more in part to Depp's portrayal than dramatic license, a small sympathy is felt for Jung and what becomes an almost comical series of bad choices. But director Demme isn't able to sustain the energy level from a good opening that nearly makes you feel for the characters. The result is a familiar jaunt down memory lane that has little else to say than it sucks to get caught. ★★ VHS: $102.99; DVD: $24.99

Blow Out

(1981, 107 min, US, Brian De Palma) *John Travolta, Nancy Allen, John Lithgow, Dennis Franz.* De Palma serves up this interesting rehash of Antonioni's *Blow-Up.* Movie sound engineer Travolta inadvertently records a car accident that turns out to be no accident. Allen costars as the accident's survivor who knows more than she should. Lithgow, in a chilling performance, is the psycho on her trail. Good use of various Philadelphia locations. ★★★ DVD: $19.99

Blow-Up

(1966, 108 min, GB/Italy, Michelangelo Antonioni) *Vanessa Redgrave, David Hemmings, Sarah Miles, Jane Birkin.* Antonioni's hypnotic and provocative film stars Hemmings as a fashion photographer in swinging 1960s London who sees a possible murder within one of his photographs. The film's lasting power lies in the way the images begin to reveal the mystery, all without the use of dialogue or sound. (Filmed in English) ★★★★ VHS: $19.99

Blown Away

(1994, 120 min, US, Stephen Hopkins) *Jeff Bridges, Tommy Lee Jones, Suzy Amis, Lloyd Bridges, Forest Whitaker.* More concerned with plot and character, *Blown Away* mixes action with a developed narrative, which is what gives its slight edge and many weaknesses. The always reliable J. Bridges plays a Boston bomb squad specialist who goes one on one with a former IRA bomber, played by the underused Jones. As Jones targets members of Bridges' force, the race is on to locate and stop the madman from blowing up half the city. For an action film,

Marlene Dietrich in *The Blue Angel*

there are surprisingly few scenes of carnage and mayhem (after all, this *is* about a psychotic bomber). ★★½ VHS: $9.99; DVD: $14.99

Blue

(1993, 76 min, GB, Derek Jarman) *Tilda Swinton, Derek Jarman, Nigel Terry.* Jarman, who died of AIDS in February 1994, had been battling the disease for six years at the time of making this film. With impaired eyesight and deteriorating health, Jarman created a startling experimental film in which he invites his audience into his sight-deprived world, creating a womb-like meditative state by employing a completely blue screen throughout the film. The cast reads from Jarman's often poetic journals, recounting the director's medical complexities, thoughts on the loss of loved ones, and reflections on his own life and art. Amazingly devoid of anger and neither sermonizing nor self-pitying, *Blue* is a fitting closure to an eventful career. ★★★

Blue

(1993, 98 min, France, Krzysztof Kieslowski) *Juliette Binoche, Benoit Regent.* A haunting and visually stunning film, *Blue* is the first in director Kieslowski's "color" trilogy, which would be followed by *White* and *Red.* Binoche is compelling as a grieving widow who withdraws from life after the sudden loss of her husband and daughter. Despite her efforts to remain detached from her past and present, she slowly regains her emotional balance when she uncovers her husband's secret life. The film boasts wonderful acting and beautiful cinematography, but at times gets bogged down in its overladen visual symbolism. (French with English subtitles) ★★★ VHS: $19.99

The Blue Angel

(1930, 90 min, Germany, Josef von Sternberg) *Marlene Dietrich, Emil Jannings.* Jannings seems a paragon of order and control, a diligent and respected schoolteacher who commands attention and obedience. But behind this facade is a repressed man, a man so needy for simple human contact that he falls prey to the almost violent sensuality of Lola-Lola (Dietrich, in the role which brought her international recogni-

tion), an earthy cabaret singer. He exchanges his security for the illusion of warmth and caring, and pays for his obsession with every shred of dignity and purpose he'd ever attained. Jannings is devastating, Dietrich is mesmerizing, and von Sternberg guides the performers through Expressionistic set designs with a sure hand and an unerring eye for human foibles. A film worthy of its classic status. ★★★★

Blue Chips

(1994, 108 min, US, William Friedkin) *Nick Nolte, Mary McDonnell, J.T. Walsh, Ed O'Neill, Shaquille O'Neal, Robert Wuhl.* Nolte is a grumpy old basketball coach in this authentic if familiar sports story. When Nolte's college team experiences a slump, he takes to the road to recruit players who expect new cars, bags of cash and even tractors in return for their premium services, all of which are, of course, illegal. With rousing basketball scenes, the film debut of NBA superstar O'Neal, a good performance by Nolte and a moving ethical dilemma, *Blue Chips* lacks a cast of interesting supporting characters to round out the story. This is surprising since it was written by Ron Shelton, who penned *Bull Durham* and *White Men Can't Jump.* ★★½ VHS: $9.99

Blue Collar

(1978, 114 min, US, Paul Schrader) *Richard Pryor, Harvey Keitel, Yaphet Kotto, Cliff De Young.* A searing drama with Pryor and Keitel as auto workers up against their corporate bosses, and their own union, in a losing battle. Pryor and Keitel are both outstanding in what may be their best screen performances. As a fellow worker also caught up in their ill-fated fight, Kotto gives a mesmerizing performance. (Letterboxed) ★★★ VHS: $14.99; DVD: $24.99

Blue Country

(1978, 104 min, France, Jean-Charles Tacchella) *Brigitte Fossy, Jacques Sernas.* Following his success with *Cousin, Cousine,* Tacchella directed this enchanting romantic comedy about two free souls who leave the troubles of city living behind to renew their love and begin a new life amidst the idyllic French countryside. (French with English subtitles) ★★★

The Blue Dahlia

(1946, 99 min, US, George Marshall) *Alan Ladd, Veronica Lake, William Bendix, Howard da Silva, Hugh Beaumont.* Raymond Chandler wrote the screenplay for this tense, well-produced noir thriller with Ladd suspected of murdering his unfaithful wife. ★★★ VHS: $14.99

Blue Desert

(1991, 98 min, US, Bradley Battersby) *Courteney Cox, Craig Sheffer, D.B. Sweeney, Philip Baker Hall.* Cox stars as a New York City comic book artist who finds herself hitting the road after being victimized by crime one time too many. Unfortunately, life in the small Southwestern town where she ends up proves no friendlier than the big city when Cox attracts the attentions of a troubled ex-con (Sheffer) and a local cop (Sweeney). Director Battersby creates an ominous, uneasy tone from start to finish. This above-average thriller is uniformly well-acted and provides a good look into the psychology of a victim while also making a statement about the position of an attractive single woman in a world where men call the shots. ★★★

The Blue Gardenia

(1953, 90 min, US, Fritz Lang) *Anne Baxter, Richard Conte, Ann Sothern, Raymond Burr, George Reeves, Nat "King" Cole.* Hack producer Alex Gottlieb cynically titled this standard-issue Hollywood murder mystery to exploit the public's fascination with the "Black Dahlia" murder of 1947. What director Lang gave him was a classic noir. Baxter wakes up from a drunken night on the town with lothario Burr only to find the playboy murdered at her feet. Newspaper gossip columnist Conte and her wise-cracking roommate Sothern try to prove her innocence. Invoking a great atmosphere, Lang livens things up with his usual visual flair, penchant for long takes, and brilliant mise-en-scène. ★★★½ VHS: $24.99; DVD: $24.99

Blue Hawaii

(1961, 101 min, US, Norman Taurog) *Elvis Presley, Joan Blackman, Angela Lansbury.* Pleasant Presley musical with Elvis as a returning soldier who bypasses the family business to work for a local tourist agency. Blackman is the love interest, and Lansbury adds a touch of class as Presley's mom. Elvis sings "Can't Help Falling in Love" and the title tune. ★★½ VHS: $14.99; DVD: $19.99

The Blue Hour

(1992, 88 min, Germany, Marcel Gisler) *Andreas Herder, Dina Lepizig.* The vulnerability and loneliness of a pretty "rent boy" and a flighty salesgirl is the theme of this absorbing drama. Theo is a Berlin hustler, a handsome young man who, despite selling his body, retains an amazingly sweet and trusting nature. Despite living the "good life," Theo begins feeling a little old, tired and alienated. His sadness is relieved a bit when he strikes up an uneasy relationship with his next-door neighbor, Marie, a punkishly outlandish French woman. Their friendship is not the stuff of high drama, but it is a simple, surprisingly touching tale of an unlikely love between two social outcasts. (German with English subtitles) ★★★ VHS: $29.99

Blue Ice

(1993, 96 min, GB, Russell Mulcahy) *Michael Caine, Sean Young, Ian Holm, Bob Hoskins, Bobby Short.* An appealing espionage drama with the ubiquitous Caine as a spy who came in from the cold, only to find himself frost-bitten when his oldest friends start turning up dead — with the only link being the beautiful femme fatale (Young) who recently entered his life. Caine's faithful performance harkens back to his old "Harry Palmer" days in *The Ipcress File* and *Funeral in Berlin.* Worth the price of a rental for the mental torture sequence alone. ★★★ VHS: $9.99

Blue in the Face

(1995, 90 min, US, Wayne Wang & Paul Auster) *Harvey Keitel, Mel Gorham, Lou Reed, Roseanne, Lily Tomlin, Michael J. Fox, Giancarlo Esposito, Jim Jarmusch, Madonna, Mira Sorvino, RuPaul.* Not really a sequel, the ingratiating *Blue in the Face* is a new collection of stories which concentrate on the customers of a Brooklyn smoke shop which was first featured in *Smoke.* Keitel returns as Auggie, the gregarious sales clerk who acts as both father confessor and camp counselor to a fresh crop of playmates. Told in a semidocumentary and more fragmented style than the previous film, *Blue in the Face,* as with *Smoke,* revels in the diversity of its Park Slope neighborhood, here through the many talking-heads interviews, anecdotes, monologues and fictionalized stories which populate this funny film. An eclectic, engaging cast weaves its way through the skimpy narrative. ★★★½ VHS: $9.99

Blue Jeans

(1981, 101 min, France, Hugues Burin des Roziers) This interesting curiosity follows the first loves of a 13-year-old boy who is sent to England one summer to study English. His tentative advances with a young girl are charming. However, she is soon lured away from him by another, older boy, which leaves our hero alone. The strange twist is that he also becomes attached to the other boy and develops a crush on the unresponsive young man. A touching and sensitive look at the heartache of first love. (French with English subtitles) ★★★

The Blue Kite

(1993, 138 min, China, Tian Zhuangzhuang) *Lu Liping, Pu Quanxin.* This harrowing tale of a family's struggle to survive in revolutionary China is told from the perspective of a young boy, Tietou, who witnesses firsthand the cruelty of class struggle. Banned by the Chinese authorities and ultimately resulting in the exile of filmmaker Tian, the film is strikingly similar to Zhang's *To Live,* in that it tells the story of one family from the Great Leap Forward through the Cultural Revolution. But where *To Live* succeeded in drawing the viewer into the intimate lives of a small family, *The Blue Kite* introduces too many players and it is hard to keep them all straight. The result is a dispassionate distancing from the characters as their lives fall victim to unwarranted punishments. (Mandarin with English subtitles) ★★½ VHS: $29.99

Blue Lagoon

(1980, 104 min, US, Randal Kleiser) *Brooke Shields, Christopher Atkins, Leo McKern, William Daniels.* Two young children (Shields, Atkins) come of age on a desert island after being ship-wrecked there. The facts of life are presented through effective (yet gooey) soft-focus cinematography. Cheesy dialogue and bad acting add to the mess. Not a film to take to a desert island. (Sequel: *Return to the Blue Lagoon*) ★½ VHS: $9.99; DVD: $24.99

The Blue Max

(1966, 157 min, US, John Guillermin) *George Peppard, Ursula Andress, James Mason.* Peppard does an able job in this high-flying romance/adventure story portraying a German WWI pilot who has a steamy love affair with Andress. Excellent aerial photography punctuates the dogfight scenes. ★★★ VHS: $19.99

Blue Sky

(1994, 101 min, US, Tony Richardson) *Jessica Lange, Tommy Lee Jones, Powers Boothe, Carrie Snodgress, Chris O'Donnell.* Shot in 1990 and on the shelf for four years, Richardson's final film is an affecting melodrama of a family in crisis which is further enhanced by two exceptional performances by Lange and Jones. Set in the early 1960s, the story concerns military nuclear engineer Jones, wife Lange and their family who move to a new Army base where infidelity, betrayal and conspiracy await them. A flirtatious Southern belle in the Blanche DuBois/Scarlett O'Hara mold, Lange's Oscar-winning portrayal of Carly is a revelation of sexuality and naiveté, and as Carly is the heart of the story, Lange's smoldering portrait is very much the centerpiece of the film. ★★★ VHS: $14.99; DVD: $19.99

Blue Steel

(1990, 95 min, US, Kathryn Bigelow) *Jamie Lee Curtis, Ron Silver, Clancy Brown, Louise Fletcher, Tom Sizemore.* Curtis delivers a coolly understated performance in this atmospheric police thriller as a rookie cop who empties her gun into an armed robber, and is promptly suspended when the dead man's gun cannot be found. Unbeknownst to her, the witness who stole the weapon is the same man she has just started dating — the man responsible for a series of killings using bullets with her name on them. Silver is effective as the serial killer. Director Bigelow suffuses the film with the noir glow that permeated her acclaimed vampire saga, *Near Dark.* ★★½ VHS: $9.99

Blue Streak

(1999, 94 min, US, Les Mayfield) *Martin Lawrence, Luke Wilson, Dave Chappelle, William Forsythe.* A case of a good comedian being sabotaged by bad material, *Blue Streak* is an ill-paced and very frantic action-comedy which isn't half as funny as it thinks it is. Lawrence (who was much better in his other 1999 film *Life*) stars as a jewel thief who must impersonate a cop in order to retrieve his stolen, hidden stash. In the process, he solves a few cases while earning the admiration of his "fellow officers," all the while trying desperately to grab the diamond and run. The premise isn't a bad one, but in the hands of director Mayfield and the screenwriters Lawrence is reduced to shrieking and flailing and horrible mugging — no one lets the funny setup play out. Forget the fact the everyone around him acts like idiots; in the process, Lawrence becomes one too, and he's too talented a comedian to be reduced to such mindless shenanigans. ★½ VHS: $14.99; DVD: $19.99

Blue Thunder

(1983, 108 min, US, John Badham) *Roy Scheider, Malcolm McDowell, Daniel Stern, Candy Clark, Warren Oates.* Fascism was never so much fun as in this movie with grown-up little boys playing with their war toys. Scheider is the Vietnam vet who, after a particularly bad psychotic episode, steals the government's surveillance helicopter. McDowell is the unhappy government rep out for Scheider's blood. Amazing aerial chases over Los Angeles heighten the suspense of this otherwise silly thriller. ★★ VHS: $9.99; DVD: $14.99

Blue Velvet

(1986, 120 min, US, David Lynch) *Kyle MacLachlan, Laura Dern, Isabella Rossellini, Dennis Hopper, Dean Stockwell, Jack Nance.* Director Lynch unleashes his demented imagination with all its perversely poetic force. Both witty and luridly beautiful, the film is part mystery, part surrealist dream. Lynch uses the postcard-perfect town of Lumberton to plunge into an all-embracing ritual of sinful crime, sadism and redemption. MacLachlan innocently discovers a human ear in his backyard one day and is quickly drawn into the sordid, masochistic world of a nightclub singer (Rossellini). Hopper is at his lunatic best as the all-powerful psychotic drug thug Frank Booth. *Blue Velvet* is a piece of primal pop art, an erotic parable with trance-like power. ★★★★ VHS: $14.99; DVD: $24.99

Bluebeard's Eighth Wife

(1938, 80 min, US, Ernst Lubitsch) *Claudette Colbert, Gary Cooper, David Niven, Edward Everett Horton.* Billy Wilder and Charles Brackett wrote the screenplay for this sophisticated Lubitsch sex comedy with Cooper as a playboy millionaire who meets his match in Colbert. ★★★ VHS: $14.99

The Blues Brothers

(1980, 133 min, US, John Landis) *James Belushi, Dan Aykroyd, Carrie Fisher, Kathleen Freeman, Cab Calloway, James Brown, John Candy, Henry Gibson, Aretha Franklin, Ray Charles.* From their "Saturday Night Live" sketch, Belushi and Aykroyd are Jake and Elwood Blues, good-hearted petty criminals and dedicated bluesmen. The story about a quest to find the money to save an orphanage and the possible consequences of running a red light is really just an excuse to string together as many hilarious episodes as the filmmakers can. This movie has it all: monumental car chases (and car crashes), a mysterious killer stalking the duo, a mission from God, raucous concert scenes, but also full musical performances by Franklin, Charles, Brown and Calloway. The movie is briskly paced, filled equally with action and musical scenes, tremendously funny and is a virtual tour of the city of Chicago. (Letterboxed VHS is available for $19.99) (Sequel: *Blues Brothers 2000* ★★★½ VHS: $14.99; DVD: $34.99

Blues Brothers 2000

(1998, 124 min, US, John Landis) *Dan Aykroyd, John Goodman, Joe Morton, J. Evan Bonifant, Aretha Franklin, James Brown, B.B. King.* Eighteen years after the fact, this surprisingly bad sequel to the hilarious 1980 comedy brings the Blues Brothers back to the screen — minus John Belushi, of course. Released from prison, Elwood (Aykroyd) is "appointed" mentor to a young ne'er-do-well and decides to get the band back together. An embarrassing Morton as a policeman is in hot pursuit the whole way, until he has a change of heart in an insipid scene inspired by the gospel number in the first film. In fact, 95% of *2000* is a fifth-rate rip-off of its predecessor with absolutely none of the joy, humor or timing which made that film terrific. What's more, the musical numbers are lousy. The only real spark comes from a genuinely fun all-star Blues Band at the very end of the film; it's too little, too late. Goodman is good as a bartender along for the ride, but he's no substitute for Belushi. ★½ VHS: $14.99; DVD: $34.99

Blume in Love

(1973, 117 min, US, Paul Mazursky) *George Segal, Susan Anspach, Kris Kristofferson, Marsha Mason, Shelley Winters.* Mazursky's perceptive and engaging comedy-drama about love and rejection stars Segal as a divorce lawyer whose life is turned upside-down when his wife (Anspach) walks out on him. ★★★ VHS: $14.99

Blunt: The Fourth Man

(1992, 86 min, GB, John McGlasham) *Anthony Hopkins, Ian Richardson.* Hopkins is a delight as Guy Burgess, the British government official who fled England before the discovery that he and several others were spies for the Soviets. (Knowledge of this story is beneficial.) At the center of the tale is Burgess' fellow spy, Anthony Blunt (wonderfully played by Richardson), who recruited Burgess while attending Cambridge in the 1930s. Set in the early 1960s, the film shows Blunt as a well-respected art historian. When his well-ordered life is threatened, Blunt begins an elaborate cover-up and damage control campaign. His biggest challenge is protecting Burgess, his former lover and close friend. An inviting and well-produced tale whose characters can also be seen in *Another Country* and *An Englishman Abroad.* ★★★ VHS: $19.99

The Boat

See: Das Boot

The Boat Is Full

(1981, 104 min, Switzerland, Markus Imhoof) *Tina Engel, Curt Bois.* A haunting account of a group of Jewish refugees who attempt to seek asylum in Switzerland, despite that country's strict and subtly prejudiced immigration laws. Their struggle for freedom and life provides the emotional center to this film that is both horrifying in the depiction of a people's racial attitudes and heartrending in another's efforts to overcome them. (German with English subtitles) ★★★½ VHS: $29.99

Bob & Carol & Ted & Alice

(1969, 104 min, US, Paul Mazursky) *Robert Culp, Natalie Wood, Elliott Gould, Dyan Cannon.* Mazursky's breakthrough directorial debut is a somewhat dated but nevertheless enjoyable treatise on marriage and sex (but not necessarily in that order). Culp and Wood are a married couple who try to convince friends Gould and Cannon to express themselves sexually — by wife-swapping. Both Gould and Cannon received Oscar nominations for their delightful performances. ★★★ VHS: $9.99

Bob le Flambeur

(1955, 102 min, France, Jean-Pierre Melville) *Roger Duchesne, Isabel Corey.* Melville, the Father of the French New Wave, has made a quirky, highly stylized film which revolves around Bob, an aging but elegant gangster who plans a daring robbery of the Deauville Casino. The tension builds as Bob recruits his Montmarte cohorts, plans the break-in and attempts to execute "the biggest heist of the century." An entertaining comedy of manners as well as an exciting drama. (French with English subtitles) ★★★½ VHS: $29.99

Bob Roberts

(1992, 103 min, US, Tim Robbins) *Tim Robbins, Giancarlo Esposito, Alan Rickman, Gore Vidal, David Strathairn, James Spader, Susan Sarandon, Lynne Thigpen, John Cusack, Bob Balaban.* Robbins wrote, directed and stars in this scathingly brilliant political satire about the senatorial campaign of a right-wing candidate. Told in a mockumentary style, reminiscent of *This Is Spinal Tap*, the film often recalls *The Player*, introducing a gallery of characters who weave in and out of the story, many of whom are portrayed by terrific celebrity cameos. But Robbins, as an actor, writer and director, has an instinctive and incisive wit which gives the film a definition all its own. As the country music-singing, neo-fascist, laissez faire-invoking Roberts, Robbins gives a priceless performance; there are few of his generation who can handle comedy with such finesse. ★★★★ VHS: $9.99; DVD: $24.99

Bobby Deerfield

(1977, 124 min, US, Sydney Pollack) *Al Pacino, Marthe Keller.* Pacino makes a valiant effort to breathe some life into this turgid romantic drama, but even his talents can't save this story of a race car driver who falls in love with socialite Keller, who's suffering from "Ali MacGraw's Disease." (And Al, next time, leave the impressions to Rich Little.) ★ VHS: $14.99

La Boca del Lobo

(1988, 111 min, Peru, Francisco J. Lombardi) The human tragedy of the Peruvian Civil War is explored in this intense drama. Set in a poor Indian village in the Andes, the bucolic calm of the town is disturbed when a small army patrol is sent to investigate possible insurgent activity. The soldiers, like the American forces in Vietnam, soon become entrenched in a bloody, morally ambivalent and increasingly frustrating guerrilla war of attrition. The desperate situation explodes after a newly appointed lieutenant declares the entire village guilty of treason and leads his forces toward a horrible atrocity. A young soldier in the group must choose between blind obedience of his superior and following the dictates of his conscience to oppose him. (Spanish with English subtitles) ★★★ VHS: $39.99

Bodies, Rest & Motion

(1993, 93 min, US, Michael Steinberg) *Bridget Fonda, Eric Stoltz, Tim Roth, Phoebe Cates, Alicia Witt, Peter Fonda.* A loosely structured drama about four disillusioned twentysomethings looking for themselves. Fonda plays a young woman who finds herself in a dilemma when her estranged boyfriend (Roth) just takes off one day. Stoltz (the film's coproducer) is a house painter, quite content with life in the nowhere Arizona town where the film takes place, who meets and falls in love with stressed-out Fonda. Steinberg lets things unfold simply and slowly, which is much to the film's benefit. ★★★ VHS: $19.99

Body and Soul

(1947, 104 min, US, Robert Rossen) *John Garfield, Lilli Palmer, Anne Revere, Canada Lee.* Garfield gives a career performance in this hard-hitting, sometimes brutal but always mesmerizing boxing drama. Garfield plays Charlie Davis, a tough, ambitious kid from the poor part of town who makes a name for himself in the boxing world. As his career takes off, he loses sight of his dreams and honor and succumbs to the easy money supplied by his gangster manager. In support, Revere and Lee, as Davis's mother and opponent-turned-trainer, respectively, are excellent. With a taut and polished screenplay by Abraham Polonsky, *Body and Soul* is an uncompromising tale of greed, corruption and redemption, brilliantly realized by director Rossen. One of the greatest of all boxing films. ★★★★ VHS: $9.99; DVD: $24.99

Body Bags

(1993, 95 min, US, John Carpenter & Tobe Hooper) *Stacy Keach, Mark Hamill, Deborah Harry, Sheena Easton, Twiggy.* This fun horror anthology is hosted by Carpenter and features buckets of gore and bizarre humor. Highlights include "The Gas Station," a grim slasher tale and the incredibly funny "Hair" starring Keach as a middle-aged balding man with an overwhelming desire for a full head of hair. Some fright fans may be turned off by the sometimes heavy-handed attempts at comedy, but inventive casting combines with good brisk pacing to provide for plenty of shocks and yucks. ★★½ VHS: $9.99; DVD: $19.99

Body Double

(1984, 109 min, US, Brian De Palma) *Craig Wasson, Melanie Griffith, Deborah Shelton, Dennis Franz.* De Palma's acclaimed sleazy thriller about a voyeuristic actor (Wasson) whose penchant for peeping involves him in the grisly murder of a woman (Shelton) on whom he's been spying. A pre-stardom Griffith also stars as a porn star. De Palma borrows from Hitchcock (here *Rear Window*) once again, with successful results. ★★★ VHS: $9.99; DVD: $14.99

Body Heat

(1981, 113 min, US, Lawrence Kasdan) *William Hurt, Kathleen Turner, Ted Danson, Richard Crenna, Mickey Rourke.* Simmering passions and deadly schemes are ignited under the hot Florida sun in Kasdan's remarkable, sensuous thriller which almost single-handedly brought noir back to vogue. With nods to *Double Indemnity* and *The Postman Always Rings Twice*, Kasdan's riveting tale stars Hurt as a second-rate lawyer who begins an affair with sultry and very married Turner (her memorable debut). Only her husband (Crenna) stands in the way of their happiness. Kasdan takes the traditional femme fatale tale and spices it up with sexy lovemaking scenes, crackling dialogue and twist upon twist. In their first appearance together, Hurt and Turner are simply dynamite. ★★★★ VHS: $9.99; DVD: $14.99

Body Melt

(1993, 82 min, Australia, Philip Brophy) *Gerard Kennedy, Andrew Daddo.* A scientific experiment turns an Australian community into melting zombies. The plot is weak. The acting is weaker. The special effects are truly disgusting and the film boasts a shameless group of backwoods *Deliverance*-type hicks who are more repulsive than any melting zombies. *Body Melt* tries to ride on the coattails of Peter Jackson's successful *Dead Alive*, but misses the mark by a mile. ★

Body of Evidence

(1992, 99 min, US, Uli Edel) *Madonna, Willem Dafoe, Anne Archer, Joe Mantegna.* Madonna and Dafoe star in this lethargic psycho-sexual mystery that makes *Basic Instinct* look like the *Citizen Kane* of the whodunit-in-the-sack thrillers. The "body" in question is Madonna's over-exposed corpus, the lethal weapon in a classic case of come-and-gone lovemaking. Dafoe is Frank Delaney, the morally dubious lawyer who must prove that while S&M hellcat Madonna is a "killer" in bed (wielding handcuffs, candles and mega-developed inner thighs), she's not actually a murderer. But can he maintain professional distance and resist the pint-sized dynamo who "does it like animals do it?" Madonna's acting doesn't amount to much, but she still out-acts Dafoe, who gives the worst performance of his career. As the prosecuting attorney, Mantegna can barely conceal his disdain for the entire affair. ★ VHS: $14.99

Body Parts

(1991, 88 min, US, Eric Red) *Jeff Fahey, Kim Delaney, Brad Dourif.* Fahey loses an arm in an auto accident and his distraught wife approves emergency surgical replacement with a donated limb. The surgery is a success, but the donor — an executed murderer — wants his arm back! While the movie occasionally slips into hackneyed horror contrivance, it is often surprisingly effective in its treatment of Fahey's bizarre predicament. Where does consciousness reside? In the mind? In the soul? Or in individual body parts? ★★½ VHS: $9.99

Body Shots

(1999, 106 min, US, Michael Cristofer) *Sean Patrick Flanery, Jerry O'Connell, Amanda Peet, Tara Reid, Ron Livingston, Emily Procter, Brad Rowe.* This annoying twentysomething "exposé" deals with date rape and barhopping in the most superficial manner possible. A gaggle of attractive young adults — who run the gamut from merely shallow to completely excruciating — get together for a night on the town, pausing only to turn to the camera and share their "feelings" and "insights" with the audience. With the look and feel of a lower-end Fox-TV flick, phoned-in performances from its "hip" young cast, and an embarrassing reach for style and meaning by its director, *Body Shots* is a painful experience. Any thirty seconds of a "Buffy the Vampire Slayer" episode has more depth and insight. ★ VHS: $14.99; DVD: $24.99

The Body Snatcher

(1945, 77 min, US, Robert Wise) *Boris Karloff, Bela Lugosi, Henry Daniell.* Wise's second film for producer Val Lewton (the first being *Curse of the Cat People*) is an exceptionally atmospheric thriller about a 19th-century medical school professor in league with a grave robber. Based on a Robert Louis Stevenson story. ★★★

Body Snatchers

(1993, 96 min, US, Abel Ferrara) *Forest Whitaker, Meg Tilly, Gabrielle Anwar, Billy Wirth.* From the director of such hard-hitting hits as *Bad Lieutenant* and *King of New York* comes this eerie but redundant second remake of the 1956 sci-fi classic *Invasion of the Body Snatchers*, about soul-stealing seed pods from space. Anwar toplines as a divorce-brat whose unsuspecting father accepts a job assignment relocating him to a military base now being used as an alien stronghold. ★★½ VHS: $19.99; DVD: $19.99

The Bodyguard

(1992, 129 min, US, Mick Jackson) *Kevin Costner, Whitney Houston, Gary Kemp, Ralph Waite, Robert Wuhl.* Costner plays the title character to Houston's big, big movie star in this idiotic romantic thriller. When she is plagued by death threats, Houston's manager signs on rambling man Costner, tops in his profession, but who never stays in one place too long (he's probably in constant search for a good barber). At odds from the beginning, Costner and Houston become enraptured with each other, leading to an inevitable fling. It won't take long to figure out who hired the hit man. There's a good lakeside sequence, but nothing else in the film nears the level of its short-lived excitement. (Letterboxed VHS available for $19.99) ★½ VHS: $14.99; DVD: $19.99

Boeing, Boeing

(1965, 102 min, US, John Rich) *Jerry Lewis, Tony Curtis, Thelma Ritter.* Curtis and Lewis team in this frantic sex farce which — even for the '60s — is particularly anti-feminist. Curtis hams it up royally as a journalist who literally has his hands full juggling the simultaneous relationships with three live-in fiancées, all stewardesses and strangers to each other. Enter fellow reporter Lewis, who is forced to help Curtis in keeping the three women from meeting when all unexpectedly arrive at the same time. Ritter proves to be a saving grace, providing most of the laughs as Curtis' exasperated housekeeper. ★★ VHS: $14.99

Bogus

(1996, 111 min, US, Norman Jewison) *Whoopi Goldberg, Gérard Depardieu, Haley Joel Osment, Nancy Travis, Andrea Martin, Sheryl Lee Ralph.* Disarming despite its own shortcomings, *Bogus* is a children's fantasy which tells children the world is not always a nice place — so that's why there are such things as invisible childhood friends. Bogus is one such presence. He appears to Albert (Osment), a seven-year-old boy whose mother has been killed in a car accident. With no family, the youngster is sent to live with his mother's foster sister, Harriet (Goldberg). The story concentrates on their efforts to learn to love each other. The scenes between Bogus and Albert are the film's most appealing moments, and, as Bogus, Depardieu has rarely demonstrated such a light side. More demanding, Albert and Harriet's scenes are more difficult to watch, and they underscore the story's sparseness. ★★½ VHS: $9.99

Boiler Room

(2000, 120 min, US, Ben Younger) *Giovanni Ribisi, Vin Diesel, Nia Long, Ben Affleck, Nicky Katt, Scott Caan, Ron Rifkin.* Bristling with a vibrant rhythm that sets it apart from the pack, writer-director Younger's compelling *Boiler*

Room has a take-no-prisoners attitude in telling its story of innocence lost, shady dealings and eventual redemption. Ribisi gives a super-charged performance as Seth, a naïve young man looking to make his mark as a stock broker. Things spiral out of control when he joins a company involved in illegal tradings. Caught in a crisis of conscience, Seth is torn between easy money and doing the right thing. His decision and the film's outcome isn't as predictable — nor as black and white — as you'd think. Ribisi is terrific as the young go-getter, a Duddy Kravitz for the millennium. His scenes with his father (expertly played by Rifkin) are masterful, creating a sublime dichotomy between Seth's two equally important worlds — family and business. Seth briefly enjoys the sweet smell of success, but the cost is high in this uncompromising, whirlwind look at ambition and corruption. Diesel is especially good in support as a rival broker. ★★★ VHS: $14.99; DVD: $24.99

Boiling Point

(1990, 98 min, Japan, Takeshi Kitano) *Takeshi Kitano, Masahiko Ono.* A stately, arty film with occasional bursts of graphic violence, *Boiling Point* is extremely brutal, deadpan, blackly comic, and Kitano's first fully realized film as director (his earlier *Violent Cop* was picked up by him in mid-production). A young baseball player/car wash attendant offends the local crimelord, and enlists the help of a seasoned, amoral criminal (Takeshi), a cold-blooded psychopath who's so bad that he's been booted from the yakuza. While it's certainly too slow for the "kill-'em-all" action crowd, *Boiling Point* may appeal to more patient crime film fans, with its elegant, at times, eerie atmosphere, fascinating characters, and unusual outlook. Not as engrossing as *Hana-Bi (Fireworks)*, but still worthwhile in its own right, this is rewarding for those with stamina. (Japanese with English subtitles) ★★★ VHS: $19.99; DVD: $19.99

Boiling Point

(1993, 93 min, US, James B. Harris) *Wesley Snipes, Dennis Hopper, Lolita Davidovich, Viggo Mortensen, Dan Hedaya, Seymour Cassel, Valerie Perrine.* Snipes heads an eclectic cast as a treasury agent out to avenge his partner's death (how original) at the hands of a shifty grifter (Hopper) and his trigger-happy henchman (Mortensen). While the film garnered many favorable reviews for its focus on character rather than gunplay, it is by no means the *Lethal Weapon* derivative it might have been. As a result, the movie simmers when it should have boiled. ★★½ VHS: $9.99; DVD: $14.99

Bolero

(1984, 104 min, US, John Derek) *Bo Derek, George Kennedy, Olivia d'Abo.* Derek takes her clothes off in the quest to lose her virginity. Surely there must have been one immediate taker so we wouldn't have had to suffer for 104 minutes. ★

Bombay Talkie

(1970, 108 min, India, James Ivory) *Jennifer Kendal, Shashi Kapoor.* Lucia, an American novelist, arrives in India in a desperate search for new sensations and experiences which will help her forget her approaching middle age. She soon meets and begins an affair with Vikram, a dazzling movie actor. Vikram eventually leaves his wife and

family and destroys his life and career in a futile pursuit of an image that does not exist. Director Ivory and writer Ruth Prawer Jhabvala present an interesting look at culture clash, but the romantic dramatics are very much in the range of the familiar. (Letterboxed) ★★½ VHS: $19.99

Bombshell

(1933, 95 min, US, Victor Fleming) *Jean Harlow, Lee Tracy, Frank Morgan.* This fast-paced, early satire on Hollywood hasn't lost a bit of its bite over the years. Harlow stars as the used and abused Hollywood starlet whose face and name are plastered across the country. And now she wants to change her image. The snappy dialogue keeps this film rolling along. Harlow, who could have been playing herself, gives one of her best performances in this hysterical film. ★★★½ VHS: $19.99

Bon Voyage & Aventure Malgache

(1944, 26/31 min, France, Alfred Hitchcock) During World War II, Alfred Hitchcock made these two shorts in an effort to boost morale, particularly that of the French Resistance. *Bon Voyage* is classic Hitchcock, a taut spy story about an RAF pilot who escapes from a POW camp that grows more and more intense with each plot twist. *Aventure Malgache* tells the story about the Resistance fighting a corrupt government in Madagascar. Though it is not as suspenseful as the first film, it is especially intriguing because it is based on a true story. Both films showcase many of the director's stylish and thematic trademarks and should not be missed by die-hard fans of the Master of Suspense. (French with English subtitles) ★★★ VHS: $39.99; DVD: $24.99

The Bone Collector

(1999, 118 min, US, Phillip Noyce) *Denzel Washington, Angelina Jolie, Queen Latifah, Michael Rooker, Ed O'Neill, Luis Guzman.* The fact that Washington is stuck in a bed for 99% of the film surprisingly takes nothing away from this intense, involving thriller. He plays a seasoned police criminologist who is paralyzed from the neck down while on a case. Contemplating suicide, he is temporarily distracted, and a little enthused to be working again, when he's asked to help in an especially difficult case — a serial killer is picking up passengers in a cab and brutally skinning them. Jolie is the cop who finds the first body and is brought in to be Washington's eyes, ears and legs. A straightforward mystery that doesn't rely on convoluted twists and turns, *The Bone Collector* is a taut, efficient exercise in terror that is rarely gruesome. It's able to maintain its momentum without much blood and guts, relying on good, old-fashioned suspense to produce those goose bumps. Latifah is well-cast as Washington's no-nonsense nurse. ★★★ VHS: $14.99; DVD: $24.99

The Bonfire of the Vanities

(1990, 125 min, US, Brian De Palma) *Tom Hanks, Melanie Griffith, Bruce Willis, Kim Cattrall, Morgan Freeman, Saul Rubinek, Andre Gregory.* Based on Tom Wolfe's runaway best-seller, this absurdly uneven film adaptation by De Palma was one of the most anticipated releases of 1990, and created one of that year's loudest thuds. This satire on greed and justice is a disappointment on numerous levels. In one of the many ill-advised changes from the book, the

miscast Hanks plays a basically likable Sherman McCoy, the Wall Street wizard who is thrust into the media spotlight when he and his mistress (Griffith) are involved in the hit-and-run of a black man. Willis makes an earnest stab at the now-American author Peter Fallow, the down-on-his-heels journalist who lucks into the story of the year. ★½ VHS: $14.99; DVD: $19.99

Bongo Man

(1982, 89 min, Jamaica/West Germany, Stefan Paul) The normally peaceful island of Jamaica, rocked with dissension and bloodied by riots during the presidential elections of the early 1980s, provides the dramatic backdrop to this Reggae Sunsplash-styled concert film featuring Jimmy Cliff. The potentially explosive situation is intercut with the Rasta and reggae music of Cliff and Bob Marley and the Wailers in an effort to promote the idea that "politicians divide, musicians unite." ★★★

Bonjour Tristesse

(1958, 94 min, US, Otto Preminger) *Jean Seberg, David Niven, Deborah Kerr.* The French Riviera is the setting of this skillful adaptation of Françoise Sagan's novella about a young girl (Seberg) who drives a wedge between her rake father (Niven) and his mistress (Kerr). Captivating performances from both Niven and Kerr. ★★★ VHS: $19.99

Bonnie and Clyde

(1967, 111 min, US, Arthur Penn) *Faye Dunaway, Warren Beatty, Gene Hackman, Estelle Parsons, Michael J. Pollard, Denver Pyle.* Bonnie and Clyde marked the arrival of the New Hollywood in the late Sixties with a burst of creative energy. An exceptional script by David Newman and Robert Benton, stylish direction by Penn, Dede Allen's brilliant editing and great performances from the entire cast (including Beatty and Dunaway as the title characters) combine to make this one of the most daring and successful of all mainstream American productions. Based on the exploits of the real-life pair who went on a crime spree through the Midwest, the movie is by turns humorous, thrilling, romantic and shocking. The climactic sequence is a tour de force of visceral filmmaking impossible to dismiss. ★★★★ VHS: $14.99; DVD: $19.99

The Boogey Man

(1980, 86 min, US, Ulli Lommel) *Suzanna Love, Ron James, John Carradine.* This boring and pointless low-budget production begins as a pair of siblings murder their mother's abusive boyfriend. Shift forward twenty years (the first, but not the last horror-film cliché employed in this movie) to the brother and sister, now grown but still suffering the psychological consequences of that terrible night. In an attempt to overcome her fears, the sister returns to the scene of the crime, and the vengeful spirit of the murdered boyfriend is released. You can guess the rest. Amateurish and routine. (Letterboxed) ★ VHS: $14.99

Boogie Boy

(1998, 104 min, US, Craig R. Hamann) *Mark Dacascos, Emily Lloyd, Jaimz Woolvett, Traci Lords, Frederic Forrest, Joan Jett.* Part Tarantino-esque pulp drama, part drug exposé, and part bloody murder thriller, this weird flick tries for greatness and settles for being a mildly intriguing find. Jessie (Dacascos) is a hunky ex-con who is reunited with his ex-cellmate (and prison lover) Larry (Woolvett) in a dark, drug-infested area of Los Angeles. Jessie has been trying to go straight: He's successful in not continuing the relationship with Larry but fails miserably when it comes to the law. A drug deal goes sour and the result is a lot of dead bodies. Jessie and Larry flee the city. They end up in an barren motel in the desert operated by a crazed codger (Forrest) and his sexpot girlfriend (Lloyd). Hell, it's ridiculous, but the violence, offbeat characters and appearances by Jett and Lords may make it of interest. ★★½ VHS: $102.99; DVD: $14.99

Boogie Nights

(1997, 155 min, US, Paul Thomas Anderson) *Mark Wahlberg, Julianne Moore, Burt Reynolds, Don Cheadle, William H. Macy, Heather Graham, John C. Reilly, Alfred Molina, Philip Seymour Hoffman, Luis Guzman, Philip Baker Hall.* Wahlberg sparkles in this immensely enjoyable and decidedly over-the-top trip through the '70s as seen through the filter of the adult film industry. Wahlberg is Eddie Adams, an unassuming busboy at a seedy L.A. discotheque where he is approached by XXX-porn director Jack Horner (Reynolds, in a role that should have won him an Oscar). Within weeks our winsome hero is transformed from hayseed Valley Boy into the latest 100%-grade AAA beef packin' superstar...Dirk Diggler! Director Anderson (*Hard Eight*) does a masterful job of piecing together this cinematic expedition from the giddy innocence of the early '70s to the paranoiac, cocaine-addled violence at the beginning of the Reagan era. Moore is stunning as Reynolds' porn-star wife Amber Waves, the veteran starlet who helps initiate Dirk into the tight-knit family that lives and parties in and around their Valley bungalow. Includes 20 minutes of censored scenes not shown theatrically. (VHS available letterboxed or pan & scan) ★★★★ VHS: $19.99; DVD: $29.99

Book of Shadows: Blair Witch 2

(2000, 90 min, US, Joe Berlinger) *Jeffrey Donovan, Stephen Barker Turner, Kim Director, Erica Leerhsen, Tristen Skylar.* Invention and filmic chicanery are replaced with silliness and clichés in this tired sequel to the surprise 1999 box-office hit. Noted documentarian Berlinger (*Brother's Keeper, Paradise Lost*) is able to give this film an improved visual style over the original, but the screenplay he and Dick Beebe has concocted is trapped somewhere in the backwoods of mediocrity. Four fans of the first film spend a night in the Black Hills of Burkittsville, Maryland, courtesy of a local tour guide. It soon becomes apparent that there's something out there when they all descend into a nightmare of madness and murder. Too many jump-cuts add to the confusion of too many flashbacks, resulting in stock scares and little tension. A decent twist ending is lost amongst the one-dimensional characters and convoluted story. ★½ VHS: $14.99; DVD: $24.99

Boomerang

(1992, 118 min, US, Reginald Hudlin) *Eddie Murphy, Robin Givens, Halle Berry, David Allen Grier, Eartha Kitt, Geoffrey Holder, Martin Lawrence.* Murphy stars in this entertaining comedy about a way smooth, way charming advertising man in search of the ideal woman. But his cavalier use of sex to avoid communicating and his overem-

phasis on a woman's appearance come back at him when he meets his new boss, Givens. The film's amiable "buppy" characters and romantic sentiment put its heart in the right place, but the level of the humor rarely rises above the belt. ★★½ VHS: $14.99

The Boost

(1988, 95 min, US, Harold Becker) *James Woods, Sean Young, Steven Hill.* A totally mishandled "say no to drugs" treatise about a hotshot salesman and his wife whose fresh new start in L.A. becomes a cocaine nightmare. Of value only as the film that sparked the real-life "fatal attraction" skirmish between stars Young and Woods. ★★ VHS: $14.99

Das Boot (The Boat)

(1981, 209 min, West Germany, Wolfgang Petersen) *Jurgen Prochnow, Herbert Gronemeyer.* Few films convey the horror of war as powerfully as Petersen's claustrophobic account of a German U-boat's passage through hostile waters. Dispelling traditional film images of war heroism, *Das Boot* substitutes a truer vision of the waste and inhumanity inherent in battle. This is the full-length director's cut. (Letterboxed) (German with English subtitles) ★★★★ VHS: $19.99; DVD: $27.99

Booty Call

(1997, 77 min, US, Jeff Pollack) *Jamie Foxx, Tommy Davidson, Vivica A. Fox, Tamala Jones, Gedde Watanabe.* Infectiously silly and sporadically amusing, *Booty Call* isn't nearly as tasteless as its title would suggest. Buppie Davidson and his girlfriend of seven weeks bring along their respective best friends (who have never met) for a double date. The men make a "gentleman's bet" to see who will bed his girl first. Not at all original but still able to produce a few laughs, *Booty Call* contains annoying gay and immigrant stereotyping, sloppy editing and moronic, subsitcom situations. And even at a scant 77 minutes, it feels too long. Still, the four leads are enthusiastic and appealing, and the film is marginal, dumb fun. ★★ VHS: $9.99; DVD: $19.99

Bopha!

(1993, 120 min, US, Morgan Freeman) *Danny Glover, Alfre Woodard, Maruis Weyers, Malcolm McDowell.* Actor Freeman makes his directorial debut with this solemn and powerful anti-Apartheid drama based on the play by Percy Mtwa. Glover stars as a black South African police sergeant whose position requires him to unwittingly enforce the country's racist laws. Labeled a traitor by his community, his world further deteriorates when he comes in conflict with his student rebel son (Weyers), who helps open his eyes to the injustices around them. As a study of racism, *Bopha!* doesn't instill anger but rather succinctly explores the ways this practice tears apart the fabric of black families. Slowly paced at times, the film helps bring to light the reality of South Africa. ★★★ VHS: $19.99

Bordello of Blood

(1996, 87 min, US, Gilbert Adler) *Dennis Miller, Angie Everhart, Erika Eleniak, Chris Sarandon, Corey Feldman, Whoopi Goldberg.* Producer Robert Zemeckis and the other slumming talent behind the "Tales from the Crypt" series have given us another bloodless vampire movie, starring Everhart as the legendary Queen of the

Mark Wahlberg (l.) and Burt Reynolds in *Boogie Nights*

Undead. Accidentally resurrected, she sets up residence in a mortuary, playing madam to a group of undead ladies of the night. When a young Christian crusader (Eleniak) loses her brother (Feldman) to the vampiric legions, she enlists the aid of a private detective (Miller) to help find him. The gore scenes are lame and bloodless and much of the script is reminiscent of *From Dusk Till Dawn*. Even the usually funny Miller seems embarrassed. ★½ VHS: $14.99; DVD: $29.99

The Border

(1982, 107 min, US, Tony Richardson) *Jack Nicholson, Harvey Keitel, Valerie Perrine, Warren Oates.* Nicholson stars as a U.S. border guard who gets caught up in the business of transporting illegal aliens to pay for the materialistic lifestyle his wife craves. His morals come to haunt him in the form of a young Mexican mother and her child, about whom he comes to care. An engrossing film with excellent performances. ★★★ VHS: $14.99

Boris and Natasha

(1991, 88 min, US, Charles Martin Smith) *Dave Thomas, Sally Kellerman, Paxton Whitehead.* When we last left our evil villains, Boris Badenov and Natasha Fatale, they were two-dimensional characters drawn on paper — and still they had more depth than these live-action blow-ups made flesh by Thomas and Kellerman. True, Kellerman puts in a nice turn as the old-fashioned Pottsylvanian moll, and the script does retain some of the original cartoon nuttiness, but the plot...the animated Boris came up with better ideas. The theme song sums it up: "It's good to be bad" — but it's bad to be mediocre. ★★

Born in Flames

(1983, 78 min, US, Lizzie Borden) A science fiction tale of feminist activism and "women's empowerment from the underground," *Born in Flames* is set in an imagined future, ten years after a socialist revolution that had left the patriarchal power structure intact. A band of female anarchists, led by a black lesbian and her advisor, do battle against an unresponsive government. This unusual, engaging and controversial independent feature has a cinema verité quality which lends the story the raw power of documentary while conveying a hopeful fantasy of women of different races and sexual orientations working together against oppression. ★★★ VHS: $29.99

Born on the Fourth of July

(1989, 144 min, US, Oliver Stone) *Tom Cruise, Willem Dafoe, Raymond J. Barry, Caroline Kava, Frank Whaley, Jerry Levine, Kyra Sedgwick, Stephen Baldwin, Lili Taylor, Tom Berenger.* Stone won a much-deserved Oscar as Best Director for this brilliant, gut-wrenching adaptation of Vietnam vet Ron Kovic's autobiography. Cruise gives a remarkable performance as the initially gung-ho soldier, whose life is covered in various, almost-episodic scenes, from his tour of duty and injury to the horrendous healing process to Kovic's gradual political awakening and activism. Although Stone's *Platoon* is generally acknowledged as a landmark in the myriad of war movies, *Born* is the definitive Vietnam film to date: for Kovic, like our country itself, began the war with undying faith, and endured a painful crippling and anguishing soul-searching which ultimately suggested we hadn't done the right thing. (Letterboxed VHS available for $19.99) ★★★★ VHS: $14.99; DVD: $26.99

Born to Dance

(1936, 105 min, US, Roy Del Ruth) *James Stewart, Eleanor Powell.* That national treasure from the 1930s, Powell, stars with Stewart in this Cole Porter musical. The story, concerning a sailor in love, is routine; but Powell's musical numbers are sensational. Score includes "Easy to Love" and "I've Got You Under My Skin." ★★½ VHS: $19.99

Born to Kill

(1947, 97 min, US, Robert Wise) *Lawrence Tierney, Claire Trevor.* Born to Kill is a tough and gritty film noir, directed by Wise early in his career when he was just beginning to explore the possibilities of the genre. This hard-boiled melodrama probes the dark side of human nature and shows the results of giving in to those urges. Tierney is harrowing as a murderer who will do anything to get what he wants — and what he wants is his wife's sister. ★★★

Born Yesterday

(1950, 103 min, US, George Cukor) *Judy Holliday, William Holden, Broderick Crawford.* Though director Cukor's staging is more stage-bound than most of his stage-to-screen adaptations, *Born Yesterday* is nonetheless a thoroughly delightful comedy which earned Holliday an Oscar for her first starring role. Re-creating the part of Billie Dawn which she played on stage, Judy gives one of the classic "dumb blonde" portrayals as a gangster's moll who comes under the tutelage of "cultured" writer Holden. Crawford is her slobbish boyfriend negotiating unsavory political connections in the nation's capitol. It was a remarkable win for Holliday, besting that year both Bette Davis (*All about Eve*) and Gloria Swanson (*Sunset Boulevard*). Garson Kanin adapted his own stage hit. ★★★½ DVD: $24.99

Born Yesterday

(1993, 101 min, US, Luis Mandoki) *Melanie Griffith, John Goodman, Don Johnson, Edward Herrmann, Max Perlich.* More appropriately titled *Born Again Yesterday*, this by-the-book remake of the 1950 Judy Holliday classic casts squeakbox Griffith as the airhead consort of a loutish tycoon (Goodman). When she goes along with Goodman's plans to smarten her up, she falls for the teacher: yummy Washington columnist

Johnson. The updated screenplay doesn't stray too much from the original text, which accounts for the film's few laughs. Griffith and Johnson only go through the motions, though Goodman captures the spirit of the crooked businessman. ★★½

The Borrower

(1991, 97 min, US, John McNaughton) *Rae Dawn Chong, Don Gordon, Antonio Fargas.* Director McNaughton follows up his *Henry: Portrait of a Serial Killer* with this gory revamping of 1987's *The Hidden*, wherein an alien psycho-killer is sent to Earth for a lifelong prison sentence. This time, our other-worldly friend survives by tearing off and borrowing the heads of his victims, thereby acquiring personalities and memories as a side effect. ★★½ VHS: $14.99

The Borrowers

(1998, 86 min, GB, Peter Hewitt) *John Goodman, Jim Broadbent, Celia Imrie, Mark Williams, Hugh Laurie.* Based on the classic children's novels by Mary Norton, *The Borrowers* is the totally delightful story of 4-inch tall people who live under the floorboards of a huge house and survive by "borrowing" from the humans who live upstairs. The humans, or human "beans" as they're called, are the Clock family, who have just been kicked out of their house by conniving lawyer Ocious P. Potter (Goodman). Not to worry, because the borrowers are on the case. Told with skill, *The Borrowers* features wonderful special effects, but the film is much more than that. Children will marvel at the well-paced and imaginative story; adults will appreciate the film's good humor, which all ages will get. Goodman is particularly good-spirited as the mean-spirited Potter. ★★★½ VHS: $22.99; DVD: $19.99

Bossa Nova

(2000, 95 min, Brazil, Bruno Barreto) *Amy Irving, Antonio Fagundes, Alexandre Borges, Débora Block, Stephen Tobolowsky.* Mary Ann (Irving) is a widowed, fortysomething English teacher living in Rio de Janeiro. She is wooed by Pedro (Fagundes), a handsome, middle-aged lawyer, and Acacio (Borges), a studly soccer star — both of whom are students of hers. Meanwhile, Pedro's brother has the hots for the new legal intern, who has the hots for Acacio, and so on and so on. The charming *Bossa Nova* is a beguiling romantic comedy that may contain a few clichés of the genre (silly fantasy sequences, last-minute chases to the airport), but its very appealing leads and the gorgeous locale erase any concerns about such familiarity. A genuinely entertaining lark, this is as fun (and frothy) as the bossa nova itself. (English and Portuguese with English subtitles) ★★★ VHS: $21.99; DVD: $24.99

The Boston Strangler

(1968, 120 min, US, Richard Fleischer) *Tony Curtis, Henry Fonda, George Kennedy, Murray Hamilton.* Curtis' gripping performance as the infamous psychopath dominates this intense story — told in quasi-documentary style — of his insidious campaign of fear and subsequent capture and trial. Fonda also stars as the police detective on the case. ★★★

The Bostonians

(1984, 122 min, GB, James Ivory) *Vanessa Redgrave, Christopher Reeve, Jessica Tandy, Linda Hunt, Wallace Shawn.* An exceptionally strong

performance by Redgrave and a commendable portrayal from Reeve highlight this Merchant Ivory adaptation of Henry James' novel. Set in 19th-century New England, the story concerns a love triangle in which Redgrave, an early feminist heroine, and Reeve, a reactionary Southern lawyer, battle for the love (and political soul) of a young girl. Ruth Prawer Jhabvala (who has scripted most Merchant Ivory productions) gleaned the emotional core out of James' work and her screenplay unearths the story's underlying passion. ★★★½ VHS: $12.99; DVD: $24.99

Bottle Rocket

(1996, 91 min, US, Wes Anderson) *Owen C. Wilson, Luke Wilson, Robert Musgrave, James Caan.* In a world of diminished expectations, three disaffected misfits tackle Goal #1 of the master plan of the trio's least stable member. Too old for adolescent rebellion but with no clue of adulthood, they embark on a multi-decade program for a life of crime. This dark comedy employs engaging performances from a cast of mostly unknowns in a well-paced, quirky and surprisingly poignant tale of modern-day rites of passage. A bittersweet tale of unfocused desires and misspent energy, creating an oddly affecting and ingratiating parable about the dangers of self-delusion and misplaced trust. Caan has an extended cameo as a consummate con artist, the ill-chosen guru of the master plan's author. ★★★ VHS: $14.99; DVD: $29.99

Le Boucher

(1969, 94 min, France, Claude Chabrol) *Stéphane Audran, Jean Yanne.* The countryside in and around a small French village is the deceivingly bucolic setting for this well-paced and compelling Hitchcockian murder thriller. The stunning Audran stars as Hélène, a sophisticated schoolteacher. Emotionally scarred by a spurned love affair, she befriends a shy butcher who is tortured by his experiences in the Indochina war. Tensions mount and tragedy strikes after Hélène begins to suspect that the man is responsible for a series of sadistic killings of young women. (French with English subtitles) ★★★½ VHS: $79.99

Boudu Saved from Drowning

(1932, 87 min, France, Jean Renoir) *Michel Simon, Charles Granval.* A humane book seller saves the life of a tramp (the wonderful Simon) who tries to commit suicide in the Seine. Disastrous results are his thanks when the uninhibited Simon moves into the man's home and proceeds to seduce his wife and maid. Unlike the 1986 remake, *Down and Out in Beverly Hills*, Renoir's tramp evades encroaching "respectability" and stays true to his anarchistic ways. (French with English subtitles) ★★★½ VHS: $29.99

Boulevard

(1994, 96 min, US/Canada, Penelope Buttenhuis) *Kari Wuhrer, Rae Dawn Chong, Lou Diamond Phillips, Lance Henriksen.* A battered teen leaves her small town for the rough 'n' tumble streets of the big city. A frail, bruised but still beautiful Jennifer (Wuhrer) runs off to Toronto in an effort to escape from her abusive white-trash boyfriend. Penniless and friendless, she is clutched from the city's mean streets by Ola (Chong), a tough-talking prostitute (yes, with a heart of gold). The tired plot features an

B

over-acting Phillips as the bad pimp, a seen-it-all cop (Henriksen) and a bevy of stereotypical whores. ★★½

Boulevard of Broken Dreams

(1993, 95 min, Australia, Pino Amenta) *John Waters, Kim Gyngell.* Experiencing a mid-life crisis, Tom Garfield (Waters) returns to his native Australia after a ten-year absence. Having found great success in New York and Hollywood as a writer, he's back home to try to pick up the pieces of his scattered life — including reconciling with his estranged wife and daughter. Filmed at a snail's pace, *Boulevard of Broken Dreams* unfolds so slowly that it's rough going to get to the story's touching, second-half revelation. ★★

La Boum

(1981, 100 min, France, Claude Pinoteau) *Sophie Marceau, Claude Brasseur, Brigitte Fossey.* This charming French farce stars Marceau as a 13-year-old girl who auspiciously encounters the rites of teendom and the rituals of adulthood. An ingenious and graceful depiction of adolescent growth and familial affairs. (French with English subtitles) ★★★

Bounce

(2000, 106 min, US, Don Roos) *Ben Affleck, Gwyneth Paltrow, Joe Morton, Natasha Henstridge, Tony Goldwyn, Johnny Galecki, David Paymer, Alex D. Linz, Jennifer Grey.* Affleck plays a hotshot ad executive who gives a plane ticket to a pleasant writer (Goldwyn) who wants to see his wife (Paltrow). Not out of pity, mind you, but so he can woo a hot babe (Henstridge, playing to type) at the bar. The plane then goes down, and while Death doesn't chase Affleck *Final Destination* style, the bottle and guilt do. A year later, he tracks down Paltrow, to see how she's doing. But while not revealing himself as the guy who kinda killed her husband, he falls in love with her. An unlikely plot to be sure, but writer-director Roos (*The Opposite of Sex*) takes the trappings and creates a truly winning romance between an unsavory (but with room for improvement) man and an ideal (but hurting) woman. The two leads deal with their deep and conflicting emotions in a most human way, with pain and humor organically bursting from the situation. Real-life exes Affleck and Paltrow bring whatever they learned from their relationship to the screen and the film is better for it. ★★★ VHS: $14.99; DVD: $29.99

Bound

(1996, 108 min, US, Andy Wachowski & Larry Wachowski) *Jennifer Tilly, Gina Gershon, Joe Pantoliano.* In this stunning debut feature, the brothers Wachowski have accomplished a remarkable feat: They've taken a tried-and-true cinematic formula (film noirish plans, scams and betrayal) and added a very '90s sensibility to it, not to mention a major lesbian plot angle, without losing any of the thrill, intrigue, or snappy dialogue which characterized its '40s counterparts. Gershon and Tilly star as neighbors who become lovers first, then partners in crime. Or as Gershon says, "I can fuck somebody when I've just met them; but to steal with them, I have to know them better than myself." The question for the rest of the film then becomes who will betray whom. The intelligent script avoids every cliché it approaches and is

constantly taking the viewer into new angles of the familiar story line. *Bound* is an unexpected accomplishment, stylishly shot and edge-of-your-seat tense, and both actresses give their best performances to date. Pantoliano is great in support as Tilly's mob-connected boyfriend. (Letterboxed VHS available for $14.99) ★★★★ VHS: $9.99; DVD: $14.99

Bound and Gagged: A Love Story

(1993, 96 min, US, Daniel Appleby) *Elizabeth Saltarrelli, Ginger Lynn Allen, Chris Denton, Karen Allen, Chris Mulkey.* This frantic "My girlfriend's left me, but I'm gonna get her back" lesbian comedy is an amazingly self-assured independent feature by Appleby. Cliff (Denton) is a hetero slacker who is thrown into a suicidal funk by his wife's gleeful, vindictive departure. His best friend is Elizabeth (Saltarrelli), a fun-loving but irrational bisexual who sleeps with men but is hopelessly in love with Leslie (former porn queen Lynn Allen), a young woman stuck in a marriage with an abusive husband (Mulkey). When Leslie's hubby demands that the two stop seeing each other, Elizabeth, with a befuddled Cliff in tow, abducts Leslie and goes on the road, roaming the Midwest in a queer *Thelma and Louise* fashion. A snappily bizarre romp filled with weird, zany, and not always likable characters which mischievously explores the mysteries of obsessive but elusive love. ★★★ DVD: $19.99

Bound for Glory

(1976, 149 min, US, Hal Ashby) *David Carradine, Melinda Dillon, Ronny Cox, Randy Quaid, Gail Strickland.* A Best Picture nomination went to this acclaimed biography of the great singer-composer Woody Guthrie. Carradine gives an exceptional performance as Guthrie, whose travels across the country during the Depression would inspire his legendary folk songs. Superb cinematography by Haskell Wexler. ★★★½ VHS: $14.99; DVD: $19.99

The Bounty

(1984, 130 min, Australia, Roger Donaldson) *Anthony Hopkins, Mel Gibson, Laurence Olivier, Edward Fox, Daniel Day-Lewis, Bernard Hill.* Donaldson's lavish and sensual production presents a decidedly different and allegedly more authentic version of the infamous nautical mutiny. Hopkins as Captain Bligh is not a tyrannical madman, but rather a puritanically moral and unflinchingly formal seaman. Gibson is Fletcher Christian, former friend of the captain, who becomes a reluctant figurehead in the takeover. ★★★ DVD: $19.99

Bowfinger

(1999, 94 min, US, Frank Oz) *Steve Martin, Eddie Murphy, Heather Graham, Christine Baranski, Terence Stamp.* Martin wrote and stars in this good-spirited, funny look at a hack Hollywood producer who will go to any lengths to get his film made. Martin is Bobby Bowfinger, a 49-year-old movie producer who has some pathetic titles under his belt. He is convinced that he can sell his newest picture with superstar Kit Ramsey's (Murphy) participation. Ramsey won't do it, so Bowfinger hires a lookalike (Murphy again) and edits him with surreptitious footage of the real star. Some good-hearted laughs occur as Bowfinger resorts to every trick in the book, and Ramsey sees conspiracy all around him; though

the thinly veiled digs at Scientology (here called "Mind Head") aren't as sharp as they could have been. Martin resorts to his manic personality with good results, and Murphy — certainly in on the joke — has a great time as the pampered movie star and his slow-witted double. Graham is wasted in a redundant "sleeping your way to the top" role. ★★★ VHS: $14.99; DVD: $26.99

Box of Moonlight

(1997, 111 min, US, Tom DiCillo) *John Turturro, Sam Rockwell, Catherine Keener, Lisa Blount, Dermot Mulroney.* On the heels of DiCillo's uproarious comedy *Living in Oblivion*, this bizarre existential amusement is a disappointment. Turturro stars as Al Fountain, an anal-retentive electrical engineer who's overseeing the installation of a generating turbine in a small Appalachian hamlet. Al begins to see odd hallucinations (coffee pouring out of a cup backwards, etc.), and when the plug gets pulled on his project, he decides to go on a capricious search for a lake resort of childhood memory. His quest ultimately lands him in the lap of a twisted Peter Pan–like oddball (Rockwell) who refers to himself only as Kid. It's all too obvious that this imp is going to be Al's spiritual mentor and that's precisely what makes *Box of Moonlight* dissatisfying; it's all too obvious. Turturro gives an uncharacteristically wooden performance that is thankfully offset by Rockwell's spirited turn. ★★ VHS: $14.99; DVD: $24.99

Boxcar Bertha

(1972, 97 min, US, Martin Scorsese) *Keith Carradine, Barbara Hershey, John Carradine.* Scorsese's second feature-length film is not what you'd expect from a Roger Corman production with a title like this. Hershey gives a fine performance as a Depression-era orphan whose life is radicalized through association with renegade K. Carradine. ★★★

The Boxer

(1997, 109 min, Ireland, Jim Sheridan) *Daniel Day-Lewis, Emily Watson, Ciaran Fitzgerald, Brian Cox.* This third collaboration between director Sheridan and actor Day-Lewis (*My Left Foot, In the Name of the Father*) is an engaging drama but is by far the least accomplished of their three films together. Day-Lewis plays Danny Flynn, a thirtyish Irish boxer and former IRA member recently released from prison after 14 years who tries to make a new start by reopening his old gym and allowing both Catholics and Protestants to join. Predictably, things don't go as smoothly as hoped, with Flynn's old IRA cronies unable to lay down the sword, and Danny involved in a forbidden romance with his old flame Maggie (Watson), whose husband is in prison for an IRA bombing. The acting is uniformly excellent; Lewis, Watson and Cox give strong portrayals. The film also has the pleasantly nostalgic feel of an early '80s British crime thriller, but like many of those films, the end result is involving, unremarkable entertainment. ★★★ VHS: $14.99; DVD: $34.99

The Boxer and Death

(1962, 107 min, Czechoslovakia, Peter Solan) *Stefan Kvietik.* A Polish amateur boxer, imprisoned in a German concentration camp, is forced to literally fight for his life after the camp's burly commandant, a boxer himself, spares him from death, but forces him into pummeling fighting matches. Initially stunned

Boys Don't Cry

when he begins to receive special treatment while the commandant "fattens" him up for the kill, the prisoner faces not only the resentment of his fellow prisoners, but must decide whether to continue playing the patsy or risk his life by beating the egocentric commandant. Holding little back in depicting the wretched conditions of the death camps, the film is an unforgettably harrowing tale of bitter survival. (Czech and German with English subtitles) ★★★ VHS: $29.99

Boxing Helena

(1993, 95 min, US, Jennifer Lynch) *Julian Sands, Sherilyn Fenn, Bill Paxton, Art Garfunkel, Kurtwood Smith.* Only a child of the '80s, who was raised on "Dallas" and MTV, could think it acceptable to resolve a dramatic conflict with an "it was all a dream" sequence disguised as a music video. And twentysomething director Lynch shows her age in this immature study of love and image. Though the leads (Sands and Fenn) are undoubtedly physically attractive, Sands' twitchy, insecure performance makes the film extremely difficult to watch, even before the "dismember the one you love" theme comes to bear. ★½ VHS: $14.99; DVD: $19.99

A Boy and His Dog

(1975, 87 min, US, L.Q. Jones) *Don Johnson, Jason Robards, Jr.* A quirky sci-fi comedy that envisions a future of roving scavengers and secluded townspeople. A young Johnson, accompanied by his highly intelligent talking dog, enters a surreal world of Americana only to be faced with imprisonment and the spectre of becoming a semen-producing machine for the women of the town. A cult favorite based on Harlan Ellison's WWIII sci-fi novel. ★★★ VHS: $29.99; DVD: $19.99

The Boy with Green Hair

(1948, 82 min, US, Joseph Losey) *Dean Stockwell, Pat O'Brien, Robert Ryan.* An involving WWII drama about a young war orphan who becomes a social outcast when overnight his hair turns green. A very young Stockwell stars as the youth who is passed around from relative to relative, and ultimately becomes a symbol of the futility of war. ★★★

The Boyfriend

(1971, 141 min, GB, Ken Russell) *Twiggy, Christopher Gable, Tommy Tune, Glenda Jackson.* All-out musical numbers and spectacle abound in this lavishly entertaining musical, a glamorous tribute to Busby Berkeley. In a cameo

appearance, Jackson is the star who, before opening night of the "big show," breaks her leg, forcing her mousy understudy (Twiggy) into the spotlight and onto the road to superstardom. The film was recently restored with additional footage. ★★★

Boyfriends

(1997, 82 min, GB, Neil Hunter & Tom Hunsinger) *James Dreyfus, Mark Sands, Michael Urwin, Andrew Abelson.* This insightful and entertaining comedy-drama, depicting three troubled gay male couples, is both knowingly funny and unflinchingly on-target. The story revolves around an Easter weekend country retreat arranged for six young gay friends and bedmates. But what begins as a relaxing time soon unravels into a series of bed-hopping, ego-bruising episodes of emotional turmoil to rival the grand-daddy of gay male angst films, *The Boys in the Band*. ★★★ VHS: $29.99; DVD: $29.99

Boyfriends and Girlfriends
(L'Ami de Mon Amie)

(1987, 103 min, France, Eric Rohmer) *Emmanuelle Chaulet, Sophie Renoir.* This, Rohmer's sixth in his series of "Comedies & Proverbs," comes dangerously close to being a parody of his best work. Intellectually lightweight with only a wisp of a plot, the film revolves around a group of young, attractive and rich friends who, when not being shallow and self-centered, are on the prowl for sex. Blanche, a shy, lonely civil servant befriends the carefree Lea, who attempts to find her a lover only to see it backfire when Blanche becomes involved with Fabian, Lea's boyfriend. Set in the beautifully designed but emotionally cold new city of Cergy outside of Paris, Rohmer observes these people's love follies with his usual detached amusement. (French with English subtitles) ★★ VHS: $19.99; DVD: $29.99

Boys

(1996, 87 min, US, Stacy Cochran) *Winona Ryder, Lukas Haas, James LeGros, Skeet Ulrich, John C. Reilly, Chris Cooper, Jessica Harper.* As *Boys* illustrates through rather clichéd dramatics: Left to their own devices, boys will be boys. This film also illustrates: A contrived script left underdeveloped will soon be forgotten. *Boys* is based on a short story by James Salter, and the premise would stretch the limits of a 20-minute short. In his first "grown-up" role, Haas plays a high school senior at a boys' academy who shelters injured Ryder, who's avoiding the authorities, though why is a mystery. As the school becomes abuzz about a girl on campus, the young teen falls for the hard-partying, "older" woman. Scenes are dragged on too long, and it takes forever to get to the puzzle of what happened — by then you just won't care. ★½ VHS: $14.99; DVD: $24.99

The Boys

(1997, 85 min, Australia, Rowan Woods) *David Wenham, Toni Collette, Lynette Curran, John Polson.* Reminiscent of the smashing *Once Were Warriors*, *The Boys* is a well-wrought study of a brutal family dynamic. Brett (Wenham) returns from a stint in jail to the bleak poverty of home. He sees himself as the head of the household, but is actually the catalyst for its dissolution, imposing the illusion of order and normalcy through fear and intimidation. The family feeds on shared distrust and a casual, base violence that

erupts with regularity and explosive force. These episodes punctuate an ongoing, numbing inertia, an entrapping cycle of helplessness and hopelessness. The film's power lies in its ability to strip away all pretense from raw emotion and resonate with the primordial, blind fury of its protagonists. The on-target performances are utilized to good effect by director Woods in this potent examination of a volatile, corrosive domestic matrix. ★★★ VHS: $9.99

Boys and Girls

(2000, 95 min, US, Robert Iscove) *Freddie Prinze, Jr., Claire Forlani, Jason Biggs, Amanda Detmer, Heather Donahoe.* An awful teen comedy, the generically titled *Boys and Girls* reteams the star and director of *She's All That*, but cannot duplicate that film's meager charms. The "plot" finds Prinze dumped by his girlfriend — or rather, she asked her roommate (Forlani) to tell him he's dumped. Shockingly, Prinze and Forlani start to fall in love, and that's when boredom sets in. Annoying, moldy one-liners alternate with crappy bubble-gum music to grate on your last nerve, while the one surefire scene in these things — the dance/musical number — is overdone and infantile, with a song that desperately wants to be Fatboy Slim's "Rockafella Skank," which was used in the dance scene in *She's All That*. Forlani is terribly miscast and Prinze is merely terrible. ★ VHS: $19.99; DVD: $32.99

Boys Don't Cry

(1999, 116 min, US, Kimberly Peirce) *Hilary Swank, Chloë Sevigny, Peter Sarsgaard, Brendan Sexton III, Alison Folland, Alicia Goranson, Matt McGrath.* A brutal, enthralling examination of sexual identity, this fictionalized drama focuses on the tragic real-life story of Brandon Teena, a woman (Teena Brandon) who decided quite early to live her life as a man — a decision he paid for with his life. Oscar winner Swank is riveting as Brandon, a sweet but far-from-perfect 21-year-old drifter who simply wanted to be a boy and love women — and have them love him. The harrowing tale, set in a trailer-trash Nebraska town, follows Brandon as he befriends and moves in with a group of poor but fun-loving people. He also falls in love with Lana (Sevigny in an equally impressive performance), a tough-talking gal who finally meets a man who respects her and treats her right. But when Brandon is exposed as a woman, ignorance, fear and homophobia drives two of Lana's male friends to violently confront him. Unflinching in its depiction of the working-class environment and complex in its handling of all of the characters, the film humanizes a person whose only crime was to express his true sexual identity. An unforgettable film experience. After watching *Boys Don't Cry*, you'll be equally moved by the true-life documentary on Brandon, *The Brandon Teena Story*. ★★★★ VHS: $14.99; DVD: $34.99

The Boys from Brazil

(1978, 123 min, US, Franklin J. Schaffner) *Laurence Olivier, Gregory Peck, James Mason, Uta Hagen, Lilli Palmer, Steve Guttenberg, Denholm Elliott.* Olivier stars in this high-tension political thriller as a Nazi-hunter who uncovers the existence of a war criminal (Peck) and his plans to resurrect the Third Reich by cloning Adolf Hitler. Based on the novel by Ira Levin. ★★★ VHS: $9.99; DVD: $24.99

B

The Boys in the Band

(1970, 118 min, US, William Friedkin) *Kenneth Nelson, Leonard Frey, Cliff Gorman, Laurence Luckinbill, Frederick Combs, Robert La Tourneaux.* Historically and politically significant despite (or because of) the pervading self-loathing and wallowing self-pity of its gay characters, *The Boys in the Band* is a stage-bound, hyperventilating comedy-drama about eight friends who get together for a simple birthday party. What ensues during the course of the evening is enough emotion, acid-laced barbs and self-analysis to last a lifetime. Michael (Nelson), a guilt-ridden Catholic with a drinking problem, is the host of the party. Harold (marvelously played by Frey) is the birthday boy. And the guests include a bickering couple, a hustler (a present for Harold), and a limp-wristed, lisping interior designer (immortally played by Gorman). With a screenplay peppered with many memorable lines, *The Boys in the Band* is a pre-liberation classic which is dated but hilarious and at times surprisingly offensive to '90s gay sensibility. It's also an important step in the depiction of gays in film. ★★★

The Boys Next Door

(1985, 91 min, US, Penelope Spheeris) *Charlie Sheen, Maxwell Caulfield, Christopher McDonald, Patti D'Arbanville, Moon Zappa.* Sheen and Caulfield are Bo and Roy, respectively, two California high school grads who went their frustrations by going on a killing spree. In a hard-hitting, semidocumentary-like style, the film examines the damaged psyches of these two killers as they wend their way throughout Los Angeles randomly choosing and then murdering their victims. The murder scenes are especially brutal, but don't border on the gratuitous as they serve to illustrate the duo's twisted minds. There's a subplot of gay bashing (one of the film's most disturbing sequences) which brings to light Roy's closeted homosexual feelings. ★★★ DVD: $24.99

The Boys of St. Vincent

(1992, 184 min, Canada, John N. Smith) *Henry Czerny, Johnny Morina, Sebastian Spence.* This compelling two-part drama of physical and sexual abuse at a Canadian boys' orphanage unravels like a wrenching visual horror film and makes for a riveting, if uncomfortable, viewing. Part One, set in a Newfoundland school in 1975, centers on a withdrawn ten-year-old boy who is the sexual pet of Brother Lavin (Czerny), the dictatorial and devil-like principal. It takes a sympathetic janitor to call the police, but Church complicity and police reluctance to interfere conspire to cover up the problem in a veil of secrecy. Part Two, set 15 years later, finds the boys, now emotionally scarred men, successfully initiating charges against the brothers involved. The story, based on true events, is quite disturbing, and the scenes of physical and sexual abuse are almost too painful to watch. ★★★ VHS: $29.99

Boys on the Side

(1995, 117 min, US, Herbert Ross) *Whoopi Goldberg, Mary-Louise Parker, Drew Barrymore, James Remar, Matthew McConaughey, Estelle Parsons, Billy Wirth.* Singer-musician Joan (Goldberg), reeling from the break-up of her latest band, takes a ride-share to L.A. with Robin (Parker), a seemingly pristine yuppie who bemoans the crash of the real estate market. En route, they stop to visit Joan's friend Holly (Barrymore), interrupting her savage beating at the hands of her scummy boyfriend. The swiftly moving odyssey which follows is punctuated by strong characterizations. Fine cinematography indulges the glowing desert vistas of Tucson, a pit stop which extends to include birth and death. The film flirts with mawkishness during the last half-hour, only momentarily crossing the line. While comparisons to *Thelma and Louise* are to be made, the film's more about survival than allegory. And that's its gritty strength. ★★★ VHS: $14.99; DVD: $19.99

Boys Town

(1938, 96 min, US, Norman Taurog) *Spencer Tracy, Mickey Rooney.* Fine sentimental drama with Tracy winning an Oscar for his poignant portrayal of Father Flanagan, the founder of a school and community for troubled youths. Rooney is a street-wise delinquent. ★★★ VHS: $19.99

Boyz N the Hood

(1991, 107 min, US, John Singleton) *Cuba Gooding, Jr., Ice Cube, Morris Chestnut, Laurence Fishburne, Nia Long, Tyra Ferrell, Angela Bassett.* Singleton's powerful directorial debut is a brilliant examination of the crises facing young black men in the '90s, as well as a searing indictment of the culture of violence which holds sway in American ghettoes today. Set in the rough-and-tumble of South Central Los Angeles, the film tells the story of three black teens who face the unrelenting, and often deadly, realities of urban life. Singleton successfully avoids stereotyping his three heroes as inner-city misfits and instead portrays them as average American youth caught in an untenable situation. ★★★★ VHS: $12.99; DVD: $19.99

The Brady Bunch Movie

(1995, 89 min, US, Betty Thomas) *Shelley Long, Gary Cole, Christine Taylor, Jennifer Elise Cox, RuPaul, Jean Smart.* The millions who loved — or hated — "The Brady Bunch," have reason to rejoice in this hilarious polyester and plaid restoration that asks the question, "What would happen if America's favorite family of the '70s ever collided with the naughty '90s?" In true sit-com fashion, this week's episode finds the Bradys on the verge of losing their groovy pad unless they can raise the $20,000 they owe in back taxes. And to add to the stew, Jan's sibling rivalry with "Marcia! Marcia! Marcia!" reaches fever pitch; and Marcia's best friend at school has a lesbian crush on her. Long and Cole appear as parents Carol and Mike, but it's Taylor and especially Cox who shine as Marcia and Jan, respectively. Chock-full of in-jokes and laughs, this double-knitted comedy strikes a nostalgic chord even as it hits the funny bone. (Sequel: *A Very Brady Sequel*) ★★★ VHS: $9.99

Brain Damage

(1988, 94 min, US, Frank Henenlotter) *Rick Herbst, Gordon MacDonald.* If you loved *Frankenhooker* or *Basket Case*, then this offbeat gem is for you. In a sharp parable about drug addiction, Herbst must cater to his talking parasite's every whim, or be deprived of its euphoria-inducing excreta. Horror show host Zacherley supplies the voice for the wise-cracking slug. ★★★ VHS: $14.99; DVD: $29.99

Brain Dead

(1989, 85 min, US, Adam Simon) *Bill Pullman, Bill Paxton, Bud Cort.* Well-intentioned psychological thriller that asks the question, "Are we the dreamer, or the dream?" Pullman stars as a scientist whose brain research leads to the recesses of his own mind. To say more would be to give the show away, but suffice it to say that the film is highly original and well-staged. ★★★ VHS: $14.99; DVD: $19.99

Brain Donors

(1992, 79 min, US, Dennis Dugan) *John Turturro, Bob Nelson, Mel Smith, Nancy Marchand.* Anyone who has been blown away by the intensity of Turturro must also have been impressed by the actor's versatility. From a snivelling traitor in *Miller's Crossing* to a self-important playwright with nothing to say in *Barton Fink*, Turturro's cutting-edge performances invariably leave one asking, "What does he do for an encore?" Well, try this for size, as he takes on the ambitious role of Groucho Marx. Updated and restaged to the world of ballet, this well-meaning remake of the Marx Brothers' classic *A Night at the Opera* benefits from Turturro's frenetic turn as an ambulance-chasing shyster masquerading as an impresario of the dance. Marchand pays ample tribute to Margaret Dumont. ★★½ VHS: $14.99

The Brain from Planet Arous

(1958, 70 min, US, Nathan Juran) *John Agar, Joyce Meadows.* In this precursor to *The Hidden*, a lascivious criminal brain from another galaxy commandeers the body of nuclear scientist Agar. Another brain from Arous, this one benevolent, comes to Earth and enlists the help of Agar's girlfriend, her father and her dog (which it inhabits), in an attempt to foil the plans of the evil brain, named Gor. Agar makes an appropriately insane, if overacting, villain when he is being controlled by Gor, and the brisk movie is engaging in a campy way, but overall it is 1950s sci-fi schlock, complete with cheesy special effects and one-dimensional plot and characters. It's fun to watch, however. ★★ VHS: $19.99

The Brain That Wouldn't Die

(1963, 81 min, US, Joseph Green) *Herb (Jason) Evers, Virginia Leith.* A scientist wants to graft the body of a hooker onto the decapitated head of his girlfriend. The seven-foot tall mutant in the closet doesn't think that's such a good idea. With occasional moments of gore, this is so bad, it's...well, bad. It's also cheesy, late-nite fun. ★½ VHS: $12.99; DVD: $24.99

Brainscan

(1994, 96 min, US, John Flynn) *Edward Furlong, Frank Langella, T. Ryder Smith, Amy Hargreaves.* This high-tech horror yawn fest shamelessly borrows from the *Nightmare on Elm Street* films. A teenage video game addict (Furlong) orders a new interactive game which penetrates his subconscious. When friends and neighbors start turning up dead, he becomes the center of an investigation, while at the same time he's coaxed by a CD-ROM–spawned villain named the Trickster (Smith). Long on dazzling special effects but lacking in plot. ★★ VHS: $9.99

Brainstorm

(1983, 106 min, US, Douglas Trumbull) *Natalie Wood, Christopher Walken, Louise Fletcher, Cliff Robertson.* Forever to be remembered chiefly as Wood's last film (a double was used to finish some scenes), this energetic, highly original sci-fi yarn covers a lot of the same ground as *Flatliners*, but with better special effects (director Trumbull did the magic for *2001: A Space Odyssey*, after all). Fletcher is a knockout as a scientist grappling with the moral repercussions of a euphoria-making sensory device. ★★★ VHS: $14.99; DVD: $19.99

Bram Stoker's Dracula

(1992, 127 min, US, Francis Ford Coppola) *Gary Oldman, Winona Ryder, Anthony Hopkins, Keanu Reeves, Cary Elwes, Richard E. Grant, Bill Campbell, Tom Waits, Sadie Frost.* Coppola's extravagant adaptation of the literary classic delivers the goods with visceral, almost apocalyptic images of carnage juxtaposed with lush, Gothic visuals befitting an Anne Rice novel. These elements coupled with a truly seductive performance by Oldman as the bloodsucking antihero makes for a riveting journey through time. The film opens in the 14th century where Vlad the Impaler (sometimes thought to be Stoker's inspiration for his novel) renounces God in favor of evil following his beloved's premature death. The film then jumps to 19th-century England where Vlad, now known as Count Dracul, finds his eternal love reincarnated as a young beauty, portrayed by Ryder. A boldly original and satisfying interpretation of vampire lore. ★★★½ VHS: $14.99; DVD: $19.99

Branded to Kill

(1967, 91 min, Japan, Seijun Suzuki) *Jo Shishido, Mariko Ogawa, Annu Mari.* This bizarre gangster thriller is a remarkable, audacious piece of filmmaking. It tells the story of Hanada (Shishido), the underworld's "Number Three Killer," a dead shot with either pistol or rifle who also becomes sexually aroused when he sniffs boiled rice. After he shoots Number Two Killer, he is given four extremely difficult assassinations to save face. He carries out three of them (all imaginatively staged), but the fourth is bungled, so he is marked for death. Eventually, Number One Killer comes out of the shadows and begins

Branded to Kill

a long, tense showdown with Hanada. Highly original, the film thumbs its nose at both linear storytelling and Japanese filmmaking (especially the yakuza genre). However, director Suzuki's compositions are brilliant, using the black-and-white widescreen frame in new, inventive ways. While not for everyone — its story is very confusing and impressionistic — the film is a wild piece of entertainment. (Letterboxed) (Japanese with English subtitles) ★★★½ VHS: $29.99; DVD: $29.99

The Brandon Teena Story

(1997, 88 min, US, Susan Muska and Greta Olafsdottir) A powerful and emotionally moving documentary that delves into the nature of sexual identity as it relates to the senseless injustice of the brutal murder of a young female-to-male transsexual. In 1993, Brandon Teena was a fresh-scrubbed young man of twenty who moved to the small town of Falls City, Nebraska. He soon began dating girls. But the truth came out that he was biologically a woman, a discovery that prompted two of his former friends to beat and rape him. After going to the shockingly indifferent authorities, she went into hiding, only to be discovered and then killed, along with two friends. A bleak tale, but one that is given exhaustive and heartfelt handling by the filmmakers who had extraordinary access to all of the involved; Brandon's mother and sister, his female lovers (who claim "he knows how to treat a lady"), friends, the police and even the imprisoned killers. Much of the information in the film formed the basis of the 1999 fiction film *Boys Don't Cry.* ★★★★ VHS: $24.99; DVD: $29.99

Brassed Off

(1997, 107 min, GB, Mark Herman) *Pete Postlethwaite, Ewan McGregor, Tara Fitzgerald, Stephen Tompkinson.* In the wonderful tradition of "small" British social comedies comes this unexpected pleasure with one of the most unlikely topics for a ravishing and delectable comedy: a brass band competition. In the small Northern England mining town of Grimley, miners have proudly played in the town's brass band for over a century. But the imminent closing of the mines threatens not only the livelihood of an entire town, but the band as well. Under the direction of Postlethwaite, the band tries to persevere as the championship and an uncertain future lie ahead. Writer-director Herman has created an absolute joy — its humor is sharp, its political observations sharper, and the film is peopled with most appealing and nicely defined characters. ★★★½ VHS: $14.99; DVD: $29.99

The Brave Little Toaster

(1987, 90 min, US, Jerry Rees) *Voices of: Jon Lovitz, Phil Hartman.* Cute animated musical adventure of a dejected toaster who rounds up the other household appliances — the vacuum cleaner, electric blanket, bedside lamp and radio — and leaves their country cottage for the big city in search of their beloved owner. ★★★ VHS: $14.99

Braveheart

(1995, 180 min, US, Mel Gibson) *Mel Gibson, Sophie Marceau, Patrick McGoohan, Catherine McCormack, Ian Bannen, Brendan Gleeson.* Gibson's second feature film as director is an accomplished, realistically staged historical epic about 13th-century Scottish patriot and free-

dom fighter William Wallace. Written by Randall Wallace, reportedly a descendant of the hero himself, it shows us William's youth, the courtship of his wife, his reluctant entry into "the Troubles" with the English King Edward the Longshanks (McGoohan), and his eventual embrace of the military leadership of his country. Three hours in length, *Braveheart* is remarkably never dull — a credit to Gibson's direction since the script must juggle several story lines. The most amazing thing about the film, however, is its savagely authentic battle scenes, two of which are of an epic scale not seen in film since *Spartacus.* But Wallace's psychological transition from revenge to revolution and his courage in the face of death lift the film above the limitations of an action/adventure movie. (VHS available letterboxed or pan & scan) ★★★½ VHS: $24.99; DVD: $29.99

Brazil

(1985, 131 min, US, Terry Gilliam) *Jonathan Pryce, Kim Greist, Robert De Niro, Katherine Helmond, Ian Holm, Bob Hoskins.* The second in Gilliam's "trilogy" about the realm of fantasy intruding into everyday life (the first being *Time Bandits*, the last *The Adventures of Baron Munchausen*), this darkly comic film is the best of the three. Pryce is a bureaucrat stuck in a chaotic government styled in equal parts after *1984* and *Modern Times.* He accidentally discovers a mistake made by an authoritarian wing of the government where a man was tortured to death because of a clerical error. His struggle with both his conscience and with the authorities who are now after him is interwoven with his increasingly frequent flights of fancy involving a mysterious stranger he loves and a huge samurai-like demon he must defeat to save her. Gilliam's vision is perfectly realized here; his futuristic society is a black, towering megalith of ductwork, fascist architecture and machinery crammed into every possible space. A towering achievement for Gilliam, especially considering the struggle he reportedly had to have the film released in its original form — a struggle with a mindless bureaucracy not unlike the one experienced by Pryce in this work of "fiction." ★★★★ VHS: $14.99; DVD: $24.99

Break of Hearts

(1935, 80 min, US, Philip Moeller) *Katharine Hepburn, Charles Boyer.* Hepburn and Boyer offer good performances in this gentle romantic drama about a young composer (Kate) and her love affair with a famous conductor (Boyer). ★★½ VHS: $19.99

Breakdown

(1997, 93 min, US, Jonathan Mostow) *Kurt Russell, Kathleen Quinlan, J.T. Walsh.* Somewhere in the Texas desert, a husband and wife (Russell and Quinlan) are "taking the scenic route" on their way to San Diego and a new life. The financial worry they share is nothing compared to the trouble that lay ahead when she disappears in this tension-filled thriller. Stranded in the middle of nowhere, Quinlan accepts a ride from a friendly trucker (Walsh) while Russell stays with the car. But when Russell meets up with Walsh, he insists they've never met and knows nothing about his wife. The story follows Russell as he desperately tries to piece the puzzle together and locate his wife. Director Mostow creates quite a lot of suspense from the

B

simple premise, and manages to do so with only barren landscape and narrative thrift. (Letterboxed VHS available for $14.99) ★★★ VHS: $9.99; DVD: $24.99

Breaker Morant

(1979, 107 min, Australia, Bruce Beresford) *Edward Woodward, Bryan Brown, Jack Thompson, John Waters.* "Breaker" Morant, a cavalry officer serving in South Africa's Boer War, was tried for war crimes and murder along with two other Australian soldiers. They were defended by an inexperienced but spirited military defense attorney who valiantly tried to expose the political nature of the trial. This fact-based drama stars Woodward, in a sterling performance, as Morant, a heroic soldier who also happened to be a sensitive poet and sometime philosopher. Contrasted with him are the other two soldiers on trial: one a rowdy ne'er-do-well (Brown) and the other an inexperienced introvert. Beautifully filmed, *Breaker Morant* incorporates exciting flashbacks as the facts are presented in the courtroom. It's also profoundly moving, a riveting exposition of a series of events open to many interpretations which lead to a definite conception of what truth is. ★★★★ VHS: $14.99; DVD: $19.99

Breakfast at Tiffany's

(1961, 114 min, US, Blake Edwards) *Audrey Hepburn, George Peppard, Patricia Neal, Mickey Rooney.* Based on a Truman Capote story, this winning romantic comedy stars Hepburn as small-town Texas girl Holly Golightly, who leaves home to conquer the Manhattan party scene. There's zesty direction by Edwards and a fanciful Henry Mancini score including the Oscar-winning "Moon River." (VHS available letterboxed or pan & scan) ★★★½ VHS: $14.99; DVD: $29.99

The Breakfast Club

(1985, 92 min, US, John Hughes) *Emilio Estevez, Anthony Michael Hall, Judd Nelson, Molly Ringwald, Ally Sheedy.* Perceptive and entertaining teen drama written and directed by Hughes. Five high school students spend a Saturday detention at the school library. All of the students come to learn a little about themselves, as well as their newly acquainted classmates. This young cast has rarely been better. ★★★ VHS: $9.99; DVD: $24.99

Breaking Away

(1979, 100 min, US, Peter Yates) *Dennis Christopher, Daniel Stern, Dennis Quaid, Paul Dooley, Barbara Barrie.* A funny, exhilarating ode to growing up. Four recent high school graduates compete against insecurity, frustration and an Italian bicycle racing team. Sensitively directed by Yates. ★★★★ VHS: $9.99

Breaking Glass

(1980, 104 min, GB, Brian Gibson) *Hazel O'Connor, Phil Daniels, Jonathan Pryce.* The rise to stardom is old fodder for the story mill and this unexceptional punk/new wave success story does nothing to give it new life. This is a fairly predictable tale of the exploits of Hazel O'Connor as she works her way out of the dingy clubs and into the clubs of London to become a punk superstar. Only exceptional performances save this film from complete mediocrity. ★★

Breaking In

(1989, 91 min, US, Bill Forsyth) *Burt Reynolds, Casey Siemaszko, Sheila Kelley, Maury Chaykin.* This heist comedy by Forsyth was anticipated by many in the film community with great relish. Couple Forsyth's knack for putting together charming, off-kilter comedies and the screenwriting genius of John Sayles; add to the mix the inimitable talents of Reynolds and the youthful energy of newcomer Siemaszko, and it's easy to see why so many people were expecting so much from this story about an aging safecracker (Reynolds) and his overly enthusiastic apprentice (Siemaszko). The result, however, is a somewhat mild, not overly ambitious comedy of errors. ★★½ VHS: $14.99

Breaking the Code

(1986, 90 min, GB, Herbert Wise) *Derek Jacobi, Harold Pinter, Prunella Scales, Amanda Root, Alun Armstrong, Richard Johnson.* Re-creating his Tony Award—winning performance for this exceptional play-on-film, Jacobi is outstanding as mathematician and WWII hero Alan Turing, who was naively open about his homosexuality in an intolerant society. A mathematical genius, Turing was responsible for single-handedly breaking the near-impenetrable Nazi Enigma code, a breakthrough which virtually guaranteed an Allied victory against the German navy. Hugh Whitemore's intelligent screenplay traces Turing's life as a university student, his time working for British intelligence, and his postwar years as a government researcher in crystal-clear flashbacks. Complex, often humorous, and intellectually satisfying, Whitemore's story, while paying tribute to Turing, is a stinging indictment of homophobia and its often high cost. As the stuttering, nail-biting, completely candid Turing, Jacobi mesmerizes with a stunning portrayal rich in subtle shadings, honest emotions and profound compassion. ★★★★ VHS: $19.99

Breaking the Rules

(1992, 100 min, US, Neal Israel) *Jason Bateman, Jonathan Silverman, C. Thomas Howell, Annie Potts.* A tedious tale of three young men who reunite a few years after college to confront their pasts and their futures which sadly breaks no rules and blazes no new trails. In all fairness, the three young leads do their best with a lethal script which follows the trio as they set off on a cross-country road trip after Bateman reveals to them that he is dying of cancer. Potts enlivens things up as a small-town waitress who joins them on their trail of tears. (Filmed in 1989 but released three years later.) ★½ VHS: $14.99

Breaking the Waves

(1996, 156 min, GB/Scotland, Lars von Trier) *Emily Watson, Stellan Skarsgård, Katrin Cartlidge, Jean-Marc Barr, Udo Kier.* Danish director von Trier has managed to tightrope his way toward straight narrative while at the same time making a thoroughly unconventional movie. And it must be said at the outset that this 156-minute marathon is definitely not for all tastes. But for those who are not put off by a claustrophobic, hand-held, ultra-intimate character study of the pitiful lives of a few hardy souls in an inhospitable Scottish hamlet on the North Sea coast, the result is a riveting and thought-provoking examination of obsessive love and one's relationship to God. Bess (Watson) is an emotional-

ly unstable young woman who breaks the village taboo by marrying an outsider, Jan (Skarsgård). Jan, a big bear of an oil rig worker with a heart of gold, seems bent on seeing her passions flower beyond her strict religious background. But on the fateful day that he must return to his rig, she breaks apart mentally and thus begins her slide into all-out obsession. Bess regularly throughout the film holds intimate two-way conversations with God — as hokey as they could have been, Watson miraculously pulls them off. Ultimately the film seems as confused about faith as its characters are, but that by no means diminishes its effectiveness as a philosophical puzzler. (VHS available letterboxed or pan & scan) ★★★★ DVD: $14.99

Breaking Up

(1997, 89 min, US, Robert Greenwald) *Russell Crowe, Salma Hayek.* Though played engagingly by both Crowe and Hayek, this minor romantic comedy has some good ideas and inventive visuals, but is sabotaged by a rambling screenplay and sometime static direction. The story follows the ups and downs of a relationship — they love, they split, they argue, they reconcile, they make love, they split. Much more suited to the stage than the screen, *Breaking Up* has an energy level that is almost exhausting — detailing a break-up and reconciliation doesn't necessarily need to make the viewer feel they, too, have sweated the anxiety of this volatile affair. ★★ VHS: $19.99

A Breath of Scandal

(1960, 98 min, US, Michael Curtiz) *Sophia Loren, John Gavin, Maurice Chevalier.* The ghost of Ernst Lubitsch was vainly resurrected for this uneven adaptation of the Ferenc Molnar play. Loren gives a gallant attempt to be sexy and funny, playing an Austrian princess. Unfortunately, she's cast opposite the monotonous Gavin as an American businessman who enters her life and with whom she falls in love. Director Curtiz evokes a small degree of playfulness, but misses many comic opportunities. However, former Lubitsch leading man Chevalier appears as Loren's father, and he elevates every scene in which he appears. ★★ VHS: $9.99

Breathless (À Bout de Souffle)

(1959, 89 min, France, Jean-Luc Godard) *Jean-Paul Belmondo, Jean Seberg.* Godard shook the film world with his dynamic style of editing, sound usage, character development and plot progression in this, his first feature film. Belmondo is the two-bit, existential hood engaged in a fateful affair with Seberg. (Remade in 1983) (French with English subtitles) ★★★★ VHS: $19.99

A Breed Apart

(1984, 101 min, US, Philippe Mora) *Donald Pleasence, Powers Booth, Rutger Hauer, Kathleen Turner.* Millionaire egg collector Pleasence wants two rare Bald Eagle eggs, even if it means extinguishing the species. He offers $150,000 to world-famous mountain climber Boothe to scale the rock face on which the nest sits, on an island owned by Vietnam vet back-to-nature survivalist Hauer. An idiosyncratic little film saved from its shortcomings by the performances of its cast. ★★½

Brenda Starr

(1992, 94 min, US, Robert Ellis Miller) *Brooke Shields, Timothy Dalton, Tony Peck, Diana Scarwid, Charles Durning, Eddie Albert, Henry Gibson.* It took four painstaking years to bring Dale Messick's popular comic strip character straight to home video, and this is so bad it's easy to see why it was never released theatrically. Shields headlines as the star reporter for the *Flash* who, along with her dashing mystery man Basil St. John (Dalton), is hot on the trail of the scoop of the century: a new, secret formula created by an ex-Nazi scientist which could open the door to star travel. It has to be seen to be disbelieved. (Letterboxed) ★ VHS: $14.99; DVD: $24.99

Brewster McCloud

(1970, 101 min, US, Robert Altman) *Bud Cort, Sally Kellerman, Shelley Duvall, Michael Murphy, Margaret Hamilton.* A quirky oddity that, although seemingly dated today, still should please fans of fantasy as well as devotees of director Altman. Cort stars as the misunderstood young man who lives within the catacombs of Houston's Astrodome and dreams of flying on his own. Kellerman is his fairy godmother who helps make it happen, and the delightful Duvall plays a Dome tour guide who befriends him. A funny fable about man's lofty ambitions as well as the forces of self-destruction. ★★★ VHS: $19.99

Brewster's Millions

(1985, 101 min, US, Walter Hill) *Richard Pryor, John Candy, Lonette McKee, Hume Cronyn.* Though Pryor and Candy are appealing performers, and work rather well together, there's not much to recommend in this oft-told tale. Pryor plays a baseball player who stands to collect $300 million — but only if he can spend $30 million in exactly one month. ★★ VHS: $9.99; DVD: $19.99

Brian's Song

(1970, 73 min, US, Buzz Kulik) *James Caan, Billy Dee Williams, Jack Warden.* Well-made and moving TV drama about Chicago Bears player Brian Piccolo, and his special friendship with teammate Gale Sayers when the former is diagnosed with cancer. Caan as Piccolo and Williams as Sayers bring remarkable heartfelt conviction to their roles. ★★★ VHS: $9.99; DVD: $24.99

The Bride

(1985, 118 min, US, Franc Roddam) *Sting, Jennifer Beals, Clancy Brown, David Rappaport, Quentin Crisp, Geraldine Page, Cary Elwes.* Sting plays Dr. Frankenstein, whose monster (Brown) runs away from the lab after being rejected by his newly created bride-to-be (Beals). On the road, the goodhearted but muddled monster is befriended by a conniving midget (Rappaport). The friendship that develops is both funny and touching and makes the film worth watching despite the inane activities going on back at Frankenstein's castle. ★★½ VHS: $9.99

The Bride Came COD

(1941, 92 min, US, William Keighley) *Bette Davis, James Cagney, Jack Carson, George Tobias.* Though neither was known specifically for comedy, Davis and Cagney bring a lot of life to this zesty 1940s romp about flier Cagney kidnapping bride-to-be Davis at her millionaire father's request. The

fireworks start when they crash land in the desert. ★★★ VHS: $19.99

Bride of Chucky

(1998, 89 min, US, Ronny Yu) *Jennifer Tilly, Brad Dourif, John Ritter, Katherine Heigl, Nick Stabile, Alexis Arquette.* Chucky gets lucky in this third installment of the popular horror franchise, but so, too, does the viewer as director Yu and writer Don Mancini have created a campy, over-the-top horror comedy which piles on the laughs as much as the scares. Tilly is priceless as Tiffany, a black magic woman who brings Chucky back to life (after his demise in *Child's Play 2*). But Chucky has other plans, and soon, Tiffany is a pint-sized dolly herself, and the deadly duo are on the road on a fun-packed killing spree. The deaths are imaginatively staged (though bloody and sick), and Chucky and Tiffany have a most amusing time with bad puns and badder attitudes. Put the logic on hold, and enjoy this for what it is — a crazy, funny, irreverent gross-out fest. Better than either of its predecessors. ★★★ VHS: $14.99; DVD: $24.99

The Bride of Frankenstein

(1935, 75 min, US, James Whale) *Boris Karloff, Colin Clive, Elsa Lanchester.* Dr. Frankenstein (Clive) makes a bride for his creature (Karloff), and all hell breaks loose. Arguably better than the orginal — both emotionally and stylistically — Whale's moody sequel to his 1931 classic *Frankenstein* best illustrates the director's macabre sense of humor and filmmaking talent. Lanchester plays a dual role as "the bride" and as author Mary Shelley. Whale personally designed Lanchester's spiffy hair-do. ★★★★ VHS: $14.99; DVD: $29.99

Bride of Re-Animator

(1990, 99 min, US, Brian Yuzna) *Jeffrey Combs, Bruce Abbott.* This sequel to the horror cult classic *Re-Animator* carries on the tradition of presenting graphic bloodshed so outrageous it's goofy. Combs reprises his role as Herbert West, the thoroughly demented medical student who is obsessed with reanimating dead tissue. Here, Herbert launches a new project at med school. Filled with hilarious one-liners and ludicrous scenarios only possible in films like this, *Bride of Re-Animator* is silly and entertaining, equal parts comedy and horror. ★★½ VHS: $9.99; DVD: $29.99

Bride of the Monster

(1956, 69 min, US, Ed Wood, Jr.) *Bela Lugosi, Tor Johnson, Loretta King, Tony McCoy, Harvey Dunn, Dolores Fuller, Paul Marco.* Bela's last screen appearance, where he conducts radiation experiments on men (and creates a giant killer rubber octopus). Tor plays his monstrous servant. Low-grade, low-budget craziness from Wood. ★ VHS: $19.99; DVD: $24.99

The Bride with White Hair

(1993, 111 min, Hong Kong, Ronny Yu) *Leslie Cheung, Brigitte Lin.* Set in a fantasy world which sometimes resembles feudal China and sometimes looks like Rudyard Kipling on acid, this expensive Hong Kong film is about a young warrior (Cheung), the successor to the leadership of the clan Wu Tang, who falls in love with a powerful warrior/witch (Lin) who is the bound slave of a pair of evil siblings whose intent is to destroy Wu Tang and rule the world. These star-

crossed lovers make a pact to run away together, but things naturally go awry, leaving bloodshed in their wake. Filled with the usual Hong Kong action setpieces, *Bride* is distinguished by its adult tone and heartfelt love story. (Cantonese with English subtitles) ★★★★ VHS: $19.99; DVD: $29.99

The Bride with White Hair 2

(1993, 80 min, Hong Kong, David Wu) *Brigitte Lin, Sunny Chan, Christy Chung, Leslie Cheung.* Made right on the heels of *Bride* part one, this dull and pointless sequel picks up ten years after the events of the original. Ni-chang (Lin), the white-haired witch, is now inexplicably the leader of a man-hating cult populated by women who have been cheated on or betrayed by their lovers and confidants. Seeking to destroy the remnants of the Wu Tang clan, Lin kidnaps the bride of the nephew of Cho Yi-hang (Cheung), the man who originally betrayed her. Tepid, lackluster and sorely missing the style of the first production, *Bride 2* only becomes worthwhile during its last ten minutes, when Lin and Cheung are finally (and inevitably) reunited. Unfortunately, it's too long a wait. (Cantonese with English subtitles) ★½ VHS: $19.99; DVD: $29.99

The Bride Wore Black

(1967, 107 min, France, Francois Truffaut) *Jeanne Moreau, Claude Rich, Jean-Claude Brialy.* Moreau stars as the inscrutable femme fatale with a murderous mission in Truffaut's haunting, suspense-filled homage to Hitchcock. Widowed on her wedding day, Moreau vows vengeance on her husband's killers. Stylish and extremely satisfying with a score by Bernard Herrmann. (French with English subtitles) ★★★½ VHS: $19.99; DVD: $19.99

The Bride Wore Red

(1937, 103 min, US, Dorothy Arzner) *Joan Crawford, Franchot Tone, Robert Young.* In a nod to "Pygmalion" and with a touch of "Cinderella," an eccentric count, trying to prove his theory about class difference, sends nightclub singer Crawford off to a posh Austrian resort. There she poses as royalty, meets postman Tone and rich playboy Young. Director Arzner isn't afforded the luxury of a classic screenplay, but manages to infuse a degree of high spirits into her social comedy. Crawford is well cast and looks great. ★★★ VHS: $19.99

Brides of Dracula

(1960, 85 min, GB, Terence Fisher) *Peter Cushing, David Peel.* Dracula's back and this time he's a blond! Peel stars in this quasi-Freudian take on the vampire legend as a bloodthirsty count whose dining-out privileges are revoked by his mother, who keeps him locked in the castle tower. Who says blonds have more fun? Cushing reprises his role as Professor Van Helsing. ★★★ VHS: $14.99

Brideshead Revisited

(1980, 581 min, GB, Charles Sturridge/Michael Lindsay-Hogg) *Jeremy Irons, Anthony Andrews, Claire Bloom, Laurence Olivier, John Gielgud, Diana Quick.* A brilliant and haunting adaptation of Evelyn Waugh's best-loved novel. Don't be put off by the length of this miniseries, as it is divided into six easily viewed and totally captivating episodes which chronicle a young man's enigmatic and obsessive relationship with a rich, aristocratic British family. Spanning three decades from the early 1920s to the end of WWII, the story begins as a disenchanted British army captain, Charles Ryder (Irons), looks back on his earlier life, in happier days. It was then he first encountered Sebastian Flyte — the dazzling ill-starred son of Lord and Lady Marchmain. Sebastian brings Charles to the family home of Brideshead, beginning Charles' compulsive love affair with this strange, doomed family. Irons is outstanding in what may be the finest miniseries on video. ★★★★ VHS: $119.99

The Bridge

(1959, 102 min, West Germany, Bernhard Wicki) *Volker Bohnet, Fritz Wepper.* Based on the autobiography of one of the participants, *The Bridge* is set during the final days of WWII, when Allied armies were triumphantly advancing across the German countryside and the Nazi war machine was grinding to a halt. In desperation, Hitler and his generals tapped the last resource available to defend their homeland: children. The film tells the story of a group of boys who enthusiastically take up rifles and don uniforms to defend their hometown. Due to an unfortunate set of coincidences, their adult commander is accidentally killed and they are left, leaderless, to guard the bridge leading into their town. After the rest of the nearby German army retreats past them, they remain at their posts to face the approaching Americans, without a wiser, guiding force to tell them when to retreat or surrender. A strong antiwar film which paradoxically contains some remarkable battle sequences. You won't soon forget its harsh picture of children forced to die like men. (German with English subtitles) ★★★½

The Bridge on the River Kwai

(1957, 161 min, GB, David Lean) *Alec Guinness, William Holden, Jack Hawkins, Sussue Hayakawa.* This magnificent wartime drama won seven Academy Awards and stands out as one of the greatest and most powerful films ever made about war and its degenerative effect on the minds of men. Filled with high-powered action sequences and intense psychological torture. ★★★★ VHS: $14.99; DVD: $24.99

Bridge to Nowhere

(1986, 82 min, Australia, Ian Mune) *Bruno Lawrence, Alison Rutledge.* A tense action-adventure film about five teenagers who, on an outdoor camping trip, cross paths with a psychotic hermit. Their struggle for survival reminds one of an Aussie *Deliverance.* ★★★

A Bridge Too Far

(1977, 175 min, GB, Richard Attenborough) *Dirk Bogarde, James Caan, Sean Connery, Robert Redford, Gene Hackman, Laurence Olivier, Liv Ullmann.* Though most will regard this as "a film too long," Attenborough's adaptation of Cornelius Ryan's book about a disastrous raid behind German lines in WWII Holland does offer a meticulous examination of the ill-fated mission. ★★★ VHS: $24.99; DVD: $14.99

The Bridges at Toko-Ri

(1954, 103 min, US, Mark Robson) *William Holden, Grace Kelly, Fredric March, Mickey Rooney.* Holden stars in this powerful Korean War drama based on James Michener's novel about a civilian lawyer recalled to military duty overseas.

Kelly also stars as his wife who patiently waits at home. Holden and Kelly give fine performances, as do March, as a world-weary admiral, and Rooney as a fellow pilot. ★★★½ VHS: $9.99; DVD: $29.99

The Bridges of Madison County

(1995, 135 min, US, Clint Eastwood) *Clint Eastwood, Meryl Streep, Annie Corley, Victor Slezak, Jim Haynie.* Robert James Walker's best-selling novel makes for a grand love story, beautifully evoking the romanticism of the novel and further illustrating the lyricism and range of director Eastwood. Streep plays Francesca Johnson, a Iowa housewife and Italian émigré whose children, upon her death, discover that their seemingly staid mother was involved in an extramarital affair. As the film flashbacks to the mid-1960s, the story focuses on the four-day romance between Francesca and a photojournalist, Robert Kincaid (Eastwood). *Bridges...* is a truly romantic, knowing drama which is as intimate as two lovers. Only one or two slowly paced scenes which interrupt the movement of the story keep this from being the romantic masterwork it very nearly is. The remarkable Streep has a rapport with Eastwood like no other actress with whom he's appeared. And he is commendable in a role which seems to have the Robert Redford stamp all over it. ★★★½ VHS: $14.99; DVD: $19.99

Bridget Jones's Diary

(2001, 95 min, GB, Sharon Maguire) *Renee Zellweger, Colin Firth, Hugh Grant, Jim Broadbent, Gemma Jones, Embeth Davidtz.* It doesn't take long for the clichés to start. Not even minutes into the film, the main character, Bridget (Zellweger), an ever-so-slightly overweight single woman approaching her 30s, lip-synchs a song (in this case, "All By Myself"). It's been done to death for decades, now. But damn if Zellweger doesn't make it seem fresh and new; bestowing that scene and others to follow with such charm as to make anyone forget that we've seen all this before. Based on the best-seller by Helen Fielding, the story follows Bridget and her search for Prince Charming. Whereas the book was a series of personal journals, the film is more traditional in its narrative as Bridget meets Mr. Right and Mr. Maybe Right, just not knowing that she has them turned around. Firth is the stuffy lawyer with whom it's hate-at-first-sight, and the debonair Grant is Bridget's womanizing boss with whom she thinks she's found true love. They complete a most agreeable threesome. Though not able to fully establish Bridget's multifaceted personality so clearly delineated in the book, this whimsical adaptation is nevertheless abundant with good humor, quality laughs, and features a first-rate performance by the adorable Ms. Zellweger. ★★★ VHS: $102.99; DVD: $29.99

Brief Encounter

(1946, 86 min, GB, David Lean) *Trevor Howard, Celia Johnson.* A masterpiece from Britain's postwar cinema, this extraordinary romantic drama stars Howard and Johnson, both giving impeccable performances, as two ordinary, middle-aged people involved in a short but compassionate extramarital affair. Subtle, masterful direction from Lean. Based on Noël Coward's one-act play, "Still Life." ★★★★ DVD: $39.99

Renee Zellweger in *Bridget Jones's Diary*

A Brief History of Time

(1992, 80 min, US, Errol Morris) *Stephen Hawking.* This fascinating, intellectually demanding documentary examines the life of British theoretical physicist Hawking, based on his own best-selling book. Interweaving biographical and academic information, the film balances its time between insightful glimpses into Hawking's past and colleagues expounding on his scientific theories. A victim of ALS (Lou Gehrig's disease), Hawking is completely paralyzed and confined to a wheelchair, but his amazing inner strength and incredible intellect shine through, making his ideas and the film itself all the more mesmerizing. It's the most stimulating Advanced Physics class you'll never attend. ★★★½ VHS: $19.99

Brigadoon

(1954, 109 min, US, Vincente Minnelli) *Gene Kelly, Van Johnson, Cyd Charisse.* Kelly and Johnson play two American hunters who stumble upon a magical 18th-century village in the Scottish Highlands — a village that comes alive only once every 100 years. Charisse also stars in this enchanting adaptation of the Broadway musical. ★★★ VHS: $14.99; DVD: $19.99

Bright Eyes

(1934, 83 min, US, David Butler) *Shirley Temple, James Dunn, Jane Withers.* Temple sings "On the Good Ship Lollipop." Who could ask for anything more? The story has to do with a custody battle over little Shirley. ★★★ VHS: $9.99

Bright Lights, Big City

(1988, 110 min, US, James Bridges) *Michael J. Fox, Kiefer Sutherland, Phoebe Cates, Frances Sternhagen, Swoosie Kurtz, Dianne Wiest.* Uptown boy Fox doesn't realize that he should just say "no" in this fair adaptation of Jay McInerney's best-seller. Fox gives an earnest performance as the young magazine editor whose life becomes entrapped in an endless cycle of work, drugs and decadent nightlife. Sutherland is well-cast as Fox's sleazy bar pal, Tad. ★★½ VHS: $9.99

B

A Bright Shining Lie

(1998, 120 min, US, Terry George) *Bill Paxton, Amy Madigan, Eric Bogosian, Donal Logue.* Episodic docu-drama based on Neil Sheehan's acclaimed account of the slipshot machinations — of both the U.S. and South Vietnamese governments — behind the Vietnam War. Paxton stars as a lt. colonel who resigns in disgust over the U.S. military's botched handling of the war, only to resurface as a civilian advisor to the military. What could have been a searing, fascinating exposé or a compelling tragedy of one man's misguided passion (or, in the right hands, both), is instead a middle-of-the-road, only occasionally interesting cop-out. Aside from several fly-on-the-wall sequences depicting the decision-makers at work, there's precious little you haven't seen before. ★★½ VHS: $14.99; DVD: $14.99

Brighton Beach Memoirs

(1986, 108 min, US, Gene Saks) *Jonathan Silverman, Blythe Danner, Bob Dishy, Judith Ivey, Jason Alexander.* The first of playwright Neil Simon's autobiographical trilogy on his coming of age. The story focuses on the Jeromes, a tight-knit Jewish family living in a poor Brooklyn neighborhood in the late 1930s. Silverman makes a personable young Simon, and Danner has some good moments as his mother. Not as successful as the second film, *Biloxi Blues*, but entertaining all the same. ★★★ VHS: $9.99

Brighton Rock

(1947, 87 min, GB, John Boulting) *Richard Attenborough, Carol Marsh, Hermione Baddeley.* A tense drama, based on the novel by Graham Greene, examining the criminal underworld in Brighton. A young and menacing Attenborough is Pinky, an inexperienced but ambitious thug who, with his rag-tag gang of hooligans, begins to stake out his turf on the bustling streets of Brighton. Marsh is the innocent waitress who tragically falls in love with the soulless, immoral killer. ★★★½ VHS: $39.99

Brimstone and Treacle

(1982, 85 min, GB, Richard Loncraine) *Sting, Denholm Elliott.* A satanic young man (Sting) methodically forces his way into the lives of a middle-class suburban family by claiming to be the suitor of their mute and immobilized daughter. This unusual and malevolent thriller

is not for the faint of heart, but will pay off for those with a need for something out of the ordinary. ★★★ VHS: $14.99

Bring It On

(2000, 99 min, US, Peyton Reed) *Kirsten Dunst, Gabrielle Union, Eliza Dushku, Jesse Bradford, Ian Roberts.* Dunst is voted captain of her cheerleading squad, and must defend their first-place status in the all-important squad competition. This year, however, they may have to face off against the superb Compton squad — whose routines Dunst's group have been "borrowing" — if the Comptons can afford the entry fee. A lightly amusing teen film, *Bring It On* is bolstered by assured direction, some surprisingly sharp satire and Dunst's solid performance (the rictus on her face when she's forced to perform a stolen routine is at once hilarious and agonizing to watch). With fun support from "Buffy"'s Dushku as the tough-ass new chick on the squad, this is a touch more sophisticated than one might expect. ★★★ VHS: $14.99; DVD: $26.99

Bring Me the Head of Alfredo Garcia

(1974, 112 min, US, Sam Peckinpah) *Warren Oates, Isela Vega, Gig Young, Robert Webber.* Oates is a piano player who becomes a bounty hunter when the title command is proclaimed by a rich Mexican landowner. Oates sets off across the dirty, dusty modern landscape to find and deliver that head, which belongs to the father of the landowner's child. Oates is helped by Vega, his sometimes lover who knows Garcia's last whereabouts. They plan to deliver the head, accept the bounty and make a better life for themselves together. As is not common in Peckinpah's films, this happy, nonviolent outcome is unlikely. An uncharacteristic film for Peckinpah — it harkens back to his earlier *Ride the High Country* — *Alfredo Garcia* is somber and rather downbeat, but it will please those who are willing to take a brief interest in the struggling lives of its unhappy characters. ★★★ VHS: $14.99

Bringing Out the Dead

(1999, 121 min, US, Martin Scorsese) *Nicolas Cage, Patricia Arquette, John Goodman, Ving Rhames, Tom Sizemore.* Director Scorsese brings his usual gritty eye to this story of an EMT worker (Cage) who becomes haunted by the

spirit of a woman he could not save. As the hallucinations (or are they?) continue, he spirals out of control in a binge of alcohol, drugs and recklessness. Scorsese's visuals compensate for the sporadic dramatic lapses, and a great supporting cast is in good form. (VHS available letterboxed or pan & scan) ★★★ VHS: $14.99; DVD: $29.99

Bringing Up Baby

(1938, 102 min, US, Howard Hawks) *Katharine Hepburn, Cary Grant, Charlie Ruggles, May Robson, Barry Fitzgerald, Fritz Feld.* The definitive screwball comedy, and one of the funniest films ever made. Grant gives his best comic performance as a hilariously befuddled, bespectacled anthropologist who becomes mixed up with daffy but determined heiress Hepburn (also in one of her funniest performances). Together, they tear apart the Connecticut countryside searching for leopards, pet terriers and an intercostal clavicle, all the while being mistaken for the notorious "Leopard Gang," big game hunters and nuts from Brazil. Grant and Hepburn's flawless comic timing and Hawks' inspired direction combine to make this a timeless and much-adored classic. ★★★★ VHS: $19.99

Brink of Life

(1958, 82 min, Sweden, Ingmar Bergman) *Eva Dahlbeck, Ingrid Thulin, Bibi Andersson, Max von Sydow.* A simple direct drama by Bergman with a great "Bergman cast." The film focuses on three women facing childbirth during a 24-hour period in a maternity ward. Bergman won the Best Director prize at Cannes for this effort. (Swedish with English subtitles) ★★½ VHS: $29.99

The Brinks Job

(1978, 103 min, US, William Friedkin) *Peter Falk, Peter Boyle, Gena Rowlands, Warren Oates, Allen Garfield, Paul Sorvino.* One of director Friedkin's most entertaining films, this splendid caper comedy re-creates the famous heist which rocked Boston in 1950. ★★★ VHS: $12.99

Britannia Hospital

(1982, 115 min, GB, Lindsay Anderson) *Leonard Rossiter, Graham Crowden, Malcolm McDowell, Joan Plowright.* This scathingly funny and winningly absurd black comedy sums up the ailing state of the once mighty British Empire. Preparations for a visit by the Queen Mother to a floundering medical institution are set against the backdrop of violent protests against the specialized care given to a ruthless African dictator. In the midst of the melee, every possible (and impossible) catastrophe arises until Crowden (as the inimitably insane Dr. Millar) eloquently sums up the meaning of human existence. ★★★½ VHS: $9.99

Broadcast News

(1987, 131 min, US, James L. Brooks) *Holly Hunter, Albert Brooks, William Hurt, Jack Nicholson, Joan Cusack.* An extraordinary study of the ethical proprieties of television journalism, this is a surgically fine and remarkably funny dissection of the daily goings-on of a TV newsroom. Hunter is nothing short of brilliant as the slightly neurotic but talented producer who is saddled with undisciplined newcomer Hurt, a superficial neophyte with whom she begins an affair. As Hunter's coworker and pal, A. Brooks gives one of the great comic performances of

Bringing Up Baby

recent years. J. L. Brooks has written a superbly detailed and intelligent screenplay, and his direction is equally as commanding. ★★★★ VHS: $14.99; DVD: $29.99

Broadway Damage

(1997, 110 min, US, Victor Mignatti) *Michael Shawn Lucas, Aaron Williams, Mara Hobel, Hugh Panaro.* Catching the recent wave of gay-themed films which eschew troubling subjects like AIDS, homophobia and coming out for a more sunny, cute-boys-in-love romanticism is this sugary, determinedly optimistic love story. The story revolves around the ambitions and loves of three wide-eyed dreamers trying to become a success in Manhattan. They include aspiring actor Marc (Lucas); his mop-headed best friend and would-be musical composer Robert (Williams), who's secretly in love with Marc; and Marc's ditsy Greenwich Village roommate Christina (Hobel). Will the two young men get together, or will the sexy new stud in town steal Marc's heart? Lacking any real insight, the film is at times funny, and occasionally charming in its innocence. ★★½ VHS: $29.99; DVD: $24.99

Broadway Danny Rose

(1984, 83 min, US, Woody Allen) *Woody Allen, Mia Farrow, Nick Apollo Forte, Milton Berle.* Allen stars as a hopelessly inept talent agent in this charming comedy, doggedly plugging his fourth-rate clients on the borscht circuit. Forte, as a beefy lounge crooner, is his prize attraction, and Farrow is a gum-chewing moll in distress. ★★★½

The Broadway Melody

(1929, 104 min, US, Harry Beaumont) *Bessie Love, Anita Page.* The first musical to win a Best Picture Oscar, this backstage tuner shows its age. The story is about two sisters trying to make it on Broadway. Love and Page play the starstruck siblings, and there's a pleasant score. Billed as "The First All-Talking, All-Singing, All-Dancing Musical" — and it was. ★★½ VHS: $14.99

Broadway Melody of 1940

(1940, 102 min, US, Norman Taurog) *Fred Astaire, George Murphy, Eleanor Powell.* A sparkling backstage musical. Excellent dance numbers, and a lovely Cole Porter score including "Begin the Beguine" and "I've Got My Eyes on You" set the tone. ★★★

Brokedown Palace

(1999, 100 min, US, Jonathan Kaplan) *Claire Danes, Kate Beckinsale, Bill Pullman, Lou Diamond Phillips, Jacqueline Kim.* It's *Clueless* meets *Midnight Express* as Danes and Beckinsale play a couple of young, naïve travellers and recent high school grads who soon find themselves trapped in a Thai prison, trying desperately to get a hearing before the nation's kangaroo-court justice system. There are attempted escapes, and the women's friendship is strained by the prison experience. The territory feels too well-trodden here, but the performances are convincing and there are undeniable moments of tension throughout. Pullman is the American lawyer who defends the two girls. ★★ VHS: $14.99; DVD: $34.99

Broken Arrow

(1950, 93 min, US, Delmer Daves) *James Stewart, Jeff Chandler, Will Geer, Jay Silverheels.* After his great success in *Winchester 73*, Stewart jumped back in the saddle for this acclaimed "pro-Indian" saga with Stewart as an ex-military officer acting as mediator between the Army and Apache chief Cochise (well played by Chandler). One of the first of those great '50s westerns to sympathetically portray Native Americans. ★★★ VHS: $14.99

Broken Arrow

(1996, 110 min, US, John Woo) *John Travolta, Christian Slater, Samantha Mathis, Delroy Lindo, Bob Gunton, Frank Whaley, Howie Long.* Woo's second American film is a moderately successful, big-budget action adventure, but it will be a letdown to the director's fans who have followed his transition from Hong Kong to the United States. Travolta and Slater star as Air Force pilots and steadfast buddies who fly a test run of a new B3 bomber. With nuclear weapons aboard the plane, Travolta ejects them and then himself, leaving his friend aboard the plummeting aircraft. Slater survives and teams up with a park ranger (Mathis), together going after Travolta who is in league with terrorists who plan to sell the weapons back to the government. Much of *Broken Arrow* is undermined by an inane script which eventually throws logic out the window to facilitate its major action sequences. Though somewhat (if brainlessly) entertaining, the film is indistinguishable from any other garden-variety action flick. (Letterboxed VHS available for $19.99) ★★½ VHS: $9.99; DVD: $24.99

Broken Blossoms

(1919, 95 min, US, D.W. Griffith) *Lillian Gish, Richard Barthelmess, Donald Crisp.* Griffith directed this silent classic of a self-appointed Asian emissary of peace (Barthelmess) and his efforts to protect a young girl (Gish) from exploitation and abuse by her London thug father (Crisp). This sepia and blue-tinted video contains a short introduction by Ms. Gish. The original musical score strongly supports the film's dramatic undercurrents. ★★★½ VHS: $24.99; DVD: $29.99

Broken English

(1997, 92 min, New Zealand, Gregor Nicholas) *Aleksandra Vujcic, Rade Serbedzija, Julian Arahanga.* A somber drama about having to choose between love and family, *Broken English* depicts the sensitive relationship between Nina (Vujcic), a former Yugoslavian living in New Zealand, and Eddie (Arahanga), a Maori. This gritty film wants to make a powerful statement about the way cultures are assimilated and/or vanished, only it lacks the impact of the producer's previous film, *Once Were Warriors.* The idea of remembering one's roots is important, but director and cowriter Nicholas employs some rather heavy-handed symbols to emphasize the point. Although *Broken English* earned a NC-17 rating for one graphic sexual encounter, viewers not looking for a worthwhile but heated sociopolitical film may be disappointed. ★★★ VHS: $24.99

The Broken Hearts Club

(2000, 91 min, US, Greg Berlanti) *Timothy Olyphant, Dean Cain, Matt McGrath, Ben Weber, Zach Braff, Billy Porter, Nia Long, John Mahoney, Andrew Keegan.* In his feature film debut, writer-director Berlanti (producer of "Dawson's Creek") has crafted an often funny, touching

Brother's Keeper

slice-of-life portrait of the lives, loves and dramas of a group of gay West Hollywood friends. The characters include Dennis (Olyphant), a promising photographer and his often dysfunctional friends: his housemate Cole (Cain), a charming man-stealing actor; Benji (Braff), a punkish gym bunny fancier; analytical grad student Howie (McGrath); and cynical quipster Patrick (Weber). They all hang out together at a restaurant run by the group's unofficial patriarch, Jack (Mahoney) and play together on a softball team coached by Jack (a part-time drag performer). Dramas abound, especially when Cole seduces and abandons the fragile, just-out-of-the-closet Kevin (Keegan), leaving Dennis to help pick up Kevin's emotional pieces. The film loses steam towards the end as Berlanti isn't quite sure how to wrap things up, but his film is witty and always entertaining. ★★★ VHS: $14.99; DVD: $29.99

Broken Lance

(1954, 96 min, US, Edward Dmytryk) *Spencer Tracy, Richard Widmark, Robert Wagner.* This remake of *House of Strangers* has been transferred out West, and bears more than a little resemblance to "King Lear." Tracy is dynamic as the patriarch of a cattle dynasty whose three sons become at odds with their father and each other. ★★★

Broken Noses

(1987, 75 min, US, Bruce Weber) *Andy Minsker.* The provocative photographer famed for his salacious Calvin Klein underwear ads, Weber has produced, in this low-budget short feature, a surprisingly touching and strikingly provocative documentary on Golden Gloves Champion Andy Minsker and the pre-pubescent and teenage boys of the Mount Scott Boxing Club. Weber takes his camera into Andy's home, where we watch and listen to his family and friends as well as Andy's own thoughts on the rigors of professional boxing and his obvious role as another "Great White Hope." The camera captures the romantic and sensual machismo of the young boxers and the film features the music of Julie London, Chet Baker and Gerry Mulligan. ★★★ VHS: $29.99

Broken Vessels

(1999, 91 min, US, Scott Ziehl) *Jason London, Todd Field, Roxanna Zal, Susan Traylor.* While it will invariably be compared to Martin Scorsese's *Bringing Out the Dead* for traversing the same territory — the nervewracking lives of EMT workers — *Broken Vessels* is, nevertheless, an astonishing film in its own right. London plays Tom, a guy from Altoona who relocates to Los Angeles to escape a tragedy in his past. Working as a lifesaver, Tom is soon fighting another personal battle when his partner Jimmy (the excellent Field) hooks him on copious amounts of drugs as an antidote to their thankless profession. As Tom and Jimmy descend further into addiction, it is only a matter of time before they crash and burn. Director Ziehl starts the film out episodically before it culminates in its harrowing finale. There is fine support by Zal as Tom's potential girlfriend, and the manic Traylor as Susy, the crazy next-door neighbor who offers the two men drugs and trouble. ★★★ VHS: $14.99; DVD: $9.99

Broken Vows

(1986, 95 min, Canada, Jud Taylor) *Tommy Lee Jones, Annette O'Toole, M. Emmet Walsh, Frances Fisher, David Strathairn, Milo O'Shea.* This atrocious religious drama stars Jones as a priest who undergoes a spiritual conflict when he falls in love. His troubles begin when he becomes obsessed with finding a killer. He befriends the deceased man's girlfriend (O'Toole), and while trying to piece together the puzzle, they fall in love. Jones must have needed rent money, for he walks through his role with little conviction. The direction is sluggish and the script astonishingly bad. ★ VHS: $19.99

Bronco Billy

(1980, 119 min, US, Clint Eastwood) *Clint Eastwood, Sondra Locke, Geoffrey Lewis, Scatman Crothers.* One of Eastwood's most underrated films, this endearing western fable follows the adventures of a traveling Old West show run by cowboy Clint. ★★★ VHS: $14.99; DVD: $19.99

A Bronx Tale

(1993, 122 min, US, Robert De Niro) *Robert De Niro, Chazz Palminteri, Lillo Brancato, Francis Capra, Joe Pesci.* In his directorial debut, De Niro recalls the films of his longtime director Martin Scorsese with this beautifully shot and eloquent crime drama based on the play by Chazz Palminteri. Set in the early 1960s, the story traces the relationship between a Bronx youth, Calogero, and a local gangster, Sonny (effectively played by Palminteri), whom the boy refused to identify in a gangland slaying. As "Cee" grows up, he forms a bond with Sonny, much to the dismay of his ethical father (De Niro in a subtle performance). Against the backdrop of petty crime, camaraderie, murder and good times, Cee must decide which path to take, which "father" to emulate. Capra and Brancato as the child and teenaged Cee, respectively, both create memorable characterizations. (Letterboxed VHS available for $14.99) ★★★½ VHS: $9.99; DVD: $19.99

The Brood

(1979, 90 min, Canada, David Cronenberg) *Samantha Eggar, Oliver Reed, Art Hindle.* The shape of rage is the subject of Cronenberg's fourth visceral medical horror feature — and also the title of the book written by Reed's character, a renowned but controversial psychiatrist whose "psychoplasmics" method of therapy encourages patients to give physical form to their emotions and fears. Eggar, Reed's star patient, is undergoing intensive treatment at his New Age—type colony in the woods. It is there she gives life to a bizarre group of mutant children who murder her enemies. *The Brood* has the framework of an ordinary horror film, but it is distinguished by an intelligent exploration of the darkest pathologies of the human psyche. ★★★

The Brother from Another Planet

(1984, 110 min, US, John Sayles) *Joe Morton, Darryl Edwards, Maggie Renzi, David Strathairn, John Sayles.* After his spaceship plummets into New York harbor, a mute black alien (Morton) stumbles into Harlem and learns the earthly ropes. Sayles' comic version of a stranger in a strange land is slyer than *Starman*, earthier than *E.T.* and a potent commentary on the everyday alienation of urban inhabitants. ★★★½

Brother of Sleep

(1996, 127 min, Austria, Joseph Vilsmaier) *Andre Eisermann, Dana Vavrova, Ben Becker.* A hypnotic tale set in a remote Alpine village, *Brother of Sleep* is a strange combination of religious parable and tragic love story. Writer-director-cinematographer Vilsmaier has succeeded admirably in capturing the film's palpable atmosphere, but the magnificent visuals are sadly diminished on video. Screenwriter Robert Schneider adapted his own novel depicting the jealousies and prejudices of the residents of Eschberg, a hateful little hamlet that is blessed — or cursed — with the bastard birth of Elias Alder (Eisermann). Elias possesses exceptional hearing and he soon becomes the town's celebrated church organist. Complicating Elias' natural gift is his love for his half-sister, Elsbeth (Vavrova), and the bitter rivalry of his friend Peter (Becker) for her affection. Although the film is slow going at times, the unerring performances keep the film focused when the action sags. (German with English subtitles) ★★★ VHS: $79.99

Brother Sun, Sister Moon

(1973, 110 min, GB/Italy, Franco Zeffirelli) *Graham Faulkner, Alec Guinness, Valentina Cortese.* Sappy, meandering, hippie-esque (in the bad sense of the word) and plagued by a soundtrack by Donovan, Zeffirelli's romantic story of 13th-century St. Francis of Assisi is quite enjoyable nonetheless. A young man from a wealthy family has a burning quest for spiritual fulfillment which causes him to abandon all worldly possessions and pleasures and live a simple life among nature and the poor. Spectacularly beautiful scenery and sumptuous costumes highlight the tale. ★★½ VHS: $14.99

Brother's Keeper

(1992, 105 min, US, Joe Berlinger & Bruce Sinofsky) The quiet, nearly impoverished farming community of Munnville, New York, became the center of a media barrage in 1990 when semi-illiterate farmer Delbert Ward was arrested for killing his 60-year-old brother while his two brothers slept nearby. Having been arrested and signed a confession under duress, Delbert was subsequently released on bail with the support of the local townspeople who believed in his innocence. This award-winning documentary, while scrutinizing the particulars of the case, becomes a fascinating probe into the mindset of rural America. It becomes painfully obvious that Delbert was a disoriented victim railroaded into a plainly false confession, which is the one very minor drawback of the film, as it lacks none of the dramatic tension of *The Thin Blue Line*. However, it's a mesmerizing sociological and legal look at an almost forgotten piece of the American pie. ★★★★ VHS: $19.99

A Brother's Kiss

(1996, 93 min, US, Seth Zvi Rosenfeld) *Nick Chinlund, Michael Raynor, Talent Harris, John Leguizamo, Cathy Moriarty, Rosie Perez, Michael Rapaport.* A hard-hitting and absorbing debut from writer-director Rosenfeld, *A Brother's Kiss* astutely develops the bond between two siblings on opposite sides of the law. Lex (Chinlund) is the older brother, whose failures in hoops and marriage lead him to a life of crime. Mick (Raynor) is the baby, a sensitive cop devoted to keeping their broken family together. The story, told in a lengthy flashback, shows the terrible event that forces Lex to protect Mick as a kid, and the efforts the adult Mick takes to save Lex when the world starts closing in on him. Although some of the plotting is a bit contrived, both leads are given an opportunity to show their tremendous range as actors. Tough, but tender, *A Brother's Kiss* is an affecting urban drama. ★★★ VHS: $9.99; DVD: $9.99

The Brothers Karamazov

(1958, 146 min, US, Richard Brooks) *Yul Brynner, Lee J. Cobb, William Shatner, Maria Schell.* Epic adaptation of Fyodor Dostoyevsky's novel set in 19th-century Russia. Four brothers of disparate temperament react to the death of their tyrannical father. A psychological study well-scripted by director Brooks and competently acted by its cast. ★★★ VHS: $24.99

The Brothers McMullen

(1995, 97 min, US, Edward Burns) *Jack Mulcahy, Edward Burns, Mike McGlone, Connie Britton, Maxine Bahns, Elizabeth P. McKay.* Burns' directorial debut is an unaffected, refreshing and surprisingly involving look at three Irish-American brothers. As they bury their abusive, alcoholic father, they are advised by their mom not to make the same mistakes she did. She leaves from the cemetery to catch a plane to Ireland to be with the man she's always loved. Commitment is a struggle for the three siblings — one married, one engaged, one adamantly unattached — a struggle made no easier by their mother's revelation after their lifelong witness to the pain of an unhappy union. Mulcahy, McGlone and Burns convey the relaxed familiarity of brothers, giving subtle and natural performances. The women in their lives don't get as much screen time, but their presence rings as affably true as the men's. This small, pleasant, bemusing comedy opens a window on life's foibles, offering a view both engaging and endearing. ★★★ VHS: $14.99; DVD: $29.99

The Browning Version

(1951, 93 min, GB, Anthony Asquith) *Michael Redgrave, Jean Kent, Nigel Patrick.* Redgrave gives a stirring performance in this outstanding drama about a stodgy English boarding school-teacher who finds himself being forced out of his teaching position and discovers his wife's infidelity. He finds redemption in an unexpected act of kindness when one of his young students gives him a copy of "The Browning Version" of Aeschylus' "Agamemnon," a play which he has translated. Terence Rattigan scripted this adaptation of his own play, and his poignant screenplay, Redgrave's classic portrayal and a splendid supporting cast make this must-viewing. (Remade in 1994 with Albert Finney) ★★★★ VHS: $19.99

The Browning Version

(1994, 97 min, US, Mike Figgis) *Albert Finney, Greta Scacchi, Matthew Modine, Michael Gambon, Julian Sands, Ben Silverstone.* This elegantly produced and deliberately paced film explores the sterile isolation of a profoundly unhappy professor at what appears to be the anticlimactic end of his career. Finney is a marvel of nuance and understatement as the tightly controlled and rigidly repressed teacher. WWII has ended, and Finney is the victim of modernization — he's being transferred to another school. His departure marks a loss of prestige and place, mirrored with intense disdain in the eyes of his embittered, spiteful wife (Scacchi). A chance gift from an appreciative student serves as catharsis for the beleaguered scholar, precipitating a reevaluation of a life hitherto defined by unspoken recriminations and calcified regrets. Finney's performance is matched by his supporting cast, especially Silverstone as the young student whose compassion and understanding greatly exceeds his years. ★★★ VHS: $19.99

Brubaker

(1980, 132 min, US, Stuart Rosenberg) *Robert Redford, Jane Alexander, Yaphet Kotto, Morgan Freeman.* Based on a true story, Redford stars as a newly appointed warden of an Arkansas prison whose humane reforms uncover a web of corruption and murder. Slightly overlong, this is nevertheless compelling drama with earnest performances. ★★★ VHS: $9.99

Brussels-Transit

(1980, 90 min, Belgium, Samy Szlingerbaum) With blurry images of a cold, impersonal subway station and tram cars slowly moving through the fog of a northern European city, a woman's voice begins to sing a heartfelt poem in Yiddish. So begins this fascinating "art" film that delves into one Jewish family's life when they leave Lodz, Poland, after WWII. Narrated by the director's mother, the film uses her reminiscences of her family's life as she, her tailor husband and their two small children eventually settle in Brussels and attempt to eke out an existence despite a devastated Europe and ignorance of the language and customs. Spanning the years 1947 through the early 1950s, this is an unusual, somber yet touching document of one family's determination to survive. (Yiddish with English subtitles) ★★★

El Bruto (The Brute)

(1952, 83 min, Mexico, Luis Buñuel) *Pedro Armendariz, Katy Jurado, Andres Soler, Rosita Arenas.* This is the ironic tale of a not-too-bright but tender-hearted brute who is hired by a rich landlord to evict a group of striking tenants. He does his job only too well, resulting in the death of an elderly man. The young wife of the landlord, like a moth to flame, is fatally attracted to this "primeval man" and in quick succession seduces the hulking worker, abandons her husband and runs off with her lover. The price for her infidelity is increasing sexual torment and a descent into madness. A passionate exploration of the mechanisms of desire and the potential consequences of its fulfillment. (Spanish with English subtitles) ★★★ VHS: $24.99

The Brylcreem Boys

(1996, 106 min, Ireland, Terence Ryan) *Bill Campbell, Angus MacFadyen, Gabriel Byrne, Jean Butler, William McNamara.* Dramatizing a little-known historical fact, *The Brylcreem Boys* is set in an Irish P.O.W. camp during WWII. In an effort to keep its neutrality during the war, Ireland interned both Allied and German soldiers captured on Irish soil. The two enemies were kept in separate camps, very visible to each other. Escape was discouraged on both sides because both the English and German governments considered Irish waterways vital. Even prisoners on day passes did not attempt escape. An often interesting war drama which is sometimes hindered by subpar production values and a frivolous romantic subplot, *The Brylcreem Boys* follows two pilots, one Canadian (Campbell) and the other German (MacFadyen), as they — after downing each other's planes — adapt to captivity, sitting out the war, and eventually face each other. ★★½ VHS: $9.99; DVD: $9.99

Buck Privates

(1941, 84 min, US, Arthur Lubin) *Bud Abbott, Lou Costello, the Andrews Sisters.* One of Abbott and Costello's funniest comedies. The Andrews Sisters also star. Bud and Lou join the Army, with predictable comedic results; Patty, Maxine and Laverne sing. ★★★½ VHS: $14.99

A Bucket of Blood

(1959, 66 min, US, Roger Corman) *Dick Miller, Barboura Morris.* With exception to *Little Shop of Horrors*, this sly horror parody is director Corman's best work from his early and extremely low-budget days. That great character actor Miller is center stage as a beatnik coffeehouse waiter whose newly found prominence as a sculptor is helped greatly by the dead bodies underneath his clay. ★★★ VHS: $12.99; DVD: $19.99

The Buddha of Suburbia

(1993, 222 min, GB, Roger Michell) *Naveen Andrews, Roshen Seth, Brenda Blethyn, Steven MacKintosh.* Hanif Kureishi's (*My Beautiful Laundrette*) serio-comic novel of life among the bohemians and bohemian-wannabes in 1970s London is the basis for this accomplished BBC miniseries. The story focuses on handsome Karim (Andrews), a bisexual teenager of an unconventional English mother (Blethyn) and a surprisingly eccentric Indian father (Seth) who longs to escape the confines of suburban Bromley and experience life. Karim finally gets his wish — and the film comes into its own — and moves to a frenetic, punk-filled London when his father becomes a guru in the '70s Buddhist scene. Sort of an English *Tales of the City*, this sprawling slice-of-life story features music by David Bowie. ★★★

Buddy

(1997, 84 min, US, Caroline Thompson) *Rene Russo, Robbie Coltrane, Alan Cumming, Paul Reubens, Irma P. Hall.* Based on the book by Gertrude Lintz ("Animals Are My Hobby"), this alternately appealing and shmaltzy true story chronicles the history of Buddy, a gorilla who spent most of his 54 years in the Philadelphia Zoo, living longer than any other gorilla. Trudy (warmly portrayed by Russo) is a true animal lover lucky enough to live in a large mansion where, with the support of her loving husband (Coltrane), she keeps hundreds of animals. Buddy is an infant and near death when she rescues him from the zoo. She nurses him back to health and he matures on their estate. ★★½ VHS: $14.99; DVD: $24.99

Buddy, Buddy

(1981, 96 min, US, Billy Wilder) *Jack Lemmon, Walter Matthau, Paula Prentiss, Klaus Kinski.* This American version of the French film *A Pain in the A* — is a low-key black comedy highlighted by the pairing of Lemmon and Matthau. Lemmon plays a hit man whose job is interrupted by an obnoxious hotel neighbor played by Matthau. The magic between them makes up for the fair script. ★★★ VHS: $19.99

The Buddy Holly Story

(1978, 113 min, US, Steve Rash) *Gary Busey, Charles Martin Smith, Don Stroud.* The life of Buddy Holly, the legendary rockabilly king, is brought to the screen with Busey in the title role. In an amazing metamorphosis, Busey transforms himself into the rock 'n' roll pioneer, not only in looks, but also with his singing. Songs include "That'll Be the Day," "Peggy Sue," "Rave On," "Maybe Baby" and more. ★★★½ VHS: $9.99; DVD: $24.99

The Buddy System

(1984, 110 min, US, Glenn Jordan) *Susan Sarandon, Richard Dreyfuss, Wil Wheaton, Nancy Allen.* Wheaton plays matchmaker for his mom (Sarandon) and his school security guard (Dreyfuss). The couple experience hate at first sight but, of course, they eventually fall in love. The story here is obviously nothing new, but the performances are the main attraction. ★★½ VHS: $59.99

Buena Vista Social Club

(1999, 105 min, US/Cuba, Wim Wenders) *Ry Cooder, Ibrihim Ferrer, Rubén González.* One would assume that a Wim Wenders documentary about some old-time Cuban musicians would be an all-out celebration of the joy and swagger of the Afro-Caribbean beat — and *Buena Vista Social Club* is that. But more to the core of this riveting peek into the world of old and new Havana is a fascination with the human spirit. What Wenders and guitarist Cooder uncover is a group of men (and one woman), mostly in their late 70s and early 80s (they were all world-class musicians of the 1930s and '40s), who have survived decades of neglect and obscurity, and whose inextinguishable passion for their music is as palpable today as it was 40 years ago. These guys jump into their adoration of music and take off as if a fire that had smoldered for 30

Buena Vista Social Club

years just got doused by a barrel of gasoline. Wenders weaves back and forth from interviews with his principals, a recording session in Havana, and a triumphant Carnegie Hall performance, creating a tapestry that owes as much to the fortitude and joie de vivre of these remarkable troubadours as it does to the music. It will leave one wanting to own the album (worth every penny) and mindful that no matter how tough life can be, just sit down and enjoy the music — life is beautiful! ★★★★ VHS: $9.99; DVD: $19.99

Buffalo Bill and the Indians

(1976, 135 min, US, Robert Altman) *Paul Newman, Burt Lancaster, Geraldine Chaplin, Joel Grey, Harvey Keitel, Shelley Duvall.* The wild, wild West — Robert Altman style. Based on the off-Broadway hit "Indians" by Arthur Kopit, Newman stars as the legendary Buffalo Bill, who is now a carnival attraction reliving the mythic adventures of his youthful Indian-fighting days, and believing it's all true. A cynical examination of heroes, legends and show business. ★★★ VHS: $14.99; DVD: $19.99

Buffalo '66

(1998, 110 min, US, Vincent Gallo) *Vincent Gallo, Christina Ricci, Ben Gazzara, Rosanna Arquette, Anjelica Huston, Kevin Corrigan, Mickey Rourke, Jan-Michael Vincent.* An impressive directorial debut for actor Gallo, this is the kind of personal filmmaking that hasn't been seen since the '70s. Rampantly experimental, with multiple screens, bizarre freeze frames and ersatz, Dennis Potteresque musical interludes, *Buffalo '66* was shot on color reversal film stock, giving the film a grainy, contrasty look. A bit off-putting initially, the film begins as a just-released ex-con (Gallo), a seemingly repellent character, kidnaps trailer-park nubile Ricci from her tap-dancing class and forces her to pretend to be his wife (he's visiting his estranged parents, and wants to make a good impression). After meeting his horrifying parents (Gazzara and Huston), and getting to know Gallo more fully, both the viewer and Ricci (terrific, as always) gain a bit more sympathy for this loser. Completely unpredictable, with a smashing set-piece finale. ★★★½ VHS: $14.99; DVD: $24.99

Buffet Froid (Cold Cuts)

(1979, 102 min, France, Bertrand Blier) *Gérard Depardieu, Genevieve Page, Bernard Blier, Michel Serrault.* A surrealist urban landscape is the setting for this absurdist comedy of despair in which violence is a way of life and everyone is either a murderer or his victim. Depardieu stars as a drifter who is obsessed with death. After stabbing a man, he runs home to his wife and confesses the crime. Unperturbed, she simply throws the knife into the dishwasher. But before the machine completes its last cycle, she, in turn, is killed by an intruder. In the bewildering course of events that follow, Depardieu meets and befriends both an amoral police chief as well as his wife's killer. Director Blier maliciously blends elements of urban terror gone berserk with a Kafka-esque sense of an individual trapped in a world of desensitized and twisted logic. (French with English subtitles) ★★★ VHS: $19.99; DVD: $19.99

Buffy the Vampire Slayer

(1992, 86 min, US, Fran Rubel Kuzui) *Kristy Swanson, Luke Perry, Donald Sutherland, Paul Reubens, Rutger Hauer, Hilary Swank, David Arquette.* A potentially amusing horror spoof which unfortunately gets mired in an internal confusion over whether to be *Bill & Ted* meets *The Lost Boys* or *Heathers* meets *Dracula*, *Buffy* is a vampire saga in search of some bite. Buffy (Swanson) is an average airhead California cheerleader before Sutherland shows up to inform her that it is her destiny to rid the earth of the evil bloodsucking undead. *Buffy* is about as stimulating as a weekend at the mall, though at least it has the good sense to visit the nicer clothing stores. ★★ VHS: $9.99

A Bug's Life

(1998, 95 min, US, John Lasseter) *Voices of: Dave Foley, Kevin Spacey, Julia Louis-Dreyfus, Denis Leary, Phyllis Diller.* The guys at Disney and Pixar, who gave us the (first) all-computer-animated film *Toy Story*, have struck paydirt again, with this jubilant, bedazzling family feature. The story begins when a loner ant, Flik (Foley), accidentally ruins the colony's sacrificial food tribute to the local grasshopper gang, led by the nasty

Hopper (voiced with gleeful menace by Spacey). Flik is sent on a scouting mission and finds a gaggle of "tough bugs" to help — only he doesn't know they're actually circus performers. A little livelier and funnier than the similarly themed *Antz*, most of the humor here is aimed at the kids. There's plenty of clever visual and verbal gags flying around, which helps hide the fact that the script — while full of adventure and humor — lacks a little of the emotional core that make Disney's best animated films so resonant. ★★★½ VHS: $22.99; DVD: $29.99

Bugis Street (Yao jie huang hou)

(1994, 101 min, Singapore, Yonfan) *Hiep Thi Le, Michael Lam, Grego, David Knight.* The teeming (and often steamy) world of transvestite and transsexual prostitution in 1970s Singapore is vividly brought to the screen in this deliciously tawdry and campily funny melodrama. A wide-eyed and naïve country girl (Li of Oliver Stone's *Heaven and Earth*) comes to the big city and begins work as a maid in what she thinks is a classy hotel — but reality (helped by a few "scenes") makes her realize that the Sin Sin Hotel is actually the sleazy home and work site for a bevy of gorgeously attired, lovelorn transvestite prostitutes. In this wonderfully hyperventilating film, the director obviously has a soft spot for these tough but tender gals whose romanticism remains undimmed on this street of cheap sex and unrealized dreams. (Cantonese with English subtitles) ★★★

Bugsy

(1991, 135 min, US, Barry Levinson) *Warren Beatty, Annette Bening, Ben Kingsley, Harvey Keitel, Elliott Gould, Joe Mantegna, Bebe Neuwirth, Robert Beltran.* Though *Bugsy* boasts an intelligent screenplay, outstanding production values and strong direction, it's Beatty's fascinating and remarkably complex performance which dominates and distinguishes Levinson's taut, colorful gangster saga. Beatty is "Bugsy" Siegel, a New York crime lord who was sent by the mob to Hollywood in the 1940s, eventually helping to found Las Vegas and its first casino, the Flamingo. Bening (whose offscreen romance with Beatty was highly publicized) is terrific as Virginia Hill, an aspiring actress who becomes involved with Bugsy. The film evenly — and quite successfully — divides its time between the volatile relationship between Bugsy and Virginia, and Bugsy's near-obsessive quest to build his desert resort. ★★★½ VHS: $9.99; DVD: $14.99

Bugsy Malone

(1976, 93 min, GB, Alan Parker) *Scott Baio, Jodie Foster, Florrie Augger.* Doing a mean Joan Blondell imitation, Foster steals the show in this charming children's musical which features an all-child cast. This parody of 1930s gangster flicks pits two crime bosses against each other for control of the town. Baio is the likable hero who falls in with the wrong crowd. Foster plays a nightclub headliner who can zing a one-liner with the best of them. Paul Williams wrote the unmemorable score. And parents, don't worry — there are no bullets, only whipped cream. ★★★ VHS: $14.99

Bull Durham

(1988, 108 min, US, Ron Shelton) *Kevin Costner, Susan Sarandon, Tim Robbins, Robert Wuhl.*

Costner stars in this entertaining, literate and very sexy comedy as a veteran catcher who joins the minor league Durham Bulls and is relegated to playing baby-sitter to a hotshot pitcher (Robbins). Both become involved with the town's leading baseball authority/groupie, the ever-incredible Sarandon. A major achievement from first-time director Shelton. ★★★½ VHS: $14.99; DVD: $24.99

Bulldog Drummond

(1929, 85 min, US, F. Richard Jones) *Ronald Colman, Joan Bennett, Montagu Love.* In his first sound film, Colman's splendid performance illustrates why he was one of the most popular actors of his time. Colman is the ever-glib and suave Capt. "Bulldog" Drummond, the ex-British Army officer looking for excitement. He finds it when he places an ad offering his services to anyone for anything. It's Bennett who answers, involving Drummond in a kidnapping, blackmail and murder scheme, as her uncle is being held against his will. The film holds up surprisingly well, and features a nifty plot, good humor and fun characters. ★★★½ VHS: $14.99

Bullet in the Head

(1990, 118 min, Hong Kong, John Woo) *Tony C W Leung, Jacky Cheung, Waise Lee.* Woo's dark, grim, brutally violent tale of three friends in 1967 Hong Kong, whose exploits include smuggling, gang-turf wars, gold theft, greed-induced betrayal and more. With the Vietnam War, political unrest, cold-blooded assassinations and merciless executions serving as a backdrop, this must-see departure from Woo's "spaghetti Eastern" style of filmmaking leaves one drained, emotionally and physically. (Letterboxed) (Cantonese with English subtitles) ★★★½ VHS: $19.99; DVD: $49.99

Bullet to Beijing

(1997, 105 min, GB, George Mihalka) *Michael Caine, Jason Connery.* This latter-day installment in the Henry Palmer series is a truly disappointing and flat entertainment. Caine sleepwalks through his role as the bespectacled thief-turned-agent, who, in '60s espionage thrillers such as *The Ipcress File* and *Billion Dollar Brain*, provided a fun, slightly intellectual alternative

to the James Bond films. Here, we're treated to an uninvolving story about laid-off superagents-for-hire (due to budget cuts — the only stab at political commentary) searching for a deadly gas. Or something like that. The slack pacing, metronome editing, listless action scenes and endless parade of talking heads make for grueling viewing. ★ VHS: $7.99

Bulletproof

(1996, 85 min, US, Ernest Dickerson) *Adam Sandler, Damon Wayans, James Caan.* An annoying, screechy comedy, *Bulletproof* is barely watchable even for hard-core fans of the two leads. Sandler and Wayans are good friends who steal expensive cars for a living, and wish to move up the ladder by working for TV car huckster Caan (in another phoned-in, sleazy villain role). It's soon revealed, however, that Wayans is an undercover cop, earning Sandler's trust so he can nail Caan. During a bust gone bad, Sandler shoots Wayans in the head (don't ask); Wayans rehabilitates himself and is forced to join Sandler again as the two are chased by the bad guys, bickering the whole time. Badly plotted, this infantile movie is unexciting, uninvolving and virtually laughless. ★ VHS: $9.99; DVD: $24.99

Bulletproof Heart

(1995, 96 min, US, Mark Malone) *Anthony LaPaglia, Mimi Rogers, Matt Craven, Peter Boyle.* LaPaglia and Rogers dance a lethal *pas de deux* in this sly if formulaic thriller about a cold-hearted hit man hired to kill a gorgeous socialite/dominatrix who, for mysterious reasons, is quite ready and willing to die. Intrigued by his latest "client," he sets out to unlock the secret of her past and ends up in a torrid affair that leads to a twist ending. Malone's film is an interesting addition to the so-called "cinema of amorality" heralded by such films as *The Last Seduction* and *Red Rock West.* ★★½ VHS: $9.99

Bullets over Broadway

(1994, 99 min, US, Woody Allen) *John Cusack, Dianne Wiest, Chazz Palminteri, Jennifer Tilly, Jim Broadbent, Tracey Ullman, Rob Reiner, Mary-Louise Parker.* Set in 1920s New York City, one of Allen's brightest and funniest films blends his own

comic sensibilities with a touch of Damon Runyon to tell the tale of a political idealist and playwright (Cusack) desperate to get his play on Broadway. His only source of funding is a mobster who insists that his moll (a perfectly cast Tilly) star in the show. Pride tossed aside, he begins rehearsals only to find his leading lady accompanied by a nettlesome and opinionated bodyguard (Palminteri). His oddball cast is rounded out by a wifty stage legend (Wiest, who won a much-deserved Oscar) and an overeating leading man (Broadbent). While Wiest received the Academy's recognition, kudos must also go to Palminteri, who dominates his interactions with Cusack and gives the film a solid narrative anchor. ★★★★ VHS: $14.99; DVD: $29.99

Bullitt

(1968, 113 min, US, Peter Yates) *Steve McQueen, Jacqueline Bisset, Robert Duvall.* Yates' exceptionally exciting police thriller redefined the chase sequence for years to come. McQueen is a tough San Francisco detective on the trail of a witness' killers. Though the film is noted for the classic car chase scene, there's much more to recommend here. ★★★ VHS: $14.99; DVD: $19.99

Bulworth

(1998, 109 min, US, Warren Beatty) *Warren Beatty, Halle Berry, Oliver Platt, Don Cheadle, Paul Sorvino, Jack Warden, Joshua Malina, Isaiah Washington, Laurie Metcalf, Sean Astin, Christine Baranski.* A blistering, hilarious, razor-sharp social comedy which takes aim at American politics and political correctness and skewers them both with equal contempt and veracity, *Bulworth* hits new heights in American political comedies. In this frontal assault on the contemporary political scene, Beatty is Senator Jay Bulworth: a Democrat, near financial ruin, in the midst of a nervous breakdown, and who has just hired an assassin to kill him. But before the inevitable hit happens, Bulworth's sleepless, alcohol-driven delirium has an unexpected effect and he starts shooting from the hip, telling the truth and spouting un-PC remarks to and about one and all. In remarkable, non-gimmicky set pieces of rap and rhyme which escalate in brilliantly written and performed barrages, Bulworth discovers a voice inside him which gives him the will to live — but is it too late? Not merely content to just poke fun with an insider's wink of an eye, Beatty voice is clear and assured. His performance is an absolute marvel; the actor's never been this funny, and his dramatic instincts serve him well. No tail wagging this dog, *Bulworth* is an original. (Letterboxed VHS available for $19.99) ★★★★ VHS: $9.99; DVD: $22.99

Buona Sera, Mrs. Campbell

(1968, 113 min, US, Melvin Frank) *Gina Lollabrigida, Peter Lawford, Phil Silvers, Telly Savalas, Shelley Winters, Lee Grant.* The premise reeks of '60s dreck: Lollabrigida plays an Italian mother who has been accepting child support for 20 years from three American WWII vets — who each thinks her daughter is his — and now they are all returning for a reunion to her small village. But this one-joke comedy is a lot funnier than it has a right to be, for it is a constant source of well-earned laughs. Lollabrigida has probably never been funnier on screen, and she has the good fortune to play off the considerable comedic skills of a skilled supporting cast. ★★★ VHS: $14.99

Bulworth

The 'burbs

(1989, 103 min, US, Joe Dante) *Tom Hanks, Carrie Fisher, Bruce Dern, Henry Gibson.* This sometimes humorous, shallow comedy plays like "Leave It to Beaver" meets "The Munsters" rather than the dark, crazy romp it could have been. Hanks plays the suburban Everyman whose voice of sanity amongst the insanity around him is soon stifled when he and his neighbors begin to suspect that the new and very strange family who just moved in are cannibalistic murderers. ★★ VHS: $9.99; DVD: $24.99

Burden of Dreams

(1982, 94 min, US, Les Blank) Blank's revealing documentary of Werner Herzog's inexorable pursuit in filming *Fitzcarraldo* is a gripping portrait of artistic obsession and the creative process. Captured in this absorbing film are the moments of frustration and boredom, elation and prophecy which seized Herzog's crew (and himself) during their stay in the South American wilderness. ★★★ VHS: $59.99

Burglar

(1987, 102 min, US, Hugh Wilson) *Whoopi Goldberg, Bobcat Goldthwait, Lesley Ann Warren, John Goodman.* Though Goldberg tries her best with this mediocre material, and Goldthwait is a very appealing supporting character, there's not much to recommend in this comic mystery with Whoopi as a second-rate burglar who witnesses a murder and, being the number one suspect, tries to solve it herself. ★★ VHS: $14.99; DVD: $14.99

The Burglar

(1987, 83 min, USSR, Valery Ogorodnikov) *Konstantin Kinchev.* Soviet rock star Kinchev stars as a Western-influenced rocker determined to make it big at any cost. His ambition gets him in trouble after he steals a synthesizer for his group. The situation gets even more complicated after Senka, his "good brother," tries to take the heat by claiming that he stole the instrument. An unusual post-glasnost slice-of-life drama. (Russian with English subtitles) ★★★ VHS: $59.99

Burke and Wills

(1987, 140 min, Australia, Graeme Clifford) *Jack Thompson, Nigel Havers, Greta Scacchi.* This may not be the film that you'll want to watch on a hot summer's day — an epic retelling of an expedition into the searing heat of the Australian Outback. Thompson and Havers star as the 19th-century explorers whose ambition it is to cut a path through uncharted South Australian territory — distancing over 1,000 miles. Both actors give bravura performances as a pair of men determined to chart the uncharted no matter what the cost. The film's dazzling Cinemascope images may be lost on video, but the taut drama and heroic vision will not. ★★★½

The Burmese Harp

(1956, 116 min, Japan, Kon Ichikawa) *Shoji Yasui, Rentaro Mikuni.* A magnificent, poetic piece of filmmaking. The action takes place during the closing stages of the war in Burma. A young Japanese soldier, a musician and mystic, hears a call to remain behind with his harp to minister to the dead, both friend and foe alike.

(aka: *Harp of Burma*) (Japanese with English subtitles) ★★★½ VHS: $29.99

Burn! (Queimada)

(1969, 112 min, Italy/France, Gillo Pontecorvo) *Marlon Brando, Evarist Marquez.* Brando is brilliant as the Machiavellian Sir William Walker, a soldier-of-fortune sent by a British company to investigate a slave uprising on a sugar-producing Caribbean Island governed by repressive Portuguese colonials during the mid-1800s. After witnessing the brutal exploitation of the peasants and feeling that he can offer a better deal, Walker helps instigate a successful native rebellion. But when the revolt turns financially sour for the British, he switches sides and battles the leaders of the fledgling nation. A complex, anti-colonial political drama. ★★★ VHS: $19.99

Burn Hollywood Burn

(1998, 86 min, US, Alan Smithee) *Ryan O'Neal, Coolio, Chuck D, Eric Idle, Sylvester Stallone, Whoopi Goldberg, Jackie Chan.* Macho screenwriter Joe Eszterhas must have decided he had enough. After raking in millions for scripts like *Showgirls* and *Basic Instinct*, he decided to bite the hand that feeds him and write and produce this satire of the way Tinseltown works. *Burn Hollywood Burn* is meant to be a hip, guerilla black comedy, but Eszterhas' hipness quotient appears to be up there with Newt Gingrich's, thanks to the weary salvos hurled at Hollywood here. The story posits Idle as Alan Smithee, whose first directorial effort is *Trio*, a $212 million actioner. When evil producer O'Neal threatens to re-edit it, Idle responds by threatening to torch the film's only existing print. A similar premise worked in *S.O.B.*, but Eszterhas, who actually wrested control of this film from original helmer Arthur Hiller (who, in turn, replaced his name with "Alan Smithee" on the final credits!), has a penchant for chaos in his comedy, and this has the comic subtlety of a Godzilla rampage. ★½ VHS: $9.99

The Burning Season

(1994, 100 min, US, John Frankenheimer) *Raul Julia, Edward James Olmos, Sonia Braga, Kamala Dawson, Luis Guzman, Esai Morales.* Julia delivers his final performance, giving a pristine portrayal of Chico Mendes, the Brazilian union leader murdered while trying to preserve the rain forest and, with it, his way of life. The HBO docudrama opens with Mendes as a young boy getting his first lesson in exploitation by watching his father be grossly underpaid for a rubber delivery. In later years, the conflict between the rubber harvesters and the land barons is delineated in the larger stories of international investments and ecological issues; but the focus never strays too far from one man's passion to protect and serve his community. An impassioned, successful piece of filmmaking. Julia won a posthumous Best Actor Emmy for his work here. ★★★½ VHS: $19.99

Burning Secret

(1988, 110 min, GB, Andrew Birkin) *Faye Dunaway, Klaus Maria Brandauer, David Eberts.* Dunaway and Brandauer give affecting performances in this beautifully filmed period piece set in 1919 Vienna about the love affair between the repressed wife of an American diplomat (Dunaway) and a war-battered Austrian nobleman (Brandauer). Most remarkable is Eberts as Dunaway's young, asthmatic son, who intro-

duces the two lovers and becomes an unlikely protagonist in a most unusual triangle. ★★★

Burnt by the Sun

(1994, 134 min, Russia, Nikita Mikhalkov) *Nikita Mikhalkov, Oleg Menshikov, Nadia Mikhalkov.* The simplicity of a family outing on a tranquil Sunday afternoon is a potent and deceiving backdrop for betrayal and corruption in Mikhalkov's powerful yet lyrical Oscar-winning drama. An allegory for Stalin's clandestine reign of terror which engulfed the Russian landscape in the mid-1930s, the Chekhovian *Burnt by the Sun* tells the story of a Russian civil war hero (played with gusto by the director), his wife and child (Mikhalkov's real-life daughter, and she's a real charmer). Set during one summer's day, the action takes place at the family's dacha where the wife's former lover (the appealing Menshikov) has returned. A clownish, beguiling man, Menshikov's presence is greeted with delight by all, and as he reminisces and charms, it soon becomes clear he has a sinister but ulterior motive. Director Mikhalkov's success lies in both his leisurely pacing, which is cunning, and his sharp, subtle portrait of malevolence, which is unexpected. (Russian with English subtitles) ★★★½ VHS: $19.99

Burnt Offerings

(1976, 115 min, US, Dan Curtis) *Bette Davis, Karen Black, Oliver Reed, Lee Montgomery.* A chilling haunted house film from the director of "Dark Shadows." A family moves into a luxurious country estate, where one by one they succumb to the unknown force surrounding the house. ★★★ VHS: $14.99

Burroughs

(1983, 87 min, US, Howard Brookner) *William Burroughs.* Celebrated novelist William S. Burroughs is vividly profiled in this informative and fascinating study of his life and work. The author of "Junkie," "Naked Lunch" and "Nova Express" recounts with several of his friends the momentous episodes of a wildly eventful existence. A splendid glimpse into the mind of a true literary maverick. ★★★½ VHS: $41.99

Bus Stop

(1956, 96 min, US, Joshua Logan) *Marilyn Monroe, Don Murray, Arthur O'Connell, Eileen Heckart.* Monroe displays her usual sex appeal as well as surprising pathos in this delightful adaptation of the William Inge comedy. MM stars as a torchy cafe singer who becomes the object of affection — and obsession — of young naive cowpoke Murray (who received an Oscar nomination for his sensationally wild performance). ★★★½ VHS: $9.99; DVD: $24.99

The Bushido Blade

(1979, 104 min, Japan, Tom Kotani) *Richard Boone, James Earl Jones, Toshiro Mifune, Mako, Sonny Chiba.* In his final performance, Boone is exceptionally hammy as the leader of a group of Shogun warriors. Their mission is to search for a coveted sword through 19th-century Japan. A pretty but not very satisfying kung-fu action tale. Lots of beheadings keep you from falling asleep. Filmed in English. ★½ VHS: $69.99

Bushwhacked

(1995, 90 min, US, Greg Beeman) *Daniel Stern, Jon Polito, Brad Sullivan.* An inferior, terribly con-

The Butcher Boy

ceived family comedy in which Stern's wild-eyed antics and bumbling, slapstick acting style wear thin quickly. He plays a package delivery man who is framed for murder and chased by the FBI. He sets off for Devil's Peak, a remote mountaintop, upon learning that proof of his innocence may be there. Along the way, he is mistaken for a top-notch scout leader and forced to lead four boys and a girl on an overnight hike. ★½ VHS: $9.99

Business as Usual

(1987, 89 min, GB, Lezli-An Barrett) *Glenda Jackson, Cathy Tyson.* Jackson delivers a typically strong performance in this interesting but somewhat preachy discourse on sexual harassment in the workplace. Jackson plays a Liverpool boutique manager who is fired after she files a complaint against her boss on behalf of a coworker (Tyson). Based on a true story which became a cause célèbre in England. ★★ VHS: $19.99

Buster

(1988, 102 min, GB, David Green) *Phil Collins, Julie Walters.* Collins makes his film debut as Buster Edwards, the only conspirator in the Great Train Robbery (the biggest heist in British history) who managed to elude police. Both Collins and Walters (as his neglected wife) are good in this otherwise ordinary caper film. ★★½ VHS: $6.99

Bustin' Loose

(1981, 94 min, US, Oz Scott) *Richard Pryor, Cicely Tyson.* Pryor is in splendid comic form as an ex-con who drives teacher Tyson and a busload of orphaned and problem children cross-country. Pryor and Tyson make an appealing team. ★★★ VHS: $9.99; DVD: $19.99

Busting

(1973, 89 min, US, Peter Hyams) *Elliott Gould, Robert Blake, Antonio Fargas, Allen Garfield, Michael Lerner.* Patently offensive to gays, lesbians, blacks and other members of the disenfranchised, this standard police comedy-drama doesn't pit cops against robbers, but rather cops against the "socially and sexually deviant." Gould and Blake are two out-of-control vice cops, rampaging through the underworld of prostitution and gay bars undeterred by the Bill

of Rights and basic justice. Though this was probably intended to be more of a social comedy "exposing" the misdirection of a corrupt police force, antigay slurs abound, and over time its noxious depiction of gays is what one remembers. ★

But I'm a Cheerleader

(2000, 90 min, US, Jamie Babbit) *Natasha Lyonne, Cathy Moriarty, Clea DuVall, RuPaul Charles, Mink Stole, Bud Cort.* A high-spirited if sometimes forced comedy that pokes fun at homophobia as well as lesbian and gay stereotypes — but all in good fun. Poor Megan (Lyonne); she may be a pretty high schooler, model student and cheerleader who's dating the captain of the football team, but her loving parents think otherwise. You see, she's a vegetarian, she doesn't like kissing her boyfriend, and one can't ignore those Melissa Etheridge records. She is quickly carted off to True Directions, a scarily cheerful five-step de-homofication rehab camp. Sapphic sparks fly when Megan locks eyes with Graham (DuVall), a tomboy beauty with no intention of going straight. Director Babbit aims for anarchic, John Waters–like hijinks, which don't always hit the bull's-eye, but nevertheless the film is marked by good humor and just a touch of subversion. ★★½ VHS: $14.99; DVD: $24.99

Butch Cassidy and the Sundance Kid

(1969, 110 min, US, George Roy Hill) *Paul Newman, Robert Redford, Katharine Ross.* Classic western (and box-office smash) with Newman and Redford as outlaws on the run from a relentless posse. Told with great humor and infinite style. Winner of four Academy Awards, including William Goldman's screenplay, Score and Song ("Raindrops Keep Falling on My Head"). ★★★★ VHS: $14.99; DVD: $29.99

The Butcher Boy

(1998, 106 min, Ireland, Neil Jordan) *Eammon Owens, Stephen Rea, Alan Boyle, Fiona Shaw, Sinéad O'Connor, Ian Hart, Milo O'Shea.* A remarkable tale of troubled youth told with the utmost authority, intelligence and imagination, *The Butcher Boy*, ripe with dark humor and darker insights, tells the story of a misfit 12-year-old, Francie (Owens). It's the height of the Cold

War, and even in his rural Irish village, the events of the Cuban Missile Crisis have their toll on Francie's fellow townspeople. But Francie is more concerned with having good times with his best friend Joe, the only distraction from his mentally unstable mum and his abusive dad (Rea). As his family life worsens, Francie's own mental state begins to deteriorate. He begins seeing neighbors as villains and having visions of the Virgin Mary (O'Connor), until his fill of loneliness and confusion lead to their inevitable climax. Though essentially a story of mental breakdown, *The Butcher Boy* is surprisingly effervescent, sweetened by a startling astute screenplay by Jordan and Patrick McCabe (based on McCabe's novel), and fine, literate direction. As Francie, young Owens is exceptional. ★★★★ VHS: $14.99

The Butcher's Wife

(1991, 107 min, US, Terry Hughes) *Demi Moore, George Dzundza, Jeff Daniels, Frances McDormand, Mary Steenburgen, Max Perlich, Miriam Margolyes.* Moore has the title role in this whimsical romantic comedy as a Southern clairvoyant who impulsively marries a doughy butcher (Dzundza) from Greenwich Village. In her new surroundings, she sets off a farcical chain reaction of sexual trysts through her predictions of love to a neighborhood starving for it. She also finds romance with neighbor/psychiatrist Daniels. Moore is actually quite appealing here, making the most of the material. ★★★ VHS: $14.99

Butterfield 8

(1960, 109 min, US, Daniel Mann) *Elizabeth Taylor, Laurence Harvey, Eddie Fisher.* Taylor won an Oscar (though many say it was because of her nearly dying of pneumonia) for her sultry portrayal of an expensive call girl who lives with her mom and doesn't think she's a prostitute. The film features great histrionics and a swell supporting cast. A good, old-fashioned soaper with some fine, campy dialogue. ★★★ VHS: $14.99; DVD: $19.99

Butterflies Are Free

(1972, 109 min, US, Milton Katselas) *Goldie Hawn, Eileen Heckart, Edward Albert.* Based on the Broadway play, *Butterflies are Free* is a sensitive and touching comedy-drama about a blind young man (Albert) who is determined to be independent. Leaving his family home, he ventures to San Francisco where he befriends his eccentric next door neighbor, played by Hawn. They become friends and lovers, only to have their burgeoning relationship hampered by the over-protective mom, played by Heckart, who won an Academy Award for her work. ★★★ VHS: $9.99

Butterflies on the Scaffold
(Mariposas en el Andamio)

(1996, 75 min, Cuba, Margaret Gilpin & Luis Bernaza) A rare view of what day-to-day life is like for the gay and drag community in modern Cuba. It is a highly unusual look at how a group of working-class drag queens in a small town have become an integral part of their neighborhood. Glamorous gowns fashioned from sugar sacks and eyelashes made of carbon paper are the reality of drag in Cuba. The journey moves from on-stage action and backstage preparation to insightful interviews with community leaders, the performers themselves, and their families. An engaging film about social, human and cultural transformation. (Spanish with English subtitles) ★★★ VHS: $39.99

Butterfly Kiss

(1995, 88 min, GB, Michael Winterbottom) *Amanda Plummer, Saskia Reeves.* Plummer joins the ranks of film's most notorious lesbian killers in this disturbing and hypnotically black psycho/comedy. Obsessed with Judith, the only woman to have really loved her, Eunice (Plummer), a tough North of England lass, goes on a bloody search for her. On the way she meets, captivates and seduces a female gas station attendent (Reeves) who quickly becomes her accomplice. An intelligent, quirky tale that will be sure to upset some and entrance others. ★★★ VHS: $29.99

By Dawn's Early Light

(1990, 100 min, US, Jack Sholder) *Powers Boothe, Rebecca De Mornay, Martin Landau, James Earl Jones.* This made-for-cable nuclear drama is a classy, edge-of-your-seat thriller combining elements of *Fail Safe* and *The Hunt for Red October.* Boothe and De Mornay star as romantically involved pilots who face a moral and personal dilemma when they are assigned to drop the bomb against the "enemy" when Washington D.C. is devastated in an accidental attack. Landau is the cautious and concerned President whose presumed death brings the country to the brink of nuclear catastrophe. ★★★½ VHS: $9.99

By Design

(1981, 88 min, Canada, Claude Jutra) *Patty Duke Astin, Sara Botsford.* The sexual revolution travels north in this quirky comedy directed by Quebecer Jutra. Duke Astin (Helen) and Botsford (Angel) star as two fashion designers, business partners and lovers who decide they want to have a baby. Rejected by the adoption agency and finding artificial insemination "gross," the frustrated pair decide that a stud is needed. After slapstick encounters cruising the straight discos, bars and construction sites of Vancouver, Helen and Angel choose Terry, an oafish photographer who eagerly accepts the mission. The deft handling of the relationship among the trio makes this an offbeat and touching comedy. ★★½

Bye, Bye Birdie

(1963, 112 min, US, George Sidney) *Dick Van Dyke, Ann-Margret, Paul Lynde, Janet Leigh.* It's like an episode of "Dobie Gillis" with songs in this rather benign satire on the foibles of rock 'n' roll. Before reporting for his military service, an Elvis-like character makes a visit to a small Midwestern town. And wouldn't you know it, those darn teenagers just get all silly. Van Dyke repeats his star-making Broadway role, and is helped by pleasant performances from Ann-Margret and Lynde. Enjoyable tunes like "Put on a Happy Face" and "Kids" enliven this ever-so-amusing confection. (Remade in 1999) ★★★ VHS: $14.99; DVD: $29.99

Bye Bye Blues

(1990, 110 min, US, Anne Wheeler) *Rebecca Jenkins, Luke Reilly, Stuart Margolin, Michael*

Ontkean, Kate Reid. A provocative romantic drama set during WWII. The wife of a military doctor captured by the Japanese, in an effort to make ends meet, takes a job with a local swing band and falls in love with the lead singer. A stylish and tuneful exploration of one woman's liberation. ★★★ VHS: $29.99

Bye Bye Brazil

(1979, 110 min, Brazil, Carlos Diegues) *Jose Wilker, Betty Fario, Fabio Junior.* Diegues' lyrical journey across Brazil is part road movie, part travelogue sprinkled with hints of political message and a touch of magical realism. Wilker stars as Lord Gypsy, the leader of a troupe of traveling performers known as Caravana Rolidei. The film follows this group in a quasi-documentary style on a revelatory trip across the Trans-Amazon highway and beyond. Faria costars as Salome, Queen of the Rumba. Diegues and his cast and crew actually embarked on a 9,000-mile journey to make the film, letting much of the material come to them along the way. The resulting "journal" is not always successful, but is at times mesmerizing and offers a unique look at the rapidly changing face of Brazil. ★★★ VHS: $19.99

Bye Bye, Love

(1995, 107 min, US, Sam Weisman) *Matthew Modine, Paul Reiser, Randy Quaid, Janeane Garofalo, Rob Reiner.* Thanks to three appealing performances by Modine, Reiser and Quaid and an involving screenplay, *Bye Bye, Love* is a most pleasant surprise. Three divorced fathers meet regularly at McDonald's for the exchange of children with the ex-wives. In the course of a weekend, the story follows them as they toss one-liners, date, commiserate and fulfill their parental duties. To its credit, the film never trivializes divorce, only finding comic and sometimes touching fallout from it; though to its discredit, the wives' parts are sketchily written. Quaid is extremely funny, and his scenes with blind date Garofalo, herself hilarious, are among the film's best. ★★★ VHS: $19.99

Cabaret

(1972, 124 min, US, Bob Fosse) *Liza Minnelli, Michael York, Joel Grey, Helmut Griem, Marisa Berenson.* Fosse's savory depiction of Christopher Isherwood's '30s Berlin stars an effervescent Minnelli as nightclub singer and carefree bohemian Sally Bowles and York as Isherwood's alter ego Brian Roberts. The short-lived decadent world of pre-Hitler Berlin as well as the rising nationalistic tide of Fascism are effectively captured in this trendsetting musical. Griem is a wealthy and debonair baron who sweeps both Sally and Brian off their feet. The musical numbers performed at the Kit Kat Klub are just some of the film's rousing highlights, a collection of great songs belted by Academy Award winners Minnelli and Grey as the devilishly cynical Master of Ceremonies. ★★★★ VHS: $14.99; DVD: $19.99

Cabaret Balkan

(1999, 102 min, Serbia, Goran Paskaljevic) *Nikola Ristanovski, Lazar Ristovski, Mirjana Jokovic.* Belgrade is a rough town, almost like the Wild West, and this is a rough Wild West movie. With five parallel stories of post-war Balkan life, this biting comedy doesn't have a clear plot line, but as a pastiche it works beautifully. Like Kusterica's *Underground,* there is a horn band serenading us, but it surrounds a bus about to be highjacked by a slightly deranged anarchist. The Cabaret Balkan of the title features another slightly deranged man, but this one is performing an anarchist political cabaret act. Cascading from tale to tale without warning, there's one constant: a dark aura, almost surreal. The film contains senseless vio-

Cabaret: Liza Minnelli and Joel Grey know that "money makes the world go 'round"

lence, but that is life in Belgrade. The story reeks of a corrupt society where people are questioning the moral thread that has held them together for centuries. It's amazing that such a significant message is delivered in a film that manages to amuse as well as enlighten. (Serbo-Croatian with English subtitles) ★★★½ VHS: $102.99

Cabeza de Vaca

(1992, 108 min, Mexico, Nicholas Echevarria) *Juan Diego, Daniel Gimenez Cacho.* In 1528, a Spanish expedition shipwrecks off the coast of Florida — 600 of the men aboard die. One survivor roams the countryside searching for his comrades, but instead finds the Iguase, an ancient Indian tribe. Over the next eight years, the survivor, Cabeza de Vaca, learns their alien culture, becoming a healer and a leader. But he soon has to confront his past when newly arriving conquistadors seek to enslave the Indians. A vividly entertaining, large-scale film with stunning visuals and a sometimes surrealistic story which at times drifts into territory blazed by films such as *El Topo* and *A Man Called Horse*. (Spanish with English subtitles) ★★★½

Cabin Boy

(1994, 81 min, US, Adam Resnick) *Chris Elliott, Ann Magnuson, David Letterman.* A television skit stretched to a barely feature-length 81 minutes, this initially funny but ultimately tedious comedy stars Elliott as an obnoxious rich boy (forget the fact that he's balding and in his thirties) who mistakenly embarks on an "it's gonna make you a man" high-seas adventure. Playing the self-centered, moronic innocent character to the hilt, Elliott brings some antic humor to the otherwise disappointing tale. Letterman has some fun in an early cameo (you get to see him before slumber sets in) and Magnuson is featured as a vampish, six-armed creature from the sea. ★½ VHS: $19.99

The Cabin in the Cotton

(1932, 77 min, US, Michael Curtiz) *Bette Davis, Richard Barthelmess, Dorothy Jordan.* Okay trivia buffs, one of Davis' most repeated lines is: "Ah'd love to kiss ya but I just washed my hay-uh." And it's said in this period melodrama, an important step in Davis' rise to stardom. In a supporting part, Davis had her first "bad girl" role as a Southern vixen out to set honest sharecropper's son Barthelmess (a silent screen actor whose star was fading) on the road to ruin. Bette is terrific in this otherwise routine drama. ★★ VHS: $19.99

Cabin in the Sky

(1943, 99 min, US, Vincente Minnelli) *Eddie Anderson, Lena Horne, Louis Armstrong, Ethel Waters, Duke Ellington.* A stellar black cast is featured in Minnelli's musical fable about the forces of good and evil vying for the soul of Little Joe (Anderson). ★★★ VHS: $19.99

The Cabinet of Dr. Caligari

(1919, 69 min, Germany, Robert Wiene) *Conrad Veidt, Werner Krauss.* Setting in motion the wave of German Expressionism, director Wiene created this nightmarish universe which lies beneath the facade of order and reason. This horror classic employs dazzling use of art direction, lighting and cubist set design to tell its

Cabin in the Sky

chilling tale of a carnival hypnotist using a somnambulist for the former's evil purposes. (Silent with musical accompaniment) ★★★★ VHS: $24.99; DVD: $24.99

Cabiria

(1914, 123 min, Italy, Giovanni Pastrone) The most ambitious and spectacular of the historical epics for which Italy was famous before WWI, *Cabiria* set the standard for big-budget feature-length movies and opened the way for D.W. Griffith and Cecil B. DeMille. During the war between Carthage and Rome, a girl — Cabiria — is separated from her parents. In her odyssey through the world of ancient Rome, she encounters an erupting volcano, the barbaric splendor of Carthage, human sacrifice and Hannibal crossing the Alps. Mastered from a 35mm archive, *Cabiria* features a newly recorded soundtrack from the original 1914 score. ★★★ VHS: $24.99; DVD: $29.99

The Cable Guy

(1996, 91 min, US, Ben Stiller) *Jim Carrey, Matthew Broderick, Leslie Mann, Jack Black, George Segal, Diane Baker, Ben Stiller, Eric Roberts, Janeane Garafalo, Andy Dick.* Carrey attempts the difficult genre of black comedy stamped with his own unique brand of humor. However, humor is not what you get with this unfunny, undisciplined comedy. Carrey plays an obnoxious cableman whose present of free cable to customer Broderick turns the latter's life upside-down. As Carrey latches onto — even stalks — the protesting Broderick, his family and friends only see one swell guy. The scenario can lend itself to many humorous situations, as *What about Bob* proved; however, the result here is mean-spirited, its malice underscored by a deficiency of laughs. (Letterboxed VHS available for $19.99) ★½ VHS: $9.99; DVD: $19.99

Cactus

(96 min, Australia, Paul Cox) *Isabelle Huppert, Norman Kaye, Robert Menzies.* Huppert stars as a young French woman visiting Australia who begins to lose her sight after a car accident. Her acceptance of the possibility of total blindless is difficult until she meets Robert, a wise and witty young man who was born blind. They fall in love and they both help each other accept their limitations and handicaps. While not totally success-

ful, this film does feature a hypnotic score and many affecting scenes between the lovers. ★★½

Cactus Flower

(1969, 103 min, US, Gene Saks) *Walter Matthau, Ingrid Bergman, Goldie Hawn, Jack Weston.* The enchanting performances of the three leads make this lackluster screen version of Abe Burrows' Broadway hit tolerable. Walter plays a dentist secretly in love with his nurse Ingrid, though he's having an affair with Goldie. Hawn won the Oscar for her delightful screen debut. ★★½ VHS: $9.99

Caddie

(1976, 107 min, Australia, Donald Crombie) *Helen Morse, Jack Thompson.* An affectionate account of a determined woman struggling for independence in Sydney during the 1920s and '30s. Morse excels as the strong-willed heroine. ★★★

The Caddy

(1953, 95 min, US, Norman Taurog) *Jerry Lewis, Dean Martin, Donna Reed.* Lewis supplies most of the laughs in this minor Lewis and Martin comedy. Jerry is the son of a golf pro who's afraid of crowds. Dino sings "That's Amore." ★★½ VHS: $14.99

Caddyshack

(1980, 98 min, US, Harold Ramis) *Michael O'Keefe, Chevy Chase, Rodney Dangerfield, Bill Murray, Ted Knight.* Depending on your comedic tastes, this wacky comedy will either cause moments of silly hysteria or pains of anguish. Either way, good taste is thrown by the wayside. Chase and Dangerfield (in a terrifically funny performance) are just two of the crazy members of an exclusive country club. Murray chases gophers a lot. (Sequel: *Caddyshack II*) ★★½ VHS: $14.99; DVD: $19.99

Caddyshack II

(1988, 93 min, US, Allan Arkush) *Chevy Chase, Dan Aykroyd, Dyan Cannon, Jackie Mason, Robert Stack.* As in the original *Caddyshack*, a seasoned comedian (Rodney Dangerfield in the first, Mason in the sequel) is the only reason to even consider this otherwise sophomoric comedy. For the rest of the cast, it's merely career lowpoints. ★½ VHS: $14.99; DVD: $14.99

Cadillac Man

(1990, 97 min, US, Roger Donaldson) *Robin Williams, Tim Robbins, Pamela Reed, Annabella Sciorra, Lori Petty.* Williams is a fast-talking, womanizing car salesman and Robbins is the gun-toting jealous husband who decides to take Williams and his dealership hostage. Williams does his usual schtick, but this one should have been better. ★★½ VHS: $9.99

Caesar and Cleopatra

(1946, 127 min, GB, Gabriel Pascal) *Vivien Leigh, Claude Rains, Flora Robson.* No, this isn't Shakespeare, this is Shaw. Rains and Leigh star in this sluggish rendition of George Bernard Shaw's play about the aging Roman conqueror and the beautiful, soft-headed Queen of the Nile. Great performances capture some of Shaw's unique wit, but the plot has a tendency to drag. ★★½ VHS: $14.99

Café au Lait

(1993, 94 min, France, Mathieu Kassovitz) *Julie Mauduech, Hubert Kounde, Mathieu Kassovitz.* Kassovitz has put together a racially charged but ultimately tame tale about an interracial ménage à trois. The film's impressive opening credits take place over a lightning-paced bicycle-wheel's-eye ride through Paris that leads to the collision of Felix (Kassovitz), a gawky Jewish bicycle messenger, and Jamal (Kounde), a handsome, well-groomed son of an African ambassador. Unbeknownst to either, they have the shared affections of Lola (Mauduech), a light-skinned beauty of Caribbean descent. The two men wind up on her doorstep together, whereupon she informs them that she is pregnant and doesn't know, much less care, who the father is. Needless to say, for the rest of the film, the men joust over race and ego, tossing epithets at each other with little reserve. *Café au Lait*'s problem is that while it tries to be light-hearted comedy, the slurs are laid on a little too thick. Kassovitz fails to take a serious subject and inject humor into it; he simply turns comedy serious. It doesn't work. (French with English subtitles) ★★ VHS: $29.99

Café Express

(1981, 89 min, Italy, Nanni Loy) *Nino Manfredi, Gigi Reder, Adolfo Celi.* Manfredi stars in this top-notch Italian comedy about a charming flim-flam man's attempts to aid his ailing son, outwitting the dim-witted police in the process. A lovable, compassionate portrait by Italy's most inventive comedy director, Loy. (Italian with English subtitles) ★★★

Cafe Flesh

(1982, 80 min, US, Rinse Dream) *Pia Snow, Marie Sharp, Andrew Nichols, Kevin James.* "Post-nuke thrill freaks looking for a kick!" Decadent hardly suffices in describing this concoction of tongue-in-cheek punk pornography. In the post-apocalyptic future, those capable of engaging in sex (positives) are employed to perform for the vast majority of impotent onlookers (negatives), who succumb to nausea at the very outbreak of foreplay. Demented, you say? You'll never take sex for granted again. ★★ VHS: $39.99; DVD: $39.99

Café Society

(1995, 104 min, US, Raymond DeFelitta) *Frank Whaley, Peter Gallagher, Lara Flynn Boyle, Anna Thomson, David Patrick Kelly.* Fact-based drama about Mickey Jelke (Whaley), a sophisticated New York playboy whose cushy lifestyle of booze and broads is brought to a screeching halt by a headline-grabbing scandal. When Jelke declares his love for the sultry but subpar Patricia Ward (Boyle), his mother cuts him off without a cent. To maintain his extravagant standard of living, Jelke begins to prostitute Pat, and his downfall really begins. This stylish film captures the essence of how the 1950s could not tolerate the socially irresponsible, especially if they were monied. DeFelitta films *Café Society* in a manner that is right out of the era it depicts, and it couldn't be more appropriate. ★★★ VHS: $24.99

La Cage aux Folles

(1978, 91 min, France/Italy, Edouard Molinaro) *Ugo Tognazzi, Michel Serrault, Michel Galabru, Benny Luke.* This frolicsome farce that finally made drag respectable stars Tognazzi and Serrault as gay lovers who must, amid mounting complications, pose as mom and dad for the sake of a prospective daughter-in-law and her straight-laced parents. The laughs are plentiful, and Serrault creates an endearing, even resilient characterization of the drag queen Alban. Followed by two sequels, an American remake (*The Birdcage*), and adapted into an award-winning Broadway musical. (French with English subtitles) ★★★½ VHS: $14.99; DVD: $19.99

La Cage aux Folles II

(1980, 101 min, France, Edouard Molinaro) *Ugo Tognazzi, Michel Serrault, Marcel Bozzuffi, Benny Luke.* This sequel to the popular comedy reunited the original stars (Tognazzi and Serrault) who, as gay lovers Alban and Renato, become involved with spies and are forced to flee the country. Alban's valiant attempts to masquerade as a Sicilian peasant woman is one of the hilarious highlights to this otherwise uneven sequel. (French with English subtitles) ★★½ VHS: $14.99; DVD: $19.99

La Cage aux Folles III: The Wedding

(1985, 88 min, France, Georges Lautner) *Michel Serrault, Ugo Tognazzi, Michel Galabru, Benny Luke, Stephane Audran.* Who saw this film when it came out theatrically? Judging from the box office receipts, not many. Gay cabaret star Alban learns he is to inherit a fortune — but only on the condition that he marry and provide an heir in 18 months. The magic is gone, though Tognazzi and Serrault are still a joy to watch. (Dubbed) ★½ VHS: $19.99

Caged Heat

(1974, 84 min, US, Jonathan Demme) *Juanita Brown, Erica Gavin, Barbara Steele.* This ain't no party, this ain't no disco, this ain't no *Stop Making Sense.* Demme's first-time directorial touch raises this women-behind-bars low-budget potboiler above the norm. Surprisingly competent performances in this semi-skin-flick morality tale. Remember: It is unlawful to transport weapons or narcotics into a federal penal institute. ★★½ VHS: $14.99

The Caine Mutiny

(1954, 125 min, US, Edward Dmytryk) *Humphrey Bogart, Fred MacMurray, Van Johnson, Jose Ferrer, Lee Marvin.* In his last great role, Bogart stars as the neurotic Captain Queeg in this sensational screen version of Herman Wouk's Pulitzer Prize—winning novel. During a fierce typhoon, the men of the USS *Caine* relieve their captain of command when he suffers a breakdown, leading to a court-martial of the executive officers behind the "mutiny." ★★★★ VHS: $19.99; DVD: $29.99

The Caine Mutiny Court-Martial

(1988, 100 min, US, Robert Altman) *Brad Davis, Jeff Daniels, Peter Gallagher, Eric Bogosian.* Altman's made-for-TV movie is a solid translation of the Herman Wouk play. Altman briskly takes us through 100 minutes' worth of interrogation, all the while building and never losing the dramatic tension. Featuring some trademark Altman touches including, of course, multi-layered dialogue, the film includes a number of powerful performances. Davis plays the infamous Lt. Commander Queeg, Daniels is the lieutenant on trial for mutiny, and Bogosian puts in a brilliant performance as the complex, first-time defense lawyer. ★★★½

Cal

(1984, 94 min, Ireland, Pat O'Connor) *Helen Mirren, John Lynch, Donal McCann.* A Catholic youth (Lynch) who lives in a predominantly Protestant section of Ulster becomes romantically involved with the widow of a Protestant policeman. His political belief structure is severely tried when he realizes that he was a participant in her husband's death. This powerful, gut-wrenching drama features Mirren in a superlative performance. ★★★½ VHS: $19.99

Calamity Jane

(1953, 101 min, US, David Butler) *Doris Day, Howard Keel.* Day gives one of her most appealing performances as the legendary Calamity Jane, the tomboyish sharpshooter who changes her ways when she falls for Wild Bill Hickok (Keel). Musical score includes the Oscar-winning "Secret Love." ★★★ VHS: $14.99

Calendar

(1993, 74 min, Canada/Armenia/Germany, Atom Egoyan) *Arsinée Khanjian, Ashot Adamian, Atom Egoyan.* Egoyan directed and stars in this hypnotic tale as a photographer whose wife leaves him for another while they are on assignment in Armenia. *Calendar* explores the nature of voyeurism and sexual obsession with an inventive, compelling structure. (English and Armenian with English subtitles) ★★★

Calendar Girl

(1993, 90 min, US, John Whitesell) *Jason Priestley, Jerry O'Connell, Emily Warfield, Maxwell Caulfield.* Priestley tries to shed his "90210" image with a fast-talking, tough-guy numbers-runner characterization in this tiresome comedy. Set in 1962, the film follows the misadventures of a group of boyhood friends who decide to take a road trip to Hollywood to try and get Marilyn Monroe in the sack. ★½ VHS: $9.99

C

California Suite

(1978, 102 min, US, Herbert Ross) *Jane Fonda, Alan Alda, Maggie Smith, Michael Caine, Walter Matthau, Elaine May, Richard Pryor, Bill Cosby.* An often very funny film version of Neil Simon's stage hit, which focuses on four disparate groups of families and friends who stay at the Beverly Hills Hotel. Here the stories are interwoven, so the weaker of the four never really drags the film down. The best of the chapters is the touching and extremely well-acted tale of Britishers Smith and Caine coming to town for the Oscars. Ironically, Smith won an Academy Award for her wonderful portrayal of a nominated actress; Caine plays her bisexual husband with depth and conviction. ★★★ VHS: $9.99

Caligula

(1979, 156 min, US, Tinto Brass & Bob Guccione) *Malcolm McDowell, John Gielgud, Peter O'Toole, Helen Mirren.* No, this isn't an ersatz PBS documentary. Despite its prestigious cast, this controversial production manages to steer clear of most socially accepted standards of decency. But for those chagrined at having missed the decadence and excess of the Roman Empire, this X-rated epic is as satisfying as a day of debauchery. ★ VHS: $79.99; DVD: $29.99

Call Northside 777

(1948, 111 min, US, Henry Hathaway) *James Stewart, Lee J. Cobb, Richard Conte, Helen Walker.* This true story stars Stewart as a 1940s Chicago newspaperman whose investigation into an 11-year-old crime helps set free an innocent man. Directed in fascinating semidocumentary style by Hathaway, the film traces the route taken by Stewart as he slowly uncovers evidence of police corruption and conspiracy. Cobb is very good as Stewart's editor, and Conte is the unjustly convicted prisoner. Hathaway creates a tension throughout even though the outcome is obvious. ★★★½ VHS: $19.99

Came a Hot Friday

(1985, 101 min, New Zealand, Ian Muneli) *Philip Gordon, Peter Bland.* A rollicking comic adventure about two con men who roam through the New Zealand countryside, cheating bookmakers and hustling the locals. As their fortunes turn bad, they form an alliance with an insane eccentric with a pronounced Zorro fetish. A silly and mirth-filled examination of the underbelly of the capitalistic urge. ★★★

Camelot

(1967, 175 min, GB, Joshua Logan) *Richard Harris, Vanessa Redgrave, Franco Nero, David Hemmings, Lionel Jeffries.* This big-budget film version of the Lerner and Loewe Broadway hit is tragically short on excitement and none of those in the cast can really sing. Harris (who would go on to perform the role in a successful revival in the '80s) is a capable King Arthur, who recounts his story of chivalry, romance and betrayal. Redgrave, though miscast, is a lovely Guinevere, Arthur's betrothed and future queen. Jeffries is an almost amusing Merlin. (VHS available letterboxed or pan & scan) ★★ VHS: $19.99; DVD: $19.99

The Cameraman

(1927, 70 min, US, Edward Sedgwick) *Buster Keaton, Marceline Day.* In his first film under the constricting dictates of the M-G-M front office (read: Mayer, Thalberg), Keaton still manages many fine moments of comedic poetry as an inept newsreel photographer who gets mixed up with gangsters. ★★★ VHS: $29.99

The Cameraman's Revenge & Other Fantastic Tales

(1912-1958, 80 min, Russia/France, Ladislaw Starewicz) A treat for everyone in the family, this is truly a treasure-trove of animation. There is much to be said for Starewicz's art, the influence of which is evident in the work of Tim Burton, the Brothers Quay and other surrealist animators. Each piece in this collection shows a growing understanding of manipulating the media, culminating in true mastery of the craft in works like *Mascot* and *Voice of the Nightingale*. The musical accompaniment of the earlier works is sloppy and undistinguished, but with the advent of sound in the later works, the true richness of music fully complements his work. It is interesting to note that in Starewicz's "relocation" to Paris in the early '20s, he changed his name and became much more commercial and made his allegories less striking. (Russian with English subtitles) ★★★★ VHS: $59.99

Camila

(1984, 105 min, Argentina, Maria Luisa Bemberg) *Susu Pecararo, Imanol Arias.* Taken from a true story that was one of Argentina's most notorious scandals, *Camila* tells the haunting tale of a doomed and forbidden love. In 1847, Camila, the daughter of a wealthy politican, falls in love with a Jesuit priest. Unable to suppress their desire, the couple are forced to flee. However, the government, her family and the Church, outraged by their "sacrilege," unite in an effort to hunt them down. A gripping, elegant and erotic love story. (Spanish with English subtitles) ★★★ VHS: $29.99

Camilla

(1994, 90 min, Canada, Deepa Mehta) *Jessica Tandy, Bridget Fonda, Elias Koteas, Maury Chaykin, Hume Cronyn, Graham Greene.* The last theatrical film of the great Tandy is an appealing road movie with the actress in wonderful form. She plays the title character, a retired concert violinist who lives in a past of accolade and romance.

Slightly scandalous and given to exaggeration more than not, she begins a cross-country trip from her Georgia home to Toronto with Fonda, a fellow if untalented musician with an uncertain future. On the way, they meet a select group of eccentrics and try to come to terms with their individual concerns. Both actresses are delightful, and it's to their credit that each is able to overcome the generic dialogue and predictable dramatics. ★★½ VHS: $19.99

Camille

(1936, 110 min, US, George Cukor) *Greta Garbo, Robert Taylor, Henry Daniell.* Classic 1930s tearjerker with Garbo in one of her best roles (most Garbo-ites feel this is her definitive portrayal) as Alexander Dumas' doomed courtesan. One of the better examples of those opulent M-G-M productions which the studio either excelled at (as in this instance) or overproduced and ultimately butchered. They could have found a better Armand than Taylor, but Daniell is sensational as the villainous Baron de Varville. ★★★½ VHS: $19.99

Camille 2000

(1969, 115 min, Italy, Radley Metzger) File this cheesy Italian soap opera under campy sexploitation! Poor Dumas' classic tale gets trashed in this "naughty" exposé of heated passions, duplicitous lovers, cheating wives, horny but handsome men and sexually overcharged women and, last but not least, true love. The poor acting actually helps in giving this trash some camp value. (Dubbed) ★ VHS: $19.99; DVD: $24.99

Camille Claudel

(1988, 149 min, France, Bruno Nuytten) *Isabelle Adjani, Gérard Depardieu, Laurent Grevill.* The twin titans of French cinema, Adjani and Depardieu, star in this stirring look at the troubled life of the young sculptress Camille Claudel and her fateful relationship with Auguste Rodin. The movie examines the young artist and the creative fire which burned in her soul and eventually thrust her to the perilous heights of the male-dominated and very misogynist Parisian art world. Her romantic obsession with her mentor and lover, Rodin, eventually plunged her into a world of loneliness and madness. A

Isabelle Adjani in *Camille Claudel*

haunting love story featuring a mesmerizing performance by Adjani. (French with English subtitles) ★★★ VHS: $19.99; DVD: $19.99

Camp Nowhere

(1994, 96 min, US, Jonathan Prince) *Christopher Lloyd, Jonathan Jackson, M. Emmet Walsh, Tom Wilson, Wendy Makkena.* A zany and surprisingly funny romp which borrows just a little from the semi-classic British comedy *The Happiest Days of Your Life.* A group of adolescents, who are all being shipped off to various theme camps for the summer (military, diet, computer, etc.), unite their resources and rent a run-down location all their own. This is done with the help of flaky drama teacher Lloyd. The kids enjoy their adult-free vacation until the moms and dads decide to visit, prompting a wacky, complicated ruse. Silly shenanigans and a deft directorial touch make this as fun as a child's summer day. ★★★ VHS: $9.99

Can-Can

(1960, 131 min, US, Walter Lang) *Shirley MacLaine, Frank Sinatra, Louis Jordan, Maurice Chevalier.* A powerhouse cast isn't enough to offset the many lethargic moments in this only occasionally entertaining Cole Porter musical. Shirley wants to dance the "shameful" title dance; the police say no, lawyer Frank says she can-can. Songs include "I Love Paris" and a few not in the original stage production. ★★½ VHS: $9.99

Can She Bake a Cherry Pie?

(1983, 90 min, US, Henry Jaglom) *Karen Black, Michael Emil, Frances Fisher.* As quirky comedies go, this one takes the cake, so to speak. Jaglom delivers an eccentric love story among a group of decidedly peculiar New York neurotics. Black is Zee, an emotional wreck, frazzled by her recent break-up with her husband and starved for affection. She meets Eli (Emil), a balding, opinionated, health-obsessed rationalist, who goes so far as to measure her pulse during sex to gauge the strength of his orgasms. Pure emotion meets pure logic and the result is an oddly charming couple. ★★★ VHS: $29.99

Can't Buy Me Love

(1987, 94 min, US, Steve Rash) *Patrick Dempsey, Amanda Peterson, Dennis Dugan.* Dempsey and Peterson make for an attractive twosome in this well-played though slight teen comedy with Dempsey as a high school nerd paying school beauty Peterson to pretend to be his girlfriend. ★★½

Can't Hardly Wait

(1998, 101 min, US, Deborah Kaplan & Harry Elfont) *Ethan Embray, Jennifer Love Hewitt, Charlie Korsmo, Seth Green, Lauren Ambrose, Peter Facinelli.* *Can't Hardly Wait* takes its cue from those John Hughes films of the '80s and puts a '90s spin on it. For the most part, it succeeds. The majority of the action takes place on graduation night at what will be the biggest party of the year. Preston (Embray), an aspiring writer, attempts a last-ditch effort to let Amanda (Hewitt) know how he feels about her. The film is more a series of situations, some funnier than others, some not very funny at all. What the directors have captured is, in some cases, a dead-on parody of the many social cliques rampant in today's high schools. It's hard to imagine any of these groups attending the same social gathering, but the writers seem to

know this and have a lot of fun with the improbability of the situation. Ducky would no doubt approve. ★★½ VHS: $9.99; DVD: $14.99

Canadian Bacon

(1994, 91 min, US, Michael Moore) *John Candy, Alan Alda, Rhea Perlman, Kevin Pollak, Steven Wright, James Belushi.* After a terrific debut with *Roger & Me,* director Moore misfires with this silly political farce about the U.S. President (Alda) declaring war on Canada in order to win support for his reelection campaign. ★½ VHS: $14.99; DVD: $14.99

The Candidate

(1972, 109 min, US, Michael Ritchie) *Robert Redford, Peter Boyle, Melvyn Douglas, Allen Garfield, Don Porter.* Potent and vastly entertaining political satire and exposé. Redford stars as an idealistic, dark-horse senatorial candidate running against a powerful, conservative incumbent. The extremely authentic flavor to the behind-the-scenes meetings and pow-wows, and an incisive screenplay by Oscar-winner Jeremy Larner add greatly to the success of the film. Great supporting cast. ★★★½ VHS: $19.99; DVD: $19.99

Candide

(1991, 147 min, US/GB, Humphrey Burton) *Jerry Hadley-Land, June Anderson.* Performed in 1989 at London's Barbican Centre, Leonard Bernstein's rousing musical — first performed on Broadway in 1956 — is based on Voltaire's satiric book. With a youthfully animated Bernstein conducting, this production stars Hadley-Land as Candide and Anderson as Cunegonde. With lyrics by Lillian Hellman, Dorothy Parker and Stephen Sondheim, the show follows the adventures that befall Candide in his search for "The Best of All Possible Worlds." ★★★ VHS: $34.99

Candy

(1968, 124 min, US/France/Italy, Christian Marquand) *Ewa Aulin, Richard Burton, Marlon Brando, Charles Aznavour, James Coburn, Ringo Starr, John Astin, Walter Matthau, John Huston.* A cause célèbre in the 1960s, this often funny but quite silly sex comedy follows naïve high school student Candy and her many sexual adventures with the opposite sex. Some good cameos (especially Burton as a drunken poet and Starr as the Mexican gardener) propel a far-out blend of '60s sexual liberation and hippie hijinks. Astin gets the best marks in the dual roles of Candy's staid father and lecherous uncle. Buck Henry adapted the novel by Terry Southern. (Letterboxed) ★★½ VHS: $14.99; DVD: $29.99

Candy Mountain

(1988, 91 min, US, Robert Frank & Ruth Wurlitzer) *Kevin J. O'Connor, Tom Waits, David Johansen, Leon Redbone.* Infused with a '50s Beat mentality, *Candy Mountain* is an engagingly charming and funny road movie. O'Connor plays an impassive, down-on-his-heels rocker who hits the road in search of the mythical master guitar maker Elmore Silk. His travels are punctuated with a bevy of oddball, on-the-fringe characters. A quirky, decidedly American low budgeter reminiscent of such road sagas as *Easy Rider* and *Stranger Than Paradise.* ★★★ VHS: $14.99

Candyman

(1992, 101 min, US, Bernard Rose) *Virginia Madsen, Tony Todd, Xander Berkeley, Vanessa Williams.* Rose follows up his 1988 film *Paperhouse,* a psychologically astute horror film, with this solid adaptation of goremeister Clive Barker's short story, "The Forbidden." Madsen gives a gutsy performance as a graduate student whose research into contemporary myths and legends summons the vengeful hook-handed spirit of a slave (Todd) who was murdered for daring to love a white woman. In possibly the first horror movie with an interracial love theme, Rose sacrifices cheesy special effects in favor of interesting characterizations and bizarre set designs, making this an enduring horror movie for the art-house set. (Followed by 2 sequels) ★★★ VHS: $9.99; DVD: $19.99

Candyman 2: Farewell to the Flesh

(1995, 95 min, US, Bill Condon) *Tony Todd, Kelly Rowan, Veronica Cartwright.* When a young woman (Rowan) loses both her father and husband to the Candyman (Todd), she comes to realize that maybe the two are bound by more than just coincidence. Clive Barker's hook-handed menace returns in this savage sequel that explains how the urban legend came to be. Taking place as though the original never happened, Condon's film more directly tackles the topic of racial harmony and intolerance, though it relies less on mysticism than on sheer blood-and-guts horror — a combination that may or may not please the original audience. Philip Glass' mesmerizing and passionate score adds just the right note of poetic justice to this tragic tale. ★★½ VHS: $9.99

Cane Toads

(1987, 47 min, US, Mark Lewis) Sardonic wit and imaginative direction elevate this unusual documentary above the level of mere agricultural travelogue. The film details the introduction of cane toads from Hawaii to North Queensland, Australia, in 1935 to combat a cane grub infestation that was ravaging the sugar industry. Prolific breeders who lacked natural enemies in their new home, the toads quickly overwhelmed over 40% of Queensland and, at the time of filming, were expanding down the coast, rapidly adapting to new environments and killing off natural wildlife. This film is a fascinating look at a man-made catastrophe, a magnificently bungled attempt to alter the natural order. ★★★ VHS: $19.99

Cannery Row

(1982, 120 min, US, David S. Ward) *Nick Nolte, Debra Winger, M. Emmet Walsh, Audra Lindley.* Nolte and Winger are well-matched in this appealing if unusual romantic comedy-drama based on the John Steinbeck stories "Cannery Row" and "Sweet Tuesday." Nolte is a former baseball player-turned-biologist who is thrown together with feisty good-time girl Winger, thanks to the denizens of Cannery Row. Directorial debut for writer Ward (*The Sting*). ★★★ VHS: $19.99

Cannibal Man (La Semana del Asesino)

(1971, 98 min, Spain, Eloy de la Iglesia) *Vincent Parra, Emma Cohen, Eusebio Poncela, Vicky Lagos.* A creepy, grisly and disturbing horror film and quite an unusual departure for director de la Iglesia. Parra is Marcos, a slaughterhouse worker who, after killing a cab driver in self-defense, loses his grip on sanity and begins a murderous rampage throughout the city. But what to do with the bodies? Banned in many countries for its graphic violence, this intense study of a decent man driven to obscene murder is being released in its original uncut and uncensored version. (Letterboxed) (English dubbed) (aka: *The Apartment on the 13th Floor*) ★★★ VHS: $14.99; DVD: $29.99

Cannibal! The Musical

(1996, 90 min, US, Trey Parker) *Trey Parker, Dian Bachar, Ian Hardin, Jason McHugh, Toddy Walters.* The sole survivor of an ill-fated mining expedition tells how his taste for gold was replaced by that of human flesh and, yes, Virginia, it is a musical. You'll have a perfectly schpedoikle time with this bizarre, intentionally campy blend of showtunes and fresh, raw meat. Made way before Parker (billed here as "Juan Schwartz") hit it big with "South Park." ★★★ VHS: $14.99; DVD: $24.99

The Cannonball Run

(1981, 95 min, US, Hal Needham) *Burt Reynolds, Roger Moore, Farrah Fawcett, Dom Deluise, Dean Martin, Sammy Davis, Jr., Jamie Farr.* It's *Gumball Rally* gone smug, as Reynolds and his former in-crowd stage a cross-country race. Much ad-libbing, mugging, and car crashes. After watching Reynolds almost break up laughing at his own lines for the tenth time, you'll put up the red flag. (Sequel: *Cannonball Run II*) ★½ VHS: $9.99; DVD: $14.99

A Canterbury Tale

(1944, 123 min, GB, Michael Powell & Emeric Pressburger) *Eric Portman, Sheila Sim, Sergeant John Sweet, Dennis Price.* One of the most original films to come out of wartime Britain, this Powell/Pressburger tale bears no relation to the Chaucer story. It is, instead, an offbeat tale about a young woman, a British officer and an American sergeant who arrive in the small village in Kent, befriend each other and become involved in an effort to apprehend the "glue man" — a mysterious individual who has been pouring glue on the heads of young ladies escorting soldiers. Filled with interesting commentary on the effects of war on a small community, this film is a very entertaining and thought-provoking WWII classic. ★★★½ VHS: $29.99

The Canterbury Tales

(1971, 109 min, Italy, Pier Paolo Pasolini) *Laura Betti, Ninetto Davoli, Hugh Griffith.* Pasolini's second film in his "Trilogy of Pleasure" adopts six of the ribald stories contained in Chaucer's classic. Set in England and featuring the director as Chaucer himself, the film seeks out the raciest, most exotic and controversial aspects of life in the Middle Ages. Rumor has it that Pasolini, long known for working with non-professionals in his films, even used hitchhikers he picked up during his travels in England for major roles in the film. (Italian with English subtitles) ★★★

The Canterville Ghost

(1944, 96 min, US, Jules Dassin) *Charles Laughton, Robert Young, Margaret O'Brien, Una O'Connor.* He may be a hambone, but what great fun when Laughton is on the screen as the haunter of a 17th-century castle. He can't leave until descendant Young does one heroic act — besides not murdering O'Connor to stop her incessant screeching. Adapted from an Oscar Wilde tale. ★★★ VHS: $19.99

Cape Fear

(1962, 105 min, US, J. Lee Thompson) *Gregory Peck, Robert Mitchum, Polly Bergen, Martin Balsam, Telly Savalas.* One of the most nerve-wracking and suspenseful films of all time, this thriller is set in the seemingly tranquil Louisiana bayous. The story centers around Peck, an upstanding criminal prosecutor whose family falls under the terror of a man whom Peck sent to jail years earlier — the menacing Mitchum. Through a series of chilling yet all-too-believable scare tactics, Mitchum enacts his revenge on Peck's family with such cool-headedness that the film at times becomes almost too intense to watch. Brilliant cinematography, a terrific score and outstanding performances elevate this often-imitated thriller to an almost unbearable level of tension. (Remade in 1991) ★★★½ VHS: $14.99

Cape Fear

(1991, 130 min, US, Martin Scorsese) *Robert De Niro, Nick Nolte, Jessica Lange, Juliette Lewis, Robert Mitchum, Gregory Peck, Martin Balsam.* Scorsese's masterful updating of the 1962 thriller. Upon his release from a 14-year prison term, Max Cady (De Niro) travels to the hometown of his former defense attorney, Sam Bowden (Nolte). Because of the atrocious nature of the crime, Bowden suppressed information and lost the case. And now Cady has come to instruct his counselor on the meaning of loss. As the sociopath Cady, De Niro, with his patented ability to convey tightly controlled rage, delivers an intense, breathtaking portrait of evil. As the family he terrorizes with half-truths and innuendo, Nolte, Lange (as his wife) and Lewis (as their daughter) are uniformly fine. Lewis and De Niro's scene set in a school auditorium is a mesmerizing exercise in corruption. The visual potency may be lost on the small screen; but the searing characterizations maintain full strength. This can be added to Scorsese's list of classics. (VHS letterboxed available for $14.99) ★★★½ VHS: $9.99

Capitaine Conan

(1996, 130 min, France, Bertrand Tavernier) *Philippe Torreton, Samuel Le Bihan, Bernard Le Coq, Catherine Rich.* In the hell of WWI trench warfare, Capitaine Conan (Torreton) leads an elite squad expert in hand-to-hand, guerrilla combat. He's a man with no illusions, infinitely adaptable, his own code of ethics carved in stone. The film opens on the eve of the big push into no-man's-land — battlefields of orchestrated slaughter and mass insanity. As the dead are carried off, military bureaucracy gets bogged down in the war after the war. The system turns against its own, and those who've risked their lives in battle face the firing squad for the "theft" of a few blankets. Director Tavernier crafts a sweeping indictment of man's capacity for savagery with finely etched, sharply honed portrayals. The haunted visage of an aging, diminished Conan is testament to the price of war. (Letterboxed) (French with English subtitles) ★★★½ VHS: $24.99; DVD: $29.99

Captain Blood

(1935, 99 min, US, Michael Curtiz) *Errol Flynn, Olivia de Havilland, Basil Rathbone.* The first of the many Curtiz-Flynn-de Havilland swashbucklers; and an immensely entertaining film. Flynn stars as an Irish doctor who is sentenced to life-long servitude in the Americas after treating a wounded rebel. He later escapes to captain a pirate ship. Contains one of the best sword fight scenes in the movies: Flynn and Rathbone dueling it out on a rocky beach. ★★★½ VHS: $14.99

Captain Horatio Hornblower

(1951, 117 min, GB, Raoul Walsh) *Gregory Peck, Virginia Mayo, Christopher Lee.* Peck is appropriately gallant in the title role as Britain's dashing naval hero in this lively adaptation of the C.S. Forester novels. It's the Napoleonic Wars, and England is at a crisis. Not to worry, though, for Capt. Hornblower is at the helm. The good captain takes on the French, a Spanish rebel, and saves the day. Things really get explosive when he rescues her ladyship Mayo, who's adrift at sea. There are a couple of nifty battle scenes, and even a romantic subplot doesn't drag the action. Hornblower looks good in his early 19th-century costumes; he's got a funny name, though. ★★★ VHS: $19.99

Captain January

(1936, 75 min, US, David Butler) *Shirley Temple, Guy Kibbee, Buddy Ebsen.* Little Shirley sets the tears flow in this sentimental tale of a young orphan being taken away from her adoptive father (Kibbee). She sings "The Codfish Ball." ★★½ VHS: $14.99

Captain Newman M.D.

(1963, 126 min, US, David Miller) *Gregory Peck, Tony Curtis, Angie Dickinson, Bobby Darin.* Compelling comedy-drama starring Peck as a dedicated military doctor treating mentally disturbed soldiers stateside during WWII. ★★★ VHS: $14.99

Captain Ron

(1992, 99 min, US, Thom Eberhardt) *Kurt Russell, Martin Short, Mary Kay Place.* In this amiable variation of *What about Bob?*, Short is a mild-mannered family man who inherits a boatload of trouble when he takes his family sailing with the help of lovable, ne'er-do-well Captain Ron (Russell). Like Richard Dreyfus' psychiatrist, Short's exasperated father is the only one to notice a bumbler's shortcomings to which the rest of the family is blind. Short's comic instincts are still on the mark, but it is Russell's surprising flair for comedy which makes these hijinks seaworthy. ★★½

The Captain's Paradise

(1953, 80 min, GB, Anthony Kimmins) *Alec Guinness, Yvonne De Carlo, Celia Johnson.* Guinness is true to form in this romping farce about a ferry boat captain who gives life to the saying "a woman in every port." Thinking he has conquered life's ills, he shuttles merrily back and forth between his betrothed, one in Tangier and one in Gibraltar. But the comedy heats up when his scheme begins to unravel. ★★★½

Captains Courageous

(1937, 116 min, US, Victor Fleming) *Spencer Tracy, Freddie Bartholomew, Melvyn Douglas, Lionel Barrymore, Mickey Rooney.* Well-produced, exciting adaptation of Rudyard Kipling's adventure story. A rich, pampered youth falls off a ship and is rescued by a Portuguese fisherman, teaching the boy his love for the sea. Spencer Tracy won the first of his two Oscars as the fisherman. ★★★½ VHS: $19.99

Career Girls

Captives

(1996, 99 min, GB, Angela Pope) *Tim Roth, Julia Ormand, Keith Allen, Siobhan Redmond, Peter Capaldi.* When she accepts a part-time position as dentist at a maximum security prison in London, a newly divorced woman begins a hesitant affair with a prisoner and is thrust into perilous circumstances. *Captives* may not feature the most original plot line, but thanks to extremely appealing performances from its two leads, and a well-versed screenplay, this romantic drama/thriller is consistently engaging. Ormand is captivating as a woman caught off guard, whose act of kindness leads her to a road she never anticipated. Roth plays her lover with smoldering intensity, a victim to his surroundings and loneliness as much as the woman with whom he falls in love. *Captives* never relies on the obvious, instead creating a believable and sensual relationship between the two characters while pitting them against outside forces. ★★★ VHS: $79.99

The Car

(1977, 96 min, US, Eliot Silverstein) *James Brolin, Kathleen Lloyd, John Marley, R.G. Armstrong.* A rather dour black sedan, seemingly out of a Bergman movie, has some existential problems — no driver, no purpose in life, no license plates. So can you blame it when it decides to terrorize the residents of a small New Mexico town? One of the more preposterous villains in cinema is treated as a dead-serious menace, especially by our hero Brolin. Bizarre stuff indeed. ★★ VHS: $14.99; DVD: $24.99

Car Trouble

(1985, 93 min, GB, David Green) *Ian Charleson, Julie Walters.* Vicious *War of the Roses*-style comedy about a harried air-traffic controller and his long-suffering wife of nine years whose lives become a nightmare when he takes on a mistress — a jazzy red sports car! A caustic comedy of the blackest sort, marred only by its implausible ending. ★★½

Car Wash

(1976, 97 min, US, Michael Schultz) *Richard Pryor, Antonio Fargas, Ivan Dixon, Franklin Ajaye, Sully Boyar, George Carlin, Melanie Mayron.* Appealing and often funny, this episodic, hit-or-miss comedy follows the comic exploits of a group of Los Angeles car wash employees in the disco-swinging '70s. A good musical score and some hearty laughs await. Written by Joel Schumacher. ★★½ VHS: $9.99; DVD: $19.99

Caravaggio

(1986, 93 min, GB, Derek Jarman) *Nigel Terry, Sean Bean, Tilda Swinton.* Michelangelo Merisi Caravaggio (1573-1610) was the last, perhaps the greatest, and certainly the most controversial painter of the Italian Renaissance. This stylish, adventurous tribute to the outlandish artist is directed by Jarman and is further proof of his ability to stretch artistic invention. The temperaments of Jarman and Caravaggio are well-suited; the result is a bold and quirky film with contemporary touches, spectacular camera work and an impressionistic feel. ★★★ VHS: $39.99

Career Girls

(1997, 87 min, GB, Mike Leigh) *Katrin Cartlidge, Lynda Steadman, Mark Benton, Kate Byers.* In this wry, nicely crafted character study, Cartlidge and Steadman costar as Hannah and Annie, respectively, a pair of college roommates who meet up in London years later for a personal reunion. Through a series of flashbacks, Leigh depicts the wild days of their raucous, punked out youth living in a seedy London flat, pursuing their studies and loves, and consulting Emily Brontë's "Wuthering Heights" as an oracle. The young Hannah is frenetic and high-strung, while Annie is a study in timidity — a strange pair, but they form a deep bond nonetheless. A decade later, both have matured, yet they awkwardly circle around each other searching for that nexus that brought them together in the first place. Leigh is a master of portraying the complex subtleties of the human condition as he delves into his protagonists' fragile psyches. ★★★½ VHS: $14.99

Career Opportunities

(1991, 85 min, US, Bryan Gordon) *Frank Whaley, Jennifer Connelly, Dermot Mulroney, John Candy.* John Hughes wrote the screenplay for this far-fetched, underdeveloped comedy, sort of an adult *Home Alone.* Whaley plays a night janitor at a discount store who comes across rich kid Connelly, who got locked in. Together they defend the store against two burglars who are about to clean the place out. ★½ VHS: $19.99; DVD: $24.99

Carefree

(1938, 80 min, US, Mark Sandrich) *Fred Astaire, Ginger Rogers, Ralph Bellamy, Luella Gear, Jack Carson, Franklin Pangborn.* Though this Astaire-Rogers musical's dance sequences can't compare to some of their 1930s contemporaries, *Carefree* boasts one of the duo's strongest screenplays. A lively screwball outing, the story deals with radio star Ginger falling for psychiatrist Fred, even though she's engaged to his best friend (perennial best friend Bellamy). Ginger, probably because she's the romantic aggressor for once, is at her most spirited as she lets her subconscious roam wild to remain a patient. Irving Berlin's score is pleasant but not among his best, though "Dancing in the Dark" and an elaborately choreographed tour through a country club are sublime. ★★★ VHS: $14.99

Careful

(1992, 100 min, Canada, Guy Maddin) *Kyle McCulloch, Gosia Dobrowolska, Sarah Neville, Brent Neale.* A culture of repression and paranoid caution inhabits a small mountain valley community living in stringently enforced guilt, guarding against the threat of avalanche. This alternate world is described by director Maddin (*Tales of Gimli Hospital*) in saturated colors and stark imagery coupled with kitschy detail, creating a hyperreality of repressed passions, a rigidly organized hotbed of Freudian conflicts where dead fathers try to caution Oedipal sons, and daughters vie for fathers' affections. Visually sumptuous, witty and truly unique, *Careful* can be described as "David Lynch meets German Expressionism" via dream therapy. It's both stimulating and adventurous. ★★★ VHS: $24.99; DVD: $29.99

Careful, He Might Hear You

(1983, 116 min, Australia, Carl Schultz) *Wendy Hughes, Robyn Nevin, Nicholas Gledhill, John Hargreaves.* This poignant and emotionally charged drama digs deep to expose the underlying spitefulness of a quietly waged battle between two sisters vying for the custody of their displaced nephew. Directed by Schultz with epicurean zeal, the film benefits from brilliant performances by the ensemble. ★★★

Caresses (Caricies)

(1997, 96 min, Spain, Ventura Pons) *David Selvas, Laura Conejero, Julieta Serrano, Mercè Pons.* Fasten your seatbelts for this visually torrid tour through the streets of Barcelona and into the violently emotional world of its love-starved inhabitants. Director Pons proves to be a daring and original filmmaker as he weaves several seemingly unconnected stories into a complex tapestry of people trapped by their sexual desires and who find their passions both ignited and muted — all in an effort for some kind of human tenderness. The cutting is rapid, the images glossy, and the issues lurid and controversial. A drama of human detachment that will excite and mesmerize the viewer. (Catalan with English subtitles) ★★★½ VHS: $79.99

Carla's Song

(1996, 127 min, Scotland/Nicaragua, Ken Loach) *Robert Carlyle, Oyanka Cabezas, Scott Glenn, Salvador Espinoza.* Carlyle evidences the same earthy naturalism he brought to *The Full Monty* as George, a Glasgow bus driver whose simple act of kindness precipitates an unexpected journey. George is enthralled by Carla (Cabezas, in a mesmerizing performance), a beautiful, impoverished woman with a troubled history. The petty bureaucracy faced by George fades to insignificance compared to the stark horror of Carla's past in her native Nicaragua. They return there together to confront the memories that haunt her sleep. The war zone of 1987 Nicaragua is stark counterpoint to the profound and deeply held affection shared by Carla and her companeros. Director Loach again offers many crystalline moments of human interaction, from a debate on movie dialogue to the full disclosure of Carla's traumatic experiences. A surprising film of power and kind regard for its two main protagonists, each of whom experiences self-discovery and some degree of closure. ★★★ VHS: $19.99; DVD: $14.99

Carlito's Way

(1993, 141 min, US, Brian De Palma) *Al Pacino, Penelope Ann Miller, Sean Penn, John Leguizamo, Luis Guzman, Adrian Pasdar.* Scarface star Pacino and director De Palma reunite to create another Hispanic gangster drama. But unlike that film's Tony Montana, Carlito Brigante (Pacino) is a man defined by romanticism and simplicity. After serving five years in prison, Carlito simply wants to go to the Bahamas to start a car-rental agency. However, loyalties to his friend David Kleinfeld (stunningly portrayed by Penn), a corrupt and double-dealing lawyer, threaten to drag him down. Pacino delivers a solid performance, and there's amazing camerawork; though one can only feel that this territory has already been heavily traveled. (VHS letterboxed available for $14.99) ★★½ VHS: $9.99; DVD: $26.99

Carlton-Browne of the F.O.

(1959, 88 min, GB, Jeffrey Dell & Roy Boulting) *Peter Sellers, Terry-Thomas.* A hilarious screwball farce about the Island of Gallardia — a British protectorate which was somehow forgotten for 50 years. When this embarrassing circumstance is uncovered, the blundering Terry-Thomas is sent to lead the Foreign Office. A scathing satire on diplomacy. ★★★

Carmen Jones

Carmen

(1984, 130 min, Italy/France, Francesco Rosi) *Placido Domingo, Julia-Migenes Johnson.* In a season of several Carmens, Rosi's stirring version is certainly truest to the Bizet opera. As the gypsy heroine, Johnson is a lusty fireball of unkempt urges. Domingo brings his robust tenor to the role of the soldier broken by her powerful allure. (French with English subtitles) ★★★ VHS: $19.99; DVD: $27.99

Carmen Jones

(1954, 105 min, US, Otto Preminger) *Dorothy Dandridge, Harry Belafonte, Pearl Bailey, Diahann Carroll, Brock Peters.* Directed by Preminger (who also directed *Porgy and Bess*) and scored by Oscar Hammerstein, Bizet's famous opera is transformed into an all-black musical starring Dandridge as a flirtatious party girl who causes soldier Belafonte to go off the deep end because of his passion for her. Laced with many fine performances, this highly entertaining songfest also made Dandridge the first black performer nominated for an Oscar in a leading role. ★★★ VHS: $19.99

Carnal Knowledge

(1971, 97 min, US, Mike Nichols) *Jack Nicholson, Art Garfunkel, Candice Bergen, Ann-Margret, Rita Moreno.* Director Nichols collaborated with Jules Feiffer to create this brutally honest and surprisingly perceptive examination of American sexual politics, seen over the course of two decades through the eyes of two college buddies and their relationships with various women. The camera is unflinching and revelatory, capturing the most ephemeral of moments: the awkward tentativeness of youthful encounters, the exploitative cynicism of middle-aged desperation, the self-deceptive smug assuredness which accompanies the acquisition of a new partner — nothing is glossed over or ameliorated. Nicholson is brutally honest in his depiction of a man for whom women are at best a pleasure and at worst an alimony payment. Garfunkel is the best friend who likes to think of himself as more highly evolved. Bergen and Ann-Margret are two of the women who pass through their lives. All give superior performances in a remarkable piece of work. ★★★★ VHS: $14.99; DVD: $19.99

Carnival of Souls

(1962, 83 min, US, Herk Harvey) *Candace Hilligoss, Sidney Berger.* This eerily chilling and angst-ridden cult classic follows Mary Henry (icily portrayed by Hilligoss) a taciturn organist who miraculously survives a near-fatal car accident. Shaken, she decides to start life anew, and sets out for new pastures. No sooner has she hit the road than she is haunted by a ghoul who is invisible to all but her. Filmed in shadowy black and white, the film's visual power — which set precedent for such chillers as *Night of the Living Dead*, etc. — evokes an undeniably menacing and twisted tone. *Carnival of Souls* takes us back to an era when the horror genre probed the supernatural with an eye to the psyche and spirit rather than gut-bucket gore. (Remade in 1998) ★★★ VHS: $12.99; DVD: $39.99

Carnival Rock

(1958, 80 min, US, Roger Corman) *Susan Cabit, Dick Miller, The Platters.* Thrill-seeking kids, grimy

gangsters and psychopathic teens clash in a rockabilly, rhythm 'n' blues, rock 'n' roll nightclub. ★★ VHS: $7.99

Carnosaur

(1993, 83 min, US, Adam Simon) *Diane Ladd, Rapheal Sbarge, Jennifer Runyan.* Roger Corman produced this shocker with Ladd as a genetic engineer who develops a virus that can turn a mild-mannered chicken embryo into a bloodthirsty Tyrannosaurus Rex. Fueled by the amphetamine-overdrive performance of Ladd, well-paced snatches of humor, cheesy special effects that can only be rivaled by the children's show "Land of the Lost," and jabs at *Jurassic Park*, this entertaining schlock-fest is sure to appeal to those who like heavy doses of vitamin "B" in their viewing diet. (Followed by 2 sequels) ★★½ VHS: $14.99

Carnosaur 2

(1994, 83 min, US, Louis Morneau) *John Savage, Cliff DeYoung, Rick Dean, Don Stroud.* This dreadfully misconceived sequel to the charmingly cheap and fun *Carnosaur* is a humorless excursion. Little more than an attempt to clone *Aliens*, *C2* follows the exploits of an irreverent group of wise-cracking mercenaries enlisted by a corrupt bureaucrat to do battle with the mutant chicken dino beasts from *C1*. ★ VHS: $14.99

Carny

(1980, 107 min, US, Robert Kaylor) *Jodie Foster, Gary Busey, Robbie Robertson, Kenneth McMillan, Meg Foster, Craig Wasson.* A quirky, moody drama about life on the road with a carnival. Busey and Robertson are carnival hustlers, or "carnies," whose lives are interrupted when they take in teenage runaway Jodie. Unusual and offbeat, though very satisfying. ★★★ VHS: $19.99

Caro Diario (Dear Diary)

(1994, 142 min, Italy, Nanni Moretti) *Nanni Moretti, Jennifer Beals, Alexandre Rockwell.* An endearing and delightful odyssey in three parts based on director Moretti's personal diaries, *Caro Diario* ("Dear Diary") is an amusing, insightful and illuminating journey. In the first segment, "On My Vespa," Moretti zooms around Rome and its adjoining neighborhoods making wry commentary on the architectual styles, inhabitants and social trends. "Islands" finds Moretti and a friend traveling to Italy's Lipari Islands in search of a relaxing place to work, only to be put off by the increasing eccentricities of each successive archipelago. In the final tale, "Doctors," Moretti comes face to face with the medical profession in an attempt to root out the cause of a mysterious skin ailment — any who have suffered at the hands of "specialists" will find this particularly humorous. (Italian with English subtitles) ★★★½ VHS: $19.99

Carousel

(1956, 128 min, US, Henry King) *Gordon MacRae, Shirley Jones, Cameron Mitchell.* Invigorating screen version of the Rodgers and Hammerstein musical (based on Molnar's "Liliom") about a roguish carnival barker (MacRae) who tries to change his ways when he falls for Jones. Songs include "Soliloquy (My Boy Bill)," "June Is Busting Out All Over" and "You'll Never Walk Alone." (VHS letterboxed available for $19.99) ★★★ VHS: $14.99; DVD: $24.99

Carpool

(1996, 90 min, US, Arthur Hiller) *Tom Arnold, David Paymer, Rhea Perlman, Rod Steiger.* This icky "family comedy" equates reckless driving and the mass destruction it causes with getting in touch with your inner child. Or that may be, at least, one subtext to think about to keep yourself awake while watching this almost laughless, frequently annoying mess. Arnold plays a would-be thief who takes ad exec Paymer and the five kids in his carpool hostage after a botched robbery. But of course he's a friendly criminal, and everybody ends up smiling in one of those warm and fuzzy, artificial endings that's actually quite depressing. ★½ VHS: $19.99

Carrie

(1952, 118 min, US, William Wyler) *Jennifer Jones, Laurence Olivier, Miriam Hopkins, Eddie Albert, Basil Rathbone.* A turn-of-the-century country girl (Jones) comes to Chicago to pursue a life on the stage. There she becomes involved with wealthy, married man (Olivier), whose relationship with the actress leads to his downfall. Based on Theodore Dreiser's satirical novel. Olivier is simply brilliant, and Jones gives one of her most accomplished performances. ★★★

Carrie

(1976, 97 min, US, Brian De Palma) *Sissy Spacek, Piper Laurie, Amy Irving, John Travolta, William Katt, Nancy Allen, Betty Buckley.* De Palma's chilling adaptation of the Stephen King novel tells the story of a mousy high school girl taunted by classmates. What her tormentors don't know is that Carrie possesses frightening telekinetic powers, eliciting film's most famous temper tantrum. Perhaps the worst mother-daughter relationship since Joan and Christina, Spacek and Laurie, as Carrie and her bible-thumping mother, respectively, were both nominated for Oscars and deservedly so. (VHS available letterboxed or pan & scan) ★★★½ VHS: $9.99; DVD: $19.99

Carried Away

(1996, 105 min, US, Bruno Barreto) *Dennis Hopper, Amy Irving, Amy Locane, Julie Harris, Hal Holbrook, Gary Busey.* A low-key but quite involving romance based on the novel "Farmer" by Jim Harrison. Hopper plays a small-town farmer and schoolteacher who can't quite commit to marrying longtime girlfriend Rosealee (Irving). When a young, sexy student (Locane) enters his classroom, his life changes irrevocably. What sounds like a *Fatal Attraction* ripoff is actually an understated, quietly powerful sleeper about a man's midlife crisis, handled with sensitivity and a minimum of clichés. *Carried Away* unfolds with the tempo of a rich novella — it's not epic in scope but nevertheless creates moments of unexpected joy. ★★★ VHS: $19.99

Carrington

(1995, 123 min, GB, Christopher Hampton) *Jonathan Pryce, Emma Thompson, Steven Waddington, Rufus Sewell, Samuel West, Penelope Wilton, Janet McTeer, Jeremy Northam.* Based on the book "Lytton Strachey" by Michael Holyroyd, *Carrington* is the story of the relationship and attraction between artist Dora Carrington (Thompson) and gay Bloomsbury Group writer Lytton Strachey (Pryce). Their unconventional but enduring friendship and love story begins when Strachey becomes attracted to what he thinks is a boy. He is embarrassed to find out the "boy" is actually Dora Carrington. A tentative kiss by Strachey does not lead to sexual relations, but Carrington does fall in love with him. They eventually move in together and sleep together and even find themselves attracted to the same men, including Carrington's future husband (Waddington). Bearded, painfully thin and always ready with the satiric quip, Pryce's Strachey is a revelation. Director Hampton has fashioned a fine, sometimes dark period piece, complete with lush surroundings, and it is well-served by an intelligent screenplay. ★★★½ VHS: $14.99

Casablanca

Carry Me Back

(1982, 93 min, Australia, John Reid) *Grant Tilly, Kelly Johnson.* Two brothers and their cantankerous father venture from their family farm to watch a rugby match hundreds of miles from home. During the match the old codger dies in the hotel room. Problems arise when the brothers discover that in order to inherit the family estate, the father must die on the family's property. What ensues is a series of sometimes funny complications as the two attempt to smuggle old dad home without anyone knowing he's a stiff. ★★½

Carry on Cleo

(1968, 92 min, GB, Gerald Thomas) *Sidney James, Amanda Barrie, Kenneth Williams, Jim Dale.* One of the best of the "Carry On" series. This is admittedly a qualified endorsement which can only be taken with so much seriousness, but this witty reworking of ancient history features lots of silly hijinks, along with Cleopatra, Caesar, Marc Antony and lots of vestal virgins. ★★½

Carry on Cruising

(1962, 89 min, GB, Gerald Thomas) *Sidney James, Kenneth Williams, Liz Fraser.* The zany, pre-Python "Carry On" gang unleash themselves on a Mediterranean cruise ship. Though not a serious thesis on the state of human existence, the film has lots of slapstick gags and lowbrow humor, which in most cases will suffice. ★★½

Carry on Doctor

(1968, 95 min, GB, Gerald Thomas) *Frankie Howard, Kenneth Williams, Jim Dale.* More hijinks from the "Carry On" crew with their sights set this time on the medical profession. This romping farce is set at an English hospital filled with crazy doctors, crazier patients and a bevy of sex-starved nurses. ★★

The Cars That Ate Paris

(1974, 92 min, Australia, Peter Weir) *Terry Camillieri, Kevin Miles.* A bizarre horror tale of a mutated town struggling to survive by cannibalizing the vehicles of unsuspecting travelers and leaving the inhabitants either dead or "veggies" for medical experimentation. A tongue-in-cheek shot at automotive madness. Original full-length version. (aka: *The Cars That Eat People*) ★★★ VHS: $19.99

Cartouche

(1961, 115 min, France, Philippe de Broca) *Jean-Paul Belmondo, Claudia Cardinale.* He robs from the rich and gives to the poor. Sound familiar? Director de Broca presents his variation of the Robin Hood legend with the always suave Belmondo as Cartouche, the once-petty thief turned avenger of the poor. This slapstick adventure has Belmondo fighting the foes with a quick sword and a witty tongue and romancing the women with pretty much the same. Slow and dated, it's fairly enjoyable nevertheless. (French with English subtitles) ★★ VHS: $29.99

Casablanca

(1942, 102 min, US, Michael Curtiz) *Humphrey Bogart, Ingrid Bergman, Claude Rains, Paul Henreid, Peter Lorre, Sydney Greenstreet.* As time goes by, no film equals the popularity of this indisputable classic. In quintessential roles, Bogart and Bergman are former lovers reunited in wartorn Casablanca. Bogey is the cynical cafe owner who lives by his own moral code and sticks his neck out for "no one." Bergman, as the beautiful wife of Resistance leader Paul Henried, finds herself torn between two lovers when she reenters Bogey's life. The film's great success lies in the inimitable pairing of its two stars, a thoroughly romantic story line, terrific humor and numerous moments of suspense. Of course, that great ending helps, too. Studio filmmaking from the 1940s doesn't come better than this, and director Curtiz masterfully handles the action, comedy and romance. Nearly stealing the film is Rains as a "poor, corrupt official" who as a Nazi puppet soon discovers the beginning of a beautiful friendship. Academy Award winner for Best Picture. ★★★★ VHS: $14.99; DVD: $19.99

Casanova's Big Night

(1954, 86 min, US, Norman Z. McLeod) *Bob Hope, Joan Fontaine, Basil Rathbone, Raymond Burr, Vincent Price.* The laughs are plentiful in this engaging Hope spoof with Bob mistaken as the legendary ladies' man and doing nothing to correct the error. No one plays ham like Hope. ★★★ VHS: $14.99

C

Tom Hanks goes solo in *Cast Away*

Casino

(1995, 177 min, US, Martin Scorsese) *Robert De Niro, Sharon Stone, Joe Pesci, James Woods, Don Rickles, Alan King, Kevin Pollak, Dick Smothers.* A gangster who lives by his own moral code; a hot-headed hit man with a hair-trigger temper; a fascinating peek into the inner-workings of under-world crime; these are all familiar trappings of director Scorsese's best-known works. And in *Casino*, his ambitious examination of a mob-controlled Las Vegas, these familiarities both enhance and hinder the director's epic story of love among the slots. De Niro plays a crafty casino manager whose life is intruded upon by two opposing forces — a volatile mob associate (Pesci) who invades his business and a gorgeous ex-prostitute (Stone) who captures his heart. *Casino* is at its best during the first half, introducing its gallery of players and detailing the daily operation of the casino; it eventually somewhat loses its balance and momentum. Stone is terrific in a breakthrough role, though, truthfully, we've seen De Niro and Pesci do all this before. (VHS available letterboxed or pan & scan) ★★★ VHS: $14.99; DVD: $26.99

Casino Royale

(1967, 130 min, GB, John Huston, Ken Hughes, Robert Parrish, Joseph Mc) *Peter Sellers, David Niven, Ursula Andress, Woody Allen, Orson Welles, Jacqueline Bisset, Deborah Kerr, Peter O'Toole, Jean-Paul Belmondo, William Holden, Charles Boyer.* A grand spoof of the James Bond genre. Often muddled, perhaps by the multitude of talents more than anything else, the film is nonetheless filled with hilarious moments and is guaranteed to please comedy buffs. ★★½

Casper

(1995, 95 min, US, Brad Silberling) *Bill Pullman, Christina Ricci, Cathy Moriarty, Eric Idle, Malachi Pearson, Dan Aykroyd, Clint Eastwood, Mel Gibson.* Children of all ages should delight in this special effects charmer filled with spiffy cameos, amazing ghostly creatures and a dash of mischief. Pullman and Ricci are a ghostbusting father and his unconventional daughter who move into a haunted house to rid it of prankish poltergeists. Though the screenplay is very much on a sit-comish level, the film exhibits great effects as Casper and his three devilish uncles haunt, eat, fight, drink and fly about. Casper is a "fleshed"-out kid with humor and spunk, and Ricci is adorable (though she's not given the wondrous zingers like in the *Addams Family* films). ★★★ VHS: $14.99

Cass

(1981, 90 min, Australia, Chris Noonan) *Michelle Fawden, John Waters, Judy Morris.* This wrenching drama deals with a young female filmmaker whose life is thrown in crisis after making a film about a primitive, tribal society. She returns to "civilized society" and her husband, but becomes isolated from him. She soon falls in love with another woman. The film focuses on her attempts to resolve her newly discovered inner conflicts. ★

Cass Timberlane

(1947, 119 min, US, George Sidney) *Spencer Tracy, Lana Turner, Zachary Scott.* A very standard 1940s romantic drama based on Sinclair Lewis' novel of class distinction and self-discovery. In a

small Midwestern town, a middle-aged, widowed judge (Tracy) is charmed by a young artist (Turner) who's from the wrong side of the tracks. The story focuses on their May-December romance. Tracy and Turner are a compatible couple, but neither is helped by clichéd situations and characters. ★★ VHS: $19.99

Cast a Deadly Spell

(1991, 92 min, US, Martin Campbell) *Fred Ward, David Warner, Julianne Moore, Clancy Brown.* Ward is a delight as H. Philip Lovecraft, the only private eye in 1948 Los Angeles who does *not* use magic in his daily life. Lovecraft is hired by Warner (who has come to wear sinister as a favorite suit) to retrieve a pilfered book...a large, ornate book containing the secrets of ultimate power and world domination. Warner's daughter, when not hunting unicorns on the estate grounds, complicates Lovecraft's quest for the tempting tome and alters the fate of mankind. There's also a femme fatale chanteuse, really spiffy clothes, great noirish dialogue and enticing special effects. Made for cable with tongue in cheek, *Cast a Deadly Spell* pays loving homage to the horror and supernatural genre. ★★★½ VHS: $9.99

Cast Away

(2000, 143 min, US, Robert Zemeckis) *Tom Hanks, Helen Hunt, Nick Searcy, Jenifer Lewis, Chris Noth.* In *Cast Away*, an ultimately satisfying adventure, Hanks gets an actor's dream of a lifetime — to be solo for most of a film — and single-handedly transforms it into a compelling, sometimes spellbinding tale of survival. Chuck Noland (Hanks) is a workaholic Federal Express systems engineer who says goodbye to his fiancée (Hunt), boards a plane and en route to his next assignment crash lands (in one helluva scene) on a deserted island. Alone and ill-prepared, Chuck must summon all the courage and shrewdness deep down inside to survive this new ordeal. How he manages to discover both makes for often rousing entertainment. The scenes on the island, which make up most of the film's running time, are stunning. Blessed with gorgeous cinematography, *Cast Away* is able to fully maintain interest even as Chuck goes about the most

mundane tasks. The scenes off the island, however, are routine and even trite. These bookend sequences display none of the ingenuity displayed on the island. Thanks to Hanks, though, it hardly matters; he's so good he can make an emotional attachment to a volleyball seem the norm. ★★★ VHS: $102.99; DVD: $29.99

The Castle

(1968, 89 min, West Germany, Rudolf Noelte) *Maximilian Schell, Cordula Trantow.* A stylized if somewhat indistinct version of Franz Kafka's novel. Schell stars as a stranger known as "K" who arrives at a small village claiming he is the new land surveyor for a nearby castle. However, in true Kafka-esque fashion, K, confronted with a sinisterly bureaucratic and regimented populace, cannot gain admittance to the fortress. (Filmed in English) ★★½

Casual Sex?

(1988, 97 min, US, Genevieve Robert) *Lea Thompson, Victoria Jackson, Andrew Dice Clay.* Harmless, diverting sex comedy with Thompson and Jackson as single women in search of more than a one-night stand in the age of AIDS. Clay plays a sexist creep who turns out to be Mr. Nice Guy. ★★½ VHS: $9.99

Casualties of War

(1989, 113 min, US, Brian de Palma) *Michael J. Fox, Sean Penn, John C. Reilly, John Leguizamo, Thuy Thu Le.* Set in 1966 Vietnam, this harrowing, fact-based story is about a Vietnamese woman who is kidnapped, raped and murdered by four soldiers. Fox stars as a newly arrived private who is forced to participate; Penn is the near-maniacal platoon sergeant who heads the assault. Superbly directed by De Palma, the film divides its running time between the horrific act and its aftereffect; the focus is on Fox in particular, who, though passively resistant during the ordeal, ultimately brings the men to trial. Le is heartbreaking as the murdered woman. ★★★½ VHS: $9.99

Cat and Mouse

(1975, 107 min, France, Claude Lelouch) *John-Pierre Aumont, Michele Morgan.* This mesmerizing and ingenious Parisian murder mystery is full of unexpected twists and humorous turns as an unorthodox detective delves into the death of a millionaire. The murder, thinly disguised as suicide, leads the detective to a variety of suspects and many baffling questions. (French with English subtitles) ★★★1/2

The Cat and the Canary

(1927, 81 min, US, Paul Leni) *Laura La Plante, Creighton Hale, Tully Marshall*. This delightfully eerie thriller — to which director Leni brings the Gothic sensibilities of his native Germany — is a classic of the horror genre and set the style for the famous Universal horror films of the 1930s. A group of relatives gather at midnight in an abandoned mansion to read the will of an old man. The dead man's niece is the heiress, but only if she spends the night in the house. During the course of the spooky night, she encounters clutching hands, sliding panels, revolving bookcases and a cat-like apparition. Also includes a good Harold Lloyd short, 1920's *Haunted Spooks*. (Silent with musical accompaniment) ★★★1/2 VHS: $29.99; DVD: $24.99

Cat Ballou

(1965, 96 min, US, Elliot Silverstein) *Jane Fonda, Lee Marvin, Michael Callen, Dwayne Hickman, Stubby Kaye, Nat King Cole*. Fonda sparkles in the lead role in this wonderful western spoof as a schoolteacher who turns outlaw to avenge her father's murder. But it's Marvin who walked away with an Oscar for his performance in dual roles — he plays both the film's villain and the washed-up, alcoholic gunman who is forced out of retirement to hunt him down. Cole and Kaye spice up the film with intermittent musical numbers as a pair of wandering minstrels. A breezy, comedic homage to the classic western take on the conflict between good and evil. ★★★1/2 VHS: $14.99; DVD: $24.99

The Cat O'Nine Tails

(1971, 89 min, Italy, Dario Argento) *Karl Malden, James Franciscus, Catherine Spaak*. Argento's second neo-Hitchcockian thriller is a confusing murder mystery involving industrial espionage in the world of experimental genetics. Malden is a blind ex-newspaper reporter who may hold some important information about the mysterious accidental death of a scientist. He contacts Franciscus, himself a reporter, and the two of them begin an investigation which leads them closer to the truth and into a deadly race with the killer. Malden and Franciscus are both good, but the story is needlessly confusing and not very engaging even when it is clarified at the end. This, however, is hardly surprising, as the U.S. video release of *Cat* is missing nearly 22 minutes from the original edit. (Filmed in English) ★★ VHS: $12.99

Cat on a Hot Tin Roof

(1958, 108 min, US, Richard Brooks) *Elizabeth Taylor, Paul Newman, Burl Ives, Judith Anderson, Madeleine Sherwood, Jack Carson*. Everyone has a skeleton in the closet in Tennessee Williams' Pulitzer Prize—winning drama. Taylor sinks her claws into the role of Maggie the Cat, the tormented, sexually frustrated wife of guilt-ridden ex-jock Brick (Newman). The prototypic tale of family conflict and confrontation. ★★★★ VHS: $14.99; DVD: $19.99

Cat on a Hot Tin Roof

(1984, 122 min, US, Jack Hofsiss) *Jessica Lange, Tommy Lee Jones, Rip Torn, Kim Stanley, David Dukes, Penny Fuller*. An excellent made-for-TV adaptation of the Tennessee Williams play, with particularly strong performances from Lange as Maggie the Cat; Torn as Big Daddy; and Jones as Brick, Big Daddy's favorite son, an alcoholic ex-jock with a burden from his past that he cannot resolve. ★★★1/2 VHS: $19.99; DVD: $29.99

Cat People

(1942, 70 min, US, Jacques Tourneur) *Simone Simon, Kent Smith, Jane Randolph*. Of the eight horror films Val Lewton produced for RKO Pictures in the 1940s, this moody and suspenseful thriller — awash in stark shades of black and white — is his classic. Simon stars as a mysterious woman who refuses to consummate her marriage to architect Smith on the belief that she is descended from a race of cat people and if sexually aroused, she will transform into a panther. (Remade in 1982) ★★★1/2

Cat People

(1982, 118 min, US, Paul Schrader) *Nastassja Kinski, Malcolm McDowell, John Heard, Annette O'Toole, Ruby Dee*. Schrader's gory remake of the 1942 classic chiller is shameless fun, even more so with the director's psychological baggage to laugh at. McDowell and Kinski play kissin' cousins who can't get down from their family tree. The whole production exudes an all-pervasive air of fetid evil, perversity and eroticism — much like the city in which it is set: New Orleans. ★★1/2 VHS: $9.99

Cat's Eye

(1985, 94 min, US, Lewis Teague) *Drew Barrymore, James Woods, Alan King, Robert Hays, Alan King, James Naughton*. Stephen King's uneven horror trilogy about a clinic that helps smokers quit; a mobster who gets even with his wife's lover; and (the best sequence) a cat who protects a young girl from a deadly troll. ★★1/2 VHS: $9.99

Cat's Play

(1974, 115 min, Hungary, Karoly Makk) *Margit Dayka, Margit Makay*. A contemplative drama about rekindled passion, love, friendship and growing old. Two sisters, living in different regions of the country, continue to communicate through letters and phone calls. The correspondence, usually centering on earlier, happier times, turns darker when one of them falls desperately in love with her old flame. Despite her sister's imploring, the normally sedate woman becomes girlish in her efforts to restart the affair, and despondent and self-destructive when it fails. Told in the form of an epistolary novel and utilizing vivid images to convey the character's innermost thoughts, the film is a serious, stylistically daring and deeply involving drama. (Hungarian with English subtitles) ★★★1/2 VHS: $29.99

Catamount Killing

(1974, 93 min, US/West Germany, Krzystof Zanussi) *Horst Bucholz, Ann Wedgeworth*. Polish director Zanussi (*A Year of the Quiet Sun*) tries his hand at film noir in this English-speaking thriller set in a bucolic Vermont town. Bucholz stars as a newly arrived bank manager who seduces an older woman and then involves her

in the faking of a robbery at his bank. Their plans go awry, however, resulting in murderous cover-ups. It has its moments, but there's nothing new here. ★★1/2 VHS: $79.99

Catch-22

(1970, 121 min, US, Mike Nichols) *Alan Arkin, Jon Voight, Martin Sheen, Orson Welles, Art Garfunkel, Richard Benjamin, Paula Prentiss, Bob Newhart, Anthony Perkins, Jack Gilford, Buck Henry*. Brilliant screen adaptation of Joseph Heller's best-selling antiwar novel. Arkin heads a first-rate all-star cast as a WWII Army pilot caught up in the absurdities of military life. What a cast. A powerful and subversively funny black comedy. ★★★★ VHS: $14.99; DVD: $29.99

The Catered Affair

(1956, 93 min, US, Richard Brooks) *Bette Davis, Ernest Borgnine, Debbie Reynolds*. Good performances distinguish this absorbing family drama. Davis is in fine form as the wife of Bronx cabbie Borgnine, whose determination to give daughter Reynolds an elegant wedding far exceeds the family's income. ★★★ VHS: $19.99

Cats Don't Dance

(1997, 75 min, US, Mark Dindal) *Voices of: Scott Bakula, Jasmine Guy, Natalie Cole, Kathy Najimy, Don Knotts*. A good vocal cast adds depth and character to this wonderful animated musical. Danny is a small-town cat seeking fame and fortune in Hollywood. There he meets Sawyer, the charming secretary of the animal talent agent. Danny's big dreams are soon crushed when he finds out that animals are limited to bit parts and are not allowed to speak or sing. Danny and Sawyer eventually overcome the odds and triumphantly sing and dance their way to the top, taking lots of other underappreciated animals with them. ★★★1/2 VHS: $19.99

Caught

(1949, 88 min, US, Max Ophüls) *Barbara Bel Geddes, Robert Ryan, James Mason*. Intriguing film noir psychodrama with Bel Geddes as a mistreated wife caught between her villainous millionaire husband (Ryan) and a caring doctor (Mason). ★★★ VHS: $19.99

Caught

(1996, 109 min, US, Robert M. Young) *Edward James Olmos, Maria Conchita Alonso, Arie Verveen, Steven Schub*. Nick (Verveen), a "mysterious drifter," is taken in by Joe (Olmos), a fish shop owner, and his wife Betty (Alonso). He's given a job and the bedroom of their son, who's in Hollywood trying to break into movies. Things are rosy until Betty and Nick start having an affair, and things get really tense when son Danny pays a surprise visit. While the scenario and conclusion fit neatly into the glib "adultery-never-pays" agenda of most erotic thrillers, *Caught* is far more believable and involving than one would expect, with good performances and a deliberate pace that allows scenes to unfold naturally. ★★★ VHS: $14.99

Caught in the Draft

(1941, 82 min, US, David Butler) *Bob Hope, Eddie Bracken, Dorothy Lamour, Lynne Overman*. Hope gets *Caught in the Draft* and the service will never be the same. Congress has just legalized the draft, and movie star Hope schemes to avoid both induction into the Army and marriage to colonel's daughter Lamour. Of course, it all backfires, and Hope, who faints at the sound of a gunshot, is thrust on an unsuspecting military. This winning comedy is an arsenal of one-liners and sight gags, and its screenplay adheres to a much tighter structure than the standard Hope comedy. Lamour isn't given much to do but react to Hope, but she looks great; Bracken and Overman are tops in support as Hope's henchmen. ★★★ VHS: $14.99

Caught Up

(1998, 98 min, US, Darin Scott) *Bokeem Woodbine, Cynda Williams, Clifton Powell, Tony Todd, Jeffrey Combs, Snoop Doggy Dogg, L.L. Cool J.* A poorly written urban crime drama that would work better as a sketch in *Hollywood Shuffle, Caught Up* stars Woodbine as an ex-con trying to go straight. Shortly after his release from prison, he meets Trish (a mediocre Williams), a psychic being chased by an evil Rastafarian (don't ask). Instead of staying the hell away from her (she's beautiful, you see) and trying to connect with his former squeeze, he agrees to help her. Every stereotype and cliché is here, not to mention howlingly bad dialogue ("Nobody was waiting for me but a dude named destiny") and cameos from yesterday's heroes. ★ VHS: $9.99; DVD: $14.99

Cavalcade

(1933, 110 min, US, Frank Lloyd) *Clive Brook, Diana Wynyard, Una O'Connor.* Noël Coward's 1930s stage hit is given superior treatment in this Oscar-winning adaptation. Brook and Wynyard head an upper-class British family at the turn of the century. The film follows their lives through the first World War and into the 1930s. Wynyard's performance seems exaggerated and dated, but the film does not. First-rate production values and an engrossing story make this one of the classics from its era. ★★★½ VHS: $19.99

The Caveman's Valentine

(2001, 100 min, US, Kasi Lemmons) *Samuel L. Jackson, Colm Feore, Ann Magnuson, Damir Andrei, Aunjanue Ellis, Anthony Michael Hall.* In her second directorial outing (after the exceptional *Eve's Bayou*), Lemmons treads a fine line between bravura and excess but is able to find middle ground thanks to a fascinating, concrete performance by Jackson. With a screenplay by George Dawes Green, who adapted his own novel, *The Caveman's Valentine* features Jackson as Romulus Ledbetter, a once-promising pianist whose severe schizophrenia has made him a resident of the streets. When he discovers a dead body near his home (a cave in Central Park), he begins an investigation into the death, which may have been murder. A quite unusual detective story, the film is a hallucinatory odyssey in which our Columbo is quite mad and we're not sure as to the validity of his findings or when his next outburst will surface. This only adds to the unique pleasures of this absorbing, novel film. However, it's hard to imagine this working at all without the presence of Jackson. His is a bold, passionate performance that anchors this tricky, even illuminating puzzle. ★★★ VHS: $102.99; DVD: $26.99

CB4

(1993, 83 min, US, Tamra Davis) *Chris Rock, Allen Payne, Chris Elliott, Phil Hartman, La Wanda Page.* "Saturday Night Live"'s Rock stars in this hiphop, gangsta rap parody, which he cowrote with former music critic and author Nelson George. The film, which starts out as a hysterically funny pseudo-documentary, strays from its course by turning into a narrative tale and morality play. The film is filled with hilarious moments that are sharp-witted comments on African-American, B-Boys stereotypes, but all of that is lost in a weak story. ★★½ VHS: $9.99

Cecil B. DeMented

(2000, 87 min, US, John Waters) *Stephen Dorff, Melanie Griffith, Patricia Hearst, Mink Stole, Ricki Lake, Alicia Witt, Kevin Nealon.* Waters returns to the guerrilla moviemaking style of his earlier, unconventional days, but the result is far from revolutionary — or even competent, for that matter. Ostensibly a broad farce on Hollywood filmmaking, the lifeless *Cecil B. DeMented* is so scattershot and devoid of direction that it's difficult to tell exactly what it wants to be. Dorff is the titular underground filmmaker who kidnaps superstar Honey Whitlock (Griffith) and forces her to appear in his independent film, *Raving Lunatic.* Waters uses this setup as a frontal assault on mainstream cinema, as characters go about attacking the system and anyone in their way. Anarchy and mayhem prevail. You'd think Waters would be inspired by this premise, but he's unable to deliver on hardly any of his punchlines, making this unfunny mess the director's least satisfying work. Sure *Patch Adams: The Director's Cut* is humorous, but *Cecil B. DeMented* is in need of more substance and less throwaways. ★½ VHS: $14.99; DVD: $24.99

The Celebration

(1998, 106 min, Denmark, Thomas Vinterberg) *Ulrich Thomsen, Henning Moritzen, Thomas Bo Larsen, Paprika Steen.* A hugely dysfunctional family arrives at a secluded hotel for a 60th birthday party for the family patriarch. Suffice it to say, things don't go as cheerily as hoped. A searing, uncompromising drama, *The Celebration* is also incredibly involving and highly entertaining, and despite the subject matter (alcoholism, incest, rape, racism, to name a few), it sidesteps heavy artiness and Jerry Springer-like wallowing. Amazing performances, incisive writing and spot-on direction combine to make this quite memorable. Under the tenets of the "Dogma '95" idea, which sets strict rules about realism in cinema and is espoused by a number of European directors, *The Celebration* achieves an almost unbearable, in-your-face tension — it cuts right to the bone. (German with English subtitles) ★★★½ VHS: $14.99

Celebrity

(1998, 113 min, US, Woody Allen) *Kenneth Branagh, Judy Davis, Winona Ryder, Leonardo DiCaprio, Joe Mantegna, Melanie Griffith, Bebe Neuwirth, Charlize Theron, Famke Janssen, Hank Azaria, Dylan Baker.* Woody asks "What price fame?" and then comes up with a few desirable and not-so desirable answers in this often amusing, scattershot comedy that is Allen's first film since *Shadows and Fog* shot in black and white. Taking over the "Woody" role (neurotic, stammering author), Branagh plays Lee Simon, a self-absorbed writer who falls down the celebrity rabbit hole. The assorted people he meets on his crazy journey include Griffith (as a pampered actress who will only have oral sex with our hero), DiCaprio (very effective as a spoiled DiCaprio-like superstar), Theron (as a fun-

Celebrity

loving supermodel) and Ryder (as a more down-to-earth actress). Woody's dialogue is zesty, and though the story isn't quite as developed as one would like, the humor and a good cast certainly compensate. Davis sparkles as Simon's ex-wife who achieves her own unexpected fame. ★★★ VHS: $19.99; DVD: $29.99

Celeste

(1981, 107 min, Germany, Percy Adlon) *Eva Mattes, Jurgen Arndt.* With no plot to speak of, this subtle yet involving and ultimately inspiring love story chronicles the daily routine of an uneducated peasant girl (the wonderful Mattes) who is hired as the housekeeper for the ailing author Marcel Proust. The film's power lies in the evolving relationship between the intellectual Proust and the simple, caring woman who in the course of nine years not only tends to his house but becomes his companion, secretary, friend and surrogate mother. Based on the memoirs of the real Céleste Albaret. (German with English subtitles) ★★★ VHS: $29.99

Celestial Clockwork

(Mécanicas Célestes)

(1994, 86 min, France/Venezuela, Fina Torres) *Ariadna Gil, Arielle Dombasle, Evelyne Didi.* Exuberant, fanciful and infused with magical realism, this "Alice in Wonderland/Cinderella"-like comedy is a delightful celebration of the pursuit of individual happiness and sexual open-mindedness. In dusty Caracas, the lovely Ana suddenly comes to her senses on the altar and flees, leaving her stunned husband-to-be and her former life behind. She jumps aboard the next Paris-bound plane and takes up residence in a funky crash pad with her old friend Alma. The apartment is right out of Almódovar, populated by a bevy of Latina exiles aggressively excercising their free will and indulging in outrageous Parisienne chic. Brimming with oddball characters and loopy plot twists, the film is a highly entertaining ride with Ana on her picaresque journey to self-fulfillment. (Spanish and French with English subtitles) ★★★½

Celine and Julie Go Boating

(1974, 193 min, France, Jacques Rivette) *Dominque Labourier, Juliet Berto.* A truly magical cinematic journey, this 1970s art-house classic is "Alice in Wonderland" meets Cocteau. Celine (Berto) is a magician who becomes fast friends with librarian Julie (Labourier) after they meet at the steps of Montmarte. Forming an uncanny, symbiotic bond, they move into the same flat and begin sharing completely of each others' lives: bed, clothes, boyfriend, etc. Ultimately, they begin sharing the same alternate reality when they partake of a magic candy that transports them into an imaginary (or is it) haunted house, where they become involved in the drama of its inhabitants. Just as this reaches a climax, the hallucination ends and Celine and Julie must begin again. Rivette commits a huge cinematic risk by presenting this scene again and again as each time it inches closer to its conclusion (hence the 193-minute running time) and voila! It pays off. As delightful and engaging as its two main characters. (French with English subtitles) ★★★★ VHS: $29.99

The Cell

(2000, 107 min, US, Tarsem Singh) *Jennifer Lopez, Vincent D'Onofrio, Vince Vaughn, Dylan Baker, Marianne Jean-Baptiste.* The plot, and any attempt at describing *The Cell*, sounds quite tired. A psychologist (Lopez) must enter the mind of a serial killer (D'Onofrio) to find a dying victim (*Silence of the Lambs*); she does this by infiltrating his dream state (*Dreamscape*), and must learn to control this false reality (*The Matrix*). Knowing all that, it's all the more incredible to find how original this thriller is. Breathtaking stream-of-conciousness sequences through a tense carnival-of-horrors fantasy world are the highlight of this trippy film destined for cult status. With bizarre violence and an experimental technique, director Singh is superficially reminiscent of David Fincher, but this big-screen debut is full of hope and lacks Fincher's nihilistic tendencies. A music video director (R.E.M.'s "Losing My Religion"), Singh shows he can sustain his vision; armed with a more substantial script, not even the sky would be his limit. ★★★ VHS: $14.99; DVD: $24.99

The Celluloid Closet

(1995, 102 min, US, Rob Epstein & Jeffrey Friedman) *Narrated by and featuring: Lily Tomlin, Susan Sarandon, Whoopi Goldberg, Shirley MacLaine, Tony Curtis, Tom Hanks, Gore Vidal, Quentin Crisp.* Inspired by Vito Russo's seminal book on the depiction of homosexuality in Hollywood cinema, this funny, informative and occasionally moving documentary offers — through interviews and a vast assortment of film clips — a candid mini-history of gays and lesbians on-screen. *The Celluloid Closet* takes a chronological approach to the subject, offering clips from the turn of the century (*The Gay Brothers*) through the silents to the effeminate caricatures of the 1930s (*Broadway Melody*), the pitiful homosexual of the 1950s and '60s, the violently deviant homosexual of the '70s and '80s, and concluding with the squeaky clean image of recent times. While encompassing in scope, the film is too simplistic and suffers from the lack of critical analysis and a central point of view. And too many actors have nothing really to say — only Tony Curtis and Susan Sarandon offer insight into the queer roles they have played. With that said, however, *The Celluloid Closet* is more than recommended, but for something deeper, it is best to read Russo's book. ★★★ VHS: $24.99; DVD: $29.99

Celtic Pride

(1996, 91 min, US, Tom De Cerchio) *Damon Wayans, Daniel Stern, Dan Aykroyd, Christopher McDonald, Deion Sanders, Larry Bird.* Horrible, obnoxious and unfunny, *Celtic Pride* casts an irritating Aykroyd and a killable Stern as two pathetic Boston Celtic fans who kidnap the opposing team's star player (a bored Wayans) to ensure their beloved team's victory. What should have been a vicious, wicked satire on professional sports and their more obsessive fans instead is a grueling debut by a film student-like director who has little knowledge of direction, sports or comic timing. Every potentially interesting exchange or insight is diverted to a cheap insult or unnecessary pratfall. ★ VHS: $19.99

The Cement Garden

(1996, 108 min, GB, Andrew Birkin) *Andrew Robertson, Charlotte Gainsbourg, Alice Coultard, Ned Birkin.* Based on a novel by Ian McEwan ("The Comfort of Strangers"), this bizarre and twisted tale of adolescence run amok is at once fascinating and seductively repulsive. On the edge of some barren, unidentified British city stands a lone remaining house. Its four young occupants suddenly find themselves orphaned. Julie (Gainsbourg), the eldest, becomes the de facto leader of the clan. Her brother Jack (Robertson), when his head's not lost in a sci-fi fantasy novel, is usually masturbating. Tom (Birkin) is an 8-year-old cross-dresser, and Sue (Coultard) is a 13-year-old conformist. They decide to dispose of mum's body and avoid the orphanages and thus begins a summer of complete descent into childish fantasy that's a pointed allegory — à la "Lord of the Flies" — about the decay of social behavior in a crumbling industrial society. The film teases the viewer with snippets of coherency only to settle back into an infuriatingly alluring moral ambiguity. ★★★ VHS: $29.99; DVD: $29.99

The Cemetery Club

(1992, 106 min, US, Bill Duke) *Ellen Burstyn, Olympia Dukakis, Diane Ladd, Danny Aiello, Lainie Kazan, Christina Ricci, Wallace Shawn.* A talented cast attempts to breathe life into this sappy adaptation of the failed Broadway comedy. Sadly, this meandering saga of three middle-aged widows who gather at the cemetery to toss one-liners at their husbands' graves falls well wide of its mark — straddling the line between comedy and drama, and failing to be either funny or dramatic. Burstyn gives the most charming performance of the film as a widow who finds romance. ★★ VHS: $9.99

Cemetery Man

(1994, 100 min, Italy/US, Michele Soavi) *Rupert Everett, Anna Falchi, Francois Hadji-Lazaro.* Dario Argento's protégé Soavi comes wholly into his own with this highly original adaptation of a novel by Italian pop writer Titiano Sclavi. Everett stars as Francesco Dellamorte, caretaker of the Buffalore Cemetery. What would seem a quiet job has recently become quite a problem, however, as the dead have been returning to life soon after burial, and it is up to Dellamorte to put them permanently back into their graves. Soon he's killing the living in order to keep them from rising from the dead and he can no longer distinguish between fantasy and reality. Though the film is somewhat convoluted and definitely unreal, Soavi's camera rarely stops moving. Entertaining and enticing, the film is not for the casual viewer, but those who visit the graveyard several times a week will find rewards in store. (Filmed in English) ★★★ VHS: $29.99

Center Stage

(2000, 116 min, US, Nicholas Hytner) *Amanda Schull, Peter Gallagher, Susan May Pratt, Ethan Stiefel, Donna Murphy.* Best of the best in ballet students vie for positions in the American Ballet Academy, while dealing with the usual mélange of personal troubles. Slow-paced, overlong but mildly involving, *Center Stage* benefits greatly from decent performances and an appealing lead (the beautiful-in-a-perky-way Schull), but the film is terminally shallow and derivative. There's nothing here you haven't seen in countless "gotta-be-the-best" films (whether about singers, athletes, chess players or dancers), but like its antecedents, *Center Stage* shines in its performance scenes. Some of these include spectacular performances of "Swan Lake" choreographed by Lee Ivanov, "Romeo and Juliet" choreographed by Sir Kenneth MacMillan, and "Stars and Stripes" choreographed by George Balanchine. Dance fans and teenage girls should love the film; everyone else should approach with caution. ★★½ VHS: $14.99; DVD: $19.99

Central Station

(1998, 115 min, Brazil, Walter Salles) *Fernanda Montenegro, Marilia Pera, Vinicius de Oliveira.* Heartrending without being maudlin, *Central Station* is a poignant, accomplished drama featuring an outstanding performance from Brazil's grand dame of theatre, Montenegro. At the Rio De Janeiro central train station, Dora (Montenegro), a retired schoolteacher, writes and posts letters for the illiterate to "make ends meet." Often they end up in her bureau at home, or the trash can. When a woman is killed in a bus accident, Dora begins an odyssey of self-awakening when she reluctantly escorts the deceased woman's nine-year-old son Josué (de Oliveira) to his long-lost father hundreds of miles cross-country. Montenegro has made Dora a fascinating character: this is a portrayal that is intense and nuanced, and Montenegro can say

Celine and Julie Go Boating

more with her eyes than a page of dialogue. Young de Oliveira is a heartbreaker as Josué; he's adorable without the precociousness. A beguiling and touching journey, *Central Station* is rich in emotion and honesty, and marvelously done. (Portuguese with English subtitles) ★★★★ VHS: $21.99; DVD: $29.99

La Cérémonie

(1996, 111 min, France, Claude Chabrol) *Isabelle Huppert, Sandrine Bonnaire, Jacqueline Bisset, Jean-Pierre Cassel.* Director Chabrol casts a sideways glance at class warfare in this somewhat off-center thriller that examines the tentative relationship between the modern aristocracy and their domestics. Bonnaire stars as the newly appointed maid for Bisset and her industrialist husband Cassel. She seems a perfect new hire. But what seems like coy respect for her new employers slowly gives way under the strain of bitter secrets and a spotted past. Into the picture walks Huppert (radiant as ever), as a smart-ass postal worker with a rocky past of her own. The atmosphere is tense throughout as Bonnaire's perfect veneer begins to crack and the family becomes increasingly intolerant of her rebelliousness and her budding friendship with Huppert. Chabrol explores this territory with characteristic understatement and a "classical" panache that makes the film feel more "arty" than it really is, but his intricate study of character makes this captivating viewing nonetheless. (French with English subtitles) ★★★½ VHS: $29.99

César

(1936, 117 min, France, Marcel Pagnol) *Raimu, Pierre Fresnay.* Emboldened by the success of *Marius* and *Fanny*, Pagnol decided to direct the final installment of his stage trilogy himself. Once again Raimu steals the film as Marius' father, but this time the film bears his name so it's all right. Short on plot but long on everything else (especially running time), *César*, like all of the films to come out of Pagnol's studio, is full of people whose company one enjoys, all of whom inhabit a little village in which one would love to have lived. The plot concerns Fanny's young son who discovers that Marius is his real father. Through his efforts, they are reunited after 20 years. (French with English subtitles) ★★★ VHS: $39.99

César and Rosalie

(1972, 110 min, France, Claude Sautet) *Yves Montand, Romy Schneider, Sami Frey.* Montand and Schneider give compelling performances in this charming comedy, a bittersweet tale of friendship and love. Schneider plays a divorcée living with tycoon Montand who becomes involved with young artist Frey. Quite unexpectedly, however, the two men, who at first see each other as nothing more than rivals, become friends, laying the framework for an unusual and caring relationship among the three lovers. (French with English subtitles) ★★★½

Chain Lightning

(1950, 95 min, US, Stuart Heisler) *Humphrey Bogart, Eleanor Parker, Raymond Massey.* Actual war and aerial footage highlight this routine aviation adventure, with Bogart hitting the skies as a former WWII bomber pilot who tests the new jets. Massey is the multibillionaire with a fascination for airplanes who funds the tests. ★★½ VHS: $19.99

Chain of Desire

(1992, 105 min, US, Temistocles Lopez) *Linda Fiorentino, Malcolm McDowell, Seymour Cassel, Kevin Conroy, Elias Koteas, Patrick Bauchau, Grace Zabriskie.* From the director of the intriguing *Exquisite Corpses* comes this stylistically inventive and wittily droll observation and AIDS allegory on sexual yearning and unrequited love. Fiorentino is Alma, a singer in a slick New York nightclub who sleeps with Jesus, a married Hispanic worker. This successful coupling begins a humorous but sexually frustrating daisy chain of purely sexual encounters with a succession of New York characters. McDowell is featured as a cheesy closeted journalist with a taste for street urchins, and Cassel plays a philandering artist. A titillating highlight is a three-way, voyeuristically charged masturbation scene (both gay and straight) among three people in three different curtain-less high-rise apartments. An erotic updating of *La Ronde* exploring sexual desire. ★★★

Chain Reaction

(1996, 100 min, US, Andrew Davis) *Keanu Reeves, Morgan Freeman, Rachel Weisz, Fred Ward.* Reeves takes his turn as the unjustly accused in Davis' attempted reworking of *The Fugitive*. Reeves stars as a young machinist working on a university physics project attempting to find a new, cheap source of energy. Once the team makes its discovery, dark forces take over and the lab is blown to smithereens. Only Reeves and a young associate hold the secret to the discovery. Framed for murder, they must run for their lives, both from the police and from the nefarious forces behind the set-up. Tedious, overlong and full of gaping plot holes. ★ VHS: $9.99; DVD: $22.99

Chained

(1934, 76 min, US, Clarence Brown) *Clark Gable, Joan Crawford, Otto Kruger.* Gable and Crawford enjoy a brief encounter aboard a cruise ship in this familiar romantic drama. Gable pursues Crawford until she gives in, but when she returns to New York and lover Kruger, she becomes torn between the two men. ★★

Chained Heat

(1983, 97 min, US, Paul Nicholas) *Linda Blair, Sybil Danning, John Vernon, Tamara Dobson, Stella Stevens.* Sex, violence, showers, sex, drugs, prostitution, white slavery, sex, corruption (did we mention sex?) from the producer of *The Concrete Jungle*. One of the great treats (meaning sleaziest) in the women-in-prison genre, this violent and sexually explicit exploitation film stars the genre's reigning queens: Blair and Danning. Blair plays the innocent who's in for a quick and brutal education, as the prison is run by a drug-dealing wretch of a warden, and populated with hard-as-nails, knife-wielding peroxide babes. If Blair thought being possessed by the Devil was tough, she's never spent time in a women's prison. ★★½

Chained Heat 2

(1993, 98 min, US, Lloyd Simani) *Brigitte Nielsen, Paul Koslo.* All hope seems lost for pretty strawberry blonde Alex when she is unjustly imprisoned in a hellish all-female Czechoslovakian prison for drug smuggling. The hell-hole is ruled by a suit-and-tie attired warden (played by Nielsen), aided by her knife-wielding, cigar-chomping, Lotte Lenya wannabe henchwoman. Will our heroine ever escape? Will any of the

actresses ever attend acting classes? Filmed in an actual Prague prison, the film is laughably bad, featuring the requisite bevy of beauties, plenty of gratuitous flesh and several lesbian lovemaking scenes. How would you like your exploitation? With cheese, please. ★½ VHS: $14.99

Chairman of the Board

(1998, 95 min, US, Alex Zamm) *Carrot Top, Courtney Thorne-Smith, Larry Miller, Raquel Welch, Jack Warden, Bill Erwin, M. Emmet Walsh.* It's tempting to simply call this: "Pee-wee Herman *is* the *Hudsucker Proxy*." What an insult to both comedian and film. Carrot Top is a surfer dude (ugh!) who strikes up a brief friendship with tycoon Warden. When the latter dies, Mr. Top is left the (cue: film title) of his huge invention business. But Warden's nephew (Miller) wants the seat, and he'll be boss if the company stock drops too far. Despite some cool doodads, and maybe a few amusing scenes, *Chairman of the Board* does star Carrot Top and his screechy voice. And the jokes, well, they seem to have been written during the Bush (Sr.) administration. ★½ VHS: $14.99; DVD: $24.99

The Chalk Garden

(1964, 106 min, GB, Ronald Neame) *Deborah Kerr, Hayley Mills, John Mills, Edith Evans.* Kerr gives a beautiful performance as a governess who helps a troubled youngster coming of age. Hayley is affecting as the young girl; her father John and Evans offer solid support. ★★★ VHS: $19.99

The Chamber

(1996, 110 min, US, James Foley) *Chris O'Donnell, Gene Hackman, Faye Dunaway, Lela Rochen, Robert Prosky.* In *A Time to Kill*, race relations is the focal point in a complex and involving tale. In this Grisham adaptation, race relations once again plays a major role in the story, but it's watered down and merely a plot device to a uneventful drama. O'Donnell sleepwalks through his role as a young lawyer who attempts to get a stay of execution for his grandfather (Hackman), a KKK member and convicted murderer sentenced to death. As he races against the clock, he tries to get to know a man he never knew who is unwilling to either defend himself or reconcile. Not a lot happens — O'Donnell rushes here and there, and Hackman breaks into choruses of epithets every other scene. Hackman's good performance is offset by the film's flat character development and a plodding pace. ★★ VHS: $7.49; DVD: $26.99

The Chambermaid on the Titanic

(1998, 96 min, France, Bigas Luna) *Olivier Martinez, Romane Bohringer, Aitana Sánchez-Gijón, Didier Bezace.* This tragi-comic love story about the fictionalized, nonsexual relationship between the handsome foundry worker Horty (Martinez) and the beautiful chambermaid of the title, Marie (Sanchez-Gijon), is all promise and no payoff. Director Lunas tries to create a charming period piece about love, trust, and truth, but this joyless film lacks depth and passion. As Horty recounts his adventures to his friends about how he helped Marie when she was stranded the night before the ocean liner sails, the excitement his coworkers feel hearing his tale is not shared by the viewer. The two leads ooze sex appeal, and a scene in which they share kisses under a dining room table generates some heat, yet there is little else of interest in their chaste relationship. Horty's wife Zoe (Bohringer) complicates matters in the final third, but by that time, *The Chambermaid on the Titanic* has capsized almost completely. (French with English subtitles) ★★ VHS: $29.99

Chameleon Street

(1988, 98 min, US, Wendell B. Harris, Jr.) *Wendell B. Harris, Jr., Angela Leslie, Richard Kiley.* One of the merits of video is that it allows such overlooked gems as this to finally have their day in the sun. Fledgling filmmaker Harris wrote, directed and stars in this hip comedy (based on a true story) about a man who attempts to beat the system by impersonating various upstanding members of society — and getting away with it! Harris' witty, world-weary narration adds just the right touch, imbuing the film with a '90s attitude offset by '70s sensibilities. ★★★ VHS: $19.99

Champion

(1949, 90 min, US, Mark Robson) *Kirk Douglas, Arthur Kennedy, Marilyn Maxwell, Ruth Roman.* Hard-nosed boxing tale without *Rocky* schmaltz about a nasty fighter (Douglas) who sacrifices everything as he punches his way to the top. Douglas gives an exceptional performance as the would-be champ. ★★★½ VHS: $14.99; DVD: $24.99

Chan Is Missing

(1982, 80 min, US, Wayne Wang) *Wood Moy, Marc Hayashi.* Wang's first feature film was shot in the director's hometown of San Francisco for a mere $20,000. The film follows the wanderings of a middle-aged cab driver and his wise-cracking nephew as they search all over Chinatown for Chan — who has mysteriously disappeared with the $2,000 meant to buy their taxi permit. A sophisticated statement about the trials and tribulations of ethnic assimilation. ★★★½ VHS: $79.99

Chances Are

(1989, 108 min, US, Emile Ardolino) *Robert Downey, Jr., Cybill Shepherd, Mary Stuart Masterson, Ryan O'Neal.* A routine "switch" comedy saved by Downey's charming performance. The spirit of Shepherd's deceased husband turns up in her daughter's boyfriend (Downey). With Masterson and O'Neal as the confused partners of Downey and Shepherd respectively. ★★ VHS: $9.99; DVD: $29.99

Chanel Solitaire

(1981, 120 min, France, George Kaczender) *Karen Black, Rutger Hauer, Marie-France Pisier, Timothy Dalton.* This melodramatic biopic stars Pisier as Coco Chanel, the famous couturiere who overcame a poor childhood to conquer Paris and the world with her fabulous designs. (Filmed in English) ★★ VHS: $19.99

Chang

(1927, 67 min, US/Siam, Merian C. Cooper & Ernest B. Schoedsack) Remastered from an original negative, this entertaining and exciting documentary/fiction film was shot entirely in the jungles of Siam. The story follows a native family who lives in a tree house on the edge of the dark, potentially dangerous jungle. The film depicts their everyday routine of farming, hunting and family life, until disaster strikes when a spectacu-

larly filmed elephant stampede overruns their village. A tender tale of survival that features a new musical score by composer Bruce Gaston. ★★★ VHS: $39.99

The Changeling

(1979, 109 min, Canada, Peter Medak) *George C. Scott, Melvyn Douglas, Trish Van Devere.* Creepy and very effective ghost story/murder mystery about a composer (Scott) whose recent loss of wife and daughter make him receptive to the hauntings of a murdered child. You would never think a wheelchair could be so frightening. ★★★ VHS: $9.99; DVD: $14.99

Chaplin

(1992, 140 min, GB/US, Richard Attenborough) *Robert Downey, Jr., Dan Aykroyd, Kevin Kline, Geraldine Chaplin, Anthony Hopkins, Diane Lane, Penelope Ann Miller, Marisa Tomei, James Woods.* Director Attenborough's bio-pic of Charlie Chaplin aspires towards the sweep of his many epics and, while it's fine for the bigger scenes, it leaves the smaller, more personal moments lacking emotion. As Chaplin, Downey dons astonishingly accurate movements, gestures and expressions (and earned an Oscar nomination for it), but never really gets into Chaplin's mind or soul. The story covers Chaplin's poor childhood in England to his arrival in America and eventual stardom to his many ups and downs throughout his career. Though the screenplay is, for the most part, extremely witty, so much screen time is given to Chaplin's numerous love affairs and ongoing feud with J. Edgar Hoover, one has to wonder when the immortal tramp ever had time to devote to his own brilliant films. (Letterboxed VHS available for $14.99) ★★½ VHS: $9.99; DVD: $14.99

Character

(1997, 114 min, The Netherlands, Mike van Diem) *Jan Decleir, Fedja van Huet, Betty Schuurman, Tamar Van Den Dop, Victor Low, Hans Kesting.* This outstanding, Oscar-winning period drama about a son in 1920s Rotterdam trying to reconcile his relationship with his abusive father is eerily compelling. Directed and adapted by Van Diem, the film opens with the murder of Dreverhaven (Decleir), but the story is more of a whydunnit than a whodunnit. Flashbacks reveal the hateful Dreverhaven as a powerful, controlling man who is feared by all and loved by none. His illegitimate son Katadreuffe (van Huet) is the most likely suspect, as he has spent his entire life trying to get out from under his father's oppressive thumb. Much of the film traces Katadreuffe's struggle to find his place in the world, only to find each triumph undermined by his father's evil influence. The film is full of anguish, but the cruel moments are offset by Katadreuffe's few achievements. Van Diem has crafted a highly stylized, emotional film, with a mesmerizing look: the chiaroscuro lighting, the roving camera and the period detail all contribute to the film's beautiful but stark atmosphere. Likewise, the full-bodied performance by Decleir is well balanced by van Huet's reluctant hero. (Dutch with English subtitles) ★★★★ VHS: $21.99

Charade

(1963, 114 min, US, Stanley Donen) *Cary Grant, Audrey Hepburn, Walter Matthau, James Coburn, George Kennedy.* The ever radiant Hepburn and

the dapper Grant star in this delightfully comic ode to Hitchcock. The recently widowed Hepburn finds herself terrorized by the gang of her late husband's ex-associates all bent on finding his missing fortune. Not knowing where to turn, she seeks safety with Grant, but is he all he's cracked up to be? A twisting tale of intrigue. ★★★½ VHS: $19.99; DVD: $39.99

The Charge of the Light Brigade

(1936, 116 min, US, Michael Curtiz) *Errol Flynn, Olivia de Havilland, David Niven, Nigel Bruce.* Rousing Flynn adventure inspired by Tennyson's poem about the famous British infantrymen fighting to the death in 19th-century India. De Havilland (who else?) plays Flynn's love interest. ★★★ VHS: $19.99

Chariots of Fire

(1981, 123 min, GB, Hugh Hudson) *Ben Cross, Ian Charleson, Ian Holm, Nigel Havers, Dennis Christopher, John Gielgud, Alice Krige, Brad Davis.* This occasionally heavy-handed portrait of the passionate careers of British track stars Eric Liddell and Harold Abrahams is nonetheless an elegant and poignant drama about religious and social differences in the England of 1924. The stories of Liddell, a deeply religious Scotsman, and Abrahams, one of the first Jews to attend Cambridge, unfold with a depth and grace which made this film a rousing international success. Academy Award winner for Best Picture. ★★★½ VHS: $14.99; DVD: $19.99

Charleen/Backyard

(1978/1976, 59/40 min, US, Ross McElwee) Die hard fans of director McElwee (*Sherman's March*) should appreciate these two early documentaries focusing on his friends and family in North Carolina. *Charleen* (1978) is a personal portrait of a chatty, and, at times, remarkable woman who teaches poetry to poor children and who had befriended Ezra Pound and e.e. cummings. *Backyard* (1976) chronicles the minidramas of McElwee's friends, family and their (indentured?) household staff back in Charlotte, North Carolina. Mildly interesting stuff. ★★ VHS: $29.99

The Charles Bukowski Tapes

(1987, 240 min, US, Barbet Schroeder) *Charles Bukowski.* Bukowski, the grizzled, drunken Beat poet whose writings ("Barfly," "Tales of Ordinary Madness") as well as his own life reflect the tragic beauty and painful loneliness of the "defeated, demented and damned," is profiled in this stimulating documentary/interview. Broken up into numerous segments, the film lets Bukowski ramble on, usually tanked up on beer or wine, about everything: his travels throughout the seedy terrain of American cities, the forces behind creativity, sleazy sex, even the pleasures of pollution. Whether in his run-down L.A. home or in his old childhood home, Bukowski proves to be both a pontificating drunk and chronicler of the losers as well as a fascinating if self-indulgent philosopher — an American original. ★★★★ VHS: $79.99

Charles et Lucie

(1979, 96 min, France, Nelly Kaplan) *Daniel Ceccaldi, Ginette Garcin.* This Gallic comedy is the rags-to-riches-to-rags story of a poor Parisian couple who find that they have inherited a beautiful mansion on the Riviera. The only catch is that they must sell all their furniture in order to pay the lawyer fees. But sell they do, as they go driving off to the Riviera with their dreams of riches. The couple confronts a series of adventures that rekindle their love and taste for living. A delightfully refreshing love story. (French with English subtitles) ★★★½

Charlie's Angels

(2000, 95 min, US, McG) *Cameron Diaz, Drew Barrymore, Lucy Liu, Bill Murray, Sam Rockwell, Tim Curry, Kelly Lynch, Crispin Glover, Matt LeBlanc, LL Cool J, Tom Green, Luke Wilson; Voice of: John Forsythe.* Or, *The Powerpuff Girls: 20 Years Later.* Except for that omnipresent speakerphone, you'd never know this was based on the TV show, and unlike the many TV adaptation bombs, *Charlie's Angels* is remarkably unforced and damn fun. Hey, you've got Cameron Diaz dancing in her Underoos, why not let the scene linger a little? The sweet ditzy blond (Diaz), the bad red-headed grrl (Barrymore) and the brainy brunette (Liu) all know how to use their hair and their kung-fu to fight crime on behalf of benevolent Charlie. They get Hong Kong–style showdowns with plenty of wirework, in a serviceable and self-aware plot that doesn't get in the way of the girl power and T&A (an effective mix, pleasing to all sexes and orientations). McG knows it's cheesy, but the Angels don't, and that makes them even more charming. A rare case of the cast and crew's fun spilling onto the screen, these *Angels* are an infectious if lightweight delight. ★★★ VHS: $19.99; DVD: $27.99

Charlotte's Web

(1973, 94 min, US, Charles A. Nichols) *Voices of: Debbie Reynolds, Henry Gibson, Paul Lynde, Charles Nelson Reilly.* Captivating animated feature based on the writings of E.B. White, centering on the friendship of a spider and pig. Reynolds is the voice of Charlotte. ★★★ VHS: $14.99; DVD: $24.99

The Chase

(1966, 135 min, US, Arthur Penn) *Marlon Brando, Jane Fonda, Robert Redford, Angie Dickinson, James Fox, Janice Rule, Robert Duvall.* Redford is an escaped prisoner who returns to his small Texas town, stirring up both trouble and passions. Brando is the sheriff, and Fonda the old girlfriend. Screenplay by Lillian Hellman, based on Horton Foote's novel. Though there's a lot of talent involved here, this notoriously troubled production suffers from too-many-chiefs (producer Sam Spiegel's constant interference); however, there are some interesting moments. ★★½ VHS: $9.99

The Chase

(1994, 87 min, US, Adam Rifkin) *Charlie Sheen, Kristy Swanson, Ray Wise, Cary Elwes, Henry Rollins.* When not dwelling on the sappy romance at its core, *The Chase* is almost remarkable in its skewering of the feeding frenzy network news has become. Sheen stars as a wrongly accused fugitive who accidentally takes a millionaire's daughter (Swanson) hostage, thereby setting off a high-speed run for the border — with full media circus in tow. Rifkin's satire mixes hip, self-assured MTV-style photography with dead-on lampoons of media-ocrity to create an intermittently appealing comedy. ★★½ VHS: $9.99

Chasers

(1994, 102 min, US, Dennis Hopper) *Tom Berenger, William McNamara, Dennis Hopper, Dean Stockwell, Gary Busey, Crispin Glover.* McNamara plays a wise-cracking naval officer who gets paired up with a tough sergeant (Berenger) in order to escort a "sexy and sassy" prisoner (Eleniak) in this *Last Detail* rip-off. If you used your imagination to predict wild and wacky misadventures for the three to encounter, you'd be doing more than the screenwriters. With this cast you'd think there would be something of interest here. This film does prove one positive thing: Hopper must have a lot of devoted friends. ★ VHS: $9.99; DVD: $19.99

Chasing Amy

(1997, 105 min, US, Kevin Smith) *Ben Affleck, Joey Lauren Adams, Jason Lee, Dwight Ewell, Jason Mewes, Kevin Smith, Matt Damon.* Making a hyperspace jump from his previous two efforts, writer-director Smith has fashioned a very funny, insightful and painfully honest romantic comedy for the '90s. Affleck plays a popular comic book artist who befriends Alyssa (Adams), a lesbian, at a comic book convention. Their friendship develops, but he finally breaks down and confesses his love for her. At first angry, she soon declares similar feelings and they begin a relationship. That is, until he discovers her sordid, straight past, which he can't stop obsessing over. Some remarkably mature observations about love and relationships are made by Smith, particularly in his recurring role as "Silent Bob." Gone are the bathroom jokes and farcical nonsense which ruined *Mallrats*. This is an accomplished, enjoyable movie which accurately pokes fun at a variety of modern relationships (straight, gay and bi) and even manages a few honestly tearjerking sequences. Lee has also come a long way from *Mallrats*, bringing humor and texture to the role of the "other man." And look for Matt Damon in a tiny role. ★★★½ VHS: $14.99; DVD: $32.99

Le Chat (The Cat)

(1970, 88 min, France, Pierre Granier Deferre) *Simone Signoret, Jean Gabin.* Signoret and Gabin are an elderly married couple of 25 years whose early love has turned into a silent hate. Set in a decaying and soon-to-be-demolished apartment house, the film explores the relationship of the two, who have no one else and who refuse to talk to each other. The probing of the reasons for the embittered separation are acted out in this sad yet unforgettable drama. Brilliantly acted. (French with English subtitles) ★★★

Chattahoochee

(1990, 98 min, US, Mick Jackson) *Gary Oldman, Dennis Hopper, Frances McDormand, Pamela Reed.* When a Korean War veteran (Oldman) disrupts life in his sleepy, small Florida town by firing off a barrage of ammunition in a clumsy attempt to get himself killed, he's promptly shipped off to an asylum that makes *The Snake Pit* look like a politician's prison. Oldman is remarkable as the incarcerated vet who rediscovers himself as he opposes the insanity of the institution that confines him. ★★★ VHS: $14.99

The Cheap Detective

(1978, 92 min, US, Robert Moore) *Peter Falk, Eileen Brennan, Ann-Margret, Madeline Kahn, Dom DeLuise, Stockard Channing, James Coco, Sid Caesar, Phil Silvers.* There are lots of laughs in Neil Simon's follow-up to *Murder by Death.* Falk stars in this private-eye parody, *The Maltese Falcon* in particular, ably assisted by a great comic cast. Who cares if some of the jokes are forced; the film is in good humor, and what a cast! ★★★ VHS: $14.99

Cheaper by the Dozen

(1950, 85 min, US, Walter Lang) *Clifton Webb, Myrna Loy, Jeanne Crain.* Webb is well cast in this charmingly sweet comedy as an efficiency expert and father of twelve. The ever-classy Loy is his wife, who really keeps the household going. (Sequel: *Belles on Their Toes*) ★★★

Chicken Run: Making the great escape

Un Chien Andalou

The Cheat

(1915, 59 min, US, Cecil B. DeMille) *Sessue Hayakawa, Fannie Ward.* Racist — racy — DeMille at his best, before his bombast interfered with his pandering to his middle-class clientele. A vivacious socialite becomes the Occidental tourist when she loses the community chest fund in a bad stock deal. Salvation comes in the form of a wily Asian gentleman who prefers to take his interest out in trade, branding her — literally — a scarlet woman. Hayakawa gives a wonderfully modulated performance, his Zen-like calm evoking still waters against the raging torrents of stock company histrionics. Also: *A Girl's Folly* (1917, 30 min, US, Maurice Tourneur), a behind-the-scenes look at the day-by-day workings of a film studio. A gentle satire of a nascent industry, the film is alive with warmth and it is that which survives the intervening decades. ★★★½ VHS: $29.99; DVD: $29.99

Checking Out

(1989, 90 min, US, David Leland) *Jeff Daniels, Melanie Mayron, Michael Tucker.* Hypochondriac Daniels thinks he's going to die — after 15 minutes, you wish he would. Disappointing comedy wastes its intriguing premise. You know you're in trouble when the film's best joke is "Why don't Italians barbecue?" (Because the spaghetti falls through the grill.) ★ VHS: $14.99

Cheech & Chong's Next Movie

(1980, 99 min, US, Thomas Chong) *Cheech Marin, Thomas Chong, Evelyn Guerrero, Edie McClurg, Paul Reubens, Phil Hartman.* Cheech and Chong appear in the follow-up to their hit *Up in Smoke*, with lots more dope jokes. The duo hits the road for a series of rather crude adventures, which are only intermittently amusing. Not nearly as funny as *Smoke*. ★★ VHS: $9.99

A Chef in Love

(1996, 98 min, France/Georgia, Nana Dzhordzadze) *Pierre Richard, Nino Kirtadze.* This amusing, but ultimately meandering, yarn makes a trek through the Caucuses circa the 1920s on the heels of a happy-go-lucky French chef known as Pascal Ichak (Richard). The film begins in the 1990s: A young Franco-Georgian is introduced to a mysterious woman who claims she has papers written by her mother (portrayed in her youth by a radiant Kirtadze) that she would like him to translate. This precipitates a series of flashbacks describing his mother's pre-Communist life in Georgia. Richard is a pleasure to watch, and his sexual chemistry with Kirtadze is surprisingly easy-going and believable. But none of this can overcome the film's rambling lack of focus as it tries to be both uplifting tale of culinary and lustful delight and cautionary tome on the evils of armed revolution. (French and Georgian with English subtitles) ★★ VHS: $24.99

Cherry Falls

(2000, 92 min, US, Geoffrey Wright) *Brittany Murphy, Michael Biehn, Jay Mohr.* A neat, witty inversion of the usual slasher film cliché: In the small town of Cherry Falls, a serial killer appears to be targeting a very specific demographic — virgins. The town's sexually inexperienced teens then schedule a sex party, all in the name of self-preservation. *Cherry Falls* is an accomplished mix of black humor, satire and horror, making it a better-than-average slasher, with muscular direction from Wright (*Romper Stomper*), good performances by Biehn and Murphy, and a terrifically funny/brutal wrap-up at the aforementioned party. Don't be put off by the fact this went straight to video; *Cherry Falls* is the real deal. ★★★ VHS: $89.99

Cherry, Harry & Raquel

(1969, 71 min, US, Russ Meyer) *Uschi Digard, Astrid Lillimor, Linda Ashton, Charles Napier.* Set in a dusty Arizona border town, *Cherry, Harry & Raquel* depicts double-crossing drug smugglers involved in power struggles, interspersed with various sexual encounters both lesbian and heterosexual. ★★ VHS: $79.99

Cherry 2000

(1988, 93 min, US, Steve DeJarnatt) *Melanie Griffith, Ben Johnson, Harry Carey, Jr., Tim Thomerson, Laurence Fishburne.* Futuristic, post-apocalyptic adventure with Griffith as a mercenary who helps a husband looking for the prototype of his robot-wife — stored in a factory located in a forbidden zone. An enjoyable sci-fi outing which wants to please, and for the most part succeeds. ★★½ DVD: $14.99

Le Chêvre (The Goat)

(1981, 91 min, France, Francis Véber) *Gérard Depardieu, Pierre Richard.* Richard and Depardieu, the hilarious sleuthing duo of *Les Compares*, are reunited in this "prequel." Private-eye Depardieu reluctantly teams up with the bungling Richard as they travel to Mexico to find a missing woman. What follows is a series of misadventures of epic proportions. The stone-faced Depardieu is surprisingly delightful as the straight man to Richard's never-ending encounters with slamming doors, crashing planes and even lethal drinking straws in this comedy for all ages. (American remake: *Pure Luck*) (French with English subtitles) ★★★

Cheyenne Autumn

(1964, 158 min, US, John Ford) *Richard Widmark, Carroll Baker, Karl Malden, Edward G. Robinson, James Stewart, Sal Mineo.* Ford's last western is a sprawling account of the Cheyenne Nation's 1,500-mile journey from the arid Southwest to their northern homeland. Ford depicts multiple aspects of the story: the influence of land speculators in Washington, sensationalization by the press, the varying attitudes of Army personnel, and the overwhelming hardships of the Cheyenne. Fine performances throughout. Shot in 70mm, the visual impact of the landscapes is retained on the small screen. Note: The Dodge City sequence, with a very funny James Stewart, was cut after first release; it's restored on video. ★★★ VHS: $19.99

The Cheyenne Social Club

(1970, 103 min, US, Gene Kelly) *Henry Fonda, James Stewart, Shirley Jones.* Fonda and Stewart dusted off their spurs to team together in this appealing though formula western comedy with the two Hollywood legends playing aging cowpokes who hang their hats at a new home — Stewart's newly acquired bordello. Jones runs the place. ★★½ VHS: $14.99

Chicken Run

(2000, 84 min, GB, Nick Park & Peter Lord) *Voices of: Mel Gibson, Miranda Richardson, Julia Sawalha.* Masters of the claymation short Park and Lord (from Aardman studios, home of "Wallace & Gromit") find none of their whimsy diluted in their first full-length entry. The plot is an homage/take-off of prisoncamp movies, from *The Great Escape* to *Stalag 13*, that will literally fly over the heads of rapt youngsters who are just in it for the chickens. Ginger (voiced by Sawalha) is a headstrong hen on evil Mrs. Tweedy's farm, whose plots to escape become more urgent upon the arrival of an on-site chicken pie factory. Enter American flyboy rooster Rocky (Gibson), who can teach them to fly the coop (he hopes). A colorful cast of supporting fowl add to the humor, along with such Aardman trademarks as complicated machinery, veddy British creatures, and warm and expressive claymation. Richly detailed, *Chicken Run* is grand entertainment that invites repeat viewing for all ages. ★★★★ VHS: $22.99; DVD: $26.99

Un Chien Andalou/ Land without Bread

(1928/1932, 17/45 min, France/Spain, Luis Buñuel & Salvador Dali) Beginning with a pristine copy of *Un Chien Andalou*, this video of two of Buñuel's earliest film work also includes his documentary on the unbelievably impoverished Spanish region of Hurdanos. Told with English narration, this moving and sad account of these stoic people is an unusual departure for Buñuel, for he forsakes his trademark humor and surrealism and instead takes the job of a social realist as he photographs the parched, mountainous area and films the people in their medieval-like towns, virtually untouched by the wealth and conveniences offered in the 20th century. An unrelenting and somber portrait of a people and one that was immediately banned by the Franco government. VHS: $24.99

La Chienne

(1931, 100 min, France, Jean Renoir) *Michel Simon, Janie Mareze.* This somber, naturalistic melodrama, whose surprisingly modern theme of sexual obsession and violence created tremendous controversy when first released in France, did not receive its American premiere until 1976. Realistically filmed on the noisy streets of Montmartre, this story of uncontrolled passion is about an unhappily married clerk (Simon) who falls in love with a prostitute, steals for her, then, in a fit of rage, murders her and keeps quiet while her pimp goes to the guillotine. Unsentimental, this amoral story, whose film translation is *The Bitch*, was remade by Fritz Lang in *Scarlet Street* (1945). Reportedly, the film's producer vainly attempted to re-edit the film;

C

Children of the Revolution

Renoir regained control. (French with English subtitles) ★★★½ VHS: $59.99

A Child Is Waiting

(1962, 102 min, US, John Cassavetes) *Judy Garland, Burt Lancaster, Gena Rowlands.* Garland is splendid in this poignant tale of a sympathetic woman's relationship with a mentally retarded boy. *A Child Is Waiting* pulls no punches in portraying the inadequacy and frustration teachers feel in trying to reach the youngsters, and the guilt parents bear in surrendering their children to mental hospitals. Most touching of all, though, are the performances of the children; they are joyous and innocent, and truly in the heart of everyone they touch. ★★★ VHS: $19.99

Child's Play

(1988, 87 min, US, Tom Holland) *Catherine Hicks, Chris Sarandon, Alex Vincent, Brad Dourif.* Chucky is a popular talking doll, sweet as peaches and cream (and a complexion to match). That is, until one of the dolls is possessed by the spirit of a murderer; then little Chucky is spewing forth naughty words and hacking people to death. Unchallenging, silly and slickly-made, it does manage to produce a few chills. (Sequel: *Child's Play 2*) ★★½ VHS: $14.99; DVD: $19.99

Child's Play 2

(1990, 85 min, US, John Lafia) *Alex Vincent, Jenny Agutter, Gerrit Graham, Grace Zabriskie.* Chucky's back, and this time he's powered by an even more insidious force: capitalism! Chucky tries to take possession of young Andy's body, once again, lest he remain in the valley of the dolls forever. Enter Zabriskie as a child welfare worker who won't believe Andy's "boy who cried doll" stories. A bad *Fatal Attraction* for the pre-school set. (Sequel: *Bride of Chucky*) ★ VHS: $19.99; DVD: $24.99

The Children Are Watching Us
(I Bambini Ci Guardano)

(1942, 89 min, Italy, Vittorio De Sica) *Luciano de Ambrosis, Isa Pola.* One of De Sica's most heartrending films as well as an unusually critical look at Mussolini's Italy. The story focuses on the effects that a marital breakup and a suicide have on a lonely and unwanted four-year-old boy. A sad and touching story from the master of Italian neorealism. (Italian with English subtitles) ★★★½ VHS: $29.99

Children of a Lesser God

(1986, 119 min, US, Randa Haines) *Marlee Matlin, William Hurt, Piper Laurie, Philip Bosco.* Matlin won an Oscar for her immensely moving portrait of an embittered deaf woman reluctant to commit herself to a relationship. Hurt is equally as compelling as the idealist special education teacher who falls in love with her. ★★★ VHS: $14.99; DVD: $29.99

Children of Heaven

(1998, 88 min, Iran, Majid Majidi) *Mohammad Amir Naji, Mir Farrakh Hashemian, Bahareh Seddiqi.* A simple but outstanding film, *Children of Heaven* — like *The White Balloon* before it — shows life in a very foreign country through the eyes of a child. Ali (Hashemian) is a nine-year-old boy who loses his sister Zara's sneakers on the way home from the repair shop. Rather than incur their poor father's wrath, they agree to share Ali's shoes to get to and from school. This arrangement soon causes both children grief. The solution to their problem comes in the form of a race, which Ali enters, hoping to win the third place prize — a new pair of sneakers. A deserved Academy Award nominee for Best Foreign-Language Film, *Children of Heaven* features heartbreaking performances by the two children, and its poetic imagery — particularly a scene in which Ali soaks his feet in a fountain full of goldfish — make writer-director Majidi a talent to watch. (Farsi with English subtitles) ★★★★ VHS: $19.99

Children of Nature

(1991, 85 min, Iceland, Fridrik Thor Fridriksson) *Gisli Halldorsson, Sigridur Hagalin, Bruno Ganz.* Nominated for a Best Foreign Film Oscar, this lushly photographed and deliberately paced film follows the odyssey of a man nearing the end of his life. After an uncomfortable attempt at living with his daughter and her family, he enters a nursing home, where he meets a woman he knew in his youth. Her feisty exuber-ance complements his stoic strength; their shared desire for independence unites them in a journey of adventure and discovery. These two protagonists are portrayed with warmth and gentle vigor in a film peppered with telling moments of quiet revelation. A lyrical meditation on humankind's relationship with nature and society. (Icelandic with English subtitles) ★★★ VHS: $19.99

Children of Paradise
(Les Enfants du Paradis)

(1945, 189 min, France, Marcel Carné) *Jean-Louis Barrault, Arletty, Pierre Brasseur.* Considered by many to be one of the greatest films ever made, this intensely romantic melodrama wonderfully re-creates the teeming excitement of the early 1800s — both for the French theatre as well as Paris' *Boulevard du Crime.* In a complicated series of events, the film follows the interlocking fates of four central characters: Frederick (Brasseau), a haughty actor who communicates through words; Baptiste (Barrault), a sensitive pantomimist; Garance (Arletty), an elusive, glamorous woman of easy virtue who stands between them and the fourth character, a murderous thief. Using the theatre as a metaphor for life, the Jacques Prévert-scripted story is a richly entertaining, immense masterpiece of postwar cinema. (French with English subtitles) ★★★★ VHS: $39.99

Children of the Corn

(1984, 93 min, US, Fritz Kiersch) *Peter Horton, Linda Hamilton, R.G. Armstrong.* Silly Stephen King horror story about a young couple who arrive in a small Iowa town controlled by demonic children. (Followed by five atrocious sequels) ★ VHS: $9.99; DVD: $24.99

Children of the Revolution

(1997, 102 min, Australia, Peter Duncan) *Judy Davis, Geoffrey Rush, Sam Neill, F. Murray Abraham, Richard Roxburgh, Rachel Griffiths.* A boisterous political farce/satire that supposes what might become of Joseph Stalin's illegitimate son if he were raised by an ardent Communist mom in middle-class Australia. Davis is in top form as Joan Fraser, a vociferous 1950s era radical who writes love letters to "Uncle Joe." The aging and lonely Stalin (Abraham) catches wind of her ardor and invites her to the Kremlin for a bit of a dialectical frolic. The rest, as they say, is history. Davis returns to Oz pregnant, but is the child Stalin's or that of Australian double agent spy Neill? Needless to say, the fun is just getting started as the film follows little Joe through childhood to his adult years through a series of nicely strung together vignettes. Writer-director Duncan takes his narrative over the top with conviction and gusto, making *Children of the Revolution* a capricious and thoroughly agreeable romp through a mock history as seen through a fun house mirror. ★★★½ VHS: $19.99

Children Shouldn't Play with Dead Things

(1972, 85 min, US, Benjamin [Bob] Clark) *Alan Ormsby, Anya Ormsby, Jane Daly.* Cheapie horror film (from the director of *Porky's*, no less) about young film students making a movie in a graveyard and resurrecting the dead. Eeek. ★½ VHS: $14.99; DVD: $24.99

The Children's Hour

(1961, 107 min, US, William Wyler) *Shirley MacLaine, Audrey Hepburn, James Garner, Miriam Hopkins, Veronica Cartwright.* Wyler's compelling though stagey second treatment of Lillian Hellman's play (1936's *These Three* was the first) tells of the devastating effects of gossip and scandalous rumors about two women. Hepburn and MacLaine are teachers at an all-girls' boarding school. When a vindictive little girl accuses the two of having an affair, their lives (and their careers) are ruined after a self-righteous community believes the unsubstantiated allegations (shades of McCarthyism!). However, the rumor also forces MacLaine to come to terms with her closeted lesbian feelings. Attempting to right the wrong of his original film which was not allowed to discuss the theme of lesbianism, Wyler rather flimsily addresses it here. ★★½ VHS: $19.99

Chill Factor

(1999, 102 min, US, Hugh Johnson) *Cuba Gooding, Jr., Skeet Ulrich, Peter Firth, David Paymer, Kevin J.O'Connor.* Military scientist Paymer is developing a new chemical weapon which becomes colossally deadly when its temperature drops below 50 degrees. A major accident occurs (of course) and many soldiers are killed, but since Paymer is valuable to the military, the conscientious colonel of the mission is the fall guy. Ten years later he is released from prison, with revenge on his mind. It's up to ice-cream truck driver Gooding and night clerk Ulrich to put a stop to him. At times insultingly stupid, at times a *Speed* ripoff, *Chill Factor* is still sorta fun, in a *completely* mindless, cliffhanger serial way. The potential for Firth's character to be a morally conflicted bad guy (à la Ed Harris in *The Rock*) is scrapped early on to give us yet another cruel, colorless villain. And Gooding and Ulrich's banter becomes annoying after while. But while never dull, it's easily forgotten ten minutes after the credits roll. ★★ VHS: $14.99; DVD: $14.99

Chilly Scenes of Winter

(1982, 99 min, US, Joan Micklin Silver) *John Heard, Mary Beth Hurt, Peter Riegert, Kenneth McMillan, Griffin Dunne.* Silver's bittersweet comedy on the trials and triumphs of love. Heard portrays the quirky but amiable civil servant whose desperate passion confuses the reluctant object of his adoration (Hurt). A warm, beguiling film on the fragile bliss of romance. ★★★½ VHS: $19.99

China Girl

(1987, 88 min, US, Abel Ferrara) *James Russo, Sari Chang.* Absorbing, gritty update of "Romeo and Juliet" set in New York's Little Italy and Chinatown, with Italian Russo and Chinese Chang falling in love against a gangland backdrop. ★★★

China Moon

(1994, 99 min, US, John Bailey) *Ed Harris, Madeleine Stowe, Benicio Del Toro, Charles Dance.* Q: What do you get when you mix a rich husband, a beautiful wife and a tough guy who should know better? A: This umpteenth steamy, hard-boiled film noir *Body Heat* rip-off. Harris stars as a savvy police detective who becomes involved with rich banker's wife Stowe. When her husband (Dance) turns up dead, Harris must help her erase any clues to the crime. But is he being set up as patsy? *China Moon* has its moments, but this is mostly run of the mill material. ★★ VHS: $9.99

China, My Sorrow

(1989, 86 min, China, Dai Sijie) *Guo Yiang Yi, Tieu Quan Nghieu.* A wonderful story of imprisoned men in a mountain camp for noncompliant citizens under Chairman Mao. The story follows young "Four-eyes" as he is sent to the re-education center for playing music unsuitable to a young comrade (oddly enough, the song sounds much like the patriotic tune from *Yellow Earth*). "Four-eyes" and the other undesirables are put through grueling days of hard labor and dehumanizing treatment in hopes of turning them into "good workers." The story line is deeply spiritual and the photography rivals Zhang Yimou's works. (Mandarin and Shanghaiese with English subtitles) ★★★ VHS: $29.99

China Seas

(1935, 88 min, US, Tay Garnett) *Clark Gable, Jean Harlow, Rosalind Russell, Wallace Beery, Hattie McDaniel.* A good cast highlights this box-office hit with Gable as a steamship captain — transporting a secret cargo to China — who becomes romantically involved with passengers Harlow and Russell. ★★★ VHS: $19.99

The China Syndrome

(1979, 123 min, US, James Bridges) *Jane Fonda, Jack Lemmon, Michael Douglas, Wilford Brimley, Scott Brady, James Karen.* Though this nuclear thriller greatly benefitted from the timely publicity from the Three Mile Island accident, this outstanding drama would have succeeded without it. Fonda is excellent as a television reporter who inadvertently films an accident at a nuclear power plant, involving her in political intrigue. Lemmon gives a superlative portrayal of a loyal plant supervisor whose search for the truth leads to tragedy. Douglas is well-cast as Fonda's radical cameraman who helps in the investigation. A tension-filled examination of corporate cover-up which is both cautionary and unrelentingly suspenseful. Special mention goes to Brimley for his first-rate turn as Lemmon's longtime coworker. ★★★★ VHS: $9.99; DVD: $24.99

Chinatown

(1974, 131 min, US, Roman Polanski) *Jack Nicholson, Faye Dunaway, John Huston, Perry Lopez.* A superb, Oscar-winning script and consistently outstanding peformances are supported by meticulous production values to deliver a classic tale of intrigue, conflicted loyalties, overwhelming greed and the futility of honor in a corrupt world. Nicholson plays Jake Gittes, a Los Angeles private eye called into what at first appears to be a simple case of marital infidelity. Dunaway arrives at his offices to declare that she is the real wife of the man Gittes has been paid to follow, and she has no desire to see her husband tailed. Gittes, with more curiosity than forethought, delves even deeper into the mystery; the governmental malfeasance he uncovers is child's play compared to the murky family secrets lying even deeper below. Especially arresting is Huston's portrayal of Dunaway's father, a man who accepts no limits to his power and position, whether in business or in his homelife. A contemporary American film classic featuring one of Nicholson's best performances. (Sequel: The

Two Jakes) (VHS available letterboxed or pan & scan) ★★★★ VHS: $14.99; DVD: $24.99

Chinese Boxes

(1984, 87 min, GB, Chris Petit) *Will Patton, Robbie Coltrane.* An unusual though compelling thriller about an American tourist (Patton) caught up in international intrigue in West Berlin after the death of a drug pusher. ★★½ VHS: $69.99

A Chinese Ghost Story

(1987, 95 min, Hong Kong, Siu-Tung Ching) *Leslie Cheung, Joey Wong, Ma Wu, Dawei Hu, Jin Liang.* Moving from his commercially successful martial arts flicks, director Ching has gone the way of *Ghost* with this entertaining and atmospheric supernatural love story with surprisingly impressive special effects. Set during the Ming Dynasty, the story features a wandering scholar who, while visiting a haunted temple, meets and falls in love with a glamorous female ghost. But their love is never tranquil as he soon finds that he must do battle with a horde of hellish creatures to come out and end their relationship. (Cantonese with English subtitles) ★★★ VHS: $19.99; DVD: $49.99

Chinese Roulette

(1976, 86 min, West Germany, Rainer Werner Fassbinder) *Margit Carstensen, Ulli Lommel, Anna Karina, Brigitte Mira, Andrea Schober, Volker Spengler.* Set during a weekend retreat in a castle, this elegant Gothic thriller follows the consequences when a crippled girl (Schober) organizes a bizarre and fiendish truth game in order to psychologically attack her philandering parents and their respective lovers. With sweeping camera movement, lush scenery and music, this cruelly humorous melodrama is pure Fassbinder. (German with English subtitles) ★★★

Chitty Chitty Bang Bang

(1968, 143 min, US, Ken Hughes) *Dick Van Dyke, Sally Ann Howes, Lionel Jeffries.* Dyke stars as a slightly crackpot scientist who turns an old racing car into a magical flying machine. Unmemorable songs dampen the amiable spirits of this otherwise genial children's musical, which should entertain those in the pre-teen years. ★★½ VHS: $14.99; DVD: $19.99

Chloë in the Afternoon

(1972, 97 min, France, Eric Rohmer) *Bernard Verley, Zou Zou, Francoise Verley, Marie-Christine Barrault.* Rohmer's final entry in his series of

Jack Nicholson in *Chinatown*

C

"Moral Tales" continues with the theme of temptation met and mastered in this fascinating story of a happily married suburban man who struggles to stay faithful after he meets an unstable woman out of his past. Although constantly harboring lecherous tendencies, our chaste Don Juan must decide between fidelity and the rueful charms of Chloë, a young, attractive free spirit intent on seducing him. An elegant comedy of sexual mores. (French with English subtitles) ★★★★ VHS: $19.99; DVD: $29.99

Chocolat

(1988, 105 min, France, Claire Denis) *Mireille Perrier, Emmet Judson*. This surprisingly assured and quietly emotional film is a most impressive debut for director Denis. The story centers around a young white woman who returns to Cameroon, recalling her life there as a child of the French colonial governor. Her reminiscences — that of a young girl isolated in an exotic but foreign land — evoke the repression of the people, but focus primarily on the special relationship she had with the family's black houseboy. (French with English subtitles) ★★★ VHS: $19.99; DVD: $19.99

Chocolat

(2000, 121 min, GB, Lasse Hallström) *Juliette Binoche, Johnny Depp, Judi Dench, Alfred Molina, Lena Olin, Victoire Thivisol, Carrie-Anne Moss, Peter Stormare, Hugh O'Conor, Leslie Caron, John Wood*. A sweet confection whose ingredients of romantic lyricism and magical culinary delights provide a tasty complement to a trifling story of social oppression, *Chocolat* is a lightweight fable that charms through sheer determination. The alluring Binoche is Vianne, a single mother and chef who arrives at a small French village with her young daughter. Opening a chocolate shop featuring a selection of mouth-watering creations, Vianne soon becomes embroiled in the town's political bureaucracy when she stands up to the petty-minded mayor (Molina) who wants the free-spirited entrepreneur run out of town. Binoche is captivating as the winsome Vianne, who slowly wins over many of the townspeople. These include Dench as a curmudgeon who finds her heart, Olin as an abused wife who finds the strength to leave her husband, and Depp as a handsome gypsy who finds Vianne irresistible. Like the delicious concoctions that Vianne prepares, *Chocolat* is sure to please — just don't expect anything too filling. ★★★ VHS: $102.99; DVD: $29.99

The Chocolate War

(1988, 106 min, US, Keith Gordon) *Ilan Mitchell-Smith, John Glover, Bud Cort, Adam Baldwin*. First-time director Gordon has fashioned a somber but thoughtful version of the "high school hell" film. Set in an oppressive Catholic school, young Jerry (Mitchell-Smith) refuses to conform with his classmates by declining to participate in the school's annual fund-raising effort — the chocolate bar sale. In response, the entire student body bombards him with both physical and emotional retribution. At first glance, *The Chocolate War* appears to be a simple us-against-them film, but on a deeper level, it is a scathing comment on fascism and authoritarian rule. ★★★

Choice of Arms

(1983, 117 min, France, Alain Corneau) *Gérard Depardieu, Yves Montand, Catherine Deneuve*.

Reminiscent of the best works of Claude Chabrol and Jean-Pierre Melville, this classy gangster film adroitly explores the complex and often-times violent relationship between a reformed underworld chieftain (Montand) and his recently paroled crony: a wonderfully bestial and explosive Depardieu. A taut, psychologically charged thriller. (French with English subtitles) ★★★½

The Choirboys

(1977, 120 min, US, Robert Aldrich) *James Woods, Charles Durning, Louis Gossett, Jr., Burt Young, Randy Quaid, Don Stroud, Blair Brown, Charles Haid*. An awful screen adaptation of Joseph Wambaugh's novel, this low-brow, homophobic, rambling piece of trash follows the supposedly comic exploits of a group of L.A. cops who violate civil rights and generally act like a bunch of morons to help alleviate the pressures of the job. Arguably the worst mainstream film of the 1970s. ★

Choose Me

(1984, 114 min, US, Alan Rudolph) *Keith Carradine, Genevieve Bujold, Lesley Ann Warren, Rae Dawn Chong*. Rudolph looks at the mate-swapping, bed-hopping antics of L.A. singles looking for love under all the wrong sheets. Carradine is the sinuous Lothario pursuing various women with amorous abandon. ★★★½ VHS: $14.99

A Chorus Line

(1985, 113 min, US, Richard Attenborough) *Michael Douglas, Terrence Mann, Alyson Reed, Audrey Landers*. Those who did not see the Broadway production of this Pulitzer Prize- and Tony Award-winning musical may appreciate Attenborough's lifeless adaptation. All others will long for the class of the original. The story, of course, is about a group of dancers auditioning for the chorus of a Broadway musical. The show's famous song, "What I Did for Love" (the song, a dancer's anthem, has been changed from "What if I couldn't dance anymore" to a whiny lovers' lament), is thrown away by Attenborough's over-the-shoulder, off-handed nonchalance; and the classic finale "One" is considerably less show-stopping. ★★ VHS: $14.99

A Chorus of Disapproval

(1989, 92 min, GB, Michael Winner) *Jeremy Irons, Anthony Hopkins, Prunella Scales, Jenny Seagrove*. Alan Ayckbourn's award-winning play about the comic transformation of a timid widower into a heart-breaking Lothario is brought to the screen in this humorous, engaging and finely acted farce. Irons plays Guy Jones, a reserved and recently widowed young man who moves into a new town in northern England and, in an effort to "have fun and meet friends," joins the local amateur acting company's production of "The Beggar's Opera." The heads (and pelvises) of the ladies in the troupe are all turned on young Guy as he sheds his shyness and becomes entangled in a few love affairs. Hopkins is wonderful as the play's blustering and tempestuous director. ★★★ VHS: $19.99

The Chosen

(1981, 108 min, US, Jeremy Paul Kagan) *Robby Benson, Barry Miller, Rod Steiger, Maximilian Schell*. An extraordinarily tender and moving screen version of Chaim Potok's novel about the friendship and conflicting loyalties of two Jewish teenagers: Hasidic Benson and liberalized Miller. The film is a loving re-creation of 1940s Brooklyn, and features a stellar cast. ★★★½

Les Choses de la Vie
(The Things of Life)

(1969, 90 min, France, Claude Sautet) *Michel Picoli, Romy Schneider, Lea Massari*. This appealing romantic comedy centers on an architect who, after suffering a near fatal auto accident, takes the time to reflect on his life and loves. The always capable, ubiquitous Picoli stars as a sensitive man torn between his love for his estranged wife (Massari) and his mistress (Schneider). A nicely observed tragi-comedy that builds to a moving examination of the fragility of life and relationships. (American remake: *Intersection*) (French with English subtitles) ★★★ VHS: $29.99

Christ Stopped at Eboli

(1979, 118 min, Italy, Francesco Rosi) *Irene Papas, Gian Maria Volonte*. Rosi's award-winning adaptation of Carlo Levi's classic is a rich, reso-

Juliette Binoche radiates in *Chocolat*

nant film about a writer/artist and political exile, who is banned to a village in southern Italy by Mussolini in 1935. The exile's experiences in this world of poverty and quiet despair open his eyes to the unshakable values of the resolute villagers. A film full of faith in human values, stunningly directed. (Italian with English subtitles) ★★★½ VHS: $59.99

Christabel

(1989, 149 min, GB, Adrian Shergold) *Elizabeth Hurley, Stephen Dillon.* This outstanding BBC production tells the true-life story of Christabel Bielenberg, an aristocratic English woman who marries a German lawyer and finds herself plunged into the nightmare of Nazi Germany. Having joined the Resistance, her husband is arrested and sent to the notorious Ravensbruck concentration camp. Based on her autobiography, the film follows Bielenberg as she travels across war-ravaged Germany and takes on the Nazi beauracracy and the Gestapo in an effort to free her husband. Written by Dennis Potter. ★★★½ VHS: $19.99

Christiane F.

(1981, 124 min, Germany, Ulrich Edel) *Natja Brunhurst, Thomas Haustein, David Bowie.* The spine-tingling account of a young German girl lost in the dark abyss of drug dependency and prostitution. Based on a true story, the film has a striking authenticity acquired through the use of actual locales (Berlin's seamiest junkie havens) and a pallid-complexioned cast. Bowie provides the soundtrack music. ★★★

Christine

(1983, 111 min, US, John Carpenter) *Keith Gordon, Robert Prosky, Harry Dean Stanton, John Stockwell.* Horror mavens Carpenter and Stephen King joined forces for this stylish though basic adaptation of King's novel with Gordon making the most of a shy teenager who is under the spell of a demonic '58 Plymouth. ★★ VHS: $9.99; DVD: $19.99

A Christmas Carol

(1951, 86 min, GB, Brian Desmond Hurst) *Alastair Sim, Kathleen Harrison, Michael Hordern, Patrick Macnee.* A wonderful, heartwarming rendition of Charles Dickens' classic tale, featuring a terrific performance by the delightful Sim as Scrooge. A hardy perennial that has become a well-loved part of the Christmas experience. ★★★★ VHS: $14.99; DVD: $19.99

Christmas in Connecticut

(1945, 101 min, US, Peter Godfrey) *Barbara Stanwyck, Dennis Morgan, Sydney Greenstreet, S.Z. Sakall, Reginald Gardiner, Una O'Connor.* A breezy if lightweight comedy of mistaken identity. Stanwyck plays a successful writer for a women's magazine who's been faking her housekeeping abilities. When a war hero (Morgan) is to stay on "her" farm for the weekend, Stanwyck is forced to impersonate the woman her readers think she is. Of course, love blossoms between Stanwyck and Morgan, even though he thinks she is really married (an unusual comedic swipe at adultery for the '40s). Stanwyck's funny and effortlessly charming, Morgan doesn't make much of a presence, though Greenstreet and the delightful Sakall supply good support. The laughs aren't consistent but it's fun nonetheless. ★★½ VHS: $14.99

Christmas in July

(1940, 67 min, US, Preston Sturges) *Dick Powell, Ellen Drew, William Demarest.* A practical joke escalates into a frenzy of consumerism and wish-fulfillment in this whimsical Sturges look at the American Dream. Powell thinks he's won $25,000 in a slogan contest; but does money really buy happiness? Or, as the boss said to Jimmy, "Now that you're a capitalist, I don't know how you feel about working for a living..." ★★★½ VHS: $9.99

A Christmas Story

(1983, 98 min, US, Bob Clark) *Darren McGavin, Melinda Dillon, Peter Billingsley.* An absolutely charming adaptation of Jean Shepherd's short story. A delight for both children and adults, this endearing reminiscence of the holiday season circa 1940 captures the everyday life of the era, as young Billingsley hopes (anguishes is more accurate) for a Red Ryder BB gun. McGavin and Dillon are simply wonderful as his somewhat unconventional parents. A perennial. ★★★½ VHS: $14.99; DVD: $19.99

Christopher Columbus: The Discovery

(1992, 121 min, US, John Glen) *Marlon Brando, Tom Selleck, Rachel Ward, George Corraface, Nigel Terry.* From the production team that brought us *Superman* (Alexander and Ilya Salkind) comes this equally mythological depiction of the seafaring Genoan of American folklore, Cristóbal Colón. Brimming with lots of overblown production values, the film sets sail into the murky waters of historical narrative with its compass askew and its rigging tangled. Despite these failings, however, the film will still be satisfying viewing to lovers of melodramatic adventure on the high seas. Corraface performs ably in the title role, making the best of a bad script. ★★

Christopher Strong

(1933, 77 min, US, Dorothy Arzner) *Katharine Hepburn, Colin Clive, Billie Burke.* One of the few female directors of her time, Arzner brings an enchanting perspective to this capable romantic drama with Hepburn in her element as an aviatrix in romantic and professional conflict. Clive is one of the reasons for both. ★★★

Chuck & Buck

(2000, 99 min, US, Miguel Arteta) *Mike White, Chris Weitz, Lupe Ontiveros, Beth Colt, Paul Weitz, Paul Sand.* At times weird, at times disturbing, but ultimately and unexpectedly poignant, the highly original and sometimes creepy *Chuck & Buck* plays like a gay *Fatal Attraction* as interpreted by Forrest Gump. In a story both lean and complex, screenwriter White has given himself quite a part. Buck is an emotionally stunted 27-year-old man who is fixated on his childhood friend (and possible lover) Chuck. Buck sucks lollypops and has childish taste in fashions, including a penchant for Members Only jackets. When Buck's mother dies, he travels to Los Angeles in an attempt to reestablish a relationship with Chuck. In between finding work with a downtown theatre group, Buck begins stalking his former friend who no longer wants anything to do with him. Told with a delightfully twisted sense of humor and an even stranger perspective, *Chuck & Buck* will never win awards from gay activist groups. However, for a sardonic look

at obsessive love and emotional instability, director Arteta's no-he-didn't-say-that comedy is hard to beat. ★★★½ VHS: $14.99; DVD: $24.99

Chuck Jones Extremes & Inbetweens: A Life in Animation

(2000, 85 min, US, Margaret Selby) *Chuck Jones; Celebrity appearances by: Whoopi Goldberg, Matt Groening, Ron Howard, John Lasseter, Leonard Maltin, Steven Spielberg, Robin Williams.* A joyous celebration of the life of animator Chuck Jones, the creative genius behind Bugs Bunny, Porky Pig, Daffy Duck and all their friends from the Warner Brothers lot. Includes interviews with celebrity fans (Spielberg accurately calls Jones' 1955 *One Froggy Evening* "the *Citizen Kane* of animated shorts"), as well as insight from Jones himself. And, of course, numerous clips from his great cartoons. ★★★½ VHS: $19.99

C.H.U.D.

(1984, 88 min, US, Douglas Cheek) *John Heard, Daniel Stern, Kim Greist, John Goodman, Jay Thomas, Patricia Richardson.* If you're a fan of spoofy-played-for-straight horror films, then this *C.H.U.D.*'s for you. All others, however, may not enjoy this tale of street people becoming Cannibalistic Humanoid Underground Dwellers when they become exposed to radioactive gunk and begin a murderous rampage. (Sequel: *C.H.U.D. II: Bud the Chud*) ★★ VHS: $9.99; DVD: $24.99

C.H.U.D. II: Bud the Chud

(1989, 84 min, US, David Irving) *Brian Robbins, Gerrit Graham, Robert Vaughn, Bianca Jagger, June Lockhart.* The Cannibalistic Humanoid Underground Dwellers are back with less intelligence, less chills, less wit...you get the picture. ★

Chungking Express

(1994, 103 min, Hong Kong, Wong Kar-Wai) *Brigitte Lin, Takeshi Kaneshiro, Tony Leung, Faye Wong.* The stories of two Hong Kong police officers who are dumped by their girlfriends are interwoven in this brilliant, engrossing, yet low-budget pastiche. Made while working in postproduction on his angst-ridden swordsman movie *Ashes of Time*, *Chungking*'s swift genesis and execution shows. It is vibrant, immediate and exudes a truthfulness and poignancy which can be attributed to its lack of rewrites and production tinkering. Slow motion, jump cuts, pixellated movement and the recurrent use of a handful of pop tunes all combine to make the film very different from its Hong Kong brethren, yet it is set firmly within that diverse genre. There is also at least a kernel of truth for most people in this film about romantic relationships and how we adapt to their beginnings as well as their ends. (Cantonese with English subtitles) ★★★★ VHS: $79.99

The Church

(1990, 110 min, US/Italy, Michele Soavi) *Tomas Arana, Hugh Quarshine.* Dario Argento produced this so-so chiller about a group of people trapped in a church built on top of a satanic burial ground. Director Soavi delivers all the style of the master, but few of the shocks. This is the unrated version. ★★ VHS: $79.99

Ciao! Federico!

(1970, 62 min, US, Gideon Bachmann) This absorbing look at the great Italian filmmaker Federico Fellini was recorded during the making of *Fellini's Satyricon*. Includes interviews with the director and scenes from the classic film. (Italian with English subtitles) ★★★ VHS: $19.99

Ciao! Manhattan

(1965-1971, 84 min, US, John Palmer & David Weisman) This kaleidoscopic journey through the life of Warhol superstar Edie Sedgwick is both a searing psychodrama of burn-out syndrome and a dynamic potpourri of sixties cultural paraphernalia. From Edie's rise to the throne of the pop underground to her tragic plummet into drug abuse and mental illness, *Ciao!* manages to be comical, perplexing and poignant. Filming began in 1965, capturing the orgiastic frenzy of the Warhol Factory's heyday. Work resumed years later with a crumbling Edie living at the bottom of a swimming pool on the West Coast. Only months after the completion of filming, Edie died of a barbiturate overdose. She was 28 years old. ★★★½

Ciao, Professore!

(1994, 99 min, Italy, Lina Wertmüller) *Paolo Villaggio, Isa Dabieli.* A flip soundbite for this breezy comedy-drama would be to call it a pubescent spaghetti *To Sir with Love.* A portly middle-aged teacher (Villaggio) from northern Italy is accidentally sent to a poverty-stricken seaside town near Naples. What he finds when he arrives is a beleaguered school and a class full of truant third graders. His formidable task is to round up the group of streetwise kids, gain their trust and begin to teach them. Wertmüller overcomes the hackneyed and predictable plot through the inspired casting of the children — all of them tough but cute mini-adults, each with a personality that would soften the most curmudgeonly heart. A decidedly different but quite enjoyable film. (Italian with English subtitles) ★★★

The Cider House Rules

(1999, 131 min, US, Lasse Hallström) *Tobey Maguire, Charlize Theron, Michael Caine, Delroy Lindo, Paul Rudd, Jane Alexander, Kathy Baker, Erykah Badu, Kieran Culkin, Heavy D.* Heartwarming and inspiring aren't exactly the first two sentiments you'd expect from a filmization of a John Irving novel, but that's precisely what you do get with this moving, beautifully acted adaptation of the author's best-seller. A marvelously understated Maguire is Homer, a serious young man who has spent his entire life in an orphanage in rural Maine. The orphanage is run by the kindly Dr. Larch (Caine in his poetic Oscar-winning performance), who looks upon each orphan as his charge, and who anoints them each night with his majestic blessing, "Good night you princes of Maine, you kings of New England." Dr. Larch has prepared Homer to take over as caregiver for the orphans, even though Homer isn't schooled in medicine. However, when Homer meets a stranded couple, it prompts him to leave his life-long home and head out into an unchartered country awash in turmoil from poverty, racism and the second world war. Irving has adapted his own novel, which may explain why the characters resonate with such emotional clarity. Director Hallström's exquisite pacing and superior evocation of wartime America certainly add to the film's overall sense of accomplishment, but it is those trenchant characters, and the great ensemble who brings them to life, which elevates *The Cider*

House Rules to near-classic status. ★★★½ VHS: $14.99; DVD: $32.99

The Cigarette Girl of Mosselprom

(1924, 78 min, USSR, Yuri Zhelyabuzhsky) A delightful and boisterous comedy satirizing Soviet life and filmmaking in the 1920s. The story follows the exploits of a young woman who is tossed from street vending into the movies when she is cast in a romantic melodrama. (Silent with orchestral accompaniment) ★★★ VHS: $29.99

Cimarron

(1931, 124 min, US, Wesley Ruggles) *Irene Dunne, Richard Dix.* The first western to win an Oscar for Best Picture is a severely dated and rather lumbering period piece based on an Edna Ferber story about American pioneers in the Old West. Dix gives the kind of performance which is subject to parody, though Dunne's solid portrait certainly elevates the production. (Remade in 1960) ★★ VHS: $19.99

Cinderella

(1950, 74 min, US, Wildred Jackson) Walt Disney's classic animated feature is a remarkable achievement, and one of his best loved. The story, of course, follows "poor Cinderella" from abused stepsister to belle of the ball. It is the combination of the superb animation, the enchanting songs and a wonderful gallery of characters which makes *Cinderella* a timeless masterpiece. ★★★★

Cinderella

(1964, 77 min, US, Charles S. Dubin) *Lesley Ann Warren, Ginger Rogers, Walter Pidgeon, Stuart Damon, Celeste Holm.* Rodgers and Hammerstein wrote the score for this enchanting musical based on the fairy tale classic, and it's ideal for younger viewers. Warren sweetly plays the title character. ★★★

Cinderella Liberty

(1973, 117 min, US, Mark Rydell) *James Caan, Marsha Mason, Eli Wallach, Kirk Calloway.* Two strong performances from Caan and Oscar-nominee Mason highlight this touching drama about a sailor who becomes involved with a prostitute and her illegitimate black son. Caan has never been better, here playing the good-natured seaman who falls for the hard-bitten Mason. The film effectively combines the gritty realism of the surroundings and the classic elements of the star-crossed romantic melodrama. ★★★ VHS: $29.99

Cinema Paradiso

(1990, 123 min, Italy, Giuseppe Tornatore) *Philippe Noiret, Salvatore Cascio.* A wonderfully endearing and emotionally satisfying story of remembrance and love. The story is about the developing relationship and love between a precocious fatherless boy of eight, Toto (engagingly played by Cascio), and a crusty old projectionist, Alfredo (a perfectly cast Noiret). Set mostly in a movie theater in a dusty Sicilian town after WWII, these two characters, seemingly so different, are drawn together and soon develop an unusual attachment. The movie is told in a series of flashbacks when Toto, now a successful film director in Rome, prepares to return to his boyhood village for the funeral of Alfredo. His loving memories of early childhood and adolescence provide the emotional core. For all but the most jaded,

Cinema Paradiso will prove to be a rare, tender and unforgettable film. (Italian with English subtitles) ★★★★ VHS: $14.99; DVD: $19.99

Circle of Friends

(1995, 114 min, Ireland, Pat O'Connor) *Chris O'Donnell, Minnie Driver, Colin Firth, Geraldine O'Rawe.* Director O'Connor is in a sweetly romantic mood and creates a picturesque atmosphere for an improbable love story with this beguiling adaptation of Maeve Binchy's novel. Benny (Driver) could probably be called the "ugly duckling" among her group of childhood friends, and growing up in a small Irish town in the late 1950s hasn't exactly given her the opportunity for romantic or social encounters. But that's all about to change when Benny enters university and falls under the spell of the soccer team's handsome star player (O'Donnell). While "plain Jane" Cinderellas have found their Prince Charmings before, this one's done with a refreshing voice and a very grounded view of the world. Driver is wonderful as Benny, imbuing her character with sensibility and spirit. ★★★½ VHS: $9.99; DVD: $14.99

Circle of Iron

(1979, 102 min, US, Richard Moore) *David Carradine, Jeff Cooper, Roddy McDowall, Eli Wallach, Bruce Lee.* Offbeat martial arts adventure (filmed in Israel and started by Bruce Lee before his death) about a young karate master in search of spiritual perfection and a sacred book of knowledge. ★★½

Circle of Passion

(1996, 94 min, GB/France, Charles Finch) *Sandrine Bonnaire, Jane March, Charles Finch, Jean Rochefort, James Fox.* This sappy love story overcomes a wretched opening titles montage to become a palatable if slightly cheesy romance. A British banker, working in his father-in-law's Paris branch, puts his job, reputation and loveless marriage on the line when he has a torrid affair with a French beauty (the luminous Bonnaire). Will he do the responsible thing, or follow his bliss? Swank Parisian locations and decent performances go a long way toward making this non-vanity production watchable. This is classy trash, though — beautiful faces and scenery can't completely disguise the cliché-ridden story and overbaked dialogue. (aka: *Never Ever*) ★★½ VHS: $79.99

Circuitry Man

(1989, 85 min, US, Steven Loy) *Vernon Wells, Dana Wheeler-Nicholson.* Cheap sci-fi actioner about a post-apocalyptic age where the Earth's oxygen has been depleted, everybody lives underground, and the last remaining frontier is the human mind. ★½ VHS: $19.99

The Circus

(1928, 71 min, US, Charles Chaplin) *Charlie Chaplin, Merna Kennedy, Allan Garcia, Henry Bergman.* The Circus has the Little Tramp as a member of the greatest show on Earth. This rarely seen gem features fantastic sight gags and lots of Chaplin's trademark physical humor. ★★★★ DVD: $29.99

The Cisco Kid

(1993, 95 min, US, Luis Valdez) *Jimmy Smits, Cheech Marin.* Mildly entertaining action-comedy which tells the story of the famous south of the border bandit with about as much accuracy as a counterfeit Rolex. The suave Smits stars as the Cisco Kid, who teams up with Pancho (Marin) as he tries to save Mexico from corrupt politicians and nefarious Frenchmen. Spiced with many stunts and ill-placed jokes for lack of a real story. ★★ VHS: $14.99

The Citadel

(1938, 112 min, US/GB, King Vidor) *Robert Donat, Rosalind Russell, Ralph Richardson, Rex Harrison.* An extraordinary retelling of A.J. Cronin's novel featuring superior performances by Donat and Russell. Donat is an idealistic and hard-working London doctor whose flirtation with the rich (and an easier case load) leads him to ignore his principles and his wife (Russell). Richardson is terrific in support as an old family friend. ★★★★ VHS: $24.99

Citizen Cohn

(1992, 112 min, US, Frank Pierson) *James Woods, Joe Don Baker, Ed Flanders, Frederic Forrest, Joe Bologna, Lee Grant.* Based on the novel by Nicholas von Hoffman, this engrossing biographical and political drama on the life of Roy Cohn — Communist headhunter, ruthless lawyer and closeted homosexual who died of AIDS in 1986 — is great explosive fun. Using his trademark hyper-energy coupled with his on-edge, often grating on-screen personality to unforgettable use, a seemingly possessed Woods stars as the charismatic, but at times demonic Cohn. Made for HBO, the film is structured in a series of flashbacks, as the now disbarred Cohn lies semi-conscious in a hospital bed, dying of AIDS and hallucinating on many of the contentious incidents from his life. Pulling no punches, the story includes Cohn's early triumphs as the prosecutor at the Rosenbergs' trial, and his work as henchman/conciliator to Joe McCarthy during the Communist witch-hunts. ★★★½ VHS: $9.99; DVD: $19.99

Citizen Kane

Citizen Kane

(1941, 119 min, US, Orson Welles) *Orson Welles, Joseph Cotten, Everett Sloane, Agnes Moorehead.* This masterful union of form and content stretched the boundaries of cinema with its ingeniously crafted narrative and stunning shot construction. The tale of Charles Foster Kane contains all the vital elements of epic tragedy: greed, jealousy, scandal and failure. A devastating critique of the American Dream and an unmatched singular tour de force by producer, director, star and coauthor Welles. ★★★★ VHS: $19.99

Citizen Ruth

(1996, 104 min, US, Alexander Payne) *Laura Dern, Swoosie Kurtz, Mary Kay Place, Kelly Preston, Burt Reynolds, Tippi Hedren, Diane Ladd.* A scathingly funny satire that dares to take on the super-charged issue of abortion. Dern is Ruth Stoops, a hard-core skid-row regular. Pregnant and hauled before a local magistrate, she's ordered by the court to have an abortion. Just like that she finds herself at the center of a mushrooming controversy. The first to "adopt" her are local pro-lifers Place and Smith, who attempt to make a good Christian of her. Eventually, the other side catches wind and she's stolen away by a couple of radical lesbians (Kurtz and Preston). With both sides wanting to make her their respective "abortion poster child," Ruth smells opportunity. Though writer-director Payne seems to express a mildly pro-choice point of view, he leaves no one unscathed as he lampoons both sides for their unyielding zealotry with hilarious results. ★★★½

Citizen X

(1995, 103 min, US, Chris Gerolmo) *Stephen Rea, Donald Sutherland, Max von Sydow, Joss Ackland.* Made for HBO, *Citizen X* is a tense, carefully detailed thriller about Russia's most horrific serial killer and the years-long search for him. Rea is a forensics expert and amateur detective who, upon the discovery of several bodies in a secluded wooded area, is assigned to head the investigation to track the killer. His task is made all the more difficult by an uncooperative Russian bureaucracy and antiquated investigatory procedures. Sutherland is well-cast as Rea's superior who may or may not be on his side. Adult in nature, the story doesn't flinch from the realities of its subject, and writer-director Gerolmo casts an eerie, ominous spell. ★★★½ VHS: $9.99; DVD: $14.99

Citizen's Band

(1977, 98 min, US, Jonathan Demme) *Paul Le Mat, Candy Clark, Ann Wedgeworth, Marcia Rodd.* A delightful slice of Americana, this satire on the CB craze interweaves several stories revolving around an odd and lovable assortment of characters, all obsessed with their short wave radios. A quirky original from director Demme. (aka: *Handle with Care.*) ★★★½ VHS: $59.99

The City (La Ciudad)

(1999, 88 min, US, Davd Riker) Filming in gritty black and white over a five-year period (1992-1997), director Riker used immigrant workers in New York City to shoot a series of vignettes, creating a timeless metaphor on survival and the quest for opportunity and a better life. With images as earthy as Eisenstein in Mexico, several short stories link together to reveal the reality of the underclass; day laborers scrambling for work

or crammed into sweltering factories for hours of tedious, low-paying piece work. One man, living in a car with his daughter, cannot enroll her in school because he can't prove residency. Another, a fresh arrival to the city, cannot find his way back to a new-found friend in a maze of high-rise buildings. Riker tells his stories of the displaced trying to find roots in an alien environment with a documentary directness and a neo-realist compassion. (English and Spanish with English subtitles) ★★★½ VHS: $89.99

City Hall

(1996, 110 min, US, Harold Becker) *Al Pacino, John Cusack, Bridget Fonda, Danny Aiello, David Paymer, Martin Landau, Anthony Franciosa.* The story of a small-town boy's adventures in the big city gets another telling in this occasionally gritty political drama. Cusack plays the Deputy Mayor of New York City, an idealistic, loyal foot soldier to Pacino's gregarious and often charming mayor. When a young child is killed during a gangland/police shootout, the administration gets into high gear investigating the murder and playing damage control. As Cusack digs deeper, he discovers a trail of cover-ups and widespread corruption — but how high does it go? Cusack ably conveys the turmoil of a naive politico suddenly learning how to play hard ball. Pacino is able to carve emotion from a rather one-dimensional character, and he's given to less theatrical outbursts. *City Hall* presents an intriguing view of a machine at work; it's just so indifferent about it all it's hard to get really excited. ★★½ VHS: $9.99; DVD: $14.99

City Heat

(1984, 98 min, US, Richard Benjamin) *Clint Eastwood, Burt Reynolds, Jane Alexander, Madeline Kahn, Irene Cara, Richard Roundtree, Rip Torn.* A good cast is, sadly, not enough to elevate the enjoyment level of this disappointing '30s-style gangster take-off. ★★ VHS: $14.99

City Lights

(1931, 90 min, US, Charles Chaplin) *Charles Chaplin, Virginia Cherrill, Harry Myers, Hank Mann.* Chaplin's final silent film is one of the screen's true masterworks. Charlie plays the Little Tramp, who falls in love with a blind flower girl and vows to obtain the money needed for an operation to restore her sight. Filled with great humor and overwhelming emotional poignancy. ★★★★ VHS: $14.99; DVD: $29.99

City Limits

(1985, 85 min, US, Aaron Lipstadt) *Rae Dawn Chong, Kim Cattrall, Robby Benson, James Earl Jones.* It's another post-apocalyptic thriller with gangs of youths roving barren cities on motorcycles. This second feature from the team which produced *Android*, while not as successful as its earlier effort, still manages to rise slightly above its overworked premise. ★★ VHS: $79.99

City Lovers/Country Lovers

(1982, 105 min, South Africa, Barney Simon, Mamie van Rensberg) Two works by South African dramatist Nadine Gordimer. In *City Lovers,* a middle-aged white geologist begins an affair with a black cashier; in the latter story, the son of a wealthy white farmer and the daughter of a black farmhand, who have grown up together, are secret lovers. The unifying theme in both of Gordimer's works is that the lovers must suffer the consequences of their relationships from the strict, oppressive South African government. ★★★ VHS: $69.99

City of Angels

(1998, 114 min, US, Brad Silberling) *Nicolas Cage, Meg Ryan, Dennis Franz, Andre Braugher, Colm Feore.* In remaking Wim Wenders' *Wings of Desire,* director Silberling had a difficult choice to make: keep the flavor of the original or totally Americanize it for the romantic crowd. The end result of his *City of Angels* is a little of both, which is why the film is successful and unsatisfying at the same time. The morose Cage plays Seth, an angel who is one of many in Los Angeles who look after and hear the thoughts of the mortals around them. When Seth crosses paths with Dr. Maggie Rice (Ryan), a determined, attractive surgeon, he begins to fall in love and question his role as an angel. The film's first half manages to capture the pacing, style, and even the melonchaly of *Wings,* albeit the L.A. sun gives the city a rosier look. The second, and more conventional, half is strictly a by-the-books Hollywood romance haunted by the predictability and essence of other melodramas. (VHS available letterboxed or pan & scan) ★★½ VHS: $19.99; DVD: $19.99

City of Hope

(1991, 129 min, US, John Sayles) *Vincent Spano, Tony Lo Bianco, Joe Morton, John Sayles, Angela Bassett, David Strathairn.* Sayles' take on the decline of the American city during the Reagan-Bush years is a masterfully layered exposé of corruption, greed, political favoritism, street crime and neighborhood vigilantism. Spano stars as the disillusioned son of a corrupt city contractor who, fed up with graft, quits his "ghost job" on a high-rise construction project only to find himself at the center of a swirling web of local political intrigue. Sayles manages to tinge his story with just about every major news item of the early '90s and then some. Spano is well-cast as the enlightened thug, and Morton puts in a fine turn as an idealistic City Councilman. Another Sayles veteran, Strathairn, is terrific as a street person witness to it all. ★★★½ VHS: $19.99

City of Industry

(1997, 97 min, US, John Irvin) *Harvey Keitel, Timothy Hutton, Stephen Dorff, Famke Janssen.* Keitel is Roy Egan, a retired criminal brought into one last jewel heist by his brother Lee (Hutton). To realize the American Dream of the last big score, Lee calls in Skip Kovich (Dorff), whose edgy near-psychosis and lack of allegiance sharply contrast with both Roy, a centered old warrior, and Lee, a journeyman thief worried about Mom going into a nursing home. Planned with precision and executed with exactly orchestrated violence, the job goes as planned. But Skip is greedy. Roy literally crawls away from death to scour the infested maze of L.A. in a personal quest for vengeance and honor. Director Irvin seeds the violence with small personal moments which reveal intimate aspects of the protagonists' personalities, humanizing a world in which grand theft auto, gun sales in parking lots, and jail terms are a way of life. Immersed in a desperate milieu, the film is an examination of a man alone, shouldering the burden of retribution, propelled by a pristine desire for absolute

justice. An intriguing character study adeptly handled by the cast. ★★★ DVD: $14.99

City of Joy

(1992, 134 min, GB, Roland Joffé) *Patrick Swayze, Pauline Collins, Om Puri.* An aimless and disillusioned American surgeon (Swayze) attempts to lose himself in the back streets of Calcutta. Against his will, he's drawn into the operations of a health clinic run by a nurse (Collins), who's committed to the clinic's survival with pragmatic optimism and iron will. Together, they battle against the overwhelming need and abject poverty of their patients, and confront a brutal and exploitive local boss. Some engaging performances and arresting location shooting elevate the film above its predictable story line. ★★½ VHS: $9.99

The City of Lost Children

(1995, 112 min, France, Marc Caro & Jean-Pierre Jeunet) *Ron Perlman, Daniel Emilfork, Judith Vittet, Dominique Pinon.* A fascinating, engrossing and disturbing fractured fairy tale. Set in and around an eerie, oddly futuristic yet late 19th-century waterfront (it's a setting seemingly inspired by Samuel Beckett and Fritz Lang), the film follows a hulking but pea-brained circus strongman (Perlman) known only as "One," who is on a desperate search to find his abducted ward, Little Brother. Along the way, he joins forces with a group of street urchins who steal for a Faginesque Siamese twin. The search ultimately leads to a sea-platform/laboratory where Krank, the genetically created orphan of a mad scientist, lords over his siblings (including a talking brain in a box) and conducts diabolical dream experiments. Though not as seamless as their previous *Delicatessen,* the directors have crafted a truly unique tale that is complemented by good performances, mind-blowing imagery and superb special effects. (Available dubbed and in French with English subtitles) ★★★½ VHS: $24.99; DVD: $24.99

City of Women

(1981, 139 min, Italy, Federico Fellini) *Marcello Mastroianni, Ettore Manni, Anna Prucnall.* Mastroianni stars as the bruised, baffled and bedazzled man who stumbles into a feminist convention, which sets off a series of wild, surrealistic fantasies. Fellini continues his eternal search into his psyche with an eloquent flourish. (Italian with English subtitles) ★★★ VHS: $19.99; DVD: $29.99

City Slickers

(1991, 108 min, US, Ron Underwood) *Billy Crystal, Daniel Stern, Jack Palance, Bruno Kirby, Patricia Wettig, Helen Slater, David Paymer, Josh Mostel.* An often hilarious and heartwarming farce about three adventure-seeking Manhattanite buddies who sign up for an "authentic" Western cattle drive. Along the way, they confront their fears, unfulfilled childhood fantasies, and their respective mid-life crises. This may sound like a recipe for cheap sentimentality, but thanks to solid performances and razor-sharp, quick-witted dialogue, the film is a fun-filled and poignant examination of the disillusionment of middle age. Palance (who won an Oscar) steals the show as the real-life cowboy who leads the round-up. (Sequel: *City Slickers II*) ★★★½ VHS: $9.99; DVD: $19.99

City Slickers II: The Legend of Curly's Gold

(1994, 105 min, US, Paul Weiland) *Billy Crystal, Daniel Stern, Jack Palance, Jon Lovitz, Patricia Wettrig.* A genial sequel which is less a continuation and more a carbon copy of the original. Crystal learns that Curly (the Palance character who died in the first film) may have left behind a fortune in gold. He, Stern and brother Lovitz head west to search for it. On the way, Curly's twin brother shows up (Palance) and all face the same series of western misadventures as in the first film. Though there's no lack of funny lines, and Crystal is a delight to watch, the sorry subplot of Lovitz and Crystal's strained relationship and an overwhelming feeling of déjà vu make this only intermittently entertaining. ★★½ VHS: $14.99

La Ciudad y los Perros
(The City and the Dogs)

(1987, 135 min, Peru, Francisco J. Lombardi) Although very few of its films reach the United States, this powerful drama of personal honor amidst rampant terror proves that Peruvian cinema is quite vibrant. The story is set in a boy's military academy outside Lima. Within the confines of the repressive structure, four angry cadets form a private circle that begins to victimize and dominate the other cadets. It is only after a theft escalates into possible murder that a brave young man confronts the group. A hard-hitting and absorbing drama from Mario Vargas Llosa's classic novel. (Spanish with English subtitles) ★★★

A Civil Action

(1998, 113 min, US, Steve Zaillian) *John Travolta, Robert Duvall, Kathleen Quinlan, William H. Macy, Tony Shalhoub, John Lithgow, James Gandolfini, Dan Hedaya.* What's this: An intriguing, complex courtroom drama *not* penned by John Grisham? Based on the best-seller by Jonathan Harr, this classy production, which is based on a true-life incident, shares with Grisham a judicial setting, but *A Civil Action* has its own, distinctive flavoring in which justice may not always be served. Travolta is commendable as Jan Schlichtmann, a hot-shot, cynical personal injury lawyer who agrees to represent eight families from a small Massachusetts town against two large corporations whose dumping of toxic materials may have caused a breakout of leukemia. At first eager to take on the big guys, Schlichtmann meets his match in a seasoned attorney (Duvall) from the other side. The outcome is unexpected, and director Zaillian's screenplay adaptation contains many sharp observations of the legal profession, and on ethics vs. the law. ★★★ VHS: $14.99; DVD: $29.99

Civilization

(1916, 86 min, US, Raymond B. West) *Howard Hickman, Enid Markey.* Contemporary with Griffith's *Intolerance,* producer Thomas Ince proved himself every bit the director's equal with this impressive silent exhibiting strong plot construction and narrative economy. Set in the mythical kingdom of Teutonic, the story depicts that country's plunge into the surreal madness of war. Only when Christ himself returns to take the sovereign on an amazing journey to see the resulting carnage is the country saved. *Civilization* was both a commercial and critical success upon its release in 1916, and was not only used to help re-elect President Wilson but also was a rallying cry against America's entry into WWI. The film became frightfully out of fashion when America entered the war. ★★★ VHS: $29.99

Claire Dolan

(1998, 95 min, US, **Lodge Kerrigan**) *Katrin Cartlidge, Vincent D'Onofrio, Colm Meaney.* Employing the same disciplined, spare style as his debut film *Clean, Shaven*, Kerrigan's follow-up is another cold film with a warm center. Featuring characters and a narrative a little less compelling than his debut work, the challenging *Claire Dolan* follows the story of an Irish immigrant (Cartlidge), a high-class prostitute who owes her sleazy pimp (Meaney) money and is working only until her debt is paid. She attempts to escape her existence by moving to Long Island, where she begins dating a kindly cabbie (an excellent D'Onofrio). Her past, of course, catches up with her. Some terrific individual moments, sturdy performances and an effective score give relief from the film's depressing tone; ultimately, this unusual character study moves in unexpected ways. ★★★ VHS: $49.99

Claire of the Moon

(1992, 106 min, US, **Nicole Conn**) *Trisha Todd, Karen Trumbo, Faith McDevitt.* While not the breakthrough lesbian film for which many had hoped, *Claire of the Moon* is an earnest if amateurish drama of simmering female sexual desire and equally strong denial. At an oceanside women writers' retreat in Oregon, Dr. Noel Benedict (Trumbo), a brooding psychologist and lesbian author of "serious" books, finds herself rooming with her opposite — Claire (Todd), a willowy, cynical straight blonde woman who is determinedly messy and fun-loving. Their budding relationship becomes a tense and inadvertently amusing cat-and-mouse game of "I want you...I don't want you" as they alternately try to overcome their insecurities and accept their true feelings. A refreshingly intimate lesbian romance that works as a love story despite being a talky and didactic soap full of typical lesbian stereotypes and featuring a wooden script, stilted acting, and an overload of lingering glances. ★★ VHS: $29.99; DVD: $29.99

Claire's Knee

(1970, 106 min, France, **Eric Rohmer**) *Jean-Claude Brialy, Aurora Cornu, Beatrice Romand, Laurence de Monaghan.* The fifth in director Rohmer's series of "Moral Tales," *Claire's Knee* is

Clay Pigeons

a sophisticated comedy of lust, unfulfilled desire and fidelity. The film tells the story of a young diplomat, recently engaged, who harbors a peculiar obsession with the teenage sister of his fiancée. A literate satire on sexual temptations with fine cinematography by Nestor Alemendros. (French with English subtitles) ★★★ VHS: $19.99; DVD: $29.99

Clara's Heart

(1988, 108 min, US, **Robert Mulligan**) *Whoopi Goldberg, Neil Patrick Harris, Michael Ontkean, Kathleen Quinlan, Spalding Gray.* A heartwarming performance by Goldberg dominates this uneven drama about a Jamaican maid whose loving influence on a young boy (Harris) helps him through family difficulties. Ontkean and Quinlan are the youth's parents — grief-stricken over the death of their infant — who inadvertently ignore their other child. ★★ VHS: $14.99

Clash by Night

(1952, 105 min, US, **Fritz Lang**) *Barbara Stanwyck, Robert Ryan, Paul Douglas, Marilyn Monroe, Keith Andes.* Stanwyck gives a dynamic performance in this steamy psychodrama as the penned-up wife of a boring fishing boat captain (Douglas) whose yearning for excitement leads her to her husband's best friend (Ryan). ★★★ VHS: $14.99

Clash of the Titans

(1981, 118 min, GB, **Desmond Davis**) *Harry Hamlin, Judi Bowker, Laurence Olivier, Maggie Smith.* Special effects by Ray Harryhausen (his final film before retirement) highlight this appealing if listless Greek mythology adventure set during ancient times. ★★ VHS: $14.99

Class

(1983, 98 min, US, **Lewis John Carlino**) *Jacqueline Bisset, Rob Lowe, Andrew McCarthy, Cliff Robertson, John Cusack, Alan Ruck, Casey Siemaszko, Joan Cusack.* Bisset finds herself unknowingly involved with her son's college roommate. Lowe is her offspring, McCarthy is her youthful lover. Bisset brings more class to this uninspired teen comedy than it deserves. ★½ DVD: $19.99

Class Act

(1992, 98 min, US, **Randall Miller**) *Christopher Reid, Christopher Martin, Meshach Taylor, Doug E. Doug.* Blend the hip-hop hijinks of Kid 'n' Play's previous hit, *House Party*, throw in a little of the antic, slap-and-ouch comedy of the Three Stooges and a 1990s black version of Hope and Crosby, and you get some idea of what is in store in this agreeably inane teen comedy. Teen genius Kid (Reid) finds himself in a foul-up that has him changing places with one of his school's fun-loving bums, Play (Martin). Although all of the goings-on are predictable, the film's infectious desire to entertain and amuse pays off, creating a harmless anti-drug comedy that is pure fun. ★★★ VHS: $19.99

Class Action

(1991, 110 min, US, **Michael Apted**) *Gene Hackman, Mary Elizabeth Mastrantonio.* Hackman's dominant performance highlights this routine though intriguing courtroom drama — though he's not on screen nearly enough. He plays a dedicated attorney who, on behalf of an injured motorist, takes a powerful corporation to court — with his daughter Mastrantonio as

opposing counsel. Part mystery and part courtroom intrigue, the film has moments of interest, but some of the twists are rather contrived. ★★

The Class of Miss MacMichael

(1978, 93 min, GB, **Silvio Narizzano**) *Glenda Jackson, Oliver Reed, Michael Murphy, Rosalind Cash.* Jackson stars as a feisty trade schoolteacher who struggles to gain the respect of her unruly students. Reed plays the school's menacing principal. The combination of comedy and melodrama is ill-served here. ★½

Class of 1984

(1982, 93 min, US, **Mark L. Lester**) *Perry King, Timothy Van Patten, Roddy McDowall, Michael J. Fox.* The new teacher (King) gets tormented by his students — and by Van Patten in particular — at an inner-city high school. Without the pretentions of a serious-minded examination of teacher-student relations, this half-baked, violent actioner is strictly for thrills — though it produces only a few. ★★

Class of 1999

(1989, 99 min, US, **Mark L. Lester**) *Malcolm McDowell, Stacy Keach, Pam Grier.* In the wake of *The Terminator* comes this not-too-shabby ripoff (but ripoff nonetheless) about a high school from hell where gang-bangers meet their match in a group of malfunctioning renegade robot teachers. ★★½ VHS: $14.99

Class of Nuke 'Em High

(1986, 84 min, US, **Richard W. Haines & Samuel Weil**) *Janelle Brady, Gilbert Brenton.* From the cinematic genii who gave us *The Toxic Avenger* comes their greatest masterpiece yet. High school students exposed to toxic waste become hideous mutants. Oh, the horror of it all. Is there no one who can save them? ★½ VHS: $14.99; DVD: $14.99

Clay Pigeons

(1998, 104 min, US, **David Dobkin**) *Vince Vaughn, Janeane Garofalo, Joaquin Phoenix, Georgina Cates, Scott Wilson.* A playful noir thriller which ambles at its own speed but has a few nice surprises along the way. Both comic and dark, the story follows down-on-his-luck Clay (an engaging Phoenix), a small-town cowboy who's having an affair with his best friend Earl's wife. But Earl has a plan and he's gone through with it — commit suicide and frame Clay for murder. With no help or sympathy from the new widow, Clay is left alone to straighten things out. Enter Lester Long (Vaughn), an enigmatic stranger who befriends Clay. In no time, more dead bodies, the FBI and a serial killer who may or may not be Lester cross Clay's path. Making a solid feature debut, director Dobkin makes good use of the dusty locale, nicely capturing the pace and environment for their satiric and atmospheric qualities. Garofalo is especially appealing as an FBI agent on the case, and Vaughn mixes menace with charm to make a most believable scoundrel. ★★★ VHS: $9.99; DVD: $19.99

Clean and Sober

(1988, 122 min, US, **Glenn Gordon Caron**) *Michael Keaton, Morgan Freeman, Kathy Baker, M. Emmet Walsh.* Keaton, in a departure from his comic portrayals, gives a first-rate performance as a drug-addicted businessman who hides out in a drug rehab; this forces him to come to terms with his addiction. While lacking the strong narrative of *The Lost Weekend* or *The Days of Wine and Roses*, the film nevertheless is a forceful drama told in a truthful, no-holds-barred manner. Excellent support from Freeman as a dedicated counselor and Baker as a weary addict. ★★★ VHS: $14.99; DVD: $14.99

Clean, Shaven

(1995, 109 min, US, Lodge Kerrigan) *Peter Greene, Robert Albert, Jennifer MacDonald.* Kerrigan's first film is a vivid, gut-wrenching study of paranoid schizophrenia, told from the point of view of the disturbed individual. Greene stars as a recently released mental patient who begins an obsessive quest to find his young daughter, now living with an adopted mother. When his tortured journey takes a murderous turn, a manhunt begins and he is pursued by an equally obsessive detective. The film's soundtrack is particularly innovative, layering various elements such as radio broadcasts, overheard conversations and random noises within and around the dialogue itself. This cacophony, approximating what the mentally disturbed hear every day, is the single most powerful element contributing to the film's success. Very experimental in nature, and definitely not for the squeamish, *Clean, Shaven* is a highly original vision which succeeds as both social commentary and as a radically new method of exposition. (Letterboxed) ★★★ VHS: $19.99; DVD: $19.99

Clean Slate

(1994, 107 min, US, Mick Jackson) *Dana Carvey, Valeria Golino, James Earl Jones, Kevin Pollak, Michael Murphy, Michael Gambon.* This amusing, gimmick-ridden piffle stars Carvey as a mild-mannered private eye whose plans to testify against a crime boss are thwarted when a rare form of amnesia makes him forget everything that happened the day before. Not very memorable, and that's the point. ★★ VHS: $9.99

Clear and Present Danger

(1994, 142 min, US, Phillip Noyce) *Harrison Ford, Willem Dafoe, Anne Archer, James Earl Jones, Ann Magnuson, Joaquim de Almeida, Donald Moffat.* Ford reprises his role from *Patriot Games* in this third Jack Ryan tale. An efficient and exciting thriller, *Danger* begins as Ryan takes over as acting deputy director of the CIA. He soon finds himself in political hot water and immediate danger when he uncovers evidence of White House duplicity with a drug cartel. Though the film is slightly overlong, it never fails to entertain, and there's a slam-bang ambush scene which is breathtaking. As usual, Ford is a commanding presence and his heroic Everyman character is well served here. More thrilling than *Games* and on par with *Hunt for Red October*, *Danger* is a helluva ride. (VHS available letterboxed or pan & scan) ★★★½ VHS: $14.99; DVD: $29.99

Clearcut

(1992, 98 min, Canada, Richard Bucaski) *Graham Greene, Ron Lea, Floyd "Red Crow" Westerman.* This Native American *Deliverance* serves as an impassioned cry against environmental atrocities committed in the Canadian wilderness by big timber and paper companies. Greene plays Arthur, an irate Native who, upon learning of yet another court decision against his tribe, takes matters into his

own hands and abducts the foreman of the local paper mill and the lawyer representing his tribe and takes them to the forest for a harrowing lesson in humility. Greene gives a sturdy performance in this sometimes compelling drama. ★★½ VHS: $79.99

Cleo from 5 to 7
(Cleo de cinq à sept)

(1961, 90 min, France, Agnès Varda) *Corinne Marchand, Antoine Bourseiller, Dorothee Blanck, Michel Legrand, Anna Karina, Jean-Luc Godard, Eddie Constantine.* An intelligent and absorbing film which examines a woman at the crossroads of life. A successful Parisian songstress, fearing the worst, is forced to reevaluate her life while waiting two hours for a medical report on her health. (French with English subtitles) ★★★½ VHS: $29.99; DVD: $29.99

Cleo from 5 to 7

Cleopatra

(1963, 248 min, US, Joseph L. Mankiewicz) *Elizabeth Taylor, Richard Burton, Rex Harrison, Roddy McDowall, Hume Cronyn, Martin Landau.* Notorious epic about the queen of the Nile. Whether it's more noted for the Taylor-Burton angle (they met and fell in love) or the colossal sum spent on it, the film, though spectacular looking, is a tough four-hour viewing. However, it does feature two award-calibre performances by Harrison (who was Oscar nominated) and McDowall (who wasn't because of a clerical error). ★★ VHS: $14.99; DVD: $26.99

Cleopatra Jones

(1973, 89 min, US, Jack Starrett) *Tamara Dobson, Shelley Winters, Antonio Fargas.* There's lots of action in this violent adventure with Dobson as a lovely but lethal martial arts-trained government agent out to bust drug kingpins — including the hilariously preposterous Winters. (Sequel: *Cleopatra Jones and the Casino of Gold*) ★★½ VHS: $14.99; DVD: $14.99

Cleopatra Jones and the Casino of Gold

(1975, 94 min, US, Chuck Bail) *Tamara Dobson, Stella Stevens, Norman Fell.* Don't let an incoherent plot and ludicrous acting keep you away from this fun if less than stellar follow-up to *Cleopatra Jones*. The leggy Dobson returns as the brave and sexy drug agent out to wipe out a notorious Hong Kong drug ring. Stevens camps it up as the villainous "Dragon Lady." ★★ VHS: $14.99

Clerks

(1994, 89 min, US, Kevin Smith) *Brian O'Halloran, Jeff Anderson, Marilyn Ghigliotti, Kevin Smith, Jason Mewes.* The two-store location in *Clerks*, a ferociously entertaining gem, doesn't even count as a mall — it's just a parking lot anchored by a third-rate video store and a convenience store. To work in either establishment is more serving time than being employed. The convenience store clerk tries to maintain a sense

of direction in the face of futility; the video store guy has abandoned hope long ago — when he opens the store at all it's to show contempt for his customers. Waiting in limbo, without even the comforting illusion of Godot, these Generation Xers structure their pointless day with corpse abuse, analyses of working-class exploitation, unrequited love and sponging friends. This original, highly inventive low-budget surprise stirs its disparate elements into a '90s examination of meaning and purpose. It all culminates with the delivery of spontaneous satori in the face of existential despair. And it's damn funny, too. ★★★½ VHS: $14.99; DVD: $39.99

The Client

(1994, 124 min, US, Joel Schumacher) *Susan Sarandon, Tommy Lee Jones, Anthony LaPaglia, Mary-Louise Parker, Anthony Edwards, Brad Renfro, Will Patton.* This adaptation of John Grisham's novel falls short of its expectations. Sarandon stars as a struggling Memphis attorney who sees a golden opportunity walk in her door in the person of a young boy — a witness to the suicide of a mob lawyer — who hires her to help keep the Feds off his back. Of course, the bad guys show up, and the little guy finds himself on the run from both relentless G-man Jones and villainous underworld kingpin LaPaglia. While at times entertaining, the film suffers from too many incredulities and a slack plot full of deadly breaks in the action. ★★½ VHS: $9.99; DVD: $19.99

Cliffhanger

(1993, 118 min, US, Renny Harlin) *Sylvester Stallone, John Lithgow, Michael Rooker, Janine Turner, Paul Winfield, Caroline Goodall, Leon, Max Perlich.* An unbelievably hair-raising, excessively violent actioner which, when flexing its special effects and cinematographic muscles, is nothing short of remarkable. However, these first-rate action scenes are offset by one-dimensional characters, clichéd plot developments and flat dialogue. Stallone plays an expert mountain climber haunted by the edge-of-your-seat opening tragedy. Reluctantly, he returns to the same locale when skyjackers crash land in the mountains. Stallone and buddy Rooker are then forced to help the sadistic Lithgow retrieve stolen cash. Thrills, lots of blood, gruesome deaths, amazing climbing footage and a cave-load of bats await them. ★★½ VHS: $9.99; DVD: $19.99

The Clinic

(1984, 93 min, Australia, David Stevens) *Chris Haywood, Simon Burke.* A comedy about social disease? It may sound strange, possibly in bad taste and potentially off-putting, but *The Clinic* is a surprisingly fresh and funny frolic about one day in the life of a Sydney V.D. clinic. Chock-full of bawdy doctor/patient vignettes, the film is never derisive and maintains a gentle understanding for the afflicted denizens of this madcap milieu. ★★★

Cloak and Dagger

(1946, 106 min, US, Fritz Lang) *Gary Cooper, Lili Palmer, Robert Alda.* A routine spy thriller, which is more cloak than dagger. Cooper stars as an American scientist who is sent to Germany during WWII to uncover military secrets. Palmer is the femme fatale with whom he becomes involved. ★★½ VHS: $19.99

Cloak and Dagger

(1984, 101 min, US, Richard Franklin) *Henry Thomas, Dabney Coleman, Michael Murphy.* Enjoyable and even suspenseful children's thriller with Thomas as a young boy who becomes involved with spies when he obtains secret microfilm. Coleman plays dual roles as his father and his imaginary James Bond-ish playmate. ★★½ VHS: $19.99

The Clock

(1945, 90 min, US, Vincente Minnelli) *Judy Garland, Robert Walker, James Gleason.* A lovely romantic drama featuring one of Garland's best dramatic performances. Judy plays an office worker who meets soldier Walker while he's on a two-day pass; the two fall in love while spending the day together. ★★★½ VHS: $19.99

Clockers

(1995, 129 min, US, Spike Lee) *Harvey Keitel, Delroy Lindo, John Turturro, Keith David, Mekhi Phifer.* Lee collaborated with Martin Scorsese (he produced) on this adaptation of Richard Price's best-selling novel. In a very good debut performance, Phifer plays Strike, a smart youth who has gotten involved with a local crime lord, Rodney (Lindo). Strike is a "clocker," a dealer who can be found working around the clock from his perch on a park bench. When a murder occurs, a sympathetic homicide detective (Keitel) on the case

A Clockwork Orange

refuses to believe the self-defense story given by Strike's brother, who has confessed to the crime. The officer probes deeper into Strike's world, pressuring the young man to come clean and give up Rodney. A complex tale of loyalty, betrayal and honor, and powerful without being maudlin. *Clockers* may not be particularly distinguished, but it is entertaining, engrossing and enlightening. ★★★ VHS: $9.99; DVD: $24.99

The Clockmaker

(1973, 105 min, France, Bertrand Tavernier) *Philippe Noiret, Jean Rochefort, Jacques Denis.* Based on a novel by Georges Simenon, this fascinating and thought-provoking drama stars Noiret as a clockmaker in Lyon whose life is drastically changed after he learns that his son was involved in leftist terrorist acts. With the arrest of his son, the man's placid and ordered life must be reviewed as he tries to understand his role in the world. One of the finest French films of the 1970s. (Letterboxed) (French with English subtitles) ★★★★ VHS: $24.99

Clockwatchers

(1997, 96 min, US, Jill Sprecher) *Toni Collette, Parker Posey, Lisa Kudrow, Alanna Ubach, Paul Dooley.* Collette stars as an ambitious temp worker who gets a job at a credit agency. She immediately befriends three other temps there — aspiring actress Kudrow, about-to-be-married Ubach, and the eternally snappy, bitchy, energetic Posey. The surprisingly close quartet soon have their friendships and loyalties tested when they are suspected in a rash of thefts. Anyone who's ever worked as a temp will instantly recognize many dead-on details and situations, and the atmosphere captured by director Spencer is totally accurate. The first half of *Clockwatchers* is an extremely funny, lightly satiric view of office politics (Posey has all the best moments here). But when the plot mechanics start to grind, the picture becomes too self-serious, its light touch lost for good. ★★★ VHS: $14.99; DVD: $24.99

Clockwise

(1986, 98 min, GB, Christopher Morahan) *John Cleese, Penelope Wilton, Alison Steadman.* Monty Python's Cleese is in rare comic form in this delightful and uproarious comedy as a fastidious headmaster whose perfunctory life is turned upside-down when he boards the wrong train for an important conference. ★★★½ VHS: $14.99

A Clockwork Orange

(1971, 135 min, GB, Stanley Kubrick) *Malcolm McDowell, Patrick Magee, Adrienne Corri.* Little Alex and his grahzny droogs prowl the streets in search of sldky devotchkas. Kubrick's brilliant adaptation of the Anthony Burgess novel assaults the screen with snakes, Ludwig von, the old in-out and oodles more. Don't be oddy-knocky, take this film home and viddy the meaning of it all, my brothers. ★★★★ VHS: $19.99; DVD: $24.99

Close Encounters of the Third Kind

(1977, 152 min, US, Steven Spielberg) *Richard Dreyfuss, Melinda Dillon, Teri Garr, François Truffaut, Bob Balaban.* Spielberg's classic sci-fi film. Dreyfuss and Dillon are just two of the many Earthlings to see an alien craft — and are compelled to travel to Devil's Tower in Wyoming. The special effects, including the

mother ship and the aliens, are second to none, and John Williams' lush, magical score is extraordinary. (This is the "special edition," which includes scenes not in the original 1977 release.) ★★★★ VHS: $12.99; DVD: $27.99

Close to Eden

(1992, 106 min, Russia, Nikita Mikhalkov) *Badema, Byaertu, Vladimir Gostukhin.* This exquisitely rendered fable examines the effects of modernization on a family living on the Mongolian steppes just inside the Chinese border. After giving shelter to a stranded Russian truck driver, the family begins to question their own traditional lifestyles, leading the father to make a hilarious yet sobering journey to the nearest big city in search of such modern amenities as a television and condoms. Mikhalkov masterfully depicts their simple yet noble lives as contrasted with the polluted degradation of the industrialized city and keeps the pace lively despite the film's essentially static nature. At times mirthful and humorous, at other times serious and ponderous, the film charms with several marvelous flights of fantasy, one of which finds the husband coming face to face with Gunga Din. (Russian with English subtitles) ★★★★ VHS: $7.99

Closely Watched Trains

(1966, 89 min, Czechoslovakia, Jiri Menzel) *Vaclav Neckar, Jitka Bendova, Josef Somr.* This Oscar-winning Best Foreign Film is a charming, bittersweet tragicomedy about a young, naive train dispatcher and his attempts to find love during the Nazi occupation. (Czechoslovakian with English subtitles) ★★★½ VHS: $29.99

Closet Land

(1991, 95 min, US, Radha Bharadwaj) *Alan Rickman, Madeleine Stowe.* In a nameless country, a woman, the writer of children's books, is taken to a secluded room with no apparent exit or entrance. There she is interrogated by a seemingly benign officer. But when his requests for a confession to political subversion are denied, he becomes increasingly violent, inflicting mental and physical torture to achieve his goal. Stowe and Rickman give tremendous performances in this political allegory, a powerful and fascinating study of the individual struggle to control one's own thoughts, and an acknowledgment of the resiliency of the human spirit. ★★★

The Clouded Yellow

(1951, 85 min, GB, Ralph Thomas) *Trevor Howard, Jean Simmons, Kenneth More.* An exciting psychological thriller and whodunit. Howard plays a British secret agent who is forced into retirement. He accepts a job in the country looking forward to peace and relaxation. There he meets emotionally scarred Simmons, who becomes the prime suspect in the murder of a hired hand. Together, Howard and Simmons flee the countryside in a determined effort to prove her innocence. The film takes its time setting up characterization, but once the chase begins, *The Clouded Yellow* (named after an elusive butterfly) shifts gears and becomes an unpredictable Hitchcock-like chase story which stays suspenseful until the final credits. ★★★½ VHS: $39.99

Clouds over Europe

(1939, 78 min, GB, Tim Whelan) *Laurence Olivier, Ralph Richardson, Valerie Hobson.* Olivier and especially Richardson are both in terrific form in this taut espionage thriller which — à la *The Thin Man* — combines unusually witty comedy with a darn good mystery. Set in England at the start of WWII, the film stars Richardson as a government agent who is investigating the disappearance of a top secret British aircraft. Olivier is one of the pilots who helps crack both the case and the skulls of the Nazis behind the scurrilous plot. (aka: *Q Planes*) ★★★½

The Clowns

(1970, 90 min, Italy, Federico Fellini) This "documentary" within a film is a three-ring circus of spectacle, slapstick and sensation. Fellini (acting in the film as head of the camera crew) lovingly pays homage to the circus clowns of his childhood. (Italian with English subtitles) ★★★ VHS: $19.99

The Club

(1980, 93 min, Australia, Bruce Beresford) *Jack Thompson, Graham Kennedy, John Wood.* An entertaining if pedestrian sports drama. Thompson is terrific as the inspirational coach of a soccer club who must change his team's losing ways and rally them to a championship. The film's not brain surgery, but at least it's better than *The Fish That Saved Pittsburgh.* ★★½

Club des Femmes

(1936, 90 min, France, Jacques Deval) *Danielle Darrieux.* Darrieux stars as a nightclub entertainer who lives with several other women in a hotel in Paris where men are banned. The women's lives and fates unravel in this entertaining, playfully energetic farce. (French with English subtitles) ★★★

Club Extinction

(1990, 112 min, France/West Germany/Italy, Claude Chabrol) *Jennifer Beals, Alan Bates, Andrew McCarthy.* A stunning futuristic tale about a German society plagued by a series of violent, unexplained suicides. Originally titled *Dr. M.* (perhaps in homage to Fritz Lang's entropic character), the film stars Bates as the megalomaniacal Dr. Marsfeldt, head of an all-powerful media organization and self-professed "travel agent" for whom death is the ultimate solution. Beals is oddly (but effectively) cast as Marsfeldt's unwitting ally. Fans of the cerebral science fiction of the '70s will find this a welcome treat. (Filmed in English) (aka: *Doctor M*) ★★★

Club Paradise

(1986, 96 min, US, Harold Ramis) *Robin Williams, Peter O'Toole, Rick Moranis, Jimmy Cliff, Joanna Cassidy, Twiggy, Adolph Caesar.* A good cast isn't enough to totally save this water-logged comedy about a disabled firefighter (Williams) who becomes partners with a reggae nightclub owner (Cliff) in a broken-down Caribbean resort. ★★ VHS: $14.99

Clue: The Movie

(1985, 96 min, US, Jonathan Lynn) *Eileen Brennan, Christopher Lloyd, Madeline Kahn, Tim Curry, Lesley Ann Warren, Michael McKean.* A good cast is wasted in this limp, gimmicky mystery-comedy based on the popular board game. Was it Mrs. Peacock in the library with the candlestick? Or was it Col. Mustard in the hall with the rope? Who cares? ★ VHS: $14.99; DVD: $24.99

Alicia Silverstone (foreground) and Justin Walker in *Clueless*

Clueless

(1995, 97 min, US, Amy Heckerling) *Alicia Silverstone, Stacey Dash, Brittany Murphy, Paul Rudd, Julie Brown, Jeremy Sisto, Dan Hedaya, Wallace Shawn.* What writer-director Heckerling did for the 1980s with *Fast Times at Ridgemont High* she does for the '90s in this hilariously witty send-up of high school life and adolescence (California upper-middle class specifically). The superficial but naively intelligent Cher (Silverstone), a carefree 15-year-old beauty with not much on her mind but clothes, social standing and boys, comes to a life decision to use her good looks and popularity for good causes. She sets out on a glorious quest to play matchmaker and good samaritan to anyone within arm's reach — but will she herself find true love? Heckerling's delicious updating of Jane Austen's "Emma" is one mirthful exposition after another, playfully lampooning the teenage milieu — there's a gallery of funny one-liners and comic vignettes. Silverstone proves herself an impeccable comedienne, giving a cheerful, uproarious performance. ★★★½ VHS: $14.99; DVD: $29.99

Coal Miner's Daughter

(1980, 125 min, US, Michael Apted) *Sissy Spacek, Tommy Lee Jones, Beverly D'Angelo, Levon Helm.* Spacek won an Oscar for her stirring portrait of country singer Loretta Lynn in this accomplished musical biography. The film follows Lynn's rise from a poor Kentucky mining town girl to country music superstar. Jones gives a fine performance as Lynn's husband, and D'Angelo is sensational as Patsy Cline. ★★★½ VHS: $9.99

Cobb

(1994, 128 min, US, Ron Shelton) *Tommy Lee Jones, Robert Wuhl, Lolita Davidovich.* Ty Cobb was one of the greats on the field, but off it he was despised by the players and public alike. *Cobb*, Shelton's demanding adaptation of Al Stump's myth-shaking novel, makes it easy to see why. Jones gives a big, brash performance as the baseball great, now in his 70s. He's just hired second-string reporter Stump (Wuhl) to write his biography. As Stump gathers biographical information, he soon comes to realize that the legend of the player is greatly contradicted by the actions of the man. Shelton takes the chance of alienating most viewers. But it only underscores his story about the demystification of our heroes, and the price it extracts. Playing William Holden to Jones' Gloria Swanson, Wuhl's one-dimensional portrayal is the major weakness of the film. ★★½ VHS: $14.99

Cobra

(1925, 75 min, US, Joseph Henabery) *Rudolph Valentino, Nita Naldi.* One year before his death, Valentino went independent with this enjoyable melodrama about a modern-day Don Juan — a promiscuous Italian count who abandons his homeland for anonymity in New York — who becomes mesmerized by his boss' wife. Only Valentino could hold his own against the lavish sets of William Cameron Menzies and the costuming of legendary fashion maven Adrian. But he does so with aplomb. ★★★ VHS: $24.99; DVD: $24.99

Cobra

(1986, 87 min, US, George P. Cosmatos) *Sylvester Stallone, Reni Santoni, Brigitte Nielsen.* Stallone does his *Dirty Harry* bit with far less successful results as a Los Angeles detective hunting a serial killer. Dramatically sloppy and very gory. ★ VHS: $14.99; DVD: $14.99

The Coca-Cola Kid

(1985, 94 min, Australia, Dusan Makavejev) *Eric Roberts, Greta Scacchi.* Makavejev directed this strangely enjoyable, capitalist/sexual comedy which stars Roberts as an overly motivated American corporate whiz kid in search of new markets. Landing in Australia, he encounters difficulty with several stubbornly eccentric Aussies. Makavejev weaves his plot with characteristic absurdity and sensuality. ★★★ VHS: $14.99

Cocaine Cowboys

(1979, 87 min, US, Ulli Lommel) *Jack Palance, Tom Sullivan, Andy Warhol, Suzanna Love.* A strange story of a rock 'n' roll band who smuggle cocaine to help pay their expenses. They fall into trouble with their underworld financiers when a shipment of coke is lost in the ocean. Produced by Warhol. ★

El Cochecito

(1960, 90 min, Spain, Marco Ferreri) This tragi-comedy is something of a perverse one-joke film — old dad, perfectly fit, nonetheless demands from his son a motorized wheelchair in order to socialize properly with his crippled friends. This film wears thin after a while, but it does contain moments of truly bizarre black comedy while making points about the elderly and their loneliness. (Spanish with English subtitles) ★★

Cock & Bull Story

(1992, 80 min, US, Billy Hayes) *Trevor Goddard, Mark Sheppard.* "Midnight Express" author Hayes directed this potent two-man drama videotaped before a live audience. The story is set in a small English town in a gym locker room where Jacko (Sheppard), a boxer with hopes of making it big in London, trains for an upcoming event. His best mate, the fast-talking Travis (Goddard), hangs around and they engage in a series of tension-filled, sexually charged admissions and revelations about their personal feelings. Amidst the taunts and the macho posturing by the working-class youths comes the reality that the two can only express themselves through violence, despite their deep feelings to the contrary. Flat sound quality due to the live recording mars this otherwise gripping story. ★★★

Cockfighter

(1974, 83 min, US, Monte Hellman) *Warren Oates, Patricia Pearcy.* Oates stars as a trainer of fighting cocks whose illegal profession threatens his relationship with girlfriend Pearcy. A fascinating, offbeat drama from Hellman (*Two-Lane Blacktop*). ★★★ VHS: $14.99; DVD: $29.99

Cocktail

(1988, 100 min, US, Roger Donaldson) *Tom Cruise, Bryan Brown, Elisabeth Shue, Kelly Lynch, Gina Gershon.* A completely witless, slick and formulaic piece of celluloid junk food. Cruise stars as a young go-getter who arrives in the Big Apple, ready to cut himself a slice of the Wall Street action. To his dismay, he ends up working in a trendy uptown bar where — under the tutelage of master bartender and part-time philosopher Brown — he's seduced by the life of quick money and easy women. ★½ VHS: $9.99

Cocktail Molotov

(1980, 100 min, France, Diane Kurys) *Elise Caron, Philippe Lebas, François Cluzet.* Sequel to Kurys' *Peppermint Soda* has Caron encountering political students in Venice, but they all long to be back in Paris, in the midst of the student rebellions. Light and sweet, a wonderful look at 18 year olds discovering themselves while traveling through Europe. (French with English subtitles) ★★★ VHS: $29.99

The Cocoanuts

(1929, 96 min, US, Joseph Santley) *The Marx Brothers, Margaret Dumont.* The Marx Brothers' first cinematic exercise in mayhem has the feel of the Vaudeville stage where they cut their teeth. The setting is a Florida hotel rapidly losing money under Groucho's management. All the elements of inspired madness are here, not

the least of which is rapid-fire double-talk. ★★★ VHS: $14.99; DVD: $24.99

Cocoon

(1985, 117 min, US, Ron Howard) *Don Ameche, Jessica Tandy, Hume Cronyn, Wilford Brimley, Steve Guttenberg, Maureen Stapleton, Jack Gilford, Gwen Verdon.* Pleasant, sentimental sci-fi fantasy about a group of Florida senior citizens who discover a fountain of youth — courtesy of the planet-hopping aliens next door. An exceptional cast of veterans keep it endearing. Ameche won an Oscar. (Sequel: *Cocoon: The Return*) ★★★ VHS: $9.99

Cocoon: The Return

(1988, 116 min, US, Daniel Petrie) *Don Ameche, Jessica Tandy, Hume Cronyn, Wilford Brimley, Maureen Stapleton, Gwen Verdon, Steve Guttenberg.* All the stars of the highly successful *Cocoon* return in this frequently charming though ordinary sequel which brings the aging space travelers back to Earth for a four-day visit. The plot borrows greatly from the original and the story is too syrupy and heavy-handed, but the cast helps to capture a little of the magic of the first film. ★★ VHS: $9.99

Un Coeur en Hiver

(1992, 100 min, France, Claude Sautet) *Emmanuelle Beart, Daniel Auteuil, Andre Dussollier.* Sautet's emotionally cool and complex film is a startling look at love, passion and miscommunication. Dussollier plays a man who sees his wife for a young, beautiful concert violinist (Beart). After meeting her lover's business partner (Auteuil), she soon falls in love with him. Auteuil's performance as the cold and emotionally void object of affection is an underrated gem. (French with English subtitles) ★★★½

Coffy

(1973, 91 min, US, Jack Hill) *Pam Grier, Booker Bradshaw.* Duck for cover! Hipswinging Grier, the queen of blaxploitation, is packing and out for violent revenge! Spurred by her little sister's drug overdose, nurse Coffy becomes a one-woman execution squad as she seeks out the people responsible. Sexy, smart and always willing to bare her considerable assets in the line of duty, our sweet heroine poses as a prostitute as she battles crooked politicians, L.A. cops on the take, Italian drug pushers and Super Fly—attired pimps. She blows them all away in this violent, action-packed thriller. ★★½ VHS: $9.99; DVD: $19.99

Cold Around the Heart

(1997, 96 min, US, John Ridley) *David Caruso, Kelly Lynch, Stacey Dash, Chris Noth, John Spencer.* Though ultimately just another nail in the coffin of career suicide Caruso, this Jim Thompson-esque journey into amorality (written by director Ridley) can be summed up as *Bonnie and Clyde* meets *The Last Seduction*. Caruso is strangely endearing as a ponytailed, Mamet-spouting "ewok" who goes hunting for his double-crossing, ice-goddess girlfriend (Lynch) when she takes off with the loot and sticks him with the cops. Dash, on the run from an abusive father, tags along for some light sexual tension, but her character is basically an afterthought to Lynch's bleach-blonde lethal weapon in jeans. ★★½ VHS: $79.99

Cold Blood

(1978, 90 min, West Germany, Ralf Gregan & Gunter Vaesse) *Rutger Hauer, Vera Tschechowa.* This "dishonor among thieves" drama features a hot-blooded, miniskirt-clad young woman who falls for the charming but coldly opportunistic Hauer and ends up in a nightmarish adventure. The film keeps one's attention, but the ending is ridiculous. (Dubbed) ★★

Cold Comfort Farm

(1995, 99 min, GB, John Schlesinger) *Kate Beckinsale, Eileen Atkins, Ian McKellen, Rufus Sewell, Sheila Burrell, Stephen Fry, Freddie Jones, Joanna Lumley, Miriam Margolyes.* What begins as a seemingly familiar "Masterpiece Theatre"/Merchant Ivory—style upper-class English drama soon turns into a raucously funny satire that's a true delight. In the 1930s, pretty but naïve Flora Poste (Beckinsale) finds herself an orphan (and penniless), so she decides to claim her "rights" by moving to the estate of her rural relatives, the Starkadders of Sussex. And that is where the drawing room familiarity ends; for the doom-laden Starkadders, saddled by an ancient curse, are one sorry lot. They live in medieval squalor, talk in olde English and are far from accommodating to their highfalutin cousin. But Flora rolls up her sleeves and, with a smile on her pretty face, pulls the family into the 20th century. Adapted from Stella Gibbons' 1932 parody. ★★★★ VHS: $14.99

Cold Feet

(1984, 96 min, US, Bruce van Dusen) *Griffin Dunne, Marissa Chibas, Blanche Baker.* Dunne and Chibas, both involved in non-gratifying relationships, take a chance on each other in a final stab at romance. Baker has some good scenes as Dunne's ex-wife in this otherwise static comedy. ★★ VHS: $59.99

Cold Feet

(1989, 94 min, US, Robert Dornhelm) *Keith Carradine, Sally Kirkland, Tom Waits, Rip Torn, Bill Pullman.* Screenwriter and novelist Tom McGuane's engrossing comedy, set in Montana, stars Carradine as the sanest in a trio of modern-day desperadoes whose partners include his oversexed wife-to-be Kirkland and Waits as a charming but dangerous killer bent on revenge after being jilted out of the money from their last heist. The couple's attempts to settle down in anonymity with their loot prove to be as elusive as the law, and their own lust and greed finally undermine their demented idea of the American Dream. This outrageous comedy is engaging and fun, although the writing seems forced at times, with zany characters trying a bit too hard to be "weird." ★★★

Cold Fever

(1995, 85 min, Iceland, Fridrik Thor Fridriksson) *Masatoshi Nagase, Lili Taylor, Fisher Stevens, Gisli Halldorsson.* A young Japanese executive, Atsuhi Hirata (Nagase), forgoes a sunny golfing holiday in Hawaii in order to conduct a traditional memorial ceremony in honor of his dead parents. To complete this ritual, he must travel to the harsh, wintry wilderness of Iceland, where he meets an oddball assortment of eccentric characters. As Hirata travels through the frozen wasteland, his journey of making peace with the dead becomes a personal quest for

C

inner solace, made all the more powerful and mesmerizing by the film's spellbinding cinematography. Thoroughly absorbing, *Cold Fever* shifts from quirky comedy to contemplative, existential drama and coalesces into a meditative, heady comment on spirituality and an individual's place in the world. (In English and Japanese and Icelandic with English subtitles) ★★★½ VHS: $19.99

Cold Heaven

(1992, 105 min, US, Nicolas Roeg) *Theresa Russell, Mark Harmon, Talia Shire, Will Patton.* Anyone who thinks the age of chivalry is dead should take a look at the career of director Roeg, who seems content to simply make movies to keep his wife (actress Russell) employed. Case in point: this unabashedly moralistic drama that veers wildly between being a supernatural thriller and a Hallmark greeting card. Russell essays the role of an unfaithful wife who experiences extreme Catholic guilt when her husband (Harmon) is killed before she can make amends. ★ VHS: $14.99

Cold Sassy Tree

(1989, 100 min, US, Joan Tewkesbury) *Faye Dunaway, Richard Widmark, Neil Patrick Harris, Frances Fisher.* Dunaway and Widmark give affecting performances in this wonderful May-December romance about Northerner Dunaway and widower Widmark's affair shocking his turn-of-the-century Southern town. ★★★ VHS: $14.99

Cold Turkey

(1971, 99 min, US, Norman Lear) *Dick Van Dyke, Bob Newhart, Tom Poston, Vincent Gardenia, Jean Stapleton, Edward Everett Horton.* A '60s-ish comedy about a small town and their efforts to stop smoking for a month to win $25 million in prize money. A pleasant romp, with Van Dyke as the minister spearheading the campaign, and a good supporting cast. ★★★ VHS: $19.99

Colegas

(1980, 117 min, Spain, Eloy de la Iglesia) A fine drama about the friendship among three teenagers in present-day Madrid. Jose and Antonio have been friends for most of their lives, but their relationship is severely tested after it is discovered that Antonio's sister, Rosario, is pregnant by Jose. Their efforts to get an abortion in Catholic Spain lead them to Morocco and the dangerous drug trade. (Spanish with English subtitles) ★★★ VHS: $59.99

The Collection

(1978, 64 min, GB, Michael Apted) *Laurence Olivier, Alan Bates, Malcolm McDowell, Helen Mirren.* A great cast delivers outstanding performances in this gripping adaptation of Harold Pinter's critically acclaimed 1960 play. Harry (Olivier) and Bill (McDowell) are an embittered gay couple who come under attack from the menacing Bates when he accuses the younger Bill of sleeping with his wife (Mirren). Veiled threats and jealousy give way to deception, disappointment and betrayal as all four characters become trapped in a series of recriminations. ★★★½

La Collectionneuse

(1966, 88 min, France, Eric Rohmer) *Patrick Bachau, Daniel Pommereulle, Haydeé Politoff.* An interesting investigation of gender politics as well as

modern notions of art, beauty and truth, Rohmer's "fable," the fourth in a series of six, offers an unusual parable for those unschooled in the complex games of sexual pairing. The story revolves around Adrian, a self-important would-be gallery owner, his painter friend Daniel, and a Lolita-esque nymphette (Politoff). The story unfolds through Adrian's voice-over with a minimal and beautiful use of visual explication. Though the narrative is at times overbearing and didactic, the film maintains an even pace, thorough characterization and a solid story. (French with English subtitles) ★★★ VHS: $19.99; DVD: $29.99

The Collector

(1965, 119 min, GB, William Wyler) *Terence Stamp, Samantha Eggar, Mona Washbourne.* Searing psychological thriller with Stamp kidnapping Eggar and keeping his prisoner in his basement. Superior performances from the two leads. ★★★½ VHS: $19.99

College

(1927, 66 min, US, James W. Horne) *Buster Keaton, Ann Cornwall.* Keaton stars as a scholar who looks down on athletics but is forced to participate in order to win the attention of his girl. Compared to other Keaton comedies, this is minor, but it is elevated by some memorable gags. ★★★ VHS: $29.99; DVD: $29.99

College Swing

(1938, 86 min, US, Raoul Walsh) *Bob Hope, George Burns, Gracie Allen, Martha Raye, Edward Everett Horton.* Hope's second film is an intermittently amusing hodgepodge of music, laughs, swing, academia and romance. The film's palatable when the five leads are on screen. But some of the musical numbers, an icky romance subplot, and a few comic sequences are rough going. However, it's one of the few films from the 1930s to actually show living and breathing teenagers. They're the real *Swing Kids.* ★★ VHS: $14.99

Colonel Redl

(1984, 144 min, Hungary/Germany, István Szabó) *Klaus Maria Brandauer, Armin Mueller-Stahl, Gudrun Landgrebe.* Brandauer gives a bravura performance as a man driven by a lust for power to rise from the son of a poor railway worker to become head of military intelligence and commander of the 8th Army in Prague. A sweeping historical epic of intrigue, love and treason set in Austria during the turbulent years leading up to WWI. (German with English subtitles) ★★★

Color Me Blood Red

(1965, 79 min, US, Hershell Gordon Lewis) *Don Joseph, Candi Conder.* A struggling artist (Joseph) finds that blood supplies the perfect color for his newest painting. He begins getting his art supply from the dripping fingers of his girlfriend, but fingers soon turn to something much easier — simply smash her face against a canvas and instant art! With the usual bad acting and homemade (but always disturbing) gore. The final third of Lewis' blood trilogy which includes *Blood Feast* and *Two Thousand Maniacs.* ★ VHS: $29.99; DVD: $24.99

The Color of Money

(1986, 119 min, US, Martin Scorsese) *Paul Newman, Tom Cruise, Mary Elizabeth Mastrantonio, Helen Shaver, John Turturro, Forest Whitaker.*

Newman won an Oscar for re-creating his acclaimed role as *The Hustler*, "Fast Eddie" Felsen, ex-pool hustler turned liquor retailer, who vicariously relives the glory days of his youth through a hotshot pool player (Cruise). With Scorsese's inventive direction and Robbie Robertson's smoky score, this is a rare film experience. ★★★★ DVD: $29.99

Color of Night

(1994, 140 min, US, Richard Rush) *Bruce Willis, Jane March, Ruben Blades, Lesley Ann Warren, Scott Bakula, Lance Henriksen, Kevin J. O'Connor.* Sigmund Freud meets a limp *Die Hard* in this mildly diverting but far from mysterious murder mystery starring Willis as a troubled psychologist who gets caught up in a series of murders. After one of his patients throws herself from his New York penthouse, he moves to L.A. where he becomes involved in murder, car chases, a group therapy session from hell, and a mystery woman. Willis tries to play off his "tough guy" image (his character is a gun-fearing Clark Kent-type), but it doesn't last long. Includes the controversial frontal nude scenes of Willis. Be prepared to be disappointed. (Director's cut) ★★ VHS: $9.99; DVD: $29.99

The Color of Paradise

(1999, 90 min, Iran, Majid Majidi) *Hosein Mahjoob, Salameh Feyzi.* Director Majidi, who helmed the exquisite *Children of Heaven*, weaves another moving, lyrical story that is certain to touch the heart. Mohammad is a young blind boy who returns home from the Institute of the Blind for the summer. Happy to be reunited with his father and grandmother, the child maintains a wondrous perspective on life even though it becomes clear that his father plans on disowning him. A haunting look at childhood innocence and the beauty that surrounds us. (Farsi with English subtitles) ★★★½ VHS: $21.99; DVD: $29.99

The Color of Pomegranates

(1969, 80 min, USSR/Armenia, Sergei Paradjanov) *Sofiko Chiaureli, M. Aleksanian.* Shelved after being termed "hermetic and obscure" by Soviet authorities, this poetic masterpiece was the last film director Paradjanov made before his five-year imprisonment in 1974 on trumped up charges of "incitement to suicide, speculation in foreign currency, spreading venereal disease, homosexuality and speculation in art objects." *The Color of Pomegranates* focuses on the powerful works and spiritual odyssey of 17th-century Armenian poet Sayat Nova. Filled with oblique, symbolic imagery, this exotic mosaic of a film is divided into eight sections, each depicting — from childhood to death — a period of the poet's life. A tribute not only to Nova but to the spirituality of the Armenian people. (Armenian with English subtitles) ★★★½ VHS: $29.99; DVD: $34.99

The Color Purple

(1985, 153 min, US, Steven Spielberg) *Whoopi Goldberg, Danny Glover, Oprah Winfrey, Margaret Avery, Rae Dawn Chong, Adolph Caesar.* Spielberg's acclaimed though controversial screen version of Alice Walker's Pulitzer Prize—winning novel. Goldberg made a triumphant film debut as Celie, a black woman who tries to overcome the hardships of her arranged marriage to ill-tempered Mr. (Glover) to find her own identity. Winfrey and Avery are both terrific in support as, respectively, the live-in maid to an oppressive white family, and Mr.'s mistress, a cabaret singer who contributes greatly to Celie's flourishing. (Letterboxed) ★★★½ VHS: $19.99; DVD: $24.99

Colors

(1988, 120 min, US, Dennis Hopper) *Robert Duvall, Sean Penn, Maria Conchita Alonso, Damon Wayans.* A clamorous vision of gang warfare in Los Angeles directed by Hopper, with his patented flair for the unusual and bizarre. Duvall and Penn are fine in their roles as L.A. cops, but what really gives the film its edge is the presence of actual gang members whom Hopper cast to play the Bloods and the Crips — the city's largest rival gangs. Without totally departing from action movie conventions, *Colors* brims with flavor and detail and features a tremendous soundtrack. ★★★ VHS: $9.99

Coma

(1978, 113 min, US, Michael Crichton) *Genevieve Bujold, Michael Douglas, Richard Widmark, Elizabeth Ashley, Tom Selleck, Rip Torn.* Solid medical thriller adapted and directed by former med student Crichton. Bujold is a Boston doctor whose investigations into a series of inexplicable hospital deaths leads her to a horrifying conspiracy. Douglas is her disbelieving boyfriend, and Widmark is well cast as a hospital administrator. (Letterboxed VHS available for $19.99) ★★★ VHS: $14.99; DVD: $19.99

Combination Platter

(1993, 85 min, US/China, Tony Chan) *Jeff Lau, Colleen O'Brien.* Director Chan elicits finely drawn characterizations with minimal exposition in this low-budget independent feature. Centering around the efforts of a young, newly arrived Hong Kong emigré to get his green card, the deceptively simple story line allows a good ensemble cast to reveal the distinct personalities of a group of restaurant employees dealing with interpersonal conflicts, annoying customers, Department of Immigration agents and familial expectations. A small film, but knowing and direct in its execution. (English and Chinese with English subtitles) ★★★ VHS: $79.99

Come and Get It

(1936, 99 min, US, Howard Hawks & William Wyler) *Edward Arnold, Joel McCrea, Frances Farmer, Walter Brennan.* An aggressive entrepreneur in the Northwest timber country abandons true love for the boss' daughter. Many years later, he's deluded into believing that he can revoke that decision of youth. Robust performances throughout. Brennan won his first of three Oscars. ★★★ VHS: $14.99; DVD: $24.99

Come and See

(1985, 142 min, USSR, Elem Klimov) *Alexei Kravchenko, Olga Mironova.* The theatrical availability in 1987 of this remarkably powerful Russian film by the long-ostracized director Elem Klimov was one of the first tangible results of glasnost in the Soviet Union. Told with a barrage of electrifying imagery, *Come and See* is an account of the brutal invasion suffered by the Russians at the hands of Hitler. Episodes shift back and forth between the ultra-realistic and a dreamlike surrealism which borders on hallu-

cinogenic. As seen through the eyes of a young boy, the Nazi atrocities against his village burn the screen with fierce images which will linger for a long time to come. A powerful cinematic achievement. (Russian with English subtitles) ★★★★ VHS: $59.99

Come Back, Little Sheba

(1952, 99 min, US, Daniel Mann) *Burt Lancaster, Shirley Booth, Terry Moore.* Though she'll probably always be remembered as TV's "Hazel," Booth's finest hour came when she set the stage and screen afire with her unforgettable Oscar-winning performance as the downtrodden wife of an alcoholic (Lancaster). In this brilliant screen version of William Inge's play, Booth and Lancaster rent their home to young Moore, setting the stage for jealousy and recriminations. ★★★★ VHS: $14.99

Come Back to the 5 & Dime, Jimmy Dean, Jimmy Dean

(1982, 110 min, US, Robert Altman) *Cher, Sandy Dennis, Karen Black, Kathy Bates, Sudie Bond.* The stage is set for emotional warfare of a James Dean Fan Club reunion in a dust-bowl Texas town. Sandy's psyche, Cher's chest, Karen's contours and Kathy's sobriety are all in question as every skeleton tumbles from the closet in Altman's bitchy, Southern cat fight. ★★★

Come Blow Your Horn

(1963, 112 min, US, Bud Yorkin) *Frank Sinatra, Lee J. Cobb, Molly Picon, Barbara Rush, Jill St. John, Tony Bill.* Based on Neil Simon's stage play, this free-wheeling comedy charts swinging Sinatra's bachelorhood as he tries to guide his younger brother (Bill in his screen debut) on the same road. Cobb is excellent as Sinatra's traditional father not happy with the course his sons are taking. ★★★ VHS: $14.99

Come Dance with Me

(Voulez-vous danser avec moi?)

(1959, 91 min, France, Michel Boisrond) *Brigitte Bardot, Henry Vidal.* In this fluffy comedy-thriller, Bardot does some Nancy Drew-like sleuthing into the murder of a female dance studio owner, a murder that the police believe was committed by her dentist husband. Shot in bright colors and in a breezy style, the film follows Virginia (BB) as she gets a job as a dance instructor at the studio and tries to figure out whodunit. (Letterboxed) (French with English subtitles) (aka: *Do You Want to Dance with Me?*) ★★½ VHS: $14.99; DVD: $29.99

Come See the Paradise

(1990, 138 min, US, Alan Parker) *Dennis Quaid, Tamlyn Tomita, Sab Shimono.* In this story of the internment of Japanese-Americans in camps during WWII, Parker gets credit for tackling a subject heretofore untouched by any American film, though one wishes the story had more dramatic structure. The first half of the film follows the love affair between a projectionist (Quaid) and his Asian boss' daughter (Tomita). Married for only a short time, they are separated after the bombing of Pearl Harbor. Quaid is drafted, and Tomita and her entire family are uprooted and sent to the camps. The remainder of the film centers on the heart-breaking conditions they face. ★★★ VHS: $19.99

The Comedy of Terrors

(1963, 84 min, US, Jacques Tourneur) *Boris Karloff, Vincent Price, Peter Lorre, Basil Rathbone.* A real treat from Val Lewton's disciple Tourneur. Two bumbling undertakers (Price, Lorre) supplement their business by murdering elderly potential clientele. Karloff is Price's father-in-law, and Rathbone plays a vengeful landlord who accidentally becomes an on-again, off-again customer. With a hilarious and extremely literate script by Richard Matheson, superb art direction, beautiful cinematography and an impressive score, *The Comedy of Terrors* stands alongside Roger Corman's best Price/Poe films. It's a devious send-up of the best Shakespearean tragedies which succeeds as both black comedy and tongue-in-cheek horror camp. ★★★½ VHS: $12.99

Comes a Horseman

(1978, 118 min, US, Alan J. Pakula) *Jane Fonda, Jason Robards, James Caan, Richard Farnsworth, George Grizzard.* In Montana after the second world war, ranch owner Robards wants Fonda's spread because he knows something she doesn't — there's oil under her land. The only thing stopping him: tough cowboy Caan. Farnsworth is terrific as Fonda's dedicated ranch hand. (Available letterboxed or pan & scan) ★★★ VHS: $9.99

Comfort and Joy

(1984, 90 min, Scotland, Bill Forsyth) *Bill Paterson, Eleanor David.* Forsyth's whimsical mixture of "Alice in Wonderland" and *Sullivan's Travels.* When his kleptomaniacal, live-in lover abandons him, Alan (a cheerfully bland Glasgow radio personality) falls into a frightful funk and, aimlessly searching for salvation, stumbles into the midst of a gangland battle between rival factions of an ice cream cartel. ★★★ VHS: $9.99

The Comfort of Strangers

(1991, 102 min, GB, Paul Schrader) *Rupert Everett, Natasha Richardson, Christopher Walken, Helen Mirren.* Director Schrader delves into the dark side of human nature with this visually exquisite production of Harold Pinter's screenplay about a young English couple (Everett, Richardson) who retreat to Venice to re-evaluate their relationship, and find themselves pawns in the twisted games of an Italian nobleman and his invalid wife (Walken, Mirren). Marred only slightly by a seemingly unmotivated shock ending, this is quirky entertainment. ★★★

Comic Book Confidential

(1990, 85 min, US, Ron Mann) For devotees of animation, comic books and the creative forces behind them, this fascinating and delightful documentary is required viewing. The film combines historical footage, montages of comic art and a series of amusing interviews with many of the leading independent animators of the last 20 years, including William M. Gaines (of *Mad* magazine fame), Stan Lee, Robert Crumb, Linda Barry, Art Spiegelman and many others. From the very first comic, "Funnies on Parade," to the very latest, "Raw," the film provides an entertaining and informational peek behind the animated doors of comics and their creators. ★★★ VHS: $19.99

Coming Home

(1978, 127 min, US, Hal Ashby) *Jane Fonda, Jon Voight, Bruce Dern, Penelope Milford, Robert Carradine.* The stunning, Oscar-winning perfor-

C

mances of Voight and Fonda dominate this moving Vietnam war drama about disabled Voight beginning an affair with married Fonda, whose husband Dern is overseas. A poignant love story and gripping anti-war film which unfortunately over-dramatizes some of its key scenes. ★★★ VHS: $9.99

Coming Out

(1989, 109 min, East Germany, Heiner Carow) *Matthias Freihof, Dirk Kummer, Michael Gwisdek, Dagmar Manzel.* This was East Germany's first and only gay-themed film, which reportedly received its premiere on the same night the Berlin Wall came down. It is a gripping study of a man searching for his true sexual identity. Philip is a "straight" schoolteacher whose repressed homosexuality is ignited after meeting an old school chum with whom he had a gay affair. Reminiscent of quasi-autobiographical films (and all involving schoolteachers) like *Taxi Zum Klo* and *Nighthawks*, this is a sentimental but frank tale which offers a rare glimpse into the "perils" of homosexuality behind the now-destroyed Iron Curtain. (German with English subtitles) ★★★ VHS: $79.99

Coming Out under Fire

(1994, 71 min, US, Arthur Dong) This entertaining and eye-opening documentary centers on nine lesbians and gay men and their experiences as "undesirables" in the armed forces during WWII. Based on Allen Berube's book "Coming Out under Fire: The History of Gay Men and Women in World War II," the film provides a historical overview of the American government's shifting attitudes towards gays in the military and allows the interviewees to describe vivid personal experiences of the discriminatory practices of their own government. The film comes alive when the often eloquent vets recount both their good times and bad living as closeted homosexuals in an organization that viewed them as unfit for service, morally suspect or potentially hazardous to morale. ★★★ VHS: $14.99

Coming to America

(1988, 116 min, US, John Landis) *Eddie Murphy, Arsenio Hall, James Earl Jones, Samuel L. Jackson, Cuba Gooding, Jr.* Only sporadically funny, this Murphy comedy is surprisingly good-natured, a change of pace for the comic. An African prince (Murphy) engaged to a native woman decides to leave his home and head to New York in search of true love. Hall is his "man Friday" who accompanies the prince on his quest. What ensues is a rather formulaic fish-out-of-water tale with most of its jokes telegraphed hours before they arrive. ★★½ VHS: $14.99; DVD: $29.99

Coming Up Roses

(1986, 93 min, Wales, Stephen Bayly) *Dafydd Hywel, Iola Gregory.* A mildly amusing updating of *The Smallest Show on Earth*. Against the grim landscape of Thatcher's England, three employees of a dilapidated movie theatre struggle to save the old house. (Welsh with English subtitles) ★★½

Command Decision

(1949, 113 min, US, Sam Wood) *Clark Gable, Walter Pidgeon, Van Johnson, Brian Donlevy.* Gable stars as an Air Force general wrestling with his conscience about sending young men off to a certain death in order to achieve a strategic victory. Pidgeon plays Gable's superior officer;

Johnson is a raw recruit. A gripping and thoughtful war adventure based on the '40s stage hit. ★★★ VHS: $19.99

Commandments

(1997, 87 min, US, Daniel Taplitz) *Aidan Quinn, Courteney Cox, Anthony LaPaglia, Pamela Gray.* An ambitious but misguided quasi-religious comedy-drama, *Commandments* features the underrated Quinn as an emotionally troubled physician who attempts to come to terms with his life after facing a series of traumatic experiences. Losing his wife, job, house and even his dog, Quinn tries to commit suicide, but even that doesn't work out. He lands in a hospital where he recounts his mess of a life and decides the only retribution for his problems is breaking all his Ten Commandments. These elements are certainly enough for an interesting film, and *Commandments* is for a while. Eventually, however, first-time director Taplitz (who also scripted) has trouble juggling all of the elements, resulting in a muddle of a movie. ★★ VHS: $9.99

Commando

(1985, 90 min, US, Mark L. Lester) *Arnold Schwarzenegger, Rae Dawn Chong, Dan Hedaya.* This fast-paced, often amusing adventure thriller (though violent and cluttered) is one of Schwarzenegger's best action films from the early part of his career. Arnold plays a retired Army colonel who sets out to rescue his young daughter, kidnapped by an exiled Latin American dictator. ★★½ VHS: $9.99; DVD: $29.99

Commissar

(1967, 105 min, USSR, Alexander Askoldov) *Nonna Mordyukova, Rolan Bykov.* Banned for 21 years by Soviet authorities, this remarkable human drama shocked the censors with its bold themes of anti-Semitism and women's rights. Set in 1920 during the Russian Civil War, the story follows the austere Claudia, whose military career as a Red Army commander is jeopardized when she becomes pregnant by a comrade. She moves in with a poor Jewish family in the countryside until the child is born. Initially hostile to the family's religion and peasant ways, she soon finds herself softening and appreciating the cultural differences they have as well as the common bonds they all share. After the child is born, she faces the difficult choice of staying or rejoining the army. (Russian with English subtitles) ★★★½ VHS: $59.99

Commissioner of the Sewers

(1986, 60 min, US, Klaus Maeck) *William Burroughs.* From the publication of his novel "Junky" in 1963 through the present with the Hollywood-backed film version of his "Naked Lunch," William S. Burroughs has remained a controversial and fascinating figure. This documentary doesn't uncover anything new for seasoned Burroughs-philes, but for the uninitiated, it will prove to be enlightening as Burroughs — with his deadpan wit and outlandish theories — pontificates on everything from his beliefs on death after life, art and artists, to the meaning of his cut-up style of writing. He concludes with a reading of his now famous, and bitterly sarcastic, "Thanksgiving Prayer." ★★½ VHS: $29.99

The Commitments

(1991, 116 min, Ireland, Alan Parker) *Robert Arkins, Michael Aherne, Colm Meaney, Angeline Ball.* Parker's exuberant homage to the Dublin music

scene has at its heart a highly talented cast of non-actors recruited for their musical skills. The story follows Jimmy, a determined young hustler who can't rest until he realizes his dreams of putting together a soul group. What the film lacks in plot is more than amply made up for in raw energy and outstanding musical numbers, all of which were actually performed by the cast. Some of the versions of soul standards ("Try a Little Tenderness," "Mustang Sally") compare very favorably with the originals. ★★★½ DVD: $29.99

Committed

(1984, 77 min, US, Sheila McLaughlin & Lynne Tillman) *Committed* tells the striking story of film star/leftist iconoclast Frances Farmer. While dealing with the same subject as *Frances*, with Jessica Lange, this independent production avoids some of the theatrics in this feminist interpretation of her life. In 1935, Farmer was an overnight Hollywood sensation; within ten years she was in a state mental hospital. From stardom to a locked ward to a lobotomy, the film reconstructs a compelling and many-layered look at the life and repression of this culturally defiant woman. ★★★ VHS: $29.99

Common Threads: Stories from the Quilt

(1989, 79 min, US, Robert Epstein & Jeffrey Friedman) *Narrated by: Dustin Hoffman, Cleve Jones.* In this Academy Award—winning documentary, Epstein and Friedman talk with surviving relatives and friends of five people who died of AIDS and were memorialized by the AIDS Quilt. The film presents an emotionally charged look into their lives, as told by those left behind through recollection, photographs and film. Of course, there is great poignancy to these stories. But the storytellers also infuse a spirit of being to the departed which obviously helps keep the memory of those loved ones alive. Not a eulogistic memorial, but rather personal and heartfelt reminiscences. ★★★½ VHS: $24.99

Communion

(1989, 109 min, US, Philippe Mora) *Christopher Walken, Lindsay Crouse, Frances Sternhagen.* Based on Whitley Strieber's best-seller, which detailed his experiences with alien beings, this serious-minded science-fiction thriller is far more interesting for the allegations presented by the author than for the outcome of the film. Walken, usually adept at playing eccentric characters, gives a truly strange performance as Strieber. The only cast member to really come out of this muddle totally unscathed is Sternhagen, who plays a psychiatrist all too familiar with close encounters of the third kind. ★★ VHS: $14.99; DVD: $29.99

The Company of Wolves

(1985, 95 min, GB, Neil Jordan) *David Warner, Angela Lansbury, Stephen Rea.* An offbeat Freudian adaptation of "Little Red Riding Hood" which intriguingly explores some of the adult subtexts of the classic story. An atmospheric mixture of dreams and fantasy, the film teeters on the edge of the downright bizarre, but it remains a frighteningly mysterious and slightly sexy thriller. ★★★

Company: Original Cast Album

(1970, 58 min, US, D.A. Pennebaker) *Elaine Stritch, Dean Jones, Barbara Barrie, Charles Kimbrough, Harold Prince.* Behind-the-scenes look at the recording sessions of Stephen Sondheim's Tony Award–winning Broadway musical "Company." The original Broadway cast, including Stritch, Barrie, Kimbrough, and Jones (who replaced lead Larry Kert after three weeks), shine and grind it out in this truly revealing documentary of the creative process at work. For anyone who cherishes the cast recording, especially Stritch's classic rendering of "The Ladies Who Lunch," this is a must. ★★★½ VHS: $24.99; DVD: $29.99

Les Comperes

(1983, 92 min, France, Francis Vèbor) *Gérard Depardieu, Pierre Richard, Anny Duperey*. This very funny farce features the odd-couple Depardieu and Richard as the two former lovers of a woman who is desperately looking for her runaway son, and who enlists each of them to help find him by telling each that he is the child's father. Depardieu, as an ox-like journalist, and Richard, as a bumbling depressive, prove to be a winning combo. (American remake: *Father's Day*) (French with English subtitles) ★★★½

The Competition

(1984, 129 min, US, Joel Olianski) *Richard Dreyfuss, Amy Irving, Lee Remick, Sam Wanamaker*. Concert pianists Irving and Dreyfuss compete against one another for the same prize — only to find romance blossoming between them. It's predictable melodramatics, but the two stars are sincere and the concert footage nicely balances the film. ★★½ VHS: $9.99

Le Complot

(1973, 120 min, France, René Granville) *Jean Rochefort, Michel Bouquet*. This taut espionage thriller is not in the same class as *Z* or *Day of the Jackal* (based on the same historical episode), but is still gripping entertainment. In 1960, Charles DeGaulle, frustrated by its bloody insurrection, granted Algeria independence, much to the shock of millions of Frenchmen who viewed Algeria as an integral part of French domain. The political unrest spawned by DeGaulle's actions resulted in an underground terrorist movement, organized by French-Algerians, fanatical right-wing patriots and disillusioned officers formerly stationed in the North African colony. The labyrinthine webs of alliances, surveillance, deceit and betrayal are revealed as the film follows police and government agencies seeking to destroy the terrorist organization before the Republican order is threatened. (French with English subtitles) ★★★

Compromising Positions

(1985, 98 min, US, Frank Perry) *Susan Sarandon, Judith Ivey, Raul Julia, Joe Mantegna, Edward Herrmann, Mary Beth Hurt*. This offbeat comic mystery is, for the most part, an entertaining sleeper with the terrific Sarandon as a Long Island housewife who sets out to find just who killed dentist Mantegna. As her investigation ensues, she discovers the womanizing doctor could have been done in by any one of his female patients. Though the film's resolution is not up to par, it's certainly fun getting there. Among the supporting cast, Ivey is terrific as Sarandon's acerbic friend. ★★★ VHS: $14.99

Compulsion

(1959, 105 min, US, Richard Fleischer) *Dean Stockwell, Bradford Dillman, Orson Welles, E.G.*

Marshall. An outstanding, thought-provoking and ultimately suspenseful account of the Leopold-Loeb murder case, *Compulsion* is an enthralling, three-part, fictionalized telling of the notorious murder trial (also told in *Rope* and *Swoon*). Stockwell and Dillman as Judd and Artie, two rich geniuses who, seemingly friendless, are involved in a "dangerously close" relationship ('50s code for gay). The first third of the film examines their friendship, in which they kidnap a local boy and murder him. The murder investigation fills the middle third of the film, and the inevitable murder trial follows. Welles appears as their agnostic defense attorney, who is based on Clarence Darrow. In a magnificent portrayal, Welles delivers some of the most moving courtroom speeches outside of *Inherit the Wind*. ★★★★ VHS: $19.99

Con Air

(1997, 115 min, US, Simon West) *Nicolas Cage, John Malkovich, John Cusack, Steve Buscemi, Ving Rhames, Colm Meaney, Mykelti Williamson*. Producer Jerry Bruckheimer calls on Cage to deliver more of the same high-octane excitement of their previous smash, *The Rock*. More of the same is what you get with *Con Air*, a high-voltage ride which copies much of *The Rock*'s action framework without necessarily improving upon it. Cage plays a former Army ranger unjustly sentenced to prison. Upon his parole and flight home, his plane is commandeered by a group of ruthless criminals en route to maximum security. Under the leadership of psycho Malkovich, they plan their getaway, unaware that Cage is trying to sabotage their every move. Though engaging and offering many slam-bang action sequences, the film suffers from the lack of truly inventive action set pieces — we've seen all this elsewhere. But *Con Air* also has a hip sense of humor, and maintains a good degree of tension throughout. (VHS available letterboxed or pan & scan) ★★½ VHS: $14.99; DVD: $29.99

Conan the Barbarian

(1981, 130 min, US, John Milius) *Arnold Schwarzenegger, Sandahl Bergman, James Earl Jones*. Robert E. Howard's pulp fantasy hero is given full fleshy form by Schwarzenegger. The story, very faithful to the tone of the original novels, takes us from Conan's barbarian boyhood and his enslavement and training as a pit fighter through sundry minor adventures and escapades, bringing it full circle as he confronts the murderer of his parents and destroyer of his village, the evil sorcerer Thulsa Doom (Jones). *Conan* is a rousing adventure with plenty of chest-thumping, sword-hacking, male-bonding fun. The testosterone-laden script, by cowriters Milius and Oliver Stone, wisely gives most of the lines to everyone *but* Arnold, and moves briskly along. Add to this an adventurous musical score and Ron Cobb's outstanding "period fantasy" production design, and *Conan* is sure to please. ★★★ VHS: $9.99; DVD: $29.99

Conan the Destroyer

(1984, 103 min, US, Richard Fleischer) *Arnold Schwarzenegger, Grace Jones, Mako, Wilt Chamberlain*. The emphasis is on comedy, rather than revenge, in this disappointing sequel. This time around, Conan and cohorts (including a laughable Chamberlain) must rescue a princess from the clutches of an evil wizard. This story, however, is needlessly complicated, lacking the

simplicity and economy of the original film's script, which was its saving grace. *Destroyer*, however, is not without its pleasures: Jones and Mako are among them. Arnold is given too many lines to say this time around, but manages an admirable performance when he sticks to swinging a sword and flexing his pecs. Though the final fight is in the adventurous spirit of Robert E. Howard's original stories, it is not really worth the wait. ★½ VHS: $9.99; DVD: $24.99

The Conductor

(1979, 110 min, Poland, Andrzej Wajda) *John Gielgud, Krystyna Janda*. Dubbed with a jarringly inappropriate Polish voice, Gielgud nevertheless is quite commanding as an elderly Polish émigré and internationally renowned maestro who returns to his homeland after a 50-year absence. There, he rouses the provincial Gdansk Orchestra with a stirring version of Beethoven's "Fifth Symphony." Gielgud is believable as the baton-twirling conductor, although the film never comes together. (Polish with English subtitles) ★★ VHS: $79.99

Coneheads

(1993, 87 min, US, Steve Barron) *Dan Aykroyd, Jane Curtin, Jason Alexander, David Spade, Phil Hartman, Michelle Burke, Michael McKean, Jon Lovitz, Sinbad, Chris Farley, Ellen DeGeneres*. Surprisingly sophisticated humor, winning performances and neat special effects redeem what might have been just another bastard child sprung from the loins of "Saturday Night Live." Aykroyd and Curtin reprise their roles as Beldar and Primaat Conehead, who become trapped in suburbia USA. What initially reads as a one-joke premise (and one of the more tedious of the SNL sketches) is adroitly expanded into ideal entertainment for those who like their comedy off the wall. ★★★ VHS: $14.99; DVD: $29.99

Confidential Report

(1955, 99 min, GB, Orson Welles) *Orson Welles, Michael Redgrave, Akim Tamiroff*. Welles takes a factual mysterious occurrence and weaves a mesmerizing, convoluted tale of intrigue, deception and false identity. Welles plays Gregory Arkadin, a man of immense wealth and power, who commissions a petty gangster to compile a dossier on the origins of… Gregory Arkadin. Pay attention: the action moves very swiftly. Remastered print. (aka: *Mr. Arkadin*) ★★★ VHS: $29.99

Confidentially Yours

(1984, 111 min, France, François Truffaut) *Fanny Ardant, Jean-Louis Tringtignant*. Truffaut's final film is a joyously spirited blend of screwball antics and film noir intrigue. The zesty Ardant is an intrepid Girl Friday determined to clear her boss of a murder charge. This supremely stylish romantic comedy sparkles with the director's joie de vivre. (French with English subtitles) ★★★½ VHS: $19.99; DVD: $29.99

Conflict

(1945, 86 min, US, Curtis Bernhardt) *Humphrey Bogart, Sydney Greenstreet, Alexis Smith*. An interesting misfire for Bogart. He plays a wife-killer who becomes involved in a psychological cat-and-mouse game with psychiatrist Greenstreet, who devises a scheme to get the murderer to admit his guilt. Smith is especially good as the younger sister of Bogart's deceased wife. ★★ VHS: $19.99

C

The Conformist

(1969, 115 min, Italy, Bernardo Bertolucci) *Jean-Louis Trintignant, Dominique Sanda, Stefania Sandrelli.* This fascinating exploration of the emotional roots of Fascism in pre-war Italy ranks as one of the best Italian films of the 1970s. Trintignant stars as Marcello, a repressed homosexual traumatized by a childhood incident in which he shot the family chauffeur after a seduction attempt. Now an adult, Marcello longs for conformity and appears to find it when he joins the Italian Fascist secret service and tries to hide his homosexuality by marrying a vapid, petite bourgeois woman he barely tolerates. Sent to assassinate his former professor, who is now a leading dissident, he meets and is "attracted" to a lesbian and anti-fascist (the alluring Sanda), who eventually develops into the moral adversary to Marcello's perverted beliefs. Sanda, who performs an exhilarating tango with Sandrelli, is a strong counterweight to Trintignant's Marcello. (Italian with English subtitles) ★★★★

Congo

(1995, 109 min, US, Frank Marshall) *Dylan Walsh, Ernie Hudson, Tim Curry, Laura Linney, Joe Don Baker, Bruce Campbell.* An expedition into the Congo to return a talking ape (don't ask!) to her native habitat turns deadly when the troop stumbles across a legendary diamond mine guarded by a race of killer gorillas. One might expect that such a premise by the author of *Jurassic Park* would have some degree of style and suspense. Look elsewhere. Marshall's uninspired direction and a hodgepodge screenplay strips away all but the barest of sci-fi nuance. The result is a frivolous Disney-style adventure which plays like *Swiss Family Robinson*. Only Hudson's tongue-in-cheek portrayal of a "great white hunter" provides enjoyment. (Letterboxed VHS available for $14.99) ★★ VHS: $9.99; DVD: $24.99

A Connecticut Yankee

(1931, 95 min, US, David Butler) *Will Rogers, Maureen O'Sullivan, Myrna Loy.* Mark Twain's novel gets the Hollywood treatment once over. Rogers was a force to be reckoned with back in the 1930s, with his "I only know what I read in the papers" attitude softening the sting of his satire that would have gotten him branded a "fellow traveler" in the dark ages of the '50s. This version starts in a haunted house with radio repairman

A Connecticut Yankee

Rogers getting blasted back to the 6th century and ends with Model Ts riding to the rescue of King and country. Unlike the Bing Crosby version, Rogers never sings. ★★★ VHS: $19.99

A Connecticut Yankee in King Arthur's Court

(1949, 107 min, US, Tay Garnett) *Bing Crosby, Rhonda Fleming, William Bendix, Cedric Hardwicke.* Musicalized, pleasant third screen version of the Mark Twain tale, with Crosby as a 20th-century blacksmith who is transported back in time to the court of King Arthur. Bing croons a couple of tunes. ★★½ VHS: $14.99

The Conqueror Worm

(1968, 88 min, GB, Michael Reeves) *Vincent Price, Ian Ogilvy.* Price stars as Matthew Hopkins in this fascinating historical drama. In the 17th-century England during the struggle between Cromwell and the Crown, Hopkins and his associates seek out and persecute "witches," as well as anyone else who incurs their wrath. When Hopkins executes the priest of a small town for being a warlock, he and his partner find themselves the target of a young soldier who leaves his post in Cromwell's army to hunt down and kill the pair. The movie is immensely engrossing and captures the English period detail remarkably well for a low-budget production. Price is at his menacing, sadistic best. The only complaint with the film is that it has been released on video with its original orchestral score replaced by a totally inappropriate and repetitive synthesizer track. (aka: *Witchfinder General*) ★★★½ VHS: $12.99

Conquest

(1937, 112 min, US, Clarence Brown) *Greta Garbo, Charles Boyer.* Good romantic costumer with Garbo as Napoleon's Polish mistress, Marie Walewska. Boyer effectively plays the French conqueror. ★★★ VHS: $19.99

Conquest of the Planet of the Apes

(1972, 87 min, US, J. Lee Thompson) *Roddy McDowall, Ricardo Montalban, Natalie Trundy, Don Murray.* Fourth in the *Apes* series. Back on present-day Earth, domesticated apes, who have been made slave-like servants, begin to rebel against the humans. The appeal of the series had begun to run its course, but this still manages to entertain in spite of itself. ★★½ VHS: $14.99

Consenting Adult

(1985, 100 min, US, Gilbert Cates) *Martin Sheen, Marlo Thomas, Barry Tubbs.* A compelling, well-made if ever-so-sincere TV movie based on the Laura Hobson ("Gentlemen's Agreement") bestseller, and updated by a decade to include such topics as AIDS and anti-gay crime. Thomas has one of her best roles as the mother of a college athlete who must come to terms with her son when she discovers he is gay. ★★★

Consenting Adults

(1993, 99 min, US, Alan J. Pakula) *Kevin Kline, Mary Elizabeth Mastrantonio, Kevin Spacey, Forest Whitaker.* Yet another in the glut of "steamy erotic thrillers," this one from the director of *Presumed Innocent.* A night of passion erupts into murder and betrayal when a married man (Kline) finds his neighbor's wife too tempting to

Jodie Foster in Contact

resist. Mastrantonio is the betrayed wife, and a creepy Spacey is the cuckold husband — or is he? What could have been an A-1 thriller is defeated by ridiculous plot contrivances and oh-so-predictable twists and turns. ★½

Consolation Marriage

(1931, 82 min, US, Paul Sloane) *Irene Dunne, Pat O'Brien.* Dunne and O'Brien offer appealing performances in this standard romantic drama about jilted lovers who meet and marry, only to question their love when their former partners return. ★★½ VHS: $19.99

Conspiracy Theory

(1997, 135 min, US, Richard Donner) *Mel Gibson, Julia Roberts, Patrick Stewart.* Jerry Fletcher (Gibson) is a slightly paranoid New York cab driver who has an opinion on everything from a government conspiracy to assassinate the president by earthquake to Oliver Stone being a Republican pawn. You can read all about them in his newspaper, which has a circulation of five. However, when he's kidnapped by mysterious government agents, he may not be as paranoid as he, we, or Alice (Roberts), a Justice Department lawyer in whom he continually confides, may think. Crisply directed by Donner, *Conspiracy Theory* is an exciting, well-paced thriller that doesn't always follow logic but is fun nevertheless as it wends its way through intricate plot developments, unexpected twists and a dose of some good old-fashioned suspense. (Letterboxed VHS available for $19.99) ★★★ VHS: $14.99; DVD: $19.99

Consuming Passions

(1988, 98 min, GB, Giles Foster) *Vanessa Redgrave, Jonathan Pryce, Sammi Davis.* A floundering family-owned chocolate factory finds the recipe for success when three employees take an accidental dip in the mixing vats. If this sounds like an absurd premise, it is, but still there are occasional flashes of hilarity. Based on a short play by Terry Jones and Michael Palin. ★★½

Contact

(1997, 150 min, US, Robert Zemeckis) *Jodie Foster, Matthew McConaughey, Tom Skerritt, Angela Bassett, John Hurt, David Morse, James Woods, William Fichtner, Rob Lowe.* Director Zemeckis' take on Carl Sagan's novel is easily one of the most thoughtful films to make its way out of Hollywood in the last several years and, depending on one's spiritual point of view, one of the most profound. *Contact* follows Foster on a mythic journey that would make even Joseph Campbell proud as Dr. Eleanor Arroway, an astrophysicist whose life's work involves searching infinitesimal radio bandwidths for signs of extraterrestrial intelligence. Sagan's screenplay (he worked arduously on the filming until his death of cancer just prior to its completion) brilliantly intertwines Foster's endeavor with her almost desperate need for resolution around her father's death as she struggles with a sense of existential alienation and spiritual ambiguity. As directed by Zemeckis, the film is briskly paced (even at 150 minutes running time) and delivers its share of high-tech sci-fi wizardry which, combined with its lofty contemplations on life, the universe and everything, makes *Contact* a rare cinematic treat that tickles multiple pleasure zones. (VHS available letterboxed or pan & scan) ★★★★ VHS: $14.99; DVD: $19.99

Contempt

(1963, 103 min, France/Italy, Jean-Luc Godard) *Brigitte Bardot, Jack Palance, Fritz Lang, Michel Piccoli.* A piercing, alienating film about film. Godard tackles communication problems and the difficulties of creating a motion picture — the compromises, frustration, idiocy and sacrifice. Bardot is the contemptuous wife of a writer (Piccoli) who sells out. (French with English subtitles) ★★★½

The Contender

(2000, 125 min, US, Rod Lurie) *Joan Allen, Gary Oldman, Jeff Bridges, Christian Slater, Sam Elliott, William Petersen, Philip Baker Hall, Saul Rubinek, Mariel Hemingway.* With his sophomore production, writer-director Lurie continues exploring the political themes found in his first film *Deterrence*, but here they resonate much further to coalesce into a profound, moving study of honor and backroom political maneuverings. In a controlled, exemplary performance, Allen is Laine Hanson, a U.S. Senator who is chosen by the President (an exceptional Bridges) to fill the vacancy of Vice President when the V.P. dies in office. What should be a smooth appointment becomes political wheeling and dealing when the head of the confirmation committee (Oldman) — in an attempt to discredit the candidate — uncovers a sex scandal which Hanson may have been involved in years earlier. On the heels of the Clinton-Lewinsky affair, this discourse on the blurring of public service and private lives takes aim at a contemporary phenomena, squarely finding fault with ambitious politicians, a hungry press and a nation eager to learn the next dirty little secret. Oldman (who also executive produced) is outstanding as the vengeful Congressman, shading his McCarthy-like politico with equal parts venom, intelligence and humor. That he is a Republican to a Democratic administration may give evidence of the filmmaker's leanings, but it takes nothing away from this gripping, smart (and in the end even Capra-esque) morality play. ★★★★ VHS: $14.99; DVD: $26.99

Continental Divide

(1981, 103 min, US, Michael Apted) *John Belushi, Blair Brown, Allen Garfield.* Belushi shows his acting range in this likable little romantic comedy about a hard-nosed, cynical urbanite who travels to the Rockies to interview a reclusive, self-reliant ornithologist (Brown). Written by Lawrence Kasdan. ★★½ VHS: $7.49

Contraband

(1940, 88 min, GB, Michael Powell) *Conrad Veidt, Valerie Hobson, Esmond Knight, Leo Glenn.* Powell directs this Emeric Pressberger screenplay and the result is a briskly paced thriller in the edge-of-the-seat tradition of early Alfred Hitchcock. Set in 1939, the story begins on a commercial boat captained by Veidt. The chase is on when two of his passengers (one being Hobson) jump ship when docked for an inspection. Veidt follows the two into a blackout shrouded London where intrigue and murky dangerous characters seem to be at every corner. Th film is set in flashy Soho nightclubs and dank warehouses, as he unwittingly becomes ensnared in a Nazi espionage ring. Originally titled *Blackout* in the U.S., the film offers a light, even humorous approach while still keeping the viewer wide-eyed in the labyrinthine spy world. Veidt is especially memorable as the crusty but resourceful captain. ★★★★ VHS: $24.99; DVD: $29.99

The Conversation

(1974, 113 min, US, Francis Ford Coppola) *Gene Hackman, Robert Duvall, Frederic Forrest, Harrison Ford, Allen Garfield.* This harrowing and brilliant film on the ethical and moral dilemmas of wiretapping and its consequences on personal liberties is Coppola's best film outside of the *Godfather* series. Hackman gives a bravura performance as a surveillance specialist who comes to question the propriety of his profession, only to become a victim himself. Hackman tearing his apartment to shreds is one of the most devastating sequences ever put to film. ★★★★ VHS: $14.99; DVD: $29.99

Conversation Piece

(1974, 122 min, Italy, Luchino Visconti) *Burt Lancaster, Silvana Mangano, Helmut Berger, Claudia Marsani.* Lancaster is memorable as a retired intellectual whose life of solitude amid his books, paintings and art is abruptly invaded by the arrival of a garish "modern" family who move in upstairs. His old-world comforts are shattered as he is both drawn to and forced to participate in their tawdry and hedonistic lifestyle. The invading family (which brings a breath of fresh air, life and love into the professor's life) includes the enchanting countess (Mangano), her daughter (Marsani) and the Countess' student revolutionary boy-toy (Berger). (Filmed in English) ★★★

The Conviction

(1993, 92 min, Italy, Marco Bellocchio) *Vittorio Mezzogiorno, Claire Nebout, Andrzej Seweryn.* Attempting to capture some of the money-generating controversy of his sexually explicit *Devil in the Flesh*, Bellocchio's *The Conviction* tackles the murky but volatile subject of sexual harassment. A man and a woman get locked in a castle/museum after closing. The man, Lorenzo, and the woman, Sandra, play out a cat-and-mouse dance of domination and submission that eventually leads to a furious sexual conclusion. When the passions are spent, Lorenzo produces a key, prompting Sandra to feel used and abused. She initiates legal action claiming she was raped. What follows is a debate on sexuality and the problems between the sexes. (Italian with English subtitles) ★★½ VHS: $19.99

Coogan's Bluff

(1968, 100 min, US, Don Siegel) *Clint Eastwood, Lee J. Cobb, Susan Clark, Tisha Sterling.* Siegel directs with his usual manic pace as Arizona sheriff Clint becomes a fish out of water when he comes to the Big Apple to capture an escaped hood convicted of murder. ★★★ VHS: $14.99

The Cook, the Thief, His Wife & Her Lover

(1990, 126 min, GB, Peter Greenaway) *Helen Mirren, Michael Gambon, Richard Bohringer, Alan Howard, Tim Roth.* One of the most controversial films in years, the title of this Jacobean revenge-tragedy, set in an upscale French restaurant, says it all. The restaurant is visited nightly by the sadistic Thief (played ferociously by Gambon). His battered Wife (Mirren in a heartbreaking performance) seeks solace in her secret Lover whom she meets one evening while dining. The sympathetic Cook rounds out the cast. A surreal theatre piece combining moments of tender tragedy and stomach-turning physical and mental cruelty, the film suggests that revenge is not always sweet: It sometimes has a few bones. (Unrated) (Letterboxed) ★★★½ VHS: $14.99; DVD: $29.99

Cookie

(1989, 93 min, US, Susan Seidelman) *Peter Falk, Emily Lloyd, Dianne Wiest, Brenda Vaccaro, Jerry*

Bardot abed in *Contempt*

Lewis, Rikki Lake, Adrian Pasdar. Seidelman gets a couple of spirited performances in this cute tale by Nora Ephron. Smart-ass teenager Lloyd finally hooks up with the father (Falk) she never knew when she becomes his chauffeur after he is released from jail. ★★½ VHS: $14.99

Cookie's Fortune

(1999, 118 min, US, Robert Altman) *Glenn Close, Charles S. Dutton, Julianne Moore, Liv Tyler, Chris O'Donnell, Patricia Neal, Ned Beatty, Courtney B. Vance, Donald Moffat, Lyle Lovett.* Lyrical, endearing and as satisfying as a cool lemonade, Altman's playful comedy set in a most inviting small Mississippi town finds the director not only in top form but also in a most unusually good mood. The master of the ensemble, Altman utilizes a sublime cast for this Gothic parable about deception, loyalty and great catfish enchiladas. The elegant Neal is Cookie, a widow whose closest friend is her caretaker, Willis (Dutton). Estranged from family and missing her husband, Cookie commits suicide. The body is found by her conniving niece Camille (Close), who, rather than have a public scandal, makes it look like a murder/robbery. In doing so, Willis becomes the prime suspect. Altman takes his sweet time with this deceptive tale, allowing the characters to grow on you as the story unfolds. Each has their quirks that bring laughter to the outwardly dark proceedings. The cast is exemplary, though Dutton steals the show as the Wild Turkey-swilling, down-home Willis. ★★★½ VHS: $14.99; DVD: $19.99

A Cool, Dry Place

(1999, 120 min, US, John N. Smith) *Vince Vaughn, Joey Lauren Adams, Monica Potter, Bobby Moat.* Russ, a Midwestern lawyer, basketball coach and single father, is an atypical role for the magnetic Vaughn, but he still turns in another charming performance. In fact, he is the best reason to watch this thinly plotted domestic drama that has Russ vacillating between Beth (Adams), his potential new girlfriend, and Kate (Potter), the wife who left him. Smith has made a largely unremarkable slice of life, but *A Cool, Dry Place* is absorbing, and its heart is in the right place. Much of the film's action involves Russ caring for Calvin (Moat), his five-year-old son, who's a handful, and these scenes are very appealing, thanks mostly to Vaughn. The actor effortlessly conveys the stress of a single father who is dedicated to his son but is hoping to get more out of life. Moat is a real find, though the film strains when Potter is on-screen — her character is the weakest element in the film. ★★½ VHS: $102.99

Cool Hand Luke

(1967, 126 min, US, Stuart Rosenberg) *Paul Newman, George Kennedy, Strother Martin, Anthony Zerbe, Harry Dean Stanton, Dennis Hopper.* Newman is splendid as the chain gang convict who's always in trouble with the boss and subsequently becomes hero to all of his fellow prisoners. The film is highlighted by the now famous egg eating scene. An excellent supporting cast is headed up by Martin ("What we got here is a failure to communicate"). (VHS available letterboxed or pan & scan) ★★★★ VHS: $14.99; DVD: $19.99

Cool Runnings

(1993, 98 min, US, Jon Turteltaub) *Leon, Doug E. Doug, John Candy, Rawle D. Lewis, Malik Yoba.*

Charles Dutton (l.) and Liv Tyler enjoy a little Southern comfort in *Cookie's Fortune*

Disney's interpretation of the true-life story of the Jamaican bobsled team is a slightly trivial but amusing and uplifting saga. Relying on the tried-and-true formula of the underdog competing against all odds, the story follows Derice, a determined young Jamaican sprinter whose bid for the Jamaican track team is tragically dashed. Intent on becoming an Olympian at any cost, he turns to the unlikely sport of bobsledding, assembling a rag-tag crew to man his chariot and turning to ex-Olympian Candy for coaching. Briskly paced and well stocked with both funny and touching moments. ★★★ VHS: $14.99; DVD: $29.99

Cool World

(1992, 101 min, US, Ralph Bakshi) *Gabriel Byrne, Brad Pitt, Kim Basinger.* Byrne stars as an ex-con and cartoonist who discovers that his cartoon creations have a life of their own in a parallel universe known as Cool World. Director Bakshi follows the Roger Rabbit lead and combines live-action actors with his visually wild animation. On a technical level, the film is fascinating; Bakshi's trademark dark and leering imagery is as hip as ever. But film is curiously unsatisfying — the story is muddled and the action unfocused. Byrne and costar Pitt are competent in their roles, but Basinger is sadly out-gunned by her cartoon alter ego. ★ VHS: $14.99

Cooley High

(1975, 107 min, US, Michael Schultz) *Glynn Turman, Lawrence Hilton-Jacobs.* Affectionate reminiscence about a group of black high school students in mid-1960s Chicago. The basis for the TV series "What's Happening." ★★★ VHS: $9.99; DVD: $14.99

Cop

(1987, 110 min, US, James B. Harris) *James Woods, Leslie Ann Warren, Charles Durning.* Routine suspense thriller is given a boost by Woods' over-the-top portrayal of a cop whose domestic strife interferes with his pursuit of a serial killer. Based on the novel "Blood on the Moon" by James Ellroy. ★★

Cop and a Half

(1993, 93 min, US, Henry Winkler) *Burt Reynolds, Norman D. Golden III, Ruby Dee, Ray Sharkey.* This unbearably wooden action comedy has more troubles than its star Reynolds had in divorce court. Devon (Golden) is a precocious eight-year-old who idolizes policemen. When he becomes the sole witness to a mob hit, he strikes a deal with the local police: If they make him a cop, he'll tell them everything he knows. Reynolds plays the hard-nosed, rule-busting detective who is given the task of taking young Devon on patrol — and wouldn't you know it, Burt hates kids. ★ VHS: $7.49; DVD: $24.99

Cop Land

(1997, 105 min, US, James Mangold) *Sylvester Stallone, Harvey Keitel, Robert De Niro, Ray Liotta, Peter Berg, Michael Rapaport, Janeane Garofalo, Robert Patrick, Cathy Moriarty, Annabella Sciorra.* An enthralling police drama about corruption and redemption, *Cop Land* also marks the best performance of Stallone's career. Splendidly written and directed by Mangold (*Heavy*), the film is set in fictional Garrison, New Jersey, a small town mostly populated by New York City police officers. Stallone plays Freddie Heflin, Garrison's half-deaf sheriff who has unsuccessfully applied for the NYC police department and who is merely tolerated by those he most wants to be one of. When a young officer (Rapaport) is involved in an off-duty shooting, cover-up, betrayal and murder force Freddie to re-evaluate loyalties and he must summon the courage to stand up against men he has long admired. Stallone's characterization of Freddie is a subtle combination of frustration, longing, self-doubt and decency, and the actor manages to make Freddie sympathetic, pathetic and believable. Liotta steals the film with his gritty, dynamic portrait of a cop on the edge. (Letterboxed VHS available for $19.99) ★★★½ VHS: $14.99; DVD: $29.99

Copacabana

(1947, 92 min, US, Alfred E. Green) *Groucho Marx, Carmen Miranda.* Miranda can't get a gig, until manager and erstwhile boyfriend Marx lands two jobs for her. At the same club. As two different people. It becomes a bit of a strain, what with one being Brazilian and the other French. There's lots of flashy musical production numbers, and the usual wise-cracking encounters with officious officials. ★★½ VHS: $19.99

C

Cops and Robbers

(1973, 93 min, US, Aram Avakian) *Joseph Bologna, Cliff Gorman.* Two fine performances from Bologna and Gorman as two cops who decide to pull off one perfect heist and then retire highlight this caper film that manages to be both funny and suspenseful. From the novel by Donald Westlake. ★★★ VHS: $14.99

Cops and Robbersons

(1994, 95 min, US, Michael Ritchie) *Chevy Chase, Jack Palance, Dianne Wiest, Robert Davi.* Chase is a suburban dad (and would-be detective) who sees his big break in the form of a crotchety ol' police captain (Palance) who moves in with the family to stake out the murderous counterfeiter next door. There are a few amusing gags, and Palance's patented sneering and growling makes this tolerable, but it's predictable and routine. ★★ VHS: $9.99; DVD: $19.99

Copycat

(1995, 123 min, US, Jom Amiel) *Holly Hunter, Sigourney Weaver, Dermot Mulroney, Harry Connick, Jr., William McNamara, Will Patton.* Despite its derivative shocks and improbabilities, *Copycat* manages to serve a few chills which should give less-than-demanding thriller fans a cheap scare or two. Weaver is a renowned author and criminologist who is nearly killed by a psycho (Connick). When a copycat serial killer begins terrorizing the city, cops Hunter and Mulroney convince the agoraphobic and homebound expert to help track him. The film is full of twists (some predictable, some not), but a few of the sequences needed to set up the next scare lack either credibility or depth. Weaver and Hunter play well off each other. ★★½ VHS: $9.99; DVD: $19.99

Coquette

(1929, 75 min, US, Sam Taylor) *Mary Pickford, Johnny Mack Brown.* Pickford was the second recipient of a Best Actress Oscar, and with her win came the Academy's first controversy. Complaints were made that it was merely a popularity contest, and Pickford's histrionic portrayal of a flirtatious Southern belle only confirms those critics' charges. Pickford does get to break down on the stand, and grieve over her lover's dead body, but this tale of the Old South creaks at the seams. Beware of poor sound quality in certain scenes. ★★ VHS: $19.99

Le Corbeau (The Raven)

(1943, 90 min, France, Henri-Georges Clouzot) *Pierre Fresnay, Noel Roquevort.* A pessimistic thriller about a small-town physician who becomes the victim of a poison letter campaign that sets his entire town into a frenzy of paranoia. This uncompromising depiction of the French middle class caused quite a storm when it was released because it was made with the assistance of the Germans and was viewed by many as an anti-French propaganda film. (French with English subtitles) ★★½

The Corn Is Green

(1945, 114 min, US, Irving Rapper) *Bette Davis, John Dall.* Davis shines in one of her most heartfelt performances as Miss Moffat, a lonely schoolteacher in a small Welsh mining town who dedicates herself to a gifted student (Dall), with the hope that the youth will leave his oppressive environment and one day enter Oxford. A superior, sentimental adaptation of Emlyn Williams' play. Davis would reprise the role in the ill-fated musical "Miss Moffat." (Remade in 1979) ★★★ VHS: $19.99

Cornered

(1945, 102 min, US, Edward Dmytryk) *Dick Powell, Walter Slezak.* Powell reaffirmed his tough-guy persona (after *Murder My Sweet*) with this taut thriller set post-WWII. Powell plays a war veteran whose wife died at the hands of Nazi collaborators. He winds up in Buenos Aires after circling the globe in search of a group of escaped fascists — his wife's killer among them. ★★★ VHS: $19.99

Corrina, Corrina

(1994, 115 min, US, Jessie Nelson) *Whoopi Goldberg, Ray Liotta, Tina Majorino, Joan Cusack, Don Ameche, Larry Miller, Patrika Darbo.* In an impressive debut as both writer and director, Nelson has fashioned a charming, sweet and intelligent romantic comedy-drama and semiautobiography set in the 1950s. Liotta is a single father coping with both the recent death of his wife and raising his traumatized seven-year-old daughter (marvelously played by Majorino). Goldberg costars as their new housekeeper Corrina, who takes the young girl under her wing, and who eventually becomes involved in an interracial romance with Liotta. Both Liotta and Goldberg offer sensitive, understated performances; and the film is thankfully devoid of any hokiness and sentimentality which characterize most heartwarming stories. ★★★ VHS: $14.99; DVD: $14.99

Corrupt

(1983, 99 min, Italy, Roberto Faenza) *Harvey Keitel, Johnny Lydon.* An auspicious film debut by the notorious Lydon (aka Rotten). A sleazy heir to wealth, Lydon insinuates himself into a sadomasochistic relationship with a NYC police inspector (Keitel), stripping his personality to the bone. Relentlessly demented and frequently bristling with hostile humor, this is a kinky, punky policer. (aka: *Cop-Killer* and *Order of Death*) ★★★ VHS: $79.99

The Corruptor

(1999, 110 min, US, James Foley) *Chow Yun-Fat, Mark Wahlberg, Ric Young.* Stylish and ultra-violent, *The Corruptor* comes close to being a Hong Kong action film, right down to the central themes of male friendship and betrayal. Unfortunately, it also tries to be a cop-buddy movie, a car chase fest, and a murder mystery. The smashing opening, reminiscent of *A Better Tomorrow*, is Yun-Fat at his best, gunning down Fuk gang members in an antique shop. Against charisma like his, Wahlberg looks a bit lost. There's a great car chase in the middle, with pedestrians at the mercy of blazing guns, but like the other elements, the parts never gel into a solid film. ★★½ VHS: $14.99; DVD: $19.99

Cosi

(1997, 100 min, Australia, Mark Joffe) *Toni Collette, Ben Mendelsohn, Barry Otto, Colin Friels, Rachel Griffiths.* This whimsical little fairy tale follows Lewis (Mendelsohn), a young man who, having lost his sense of purpose in life, takes the first job he can get — directing a theatre troupe in a mental institution. On his first day, he is immediately besieged by Roy (Otto, in a gorgeously over-the-top role), a hyperkinetic, compulsive psychopath whose life's dream is to produce Mozart's comic opera "Cosi Fan Tutte." Bereft of his own ideas, Lewis goes along with Roy's obsession, making practical cuts along the way and slowly learning to interact with his band of zanies. The film refreshingly does not try to portray its mental patients as spiritually transcendent or morally superior to their "sane" counterparts. Instead the focus is on Lewis' slow awakening to a sense of self-confidence. At times scattered and unfocused, *Cosi* nonetheless is an enjoyable and even uplifting oddity. ★★★ VHS: $14.99; DVD: $29.99

The Cosmic Eye

(1985, 76 min, US, Faith Hubley) *Voices of: Maureen Stapleton, Dizzy Gillespie, Linda Atkinson.* A charming feature from one of our great animators. Expanding on the work she did with her late husband John, Hubley creates a free-form visual poem about the rights and responsibilities of humankind. Its positive message never gets old, and it seems so simple, too. ★★★ VHS: $19.99

Cosmic Slop

(1994, 90 min, US, Reginald Hudlin, Warrington Hudlin & Kevin Rodney) The creators of the *House Party* series and *Boomerang* succeed on all levels with this hip, Afro-centric "Twilight Zone"-inspired trilogy hosted by master funkateer George Clinton. Provocative, funny and always socially aware, this trio of tales tackles many of today's important issues such as domestic violence, gun control, religion and racism in a light-handed and sometimes humorous fashion. Despite its casual attitude, this clever and offbeat film manages to provide enough entertainment to satisfy those in search of something a little different. ★★★ VHS: $14.99

Costa Brava

(1995, 92 min, Spain, Marta Balletbo-Coll) *Marta Balletbo-Coll, Desi del Valle.* Director Balletbo-Coll stars in this breezy English-language romantic comedy as a ditsy-esque tour guide and aspiring stand-up comedienne/playwright who falls in love with a beautiful not-ready-yet-ready-for-full-time-lesbianism university instructor from Israel (del Valle). Quirky, funny, endearing and fresh with realistic dialogue — it feels a lot like a lesbian *Annie Hall*. ★★★

The Cotton Club

(1984, 127 min, US, Francis Coppola) *Richard Gere, Diane Lane, Bob Hoskins, Lonette McKee, Gregory Hines, James Remar, Nicolas Cage, Allen Garfield, Gwen Verdon, Laurence Fishburne, Joe Dallesandro.* Coppola's musical gangster film is a visual tour de force betrayed by a lack of dramatic substance. A good supporting cast totally overshadows leads Gere and Lane. ★★½ VHS: $14.99; DVD: $19.99

Cotton Comes to Harlem

(1970, 97 min, US, Ossie Davis) *Godfrey Cambridge, Raymond St. Jacques, Redd Foxx, Cleavon Little.* Made just prior to the explosion of blaxploitation films in the '70s, this fine adaptation of the Chester Himes novel stars Cambridge and St. Jacques as policemen Coffin Ed Johnson and Gravedigger Jones. Actor-turned-director Davis does a fine job in telling their story as they try to expose a radical back-to-Africa preacher who they believe "ain't nothing but a cheat." A splendid blend of action and comedy, the film is also

a spirited re-creation of 1950s Harlem. ★★★
VHS: $9.99; DVD: $19.99

A Couch in New York

(1997, 104 min, US, Chantal Akerman) *William Hurt, Juliette Binoche.* New York psychoanalyst Hurt, needing a change of pace, swaps apartments with Parisian Binoche. She's barely unpacked in his apartment when she's mistaken for Hurt's analyst fill-in by one of his more neurotic patients, an error she doesn't clear up. Things get even wackier when Hurt comes home earlier than expected. Abandoning her experimental filmic techniques but maintaining the same light touch evident in her earlier films, Akerman has made an uneven yet disarming romantic comedy. Hurt's tight-lipped coldness works to advantage, and Binoche — despite a few awkward moments — exudes charm in abundance. Though it's fluff, there's an unexpected frothiness, and at the odd moment it beguiles. ★★½ VHS: $14.99; DVD: $24.99

The Couch Trip

(1988, 97 min, US, Michael Ritchie) *Dan Aykroyd, Walter Matthau, Charles Grodin, Donna Dixon.* Aykroyd brings a charm to this standard comedy about a mental patient who escapes by impersonating a radio talk show psychologist in Beverly Hills. ★★½ VHS: $9.99

Count Dracula

(1970, 98 min, Italy/Spain/West Germany, Jesse Franco) *Christopher Lee, Herbert Lom, Klaus Kinski.* Lee dons tooth and cape in this slowly paced but faithful updating of Bram Stoker's "Dracula." A lawyer and his fiancée encounter the prince of darkness in Transylvania. ★★½ VHS: $14.99

The Count of Old Town

(1935, 75 min, Sweden, Edvin Aldolphson & Sigurd Wallen) *Ingrid Bergman, Edvin Adolphson.* Bergman made her film debut in this buoyant comedy as a maid in a cheap hotel who falls in love with a roguish thief. (Swedish with English subtitles) ★★★ VHS: $19.99

Country

(1984, 109 min, US, Richard Pearce) *Jessica Lange, Sam Shepard, Wilford Brimley, Matt Clark.* Lange and Shepard star as farmers who fight to save their land when the government threatens foreclosure and who struggle to save their family from the ravages of crisis. A well-

made and topical film. Lange's performance is remarkable. ★★★

The Country Girl

(1954, 104 min, US, George Seaton) *Grace Kelly, William Holden, Bing Crosby, Gene Reynolds.* Three stand-out lead performances distinguish this absorbing Clifford Odets adaptation with Kelly in her Oscar-winning role as the wife of alcoholic actor Crosby. Holden is the dedicated director trying to help him in his comeback, becoming romantically involved with Grace in the process. ★★★½ VHS: $14.99

Country Life

(1995, 115 min, Australia, Michael Blakemore) *Sam Neill, Greta Scacchi, John Hargreaves, Kerry Fox, Michael Blakemore.* On the heels of Louis Malle's *Vanya on 42nd Street* comes another, delectable interpretation of Chekhov's "Uncle Vanya." Concentrating more on the comedy of culture clash and romantic escapades than the drama of emotional chasms and interpersonal relationships, this sometimes giddy concoction is set on a sheep ranch in post-WWII Australia. A sweetly romantic Neill stars as Dr. Askey, an idealistic boozer who falls in love with Deborah (Scacchi), the young wife of the estate's owner (director Blakemore in a smashing performance) who has returned after a long absence. Unrequited love, social upheaval, and regret are themes still present, though this comedy of manners treads softly. Not every scene of this liberal translation reaches its potential, but as an immensely appealing ensemble proves, *Country Life* has its merits. ★★★½ VHS: $9.99

Countryman

(1982, 100 min, Jamaica/GB, Dickie Jobson) *Hiram Keller, Kristine Sinclair.* Although laden with a poor script, unprofessional acting and muddled politics, this lively story of the power of the Rastafarian is still good entertainment. A peaceful Rastafarian fisherman (Keller) rescues two Americans from a plane crash. But instead of being given a simple thanks, he is thrown into a caldron of political intrigue which forces him to flee into the lush Jamaican jungle. It is there that he attains supernatural powers and is able to battle the elements and foe alike. The film is highlighted with a sampler-style reggae soundtrack featuring the music of Bob Marley, Toots and the Maytals, Scratch Perry, Aswad and Steel Pulse. ★★½

Le Coup de Grâce

(1976, 98 min, West Germany, Volker Schlöndorff) *Margarethe von Trotta, Matthias Habich, Matthieu Carriere.* Understated yet subtly disquieting, this drama explores destructive human behavior — in personal relationships as well as politics. Set in 1919 in a forlorn Baltic country estate, the story traces the lives of a middle-aged woman (von Trotta), her brother, and a German lodger who find themselves slowly impoverished by the civil war and anxious over the advancement of Red troops on their land. The woman, desperate for affection, falls obsessively in love with a Soviet soldier, a man who does not return the love and is soon driven away by her erratic and at times virulent behavior. A serious portrait of bitterly restrained people caught in the whirlwind of change. (Letterboxed) (German with English subtitles) ★★★ VHS: $29.99

Coup de Tête (Hothead)

(1978, 100 min, France, Jean-Jacques Annaud) *Patrick Dewaere, Jean Bouise, Michel Aumont.* This engaging comedy follows the exploits of a crazed soccer player whose antics on and off the field cause him to lose his position, get fired and end up in jail. He gets out, however, and soon exacts his "revenge." A bristling comedy with Dewaere in one of his best roles. ★★★

Coup de Torchon (Clean Slate)

(1981, 128 min, France, Bertrand Tavernier) *Philippe Noiret, Isabelle Huppert, Stéphane Audran, Guy Marchant.* A diabolical black comedy which spits in the face of morality. Noiret is the ineffectual law enforcer in an African village who one day abandons his policy of nonconfrontation and embarks on a systematic shooting spree. Based on the novel "Pop. 1280" by Jim Thompson. (Letterboxed) (French with English subtitles) ★★★½ VHS: $29.99; DVD: $29.99

Coupe de Ville

(1990, 99 min, US, Joe Roth) *Alan Arkin, Daniel Stern, Patrick Dempsey, Ayre Gross, Joseph Bologna, Annabeth Gish.* A sentimental though engaging road movie — and a heart-on-the-sleeve tribute to Dad. Three estranged brothers are reunited on a cross-country trip to deliver a birthday present, a 1954 Coupe de Ville, to their mom. Of course, en route, the boys not only discover a little something about each other, but about themselves as well. Though the film tries to be insightful, it borders on manipulative and, at times, heavy-handed sentimentality. However, there are some funny lines and attractive performances. ★★½ VHS: $9.99

Courage Mountain

(1990, 96 min, US, Christopher Leitch) *Charlie Sheen, Leslie Caron, Juliette Caton.* A beautifully photographed family film, this new version of the famed "Heidi" story won't make anyone forget the beloved 1937 Shirley Temple classic, but it is nevertheless an earnest, well-paced and sincerely acted adventure which should more than entertain pre-adolescent viewers. Young Caton ably plays the little heroine who, on the eve of WWI, moves from her Swiss Alps home to a fancy boarding school across the border in Italy. Once there, however, Heidi and a group of friends are separated from their headmistress and are taken to a local orphanage and used for slave labor. ★★★ VHS: $14.99

Marie-France Pisier in *Cousin, Cousine*

Rita Hayworth in a pose from *Cover Girl*

Courage Under Fire

(1996, 115 min, US, Edward Zwick) *Denzel Washington, Meg Ryan, Lou Diamond Phillips, Michael Moriarty, Matt Damon, Bronson Pinchot, Scott Glenn, Zeljko Ivanek, Sean Astin.* Addressing themes previously unrepresented in serious filmmaking from Hollywood — the Gulf War and women in the military — the intelligent and perceptive *Courage Under Fire* is more than up to the challenge of either. In a solid characterization, Washington plays an Army commander who is investigating the case of a posthumous Medal of Honor going to a female pilot (a very effective Ryan) killed in action. What should be a simple process soon becomes complicated when witnesses begin to contradict each other's stories — and it's uncertain if she died a hero or a coward. As Washington digs deeper to uncover the truth (which places him in conflict with military brass), Ryan's story is told in riveting, *Rashomon*-like flashbacks. (Letterboxed VHS available for $19.99) ★★★½ VHS: $14.99; DVD: $29.99

The Court Jester

(1956, 101 min, US, Norman Panama & Melvin Frank) *Danny Kaye, Basil Rathbone, Angela Lansbury, Glynis Johns.* Kaye has one of his best roles in this beloved comedy classic which rates as one of the funniest comedies of all time. To help restore the throne to its rightful heir, Kaye goes undercover, posing as a court jester, and in the process, of course, turns the palace upside-down. Basil Rathbone and young Johns and Lansbury also star. And don't forget: "The pellet with the poison's in the vessel with the pestle." Or is that "the flagon with the dragon?" ★★★★ VHS: $14.99; DVD: $29.99

The Courtesans of Bombay

(1974, 74 min, India, Ismail Merchant) *Kareem Samar, Zohra Segal, Saeed Jaffrey.* An intriguing and entertaining story which follows the inhabitants of Pavanpul, the courtesan quarters, who by day carry on their daily domestic lives and by night thrill and delight with exuberant singing, dancing and sex. Filmed in a pseudo-documentary style, the film is more of interest for its sociological stance than for entertainment value. Merchant's directorial debut. ★★½

Cousin Bette

(1998, 108 min, GB, Des McAnuff) *Jessica Lange, Elisabeth Shue, Bob Hoskins, Geraldine Chaplin, Hugh Laurie.* Skating dangerously close to *Dangerous Liaisons* territory, director McAnuff tackles Balzac's story of class rivalry, sexual treachery and revenge, and though his production lacks the sizzle of Stephen Frears's classic, this poor cousin manages to stand on its own. Betraying her good looks, Lange stars as the uncomely title character, poor relations to the wealthy Hulot family in 19th-century France. Rebuffed by Hector Hulot (Laurie), she plots vengeance upon the family. Taking a job as seamstress to the theatrical belle of Paris, Jenny Colson (wonderfully played by Shue), Bette lets loose her wrath on the family one by one, with a little help from the Hulots' individual vices and a lot of help from Jenny. Lange settles into the role nicely, though she's rarely given the opportunity to strut her stuff. ★★★ VHS: $102.99; DVD: $34.99

Cousin Bobby

(1992, 69 min, US, Jonathan Demme) A provocative and sincere documentary about director Demme's long-lost cousin Bobby Castle, a politically radical Episcopal priest who militantly crusades for the poor parishioners of his Harlem church. Demme goes about filming his story as if it were a home movie, documenting his own rediscovery of a distant relation with hand-held camera work and microphone booms exposed. Demme splits the film between this familial reunion and Castle's history as a civil rights leader, concentrating especially on his close friendship in the '60s with Black Panther Party member Isaiah Rowley. Eloquent and outspoken, Castle, along with cousin Jonathan, makes a powerful and compelling case for economic equality and social justice. ★★★½ VHS: $19.99

Cousin, Cousine

(1975, 95 min, France, Jean-Charles Tacchella) *Marie-Christine Barrault, Marie-France Pisier, Victor Lanoux, Guy Merchant.* An engaging look at love among the members of a large French family. Trouble brews when two cousins by marriage discover they have more in common than their in-laws. A sexy, romantic comedy. (American remake: *Cousins*) (French with English subtitles) ★★★½ VHS: $29.99

Cousins

(1989, 110 min, US, Joel Schumacher) *Ted Danson, Isabella Rossellini, William L. Petersen, Norma Aleandro, Lloyd Bridges.* An amiable if unremarkable rehash of *Cousin, Cousine* highlighted by a handful of sincere and appealing performances, including Danson and Rossellini as two cousins who fall in love. Bridges and Aleandro both give the film a dash of vitality — which keeps it afloat — as a pair of high-spirited sexagenarian lovers. ★★½ VHS: $19.99

Cover Girl

(1944, 107 min, US, Charles Vidor) *Gene Kelly, Rita Hayworth, Eve Arden, Phil Silvers.* This delightful Kern-Gershwin musical has Kelly's brilliant dancing, Silvers' burlesque routines, Arden's wisecracks and Hayworth's beauty, all packaged in lush Technicolor by the sure hand of director Vidor. ★★★½ VHS: $19.99

Cover Me

(1995, 94 min, US, Michael Schroeder) *Stephen Nichols, Courtney Taylor.* Playboy Films' first video release is this tepid, seen-it-before murder mystery set amidst the sex industry of L.A. in which a serial killer stalks models who have appeared on the cover of a local skin magazine. Demi/Dimitri's (Nichols) MO is to don women's clothing, go to a strip club, pick up a prostitute/dancer and take her home, presumably for a night of paid lesbian sex. But girl-girl lovemaking soon turns to boy-girl killing and it takes a sultry policewoman (Taylor) to go undercover to capture the sicko. ★ VHS: $79.99

Cover-Up

(1988, 76 min, US, Barbara Trent) After releasing the right-wing documentary *Oliver North*, distributor MPI Video then produced this left-leaning probe into the shady dealings of the Iran-Contra Affair. The story alleges that the 1980 Reagan-Bush campaign bargained with the Iranians to delay the hostages' release to insure a victory over President Carter. ★★★ VHS: $14.99

The Covered Wagon

(1923, 60 min, US, James Cruze) *J. Warren Kerrigan, Lois Wilson, Alan Hale.* Beautifully photographed epic of the Old West, introducing some of the elements of the genre that others would later exploit more fully. One of the biggest box-office smashes of the 1920s. ★★★ VHS: $9.99

Coyote Ugly

(2000, 101 min, US, David McNally) *Piper Perabo, Adam Garcia, Maria Bello, Melanie Lynskey, John Goodman.* A young waitress (Perabo) leaves behind her small Jersey town to pursue her dreams of a songwriting career in the Big Apple. Sadly, she is shocked to find that the big city is cold and heartless, and she's forced to take a job at the title bar, where she must wear skimpy clothes and serve drinks to horny men. Surprisingly retro (in the worst sense), this film plays its Horatio Alger story line straight — this is a squeaky-clean movie, with not a whiff of nudity or sexuality (contrary to the impression the trailers leave, *Coyote Ugly* is *not* a strip club). It plays like *Showgirls* remade as an "Afterschool Special" — only it's not even as fun as that might sound. *Coyote Ugly* is ragingly artificial, predictable and annoying, with Goodman providing the only glimpse at recognizable human behavior. Possibly producer Jerry Bruckheimer's worst, and that's saying something. ★ VHS: $14.99; DVD: $29.99

Le Crabe Tambour

(1977, 120 min, France, Pierre Schoendoerffer) *Jacques Perrin, Jean Rochefort, Claude Rich.* Haunting and provocative, Schoendoerffer's unconventional war drama lays bare the primitive sentiments of men in battle. Based on the actual exploits of a legendary French officer, nicknamed Le Crabe Tambour (the Drummer Crab), the film furrows through the complexities of honor and military chivalry. Perrin portrays the title character with a fascinating elusiveness — projecting the oblique demeanor of a perennial soldier. Accentuating the rich performances is Raoul Coutard's boldy adventurous cinematography, with its many spellbinding evocations of the elements. (French with English subtitles) ★★★½ VHS: $59.99

Crackers

(1983, 91 min, US, Louis Malle) *Donald Sutherland, Jack Warden, Sean Penn, Wallace Shawn.* Malle's remake of the Italian classic *Big Deal on Madonna Street* is long on charm, but falls short when it comes to delivering either story or laughs. The film centers around a group of losers who keep off the mean streets of San Francisco by hanging out at a local pawn shop. When they concoct a scheme to crack the safe in the shop, the comedy is supposed to gear up, but somehow, the film never really gets on track. ★★ VHS: $59.99

Cradle Will Rock

(1999, 133 min, US, Tim Robbins) *Hank Azaria, Rubén Blades, Joan Cusack, John Cusack, Cary Elwes, Philip Baker Hall, Cherry Jones, John Angus MacFayden, Bill Murray, Vanessa Redgrave, Susan Sarandon, Jamey Sheridan, John Turturro, Emily Watson.* It's 1937 in America. The poor form bread lines, the rich rail against Communism, and 22-year-old upstart Orson Welles joins John Houseman to put on a show — a Federal Theatre production of Marc Blitzstein's musical "Cradle Will Rock." What Welles and Houseman see as a play, others see as an arm of the Red Menace. The Federal Theatre Project itself is under attack as un-American, foreshadowing NEA struggles today. Director Robbins weaves multiple story lines in this complex exploration of an era of social upheaval and ideological confrontation. A gifted ensemble delivers spirited performances: MacFayden and Elwes delight as Welles and Houseman; Blades carries the role of Diego Rivera with the requisite bravado; Murray's red-baiting Crickshaw inspires poignant revulsion; Jones' battling head of the Federal Theatre dazzles. In fact, there's not a bad performance in the lot. Robbins' evocation of 1930s New York City is complete and convincing. The film's structure, while at times somewhat cumbersome, allows the protagonists to reflect each other, like facets of a prism. It's a story ideally fitted to Robbins' political leanings, and he has fully utilized his cast to give voice to the myriad opinions of the day, capturing a sense of excitement and urgency. The film's final shot is wry and cautionary and pretty damn sobering. An entertaining and thought-provoking film. ★★★½ VHS: $14.99; DVD: $29.99

The Craft

(1996, 100 min, US, Andrew Fleming) *Robin Tunney, Fairuza Balk, Neve Campbell, Rachel True, Cliff De Young, Helen Shaver. Heathers* meets *Carrie* in this psychologically mature tale of teen angst and retribution about a circle of student misfits whose prankish use of witchcraft against their tormentors gets out of hand when one of them (Balk) loses control of her own personal demons and becomes a bitch of a witch. Director Fleming takes what might have been more Gen-X drivel and invests it with surprisingly keen insight and malicious wit. ★★★ VHS: $14.99; DVD: $24.99

Craig's Wife

(1936, 75 min, US, Dorothy Arzner) *Rosalind Russell, John Boles, Jane Darwell, Billie Burke.* Russell is outstanding as the selfish, materialistic wife whose obsessive social climbing ruins her marriage. (Remade in 1950 as *Harriet Craig*) ★★★ VHS: $19.99

Cary Elwes (l.), Hank Azaria (c.) and John Angus MacFayden in *Cradle Will Rock*

The Cranes Are Flying

(1957, 94 min, USSR, Mikhail K. Kalatozov) *Tatyana Samoilova, Alexei Batalov.* Made during the "thaw" of the Cold War that resulted in greater liberty for filmmakers, this lyrical and poignant love story is set during WWII and follows the sad tale of two young lovers who are separated by the war. Tragedies soon befall the girl after her sweetheart volunteers to fight, leaving her in the hands of his brutish cousin. With sweeping and lush camera work, moving performances and an unusual absence of political propaganda, this is a tender, realistic portrayal of a love that triumphs in the face of adversity. (Russian with English subtitles) ★★★½

Crash

(1997, 100 min, Canada, David Cronenberg) *James Spader, Holly Hunter, Elias Koteas, Debra Unger, Rosanna Arquette.* Banned in London and cheered and hissed at the Cannes Film Festival, Cronenberg's controversial adaptation of J.G. Ballard's novel rumbles on the fumes of its outlaw reputation. Like *Naked Lunch* and *Videodrome*, this eerie effort finds a netherworld where technology, obsession and sex meet; then it sets them against each other in the horrific battlefield of the mind. Spader plays a Toronto film producer whose unquenchable sexual desires take a new turn after he's involved in a car accident that kills the husband of passenger Hunter. Despite the tragedy and subsequent injuries, Hunter and Spader begin a carnal relationship that eventually leads to an unusual medical researcher (Koteas), who gets his kicks staging the car accidents of the deceased and famous (James Dean, Jayne Mansfield). Spader eventually brings wife Unger into the fray. Story line and character development take a backseat to mood and the psychological surveying going on here. Cronenberg goes boldly where few directors have ever gone before. If you follow him, make sure your seatbelts are on tight. ★★★ VHS: $19.99; DVD: $24.99

Crash Dive

(1943, 105 min, US, Archie Mayo) *Tyrone Power, Dana Andrews, Anne Baxter.* Power stars as a naval officer who is assigned to commander Andrews' sub. In between daring attacks on the Germans, he falls in love with Andrews' fiancée Baxter. The story nicely mixes romance, comedy and

wartime heroics, the special effects are commendable, and the film's rich color is an asset. ★★★ VHS: $19.99

The Crazies

(1973, 103 min, US, George Romero) *Lane Carroll, W.G. McMillan, Harold Wayne Jones.* An early thriller from director Romero about a bungled Army experiment contaminating a small town's water supply, turning its citizens into crazed killers. ★★ VHS: $14.99

Crazy from the Heart

(1991, 94 min, US, Thomas Schlamme) *Christine Lahti, Ruben Blades, William Russ.* A compelling drama about a high-school teacher who falls for a Hispanic janitor, causing an uproar in their small town. Both Lahti and Blades give convincing performances in this examination of self-confidence and individuality. ★★★ VHS: $79.99

Crazy in Alabama

(1999, 113 min, US, Antonio Banderas) *Melanie Griffith, Lucas Black, Meat Loaf, Rod Steiger, David Morse, Cathy Moriarty, Elizabeth Perkins, Robert Wagner, Richard Schiff.* Banderas' directorial debut, starring wife Griffith, is not just a Hollywood vanity production. Evidencing influences from his early work with Pedro Almodóvar, Banderas balances with agility broad farce and considerable gravity. It's summer in Alabama, 1965, and Lucille (Griffith) has just poisoned and decapitated her brutish husband and deposited her 7 children on her mother's doorstep to leave to pursue her dream of appearing on an episode of "Bewitched." The story is seen through the eyes of her nephew Peejoe (a rock-solid Black), who, through the simple expedient of truth, becomes a participant in the burgeoning Civil Rights movement. The film is snappily paced as it contrasts Lucille's road trip insanity with the societal insanity of segregation. Credit goes to Banderas for maintaining two such dissimilar tones with the same film which, with the exception of a bogged-down courtroom finale, he does with surprising success. ★★★ VHS: $14.99; DVD: $24.99

Crazy in Love

(1992, 93 min, US, Martha Coolidge) *Holly Hunter, Gena Rowlands, Bill Pullman, Julian Sands, Frances McDormand.* Director Coolidge has crafted a lyrical and mature examination of the bonds of family and the complications which arise out of compulsive passions. Hunter fears her husband (Pullman) is losing interest in their marriage when she meets an enchanting photographer, Sands. Filmed to good effect in and around Seattle, the film sports earnest dialogue and characterizations along with moments of touching intimacy. ★★½ VHS: $79.99

Crazy Mama

(1975, 82 min, US, Jonathan Demme) *Ann Sothern, Cloris Leachman, Linda Purl, Stuart Whitman.* Director Demme's talents are very much in evidence in this early exploitation film made for Roger Corman. Three generations of women go on a riotous crime spree from California to Arkansas. An action/comedy/drama similar to Demme's later *Married to the Mob.* ★★½

Crazy Moon

(1987, 98 min, Canada, Allan Eastman) *Kiefer Sutherland, Vanessa Vaughn.* An innocuous variation on the *Harold and Maude* theme (society misfits in love). Sutherland stars as an '80s teenager caught up in '40s nostalgia who falls in love with a deaf girl. Cinema from the Great White North does not send Hollywood packing, but it's entertaining nonetheless. ★★½

Crazy People

(1990, 90 min, US, Tony Bill) *Dudley Moore, Daryl Hannah, Paul Reiser, Mercedes Ruehl, J.T. Walsh.* Moore stars as an advertising executive whose policy of "truth in advertising" lands him in the loony bin. There he becomes mixed up with a group of fellow patients. This is simply *The Dream Team* on Madison Avenue. When it is lampooning TV and print advertising, it is funny. But unfortunately, the rest of it is awkward and maudlin. ★★ VHS: $14.99

The Crazy Ray/Entr'acte

(1923/1924, 40/20 min, France, René Clair) *The Crazy Ray*, Dadaist Clair's first film, is a fanciful and amusing story of a mad scientist who invents a ray gun and puts the entire city of Paris in suspended animation. *Entr'acte*, conceived as a filmic intermission to be shown during the Dada ballet "Relache," has endured well beyond the original intention to become one of the important surrealist films of the period. Plotless, the film, in frantic movements designed to offend its original audience, includes a chase through Paris with a runaway hearse. (Silent with musical accompaniment) ★★★ VHS: $39.99

Creation of Adam

(1993, 93 min, Russia, Yuri Pavlov) *Alexander Strizhenov, Anzhelika Nevolina.* The first gay-themed film from Russia, this mystical drama will disappoint many with its oblique handling of the gay angle. Set in the industrialized port of St. Petersburg, the story follows handsome designer Andrei (Strizhenov) who is stuck in an unfulfilling relationship with his equally unhappy wife. After saving an effeminate teen from a group of queer-bashers, he is quickly accused — by both the thugs and his wife — of being homosexual. His life is transformed when he meets Philip, a mysterious, self-assured young man. Their ensuing relationship, handled in a weird, dreamlike manner, is one of both seduction and brotherly guidance. (Russian with English subtitles) ★★½ VHS: $39.99

Creation of the Humanoids

(1962, 75 min, US, Wesley E. Barry) Andy Warhol's favorite film features Forrest J. Ackerman (creator of "Famous Monsters of Filmland") and makeup by Jack Pierce, who created all the great monsters like Frankenstein and The Wolfman. After the next big one, humanoids are created to replace all the dead Third World people who used to do our menial work. ★

Creator

(1985, 108 min, US, Ivan Passer) *Peter O'Toole, Mariel Hemingway, Vincent Spano, Virginia Madsen.* Middling sci-fi comedy with O'Toole as a Nobel Prize—winning biologist who attempts to clone his long-deceased wife with the help of a young med student (Spano). ★★ VHS: $9.99

Creature Comforts

(1990, 30 min, GB, Nick Park, Peter Lord & Boris Kossmehl) Park and the Aardman studios, burst onto the animation scene with "Creature Comforts," a hilariously dry five-minute claymated short so bursting with detail and humor that it must be watched more than once. Taking the form of a BBC news item, clay-animated animals are interviewed in their zoo cages, but they're voiced by real-life British citizens complaining about their dwellings! But this Oscar-winner for Best Animated Short isn't the only piece on the tape; also included is Kossmehl's hilarious, expressionistic "Not Without My Handbag," showing materialistic folk in the afterlife, and Lord's "Wat's Pig" and "Adam," the first a fable about twins separated into different class structures, the latter a Bill Plympton-esque stream-of-consciousness take on evolution. ★★★★ VHS: $9.99; DVD: $9.99

Creature from the Black Lagoon

(1954, 79 min, US, Jack Arnold) *Richard Carlson, Richard Denning, Whit Bissell, Julie Adams.* What '50s monster movie could be any good without Carlson, Denning or Bissell? Well, this film's got all three! Plus the neatest monster this side of the sushi bar. The film exhibits a surprising lyricism in its underwater sequences, especially the aquatic *pas de deux* with the heroine. Features the classic line, "David, you still don't look like an ekistiologist." Originally shown in 3-D. (Sequel: *Revenge of the Creature*) ★★★ VHS: $14.99; DVD: $29.99

The Creeper

(1948, 64 min, US, Jean Yarbrough) *Onslow Stevens, Eduardo Ciannelli.* A surprisingly stylish low-budget horror film about a mad doctor whose nostrum turns men into killer cats. ★★½

The Creeping Flesh

(1970, 89 min, GB, Freddie Francis) *Peter Cushing, Christopher Lee.* A lesser Hammer Studios production perhaps, but any horror film with Cushing and Lee is bound to provoke a few chills. The plot features (you guessed it) a mad scientist who is obsessed with harnessing the "essence of evil." It's an old-fashioned affair, filled with monsters, evil spirits and numerous subplots. ★★★ VHS: $49.99

Creepshow

(1982, 120 min, US, George Romero) *E.G. Marshall, Hal Holbrook, Adrienne Barbeau, Ted Danson, Leslie Nielsen, Ed Harris.* Five horror stories

written by Stephen King offer a few chills, especially the final one about paranoid high-rise dweller Marshall and his newly arrived guests — hundreds of cockroaches. ★★★ VHS: $9.99; DVD: $19.99

Creepshow 2

(1987, 89 min, US, Michael Gornick) *Lois Chiles, George Kennedy, Tom Savini, Dorothy Lamour.* Three more Stephen King stories, here adapted by George Romero. Doesn't deliver the same number of chills as the original, but undemanding horror fans shouldn't mind. ★★ VHS: $9.99; DVD: $24.99

The Crew

(1994, 99 min, US, Carl-Jan Colpaert) *Viggo Mortensen, Jeremy Sisto, Pamela Gidley, Donal Logue.* Funny, nasty and suspenseful, this psychological thriller revolves around a group of five people whose Caribbean cruise turns into a nightmare after their boat is hijacked by two men, including a pre-op transsexual out to raise enough money for his sex change. A richly detailed action/drama which touches upon homophobia, and offers one of the least likely heroes one will ever encounter. ★★★ VHS: $39.99

The Crew

(2000, 88 min, US, Michael Dinner) *Burt Reynolds, Richard Dreyfuss, Seymour Cassel, Dan Hedaya, Carrie-Anne Moss, Jennifer Tilly, Lainie Kazan, Miguel Sandoval, Jeremy Piven.* A seasoned cast makes the most of this amiable comedy about four aged small-time hoods and their last hurrah. Sort of a *Grumpy Old Wiseguys*, the story follows the comic exploits of Reynolds, Dreyfuss, Cassel and Hedaya, former Jersey boys now retired and living in South Beach. When it appears they will lose their retirement home, they band together for a little con. While a lot of this is familiar territory, the grouping of these four pros and some genuinely amusing moments make *The Crew* a likable, entertaining bit of nonsense. ★★½ VHS: $14.99; DVD: $32.99

Cria!

(1975, 107 min, Spain, Carlos Saura) *Geraldine Chaplin, Ana Torrent.* This beautifully acted, haunting film stars Torrent as a nine-year-old heroine with an uncanny talent for observing scenes not meant for her eyes, specifically the death of her father. An evocative film about the darker side of childhood, superstition, knowledge and the inevitable loss of innocence. (Spanish with English subtitles) ★★★½ VHS: $29.99

Cries and Whispers

(1972, 106 min, Sweden, Ingmar Bergman) *Liv Ullmann, Ingrid Thulin, Harriet Andersson, Kary Sylwan, Erland Josephson.* Bergman delves into the tumultuous world of familial hates, longings and frustrations in this beautifully rendered, multilayered classic. Ullmann is superlative as a repressed woman unable to cope with her sister's slow death from tuberculosis. An unforgettable, shattering portrait of the conscious and subconscious. (Swedish with English subtitles) ★★★★ VHS: $29.99; DVD: $29.99

Crime and Punishment

(1935, 110 min, France, Pierre Chenal) *Harry Baur, Pierre Blanchar.* Dostoyevsky's complex, brooding novel is brilliantly brought to the screen in this haunting and menacing adaptation. Baur stars as Raskolnikov, a tormented student who murders a money lender and her daughter and soon finds himself stalked by the cunning magistrate Porfiry. Light years ahead of Josef von Sternberg's Hollywood version released that same year, director Chenal stages most of the action in a claustrophobic and atmospheric studio set — the result being an almost airless and unrelentingly intense drama. (French with English subtitles) ★★★★

Crime and Punishment

(1935, 88 min, US, Josef von Sternberg) *Peter Lorre, Edward Arnold, Marian Marsh.* Not as intense as the French adaptation of Dostoyevsky's existential novel, von Sternberg's version is at least more palatable entertainment. Lorre gives a stellar performance as the brooding intellectual, Raskolnikov, who murders a greedy pawnbroker, deeming her "unfit to live." The omission of the accidental killing of the pawnbroker's retarded daughter lessens the guilt Raskolnikov battles in the novel. The story is lightened just a bit by this and Lorre's character appears a little more amiable because of it. ★★½ VHS: $19.99

Crime and Punishment

(1970, 200 min, USSR, Lev Kulidzhanov) *Georgi Taratorkin, Victoria Fyodorova.* This Russian version of the Dostoyevsky's literary classic about a student who murders a pawnbroker and her daughter is an authentic and brilliant translation of the much-filmed novel. The impoverished Raskolnikov, racked by guilt for his crimes, is eventually hunted by Police Inspector Porfiry and confesses. Much longer than the U.S., English and French versions, the film probes the intense mental anguish of Raskolnikov and provides a haunting image of the man's tortured soul. (Russian with English subtitles) ★★★½ VHS: $29.99

Crime of the Century

(1996, 110 min, US, Mark Rydell) *Stephen Rea, Isabella Rosselini.* In the 1930s, the Lindbergh baby kidnapping/murder case and its subsequent trial was an unprecedented media event. An entire nation pored over every word, clue and witness' account. When the trial was over, a German emigrant named Hauptmann was found guilty and executed. But through the years, many historians have speculated that Hauptmann may have been innocent, a victim of an inferior defense, a zealous police investigation and a prejudiced court system. The methodically paced but riveting *Crime of the Century*, a made-for-HBO drama, takes this view and succinctly presents the facts as they *could* have been. It not only makes for great viewing, but a damn good argument for a miscarriage of justice as well. Rea is perfectly subdued as Hauptmann, whose only crime may have been a poor choice of a business partner. ★★★½ VHS: $14.99

Crime Story

(1993, 90 min, Hong Kong, Kirk Wong) *Jackie Chan, Kent Cheng.* A real-life incident serves as the inspiration for a rare dramatic turn by Chan. Jackie is an ace Hong Kong cop called in to work on a tough kidnapping case. Little does he know that his own partner (Cheng) is involved in the scam. Featuring almost no comedy, *Crime Story* is as serious as a heart attack. Jackie's frustration at the escalating human cost of the case burns stronger, reaching a fever pitch at the climax when he confronts his partner in a burning tenement building. Very few Hong Kong action films reach the emo-

tional intensity of this film. Unfortunately, the film has been released in an atrociously dubbed version which severely detracts from its serious tone. (Dubbed) ★★★½ VHS: $9.99

Crime Zone

(1988, 93 min, US, Louis Llosa) *Sherilyn Fenn, David Carradine, Peter Nelson.* A low-budget, futuristic *Bonnie and Clyde, Crime Zone* tells the tale of two young "sub-grades," Bone (Nelson) and Helen (Fenn). They are hired by a mysterious man (Carradine) to steal an important government computer disk and soon find themselves the targets of an all-out police dragnet. Roger Corman produced this imaginative and entertaining if somewhat cheesy sci-fi thriller. ★★½ VHS: $79.99

Crimes and Misdemeanors

(1989, 97 min, US, Woody Allen) *Woody Allen, Mia Farrow, Martin Landau, Anjelica Huston, Alan Alda, Jerry Orbach.* Allen's fascinating blend of humor and gripping melodrama follows the intersecting stories of two men: a successful opthalmologist (Landau) who arranges the murder of his mistress, and an out-of-work filmmaker (Allen) who falls in love with his producer (Farrow). It is Allen's remarkable irony that one man's deep-rooted religious principles are betrayed at an insignificant cost, and integrity is ill-rewarded. ★★★★ VHS: $14.99; DVD: $19.99

The Crimes of M. Lange

(1935, 85 min, France, Jean Renoir) A delightfully droll black comedy, scripted by Jacques Prévert and Renoir, that mixes fantasy and politics in its story of a worker uprising. When the crooked and lecherous boss of a publishing house suddenly disappears, the exploited workers of the company unite to form a co-operative and succeed in making the company a huge success. When the boss returns to take over, he finds the workers, led by M. Lange, a timid writer of pulp westerns, united in opposition. (French with English subtitles) ★★★★ VHS: $59.99

Crimes of Passion

(1984, 107 min, US, Ken Russell) *Anthony Perkins, Kathleen Turner, John Laughlin.* This sizzling tale of a sexually repressed street preacher and a mysterious prostitute carries as resounding a wallop as could only come from the inimitable talents of Russell. Perkins stars as the deranged reverend who's hell-bent on saving the soul of China Blue (Turner) — a well-respected fashion designer by day who becomes a slinky streetwalker at night. Overflowing with camp humor and bizarre twists, the film is a visual treat in which seductive waves of saturated neon splash across the screen. Definitely one of Russell's more unique (a term which may be redundant when describing his work) and unforgettable ventures. ★★★

Crimes of the Heart

(1986, 105 min, US, Bruce Beresford) *Sissy Spacek, Diane Keaton, Jessica Lange, Tess Harper.* In the 1940s, this offbeat comedy would have been classified as a "woman's picture"; today, it is called a "star vehicle." Spacek, Keaton and Lange breathe life into Beth Henley's Pulitzer Prize—winning play about three Southern sisters reunited in time of crisis, and of their estrangement and reconciliation. A sweet-natured film which garnered Oscar nominations

for Spacek, costar Harper and its screenplay adaptation. ★★★ VHS: $14.99

Crimetime

(1996, 95 min, GB, George Sluizer) *Stephen Baldwin, Pete Postlethwaite, Sadie Frost, Geraldine Chaplin, Karen Black.* Tabloid TV gets the *Network* treatment with this stylish looking thriller which very nearly sinks in its own smartness. With Marianne Faithull singing two songs in the opening scene, the film gets off to a good start. Postlethwaite plays a serial killer who picks up his first victim. A rather gruesome murder, it catches the attention of a TV magazine show (run by Black doing her worst Faye Dunaway imitation) which re-stages sensationalistic crimes. Baldwin is the actor who gets his 15 minutes playing the murderer. Alternating between black comedy and suspense, *Crimetime* becomes more bizarre as the murders continue and Baldwin and Postlethwaite form a bond. ★★ VHS: $79.99

Crimewave

(1986, 83 min, US, Sam Raimi) *Louise Lasser, Paul L. Smith, Bruce Campbell.* Long before *Darkman* or *Miller's Crossing,* Raimi and the Coen Brothers — Joel and Ethan — joined forces to make this intermittently amusing black farce about a couple of bungling rat exterminators who set their sights on two-legged mammals instead. ★★½

Criminal Law

(1989, 117 min, US, Martin Campbell) *Gary Oldman, Kevin Bacon, Joe Don Baker, Karen Young, Tess Harper.* Oldman and Bacon dance a psychotic *pas de deux* in this muddled thriller about a rich-kid serial killer (Bacon) who, having been caught, tried, and found not guilty, taunts his defense attorney (Oldman) with the knowledge that he's really guilty and plans to kill again. Britisher Oldman does a knock-out American accent, but it's not enough to overcome the shaky story line and plotting. ★★½ VHS: $9.99

The Criminal Life of Archibaldo de la Cruz

(1955, 91 min, Mexico, Luis Bunuel) *Ernesto Alonso, Ariadne Welter.* Director Buñuel ended his self-exile in Mexico with this slyly humorous black comedy of one man's dark, sexual and murderous obsessions. After a traumatic experience in which a boy enjoys a secret sexual thrill on the accidental death of the family maid, he grows up one sick little pup. Years later he is an aristocratic gentleman, and Archibaldo's secret thoughts harbor a guilt-fueled fantasy of sexual kinkiness, crime and murder against women; but, in true Buñuelian fashion, his criminal desires are thwarted at every turn. With surrealistic touches and macabre fetishism, Buñuel pokes wicked fun at the bourgeoisie, Catholicism and the Latino male. (Spanish with English subtitles) ★★★★ VHS: $29.99

The Crimson Pirate

(1952, 104 min, US, Robert Siodmak) *Burt Lancaster, Nick Cravet, Eve Bartok, Christopher Lee.* Lancaster is in top form, both as actor and athlete, in this supremely entertaining swashbuckler with Lancaster and fellow acrobat Cravat fighting the bad guys in the Mediterranean. ★★★

Crimson Tide

(1995, 113 min, US, Tony Scott) *Denzel Washington, Gene Hackman, Matt Craven, George Dzundza, Viggo Mortensen, Lillo Brancato, Jr., Jason Robards.* If *The Hunt for Red October* brought an end to the Cold War at a theatre near you, then another submarine thriller, *Crimson Tide*, certainly tries to rekindle the sleepy politics of paranoia. And it does so in an exceedingly efficient manner. Washington stars as the newly appointed second-in-command of the nuclear submarine *USS Alabama*. He and the crew serve under the watchful eye of hard-nosed captain Hackman (giving one of his patented blustery performances). Things heat up, however, when a renegade Russian general takes control of a Soviet sub and threatens nuclear war. In no time, Washington and Hackman are at odds with each other over possible retaliation. Fairly authentic and exciting throughout, *Crimson Tide* is more credible than Scott's other military saga *Top Gun*. ★★★ VHS: $14.99; DVD: $29.99

Criss Cross

(1949, 87 min, US, Robert Siodmack) *Burt Lancaster, Yvonne DeCarlo, Dan Duryea, Stephen McNally.* Lancaster returns from prison looking to go straight. Plans go awry when he runs into ex-wife DeCarlo and her double-crossing plan for an armored car stick-up. A terrific sense of atmosphere and shadowy suspense make this "B" noir one not to miss. ★★★ VHS: $14.99

Critical Care

(1997, 109 min, US, Sidney Lumet) *James Spader, Kyra Sedgwick, Albert Brooks, Helen Mirren, Anne Bancroft, Jeffrey Wright, Wallace Shawn.* The Clintons may not have pushed through their health care package during their first term, but the subject of health care, insurance companies and modern medicine is certainly alive and kicking in 1997, first with *The Rainmaker*, and now with Lumet's consistently entertaining satire. Spader plays a callous, burned-out doctor at a major hospital who gets caught between two sisters fighting over their comatose father. One, a spacey holy roller, wants him kept alive; the other, a manipulative fashion model, wants to pull the plug. Several subplots wind their way through the central story, making some caustic observations on the business of saving lives. The film has an otherworldly story line involving the afterlife which completely misfires, and the ending may be too pat, but there are a great many delicious moments to savor. ★★★ VHS: $9.99; DVD: $9.99

Critical Condition

(1987, 100 min, US, Peter Faiman) *Richard Pryor, Rachel Ticotin, Ruben Blades, Joe Mantegna, Joe Dallesandro.* Harmless though silly Pryor comedy with Pryor as a developer who feigns insanity to stay out of jail. But when he escapes from the mental ward, he is mistaken for a doctor and proceeds to turn the hospital topsy-turvy. ★★ VHS: $14.99

Critters

(1986, 86 min, US, Stephen Herek) *Dee Wallace Stone, M. Emmet Walsh, Billy Zane, Don Opper, Terrance Mann.* Offbeat comic horror film about some hairy tumbleweed-like monsters who arrive from another planet and terrorize a small Kansas town. An enjoyable, silly romp with both laughs and chills going for it. (Followed by 3 sequels) ★★½ VHS: $14.99

"Crocodile" Dundee

(1986, 95 min, Australia, Peter Faiman) *Paul Hogan, Linda Kozlowski.* A surprise and huge box-office hit, *"Crocodile" Dundee* is a tepid comedy about an Australian Everyman (played by Hogan), which would be like saying that Sylvester Stallone is an American Everyman) who finds adventure in the wilds of New York City. Dundee is an Aussie crocodile poacher and local legend who becomes the subject of an article written by American reporter Kozlowski. She invites him back to the States, and together they become involved in urban intrigue and romance. Admittedly, Hogan has a genial charm to him (if you can ignore his homophobia), but the film casts him in too many clichéd antics, and most of the comedy just isn't funny. (Sequel: *"Crocodile" Dundee II*) ★★ VHS: $9.99

"Crocodile" Dundee II

(1988, 111 min, US/Australia, John Cornell) *Paul Hogan, Linda Kozlowski.* For the record, Mick "Crocodile" Dundee (Hogan) must save his girlfriend (Kozlowski) from ruthless drug dealers. For the record, this is a witless, though very profitable sequel. For those who liked the original, there's probably nothing we can say to dissuade you from watching this (and there's a lot of you). For those who didn't, avoid this at all costs. (Sequel: *"Crocodile" Dundee in L.A.*) ★ VHS: $9.99

Cronica del Alba

(1982, 82 min, Spain, Antonio J. Betancor) Like Truffaut's Antoine Donel series, *Cronica del Alba* is the second film on the life story of a young boy growing into manhood. Jose Garces, or "Pepe," last seen in *Valentina*, is now 15 years old and in his first year at the university. The setting is Zaragoza in 1919, on the eve of the anarchist rebellion, and our hero is caught among his continued love for the now ravishing Valentina, his bourgeois origins, and his developing revolutionary ideals. Adapted from the novel by Ramon J. Sender. (Spanish with English subtitles) ★★★

Cronos

(1993, 92 min, Mexico, Guillermo Del Toro) *Federico Luppi, Ron Perlman, Claudio Brook, Margarita Isabel.* This delicious and chilling little oddity from Mexico tells the tale of an aging antique dealer who happens upon an ancient device, built by an alchemist bent on achieving immortality, which transforms its user into a vampire. Upon accidentally discovering the scarab-shaped machine's purpose, the old man becomes addicted to its power and is soon on the road to ruin. Into the picture comes a wealthy American industrialist who is dying of cancer and will stop at nothing to get his hands on the box. Though at times gruesome and grisly, the film has a fair share of good humor and at its core is a touching tale about the relationship between the old man and his grandchild. (Spanish with English subtitles) ★★★ VHS: $9.99

Crooklyn

(1994, 114 min, US, Spike Lee) *Alfre Woodard, Spike Lee, Zelda Harris, Delroy Lindo.* Occasionally funny and at times abrasive, this semiautobiographical film directed by Spike and cowritten by Lee and his siblings focuses on the Carmichael family as they experience a summer in their crowded but comfortable Brooklyn neighborhood. Centering on the relationship between the

Carmichaels' matriarch (Woodard) and her young daughter (skillfully played by Harris), this patchwork quilt pieced together with vintage "Soul Train" footage and Afro Sheen commercials has wonderful moments, but may be a little on the long side for those with short attention spans. Note: One painfully long sequence is shot in Cinemascope, so do not attempt to adjust your sets. ★★★ VHS: $9.99; DVD: $24.99

Cross Creek

(1983, 122 min, US, Martin Ritt) *Mary Steenburgen, Rip Torn, Alfre Woodard, Peter Coyote, Dana Hill.* Based on the memoirs of Marjorie Rawlings ("The Yearling"), this compelling drama stars Steenburgen as the author who ventures into Florida's backwoods and composes the novel which life there inspired. Sterling support from Torn and Woodard. ★★★ VHS: $9.99

Cross My Heart

(1987, 100 min, US, Armyan Bernstein) *Martin Short, Annette O'Toole, Paul Reiser.* Short and O'Toole are well cast as two romantics on a first date — where everything goes wrong. An insightful though slow-moving comedy not without a considerable charm. ★★½ VHS: $9.99

Cross My Heart

(1990, 105 min, France, Jacques Fansten) French films don't come any sweeter than this charming, offbeat story about a group of classmates united in protecting a fellow student after his mother suddenly dies. When his young mother inexplicably dies one evening, 12-year-old Martin, fearful that he will be sent to an orphanage, tries to cover up her death. His resourceful classmates soon discover the situation, swear secrecy and begin an elaborate plan to keep Martin away from the authorities by tutoring him, supplying food and money, forging letters to an increasingly suspicious principal and even burying mom in an old grandfather clock! A heartwarming and winsome tale of growing up. (French with English subtitles) ★★★ VHS: $19.99

Cross My Heart and Hope to Die

(1994, 96 min, Norway, Marius Holst) *Martin Dahl Garfalk, Jan Kornstad.* A haunting Norwegian film about a young boy's coming of age. When Otto (Garfalk) is the only child left in town during summer vacation, he befriends Frank (Kornstad), a mysterious stranger who shows up one day out of nowhere. Almost immediately, weird things start happening: they find a body in the lake; Otto's mother may be having an affair with Frank; and the boy's father is crippled in an accident. The tension builds inexorably as Otto suspects his new friend of foul play — but do his eyes decieve him? Director Holst films everything impeccably, slowly revealing the truth. *Cross My Heart* is at times unsettling — there is an awful incident with a rat — but it is hypnotic nonetheless. Garfalk gives an exceptional performance as Otto, and he is well supported by Kornstad as the seductive, secretive Frank. (Norwegian with English subtitles) ★★★½ VHS: $79.99; DVD: $29.99

Cross of Iron

(1977, 120 min, GB/West Germany, Sam Peckinpah) *James Coburn, Maximilian Schell, James Mason, David Warner, Senta Berger.* Notable for being the great action director Peckinpah's first war film, this nonetheless represents the director's decline and is only intermittently interesting. It tells the story of a group of German soldiers on the Russian front in 1943 — a compelling idea which isn't given its full due. There is, however, a brilliantly staged battle scene near the end of the film which may, or may not, make it worth sitting through. ★★ DVD: $29.99

Crossfire

(1947, 85 min, US, Edward Dmytryk) *Robert Mitchum, Robert Ryan, Robert Young, Gloria Graham.* One of the first Hollywood films to deal with racial bigotry, this low-budget but engrossing thriller was shot entirely at night. In a New York City hotel, a Jewish man is murdered and three G.I.s just back from the war are suspected. Interestingly, the original victim in the Richard Brooks novel, "The Brick Foxhole," on which the film is based, was a homosexual. Ryan (in an Oscar-nominated role) is especially good as a bigoted soldier. ★★★★ VHS: $14.99

Crossing Delancey

(1988, 97 min, US, Joan Micklin Silver) *Amy Irving, Peter Riegert, Reizl Bozyk, Jeroen Krabbe, Sylvia Miles.* A charming tale of a "modern" woman searching for love and identity in an all-too-often inhumane "modern" world. Irving is radiant as a young urbanite who has fled her ethnic roots to become a member of the "in" Greenwich Village literary scene. When her aging Lower East Side Jewish grandmother, Bubbie, hires a matchmaker to find her a hubbie — a local pickle maker (wonderfully portrayed by Riegert) — her flight becomes all the more urgent. But despite all of her efforts to deny him, he possesses an undeniably sincere charm which plunges her into a true crisis of identity. Bozyk is a delight as the overbearing but lovable Bubbie. ★★★ VHS: $14.99

The Crossing Guard

(1995, 114 min, US, Sean Penn) *Jack Nicholson, David Morse, Anjelica Huston, Robin Wright, Piper Laurie, Richard Bradford, Robbie Robertson, John Savage.* Writer-director Penn has crafted an actors' vehicle in this somber treatment of guilt and redemption. The story opens on the day John Booth (Morse) is released from prison after serving his sentence for the drunk driving death of a young girl, whose father Freddy Gale (Nicholson) has vowed revenge. Both Morse and Nicholson deliver powerful yet nuanced performances as each struggles with his own personal hell. Huston is equally compelling as Mary, the child's mother, who has attempted to move beyond her own numbing loss and reconnect with life. As the characters confront and rebuff each other, a more complete version of their lives emerges. A solid supporting cast and exquisite cinematography propel a sometimes lumbering story line to its resolution, unexpected in its emotional release. ★★★ VHS: $9.99; DVD: $29.99

Crossing the Bridge

(1992, 103 min, US, Mike Binder) *Josh Charles, Jason Gedrick, Stephen Baldwin, Cheryl Pollak, Richard Edson.* Detroit, 1975, is the setting for this rambling, finally-coming-of-age drama about three high school buddies drifting nowhere three years after graduation. Told through the eyes of Mort (an aspiring Jewish writer who sleeps until noon and hangs out with his dopey ex-jock friends), the story concerns the growing up that occurs when the gang considers smuggling drugs from Canada. Writer-

The extraordinary Zhang Ziyi in *Crouching Tiger, Hidden Dragon*

director Binder's film comes off as a dramatically enhanced autobiography depicting what might have been his "good old days," but the screenplay at its worst gives way to clichés about tough young adulthood. ★★

Crossover Dreams

(1985, 85 min, US, Leon Ichaso) *Rubén Blades, Shawn Elliott, Elizabeth Peña.* Although American made, the Latin setting in New York's Spanish Harlem gives a feel of America as a foreign land. Blades delivers a mesmerizing acting and singing performance in this gritty, bittersweet comedy about a musician who vainly strives to "cross over" to the pop music mainstream. This is a compelling tale about betraying one's roots and friends for the sake of success, and marks an impressive screen introduction for Blades. ★★★

Crossroads

(1986, 100 min, US, Walter Hill) *Ralph Macchio, Joe Seneca, Jami Gertz, Joe Morton.* Macchio is a musical prodigy who, with the help of a legendary bluesman, hits the road for fame and fortune. He also battles the Devil for his immortal soul. Ry Cooder wrote the score; good as it may be, it doesn't help. ★½ VHS: $19.99

Crouching Tiger, Hidden Dragon

(2000, 119 min, Taiwan, Ang Lee) *Chow Yun-Fat, Michelle Yeoh, Zhang Ziyi, Chang Chen, Cheng Pei Pei.* With one master stroke, director Lee has simultaneously made the art film accessible, the martial arts film artful, and combined several genres to create one of the most poetic, exciting and awe-inspiring films in recent memory. A stunning achievement of immeasurable beauty, *Crouching Tiger, Hidden Dragon* finds director Lee — who helmed such great English-language films as *Sense and Sensibility* and *The Ice Storm* — back home in his native Taiwan to tell the thrilling story of master warriors, gravity-defying fights and the ultimate battle for the legendary Green Destiny sword. Yun-Fat is Li Mu Bai, the land's most celebrated soldier, who returns to his village to leave behind the ways of the samurai. Fate, however, has other plans as Li comes face to face with his fiercest of enemies, the Jade Fox (Pei). Caught in the middle is Jen (an extraordinary Ziyi), the

daughter of the local governor who is promised in an arranged marriage. Destinies and passions soon collide in a beautiful, swirling mixture of acrobatics and romantic sweep. The fight scenes, choreographed by Yuen Wo-Ping (*The Matrix*), are simply astonishing, bordering on the fantastic but possessing such grace as to never appear absurd. The story, based on the novel by Wang Du Lu, stands on its own as a study of tradition and defiance; with the Hong Kong-style fight scenes, it's a perfect blending of action and grand drama. Winner of 4 Academy Awards, including Best Foreign-Language Film. (Mandarin with English subtitles) ★★★★ VHS: $22.99; DVD: $27.99

Croupier

(1998, 91 min, GB, Mike Hodges) *Clive Owen, Kate Hardie, Alex Kingston, Gina McKee, Nicholas Ball.* Jack Manfred (Owen) suffers writer's block by day and deals cards by night, the croupier job suggested by his small-time-hood dad. Jack dyes his bleached hair black and recedes behind his tuxedo, unreadable, while unerringly reading the gamblers. He uses a keen perception of human nature while dealing that he cannot harness for writing. He lives with an ex-cop store detective who loves him, of whom he's fond; he's either incapable of commitment or was weaned early from that weakness. He never gambles until he bets the farm. Breaking a cardinal rule, Jack gets involved with a beautiful player (Kingston), who leads him down a crooked path. Addiction lives on both sides of the betting table, inducing lapses of judgment and enabling convoluted patterns of betrayal. *Croupier* is an intriguing, devastatingly cynical meditation on loyalty, allegiance and the mathematics of risk, delivered with a delicious noir sentiment and an appropriate lack of sentimentality. ★★★½

The Crow

(1994, 105 min, US, Alex Proyas) *Brandon Lee, Ernie Hudson, Michael Wincott, David Patrick Kelly, Rochelle Davis, William H. Macy.* *The Crow* was expected to be Lee's breakout film. Instead, he was killed on the set. He was 28. Ironically, his father, Bruce Lee, also died at an early age when his film career was expected to explode. The film itself is almost overshadowed by these events, but stands on its own as an entertaining actioner with a driving love story. In a darkly luminous, decaying

C

inner city, Lee and his fiancée are brutally murdererd for standing up to a slimy urban developer. Lee emerges from his grave after a year's regeneration, seeking vengeance to gain his final peace. Lee exhibits an engaging screen presence in this well-paced, starkly shot neo-noir. His future work would have been eagerly anticipated. (Followed by 2 sequels) (VHS letterboxed available for $19.99) ★★★½ VHS: $14.99; DVD: $29.99

The Crow: City of Angels

(1996, 86 min, US, Tim Pope) *Vincent Perez, Mia Kirshner, Iggy Pop, Richard Brooks.* Using the same mythology created in the original but building a completely separate story from it, a new team of filmmakers has made a darker vision of the undead avenger. Ash (Perez), a single father, is killed for accidentally witnessing a murder one night — the vengeance of the Crow rises. Ash is informed of his dark purpose by Sarah (Kirshner), the only character to appear in both films, and soon sets his sights on a drug lord his crew. Looking like a music video spawned in Clive Barker's nightmares, this sequel is filled with ritualistic tattoos, piercings, and enough religious imagery and symbolism to elevate it above its pulp-action roots. (VHS letterboxed available for $19.99) ★★★ VHS: $14.99; DVD: $29.99

The Crowd

(1928, 104 min, US, King Vidor) *Eleanor Boardman, James Murray.* This classic silent drama tells the tale of a newlywed couple's hard times in New York City. Boardman and Murray give refreshingly subtle performances as the young lovers who learn that it is their love for each other that prevents them from being swallowed up by the big city's faceless crowd. ★★★★ VHS: $29.99

The Crucible

(1996, 123 min, US, Nicholas Hytner) *Daniel Day-Lewis, Winona Ryder, Paul Scofield, Joan Allen, Bruce Davison.* Arthur Miller's 1953 play about the Salem witch-hunts was a thinly veiled allegory on McCarthyism, and the critical reception to it was lukewarm at best, what with the hearings still going on. In time, McCarthyism died along with McCarthy, and the play was recognized as a masterwork of the American theater. Adapted for the screen by Miller himself, this ominous, viscerally powerful film version is faithful to the text and maintains a larger-than-life feel. The story centers on the hysteria which results when lovestruck teen Abigail Williams (Ryder) falsely accuses neighbors of witchcraft — which ultimately leads to the accusation of John Proctor (Day-Lewis) and his wife Elizabeth (the terrific Allen). There needn't be a topical political or social relevance to appreciate this remarkable film; *The Crucible* provides an acidly ironic contrast to contemporary trials in which, rather than the innocent being persecuted, the guilty are set free. (VHS letterboxed available for $19.99) ★★★★ VHS: $9.99

Cruel Intentions

(1999, 97 min, US, Roger Kumble) *Sarah Michelle Gellar, Ryan Phillippe, Reese Witherspoon, Selma Blair, Sean Patrick Thomas, Joshua Jackson.* Choderlos de Laclos's novel "Les Liaisons Dangereuses" has been made into three great movies already; this fourth leads one to believe that it can do no wrong. The exploits of Valmont (Phillippe) and Merteuil (Gellar) are updated to the politically incorrect '90s in Manhattan, and given a terrifically trashy twist by writer-director Kumble. The

step-siblings set up a wager for Phillippe to seduce Witherspoon (cast against type as a goody-goody virgin); Merteuil's prize? "I'll fuck your brains out." No pretentiousness here, just catty talk and vile acts — get out the popcorn! *Cruel Intentions* is a fun hoot from start (the ruin of a psychiatrist) to inevitable finish (the slow-motion comeuppance of Merteuil). (Sequel: *Cruel Intentions 2*) ★★★ VHS: $14.99; DVD: $24.99

Cruel Intentions 2

(2000, 87 min, US, Roger Kumble) *Robin Dunne, Amy Adams, Sarah Thompson, Mimi Rogers.* Cruel Intentions 2, the fifth retelling of *Les Liaisons Dangereuses*, is the weakest by far. But this oddball, straight-to-video trash could be enjoyable to die-hard fans of the first *Cruel Intentions*, for this follows in the footsteps of Gus Van Sant's *Psycho* in an almost scene-for-scene remake of the original. This scenario is made even more absurd than Van Sant's guilty pleasure, because this is made by the same writer-director as the first film (couldn't he have found any other projects to keep him busy?). The characters are all the same in this sequel (even though not all of them survived last time), and the situations are almost identical, with some tiny variations here and there. A half-hearted, junior high drama class run-through of the first film. ★½ VHS: $102.99; DVD: $24.99

The Cruel Sea

(1953, 121 min, GB, Charles Frend) *Jack Hawkins, Donald Sinden, Denholm Elliott, Stanley Baker, Virginia McKenna, Alec McCowen.* Recalling the 1940s classic British war films in both its pacing and structure, the sometimes riveting *The Cruel Sea* follows the wartime experiences of the crew of a British warship patrolling the Atlantic during WWII. Hawkins stars as the ship's captain, who witnesses the sacrifice and dehumanizing effect of combat as he and his men battle a literally unseen enemy, the German U-boats underneath the ocean. From the young faces of the dead to a mesmerizing sequence of a ship sinking, the film delves into the often harsh daily lives of men at war, on the sea and, to a lesser extent, on land. The film features stunning cinematography, and its location shooting and actual war footage only accentuates the realism the film successfully conveys. ★★★½

Cruel Story of Youth

(1960, 97 min, Japan, Nagisa Oshima) *Yusuke Kawazu, Miyuki Kuwano.* Dazzling, audacious and strangely contemporary, Oshima's searing depiction of youthful alienation centers around the doomed affair of two teenaged lovers. The film shows a perversely Americanized post-WWII Japan and a disillusioned generation of reckless thrill-seekers. Behind his Ray Bans and his cat-that-ate-the-bird grin, the lead character charts a course toward a tragic end and drags his sexually exploited girlfriend down with him. (Japanese with English subtitles) ★★★★ VHS: $29.99

The Cruise

(1998, 76 min, US, Bennett Miller) Plato had it wrong: Some lives *should* be unexamined. Case in point: one Timothy "Speed" Levitch, a tour bus guide with a penchant for free associating like a mental patient. Now share the insanity with family and friends with this engaging documentary. Enjoy the musings of a typical "colorful character" as he waylays the unsuspecting onto a double deck

bus for a ride 'round the ninth circle of Hell — with his own ego at the center. Be amazed as this autodidact (who must have been his own worst student) preens and poses, whines and rails, offering insights of the myopic. Few street philosophers have ever been more pedestrian — or in his own odd way, entertaining. In an unsurprising twist, the tour bus company, after viewing this documentary, fired Levitch. ★★★ VHS: $102.99

Cruising

(1980, 106 min, US, William Friedkin) *Al Pacino, Paul Sorvino, Karen Allen.* Pacino goes undercover in the Village's gay community and director Friedkin lets loose a homophobic assault. Pacino plays a police officer assigned to investigate a series of murders committed against gay men. So he dons leather cap and jacket and hits the clubs. This thriller has been aptly described as a "gay horror story," for Friedkin's vision of the gay world is both horrific and inaccurate. ★ VHS: $14.99

Crumb

(1995, 119 min, US, Terry Zwigoff) R. Crumb certainly never wore any flowers in his hair that Summer of Love when he invented underground comics. Indeed, in each succeeding issue of *Zap* he spewed forth page after foolscap page of Hogarthian bile documenting the delusional nature of our Aquarian innocence. Director Zwigoff has captured the complexity of this man in his straightforward, riveting documentary, allowing the helplessly voluble Crumb to tell us more than he ever meant to — just like he does in his comics. Only his art has allowed him to come to terms with his "eccentricities," an outlet not available to his two brothers, one of whom finally killed himself after many attempts. The two family members who make the strongest impression by their absence are Crumb's sisters, who wisely declined to participate. ★★★½ VHS: $19.99; DVD: $29.99

Crush

(1992, 97 min, New Zealand, Alison MacLean) *Marcia Gay Harden, Donough Rees, Caitlin Bossley.* This unnerving psychological thriller is infused with a brooding sense of doom. Set against the bubbling geysers of rural New Zealand, the story

Crumb

examines themes of passion, betrayal, desire, jealousy, seduction, and revenge. Two women, Lane (Harden) and Christina (Rees), are involved in a car accident, leaving Christina severely injured and Lane (whose carelessness was the cause of the accident) unscathed. Lane inexplicably abandons her comatose friend, eventually befriending a novelist, Colin, and his 15-year-old boyish daughter, Angela. Angela, in turn, befriends the slowly recovering Christina, thereby precipitating an emotional showdown among the characters. A twisted, stylish, tension-filled feature which works best when delving into the three women's constantly shifting relationships and subtle sexual games. ★★★ VHS: $14.99

The Crush

(1993, 89 min, US, Alan Shapiro) *Cary Elwes, Alicia Silverstone, Jennifer Rubin, Kurtwood Smith.* When a handsome young journalist (Elwes) rents the guest house of an affluent couple, he becomes the object of their precocious teenage daughter's (Silverstone) dangerously obsessive affections. With a sexy 14-year-old seductress as the protagonist, a victim who is so clueless that one is tempted to yell "just get out of the house already, stupid," and a wonderfully inane plot twist involving a used condom, *The Crush* has a sort of shamelessness about its own cheesiness. Silverstone bats her eyes, flirts and connives like a pint-sized Sharon Stone. ★★½ VHS: $14.99; DVD: $14.99

Crusoe

(1989, 95 min, US, Caleb Deschanel) *Aidan Quinn, Ade Sapara, Timothy Spall.* "Just sit right back and you'll hear a tale, the tale of a fateful trip..." This is indeed a fateful trip into the darkened heart of the colonial imperialist, a trip on which director Deschanel perilously sets out to explore the moral ineptitude of a 19th-century slave trader. Not that this isn't a noble purpose, but what results here is an overburdened and laboring rendition of the Robinson Crusoe story. The film is not entirely without merit, however: the cinematography delivers a splendid view of the Seychelles and Quinn is compelling as a Crusoe who is forced to reevaluate his assumptions about life, power and greed. ★★

Cry-Baby

(1990, 85 min, US, John Waters) *Johnny Depp, Amy Locane, Willem Dafoe, Polly Bergen, Patricia Hearst, Traci Lords, Ricki Lake, Susan Tyrrell, Joe Dallesandro.* Waters' musical spoof of 1950s teen flicks is set (where else?) in Baltimore and stars Depp as "Cry-Baby" Walker, a tough-as-nails, pretty-boy delinquent and leader of the ultracool Drapes, who falls in love with Allison, a squeaky clean rich girl who has that itch to go "bad." But for those of us who were teased by the uproarious *Hairspray* and have been waiting for his definitive "suburban mall period" classic, sadly, this is not the one. Although it falls a little flat, it is still enjoyable, especially for its many Waters touches. ★★★ VHS: $9.99

Cry Freedom

(1987, 157 min, GB, Richard Attenborough) *Kevin Kline, Denzel Washington, Penelope Wilton, Kevin McNally, John Thaw, Timothy West, Zakes Mokae, Alec McCowen.* Attenborough's superbly rendered film about the life and death of South African activist Stephen Biko is a compelling vision of the violence and strife which tears at the heart of the black townships. The story is told through the eyes of Biko's white journalist friend, Donald Woods (excellently portrayed by Kline). As Biko, Washington delivers a moving performance. The film was criticized for concentrating more on the plight of Woods and his family than on black South Africa, but in fact, the film stands as a stirring portrait of how injustice for some leads to injustice for all. ★★★½ VHS: $9.99; DVD: $26.99

A Cry in the Dark

(1988, 121 min, Australia, Fred Schepisi) *Meryl Streep, Sam Neill, Bruce Myles.* With an astonishing characterization, here portraying a mother on trial for the murder of her child, Streep once again gives proof that she is the finest actress of her generation. Lindy Chamberlain (Streep), a housewife and mother, is wrongfully arrested when her baby is killed by a dingo. The film recounts the tragedy and its aftermath, and not only explores the unbelievable strain on the Chamberlain household during the trial, but also the power of public opinion and a cynical press. A serious and intelligent film directed with a subtle hand. Neill is excellent as Streep's husband. ★★★½ VHS: $14.99; DVD: $14.99

Cry of the Banshee

(1970, 92 min, GB, Gordon Hessler) *Vincent Price, Elisabeth Bergner, Hugh Griffith.* This bad period horror film has virtually no redeeming value save the performance of Price, who is clearly working well below his talent here. He plays a village magistrate who sadistically persecutes those he suspects of witchcraft. When Price exterminates a group of heathens who turn out to be Satan-worshippers, he has a curse placed upon his household by the leader of the group. The film then turns into a sort of slasher/monster movie, with various members of his household being dispatched in various gory ways. Good production design is offset by a ludicrous and offensive script, which includes lots of nudity and gore to appeal to a mass market crowd. ★ VHS: $12.99

Cry, the Beloved Country

(1951, 111 min, GB, Zoltan Korda) *Canada Lee, Sidney Poitier, Charles Carson.* One of the first films to confront the injustices of Apartheid in South Africa, this Korda classic, based on the Alan Paton novel, tells the tale of a black rural priest (Lee) who travels to Johannesburg to find his son. Once there, he is confronted by the brutal realities of urban crime and the dehumanizing conditions of the segregationist townships. Poitier costars as an urban cleric who helps Lee in his search. (Remade in 1996) ★★★½ VHS: $69.99

Cry, the Beloved Country

(1996, 109 min, US/South Africa, Darrell James Roodt) *James Earl Jones, Richard Harris, Vusi Kunene, Charles S. Dutton.* A second screen version of Alan Paton's novel of racial inequality in 1940s South Africa, *Cry, the Beloved Country* is compassionate storytelling which is lacking a thoroughly fluid narrative but is enriched by two terrific actors. Jones plays Rev. Stephen Kumalo, a rural priest who embarks on an odyssey of discovery when he travels to Johannesburg in search of his lost son and sister. Through a little detective work, he soon learns his son is on trial for killing a white man in a robbery attempt. Harris plays James Jarvis, the victim's father, a supremacist and neighbor of Rev. Kumalo. The story constructs each grieving father's journey, eventually leading to their paths crossing. A reverent, almost solemn adaptation, the film's strengths lie in Jones and Harris' remarkable performances, and from a dramatically involving story which examines the plight of both fathers and their eventual reconciliation with their sons. ★★★ VHS: $19.99

The Crying Game

(1992, 112 min, GB, Neil Jordan) *Stephen Rea, Jaye Davidson, Forest Whitaker, Miranda Richardson, Jim Broadbent, Adrian Dunbar.* In a brilliant marketing coup, the folks at Miramax Films released this film strongly advising people not to give away its "secret." Word of this "secret" quickly swept the nation and everybody was dying to see what would have otherwise been another *Defence of the Realm* or *Hidden Agenda.* Thankfully, director Jordan's tautly realized political thriller is worthy of all the praise and press it generated. Rea received an Oscar nomination for his role as an IRA terrorist with a troubled conscience who promises a captured British soldier (Whitaker) that he'll look after his girlfriend. Sometime later, Rea has opted out of the terror game and is trying to lead a quiet life of obscurity in London, where he decides to look her up. Newcomer Davidson's portrayal of the slender and exotic hairdresser is a knockout and also garnered an Oscar nomination. Trouble comes in spades when one of Rea's old Republican comrades (the exhilarating Richardson), shows up to test his loyalties. An exciting and highly entertaining story sprinkled with drama, comedy and plenty of intrigue. ★★★★ VHS: $9.99; DVD: $14.99

Cuba

(1979, 126 min, US, Richard Lester) *Sean Connery, Brooke Adams, Hector Elizondo, Denholm Elliott, Jack Weston, Chris Sarandon, Lonette McKee.* Director Lester imbues a high style to this political thriller about a doomed love affair between Connery and Adams as the Batista government collapses around them. ★★★ VHS: $6.99

Cube

(1998, 90 min, Canada, Vincenzo Natali) *Nicole DeBoer, Nicky Guadagni, David Hewlett, Maurice Dean Wint.* A taut little paranoid suspense thriller, the low-budget *Cube* follows a handful of diverse people who wake up inside a uniquely designed prison — a gigantic cube with individual chambers that are constantly changing configuration, much like a rotating Rubik's Cube. It's a simple Darwinian tale of survival of the fittest as the prisoners ponder the nature and identity of their jailors and struggle to find a way out. Despite a rather predictable screenplay full of randomly stilted dialogue and some shakily amateurish performances, *Cube* is salvaged by a terrific production design, some inventive and very convincing visual effects, and a rich soundtrack. Even though the ending is somewhat of a letdown, *Cube* is still very much worth a look. ★★½ VHS: $14.99; DVD: $24.99

La Cucaracha

(1999, 95 min, US/Mexico, Jack Perez) *Eric Roberts, Joaquim De Almeida, Tara Crespo, Victor Rivers, James McManus.* Roberts is a desperate drifter stranded south of the border who's given a second chance when a Mexican monarch offers him $100,000 to kill the man who raped and murdered his 16-year-old son. As he debates whether or not to do it, his life is put in danger by the very men offering him the contract. Costar McManus wrote this strangely moving tale of revenge and redemption that's a notch above the usual B-movie actioner. ★★½ VHS: $102.99; DVD: $29.99

Cujo

(1983, 91 min, US, Lewis Teague) *Dee Wallace, Danny Pintauro, Ed Lauter.* Only Stephen King could write a book about a mother and son trapped in a broken-down car and being terrorized by a rabid St. Bernard and get away with it. If you think this premise sounds silly, think again, because this ably made film adaptation is at times terrifying and filled with tension, which builds to an excellent climax. ★★★ VHS: $9.99; DVD: $19.99

The Cup

(2000, 94 min, Bhutan, Khyentse Norbu) *Jamyang Lodro, Orgyen Tobgyal, Neten Chokling.* In a Tibetan monastery in exile in the mountain regions of India, two young cousins safely arrive after a perilous journey from Tibet. Their adaptation to austere monastic life includes an unexpected wrinkle — their introduction to World Cup soccer! Even in this isolated, ethereal locale, soccermania is rampant. When, just before the 1998 World Championship match, it becomes necessary to obtain a TV and satellite dish, the entire monastery gets involved with the project. *The Cup* maintains a wacky, caper ambience while never losing sight of the circumstances that brought these Tibetan Buddhists to their present location. Delightful character portrayals and sure-handed direction combine to deliver an engrossing entertainment in which exotic ritual coexists with a contemporary sports milieu. Based on actual events. (Bhutanese with English subtitles) ★★★½ VHS: $19.99

Cup Final

(1991, 107 min, Israel, Brian Riklis) *Moshe Ivgi, Muhamad Bakri.* A quiet, slightly comic and refreshing examination of the futile hatred between Israelis and Palestinians. The story follows Cohen, a young, nebbishy Jewish soldier whose planned trip to Spain for the World Cup soccer finals is dashed when he is captured by a PLO band. Forced to join them on their trek to Beirut, where they hope to find safe haven, he slowly overcomes his resentment towards his captors and even finds room to bond with them when he discovers that he and their charismatic commander, Ziad, are both rooting for the Italian team in the Cup Final. Filled with irony and gentle humor, the film exploits the situation to expose the prejudices of both sides while offering a glimmer of hope that their conflict is not intractable. (Hebrew and Arabic with English subtitles) ★★★ VHS: $59.99

Curdled

(1996, 94 min, US, Reb Braddock) *William Baldwin, Angela Jones, Lois Chiles, Daisy Fuentes, Mel Gorham, Barry Corbin.* In an enticing but bizarre performance, Jones stars as Gabriela, a young woman fascinated by the sight and smell of human blood. In order to satisfy her craving for gore, she takes a job with a cleaning service specializing in post-forensic jobs. Their latest moneymaker is cleaning up after the "Blueblood Killer," a serial killer preying on wealthy socialites. After she finds a clue to his identity lurking beneath a pool of coagulated blood, she

becomes the target of the murderer. Brilliant in its conception but flawed in execution, *Curdled* nevertheless remains satisfying for those who can stomach its subject matter. One could complain, however, that the filmmakers did not take the premise far enough; instead they make Gabriela a garden-variety Nancy Drew. ★★½ VHS: $14.99

The Cure

(1995, 95 min, US, Peter Horton) *Brad Renfro, Joseph Mazzello, Annabella Sciorra, Diana Scarwid, Bruce Davison.* A surprisingly heartwarming story of a boy with AIDS and his friendship with a precocious neighbor. Renfro and Mazzello are the kids of single mothers who happen to be as different as water and wine. Scarwid, in a role which has her paralleling the bitchy, jilted mother she hated in *Mommie Dearest*, and Sciorra are the flatly drawn mothers. Mazzello has that likable quality and wins over not only the friendship of the punky Renfro, but also the viewer's heart. On a quest to find a cure, the story ends up as almost a pre-teen version of *Midnight Cowboy* complete with bus rides and sickness, stealing and shivering. ★★★ VHS: $19.99

Curly Sue

(1991, 102 min, US, John Hughes) *James Belushi, Alisan Porter, Kelly Lynch.* Hughes butchers the memory of *Paper Moon* in this maudlin rehash about a father and daughter con artist team on the grift. Drifter Belushi and young Porter hit Chicago and immediately put the sting on yuppie lawyer Lynch. After hitting Belushi twice with her car, she invites them to stay at her luxury penthouse. Once together, of course, she falls victim to their charm, and vice versa. Hughes' screenplay is ludicrous and manipulative (even for him), and his attempts to mix the bittersweet with slapstick are ill-served. He's gone to the same well once too often. ★ VHS: $9.99

The Curse

(1987, 92 min, US, David Keith) *Wil Wheaton, Claude Akins, Cooper Huckabee, David Keith.* An alien meteorite lands on a Tennessee farm, setting off a battle between the young boy who lives there and the surrounding neighbors, who have now been driven crazy from the meteor's effects. An interesting if flat sci-fi tale based on H. P. Lovecraft's "The Color out of Space," which was previously filmed as *Die, Monster, Die*. ★★

The Curse of Frankenstein

(1957, 93 min, GB, Terence Fisher) *Peter Cushing, Christopher Lee, Hazel Court.* When their programmer *The Quatermass Experiment* became a "monster" hit, Hammer Studios wanted to know why. Was it the sci-fi? Or the monster? Marketing research came back with charts to prove that it was the latter, so Fisher was assigned to direct a new version of Mary Shelley's classic — this time with all the blood and guts that Eastman color and an X certificate would allow. The results made Cushing and Lee stars and Hammer Studios the Universal of the Thames. This doctor is no madman, just intellect personified; and in this series of films it is he, not the monster, that is the unifying thread. ★★★½ VHS: $14.99

The Curse of Her Flesh

(1968, 75 min, US, Michael Findlay & Roberta Findlay) Take a little New York avant-garde the-

atre, blend in some psychedelic '60s sexual revolutionism and some purely gratuitous "T&A" action, and the result is this entertainingly weird low-budgeter. For those who appreciate lines like, "I was once told by a girlfriend that my big toe was better than any man's," this video was made for you. Oh, and the plot? Something about a nightclub owner on a killing spree. ★★ VHS: $24.99

The Curse of the Blair Witch

(1999, 60 min, US) The *Blair Witch* phenomena takes a bizarre turn, as the pseudodocumentary gets its own pseudodocumentary with this spinoff. Scenes from the original movie, as well as outtakes, are interspersed with talking-head interviews of the locals around the site of the disappearance. The more conventional structure closely resembles that of *The Last Broadcast*, an indie flick about the search for the Jersey Devil. Originally aired on the Sci-Fi channel to drum up interest in the movie, *Curse* still holds up pretty well on its own, especially as an appetizer before the main dish. ★★½ VHS: $9.99

The Curse of the Cat People

(1944, 73 min, US, Robert Wise & Gunther von Fritsche) *Simone Simon, Kent Smith, Jane Randolph.* This moody sequel to the classic *Cat People* is an effective psychological thriller about a young girl who is befriended by the spirit of her father's deceased first wife. Simon returns from the original as the ghostly visitor. ★★★ VHS: $19.99

Curse of the Demon

(1957, 82 min, GB, Jacques Tourneur) *Dana Andrews, Peggy Cummins.* From the director of the original *Cat People* comes this low-budget, terrifying tale about a psychologist who investigates the death of a colleague, who may have been the victim of an ancient curse. Andrews is the sleuthing shrink. A wonderfully atmospheric film which is marred only by its wooden-looking monster, included at the insistence of its American distributors. ★★★½ VHS: $14.99

Curse of the Queerwolf

(1987, 90 min, US, Mark Pirro) *Michael Palazzolo, Kent Butler.* One of the funnier (if lamebrained) low-budget horror/sexploitation flicks to come around in some time, this wacky variation on the werewolf legend is marred only by an insidious streak of homophobia. The story follows Larry, a typical straight-as-an-arrow guy who, much to his horror, is bitten on the ass by a pretty "girl," turning him into a queerwolf — male by day and tarty, heavily rouged "lady" by full moon. The target of the film's antic humor is primarily gay men and innocent little dogs. But while offensive to some, it is more harmless camp than incendiary hatred. ★★ VHS: $19.99

The Curse of the Starving Class

(1994, 102 min, US, J. Michael McClay) *James Woods, Kathy Bates, Henry Thomas, Randy Quaid, Louis Gossett, Jr., Kristin Fiorella.* Ostensibly a quirky, comedy-tinged family melodrama about a clan of failing Nevada farmers, this adaptation of Sam Shepard's stage play feels mushy, contrived and disjointed in its examination of a po' white trash family. Woods is the alchoholic, good-fornothing dad, who has been exiled from home by his more sober but no-less-dysfunctional wife (Bates). Both seem to derive sick pleasure from not only tormenting each other, but their cowboy son (Thomas) and precocious daughter

Cyclo

(Fiorella) as well. At issue is the family farm, which both parents are plotting to sell behind each other's backs. ★★ VHS: $14.99

The Custodian

(1993, 110 min, Australia, John Dingwall) *Anthony LaPaglia, Hugo Weaving, Barry Otto.* This stinging indictment of police corruption stars LaPaglia as an honest cop who implicates himself in an internal affairs investigation as part of a scheme to bring down his crooked partner (Weaving). Top-notch performances and nail-biting suspense make this a most pleasant surprise. ★★★ VHS: $79.99

Cutter's Way

(1981, 105 min, US, Ivan Passer) *Jeff Bridges, John Heard, Lisa Eichhorn.* Passer's taut and complex thriller has a trio of social misfits stalking a possible murderer for their own muddled purposes. Heard lends poignancy to the role of a crippled Vietnam War vet and Bridges is his drifting Ivy League buddy. ★★★ VHS: $19.99; DVD: $19.99

Cutthroat Island

(1995, 118 min, US, Renny Harlin) *Geena Davis, Matthew Modine, Frank Langella, Maury Chaykin, Stan Shaw.* Director Harlin's attempt to make his wife Davis into a blockbuster action heroine is fun for awhile, but this pirate adventure is without a brain in its well-costumed head. A return to the swashbuckling sagas and serials of the 1930s, *Cutthroat Island* is the familiar story of buried treasure, coded maps, uneasy alliances, treacherous kin, barroom brawls and narrow escapes, capped by a big sea battle at the end. The real draw of the movie is not its script, but its spectacle. And the film succeeds in its several set-piece action scenes. Unfortunately, the few merits the film does have will probably be lost on the small screen. Davis and Modine do most of their own stunts, which the director — in Jackie Chan-style — makes obvious with a zooming camera. (Letterboxed VHS available for $14.99) ★★ VHS: $9.99; DVD: $14.99

Cyber Ninja

(1991, 80 min, Japan, Keita Amemiya) Non-stop cartoon-like action and outrageous special effects are sure to keep you on your toes in this highly original and bizarre *Star Wars*–inspired sci-fi/martial arts epic. With the story taking place amid the chaos of a destructive war, a warrior princess is kidnapped by the underlings of a dark overlord. Intended to be the main course in a blood sacrifice which will unleash evil upon the land, the princess' only hope is a rebel band of soldiers and the mysterious Cyber Ninja to rescue her before it's too late. The film manages to save itself by spicing things up with the use of some truly hallucinatory visuals and unexpected twists. ★★★

Cyborg

(1989, 86 min, US, Albert Pyun) *Jean-Claude Van Damme, Deborah Richter.* Silly and violent sci-fi actioner with Van Damme fighting vicious gangs in the post-apocalyptic future. (Followed by 3 sequels) ★ VHS: $9.99; DVD: $24.99

Cyborg 2

(1993, 99 min, US, Michael Schroeder) *Elias Koteas, Angelina Jolie, Jack Palance.* Once again a cyborg (Jolie) chooses a hero (Koteas) to be her protector as she tries to escape her creators. Koteas is no Van Damme, and this time it's the cyborg who's the fighting machine and routinely helps the hero out of hot spots. The good effects make this slightly more enjoyable than the first film. ★★ VHS: $9.99; DVD: $14.99

Cyclo

(1995, 124 min, Vietnam, Tran Anh Hung) *Le Van Loc, Tony Leung-Chiu Wai, Tran Nu Yen Khe.* As he did in his previous film *The Scent of Green Papaya,* writer-director Hung unfolds a tale of corruption and redemption in a world that is both beautiful and dangerous. The result is a mesmerizing glimpse into the lives of a handful of characters on the brink of despair. The bustle of Ho Chi Minh City proves almost too difficult for a cyclo (pedicab) driver to earn his living, and he soon gets mixed up with a tough crime lord. To complicate matters, his sister, working as a prostitute, falls in love with the gangster, and a power struggle ensues. Often lush and disturbing at the same time, Hung evokes a very distinctive, albeit depressing environment for his unusual character study. Though at times slow moving (and unapologetically violent), *Cyclo* is an extraordinary, highly charged drama that builds inexorably to its stunning conclusion. (Vietnamese with English subtitles) ★★★½ VHS: $29.99

Cyrano de Bergerac

(1950, 113 min, US, Michael Gordon) *Jose Ferrer, Mala Powers, William Prince.* Ferrer won an Oscar for his stirring portrayal of one of literature's favorite heroes: the swashbuckling poet with the protruding proboscis — Cyrano de Bergerac. Though the film is technically uneven, it is more than made up for by Ferrer's classically flamboyant performance. Steve Martin (*Roxanne*), Gérard Depardieu and Derek Jacobi all appear in other versions of the Edmond Rostand classic and each actor is singularly brilliant. ★★★ VHS: $9.99

Cyrano de Bergerac

(1984, 176 min, GB, Terry Hands) *Derek Jacobi, Sinead Cusack, Pete Postlethwaite.* The Royal Shakespeare Company's elaborate and stunning 1984 Broadway production of Edmond Rostand's classic. Jacobi is mesmerizingly brilliant in the title role, and there's an exceptional supporting cast. ★★★★

Cyrano de Bergerac

(1990, 135 min, France, Jean-Paul Rappeneau) *Gérard Depardieu, Jacques Weber, Anne Brochet, Vincent Perez.* Rappeneau's outstanding realization of Edmond Rostand's classic play is an overwhelming cinematic achievement, made only more so by the monolithic screen presence of Depardieu in the title role. For his part, Depardieu delivers the performance of a lifetime as he sinks into the romantic heart of Cyrano with panache and punctuates every action with a flourish. Everything else in the film falls into place around him: the lavish set pieces, the swashbuckling action, the beautiful rhyming verse and the brilliant cinematography. A most exciting and emotionally rewarding film experience. (French with English subtitles) ★★★★ VHS: $19.99

Da

(1988, 102 min, US, Matt Clark) *Martin Sheen, Barnard Hughes, William Hickey.* Hughes reprises his award-winning stage role in this endearing adaptation about a man (Sheen) who returns to his native Ireland for his estranged father's funeral; coming to terms with his deceased parent when the man materializes after the funeral. A rewarding, funny examination of familial responsibilities and misgivings. ★★★

Dad

(1989, 117 min, US, Gary David Goldberg) *Jack Lemmon, Ted Danson, Olympia Dukakis, Ethan Hawke, Kevin Spacey, Zakes Mokae.* As with the similarly themed *Da,* a son attempts to reconcile himself with his father, though in this instance his dad is not deceased but dying. Though not as successful as Matt Clark's comedy, Lemmon's terrific performance compensates for the film's occasional dramatic lapses. ★★½ VHS: $7.49

Daddy Long Legs

(1955, 126 min, US, Jean Negulesco) *Fred Astaire, Leslie Caron, Terry Moore, Thelma Ritter.* An enchanting musical romance with playboy Astaire anonymously sponsoring orphan Caron's education, the two eventually falling in love. Score includes "Something's Got to Give." ★★★ VHS: $19.99

Daddy Nostalgia

(1990, 105 min, France/GB, Bertrand Tavernier) *Dirk Bogarde, Jane Birkin, Odette Laurie.* In this tender and wise story of the complex relationship between an aging, sick father, his wife and their daughter, Bogarde — in what may be his valedictorian performance — is simply brilliant as the fastidious and at times insufferable father. Birkin plays his gangly screenwriter daughter who travels to her parents' sun-splashed Côte d'Azur villa when her father takes ill. Completing the trio is Bogarde's wife (Laurie), a French woman who has become distant after enduring years with her grouchy, emotionally diffident husband. Director Tavernier insightfully delves into the characters' lives, thoughts and feelings as they attempt to understand each other and express their love. ★★★★ VHS: $29.99

Daddy's Dyin'...Who's Got the Will

(1990, 97 min, US, Jack Fisk) *Beau Bridges, Beverly D'Angelo, Tess Harper, Judge Reinhold, Amy Wright, Keith Carradine.* A wacky Texas family reunites at Daddy's deathbed, where secrets, accusations and grudges spew forth as its members wait to see exactly what they're gonna git. Amiable shenanigans. ★★½ VHS: $14.99

Daisy Miller

(1974, 93 min, US, Peter Bogdanovich) *Cybill Shepherd, Cloris Leachman, Eileen Brennan, Mildred Natwick.* Visually striking adaptation of Henry James' novel with Shepherd as the 19th-century heroine Daisy, a young American woman who shocks European high society with her liberated sexual attitudes. Though Shepherd's flirtatious performance fails to fully capture the spirit and complexity of James' character, she is surrounded by a first-rate supporting cast, including Leachman as Daisy's mother, and especially Brennan as a snobbish socialite. ★★★ VHS: $14.99

Damage

(1993, 112 min, GB, Louis Malle) *Jeremy Irons, Juliette Binoche, Miranda Richardson, Rupert Graves, Ian Bannen, Leslie Caron. Damage* is an arousing film, not just for the voyeuristic thrill of the much ballyhooed sex scenes between Irons and Binoche, but for the peek into the sumptuous London flats, elegant country estates and luxurious antiqued European hotels which serve as the film's backdrop. Irons plays an English cabinet minister who finds himself drawn to his son's exquisite and emotionally bruised new lover (Binoche). Richardson is Irons' restrained but ultimately tortured wife, and Graves is the betrayed son and lover. Not much in terms of plot, but high on atmosphere and tension (both carnal and familial), *Damage* is at times an almost savage look into the sexual psyche. (Unrated) ★★★ VHS: $19.99; DVD: $24.99

Dame Edna's Neighbourhood Watch

(1992, 144 min, GB) *Dame Edna (Barry Humphries).* Gorgeously attired, fabulously successful and bitingly sarcastic, Dame Edna (played by Humphries), everyone's favorite drag queen and Australia's most startling export since koala steaks, is a riotous hoot in this three-tape TV series. Each tape has two episodes and the premise is simple: Dame Edna, with the aid of her heat-seeking gladiolas, chooses three contestants from the all-female studio audience. Unbeknownst to one of them, the mischievous Edna has secretly sent a film crew to one of their homes, gotten into it and now for the entire audience to watch, rummages through drawers, rooms, closets and bathrooms, wittily commenting on the tacky, the obscene and the just plain ordinary. With her pale purple hair and rhinestone-encrusted spectacles and dresses that only a mad gay designer could have envisioned, Dame Edna is one unforgettable character. So possums, relax and enjoy this riotous comedy tape. (Two volumes available) ★★★ VHS: $59.99 each DVD: $29.99 each

Dames

(1934, 90 min, US, Ray Enright) *Dick Powell, Ruby Keeler, Joan Blondell, Zasu Pitts.* One of the best of the 1930s musicals, this backstage tuner features some great standards ("I Only Have Eyes for You," and the title tune among them) and those terrific Busby Berkeley dance routines. Forget the plot — it's another "let's put on a show" — it's the singing and dancing and comedy that's the main attraction here, and it's a hoot. Blondell is a standout as a wise-cracking chorine. ★★★ VHS: $19.99

Damn the Defiant!

(1962, 101 min, GB, Lewis Gilbert) *Alec Guinness, Dirk Bogarde, Anthony Quayle.* Guinness is stellar as a British naval captain who must fend off a challenge for power by his first mate (Bogarde), a fierce and merciless officer who is reviled by the crew. Set during the Napoleonic wars, the movie was filmed with an acute sense of historical detail. ★★★ VHS: $14.99; DVD: $24.99

Damn Yankees

(1958, 110 min, US, George Abbott) *Gwen Verdon, Ray Walston, Tab Hunter, Jean Stapleton.* "Whatever Lola wants, Lola gets," and what Lola gets is this sparkling screen adaptation of the Tony Award—winning Broadway musical. Hunter is Joe Hardy, the youthful reincarnate of a middle-aged die-hard Washington Senators fan who makes a pact with the Devil so he can help beat those damn New York Yankees. Re-creating their award-winning stage roles are the miraculous Verdon as Lola, who helps tame Joe, and Walston, who gives an irrepressible comic performance as the Devil. With splashy choreography by Bob Fosse (who also appears in one dance sequence), a good-natured and memorable score and appealing characters, *Damn Yankees* is a definite winner. ★★★½ VHS: $14.99

The Damned

(1969, 155 min, Italy/Germany, Luchino Visconti) *Dirk Bogarde, Ingrid Thulin, Helmut Berger, Charlotte Rampling.* A frantic international cast depicts Visconti's panorama of pre-war German decadence and Nazi narcissism. Visconti captures all the horrors of the era, culminating with the infamous slaughter of the "Night of the Long Knives." Berger is exceptional with his elaborate impersonation of Marlene Dietrich. (Filmed in English) ★★★½ VHS: $59.99

A Damsel in Distress

(1937, 101 min, US, George Stevens) *Fred Astaire, Joan Fontaine, George Burns, Gracie Allen.* Astaire's best musical of the 1930s made without Ginger Rogers. Though Fontaine lacks Ginger's musical skill and screen charm, costars Burns and especially Allen make one forget about the leading lady with their delightful supporting turns. Fred plays a famous dancer performing in London who falls for Lady Joan. The film contains one of the most remarkable musical production numbers ever conceived, "The Funhouse" sequence, and other

George Burns and Gracie Allen join Fred Astaire in *A Damsel in Distress*

Gershwin numbers include "A Foggy Day" and "Nice Work If You Can Get It." ★★★½ VHS: $14.99

Dance, Girl, Dance

(1940, 90 min, US, Dorothy Arzner) *Maureen O'Hara, Lucille Ball, Louis Hayward.* In possibly her most explicitly feminist film, director Arzner pairs O'Hara, as an idealistic young woman who dreams of becoming a ballerina, with Ball, the tough-as-leather show girl who doesn't take any shit from her leering, drunken audience. Ball convinces O'Hara to become partners in a burlesque troupe in this entertaining "the vamp and the virgin" comedy-drama. As "Bubbles," Ball is in great form. ★★★

Dance Me Outside

(1994, 91 min, Canada, Bruce McDonald) *Ryan Black, Adam Beach, Lisa LaCroix, Michael Greyeyes, Kevin Hicks, Sandrine Holt.* Energized and completely unaffected performances from a talented young cast imbue a finely crafted coming-of-age story with gritty realism. Set in the present day on a Canadian Indian reservation, a young woman's murder is the focal point of many intertwining stories of relationship, family, friendship, racial prejudice and the search for identity and purpose. Black and Beach play two young men trying to get into an auto mechanics school in Toronto. They need to write an essay as part of the entrance exam, but have nothing to say until the brutal murder of one of their friends provides the material — not only for the essay, but for their own personal quests for definition and adulthood. This independent winner details the course of many lives with humor, insight and compassion, without maudlin sentimentality or gilded heroics. ★★★ VHS: $79.99

Dance of Hope

(1990, 75 min, US, Deborah Shaffer) The brutal excesses of power of the Argentine military government and the heart-rending plight of *los desaparacidos* have been well documented. But the equally repressive actions of the Pinochet regime in neighboring Chile is only now being uncovered. This film by Academy Award—winning director Shaffer probes the sad story of the relatives of the thousands of people who "disappeared" and their efforts to get the government to provide answers. The title of the film refers to the *cueca*, Chile's national dance of passion and courtship: the mothers, wives and relatives of the missing citizens perform this dance alone to emphasize the loss of their partner. (Spanish with English subtitles) ★★★ VHS: $59.99

Dance with a Stranger

(1985, 101 min, GB, Mike Newell) *Miranda Richardson, Rupert Everett, Ian Holm, Joanne Whalley.* This critically acclaimed tale of passion and mystery follows the path of the romantic self-destruction of Ruth Ellis, the last woman to be executed in Great Britain. This gripping examination of a murderous romance stars Richardson (in a sensational film debut) as a dance hall girl who murders her abusive lover. As the selfish murdered boyfriend, Everett gives a convincing and sensual performance of an emotionally shallow upperclass beauty whose slumming leads to his demise. Holm is outstanding in support as another of Ellis' men. ★★★½ VHS: $14.99; DVD: $19.99

Dance with Me

(1998, 126 min, US, Randa Haines) *Vanessa L. Williams, Chayanne, Kris Kristofferson, Joan Plowright.* An insipid attempt at a fluffy date movie as both romance and dance film. Chayanne plays a Cuban dancer who comes to Texas to work in a dance studio owned by Kristofferson, an old flame of his mother's. Although he's hired as a handyman, our studly hero quickly displays his rug-cutting prowess and is invited to take part in a national dance contest in Vegas. While waiting for the big event, he starts a charmless relationship with sexy dancer Williams, and bonds with Kris, who can't seem to figure out Chayanne's obvious "big secret." Hokey dialogue, lame humor, stilted acting and unexciting dancing sink this snoozer quick. ★½ VHS: $9.99; DVD: $24.99

Dance with the Devil

(1998, 121 min, US, Alex de la Iglesia) *Rosie Perez, Javier Bardem, James Gandolfini, Harley Cross, Aimee Graham, Don Stroud, Alex Cox.* Violent and weird for weird's sake, this noir thriller follows the road adventures of a deranged couple: a fiery Mexican-American (Perez) and her cult-leader boyfriend (Bardem). They kidnap a young couple and plan to use them in a bizarre religious sacrifice, but not before intercepting a truckload of fetuses for a mob boss. (aka: *Perdita Durango*) ★★ VHS: $14.99

Dancer in the Dark

(2000, 139 min, US/Denmark, Lars Von Trier) *Björk, Catherine Deneuve, David Morse, Peter Stormare, Vladan Kostic, Jean-Marc Barr, Joel Grey, Udo Kier, Zeljko Ivanek.* Björk imparts a strong, naturalistic presence as Selma, a displaced Czech in small-town, 1960s America. Going blind from a hereditary disease, Selma is fighting an unrelenting deadline, working backbreaking and tedious jobs, scrounging for money for her son's eye operation, armed only with steely determination and an unbreakable code of honor. She can transmute the noises of her factory job into music, imagining elaborate dance numbers like those she barely sees on the silver screen. She's an innocent in a world of opportunistic betrayal, a grounded element in a broad allegory of sacrifice. The film presents a premise with strong potential but suffers somewhat from a rambling self-indulgence. Yet, while the narrative structure could have been tighter, there are moments of charming whimsy and moments of gut-wrenching anguish, delivered with a sure hand by a remarkable cast who prevent the pathos from devolving into bathos. Watch it knowing that it will rip your heart out. ★★★½ VHS: $14.99; DVD: $24.99

Dancer, Texas Pop. 81

(1998, 97 min, US, Tim McCanlies) *Breckin Meyer, Peter Facinelli, Ethan Embry, Eddie Mills, Patricia Wettig.* Good-natured slice-of-life tale about four young men, graduating from high school in their small Texas town, attempting to keep their promise to each other to move to L.A. together, despite pressures from family and friends. This lightweight though compelling drama unfolds at just the right pace, nicely juggling the four men's stories, leading to a satisfying, though not too schmaltzy or pat, conclusion. All four leads are quite good, as are the supporting players, and writer-director McCanlies captures the feel and attitude of a small town, highlighting both the

positive and negative aspects of growing up in such a place. In addressing leaving home for the first time, the film does a fine job detailing the fear and excitement of that time in one's life. ★★★ VHS: $14.99; DVD: $29.99

Dancers

(1987, 98 min, US, Herbert Ross) *Mikhail Baryshnikov, Leslie Browne, Mariangela Melato, Tommy Rall.* From the director and star of *The Turning Point* comes this inferior tale of an egocentric ballet star (Baryshnikov) who tends to seduce every young woman with whom he dances. When he turns his eye towards a young ballerina, he gets an unexpected lesson in love. ★ VHS: $14.99

Dances with Wolves

(1990, 183 min, US, Kevin Costner) *Kevin Costner, Mary McDonnell, Graham Greene, Rodney A. Grant.* Costner's directorial debut is this emotionally charged Academy Award—winning tribute to the Sioux Indians of the Dakota plains. Costner himself stars as Lt. John Dunbar of the Union Army, a man whose life is changed forever when he befriends the Lakota. At the close of the Civil War, Costner applies for service in the Western frontier. When he finally arrives at his outpost, finding it deserted, he settles in and begins to explore the territory. It is here that he makes contact with the Lakota. Beautifully photographed and filled with amazing stunts, *Dances with Wolves* presents a majestically sweeping vision of the grandeur of the great American West. The acting throughout is wonderful with Greene particularly memorable as Kicking Bird. A wonderful cinematic achievement in which Costner brings back the epic western. (English and Lakota with English subtitles) ★★★★ VHS: $14.99

Dancing at Lughnasa

(1998, 94 min, Ireland, Pat O'Connor) *Meryl Streep, Catherine McCormack, Michael Gambon, Kathy Burke, Sophie Thompson, Brid Brennan, Rhys Ifans.* As captivating as the Irish hills in which it is set, *Dancing at Lughnasa* is a poetic memory piece based on the award-winning play by Brian Friel. Set in the 1930s, it's about the last summer one family will spend together. Heading a remarkably fine cast is Streep, who absolutely shines as Kate, the eldest of five sisters who, at the story's beginning, are preparing for the return of their beloved brother Jack, a missionary who has been abroad for 25 years. The reunion, however, is tinged with melancholy when it becomes apparent he has suffered a mental breakdown. The pulse of Friel's story is the poignant relationship of the sisters, who are ruled over by Kate. Eventually, each sister — including Kate herself — breaks free of some form of repression. This culminates in a thrilling dance performed by the sisters which ultimately bonds and then separates them. With her rich Irish accent, Streep is a marvel of subtle inclination, and she's ably matched by a marvelous group of actresses. ★★★ VHS: $21.99; DVD: $29.99

Dancing in the Dark

(1986, 98 min, Canada, Leon Marr) *Martha Henry, Neil Munro.* Henry gives a mesmerizing performance as a woman whose life is defined by the minutiae of her 20-year marriage. When her protective shell of illusion cracks, she forfeits her tenuous grasp on reality for a moment of catharsis. Well-crafted and somber, with thoughtful direction by Marr. ★★★ VHS: $14.99

Dancing Lady

(1933, 94 min, US, Robert Z. Leonard) *Joan Crawford, Clark Gable, Franchot Tone, Nelson Eddy, The Three Stooges.* An appealing if ordinary M-G-M musical about chorus girl Crawford making it to the top while involved with stage director Gable and playboy Franchot Tone. Astaire made his film debut. ★★½ VHS: $19.99

Dandelions

(1974, 92 min, The Netherlands, Adrian Hoven) *Rutger Hauer, Dagmar Lassander.* A young Hauer stars in this cartoonish sex drama that is dubbed in a style reminiscent of *What's Up, Tiger Lily?* Rutger appears as a boozing, womanizing, self-hating low-life — or as one of the women he torments in the film calls him, "a cesspool of depravity." The characters, when they are not naked or gyrating in sexual contortions, are clothed in outlandish '70s mod outfits. Did people really dress like that? ★★

Dangaio

(1988, 45 min, Japan, Toshihiro Hirano) With names like Ramba and Pi Thunder, this cross-cultural animated space story involves four Esper-Warriors (three teenage girls and a boy), who are brainwashed and then altered into "augmented humans" or androids by a cunning scientist. This samurai-influenced story follows their adventures through space as they fight a powerfully evil blond cyborg as well as other galactic despots, all the while seeking the truth of their actual identities. The battles are mostly in space, but in one funny sequence, poor Tokyo again finds itself an impotent victim to a Godzilla-like thrashing. ★★★ VHS: $34.99

Danger Diabolik

(1968, 99 min, Italy, Mario Bava) *John Phillip Law, Marisa Mell, Michel Piccoli, Terry-Thomas.* In this campy, colorful, wild adaptation of a popular Italian comic book, director Bava has created a fun romp which echoes and spoofs everything from James Bond to those "big heist" films of the early 1960s. Law plays Diabolik, a master criminal who surrounds himself with electronic gadgets, beautiful women and wealth. During the course of the film, he steals ten million dollars, a priceless emerald necklace and a twenty-ton ingot of gold — and he manages to elude both the police and the underworld syndicate which has put a price on his head. Too much fun to seriously criticize and too ludicrous to take too seriously, the movie succeeds at just the level it was meant to: as a live-action comic book which has the viewer constantly rooting for its ultimate super (anti)hero. (Filmed in English) ★★★ VHS: $9.99

Dangerous

(1935, 72 min, US, Alfred E. Green) *Bette Davis, Franchot Tone.* Davis won an Oscar for her performance in this glossy soaper, but it was more for the snub the year earlier when she was overlooked for *Of Human Bondage.* However, Davis is quite good as an actress on the skids who captivates architect Tone. ★★½ VHS: $19.99

Dangerous Beauty

(1998, 112 min, US/GB, Marshall Herskovitz) *Catherine McCormack, Rufus Sewell, Oliver Platt, Moira Kelly, Fred Ward, Jacqueline Bisset.* McCormack stars as a strong-willed woman of lower station in 16th-century Venice who, when spurned by her true love (who refuses to marry below his station), becomes a very popular courtesan. The first of a recent spate of "feminists from the past" films, *Dangerous Beauty* is artless art-house lite, a frequently dull and pandering film with a potentially intriguing premise: how does an intelligent, independent woman get by in a society where women are treated as little more than objects? The clichéd answer that a whore is master of the man is given a spirited reading by McCormack, but the film as a whole can't transcend the mundane. Fans of costume dramas should enjoy this more, but even they will most likely be underwhelmed. ★★ VHS: $14.99; DVD: $19.99

Dangerous Game

(1993, 107 min, US, Abel Ferrara) *Harvey Keitel, Madonna, James Russo.* Ferrara continues his examination of moral ambiguity (*Bad Lieutenant*) with this verité *pas de trois* among a film director (Keitel) and his two leads (Madonna and Russo). They're working on a nauseating little film in which Russo plays a husband who continually abuses his wife (Madonna) and subsequently both attempt to escape their life of drug abuse and debauchery. Using the device of a film within a film, Ferrara warps the distinction between illusion and reality as the three principals become ever more enmeshed in their on- and off-the-set shenanigans. Ferrara shows a deft directorial hand, but that won't help most viewers overcome the film's repugnant core and unrelentingly nihilistic viewpoint. (Unrated) ★½ VHS: $79.99

Dangerous Ground

(1997, 96 min, US/South Africa, Darrell James Roodt) *Ice Cube, Elizabeth Hurley, Ving Rhames, Eric Miyeni.* Rapper-turned-actor Cube plays a native of South Africa who returns home from his adopted United States after his father dies. Now a San Francisco social worker, Cube finds the old neighborhood ain't like it used to be: instead of white pro-Apartheid thugs, he now has to face black mobsters dealing in drugs, carjackings and other illicit activities. He also discovers that his brother is indebted to a Nigerian druglord (Rhames), and tries to locate and help his sibling. Despite the potentially interesting background and political milieu, *Dangerous Ground* isn't much better than most direct-to-video thrillers. Roodt just can't get the mix of action and intrigue right; this ground is not only dangerous, but shaky as well. ★½ VHS: $79.99; DVD: $19.99

Dangerous Liaisons

(1960, 111 min, France, Roger Vadim) *Jeanne Moreau, Gérard Philip, Jean-Louis Trintignant.* Vadim's version of Choderlos De Laclos' decadent tale of the sexual games of the morally bankrupt is set within the chic and smoky jazz clubs of modern-day Paris. Moreau and Philip are the wealthy couple in a marriage where adultery and deceit are allowed and even encouraged just as long as love is absent. Philip's Valmont is a debonair, mysterious manipulator whose conquests are recounted to and equalled by, Moreau — his wickedly duplicitous wife Juliette. The film, possibly Vadim's best, pulsates with sexual energy and excitement with its cool mood enhanced by a sultry jazz score by Thelonious Monk with Art Blakey and the Jazz Messengers. "C'est la guerre." "Tres bien, la guerre!" (French with English subtitles) ★★★½ VHS: $79.99

Dangerous Liaisons

(1988, 120 min, US, Stephen Frears) *Glenn Close, John Malkovich, Michelle Pfeiffer, Swoosie Kurtz, Keanu Reeves, Uma Thurman, Mildred Natwick, Peter Capaldi.* Sexual corruption, insidious power games, deceitful duplicity and seductively witty dialogue are some of the unusual ingredients in this sumptuously enticing film. Close stars as the Marquise de Merteuil, an elegantly detached woman who along with her former lover, the similarly cunning Valmont (Malkovich), enters into a wager on whether he can seduce the innocent Pfeiffer. Their amoral sexual sport entangles them and all who enter their lives as it follows its inevitably destructive course. Close revels in the role of the acrimonious aristocrat, and Malkovich, although cast against type, still captures the dangerously seductive charms of a snake dressed in gentleman's clothing. A special cinematic treat that should entertain the entire spectrum of tastes — from the romantic to the Machiavellian. (Letterboxed) ★★★★ VHS: $9.99; DVD: $14.99

A Dangerous Man: Lawrence After Arabia

(1990, 104 min, GB, Christopher Menaul) *Ralph Fiennes, Denis Quilley, Paul Freeman, Nicholas Jones, Siddig el Fadil.* Rarely blinking or moving his lips, Fiennes does little to liven up this filmed history lesson. *A Dangerous Man,* picking up after the events of David Lean's *Lawrence of Arabia,* chronicles Lawrence's attempts to convince the British and French governments to bestow the countries of Syria and Damascus unto his close friend, the Emir Faisel (who gave Lawrence *that* robe). Chock full of historical facts and figures, this would be a suitable film to show in history class, but nowhere else. ★½ VHS: $19.99

Dangerous Minds

(1995, 94 min, US, John N. Smith) *Michelle Pfeiffer, George Dzundza, Courtnay B. Vance, Robin Bartlett.* As gritty as a high school prom, *Dangerous Minds,* based on LouAnne Johnson's autobiography "My Posse Don't Do Homework," treads the well-worn hallways and classrooms of nearly every self-sacrificing teacher film from *Blackboard Jungle* to *Stand and Deliver.* And while *Minds* is clichéd, predictable and sentimental, it offers Pfeiffer as Johnson a chance to deliver an affecting performance — it helps gloss over the film's otherwise formulaic structure. The unruly students are mostly Screenplay 101 concoctions — their tongues may be sharp, but what makes them tick is noticeably absent. ★★½ VHS: $14.99; DVD: $29.99

Dangerous Moonlight

(1941, 83 min, GB, Brian Desmond Hurst) *Anton Walbrook, Sally Gray, Cecil Parker.* This wartime classic tells the story of a Polish concert pianist (Walbrook) who, against the strenuous objections of his wife, puts aside his music and flies for the RAF. Wonderfully directed and superbly acted, the film makes excellent use of its classical music score. ★★★½

Dangerous Moves

(1983, 110 min, Switzerland, Richard Dembo) *Michel Piccoli, Leslie Caron, Liv Ullmann.* Set amid the tranquil lakeside of Geneva at the site of an international chess match, this Academy Award—winning film is imbued with a power, literacy and complexity that belies its sedate environment. The physical movements may be minimal, but the tension between the two grand masters is visceral and exciting. ★★★

A Dangerous Woman

(1993, 99 min, US, Stephen Gyllenhaal) *Debra Winger, Gabriel Byrne, Barbara Hershey, David Strathairn, Chloe Webb, Laurie Metcalf, Jan Hooks.* Winger is riveting as an innocent, child-like woman living in a small Southern town. Though somewhat shielded by her aunt's (Hershey) position of power and influence, her naive inability to tell socially expected lies throws her into conflict with others in her community. She is also ill-equipped to deal with the emotional upheaval she experiences at the hands of an itinerant laborer (Byrne). Ironically, her turmoil mirrors that of her sister's conflicted relationship with a married man, offering acerbic commentary on our lack of control in affairs of the heart. Though the narrative gets somewhat muddled, the film is ably carried by a fine ensemble cast. ★★½ VHS: $14.99

Daniel

(1983, 129 min, US, Sidney Lumet) *Timothy Hutton, Mandy Patinkin, Lindsay Crouse, Ed Asner, Amanda Plummer.* This gripping political drama based on the Julius and Ethel Rosenberg case divides its story between two eras: the 1950s, when the Rosenbergs were (unjustly?) sentenced to death; and the late 1960s, where their surviving children grapple with the memory of their parents (Patinkin, Crouse). Hutton plays the title character, whose search for the truth about his mom and dad (here called the Isaacsons) ushers a wave of recollections about them. Expertly acted, this rewarding film moves slowly, but never fails to move the viewer. ★★★ VHS: $59.99

Danny Boy

(1984, 92 min, Ireland, Neil Jordan) *Stephen Rea, Veronica Quilligan, Donal McCann, Ray McAnally.* This bleak Irish drama is a taut portrait of a young saxophone player who witnesses the murder of his manager. Haunted by violent images of one of the assailants, he sets out to hunt him down and avenge the atrocity. A dark and moody character study whose style is too self-serving and which is only occasionally intriguing. Rea appears in his film debut as the young musician. ★★ VHS: $59.99

Dante's Inferno

(1969, 90 min, GB, Ken Russell) *Oliver Reed.* Russell's filmic fascination with artists tortured by personal weaknesses (*The Music Lovers, Mahler, Valentino*) is amply evident in this early, rarely seen film. Reed plays Dante Gabriel Rossetti — a morose, brilliant and drunken painter-poet who, as Russell sees it, was more interested in his flamboyant and excessive lifestyle than his artistic output. Russell re-creates the period wonderfully in this engrossing tale of art, poetry, booze and sex. ★★★

Dante's Peak

(1997, 100 min, US, Roger Donaldson) *Pierce Brosnan, Linda Hamilton.* Following *ID4* and *Twister*, *Dante's Peak* should have been an F/X blast. But with only adequate effects and a transparent and cluttered story, this disaster adventure disappoints on all levels. Clearly needing lunch money, Brosnan plays a scientist who predicts a major volcanic eruption in the Pacific

Northwest. No one believes him, except the spunky mayor (Hamilton) of the town located next to the mountain he thinks is ready to blow. The film teases throughout until the eventual explosion, but only after a stockpile of clichéd characters and plot lines limp across the screen. (VHS letterboxed available for $14.99) ★ VHS: $9.99; DVD: $34.99

Danton

(1982, 136 min, Poland/France, Andrzej Wajda) *Gérard Depardieu, Wojciech Pszoniak.* Wajda directs his camera toward the social upheaval and political treachery of the French Revolution, and by doing so, draws an obvious allegory to the political situation in his native Poland in the 1980s. Depardieu is the boisterous people's champion, Danton, who is betrayed by the coldly civilized Robespierre as they maneuver for leadership of the new Republic. (French with English subtitles) ★★★★ VHS: $29.99

Danzón

(1991, 103 min, Mexico, Maria Novaro) *Maria Rojo, Carmen Salinas, Blanca Guerra.* The sudden disappearance of her longtime dancing partner compels Julia (the endearing Rojo), a demure Mexico City telephone operator, to begin a search which escalates into a personal odyssey. She begins her road trip guarded and aloof, but before long is getting invaluable fashion advice from a cabaret-performer transvestite and warm emotional support from her hotel's craggy conciérge as well as the resident ladies of the evening. She greets this cavalcade of intriguing characters and exotic circumstances with a newly informed independence and a revitalized sense of self. Dance music pulsates throughout the film; the cultural significance of the dancehall is especially evident in one scene in which Julia explains the nuances of *danzón* (a particular kind of dance) to an admiring young man. A grown-up fairy tale awash with light and vibrant color. (Spanish with English subtitles) ★★★ VHS: $19.99

Darby O'Gill and the Little People

(1959, 93 min, US, Robert Stevenson) *Albert Sharpe, Sean Connery, Janet Munro, Estelle Winwood.* Sharpe is the Irish caretaker whose tendency to spin the blarney causes no one to believe him when he becomes the guest of the Leprechauns in their underground home. Great special effects create a timeless atmosphere of charm and fantasy. ★★★

Dario Argento's Phantom of the Opera

(1998, 100 min, Italy, Dario Argento) *Julian Sands, Asia Argento, Andrea Di Stefano, Nadia Rinaldi.* Dario's beautiful daughter Asia plays opera singer ingenue Christina and Sands is the Phantom in this disappointing period adaptation of the oft-filmed classic. The pace is leaden, Argento's trademark visual flair is largely absent, and the film has no spark. There are some bizarre changes to the original story — the surprisingly handsome, unscarred Phantom has been raised by rats(!), and a pair of comic-relief rat-catchers make their jobs easier by building a rat-catching mobile. Asia and Sands are unremarkable, the music is good, and the period atmosphere is convincing, though there isn't any of the bravura setpieces fans have come to expect from Dario. ★★ VHS: $9.99; DVD: $24.99

The Dark Angel

(1935, 110 min, US, Sidney Franklin) *Fredric March, Merle Oberon, Herbert Marshall, Janet Beecher, John Halliday.* Lillian Hellman cowrote the screenplay for this affecting melodrama of three childhood friends, and their experiences after one is injured in World War I. Based on the 1925 silent starring Ronald Colman and Vilma Banky. ★★★ VHS: $14.99

The Dark Angel

(1987, 148 min, GB, Peter Hammond) *Peter O'Toole, Jane Lapotaire, Beatie Edney.* O'Toole is an indulgent study of heavy-lidded menace in this wonderfully Gothic tale of a trusting maiden, a tragic death, a large inheritance, a mysterious and nasty Frenchwoman, and a deceptively helpful uncle. This is all based on J.S. LeFanu's "Uncle Silas," written in 1864, which is generally regarded as the first psychological thriller. Encroaching danger is presaged by the strange French governess' incessant probing of her innocent charge, Maude (Lapotaire), regarding the existence of her father's will. Maude's father reveals to her the key to the chest in the library, but not enough family secrets to save her from horrific malice from those she's been told to trust. The cast revels in their deliciously exaggerated characterizations, and the production is a feast of fine detail. ★★★ VHS: $19.99

The Dark at the Top of the Stairs

(1960, 123 min, US, Delbert Mann) *Robert Preston, Dorothy McGuire, Angela Lansbury, Eve Arden, Shirley Knight.* An expertly acted, deeply affecting film version of William Inge's Pulitzer Prize-winning play. Preston heads an exceptional cast as the patriarch of an Oklahoma family in the 1920s. As seen through the eyes of a young boy coming of age, the story focuses on a family's fortunes and misfortune, misunderstandings and prejudice. ★★★

Dark City

(1990, 98 min, Zimbabwe/GB, Chris Curling) The struggle of black South Africans for justice and equality in their own land is the theme of this impassioned political thriller filmed entirely in Zimbabwe with a cast made up primarily of the members of Johannesburg's Market Theatre. When a peaceful march to the mayor's house of a black township turns violent, the police begin a crackdown, arresting seven innocent people. As they are put on trial in a kangaroo court, the black leaders are faced with accepting the injustice or fighting back. The film examines the rifts within the black independence movement which often foment violence within the community, pitting black against black and rarely involving the true antagonists: the white authorities. ★★★ VHS: $29.99

Dark City

(1998, 100 min, US, Alex Proyas) *Rufus Sewell, Kiefer Sutherland, Jennifer Connelly, William Hurt.* In an unnamed city with striking architectural design — an amalgam of *M, Metropolis* and Tim Burton's *Batman* — a young man (Sewell) wakes up in a bathtub, a corpse in the next room. All evidence points to his being a serial killer, but he has no memory whatsoever. Did he really do it? And who are those weird bald men who are trailing him? Aided in his investigation by an initially antagonistic police detective (Hurt) and a wife

Darling

he can't remember (Connelly), Sewell begins to unravel the truth behind the mysteries. Director-cowriter Proyas' superior follow-up to *The Crow* is a riveting sci-fi thriller, as well as a fascinating examination of memory, identity and free will. Some may feel the eye-popping effects overwhelm a thin story, but the visuals are truly in the service of a well-crafted tale. (VHS available letterboxed or pan & scan) ★★★½ VHS: $14.99; DVD: $19.99

The Dark Corner

(1946, 99 min, US, Henry Hathaway) *Lucille Ball, Clifton Webb, Mark Stevens.* An unfairly neglected film noir mystery which is both exciting and well-acted. Lucy plays a secretary who sets out to prove the innocence of her private detective boss (Stevens), who's been framed for murder. Webb costars as the caustic, wealthy art dealer who's behind the frame-up. ★★★ VHS: $59.99

The Dark Crystal

(1983, 94 min, GB, Jim Henson & Frank Oz) *The Muppets.* Muppet masters Henson and Oz deliver their take on a Tolkien-esque world peopled with furry dwarf creatures and evil sorcerers with their unmistakable zaniness and a healthy dose of plain-old good storytelling. The story concerns Jen, a young male "Gelfling," who sets out on a harrowing and heroic journey to rid his magical realm of the evil rule of the "Skeksis," a bilious and physically repugnant race that resemble decaying vultures. While a little short on plot, the film's characterizations are top-notch and should delight adults as well as kids. ★★★ VHS: $14.99; DVD: $24.99

Dark Eyes

(1987, 115 min, Italy, Nikita Mikhalkov) *Marcello Mastroianni, Silvana Mangano, Marthe Keller.* Mastroianni is nothing short of brilliant as Romano, an irresolute dreamer seduced by both love and money in this charming romantic fable by Russian émigré Mikhalkov. The story begins on an ocean liner where the garrulous Romano recounts his tumultuous and tragic life story to a rapt elderly newlywed. His tale is one of lost ambitions, luxury and boredom changed forever after he meets and falls deliriously in love with a mysterious Russian beauty. A funny, enchanting and, most of all, entertaining film. (Italian with English subtitles) ★★★½

Dark Habits

(1983, 96 min, Spain, Pedro Almodóvar) *Carmen Maura, Julieta Serrano, Christina Pascual.* While not Almodóvar's best work, *Dark Habits* nonetheless manages to carry the director's unparalleled sense of twisted, subversive and blacker-than-black humor. When Yolanda's boyfriend dies of an overdose of heroin, she decides it's better to run and hide than face the law. She winds up at the doorstep of the "Humble Redeemers," an order of heroin-addicted nuns who specialize in cases like hers — indeed, they were all once cases like her! The cast includes some of the familiar Almodóvites: Serrano stars as the Mother Superior and Maura appears as the cloister's resident tiger keeper, Sister Sin. (Spanish with English subtitles) ★★½ VHS: $39.99

The Dark Half

(1993, 121 min, US, George Romero) *Timothy Hutton, Amy Madigan, Michael Rooker, Julie Harris, Robert Joy.* Hutton stars in this well-mounted but uninvolving story from the undisputed master of recycled horror, Stephen King. Hutton is adequate in the role of a "serious" author who is forced by a blackmailer to publicly bury his cheesy pulp fiction-writing pseudonym, "George Stark." But, like most dead things in horror movies, Stark doesn't take extinction lying down; he springs to life and goes on a killing spree. Romero's sure-footed direction is light-years away from the low-budget material that he has come to be associated with; it just isn't very scary. ★★½ VHS: $9.99; DVD: $19.99

Dark Journey

(1937, 79 min, GB, Victor Saville) *Vivien Leigh, Conrad Veidt, Joan Gardner.* An efficient espionage yarn, *Dark Journey* features the luminous Leigh as a Stockholm dress shop owner whose successful business is really a front for her spying for the German government. It's through her dresses that she dispatches secret information. Veidt is a German playboy who courts her. Of course, there's more than that going on here. Is Leigh really in league with the Germans? Is Veidt the fop he pretends to be? Through the years we've seen so many films of this sort that the answers may not be all that difficult to come up with. But *Dark Journey* keeps your interest throughout, is well played by the entire cast, and a couple nightclub scenes offer a keen look at trendy high society in the late teens. ★★★ VHS: $19.99

The Dark Mirror

(1946, 85 min, US, Robert Siodmak) *Olivia de Havilland, Lew Ayres, Thomas Mitchell.* De Havilland, in a dual role, gives an entertainingly over-the-top performance as identical twins: one a virtuous young lady, the other a psychotic, deranged murderer. This Freudian thriller, both tense and fast-paced, revolves around the police and a psychiatrist's baffled efforts to determine which of the two women is innocent and which is the killer. ★★★ VHS: $14.99

Dark Passage

(1947, 106 min, US, Delmer Daves) *Humphrey Bogart, Lauren Bacall, Agnes Moorehead.* Bogart stars in this stylish film noir as a falsely accused convict who escapes prison and changes his appearance (via plastic surgery) in order to smoke out the real culprit. Bacall is on hand as the socialite who believes in him. Good use of subjective camerawork, in which the first half hour of the film is shown from the point of view of the escaped con — whose face we don't see until he becomes Bogart. Moorehead is especially good in support. ★★★ VHS: $19.99

Dark Victory

(1939, 106 min, US, Edmund Goulding) *Bette Davis, George Brent, Geraldine Fitzgerald, Humphrey Bogart, Ronald Reagan.* In one of her greatest triumphs, Davis stars in this classic soaper as a jet-setting socialite who discovers she has only a few months to live. As she slowly accepts her fate, she becomes more responsible, living her remaining months "beautifully and finely," as her doctor/lover (Brent) suggests. ★★★½ VHS: $14.99; DVD: $19.99

The Dark Wind

(1993, 111 min, US, Errol Morris) *Lou Diamond Phillips, Gary Farmer, Fred Ward, Guy Boyd.* Director Morris imbues *Dark Wind* with the same hypnotic realism which permeated his *The Thin Blue Line.* Phillips is at his best as Jim Chee, the Navajo cop who studies to be a medicine man. A corpse mutilated by a Navajo skinwalker is found on Hopi ground, involving the police in intertribal politics and the spectre of witchcraft. The FBI and major drug transactions rapidly surface in this tale of a long-festering lust for revenge and rampant greed. Neil Jiminez (*The Waterdance*) cowrote the story based on one of Tony Hillerman's many books set in the Arizona territories. ★★★

Darkman

(1990, 120 min, US, Sam Raimi) *Liam Neeson, Colin Friels, Frances McDormand, Larry Drake.* Spectacular stunts and excellent special effects highlight this superhero adventure story. Neeson stars as a scientist whose unfortunate run-in with the mob leaves him horribly disfigured and transforms him into a shadowy crime fighter. Director Raimi (the *Evil Dead* trilogy) continues to impress with his inventiveness as he and his scriptwriters unleash a slew of clever plot twists and come up with at least a half-dozen new ways to dispose of the bad guys. Friels and McDormand offer fine support as, respectively, an evil real estate tycoon and Neeson's lawyer girlfriend. (Followed by 2 sequels) ★★★ VHS: $14.99; DVD: $24.99

Darling

(1965, 122 min, GB, John Schlesinger) *Julie Christie, Dirk Bogarde, Laurence Harvey.* This highly influential classic brilliantly captures many of the manners, morals, and mores of mod mid-'60s London. Christie, who is nothing less than radiant, deservedly won an Oscar for her portrayal of a young London model who quickly climbs the social ladder by strategically jumping in and out of assorted beds. Bogarde also stars as one of her conquests, and Harvey is featured as one who escapes her enticing trap.

D

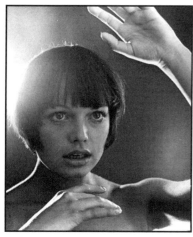

Daughters of Darkness

Schlesinger received an Oscar nomination for his perceptive direction, and the film itself was a Best Picture nominee. ★★★★ VHS: $19.99

D.A.R.Y.L.

(1985, 99 min, US, Simon Wincer) *Mary Beth Hurt, Michael McKean, Barret Oliver, Colleen Camp.* An engaging if low-keyed children's fantasy about a young boy, half android, who runs away from his government lab and is befriended by a childless couple. Oliver nicely plays the youth. ★★½ VHS: $14.99

Daughters of Darkness

(1971, 96 min, Belgium, Harry Kumel) *Delphine Seyrig, Daniele Ouimet, John Karlen.* One from the vaults! Seyrig stars as a Hungarian countess and present-day vampiress who, in order to continue her daily blood baths (a youth and beauty preservative), must continually prowl for nubile virgins. Her blood-gathering soirees take her to Belgium where she, along with her lesbian secretary, seductively stalks the hotel for a quick fix. Bela Lugosi she's not. Campy, funny and erotic, this Gothic tale explores the darker side of sexuality with shocking frankness. (Filmed in English) ★★★ VHS: $14.99; DVD: $24.99

Daughters of the Dust

(1991, 114 min, US, Julie Dash) *Cora Lee Day, Alva Rodgers, Barbara O.* Independent filmmaker Dash has fashioned a lyrical, visually stunning drama about an African Gullah family off the coast of Georgia, circa 1902. Centering on the family's struggles, the film shows how half the family wants to move to the mainland, while the other half worry that their traditional African culture will be forever lost. Gorgeous and exquisite. ★★★½ VHS: $24.99; DVD: $34.99

Dave

(1993, 110 min, US, Ivan Reitman) *Kevin Kline, Sigourney Weaver, Frank Langella, Kevin Dunn, Ving Rhames, Charles Grodin, Ben Kingsley, Arnold Schwarzenegger.* A crowd-pleaser in every sense of the word, *Dave* is a fabulously funny comedy worthy of bipartisan support. In a particularly appealing performance, Kline plays Dave, a likable, good-hearted schmoe who's a dead-ringer for the President of the United States. Which is why,

when the Commander in Chief suffers a stroke, he's chosen to impersonate him. Under the tutelage of the scheming Chief of Staff (a wonderfully nasty Langella), Dave charms all, including his First Lady (Weaver), as he sets forth his own political agenda. Writer Gary Ross revels in the fish-out-of-water scenario, and taps into a Capra-esque tone — minus the sentimentality — in celebration of the Average Joe. There's also four score and seven cameo appearances — and to give one of them away is grounds for impeachment. ★★★½ VHS: $9.99; DVD: $19.99

David

(1979, 106 min, West Germany, Peter Lilienthal) *Mario Fischel, Walter Taub, Eva Mattes.* A suspenseful, understated account of the devastating rise of fascism and its effect on one particular family. David, a Jewish teenager growing up in Berlin in the 1930s, is temporarily insulated from the Nazis' horrific policies by his naively optimistic middle-class family. Told on a human scale, the film follows David as he witnesses the destruction of his community and home; is separated from his parents; and experiences personal persecution by brutal authorities and neighbors. His will to survive is well-portrayed in this moving drama. (German with English subtitles) ★★★ VHS: $79.99

David and Lisa

(1962, 94 min, US, Frank Perry) *Keir Dullea, Janet Margolin, Howard da Silva.* Perry's acclaimed drama about the relationship between two mentally ill teenagers, played with great sensitivity by Dullea and Margolin, is a sympathetic, rewarding look at young love and institutionalization. Da Silva gives a wonderful performance as their sympathetic doctor. ★★★½ VHS: $29.99; DVD: $29.99

David Copperfield

(1935, 130 min, US, George Cukor) *Freddie Bartholomew, W.C. Fields, Edna May Oliver, Lionel Barrymore, Maureen O'Sullivan, Roland Young, Basil Rathbone.* Cukor's superbly crafted adaptation of Charles Dickens' classic novel (the author's favorite among his own work) was one of the box-office giants of the 1930s, and with good reason. Bartholomew, in perhaps his finest role, heads a stellar all-star cast as Dickens' young hero, experiencing the hardships and sorrows of orphaned life in 19th-century England. Fields is the perfect incarnation of Micawber, David's ne'er-do-well mentor, and Oliver is splendid as David's eccentric Aunt Betsy. One of the finest filmic interpretations of classic literature. ★★★★ VHS: $19.99

David Holzman's Diary

(1967, 74 min, US, Jim McBride) *L.M. Kit Carson, Louise Levine.* Selected as one of the American cultural treasures in the Library of Congress' National Film Registry, this amazingly self-assured and uncomfortably perceptive first film by McBride (*The Big Easy*) is an audacious, groundbreaking independent film. David, an obsessively neurotic aspiring filmmaker attempting to unravel the mysteries of life, decides to make a movie on his life — to record on film "truth at 24 frames a second" and thereby capture the essence of his everyday events and people. But instead of learning from the study, the

young man's film diary becomes his undoing, alienating his friends and girlfriend, distorting any real meaning and finally turning him into an alienated, frustrated and voyeuristic basketcase. Filmed in a wickedly *faux* cinema verité style, this clever satire captures both the feeling of the tumultuous '60s era and the folly of its self-seeking "artists." ★★★★ VHS: $19.99

David Lynch's Hotel Room

(1992, 100 min, US, David Lynch/James Signorelli) *Harry Dean Stanton, Glenne Headly, Griffin Dunne, Chelsea Field, Crispin Glover, Alicia Witt, Deborah Unger.* A documentary about the places director Lynch stays when he travels — now *that* would be interesting! Here, rather, is a collection of three odd tales set in the same hotel room in various eras. *Tricks* is a basic weird-for-the-sake-of-weird story involving Stanton, hooker Headly and an unexpected guest checking into room 603 in 1969. An ominous tone and mysterious mood permeate, but nothing really adds up. *Blackout*, the third segment and set in 1936, finds Lynch mining the spirit, but not the style, of *Eraserhead* to produce an awkward conversation between a young Oklahoma couple (Witt, Glover). The second segment provides the only real spark in the program. Directed by Signorelli, *Getting Rid of Robert* is a campy black comedy concerning three young socialites as they anticipate the arrival of a soon-to-be ex-boyfriend. ★★

Dawn of the Dead

(1979, 125 min, US, George Romero) *David Emge, Ken Foree, Scott Reiniger.* In this second installment of the *Night of the Living Dead* trilogy, the zombies get their just deserts when a Philadelphia SWAT team gets trapped in their hangout — a large suburban shopping mall. There's lots of sly humor, blood and guts, making this bizarrely entertaining horror film a classic of the genre. (Director's cut)(Letterboxed) (Sequel: *Day of the Dead*) ★★★½ VHS: $14.99; DVD: $24.99

The Dawn Patrol

(1938, 103 min, US, Edmund Goulding) *Errol Flynn, Basil Rathbone, David Niven, Donald Crisp.* Flynn had one of his best roles as a WWI flying ace assigned to keep the Germans behind enemy lines. Rathbone is in good form as a tough officer who must send new recruits to almost certain death. ★★★ VHS: $19.99

The Dawning

(1991, 96 min, Ireland, Robert Knights) *Anthony Hopkins, Rebecca Pidgeon, Jean Simmons, Hugh Grant, Trevor Howard.* An affecting tale about a young woman coming of age in 1920s Ireland and a mysterious man who she thinks may be her long-lost father. Set just outside Dublin at the height of the Republican campaign for independence, the story centers around Nancy, who, surrounded by wealth, has little knowledge of the political violence and turmoil engulfing her country. On her 18th birthday, she enounters a rough-hewn rogue (Hopkins) in his secret hideaway by the beach. Reminiscent of many a "Masterpiece Theatre" production, the film sports some able performances and is thoroughly enjoyable viewing, although ultimately it glosses over the political and emotional issues it purports to address. ★★ VHS: $79.99

The Day After

(1983, 126 min, US, Nicholas Meyer) *Jason Robards, JoBeth Williams, John Lithgow, Steve Guttenberg, Amy Madigan, John Cullum.* Powerful made-for-TV movie detailing life in a small Kansas town before and after a nuclear strike. Powerful images fill the screen with what Americans would have to look forward to in the case of the unthinkable. Though not as subtle as the similarly themed *Testament*, it is, however, not as devastatingly graphic as its haunting British counterpart, *Threads*. ★★★

The Day after Trinity

(1980, 89 min, US, Joe Else) The scientific research which ushered in the dawn of the nuclear era is examined in this penetrating documentary. The site is Los Alamos, New Mexico, where, in 1941, J. Robert Oppenheimer and a group of brilliant scientists worked on a government project to end the war — with the results being a weapon of such power and destructive capability that its use in 1945 irrevocably changed the world. With footage of actual explosions and interviews with the people involved in the research, the film explores the moral anguish experienced by the naive scientists whose peace-inspired work resulted in the creation of a new generation of terrifying weapons. ★★★ VHS: $39.99

A Day at the Races

(1937, 111 min, US, Sam Wood) *The Marx Brothers, Margaret Dumont, Maureen O'Sullivan.* Fair maiden O'Sullivan is about to lose her health spa unless she receives financial assistance from hypochondriac millionairess Dumont. And who best to woo the symptomladen lady than the ever-amorous Dr. Hugo C. Hackenbush, played by — guess who? — Groucho Marx. Chico and Harpo masquerade as his medical assistants, and the day is saved by a horse. ★★★½

Day for Night

(1973, 120 min, France, François Truffaut) *François Truffaut, Jean-Pierre Léaud, Jacqueline Bisset, Jean-Pierre Aumont, Valentina Cortese.* A loving ode to the intricacies of filmmaking. Truffaut portrays the compassionate director of a beleaguered production. Léaud is a spoiled young actor and Bisset is the beautiful heroine of the film within a film. Cortese is splendid as an actress who just can't get that one take right. An exhilarating and affectionate satire that captured the Best Foreign Film Oscar. (English language version) ★★★★ VHS: $59.99

A Day in the Country

(1936, 40 min, France, Jean Renoir) *Sylvia Bataille, Georges Darnoux, Jane Marken, André Gabriello, Paul Temps.* A Parisian mother and daughter are seduced during an afternoon outing, but what exhilarates one proves to be a rude awakening for the other. Renoir's lyrical, impressionistic work is taken from a de Maupassant short story. (French with English subtitles) ★★★★ VHS: $39.99

A Day in the Death of Joe Egg

(1972, 106 min, GB, Peter Medak) *Alan Bates, Janet Suzman, Elizabeth Robillard.* Bates and Suzman give intense performances as a couple whose marriage is coming undone by the stress of caring for their spasmodic daughter. A black comedy of the darkest imaginable shade. ★★★ VHS: $69.99

Day of the Beast

(1996, 99 min, Spain, Alex de la Iglesia) *Alex Angulo, Armando de Razza, Santiago Segura, Terele Pavez.* Spanish cult director de la Iglesia follows his black comedy *Accion Mutante* with this horror satire. Father Angel, a laconic, devout priest, is convinced that Satan has come to Earth to claim it as his own, and, with the help of a beefy music store clerk, decides to stop him. Very Catholic and very Spanish, *Day of the Beast* is an effectively offbeat film that will strongly appeal to fans of outrageous humor. Not for all tastes, certainly (hardcore horror fans may find it too jokey, mainstream audiences will find it too over the top and bizarre), this is a flawed but original and entertaining work. It's a certain contender for cult favorite status. Winner of 6 Spanish Goya awards. (Spanish with English subtitles) ★★★ VHS: $69.99

Day of the Dead

(1985, 102 min, US, George Romero) *Lori Cardille, Terry Alexander, Joseph Pilato.* Romero's final entry in his "zombie" series, following *Night of the Living Dead* and *Dawn of the Dead.* A group of scientists and military personnel become trapped in an underground missile silo, and hordes of the living dead lie between them and freedom. This claustrophobic horror film lacks the suspense of the first film and the special effects wizardry of the second. (Letterboxed) ★½ VHS: $14.99; DVD: $29.99

The Day of the Jackal

(1973, 141 min, GB, Fred Zinnemann) *Edward Fox, Alan Badel, Cyril Cusack, Delphine Seyrig, Derek Jacobi.* Zinnemann's taut political thriller chronicles the international manhunt for a professional assassin (Fox) on assignment to kill Charles DeGaulle. Though history tells us of the assassin's failure, the film maintains a remarkable tension throughout, and builds to an incredibly suspenseful ending. (American remake: *The Jackal*) ★★★½ VHS: $14.99; DVD: $24.99

The Day of the Locust

(1975, 144 min, US, John Schlesinger) *Donald Sutherland, Karen Black, William Atherton, Burgess Meredith, Geraldine Page.* A powerful, beautifully filmed screen version of Nathanael West's novel of aspirations and forgotten dreams in 1930s Hollywood. Black gives one of her best performances as an opportunistic, aspiring actress involved with both young studio set director Atherton and lonely, slightly slow-witted Sutherland (in a mesmerizing portrayal). Meredith received a well-deserved Oscar nomination as Black's boozing, sickly ex-vaudevillian father. An unforgettable though demanding film experience; the Hollywood premiere at the finale remains one of the most chilling sequences ever put to film. ★★★½ VHS: $14.99

The Day of the Triffids

(1963, 95 min, GB, Steve Sekely) *Howard Keel, Nicole Maurey, Janet Scott.* Lying in a London hospital bed with bandages around his eyes, Keel is one of the few people on Earth to miss a spectacular meteor display in the skies. He wakes up the next morning to discover that most of the population has disappeared and the few remaining people have lost their sight. And to make matters worse, man-eating plants are slowly taking over the city. This is the fascinating premise of this low-budget but smart sci-fi thriller which puts as much accent on characterization and plot as it does on chills. The killer plants are kind of cheesy, but that only adds to the fun. ★★★ VHS: $19.99

The Day the Earth Stood Still

(1951, 92 min, US, Robert Wise) *Michael Rennie, Patricia Neal, Hugh Marlowe, Sam Jaffe, Billy Gray.* 1950s science fiction doesn't come any better than this classic tale of alien beings and Earth's redemption. Rennie plays Klaatu, an emissary from outer space who arrives in the nation's capital to deliver a message of doom. Shot on sight and tiring of lip service from the political hacks (it *is* Washington, D.C.), he decides to mingle with the general population, and befriends widow Neal and her precocious son Gray. Meanwhile, there's the matter of the eight-foot robot, Gort, standing guard of Klaatu's spaceship, and his mission of peace. Made at a time when most sci-fi stories featured killer aliens, Wise's poetic, cautionary film presented a benevolent spaceman, and it did so in a suspenseful manner with touches of wit and political awareness. Jaffe's enlightened scientist is particularly appealing. Klaatu Barada Nikto. ★★★★ VHS: $14.99

The Day the Sun Turned Cold

(1994, 99 min, China/Hong Kong, Yim Ho) *Siqin Gowa, Tuo Zhong Hua.* This coproduction between mainland China and Hong Kong filmmakers is a powerful and sad exploration of grief, regret and responsibility which is haunting in its stark emotions. Set in a tiny rural area in northern China, the story centers on a patriotic young factory worker and good Communist who goes back to his childhood village to accuse his mother of secretly poisoning his father many years before. Through flashback, we learn of the stern habits of the father, a possible extramarital affair by the mother, and a kindly stranger who may have been a catalyst for the supposed murder. *The Day the Sun Turned Cold* moves at a languid pace, allowing the time to savor all its emotions. While uninvolving on a visual level, the film is thoroughly engrossing through its well-developed characters and thought-provoking story. (Mandarin with English subtitles) ★★★½ VHS: $79.99

Daybreak

(1993, 91 min, US, Stephen Tolkin) *Moira Kelly, Cuba Gooding, Jr., Martha Plimpton, Omar Epps, Alice Drummond.* Tolkin's adaptation of the off-Broadway play "Beirut" is set in the near future of New York City as an epidemic sweeps across the nation, infecting hundreds of thousands of individuals. The government places the "positive" individuals into isolation camps. Kelly plays a young woman whose eyes are opened to what really is happening when she meets a group of resistance fighters led by Gooding, who tend and care for the infected. While this made-for-cable film is an obvious AIDS metaphor, it never really etches itself into believability, despite competent performances by the leads. ★★ VHS: $9.99

Daylight

(1996, 115 min, US, Rob Cohen) *Sylvester Stallone, Amy Brenneman, Viggo Mortensen, Dan Hedaya, Claire Bloom, Stan Shaw.* Dull and dreary from start to finish, this is less "*Die Hard in a tun-*

nel" and more "*The Poseidon Adventure* underground." Stallone is a former New York emergency services specialist (and now cab driver) who's on the scene when the Lincoln Tunnel collapses, killing dozens of motorists and trapping a handful of commuters inside. Sly must enter the tunnel (the best sequence in the film, unfortunately at the very beginning) and lead the dazed survivors out. The victims are a mixed bag of stereotypical disaster movie characters. (Letterboxed VHS available for $14.99) ★½ VHS: $9.99; DVD: $34.99

The Days of Being Dumb

(1992, 98 min, Hong Kong) *Jacky Cheung, Tony Leung*. This charmingly slapdash comedy is a fun example of Hong Kong action/comedy features. Fred (Cheung) and Keith (Leung) are inseparable boyhood friends and inept gangster wannabes. Their attempts to join the Hong Kong underworld are hampered because every time they join, they accidentally cause the quick death of their crime boss. Try as they might, the two just can't stay in a gang and soon earn the reputation as jinxes. They decide to go independent, but their first scheme — pimping — turns into a disaster when their first prostitute from Singapore turns out to be a lovelorn lesbian. Not of "international" standards, the film is nonetheless great, mindless fun. ★★½ VHS: $59.99

Days of Heaven

(1978, 95 min, US, Terrence Malick) *Richard Gere, Brooke Adams, Sam Shepard, Linda Manz*. Malick's lyrical film of a triangular love affair is set in the Eden-like vistas of the golden wheat fields of Texas. Gere stars as a Depression-era drifter who, with his sister Manz and girlfriend Adams, finds employment on the farm of lonely landowner Shepard. A beautiful, haunting version of the pastoral dream. (Letterboxed VHS available for $14.99) ★★★★ VHS: $9.99; DVD: $29.99

Days of Thunder

(1990, 107 min, US, Tony Scott) *Tom Cruise, Robert Duvall, Nicole Kidman, Cary Elwes, Michael Rooker*. Cruise, who acquired Paul Newman's fascination for race driving when they appeared together in *The Color of Money*, takes to the track in this heavily clichéd racing drama. Cruise plays a boy wonder behind the wheel and under the sheets. Duvall and Kidman benefit from his areas of expertise. ★★ VHS: $14.99; DVD: $29.99

Days of Wine and Roses

(1962, 117 min, US, Blake Edwards) *Jack Lemmon, Lee Remick, Charles Bickford, Jack Klugman*. Though he is mainly considered a comedic filmmaker, Edwards directed two impressive dramas in the early 1960s: *Experiment in Terror*, and this harrowing story about alcohol abuse. Lemmon and Remick give outstanding performances as a newly married couple whose lives are devastated by the rigors of their incessant drinking bouts. On par with Billy Wilder's *The Lost Weekend*. ★★★½ VHS: $19.99

The Daytrippers

(1997, 87 min, US, Greg Mottola) *Hope Davis, Stanley Tucci, Parker Posey, Liev Schreiber, Anne Meara, Pat McNamara, Campbell Scott*. Writer-director Mottola's first film is a prime example of what independent filmmaking should be. Take a simple story about a highly dysfunctional family

Hope Davis is joined by Liev Schreiber and Parker Posey in *The Daytrippers*

and shoot it on location for next to no money, and put together a compelling little comedy drama. The action begins when Davis discovers a cryptic postcard — which suggests an extramarital affair — that's fallen from husband Tucci's night stand. She takes the card to her mother and father (Meara and McNamara), and they in turn suggest they all go into the city and confront Tucci with it. Hope's younger sister Posey and her boyfriend Schreiber tag along and thus begins a smartly concocted and at times hilarious, picaresque ride from Long Island to Manhattan and environs. Whenever things seem about to fizzle, Mattola's ingeniously written script unveils another intricate exploration of family dynamics as it heads towards a couple of dramatic denouements. ★★★½ VHS: $14.99; DVD: $24.99

Dazed and Confused

(1993, 113 min, US, Richard Linklater) *Wiley Wiggins, Jason London, Sasha Jenson, Rory Cochrane, Milla Jovovich, Anthony Rapp, Matthew McConaughey*. The second film by director Linklater moves at a slacker's pace, ambling here, ambling there, all the while telling the eclectic and engaging tale of a group of teenagers celebrating the last day of school in 1976. The pacing befits the film's message, which basically says that "the '70s suck and nothing happens." With a virtually nonexistent plot, the story follows a core cast of eight teenagers through their haze of alcohol, music, drugs (lots-o-pot), minor rebellions and bizarre school initiations. The young actors, most notably newcomer Wiggins, have understated styles that make their boredom seem genuine and their anticipation of the "coolness of the eighties" seem slightly pathetic. If none of the characters in this film seem familiar to you, your teenage years were definitely spent pre-Woodstock. ★★★ VHS: $14.99; DVD: $24.99

The Dead

(1987, 88 min, Ireland, John Huston) *Anjelica Huston, Donal McCann, Donal Donnelly*. Director Huston's last film is a remarkable tribute to the poetic mastery of James Joyce. Deftly capturing the essence of Joyce's prose, Huston has fashioned a film brimming with incredible detail and richly imbued with the Irish spirit. The story may be a disappointment to some, however; for no matter how one approaches it, the viewer is simply an uninvited guest to a Christmas dinner party

at which nothing really happens. Huston saves any emotional wallop for the film's ending passage, in which the narrative poetry finally draws the audience into a long-awaited catharsis; considering the film's rich atmosphere, it's a worthwhile wait. ★★★½

Dead Again

(1991, 107 min, US, Kenneth Branagh) *Kenneth Branagh, Emma Thompson, Derek Jacobi, Robin Williams, Hanna Schygulla*. Following his triumphant interpretation of Shakespeare's *Henry V*, actor-director Branagh goes giddy in this wildly imaginative comedy-thriller. He stars as Mike Church, a Los Angeles detective who comes to the aid of a mysterious amnesiac woman (Thompson). She is haunted by memories from 40 years earlier in which a renowned composer (Branagh again) may have murdered his wife (Thompson again). Jacobi costars as a psychic who tries to help them sort things out. Branagh uses this preternatural premise and runs it over the top, taking the audience on a wonderfully tongue-in-cheek rollercoaster ride replete with surprise twists and a Hitchcockian ending. ★★★½ VHS: $9.99; DVD: $29.99

Dead Ahead: The Exxon Valdez Disaster

(1992, 90 min, US/GB, Paul Seed) *John Heard, Christopher Lloyd, Rip Torn, Michael Murphy, Bob Gunton*. Meticulously researched, superbly acted and thoroughly engrossing, this HBO/BBC production is a fast-paced exposé on the chain of events set in motion when the Exxon tanker *Valdez* dumped millions of gallons of crude oil into the pristine Alaskan waters of Prince Williams Sound. The accident itself, caused by drunken carelessness, was horrible enough; even more terrifying was the response to it. The film presents a parade of company executives and government and military officials more interested in spin-doctoring than solving the problem at hand. ★★★½ VHS: $79.99

Dead Alive

(1991, 97 min, New Zealand, Peter Jackson) *Timothy Balme, Elizabeth Moody*. Before *Heavenly Creatures*, Jackson made this wild zombie-splatterthon that ranks without a doubt as the goriest film ever made, bar none! Originally filmed as

Brain Dead, this coal-black comedy barrage of pus-spewing, entrail-eating wackiness follows the story of an overbearing mother, her charming but somewhat wimpy son, his spicy Latina lover, a kung fu-fighting priest and a very rabid Sumatran rat-monkey. This highly entertaining, limb-shredding homage to such directors as George Romero and Sam Raimi is a must-see for those who like heavy doses of slapstick mixed with their horror. ★★★½ VHS: $9.99; DVD: $19.99

Dead Calm

(1989, 96 min, Australia, Phillip Noyce) *Sam Neill, Nicole Kidman, Billy Zane.* Nail-biting suspense abounds in this high-seas thriller about a married couple who take to the Pacific in their yacht to find peace of mind after the death of their infant son. Their tranquility is shattered, however, when they take aboard the lone passenger of a sinking yacht, unaware that the man is a psychopath. Director Noyce effectively uses the tiny confines of the boat to develop a frenzied atmosphere of claustrophobia and terror. Neill and Kidman give grounded performances as the victimized couple, and Zane is a perfect embodiment of evil as the maniacal visitor. ★★★ VHS: $14.99; DVD: $19.99

Dead Connection

(1993, 93 min, US, Nigel Dick) *Michael Madsen, Lisa Bonet, Gary Stretch.* Madsen is a cop on a mission in this mean-spirited suspenser about a vicious psychopath (Stretch) who uses his exceptional good looks to attract women; then, he beats them to death and rapes them (in that order). Interesting characterizations and a few twists can't distract from the formulaic story and of its execution. ★★

Dead End

(1937, 93 min, US, William Wyler) *Humphrey Bogart, Sylvia Sidney, Joel McCrea, Claire Trevor, Dead End Kids.* Director Wyler elicits remarkable performances from his entire cast in this classic drama, based on Sidney Kingsley's Broadway hit, about life in a New York City tenement. Lillian Hellman wrote the screenplay adaptation. ★★★½ VHS: $14.99

Dead Heat

(1988, 86 min, US, Mark Goldblatt) *Treat Williams, Joe Piscopo.* Two L.A. cops investigate a series of robberies only to discover the culprits are the living dead. The criminals may have been brought back to life, but this film is dead and buried. An embarrassment for the otherwise respectable Williams. ★ VHS: $14.99

Dead Man

(1996, 120 min, US, Jim Jarmusch) *Johnny Depp, Gary Farmer, Lance Henriksen, Gabriel Bryne, Robert Mitchum, John Hurt, Iggy Pop, Billy Bob Thornton, Crispin Glover.* Director Jarmusch uses the elements of the traditional western to craft a grim and gritty tale of one man's odyssey through a harrowing, alien environment to his inevitable resolution. Depp is the perfect embodiment of a wanderer adrift in a world he never made, searching for meaning and direction in a hostile landscape fraught with danger, studded with pitfalls, and muddled by one miscommunication after another. *Dead Man* is part existential allegory, part fairy tale; and in it Depp is basically the knight errant who must overcome a series of trials on his path. In its starkness and simplicity, *Dead Man* returns to the crystalline laconicism of

Jarmusch's *Stranger Than Paradise*; and though we may sense that this saga is essentially without hope, we are still wryly bemused and frequently amused. (VHS available letterboxed or pan & scan) ★★★ VHS: $19.99; DVD: $32.99

Dead Man on Campus

(1998, 94 min, US, Alan Cohn) *Tom Everett Scott, Mark-Paul Gosselaar, Alyson Hannigan.* Two college roommates, failing their classes, decide to save their skins by taking advantage of a university rule that grants a 4.0 average to anyone whose roommate commits suicide. They search for the perfect candidate. Gosselaar and Scott give engaging performances under trying circumstances, and there's a few more laughs than would be expected. Still, this is an unpleasant, tasteless premise, and irresponsible partiers are amusing for only so long. John Waters or Mel Brooks may have been able to mine this dangerous comic field, but Cohn doesn't have a first clue. ★★ VHS: $14.99; DVD: $29.99

Dead Man Walking

(1995, 125 min, US, Tim Robbins) *Susan Sarandon, Sean Penn, Robert Prosky, Raymond J. Barry, R. Lee Ermey, Lois Smith.* Powerful performances from Penn and Sarandon and the deft directorial touch of sophomore helmer Robbins distinguish this gripping examination of capital punishment. Sarandon stars as Sister Helen Prejean (upon whose book the film is based), a Louisiana nun, who, having devoted her life to ministering to the poor, receives a plea for help from death row inmate Matthew Poncelet (Penn). Most of the film revolves around these two characters as Sister Helen tries to draw out some shred of humanity and redemption from the remorseless Poncelet. As an analysis of a hot political issue, *Dead Man Walking* manages, remarkably, to find the center by concentrating on the totality of the human tragedy in both the initial crime and the concept of execution — ultimately, there are no winners in this story. Sarandon and Penn play off each other brilliantly, both giving career performances (Sarandon won an Academy Award) in a film that depends heavily on the intimate and emotionally gut-wrenching scenes between the two of them. A thought-provoking film that will

spark many a debate rather than settle them. ★★★★ VHS: $9.99; DVD: $19.99

Dead Men Don't Wear Plaid

(1982, 90 min, US, Carl Reiner) *Steve Martin, Rachel Ward, Reni Santoni, George Gaynes.* A vastly entertaining and clever mystery spoof with Martin as a private eye who mixes it up on screen with Humphrey Bogart, Bette Davis, Barbara Stanwyck, Burt Lancaster and Alan Ladd — thanks to old movie clips and ingenious editing. ★★★ DVD: $24.99

Dead of Night

(1945, 102 min, GB, Basil Dearden/Robert Hamer/Charles Crichton/Albert) *Michael Redgrave, Basil Radford, Sally Ann Howes.* An eerie and chilling horror masterpiece about five people gathered together to tell strange tales. Made in 1945, the film was the standard for all subsequent horror anthologies to follow. The highlight is the final tale with Redgrave as a ventriloquist — it'll definitely leave you hearing all of those things that go bump in the night. ★★★★

Dead of Winter

(1987, 100 min, US, Arthur Penn) *Mary Steenburgen, Roddy McDowall, Jan Rubes.* Steenburgen is in good form playing three roles in this tense chiller. An out-of-work actress must fight for her life when she accepts a part in a movie being produced by an eccentric recluse (Rubes) at his remote country mansion. McDowall is splendid as a mild-mannered though psychotic henchman. ★★★ VHS: $14.99

Dead Poets Society

(1989, 128 min, US, Peter Weir) *Robin Williams, Robert Sean Leonard, Ethan Hawke, Josh Charles, Kurtwood Smith, Lara Flynn Boyle, Al Ruggiero.* Director Weir's surprise hit is an often hilarious, sometimes deeply moving and somber treatise on the fires of youth and the creative spirit which they enkindle. Williams gives a spirited performance as Jack Keating — an unconventional English teacher at a New England boarding school for boys who finds himself at odds with the school's administration. And while no one here will deny the brilliance of

Sean Penn and Susan Sarandon in *Dead Man Walking*

Williams' work, the movie really doesn't belong to him: it belongs to the young actors who play his students. Leonard and Hawke head the ensemble of talented teenagers who make this movie a true success; their performances, as a group, are nothing less than marvelous. ★★★ VHS: $9.99; DVD: $29.99

The Dead Pool

(1988, 91 min, US, Buddy Van Horn) *Clint Eastwood, Liam Neeson, Patricia Clarkson, Jim Carrey.* In his fifth appearance as detective Harry Callahan, Eastwood finds himself hunting down the perpetrator(s) of a hit list known as the "dead pool." Not as exciting as its predecessors, still the film has all of the action and gunplay one comes to expect from *Dirty Harry* movies. ★★½ VHS: $14.99

Dead Presidents

(1995, 119 min, US, Allen and Albert Hughes) *Larenz Tate, Keith David, Chris Tucker, Rose Jackson, Bokine Woodbine, N'Bushe Wright, Seymour Cassel.* The Hughes Brothers follow their scintillating debut *Menace II Society* with this less impressive though not uninteresting morality tale about a young black Vietnam vet trying to build a life after the war. The film has all the elements required to be a fascinating study of this young man's struggle to reintegrate, and his fall from virtue to disgrace. But the film can't seem to decide what to be: Is it a touching ghetto melodrama; harrowing Vietnam War exposé; or shoot-'em-up heist flick? Alternately, it tries to be each of these things, but the transitions are not smooth and many of the characters are one-dimensional stereotypes. Tate imbues his role with more complexity than seems to have been in the script. ★★½ VHS: $9.99

Dead Reckoning

(1947, 100 min, US, John Cromwell) *Humphrey Bogart, Lizabeth Scott.* Departing slightly from his tough guy roles, Bogart plays a noir hero who, when he investigates the disappearance of an Army buddy, becomes entangled in a web of intrigue well beyond his control. A cynical tale where the hunter becomes the hunted. Scott is luminously attractive as the duplicitous young lady who entraps Bogie. A taut mystery which will keep you guessing right up to the end. ★★★ VHS: $19.99

Dead Ringer

(1964, 115 min, US, Paul Henreid) *Bette Davis, Peter Lawford, Karl Malden.* Davis' follow-up to her smash hit *What Ever Happened to Baby Jane?* may be a silly psychological thriller, but thanks to Davis' histrionics, it's certainly a lot of fun. Bette chews the scenery as estranged twins: one good and one evil. When the latter kills the former, she changes places with her wealthy sister to live the good life. Will anyone suspect the imposter? Police inspector Malden has his doubts. ★★★ VHS: $14.99

Dead Ringers

(1988, 115 min, Canada, David Cronenberg) *Jeremy Irons, Genevieve Bujold, Heidi von Palleske.* The good twin-bad twin genre gets an unusual and fascinating once-over in this intense, often gruesome and quite disturbing psychological horror film based on an actual incident. Irons stars as identical twin brothers whose drug dependency and romantic involvement with the same woman (Bujold) triggers their emotional and professional decline. Irons gives a truly magnificent performance as the two doctors, giving each brother a

distinctive and subtle shading. Bujold is excellent as the actress caught between them. Masterfully directed by Cronenberg, the faint of heart should beware. ★★★½ VHS: $14.99; DVD: $24.99

Dead Tired (Grosse Fatigue)

(1994, 85 min, France, Michel Blanc) *Michel Blanc, Carole Bouquet, Philippe Noiret, Charlotte Gainsbourg, Thierry L'Hermitte, Roman Polanski.* Director and writer Blanc plays dual roles as himself and a mischievous double in this wicked little farce dotted with actors, directors and the occasional agent, all playing themselves. Blanc finds himself in a waking nightmare, accused of nefarious deeds by friends and acquaintances of long standing. He retreats to the countryside to regain his composure, but that only leads him deeper into the abyss. Spurred into action by his friend Bouquet, they embark on an odyssey to discover the source of his inexplicable predicament. A delightful romp with many sly observances on fame and the cult of celebrity. (French with English subtitles) ★★★ VHS: $19.99

The Dead Zone

(1983, 103 min, US, David Cronenberg) *Christopher Walken, Martin Sheen, Brooke Adams, Herbert Lom, Colleen Dewhurst, Anthony Zerbe.* From "goremeister" Cronenberg comes this unusually tame yet excellent adaptation of the Stephen King novel about an average Joe (Walken) who wakes from a five-year coma with the ability to see the future of anyone he touches. ★★★ VHS: $14.99; DVD: $29.99

Deadline at Dawn

(1946, 83 min, US, Harold Clurman) *Susan Hayward, Bill Williams, Paul Lukas.* With a crackling screenplay by Clifford Odets and an ominous and steamy New York-at-night backdrop, this fast-paced murder mystery stars Hayward as a streetwise but soft-hearted dance hall girl who gets involved with a naive sailor in their frantic search for the killer of a female blackmailer. She soon becomes enmeshed in a maze of suspects and seedy characters, all offering good reasons for having knocked off the broad. ★★★ VHS: $19.99

Deadlock

(1991, 103 min, US, Lewis Teague) *Rutger Hauer, Mimi Rogers, Joan Chen, James Remar. The Defiant Ones* with a twist: Hauer and Rogers costar in this slick, entertaining made-for-cable thriller as a pair of criminals, shackled together at their necks by an explosive collar. They escape from an experimental maximum security prison to recover $25 million in stolen diamonds from Hauer's double-crossing partners in crime. ★★★ VHS: $19.99

The Deadly Companions

(1961, 90 min, US, Sam Peckinpah) *Maureen O'Hara, Brian Keith, Chill Wills.* Peckinpah's first film lacks the director's later accomplished visual style, but this is nevertheless an interesting western drama. O'Hara is a pioneer woman whose young son is accidentally killed; Keith is the ex-Army officer responsible for the boy's death, who escorts the woman cross-country for the boy's burial. ★★★ VHS: $14.99

Deadly Currents

(1991, 114 min, Canada, Simcha Jacobovici) An involving documentary concerning the Israeli-Palestinian conflict, this surprisingly evenhanded examination gives equal time to both sides, as well

as to three people caught in the middle. Soldiers, policemen, children, political leaders and terrorists all have their say — and the film avoids both sentimentality and a politically correct viewpoint. An intimate look at everyday life in the West Bank, an existence marked by the commonality of violence and hatred. No pat resolutions, here; no one offers a viable solution to the conflict, and few offer any hope. (Hebrew and Arabic with English subtitles) ★★★½ VHS: $29.99

Deadly Friend

(1986, 99 min, US, Wes Craven) *Matthew Laborteaux, Kristy Swanson.* Teenage genius implants a chip into the brain of a dead friend, bringing her back to life — as a rampaging killer. Craven has certainly done better. ★ VHS: $14.99

The Deadly Mantis

(1957, 78 min, US, Nathan Juran) *Craig Stevens, William Hopper.* Released by an earthquake in the Arctic, a giant praying mantis hops to the East Coast, causing destruction in Washington, D.C. and New York City before being gassed to death in the Holland Tunnel. Fun 1950s schlock with good F/X and lots of stock footage. ★★½ VHS: $14.99

Deadtime Stories

(1986, 83 min, US, Jeffrey S. Delman) *Scott Valentine, Michael Mesmer.* An average horror trilogy, whose stories of witches, werewolves and murderesses is highlighted by the final and funny "Goldilocks" story. ★★

Deal of the Century

(1983, 99 min, US, William Friedkin) *Chevy Chase, Sigourney Weaver, Gregory Hines, Wallace Shawn.* An embarrassing political comedy about weapons dealers involved with the Third World. ★

Dear God

(1996, 112 min, US, Garry Marshall) *Greg Kinnear, Laurie Metcalf, Hector Elizondo, Maria Pitillo, Tim Conway, Roscoe Lee Browne, Nancy Marchand, Jack Klugman.* Very nearly smirking his way to cynically cool, Kinnear is nevertheless submerged in the same sap and nonsense he so adroitly lampooned on "Talk Soup." He plays a scam artist who is forced to take a job at the post office's dead letter department. There, he begins reading letters written to God — and inadvertently helps the beleaguered authors (the letter writers, not the script writers) in an escalating "do-good" campaign. Marshall's wooden direction only underscores the screenplay's lack of laughs. ★★ VHS: $14.99

Death and the Maiden

(1994, 103 min, GB, Roman Polanski) *Sigourney Weaver, Ben Kingsley, Stuart Wilson.* A grim, involving chamber piece based on Ariel Dorfman's stage play, *Death and the Maiden* stars Weaver as a former brutalized political prisoner. Now living peacefully with her husband (Wilson), whom she had protected, Weaver's seemingly calm exterior is shattered one night when she hears the voice of an acquaintance of her husband — the man who had tortured her. Thus sets in motion a game of revenge as the man (a marvelously controlled Kingsley), now being held hostage, firmly denies being him. Weaver will do anything to prove that he is. But who is right? Weaver's forceful but one-note portrayal and Polanski's stage-bound direction don't completely undermine an otherwise compelling scenario. ★★½ VHS: $19.99

Death Becomes Her

(1992, 115 min, US, Robert Zemeckis) *Meryl Streep, Goldie Hawn, Bruce Willis, Isabella Rossellini, Sydney Pollack.* Vanity, thy name is woman — or, more specifically, Streep and Hawn in this hilariously vicious black comedy. Youthful lovers Hawn and Willis are engaged; that's until Broadway star Streep gets in the way. Years later, Hawn plots her revenge: Streep's death. But there's a catch — Streep has found the secret to immortality. Black comedy doesn't often get sharper than this, and there are some staggering special effects to help underscore the film's delightful nastiness. Streep once again amazes as she revels in the role of a vain, aging actress; her satiric performance is at once subtle, cunning and totally brilliant. And wait until you see Goldie as a 400-pound eating machine — it alone is worth the rental fee. ★★★½ VHS: $7.49; DVD: $24.99

Death in Brunswick

(1990, 106 min, Australia, John Ruane) *Sam Neill, Zoe Carides, John Clarke.* Neill is Cal, a 34-year-old unemployed cook under the thumb of his meddling mom and living in squalor with no clear ambitions. A job in a sleazy nightclub introduces him to a vibrant young woman and a set of circumstances which transform his muddle through life into a dead-long propulsion for survival. A darkly funny, low-budget surprise, with the gritty sense of realism often present in Australian films. Neill is matched by the supporting cast in whimsical portrayals of marginal small-town characters who handle life's eccentricities with more heart than reason. ★★★ VHS: $102.99

Death in the Garden

(La Mort en ce Jardin)

(1956, 90 min, Mexico, Luis Buñuel) *Georges Marchal, Simone Signoret, Charles Vanel.* Using a more conventional narrative, Buñuel's *Death in the Garden* may prove a disappointment to fans of the great surrealist director. Based on a novel by Jose Andre Lacour, the film tells the story of diamond miners in post-WWII South America. When military officials announce that all mining will be controlled by the government, the town erupts into riotous chaos. A motley group of refugees eventually flees the militia on a riverboat for Brazil. Ultimately the film's structure breaks down to reveal what is an existential polemic, rather than a social critique — and at best, an interesting historical document that testifies to the dangers of colonialism. (French and Spanish with English subtitles) ★★½ VHS: $24.99

Death in Venice

(1971, 130 min, Italy, Luchino Visconti) *Dirk Bogarde, Björn Andresen.* Visconti's adaptation of the Thomas Mann novella of an artist in search of purity and beauty but who ultimately becomes fatally obsessed with an exquisite teenaged boy is a melancholy experience. Set in turn-of-the-century Venice, this languidly paced, darkly atmospheric film stars Bogarde as Aschenbach, an older man enamored with a flirtatious but unattainable blond youth (Andresen), who is gradually weakened by the cholera epidemic sweeping

the city. Visconti changed Aschenbach's profession from writer to composer, enabling him to fill a largely wordless film with the wondrous music of Gustav Mahler. (Filmed in English) ★★★ VHS: $59.99

Death of a Bureaucrat

(1966, 87 min, Cuba, Tomás Gutiérrez Alea) *Salvador Wood, Silvia Planas.* When it comes to uproarious comedies, one rarely identifies the films of the Communist bloc, in general, and Castro's Cuba, in particular, as a source. But this madcap comedy is nothing if not a joy from beginning to end. Paying homage to the surrealist humor of Luis Buñuel and the pratfall antics of Harold Lloyd and Buster Keaton, Alea's story concerns a young man whose recently widowed mother finds that she cannot receive her pension without his father's union card — which was buried with him! He finds himself in a classic catch-22 as he tackles an endless array of red tape in his bewildering efforts to first get his father exhumed and then to get him reburied. A very funny black comedy which pokes wildly subversive fun at the powers that be. (Spanish with English subtitles) ★★★½ VHS: $59.99

Death of a Salesman

(1985, 150 min, US, Volker Schlöndorff) *Dustin Hoffman, John Malkovich, Kate Reid, Stephen Lang, Charles Durning.* Remarkably successful play-on-film version of Arthur Miller's classic drama, with Hoffman giving a stunning performance as Willy Loman, the aging Brooklyn salesman whose career and home life slowly unravel about him. A superior supporting cast includes Malkovich and Lang as his sons, and Reid as his loyal wife. ★★★★ VHS: $29.99

Death of a Soldier

(1985, 93 min, Australia, Philippe Mora) *James Coburn, Reb Brown, Bill Hunter.* A well-mounted recounting of the true story of a U.S. Army private stationed in Australia during WWII who murders three local women, and of his subsequent trial and execution. ★★½ VHS: $79.99

Death on the Nile

(1978, 135 min, GB, John Guillermin) *Peter Ustinov, Bette Davis, David Niven, Angela Lansbury, Maggie Smith, Mia Farrow, Simon MacCorkindale, Jack Warden.* Lavish Agatha Christie mystery highlighted by sumptuous locales and a solid cast. Ustinov is a delightful Hercule Poirot, who investigates the shipboard murder of a spoiled heiress. Who done it? We'll never tell. Lansbury is a standout among these accomplished performers. (Letterboxed) ★★★ VHS: $9.99; DVD: $24.99

Death Race 2000

(1975, 80 min, US, Paul Bartel) *David Carradine, Sylvester Stallone, Mary Woronov.* Frankenstein (Carradine) is the survivor of a number of deadly crashes, outfitted with a number of artificial limbs and devices, taking on his challenger Machine Gun Viterbo (Stallone) in this funny, somewhat campy but exciting action-satire. ★★★ VHS: $14.99; DVD: $24.99

Death Takes a Holiday

(1934, 78 min, US, Mitchell Leisen) *Fredric March, Evelyn Venable, Guy Standing, Gail Patrick.* Maxwell Anderson's acclaimed Broadway drama makes for a fascinating and surreal film adaptation. March

plays Death, who decides to take a three-day holiday. Disguising himself as royalty, he stays at a Spanish villa where he observes humans up close for the first time and, to his surprise, falls in love. (Remade as *Meet Joe Black*) ★★★½ VHS: $14.99

Death Warrant

(1990, 90 min, Canada, Deran Sarafian) *Jean-Claude Van Damme, Cynthia Gibb, Robert Guillaume.* A cop (Van Damme) goes undercover in a violent penitentiary, seeking out those responsible for a series of brutal prison murders. Violent and only sporadically interesting. ★★ VHS: $9.99; DVD: $14.99

Death Wish

(1974, 93 min, US, Michael Winner) *Charles Bronson, Vincent Gardenia, Hope Lange, Steven Keats, Olympia Dukakis, Jeff Goldblum, Christopher Guest.* In the film which started the "vigilante" action genre, Bronson stars as a New York businessman who seeks vengeance against society's criminal underworld for the death of his wife and the rape of his daughter. The film tries to balance gritty, violent action sequences with a supposedly thoughtful treatise on crime and punishment, but it's nothing more than an excuse for Bronson to blow away punks and street scum and having the audience cheer him while he's doing it. As a detective on Bronson's trail, Gardenia is actually quite good, giving more conviction to his part than it deserves. (Followed by 4 sequels) ★★½ VHS: $14.99; DVD: $29.99

Deathtrap

(1982, 116 min, US, Sidney Lumet) *Michael Caine, Christopher Reeve, Dyan Cannon, Irene Worth.* Ira Levin's hit Broadway murder mystery is brought to the screen in only a satisfactory adaptation. Caine plays a down-on-his-luck playwright who sees a chance at reclaiming success when a former student (Reeve) shows up with a sure hit script. Caine plots to murder him and take the play as his own. But plot twists and red herrings await them. The two twist endings are neatly written, but the entire production suffers from a dreariness due, in most part, to Lumet's stage-bound direction. ★★½ VHS: $19.99; DVD: $14.99

Deathwatch

(1980, 128 min, France/West Germany, Bertrand Tavernier) *Romy Schneider, Harvey Keitel, Max von Sydow, Harry Dean Stanton.* This unusual, present-day science-fiction film features Schneider as a terminally ill woman whose slow death is being witnessed by a mass audience through a tiny video camera implanted in the eyes of an undercover TV reporter (Keitel). A fascinating film which speculates on the abuses of the media as well as the rise of Big Brother. (Filmed in English) ★★★

The Decalogue

(1988, 571 min, Poland, Krzysztof Kieslowski) The director of the "Three Colors" trilogy (*Blue, White* and *Red*) had already created his masterpiece by the time those films hit these shores. In fashioning ten short films for Polish television, each inspired by one of the Ten Commandments, Kieslowski explores dark, difficult moral and ethical dilemmas in his trademark brooding, moody style. Each episode is deeper than it appears; the fifth film, "Thou Shalt not Kill," is not merely a murder story but a treatise on capital punishment. And the ten films, while working individually, are most pow-

The Decalogue

erful as a whole; all taking place in the same area, characters from some episodes make cameo appearances in others. This is a fully realized masterwork, worthy of its legendary status. ★★★★ VHS: $99.99

The Decameron

(1970, 111 min, Italy, Pier Paolo Pasolini) *Franco Citti, Ninetto Davoli.* Boccaccio's bawdy and earthy stories of sexual adventures during the 14th century receive the Pasolini treatment. Told in several episodes, the stories illustrate the different facets of uninhibited human sexuality. The film takes special pleasure in depicting the Church's sexually repressed clerics frolicking lecherously amongst their flocks. *The Decameron,* Pasolini's first film in his trilogy of medieval tales, is perhaps his funniest and is certainly one of the director's best films. (Italian with English subtitles) ★★★½

Deceived

(1991, 103 min, US, Damian Harris) *Goldie Hawn, John Heard, Jan Rubes, Beatrice Straight, Kate Reid.* Hawn delivers an understated performance as a woman who slowly comes to discover that her recently deceased husband (perennial yuppie bad-guy Heard) may not have been all the good things that she thought he was. In fact, he may not even be dead. Crisp direction and stylish settings keep a predictable plot moving briskly. ★★½

Deceiver

(1998, 102 min, US, Jonas & Joshua Pate) *Tim Roth, Renee Zellweger, Chris Penn, Michael Rooker, Rosanna Arquette, Ellen Burstyn.* A twisty bit of trickery, *Deceiver* is gripping without ever being really good. Slickly written and directed by twins Joshua and Jonas Pate, this psychological mystery concerns two cops, Braxton (Penn) and Kennesaw (Rooker), who are administering a polygraph test to murder suspect James Walter Wayland (Roth). James suffers from temporal lobe epilepsy, and he may have killed, halved, and discarded a prostitute during one of his seizures. However, while the cops do not have any hard evidence, James has some dirt on them. This overly arty film has only some bravura acting by Roth and Rooker to recommend it. ★★½ VHS: $9.99

The Deceivers

(1988, 112 min, GB, Nicholas Meyer) *Pierce Brosnan, Saeed Jaffrey, Shashi Kapoor, Keith Michell.* Brosnan stars as a 19th-century British officer who goes undercover to investigate a series of ritual killings by the secret brotherhood of the Thuggees. Posing as an Indian, the officer infiltrates the fiendish sect and finds himself mysteriously drawn into its power, endangering not only his mission, but his life as well. At times a bit muddled, the film nonetheless is an often exciting and interesting sojourn to a little-traveled time in history. ★★½

December Flower

(1984, 650 min, GB, Judy Allen) *Jean Simmons, Mona Washbourne.* This tender story about the flowering relationship between a middle-aged widow and her aging aunt is a beautiful tribute to the resilience of the elderly. ★★★ VHS: $14.99

Deception

(1946, 112 min, US, Irving Rapper) *Bette Davis, Paul Henreid, Claude Rains.* Davis is in great form as a suffering pianist torn between Rains and Henreid. Rains matches La Davis every step of the way with a grand portrayal of her mentor. One of Davis' most entertaining soaps. ★★★ VHS: $19.99

Deception

(1992, 90 min, US, Graeme Clifford) *Andie MacDowell, Liam Neeson, Viggo Mortensen, Jack Thompson.* What could elevate this by-the-book mystery about a harried housewife (MacDowell) who crisscrosses the globe in search of answers after her flyboy husband dies surrounded by shady dealings? Why, Neeson, as a shyly charismatic "Feed the World" worker, of course. MacDowell gives, as usual, a one-note performance. ★★ VHS: $9.99

The Decline of the American Empire

(1986, 101 min, Canada, Denys Arcand) *Dominique Michel, Dorothee Berryman, Louise Portal, Genevieve Rioux, Pierre Curzi.* Arcand's comically incisive film examines a group of male and female French Canadian academicians as they analyse the worlds of sex and human mortality. As their discussion

unfolds, many in the group arrive at varying degrees of self-discovery. Arcand skillfully weaves his way through the many viewpoints and compassionately presents his characters as they turn to sexuality as a hedge against death. (French with English subtitles) ★★★ VHS: $79.99

The Decline of Western Civilization

(1980, 100 min, US, Penelope Spheeris) Spheeris' absorbing, close-up look at the hardcore lifestyle on the wild and wooly West Coast features the serene sounds of X, Black Flag, Fear, Germs and Catholic Discipline. ★★★

The Decline of Western Civilization, Pt. 2: The Metal Years

(1988, 90 min, US, Penelope Spheeris) Director Spheeris' raucous follow-up to her acclaimed docu-musical probes the headbanging fans and fast-living stars of the heavy metal world. Plenty of music and amusing interviews with demi-gods Ozzy Osbourne, Aerosmith, Gene Simmons and Alice Cooper. ★★½

Deconstructing Harry

(1997, 96 min, US, Woody Allen) *Woody Allen, Kirstie Alley, Elisabeth Shue, Judy Davis, Demi Moore, Billy Crystal, Robin Williams, Julia Louis-Dreyfus, Mariel Hemingway, Eric Bogosian, Julie Kavner, Amy Irving, Bob Balaban, Hazelle Goodman.* With the most infuriatingly honest, dark and derisive film of his career, Allen's funny comedy finds the writer-director in new territory as he opens the wounds of his private life in language, situation and character. Woody plays Harry Block, a writer in the throes of crisis with ex-wives, ex-girl-friends, career and conscience. These themes are presented in such an in-your-face cinematic style and bantered about with uncharacteristic off-color dialogue, that Woody's self-revelatory exploration of an unapologetically immature husband, father and artist will certainly divide even his most loyal fans. The story, which inventively and successfully mixes past and present, and reality and fiction, follows Block as he prepares to accept an award from his alma mater. In support, Alley as an ex-wife, Davis as a former in-law, Crystal as the Devil, and Williams as a fictional character whose life becomes literally blurred, stand out among the large, cameo-like all-star cast. (VHS available letterboxed or pan & scan) ★★★½ VHS: $19.99; DVD: $24.99

Decoration Day

(1990, 99 min, US, Robert Markowitz) *James Garner, Bill Cobbs, Judith Ivey, Ruby Dee, Laurence Fishburne.* Garner stars in this made-for-TV drama about a retired Georgia judge who reluctantly searches for his estranged boyhood friend, a black WWII vet who refuses to accept a long overdue Congressional Medal of Honor. An intelligent screenplay, incisive direction and exceptional performances contribute to elevate this well above standard TV-movie fare. ★★★½ VHS: $14.99

The Deep

(1977, 123 min, US, Peter Yates) *Nick Nolte, Jacqueline Bisset, Lou Gossett, Jr., Robert Shaw.* Nolte and Bisset play lovers on a romantic vacation in Bermuda who stumble upon a sunken wreck from WWII and get entangled with a Haitian drug dealer (Gossett) and an old treasure hunter (Shaw). The cinematography captures the lushness of the surroundings, but a flat screenplay sinks to the bottom. ★★ VHS: $9.99; DVD: $19.99

Deep Blue Sea

(1999, 105 min, US, Renny Harlin) *Saffron Burrows, Thomas Jane, Samuel L. Jackson, L.L. Cool J, Michael Rapaport, Stellan Skarsgård.* Borrowing quite liberally from just about every popular horror/thriller of the last couple decades, this underwater thriller still manages to entertain in spite of its creaky story, cartoonish effects and one of the most wooden performances from a lead in quite some time. Scientist Burrows is searching for an Alzheimer's cure by toying with shark DNA. Only thing is, her tests have elevated the sharks up the evolutionary scale a notch or two. And now the great whites have flooded the underwater lab the small crew inhabits — and they're pissed. The production design is actually quite good, but is offset by the less-than-menacing sharks. At least it's fun to watch each member become dinner in a wide variety of attacks. Jackson has his usual commanding self (keep your eyes wide open for his "rallying the troops" speech), though Burrows must have taken acting lessons from Steven Seagal. ★★½ VHS: $14.99; DVD: $19.99

Deep Cover

(1980, 81 min, GB, Richard Loncraine) *Donald Pleasence, Denholm Elliott, Tom Conti.* Dennis Potter wrote the screenplay for this brooding made-for-TV drama which mixes cryptic dialogue, paranoia, sexual duplicity and a notorious 1930s British scandal. Pleasence stars as a reclusive former Cambridge professor and author whose home is visited by an enigmatic stranger (Conti), claiming to be writing his thesis on one of his books. As he ingratiates himself into the household, including tempting the author's wife and daughter, it becomes apparent that he has ulterior motives. Potter sets the pace of his scenario slowly as characters playfully banter back and forth, with the author playfully giving bits of information only when needed. The cinematography gives the film a storybook glow which belies the characters' malevolent intents. (aka: *Blade on the Feather*) ★★½

Deep Cover

(1992, 107 min, US, Bill Duke) *Laurence Fishburne, Jeff Goldblum, Victoria Dillard, Charles Martin Smith, Clarence Williams III, Glynn Turman.* In this gritty urban thriller, Fishburne is magnetic as a cop who finds himself being seduced by a life of crime when he is sent into "deep cover" as a drug dealer. With a story as streetwise as anything this side of Scorsese, the screenplay by maverick writer Michael Tolkin (*The Player*) adds an extra level of depth and decadence to the characterizations — particularly Goldblum's turn as an ultra-smarmy attorney who wants to market his own designer drug. ★★★½ VHS: $9.99; DVD: $14.99

Deep Crimson

(1996, 110 min, Mexico, Arturo Ripstein) *Daniel Giménez Cacho, Regina Orozco, Marisa Paredes.* This is a truly odd film, based on the same ultra-strange true case that inspired the cult movie *The Honeymoon Killers*. There's no camp in this one, just a straightforward retelling of the tale of the doomed lovers and their nasty scheme to rip various spinsters and widows out of their fortunes after marrying and murdering them. Fans of *Honeymoon Killers* will either enjoy this for its different take on the case or be put off by the film's rather sluggish pacing. (Spanish with English subtitles) ★★ VHS: $29.99

The Deep End of the Ocean

(1999, 106 min, US, Ulu Grosbard) *Michelle Pfeiffer, Treat Williams, Whoopi Goldberg, Jonathan Jackson, Ryan Merryman.* A minor, TV movie-of-the-week story elevated by its cast, this earnest drama follows the hardships endured by a family after their youngest child disappears. In an engaging portrayal which manages to overcome the clichés of the story, Pfeiffer is Beth who, while attending her high school reunion, loses her son Ben in a crowded lobby. Though the police (led by Goldberg) follow every lead, young Ben is never found. The story then examines the strain on husband and wife, who soon engage in a series of accusations. A few years later, however, Beth sees a neighborhood boy who she thinks may be Ben. Is he? By then it won't matter much, for the story becomes strained as it pretends to examine the moral dilemma — but it's all so superficial. ★★ VHS: $9.99; DVD: $19.99

Deep Impact

(1998, 121 min, US, Mimi Leder) *Robert Duvall, Téa Leoni, Morgan Freeman, Maximilian Schell, Elijah Wood, Vanessa Redgrave.* The first of 1998's two disaster films to the gate, *Deep Impact* is a visually striking end-of-the-world flick which is focused more on human emotion than special effects. Its counterpart, *Armageddon*, has much more action and F/X fun going for it, but that Disney-backed space saga is certainly inferior in the drama department. Young astronomer Wood discovers a huge comet hurtling towards Earth. This sets in motion the inevitable panic as the President (a stately Freeman) responds accordingly. Leoni is a TV reporter who breaks the news, and the story shuttles between her private and professional lives, the emotional toll the impending doom takes on everyone, and the space mission which attempts to destroy the comet. The effects at the end are good, but there's little of them, which could make one feel cheated. (VHS available letterboxed or pan & scan) ★★½ VHS: $14.99; DVD: $24.99

Deep in My Heart

(1954, 132 min, US, Stanley Donen) *Jose Ferrer, Merle Oberon, Paul Henreid, Gene Kelly, Cyd Charisse.* Entertaining production numbers highlight this otherwise by-the-books musical biography of Hungarian composer Sigmund Romberg ("The Student Prince," "The Desert Song"), with Ferrer as the songwriter. ★★½

Deep Red

(1975, 98 min, Italy, Dario Argento) *David Hemmings, Daria Nicoldi, Gabriele Lavia.* Hemmings stars in this chilling horror-mystery as a British musician in Rome who witnesses the "Hatchet Murder" of a psycho. He then becomes obsessed with solving the case, finding clues, corpses and some bizarre drawings along the way. Filled with tension and atmosphere. (Letterboxed) ★★★ VHS: $14.99; DVD: $29.99

Deep Rising

(1998, 106 min, US, Stephen Sommers) *Treat Williams, Famke Janssen, Anthony Heald, Kevin J. O'Connor, Wes Studi, Djimon Hounsou.* A perfect example of cookie-cutter movie-making, *Deep Rising* is an odd, uneven though strangely enjoyable hybrid of *The Poseidon Adventure, Die Hard, Predator* and all four *Alien* films. Defying logic and coherence, the film puts a colorful assortment of gleefully underwritten characters in jeopardy when a luxurious cruise ship is undertaken by bad guys with guns. The twist is that a gigantic underwater creature has come up from the depths for supper. Lots of pre-fab suspense and bloody mayhem ensues, though the effects are distractingly cheesy. Still, there's lots of campy B-movie fun to be had. ★★ VHS: $9.99; DVD: $29.99

DeepStar Six

(1988, 103 min, US, Sean S. Cunningham) *Greg Evigan, Nancy Everhard, Miguel Ferrer, Taurean Blacque.* A group of deep-sea explorers attempt to establish a secret naval base on the ocean floor, but they discover there's a terror in the ocean depths. Nothing could be as scary, though, as this film's screenplay, acting and directing. ★ VHS: $14.99; DVD: $14.99

The Deer Hunter

(1978, 183 min, US, Michael Cimino) *Robert De Niro, Christopher Walken, Meryl Streep, John Cazale, John Savage, George Dzundza, Shirley Stoler.* This Oscar-winning Best Picture is an unusual Vietnam War film in that it shows its characters before, during and after their war experience. The Vietnam episode is only a third of the film, but it is so devastating that it stays with you until the film's end. Among the extraordinary ensemble, Walken won an Oscar for his emotionally scarred soldier. (VHS available letterboxed or pan & scan) ★★★★ VHS: $14.99; DVD: $26.99

Def by Temptation

(1990, 95 min, US, James Bond III) *Cynthia Bond, Kadeem Hardison, James Bond III, Bill Nunn, Melba Moore, Samuel L. Jackson.* An all-black cast invigorates this original treatment about a virginal "man of God" (Bond) who must avenge his father's downfall by doing battle with a demon (Cynthia Bond, the director's sister) who preys on sexually dishonest souls. Director Bond makes the most of his low, low budget while serving up a horror treat that harks back to the "blaxploitation" era of *Blacula*, but without the gratuitous exploitation of that genre. ★★★ VHS: $14.99; DVD: $14.99

Defence of the Realm

(1987, 96 min, GB, David Drury) *Gabriel Byrne, Greta Scacchi, Denholm Elliott, Ian Bannen.* Engrossing political thriller about a journalist who uncovers an explosive sex scandal involving a Member of Parliament and a KGB agent, which leads the reporter on the trail of a governmental cover-up of a nuclear mishap on an American military base. Elliott gives a smashing performance as Byrne's seasoned editor. ★★★ VHS: $14.99

The Defender

(1994, 100 min, Hong Kong, Corey Yuen) *Jet Li, Christy Chung.* The inimitable Li is saddled with third-rate material here. Basically a Hong Kong remake of *The Bodyguard*, *The Defender* has Beijing bodyguard Li assigned to protect lovely young Chung from a bunch of baddies. The usual dull antagonism between the two is protracted, and it's nearly an hour before the first real action scene (an acceptable shootout in a shopping mall). Li's charisma is the only thing holding one's attention until the terrific climax, with Li going mano-a-mano with the baddest of the bad guys. It's tough going until then, so if you're unfamiliar with Li (and shame on you if you are!), check out *Twin Warriors* or *Fist of Legend* for first-rate Jet action. (Dubbed) (aka: *The Bodyguard from Beijing*) ★★ VHS: $102.99; DVD: $29.99

Defending Your Life

(1991, 112 min, US, Albert Brooks) *Albert Brooks, Meryl Streep, Rip Torn, Lee Grant, Buck Henry.* One of the most innovative and freshest comedies of the '90s, this low-key, quirky and very funny fantasy follows businessman Brooks' adventures in the hereafter. Killed in a car accident, he goes on trial to determine his next plane of existence. During his stay at Judgment City — where you can eat as much as you like and never gain weight — he falls in love with Streep, who is certainly on a higher spiritual plateau. The film, written and directed by Brooks, finds most of its humor with our conceptions concerning death, love and commitment. A particular highlight is Streep eating pasta, and there's a cameo which alone is worth the price of the rental. ★★★½ VHS: $9.99; DVD: $19.99

The Defiant Ones

(1958, 97 min, US, Stanley Kramer) *Tony Curtis, Sidney Poitier, Theodore Bikel, Lon Chaney, Jr.* Kramer had a thing for films about prejudice (*Guess Who's Coming to Dinner, Judgment at Nuremberg*), but this taut drama is probably the best of them all. Curtis and Poitier play two escaped convicts cuffed to each other, fleeing the police in the South. Their performances are remarkably well-defined. ★★★★ VHS: $14.99

Déjà Vu

(1998, 115 min, GB/US, Henry Jaglom) *Stephen Dillane, Victoria Foyt, Vanessa Regrave, Rachel Kempson, Noel Harrison, Anna Massey.* Another anxious romance from writer-director Jaglom, *Déjà Vu* will please his dedicated fans, and it may actually earn him some new ones. Foyt (Jaglom's wife, and the film's cowriter) stars as Dana, a woman who believes — based on a set of coincidences — that her soulmate is Sean (Dillane), a painter. As the couple hopscotch around the globe and each other's hearts, they allow fate and destiny to take control of their lives. *Déjà Vu* has some lovely, romantic moments when its characters' neuroses are not too overbearing, and happily, Jaglom's direction is a bit less intrusive than usual. Dillane is an engaging romantic hero, and the film is graced with the elegant presence of Redgrave. ★★★ VHS: $14.99

The Delicate Delinquent

(1957, 90 min, US, Don McGuire) *Jerry Lewis, Darren McGavin, Martha Hyer.* Lewis plays a bumbling (what else?) janitor who hangs out with the crowd from the wrong side of the tracks but ends up becoming a police officer. His first movie without Dean. ★★★ VHS: $14.99

Delicatessen

(1991, 97 min, France, Jean-Pierre Jeunet & Marc Caro) *Dominique Pinon, Marie-Laure Dougnac, Jean Claude Dreyfus.* Displaying a playfully inventive virtuosity with the camera, and offering as its theme the socially indigestible subject of cannibalism, *Delicatessen* is a hilariously witty and sweetly outrageous story of a fairy-tale romance set amidst the ruins of a post-apocalyptic world. The story revolves around an enterprising butcher who stays in business by adding some human flesh to his meats and sausages. Life changes for the butcher and the oddball tenants in the ramshackle flats above his shop when Louison (Pinon), a sweet-natured clown-on-the-lam comes looking for a job and then

falls in love with Julie, the butcher's willowy, near-sighted daughter. As poor Louison has to stay one step ahead of the butcher's cleaver, the directors gleefully notch up the speed and unleash a flurry of chaos as the film races to an inspired comic-book conclusion. While not for all tastes, this furiously paced tale is a deliciously outrageous comedy which brims with mischievous visual lunacy. (French with English subtitles) ★★★★ VHS: $7.99

Delirious

(1983, 70 min, US) *Eddie Murphy.* Murphy live in concert, recorded in Washington, D.C. in 1983, at the beginning of his phenomenal film career. Brimming with the humor — adult-oriented, often side-splitting and usually offensive — which has become the comic's trademark.

Deliverance

(1972, 109 min, US, John Boorman) *Jon Voight, Burt Reynolds, Ned Beatty, Ronny Cox.* James Dickey's best-seller makes for a stirring adventure-drama about four business associates whose weekend in the wilds turns tragic. Voight and Reynolds are fine as two of the execs, and completing the quartet, Beatty and Cox both make impressive film debuts. (VHS available letterboxed or pan & scan) ★★★½ VHS: $14.99; DVD: $19.99

The Deluge

(1974, 183 min, Poland, Jerzy Hoffman) Set in the mountainous ravines of the Carpathians and filled with burning villages, opulent castles and spurting blood, this 17th-century war epic chronicles the patriotic glory and bloody violence during the Polish-Swedish War. The story is told through the romantic eyes of Andrzej, a courageous adventurer who finds more than a little time for amorous interludes. Based on the novel by Henryk Sienkiewicz, this Polish *Tom Jones* was nominated for the Academy Award for Best Foreign Language Film. (Polish with English subtitles) ★★★ VHS: $79.99

Delusions of Grandeur

(1976, 85 min, France, Gerard Oury) *Yves Montand, Louis De Funes.* A delightful, fast-paced comedy of royal intrigue in 17th-century Spain. Louis De Funes is an evil, all-powerful minister of the king who, when exiled by the queen, plots to get even. He is aided by his clever, good-natured servant, Blaze (Montand). (French with English subtitles) ★★★

Dementia 13

(1963, 81 min, US, Francis Ford Coppola) *William Campbell, Luana Anders.* Coppola made his feature film debut with this Roger Corman cheapie about an ax-murderer on the loose in an Irish castle. Often very gory, Coppola effectively uses black and white to enhance the horror of this Gothic thriller. Worth a look as both low-budget horror film and as first film for a major American director. ★★★ DVD: $9.99

Demetrius and the Gladiators

(1954, 101 min, US, Delmer Daves) *Victor Mature, Susan Hayward, Anne Bancroft, Ernest Borgnine, Michael Rennie, Debra Pagent.* A good cast is featured in this inferior sequel to 1953's *The Robe*, which centers on the search for the robe that Christ wore before he was crucified. ★★ VHS: $9.99; DVD: $24.99

Demolition Man

(1993, 114 min, US, Marco Brambilla) *Sylvester Stallone, Wesley Snipes, Sandra Bullock, Denis Leary, Rob Schneider.* In this surprisingly effective and comical action film, Stallone plays a renegade cop whose battle with bad-guy Snipes leads to the deaths of innocent civilians. Both are frozen as punishment. Thirty-five years later, in a grotesquely funny fascist utopian society, Snipes escapes, and an ill-equipped police department defrosts Sly to help them catch him. First-time director Brambilla has a good eye in creating an off-center future, and his action sequences are well-staged. As the over-the-top villain, Snipes clearly seems to be enjoying himself. ★★★ VHS: $9.99; DVD: $19.99

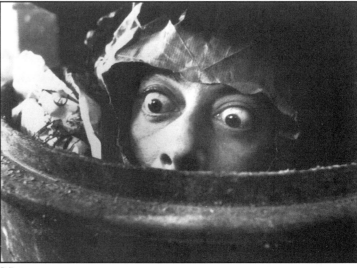

Delicatessen

Demon Barber of Fleet Street

(1936, 68 min, GB, George King) *Tod Slaughter, Bruce Seton, Stella Rho, Eve Lister.* The cruelties of man are more wondrous than Peru in this true story of barber Sweeney Todd, who would kill bad-tipping customers and turn them into meat pies. (No singing in this film.) Slaughter's most famous exercise in the Grand Guignol, rumored to feature asylum inmates in minor roles (mostly in front of the camera). ★★½ VHS: $9.99

Demon Knight

(1995, 93 min, US, Ernest Dickerson) *Billy Zane, William Sadler, Jada Pinkett, Brenda Bakke, Thomas Haden Church, CCH Pounder, Dick Miller.* The Crypt Keeper from TV's "Tales from the Crypt" makes his way to the big screen in this tongue-in-cheek tale. The film, like the series, is alternately ghoulish, coolish and humorous, but it doesn't quite succeed in becoming the triple threat it so wants to be. Director Dickerson creates a chilling atmosphere, but he's working from an undeveloped script. It has to do with the Devil (Zane) battling the mortal guardian (Sadler) of a key containing the blood of Christ. Zane has a devilishly good time hunting his prey to a small New Mexico hotel and then tormenting all within his reach. ★★ VHS: $14.99; DVD: $29.99

Demon Seed

(1977, 97 min, US, Donald Cammell) *Julie Christie, Fritz Weaver; Voice of: Robert Vaughn.* Christie plays a housewife who's caught in the deadly plot of a powerful computer system as it attempts to secure immortality and take over the world. ★★½ VHS: $14.99

Demons

(1986, 89 min, Italy, Lamberto Bava) *Urbano Barberini, Natasha Hovey.* Stylish, eerie (if somewhat implausible) horror film cowritten and produced by Italian horror master Dario Argento about a movie preview audience watching a slasher film, while the horror on screen extends itself into the real world. (Letterboxed) (Sequel: *Demons 2*) ★★★ VHS: $14.99; DVD: $29.99

Demons in the Garden

(1982, 100 min, Spain, Manuel Gutiérrez Aragón) *Angela Molina, Ana Belen, Eusabio Lazáro.* A child's magical memory of his father's hypocrisy and deceit is the subject of this engrossing tale about life after the end of the Spanish Civil War. A young boy grows up spoiled and manipulative as his mother, aunt and grandmother vie for influence over him. A trio of Spain's finest actresses etch memorable portraits that embody the divided nature of the Spanish character. (Spanish with English subtitles) ★★★ VHS: $79.99

Dennis Potter:
The Last Interview

(1996, 70 min, GB) Betrayed by his body, sipping morphine from a flask, Dennis Potter, writer of such masterworks as "The Singing Detective," "Pennies from Heaven" and "Brimstone and Treacle," talks about his life, his art and his impending death in this often fascinating interview. The location for this gentle interrogation is appropriate: a TV studio empty save for two chairs, a small table, the interviewer and his clipboard, and Potter himself. Only

minutes into the program, the playwright can no longer maintain his adopted role as Britain's bitterish curmudgeon — or perhaps, like so many of the characters who populate his plays, he just gives it more complexity and greater depth. ★★★ VHS: $29.99

Dennis the Menace

(1993, 94 min, US, Nick Castle) *Walter Matthau, Joan Plowright, Mason Gamble, Christopher Lloyd, Lea Thompson, Paul Winfield.* This updating of the "Dennis the Menace" saga has its moments, like the one where Dennis (Gamble) explains to Mrs. Wilson why his parents want to be left alone for their weekly Sunday morning "wrestling" sessions. Unfortunately, moments like these are few and far between and the story consequently sags around John Hughes' by now worn-out plot involving a burglar (Lloyd) who gets nailed by a precocious eight-year-old. Most of the performances are bland, with the exception of Matthau as the curmudgeonly Mr. Wilson and Plowright as his understanding wife. ★★ VHS: $14.99

The Dentist

(1996, 93 min, US, Brian Yuzna) *Corbin Bernsen, Linda Hoffman.* Rather than being a *Dr. Giggles*-like slasher movie, this ambitious but failed project is more along the lines of a psychological thriller with teeth. Bernsen stars as a successful dentist with a beautiful wife, luxurious home and lucrative practice. This, however, is all an illusion, as he's slowly losing it all. While there is some effective satire, the film unfortunately concentrates too much on the collapse of the doctor's mind. Fans expecting a slasher pic will be sorely disappointed. Dentistry was more chilling in *Marathon Man*. (Sequel: *The Dentist 2*) ★★ VHS: $9.99; DVD: $14.99

Le Départ

(1966, 90 min, Belgium, Jerzy Skolimowski) *Jean-Pierre Léaud, Catherine Duport.* Mark (Léaud) is a 19-year-old with a mania for Porsches and car racing. His determination to enter a race (and find a Porsche in the process) is undermined when he meets and falls in love with Michele. A funny, visually eclectic story of one's dreams confronting reality. (French with English subtitles) ★★★

Deranged

(1974, 88 min, US, Bob Clark & Alan Ormsby) *Roberts Blossom, Cosette Lee.* Based on the real-life activities of Wisconsin necrophile/murderer Ed Gein, *Deranged* stars Blossom as "the butcher of Woodside," a mother-obsessed weirdo who digs up his mom, stuffs her and soon begins to kill other women to keep her company. Shocking, graphic, and at times semi-humorous, this unusual release is truly a "you've got to see it to believe it," but is recommended only to horror fans with a strong stomach. ★★

Le Dernier Combat
(The Last Battle)

(1983, 93 min, France, Luc Besson) *Pierre Jolivet, Jean Bouise, Jean Reno, Fritz Wepper.* Besson makes an impressive directorial debut with this offbeat, black-and-white sci-fi adventure set in a post-nuclear world where the few surviving men battle each other over territory and the last remaining women on Earth. Though Besson's film, which has no dialogue, follows the conventions of the post-apocalyptic genre, his visuals are striking and he creates a disturbing sense of atmosphere. ★★★

Dersu Uzala

(1975, 160 min, Japan/USSR, Akira Kurosawa) *Yuri Solomin, Maxim Munzuk.* Kurosawa's Oscar-winning epic, a magnificent and sweeping production, explores the tremendous bond between an early 20th-century Russian explorer and his faithful guide Dersu. Kurosawa's immense visual artistry vividly captures nature's beauty and wrath. (Japanese with English subtitles) ★★★★ VHS: $39.99; DVD: $39.99

Desecration

(1999, 88 min, US, Dante Tomaselli) *Irma St. Paule, Christie Sanford, Danny Lopes.* Weird and dreamlike, the intriguing *Desecration* from first-time director Tomaselli is loaded with atmosphere and bizarre Catholic/mother imagery once the silly plot kicks in. A young ne'er-do-well at a Catholic school accidentally kills a nun — with his remote control airplane! That unintentionally funny scene out of the way, *Desecration* becomes a rather likable guilt-trip nightmare that, at its best, recalls classic dream/horror films like *Phantasm*. Very uneven, very low-budget, and very goofy, one wishes *Desecration* were a little scarier, a bit more outrageous but, all things considered, it's a nice surprise. ★★½ VHS: $19.99; DVD: $24.99

Desert Bloom

(1986, 103 min, US, Eugene Corr) *Jon Voight, Annabele Gish, JoBeth Williams, Ellen Barkin.* This underrated, extremely well-acted drama is set in 1950s Nevada at the dawn of the A-Bomb testing. Gish offers a sincere performance as a young girl coming of age living with her mom (Williams) and troubled stepdad (Voight). Barkin is terrific as Gish's sympathetic, flamboyant aunt. ★★★½ VHS: $14.99

Desert Blue

(1999, 90 min, US, Morgan J. Freeman) *Christina Ricci, Brendan Sexton III, Casey Affleck, Kate Hudson, Sara Gilbert.* A fine indie film about a handful of characters living in Baxter, California, *Desert Blue* deals with a quarantine imposed on the small roadside town. When a trucker spills a feared contaminant and dies, the entire town is contained. Blue (Sexton) is the son of the town's founder, and he falls in love with Skye (Hudson), a TV actress stranded in the town during an ill-timed visit. Meanwhile, Ely (Ricci), who likes to blow things up, and her boyfriend Peter (Affleck), have run-ins with the FBI. While the drama — in which hopes and dreams of the residents are explored — is nothing special, the natural performances by the young cast make this minor film worthwhile. As tempers flare, secrets are revealed, and love blossoms in the desert, writer-director Freeman (*Hurricane Streets*) makes things compelling even when they get contrived. ★★★ VHS: $14.99; DVD: $24.99

The Desert Fox

(1951, 88 min, US, Henry Hathaway) *James Mason, Cedric Hardwicke, Jessica Tandy.* A tour de force performance by Mason highlights this standout WWII war drama about Field Marshall Rommel and the Nazi general's defeat in the African campaign. ★★★½ VHS: $19.99

Desert Hearts

(1985, 93 min, US, Donna Deitch) *Helen Shaver, Patrice Charbonneau, Audra Lindley, Gwen Welles.* Truly a landmark film in its positive and very realistic depiction of a love affair between two attractive and intelligent women, offering the viewer a human-scale, tender treatment of two women in love. A dude ranch in Reno, Nevada, in 1959 is the setting for the meeting of an uptight Columbia University professor awaiting her divorce and a free-spirited and openly gay sculptress who lives on the ranch. Shaver and Charbonneau both give warm, expansive performances. ★★★½ VHS: $14.99; DVD: $19.99

The Desert Rats

(1953, 88 min, US, Robert Wise) *Richard Burton, Robert Newton, James Mason.* Mason repeats his role from *The Desert Fox* as Field Marshal Rommel in this exciting WWII actioner. Set in North Africa, Rommel wages a battle of wits with a British commander (Burton) in the Allied offensive at Tobruk. ★★★ VHS: $19.99

Design for Living

(1933, 90 min, US, Ernst Lubitsch) *Miriam Hopkins, Fredric March, Gary Cooper, Edward Everett Horton.* A smart and very funny adaptation of Noël Coward's stage play, substantially rewritten for the screen by Ben Hecht. The story involves three struggling bohemian artists in 1930s Paris. Cooper is a painter, March is a writer, and the enchanting Hopkins is in love with both of them. Even though much of Coward's sexual innuendo has been removed, this is still enjoyable in part to the great lead performances and the director's deft "touch." Horton stands out as Hopkins' fussy cliché-spouting husband. ★★★½

Designing Woman

(1957, 118 min, US, Vincente Minnelli) *Gregory Peck, Lauren Bacall, Mickey Shaughnessy.* This pleasant romantic comedy is reminiscent of *Woman of the Year.* Sportswriter Peck and fashion designer Bacall fall in love and marry while visiting California. Once back in their native New York, however, the honeymoon is over as the mismatched couple must contend with each other's crazy friends, jealous former partners and big city thugs. It's an engaging romp brightened by two star performances, but lacks the depth of the Spencer Tracy-Katharine Hepburn comedies it imitates. The film features (probably) the first choreographed kickboxing scene — by a fey dancer, no less. ★★★ VHS: $19.99

Desire

(1993, 108 min, Canada/France/West Germany, Andrew Birkin) *Greta Scacchi, Vincent D'Onofrio, Claudine Auger.* With its gorgeous multicontinental locales, attractive cast, and the beginnings of a passionate "lost love"-type story, *Desire* starts off with a romantic bang, but slowly peters out into just another repetitive romp in the proverbial sand. Scacchi plays the daughter of European intellectuals who spend their holidays in the Scottish countryside. One summer Scacchi experiences a sexual awakening with farmer/fisherman D'Onofrio. Their subsequent brief encounters haunt Scacchi throughout her marriage, divorce and move to America. ★★ VHS: $89.99

Desire and Hell at Sunset Motel

(1992, 87 min, US, Alien Castle) *Sherilyn Fenn, Whip Hubley, Paul Bartel, David Johansen, David Hewlett.* A bickering young couple (Fenn, Hubley) take a room in a moderately sleazy motel in sun-baked Southern California in 1958. Their contemptuous combat is punctuated with

periods of blackout, flashbacks (flashforwards?), illicit and would-be lovers, a peeping-tom motel manager and a disappearing body in the pool. You won't know who's loyal to whom until the very end. An intriguing look at the dark side of Ozzie and Harriet America. Director Castle also wrote the satisfyingly convoluted script. ★★½ VHS: $19.99

Desire Under the Elms

(1958, 111 min, US, Delbert Mann) *Anthony Perkins, Sophia Loren, Burl Ives.* A curiously uneven but seductive adaptation of Eugene O'Neill's drama. Set in mid-19th-century New England, the film stars Perkins as the son of farmer Ives. He begins an affair with his stepmother (the miscast but alluring Loren). ★★½ VHS: $19.99

Desiree

(1954, 110 min, US, Henry Koster) *Marlon Brando, Jean Simmons, Merle Oberon, Michael Rennie.* A rather muddled costume drama chronicling the love affair between young officer Napoleon and his mistress Desiree. More attention was paid to sets and costumes than historical accuracy, and the film suffers for it. Brando is an animated Napoleon, Simmons is a lovely Desiree, and Oberon is quite stunning as Josephine, but even these talents can't help salvage this production from mediocrity. ★★ VHS: $19.99

Desk Set

(1957, 103 min, US, Walter Lang) *Katharine Hepburn, Spencer Tracy, Joan Blondell, Gig Young.* Tracy and Hepburn, in their eighth film together, are both splendid in this spirited version of the Broadway hit. Kate runs the research department of a TV network; Spence is the efficiency expert whose computer is about to replace her and her staff. And though they're initially at odds, romance ensues. Blondell is particularly snappy in support. ★★★½ VHS: $14.99

Desolation Angels

(1995, 90 min, US, Tim McCann) *Michael Rodrick, Peter Bassett, Jennifer Thomas, Quentin Crisp.* It seems nearly every independent film released these days falls into one of two camps — the touchy-feely twentysomething relationship movie, or the gritty, cynical "this-is-reality" cinema verité. *Desolation Angels,* detailing a working-class man's pursuit of vengeance for the alleged rape of his girlfriend, falls into the latter category. With its constant handheld camerawork, real locations and unpleasant situations, the film aims for harsh realism, and succeeds much of the time. But the two male leads are thinly drawn and uninteresting, and the supporting characters are stock; only Thomas gives a performance of merit. ★★½ VHS: $9.99; DVD: $9.99

Despair

(1978, 119 min, Germany, Rainer Werner Fassbinder) *Dirk Bogarde, Andrea Ferreol, Volker Spengler.* This critically maligned psychological drama, based on Tom Stoppard's adaptation of a Vladimir Nabokov novel, is an interesting, even riveting but ultimately muddled puzzle. Bogarde stars as Russian émigré Hermann Hermann, a 1930s chocolate manufacturer who attempts to elude the Nazis by exchanging identities with a working-class double. The French title, *The Mistake,* might better describe Hermann's unbal-

anced schizoid state of mind when he concocts a plan of murdering his "double," collecting the insurance and then fleeing to Switzerland using the dead man's identity papers. (Filmed in English) ★★½ VHS: $29.99

Desperado

(1995, 106 min, US, Robert Rodriguez) *Antonio Banderas, Salma Hayek, Joaquim de Almeida, Cheech Marin, Steve Buscemi, Quentin Tarantino.* Sophomore director Rodriguez returns to the scene of the crime with this occasionally dazzling sequel to his refreshing low-budget debut, *El Mariachi.* Rodriguez has all the right elements in place: sexy Banderas; a strikingly beautiful yet uncharacteristically strong female lead in Hayek; and a budget for enough pyrotechnics to blow up an entire city block. Sadly, however, *Desperado,* though flawlessly filmed and edited, fails to capture the good-humored slapstick zaniness of its predecessor and commits the sin of taking itself too seriously. Banderas (taking up the role of the Mariachi from the first film) breezes into town seeking vengeance. The ensuing gun battles will stand up proudly against the best of John Woo for their outstanding choreography and bubblegum hilarity. But Rodriguez blows all his ammunition in the first 40 minutes and the remaining hour sees the action become increasingly sporadic and inane. Still, Banderas exudes pure charisma and is a savory pleasure to watch. ★★½ VHS: $9.99; DVD: $19.99

Desperate

(1947, 74 min, US, Anthony Mann) *Steve Brodie, Audrey Long, Raymond Burr.* Refusing to take the rap for a fur heist he was conned into, honest ex-vet Brodie is forced to flee from both the police as well as the thug ringleader (the unsettlingly villainous Burr). His life on the lam is fraught with danger for him and his pregnant wife until he decides to fight back. A taut and engrossing low-budget film noir. ★★★

Desperate Characters

(1971, 88 min, US, Frank D. Gilroy) *Shirley MacLaine, Kenneth Mars, Gerald S. O'Loughlin, Sada Thompson.* As seen through the eyes of the characters of this edgy drama, New York City seems to be a breeding ground of lives of quiet desperation. Addressing burgeoning themes whose topicality have not faded, Gilroy's adaptation of Paula Fox's novel is a moody character study which taps into the white fears of urban living in the early 1970s. The story follows the tedium that is the life of married couple MacLaine and Mars as they eke out a daily existence. That the film is never tedious is as much a credit to director Gilroy's deft touch as it is to the two excellent performances by MacLaine and Mars. ★★★

The Desperate Hours

(1955, 112 min, US, William Wyler) *Humphrey Bogart, Fredric March, Martha Scott, Arthur Kennedy, Gig Young.* A suburban nightmare movie that pre-dates *Blue Velvet.* Bogart is an ex-con who holds a perfect Eisenhower-era family (suit-and-tie dad, doting mom, attractive daughter and precocious young son) hostage in their own home. March is the strong-willed father, afraid for his family's safety, who wages a battle of wits and guts with Bogey. (Remade in 1990) ★★★½ VHS: $14.99

Marlene Dietrich (r.) in *Destry Rides Again*

The Desperate Hours

(1990, 105 min, US, Michael Cimino) *Mickey Rourke, Anthony Hopkins, Lindsay Crouse, Mimi Rogers, Kelly Lynch.* A disappointing remake of the 1955 Humphrey Bogart thriller. Rourke stars as a psychotic who, with the help of his laywer, busts out of jail. They hide out in the house of a recently separated couple (Hopkins, Rogers). Crouse is a tough-talking FBI agent hot on Rourke's tail. Cimino fails to deliver on what could have been a taut little thriller, choosing unwisely to "open" the film up; but he does manage to keep the suspense high and deliver some jarring moments. ★★ VHS: $14.99

Desperate Journey

(1942, 107 min, US, Raoul Walsh) *Errol Flynn, Raymond Massey, Ronald Reagan, Alan Hale.* A rather exciting war adventure which mixes suspense, comedy and patriotism. Flynn plays an Australian commander who leads a group of Allied airmen (including wise-cracking Reagan) on a bombing mission in Germany. When they're shot down over enemy territory, he leads them on a perilous journey across Germany — in between acts of sabotage and imprisonment — to England and freedom. Hale provides the comic relief, and Massey is a relentless Nazi officer on their trail. ★★★ VHS: $19.99

Desperate Living

(1977, 90 min, US, John Waters) *Mink Stole, Edith Massey.* A motion picture malignancy which "spread like cancer in Waters' brain." Stole stars as a society dame who kills her hubby and goes on the lam with her 400-pound black maid Grizelda. They find refuge in Mortville, a haven for perverts, murderers and worse, ruled over by porcine despot Queen Carlotta (Massey). A high-volume, determinedly offensive camp comedy. ★★★ VHS: $19.99

Desperate Measures

(1997, 100 min, US, Barbet Schroeder) *Michael Keaton, Andy Garcia, Brian Cox, Marcia Gay Harden.* Utterly preposterous suspense yarn with Keaton as an imprisoned psycho-killer who just happens to be the sole match for a bone marrow transplant that will save the life of a cop's

(Garcia) 10-year-old son. During the operation, Keaton stages a daring breakout, and the rest of the film is basically a cat-and-mouse chase throughout a hospital. Several pyrotechnic sequences are well-staged and edited, and the climax heats up a bit with an energetic highway chase, but the thrills are canned and the one-liners flat. ★½ VHS: $9.99; DVD: $29.99

Desperate Remedies

(1993, 92 min, New Zealand, Stewart Main & Peter Wells) *Jennifer Ward-Lealand, Cliff Curtis, Kevin Smith.* Campy to an outrageously shameless fault, this deliriously enjoyable and visually explosive costume romp is presented in blinding colors and with a convoluted plot that seems to have combined a dozen Harlequin romance novels. Set in Hope, a rugged 19th-century New Zealand pioneer seaport, the story revolves around the efforts of Doretha (Ward-Lealand), a strong-willed rich girl, and a sneering fop, Fraser (Curtis), to set up her pregnant opium-and-love-addicted sister Anna with the newly arrived but befuddled hunk Lawrence (Smith). The operatic plot soon falls to the background as the heaving breasts, lust-filled eyes and seething passions of all concerned envelop the viewer. A delightful romp that should have all howling with laughter. ★★★ VHS: $7.99

Desperately Seeking Susan

(1985, 104 min, US, Susan Seidelman) *Rosanna Arquette, Madonna, Aidan Quinn, Laurie Metcalf, Steven Wright, Ann Magnuson, John Turturro.* This hip comic adventure stars Arquette as a bored New Jersey housewife thrust into the heart of Greenwich Village bohemianism by a konk on the head. Madonna made her feature film debut as Susan, the free spirit whose life Arquette follows through the personals in *The Village Voice.* ★★★ VHS: $9.99; DVD: $19.99

Destination Tokyo

(1943, 135 min, US, Delmer Daves) *Cary Grant, John Garfield, Alan Hale, Dane Clark.* Grant heads a good cast in this taut WWII submarine tale about the crew whose invasion of mainland Japan laid the groundwork for the aerial strike of Tokyo (for that story, see *Thirty Seconds over*

Tokyo). Though the characters are pure 1940s caricatures of fighting men, the sincerity of the actors portraying them and the solid action and suspense more than compensate. ★★★½ VHS: $19.99

Destiny (al Massir)

(1997, 135 min, Egypt, Youssef Chahine) *Nour el-Cherif, Laila Eloui, Mahmoud Hemeida.* When a disciple of Averroes (a 12th-century philosopher) is burned at the stake for heresy, his young son journeys to Andalusia to study with his father's mentor. There, the teenager becomes involved in romance, adventure, musical dance numbers, and a rip-roaring fight against an evil sheik. The exotic locales, frenzied plot and vibrant storytelling help make this a real discovery and treat. (Letterboxed) (Arabic with English subtitles) ★★★ VHS: $89.99

Destiny Turns on the Radio

(1995, 101 min, US, Jack Baran) *Dylan McDermott, Nancy Travis, James LeGros, James Belushi, Quentin Tarantino, Allen Garfield, Bobcat Goldthwaite, Richard Edson.* Julian (McDermott) breaks out of jail after three years to find out from his partner in crime Thoreau (LeGros) that the money from their bank job is gone and his girl (Travis) has taken up with another (Belushi). Reality is heightened by confluences of chance and predestination; forays into the supernatural can be initiated by filling up the pool, and maintaining a healthy respect for animistic spirits and 20th-century rituals. And everyone agrees that Las Vegas is a town of limitless possibilities — a man can make his mark with a fair degree of patience and a pair of non-conducting rubber-soled boots. The cast is uniformly engaging, and Baran provides some witty directorial touches to the tragically hip script. ★★½ VHS: $9.99

Destry Rides Again

(1939, 94 min, US, George Marshall) *James Stewart, Marlene Dietrich, Brian Donlevy, Mischa Auer.* A gunslinger spoof — with a serious side — starring Stewart as a non-violent sheriff who tames a Wild West town. There's plenty of action, lots of laughs and Dietrich, as a sexy saloon singer, even gets to sing a song or two. ★★★★ VHS: $14.99

Details of a Duel

(1989, 97 min, Argentina, Sergio Cabera) A teacher and a butcher leave home to go about their business of the day, including preparing for death. Contrary to their true nature, one must kill the other by mid-afternoon. Egged on by the clergy, the militia and the town's bureaucrats, the private conflict between the two men is soon escalated into a gladiatorial spectacle. Set in the Argentine Andes in the 1950s, this wry and subtle comedy mischievously exposes the machismo code of honor, a tradition that dictates a duel and possible death — all in the name of manly protocol. (Spanish with English subtitles) ★★★ VHS: $59.99

Detective

(1985, 95 min, France, Jean-Luc Godard) *Claude Brasseur, Nathalie Baye, Johnny Hallyday, Laurent Terzieff, Jean-Pierre Léaud, Julie Delpy.* Another one of Godard's difficult films, *Detective* has all of the hallmarks of the famed French New Wave director's later works: repetitive images, intermittent music and sound, and inscrutable scenes depicting the relationships among art, sex, death and culture. While the twin plotlines have something to do with an unsolved murder, and a couple's attempt to recover money owed to them by a boxing manager, the film is really about stylistic excess and the creation of desire. Godard constantly toys with the audience, occasionally filling the frame with static shots that are nice to look at, but ultimately meaningless. (French with English subtitles) ★★½ VHS: $19.99

The Detective

(1954, 91 min, GB, Robert Hamer) *Alec Guinness, Peter Finch, Joan Greenwood, Cecil Parker.* A sterling adaptation of the G.K. Chesterton novel. Guinness is in masterful form in this lively detective-thriller as the priest-turned-sleuth on the trail of stolen religious artifacts. (aka: *Father Brown*) ★★★ VHS: $19.99

Deterrence

(2000, 104 min, US, Rod Lurie) *Kevin Pollak, Timothy Hutton, Sheryl Lee Ralph, Sean Astin.* Former *L.A. Magazine* film critic Lurie makes a promising directorial debut with this thinking person's thriller that's sort of a cross between *Miracle Mile* and *Fail-Safe*. During a severe snowstorm, the U.S. President (Pollak), a couple of his advisors, and some locals are stranded at a roadside diner in a small Colorado mountain town. While there, the President becomes involved in a showdown with the Iraqi government, a confrontation that could lead to global nuclear war. A one-setting piece, the film is rarely claustrophobic. Instead, Lurie keeps the camera and — for the most part — the story moving. And though the limitations of a one-room setting are apparent, the ensemble is effective in giving a for-the-most-part actionless story the impression of action. ★★½ VHS: $14.99; DVD: $29.99

Detour

(1945, 68 min, US, Edgar C. Ulmer) *Tom Neal, Ann Savage.* Made for almost nothing in only five days by a small-time studio, this film noir classic probes the plight of an "innocent" man trapped in circumstances beyond his control. While hitchhiking across the U.S. to meet his girlfriend in Los Angeles, a man is accused of murder by a tough-talking tomato, who threatens to tell the police if he does not follow her every demand. Entrapped by this increasingly dangerous psychopath, the man must plot his escape. Infused with snappy dialogue, fog-shrouded city streets and a wonderfully evil femme fatale, this dark drama will prove to be a delight for all noir fans. ★★★½ VHS: $24.99; DVD: $24.99

Detroit 9000

(1973, 106 min, US, Arthur Marks) *Alex Rocco, Hari Rhodes, Vonette McGee, Scatman Crothers.* This blaxploitation crime thriller is a moderately entertaining (if overlong) entry in the '70s nostalgic sweepstakes. Rocco plays the "white cop" on a major racially charged case — masked men rob the wealthy (mostly African-American) crowd at a fundraiser for a Detroit politician. He's paired with a black cop (Rhodes) to help smooth things over, and the duo chase suspects, have some shootouts, and wear stylin' clothes. The mastermind is revealed in the beginning, so there's no real suspense, and the story is uneven. But there's some funky music, Rocco's solid

turn, and a few decent action scenes. It can be pretty nifty. ★★½ VHS: $14.99; DVD: $32.99

Detroit Rock City

(1999, 95 min, US, Adam Rifkin) *Edward Furlong, Natasha Lyonne, Sam Huntington, James DeBello.* From the director of *The Chase* comes another rambunctious party suited for late-night basic cable broadcast. Four high school friends head to the Motor City for a Kiss concert in 1978. When they lose their tickets, they go about scoring new ones. *Detroit Rock City* is more about the fans than the band (these over-the-hill musicians appearing as themselves are no more than a cameo), and the humor is gross and silly. The film does have a nice '70s vibe to it, and the credit sequence is kinda cool. ★★ VHS: $14.99; DVD: $19.99

Deuce Bigalow: Male Gigolo

(1999, 88 min, US, Mike Mitchell) *Rob Schneider, William Forsythe, Eddie Griffin, Arija Bareikis, Oded Fehr.* There are some comics for whom it should be unlawful to star in their own films. Tom Arnold is one of these. Rob Schneider is another. The former "Saturday Night Live" comedian actually has made an impression for himself as a comic foil in supporting roles, but carrying an entire film is a whole other matter. Case in point is this horrid little comedy with Schneider as a fish-out-of-water fish-tank cleaner who stumbles into male prostitution — and succeeds! A sardonic, even silly take on male hustling could have been just what the housewife ordered, but the filmmakers have forgotten the first rule of comedy: It's gotta be funny. The jokes are tired, the story ridiculous, and even the dumb-dumber schtick fails to produce even the mildest of groans. ★ VHS: $14.99; DVD: $32.99

Devi

(1960, 96 min, India, Satyajit Ray) *Chhabi Biswas, Sharmila Tagore, Soumitra Chatterjee.* Ray's dreamily sensual film is about a Bengalese girl of astounding beauty who is declared to be a reincarnation of a goddess by her wealthy father-in-law. When he starts a cult of worship in her honor, she gradually becomes convinced of her own divinity. This ironic examination of India's decadent upper classes was banned from export until the intercession of Nehru. (Bengali with English subtitles) ★★★ VHS: $24.99

The Devil and Daniel Webster

(1941, 109 min, US, William Dieterle) *Edward Arnold, Walter Huston, James Craig, Simone Simon.* Terrific screen version of Steven Vincent Benet's novel with Arnold and Huston giving terrific performances as Daniel Webster and Mr. Scratch (aka the Devil), respectively. The famous statesman defends a farmer who has sold his soul. The case is prosecuted by Scratch and the jurors are the cursed from Hell. (aka: *All That Money Can Buy*) ★★★½ VHS: $24.99

The Devil and Max Devlin

(1981, 95 min, US, Steven Hillard Stern) *Elliott Gould, Bill Cosby.* After getting pummeled by a bus, the deceased Max Devlin (Gould) strikes a deal with the Devil (Cosby) to have his life restored if he can convince three people to sell their souls. An unexciting execution of a time-worn premise. ★★ DVD: $24.99

The Devil and Miss Jones

(1941, 92 min, US, Sam Wood) *Charles Coburn, Jean Arthur, Robert Cummings, Edmund Gwenn.* Captivating Capra-esque comedy about a millionaire (Coburn) who goes undercover at his own department store to find out what his disgruntled employees are complaining about. The strength of Norman Krasna's script and the charm of stars Arthur, Cummings and Coburn transcend the clichés and make for a most enjoyable romp. ★★★ VHS: $14.99

The Devil Bat

(1941, 69 min, US, Jean Yarbrough) *Bela Lugosi, Dave O'Brien.* Lugosi charges up his giant bats with electricity and then sics them on people wearing his specially formulated cologne, only to be done in by a father of three wearing too much Old Spice. (Sequel: *The Devil Bat's Daughter*) ★★½ VHS: $12.99

The Devil-Doll

(1936, 79 min, US, Tod Browning) *Lionel Barrymore, Maureen O'Sullivan.* Barrymore has a field day in this fun horror film as a scientist who shrinks humans to the size of dolls to get even with his enemies. ★★★ VHS: $19.99

Devil Girl from Mars

(1954, 77 min, GB, David MacDonald) *Patricia Laffan, Hugh McDermott.* A Scottish inn and its inhabitants are terrorized by a beautiful but ruthless Martian (Laffan) in black leather. One of the first films with aliens seeking Earthlings for breeding stock. ★★ VHS: $14.99; DVD: $24.99

Devil in a Blue Dress

(1995, 102 min, US, Carl Franklin) *Denzel Washington, Tom Sizemore, Jennifer Beals, Don Cheadle.* Washington, that master of subtle characterization, has created another persona rooted in a specific time and place with striking authenticity. Washington is Easy Rawlins (the character in Walter Mosley's books), a WWII vet whose recent unemployment coupled with mortgage payments induces him to agree to DeWitt Albright's (Sizemore) request to locate Daphne Money (Beals). She's an enigmatic beauty publicly tied to a local politico, and she's recently dropped out of sight. Soon Rawlins finds that he's fallen down the rabbit hole. He calls on an old acquaintance for support, Cheadle in a hyperkinetic turn as Mouse, who shoots first and rarely asks questions. Director Franklin has meticulously re-created late 1940s Los Angeles, allowing it to bathe in the golden glow of reminiscence. ★★★½ VHS: $9.99; DVD: $14.99

Devil in the Flesh
(Le Diable au Corps)

(1947, 110 min, France, Claude Autant-Lara) *Gérard Philipe, Micheline Presle.* A beautifully acted and exquisitely filmed tale of the passionate and tragic involvement between a young student and a mature married woman set during World War I. While relatively calm by today's jaded standards, this shocking love story caused quite a controversy when it was first released. (Remade in 1987) (Dubbed) ★★★½ VHS: $34.99

Devil in the Flesh

(1987, 110 min, Italy/France, Marco Bellocchio) *Maruschke Detmers, Federio Pitzalis.* Bellocchio's notorious updating of the classic Maurice

Grace Kelly caught unaware in
Dial M for Murder

Radiquet novel tells the story of a sizzling love triangle among an imprisoned terrorist, his sultry girlfriend, and a teenage boy she lures right from the schoolyard. The themes of political intrigue, betrayal and madness take a back seat to the erotic couplings and explicit oral sex scenes between the sensuous young woman (Detmers), and her handsome, enamored young victim (Pitzalis). The unedited version. (Italian with English subtitles) ★★★

The Devil Is a Woman

(1935, 83 min, US, Josef von Sternberg) *Marlene Dietrich, Cesar Romero, Lionel Atwill, Edward Everett Horton.* Fans of Dietrich and director von Sternberg have long waited for this breathtaker. Its history is marked by legend: The Franco government demanded that every copy be destroyed lest diplomatic ties be strained. Long thought lost, a copy was supplied by Dietrich herself for a 1960s retrospective. Outdoing himself with costumes and sets, von Sternberg tells a rich tale, set during Carnival in Seville, Spain, of love's dark side. An older man (Atwill) recounts his humiliation at the hands of a siren (Dietrich), and warns his young friend (Romero) vainly to save himself from wreckage. Dietrich's beauty and humor and the director's eye for contrast inspire a reverence akin to that which one feels in a great cathedral. ★★★½ VHS: $14.99

The Devil, Probably

(1977, 95 min, France, Robert Bresson) *Antoine Monnier, Tina Irissari, Henri de Maublanc, Laetitia Carcano.* In a world dying from human pollution, young, angelic Charles (Monnier) finds no solace in radical politics, religion, sex, psychology or the arts. Unanchored, he vacillates between two women who love him: Edwige (Carcano), who waits for him stoically, and Alberte (Irissari), who leaves her lover Michel (de Maublanc) to care for the increasingly alienated Charles. His death wish is a microcosm of the planet's unraveling, and the combined support and caring of his friends and lovers have no impact on his downward spiral. Bresson's polemic on the human penchant for self-destruction and inability to commit is kaleidoscopic, visionary; at once frenetic and stilted, energized and stolid, blistering and melancholy. (French with English subtitles) ★★★½ VHS: $29.99

Devil's Advocate

(1997, 140 min, US, Taylor Hackford) *Al Pacino, Keanu Reeves, Charlize Theron, Judith Ivey, Craig T. Nelson, Jeffrey Jones.* Pure pulp fiction here, with Pacino in rabid scene-chewing mode as Lucifer himself. In what amounts to Grisham's *The Firm* on a theological scale, a young hotshot lawyer (Reeves) is seduced by the money and allure of a high-powered New York law firm and discovers that the price for selling out is his soul. This crackerjack thriller is given a boost not only from Pacino's deliciously over-the-top histrionics, but from Hackford's clever direction, a slick production design, some eye-popping special effects, and an effectively creepy musical score. It also helps that just beneath the high-gloss surface, nobody is taking this preposterous fluff too seriously. (Available letterboxed or pan & scan) ★★★ VHS: $14.99; DVD: $24.99

The Devil's Disciple

(1959, 83 min, US, Guy Hamilton) *Burt Lancaster, Kirk Douglas, Laurence Olivier, Harry Andrews, Janette Scott, George Rose.* Lancaster, Douglas and Olivier bring splendor to the words of George Bernard Shaw in this glorious Revolutionary tale based on Shaw's play. Lancaster plays a small-town pastor, indifferent to the war around him, who gets a loud wake-up call to arms when he crosses paths with an American rebel (Douglas) and British General Burgoyne (Olivier). There's wit and vitality to Shaw's clever dialogue: no boring discourse here. The performances of the three actors befit their legendary stature. ★★★½ VHS: $19.99

The Devil's Eye

(1960, 90 min, Sweden, Ingmar Bergman) *Bibi Andersson, Gunnar Björnstrand.* One of Bergman's few comedies, this captivating adaptation of G. B. Shaw's "Don Juan in Hell" begins with the old Irish proverb, which says, "A maid's chastity is a sty in the eye of the Devil." We follow the determined efforts of Satan who, on a promise of reduced time in Hell, sends Don Juan to earth in order to rob the virginity of bride-to-be Andersson. Will the Devil's eye problem clear up, or will human goodness triumph? (Swedish with English subtitles) ★★★ VHS: $29.99

The Devil's Own

(1997, 110 min, US, Alan J. Pakula) *Harrison Ford, Brad Pitt, Margaret Colin, Ruben Blades, Treat Williams, George Hearn.* The teaming of Ford and Pitt works surprisingly well to create an absorbing if somber drama which balances social and moral issues, good action sequences, and an affecting tale of a surrogate father and son. Showing few signs of its high-profile on-set difficulties, *The Devil's Own* casts Pitt as an IRA commander whose latest battle with the British forces him into hiding in America. He is placed with unsuspecting New York cop Ford, and while playing the part of the gracious visitor he is actually preparing a return to Ireland with a boatload of missiles. The strong performances by Ford and Pitt firmly establish their bond of friendship and the sting of its eventual betrayal. The screenplay sometimes looks patchy (it was often written daily), but the overall finished product is sleek and engrossing. ★★★ VHS: $9.99; DVD: $14.99

The Devil's Playground

(1976, 105 min, Australia, Fred Schepisi) *Arthur Dignam, Nick Tate, Simon Burke.* This compelling drama, set in a boys' seminary, probes the torment of young students and their instructors as they grapple with sexual yearning and the harsh codes of religious discipline. The story concerns one particular boy's struggle to deal with both his divine calling and his pent-up sexual needs. A sometimes funny, always hard-hitting indictment of repression. ★★★ VHS: $29.99

The Devil's Wanton

(1949, 78 min, Sweden, Ingmar Bergman) *Doris Svedlund, Eva Henning.* Bergman's sober interpretation of hell on earth, told from the point of view of a girl trying to find happiness with a man who was deserted by his wife after her lover had their baby killed. This arty drama is filled with many of the master's signatures and cinematic techniques. (Swedish with English subtitles) ★★½

The Devils

(1971, 109 min, GB, Ken Russell) *Oliver Reed, Vanessa Redgrave, Dudley Sutton, Gemma Jones, Max Adrian.* Reed is the martyred cleric and Redgrave is the sexually repressed nun in Russell's gruesome and graphic account of witchcraft hysteria in the 17th-century. Both Reed and Redgrave are superb in this frenzied adaptation of Aldous Huxley's book "The Devils of Loudon." Filmed with Russell's usual sobriety and reserve. ★★★½ VHS: $19.99

Diabolically Yours

(1967, 94 min, France, Julien Duvivier) *Alain Delon, Senta Berger.* Rivaling Brigitte Bardot for the title for the greatest number of forgettable, grade-B French films, dashing Delon gives his all in this psycho thriller about a man's desperate search for his sanity. After a near-fatal car accident that left him in a coma for three weeks, Delon awakens to find that his memory is completely lost. Paranoia overwhelms him when he begins to suspect that the woman who claims to be his loving wife, the doctor who is supposed to be his best friend and the relatives who visit are merely staging an elaborate charade in some kind of secret conspiracy to drive him crazy. (Dubbed) ★★½ VHS: $59.99

Diabolique (Les Diaboliques)

(1954, 107 min, France, Henri-Georges Clouzot) *Simone Signoret, Vera Clouzot, Paul Meurisse, Michel Serrault.* This white-knuckled thriller is set in a shabby boys' school and stars Signoret as a battered mistress who plots a murder with her lover's wife (Clouzot). In grisly fashion, they drug the husband, drown him in the tub and dump the corpse in a pool. But mysteriously, the body disappears and evidence of their crime begins to haunt them. The heart-stopping climax and twist ending will have you on the edge of your seat. (aka: *The Fiends*) (American remake: *Diabolique*) (French with English subtitles) ★★★★ VHS: $29.99; DVD: $29.99

Diabolique

(1996, 105 min, US, Jeremiah C. Chechik) *Sharon Stone, Isabelle Adjani, Chazz Palminteri, Kathy Bates, Spalding Gray, Shirley Knight.* An inferior, lifeless remake of the 1954 classic French thriller. Stone and Adjani are teachers at a boarding school who plot and kill Adjani's tyrannical husband (Palminteri), the school's headmaster. They get away with it, but when the body turns up missing, it appears he may not be dead.

Michelle Williams (l.) and Kirsten Dunst expose tricky *Dick*

Bates adds a little life as a detective investigating the disappearance. Not even a '90s bent on the two women's sexual relationship makes this of interest. ★½ VHS: $19.99; DVD: $19.99

Dial M for Murder

(1954, 105 min, US, Alfred Hitchcock) *Grace Kelly, Ray Milland, Robert Cummings, John Williams.* Kelly is the rich and beautiful wife of the diabolical Milland. He hires a hit man to bump her off, but she kills the would-be assassin and faces the electric chair. In his inimitable fashion, Hitchcock forces the culprit husband to reveal his guilt. (Originally filmed in 3-D) (Remade as: *A Perfect Murder*) ★★★ VHS: $14.99

Diamonds Are Forever

(1971, 119 min, GB, Guy Hamilton) *Sean Connery, Jill St. John, Charles Gray, Jimmy Dean.* Connery returns for his next-to-last appearance as 007. His mission: to track down a diamond smuggler; which, of course, requires a whirlwind, world-wide adventure through Amsterdam, Los Angeles and Las Vegas. Lots of fun. (Sequel: *Live and Let Die*) ★★★ VHS: $9.99; DVD: $26.99

Diary of a Chambermaid

(1946, 86 min, US, Jean Renoir) *Paulette Goddard, Burgess Meredith, Judith Anderson, Hurd Hatfield.* This bewitching but distinctively odd adaptation of the Octave Mirbeau novel was one of Renoir's last films made during his sojourn in Hollywood during the war. Coproduced and scripted by Meredith, this romantic comedy stars Goddard as the keyhole-peeping, gold-digging chambermaid whose arrival at a provincial mansion brings havoc to its decadent inhabitants. The films features Meredith as an eccentric, flower-eating neighbor, and Anderson as the matriarch of the household who rules with an iron fist. Though not as bitterly savage as the Luis Buñel version, Renoir's film is still sharp in its satire of the upper classes. ★★½ VHS: $14.99

Diary of a Chambermaid

(1964, 79 min, France, Luis Buñuel) *Jeanne Moreau, Michel Piccoli, Georges Geret.* Moreau stars as a reserved and well-cultured woman from Paris who begins to work for an upper-class family in the Provinces in 1939. The new maid soon

discovers that the family is a thoroughly decadent group of characters as she finds herself enmeshed in the midst of a hotbed of hypocrisy and perversion. Their seemingly innocuous habits, like the grandfather's foot fetish, prove to be not-so-harmless when a young girl is found murdered and Moreau becomes obsessed with exposing the killer. Buñuel's sly comic touches are in evidence, but the film retains a biting edge as he equates the gentry's oppression with the rise of fascism. (French with English subtitles) ★★★½ VHS: $29.99; DVD: $29.99

Diary of a Country Priest

(1950, 120 min, France, Robert Bresson) *Claude Layou, Jean Riveyre.* Bresson's uniquely austere style of filmmaking is beautifully rendered in this somber work on the life and death of a young priest and his unsuccessful attempts to minister his first parish. (French with English subtitles) ★★★½ VHS: $39.99

Diary of a Hitman

(1991, 90 min, US, Roy London) *Forest Whitaker, Sherilyn Fenn, James Belushi, Seymour Cassel.* Though miscast, Whitaker makes a good showing as a hit man who studiously saves the earnings from his murderous profession for a down payment on his co-op apartment. Fenn is a drug-addicted cheerleader wannabe who stands in Whitaker's way for one last completed assignment. An intriguing premise executed with style, and it's fairly suspenseful. ★★★ VHS: $14.99

Diary of a Lost Girl

(1929, 100 min, Germany, G.W. Pabst) *Louise Brooks, Fritz Rasp.* The alluring and enigmatic Brooks stars in this parable of a woman's road to ruin. Brooks is a wronged innocent who is banished from respectability for having a baby out of wedlock. Forced to live in a hellish house of correction, she escapes only to land in a brothel where she finds her ultimate redemption. (Silent with musical soundtrack) ★★★½ VHS: $24.99

Diary of a Mad Housewife

(1970, 94 min, US, Frank Perry) *Carrie Snodgress, Richard Benjamin, Frank Langella.* A perceptive study of housewife Snodgress' psychological deterioration at the hands of social climbing, philandering husband Benjamin and charmingly ego-

centric writer Langella, with whom she has a brief, tempestuous affair. Superb performance by Snodgress and good support from Langella. ★★★

Diary of a Mad Old Man

(1987, 90 min, France/Belgium, Ralph Michael) *Derek De Lint, Ralph Michael, Beatie Edney.* This Ingmar Bergman-influenced drama is a tepid examination of an old man as he nears the end of his life. Marcel is a rich and self-absorbed businessman who forsakes the love of his devoted wife for a never-consummated sexual obsession with his son's attractive wife. The indignities of the aging process do not stop him from pursuing the young woman, even at the expense of his family and health. For a better look at an old man's reflection on his nearly completed life, watch *Wild Strawberries.* (Filmed in English) ★½

Diary of a Seducer

(1995, 95 min, France, Daniele Dubroux) *Chiara Mastroianni, Jean-Pierre Léaud, Melvil Poupaud.* A near-deadly boring film, *Diary of a Seducer* derives its plot from a magic book that forces its readers to fall in love with the giver. While this story line has the potential for a *La Ronde*-type of farce, writer-director Dubroux shuns this approach and instead labors to feature bizarre characters and a dead body. These elements would have benefitted from a subversive touch á la Buñuel, but Dubroux opts for a too-cool tone. When Claire (Marcello's daughter Chiara) is given the Kierkegaard book of the title by Gregoire (Poupaud), she becomes entranced by him. Meanwhile, various acquaintances, including her therapist, develop an interest in Claire. There are the inevitable misunderstandings, but there is no real tension among the characters or their predicaments. *Diary of a Seducer* is billed as a comic thriller, but it is neither funny nor thrilling. And what's more, it's not even seductive. (French with English subtitles) ★★ VHS: $79.99

The Diary of Anne Frank

(1959, 156 min, US, George Stevens) *Millie Perkins, Joseph Schildkraut, Shelley Winters, Ed Wynn, Richard Beymer, Lou Jacobi.* One of the most gripping and heartfelt stories to emerge from the Holocaust, this magnificent adaptation of the acclaimed play is based on the writings of Dutch teenager Anne Frank, whose diaries documenting years of hiding during WWII captured the hearts of millions around the world. Perkins deftly plays Anne, who hid with her family in the attic of an Amsterdam warehouse to elude the Nazis. A superior supporting cast (including Oscar winner Winters). *Diary* is a testament to individual courage and a bitter history lesson we should never forget. ★★★★ VHS: $14.99

Diary of Forbidden Dreams

(1972, 94 min, Italy, Roman Polanski) *Marcello Mastroianni, Sydne Rome.* Originally titled *What?*, this Polanski oddity is a ribald comedy about the sexual misadventures of an innocent but irresistible young woman. Her bizarre ordeal begins when she seeks shelter in an eccentric's mansion on the Italian Riviera. Her docile host turns lecherous tiger — but that only opens up a can of sexual worms as several other weird men descend for a bite. Funny and just a bit strange. ★★½

Dick

(1999, 92 min, US, Andrew Fleming) *Kirsten Dunst, Michelle Williams, Dan Hedaya, Will Ferrell, Bruce McCulloch, Teri Garr, Dave Foley, Jim Breuer, Harry Shearer, Saul Rubinek.* "Muckraking bastard journalists" Bob Woodward and Carl Bernstein won a Pulitzer Prize for breaking the Watergate scandal, relying heavily on a source named "Deep Throat." But who was this source? According to *Dick*, it was two 15-year-old girls who were in the wrong place at the right time. This theory is not Oliver Stone's however; as directed by Fleming, it is given a light, even cute satirical touch that hits lots of easy targets without saying anything deep. Dunst and Williams, making a winning couple, witness the burglary at the hotel and later see paper shredding and even Dick's recording system (on which Williams leaves an 18½-minute love paean to him). They're kind of the Forrest Gumps of Watergate. Anyone familiar with the scandal will enjoy the references, but the jokes are predictable, until the film thuds to an ending with a labored *Dick* joke. ★★½ VHS: $9.99; DVD: $24.99

Dick Tracy

(1990, 104 min, US, Warren Beatty) *Warren Beatty, Al Pacino, Dustin Hoffman, Glenne Headly, Madonna.* Beatty's colorful adaptation of the Chester Gould comic strip is a dazzling display of costumery and scenery. The performances in the film are, for the most part, splendid. Pacino's rendition of Tracy's arch-rival Big Boy Caprice is sensational. In the title role, Beatty delivers an appropriately heroic performance; Headly is charming as his girlfriend Tess Trueheart; and Madonna gets to sing a couple of breathy show tunes penned by the inimitable Stephen Sondheim, and all of her other attributes are used to perfection. A highly entertaining romp — maybe now we can forget about *Ishtar*. ★★★

Die! Die! My Darling!

(1965, 97 min, GB, Silvio Narizzano) *Tallulah Bankhead, Stephanie Powers, Peter Vaughan, Donald Sutherland.* The legendary Bankhead stars in this campy *Baby Jane*-style thriller about a psychotic old woman who keeps her son's fiancée (Powers) hostage in her attic. Screenplay by Richard Matheson. (aka: *Fanatic*) ★★½ VHS: $9.99

Die Hard

(1988, 132 min, US, John McTiernan) *Bruce Willis, Bonnie Bedelia, Alan Rickman, Alexander Godunov, Reginald Vel Johnson, Hart Bochner, William Atherton.* First-rate action thriller starring Willis as a tough New York City policeman whose L.A. vacation is cut short when he finds himself — armed only with his wits — up against a group of terrorists who have taken control of a 40-story office building, among whose hostages include his wife. The action scenes are extremely well-directed and maximize suspense, and Willis' cynical cop is afforded some great one-liners as he battles the bad guys. (Followed by two sequels) (Letterboxed VHS available for $19.99) ★★★½ VHS: $14.99; DVD: $29.99

Die Hard 2

(1990, 122 min, US, Renny Harlin) *Bruce Willis, Bonnie Bedelia, William Atherton, Franco Nero, John Amos, Reginald Vel Johnson, John Leguizamo, Robert Patrick.* Willis is back in this fast-paced pyrotechnic sequel. This time, he's at Dulles Airport in Washington, D.C. waiting for his wife (Bedelia) to land, when the place is taken over by a mercenary commando squad trying to hijack a Noriega-like dictator to safety. Not as tense, or as comprehensible, as the first film, but the large scale special effects and stunt work are amazing and the film packs a visceral jolt. (Letterboxed VHS available for $19.99) ★★★ VHS: $14.99; DVD: $29.99

Die Hard with a Vengeance

(1995, 112 min, US, John McTiernan) *Bruce Willis, Samuel L. Jackson, Jeremy Irons, Graham Greene, Colleen Camp.* Willis' New York City cop John McClane gets to play on his home turf in this action-packed if derivative third entry. McClane is called into a terrorist bombing case when the brother of one of McClane's victims is out for revenge by playing cat-and-mouse all over the city with our hapless hero. Before you can say *Lethal Weapon*, McClane is partnered with a Harlem store owner (Jackson) who is now forced to help track down the bomber. *With a Vengeance* features some extraordinary action sequences; but even in light of the likable pairing of Willis and Jackson, the film has less to offer than the first two. (VHS available letterboxed or pan & scan) ★★½ VHS: $19.99; DVD: $29.99

Different for Girls

(1996, 97 min, GB, Richard Spence) *Rupert Graves, Steven Mackintosh, Miriam Margolyes, Saskia Reeves, Charlotte Coleman.* An endearing, highly enjoyable and offbeat romantic transgender comedy. Paul (Graves, who played Scudder in *Maurice*) and Karl (Mackintosh) were childhood best friends. Separated after nearly 20 years, they meet up again in London. But things have changed a bit: Karl has undergone a sex change operation and is now called Kim. She is organized and genteel, with a career as a writer in a greeting card company. Paul has become a rebellious character, working as a motorcycle courier by day and a pub crawler at night. How they overcome society's prejudices and, more importantly, their own differences, is executed in a breezy, refreshingly warm fashion. ★★★ VHS: $14.99; DVD: $19.99

A Different Story

(1978, 108 min, US, Paul Aaron) *Perry King, Meg Foster, Valerie Curtin.* A gay man (King) and a lesbian (Foster) marry to prevent his deportation, and then fall in love, have kids and go straight — each surrendering his/her sexual identity. The film uses the gay subtext simply as a gimmick, dwelling little on their original sexual orientation and more on their affair. Curtin is shrill and offensive as Foster's former lover; some of the other characters are merely stereotypes, as well. Addressing the sexual politics, the film is questionable in the notion that queers can be cured with a good heterosexual fuck. Politics aside, it's just not funny. ★½

Digging to China

(1998, 103 min, US, Timothy Hutton) *Kevin Bacon, Mary Stuart Masterson, Cathy Moriarty, Evan Rachel Wood.* Sentimental without being cloying, *Digging to China* is the fine directorial debut by actor Hutton, who coaxes a wonderful lead performance from young Wood. Harriet, a loquacious 10-year-old who marches to the beat of a different drummer, lives in a North Carolina cabin lodge operated by her mother (Moriarty) and her older sister Gwen (Masterson). Constantly dreaming of escape, Harriet meets Ricky (Bacon), a mentally retarded man, she finds a co-conspirator for her projects. Their adventures allow them some control over their lives, but fearing more than just friendship, Gwen tries to keep them apart. The screenplay, by Karen Janszen, intelligently addresses the way love can overcome grief, though the film is only slightly marred when the drama and Bacon's performance feel forced. ★★★ VHS: $9.99; DVD: $9.99

Diggstown

(1992, 98 min, US, Michael Ritchie) *James Woods, Louis Gossett, Jr., Oliver Platt, Bruce Dern, Heather Graham.* Woods offers a sturdy performance in this familiar but likable Runyon-esque comedy about a grifter par excellence, his semi-retired partner (Gossett), and their screwball scheme to swindle an entire town. Though not as intricately plotted as *The Sting*, nor as stylish, the film offers good performances and some nice action sequences. ★★½ VHS: $6.99; DVD: $14.99

Dim Sum: A Little Bit of Heart

(1984, 89 min, US, Wayne Wang) *Laureen Chew, Kim Chew, Victor Wong, Joan Chen.* Once again, director Wang reveals the communality of human experience through a sharply focused examination of a distinctive culture. The relationship between a Chinese-American mother and daughter is central to this warm observation of the familial bonds and cultural strengths of an Asian family in San Francisco. ★★★

Diner

(1982, 110 min, US, Barry Levinson) *Kevin Bacon, Steve Guttenberg, Daniel Stern, Mickey Rourke, Ellen Barkin, Timothy Daly, Paul Reiser, Michael Tucker.* A scintillating slice-of-life served with a sprinkling of '50s nostalgia and a robust helping of male camaraderie. Levinson has created one of the most charming and humorous documentations of the often awkward transition from youth to adulthood. Impeccable ensemble acting. ★★★★ VHS: $14.99; DVD: $19.99

Dinner at Eight

(1933, 111 min, US, George Cukor) *Lionel Barrymore, Billie Burke, John Barrymore, Marie Dressler, Wallace Beery, Jean Harlow, Edmund Lowe.* An all-star cast highlights this elegant Cukor classic based on George S. Kaufman and Edna Ferber's stage hit. Park Avenue shipping magnate Barrymore and his social-climbing wife Burke throw a dinner party for a visiting British lord. On the guest list are fading screen idol Barrymore (before his own decline); aging stage legend Dressler; and obnoxious financier Beery and his blowsy wife Harlow. How their lives and problems intertwine is the stuff that great moviemaking is made of. Dressler and Harlow steal the show. (Remade in 1996) ★★★★ VHS: $19.99

The Dinner Game

(1999, 81 min, France, Francis Veber) *Thierry Lhermitte, Jacques Villeret, Francis Huster, Catherine Frot.* In this biting French comedy, a group of friends meet each week for a dinner party in which each tries to bring the most boring dinner guest. When Pierre thinks he has a winner in unsuspecting accountant François, the tables are soon turned on the unsuspecting Pierre as he can't get rid of François no matter how hard he tries. Hilarious jokes and sight gags punctuate this subversive gem. (French with English subtitles) ★★★½ VHS: $14.99; DVD: $24.99

D

Dinosaur

(2000, 82 min, US, Eric Leighton & Ralph Zondag) *Voices of: D.B. Sweeney, Julianna Margulies, Joan Plowright, Ossie Davis, Alfre Woodard, Della Reese*. Cool computer animation of dinosaurs trying to avoid the effects of a meteor crashing into the Earth highlight this uneven animated rip-off of *Land Before Time*. Since it's a Disney film, the dinos talk (though don't sing), and band with lemurs to save themselves from extinction while on a march to their breeding ground. Unfortunately, the $125 million movie is at the service of a 98¢ script, a clichéd road movie that goes nowhere new. ★★ VHS: $26.99; DVD: $39.99

Diplomaniacs

(1933, 63 min, US, William A. Seiter) *Bert Wheeler, Robert Woolsey, Marjorie White*. The comedy team of Wheeler and Woolsey star in one of their best comic outings, a totally crazy and hilarious romp (in every sense of the word) as barbers on an Indian reservation, being mistaken for diplomats and sent to Geneva to attend a peace conference. Silly and quite enjoyable fun. ★★★ VHS: $19.99

El Diputado (The Deputy)

(1979, 110 min, Spain, Eloy de la Iglesia) *Jose Sacristan, Maria Luisa San Jose, Jose Alonso*. This highly praised and powerful thriller follows the political and sexual coming out of a young married politician in post-Franco Spain. A Congressman's repressed homosexual desires are awakened while serving a brief prison term for a political matter. After a first encounter, he furtively seeks out sexual partners until he falls in love with a 16-year-old street hustler. The film deals with the delicate balance between his life, his loving wife and his political goals. (Spanish with English subtitles) ★★★ VHS: $59.99

Directed by Andrei Tarkovsky

(1988, 105 min, USSR, Michel Leszcylowski) This "investigative" documentary into the life and works of the Soviet Union's greatest modern director was produced by the Swedish Film Institute and directed by Tarkovsky's longtime friend and editor Leszcylowski. Filmed in Sweden during the making of his final feature, *The Sacrifice*, and while he was gravely ill with cancer, the film attempts to capture, through interviews and footage from his films, the essence behind this brooding intellectual genius. ★★★ VHS: $29.99; DVD: $39.99

Dirty Dancing

(1987, 105 min, US, Emile Ardolino) *Patrick Swayze, Jennifer Grey, Jerry Orbach, Cynthia Rhodes, Jack Weston*. This sleeper hit of 1987 is a wonderfully nostalgic coming-of-age tale set in a Catskill Mountains resort in 1963. Swayze became a star thanks to his role as the handsome dance instructor who becomes involved with innocent teenager Grey. Some good dancing and golden oldies highlight the film. ★★★ VHS: $14.99; DVD: $29.99

Dirty Dishes

(1982, 99 min, France, Joyce Buñuel) *Carol Laurie, Pierre Santini*. After ten years of cooking, cleaning and taking care of her husband, a housewife's life has become so dulled by these domestic chores that even an affair with a younger man and other incidents cannot seem to break her out of her crazed boredom. A deceptively comic *Diary of a Mad Housewife*. The director is Luis Buñuel's daughter-in-law. (French with English subtitles) ★★★

The Dirty Dozen

(1967, 150 min, US, Robert Aldrich) *Lee Marvin, Charles Bronson, John Cassavetes, Donald Sutherland, Robert Ryan, Ernest Borgnine, George Kennedy, Telly Savalas, Jim Brown*. Classic WWII adventure with Marvin leading 12 condemned prisoners on a daring raid of a Nazi stronghold. Not a dull moment in its two-and-a-half hours, the first half of the film follows the rigorous training the men go through, and the second covers the cracker-jack assault. (VHS available letterboxed or pan & scan) ★★★½ VHS: $14.99; DVD: $19.99

Dirty Hands

(1976, 102 min, France/Italy/Germany, Claude Chabrol) *Romy Schneider, Rod Steiger, Paoli Giusti, Jean Rochefort*. Chabrol, France's master of the suppressed but always torrid urges and desires of the bourgeoisie, directed this familiar though atmospheric tale of treachery, murder and mystery. A woman and her lover plot to murder her husband — but with unexpected results. ★★

Dirty Harry

(1971, 103 min, US, Don Siegel) *Clint Eastwood, Harry Guardino, Andy Robinson, John Vernon*. The first of Eastwood's *Dirty Harry* series is a classic action-thriller. In this flavorful and exciting police story, Harry Callahan chases after a psychopathic rooftop sniper. (Sequel: *Magnum Force*) ★★★ VHS available letterboxed or pan & scan) ★★★ VHS: $14.99; DVD: $19.99

Dirty Rotten Scoundrels

(1988, 110 min, US, Frank Oz) *Michael Caine, Steve Martin, Glenne Headly, Barbara Harris*. Caine and Martin make an unlikely but very funny and effective comic duo in this hilarious yarn about a couple of con men competing for control of a town on the French Riviera. Caine is superb as the established swindler who masquerades as a deposed prince. When rival Martin (who is in his element as the rude and crude American) lands on the scene, Caine is faced with a serious challenge to the control of his turf, where the two become enmeshed in a wacky series of attempts to outscheme each other. Headly more than holds her own as their mutual target. (Remake of 1962's *Bedtime Stories*) ★★★½ VHS: $9.99

Dirty Work

(1998, 82 min, US, Bob Saget) *Norm Macdonald, Jack Warden, Artie Lange, Christopher McDonald, Chevy Chase, Don Rickles, Adam Sandler, Chris Farley*. Dirty work, indeed. The only serious problem with this movie is dealing with Norm Macdonald being on-screen for about eighty-two minutes. As a TV comic-type, Macdonald gets his smart-ass stream-of-consciousness shtick to work in little five-minute bits — but in his own movie? Yikes. Basically, wacky stuff happens to Norm and fat-guy sidekick Lange when they open a Revenge-for-Hire business. The jokes are all Norm's and they all seem to be related to his "note to self" mini tape-recorder bit from "Saturday Night Live." The funniest bits then become the numerous cameos like Sandler (as Satan) and Farley. Unless you're into this sort of thing, let someone else watch it for you. ★½ VHS: $14.99; DVD: $24.99

The Disappearance of Garcia Lorca

(1997, 113 min, US/Spain, Marcos Zurinaga) *Andy Garcia, Esai Morales, Edward James Olmos, Jeroen Krabbe, Giancarlo Giannini, Miguel Ferrer*. Poet Federico Garcia Lorca was one of the first victims of Franco's fascist regime, which took power after winning the Spanish Civil War in 1939. *The Disappearance of Garcia Lorca* follows a journalist who returns to his boyhood home in Spain to uncover the mystery surrounding the death of Lorca, whose writings and homosexuality branded him as a subversive by the government. The cast, including Olmos and Ferrer, is uniformly good, but it is Garcia's stand-out performance as Lorca which elevates the film. Morales portrays Ricardo Gonzales, the journalist who idolized Lorca as a child and who ignores the countless threats in his quest for the truth. The flashbacks are confusing at times, but overall, the film is compelling. (Filmed in English) ★★★ VHS: $24.99

The Disappearance of Kevin Johnson

(1995, 105 min, US, Francis Megahy) *Michael Brandon, Pierce Brosnan, James Coburn, Dudley Moore, Kari Wuhrer*. If you thought *The Player* was a hoot, this mockumentary is just what the doctor ordered: a dark, witty Hollywood biz satire with some interesting curves to boot. A TV crew from England working on a documentary on Brits living in L.A. discovers that Kevin Johnson, a millionaire British film producer, has mysteriously disappeared. Led by an anonymous, off-screen filmmaker-narrator, the TV crew decides to find out what happened to Johnson. While writer-director Megahy has lots of fun with this premise, aping real-life documentarian Nick Broomfield's *Heidi Fleiss: Hollywood Madam* with his accent and persistent, probing questions, he relies a little too much on talking heads to supply the story's information. Still, anyone who reads *Variety* on a regular basis or has surfed the Ain't It Cool News website should enjoy watching Tinseltown jerks get theirs one more time. ★★★ VHS: $79.99

Disclosure

(1994, 128 min, US, Barry Levinson) *Michael Douglas, Demi Moore, Donald Sutherland, Dennis Miller, Caroline Goodall, Roma Maffia*. Douglas, the self-appointed spokesman for the victimized white heterosexual male, is cast as such once again as a successful computer engineer and all-around good guy who is sexually harassed by his new boss and ex-flame Moore. She in turn brings charges against him. Thus sets in motion a battle to prove his innocence. Forgetting the obvious complaint of a female aggressor in Hollywood's first film about sexual harassment, there are other points that make *Disclosure* an irritating piece of trash. Though slickly made by Levinson, the film is a cheap sleight of hand which is no more about harassment than *Philadelphia* is about AIDS. Lacking the courage of its convictions, the film is ultimately about corporate intrigue, and even then misses the mark as a biting indictment. ★★ VHS: $9.99; DVD: $19.99

The Discreet Charm of the Bourgeoisie

(1972, 100 min, France, Luis Buñuel) *Fernando Rey, Delphine Seyrig, Jean-Pierre Cassel, Bulle Ogier,*

Diva

Michel Piccoli, Stéphane Audran. A witty anarchistic social comedy about six upper-crust Parisians and their unsuccessful attempts to dine in a civilized manner. Buñuel's sardonic statement on the amoral world of the ruling class. (Letterboxed) (French with English subtitles) ★★★★ VHS: $29.99; DVD: $39.99

The Disenchanted
(La Désenchantée)
(1990, 78 min, France, Benoit Jacquot) *Judith Godreche, Marcel Bozonnet.* Slight but not uninteresting, *The Disenchanted* concerns the 17-year-old Beth (Godreche) as she grapples with her sexuality. This sparse, not entirely revealing character study opens with Beth's boyfriend challenging her to sleep with ugly men, and ends with Beth being the unwilling object of a sugar daddy's attention. In between, she meets A.D. (Bozonnet), a potential suitor who forces her to reevaluate her feelings and goals in life. Writer-director Jacquot deliberately keeps the drama subtle, but the tension is often quite palpable. The lovely Godreche gives a finely nuanced performance, but the film is detached and uninvolving, and this moodiness casts a pall over the entire film. (French with English subtitles) ★★½ VHS: $24.99; DVD: $29.99

Dish Dogs
(1998, 96 min, US, Robert Kubilos) *Sean Astin, Brian Dennehy, Matthew Lillard, Shannon Elizabeth.* Astin's winning performance is the sole saving grace of this mostly uninvolving comedy about a philosophy-spouting "career dishwasher" who is unwilling to let anything — even a beautiful stripper (Elizabeth) — interfere with his quest for spiritual "epiphany." Lillard puts in his usual overbearing act as the best friend who gives it all up for love, and Dennehy has a limited role as the boys' mentor. Released in time to cash in on the *American Pie* craze. ★★ VHS: $69.99; DVD: $24.99

The Disorderly Orderly
(1964, 90 min, US, Frank Tashlin) *Jerry Lewis, Glenda Farrell, Kathleen Freeman.* Lewis is a young practicing med student who seems to have more of a flair for comedy than healing (unless you believe in the healing power of laughter). ★★★ VHS: $14.99

Disorganized Crime
(1989, 101 min, US, Jim Kouf) *Lou Diamond Phillips, Fred Gwynne, Corbin Bernsen, Ruben Blades, William Russ.* Disorganized comedy about a group of small-time criminals who attempt the ultimate heist, but who are faced with a few problems, such as the loss of their leader and no plan whatsoever. ★★

Disraeli
(1929, 87 min, US, Alfred E. Green) *George Arliss, Florence Arliss, Joan Bennett.* Arliss, such a distinguished actor of his day that in this film he is billed "Mr. George Arliss," won a much-deserved Best Actor Oscar for recreating his legendary Broadway performance. This intelligent if stagey adaptation centers on England's Jewish Prime Minister of the late 19th century and his efforts to secure the Suez Canal for Britain — which includes going head-to-head with Russian spies and anti-Semitism. Arliss' wife Florence is ideally cast as Disraeli's spouse. Arliss had played the role once before in a 1921 silent. ★★★½ VHS: $19.99

Distant Thunder
(1973, 92 min, India, Satyajit Ray) *Soumitra Chatterjee, Sandhya Roy.* Set in a remote village in Bengal during the outbreak of WWII, this harsh and vividly filmed story chronicles the lives of several families when the area is shaken by a famine and their world is disastrously uprooted. A riveting drama of great scope and power. (Hindi with English subtitles) ★★★½ VHS: $39.99

Distant Thunder
(1988, 114 min, US, Rick Rosenthal) *John Lithgow, Ralph Macchio, Janet Margolin.* An emotionally scarred Vietnam vet (Lithgow) leaves his secluded life in Washington's rain forest to see the son (Macchio) he hasn't seen in fifteen years. Lithgow's sensitive performance can't offset the sentimental melodramatics and clichéd characterizations. ★★ VHS: $14.99

Distant Voices, Still Lives
(1988, 85 min, GB, Terence Davies) *Freda Dowie, Pete Postlethwaite, Angela Walsh.* Davies' autobiographical and unblinking account of a family's oppressive lifestyle in pre- and post-war England.

A timeworn photo album on film, the story traces the adolescence of Davies and his older sisters struggling to mature despite their abusive father's tyranny; and also the grown children's disenchantment, told through song at the local pub. *Distant Voices, Still Lives* is a passionate and rich film. ★★★½ VHS: $89.99

The Distinguished Gentleman
(1993, 112 min, US, Jonathan Lynn) *Eddie Murphy, Sheryl Lee Ralph, Joe Don Baker, Lane Smith, Grant Shaud.* More homogenized humor from former four-letter-wordsmith Murphy. This time out he tackles the role of a grifter who scams his way into Congress in search of streets paved with gold, only to discover that he has a heart of gold himself. Awww, shucks. It's pretty funny, though, even without the profanity. ★★½ DVD: $29.99

Le Distrait (The Daydreamer)
(1978, 101 min, France, Pierre Richard) *Pierre Richard, Bernard Blier, Maris-Christine Barrault.* Richard continues his bungling and frantically funny misadventures in this Gallic farce about an ad executive who just can't keep fantasy away from reality. Richard himself directed this funny escapade. (French with English subtitles) ★★★

Disturbing Behavior
(1998, 84 min, US, David Nutter) *James Marsden, Katie Holmes, Nick Stahl, Bruce Greenwood, William Sadler. Disturbing Behavior* is an underachieving thriller that is, at best, a passable adolescent tragic melodrama. A mildly dysfunctional family, recovering from the suicide of their 11-year-old son and brother, move to the all-American town of Cradle Bay. Before you can say *The Stepford Wives,* our teen heroes discover a bizarre conspiracy by the adults to turn their rebellious kids into obedient, scholarly model citizens. While hardly original, the premise is at least intriguing, though more certainly could have been expected. Last-minute studio cuts may be to blame for the lack of coherence and character motivation. ★★ VHS: $9.99; DVD: $19.99

Diva
(1981, 123 min, France, Jean-Jacques Beineix) *Wilhemina Fernandez, Frederic Andrei, Richard Bohringer, Dominique Pinon.* Beineix's stunning film debut is a dashing, eclectic adventure that shimmers with style and humor. The unpredictable escapades begin when a young postal messenger secretly tapes the performance of a determinedly unrecorded operatic star. The chase begins when he flees from a skinhead punk, a pair of inescapable Taiwanese record pirates, and the police. A rapturous thriller that is an amalgam of pop culture paraphernalia, B-movie clichés and prodigious flair. (French with English subtitles) ★★★½ VHS: $9.99; DVD: $24.99

Dive Bomber
(1941, 130 min, US, Michael Curtiz) *Errol Flynn, Fred MacMurray, Ralph Bellamy.* A dashing young Navy flight doctor (Flynn) attempts to discover a way to prevent "pilot blackout" at the end of a powerdive. MacMurray and Bellamy are a veteran pilot and chief flight doctor, respectively. Their interaction with Flynn is good, but this film follows conventions like there's no tomorrow. Spectacular aerial photography highlight an otherwise solid by-the-numbers film. ★★★ VHS: $19.99

Divine Madness

(1980, 95 min, US, Michael Ritchie) *Bette Midler.* La Belle Bette, the Divine Miss Midler, in concert. No joke is too cheap, no gag too crass as evidenced by the raunchy stage performance of Bette and her Harlettes. And she sings, too. There is no other, why should there be? ★★★ VHS: $14.99; DVD: $14.99

The Divine Nymph

(1979, 90 min, Italy, G.P. Griffi) *Laura Antonelli, Marcello Mastroianni, Terence Stamp.* This sexy romp features Laura Antonelli as a young and sensuous woman who becomes involved in a tragic love triangle with Mastroianni and Stamp. A predictable story of decadence, obsession and deception. ★★

Divorce — Italian Style

(1961, 104 min, Italy, Pietro Germi) *Marcello Mastroianni, Daniela Rocco.* Mastroianni is pure magic in this frantic satire on love and marriage — the first, and best, of the Italian sex comedies of the 1960s. Mastroianni plays an aging nobleman who, in order to marry his vivacious teenage cousin, must first get rid of his wife — a difficult task in a no-divorce country. His convoluted plan soon involves him acting as a jealous husband who, on finding his wife in bed with another man, kills her off in a fit of passion — the only problem is finding the "other man." A delightful comedy that was nominated for three Academy Awards and won for Best Original Screenplay. (Italian with English subtitles) ★★★★ VHS: $24.99; DVD: $29.99

The Divorce of Lady X

(1938, 92 min, GB, Tim Whelan) *Laurence Olivier, Merle Oberon, Ralph Richardson.* This witty, sophisticated comedy examines the problems of a London barrister who allows a pretty young lady to spend an "innocent" night in his flat, only to later be named as a correspondent in a subsequent divorce action. A frothy comedy. ★★★

The Divorcee

(1930, 83 min, US, Robert Z. Leonard) *Norma Shearer, Chester Morris, Conrad Nagel, Robert Montgomery.* Shearer won an Oscar for her portrayal of a married woman who suffers through her husband's infidelity before deciding to give him a taste of his own medicine. Shearer's performance makes this hoary melodrama of interest. ★★½ VHS: $19.99

Do the Right Thing

(1989, 120 min, US, Spike Lee) *Danny Aiello, Ossie Davis, Ruby Dee, Spike Lee, John Turturro, Giancarlo Esposito, Bill Nunn, Richard Edson, Paul Benjamin, Samuel L. Jackson, John Savage, Rosie Perez, Martin Lawrence.* Lee's brilliant, controversial and thought-provoking *Do the Right Thing* bulldozed its way into the American consciousness — forcing people to take sides on many of Lee's radical assertions and making race relations the hot topic of the summer of '89. The story revolves around a single street in the Bed-Stuy section of Brooklyn during one of the hottest days of summer. Spike's attention is given to the citizens of the street from da Mayor (Davis is terrific as the suds-soaked elder who offers snatches of street wisdom) and Momma Preacher (wonderfully rendered by Dee) to Mookie (Lee is his rambunctious self as the un-enlightened delivery boy for Sal's

Pizzeria). Aiello also shines as Sal. Superbly acted and filmed, *Do the Right Thing* is not simply incendiary — it is downright great filmmaking. ★★★★ VHS: $9.99; DVD: $24.99

Do You Remember Dolly Bell

(1981, 105 min, Yugoslavia, Emir Kusturica) Made a a few years before his highly successful *When Father Was Away on Business*, director Kusturica's perceptive and amusing coming-of-age drama is set in 1960s Sarajevo. The story centers around the family life of Dino, an amiable 16-year-old who befriends a caustic but engaging young prostitute, nicknamed Dolly Bell. An engrossing film which delves into Yugoslavia's ever-shifting nature of nonaligned Communism and its effect on the family, especially the young. (Serbian with English subtitles) ★★★

D.O.A.

(1950, 83 min, US, Rudolph Mate) *Edmond O'Brien, Pamela Britton, Luther Adler, Beverly Garland.* O'Brien walks into a police station and reports a murder: his own. Thus begins Mate's tense, enthralling mystery about a man who only has three days to find out who gave him a slow-acting lethal poison. Filmed on location in Los Angeles and San Francisco, this classic film noir will have you on the edge of your seat right up to the end. (Remade in 1988) ★★★½ VHS: $19.99; DVD: $19.99

D.O.A.

(1988, 96 min, US, Rocky Morton & Annabel Jankel) *Dennis Quaid, Meg Ryan, Charlotte Rampling, Daniel Stern.* Codirectors Morton and Jankel's music video background is much in evidence in this slick style-over-substance remake of the 1950 film noir classic about a man (Quaid) who spends his final hours of life looking for the person who slipped him a slow-acting poison. Though much maligned as a remake, the film is a fairly enjoyable thriller in its own right. ★★½

Doc Hollywood

(1991, 105 min, US, Michael Caton-Jones) *Michael J. Fox, Bridget Fonda, Woody Harrelson, Julie Warner, Barnard Hughes, David Ogden Stiers, Frances Sternhagen.* A hotshot big-city doctor is forced to offer his services to a small, backwoods town populated with a collection of offbeat and endearing characters. No, it's not "Northern Exposure." It's *Doc Hollywood*, a surprisingly charming comedy with Fox as the doctor in question, a Washington, D.C. surgeon waylaid in a Southern community on his trek west. Fox gives an attractive performance as the Doc; he maintains his boyish qualities while discovering a maturity on-screen heretofore unseen. ★★★ VHS: $9.99; DVD: $14.99

Docks of New York

(1928, 76 min, US, Josef von Sternberg) *George Bancroft, Betty Compson.* Lacking the mannered bombast of his later melodramas, von Sternberg's efficient, superb drama chronicles a stevedore's developing love for a woman he saved from suicide. The director's mastery of the language of silent film is most evident in his slow dissolves — either to compress time, or to accentuate the internal turmoil of a character. ★★★★ VHS: $29.99

The Doctor

(1991, 125 min, US, Randa Haines) *William Hurt, Christine Lahti, Elizabeth Perkins, Mandy Patinkin, Adam Arkin, Charlie Korsmo.* Yet another

in 1991's spate of moral redemption films (*Regarding Henry, The Fisher King, Doc Hollywood*), *The Doctor* features a solid performance by Hurt, who again teams up with *Children of a Lesser God* director Haines. Hurt plays Jack McKee, a successful and respected heart surgeon who finds himself on the other side of the emergency room door when he is diagnosed with throat cancer. In coming to grips with both his illness and the indifference of his colleagues, he soon realizes his own shortcomings as a doctor and husband. Hurt's performance is incredibly nuanced; even at his most glib, McKee is a sympathetic and all-too-real character. Perkins also excels as a terminally ill woman. ★★★

The Doctor and the Devils

(1985, 93 min, GB, Freddie Francis) *Timothy Dalton, Jonathan Pryce, Twiggy, Julian Sands, Stephen Rea, Patrick Stewart, Phyllis Logan.* Another unusual production from Brooksfilms (Mel Brooks' production company) is based on a 1940s screenplay by Dylan Thomas. It concerns two of the most famous villains in British history, Broom and Fallen, who provided corpses for the anatomical research of Dr. Thomas Rock. A grisly tale which evokes images of the old Hammer classics. ★★★ VHS: $79.99

Dr. Bethune

(1990, 115 min, Canada/China/France, Phillip Borsos) *Donald Sutherland, Helen Mirren, Helen Shaver, Anouk Aimée.* In a mesmerizing performance, Sutherland brings subtle shading to the many facets of Dr. Norman Bethune, a complex man whose rude arrogance is tempered by his compassionate devotion to the cause of universal medical treatment. With a history as social and medical crusader, Bethune is summoned in 1938 to Yunan by Chairman Mao to be chief medical advisor to 100,000 troops. In flashbacks, the film concentrates on his efforts there, and his prior achievements, as well. Beautifully photographed and finely crafted. ★★★½ VHS: $19.99

Dr. Caligari

(1991, 80 min, US, Stephen Sayadian) *Madeleine Reynal, Fox Harris.* The director of the stylish porno-punk *Cafe Flesh* goes "legit" with this colorful takeoff on the classic German silent *The Cabinet of Dr. Caligari.* Now it is his granddaughter who is in charge of the asylum and her radical new form of therapy consists of gender bending until the patient snaps from severe mental fatigue. ★★

Dr. Cyclops

(1945, 75 min, US, Ernest Schoedsack) *Albert Dekker, Janice Logan.* Until the late 1950s, it was rare for color films to have many special effects. It was even rarer for a horror film to be made in color. Dekker plays a mad doctor living in the jungle who shrinks anyone who visits him for no other reason than because he can. Good premise and nicely done. ★★★ VHS: $14.99

Doctor Detroit

(1983, 91 min, US, Michael Pressman) *Dan Aykroyd, Donna Dixon, Fran Drescher, Howard Hesseman, Lynn Whitfield, Glenne Headly.* Aykroyd plays a mild-mannered college professor who finds himself caught up in a power struggle with the Chicago mob when he takes care of five beautiful prostitutes. Some good laughs in this playful comedy. ★★½ VHS: $9.99

D

Doctor Dolittle

(1967, 151 min, US, Richard Fleischer) *Rex Harrison, Samantha Eggar, Anthony Newley, Richard Attenborough, Geoffrey Holder.* Harrison talks to the animals and sails around the world in a giant snail. Children may enjoy this musical fable, though adults will find some of it difficult to take. A beguiling score includes "Talk to the Animals" (Oscar winner). (Remade in 1998) ★★½ VHS: $9.99; DVD: $22.99

Dr. Dolittle

(1998, 85 min, US, Betty Thomas) *Eddie Murphy, Ossie Davis, Oliver Platt, Peter Boyle, Jeffrey Tambor; Voices of: Chris Rock, Norm Macdonald, Ellen DeGeneres, Albert Brooks, John Leguizamo, Paul Reubens.* Murphy proves he *can* talk to the animals in this very funny and entertaining family comedy based on the 1967 Rex Harrison musical. As with his successful *The Nutty Professor*, Murphy has updated a '60s semi-classic to produce a laugh-laden hit which stands on its own. Eddie plays Dr. Dolittle, a talented physician who, much to his regret, learns he has the ability to understand animals — all animals. Unlike Rex Harrison's Dolittle, Murphy's doc is not happy about his gift, and it wreaks havoc with family and business associates. Though some of the family segments border on the sappy, the humor is much more broad and cutting. Director Thomas (*The Brady Bunch Movie*) has once again created a winning comedy for the whole family. (Sequel: *Doctor Dolittle 2*) ★★★ VHS: $9.99; DVD: $29.99

Dr. Faustus

(1968, 93 min, GB, Richard Burton) *Richard Burton, Andreas Teuber, Elizabeth Taylor.* Colorful rendering of the Faustus legend with first-time director Burton in the title role as a man who sells his soul to the Devil for personal gain. While not the best telling of the tale, the film is notable for a cameo appearance by the director's wife in the role of "Helen of Troy." ★★ VHS: $19.99

Dr. Giggles

(1992, 96 min, US, Manny Coto) *Larry Drake, Holly Marie Combs, Glenn Quinn.* With a razor-thin scalpel in hand, a menacingly diabolical giggle and a penchant for involuntary organ transplants, Dr. Giggles is no ordinary Marcus Welby. Drake draws more than just a few chuckles as the deranged son of a mad doctor who escapes from an asylum and sets out to exact vengeance on the town that killed his father. While it fails to deliver the goods for hardcore splatter aficionados, this amusing horror spoof will have some viewers placing their hands over their eyes...when not holding on to vital organs. ★★ VHS: $19.99

Doctor in the House

(1954, 92 min, GB, Ralph Thomas) *Dirk Bogarde, Muriel Pavlow, Kenneth More, Donald Sinden, Kay Kendall.* Bogarde stars in this hilarious farce about medical school students based on the story of Richard Gordon. This was the first of a series of sophisticated takeoffs on the *Carry On* films. ★★★

Dr. Jekyll And Mr. Hyde

(1920, 96 min, US, John S. Robertson) *John Barrymore, Martha Mansfield.* Barrymore gives a virtuoso performance as Robert Louis Stevenson's tormented doctor in this silent classic. Filmed many times since, including the 1932

Fredric March version, which has yet to be surpassed. ★★★ VHS: $24.99; DVD: $24.99

Dr. Jekyll and Mr. Hyde

(1932, 82 min, US, Rouben Mamoulian) *Fredric March, Miriam Hopkins, Halliwell Hobbes.* Robert Louis Stevenson's classic thriller of split personality and dementia has been done so many times and on so many different levels that it, like "Frankenstein," has somehow lost not only its freshness, but also its ability to cause fear or to shock. This 1932 version is an exception. March, who won the Oscar for Best Actor, brings both tenderness and ferocity to the character that, despite the film's age, makes it hard to imagine anyone else in the role. Hopkins is unforgettable as the doomed prostitute who takes up with Mr. Hyde, and had there been a Supporting Actress category in 1932, she probably would have been an Oscar winner as well. Armenian-born director Mamoulian used his innovative camerawork and direction to create a truly tragic figure. One of the all-time greats in horror. ★★★★ VHS: $19.99

Dr. Jekyll and Mr. Hyde

(1941, 114 min, US, Victor Fleming) *Spencer Tracy, Ingrid Bergman, Lana Turner.* Slick remake of the Robert Louis Stevenson story with Tracy as the mad doc, Bergman as Hyde's ill-fated Cockney mistress and Turner as Jekyll's bride-to-be. ★★★ VHS: $19.99

Dr. Jekyll & Ms. Hyde

(1995, 95 min, US, David Price) *Tim Daly, Sean Young, Lysette Anthony, Harvey Fierstein.* When network TV shows nothing but "Hee-Haw," when an ushers' strike closes down the cinema, and when video stores are stocked with only Sylvester Stallone flicks, only then should this ludicrous film be watched. A tired variation of the Jekyll and Hyde tale, this insipid comedy features Daly as an eccentric scientist who accidentally turns into a power-hungry woman (Young). Yes, sexual hijinks ensue as men fall under his/her murderous attractiveness. The best thing that can be said about this film is that it does not cause cancer (although not all of the studies are in). ★ VHS: $14.99

Dr. Jekyll and Sister Hyde

(1972, 94 min, GB, Roy Ward Baker) *Ralph Bates, Martine Beswick.* Friends of Freud should have a field day with this intriguing, but at times lifeless, variation of the Robert Louis Stevenson chiller with Bates as the insanely curious doctor who manages to isolate his dark side only to find that it is actually feminine! As with most treatises on the nature of good and evil, evil is more fun, as evidenced by Beswick's villainous performance as Sister Hyde. ★★★ VHS: $9.99

Dr. No

(1963, 111 min, GB, Terence Young) *Sean Connery, Ursula Andress, Joseph Wiseman.* Connery stars in the first and foremost James Bond adventure. There's sex, violence, exotic locales and the master-fiend Dr. No. This is agent 007 at his finest. (Sequel: *From Russia with Love*) ★★★½ VHS: $14.99; DVD: $34.99

Dr. Phibes Rises Again

(1972, 89 min, GB, Robert Fuest) *Vincent Price, Peter Cushing, Terry-Thomas, Beryl Reed.* A disfigured madman (Price) and his deceased wife go boating down the Underground River of the Dead in this sequel to *The Abominable Dr. Phibes.*

Everybody's in it for the laughs — even the set designer. ★★½ VHS: $12.99; DVD: $14.99

Dr. Strangelove

(1964, 93 min, GB, Stanley Kubrick) *Peter Sellers, George C. Scott, Sterling Hayden, Slim Pickens, Keenan Wynn.* Kubrick's unforgettable and hilarious black comedy is undeniably one of the greatest indictments of the Cold War ever to be seen in the cinema. From the legendary performances of the cast to Kubrick's brilliant use of the cinematic form, the film is an undaunted piece of mastery. The film's profound message about the dangers of aggression in the nuclear age is as timely now as it was when it was released — a superior cinematic achievement. ★★★★ VHS: $19.99; DVD: $29.99

Dr. T & the Women

(2000, 121 min, US, Robert Altman) *Richard Gere, Helen Hunt, Laura Dern, Farrah Fawcett, Shelley Long, Tara Reid, Kate Hudson, Liv Tyler, Lee Grant, Janine Turner, Robert Hays, Andy Richter, Matt Malloy.* Director Altman has always brought out the best in his actors, and here he has done the impossible: coaxed a smart, rich and winning performance out of old stoneface, Richard Gere. He plays an obstetrician/gynecologist around whom many Dallas women's lives seem to revolve, in typical multicharactered Altman style. While he's the object of some misplaced affection, he is wholly devoted to his wife; when she has a mental breakdown and reverts to childish ways (appropriately, she's played by nutty-and-nuttier Fawcett), his formerly perfect life is thrown into turmoil. His wife now institutionalized, Dr. T fills his loneliness with golf pro Hunt, who proves a tantalizing seductress. However, the emphasis is on humor, as Altman's positive outlook sees no difference between quirky little problems (Dern's tipsy sister-in-law) and the ones that initially seem huge (engaged daughter Hudson's lesbian affair) — in the end, life goes on. Long is a particular comic standout as Dr. T's harried and too-devoted head nurse. ★★★ VHS: $14.99; DVD: $24.99

Dr. Terror's House of Horrors

(1965, 98 min, GB, Freddie Francis) *Peter Cushing, Christopher Lee, Donald Sutherland.* Intriguing, episodic horror film from the director of *The Doctor and the Devils.* Five fellow travelers have their tarots read by a mysterious doctor as they ride on a train headed — where? Francis directs a strong cast. ★★★ VHS: $14.99

Doctor Zhivago

(1965, 197 min, US, David Lean) *Julie Christie, Omar Sharif, Geraldine Chaplin, Rod Steiger, Alec Guinness, Tom Courtenay, Rita Tushingham, Ralph Richardson.* Through his retelling of Boris Pasternak's novel of the Russian Revolution, Lean succeeds in creating both a mammoth spectacle and an impressive and absorbing account of one of the most fascinating and important periods in human history. An incredible ensemble is headed by the exceptional Christie and handsome Omar, with Steiger and Courtenay excelling among the fine ensemble cast. (VHS available letterboxed or pan & scan) ★★★½ VHS: $24.99

Dodes'ka-den

(1970, 140 min, Japan, Akira Kurosawa) *Yoshitaka Zushi, Junzaburo Ban.* A stunning and masterful examination of the downtrodden lives and glorious dreams of a number of Tokyo slum dwellers. Kurosawa's first film in color is an eloquent and impassioned affirmation of life and the awesome power of hope. Oddly, the film was not very well received by the critics and was a big disappointment at the box office, causing Kurosawa to abandon filmmaking for several years. (Japanese with English subtitles) ★★★ VHS: $29.99

Dodge City
(1939, 101 min, US, Michael Curtiz) *Errol Flynn, Olivia de Havilland, Ann Sheridan, Bruce Cabot, Alan Hale.* Flynn trades in his sword and tights for a pistol and cowboy boots as the new sheriff in a trigger-happy town. Flavorful western fun. ★★★ VHS: $14.99

Dodsworth
(1936, 101 min, US, William Wyler) *Walter Huston, Mary Astor, Ruth Chatterton, David Niven, Paul Lukas, Maria Ouspenskaya.* Superb film version of Sinclair Lewis' novel about a retired industrialist and his wife who travel abroad, each coming to re-examine the purpose and value of their lives. Huston, Chatterton and Astor all give outstanding performances. ★★★★ VHS: $14.99

Dog Day (Canicule)
(1983, 101 min, France, Yves Boisset) *Lee Marvin, Miou-Miou, Jean Carmet.* This gritty, macabre little gem is a pristine manifestation of the Gallic infatuation with American gangsters. Marvin stars as Jimmy Cobb, a chiseled-faced personification of the amoral yet honorable hood, who is on the run after a botched stick-up job. He finds himself at the dubious mercy of a farming family, whose interrelationships and sense of loyalties make the word "criminal" inoperative. Like Godard's *Alphaville* and Melville's *Bob le Flambeur*, this is a parable of existential man told against the backdrop of the chimerical safety of small-caliber weapons and the elusive salvation of the big score. ★★★½

Dog Day Afternoon
(1975, 130 min, US, Sidney Lumet) *Al Pacino, Charles Durning, Chris Sarandon, John Cazale, Carol Kane.* Before Pacino embarrassed himself *Cruising* the leather bars, he gave a first-rate performance as a gay thief whose attempt to rob a bank (to pay for his lover's sex change) brings the city of New York to a standstill. An often delightful comedy, director Lumet flavors his film with warm characters and deft humor. In supporting roles, Durning as a police liaison and Oscar-nominee Sarandon as Pacino's lover are standouts. Based on a true incident. ★★★½ VHS: $14.99; DVD: $19.99

Dogfight
(1991, 92 min, US, Nancy Savoca) *River Phoenix, Lili Taylor, Brendan Fraser.* The heavily anticipated second effort from director Savoca is every bit as marvelous as her debut, *True Love*. Phoenix stars as a young marine who sets out with his buddies on a dogfight — a search for the ugliest girl in town to escort her to a dance. He charms Taylor, a plump and awkward aspiring folk singer who soon discovers his cruel deception. To make amends, he convinces her to go on a "real" date and they wind up spending the night together — a night of revelation and intimacy which neither would soon forget. Phoenix, as always, is first-rate, but it is Taylor's superb portrayal which elevates the film.

An honest slice-of-'60s life captured with sensitivity and awareness. ★★★½ VHS: $19.99

Dogma
(1999, 125 min, US, Kevin Smith) *Linda Fiorentino, Chris Rock, Salma Hayek, Jason Lee, Alan Rickman, Matt Damon, Ben Affleck, Jason Mewes, Kevin Smith.* Protests surrounding "sacrilegious" Catholic movies are generally a good sign (i.e. *Last Temptation of Christ, Priest*); Smith's *Dogma* lives up to the obvious protests. Smith's story concerns Bethany (Fiorentino), an abortion clinic worker, who must go on a pilgrimage to New Jersey to save the world from two fallen angels (Damon and Affleck, natch) who plan on exploiting a dogmatic loophole to get back into heaven. It seems God has gone missing after a skee-ball expedition, so Bethany will need the help of stoner prophets Jay and Silent Bob, and Rufus (Rock), the black 13th apostle. Wait, wait, put your pickets down. . . Smith has done his homework. Within these outrageous trappings are reverent ideas that preach a personal relationship with God, rather than simple servitude before a church (or other organization). These mature themes are presented in an often hilarious package, with Rock at his best delivering fall-down-funny dialogue guaranteed to spark conversation. Smith has also matured cinematically, tackling the widescreen format in a subtle homage to the bibilical epics of the 1950s. The plot becomes a bit ponderous, and the torrent of ideas slows to a trickle as the film wraps. But after seeing God do a handstand and explain the meaning of life, all is forgiven in this ambitious, fantastic parable. ★★★½ VHS: $14.99; DVD: $24.99

Dogs in Space
(1987, 109 min, Australia, Richard Lowenstein) *Michael Hutchence, Saskia Post.* This "drugged-up punks in love" picture explores the underground subculture of Australia's alienated youth, circa 1978. Hutchence, lead singer of INXS, stars as the immovably passive leader of a commune of punks and hangers-on living in comfortable squalor in a ramshackle house in Melbourne. Infused with loud music, countless subplots and characters, the film, like its denizens, is incoherent and rambling. Yet, despite the problems, it is entertaining and amusing. ★★½

The Dogs of War
(1980, 101 min, GB, John Irvin) *Christopher Walken, Colin Blakely, Tom Berenger, JoBeth Williams.* This film stretches the boundaries of political reason by idolizing a group of mercenaries who are hired to overthrow the dictator of a newly formed West African nation. A somber but solid adaptation of Frederick Forsythe's novel. ★★★ VHS: $9.99

Doin' Time on Planet Earth
(1988, 83 min, US, Charles Matthau) *Matt Adler, Adam West, Candy Azzara.* A harmless, dopey comedy about teenage alienation — as in alien from outer space. Adler is trapped in a dull, small Arizona town. Life seems aimless until he comes to the conclusion he's really from another planet. He meets up with West and Azzara, who convince him not only that he is right, but he's their leader who's destined to take them home. The film pokes fun at the extraterrestrial craze, and produces a few smiles. ★★½ VHS: $19.99

La Dolce Vita
(1960, 176 min, Italy, Federico Fellini) *Marcello Mastroianni, Anita Ekberg, Anouk Aimée, Lex Barker.* A staggering, trendsetting film that examines the hollow lives of Rome's decadent upper crust through the eyes of a cynical columnist. Mastroianni became an international star thanks to his swaggering portrayal of the lustful gossip columnist, and Fellini sharply observes the mores and morals of a generation. (Italian with English subtitles) ★★★★ VHS: $24.99

Dolemite
(1974, 88 min, US, D'Urville Martin) *Rudy Ray Moore.* He's bad, the man is out-a-sight...he's Dolemite! Spewing hilarious invective-filled poetry that would make Eddie Murphy blush, Moore single-handedly brings back those halcyon days at the Goldman Theatre when pimps in fluorescent polyester jumpsuits, fur hats and gravity-defying Afros ruled the cinematic land. Ignore the ludicrous acting and production values and just sit back and enjoy Dolemite as he faces crooked white cops, double-dealing thugs and scantily clad "hos" in this blaxploitation classic. Can you dig it? ★★★ VHS: $19.99; DVD: $19.99

Matt Damon and Ben Affleck as fallen angels in *Dogma*

A Doll's House

(1973, 87 min, GB, Joseph Losey) *Jane Fonda, Edward Fox, Trevor Howard, David Warner, Delphine Seyrig.* Fonda's controversial interpretation of Henrik Ibsen's 19th-century liberated woman is the centerpiece of Losey's cinematic adaptation of the classic play. Fonda plays Nora, who risks destruction in order to save her husband, only to suddenly and dramatically have to assert her independence when he confronts her with unabashed male arrogance. ★★★

Dollar

(1938, 78 min, Sweden, Gustaf Molander) *Ingrid Bergman.* An uncharacteristically light *Rules of the Game*-like comedy about three society couples who set out on a group skiing vacation. (Swedish with English subtitles) ★★½ VHS: $19.99

The Dollmaker

(1984, 140 min, US, Daniel Petrie) *Jane Fonda, Geraldine Page, Amanda Plummer, Levon Helm.* Fonda won an Emmy Award for her stirring performance in this first-rate TV drama as an impoverished farm woman who moves her family to Detroit when her husband lands a factory job. The film evokes a fine feel for 1940s America, and there's a stellar supporting cast. ★★★½

Dolores Claiborne

(1995, 125 min, US, Taylor Hackford) *Kathy Bates, Jennifer Jason Leigh, Christopher Plummer, David Strathairn, Eric Bogosian.* This heartfelt adaptation of Stephen King's best-seller is distinguished by yet another Oscar-caliber performance by Bates as a downtrodden New England housewife who must vindicate herself in the murder of her employer even as she unlocks the secrets that separate her from her neurotic, chain-smoking daughter (Leigh). Hackford deftly and seamlessly switches from present day to flashback, creating a richly woven tapestry of mystery and suspense. As was demonstrated by *Stand by Me* and *The Shawshank Redemption*, it seems King's best screen adaptations are those which concentrate more on intimate relationships and less on horror. (VHS available letterboxed or pan & scan) ★★★½ VHS: $9.99; DVD: $19.99

The Dolphin (O Boto)

(1987, 95 min, Brazil, Walter Lima, Jr.) *Carlos Alberto Riccelli, Cassia Kiss.* This steamy fantasy is derived from a Brazilian myth about "O Boto," a lustful "were-dolphin" who, on the night of the full moon, becomes a handsome young man and lures unsuspecting women to the water, where he bewitches and seduces them. Set in a small village on the northern coast of Brazil, the film tells the tale of Tereza, the daughter of a fisherman who falls under "O Boto"'s spell. When she gives birth to his son, the town becomes victim to a terrible curse in which the local waters become devoid of fish. Tinged with a smattering of black humor, this erotic drama is filmed in sensuous shades of midnight blue and is reminiscent in tone, though not on the same level, as the classic *Dona Flor and Her Two Husbands.* (Portuguese with English subtitles) ★★★ VHS: $19.99

Dominick & Eugene

(1988, 111 min, US, Robert M. Young) *Tom Hulce, Ray Liotta, Jamie Lee Curtis, Todd Graf. Rain Man* has nothing on this similarly themed, criminally neglected drama. Set in Pittsburgh, the film details

La Dolce Vita

the complex relationship between twin brothers who have a dark secret buried in their past. Dominick (Hulce) is a slow-witted man-child whose job as a trash collector subsidizes his brother's medical school tuition. Eugene (Liotta) realizes his financial dependence on his brother — and Dominick's emotional dependence on him — is becoming burdensome, forcing him to consider some tough decisions about their future. Hulce gives a brilliantly textured performance and it probably should have been him, not Dustin Hoffman, to win that year's Oscar for a portrayal of a mentally disabled sibling. ★★★★ VHS: $14.99

Don Giovanni

(1979, 186 min, France/Italy, Joseph Losey) *Ruggero Raimondi, Jose van Dam, Kiri Te Kanawa, Teresa Berganza.* Losey's brilliant screen adaptation of Mozart's operatic masterpiece features what amounts to an all-star cast of singers including van Dam, Te Kanawa, Raimondi and Berganza. Using a subtle blend of commedia dell'arte and morality play, Losey's interpretation of this Don Juan-based legend is a beautiful and bold marriage of opera and cinema. (Italian with English subtitles) ★★★★ VHS: $24.99

Don Juan

(1926, 111 min, US, Alan Crosland) *John Barrymore, Mary Astor, Myrna Loy.* The first sound feature (only music and sound effects, no dialogue, thus no mention in the history books). Barrymore is at his swashbuckling best, running when others would walk, jumping when others would sit down. If he weren't such a kinetic ball of energy, he would get lost in the sumptuous sets. ★★★½ VHS: $29.99

Don Juan deMarco

(1995, 90 min, US, Jeremy Leven) *Johnny Depp, Marlon Brando, Faye Dunaway, Rachel Ticotin.* In this deliriously romantic fable about the power and magic of love, Depp stars as a possibly delusional young man who, insisting that he is the legendary lover Don Juan, decides to end his life because he cannot have the one woman he truly loves. Enter Brando as the retiring psychiatrist who tries to unlock the mystery of "the greatest lover that ever lived," all the while being seduced by the rhapsodic tales Depp spins during his therapy. First-time director Leven serves up a most delicious mixture of erotic love and come-

dy. Even in light of Brando's sometimes cumbersome presence, *Don Juan* is a natural charmer — as only Depp could play him. ★★★ VHS: $9.99; DVD: $14.99

Don Juan My Love

(1990, 96 min, Spain, Antonio Mercero) *Juan Luis Galiardo, Rossy de Palma.* This delightful fable is a thoroughly enjoyable and, at times, hilariously wicked comedy. The tormented ghost of the womanizing Don Juan rises from his grave and, as he has been doing for hundreds of years, begins a 24-hour attempt to end his term in purgatory by doing a good deed. The comedy of errors begins when he is mistaken for an obnoxious actor who is playing Don Juan in a theatrical production. Drug-smuggling actors, corpulent knife-wielding grandmothers, castanet-speaking production assistants and coke-filled angels all pop up in this wild romp which juxtaposes the romantic memory of old Spain with the harsh reality of a modern one. (Spanish with English subtitles) ★★★ VHS: $19.99

Don King: Only in America

(1997, 112 min, US, John Herzfeld) *Ving Rhames, Vondie Curtis-Hall, Jeremy Piven, Loretta Devine, Keith David.* HBO's free-wheeling, wholly enjoyable account of the life and times of the badass promoter, Don King. Based on Jack Newfield's controversial book, this production is a showcase for Rhames, boldly bald in past roles, now electri-follicled as the motor-mouthed huckster. Director Herzfeld and screenwriter Kario Salem chronicle the events that put King on boxing's throne, beginning with his numbers running days in 1950s Cleveland and two jail stints before emphasizing his relations with boxing's greats, his wheelings and dealings behind the scenes, arranging TV deals, and duping business rivals and fighters alike. At one point towards the film's end, Rhames, in all of his galvanizing glory, addresses the camera from inside the boxing ring. He says, "I made you HBO motherfuckers a lot of money." Talk about guts and glory. ★★★½ VHS: $9.99

Don Quixote

(1973, 110 min, US, Rudolf Nureyev/Robert Helpmann) *Robert Helpmann, Rudolf Nureyev.* The film version of Marius Petipas' colorful ballet was codirected by Nureyev (who also plays Basilio) and Helpmann (who appears in the title role). Featuring the Australian Ballet, scored by Ludwig Minkus and lavishly filmed by cinematographer Geoffrey Unsworth. ★★★½ VHS: $39.99

Don Segundo Sombra

(1969, 110 min, Spain, Manuel Antin) *Juan Carballido, Juan Carlos Gene.* Based on Ricardo Guiraldes' novel, the title character narrates the story of Fabio Caceres as he grows into adulthood. Don Segundo Sombra, an old "gaucho," is his mentor and model: he teaches the youth moral and human values through his behavior, his stories and his example. (Spanish with English subtitles) ★★½ VHS: $29.99

Doña Flor and Her Two Husbands

(1976, 106 min, Brazil, Bruno Barreto) *Sonia Braga, Jose Wilker.* The humorous account of a young woman (Braga) whose first husband is beckoned from the grave when her second fails to satisfy her sexual needs. Barreto's hedonistic excursion simmers with the sights and sensuality of Brazil. (American remake: *Kiss Me Goodbye*) (Portuguese with English subtitles) ★★★ VHS: $19.99

Doña Herlinda and Her Son

(1986, 90 min, Mexico, Jaime Humberto Hermosillo) *Guadalupe del Toro, Marco Antonio Trevino, Arturo Meza.* A funny and subversively heartwarming love story about Doña Herlinda, a shrewd yet always placid mother who wishes for her son only that he live happily with Mom, his wife... and another man if need be. Her son, a sexually confused surgeon, is having a relationship with Ramon, a handsome music student. When Mom realizes that their relationship is romantic and deep, she helps things out by inviting her son's lover to stay with them, reasoning "Rodolfo has such a large bed!" A wickedly funny and uplifting Mexican comedy of manners which sympathetically portrays gay love. (Spanish with English subtitles) ★★★½ VHS: $39.99

Donkey Skin

(1970, 90 min, France, Jacques Demy) *Catherine Deneuve, Jean Marais, Delphine Seyrig.* This enchanting and lyrical fairy tale is set in a small kingdom where the beloved queen is dying. Her final wish is that her husband, the king, only marry someone who is as beautiful as she. To the king's consternation, the only woman is his daughter! Filmed in sumptuous color, this adaptation of Charles Perrault's story is consistently entertaining. (French with English subtitles) ★★★

Donnie Brasco

(1997, 115 min, US, Mike Newell) *Al Pacino, Johnny Depp, Anne Heche, Michael Madsen, Bruno Kirby, James Russo, Zeljko Ivanek.* Director Newell captures the nuance and flavor of 1970s gangland New York in this crisp, extremely well-acted gangster drama based on the real-life experiences of undercover FBI agent Joe Pistone. Depp is Donnie Brasco (alias Pistone), who infiltrates the mob. Befriending mid-level wiseguy Lefty Ruggiero (Pacino), Donnie secures a place for himself with Lefty as his mentor, all the while dispatching vital information. The strength of the film is the human face placed on all its characters. The best of these is Pacino's Lefty, an anonymous foot soldier who sees in Donnie a chance to pass along his limited worldly wisdom. Michael Corleone he's not, and Pacino is superb in etching the fragile shadings of unfulfilled ambition. Absorbing and vigorous, *Donnie Brasco*

brings a fresh attitude to an often overplayed genre. ★★★½ VHS: $9.99; DVD: $29.99

Donovan's Brain

(1953, 83 min, US, Felix Feist) *Lew Ayres, Gene Evans, Nancy Davis.* Another scientist with a social problem. This one is Ayres, and he's being controlled by the disembodied and quite living brain of an evil industrialist. ★★★ VHS: $14.99; DVD: $14.99

Don's Party

(1976, 91 min, Australia, Bruce Beresford) *John Hargraves, Pat Bishop, Graham Kennedy.* A hilariously vulgar, 100-proof comedy which directs an unrelenting attack on Australian politics and suburbia. Don invites his friends over for an election night party but what begins as a quiet victory celebration soon succumbs to riotous boozing, arguments, partner-swapping, fights and marriages crumbling. Great fun! ★★★ VHS: $19.99; DVD: $29.99

Don't Bother to Knock

(1952, 76 min, US, Roy Baker) *Marilyn Monroe, Richard Widmark, Anne Bancroft, Jim Backus.* Billed for the first time above the title, Marilyn plays an emotionally disturbed baby-sitter who's a danger to herself and the young girl she's watching. Widmark lives across the courtyard and comes to the rescue. As a lounge singer involved with Widmark, Bancroft makes her film debut. A contrived melodramatic suspenser that's made bearable thanks to a few exciting scenes, and MM and her durable costar. ★★½

Don't Do It

(1994, 95 min, US, Eugene Hess) *Alexis Arquette, Heather Graham, James LeGros, Sheryl Lee, James Marshall, Esai Morales, Balthazar Getty.* Essentially a series of vignettes, this uninspired look at twentysomething relationships advertises itself as "the Generation X Comedy," with a display box that says more about the musical score than the story line. For good reason. Ill-using its large group of up-and-coming actors, many of whom have previously given competent performances, the film tries to be a contemporary comedy of manners, complete with requisite AIDS reference; but it collapses in on itself with derivative tedium. Don't Watch It! ★ DVD: $24.99

Don't Drink the Water

(1969, 100 min, US, Howard Morris) *Jackie Gleason, Estelle Parsons, Ted Bessell.* Mildly entertaining version of Woody Allen's hit play with Gleason and Parsons as American tourists on European vacation who are accused of spying and held captive in the Iron Curtain country of Vulgaria. (Remade in 1999) ★★½

Don't Let Me Die on a Sunday

(1999, 86 min, France, Didier Le Pecheur) *Elodie Bouchez, Jean-Marc Barr, Martin Petitguyot, Patrick Catalifo.* A handsome morgue worker eyes a hot young woman on the slab; he locks the door and does the unmentionable. Teresa, the young woman, had a drug overdose at a rave, and she comes

back to life after the experience. She befriends Ben, the morgue worker, and they go on a journey of bisexual S&M orgies where anything goes. The uneven film is difficult to follow, with little reward at the end. (French with English subtitles) ★★ VHS: $79.99; DVD: $29.99

Don't Look Back

(1967, 96 min, US, D.A. Pennebaker) D.A. Pennebaker's intimate portrait of a young Bob Dylan follows the iconoclastic troubadour on his 1965 British tour as he encounters adoring fans, skeptical critics and bothersome comparisons to Donovan. ★★★½ VHS: $19.99; DVD: $24.99

Don't Look Now

(1973, 110 min, GB, Nicolas Roeg) *Donald Sutherland, Julie Christie, Hilary Mason.* This stylish, visually beautiful mystery based on a novel by Daphne du Maurier established Roeg as a leading auteur. In addition to creating one of the most famous sex scenes in the history of the cinema, Roeg brilliantly taps into one of the most primal fears of many adults — the death of a child. Christie and Sutherland are the bereaved parents who attempt to contact their child through a medium. Roeg's haunting imagery of winter in Venice is breathtaking. ★★★½ VHS: $49.99

Don't Play Us Cheap

(1972, 95 min, US, Melvin Van Peebles) *Esther Rolle, Avon Long, Mabel King, Rhetta Hughes, Joe Keyes, Jr.* Based on Van Peebles' endearing stage musical celebrating through song and dance the resilience of the African-American culture, this slightly dated and stagey filmic adaptation nicely captures the essence of the original piece. Featuring the original cast, the film is the playful and comic tale of two minions of the Devil whose perpetual assignment of breaking up parties leads them to crash a festive Saturday night get-together in Harlem. Van Peebles experiments with editing and over-lapping, which he sometimes allows to go on too long. He also wrote the music: Some songs are energetic and tuneful, others are laborious. ★★★ VHS: $79.99

Don't Tell Mom the Babysitter's Dead

(1991, 105 min, US, Stephen Herek) *Christina Applegate, Joanna Cassidy, Keigh Coogan,*

Fred MacMurray and Barbara Stanwyck in *Double Indemnity*

Christopher Plummer. Left in the care of a tyrannical baby-sitter for the summer while their mother is away, Applegate and siblings get a reprieve when nanny unexpectedly dies. With no money to live on, sis is sent into the working world. There are a few laughs, but this amiable comedy is very one-note. Nice turn by Cassidy as Applegate's boss. ★★ VHS: $9.99; DVD: $14.99

The Doom Generation

(1995, 85 min, US, Gregg Araki) *Rose McGowan, James Duval, Johnathon Schaech, Parker Posey, Heidi Floss, Margaret Cho, Amanda Bearse.* Araki's self-acknowledged "heterosexual film," a teens-on-the-run epic, is dripping with homoerotic undertones, foul language, and violence that borders on the sadistic. On what was supposed to be a simple date, the tough-as-nails Amy (McGowan), an angry Valley Girl with a checkered past, and Jordan (Duval), a sweetly naïve cutie, meet up with the dangerously sexy X (Schaech). He soon gets them involved in a Quickie Mart robbery that turns deadly. And with bloody Twinkies in hand, the three escape into the neon night. Of course, just like those horny mall rats of suburbia, sex is always on the minds of our attractive protagonists, resulting in various couplings. *The Doom Generation* is a viciously funny, tumultously nihilistic ride through a hellish California. Buckle up. ★★★½ VHS: $14.99; DVD: $24.99

The Doors

(1991, 141 min, US, Oliver Stone) *Val Kilmer, Meg Ryan, Kyle MacLachlan, Kevin Dillon, Frank Whaley.* A daring, provocative and hallucinogenic tribute, ostensibly a biography but much more, of the founding member of the 1960s rock group The Doors — Jim Morrison. Director Stone sees Morrison as a lost poet of his generation, which he probably was, and the film never condescends to either the era (which is difficult to recapture on film, but Stone has done so amazingly) or Morrison himself. Kilmer is an uncanny look-alike of the singer, but his portrayal goes far beyond simple impersonation. Kilmer embodies the passion and the firebrand of the pop star which was Jim Morrison. The live performances are particularly impressive, featuring most of the group's classic material. ★★★½ VHS: $14.99; DVD: $34.99

Double Dragon

(1994, 96 min, US, James Yukich) *Robert Patrick, Mark Dacascos, Scott Wolf, Alyssa Milano.* Another witless, empty attempt to cash in on the success of a video game. The results are just a cut above a Saturday morning cartoon. In postapocalyptic Los Angeles where street gangs rule and even the cops are afraid to go out after dark, the nefarious Koga Shuko (Patrick, looking like a refugee from a Prince video) attempts to wrest the second half of a mystical medallion from the two perky kickboxing orphans (Dacascos and Wolf) charged with protecting it. Strictly for the pre-teen set. ★½ VHS: $19.99; DVD: $19.99

Double Face

(1977, 84 min, Italy/West Germany/GB, Robert Hampton) *Klaus Kinski.* Atrocious in so many ways — cheesy special effects, cartoonish acting, overly serious plot and the just-not-quite-right dubbing — this baffling and hyperventilating murder mystery is nevertheless strangely enjoyable. Kinski gives a wonderfully constipated, clenched-jaw performance as the cuckold husband of a wealthy industrialist who dies in a suspicious car accident. Did she die innocently or was she killed or better yet, was her death faked with her lesbian lover? Not content to simply run the company and enjoy the money, our hero begins his own investigation into the byzantine circumstances and finds out more than he ever wanted to know. Great trash. (Dubbed) ★★ VHS: $49.99

Double Happiness

(1995, 87 min, Canada/China, Mina Shum) *Sandra Oh, Alannah Ong, Stephen Chang, Frances You, Johnny Mah, Callum Rennie.* This delightfully offbeat drama-comedy is a promising feature film debut from writer-director Shum. Set in Vancouver, the story follows Jade Li (Oh), a spunky 22-year-old Chinese-Canadian woman who, when not working for her big break in acting, tries to find romance — two goals that upset her traditional-minded parents who just want her to find a "nice Chinese man and settle down." Interracial romance blooms when Jade falls for a cutely dorky white guy (Rennie) while her parents (Chang, Ong) desperately try to set her up with a handsome, debonair and Chinese (but gay) lawyer (Mah). The complex family dynamics of an immigrant family clinging to the ways of the old world are wonderfully exposed in this spirited, thoughtful film. ★★★ VHS: $19.99

Double Impact

(1992, 107 min, US, Sheldon Lettich) *Jean-Claude Van Damme.* Van Damme really cuts his acting teeth (okay, maybe not) in this predictable kickfest as twin brothers separated at birth who reunite years later to avenge the brutal murder of their parents. Though not a horror movie, it's scary to think Jean-Claude actually does seem to be two different people. ★★ VHS: $14.99; DVD: $14.99

Double Indemnity

(1944, 106 min, US, Billy Wilder) *Barbara Stanwyck, Fred MacMurray, Edward G. Robinson.* Considered to be the definitive film noir. The stunning Stanwyck plays an alluring vixen who cons unsuspecting insurance investigator MacMurray into a murderous web of intrigue. A very sexy film, rich in subtlety. Robinson is especially good as a wily investigator. Director Wilder at his best. ★★★★ VHS: $14.99

Double Jeopardy

(1999, 105 min, US, Bruce Beresford) *Ashley Judd, Tommy Lee Jones, Bruce Greenwood, Annabeth Gish.* If you've seen the trailers, you've seen the movie. Framed for murdering her husband, a woman (Judd) serves seven years for the crime. When she discovers that he isn't dead, she breaks parole and goes hunting for him. Jones, who doesn't appear until a half-hour into the film, plays her embittered parole officer who chases her across the country. There's one especially good scene involving handcuffs, a car, a ferry and both Judd and Jones going overboard. But other than that, this thriller is standard issue, by-the-books and often implausible. The film's twist ending would have been mildly diverting had it not been given away in the coming attractions. ★½ VHS: $14.99; DVD: $29.99

A Double Life

(1947, 104 min, US, George Cukor) *Ronald Colman, Shelley Winters, Edmond O'Brien.* Colman won an Oscar for his triumphant performance as an acclaimed stage actor who can no longer separate his on- and offstage lives — and now he's playing "Othello." Winters is terrific in support as his fateful girlfriend. A superior suspense drama directed with great relish by Cukor. ★★★½ VHS: $14.99

The Double Life of Veronique

(1991, 97 min, Poland/France, Krzysztof Kieslowski) *Irene Jacob, Philipe Volter.* Jacob is mesmerizing in dual roles in this beautifully photographed, dream-like exploration of psychic bonds and parallel lives. Jacob plays two women, born at the same time but a thousand miles apart, who are as inextricably bound as Siamese twins. Lush, golden lighting imparts an ethereal sense of myth and fairy tale as Veronique/Veronika searches for an understanding of her pervasive emotional reality. A revelatory inquiry into the transience of human existence and the devastation of loss. (French and Polish with English subtitles) ★★★½ VHS: $7.99

Double Suicide

(1969, 105 min, Japan, Masahiro Shinoda) *Kichieman Nakamura, Shima Iwashita, Hosei Komatsu.* Set in 18th-century Japan and faithful to the Bunraku puppet theatre tradition for which it was originally written, this delicate, stylistic and erotic film tells the tragic tale of a middle-class merchant who, blinded by passion, loses his family and business in his relentless pursuit of an alluring prostitute. *Double Suicide* moves continually between the realistic and the formality of the Banruku Puppet Theatre which links it to the original play. (Japanese with English subtitles) ★★★ VHS: $29.99; DVD: $29.99

Double Take

(1997, 86 min, US, Mark L. Lester) *Craig Sheffer, Costas Mandylor, Brigitte Bako.* Sheffer (sporting a truly distracting haircut) plays a respected novelist with a serious case of writer's block who witnesses the shooting death of a jeweler friend. He testifies against the suspect, certain of the man's guilt. But, several days after the conviction, Sheffer sees the guy's double on the street — could he have nabbed the wrong guy? Halfway intriguing premise holds one's attention for about half the running time, but the film has no surprises or twists. While one wouldn't expect depth from the premise, *Double Take* is *really* empty, with neither the scintillating style of DePalma nor the witty ironic commentary of a Larry Cohen to compensate. ★★ VHS: $79.99

Double Team

(1997, 91 min, US, Tsui Hark) *Jean-Claude Van Damme, Dennis Rodman, Mickey Rourke, Paul Freeman.* Lightning strikes a fourth time, as an extremely talented Hong Kong action director (Hark) succumbs to the dubious talents of star Van Damme (Yuen Kwai, John Woo and Ringo Lam were before him). Van Damme is a covert agent and assassin who is wounded while trying to off a particularly nasty terrorist. His identity is erased and he is sent to a top-secret island facility called the Colony. In the movie's only moderately well-written action setpiece, he escapes; thus begins the hunt for his nemesis, this time with the aid of a tattooed weapons expert (the similarly attired Rodman). Despite a surprisingly okay performance by Rodman, the movie goes nowhere. Only a furious kung fu fight between Van Damme and Chinese stuntman and movie villain Xiong Xin-Xin will quicken the pulse. ★½ VHS: $9.99; DVD: $14.99

Double Wedding

(1937, 87 min, US, Richard Thorpe) *William Powell, Myrna Loy, Florence Rice, John Beal, Jesse Ralph.* Asking the probing question, "Why do Bohemians have to stay up all night?," this breezy screwball comedy stars Powell as an eccentric artist who crosses paths with rigid businesswoman Loy when she thinks he's in love with her younger sister (Rice). A slew of zany characters are thrown into the stew as the two slowly fall in love. These include Beal, a catatonic wonder, as Rice's real fiancé, and Ralph as a fiery old broad and friend to Powell. The ending is right out of a Marx Brothers film. Based on the play "Great Love" by Ferenc Molnar ("The Guardsman"). ★★★ VHS: $19.99

Doubting Thomas

(1935, 78 min, US, David Butler) *Will Rogers, Billie Burke.* It's comedy of a high order when Rogers' wife Burke gets the lead in a small-town amateur theatrical production. One of Rogers' best films is a truly funny adaptation of George Kelly's play, "The Torch Bearers." A good starter for those unfamiliar with the wonderful, homespun Rogers. ★★★ VHS: $19.99

Le Doulos

(1962, 108 min, France, Jean-Pierre Melville) *Jean-Paul Belmondo, Michel Piccoli, Serge Reggiane, Jean Dessaily.* Melville's remarkable 1962 "nocturnal western" is adapted from a French detective novel and set in the French underworld. Belmondo stars as a mysterious, cryptic informer caught up in the complex relationship between criminal and policeman. In this tightly written and subtly acted film, Melville has created a man's world rich with male rituals and solidly sensuous women, all involved in a Pirandellian plot that none of the characters fully understands. Stylishly and brilliantly photographed in black and white, and filled with Melville's passionate love of film noir and the language of film. (French with English subtitles) ★★★ VHS: $24.99

Down and Dirty

(1976, 115 min, Italy, Ettore Scola) *Nino Manfredi, Francesca Anniballi.* Can you believe that Scola, the esteemed director of such highbrow hits as *Passion D'Amore* and *La Nuit de Varennes*, would also be responsible for this hilarious Italian "version" of *Pink Flamingos!*? Italy's urban poor, long ennobled in neorealist films, are seen in an entirely different light in this demented and scathing black comedy. Manfredi stars as the brutish patriarch of a morally depraved family whose interests include adultery, murder, revenge and incest. This thoroughly sick, no-holds-barred romp about Rome's low-life will have you crossing the street screaming the next time you are approached by a vagrant. (Italian with English subtitles) ★★★ VHS: $29.99

Down and Out in Beverly Hills

(1986, 97 min, US, Paul Mazursky) *Nick Nolte, Richard Dreyfuss, Bette Midler, Little Richard, Elizabeth Pena, Alexis Arquette.* Mazursky's boister-

ously funny social comedy stars Nolte as a street person who is taken in by a nouveau riche Beverly Hills family when he tries to drown himself in their swimming pool. Dreyfuss and Midler are in top form as the husband and wife whose lives are turned upside-down by their new boarder. Modern remake of the Jean Renoir 1932 classic *Boudu Saved from Drowning.* ★★★

Down by Law

(1986, 107 min, US, Jim Jarmusch) *John Lurie, Tom Waits, Roberto Benigni, Ellen Barkin.* Jarmusch continues on the theme of alienated outsiders in this razor-sharp and decidedly different "road picture." Lurie and Waits (wonderfully cast as a gravel-voiced D.J./hipster) meet up in a Louisiana prison, where they team with an irrepressible Italian tourist who leads them on a jailbreak through a stark eerie swamp and beyond. An offbeat comedy from one of the most original American filmmakers of today. ★★★

Down in the Delta

(1998, 115 min, US, Maya Angelou) *Alfre Woodard, Al Freeman, Jr., Wesley Snipes, Esther Rolle, Mary Alice.* Poet Maya Angelou's stellar directorial debut is a beautifully realized portrait of the highs and the lows of African-American life. Woodard stars as Loretta, a screwed-up, boozing mom living in the projects of Chicago. Her son and daughter are under the kindly supervision of Grandma (Alice, graceful as always) who finally has enough of Loretta's addictive ways — she sends Loretta and her kids on a bus for the Mississippi Delta to spend a summer with Uncle Earl (Freeman). Once there, of course, Loretta undergoes a slow transformational healing. If this sounds a bit trite and smacking of "Afterschool Special," it is; but it doesn't deter a splendid cast (which also features Rolle in her swansong) from elevating this into a serious and sensible family drama that is filled with a sense of triumph and a profound connection to history. ★★★ VHS: $14.99

Down Periscope

(1996, 92 min, US, David S. Ward) *Kelsey Grammer, Lauren Holly, Bruce Dern, Rob Schneider, Rip Torn, Harry Dean Stanton.* Another small-to-big screen casualty, "Frasier"'s Grammer forgoes his very funny TV persona for a smug submarine commander on his first, disaster-prone mission. The usual assortment of misfits and slackers are on hand, with a slightly bemused Grammer enduring his crew's shenanigans; after all, damn it, they're a great bunch of guys. Director Ward does manage to inject some humor, though for the most part the laughs are infrequent, and when they do occur, they are of the knucklehead variety. ★★ VHS: $9.99

Down to You

(2000, 89 min, US, Kris Isacsson) *Freddie Prinze, Jr., Julia Stiles, Selma Blair, Shawn Hatosy, Henry Winkler.* A romantic comedy that lives up — or is it down? — to its title, *Down to You* benefits from having two cute stars, but it gives them little to do. Al (Prinze) is a chef in college who meets and falls in love with Imogen (Stiles), a designer. They have friends who direct porn films (Orth) or star in them (Blair), and they stay generally smitten except when Al suspects Imogen of having an affair, and then he actually has one himself. While little of the film is realistic, which is OK, the characters on the WB network are just as pretty and much more fun to watch. This is a

Alfre Woodard in *Down in the Delta*

shame because Prinze and Stiles are engaging performers. Unfortunately, they are stuck in a futile film that fails to fully take advantage of their talents. ★½ VHS: $14.99; DVD: $29.99

Downhill Racer

(1969, 102 min, US, Michael Ritchie) *Robert Redford, Gene Hackman, Dabney Coleman.* Redford is the ski bum who gets a chance for an Olympic tryout. Hackman is the compassionate coach. An involving drama heightened by superior ski sequences. ★★★ VHS: $14.99

Downtown

(1990, 96 min, US, Richard Benjamin) *Anthony Edwards, Forest Whitaker, Joe Pantoliano, Penelope Ann Miller.* Though Edwards and Whitaker are extremely likable actors, there's little to recommend in this buddy-cop comedy set in urban Philadelphia (though locals may not recognize all the scenery). Edwards is the naïve white cop partnered with streetwise black cop Whitaker, together tracking down a stolen-car ring. ★★ VHS: $19.99

Dracula

(1931, 75 min, US, Tod Browning) *Bela Lugosi, Dwight Frye, David Manners, Helen Chandler.* Classic Hollywood horror film with Lugosi as the quintessential Count Dracula, that pain-in-the-neck vampire who here is on the loose in foggy old London. Director Browning creates an effectively eerie atmosphere to play out his tale, played to the hilt by Lugosi. Frye makes a memorable Renfield. (Also available in a Spanish-language version and one with a new score composed for the film) (Sequel: *Dracula's Daughter*) ★★★½ VHS: $14.99; DVD: $29.99

Dracula: The Spanish Version

(1931, 104 min, US, George Melford) *Carlos Villarias, Lupita Tovar.* One from the vaults! Filmed simultaneously with the original 1931 Bela Lugosi classic, this long-lost gem features the same sets and script translated into Spanish. Ripe with sensuality and atmosphere, many feel this version is more chilling than its English-language counterpart. With Villarias as the infamous Count. (Spanish with English subtitles) ★★★½ VHS: $14.99; DVD: $29.99

Dracula

(1973, 100 min, US, Dan Curtis) *Jack Palance, Simon Ward, Nigel Davenport.* Having made a fortune serializing the vampire legend with "Dark Shadows," producer-director Curtis returns to the original source with this made-for-TV adaptation of the Bram Stoker novel. Hollywood ham Palance dusts off his formal attire for the title role of the Count who...well, you know the story. Teleplay by Richard Matheson. ★★½ VHS: $59.99; DVD: $24.99

Dracula

(1979, 109 min, US, John Badham) *Frank Langella, Kate Nelligan, Laurence Olivier, Donald Pleasance, Trevor Eve.* This cinematic interpretation of the Broadway hit highlights the sexual subtext which is really at the heart of the vampire legends. Still, director Badham doesn't ignore the frights in this dark romance featuring Langella as the sensual count locked in immortal combat with Dr. Van Helsing (Olivier). Features an excellent score by John Williams. ★★★ VHS: $14.99; DVD: $24.99

Dracula: Dead and Loving It

(1995, 90 min, US, Mel Brooks) *Leslie Nielsen, Peter MacNicol, Steven Weber, Harvey Korman, Amy Yasbeck, Mel Brooks, Lysette Anthony, Anne Bancroft.* After a few comic misfires, Brooks is close to speed once more with this funny if sometimes obvious spoof on vampire films. Nielsen clearly is enjoying himself as the Count, neatly satirizing every vamp from Lugosi to Oldman. The story is basically the same: Dracula comes to England, and becomes a real pain in the neck until Professor Van Helsing (Brooks) gets on his trail. Brooks and his cowriters aren't on target with every joke, but many of the ones which do work are surprisingly fresh (such as Dracula dancing in front of a mirror or a hysterical scene of a staking). ★★½ VHS: $14.99

Dracula Has Risen from the Grave

(1968, 92 min, GB, Freddie Francis) *Christopher Lee, Rupert Davies, Veronica Carlson.* In this Hammer vampire horror tale, Lee emerges from a watery hibernation — looking more constipated than usual — to take sweet vengeance on a haughty monsignor (Davies) by claiming his beautiful niece. Hokey, campy fun. ★★½

Dracula's Daughter

Dracula: Prince of Darkness

(1965, 90 min, GB, Terence Fisher) *Christopher Lee, Andrew Keir, Barbara Shelley.* Lee is back as the epitome of evil. Only this time around, he doesn't say one word! Not to worry, however: his physical presence speaks volumes. A group of four English travelers stumble upon Castle Dracula in the mountains of Transylvania and unwittingly participate in his resurrection by a faithful human servant. More atmospheric than previous entries in the cycle, *Prince of Darkness* is another subtle masterwork by director Fisher. (Letterboxed) ★★★ VHS: $14.99

Dracula's Daughter

(1936, 70 min, US, Lambert Hillyer) *Gloria Holden, Otto Kruger.* With a decided taste for female blood, the screen's first vampire of the fairer sex, Holden, stars in this moody sequel to the Bela Lugosi classic. Holden stars as the titular vampire, whose attempts to escape her bloodthirsty inclinations (through the help of a sympathetic doctor) are dashed when she develops an affinity for a young woman whom she seduces and vampirizes. The first of what would be a long line of lesbian-themed vampire films. ★★★ VHS: $14.99

Dragnet

(1954, 89 min, US, Jack Webb) *Jack Webb, Ben Alexander.* Webb is Sergeant Joe Friday and Alexander is Officer Frank Smith in this first film version of two Los Angeles detectives, here investigating a mob slaying. Webb teamed up with Harry Morgan in the original TV series. (Remade in 1987 as a comedy) ★★½ VHS: $14.99

Dragnet

(1987, 106 min, US, Tom Mankiewicz) *Tom Hanks, Dan Aykroyd, Harry Morgan, Christopher Plummer, Elizabeth Ashley, Dabney Coleman.* "Just the facts..." Okay, this mediocre comic remake of the movie and famed TV series is a bust. Hanks and Aykroyd try their best to bring some lightheartedness into their roles, but they just aren't given any good material. ★½ VHS: $14.99; DVD: $24.99

Dragon Chow

(1987, 75 min, Germany, Jan Schütte) *Ric Young, Bhasker, Buddy Uzzaman.* Schütte's evocative and moving study of the hopes and ambitions of a pair of immigrant Pakistanis in Hamburg, West Germany, is as unpretentious and pristine as its simple black-and-white photography. The story follows Shezad and Rashid, who live in a barren welfare hotel filled with Hamburg's *gastarbeiter* (guest workers). Shezad's dream is to break into the restaurant business. He gets his start when he lands a job at a local Chinese restaurant and joins forces with one of the waiters. Schütte's story is simple and understated, but his treatment of this stranger-in-a-strange-land theme is flavorful and at times captivating. (German with English subtitles) ★★★½ VHS: $69.99

Dragon Fist

(1984, 95 min, Hong Kong, Lo Wei) *Jackie Chan.* Chan stars as kung fu artist Yuan, who seeks vengeance for the death of his master. Traveling with the master's widow and her daughter, they journey to a distant village where they uncover the killer. To their surprise, however, he has mutilated himself out of guilt for his deed. Revenge, honor, soap-opera melodrama and great fight scenes galore make this an above-average martial arts film. ★★★ VHS: $19.99

Dragon Inn

(1992, 105 min, Hong Kong, Raymond Lee) *Maggie Cheung, Brigitte Lin, Tony Leung, Donnie Yen.* A needlessly dense and lengthy prologue sets up the premise for this Hong Kong actioner: bad guys want to kill the good guys. Most of the film takes place in the titular locale: the only shelter for many miles in a vast desert. After a sluggish first half (which prompts one to wonder if this should have been called *Draggin Inn*), the film kicks into high gear with the type of kinetic and imaginative fight scenes fans have come to expect from producer Tsui Hark. With a lot of trimming (this cut is actually longer than the original), this could have been first-rate. As is, it's uneven and mildly enjoyable. (Letterboxed) (Cantonese with English subtitles) ★★½ VHS: $59.99; DVD: $29.99

Dragon Seed

(1944, 149 min, US, Jack Conway & Harold S. Bucquet) *Katharine Hepburn, Walter Huston, Agnes Moorehead.* Pearl S. Buck's novel of patriotism and heroism in war-torn China is the basis for this Hepburn vehicle. Kate plays a young Chinese peasant who becomes a guerrilla fighter when the Japanese army invades her small village. Anglo-Americans portraying Asians may disturb some viewers, but this well-intentioned war drama did serve as allegory and morale booster for the American fight against Nazism at the time. ★★½ VHS: $14.99

Dragon: The Bruce Lee Story

(1993, 119 min, US, Rob Cohen) *Jason Scott Lee, Lauren Holly, Robert Wagner, Michael Learned, Nancy Kwan.* This rousing chop-socky story of Bruce Lee rises above its mediocre bio-pic roots thanks to the winning combination of its undeniably exciting subject, a breezy and witty screenplay, elaborately staged fight sequences, and the riveting presence of Jason Scott Lee in the lead role. The film follows B. Lee from his early days in Hong Kong to his life as an ambitious American immigrant and movie superstar who dies suddenly at the age of 32. J.S. Lee's winning smile, chiseled body and effervescent personality carry the adulatory movie, adapted from the book by Lee's widow, Linda Lee Cadwell. While the film's love story is "nice," it is the fight sequences that are mesmeric — capturing the exaggerated look of kung fu fights, with their gravity-defying leaps, flailing legs and fists, hissing and crowing noises, and physical punishment that would pulverize any mere mortal. ★★★½ VHS: $9.99; DVD: $24.99

Dragonheart

(1996, 108 min, US, Rob Cohen) *Dennis Quaid, David Thewlis, Pete Postlethwaite, Julie Christie; Voice of: Sean Connery.* This film will be remembered, at the very least, for featuring the first completely computer-generated main character, Draco the Dragon (voiced by Connery). It is unfortunate, however, that this is the best thing about the movie. Quaid stars as an errant knight who lives to slay dragons. He meets his match in

Draco, whom he discovers is the last of his kind. They soon join forces to destroy the evil king and restore goodness to the land. While the computer effects are stupendous and the scenes between Draco and Quaid are the best of the film, the overall tone of the movie is far too juvenile for adults and too heavy, even dull at times, for kids. (VHS available letterboxed or pan & scan) ★★½ VHS: $14.99; DVD: $34.99

Dragonslayer

(1981, 108 min, US, Matthew Robbins) *Ralph Richardson, Peter MacNicol, Caitlin Clarke.* When his mentor (Richardson) suddenly shuffles off his mortal coil, a young sorcerer's apprentice (MacNicol) finds himself thrust into battle with a massive serpent. This exciting tale will be sure to please fans of medieval myth and fantasy as well as lovers of good action-adventure. The dragon sequences are terrific. ★★★ VHS: $14.99

The Draughtsman's Contract

(1982, 103 min, GB, Peter Greenaway) *Anthony Higgins, Janet Suzman, Joss Buckley, Steve Ubels, Anne Louis Lambert, Hugh Fraser.* This bizarre tale of adultery, blackmail and murder is set amidst the genteel countryside of late 17th-century England. An early effort from director Greenaway (*The Cook, The Thief...*), this provocative and ribald puzzle of a film concerns an artist's rather unusual bargain to sketch the estate of a wealthy landowner: £8 per drawing and the use of the man's wife for sexual favors. ★★★ VHS: $29.99; DVD: $29.99

Dream for an Insomniac

(1997, 87 min, US, Tiffanie Debartolo) *Ione Skye, Jennifer Aniston, Mackenzie Astin, Michael Landes, Seymour Cassel.* This dopey little story could be called *Cure for Insomnia*. With a sanitized San Francisco as backdrop, the movie borrows its unnaturally tidy coffee-shop setting from "Friends," the TV home of Aniston, and contains a lot of inane banter about caffeine. And don't adjust your sets: the first quarter is in black and white, building to one of the worst abuses of the "Oz effect." This cream puff is overstuffed with an almost uninterrupted soundtrack of goofy swing instrumentals or tunes by alterna-bands of the moment, so that in some scenes the wannabe-witty dialogue is all but drowned out. This is ultra-light romantic comedy for 17-year-olds on a date. ★★ VHS: $14.99

Dream Lover

(1994, 103 min, US, Nicholas Kazan) *James Spader, Madchen Amick, Bess Armstrong, Larry Miller.* Spader plays a successful architect who meets in the person of Amick his dream woman. Low-keyed and set at a lethargic pace, the film (ever so) slowly has Spader soon wondering if his new wife and the mother of his child is not only having an affair but if she is really who she says she is. *Dream Lover* does become mildly interesting when the con becomes evident, and builds to a rather neat twist ending. ★★

A Dream of Passion

(1978, 106 min, Germany, Jules Dassin) *Ellen Burstyn, Melina Mercouri, Irene Emirza, Andreas Filippides.* This interesting film focuses on the parallel Medea-like lives of two women in modern-day Athens. Burstyn delivers a powerful performance as an American woman jailed in Greece for murdering her three children in a fit of rage over her unfaithful husband. Mercouri is an international actress who returns to Greece to play the role of Medea in a play. She soon becomes obsessed with Burstyn's plight and the two women's lives become inextricably connected through tragedy. (Filmed in English) ★★

The Dream Team

(1989, 113 min, US, Howard Zieff) *Michael Keaton, Christopher Lloyd, Peter Boyle, Stephen Furst, Lorraine Bracco.* Keaton heads a solid cast in this literally crazy comedy about the misadventures of four mental patients on the loose in New York City. They're left to fend for themselves on the mean streets when their doctor witnesses a murder and is left for dead. ★★★

Dream with the Fishes

(1997, 96 min, US, Finn Taylor) *David Arquette, Brad Hunt, Cathy Moriarty, Kathryn Erbe, Patrick McGaw.* Arquette stars as a voyeuristic, suicidal schlub who becomes involved with his low-life, terminally ill neighbor. Not at all the "Afterschool Special" it may sound like, *Dream with the Fishes* allows the excellent Arquette and the rest of the fine cast to flesh out the characters, warts and all. The basic story, of an introvert who is brought out of his shell by his opposite, is a well-worn tale; but Arquette, Hunt and writer-director Taylor bring an individuality to the film that makes it seem *almost* fresh. Marred by a sometimes trendy soundtrack and a near-absence of narrative drive, the film arouses real sympathy for the characters without becoming maudlin. Unfortunately, Taylor's screenplay doesn't cut deep enough. ★★½ VHS: $24.99

Dreamchild

(1985, 94 min, GB, Gavin Millar) *Ian Holm, Coral Brown, Peter Gallagher, James Wilby.* This lavish fantasy/drama tells the story of the 80-year-old Alice Hargreaves who, as a child, had inspired Lewis Carroll to write his immortal "Alice in Wonderland." As Mrs. Hargreaves prepares to attend a symposium at Columbia University celebrating the 100th anniversary of Carroll's birth, she becomes haunted by fantastic images of the classic story, her youth, and her relationship with Mr. Carroll. Holm is superb as the stuttering Carroll, and Brown is unforgettable as the elder Alice. ★★★½ VHS: $14.99

Dreamers of the Day

(1990, 94 min, Canada, Patricia Spencer & Philip Wood) *Lorna Harding, Julie Lemieux.* From the *Claire of the Moon* school of lesbian love and sexual coming out is this enjoyable if a bit amateurish drama. Set in Toronto, the story revolves around the friendship between openly lesbian Andra (Harding), an aspiring filmmaker, and Claire (Lemieux), a married, professionally successful film producer. The film follows their budding friendship, which is undermined by Andra's attraction to the "straight" Claire, and their eventual romantic relationship. A tender and believable love story, the film suffers a bit from a standard story line, often stilted acting, and a static camera. ★★

Dreaming of Joseph Lees

(1999, 114 min, GB, Eric Styles) *Samantha Morton, Lee Ross, Rupert Graves.* A somber drama about an unhappy love triangle, *Dreaming of Joseph Lees* is set in dreary Somerset, England circa 1958. Eva (Morton) is a young girl who loves her cousin Joseph (Graves), but sees little of him. She is courted by Harry (Ross), a young man who offers her temporary happiness, and she eventually moves in with him. Yet, when Eva reunites with Joseph, she finds her feelings for him cannot be denied. *Dreaming of Joseph Lees* deliberately paces its first hour, where very little happens, only to gum up the works by rushing things in the last thirty minutes. The film captures the stifling atmosphere well, but like the characters, the audience suffers. ★★ VHS: $102.99

Dreaming of Rita

(1994, 108 min, Sweden, Jon Lindstrom) *Per Oscarsson, Marika Lagercrantz.* From the less serious side of Swedish filmmaking comes this wacky, but sadly not entirely successful, road comedy. The action kicks off when the recently widowed Bob (Oscarson) flips his lid, and runs off in search of a Danish sweetheart of some thirty years earlier. This precipitates a chase in which his daughter, Rita (named after Miss Hayworth), tracks him down and together they journey on to Copenhagen, all the while exploring their past à la *Wild Strawberries*. Along the way they all get the loopy advice of Eric XIV, a latter-day computer-hacking roadside prophet who seems bent on getting Rita into bed. The film ultimately lands nowhere and its pat ending leads to no revelations; still, *Dreaming of Rita's* amiable atmosphere and curious characters make it amusing, if not wholly worthwhile, viewing. (Swedish with English subtitles) ★★½ VHS: $29.99

The Dreamlife of Angels

(1999, 113 min, France, Erick Zonca) *Elodie Bouchez, Natacha Regnier, Gregoire Colin.* An intimate and deceptively simple film, *The Dreamlife of Angels* nevertheless packs an indelible emotional wallop. Isa (Bouchez) is a wanderer who meets factory-worker Marie (Regnier) when she stops in the northern French town of Lille. The two very different women soon forge a complex and unlikely friendship. Director Zonca chronicles the survival instincts and self-destructive tendencies of both Isa and Marie as they conduct their affairs, filming much of the action in real time. The naturalistic performances by the three leads are uniformly outstanding, and the film's stark directorial style only reinforces the despair of the lives on display. Emotionally complex and ultimately devastating. (French with English subtitles) ★★★½ VHS: $14.99; DVD: $29.99

Dreams

(1955, 87 min, Sweden, Ingmar Bergman) *Harriet Andersson, Gunnar Bjornstrand, Eva Dahlbeck.* This probing study into the psychology of desire follows the activities of a photography agency head and her top model who, while visiting another city for work, each have an affair. The setting is but a pretense for Bergman to explore women's dreams, torments and sexual obsessions, and how all of this affects their relationships with men. (Swedish with English subtitles) ★★★ VHS: $29.99

Dreamscape

(1984, 99 min, US, Joseph Ruben) *Dennis Quaid, Kate Capshaw, Max von Sydow, Christopher Plummer.* Telepathic spies romp through the president's nightmares in this imaginative sci-fi thriller. Good dream sequences. ★★★ VHS: $19.99; DVD: $24.99

Dress Gray

(1986, 208 min, US, Glenn Jordan) *Alec Baldwin, Hal Holbrook, Lane Smith, Lloyd Bridges, Patrick Cassidy, Timothy Van Patten.* This riveting murder mystery set in a military academy during the Vietnam War is based on the novel by Lucian K. Truscott IV and adapted by Gore Vidal. Baldwin stars as a cadet who becomes embroiled in a cover-up over the mysterious death of another cadet who had been raped before his murder. Fearing a scandal, the embarrassed commandant (Holbrook) and his staff cover up the death as a simple drowning. But as the truth slowly begins to unravel, Baldwin becomes a suspect and, like a high stakes Hardy Boys mystery, he attempts to clear his name and uncover the real killer with the mystery unraveling in a genuinely tense and exciting fashion. *Dress Gray* is both a well-told story and a well-developed allegory for America's involvement in Vietnam. ★★★½ VHS: $24.99

Dressed to Kill

(1979, 105 min, US, Brian De Palma) *Michael Caine, Angie Dickinson, Nancy Allen, Keith Gordon, Dennis Franz.* De Palma's homage to Hitchcock stars Caine as an inquisitive psychiatrist and Dickinson as a woman whose promiscuity leads her to become the first victim of a schizophrenic transvestite murderer. De Palma succeeds in creating both atmosphere and suspense. ★★★ VHS: $19.99; DVD: $19.99

The Dresser

(1983, 118 min, GB, Peter Yates) *Albert Finney, Tom Courtenay, Edward Fox, Michael Gough.* Finney and Courtenay are both outstanding as, respectively, a grandiloquent, aging actor and his devoted dresser. Finney is the head of a second-rate touring company besieged by financial and wartime woes; Courtenay is his gay confidant/secretary/valet who watches over him with the eye of a hawk and the perseverance of a den mother. A brilliant, moving and often funny peek behind the curtain of theatre life. ★★★½ VHS: $9.99

The Dressmaker

(1989, 92 min, GB, Jim O'Brien) *Joan Plowright, Billie Whitelaw, Pete Postlethwaite, Jane Horrocks.* Set in Liverpool in 1944, this intricate character study subtly probes the complexities of three women. When Rita, a timid, young waif, befriends a randy American soldier who is stationed in town, a bitter struggle for her soul ensues between her two aunts: the fun-loving Margo (beautifully played by Whitelaw) and the disapproving, repressed spinster Nellie (icily portrayed by Plowright). Based on the novel by Beryl Bainbridge, this extremely well-acted and absorbing family drama is taunt with sexual tensions and impending disaster. ★★★ VHS: $79.99

Drifting

(1983, 80 min, Israel, Amos Gutman) *Jonathan Sagalle, Ami Traub.* Gutman's acclaimed first feature is also the first gay film made in Israel. The story follows Robi, a 24-year-old would-be filmmaker who isolates himself completely in the gay world and grows increasingly troubled — not by the political turmoil in his country, but by his increasingly aimless and frustrated life. His ennui causes him to reject his friends and lover and withdraw into self-destruction. A sensitive and moving drama. (Hebrew with English subtitles) ★★★

Drifting Weeds

(1959, 119 min, Japan, Yasujiro Ozu) *Ganjiro Nakamura, Machiko Kyo.* A remake of his own silent film *A Story of Silent Weeds*, Ozu's lyrical drama is about rivalries among a traveling acting troupe. The film is marked by Ozu's spare directorial style and the beautiful photography by Daiei cameraman Miyagawa. (Japanese with English subtitles) (aka: *Floating Weeds*) ★★★½

Drive Me Crazy

(1999, 91 min, US, John Schultz) *Melissa Joan Hart, Adrian Grenier, Stephen Collins, Susan May Pratt.* Attractive opposites Nicole (Hart) and Chase (Grenier) are next-door neighbors and seniors in high school. When their respective partners dump them before the big centennial dance, Nicole and Chase pose as a couple to win back their true loves. Of course, while they "scam" everyone with their act, the pair end up falling for each other. Never mind the contrived plot; these two cuties exude some major charm in the process of learning to be "themselves." *Drive Me Crazy* is that rarity in teen films, a combination of hip and smart that's consistently amusing and never insulting. Hart is adorable as the perky go-getter with the crush on the jock but the heart for the rebel while Grenier is endearing as the social outcast who bonds with the in-crowd. ★★★ VHS: $14.99; DVD: $34.99

The Driver

(1978, 131 min, US, Walter Hill) *Bruce Dern, Ryan O'Neal, Isabelle Adjani.* Some spectacular car chase sequences highlight this unusual action-adventure with Dern as a cop obsessed with catching jewel thief O'Neal. ★★★ VHS: $59.99

Driving Miss Daisy

(1989, 99 min, US, Bruce Beresford) *Morgan Freeman, Jessica Tandy, Dan Aykroyd, Esther Rolle, Patti LuPone.* Based on Alfred Uhry's play, this is an extremely well-acted and literate examination of the four-decade relationship between an elderly, Southern Jewish widow and her ever-patient black chauffeur. Oscar-winner Tandy and Freeman give magnificent performances as Daisy and Hoke, whose working relationship, beginning in 1948, slowly develops into one of friendship, reflecting the changing social mores around them. Oscar winner for Best Picture, though there were far more worthy films nominated that year. ★★★½ VHS: $14.99; DVD: $19.99

Drop Dead Fred

(1991, 98 min, US, Ate De Jong) *Phoebe Cates, Rik Mayall, Marsha Mason.* A poor man's *Beetlejuice*, this sporadically funny though annoying comedy manages to entertain in spite of itself. Cates returns home to her shrewish mother (Mason) after her husband dumps her. There she is revisited by her "imaginary" childhood friend, Drop Dead Fred. As played by Mayall (of "The Young Ones"), Fred is a nose-picking, mischievous tornado of activity, eager to help straighten out the life of his former friend. Mayall's over-the-top mugging will either cause chuckles or spasms, but there's no denying that when he's on the screen, the film comes alive. ★★ VHS: $9.99

Drop Dead Gorgeous

(1999, 99 min, US, Michael Patrick Jann) *Kirstie Alley, Kirsten Dunst, Denise Richards, Ellen Barkin, Allison Janney.* A scintillating premise is allowed to be flushed down the drain thanks to static direction and a script that doesn't live up to its potential. Told as a faux documentary, the story sends up beauty pageants and the mothers and daughters who live for them — and would kill for them. That the film hits a few of its targets in parodying the contestants and their families makes it only more disappointing that it begins to fizzle midway through. Alley and Richards are in good form as the prim and haughty mother and daughter determined to win at any cost. Dunst gives a lively portrayal of a down-to-earth contestant who uncovers a murder plot during state finals, and Barkin is just right as her trailer-trash mom. Too bad the satire they've all been given to do is so obvious. ★★ VHS: $14.99; DVD: $19.99

Drop Zone

(1994, 101 min, US, John Badham) *Wesley Snipes, Gary Busey, Michael Jeter, Yancy Butler, Grace Zabriskie.* Exhilarating aerial photography punctuates this otherwise by-the-numbers rehash of *Die Hard* and *Point Break.* Snipes stars as a U.S. marshall who goes undercover in the world of skydiving to locate a gang of gonzo parachutists (headed by *ubervillain* Busey) planning to "drop in" on

The Three Cissies: *Drowning by Numbers*

Duck Soup

the DEA, steal the names of every undercover agent working in the field, and sell them to the highest bidder. Obviously this is the kind of film where macho posturing replaces acting, and stuntwork supplants action, but Snipes and Busey make the best of it. ★★½ VHS: $9.99; DVD: $24.99

Drowning by Numbers

(1987, 121 min, GB, Peter Greenaway) *Joan Plowright, Juliet Stevenson, Joely Richardson, Bernard Hill.* Wildly imaginative and entertaining, this offbeat comedy is a decidedly different twist on the battle between the sexes. The film follows the saga of three women (all named Cissie) who drown their husbands and then, attempting to cover up their crimes, engage in a bizarre game of sexual innuendo with the local coroner, Madgett. This outrageous tryst becomes the centerpiece of Greenaway's operative metaphor, namely, the games people play. The film is literally filled with games, mostly played by Madgett and his pre-pubescent son. Additionally, the film itself is one long game of numerical hide-and-seek — video viewers beware, the small screen may make it difficult to participate. A terrific ensemble is featured. ★★★½ VHS: $14.99

Drowning Mona

(2000, 107 min, US, Nick Gomez) *Danny DeVito, Bette Midler, Neve Campbell, Jamie Lee Curtis, Casey Affleck, Will Ferrell, William Fichtner, Marcus Thomas.* A good premise that is rarely fulfilled, *Drowning Mona* tries desperately to recapture the fun and dark humor of *Ruthless People*, DeVito and Midler's hilarious first film together, but their reunion unfortunately lacks that film's wit, timing and discipline. Midler is Mona Dearly, who at the film's beginning sails off a cliff in her new Yugo into the depths of a local lake. It soon becomes apparent it was murder. But who did it? Through a series of flashbacks, it looks as if the whole town had reason to bump the mean-spirited Mona off. It's up to DeVito as the town's sheriff to figure it out. The scenario is ripe for black comedy, but director Gomez has little command for either frantic farce or subtle comedic escapades, and as such most of the comedy just sits there — despite an eager cast. ★★ VHS: $14.99; DVD: $24.99

The Drowning Pool

(1976, 108 min, US, Stuart Rosenberg) *Paul Newman, Joanne Woodward, Anthony Franciosa, Melanie Griffith.* This sequel to *Harper* finds Newman deep in the heart of Dixie trying to help old lover Woodward out of a jam and only making matters worse. Griffith makes a delightful film debut as Woodward's precocious daughter. ★★½ VHS: $14.99

Drugstore Cowboy

(1989, 100 min, US, Gus Van Sant) *Matt Dillon, Kelly Lynch, James LeGros, Heather Graham, William S. Burroughs.* Van Sant's gritty and provocative exposé of the down-and-out lives of four drug addicts living in the Pacific Northwest in the 1970s is highly original and profoundly honest. Dillon is perfectly cast as an icy-cool and unrepenting "drug fiend" who plays daddy to a rogue family of three fellow junkies — Lynch as his statuesque wife and LeGros and Graham as his mindless junkie pals. Drawing its power from a surprisingly wry sense of humor and its wholly unapologetic tone, the film follows Dillon and crew as they wantonly romp from town to town and burgle the drugs they need from local apothecaries. It seems inconceivable that in the Reagan-Bush era of rampant antidrug hysteria a film as brazenly nonjudgmental on this issue could have been made, much less enjoy the tremendous acclaim this film deservedly received. Burroughs has a terrific cameo as a weathered drug addict. ★★★★ VHS: $9.99; DVD: $24.99

Drums

(1938, 104 min, GB, Zoltan Korda) *Roger Livesey, Raymond Massey, Sabu, Valerie Hobson.* Korda's beautifully filmed colonial adventure features Livesey as a patriotic British officer who forms an alliance with a young Indian prince (Sabu) to help him battle his scheming uncle (Massey). ★★★ VHS: $19.99

Drums Along the Mohawk

(1939, 103 min, US, John Ford) *Henry Fonda, Claudette Colbert, Edna May Oliver, John Carradine.* Released the same year as his classic western *Stagecoach*, Ford heads East with this sumptuous historical drama mixed with humor and rousing adventure sequences. Fonda and Colbert star as colonists during the Revolutionary War who must protect themselves from Indian uprisings in the backwoods of upstate New York. Gorgeous cinematography in glorious Technicolor. ★★★ VHS: $19.99

Drunken Angel

(1948, 102 min, Japan, Akira Kurosawa) *Toshiro Mifune, Takashi Shimura.* An older doctor attempts to cure and rehabilitate a tubercular young gangster (Mifune) in this sinister and disturbing allegory on the human condition. This early Kurosawa work pays tribute to American film noir. (Japanese with English subtitles) ★★★ VHS: $19.99

Drunken Master II

(1994, 102 min, Hong Kong, Chia-Liang Liu) *Jackie Chan, Anita Mui, Andy Lau.* In this terrific action comedy (many fans think this may be Jackie's best), the martial arts superstar plays Wong Fei Hun, a ne'er-do-well who battles the bad guys with a bizarre secret weapon: the more he drinks, the more amazing a fighter he becomes. This film contains two of the greatest fight scenes ever filmed: an extremely energetic bamboo-stick fight, and the lengthy, climactic mano-a-mano. This is a must-see for action nuts,

and a must-own for Jackie fans. (Letterboxed) (Cantonese with English subtitles) (A dubbed, pan & scan version is available called *The Legend of Drunken Master*. The VHS retails for $102.99; DVD retails for $29.99) ★★★★ VHS: $19.99

Drunks

(1997, 88 min, US, Peter Cohn) *Richard Lewis, Faye Dunaway, Dianne Wiest, Amanda Plummer, Howard Rollins, Jr., Parker Posey, Spalding Gray.* A small group of recovering alcoholics gather in the basement of a Times Square church for an intense AA meeting. One member (Lewis) ducks out early to walk the streets of New York City — will he revert to his old ways? Well-intentioned but rather flat, *Drunks* barely qualifies as a movie; it's basically a succession of talking heads, each giving his or her story of addiction and misery. This is an adaptation of the play "Blackout," and its theatrical origins show. The acting is uniformly good, with individual moments of power, but the overall effect is artificial and unconvincing. It has the feel of an actor's workshop, and screams to be left on the stage. ★★ VHS: $14.99; DVD: $24.99

Dry Cleaning (Nettoyage à sec)

(1999, 97 min, France, Anne Fontaine) *Miou-Miou, Charles Berling, Stanislas Merhar.* This unusually compelling French psychosexual drama revolves around a staunchly "normal" married couple and how their dormant sexuality is ignited when a young man — a bisexual drag queen performer — enters their lives. Nicole (Miou-Miou) and Jean-Marie (Berling) are a strait-laced married couple who operate a small-town dry cleaning shop. On a rare night out, they visit a club where they become enthralled by a brother-sister drag act. Through circumstances, the brother, Loic — an enigmatic but sexily androgynous young man — begins to work at the couple's shop. The story focuses on how both Marie and Jean-Marie are attracted to him. The drama provocatively probes the shifting emotions, pent-up sexual longings and fears of the three. (French with English subtitles) ★★★ VHS: $59.99; DVD: $29.99

A Dry White Season

(1989, 97 min, US, Euzhan Palcy) *Donald Sutherland, Zakes Mokae, Jurgen Prochnow, Susan Sarandon, Marlon Brando.* South African director Palcy powerfully confronts the violence and inhuman brutality of Apartheid. Sutherland is excellent as Ben du Toit, a well-respected Afrikaner schoolteacher asked to use his influence to help find his gardener's missing son. Du Toit quickly finds himself entangled with the dreaded Special Branch — a rather noxious element of the South African security system. The movie draws its power as we witness du Toit, ostracized, humiliated and beaten, in his transformation from ignorant patriot to outraged citizen. Excellent supporting cast. ★★★½

DuBarry Was a Lady

(1943, 100 min, US, Roy Del Ruth) *Red Skelton, Lucille Ball, Gene Kelly, Zero Mostel.* Those two crowned heads of comic tomfoolery, Skelton and Ball, take over the Bert Lahr and Ethel Merman roles in this entertaining adaptation of the Cole Porter musical. And though Red and Lucy are just fine, Hollywood once again outsmarted itself in the translation of a stage musical, here keeping only three of Porter's songs ("Friendship,"

D

"Do I Love You" and "Katie Went to Haiti"). Red's in love with nightclub entertainer Lucy. He sips a mickey and dreams he's Louis XV of France to Lucy's Madame DuBarry. ★★★ VHS: $19.99

duBEAT-E-O

(1984, 84 min, US, Alan Sacks) *Ray Sharkey.* Punky, irreverent and cocky, but marred by a nasty misogynist, violent and antigay streak, this low-budget musical-comedy is a wonderful illustration of the vastly different independent filmmaking worlds of L.A. and New York. Sharkey plays a sleaze-ball filmmaker who, on the "forceful" insistence of his producer, must finish his rock opus on Joan Jett within 31 hours. With offscreen narration and commentary by the actual filmmaker and his friends, the film's hipper-than-thou approach will remind many of the much funnier and similarly themed *Tapeheads.* Featuring the music of Joan Jett, Social Distortion and The Lounge Lizards. ★★½ VHS: $59.99

Duck Soup

(1933, 70 min, US, Leo McCarey) *The Marx Brothers, Margaret Dumont.* The best Marx Brothers by most standards, this wacky tale follows the boys' exploits in the tiny country of Freedonia (Land of the Spree and Home of the Knave). Groucho is memorable as the celebrated Rufus T. Firefly, newly appointed president; Harpo and Chico are enemy spies, and Zeppo is a tenor. Dumont is her usual resilient self. ★★★★ VHS: $14.99

Dude, Where's My Car?

(2000, 83 min, US, Danny Leiner) *Ashton Kutcher, Seann William Scott, Jennifer Garner, Marla Sokoloff, Kristy Swanson.* Two stoners, Chester and Jesse (Kutcher, Scott), have such a wild night partying they wake up not remembering a thing. They spend the entire film trying to piece together what happened. Not exactly a premise that would have had Billy Wilder jumping up and down, but one that has a certain amount of promise in the dumb slacker comedy genre. What transpires is a curiously sweet but laughless exercise in pot jokes, sex jokes and alien encounters. A lesser Bill and Ted, Kutcher and Scott are agreeable enough, but the tame screenplay reduces them to stealing from Abbott and Costello, Cheech and Chong, Parker and Stone, without any identity of their own. ★½ VHS: $102.99; DVD: $26.99

Dudley Do-Right

(1999, 83 min, US, Hugh Wilson) *Brendan Fraser, Alfred Molina, Sarah Jessica Parker, Eric Idle, Robert Prosky, Alex Rocco.* Trying to capture the same sense of silly fun that made *George of the Jungle* such a hit, this amiable comedy — based on another Jay Ward cartoon — certainly gets the silly part down. With the same toothy enthusiasm he brought to *George*, Fraser is Dudley Do-Right, that luckless Canadian Mountie who forever is being outsmarted by that dastardly villain Snidely Whiplash. The story, which is backseat to pratfalls and goofy shenanigans, has to do with Snidely faking a gold rush so that his town can reap the rewards. Only Dudley can stop him — or can he? There are quite a few laughs, most at the expense of Dudley, but the silliness ratio becomes a little too high after a while. ★★½ VHS: $14.99; DVD: $24.99

Duel

(1971, 90 min, US, Steven Spielberg) *Dennis Weaver, Lucille Benson.* Spielberg's career-launching film is a first-rate made-for-TV thriller starring Weaver as a businessman being terrorized by an unseen truck driver who is apparently, and for no known reason, out to kill him. Inventive and highly suspenseful. ★★★ VHS: $9.99

Duel at Diablo

(1966, 103 min, US, Ralph Nelson) *Sidney Poitier, James Garner, Bibi Andersson, Dennis Weaver.* An exciting western with Garner as an Indian scout, seeking revenge for the murder of his wife, who helps transport guns across Indian territory. Poitier is an ex-Army officer. Together, they hold off an Indian attack. ★★★ VHS: $19.99

Duel in the Sun

(1946, 130 min, US, King Vidor) *Gregory Peck, Jennifer Jones, Joseph Cotten, Lillian Gish, Lionel Barrymore, Butterfly McQueen.* Producer David O. Selznick's sexy epic western about the rivalry between two brothers (Peck, Cotten) for the love of a beautiful half-breed Indian girl, played with sultry authority by Jones. One of the most popular films of the 1940s, the film, though very entertaining, sometimes seems to border on high camp. (Letterboxed) ★★★ VHS: $14.99; DVD: $14.99

Duel to the Death

(1982, 100 min, Hong Kong, Ching Siu-Tung) *Damian Lau, Flora Cheung, Norman Tsui.* Two outstanding swordsmen from rival schools, one Japanese and one Chinese, are forced to do battle in a traditional tournament which is held once every 100 years. Unexpectedly, the two become friends, combining their awesome abilities to defeat their enemy. This debut film from director Ching features all the trademark attractions of his later works: gravity-defying swordsmen, chaotic camerawork, themes of loyalty and duty, a bit of humor to lighten the drama and sumptuous visuals. (Letterboxed) (Cantonese with English subtitles) ★★★½ VHS: $59.99; DVD: $29.99

The Duellists

(1977, 100 min, GB, Ridley Scott) *Keith Carradine, Harvey Keitel, Albert Finney, Edward Fox,* *Tom Conti.* Scott's first feature film is an eccentric rendering of the Joseph Conrad story about an inexplicable feud between two officers of the Napoleonic army. Carradine and Keitel personify the passion, honor and violence which are the heart of Conrad's story. A visually stunning film. ★★★½ VHS: $14.99

Duet for One

(1986, 107 min, GB, Andrei Konchalovsky) *Julie Andrews, Alan Bates, Max von Sydow, Rupert Everett.* Andrews, taking a break from musical comedy, gives a sensitive performance in this routine tragic tale of a world-renowned concert violinist whose career is brought to an abrupt end with the onset of multiple sclerosis. Adapted from the play by Tom Kempinksi, who based his story on Jackie du Pre (whose own story would be told in *Hilary & Jackie*). ★★½ VHS: $14.99

Dulces Navajas (Navajeros)

(1981, 100 min, Spain, Eloy de la Iglesia) *Isela Vega.* Within the slums and bordellos of Madrid, an illiterate 16-year-old gang leader battles police, prison authorities and rival youth gangs for love and acceptance. A hard-hitting, sexually charged film based on a true story. (Spanish with English subtitles) ★★★

Dumb and Dumber

(1994, 106 min, US, Peter Farrelly) *Jim Carrey, Jeff Daniels, Teri Garr, Lauren Holly, Charles Rocket.* This sophomoric, scatological road comedy and box-office success follows Lloyd and Harry, two bumbling, dimwitted roommates who travel cross-country to locate Lloyd's dream woman (Holly). On the way, their stupid shenanigans involve them with blackmailers, murderers and high society. Anyone who has seen a Jerry Lewis or Bob Hope comedy has seen this all before. Ironically, for a Carrey vehicle it's Daniels as Harry who supplies most of the laughs, including a hilarious sequence set on the slopes of Aspen with Holly as a Margaret Dumont–like foil. Carrey, in turn, gives a hammy performance which captures none of the golden timing demonstrated in *The Mask.* (Letterboxed VHS available for $19.99) ★½ VHS: $14.99; DVD: $24.99

Dude, Where's My Car?

Dumbo

(1941, 64 min, US, Ben Sharpsteen) After the (initial) financial disappointment of *Fantasia*, Disney needed some cash, and fast, or his studio was going to be converted into a hospital. This film was made quick and cheap, and that's what gives it its energy and charm. With clean and simple design, charming songs, and all the vitality of the classic shorts, *Dumbo* found Disney returning to form. ★★★★ VHS: $22.99

Dune

(1984, 137 min, US, David Lynch) *Kyle MacLachlan, Jose Ferrer, Francesca Annis, Sting, Max von Sydow, Brad Dourif, Patrick Stewart.* Lynch brings Frank Herbert's sci-fi classic to the screen in this wildly uneven but thought-provoking adaptation. In the distant future, the most coveted substance is the drug-like spice known as Melange. Valued for its mind-expanding properties, the sole source of the spice is the desert planet Arrakis, or Dune. Thus, the superpowers clash over the control of Arrakis; for whoever owns the spice owns the universe. Although inconsistent, the set and costume design, as well as Lynch's directorial touches, make *Dune* a film that challenges the imagination. (VHS available letterboxed or pan & scan) ★★½ VHS: $14.99

Dune

(2000, 270 min, US, John Harrison) *William Hurt, Alec Newman, Giancarlo Giannini, Uwe Ochsenknecht, Ian McNiece, Matt Keeslar, Saskia Reeves.* One of the most damning criticisms of David Lynch's trippy 1984 adaptation of Frank Herbert's classic sci-fi saga is that Lynch's film is too muddled and compressed, shoehorning a dense, labyrinthine plot into 140 minutes of movie. Produced for the Sci-Fi Channel, this new miniseries runs a marathon four-and-a-half hours, yet despite the opportunity to flesh out characters and expound on shady alliances and secret betrayals, this longer *Dune* is just as confounding — only far more tedious. Some truly cool special effects are offset by shoddy visuals, and the semi-impressive production design is wrecked by the overuse of colored lighting effects to establish locale and mood. On a technical level, this new *Dune* doesn't even compare to the Lynch version, begging the all-important question: "Why bother?" ★★ VHS: $39.99

The Dunera Boys

(1985, 150 min, Australia, Sam Lewin) *Bob Hoskins, Joe Spano.* Hoskins stars in this film about a group of Jewish refugees during WWII who are suspected of being Nazi informants by the British army. They are deported to a prison camp in Australia. Hoskins is absolutely brilliant as one of the refugees who is forced to prove his loyalty to England. Marred only by its length, this is an intelligently written and powerfully acted film. ★★★ VHS: $79.99

Dunston Checks In

(1995, 85 min, US, Ken Kwapis) *Jason Alexander, Faye Dunaway, Eric Lloyd, Rupert Everett, Paul Reubens, Glenn Shadix.* Parents, beware: When Dunston checks in, your brain checks out. Dunston is an orangutan whose owner (Everett) passes for a British lord but who is in fact a thief with a primate assistant. The two of them check into a five-star hotel run by Alexander. And then

the shenanigans begin. Neither the strong cast nor the excellent production values can overcome the convoluted and drawn out story line. ★★ VHS: $9.99

The Dunwich Horror

(1969, 90 min, US, Daniel Haller) *Dean Stockwell, Sandra Dee, Ed Begley.* Roger Corman produced this effective adaptation of the classic H.P. Lovecraft story. Stockwell's interest in a rare book called "The Necronomicon" soon requires more than an attentive reading and begins to impinge on his relationship with girlfriend Dee. Begley, in his last role, is the professor who puts a stop to all this evil. ★★½ VHS: $12.99

Dust

(1985, 88 min, Belgium/France, Marion Hansel) *Jane Birkin, Trevor Howard.* Set on an isolated South African farm, this Venice Film Festival winner charts, with fearful precision, the mental disintegration of a lonely and sexually desperate young woman (Birkin) who murders her tyrannical father (Howard). Based on J. M. Coetzee's novel "In the Heart of the Country." ★★★

Dusty

(1985, 89 min, Australia, John Richardson) *Bill Kerr, Noel Trevarthen.* A heartwarming tale of an aging Outback prospector, played by Kerr, who befriends a half-wild sheepdog named Dusty. A moving family adventure in the tradition of *Old Yeller*. ★★★ VHS: $39.99

Dutch

(1991, 105 min, US, Peter Faiman) *Ed O'Neill, JoBeth Williams, Ethan Randall.* John Hughes returns to one of his successful formulas (*Planes, Trains and Automobiles*) with considerably less successful results. Working-class stiff O'Neill is engaged to upper-crust Williams. It's Thanksgiving vacation, and Williams' preppy teenage son (Randall) is stuck at school. So O'Neill is sent to escort the lad home. You won't need a crystal ball to predict plot developments, such as the two of them won't hit it off, or the cross-country trip becomes a comedy of errors, or they become best buddies. Randall is appropriately obnoxious — to the point of wanting to hit him with a snow shovel. ★½

Dying Young

(1991, 105 min, US, Joel Schumacher) *Julia Roberts, Campbell Scott, Colleen Dewhurst, Vincent D'Onofrio, Ellen Burstyn.* Director Schumacher and star Roberts reunite after their successful *Flatliners*, though their experience with near-death heroics is catatonic. In a terribly written role (which shamelessly copies her *Pretty Woman*), Roberts is a working-class woman who takes a job as nurse to a terminally ill man (Scott). As the rich man intellectually enlightens her, she brings a much-needed spark of energy to an otherwise privileged, lonely person. Set in San Francisco and full of AIDS awareness messages in the background, the film is a tedious allegory for that disease and its wasting of young lives — if only the filmmakers had the guts to make the movie which this self-consciously tries to be. ★ VHS: $9.99

Each Dawn I Die

(1939, 92 min, US, William Keighley) *James Cagney, George Raft, George Bancroft.* Cagney plays a reporter who is framed and sent to prison. Raft is the tough con he tangles with. This routine Warner programmer features its stars in good form but is mired by a convoluted second half. ★★½ VHS: $19.99

The Eagle

(1925, 77 min, US, Clarence Brown) *Rudolph Valentino, Louise Dresser, Vilma Banky.* Full of romance, action and adventure, this silent costume adventure yarn was adapted from an Alexander Pushkin story. Valentino plays a young Russian officer who rejects the advances of the evil Czarina (Dresser). As a result, he is banished. But he returns as the Eagle, a Tartar Robin Hood out to take vengeance against the Czarina as well as win the hand of the woman (Banky) he loves. Great fun and Valentino cuts a fine swash. ★★★½

The Eagle and the Hawk

(1933, 68 min, US, Stuart Walker) *Fredric March, Cary Grant, Carole Lombard.* March and Grant make a formidable team in this first-rate anti-war film set during WWI. They play American pilots stationed in France, each learning a lesson about heroism and friendship. Lombard is the society girl torn between them. ★★★½ VHS: $14.99

The Eagle Has Landed

(1977, 123 min, GB, John Sturges) *Michael Caine, Donald Sutherland, Robert Duvall, Donald Pleasence, Treat Williams, Larry Hagman.* Fast-moving, intricately plotted and solidly entertaining, this WWII action-adventure makes full use of an excellent cast. Based on the novel by Jack Higgins about an attempt by the Germans to kidnap Winston Churchill. ★★★ VHS: $9.99; DVD: $14.99

The Eagle Has Two Heads

(L'Aigle à Deux Têtes)

(1947, 99 min, France, Jean Cocteau) *Jean Marais, Edwige Feuillere.* This extravagant and romantic melodrama was adapted from Cocteau's hugely successful play. Set in the 19th century, the film stars Marais as a lederhosen-clad poet/anarchist (and double for the dead king) who sets out to assassinate the beautiful queen (Feuillère), but when the two lock eyes, it is love at first sight. In keeping with Cocteau's passion for linking love with death, the couple meets a tragic end. Probably the least successful of Cocteau's films. (French with English subtitles) ★★½ VHS: $29.99

An Early Frost

(1985, 100 min, US, John Erman) *Aidan Quinn, Gena Rowlands, Ben Gazzara, Sylvia Sidney, D.W. Moffett, John Glover.* The first TV movie to deal with the subject of AIDS, *An Early Frost* is a thoughtful and undeniably powerful drama.

Quinn stars as Michael, a successful gay lawyer who learns he has been infected with the HIV virus. He decides to tell his family, who do not even know he is gay. The effect of his announcement on him and his family is at the core of the heartfelt story. Quinn gives a sensitive though commanding performance, and Rowlands, Gazzara and especially Sydney offer strong support as his parents and grandmother. Glover is remarkable as a dying patient Michael befriends. An Emmy Award winner for Best Screenplay. ★★★½ VHS: $19.99

Early Summer (Bakushu)

(1951, 135 min, Japan, Yasujiro Ozu) *Ichiro Sugai, Chishu Ryu.* The essence of Japanese family life is masterfully captured in this illuminating, passionate and, at times, humorous work that must be considered one of director Ozu's best post-war films. Noriko, an intelligent and independent woman of 28, is faced with an arranged marriage to an unloved and unloving man, but her sense of individualism conflicts with her feelings of obligation towards her family. A restrained, succinct observation on the inevitable tides of change on family traditions and bonds, and their effect on Japanese culture. (Japanese with English subtitles) ★★★★ VHS: $29.99

The Earrings of Madame de

(1945, 105 min, France, Max Ophüls) *Charles Boyer, Danielle Darrieux, Vittorio De Sica.* This wonderfully captivating film tells the ironic and ultimately tragic tale of a woman and a set of diamond earrings which are given to her by her husband, pawned by him when in debt, and then given again to her, but this time by her lover. A remarkable portrait of the vanity and frivolous nature of the upper classes in 19th-century Paris. (French with English subtitles) ★★★ VHS: $14.99

Earth

(1930, 90 min, USSR, Alexander Dovzhenko) *Semyon Svashenko, Mikola Nademsy.* One of the last silent movies and a masterpiece in Soviet cinema, *Earth* is a lyrically-told poem about man's love of nature, his endeavors to adapt it to his needs, and of man's death as part of the cycle of life. In Ukraine, a collective of poor peasants attempt to farm the vast lands of the Kulaks, the landed gentry, who in turn oppose them. Dovzhenko paints an indelible portrait of a people's struggle against superstition, rich landowners and nature itself in their fight to make their dreams reality. (Silent with orchestral accompaniment) ★★★★ VHS: $29.99

Earth Girls Are Easy

(1989, 102 min, US, Julien Temple) *Jeff Goldblum, Geena Davis, Jim Carrey, Damon Wayans, Julie Brown.* After dissecting 1950s London with a rock beat in the brilliant *Absolute Beginners*, director Temple takes a look at 1980s California, complete with Valley girls, dudes and aliens — from outer space. Davis awakens to find a spaceship in her swimming pool, a ship with shaggy Goldblum, Carrey and Wayans aboard. Doing her best for interplanetary relations, she takes the visitors under her wing, and in the process falls in love with Captain Jeff. The film never reaches the comic fever pitch it sets out to capture, though the cast manages to make the most

East Is East

of the uneven screenplay. ★★½ VHS: $9.99; DVD: $14.99

Earth vs. the Flying Saucers

(1956, 83 min, US, Fred F. Sears) *Hugh Marlowe, Joan Taylor.* Splendid special effects by wizard Ray Harryhausen highlight this sci-fi favorite about aliens demanding Earth's surrender. ★★★ VHS: $9.99

Earthquake

(1974, 129 min, US, Mark Robson) *Charlton Heston, Genevieve Bujold, George Kennedy, Ava Gardner, Richard Roundtree, Lorne Greene, Marjoe Gortner, Victoria Principal.* Well, it *did* win an Oscar for some outstanding special effects, but aside from a dexterity at leveling miniature models of L.A., the film offers little else. Greene plays Gardner's father! ★★ VHS: $9.99; DVD: $19.99

East Is East

(2000, 96 min, GB, Damien O'Donnell) *Om Puri, Linda Bassett, Jordan Routledge, Archie Panjabi, Emil Marwa.* A highbrow cultural comedy with a penchant for gross-outs, this curiously entertaining import beat out *Notting Hill* for the British Academy Award for Best British Picture. The legendary (in the right circles) Puri plays George, a Pakistani immigrant in Manchester. His family, including Anglo wife Ella (Bassett) and their seven kids, is growing up in the early '70s; circumcision, arranged marriage, and George's other Muslim family values don't rub well in this time of cultural upheaval. Likewise, neither does their mixed family fit in with the xenophobic locals. The comedy is excellent; from subtle commentary to broad strokes, it's all winningly acted by the young ensemble and especially Puri. However, when the script takes occasional sharp turns to the serious (and George's monstrous, domineering side appears), the tone shift is so jarring as to take you out of the movie. There's a good little comedy in here; the attempt at something more relevant taints the film as much as it tarnishes Puri's character. ★★★ VHS: $19.99; DVD: $29.99

The East Is Red

(1992, 95 min, Hong Kong, Ching Siu-Tung) *Brigitte Lin-Ching Hsia.* Move over, Supergirl. Your days are numbered, Wonder Woman. Asia the Invincible, the first transsexual lesbian superhero, is now the reigning queen. This spectacular kung-fu fantasy is 95 minutes of nonstop action featuring awesome special effects and enough flailing bodies and exhilarating fight sequences to keep any fan of the genre enthralled. With magical powers, Asia (Ching-Hsia) is a fiery villain/hero who goes on a rampage, fighting neighboring armies, Spanish conquistadors and even a bevy of fake Asias, to regain the hand of Snow, the woman she loves. ★★★ VHS: $39.99; DVD: $29.99

East of Eden

(1955, 115 min, US, Elia Kazan) *James Dean, Julie Harris, Raymond Massey, Jo Van Fleet.* Dean gives an affecting and sincere performance as a rebel with a cause in this Kazan classic. Based on John Steinbeck's novel, this was Dean's starring debut as a misunderstood youth, yearning for his father's approval while searching for the truth about his mysteriously absent mother. Harris and Massey give fine performances in support, and Van Fleet was an Oscar winner for her portrayal of Dean's bitter mom. ★★★★

East Side Story

(1997, 78 min, Germany, Dana Ranga) A terrific documentary which offers a history of the Communist musical. Told through narration, interviews and wonderful film clips, it's a fascinating history indeed. We see scenes from Stalin's favorite film — a cheesy "song for the common man"; clips from films considered subversive by censorious governments; and hilariously campy '60s teen musicals influenced by U.S. and British films. While the clips themselves are the real draw here, the interviews provide an enticing inside look at how artists worked within the heavy constraints of a Communist regime. The only real drawback is that it is an inadvertent tease: these tantalizing clips are likely the only glimpses we'll get of these films. (German and various other languages with English subtitles) ★★★★ VHS: $24.99; DVD: $29.99

East Side, West Side

(1949, 108 min, US, Mervyn LeRoy) *Barbara Stanwyck, James Mason, Ava Gardner, Van Heflin.* The foibles of New York's society darlings are under scrutiny in this capable though shallow melodrama based on the Marcia Davenport novel. Stanwyck and Mason are a wealthy couple whose marriage is coming apart, especially with Gardner and Heflin waiting for them in the wings. Good performances by all help gloss over the occasional dramatic potholes. ★★½ VHS: $19.99

East/West (Est/Ouest)

(1999, 125 min, France/Russia, Régis Wargnier) *Sandrine Bonnaire, Oleg Menchikov, Catherine Deneuve, Sergi Bodrov Jr.* Alexei Golovine (Menchikov) is a young Russian doctor living in France in 1946, when Stalin issues an open invitation to all expatriates to return to Mother Russia. With his French wife Marie (Bonnaire) and their young son, he joins the last wave of the WWII diaspora. Like the Romanovs, the Golovine family speak French better than Russian when their ship reaches port and they receive their first lesson in the institutional insanity that is Stalinist Russia. Essentially hijacked and shipped to Kiev, they are little more than prisoners, under constant surveillance, under constant suspicion. Alexei is more fully aware of his family's peril; as he struggles with the guilt of placing them in this situation, he plays to the country's need for medical practitioners. As he did in *Indochine*, director Wargnier explores epic, historical events through personal, intimate human moments. The performances are excellent, especially Menchikov's turn as the father who never lost sight of the long view regarding his family's safety. (French and Russian with English subtitles) ★★★½ VHS: $21.99; DVD: $29.99

Easter Parade

(1948, 104 min, US, Charles Walters) *Judy Garland, Fred Astaire, Ann Miller, Peter Lawford.* Tuneful Irving Berlin musical with Astaire and Garland as a song-and-dance team during the early 1900s. Songs include "Steppin' Out with My Baby," "A Couple of Swells" and the title tune. ★★★½ VHS: $14.99

The Easy Life (Il Sorpasso)

(1963, 105 min, Italy, Dino Risi) *Vittorio Gassman, Jean-Louis Trintignant.* Capturing the optimistic and carefree outlook in a rapidly modernizing Italy, this comedy-drama stars Gassman as a pleasure-seeking middle-aged playboy who meets his opposite in a young Trintignant, a meek, serious law student whom he takes under his wing. The fast-talking and equally fast-driving Gassman convinces the young man to accompany him on a trip to northern Italy and taste life's sweet offerings. A likable, offbeat film, well-played by the two charming leads. (Letterboxed) (Italian with English subtitles) ★★★

Easy Living

(1937, 88 min, US, Mitchell Leisen) *Jean Arthur, Ray Milland, Edward Arnold, Franklin Pangborn, William Demarest.* Preston Sturges wrote the screenplay for this consistently funny screwball comedy. In a wonderfully wacky performance, Arthur sparkles as a working girl whose life turns upside-down when tycoon Arnold throws his wife's mink out the window, landing on

Arthur. Milland costars as Arnold's son who romances her. There's a great slapstick scene at an automat, and Pangborn, as a catty salesclerk, proves that when it comes to dishing the dirt, he's second to none ("Where there's smoke, there must be. . . somebody smoking"). ★★★½ VHS: $14.99

Easy Living

(1949, 77 min, US, Jacques Tourneur) *Victor Mature, Lucille Ball, Lizabeth Scott.* Mature plays an aging football star facing retirement. Ball plays the team secretary in love with him. Scott plays Mature's possessive wife. A compelling and thoughtful drama accented by three smart performances. ★★★

Easy Money

(1983, 95 min, US, James Signorelli) *Rodney Dangerfield, Joe Pesci, Candy Azzara, Geraldine Fitzgerald.* Dangerfield delivers some good laughs in this easygoing comedy about a slobbish baby photographer who stands to inherit millions — if he can give up drinking, smoking, gambling and over-eating. ★★★ DVD: $19.99

Easy Rider

(1969, 94 min, US, Dennis Hopper) *Peter Fonda, Dennis Hopper, Jack Nicholson.* This low-budget phenom sent shock waves through Hollywood and the nation. Fonda and Hopper are the hippie bikers whose trek across America blithely caught the mood of the times. Nicholson is unforgettable as the alcoholic lawyer with an itch to drop out. ★★★½ VHS: $14.99; DVD: $24.99

Easy Virtue

(1927, 79 min, GB, Alfred Hitchcock) *Isabel Jeans, Ian Hunter.* Hitchcock meets Noël Coward. It's tempting to simply leave it at that. Based on a story by Coward, this early silent Hitchcock feature comes up a little short dramatically, but it does have flashes of the director's later style. The story has to do with the melodramatic sufferings an alcoholic's wife (Jeans) endures. ★★½ VHS: $12.99

Eat a Bowl of Tea

(1989, 102 min, US, Wayne Wang) *Cora Miao, Russell Wong, Victor Wong, Jessica Harper.* Shortly after WWII, young Ben Loy is sent to Hong Kong by his father, Wah Gay, to find a bride. He returns with Mei Oi — a very modern and independent young woman with whom he has fallen deeply in love. Unfortunately, the choice is not one which sits so well with Wah Gay. What follows is a wry and irreverent, often offbeat and always endearing treatise on the struggle between old and new in the Chinese community. It is pulled together with the dizzyingly frantic pace of a 1930s screwball comedy. Once again, Wang has succeeded in making a purely Chinese-American movie which will appeal to all. (English and Mandarin with English subtitles) ★★★ VHS: $19.99

Eat Drink Man Woman

(1994, 120 min, Taiwan, Ang Lee) *Sihung Lung, Ah-Leh Gua, Winston Chao, Yu-Wen Wang, Chien-Lien Wu.* A heartfelt and humorous examination of the romantic aspirations of an aging widower and his daughters. Featuring the most visually sumptuous cinematic food since *Like Water for Chocolate* and *Babette's Feast*, the film

opens with a bang — the viewer being drawn into an ornate ritual of food prep as old Tao Chu (once *the* master chef of all Taipei) readies an "average" Sunday family dinner. His three daughters are a study in diversity: Jia-Jen, the eldest, is a devoutly Christian schoolteacher; Jia-Chien, the middle, is a rebellious spitfire and successful businesswoman; Jia-Ning, the youngest, seemingly infatuated with American "mall culture," works at Wendy's and is caught in the throes of puppy love. Lee's acute eye for character uses this quartet to paint a stirring and highly humorous picture of emotional isolation against a backdrop of Taiwan's rapidly modernizing culture. (Mandarin with English subtitles) ★★★★ VHS: $14.99

Eat the Peach

(1986, 95 min, Ireland, Peter Ormrod) *Stephen Brennan, Eamon Morrissey.* Two unemployed Irish fellows, inspired by a scene in Elvis Presley's bike movie, *Roustabout*, conspire to construct a "Wall of Death" upon which they will ride their cycles and defy gravity. Of course, their families and friends think they've gone mad, but Vinnie and Arthur persevere, resorting to smuggling and petty theft to realize their dream. An amiable comedy, filled with down-home Irish charm. ★★½ VHS: $79.99

Eat the Rich

(1988, 92 min, GB, Peter Richardson) *Nosher Powell, Lanah Pellay, Miranda Richardson.* The outrageous British comedy troupe The Comic Strip (*The Supergrass*) serves some heaping portions of over-the-top comedy in this biting attack on England's class system. Having been fired from a very posh and unbearably snobby London restaurant, a transsexual waiter gangs up with a couple of fellow disenfranchised citizens and vows to start the revolution. They begin by taking over the restaurant and renaming it "Eat the Rich" — which, as it turns out, is exactly what the patrons unwittingly do. A marvelous example of Thatcher-era humor. ★★★ VHS: $19.99

Eaten Alive

(1976, 96 min, US, Tobe Hooper) *Neville Brand, Mel Ferrer, Carolyn Jones, Robert Englund.* From the director of *The Texas Chainsaw Massacre* comes this horror outing about a psychopathic hotel owner who has a bad habit of feeding his guests to his pet crocodile. Hooper's debut feature is bizarre though occasionally scary. ★★ DVD: $24.99

Eat Drink Man Woman

Eating

(1990, 110 min, US, Henry Jaglom) *Frances Bergen, Lisa Richards, Gwen Welles.* Jaglom takes us on a wonderfully entertaining afternoon outing to a fine suburban L.A. home where a group of women come together for a birthday party and where everyone's favorite topic of discussion is food, food, food. Filmed with an all-female cast, the comedy is much more consistent and funnier than Jaglom's previous outings as the wacky cast of Left Coast caricatures chatter, bemoan and marvel in their collective guilt for and obsession with food and eating. The film is loosely structured, allowing the actresses to improvise, with the results being many hilariously memorable and perceptive lines. ★★★½ VHS: $79.99

Eating Raoul

(1982, 83 min, US, Paul Bartel) *Paul Bartel, Mary Woronov, Robert Beltran, Buck Henry, Ed Begley, Jr., Edie McClurg.* Paul and Mary Bland, a mild-mannered couple, devise a diabolical scheme to raise funds for their entrepreneurial dreams. Placing an ad in the local sex publication, they lure unsuspecting degenerates to their abode, club them with a frying pan and empty their wallets. Hunky Beltran also stars as the not-as-clever-as-he-thinks-he-is hustler Raoul, who may become their next victim. Bartel's cannibalistic farce serves up a healthy portion of laughs in his most consistently outrageous comedy. ★★★½

The Ebony Tower

(1987, 80 min, GB, Robert Knights) *Laurence Olivier, Greta Scacchi, Roger Rees, Toyah Wilcox.* Olivier stars as an aging painter who, out of disdain for the art world, cloisters himself with two beautiful female art students in a remote French chateau. Their peaceful retreat is sent into chaos, however, by the arrival of a young artist (Rees). John Mortimer adapted the John Fowles novel. ★★★

Echo Park

(1986, 92 min, US, Robert Dornhelm) *Tom Hulce, Susan Dey, Michael Bowen, Christopher Walken, Cheech Marin.* An offbeat charmer about a would-be actress (Dey) and her relationship with two boarders, a songwriting pizza delivery man (the very likable Hulce) and a budding body-builder (Bowen), both of whom share her rundown duplex in East Los Angeles. ★★★ VHS: $14.99

Echoes of Paradise

(1987, 92 min, Australia, Phillip Noyce) *Wendy Hughes, John Lone.* Hughes stars as a happily married mother of three whose idyllic suburban life is shattered after she discovers that her husband has been in a series of affairs for years. In an effort to escape the emotional turmoil at home, she travels with a friend to exotic Thailand where she meets a handsome Balinese dancer (Lone). Her repressed desires and attitudes are slowly shed (as are her clothes) as she enters into a liberating relationship with the worldly and sweet-as-honey Lone. The film treads no new territory; and with seductive lines like, "You look tense. Let me give you a massage," the viewer should take the film more as a beautiful travelogue and less as anything insightful. ★★

The Eclipse (L'Eclisse)

(1962, 123 min, Italy, Michelangelo Antonioni) *Monica Vitti, Alain Delon.* The concluding film in Antonioni's existential trilogy, which includes *L'Avventura* and *La Notte*, continues with the theme of the barriers to human communication as part of an increasingly stark contemporary world. Vitti stars as a young woman who, hours after leaving her old lover, meets a passionate young man (Delon). Whether she'll really end her old affair or if the fledgling new one will even begin is at the heart of the conflict in this existential "art" film. The plot, however, takes a back seat to Antonioni's experimental film techniques and abstract style. (Letterboxed) (Italian with English subtitles) ★★★

Ecstasy

(1933, 82 min, Czechoslovakia, Gutsav Machaty) *Hedy Lamaar, Jaromir Rogoz.* A true curiosity! This slow-moving, predictable Czech film would have long been used for landfill had it not been for its scandalizing nude scenes of a pre-Hollywood Lamarr. This uncut version has Lamarr in all her natural beauty as a young woman whose marriage to a fastidious older man sours on their wedding night. She soon leaves him and finds solace in the arms of a handsome young engineer. Filmed mostly as a silent film, with only about 20 words spoken, the acting is overly expressive by today's standards. (German with English subtitles) ★ VHS: $29.99

Ed Wood

(1994, 128 min, US, Tim Burton) *Johnny Depp, Martin Landau, Sarah Jessica Parker, Bill Murray, Patricia Arquette, Vincent D'Onofrio, Jeffrey Jones.* Depp stars as the titular character in this ideally crafted biopic of the 1950s film director who single-handedly molded the grade-B aesthetic. Shot in black and white and imitating the cheesy production values of Wood's immortal cult classics, the film is a perfect tribute to the man whose charming incompetence as a filmmaker was equally matched by an unrelenting enthusiasm for the medium. Depp's portrayal of Wood, a WWII vet with an insatiable appetite for angora and women's clothing, is right on the money, but it is Landau's astonishing portrait of Bela Lugosi that steals the show. As the drug-addicted fallen star, Landau's Oscar-winning performance transforms the film from simple biography to an inspirational tale of friendship and redemption. Fortunately, director Burton tempers the film's serious underbelly with generous doses of hilarity and wit, or to quote Depp as Wood, "Transvestites! Get me transvestites!" ★★★★

Ed Wood, Look Back in Angora

(1994, 51 min, US, Ted Newsom) A fitting companion piece to Tim Burton's *Ed Wood*, this engagingly frenetic examination of the blazingly eccentric director-writer-actor crosscuts clips from his one-of-a-kind movies with interviews from those who knew him. Interviewees include an ex-Marine who fought with him in the Pacific during WWII; movie industry types of the most marginal sort; and his long-suffering, ever-devoted wife. Director Newsom lets Wood's films speak for the tormented, would-be auteur, creating an affectionate and intimate biography of an obsessive whose ambitions greatly exceeded his talents. A stirring tribute to the man who created some of the worst movies ever made. ★★★½ VHS: $9.99

Eddie

(1996, 100 min, US, Steve Rash) *Whoopi Goldberg, Frank Langella, Dennis Farina, Richard Jenkins.* In this predictable though amiable sports comedy, Whoopi plays a die-hard New York Knicks fan who becomes the slumping team's head coach. *Eddie* bears no more originality than similarly themed kids' films like *Rookie of the Year* and *Little Big League*, and it unfortunately promises more than it can deliver. Whoopi is agreeable and often amusing, but her comic prowess alone cannot keep this comedy courtside. ★★½ VHS: $9.99; DVD: $29.99

Eddie and the Cruisers

(1983, 92 min, US, Martin Davidson) *Tom Berenger, Michael Paré, Ellen Barkin.* A popular 1960s rock band leader presumably died in an accident — but he may have faked his death and returned to his old neighborhood. Barkin is the TV reporter investigating the story; Paré is the legendary Eddie. (Sequel: *Eddie and the Cruisers II*) ★★½ VHS: $9.99

Eddie Murphy: Raw

(1987, 90 min, US, Robert Townsend) *Eddie Murphy.* This aptly titled movie is Murphy's first concert film. He's often very funny and has a great deal of energy, but he's as enamored with his anatomy as ever. If you like Murphy and enjoy his style of humor, this R-rated (well-justified) romp is the one for you. ★★ VHS: $14.99

Eden

(1998, 106 min, US, Howard Goldberg) *Joanna Going, Dylan Walsh, Sean Patrick Flannery.* No more than a TV movie of the week with a handful of four-letter words, *Eden* concerns a housewife, Helen (Going), who is having out-of-body experiences. This film tries to address the mind/body/spirit problem, but like its heroine, it has no real energy. Helen, who suffers from multiple sclerosis, has a series of dream-flights where she can see and feel the lives of others. As Helen starts to follow her own path, she inspires a student, an underachiever, to grow. Frankly, none of this is very moving, since the film touches on the issues rather than tackling them. At least *Eden* is never offensive or insulting. ★½ VHS: $19.99; DVD: $14.99

The Edge

(1997, 117 min, US, Lee Tamahori) *Anthony Hopkins, Alec Baldwin, Elle Macpherson, Harold Perrineau.* Set against the beautiful mountaintops and lakes of remote Alaska, *The Edge* is a taut action adventure that pits man against beast, man against man, and it's not only the strongest who survives but the smartest, as well. Hopkins plays a multimillionaire who travels along with his model wife on a fashion shoot. When he and photographer Baldwin become trapped in the wilderness after a plane crash, they must use their wits to fight the elements and eventually each other. David Mamet's screenplay is terse and economical, providing a believable tension between the two men. If the pacing falls apart somewhat by story's end, *The Edge* has still provided some fine, chilling moments. (Letterboxed VHS available for $19.99) ★★★ VHS: $9.99; DVD: $29.99

E

EDtv

of the cynical and boozy Caine. Driven by her thirst for knowledge, Rita exchanges the chatter of the ladies' hair salon for discussions on Chekov and Blake, while at the same time breathing new life into her moribund teacher. A warm and witty comedy from Willy Russell's hit West End play. ★★★½ VHS: $9.99

The Education of Little Tree

(1998, 117 min, US, Richard Friedenberg) *James Cromwell, Tantoo Cardinal, Joseph Ashton, Graham Greene.* An adaptation of Forrest Carter's novel, the beautifully made *The Education of Little Tree* tells the story of Little Tree, a Cherokee boy (Ashton) who leaves the confines of his rural town to live with his grandparents (Cromwell and Cardinal) in the hills of Tennessee's Smoky Mountains during the Depression. There, the grandfather teaches Little Tree the ways of "mountain folk" and instills in him a cultural pride with the help of a spiritual Indian friend, Willow John (Greene). More than just a quaint slice of Americana, *The Education of Little Tree* brings the attitudes of the era and its people into sharp perspective. Brought to marvelous life by the cast and exquisite cinematography, *The Education of Little Tree* is an affecting vision of a time when people's bitter life lessons are often peppered with steps toward belief in oneself. ★★★½ VHS: $9.99

Edvard Munch

(1974, 168 min, Norway, Peter Watkins) *Geir Westby, Gro Fraas.* Though labeled by his contemporaries as a sick madman, Edvard Munch (1863-1944) is considered one of the most important and influential painters in the Expressionistic Movement. This abstract examination into the psyche of the artist traces Munch's professional and private lives through the combination of narrative and dialogue (some taken directly from his diary), reenactments, and documentary-like interviews. The collage design of the film produces an overlaying of image and sound, a hodgepodge of short scenes and repetition of events that its running time of 167 minutes may push some viewers to wonder if they could be the model for Munch's most famous work: The Scream. (Norwegian and German with English subtitles) ★★½ VHS: $29.99

Edward II

(1991, 91 min, GB, Derek Jarman) *Steven Waddington, Andrew Tiernan, Tilda Swinton, Nigel Terry.* Director Jarman has reworked Christopher Marlowe's play into a homoerotic, sexually charged, radically relevant work for our times. Graphically brutal, moving, surprisingly funny and always erotic, Jarman blends Marlowe's prose with contemporary jargon and costumes, replete with surprising portrayals of queer sex, profanity and ACT-UP activists for a truly mesmerizing experience. One of the film's most surprising sequences occurs when Annie Lennox appears crooning Cole Porter's classic "Ev'ry Time We Say Goodbye," the piece she performed in the AIDS benefit "Red, Hot and Blue." Brilliant, daring and innovative, *Edward II* is contemporary filmmaking at its finest, and one of the best examples of modern queer cinema. A must see. ★★★★ VHS: $19.99

Edge of Darkness

(1943, 120 min, US, Lewis Milestone) *Errol Flynn, Ann Sheridan, Walter Huston, Ruth Gordon, Judith Anderson.* From the director of the classic antiwar film *All Quiet on the Western Front* comes that film's antithesis, a gripping WWII drama and passionate call-to-arms. Flynn and Sheridan head a splendid ensemble cast as leaders of the underground movement of their small Norwegian village, which the Nazis occupy. Featuring exceptional cinematography, this well-detailed film examines daily life under oppressive German rule and the birth of the town's Resistance movement. A dashing Flynn, a no-nonsense Sheridan and a heart-tugging performance by Gordon all contribute to make *Edge of Darkness* stand out among other war-era films. ★★★½ VHS: $19.99

Edge of Darkness

(1986, 307 min, GB, Martin Campbell) *Bob Peck, Joanne Whalley, Joe Dan Baker.* This stylishly produced BBC thriller is filled with espionage and intrigue and won six British "Emmy" awards. Peck stars as a London police detective whose life is brutally torn apart when his young daughter is found murdered. As he follows the trail of her killer(s), he uncovers a tangled web of conspiracy involving government agents, a maverick CIA operative, multinational corporations and a radical environmental group. Good, solid action entertainment. ★★★ VHS: $29.99

Edge of Sanity

(1988, 90 min, GB, Gerald Kikoine) *Anthony Perkins, Glynis Barber.* Turgid, uninvolving and ineptly directed, this Dr. Jekyll and Mr. Hyde horror spin-off features a bug-eyed Perkins as a doctor who accidentally concocts a mixture that turns him into a pasty-faced killer with a predilection for sleazy prostitutes. Set in Victorian London, this updated version of the Stevenson classic is a disappointment that is not enjoyable even on a camp level. ★

Edison the Man

(1940, 107 min, US, Clarence Brown) *Spencer Tracy, Rita Johnson, Charles Coburn.* Fine sequel to *Young Tom Edison* (which starred a youthful Mickey Rooney) with Tracy as the adult inventor. The film follows Edison's fascination with devices, and though some of the story is Hollywood-ized, it's a rewarding homage to the American genius. ★★★ VHS: $19.99

Edith and Marcel

(1983, 140 min, France, Claude Lelouch) *Marcel Cerdan, Jr., Evelyne Bouix, Charles Aznavour.* The love affair between singer Edith Piaf and boxing champion Marcel Cerdan, who died in a plane crash in 1944, is romantically brought to the screen by Lelouch. The entrancing music of actual Piaf recordings and the casting of real-life son Cerdan, Jr. in the lead role adds pathos to this tragic love story. (French with English subtitles) ★★½

EDtv

(1999, 122 min, US, Ron Howard) *Matthew McConaughey, Jenna Elfman, Woody Harrelson, Ellen DeGeneres, Martin Landau, Sally Kirkland, Rob Reiner, Dennis Hopper, Elizabeth Hurley, Clint Howard.* EDtv is no *Truman Show* — oh, wait, yes it is. Similar in premise though not in accomplishment, Howard's lively though unremarkable comedy has video store clerk McConaughey having his every move televised for the amusement of his home viewing audience — 24 hours a day. Whereas Jim Carrey's Truman was an innocent dupe, Ed is a willing participant, that is, until it starts to interfere with the romance with his brother's girlfriend. Good fodder for TV, though. *EDtv* sometimes drags between the often very funny scenes of Ed's latest TV melodramas, which are lapped up by fans across the nation. McConaughey is quite appealing with his aw-shucks, average-guy bit, and Harrelson has a few good scenes as his brother. However, it's DeGeneres who gives the film's best performance as the series' producer. You often find yourself rooting more for her than for Ed. That's show biz. ★★½ VHS: $9.99; DVD: $34.99

Educating Rita

(1983, 110 min, GB, Lewis Gilbert) *Michael Caine, Julie Walters.* Walters is delightful as the Cockney dynamo who enrolls in a course at the Open University and comes under the tutelage

Edward Scissorhands

(1990, 98 min, US, Tim Burton) *Johnny Depp, Winona Ryder, Dianne Wiest, Alan Arkin, Vincent Price, Kathy Baker, Anthony Michael Hall, Conchata Ferrell.* Having paid his dues to Hollywood several times over with *Batman*, director Burton presents this small-scale gem about a boy with scissors for hands. This heartbreaking and highly original parable on conformity casts Depp as a social misfit who's taken by Wiest to live in her "average suburban household," where he falls in love for the first time, becomes all the rage as a hairdresser to the neighborhood's wives, and learns the high cost of societal conventions. Burton has fashioned in this beautifully filmed and comic fantasy the ultimate tale of the outsider as misunderstood and victimized innocent. ★★★½ VHS: $14.99; DVD: $29.99

The Eel

(1997, 117 min, Japan, Shohei Imamura) *Koji Yakusho, Misa Shimizu.* As he commutes home, a workaday Everyman (Yakusho of *Shall We Dance?*) reads a poison pen letter informing him of his wife's infidelity. Later, he returns home early from a fishing trip to find the allegations are true. He seems quietly surprised when he brutally stabs his wife to death, and hums a gentle tune as he bicycles to the police station to turn himself in. Eight years later, he is released to the care of his parole officer, with the pet eel that had been his best companion during his incarceration. He has a hard time unlearning the habits of his confinement, but his intervention in a young woman's suicide attempt proves the catalyst that enables him to reconnect with life. A compassionate yet unsentimental look at base cruelty and exalted empathy, containing moments of stunning revelation, exposing human foibles and graces. Director Imamura (*Black Rain*) has constructed a sagacious consideration of the societies we construct and the raw emotion always lying just beneath the surface. Winner of the Palme d'Or at the 1997 Cannes Film Festival. (Japanese with English subtitles) ★★★ VHS: $89.99

Effi Briest

(1974, 140 min, Germany, Rainer Werner Fassbinder) *Hanna Schygulla, Wolfgang Schneck,* *Ulli Lommel.* Schygulla is luminous as the title character in Fassbinder's accomplished adaptation of the 1895 novel by Theodore Fontane. Fassbinder once again explores the subject of societal restraints in this beautifully photographed and elegantly mounted production. When Effi's much-older husband finds evidence of a long-dead affair, a chain of events is inexorably initiated, and Effi is its primary victim. Schygulla's performance is subtle, delicately layered and compelling. One of the director's best works. (German with English subtitles) ★★★★

Marcello Mastroianni in *8½*

The Efficiency Expert

(1992, 85 min, Australia, Mark Joffe) *Anthony Hopkins, Alwyn Kurts, Angela Punch McGregor, Bruno Lawrence.* In the tradition of *Local Hero* comes this warm, low-key comedy from Australia. Set in 1960s Melbourne, the film is about a management specialist's (Hopkins) efforts to "update and modernize" a small, family-run moccasin company. Instead of focusing on the ins-and-outs of the efficiency business, director Joffe's film is about decent working people trying to treat each other decently. In a richly textured but subtly moving performance, Hopkins plays a man in the midst of both a personal and a professional crisis of ethics. While the film may not break any new ground, it treads familiar territory gently and pleasantly. ★★★ VHS: $14.99

Egg

(1988, 58 min, The Netherlands, Danniel Danniel) *Johan Leysen, Marijke Vengelers.* This engaging and delightful short film centers around a sweet but lonely 35-year-old baker whose quietly efficient life is put into turmoil after a personal ad he placed in an out-of-town newspaper produces a determined woman at his doorstep. Their tenuous attempts at a relationship soon involve the entire town's population. A humorous fable that takes a subdued approach and relies more on the actions of the characters than dialogue to tell its tale. (Dutch with English subtitles). ★★★ VHS: $59.99

The Egg and I

(1947, 108 min, US, Chester Erskine) *Claudette Colbert, Fred MacMurray, Marjorie Main, Percy Kilbride.* Big city socialite Colbert experiences culture shock at new hubby MacMurray's chicken farm. Colbert sparkles; she and MacMurray highlight a strong supporting cast of seasoned character actors in this delightful, witty and fun excursion into the green acres of the American heartland. One of the smash hits of the 1940s, the film introduced Main and Kilbride as "Ma and Pa Kettle." ★★★ VHS: $14.99

The Egyptian

(1954, 140 min, US, Michael Curtiz) *Victor Mature, Edmund Purdon, Jean Simmons, Peter Ustinov.* Hollywood doesn't make 'em like this anymore — and for most of us that's probably good news. An abandoned baby grows up to be the Pharaoh's physician. Based on a true story. A lifeless biblical epic. ★ VHS: $19.99

The Eiger Sanction

(1975, 128 min, US, Clint Eastwood) *Clint Eastwood, George Kennedy, Jack Cassidy.* Eastwood is a college art professor and part-time government assassin in this somewhat "Bond-esque" movie of spies and espionage. Features some splendid mountain climbing scenes. Cassidy's fag routine grows tiresome very quickly. ★★ VHS: $9.99; DVD: $24.99

8½

(1963, 135 min, Italy, Federico Fellini) *Marcello Mastroianni, Claudia Cardinale, Anouk Aimée.* Fellini's masterful statement on his life and art stars Mastroianni as a filmmaker paralyzed by creative block and slipping deeper into a world of dream and fantasy. Cardinale portrays his sensuous apparition. (Italian with English subtitles) ★★★★ VHS: $29.99

8 Heads in a Duffel Bag

(1997, 95 min, US, Tom Schulman) *Joe Pesci, Andy Comeau, Kristy Swanson, David Spade, Todd Louiso, George Hamilton, Dyan Cannon.* Anyone expecting a dark comedy hybrid of *Weekend at Bernie's* and *Goodfellas* will be horribly disappointed by this strained and unfunny comedy about a mobster (Pesci) whose bag containing the heads of his boss' rivals is accidentally switched with that of a college schmoe (Comeau) trying to make a good impression on his fiancée's parents. Pesci has the thankless task of having to rehash his mobster schtick, and spends the entire movie bullying and torturing Comeau's roommates (Spade and Louiso) into revealing their whereabouts. ★½ VHS: $9.99

Eight Men Out

(1988, 119 min, US, John Sayles) *John Cusack, D.B. Sweeney, Christopher Lloyd, John Mahoney, Charlie Sheen, Michael Lerner, David Strathairn, Michael Rooker.* A beautiful period piece rich in emotion about the infamous "Black Sox Scandal" of 1919. It was a time when baseball players were the heroes of the day, until the underpaid and underappreciated players of the Chicago White Sox threw the World Series and brought shame to our national pastime. Examining the events which led up to the darkest days in the history of American sports, Sayles has assembled a fine team of young, talented actors. Sayles should be commended as both writer and director for the depth and clarity he brings to the almost 20 characters whose individual stories seem to effortlessly intertwine to tell this fascinating and sorrowful tale. ★★★★ VHS: $14.99; DVD: $19.99

8MM

(1999, 119 min, US, Joel Schumacher) *Nicolas Cage, Joaquin Phoenix, Peter Stormare, James Gandolfini, Catherine Keener, Anthony Heald, Chris Bauer.* An instance in which *8* isn't greater than *Seven*, this slick but lurid thriller attempts to be sexually provocative with its adult movies backdrop, but ultimately disintegrates into a formulaic, tired revenge flick out for blood. The dark-hued, somber *8MM* opens promisingly. Private investigator Tom Welles (a sullen Cage) is hired by a millionaire's widow to determine if a "snuff movie" found in his safe is real or not. This takes him on a journey to Hollywood and the much darker side of the pornography industry. From there, it gets ugly as Welles soon finds what he's looking for. *8MM* works as a detective story, and the first half of his chase can be involving. But the story lacks in the human element it pretends to care about. The film does offer some bloody thrills, but they're neither edgy nor satisfying. ★★ VHS: $9.99; DVD: $19.99

8 Million Ways to Die

(1986, 115 min, US, Hal Ashby) *Jeff Bridges, Rosanna Arquette, Andy Garcia.* Slick though unremarkable crime thriller with Bridges as an ex-Los Angeles sheriff who tries to crack a cocaine ring and help a prostitute (Arquette) break free of her obsessive pimp. Garcia is terrific as Arquette's menacing pimp. ★★★ VHS: $19.99

1860

(1933, 80 min, Italy, Alessandro Blasetti) *Aida Bellia, Andrea Checchi, Vasco Crepi.* The struggle for the unification of Italy, and especially the Sicilian peasant revolt against the Prince of Naples, provide the historical backdrop to this elegant war drama. Using non-professional actors, location shooting and natural lighting, the film brings an almost documentary feel to the story of one peasant's role during the battles and is considered a stylistic precursor to the Italian neorealist movement of the 1940s. (Italian with English subtitles) ★★★ VHS: $29.99

The 18th Angel

(1998, 100 min, US, William Bindley) *Christopher McDonald, Rachael Leigh Cook, Stanley Tucci, Maximilian Schell, Wendy Crewson.* A group of kooky Etruscan monks, led by Schell, are looking for eighteen "angels" — children and young teens whose innocence and beauty, along with the aid of an evil ancient clock, will bring about the ascendance of Satan and his reign of darkness over the universe. How? Who knows? Who cares? Certainly not *Omen* scribe David Seltzer, who wrote this dreck. The main story centers around a young beauty and her widower father, who are invited to Rome under odd circumstances; of course, those nasty Etruscans want the beautiful girl as the 18th angel. Clichéd, moronic, unsuspenseful, *The 18th Angel* is a slap in the face of horror fans and an insult to everyone else. ★ VHS: $9.99

The Eighth Day

(1996, 114 min, France, Jaco van Dormael) *Daniel Auteuil, Pascal Duquenne, Miou-Miou.* Optimistic Belgian director van Dormael is given over to some wonderful flights of fancy, but his message about living life to the fullest is still cliché no matter how he dresses it up. George (Duquenne), a young man with Down's Syndrome, has a childlike sense of wonder. Harry (Auteuil), an uptight salesman, fails to appreciate what he has. When these two characters meet in an accident one stormy night, they, of course, have a transforming effect on one another. Van Dormael can achieve great moments of sadness and magic in the film, much like his previous *Toto the Hero*, but there is too much filler between the scenes that truly captivate. However, the acting is superb. Duquenne is truly inspired as George, and Auteuil deftly shows how Harry melts from his cold, unfeeling personality into a caring human being. (French with English subtitles) ★★½ VHS: $9.99

The Eighties

(1983, 82 min, Belgium/France, Chantal Akerman) *Aurore Clement, Lio.* The creative genesis of art and the filmmaking process is examined and deconstructed in this unusually fascinating and pleasurable film. Unlike director Akerman's previous somber films, this is a giddy work: a musical set in a suburban shopping mall, and nothing like the Hollywood musicals of the past. The first part of the film features a series of confusingly repetitive and jumbled scenes of a group of women singing, talking, discussing and arguing. Pushing the viewer's tolerance, the film changes direction completely in the second half to reveal the end result of all this confusion — a deliriously fun and lively musical extravaganza. (French with English subtitles) ★★★ VHS: $79.99

84 Charing Cross Road

(1987, 97 min, GB/US, David Jones) *Anne Bancroft, Anthony Hopkins, Judi Dench, Mercedes Ruehl.* Bancroft and Hopkins give spendid performances in this lovely film version of Hugh Whitemore's play (based on the memoirs of Helen Hanff) about the 20-year, transatlantic correspondence between a London bookseller (Hopkins) and one of his customers, a New York City woman (Bancroft). ★★★½ VHS: $19.99

Eijanaika

(1981, 151 min, Japan, Shohei Imamura) *Ken Ogata, Shigeru Izumiya.* This chaotic portrait of Japanese society in the throes of a violent transition is masterfully directed by Imamura. Set in a bustling 19th-century Tokyo, the film depicts the loss of power by the Samurai Class at the hands of the new Imperial forces as well as outside business interests. Filmed against a backdrop of corruption, anarchy, bloodshed and eroticism, the story follows Genji, who returns to Tokyo after a five-year absence and finds that his wife has run off with a gangster. This mosaic portrait of Japanese culture run amok climaxes in a revolutionary frenzy and one of the most highly charged and dramatic spectacles in modern Japanese cinema. (Japanese with English subtitles) ★★★½ VHS: $24.99

El (This Strange Passion)

(1952, 82 min, Mexico, Luis Buñuel) *Arturo de Cordova, Delia Garces.* This overheated story of passion, jealousy and violence is one of Buñuel's most entertaining films from his Mexican period. A biting anticlerical satire full of bizarre touches and one that continues his theme of *amour fou*, which he first dealt with in *L'Age D'Or*. Francisco, a seemingly normal and devout aristocrat (but secret foot fetishist), becomes obsessed with a woman he sees in church. He pursues her and eventually marries the woman, but soon changes from a loving husband to a man crazed with murderous and unjustifiable jealousy. Buñuel's wry sense of humor is clearly intact in this memorable black comedy. Please note that there is a slight problem with reading the white subtitles when there is a white background. (Spanish with English subtitles) ★★★ VHS: $59.99

El Cid

(1961, 185 min, US, Anthony Mann) *Charlton Heston, Sophia Loren, Raf Vallone, Genevieve Page.* Sprawling historical epic with Heston as the legendary Spanish hero who drove the Moors from his homeland. A smart costume epic complete with impressive battle sequences, a better-than-average romance, and a story line none too difficult to follow. ★★★

El Dorado

(1967, 126 min, US, Howard Hawks) *John Wayne, Robert Mitchum, James Caan, Edward Asner, Christopher George.* Hawks' follow-up to his classic western *Rio Bravo*, *El Dorado* is an exciting western adventure with fine touches of comedy. Aging gunfighter Wayne and sheriff Mitchum team up against a ruthless cattle baron. ★★★ VHS: $9.99; DVD: $24.99

El Norte

(1983, 139 min, US, Gregory Nava & Anna Thompson) *David Villalpando, Zaide Silvia Gutierrez, Ernesto Cruz.* After their parents are murdered by a government death squad, a brother and sister flee their remote Guatemalan village and begin a hazardous trek to the "promised land" of America. A stunning, poetic tale of survival. ★★★½

El Super

(1979, 80 min, US, Leon Ichaso & Orlando Jiminez-Leal) *Raymundo Hidalgo-Gato, Orlando Jiminez-Leal, Elizabeth Peña.* Made in New York, this humorous, unsentimental story of the trials of a homesick Cuban immigrant is both accomplished and heartwarming. Roberto, a Cuban exile for 10 years, works as a super in a New York apartment house and lives in its basement. Still not assimilated into this strange new land of snow, garbage and crime, he dreams of the palm trees, warmth and friendliness of his former land. This comically sad tale of a reluctant émigré is reminiscent of *Bread and Chocolate*. (Spanish with English subtitles) ★★★ VHS: $19.99

The Eleanor Roosevelt Story

(1965, 90 min, US, Richard Kaplan) When a Boswell, due to propriety, chooses to ignore the defining crisis in its subject's life, then any possibility of framing a coherent profile is relinquished. This by-the-numbers collage of newsreel footage and snapshots narrated with an almost comically stentorian voice-over by Eric Severeid won an Academy Award for Best Documentary in 1965. Now "freshened up" for home video with a few pointless words from Hillary Rodham Clinton, *The Eleanor Roosevelt Story* is hindered by an incessant tone of veneration, endemic of its era before Watergate. We only learn what she did, never really *why*. What was it that caused this sheltered woman of privilege to suddenly betray her class and become a rare advocate for the poor and disenfranchised? And nothing is mentioned about her husband's infidelities, nor her longtime relationship with Lorena Hickok. Maybe such things weren't discussed during the mid-'60s, but in ignoring the more controversial issues, their absence is only magnified. ★★ VHS: $29.99

Election

(1999, 105 min, US, Alexander Payne) *Matthew Broderick, Reese Witherspoon, Chris Klein, Jessica Campbell, Colleen Camp. Citizen Ruth* director Payne once again tackles political processes, this time within a public high school. Running for school president is perky overachiever Witherspoon; her nemesis here is Broderick, as a teacher (not a Bueller) who looks for ways to defeat her (including pressuring a dim jock into the race). No one in this scattershot satire is safe, with teacher-student sex, budding lesbianism, campaign politics and perfectionist parents

Joseph Fiennes and Cate Blanchet in *Elizabeth*

among the dozens of targets. It's completely hilarious, and even when the viciousness is shocking, it rings very true. Witherspoon once again shines as the public school equivalent of *Rushmore*'s Max, but it's Broderick who's the revelation, playing the most complex and adult (if not exactly grown-up) part of his career. *Election* may not have *Rushmore*'s lethal dose of comedic poison, but it's a damn funny, scintillating slap at the forces of comformity, cheer and good fortune. ★★★½ VHS: $14.99; DVD: $29.99

The Electric Horseman
(1979, 120 min, US, Sydney Pollack) *Robert Redford, Jane Fonda, Valerie Perrine, John Saxon, Willie Nelson, Wilford Brimley*. An unusual though entertaining drama about a cowboy (Redford) who steals a $12 million horse and escapes into the Nevada desert. There he is followed by a TV reporter (Fonda) and romance ensues. ★★★ VHS: $9.99

The Elegant Criminal
(1991, 120 min, France, Francis Girod) *Daniel Auteil, Jean Poiret*. Long dependent on Hollywood for its cinematic diet of lurid depictions of evil (*Silence of the Lambs, Cape Fear*, etc.), the French now have an evil genius to call their own. In this fascinating portrait, based on the true story of the notorious 19th-century murderer Pierre-Francois Lacenaire, director Girod has avoided the cheap, gory route and instead has fashioned an intimate, witty and complex look into the dark abyss of unrepentant evil. Auteil is riveting as Lacenaire — a failed playwright, refined gentleman, persuasive conversationalist, and homosexual, as well as thief, con man and knife-wielding mass murderer — who despite (or because of) it all, received the respect of his jailers and became a national celebrity. (French with English subtitles) ★★★ VHS: $19.99

The Element of Crime
(1989, 104 min, Denmark, Lars Von Trier) *Michael Elphick, Esmond Knight, Jerold Wells*. This dark and brooding police thriller follows the story of an emotionally fragile cop who, after spending years in self-exile in Egypt, returns to a post-nuclear Europe — a continent plunged into inexplicable darkness, constant rain, and which is crumbling into chaos and senseless crime. Hired to track down the elusive killer responsible for a series of horrifying mutilations of young girls, the detective attempts to solve the killings by using the revolutionary theory of his former mentor: re-creating the exact events leading up to each murder. Filmed in mute black and white, the film's labyrinthine plot and bizarre imagery combine to make this a beguiling yet satisfying murder-mystery. (Filmed in English) ★★★ VHS: $19.99; DVD: $39.99

The Elementary School
(1991, 100 min, Czechoslovakia, Jan Svêrák) *Jan Triska, Libuse Safrankova*. Six years before the astounding *Kolya*, director Svêrák tells another story through the eyes of children. In a small Czech village at the end of WWII, young boys use abandoned tanks as jungle gyms and drive their teacher to distraction. Their overwrought instructor is replaced by a man of military bearing with many stories of brave exploits to tell. The students' childhood confidences and explorations are juxtaposed against the ambiguous realities of the adult world, where no truth is pristine and the behavior of a perceived hero is often questionable. What the film may lack in cohesion is more than compensated for in its warmth and compassion. A series of youthful reminiscences told in golden glow of adult reflection on that time when Czechoslovakia basked in the expectation of socialism with a human face. (Czech with English subtitles) ★★★ VHS: $79.99

Eléna and Her Men
(1956, 98 min, France, Jean Renoir) *Ingrid Bergman, Jean Marais, Mel Ferrer*. A blithely old-fashioned, highly stylized creation from director Renoir starring Bergman as an impoverished 1880s Polish countess. On Bastille Day in Paris, Bergman becomes romantically involved with a debonaire count and a high-ranking soldier. This lush *fantaisie musicale* follows the countess' days as she must choose between the men and, of course, live happily ever after. This film, which Bergman specifically asked the director to make for her, was long thought lost. (French with English subtitles) (aka: *Paris Does Strange Things*) ★★★ VHS: $24.99

Eleni
(1985, 117 min, US, Peter Yates) *John Malkovich, Kate Nelligan, Linda Hunt, Dimitra Arliss*. Based on Nicholas Gage's autobiographical best-seller, this uninvolving adaptation stars Malkovich as a *New York Times* reporter who returns to his native Greece to investigate the death of his mother at the hands of Communist guerrillas 30 years earlier. Nelligan is excellent as Gage's mother, whose story is told in flashback. ★★

The Elephant Man
(1980, 125 min, US, David Lynch) *John Hurt, Anthony Hopkins, Anne Bancroft, John Gielgud, Wendy Hiller*. An eerie and hypnotic account of the life of John Merrick — a man so hideously deformed by disease that he was forced to make a living as a sideshow freak. Filmed in stark black and white, Lynch's camera acutely captures the darker corners of Victorian London and draws us into a world of shadows and despair. (Not associated with the Tony Award-winning play.) ★★★★ VHS: $14.99

Elephant Walk
(1954, 103 min, US, William Dieterle) *Elizabeth Taylor, Peter Finch, Dana Andrews*. A new wife travels to her husband's exotic plantation, where a battle ensues with nature. No, it's not *The Naked Jungle*, which had those neat killer ants, but the inferior *Elephant Walk*, which can only boast rampaging elephants. Taylor joins husband Finch on his Ceylon tea plantation. There, she falls for foreman Andrews, and contends with epidemic, drought, her husband's wrath and the aforementioned pachyderms. (Taylor replaced Vivien Leigh, who can be seen in certain shots.) ★★ VHS: $14.99

11 Harrowhouse
(1974, 95 min, GB, Aram Avakiam) *Charles Grodin, Trevor Howard, Candice Bergen, James Mason, John Gielgud*. Grodin stars as a diamond salesman enlisted by a crazy millionaire (Howard) to steal one million dollars' worth of diamonds. An unusual action spoof. ★★½ VHS: $29.99

Elizabeth
(1998, 124 min, GB, Shekhar Kapur) *Cate Blanchett, Geoffrey Rush, Joseph Fiennes, Richard Attenborough, Christopher Eccleston, Fanny Ardant*. With its graphic and gruesome opening sequence of a trio of Protestant heretics being burned at the stake, one knows right away that this look at the tumultuous rise to power of one of England's most beloved monarchs will not be the fluff of light costume drama. The year is 1554 and Elizabeth's Catholic half-sister Mary is on the throne. She's dying of cancer and amidst the religious strife that's tearing England apart, Elizabeth becomes the last hope for the country's Protestants. Naturally, the palace is awash in intrigue, and everyone's being carted off to the Tower — including Elizabeth. Blanchett is a dazzling Elizabeth, offering a radiant portrayal of a young woman who through cunning and guile is struggling to hang onto every shred of her independence — it's a riveting portrayal. Moody, gloomy and ultimately triumphant, *Elizabeth* is also adorned by a number of notable supporting turns including Rush as the unscrupulous Walsingham and Fiennes as Elizabeth's exuber-

ant young lover Robert Dudley. As would be expected, the evocation of 16th-century England is flawless. ★★★★ VHS: $14.99; DVD: $19.99

Elmer Gantry

(1960, 146 min, US, Richard Brooks) *Burt Lancaster, Jean Simmons, Shirley Jones, Dean Jagger.* Lancaster won a Best Actor Oscar for his dynamic portrayal of a shady evangelist who charms himself into a religious troupe and the heart of Simmons. Jones also won an Oscar for her sensational performance as Lancaster's former girlfriend-turned-prostitute. Based on Sinclair Lewis' best-seller. ★★★½ VHS: $14.99; DVD: $19.99

The Elusive Corporal

(1962, 106 min, France, Jean Renoir) *Jean-Pierre Cassel, Claude Brasseur.* This intentionally lighthearted comedy about various attempts of three French soldiers to escape from a POW camp during World War II may bring to mind Renoir's antiwar classic *La Grande Illusion.* But the intent of the director was less an examination of class and regional differences and more an exploration of the solidarity and friendship of his characters. Cassel is the charming and educated corporal who dedicates himself to breaking out of prison by any means possible. A wry, gentle comedy, featuring lively performances, and one of Renoir's most entertaining films. (French with English subtitles) ★★★½ VHS: $59.99

The Elusive Pimpernel

(1950, 107 min, GB, Michael Powell & Emeric Pressburger) *David Niven, Margaret Leighton, Cyril Cusack.* Longtime collaborators Powell and Pressburger's excellent version of the daring exploits of Baroness Orczy's famous character is every bit as entertaining as the 1935 original, *The Scarlet Pimpernel.* Niven is excellent as the heroic adventurer who rescues French aristocrats from the guillotine while doubling as an "indolent dandy of London." Originally filmed as a musical, all of the numbers were edited out, which is probably all the better. ★★★ VHS: $29.99

Elvira Madigan

(1967, 89 min, Sweden, Bo Widerberg) *Pia Degermark, Thommy Berggren.* Considered one of the cinema's most beautiful films, this tale of star-crossed love follows a young officer who meets a beautiful circus dancer and takes off to create a fragile life in isolation which must surely destroy them both. This exquisitely photographed, superbly performed film explores the consequences of love in a lyrical, poignant manner. (Swedish with English subtitles) ★★★★ VHS: $19.99

Elvira, Mistress of the Dark

(1988, 96 min, US, James Signorelli) *Cassandra Peterson, Jeff Conaway, Edie McClurg.* A feature film may seem like an unlikely vehicle for Elvira, the late night horror show hostess. It does not take long, however, for this disarming comedy to win you over. In the same vein as Pee-wee Herman, Cassandra Peterson's outrageous alter ego travels to Salem, Massachusetts, to collect an inheritance. Her confrontations with the straight-laced residents are funny and surreal. ★★½

The Emerald Forest

(1985, 113 min, US, John Boorman) *Powers Boothe, Charley Boorman, Meg Foster.* Director Boorman's son Charley plays the kidnapped child of an American engineer stationed deep within the Amazon. Boorman captures the beauty and mystery of these precious rain forests, while weaving subtle messages of the importance of cultural diversity and environmental respect into this taut action-packed adventure. Boothe plays the father who spends ten years searching for his son. ★★★½ VHS: $14.99; DVD: $19.99

Emily Brontë's Wuthering Heights

(1992, 107 min, GB, Peter Kosminsky) *Ralph Fiennes, Juliette Binoche.* The idea of Fiennes and Binoche, who were so lovely together in *The English Patient,* appearing as star-crossed lovers Heathcliff and Cathy certainly demands a certain amount of expectations while at the same time making the cinematic mouth water. But unfortunately, neither performer is allowed to really shine under the misguided direction of Kosminsky. Fiennes plays Heathcliff with passionate despair and anger, but forgets that ultimately this is a man driven by loss of love, not hate. Binoche plays Cathy more as a flirt while not fully exploring her divided romantic loyalty. The film never establishes its own tempo and finally is nothing more than a collection of beautiful set pieces unable to fully capture the story's splendor and romanticism. ★★ VHS: $14.99

Emma

(1996, 107 min, GB, Diarmuid Lawrence) *Kate Beckinsale, Mark Strong, Prunella Scales, Samantha Morton.* In this sterling television adaptation, Beckinsale upstages Gwyneth Paltrow's recent take on the title character (though Paltrow brings her own sparkle) with a very mannered but nonetheless mischievous look at Austen's would-be Cupid. Having found true love for her one-time nanny, Emma Woodhouse declares herself a bonafide matchmaker and sets out to sow the seeds of amorous bliss for her best friend. Her plan goes terribly awry, however, and in the end, she's squarely confronted with her own shortcomings. It's a marvelously moral tale that is presented here with all the manners and propriety that Austen herself could have hoped for. ★★★★ VHS: $14.99; DVD: $19.99

Emma

(1996, 111 min, GB, Douglas McGrath) *Gwyneth Paltrow, Jeremy Northam, Greta Scacchi, Toni Collette, Alan Cumming, Juliet Stevenson, Ewan McGregor, Polly Walker.* An absolutely charming, albeit commercial, rendition of Jane Austen's novel about a meddlesome young woman whose attempts to sow the seeds of romance go hopelessly awry. A radiant Paltrow brings an abundance of youthful exuberance to the title role while exceeding all expectations of her American pop film pedigree. And while her Emma is a peppy, somewhat modernized interpretation (unlike Kate Beckinsale's truly Austenesque turn in the A&E version), in the context of director McGrath's fanciful take on the tale, it's right on the money. There's no reason for anyone not to be swept up in the sheer fun of it all. ★★★½ VHS: $19.99; DVD: $29.99

Gwyneth Paltrow as *Emma*

Emma's Shadow

(1988, 93 min, Denmark, Soeren Kragh-Jacobsen) *Bjorje Ahistedt, Line Kruse.* The unlikely friendship between a willful, lonely 11-year-old girl with a slow-thinking, middle-aged sewer worker is the center of this small but affecting drama set in 1930s Copenhagen. Little rich girl Emma, frustrated by her parents' inattention, stages her own kidnapping and runs away from home, eventually hiding out at Malthe's ramshackle flat in the poor section of town. They form an unlikely alliance — with the clumsy but affectionate man passing the little girl off to his friends and neighbors as his niece. This Cannes Film Festival winner is a touching, gentle, lyrical movie about two lonely outcasts who find love and understanding. (Danish with English subtitles) ★★★

Emmanuelle

(1974, 94 min, France, Just Jaeckin) *Sylvia Kristel, Alain Cuny.* Until Perrier hit these shores, director Jaeckin's classy come-on reigned as France's most popular export. Kristel plays the inquisitive neophyte who sets out to satiate her carnal desires. A film classic which depicts virtually every variation on sexual activity as the heroine pursues the peaks of pleasure and desire. (Available dubbed or French with English subtitles) ★★½ VHS: $19.99; DVD: $29.99

The Emperor Jones

(1933, 72 min, US, Dudley Murphy) *Paul Robeson, Dudley Digges.* Robeson plays Brutus Jones, a strong-willed, egotistical railroad pullman who becomes king on a small island in the South Seas. Though this screen adaptation of Eugene O'Neill's acclaimed stage play is rather stagey, it is well worth a look for Robeson's incredibly commanding performance. ★★★ VHS: $19.99

The Emperor's New Groove

(2000, 77 min, US, Mark Dindal) *Voices of: David Spade, John Goodman, Eartha Kitt, Patrick Warburton.* Though its animation isn't up to Disney's usual standards, this madcap romp is elevated by a bouncy screenplay whose accent is most definitely on jokey one-liners and spirited hijinks. Spade provides good vocals for Kuzco, a self-centered king nearing his 18th birthday. When he fires his advisor Yzma (Kitt), she retaliates by turning him into a llama. In the kingdom's dark forests, Kuzco teams with peasant Pacha (Goodman) to return to the castle and his former self. The jokes are lively and keep coming, thanks to Spade's vainglorious reading and general silliness all around. Though it could have used more (and better) songs, *The Emperor's New Groove* is fun through and through. ★★★ VHS: $26.99; DVD: $29.99

Empire of the Sun

(1987, 152 min, US, Steven Spielberg) *Christian Bale, John Malkovich, Miranda Richardson, Nigel Havers, Joe Pantoliano, Ben Stiller.* Spielberg's ambitious project is an enthralling and spectacularly filmed if not totally successful tale of a young, privileged British boy (Bale) living in 1940s China who is separated from his parents when the Japanese invade. Sent to an internment camp, the youth quickly adapts to his environment, aided, in part, by sleazy American Malkovich and frustrated Richardson. Tom Stoppard adapted J. G. Ballard's autobiographical novel. ★★★½ VHS: $14.99

Empire State

(1987, 104 min, GB, Ron Peck) *Cathryn Harrison, Martin Landau, Ray McAnally.* An underworld crime thriller set amidst the 1980s boom of the rapidly gentrifying docklands of London's East End. Seemingly countless characters and subplots are woven through this violent tale of drugs, scheming real estate speculation, greedy yuppies, bruising boxers, male prostitutes and elegant moles. The central story follows the attempt of a young Turk and former male prostitute to try to take over a glitzy gay/straight nightclub. The provocative though uneven film opens promisingly, but concludes in a mess of unanswered questions. ★★½ VHS: $79.99

The Empire Strikes Back

(1980, 124 min, US, Irvin Kershner) *Mark Hamill, Harrison Ford, Carrie Fisher, Billy Dee Williams, Anthony Daniels, David Prowse, Alec Guinness, Clive Revill, James Earl Jones.* This second and arguably best installment of George Lucas' *Star Wars* trilogy picks up the story as the Rebellion, fresh from its destruction of the Death Star, is consolidating its power and internal structure. An Imperial probe droid soon interrupts their work and puts them on the defensive against a newly reorganized and newly vengeful Empire, led by the evil Darth Vader. The Rebel leaders disperse, Luke heading off to a swamp planet to complete his Jedi training, in order to be prepared for the inevitable confrontation with Vader, and Han and Leia taking an extended detour with the droids through an asteroid belt and a city in the clouds. By far the darkest of the trilogy, *Empire* sustains a high level of tension throughout the film, especially since there exists the real possibility of evil triumphant. Discarding the western clichés of the first film, *Empire* improves upon the original and leaves the viewer wanting more, more, more. ★★★★

Employees' Entrance

(1933, 75 min, US, Roy Del Ruth) *Warren William, Loretta Young, Wallace Ford.* This Depression-era melodrama puts *Wall Street* to shame. William stars as a department store manager who fires employees at the drop of a hat and is constantly fighting the managing directors, but he also keeps profits up. Young is a new employee who finds herself at odds with him when her fiancé becomes his assistant. Can she keep him from becoming as unscrupulous as the boss? With some racy dialogue and humorous moments, this is a thinly veiled debate about management's treatment of labor and its lack of morality. ★★★ VHS: $19.99

Empty Canvas

(1964, 118 min, Italy, Damiano Damiani) *Bette Davis, Horst Bucholtz, Catherine Spaak.* International casting of stars for film productions was quite the rage in Europe in the mid-Sixties. Which explains how Davis, with a Southern accent and blond Dutchboy wig, ended up in this interesting but convoluted Italian production. Art student Bucholtz's love for a seductive model is frustrated by his domineering and blustery and immensely wealthy mother (Davis). A treat for Davis fans, but overall the story fails to excite. (Filmed in English) ★★

The Empty Mirror

(1996, 118 min, US, Barry J. Hershey) *Norman Rodway, Camilla Soeberg, Joel Grey, Peter Michael Goetz, Doug McKeon.* Through archival footage, hallucinatory flashbacks, and subjective self-analysis, history's most notorious mass murderer, Adolf Hitler, lays bare his own psyche while reveling in his own genius. Rodway's powerful performance (shot basically in the form of a one-man show) and Hershey's mesmerizing camera cannot overcome the unpleasantness of having to spend two hours inside the mind of an unrepentant monster. As the title suggests, the mirror — and indeed the experience — is truly quite empty. ★½ VHS: $19.99

Enamorada (In Love)

(1965, 81 min, Mexico, Emilio Fernandez) A classic of the Mexican cinema. Beatriz is the beautiful daughter of a very wealthy man. Jose, a general committed to social and political change, is deeply in love with her. But the woman, blinded by a life's teaching that class is more important than love, has only contempt for this peasant-born young man. A fiery and passionate tale of love overcoming social pressures. (Spanish with English subtitles) ★★★½

Enchanted April

(1991, 104 min, US, Mike Newell) *Miranda Richardson, Josie Lawrence, Joan Plowright, Polly Walker, Alfred Molina, Jim Broadbent, Michael Kitchen.* A heartwarming adaptation of Elizabeth von Arnim's 1922 romantic comedy about four English women who run off to an Italian seaside castle for emotional revitalization. The theme is a familiar one to English literature (uptight Brits flee their rainy island to the Italian sun where they finally let loose, a little) and it's done full justice here. Filmed in the actual villa in Portofino, Italy, where von Arnim penned her book, the film lovingly re-creates the ambience of the era while telling its charming tale of four women who start off as unlikely traveling com-

panions and wind up best of friends. The acting is uniformly excellent. ★★★★ VHS: $19.99

The Enchanted Cottage

(1945, 92 min, US, John Cromwell) *Dorothy McGuire, Robert Young, Herbert Marshall, Mildred Natwick.* Isolated from society by physical deformities resulting from different sets of circumstances, a young man and woman learn to see themselves through each other's eyes. Touching performances from McGuire and Young elevate what could have been mawkish melodrama. Instead, this is a fantasy parable about the healing power of unconditional love. This film was used as an allegorical reference in Joseph Wambaugh's "The Secrets of Harry Bright." ★★★

Encino Man

(1992, 88 min, US, Les Mayfield) *Pauly Shore, Brendan Fraser, Sean Astin, Megan Ward.* In a move that might seem tantamount to box-office suicide, Hollywood has given us a movie starring quite possibly the most irritating creature ever put before the camera: MTV's Shore. The punchline is...for the most part, it works. Shore plays the world's oldest-looking high school student who becomes part of the in-crowd when his best friend (Astin) unearths a prehistoric man in his backyard. Though a wee bit lethargic in the laughs department, a debuting Fraser steals the pic hands down with his money's-worth performance as the title character. ★★½ DVD: $29.99

Encore

(1952, 87 min, GB, Pat Jackson, Anthony Pelissier & Harold French) *Glynis Johns, Kay Walsh, Nigel Patrick.* An intriguing trilogy based on three short stories by W. Somerset Maugham. In the first, a playboy battles with his brother over money; in the second, an irascible spinster makes life miserable for the unfortunate passengers on an ocean crossing; in the third, a circus high-diver gets the jitters. ★★★½

The End

(1978, 100 min, US, Burt Reynolds) *Burt Reynolds, Dom DeLuise, Sally Field, Joanne Woodward, Carl Reiner, David Steinberg, Kristy McNichol, Robby Benson, Myrna Loy.* Scandalously funny, this wicked black comedy features Reynolds as a man who is told that he has only a few months to live and decides to commit suicide. Featuring hilarious appearances by the entire cast, especially DeLuise who is wonderfully deranged as Reynolds' schizophrenic best friend. The film takes a sharp satiric swipe at the hypocrisy of compassion as well as the sanctity of life. ★★★ VHS: $14.99; DVD: $14.99

End of Days

(1999, 118 min, US, Peter Hyams) *Arnold Schwarzenegger, Gabriel Byrne, Robin Tunney, Kevin Pollak, Rod Steiger.* After a two-year absence from movie screens, "Ah-nuld" is back with a medium bang in this bizarre mix of generic action flick and fire-and-brimstone apocalyptic thriller. Arnold (looking noticeably trim in his first outing since his heart surgery) is a scruffy, faithless New York cop who must protect a cynical woman from the vile clutches of Satan himself (Byrne, whose sinister leer and malevolent pranks provide the only source of much-needed humor in this otherwise grim and heartless movie). Tired cop-movie clichés and digital special effects dominate as the forces of evil threaten the forces of light, and it's up to the intrepid policeman to renew his faith and save the world. Knowing what he's up against, the film flirts with ludicrousness far too often by making him blast away at Beelzebub with a Rambo-sized arsenal. Steiger has some fun chewing his and everyone else's scenery. ★★ VHS: $14.99; DVD: $24.99

End of St. Petersberg

(1927, 69 min, USSR, Vsevolod Pudovkin) *Ivan Chuvelov*. Made on the commemoration of the Tenth Anniversary of the 1917 Revolution, this ambitious drama follows the plight of a common laborer who is forced to leave his failing farm only to then suffer at the hands of capitalist factory owners and eventually witness the horrors of war. The film, in not a subtle fashion, details the pains and humiliation the people had to endure before experiencing the social upheavals and resulting freedoms of the Revolution. (Silent with orchestral accompaniment) ★★★ VHS: $29.99

The End of the Affair

(1999, 101 min, GB, Neil Jordan) *Ralph Fiennes, Julianne Moore, Stephen Rea, Ian Hart*. Jordan's exquisite and mostly faithful adaptation of Graham Greene's semiautobiographical novel, *The End of the Affair* features remarkable performances, gorgeous cinematography, and an outstanding Michael Nyman score. Maurice Bendrix (Fiennes) begins an erotic affair with Sarah Miles (Moore), who ends things for no apparent reason. Two years after this divisive break, Maurice and Sarah reunite through her cuckolded husband, Henry (Rea), and emotions begin to simmer again. Jordan keeps the tension mounting as Maurice slowly discovers what changed in his relationship with Sarah. Yet what makes the film so passionate is that in the present or in the past, every touch between the lovers is palpable and heartfelt. The second screen version of Greene's novel, this *End of the Affair* is heartbreaking and very moving. ★★★½ VHS: $19.99; DVD: $27.99

The End of Violence

(1997, 122 min, US, Wim Wenders) *Bill Pullman, Andie MacDowell, Gabriel Byrne, Loren Dean, Udo Kier, Sam Fuller*. Director Wenders' disdain for contemporary Hollywood and fear of Los Angeles is evident in almost every scene of *The End of Violence*. Pullman plays a producer specializing in blood-and-bullets epics who is so absorbed in financing his latest movie that when wife MacDowell announces she's leaving him, he barely reacts. Soon, Pullman leaves his big pool and Malibu estate, too; he's carjacked by two thugs who can't figure out what to do with their high-profile victim. While trying to decide, they're murdered, giving Pullman a chance to start a new life for himself. At the same time, Byrne, a former government scientist, is busy on his new assignment, developing a surveillance system for the L.A. area. Strange things start to occur when both men's lives eventually cross. Part thriller, part Hollywood business satire and part marital drama, *The End of Violence* is a haunting meditation on living and dying in L.A., a place where a wife uses a cell phone to tell her husband she wants a divorce while sitting a few feet away. ★★★ VHS: $14.99; DVD: $19.99

Enemy at the Gates

Endangered Species

(1982, 92 min, US, Alan Rudolph) *Robert Urich, JoBeth Williams, Hoyt Axton, Paul Dooley, Peter Coyote, Dan Hedaya*. Low-keyed performances enhance this fact-based suspense thriller about a New York detective (Urich) assigned to investigate a string of bizarre cattle mutilations out West. Williams costars as the country sheriff also on the case. Slow-moving at times, but the patient viewer will be rewarded. ★★★

Endless Love

(1981, 115 min, US, Franco Zeffirelli) *Brooke Shields, Martin Hewitt, Don Murray, Shirley Knight, Richard Kiley, Beatrice Straight, Tom Cruise, James Spader*. The film which will always be remembered as the butt of Bette Midler's classic Oscar-night joke: "That endless bore — *Endless Love*." It's about two teenagers (Shields, Hewitt) with the hots for each other. Despite being in one of the worst films of its decade, debuting actors Cruise and Spader were able to get work after this. ★

Endless Night

(1971, 95 min, GB, Sidney Gilliat) *Hayley Mills, Hywel Bennett, Britt Ekland, George Sanders, Per Oscarsson*. Suspenseful Agatha Christie thriller about a rich American girl (Mills) who marries her chauffeur (Bennett). When they move into her mansion, their new life is anything but blissful when blackmail and murder enter the scene. (Letterboxed) ★★★ VHS: $9.99; DVD: $24.99

Enemies: A Love Story

(1989, 119 min, US, Paul Mazursky) *Ron Silver, Anjelica Huston, Lena Olin, Margaret Sophie Stein, Paul Mazursky, Alan King*. Featuring a superb evocation of post-WWII New York, director Mazursky has created a career milestone with this darkly comic tale about a Jewish immigrant (Silver), scarred from his wartime experiences, who suddenly finds himself with three wives. An extraordinary cast includes Huston as his strong-willed first wife thought killed in the camps; Stein as his gentile, slave-like second; and the remarkable Olin as a lusty socialist whose passion most ignites the stolid Silver. ★★★★

Enemy at the Gates

(2001, 131 min, GB, Jean-Jacques Annaud) *Jude Law, Joseph Fiennes, Rachel Weisz, Ed Harris, Bob Hoskins, Ron Perlman, Eva Mattes*. Battle sequences nearly as stunning as those in *Saving Private Ryan* collide with the familiar subplot of two soldiers in love with the same woman, making the visually exciting *Enemy at the Gates* a rousing if routine war film. Based on the experiences of real-life Russian hero Vassili Zaitsev (Law), the story begins as inexperienced youngsters recruited by Stalin's demoralized army are immediately thrown into deadly battle at the strategic location of Stalingrad (as realized in a brilliantly staged opening sequence). One of these is Vassili, who demonstrates a rare talent for marksmanship. In an effort to bolster morale, a writer follows Vassili's successful sniper attacks on German officers, turning him into a national hero. This also attracts the attention of the Nazis, who send a cold-blooded assassin (a sensational Harris) to hunt him down, setting in motion a thrilling cat-and-mouse game between the two marksmen. *Enemy at the Gates* is at its best detailing the components of war, from bloody battle to the final hunt. It loses much of its dramatic momentum by giving equal time to an uninvolving love triangle. ★★½ VHS: $102.99; DVD: $29.99

The Enemy Below

(1957, 98 min, US, Dick Powell) *Robert Mitchum, Curt Jurgens, David Hedison, Theodore Bikel*. Solid WWII yarn with Mitchum as an American warship commander and Jurgens as a Nazi U-boat captain engaged in a battle of wits as the Yanks hunt down a German sub. As in the much-later *The Hunt for Red October*, the film explores the interpersonal relationships between the men of both crews, and also features Oscar-winning special effects. ★★★ VHS: $9.99

Enemy Mine

(1985, 108 min, US, Wolfgang Petersen) *Dennis Quaid, Lou Gossett, Jr.* From the director of *Das Boot* comes this visually striking sci-fi adventure about two interplanetary enemies, a pilot from Earth and a warrior from the planet Drac, who become stranded together on a distant, deserted planet. A space-age *Hell in the Pacific.* ★★★ VHS: $9.99; DVD: $24.99

Enemy of the State

(1998, 127 min, US, Tony Scott) *Will Smith, Gene Hackman, Jon Voight, Regina King, Loren Dean, Jason Lee, Gabriel Byrne, James Le Gros, Ian Hart.* Producer Jerry Bruckheimer reteams with director Scott (*Crimson Tide*) for this exciting political thriller — and fortunately they had the good sense to cast Smith as the Everyman running for his life. The engaging Smith is Robert Dean, a wily lawyer who is forced to use all his wiles when government goons mistake him for an agent with damaging evidence against their covert syndicate. Dean then spends the rest of the film dashing in and out of trouble in tense, even plausible cat-and-mouse games. He gets a little help from a reclusive surveillance expert (Hackman in another saving-grace supporting turn) who teaches him a few tricks in the book. The film starts a little slow in setting up the game, but once the game's afoot, *Enemy of the State* is an often crackerjack espionage tale. ★★★ VHS: $14.99; DVD: $29.99

Enemy Territory

(1987, 90 min, US, Peter Manoogian) *Gary Frank, Ray Parker, Jr., Jan-Michael Vincent.* Effective urban thriller about a naive insurance salesman and a street-smart phone workman who join forces when they become trapped in a ghetto apartment building under siege by a neighborhood gang. ★★½ VHS: $79.99

The Enemy Within

(1994, 86 min, US, Jonathan Darby) *Forest Whitaker, Sam Waterston, Dana Delany, Jason Robards, George Dzundza, Josef Sommers.* In this updated remake of *Seven Days in May*, the president (Waterston) has seven days to sign a bill which increases the military budget by 30%. He does not intend to sign it. Whitaker turns in a solid performance as the colonel who inadvertently uncovers a plot to overthrow the presidency — perpetrated by the U.S. military. Robards exudes controlled mania as the general who orchestrates the military maneuvers. A tautly paced and finely detailed HBO production. ★★★ VHS: $9.99

Les Enfants Terribles

(1950, 107 min, France, Jean-Pierre Melville) *Edouard Dermithe, Nicole Stephane.* A landmark of French cinema and a strong influence on the New Wave filmmakers, this collaboration with Jean Cocteau (who scripted the film and oversaw its production) is a haunting cinematic poem about the love and confused narcissism of a brother and sister, whose passion for each other is so intense that it flowers into perversity and eventual death. Please note that the only available videos of this classic, taken from a 16mm film, are in only fair condition. (French with English subtitles) ★★★ VHS: $29.99

L'Enfer

(1993, 100 min, France, Claude Chabrol) *Emmanuelle Béart, François Cluzet.* There's an unsettling discord between the open, sun-drenched country inn where *L'Enfer* is set, and the spiralling descent into madness which the film depicts. A husband (Cluzet) becomes increasingly obsessional regarding his wife's

(Béart) supposed infidelities. While the film is sometimes ambivalent about her actual culpability, there is no doubt that Cluzet has crossed into a reality of his own making. Chabrol's masterly command of the medium allows the viewer to enter the mind of a man driven to hallucinatory extremes fueled by his paranoid distrust. The great director Henri-Georges Clouzot wrote the screenplay in 1963 with the intent of directing it. Although this rendition is different in tone from what we could have expected from that treatment, *L'Enfer* still retains Clouzot's dark edge. (French with English subtitles) ★★★★ VHS: $19.99; DVD: $29.99

The Enforcer

(1951, 87 min, US, Bretaigne Windust) *Humphrey Bogart, Zero Mostel, Everett Sloane.* Tough Bogart drama with Bogey as a hard-boiled district attorney out to break a crime ring. ★★★ VHS: $9.99

The Enforcer

(1976, 96 min, US, James Fargo) *Clint Eastwood, Tyne Daly, Harry Guardino.* Eastwood encores as Dirty Harry in this third installment of the series. Daly costars as his partner as they comb San Francisco in search of a terrorist group. (Sequel: *Sudden Impact*) ★★★ VHS: $14.99

The English Patient

(1996, 162 min, US, Anthony Minghella) *Ralph Fiennes, Kristin Scott Thomas, Juliette Binoche, Willem Dafoe, Colin Firth, Naveen Andrews, Jürgen Prochnow.* From its opening frames, *The English Patient* evokes an exhilarating sense of time and place. Told with sweeping economy and the lyricism and tempo that only great art can author, this breathlessly romantic and impassioned epic is a rare reminder of the pleasures made available from consummate filmmaking. The story effortlessly narrates two time periods: pre-war Northern Africa and war-torn WWII Italy. The superb Fiennes plays a severely burned amnesiac whose love affair with a married woman is told through flashback. Scott Thomas revels in the role of the beautiful sophisticate, giving a smart, alluring performance. Adapted from Michael Ondaatje's celebrated novel by director Minghella, *The English Patient* is keenly observed and replete with the kind of romanticism and intelligent dialogue audiences ache for. Winner of 9 Academy Awards, including Best Picture and Best Director. (VHS available letterboxed or pan & scan) ★★★★ VHS: $14.99; DVD: $29.99

An Englishman Abroad

(1985, 63 min, GB, John Schlesinger) *Alan Bates, Coral Browne.* Bates gives a riveting performance in this brilliantly staged drama based on a true incident. Guy Burgess (Bates), the infamous British spy, traitor and gay outcast, defected to Russia in the 1940s. During a 1958 theatrical performance in Moscow featuring visiting actress Browne (appearing as herself), a drunken Burgess promptly crashes backstage and sets up a friendship with the actress. Browne, who is intrigued by this disheveled and eccentric outsider, comes to pity, despise and assist him after he invites her to his shabby flat — and comes to understand this almost broken man. A touching and humorous film with a witty, concise screenplay. ★★★★

The Englishman Who Went Up a Hill, But Came Down a Mountain

(1995, 99 min, GB, Christopher Monger) *Hugh Grant, Tara Fitzgerald, Colm Meaney, Ian Hart, Kenneth Griffiths.* Recalling the whimsy of those wonderful Ealing comedies of the '50s and '60s, this is a thoroughly engaging if understated romp which charms at the most unexpected moments. Set in 1917, the film stars Grant as an English mapmaker who travels to a small Welsh village to measure the town's mountain, which appears to be the only source of pride for the villagers. When they discover their mountain's height only qualifies as a hill, and will therefore be ineligible to be included on the map, the entire populace engages in a crazy scheme to make up the difference and to keep Grant in town to remeasure it. Director Monger sets an easygoing pace which befits the story's unconventional comedy, and an excellent supporting cast displays an abundance of character and wit. ★★★ VHS: $14.99; DVD: $29.99

Enjo

(1958, 98 min, Japan, Kon Ichikawa) *Raizo Ichikawa, Ganjiro Nakamura.* Although *Enjo* takes place in a foreign world, there are emotions explored that transcend all boundaries. Goichi Mizoguchi (Ichikawa) is a young monk who is lonely and misunderstood. After his father's death, Mizoguchi leaves his poor temple and arrives at the famous Shukaku temple. Mizoguchi soon proves to be inept at most everything he tries, with exception to his love for the temple. While political infighting and scandal dominate the rest of the monks' time, the ostracized Mizoguchi only wants to care for Shukaku. Beautifully shot, *Enjo* is another masterpiece from Ichikawa (*The Burmese Harp*). Based on Yukio Mishima's novel. (Japanese with English subtitles) ★★★½ VHS: $19.99

Enormous Changes at the Last Minute

(1983, 115 min, US, Mirra Bank & Ellen Hovde) *Ellen Barkin, Kevin Bacon, Maria Tucci, Lynn Milgran.* Based on the charming, humanistic tales of novelist Grace Paley, *Enormous Changes* unites a crisp John Sayles—Susan Rice script and glorious performances. This trilogy from Paley's second collection glistens with the dignity of contemporary urban women struggling against setbacks but determined to get their fair share from life. A funny, gracefully optimistic work. ★★★ VHS: $79.99

The English Patient

Ensign Pulver

(1964, 104 min, US, Joshua Logan) *Robert Walker, Walter Matthau, Tommy Sands, Larry Hagman, James Coco, Jack Nicholson.* Inferior sequel to *Mister Roberts* with Walker taking over the Jack Lemmon role. Ensign Pulver continues his wartime shenanigans aboard a naval ship. ★★ VHS: $14.99

Enter the Dragon

(1973, 103 min, US, Robert Clouse) *Bruce Lee, John Saxon, Jim Kelly.* The first American/Hong Kong coproduction is arguably the best martial arts film ever made. Lee (appearing in his final film) goes underground to track down an opium ring. This Special Edition includes 3 minutes of martial arts scenes previously unseen, a 20-minute documentary featuring Lee, and a collectable lobby card. (VHS available letterboxed or pan & scan) ★★★½ VHS: $14.99; DVD: $19.99

The Entertainer

(1960, 100 min, GB, Tony Richardson) *Laurence Olivier, Joan Plowright, Daniel Massey, Alan Bates, Albert Finney.* Olivier gives an extraordinary performance in Richardson's depiction of a seedy vaudevillian on the skids who unwittingly destroys those around him. As the egotistical Archie Rice, Olivier captures the grotesque demeanor and futile yearnings of a defeated man. Based on John Osborne's play. ★★★½ VHS: $24.99; DVD: $19.99

Entertaining Mr. Sloane

(1970, 94 min, GB, Douglas Hickox) *Beryl Reid, Harry Andrews, Peter McEnery.* Playwright Joe Orton's scathing black comedy about a young stud's entry into the lives of a middle-aged brother and sister. Reid is the sex-starved, man-hungry sister, Andrews is her latently homosexual brother and McEnery is the menacing hustler. This is a superbly acted and boldly presented rendition of one of Britain's most daring late-great playwrights. ★★★

Entrapment

(1999, 120 min, US, Jon Amiel) *Sean Connery, Catherine Zeta-Jones, Ving Rhames, Will Patton.* A tame thriller given much more class by its two stars than it really deserves, *Entrapment* stars the beautiful Zeta-Jones as an insurance investigator who tracks down world-class thief Connery when a priceless painting is stolen. She cons her way into a scheme with him, but is she really there to trap him? The story has a twist every half-hour or so, but none will produce more than a mild "oh" as director Amiel approaches the material with a nonchalant ambivalence. The two elaborate thefts that bookend the film sustain interest and even generate a moment or two of suspense, but the cat-and-mouse games between Connery and Zeta-Jones, Connery and Rhames (as his mysterious partner), and Zeta-Jones and Patton (as her boss) go nowhere. ★★ VHS: $14.99; DVD: $26.99

Entre Nous

(1983, 110 min, France, Diane Kurys) *Miou-Miou, Isabelle Huppert, Guy Marchand.* Kurys' largely autobiographical work is a beautiful rendering of the strength and complexity of friendship. Huppert portrays Lena, a reticent housewife resigned to the numbing security of her husband and family. Through a chance encounter, she meets Madeleine (Miou-Miou), a vibrantly bohemian sculptress whose love and companionship open the door to Lena's self-discovery. The film radiates with the delicate nuances of a woman's sensibility and sensuality. (French with English subtitles) ★★★★ VHS: $19.99; DVD: $29.99

Equinox

(1993, 107 min, US, Alan Rudolph) *Matthew Modine, Lara Flynn Boyle, Fred Ward, Tyra Ferrell, Marisa Tomei, Kevin J. O'Connor, Tate Donovan, M. Emmet Walsh.* An elderly, indigent woman lies dying in a New York City street. She clutches a scrap of paper, closed with sealing wax, which catches the eye of a curious, would-be-writer morgue attendant, initiating a quest to uncover the truth behind a 30-year-old blind trust. Director Rudolph's relentless pacing is magnified by the constant, pounding ambient noise which underscores the desperation of characters tightly interwoven by proximity but with no emotional contact. As is usual with Rudolph films, there's an eclectic mix of talented players. Every element of the production is on-target and highlighted by a mesmerizing soundtrack. ★★★½ VHS: $19.99

Equinox Flower

(1958, 118 min, Japan, Yasujiro Ozu) *Shin Saburi, Kinuyo Tanaka.* Ozu's deceptively serene style of filmmaking is showcased in this family drama about the post-war generation gap between a tradition-bound businessman and his more modern-minded daughter. Although sympathetic to the independence of his friends' children, Hirayama confronts rebellion in his own family after his daughter announces her engagement to a young man without seeking his approval. Shooting from about three feet from the ground with a rock-steady camera and featuring a bold use of color (his first film in color), Ozu provides a gentle drama of familial misunderstanding and reconciliation, a beautifully designed and moving work. (Japanese with English subtitles) ★★★ VHS: $19.99

Equus

(1977, 138 min, US, Sidney Lumet) *Richard Burton, Peter Firth, Jenny Agutter, Joan Plowright.* Peter Shaffer's shattering play is faithfully brought to the screen with Burton as the troubled psychiatrist who attempts to unlock the secret which triggered a disturbed stable boy (Firth) to blind six horses. Both Burton and Firth are especially good. ★★★ VHS: $14.99

Eraser

(1996, 115 min, US, Charles Russell) *Arnold Schwarzenegger, James Caan, Vanessa Williams, James Coburn, James Cromwell.* Arnold's megabudget action movies have nearly attained a status not unlike Greek mythology: Everybody knows the stories and how they'll end, so just add explosions. This story-lite, gun-heavy vehicle is one of the worst offenders. Combining plot elements from a half-dozen earlier (and better) Schwarzenegger efforts, *Eraser* gives us Arnold as a U.S. marshal charged with protecting star witness Williams pitting him against one of his own guys. *Eraser* is full of by-the-numbers stunts and explosions — it's all been done before, and will only entertain diehard fans. (VHS available letterboxed or pan & scan) ★★ VHS: $9.99; DVD: $19.99

Eraserhead

(1977, 90 min, US, David Lynch) *Jack Nance, Charlotte Stewart, Jeanne Bates.* Lynch's fiendish cult classic adopts the logic of dreams and nightmares as layers of reality dissolve, sucking you into the eerie world of a warped mind. The befuddled "hero" Henry struggles against the powers of the shrinking mutant slab in this demented gem which promises that in heaven, everything is fine. Based, in part, on the director's brief stay in Philadelphia. ★★★½

Erendira

(1982, 103 min, Mexico/France/West Germany, Ruy Guerra) *Irene Papas, Claudia Ohana, Michael Lonsdale.* Director Guerra paints a surreal fresco of passion and revenge in this darkly humorous tale of a young girl forced into prostitution by her demented grandmother (Papas). Based on a short story by Gabriel García Márquez. (Spanish with English subtitles) ★★★ VHS: $24.99

Erik the Viking

(1989, 100 min, GB, Terry Jones) *Tim Robbins, Mickey Rooney, John Cleese, Terry Jones, Antony Sher, Eartha Kitt.* Monty Python-ite Jones directed this funny, offbeat comic adventure which dares to ask the pertinent question, "Why rape, pillage and kill if you don't really feel like it?" Robbins stars as the sensitive Norseman, Erik, who questions the rather violent way of life of a 12th-century Viking after he is affected by a woman he has accidentally killed. The director appears as the king of an island teeming with Julie Andrews wannabes. ★★½

Erin Brockovich

(2000, 126 min, US, Steven Soderbergh) *Julia Roberts, Albert Finney, Aaron Eckhart, Peter Coyote, Marg Helgenberger, Cherry Jones.* Roberts (who won a Best Actress Oscar) absolutely shines as the title character, a single mother of three with no formal training who was instrumental in a class-action lawsuit against California's powerful electric company PG&E. Based on a true story, this always compelling, often funny and unexpectedly touching film traces Erin's road in helping score the largest settlement in U.S. history. Talking her way into a job with a law firm run by her ex-attorney (Finney in a sensational turn), she stumbles accidentally onto medical files which hint at cover-up. Beginning an exhausting investigation, she learns the giant power company has been dumping pollutants in a small town's water supply, causing devastating health problems for local residents. Director Soderbergh's first commercial film is a winner — the king of the independents is right at home with the rhythm of an underdog story, the demands of a big-budget film, and showcasing to great effect Hollywood's biggest female star of the '90s. This is a Julia Roberts movie for those who don't like Julia Roberts movies. ★★★½ VHS: $14.99; DVD: $26.99

Ermo

(1995, 93 min, China, Zhou Xiaowen) *Alia, Liu Peiqi, Ge Zhijun.* Not the uproarious comedy the video box would imply, *Ermo* is actually a scathing social satire on the rapidly changing

E

Julia Roberts in *Erin Brockovich*

economic and political changes currently underway in Communist China. Set in that country's impoverished rural interior, the story focuses on Ermo, a pretty young woman who, despite a husband and children, becomes determined to "keep up with the Joneses" in her effort to own the biggest (and almost only) television in the village. For the politicos, it can be seen as an indictment on the encroaching (and soulless) consumerism and for others less didactically inclined, simply a wry comedy-drama about ambition, family and the hidden joys of the simple ways of life. (Mandarin with English subtitles) ★★★

The Ernest Green Story

(1991, 101 min, US, Eric Laneuville) *Morris Chestnut, CCH Pounder, Ossie Davis, Ruby Dee.* This stirring, superb production from the Disney family entertainment line tells the true story of the first black student to graduate from a white high school in the South. Battling intense hatred, the Arkansas government and even the Arkansas National Guard, nine brave teenagers chose to take a stand for equal education by leaving the safety of their black high school to enroll in a prestigious white Little Rock school. ★★★★ VHS: $39.99

Ernesto

(1979, 95 min, Italy, Salvatore Samperi) *Michele Placido, Martin Halm.* This lush period drama revolves around the emotional and sexual coming of age of an impetuous Italian teenager who quickly discovers the power of youth, beauty and money. Set in the town of Trieste in 1911, the story follows Ernesto, the son of a wealthy merchant who, wielding his emerging sexuality with wanton abandon, becomes involved with a hunky stevedore, only to cruelly discard him. The lad immediately enters into an unlikely love triangle with a younger boy and his twin sister. Throughout his amorous romps, Ernesto — not a particularly likable youth — remains a figure of vacillating loyalties and reckless sexuality. The handsome Placido is perfectly cast as the helplessly infatuated workman. (Italian with English subtitles) ★★★ VHS: $49.99

Ernesto Che Guevara: The Bolivian Diary

(1997, 94 min, Switzerland/France, Richard Lindo) In a quietly moving documentary portrait, director Lindo has succeeded in delicately mythologizing one of the century's great idealists. *The Bolivian Diary* begins with Ernesto "Che" Guevara's exile from the state he helped revolutionize. Building a narrative from Che's own handsomely scripted journal entries, the viewer travels within Bolivian underbrush, down narrow river canyons and through one-street villages in the footsteps of the guerillas. Archival films and stills of Fidel and party officials are complemented by grainy, sun-washed and lyrical video footage of testimony from surviving guerillas and Bolivian soldiers, as well as the peasants with whom Che interacted during his 11 months as leader of the revolution run aground. ★★★ VHS: $29.99

The Escape

(1995, 91 min, Canada/US, Stuart Gillard) *Patrick Dempsey, Brigitte Bako, Colm Feore.* A routine escaped convict tale with artsy pretenses, *The Escape* is a stylishly made thriller which can't escape the formula of the genre. Dempsey is a convicted murderer who becomes a fugitive when he runs away from his brutal guards while working in a remote wooded area. During a thunderstorm, he hides out in an abandoned house, only to save the life of a young, beautiful cellist (Bako) whose car has careened into a nearby lake. Together they wait out the storm, and Dempsey — the object of a manhunt — finds romance and possible redemption with the young woman. The film starts briskly, but the romantic angle slows things considerably. ★★½ VHS: $59.99

Escape from Alcatraz

(1980, 112 min, US, Don Siegel) *Clint Eastwood, Patrick McGoohan, Fred Ward, Danny Glover, Roberts Blossom.* A true story of the only three men ever to escape from Alcatraz. Eastwood stars as Frank Morris, the bank robber who masterminds the escape. An exciting and accomplished thriller. ★★★½ VHS: $14.99; DVD: $24.99

Escape from L.A.

(1996, 100 min, US, John Carpenter) *Kurt Russell, Steve Buscemi, Stacy Keach, Peter Fonda, Cliff Robertson, Pam Grier, Bruce Campbell, Paul Bartel.* Both a remake of and a sequel to his 1981 cult classic *Escape from New York,* Carpenter's *Escape from L.A.* marks the return of the world's most unlikely one-eyed hero, Snake Plissken (Russell). This time, he must enter the island of Los Angeles, now serving as a spot of exile for those deemed undesirable by the fascist regime ruling what remains of the United States. There he has to retrieve both a lethal satellite control mechanism and the president's loony daughter, in that order. Fans of the first film may be entertained as Carpenter and Russell cover much of the same ground, but overall a sense of "we've seen all this before" works against it. ★★½ VHS: $9.99; DVD: $24.99

Escape from New York

(1981, 106 min, US, John Carpenter) *Kurt Russell, Lee Van Cleef, Ernest Borgnine, Donald Pleasence, Isaac Hayes, Adrienne Barbeau.* In 1997,

New York City is a walled, barricaded maximum security prison. Air Force One, with the president aboard, is hijacked and crash lands inside the prison. Snake Plissken (Russell), one-time war hero and just sentenced to life, is volunteered as a one-man rescue team. *Escape from New York* effectively blends action-adventure and tongue-in-cheek comedy with consistently engaging performances from its cast. Imbued with trademark Carpenter directorial touches, not the least of which is the musical score. (Director's cut) ★★★½ VHS: $9.99; DVD: $19.99

Escape from the Planet of the Apes

(1971, 97 min, US, J. Lee Thompson) *Roddy McDowall, Kim Hunter, Ricardo Montalban, Sal Mineo.* In the third entry of the *Apes* series, futuristic apes McDowall and Hunter travel back in time to present-day Los Angeles. Though all the *Ape* sequels lack the energy and creative spark of the first film, this is nevertheless a lot of fun and the simian cast is clearly enjoying itself. ★★★ VHS: $14.99

Escape Me Never

(1947, 103 min, US, Peter Godfrey) *Errol Flynn, Ida Lupino, Alexis Smith.* Lupino sparkles as the waif with a heart o' gold in this musical melodrama set in northern Italy. She's a single mother crooning for her cappuccino while her beau, charming composer Flynn, smooth-operates on aristocrat Parker. Even after making an honest woman out of Lupino, Flynn can't curb his lust. Predictable yes, but Lupino is a delight. ★★½ VHS: $19.99

Escape to Witch Mountain

(1975, 97 min, US, John Hough) *Eddie Albert, Donald Pleasence, Ray Milland.* Two orphans with psychic powers search for their origins with the help of Albert, in one of Disney's better mystery/fantasies. Pleasence is a psychic investigator and Milland plays an evil tycoon. ★★★ VHS: $19.99

E.T., The Extra-Terrestrial

(1982, 115 min, US, Steven Spielberg) *Henry Thomas, Dee Wallace, Drew Barrymore, Robert MacNaughton, Peter Coyote.* A classic sci-fi adventure, and one of the most popular pictures of all time. An alien lands in suburban California and is befriended by a ten-year-old boy (Thomas), who helps the space traveler return home. It's magical, mystical, funny and extremely touching; and E.T. itself is a marvel of makeup and effects. Barrymore is a delight as Thomas' younger sister. This is our generation's *The Wizard of Oz.* ★★★★

L'État Sauvage

(1978, 111 min, France, Francis Girod) *Jacques Dutronc, Marie-Christine Barrault, Michel Piccoli.* An unusually hard-hitting French political thriller that deals with the ambiguous relationship and underlying racism between France and one of her former colonies — a developing central African country. Set in the early 1960s, the story revolves around a young French couple who find themselves adrift in the politically charged atmosphere of a recently established black state. The man (Dutronc) is an UNESCO official who finds that his wife (Barrault) is having an illicit affair with the powerful Minister of

Health. A taut drama of corruption, hatred and deceit. (French with English subtitles) ★★★

L'Été Meurtrier
(One Deadly Summer)

(1983, 134 min, France, Jean Becker) *Isabelle Adjani, Alain Souchon.* This sizzling psychological drama captured four Césars in 1983, including the Best Actress Award for Adjani. The story is set in a provincial village where a cartoonish tramp, played to the hilt by Adjani, struts into town, throwing male libidos into a frenzy. Though dismissed as a whore by the townsfolk, little do they know that beneath the unpredictable exterior lurks a cunningly vengeful woman, determined to wipe away the remembrances of a haunting personal tragedy. (French with English subtitles) ★★★

The Eternal

(1999, 95 min, US/Ireland, Michael Almereyda) *Alison Elliot, Jared Harris, Christopher Walken, Lois Smith.* An alcoholic couple (Elliot and Harris, who are both good) with a young son decide to kick the bottle by visiting Elliot's family in Ireland. They arrive to meet crazy Uncle Bill (Walken), who's keeping a mummified witch in the basement. The set-up promises to be a funny/creepy variation of the classic *The Old Dark House.* Unfortunately, it's just a moderately interesting mishmash. While there's a little humor (thanks to Walken), the film mostly opts for murky pretension and vague "scares," neither of which work. (aka: *Trance*) ★★ VHS: $79.99; DVD: $24.99

The Eternal Return (L'Eternel Retour)

(1943, 100 min, France, Jean Delannoy) *Jean Marais, Madeleine Sologne.* Written by Jean Cocteau, this modern retelling of the Tristan and Isolde legend is a lavishly romantic and tender love story. Marais is Patrice, the nephew of a wealthy widower, who arranges a marriage (albeit loveless) between Nathalie, a beautiful young woman he meets, and his uncle. With the help of a love potion, Patrice and Nathalie are irrevocably attracted to each other, threatening the family with their forbidden love. A poetic fable of tragic love. (French with English subtitles) (aka: *Love Eternal*) ★★★ VHS: $24.99

Ethan Frome

(1993, 107 min, US, John Madden) *Liam Neeson, Patricia Arquette, Joan Allen, Tate Donovan.* Anyone who has read Edith Wharton's bleak tale of one man's catastrophic grasp at passion knows its movie adaptation is not destined to be "the feel-good hit of the season." Neeson is perfectly cast as the poor farmer whose desire for his wife's cousin (Arquette) ends in a tragic accident. Neeson's face transforms from twisted and bitter to smooth and handsome as this classic tale flashes between post- and pre-accident. Arquette is similarly well-suited, eschewing coquettishness for a more heart-pounding, lump-in-your-throat, clumsy sense of desire. The pace is slow and there is rarely any relief from the oppressiveness of the story, but the superb acting and intensity of its emotions more than compensate. ★★★

Eureka

(1983, 130 min, GB, Nicolas Roeg) *Gene Hackman, Rutger Hauer, Theresa Russell, Mickey Rourke.* Roeg's tale of a gold prospector (Hackman) who strikes it rich in the Yukon and, years later, must fight gangsters and a son-in-law who might be a sorcerer is told in the director's familiar mythic style. His trademarks — breathtaking cinematography, jagged editing, and temporal jumps — are all present in this mystical story of greed and lust. ★★½ VHS: $14.99

Europa, Europa

(1991, 110 min, Germany/France, Agnieszka Holland) *Marco Hofschneider, Klaus Abramowsky, Julie Delpy.* This sweeping statement on the resilience of the human spirit is one of the most powerful films to address the Holocaust. A brilliant mix of gut-wrenching drama and dark humor, *Europa, Europa* is based on the harrowing true story of Solomon Perel, a Jewish teenager who miraculously survived the war by passing himself off as Aryan; so well, in fact, that he unwittingly wound up in the Nazi Youth. Set adrift in a historical tide of events beyond his control, young Solomon desperately clings to his identity while at the same time having to forsake it. It's a moral dilemma which would push most to the breaking point. Holland adeptly seizes Perel's story and punctuates the horror of his situation without overemphasizing the psychological strain such an ordeal might have had on its young hero. (German and Russian with English subtitles) ★★★★ VHS: $19.99

The Europeans

(1979, 92 min, US, James Ivory) *Lee Remick, Lisa Eichhorn, Robin Ellis.* A lush adaptation of Henry James' novel about a 19th-century New England family whose lives are disrupted by the arrival of two European cousins — one a meddlesome, fortune-hunting countess. (Letterboxed) ★★★ VHS: $19.99

Eve and the Handyman

(1960, 65 min, US, Russ Meyer) At times reminiscent of a Buster Keaton silent comedy, this early work by Meyer emphasizes sight gags and features a detective novel-style narrative by Eve Meyer as she tracks her man through his daily routine, noting his attempts to ignore a series of trademark Meyer women. Filmed on location in San Francisco, and featuring a thumping striptease soundtrack, *Eve and the Handyman* comments on sex and society in a lighter fashion than Meyer's later works. ★★½ VHS: $79.99

Eve of Destruction

(1991, 95 min, US, Duncan Gibbons) *Renee Soutendijk, Gregory Hines, Kevin McCarthy.* The sexy Soutendijk is superbly preposterous as a spike-heeled, nuclear warhead-equipped humanoid in this otherwise disappointing sci-fi thriller. Eve VIII, an experimental cyborg invented by a sexually repressed doctor (also played by Soutendijk), is accidentally activated and becomes stuck in her "Battlefield mode" of programming. Our supercharged heroine is every misogynist's worst nightmare as she plows her way cross country, destroying all in her path. A great idea never realized. ★½ VHS: $6.99

Eve's Bayou

(1997, 109 min, US, Kasi Lemmons) *Samuel L. Jackson, Jurnee Smollett, Lynn Whitfield, Debbi Morgan, Meagan Good, Diahann Carroll.* Making a most impressive directorial debut, Lemmons has created a stunning, bittersweet and good-humored memory piece which evokes the wistful recollections of youth as wisely as *To Kill a Mockingbird.* An adult narrator looks back at her youth in the South and on her relationship with her father. As ten-year-old Eve (Smollett) recalls in the film's opening, it is 1962 and the year "I killed my father." In the small Louisiana town of Eve's Bayou, young Eve's father, Dr. Batiste (Jackson), appears to be the idol of all the women in the area. When she spies him having sex with a neighbor, the entire family is thrown into emotional turmoil which eventually brings to light sibling rivalry, patricide, voodooism, parapsychology and incest. Jurnee is an absolute wonder as Eve; rarely has a child actor demonstrated such range and understanding. As Eve's psychic and emotionally scarred aunt, Morgan gives a knockout performance which is all at once touching, majestic, persuasive and, most of all, full of grace. ★★★★ VHS: $14.99; DVD: $19.99

Ever After

Even Cowgirls Get the Blues

(1994, 100 min, US, Gus Van Sant) *Uma Thurman, John Hurt, Rain Phoenix, Lorraine Bracco, Keanu Reeves, Crispin Glover, Roseanne, Udo Kier, Faye Dunaway, Steve Buscemi.* A disappointingly vapid and lifeless misfire, this attempt to capture the hippie-dippy effervescence of Tom Robbins' 1976 novel completely fails to come to cinematic life. Thurman plays the pleasant if vacuous Sissy Hankshaw, a young beauty who is blessed/cursed with abnormally large thumbs and who lives the free life of the road. Encouraged by "The Countess" (an over-the-top faggy Hurt) to visit his dude ranch, Sissy soon becomes embroiled in a cowgirl uprising headed by the "charismatic" Bonanza Jellybean (the catatonic Phoenix). A high point is the psychedelic country score by k.d. lang. Saddled by its attempts to be both post-modern camp and politically and sexually relevant, *Cowgirls* is nonetheless does sport moments of fun. ★★ VHS: $19.99

The Evening Star

(1996, 129 min, US, Robert Harling) *Shirley MacLaine, Juliette Lewis, Bill Paxton, Miranda Richardson, Marion Ross, Ben Johnson, Jack Nicholson, Scott Wolf.* MacLaine repeats her *Terms of Endearment* Oscar-winning role as Aurora Greenway in this strained if occasionally compelling sequel. *The Evening Star* takes place 13 years after the death of Aurora's daughter Emma. Aurora has raised her three grandchildren, but they are mostly problem kids who have little time or affection for their meddling grandmother. As the jagged, episodic story introduces its characters, Aurora tentatively initiates an affair with a younger man (Paxton) while her teenaged granddaughter (Lewis) is ready to run away to Los Angeles. *The Evening Star* doesn't have the original's rich material exploring the complex relationship between mother and daughter, but it does have a very able cast. ★★½ VHS: $9.99; DVD: $29.99

Event Horizon

(1997, 97 min, US, Paul Anderson) *Laurence Fishburne, Sam Neill, Kathleen Quinlan, Joely Richardson.* Innovative visuals and an inspired production design can sometimes save an otherwise mediocre film. This is almost true in the case of *Event Horizon*, but not quite. Its lamebrained script, underdeveloped characters and seen-it-all-before feel work too strongly against it. Fishburne stars as the commander of an interstellar rescue team which is sent to investigate a previously "lost" ship, the *Event Horizon*. Once on site, they find out that it's sort of ghost ship which begins to exert harmful psychological influences over the rescue team. ★★ VHS: $9.99; DVD: $24.99

Ever After

(1998, 121 min, GB, Andy Tennant) *Drew Barrymore, Anjelica Huston, Dougray Scott, Jeroen Krabbé, Jeanne Moreau.* An absolutely delightful film. Barrymore drops the Gen-X bad-girl image and delivers a bravura performance (faltering fake accent notwithstanding) as the Cinderella-inspired heroine. Barrymore is Danielle, a servant girl whose loving father (Krabbé) kicks the bucket only days after bringing home his new wife (Huston, who's tailor-made to play the evil stepmom) and her two daughters. It's all done with a healthy sense of good-natured fun and the result is alternately touching, hilarious, romantic and thought-provoking. ★★★½ VHS: $14.99; DVD: $24.99

Everest

(1998, 48 min, US, MacGillivray Freeman) *Narrated by: Liam Neeson.* Meant for a huge IMAX screen, this will certainly lose its impact on the viewer's home TV. Though flawed, it's a worthwhile experience, filmed during the 1996 climbing disaster which cost several lives (and was the inspiration for the film *Into Thin Air*). The footage of Mt. Everest is impressive (even on the small screen), and the minutiae of the climbers' preparation and actual climb are fascinating. Far from accomplished filmmaking, as documentary it owes more to "Hard Copy" and less to the Maysles brothers, and Neeson's narration tends to be intrusive. Talk about making a molehill out of a mountain. ★★½ VHS: $19.99; DVD: $39.99

Evergreen

(1934, 91 min, GB, Victor Saville) *Jessie Matthews, Sonnie Hale.* Saville's musical comedy features a dazzling performance from Matthews as a young unemployed chorus girl who rises to fame by imitating her long-retired, but once-famous, mother. Fabulous set pieces make a wonderful backdrop for Matthews' splendid dancing. Punctuated by a lively Rodgers and Hart score. ★★★½

The Everlasting Secret Family

(1987, 93 min, Australia, Michael Thornhill) *Mark Lee, Arthur Dignam.* With an outrageous premise — a highly organized secret society of pederasts stalk area schools for young male victims whom they then ravage and reprogram to their way of life — this is an enjoyably ludicrous drama that, despite its sinister idea, still makes for strangely riveting, erotically charged entertainment. Lee plays a gorgeous young boy who is spirited away by a wealthy middle-aged senator. He soon tolerates the sex and begins to enjoy the power and prestige he attains as the "boy-toy" of the politician. But as is wont for a finicky pederast, the senator soon drops him for younger flesh. Now fully indoctrinated into the society, and aging rapidly, Mark must go off himself in search of an innocent victim; and the boy he chooses is the senator's young son! Enjoyable camp once you ignore its incendiary harangues. ★★

Every Day's a Holiday

(1937, 79 min, US, A. Edward Sutherland) *Mae West, Edmund Lowe, Charles Winninger, Louis Armstrong.* The imitable West tips her hat to the screwball genre with this amusing romp set at the turn of the century. Written by West, the story follows Mae as con artist/performer Peaches O'Day and her series of misadventures trying to elude the police, masquerade as a dark-haired French chanteuse, and organize a mayoral race. Mae manages to turn a catchphrase or two ("Keep a diary, and someday it'll keep you"), but most of the film's comedy is courtesy of lots of hair-brained hijinks. Mae proves herself quite handy with a pair of drumsticks. ★★★ VHS: $14.99

Every Girl Should Be Married

(1948, 84 min, US, Don Hartman) *Cary Grant, Betsy Drake, Diana Lynn, Franchot Tone.* In a role reversal from most '30s and '40s comedies, shopgirl Drake sets her eyes on eligible bachelor Grant, and *she* pursues *him*. Of course, Grant is happily unmarried with a preference to stay that way. Grant's charm makes this ordinary comedy more frothy than it really is. ★★½ VHS: $19.99

Every Man for Himself and God Against All

(1974, 110 min, West Germany, Werner Herzog) *Bruno S., Brigitte Mira, Walter Ladengast.* A young man, imprisoned in a cellar and locked away from society for most of his life, reemerges and must begin the arduous task of readjusting to an illogical and iniquitous world. Bruno S. gives an astounding performance as Kasper Hauser. (German with English subtitles) (aka: *The Mystery of Kasper Hauser*) ★★★½

Every Which Way But Loose

(1978, 115 min, US, James Fargo) *Clint Eastwood, Sondra Locke, Ruth Gordon, Geoffrey Lewis.* Amazingly, this boisterous, feeble backwoods comic adventure of a barroom brawler and his pet orangutan is Eastwood's most successful film to date. Go figure. Clint has certainly done better (and so has Clyde). (Sequel: *Any Which Way You Can*) ★½ VHS: $14.99

Everybody Wins

(1990, 98 min, US, Karel Reisz) *Nick Nolte, Debra Winger, Will Patton, Jack Warden.* Nolte is a small-town private investigator hired by local free-spirit Winger to prove a friend innocent of murder. Ill-conceived from the start, the ludicrous screenplay is by Arthur Miller. ★ VHS: $9.99

Everybody's All-American

(1988, 127 min, US, Taylor Hackford) *Jessica Lange, Dennis Quaid, Timothy Hutton, John Goodman, Carl Lumbly.* An involving drama about love and broken dreams with Quaid as a college football star and Lange as his beauty queen girlfriend; they marry and search for the American Dream. ★★★ VHS: $14.99

Everybody's Fine

(1991, 115 min, Italy, Giuseppe Tornatore) *Marcello Mastroianni, Salvatore Cascio.* Much less saccharine than his delightful art-house hit *Cinema Paradiso*, director Tornatore's family drama is a bittersweet tale of illusion and disenchantment. Mastroianni stars as a simple old man who decides to visit his five "successful and happy" grown children who are dispersed throughout Italy. Unprepared for his surprise visits, his children try to bolster his mistaken belief that they lead problem-free lives, but their charades quickly fall apart, forcing him to come to grips with reality and let go of his cherished and idealized images of their childhoods. (Italian with English subtitles) ★★★

Everyone Says I Love You

(1996, 100 min, US, Woody Allen) *Woody Allen, Goldie Hawn, Alan Alda, Julia Roberts, Edward Norton, Drew Barrymore, Tim Roth, Lukas Haas, Gaby Hoffmann, Natalie Portman.* Not everyone will be echoing the sentiments of the title of Allen's musical comedy valentine to New York,

Paris and big city neurotics. Often entertaining and funny though insubstantial with lightweight character development, the film is a pastiche of bygone Hollywood musicals where characters just break into song. But whereas those musicals featured performers with good voices, here actors not known for their singing talents (and for good reason) use their own voices. A few are used to good effect (Hawn, Norton), but most are not. It's a distracting gimmick. Hawn is radiant as Allen's ex-wife, and the two engage in a wonderful dance sequence on the banks of the Seine. ★★½ VHS: $14.99; DVD: $29.99

Everything You Always Wanted to Know about Sex. . . But Were Afraid to Ask

(1972, 87 min, US, Woody Allen) *Woody Allen, Burt Reynolds, Gene Wilder, Tony Randall, Lynn Redgrave, Lou Jacobi.* Allen's hilarious assault on Dr. David Reuben's ridiculous best-seller is full of crude jokes, potentially obscene skits and Woody's unforgettable portrayal of the reluctant, existential sperm. ★★★ VHS: $14.99; DVD: $19.99

Evil Cat

(1987, 90 min, Hong Kong, Dennis Yu) *Chow Yun-Fat.* Incredible fantasy-based martial arts/horror flick where an ancient cat-like being enters our world from a subterranean home to unleash its destruction of our society. ★★★½ VHS: $59.99

The Evil Dead

(1983, 85 min, US, Sam Raimi) *Bruce Campbell, Helen Sandweiss, Betsy Baker.* This low-budget horror film has more scares in it than all the *Friday the 13th*s put together. Five friends head to the woods for a secluded, quiet weekend. However, things are anything but quiet when they awaken a demonic spirit. Director Raimi concentrates more on the suspense than the gore (though there's plenty of that, too), which immediately separates it from the usual, mindless horror film. (Letterboxed) (Sequel: *Evil Dead 2*) ★★★ VHS: $14.99; DVD: $24.99

Evil Dead 2: Dead by Dawn

(1987, 85 min, US, Sam Raimi) *Bruce Campbell, Sarah Berry, Dan Hicks.* In this spectacularly entertaining and frightening horror sequel, director Raimi accomplishes the near-impossible: he tops his terrific original. Campbell returns once again to battle the demonic spirits at that secluded cabin in the woods. There's a lot more humor here, and the special effects are sensational. Campbell gives an over-the-top performance which helps immensely in the enjoyment of this outrageously original chiller. (Letterboxed) (Sequel: *Army of Darkness*) ★★★½ VHS: $14.99; DVD: $29.99

The Evil of Frankenstein

(1964, 98 min, GB, Freddie Francis) *Peter Cushing, Duncan Lamont.* Dr. Frankenstein discovers that his monster has been preserved in ice, but has fallen under the spell of a hypnotist and is rampaging once again. Cushing plays Doctor Frank in this entertaining though familiar Hammer Films production. ★★ VHS: $14.99

Evil Under the Sun

(1982, 112 min, GB, Guy Hamilton) *Peter Ustinov, James Mason, Maggie Smith, Roddy McDowall, Diana Rigg, Sylvia Miles.* Ustinov returns as Hercule Poirot in this Agatha Christie mystery. Though not up to par with *Murder on the Orient Express* or *Death on the Nile*, this effective whodunit will nevertheless keep you guessing right up to the end. Poirot investigates the murder of a bitchy actress. (Letterboxed) ★★½ VHS: $9.99; DVD: $24.99

Evita

(1996, 135 min, US, Alan Parker) *Madonna, Antonio Banderas, Jonathan Pryce, Jimmy Nail.* Madonna gives an extremely capable performance as Argentina's first lady Eva Peron in this big, splashy, well-crafted adaptation of Andrew Lloyd Webber's musical. Though Parker's direction sometimes teeters on overkill, he has staged some knockout musical sequences. Closely following the stage show, the story follows the rise of Eva Duarte from poor beginnings to stardom as a (second-rate) actress to becoming her country's first lady and sometimes spiritual voice. Webber acknowledges Eva's status as a controversial figure, but straddles the fence in political terms. Still, the music is his best. The real surprise is Banderas, who is splendid in both voice and performance as the story's narrator and social conscience. (VHS letterboxed available for $19.99) ★★★½ VHS: $14.99; DVD: $29.99

The Ex-Mrs. Bradford

(1936, 80 min, US, Stephen Roberts) *William Powell, Jean Arthur, James Gleason.* Powell goes sleuthing with ex-wife Arthur. Is Powell ever not suave and debonair? Is Arthur ever not sparkling and charming? Apparently not. Stylish, witty fun, with a darned clever resolution to the murders at hand. Powell is in familiar Nick Charles territory here. ★★★

Excalibur

(1981, 140 min, GB, John Boorman) *Nigel Terry, Nicol Williamson, Helen Mirren, Gabriel Byrne, Liam Neeson, Patrick Stewart.* This spellbinding saga is steeped in the rich lore of gallant knights and sinister sorcery. A lavish production, aswirl with sensuous colors and breathtaking imagery, *Excalibur* is a superlative rendition of the Arthurian legend with added mystical and sexual overtones. It is a brilliant illumination of why these tales have survived so vividly in our imaginations. Williamson steals the show as Merlin. ★★★★ VHS: $9.99; DVD: $14.99

Excess Baggage

(1997, 101 min, US, Marco Brambilla) *Alicia Silverstone, Benicio Del Toro, Christopher Walken, Harry Connick, Jr., Jack Thompson.* An unappealing Silverstone stars in the equally unappealing *Excess Baggage.* She plays Emily Hope, an heiress who fakes her own kidnapping to garner the attention of her power-hungry father (Thompson). More interested in his business deals, he sends old friend Uncle Ray (Walken) to deal with the mess. Meanwhile, Emily's "captor" is Vincent (the deliciously bizarrre Del Toro), who comes off more as sociopath than thief-with-a-heart-of-gold. The only chemistry on-screen is between Vincent and Ray, and these scenes are all too brief. If the writers had them

ditch Emily at a truck stop and head off as a duo, there could've been a decent road movie in the making. ★★ VHS: $9.99; DVD: $29.99

Executioners (The Heroic Trio 2)

(1993, 90 min, Hong Kong, Ching Siu-Tung & Johnny To) *Anita Mui, Michelle Yeoh, Maggie Cheung, Anthony Wong.* The female superhero trio is back, but this time in a sober, nihilistic post-apocalyptic world of the future where water is a precious commodity and power-mad politicians vie for the support of the beleaguered population. De-emphasizing the comedy almost to an extreme, this sequel is satisfying in its own way, but lacks the campy fun and vivaciousness of the first film. Without as much action or comedy as its predecessor, *Executioners* relies instead on its bleak tone and future-noir art direction to retain interest; it is, however, more stylishly shot and edited than the first *Trio* film. (Cantonese with English subtitles) ★★½ VHS: $19.99

Executive Decision

(1996, 133 min, US, Stuart Baird) *Kurt Russell, Halle Berry, John Leguizamo, Oliver Platt, Steven Seagal, Joe Morton, Len Cariou, B.D. Wong, J.T. Walsh.* It would be easy to call *Executive Decision* another *Under Siege* clone, for it does bear many similarities: terrorists have taken control of a mode of transportation and it's up to our hero (Russell) to set things right. But this exciting actioner relies less on explosions and more on suspense, paying greater attention to how they do it. Mideast terrorists have taken control of an American airliner, and in a daring mid-flight link-up, the good guys board the plane in their effort to thwart the bad guys' plans to bomb the Eastern seaboard. As a think-tank specialist out of his league, Russell carries much of the action by giving an understated characterization rather than playing it like, say, Steven Seagal, who appears briefly as a commando. (Letterboxed VHS available for $19.99) ★★★ VHS: $9.99; DVD: $19.99

Executive Suite

(1954, 104 min, US, Robert Wise) *Barbara Stanwyck, William Holden, Fredric March, June Allyson, Walter Pidgeon, Shelley Winters, Paul Douglas.* When the president of a major furniture-manufacturing company suddenly dies, the members of the Board scramble to replace him quickly and quietly. Each man is driven by his own motives, be it avarice or altruism. An all-star cast is entangled in many subplots, which complement the big business focus. A very involving drama adapted from Cameron Hawley's best-selling novel. ★★★ VHS: $19.99

eXistenZ

(1999, 97 min, Canada, David Cronenberg) *Jennifer Jason Leigh, Jude Law, Willem Dafoe, Ian Holm, Sarah Polley, Christopher Eccleston.* Allegra Geller (Leigh) has created her newest game, eXistenZ, whose virtualism is so real that players need to attach the game directly to their spines. Once hooked up, players can touch, taste, feel the environment; but what effect does this have on their reality? Complicating matters is the self-reflexivity of eXistenZ, where players hook up to new games within the game. Ostensibly a meditation on our decreasing grip on reality, it seems more an excuse for Cronenberg to explore orifices (the anus-like "bio-ports" that the game hooks up to), gore, and other favorite themes. It's a fun ride, and certainly very creepy, especially the game unit and umbilical cord that are made from flesh and blood. But the later plot twists betray the characters' previous actions, and following the story can become a chore rather than a pleasure. ★★½ VHS: $14.99; DVD: $29.99

Exit to Eden

(1994, 113 min, US, Garry Marshall) *Dan Aykroyd, Rosie O'Donnell, Dana Delany, Paul Mercurio, Iman, Stuart Wilson, Hector Elizondo.* Based on the Anne Rice novel, with a new sub-plot thrown in for not-so-good measure, *Exit to Eden* is a tedious comedy which mixes mild S&M fantasy with a ridiculous story of jewel thieves. Mercurio stars as a hunky photographer with specialized sexual tastes (read: S&M) who unknowingly takes photos of two thieves in the middle of a heist. Pursued by cops Aykroyd and O'Donnell, the bad guys follow Mercurio to a tropical island resort named Eden, a kinky sexual Disneyland run by dominatrix Delany. Director Marshall tries to create a sophisticated, wacky romp when all the characters come together, but this contrived flop is enough to give sex a bad name. ★ VHS: $9.99

Exodus

(1960, 213 min, US, Otto Preminger) *Paul Newman, Eva Marie Saint, Ralph Richardson, Sal Mineo, Lee J. Cobb, Peter Lawford.* An epic version of Leon Uris' mammoth novel detailing the struggles of the new Israeli state. Newman plays an Israeli resistance leader, involved with Army nurse Saint. ★★★ VHS: $24.99

The Exorcist

(1973, 121 min, US, William Friedkin) *Ellen Burstyn, Max von Sydow, Lee J. Cobb, Linda Blair, Jason Miller.* The film that brought the devil back into vogue and spurred a host of imitations. Blair gives her all in a role that requires her to turn green and rotate her head 360 degrees. Don't say we didn't warn you. (Followed by 2 sequels) ★★★½ DVD: $24.99

The Exorcist: The Version You've Never Seen

(2000, 132 min, US, William Friedkin) *Ellen Burstyn, Max von Sydow, Lee J. Cobb, Linda Blair, Jason Miller.* Friedkin and writer William Peter Blatty have restored some cut scenes, pumped up the sound and added some visual effects in what may best be described as a "writer's cut" of the film. Some of the cut scenes were previously available on video, but here they're integrated into the film, adding to the story but crippling the pace in parts. The new effects are pretty spiffy. A nice companion to the original, as neither version is definitive. ★★★ VHS: $14.99; DVD: $24.99

Exorcist II: The Heretic

(1977, 110 min, US, John Boorman) *Richard Burton, Linda Blair, Ellen Burstyn, Max von Sydow, Lee J. Cobb.* It's a few years after the infamous possession, and Blair's being visited by unwanted guests again. Burton is the priest who tries to evict 'em in Boorman's over-the-top sequel featuring some really wild special effects, campy performances and lots of silly religious mumbo-jumbo. ★½ VHS: $9.99

The Exorcist III

(1990, 110 min, US, William Peter Blatty) *George C. Scott, Ed Flanders, Jason Miller, Nicol Williamson, Scott Wilson, Brad Dourif.* Author William Peter Blatty takes matters into his own (directorial) hands with this adaptation of his "Exorcist" sequel, "Legion." Police detective Lt. Kinderman returns (now in the persona of Scott), and is on the trail of a serial killer. When evidence suggests that the killings are the handiwork of more than one person (including an executed murderer), he begins to suspect the presence of greater evil (could it be. . . oh, I don't know. . . Satan?). The plot, undone by its own complexity, does manage to work up a good chill. ★★½ VHS: $9.99; DVD: $14.99

Exotica

(1995, 104 min, Canada, Atom Egoyan) *Bruce Greenwood, Mia Kirshner, Elias Koteas, Victor Garber.* A beguilingly cryptic, haunting psychological thriller. In Robert Altman-style, Egoyan weaves several characters and their stories together as he explores such ominous themes as voyeurism, grief, betrayal and the search for healing, forgiveness and salvation. There is Thomas, a gay pet shop owner involved in illegal importation of exotic bird eggs; Francis (Greenwood), a tax advisor who spends his sullen nights at a strip club called Exotica where he quietly obsesses over one particular dancer, Christina (Kirshner). She, in turn, is involved in a relationship with Zoe, the club owner and object of jealous affection by the violent D.J., Eric (Koteas). Nothing is as it seems as Egoyan stingily offers bits of information to the byzantine connections that thread the characters together. An intelligent, even mesmerizing black comedy, *Exotica* will entrance those with the patience to consider the complexities of this demanding film. ★★★½ VHS: $19.99; DVD: $29.99

Experience Preferred. . . But Not Essential

(1983, 80 min, Wales, Peter Duffell) *Elizabeth Edmonds, Sue Wallace.* A delightful little comedy about a schoolgirl's summer experiences at a resort hotel on the Welsh coast. Annie (Edmonds) begins her life's education when she encounters the eccentric and slightly daft employees of the Hotel Grand. Included in the colorful crew are the Scottish cook who romances her out of her "wellies" and a burly somnambulist prone to nocturnal wanderings in the nude. A warm, charming film with unexpectedly good performances. ★★★

Experiment in Terror

(1962, 123 min, US, Blake Edwards) *Glenn Ford, Lee Remick, Stephanie Powers, Ross Martin.* Good performances highlight this exciting thriller about a psychopath who kidnaps a bank teller's sister, thus blackmailing the woman into stealing from her employer. Ford is the agent assigned to the case, and Powers is the abducted sister. As the cashier, Remick is first-rate, and Martin — long before his celebrated "Wild Wild West" good-guy role on TV — is chilling as the killer. ★★★ VHS: $14.99

Explorers

(1985, 100 min, US, Joe Dante) *River Phoenix, Ethan Hawke, Jason Presson, Amanda Peterson,* *Dana Ivey, James Cromwell.* This lighthearted and wacky sci-fi comedy follows the adventures of three young boys who build a makeshift spacecraft and head for the stars. Phoenix (as the brainy nerd!), Hawke and Presson are the kids, and their confrontation with alien creatures is delightful. ★★★ VHS: $14.99

Expresso Bongo

(1959, 101 min, GB, Val Guest) *Laurence Harvey, Cliff Richard, Sylvia Syms.* Director Guest brings lots of energy and panache to this fast-moving teen pic. *Expresso Bongo* follows the exploits of an opportunistic music agent (played with speed freak freneticism by Harvey), who "discovers" singer/bongo player Richard and proceeds to make him a star, at the expense of his girlfriend/client, a stripper who spies greener pastures. Like most studio-financed, trendy teen flicks, this is more square than it thinks it is, with all the "teens" played by actors in their late 20s and early 30s, and featuring kitschy (but catchy) musical numbers. For a happy-go-lucky piece of fluff, though, there are some witty barbs, snappy dialogue and snazzy visuals to spare. ★★★ VHS: $24.99

Exquisite Corpses

(1989, 95 min, US, Temistocles Lopez) *Zoe Tamerlaine Lund, Gary Knox, Daniel Chapman.* A young man with a trombone and a stetson, fresh from the American heartland, gets off the bus in New York City. In no time at all, he's had his luggage stolen and found out that his fiancée is shacked up with another guy. In not very much more time, he's subjected to every con and con artist in the book (all those guys in ponytails); but he also gets a dose of urban myth and magic. Before long, our newly issued midnight cowboy is *the* hot new cabaret star. But the path of our hero's quest to become the new idol for the jaded masses is littered with dead bodies. Writer-producer-director Lopez has fashioned a witty, sly, sardonic little gem, peopled with characters only slightly exaggerated. ★★★

The Exterminating Angel

(1962, 95 min, Mexico, Luis Buñuel) *Silvia Pinal, Enrique Rambal.* Buñuel's scathing wit is amply displayed in one of his most complex works. The guests of a dinner party are simply unable to leave their host's home when they are ready to depart. Within this claustrophobic microcosm, Buñuel lampoons society's decadence and corruption. (Spanish with English subtitles) ★★★★ VHS: $24.99

Extramuros (Beyond the Walls)

(1985, 120 min, Spain, Miguel Picazo) *Carmen Maura.* A fascinating and often strange story of lesbian love and lusty ambition behind a convent's walls. While the Plague ravages all around, a poverty-stricken convent becomes the center of attention after Sister Angela injures her hands and fakes the miracle of Stigmata. The nun, with her lover Sister Ana (Maura), staves off the despotic Mother Superior to eventually become prioress herself, until the members of the Inquisition pay a not-so-friendly visit to the "saint." An unusual melodrama that borders on the deliriously unreal — a curious mix of the combined excesses of Ken Russell's *The Devils* and the Watergate conspiracy. (Spanish with English subtitles) ★★★ VHS: $19.99

The Extraordinary Adventures of Mr. West in the Land of the Bolsheviks

(1924, 78 min, USSR, Lev Kuleshov) *Vsevolod Pudovkin, Boris Barnet.* This sharply satiric comedy has all of the action and pratfalls of a Chaplin film in telling its story about the wildly misconceived notions Americans had (and still possess) of Soviet Russia. Mr. West, a naïve and nervous American, travels to Russia to see firsthand this nation of raging Bolsheviks and deranged radicals. But with the "help" of some mischievous pranksters, his travels turn into a wild adventure peopled by an increasingly strange procession of weirdos. An inspired and still timely farce. (Silent with orchestral accompaniment) ★★★ VHS: $29.99

Extreme Justice

(1993, 105 min, US, Mark L. Lester) *Lou Diamond Phillips, Scott Glenn, Chelsea Field, Yaphet Kotto.* Interesting but highly uneven — and at times wooden — drama about the LAPD's unique crime-fighting task force, the S.I.S. (Special Investigation Squad) and their highly unorthodox methods of taking hard-core criminals off the streets. ★★ VHS: $6.99; DVD: $14.99

Extreme Measures

(1996, 117 min, US, Michael Apted) *Gene Hackman, Hugh Grant, Sarah Jessica Parker, David Morse, Debra Monk, Bill Nunn.* A blurry look at the halls of medicine, *Extreme Measures* asks if the ends can justify the means when one prominent doctor (Hackman in another skilled portrayal) takes both lives and shortcuts to find a cure for the incurable. Grant is the unknowing physician caught in the conspiracy. This stunted wandering never reaches a vastness of any thrill, with its frequent plot turns leaving viewers knowing where it will lead without a proper explanation of how it arrived there. ★★ VHS: $19.99; DVD: $19.99

Extreme Prejudice

(1987, 104 min, US, Walter Hill) *Nick Nolte, Powers Boothe, Maria Conchita Alonzo, Rip Torn.* Appealing actioner with boyhood friends Nolte and Boothe finding themselves at odds when one grows up to be a drug king and the other a Texas Ranger. ★★½ VHS: $9.99; DVD: $14.99

Extremities

(1986, 90 min, US, Robert M. Young) *Farrah Fawcett, Alfre Woodard, Diane Scarwid, James Russo.* Fawcett, who appeared in William Mastrosimone's hit off-Broadway play, repeats her stage role as an attempted rape victim who overcomes her attacker and holds him hostage. Farrah's attempt to prove herself a serious actress, for the most part, is a success: she gives a compelling performance. Woodard and Scarwid ably play Farrah's roommates caught in the moral dilemma, and Russo makes an intense psycho. ★★½

Eye for an Eye

(1996, 105 min, US, John Schlesinger) *Sally Field, Ed Harris, Kiefer Sutherland, Joe Mantegna, Beverly D'Angelo, Charlayne Woodard.* Field assumes the Charles Bronson role from the *Death Wish* series as a mother who seeks vengeance against the man who raped and murdered her daughter, and then walked free. About as dramatically defined as any of the Bronson sequels, *Eye for an Eye* features incredibly overdrawn characters

Eyes Wide Shut: Tom and Nicole's last date?

who all wear their caricatures on their sleeves. The film could have veered into an interesting examination of the mother's dilemma, but opts for the ridiculous scenario of a gun-toting Field stalking the low-rent district of L.A.'s downtown (rich people = good; poor people = bad). ★½ VHS: $9.99

Eye of God

(1997, 88 min, US, Tim Blake Nelson) *Martha Plimpton, Kevin Anderson, Hal Holbrook, Nick Stahl, Margo Martindale, Richard Jenkins.* The chilling *Eye of God* uses the biblical tale of Abraham and Isaac to dovetail two riveting stories — Ainsley Dupree's (Plimpton) increasingly repressive marriage to an ex-con (Anderson), and a devastated young boy's (Stahl) response to witnessing a gruesome murder. Writer-director Nelson has a remarkable grasp of the dead-end lives of his characters, and the performances are uniformly excellent. Using an ominous flash-forward/flash-back time sequence to create a brilliant mosaic that shows how these very different characters' lives intersect. The only drawback to this simple yet extraordinarily powerful film is the graphic, disturbing ending which reinforces the evil that prompts the grisly murder. A haunting, unforgettable experience. ★★★½

Eye of the Beholder

(2000, 101 min, US, Stephan Elliott) *Ashley Judd, Ewan McGregor, Jason Priestley, Genevieve Bujold, Patrick Bergen, k.d. lang.* A film so bad it will bring a greater appreciation of grade-B, direct-to-video thrillers, *Eye of the Beholder* takes a ludicrous story and then makes it totally incomprehensible with flashy camerawork, weird editing and weirder plot developments. A comatose McGregor plays a British intelligence officer (named "The Eye"!) haunted by his wife and daughter leaving him. While on assignment, he witnesses a woman (Judd) kill a man. Instead of turning the sexy suspect in, he tracks her across the country as she goes on a killing spree. Then things get even sillier. The two lead roles are impossible to flesh out, though the supporting characters are slightly more interesting. ★ VHS: $14.99; DVD: $19.99

Eye of the Needle

(1981, 112 min, US, Richard Marquand) *Donald Sutherland, Kate Nelligan, Ian Bannen.* Excellent WWII spy thriller starring Sutherland (in one of his best roles) as the notorious Nazi assassin "The Needle," who must keep his identity secret when he becomes stranded on an island inhabited by a war-wounded Brit and his lonely and frustrated wife (Nelligan). Based on the best-selling novel by Ken Follett. Riveting from start to its pulse-pounding finish. ★★★½ VHS: $14.99

Eye of the Storm

(1991, 98 min, US, Yuri Zeltser) *Lara Flynn Boyle, Dennis Hopper, Craig Sheffer, Bradley Gregg.* Adequate performances and a flashy build-up somehow can't quite sustain this stylish exercise in suspense. A downtrodden wife (Boyle) takes a wrong turn when she and her abusive husband (Hopper), pull into a lonely desert hotel run by a strange young man (Sheffer) and his blind brother (Gregg). ★★ VHS: $14.99

Eyes of Laura Mars

(1978, 104 min, US, Irvin Kershner) *Faye Dunaway, Tommy Lee Jones, Brad Dourif, Rene Auberjonois, Raul Julia.* Bondage chic goes commercial in Kershner's tale of a psychic fashion photographer (Dunaway) and a troubled policeman (Jones) searching for the identity of an ice pick murderer. A few good scares are interspersed with a muddled story. ★★½ VHS: $9.99

The Eyes of Tammy Faye

(2000, 79 min, US, Fenton Bailey & Randy Barbato) *Tammy Faye Bakker, Jim Bullock, Jerry Falwell, Pat Robertson; Narrated by: RuPaul.* This wonderfully original, surprisingly sympathetic and oftentimes-hilarious documentary is narrated by none other than RuPaul. Young Tammy had it all: she was a Southern beauty, she had a handsome, adoring husband, and they together produced a theme park and a highly rated television show that generated enough money to keep her in blush and eyelashes well into the next millennium. Yet, it all fell apart. Husband number one (Jim) is in jail, number two in jail, daughter a runaway, son wallowing in booze and drugs and the religious cash cow empire destroyed. It's a *Citizen Kane* for the Right Wing religious sect, one hell of a documentary as Bailey and Barbato capture the many facets of a surprisingly complex, misunderstood personality. This human chronicle — featuring strange hand puppets that introduce each segment — is beyond fascinating, almost beyond believability. ★★★½ VHS: $102.99; DVD: $24.99

The Eyes, the Mouth

(1982, 100 min, Italy/France, Marco Bellocchio) *Lou Castel, Angela Molina, Emmanuelle Riva.* A compelling examination of a family ravaged by the suicide of a brother, and of the lengths that the brother's twin must go to to separate himself from the crippling ties of the past. (Italian with English subtitles) ★★★ VHS: $19.99

Eyes Wide Shut

(1999, 159 min, GB, Stanley Kubrick) *Tom Cruise, Nicole Kidman, Sydney Pollack, Marie Richardson, Rade Sherbedgia.* Cruise and Kidman are William and Alice Harford, a physically beautiful, emotionally stunted, psychologically impaired couple living in opulence in New York City. He is a top-dollar doctor, she once ran an art gallery; their outward veneer of perfection covers an essential, existential emptiness. William finds himself drawn into an underground world of sexual excess while obsessed by his wife's disclosure of an unfulfilled fantasy — a fantasy that becomes as real to him as his waking life. He crashes a party to find a ritual mass of depravity, precipitating a series of events which seems to threaten his very life. Kubrick has crafted an exploration of how our internal lives inform our perception of reality, warping our view of the world to mirror our lust and shame and fear. In his final opus, the director utilizes to great effect his signature striking visual imagery in constructing a mystery both visceral and abstract. The film requires attention and is sometimes slow-moving; but it is ultimately most rewarding as it choreographs the interplay between sex and death, love and need. ★★★½ VHS: $19.99; DVD: $24.99

Eyes without a Face

(1959, 90 min, France, Georges Franju) *Alida Valli, Pierre Brasseur.* This elegantly moody horror film concerns a deranged plastic surgeon who, after being responsible for a car accident that leaves his young daughter hideously disfigured, becomes determined to give her a new face — a face whose skin is grafted from the bodies of beautiful women his assistant kidnaps off the streets of Paris. A macabre and frightening story that creates its horror not through histrionics or blood but through an elegantly dark style, similar to the works of Jean Cocteau and the early German expressionists. (French with English subtitles) (aka: *The Horror Chamber of Dr. Faustus*) ★★★½ VHS: $29.99

Eyewitness

(1981, 102 min, US, Peter Yates) *William Hurt, Sigourney Weaver, James Woods, Christopher Plummer, Irene Worth.* A slickly produced murder mystery about a janitor (Hurt) who pretends to have knowledge of a murder being investigated by a hotshot reporter (Weaver), in order to become involved with the beautiful journalist. ★★★ VHS: $14.99

F/X

(1986, 106 min, US, Robert Mandel) *Bryan Brown, Brian Dennehy, Cliff deYoung, Diane Venora, Jerry Orbach.* Imaginative and taut thriller with Brown as a movie special effects expert who is hired by the Justice Department to fake the assassination of a mobster, only to be framed for the murder. The film features fine F/X, and makes good use of New York City locales. Dennehy is particularly good as a cop on Brown's trail. ★★★ VHS: $9.99; DVD: $19.99

F/X 2

(1991, 109 min, US, Richard Franklin) *Bryan Brown, Brian Dennehy, Rachel Ticotin, Joanna Gleason, Philip Bosco, Kevin J. O'Connor, Jose DeGuzman.* This more-than-capable sequel to the 1986 hit picks up five years later. F/X expert, and now toy manufacturer, Brown is convinced to help his girlfriend's ex-husband in a police sting. But when the latter is killed, Brown discovers a cover-up and enlists the help of pal Dennehy to find out what happened. Though not entirely as successful as the original, the film nevertheless is an exciting mystery story peppered with some good special effects. Watch out for a real killer clown. ★★½ VHS: $9.99; DVD: $19.99

The Fable of the Beautiful Pigeon Fancier

(1988, 73 min, Brazil/Spain, Roy Guerra) *Claudia Ohana, Tonia Carrero.* From Gabriel García Márquez comes this lyrical, dreamlike fable, filled with mystical foreboding, dealing with the love of an older man for an alluringly mysterious woman. Don Orestes, a Dali-esque dandy of a man, lives off the wealth of his family in a poverty-stricken town in 19th-century Brazil. His highly structured life, dominated by

his mother, is thrown into a whirlwind after he meets and falls in love with Fulvia (Ohana), a beautiful dark-haired woman who tends pigeons and lives in seclusion on the edge of town with her husband and baby. The two are inexplicably drawn together, culminating in a fateful conclusion. Note: This film, made for Spanish television, was filmed in Brazil. The actors spoke Portuguese, which was then dubbed into Spanish. (Spanish with English subtitles) ★★★

The Fabulous Baker Boys

(1989, 113 min, US, Steve Kloves) *Jeff Bridges, Michelle Pfeiffer, Beau Bridges, Jennifer Tilly.* This vibrant and sexy romantic comedy-drama is an extremely well-written, -acted and -executed adult entertainment set against the sometimes tacky world of the lounge act. Pfeiffer, an actress of stunning beauty and incomparable talent, gives an intelligent, smoldering performance as Susie Diamond, the singer who enters the lives of two brothers (the fabulous Bridges boys) whose piano act is dying a slow death. The film follows the love affair between cynical Jeff and sultry Michelle, almost effortlessly evoking the mood of those great 1940s screen romances. The smoky atmosphere is further enhanced by Dave Grusin's outstanding jazz score. (VHS available letterboxed or pan & scan) ★★★½ VHS: $14.99; DVD: $24.99

Face

(1997, 107 min, GB, Antonia Bird) *Robert Carlyle, Ray Winstone, Steven Waddington, Philip Davis, Lena Headey.* A moderately intriguing British crime drama, *Face* proves that old adage: There is no honor among thieves. When a gang of five men, led by Ray (Carlyle), commit armed robbery, the take is less than expected. Then, when the money that has been divided up equally starts to disappear, Ray and his pals have to figure out who is taking the cash and leaving bodies behind. *Face* has a few tense action sequences to recommend it, but the pacing is sometimes slow and the thick accents occasionally troublesome. A subplot involving Ray's failing romance with a pretty activist (Headey) doesn't make the film any more involving. Director Bird has made a gritty little picture, and Carlyle is quite effec-

Face/Off: John Travolta (l.) and Nicolas Cage trade identities

tive in the lead role, but anyone looking for another *Lock, Stock and Two Smoking Barrels* will be mildly disappointed.Carlyle stars as the leader of a motley group of East End armed robbers who must hunt down a traitor among them after the money from a big heist goes missing. ★★½ VHS: $19.99

A Face in the Crowd

(1957, 126 min, US, Elia Kazan) *Andy Griffith, Patricia Neal, Walter Matthau, Lee Remick, Tony Franciosa.* The writer (Budd Schulberg) and director of *On the Waterfront* were reunited for this compelling drama about a homespun hillbilly entertainer whose TV success transforms him into a power-hungry demagogue. Griffith is quite good in his film debut. ★★★½ VHS: $19.99

Face of Another

(1966, 124 min, Japan, Hiroshi Teshigahara) *Tatsuya Nakadai, Machiko Kyo.* A scientist, his face horribly disfigured in an industrial accident, is fitted with a handsome mask; but instead of gaining renewed confidence and self-esteem, he retreats into self-pity and mistrust, eventually seducing his wife and then accusing her of adultery. Using surreal techniques, this psychological drama examines the dehumanization and isolation of man in present-day Japan. A chilling and fatalistic tale of alienation that was coscripted by Teshigahara and Kobo Abe, whose previous collaboration was *Woman in the Dunes.* (Japanese with English subtitles) ★★★ VHS: $59.99

Face/Off

(1997, 138 min, US, John Woo) *John Travolta, Nicolas Cage, Joan Allen, Gina Gershon, Nick Cassavetes, Harve Presnell, Margaret Cho, CCH Pounder, Colm Feore.* A highly textured, complicated film which nearly equals the excellent work director Woo accomplished in Hong Kong. The inventive script sets up a situation that, although it is completely implausible, plays right into Woo's strength: an intimate conflict between two inextricably connected men of action. Travolta is Sean Archer, an FBI agent committed to the capture of terrorist Castor Troy (Cage), who murdered Archer's son in a botched assassination attempt. Troy is captured, but put into a coma, and Archer assumes his identity. But Troy soon wakes up, assumes Archer's identity and takes over his old life. They soon share a bond which is more complex than that of traditional hero and villain. The action sequences are brilliantly staged and the dramatic content of the film — Allen brings a quiet strength to the role of Archer's wife — finally lives up to Woo's famous pyrotechnic sequences. (VHS available letterboxed or pan & scan) ★★★½ VHS: $14.99; DVD: $29.99

Faces

(1968, 129 min, US, John Cassavetes) *Gena Rowlands, John Marley, Lynn Carlin, Seymour Cassel, Fred Draper.* Cassavetes was a master of truth-telling without compromise, whose unrepentant exposure of human hypocrisy was tempered by his astounding empathy for human suffering — even when self-inflicted. This is an unflinching examination of a middle-aged, middle-class couple in the throes of marital breakup, and the emotionally ravaging effects of their mid-life attempts to establish new rela-

tionships. The couple (Carlin, Marley), and their friends and acquaintances (Rowlands is devastating as the other woman) are fully revealed as they confront the artificial confines of their societal roles. An arresting drama that pulls no punches as it divulges one couple's painful confrontation with stifling confinement and lack of communication — a confrontation which acts as metaphor for the social structures of the era. ★★★½ VHS: $14.99; DVD: $24.99

Faces of Women

(1987, 103 min, Ivory Coast, Désiré Ecaré) *Eugénie Cissé Roland, Sidiki Bakaba.* This debut effort by director Ecaré is an exuberant blend of raucous comedy, pulsating African music and dance, and steamy eroticism. Two stories, filmed ten years apart with two separate casts, are woven together with the chants and dances of an energetic female chorus. Both segments concern the place of African women in marriage, sex and society. The first and pivotal story offers an erotic, feminist slant on lust and cuckolding, with lovemaking so candid that the film was barred for many years from its native country. Having created a bold, vibrant film, Ecaré uses a New Wave-influenced directorial style to examine the eternal battle of the sexes. (French with English subtitles) ★★★ VHS: $79.99

The Faculty

(1998, 105 min, US, Robert Rodriguez) *Elijah Wood, Clea DuVall, Jordana Brewster, Josh Hartnett, Laura Harris, Robert Patrick, Piper Laurie, Bebe Neuwirth, Salma Hayek, Jon Stewart.* If Shakespeare, Jane Austen and Laclos can return to high school, why not those damn pod people? In another teenage updating, this time of *Invasion of the Body Snatchers*, teens take on a group of aliens who are taking control of their small town. The story has been told three times already, so there's very little new to add here — in fact, hardly anything at all. But director Rodriguez at least has a degree of fun with the tale. Wood and several classmates stumble upon the fact that the faculty are now body-snatching aliens. There are a couple of swiftly paced scenes, and a cast obviously enjoying themselves helps gloss over the slow patches and obligatory pop culture references. ★★½ VHS: $14.99; DVD: $29.99

Fahrenheit 451

(1967, 111 min, France, François Truffaut) *Julie Christie, Oskar Werner, Cyril Cusack.* This intriguing adaptation of the famed Ray Bradbury novel is a frightening vision of a not-too-distant future where books are outlawed and firemen incinerate "anti-social rubbish." Truffaut creates an eerie atmosphere of repression in this intelligent sci-fi tale. (Filmed in English) ★★★ VHS: $14.99; DVD: $29.99

Fail-Safe

(1964, 111 min, US, Sidney Lumet) *Henry Fonda, Larry Hagman, Walter Matthau, Dan O'Herlihy, Dom DeLuise, Fritz Weaver.* One of the most effective films yet made about the futility and horror of nuclear war, this taut and suspenseful adaptation of Burdick-Wheeler's best-seller is a nightmare "what-if" scenario: Through computer error, we have sent a plane to bomb Moscow — and the President must convince the Russians it was an accident and also decide how to rectify the situation. Fonda is appropriately low-keyed

Fahrenheit 451

as the Commander-in-Chief, and a young Hagman ably plays the interpreter. This is the serious side of *Dr. Strangelove*, and every bit as gripping. (Remade in 2000) ★★★½ VHS: $14.99; DVD: $24.99

Fair Game

(1985, 88 min, Australia, Mario Andreacchio) *Cassandra Delaney, Peter Ford, David Sandford.* Mindless revenge flick about an outback animal preservationist who finds herself in a sadistic game of one-upmanship with a psychotic poacher and his brain-dead cohorts. ★ VHS: $29.99; DVD: $29.99

Fair Game

(1995, 90 min, US, Andrew Sipes) *William Baldwin, Cindy Crawford, Steven Berkoff, Jenette Goldstein.* Acting more with the variety of T-shirts she wears than with her emotions, Crawford makes her acting debut as a divorce lawyer who is hunted by a renegade ex-KGB agent. This latest Eurotrash villain (Berkoff) and his gang of thugs try to blow up Cindy because she is inadvertently delving too deep into their business. Baldwin is the chummy cop-on-the-edge who rescues her, and the two run for their lives, pursued by the bad guys. The action sequences are boring, the acting is bad, and even the sight of a villain targeting Baldwin's ass-crack with a laser while in *in flagrante delicto* with Crawford in a moving boxcar cannot enliven this bloated mess. ★ VHS: $9.99; DVD: $14.99

Fairy Tale: A True Story

(1997, 99 min, GB, Charles Sturridge) *Florence Heath, Elizabeth Earl, Phoebe Nicholls, Peter O'Toole, Harvey Keitel, Mel Gibson.* At the turn of the century, well before New Age hung from shoppes in every city's version of Greenwich Village, spiritualism was all the rage. In post-WWI England, theosophy stepped out of dark parlour trickery and into the light of the headlines via a series of photographs — of fairies. *Fairy Tale* is the true story of two young girls who supposedly took these photographs. O'Toole materializes as an old Sir Arthur Conan Doyle, whose jaw-agaped amazement brings the magic and hope of the story into the public's tea hour. This wonderful family film, awash in playful special effects, will surely entertain both child and adult alike. ★★★½ VHS: $14.99

The Falcon and the Snowman

(1985, 131 min, US, John Schlesinger) *Sean Penn, Timothy Hutton, Lori Singer, Pat Hingle.* Acclaimed espionage thriller based on the true-life story of Christopher Boyce and Dalton Lee, who sold national secrets to the Soviets. Hutton and Penn are both outstanding as the accused, conflicted teens. (VHS letterboxed available for $19.99) ★★★ VHS: $14.99; DVD: $24.99

Fall

(1997, 90 min, US, Eric Schaeffer) *Eric Schaeffer, Amanda De Cadenet, Francie Swift, Lisa Vidal, Rudolf Martin, Roberta Farnham Maxwell.* It is perhaps damning with faint praise to say that Schaeffer's vanity production *Fall*, which he wrote, produced, directed and stars in, is better than his last film, *If Lucy Fell*. As Michael Shiver, a cab driver who begins a heated affair with married supermodel Sarah Easton (De Cadenet), Schaeffer will either charm or annoy viewers with his cutesy-poo petulance. Chronicling this unlikely relationship, Schaeffer seems to be bringing his sexual fantasies to the screen, allowing Michael to sex-talk Sarah to orgasm in one scene followed by Sarah tying up and screwing Michael in another. At least this boy-meets-supermodel romance has a terrific soundtrack to keep it moving, since there is too much dialogue and too little plot. ★★½

The Fall of the House of Usher

(1960, 85 min, US, Roger Corman) *Vincent Price, Myrna Fahey, Mark Damon.* Corman graduated (for a time, anyway) from quickly produced exploitation pictures to heavily atmospheric, adult-themed horror films with this, his first of eight film adaptations of the works of Edgar Allan Poe. Price stars as the tragic Roderick, last in the doomed line of Ushers. Philip Winthrop (Damon) arrives at the House of Usher to sweep away his fiancée Madeline, Roderick's sister. Roderick, however, will not allow her to leave, and Damon becomes a hopeless bystander. An unusually realized Gothic horror story; Richard Matheson's chilling screenplay was also a remarkable beginning in a line of Poe adaptations. ★★★ VHS: $14.99; DVD: $14.99

Fall of the Romanov Dynasty

(1927, 90 min, USSR, Ether Shub) With innovative editing of remarkable archival footage, this is the first historical documentary produced in the Soviet Union. It's a stirring account of the events that led up to the overthrow of the Czarist regime and the subsequent rise of the people's republic. Director Shub skillfully utilizes newsreel footage as well as Czar Nicholas' home movies in bringing to life those fateful years between 1912 and 1917. (Silent with piano accompaniment) ★★★ VHS: $29.99

Fall Time

(1994, 88 min, US, Paul Warner) *Mickey Rourke, Stephen Baldwin, David Arquette, Jonah Blechman, Jason London.* This kinky crime thriller uses Tarantino-style violence and a bevy of pretty boys to create an improbable tale dripping with homoerotic undertones. Leon (Baldwin) and Florence (Rourke) are two gun-toting crooks (and possible lovers) looking to hit a bank in a Southern town. Their scheme is foiled when three freshly scrubbed teens get in the way. The boys — ringleader David (Arquette), cute Joe (Blechman) and chiseled beauty Tim (London)

— are soon held hostage by the hoods. The film then takes a decidedly S&M bent as knives and guns are brandished (often times towards their captives' mouths — duh, symbolism?), pants are dropped and a bondage fantasy right out of a violent porn novel is acted out as Leon and Florence torment the youths while figuring out their next move. ★★★ VHS: $9.99; DVD: $24.99

Fallen

(1998, 115 min, US, Gregory Hoblit) *Denzel Washington, John Goodman, Donald Sutherland, Embeth Davidtz, James Gandolfini, Elias Koteas, Robert Joy, Al Ruggiero.* In this not altogether unsuccessful merging of supernatural thriller and police procedural, Washington plays a Philadelphia detective who, in the film's opening, watches the vicious serial killer (Koteas) he captured sizzle in the electric chair. Shortly thereafter, several murders take place with the very same M.O. as before — are they copycat killings, or is the explanation supernatural? Director Hoblit and screenwriter Nicholas Kazan approach their well-worn premise with a realistic, earthbound feel, à la *Rosemary's Baby* and *The Exorcist*, but with mixed results. Ironically, the gritty atmosphere Hoblit brings to the picture allows the already silly scare scenes to appear even sillier. However, *Fallen* is reasonably compelling, admirably dark and creepy, and has a nice twist ending. (VHS available letterboxed or pan & scan) ★★½ VHS: $14.99; DVD: $19.99

Fallen Angels

(1995, 96 min, Hong Kong, Wong Kar-Wai) *Leon Lai Ming, Michele Reis, Takeshi Kaneshiro.* A companion piece to his terrific *Chungking Express*, director Kar-Wai's *Fallen Angels* is a similarly atmospheric, stunningly visual treat. Two tenuously related story lines are interwoven here: a young hit man considers a career change, and a slacker who lives with his pop earns a living by breaking into shops after hours and selling the goods. As with *Chungking*, the stories in *Angels* aren't as important as the characters and the details of their day-to-day lives, their feelings, outlooks and relationships. Kar-Wai's restless camerawork and editing, multiple film stocks, ultra-cool soundtrack and stylized — though brief — gunfights signal the emergence of a hip, very talented craftsman and artist; it's his humanism and warmth that really stand out and set him apart. (Cantonese with English subtitles) ★★★½ VHS: $24.99; DVD: $29.99

Fallen Champ: The Mike Tyson Story

(1993, 93 min, US, Barbara Kopple) Mike Tyson went from Brownsville, Brooklyn, welfare kid to Heavyweight Champion of the World to convicted rapist, all before his 25th birthday. Kopple traces the many influences in his life which led him from obscurity to adulation, and ultimately, to his incarceration. Powerful, lucid and unflinching, this documentary offers compelling commentary on Tyson as an individual as well as on being black in America. ★★★ VHS: $14.99

The Fallen Idol

(1948, 95 min, GB, Carol Reed) *Ralph Richardson, Bobby Henrey, Michele Morgan, Jack Hawkins.* Richardson stars in this outstanding realization of Graham Greene's story about the friendship between an upper-class boy and a

house servant who is suspected of murder. Reed skillfully probes the psychological depths of his characters while creating a fascinating examination of the schism between adults and children in their views of reality. ★★★★ VHS: $29.99

Falling Down

(1993, 112 min, US, Joel Schumacher) *Michael Douglas, Robert Duvall, Barbara Hershey, Frederic Forrest, Tuesday Weld, Rachel Ticotin, Lois Smith.* In this over-the-edge, misanthropic black comedy, Douglas plays a slightly psychotic, unemployed defense worker whose pent-up hostilities against what he perceives as an increasingly foreign society explode in the sweltering heat and insufferable traffic jams of Los Angeles. At times wildly entertaining, at others shockingly violent and disturbing, the film follows Douglas as he treks across L.A. towards the home of his estranged wife, unleashing his fury on Latinos, Asians, neo-Nazis and other "bogeymen" standing between him and the American dream. Duvall injects a voice of reason in the film as a henpecked cop who must come to grips with his own sense of inadequacy before confronting Douglas. A reactionary though simple message of white fear in an increasingly non-white society. ★★★ VHS: $9.99; DVD: $14.99

Falling in Love

(1984, 107 min, US, Ulu Grosbard) *Meryl Streep, Robert De Niro, Harvey Keitel, Dianne Wiest.* A curiously unaffecting film, given the high-power cast. De Niro and Streep allow a chance encounter on a commuter train to blossom into an affair. They provide their usual professional performances, as do supporting players Keitel and Wiest, among others. There just isn't very much to work with. Interesting as evidence of a seldom-exposed aspect of the De Niro persona and a chance to see Streep do a toned-down, suburban Annie Hall. ★★½ VHS: $14.99

Fame

(1980, 134 min, US, Alan Parker) *Irene Cara, Barry Miller, Paul McCrane, Lee Curreri, Anne Meara, Richard Belzer.* Parker follows a group of students at the New York High School of the Performing Arts from their auditions in dance, voice, drama and music through their graduation ceremony. Hot lunches, hard lessons and dancing in the street. Cara sings the Oscar-winning title song. ★★★

The Family

(1987, 130 min, Italy, Ettore Scola) *Vittorio Gassman, Fanny Ardant, Philippe Noiret.* Utilizing a relaxed and intimate filmmaking style, Scola chronicles the 80 years of one typical family's life, loves and losses. By confining the entire story within the walls of a grand Roman apartment, Scola's attention is not on the tumultuous events of the 20th century but rather on the more mundane but equally compelling story of a middle-class family headed by Gassman. A touching and finely detailed soap opera. (Italian with English subtitles) ★★★ VHS: $19.99

Family Business

(1989, 115 min, US, Sidney Lumet) *Sean Connery, Dustin Hoffman, Matthew Broderick, Rosana De Soto.* Endearing misfire written by Vincent Patrick (*The Pope of Greenwich Village*) about three generations of small-time crooks

(Connery, Hoffman, Broderick) who decide to pull one last heist together. Though Patrick's screenplay has the same "homespun" feel that made *Pope* such a joy, the three strong leads tend to overpower the material. Efficiently directed by Lumet, though. ★★ VHS: $9.99

The Family Game

(1983, 107 min, Japan, Yoshimitsu Morita) *Junichi Tsujita, Yusaku Matsuda.* The contemporary Japanese middle class are mercilessly lampooned in this hilarious farce. The story, brimming with style and invention — from its extraordinary visual design to its incredibly quirky soundtrack — revolves around a family's decision to hire a tutor for their academically troubled son. The unorthodox and anarchistic instructor proceeds to wreak havoc in their previously tranquil lives. A wickedly satiric and endlessly surprising film. (Japanese with English subtitles) ★★★ VHS: $59.99

Family Life

(1971, 108 min, GB, Ken Loach) *Sandy Ratcliff, Grace Cave, Bill Dan, Hilary Martyn.* An indictment of the generation gap, the mental health care system and society at large. This fictional documentary by Loach details the deteriorating mental state of a severely disturbed 19-year-old girl with an identity crisis, who becomes pregnant and is forced by her parents into an abortion. A harrowing portrait of mental illness and one that comes down hard against drug treatments and electro-shock therapy. (aka: *Wednesday's Child*) ★★★ VHS: $19.99

The Family Man

(2000, 125 min, US, Brett Ratner) *Nicolas Cage, Téa Leoni, Don Cheadle, Jeremy Piven, Saul Rubinek.* Sharing more in common with *Mr. Destiny* than with *It's a Wonderful Life* for which it so desperately strives, this moderately enjoyable fantasy benefits greatly from a nice turn by Leoni. Cage plays Jack, a very successful Wall Street businessman who awakens on Christmas day to find himself in a parallel life: husband to Kate (Leoni), the woman he left behind 13 years earlier. Trapped in this new existence with no history of his former self, Jack lives out this new life all the

The Family Man

while trying to return to his reality. Balancing family comedy, sentimental dramatics and flights of fancy is a tall order, and director Ratner has difficulty in fully realizing and juggling these various tones. What success the film does achieve comes from the genial performances and a cute premise that delivers half of the time. ★★½ VHS: $102.99; DVD: $26.99

Family Plot

(1976, 120 min, US, Alfred Hitchcock) *Bruce Dern, Barbara Harris, William Devane, Karen Black, Ed Lauter, Katherine Helmond.* The 53rd and final film in Hitchcock's illustrious career is a quirky blend of sinister humor and mystery. Harris, in a wonderfully kooky performance, is a phony (?) medium who, along with boyfriend Dern, stumbles onto the kidnapping pastime of diabolical Devane and Black. A supremely droll study of coincidence and the criminal urge. ★★★½ VHS: $14.99; DVD: $29.99

A Family Thing

(1996, 110 min, US, Richard Pearce) *James Earl Jones, Robert Duvall, Michael Beach, Irma P. Hall, David Keith, Grace Zabriskie, Regina Taylor.* Jones and Duvall deliver subtle, finely drawn characterizations as half-brothers who are reunited after a separation of many decades, hundreds of miles, and the chasm of American racial relationships. Raised as white in a small Arkansas town, Duvall receives a posthumous letter from his mother informing him that in fact his birth mother was a black woman. In unacknowledged, tightly controlled emotional upheaval and within shouting distance of old age, he embarks on an odyssey of self-discovery, traveling to Chicago to find his brother and his history. The supporting cast is uniformly competent, with Hall in a standout performance as Aunt T., the family's backbone and historian. *A Family Thing* is a small gem of surprising emotional impact, a story of ordinary people which encapsulates larger issues in a personal framework. ★★★½ VHS: $6.99; DVD: $19.99

Family Viewing

(1987, 86 min, Canada, Atom Egoyan) *David Hemblen, Aidan Tierney, Arsinée Khanjian.* Told with salacious humor and effective drama, this unusual black comedy is a droll observation of the goings-on of a de-nuclearized family. Dad is a middle-class, sadomasochistic VCR repairman who, after driving his wife away with his obsession with kinky phone sex, lives in domestic bliss with his sexy bimbo. His son, Stan, is a pasty-faced teenage couch potato. The son finally escapes from his father and moves in with his girlfriend who, unbeknownst to him, works at the phone sex company and has a peculiar sexual relationship with his father. This story of contemporary familial corruption is an intelligent and promising start for a talented filmmaker. ★★★

The Fan

(1981, 95 min, US, Edward Bianchi) *Lauren Bacall, James Garner, Maureen Stapleton, Michael Biehn, Hector Elizondo, Griffin Dunne.* Bacall plays a legendary stage and screen star who is stalked by a psychotic fan. A creepy and rather unlikable thriller based on Bob Randell's novel. ★½ VHS: $14.99

The Fan

(1996, 116 min, US, Tony Scott) *Robert De Niro, Wesley Snipes, Ellen Barkin, John Leguizamo, Benicio Del Toro, John Kruk.* As slick, cold and transparent as ice, *The Fan* is a twisted, by-the-books thriller which offers few thrills or any redeeming qualities. De Niro is a Willy Loman–like salesman and obsessed San Francisco Giants fan about to lose his grip. Snipes is the Ken Griffey–like superstar who becomes De Niro's object of obsession. The suspense supposedly starts when they cross paths, but it's more like a lesson in Screenplay Coincidence 101. Barkin has little to do as a sports announcer. The background baseball sequences, even with the addition of real players such as Kruk, add little excitement and offer no rebuttal to the complaint that baseball in movies is boring. ★½ VHS: $9.99; DVD: $24.99

Fancy Pants

(1950, 92 min, US, George Marshall) *Bob Hope, Lucille Ball, Bruce Cabot.* Hope and Ball are in good form in this spirited remake of *Ruggles of Red Gap.* Bob is the cowardly valet who heads West with wild-and-woolly Lucy. She also sings the title song. ★★★ VHS: $14.99

Fandango

(1985, 91 min, US, Kevin Reynolds) *Kevin Costner, Judd Nelson, Sam Robards, Chuck Bush, Suzy Amis, Glenne Headly.* Five college roommates, having just graduated, go on a last fling together across the Texas Badlands. An interesting youth drama with good performances from its cast. ★★½ VHS: $9.99

Fanny

(1932, 120 min, France, Marc Allégret) *Raimu, Charpin, Orane Demazis, Pierre Fresnay.* In this second segment of the remarkable Pagnol Trilogy, Marius' father César (played by the unforgettable character actor Raimu) comforts Fanny after being deserted by his son. Pregnant, she accepts the hand of Panisse, a kindly but older friend of César's. The film provides a rich portrait of complex familial relationships. (French with English subtitles) ★★★½ VHS: $24.99

Fanny

(1961, 133 min, US, Joshua Logan) *Leslie Caron, Maurice Chevalier, Charles Boyer, Horst Buchholz.* Acclaimed reworking of Marcel Pagnol's timeless story, based on the Broadway musical but *without* the songs (similar to 1963's *Irma La Douce*), with Caron as the young waif abandoned by a sailor. Enchanting performances. ★★★ VHS: $14.99

Fanny and Alexander

(1982, 197 min, Sweden, Ingmar Bergman) *Pernilla Allwin, Bertil Guve, Gunn Wallgren, Erland Josephson, Harriet Andersson.* Bergman's joyous and engrossing portrait of a civilized Swedish family gracefully details the trauma and triumphs they encounter over the course of a year. Abandoning the dour tone of his earlier works, Bergman creates an enchanting tapestry of life's amplitude in this wise and witty Academy Award winner. (Swedish with English subtitles) ★★★★ VHS: $19.99

Fanny and Alexander

Fantasia

(1940, 120 min, US, Joe Grant & Dick Huemer) This Walt Disney masterpiece is a consummate collection of seven animated shorts, each utilizing a classical score for their background, and all under the direction of Leopold Stokowski. The selections include "The Sorcerer's Apprentice," starring Mickey Mouse; the brilliantly animated "The Rites of Spring"; and the stirring finale, "A Night on Bald Mountain." ★★★★ DVD: $29.99

Fantasia 2000

(2000, 75 min, US, Various Directors) Hosts: Steve Martin, Itzhak Perlman, Quincy Jones, Bette Midler, James Earl Jones, Penn & Teller, James Levine, Angela Lansbury. Despite the inclusion of "The Sorcerer's Apprentice," this is not a reworking of the original *Fantasia* (as Walt Disney originally intended) so much as a brand new film in the same spirit, using computer technology and IMAX to make it as technically up-to-date as the original was in 1940. Astonishingly rich in detail, with a surround-sound score by the Chicago Symphony that makes the most tired pieces feel fresh, *Fantasia 2000* is a worthy successor, and at a too-brief 75 minutes, leaves one begging for a third installment. Like the original, it's a little heavy on dancing animals. Refreshingly, there's some new style here, too: an urban, Abe Hirschfeld-inspired "Rhapsody in Blue" is closer to Warner than Disney and is most welcome. What a trip. Best experienced in the original IMAX big-screen format. ★★★½ VHS: $26.99; DVD: $29.99

Fantastic Planet

(1973, 74 min, France, René Laloux) An unusual and provocative combination of science fiction and animation. Jammed with original ideas and visualizations, this French production is an imaginative allegorical tale about a futuristic planet where men are tolerated as tame, tiny pets. Also included are three shorts from Laloux: *Les Dents du Singe (Monkey's Teeth)*, *Les Temps Morts (Idle Time)* and *Les Escargots (The Snails)*. (In English) (Letterboxed) ★★★ VHS: $14.99; DVD: $24.99

Fantastic Voyage

(1966, 100 min, US, Richard Fleischer) *Stephen Boyd, Raquel Welch, Donald Pleasence, Edmond O'Brien.* The special effects in this highly entertaining mid-'60s sci-fi classic may seem simple by today's standards, but at the time, they were nothing less than breathtaking. Members of a medical team are miniaturized and then injected into the body of the president in order to perform some truly up-close surgery. ★★★ VHS: $14.99; DVD: $24.99

Far and Away

(1992, 140 min, US, Ron Howard) *Tom Cruise, Nicole Kidman, Robert Prosky, Thomas Gibson, Barbara Babcock, Colm Meaney.* Cruise and Kidman manage to ignite a few sparks in this handsomely produced romantic epic set in late 19th-century Ireland and America. Essentially a three-act story, the first part, set in Ireland, finds poor farmer Cruise and rich landowner's daughter Kidman meeting after he attempts to murder her father. The second act takes place in Boston, where the two have emigrated, finding only poverty and corruption. The final is set in the Old West, where all have surfaced to strike a claim. Though the film's Boston scenes are overly melodramatic, the lush Irish landscapes and the vast Western skies provide a thrilling backdrop for what becomes, ultimately, a surprisingly rousing entertainment. (Letterboxed VHS available for $14.99) ★★★ VHS: $9.99; DVD: $29.99

Far Away, So Close

(1993, 140 min, Germany, Wim Wenders) *Otto Sander, Peter Falk, Willem Dafoe, Lou Reed.* Wenders continues his "Angels over Berlin" saga with this less-than-successful follow-up to the brilliant *Wings of Desire*. Where Bruno Ganz's Ariel in *Wings* was an angel whose selfish need to be human made him physically manifest, *Far Away's* Cassiel (Sander) comes down to earth because he wants to make things better. Instead, he falls victim to all of the human ailments he had hoped to remedy. Wenders takes a very grim view of the post-Cold War world, using Berlin as the perfect setting for a tale of impending social anarchy brought about by the collapse of old systems. Too often, however, Wenders allows his narrative to run wild. Dafoe appears as a sleazy devil figure named Emit Flesti (*time itself* spelled backwards). (German with English subtitles) ★★ VHS: $14.99; DVD: $29.99

The Far Country

(1955, 97 min, US, Anthony Mann) *James Stewart, Ruth Roman, Walter Brennan.* A sturdy western adventure with Stewart in typically good form as a cowboy whose cattle drive to Alaska turns disastrous when he is swindled by outlaws. Good scenery and character interplay highlight this exciting tale. ★★★ VHS: $14.99

Far East

(1982, 90 min, Australia, John Duigan) *Bryan Brown, Helen Morse.* Tepid drama about the owner of a sleazy tourist bar in Southeast Asia and his relationship with the wife of a crusading journalist. This mixture of political intrigue and romance has been done time and time again — with better results. ★

Far from Home

(1989, 86 min, US, Meiert Avis) *Drew Barrymore, Matt Frewer, Richard Masur, Susan Tyrrell, Jennifer Tilly.* Barrymore headlines this standard B-thriller about a budding teenaged nymphet who is stalked by an unknown killer while vacationing with her estranged father (Frewer). Nothing special, but a few unexpected touches (including a well-handled lesbian couple) spice things up. ★★ VHS: $9.99; DVD: $14.99

Far from Home: The Adventures of Yellow Dog

(1995, 81 min, US, Phillip Borso) *Mimi Rogers, Bruce Davison, Jesse Bradford.* An adolescent boy is lost in the wilds and faces certain horrors as he attempts to find his way back home. Set at a lethargic pace and given to clichés of the genre, *Far from Home's* main appeal is the "boy and his dog" story which punctuates the survival dramatics. Bradford stars as the 14-year-old who becomes separated from his father's boat excursion during a storm. The film offers beautiful scenery (shot on location in British Columbia), but fails to maintain any excitement in the boy's rescue attempts. ★★ VHS: $9.99

Far from Poland

(1984, 106 min, US, Jill Godmilow) Denied a visa to shoot a film in Poland, left-leaning independent filmmaker Godmilow (*Waiting for the Moon*) is forced to construct her documentary on the Solidarity movement from her studio in New York. This serious nonfiction film delves into the perception and representation of "truth" as it charts the rise of the Solidarity movement in the shipyards of Damansk in early 1980 to its suppression by martial law in December 1981. From a number of various angles, Godmilow aims to present the reality of the situation without succumbing to easy, prejudicial conclusions. ★★★ VHS: $69.99

Far from the Madding Crowd

(1967, 169 min, GB, John Schlesinger) *Julie Christie, Alan Bates, Peter Finch, Terence Stamp.* Christie stars as a ravishing femme fatale who manages to make emotional mincemeat out of three men's lives (Bates, Finch, Stamp). Director Schlesinger's masterful touch combined with the brilliant cinematography of Nicolas Roeg make this an extraordinary viewing experience. (Letterboxed VHS available for $24.99) ★★★½ VHS: $19.99

Far North

(1988, 92 min, US, Sam Shepard) *Jessica Lange, Charles Durning, Tess Harper, Patricia Arquette, Donald Moffat, Ann Wedgeworth.* Lange and Durning head a strong cast in this allegorical tale written by Shepard, here making his directorial debut. When the head of a Minnesota farming family is almost killed by one of his most obstinate horses, he wants his strong-willed daughter to destroy the dangerous animal, with unexpected consequences. ★★★ VHS: $9.99

A Far Off Place

(1993, 105 min, US, Mikael Salomon) *Reese Witherspoon, Ethan Randall, Sarel Bok, Maximilian Schell, Jack Thompson.* Based on a pair of novels by Laurens van der Post, this passable Disney adaptation recounts the adventures of a pair of white teenagers and their Bushman friend who, in order to evade a gang of murderous poachers, flee into southern Africa's Kalihari Desert. The story of orphaned children fleeing evil adults appears to be the perfect Disney fit; but despite this, or perhaps because of it, the film occasionally gets bogged down in formulaic predictability. ★★½ VHS: $14.99

Farewell My Concubine

(1993, 155 min, China, Chen Kaige) *Leslie Cheung, Zhang Fengyi, Gong Li.* Told on an epic scale, this big-budget spectacle recounts the tempestuous relationship between two Peking Opera stars as they live through five decades of turbulent Chinese history. In a repressive 1920s opera school, an androgynous young boy, Dieyi, begins a life-long involvement with another student, Xiaolou. Years later, the two achieve national stardom, best known for their rendition of the tragic opera "Farewell My Concubine," in which the now-adult Dieyi (Cheung) plays the part of a woman. As their professional lives soar, their relationship becomes strained as the gay Dieyi falls in love with his affectionate but heterosexual costar. Even after Xiaolou (Zhang) marries a fiery former prostitute (superbly played by Gong), the two men's lives remain intractably intertwined. Exotic locations, sweeping photography, colorful costumes and an emotional story line make this a riveting experience. (Mandarin with English subtitles) ★★★★ DVD: $29.99

Farewell, My Lovely

(1975, 98 min, GB, Dick Richards) *Robert Mitchum, Charlotte Rampling, Sylvia Miles, Anthony Zerbe, Sylvester Stallone.* Wonderfully evoking the time and mood of Raymond Chandler's 1940s Los Angeles, this film noir detective drama stars Mitchum as an aging, down-on-his-heels Philip Marlowe who is persuaded to take on a case involving a nightclub singer missing for six years. Rampling is confusingly and destructively alluring as the femme fatale and Miles is unforgettable as an alcoholic floozy who "sings" for a bottle. A complex, dark and entertaining film that more than holds its own with the original, *Murder My Sweet.* ★★★½ VHS: $14.99; DVD: $24.99

A Farewell to Arms

(1932, 78 min, US, Frank Borzage) *Gary Cooper, Helen Hayes, Adolph Menjou.* Hemingway's nihilistic novel of profane love and war deflated the 1920s' romantic ideals, but Depression-era Hollywood wanted something to believe in after the death of God and Country. Enter director Borzage, whose faith in the transcendence of physical love elevates Hemingway's bumbling paramours, finding something sacred in their union. Everything is painted in extremes: candid, naturalistic dialogue bumps into silent-era expressionism; tiny thespian Hayes and huge hunk Cooper cut iconic figures; squint-inducing darks of warfare open to blinding heavenly lights of love. A remarkable achievement, for those with a stomach for it, less a literal translation than a metamorphosis to fit the medium, and a taste of what hot, steamy places were American cinemas in that desperate year of 1932. (Remade in 1957) ★★★½ DVD: $24.99

Farewell to the King

(1989, 117 min, US, John Milius) *Nick Nolte, James Fox, Nigel Havers.* From the macho writer-

director Milius (*The Wind and the Lion, Red Dawn*) comes this visually stunning, thematically stunted adventure epic of a WWII Army deserter (Nolte) who faces a crisis of conscience when the island paradise he has ruled in peace is invaded by the British-Japanese conflict. Based on a novel by Pierre Schoendoerffer. ★★

Fargo

(1996, 90 min, US, Joel Coen) *Frances McDormand, William H. Macy, Steve Buscemi, Peter Stormare, Harve Presnell.* The peculiarly heightened reality that is a trademark of Coen Brothers' films is well-suited to this bizarre, true-life tale of a seemingly solid, middle-class man (Macy) whose proximity to financial ruin precipitates a hair-brained scheme for quick monetary reward. His plan — to arrange his wife's kidnapping, thereby splitting the ransom to be paid by his wealthy father-in-law — culminates in horrific tragedy imbued with macabre humor. Macy is an accomplished journeyman actor, and he renders an authentic and pathetic character. But the absolute delight is Oscar-winning McDormand as Margie the pregnant police chief, offhandedly battling morning sickness as she examines a triple-homicide crime scene. Minnesota's vast frozen expanses endow physicality to the desperate isolation which underlies this winter's tale. An unnerving study of human frailty and deception. (Letterboxed VHS available for $19.99) ★★★★ VHS: $14.99; DVD: $19.99

Farinelli

(1994, 110 min, Belgium, Gerard Corbiau) *Stefano Dionisi, Enrico Lo Verso, Jeroen Krabbé.* The tumultuous life of castrato singer Farinelli (née Carlo Broschi), along with his co-dependent relationship with his brother, is bombastically explored in this absorbing if predictable period drama. Set in 18th-century France, the story revolves around the passionate, ambitious and handsome singer (Dionisi), whose beautiful voice — preserved through a traumatic castration as a boy — becomes his instrument for success. Riding the coattails of that success is his brother Ricardo (Lo Verso), a much less talented composer, and their intense love/hate relationship extends to their careers and romantic affairs. An elegant drama of unchecked ambition that sadly suffers from operatic excess, *Farinelli* could be called the *Lisztomania* for the opera set. (French and Italian with English subtitles) ★★½ VHS: $19.99; DVD: $29.99

The Farmer's Daughter

(1947, 97 min, US, H.C. Potter) *Loretta Young, Joseph Cotten, Ethel Barrymore, Charles Bickford.* Young won an Academy Award for her enchanting performance as a Swedish farm girl who takes a job as a maid for a Congressman's family and finds love and political career opportunities. A charming comedy with sublime performances from the cast. (Basis for a 1960s TV series.) ★★★ VHS: $14.99

Fast, Cheap, & Out of Control

(1997, 82 min, US, Errol Morris) Another quirky factual film from maverick documentari-

Frances McDormand takes aim in *Fargo*

an Morris (*The Thin Blue Line, A Brief History of Time*), this look at four men who have found infatuation and fascination with their eccentric lines of work is the story of obsession by an obsessive. They include: Hoover, an animal trainer, whose mentor was circus impressario Clyde Beatty; Mendez, a naked mole rat researcher working out of the Philadelphia Zoo; inventor Brooks, who developed an insect-like robot; and Mendonca, a topiary gardener with the ability to shape bushes into spitting images of animals. On the surface, they seem like regular guys. Delve a little deeper, however, and their obsessive streaks become more apparent, as they espouse on their particular field of expertise while tinkering with science and nature. Morris' inventive flourishes help show us that even the most ordinary people can be extraordinary at times. ★★★ VHS: $24.99

Fast Talking

(1986, 93 min, Australia, Ken Cameron) *Steve Bisley, Tracey Mann.* A sensitive comedy about the coming of age of a streetwise Australian youth who yearns to break out of the restricting confines of school and family life. A movie about hope, defiance and emotional honesty. ★★½

Fast Times at Ridgemont High

(1982, 92 min, US, Amy Heckerling) *Jennifer Jason Leigh, Judge Reinhold, Sean Penn, Phoebe Cates, Forest Whitaker, Eric Stoltz, Anthony Edwards.* "Hey, dude, let's party." With these infamous four words, Penn introduced the California Valley boy in this entertaining, wacky comedy whose moments of insight into the rigors of growing up elevate it far above the usual teenager-obsessed-with-sex flick. A few of these students would go on to make names for themselves. Heckerling's directorial debut. ★★★ VHS: $14.99; DVD: $29.99

Faster, Pussycat, Kill! Kill!

(1966, 83 min, US, Russ Meyer) *Tura Satana, Lori Williams, Haji.* Tura Santana stars as Varla, the tough-talking ringleader of a wild gang of out-of-control go-go girls(!) in this thoroughly outrageous cult classic. Varla, the proto-lesbian killer with a taste for fast cars and helpless girls, rules with a leather-gloved fist over blonde beauty Billie (aka Boom Boom) (Lori Williams) and dark toughie Josie (Haji), two hot-rodding chicks in skin-tight clothes (calling them buxom would be redundant when talking about a Russ Meyer babe). Set in the California desert, these violent femmes kill a man and kidnap his bikini-wearing cutie pie girlfriend and go on a reckless road to inevitable ruin. Filled with hilarious dialogue and hellacious catfights, this potboiler is one of Meyers' best. ★★★ VHS: $79.99

Fat City

(1973, 96 min, US, John Huston) *Stacy Keach, Jeff Bridges, Susan Tyrrell, Candy Clark.* After a period of intermittent critical and commercial success, Huston delivered this powerful portrayal of lonely outcasts on the fringes of the boxing world in California. Keach plays a down-and-out veteran of the ring and Bridges is a hungry newcomer. Tyrrell is outstanding in support, giving a heartbreaking performance as a boisterous barfly. ★★★½ VHS: $19.99

Fat Man and Little Boy

(1989, 126 min, US, Roland Joffé) *Paul Newman, Dwight Schultz, Bonnie Bedelia, John Cusack, Natasha Richardson, Laura Dern.* Newman, in an uncharacteristically unsympathetic and cold portrayal, stars as General Leslie Groves, the military leader who oversaw the project headed by the scientist J. Robert Oppenheimer. From this project would come the bombs which would be dropped on Hiroshima and Nagasaki. The film tries to create a mood of suspense in whether the scientists will succeed, but is far more interesting for the psychological games played between Groves and Oppenheimer in their race to develop and ultimately use the bombs. ★★½ VHS: $14.99

Fatal Attraction

(1987, 119 min, US, Adrian Lyne) *Michael Douglas, Glenn Close, Anne Archer, Fred Gwynne.* A box-office sensation, this psychological thriller is a not-too-subtle cautionary tale about adultery in the age of AIDS. Married exec Douglas has a one-night stand with Close and lives to regret it. Archer is the wife who is most hurt (literally) by the indiscretion. The film received a Best Picture nomination — a nod more to the sociopolitical impact of the story than a recognition of great filmmaking. (The Director's Cut, which runs 159 minutes, is available for $19.99 in a letterboxed format) ★★★ VHS: $14.99

Fatal Beauty

(1987, 104 min, US, Tom Holland) *Whoopi Goldberg, Sam Elliott, Ruben Blades, Jennifer Warren, Brad Dourif, Cheech Marin.* This attempt to cash in on the success of *Beverly Hills Cop* stars Goldberg as an L.A. cop who's tracking down the source of a lethal batch of cocaine known as "Fatal Beauty." Very few thrills and an inferior story line is only partially offset by Goldberg's mugging. ★½ VHS: $9.99; DVD: $14.99

Fatal Instinct

(1993, 85 min, US, Carl Reiner) *Armand Assante, Sean Young, Kate Nelligan, Sherilyn Fenn, Christopher McDonald, James Remar, Tony Randall.* Unjustly maligned upon its release, *Fatal Instinct* is a sometimes very funny takeoff on film noir — and some of the targets include *Body Heat, Basic Instinct* and *Double Indemnity.* Though no Leslie Nielsen, Assante proves himself quite adept at parody, playing a cop/lawyer whose work for client Young puts him on the road to danger. Nelligan is his wife, who's planning to knock off her husband and run off with her mechanic. As with most comedies of this sort, not all the gags work, but there's an abundance of laughs which

do, thanks to a cast which clearly is having a lot of fun. Our favorite gag: Young's *Fatal Attraction* roller coaster ride. ★★★ VHS: $14.99

Fatal Vision

(1984, 192 min, US, David Greene) *Karl Malden, Eva Marie Saint, Gary Cole, Barry Newman, Andy Griffith.* Critically acclaimed adaptation of the Joe McGinniss best-seller in which an ex-Green Beret is accused of murdering his pregnant wife and two young daughters, and his in-laws' relentless search for justice. Based on a true story. ★★★

Father

(1966, 89 min, Hungary, István Szabó) *Andras Balint, Miklos Gabor.* A sensitive and involving look at a young man's maturation as he searches for the real conditions that caused his father's death in World War II. (Hungarian with English subtitles) ★★★ VHS: $24.99

Father

(1991, 106 min, Australia, John Power) *Max von Sydow, Carol Drinkwater.* Set in modern-day Melbourne, this touching, emotional story concentrates on a middle-class family, including a young mother, her husband and their young daughters, who run a small hotel and restaurant, along with her aging father who built the place many years ago. An anonymous phone call urges the woman to watch a TV documentary one night, so as to learn the "real past" of her father. In a riveting moment, the woman is forced to delve into her father's questionable past. Reminiscent of Costa-Gavras' much slicker *Music Box, Father* is smaller in scale, but packs more power, due in large part to von Sydow's tortured and pained portrayal. ★★★ VHS: $19.99

Father Goose

(1964, 116 min, US, Ralph Nelson) *Cary Grant, Leslie Caron, Trevor Howard.* Grant goes beach bum in this entertaining, sporadically funny comic adventure, the next-to-the-last film the actor would make. Set during WWII, the film casts Grant as a beachcomber living alone on a small South Seas island who is "drafted" by the Australian navy as a lookout. Complications, romance and some laughs arise when he rescues a French schoolmistress and six refugee children adrift at sea. (Letterboxed) ★★★ VHS: $19.99; DVD: $29.99

Father of the Bride

(1950, 93 min, US, Vincente Minnelli) *Spencer Tracy, Joan Bennett, Elizabeth Taylor, Billie Burke, Leo G. Carroll, Russ Tamblyn.* In this delightful family comedy, Tracy may have proved the inspiration for every sitcom father who has ever had to deal with a teenager. But few have done it better; it's hard to believe someone could be so funny just lifting an eyebrow. The story follows father Tracy and mother Bennett readying for daughter Taylor's wedding. (Sequel: *Father's Little Dividend*) (Remade in 1991) ★★★½ VHS: $14.99

Father of the Bride

(1991, 105 min, US, Charles Shyer) *Steve Martin, Diane Keaton, Martin Short, B.D. Wong, Kimberly Williams.* Martin takes over the Spencer Tracy role from the 1950 classic comedy about a family preparing for their eldest daughter's wedding. Martin, who doesn't attempt to compete

with Tracy, gives a very funny performance as the exasperated dad, but the film manages to be only mildly amusing. As with the original, Mom (played endearingly by Keaton) and Dad become overwhelmed by all the arrangements. From the in-laws to the caterers (Short and Wong in stereotypes), it's a never-ending calamity which the father of the bride handles with one-liners, pratfalls and humiliation. Ultimately, this *Father* is only a stand-in for the original. (Sequel: *Father of the Bride, Part II*) ★★½ VHS: $9.99; DVD: $29.99

Father of the Bride, Part II

(1995, 106 min, US, Charles Shyer) *Steve Martin, Diane Keaton, Martin Short, Kimberly Williams, Kieran Culkin, B.D. Wong.* This painfully unfunny, sugar-coated "comedy" about the travails of a rich family will send hypoglycemics into shock and anyone else possessing an even mildly cynical nature to seek out a large barf bag. A follow-up to the 1991 hit and based on the screenplay of the 1951 film *Father's Little Dividend,* this flimsy excuse for a movie stars Martin as George Banks, the grumpy and whiny husband of Nina (an often-in-soft-focus Keaton), the 1950s idea of the perfect wife. The premise is that both his wife and daughter become pregnant (and that's it folks — that's the plot — they each deliver a baby and then the movie ends!). Short and Wong return from the '91 original reprising their offensive roles as swishy and shrill decorators. ★ VHS: $14.99; DVD: $32.99

Father's Day

(1997, 98 min, US, Ivan Reitman) *Robin Williams, Billy Crystal, Nastassja Kinski, Charlie Hofheimer, Julia Louis-Dreyfus, Bruce Greenwood.* Admittedly, the thought of Williams and Crystal costarring in their first film together would seem almost heaven-sent. Expectations aside, however, their first joint venture is only occasionally funny, and director Reitman doesn't give his stars ample room in which to explore the comic possibilities of the scenario. Based on the French comedy *Les Comperes,* the story begins when former lover Kinski tells both Williams and Crystal that her missing son is his. They eventually unite to locate the teenager, and their incompatability sets the stage for a few laughs. The two stars — as would be expected — have a great rapport. But the screenplay just isn't consistently funny. Instead of nonstop hilarity, we get two incredibly gifted but underused leads. ★★½ VHS: $9.99; DVD: $19.99

Father's Little Dividend

(1951, 82 min, US, Vincente Minnelli) *Spencer Tracy, Elizabeth Taylor, Joan Bennett, Billie Burke.* Cheerful sequel to the hit comedy *Father of the Bride.* All the main leads repeat their roles as newlywed Taylor returns home — expecting. ★★★ VHS: $19.99

Fatherland

(1994, 100 min, US, Christopher Menaue) *Rutger Hauer, Miranda Richardson, Peter Vaughan, Jean Marsh, Michael Kitchen.* It's 1964. Hitler, having won WWII, dominates Europe (now known as Germania), but is still battling guerrillas in Russia. Needing an alliance with the United States, Germany opens its borders to American journalists for the first time since the war. The Reich readies for a celebration of the Fuhrer's 75th birthday, and there are rumors of a summit with U.S. President Joseph Kennedy, Sr. Through unusual elements in a murder investigation, SS Major Hauer (the SS is now the peacetime police) and U.S. journalist Richardson cross paths while tracking down a decades-old mystery. This HBO production is a well-executed thriller which makes good use of an intriguing premise and is uncomfortably effective in imagining life in a prosperous authoritarian state. ★★★½ VHS: $19.99

Fatso

(1980, 94 min, US, Anne Bancroft) *Dom DeLuise, Anne Bancroft, Ron Carey, Candice Azzara.* First-time director Bancroft treads into husband Mel Brooks' territory with this occasionally amusing though disappointing comedy about an obese man's attempts to diet. DeLuise makes the most of the material ("Get the honey!"), but even his larger-than-life comedic talents aren't enough to warrant a recommendation. ★★ VHS: $14.99

Faust

(1926, 116 min, Germany, F.W. Murnau) *Emil Jannings, Gosta Ekman, Camilla Horn, Wilheim (William) Dieterle.* This lavishly produced expressionistic fable is one of the classics of silent film. The story begins with a wager: a wager between God and the Devil over one of earth's souls, an elderly scientist named Faust. Jannings stars as Mephistopheles, a conniving evil-doer sent to a plague-stricken Europe to convince Faust to sell his soul in exchange for youth, pleasure and power. Jannings is superb as the wide-eyed, satin-caped Mephisto — an impish figure who takes malicious delight in destroying people's lives. With elaborate, medieval *Caligari*-like sets, experimental special effects, vivid imagery and a timeless tale, the film is Murnau's masterpiece and one that is just as striking when viewed today. ★★★½ VHS: $24.99; DVD: $29.99

Faust

(1994, 97 min, Czech Republic, Jan Svankmajer) A warped, hypnotic retelling of the Faust legend. Anyone familiar with Czech animator Svankmajer knows he's not going to helm the next *Winnie the Pooh* episode. His films are adult, dark, obsessive and truly surreal. *Faust* is definitely no exception. Making use of marionettes, live action and stop-motion animation, Svankmajer arguably has made his most mature, haunting and affecting film to date — after a slow start, this becomes fascinating and enthralling. Svankmajer is able to take clay figures and clunky puppets and create memorable images that are disturbing and hilarious, revolting and gorgeous. A real pleasure for fans of the bizarre. ★★★½ VHS: $24.99; DVD: $29.99

The Favor

(1994, 97 min, US, Donald Petrie) *Harley Jane Kozak, Elizabeth McGovern, Bill Pullman, Brad Pitt, Larry Miller, Ken Wahl.* When married Kathy (Kozak) can't get her old flame (Wahl) out of her amorous fantasies, she convinces her semi-single friend Emily (McGovern) to act as her, well, as her proxy in love, thereby being able to enjoy an extramarital affair vicariously. Of course, a few problems arise, like the protests of Emily's young beau (Pitt). A tepid comedy buoyed by McGovern's quirky charms. ★★ VHS: $9.99

The Favor, the Watch and the Very Big Fish

(1991, 89 min, GB, Ben Lewin) *Bob Hoskins, Jeff Goldblum, Natasha Richardson, Michel Blanc, Jean-Pierre Cassel.* Hoskins photographs religious tableaus for the greater glory of the Mother Church. He's given the assignment to find a new Christ on the same day a friend asks a favor, in the execution of which he meets Richardson, an enchanting young woman with an incredible story about a watch. Blanc and Goldblum join them in this fanciful and irreverent tale of the foibles of belief and the dangers of misplaced faith. Lewin directs his delightful script with wit and vigor, and the cast is engaging. As the two guys at the riverbank note, "I just saw someone trying to walk on the water." "It happens. Go to sleep." ★★★ VHS: $9.99

Fear (La Paura)

(1954, 84 min, Italy, Roberto Rossellini) *Ingrid Bergman, Mathias Wiedman.* Rossellini's last and darkest film shows a marriage stumbling across lines of suspicion, mistrust and fear. An unfaithful wife (Bergman) is blackmailed by her lover's ex-girlfriend (and husband?). Her guilt drives her further into a series of lies leading to tragedy. (Filmed in English) ★★½

Fear

(1996, 95 min, US, James Foley) *Mark Wahlberg, Reese Witherspoon, William L. Petersen, Amy Brenneman.* When adorable adolescent Witherspoon finds herself the object of obsession of bad-boy Wahlberg, bad things ensue, especially bad things for — surprise — the family pet and the sensitive best friend. The screenplay appears to have been written with much help from a psychology textbook as there is no shortage of *quien es mas macho* posturing between boyfriend and Mr. Father Knows Best (Petersen) and a "You're not my mother" conflict between daughter and stepmom. A standard, predictable genre thriller. ★½ VHS: $9.99

Fear and Loathing in Las Vegas

(1998, 119 min, US, Terry Gilliam) *Johnny Depp, Benicio Del Toro, Ellen Barkin, Cameron Diaz, Gary Busey, Christina Ricci, Lyle Lovett.* A hallucinatory, extravagantly funny and unapologetic look at writer Hunter S. Thompson's drug-induced haze in late-1960s Las Vegas. The film was ripped apart by most critics, which could lead one to speculate that maybe its non-antidrug posture was too much; that maybe the film became confused with its subject matter. At any rate, it's a crime that Gilliam's imaginative sojourn was overlooked. Depp is remarkable as Thompson, who is assigned to cover a sporting event for an unnamed magazine. Accompanied by his overweight Samoan lawyer (an almost unrecognizable Del Toro), Thompson begins a descent into cultural hell as the backyard of America's playground lays waste to unceasing drug and alcohol binges. *Fear and Loathing* is a visual tour de force of acid trips, tacky art direction and oblivious destruction, and Gilliam and his cowriters have taken all prisoners in translating the essence of a counterculture classic. This wild, dizzying ride sputters now and then, but like any good amusement, it takes us by the throat and rattles us around till we're not sure which way is up. (VHS letterboxed available for $14.99) ★★★½ VHS: $9.99; DVD: $26.99

Fear City

(1984, 93 min, US, Abel Ferrara) *Tom Berenger, Melanie Griffith, Billy Dee Williams, Rae Dawn Chong.* From the director of *King of New York* comes this grade-B thriller about New York City strippers getting sliced and diced by a self-righteous martial arts expert hell-bent on cleansing the city. ★★½ VHS: $9.99; DVD: $24.99

The Fear Inside

(1992, 100 min, US, Leon Ichaso) *Christine Lahti, Dylan McDermott, Jennifer Rubin, Thomas Ian Nicholas.* The ever-underrated Lahti headlines this sterling nail-biter about a woman suffering from acute agoraphobia, making it impossible for her to leave the house — even when it is taken over by a psychotic couple on the run. Nostalgia fans will undoubtedly recognize this as an updating of the 1964 cult classic *Lady in a Cage.* By changing the prison from a physical one to one of the mind, the terror and helplessness are made all the more real. ★★★

Fear of a Black Hat

(1994, 86 min, US, Rusty Cundieff) *Mark Christopher Lawrence, Larry B. Scott, Rusty Cundieff, Kasi Lemmons.* First-time director Cundieff wears many hats, including writer and star, in this often hilarious, sophisticated *This Is Spinal Tap*-like parody about the making of a documentary of a "rags to riches" Public Enemy-like rap group called N.W.H. ("Niggaz with Hats"), whose members display an obscene fascination with "booty," guns and hats. The insipid head of the group, Ice Cold (Cundieff), and his daffy cohorts are seen in interviews and personal moments, all of them blistering funny. But the film's true genius lies in its scathing skewering of rap industry infighting, as well as the group's off-the-cuff, outlandish "PC" justifications for the sexism, misogyny, racism and violence strewn throughout their music. ★★★½

Fear Strikes Out

(1957, 100 min, US, Robert Mulligan) *Anthony Perkins, Karl Malden.* Unflinching examination of baseball player Jimmy Piersall, whose battle with mental illness is tensely brought to the screen by a stand-out portrayal from Perkins. Another strong performance from veteran Malden as Piersall's father. ★★★ VHS: $14.99

Fearless

(1993, 122 min, US, Peter Weir) *Jeff Bridges, Rosie Perez, Isabella Rossellini, Tom Hulce, John Turturro, Benicio Del Toro.* Weir returns to form with this unnerving character study, reminiscent of the director's more complex Australian works. Bridges is remarkable as an airplane crash survivor who undergoes a dramatic change of personality. Having saved several lives on the plane, Bridges begins to assume a Christ-like persona as he moves further away from his loved ones and forms a bond with another survivor (Perez in a controlled and riveting performance), a mother whose two-year-old died in the crash. Perez and Bridges' scenes together possess a rare intensity, and both actors are the driving force of the film. Weir is successful in both examining the damaged psyches of his characters, and keeping a firm hand on an extremely well-directed crash sequence, told mostly through flashback. ★★★½ VHS: $14.99; DVD: $14.99

F

The Fearless Vampire Killers

(1967, 107 min, GB, Roman Polanski) *Roman Polanski, Jack MacGowran, Sharon Tate, Alfie Bass.* The restored version of this horror comedy adds over fifteen minutes of material to Polanski's loving tribute to the vampire films of Hammer Studios. Polanski himself plays one of the hunters out to rid the world of vampirism. The full title is: *The Fearless Vampire Killers or Pardon Me, But Your Teeth Are in My Neck.* ★★★ VHS: $14.99

Feast of July

(1995, 118 min, GB, Christopher Menaul) *Embeth Davidtz, Tom Bell, Gemma Jones, Greg Wise, James Purefoy.* While this Ismail Merchant production would be but a minor addition to the oeuvre of his directing partner James Ivory, it is a decent first outing for British TV helmer Menaul. True to decorative detail and languid rhythms we associate with that era, *Feast of July* is a wistful pleasantry, needing only Alastair Cooke's gently guiding introduction to make one feel certain that "Masterpiece Theatre" is on the telly. Davidtz embodies the broken and battered Bella Ford, a woman led astray in a town and a time not known to be forgiving. She is forced to bury her stillborn baby in the rough earth and seek sanctuary in the house of a lamplighter and his marriageable sons. ★★½ VHS: $19.99

Fedora

(1978, 114 min, US/West Germany, Billy Wilder) *William Holden, Marthe Keller, Jose Ferrer, Frances Sternhagen, Henry Fonda, Michael York.* This fascinating curiosity from Wilder, towards the end of his career, stars Holden as an independent film producer who goes to Greece in search of Fedora, an actress from Hollywood's glamour years who now lives in a secluded villa. The film demonstrates a more romantic side of Wilder, but his potshots at contemporary Hollywood lack the bite of his more classic turns in the director's chair, most notably *Sunset Boulevard.* ★★★

Feeling Minnesota

(1996, 95 min, US, Steven Baigelman) *Keanu Reeves, Vincent D'Onofrio, Cameron Diaz, Delroy Lindo, Courtney Love, Tuesday Weld, Dan Aykroyd.* As pseudo-hip and annoying as the worst Tarantino rip-off, *Feeling Minnesota* fails as thriller, Generation X road movie, and Tarantino-wannabe. The dull plot concerns a prodigal son named Jjaks (gosh, how cool!) who returns home for his loathsome brother's wedding to a bombshell (Diaz, who's forced to marry the lout as punishment for stealing from the local baddie), only to run off with his sister-in-law. With the exception of Love's waitress, all the characters are scum, and the "big twist" is as illogical and obvious as the surprise ending of a minor "Hart to Hart" episode. ★½ VHS: $14.99; DVD: $19.99

Felicia's Journey

(1999, 111 min, GB, Atom Egoyan) *Bob Hoskins, Elaine Cassidy, Arsinée Khanjian.* A young runaway is befriended by a gentlemanly chef, a serial killer who has been murdering young women who find themselves in desperate situations. Director Egoyan (*The Sweet Hereafter*) explores the psyche of a mass murderer with restraint, concentrating on emotional conflict rather than violence. ★★★ VHS: $9.99; DVD: $19.99

Fellini Satyricon

(1969, 129 min, Italy, Federico Fellini) *Martin Potter, Capucine, Hiram Keller, Salvo Randone.* A wild and shocking phantamagoria set in a world of hermaphrodites, dwarves, prostitutes, nymphomaniacs, and homosexual youths. Boldly bizarre in the unmistakable Fellini manner. (Italian with English subtitles) ★★★½ VHS: $19.99; DVD: $19.99

Fellini's Roma

(1972, 128 min, Italy, Federico Fellini) *Peter Gonzales, Fiona Florence, Anna Magnani, Gore Vidal.* Nostalgic and lavishly impressionistic, this "story of a city" is an engrossing tour of the Eternal City. Spanning from the '30s to the turbulent Rome of the '70s, Fellini offers a diverse view of his home through a mélange of deeply personal images of this vital, passionate land. (Italian with English subtitles) ★★★ VHS: $19.99; DVD: $19.99

Fellow Traveler

(1989, 97 min, GB, Philip Saville) *Ron Silver, Hart Bochner, Daniel J. Travanti, Imogen Stubbs.* *Fellow Traveler* is a totally engrossing psychological mystery about a blacklisted Hollywood writer living in England who learns of the suicide of his best friend. Silver is splendid as the writer who, haunted by the memory of his friend (Bochner), tries to piece together the reason and circumstance of his death — even at the risk of his own safety. Travanti is fine as Silver's former psychiatrist who may hold the key to the tragedy. An intriguing glimpse into the days of blacklisting and anti-Communist hysteria, and of the pain endured by those blacklisted. ★★★

Female

(1933, 60 min, US, Michael Curtiz) *Ruth Chatterton, George Brent.* This early directorial effort by Curtiz is a foreshadowing of his greatness to come (*Casablanca*, etc.). Chatterton is the head of an automobile factory. She's never found a man who's an equal match, although she's had some fun along the way. Brent plays a new employee who's not afraid to say no to her. Looking for a man who wants her for herself and not her money, she struggles with her identity: can she be a hard-working woman and still be "feminine?" Never too melodramatic and surprisingly explicit, the film's subject matter is still relevant today. ★★★½ VHS: $19.99

Female Perversions

(1996, 113 min, US/Germany, Susan Streitfeld) *Tilda Swinton, Amy Madigan, Karen Sillas, Clancy Brown, Frances Fisher, Paulina Porizkova.* *Female Perversions* is pretentious, arty and angry — three qualities which make it both intriguing and tough going. Swinton stars as Eve, a high-profile lawyer preparing for an interview with the governor in the hopes of being appointed a judge. In the meanwhile, she must contend with her estranged, kleptomaniac sister (Madigan), a workaholic boyfriend (Brown), a somewhat hesitant female lover (Sillas), and her own inner demons. Though heavy-handed, the material offers strong compensations — solid acting (Swinton in particular, playing the definitive neurotic), some insightful dialogue and a thoughtful ending. ★★½ VHS: $14.99

Female Trouble

(1974, 95 min, US, John Waters) *Divine, Edith Massey, Mink Stole.* Follow the trials and tribulations of Dawn Davenport (Divine): from cha-cha heel obsessed teen to rape victim to murderess to electric chair victim. Waters' ode to misguided teen traumas and prison melodrama includes satirical blasts at middle-class values, performance art, and really bad makeup. ★★★

La Femme Nikita

(1990, 117 min, France, Luc Besson) *Anne Parillaud, Jean-Hugues Anglade, Tcheky Karyo, Jean Reno, Jeanne Moreau.* Action-packed and filled with mega-violence, Besson's wonderfully entertaining romantic thriller is one part *Clockwork Orange* and two parts "Pygmalion." The seductively pouty and dazzlingly leggy Parillaud debuts as Nikita, a modern-day Eliza Doolittle with a vicious mean streak. Besson's story fol-

Anne Parillaud in *La Femme Nikita*

lows her somewhat Orwellian transformation from savagely criminal, punked-out heroin addict to well-groomed, statuesque and cold-blooded assassin for the French government. Soon, however, she begins to experience stirrings of humanity, which elevates *La Femme Nikita* above its action-adventure status. Besson bathes his visuals in neon-drenched colors and captures the action with a high-fashion, nouveau-chic panache. (American remake: *Point of No Return*) (French with English subtitles) ★★★½ VHS: $19.99; DVD: $19.99

Les Femmes (The Women)

(1969, 86 min, France, Jean Aurel) *Brigitte Bardot, Maurice Ronet, Kristina Holm.* A racy romantic comedy starring the petulant Bardot as a very personal secretary to a handsome writer who needs some special inspiration to get his creative juices flowing. Silly and unimportant but fun, this look into the amorous exploits of the French should entertain BB fans who are determined to trudge through her entire filmography. (French with English subtitles) ★★½ VHS: $14.99; DVD: $29.99

Femmes de Paris (Peek-a-Boo)

(1953, 83 min, France, Jean Loubignac) *Robert Dhery, Collette Brosset.* A delightful backstage comedy set in a burlesque hall and featuring the "Bluebell Girls" who provide the beauty (and some daring nudity!) and Louis de Funes who delivers the comedy. Adapted from the play "Ah, Les Belles Bacchantes." (French with English subtitles) ★★★

Ferngully: The Last Rainforest

(1992, 72 min, US, Bill Kroyer) *Voices of: Robin Williams, Tim Curry, Samantha Mathis, Christian Slater.* Excellent animation and a timely message more than compensate for the relatively weak tale of fairies and humans engaged in a power struggle over the valuable rainforest. The fairies and their friends are happily living in a magical rainforest until the humans, while thoughtlessly cutting down trees, unleash the mysterious, evil monster Hexxus. While oversimplistic, the themes serve to promote ecological awareness at an early age. (Sequel: *Ferngully 2: The Magical Rescue*) ★★★ VHS: $9.99

Ferris Bueller's Day Off

(1986, 103 min, US, John Hughes) *Matthew Broderick, Alan Ruck, Mia Sara, Jeffrey Jones, Jennifer Grey.* Often hilarious Hughes teen comedy with Broderick in great form as a high school student whose charm and ingenuity are able to get him into — and out of — any situation of his choosing. The story follows Bueller and his friends playing hooky and visiting downtown Chicago. ★★★½ VHS: $9.99; DVD: $24.99

A Few Good Men

(1992, 138 min, US, Rob Reiner) *Tom Cruise, Demi Moore, Jack Nicholson, Kevin Pollak, Kiefer Sutherland, Cuba Gooding, Jr., Kevin Bacon.* Cruise's high-octane performance as a cocky but lovable underdog helps energize an already compelling courtroom drama and murder mystery. Cruise plays a Navy lawyer who is chosen to defend two Marines accused of killing a fellow soldier. The question is: Were the two young cadets acting on their own, or were they under orders from a superior officer? As Cruise and fellow lawyers Moore (who is actually fully

clothed here) and Pollak feverishly investigate the killing, they are thwarted by military red tape and uncooperative soldiers at every turn. In a small but pivotal role, Nicholson is the essence of the quintessential military mindset and gives a spellbinding performance as an overzealous commander. ★★★½ VHS: $14.99; DVD: $29.99

ffolkes

(1980, 99 min, GB, Andrew V. McLaglen) *Roger Moore, Anthony Perkins, James Mason.* A surprisingly entertaining high-seas actioner with Perkins chewing the scenery as the leader of a group of terrorists who have taken over a supply ship. Moore, in a playful mood, is the disheveled hero out to stop them. ★★★ VHS: $59.99

Fiddler on the Roof

(1971, 181 min, US, Norman Jewison) *Chaim Topol, Norma Crane, Leonard Frey, Molly Picon.* Magnificent screen version of the smash Broadway musical based on the stories of Sholem Aleichem. Topol plays Tevye the milkman (and he almost makes one forget about Zero Mostel), a poor Jewish husband and father of five who grapples with changing religious and social mores in Czarist Russia. The musical sequences are outstanding, and the classic score includes "If I Were a Rich Man" and "Sunrise, Sunset." ★★★★ VHS: $24.99; DVD: $24.99

The Field

(1990, 110 min, Ireland, Jim Sheridan) *Richard Harris, Brenda Fricker, Tom Berenger, John Hurt, Sean Bean.* Harris' excellent performance dominates this emotionally satisfying, leisurely paced and beautifully filmed story of obsession and murder. Harris plays (appropriately named) Bull McCabe, a poor farmer working the fields of the gorgeous Irish countryside, whose determination and inflexibility towards acquiring a piece of land — one he had been cultivating for decades — leads to tragedy. ★★★½ VHS: $14.99; DVD: $24.99

Field of Dreams

(1989, 106 min, US, Phil Alden Robinson) *Kevin Costner, James Earl Jones, Amy Madigan, Burt Lancaster, Ray Liotta, Frank Whaley, Gaby Hoffmann.* "If you build it, he will come." This is what novice farmer Costner hears in his cornfield one day, accompanied by a vision for him to build a baseball field. Acting on faith alone,

he builds it, and "he" does come, he being the ghost of the great "Shoeless" Joe Jackson. This warm and humorous fantasy is a profoundly moving and magical fable about faith, redemption and our national pastime. An idealistic Costner excels as the farmer; so does Jones as a reclusive, iconoclastic 1960s author who journeys with Costner. This is our generation's *It's a Wonderful Life.* (Letterboxed VHS available for $14.99) ★★★★ VHS: $9.99; DVD: $34.99

Field of Honor

(1988, 87 min, France, Jean-Pierre Denis) *Cris Campion, Eric Wapler.* Set in 1870 France, this subtle but moving drama concerns a naïve farm boy who, as was common at the time, is paid by a rich merchant to take the place of his son in the army. But he is soon disillusioned once he witnesses the horrors of war. (French with English subtitles) ★★★ VHS: $19.99

Fiend without a Face

(1958, 74 min, GB, Arthur Crabtree) *Marshall Thompson, Kim Parker.* Lifting a lesson from the Krell, a scientist using simple everyday objects manages to materialize his thoughts. Unfortunately, he's thinking about brains that crawl around on their spinal cords and suck the mental matter out of the heads of the local villagers who are revolted and revolt. The special effects are surprisingly good, and the film is both very effective and frightening. ★★★ DVD: $39.99

Fierce Creatures

(1997, 98 min, GB,US, Robert Young & Fred Schepisi) *John Cleese, Jamie Lee Curtis, Kevin Kline, Michael Palin.* The cast of 1988's classic *A Fish Called Wanda* reunites for this not-really-a-sequel. The plot concerns a rich Australian tycoon (Kline) who overtakes a British company that controls, among other things, a zoo. Kline also plays the tycoon's oversexed, ne'er-do-well son, and he and the sexy Curtis supervise the promotional overhaul of the zoo, set in motion by the rigid and seemingly animal-hating new director (Cleese). The film has a few clever bits but, ultimately, it's not nearly as funny as *Wanda*, simply because the pitch-black humor and cheerful malevolence of the first film are substituted with cute, family-friendly hijinks. (Letterboxed VHS available for $19.99) ★★½ VHS: $14.99; DVD: $24.99

The Fifth Element

Brad Pitt and Ed Norton in *Fight Club*

The Fifth Element

(1997, 127 min, US, Luc Besson) *Bruce Willis, Gary Oldman, Ian Holm, Milla Jovovich, Chris Tucker, Luke Perry.* Besson's Gallic sensibilities serve him well in this sci-fi near-epic starring Willis as a cab driver who saves the world. Corbin Dallas, a decorated ex-soldier, is called upon to do his duty again when a gigantic, indestructible black flame is discovered to be advancing toward the Earth. Luckily, Corbin has the assistance of the Fifth Element, the Supreme Being of the Universe, a very cute, and very deadly, orange-haired alien (Jovovich). Standing in their way is a weapons magnate (Oldman) with big buck teeth and an accent to rival Foghorn Leghorn's. The effects and overall visual design of the film are stunning. Unfortunately, the story itself does not live up to its look and feel. It succeeds as fantastic popcorn entertainment, but falls short of being a speculative science fiction classic. ★★★ VHS: $14.99; DVD: $29.99

The Fifth Monkey

(1990, 93 min, GB/Brazil, Eric Rochat) *Ben Kingsley.* A lushly photographed though slow-moving version of Jacques Zibi's novel "Le Cinquième Singe." Kingsley plays a peasant animal trader whose discovery of four chimpanzees in the Brazilian wilderness seems to be the answer to his matrimonial money problems. En route through the jungles to sell the animals, however, Kingsley comes up against mercenaries and corrupt officials. ★★

Fifth of July

(1983, 120 min, US, Marshall W. Mason & Kirk Browning) *Richard Thomas, Jeff Daniels, Swoosie Kurtz, Jonathan Hadary.* An extremely well-acted, first-rate adaptation of Lanford Wilson's acclaimed Broadway comedy-drama, with most of the original cast reprising their roles. The show is slightly opened up yet still retains its intimate theatricality. In a splendid performance, Thomas plays a gay schoolteacher and disabled Vietnam vet who faces an emotional crisis upon returning to the classroom. Daniels is his sup-portive lover whose even temper and good will are put to the test when Thomas' college friend Kurtz (who won a Tony Award), a free-spirited and now successful singer, arrives with her entourage for a short stay. As the characters recall the past and face the future, secret passions, betrayals and insecurities are brought to the surface. Wilson's poetic dialogue is funny, tender, intelligent and remarkably assured. ★★★★ VHS: $29.99

55 Days at Peking

(1963, 154 min, US, Nicholas Ray) *Charlton Heston, Ava Gardner, David Niven, Flora Robson, Paul Lukas.* Sprawling, exciting epic about a group of Europeans involved in the Chinese Boxer Rebellion of 1900. ★★★ VHS: $19.99

54

(1998, 96 min, US, Mark Christopher) *Ryan Phillippe, Salma Hayek, Mike Myers, Sela Ward, Breckin Meyer, Neve Campbell, Heather Matarazzo, Michael York, Lauren Hutton.* There's another reason to hate the disco era: writer-director Christopher's *54*, a clichéd morality tale of dance, drugs and redemption. In yet another boy-comes-to-the-big-city plot line, Phillippe stars as Shane, a naïve, good-looking 19-year-old from Jersey City whose dream of getting into Studio 54, the shining star of New York dance clubs, becomes a reality when he becomes employed there. Quicker than you can snort a hit of coke, he's doing drugs and having anonymous sex. As a story of corrupted youth, *54* has little to offer; its limited appeal lies in the peripheral characters who populate the club. Best of these is Myers, who gives an engaging performance as Steve Rubell, 54's owner. He should have been the main focus of the film. ★★ VHS: $14.99; DVD: $29.99

52 Pick-Up

(1986, 114 min, US, John Frankenheimer) *Roy Scheider, Ann-Margret, Vanity, John Glover, Clarence Williams III.* Elmore Leonard's best-selling novel makes for an exciting screen thriller. Scheider plays a successful businessman who takes on a group of blackmailing pornographers. Solid support from Glover as the villainous ringleader. ★★★

Fight Club

(1999, 139 min, US, David Fincher) *Brad Pitt, Edward Norton, Helena Bonham Carter, Meat Loaf, Jared Leto.* A smart and sexy adrenaline rush, the subversive *Fight Club* bids farewell to the old millennium and greets the new as it tears apart the mores and morals of the great, late 20th century. *Seven* director Fincher brings the same kind of gut-level tension that distinguished that film to this nihilistic tale of white, disenfranchised blue-collar men who find emotional release in nightly bareknuckle fighting — but in the form of a vibrant, hyperventilating black comedy. Norton is the Narrator, an angst-ridden businessman whose life dramatically changes when he meets the mysterious Tyler Durden (Pitt). Together they start Fight Club, a movement that catches on like wildfire. Violent and vibrant, the film is a ravaging attack on consumerism and a bloody exercise in machismo, as members beat each other senseless in superbly choreographed fight scenes. But this is a film where not everything is as it appears, and Fincher takes delight in confounding and provoking. Norton and Pitt are excellent, each submerging themselves into their roles with bravado and verve. ★★★½ VHS: $14.99; DVD: $34.99

Fight for Us

(1989, 92 min, The Philippines, Lino Brocka) *Phillip Salvador, Dina Bonnevie.* Filmed clandestinely, director Brocka's stirring drama explores the political chaos and repression in The Philippines after a bloody revolution brings down a dictator only to install an equally corrupt "democracy." Jimmy Cordero is a former priest and dissident freed from jail after Marcos' downfall. He finds his efforts to resume a normal life interrupted when he is forced to confront a group of vigilantes who commit mass murders all in the name of democracy and anti-Communism. His efforts to bring these men to justice and to expose their connection to the government embroils him in a bloody fight that threatens an entire village as well as his wife, friends and children. ★★★ VHS: $79.99

The Filth and the Fury

(2000, 103 min, GB, Julien Temple) *John Lydon, Paul Cook, Sid Vicious, Glen Matlock, Steve Jones, Malcolm McLaren.* The Filth and the Fury opens with newsreel footage of the violent street protests which permeated Great Britain in the late 1970s. It now seems inevitable that the band The Sex Pistols would skyrocket to infamy during this period of profound social unrest. Director Temple has brilliantly documented the period's social chaos with an intimate portrait of the band — delivered with affection and without blinders on. In only 26 months, The Sex Pistols were hired and fired by three major record companies, banned and condemned throughout England, and, in the process of disintegration from internal dissention, broken apart by a junkie whore. As punk is absorbed into the mainstream and shredded fabric held together by safety pins shows up on haute couture runways, The Sex Pistols descend into their final dissolution. A very entertaining documentary for both lovers and haters of punk. ★★★½ VHS: $14.99; DVD: $24.99

Final Analysis

(1992, 124 min, US, Phil Joanou) *Richard Gere, Kim Basinger, Uma Thurman, Eric Roberts, Keith David.* First teamed in *No Mercy,* where they caused very few sparks, Gere and Basinger are together again in this routine but flashy thriller. A low-key Gere plays a successful San Francisco psychiatrist who, faster than you can say "Prince of Tides," becomes involved with a relative of one of his patients. The patient: Thurman, who shows up with new and interesting stories. The relative: Basinger, a beauty who could use a few hours on the couch herself. As Gere becomes spellbound by Basinger, he finds himself caught in a deadly game of cat and mouse between Basinger and her gangster husband Roberts. ★★½ VHS: $9.99; DVD: $14.99

The Final Countdown

(1980, 104 min, US, Don Taylor) *Kirk Douglas, Martin Sheen, Katharine Ross, James Farentino.* Intriguing and imaginative sci-fi outing with Douglas as the commander of an aircraft carrier who is suddenly transported — with his ship and crew — back to the Pacific just days before the Pearl Harbor attack. ★★★

Final Destination

(2000, 93 min, US, James Wong) *Devon Sawa, Ali Larter, Kerr Smith, Kristen Cloke, Daniel Roebuck.* An overacting high-schooler (Sawa) has a premonition that the plane he and his classmates are on will explode. He makes a scene, and is thrown off, along with several of his friends and one teacher. The plane does explode, but Death is unhappy that Sawa has ruined his Design, and proceeds to pick off the survivors one by one. Wong and his cowriter Glen Morgan wrote some of the best episodes of "Millennium" and "The X-Files"; here, despite a very silly but interesting premise, they come up with one or two creepy/funny touches, but basically settle for snooze-inducing teen slasher clichés, dorky "philosophical" discussions, and an idiotic (though, to be fair, studio-imposed) ending. They're capable of much more. ★½ VHS: $14.99; DVD: $24.99

Finders Keepers, Lovers Weepers

(1968, 72 min, US, Russ Meyer) *Ann Chapman, Lavelle Roby, Jan Sinclair.* Inspired by Don Siegel's gangster movies, *Finders Keepers, Lovers Weepers* is about a robbery attempt in a go-go dance bar that gets out of hand. There's a memorable sequence of a couple making love out with a demolition derby. ★★ VHS: $79.99

Finding Forrester

(2000, 136 min, US, Gus Van Sant) *Sean Connery, Rob Brown, F. Murray Abraham, Anna Paquin, Busta Rhymes.* Connery gives a career-topping performance as a brilliant, reclusive writer in this compelling drama from the director of *Good Will Hunting.* Sharing in common with that film the themes of mentorship and academia, *Finding Forrester* follows the friendship of 16-year-old Jamal (Brown), a high-school basketball star with a secret passion for writing, and William Forrester (Connery), a celebrated author who's as famous for his privacy as he is for his artistic output of one (Pulitzer Prize-winning) novel. The touching, often humorous story explores the bond which grows between them, and how each has something to teach the other. Connery

is nothing short of great as the ultimately vulnerable Forrester, shading the writer with just the right mixture of arrogance and anxiety. Young Brown — in his film debut — keeps pace nicely with the seasoned cast around him. ★★★ VHS: $19.99; DVD: $24.99

A Fine Madness

(1966, 104 min, US, Irvin Kershner) *Sean Connery, Joanne Woodward, Jean Seberg, Colleen Dewhurst.* Elliot Baker did a fine adaptation of his own satiric novel, retaining much of its bite and a lot of its slapstick. Taking a break from his role as 007, Connery plays an egocentric poet at odds with the world, including wife Woodward. ★★★ VHS: $14.99

A Fine Mess

(1986, 100 min, US, Blake Edwards) *Ted Danson, Howie Mandel, Richard Mulligan.* Danson and Mandel are two get-rich-quick schemers chased throughout Los Angeles by two petty, inept thieves. Unfortunately, there is nothing worth recommending in this stupid and unfunny comedy. ★ VHS: $19.99

Fingers

(1978, 91 min, US, James Toback) *Harvey Keitel, Jim Brown, Tisa Farrow, Danny Aiello, Michael V. Gazzo.* Gritty Scorsese-esque character study of an aspiring concert pianist (Keitel) who moonlights as a debt collector for his aging mafioso father. Though favorably reviewed upon its initial release, the film failed to receive audience support, and over the years has attained a certain cult status. ★★★ VHS: $29.99

Finian's Rainbow

(1968, 145 min, US, Francis Ford Coppola) *Fred Astaire, Tommy Steele, Petula Clark, Keenan Wynn, Al Freeman, Jr.* Coppola's glossy but rather stilted song-and-dance is based on the Burton Lane—E.Y. Harburg Broadway musical. Astaire, bringing a touch of dignity and immeasurable charm, the scene-stealing Steele, and Clark as Astaire's spirited daughter, star in this story of racism, leprechauns and a stolen crock of gold. ★★½ VHS: $19.99

Finnegan Begin Again

(1984, 112 min, US, Joan Micklin Silver) *Mary Tyler Moore, Robert Preston, Sam Waterston, Sylvia Sydney.* Moore and especially Preston offer strong performances in this delightful made-for-cable movie about the relationship between a sixtysomething newspaper man and a 40-ish schoolteacher. ★★★ VHS: $9.99

Fiorile

(1992, 118 min, Italy, Paolo & Vittorio Taviani) *Michael Vartan, Galatea Ranzi.* A wonderful tale spanning three hundred years in a family's history of unrequited love. A poor farmer's daughter, Fiorile Benedetti, falls in love with a soldier of Napoleon's troops sent to insure safe passage of a chest of gold. While they tryst, her brother finds the gold on the back of a stray mule. Rather than return the gold, the brother keeps it, prompting the French to kill the soldier; which, in turn, leaves Fiorile listless and pregnant. She places a curse on the person who caused her lover to be killed. This sets off the continuation of the theme through every other generation of Benedettis. Sibling rivalry, greed, power and the rest of the expected fare are fea-

tured in this beautifully photographed, sweeping costume drama. (Italian with English subtitles) (aka: *Wildflower*) ★★★ VHS: $19.99

Fire

(1997, 104 min, Canada/India, Deepa Mehta) *Shabana Azmi, Nandita Das.* The newly wed Sita (Das) is a young and beautiful woman who comes to live with her husband's brother and his wife Radha (Azmi) in New Dehli. Restless and independent and realizing that her arranged-marriage husband is far from faithful, Sita quickly finds her new world stifling. The older Radha, on the other hand, offers the face of complacency, all the while holding within her rage and loneliness. Within this volatile atmosphere the two women strike up a natural friendship which leads to smoldering passions and a sensual but secretive romance. Mehta has created a taut, brave and invigorating love story that challenges the place of women in Indian society. (Filmed in English) ★★★½ VHS: $29.99; DVD: $29.99

Fire and Ice

(1983, 83 min, US, Ralph Bakshi) This animated sword & sorcery film is many cuts above its live-action brethren thanks to a fine script from ace comic writers Roy Thomas and Gerry Conway, striking graphic designs by Frank Frazetta, and powerful animation by Bakshi. ★★★

Fire Down Below

(1957, 116 min, US, Robert Parrish) *Jack Lemmon, Robert Mitchum, Rita Hayworth, Herbert Lom, Anthony Newley.* Solid performances from Lemmon and Mitchum and the particularly hypnotic presence of Hayworth barely compensate for the wooden direction from Parrish in what should have been a rollicking scorcher of a movie. Refugee Hayworth has no papers. Seafaring buddies Lemmon and Mitchum are paid to smuggle her from one Carribean island to another. During the voyage, both fall for her. Hard. ★★½ VHS: $19.99

Fire Down Below

(1997, 103 min, US, Felix Enriquez Alcala) *Steven Seagal, Marg Helgenberger, Kris Kristofferson, Harry Dean Stanton, Randy Travis.* If Dylan could go electric, why can't Seagal go country? Well, Seagal does go country in this, the monosyllabic martial arts maven's second ecological action-er. It's actually not intolerable, especially if you like to see some ornery hillbilly ass kicked by the often silent-but-deadly Seagal. He's an EPA agent sent to Kentucky to find out who killed a former compadre who discovers that the environment is being polluted by Kristofferson, a good ol' boy tycoon. This is decent genre fodder, until the end when the pony-tailed palooka makes like Superman and Al Gore at the same time, getting all political about the hazards of pollution. Didn't he get all that out of his system in his laughable *On Deadly Ground?* ★★ VHS: $9.99; DVD: $19.99

Fire in the Sky

(1993, 111 min, US, Robert Lieberman) *Robert Patrick, D.B. Sweeney, James Garner, Peter Berg, Craig Sheffer, Henry Thomas.* In a small Southwestern town, five loggers report the disappearance of their coworker. But what has the police and community up in arms is their story — that he was abducted by a UFO. Based on an actual sighting, *Fire in the Sky* is a surprisingly engrossing and credible recounting of the young man's story and the dilemma faced by his friends. The film's success is due in large part to its focus on the community and its reactions to the alleged event. Well-crafted and nicely acted by a strong cast, this underrated and unexpectedly engaging film is worth checking out by skeptics and believers alike. The scenes aboard the spacecraft are particularly effective. ★★★ VHS: $19.99

Fire over England
(1937, 89 min, GB, William K. Howard) *Laurence Olivier, Flora Robson, Vivien Leigh, Leslie Banks, Raymond Massey, James Mason.* A handsomely produced costume epic set during the 1500s British-Spanish naval conflict, *Fire over England* is a forcefully acted, well-written historical drama highlighted by the outstanding performance by Robson as Queen Elizabeth. Though stagey in parts, the action moves swiftly as the story follows British loyalist Olivier trying to uncover an assassination plot on the queen, eventually being sent to Spain to impersonate a traitor. A young and vibrant Leigh plays one of the queen's ladies who is in love with Olivier. Both give sincere portrayals which hint at the greatness to come; though it is Robson as the willful, self-pitying but ever-commanding monarch who anchors the film. ★★★ VHS: $19.99

The Fire Within (Le Feu Follet)
(1963, 104 min, France, Louis Malle) *Maurice Ronet, Lena Skerla.* Stylish photography — perfectly capturing the "Swinging Paris" so familiar in the New Wave films of Godard, Truffaut and Rivette — is contrasted with an austere, melancholy account of a young man's final 48 hours in this, one of Malle's best works. Alain (Ronet), a handsome man of about thirty, is a recovering alcoholic about to release himself from a clinic. Disinterested in his former lifestyle as a bon vivant, and infused with an existential angst, he seeks out his friends in a dispirited attempt in finding some reason to live. A serious, somber drama of emptiness, regret and lost love. (French with English subtitles) ★★★½ VHS: $29.99

Vivien Leigh in *Fire over England*

Firefox
(1982, 124 min, US, Clint Eastwood) *Clint Eastwood, Freddie Jones, Nigel Hawthorne.* Eastwood's lukewarm espionage thriller concerns a retired U.S. pilot who sneaks behind Russian lines to steal their latest MiG. The film is peppered with occasional sparks of high-flying action and, despite its plodding pace, provides some entertaining moments. ★★ VHS: $14.99

Firelight
(1998, 104 min, GB/France, William Nicholson) *Sophie Marceau, Stephen Dillane, Kevin Anderson, Joss Ackland, Lia Williams.* A predictable, barely fresh story of passion's power which manages to involve nonetheless. A Swiss woman, Elizabeth, is paid to surrogate a child for a secretive wealthy Englishman, Charles. Of course, during the fun part of their "transaction," sparks begin flying and they fall in love. However, circumstances dictate they must part, and the baby is shipped off. Seven years later, Elizabeth tracks her child — Louisa, a spoiled brat from hell, whom daddy merrily enables. Elizabeth then becomes the child's governess, and soon old feelings are reignited. There's little grit or grime in the story telling, which could have been used to avoid the Hallmarkesque atmosphere. An ultimately average period piece. ★★ VHS: $19.99

Fireman's Ball
(1967, 73 min, Czechoslovakia, Milos Forman) *Vaclav Stockel, Josef Svet.* Forman aims his satiric wit at Slavic bureaucracy in this, one of his earliest films. The setting is a ball honoring an aged fire chief, but he is quickly forgotten and it gives way to a torrent of disasters, including one of the funniest and most wonderfully demoralizing beauty contests ever conceived. (Czech with English subtitles) ★★★ VHS: $29.99

Fires on the Plain (Nobi)
(1959, 105 min, Japan, Kon Ichikawa) *Eiji Funakoshi, Osamu Takizawa.* This hard-hitting antiwar outcry revolves around the retreat of a group of Japanese soldiers in the Philippines during WWII. Hiding in the hills, the soldiers must resort to cannibalism in order to survive. A harrowing, depressing and graphic account of the horrors of war. (Japanese with English subtitles) ★★★ VHS: $29.99

Fires Within
(1991, 90 min, US, Gillian Armstrong) *Jimmy Smits, Greta Scacchi, Vincent D'Onofrio.* Smits and Scacchi score high marks based on sex-appeal quotient with this slow-moving though compelling romantic love triangle set against the backdrop of political imprisonment and social injustice. Having just been released from eight years of prison in Castro's Cuba, Smits joins his family in Miami only to find that his wife (Scacchi) has become involved with a local (D'Onofrio) and his young daughter cannot remember him. In his struggle to assimilate and win back his family's love, Smits finds he must choose between his new life and the old comrades of his homeland. ★★½ VHS: $14.99

Firestarter
(1984, 115 min, US, Mark Lester) *George C. Scott, Drew Barrymore, Martin Sheen, Louise Fletcher, Art*

Carney. Scott and Barrymore strike sparks in this Stephen King horror story about a little girl who can induce a conflagration through mere thought. ★★½ VHS: $9.99; DVD: $29.99

Firestorm
(1998, 89 min, US, Dean Semler) *Howie Long, Scott Glenn, Suzy Amis, William Forsythe.* This moronic trash exemplifies Hollywood's contempt for action fans. Ex-NFL star Long plays a gung-ho firefighter who must battle a raging forest fire and the prison-breaking convicts who started it as a cover for their escape. After a hilariously idiotic opening rescue scene, *Firestorm* becomes *so* ludicrous that it ceases to be even unintentionally amusing. The action scenes are listless, the dialogue despicable, and the comic relief just plain sad. Long is akin to a live-action Dudley DoRight. ★ VHS: $9.99; DVD: $24.99

Fireworks (Hana-Bi)
(1998, 103 min, Japan, Takeshi Kitano) *Takeshi Kitano, Ren Osugi, Kayoko Kishimoto.* The Japanese cryptogram for "fireworks" contains the symbol for "flower" and the symbol for "fire"; creation and destruction, an apt metaphor for this action-packed chamber piece of three people searching for a "furious peace." While visiting his dying wife in the hospital, a tough detective (played with Rayband stoicism by writer-director Kitano) escapes an ambush of his partners by a gang of ruthless criminals. Now he must find justice and redemption for sins he did not commit yet that haunt him still. By choosing to tell a tale as familiar as a Noh play, Kitano is free to concentrate on the characters, slowly revealing their scarred souls in a exhilarating, non-linear fashion, letting images play off one another in a uniquely cinematic, pyrotechnic display. A bad-boy filmmaker/actor/pop icon known as "Beat" in his native Japan, Kitano displays an uncanny ability to mix action, comedy and attitude; his film has style to spare. (Japanese with English subtitles) ★★★½ VHS: $29.99; DVD: $29.99

The Firm
(1993, 153 min, US, Sydney Pollack) *Tom Cruise, Gene Hackman, Jeanne Tripplehorn, Holly Hunter, Ed Harris, Wilford Brimley, Hal Holbrook, David Strathairn, Gary Busey.* In this exciting adaptation of John Grisham's best-selling novel of corporate intrigue, Cruise plays a Harvard law graduate who accepts a golden opportunity job with an upscale Memphis firm. However, Cruise soon learns all is not as it appears when the Orwellian company not only has a firm grasp on his life, but may have even murdered employees. *The Firm* is a constant source of pulse-pounding suspense, and benefits greatly from an outstanding ensemble cast. Hackman heads this group as a seasoned lawyer who takes Cruise under his wing, and the shimmering Hunter is a helpful and wily secretary. Director Pollack keeps the action at a brisk pace which belies the two-and-a-half-hour running time. ★★★½ VHS: $14.99; DVD: $29.99

First Blood
(1982, 97 min, US, Ted Kotcheff) *Sylvester Stallone, Brian Dennehy, David Caruso, Richard Crenna.* The film that introduced Rambo. Stallone plays an ex-Green Beret who is falsely arrested by small town authorities (led by

Dennehy); he exacts his revenge in particularly violent ways. Though it's not saying much, this mindless, violent actioner is the "best" of the trilogy. (Letterboxed VHS available for $14.99) (Sequel: *Rambo: First Blood Pt. 2*) ★★ VHS: $9.99; DVD: $19.99

The First Deadly Sin

(1980, 112 min, US, Brian G. Hutton) *Frank Sinatra, Faye Dunaway, Brenda Vaccaro, David Dukes, James Whitmore.* Sinatra stars as a New York City police detective trying to uncover a serial killer while at the same time trying to cope with his wife's impending death. Dunaway plays his bedridden spouse. Too sluggish to be an interesting action film and too convoluted to be of interest as a thriller. ★★ VHS: $14.99; DVD: $14.99

...First Do No Harm

(1996, 94 min, US, Jim Abrahams) *Meryl Streep, Fred Ward, Seth Adkins.* A middle-class couple's (Streep, Ward) emotional and economic hardships when faced with the news that their youngest son has epilepsy is at the center of this earnest, moving made-for-TV drama. At first, the family is able to offer one another support and everything seems fine on the surface, but when Ward's health insurance is discontinued, tensions rise. While it occasionally conforms to its TV "disease of the week" roots, this is believable and well made, helped immeasurably by the Ward, Streep and young Adkins as the young boy, whose realistic performance makes the seizures especially wrenching. An effectively somber yet hopeful drama. ★★★ VHS: $19.99

First Family

(1980, 104 min, US, Buck Henry) *Bob Newhart, Madeline Kahn, Gilda Radner, Rip Torn, Julie Harris, Harvey Korman.* Henry wrote and directed this aimless political satire about a time in our not-too-distant future (perhaps even in your lifetime) when we have an ineffectual president (Newhart), with a dipsomaniac first lady (Kahn) and a promiscuous daughter (Radner), and his funny adventures with that ever-wacky Third World. ★★ VHS: $14.99

First Kid

(1996, 101 min, US, David Mickey) *Sinbad, Brock Pierce, Robert Guillaume, Timothy Busfield, James Naughton, Zachary Ty Bryan.* A mildly amusing family comedy, *First Kid* is sort of a *Guarding Tess* for the prepubescent set. Sinbad plays a Secret Service agent who wants to guard the president. But he's assigned to the commander-in-chief's bratty, trouble-making adolescent son instead. The film manages to produce a few laughs at the expense of Sinbad and his efforts to hide his charge's mischievous nature. But a lot of time is also spent on the youth's self-pitying, which would bore even its target audience. ★★ VHS: $19.99

First Knight

(1995, 132 min, US, Jerry Zucker) *Sean Connery, Richard Gere, Julia Ormond, Ben Cross, John Gielgud.* With *First Knight*, one actually gets two movies in one sitting. The first is the familiar though nicely played story of King Arthur (played with gusto by Connery) and his reign at Camelot, fighting evil knights for the sake of queen and country. The second concentrates on the love story between Lancelot and

Guinevere — and it's a preposterous one at that. Gere stars as Lancelot, and his knight is a swaggering *Yankee in King Arthur's Court* who acts more like Fred Astaire pursuing Ginger Rogers than a man burnt by the embers of love. Set against an impressive evocative backdrop, it's still not quite enough to offset Gere's miscasting and an uneven screenplay. ★★½ VHS: $9.99; DVD: $19.99

First Love

(1970, 90 min, GB, Maximilian Schell) *Maximilian Schell, Dominique Sanda, John Moulder-Brown.* Based on a story by Russian novelist Ivan Turgenev, this lyrical drama — photographed by Sven Nykvist — features a very attractive love interest in Sanda and Moulder-Brown. Set in a Russian dacha during the calm before World War I, the story involves a teenager's (Moulder-Brown) first love with the lovely yet bedeviling daughter of an impoverished and eccentric old woman who moves in next door. Our lovesick young man's attempts to capture her interest are thrown into confusion when he discovers that she is his father's mistress! The excitement, pain and mystery of young love are captured in this Barry Levinson–produced film. ★★★ VHS: $49.99

First Love Last Rites

(1998, 94 min, US, Jesse Peretz) *Natasha Gregson Wagner, Giovanni Ribisi, Donal Logue, Robert John Burke.* Ribisi and Wagner are young lovers who, after some arousing sex scenes, start to finally learn about each other. And what could be more terrifying than learning that her dad is Robocop 3? *First Love Last Rites* attempts to build drama out of eel fishing, a mysterious rat, and a woman who has such winning lines as "You've got such long eyelashes; they remind me of my dog." At least he has good taste in music; a toy record player in his pad is always spinning Shudder To Think 45s. Wagner continues to prove that while beauty is inherited, talent is not. Ribisi has something going on, however, from his nervous little laugh to his fleeting full frontal. Still, the distinct lack of significant events makes this a snoozer. ★★ VHS: $79.99

First Men in the Moon

(1964, 103 min, GB, Nathan Juran) *Lionel Jeffries, Edward Judd, Martha Hyer.* Master stop-motion animator Ray Harryhausen adapts H.G. Wells' speculative novel to his own needs adding lots of grasshopper-like moonmen, giant slug-cows and huge underground factories. Jeffries gives an amusing performance as the bumbling scientist, as does Judd as his unwilling compatriot. ★★★ VHS: $14.99

First Name: Carmen

(1983, 87 min, France/Switzerland, Jean-Luc Godard) *Maruschka Detmers, Jacques Bonnaffe, Jean-Luc Godard.* This deconstructionist version of Merimee's classic tale finds Godard, loopy and pithy as ever, transforming the gypsy femme fatale into a filmmaker-cum-bank-robbing-revolutionary whose politics aren't nearly as well developed as her libidinal urges. Joseph is the befuddled bank guard who is captivated by her sexual charms in the midst of a botched heist. Offering his asides and snide observations is her uncle, a washed-up fraud of a film director named Jean-Luc Godard, played with understated conviction by Godard himself!

(French with English subtitles) ★★★ VHS: $19.99; DVD: $19.99

The First Power

(1990, 99 min, US, Robert Resnikoff) *Lou Diamond Phillips, Tracy Griffith, Mykelti Williamson.* Lackluster horror film offers little in chills or originality as L.A. cop Phillips is up against the spirit of a recently executed murderer. ★ VHS: $14.99; DVD: $14.99

The First Wives Club

(1996, 102 min, US, Hugh Wilson) *Bette Midler, Goldie Hawn, Diane Keaton, Maggie Smith, Sarah Jessica Parker, Dan Hedaya, Stephen Collins, Victor Garber.* If Hell hath no fury like a woman scorned, then the three divas of comedy hath more than their fair share of fun in *The First Wives Club*, a funny, spirited romp which postulates that revenge is not only sweet but profitable. With not an ego in sight, Midler, Hawn and Keaton play former college roommates who are reunited after 25 years when a friend commits suicide. Sharing in common insensitive, philandering ex-husbands, they form a bond (and later a company) to get even with their not-so-better halves. Based on Olivia Goldsmith's best-seller, the buoyant screenplay mixes physical comedy with sharp one-liners which fire bullets into the body-bag residue of male-female relationships. Midler, Hawn and Keaton ignite the film with sparkling energy and wit. ★★★ VHS: $9.99; DVD: $24.99

A Fish Called Wanda

(1988, 108 min, GB, Charles Crichton) *Kevin Kline, Jamie Lee Curtis, John Cleese, Michael Palin.* What happens when two scheming American jewel thieves join forces with a pair of double-crossing British thugs? All hell breaks loose, that's what. This slapdash, high-speed comedy is certainly one of the funniest film of the 1980s. Cleese is wonderful as an uptight barrister who inadvertently gets tangled in the mess. Palin has some very funny scenes as the bumbling, stuttering sidekick, and Curtis simply enchants as the manipulative American bombshell. But the laurels go to Oscar winner Kline, who, as Curtis' psychotic boyfriend ("Don't call me stupid"), climbs all over the screen in one of the finest comic performances in years. A fabulously entertaining caper comedy featuring a wickedly funny running gag about some very unlucky dogs. ★★★½ VHS: $9.99; DVD: $14.99

The Fisher King

(1991, 138 min, US, Terry Gilliam) *Jeff Bridges, Robin Williams, Mercedes Ruehl, Amanda Plummer, Michael Jeter.* Gilliam's magical fable for modern times is an original and delightful masterwork complete with love, desperation and redemption. A hypnotic and exceptionally funny parable, the film stars Bridges as a hotshot D.J. whose world collapses when he feels responsible for a restaurant shooting. A few years later, he finds possible salvation in the form of street person Williams, a former professor whose wife was killed in the slayings. In a quest worthy of the Holy Grail, Bridges sets out to make amends for the two lives touched by the tragedy. Williams gives one of his best performances, demonstrated vulnerability and tenderness. Bridges, in a very subdued role, is equally impressive and Oscar-winner Ruehl is smashing as his lusty girlfriend. ★★★★ VHS: $9.99; DVD: $29.99

F

Richard Gere and Sean Connery in *First Knight*

A Fistful of Dollars

(1964, 96 min, Italy, Sergio Leone) *Clint Eastwood, Gian Marie Volante.* The first of Leone's "spaghetti westerns" is an exciting and entertaining working of Kurosawa's *Yojimbo*. Eastwood became a star thanks to his role as the "Man with No Name," a mysterious stranger who gets involved in a feud between two rival families. ★★★ VHS: $14.99; DVD: $14.99

A Fistful of Dynamite

(1971, 138 min, Italy, Sergio Leone) *James Coburn, Rod Steiger, Romolo Valli.* Coburn stars in this high-voltage war adventure as an Irish terrorist who hooks up with peasant Steiger during the Mexican Revolution. (aka: *Duck You Sucker*) ★★★ VHS: $14.99

Fitzcarraldo

(1982, 157 min, West Germany, Werner Herzog) *Klaus Kinski, Claudia Cardinale.* Herzog chronicles the bizarre history of a strong-willed visionary whose dream is to construct an opera house in the heart of the Peruvian jungle. A beguiling tale laced with the director's usual dose of mysticism and madness and featuring yet another appropriately lunatic performance by Herzog favorite Kinski in the title role. (Letterboxed) ★★★★ VHS: $19.99; DVD: $34.99

Five Card Stud

(1968, 103 min, US, Henry Hathaway) *Robert Mitchum, Dean Martin, Inger Stevens, Roddy McDowall.* A tame western adventure with Martin as a gunslinger (and part-time gambler) investigating the murders of the members of a lynch gang. ★★ VHS: $9.99

Five Corners

(1988, 98 min, US, Tony Bill) *Tim Robbins, Jodie Foster, John Turturro, Elizabeth Berridge, Todd Graff.* With plot developments as capricious as life itself, this story of five teenagers living in the Bronx in 1964 is writer John Patrick Shanley's follow-up to *Moonstruck*. Turturro gives a standout performance as a psychotic ex-con whose infatuation with Foster leads to an evening of tragedy. ★★★ VHS: $14.99

Five Days One Summer

(1983, 108 min, US, Fred Zinnemann) *Sean Connery, Betsy Brantley.* Connery plays a middle-aged doctor vacationing in a remote Swiss village in the early 1930s. There he is accompanied by a young woman (Brantley), who is posing as his wife. However, as their relationship is explored, their dark secrets soon surface. This soap opera is set at a lethargic pace, and even Connery can't make you feel for the characters' plight. ★★ VHS: $14.99

Five Easy Pieces

(1970, 98 min, US, Bob Rafelson) *Jack Nicholson, Karen Black, Lois Smith, Susan Anspach.* This fascinating character study follows an aimless drifter who abandons the accoutrements of middle-class existence (and a promising musical career) for a life on the road spent amongst the squalor of cheap bars and shabby motels. Nicholson gives a virtuoso, career-making performance, and Black and especially Smith as Nicholson's sister are outstanding in support. ★★★★ VHS: $9.99; DVD: $24.99

Five Fingers

(1952, 108 min, US, Joseph L. Mankiewicz) *James Mason, Michael Rennie, Danielle Darrieux.* The allegedly true story of how the Nazis came upon the plans for the Allied's Normandy invasion makes for a riveting and witty spy story which forgoes cloak and dagger in favor of an intelligent character study. Mason is excellent as the suave valet to a high-ranking British diplomat who finances his planned retirement by selling secrets to the Germans. Rennie is the agent on his trail. A complex tale of espionage which explores class differences as well, *Five Fingers* has not one but two great twists at its exciting finale. ★★★★ VHS: $19.99

Five Graves to Cairo

(1943, 96 min, US, Billy Wilder) *Franchot Tone, Anne Baxter, Akim Tamiroff, Erich von Stroheim.* With a wit and style usually not associated with WWII dramas, director Wilder has crafted a suspenseful espionage tale that is at once taut and relaxed. Tone stars as a British corporal who is stranded in the North African desert.

Stumbling upon a hotel run by Tamiroff and Baxter, he is forced to impersonate a German agent when Field Marshal Rommel arrives in his push towards Cairo. Von Stroheim ably plays Rommel as a blustery, egocentric militarist. Tone is quite affable as an ordinary man thrust into danger — he would have been quite at home in *The 39 Steps* or *The Lady Vanishes*. In fact, Wilder's splendid blend of action, humor and intrigue is very Hitchcockian — though Wilder's celebrated cynicism was firmly taking root, and his gift for dialogue distinguishes the film. ★★★½ VHS: $14.99

The Five Heartbeats

(1991, 122 min, US, Robert Townsend) *Robert Townsend, Michael Wright, Tico Wells, Diahann Carroll.* Townsend's flavorful but uneven musical drama is about the rise and fall of a black singing group in the 1960s. Townsend, who wrote the screenplay with Keenan Ivory Wayans, plays the group's leader and songwriter, who takes The Five Heartbeats from obscurity to stardom. There are many fine moments, especially the musical sequences, which have an indestructible energy; but some of the film's dramatic scenes are heavy-handed and border on music industry cliché. ★★½ VHS: $19.99

The 5,000 Fingers of Dr. T

(1953, 88 min, US, Roy Rowland) *Peter Lind Hayes, Hans Conreid.* Dr. Seuss wrote this imaginative and unusual children's entertainment about a young boy (Hayes) who fantasizes that his piano teacher (Conreid) is really the diabolical Dr. T., who kidnaps and imprisons youths, forcing them to participate in daily piano rehearsals. Clever set designs, wild choreography and an abundance of youthful escapades make this curiosity all the more intriguing. ★★★ VHS: $14.99; DVD: $24.99

Flamenco

(1997, 100 min, Spain, Carlos Saura) *Joaquin Cortes, Paco de Lucia, Lole y Manuel, Farruco.* As he proved with his trilogy *Blood Wedding, Carmen,* and *El Amor Brujo,* director Saura is the undisputed master of filming flamenco. This new documentary, which showcases the music and dance of Spain, will thrill fans of his work as well as those viewers interested in watching this stunning art form. Through 20 episodes, musicians play guitar in silhouette while singers and dancers perform various bulerias. While the fast-paced clapping and clacking of heels is mesmerizing, some of the slower numbers may cause viewers to fidget. Nevertheless, the dazzling costumes and expressive faces of the performers will keep viewers attentive. ★★★ VHS: $29.99

The Flamingo Kid

(1984, 98 min, US, Garry Marshall) *Matt Dillon, Hector Elizondo, Richard Crenna, Jessica Walter.* Dillon is well-cast in this endearing teen comedy about a Brooklyn high school grad who takes a summer job at an exclusive Long Island club. The film abandons the usual sex-obsessed hijinks of most teen comedies, opting instead for a surprisingly sweet reminiscence of the times. An excellent supporting cast includes Elizondo as Dillon's dad, Walter as a snobbish patron, and, in a dynamic performance, Crenna as an unscrupulous car salesman whose influence on the naïve Dillon proves to be an eye-opener. ★★★ VHS: $14.99; DVD: $14.99

Flamingo Road

(1949, 94 min, US, Michael Curtiz) *Joan Crawford, Zachary Scott, Sydney Greenstreet.* Crawford gives one of her better performances in this highly entertaining melodrama which skewers small town Americana and the political process. Crawford plays a carnival dancer who becomes stranded in Smalltown, USA. There, she falls in love with the town deputy (Scott), but the sheriff and town boss (the ever-evil Greenstreet) have other ideas. When the latter frames Joan and sends her to prison, it's get-even time when Joan is released. Crawford suffers gallantly, and is ever-ready with the next witty barb. ★★★ VHS: $19.99

Flash Gordon

(1980, 110 min, US, Mike Hodges) *Sam J. Jones, Melody Anderson, Max von Sydow, Topol, Timothy Dalton, Mariangela Melato, Ornella Muti, Brian Blessed.* Though this updated sci-fi adventure failed to set a spark at the box office, it's a guaranteed fun ride as football hero Flash Gordon (Jones) and reporter Dale Arden (Anderson) travel to the planet Mongo with Dr. Zarkov (Topol) to stop the destruction of Earth at the hands of evil emperor Ming (the Merciless, that is), played with great relish by von Sydow. Features splendid sets and costumes, good special effects and a wonderful comic touch to the action. Score by Queen. ★★★ VHS: $9.99

A Flash of Green

(1985, 122 min, US, Victor Nunez) *Ed Harris, Blair Brown, Richard Jordan, John Glover.* In this compassionate tale of corruption and greed, an investigative journalist (Harris) becomes involved in a local real estate dispute between a corrupt politician and a homeowner. ★★★

Flashback

(1990, 108 min, US, Franco Amurri) *Dennis Hopper, Kiefer Sutherland, Carol Kane, Richard Masur.* Hopper makes the most of his role as a '60s fugitive captured by the FBI in this slight comedy. It's Hopper's show all the way, actually, as he plays an Abbie Hoffman–like radical who is being transported by uptight agent Sutherland. It's sort of a poor man's *Midnight Run* with a political flavor as Hopper continually outwits his guardian till each discovers a respect for the other. ★★½ VHS: $14.99

Flashdance

(1983, 96 min, US, Adrian Lyne) *Jennifer Beals, Michael Nouri, Belinda Bauer, Lilia Skala.* Gnash your teeth if you will, but there's no denying this film's impact on Hollywood and pop culture (not to mention the welding industry). You certainly didn't find torn sweatshirts at Bloomie's before. In spite of its stilted plot, *Flashdance* is a viscerally entertaining musical with imaginative dance routines and a pulsating score. C'mon now, "What a feeling." ★★ VHS: $14.99

Flawless

(1999, 110 min, US, Joel Schumacher) *Robert De Niro, Philip Seymour Hoffman, Barry Miller, Joey Arias, Jackie Beat.* Flawless might be better titled *Shameless* for its story rips-off *Outrageous!* and *The Queen.* Director Schumacher takes a true incident that happened to a friend of his and turns it

into a second-rate melodrama, complete with stereotypes and ridiculous subplot. De Niro is Walt, a retired security guard living in the same run-down East Village building as Rusty, a flamboyant drag queen. When Walt suffers a stroke that partially paralyzes his speech, he takes singing lessons from Rusty to strengthen his vocal cords. As expertly played by Hoffman, Rusty is a larger-than-life, line-quoting, all-out drag queen who doesn't seem to stop "being on" for a minute. But his performance isn't quite enough to compensate for all the clichés, misguided sincerity and the eventual tacky run-in with small-time crooks. ★★ VHS: $14.99; DVD: $24.99

Fled

(1996, 98 min, US, Kevin Hooks) *Laurence Fishburne, Stephen Baldwin, Will Patton, Salma Hayek, Robert Hooks.* A low-rent knock-off of *The Defiant Ones*, Fled pits a black and white man against each other, both of whom are escaped convicts and handcuffed together. But wait — this isn't an old boring examination of moral conflict or a complex story of two men grappling with prejudice and inner pain. This is an action movie. Set in the high-tech '90s. Where computer software replaces human interest. Fishburne is saddled with dopey Baldwin, together fleeing police and mysterious underworld figures on their trail. They bicker, they argue, they fight, they fall down a lot — they do everything but walk into the sunset together. ★★ VHS: $102.99; DVD: $14.99

Flesh

(1968, 89 min, US, Paul Morrissey) *Joe Dallesandro, Candy Darling, Jackie Curtis, Patti D'Arbanville, Maurice Braddell.* A true artifact of the '60s sexual revolution as well as a great example of the quirky New York independent filmmaking that came out of the Warhol film factory. The film is an homage to the personality and body (with the emphasis on body) of Dallesandro. The plot is simply a day in the life of gay hustler Joe, who utters immortal lines such as, "How am I going to make any money without clean underwear!" The story is told in vignettes and features old Warholian favorites Darling and Curtis. There are priceless drug-induced dialogues throughout including the great philosophical thought, "The more you learn the more depressed you get." ★★★ VHS: $19.99; DVD: $24.99

Flesh & Blood

(1985, 126 min, The Netherlands, Paul Verhoeven) *Rutger Hauer, Jennifer Jason Leigh, Tom Burlinson, Susan Tyrrell, Jack Thompson, Bruno Kirby.* Given a big budget for the first time, Verhoeven weaves a colorful, erotic and gritty story of a rag-tag group of mercenary soldiers during Europe's feudal wars. This rowdy adventure tale lives up to its title and fascinates us with battles at castle gates, treacherous kings and princesses in distress. Don't miss this one. (Filmed in English) ★★★½

Flesh and Bone

(1993, 124 min, US, Steve Kloves) *Dennis Quaid, Meg Ryan, James Caan, Gwyneth Paltrow, Scott Wilson.* From its intense opening sequence to its haunting end, *Flesh and Bone* manages to be stylish and suspenseful without being flashy or shocking. Quaid is mesmerizing as a lonely Texas vending-machine suppli-

er whose dark past suddenly sneaks up on him. As in his first film, *The Fabulous Baker Boys*, writer-director Kloves frames his eye just below the surface of the ordinary to reveal secret things we wish we hadn't seen. Paltrow gives a delightfully droll and dangerous performance. ★★★ VHS: $19.99

Flesh and the Devil

(1926, 95 min, US, Clarence Brown) *Greta Garbo, John Gilbert, Lars Hanson.* Garbo gives a seductive performance in her first American film as a beautiful schemer who comes between life-long friends Gilbert and Hanson. Garbo and Gilbert are an inspired romantic duo. ★★½ VHS: $29.99

Flesh for Frankenstein

See: Andy Warhol's Frankenstein

Flesh Gordon

(1974, 90 min, US, Howard Ziehm & Michael Benveniste) *Jason Williams, Suzanne Fields, Joseph Hudgins, William Hunt, John Hoyt.* Flesh and his companions Prince Precious and Dr. Jerkoff explore the inner and outer regions of space. Late-nite cult fun which parodies the story's sci-fi origins, and includes lots of sex and cheesy sets and F/X. ★★ VHS: $29.99; DVD: $29.99

Fletch

(1985, 98 min, US, Michael Ritchie) *Chevy Chase, Tim Matheson, Geena Davis, M. Emmet Walsh, George Wendt.* This may be Chase's funniest screen comedy. Chevy plays an investigative reporter who, while undercover, is offered $50,000 by a millionaire (Matheson) to murder him. Plenty of sharp dialogue and Chase is very funny. (Sequel: *Fletch Lives*) ★★★ VHS: $9.99; DVD: $24.99

Fletch Lives

(1989, 95 min, US, Michael Ritchie) *Chevy Chase, Hal Holbrook, Cleavon Little, R. Lee Ermey.* In this surprisingly funny sequel, Chase returns as the glib, wise-cracking reporter Fletch who here travels to the heart of Dixie when he inherits an old Southern mansion. There, he quickly becomes involved with the Klan, toxic waste, a TV evangelist, and murder. Chase can deliver a put-down with the best of them, and his impersonations of an array of characters are quite amusing. ★★★ VHS: $9.99

A Flight of Rainbirds

(1981, 94 min, The Netherlands, Ate de Jong) *Jeroen Krabbé.* From the director of *Drop Dead Fred* and *Highway to Hell* comes this serio-comedy about love, sex and religion. Reportedly one of the highest grossing films in Dutch history, *A Flight of Rainbirds* stars Krabbé in dual roles. In one, he is a timid and repressed scientist who one night dreams that he must lose his virginity in seven days or die. His more debonair alter ego is hence forced to come to the rescue. (Dutch with English subtitles) ★★½ VHS: $29.99

The Flight of the Eagle

(1982, 139 min, Sweden, Jan Troell) *Max von Sydow, Goran Stangertz.* This Swedish epic by Troell chronicles the brave but foolhardy trek of several men who attempt a balloon mission to the North Pole in 1897. Von Sydow heads the group, who are stranded in the frozen North and are confronted with eerie silence and the very real possibility that they will not survive. A gripping existential drama. (Swedish with English subtitles) ★★★

Flight of the Innocent

(1993, 105 min, Italy, Carlo Carlei) *Manuci Colao, Francesca Neri*. When a loving 10-year-old boy witnesses the murder of his entire gangster family by a rival crime syndicate, the stage is set for this edge-of-your-seat, run-for-your-life thriller that marks the auspicious debut of director Carlei. While inarguably the best foreign actioner to come out of Europe since *La Femme Nikita*, the film also merits strong praise as an art film for its masterful juxtaposition of gorgeous dreamlike imagery with scenes of horrendous violence reminiscent of Peckinpah at his peak. Young Colao gives a striking performance as the boy evading both the mob and the police. (Italian with English subtitles) ★★★★ VHS: $19.99

Flight of the Intruder

(1991, 115 min, US, John Milius) *Danny Glover, Willem Dafoe, Brad Johnson, Rosanna Arquette, Tom Sizemore*. Vietnam War adventure film with Glover as a Navy commander saddled with hotshot pilots Johnson and Dafoe, who disobey orders and fight the enemy in the way they think they should be fought. Plays like a right-wing fantasy, and a boring one, at that. ★ VHS: $14.99

Flight of the Navigator

(1986, 90 min, US, Randal Kleiser) *Veronica Cartwright, Joey Cramer, Cliff de Young; Voice of: Paul Reubens*. Enjoyable if lightweight science-fiction tale about a 12-year-old boy (Cramer) who is kidnapped by an alien spacecraft and accidentally returned — unchanged — eight years later. ★★½

The Flight of the Phoenix

(1965, 147 min, US, Robert Aldrich) *James Stewart, Richard Attenborough, Peter Finch, Ian Bannen, Hardy Kruger, Ernest Borgnine*. First-rate adventure film about a group of plane crash survivors stranded in the Sahara Desert. Stewart heads a good cast. ★★★½ VHS: $19.99

The Flintstones

(1994, 92 min, US, Brian Levant) *John Goodman, Rick Moranis, Rosie O'Donnell, Elizabeth Perkins, Kyle McLachlan, Elizabeth Taylor*. With as much about it to like as to dislike, *The Flintstones* is an appropriately cartoonish live-action version of the adored 1960s animated TV series. Featuring some neat special effects, playful performances and a less-than-beguiling script, the film is aided by the near-perfect casting of Goodman and Perkins as Fred and Wilma, and Moranis and O'Donnell as Barney and Betty. The sluggish story has to do with Fred being promoted and used as a patsy by his devious supervisor. (Sequel: *The Flintstones in Viva Rock Vegas*) ★★½ VHS: $9.99; DVD: $29.99

The Flintstones in Viva Rock Vegas

(2000, 91 min, US, Brian Levant) *Mark Addy, Stephen Baldwin, Kristen Johnston, Jane Krakowski, Thomas Gibson, Alan Cumming, Harvey Korman, Joan Collins*. They may be a modern stone-age family, but the dialogue Fred, Wilma, Barney and Betty are forced to recite is old hat indeed. In this prequel, the story follows the adventures

of a younger, unmarried Fred and company as they meet and fall in love with their soon-to-be spouses. Addy is an able Fred, playing him more like Ralph Kramden, which is okay because he was the inspiration for Fred, anyway. Barney is played by a limber Baldwin, who actually moves like a cartoon character. But the screenplay works against the fun the entire cast tries to have. The film does feature outstanding set design and one or two funny jokes, but not enough to make you want to "meet the Flintstones" again anytime soon. ★★ VHS: $14.99; DVD: $24.99

Flipper

(1996, 96 min, US, Alan Shapiro) *Paul Hogan, Elijah Wood, Chelsea Field, Jonathan Banks, Isaac Hayes*. Originally a feature film in 1963, then a popular TV series, the story of a boy and his dolphin is back in this updated, benign family adventure. No longer a tale of a father and his sons, this time a young divorce orphan spends a summer with his bohemian uncle on a remote Caribbean island. It is here he befriends Flipper, who has lost his mate due to an evil fisherman. Of course, Flipper helps in exposing him, and makes new friends in the process. The underwater sequences of *Flipper* are rather impressive, and the locales are beautiful. ★★½ VHS: $9.99

Flirt

(1995, 85 min, US, Hal Hartley) *Bill Sage, Parker Posey, Martin Donovan, Dwight Ewell, Miho Nikaidoh*. Hartley tells a short story of a love affair at the brink of commitment. He tells it three times, in three cities with three casts, using much of the same dialogue each time. In each retelling, there's a gun and a defining moment, changing one protagonist's life unalterably. And yet, it's a commonplace occurrence, whether in New York or Berlin or Tokyo. The repetition, across cultural boundaries, across issues of sexual orientation and class identity, serves to emphasize the story's universality. Daffy and romantic, *Flirt* is about love's pain and exaltation, its nature as solid as a rock and as ephemeral as happiness; it's also about flirting and flirting's role in human relations. Godardian in nature, *Flirt* is an energetic delight, filled with wry observance and urbane compassion. ★★★ VHS: $24.99

Flirtation Walk

(1934, 98 min, US, Frank Borzage) *Dick Powell, Ruby Keeler, Pat O'Brien*. With more in common with *This Is the Army* than *42nd Street*, this cornball musical is a singing Armed Forces advertisement for a peacetime America. Powell plays a flip Army private who falls for the general's daughter, the non-dancing Keeler. Powell's repartee and most of the comedy are passable, but when buddy O'Brien starts crying amid an extended military parade, it's all too much. ★★½ VHS: $19.99

Flirting

(1990, 100 min, Australia, John Duigan) *Noah Taylor, Thandie Newton, Nicole Kidman*. Director Duigan's follow-up to *The Year My Voice Broke* is one of those purely delightful cinematic surprises — an insightful, intelligent and superbly crafted tale of coming of age. Set in early 1960s Australia, the story follows Danny Embling, a pimply-faced youth with leftist leanings and a commanding intellect who is suffering

through his time at a posh, all-boys boarding school. Scandal ensues when he becomes involved with Thandiwe Adjewa, a Ugandan student (whose father is fleeing the regime of Idi Amin) from the sister school across the lake. Kidman is solid in support as a bitchy student who tries, at first, to sabotage their relationship. Filled with humor, mirth and unwavering humanism, *Flirting* is a small gem of a movie. ★★★★ VHS: $9.99

Flirting with Disaster

(1996, 92 min, US, David O. Russell) *Ben Stiller, Patricia Arquette, Téa Leoni, Mary Tyler Moore, George Segal, Lily Tomlin, Alan Alda, Josh Brolin, Richard Jenkins*. A relentlessly funny film about a young couple who set out on a cross-country drive in search of a name for their new baby. The trouble begins when Stiller (an adoptee) becomes obsessed with finding his birth parents before bestowing his newborn son with an appellation. In steps Leoni, a long-legged, ravishing, and slightly batty psychology student who's sent by the adoption agency to help him in his search. Along the way several uproarious blunders and mistaken identities are made and Stiller and Leoni do a little of their own "flirting with disaster." As written and directed by Russell, the film is a rollicking, quixotic journey that unleashes a barrage of side-splitting gags and awkward situations, culminating in a mind-bending denouement that will warm the cockles of any ex-hippie's heart. ★★★★ VHS: $14.99; DVD: $29.99

The Florentine

(1999, 104 min, US, Nick Stagliano) *Michael Madsen, Hal Holbrook, Virginia Madsen, Tom Sizemore, Mary Stuart Masterson, Jeremy Davies, Luke Perry, James Belushi*. The day-to-day dramas of a handful of friends in a dying steel town are trotted out in this cliché-ridden film, executive produced by Francis Ford Coppola. M. Madsen is Whitey, owner of the local hangout bar the Florentine, whose sister (real-life sister Virginia) is to be married in a few days. Things get "complicated" when Virginia's old flame returns to town. A game cast and nice location work (in and around the Lehigh Valley in Pennsylvania) almost compensate for a deadeningly familiar, artificial script. ★★ VHS: $94.99

A Florida Enchantment

(1914, 64 min, US, Sidney Drew) *Edith Storey*. Considered one of the earliest films to feature ambiguous sexual attraction, this cross-dressing comedy, based on an 1896 Broadway play, is set at an elegant Florida resort. A young woman (Storey), frustrated with her fiancé's philandering, ingests magic seeds from the African Tree of Sexual Change which quickly transforms women into men and vice versa. While she remains feminine looking (though she does sprout a cute mustache), she immediately assumes the behavior of a man: swaggering belligerently, smoking furiously and making repeated advances on other women. The seeds ultimately fall into the hands of her former fiancé, who becomes an effeminate female in a male body. An ahead-of-its-time comedy which humorously explores men and women's sexual roles. ★★★ VHS: $39.99

F

Floundering

(1994, 97 min, US, Peter McCarthy) *James LeGros, John Cusack, Ethan Hawke, Lisa Zane, Steve Buscemi, Jeremy Piven, Viggo Mortensen, Alex Cox.* Set in the seedy surroundings of Venice Beach, California, the film stars LeGros as John Boyz, a twentysomething slacker who aimlessly wanders the streets of Venice. As friends pretentiously philosophize the meaning of their existence, the possibility of a plot rears its ugly head — John's failing attempts to find work. The film has some very funny moments, especially the cameos by Cusack and Buscemi. But the generic screenplay is hit-or-miss, turning the film into a series of vignettes rather than a full-length feature. ★★ VHS: $14.99; DVD: $14.99

Flower Drum Song

(1961, 133 min, US, Henry Koster) *Nancy Kwan, James Shigetta, Jack Soo, Miyoshi Umeki, Juanita Hall.* Though not one of Rodgers and Hammerstein's best musicals, this pleasant adaptation of their Broadway show manages to capture some lightheartedness and whimsical spirits. It's a tale about the conflict of old and new traditions in San Francisco's Chinatown district. The score's best songs include "I Enjoy Being a Girl" and "A Hundred Million Miracles." ★★½ VHS: $19.99

The Flower of My Secret

(1995, 105 min, Spain, Pedro Almodóvar) *Marisa Paredes, Juan Echanove, Chus Lampreave, Rossy De Palma, Joaquin Cortes.* Almodóvar continues his fascination with women on the verge in this uncharacteristically serious, even somber tale of lost love. The gorgeous and wealthy Leo (Paredes), a disenchanted writer of trash romance novels, is in the midst of the painful dissolution of her marriage. To make matters worse, her best friend is having an affair with Leo's husband; and her mother and sister — played with true familial tragicomedy by Lampreave and De Palma — are perennially at each other's throats. Needing a change in her life, Leo becomes a literary critic, but under a pseudonym. Her first assignment: do a negative review of her most recent novel. While short on a coherent plot, the characters are engaging, as Almodóvar takes a more mature approach to love and the lack of it. (Spanish with English subtitles) ★★½ VHS: $22.99

Flowers in the Attic

(1987, 95 min, US, Jeffrye Bloom) *Louise Fletcher, Victoria Tennant, Kristy Swanson.* Four children are brought by their mother to stay at their grandmother's and are locked in the attic, presumedly not to be let out again. The best-selling novel is given a flat screen translation, and the drab performances of Tennant and Fletcher (who can be tremendous in these types of roles) dampen an already preposterous film. ★ VHS: $14.99; DVD: $24.99

Flubber

(1997, 93 min, US, Les Mayfield) *Robin Williams, Marcia Gay Harden, Christopher McDonald, Clancy Brown, Ted Levine, Wil Wheaton.* Disney updates another one of its comedies, this time the popular 1961 film *The Absent Minded Professor.* Like the original, it's about a scientist who invents flubber — flying rubber. Taking over the Fred MacMurray role with considerable comedic splash is Williams,

The Flower of My Secret

who is able to somewhat control his manic personality. Unfortunately, the writers haven't given him too much to do, and ultimately *Flubber* is no more than an occasionally amusing family comedy that lets down throughout. Unlike the original, the flubber has been given human characteristics, and that's kinda cute. But there's not enough whimsical comedy and slapstick, and a subplot involving two thugs is silly. ★★½ VHS: $22.99; DVD: $29.99

Fluke

(1995, 96 min, US, Carlo Carlei) *Matthew Modine, Nancy Travis, Eric Stoltz, Max Pomeranc; Voice of: Samuel L. Jackson.* Modine dies in the first scene in a fiery car crash and, in a bizarre twist on *Ghost* and *The Incredible Journey,* is reincarnated — as a puppy. After befriending a bag lady (who names him Fluke), he finds a mentor in a big old mutt named Rumpo. Life goes on for Fluke, but he is continually haunted by thoughts of his former wife (Travis) and son (Pomeranc) and by some foreboding evil that seems linked to his former business partner (Stoltz). At times supremely silly, the film straddles the line, with varying degrees of success, between kid's fantasy comedy and adult melodrama. Still, it's all such feel-good fun, you can't help but like it. Jackson gives a goofy and garrulous turn as the voice of the streetwise Rumpo. ★★½ VHS: $14.99; DVD: $14.99

The Fly

(1958, 94 min, US, Kurt Neumann) *Vincent Price, Al (David) Hedison, Herbert Marshall, Patricia Owens.* In perhaps the ultimate sci-fi shocker of its day, Hedison stars as a scientist whose matter transference experiments go horribly awry when he accidentally integrates his own gene patterns with those of a common housefly. Contains the famous spider scene ("Help me, help me"). Screenplay by "Shogun" author James Clavell. (Remade in 1986) ★★★ VHS: $9.99; DVD: $34.99

The Fly

(1986, 96 min, US, David Cronenberg) *Jeff Goldblum, Geena Davis, John Getz.* Cronenberg's remake of the 1958 semi-classic is a terrifying thriller highlighted by both Goldblum's virtuoso performance as the scientist experiencing a metamorphosis and incredible makeup effects. An intense and gory horror film, and not for

everyone. (Sequel: *The Fly II*) ★★★½ VHS: $9.99; DVD: $34.99

Fly Away Home

(1996, 105 min, US, Carroll Ballard) *Jeff Daniels, Anna Paquin, Dana Delany, Terry Kinney.* After her mother is killed in an auto accident, a 13-year-old Australian girl (Paquin) is sent to Canada to live with her estranged father (Daniels), an eccentric inventor. What follows is an uplifting and endearing family drama that celebrates life and its wayward souls. The story has to do with Paquin raising a family of orphaned geese who think the youngster their mother. When they are threatened with possible captivity or worse, father and daughter devise an improbable plan to allow the domesticated geese to migrate over a thousand miles away. *Fly Away Home* is enhanced by extraordinary cinematography and a lovely score. A genuinely satisfying family film. ★★★½ VHS: $14.99; DVD: $29.99

Flying Down to Rio

(1933, 89 min, US, Thornton Freeland) *Delores Del Rio, Gene Raymond, Fred Astaire, Ginger Rogers, Eric Blore, Franklin Pangborn.* The film that first paired Astaire and Rogers. Del Rio and Raymond are the stars in this lively tuner about a dance band in Rio. Fred and Ginger's dancing is tops, and there's a knockout of a finale with chorines dancing on the wings of a moving plane. ★★★ VHS: $14.99

The Fog

(1980, 90 min, US, John Carpenter) *Jamie Lee Curtis, Adrienne Barbeau, Hal Holbrook, Janet Leigh, John Houseman.* Carpenter's follow-up to *Halloween* reunites him with that film's star, Curtis, in this effective horror tale about a New England coastal town terrorized by a mysterious killer fog. ★★★ VHS: $9.99

Follow Me Quietly

(1949, 59 min, US, Richard Fleischer) *William Lundigan, Dorothy Patrick.* The eternal confrontation between good and evil is re-enacted in this well-made crime melodrama. In the dark heart of a big city, a psychopathic serial killer, called "The Judge," stalks his innocent prey, leaving only a trail of corpses in his wake. The police are stymied until one detective uses an unorthodox method of constructing a dummy of the suspect, culled from evidence and witnesses, to trap the maniacal killer. ★★★ VHS: $19.99

Follow the Fleet

(1936, 110 min, US, Mark Sandrich) *Fred Astaire, Ginger Rogers, Randolph Scott, Harriet Hilliard, Lucille Ball.* Sheer musical enchantment as sailors Astaire and Scott court sisters Rogers and Hilliard (aka Harriet Nelson). Irving Berlin songs include "Let Yourself Go" and "Let's Face the Music and Dance." ★★★½ VHS: $14.99

Fool for Love

(1986, 105 min, US, Robert Altman) *Sam Shepard, Kim Basinger, Harry Dean Stanton, Randy Quaid.* Shepard's raw, elemental tragicomedy has been skillfully transferred from the stage to the screen by the ever-inventive Altman. This tale of obsessive love, set in a neon-drenched motel at the edge of the Mojave Desert, features the gorgeous and hot-tempered Basinger in a lively turn. ★★★ VHS: $14.99

The Fool Killer

(1965, 100 min, US, Servando Gonzalles) *Anthony Perkins, Edward Albert, Dana Elcar.* Shortly after the American Civil War, an abused child (Albert) runs away from home and befriends an amnesiac war veteran (Perkins) — who may or may not be a mythical killer. A moody, provocative mystery drama. ★★★ VHS: $19.99

Foolish

(1999, 84 min, US, Dave Meyers) *Master P, Eddie Griffin, Marla Gibbs, Andrew Dice Clay, Traci Bingham.* Griffin plays Foolish Waise (if the name is too obvious for your taste, please move on to another movie), an aspiring stand-up comic who's squandering his life on booze, drugs and other clichés that affect our urban youth. His brother is played by Master P, who gives a horrible performance as a minor drug dealer, exactly the life that Foolish doesn't want for himself. That said, within this tired framework, there is the remarkable talent of Griffin, who spends roughly a third of the film (and the entire climax) doing his stand-up routines. It's Richard Pryor-style observation comedy; outrageously profane and obscenely funny. No, it's not a good movie by any means, but it can be entertaining. ★★½ VHS: $9.99; DVD: $14.99

Foolish Wives

(1922, 95 min, US, Erich von Stroheim) *Erich von Stroheim, Maud George, Mae Busch.* Set in a Monte Carlo we have never known, von Stroheim's third film is chock full of adultery, seduction, blackmail, lechery and suicide, all seasoned with a heavy hand of symbolism. Would be high camp if it weren't for the perceptive characterizations with real psychological depth. ★★★ VHS: $24.99; DVD: $29.99

Fools of Fortune

(1990, 104 min, Ireland, Pat O'Connor) *Mary Elizabeth Mastrantonio, Iain Glen, Julie Christie, Michael Kitchen.* Set against the backdrop of the bloody battle for Irish independence, this engrossing film tells the tale of a family ruined by war and reunited by courage and faith. Mastrantonio stars as a young English woman whose love for her Irish cousin (Glen) draws her into the midst of the fray. Christie costars as her aunt, a British woman fighting for the Republican cause. ★★★ VHS: $19.99

Fools Rush In

(1997, 109 min, US, Andy Tennant) *Matthew Perry, Salma Hayek, Jon Tenney, Carlos Gomez, Jill Clayburgh, Tomas Milian.* Perry plays a New Yorker working in a nightclub in Las Vegas who has a one-night stand with Hayek, an earthy, aspiring photographer. Before the bacon and eggs are made in the morning, she takes off, only to reappear a few months later, pregnant. They marry (at the sort of Vegas where Elvis is sighted daily), and problems immediately kick in: culture clashes, coastal clashes, religious clashes. There's no way this relationship should work. And, until the screenwriters settle for a syrupy, storybook finale, it doesn't. There are so many differences between the characters, you wonder where the romance comes into this romantic comedy. Hayek steals the show as a hot tamale; Perry plays it befuddled throughout. ★★ VHS: $9.99; DVD: $19.99

Footlight Parade

(1933, 104 min, US, Lloyd Bacon) *James Cagney, Joan Blondell, Ruby Keeler, Dick Powell, Guy Kibbee.* Cagney is in *42nd Street* territory as a stage director putting on a Broadway show. Blondell is the faithful secretary, and she's a delight. Great musical numbers (by Busby Berkeley) include "Honeymoon Hotel," "By a Waterfall" and Cagney in "Shanghai Lil." Kibbee makes a most amusing angel (that's theatrical parlance for a show's financial backer). ★★★½ VHS: $14.99

Footloose

(1984, 107 min, US, Herbert Ross) *Kevin Bacon, John Lithgow, Lori Singer, Dianne Wiest, Christopher Penn, Sarah Jessica Parker.* Clichéd musical drama about a city boy (Bacon) who moves to Iowa and comes up against the town's powerful minister (Lithgow), who was instrumental in banning school dances. ★★ VHS: $14.99

For a Few Dollars More

(1964, 130 min, Italy, Sergio Leone) *Clint Eastwood, Lee Van Cleef, Klaus Kinski.* Eastwood stars as "The Man with No Name," who forms an uneasy alliance with Van Cleef in a search for the bandit "Indio." The good guys and bad guys, so easy to identify in the Hollywood western thanks to the wardrobe department, become as ambiguous as the landscape yet as omnipresent as Ennio Morricone's haunting score. ★★★ VHS: $14.99; DVD: $14.99

For a Lost Soldier

(1993, 92 min, The Netherlands, Roeland Kerbosch) *Andrew Kelley, Maarten Smit.* The potentially explosive subject of man-boy love is delicately handled in this touchingly romantic drama of a boy's coming of age during WWII. Jeroen (Smit), a handsome 13-year-old, is sent by his mother to the countryside. It is there that his adolescent sexual yearnings for those of his own sex begin to take hold. Initially interested in his girl-crazy best friend, Jeroen finds true love with the older Walt (Kelley), a Canadian soldier stationed in the area. A gay version of *Summer of '42*, this wonderful love story is never sexually graphic, but the achingly romantic lovemaking scene between Jeroen and Walt is certain to shock, especially with its cavalier, naturalistic view of their tender love. (Dutch with English subtitles) ★★★½ VHS: $19.99

For Colored Girls Who Have Considered Suicide/ When the Rainbow Is Enuf

(1982, 80 min, US, Oz Scott) *Alfre Woodard, Ntozake Shange, Lynn Whitfield, Trazana Beverly.* A filmed enactment of Ntozake Shange's stage production, originally presented by the New York Shakespeare Festival, *For Colored Girls* is a linked series of vignettes, choreographed and orchestrated blank verse poems, in which black women share stories of their lives, loves, betrayals and triumphs. Shange fashions a stylized codification of oral herstory, truths told in parable, passed down from mother to daughter, shared sister to sister, to ease hardships and trials, to celebrate moments of glory. The ensemble cast is potent and accessible, with special mention to Woodard, Whitfield and author Shange. An unusual and powerful film that retains the immediacy of its theatre origins. An American Playhouse production. ★★★½ VHS: $29.99

For Keeps

(1988, 98 min, US, John G. Avildsen) *Molly Ringwald, Randall Batkinoff, Kenneth Mars.* Straight-A student Ringwald lets her high school crush on fellow student Batkinoff lead her to the altar and the maternity ward as she learns that life can be a good deal harder than college prep algebra. ★ VHS: $9.99

For Love of Ivy

(1968, 102 min, US, Daniel Mann) *Sidney Poitier, Abbey Lincoln, Beau Bridges, Carroll O'Connor, Lauri Peters.* When their maid Ivy (Lincoln) announces she's leaving, O'Connor's children (Bridges and Peters) try to fix her up with small-time gambler Poitier in this charming comedy-drama. (Letterboxed) ★★★ VHS: $14.99; DVD: $14.99

For Love of the Game

(1999, 137 min, US, Sam Raimi) *Kevin Costner, Kelly Preston, John C. Reilly, Jena Malone, Brian Cox.* Kevin Costner must have been a baseball player in his previous life. For when he's on-screen and anywhere near a baseball diamond, he comes alive and performs with an intensity he rarely duplicates in his other films. He's right at home in this romantic drama with a baseball backdrop. And the baseball scenes here are terrific. Unfortunately, they only make up about a third of the film; the other two-thirds are occupied by a run-of-the-mill, predictable romance. Costner is Billy Chapel, a 40-year-old star veteran pitching what could be his last game. As he faces the Yankees and finds himself in a perfect game, Billy flashes back to the significant moments in his life. Raimi's camera captures the excitement and the authenticity of a major league game in remarkable fashion, but neither he nor Costner are able to flesh out the film's soggy romantic angle. ★★ VHS: $14.99; DVD: $24.99

For Love or Money

(1993, 96 min, US, Barry Sonnenfeld) *Michael J. Fox, Gabrielle Anwar, Anthony Higgins, Michael Tucker, Udo Kier, Bob Balaban.* In this stylish, old-fashioned romantic comedy, Fox plays a concierge extraordinaire whose dream of owning his own hotel is jeopardized when he falls for his principal investor's mistress (Anwar).

Sure, it's been done before, but this fun frolic should warm many a heart. ★★★ VHS: $7.49

For Me and My Gal

(1942, 104 min, US, Busby Berkeley) *Judy Garland, Gene Kelly, George Murphy.* Kelly made his film debut opposite Garland in this enjoyable backstage musical. They play a vaudeville couple during WWI hoping to make it big — which, of course, they do. Songs include "After You've Gone" and the title tune. ★★★ VHS: $19.99

For Richer or Poorer

(1997, 116 min, US, Bryan Spicer) *Kirstie Alley, Tim Allen, Jay O. Sanders, Michael Lerner, Wayne Knight, Larry Miller.* Alley and Allen star as a bickering and very rich Manhattan couple who are on the run from the IRS and prison after their accountant takes off with millions. They hide out in the Pennsylvania Amish country and masquerade as kinfolk to a hard-working Amish family. Featuring broad caricatures, *For Richer or Poorer* delivers a few hearty laughs at the expense of Alley and Allen's misfortunes; but most of this is silly, unfunny, and surprisingly maudlin at times. If there's really the need to see a film about hiding out in the Amish country, rent *Witness* again. ★½ VHS: $14.99; DVD: $24.99

For the Boys

(1991, 148 min, US, Mark Rydell) *Bette Midler, James Caan, George Segal, Patrick O'Neal, Arye Gross, Arliss Howard.* Midler is paired with the miscast Caan in this hit-or-miss tale about the turbulent partnership of a song and dance duo — from their meeting during WWII to the present. When set in the '40s, the film has vitality and purpose, but it is overly ambitious and none too successful in tackling the Hollywood blacklist, and the Korean and Vietnam wars. As the bawdy Dixie Leonard, Midler is in excellent voice and her acting far outshines the rest of the cast, thereby propelling this otherwise mediocre film. A good soundtrack is amongst the film's few other outstanding attractions. ★★½ VHS: $9.99; DVD: $24.99

For the Moment

(1993, 120 min, Canada, Aaron Kim Johnston) *Russell Crowe, Christianne Hirt.* This softly romantic film is set in Manitoba in 1942, and explores the relationship between a young woman (Hirt), whose husband of one week has been overseas for two years, and an equally young fighter-pilot-in-training (Crowe). Their mutual attraction is conflicted by her loyalty to her absent husband and the tenuous nature of their current circumstances. There's not much new ground here, but the film does possess an authentic feel for the era. Crowe and Hirt's strong performances counteract some hackneyed stereotypes and clichéd vignettes. A gentle and affectionate reminiscence of a time of great sacrifice and personal loss. ★★½ VHS: $14.99

For Whom the Bell Tolls

(1943, 188 min, US, Sam Wood) *Gary Cooper, Ingrid Bergman, Katina Paxinou, Akim Tamiroff.* A critical and commerical hit upon its initial release, *For Whom the Bell Tolls* is a beautifully photographed adaptation of Ernest Hemingway's novel, which hasn't held up quite as well as other films from its era. Shot in a stylized and fragmented fashion, the film stars

Cooper as an American fighting with the Spanish partisans in 1937 during their civil war. Assigned to blow up a strategic bridge, he's teamed with peasant guerrillas, led by Tamiroff and his stalwart wife Paxinou (in a dynamic Oscar-winning performance), and including refugee Bergman. As Cooper and Bergman fall in love, their future is threatened by the severity of their mission. Bergman looks impossibly beautiful, complemented by the gorgeous Technicolor. ★★★ VHS: $19.99; DVD: $26.99

For Your Eyes Only

(1981, 128 min, GB, John Glen) *Roger Moore, Carole Bouquet, Chaim Topol.* The 12th James Bond thriller marked a deliberate return to a trimmed down plot and a minimum of histrionic gadgetry. While subsequent productions have been prone to such diversions, this effort is much closer to the stylistic intentions of the series' creator Ian Fleming. The film still features many of the Bond trademarks — spectacular chase scenes, mind-boggling stunts and a bevy of beautiful women. (Sequel: *Octopussy*) ★★★ VHS: $14.99; DVD: $34.99

Forbidden Choices

(1994, 109 min, US, Jennifer Warren) *Rutger Hauer, Martha Plimpton, Kelly Lynch, Patrick McGaw.* Based on Carolyn Chute's novel "The Beans of Egypt, Maine," which was the title when released in theatres, this drama of love and poverty can be aptly described as second-rate Dickens for 20th-century America. Plimpton stars as Earlene, an alienated, waifish young woman whose fascination with her white-trash neighbors, the Bean family, forms the core of the story. Hauer is Reuben, the unlikely Bean patriarch, and McGaw is Beal, the handsome rogue who initially inspires Earlene's romantic fantasies and who eventually becomes her husband. Director Warren seems to wallow in the misfortune of the characters' lives to such an extent that you'll hear yourself saying "now what" with each passing plot development. ★★ VHS: $89.99

Forbidden Games

(1952, 87 min, France, René Clément) *Brigitte Fossey, Georges Poujouly.* Clément's poignant antiwar outcry which follows two French children who become playmates during the German occupation in 1940 and soon begin to imitate the cruelty of the adult world that surrounds them. An unforgettable film experience. (French with English subtitles) ★★★★ VHS: $29.99

Forbidden Planet

(1956, 98 min, US, Fred McLeod Wilcox) *Leslie Nielsen, Walter Pidgeon, Anne Francis, Earl Holliman.* Nielsen heads a group of space travelers who land on the planet Altair Four and encounter a "mad" scientist (Pidgeon), his alluring daughter (Francis), Robbie the Robot and the power of Id. An unusually intelligent sci-fi yarn with nifty F/X, good scenic design, and a plot borrowed from Shakespeare's "The Tempest." (Letterboxed VHS available for $19.99) ★★★½ VHS: $14.99; DVD: $19.99

Forbidden Zone

(1980, 76 min, US, Richard Elfman) *Susan Tyrrell, Hervé Villachaize, Marie-Pascale Elfman, Viva.* Horny midgets, transvestite schoolteach-

ers, a half-chicken/half-boy, savage nymphomaniacs, obese maidens in bikinis, and a dancing frog all inhabit the Forbidden Zone! Little Frenchy should never have opened that door. This ferocious farce defies description and promises to render you speechless. Original music by Danny Elfman and the Mystic Knights of the Oingo Boingo. ★★½

Force of Evil

(1948, 78 min, US, Abraham Polonsky) *John Garfield, Thomas Gomez, Marie Windsor.* Blacklisted director Polonsky's last film for over twenty years casts Garfield as a corrupt lawyer working for the mob in this powerful film noir classic. ★★★½ VHS: $9.99

Force 10 from Navarone

(1978, 118 min, GB, Guy Hamilton) *Robert Shaw, Harrison Ford, Carl Weathers, Barbara Bach, Edward Fox, Franco Nero.* Inferior sequel to *The Guns of Navarone* finds the likes of Shaw, Ford and Weathers teaming up with other members of Allied forces to blow up a bridge crucial to the Nazi war effort. ★★ VHS: $14.99; DVD: $24.99

Forced March

(1989, 104 min, US, Rick King) *Chris Sarandon, Renée Soutendijk, Josef Sommer.* Sarandon plays an actor who finds the walls dissolving between himself and the character he is playing, Hungarian poet Mikilos Radnoli, who was killed in a Nazi concentration camp. The film evokes a certain power but the ambitious story line cannot fully explore the various subjects it presents. ★★½

Forces of Nature

(1999, 104 min, US, Bronwen Hughes) *Sandra Bullock, Ben Affleck, Maura Tierney, Steve Zahn, Blythe Danner, Ronny Cox, Richard Schiff.* An engaging romantic comedy that doesn't aim straight for the heart, *Forces of Nature* benefits greatly from the very appealing chemistry between its two stars Bullock and Affleck. Ben (Affleck) is a writer on his way from New York to Savannah where he is to be married the next day. When the plane nearly crashes on takeoff, he "rescues" Sarah (Bullock), who is knocked unconscious. They head to Savannah, experiencing a series of setbacks and misadventures. Of course, Ben is soon uncertain of his marriage as he's "never met a woman" quite like Sarah. Director Hughes and writer Marc Lawrence bring a certain breeziness to their story while not going overboard in the how-nature-affects-the-two-lovers department. The ending isn't quite what you'd expect, but then neither are Sarah and Ben. They are both brought to life by two good actors in good form. ★★★ VHS: $9.99; DVD: $24.99

A Foreign Affair

(1948, 116 min, US, Billy Wilder) *Jean Arthur, Marlene Dietrich, John Lund, Millard Mitchell.* A witty script and lively performances highlight Wilder's funny satire on the military and postwar relations. Things heat up when a straight-laced Congresswoman (Arthur) — sent to investigate the morals of G.I.s overseas — discovers that a U.S. Army Captain (Lund) is more than allies with a Berlin bombshell (Dietrich). ★★★½ VHS: $14.99

Foreign Body

(1986, 108 min, GB, Ronald Neame) *Victor Banerjee, Warren Mitchell, Trevor Howard, Amanda Donohoe, Denis Quilley.* Banerjee plays an Indian immigrant in London who, upon the prodding of a friend, finds himself posing as a chiropractor. Banerjee displays a cunning knack for comedy as he is overcome by the advances of his wealthy female patients. ★★½

Foreign Correspondent

(1940, 119 min, US, Alfred Hitchcock) *Joel McCrea, Laraine Day, George Sanders, Herbert Marshall, Robert Benchley, Albert Basserman.* McCrea is an American newspaperman stationed in London who becomes involved with a Nazi spy ring and is plunged into a series of terrifying adventures. This enthralling suspenser features a host of Hitchcock's most imaginative scenes, including the windmills that turn backward, an assassination attempt in Westminster Cathedral, and a spectacular plane wreck at sea. Splendid performances. ★★★★ VHS: $14.99

A Foreign Field

(1993, 90 min, GB, Charles Sturridge) *Alec Guinness, Lauren Bacall, Jeanne Moreau, Edward Herrmann, Leo McKern, Geraldine Chaplin, John Randolph.* An enchanting international cast distinguishes this impeccably produced made-for-TV BBC drama which, though subdued and deliberately paced, is charming nonetheless. Infused with amiable moments of comedy, the film follows the connecting stories of several people visiting the shores of Normandy 50 years after D-Day. The ensemble includes McKern as a former British infantryman, Guinness as a mentally disabled veteran, Bacall as a different kind of war widow, and Moreau as a former flame of both McKern and ex-G.I. Randolph. ★★★

Foreign Student

(1994, 96 min, US/GB, Eva Sereny) *Marco Hofschneider, Robin Givens, Edward Herrmann, Hinton Battle, Charles Dutton.* Based on the novel by Philippe Labro, this low-key adaptation examines an interracial romance in the 1950s. Hofschneider plays a Parisian exchange student who spends a semester at a Southern college. There he meets a beautiful black woman (Givens), a teacher who works as a maid at the

home of one of his professors. Blind to the segregation and racism of the times, he pursues her, and the two fall in love. Any interesting dramatics are countered by rather listless pacing. ★★ VHS: $9.99

Forever and a Day

(1943, 105 min, US, René Clair, Edmund Goulding, Cedric Hardwicke,) *Ray Milland, Merle Oberon, Charles Laughton, Robert Cummings, Nigel Young, Buster Keaton, Claude Rains, Victor McLaglen, Elsa Lanchester, Gladys Cooper, Roland Young.* This impressive episodic drama chronicles the lives of several generations of a family and their London home. Spanning the century and a half from 1804 to the German Blitz, the film was produced as a post-war fundraiser for British reconstruction and features just about every Hollywood actor with English roots. ★★★½ VHS: $19.99; DVD: $24.99

Forever Female

(1953, 93 min, US, Irving Rapper) *Ginger Rogers, William Holden, Paul Douglas, Pat Crowley.* An engaging cast adds sparkle to this pleasant backstage comedy, written by Julius and Philip Epstein (*Casablanca*). Rogers plays a middle-aged Broadway actress still playing the ingénue. She meets writer Holden, whose new play's characters include a 19-year-old daughter and a 50-year-old mother. Guess which one Rogers wants to play. As Rogers' ex-husband, Douglas gives the film's best performance; he can sling a one-liner with the best of them. ★★★ VHS: $9.99

Forever Lulu

(1987, 85 min, US, Amos Kollek) *Hanna Schugulla, Debbie Harry, Alec Baldwin.* Baldwin made his theatrical film debut in this tale about a New York City novelist (Schugulla) who begins investigating the goings-on of a gangster's moll (Harry). A forgettable, sloppy ripoff of *Desperately Seeking Susan* with no originality of its own. ★ VHS: $14.99

Forever Mary

(1990, 100 min, Italy, Marco Risi) *Michele Placido, Alesandro DiSanzo.* A tougher look into modern urban Italian life than one usually sees. This hard-hitting prison drama, set in a Palermo juvenile detention center, takes an unflinching look at the "rehabilitation" of a group of teenagers. Essentially a spaghetti *To Sir with Love*, the story follows Marco (Placido), a taciturn yet dedicated teacher who volunteers to spend some time trying to educate a clamorous group of teenagers. Their initial scorn soon turns to respect and, much to the director's credit, the story avoids sentimental pitfalls and retains its hard edge. The title refers to Mario, a transvestite prostitute who falls in (puppy) love with the teacher. (Italian with English subtitles) ★★★ VHS: $39.99

Forever Mine

(1999, 117 min, US, Paul Schrader) *Joseph Fiennes, Ray Liotta, Gretchen Mol.* A towel boy (Fiennes) at a posh resort falls in love with a politician's beautiful young wife and they begin a torrid affair. When the husband finds out about it, he has the young man killed. Miraculously, the man survives the attempt on his life and. . . oh, never mind. If you stick with the film past this point, you may get a few unintentional chuckles out of it, but it's

hardly worth the wait. The acting is across-the-board wretched, the story interminable and at times embarrassing, and the only evidence that Schrader's behind this is the Catholic guilt of Mol's character and the sporadic spiritual musings from Fiennes. ★ VHS: $102.99; DVD: $24.99

Forever Young

(1983, 85 min, GB, David Drury) *James Aubrey, Nicholas Gecks, Alec McCowen.* David Putnam produced this intimate and compelling story about the relationship between a 12-year-old boy and a young priest who attempts to shield him from a painful secret. ★★★

Forever Young

(1992, 115 min, US, Steve Miner) *Mel Gibson, Jamie Lee Curtis, Elijah Wood, Joe Morton, George Wendt.* Following in the footsteps of the charming independent feature *Late for Dinner* comes this likable comedy-drama of cryogenics and lost love. Gibson plays a nice-guy test pilot in 1939 who, after his fiancée becomes comatose, agrees to be a human guinea pig for scientist/pal Wendt's experiment — to be frozen alive for a year. Fifty years later, Gibson is awakened by young Wood. As Gibson acclimates to life in the '90s, he tries to track down his long-lost friend. Alternately funny and shamelessly sentimental, *Forever Young* is the kind of popular mainstream entertainment that can unapologetically make one laugh and cry. It's a good time without having to feel too guilty for enjoying such manipulative Hollywood fare. ★★½ VHS: $9.99; DVD: $14.99

Forget Mozart

(1985, 93 min, Germany, Slavo Luter) *Armin Mueller-Stahl, Caterina Raacke.* Mueller-Stahl stars in this intellectual music lover's answer to *Amadeus* which pays far more attention to historical fact than Hollywood passions. The character of Salieri is again prominent in this story, but blame for Mozart's death is attributed to disease, a failed marriage, alcoholism and the government's inattentiveness. Mueller-Stahl is perfect as the state's investigator into Mozart's untimely demise. Focusing on the historical and political backdrop to Mozart's life, the film explores Mozart's connections with the Freemasons and their influence in this era of revolutionary change in Europe. (German with English subtitles) ★★★ VHS: $29.99

Forget Paris

(1995, 101 min, US, Billy Crystal) *Billy Crystal, Debra Winger, Joe Mantegna, Cynthia Stevenson, Richard Masur, Julie Kavner, Cathy Moriarty.* Crystal wears several hats as producer/director/writer/star of this amiable romantic comedy that offers quite a few laughs in Crystal's inimitable comedic style but is also very familiar. The on-again, off-again love affair of Crystal and Winger is told in flashbacks as friends' dinner conversation. He's an NBA ref, she's an airline manager. They meet in Paris, fall in love, marry and return to the States. But conflicting schedules and misunderstandings sabotage their happiness, and what follows is a series of breakups and reconciliations. More serious in tone than his other romances, Crystal's film does offer many laughs, but it takes longer to get to them. Winger is a delight. ★★½ VHS: $9.99; DVD: $19.99

Hervé Villechaize and Susan Tyrrell in *Forbidden Zone*

Forgotten Silver

(1996, 55 min, New Zealand, Peter Jackson & Costa Botes) *Peter Jackson, Costa Botes, Marguerite Hurst, Leonard Maltin, Sam Neill.* New Zealand, it seems, has some issues with its self-image. After being dumped by Britain following WWII, the country was forced to develop its own societal identity. Director Jackson uses this cultural blank slate as an opportunity to manufacture his own film history. With the pretense of a newly discovered trunk of rapidly disintegrating films, Jackson and cowriter/director Botes invent a "nearly forgotten" chapter in Kiwi film history. Their discovery, director Colin McKenzie (Botes), is ostensibly the most important film innovator in New Zealand history. Suffering slightly from the *Forrest Gump*-ism of McKenzie's responsibility for every major advance in film history, the film is an ingeniously convincing, deeply humorous and richly woven fabrication. When this mockumentary was first presented on New Zealand television, it prompting the network to issue an apology to those who thought it true. ★★★½ VHS: $19.99; DVD: $29.99

Forgotten Tune for a Flute

(1987, 131 min, USSR, Eldar Ryazanov) *Leonid Filatov, Tatiana Dogileva.* A breezy Soviet comedy about a bureaucrat who rediscovers a lost and suppressed part of his life. Lenny is a high-ranking government employee "happily" married to the daughter of another functionary who, after a mild heart attack, begins an affair with a sensible nurse. She, in turn, encourages him to broaden his life and take up another passion long forgotten: playing the flute. A delightful, post-*glasnost* social satire. (Russian with English subtitles) ★★★ VHS: $19.99

Forrest Gump

(1994, 142 min, US, Robert Zemeckis) *Tom Hanks, Sally Field, Gary Sinise, Robin Wright, Mykelti Williamson.* With the nugget of folk wisdom "Life is like a box of chocolates," Hanks launches into the epic telling of the life of Forrest Gump, a small-town simpleton who finds himself at the center of just about every significant cultural event in the latter half of the 20th century. It's a fine premise, and it leads to a host of entertaining moments. But it's all so shallow. Hanks' Gump is more than just an "enlightened idiot" of the Chauncy Gardner variety; he's a pure-of-heart all-American boy who never questions authority and prospers as a result. And therein lies its fundamental message, which seems to offer absolution to boomers in a sweeping apology for the bad old days of the 1960s. In support, Sinise stands out as Gump's sergeant. Forget the Gump-isms and their residue, for though you may hate some of the contents, you may appreciate the packaging. (VHS available letterboxed or pan & scan) ★★½ VHS: $14.99

Forsaking All Others

(1934, 84 min, US, W.S. Van Dyke) *Joan Crawford, Clark Gable, Robert Montgomery.* Always an intoxicating duo, Crawford and Gable reteam for this satisfying romantic melodrama. Crawford finds her marriage to Gable on the dull side (Gable dull?), so she looks for excitement in the arms of dashing Montgomery. Will she leave her husband or realize they were

meant for each other all along? The stars outperform their material. ★★½ VHS: $19.99

Fort Apache

(1948, 125 min, US, John Ford) *Henry Fonda, John Wayne, Shirley Temple, Victor McLaglen.* The first of director Ford's cavalry trilogy (followed by *She Wore a Yellow Ribbon* and *Rio Grande*) stars Fonda as a strict military commander at odds with both his men and neighboring Indians. Wayne is the more compassionate officer caught between loyalty to the soldiers in his command and duty to the martinet under whom he serves. ★★★ VHS: $14.99

Fort Apache, the Bronx

(1981, 125 min, US, Daniel Petrie) *Paul Newman, Edward Asner, Ken Wahl, Pam Grier.* Newman is the cop facing a conflict of conscience when he witnesses two policemen throw a Hispanic man off a tenement roof. Asner is the precinct captain trying to hold on to his outpost in the center of the crime-torn South Bronx (where the film was shot with much protest from the community, who didn't care for the portrayal of their neighborhood). Grier steals the film with her performance as a drug-crazed prostitute. ★★★ VHS: $9.99; DVD: $24.99

Fortress

(1993, 92 min, US, Stuart Gordon) *Christopher Lambert, Loryn Locklin, Kurtwood Smith, Jeffrey Combs.* In an authoritarian world, couples are limited to one child, and offenders are duly sentenced to lengthy stays in corporate-managed, computer-controlled prisons. Lambert and Locklin play a husband and wife who find themselves imprisoned. She must fend off the obsessive advances of the bioengineered warden (a creepy Smith), while he has to contend with the wrath of some violent fellow inmates. Lambert soon assembles a group of prisoners to help him rescue his wife and escape the fortress. Gordon showers the set with blood, and introduces a few grisly futuristic innovations. (Sequel: *Fortress 2: Re-Entry*) ★★½ VHS: $9.99; DVD: $9.99

Fortress 2: Re-Entry

(1999, 92 min, US, Geoff Murphy) *Christopher Lambert, Pam Grier.* Belated (but not really anticipated) sequel to Stuart Gordon's 1993 film is nearly on par with its passable original. Lambert is once again a rebel in the future, hiding out from the totalitarian government and raising his "illegal" son (births must be sanctioned by the state) in a log cabin in the woods with his wife. Alas, he's captured again, and sent back to an impenetrable prison that doubles as a space station. This predictable retread is still violent and fast-paced enough to please undiscriminating fans. ★★ VHS: $14.99; DVD: $24.99

Fortunata y Jacinta

(1969, 108 min, Spain/Italy, Angelino Fons) Based on the 1877 novel, "Historia de Dos Casadas," by Benito Perez Galdos, this elegant but shrill melodrama recounts the tragic story of two very dissimilar women who vie for the love of the same man. Juan, a young Rock Hudson look-alike, leads a privileged life, with his future assured by the planned marriage to his beautiful cousin Jacinta. Then he meets and becomes obsessed with the earthy, sexually charged peasant woman Fortunata. Their entangled loves and passions lead inevitably to

heartbreak and loss. The attempt by the filmmaker to tell the entire novel in the span of two hours gives the film a frantic, Cliff-Notes feel, but regardless, this ageless story of insuppressible passion is still engaging. (Spanish with English subtitles) ★★½

The Fortune

(1975, 88 min, US, Mike Nichols) *Jack Nicholson, Warren Beatty, Stockard Channing, Scatman Crothers, Florence Stanley, Richard B. Shull.* Broad satire with Nicholson and Beatty as grifters out to murder heiress Channing for her money. Funny, fast-paced and featuring great performances (especially Channing as the hapless target). ★★★½ VHS: $14.99

Fortune and Men's Eyes

(1971, 102 min, US/Canada, Harvey Hart) *Wendell Burton, Zooey Hall, Michael Greer.* John Hubert's play about homosexual brutality in prison comes to the screen in this taut, claustrophobic, and sensationalistic drama. The story follows young first-timer Smitty (Burton) who finds himself the prized sexual catch of a thuggish Rocky (Hall). Sexual humiliation, domination and abuse fill the halls of the seemingly guardless prison as the inmates enact a frenzied dance for power and gratification. Greer is alternately hilarious and terrorizing as Queeny, the affectionate, limp-wristed fairy cell mate who, when threatened, turns into a dangerously violent psychopath. ★★★ VHS: $19.99

The Fortune Cookie

(1966, 125 min, US, Billy Wilder) *Jack Lemmon, Walter Matthau, Ron Rich.* Matthau won an Oscar for his performance as a shyster lawyer out to parlay Lemmon's minor injury into some really big bucks. A funny, biting comedy from the pens of Wilder and partner I.A.L. Diamond. ★★★ VHS: $14.99; DVD: $19.99

Fortunes of War

(1987, 180 min, GB, James Cellan Jones) *Kenneth Branagh, Emma Thompson, Rupert Graves, Robert Stephens.* This BBC production follows a British couple swept up in the struggle against Fascism in 1939 Romania. Based on the autobiographical accounts of Olivia Manning, the story follows the pair as they reluctantly and increasingly become involved with the British Secret Service. With Branagh and Thompson in the leads, the acting is, as would be expected, top-notch, and this epic production whisks the viewer through such exotic locales as Bucharest, Athens, and Cairo. ★★★ VHS: $29.99

Forty Carats

(1973, 110 min, US, Milton Katselas) *Liv Ullmann, Edward Albert, Gene Kelly, Binni Barnes.* Lackluster version of the Broadway hit with Ullmann as a 40-ish New Yorker who begins an affair with 20-ish Albert while on holiday in Greece. Though Ullmann is miscast and Albert is rather emotionless, there's good support from Kelly and Barnes. ★★ VHS: $59.99

48 Hrs.

(1983, 97 min, US, Walter Hill) *Eddie Murphy, Nick Nolte, James Remar, Annette O'Toole.* Murphy's dazzling big-screen debut elevates this cop and convict caper above the usual urban action-drama. Murphy and the comically gruff Nolte join forces to track a pair of homi-

The Fountainhead

cidal heavies in Hill's jagged-edged comedy-thriller. (Sequel: *Another 48 Hrs.*) ★★★½ VHS: $9.99; DVD: $24.99

The 49th Parallel

(1941, 107 min, GB, Michael Powell) *Leslie Howard, Laurence Olivier, Eric Portman, Raymond Massey, Glynis Johns.* A stirring WWII suspense drama which was one of the first of the great 1940s British films detailing both the physical and moral fight against the Nazis. When a German U-boat is sunk off the coast of Canada, its five survivors embark on a murderous, ruthless trail from one community to another in their quest to cross into the United States. This political allegory follows the stalwart fight of civilians and servicemen alike to keep the German soldiers from accomplishing their mission. (aka: *The Invaders*) ★★★★ VHS: $14.99

42nd Street

(1933, 89 min, US, Lloyd Bacon) *Warner Baxter, Ruby Keeler, Bebe Daniels, George Brent, Dick Powell, Ginger Rogers.* Classic backstage musical with Baxter as the driven director and Keeler as the chorine who subs for the injured leading lady and "comes back a star." It's a little creaky by today's standards, but who cares — it's got those terrific Busby Berkeley dance numbers and a fine Warren-Dubin score. ★★★★ VHS: $14.99; DVD: $19.99

The 47 Ronin: Parts 1 & 2

(1942, 112 min, Japan, Kenji Mizoguchi) Taking his inspiration from one of the most admired tales of Japanese folklore, Mizoguchi adapts for the screen the true story of the 47 masterless samurai who, in 1703, all mysteriously killed themselves by committing *seppuku*. The two-part film begins with the Lord Asano who, in anger, draws his sword and strikes an arrogant but superior lord. With this act of insolence, he must kill himself, which leaves his loyal samurai without a leader. The ronin vow to avenge their young lord's death. And with this background our story takes off. Successfully created to inspire wartime patriotism for the war-weary public, the film reinforces traditional Japanese values, as well as reminding the people of their heroism and warrior spirit. (Japanese with English subtitles) (Each VHS volume sells singularly for $29.99) ★★★ VHS: $49.99; DVD: $34.99

Foul Play

(1978, 116 min, US, Colin Higgins) *Goldie Hawn, Chevy Chase, Dudley Moore, Burgess Meredith, Rachel Roberts, Brian Dennehy.* Hawn stars in this funny mystery comedy as a San Francisco librarian who becomes involved with detective Chase and a plot to assassinate the Pope. ★★★ VHS: $14.99

The Fountainhead

(1949, 114 min, US, King Vidor) *Gary Cooper, Patricia Neal, Raymond Massey.* This highly stylized film version of the Ayn Rand novel stars Cooper as an architect, modeled after Frank Lloyd Wright, whose ideas are ahead of their time. A rugged individualist, Cooper takes on a group of federal housing bureaucrats in a struggle over the perversion of his designs. ★★★ VHS: $19.99

Four Adventures of Reinette and Mirabelle

(1986, 95 min, France, Eric Rohmer) *Joelle Miquel, Jessica Forde, Beatrice Romand.* Sophisticated humor and two disarmingly charming leads highlight this low-budget account of the up-and-down relationship between two young students. Reinette, a rigorously principled, naïve country girl who is studying ethnology at the Sorbonne, meets Mirabelle, a pragmatic, worldly Parisian art student, and they decide to become flatmates. Together, they have four adventures involving several characters from the streets of Paris. As always, this Rohmer tale is a talk-fest (but entertainingly so) as the two unknown teenage actresses give beguilingly naturalistic performances. An intelligent drama filled with wisdom, idealism and beauty. (French with English subtitles) ★★★½ VHS: $29.99

Four Days in July

(1984, 99 min, Ireland, Mike Leigh) *Des McAleer, Brid Brennan, Stephen Rea.* This quirky comedy-drama is set in Northern Ireland during the middle of July, when the Protestants celebrate their national pride. Director Leigh deftly interweaves the lives of two couples, one Protestant and the other Catholic, and both expecting their first child. In his typical cinema verité manner, Leigh gently exposes the nuances of these disparate elements of Ulster society employing only simple living room conversation and other trivial daily chores — it is a quietly evocative exposé on a territory torn by strife. ★★★½ VHS: $29.99

Four Days in September

(1997, 113 min, Brazil, Bruno Barreto) *Alan Arkin, Pedro Cardoso, Fernando Torres, Fisher Stevens.* After making two interesting but uneven films in the U.S. (*A Show of Force, Carried Away*), director Barreto returned to his native Brazil for this superior thriller. In the tradition of *State of Siege* and *Missing*, this true-life tale focuses on the people caught in the middle of perilous political turmoil. The case here is Brazil in 1969, when a group of young radicals rebelling against an oppressive military government kidnap Charles Elbrick (Arkin), the U.S. Ambassador to the country. Tightly wound, marvelously acted and filled with moments of bare-knuckle suspense, the film belongs on the shelf next to the best of Costa-Gavras. (In English and Portuguese with English subtitles) ★★★½ VHS: $102.99

Four Eyes and Six-Guns

(1992, 92 min, US, Piers Haggard) *Judge Reinhold, Fred Ward, Patricia Clarkson, Dan Hedaya.* This entertaining family fare features an engaging performance from Reinhold as Ernest Allbright, a naïve, idealistic New York City optometrist who follows his dream to Wyatt Earp's Tombstone, Arizona. Before he gets there, his examination equipment is trashed while he's brutalized in a train robbery; after he arrives, he's bilked out of his life savings and winds up broke in a tumble-down shack. Of course, goodness and righteousness eventually triumph over adversity and deceit — aided in large part by Allbright's uncanny and unorthodox expertise with a six-gun. Trusty Ward delivers a workmanlike portrayal of Marshall Earp. ★★½ VHS: $9.99

The Four Feathers

(1939, 115 min, GB, Zoltan Korda) *Ralph Richardson, John Clements.* A.E.W. Mason's story about a young aristocrat who resigns his military commission on the eve of an expedition to the Sudan. He is subsequently branded a coward by friends and lover alike. To prove his worthiness he joins the group and helps battle the Sudanese uprising. A great epic of British imperialism. ★★★½ VHS: $14.99

Four Friends

(1981, 116 min, US, Arthur Penn) *Craig Wasson, Jodi Thelen, Michael Huddleston, Jim Metzler.* Powerful stuff from director Penn. This tale of growing up in the sixties is a classic story of the son of a steelworker who falls in love with the girl his best friends have fallen for. It takes a decade to work out, but they figure it out. The car crashing onto the disco finale is one of the most memorable scenes in all of Penn's films. Magical score by Elizabeth Swados. ★★★½ VHS: $14.99; DVD: $19.99

Four Horsemen of the Apocalypse

(1961, 153 min, US, Vincente Minnelli) *Glenn Ford, Charles Boyer, Lee J. Cobb, Ingrid Thulin, Paul Henreid.* Remake of the Rudolph Valentino silent box-office hit, with much less success, about brothers fighting on opposite sides of the war, here updated to WWII. ★★ VHS: $19.99

The 400 Blows

(1959, 99 min, France, François Truffaut) *Jean-Pierre Léaud, Claire Maurier, Jeanne Moreau.* Arguably the finest in a long line of cinematic coming-of-age efforts, *The 400 Blows* marked the emergence of a brilliant young directorial talent. Truffaut's largely autobiographical feature film debut commenced the wonderful saga of Antoine Doinel (Léaud), the director's alter ego. Oppressed by the demands of parents and teachers, the young Antoine ventures out on his own, only to discover the unsettling bleakness of personal freedom. (French with English subtitles) ★★★★ VHS: $29.99; DVD: $29.99

F

F

4 Little Girls

(1997, 102 min, US, Spike Lee) Told with present-day interviews and archival footage, the riveting *4 Little Girls* recounts the story of the title teens who were killed by a racist's bomb while they attended Sunday school in early 1960s Birmingham. The film also examines the attitudes of the people — both black and white — in that city at the time, and how the rest of the country reacted. Several of the interviews may move you to tears, and there's a jaw-dropping, and rather sad, talk with former Alabama Governor George Wallace. But what one comes away with most from this fascinating film is the astonishing courage and depth of spirit of the families and friends of the victims in the face of such unspeakable hatred. ★★★★ VHS: $14.99; DVD: $19.99

The Four Musketeers

(1974, 106 min, GB, Richard Lester) *Oliver Reed, Raquel Welch, Richard Chamberlain, Frank Finlay, Michael York, Christopher Lee.* Lester's impressive follow-up to *The Three Musketeers*, his romping vision of the Dumas classic, was filmed simultaneously with the original. While darker in tone than the first film, and less emphatic in its physical comedy, it is still filled with incisive period wit and lots of rollicking adventure. ★★★ VHS: $14.99; DVD: $19.99

Four Rooms

(1996, 98 min, US, Allison Anders, Alex Rockwell, Robert Rodriguez & Quentin Tarantino) *Tim Roth, Antonio Banderas, Jennifer Beals, Marisa Tomei, Madonna, Bruce Willis, Quentin Tarantino.* While two of the four segments in this anthology film are moderately good, the other two are so abysmally bad that they very nearly make the entire project a failure. The film takes place on New Year's Eve and tells four different bizarre stories, happening in four different rooms of a hotel serviced by one very overworked bellboy (Roth in an ingratiatingly mugging performance). Anders' segment concerns a coven of witches; it's boring from start to finish. Rockwell's bit is equally bad: It stars Beals as the victim of a twisted bondage and power game and is actually painful to watch. The film livens up substantially in Rodriguez's segment, about two children in a room by themselves, nominally supervised by Roth. And Tarantino's segment tops off the weird mix with a macabre tale of a bet made in flesh. ★½ VHS: $14.99; DVD: $29.99

The Four Seasons

(1981, 107 min, US, Alan Alda) *Alan Alda, Carol Burnett, Rita Moreno, Jack Weston, Len Cariou, Sandy Dennis.* A genuinely funny comedy on romance and relationships; director Alda has yet to equal this story about a group of friends who spend their vacations together. As the couples, Alda and Burnett, Weston and Moreno, and Cariou and Dennis and then Armstrong, all offer delightful performances. A witty, even perceptive script by Alda. ★★★

Four Weddings and a Funeral

(1994, 116 min, GB, Mike Newell) *Hugh Grant, Andie MacDowell, Kristin Scott Thomas, Simon Callow, John Hannah, Rowan Atkinson.* Grant is effortlessly charming in this enchanting romantic comedy playing a likable Britisher whose biggest flaw seems to be his fear of commitment. Fulfilling its titular promise, the film follows Grant and a wonderful group of friends as they wind their way from one ceremony to another imparting blithe observations on love, relationships and fear of both. Featuring a marvelously written screenplay, the film only loses control at its finale with an abrupt, simplistic ending which belies the intelligence that came before it. Callow and Hannah, as devoted lovers, and Atkinson, immensely funny as a tongue-tied priest, are exceptional in support. ★★★½ VHS: $9.99; DVD: $14.99

1492: Conquest of Paradise

(1992, 150 min, GB/France/US, Ridley Scott) *Gérard Depardieu, Sigourney Weaver, Armand Assante, Frank Langella, Loren Dean, Angela Molina.* The better of 1992's two dramatizations (the other being *Christopher Columbus: The Discovery*) about Christopher Columbus being discovered by Native Americans when he got lost trying to find a quicker trade route to Asia. Depardieu gives a fine performance as the explorer who betrays and is eventually betrayed, ultimately ending his years in obscurity and poverty. Director Scott's eye for the striking visual serves him well in enlivening this revisionist epic, which unfortunately suffers from delusions of profundity. (VHS available letterboxed or pan & scan) ★★ VHS: $24.99

The 4th Man

(1983, 110 min, The Netherlands, Paul Verhoeven) *Jeroen Krabbé, Renée Soutendijk, Thom Hoffman.* A wonderful hallucinatory thriller that bristles with dark, forboding humor and sexual paranoia. The story concerns a brooding novelist (Krabbé) entwined in the web of a mysterious beautician and her handsomely sculpted lover. Starring the hauntingly beautiful Soutendijk. (Dutch with English subtitles) ★★★½ VHS: $14.99; DVD: $29.99

The Fourth Protocol

(1987, 100 min, GB, John MacKenzie) *Michael Caine, Pierce Brosnan, Joanna Cassidy.* A superior political thriller with Caine as a government agent who stumbles upon a plot by a renegade Soviet general to destroy an American airbase in England. Based on Frederick Forsyth's novel, the film, as with the author's *The Day of the Jackal*, builds an unrelenting tension until its shattering conclusion. Brosnan is the KGB agent assigned to the deadly task, and Cassidy is radiant as his contact. ★★★½

The Fourth War

(1990, 91 min, US, John Frankenheimer) *Roy Scheider, Jurgen Prochnow, Tim Reid, Harry Dean Stanton.* Scheider and Prochnow battle it out as the last of the Cold War militarists in this competent though unexciting thriller. Scheider plays an American colonel and Prochnow is a Russian commander, both willing to start WWIII for the sake of psyching out the other. ★★½ VHS: $9.99

Fox and His Friends

(1975, 123 min, Germany, Rainer Werner Fassbinder) *Rainer Werner Fassbinder, Peter Chatel, Harry Baer, Kurt Raab.* Fassbinder's first specifically male gay-themed film is a richly textured and powerful drama of the relationship between two gay men of vastly different

The 400 Blows

social backgrounds. A lower-class carnival entertainer, Fox (played by Fassbinder), finds himself suddenly flush after winning 500,000DM in a lottery. He soon becomes involved in an ill-fated romance with gold-digging Eugen, a rich, manipulative young man. The eternal class struggle and the continued exploitation of the poor and working class is tragically played out as the unwitting Fox is swindled out of his money and self-respect by his bourgeois lover and his family. (German with English subtitles) ★★★★

The Fox and the Hound

(1981, 83 min, US, Art Stevens, Ted Berman & Richard Rich) *Voices of: Kurt Russell, Mickey Rooney, Sandy Duncan, Corey Feldman.* While the music of this potential classic is not up to Disney's current standards, this tale of friendship between the hunter and the hunted is timeless and timely. Tod is an orphaned fox cub who befriends Copper, a hound puppy who will eventually be trained to hunt foxes. Although they become best friends, their relationship is threatened by Copper's owner, who is determined to kill Tod. The thrilling climax proves that friendship is indeed more powerful than hate or revenge, and reminds kids that differences need not be dividers. The animation is first-rate. ★★★ VHS: $22.99; DVD: $29.99

Foxes

(1980, 106 min, US, Adrian Lyne) *Jodie Foster, Sally Kellerman, Randy Quaid, Laura Dern.* Foster stars as one of four girls who share an apartment in the Los Angeles suburbs in this sociological study which poignantly examines the restless lives of today's youths, although it presents more questions than answers. ★★½ VHS: $9.99

Foxfire

(1996, 102 min, US, Annette Haywood-Carter) *Hedy Burress, Angelina Jolie, Jenny Lewis, Jenny Shimizu, Sarah Rosenberg, Cathy Moriarty.* A disappointing adaptation of Joyce Carol Oates' novel about a girl gang, *Foxfire* waters down important issues such as sexual harassment, drug addiction, and female teenage angst as it depicts the actions of five rebellious high school girls coming to terms with their identities. Suspended from school for attacking a teacher, these disparate teens embark on a series of crimes that escalate in their severity. Director Haywood-Carter succeeds in generating a palpable sexual tension between two of the girls, but is unable to coax a single decent performance from the cast. What could have been a fiery display of female solidarity quickly becomes a frustrating one. ★★ VHS: $14.99; DVD: $24.99

Foxy Brown

(1974, 94 min, US, Jack Hill) *Pam Grier, Terry Carter, Antonio Fargas.* Mob queenpin Miss Katherine finds her harem reduced to mincemeat when Grier goes after those responsible for her brutal rape and the death of her brother. Grier is certainly a sight, but this early blaxploitation actioner is very violent and muddled. ★★ VHS: $9.99; DVD: $14.99

Frameup

(1993, 91 min, US, Jon Jost) *Howard Swain, Nancy Carlin.* It's no big secret that the works of Jost are an acquired taste: his minimalistic, freeform films test the patience of most viewers and are probably of interest only to experimental filmmakers and fans thereof. *Frameup*, a monotonous, pretentiously artsy examination of a *Badlands*-like couple, holds true to the director's reputation. Husband and wife Swain and Carlin star as the ill-fated couple, who meet in Idaho and head West for relaxation, sex and murder. Comprised of a series of narrations framed by a motionless camera, the film is all talk and very little action. Carlin gives a grating performance; Swain nearly captures the essence of a bad guy. ★ VHS: $24.99

Frances

(1982, 140 min, US, Graeme Clifford) *Jessica Lange, Kim Stanley, Sam Shepard.* Lange gives a powerful performance as Frances Farmer, the radiant Hollywood starlet of the '30s whose nonconformity launched a tragic succession of injustices. This chilling bio-pic delineates the demise of Farmer's promising film career and discloses the terrifying conditions of her imposed institutionalization. ★★★

Francesco

(1989, 105 min, Italy, Liliana Cavani) *Mickey Rourke, Helena Bonham Carter.* A pre-puffy faced, before-his-boxing-career-skids-days Rourke is featured in this religious drama giving an emotionally raw and stirring performance as Francesco, the egotistical son of a wealthy merchant. After reading one of the first non-Latin translations of the Bible, Francesco takes the gospels literally. He gives up everything to live and suffer with the poor, gains "peace," starts the Franciscan order and becomes a saint. An elegantly told biblical epic that proves captivating even for non-believers. ★★★ VHS: $79.99

Francis

(1950, 91 min, US, Arthur Lubin) *Donald O'Connor; Voice of: Chill Wills.* The first in the popular 1950s comedy series about the comic hijinks of Francis, the talking mule. Before dazzling audiences with his fancy footwork in *Singin' in the Rain*, O'Connor had one of his first big hits as a G.I. who is befriended by the chatty and wise-cracking animal. The entire series is dated but mindless fun, and this first entry is the best of them. Director Lubin went

on to direct TV's "Mr. Ed." (Sequels: *Francis Covers the Big Town, Francis Goes to the Races, Franics Goes to West Point, Francis in the Haunted House, Francis in the Navy* and *Francis Joins the WACS*) ★★½ VHS: $9.99

Frankenhooker

(1990, 85 min, US, Frank Henenlotter) *James Lorinz, Patty Mullen, Louise Lasser.* From the director of *Basket Case* and its sequels comes this tale of a girl who is dismembered by a lawn mower at her own birthday party and the efforts of her boyfriend to get her back together. While keeping her head on ice in the family freezer, he goes shopping for parts on 42nd Street to see what he can pick up. Great sick fun. (Unrated) ★★½

Frankenstein

(1931, 72 min, US, James Whale) *Boris Karloff, Colin Clive, Mae Clark, Dwight Frye.* The granddaddy of all horror films. This classic stars Karloff as the man-made monster, Clive as the scientist who creates him ("It's alive!"), and Clark as the requisite damsel in distress. A masterpiece of suspense, atmosphere and design. (Sequel: *The Bride of Frankenstein*) ★★★★ VHS: $14.99; DVD: $29.99

Frankenstein Meets the Wolf Man

(1942, 73 min, US, Roy William Neill) *Lon Chaney, Jr., Bela Lugosi, Patric Knowles, Maria Ouspenskaya.* It's Lugosi meets Chaney in this fifth entry in the *Frankenstein* series, and sequel to *The Wolf Man*. This eerie, well-made story has Chaney searching to end his curse, only to do battle with the monster. As with the majority of the Universal horror films of the '30s and '40s, it's chilling to the bone. (Sequel: *House of Frankenstein*) ★★★ VHS: $14.99

Frankenweenie

(1984, 27 min, US, Tim Burton) *Shelley Duvall, Daniel Stern, Barret Oliver.* Director Burton gives his special treatment to a young boy's undying devotion to his dog. Duvall and Stern are Oliver's parents in this dark, brooding examination of heartfelt loyalty in the face of rabid persecution. You'll see early glimmerings of *Edward Scissorhands* and *Batman*, evidence of Burton's already-strong signature. A very polished effort and O.K. for kids despite its somber tone. ★★★½

Frankie and Johnny

(1991, 118 min, US, Garry Marshall) *Al Pacino, Michelle Pfeiffer, Kate Nelligan, Hector Elizondo, Nathan Lane.* Pacino and Pfeiffer turn in a pair of charming performances in this pleasing romantic comedy about an ex-con (Pacino) who takes a job as a short order cook in a greasy-spoon diner and falls for the waitress (Pfeiffer). Excellent support includes Nelligan as an oversexed waitress, and Lane as Pfeiffer's gay best friend. Marshall's directing is overly sentimental and TV-ish, as with his previous outing, *Pretty Woman*, but Terrence McNally's adaptation of his own stage play, "Frankie and Johnny in the Claire de Lune," is strong enough to make this an enjoyable outing. ★★★ VHS: $14.99

Frankie Starlight

(1995, 101 min, Ireland, Michael Lindsay-Hogg) *Anne Parillaud, Matt Dillon, Gabriel Byrne, Georgina Cates, Corban Walker, Alan Pentony.* This

bittersweet Irish yarn tells the tale of a slightly psychic young French girl (Parillaud) and her Irish-born dwarf son, Frankie. Weeks before D-Day, Parillaud makes the disastrous error of predicting the invasion a day early. Stricken with grief, she stows away on an American troop ship only to be dropped off in Ireland, pregnant. She finds a benefactor in a kindly customs officer (Byrne) who helps her through hard times and becomes a surrogate father to Frankie, and plants in the young boy a love of stargazing. Not a lot transpires in *Frankie Starlight*, but its likable characters and generally mirthful outlook make it a completely enjoyable lark. ★★★ VHS: $19.99

Frantic

(1958, 94 min, France, Louis Malle) *Jeanne Moreau, Maurice Ronet.* Malle's first film is an elegant thriller about what can happen to the perfect crime. Moreau's lover is trapped in an elevator after murdering her husband. Subsequently, they become incriminated in a series of crimes they neither committed nor can deny, when their getaway car is stolen by a delinquent Parisian couple and is used for a rampage. A stylish film noir with a great Miles Davis score. (French with English subtitles) ★★★

Frantic

(1988, 120 min, US, Roman Polanski) *Harrison Ford, Emmanuelle Seigner, Betty Buckley, John Mahoney.* Ford gives a controlled but compelling performance as an American whose wife (Buckley) disappears the first day of their French vacation. He discovers the sleazy underbelly of Paris at night as he unrelentingly searches for his missing wife. ★★★ VHS: $9.99; DVD: $14.99

Frauds

(1993, 94 min, GB, Stephan Elliott) *Phil Collins, Hugo Weaver, Josephine Byrnes.* Guilt, fate and the "Peter Pan Syndrome" collide in this dark British comedy that gives new meaning to the term "death by misadventure." Collins earns his acting wings as a game-playing insurance investigator who makes out like a bandit blackmailing a young couple (Weaver, Byrnes) who are guilty of insurance fraud — until the two find the prankster's own Achilles' heel. Good set design, winning performances and coal-black humor easily elevate this film above the level of standard "B-movie" fare. ★★★ VHS: $49.99

Freaked

(1993, 85 min, US, Tom Stern & Alex Winter) *Alex Winter, Randy Quaid, Brooke Shields, Mr. T, Bobcat Goldthwait.* Winter (the *other* guy from *Bill & Ted's Excellent Adventure*) codirected and cowrote this highly original, laugh-laden comedy. He plays a self-absorbed TV star who, upon being named spokesperson for the nefarious E.E.S. Corporation (Everything Except Shoes), is sent to the tropical paradise Santa Flan to curb rumors about the side effects of the company's toxic product. It is there he and a group of innocents are turned into sideshow freaks by a demented scientist/carnival owner (Quaid). Amazingly creative in its use of special effects. ★★★½ VHS: $89.99

Freaks

(1931, 64 min, US, Tod Browning) *Wallace Ford, Olga Baclanova.* Browning's shocking story of circus freaks who wreak vengeance against their

217

cruel exploiters. Sometimes gruesome, yet a sympathetic look at society's outcasts driven by abuse to an act of terror. ★★★ VHS: $19.99

Freaky Friday

(1977, 95 min, US, Gary Nelson) *Barbara Harris, Jodie Foster, Patsy Kelly.* Long before the body-switching craze of the late 1980s, Harris and Foster played mother and daughter who switched identities for predictable comic results. This Disney comedy is charmingly done and benefits greatly from sparkling performances from the two ladies. ★★★

Freddy Got Fingered

(2001, 92 min, US, Tom Green) *Tom Green, Rip Torn, Marisa Coughlan, Eddie Kaye Thomas, Julie Hagerty, Anthony Michael Hall.* Tom Green, "le roi du *gross* de 2000," starts off his debut as auteur recklessly skateboarding through a mall. This is apt, as *Freddy Got Fingered* owes its origins not to surrealism or gross-out comedy but punk skateboard videos, with their mix of loud music and outrageous antics. As such, Green is forgiven for not having much of a plot (a dolt's half-assed quest to become an animator); what's unforgivable is how shockingly unfunny and mean-spirited the episodic setups are. A master of confrontational humor, Green seems to feed off of unwilling participants on his TV show; here, the gags are left hanging lifeless on the scripted characters. In the process, he's reduced to a mere buffoon, performing for an audience of one. Undeniably bizarre, and a disturbing personal peek into what Green finds funny, *Freddy* might have worked if foisted upon the actors without a script; instead, it's exceedingly unpleasant and suprisingly incompetent. ★½ VHS: $102.99; DVD $29.99

A Free Soul

(1931, 91 min, US, Clarence Brown) *Clark Gable, Lionel Barrymore, Norma Shearer, Leslie Howard, James Gleason.* Barrymore won an Oscar for his solid portrayal of a lawyer defending mobster Gable on a murder charge. Shearer plays the attorney's daughter, who falls in love with Gable. The film is impeccably acted, and helped launch Gable on the road to stardom. ★★★ VHS: $19.99

Free Willy

(1993, 111 min, US, Simon Wincer) *Jason James Richter, Lori Petty, Michael Madsen.* Director Wincer pulls every cheap emotional trick out of his bag in this tale of a boy and his whale and, for the most part, he succeeds in his efforts. Kind of an *E.T.* of the sea, the film follows a runaway (Richter) from the foster care system who is taken under the wing of the park's employees and befriended by their charge, an unhappy whale named Willy. When the park's greedy owner sees profits in killing the whale and collecting the insurance, our young hero is pressed into action to save his friend. Yes, it reeks of tearjerking formulaity, but the film is nevertheless a winner among its target audience — kids. (Followed by 2 sequels) ★★½ VHS: $14.99; DVD: $14.99

Free Willy 2: The Adventure Home

(1995, 96 min, US, Dwight Little) *Jason James Richter, August Schellenberg, Jayne Atkinson, Michael Madsen, Elizabeth Peña, Mykelti Williamson, M. Emmet Walsh, Francis Capra.* Jesse (Richter) and

his whale pal Willy are reunited for more adventure in this amiable sequel which ambitiously tackles ecological, Native American and coming-of-age themes. While on a family camping trip, Jesse makes contact with Willy, who has been reunited with his family. When an oil tanker runs aground and spills its contents, Willy and his family's lives are threatened by the spill. Though the first half of the film is maudlin, the scenes with Jesse and Willy have an excitement to them, especially the film's finale which pits Jesse against greedy industrialists and a deadly oil fire. ★★½ VHS: $14.99

Free Willy 3: The Rescue

(1997, 86 min, US, Sam Pillsbury) *Jason James Richter, August Schellenberg, Annie Corley, Vincent Berry.* Young Max (Berry) finds out that he is the son of a whale poacher when he accompanies his father for the first time on a fishing trip. Jesse (Richter), back from the first two *Willy* films and now a teenager, has followed Willy to Alaska and is on a whale tracking research team. The team comes upon the whalers just as they are about to make a kill, but fail to obtain hard evidence of their crime. Max and Jesse become friends and work together to stop the poaching. Simplistic in its story and execution, there's a good ecological message for kids, but the film veers towards overkill. ★★½ VHS: $14.99

Freedom Is Paradise

(1989, 75 min, Russia, Sergei Bodrov) The innocent young boy in search "of freedom" or "of his father" has been a consistent theme in Russian filmmaking. Films like *Freeze, Die, Come to Life* and *Come and See* all use the boy as a symbol of a new, true Russia lost in a harsh post-Communist world. This harrowing yet lyrical drama centers on 13-year-old Sasha who, after his mother dies, begins a journey through the barren worlds of Alma Ata in middle Asia to the outskirts of Leningrad, all in a determined quest to find his long-imprisoned father. The story follows the boy as he is put in a reform school for orphans, escapes and, finally, through the intervention and help of strangers, arrives at a Gulag-like prison. A serious and gripping tale of persistence and perseverance. (Russian with English subtitles) ★★★½ VHS: $59.99

Freejack

(1991, 110 min, US, Geoff Murphy) *Emilio Estevez, Mick Jagger, Anthony Hopkins.* An insipid sci-fi thriller from the producer/cowriter of *Alien* and *Total Recall.* With special effects which far outshine the acting, the film features a catatonic Estevez as a cocky race car driver who is taken from the 20th century into the future by the lunar-faced Jagger, who sports a smirk throughout the film as if to say, "And I get paid plenty for this!" Jagger is the hired hand of an evil industrialist who wants to prolong his life by transferring the life juices of our young hero into his dying body. Hopkins lends some class to the production in a small role. ★½ VHS: $14.99; DVD: $14.99

Freeway

(1996, 101 min, US, Matthew Bright) *Kiefer Sutherland, Reese Witherspoon, Wolfgang Bodison, Dan Hedaya, Amanda Plummer, Brooke Shields.* Witherspoon is a revelation as Vanessa, a white-trash gal with morals, guts and spunk who gets into a load of trouble when she decides to visit

her grandmother. This darkly funny indie — written and directed by Bright — features the often miscast Sutherland as Bob, a demented psychologist who picks up the stranded Vanessa on the highway. But is he a notorious serial rapist/murderer, or just a horny guy who gets kinky with a hot teen in his car? Well, Witherspoon doesn't wait for the 6:00 news to find out and her decision leads to violence, revelations and a manhunt. Funny, vicious and quite unusual (the body count is surprisingly high). (Sequel: *Freeway 2: Confessions of a Trickbaby*) ★★★½ VHS: $9.99; DVD: $24.99

Freeway 2: Confessions of a Trickbaby

(1999, 90 min, US, Matthew Bright) *Natasha Lyonne, Vincent Gallo, Maria Celedonio, David Alan Grier, Michael T. Weiss, John Landis, Max Perlich.* Bright's follow-up is unrelated to the original, except for its twisted tone and over-the-top grotesqueness. Yes, that's a compliment. The opening scenes show White Girl (Lyonne), a hardened criminal not even 20 years of age, being incarcerated, where she immediately indulges her bulimic tendencies with the longest sustained vomit in memory. There she befriends psychotic Cyclona (Celedonio); they escape and set out on a road trip to find a mystic nun (Gallo). Loosely paralleling the Hansel and Gretel fairy tale (like *Freeway*'s Red Riding Hood connections), *Freeway 2* plays even more like Bright's fetish reel: girls killing, girls injecting, girls masturbating. It's all done with outrageous humor and style, and somehow Bright still pulls compelling, inhibition-free performances from his female leads. Great late-night fun. ★★★ VHS: $89.99; DVD: $24.99

Freeze, Die, Come to Life

(1990, 105 min, Russia, Vitaly Kanevski) *Pavel Nazarov, Dinara Drukarova.* A brutal and uncompromising look at Soviet life under the Stalin regime as seen through the eyes of a young boy. The Party faithful are rallying villagers for a May Day celebration amid the abysmal poverty and unceasingly overcast skies in a remote Siberian outpost. The young protagonist, a pint-sized rebel and unwilling scapegoat, struggles gamely against hypocrisy, toadyism and bureaucratic myopia while maintaining his high spirits and fierce sense of individuality. Filmed with a raw, documentary-like feel, the film is sometimes bitter, often funny and insightful, and has moments of touching tenderness. It's also reminiscent of the equally superlative *Come and See.* ★★★½

French Can-Can

(1955, 102 min, France, Jean Renoir) *Jean Gabin, Françoise Arnoul, Edith Piaf.* Set during La Belle Epoque in Paris' lively Montmartre, Renoir gloriously vibrant tribute to the music hall shimmers with the brilliant colors of the director's palate. *French Can-Can* weaves a tale of jilted lovers, ambitious artists and scheming "angels." Gabin, the Gallic Bogart, portrays an amorous impresario with a dream to revive the can-can in a renovated nightclub, which will become the legendary Moulin Rouge. Surrounding him is a circus of dance, love and music, and the people swept up in the exhilarating rhythms of the theater. (French with English subtitles) ★★★★ VHS: $59.99

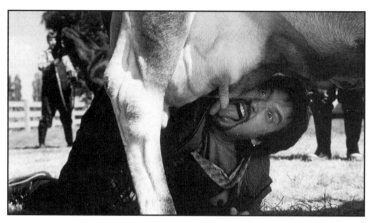

Proof that there is no low too low for Hollywood: Tom Green in *Freddy Got Fingered*

The French Connection

(1971, 104 min, US, William Friedkin) *Gene Hackman, Roy Scheider, Fernando Rey*. Hackman's tour de force performance as real-life New York City detective Popeye Doyle dominates this slam-bang police adventure about Doyle hunting down an international narcotics ring. Scheider also stars as Hackman's partner. Winner of five Academy Awards, including Best Picture. (Sequel: *French Connection II*) ★★★½

French Connection II

(1975, 119 min, US, John Frankenheimer) *Gene Hackman, Fernando Rey, Bernard Fresson*. Hackman returns in this exciting sequel to the original Oscar winner. Popeye Doyle continues his search for an international drug ring, headed by Rey (who also returns from the first film). ★★★

The French Detective

(1975, 100 min, France, Pierre Granier-Deferre) *Lino Ventura, Patrick Dewaere, Victor Lanoux*. An entertaining police story which pits a determined middle-aged cop (Ventura) and his cynical young partner (Dewaere) against a ruthless and elusive politician. (French with English subtitles) ★★★

French Exit

(1996, 92 min, US, Daphna Kastner) *Jonathan Silverman, Madchen Amick, Molly Hagan*. A lightweight set-in-Hollywood romantic farce, this first-time effort from actress Kastner plays like "Four Parties and a Reconciliation." Silverman and Amick are both screenwriters. They meet when her car plows into his during one of those legendary L.A. traffic jams. At first they're at odds, competing for the writing assignment on a remake of *Mutiny on the Bounty* (her take: all female). Then they fall in love. Then they break up. And so on. All of this occurs against the backdrop of Hollywood parties. Some of the inside industry stuff is enjoyable on an elementary level, but few sparks fly between the two leads. This routine film is at its best when it tires to be daring, like having Timothy Leary (in a cameo) handing out Ecstasy-laced cups of tea at one of those schmooze fests. ★★ VHS: $86.99

French Kiss

(1995, 111 min, US, Lawrence Kasdan) *Kevin Kline, Meg Ryan, Timothy Hutton, Jean Reno, François Cluzet*. Ryan plays an American émigré who's engaged to Canadian doctor Hutton. He flies to Paris for a business trip. Since she's afraid to fly, she stays home. Bad move. He meets a beautiful French woman and breaks the engagement. This sends her abroad. On the flight, she meets French jewel thief Kline, who uses her to help smuggle his latest booty. In an effort to keep track of her and the jewels, he pretends to help her win Hutton back. Of course, love blossoms. *French Kiss* is a lot more funny and endearing than the formulaic plot suggests, thanks to the frothy pace set by director Kasdan and the pleasant performances by its two stars. Ryan and Kline wrangle fresh interpretations of parts they've played before. ★★★ VHS: $14.99; DVD: $29.99

French Lesson

(1986, 90 min, GB, Brian Gilbert) *Jane Snowden, Alexandre Sterling*. Snowden stars in this amusing little comedy of manners about a young English woman who sojourns to France where she receives a schooling in affairs of the heart. ★★½ VHS: $14.99

The French Lieutenant's Woman

(1981, 124 min, GB, Karel Reisz) *Meryl Streep, Jeremy Irons, Leo McKern*. This passionate tale of a mysterious woman's obsession shines with the excellent acting of Streep and Irons, and the intriguingly complex screenplay by Harold Pinter. ★★★ VHS: $9.99

French Twist

(1995, 100 min, France, Josiane Balasko) *Josiane Balasko, Victoria Abril, Alain Chabat*. This whimsical French farce with a lesbian twist nicely blends all the outrageousness of its genre with some frothy subtleties to create a highly amusing *divertimento*. Abril is Loli, the dutiful Spanish wife of a boorish French real estate broker (Chabat). Marijo (Balasko), a bohemian, cigar-smoking dyke from Paris, lands on their doorstep in the South of France with a broken-down VW minivan and, after a bit of small talk, makes a pass at Loli. Starved for the attentions of her philandering husband, Loli responds warmly to these advances. Filled with the stan-dard burlesque guffaws, *French Twist* is most impressive for its even-handed treatment of its characters. Balasko is quite fetching as a boyishly macho lesbian, Abril's range of emotion is sensational and her radiance is enough to capture the heart of any sexual persuasion. (French with English subtitles) ★★★ VHS: $19.99

The French Way

(1952, 72 min, France, Michel Deville) *Josephine Baker, Micheline Presle*. This wartime musical comedy is generally pedestrian fare, but the presence of Baker helps make it of interest. Ms. Baker, who sings five songs in the film, plays cupid to two young lovers who cannot marry because of their feuding parents. (French with English subtitles) ★★

Frenzy

(1972, 116 min, GB, Alfred Hitchcock) *Jon Finch, Alec McCowen, Barry Foster, Vivien Merchant, Anna Massey, Billie Whitelaw*. Brilliant latter-day Hitchcock. A suave London strangler ingeniously incriminates an innocent man in a wave of murders. A bold and crafty reassertion of Hitch's mastery of the suspense genre. ★★★★ VHS: $14.99; DVD: $29.99

Frequency

(2000, 119 min, US, Gregory Hoblit) *Dennis Quaid, Jim Caviezel, Andre Braugher, Elizabeth Mitchell, Noah Emmerich*. Mixing equal parts sentiment, fantasy, thrills and the most moving father-son bond since *Field of Dreams*, *Frequency* takes a rather implausible premise and makes it work with a little bit of heart, a touch of cleverness, and plenty of "spirit and guts." Quaid plays Frank Sullivan, a heroic fireman living with his wife and young son John in 1969 Queens. Caviezel is a grown-up John, a police officer in the year 2000. When they are able to contact each other on Frank's ham radio 30 years apart (the presence of the Aurora Borealis presumably causing this time warp), it sets in motion a remolding of fate and the hunt for a serial killer. Screenwriter Toby Emmerich plays a little fast and loose with the concepts of time and space (even for a fantasy), but he's also created a handful of characters that should win over even the most skeptical. ★★★ VHS: $14.99; DVD: $24.99

Fresh

(1994, 115 min, US, Boaz Yakin) *Sean Nelson, Giancarlo Esposito, Samuel L. Jackson, N'Bushe Wright*. Starkly realized and ingeniously crafted, this urban coming-of-age drama follows an inner-city youth as he struggles to ride out life in the mean streets of Harlem. Nelson delivers a disturbing portrayal as Fresh, a tensoming chess wizard (and a hardened drug runner) who is teetering on the edge of a life of crime. His dispassionate, calculating approach to life offers the viewer a sobering look at a vanquished generation, and his Machiavellian maneuvers and innovative survival skills make this much more than just another blighted urban/teen melodrama. Jackson is excellent in support as Fresh's unemployed father, a fallen chess master to whom the boy regularly turns for advice. ★★★½ VHS: $14.99

Fresh Horses

(1988, 105 min, US, David Anspaugh) *Molly Ringwald, Andrew McCarthy, Patti D'Arbanville,*

Ben Stiller. After she turned on *The Pick-Up Artist* and he scored *Less Than Zero*, it was uncertain if Ringwald and McCarthy could sink any lower in their careers. Well, they could. Essentially a wrong-side-of-the-tracks romantic drama, this totally contrived and suprisingly moribund film, about rich college student McCarthy falling for poor but sexy Ringwald, isn't even for fans of the two stars. ★ VHS: $14.99

The Freshman

(1990, 102 min, US, Andrew Bergman) *Marlon Brando, Matthew Broderick, Maximilian Schell, Bruno Kirby*. This delightfully droll comedy stars Broderick as a film student who takes a job as a messenger for a presumed Mafia don (Brando). Brando, with no apologies, patterns his role after another Mafia don he made famous in a cinema classic back in the '70s — and he's terrifically funny. Look for a show-stopping cameo by Bert Parks. ★★★½ VHS: $9.99; DVD: $19.99

Frida

(1984, 108 min, Mexico, Paul Leduc) *Ofelia Medina, Juan Jose Gurrola*. The life of painter, revolutionary and woman-of-the-world Frida Kahlo is brilliantly brought to the screen in this insightful and poetic biography. Told from her deathbed in surreal flashbacks reminiscent of her own canvases, the film recalls Frida's stormy relationship with muralist Diego Rivera, her dealings with Leon Trotsky, her involvement with the cultural renaissance in Mexico in the 1930s, as well as captures the spirit and determination of one of the dominant painters of the 20th century. (Spanish with English subtitles) ★★★ VHS: $29.99

Friday

(1995, 96 min, US, F. Gary Gray) *Ice Cube, Chris Tucker, Johnny Witherspoon, Tiny Lister, La Wanda Paige*. This well-written (by Cube and DJ Pooh) hip-hop comedy chronicles a day-in-the-life of a pair of homeboys in South Central Los Angeles who try to raise enough money to pay a debt to a pot dealer. Spiced with acid-tongued dialogue, *Friday* is a most amusing, energetic romp. ★★★ VHS: $14.99; DVD: $24.99

Friday the 13th

(1980, 96 min, US, Sean S. Cunningham) *Betsy Palmer, Adrienne King, Kevin Bacon*. Director Cunningham started the slasher genre with this gory though unexciting thriller about an unknown killer stalking camp counselors at Camp Crystal Lake. Jason would come back for seven more helpings. ★★ VHS: $9.99; DVD: $24.99

Fried Green Tomatoes

(1991, 130 min, US, Jon Avnet) *Kathy Bates, Mary Stuart Masterson, Mary-Louise Parker, Jessica Tandy, Cicely Tyson, Chris O'Donnell, Stan Shaw, Lois Smith*. Based on Fannie Flagg's novel, this heartwarming, touching and funny film revolves around two separate stories: one present-day and one set in the 1930s. Ignored housewife Bates meets charmer Tandy at a retirement home. It is there Tandy tells her the story of Idgy and Ruth, two friends from her youth in a small, nearby Alabama town. It is the latter story which is at the core of this tender, remarkable film. And as these two women, the incredible Masterson and the wonderful Parker deliver multilayered performances worthy of their sto-

ryteller's adulation. A lovely piece of pop filmmaking with indelible performances by a gifted cast. (Letterboxed VHS available for $14.99) ★★★½ VHS: $9.99; DVD: $29.99

A Friend of the Deceased

(1998, 100 min, Ukraine, Vyacheslav Krishtofovich) *Alexandre Lazarev, Tatiana Krivitska, Eugen Pachin, Elena Korikova*. This Ukrainian twist on *It's a Wonderful Life* is poignant, funny, and, ultimately, romantic. Anatoli (Lazarev) is an unemployable translator who's wife has left him, and who has lost the will to live. Deciding to commit suicide, he hires a hit man to kill him, but a series of encounters with an old friend (Pachin), a kindhearted prostitute (Krivitska) and a recent widow (Korikova), force Anatoli to reconsider his decision. What makes *A Friend of the Deceased* special is that Anatoli is a kind Everyman, dissatisfied with his place in the world, yet also unable to change it. Director Krishtofovich has created a resonant drama that speaks to anyone who has ever found himself trapped in an inescapable rut. As Anatoli, the handsome Lazarev gives a great performance in this highly affecting film. (Russian with English subtitles) ★★★½ VHS: $102.99

Friendly Persuasion

(1956, 138 min, US, William Wyler) *Gary Cooper, Dorothy McGuire, Anthony Perkins, Marjorie Main*. Wyler's absorbing and sensitive adaptation of Jessamyn West's novel is about a Quaker family trying to maintain their religious beliefs during the days of the Civil War. An exceptional cast. ★★★½ VHS: $14.99; DVD: $19.99

Fright Night

(1985, 105 min, US, Tom Holland) *Chris Sarandon, William Ragsdale, Roddy McDowall, Amanda Bearse, Stephen Geoffreys*. Writer-director Holland takes the Gothic out of vampire lore and plops it right down in the middle of the American suburbs. In this wonderfully toothsome twist on the "Boy Who Cried Wolf" story, a young teen desperately trys to convince people that his new neighbor is not the handsome ladykiller he seems to be. He finally enlists the reluctant help of a washed-up TV horror show host (McDowall). Ragsdale lends an over-the-top urgency to the young ghoul-chaser, Geoffreys is particularly effective as Ragsdale's hapless cohort. (Sequel: *Fright Night Pt. 2*) ★★★ VHS: $9.99; DVD: $19.99

Fright Night Pt. 2

(1988, 101 min, US, Tommy Lee Wallace) *Roddy McDowall, William Ragsdale, Traci Lind*. The sister of the vampire killed in the original is out for blood against those who killed him — including TV horror film host Peter Vincent (McDowall); until she finally sees the light about what's at stake with her degenerate lifestyle. ★★ VHS: $14.99

The Frighteners

(1996, 110 min, US, Peter Jackson) *Michael J. Fox, Trini Alvarado, Jeffrey Combs, Dee Wallace Stone, Jake Busey, R. Lee Ermey*. Jackson proves once again that he's an original with this horror/suspense/private eye/love story/serial killer/ghost comedy. Fox is Frank Bannister, a con man ghost-hunter who has the unique power to see the dearly departed. He stumbles

into the middle of a series of murders being committed by a ghastly apparition only he can see. Able to determine who will be next on this soultaker's list, he decides to use his gift to stop the malevolent spirit when a beautiful young widow (Alvarado) shows up with a number on her head. Exhilarating from start to finish, *The Frighteners* features terrific computer-generated special effects and is a brilliant fusion of comedy and horror, alternately hilarious and downright shocking. (Letterboxed VHS available for $19.99) ★★★½ VHS: $14.99; DVD: $24.99

The Fringe Dwellers

(1986, 101 min, Australia, Bruce Beresford) *Kristina Nehm, Justine Saunders*. This exotic film concerns Australia's Aborigines, whose story is similar to that of the American Indian, and the sad and frustrating fact that their tribal roots are disintegrating as they become displaced in their own land. The story follows Trilby, an Aborigine who seeks to leave her community to live out her dreams of romance and high living in the big city. ★★★ VHS: $79.99

The Frisco Kid

(1979, 122 min, US, Robert Aldrich) *Harrison Ford, Gene Wilder*. Aldrich captures the warmth and poignancy that could have so easily been lost in this tale of the Old West set in the 1850s. Bank robber Ford becomes the reluctant guide for rabbi Wilder on his way to join his congregation in California. A nice mixture of comedy and sentimental dramatics. ★★★ VHS: $14.99

Frisk

(1995, 83 min, US, Todd Verow) *Michael Gunther, Craig Chester, Jaie Laplante, Raoul O'Connell, Parker Posey, Alexis Arquette*. Verow makes a memorable if controversial feature film debut with this adaptation of Dennis Cooper's novel of homosexuality, sadism and murder. Dennis (Gunther) is a young gay man who experiences problems with his sexual persona. He meets Henry (Chester), a drugged-out masochist with no self-esteem. What begins as playfully violent sexual antics culminates in murder. Graphic in its gay sex scenes, the film escalates to an almost unwatchable intensity as the violence becomes all too real — or is it simply imagined? Technically proficient and intelligently made, *Frisk*'s ominous content prompts the question of what is being said about gay men. No easy answers here. ★★★ VHS: $29.99

Fritz the Cat

(1972, 78 min, US, Ralph Bakshi) R. Crumb's raunchy feline comes to life in this full-length X-rated cartoon crammed with good humor and bad taste. Whips up more obscenity and violence than Disney dared dream of. ★★★

Frogs for Snakes

(1999, 98 min, US, Amos Poe) *Barbara Hershey, Robbie Coltrane, Harry Hamlin, Ian Hart, John Leguizamo, Lisa Marie, Clarence Williams III, Debi Mazar*. Indie crime drama is an interesting failure — an attempt to meld a low-key gangster flick with an acting class. A group of New Yorkers — all acting students from the same class who moonlight as hit men and the like for off-Broadway producer and crime boss Coltrane — double-cross and murder each other, mostly in the name of securing a good stage role. While the satire is fairly original though obvious, it does get a little tiresome by the end, what with every member of the cast doing at least one monologue from a classic film or play. ★★ VHS: $14.99

From Beyond

(1986, 85 min, US, Stuart Gordon) *Jeffrey Combs, Barbara Crampton.* Gordon's effective follow-up to his acclaimed *Re-Animator.* Once again borrowing from the works of H. P. Lovecraft, Gordon fills his film with outstanding and quite eerie special effects for his story about a doctor, investigating the death of a scientist, who becomes obsessed with the dead man's experiments with the "beyond." ★★★

From Beyond the Grave

(1973, 97 min, GB, Kevin Connor) *Peter Cushing, Donald Pleasence, David Warner, Ian Bannen, Margaret Leighton.* Four customers each try to rip off antique dealer Cushing in some way, and — as is always the case in these kinds of films — get their just desserts in various macabre and supernatural ways. The best story involves an old doorway that opens a portal into a sinister world which threatens to suck in and destroy a young married couple. Lots of ghoulish fun and great entertainment on a dark night. ★★½ VHS: $14.99

From Dusk Till Dawn

(1996, 107 min, US, Robert Rodriguez) *George Clooney, Quentin Tarantino, Harvey Keitel, Juliette Lewis, Cheech Marin, Fred Williamson, Salma Hayek, Tom Savini, Michael Parks.* The beleaguered horror genre receives a welcome shot from screenwriter Tarantino and director Rodriguez. It's easily the most entertaining horror/action/comedy since *Evil Dead 2.* Two homicidal brothers (Clooney, Tarantino) take a lapsed Baptist minister (Keitel) and his family hostage on their run to the Mexican border. The only thing that stands between them and freedom is one night is the Titty Twister, home to a horde of shape-shifting vampires (including gorgeous vampiress Hayek). Screenwriter Tarantino effortlessly combines the best elements of two genres — the film begins as an escaped-convicts road movie and turns on a dime into the realm of zombie and vampire flick. Gory and very adult themed, it will leave

you screaming and laughing. (Letterboxed VHS available for $19.99) (Sequel: *From Dusk Till Dawn 2: Texas Blood Money*) ★★★½ VHS: $14.99; DVD: $32.99

From Dusk Till Dawn 2: Texas Blood Money

(1998, 88 min, US, Scott Spiegel) *Robert Patrick, Bo Hopkins, Duane Whitaker, Raymond Cruz, Bruce Campbell, Tiffani-Amber Thiessen.* A straight-to-video sequel executive-produced by Quentin Tarantino and Robert Rodriguez, this blood-soaked vampire tale lacks the visceral thrills and comic punch of the original, but fans of the genre looking for gory fun may not mind its by-the-numbers (though stylized) bloodletting. A group of good ol' boys look to knock off a bank, but vampires from the local Titty Twister have other ideas. The story takes forever to get started, but when the carnage commences, *Dawn 2* is quite over-the-top. It's not all that suspenseful, but it certainly has its share of vampiric activity. ★★ VHS: $102.99; DVD: $29.99

From Dusk Till Dawn 3: The Hangman's Daughter

(1999, 94 min, US/Mexico, P.J. Pesce) *Sonia Braga, Michael Parks, Rebecca Gayheart, Marco Leonardi, Danny Trejo.* Direct-to-video prequel to the highly entertaining 1996 crime/horror hybrid is mostly a wash. Inspired by the real-life disappearance of writer Ambrose Bierce in Mexico, *FDTD3* follows Bierce as he tangles with a variety of stereotypes before ending up at a brothel run by vampires. Unlike *FDTD2*, this film follows the exact structure as the original: it's a straight-faced (if over-the-top) western for the first hour before shifting gears and becoming a flat-out horror film. The problem is, this time we expect the horror, so surprise is nil, and while the horror scenes are OK, the buildup is not, lacking the much-needed Tarantino wit and George Clooney charisma. Overall, *FDTD3* is pointless and weak. ★½ VHS: $102.99; DVD: $29.99

From Here to Eternity

(1953, 118 min, US, Fred Zinnemann) *Burt Lancaster, Deborah Kerr, Montgomery Clift, Donna Reed, Frank Sinatra, Ernest Borgnine.* A brilliant cast brings to the screen James Jones' novel of

pre-WWII life in an outstanding adaptation in which everything clicks — from the multi-layered screenplay to director Zinnemann's focused eye to a gallery of indelible performances. Set in Pearl Harbor just before the Japanese attack, the film follows the lives of a group of soldiers stationed in Hawaii. Lancaster excels as the impassioned sergeant involved with commander's wife Kerr. In what is the performance of his career, Clift plays a trumpet-playing G.I. whose soul-searching is at odds with military sensibility. Sinatra and Reed both won Oscars in support as, respectively, a private and a dance-hall hostess. Lancaster and Kerr appear in one of the most famous lovemaking scenes of all time: sand, saltwater and seaweed never looked so good. ★★★★ VHS: $19.99

From Russia with Love

(1964, 118 min, GB, Terence Young) *Sean Connery, Lotte Lenya, Robert Shaw, Daniela Bianchi.* Super spy James Bond (Connery) must retrieve a top secret decoder machine and return it to England. The second, and many say the best, of the Bond adventures has Lotte Lenya as a sinister spy determined to terminate Agent 007. Plenty of suspense and hair-raising encounters. (Sequel: *Goldfinger*) ★★★½ VHS: $9.99; DVD: $26.99

From the Earth to the Moon

(1958, 100 min, US, Byron Haskin) *Joseph Cotten, George Sanders, Debra Pagent.* Cotten and Sanders play rival munitions manufacturers teaming up to reach the moon in this unusually faithful adaptation (except for the stowaway love interest) of the Jules Verne story. Director Haskin (*War of the Worlds*) captures a good sense of place and era that imbues the film with charm, if not scientific accuracy. ★★½

From the Hip

(1987, 111 min, US, Bob Clark) *Judd Nelson, Elizabeth Perkins, John Hurt, Ray Walston.* From the director of *Porky's* comes this courtroom comedy that turns rather suspenseful at the end. Nelson is the brash upstart lawyer whose courtroom theatrics would embarrass even F. Lee Bailey, as he is faced with defending a repellent murder suspect (Hurt at his most flamboyant). ★★½

From the Life of Marionettes

(1980, 104 min, West Germany, Ingmar Bergman) *Robert Atzorn, Christine Buchegger, Martin Benrath.* This harrowing and provocative film was made in West Germany during Bergman's celebrated self-exile from Sweden for tax-evasion charges. His troubled mental state could be a clue to his harrowing story of a successful but dangerously psychotic businessman who is obsessed with killing his unfaithful wife. This obsession leads him into the sleazy world of sex clubs where he brutally murders a prostitute. An unsettling film, not for everyone, but insightful for Bergman-philes. (German with English subtitles) ★★½ VHS: $29.99

The Front

(1976, 94 min, US, Martin Ritt) *Woody Allen, Zero Mostel, Herschel Bernardi, Joshua Shelley, Lloyd Gough.* This dramatization doesn't stray from the real-life situation that too many American artists found themselves in during the Truman and Eisenhower years — a reality that seems to be re-emerging in other forms today. In this drama with comedic

Burt Lancaster and Deborah Kerr's quintessential embrace in *From Here to Eternity*

overtones, director Ritt captures an era permeated with fear, necessitating Allen to front for desperate writers blacklisted for having Communist associations. The film is all the more powerful knowing that director Ritt, costars Mostel (in a terrific supporting turn), Bernardi, Shelley, Gough and writer Walter Bernstein were all victims of the Hollywood witchhunt. ★★★½ VHS: $9.99

The Front Page

(1931, 103 min, US, Lewis Milestone) *Adolphe Menjou, Pat O'Brien, Mae Clarke, Edward Everett Horton.* This early talkie starts talking and doesn't stop. Menjou plays the ruthless newspaper editor who will do anything to beat the rival papers covering the execution of a convicted murderer. O'Brien is his reporter who will abandon his fiancée and his ethics to get that interview by helping the convict escape. This first filming of the Hecht/MacArthur comedy — later gender-switched into *His Girl Friday*, then remade by Billy Wilder, and updated as *Switching Channels* — is fast and funny and as cynical as a *National Enquirer* headline. ★★★½ VHS: $19.99

Frozen Assets

(1992, 96 min, US, George Miller) *Shelley Long, Corbin Bernsen, Larry Miller, Matt Clark.* This thematic mishmash manages somehow to combine plot lines about a bordello-like sperm bank, a stud-of-the-year contest and frustrated unemployed prostitutes into what appears to be a family comedy. Bernsen is a low-level executive sent to a small town to improve the finances of the community sperm bank. Long is the uptight biochemical engineer in charge of the "bank." ★ VHS: $79.99

The Fugitive

(1947, 104 min, US, John Ford) *Henry Fonda, Dolores Del Rio, Pedro Armendiaz, Sr.* Affecting political allegory set in an anti-clerical, totalitarian Mexican state about a priest (Fonda) on the run from zealous government officials. Director Ford's classic tale, told with foreboding and awash with shadows, is a subdued but nevertheless arresting portrait of a corrupt state versus the indomitable faith of its people. Filmed on location in Mexico. ★★★½ VHS: $19.99

The Fugitive

(1993, 127 min, US, Andrew Davis) *Harrison Ford, Tommy Lee Jones, Jeroen Krabbé, Joe Pantoliano, Julianne Moore, Sela Ward.* Though not the first, nor last, film of TV-to-big-screen adaptations, *The Fugitive* is certainly the final word. Ford takes over the part once immortalized by David Janssen in the classic 1960s TV show: Dr. Richard Kimble, a successful surgeon falsely convicted of murdering his wife. En route to prison, Kimble escapes, setting into motion a massive manhunt led by the relentless Det. Gerard (marvelously played by Oscar winner Jones). Rather than simply rehash the original series, director Davis and his writers have updated and re-energized a quintessential TV drama with remarkable success. A breathtaking adventure and a fascinating detective story told at breakneck speed, *The Fugitive* also features some of the best chase sequences in recent memory. (VHS available letterboxed or pan & scan) ★★★★ VHS: $14.99; DVD: $24.99

The Fugitive Kind

(1959, 135 min, US, Sidney Lumet) *Marlon Brando, Anna Magnani, Joanne Woodward, Maureen Stapleton.* Disappointing though gritty version of Tennessee Williams' play, "Orpheus Descending." Brando stars as a Mississippi drifter who becomes involved with two women (Magnani and Woodward) while staying at a small Southern town. Tallulah Bankhead may have said it best: (to Williams) "Dahling, they've absolutely ruined your perfectly dreadful play." ★★ VHS: $19.99

Full Contact

(1992, 99 min, Hong Kong, Ringo Lam) *Chow Yun-Fat, Simon Yam, Anthony Wong.* In this brutal Hong Kong action film, Chow plays Jeff, a petty thief who teams up with Judge (Yam), a creepy associate of his cousin (Wong), for a big heist. They pull off the heist, but Judge double-crosses Jeff and kills his young friend and partner, leaving Jeff for dead in an unfortunate bystander's burning home. Jeff slowly recovers, building his strength and wrath for another confrontation with Judge and his traitorous cousin. A radical departure for American audiences used to John Woo's highly stylized, melodramatic and tragic story-driven operas. Lam's work is more Western and story-driven. His eruptions of violence are filmed in a less balletic way, particularly in this film, where the final showdown between Jeff and Judge involves point-of-view shots of the bullets speeding across the room into furniture and human skulls. (Cantonese with English subtitles) ★★★ VHS: $19.99; DVD: $49.99

Full Metal Jacket

(1987, 120 min, US, Stanley Kubrick) *Matthew Modine, Alan Baldwin, Vincent D'Onofrio, R. Lee Ermey, Dorian Harewood, Arliss Howard.* Kubrick's brilliantly realized Vietnam War drama, told with such grace and subtlety it practically discredits all similarly themed films which precede it. Kubrick divides his film into two equally devastating parts: a brutal boot camp training sequence and a horrific war piece set amidst the rubble of the 1968 Tet Offensive. Outstanding in support are D'Onofrio (who à la Robert De Niro gained 60 pounds for the part) as a dimwitted recruit, and Ermey as a merciless drill sergeant. ★★★★ VHS: $19.99; DVD: $24.99

The Full Monty

(1997, 95 min, GB, Peter Cattaneo) *Robert Carlyle, Tom Wilkinson, Mark Addy, Paul Barber, Steven Huison, Hugo Speer, Lesley Sharp.* This hard-edged but still quite funny and endearing hit follows the misadventures of a group of unemployed steelworkers who band together to take it all off! When a local performance of the Chippendales sells out, divorced dad Gaz (Carlyle) reasons anything they can do, he can do almost as well. He rounds up a group of cohorts — all suffering under Northern England's economic crunch — to form their own strip group, including best friend Dave (Addy), who's endearingly slow-witted and a bit overweight; Guy (Speer), a looker whose endowment is perfect for the job; and Gerald (Wilkinson), an uptight, middle-aged former foreman. The group is the unlikeliest candidates to draw a sell-out crowd, but their antics together most definitely are charming, often hilarious and guaranteed to keep a smile on one's face. (Letterboxed VHS available for $19.99) ★★★½ VHS: $14.99

Full Moon in Blue Water

(1988, 95 min, US, Peter Masterson) *Gene Hackman, Teri Garr, Burgess Meredith, Elias Koteas.* Playwright Bill Bozzone wrote this muddled screenplay about a widower (Hackman) haunted by the past and the effect it has on his relationship with his girlfriend (Garr), his father-in-law (Meredith) and his failing business on the coast of Texas. ★★

Full Moon in Paris

(1984, 102 min, France, Eric Rohmer) *Pascale Ogier, Tcheky Karyo.* Sharp dialogue and the beguiling presence of Ogier help make this Rohmer philosophical romance a gem. A headstrong self-absorbed woman, bored of her live-in lover, finds a second flat and begins another affair. (French with English subtitles) ★★★½ VHS: $19.99; DVD: $29.99

Full Speed (À Toute Vitesse)

(1996, 85 min, France, Gael Morel) *Mezziane Bardadi.* An assured feature debut for actor Morel (*Wild Reeds*), *Full Speed* delves into the tangled sexual lives of several young people in rural France. Samir (Bardadi), a handsome teenager of Arab descent, becomes moody and alienated after his intensely close friend dies in an accident. He rediscovers happiness when he befriends a group of young people, including Quentin, a writer, his twenty-year-old free-spirited girlfriend, and eighteen-year-old Jimmy, a gorgeous tough guy who's always in trouble. While Julie and Jimmy begin to have an affair, Samir falls violently in love with a tentatively accepting Quentin. Director Gael borrows more than he should have from his mentor André Téchiné's classic film. The similarities are so obvious as to be embarrassing, but if taken alone, Morel's film successfully captures the drama of young lust, bisexuality, unrequited love and racial prejudice. ★★★ VHS: $29.99

Full-Tilt Boogie

(2000, 100 min, US, Sarah Kelly) This entertaining feature-length documentary covers the making of the crime thriller/horror hybrid *From Dusk Till Dawn*. Beginning with an announcement of the project at a horror convention, and concluding with the final day of filming, *Full-Tilt Boogie* offers an intriguing look at the incredible amount of work that goes into the creation of a film. It could be argued that *From Dusk Till Dawn* isn't deserving of a making-of feature, but this is invaluable as a peek into the day-to-day grind of a film shoot. While the film is a bit ragged, and certainly isn't a fascinating portrait of a passionate artist like the terrific *Hearts of Darkness* or *The Hamster Factor*, for fans of collaborators Quentin Tarantino and Robert Rodriguez — and *From Dusk Till Dawn* in particular — *Full-Tilt Boogie* is a must. ★★★ VHS: $102.99

The Fuller Brush Girl

(1950, 85 min, US, Lloyd Bacon) *Lucille Ball, Eddie Albert.* A hilarious follow-up to *The Fuller Brush Man*. Ball and Albert play a pair of young lovers trying to scrape together enough money to buy their dream house. Desperate for money, Lucy jumps into door-to-door cosmetics sales with disastrous results. The plot is slight and some of the hijinx are a little too over-the-top, but Ball's talent for outrageous slapstick carries the day, making this an all-around good time. Red Skelton has a cameo, reprising his role as the Fuller Brush Man. ★★★ VHS: $19.99

The merry pranksters of *Funny Bones*

The Fuller Brush Man

(1948, 93 min, US, S. Sylvan Simon) *Red Skelton, Janet Blair*. Skelton gets a lot of mileage from this wacky, slapstick comedy with the gifted comedian uncovering a murder while going door-to-door. (Sequel: *The Fuller Brush Girl*) ★★★ VHS: $14.99

Fun with Dick and Jane

(1977, 95 min, US, Ted Kotcheff) *Jane Fonda, George Segal, Ed McMahon*. Fonda and Segal bring a lot of life to the 1970s social comedy as a married couple who turn to robbery to maintain their way of life after hubby Segal gets fired. ★★★ VHS: $9.99

The Funeral

(1996, 99 min, US, Abel Ferrara) *Christopher Walken, Chris Penn, Annabella Sciorra, Vincent Gallo, Benicio Del Toro, Isabella Rossellini*. Director Ferrara and screenwriter Nicholas St. John continue their exploration of morality and personal responsibility, but with a much greater degree of success than their previous collaboration, the awful *The Addiction*. This time around, the gangster genre is the target, and the pair fashion a tale of organized crime in the 1930s, where the families of two surviving brothers (Walken, Penn) come together at the untimely funeral of a third. While *The Funeral* is interesting and its ensemble achieves an almost Coppola-level of success in the period gangster film genre, the film is overburdened with moralizing philosophy. ★★½ VHS: $14.99; DVD: $24.99

Funeral in Berlin

(1966, 102 min, GB, Guy Hamilton) *Michael Caine, Eva Renzi, Oscar Homolka*. Caine is the British operative who must arrange the defection of a top-level Russian military officer in Berlin. The second of the "Harry Palmer" spy thrillers, filmed on location in Berlin, has a few exciting scenes but isn't as effective as *The Ipcress File*. Based on the novel by Len Deighton. (Sequel: *Billion Dollar Brain*) ★★½ VHS: $14.99

The Funhouse

(1981, 96 min, US, Tobe Hooper) *Elizabeth Berridge, Shawn Carson, Cooper Huckabee, Sylvia Miles*. A group of teenagers decides to spend a night in a carnival funhouse and is stalked by a ghoulish creature. Not very spooky, the film relies on the occasional shock for its chills. ★★ VHS: $14.99

Funny Bones

(1995, 128 min, GB, Peter Chelsom) *Oliver Platt, Lee Evans, Jerry Lewis, Leslie Caron, Oliver Reed, Richard Griffiths*. Tommy Fawkes (Platt) is a failing comic who lives in the shadow of his near-legendary father George (Lewis). When Tommy's act bombs in Las Vegas, he immediately disappears, only to turn up in a small coastal town in England where he grew up. But what does this have to do with the opening sequence of a half-witted comedian (Evans) who's left adrift at sea? Well, to tell any more would be to give away some of the zaniest jokes, sight gags and plot developments since Mel Brooks was in his prime. An alternately hilarious and dark comedy which seems to revel in both typical British drollness and over-the-edge Pythonish pranks, *Funny Bones* is a boldly original if lunatic peek into the artistic process which at the same time tries to answer that age-old question: What is funny? As the talented nut case, Evans gives an uproarious performance combining superlative physical schtick with a sympathetic portrait of a fragile mind. ★★★★

Funny Dirty Little War

(1983, 80 min, Argentina, Hector Olivera) *Federico Luppi, Julio de Grazia*. This anarchic and ruthless black comedy dissects the political absurdities and petty bureaucracy of a small Argentine village during the post-Peron years in the late 1950s. A full-scale civil war erupts in an otherwise peaceful, though disordered town when a local administrator becomes involved in a fanatical conflict with his governmental associates. As each political faction doggedly pursues victory, the corruption and dehumanization of war takes its toll when all involved increasingly become efficient in the practices of torture and murder. A blistering anti-war satire which is both witty and tragic. (Spanish with English subtitles) ★★★½ VHS: $29.99

Funny Face

(1957, 104 min, US, Stanley Donen) *Fred Astaire, Audrey Hepburn, Kay Thompson*. All Paris becomes fixated when photographer Astaire pulls out all the stops to capture the heart of his new model, the radiant Hepburn. This charm-ing musical, from the director of *Singin' in the Rain*, features a fine score by George Gershwin, including "How Long Has This Been Going On?" and "S'Wonderful." ★★★½ VHS: $14.99; DVD: $29.99

Funny Farm

(1988, 101 min, US, George Roy Hill) *Chevy Chase, Madolyn Smith*. More dumb hijinks with Chase, here as a city-bred writer whose move to the country isn't exactly what he thought it would be. Some of the jokes are very funny, but many fall flat. ★★ VHS: $14.99; DVD: $14.99

Funny Games

(1997, 108 min, Austria, Michael Haneke) *Susanne Lothar, Ulrich Mühe, Arno Frisch*. To describe this repulsive though accomplished thriller as unpleasant, horrifying or gut-wrenching would be a colossal understatement. A wealthy couple and their young son are terrorized by two preppie psychos while vacationing at a lakeside house. What might sound like a typical genre flick is anything but; while there is relatively little on-screen physical violence, the psychological brutality in *Funny Games* is intense to the nth degree. Technically polished, well-directed and acted, the film is ultimately too nihilistic, cynical and depressing except for the most adventurous, daring viewer. (German with English subtitles) ★★½ VHS: $19.99; DVD: $29.99

Funny Girl

(1968, 155 min, US, William Wyler) *Barbra Streisand, Omar Sharif, Kaye Medford, Walter Pidgeon, Anne Francis*. Streisand's Oscar-winning film debut, repeating her acclaimed stage role, as the legendary performer Fanny Brice. Though the film is somewhat melodramatic for a musical biography, Streisand's singing and clowning make it all worthwhile. Good period design, and Barbra sings "My Man," "People," and "Don't Rain on My Parade." (Sequel: *Funny Lady*) ★★★ VHS: $19.99

Funny Lady

(1975, 137 min, US, Herbert Ross) *Barbra Streisand, James Caan, Omar Sharif, Ben Vereen, Roddy McDowall*. This okay sequel to *Funny Girl* finds Barbra in excellent voice reprising her role as legendary performer Fanny Brice. With Nicky in prison, Fanny takes up with Billy Rose, who would become her second husband. Caan plays Billy, Sharif has a small role encoring as Nicky, and Vereen is a standout performing "Goodtime Charley." ★★½ VHS: $14.99

A Funny Thing Happened on the Way to the Forum

(1966, 99 min, US, Richard Lester) *Zero Mostel, Jack Gilford, Michael Crawford, Phil Silvers, Buster Keaton*. A rip-roaring, bawdy and hilarious adaptation of the hit Broadway musical. Mostel (with the exception of "Fiddler on the Roof") had his best role on-stage, and here on-screen, as a conniving Roman slave who sets out to obtain his freedom. Sexual innuendo, slapstick and feverish chases are the order of the day as Mostel uses every trick in the book in his glorious quest. Gilford also repeats his stage role as a fellow slave, and Crawford is their young, love-struck master. Score by Stephen Sondheim. ★★★½ VHS: $14.99; DVD: $19.99

F

223

Fury

(1936, 94 min, US, Fritz Lang) *Spencer Tracy, Sylvia Sidney, Walter Brennan.* Lang's masterful exposé of mob violence with Tracy in a powerful portrayal of an innocent man unjustly accused of murder. Sidney is splendid as Tracy's fiancée. ★★★½ VHS: $19.99

The Fury

(1978, 118 min, US, Brian De Palma) *Andrew Stevens, Kirk Douglas, John Cassavetes, Amy Irving, Carrie Snodgress.* Set in the paranoid post-Watergate '70s, *The Fury* tells the story of two young psychics, Stevens and Irving, who are being manipulated by a covert government agency attempting to harness their awesome powers. Stevens' father (Douglas) comes to their aid, battling the evil Cassavetes. Director De Palma's film, as with most of his work, is highly stylized and often very violent. Rick Baker's makeup wizardry is outstanding. ★★★ VHS: $9.99

Fury Is a Woman

See: Siberian Lady Macbeth

Futuresport

(1998, 89 min, US, Ernest Dickerson) *Dean Cain, Vanessa L. Williams, Wesley Snipes, Rachel Shane, Adrian Hughes, Bill Smitrovich.* In 2015, professional basketball is disbanded due to scandal. It is replaced by, no, not BASEketball, but by a violent mix of rollerball, skateboarding and hockey. Ten years later, it is the country's favorite sport, and Cain is its favorite player. Meanwhile, in Hawaii, the revolutionary group Hawaiian Liberation Front is fighting guerrilla warfare. How these two factions meet makes up *Futuresport,* an entertaining, well-made futuristic actioner made for TV. The subplot about the revolutionaries is sometimes confusing, but the scenes of futuresport are exciting, and the film doesn't drag during its non-action sequences. ★★★ VHS: $9.99; DVD: $14.99

G.I. Jane

(1997, 120 min, US, Ridley Scott) *Demi Moore, Viggo Mortensen, Anne Bancroft, Jason Beghe, Scott Wilson.* The initial reaction to a film starring Moore as the first female SEAL candidate was an expectant rush of cynical loathing. Instead, immersed in the pyrotechnics of director Scott's signature hyperactive style, substantive questions are raised in this extravagant Hollywood product. Moore is chosen with the influence of a U.S. Senator from Texas (portrayed with icy flint by Bancroft) with her own agenda. Moore is reminded that Israelis stopped using women in combat because male soldiers tarried when women were injured. Let's face it: The real male nightmare regarding women in the military is not women who *get* killed but women who *can* kill. *G.I. Jane* is a slickly made exploration of some button-pushing issues, presented with a budget rivaling some of your smaller wars. (VHS

Galaxy Quest: Not too bold about going where no man as gone before

available letterboxed or pan & scan) ★★★ VHS: $19.99; DVD: $29.99

Gabriel over the White House

(1933, 78 min, US, Gregory La Cava) *Walter Huston, Karen Morley, Franchot Tone.* In this unabashed Depression-era propaganda piece, Huston stars as the president, elected by fraud and entrenched in a corrupt party system until his conversion at the hands of God. Thereafter he sets out to dissolve Congress and institute a kind of bleeding-heart liberalist dictatorship where all of the evils of the world can be eradicated. For those of us who respect the balance of power created by a trilateral government, it's a pretty frightening picture. Still, the film offers some fascinating glimpses at the social agenda in the early days of Roosevelt as well as makes some ominous predictions about the horrors of future world wars. ★★½ VHS: $19.99

Gabriela

(1983, 102 min, Brazil, Bruno Barreto) *Sonia Braga, Marcello Mastroianni.* Brazilian beauty Braga swaggers through this dreamy sex comedy as the hard-to-hold wife of a Turkish bar owner (Mastroianni) who sets an entire two-bit town on its ear. Barreto smoothly directs Jorge Amado's tale of primitive passion and derailed amour. (Portuguese with English subtitles) ★★★ VHS: $79.99

Gal Young 'Un

(1979, 105 min, US, Victor Nunez) *Dana Preu, David Peck.* Based on a story by Marjorie Kinnan Rawlings ("The Yearling," "Cross Creek"), and set in Florida during Prohibition, this passionate film follows a lonely widow (Preu) who erupts into violence when she realizes that she has been victimized by a fast-talking con man (Peck). ★★★

Galaxy Quest

(1999, 100 min, US, Dean Parisot) *Tim Allen, Sigourney Weaver, Alan Rickman, Tony Shalhoub, Sam Rockwell, Daryl Mitchell, Enrico Colantoni.* What took this so long? Spoofing the decades-old "Star Trek" TV series may not seem the most timely of subjects, but in the hands of writers Robert Gordon and David Howard, director

Parisot, and a most engaging cast, it was definitely worth the wait. In this very funny sci-fi comedy, the cast members of a "Star Trek"-type TV show are thrust into intergalactic adventure when aliens think the TV stars to be real space heroes. There won't be a problem figuring out who's supposed to be who, and the one-liners and obvious shots at Trekkies are all done in good humor. If William Shatner hadn't made famous the role of Capt. James T. Kirk, then Allen would have been the next, clear choice. He, Weaver and Rickman (extremely funny as the "Spock" character) are surely enjoying themselves, which is why this works as well as it does. You don't have to be a "Star Trek" fan to appreciate this delight — but it sure wouldn't hurt. ★★★ VHS: $14.99; DVD: $24.99

Gallipoli

(1981, 110 min, Australia, Peter Weir) *Mel Gibson, Mark Lee, Bill Kerr.* A visually striking and emotionally jarring war drama focusing on the camaraderie of two young Australians who naïvely enlist in the army only to meet the savage realities of World War I. Gibson and Lee star as a pair of budding athletes who encounter the butchery of trench warfare up close on a stretch of godforsaken Turkish coastline known as Gallipoli. Weir holds no punches in delivering a stinging indictment of military leadership and war in general. (VHS available letterboxed or pan & scan) ★★★★ VHS: $14.99; DVD: $24.99

The Game

(1997, 128 min, US, David Fincher) *Michael Douglas, Sean Penn, Deborah Kara Unger, Carroll Baker, Armin Mueller-Stahl.* The unknown can usually be nerve-racking, from a haunting voice in the night to the nagging curiosity of what's right around the corner. Hitchcock was a master of exploiting the unknown and our fears of it. He would have no doubt smiled mischievously at Fincher's slick, tense thriller in which twists, suspense and uncertainty all come together in a chilling puzzle called *The Game.* Douglas is right at home as Nicholas Van Orton, a multimillionaire investment banker who is given a present of "the game," sort of a full-time fantasy camp where the subject lives out an unknown scenario. As life-threatening and increasingly bizarre incidents occur, Van Orton learns this game, once begun, is not easily ended. Fincher (*Seven*) is very successful in setting up his action pieces, and maintains believable, edge-of-your-seat tension throughout. ★★★ VHS: $19.99; DVD: $29.99

The Game Is Over

(1966, 96 min, France, Roger Vadim) *Jane Fonda, Michel Piccoli, Peter McEnery.* Fonda's first dramatic role features her as a neglected wife who falls passionately in love with her stepson (McEnery). Her husband (Piccoli) learns of the affair and viciously plots revenge. Swinging '60s Paris comes alive in this electrifying story of decadence directed by Fonda's then-husband. (Filmed in English) ★★★

Game of Seduction

(1985, 95 min, France, Roger Vadim) *Sylvia Kristel, Nathalie Delon, Jon Finch.* A steamy frolic amid the boudoirs and satin bedsheets of the always decadent French bourgeoisie. Kristel stars as a sultry and beautiful woman who is happily married. Her fidelity to her husband is severely tested when a cold-blooded killer and equally cunning noblewoman place a bet that he can seduce her. (Filmed in English) ★★½

Gandhi

(1982, 200 min, GB, Richard Attenborough) *Ben Kingsley, Candice Bergen, John Gielgud, Edward Fox, John Mills, Saeed Jaffrey, Trevor Howard, Daniel Day-Lewis.* Kingsley brilliantly portrays Mahatma Gandhi, the spiritual and political leader of India who, driven by his dream of an independent India and guided by principles of non-violence, struggled a lifetime to rid his country of British imperialism. A fascinating and moving portrait of a man whose commitment to non-violence has served as a shining example to people all over the world. Winner of 8 Academy Awards including Best Picture. ★★★★ VHS: $29.99

Gang in Blue

(1996, 99 min, US, Melvin Van Peebles & Mario Van Peebles) *Mario Van Peebles, Josh Brolin, Melvin Van Peebles, Cynda Williams, J.T. Walsh, Stephen Lang.* The Van Peebles — father Melvin and son Mario — team up as codirectors and costars for this made-for-cable drama. A racist band of big-city cops has been harassing — and murdering — minorities for years. One black cop (Mario) has had enough. He's then assigned a new partner — a redneck ex-Marine. This fact-based cop drama is by the numbers at times, rather heavy-handed at others, but it has some kick to it and is certainly never dull. It falls in the trap, however, of presenting racists as one-dimensional characters; a little more development would have given the film more of an edge. ★★½

Gang Related

(1997, 109 min, US, Jim Kouf) *James Belushi, Tupac Shakur, Lela Rochon, Gary Cole, James Earl Jones, Dennis Quaid, David Paymer.* Belushi and Shakur are cops and partners (in crime) who shake down a handful of drug dealers, murder them, and then dismiss the cases as "gang related." Their scheme hits a snag when their latest hit turns out to be an undercover DEA agent, and a full-blown investigation ensues. Their search for a suitable patsy leads to alcoholic, homeless Quaid, and their problems snowball even more. Writer-director Kouf does a nice job

of slowly turning the screw (and coaxing a good performance from Shakur in one of his last roles), but then drops the ball — the trite, superficial ending reveals the total lack of point of view and hollowness at the film's core. ★★½ VHS: $14.99

The Gang's All Here

(1943, 103 min, US, Busby Berkeley) *Alice Faye, Carmen Miranda, James Ellison, Edward Everett Horton, Charlotte Greenwood, Eugene Pallette, Benny Goodman.* A camp classic from the Golden Age of Hollywood! Forget about the lame love story between Faye and Ellison and pay attention to the fabulously over-the-top frocks and musical dance numbers starring Miranda, the delightful zaniness of Greenwood, and the inestimable Horton. "The Lady in the Tutti-Frutti Hat" is the film's showstopper. ★★★

The Gangster

(1947, 84 min, US, Gordon Wiles) *Barry Sullivan, John Ireland, Henry Morgan, Leif Erickson.* A cynical gangster (Sullivan) is confronted with a vicious out-of-towner who tries to muscle in on his territory. A tough, intriguing character study with Sullivan giving a commanding portrayal of a nefarious hood. ★★★ VHS: $14.99

Garbo Talks

(1984, 104 min, US, Sidney Lumet) *Anne Bancroft, Ron Silver, Harvey Fierstein, Carrie Fisher, Catherine Hicks, Steven Hill.* Bancroft's spirited performance dominates this bittersweet comedy about a son (Silver) who goes through heaven and hell to make his dying mother's last wish come true: to meet Greta Garbo. An episodic tale which features charming touches, though the film does move at a slow pace. ★★½ VHS: $19.99

The Garden

(1990, 88 min, GB, Derek Jarman) *Tilda Swinton, Johnny Mills, Philip MacDonald.* As director Jarman fitfully sleeps in his garden, his cryptic dreams — culled from his subconscious and his fevered imagination — are played out in their fullest, queerest glory. The lyrical images of male love, tenderness and art are interspersed with visions of natural beauty but col-

lide against a background of homophobia, persecution and death. An allegory for AIDS, and his friends who have died from it, the film's main narrative thrust depicts two young male lovers as they are taunted, arrested, tortured and then crucified for their beliefs. A stunningly filmed work of art, full of poetic images, and supported by a haunting score by Simon Fisher Turner. ★★★ VHS: $14.99

The Garden of Delights

(1970, 95 min, Spain, Carlos Saura) *Jose Luis Lopez Vincent, Lina Canelajas.* Saura drastically changes pace and theme with this bizarre black comedy on Spanish society. This cynical tale is about a rich and ruthless old man who loses his memory and suffers from paralysis after an auto accident. His monstrously greedy relatives, desperate to find out the location of his fortune, stage disturbing scenes from his boyhood in their efforts to shock him into remembering. All the while, the old man silently plots his revenge. (Spanish with English subtitles) ★★★

The Garden of the Finzi-Continis

(1970, 95 min, Italy, Vittorio De Sica) *Dominique Sanda, Helmut Berger, Lino Capolicchio, Fabio Testi, Romolo Valli.* Set in fascist Italy, De Sica's Oscar-winning Best Foreign Film depicts an aristocratic Jewish family's confrontation with sweeping anti-Semitism. Based on the semiautobiography by Giorgio Bassani, this exquisitely photographed film explores the horrors of pre-war and war-torn Italy, and the complacency taken by the Finzi-Continis family who lock themselves in the comfort of their mansion's garden away from the realities outside their walls. (Italian with English subtitles) ★★★½ VHS: $21.99; DVD: $29.99

Gardens of Stone

(1987, 112 min, US, Francis Ford Coppola) *James Caan, James Earl Jones, Anjelica Huston, D.B. Sweeney, Dean Stockwell, Mary Stuart Masterson, Laurence Fishburne, Lonette McKee.* Coppola's passionate though heavy-handed Vietnam War film is a showcase for some four-star acting. Caan and Jones deliver powerful performances as cynical Arlington Honor Guard officers who refer to themselves as "toy soldiers" — powerless

Gallipoli

to do anything about the onslaught of body bags except give them elegant funerals. Sweeney is the young officer itching to go to Vietnam: a gung-ho youngster who may not be ready for the experience. ★★½ VHS: $9.99

Gas Food Lodging

(1992, 102 min, US, Allison Anders) *Fairuza Balk, Brooke Adams, Ione Skye, James Brolin, Donovan Leitch.* In her debut film, director Anders tears a page out of Wim Wenders' *Paris, Texas* (on which she was an assistant director) with this heartfelt and emotionally penetrating tale of familial discord and redemption set against the backdrop of the American Southwest desert. Young Shade (winsomely portrayed by Balk) lives with her single mother (Adams) and her teenage sister (Skye). She spends her afternoons alternately haunting the town's deserted cinema (watching her favorite Mexican screen heroine in a series of cheesy romances), and hanging out with her androgynous friend. Sprinkled throughout with a wry sense of humor, the film sports some enjoyably whimsical moments, especially when Shade bridges the town's racial barrier and befriends a young Mexican boy and his deaf mother. A truly enjoyable, exquisitely rendered drama. ★★★½ VHS: $19.99

Gaslight

(1944, 114 min, US, George Cukor) *Ingrid Bergman, Charles Boyer, Joseph Cotten, Angela Lansbury.* Boyer is an effectively sinister counterpoint to Bergman's fragile, luminous innocence in Cukor's classic treatment of manipulation and betrayed love. Boyer has a hidden purpose when he woos and weds orphan Bergman; to protect his secret, he begins a systematic attempt to drive her insane. In her film debut, Lansbury is very tarty as their flirty maid. ★★★½ VHS: $14.99

The Gate

(1987, 92 min, US, Tibor Takacs) *Stephen Dorff, Christa Denton, Louis Tripp.* The Gate, which delivers a few effective frights, follows a pair of young teens who accidentally unleash a horde of demons upon their neighborhood by playing the Satanic messages of a heavy metal record. The embarrassing plot is really just an excuse to showcase the film's spectacular low-budget effects, which include a very scary walking corpse. ★★

Gate of Hell

(1953, 89 min, Japan, Teinosuke Kinugasa) *Kazuo Hasegawa, Machiko Kyo.* A handsomely photographed historical drama set during the 12th-century Japanese rebellion about a samurai warrior who invades a small town, falls in love with and is rejected by a married woman. Academy Award for Best Foreign Film. (Japanese with English subtitles) ★★★½ VHS: $29.99

Gates of Heaven

(1978, 82 min, US, Errol Morris) An appealingly funny documentary about pet owners and the trauma they face when their pet cemetary is sold and their animals' remains are transfered to another plot. A truly original meditation on the American soul. ★★★½

Gattaca

(1997, 112 min, US, Andrew Niccol) *Ethan Hawke, Uma Thurman, Alan Arkin, Jude Law, Tony Shalhoub, Blair Underwood, Loren Dean, Ernest Borgnine, Xander Berkeley, Elias Koteas.* The phrase "designer genes" takes on an entirely new meaning in this elegant, beautifully lensed drama that falls into the category of "thinking person's science fiction." Set in a future where the unborn are genetically engineered and bred to be "super yuppies," the story centers around a physically flawed genius (Hawke) who, using samples of hair, skin, blood and urine, assumes the identity of a paralyzed athlete (Law) in order to gain entrance into the elitist Gattaca Corporation space project. Director Niccol eschews the visual histrionics of, say, *The Fifth Element* for a minimalist look and feel that is strongly reminiscent of the cerebral sci-fi classics of the '60s and '70s. ★★★ VHS: $9.99; DVD: $19.99

The Gauntlet

(1977, 109 min, US, Clint Eastwood) *Clint Eastwood, Sondra Locke.* Eastwood is cop Ben Shockley who thinks he is escorting an ordinary witness (Locke) back to Phoenix for a trial. But he soon finds there are plenty who want to stop her from testifying against an organized crime family. A flavorful, exciting action tale nicely handled by director and star Eastwood. ★★★ VHS: $14.99; DVD: $19.99

The Gay Deceivers

(1969, 99 min, US, Bruce Kessler) *Michael Greer, Kevin Coughlin, Larry Casey.* What has time done to this low-budget '60s comedy about two "perfectly normal" guys who try to evade the draft by posing as homosexual lovers? Is it offensively homophobic drivel or simply a frequently hilarious, naïvely camp curiosity? Filmed in a contemporary sitcom style, the film's funniest scenes come when our hapless heroes, under investigation by a suspicious Army recruiter, must move in to a gay bungalow complex, populated by the most outrageous gay stereotypes this side of Fairyland. Greer steals the show as Malcolm, the boys' gay landlord. If you mind swishy, lisping, prancing "fags," avoid this at all costs. For others, this anachronistic sex comedy will provide some laughs and an appreciation of how much things have changed in 30 years. ★★½ VHS: $19.99; DVD: $24.99

The Gay Divorcee

(1934, 107 min, US, Mark Sandrich) *Fred Astaire, Ginger Rogers, Edward Everett Horton, Alice Brady, Eric Blore, Erik Rhodes, Betty Grable.* In their second film together, Astaire and Rogers demonstrate such chemistry in both dancing and non-musical scenes that it only makes sense that they'd be paired another eight times. Fred plays a noted dancer who meets and pursues Ginger all over London. But she's unhappily married and hires Fred's best friend, lawyer Horton, to set up an infidelity scam to initiate a divorce. That's all the plot that's needed to provide several exquisite dance numbers and very lively comedy. Among the routines, Fred and Ginger perform "The Continental" and "Night and Day." The hilariously effete Horton and scatter-brained Brady offer wonderful support, with Horton actually getting to perform a song ("Let's Knock Knees") and Brady given such amusing lines as "Divorces make me so sentimental." ★★★½ VHS: $14.99

Uma Thurman in *Gattaca*

Gay Purr-ee

(1962, 85 min, US, Abe Levitow) *Voices of: Judy Garland, Robert Goulet, Red Buttons, Paul Frees.* Garland is in exceptionally good voice as Musette, the fairest feline in all of France. This animated tale follows her flight from country abode to the big city in search of fame and fortune. Her jilted suitor (Goulet) and small friend (Buttons) prowl after her in hot pursuit and arrive just in time to save her from the clutches of the villain Meowrice (Frees). ★★½ VHS: $14.99

Gen-X Cops

(1999, 113 min, Hong Kong, Benny Chan) *Nicholas Tse, Stephen Fung, Sam Lee, Grace Ip.* Dorky Hong Kong action film is entertaining, clichéd cheese, but nothing more. A group of ne'er-do-well, "hip" rookie cops are recruited by a foul-up police officer to go undercover and stop a bunch of bad guys. Typical for a HK genre film, *Gen-X Cops* is wildly uneven, veering from sappy melodrama to violent action to silly slapstick, sometimes in the same sequence. Still, lotsa action and style, and an amusing, last-minute cameo from producer Jackie Chan. (Dubbed) ★★½ VHS: $9.99; DVD: $24.99

The Gene Krupa Story

(1959, 101 min, US, Don Weis) *Sal Mineo, Susan Kohner, James Darren, Red Nichols, Buddy Lester.* Mineo gives a good performance as the famous jazz drummer in this ordinary bio which examines Gene Krupa's professional career and his personal life, including an almost career-ending drug addiction. ★★ VHS: $19.99

The General

(1927, 74 min, US, Buster Keaton & Clyde Bruckman) *Buster Keaton, Marion Mack, Glen Cavander, Jim Farley.* Keaton plays a Confederate engineer with two great loves: a sweet Southern belle, and his train. When both are kidnapped by Yankee spies, Buster sets out on an uproarious quest to rescue them. Keaton uses his impeccable timing and acrobatic expertise to create many of silent comedy's definitive routines. The stunts here, often involving cannons and moving trains, demonstrate what a fearless performer Keaton was. ★★★★ VHS: $29.99; DVD: $29.99

The General

(1998, 124 min, GB, John Boorman) *Brendan Gleeson, Adrian Dunbar, Sean McGinley, Jon Voight, Maria Doyle Kennedy, Angeline Ball.* An adroit execution of the real-life story of Martin Cahill.

Gleeson is brilliant in his portrayal of Cahill, folk hero to some, violent master criminal to others. Born into abject poverty, he alternates charm with casual brutality as he directs his considerable talents toward the circumvention of the law. He orchestrates a daring jewel heist deemed by the IRA as too risky to attempt, yet never misses the queue for the dole. Self-defined as the ultimate outsider, bound by no laws but his own limited but deeply held loyalties, Cahill's downfall results from rebuffing the IRA and attempting a deal with the Loyalists. Voight acquits himself well as a policeman who watches Cahill grow from truant to crime lord as he himself moves from beat cop to inspector. The film succeeds in delivering not just Cahill's story, but a feeling for the country and its people. It was jarring to realize that, in the earlier days depicted, the criminals were armed but the policeman on the street was not. ★★★½ VHS: $21.99; DVD: $29.99

General Della Rovere

(1959, 129 min, Italy, Roberto Rossellini) *Vittorio De Sica, Otto Messmer, Sandra Milo.* Brilliantly acted by De Sica, this tragic story revolves around an opportunistic con man who is persuaded by the Germans to impersonate a dead Resistance leader. Their plan backfires, however, when the man begins to assume the characteristics of the general. De Sica's transformation from scoundrel to hero and martyr is riveting. (Italian with English subtitles) ★★★★

The General Died at Dawn

(1936, 97 min, US, Lewis Milestone) *Gary Cooper, Madeleine Carroll, Akim Tamiroff.* Top-notch romantic adventure with Cooper as a mercenary in the Far East who becomes involved with spy Carroll and fights treacherous warlord Tamiroff. Script by Clifford Odets. ★★★½ VHS: $14.99

The General's Daughter

(1999, 118 min, US, Simon West) *John Travolta, Madeleine Stowe, James Cromwell, James Woods, Timothy Hutton, Clarence Williams III.* With this story of murder, betrayal and cover-up, West attempts the quintessential military murder mystery tinged with social commentary. However, the director of *Con Air* has bitten off more than he can chew. Travolta is a wily investigator for the Army's Criminal Investigation Division. Having just sliced up an arms dealer with a boat engine, he's called upon to investigate the murder of a female captain found naked and tied to stakes in the ground. The fact that she's also a high-profile general's daughter only adds more pressure to an already tense case. Unfortunately, the characters aren't fully developed, and West's direction is slack. He fails at creating tension during the investigation, and his red herrings can be seen a mile away. As a comment on women in the military, which it pretends to be about, it's merely window dressing. ★★ VHS: $14.99; DVD: $29.99

A Generation

(1954, 85 min, Poland, Andrzej Wajda) *Tadeusz Lominicki, Ursula Modrzynska, Zbigniew Cybulski, Roman Polanski.* The first of Wajda's "War Trilogy" (which includes *Ashes and Diamonds* and *Kanal*), this is a compelling, exceptionally told story of the underground youth movement afoot in Nazi-occupied Poland. A young man, lured by a pretty face, helps the Resistance by aiding escapees from the Warsaw Ghetto. The naïveté of the youthful freedom fighters is shown in their understanding of war as a game. Their view is soon changed with the realities of death as their innocent lives are corrupted and forever scarred. Wajda creates a mood of urgent and threatening angst. A young Polanski is featured as one of the many youthful members of the Resistance. ★★★★ VHS: $24.99

A Gentle Woman (Une Femme Douce)

(1969, 89 min, France, Robert Bresson) *Dominique Sanda, Guy Frangin, Jane Lobre.* Bresson's first color film opens as an achingly beautiful 17-year-old Sanda leaps from her window to her death in the Paris streets below. Her husband recounts their brief courtship and marriage in a curious monotone with no emotional affect. This self-deluded, self-important man sees her (she's never given a name) only as a "sweet girl," not as an evolving personality. She is a young and impoverished orphan, leaving relatives whom she describes as sinister. He is a methodical man without spontaneity or joy, who becomes obsessive when she fails to be totally compliant. The subtle though involving film maintains a sterile atmosphere, employing no score; the only music is fragmented, ulitzed as ambient sound as she changes her records from pop to classical when he enters the room. The viewer is witness to two lives which intersect with no real connection, and the man is left with his version of the truth. (French with English subtitles) ★★★ VHS: $29.99

Gentleman Jim

(1942, 104 min, US, Raoul Walsh) *Errol Flynn, Alexis Smith, Jack Carson, Alan Hale, William Frawley.* Flynn is in good form as turn-of-the-century boxer Jim Corbett. Interesting look at the early days of boxing. ★★★ VHS: $19.99

Gentleman's Agreement

(1947, 118 min, US, Elia Kazan) *Gregory Peck, John Garfield, Dorothy McGuire, Celeste Holm, Jane Wyatt, Dean Stockwell.* Peck stars as Skyler Green, a journalist who goes undercover as a Jew in order to collect information on anti-Semitism in this Academy Award—winning Best Picture. The premise has a tendency towards preachiness but sadly many of the issues concerning prejudice brought up in this 1947 film are still raging through today's headlines. From the cynical vantage point of the 1990s, Skyler can appear overly earnest as he discovers anti-Semitism at almost every turn. Easing some of the heavier moments in the film, however, is Holm, who won a Supporting Actress Oscar for her delightful portrayal of Ann, a wisecracking, life-of-the-party fashion editor who befriends Skyler. A powerful, earnest treatise on prejudice. ★★★½ VHS: $14.99; DVD: $24.99

Gentlemen Prefer Blondes

(1953, 91 min, US, Howard Hawks) *Marilyn Monroe, Jane Russell, Charles Coburn, Elliott Reed, Tom Noonan.* Marilyn is the gold-digging Lorelei Lee, who's just a little girl from Little Rock. She and best pal Jane head to Paris in search of well-heeled husbands. Though Hawks' direction is sometimes static, and he may not fully understand the intricacies of the Hollywood musical, he nevertheless has created a bright and brassy musical comedy. Featuring unbeatable humor and the classic "Diamonds Are a Girl's Best Friend" production number, *Gentlemen*'s wonderful story line and snappy dialogue shine through. Marilyn gives one of her most endearing performances. And Russell, who has the funniest line about a hat, is at her best. ★★★ VHS: $9.99; DVD: $24.99

Genuine Risk

(1989, 86 min, US, Kurt Voss) *Terence Stamp, Michelle Johnson, Peter Berg.* A by-the-books erotic thriller involving a fatal love triangle. The lusty girlfriend (Johnson) of an underworld kingpin (Stamp) seduces his brooding bodyguard, igniting jealousy, rage and murder. ★★½ VHS: $79.99

George of the Jungle

(1997, 91 min, US, Sam Weisman) *Brendan Fraser, Leslie Mann, Thomas Haden Church, Holland Taylor, Richard Roundtree; Voice of John Cleese.* Okay, so we didn't exactly need another movie based on an animated television series; but Disney's live-action spin on the cult Saturday morning cartoon is actually amicable, innocuous fun. Fraser stars as the accident-prone, loincloth-wearing jungle boy George, and it's the sort of camp-it-up, cheerfully silly role that would humiliate an actor with either less confidence or a lesser sense of humor. Another ingredient in the film's overall enjoyment is capturing the feel of the old Jay Ward (who also did "Rocky and Bullwinkle") cartoons, down to the smart-ass narrator, bad puns, and breaking the cinematic fourth wall. It's surprising how many laughs one can milk out of George smashing face-first into a variety of objects. ★★★ VHS: $14.99; DVD: $29.99

George Stevens: A Filmmaker's Journey

(1984, 100 min, US, George Stevens, Jr.) A thoroughly engaging and heartfelt documentary written and directed by Stevens, Jr. about the life and career of his father, the noted film director. The program includes scenes from such Stevens classics as *Gunga Din, Woman of the Year, A Place in the Sun* and *Giant.* Stevens' approach to filmmaking is explored, and the film also includes rare color footage taken by the director during WWII. ★★★ VHS: $14.99

Brendan Fraser in *George of the Jungle*

Jane Russell (l.) and Marilyn Monroe in *Gentlemen Prefer Blondes*

George Washington Slept Here

(1942, 91 min, US, William Keighley) *Jack Benny, Ann Sheridan, Charles Coburn, Hattie McDaniel.* Before Cary Grant as Mr. Blandings built his dream house, or Oliver and Lisa said "goodbye city life" in "Green Acres," Benny and Sheridan tore apart the countryside in this amusing comedic romp. Antique-buff Sheridan surprises city-loving husband Benny by buying a colonial home in the country. It's dilapidated, but it's okay: for George Washington once slept there. They soon find, however, that the place hasn't been touched since then as they prepare to refurbish it. Benny delivers his one-liners with zeal; and if there is a clinker among them, don't worry — there's a better one just a few lines away. Based on the Kaufman and Hart play. ★★★ VHS: $19.99

Georgia

(1987, 90 min, Australia, Ben Lewin) *Judy Davis, Julia Blake.* Davis is an intelligent, witty, eccentric and captivating actress. And she brings all of these attributes to this slightly mystifying story of Nina Baily, an Australian tax lawyer who discovers that her biological mother was not the woman who raised her, but instead was Georgia, an erratic high society photographer who died amid tabloid rumors: "Accident or murder?" Though at times the facts are a bit hard to keep straight through the characters' thick Australian accents, the compelling story and rich charac-

terizations make *Georgia* an extremely satisfying mystery. ★★★ VHS: $19.99

Georgia

(1995, 117 min, US, Ulu Grosbard) *Jennifer Jason Leigh, Mare Winningham, Ted Levine, Max Perlich, John Doe.* Sibling rivalry achieves new heights in this courageous but ultimately disappointing musical drama which examines the fragile relationship between two sisters. Giving a no-holds-barred performance which is as gutsy as it is excessive, Leigh plays Sadie, an untalented rock singer struggling to make a name for herself in the grunge clubs of Seattle. Her sister, Georgia (Winningham), however, has made a name for herself, a success which Sadie both resents and desperately strives for. *Georgia* is at its best when exploring their unstable relationship — Georgia is somewhat intolerant but protective, Sadie constantly seeking independence and approval. But the film also seems to revel in Sadie's professional and personal inadequacies, often exposing raw emotions in a dramatically involving series of events but without benefit of much subtlety. However, Sadie's final indignity is that a film about her is named after Georgia. ★★½ VHS: $19.99; DVD: $29.99

Georgy Girl

(1966, 100 min, GB, Silvio Narizzano) *Lynn Redgrave, James Mason, Charlotte Rampling, Alan Bates.* Redgrave delivers a delightful performance in this uncommon British comedy about

a frumpy young woman who's satisfied to live life vicariously through her swinging London roommate (Rampling). A delightful adult comedy-drama of modern-day morals. Mason stars as a wealthy man who desires the ugly-duckling Georgy as his mistress. ★★★½ VHS: $19.99

Germany Year Zero

(1947, 75 min, Italy/Germany, Roberto Rossellini) *Edmund Moeschke.* This grim vision of destruction and chaos forms one of Rossellini's war trilogy which includes *Open City* and *Paisan.* The setting for this neorealist classic is the ruined city of Berlin after the war where survivors struggle to live peacefully in an environment where their self-respect, even their humanity, is destroyed. The dispassionate camera follows 12-year-old Edmund (Moeschke), a boy whose family lives in a cramped war-damaged flat with four other families. As Edmund scavenges the city for coal, money and food, he meets Mr. Enning, a creepy middle-aged man and former Nazi schoolteacher. The old man soon involves the boy in the black market and ultimately eggs the youth to a heinous crime, an act which destroys the boy's innocence and proves the pervading power of lingering fascism. (German with English subtitles) ★★★½ VHS: $79.99

Germinal

(1993, 160 min, France/Italy/Belgium, Claude Berri) *Gérard Depardieu, Miou-Miou, Renaud, Judith Henry.* Based on Emile Zola's gripping novel about coal miners in the 19th century, *Germinal* provides director Berri with yet another exquisite literary adaptation. Miou-Miou and Depardieu are wonderfully type-cast as the working-class hero and his wife who struggle through the tense conditions that lead to a workers revolt. With sweeping camerawork and a pervading sense of doom, the film expertly captures the feeling of claustrophobia as to recall the power and anxiety of *Das Boot.* Berri is a true master of detail and period work, and nowhere is it more evident than this epic saga. (French with English subtitles) ★★★½ VHS: $19.99

Geronimo: An American Legend

(1993, 115 min, US, Walter Hill) *Jason Patric, Gene Hackman, Robert Duvall, Wes Studi, Rodney A. Grant, Kevin Tighe, Matt Damon.* Patric brings intensity and intelligence to this haunting examination of Geronimo, the Apache who was the last Native American leader to elude the government's attempt to confine the Indian nations to reservations. Shot amid the dusty Utah vistas, Patric — complete with gentle Southern drawl — plays the cavalry officer who is sent to bring in Geronimo (Studi) upon his surrender. The last scenes in the film paint a vivid portrait of some of the most shameful injustices in the history of the West. ★★★ VHS: $9.99; DVD: $14.99

Gervaise

(1956, 110 min, France, René Clément) *Maria Schell, François Perier.* Based on the Emile Zola novel "L'Assommoir," this superbly acted drama of a laundrywoman's bleak life in 19th-century Paris achieves moments of brilliant realism and spellbinding dramatics but is overshadowed by the depressing lives of its characters. Nominated for Best Foreign-Language Film, *Gervaise* stars Schell in a heartbreaking performance as a crippled woman who starts life anew with her two children after her philandering husband leaves her. Happiness is short-lived, however, as her second husband turns to drink and ruins both their lives. This is a devastating tale of betrayal, revenge and star-crossed love. (Remake: *Germinal*) (French with English subtitles) ★★★ VHS: $29.99

Get Bruce!

(1999, 82 min, US, Andrew J. Kuehn) *Bruce Vilanch, Robin Williams, Billy Crystal, Bette Midler, Whoopi Goldberg, Lily Tomlin, Nathan Lane, Roseanne, Carol Burnett, Rosie O'Donnell, Shirley MacLaine.* Bruce Vilanch — with his appearances on the new "Hollywood Squares" — seems to have come out of nowhere recently; but that is far from reality as this entertaining documentary sets out to reveal. With his wildly bushy blond hair, beard, oversized glasses and roly-poly physique, Vilanch has been working behind the entertainment scene for most of his 30 years as one of the industry's top comedy writers — "everyone from Abba to Zadora." He has also been comedy writer on almost every awards show including being head writer for the Academy Awards. The film focuses on the former *Chicago Tribune* writer and features interviews with a litany of stars for whom he has been providing laugh lines. ★★★½ VHS: $19.99

Get Carter

(1971, 112 min, GB, Mike Hodges) *Michael Caine, Ian Hendry, Britt Ekland.* Ushering in the neo-noir wave of the '70s, *Get Carter* saw the future and it was bleak. The devastatingly suave Caine plays Jack Carter, a magnetic gangster with a pervasive mean streak. He heads to grimy Newcastle to track down his brother's murderer. Using intimidation (for men) and seduction (for the ladies), he gets answers and issues judgment, but revenge is rarely satisfying. Hodges provides a quiet visual flair, putting the camera right where it traditionally shouldn't be, picking up other characters and some essential mood in the process. (Remade in 1971 as *Hit Man* and in 2000 as *Get Carter*) ★★★½ VHS: $19.99; DVD: $24.99

Get Carter

(2000, 102 min, US, Stephen Kay) *Sylvester Stallone, Miranda Richardson, Rachael Leigh Cook, Mickey Rourke, Alan Cumming, Michael Caine.* Sometimes, style can indeed triumph over substance. In this inconsistently dull Americanization of *Get Carter*, though, the (lack of) substance is so prevalent that the gloss is a mere distraction, and the action scenes are so infrequent that by the time one is jolted awake, it's on to another bit of underwritten dialogue. This updating does more than move Carter (Stallone) to Seattle; it replaces the social cynicism of the original with the idea that revenge *can* buy happiness. And, yes, the brutal fights (especially with well-cast Rourke) and car chases are refreshing when they finally occur. But it leaves an empty feeling afterwards, one that the filmmakers don't recognize. Some good performances (Cumming, Cook) are wasted on the weak script. ★★ VHS: $14.99; DVD: $19.99

Get Crazy

(1983, 98 min, US, Allan Arkush) *Malcolm McDowell, Ed Begley, Jr., Lou Reed, Daniel Stern, Fabian.* The *crazy* in the title is not misleading as a rock promoter for a Fillmore East-like theatre gets more than he bargained for when he stages a New Year's Eve concert. A few "in" cameos by famous music personalities. ★★★

Get on the Bus

(1996, 121 min, US, Spike Lee) *Charles S. Dutton, Ossie Davis, Roger Guenveur Smith, Andre Braugher, Isaiah Washington.* A group of 20 or so African-American men hop on a commercial bus in Los Angeles and head to the Million Man March in Washington, D.C. Along the way, friendships are forged, fights break out, and the very purpose of this cross-country trek is discussed. Director Lee gathers together a collection of "types" (ex-gang banger, wise elder, buppie, gay couple, deadbeat dad) in an enclosed space for a period of time, and like a fascinating sociological experiment, observes the results. Lee avoids heavy moralizing for the most part, concentrating instead on delicious debates on a broad range of topics concerning black males: racism, misogyny, homophobia, upward mobility, self-respect, and even the O.J. verdict. This is a well-acted, involving, fast-paced effort marred only by a dramatically unsatisfying, clunky ending. ★★★ VHS: $9.99; DVD: $24.99

Get Out Your Handkerchiefs

(1978, 109 min, France, Bertrand Blier) *Gérard Depardieu, Patrick Dewaere, Carole Laurie.* A farcical comedy on unconventional love and sex. Depardieu is a husband aiming to please, Laurie is his enigmatic wife and Dewaere is a lover brought in to lift her out of her depression. An insightful look into the sexual roles of the modern relationship; both witty and perceptive. (French with English subtitles) ★★★½ VHS: $59.99

Get Real

(1999, 110 min, GB, Simon Shore) *Ben Silverstone, Brad Gorton, Charlotte Brittain, Stacy Hart, Kate McEnery.* A sharply observed coming-of-age story, *Get Real* is infused with charm, humor and a knowing sense of the difficulties of being a gay teen. Steven (Silverstone) is a 16-year-old living in the new British suburbia with his upper-middle-class parents. Life changes for the soft-spoken teen when he locks eyes on the school's strappingly handsome super-jock John (Gorton). The two are attracted to each other, but John's self-hating fears of others finding out about his sexuality threaten to tear apart their tentative relationship. Though the plot is too similar to *Beautiful Thing*, and there are some unnecessary melodramatic excesses, this tale should charm and captivate any audience familiar with feelings of being an outsider. The screenplay, by Patrick Wilde, is based on his play, "What's Wrong with Angry?" ★★★ VHS: $14.99; DVD: $29.99

Get Rita

(1972, 90 min, Italy, Giorgio Capitini) *Sophia Loren, Marcello Mastroianni.* In the mood for a scoop of Italian gelato? Try the cinematic equivalent in this light, endearingly terrible comedy. Loren is Poopsie, a Milanese prostitute who finds herself "bought" by Charlie (Mastroianni), an abusive, big-time gangster. Poopsie proves to be a lot tougher than her nemesis as she seeks to undermine the low-life kingpin. Sounds serious? Don't be fooled — everyone overacts in this wacky comedy whose highlight is Loren's imitation of a dancing and singing Rita Hayworth. ★½

Get Shorty

(1995, 105 min, US, Barry Sonnenfeld) *John Travolta, Gene Hackman, Rene Russo, Danny DeVito, Dennis Farina, Delroy Lindo, James Gandolfini, David Paymer, Bette Midler.* A thoroughly entertaining, hip and refreshing gangster comedy which takes aim at Hollywood and its players. Travolta gives a scintillating performance as Chili Palmer, a low-level but self-assured Miami mobster whose debt collection assignment takes him to Hollywood. An acknowledged film buff, Chili is soon pitching a movie deal to sleazy producer Harry Zimm (a hilarious Hackman) rather than collecting his debt. In an ever-spiraling comedic vortex of industry machinations, Chili becomes involved with Zimm's leading lady (Russo), a pretentious star (DeVito), a rival gangster (Lindo), and a Miami gangland boss (Farina in a wonderfully antic performance) out for revenge. Based on the novel by Elmore Leonard, *Get Shorty* is smart, cynical and fabulously funny. ★★★★ VHS: $9.99; DVD: $19.99

Get to Know Your Rabbit

(1972, 91 min, US, Brian De Palma) *Tom Smothers, John Astin, Orson Welles, Allen Garfield, Katharine Ross.* Quirky, smirky, mischievous and very '70s, this oddball comedy (actually filmed in 1970) was made during De Palma's inventive independent period. Smothers plays a '70s version of a yuppie who chucks the pressures of executive life and "drops out" to become a tap-dancing magician. Welles (who was an amateur magician) is his strange teacher, a bug-eyed Astin is his former boss and Garfield is a swinger with a brassiere fetish. The film is filled with wacky humor that does not always hit the mark, but overall it's a fine example of the kind of exuberant comedy popular at the time. ★★★ VHS: $19.99

The Getaway

(1972, 122 min, US, Sam Peckinpah) *Steve McQueen, Ali MacGraw, Ben Johnson, Sally Struthers, Slim Pickens, Jack Dodson.* McQueen and MacGraw capture on-screen the sparks they were striking offscreen in this violent tale of an ex-con hired by the mob to pull off a simple bank job. Even though the heist goes awry, the mob still wants their money — and they're holding his wife until they get it. This time out, director Peckinpah's penchant for balletic violence is subservient to the story and suspenseful action sequences. (Remade in 1994) ★★★ DVD: $19.99

The Getaway

(1994, 114 min, US, Roger Donaldson) *Alec Baldwin, Kim Basinger, James Woods, Michael Madsen, David Morse, Jennifer Tilly, Philip Seymour Hoffman.* From the director of *No Way Out* comes this glamorous, highly entertaining remake of the grungy Sam Peckinpah actioner starring real-life husband and wife Baldwin and Basinger in the roles originally played by real-life couple Steve McQueen and Ali MacGraw. Both are evenly matched as a bickering, larcenous couple on the run from a botched heist and the accomplices that set them up (including Madsen as a red-headed psycho). Special mention goes to Tilly in the comic role originally played by Sally Struthers. ★★★ VHS: $7.49; DVD: $26.99

Getting Away with Murder

(1996, 92 min, US, Harvey Miller) *Dan Aykroyd, Lily Tomlin, Jack Lemmon, Bonnie Hunt, Brian Kerwin.* What was probably intended as an acerbic commentary on contemporary morals, *Getting Away with Murder* is merely plodding and muddled. Mild-mannered history professor Aykroyd suspects next-door neighbor Lemmon to be a Nazi war criminal. His interest is misread as support by Lemmon and daughter Tomlin, leading to Aykroyd's further involvement in ensuing events. However, instead of a wry, twisting morality tale, this unfocused and weak effort telegraphs its punches way too early and without a power delivery. ★ VHS: $9.99

Getting Even with Dad

(1994, 108 min, US, Howard Deutch) *Ted Danson, Macaulay Culkin, Glenne Headly, Saul Rubinek, Hector Elizondo.* A promising premise, that of a precocious 12-year-old son blackmailing his criminal dad to go straight, hasn't been exploited at all, and both lifeless direction and an awful script make this a tedious bore. Danson plays an ex-con who masterminds a robbery which seems to be foolproof — only he didn't allow for a visitation from his estranged son (Culkin). The kid gets wise to Dad's plans, and forces him to spend time with him, hoping he'll forget his life of crime. Only Rubinek as Danson's partner and Headly as a cop rise above the material. ★½ VHS: $14.99; DVD: $14.99

Getting It Right

(1989, 105 min, GB, Randal Kleiser) *Jesse Birdsall, Lynn Redgrave, Peter Cook, John Geilgud.* This English comedy about a man's sexual and emotional awakening is a surprisingly touching and consistently funny coming-of-age film. Gavin Lamb (the perfectly cast Birdsall) is a slightly awkward but handsome 31-year-old London hairdresser who lives at home and dreams of one day losing his virginity. In a whirlwind two weeks his structured life is shattered when he is thrown into the arms, and beds, of three very different women. Redgrave is smashing as the "older woman" who introduces our young hero to the pleasures of the flesh. ★★★

The Getting of Wisdom

(1977, 100 min, Australia, Bruce Beresford) *Susannah Fowles, Alix Longman, Hilary Ryan, Barry Humphries.* A spirited girl encounters unhappiness at a snobbish Melbourne girls' academy in Beresford's pleasant if unimaginative coming-of-age drama. Set before the turn of the century, the story follows intelligent but impetuous Laura (Fowles), who leaves her rural home for higher education in the big city. There, she overcomes the school's petty regulations, schoolgirl rivalries and the authority's herd mentality. Humphries, the alter ego to Dame Edna Everage, appears as the school's principal in a wasted performance. ★★½ VHS: $19.99

Gettysburg

(1993, 254 min, US, Ronald F. Maxwell) *Tom Berenger, Jeff Daniels, Martin Sheen, Sam Elliott, Maxwell Caulfield, C. Thomas Howell, Stephen Lang, Kevin Conway, Richard Jordan.* An epic re-creation of the Battle of Gettysburg, this four-hour drama may not belie its running time, but it certainly captures the flavor of its time, and brilliantly stages in painstaking detail the endless battles which marked the Civil War.

Earnest performances from the ensemble distinguish the production, though Daniels and Jordan excel in their characterizations of ethical men caught in the confines of bloody combat. Though *Gettysburg*'s dramatic scenes aren't on par with its battle sequences, the film features outstanding production values, and also some truly awful makeup. ★★★ VHS: $24.99; DVD: $24.99

Ghost

(1990, 127 min, US, Jerry Zucker) *Patrick Swayze, Demi Moore, Whoopi Goldberg, Tony Goldwyn.* A metaphysical romance/thriller/comedy, *Ghost* is a guaranteed crowd-pleaser filled with supernatural intrigue and lots of laughs. Swayze and Moore star as Sam and Molly, a yuppie couple whose picture-perfect romance is broken up when Sam is suddenly dispatched to the other side. As he becomes stuck between dimensions, Sam's spirit roams the streets of Manhattan in search of answers. Goldberg's Oscar-winning performance as Oda Mae Brown, a storefront spiritual advisor who becomes Swayze's reluctant link to the world of the living, is hilarious. Director Zucker moves the action along at a lively pace and makes the most of Goldberg's enormous comedic talents. Aside from a simplistic version of life in the hereafter, the film has few flaws and will leave even the most skeptical viewer smiling. (VHS available letterboxed or pan & scan) ★★★ VHS: $9.99; DVD: $29.99

The Ghost and Mrs. Muir

(1947, 104 min, US, Joseph L. Mankiewicz) *Gene Tierney, Rex Harrison, George Sanders, Edna Best, Natalie Wood.* A charming fantasy about a widow (Tierney) who is romanced by a crusty if ethereal sea captain (Harrison), the once and present occupant of her New England cottage. A felicitous mixture of make-believe with an acute observation of human foibles, and requiring very little suspension of disbelief. Tierney is especially engaging. Scripted by Philip Dunne, with music by Bernard Herrmann. (Remade as a TV series in the 1960s) ★★★ VHS: $19.99

The Ghost and the Darkness

(1996, 110 min, US, Stephen Hopkins) *Michael Douglas, Val Kilmer, Bernard Hill, John Kani.* Though he doesn't appear on screen until a half-hour into the film, Douglas' big-game hunter adds just the right kick to an otherwise familiar, occasionally exciting jungle adventure. Set in late-1890s East Africa, and amazingly based on a true story, *The Ghost and the Darkness* follows the attempts to build a railroad by a British firm whose crew has come under attack by two man-eating lions. Kilmer is the engineer sent to oversee construction and the elimination of the animals. The scenery is spectacular, and the cinematography captures the beauty of the land and the terror of the beasts. Once again, nature rules. (VHS available letterboxed or pan & scan) ★★½ VHS: $14.99; DVD: $24.99

The Ghost Breakers

(1940, 85 min, US, George Marshall) *Bob Hope, Paulette Goddard, Willie Best.* Though short on plot, there's plenty of laughs to this uproarious Hope ghost comedy. Radio journalist Bob helps Paulette — who's just inherited a haunted castle in Cuba — battle the bad guys and some prankish poltergeists. And Hope's got a one-liner for every occasion ("The girls call me Pilgrim,

because every time I dance with one I make a little progress"): Some are merely funny; others are just hilarious. Best makes the most of the unflattering role of the "scared Negro" (Best does get a few zingers of his own), and Goddard is captivating. (Remade as *Scared Stiff*) ★★★½ VHS: $14.99

Ghost Dad

(1990, 84 min, US, Sidney Poitier) *Bill Cosby, Denise Nicholas, Ian Bannen.* Cosby plays a widowed father who dies and comes back to life, given a couple of days to straighten out his affairs for the sake of his children. Though Cosby hams it up, there's little that works in this tired ghost comedy. ★★ VHS: $12.99

Ghost Dog: The Way of the Samurai

(2000, 116 min, US, Jim Jarmusch) *Forest Whitaker, John Tormey, Cliff Gorman, Henry Silva, Tricia Vessey, Victor Argo.* *Ghost Dog*, a typically low-key, slow-paced Jarmusch comedy-drama, is among his best. Whitaker plays a hit man for the mob who lives his life according to the code of the Japanese samurai. When a hit goes slightly wrong, he is marked for death, leading to a war of old-school philosophies. Filled with the usual Jarmusch dry-as-toast humor, *Ghost Dog* is a surprisingly effective film, juggling hilarious insights into race relations and violence with jarring shoot-outs and dramatic moments. Whitaker is superb, the cinematography is spot-on, and the old mob guys — especially Argo and Gorman — are hysterical. Perhaps too slow for the average action fan, *Ghost Dog* is nonetheless the most accessible Jarmusch film in a while, but one that doesn't sacrifice any originality. ★★★½ VHS: $14.99; DVD: $19.99

The Ghost Goes Gear

(1966, 79 min, GB, Hugh Gladwich) *The Spencer Davis Group, Nicholas Parson, Jack Haig, Sheila White.* The popular 1960s British pop group Spencer Davis Group follows on the heels of The Beatles' *A Hard Day's Night* and *Help!* with this lively rock comedy featuring daft blokes, mod birds, groovy tunes and ghosts gone gear. (Letterboxed) ★★★ VHS: $14.99; DVD: $24.99

The Ghost Goes West

(1936, 82 min, GB, René Clair) *Robert Donat, Jean Parker, Eugene Pallette, Elsa Lanchester.* Delightful ghost comedy about a 200-year-old spirit who, refusing to leave the Scottish castle he haunts, travels to America when it is sold and shipped abroad. Written by Robert E. Sherwood, with Donat as charming as ever in dual roles as the poltergeist and his descendant. ★★★½

Ghost in the Machine

(1994, 90 min, US, Rachel Talalay) *Karen Allen, Chris Mulkey, Jessica Walter.* The Lawnmower Man meets *Shocker* meets *The Horror Show* ad infinitum ad nauseam (emphasis on "nauseam") as a serial killer on the brink of death is uploaded into a municipal mainframe enabling him to kill anyone who's paid their electric bill. State-of-the-art effects and a couple of creatively grisly deaths can't help shock this one back to life. ★½ VHS: $79.99

Ghost in the Noonday Sun

(1973, 93 min, GB, Peter Medak) *Peter Sellers, Spike Milligan, Anthony Franciosa, Peter Boyle.* It is rumored that Sellers and director Medak had a falling out which led to the demise of this blundering pirate comedy. Sellers stars as a rogue pirate who leads his men in search of hidden treasure, but finds that the booty is protected by a less than friendly ghost. ★

Ghost in the Shell

(1995, 80 min, Japan, Mamoru Oshii) Based on the cyberpunk manga by Masamune Shirow, *Ghost in the Shell* is a cerebral animated sci-fi tale that mixes philosophy with its high-octane action. In a future dominated by technology, a female cyborg is investigating a series of computer-hacking crimes with her special police unit, when it is revealed that their opponent is a new cybernetic life form. Director Oshii brings a distinct style of visual storytelling to this feature through a mix of computer and traditional cel animation. The results are breathtaking. (Japanese with English subtitles) ★★★½ VHS: $29.99; DVD: $29.99

Ghost Story

(1981, 85 min, US, John Irvin) *Fred Astaire, Melvyn Douglas, Douglas Fairbanks, Jr., John Houseman, Craig Wasson, Patricia Neal.* The old guard of Hollywood showed up to make this horror film as generic as its title. Astaire (in his last film) and pals teeter through this film about a shared secret from 50 years ago that is back for revenge. ★½ VHS: $19.99

Ghostbusters

(1984, 107 min, US, Ivan Reitman) *Bill Murray, Dan Aykroyd, Harold Ramis, Sigourney Weaver, Rick Moranis, Annie Potts, Ernie Hudson, William Atherton.* One of the highest-grossing comedies of all time. Murray, Aykroyd and Ramis play bumbling "paranormal investigators" who save the world, or at least New York City, from demonic apparitions. The special effects are state-of-the-art, and both high-brow and low-brow humor abounds. Fine comic performances from Weaver and Moranis. (Sequel: *Ghostbusters II*) ★★★ VHS: $14.99; DVD: $19.99

Ghostbusters II

(1989, 102 min, US, Ivan Reitman) *Bill Murray, Dan Aykroyd, Sigourney Weaver, Harold Ramis, Rick Moranis, Annie Potts, Ernie Hudson.* This formulaic sequel has, as in the original, an evil spirit from the past haunting the present — this time in the form of a truly ugly medieval monarch who is trapped in a less than flattering Renaissance painting. In conjunction with his imminent release the city of New York is being inundated by the now familiar ooze called "slime." All of the characters have returned from the first film — kudos go to Weaver for being the only one in the bunch to have actually developed her character from the original. ★★½ VHS: $12.99; DVD: $19.99

Ghosts of Mississippi

(1996, 123 min, US, Rob Reiner) *Alec Baldwin, Whoopi Goldberg, James Woods, Craig T. Nelson, William H. Macy, Diane Ladd, Virginia Madsen, Michael O'Keefe, Brock Peters.* In 1963, civil rights activist Medgar Evers was assassinated in front of his Mississippi home. The murderer went free after two hung juries couldn't come to a verdict.

Thirty years later, Evers' widow pushed for a new trial, eventually bringing her husband's killer to justice. This sad chapter of America's past is the focus of Reiner's commendable if unremarkable film, a detective and courtroom drama which doesn't quite have the passion of its convictions. Baldwin plays the Assistant District Attorney in charge of the case, and Goldberg is Myrlie Evers. Like so many Hollywood films about racial prejudice against African-Americans, the story is seen through the eyes of a white person — here Baldwin. But whereas a film like *Mississippi Burning* has energy and focus, *Ghosts of Mississippi* has professionalism but lacks heart. ★★½ VHS: $19.99; DVD: $19.99

Ghoulies

(1985, 81 min, US, Luca Bercovici) *Peter Liapis, Lisa Pelikan, Michael Des Barres, Jack Nance.* A young man inherits his father's mansion, and becomes obsessed with the demonic witchery that led to his parents' deaths. A ridiculous story line, inferior special effects and a lack of good scares don't even make this a campy pleasure. (Followed by 3 sequels) ★

Gia

(1998, 125 min, US, Michael Cristofer) *Angelina Jolie, Elizabeth Mitchell, Kylie Travis, Mercedes Ruehl, Faye Dunaway.* A mercurial, fact-based drama about the tragic life of supermodel Gia Carangi. Gia's rise and fall from an unruly Philadelphia teenager who becomes a top model to drug addict and AIDS victim makes for spellbinding viewing. As Gia seeks love and support from her mother (Ruehl) and her hesitant girlfriend Linda (Mitchell), she breaks all the rules, and everyone's heart. Cristofer's approach to the material is never melodramatic; however, he uses diary snippets and memories by those who knew her to depict Gia's fast life and untimely death. Although the film suffers from an overly arty style, it's mostly riveting thanks to Jolie's no-holds-barred star turn. ★★★ VHS: $9.99; DVD: $14.99

Giant

(1956, 200 min, US, George Stevens) *James Dean, Elizabeth Taylor, Rock Hudson, Sal Mineo, Mercedes McCambridge, Dennis Hopper.* Over 45 years after his tragic death, Dean remains a mythic icon of youthful rebelliousness and alienation. This sprawling saga of Texas oil aristocracy provided Dean his final and most challenging role as the arrogant ranch hand, Jett Rink. A Best Director Oscar went to Stevens while Hudson earned a nomination for his finest screen work and Taylor won acclaim as Hudson's compassionate wife. *Giant* is an epic-sized drama of greed, jealousy and loyalty, but its stars seem to outshine the penetrating screenplay and thoughtful direction. (Letterboxed) ★★★½ VHS: $24.99

The Giant Gila Monster

(1959, 75 min, US, Ray Kellogg) *Don Sullivan, Lisa Simone.* Giant Gila monsters with funny glued-on fins attack kids in New Mexico as they listen to rock 'n' roll in their hot rods. Youth wins out. ★★ VHS: $9.99

Gidget

(1959, 95 min, US, Paul Wendkos) *Sandra Dee, James Darren, Cliff Robertson.* First of the popular series with Dee as the innocent young beach

groupie in love with surfer Darren. Also with Robertson, who plays a beach bum, himself smitten by our little heroine. It's kinda sappy in a kinda cute way, but remember that it's *not* a documentary! ★★½ VHS: $9.99

The Gift

(1982, 195 min, France, Michel Lang) *Clio Goldsmith, Claudia Cardinale, Pierre Mondy.* A harried bank worker meets and falls in love with a beautiful and alluring mystery woman (Goldsmith), only to discover that his co-workers "bought" her for him as a retirement gift. Though the premise is promising, this sex farce barely ignites any sparks. ★★

The Gig

(1985, 92 min, US, Frank Gilroy) *Wayne Rogers, Cleavon Little, Warren Vache, Joe Silver, Jay Thomas.* Rogers heads a cast of wonderful actors in this engaging comedy-drama about a group of friends who get together to play jazz. All's well until they get their first professional gig. ★★★

Gigi

(1958, 116 min, US, Vincente Minnelli) *Leslie Caron, Louis Jordan, Maurice Chevalier, Hermione Gingold.* Enchanting Oscar-winning musical about a French girl (Caron), being groomed to be a courtesan, and her romance with a handsome playboy (Jordan). Chevalier is most memorable as young Gigi's guardian. Winner of nine Academy Awards, including Best Picture. Terrific Lerner & Lowe score includes "Thank Heaven for Little Girls" and "I Remember It Well." (VHS available letter-boxed or pan & scan) ★★★★ VHS: $14.99; DVD: $19.99

Gilda

(1946, 110 min, US, Charles Vidor) *Rita Hayworth, Glenn Ford, George MacReady.* A steamy, hard-boiled classic with the ravishing Hayworth driving husband MacReady and ex-lover Ford into frenzies of lust. Boldly adventurous in its day, *Gilda* holds up as a sizzling cauldron of perverse eroticism and social aberration. Featured is Rita's grinding performance of "Put the Blame on Mame," in which she loosens libidos with the removal of a single glove. ★★★½ VHS: $19.99; DVD: $29.99

Gimme Shelter

(1969, 91 min, US, David Maysles, Albert Maysles & Charlotte Zwerin) *The Rolling Stones.* Definitive film record of The Rolling Stone's 1969 U.S. Tour including footage from the infamous Altamont Speedway concert. The film starts with outstanding recordings of the Stones doing "Satisfaction," "Jumping Jack Flash," "Honky Tonk Woman" from their Madison Square Garden performances. The sense of foreboding is recorded with the Maysles usual spare elegance. The Altamont concert is infamous because the Hell's Angels were hired as security guards and they murdered four people at the concert. The Maysles have truly captured the clash of the Hell's Angels with 300,000 hippies that ended the summer of love. For lovers of rock 'n' roll films this is a necessity. (George Lucas is listed as a cameraman in the credits.) ★★★½ VHS: $29.99; DVD: $39.99

G

The Gin Game

(1982, 82 min, US, Mike Nichols) *Jessica Tandy, Hume Cronyn.* Tandy and Cronyn repeat their award-winning performances in this lovely comedy-drama, a live version of their early 1980s stage hit. Written by D. L. Coburn, the play casts Tandy and Cronyn as elderly residents at a rest home whose developing relationship is put to the test during a series of lively, almost cutthroat gin games. Though the play does occasionally lapse into heavy dramatics, it is nonetheless poignant, insightful and vastly amusing. Its two legendary performers are remarkably fine. ★★★

Ginger and Fred

(1986, 126 min, Italy, Federico Fellini) *Giuletta Masina, Marcello Mastroianni, Franco Fabrizi.* Fellini's best since *Amarcord* is a refreshingly whimsical story of two aging hoofers who are reunited after 30 years to appear on a TV variety show that is a cross between "This Is Your Life" and "The Gong Show." Both Masina and Mastroianni are entrancing as the two out-of-their-element dancers. (Italian with English subtitles) ★★★ VHS: $19.99

The Gingerbread Man

(1997, 114 min, US, Robert Altman) *Kenneth Branagh, Robert Duvall, Robert Downey, Jr., Daryl Hannah, Tom Berenger, Embeth Davidtz.* John Grisham's first opus written directly for the screen is a surprisingly well-paced mystery. A divorced attorney (Branagh) jumps into a relationship with a downtrodden divorcée (Davidtz) who's being stalked by her father (Duvall), the head of a backwoods cult. When Branagh uses all his legal might to get the old man committed, he places the lives of himself and his children in danger. This is not the ego-driven "clash of titans" one might expect from a cast and crew of this caliber, but rather a quiet ensemble piece with a few unexpected twists and turns (especially the ending). Altman's direction seems to add an extra dimension of thought to what might have been more action-packed drivel. ★★★½ VHS: $14.99; DVD: $19.99

Girl

(1999, 96 min, US, Jonathan Kahn) *Dominique Swain, Sean Patrick Flanery, Portia DeRossi, Summer Phoenix, Selma Blair, Tara Reid.* For those still mourning the cancellation of "My So-Called Life," rejoice: Swain does her best Claire Danes in *Girl*, which has the same look and tone of the beloved TV show as well. Swain plays a well-to-do high school virgin who has a spineless best friend (Blair), but wishes she were as strong as her other good friend, the inevitable crazy-maned, girl-with-attitude (Reid). Swain is also head over heels in lust for local rocker Flanery, and her slo-mo, luscious visions of the gorgeous guy provide the film's best kitsch moments. While obviously clichéd and derivative, *Girl* is blessed with good performances and is surprisingly engaging. ★★½ VHS: $14.99; DVD: $24.99

The Girl

(1987, 104 min, Sweden, Arne Mattsson) *Franco Nero, Bernice Stegers, Christopher Lee.* Cheesy softcore erotic thriller with Nero as a successful, married lawyer who falls under the alluring spell of an unusually lascivious 14-year-old girl. His Lolita-esque affair soon becomes his undoing, however, when his passion leads to cross-

European intrigue and murder. An unintentionally funny international mess. (Filmed in English) ★

The Girl Can't Help It

(1956, 99 min, US, Frank Tashlin) *Jayne Mansfield, Tom Ewell, Edmond O'Brien.* Mansfield stars as the quintessential "dumb blonde" in this classic cult musical. Ewell plays a talent agent hired by Mansfield's gangster boyfriend (O'Brien) to make her a famous singing star. Jayne's attributes are more visual than vocal, but included in the film are some wonderful vintage performances by Fats Domino, Gene Vincent and The Platters. ★★★ VHS: $29.99

Girl Crazy

(1943, 100 min, US, Norman Taurog) *Judy Garland, Mickey Rooney, June Allyson, Nancy Walker.* A terrific George and Ira Gershwin score highlight this enjoyable Judy-Mickey musical with Mickey as a rich kid who's sent to an all-male school to forget about girls, only to fall for Judy on arrival. Songs include "I Got Rhythm" and "But Not for Me." Choreography by Busby Berkeley. ★★★½ VHS: $14.99

Girl from Hunan

(1986, 99 min, China, Xie Fei & U Lan) *Na Renhua, Deng Xiaotuang.* Spectacular landscapes of Chinese villages, mountains and rice fields provide the lush backdrop to this powerful drama of a young woman struggling to overcome sexist repression in rural China at the turn of the century. Sent to a nearby village in a pre-arranged marriage, 14-year-old Xiao Xiao finds herself engaged to a little boy of two. Pampered by her future father-in-law, yet independent-minded, the girl cares for her toddling husband-to-be, but as her teenage years progress, she begins to think of him more in brotherly ways and directs her budding sexual curiosities toward older men, setting up a confrontation with clan elders. Featuring elaborately staged tribal ceremonies for marriage and death in a male-dominated society, the film's theme, that "women were born to suffer," is nevertheless quite powerful. (Mandarin with English subtitles) ★★★½ VHS: $29.99

The Girl in a Swing

(1989, 112 min, GB/US, Gorgon Hessler) *Meg Tilly, Rupert Frazer.* A repressed middle-aged businessman marries a mysterious German secretary (Tilly) after a whirlwind romance and gets more than he bargained for. Unfortunately, the viewer gets less than he/she hoped for in this tepid "sexy" drama, based on the 1979 novel by Richard Adams. The film is filled with many tedious tearful outbursts as well as some strange hallucinatory episodes. ★ VHS: $79.99

The Girl in the Picture

(1985, 90 min, GB, Cary Parker) *John Gordon Sinclair, Irina Brook.* Sinclair, the gangly star of *Gregory's Girl*, stars in this lighthearted comedy about the frailties of modern love. Sinclair plays a young photo shop clerk who is involved in a tumultuous on-again, off-again relationship with a young college student. ★★ VHS: $79.99

Girl, Interrupted

(1999, 127 min, US, James Mangold) *Winona Ryder, Angelina Jolie, Clea Duvall, Whoopi Goldberg, Jared Leto, Jeffrey Tambor, Vanessa Redgrave.*

Susanna (Ryder) is at odds with her upper middle-class, suburban existence in 1968 America. The only student in her posh school's graduating class not going on to college, she doesn't know where she fits in, except to know it's not here. A ritualistic suicide attempt lands her in an institution of overmedication and facile diagnoses by classically inept psychiatrists spouting promises of recovery — psychospeak for salvation. Susanna joins a small group of sister inmates, but within this environment is the presence of real, verifiable madness. Lisa (Jolie, in an Oscar-winning performance) is a lifer, a leader, and a predator. Through her interactions with Lisa, Susanna confronts her own life choices, rediscovers her capacity for connection, and gets outside of herself long enough to feel empathy. The actresses play well off each other: Jolie's visceral, mesmerizing performance is effective counterpoint to Ryder's cerebral, considered portrayal. Though it falters somewhat at the end, with ambivalence regarding Lisa's character and nature, this is a thoughtful exploration of an autobiographical book. ★★★ VHS: $14.99; DVD: $24.99

Girl 6

(1996, 107 min, US, Spike Lee) *Theresa Randle, Isaiah Washington, Spike Lee, Debi Mazar, Jenifer Lewis, Madonna, Peter Berg, Naomi Campbell, Quentin Tarantino, John Turturro.* Myriad cameo appearances by the terminally hip (Madonna, Quentin Tarantino, etc.) and the engaging presence of Randle can't save this disjointed morality tale. Randle plays a young woman who, to pay the rent until she gets her break in show business, accepts a phone sex job. Now a number on a switchboard — Girl 6 — not a name, she sinks into the milieu, losing sight of goals as they devolve into fantasies. Is this a parable equating acting and moviemaking with prostitution? Probably. But even such touches as the visual pun of Naomi Campbell in a T-shirt bearing the legend "Models Suck" can't salvage this unfocused amalgam of vignettes punctuated by an insistent, intrusive score by Prince. ★★ VHS: $29.99

Girl Talk

(1987, 85 min, US, Kate Davis) Pinky is a spunky 13-year-old who is continually threatened with lock-up for not going to school. Mars has found a surrogate family among fellow employees at a strip joint. Martha is a single 19-year-old with an infant son. Director Davis examines the lives of these three young women, the products of sexual and psychological abuse; and looks at the failure of the existing systems created to address these problems. Though the film suffers slightly from an occasional lack of focus, it is often searing in the pain it reveals. The director offers no solutions or panaceas, but simply exposes the realities of the daily lives of these women, inviting understanding and compassion. ★★★ VHS: $19.99

Girl with Green Eyes

(1964, 91 min, GB/Ireland, Desmond Davis) *Rita Tushingham, Peter Finch, Lynn Redgrave, T.P. McKenna.* Classic British coming-of-age drama with Tushingham giving an outstanding performance as a young farm girl who moves to the big city, Dublin, and falls in love with an older writer (Finch). Redgrave is terrific as Tushingham's roommate. ★★★½ VHS: $14.99

G

The Girl with the Hatbox

(1927, 67 min, USSR, Boris Barnet) *Anna Sten, Vladimar Fogel.* With heavily politicized diatribes being the norm in early Soviet filmmaking, it is an even greater pleasure to view this cheery "American style" comedy. Sten plays a poor, naïve factory girl who is given a seemingly worthless lottery ticket in lieu of pay by her unscrupulous boss, only to discover that she is a winner. The money, she soon discovers, elicits not only pleasure but the greed of those around her and devious lovers as well. (Silent with orchestral accompaniment) ★★★ VHS: $29.99

Girlfight

(2000, 110 min, US, Karyn Kusama) *Michelle Rodriguez, Jaime Tirelli, Paul Calderon.* A big winner at Sundance, this underdog story of a gutsy Brooklyn high school boxing chick has got enough raw energy and fiery talent to kick just about every other polished studio flick in the balls. Newcomer Rodriguez is a real find, her intense leer and street-smart chutzpah commanding the screen with a power and fragile confidence rarely seen by a rookie performer. She's a natural, and first-time filmmaker Kusama keeps the drama lean and unpredictable, despite — or in spite of — some familiar plot devices. ★★★ VHS: $102.99; DVD: $24.99

Girlfriends

(1978, 86 min, US, Claudia Weill) *Melanie Mayron, Amy Wright, Anita Skinner.* A flawless performance from Mayron as a photographer who makes it "on her own" after her best friend and roommate gets married makes this independent drama well worth watching. Susan (Mayron) finds success as an artist while Ann (Skinner) struggles to balance being a wife and mother with a writing career. Weill's film touchingly and accurately explores the two women's friendship and their singular ambitions without sentimentality or heavy-handedness. ★★★ VHS: $19.99

Girls in Prison

(1994, 82 min, US, John McNaughton) *Anne Heche, Ione Skye, Missy Crider, Bahni Turner, Jon Polito.* This spirited spoof of women-behind-bars films should delight any fan of trash cinema. Set during the "Communist Witch Hunt" of the 1950s, the film focuses on a trio of gals sent to an L.A. slammer for diverse reasons: Skye, a lesbian writer; Turner, who got all medieval on a TV commentator; and Crider, an aspiring folk singer. Since the homespun Crider is the real innocent, the other women unite to get her off the hook. Based on an AIP film from the 1950s, *Girls in Prison* may be the final film credit of tabloid great Sam Fuller, who penned the script with Christa Lang. Director McNaughton fills the frames with garish colors, steamy shower scenes, a host of hot-to-trot cartoony characters, and hardboiled dialogue. He has a unique talent of milking sordid subjects until they're downright refreshing. ★★★½ VHS: $14.99

Girls Just Want to Have Fun

(1985, 90 min, US, Alan Metter) *Sarah Jessica Parker, Helen Hunt, Ed Lauter, Shannen Doherty.* Enjoyable, better-than-average teen comedy with Parker giving a charming performance as a teenage girl determined to enter the big video dance contest despite protestations from family and church. ★★★ VHS: $9.99; DVD: $24.99

Girls Town

(1996, 90 min, US, Jim McKay) *Lili Taylor, Anna Grace, Aunjanue Ellis, Bruklin Harris, Asia Minor.* *Girls Town* rests mostly on the terrific chemistry of its ensemble cast. Touching upon issues important to young women, such as date rape, spousal abuse, teen pregnancy and abortion, the story provides an intimate look at a tight-knit band of female high school seniors anxiously awaiting their last day of educational captivity. The film initially looks as if it might become painfully aimless and meandering; but when an unexpected tragedy befalls the group, *Girls Town* comes sharply into focus and the young women set out to vent their rage at the men who have screwed up their nascent lives. Set somewhere in the quasi-urban environs of Queens, the film's heroines are an unlikely mix of race and social backgrounds that have coalesced around a pride in their citified toughness and an inane rebelliousness. The performances

are top-notch, and there's a nice hip-hop soundtrack. ★★★½ VHS: $9.99

Gladiator

(1992, 98 min, US, Rowdy Herrington) *Cuba Gooding, Jr., James Marshall, Brian Dennehy, Robert Loggia, Ossie Davis, John Heard.* A surprisingly sensitive blood-and-gutser focusing on the friendship between two inner-city youths (Gooding, Marshall) and their entanglement with a crooked underground fight promoter (Dennehy at his most demonic). It's silly and predictable, but fans of the genre should enjoy it. ★★ VHS: $9.99; DVD: $24.99

Gladiator

(2000, 155 min, US, Ridley Scott) *Russell Crowe, Joaquin Phoenix, Connie Nielsen, Oliver Reed, Richard Harris, Djimon Hounsou, Derek Jacobi.* Extraordinary spectacle and involving dramatics come together to produce the kind of epic gladiator movie that we haven't seen since the days of *Spartacus* and *Ben-Hur*. If it's sweep and action and story you're looking for, it's all here. In a performance that should finally make him a bona fide star, Crowe is Maximus, a decorated Roman general loyal to the emperor (a splendid Harris). Knowing he is about to die, the benevolent ruler decrees Maximus his successor, which doesn't sit too well with the scheming prince Commodus (Phoenix). In retaliation, Commodus murders his father and orders Maximus and his family killed. Maximus escapes, only to be captured and enslaved, eventually proving himself in the arena to become the star attraction of the Roman Colosseum. That the film works so well falls squarely on the very broad shoulders of Crowe, who creates a sympathetic, idealistic hero who never wavers in his principles. In support, Phoenix is outstanding as the sniveling Commodus, and the late Reed is cunningly funny in his valedictorian performance. Winner of 5 Academy Awards, including Best Picture and Best Actor (Crowe). ★★★★ VHS: $19.99; DVD: $29.99

The Glass Bottom Boat

(1966, 100 min, US, Frank Tashlin) *Doris Day, Rod Taylor, Arthur Godfrey, Paul Lynde, Dom DeLuise, John McGiver, Edward Andrews.* Though the times they were a changin', Day, in one of her last films, steered straight ahead with this familiar and silly slapstick comedy. Doris plays a widow whose work relationship with scientist Taylor leads to romance and spies. A good supporting cast. Fun for those wishing to wax a nostalgic good time. ★★½ VHS: $19.99

The Glass House

(1972, 91 min, US, Tom Gries) *Alan Alda, Dean Jagger, Vic Morrow, Billy Dee Williams, Clu Gulager, Luke Askew, Scott Hylands.* Truman Capote cowrote the screenplay (with Wyatt Cooper) for this harrowingly realistic depiction of prison life that was a landmark made-for-TV drama. Shot in an actual Utah state prison and using real inmates as extras, the film depicts the often savage, predatory conditions in the brutal "glass house" where control lies in the thuggish hands of Hugo Slocum (Morrow) and his gang of goons. ★★★ VHS: $19.99; DVD: $24.99

The Glass Key

(1942, 85 min, US, Stuart Heisler) *Alan Ladd, Veronica Lake, Brian Donlevy, William Bendix.*

Winona Ryder (l.) and Angelina Jolie in *Girl, Interrupted*

G

Tough-as-nails remake of the 1935 film, adapted from a Dashiell Hammett story, about a politician (Donlevy) who is implicated in a murder; Ladd is his "henchman" who tries to clear his name. ★★★½ VHS: $14.99

The Glass Menagerie

(1987, 134 min, US, Paul Newman) *Joanne Woodward, John Malkovich, Karen Allen, James Naughton.* The sterling performances of of the cast elevate this handsome production based on Tennessee Williams' classic play. Allen brings a heart-wrenching vulnerability to Laura, the lonely and lame daughter of faded Southern belle Woodward. Malkovich is well-cast as Woodward's troubled son Tom, and Naughton rounds out the cast as the Gentleman Caller. ★★★ VHS: $19.99

The Glass Shield

(1995, 101 min, US, Charles Burnett) *Michael Boatman, Lori Petty, Ice Cube, Richard Anderson, Michael Ironside, Bernie Casey, M. Emmet Walsh, Elliott Gould.* The Glass Shield begins with comic book strips of police officers on the job, but these one-dimensional figures unfortunately carry over to the live action. In this well-intentioned though heavy-handed examination of racism in police ranks, Boatman and Petty are newly placed officers (both there as tokens) who band together to expose corruption and widespread racism in their department. The story occasionally moves, but the rogue cops are drawn with such broad strokes they have about as much depth as a villain on a "Kojak" episode. ★★ VHS: $14.99

Gleaming the Cube

(1989, 105 min, US, Graeme Clifford) *Christian Slater, Steven Bauer, Ed Lauter.* This skateboard thriller is of interest because of its lead performer, Slater. With a hip delivery, reminiscent of Jack Nicholson, Slater brings a coolness to his role of the eternally rebellious youth who investigates the murder of his half-brother, a Vietnamese honor student. An interesting look at sibling rivalry and cultural clashes, with impressive skateboarding scenes. ★★½ DVD: $24.99

Glen and Randa

(1971, 94 min, US, Jim McBride) *Steven Curry, Shelley Plimpton.* A low-budget, post-apocalyptic

tale, this early feature by McBride follows the travels of a primitive "Adam and Eve" couple scrounging for survival and looking for the fabled city of Metropolis. Clearly made in the heyday of the hippie movement, this minimalist parable is slowly paced but nevertheless intriguing in director McBride's quirky visual style. (Originally rated "X" in its theatrical release — solely for a prolonged nude scene.) ★★★ VHS: $59.99

Glen or Glenda

(1953, 67 min, US, Edward D. Wood, Jr.) *Bela Lugosi, Dolores Fuller, Daniel Davis (Ed Wood, Jr.).* "Beevare the beeg green dragin!" Thus we are warned by narrator Bela Lugosi who introduces us to the hopelessly confused Glen, possessed with an uncontrollable urge to don female garb. Wood's unredeemable schlock-umentary is one of the most ill-conceived and funniest works of all time. "Vat are little boys made ov? Is it puppy dog tails? Big fat snails? Or maybe *brassieres! garters!*" (aka: *I Changed My Sex*) ★ VHS: $14.99; DVD: $24.99

Glengarry Glen Ross

(1992, 100 min, US, James Foley) *Jack Lemmon, Al Pacino, Ed Harris, Alan Arkin, Kevin Spacey, Alec Baldwin, Jonathan Pryce.* David Mamet's riveting adaptation of his own Pulitzer Prize–winning play is marvelously realized by Foley. Pacino, Lemmon, Harris, Arkin and Spacey star as a group of seedy real estate men who scratch out a living selling Florida vacation tracts to retirees, and Baldwin puts in a short but brilliant turn as a callous head honcho who gives this rag-tag sales force a merciless tongue-lashing. With the proverbial "axe" hanging over their heads, they find themselves in a dog-eat-dog fight for their jobs. Mamet's screenplay, which bristles with his usual razor-sharp dialogue, tells a compelling and timely story of greed, avarice and the rich getting richer. Special kudos go to both Lemmon and Pacino for their gutsy handling of Mamet's barrage of profanities. ★★★★ VHS: $14.99

The Glenn Miller Story

(1954, 113 min, US, Anthony Mann) *James Stewart, June Allyson, Harry (Henry) Morgan, Gene Kupra, Louis Armstrong.* Stewart had one of his more popular roles in this affectionate tribute to the great swing time bandleader Glenn

Miller. The film follows Miller's rise to become one of the major influences in popular music in the 1930s and '40s. Allyson plays Mrs. Miller, and the score includes such standards as "Chattanooga Choo-Choo" and "Pennsylvania 6-5000." ★★★ VHS: $19.99

The Glimmer Man

(1996, 92 min, US, John Gray) *Steven Seagal, Keenen Ivory Wayans, Bob Gunton, Brian Cox.* In this tired retread, Seagal plays a mysterious homicide detective who is skilled in martial arts and practices Chinese medicine. Wayans is his beleaguered partner. They happen upon the trail of a mysterious cover-up involving a serial killer, the CIA and Seagal's shadowy past. The outcome, however, is boring and unimaginative and not worth the buildup. Wayans is completely out of place and even Seagal's dubious talents are ultimately wasted. (Letterboxed VHS available for $19.99) ★½ VHS: $9.99; DVD: $19.99

Gloria

(1980, 121 min, US, John Cassavetes) *Gena Rowlands, Buck Henry, John Adames, Julie Carmen, Lupe Guarnica.* Cassavetes' whirlwind thriller features a remarkable performance from Rowlands as an ex-gangster's moll who begrudgingly takes charge of her neighbors' child after they are brutally massacred by the mob. As she and the kid flee would-be assassins, Cassavetes' camera masterfully captures the gritty underbelly of New York City. (Remade in 1999) ★★★ VHS: $9.99

Gloria

(1999, 108 min, US, Sidney Lumet) *Sharon Stone, Jean-Luke Figueroa, Jeremy Northam, Cathy Moriarty, George C. Scott.* Cockamamie. For those who found Gus Van Sant's *Psycho* remake unnecessary, this one rates as downright unlawful. Why Lumet would tamper with John Cassavetes' gritty thriller is incomprehensible. Stone (sporting an accent which suggests she's from Queens and Boston) now plays the title character originated by Gena Rowlands, a gangster's moll who's just out of prison. When a young boy's family is rubbed out by the mob looking for an incriminating disc, Gloria takes it upon herself to protect the youth, and she, the boy and the disc end up on the run. Everything from the art design to the mix of comedy, drama and suspense fails completely. Another instance to stick to the original. ★ VHS: $9.99; DVD: $29.99

Glory

(1989, 122 min, US, Edward Zwick) *Matthew Broderick, Morgan Freeman, Denzel Washington, Andre Braugher, Cary Elwes, Jane Alexander, Donovan Leitch, John Cullum.* This powerful Civil War drama is the startlingly good, impressive and long-overdue story about a little-known chapter in American history: the first black combat unit. Broderick heads a first-rate cast as the white commander of the 54th Massachusetts Regiment, an all-black fighting unit comprised of enlisted men who were initially denied the basic rights of other soldiers; they were then forced to prove themselves in order to be treated equally. Freeman offers solid support as the company's wise sergeant and Oscar winner Washington is outstanding as a former slave. Based on the letters of Colonel Robert Gould Shaw, whom Broderick portrays. ★★★★ VHS: $14.99; DVD: $29.99

Gladiator: Russell Crowe and Djimon Hounsou are the headliners at the Colosseum

Glory Daze

(1996, 99 min, US, Rich Wilkes) *Ben Affleck, Megan Ward, Sam Rockwell, French Stewart, Matthew McConaughey.* Amateurish to the extreme, *Glory Daze* is an infantile campus comedy about the last days of school for a group of graduating seniors. A collection of lifeless episodes and unfunny punch lines with a cast of characters either annoying or one-dimensional, this boggles the mind. The funny *PCU* proves there's always room for an imaginative updating of the *Animal House* genre, but this is just bad, lazy comedy. Affleck's a zombie, and even McConaughey's bizarre minute cameo misses the mark. ★ VHS: $14.99

Glory! Glory!

(1988, 152 min, US, Lindsay Anderson) *Richard Thomas, Ellen Greene, James Whitmore.* Anderson's potent satire of televangelism stars Thomas as Bobby Joe Stuckey, an electronic preacher whose ministry is in disarray. His contributions are dwindling and cash flow is low. Things are so bad, in fact, that he hires a sexy rock 'n' roll singer (Greene) to help boost profits, and that's when the word of the Lord really starts to get turned upside-down. ★★★

The Gnome-Mobile

(1967, 90 min, US, Robert Stevenson) *Walter Brennan, Matthew Garber, Karen Dotrice.* Bright Disney fluff by the director of *Mary Poppins.* Brennan, Garber and Dotrice are out to protect forest gnomes from the grasp of a greedy circus owner. ★★★

Go

(1999, 103 min, US, Doug Liman) *Desmond Askew, Taye Diggs, William Fichtner, J.E. Freeman, Katie Holmes, Jane Krakowski, Breckin Meyer, Jay Mohr, Timothy Olyphant, Sarah Polley, Scott Wolf.* *Go* takes the great characterizations and kinetic energy of director Liman's *Swingers* and ups the ante with colorful widescreen cinematography and a groundbreaking narrative style. The Möbius-looping story begins as supermarket cashier Polley begins a night on the town, scoring drugs and going to a rave. From there, people she works with and meets soon become the center of the film. Basically told in three acts, the non-linear story never loses its lightning-quick pulse and always remains in focus. Thankfully, the twists are never hokey; they're done for laughs and feel natural. Astoundingly entertaining, half the laughter is from the humor and half just from *Go*'s exhilarating rush. Of the great cast, Polley excels as Ronna, who comes full circle in this twisting, tantalizing puzzle of a film. ★★★★ VHS: $9.99; DVD: $19.99

The Go-Between

(1971, 118 min, GB, Joseph Losey) *Julie Christie, Alan Bates, Margaret Leighton, Michael Redgrave, Dominic Guard.* A brilliant, richly detailed portrait of a forbidden romance and the lasting influence it has on the young boy who served as messenger for the illicit lovers. Christie is the Lady Trinigham, involved in an affair with a farmer (Bates) down the road; Guard is the twelve-year-old who acts as go-between. A visually sumptuous, fascinating study of deception and its lingering effects. Screenplay by Harold Pinter. ★★★★ VHS: $19.99

Go Fish

(1994, 85 min, US, Rose Troche) *Guinevere Turner, V.S. Brodie.* An unlikely candidate to join the ranks of epochal lesbian-themed films, this delightful yet knowing independent romantic comedy is more than simply the *Desert Hearts* for the '90s. Made on an extremely low budget, filmed in black and white, and featuring primarily non-professionals in major roles, *Go Fish*'s grittiness helps in making its characters more honest and accessible. Seriously cute and boyishly hip Max (Turner), after a drought of ten months, is looking for love. She possibly finds it in the person of Ely (Brodie), a semi-dorky, slightly older woman. What the film lacks in professional pizzazz and slickness is more than made up by its vividly drawn characters and witty screenplay. ★★★½ VHS: $14.99; DVD: $19.99

The Go-Masters

(1982, 134 min, China, Duan Ji-Shun & Junja Sata) *Huang Zong-Ying, Du Peng.* The first Chinese-Japanese film coproduction, *The Go-Masters* is a sprawling political/historical epic spanning the turbulent years of the 1920s thru the 1950s, and a poignant exploration of love, loyalty and destiny — pitting pride against national power. The story focuses on the relationship of two families, one Japanese and the other Chinese. The son of the Chinese family is an aspiring master of Go, a chess-like strategy game, who moves to Japan under the tutelage of a Japanese Go champion. When war erupts, he is thrown into a political maelstrom, forced to choose between his allegiance to his birthplace and to his adopted land. (Mandarin and Japanese with English subtitles) ★★★½ VHS: $59.99

Go Now

(1998, 86 min, GB, Michael Winterbottom) *Robert Carlyle, Juliet Aubrey, James Nesbitt.* A tough British film about a young man who develops multiple sclerosis, *Go Now* could be just another disease-of-the-week weepie. Yet in the hands of director Winterbottom, this familiar love story becomes a highly affecting drama. Carlyle stars as Nick, a footballer who falls in love with Karen (Aubrey) and learns shortly thereafter that he has MS. Carlyle's portrayal of a man determined to understand and overcome his illness is remarkable, and his performance cements his leading man status. As his girlfriend, Aubrey is equally terrific. Her character really grapples with her feelings for Nick (and his feelings for her), and their struggle for happiness is quite moving. *Go Now* also features a great soundtrack of soul tunes, especially the haunting title track. ★★★ VHS: $14.99

Go Tell the Spartans

(1978, 114 min, US, Ted Post) *Burt Lancaster, Craig Wasson, David Clennon, Marc Singer.* Lancaster gives a well-modulated performance as an "advisory group commander" trying to keep his doubts to himself and his men alive as they traipse through the jungles of Vietnam on another pointless mission. One of the first films to look at our involvement in that war. ★★★½ VHS: $9.99

Go West

(1940, 81 min, US, Edward Buzzell) *The Marx Brothers, John Carroll, Diana Lewis.* Groucho, Chico and Harpo take Horace Greely's advice and head west to make their fortune, and find

The Glass Key

themselves in the middle of a land swindle involving property wanted by the railroad. Even if not quite up to the standard of their earlier films, there are lots of funny bits, especially the spectacular closing train scene. ★★½ VHS: $19.99

Go West, Young Man

(1936, 80 min, US, Henry Hathaway) *Mae West, Randolph Scott, Warren William.* Though this backwoods West comedy is not on par with her best known comedies, Mae's quips and a jab or two at Hollywood and stardom make this worthy of interest. West, who wrote the screenplay adaptation, plays a famous movie actress on tour promoting her newest film. En route to Harrisburg, she and press agent William become stranded in a small town where her arrival quickly turns everything topsy-turvy. Scott is the hunkish ('30s style) garage mechanic who makes Mae's weekend in the country all the more enjoyable. Those expecting a western romp will be disappointed, as the punny title refers to La West and not to geographic location. ★★½ VHS: $14.99

The Goalie's Anxiety at the Penalty Kick

(1971, 101 min, West Germany, Wim Wenders) *Arthur Brauss, Erika Pluhar.* After being suspended for missing a penalty kick, a goalie wanders around Vienna aimlessly. He picks up a cinema cashier and, for no apparent reason, kills her. While waiting for the inevitable arrest, he searches his soul, but finds only alienation and ennui. Although slow-going, this early Wenders film is a must for his fans. The filmmaker explores the existential territory of Camus' "The Stranger" and Sartre's "Nausea." (German with English subtitles) ★★★

God Is My Witness (Khuda Gawah)

(1994, 193 min, India, Mukul S. Anand) *Amitabh Bachchan, Sridevi.* This dazzling action/adventure/romance/musical/melodrama is a heady, thrilling experience for modern Westerners, but Indian audiences have been flocking to this type of hybrid for years. The epic story involves Badshah Khan (Bachchan), a cocky, noble Pathan chieftain who flips for the beautiful woman warrior Benazir (Sridevi), who won't marry him until he brings her the head of her father's murderer. *God Is My Witness* is full of song-and-dance numbers, but wisely — and beautifully — uses them to further the story and

G

flesh out characterizations. This attitude culminates in the operatic climax, a deliriously romantic, kitchen-sink crescendo rife with explosions, gunfire, reconciliations, swordplay, revenge and declarations of adulation. For those who mourn the loss of golden-age Hollywood; it didn't die, it just moved to India. (Letterboxed) (Hindi with English subtitles) ★★★★

God Told Me To

(1977, 91 min, US, Larry Cohen) *Tony LoBianco, Deborah Raffin, Sylvia Sidney, Sandy Dennis.* New York City is besieged by a series of unrelated sniper attacks, committed by seemingly ordinary citizens who said they were ordered by God to kill. LoBianco is the police detective whose investigation leads him to otherworldly powers. An imaginative if bizarre thriller which manages quite a few eerie moments. (aka: *Demon*) ★★½ VHS: $9.99

The Godfather

(1972, 175 min, US, Francis Ford Coppola) *Marlon Brando, Al Pacino, Robert Duvall, James Caan, Sterling Hayden, John Cazale, Diane Keaton, Talia Shire.* In Coppola's brilliant crime saga, the director transformed the lowly gangster drama into an American epic capable of rivaling the western. From the wedding of Connie Corleone to the end of her brother Michael's marriage, *The Godfather* is richly imbued with the texture of life, the allure of power and the basic corruptness of capitalism. Add to this the sheer visceral pleasure of watching top actors giving superlative performances and you've got one of the masterpieces of American cinema. Brando salvaged his career as the ruthless Don Corleone, and Pacino became a star playing his son Michael. Truly an all-star cast. (VHS available letterboxed or pan & scan) ★★★★ VHS: $24.99; DVD: $99.99 (for all 3 *Godfather* films)

The Godfather, Part II

(1974, 200 min, US, Francis Ford Coppola) *Al Pacino, Robert De Niro, Robert Duvall, Michael Gazzo, Lee Strasberg, Talia Shire.* Following the success of the original, Coppola felt free to delve more deeply and lyrically into the inherent roots of corruption, power and greed. By crosscutting his two major stories — the rise of Vito Corleone and the fall of Michael — Coppola creates a dialectical narrative which elevates the movie above its low genre birthright. Also, this was the first film to contradict the much abused notion that sequels must be "parts" of a larger story. De Niro is especially good as a young Vito. (VHS available letterboxed or pan & scan) ★★★★ VHS: $24.99

The Godfather III

(1990, 161 min, US, Francis Ford Coppola) *Al Pacino, Andy Garcia, Diane Keaton, Sofia Coppola, Joe Mantegna, George Hamilton, Talia Shire, Bridget Fonda.* The third and final entry in Coppola's *Godfather* trilogy is a worthy, if flawed, finale — though it certainly isn't in the same league as the two classics which came before it. Pacino, in a forceful performance, returns as the reluctant Mafia boss Michael Corleone, who is lulled back into gangland activities after trying to go "legit." If the picture has one major flaw, it is the casting of Coppola's daughter Sofia in the pivotal role of Michael's beloved daughter, Mary. The actress doesn't have the depth required, and in some scenes other actors can be noticed "hold-

ing back." Garcia, however, as Michael's illegitimate nephew, is exceptional as a low-level criminal with loftier ambitions. (VHS available letterboxed or pan & scan) ★★★ VHS: $24.99

Gods and Monsters

(1998, 105 min, US, Bill Condon) *Ian McKellen, Brendan Fraser, Lynn Redgrave, Lolita Davidovich, Kevin J. O'Connor, David Dukes.* In a performance that is nothing short of brilliant, McKellen hypnotizes as gay film director James Whale in this moving, poetic adaptation of Christopher Bram's novel "Father of Frankenstein." The story ostensibly follows the friendship between Whale — now in his early 60s and suffering the effects of a stroke — and his handsome straight gardener (Fraser); but at the core of this lyrical tale is a study of desire and self-determination. In the 1930s, Whale made a handful of Hollywood classics (including *Frankenstein*); it's now 1957, and he is no longer able to live his life on his terms. Knowing that Whale was found dead in his swimming pool, the filmmakers have concocted a probable scenario which ends in a cynical *pièce de résistance*. Bringing compassion and elegance to Whale, McKellen's portrayal is so rich in nuance and shading that he makes you forget it's acting. Fraser is excellent as the ex-marine who captures Whale's heart and, in turn, respect. Their bond is poignantly resilient. It is what gives Condon's film its power, its grace and its heart. ★★★½ VHS: $14.99; DVD: $34.99

The Gods Must Be Crazy

(1980, 89 min, South Africa, Jamie Uys) *N!xau.* All this fuss over a Coke bottle? After viewing it, one can see why this small-budget gem became such a huge international hit. On a peaceful day in Botswana's Kalahari desert, a Coca-Cola bottle falls to earth and disrupts the life of a simple tribe of Bushmen. Their efforts to return the bottle from whence it came unleashes a tide of savage satire and slapstick comedy from which virtually no one escapes. (Sequel: *The Gods Must Be Crazy II*) ★★★½

The Gods Must Be Crazy II

(1990, 97 min, South Africa, Jamie Uys) *N!xau. Crazy II* contains the same elements as the original including a propensity for sure-fire slapstick comedy. Bushman Xixo — played by N!xau, retaining the charm and genial sincerity which made the original such a success — returns, here having a series of misadventures searching for his two missing children. Meanwhile, a temperamental New York anthropologist is stranded in the desert with a local naturalist, and she's having a doozy of a time with the wildlife. Director Uys again displays a talent for precise choreographed visual comedy. ★★★ VHS: $19.99

Gods of the Plague

(1969, 92 min, West Germany, Rainer Werner Fassbinder) *Hanna Schygulla, Harry Baer, Margarethe von Trotta.* Deep in the backstreets of a sunless Munich, a den of sleazy gangsters and their molls stealthily plot their big heist only for it to end in betrayal and failure. Fassbinder has created a stunning and knowing tribute to film noir and the American gangster genre, combining swift camerawork with a suspenseful story line. (German with English subtitles) ★★★½ VHS: $29.99

The Godson

(1967, 86 min, France, Jean-Pierre Melville) *Alain Delon, Nathalie Delon.* Drained of bright colors and told in a crisp, tight style, this definitive hard-boiled gangster film features Delon as an emotionless and solitary hired killer whose airtight alibi for one of his jobs is slowly unraveled by authorities after he makes the mistake of falling in love. A classic tale of a man whose existence is as rigid, romantic and outdated as that of the Japanese samurai. (Dubbed) ★★★

Godspell

(1973, 103 min, US, David Greene) *Victor Garber, David Haskell, Lynne Thigpen, Jerry Sroka, Katie Hanley, Robin Lamont.* Based on the hit Broadway musical, this energetic, vastly entertaining adaptation which follows the last days of Jesus Christ through song came out the same time as *Jesus Christ, Superstar*. And though *Godspell's* score isn't as well known or as accomplished as Andrew Lloyd Weber's first hit, the film as a whole is much more satisfying. Includes "Day by Day." Jesus is played by veteran stage actor Garber, who most recently played the sympathetic, doomed ship designer in *Titanic*. ★★★½ VHS: $19.99; DVD: $27.99

Godzilla

(1998, 139 min, US, Roland Emmerich) *Matthew Broderick, Jean Reno, Maria Pitillo, Hank Azaria, Kevin Dunn, Michael Lerner.* This lumbering, top-heavy behemoth could have used a lot more humor and chintz. Oh, and a screenplay. With nary a hint of topicality nor an ounce of finesse, the filmmakers steal, er, pay homage to everything from those grade-Z atomic monster movies of the '50s and rubber-suit *Godzilla* movies to *Jurassic Park*. The result is an emotionally empty show. Sure the effects are cool, but the movie plays like an extended computer game — this is only intensified by the singular camera perspective. And forget about seeing one panoramic shot of Godzilla trapsing against the cityscape, a cornball tradition. And the

Gods and Monsters

humans? They're stuck with the lamest dialogue since Ed Wood cranked out a screenplay. ★★½ VHS: $9.99; DVD: $19.99

Godzilla, King of the Monsters

(1956, 80 min, Japan, Inoshiro Honda, Terry Morse) *Takashi Shimura, Raymond Burr.* This original A-bomb allegory, and the first and best Godzilla film to date, features surprisingly effective special effects for its time, and a dark and somber tone absent from its many sequels. Godzilla, not one of the good guys in this original incarnation, rises from the sea belching radioactive breath. The inadvertent by-product of a nuclear accident, he wreaks total destruction at every turn, including the entire city of Tokyo. Edited for U.S. consumption, this version features spliced-in sequences with Burr as a reporter (named Steve Martin!) covering the events. The original Japanese release is unfortunately not yet available on video. (American remake *Godzilla*) ★★½

Godzilla 2000

(2000, 96 min, Japan, Takao Okawara) *Takehiro Murata, Naomi Nishida, Mayu Suzuki, Hiroshi Abe, Shirô Sano.* So adherent to the Godzilla genre as to be virtually review-proof, this millennial entry is nothing if not a refreshing rebound from the bloated American behemoth. There's a nifty character introduction of the big guy (still a man in a suit, though it's a new suit) to a climactic showdown with a killer space squid in mini-Tokyo, there's a lot of nostalgic ooh-ahh for grownups and cool firebreathing fun for kids. The interim scenes of humans talking are boring as usual (despite somewhat campy dubbing), and Godzilla disappears for a long stretch of time as the scientists deal with a zero-personality spaceship. But when the squid comes out, and shoots energy bolts from his shoulder bursitis, the smiles come back, and you realize you got exactly what you expected. (Dubbed) ★★½ VHS: $14.99; DVD: $24.99

Godzilla vs. Biollante

(1989, 105 min, Japan, Kazuki Ohmori) Disappointing entry in the *Godzilla* series pits the monster hero against a giant plant creature constructed from his own radioactive blood cells. The film falls short of the loony campiness of other *Godzilla* films, but worst of all, Godzy barely ever roars. ★★ VHS: $9.99

Godzilla vs. The Sea Monster

(1966, 88 min, Japan, Jun Fukuda) Godzilla's on our side now (but he's still as clumsy as ever), fighting a giant shrimp that's really just a prawn in a plot to take over the world. ★★ VHS: $9.99

Godzilla vs. The Smog Monster

(1972, 87 min, Japan, Yoshimitsu Banno) Our evil ways catch up with us when the smog monster comes to dine on our dumps and draining ditches. After becoming intoxicated on factory fumes, he gets belligerent and starts biting the hands that feed him — smashing up the place and ignoring our polite entreaties to stop. So Godzilla bounces the bore out. ★★

Goin' South

(1978, 109 min, US, Jack Nicholson) *Jack Nicholson, Mary Steenburgen, Christopher Lloyd, John Belushi, Danny DeVito, Veronica Cartwright.* Nicholson is a horse thief who is saved from the noose by a little-known law, giving him the opportunity to marry a widow (Steenburgen) and take up the habits of a good prairie husband. However, he soon finds his past returning to haunt him. This is Nicholson's second directorial effort (after *Drive, He Said*). ★★★ VHS: $14.99

Goin' to Town

(1935, 71 min, US, Alexander Hall) *Mae West, Paul Cavanagh.* Here's a sight to behold: A sequined West dressed all in white riding a horse across the fruited plains. And darn if she doesn't look natural doing it. Mae plays a saloon singer who agrees to marry an oil tycoon/cattle rustler. When he gets killed on their wedding day, she inherits everything, and soon falls for a British earl who snubs her crude Western ways. So, the widow West heads to Buenos Aires for a crash course in society manners, horseracing and love. An enjoyable concoction with West in her element as a rustic flirt trying to make good. ★★★ VHS: $14.99

Going All the Way

(1997, 103 min, US, Mark Pellington) *Ben Affleck, Jeremy Davies, Jill Clayburgh, Amy Locane, Rachel Weisz, Lesley Ann Warren, Rose McGowan.* Here's a surprise — a period coming-of-age film, shot in a very trendy, music video style (flash frames, jump cuts, etc.) with a disaffected youth as the protagonist, and it's actually good. Davies gives a mannered yet ultimately moving performance as a shy, geeky Army vet who returns home to 1950s Indianapolis to live with his painfully status quo parents (including a bizarrely cartoonish Clayburgh). His sanity is kept intact by his friendship with a fellow vet (the winning, likable Affleck), a high school acquaintance who ran with a different crowd. Despite their differences, they become close friends. While both its title (it sounds like an '80s teen sex comedy) and plot suggest otherwise, *Going All the Way* is actually an intelligent comedy-drama which touches knowingly on questions of conformity, popularity, religion, morality, and especially sexuality. ★★★ VHS: $14.99; DVD: $19.99

Going in Style

(1979, 96 min, US, Martin Brest) *George Burns, Art Carney, Lee Strasberg.* Burns gives a rich performance as a senior citizen who talks his buddies Carney and Strasberg into helping him rob a bank because they feel bored and forgotten. While the humorous sequences are sitcom funny, it's the tragic subtext about growing old in America which gives this small comic gem an unexpected resonance. ★★★½ VHS: $14.99

Going My Way

(1944, 130 min, US, Leo McCarey) *Bing Crosby, Barry Fitzgerald, Gene Lockhart, William Frawley.* Crosby gives his most winning performance (it even won him an Oscar) as Father O'Malley, whose progressive ideas don't go down well with the street punks or the old parish priest. Bing sings "Swing on a Star," and there are plenty of familiar faces, including Oscar winner Fitzgerald. (Sequel: *The Bells of St. Mary's*) ★★★ VHS: $9.99; DVD: $29.99

Going Places

(1974, 117 min, France, Bertrand Blier) *Gérard Depardieu, Patrick Dewaere, Miou-Miou, Jeanne*

Godzilla 2000: Back to basics

Moreau. Blier's energetic account of two loutish drifters who steal, molest and terrorize until they encounter a beautiful ex-convict who undermines their entire lifestyle. A weirder French film you will never see. (French with English subtitles) ★★★

Gold Diggers of 1933

(1933, 96 min, US, Mervyn LeRoy) *Dick Powell, Joan Blondell, Ruby Keeler, Ginger Rogers, Aline MacMahon, Guy Kibbee.* Classic Berkeley backstage musical. Here it's Blondell, Keeler, Powell and pals putting on a Broadway show. Songs include "We're in the Money" (in pig Latin!) and "Forgotten Man." Berkeley's production numbers are sensational. ★★★½

Gold Diggers of 1935

(1935, 95 min, US, Busby Berkeley) *Dick Powell, Adolphe Menjou, Gloria Stuart, Alice Brady, Glenda Farrell.* That "let's put on a show" gang is back, here in the forms of Powell, Menjou, Stuart and pals. Berkeley's production numbers are first-rate, and included is the remarkable "Lullabye of Broadway" (one of the great musical sequences of all time). ★★★ VHS: $29.99

The Gold of Naples

(1954, 107 min, Italy, Vittorio De Sica) *Sophia Loren, Silvana Mangano, Toto.* Departing from his neorealist tradition, De Sica constructs four vignettes ranging from the comic to the tragic in this poignant, perceptive slice of Napleanic life. A 20-year-old Loren stars as a philandering wife who loses her wedding ring during a rendezvous with a lover and convinces her baker husband that she lost it in a pizza. Toto stars in another episode as a meek husband whose house is occupied by an arrogant racketeer. De Sica himself is featured in a third story of an avid gambler who is outsmarted in cards by an eight-year-old, and the final segment has Mangano as a prostitute who enters into a strange marriage with a mentally unbalanced young man. (Italian with English subtitles) ★★★ VHS: $59.99

The Gold Rush

(1925, 100 min, US, Charles Chaplin) *Charles Chaplin, Mack Swain.* This is quintessential Chaplin. This immortal comedy features some of the Little Tramp's most memorable routines, including the dance of the dinner rolls and the shoe-eating sequence. Charlie plays a lone prospector, adrift in the frenzy of the Klondike gold rush. ★★★★ VHS: $19.99; DVD: $29.99

The Golden Boat

(1993, 90 min, France/US, Râul Ruiz) *Michael Kirby, Annie Sprinkle, Barbet Schroeder, Jim Jarmusch, Kathy Acker.* Blending surrealism with avant-garde deconstructionism and dreamlike images, Ruiz's first English-language film follows a young philosophy student and part-time rock critic for *The Village Voice*, Israel, who encounters an older homeless man, Austin, in a back alley on the Lower East Side. Before Israel can respond, Austin stabs himself and, while bleeding profusely, leads Israel on a bizarre journey through the streets of New York. Along the way, philosophy is discussed even while Austin compulsively kills several people — all of whom seem to come back to life in future scenes. Beguilingly obscure yet strangely wonderful. ★★★ VHS: $59.99

Golden Boy

(1939, 99 min, US, Rouben Mamoulian) *William Holden, Barbara Stanwyck, Lee J. Cobb.* Clifford Odets's searing story of a youth (Holden in his breakthrough role) torn between his love of music and his boxing career. ★★★ VHS: $19.99

The Golden Child

(1986, 93 min, US, Michael Ritchie) *Eddie Murphy, Charlotte Lewis, Charles Dance.* A movie that doesn't attempt to go beyond a fingerpaint-user's idea of humor; but if you like Murphy, you may find it amusing. Jokes involve "boogers" and Pepsi cans, while Eddie looks for the "Golden Child," the kidnapped savior of the world. ★ VHS: $14.99; DVD: $29.99

The Golden Coach

(1952, 105 min, Italy, Jean Renoir) *Anna Magnani, Odoardo Spadaro.* Renoir peppered this luxuriant fable set in 19th-century South America, which follows the three transient loves of a tempestuous actress (forcefully played by Magnani) with an uncharacteristic tone of biting irony. Renoir joyfully expresses his love for the theater and theater life as he follows the "commedia dell'arte" through their lives and loves. (Filmed in English) ★★★½ VHS: $24.99

Golden Demon

(1953, 91 min, Japan, Koji Shina) *Jun Negami, Fujiko Yamamoto.* A spectacular look at the destructive effect of wealth in today's society. A poor young man falls in love with a middle-class woman but is rejected. Determined not to be hurt again, the man commits his life to the ruthless pursuit of wealth. After escaping a loveless marriage, the woman seeks out her old love but finds a changed person. A sensitive yet hard-hitting love story. (Japanese with English subtitles) ★★★

The Golden Voyage of Sinbad

(1974, 105 min, GB, Gordon Hessler) *John Phillip Law, Caroline Munro, Tom Baker.* A delightful rehashing of the adventures of Sinbad the sailor, which features some of Ray Harryhausen's finest "dynamation" effects including a ship's figurehead that comes to life and, even more impressive, a six-armed statue that does battle with Sinbad. A wonder-

fully entertaining throwback to the days of Saturday afternoon matinees. ★★★ VHS: $14.99; DVD: $29.99

Golden Years

(1991, 234 min, US) *Keith Szarbajka, Frances Sternhagen, Phillip Lenkowsky.* Stephen King tells the story of Harlan Williams, an elderly janitor who is accidentally exposed to a strange green dust in an explosion at a government defense lab. Shortly thereafter, he begins going through a series of mysterious changes which slowly turn him younger. Following this, of course, the big bad Feds show up and will stop at nothing to capture their newfound lab rat. Szarbajka plays the first aged, then youthful hall sweeper. Sternhagen is solid in support as his wife. Originally seven hours on TV, the continuity suffers somewhat in this heavily edited edition. ★★★ VHS: $14.99

Goldeneye

(1995, 127 min, GB, Martin Campbell) *Pierce Brosnan, Sean Bean, Izabella Scorupco, Famke Janssen, Joe Don Baker, Judi Dench, Robbie Coltrane, Michael Kitchen.* Brosnan has some pretty big shoes to fill with this, the 18th film to showcase the exploits of a certain "Bond, James Bond" — and those shoes fit like a glove. This time, it's personal as Bond goes after an "00" double agent (Bean) who plans to topple the world economy using a pirated weapons satellite (codename: Goldeneye). There are, of course, the usual death-defying stunts, beautiful women and arch humor. But Brosnan makes the film his own, creating a Bond who is more mature and introspective than his predecessors. Dench is M, the new head of MI6. (Sequel: *Tomorrow Never Dies*) ★★★ VHS: $14.99; DVD: $34.99

Goldfinger

(1964, 111 min, GB, Guy Hamilton) *Sean Connery, Honor Blackman, Gert Frobe, Shirley Eaton, Harold Sakata.* Her majesty's finest, Agent 007, combats the wicked genius with the Midas touch and his evil Asian henchman with the deadly derby. The third in the Bond series, complete with scads of gadgetry, loads of lovelies and Connery in top form. One of the very best of the series. (Sequel: *Thunderball*) ★★★½ VHS: $14.99; DVD: $34.99

The Goldwyn Follies

(1938, 120 min, US, George Marshall) *Adolphe Menjou, Andrea Leeds, The Ritz Brothers.* George Gershwin's last film score highlights this okay musical about a Hollywood producer who searches for a "typical" moviegoer to judge his work. ★★ VHS: $14.99

The Golem

(1920, 75 min, Germany, Paul Wegener & Carl Boese) A classic tale of a rabbi who conjures up a cannibalistic monster of Jewish legend in order to avert an oppressive policy against Jews in Hapsburg. But once brought to life, the Golem breaks free from his master's spell and rampages through the town, causing havoc that appears to be beyond anyone's ability to stop. (Silent) ★★★½ VHS: $39.99

Gone Fishin'

(1997, 94 min, US, Christopher Cain) *Danny Glover, Joe Pesci, Rosanna Arquette, Lynn Whitfield, Carol Kane, Willie Nelson.* In *Lethal Weapon 2*,

Glover and Pesci were two thirds of a terrific comedy team, with Mel Gibson playing Moe to their Larry and Curly. In the lame-brained *Gone Fishin'*, however, the results of their reteaming is painfully wretched, and about as appealing as cold fish. They play two klutzy childhood chums who've always been the best of friends. The two dim-witted pals win a fishing vacation in the Florida Everglades, cutting a swath of accidental destruction and comic mayhem across the Sunshine State. The sophomoric mentality to the film's slapstick physical humor is childish at best. ★ VHS: $9.99

Gone in 60 Seconds

(2000, 117 min, US, Dominic Sena) *Nicolas Cage, Giovanni Ribisi, Robert Duvall, Angelina Jolie, Delroy Lindo, Will Patton, Chi McBride, Scott Caan, Christopher Eccleston.* A puffed-up, way overproduced remake of the '70s H. B. Halicki drive-in classic, *Gone in 60 Seconds* has Cage stealing 50 cars in 24 hours to save his brother's hide. Typically loud, abrasive, faux-hip Bruckheimer nonsense skips his usual homophobia to allow room for some uncomfortable racism, while shoving Jolie into a surprisingly small role as "the ex." Lindo, Duvall and Patton lend a hint of class to this mess, but that's not what the film needs — it should be fast, gritty and exciting as hell; the original is hardly a triumph of content over style, but it's a lotta fun. This is shockingly dull; it's a movie about fast cars and is slow as molasses until the final half hour, when the car chase finally kicks in. And even that's a snooze. ★ VHS: $19.99; DVD: $29.99

Gone with the Wind

(1939, 224 min, US, Victor Fleming) *Vivien Leigh, Clark Gable, Olivia deHavilland, Leslie Howard, Hattie McDaniel, Thomas Mitchell, Butterfly McQueen.* This is the big one! Based on Margaret Mitchell's epic Civil War novel, Leigh stars as Scarlett O'Hara, a beautiful, spoiled and determined Southern belle who meets her match in Rhett Butler (Gable), a dashing and rebellious charmer. Academy Awards for Best Picture, Actress (Leigh), and eight others. *GWTW* has myriad characters, wonderful production values, and is the definitive example of old, big-studio moviemaking. Little wonder this movie has been woven into the fabric of our culture. ★★★★ VHS: $26.99; DVD: $24.99

Gonza the Spearman

(1986, 126 min, Japan, Masahiro Shinoda) *Hiromi Goh, Shima Iwashita.* Filmed with stunning visuals, Shinoda's period piece is a vivid and engrossing account of what life was like during the samurai era. Gonza, a handsome but overly ambitious samurai, breaks off his engagement with a woman in order to better his position by marrying the clan leader's daughter. The brother of Gonza's former fiancée, a fellow lanceman, vows revenge for the insult to his sister and family. A classic tale of love, honor and tragedy. (Japanese with English subtitles) ★★★ VHS: $24.99

Good Burger

(1997, 103 min, US, Brian Robbins) *Kenan Thompson, Kel Mitchell, Abe Vigoda, Shaquille O'Neal, Sinbad.* Silly and fun and family friendly, *Good Burger* is based on one of the more popular skits from Mitchell and Thompson's top-rated Nickelodeon TV show. When fast-food chain Mondo Burger opens up right across the street

Gone with the Wind

from their own emporium, the lads join forces to save it — and themselves — from certain economic ruin. Sinbad gets laughs as the once-hip high school teacher still stuck in the Black Power '70s. Holding together this airy confection is the genial comedy of Kenan and Kel, exhibiting pleasing traces of Laurel & Hardy and Martin & Lewis. And any movie sly enough to feature George Clinton as a mental patient ready to rock the ward has surely earned its street credentials — if not with the prepubescent crowd then surely with mom and pop. ★★★ VHS: $14.99

The Good Earth

(1937, 138 min, US, Sidney Franklin) *Paul Muni, Luise Rainer, Walter Connolly, Charley Grapewin, Jessie Ralph, Keye Luke.* Pearl S. Buck's novel of peasant farmers in China has been brilliantly brought to the screen to create one of the 1930s greatest films. In two magnificent performances, Muni and Oscar winner Rainer portray Wang and O-Lan, respectively, who at the story's beginning are first introduced to each other on their wedding day. In a gripping series of events, they endure famine, revolution, the death of a child, betrayal, life as refugees and, in a classic sequence, a swarm of locusts. Franklin's direction is self-assured and his epic stagings of a mass exodus, political riot and the locust swarm are superbly juxtaposed by deeply affecting scenes of interpersonal relationships and familial conflict. ★★★★ VHS: $19.99

Good Evening, Mr. Wallenberg

(1990, 115 min, Sweden, Kjell Grede) *Stellan Skarsgård, Erland Josephson, Katharina Thalbach.* An ambitious, compelling drama, *Good Evening, Mr. Wallenberg* is based on the true-life experiences of Raoul Wallenberg (Skarsgård), a Swedish diplomat who attempted to save tens of thousands of Jews in Nazi-occupied Budapest near the end of WWII. Encountering Nazi bureaucrats, Hungarian collaborators and civilian hostility, Wallenberg's difficult path is detailed, and the story in unflinching honesty depicts the brutal, anti-Semitic realities of the time. Though the film may lack the epic feel and fluid narrative of the similarly themed *Schindler's List*, a wrenching power exists all the same. (Swedish, German and Hungarian with English subtitles) ★★★ VHS: $19.99

The Good Father

(1987, 90 min, GB, Mike Newell) *Anthony Hopkins, Jim Broadbent, Simon Callow.* Hopkins gives a multilayered performance as a recently separated father exorcising his own demons through an acquaintance's custody battle. An intelligent, adult, considered exploration of male-female relationships and the dissolution of marriage. Nicely directed by Newell. ★★★

A Good Man in Africa

(1994, 93 min, GB, Bruce Beresford) *Colin Friels, Sean Connery, Joanne Whalley-Kilmer, John Lithgow, Louis Gossett, Jr., Diana Rigg.* After such films as *White Mischief* and *The Kitchen Toto*, two of the better stories exploring British imperialism in Africa, it would take a film of great skill and freshness to expound on the theme. Unfortunately, *A Good Man in Africa* is not that film. Not entirely, anyway. The affable Friels stars as a British diplomatic attaché whose disastrous attempts to keep order backfire at every turn. Connery is a dedicated doctor and the titular good man. Low-key and often flat, this nonetheless contains many small charms at the most unexpected moments. ★★½ VHS: $9.99

Good Morning Babylon

(1987, 115 min, Italy, Paolo & Vittorio Taviani) *Vincent Spano, Joaqui De Almeida.* The Taviani brothers' first film in English is a modern fable which chronicles the ambitions, dreams and loves of two brothers. Gifted artisans, the brothers leave their native Italy, emigrate to America and eventually work on the making of the sets for D. W. Griffith's *Intolerance.* Spano and De Almeida are the siblings (and alter egos of the directors) in this funny yet poetic homage to the magic of the cinema. (Filmed in English) ★★★

Good Morning, Vietnam

(1987, 120 min, US, Barry Levinson) *Robin Williams, Forest Whitaker, Bruno Kirby, Richard Edson, Robert Wuhl, J. T. Walsh.* Williams sparkles as Adrian Cronauer, a real-life radio D.J. who found himself plunked down against his will in Saigon, 1965. What Levinson's film lacks by way of plot is more than made up for by Williams' sensational talents — his on-air scenes are pure comic genius. ★★★ VHS: $9.99; DVD: $29.99

The Good Mother

(1988, 103 min, US, Leonard Nimoy) *Diane Keaton, Liam Neeson, Jason Robards, James Naughton, Ralph Bellamy, Teresa Wright, Joe Morton, Matt Damon.* Keaton's remarkable performance elevates this involving melodrama about a divorced mother who begins an affair with a free-spirited artist; her ex-husband retaliates with child abuse charges. Look for Matt Damon in an small uncredited role. ★★★

Good Neighbor Sam

(1964, 130 min, US, David Swift) *Jack Lemmon, Romy Schneider, Edward G. Robinson, Dorothy Provine.* Lemmon proves his mastery of physical comedy when he agrees to help the woman next door claim her inheritance by posing as her husband — much to his wife's annoyance. ★★½ VHS: $9.99

Good Night Michelangelo

(1989, 91 min, Canada, Carlo Liconti) *Giancarlo Giannini, Lina Sastri, Kim Cattrall.* A charming and offbeat film, this gentle comedy follows the lives of a family of immigrants in 1957 Toronto. Narrated by six-year-old Michelangelo, the film details the struggles, loves and misadventures of this boisterous family as they try to assimilate into the new English-speaking world. The family includes a grumpy grandfather, a hot-blooded widowed mother who rules with an iron fist, and an amorous Italian boarder, mischievously played by Giannini. Told with humor and a knowing nod to the family's difficulties, this Italian *Parenthood* is a pleasant portrait of a family in transition. (English language) ★★★

Good Sam

(1948, 128 min, US, Leo McCarey) *Gary Cooper, Ann Sheridan, Edmund Lowe.* A good samaritan (Cooper) has the knack for getting into trouble with each good deed he performs. A minor comedy from the otherwise sterling career of writer-director McCarey. ★★ VHS: $19.99

The Good Son

(1993, 87 min, US, Joseph Ruben) *Macaulay Culkin, Elijah Wood, Wendy Crewson, David Morse.* Director Ruben follows his muddled box-office hit *Sleeping with the Enemy* with this equally contrived thriller, which still should manage to give a few chills to those who enjoyed his previous work. Playing against his *Home Alone* image, Culkin reinterprets "The Bad Seed" for the '90s; he's a cherub-faced demon who delights in killing dogs, instigating a 12-car pileup and threatening the life and limb of his loved ones. Wood plays the young cousin who comes to live with Culkin and his family, and who soon discovers the truth about the little psycho. A startling ten-minute ending sequence is evidently the film's only excuse for being made. ★★ VHS: $9.99

The Good, the Bad and the Ugly

(1967, 161 min, Italy/Spain, Sergio Leone) *Clint Eastwood, Lee Van Cleef, Eli Wallach.* The final installment of the trilogy about "The Man with No Name" finds Eastwood reluctantly teaming up with low-life Wallach in order to beat bad guy Van Cleef to a buried fortune in Confederate gold. The film rambles along like the shaggy dog tale that it is, always visually interesting, often very funny, with *the* classic film score by Ennio Morricone. (VHS available letterboxed or pan & scan) ★★★½ VHS: $24.99; DVD: $14.99

The Good Wife

(1987, 97 min, Australia, Ken Cameron) *Bryan Brown, Rachel Ward, Sam Neill.* Set in a pre-WWII small Australian town, the story concerns the secretive love affair between an unhappily married woman and a handsome and attentive stranger. The stars keep the ordinary story of interest. ★★½

Good Will Hunting

(1997, 122 min, US, Gus Van Sant) *Matt Damon, Robin Williams, Ben Affleck, Minnie Driver, Stellan Skarsgård, Casey Affleck.* A breakthrough film in more ways than one, *Good Will Hunting* is a genuinely moving, exceptionally written and performed drama of a mathematical genius at odds with the world. Cowriter Damon (who deservedly shared a Best Screenplay Oscar with costar B. Affleck) gives a sincere performance as Will Hunting, a troubled working-class Boston youth who begins counseling with psychology professor Sean McGuire (Williams) to stay out of jail.

G

These sessions are the heart of the drama, in which both men are able to come to terms with their demons. And through extraordinary dialogue, the painful process of psychological recovery is as mesmerizing to watch as it is touching. Director Van Sant never allows the film to wallow in sentimentality; it's low-key, but it's also as tough-minded, steadfast and unexpectedly humorous as Will himself. As the determined professor, Williams won an Academy Award. ★★★★ VHS: $14.99; DVD: $29.99

Goodbye, Columbus

(1969, 105 min, US, Larry Peerce) *Richard Benjamin, Ali MacGraw, Jack Klugman, Nan Martin*. It's Benjamin (in his film debut) saying so long to university life when he falls for Jewish American Princess MacGraw in this, the best adaptation of any of Phillip Roth's books. ★★★ VHS: $14.99

The Goodbye Girl

(1977, 110 min, US, Herbert Ross) *Marsha Mason, Richard Dreyfuss, Quinn Cummings, Marilyn Sokol*. Snappy Neil Simon comedy with Mason as a divorced mother who is forced to share her apartment with an egocentric actor (Dreyfuss in his Oscar-winning role.) Cummings deftly plays Mason's sharp-tongued young daughter. ★★★ VHS: $14.99; DVD: $19.99

Goodbye Lover

(1999, 100 min, US, Roland Joffé) *Patricia Arquette, Dermot Mulroney, Ellen DeGeneres, Mary-Louise Parker, Don Johnson*. A playful noir with a few good twists, *Goodbye Lover* is a consistently enjoyable comic mystery which delights in its subversive ways. Older sibling Johnson is having an affair with his brother's wife (Arquette). Younger sibling Mulroney is at his wit's end — or is he? Conspiracy's afoot when one of them ends up dead. That's when cynical cop DeGeneres enters the scene. It's a case of scam, double cross and hoodwink as allegiances are tested, morals are reinterpreted, and only the truly cunning survive. The ensemble is obviously having a good time with the lively material, with the wily DeGeneres having the most fun with her role — she's delectable. And watch as writers Ron Peer, Joel Cohen and Alec Sokolow find a devilish use for ditties from *The Sound of Music*. ★★★ VHS: $14.99; DVD: $19.99

Goodbye, Mr. Chips

(1939, 115 min, US, Sam Wood) *Robert Donat, Greer Garson, Paul Henreid, John Mills*. Extraordinary adaptation of James Hilton's novel about the life of a dedicated, shy schoolmaster. Donat gives a remarkable Oscar-winning performance as Chips, and Garson is exceptional in her film debut as his young wife. One of the greatest achievements of the incredible film year of 1939. (Remade in 1969 as a musical) ★★★★ VHS: $19.99

Goodbye, Mr. Chips

(1969, 151 min, GB, Herbert Ross) *Peter O'Toole, Petula Clark, Michael Redgrave, Sian Phillips*. O'Toole's likable performance highlights this uninspired musical remake of the 1939 classic, based on the James Hilton novel. Updated to WWII, it's about a self-sacrificing teacher and his love for a dance-hall singer (Clark). Redgrave and Phillips are quite good in support. ★★ VHS: $19.99

Goodbye, New York

(1985, 90 min, Israel, Amos Kollek) *Julie Hagerty, Amos Kollek*. The comic talents of Hagerty are fully realized in this charming Israeli comedy about a ditsy New Yorker who leaves her unfaithful husband, quits her job and flees to Paris. Fate intervenes, however, as she oversleeps at the Paris stopover and ends up, without luggage or money, in the totally foreign land of Israel. She is soon befriended by a good-natured but lascivious cab driver who guides her through comic misadventures and her second education in the Holy Land. (Filmed in English) ★★★ VHS: $14.99

The Goodbye People

(1986, 104 min, US, Herb Gardner) *Martin Balsam, Judd Hirsch, Pamela Reed, Ron Silver*. Bittersweet tale of a 70-year-old retiree (Balsam) who decides to re-open his Coney Island beachfront hot dog stand; aided by his estranged daughter (Reed) and an eccentric artist (Hirsch). Based on director Gardner's play. ★★ VHS: $14.99

Goodbye Pork Pie

(1981, 105 min, New Zealand, Geoff Murphy) *Tony Barry, Kelly Johnson*. A wild adventure comedy about two young men and their thousand-mile excursion in a stolen car. As the police follow in hot pursuit, the two become newsmedia heroes as a result of their reckless escapades. ★★★

GoodFellas

(1990, 147 min, US, Martin Scorsese) *Ray Liotta, Robert De Niro, Lorraine Bracco, Joe Pesci, Paul Sorvino, Samuel L. Jackson*. Liotta delivers a gritty and charismatic performance as a young mob functionary in this based-on-fact, superbly crafted and high-energy look at the rise and fall of a mob insider. The film brilliantly illustrates the seduction of Liotta's early initiations, the headiness of his status as "goodfella" and the hellishness of his inevitable fall from grace. As Liotta's cold-blooded comrades, De Niro and especially Oscar-winner Pesci are mesmerizing; and Bracco sparkles as Liotta's tough-as-nails wife. Scorsese has created a modern masterpiece, as well as one of the finest gangster movies of all time. (VHS available letterboxed or pan & scan) ★★★★ VHS: $19.99; DVD: $24.99

The Goonies

(1985, 111 min, US, Richard Donner) *Sean Astin, Josh Brolin, Corey Feldman, Martha Plimpton, Anne Ramsey, Joe Pantoliano*. This fun-filled if loud children's adventure follows the comic exploits of a group of adolescents who go searching for buried treasure to save their parents' home. Strictly for kids and only for adults who have yet to lose their inner child. ★★½ VHS: $14.99; DVD: $24.99

Gore Vidal's Billy the Kid

(1989, 100 min, US, William Graham) *Val Kilmer, Wilford Brimley, Michael Parks*. Vidal's second film on the life and death of Billy the Kid, while enjoyable enough, does not come close to the complexity and nuances that were much in evidence in *The Left-Handed Gun*. Kilmer plays Billy, but a Billy who is less tormented and a bit more goofy than Paul Newman's interpretation. The story focuses primarily on the friendship between Billy and the man who finally guns him down, Pat Garrett. Kilmer is an attractive renegade, but his role is ultimately undermined by the traditional, strictly-by-the-numbers approach to the legend. ★★

Gore-Gore Girls

(1972, 70 min, US, Hershell Gordon Lewis) *Henny Youngman*. Lewis goes all out to gross out in his final and goriest film. Youngman (!) is the owner of a nightclub whose dancers are butchered in various gruesome fashions. Graphic (and relatively lengthy) mutilation sequences made this one of the first films ever to receive an X rating for violence. T&A and blood equals more squeamishly decadent late-night fun. ★

Gorgeous

(1999, 99 min, Hong Kong, Vincent Kok) *Jackie Chan, Shu Qi, Tony Leung*. The sad truth for fans is, Jackie Chan ain't a spring chicken no more. He's not able to execute the same astonishing, death-defying stunts or lightning-fast moves he used to. Still, with recent releases like *Shanghai Noon* and *Rush Hour* — which are essentially comedies first, and action films second — Jackie has been able to display his formidable comedic talents while downplaying the physically near-impossible. But with *Gorgeous*, a tepid romance/action film made in Hong Kong, Jackie makes a misstep. The accent is all on hideously cutesy romance and deadly dull story, with very little action or humor. (Dubbed) ★½ VHS: $9.99; DVD: $24.99

The Gorgeous Hussy

(1936, 102 min, US, Clarence Brown) *Joan Crawford, Robert Taylor, Melvyn Douglas, James Stewart*. Other than its catchy title, the best that can be said for this opulent costumer is that it features superior production values. Crawford stars as Peggy Eaton, the infamous "Belle of Washington" during President Andrew Jackson's administration. The film traces her rise in political circles, and the scandal she caused, though it's not as interesting as it sounds. ★½ VHS: $19.99

Gorgo

(1961, 78 min, GB, Eugene Lourie) *Bill Travers, William Sylvester, Vincent Winter, Bruce Seton*. When Toho Studios made a knock-off of director Lourie's *The Beast from 20 Thousand Fathoms* called Godzilla, he decided to return the favor by making this man-in-a-rubber-monster-suit film, to much better results. When a traveling circus captures a giant prehistoric beast off the Scottish Sea and exhibits it in London, it becomes an instant smash — until mom comes looking for Jr. ★★½ VHS: $14.99

The Gorgon

(1961, 83 min, GB, Terence Fisher) *Peter Cushing, Christopher Lee, Barbara Shelley*. In this Hammer film, Cushing's ward has a problem: this beauty's a Medusa, first breaking men's hearts, then turning them into stone — literally. ★★½ VHS: $14.99

The Gorilla

(1939, 66 min, US, Alan Dwan) *The Ritz Brothers, Anita Louise, Patsy Kelly, Bela Lugosi*. Though the brilliance of the Ritz Brothers was never captured on film, this traditional haunted house

Robin Williams (l.) mentors Matt Damon in *Good Will Hunting*

mystery is enlivened by their silly jokes, synchronized dancing and wild slapstick. ★★½

Gorillas in the Mist

(1988, 129 min, US, Michael Apted) *Sigourney Weaver, Bryan Brown, Julie Harris.* Weaver's outstanding performance is the heart and soul of this well-produced biography on anthropologist Dian Fossey. The story covers the nearly 20 years Fossey dedicated to the mountain gorillas of central Africa, from her arrival on the continent as a census taker to her unprecedented work with the animals to her tragic murder. Brown also stars as a *National Geographic* cinematographer (and Fossey's lover) whose films help bring about her international renown. Efficient, commanding direction from Apted. ★★★ VHS: $9.99; DVD: $26.99

Gorky Park

(1983, 126 min, US, Michael Apted) *William Hurt, Lee Marvin, Brian Dennehy, Joanna Pacula.* Three corpses are found in Moscow's Gorky Park with their faces removed to make identification nearly impossible. But the key word here to Russian policeman Hurt is "nearly." And he sets out to solve the murders with Sherlockian reasoning. Marvin is chillingly effective as a shady American businessman. A taut and clever thriller from the pen of Martin Cruz Smith, with gritty yet stylish direction from Apted. ★★★½ DVD: $19.99

The Gospel According to Al Green

(1984, 90 min, US, Robert Mugge) Philadelphia filmmaker Mugge directed this exultant, fascinating portrait of pop superstar-turned-Pentacostal preacher extraordinaire Al Green. Throughout his career, Green has incorporated both a spirituality and a sensuality that moves audiences to ecstatic heights of joy and release. Mugge captures Green both in concert and on the pulpit, hypnotizing his audience with the intensity and majesty of his performance. His dedication and desire to help his audience find happiness on this planet give this spine-tingling documentary an electric, revelatory energy rarely captured on film. ★★★½ VHS: $19.99; DVD: $19.99

Gospel According to Vic

(1986, 95 min, Scotland, Charles Gormley) *Tom Conti, Helen Mirren.* In this irreverent Scottish comedy, Conti brings his prototypical comic flair to the role of Father Cobb, a chaplain who is two miracles short of successfully pleading Sainthood for a certain Blessed Edith. ★★★ VHS: $79.99

The Gospel at Colonus

(1986, 90 min, US, Lee Breuer) *Morgan Freeman, Clarence Fountain and the Five Blind Boys of Alabama, Robert Earl Jones, Carl Lumbly.* Based on the stage musical, this is an exhilarating gospel version of Sophocles' "Oedipus at Colonus," following the journey of Oedipus and his children to Colonus where the elder has come to die. Music by Bob Telson. ★★★

Gossip

(2000, 90 min, US, Davis Guggenheim) *James Marsden, Lena Headey, Norman Reedus, Kate Hudson, Marisa Coughlan, Joshua Jackson.* Three journalism students (Marsden, Headey and Reedus) go too far when asked to identify the link between news and gossip. To illustrate, they create a real-life rumor about a celibate freshman (Hudson) and her boyfriend (Jackson) getting it on. When the boyfriend is wrongly arrested on date rape charges, the students realize that the rumor has gotten out of hand and has become the news. The serious issues are muddled in a pretty generic teen thriller that, like its characters, has a tenuous grip on reality. ★ VHS: $14.99; DVD: $19.99

Gotcha!

(1985, 97 min, US, Jeff Kanew) *Anthony Edwards, Linda Fiorentino, Alex Rocco.* The very likable Edwards plays a college kid on European vacation who becomes involved in political intrigue. Fiorentino is very much a part of that intrigue. The film never really connects, but the Edwards-Fiorentino teaming and some amusing espionage bits compensate. ★★½ VHS: $14.99

Gothic

(1987, 90 min, GB, Ken Russell) *Gabriel Byrne, Julian Sands, Natasha Richardson, Timothy Spall, Miriam Cyr.* Russell takes another step beyond the edge with this unusual, dreamlike psychological thriller. Set in the 1800s at Lord Byron's villa, the film depicts one hellish night spent by Byron and his guests, who included P. B. Shelley, his lover Mary, and author Dr. Polidori. The film suggests this fateful evening inspired Polidori to write "The Vampyre" and Mary (who would later marry her paramour) to pen "Frankenstein." ★★★ VHS: $14.99; DVD: $24.99

The Governess

(1998, 105 min, GB, Sandra Goldbacher) *Minnie Driver, Tom Wilkinson, Harriet Walter, Florence Hoath, Bruce Myers, Jonathan Rhys Meyers.* A handsomely mounted but largely uninvolving drama by writer-director Goldbacher, this story of an interloper and her affairs is more ambitious than it is good. Rosina (Driver) is a Jewess from London who passes herself as Mary Blackchurch, a governess. Employed by the Cavendish family, Rosina meets the bratty daughter, the brittle wife, and the robust patriarch (Wilkinson), an amateur photographer who takes a sexual interest in her. The drama is uninspired, and the passions are more tepid than torrid. It's an overheated but underwhelming romance. ★★ VHS: $24.99; DVD: $29.99

Grace of My Heart

(1996, 115 min, US, Allison Anders) *Illeana Douglas, Matt Dillon, Eric Stoltz, John Turturro, Bruce Davison, Patsy Kensit, Bridget Fonda, Chris Isaak, Peter Fonda, David Clennon.* Douglas turns in a captivating performance as a woman searching for professional achievement and personal fulfillment in the fiercely competitive music industry. Opening in 1958 and spanning a decade and a half, the film sweeps across the shifting tides of contemporary popular culture while exploring the life of Edna Buxton (Douglas): naïve, overprotected child of privilege with an unexpected reserve of strength. Director Anders successfully captures the look and feel of the varying eras and locales, as well as conveying the nature of the creative process as Edna's songs increasingly reflect her experiences and observations. The cast is uniformly strong in their portrayals, and the film is densely packed and leisurely paced, losing focus only briefly during the California segment. *Grace of My Heart* pays equal respect to Edna and the music. ★★★ VHS: $9.99; DVD: $29.99

Grace Quigley

(1985, 87 min, US, Anthony Harvey) *Katharine Hepburn, Nick Nolte, Elizabeth Wilson, Chip Zien.* Hepburn witnesses a murder committed by Nolte. Appreciating the professional touch, she hires him — to kill her. In the course of making the financial arrangements, a lucrative enterprise evolves; you might call it a growth industry. A quirky reflection on the perils of old age that fluctuates between farce and pathos, the film could have been better. Strong performances by Hepburn and Nolte seem ill-served by director Harvey. Another edit of the film exists, but not on video. In all this, one question is left unanswered: How can Hepburn still look that good? ★★

The Graduate

(1967, 105 min, US, Mike Nichols) *Dustin Hoffman, Anne Bancroft, Katharine Ross, William Daniels, Murray Hamilton, Marion Lorne, Alice Ghostley, Elizabeth Wilson, Buck Henry.* Nichols' landmark comedy made stars of Hoffman and Simon & Garfunkle, and cleared the path for the cinematic concerns of the younger generation. Effortlessly poignant and humorous, the film follows recent grad Benjamin (Hoffman) as he contemplates the future (plastics?) and becomes romantically involved with the sultry

Mrs. Robinson (Bancroft in a smashing portrayal) and then her daughter (Ross). A perceptive and double-edged examination of mores and morals in 1960s America. ★★★★ VHS: $14.99; DVD: $19.99

Graffiti Bridge

(1990, 91 min, US, Prince) *Prince, Morris Day, Jerome Benton.* Prince wrote, directed and stars in this awful sequel to his 1984 hit *Purple Rain*, detailing the further musical adventures of "The Kid." Look for Mavis Staples, George Clinton and Ingrid Chavez. ★ VHS: $14.99

Grain of Sand

(1983, 90 min, France, Promme Meffre) *Delphine Seyrig, Genevieve Fontanel.* Seyrig finds herself sinking into a morass of self-doubt when she loses her job after 14 years. Her only hope: locate an old lover from her past now living on the island of Corsica. Meffre makes a striking directorial debut, deftly handling the subtle psychology of a woman unsettled just as she comes to the precipice of encroaching old age. (French with English subtitles) ★★★ VHS: $59.99

Grand Canyon

(1991, 135 min, US, Lawrence Kasdan) *Kevin Kline, Danny Glover, Mary McDonnell, Steve Martin, Alfre Woodard, Mary-Louise Parker.* Writer-director Kasdan turns his discerning eye to the fears and frustrations facing the American society in the '90s. An epic assignment, to be sure, but Kasdan and cowriter and wife Meg have fashioned an insightful and powerful examination of our times. Kline plays a successful L.A. lawyer whose wrong turn driving home leads to an altercation with a street gang. He is rescued by truck driver Glover. The two men befriend each other, ultimately opening a wide panorama of issues and concerns facing not only them but their family and friends. The film tackles disparate themes such as racism, child abandonment, crime, violence, family mores, just to name a few, and all are handled with sensitivity and thoughtfulness. ★★★½ VHS: $9.99; DVD: $24.99

Le Grand Chemin

(1987, 104 min, France, Jean-Loup Hubert) *Anemone, Richard Bohringer, Antoine Hubert.* Poignant and tender without being maudlin, this delightful coming-of-age drama tells the story of a sensitive nine-year-old Parisian boy's experiences in the countryside after his mother leaves him with friends for the summer. The couple, a prissy but insolent woman and a rough and tumble drunkard, dote on the boy but incessantly argue as they are constantly reminded of their own child who tragically died a few years before. Rounding out the boy's education and introduction into the grown-up world is a rambunctious and wise-beyond-words tomboy. (American remake: *Paradise*) (French with English subtitles) ★★★½

Grand Hotel

(1932, 113 min, US, Edmund Goulding) *Greta Garbo, John Barrymore, Joan Crawford, Lionel Barrymore, Wallace Beery.* Garbo heads an all-star cast as the melancholic ballerina who "vants to be alone." Barrymore is the debonair jewel thief who romances her. Superior performances from the ensemble, fine direction from Goulding, and an intelligent script make this a classic from its era. ★★★★ VHS: $19.99

Grand Illusion

(1937, 114 min, France, Jean Renoir) *Jean Gabin, Erich von Stroheim, Pierre Fresnay.* Renoir's humanistic masterpiece examines the chivalry and codes of honor among French POWs during WWI and their elegant German commandant (von Stroheim), divided by nationality but united by class. A monumental indictment of the savagery of war. The first foreign-language film to be nominated for a Best Picture Oscar. (French with English subtitles) ★★★★ VHS: $29.99; DVD: $39.99

Grand Prix

(1966, 171 min, US, John Frankenheimer) *James Garner, Eva Marie Saint, Toshiro Mifune, Yves Montand, Jessica Walter.* Oscar-winning Special Effects and Editing highlight this otherwise plodding racing drama about the lives and rivalries of four drivers competing for the World Championship. (Available letterboxed and pan & scan) ★★½ VHS: $24.99

Grand Tour: Disaster in Time

(1992, 99 min, US, David Twohy) *Jeff Daniels, Ariana Richards.* Science-fiction buffs have reason to cheer in this edge-of-your-seat thriller penned (and directed) by Twohy, one of the legion of screenwriters credited on *Alien3*. Daniels stars as "the boy who cried aliens" when his quaint New England town is visited by time-traveling "disaster groupies" who get their kicks playing spectator to mankind's greatest tragedies. Nail-biting suspense makes this more than just another tedious morality play in the "Star Trek" mold. ★★★

La Grande Bouffe

(1973, 125 min, France/Italy, Marco Ferreri) *Marcello Mastroianni, Ugo Tognazzi, Michel Piccoli, Philippe Noiret.* Director Ferreri, who can be as unrelenting and as vicious as Jonathan Swift, performs an autopsy on a dying class. Four bored businessmen are all victims of a terminal case of ennui brought on by the limitations inherent in bourgeois sensibilities. These gourmets become gourmands and decide to end it all by eating themselves to death. Ferreri vividly exposes the desperation among aging males as they attempt to retain their privileged positions — if not in the real world, than one of their own creation. The big questions are asked, but only little ones are answered — unsatisfying perhaps, but then it's expected in these superficial times. (French with English subtitles) ★★★½ VHS: $19.99; DVD: $24.99

La Grande Bourgeoise

(1977, 115 min, Italy, Mauro Bolognini) *Catherine Deneuve, Giancarlo Giannini, Fernando Rey, Tina Aumont.* The repressed lust and violent emotions of the Italian upper classes in turn-of-the-century Rome make this stylish drama of love, murder and betrayal a fascinating drama. Deneuve marries older man Rey but her disturbed brother, Giannini, can't accept them and plots his murder. A lush, wonderfully photographed and costumed period piece. (Italian with English subtitles) (aka: *The Murri Affair*) ★★★

La Grande Guerra (The Great War)

(1959, 118 min, Italy, Mario Monicelli) *Vittorio Gassman, Alberto Sordi, Silvana Mangano.* A pardoned criminal (Gassman) becomes an unlikely soldier and together with his friend and fellow conscript, the cowardly Sordi, they find themselves becoming reluctant heroes in this diverting comedy set during World War I. (Italian with English subtitles) ★★½

Grandview, U.S.A.

(1984, 97 min, US, Randal Kleiser) *Patrick Swayze, Jamie Lee Curtis, C. Thomas Howell, Jennifer Jason Leigh, M. Emmet Walsh, John Cusack, Joan Cusack.* A good cast supplies the star power for a series of intertwining tales set in a small Midwestern town centering around the family-run auto derby. ★★ VHS: $19.99

The Grapes of Wrath

(1940, 129 min, US, John Ford) *Henry Fonda, Jane Darwell, John Carradine, Charlie Grapewin, John Qualen.* A monumental achievement in American film history, this superb adaptation of John Steinbeck's novel received compassionate and visionary guidance from director Ford, and remarkable contributions from the entire cast. Set during the Depression, the unforgettable story follows the hardships of a poor Oklahoma family, the Joads, who migrate from their dust-bowl farm to California and the promise of a better future. The outstanding cast includes Fonda, in the performance of his career, as the Joads' idealistic son, Tom; and Darwell as the stalwart matriarch. Oscars went to Ford and Darwell. ★★★★ VHS: $14.99

Grass

(2000, 79 min, US, Ron Mann) *Narrated by Woody Harrelson.* Staunch hemp lobbyist Harrelson narrates this brisk but ultimately bland documentary about our society's ever-shifting views on marijuana. Weaving together early government anti-drug propaganda films with funky stock footage of the counterculture revolution, *Grass* charts the relatively short history of the drug in American culture and recounts the growing hysteria within the government apparatus that's kept dope illegal for generations. Though not as fiendishly subversive as its subject matter would suggest, this documentary nonetheless hits some irreverent, er, highs (the ludicrous government "shock" films used out of context are especially hilarious). ★★½ VHS: $59.99

The Grass Harp

(1996, 107 min, US, Charles Matthau) *Piper Laurie, Sissy Spacek, Walter Matthau, Jack Lemmon, Edward Furlong, Mary Steenburgen, Nell Carter, Roddy McDowall, Charles Durning.* An affecting adaptation of Truman Capote's touching novel of life in the South a couple generations ago, *The Grass Harp* is as tranquil as a calm summers' eve, which doesn't always accentuate the story's plucky characters or whimsical situations. Partly autobiographical, Capote's warm tale centers on Collin, an orphaned youth who is sent to live with his two maiden aunts. Spacek plays Verena, the younger but controlling sister, and Laurie is Dolly, a cheerful, childlike recluse. One of the strengths of *The Grass Harp* is the fine ensemble cast director Matthau has assembled, including his father Walter in a wonderful turn as Dolly's suitor. The film's gentle motion befits Capote's wistful recollections. ★★★ VHS: $19.99

The Grass Is Greener

(1961, 105 min, US, Stanley Donen) *Cary Grant, Deborah Kerr, Robert Mitchum, Jean*

Simmons. Stagey but mostly entertaining drawing room comedy with Grant as an English earl whose jealousy sparks a calamitous weekend affair when wife Kerr is given the royal treatment by visiting American millionaire Mitchum. Simmons is Mitchum's wife who has her own designs on Grant. Music and lyrics by Noël Coward. (Letterboxed) ★★½ VHS: $9.99

Grave Indiscretion

(1995, 99 min, GB, J.P. Davidson) *Alan Bates, Sting, Theresa Russell, Lena Headey, Anna Massey.* Known as *The Grotesque* in Britain and the awfully titled *Gentlemen Don't Eat Poets* in its theatrical release in America, this kinky but ultimately flaccid murder-mystery is far from being a total waste of time. Reminiscent of *The Servant* and *Teorema,* the film stars Bates (wonderful in a bombastic performance) as Sir Hugo Cole, an eccentric paleontologist trapped in a sexless marriage with his American wife (Russell, in an amusing miscast role) who comes under the suspicious antics of his new butler Fledge (the arch-browed, nearly silent Sting). Set in an opulent home in late 1940s England, *Grave Indiscretion* should be enjoyed for its campy and sinister sexual encounters rather than for its feeble attempt at creating mystery and an air of foreboding. ★★ VHS: $14.99

Gray's Anatomy

(1997, 80 min, US, Steven Soderbergh) *Spalding Gray.* America's premiere monologist Gray takes on the terror of physical trauma and myriad alternative healing beliefs in *Gray's Anatomy,* in which the author/protagonist reacts to retinal damage in his left eye by embarking on yet another journey of thousands and thousands of miles. Advised to have surgery, this child of Christian Science runs the idea by his existential realist therapist, an astral-projecting sweat lodge overseer, a nutritional optometrist, and a Filipino psychic surgeon. The staged performance piece is opened up with creative direction, and interspersed with interviews with some people who've had their own encounters with medical emergencies threatening that most-precious sense: sight. As in his past theatrical forays (*Swimming to Cambodia* most notably), Gray bares his soul and psyche with self-deprecating wit and flippant awareness of the human condition. ★★★ VHS: $14.99; DVD: $14.99

Grease

(1978, 110 min, US, Randal Kleiser) *John Travolta, Olivia Newton-John, Stockard Channing, Eve Arden, Sid Caesar, Joan Blondell, Alice Ghostley.* Travolta and Newton-John created a small sensation in the late 1970s with this lively version of the drippy long-running Broadway musical. Set in the late 1950s, the film brought Travolta fame as a high school "greaser" who tries to hide his romance with "uncool" new girl Newton-John. Spirited dance numbers and a pleasant score are the main attraction here. Channing steals the show as the leader of the girl greasers, and it's always nice to see the likes of Arden, Caesar, Blondell and Ghostley. (VHS available letterboxed or pan & scan) (Sequel: *Grease 2*) ★★½ VHS: $14.99

The Great Dictator: Charlie Chaplin and Jack Oakie knock Hitler and Mussolini on their Axis

Grease 2

(1982, 114 min, US, Patricia Birch) *Maxwell Caulfield, Michelle Pfeiffer, Lorna Luft, Eve Arden, Sid Caesar.* Birch, who choreographed the appealing dance sequences in the original *Grease,* directed this very unappealing sequel. Caulfield and a young Pfeiffer are the high school kids in love. ★ VHS: $14.99

Greaser's Palace

(1972, 91 min, US, Robert Downey) *Albert Henderson, Allan Arbus.* Downey's irreverent version of the Christ Story set in the Wild West. Our Savior's descent comes in the form of Zoot Suit, a gentle song-and-dance man who arrives by parachute to work miracles and bring peace and harmony to the world. ★★½ VHS: $19.99; DVD: $24.99

Great Balls of Fire

(1989, 108 min, US, Jim McBride) *Dennis Quaid, Winona Ryder, Alec Baldwin, Trey Wilson, John Doe.* A high-energy, slick bio on rock 'n' roll legend Jerry Lee Lewis. Quaid, in a gutsy though rather one-dimensional performance, plays the rock pioneer, whose life is traced from his meteoric rise on the music scene to his controversial marriage to his teenage cousin to the infamous British tour which nearly ruined his career. Though the film is short on dramatic development, and its characters behave as music biz/Southern stereotypes, it is at its best (and agreeably entertaining) in the superior and razzle-dazzle musical numbers featuring some of Lewis' greatest hits. Ryder deftly plays Lewis' child bride. ★★★ VHS: $9.99

A Great Day in Harlem

(1994, 60 min, US, Jean Bach) *Quincy Jones, Dizzy Gillespie, Art Blakey, Art Farmer, Chubby Jackson, Paula Morris, Marian McPartland, Eddie Locke, Ernie Wilkins, Mona Hinton, Robert Benton, Sonny Rollins.* It was a beautiful day, that June morning in 1958, when fledgling photographer Art Kane and the film director Robert Benton, then editor of *Esquire,* assembled some of the greatest jazz legends for a group photograph. This marked the first time that many of the greatest drummers, trumpet, piano and sax players were at the same place at the same time where none of them were playing. Milt Hinton and his wife Mona took 8mm home movies of the event and other people took candid photos, never before seen of the gathering. Included are scenes of these jazz greats performing. An interesting glimpse into the after-hours "party" that took place on the front stoop of 125th St. that summer day. ★★★ DVD: $24.99

The Great Dictator

(1940, 128 min, US, Charles Chaplin) *Charles Chaplin, Paulette Goddard, Jack Oakie, Billy Gilbert.* Chaplin's first talkie stands as one of his greatest achievements. In this touching and often hilarious political spoof on the Third Reich, Chaplin plays dual roles: a poor Jew from the ghetto and Hynkel, the Hitler-inspired leader. Oakie is hilarious as Italian dictator "Napolini." ★★★★ VHS: $19.99; DVD: $29.99

The Great Escape

(1963, 168 min, US, John Sturges) *Steve McQueen, James Garner, Richard Attenborough, James Coburn, Charles Bronson, Donald Pleasence, David McCallum.* Blockbuster adventure, based on a true story, about a group of Allied POWs who plan a daring escape from a German camp during WWII. A terrific all-star cast. ★★★½ VHS: $24.99

Great Expectations

(1946, 118 min, GB, David Lean) *John Mills, Valerie Hobson, Bernard Miles, Alec Guinness, Jean Simmons.* One of the finest literary adaptations ever put to film, this stunning version of the Charles Dickens classic about a young orphan and his mysterious benefactor features masterful direction by Lean. ★★★★ DVD: $39.99

The Great Gatsby

(1974, 144 min, US, Jack Clayton) *Robert Redford, Mia Farrow, Bruce Dern, Sam Waterston, Karen Black.* Francis Ford Coppola adapted F. Scott Fitzgerald's classic for the screen with Redford as the titular character, a self-made man accepted into Long Island society back in the Jazz Age. The film captures neither the sensuality nor excitement of the novel, though it's a faithful adaptation. Redford and Farrow as Daisy are well-matched if curiously subdued. ★★½ VHS: $14.99

The Great Imposter

(1960, 112 min, US, Robert Mulligan) *Tony Curtis, Edmond O'Brien, Arthur O'Connell, Raymond Massey, Karl Malden.* Curtis stars in this true story as Ferdinand Waldo Demara, Jr., who in the 1950s successfully impersonated a monk, a college professor, a prison warden, a naval surgeon and a schoolteacher all before being caught and arrested. Curtis is in good form, though the episodic story only occasionally delivers. ★★½ VHS: $14.99

The Great Lie

(1941, 107 min, US, Edmund Goulding) *Bette Davis, George Brent, Mary Astor, Hattie McDaniel.* Competent soaper with Davis marrying Brent, who used to be involved with Astor. He disappears in a plane crash, Mary is pregnant, and Bette then raises the child as her own. Though Bette is her usual indomitable self, the acting honors go to Academy Award winner Astor. ★★½ VHS: $19.99

The Great Madcap

(El Gran Calavera)

(1949, 90 min, Mexico, Luis Buñuel) *Fernando Soler, Rosario Granados.* One of the most commercial films of his career, Buñuel's engaging and gentle social comedy takes a playful look at the insensitive and irresponsible bourgeoisie, a constant theme he explores in a much more surrealist and biting fashion in *The Discreet Charm of the Bourgeoisie.* Soler plays a wealthy industrialist who, after a period of drunken carousing and free-spending ways, suffers a heart attack. On recovery, he realizes that his ingratiating and fast-living wife, son and even servants, long accustomed to milking him of money and favors, need a good lesson on the value of money and the need to work. The plot has been done before, but the story remains fresh and lively with Buñuel's satiric touch. (Spanish with English subtitles) ★★★ VHS: $79.99

The Great Man Votes

(1939, 72 min, US, Garson Kanin) *John Barrymore, Peter Holden, Virginia Weidler.* Through an ironic bit of casting, Barrymore, whose career was virtually ruined because of his drinking, had his greatest late-career role as an alcoholic given one last chance at redemption. In this wonderful mix of comedy and pathos, Barrymore plays a former professor whose wife's death leads to his drinking and decline. As he fights for custody of his two children, the now–night watchman gets second chance: His is the deciding vote in the town's mayoral race, making him a very popular constituent. ★★★½ VHS: $19.99

The Great McGinty

(1940, 81 min, US, Preston Sturges) *Brian Donlevy, Akim Tamiroff, William Demarest, Muriel Angelus, Louis Jean Heydt.* In a flea-bitten Mexican cantina, a man who lost it all in a moment of dishonesty hears the story of a man who lost it all the first time he tried to go straight. Donlevy is terrific as McGinty, who goes from hobo to governor to bartender-on-the-lam. Sturges won an Oscar for the screenplay of this, his first directorial effort. ★★★½ VHS: $14.99

The Great Moment

(1944, 83 min, US, Preston Sturges) *Joel McCrea, Betty Field, William Demarest, Franklin Pangborn.* McCrea plays Dr. W.T.G. Morton, a 19th-century dentist who discovered anaesthesia, but was not credited with such during his lifetime. Sturges'

intriguing biography is an interesting failure, marred mostly by disorienting flashbacks and out-of-place slapstick. ★★ VHS: $14.99

The Great Mouse Detective

(1986, 74 min, US, John Musker) *Voices of Vincent Price, Barrie Ingham.* Boasting impeccable animation by Disney, this delightful detective story follows the exploits of a spirited murine sleuth. Kids of all ages and adults will enjoy this gentle parody of Arthur Conan Doyle's Sherlock Holmes. It may not be one of Disney's best, but it will certainly entertain. ★★★

The Great Muppet Caper

(1981, 95 min, GB, Jim Henson) *Charles Grodin, Diana Rigg, John Cleese, Robert Morley, Peter Ustinov, Jack Warden.* The standard Muppet buffoonery makes for loads of fun as they try to solve a jewel robbery. Miss Piggy steals the show with her musical numbers (so reminiscent of Marilyn in *Gentlemen Prefer Blondes*), but the star-studded list of cameos is still impressive. ★★★ VHS: $9.99

The Great Outdoors

(1988, 90 min, US, Howard Deutch) *John Candy, Dan Aykroyd, Annette Bening.* Very minor John Hughes–scripted comedy with Candy planning to spend a relaxing family vacation in the woods, not counting on cumbersome Aykroyd. ★½ VHS: $9.99; DVD: $24.99

The Great Race

(1965, 151 min, US, Blake Edwards) *Jack Lemmon, Peter Falk, Tony Curtis, Natalie Wood, Keenan Wynn.* Epic-sized comedy from director Edwards about an intercontinental race and of the wacky participants. Though some of the jokes don't make the grade, there are plenty that do. Lemmon and Falk are the bad guys (boo, hiss) up against good guys Curtis and Wood. ★★★ VHS: $14.99

The Great Rock 'n' Roll Swindle

(1980, 103 min, GB, Julien Temple) Our only question is why the powers that be changed the title of this film from the original *Who Killed Bambi?* The original ad campaign pictured a mutilated fawn and let's face it, what better way could one summarize the insane destructiveness of the legendary Sex Pistols? This fascinating documentary features the lunacy of Johnny Rotten, Sid Vicious, Malcolm McLaren and the rest of the gang. Temple would go on to direct *Absolute Beginners.* Trash and burn was never like this before. ★★★

The Great Santini

(1979, 116 min, US, Lewis John Carlino) *Robert Duvall, Michael O'Keefe, Blythe Danner, David Keith.* An immensely absorbing family drama starring Duvall as a no-nonsense military man whose toughest battle is waged with his troubled son. Outstanding performances by Duvall, Danner and O'Keefe. ★★★½ VHS: $14.99; DVD: $14.99

The Great Train Robbery

(1979, 111 min, US, Michael Crichton) *Sean Connery, Donald Sutherland, Leslie-Anne Down.* An outlandishly entertaining, knock-your-socks-off caper film from writer-director Crichton, based on an actual incident from the mid-1800s. Connery is well-cast as the mastermind behind a

daring train robbery who enlists the help of Sutherland and Down in the pursuit of a large gold shipment. Just try to sit still during the shaving scene! ★★★½ VHS: $14.99

The Great Waldo Pepper

(1975, 109 min, US, George Roy Hill) *Robert Redford, Susan Sarandon, Margot Kidder, Bo Svenson, Geoffrey Lewis, Edward Herrmann.* Entertaining comic adventure starring Redford as a daredevil pilot in the Roaring '20s. He's ably assisted by Sarandon and Kidder. Good aerial photography. ★★★ VHS: $14.99

A Great Wall

(1986, 100 min, China/US, Peter Wang) *Peter Wang, Sharon Iwai, Kelvin Han Yee.* The first Chinese/United States co-production is a good natured comedy about the cultural clashes confronting a Chinese-American family when they make their first trip back to the family's hometown in mainland China. (English and Mandarin with English subtitles) ★★½

The Great White Hope

(1970, 101 min, US, Martin Ritt) *James Earl Jones, Jane Alexander, Hal Holbrook.* Jones repeats his award-winning stage role in this commanding adaptation. Jones gives a truly magnificent performance as turn-of-the-century boxer Jack Johnson (called Jefferson here), facing as many challenges outside the ring as inside it. Alexander also repeats her stage role in a brilliant portrayal of Johnson's white mistress. ★★★

The Great White Hype

(1996, 87 min, US, Reginald Hudlin) *Samuel L. Jackson, Damon Wayans, Peter Berg, Jeff Goldblum, Jon Lovitz, Corbin Bernsen, Cheech Marin.* A playful if unruly racial and sports farce which at times goes over the edge of tastefulness and at others doesn't go far enough. Playing what could be Don King, Jackson stars as a shameless boxing promoter who engineers a championship bout to save his sagging empire — have a white opponent face his black champion (Wayans), thereby creating a racial climate to the fight. He picks a has-been boxer-turned-rock-singer (Berg), and proceeds to try to get the out-of-shape contender into a reasonable facsimile of a fighter. Funny when lampooning the boxing industry and skewering race relations, the film, which was written by Ron Shelton, can be undisciplined and characterizations tend to be too broad. Still, it offers many a laugh, and Jackson and his fellow cast members are highly spirited. ★★½ VHS: $9.99

The Greatest Show on Earth

(1952, 153 min, US, Cecil B. DeMille) *Charlton Heston, James Stewart, Betty Hutton, Dorothy Lamour, Cornel Wilde.* The title says it all and it's not just midway hyperbole when Cecil gives the DeMille treatment to the circus. All thrills and spectacle, with about as much of a plot as one would find in any big-top extravaganza. A huge cast (including Stewart as a clown) keep all three rings busy in this Oscar winner for Best Picture (though it really didn't deserve it over such classics as *High Noon* or *The Quiet Man*). ★★½ VHS: $24.99

The Greatest Story Ever Told

(1965, 195 min, US, George Stevens) *Max von Sydow, Charlton Heston, John Wayne, Carroll Baker,*

G

Angela Lansbury, Sidney Poitier, Shelley Winters, Ed Wynn, Telly Savalas. An all-star cast highlights this glossy though tired biblical epic about the life of Jesus. Wayne is the Roman centurian overseeing Christ's crucifixion (hope we didn't give away the ending). (Restored roadshow version) ★★ VHS: $19.99; DVD: $26.99

Greed

(1924, 239 min, US, Erich von Stroheim) *Dale Fuller, ZaSu Pitts, Jean Hersholt.* Probably the most complete version of this psychological epic we will ever get to see, von Stroheim's masterpiece achieves a depth of characterization through an almost obsessive use of objective correlatives. A love triangle with a gold filling, the film starts high in the mountains and ends on a burning desert. Originally over nine hours long, cut by the studio to just over two, Brownlow & Gill have restored only minutes — but important minutes — including the prologue in the mine (where much of the symbolism is set up). Features another fabulous score by Carl Davis. (Silent) ★★★★ VHS: $29.99

Greedy

(1994, 109 min, US, Jonathan Lynn) *Michael J. Fox, Kirk Douglas, Phil Hartman, Nancy Travis, Bob Balaban, Olivia d'Abo, Colleen Camp.* From the writers of *Parenthood* comes more dysfunctional family humor — and though the results aren't equal to that film, this is nevertheless an appealing, though predictable comedy sporting a wicked bent. Fox plays an estranged nephew who returns to the estate of his rich, dying uncle (the crotchety Douglas) at the insistence of his greedy cousins. The film is at its most entertaining when these vulturous family members (including the devilishly funny Hartman) are at each other's throats in venomous one-upsmanship. ★★½ VHS: $9.99; DVD: $24.99

The Greek Tycoon

(1978, 112 min, US, J. Lee Thompson) *Jacqueline Bisset, Anthony Quinn, James Franciscus, Edward Albert.* Bisset plays the young widow of an assassinated American president who ends up marrying the richest man in the world (played by a crusty Quinn). This little-camouflaged story of the Kennedy-Onassis affair offers little of interest save some exotic locations. ★

The Green Berets

(1968, 141 min, US, John Wayne & Ray Kellogg) *John Wayne, David Janssen, Jim Hutton, Aldo Ray, Raymond St. Jacques.* Wayne appeared in a few turkeys in his long career, but none more than this Vietnam War drama. Made at the infancy of the antiwar movement, this cliché-filled story is amazing in its stupidity, and even failed as a patronage to the titular fighting force. (And yes, that *is* the sun setting in the East!) ★ VHS: $14.99; DVD: $19.99

Green Card

(1990, 108 min, US, Peter Weir) *Gérard Depardieu, Andie MacDowell, Bebe Neuwirth, Gregg Edelman, Robert Prosky, Lois Smith.* The American debut of French superstar Depardieu is this abortive tale of illegal imigration. Depardieu, while not in peak form (possibly due to language barriers), carries the film for MacDowell who, though so wonderful in *sex, lies and video-*

tape, here, unfortunately, falls flat. A definite step backwards for Weir. ★★ VHS: $9.99

Green for Danger

(1946, 93 min, GB, Sidney Gilliat) *Alastair Sim, Trevor Howard, Leo Genn.* Sim camps it up as an eccentric Scotland Yard inspector investigating a series of murders in a WWII hospital unit somewhere in the English countryside. Great fun for aficionados of the classic "drawing room/country house" murder mysteries made famous by Agatha Christie. ★★★½

Green Grow the Rushes

(1951, 79 min, GB, Derek Twist) *Richard Burton, Honor Blackman, Roger Livesey.* Set in post-war rural England, this film of charming mannerisms takes its own good time setting up its peculiar story; but once that story is in motion it's unpredictably funny. A youthfully handsome Burton plays a fisherman involved in the local smuggling of alcohol. Onto the scene stumbles roving reporter Blackman, determined to find a story, anywhere. Also on hand for this gentle send-up of bureaucracy are various local authorities and government officials — some in on the scam, others trying to uncover it. Procedure gives way to lunacy as a routine pick-up literally lands itself in the middle of the town for all to see. As a crafty sea captain who handles any situation with a wry retort and deadpan diplomacy, Livesey steals the show. ★★★ VHS: $29.99

The Green Man

(1991, 150 min, GB, Elijah Moshinsky) *Albert Finney, Sarah Berger, Michael Hordern.* Adapted from a Kingsley Amis novel, this elegantly sexy thriller/ghost story stars Finney as a charming but overweight, sex-obsessed, middle-aged boozer. Along with his hard-working and all-too-understanding wife, he operates a cottage hotel outside of London that is famous for its reported ghostly visitations. Having used this ghost lore as an entertaining promotional lure, Finney, in a drunken haze, one day hallucinates that he actually sees a real ghost. After talking with the spectre, and doing some biddings for him, our inebriated hero discovers the apparition's evil intentions. A thoroughly entertaining, sophisticated and ghoulish delight. ★★★½

The Green Mile

(1999, 189 min, US, Frank Darabont) *Tom Hanks, David Morse, Michael Clarke Duncan, Bonnie Hunt, James Cromwell, Michael Jeter, Sam Rockwell, Patricia Clarkson, Harry Dean Stanton.* With his first film since his 1994 masterpiece *The Shawshank Redemption,* director Darabont returns with yet another stirring Stephen King adaptation. A little too long for its own good, *The Green Mile* is the mystical and powerful story of a physically large but mentally slow prisoner (Oscar nominee Duncan) who is transferred to the death row cellblock of a Louisiana penitentiary (known as the Green Mile) and how he comes to affect not only the guards there but his fellow prisoners as well. Hanks leads a splendid cast as the head guard who comes to realize that his prisoner may be blessed with extraordinary powers. Director Darabont creates a terrific evocation of the times, and maintains such a lyrical pace it often feels poetic. ★★★½ VHS: $19.99; DVD: $24.99

The Green Pastures

(1936, 92 min, US, William Keighley & Marc Connelly) *Rex Ingram, Oscar Polk, Eddie Anderson.* First he created a Broadway hit from the writings of Roark Bradford, then Connelly took them to Hollywood in this imaginative fable on how heaven *ought* to be. Today, one less generous might see the performances as your typical "Negro" stereotype — if the film made any attempt at realism. But *Green Pastures* has the benevolence of a child dreaming in Sunday school in a warm summer's day. The play's text is actually rather subversive: The Lord God Jehovah finally gets to move from the Old Testament to the New when he learns the meaning of mercy from his most disappointing creation, Man. The film features wall-to-wall spirituals, scored by Erich Wolfgang Korngold and performed by The Hal Johnson Choir. ★★★

The Green Room

(1978, 95 min, France, François Truffaut) *François Truffaut, Nathalie Baye.* Truffaut stars as a journalist obsessed with his mortality and the deaths of his WWI comrades. An eerie, atmospheric departure for the director. Based on the writings of Henry James. (French with English subtitles) ★★½ VHS: $19.99

Tom Hanks (l.) and Michael Clarke Duncan in *The Green Mile*

G

Tim Roth (l.) and Tupac Shakur in *Gridlock'd*

The Green Slime

(1968, 89 min, US/Japan, Kinji Fukasaku) *Robert Horton, Richard Jaeckel, Luciana Paluzzi.* An oozing, bubbling, slithering green slime, terrorizing an outer space station, threatens to invade Earth and wipe out civilization. Oh, the horror! ★ VHS: $19.99

The Green Wall

(1969, 110 min, Peru, Armando Robles Godoy) *Julio Aleman, Sandra Riva.* A stirring autobiographical tale of an urban family who, in a back-to-nature move, leave the pressures of Lima to hack out a new life in the challenging environment of the Peruvian jungle — the green wall. The film records their successes and obstacles, both natural and man-made, as they become determined to survive in this idyllic but cruel, rich but unyielding world. A film of spellbinding power and beauty. (Spanish with English subtitles) ★★★ VHS: $79.99

Greetings

(1968, 88 min, US, Brian De Palma) *Robert De Niro, Gerrit Graham, Allen Garfield.* The talents of De Palma are wonderfully previewed in this early directorial effort. Clearly showing his film school background, De Palma structures this witty satire on the '60s counterculture in a series of vignettes. A very young De Niro stars as one of three friends living in New York City. The story follows their resourceful attempts to keep one of them from being drafted. Consistently funny and inventive, the film was cowritten by De Palma and Charles Hirsch, and was soon followed by *Hi, Mom!* ★★★ VHS: $79.99

Gregory's Girl

(1982, 99 min, GB, Bill Forsyth) *Gordon John Sinclair, Dee Hepburn.* Teetering on the brink of adulthood, a gangly Scottish schoolboy discovers the pleasures and perils of infatuation as he falls for a leggy lass on the soccer team. Forsyth's spirited comedy deftly conveys the invigorating effects of young love. ★★★

Gremlins

(1984, 106 min, US, Joe Dante) *Zach Galligan, Phoebe Cates, Hoyt Axton, Polly Holliday, Dick Miller.* Offbeat humor and garish horror successfully blend together in this box-office hit. Young Galligan gets a pet mogwai (*mog-why*) from his dad. The cute, cuddly animal (after the three rules have been ignored) spawns terrifying gremlins which proceed to destroy the town. Lots of in-jokes and neat special effects; and more importantly, the film demonstrates the many uses for a blender. (Sequel: *Gremlins 2: The New Batch*) ★★★ VHS: $14.99; DVD: $19.99

Gremlins 2: The New Batch

(1990, 106 min, US, Joe Dante) *Zach Galligan, Phoebe Cates, Christopher Lee, John Glover, Paul Bartel.* The original *Gremlins* was a well-made thriller filled with a scathing, dark sense of humor, but much of its horror was too intense for smaller children. In *Gremlins 2*, Dante may have found what he was looking for when he made the first film. This hilarious romp is filled with hysterical self-reference and reaches such heights of absurdity that even little ones know it's all in good fun. This time around, the little nasties are set loose on a New York office tower, The Clamp Centre (aptly modeled, owner and all, after the Trump Plaza). ★★★½ VHS: $14.99

The Grey Fox

(1982, 92 min, Canada, Philip Borsos) *Richard Farnsworth, Jackie Burroughs, Wayne Robson.* Very successful western/character study of convicted stagecoach robber Bill Miner (Farnsworth) who emerges from prison after 30 years to find that the world has left him behind. With robbery his only acknowledged trade, and horses and stagecoaches having been supplanted by steam engines and trains, what's a guy to do? Though the pacing may be a little slow for some tastes, Farnsworth's portrayal of "the gentleman bandit" is in itself worth the price of rental. Director Borsos ably mixes the inherent humor of the situation (imagine, an 80-year-old train robber) with the pathos of the character to create a film that is touching without being maudlin. ★★★½

Grey Gardens

(1976, 95 min, US, David & Albert Maysles) The lives of Edith Bouvier Beale and her adult daughter Edie are the subject of this moving documentary by the Maysles brothers. Secluded in their decaying Long Island mansion, these two eccentric women allow the morbid spectacle of their private melodrama to simply play itself out in front of the camera. Some have charged the directors with exploitation, although by revealing their subjects so unsparingly they go beyond voyeurism and challenge us to feel true compassion for these lonely human beings. ★★★

Grey Owl

(1999, 117 min, GB/Canada, Richard Attenborough) *Pierce Brosnan, Annie Galipeau, Nathaniel Arcand, Graham Greene.* A $30 million production that went straight to video, this picturesque period drama is actually better than its roots suggest. Based on a true-life incident, *Grey Owl* stars Brosnan as an Indian tracker living in the Canadian wilds whose environmental advocacy makes him a cause celebre in 1930s England. The author of magazine articles and then a best-selling book, Grey Owl goes on tour to promote the protection of the wilderness. But as his celebrity grows, his secret past soon comes to light. Attenborough directs with an epic sweep, getting the most out of the lush Canadian backdrop, but the relationship between Grey Owl and his young bride is heavy-handed where it should be tender. Fortunately, this doesn't take too much away from the story itself, which can be quite compelling. ★★★½ VHS: $14.99; DVD: $24.99

Greystoke: The Legend of Tarzan

(1984, 129 min, GB, Hugh Hudson) *Christopher Lambert, Ralph Richardson, Ian Holm, James Fox, Andie MacDowell.* Director Hudson followed his Academy Award–winning *Chariots of Fire* with this liberally adapted retelling of the Edgar Rice Burroughs Tarzan tale. Richardson is captivating in his swan song performance and Lambert became an international sex symbol through his portrayal of the Lord of the Jungle. A visual treat and the first Tarzan film to try to bring a sophistication to the tale. ★★★ VHS: $14.99

Gridlock'd

(1997, 90 min, US, Vondie Curtis-Hall) *Tim Roth, Tupac Shakur, Thandie Newton, Vondie Curtis-Hall, Charles Fleischer, Howard Hesseman, John Sayles.* A frustration comedy about two junkies who run into bureaucratic roadblocks while trying to get clean, *Gridlock'd* is an engrossing but not quite heady trip. Solid performances by Roth and Newton (as a sultry overdoser) prevent this potentially downbeat film from becoming a trite antidrug message movie. Yet it is the heartbreaking presence of the late rapper Shakur that really makes this gritty, dark urban tale valuable. The film's weakest element is the subplot about buddies Spoon (Shakur) and Stretch (Roth) being chased by D-Reper (director Curtis-Hall), a gangster they wronged. But at least this story line puts the rest of *Gridlock'd*'s accomplishments in bold relief. ★★★ VHS: $9.99; DVD: $19.99

Il Grido (The Outcry)

(1957, 115 min, Italy, Michelangelo Antonioni) *Steve Cochran, Alida Valli.* A compelling, slow moving, if not totally successful film about a man and his daughter who wander about aimlessly when their lives are placed in upheaval after the sudden departure of his fiancee. One of director Antonioni's earlier works is a moody look at psychological breakdowns and the lack of personal communication. (Italian with English subtitles) ★★½ VHS: $24.99; DVD: $29.99

Grief

(1993, 92 min, US, Richard Glatzer) *Craig Chester, Alexis Arquette, Jackie Beat, Carlton Wilborn, Paul Bartel, Mary Woronov, John Fleck.* Writer-director Glatzer has taken his personal experiences as a writer for TV's "Divorce Court" and fashioned an engaging and funny comedy-drama about friendship, love, bereavement and trash TV. Set during an eventful workweek, the film follows the misadventures of Mark (Chester), a writer for a daytime TV show, as he comes to grips with his co-workers, office politics, an office crush, homophobia and the loss of his lover. Beat (in a "Divine" bit of casting) plays the show's overbearing but maternal producer. Arquette also stars as a bisexual employee involved in a secret office romance. Highlighting the film are campy renditions of the TV soap opera, which includes everything from lesbian circus performers to schizophrenic divas. ★★★ VHS: $29.99

Grievous Bodily Harm

(1988, 96 min, Australia, Mark Joffe) *Colin Friels, Bruno Lawrence, John Waters.* Don't let the artwork on the video box fool you: this gritty, nicely acted and sexy thriller is very much *not* the grade-C exploitation film which the cover suggests. Friels plays a seedy Sydney newspaper reporter covering the murder of a porn star. Lawrence is the policeman investigating the case. And Waters (not the American director), in a first-rate performance, is the killer whose search for his presumedly dead wife leads the three men on an intersecting road to danger. ★★★

The Grifters

(1990, 110 min, GB, Stephen Frears) *Anjelica Huston, John Cusack, Annette Bening, J.T. Walsh, Pat Hingle.* Director Frears' foray into the degenerate world of novelist Jim Thompson is a compelling look at life on the fringe. The story centers around a three-way power struggle between Roy, a small-time grifter, and the two women in his life: his mother and his girlfriend. Cusack sinks his teeth into the role of Roy with intense complexity. Huston dazzles as Roy's mother, Lily, a ruthless swindler who works the odds at the track for the mob. Bening is Myra, Cusack's part-time-prostitute girlfriend, who tries to lure him into the big-stakes world of the "long con." Though theirs is a world filled with mistrust and betrayal, Frears' vision of their lives is tempered with occasional moral twists and underlying humanity. Superbly acted and directed, *The Grifters* is peppered with moments of shocking brutality as it careens toward its tragic conclusion. ★★★★ VHS: $9.99; DVD: $14.99

The Grim Reaper (La Commare Secca)

(1962, 89 min, Italy, Bernardo Bertolucci) *Tisa Farrow, George Eastman.* This rarely seen work, based on a five-page outline by Pier Paolo Pasolini, was 22-year-old Bertolucci's first film as a director. Set in Rome's seedy underworld, the story involves the investigation of the police into the brutal murder of a prostitute. As they go through the list of possible suspects, the police find a beguiling maze of alibis as well as widely different recountings of the events leading up to the woman's last day. An interesting debut and one that the director admits was made by "someone who had never shot one foot of 35mm before but who had seen lots and lots of films." (Italian with English subtitles) ★★★ VHS: $29.99; DVD: $19.99

Grind

(1996, 96 min, US, Chris Kentis) *Billy Crudup, Adrienne Shelly, Paul Shulze, Frank Vincent.* In this slight, minor diversion about "Everyday, working-class Joes," ex-con Eddie (Crudup) moves in with older brother Terry (Shulze) and his pretty wife Janey (Shelly). Eddie gets involved with in a car theft ring and pursuing his dream of drag-car racing, spending his afternoons with Janey. One of *Grind*'s better accomplishments is capturing the blue collar milieu, and there are some very effective moments. But the many intimate scenes — alternative to Hollywood gloss — don't necessarily guarantee exciting dramatics. There's a host of good performances, a decent score, and an overall nice feel to the film, but much of it is scenarios revisited from often better films. ★★½ VHS: $14.99; DVD: $24.99

Groove

(2000, 86 min, US, Greg Harrison) *Lola Glaudini, MacKenzie Firgens, Denny Kirkwood, Hamish Linklater, Vincent Riverside, Rachel True, Steve Van Wormer.* Mix together the following ingredients over a low flame: Two brothers, a great techno dance track, an easy-to-follow story line, and ecstasy for the whole cast. The final result is the engaging *Groove*. The story line loosely follows two brothers, one of whom is to announce his engagement at the rave that night, and the other is to try ecstasy for the first time. The story juggles various subplots about the partyers, nicely keeping track of an eclectic cast of characters, The soundtrack is a great assortment of techno and trance music that alone should attract lovers of the scene to this sweet movie. ★★★ VHS: $14.99; DVD: $24.99

The Groove Tube

(1974, 75 min, US, Ken Shapiro) *Chevy Chase, Richard Belzer.* Goofy and sometimes very funny spoof on television, with a wide variety of skits and episodes. Chase made his film debut. ★★½ VHS: $19.99

Gross Anatomy

(1989, 107 min, US, Thom Eberhardt) *Matthew Modine, Daphne Zuniga, Christine Lahti, Zakes Mokae.* The Paper Chase goes to medical school in this uneven but appealing comedy-drama. Modine is in fine form as the initially cocky doctor-in-training who eventually comes to learn about more than just medicine. Lahti does as well as possible in the cliché-ridden John Houseman role of tormentor/supporter. ★★½

Grosse Pointe Blank

(1997, 109 min, US, George Armitage) *John Cusack, Minnie Driver, Dan Aykroyd, Alan Arkin, Joan Cusack, Jeremy Piven, Hank Azaria, Barbara Harris.* Wearing a few hats (cowriter, coproducer), Cusack plays an angst-ridden assassin in this very funny dark comedy. He plays Martin Blank, a successful hit man who returns to his high school's tenth reunion. There he is reunited with Debi (the very engaging Driver), his former sweetheart who he stood up on prom night (never to be heard from again). Having federal agents and a rival hit man (Aykroyd) on his trail is nothing compared to the task at hand in making amends with Debi. And then there's the school dance! John has become the master of understatement, and he gives a ripe, humorous performance. Sister Joan has some funny scenes as a wily secretary, and Arkin is hilariously crusty as Martin's reluctant psychiatrist. ★★★½ VHS: $14.99

Ground Zero

(1987, 109 min, Australia, Michael Pattison) *Colin Friels, Jack Thompson, Donald Pleasence.* In this suspenseful political thriller, Friels stars as a cinematographer who unwittingly becomes involved in political intrigue when he searches for the truth about the death of his father, a noted WWII cameraman killed under mysterious circumstances. In the process, he uncovers a British secret service cover-up from decades before. A thoroughly satisfying mystery with ample portions of social commentary and suspense. ★★★

Groundhog Day

(1993, 103 min, US, Harold Ramis) *Bill Murray, Andie MacDowell, Chris Elliott, Stephen Tobolowsky.* On the heels of his whimsical turn in *What about Bob?*, Murray tops himself with this extremely funny and surprisingly sweet romantic comedy, with the glib comedian giving one of his most likable and funniest performances. It's Groundhog Day, and cynical TV weatherman Murray has been sent to Punxsutawney, Pa., to cover the festivities for his Pittsburgh station. But there's one small problem: he seems to be reliving the day over and over and over again. Writer-director Ramis and cowriter Danny Rubin have milked this inventive premise for all it's worth, and they've given some hilarious and irresistible moments to Murray and his merry band of cohorts. MacDowell costars as his producer, and she's a good foil for the ever-increasing insanity that surrounds her. ★★★ VHS: $12.99; DVD: $19.99

The Group

(1966, 150 min, US, Sidney Lumet) *Candice Bergen, Joan Hackett, Elizabeth Hartman, Shirley Knight, Jessica Walter, Hal Holbrook, Richard Mulligan, Larry Hagman.* Bergen, Hackett and Holbrook made their film debuts in Lumet's adaptation of Mary McCarthy's novel. Following the intertwining lives of eight graduates of an exclusive women's college, the story examines each character's development as they enter adult life. In much the same way as George Cukor's *The Women*, the film is revelatory in exposing its underlying assumptions regarding women's nature and women's place. While it may sometimes play like a soap opera, it's an interesting document of its time. ★★★ VHS: $19.99

Grown Ups

(1980, 95 min, GB, Mike Leigh) *Philip Davis, Leslie Manville, Lindsay Duncan, Sam Kelly.* Featuring intricate characterizations and plenty of incisive humor, Leigh's comedy-drama, though slowly paced (as are most of Leigh's earlier films), is a meticulous and startling examination of Thatcher's England. The story focuses on a young lower-middle-class couple who have just moved into their first home and are besieged by the wife's batty sister. Not helping matters is the fact that their next-door neighbor is their former high school teacher. Not a lot happens as far as plot is concerned, but Leigh's camera and sly wit make this of interest. ★★★ VHS: $29.99

G

Grumpier Old Men

(1995, 100 min, US, Howard Deutch) *Jack Lemmon, Walter Matthau, Ann-Margret, Sophia Loren, Burgess Meredith, Kevin Pollak, Daryl Hannah.* This sophomoric though often funny sequel to *Grumpy Old Men* should definitely tickle the funny bone of those who found enjoyment in the first film. The film introduces a new character to the small Minnesota town: the impossibly beautiful Loren. She has taken over the local bait shop and is preparing to turn it into an Italian restaurant. Thus begins a war of wills as dedicated fishermen Lemmon and Matthau turn to every dirty trick in the book to sabotage her opening; that is until Loren turns to her feminine wiles and turns Matthau into putty. Many of the jokes are of the sexual and flatulent variety, though in the hands of this very able cast you can't help but laugh out loud. ★★½ VHS: $9.99; DVD: $19.99

Grumpy Old Men

(1993, 105 min, US, Donald Petrie) *Jack Lemmon, Walter Matthau, Ann-Margret, Burgess Meredith, Ossie Davis, Daryl Hannah, Kevin Pollack.* Lemmon and Matthau reunite for the first time in 12 years and they've lost none of the chemistry which has made them one of the screen's great comedy teams. And if the script isn't exactly on par with most of their previous works, their bouyant performances make this a lively comedy. They play neighbors who have been feuding since childhood. Into their lives breezes eccentric artist Ann-Margret (looking lovely but none-too-bohemian) and the race is on to capture her affection. Though many of the film's lines are on the Bart Simpson scale ("Eat my shorts," etc.), the entire cast manages to sustain a playful cheerfulness despite what the title may suggest. (Sequel: *Grumpier Old Men*) ★★½ VHS: $9.99; DVD: $19.99

Guantanamera!

(1995, 104 min, Cuba, Tomás Gutiérrez Alea & Juan Carlos Tabio) *Carlos Cruz, Mirta Ibarra, Jorge Perugorría, Raúl Eguren.* This brilliant and hilarious skewering of the Latin passion for sex, death and bureaucracy follows a picaresque trail across Cuba and uncovers a fascinating and intimate portrait of the country along the way. Yoyita, a world-renowned, expatriate singer, returns to her home town of Guantanamo to accept an award in her honor and dies of a heart attack. Her niece, nephew and ex-flame (along with Yoyita's corpse, of course) set off on a zany, ambling journey across the entire island to bury her. Directors Alea and Tabio prove their skill at pushing the limits of acceptable critique of Castro's government and do so with considerable good will and humor. (Spanish with English subtitles) ★★★★ VHS: $29.99; DVD: $29.99

The Guardian

(1990, 93 min, US, William Friedkin) *Jenny Seagrove, Dwier Brown, Carey Lowell.* Seagrove is the nanny from hell, offering newborns to an evil oak in this, Friedkin's first horror tale since *The Exorcist*. The story is ridiculous, the chills are non-existent, and Friedkin's pacing is lethargic. (Letterboxed) ★ VHS: $14.99; DVD: $24.99

Guarding Tess

(1994, 98 min, US, Hugh Wilson) *Shirley MacLaine, Nicolas Cage, Austin Pendleton, Edward Albert, Richard Griffiths.* Masquerading as a gentle comedy about the tumultuous relationship between a former First Lady and one of her Secret Service agents, *Guarding Tess* quickly deteriorates into an implausible, yawn-provoking thriller without the thrills. MacLaine is right at home with her role as the widow of a former president. She gets particular joy in playfully tormenting agent Cage, a serious young man who can't wait for his time to be up. As they bicker and eventually come to understand each other, it becomes clear that someone is out to kill her. ★★ VHS: $9.99; DVD: $24.99

The Guardsman

(1931, 83 min, US, Sidney Franklin) *Alfred Lunt, Lynn Fontanne, Roland Young.* Stage legends Lunt and Fontanne make a rare screen appearance in this thoroughly entertaining version of Ferenc Molnar's classic comedy. Reprising their acclaimed stage roles, the Lunts play a husband and wife acting team. Certain she is unfaithful to him, Lunt impersonates a dashing soldier and woos his own wife. And to his horror, she acquiesces. Though stage and screen require different acting styles, the very theatrical Lunts adapt to film with great skill. Young is splendid in support as a critic who watches this comedy of errors. (Remade as *The Chocolate Soldier* and *Lily in Love*) ★★★★ VHS: $19.99

Guess Who's Coming to Dinner

(1967, 108 min, US, Stanley Kramer) *Katharine Hepburn, Spencer Tracy, Sidney Poitier, Katharine Houghton, Beah Richards, Cecil Kellaway.* Hepburn and Tracy appeared together for the last time in this acclaimed social comedy whose theme of interracial marriage may seem tame by today's standards but in 1967 created quite a stir. Poitier is wed to Tracy and Hepburn's daughter Houghton, causing varying reactions from both their families. Hepburn won an Oscar for Best Actress, and this was Tracy's final film. Houghton, incidentally, is Hepburn's real-life niece. ★★★ VHS: $19.99; DVD: $14.99

Guilty as Charged

(1991, 95 min, US, Sam Irvin) *Rod Steiger, Lyman Ward, Isaac Hayes, Lauren Hutton, Heather Graham.* In this black comedy, spoofy thriller and cult film candidate, Steiger — with a nod to Mr. Joyboy from *The Loved One* — chews the scenery as the owner of a meat packing company who moonlights as a vigilante judge and executioner. Kidnapping paroled or escaped convicted murderers, Steiger imprisons and then zaps the convicts in a homemade electric chair. ★★½ VHS: $19.99

Guilty as Sin

(1993, 107 min, US, Sidney Lumet) *Rebecca DeMornay, Don Johnson, Stephen Lang, Jack Warden, Dana Ivey.* An uneven but trashily entertaining nail-biter. DeMornay is well-cast as a career-and-ego-driven defense attorney who bites off more than she can chew when she takes on the case of a sleek lothario (Johnson) accused of killing his wife. To say more would be to give too much away as this murder mystery snakes along with many more twists than DeMornay's pistol-driven swagger. Though steamy when it wants to be, *Guilty as Sin* is a little too slick and a little too obvious. ★★

Guilty by Suspicion

(1991, 105 min, US, Irwin Winkler) *Robert De Niro, Annette Bening, George Wendt, Martin Scorsese, Ben Piazza, Sam Wanamaker.* The Hollywood blacklist of the 1950s, though mostly ignored over the years until the 1970s — which produced *The Way We Were* and *The Front* — is the subject of this compassionate drama. De Niro is compelling as a successful film director whose personal and professional lives fall apart when he refuses to cooperate with the House Committee on Un-American Activities. Writer-director Winkler's film is full of remarkable detail, presenting its unsettling, effective story with finesse and subtlety. Bening is very good as De Niro's wife. ★★★ VHS: $14.99; DVD: $14.99

Guinevere

(1999, 105 min, US, Audrey Wells) *Stephen Rea, Sarah Polley, Jean Smart, Gina Gershon, Paul Dooley, Sandra Oh, Jasmine Guy.* There are moments of brilliance in *Guinevere*, writer-director Wells' thoughtful take on the uneasy relationship between a young girl and a much older man, but once the film makes its points, it has nowhere to go. Harper (Polley) is an insecure teen on the cusp of adulthood receiving life lessons from an aging photographer (Rea) who seduces her. While this sounds very salacious, Wells handles their relationship with extreme care and sensitivity. *Guinevere* contains a few real epiphanies, but there are an equal number of frustrating scenes, mostly involving his past lovers. The two leads are well cast, and in support, Smart is superb as Harper's disapproving mother. ★★½ VHS: $19.99; DVD: $29.99

Gulliver's Travels

(1996, 175 min, GB, Charles Sturridge) *Ted Danson, Mary Steenburgen, James Fox, Omar Sharif.* Like Lewis Carroll's "Alice" books, Jonathan Swift's 1726 classic defies translation into other media. The targets for his vitriol are now lost to the ages, and this biting attack against a bulging bourgeoisie has been carved down to a harmless little fairy tale. Who, then, would have imagined a made-for-TV production would be the most faithful and entertaining adaptation yet? And whoever OK'd Danson for the role of the good ship's doctor is either a man of vision or a fool for Q ratings. But Danson does give a very good performance in a very difficult role, wisely choosing not to attempt an English accent. Of course, the *real* stars are the special effects, here supplied by Jim Henson's always reliable people. While some of Swift's rapier raillery gets dulled down a bit, this bygone burlesque still manages to deliver a potent message. ★★★½ VHS: $9.99; DVD: $14.99

Gummo

(1997, 95 min, US, Harmony Korine) *Linda Manz, Max Perlich, Jacob Reynolds, Chloë Sevigny.* Like one of those desolate Calvin Klein ads for Obsession or CKOne, this extended exercise in vapidity from the writer of *Kids* traipses around the central Ohio town of Xenia, which has never recovered from the tornado that hit it several years prior. As seen from the point of view of a handful of the town's unsupervised adolescents, we are given over to extended, cloying (chicken-hawkish even) shots of these young wastrels as they go about their daily activities. All this is not to say that Korine — who has dubbed himself the Werner Herzog of the MTV generation —

is completely without talent. In fact, his film stylistically resembles early Herzog efforts. But that's actually part of the problem, this stuff isn't original. And, sure, it's rebellious, but it has no substance. ★ VHS: $19.99; DVD: $24.99

Gumshoe

(1972, 88 min, GB, Stephen Frears) *Albert Finney, Billie Whitelaw, Frank Finlay.* A capricious comedy about a small-time vaudevillian who's seen too many Bogart films and decides to try some sleuthing of his own. An intriguing little crime story. ★★★ VHS: $69.99

Gun Crazy

(1949, 87 min, US, Joseph H. Lewis) *John Dall, Peggy Cummins, Morris Carnovsky, Russ Tamblyn.* After a lifetime being obsessed with guns, a young man (Dall) meets the love of his life in the form of a sexy, gun-toting carnival performer. The tough-talking dame (Cummins), a dangerous femme fatale in the most literal sense, craves the good things in life and coaxes the man into a violent series of armed robberies and eventually murder. An entertaining cult favorite, seemingly years ahead of its time, that is stylishly filmed and offers an unflinching peek, in the *Bonnie and Clyde* tradition, at ill-fated fugitives on the lam. (Remade in 1992) ★★★½ VHS: $19.99

Gun Crazy

(1992, 97 min, US, Tamra Davis) *Drew Barrymore, James LeGros, Ione Skye, Billy Drago, Michael Ironside, Joe Dallesandro.* Like a magnum in a velvet glove, Barrymore blows away this touching love-and-bullets drama which proves that sometimes a cigar really is more than just a cigar, but a gun is just a gun. Barrymore slips comfortably into the role of a trailer park girl with a heart of lead who discovers the joys of gun play when she murders her touchy-feely stepfather (Dallesandro) and falls in love with the world's only male virgin (LeGros). This made-for-cable remake owes less to the 1949 classic than it does to *Badlands* or *Bonnie and Clyde*, but it is destined to stand in its own right as an exceptional entry into the "love-on-the-run" genre. ★★★½ DVD: $24.99

The Gun in Betty Lou's Handbag

(1992, 89 min, US, Allan Moyle) *Penelope Ann Miller, Eric Thal, William Forsythe, Alfre Woodard, Cathy Moriarity, Julianne Moore.* Disney's take on female empowerment and self-worth is very much a lightweight comedy. Miller stars as the title character, a small-town underdog who makes a desperate bid for attention by confessing to a crime she didn't commit. Then things get really out of hand when crime boss Forsythe comes looking for her. ★★ VHS: $19.99

Gunfight at the O.K. Corral

(1957, 122 min, US, John Sturges) *Burt Lancaster, Kirk Douglas, Rhonda Fleming, Jo Van Fleet, Earl Holliman, Deforest Kelly.* Expert telling of the infamous gunfight between Doc Holliday-Wyatt Earp and the Clanton gang. A good companion piece covering the same story is John Ford's classic *My Darling Clementine*. ★★★½ VHS: $9.99; DVD: $29.99

The Gunfighter

(1950, 84 min, US, Henry King) *Gregory Peck, Karl Malden, Helen Westcott, Millard Mitchell, Ellen Corby.* A splendid western tale with Peck in fine form as a former gunfighter unable to rid himself of his past. The look and feel of the film is remarkably authentic, and Peck is ably supported by a good cast. ★★★½ VHS: $14.99

Gung Ho

(1986, 111 min, US, Ron Howard) *Michael Keaton, Gedde Watanabe, George Wendt, Mimi Rogers, John Turturro.* Pleasant comedy examining the cultural clash between Japanese and American workers. Keaton is certainly in his element as a Pennsylvania auto employee who convinces a Japanese interest to reopen his town's closed plant. Made a few years before the numerous headline-making Japanese takeovers. Watanabe steals the show as a harried Japanese exec. ★★½ VHS: $14.99

Gunga Din

(1939, 117 min, US, George Stevens) *Cary Grant, Victor McLaglen, Douglas Fairbanks, Jr., Joan Fontaine, Sam Jaffe.* Three rowdy, hard-fisted British soldiers enjoy adventures in 19th-century India battling the Thugees and dropping wisecracks all the way. Grant, McLaglen and Fairbanks are wonderful foils for each other in this rousing adventure film: the one which all others are judged by. Also with the splendid Jaffe as the most famous water carrier in literature. Based on Rudyard Kipling's poem. ★★★★

Gunmen

(1993, 97 min, US, Deran Sarafian) *Christopher Lambert, Mario Van Peebles, Denis Leary, Patrick Stewart, Kadeem Hardison, Sally Kirkland.* A slightly above average adventure which excels in borrowing story lines from many other action films. A renegade DEA agent (Van Peebles) searching for $400 million belonging to a South American drug lord (Stewart) enlists the help of down-and-out Lambert, taking the pair on a wild chase with chain-smoking, wise-cracking Leary as their hunter. In spite of the fast pacing and over-the-top performances, the film is curiously aloof considering its theme and genre. ★★½ VHS: $9.99

The Gunrunner

(1984, 92 min, Canada, Nardo Castillo) *Kevin Costner, Sara Botsford.* A then-unknown Costner stars as an idealist, circa 1926, who tries to finance guns for the Chinese Nationalist Revolution by selling bootleg liquor in Montreal. A very minor gangster saga. ★ VHS: $14.99

The Guns of Navarone

(1961, 157 min, US, J. Lee Thompson) *Gregory Peck, David Niven, Anthony Quinn, Irene Papas, Richard Harris, Anthony Quayle, James Darren.* The special effects won an Oscar, and everything else about this fast-moving, involving and action-packed WWII adventure is up to the same standard. Peck, Niven and Quinn head a strong international cast as the Allies go after a strategic Nazi placement of big guns. Based on the novel by Alistair MacLean. (Sequel: *Force Ten from Navarone*) ★★★½ VHS: $14.99; DVD: $24.99

A Guy Named Joe

(1943, 120 min, US, Victor Fleming) *Spencer Tracy, Van Johnson, Irene Dunne, James Gleason, Lionel Barrymore.* Steven Spielberg liked this film so much he remade it in 1989 as *Always*. And it's hard to blame him. After being killed in action during WWII, pilot Tracy is sent back to Earth to look after young Johnson, who has become involved with Tracy's ex-girl Dunne. Okay, so the idea may sound silly, but who's to say it's not true. Pure romantic fluff, this 1940s morale booster may be sticky around the edges, but it certainly has heart. ★★½ VHS: $19.99

Guys and Dolls

(1955, 150 min, US, Joseph L. Mankiewicz) *Marlon Brando, Frank Sinatra, Jean Simmons, Vivian Blaine, Stubby Kaye.* The Broadway musical based on Damon Runyon's colorful characters and featuring the music of Frank Loesser comes to the screen in this lavish and entertaining film. The story centers on gambler and rogue Sky Masterson's (Brando) budding affair with an innocent Salvation Army volunteer (Simmons). A razor-thin Sinatra also stars as a fellow gambler who has to find a site for their crap game. Blaine is unforgettable as Sinatra's squeaky-voiced girlfriend who stops the show with her rendition of "Adelaide's Lament." Brando in a singing role, the mesmerizing Runyon dialogue and great music combine to create an unusual, fun musical. ★★★ VHS: $14.99; DVD: $19.99

Gypsy

(1962, 149 min, US, Mervyn LeRoy) *Rosalind Russell, Natalie Wood, Karl Malden, Ann Jillian.* Based on the Broadway landmark — itself based on the memoirs of stripper Gypsy Rose Lee — this stagey but entertaining musical stars Russell in the famed Ethel Merman role. Russell plays Rose, the driving force behind and mother of two child stars of the 1920s, one of whom becomes burlesque's reigning queen. Wood is the young Gypsy. Classic Stephen Sondheim–Jules Styne score includes "Everything's Coming Up Roses" and "Let Me Entertain You." (VHS available letterboxed or pan & scan) (Remade in 1993) ★★★ VHS: $14.99; DVD: $19.99

Gypsy

(1993, 140 min, US, Emile Ardolino) *Bette Midler, Peter Riegert, Cynthia Gibb, Ed Asner.* A faithful and exhilarating made-for-TV adaptation of the Broadway classic. Taking over one of the most demanding and rewarding roles in musical theatre, that of the hard-driven stage mother Rose, Midler delivers a tour de force performance. It is to her credit that with the ghosts of Ethel Merman, Rosalind Russell, Angela Lansbury and Tyne Daly circling overhead (all had previously played Rose), she is able to give a fresh interpretation of a time-honored role which more than one actress had stamped her name upon. Though this small-screen version may somewhat lack the energy and excitement of a live performance, there's little doubt that the story of Mama Rose and her daughter, actress/stripper Gypsy Rose Lee, is one of the greatest of all American musicals. ★★★½ VHS: $9.99

The Gypsy

(1975, 90 min, France, Jose Giovanni) *Alain Delon, Annie Girardot.* The eternally sexy Delon plays a gypsy Robin Hood, a dashing thief who would steal anything for his beleaguered people. His criminal exploits and his valiant attempts to stay one step ahead of the police help make this an exciting and entertaining adventure film. ★★★

G

Hackers

(1995, 105 min, US, Iain Softley) *Jonny Lee Miller, Angelina Jolie, Fisher Stevens, Jesse Bradford, Matthew Lillard, Lorraine Bracco.* Much like director Softley's terrific *Backbeat*, his cyber thriller *Hackers* has a stimulating visual style to it, but it is there all comparisons end. Neither plausible nor exciting, the film stars the sullen Miller as a gifted high school hacker who moves to New York and quickly falls in with fellow and trendy computer nerds. When one of their own accidentally hacks some private and incriminating files, a corporate bad guy (Stevens) and his goons set out to retrieve the disc and frame the kids. In spite of the film's sometimes impressive visuals, *Hackers* allows its clichéd teen characters' misfit hijinks to substitute for character development — and ultimately these kids are more hackneyed than hackers. ★★ VHS: $9.99; DVD: $14.99

Hail, Hero!

(1969, 97 min, US, David Miller) *Michael Douglas, Arthur Kennedy, Teresa Wright.* Douglas makes his film debut in this tense though plodding drama about an anti-war protester who enlists during the Vietnam War. ★★ VHS: $59.99

Hail Mary (Je Vous Salue Marie)

(1985, 90 min, France, Jean-Luc Godard) *Myriem Roussel, Thierry Rode, Juliette Binoche.* This controversal film is truly not as blasphemous or shocking as it has been made out to be. Rather, *Hail Mary* is a reverent modern retelling of the Incarnation and Virgin Birth of Christ. The setting is 1980s France where Mary works at her father's gas station. Her selection to be the Mother of Christ, and how she deals with this, provides the central theme to this religious work. (French with English subtitles) ★★★

Hail the Conquering Hero

(1944, 101 min, US, Preston Sturges) *Eddie Bracken, William Demarest, Ella Raines, Franklin Pangborn.* Sturges' miraculous satire stars Bracken as the conquering hero of the title, a medically discharged Marine whose small hometown thinks him a war hero. Sturges lets loose a comic assault on politics, mother love and popular opinion as Bracken's Woodrow Truesmith gallantly tries to set the record straight, but is sabotaged at every turn. Bracken (as in Sturges' *Miracle of Morgan's Creek*) is priceless, and Demarest shines as a "real" war hero trying to make Bracken look the part in his mother and sweetheart's eyes. ★★★★ VHS: $14.99

Hair

(1979, 121 min, US, Milos Forman) *Treat Williams, John Savage, Beverly D'Angelo, Annie Golden, Michael Jeter.* Forman's exuberant adaptation of the '60s landmark play shines with a wealth of cinematic finesse, heightened by Twyla Tharp's visceral choreography and the inspired performances of Williams, D'Angelo and Savage. They said it was unfilmable, and Forman proved them wrong. ★★★★ VHS: $14.99; DVD: $19.99

Hairspray

(1988, 94 min, US, John Waters) *Divine, Ricki Lake, Sonny Bono, Pia Zadora, Debbie Harry, Rick Ocasek.* Waters, the Prince of Puke and sleazemaster extraordinaire, put aside his odious ways to make this glorious sendup of the "teen scene" movies of the late '50s and early '60s. Set in Baltimore (where else?), the story follows Tracy Turnblad (Lake), a heavyset teen whose main ambition in life is to be on a local TV dance program. But she is soon faced with a moral dilemma when the producers ban her black friends from attending. Waters proves up to the task of exploring the racial issue, but wisely keeps the lid on all-out polemic and heavy-handedness by sticking with his strength — namely outrageous comedy. ★★★ VHS: $14.99

Half a Loaf of Kung Fu

(1985, 96 min, Hong Kong, Chen Chi-Hwa) *Jackie Chan.* The incomparable Chan stars as a buffoonish drifter looking for work, wisdom

and the ultimate kung fu master in Imperial China. From the opening credits, you'll know that this self-parodying kung fu epic approaches its subject with tongue planted firmly in cheek. ★★★ VHS: $39.99

Half-Baked

(1998, 73 min, US, Tamra Davis) *Dave Chappelle, Jim Breuer, Harland Williams, Guillermo Diaz, Rachel True, Clarence Williams III; cameos from: Janeane Garofalo, Snoop Doggy Dogg, Willie Nelson, Stephen Baldwin, Bob Saget, Jon Stewart, Tommy Chong.* Dude, this sucks. *Half-Baked* stars Chappelle as the leader of a quartet of stoners with loser jobs. When one is jailed for the murder of a cop (he fed a diabetic police horse pounds of junk food), the rest start raising his bail by selling grade-A ganja pilfered from the hospital where Chappelle works as a custodian. But the plot doesn't really matter; the point here is to string together a few movie parodies, superfluous cameos, and, of course, lots of pothead jokes, most of which Cheech and Chong would have thought dumb. ★★ VHS: $14.99; DVD: $24.99

Half Moon Street

(1986, 90 min, GB, Bob Swaim) *Sigourney Weaver, Michael Caine, Keith Buckley.* Muddled adaptation of Paul Theroux's novel "Dr. Slaughter," with Weaver in the role of a financially depressed American Ph.D. in London who tries to make ends meet by becoming an "escort" for politically influential clientele — in this case, the ubiquitous Caine as a high-powered British diplomat. Anyone who's ever fantasized about the statuesque Ms. Weaver will find this a guilty pleasure at best, as nudity seems to have been written into her contract. ★

Half of Heaven

(1987, 127 min, Spain, Gutierrez Aragon) *Angela Molina, Margarita Lozano.* This charming story of a young woman's growth, loves and successes reads like a modern-day fairy tale with characters including two mean and ugly sisters and a grandmother imbued with special powers. Set in 1960s Franco Spain, our story follows Rosa (Molina), an ambitious and self-reliant young widow who, with her daughter, leaves her family and the peasant lifestyle to find opportunities in the city. A wonderful story of one woman determined to make it on her own. While lulling you with the film's light and entertaining style, the director throws in biting commentary on Franco Spain, imbued with a fine Buñuelian sense of humor. (Spanish with English subtitles) ★★★

Hallelujah!

(1929, 90 min, US, King Vidor) *Daniel L. Haynes, Nina Mae McKinney, William Fontaine.* Though not the first film to feature an all-black cast, this simple morality tale is probably the best of its type and time, an era which saw African-American performers only fit for portraying maids and scared manservants. One must look beyond the patronizing and stereotypes, for at work here is quite an accessible story of an honest man caught in the clutches of evil and of his redemption. Haynes plays a trusting cotton-pickin' farmer who is led down the path of temptation by vixen McKinney. When tragedy strikes, Haynes turns to God, only to be once again led astray. Director Vidor has crafted a gripping work, and there are spellbinding scenes which equal or surpass any

Hail the Conquering Hero

Hamlet (Kenneth Branagh)

film of the day, including one of a crowd being worked into a religious frenzy. ★★★½

Halloween

(1978, 90 min, US, John Carpenter) *Jamie Lee Curtis, Donald Pleasence, Nancy Loomis, P.J. Soles.* Carpenter's celebrated horror film is credited with starting the "slasher" genre, which has given way to Freddy, Jason and the likes. There's more than just blood and guts here, though, in this suspenseful tale of little Michael Meyers returning to his small home town to pick off Curtis and friends. Pleasence is the alarmed doctor trying to warn anyone who will listen. (Followed by six sequels) (Letterboxed) ★★★ VHS: $14.99; DVD: $29.99

Halloween: H2O
(Twenty Years Later)

(1998, 85 min, US, Steve Miner) *Jamie Lee Curtis, Adam Arkin, Josh Hartnett, Michelle Williams, LL Cool J, Janet Leigh, Joseph Gordon Levitt.* What in the world, you might ask, would bring Curtis, the former Scream Queen of the Horror Flicks, back to the genre which she'd probably like to forget. Evidently, the answer lies in the very things which make *Halloween: H20* such an enjoyable horror outing: a credible script, an overall sense of fun, and lots of scares. Curtis returns as Laurie Strode, who back when Carter was president seemed to be having some sibling problems with brother Michael Myers. It's now 20 years later, and Laurie is still haunted by the memories of her murderous bro, who has decided to initiate a family reunion. Director Miner forgoes the splatter sensationalism and concentrates on scares and suspense. And what's more, characters aren't illogical horror drones. But the best thing is Curtis, who shows she can kick ass with the best of them. ★★★ VHS: $19.99; DVD: $39.99

Hamlet

(1948, 153 min, GB, Laurence Olivier) *Laurence Olivier, Eileen Herlie, Basil Sydney, Jean Simmons, Stanley Holloway, Peter Cushing.* Olivier directed and stars in this superlative adaptation of Shakespeare's tragedy. Olivier embodies the melancholy Hamlet, as much a victim of his lack of decisiveness as of his circumstances. The supporting players match him in their assumptions of their roles. Oscar for Best Picture; Olivier won as Best Actor. ★★★★ VHS: $14.99; DVD: $29.99

Hamlet

(1969, 114 min, GB, Tony Richardson) *Nicol Williamson, Anthony Hopkins, Marianne Faithfull, Gordon Jackson, Anjelica Huston.* Richardson's lit-

tle seen, imaginative interpretation was filmed at the Round House, London's equivalent of off-Broadway. Done in period dress, this *Hamlet* has a contemporary feel to it accented by dark, claustrophobic staging with little movement of the actors and a concentration on the intense faces of the leads, which include Hopkins and Faithfull as Ophelia. Williamson's performance of a confused Hamlet, full of neurotic twitches and personal uncertainties, is riveting. ★★½ VHS: $19.99

Hamlet

(1976, 67 min, GB, Celestino Coronado) *Quentin Crisp, Lindsay Kemp, Anthony Meyer, David Meyer, Helen Mirren.* Feverish, dreamlike and campy to a '70s fault, this outlandish interpretation of William Shakespeare's "Hamlet" is a low-budget druggy, flesh-filled drama staged by the Lindsay Kemp Company. Twin brothers play the oft-naked, much tortured lead, Mirren is both Gertrude and Ophelia, and a much made-up Crisp is Polonius. This Fellini-esque adaptation, condensed and altered a bit, takes place in front of a gauze background and is mostly suited to fans of the avant-garde. All caution is thrown to the wind as director Coronado fills the screen with erotic dances, futuristic costuming transvestites and two Hamlets running around clothed only in jockstraps. This isn't your mother's Shakespeare! ★★★ VHS: $19.99

Hamlet

(1990, 135 min, GB, Franco Zeffirelli) *Mel Gibson, Glenn Close, Alan Bates, Helena Bonham Carter, Paul Scofield, Ian Holm, Pete Postlethwaite.* In a sumptuous retelling of the classic tragedy, Gibson gives a fiery, credible and even inspired interpretation of Shakespeare's Melancholy Dane. And he is given remarkable support. Close is superlative as Hamlet's mother, Gertrude, who unknowingly marries her husband's murderer. Bates makes an arresting Claudius, Bonham Carter is a fragile Ophelia, and Holm is a most amusing Polonius. Director Zeffirelli brings great energy to the work, and his stagings are carefully conceived and executed. ★★★½ VHS: $9.99

Hamlet

(1996, 243 min, GB, Kenneth Branagh) *Kenneth Branagh, Julie Christie, Derek Jacobi, Richard Briers, Kate Winslet, Charlton Heston, Michael Maloney, Jack Lemmon, Billy Crystal, Robin Williams.* Attempting

to film the entire four-hour verse of Shakespeare's masterpiece, the first time the entire play has been adapted for the screen, director-star Branagh has created one of the most thrilling and accessible adaptations of *Hamlet* to date. It's fairly extravagant in detail but significantly intimate in emotion. Branagh is revelatory as the mad Prince of Denmark, and his performance never wavers in intensity or focus. The supporting cast for the most part is exemplary. Jacobi scintillates as the calculating Claudius, and Briers' exhilaratingly new interpretation of Polonius is more politician than fool. ★★★★ VHS: $24.99

Hamlet

(2000, 123 min, US, Michael Almereyda) *Ethan Hawke, Kyle MacLachlan, Sam Shepard, Liev Schreiber, Bill Murray, Julia Stiles.* Director Almereyda offers an imaginative and playful interpretation as he sets Shakespeare's classic amidst the skyscrapers of 21st-century Manhattan. But while he hits the mark, several of his cast are proving iambically challenged. In the title role, Hawke provides an interesting nihilistic hipness, but it doesn't quite play in the soliloquies. Murray trips all over himself as Polonious, but Schreiber and MacLachlan are dutiful as Laertes and Claudius respectively. Overall, it's an exciting revision of the tale, but for the definitive character interpretation, stick with Branagh's. ★★½ VHS: $102.99; DVD: $32.99

Hammers over the Anvil

(1992, 101 min, Australia, Ann Turner) *Russell Crowe, Charlotte Rampling, Alexander Outhred.* An occasionally sappy tale of a horse breaker who gets involved with an older married woman. Caught in the middle is a polio stricken boy named Alan whose dreams of riding are overshadowed by his idolizing of East Driscoll (Crowe). In addition, Alan's obvious attraction to the older Grace further complicates his quest for contentment in a life that he already finds to be quite frustrating. A rather impressive performance by Crowe in a very early role makes this film worth seeing, not to mention the opportunity to see him riding a horse naked. ★★½ VHS: $19.99; DVD: $24.99

Hammett

(1983, 97 min, US, Wim Wenders) *Frederic Forrest, Peter Boyle, Marilu Henner, Sylvia Sidney, Samuel Fuller.* After interminable delays in production, editing and distribution, Wenders' first

Hamlet (Ethan Hawke)

American feature is a surprisingly intriguing, hard-boiled yarn stemming from the fictional exploits of pulp novelist extraordinaire Dashiell Hammett (Forrest). As with the best gumshoe tales, the plot is a foggy series of double-crossings and blackmail schemes. The film boasts an impressive gallery of supporting players and stylish, shadowy sets. ★★★

The Hand

(1981, 104 min, US, Oliver Stone) *Michael Caine, Andrea Marcovicci, Viveca Lindfors.* When cartoonist Caine's hand is severed in a car accident, it follows him around and kills his enemies — or does it? Stone keeps his trademark stylistic flourishes well concealed in this early directorial outing. ★ VHS: $14.99

The Hand That Rocks the Cradle

(1992, 110 min, US, Curtis Hanson) *Rebecca DeMornay, Annabella Sciorra, Matt McCoy, Ernie Hudson, Julianne Moore.* A parents' nightmare makes for an enjoyably trashy if contrived thriller. Having created a sense of dread in *Bad Influence*, director Hanson resorts to all the tricks to give a potent scare or two. Sciorra and McCoy are almost the perfect new-age couple. They're madly in love, have a perfect home, perfect children, gee, the perfect life. Into their home comes what they think to be the perfect nanny, DeMornay. But she blames Sciorra for her husband's death and now has a score to settle. DeMornay is actually quite good as a demented Mary Poppins, and her effective performance is at the heart of *Cradle*'s modest success. ★★½ VHS: $9.99; DVD: $29.99

A Handful of Dust

(1988, 118 min, GB, Charles Sturridge) *James Wilby, Kristin Scott Thomas, Rupert Graves, Alec Guinness, Judi Dench, Anjelica Huston.* A delight for all fans of "Masterpiece Theatre," the books of Evelyn Waugh and of films which opulently depict the trials, tribulations and eventual decay of England's landed gentry in the early part of this century. Wilby stars as a naïvely contented land owner who unwittingly loses both his loves and his serenity when he allows his restless wife a "weekend" flat in London. The fun loving woman (Scott Thomas) soon falls for a penniless charmer in her frantic search for freedom and passion. Not as witty as Waugh's "Black Mischief" or "Decline and Fall," the story is nonetheless classy entertainment highlighted by a stellar cast. ★★★ VHS: $19.99

The Handmaid's Tale

(1990, 109 min, US, Volker Schlöndorff) *Natasha Richardson, Robert Duvall, Faye Dunaway, Elizabeth McGovern, Aidan Quinn.* Imagine a world so closely conformed to Phyllis Schlafly's dictates that even *she* couldn't get out of the house. In the near future, excessive environmental pollution has sterilized a majority of the population. The ruling reactionary theocracy therefore sends fertile females to the households of the ruling elite, where they are expected to copulate and procreate for the greater glory of God and state. Schlöndorff directs Harold Pinter's adaptation of Margaret Atwood's novel, fully utilizing the consummate talents of a gifted cast. ★★★ VHS: $14.99

The Hands of Orlac

(1960, 95 min, GB/France, Edmond T. Greville) *Mel Ferrer, Christopher Lee, Donald Pleasence.* When crippled pianist Ferrer gets new hands transplanted from an executed murderer, he picks up some bad habits with them. Unimaginative and rather boring. (aka: *Hands of a Strangler*) ★ VHS: $12.99

Hands on a Hardbody

(1998, 97 min, US, S.R. Bindler) Longview, Texas, is the setting for possibly the most bizarre car promotion in history: Every year, customers compete to see who can lay their hands on a truck for the longest period of time. Last person left touching the truck wins it. Not only does this contest draw an eclectic group of characters, but it pushes them to the brink of madness as sleep deprivation and exhaustion set in (4 or 5 days usually produces a winner). As much a study in the limits of human endurance as materialism, *Hands on a Hardbody* is hilarious without being exploitative, as the participants fall into fits of delirium-induced laughter. ★★★½ VHS: $39.99

Hang 'Em High

(1968, 114 min, US, Ted Post) *Clint Eastwood, Dennis Hopper, Ben Johnson, Alan Hale, Jr.* When his lynching doesn't take, Eastwood wants satisfaction from the guys who did such a lousy job. This American take on Leone's spaghetti westerns lacks that director's stylish flourishes, but this still manages to entertain. ★★½ VHS: $9.99; DVD: $14.99

Hangin' with the Homeboys

(1991, 89 min, US, Joseph Vasquez) *Doug E. Doug, John Leguizamo, Mario Joyner.* Four homeboys' search for a good time on a Friday night takes them from the South Bronx to Manhattan. It's a simple premise, but Vasquez uses it to good effect in chronicling the world view of disaffected black and Hispanic youths. Produced on a shoestring budget, the film suffers slightly from an unfocused script and some inconsistent performances (with the exception of Leguizamo — who offers some of the more poignant moments), but it still manages to entertain in spite of its shortcomings. ★★★ VHS: $14.99

The Hanging Garden

(1998, 91 min, Canada, Thom Fitzgerald) *Chris Leavins, Kerry Fox, Seanna McKenna, Peter MacNeill, Sarah Polley.* This impressively mature first feature from writer-director Fitzgerald examines the emotional tribulations of a family on the brink of destruction. The story is set in a Nova Scotia home where the extended family is reunited for a wedding. William, a young man who left the family as an obese, unhappy and closeted teenager, now returns for his sister's wedding after a 10-year absence. He returns thin, attractive and openly gay and with a great deal of pent-up rage towards his family. Told with biting humor, symbolism and moments of surrealism (William's memories of his schoolboy love, who is marrying his sister, begin to stir long buried memories). Reminiscent of *Sweetie*, the film adroitly balances the ranging emotions of its characters; the result being an involving, unsettling but moving story. ★★★ VHS: $14.99

The Hanging Tree

(1959, 108 min, US, Delmer Daves) *Gary Cooper, Karl Malden, Maria Schell, George C. Scott, Ben Piazza.* Cooper brings a quiet strength to this involving western which casts the legendary star as a mysterious stranger who takes residence at an 1870s Montana gold mining town. Cooper plays a doctor with an uncertain past. Among those who cross his path are blinded immigrant Schell, seedy prospector Malden, and in his film debut, Scott as a malicious preacher. ★★★

Hanging Up

(2000, 95 min, US, Diane Keaton) *Meg Ryan, Diane Keaton, Lisa Kudrow, Walter Matthau.* Ryan's appeal is almost enough to make this a tolerable experience, a forced comedy-drama that awkwardly shifts between heavy-handed dramatics and sappy humor. It's the story of three sisters (Ryan, Keaton, Kudrow) who are forced to come to terms with the aging of their father (Matthau). Director Keaton has assembled a solid cast, but they're given to hysterics and only an occasion register any true emotion. ★★ VHS: $14.99; DVD: $24.99

Hanna K.

(1983, 108 min, France, Constantin Costa-Gavras) *Jill Clayburgh, Jean Yanne, Gabriel Byrne, Mohammed Bakri.* Clayburgh stars as a lawyer torn between her conflicting involvement with an Israeli lover (the District Attorney of Jerusalem) and an enigmatic Palestinian whom she defends against him in court. Caught up in the political strife, her perceptions of herself, her relationships and Israel, her adopted land, are profoundly altered. The film presents many questions which, though well-meaning, are clumsily handled. (Filmed in English) ★★ VHS: $59.99

Hannah and Her Sisters

(1986, 107 min, US, Woody Allen) *Mia Farrow, Barbara Hershey, Dianne Wiest, Michael Caine, Woody Allen, Lloyd Nolan, Maureen O'Sullivan, Max von Sydow.* Brilliantly scripted and directed, *Hannah and Her Sisters* stands as one of Allen's greatest accomplishments. Featuring Farrow, an ascendant Hershey and the Oscar-winning Wiest as three sisters — whose lives are inextricably entwined amongst a host of friends, relatives, and lovers — *Hannah* is a skillful and subtle exploration of human interdependencies. This illuminating work features a superb supporting cast, including the wonderful, Oscar-winning Caine. ★★★★

Hannibal

(2001, 131 min, US, Ridley Scott) *Anthony Hopkins, Julianne Moore, Ray Liotta, Gary Oldman, Giancarlo Giannini, Frankie R. Faison, Zeljko Ivanek.* Moody, suspenseful and just a little too gratuitous in its gory depiction of evil genius, *Hannibal* picks up the story of Dr. Hannibal Lecter ten years after having an old friend for dinner in *The Silence of the Lambs*. With a new director on board for this third chapter in the Lecter series, *Hannibal* retains the vision of director Scott much like *Silence* was a product of Jonathan Demme. Gone is the psychological cat-and-mouse games between Lecter and FBI agent Clarice Starling (played with efficiency by Moore who replaced Jodie Foster). In its place is a visceral panorama of unbridled menace, a stylish, graphic display of

H

"Hello, Clarice" – Sir Anthony Hopkins and Julianne Moore in *Hannibal*

malevolence captured with chilling deliberation. The story follows Starling in her attempt to track down Lecter after he is returned to the FBI's Ten Most Wanted list. In the mix is a disfigured millionaire, a victim of Lecter's appetite, who will stop at nothing to apprehend him. Returning to the role which won him an Oscar, Hopkins delights in the sinister civility of Lecter once more, giving another precise portrait both controlled and cunning. It's the centerpiece of a devilishly entertaining, if sometimes unnerving film. In the end, *Hannibal* may not be as accomplished as *Silence*, but it will certainly get the heart pounding. ★★★ VHS: $102.99; DVD: $26.99

Hanover Street

(1979, 109 min, US, Peter Hyams) *Harrison Ford, Leslie-Anne Down, Christopher Plummer, Alec McCowan.* American soldier Ford finds love in war-torn Britain with a married woman (Down) in this uninspired romantic drama set during WWII. ★★ VHS: $9.99

Hans Christian Andersen

(1952, 120 min, US, Charles Vidor) *Danny Kaye, Farley Granger.* Kaye lends considerable charm to this wondrous children's tale about storyteller Hans Christian Andersen. Frank Loesser's score includes "Inch Worm" and "Ugly Duckling." ★★★ VHS: $14.99; DVD: $14.99

Hanussen

(1989, 140 min, Hungary/West Germany, István Szabó) *Klaus Maria Brandauer, Erland Josephson.* Following *Mephisto* and *Colonel Redl*, this third collaboration between Szabó and actor Brandauer features Brandauer as an Austrian soldier in WWI who acquires an unsettlingly accurate ability to foretell the future. Settling in Berlin, he becomes a successful magician and clairvoyant. His comfortable life becomes entangled when he foresees fascism's rise and the persecution of the Jews, and must decide on keeping quiet or exposing them. Nominated for an Academy Award for

Best Foreign Film, the film offers little dramatic punch but is beautifully photographed and has Brandauer giving a riveting performance as an ordinary man caught between powerful forces. (German with English subtitles) ★★★ VHS: $19.99

The Happiest Days of Your Life

(1950, 81 min, GB, Frank Launder) *Margaret Rutherford, Alastair Sim, Joyce Grenfell.* A charming example of post-war British comedy, this small yet delightfully droll and often hilarious tale stars those two British national treasures: Sim and Rutherford. It's a new school year at the Nutbourne Academy for Boys, and when 100 girls arrive to share accomodations, it's anything but business as usual. Sim smartly plays the befuddled Nutbourne schoolmaster, and Rutherford is wonderful as his girls' school counterpart. The film's first half is full of entendres and puns (some may be lost on American audiences); the second half hits a frenzied, screwball pitch as students and faculty in both camps attempt to simultaneously conceal Nutbourne's co-ed status from rival school personnel and visiting parents. ★★★ VHS: $29.99

Happily Ever After

(1986, 92 min, Brazil, Bruno Barreto) *Regina Duarte, Paul Castelli.* This electrifying drama borrows elements from such films as *After Hours* and *Montenegro* to create a slightly surreal and sexually charged atmosphere, where the unexpected can always happen and people fall prey to their own desires. Barreto fashions a humorous, suspenseful tale of a woman's unlikely experience with a man she first meets in a dream. Duarte delivers a powerfully controlled performance. Barreto's taut direction prevents the film from degenerating into just another skin flick. Menacing landscapes and Buñuelian adventures with a steady undercurrent of sexual excitement. (Portuguese with English subtitles) ★★★½ VHS: $69.99

Happiness

(1934, 69 min, USSR, Alexander Medvedkin) Subtitled "A Tale About a Hapless Mercenary Loser, His Wife, His Well-Fed Neighbor, a Priest, a Nun, and Other Old Relics," this free-wheeling slapstick farce stops at nothing in presenting its own skewed version of reality. Infused with elements of vaudeville, burlesque and even surrealism, the comedy, based on folklore, revolves around a farmer who finds a purse filled with money. Believing that he has found everlasting happiness, the farmer finds instead bizarre disaster every which way he turns. Banned in Russia for over 40 years, this satire on man's and society's greed features everything from polka-dotted horses to nuns in see-through tunics. (Silent with orchestral accompaniment) ★★★ VHS: $29.99

Happiness

(1998, 139 min, US, Todd Solondz) *Philip Seymour Hoffman, Jane Adams, Dylan Baker, Lara Flynn Boyle, Ben Gazzara, Louise Lasser, Cynthia Stevenson, Camryn Manheim, Elizabeth Ashley, Jon Lovitz.* The final word in family dysfunctionalism, *Happiness* is a gruelling, bitter, funny and insightful examination of the deterioration of a familial psyche, a brilliantly written, to-hell-and-back character piece. Effortlessly balancing the stories of its many characters, Solondz isn't wearing rose-colored glasses, for his depiction of human flaws, emotional scars and a suburban morass is brutally honest. The story follows three sisters, their family and relationships. At first we aren't even aware that most of the characters are related, but little by little Solondz gives just enough information. Each is given equal time, and none are shorted in composition. *Happiness* is often difficult to watch, but it is a riveting experience. Even in light of its integrity to character and honesty of the written word, it's not for everyone. ★★★★ VHS: $14.99; DVD: $24.99

Happy Birthday, Gemini

(1980, 107 min, US, Richard Benner) *Alan Rosenberg, Madeline Kahn, Rita Moreno, Robert Viharo, Sarah Molcomb, David Marshall Grant.* Ridiculous stereotypes, terrible acting and a tired script make this film version of Albert Innaurato's 1970s Broadway comedy "Gemini" a messy failure. Set in the row houses of Italian South Philadelphia, the story revolves around a closet case, Francis (Rosenberg), who, while in the midst of a sexual identity crisis, must contend with his wacky neighbors, overbearing father and the unexpected arrival of two of his WASPish Harvard friends. Problems arise when schoolmate Judith (Molcomb) wants to resume their tentative college affair, but Francis is actually attracted to her blond brother Randy (Grant). From the director of *Outrageous.* ★ VHS: $14.99

Happy Gilmore

(1996, 92 min, US, Dennis Dugan) *Adam Sandler, Christopher McDonald, Julie Bowen, Frances Bay, Carl Weathers, Bob Barker, Ben Stiller.* After the abysmal *Billy Madison*, Sandler grows up ever so slightly in this equally moronic golf comedy which produces but a few (insipid) laughs. Happy Gilmore (Sandler) is a hockey nut/player with no talent for the game; in fact, he has no talent for any sport except golf, which he discovers accidentally. When his grandmother is in danger of losing her house, he sets out to win a

Steve Zahn in *Happy, Texas*

few bucks in golf tournaments. Though *Happy Gilmore* is only marginally better than *Madison*, the jokes are still aimed at pre-pubescents, and in his few film appearances Sandler has only honed the skill of being annoying. ★½ VHS: $14.99; DVD: $24.99

Happy New Year (La Bonne Année)

(1973, 112 min, France, Claude Lelouch) *Lino Ventura, Françoise Fabian.* Veering away from his usual saccharine tendencies, Lelouch's bright romantic caper features a gangster (Ventura) who, although just paroled, plans a big robbery but instead of riches, finds his true love. (French with English subtitles) ★★★ VHS: $59.99

Happy, Texas

(1999, 98 min, US, Mark Illsley) *Jeremy Northam, Steve Zahn, Ally Walker, Illeana Douglas, William H. Macy.* Remember *The Gay Deceivers*, that campy little curiosity from the late '60s about two straight guys who have to pretend to be gay? It's sort of been updated for the '90s as *Happy, Texas*, a curious little comedy about two straight guys who have to pretend to be gay. Instead of trying to avoid the draft (as in *Deceivers*), here they try to avoid the law. There's a few laughs, and a wonderful performance by Macy (who gets the film's best line) as the sheriff of the small Texas town in which these two cons hide out; but ultimately it's a gay-themed comedy lacking any gay sensibility. Northam and the zany Zahn are the prison escapees who take the identity of two gay beauty pageant coordinators. Greeted with open arms by the town, they continue the charade with the intent of robbing the town's bank. It's a good premise, but the filmmakers never go so far enough with it. They're content to have Zahn prim and pose, and Northam's romance with the local banker goes nowhere. It's innocuous fun that will make you no better or worse for having seen it. ★★½ VHS: $14.99; DVD: $39.99

Happy Together (Cheun gwong tsa sit)

(1997, 98 min, Hong Kong, Wong Kar-Wai) *Tony Leung, Leslie Cheung.* The title is purely ironic in Kar-Wai's melancholy dissection of a gay relationship in the throngs of dissolution. More of a mood piece rather than a traditional narrative-driven drama, the story begins with two handsome men, Ho Po-wing (Cheung) and Lai Yiu-fai (Leung), making passionate and graphic love. That physical and emotional closeness will never appear again. The two go on a tempestuous vacation to Argentina where they argue, run out of money, and drift apart in a dark, desolate,

cold and wet Buenos Aries. One begins working in a nightclub to earn his money back home while the other goes for a more carefree playboy life. Their vain attempt at reconciliation is doomed — they can't reconnect yet they can't seem to leave. Filmed in an experimental style, the film is a bold look at the breakdown of love and intimacy. ★★★½ VHS: $24.99; DVD: $29.99

Harakiri

(1962, 134 min, Japan, Masaki Kobayashi) Set in 17th-century Japan after a long series of civil wars, *Harakiri* centers on the life of the Samurai in peacetime. Having no lord to serve and no war to fight, the Samurai can either live in poverty or commit harakiri, the suicide ritual. A young Samurai appears at the door of a rich lord's castle asking permission to perform the ritual, hoping instead the lord will offer him money to get rid of him. When the lord calls the soldier's bluff, the youth's father-in-law petitions the lord to take his son-in-law's place, but not before telling the tale of how the boy warrior came to be a Samurai. Kobayashi brilliantly weaves the many stories together as he effortlessly slips back and forth through time, aided greatly by the gorgeous black-and-white cinematography of Yoshio Miyajima. *Harakiri* is a classic waiting to find its cult. (Japanese with English subtitles) ★★★★ VHS: $29.99

Hard Boiled

(1992, 127 min, Hong Kong, John Woo) *Chow Yun-Fat, Tony Leung, Philip Chan.* After an exhilarating teaming in *The Killer*, the Chinese Scorsese and De Niro, Woo and Yun-Fat, triumph again with this spectacular amphetamine-overdriven thriller. Yun-Fat plays a renegade cop named Tequila, whose mission is to halt the operation of an ultra-violent gun smuggling ring. From the incredible opening shootout, which packs more punch than ten *Lethal Weapons*, to the everything-but-the-kitchen-sink ending, this action epic succeeds on many levels thanks to the multi-layered characterizations and story, focused and creative direction, and pulse-pounding action sequences that thrust this pulp melodrama to near-operatic grandeur. (Cantonese with English subtitles) (Available dubbed or in a letterboxed subtitled version) ★★★★ VHS: $14.99; DVD: $29.99

Hard Choices

(1968, 90 min, US, Rick King) *Gary McCleery, Margaret Klenck, John Sayles, Spalding Grey.* A teenager (McCleery) enters the criminal justice system through an innocent involvement with a robbery, and becomes involved with the social worker (Klenck) assigned to his case. An interesting look at the process of enforcement and corrections in this country, and highlighted by an intriguing portrayal by Sayles of a jaded, flippant drug smuggler. Based on a true story. ★★½ VHS: $19.99

A Hard Day's Night

(1964, 85 min, GB, Richard Lester) *John Lennon, Paul McCartney, George Harrison, Ringo Starr, Wilfrid Brambell.* Though 12 songs and filler would have made a hit, The Beatles and director Lester instead fashioned this inventive musical comedy classic filled with the frenzied emotion of early Beatlemania. Lester's early style shines through in this playful day-in-the-life look at the emerging rock stars. ★★★★

Hard Eight

(1997, 101 min, US, Paul Thomas Anderson) *Philip Baker Hall, John C. Reilly, Gwyneth Paltrow, Samuel L. Jackson, Philip Seymour Hoffman.* Mix the staccato, tough-talk style of David Mamet and the existential forcefulness of Melville's *Bob Le Flambeur* and you get *Hard Eight*, a scruffy independent winner that will appeal to those who, well, like scruffy independent winners. Although set in Las Vegas and Reno, the film really takes place in a neon twilight zone where glitz and seediness meet. Reilly, a naïve loser in desperate need of $6,000, gets a chance to change his luck when he meets Hall, a world-weary gambler who takes him under his wing. After a few successful years, the mens' friendship changes when Reilly falls for Paltrow, a cocktail waitress who turns tricks on the side. Directed with icy precision by Anderson, *Hard Eight* is more concerned with atmosphere and characters than intricate plotting, and on a more subtle level, he explores how people depend on and use each other. Hall turns in a mesmerizing career performance as the obsessively controlling gambler. ★★★½ VHS: $19.99; DVD: $27.99

Hard Rain

(1998, 98 min, US, Mikael Salomon) *Morgan Freeman, Christian Slater, Randy Quaid, Minnie Driver, Betty White, Richard Dysart, Ed Asner.* If you took *The Thomas Crown Affair* and bred it with *The Poseidon Adventure*, *Hard Rain* would be their bastard son. There's lots of water, boats and assorted money-grabbing types all trying to outsmart each other, but there's no credible plotting or characterizations. Slater and Asner are security guards transferring $3 million. They get caught in flood waters, which is lucky for Freeman and pals, who are after the money. After shooting Asner, the crooks chase Slater all over a flood-ravaged Midwestern small town. The technical aspects of this disaster thriller are impressive, as most scenes take place on flooded streets or in washed-out buildings. But there's not much going on in the script department; and while most fans don't watch action thrillers for their screenplay merits, you need a story now and then. ★★ VHS: $9.99; DVD: $24.99

Hard Target

(1993, 92 min, US, John Woo) *Jean-Clade Van Damme, Lance Henriksen, Arnold Vosloo, Wilford Brimley.* The Balanchine of Bullets, Hong Kong action-meister Woo, has his first stateside effort and the result is a mostly successful, if somewhat uneven, reworking of *The Most Dangerous Game*. Van Damme is up against bad-guy Henriksen, who sets up hunts for wealthy thrill seekers. The game: down-and-out combat veterans. Van Damme plays a hapless merchant marine who just wants to get out of New Orleans, but instead gets pulled into the intrigue when enlisted by a young woman whose father has disappeared. The film's first half is choppy, fraught with staccato dialogue and sporadic action. But once the chase is on, the action rises to a non-stop pitch. Woo finds his stride and delivers the goods with a flourish. ★★★ VHS: $9.99; DVD: $24.99

Hard Times

(1975, 97 min, US, Walter Hill) *Charles Bronson, James Coburn, Jill Ireland, Strother Martin.* Hill's directorial debut is also one of his best films. Bronson takes on all comers in bare-knuckle fights. Coburn plays his manager. Lots of action. ★★★ VHS: $9.99; DVD: $14.99

The Hard Way

(1991, 115 min, US, John Badham) *Michael J. Fox, James Woods, Annabella Sciorra, Stephen Lang, LL Cool J, Christina Ricci, Luis Guzman.* Though really nothing more than a formula buddy-cop comedy, the teaming of Fox and Woods proves to be a saving grace. Fox plays a spoiled Hollywood actor who is partnered with hard-boiled New York detective Woods when the former requests training for his next film assignment. Constantly at odds, Fox and Woods milk the situation dry; eliciting laughs even when the script doesn't warrant them. An amiable, harmless romp. ★★½ VHS: $7.49

Hardcore

(1979, 108 min, US, Paul Schrader) *George C. Scott, Peter Boyle, Season Hubley, Dick Sargent.* It's every father's nightmare when Scott, playing a Calvinist from the Midwest (as is director Schrader), finds his runaway daughter making porno movies in the big city. Schrader captures the sleazy, degrading lifestyle often associated with these sorts of enterprises, but doesn't have the courage of his convictions when it comes to the ending. ★★½ VHS: $14.99

The Harder They Come

(1973, 98 min, Jamaica, Perry Penzelle) *Jimmy Cliff.* The age-old story of a country boy seeking riches in the big city, of urban corruption and coming to a bad end — reggae style! Cliff is striking as the marijuana-running punk who kills a cop in a drug bust and becomes a folk hero. Features a hypnotic reggae soundtrack. ★★★ VHS: $19.99; DVD: $39.99

Hardware

(1990, 94 min, GB, Richard Stanley) *Stacey Travis, Dylan McDermott, John Lynch, Iggy Pop.* Style-over-substance defeats this *Alien/Terminator* derivative about a post-apocalyptic metal-worker (Travis) whose latest sculpture turns lethal when the scrap robot head given to her by her boyfriend (McDermott) reactivates and reassembles itself. Sounds great, but never manages to overcome the director's obvious music video background. ★ VHS: $9.99

Hard Eight

Harem

(1987, 107 min, GB/France, Arthur Joffe) *Ben Kingsley, Nastassja Kinski.* This curiosity has Kingsley as an OPEC oil minister who becomes enraptured by Kinski while on a business trip to America. Kingsley must have the beauty and right before he leaves, he ruthlessly kidnaps her and then places her among his 30-member harem. Passions explode when past meets present in this bizarre romantic comedy. (Filmed in English) ★ VHS: $79.99

Harlan County, USA

(1977, 103 min, US, Barbara Kopple) This Academy Award-winning documentary compellingly involves the viewer in the plight of Kentucky coal miners up against the Eastover Mining Company. The strikers are presented forthrightly, without condescension or glamorization, and with dignity. Surprisingly effective and immediate, the film retains its relevance regarding the conditions affecting American workers today. Highly recommended. ★★★★ VHS: $29.99

Harlem Nights

(1989, 115 min, US, Eddie Murphy) *Eddie Murphy, Richard Pryor, Redd Foxx, Della Reese, Arsenio Hall, Stan Shaw.* Murphy wrote, directed and stars in this gangster comedy set in late-1930s Harlem. Pryor and his "adopted" son Murphy are up against a crooked cop and a white mob kingpin who want a piece of their lucrative nightspot. Superlative sets and costumes can't mask an unfunny screenplay, in which most of the humor is one character cursing at another. Director Murphy's film lacks the energy needed to sustain the farcical romp it wants to be; however, writer Murphy is to be applauded for giving Pryor the plum part of the film — and the veteran comic makes the most of it. Shaw is especially good in support as a punch-drunk boxer. ★★ VHS: $14.99

Harley Davidson and the Marlboro Man

(1991, 98 min, US, Simon Wincer) *Don Johnson, Mickey Rourke, Daniel Baldwin, Vanessa Williams, Giancarlo Esposito, Tom Sizemore.* Director Wincer makes a valiant effort, but this tale of two outlaw misfits who join forces to save a neighborhood bar from greedy developers is lost in a whirlwind of lackluster performances, overblown action sequences and an undernourished script. Hardcore Rourke fans might enjoy this oddity — others beware. ★½ VHS: $14.99; DVD: $14.99

The Harmonists

(1999, 115 min, Germany, Joseph Vilsmaier) *Ben Becker, Heino Ferch, Ulrich Noethen, Heinrich Schafmeister.* Involving true-life story of a singing quintet — The Comedian Harmonists — who were superstars in Berlin in the '30s. Unfortunately, Hitler was coming into power, and three of the five were Jewish. This is a standard rise and fall of a music group drama, given dimension by the Nazism background. While there is some great music and a handful of good scenes, *The Harmonists* never really transcends its clichés or sentimentality, and a treacly ending leaves a bad taste. It holds the attention, though, and its heart is in the right place. (German with English subtitles) ★★½ VHS: $19.99

Harold and Maude

(1971, 90 min, US, Hal Ashby) *Ruth Gordon, Bud Cort, Vivian Pickles, Cyril Cusack.* He's 20 and obsessed with death; she's 80 and full of joie de vivre. Together they combat the doldrums of life. Gordon shines as the vivacious Maude and Cort is playfully grim as the morbid young Harold. Black comedy at its darkest, this wonderful love story features the music of Cat Stevens and features a hilarious supporting role by Pickles as Harold's daffy mother. ★★★★ VHS: $14.99; DVD: $29.99

Harper

(1966, 121 min, US, Jack Smight) *Paul Newman, Lauren Bacall, Robert Wagner, Janet Leigh, Julie Harris.* Newman stars as Louis Harper, a cynical Los Angeles detective hired for a missing persons case. A perfect '60s thriller, complete with scenery, California atmosphere and Newman's charisma. Bacall costars as the bedridden widow who hires Harper and she makes the most of her femme fatale charm. Sharp direction from Smight and a witty script by William Goldman make for a most entertaining thriller. (Sequel: *The Drowning Pool*) ★★★½ VHS: $14.99

Harriet Craig

(1950, 94 min, US, Vincent Sherman) *Joan Crawford, Wendell Corey.* In this engrossing remake of *Craig's Wife*, Crawford is in great form as she sulks and rages as the perfectionist, home-wrecking housewife who destroys her own marriage through her penchant for control. ★★★ VHS: $19.99

Harriet the Spy

(1996, 96 min, US, Bronwen Hughes) *Michelle Trachtenberg, Rosie O'Donnell, Eartha Kitt.* Harriet is a precocious 11-year-old girl whose independent outlook has made her a bit of an outcast. Her beloved nanny instills in Harriet individualism and an appreciation for life. Which explains Harriet's penchant for writing in her notebook everything she sees. It's her observations and thoughts which lead to trouble in the sweet and enjoyable *Harriet the Spy*, a spirited adaptation of the Louise Fitzhugh children's book. Trachtenberg makes a very appealing Harriet, and O'Donnell is wonderful as Harriet's nanny, who imparts on the young girl sage advice while serving as loyal best friend. A nicely paced frolic of youthful custom and a particularly encouraging portrait of one young girl who discovers the importance of just being her. ★★★ VHS: $19.99

Harry and the Hendersons

(1987, 110 min, US, William Dear) *John Lithgow, Melinda Dillon, Don Ameche, Lainie Kazan, M. Emmet Walsh.* This amusing little comedy about a suburban Seattle family who find themselves host to Bigfoot is filled with warmhearted humor. Lithgow puts in yet another solid (and yet unsung) performance as Dad. Rick Baker's makeup for the giant Harry won him an Academy Award. ★★½ VHS: $9.99

Harry and Tonto

(1974, 115 min, US, Paul Mazursky) *Art Carney, Ellen Burstyn, Larry Hagman, Geraldine Fitzgerald, Melanie Mayron.* A Best Actor Academy Award went to Carney for his portrayal of an old man who, after eviction from his apartment building (about to be torn down around his ears), sets out on a cross-country odyssey with his cat.

Touching, warm, humorous and sometimes very sad. In addition to *The Late Show*, perhaps the fullest use of Mr. Carney's mature talents. ★★★½ VHS: $14.99

Harvest

(1937, 129 min, France, Marcel Pagnol) *Fernandel, Orane Demazis.* Demazis and Fernandel, the stars of *Angèle*, are reunited in this Pagnolian human drama about a peasant family and their struggle for existence. An itinerant hunter, wishing to have a family, coaxes a down-on-her-luck cabaret singer to leave her abusive companion and set up house with him in a deserted, decaying mountain village. The unlikely lovers struggle, against all odds, to till the land and keep the village alive. Innocently told by today's standards, this film was originally banned by French censors on moral grounds. (French with English subtitles) ★★★★ VHS: $59.99

The Harvest

(1992, 97 min, US, David Marconi) *Miguel Ferrer, Henry Silva, Harvey Fierstein.* Ferrer stars as a screenwriter who travels to a Mexican resort town to get away from it all and rewrite his newest screenplay. Once there, he becomes involved in a convoluted series of events which lead to illegal organ transplants, murder and cover-ups. A finely crafted neo-noir thriller, *The Harvest* is an intricate puzzle that's fun to watch unfold. ★★★ VHS: $14.99

Harvey

(1950, 104 min, US, Henry Koster) *James Stewart, Josephine Hull, Victoria Horne, Cecil Kelloway, Peggy Dow, Charles Drake, Jesse White.* Stewart gives one of his most appealing performances as the tipsolated Elwood P. Dowd, whose best friend, Harvey, just happens to be a six-foot rabbit (he's actually a pooka, but why quibble). Based on Mary Chase's Pulitzer Prize–winning Broadway play, the film is a faithful and delightful adaptation, capturing all the warmth, humor and craziness which made the play one of the great sensations of the late 1940s. As Elwood's exasperated sister, Hull had the role of her career and won an Oscar for it. ★★★½ VHS: $14.99; DVD: $29.99

The Harvey Girls

(1946, 101 min, US, George Sidney) *Judy Garland, Ray Bolger, Angela Lansbury, John Hodiak, Marjorie Main, Virginia O'Brien, Cyd Charisse.* Garland sings "Atchison, Topeka and the Santa Fe" as she and other well-bred young ladies head West to be waitresses at the new Fred Harvey railroad station restaurants. Though the story is pure hokum, Judy and a talented cast plus enjoyable musical numbers make this a pleasant ride. ★★★ VHS: $14.99

The Hasty Heart

(1949, 104 min, GB, Vincent Sherman) *Richard Todd, Patricia Neal, Ronald Reagan.* Based on John Patrick's sentimental stage play, this affecting tearjerker is as sappy as it is captivating. Todd gives an immense performance as a proud Scottish soldier staying at a Burmese hospital during WWII. Arrogant and cantankerous, he makes enemies of all around him until it is learned he only has a few weeks to live. Neal is quite good as the nurse looking after him, and even the presence of Reagan as an American G.I.

doesn't compromise the integrity or enjoyment level of this polished, bittersweet tale. (Remade in 1986) ★★★½ VHS: $19.99

Hatchet for a Honeymoon

(1967, 93 min, Italy/Spain, Mario Bava) *Stephen Forsythe, Dagmar Lassander, Laura Berri.* Strong on visual imagery and short on plot, Italian horror master Bava tells the tale of a cross-dressing psycho killer/fashion mogul who murders brides while haunted by the ghost of his own wife. (Letterboxed) ★★½ VHS: $19.99; DVD: $24.99

Hate (La Haine)

(1995, 94 min, France, Mathieu Kassovitz) *Vincent Cassel, Hubert Kounde, Said Taghmaoui.* Three marginalized French youths — one black, one Arab, one Jew, and all unlikely friends — spend a night on the mean streets of Paris in this stunning black-and-white feature by actor-director Kassovitz. The day after a massive street riot during which a well-liked gang member was put into a coma by a police beating, the three friends set out on their normal daily activities. But there's a twist: a policeman lost his pistol during the melee and one of the three now has it. Violence lurks around every corner in *Hate*, and only after expectations have subsided does it show its ugly head. Low-budget though shot and edited remarkably well, the film is alternately harrowing and sad, and paints a very bleak picture of the future of urban society via its treatment of its youth. (French with English subtitles) (Letterboxed) ★★★★ VHS: $9.99

Haunted

(1995, 107 min, GB, Lewis Gilbert) *Aidan Quinn, Kate Beckinsale, John Gielgud, Anthony Andrews.* A slow-moving yet haunting ghost story about an arrogant turn-of-the-century college professor (Quinn) who, having been haunted as a child by the accidental death of his younger sister, has dedicated his life to proving there's no such things as ghosts. But when he takes up the challenge of exorcising a country estate, he uncovers a supernatural scandal so horrifying even Casper would run screaming. Director Gilbert is in uncharted territory with this poltergeist patchwork, but he compensates the unlively pace and familiar scare techniques with a good screenplay (based on the novel by James

Herbert) and winning performances. ★★½ VHS: $14.99

Haunted Honeymoon

(1986, 84 min, US, Gene Wilder) *Gene Wilder, Gilda Radner, Dom DeLuise, Jonathan Pryce.* A sometimes amusing mystery spoof with Wilder and Radner as two 1930s radio stars who visit Wilder's aunt (DeLuise in drag) at the family estate, becoming targets for murder. Though the pairing of Wilder and Radner is irresistible, they really aren't given any good material. ★★; DVD: $14.99

Haunted Summer

(1988, 106 min, US, Ivan Passer) *Eric Stoltz, Laura Dern, Philip Anglim, Alice Krige, Alex Winter.* Languid (read: boring), beautifully filmed (read: the countryside is more interesting that the characters), evocative period piece (read: pretentious costume drama drivel) and shocking (read: a failed attempt at titillation), this drama retreads the often-traveled grounds of the fateful summer that Percy Shelley, his lover and future wife Mary Goodwin, her half-sister Claire Claimont and the roguish poet Lord Byron spent together on the shores of Lake Geneva in 1816. For a much better film on the same subject, Ken Russell's dreamlike psychological thriller *Gothic* is a must. ★

The Haunting

(1963, 112 min, US, Robert Wise) *Julie Harris, Claire Bloom, Russ Tamblyn, Richard Johnson.* Wise's classic ghost story about a team of researchers investigating a haunted house. Harris and Bloom are both splendid as psychic investigators, and Wise can get more scares from a door than Jason or Freddy can scrape together with an assortment of knives and axes. Based on Shirley Jackson's "The Haunting of Hill House," this is a frightening, genuinely creepy and well-made chiller. (Remade in 1999) ★★★★ VHS: $14.99

The Haunting

(1999, 113 min, US, Jan de Bont) *Liam Neeson, Catherine Zeta-Jones, Lili Taylor, Owen Wilson, Bruce Dern, Marian Seldes.* Producing the kind of shivers that only a bad horror tale can deliver, this remake of Robert Wise's 1963 classic ghost story misses the mark in nearly every department.

The Haunting: Julie Harris (l.) and Claire Bloom go ghost-hunting

This second screen version of Shirley Jackson's "The Haunting of Hill House" starts promising. Neeson plays a psychologist who gathers three subjects (Zeta-Jones, Taylor and Owen) for a sleep-disorder study at the Gothic mansion Hill House. Little by little, it becomes apparent that the place may be haunted. In the original, this was accomplished through the subtle use of chills and scares; here it's done through loud noises and garish special effects. Mouths will be gaped — not by the sheer terror of it all but by the often ridiculous plot developments. Great production design and two good scares aren't enough to make this tolerable. ★½ VHS: $14.99; DVD: $24.99

The Haunting of Julia

(1976, 96 min, GB/Canada, Richard Loncraine) *Mia Farrow, Keir Dullea, Tom Conti.* Moody and seductive supernatural thriller with Farrow as a mother haunted by the death of her young daughter, whose spirit has now returned from the dead. ★★½

The Haunting of Morella

(1991, 82 min, US, Jim Wynorski) *David McCallum, Nicole Eggert.* Roger Corman strikes again, and strikes out, in this dismal Poe adaptation that's a far cry from his 1960s efforts. McCallum is the dopey, dedicated hubby of a condemned sorceress who returns to possess their virginal daughter. A campy mix of buxom starlets and T&A in lieu of talent. ★ VHS: $79.99

Havana

(1990, 145 min, US, Sydney Pollack) *Robert Redford, Lena Olin, Raul Julia, Alan Arkin, Richard Farnsworth.* The sixth collaboration between actor Redford and director Pollack features intelligent acting and competent direction, but is plagued by an insufferably poor script. The story follows the exploits of Redford as a big-stakes American gambler who's hanging around Havana on the eve of the Communist takeover. All he's interested in is a good poker game, but when he becomes smitten by the wife of a wealthy revolutionary (Olin), he is inextricably sucked into the political fray. The film borrows heavily from classics like *Casablanca*, right down to the Scandinavian-born leading lady, but falls mighty short of that film's greatness. ★★ VHS: $9.99; DVD: $26.99

Hawaii

(1966, 172 min, US, George Roy Hill) *Max von Sydow, Julie Andrews, Richard Harris, Gene Hackman, Carroll O'Connor, John Cullum.* Epic film version of James Michener's novel set in the 1800s about settlers in our 50th state and how they shaped the territory. Von Sydow is appropriately dour as a missionary, Andrews is his personable wife, and Harris is the sea captain in love with Andrews. ★★★ VHS: $24.99

The Hawk

(1993, 84 min, GB, David Hayman) *Helen Mirren, George Castigan, Owen Teale.* When a serial killer stalks the normally peaceful English countryside, an uptight housewife (Mirren) soon begins to suspect her traveling salesman husband (Castigan), due to the many similarities between her own life and the killer's victims. The tired script, which occasionally succeeds by creating suspenseful moments, fails just as often

by giving obvious clues and plot twists. Though the film rescues itself by allowing Mirren to deliver a strong performance, it's difficult to camouflage a clichéd, muddled story. ★★½ VHS: $19.99

Hawk's Vengeance

(1997, 96 min, US, Marc F. Voizard) *Gary Daniels, Vlasta Vrana, Cass Magda.* Somebody give Gary Daniels a break! The handsome action star has talent, great martial arts ability and a likable screen persona, but he is continually cast in crappy grade-Z action flicks like this one. This time, Daniels is cast as "Hawk," a British marine who comes to the U.S. to investigate the mysterious death of his half-brother, an American cop. He teams up with his ex-partner and together they take on a local ganglord. ★ VHS: $14.99

Hawks

(1988, 100 min, GB, Robert Ellis Miller) *Timothy Dalton, Anthony Edwards, Jill Bennett, Sheila Hancock, Connie Booth.* Quirky comedy-drama with Dalton and Edwards as two terminally ill cancer patients who escape from their hospital ward in search of adventure. Dalton and Edwards bring great pathos to their roles; and though the last third of the film veers on a rather strange course, this can be rewarding, if offbeat, entertainment. ★★½ VHS: $102.99

The Hawks and the Sparrows

(1965, 88 min, Italy, Pier Paolo Pasolini) *Toto, Ninetto Davoli.* This post-neorealist parable is an unconventional story featuring Italy's beloved stone-faced clown Toto as an Everyman who, with his empty-headed son, travels the road of life accompanied by a talking crow, who waxes philosophically and amusingly on the passing scene. Pasolini presents a tragic fable which shows two delightful innocents caught between the Church and Marxism. (Italian with English subtitles) ★★★ VHS: $29.99

He Got Game

(1998, 130 min, US, Spike Lee) *Denzel Washington, Ray Allen, Milla Jovovich, Ned Beatty, Bill Nunn, John Turturro.* In one of his most accomplished screen portrayals, Washington plays Jake, a man serving a lengthy prison term for killing his wife. Jake is released for one week to try to convince his estranged son Jesus (Allen), a nationally known high school basketball prodigy, to accept a scholarship at the governor's alma mater, in exchange for a shortened sentence. This pulpy, almost high-concept idea is given the customary intense yet loose treatment by director Lee. A healthy cynicism permeates the entire film, with coaches, colleges, family and friends all trying to get a piece of the young ballplayer. Beautifully edited, long but compelling and fast-paced, the only negative of the film is the less-than-defined characterizations of the women. The performances are uniformly good, with a surprisingly natural turn from real-life NBA star Allen. ★★★½ VHS: $14.99; DVD: $29.99

He Said, She Said

(1991, 115 min, US, Ken Kwapis & Marisa Silver) *Kevin Bacon, Elizabeth Perkins, Sharon Stone, Nathan Lane, Anthony LaPaglia.* Lightweight comedy which is actually two films in one. The story centers on the relationship of

journalists Bacon and Perkins — told through the eyes of each of them. Kwapis directed the "male" point-of-view, and Silver directed the "female" counterpart. ★★ VHS: $14.99

He Walked by Night

(1948, 80 min, US, Alfred L. Werker) *Richard Basehart, Scott Brady, Roy Roberts, Whit Bissell, Jack Webb.* This seminal noir policer showcases the use of forensic science as the LAPD tracks a vicious and highly intelligent cop killer. Starkly shot and tautly written, the film follows the police investigation as it pieces together minute scraps of evidence, following leads with state-of-the-art technology of the time. This focus on the technical aspect of criminal investigation was unique in films by 1949, and apparently made a big impression on the actor portraying the crime lab scientist — Webb. The film's introductory voice-over opens with a description of Los Angeles and tells us that what we are about to see is a true story — only the names have been changed. Sound familiar? It's the prototype for Webb's TV series, "Dragnet"; a term, incidentally, pointedly used several times in the film. ★★★ VHS: $29.99

Head

(1968, 86 min, US, Bob Rafelson) *The Monkees, Terry (Teri) Garr, Vito Scotti, Victor Mature, Frank Zappa, Annette Funicello, Jack Nicholson.* "Hey, hey, it's the Monkees!" The pre*fab*ricated four cavort with an all-star cast including Mature (that hunk of yore) and Nicholson (who also coscripted) in this psychedelic explosion of drug-induced humor. ★★★ VHS: $19.99; DVD: $24.99

Head above Water

(1997, 92 min, US, Jim Wilson) *Harvey Keitel, Cameron Diaz, Craig Sheffer, Billy Zane.* A truly wretched comedy with a slumming Keitel as a middle-aged judge who becomes terribly jealous when he finds the dead, naked body of the old beau of his beautiful young wife in the basement. Boring misadventures follow as husband and wife team up to try to dispose of the body, while Diaz's childhood friend (Sheffer) grows suspicious. A cutesy "comic" music score only adds to the misery as three able actors give career-low performances walking around like dull idiots. The ending is a slow death-crawl to the credits, with no buildup or climax to speak of. In fact, the ending is *so* inconsequential and casual, you may feel you have missed something. You won't want to rewind to find out what. ★ VHS: $19.99

Head Against the Wall
(La Tête Contre les Murs)

(1958, 90 min, France, Georges Franju) *Jean-Pierre Mocky, Anouk Aimée, Charles Aznavour.* Franju, along with Jean-Pierre Melville, made consistently intriguing films in the '40s and '50s that anticipated the French New Wave. Franju, cofounder of the Cinematique Française in 1938, was known mostly for his documentaries and shorts; this was his first feature. Taking the theme of repression and rebellion, the story — possibly influenced by James Dean's alienated youth films — follows a young man's (Mocky, who also wrote the script) escape from an insane asylum in his efforts to locate his girlfriend (Aimée) and avoid his father's desperate attempts to recommit him. (French with English subtitles) ★★★

Head of the Family

(1970, 105 min, Italy, Nanni Loy) *Leslie Caron, Nino Manfredi, Ugo Tognazzi, Claudine Auger.* Set in post-war Rome, this sensitive drama concerns a woman (Caron) whose marriage of ten years has become loveless. She must face the prospect of life alone, dealing with both its pleasures and anxieties. (Dubbed) ★★½ VHS: $79.99

Head Office

(1986, 90 min, US, Ken Kinkleman) *Judge Reinhold, Danny DeVito, Eddie Albert, Jane Seymour, Rick Moranis.* Lackluster parody of the financial world with Reinhold as a young idealist working his way up the corporate ladder. ★★ VHS: $9.99

Head On

(1998, 104 min, Australia, Ana Kokkinos) *Alex Dimitrades, Paul Capsis, Julius Garner, Tony Nikolakopoulas, Elena Mandalis, Eugenia Fragos, Paul Capsis.* In this adaptation of the book "Loaded" by Christos Tsiolkas, director Kokkinos has created a vivid portrait of a culturally and sexually confused youth in the person of Ari (brilliantly portrayed by Dimitrades), a Greek-Australian hunk. The exciting drama centers on 24 hours in Ari's life. A very closeted young man who lives with his traditionalist Greek family, the unemployed Ari spends his days with his fellow Greek friends (including a frustrated girlfriend), partying and taking drugs. At night he releases his insatiable homosexual desires through encounters with a variety of men. The clash of his straight world and his gay yearnings come to a head one evening when he meets and is attracted to a cute blond named Shawn. With a pulsating soundtrack and vibrant visuals, Kokkinos takes us on an intimate, narcotic ride into Ari's troubled world. ★★★½ VHS: $79.99; DVD: $29.99

Head over Heels (À Coeur Joie!)

(1967, 89 min, France, Serge Bourguignon) *Brigitte Bardot, Laurent Terzieff.* Bardot is a happily married woman who, through several years of marriage, has never cheated on her husband. Her fidelity is severely tested when, in London on a business trip, Bardot finds herself pursued by a handsome young man and must decide on staying faithful or having a "short" love affair. This drama, made for the French domestic market, is still an entertaining and knowledgeable look into the labyrinthine world of love. (French with English subtitles) ★★★

Hear My Song

(1991, 115 min, GB, Peter Chelsom) *Adrian Dunbar, Ned Beatty, Tara Fitzgerald, Shirley Ann Feld.* Made in the tradition of the Ealing Studio comedies with a splash of *Local Hero* thrown in, *Hear My Song* is a delightful frolic about a sprightly young Irishman trying to make a go of it as a nightclub operator in Liverpool. After making a series of disastrous bookings, he is forced to try and save his venue by luring the famed Irish tenor Josef Locke (Beatty) back from Ireland where he's been avoiding British tax collectors. Dunbar (who cowrote the screenplay with first-time director Chelsom) delivers a winning performance as the music promoter Mickey O'Neill. Beatty is marvelous as Locke, putting in one of his best performances. ★★★½ VHS: $19.99

Hear No Evil

(1993, 97 min, US, Robert Greenwald) *Marlee Matlin, D.B. Sweeney, Martin Sheen, John C. McGinley.* Matlin stars in this insipid thriller as a deaf aerobics instructor who inadvertently becomes involved in a murderous robbery scheme. It seems one of her clients, investigative reporter McGinley, picks up a scoop about a stolen coin worth a million dollars. And the police department of Portland, Oregon, has a rotten apple in the form of sergeant Sheen, who's involved in the heist. Sheen and his cronies then terrorize everyone in sight, and Matlin becomes the object of the bad guy's ire. Director Greenwald can't decide whether he's making a thriller or a music video as he inserts several numbers which completely break the tension. ★½ VHS: $9.99

Hearing Voices

(1990, 89 min, US, Sharon Greytak) *Erika Nagy, Stephen Gatta.* Numbed into quiet boredom by the shallow, manipulative world of fashion modeling, and physically scarred after reconstructive surgery, Erika floats aimlessly through her successful but empty life. She is saved emotionally after meeting Lee (sort of a Pauly Shore on Prozac), the gay lover of her doctor. Their relationship (sexual?) is an unusual love, which while not altogether fulfilling, and ultimately doomed, does help in their respective healing processes. This story, of a "romance" between a gay man and a straight woman, provides a great premise; but the film, hampered by languid pacing and stilted acting is reduced to an earnest but lifeless viewing experience. ★★

Heart and Souls

(1993, 103 min, US, Ron Underwood) *Robert Downey, Jr., Alfre Woodard, Charles Grodin, Tom Sizemore, Kyra Sedgwick, David Paymer, Elisabeth Shue.* While its scale may be more fitting for the small screen rather than the large one, this ghost comedy is really quite a charmer. Sedgwick, Sizemore, Woodard and Grodin are lost souls. They unexplainedly find themselves watching over a youngster, who grows up to be harried businessman Downey. As they try to put his life right, they also are given a chance to tie up the loose ends of their own lives, which each failed to do before their deaths. As he demonstrated in *Chaplin*, Downey has a real knack for physical comedy; which comes in handy since the spirits — recalling Steve Martin's *All of Me* — possess Downey's body for much of the film. ★★★ VHS: $7.49

Heart Beat

(1980, 109 min, US, John Byrum) *Nick Nolte, Sissy Spacek, John Heard, Ray Sharkey.* Fictionalized though rewarding account of the friendship of Beat poet Jack Kerouac and Carolyn & Neal Cassady. Heard is the author, and Spacek and Nolte are the Cassadys. Sharkey is a standout in support as a Ginsberg-like writer. ★★½ VHS: $19.99

Heart Condition

(1990, 98 min, US, James D. Parriott) *Bob Hoskins, Denzel Washington, Chloe Webb.* Instantly forgettable yet strangely enjoyable while it lasts, this phantasmal comedy about a racist cop who is befriended by a congenial black ghost is the perfect example of the "concept" idea of screenwriting. Hoskins, at his gruffest and most lovable, is a down-at-the-heels cop who suffers a heart attack. Washington is the recently deceased man who spectrally returns to earth after his heart is transplanted into Hoskins' body. The two form an unlikely team as they attempt to track down Washington's drug-lord killers. ★★½ VHS: $9.99

The Heart Is a Lonely Hunter

(1968, 125 min, US, Robert Ellis Miller) *Alan Arkin, Sondra Locke, Stacey Keach, Laurinda Barrett, Chuck McCann, Cicely Tyson.* Based on Carson McCullers' lyrical first novel, this poignant drama stars Arkin (in an Oscar-nominated performance) as a sensitive deaf-mute who befriends, supports, and then, in some quiet fashion, is betrayed by a small group of fellow social outcasts. Set in the South, this tender tale features Locke (also an Oscar nominee) and Keach in their screen debuts. ★★★ VHS: $19.99

Heart Like a Wheel

(1983, 113 min, US, Jonathan Kaplan) *Bonnie Bedelia, Beau Bridges, Bill McKinney, Anthony Edwards, Hoyt Axton, Leo Rossi, Dick Miller.* This triumphant, true-life saga chronicles the uphill struggle of stock car driver Shirley Muldowney (Bedelia) to gain acceptance in the male-dominated world of motorsport racing. A thrilling tale of determination and perseverance. Bedelia gives an outstanding performance; Bridges is exceptional as racer Connie Kalitte. ★★★½

Heart of Dixie

(1989, 95 min, US, Martin Davidson) *Ally Sheedy, Virginia Madsen, Phoebe Cates, Treat Williams.* Another in the long line of well-meaning social dramas about racial discrimination in our country's past. A worthy subject to be sure, but the film lacks a perspective and a strong narrative needed to make it of interest. Sheedy gives a sincere performance as a white college student given a jolting political lesson in racial injustice. ★★½ VHS: $19.99

Heart of Dragon

(1985, 85 min, Hong Kong, Samo Hung) *Jackie Chan, Samo Hung, Emily Chu.* In one of his earliest dramatic roles, Jackie is cast as a police officer who is constantly taking care of his mentally retarded brother (director Hung), and running into myriad troubles while doing so. This HK version of *Rain Man* begins slowly, but builds to a grueling twenty-minute action climax set in a construction site which finds Jackie fighting at his fiercest to rescue his kidnapped brother. But fight scenes are not what this movie is about; it is more about Jackie's recognition of his love and responsibility for his unfortunate sibling. The two actors have several tender and dramatic moments together, and Samo proves that he can be sentimental without becoming maudlin. (Cantonese with English subtitles) ★★★ VHS: $19.99; DVD: $29.99

Heartaches

(1981, 93 min, Canada, Donald Shebib) *Margot Kidder, Annie Potts, David Carradine.* This winsome romantic comedy and female buddy movie stars Potts as a woman who after finding herself pregnant, and not by her racing-car enthusiast boyfriend David Carradine, abandons him and goes on the road. It doesn't take her long to meet up with a zany, streetwise woman (Kidder) who takes her under her wing, and together they set up house in Toronto. Kidder gives an enjoyably manic performance in the plum role of the man-crazed peroxide blonde who takes the frumpy Potts on an unwilling series of adventures. ★★★

Heartbreak Hotel

(1988, 93 min, US, Chris Columbus) *Charlie Schlatter, David Keith, Tuesday Weld.* In this ficticious comedy, a teenager (Schlatter) kidnaps Elvis Presley (Keith) and brings "the King" home for his divorced mom (Weld). Easily forgettable. ★½

The Heartbreak Kid

(1972, 106 min, US, Elaine May) *Charles Grodin, Cybill Shepherd, Jeannie Berlin, Eddie Albert, Audra Lindley.* One of the best American comedies to come out of the 1970s, this Neil Simon scripted film from a Bruce Jay Friedman story features Grodin as Lenny, a nice if self-absorbed Jewish *schlemiel* who, realizing on his honeymoon that he has made a fatal mistake in marrying his sunburned, cake-guzzling wife (hilariously and pathetically played by Berlin), makes the decision to dump her for the WASPish ice-queen goddess in the body of Shepherd. His frantic efforts to bow out of his marriage and his ensuing relentless pursuit of his unattainable dream woman is mercilessly lampooned by director May. ★★★½ VHS: $14.99; DVD: $24.99

Heartbreak Ridge

(1986, 130 min, US, Clint Eastwood) *Clint Eastwood, Marsha Mason, Everett McGill, Moses Gunn, Mario Van Peebles, Eileen Heckart.* Vigorous war adventure, with an accent on humor during its well-paced boot camp sequence, stars director Eastwood as a rough-talking, old-school Marine sergeant in charge of a platoon of new recruits. ★★½ VHS: $14.99

Heartbreakers

(2001, 123 min, US, David Mirkin) *Sigourney Weaver, Jennifer Love Hewitt, Ray Liotta, Gene Hackman, Jason Lee, Anne Bancroft, Jeffrey Jones, Nora Dunn.* Max and Page, a beautiful mother and daughter con artist team portrayed by the beautiful Weaver and Hewitt, have just scored the latest in a long string of stings. The victim is the gruff Dean (Liotta), a chop-shop operator who — unknowingly duped — has dispensed $300,000 to the duo. Next, it's off to Palm Springs for these dirty rotten scoundrels, where they search for their next, rich pigeon. How they do it and what happens afterwards forms the basis for this intermittently funny con comedy, which should have been a whole lot funnier but manages to flimflam enough agreeable chuckles as to bamboozle the viewer into thinking it's better than it is. Director Mirkin gives his polished look, nearly as sparkling as his two ladies eve are glamorous, but the screenplay doesn't always hit its mark, as some of the jokes are needlessly self-conscious. But Mirkin has also assembled a game cast who know how to rise above the limitations of a script, giving seasoned performers such as Weaver, Liotta and Hackman ample room to lock their sights on a joke. They don't always succeed in finding the laugh, but when they do, *Heartbreakers* can be downright pleasing. ★★½ VHS: $102.99; DVD: $24.99

Heartburn

(1986, 108 min, US, Mike Nichols) *Jack Nicholson, Meryl Streep, Steven Hill, Richard Masur, Stockard Channing, Jeff Daniels, Maureen Stapleton, Mercedes Ruehl.* Nicholson and Streep deliver earnest performances in this faithful film version of Nora Ephron's autobiographical bestseller about a writer (Streep) who discovers that her husband (Nicholson) is having an affair both during and after her pregnancy. A grueling commentary on deception and its consequences. ★★½ VHS: $14.99

Heartland

(1979, 96 min, US, Richard Pearce) *Conchata Ferrell, Rip Torn, Lilia Skala.* Magnificent independent production set in the early 1900s about a widow (Ferrell) who heads to Wyoming to become housekeeper for a cantankerous rancher (Torn). A beautifully filmed story of pioneer life with sterling performances by Ferrell (whose film roles have been too few), Skala plays a stalwart neighbor. ★★★½ VHS: $24.99; DVD: $29.99

Hearts and Minds

(1974, 110 min, US, Peter Davis) This Oscar-winning documentary examines the American psyche in the wake of the Vietnam War. A series of heartrending interviews with veterans (and others who were sucked up into the war's madness) is intercut with some of the most horrifying footage of the war to create a brutally emotional viewing experience. ★★★★

Hearts of Darkness: A Filmmaker's Apocalypse

(1991, 96 min, US, Fax Bahr, George Hickenlooper & Eleanor Coppola) This mesmerizing documentary on the making of Francis Ford Coppola's *Apocalypse Now* was culled from over 60 hours of footage shot by Coppola's wife, Eleanor, while on location in the Philippine jungle. The film follows Coppola and crew as they wend their way up river and almost enter the eerie world of Joseph Conrad's "Heart of Darkness" themselves. Documented are all of the troubles which beset the film: Martin Sheen's near-fatal heart attack; sets being destroyed by tropical monsoons; and the delays caused when the Filipino Air Force helicopters being used as props would leave to engage in real combat with that country's Communist rebels. Coppola's quip to reporters at Cannes sums the film best, "We had access to too much money, too much equipment and we slowly went insane." ★★★½

Hearts of the West

(1975, 103 min, US, Howard Zieff) *Jeff Bridges, Andy Griffith, Alan Arkin, Blythe Danner, Donald Pleasence.* Underrated western spoof with Bridges as a farmboy who heads to Hollywood and becomes a star of grade-B cowboy movies. Arkin is hilarious as an eccentric director. ★★★ VHS: $19.99

Heat

(1995, 173 min, US, Michael Mann) *Al Pacino, Robert De Niro, Val Kilmer, Jon Voight, Tom Sizemore, Diane Verona, Amy Brenneman, Ashley Judd, Mykelti Williamson, Wes Studi, Ted Levine.* Mann's self-described "Los Angeles crime saga" features, among other pleasures, the first on-screen meeting between thespian heavyweights De Niro and Pacino. De Niro plays a cool, icily competent thief; Pacino is the weathered, equally cool L.A. homicide detective obsessed with his capture. Most of the film is a buildup to the inevitable showdown between the two men, neither of whom is willing to back down or give up. Mann's exceptional visual style shines with slickly staged chases, robberies and confrontations, making this a satisfying and moving crime drama. (VHS available letterboxed or pan & scan) ★★★ VHS: $14.99; DVD: $19.99

Heat and Dust

(1983, 131 min, GB, James Ivory) *Julie Christie, Greta Scacchi, Shashi Kapoor.* Ivory's lush and romantic tale of two British women's parallel absorption into the mystical and carnal realm of the Far East. Christie is the independent, contemporary woman tracing her roots and Scacchi makes a dazzling debut as her scandalous great aunt. ★★★

Heat & Sunlight

(1987, 98 min, US, Rob Nilsson) *Rob Nilsson.* The final 16 hours of a relationship between an aging, leather-clad photographer (Nilsson) and a beautiful young dancer is explored in this slow-moving, improvisational melodrama. Bringing new meaning to the phrase "vanity production," director Nilsson plays the brooding, jealous, obsessive man who is slow in realizing that his girlfriend is just not interested. ★½ VHS: $29.99

Heat of Desire (Plein Sud)

(1985, 91 min, France, Luc Beraud) *Clio Goldsmith, Patrick Dewaere, Guy Marchand, Jeanne Moreau.* This unexpectedly unpredictable tale of obsessive love follows university professor Dewaere as he meets sensuous siren Goldsmith and immediately throws off the life he had lived to that point. His involvement with her grows to include her shady family and an improbable scam that they are preparing. (French with English subtitles) ★★★

The Heat of the Day

(1991, 120 min, GB, Christopher Morahan) *Patricia Hodge, Michael Gambon, Michael York, Peggy Ashcroft.* Made for "Masterpiece Theatre," this romantic spy thriller, set against the backdrop of the London Blitz, stars Hodge as a middle-aged woman who is drawn into the espionage biz against her will. When a very mysterious and elusive Gambon shows up at her door and insinuates that her lover (York) is a Nazi spy, Hodge finds herself in a sticky ethical dilemma. Then, Gambon complicates things with his amorous advances. The three veteran actors breathe life into an otherwise moribund Harold Pinter screenplay. ★★½ VHS: $19.99

Heathers

(1989, 102 min, US, Michael Lehmann) *Winona Ryder, Christian Slater, Shannen Doherty, Kim Walker, Lisanne Falk.* Comedy comes no blacker than in this bitingly sharp satire on teenage suicide and murder. First-time director Lehmann and writer Daniel Waters have fashioned a refreshing antidote to all of those disgustingly sweet Brat Pack flicks that presume to tell Middle America what the white youth of today are thinking. The story revolves around three bitchy, self-obsessed beauties all named Heather who prance about their high school terrorizing the geeks and cock-teasing the jocks. Their newest member Veronica (Ryder) takes part in the pranks, but feels somehow empty until she meets J.D. (Slater), a decidedly different teen whose cool looks and demented sense of a good time propels her into a whirlwind week of murder, terrorism and funerals. When Veronica writes in her diary, "Suddenly my teenage angst has a body count," you know that this is no ordinary coming-of-age movie. (Letterboxed) ★★★★ VHS: $14.99

Heatwave

(1983, 99 min, Australia, Phillip Noyce) *Judy Davis, Chris Haywood.* Set amidst a blistering city heatwave, this complex thriller about the abuses of corporate power escalates to a stirring, nerve-shattering climax. Davis is especially good as a community organizer who opposes the uncontrolled and insensitive policies of an expansionist development company. ★★★

Heaven

(1987, 80 min, US, Diane Keaton) A lighthearted look at what lies ahead after this lifetime, from first-time director Keaton. Includes a mix of interviews and film footage addressing the subject of Heaven. ★★½ VHS: $9.99

Heaven

(1999, 95 min, US, Scott Reynolds) *Martin Donovan, Joanna Going, Richard Schiff.* In this intriguing and wholly satisfying tale of destiny and free will, Donovan plays a gambling addicted architect whose wife has left him and whose sole client is a scuzzy strip joint owner. After he befriends a clairvoyant transsexual stripper named Heaven, his life takes a very interesting turn. Fans of Steven Soderbergh's thrillers (*Out of Sight, The Limey*) will enjoy the constant flashbacks and forwards, which, while being visually engaging and clever, also build the story to an almost unbearably suspenseful climax. Slight and not very durable upon multiple viewings, *Heaven* is still an extremely enjoyable film, with excellent perfs from Donovan and character actor Schiff. ★★★ VHS: $19.99; DVD: $29.99

Heaven and Earth

(1993, 135 min, US, Oliver Stone) *Tommy Lee Jones, Hiep Thi Le, Joan Chen, Haing S. Ngor, Debbie Reynolds, Conchata Ferrell.* The third film in director Stone's Vietnam trilogy (*Platoon* and *Born on the Fourth of July*), based on the true-life perils of a Vietnamese peasant, Le Ly Hayslip (Le). Unique because this intensely melodramatic story looks at the war through the eyes of a woman, viewers will find themselves physically and emotionally drained as the film examines in minute detail the main character's trials which include torture, rape, prostitution and a failed marriage to an American G.I. (Jones). Lushly photographed and laced with fine performances by Le, Jones and Chen, this fiercely impassioned film shows another side of the Vietnam conflict with insight and understanding. ★★★ VHS: $19.99; DVD: $24.99

Heaven Can Wait

(1943, 112 min, US, Ernst Lubitsch) *Don Ameche, Gene Tierney, Charles Coburn, Marjorie Main.* Superbly entertaining comic fantasy from Lubitsch with Ameche as the recently departed, retelling the story of his youthful romantic intrigues to the Devil himself. (Not associated with the similarly titled Warren Beatty comedy.) ★★★½ VHS: $19.99

Heaven Can Wait

(1978, 101 min, US, Warren Beatty, Buck Henry) *Warren Beatty, James Mason, Julie Christie, Jack Warden, Dyan Cannon, Charles Grodin.* Beatty is in fine form as both director and star in this exceptional remake of the 1941 classic *Here Comes Mr. Jordan.* He plays a pro football player who dies before his time, and with the help of angel Mason, finds a new body to inhabit. Great supporting cast, especially Cannon and Grodin as murderous and quite excitable paramours. (Remade in 2001 as *Down to Earth*) ★★★½ VHS: $14.99; DVD: $29.99

Heaven Help Us

(1985, 104 min, US, Michael Dinner) *Andrew McCarthy, Mary Stuart Masterson, Donald Sutherland, John Heard, Kevin Dillon, Wallace Shawn, Patrick Dempsey, Stephen Geoffreys.* An above average and quite entertaining coming-of-age comedy set in a mid-1960s Brooklyn all-boys Catholic high school. The sometimes hilarious story follows the tight-knit group, each of whom is dealing with the inner turmoil of both being at the mercy of their ever-raging hormones, and being born a Catholic. In a funny turn, Geoffreys is one of the boys who just can't seem to keep "it" in his pants any longer. ★★★ VHS: $9.99

Heaven's a Drag

(1994, 96 min, GB, Peter Mackenzie Litten) *Ian Williams, Thomas Arlie.* Marketed as Britain's first gay mainstream movie, this romantic comedy about commitment, AIDS, death, mourning and recovery, though well-intentioned, disappoints on many levels. The London-set comedy is labored, the acting is shrill, and the story line shockingly familiar, seemingly lifted in chunks from such better films as *Ghost, Blithe Spirit* and *Truly, Madly, Deeply.* Stereotypical drag queen Mark (Williams) dies from AIDS but his hunky lover Simon (Arlie) seems unable to mourn his loss and proceeds to return to his life of good times, discos and anonymous sex. That is, until a "vengeful" Mark returns from the grave to offer his former lover advice — from keeping his apartment clean to expressing his true feelings. The usual "only I can see him" ghost shenanigans ensue. (aka: *To Die For*) ★½ VHS: $29.99

Heaven's Burning

(1997, 99 min, Australia, Craig Lahiff) *Russell Crowe, Youki Kudoh.* Crowe stars in this pre-*L.A. Confidential* role as the driver in a bank robbery gone wrong: to make their escape, the thieves take a hostage, a young Japanese woman (Kudoh) who has just left her husband on the last day of their honeymoon. When his cronies decide to kill the hostage, Crowe shoots one of them to save her, thus instigating an oath of vengeance from the slain lad's loony dad. With the jilted hubby and vengeful pop on their trail, Crowe and Kudoh drive through the Outback and fall in love. Their scenes are genuinely, sweetly romantic — Crowe makes a greatly appeal-

ing, chivalrous hero; and Kudoh is an incredibly cute, resilient and likable heroine. However, *Heaven's Burning* tends to be too jokey and mean-spirited at times. There's an amusing cameo by Colin Hay, formerly of seminal '80s band Men at Work. ★★½ VHS: $14.99; DVD: $24.99

Heaven's Gate

(1980, 220 min, US, Michael Cimino) *Kris Kristofferson, Jeff Bridges, Isabelle Huppert, Joseph Cotten, Christopher Walken.* Whadda you care how much this notorious $50 million bomb cost? It costs the same to rent as any of Corman's two-day wonders. Cimino lavishes his attention on the evolution of the community of Heaven's Gate — from its rough and tumble mining town origins to that of a full-blown city, as civilization begins to tame the wild frontier. ★★ VHS: $24.99; DVD: $19.99

Heaven's Prisoners

(1996, 126 min, US, Phil Joanou) *Alec Baldwin, Mary Stuart Masterson, Kelly Lynch, Eric Roberts, Teri Hatcher, Vondie Curtis-Hall.* A troubled, recovering-alcoholic ex-cop (Baldwin) and his wife (Lynch) enter a hazy world of drug trafficking, cover-up and disloyalty when a small plane crashes into the Bayou not far from their boat. The only survivor is a very young Salvadorian refugee, whom the couple take into their home. As the story progresses, layers of deceit are peeled away. Baldwin's attempts to secure the orphaned girl's safety lead him too close to the activities of a drug-smuggling ring, placing those closest to him in imminent danger. Though overly long, the film adroitly defines a mood of despondency and captures the feel of the Louisiana Bayou. ★★½ VHS: $14.99

Heavenly Creatures

(1994, 99 min, New Zealand, Peter Jackson) *Melanie Lynskey, Kate Winslet, Sarah Peirse.* The provocative, imaginative true-life story of how the intense and passionate relationship of 1950s teenagers Pauline Parker and Juliet Hulme led to the grisly murder of Pauline's mother. The film realistically and fantastically portrays the friendship of the teens with Lynskey and Winslet giving outstanding and believable performances as Pauline and Juliet, respectively. The parents of both teens worry about their daughters' "unnatural" relationship and things go terribly wrong when they are eventually separated. Only one solution remains for the two friends. Director Jackson endows the film with such vision and substance (in addition to some amazing special effects) that the viewer is easily and quickly drawn into the lives of the lead characters. It's the most thrilling story of matricide since *Psycho.* Of interest: After serving time, Juliet became a best-selling murder mystery author using the name Anne Perry. ★★★★

Heavens Above

(1963, 105 min, GB, John & Roy Boulting) *Peter Sellers, Cecil Parker, Isabel Jeans, Ian Carmichael.* Sellers displays his usual comic genius as an idealistic and naive young vicar who is accidentally assigned to a small country parish. When, upon arriving, he is met with a less-than-Christian zeal by the townsfolk, he cheerfully sets out to breed a healthier atmosphere — much to the chagrin of the local power structure. This scathing satire pointedly accuses the Anglican church of acquiescing to the establishment. The film's only drawback is its somewhat heavy-handed Christian message. ★★★½

Heavy

(1996, 105 min, US, James Mangold) *Pruitt Taylor Vince, Liv Tyler, Shelley Winters, Deborah Harry, Evan Dando, Joe Grifasi.* Like a more modest "*Marty* for the '90s," *Heavy* is a nicely observed, small slice-of-lifer, set mostly in an out-of-the-way greasy spoon in upstate New York, about the unrequited love between an overweight cook and a beautiful new waitress. Vince is excellent as Victor, the terribly shy but good-hearted mama's boy who dreams of both becoming a gourmet chef and having a relationship with the very appealing Callie (Tyler). Director Mangold captures many telling details that ring true — the silly, insecure gestures and childish fantasies we have when we're pining after someone seemingly unattainable. Many things in *Heavy* feel truthful — the dreary, small town atmosphere, for example, is spot on, but stops short of becoming oppressive. Though not as rich in character as one would want, Mangold makes a strong debut with this moody tale, and gets terrific performances from his cast. ★★★ VHS: $19.99; DVD: $27.99

Heavy Metal

(1981, 93 min, Canada, Gerald Potterton) *Voices of Richard Romanus, John Candy, Eugene Levy, Joe Flaherty.* An animated anthology film, *Heavy Metal* is a series of fantasy and sci-fi tales which have the common theme of breasts, broadswords, badass aliens and bodacious rock 'n' roll. Source of countless adolescent erotic fantasies, the film's animation is primitive compared to contemporary works, but its nostalgic charm and historical value are hard to deny. The segments range from the terrific ("B17" and Richard Corben's "Den") and funny ("So Beautiful, So Dangerous" and Berni Wrightson's "Captain Sternn") to the overlong ("Taarna") and trite ("Harry Canyon"). The best rely on animation and music to tell the story, rather than dialogue. *Heavy Metal* is a sexy, gory, violent, fun-filled ride whose qualities will not diminish on repeated viewing. ★★★ VHS: $14.99; DVD: $27.99

Heavy Metal 2000

(2000, 88 min, US, Michel Lemire & Michael Coldewey) *Voices of Michael Ironside, Julie Strain, Billy Idol.* A belated sequel to the 1981 cult hit, *Heavy Metal 2000* rates as a major disappointment. Periodically announced throughout the years as another anthology film, but this time mixing live action and animation, *HM2000* arrives as a fully animated, single-story film. The odd, much-sought-after glowy power thingy (the chamber of immortality) from the first film is the impetus for a snoozer story involving a bad guy (voiced by Ironside) being chased on a quest for vengeance by a hot chick. Punctuated by some fun gore and violence, the dull story meanders along with very little imagination. Animation buffs may want to watch this, but casual viewers should stay far away. ★½ VHS: $14.99; DVD: $24.99

Heavy Petting

(1989, 85 min, US, Obie Benz) *David Byrne, Sandra Bernhard, Ann Magnuson, Josh Mostel, Laurie Anderson, Spalding Grey.* Amusing and entertaining satire on our country's repression of and obsession with sex; chronicling those "innocent" days (when "good girls didn't") with clips from '50s "B" movies and with funny, insightful and occasionally stupid anecdotes. ★★★ VHS: $19.99

Heavy Traffic

(1973, 77 min, US, Ralph Bakshi) Animator Bakshi's most ambitious project of his early career, this boldly original and revolutionary work combines live-action and animation to

Hedd Wyn

tell the story of a New York youth who escapes the confines of his surroundings by drawing the people around him — creating a devastating portrait of the underside of city life. Rated X. ★★★ VHS: $14.99; DVD: $19.99

Hedd Wyn

(1995, 123 min, Wales, Paul Turner) *Huw Garmon, Sue Roderick, Judith Humphries, Phil Reid.* From a country where poets are revered as much as sports figures are in America comes this handsome and affecting film based on a true story. Told in a series of flashbacks remembered by a soldier wounded in battle in WWI, *Hedd Wyn* recounts the story of Ellis, a young farmer living with his large family in an impoverished Welsh village whose talent for prose has made him somewhat of a local celebrity. As he pursues the local lasses with religious fervor, Ellis — whose pen name is Hedd Wyn — tries to accomplish a poet's highest honor — winning a chair for poetry. While most of the story concentrates on Ellis' romantic and literary agendas, the film also reflects upon the Welsh tradition and speaks to the misfortunes of war (for both soldier and family left behind) in a series of carefully detailed battle scenes. Hedd Wyn's poetry frames the story which manages to also comment on the author's life. Garmon, a good-looking and efficient actor, brings to Ellis a good-natured charm. (Welsh with English subtitles) ★★★ VHS: $19.99

Hedda

(1975, 100 min, GB, Trevor Nunn) *Glenda Jackson, Timothy West, Jennie Linden, Peter Eyre, Patrick Stewart.* Jackson dominates this powerful film version of Henrik Ibsen's classic play "Hedda Gabler." Taken directly from the Royal Shakespeare Company's stage rendition, Jackson's Hedda is a Nordic femme fatale — a neurotic, iron-willed controller who is nevertheless alluring to the local men. ★★★

Heidi

(1937, 88 min, US, Allan Dwan) *Shirley Temple, Jean Hersholt, Arthur Treacher.* Little Shirley shines as the young Swiss girl taken away from her loving grandfather. ★★★

The Heidi Chronicles

(1995, 94 min, US, Paul Bogart) *Jamie Lee Curtis, Tom Hulce, Kim Cattrall.* Based on a play by Wendy Wasserstein (who also wrote this made-for-cable adaptation), this bittersweet drama chronicles the maturation of art historian Heidi Holland (Curtis), a tirelessly average woman naïvely caught up in the politics and fads of American life. The story begins with her high school prom in the early 1960s and then fastforwards her through the hippie and antiwar periods, the feminist decade of the '70s, and the '80s "Me Generation." Through the years, she sets forth on a voyage of self-discovery, though to her regret she doesn't always find the most satisfactory romances. Curtis gives a pleasing performance as the sometimes hapless Heidi. Hulce gives a solid performance in support as Heidi's gay friend Peter, who approaches his complex character with good humor and a level-headedness. ★★★ VHS: $14.99

Heidi Fleiss: Hollywood Madam

(1995, 106 min, US, Nick Broomfield) This weirdly funny, satirical documentary — a perhaps unintentional parody of the exploitative TV newsmagazines whose clips it uses — is the perfect vehicle for this tale of Hollywood's swarmy excesses. The film concentrates on convicted panderer Heidi Fleiss' relationships with Ivan Nagy, her lover, nemesis and alleged pimp; and Madam Alex, Hollywood's grand madam for 20 years and Heidi's one-time employer and mentor. Each of the three refutes allegations from the other two, yet they all seem inextricably linked. Wickedly enjoyable yet ultimately unsettling, it demonstrates wretched excess permeates every aspect of this latest entry into the annals of Babylon. You'll feel the need to bathe after viewing. ★★★ VHS: $14.99

Held Up

(2000, 88 min, US, Steve Rash) *Jamie Foxx, Nia Long, Barry Corbin, John Cullum, Jake Busey, Eduardo Yañez.* A moronic "action-comedy" about a loud-mouthed idiot (Foxx) whose macho-man antics cost him his new car, his girlfriend (Long, in a wasted role), and nearly his life. This feeble attempt at screwball comedy is never funny even once, and will be a major disappointment to anyone expecting the comic agility displayed by Foxx in "In Living Color." ★ VHS: $14.99; DVD: $24.99

Hell Comes to Frogtown

(1988, 86 min, US, R.J. Kizer) *Roddy Piper, Sandahl Bergman, Rory Calhoun.* Enjoyable low-budget sci-fi adventure starring Piper as a post-apocalyptic mercenary (and one of the few remaining fertile men) who must rescue a group of similarly potent women. ★★½ VHS: $9.99

H

Hell in the Pacific

(1968, 103 min, US, John Boorman) *Lee Marvin, Toshiro Mifune.* Director Boorman takes a microcosm of WWII and extrapolates a parable on the insanity of war. An American and a Japanese soldier find themselves washed up on a deserted island in the Pacific. Their mutual dependence necessitates the suppression of their hostilities. Both Marvin and Mifune are superb, managing to be both ethnic representatives and universal Everymen. Boorman directs with a sure hand. (Letterboxed) ★★★½ VHS: $14.99; DVD: $14.99

Hell Is for Heroes

(1962, 90 min, US, Don Siegel) *Steve McQueen, Bobby Darin, Harry Guardino, James Coburn, Nick Adams, Bob Newhart.* A fine cast of young actors is featured in this taut WWII drama about a small American company caught behind enemy lines. ★★★ VHS: $14.99; DVD: $29.99

Hell Up in Harlem

(1973, 96 min, US, Larry Cohen) *Fred Williamson, Julius W. Harris, Margaret Avery.* Williamson sets out, in his own annihilating way, to make the ghetto safe from detestable murderers and druggies in this entertainingly violent sequel to *Black Caesar*. One of the best scenes features black maids force-feeding soul food to Mafia children. ★★ VHS: $9.99

Hell's Angels on Wheels

(1967, 95 min, US, Richard Rush) *Jack Nicholson, Adam Roarke.* Four bikers tangle with rival roadies and local thugs. A young Nicholson plays a brooding gas station attendant named Poet who discovers the joys of a hog. Trashy biker pic still manages to entertain in a guilty pleasure sort of way. ★★

Hellbound: Hellraiser II

(1988, 97 min, GB, Tony Randel) *Ashley Laurence, Clare Higgins.* With this extremely gruesome sequel, British author Clive Barker continues to redefine the modern horror genre. Picking up where the original left off, Kirsty wakes up in a mental hospital. Intent on saving her father's damned soul, she enlists the help of a fellow patient, and together they descend into the bowels of Hell. Very graphic and violent — not suggested for the faint-hearted. (Sequel: *Hellraiser 3: Hell on Earth*) ★★★ VHS: $14.99

Hello, Dolly!

(1969, 146 min, US, Gene Kelly) *Barbra Streisand, Walter Matthau, Tommy Tune, Michael Crawford, Louis Armstrong.* Streisand shines in this elaborate and entertaining screen version of the hit Broadway musical comedy. Streisand plays turn-of-the-century matchmaker Dolly Levi, who sets her own sights on grocery store owner Horace Vandergelder (the agreeably gruff Matthau). There are wonderful dance numbers, and a whimsical score by Jerry Herman. Though some of the production is rather overblown, it detracts nothing from the film's enjoyment. Based on Thornton Wilder's comedy, "The Matchmaker." ★★★½

Hellraiser

(1987, 93 min, GB, Clive Barker) *Andrew Robinson, Clare Higgins, Ashley Laurence.* Barker's riveting directorial debut is unquestionably one of the most serious and intelligent horror films

in recent memory. Told from the perspective of Kirsty, our teenage heroine, this phantasmagorical tale of gruesome family secrets finds its beginnings with her Uncle Frank, a sinister sensualist who cracks the code of a mysterious Chinese puzzle box and thereby opens the door to another dimension. Through this threshold come the dreaded Cenobites (led by the menacing Pinhead), a punked-out crew of otherworldly sadists with a penchant for ripped flesh and steaming entrails. (Sequel: *Hellbound: Hellraiser II*) ★★★½ VHS: $14.99; DVD: $29.99

Hellraiser: Bloodline

(1996, 90 min, US, Alan Smithee) *Doug Bradley.* Makeup effects artist Kevin Yagher originally conceived and directed this fourth installment in the *Hellraiser* series as a three-part anthology film, showing the various problems that people throughout the ages have gotten into when they irresponsibly play with a Lament Configuration (the infamous puzzle box of the inventor Lemarchand). Studio executives, however, decided to re-edit the film into a linear narrative with flashbacks. Primarily set in the future, the film is now about the current Lemarchand's attempt to destroy Pinhead forever. While undoubtedly better in its original form, the studio version has its moments of interest and terror—it is still fascinating to see *Hellraiser* stories set in 19th century France and in a space station in the future. Mildly atmospheric and definitely better than the third installment of the series (*Hellraiser 3 — Hell on Earth*), *Bloodline* is worth a die-hard horror fan's passing glance, but no more. ★★ VHS: $14.99

Hellraiser: Inferno

(2000, 99 min, US, Scott Derrickson) *Craig Sheffer, Nicholas Turturro, James Remar, Doug Bradley.* The awful *Hellraiser: Inferno* is only a reminder of a better time when horror films were truly frightening and their cheap-ass knockoff sequels at least had *chapter numbers* in the titles. In case you're counting, *Inferno* is the fifth installment of the goth-horror series spawned by Clive Barker. Iconic boogeyman Pinhead pops up in a mere cameo in a yawningly uninspired tale of a bad cop who unlocks the mysterious puzzle box and takes a mind-bending plunge into Hell. Cheap production values and brittle performances wreck an already lousy script, resulting in a movie so devoid of surprise and tension it's no wonder it was condemned straight to video. Another horror series officially bites the dust. ★ VHS: $14.99; DVD: $32.99

Help!

(1965, 90 min, GB, Richard Lester) *John Lennon, Paul McCartney, George Harrison, Ringo Starr, Leo McKern, Eleanor Bron, Victor Spinetti.* It's hard to top a masterpiece. Lester and The Beatles united again in this attempt to recapture the madcap brilliance of *A Hard Day's Night*, and while the effort is a decidedly good one, it falls short of its predecessor. Still, any fan of The Beatles or Lester's slap-dash comic style will revel in this rockin' romp. ★★★½

Helter Skelter

(1976, 119 min, US, Tom Gries) *Steve Railsback, Nancy Wolfe, George DiCenzo.* Based on the best-selling novel by prosecuting attorney Vincent Bugliosi, this exceptional made-for-TV movie is

Pinhead in *Hellraiser*

a truly disturbing docu-drama about Charles Manson and his family of disciples. Railsback's intense portrayal of Charlie is stunning. ★★★½

Henessey

(1957, 103 min, GB, Don Sharp) *Rod Steiger, Lee Remick, Trevor Howard.* Steiger stars in this high-paced political thriller as an Irish demolitions expert who sets out to avenge his daughter's death by bombing the Parliament on opening day — when the Royal Family attends. The action gets hot when both the IRA and the British Secret Service try to stop him. ★★★ VHS: $19.99

Henry V

(1946, 137 min, GB, Laurence Olivier) *Laurence Olivier, Robert Newton, Leslie Banks, Renee Asherson.* A stirring version of Shakespeare's historical drama. Olivier directed as well as stars as the heroic king who fights for his kingdom in France. Filmed in Technicolor, Olivier introduces the viewer to his play on film by opening with an impressive aerial shot of a re-creation of London's 17th-century Globe Theatre. ★★★★ DVD: $39.99

Henry V

(1989, 137 min, GB, Kenneth Branagh) *Kenneth Branagh, Ian Holm, Paul Scofield, Derek Jacobi, Brian Blessed, Alec McCowan, Judi Dench, Michael Maloney, Emma Thompson.* Branagh's astonishing directorial debut remakes Shakespeare's classic which Laurence Olivier had all but stamped his name upon. Everything about this film works. Branagh delivers a bravura performance as the young King Henry which is nothing short of inspirational. His supporting cast is as good as they come. Branagh's direction is crisp and clean, his command of the dialogue is perfect and he masterfully works Shakespeare's subtle sense of humor into the movie. ★★★★ VHS: $14.99; DVD: $19.99

Henry Fool

(1998, 137 min, US, Hal Hartley) *Thomas Jay Ryan, Parker Posey, James Urbaniak, Maria Porter.* Can a lying con man be a mentor to a repressed sanitation worker? Henry Fool (Ryan) rents a room in the unhappy household of Simon Grim (Urbaniak), a young man ridiculed by clinically depressed mom Mary (Porter), slutty sister Fay (Posey) and an assortment of neighborhood toughs. Henry assumes control of these lives teetering between pointlessness and dispair, mixing unabashed admiration for Simon's poetry with tales of high adventure in South American jungles. Resistance to Henry's influence is never a consideration for Simon, whose unabating sense of futility is for once pushed aside by glimmerings of self-worth. Bringing his characters to the edge of caricature, director Hartley uses their particular idiosyncrasies to make broader statements about American cultural anomalies. ★★★ VHS: $24.99

Henry IV

(1985, 94 min, Italy, Marco Bellocchio) *Marcello Mastroianni, Claudia Cardinale.* Driven mad by unrequited love, a man (Mastroianni) spends 20 years believing himself to be a medieval emperor. A finely crafted tale of passion and illusion from Nobel Prize—winner Luigi Pirandello. (Italian with English subtitles) ★★★

Henry: Portrait of a Serial Killer

(1986, 105 min, US, John McNaughton) *Michael Rooker, Tracy Arnold, Tom Towles.* Initially dismissed by its producers as not having enough blood and action to please the *Friday the 13th* horror crowd, this harrowing portrait of a psychotic killer was not successful until the art audience discovered it. Henry, recently released from prison for killing his mother, moves in with his old buddy Otis and his sister, Becky. Henry soon resumes his random killings, eventually initiating a more-than-willing Otis in his frenzied rampages. The real horror in the film is not the actual killings, but rather in the sympathetic and non-judgmental approach the film takes as it follows Henry on his cooly detached and senseless pursuit of death. ★★★ VHS: $19.99; DVD: $24.99

Hercules

(1959, 107 min, Italy, Pietro Francisci) *Steve Reeves, Sylvia Koscina.* Muscleman Reeves stars in this sleek adventure film as the Greek hero Hercules. The film which started the "gladiator" genre which was so popular in the early '60s. ★★½

Hercules

(1997, 93 min, US, John Musker, Ron Clements) *Voices of Danny DeVito, Tate Donovan, James Woods, Bobcat Goldthwait, Paul Shaffer, Rip Torn, Charlton Heston.* While this Disney animated feature doesn't come close to matching the magical splendor of the studio's best classics, *Hercules* is brisk, breezy fun. The animation is a bit clunky, despite the liberal use of computer-enhanced effects, and the songs are downright forgettable (something that has characterized *Pocahontas* and *Hunchback of*

Notre Dame which came before this), but the instrumental score is strong, and the vocal contributions are top-notch — including Torn as Zeus, Donovan as Herc, and, in a standout bit of cheerful malevolence, Woods as Hades, the leader of the Underworld. ★★★ VHS: $22.99; DVD: $29.99

Hercules in New York

(1970, 91 min, US, Arthur Allan Seidelman) *Arnold Schwarzenegger, Arnold Stang.* Schwarzenegger's film debut finds him pitted against Stang in a grade-Z *Clash of the Titans*-like production. The picture cuts between New York and Mt. Olympus (actually a mound of rock in Central Park) as Arnie disobeys Zeus' order not to hang out with mortals. The spectacular production values in this one might have even cost as much as $100. Yes, it's trash, but hey, you must admit, this is the ultimate Saturday night party tape as well as a prime candidate for "Mystery Science Theater 3000." ★ VD: $19.99

Herdsmen of the Sun

(1988, 52 min, France, Werner Herzog) Narrated in English by director Herzog, this fascinating, anthropologic documentary focuses on the Woodabes, a Saharan nomadic tribe. The highlight of the film is the strange mating ceremony staged by the young male members, all with exotically handsome, mesmeric features, who don fancy dress and elaborate makeup for an unusual beauty pageant that is judged by the women of the tribe. ★★★ VHS: $24.99

Here Comes Mr. Jordan

(1941, 93 min, US, Alexander Hall) *Robert Montgomery, Claude Rains, James Gleason, Evelyn Keyes, Edward Everett Horton.* Classic supernatural comedy with Montgomery in a splendid performance as a boxer who dies before his time; forced to look for another body to inhabit with the help of heavenly Mr. Jordan (Rains). Special mention goes to Gleason as Montgomery's exasperated coach. (Remade in 1978 as *Heaven Can Wait* and in 2001 as *Down to Earth*) ★★★½ VHS: $19.99

Here on Earth

(2000, 97 min, US, Mark Piznarski) *Chris Klein, Leelee Sobieski, Josh Hartnett, Bruce Greenwood, Annette O'Toole, Michael Rooker.* A teen *Love Story*, without much story, this near-nauseating romantic drama is enough to put anyone off romance at least into the next century. When his drag racing leads to a local diner burning to the ground, an affluent high school student (Klein) must spend the summer helping rebuild it. There he falls for the owner's daughter (Sobieski), already involved with the other drag racer (Hartnett). By-the-numbers characters populate this turgid triangle, and even though its cast has done good work elsewhere, there's zero chemistry between any of the leads. ★ VHS: $14.99; DVD: $24.99

Hero

(1992, 112 min, US, Stephen Frears) *Dustin Hoffman, Geena Davis, Andy Garcia, John Cusack, Tom Arnold, Chevy Chase, Kevin J. O'Connor.* There's a lot to like,

and a lot to digest, in Frears' satire on heroism and the media. Hoffman returns to Ratso Rizzo territory with a glorious slimy performance as a petty crook who, in spite of himself, rescues a planeload of passengers after an aircraft crashes right in front of him. One of those he saves is TV reporter Davis, who turns the city topsy-turvy looking for the "hero" who vanished into the night. When a substantial award is offered for him to come forward, onto the scene comes grifter and too-good-to-be-true Garcia. Not getting his due, Hoffman tries to convince anyone who will listen that he really is the hero, but no one will believe him. ★★★ VHS: $14.99; DVD: $24.99

Heroes Shed No Tears

(1985, 93 min, Hong Kong, John Woo) *Eddy Ko, Lam Ching Ying, Phillip Loffrede.* Ko plays a mercenary sent to retrieve a wanted druglord from Thailand and bring him back to Hong Kong. He captures the general safely, but things go badly when he and his men try to escape the jungle. Not only are the general's men after him, but Ko is soon the object of vengeance of a mad colonel (Lam, in a terrific turn as the villain). Distinguished mainly by the excellent end fight scene between Ko and Lam, the remainder of the film is a by-the-books action flick. None of Woo's trademarks are evident in any abundance, but it's worth watching. (Cantonese with English subtitles) ★★½ VHS: $19.99

The Heroic Trio

(1993, 87 min, Hong Kong, Ching Siu-Tung & Johnny To) *Anita Mui, Michelle Yeoh, Maggie Cheung, Anthony Wong, Damien Lau.* Only the wild world of Hong Kong action cinema could have produced this dizzying comic book-style movie about three female superheroes and their battle against an androgynous demon which is trying to breed a new, evil emperor of China. Mui is the mask-wearing Wonder Woman, who runs across electrical power lines and throws razor-sharp darts into her foes. The astonishing Yeoh is the kung fu mistress Invisible Girl, who is at first allied with the demon, but who soon learns she has a mysterious past connection with Wonder Woman. Cheung plays Thief Catcher, a motorcycle-riding, shotgun-toting, leather-clad tough chick who only does good when the pay is right. An outrageous, colorful and campy romp, *Heroic Trio* is cinema for the sheer fun of it, with flying heroes/heroines and villains and gravity-defying fight scenes. (Cantonese with English subtitles) (Sequel: *Executioners*) ★★★ VHS: $19.99; DVD: $29.99

Hester Street

(1975, 90 min, US, Joan Micklin Silver) *Carol Kane, Steven Keats, Doris Roberts.* The first feature by Silver weaves a rich tapestry of ghetto life in New York City's Bowery at the turn of the century. Kane was given a well-deserved Academy Award nomination for her performance as Gilt, a Jewish émigré trying to assimilate as quietly as possible into her new country while still being supportive of her husband as he experiences a cultural identity crisis. ★★★ VHS: $29.99

Hexed

(1993, 91 min, US, Alan Spencer) *Arye Gross, Claudia Christian, R. Lee Ermey.* Gross stars as a nerdish hotel clerk who fancies himself a trendy

Lawrence Olivier's *Henry V*

H

The Hidden Fortress

big-wig. Telling fellow workers of his famous (albeit ficticious) associations with celebs, he's put to the test when one of them shows up at the hotel. She's a model with secrets of her own — one of them being that she's a murderess. Too bad she didn't take aim at the script. Director-writer Spencer tries to create a frantic farce in the mistaken identity, door-slamming tradition; what he gives life to, however, Dr. Frankenstein wouldn't lay claim to. ★ VHS: $14.99

Hey Babu Riba

(1986, 109 min, Yugoslavia, Jovan Acin) *Gala Videnovic, Nebojsa Bakocevic.* Set in 1950s Yugoslavia, this charming and funny film recounts the days of innocence of four close friends and rowing partners who all fall in love with the same girl, their beautiful blonde coxswain. The young girl, flattered by all of the attention, likes them all and wishes to remain friends but rejects their advances only to unwisely fall in love with an ambitious member of the Communist Party. A decidedly different coming-of-age film: one that explores the tender pain of first love and the bonds of loyal friendship, yet set against the political turmoil of a recently formed Communist government. (Serbo-Croatian with English subtitles) ★★★½ VHS: $19.99

Hi, Mom!

(1970, 87 min, US, Brian De Palma) *Robert De Niro, Charles Durnham, Allen Garfield, Lara Parker, Jennifer Salt.* Anarchy reigns in De Palma's frenzied sequel to *Greetings.* De Niro stars as a returning Vietnam vet who takes on the roles of urban guerrilla, porno filmmaker and insurance salesman. Add to the fray a spoof of 1970s "encounter theater" called "Be Black Baby," in which a group of black militants terrorize their white audience, and you've got a loopy and totally frantic vision of New York at the height of the counterculture generation. ★★★ VHS: $14.99

The Hidden

(1987, 98 min, US, Jack Sholder) *Kyle MacLachlan, Michael Nouri, Clu Gulager.* Alien MacLachlan gives L.A. cop Nouri a hand in capturing an incredibly violence-prone extraterrestrial hiding out in the bodies of various citizens. Stylish, clever and full of action. (Sequel: *The Hidden 2*) ★★★ VHS: $14.99; DVD: $24.99

The Hidden 2

(1994, 91 min, US, Seth Pinsker) *Raphael Sbarge, Kate Hodge, Jovin Montanaro.* Fans of the 1987 cult fave have little to cheer in this unworthy sequel that features none of the original cast and none of the originality. This time around, Sbarge stars as an alien cop sent to Earth as backup to stop the original alien from reproducing and turning the world into a party planet (darn!). Though it's as bad as it sounds, it may be worth a look for fans of the horror genre. ★★ VHS: $14.99

Hidden Agenda

(1990, 106 min, GB, Ken Loach) *Brian Cox, Frances McDormand, Brad Dourif, Mai Zetterling.* Based on an amalgamation of actual scandals, this fictionalized account of official corruption in Northern Ireland is a superb addition to the already substantial library of British films which explore the machinations of the "secret" government. The tightly woven thread of intrigue begins when an American civil rights activist (Dourif) is assassinated in Belfast. McDormand and Cox are both excellent as, respectively, Dourif's girlfriend and an incorruptible Scotland Yard detective who together uncover the biggest political scandal since Watergate and Iran/Contra. ★★★½ VHS: $14.99

The Hidden Fortress

(1958, 139 min, Japan, Akira Kurosawa) *Toshiro Mifune, Misa Vehara.* One of Kurosawa's most entertaining works, *The Hidden Fortress* concerns a shrewd general (Mifune) attempting to smuggle a petulant princess and her treasure trove of gold through enemy territory. Augmented by a bungling pair of peasants, the divergent group

encounters enough hair-raising obstacles to sap the power of a light saber. Much in evidence is Kurosawa's sense of humor, largely embodied by Mifune's warrior who flails, cajoles and berates his ragtag crew. The inspiration for *Star Wars.* (Letterboxed version) (Japanese with English subtitles) ★★★½ VHS: $29.99; DVD: $29.99

Hidden Pleasures (Los Placeres Ocultos)

(1977, 95 min, Spain, Eloy de la Iglesia) Spain's first openly gay film is an impassioned drama about a closeted bank director who prowls the street of Madrid in search of male teenage prostitutes. His life is changed after he meets and falls in love with a straight young man. The controlled, placid surface of their relationship is shattered by contradictory and sometimes violent interplay concerning differences of class, intellect and convention. (Spanish with English subtitles) ★★★ VHS: $69.99

Hide and Seek

(1980, 90 min, Israel, Dan Wolman) *Gila Almagor, Doron Tavori.* A study of adolescents in the throes of self-discovery, this film explores the sensitive issue of forbidden love. Set in the late 1940s, the crucial years before the birth of the state of Israel, the film deals with the youthful quests and adjurations of a generation which would become the backbone of the new nation. (Hebrew with English subtitles) ★★★

Hide and Seek

(1999, 100 min, US, Sidney J. Furie) *Daryl Hannah, Jennifer Tilly, Bruce Greenwood, Vincent Gallo.* An ugly, uncomfortable hostage thriller, *Hide and Seek* is a ill-fated cross between *Misery* and *The Hand That Rocks the Cradle.* Ann (Hannah) is kidnapped by Frank (Gallo) and Helen (Tilly), an unhinged couple who want the baby Ann is carrying. Chained in the basement of an isolated farmhouse, Ann tries repeatedly, and unsuccesfully, to escape at any opportunity. Meanwhile, Ann's husband, Jack (Greenwood), searches for his wife, meeting frustration at every turn. Hannah suffers nobly in her role, but it is the sleazy Gallo and the extremely annoying Tilly that ham it up in this tense yet ridiculous film that ruins whatever potential this sick story had. ★★ VHS: $79.99; DVD: $24.99

Hide in Plain Sight

(1980, 98 min, US, James Caan) *James Caan, Jill Eikenberry, Robert Viharo, Kenneth McMillan, Danny Aiello.* Caan makes an impressive directorial debut with this based-on-fact story about a divorced man (Caan) who loses his children when his ex-wife's husband is relocated after testifying against the mob. ★★★ VHS: $19.99

Hideaway

(1995, 112 min, US, Brett Leonard) *Jeff Goldblum, Christine Lahti, Alicia Silverstone, Jeremy Sisto.* Goldblum stars in this uneventful thriller about a man who returns from the brink of death with the ability to see through the eyes of a serial killer (Sisto). Good thing, too, because the killer's next victim is: (ta-da!) Goldblum's daughter (Silverstone). Dean R. Koontz's best-selling novel is reduced to pop/psychobabble drivel centering around Goldblum's need to make amends for the accidental death of his youngest daughter by risking everything to save his eldest. ★½ VHS: $14.99; DVD: $24.99

Hideous Kinky

(1999, 99 min, GB, Gilles MacKinnon) *Kate Winslet, Saïd Taghmaoui, Bella Riza, Carrie Mullen.* Based on the best-selling novel by Esther Freud (a descendant of Sigmund), this sumptuously shot though emotionally distant memory piece looks at the bohemian existence and spiritual journey of a British expatriate in early-1970s Marrakech. Winslet gives a lovely performance as Julia, who — with her two young daughters in tow — has left the dreary trappings of London for the warm desert and spiritual possibilities of Morocco. Though based on the novel by the youngest child, the story is seen through Julia's eyes, which may explain why Julia is such an enigmatic character. Director MacKinnon understands the precious relationship between mother and daughters, but the film suffers somewhat from its lack of passion and uneven pacing. ★★½ VHS: $14.99; DVD: $27.99

Hiding Out

(1987, 98 min, US, Bob Giraldi) *Jon Cryer, Keith Coogan, Annabeth Gish.* Cryer's likable performance is the sole reason to see this amiable though lifeless comedy about a stockbroker who masquerades as a high school senior to hide from the mob. ★★

The Hiding Place

(1975, 145 min, US, James F. Collier) *Julie Harris, Eileen Heckert, Arthur O'Connell.* A moving true story about a Dutch family sent to a German concentration camp for hiding Jews during WWII. Produced by Billy Graham's Evangelistic Association, the film, though overtly religious, is not in any way "preachy" — and presents an unrelenting view of camp life. Good performances from the entire cast. ★★★ VHS: $19.99

High and Low

(1962, 142 min, Japan, Akira Kurosawa) *Toshiro Mifune, Kyoko Kagawa, Tatsuya Mihashi, Takashi Shimura.* This carefully paced thriller by Kurosawa stars Mifune as a business executive who is forced to pay ransom to kidnappers who mistakenly stole his chauffeur's son. Adapted from the Ed McBain novel "King's Ransom," Kurosawa vividly captures the extent to which Mifune, an innocent bystander, has to accept responsibility for the actions of the repellent kidnappers. (Letterboxed) (Japanese with English subtitles) ★★★½ VHS: $29.99; DVD: $39.99

High Anxiety

(1977, 94 min, US, Mel Brooks) *Mel Brooks, Harvey Korman, Cloris Leachman, Madeline Kahn, Ron Carey, Howard Morris.* Perceptive Hitchcock spoof from director Brooks about a psychiatrist (Brooks) who becomes the new chief of an asylum with murderously funny results. Korman and Leachman are wonderful as kinky co-conspirators, and Kahn delectably brings to life the "icy blonde" persona of a 1930s namesake, Madeleine Carroll. Great fun for playing "spot the plot" with Hitchcock scholars. ★★★ VHS: $9.99

High Art

(1998, 102 min, US, Lisa Cholodenko) *Ally Sheedy, Radha Mitchell, Patricia Clarkson, Tammy Grimes, Bill Sage.* Faulty plumbing in a Soho walk-up leads to a chance encounter between an ambitious assistant editor at a photography magazine and a once-prominent photographer, back in New York after a decade in Berlin. As the photographer Lucy, Sheedy is a glistening, jagged edge in an almost sonambulent environment, snorting smack with her ex-Fassbinder-actress lover and other denizens of her free-falling coterie. Mitchell, as the newly minted assistant editor Syd, is luminous and arresting as she tests her wings in the turbulence of the casual duplicities of the artistically evolved. Syd and Lucy develop a true bond; but it is no match for the realities of the world they inhabit. Director Cholodenko stays one step back in observation, utilizing subtle, sharply etched performances. Syd receives first-hand experience of art and artist as disposable products for mass consumption. High art, indeed. ★★★ VHS: $14.99

High Fidelity

(2000, 113 min, US, Stephen Frears) *John Cusack, Iben Hjejle, Jack Black, Todd Louiso, Lisa Bonet, Joan Cusack, Catherine Zeta-Jones, Tim Robbins, Sara Gilbert, Lili Taylor, Natasha Gregson Wagner.* A scintillating, often hilarious look at relationships, regrets and LPs. Based on the novel by Nick Hornby, and adapted by Cusack, D.V. DeVincentis, Steve Pink and Scott Rosenberg, *High Fidelity* maneuvers through the sometimes murky waters of modern romance with comic agility and uncommon insight. Cusack is Rob, a record shop owner in Chicago, who reexamines his life after his girlfriend (the very appealing Hjejle) leaves him. Prone to evaluating anything and everything of importance in iconoclastic top five lists (that any pop culture maven would have to love), Rob sets out to discover just what happened in the top five break-ups of his life. Cusack is at his absolute best, giving Rob just the right balance of geeky hipster and angst-ridden romantic. Frears elicits natural, canny performances from the entire ensemble, who are fortunate enough to have such an intuitive, witty screenplay from which to work. There's lots of reasons to see *High Fidelity*, but the top five: 1) Cusack's great turn 2) a smart screenplay 3) what it has to say about men, women and relationships 4) perceptive direction and 5) it's just so damn funny. ★★★★ VHS: $14.99; DVD: $32.99

High Heels

(1972, 100 min, France, Claude Chabrol) *Jean-Paul Belmondo, Mia Farrow, Laura Antonelli, Daniel Ivernel.* A great cast can't save this minor Chabrol comedy mystery. Playboy doctor Belmondo courts and weds Farrow, only to then meet and fall in love with her sister, Antonelli. Belmondo then goes about the task of eliminating Miss Antonelli's many suitors. ★½

High Heels

(1991, 115 min, Spain, Pedro Almodóvar) *Victoria Abril, Marisa Paredes, Miguel Bose.* Almodóvar moves into new territory by looking a bit more closely at the human motives and desires he usually savages. The story revolves around a volatile estranged mother-daughter relationship; upon reuniting, they come to realize that they have been sharing the same man. Quicker than you can say *Women on the Verge*, the film fires head-first into a series of alternately hilarious and tragic situations. Almodóvar's trademark visuals blend with tragic and comedic melodrama to wonderful effect; he continues to be one of the most original and inventive directors working today. (Spanish with English subtitles) ★★★ VHS: $7.99

High Hopes

(1989, 110 min, GB, Mike Leigh) *Philip Davis, Ruth Sheen, Edna Dore.* This bitingly sarcastic and yet poignant survival guide to Thatcher's England is often funny and always thought provoking. The story revolves around Cyril and Shirley, two lovers attempting to stay true to their leftist ideals and lifestyle despite the rising tide of heartless capitalism. The cast of memorable characters includes Cyril's embittered mother, teetering on senility; his hysterical sister, bent on obliterating her working-class roots with the plastic comforts of suburbia; and two wildly funny upper-class twits who blindly romp amidst the decay of Thatcher's New Society. ★★★½

High Fidelity: John Cusack (l.) and Todd Louiso rock Chicago

High Noon

(1952, 84 min, US, Fred Zinnemann) *Gary Cooper, Grace Kelly, Thomas Mitchell, Lloyd Bridges, Lon Chaney, Jr., Katy Jurado.* Cooper won a second Oscar for his stirring performance in this western classic as a retiring small-town marshall who is abandoned by the townspeople when a murderer he sent away to prison returns to seek vengeance. The gunfight finale is arguably the best showdown in film. ★★★★ VHS: $14.99; DVD: $24.99

High Plains Drifter

(1973, 105 min, US, Clint Eastwood) *Clint Eastwood, Verna Bloom, Marianna Hill, Mitchell Ryan.* A solid western tale from Eastwood about the title character (Eastwood) protecting a small town from a group of prison parolees out for vengeance. (Letterboxed VHS available for $14.99) ★★★ VHS: $7.49; DVD: $24.99

High Road to China

(1983, 120 min, US, Brian G. Hutton) *Tom Selleck, Bess Armstrong, Jack Weston, Robert Morley, Wilford Brimley.* Having been the first choice, and unavailable, for *Raiders of the Lost Ark*, Selleck finally starred in a big-screen, tongue-in-cheek adventure — unfortunately for him, it was this pleasant but minor film. Selleck plays a daredevil flyer hired by Armstrong to find her missing father. ★★

High School Confidential

(1958, 85 min, US, Jack Arnold) *Russ Tamblyn, Mamie Van Doren, Jan Sterling, Jackie Coogan, Jerry Lee Lewis.* The legendary cult classic featuring "the smart aleck leader of the hot rod set," "the girl who has too much too soon," and "the glamorous teacher devoted to thwarting delinquency." They don't make 'em like this anymore! ★★ VHS: $14.99

High School High

(1996, 90 min, US, Hart Bochner) *Jon Lovitz, Tia Carrere, Mekhi Phifer, Louise Fletcher.* In this *Airplane*-like parody of *Dangerous Minds* and *Stand and Deliver*, Lovitz plays the idealistic son of the snobbish headmaster of a posh private school who takes a teaching job at Marion Berry High, the worst school in the city. The first third of the film is actually funny, alternating between sharp satire and so-dumb-it's-funny humor in true Z-A-Z fashion. Unfortunately, the writers run out of ideas far too quickly, and *High School High* ends up becoming a slightly comic variation of what it started out satirizing — a cheesy, feel-good, inspirational teen drama. ★★ VHS: $9.99; DVD: $27.99

High Season

(1987, 92 min, GB, Clare Peploe) *Jacqueline Bisset, James Fox, Irene Papas, Kenneth Branagh, Robert Stephens.* First-time director Peploe cowrote (along with son Mark) this tepid mishmash about the effects of tourism on a small Greek island. The beautiful Bisset competes with the scenery in her role as a photographer whose life is complicated by obnoxious tourists, inept spies and her self-important ex-husband (Fox in a suitably hedonistic role). No doubt Britain's idea of "mindless entertainment." ★★

High Sierra

(1941, 100 min, US, Raoul Walsh) *Humphrey Bogart, Ida Lupino, Joan Leslie, Arthur Kennedy, Cornel Wilde.* Bogart is at his best in this stirring tale of a tired, aging killer on the lam from the police. The theme is an old one, but it is masterfully rejuvinated by Bogart's unforgettable performance. Also contributing to the overall excellence of the film are stand-out performances by Leslie, as Bogey's goody-goody heartthrob, and the great Lupino, as the not-so-goody moll who pines for his love. ★★★½ VHS: $19.99

High Society

(1956, 107 min, US, Charles Walters) *Grace Kelly, Bing Crosby, Frank Sinatra, Celeste Holm, Louis Armstrong.* Amiable musical remake of *The Philadelphia Story* with songs by Cole Porter (including "True Love"). Kelly, Crosby and Sinatra take over the Katharine Hepburn, Cary Grant, and James Stewart roles. ★★★ VHS: $14.99

High Spirits

(1988, 97 min, US, Neil Jordan) *Peter O'Toole, Daryl Hannah, Steve Guttenberg, Liam Neeson, Beverly D'Angelo.* O'Toole, Hannah and Guttenberg barely manage to wring a few laughs from this tepid ghost comedy with Guttenberg as an American tourist visiting an Irish castle who meets and falls in love with ghost Hannah. ★½

High Tide

(1987, 104 min, Australia, Gillian Armstrong) *Judy Davis, Claudia Karvan, Jan Adele, Colin Friels.* A well-crafted, emotionally powerful story of a woman (Davis), stranded in a small coastal town, who befriends an adolescent girl. Armstrong's fine, sensitive direction elevates this absorbing drama well above the clichéd, maudlin soap opera it very well could have been. Davis, Karvan as the young girl, and especially Adele as the girl's grandmother, all offer outstanding performances. ★★★½

Higher Learning

(1995, 127 min, US, John Singleton) *Omar Epps, Kristy Swanson, Michael Rapaport, Laurence Fishburne, Ice Cube, Jennifer Connelly, Jason Wiles.* In *Boyz n the Hood*, director Singleton shaded his story with a subtlety which belied its incendiary theme. But in an effort to punctuate his thought-provoking *Higher Learning*, about campus strife in the '90s, he has given way to stereotypes and heavy-handedness. In remarkable detail, the story shows the fractious campus life awaiting a group of college freshman. As the students come to adhere to their own agendas — racial, sexual, political — the cookie-cutter story lays the way to a tragic but inevitable climax. Best of a good cast is Fishburne as a dedicated professor. ★★½ VHS: $9.99; DVD: $19.99

Highlander

(1986, 116 min, GB, Russell Mulcahy) *Sean Connery, Christopher Lambert, Clancy Brown, Roxanne Hart.* Lambert stars as a Scottish member of a bizarre group of immortal warriors who do battle with each other down through the ages. The story skips around from 12th-century Scotland to modern-day Manhattan to 18th-century Boston (and so on) and, as a result, the film sometimes becomes narratively incoherent. But

Gary Cooper in *High Noon*

despite this shortcoming, the action is fantastic. Connery is his usual marvelous self as Lambert's mentor and Brown is his menacing adversary. (VHS available letterboxed or pan & scan) (Followed by 3 sequels and a TV series) ★★½ VHS: $9.99

Highlander 2: The Quickening

(1990, 90 min, US, Russell Mulcahy) *Christopher Lambert, Sean Connery, Virginia Madsen, John C. McGinley.* Good special effects (as well as some chintzy ones) help add to the cheesy fun of this inferior remake of the 1986 swashbuckling adventure. Connery and Lambert dust off their broadswords as they do battle with alien assassins (led by the ever-leering Ironside) out to destroy the Earth's fragile ecosystem. (Letterboxed director's cut retails for $19.99) ★★ VHS: $9.99; DVD: $14.99

Highlander: The Final Dimension

(1994, 100 min, GB, Andy Morahan) *Christopher Lambert, Mario Van Peebles, Deborah Unger, Mako.* Director Morahan should have applied the Highlander credo, "There can be only one," to the making of sequels and not served up this totally inept and unsatisfying conclusion. Lambert reprises his role as the centuries-old swordsman who must now face a recently unearthed immortal (Van Peebles in an undisciplined performance). Offscreen beheadings, major plot holes and a totally gratuitous subplot about an old flame reincarnated as an antiquitites expert (the fetching Unger) make this rehash about as ridiculous as it sounds. ★ VHS: $14.99

Highlander: Endgame

(2000, 101 min, US, Douglas Aarniokoski) *Adrian Paul, Christopher Lambert.* After an abysmal third installment, the *Highlander* film series goes back to basics, reprising its popular themes of swordplay and mentorship. In this fourth chapter, Lambert teams with his TV counterpart Paul for a good-looking, sometimes exciting if by-the-books adventure tale of immortals battling each other to be "the one." Fans of the TV show and film series should enjoy this harmless actioner. (Fourteen minutes longer than the theatrical cut.) ★★½ VHS: $19.99; DVD: $29.99

The Highest Honor

(1984, 99 min, Australia, Peter Maxwell) *John Howard, Atsuo Nakamura, Scott Wilson.* Compelling WWII drama which recounts the true story of the unique friendship between two enemies: a POW and his Japanese jailer, both torn by their sense of duty and sense of humanity. This action/drama is interesting but not as riveting as the similarly themed *Merry Christmas, Mr. Lawrence.* ★★½ VHS: $14.99

Highway 61

(1992, 99 min, Canada, Bruce McDonald) *Don McKellar, Valerie Buhagiar, Earl Pastko.* A Canadian independent feature, this road comedy contains much of the hip and anarchic humor which distinguishes Jim Jarmusch and Hal Hartley's works. Though not entirely successful in its send-ups and Lynch-like Americana admonishments, there's an abundance of offbeat and wildly satiric jabs at the denizens both on and off the road. McKellar, displaying a charmingly subdued persona, is a staid Canadian small-town barber taken on the ride of his life by "escapee from a heavy metal crew" roadie Buhagiar. En route to New Orleans transporting the dead body she claims to be her brother, the two disparate travelers wind their way down an erratic highway as loopy and disjointed as the eccentrics they meet. ★★★ VHS: $89.99

Hilary and Jackie

(1998, 124 min, GB, Anand Tucker) *Emily Watson, Rachel Griffiths, David Morrissey, James Frain, Charles Dance.* A demanding but ultimately rewarding biography, *Hilary and Jackie* features two remarkable performances from Watson and Griffiths as the two British sisters, one the world-renowned cellist Jacqueline du Pré. Divided into two parts titled after each sister, the film traces their lives from childhood (where sibling rivalry was encouraged) to Jackie's success in the music field and Hilary's departure from it to Jackie's illness from multiple sclerosis. Giving bits of information in one part and then completing the story in the next adds a dimension not always associated with "disease-of-the-week" films, and the relationship between the two sisters is well-rounded. Watson as Jackie and Griffiths as Hilary complement each other beautifully, each giving precise, singular portrayals. ★★★ VHS: $14.99; DVD: $19.99

Hill 24 Doesn't Answer

(1959, 106 min, Israel, Thorton Dickinson) *Edward Mulhare, Haya Harareet.* Hill 24 is one of the foothills dominating the approach to Jerusalem. Set in 1949, on the eve of the U.N. cease-fire imposed during the Israeli war of independence, this fiercely realistic drama follows the actions of four young Zionists who volunteer to defend the strategic hill in order to maintain access to the besieged city. A historically important film that successfully captures the tensions in the birth of a nation. (English dialogue) ★★★ VHS: $79.99

Hillbillies in a Haunted House

(1967, 88 min, US, Jean Yarbrough) *Ferlin Husky, Joi Lansing, Lon Chaney, Jr., John Carradine, Basil Rathbone.* Two country singers and their manager spend the night in a seemingly abandoned mansion. Little do they know that a gang of foreign spies is hiding out in the basement, poised to steal a secret formula for rocket propellant. Warning: Lots of songs! ★ VHS: $19.99; DVD: $19.99

The Hills Have Eyes

(1977, 89 min, US, Wes Craven) *Susan Lanier, Robert Houston, Dee Wallace Stone.* Tense and gory horror film from director Craven. A vacationing family makes a very wrong turn in the desert — and find themselves up against a group of psychotic cannibals (are there any other kind?). (Sequel: *The Hills Have Eyes, Part 2*) ★★★

The Hills Have Eyes, Part 2

(1984, 86 min, US, Wes Craven) *Michael Berryman, Kevin Blair.* Sequel to Craven's cult horror film. This time out, it's some teenagers in trouble, as they travel through the desert. Lacks the suspense and style of the original. ★★ VHS: $14.99

Himatsuri

(1985, 115 min, Japan, Mitsuo Yangimachi) *Kinya Kitaoji, Kwako Taichi.* One of the Japanese New Wave's best efforts so far, *Himatsuri* brilliantly explores the complex mental landscape of modern Japan, torn between advanced technology and the superstitions and mystical undercurrents that pervade the Japanese subconscious. Set in a fishing village, it follows the spiritual transformation of a rough-hewn but affable lumberjack (the superb Kitaoji) who moves from defiling the land to communication with the gods that inhabit it. (Japanese with English subtitles) ★★★½ VHS: $59.99

The Hindenburg

(1975, 125 min, US, Robert Wise) *George C. Scott, Anne Bancroft, William Atherton, Roy Thinnes, Gig Young, Burgess Meredith, Charles Durning.* A good cast is featured in this inflated disaster film, which speculates that the infamous Hindenburg crash of 1937 was actually sabotage. Outstanding special effects and actual footage interspersed heighten the tension at the end — and what a knockout ending it is. ★★ DVD: $24.99

The Hired Hand

(1971, 95 min, US, Peter Fonda) *Peter Fonda, Warren Oates, Verna Bloom.* Fonda's follow-up to *Easy Rider* is this elegiac and subversive western which bombed at the box office. Fonda stars as a mysterious wanderer who returns to his wife (the terrific Bloom) after a seven-year absence. Panned by critics, this lyrically filmed mood piece on loneliness, loyalty and the nature of love was lost in the flood of "trippy" films in the early '70s, but still, it compares favorably to other "modern westerns" championed by Peckinpah. ★★★

Hiroshima

(1995, 165 min, Canada/Japan, Roger Spottiswoode & Koreyoshi Kurahara) *Kenneth Welsh, Tatsuo Matsumura, Richard Masur, Saul Rubinek.* Illuminating and extremely accomplished, this is an even-handed depiction of the events leading to the dropping of the atomic bomb on Hiroshima and Nagasaki during WWII. Told in a quasi-documentary style, *Hiroshima* incorporates actual newsreel footage which has been masterfully tinted and juxtaposes it with an astonishingly authentic re-creation of the times and events to produce a jarring, fascinating narrative. The story is seen from Truman's perspective as the new commander-in-chief, and through the eyes of Japan's Prime Minister Suzuki as the Japanese high council debates their future war efforts. Welsh as Truman and Matsumura as Suzuki ground the film with their inspired portrayals. (English and Japanese with English subtitles) ★★★½ VHS: $14.99

Hiroshima Maiden

(1988, 58 min, US, Joan Darling) *Tamlyn Tomita, Susan Blakely, Richard Masur.* A young Japanese woman from Hiroshima comes to America in 1955 and stays with a family while she undergoes treatment for radiation burns. Everyone welcomes her except the oldest son, who is persuaded by his friends that she is a spy. This touching though slowly paced drama is inspired by the stories of the real-life "Hiroshima Maidens." ★★½ VHS: $29.99

Hiroshima, Mon Amour

(1959, 91 min, France, Alain Resnais) *Emmanuelle Riva, Eiji Okada.* Obsessive pasts haunt the affair of a French woman and a Japanese architect in 1950s Hiroshima. The woman's memories of her scandalous involvement with a German soldier and the piercing recollections of nuclear horror both unite and repel the two lovers. Resnais' brilliant first film was scripted by Marguerite Duras. (French with English subtitles) ★★★★ VHS: $29.99

His Girl Friday

(1940, 92 min, US, Howard Hawks) *Rosalind Russell, Cary Grant, Ralph Bellamy, Gene Lockhart, John Qualen, Roscoe Karns.* Hawks' fast-talking, wise-cracking, sex-change version of *The Front Page.* Russell is the ace reporter set to wed the less than dynamic Bellamy. Grant is her editor and ex-husband determined to thwart the match. A classic screwball comedy filmed at a machine-gun pace, the film's jokes are hilarious, the situations outlandish, and Grant and Russell are in terrific form. (Remade in 1988 as *Switching Channels*) ★★★★ VHS: $19.99; DVD: $24.99

History Is Made at Night

(1937, 98 min, US, Frank Borzage) *Jean Arthur, Charles Boyer, Colin Clive.* Intriguing blend of romance, comedy and melodrama with Arthur and Boyer in fine form in the story of Arthur divorcing husband Clive and falling in love with headwaiter Boyer. ★★½ VHS: $14.99

History of the World, Part 1

(1981, 92 min, US, Mel Brooks) *Gregory Hines, Dom DeLuise, Madeline Kahn, Harvey Korman, Cloris Leachman, Sid Caesar, Bea Arthur; Narrated by Orson Welles.* An alternately funny and fuzzy, sometimes vulgar history lesson from the not-so-professorial mind of Brooks. Vignettes tell the progress of man from primitive cave dwellers to the Roman Empire to the French Revolution. In typical Brooks fashion, the film features outrageous comic situations, unbelievably silly jokes and an all-star cast. ★★ VHS: $9.99; DVD: $29.99

Hit!

(1973, 135 min, US, Sidney J. Furie) *Billy Dee Williams, Richard Pryor, Gwen Welles.* Embittered over the drug-related death of his daughter, U.S. agent Nick Allen (Williams) teams up with an underwater warfare expert (Pryor) to seek vengence against a group of drug smugglers in Marseilles. Overly detailed and lengthy at times, but more-than-exciting action and witty dialogue help to keep this one moving. ★★½ VHS: $14.99

The Hit

(1985, 98 min, GB, Stephen Frears) *Terence Stamp, John Hurt, Tim Roth, Laura del Sol.* Willie Parker (Stamp) dropped a dime on his mobster cohorts. For his confession, the British magistrate granted him clemency and a new identity in a bucolic Spanish villa. Now, ten years later, he's being hunted down by a hired killer and appears doomed to pay for his finger-pointing. However, things go peculiarly astray when this condemned man's tranquil acceptance of his death sentence throws his edgy executioner (Hurt) for a loop. In spite of its ominous subject matter and jagged action, *The Hit* harbors a sly undertow of dark humor which distinguishes it from simpler underworld thrillers. ★★★ VHS: $14.99

The Hitch-Hiker

(1953, 71 min, US, Ida Lupino) *Edmond O'Brien, Frank Lovejoy, William Talman.* Two ordinary men are on a weekend excursion away from their wives and families when they happen to make a deadly mistake and pick up the wrong hitch-hiker, an escaped fugitive and serial killer with a lazy eye and a deadly shot. What follows is an extremely suspenseful road movie as the killer makes the men drive him into Baja Mexico. O'Brien and Lovejoy are extremely good as the unwilling passengers, one stalwart in the face of death and the other slowly cracking under the strain, but it is Talman who steals the picture with his vivid portrait of a truly three-dimensional, but nevertheless horribly menacing villain. Lupino sustains the tension throughout. Highly recommended for fans of classic film noir, directed by the only woman in the field. ★★★½ VHS: $24.99; DVD: $29.99

The Hitcher

(1986, 97 min, US, Robert Harmon) *Rutger Hauer, C. Thomas Howell, Jennifer Jason Leigh.* Hauer is evil personified in this taut thriller about a young man who is terrorized by a maniacal hitchhiker. Howell, in what may easily be his best role to date, is the innocent driver whose trek across Nevada turns into a deadly game of cat and mouse. Filled with unrelenting suspense and seething with homoerotic imagery, this film, not for the faint of heart, will electrify fans of the genre. (VHS available letterboxed and pan & scan) ★★★ VHS: $9.99; DVD: $14.99

Holiday

Hitler's Children

(1943, 83 min, US, Edward Dmytryk) *Tim Holt, Bonita Granville, Otto Kruger, H.B. Warner.* Though the title suggests *They Saved Hitler's Brain* rather than *Watch on the Rhine*, this compelling 1940s anti-Nazi propaganda drama is very much in the latter film's league in its cautionary tale of Nazi oppression. Sort of a "Romeo and Juliet" set in the Fatherland, the story follows the friendship and romance of a Nazi youth (Holt) and an American girl (Granville) living in Germany. A big hit in its day, the title refers to the dictator's army of children undergoing fascist brainwashing. ★★★ VHS: $29.99

Hobson's Choice

(1954, 107 min, GB, David Lean) *Charles Laughton, Brenda de Banzie, John Mills.* Laughton offers a priceless performance in this delicious working-class comedy about a tyrannical bootmaker who struggles to maintain his dominion over his three daughters. De Banzie plays a strong-willed daughter who defies his authority by marrying the man of her choice. ★★★½ VHS: $29.99

Hocus Pocus

(1993, 96 min, US, Kenny Ortega) *Bette Midler, Kathy Najimy, Sarah Jessica Parker, Charles Rocket, Kathleen Freeman.* This very lightweight but amiable fantasy half-heartedly recaptures the frivolity of the Fred MacMurray comedies of the 1960s. Midler, Najimy and Parker star as 17th-century witches who return to modern-day Salem and run "amok, amok, amok." With more hokum than hocus, the witches set out to steal the souls of the town's children. Their only opposition are three spunky kids. Most of the laughs are mild, and the film gives the impression of being more risque than it is — it's harmless fare. Though she's not given much to do, Midler generates some energy, and sings "I Put a Spell on You," the film's only real highlight. ★★½ VHS: $14.99

Hoffa

(1992, 100 min, US, Danny DeVito) *Jack Nicholson, Danny DeVito, Armand Assante, J.T. Walsh, Kevin Anderson.* This sprawling biography of the tough-as-nails labor leader benefits from a gutsy performance by Nicholson in the title role, but it would have been better if it were more Hoffa and less DeVito. There are few scenes here where the costar/director's presence is not apparent, and that's the big problem: after nearly two-and-a-half hours, we know more about DeVito's ficticious sidekick, Bobby Ciaro, than we do of James Hoffa. The film traces Hoffa's rise to power, from his determined attempts to enlist truckers to the union to his prominence as the no-nonsense Teamsters president. With no thanks to David Mamet's script, DeVito glosses over Hoffa's personal life in favor of *mano-a-mano* confrontations and feverish speeches that eventually grow repetitious. ★★ VHS: $9.99

The Holcroft Covenant

(1985, 112 min, Great Britain, John Frankenheimer) *Michael Caine, Anthony Andrews, Lilli Palmer, Mario Adorf.* Master suspense director Frankenheimer is not too successful in bringing Robert Ludlum's first novel to the screen. Caine is led on a globe-trotting series of adventures as he searches for a fortune left behind by his dead father (a comrade-in-arms to Hitler). ★½ VHS: $14.99; DVD: $24.99

Hold Me, Thrill Me, Kiss Me

(1993, 110 min, US, Joel Hershman) *Adrienne Shelley, Diane Ladd, Sam Young.* If one can pay homage to Pedro Almodóvar, Russ Meyer and Woody Allen in the same film, first-time director Hershman has done it with this quirky comedy. Set in a seedy trailer park, the plot is just the old "boy meets stripper, stripper handcuffs boy to bed, boy begins to fall for stripper's animal-loving little sis" story, with a little murder and mayhem thrown in for good measure. ★★★ VHS: $79.99

Hold That Ghost

(1941, 80 min, US, Arthur Lubin) *Bud Abbott, Lou Costello, Joan Davis, Mischa Auer, The Andrews Sisters.* In one of their best films, Abbott and Costello meet their comedic equal in Davis when they spend the night in a house haunted not only by ghosts but by mobsters. A wonderful romp, and Davis is a particular delight. ★★★ VHS: $14.99

A Hole in the Head

(1959, 120 min, US, Frank Capra) *Frank Sinatra, Edward G. Robinson, Eddie Hodges, Eleanor Parker, Carolyn Jones, Thelma Ritter.* Sinatra sings "High Hopes" in this Capra sentimental favorite. Frank plays a down-on-his-heels motel owner raising a young son (Hodges) and trying to make ends meet. ★★★

The Holes (Les Gaspards)

(1981, 92 min, France/US, Pierre Tchernia) *Gérard Depardieu, Philippe Noiret, Michel Serrault.* A good cast and a peculiarly un-French premise makes this fantasy/comedy a real find for Francophiles. Living in the labyrinthine maze of ancient tunnels and caves deep under the streets of Paris is a society of people who want to escape the world above. Their tranquility is disturbed, however, after an ambitious Minister of Public Works begins to dig up the city for his many pet construction projects, one being that the Seine would be paved over for conversion into a downtown highway! The mole people take matters into their own hands by kidnapping tourists, bicyclists and even policemen in a frantic effort to keep progress at bay. Laced with many funny moments, this strange film is imaginatively executed and wackily entertaining. (Dubbed) ★★★ VHS: $79.99

Holiday

(1938, 94 min, US, George Cukor) *Katharine Hepburn, Cary Grant, Doris Nolan, Edward Everett Horton, Lew Ayres.* The second and more popular version of Philip Barry's Broadway hit, this delightful comedy stars Hepburn and Grant, in their third of four films together, as non-conformists up against an ever-restrictive world. Grant, at his most charming, plays a free spirit engaged to socialite Nolan, soon discovering he has more in common with her sister Kate. Ayres stands out as the alcoholic black sheep of the family, and Horton, repeating his role from the original 1930 film, is marvelous as Grant's mentor and friend. ★★★★ VHS: $19.99

Holiday Affair

(1949, 87 min, US, Don Hartman) *Janet Leigh, Robert Mitchum, Wendell Corey.* A beautiful and young Leigh plays a war widow who must decide between Mitchum and Corey. A pleasant comedy-drama enhanced by two delightful performances by Leigh and Mitchum. ★★½ VHS: $14.99

Holiday Hotel

(1978, 109 min, France, Michel Lang) *Guy Marchand, Sophie Barjac.* The French preoccupation with both love and summer vacation is wittily explored in this sexy, cheerful comedy. Marchand is a frazzled father whose 16-year-old daughter is set loose at a small summer resort during August holiday. Lots of French skin and a giddy good time. (French with English subtitles) ★★½

Holiday Inn

(1942, 101 min, US, Mark Sandrich) *Bing Crosby, Fred Astaire, Marjorie Reynolds.* Crosby and Astaire are the top-liners (can't get any bigger than that) at Bing's holiday resort (only open during holidays, naturally). As the romantic interest, Reynolds is splendid; as is the Irving Berlin score (which includes "White Christmas"). Delightful. ★★★½ VHS: $9.99; DVD: $29.99

Hollow Man

(2000, 113 min, US, Paul Verhoeven) *Kevin Bacon, Elisabeth Shue, Josh Brolin, Kim Dickens, William Devane.* Verhoeven's cynical invisible man thriller is a case of a perfectly good genre flick suffocated by the constrictions of the wrong genre. In updating the classic sci-fi fantasy of invisibility, Verhoeven has chosen to spin the concept into a mean-spirited, gore-splattered stalker flick. Bacon plays the supremely arrogant supergenius in charge of a secret government research project. Zapping himself transparent was the easy part; getting back is the problem, and the longer he remains invisible, the more sinister his behavior becomes. Beyond the flaky characters and flimsy plot, the film features a flashy production design and some way-cool visual effects. ★★ VHS: $14.99; DVD: $19.99

Hollow Reed

(1997, 105 min, GB, Angela Pope) *Martin Donovan, Joely Richardson, Ian Hart, Jason Flemyng, Sam Bould.* A flawed but well-meaning drama, *Hollow Reed* takes a sensitive subject — the custody battle between a gay man and his ex-wife — and introduces an explosive plot element about child abuse. Martyn (Donovan) is living happily with his boyfriend (Hart) when he learns that his son Oliver (Bould) is being physically harmed by Tom (Flemyng), the new lover of his ex-wife Hannah (Richardson). Director Pope has made an engrossing film about determining which parent is more suitable to care for Oliver, but the stress Martyn has about having his homosexuality put on trial is not properly paralleled with Hannah's feelings about loving an abuser. ★★½ VHS: $19.99

Hollywood Shuffle

(1987, 82 min, US, Robert Townsend) *Robert Townsend, Anne-Marie Johnson, Keenen Ivory Wayans, Damon Wayans.* A series of side-splitting vignettes tell the tale of a struggling black actor's search for a serious role in Hollywood. Stand-up comic and first-time director Townsend redefined the term "shoestring budget" when he "maxed out" his credit cards in order to pay the final production costs for this spoof. His strategy paid off and the resulting lampoon on racial inequity in tinseltown went on to reap huge and well-deserved rewards at the box office. ★★★ VHS: $14.99; DVD: $19.99

The Holy Innocents

(1984, 108 min, Spain, Marto Camus) *Francisco Rabal, Alfredo Lando.* In Franco's Spain, 1962, the modern world has yet to arrive at many rural communities where the feudal system of landowning gentry and peasant laborers continue. This is the setting for Camus' powerful and rousing drama of oppression and revenge. Paco and Regula, husband and wife, are gatekeepers to an aristocratic family. Their struggles — raising a family, eking out a subsistence and maintaining some self-respect — provide the soul for this touching film. (Spanish with English subtitles) ★★★

Holy Man

(1998, 114 min, US, Stephen Herek) *Eddie Murphy, Jeff Goldblum, Kelly Preston, Robert Loggia, Jon Cryer.* An insipid, empty, preachy comedy, *Holy Man* is an overlong parable almost saved by Murphy's endearing performance. Goldblum plays a desperate TV exec at a Home Shopping–like network whose ratings and sales are in the basement. After accidentally hitting an enigmatic, beatific man (Murphy) with his car, Goldblum puts this "holy man" on the air with spectacular results. Heavy-handed network satire is mixed with trendy, New Age "messages." Murphy delivers a thoughtful, change-of-pace

Holy Smoke!

performance. Goldblum, however, is at his most jittery — possibly to give the unfocused direction an energetic point of view. It doesn't help. ★½ VHS: $14.99; DVD: $29.99

Holy Smoke!

(1999, 114 min, US/Australia, Jane Campion) *Kate Winslet, Harvey Keitel, Pam Grier, Julie Hamilton.* A beautiful young Australian woman (Winslet), while vacationing in India, falls hard for a religious cult leader. Her family coerces her back home, and to spend time with a macho deprogrammer. Wildly uneven, *Holy Smoke!* boasts terrific, brave performances by Winslet and Keitel and some stylish direction, but also succumbs to cartoonish stereotyping (especially Winslet's family). The film begins and ends badly, but many of the scenes between the two leads — set in a hut in the middle of the empty, sprawling Australian Outback — are compelling, even though they never rise to the enticing war-of-wills/battle-of-the-sexes free-for-all promised early on. What was presumably intended as a loosely structured character piece comes across instead as a jumble of interesting (and middling) ideas that never come into focus. ★★½ VHS: $19.99; DVD: $29.99

Hombre

(1967, 111 min, US, Martin Ritt) *Paul Newman, Richard Boone, Fredric March, Diane Cilento, Martin Balsam.* Newman has a sardonic cool about him as a white man living among the Indians who journeys with a group of travelers on a stagecoach line's final voyage. Set in the last days of the Old West, director Ritt's riveting parable (based on an Elmore Leonard story) probes racial intolerance against Indians and the price of humanism as Newman and coriders March, Cilento and Balsam are up against bad guy Boone, highwaymen and the elements. A thoroughly satisfying western, featuring a terrific performance from Cilento as a gutsy widow. ★★★½ VHS: $9.99

Home Alone

(1990, 103 min, US, Chris Columbus) *Macaulay Culkin, Joe Pesci, Daniel Stern, Catherine O'Hara, John Heard, John Candy.* John Hughes wrote the script for this box-office smash about an eight-year-old boy left behind when his family leaves for their European Christmas vacation. Little Culkin plays Kevin, whose idyllic stay home alone is interrupted by two inept burglars. Much of the film centers on Kevin's ingenious defense ploys, and the hilariously sadistic acts of sabotage he institutes against the thieves. Pesci and Stern are the unfortunate criminals. However, it's youngster Culkin who captivates with a refreshing variation on the precocious youth; and his enormous contribution to this romp should not be overlooked. (Followed by 2 sequels) ★★★ VHS: $14.99; DVD: $29.99

Home Alone 2: Lost In New York

(1992, 113 min, US, Chris Columbus) *Macaulay Culkin, Joe Pesci, Daniel Stern, Tim Curry, Rob Schneider, Dana Ivey.* The lucrative adventures of young Kevin McAllister (Culkin) continue in this by-the-numbers but amusing sequel. The action has been transplanted from the suburbs to the more exciting mean streets of Manhattan. Predictably, Kevin becomes separated from his family again, meets up with the recently escaped Wet Bandits (Pesci, Stern) and sets out to creatively foil their plot to rob a toy store. Writer-producer John Hughes sticks to his winning formula like tar to a rooftop, though this time Kevin is less an innocent child and more a preachy know-it-all. This is much more violent than the first film. ★★½ VHS: $14.99; DVD: $29.99

Home Alone 3

(1997, 102 min, US, Raja Gosnell) *Alex D. Linz, Scarlett Johansson, Haviland Morris, Marion Seldes.* While it contains no real surprises, this third installment of the popular series has a new face who's — yes, you guessed it — left home alone. This time young Alex has the chicken pox. His mom must take time off from work to care for him, but the demands of her job are such that by the third day, she has to go in for a few hours each day. Alex then becomes involved with a stolen computer chip and spies. ★★ VHS: $14.99; DVD: $29.99

The Home and the World

(1984, 130 min, India, Satyajit Ray) *Victor Banerjee, Soumitra Chatterjee.* Set in 1908 British-ruled India, this is a shattering yet measured study of emancipation, commitment and love. The story concerns a liberal man's desire to free his wife of purdah and allow her to mingle with his male friends. His plan backfires, however, when she becomes fascinated by an intelligent revolutionary politician. Ray intricately explores the shifting tides of emotion between the three in this exquisite drama. (Bengali with English subtitles) ★★★

Home for the Holidays

(1995, 105 min, US, Jodie Foster) *Holly Hunter, Robert Downey, Jr., Dylan McDermott, Anne Bancroft, Charles Durning, Geraldine Chaplin, Steve Guttenberg, Cynthia Stevenson, Claire Danes.* Foster's directorial follow-up to *Little Man Tate* continues her examination of familial conflicts and off-the-fringe characters in this sometimes funny family comedy which proves "it's all relative." The slightly neurotic but sane Hunter returns home for the Thanksgiving holiday. To anyone who has suffered through family get-togethers, her anxiety is all the more empathetic as she is greeted by a varied assortment of relatives. Bancroft and Durning are her interfering though caring parents, Chaplin is the flaky aunt, and in the film's most spirited portrayal, Downey is her jocular gay brother. While all the characters have their peculiarities, Foster and writer W. D. Richter ultimately exploit their endearing characteristics as well. The closing montage nicely brings the film together. ★★½ VHS: $9.99

Home Fries

(1998, 93 min, US, Dean Parisot) *Drew Barrymore, Luke Wilson, Catherine O'Hara, Jake Busey, Shelley Duvall.* Barrymore is appealing in this otherwise mixed-up, where-do-we-go-next romantic/murder comedy. Flyboys and brothers Wilson and Busey buzz their dad in their helicopter, but the old guy dies of a heart attack. It seems he was fooling around and mom (a shrill O'Hara) wanted to scare him. Turns out the girl he was two-timing with is the same person who may have heard the murder on her headphones: burger drive-thru cashier Barrymore. Wilson then begins working at the place to find out what she knows. Okay, class, all

who think they're gonna fall in love, raise their hands. There are a few amusing, dark scenes, but mostly this crash course in romantic cynicism runs out of gas way before the inevitable finale. ★★ VHS: $9.99; DVD: $14.99

A Home of Our Own

(1993, 104 min, US, Tony Bill) *Kathy Bates, Edward Furlong, Soon-Teck Oh, Tony Campisi, T.J. Lowther.* Bates' sturdy performance as a widowed mother of six elevates this sentimental drama, literally a poor woman's *Alice Doesn't Live Here Anymore.* In the early 1960s, the story follows Bates and her children as they leave their Los Angeles home and head east for greener pastures. En route, they settle in Idaho, where they scrape out a living in a small rural town and try to come together as a family all the while trying to make the titular dream come true. As Shayne, the eldest son of the "Lacey tribe," Furlong is impressive. ★★½ VHS: $9.99; DVD: $14.99

Home of the Brave

(1949, 86 min, US, Mark Robson) *James Edwards, Lloyd Bridges, Frank Lovejoy, Jeff Corey.* Powerful WWII drama based on Arthur Laurents' play about a black soldier (Edwards) experiencing prejudices from fellow G.I.s while fighting in the South Pacific. Produced by Stanley Kramer. ★★★½ VHS: $19.99

Homeboy

(1988, 118 min, US, Michael Seresin) *Mickey Rourke, Christopher Walken, Debra Feuer, Ruben Blades.* After his daring performance in *Barfly,* Rourke goes even further over the edge with a highly unusual portrayal of an illiterate, monosyllabic boxer competing one last time for the title. Walken plays his unsavory manager. A downbeat but curiously appealing boxing drama which unfortunately gives in to many clichés of the genre. ★★½

Homecoming

(1948, 113 min, US, Mervyn LeRoy) *Clark Gable, Lana Turner, Anne Baxter.* In post-war roles, Gable and Turner both demonstrate a dramatic maturity together in comparison to their two earlier teamings. In this compelling if familiar wartime story, Gable stars as a society doctor who enlists and is sent overseas, where he eventually falls for headstrong nurse Turner. Baxter is Gable's wife back home: she also serving who only stands and waits. Baxter's scenes are perfunctory, as Gable and Turner's romance and working relationship during the war are the film's main attraction. ★★½ VHS: $19.99

Homegrown

(1998, 102 min, US, Stephen Gyllenhaal) *Billy Bob Thornton, Hank Azaria, Kelly Lynch, Jon Bon Jovi, Ryan Phillippe, Judge Reinhold, Ted Danson, John Lithgow, Jamie Lee Curtis.* Oddly marketed as a comedy, *Homegrown* is actually a trite murder mystery set against the landscape of America's professional marijuana industry. The flimsily constructed script cashes in on both the sensationalism and the obligatory humor attached with the subject matter, and merely hedges around the larger issues connected with what is reputedly known as America's most profitable cash crop. Despite a diverse cast, the central characters are spread too thin to hide the blemishes in the predictable story line about three dopey weed farmers who become ad-hoc drug

dealers after witnessing their boss' murder. ★★ VHS: $14.99; DVD: $29.99

Homer and Eddie

(1989, 100 min, US, Andrei Konchalovsky) *Whoopi Goldberg, James Belushi, Karen Black, Anne Ramsey.* Belushi is Homer, a sheltered, child-like man. Goldberg is Eddie, an already-crazed woman who just found out she has a month to live. Together, this unlikely pair take to the road and learn about themselves and each other. ★★ VHS: $9.99

Homeward Bound: The Incredible Journey

(1993, 90 min, US, DuWayne Dunham) *Robert Hays, Kim Greist, Jean Smart; Voices of Michael J. Fox, Sally Field, Don Ameche.* Disney's remake of their classic 1963 adventure film *The Incredible Journey* is a winsome and charming experience. Three pets are left on a neighbor's ranch while their family is temporarily away. As time passes, they become convinced that the family is in trouble and decide to make their own way back to their old house, thus beginning their "incredible journey." This is indeed one of those rare family movies that will please everyone. (Sequel: *Homeward Bound 2: Lost in San Francisco*) ★★★ VHS: $19.99; DVD: $29.99

Homeward Bound II: Lost In San Francisco

(1996, 89 min, US, David R. Ellis) *Voices of Michael J. Fox, Sally Field, Robert Hays.* With most of the original cast intact, this sequel lacks the spontaneous charm of the original. On this family vacation, these three animals escape from their cages on the airport runway, fearing that they are going to a "bad place." They must then battle their way through the animalistic streets of San Francisco, making friends and saving a child and a kitten from a raging fire along the way. Not one of the better talking animal films available. ★★ VHS: $22.99

Homicide

(1991, 100 min, US, David Mamet) *Joe Mantegna, Ving Rhames, William H. Macy.* Award-winning playwright Mamet's third outing as director is a gritty crime drama about a Jewish homicide detective struggling with his ethnic identity. Mamet regular Mantegna stars as Bobby Gold, a hard-nosed inner-city cop who is hot on the trail of a dangerous fugitive, and a probable promotion. But, when a Jewish shopkeeper is murdered, he gets lassoed into working the case by the deceased's family. Disavowing his heritage, he tries to get off the case and, at first, derides the family's hysteria over the possibly anti-Semitic nature of the crime. Mamet's characteristic terse dialogue punctuates this deftly made modern-day morality play. Mantegna's raw portrayal contributes greatly to the film's dark, moody atmosphere. ★★★★ VHS: $9.99

L'homme Blesse

(1984, 105 min, France, Patrice Chereau) *Jean-Hugues Anglade.* Adrift in the French underworld of hustlers and pick-ups, the innocent Henri (Anglade) experiences a brutal awakening to his gay sexuality. He witnesses a trick being beaten in the train station toilet, surrenders to the culprit's fierce embrace and finds himself hopelessly lost in ardor for this mysteri-

H

ous thug. Suddenly drawn to rough trade, Henri undergoes a number of hardships before finding liberation in a shocking final act of conquest. A disturbing yet powerful examination of sexual obsession and one man's personal sexual odyssey. (French with English subtitles) ★★★ VHS: $39.99

Hondo

(1953, 84 min, US, John Farrow) *John Wayne, Geraldine Page, Ward Bond.* Though not on the level of Wayne's work with director John Ford, *Hondo* is an exciting and well-made western which features a sterling film debut by Page. Wayne plays a half-Indian scout who befriends Page and her young son, who have been left alone on their ranch located dangerously close to an Apache camp. Wayne gives an overly mannered performance, but is countered by Oscar nominee Page, who gives a solid portrayal of a stalwart homesteader. ★★★ VHS: $19.99

Honey, I Blew Up the Kid

(1992, 89 min, US, Randal Kleiser) *Rick Moranis, Marcia Strassman, Robert Oliveri, Lloyd Bridges.* Moranis and Strassman reprise their roles in this mildly entertaining rehash of *Honey, I Shrunk the Kids*. This time, of course, scientist Moranis blunders in the opposite direction and winds up with a 100-foot tall, two-year-old behemoth, who threatens downtown Las Vegas (temper tantrums pose a real threat now!). While the original provided entertainment for all ages, this one will be infinitely more appealing to the little ones than adults. Another disappointment is the lack of a Roger Rabbit short which preceded the original. An instance in which bigger isn't necessarily better. (Sequel: *Honey We Shrunk Ourselves*) ★★½ VHS: $14.99

Honey, I Shrunk the Kids

(1989, 93 min, US, Joe Johnston) *Rick Moranis, Matt Frewer, Marcia Strassman.* Moranis stars as a scientist dad whose attic project goes berserk one fine afternoon and miniaturizes not only his kids, but the neighbors' as well. As bad turns to worse, the little ones find themselves stranded across the backyard, and their only hope lies in trekking across the yard — which, for them, is now the size of Kansas and bears a striking resemblence to Oz. This is a pure fluff and fun comedy-fantasy which takes its simple premise and goes a long way. (Sequel: *Honey, I Blew Up the Kid*) ★★★ VHS: $14.99

Honeymoon in Vegas

(1992, 99 min, US, Andrew Bergman) *Nicolas Cage, Sarah Jessica Parker, James Caan, Anne Bancroft, Peter Boyle, Seymour Cassel, Tony Shalhoub.* Can a film which features 34 Flying Elvises be all bad? Writer-director Bergman has taken to task this age-old question, and in his capable hands, *Honeymoon in Vegas*, featuring those same 34 Flying Elvises, is a most pleasurable comedy. Cage and Parker are madly in love, and have traveled to Las Vegas to wed. But big-time gambler Caan sees Parker, who's a dead ringer for his late wife, and promptly tricks Cage into an arrangement to spend the weekend with her. From there it's an all-out free-for-all, as Cage, now certain he has lost his love, travels through hell and high water to get her back. Cage is at his most manic, handling each successive zany setback with frenzied comic abandon.

Parker, as she was in *L.A. Story*, is a lovely and fiery comedienne. The 34 Flying Elvises, by the way, all perform admirably. ★★★ VHS: $9.99; DVD: $14.99

The Honeymoon Killers

(1970, 108 min, US, Leonard Kastle) *Shirley Stoler, Tony LoBianco.* A crazed swindler and his 250-lb. lover prey on a host of lonely, gullible women for financial gain in this sinister and subversive cult classic. ★★★

The Honeymoon Machine

(1961, 87 min, US, Richard Thorpe) *Steve McQueen, Jim Hutton, Paula Prentiss, Jack Weston, Dean Jagger.* McQueen is an American sailor stationed in Venice who joins forces with scientist Hutton in an elaborate scheme to use a Navy computer to win at the roulette table. In-between fine-tuning the system and collecting their winnings, both men find time for romance. It's slightly disorienting to see McQueen in such a farcical role, but he manages to wring a few laughs; as does the scene-stealing Weston. ★★½ VHS: $19.99

Honky Tonk

(1941, 105 min, US, Jack Conway) *Clark Gable, Lana Turner, Frank Morgan, Claire Trevor.* The first of Gable and Turner's four films together is an appealing western drama. Gable is a con artist on the run who meets up with beauty Turner en route to a small Nevada town. There, Gable takes up residence, courting Turner for romance and the locals for business. Turner makes the most of her first starring role, and the dialogue is snappy and full of double-entendres. Morgan and Trevor offer good performances in support as, respectively, Turner's drunkard father and a dance-hall girl. ★★½ VHS: $19.99

Honkytonk Man

(1982, 122 min, US, Clint Eastwood) *Clint Eastwood, Kyle Eastwood, Verna Bloom, Marty Robbins.* One of Eastwood's very few misfires. Clint plays a terminally ill, Depression-era country singer who packs up and heads on the road, hoping to make it to the Grand Old Opry. Clint's son Kyle plays his nephew who accompanies him on the trip. ★★ VHS: $14.99

Hoodlum

(1997, 122 min, US, Bill Duke) *Laurence Fishburne, Tim Roth, Andy Garcia, Vanessa Williams, Cicely Tyson, William Atherton, Loretta Devine.* The effects of crime and the efforts of a group of black crooks to control their turf in 1930s Harlem is the subject of this minor gangster outing. Fishburne is "Bumpy" Johnson, a slick con artist who wants to make his mark on New York's organized crime front. He assimilates himself into the lucrative numbers racket run by the Queen (Tyson), but soon finds the operation in trouble when veteran bad boy Dutch Schultz (Roth with a bad haircut) muscles in. Director Duke has classic aspirations, but doesn't have the chutzpah to put it all together. There's fine period production work and costumes, but this effort simply lacks the type of style needed to pull off an epic gangster movie. Bumpy? You bet. ★★ VHS: $19.99; DVD: $14.99

Hoods

(1998, 90 min, US, Mark Malone) *Joe Mantegna, Jennifer Tilly, Kevin Pollak, Joe Pantoliano, Seymour Cassel.* Another entry in the recent mob comedy subgenre, *Hoods* is too uneven in tone to be a hit with audiences. Angelo Martinelli (Mantegna, who also produced) is having one of those days. On his birthday, his ailing father (Cassel) asks him to whack someone named Carmine Dellarosa, but no one knows who he is. While the stars are well cast, and there is one rather clever plot twist, *Hoods* is ultimately disappointing because the film unwisely shifts gears from frustration comedy into poignancy. In the process, it generates too few laughs, and even less sympathy. ★★ VHS: $9.99

Hook

(1991, 144 min, US, Steven Spielberg) *Robin Williams, Dustin Hoffman, Bob Hoskins, Maggie Smith, Caroline Goodall, Charlie Korsmo, Gwyneth Paltrow.* With this update of the Peter Pan fairy tale, Spielberg has fashioned a fun-loving romp through Never-Never-Land which will delight kids and has enough depth to captivate adults. *Hook* finds Peter Pan all grown up and in the form of Peter Banning (Williams), a 40-year-old workaholic corporate raider-type who has no time for his kids let alone *being* one. When his old nemesis, Captain Hook (Hoffman), rears his ugly head and kidnaps Peter's tykes, he is forced to confront a past he doesn't even remember. The performances are splendid throughout: Williams revels in his boyish way; Hoffman camps it up as the decadent and snobbish Hook; Hoskins nearly steals the show as Hook's comical henchman Smee; and Smith is wonderful as the aging Wendy. ★★★ VHS: $9.99; DVD: $19.99

Hoop Dreams

(1994, 171 min, US, Steve James, Frederick Marx & Peter Gilbert) This compelling look at the aspirations of two talented African-American high school basketball stars, Arthur Agee and William Gates, is both highly entertaining and deeply disturbing. The film introduces the two as they are recruited to play for an exclusive suburban Catholic Academy, St. Joseph's. Their paths eventually diverge as Arthur loses his scholarship and returns to public school while William is groomed to be the team's next star. Assembled from over 250 hours of footage shot over five years, the film impressively pinpoints each young man's basketball highlights and lowlights, creating an urgent sense of athletic drama throughout. There's a bitter irony that so many young men place their hopes in basketball, and reaching the NBA, as a ticket out of the ghetto, when really it's just another level of exploitation and marketing. ★★★★ VHS: $19.99; DVD: $24.99

Hoosiers

(1986, 114 min, US, David Anspaugh) *Gene Hackman, Barbara Hershey, Dennis Hopper, Sheb Wooley, Fern Parsons, Brad Boyle.* Hackman gives a dynamic performance as the new coach to an Indiana high school basketball team, determined to get them to the championships. An exciting and involving drama, with great support from Hershey and Oscar nominee Hopper as a boozy fan. Even for those who avoid sports dramas, this is a must. ★★★½ VHS: $14.99; DVD: $19.99

H

H

Hope and Glory

(1987, 113 min, GB, John Boorman) *Sara Miles, David Hayman, Derrick O'Connor, Susan Woolbridge, Sammi Davis, Ian Bannen, Sebastian Rice-Edwards.* Boorman's sweet, finely crafted and quite humorous recollection of his childhood days in England during WWII at the time of the German Blitz. Young Rice-Edwards is Billy, the director's alter ego, through whose eyes we see a unique view of war-torn Britain. Miles is splendid as Billy's mother, who struggles to keep her family together in the wake of neighborhood bombings, extramarital affairs and indifferent adolescents. Perfectly cast and boasting outstanding production values, this reminiscence, like Woody Allen's similarly themed *Radio Days*, is a brilliant evocation of early 1940s life. ★★★★ VHS: $14.99; DVD: $19.99

Hope Floats

(1998, 112 min, US, Forest Whitaker) *Sandra Bullock, Harry Connick, Jr., Gena Rowlands, Mae Whitman, Michael Pare, Kathy Najimy.* This sentimental roller coaster delivers if you're looking for a tearjerker. All others be warned that the film pulls out all the emotional stops. Birdee (Bullock) goes on a talk show, and is told that her husband has been cheating on her with her best friend for over a year and that he is leaving her. Devastated and shamed, Birdee and her daughter Bernice take refuge with her mother (warmly played by Rowlands) in her hometown. Enter Justin (Connick), a former high school nerd, now a sexy and sympathetic house painter. There are plenty of tragic twists and turns until the inevitable happy ending. Fine acting and some heart-warming moments help elevate the film above the maudlin plot. ★★½ VHS: $14.99; DVD: $24.99

Hopscotch

(1980, 104 min, US, Ronald Neame) *Walter Matthau, Glenda Jackson, Ned Beatty, Sam Waterston.* Matthau and Jackson are reteamed (after *House Calls*) in this entertaining spy comedy with Matthau as a weary CIA agent who decides to publish his memoirs — and tell all. Beatty is his boss who's not too keen on the idea. ★★★

The Horn Blows at Midnight

(1945, 78 min, US, Raoul Walsh) *Jack Benny, Alexis Smith, Franklin Pangborn.* Though he often joked about this film being the turkey of the 1940s (and his career), Benny's ascent into the heavens is actually quite funny. Benny plays an angel who is dispatched to Earth to destroy it with one blow from Gabriel's horn. Though *To Be or Not To Be* is unquestionably Benny's one film classic, *Horn* is a pure lark with the comedian in wonderful form. ★★★ VHS: $19.99

Horror of Dracula

(1958, 82 min, GB, Terence Fisher) *Christopher Lee, Peter Cushing, Michael Gough, Melissa Stribling.* The first of the British Hammer Films to feature Lee as Count Dracula and Cushing as the tireless Dr. Van Helsing. In this outing, the Prince of Darkness ventures from Transylvania to London in search of new blood. A well-played and atmospheric horror tale that ably compares to the 1931 Bela Lugosi classic. ★★★½ VHS: $14.99

The Horror Show

(1989, 95 min, US, James Isaac) *Lance Henriksen, Dedee Pfeiffer, Brion James.* A serial killer who dies in the electric chair vows to take revenge on the cop who put him away. Now, as an unstoppable force, the killer returns to terrorize the cop and his family. ★½ VHS: $14.99

The Horse

(1983, 116 min, Turkey, Ali Ozgenturk) The incredible hardships endured by a father and son as they struggle against abject poverty is the plot of this compelling film. Reminiscent of *The Bicycle Thief*, the film, set in modern Turkey, details the father's attempts to earn enough money to send his son to school. A sensitive yet complex exposé of the grim realities of life, this film so upset the government that director Ozgenturk was sent to prison for several years. ★★★

Horse Feathers

(1932, 68 min, US, Norman Z. McLeod) *The Marx Brothers, Thelma Todd.* The password is "swordfish" as the Marx Brothers turn academia upside-down with Groucho as the head of Huxley College, preparing the school for the big game. Harpo and Chico are part-time students as well as spies. Todd is the "big girl on campus." With the exception of *Duck Soup*, this madcap romp is the funniest of all the Marx Brothers' movies. ★★★★ VHS: $14.99

Horse of Pride

(1980, 118 min, France, Claude Chabrol) *Jacques Dufilho, François Cluzet.* Chabrol, France's best-known chronicler of the foibles of the bourgeoisie, turns his cinematic eye towards a drastically different type of people: the proud but poor peasants of Brittany. Set in the early 1900s and adapted from the French best-selling novel by Pierre Jakez Helias, this earthy drama follows the rituals of birth, death, marriage and harvest in a Breton village during four seasons. Chabrol captures their values and mythology in a lifestyle that has been steadily dying. (Breton with English subtitles) ★★★½ VHS: $24.99

The Horse Soldiers

(1959, 119 min, US, John Ford) *John Wayne, William Holden, Hoot Gibson, Anna Lee.* Brooding Civil War drama with Wayne and Holden as ideologically opposed Union soldiers who are on a sabotage mission deep within Confederate territory. Not one of Ford's best, but nevertheless intriguing. ★★½ VHS: $14.99; DVD: $19.99

Horse Thief

(1986, 88 min, China, Tian Zhuangzhuang) Set in an isolated and impoverished village in Tibet, *Horse Thief* is a stirring yet simply told work of art. Nordo, a young and able man, is forced to steal in order to support his growing family. He is caught and, with family in tow, driven out of the village into nomadic life. In the harsh conditions of the countryside, his attempts to eke out an existence fail and he returns to repent. But he soon finds himself again attracted to theft. Full of mysterious religious rituals and haunted by images of death, this film eschews simple Communist doctrine and is more concerned with the ancient ways of dealing with the hardships and cruelties of life. (Mandarin with English subtitles) ★★★½ VHS: $59.99

The Horse Whisperer

(1998, 168 min, US, Robert Redford) *Robert Redford, Kristin Scott Thomas, Scarlett Johansson, Sam Neill, Dianne Wiest, Chris Cooper, Cherry Jones.* With the gorgeous mountains and fields of Montana as picturesque backdrop, Redford's emotionally satisfying and beautifully shot *The Horse Whisperer* is a stirring story of one young girl's coming of age and one woman's rediscovery of her heart. Based on the novel by Nicholas Evans, the film begins with a staggering horseback-riding accident. Thirteen-year-old Grace (Johannson) is injured in the fall, and her horse Pilgrim is about to be put to sleep. Grace's emotionally reserved mother Annie (Scott Thomas), decides to try to save the animal. She treks with Grace and Pilgrim to Montana where "horse whisperer" Tom Rooker (Redford) resides, hoping to mend both daughter and horse. It is Annie, however, who heals the most when she falls in love with Tom and regains the ability to love. (VHS available letterboxed or pan & scan) ★★★½ VHS: $14.99; DVD: $29.99

The Horse's Mouth

(1958, 93 min, GB, Ronald Neame) *Alec Guinness, Kay Walsh, Robert Coote, Michael Gough.* Guinness' flawless portrayal of Gulley Jimson, a crotchety and eccentric old artist whose love of painting leads to incessant mischief, is unquestionably one of his finest comic performances. Walsh is also brilliant as his reluctant cohabitant in this hilarious tribute to noncomformity and art. Guinness himself wrote the screenplay from a Joyce Cary novel. (Letterboxed) ★★★½ VHS: $24.99

The Horseman on the Roof
(Le Hussard sur le Toit)

(1996, 117 min, France, Jean-Paul Rappeneau) *Juliette Binoche, Olivier Martinez, Gérard Depardieu.* France's great cholera epidemic of 1832 would hardly suggest the backdrop to a gripping story of courage, loyalty and love, but with its exquisite cinematography, compelling performances and stirringly old-fashioned story line, *The Horseman on the Roof* is exactly that. Martinez stars as Angelo, handsome Colonel of the Hussards, who begins a Candide-like adventure in his attempt to return home to Italy. He is accompanied on his journey by a beautiful countess (Binoche). As small towns in Provence become ravaged with the enveloping epidemic, the two refugees encounter fear, death, intrigue, and their own hearts. Director Rappeneau (*Cyrano de Bergerac*) has crafted an ambitious epic both ravishing and penetrating which rarely falters in its intensity. Binoche offers a radiant performance, and Martinez is especially good as the dedicated soldier. (French with English subtitles) ★★★½

The Hospital

(1971, 103 min, US, Arthur Hiller) *George C. Scott, Diana Rigg, Bernard Hughes, Stockard Channing, Nancy Marchand.* Biting satire by Paddy Chayefsky with Scott as a disillusioned doctor working at a New York City hospital who finds more ills in both administrative policy and his fellow physicians than he does in his patients. Chayefsky won an Oscar for his scathing screenplay. ★★★½ VHS: $14.99

Hot Shots!

(1991, 85 min, US, Jim Abrahams) *Charlie Sheen, Cary Elwes, Valeria Golino, Lloyd Bridges, Jon Cryer, Kristy Swanson.* From one of the directors of *Airplane!* comes this often hilarious parody of military and pilot films, *Top Gun* in particular. The jokes are delivered at a machine-gun pace and most of them succeed. Sheen, satirizing his Navy SEALS role, is the Tom Cruise-ish, hotshot pilot competing against arrogant Elwes. Bridges shows up as an admiral who is obviously related to Bridges' *Airplane!* air traffic controller. Obviously, all are in *Airplane!* territory, here. And though the film doesn't reach the comic heights of that classic, *Hot Shots* is nevertheless a high-flying romp. (Sequel: *Hot Shots! Part Deux*) ★★★ VHS: $9.99

Hot Shots! Part Deux

(1993, 89 min, US, Jim Abrahams) *Charlie Sheen, Lloyd Bridges, Valeria Golino, Richard Crenna, Miguel Ferrer, Rowan Atkinson, Brenda Bakke.* More lowbrow hijinks courtesy of Abrahams and cowriter Pat Proft. Not as consistently funny as the first film, there are still quite a few funny bits to this spoof, which now sets its aim at *Rambo*-type films. Crenna even shows up to poke fun at his mentor role. And look for the cute cameo by Martin Sheen tipping his hat to his most famous role. ★★½ VHS: $9.99

Hot Spell

(1958, 86 min, US, Daniel Mann) *Shirley Booth, Anthony Quinn, Shirley MacLaine, Earl Holliman, Eileen Heckart.* Exceptional performances by Booth, Quinn and MacLaine highlight this compelling drama. Booth plays a middle-aged housewife who must contend with her husband's extramarital affairs and her children's romantic problems. ★★★

The Hot Spot

(1990, 120 min, US, Dennis Hopper) *Don Johnson, Virginia Madsen, Jennifer Connelly, Charles Martin Smith, William Sadler, Barry Corbin, Jack Nance.* Based on a Charles Williams pulp novel, this atmospheric and offbeat thriller tells a tale of robbery, murder, blackmail and "good-lookin'-but-dangerous dames" set in the dusty locales of a small Texas town. In the leading roles, Johnson as a low-life drifter and Madsen as a femme fatale fail to impress. The film is elevated, however, by a host of wonderful supporting actors and a bluesy score by John Lee Hooker and Miles Davis. ★★½ VHS: $9.99; DVD: $19.99

Hot to Trot

(1988, 83 min, US, Michael Dinner) *Bobcat Goldthwait, Dabney Coleman, Virginia Madsen; Voice of John Candy.* Goldthwait (who is a great stand-up comedian but who has yet to find a suitable film role) dons the Donald O'Connor role from the *Francis* movies of the 1950s in this tired talking horse comedy. ★ VHS: $14.99

Hotel Colonial

(1987, 103 min, US, Dinzia T.H. Torrini) *John Savage, Robert Duvall, Rachel Ward, Massimo Troisi.* Savage is called to Bogota, Colombia, to identify the body of his brother, who has supposedly committed suicide. But after trudging through the Amazonian jungle, Savage finds that his brother is actually living in a world of drugs and depravity. A dismal drama of betrayal and corruption. ★

The Hotel New Hampshire

(1984, 110 min, US, Tony Richardson) *Rob Lowe, Jodie Foster, Beau Bridges, Nastassja Kinski, Wallace Shawn, Matthew Modine, Wilford Brimley, Amanda Plummer, Anita Morris.* A felicitous actors' exercise which follows closely the John Irving novel. The serendipitous script examines the exploits of a highly unusual American family, both at home and abroad, and ranges in mood from the almost slapstick to the nearly tragic. While the direction tends to harbor self-indulgence, each actor's portrayal is inventive and endearing. ★★★ DVD: $19.99

Hotel Reserve

(1944, 79 min, GB, Peter Glenville) *James Mason, Lucie Mannheim, Herbert Lom.* Mason stars in this gripping drama about an Austrian refugee at a seaside resort in the south of France during WWII who helps the local police hunt down a Nazi spy. ★★★ VHS: $19.99

Hotel Terminus

(1988, 267 min, US, Marcel Ophüls) Winner of both the Cannes International Critics Prize in 1988 as well as the Academy Award for Best Documentary, this groundbreaking film is a meticulous investigation into the life of Klaus Barbie, the "Butcher of Lyons," whose Nazi war crimes include the ordering of the deaths of over 4,000 people as well as 44 children of Izieu. The film spans 70 years and traces the 40-year manhunt for the ruthless war criminal. An extraordinary film which is part detective story and part study of the complex web of international political deceit. *Hotel Terminus* can be considered the final chapter in Ophüls' trilogy on World War II which includes *The Sorrow and the Pity* and *Memory of Justice.* ★★★★ VHS: $14.99

The Hound of the Baskervilles

(1939, 80 min, US, Sidney Lanfield) *Basil Rathbone, Nigel Bruce, Richard Greene, Wendy Barrie, Lionel Atwill, John Carradine.* The sun never rises on the English moor; ominous foreboding permeates even broad daylight. Stark, brooding black-and-white cinematography establishes the ambience for Mr. Sherlock Holmes' unraveling of the centuries-old curse of the Baskerville family. This first pairing of Rathbone and Bruce as Sherlock Holmes and Dr. Watson clicked so powerfully that it was followed by another 13 Sherlock Holmes films. ★★★½

The Hound of the Baskervilles

(1959, 88 min, GB, Terence Fisher) *Peter Cushing, Andre Morell, Christopher Lee.* The horror masters at Hammer Studios chose Arthur Conan Doyle's most macabre mystery in what they had hoped would begin a new series for them. Cushing, though a little too aged for the role of Sherlock Holmes, does a credible job, keeping the great detective cold as ice and sharp as a tack. Effective and atmospheric. ★★★ VHS: $19.99

The Hound of the Baskervilles

(1977, 84 min, GB, Paul Morrissey) *Dudley Moore, Peter Cook, Kenneth Williams, Denholm Elliott, Spike Milligan, Terry-Thomas, Prunella Scales.* Basil Rathbone can rest easy as Morrissey's tepid spoof of Arthur Conan Doyle's classic novel falls laughlessly flat. Cowriters Moore and Cook should share the blame, as well, as their antics are deadly unfunny. Even a good supporting cast can't help. Moore slaps a happy medium, the dog runs away with the picture, and careers must be salvaged. ★

Hour of the Star

(1986, 96 min, Brazil, Suzanna Amaral) *Marcelia Cartaxo, Jose Dumont, Tamara Taxman, Fernanda Montenegro.* This deeply touching work harkens back to the grand neorealist style of *La Strada* and *The Bicycle Thief,* creating an unlikely heroine out of Macabea, an uneducated, obtuse girl from Brazil's northeastern provinces. Despite her impoverished surroundings, she carries herself with dignity and a surprising degree of wit. First-time director Amaral made the film when 52 years old, after raising nine children, then attending N.Y.U. (Portuguese with English subtitles) ★★★½ VHS: $79.99

Hour of the Wolf

(1967, 89 min, Sweden, Ingmar Bergman) *Max von Sydow, Liv Ullmann, Ingrid Thulin, Erland Josephson.* One of Bergman's most powerful works, *Hour of the Wolf* is a nightmarish drama of mental illness and creative intensity. A successful painter (von Sydow) and his loving wife (Ullmann) spend the summer on a barren island where, spurred by insomnia and haunted by demons both real and imagined, the man's sanity slowly unravels while his distraught wife helplessly watches. A haunting psychological horror film which mixes surrealistic touches with old-fashioned Gothic terror to create a brilliant and unforgettable vision of madness. (Swedish with English subtitles) ★★★★ VHS: $19.99

The Hours and Times

(1991, 60 min, GB, Christopher Münch) *Ian Hart, David Angus.* Taking the historic, seemingly unimportant fact that Beatles' manager and early guiding force Brian Epstein took John Lennon on a four-day vacation to Barcelona, Spain, just months before the meteoric rise of the Fab Four, director Münch has fashioned a fictional "what-might-have-happened" queer drama. Epstein — Jewish, upper-class and gay — and Lennon — a Liverpudlian working-class musician with unlimited but raw promise — seem an unlikely pair although their mentor/student relationship is rather intense. Their vastly different lifestyles attract and distance the two and is especially evident in Epstein's sexual attraction for the appreciative but hopelessly straight Lennon. This sexual tension provides the dramatic centerpiece in this understated and low-budget picture which works both as an engrossing exploration of the shifting nature and intensity of friendship and a touching example of unrequited love. Hart, who portrays Lennon, would play him again in *Backbeat.* ★★★½ VHS: $19.99

House

(1986, 93 min, US, Steve Miner) *William Katt, George Wendt, Richard Moll, Kay Lenz.* Tongue-in-cheek horror film about a horror novelist (Katt) who moves into the house of his deceased aunt to write about his Vietnam War experiences, and becomes terrorized by deadly, gruesome monsters. The film mixes decent horror effects with comedy, and the result is enjoyably silly. (Sequel: *House 2: The Second Story*) ★★½ VHS: $14.99; DVD: $29.99

House Arrest

(1996, 108 min, US, Harry Winer) *Jamie Lee Curtis, Kevin Pollak, Kyle Howard, Amy Sakasitz, Christopher McDonald, Wallace Shawn, Sheila McCarthy, Jennifer Tilly, Ray Walston.* On their wedding anniversary, Curtis and Pollak announce to their two children their intent to separate. Their seventh grade son Grover (Howard) decides to take radical steps and locks them in the basement in an attempt to force them to resolve their problems. Some neighborhood kids find out about the lock-up and force their parents to join the prisoners, creating a house of juvenile delinquents upstairs and disgruntled adults downstairs. *House Arrest* is too long, the ending is too pat, and there's not an abundance of funny scenes to overcome the story's banalities. ★★ VHS: $9.99

House Calls

(1978, 98 min, US, Howard Zieff) *Walter Matthau, Glenda Jackson, Art Carney, Richard Benjamin, Candice Azzara.* Matthau and Jackson make a surprisingly effective comedic team in this funny romantic romp. Swinging divorcé Walter is a surgeon who romances no-nonsense hospital administrator Glenda. Love and laughs — though not necessarily in that order — follow. Carney is great in support as an absentminded doc. ★★★

House of Angels

(1993, 119 min, Sweden/GB, Colin Nutley) *Helena Bergstrom, Rikard Wolff, Per Oscarsson.* Some would say the term "Swedish comedy" is an oxymoron, but thanks to British director Nutley, this delightful Nordic romp should sway all naysayers. A pixie-like Bergstrom stars as a young cabaret artist who returns to her mother's village to collect her inheritance, one of the town's prized estates. This, along with her leather-clad, motorcycle-straddling gay companion, Zac, turns the normally quiet little town into a beehive of gossip and curious disbelief. Sporting a wonderfully eccentric cast ranging from yokels to drag queens, the film is one of those marvelous contrivances which, though minor in scope, provides plenty of heartwarming good cheer. (Swedish with English subtitles) ★★★½ VHS: $19.99

House of Cards

(1993, 108 min, US, Michael Lessac) *Kathleen Turner, Tommy Lee Jones, Park Overall, Shiloh Strong, Esther Rolle.* While living in Mexico, seven-year-old Sally becomes influenced by the legends told to her by a native guide after her father dies in an accident at an archeological dig. Back in the States, Sally withdraws from her family, stops speaking and begins to exhibit spectacular feats of the mind and body leading doctors to diagnose her as autistic. Sally's mother (Turner) refuses to accept the diagnosis and begins to devise a cure. Besides being a tense and well-acted drama of love and mysticism, *House of Cards* asks tough questions about what's "normal" and the process involved in "curing" a child with a brilliant mind. ★★★½ VHS: $19.99; DVD: $24.99

House of Dark Shadows

(1970, 96 min, US, Dan Curtis) *Jonathan Frid, Joan Bennett, Grayson Hall.* Theatrical version of the popular 1960s daytime horror soap opera, "Dark Shadows." Frid returns as Barnabas

Collins, the 18th-century New England aristocrat-turned-vampire, here looking to end his curse. Some good chills, and recommended for fans of the TV show. ★★★ VHS: $19.99

House of Games

(1987, 102 min, US, David Mamet) *Lindsay Crouse, Joe Mantegna, Lilia Skala, J.T. Walsh.* Playright Mamet's directorial film debut is this superbly crafted story about an uptight psychiatrist (Crouse) who goes thrill-seeking with a sophisticated con artist (Mantegna). Filled with red herrings and unexpected twists, Mamet's ingenious screenplay imparts a keen sense of psychology doused with a hilarious and wry sense of humor. The acting is outstanding; Crouse is eerily emotionless as the famous shrink and Mantegna is both charming and alluring as the smooth-operating grifter. ★★★½ VHS: $19.99; DVD: $19.99

The House of Mirth

(2000, 140 min, GB, Terence Davies) *Gillian Anderson, Eric Stoltz, Dan Aykroyd, Laura Linney, Anthony LaPaglia, Elizabeth McGovern.* Ecclesiastes reads: "The heart of fools is in the house of mirth." The heroine of Edith Wharton's novel of early 20th-century high society, Lily Bart, takes residence there after a heartrending journey. A sumptuous rendering in the same mold as Martin Scorsese's earlier Wharton adaptation, *The Age of Innocence,* but far more successful in its execution, *The House of Mirth* is a sometimes staggering tale of duplicity and loss set against a chillingly repressive atmosphere imposed by Lily's gender and station. While not quite able to elaborate Lily's naïveté, Anderson is nonetheless glimmering as the orphaned society woman in search of a suitable husband (read: rich), all the while in love with a lawyer (Stoltz) of modest means. As the independent-minded but financially insecure Lily maneuvers through a maze of deception and pretense, she sets a course navigated by her own moral verisimilitude, betrayed by her honorable ideas. Marred only by abrupt character introduction, *The House of Mirth* is a superior period piece filled with gorgeous detail and exquisite performances. ★★★½ VHS: $21.99; DVD: $29.99

The House of the Spirits

(1994, 132 min, US/Sweden, Bille August) *Jeremy Irons, Meryl Streep, Glenn Close, Winona Ryder, Antonio Banderas.* Savagely received by the American film critics but embraced by the European critics, this near-epic adaptation of Isabel Allende's acclaimed novel of thwarted love and class distinction fails to fully capture the essence of the original text. But for all its shortcomings, the film possesses a sense of poetry and conviction which counter the heavy dramatics. Set against the backdrop of political upheaval in an unnamed South American country (read: Chile), the story follows the lives of the multi-generational Trueba family: including an oppressive landowner father (Irons); his innocent, clairvoyant wife (Streep); their young daughter (Ryder); and the family's repressed aunt (the remarkable Close), who has been banished by her unforgiving brother. Awash in mysticism and romantic symbolism, the film will both intrigue and infuriate with its crystalline emotions and excesses. ★★★ VHS: $19.99; DVD: $14.99

Gillian Anderson in *The House of Mirth*

House of Wax

(1953, 88 min, US, Andre de Toth) *Vincent Price, Phyllis Kirk, Charles Bronson, Carolyn Jones.* A smash hit in its day, and originally shown in 3-D, this chiller has long been a horror favorite. Price plays a sculptor who resorts to real subjects to carve after a fire mishap leaves him disfigured. ★★★ VHS: $9.99

The House of Yes

(1997, 90 min, US, Mark Waters) *Parker Posey, Josh Hamilton, Tori Spelling, Freddie Prinze, Jr., Genevieve Bujold.* Egregiously ignored in its brief theatrical run, *The House of Yes* is the most wicked comedy-incest-mental illness-melodrama of its year. Fans of *Spanking the Monkey* shouldn't miss this sharply written tale of a dysfunctional family get-together. Martin (Hamilton) brings his new fiancée Leslie (Spelling) to his bourgeois home for Thanksgiving. There they must cope with Martin's medicated, Kennedy-obsessed twin Jackie-O (Posey). Jackie-O views Leslie's presence as a very pesky distraction to their sibling bonds of sex and assassination re-enactments, and she berates her with endless biting, off-hand remarks about Leslie's poor upbringing and social standing. Posey is fabulous as always, and the rest of the ensemble is splendid. Tori doesn't even suck. Only a slightly incongruous finale mars this otherwise riotous opus to family relations. ★★★½ VHS: $14.99; DVD: $29.99

The House on Carroll Street

(1988, 100 min, US, Peter Yates) *Kelly McGillis, Jeff Daniels, Mandy Patinkin, Jessica Tandy.* Intriguing thriller set during the McCarthy era as subversive "red" McGillis mixes it up with FBI agent Daniels when she unwittingly uncovers an underground Nazi organization. ★★½ VHS: $9.99

House on Chelouche Street

(1973, 120 min, Israel, Moshe Mizrahi) *Gila Almagor, Michal Bat-Adam.* This family drama is set in Tel Aviv during the turbulent period of British rule just before the partition of

Palestine. The film successfully captures the excitement and anxiety in a rapidly evolving country. (Hebrew with English subtitles) ★★★ VHS: $19.99

House on Haunted Hill

(1958, 75 min, US, William Castle) *Vincent Price, Carol Ohmart, Richard Long.* Semi-classic haunted house story with Price as an eccentric millionaire who offers a group of strangers $10,000 each to spend a night in his haunted mansion. Good, old-fashioned, eerie fun. (Remade in 1999) ★★★ VHS: $14.99; DVD: $19.99

House on Haunted Hill

(1999, 96 min, US, William Malone) *Geoffrey Rush, Famke Janssen, Taye Diggs, Ali Larter, Bridgette Wilson, Peter Gallagher, Chris Kattan, Jeffrey Combs, Max Perlich.* This remake of Vincent Price's 1958 fun ghost story is lots of fun as well. Never taking itself too seriously (like the terrible remake of *The Haunting*), this updated ghost tale immediately pays homage to the original by naming its lead character Price. He's played by Rush, an amusement park magnate whose trophy wife (Janssen) convinces him to throw her birthday party at a supposedly haunted, now-abandoned insane asylum. Guests arrive, and all are offered a million dollars if they can live the night. Then things get spooky. It's all red herrings, shadowy figures and what's-around-the-corner boos, the kind of scares we've certainly seen before. But it's done with a certain tongue-in-cheekiness and a sense of fun that much of it is hard to resist — on a isn't-it-cheesy, seen-it-before level. ★★½ VHS: $14.99; DVD: $19.99

The House on 92nd Street

(1945, 88 min, US, Henry Hathaway) *William Eythe, Lloyd Nolan, Signe Hasso, Gene Lockhart, Leo G. Carroll.* Based on a real-life spy case during WWII, this exciting, low-keyed thriller is told in a taut semidocumentary style. Nolan stars as an FBI chief who is put in charge of the case of Nazi and Fifth Columnist infiltration after it is discovered the Germans are obtaining secrets about the atom bomb. Eythe is the American double agent setting up the Nazis, and Hasso and Carroll are two of the German agents. Beginning with a shot of J. Edgar Hoover busy at work, the film at times seems to be none-too-subtle propaganda for the government agency, but the story soon takes charge to deliver a well-detailed and crisp espionage adventure. Location footage helps in the film's general feeling of authenticity. ★★★½ VHS: $19.99

House Party

(1989, 96 min, US, Reginald Hudlin) *Christopher Reid, Christoper Martin, Robin Harris, Martin Lawrence, Tisha Campbell.* A refreshingly hip and surprisingly innocent comedy about a day in the life of a group of black suburban teenagers who simply want to throw a party without getting hassled. The story revolves around Kid (Reid, from the rap duo Kid N' Play), who must sneak out of his house and avoid a gang of thugs. Although the plot is thin, this spirited and delightful musical/dance/comedy is even more impressive in that it shows black teens having fun without resorting to the stereotypes of them being druggies, criminals or impoverished. Harris is hilari-

ous as Kid's overprotective, Dolemite-loving father. (Followed by 2 sequels) ★★★ VHS: $14.99; DVD: $19.99

House Party 2

(1991, 94 min, US, Doug McHenry & George Jackson) *Christopher Reid, Christopher Martin, Tisha Campbell, Iman, Queen Latifah, Georg Stanford Brown.* Fans of the original *House Party* might be disappointed by this politically correct, message-laden sequel to the 1990 hit starring rap stars Kid N' Play (Reid, Martin). Hip-hop hijinks ensue when Play connives to throw "the mother of all pajama parties" on the college campus where Kid is about to be expelled. ★★ VHS: $14.99; DVD: $19.99

House Party 3

(1994, 93 min, US, Eric Meza) *Christopher Reid, Christopher Martin, Tisha Campbell, Angela Means, Michael Colyar.* Kid N' Play return, here as L.A. record producers, in this truly tedious sequel. After receiving advance money from the record executive "Showboat" (Colyar), the mixed-up duo decides to squander their newfound fortune on Kid's bachelor party. Wallowing in a sea of sexist and racial stereotypical humor, this foul-mouthed feature is saved on occasion by the energetic performances of chart-toppers TLC and pint-sized rappers Immature. ★½ VHS: $14.99; DVD: $19.99

Houseboat

(1958, 110 min, US, Melville Shavelson) *Cary Grant, Sophia Loren, Harry Guardino, Martha Hyer.* Charming romantic comedy starring Grant as an overwhelmed widower who hires Loren as a maid (though she's really a socialite) to take care of his three children and their houseboat. The kind of enjoyable '50s romantic fluff which Grant seemed to have a patent on. Guardino is a scene-stealer as the handyman. ★★★ VHS: $14.99

Houseguest

(1995, 108 min, US, Randall Miller) *Sinbad, Phil Hartman, Jeffrey Jones, Kim Greist, Stan Shaw.* The premise for this genial comedy is an old one: In order to get away from the thugs looking for him, Sinbad assumes the identity of another; here, the boyhood friend of Hartman. As he is whisked away to the safe confines of suburbia, Sinbad ultimately enriches the lives of these strangers while they do the same for him. While the concept and even the execution is stale, both actors manage to wring whatever comic life is present. *Houseguest* may not be totally unwanted, but it comes dangerously close to overstaying its welcome. ★★ VHS: $9.99

Household Saints

(1993, 124 min, US, Nancy Savoca) *Lili Taylor, Vincent D'Onofrio, Tracey Ullman, Illeana Douglas.* In her previous feature-length outings (*True Love, Dogfight*), director Savoca evidenced an uncanny ability to capture the feel of the films' eras and environments. In *Household Saints*, she adds an element of the surreal which creates the mythic dimension with which we remember our childhoods and the stories our parents and grandparents told us. D'Onofrio and Ullman are winsome as the husband and wife (he wins her in a pinochle game) whose daughter (Taylor) becomes the neighborhood saint in

1950s Brooklyn. The film is delightful, funny and entertaining. ★★★½ VHS: $19.99

Householder

(1962, 101 min, India, James Ivory) *Shashi Kapoor, Leela Naidu.* The first collaboration between director Ivory, producer Ismail Merchant and writer Ruth Prawer Jhabvala (who would go on to create, among others, *The Remains of the Day*) is this delightful and warm-hearted but uneven comedy. Kapoor plays a young teacher who, pushed by his meddlesome mother, enters into an arranged marriage with a woman equally naïve and inexperienced. Troubles begin for the couple as they find themselves unprepared for the difficulties of marriage and its financial responsibilities. While not one of the trio's best works, the film provides an interesting background for their future films. ★★½ VHS: $29.99

The Housekeeper

(1986, 106 min, Canada, Ousami Rawi) *Rita Tushingham, Ross Petty, Jackie Burroughs.* Tushingham is excellent in the lead role as a dyslexic cleaning lady who goes on a murderously psychotic jag. Chilling suspense is accented by occasional forays into black humor in this sometimes confusing thriller. ★★½ VHS: $19.99

Housekeeping

(1987, 116 min, US, Bill Forsyth) *Christine Lahti, Sara Walker, Andrea Burchill.* Forsyth's first American film (shot in the Pacific Northwest) is a brilliantly quirky comedy about familial ties and individuality. Lahti gives a sensational performance as vagabond Aunt Sylvie, who comes to stay to look after her recently orphaned nieces (nicely played by Walker and Burchill). The film touchingly examines the close-knit relationship of the two sisters, and the influence Aunt Sylvie has on the two girls: one socially conscious and embarrassed by her aunt, and the other a soulmate. A film of rare sensitivity and character, with a haunting finale. ★★★★ VHS: $19.99

Housesitter

(1992, 102 min, US, Frank Oz) *Steve Martin, Goldie Hawn, Julie Harris, Dana Delany, Donald Moffat, Peter MacNicol.* A funny screwball romp about a woman who, through a web of lies and

Taye Diggs in *House on Haunted Hill* (1999)

H

deceits, squirms her way into the life of an unsuspecting architect with side-splitting results. It's a plot which is vaguely reminiscent of classics like *Bringing Up Baby* and *Ball of Fire*. Of course, Hawn, admirable a job though she does, can never be compared to the great Kate, and Martin is certainly no Cary Grant; but still, the film's outrageous humor and situations give these two modern-day comics plenty of good material to make for a thoroughly enjoyable laugh fest. ★★★ VHS: $7.49

How Green Was My Valley

(1941, 118 min, US, John Ford) *Walter Pidgeon, Maureen O'Hara, Donald Crisp, Roddy McDowall, Anna Lee, Barry Fitzgerald.* This Academy Award winner for Best Picture is a touching, expertly directed saga of a Welsh coal mining family. Crisp won an Oscar for his splendid portrayal of the family patriarch, as did Ford for his outstanding direction. ★★★★ VHS: $14.99; DVD: $24.99

How I Got into College

(1989, 89 min, US, Savage Steve Holland) *Anthony Edwards, Lara Flynn Boyle, Corey Parker, Charles Rocket, Brian Doyle-Murray.* Holland's occasionally funny but predictable and surprisingly lifeless comedy scores about a C-. Told in typical Savage Steve style, wacky characters and situations abound in this not-so-savage farce about the college entrance experience. Some of the jokes fall with a thud — but there are enough truly funny scenes to give this comedy a passing grade. Holland clearly remembers all the anxieties and hopes of the young adult years, but it's about time he grew up a little. ★★½ VHS: $9.99

How I Won the War

(1967, 109 min, GB, Richard Lester) *John Lennon, Michael Crawford, Jack MacGowran, Michael Hordern.* Lennon stars in this funny and surreal portrait of one man's less than Rambo-like military career. This often hilarious presentation of the lives of a rag-tag group of WWII soldiers taps into the somewhat naive but joyously nihilistic anti-militarism of the time. The material is certainly "dated," but the heart of the piece is in the right place. ★★★ VHS: $14.99

How Stella Got Her Groove Back

(1998, 121 min, US, Kevin Rodney Sullivan) *Angela Bassett, Whoopi Goldberg, Taye Diggs, Regina King.* Can a 40-year-old woman facing a midlife crisis find happiness in the arms of a handsome 20-year-old? If you believe this well-produced if familiar romantic drama, then the answer is yes. Bassett stars as Stella, a successful San Francisco stock broker and mother who takes an impromptu vacation to Jamaica with lifelong friend Delilah (Goldberg). There she begins a tentative affair with ex-medical student Winston (Diggs), a local with designs on the attractive Stella. Through some clichéd dramatics and out-of-date dilemmas, Stella faces an uncertain future in the arms of someone 20 years her junior. Bassett gives a competent performance but the script never really gives this terrific actress room to soar. In a nice supporting turn, Goldberg is quite good as Delilah, who ultimately succumbs to Best-Friend syndrome. ★★½ VHS: $14.99; DVD: $24.99

How Tasty Was My Little Frenchman

(1973, 80 min, Brazil, Nelson Pereira dos Santos) *Arduino Colasanti, Ana Maria Magalhaes, Ital Natur.* As the French and Portuguese swarm the Brazilian coastline in the mid-1500s, the indigenous Indian tribes align themselves with their would-be conquerers according to their own local conflicts (the friend of my enemy is my enemy). One hapless Frenchman is left to drown by a Portuguese contingent. However, he wades to shore to be found by an Indian tribe friendly to the French. Unfortunately, they mistake him for a Portuguese, and they are cannibals. Much like colonialism itself, the victim is expected to participate in the ritual of exploitation — he has a speaking part in the cooking ceremony. He is given a wife to help him learn his lines, and is well-fed during his period of instruction. He is avidly attentive to his education in tribal ways, hoping to endear himself to his captors. This delightful farce overcomes its low budget and sometimes haphazard construction with droll insight and a wicked sense of humor, courtesy of director dos Santos, a leading proponent of Brazil's Cinema Novo. (French and Tupi with English subtitles) ★★★ VHS: $79.99

How the West Was Won

(1962, 162 min, US, John Ford, Henry Hathaway & George Marshall) *Henry Fonda, John Wayne, James Stewart, Gregory Peck, Richard Widmark, Debbie Reynolds, George Peppard, Robert Preston, Agnes Moorehead.* It took three directors to bring this overblown, epic western to the screen. One of the ultimate "all-star cast" extravaganzas released during the 1960s, this mammoth production was originally shown in 3-strip Cinerama, which is lost on the small screen. The story traces the lives of three generations of a pioneer family. Some outstanding action scenes (the river raft and train sequences in particular). (VHS available letterboxed or pan & scan) ★★★ VHS: $14.99; DVD: $19.99

How to Be a Woman and Not Die in the Attempt

(1991, 96 min, Spain, Ana Belén) *Carmen Maura, Antonio Resines, Juanjo Puigcorbé, Carmen Conesa.* An episodic comedy-drama about Carmen (Maura), an Everywoman who deals with a disappointing husband, an underappreciative boss, and some thankless children, *How to Be a Woman* does a great job in setting up the frustrations of its central character, but the expected epiphany never quite arrives. Perhaps director Belén deliberately wants to leave viewers unsatisfied, because several of the story lines introduced remain unanswered. Nevertheless, viewers will care deeply about Carmen — Maura gives an outstanding, expressive performance, radiant one minute and dejected the next — as her character copes with the endless demands of work, home and family life. (Spanish with English subtitles) ★★★ VHS: $79.99; DVD: $24.99

How to Beat the High Cost of Living

(1980, 105 min, US, Robert Scheerer) *Jessica Lange, Jane Curtin, Susan Saint James, Richard Benjamin, Fred Willard, Dabney Coleman.* A trio of housewives embark on a comedic caper to nab some cash from their local shopping mall. Though a good premise, even a agreeable cast can't make sense of this muddled farce. ★½

How to Get Ahead in Advertising

(1989, 95 min, GB, Bruce Robinson) *Richard E. Grant, Rachel Ward.* A brilliant piece of rowdy leftist propoganda with shades of Monty Python, Kafka and Sigmund Freud. When ace London adman Dennis Bagley (Grant) is unable to concoct that perfect pitch for a pimple remedy, his subconscious kicks in and produces a rapidly growing pimple on his neck. Yet this is no ordinary zit! This one talks and spews a wicked venom, both at Bagley and the viewer. As the pesky pimple grows larger, its rantings on behalf of unbridled materialism become uglier and its urge to take over our hero's body becomes stronger. Where will it end? The ever shining Ward plays Bagley's wife and is the perfect foil to the boisterous boil's grotesque humor. No adventurous viewer should dare miss this fiendish satire. ★★★½; DVD: $29.99

How to Make an American Quilt

(1995, 109 min, US, Jocelyn Moorhouse) *Winona Ryder, Ellen Burstyn, Anne Bancroft, Maya Angelou, Kate Nelligan, Jean Simmons.* By no means a great film, *How to Make an American Quilt* is probably the most successful of 1995's many female ensemble pieces. Ryder is a college student who spends her summer vacation with her grandmother (the always tangy Bancroft). As the young woman looks to set her romantic and academic lives in order, she becomes enmeshed in Bancroft's quilting circle, a group of mostly older women who all share a past of secrets, pain and camaraderie. With so many stories weaving through the narrative, one or two may not be as dramatically exciting, but each member of the film's terrific cast heartens the tale with a refreshing, robust liveliness. ★★★ VHS: $9.99; DVD: $24.99

How to Marry a Millionaire

(1953, 95 min, US, Jean Negulesco) *Marilyn Monroe, Betty Grable, Lauren Bacall, William Powell, David Wayne, Cameron Mitchell.* Hollywood's first Cinemascope comedy is a witty and stylish soufflé starring Monroe, Grable and Bacall as three Manhattan gold diggers out to trap (and marry) unsuspecting millionaire bachelors. ★★★ VHS: $9.99; DVD: $24.99

How to Murder Your Wife

(1965, 118 min, US, Richard Quine) *Jack Lemmon, Virna Lisi, Claire Trevor, Mary Wickes.* Typically funny 1960s sex farce with Lemmon as a happily unmarried cartoonist who awakens one morning to find himself wed to the lovely Lisi. He quickly devises numerous plans to get rid of her. ★★★ VHS: $19.99

How to Succeed in Business without Really Trying

(1967, 121 min, US, David Swift) *Robert Morse, Michelle Lee, Rudy Vallee, Anthony Teague.* Delightful screen version of the Tony Award- and Pulitzer Prize-winning Broadway musical with Morse re-creating his acclaimed stage role. Morse stars as a mail room clerk who works his way up the corporate ladder in record time, thanks to the help of a little book and a lot of chutzpah. A terrific farce on big business, with great support from Vallee ("Groundhog!") and Lee. Frank Loesser's classic score includes "Brotherhood of Man" and "I Believe in You." Choreographed by Bob Fosse on stage, only one dance number remains. ★★★ VHS: $14.99; DVD: $19.99

How U Like Me Now

(1992, 109 min, US, Darryl Roberts) *Darnell Williams, Salli Richardson, Daniel Gardner.* First-time director Roberts proves to be a talent to be reckoned with with this charming low-budget urban comedy which recounts the professional and romantic struggles of twentysomething friends living in Chicago's South Side. The film tackles many issues, including interracial romance, buppies, back-to-Africa politics, and others, without being heavy-handed or alienating like some films of this genre. ★★★ VHS: $89.99

Howard the Duck

(1986, 111 min, US, Willard Huyck) *Lea Thompson, Jeffrey Jones, Tim Robbins.* One of the infamous duds of the 1980s, this comic fantasy isn't the worst movie ever made; however, it is an overproduced mess. Based on the comic book, it's all about an alien duck who travels to Cleveland and is befriended by rock star Thompson. In the immortal words of Groucho: "Why a duck?" ★ VHS: $7.49

Howards End

(1992, 140 min, GB, James Ivory) *Anthony Hopkins, Emma Thompson, Vanessa Redgrave, Helena Bonham Carter, Sam West, Nicola Duffett.* A sumptuous re-creation of E. M. Forster's novel of class struggle in the dying days of the Edwardian era. The story centers around the tragic confluence of three families from London's various social strata. Redgrave and Hopkins personify the upper crust as the Wilcoxes. The Schlegel sisters (Thompson and Bonham Carter) represent the liberal middle class. And Leonard Bast (West), an educated Cockney trying to make his way into the world of business, and his wife (Duffett) embody the lower depths. Filmed with all of the pomp and circumstance one has come to expect of Merchant Ivory productions, and acted with loving attention to both the mannerisms and prose of the era, *Howards End* is a truly marvelous and engaging period piece. Thompson won a well-deserved Oscar for her portrayal of the elder Schlegel, and is equally matched by Hopkins. ★★★★ VHS: $19.99; DVD: $29.99

The Howling

(1981, 91 min, US, Joe Dante) *Dee Wallace, Patrick MacNee, Dennis Dugan, Christopher Stone, Kevin McCarthy, John Carradine, Slim Pickens.* From the director who loved horror films as a kid (and then never grew up), this werewolf tale is resplendent with in-jokes, character actors and good, scary special effects. Like Dante's other works (*Gremlins 1 & 2, Explorers*), *The Howling* takes off at full gallop and doesn't stop, reflecting his years cutting trailers for Roger Corman. Co-written by John Sayles. ★★★ VHS: $9.99; DVD: $14.99

The Hucksters

(1947, 120 min, US, Jack Conway) *Clark Gable, Ava Gardner, Deborah Kerr, Sydney Greenstreet, Adolphe Menjou, Edward Arnold.* A glossy, satirical look at the business of advertising. Gable is an idealistic go-getter who finds he must virtually sell his soul in order to succeed. Kerr appears in her first American film. ★★★ VHS: $19.99

Hud

(1963, 112 min, US, Martin Ritt) *Paul Newman, Melvyn Douglas, Patricia Neal, Brandon de Wilde.* Newman gives a riveting performance as the disreputable son of Texas cattle rancher Douglas in this outstanding modern-day western. Brilliantly photographed by James Wong Howe, the film centers on Newman's volatile relationships with his estranged father (who is faced with financial ruin), impressionable nephew Brandon de Wilde, and world-weary housekeeper Neal. Oscars deservedly went to Neal as Best Actress and Douglas as Supporting Actor; in fact, the entire ensemble is superb. A film of such grit you can almost taste the dust. Based on a novel by Larry McMurtry ("The Last Picture Show," "Lonesome Dove"). ★★★★ VHS: $14.99

Hudson Hawk

(1991, 95 min, US, Michael Lehmann) *Bruce Willis, Danny Aiello, Andie MacDowell, James Coburn, Sandra Bernhard.* A major disappointment from the director of *Heathers*. Willis stars in this half-hearted comic adventure as a cat burglar who is coerced into committing a series of robberies. MacDowell is the Vatican spy he tangles with, Aiello is his partner, and Coburn is the CIA renegade trying to stop him. In all fairness, the actors try to maintain a degree of wackiness and lightheartedness, but there's too much mugging and winking; the viewer is numbed by a cast going to extremes to show the good time they're (supposed to be) having. Even the always-fun Bernhard appears lost. ★½ VHS: $9.99; DVD: $14.99

The Hudsucker Proxy

(1994, 111 min, US, Joel Coen) *Tim Robbins, Paul Newman, Jennifer Jason Leigh, Charles Durning, John Mahoney, Jim True, Bruce Campbell, Steve Buscemi.* With their usual cinematic aplomb, the Coen Brothers open the floodgates and unleash a torrent of invigorating witticisms and dizzying visuals in this spectacular, over-the-top tribute to the 1940s screwball comedy.

Robbins stars as a beamish Midwestern rube working in the Orwellian mailroom of the Hudsucker Corporation, a megalithic industrial powerhouse headed up by a heartless and power-hungry Newman. True to the genre, Robbins soon finds himself on a meteoric rise to power upon which he must learn life's hard lessons. Leigh, as a hard-nosed reporter, rat-a-tat-tats her lines at machine gun pace while paying splendid homage to Katharine Hepburn, Rosalind Russell and Barbara Stanwyck. ★★★½ VHS: $14.99; DVD: $19.99

Hugo Pool

(1997, 90 min, US, Robert Downey) *Alyssa Milano, Patrick Dempsey, Robert Downey, Jr., Richard Lewis, Malcolm McDowell, Cathy Moriarty, Sean Penn.* Misguided and inept in every department, *Hugo Pool* rivals only the pooch from *As Good as It Gets* as 1997's top dog. Milano is (inexplicably) Hugo, assigned to clean 44 pools in one day. While working her rounds, she encounters an array of "quirky" eccentrics — you know the type, the ones to give quirky a bad name. These include wheelchair-bound Dempsey, afflicted with Lou Gehrig's Disease and only capable of communicating via computerized voice; and Downey, who has a penchant for bizarre accents and gay theatrics. Given its seizure-inducing dialogue, grating score and career-nadir performances, *Hugo Pool* is an even bigger disappointment given the talented, eclectic cast (with exception of Milano, who has the screen presence of tissue paper). ★ VHS: $14.99; DVD: $24.99

Hullabaloo Over Georgie and Bonnie's Pictures

(1978, 82 min, India, James Ivory) *Victor Bannerjee, Aparna Sen, Saeed Jaffrey, Peggy Ashcroft.* This film is a lighthearted romp through royal India — a world of princesses, palaces, tourists, precious art objects and the people who wheel and deal with them. What's all the hullabaloo about? Georgie owns a priceless collection of ancient paintings which he loves, but his sister

Les Girls (Marilyn, Lauren and Betty) in *How to Marry a Millionaire*

wants more practical objects and wants him to sell. Frantic art dealers are soon in hot pursuit as the royal couple are deluged with people who want to buy. A great double twist ending concludes this exotic film. ★★★

The Human Comedy

(1943, 117 min, US, Clarence Brown) *Mickey Rooney, Frank Morgan, Fay Bainter, James Craig.* Exceptional adaptation of William Saroyan's best-seller about the trials and tribulations of small-town life during WWII. This slice-of-life drama stars Rooney in possibly his best dramatic performance as a sensitive teenager coming of age, and Morgan is terrific in support. ★★★1/2 VHS: $24.99

Human Condition, Part 1

(1959, 200 min, Japan, Masaki Kobayashi) *Tatsuya Nakadai, Michiyo Aratama.* The Human Condition is an epic chronicle of one man's struggle to retain his humanity as he descends into the hypnotic, distorted reality of war. As Part 1 (*No Greater Love*) opens, production at a mining camp in occupied Manchuria is at a standstill. With a Japan desperate for raw resources for its war machine, Kaji, a pacifist who believes that effective management requires winning the hearts and minds of the workers, is given authority. (Japanese with English subtitles) (Followed by 2 sequels) ★★★ VHS: $59.99; DVD: $29.99

Human Condition, Part 2

(1960, 180 min, Japan, Masaki Kobayashi) *Tatsuya Nakadai, Michiyo Aratama.* Part 2 (*Road to Eternity*) begins with Kaji being tortured by the military police for having treated the Chinese humanely. Allowed one memorable night with his wife, Kaji is then ordered to the front. His records brand him "red" and his superiors mistreat him zealously. (Japanese with English subtitles) ★★★ VHS: $59.99; DVD: $29.99

Human Condition, Part 3

(1961, 190 min, Japan, Masaki Kobayashi) *Tatsuya Nakadia, Michiyo Aratama.* Part 3 (*A Soldier's Prayer*) commences as Kaji awakens to a world in chaos and where the surviving Japanese soldiers savagely retreat from an equally brutal Soviet Army. Kaji's own moral standards are challenged when he is forced to kill to survive. The film's final section, set in a Russian POW camp, has our hero understanding that the socialist ideas that he has championed offer no shield to man's basest tendencies. (Japanese with English subtitles) ★★★ VHS: $59.99; DVD: $29.99

Human Traffic

(2000, 84 min, GB, Justin Kerrigan) *John Simm, Lorraine Pilkington, Shaun Parkes, Danny Dyer.* A weekend in the lives of a group of friends, as they take ecstasy, go to raves, have sex, and bitch about their dead-end jobs. First-time director Kerrigan has fashioned an infectious, ultra-stylish comedy out of potentially hackneyed material. Spot-on observations on sex, friendship, ambition, family and a slew of other topics are complimented by a fun soundtrack and some big laughs along the way. While even at a scant 84 minutes, *Human Traffic* does lose energy towards the end, but it remains an entertain-

ing, insightful film experience. ★★★ VHS: $19.99; DVD: $32.99

Humanité

(2000, 148 min, France, Bruno Dumont) *Emmanuel Schotté, Séverine Caneele. Philippe Tullier.* Pharaon De Winter (Schotté) is a quietly withdrawn, unremarkable man, a police inspector at times overwhelmed by the stark brutality he encounters in his job. Middle-aged, introspective, still wracked by a recent personal loss, he lives with his mother in a small French farming community, more as an observer than a participant in life. The savagely beautiful, uncompromising *Humanité* follows his investigation of a particularly horrific crime through a series of vignettes, each revealing a piece of the puzzle or an aspect of a protagonist's character. Director Dumont has structured a psychological portrait in the manner of *Jeanne Dielman*, a deliberately paced, thoughtfully considered examination of a man who seems sometimes somnambulistic, yet is desirous of connection; a man who stands apart yet is much like any other; a decent man capable of acts of humanity. (French with English subtitles) ★★★1/2 VHS: $79.99; DVD: $24.99

Humoresque

(1946, 125 min, US, Jean Negulesco) *Joan Crawford, John Garfield, Oscar Levant.* This superior soap opera stars Crawford as a wealthy society woman becoming romantically involved with a young, talented musician (Garfield). Crawford and Garfield (who each offer an accomplished performance) are engaging together, and the melodramatic story line is consistently entertaining. ★★★ VHS: $19.99

The Hunchback of Notre Dame

(1923, 137 min, US, Wallace Worsley) *Lon Chaney, Patsy Ruth Miller.* Chaney enthralled a generation of filmgoers in this impressive silent film of the Victor Hugo classic about the deformed bell-ringer Quasimodo, and his love for a beautiful Gypsy girl. Chaney's characterization and makeup effects are outstanding. Remade several times, including the 1939 Charles Laughton version (still the best) and even a Disney animated feature. ★★★1/2 VHS: $24.99; DVD: $24.99

The Hunchback of Notre Dame

(1939, 117 min, US, William Dieterle) *Charles Laughton, Maureen O'Hara, Edmond O'Brien, Cedric Hardwicke, Thomas Mitchell.* Outstanding version of the Victor Hugo classic with Laughton in one of his best performances as the deformed bell-ringer Quasimodo. Told with great style, the film's production values are excellent and the acting first-rate. O'Hara is a lovely Esmerelda. The best of the many screen versions. ★★★★ VHS: $19.99; DVD: $19.99

The Hunchback of Notre Dame

(1996, 95 min, US, Gary Trousdale) *Voices of Demi Moore, Tom Hulce, Kevin Kline, Jason Alexander, Mary Wickes, Charles Kimbrough.* After the high drama and pointed social lessons of the admirable *Pocahontas*, the animators at Disney have taken on an even darker text with this beautifully crafted picture film based on Victor Hugo's classic novel. Changing little of the story but reframing it to reflect Disney's traditional style of storytelling, *Hunchback* is a

brightly colored, tune-filled adaptation which manages to find quite a few laughs in a story not known for having them. Quasimodo (wonderfully voiced by Hulce) is still ugly and deformed, but here he's not quite so grotesque as to frighten little ones, and he's given three gargoyle friends to pal around with, so he's not quite as pathetic and lonely. The music by Alan Menken and Stephen Schwartz is capable but not particularly memorable as other Menken scores. ★★★1/2 VHS: $26.99

A Hungarian Fairy Tale

(1987, 95 min, Hungary, Gyula Gazdag) *David Vermes, Mária Varga, Frantisek Husák, Eszter Csákányi.* Less fairy tale and more political fable, this magical film is a startling video find. Carried away on a cloud of romance after a performance of Mozart's "Magic Flute," a beautiful young woman with a Mona Lisa smile makes love with a handsome stranger. Their union produces a child, who is lovingly raised by the woman until she suddenly dies. The young boy, Andris, lost in the impersonal world of Budapest, begins an odyssey throughout Hungary searching for his father. Told with subtle humor and imbued with poetic beauty, this story of outsiders fleeing the confines of a conformist society is a remarkable achievement. (Hungarian with English subtitles) ★★★★ VHS: $19.99

Hunger

(1966, 115 min, Denmark, Henning Carlsen) *Per Oscarsson, Gunnel Lindblom.* Oscarsson won the Best Actor Award at the Cannes Film Festival for his portrayal of a penniless and starving artist in 1890s Norway. This grim yet absorbing drama follows the young man who, despite being physically emaciated from lack of eating and prone to talking to his shoes, as well as to hallucinations, retains hope for his survival and optimism for his success as a writer as he tackles his hunger, waning self-respect and an overwhelming loneliness. The film does not have much of a plot, yet Oscarsson's performance keeps the viewer riveted. Based on the first novel by Nobel Laureate Knut Hamsun. (Danish with English subtitles) ★★★ VHS: $79.99

The Hunger

(1983, 99 min, GB, Tony Scott) *Catherine Deneuve, Susan Sarandon, David Bowie, Cliff DeYoung, Willem Dafoe.* Deneuve stars as Miriam, an icy, elegant vampiress, hundreds of years old, who goes on the prowl for a new mate after her 200-year lover (Bowie) quickly ages. Her affections find their way to Sara (Sarandon), a doctor who has written on the subject of accelerated aging. Dripping with cinematic style and chic sexual intrigue, *The Hunger* is both a chilling vampire tale and a sensuous drama of lesbian attraction and desire. The two romp, fall into each other's arms and make love — and, of course, share blood. The two stars create unprecedented sensual sizzle. (VHS available letterboxed or pan & scan) ★★★1/2 VHS: $14.99

The Hunt

(1965, 93 min, Spain, Carlos Saura) *Alfredo Mayo, Ismael Merlo.* Under a relentless sun which scorches the parched fields of central Spain, three apparently successful middle-aged men, all veterans of the Spanish Civil War, and a young man set off for a day of rabbit hunting. Fueled by the heat and long simmering ten-

Denzel Washington in *The Hurricane*

sions, the hunt escalates from petty fighting and bickering into eventual bloodshed as the men's jealousies, obsessions and hatreds rise to the surface. Saura's searing psychological thriller, spare in style, probes man's cruel nature so successfully that its tale should shock the viewer. (Spanish with English subtitles) ★★★½ VHS: $19.99

The Hunt for Red October

(1990, 135 min, US, John McTiernan) *Sean Connery, Alec Baldwin, Scott Glenn, James Earl Jones, Sam Neill, Tim Curry.* Director McTiernan's thrilling adaptation of Tom Clancy's best-seller is a well-paced and gripping Cold War drama filled with intrigue and exciting action. Connery excels as a Soviet submarine skipper who steals a state-of-the-art sub from the Russian fleet and goes AWOL. The question now facing the CIA is this: does he want to defect or is he going to single-handedly plunge the world into nuclear war? Costar Baldwin is commanding as the CIA bookworm who is convinced of the defection theory. (VHS available letterboxed or pan & scan) (Sequel: *Patriot Games*) ★★★½ VHS: $14.99; DVD: $29.99

The Hunted

(1995, 111 min, US, J.F. Lawton) *Christopher Lambert, Joan Chen, John Lone.* This hokey actioner manages lapses of excitement. Lambert stars as an American businessman in Japan who is on the run after witnessing the murder of a beautiful geisha (Chen) by a villainous ninja assassin (Lone). Violent almost to the point of slapstick, Lawton's film is yet another feeble attempt to cash in on the current "Asian cinemania" and as such features decent swordplay and a fast-paced (but ridiculous) script. ★★ VHS: $19.99; DVD: $24.99

Hurlyburly

(1998, 126 min, US, Anthony Drazan) *Sean Penn, Kevin Spacey, Robin Wright Penn, Chazz Palminteri, Garry Shandling, Anna Paquin, Meg Ryan.* David Rabe's 1984 play about drug-addled and emotionally unstable Hollywood almost-players has become something else onscreen. Could be that the cocaine-crazed scene has become passé, or that characters this desperate aren't funny anymore, just pathetic. Too bad, because the per-

formances are all fiery (possibly too fiery for the screen). Spacey comes off best as Mickey, a role he played onstage under Mike Nichols' direction, but there are also surprisingly strong (dramatic) turns by Shandling and a not-as-cute-as-usual Ryan. ★★ VHS: $19.99; DVD: $24.99

The Hurricane

(1937, 102 min, US, John Ford) *Dorothy Lamour, Jon Hall, Mary Astor, Raymond Massey, Thomas Mitchell, John Carradine.* Ford's classic adventure yarn has Lamour (complete with sarong) and Hall as tropical island lovers whose romance is interrupted by a devastating storm and island governor Massey. The film is noted for a spectacular climactic hurricane sequence. ★★★½ VHS: $14.99; DVD: $24.99

The Hurricane

(1999, 146 min, US, Norman Jewison) *Denzel Washington, Vicellous Reon Shannon, Deborah Kara Unger, Liev Schreiber, John Hannah, Rod Steiger, Debbi Morgan, Dan Hedaya, Clancy Brown, David Paymer, Harris Yulin.* With the force of one of those awesome storms which bear his name, Washington mesmerizes as champion boxer Rubin "Hurricane" Carter in this powerful, moving story of false imprisonment, racial bigotry and belated justice. In the late 1960s, Carter was a middleweight champ when he was framed and sentenced to life for three murders he didn't commit. Though celebrities from all walks of life rallied to his support, he labored in prison with writing his only outlet. In the mid-1980s, a Brooklyn youth (Shannon) studying in a Canadian commune stumbles upon Carter's book, setting in motion a series of events to set the boxer free after 22 years behind bars. The film was marred by controversy when it was learned several scenes were historically inaccurate. Despite the dramatic liberties, *The Hurricane* is a gripping reminder of the high cost of personal freedom. ★★★½ VHS: $14.99; DVD: $26.99

Hurricane Streets

(1997, 86 min, US, Morgan J. Freeman) *Brendan Sexton III, Shawn Elliott, L.M. Kit Carson.* This overrated Sundance favorite (isn't every third release a "Sundance Favorite" these days?) does have some decent moments and is an impressive debut by director Freeman (no relation to the actor). Sexton gives a wholly real performance in this more accessible, less incendiary cousin to *Kids.* Like that film, *Hurricane Streets* follows a group of ne'er-do-well teens as they commit various crimes and behave like jerks and cause adults to cluck their tongues. To his credit, Freeman coaxes fine portrayals from his cast of mostly young teens and develops strong audience sympathy for his lead character. But the whole thing has the atmosphere of an "Afterschool Special" with gun shots and curse words, and is a bit tiresome for anyone out of their teens. ★★½ VHS: $6.99

Husbands

(1970, 153 min, US, John Cassavetes) *Ben Gazzara, Peter Falk, John Cassavetes.* Perhaps nothing affects the middle-aged more profoundly than the death of a close contemporary. Director Cassavetes again utilizes his hyper-documentary style to create a reality so sharply focused that it's life mythologized; to offer moments of everyday living so individual-

istic that they're archetypal. Harry (Gazzara), Archie (Falk) and Gus (Cassavates) rail at the unnamed anxiety experienced at the death of a close friend. All the cracks and fissures in their relationships manifest during the multiday bender after the funeral. Cassavetes captures the essence of male camaraderie, deliciously choreographing testosterone flare-ups and maudlin introspection as these three embark on a transcontinental road trip. Another brilliant slap in the face from Cassavates. ★★★½ VHS: $19.99

Husbands and Wives

(1992, 110 min, US, Woody Allen) *Woody Allen, Mia Farrow, Judy Davis, Sydney Pollack, Liam Neeson, Juliette Lewis, Blythe Danner.* In an uncanny example of life imitating art, Allen's last collaboration with Farrow is an often humorous, sometimes relentless examination of disintegrating marriages and fickle attractions between older men and younger women. Made in an almost documentary, cinema verité style (complete with hand-held camera work), the film is a kind of eavesdropping on the lives of two couples: Mia & Woody and Pollack & Davis. In the opening scene, Davis and Pollack announce to Farrow and Allen that they've decided to separate and from there, the film, in typical Allen fashion, meanders through all of the intellectual and emotional ramifications of marriage, fidelity and lust. Occasionally using talking head interviews with the characters, Allen probes their thoughts on all of these matrimonial ups-and-downs. ★★★½ VHS: $19.99

Hush

(1998, 96 min, US, Jonathan Darby) *Jessica Lange, Gwyneth Paltrow, Johnathon Schaech, Nina Foch, Hal Holbrook.* Utterly ridiculous tripe about a manipulating mother (Lange) who will stop at nothing to get her son (Schaech) away from the city and back to the horse farm that is his legacy. Unfortunately, he's quite happy living in New York with his perky new wife (Paltrow). Quicker than you can say "who put that hole in my diaphragm?", Paltrow is pregnant and forced to reconsider life on the farm (especially after being mugged at knifepoint in her own apartment). Then things get really silly! This is the kind of film that relies on impossible actions and improbable reactions to proceed, and still it goes nowhere. Call it faint praise to say that the performances are good; the food on *Titanic* was good, too. ★ VHS: $9.99; DVD: $19.99

Hush. . . Hush, Sweet Charlotte

(1965, 133 min, US, Robert Aldrich) *Bette Davis, Olivia de Havilland, Joseph Cotten, Agnes Moorehead, Mary Astor, Bruce Dern.* Motivated by the success of *What Ever Happened to Baby Jane?*, this is yet another Grand Guignol thriller which was so common in the 1960s. Originally titled *What Ever Happened to Aunt Charlotte?*, Davis, again in *Baby Jane* territory, stars as a very wealthy victimized hermit, haunted by the memories of a dead lover. Moorehead received an Oscar nomination for her unrecognizable slovenly housekeeper. ★★★ VHS: $19.99

Hustle

(1975, 120 min, US, Robert Aldrich) *Burt Reynolds, Catherine Deneuve, Ben Johnson, Paul Winfield, Eileen Brennan, Eddie Albert, Ernest Borgnine.* Reynolds plays an old-fashioned L.A.

cop who spends his days investigating suicides, porn rings and the mob, and spends his nights in the arms of a sexy Parisian call girl (Deneuve). Reynolds is personable, but he's just going through the motions in this below-average police thriller. ★½ VHS: $14.99

Hustler White

(1996, 79 min, Canada, Bruce LaBruce & Rick Castro) *Tony Ward, Bruce LaBruce, Alex Austin, Kevin Kramer, Ron Athey, Vaginal Davis.* This look into the world of L.A. male prostitutes gleefully crisscrosses the lines between daring and boring; porn and art; and avant-garde satire and obnoxious gross-out. Jurgen Anger (LaBruce) is a prissy German writer who falls hard for Monti Ward (Ward), a street hustler thug. Offering half-hearted homages to such films as *Sunset Boulevard* and *Whatever Happened to Baby Jane?*, the action jerks from this brief outline of a plot to a series of disconnected sexual encounters, whose only commonality is that the sex involves everything except the loving kind. The film has a curious lifeless quality, like we're watching a film made by a director who doesn't give a fuck, featuring actors only awkwardly enacting out what they are instructed to do and a plot more interested in simple shock value. ★★ VHS: $29.99

The Hypothesis of the Stolen Painting

(1978, 78 min, France, Râûl Ruiz) *Jean Rougeul, Eva Simonet.* Made for French TV (obviously light years ahead of its American counterpart), this intriguing and meditatively intellectual mystery-thriller was directed by the highly original and beguiling avant-garde director Ruiz, a Paris-based, Chilean expatriate. The "detective" story begins with a guide showing an unseen interviewer a series of paintings by Second Empire artist Frederic Tonnerre, in an effort to solve the mystery of a seventh painting. The paintings — actually *tableaux vivants*, live stagings of the works with the people in suspended animation — are only one of the many adventurous techniques used by Ruiz in his playful unraveling of his strange whodunit. A Ruiz short, *Dog's Dialogue*, precedes the feature. (French with English subtitles) ★★★ VHS: $59.99

I, a Woman

(1966, 92 min, Sweden, Mac Ahlberg) *Essy Persson, Jorgen Reenberg, Preben Mahrt.* Unlike the more famous but equally successful *I Am Curious Yellow* that hit American shores in 1968, this groundbreaking, sexually explicit drama of a woman's yearning sexuality has survived the sexual revolution quite well. Beautiful blonde Siv (Persson) is an innocent country girl from a deeply religious family who drops her staid (no sex before marriage) boyfriend and the restrictiveness of provincial life to move to the big city and take care of her raging libido. Siv is a refreshing character — a beguilingly attractive temptress, she rejects conventional relationships and their obligations in a pursuit of simple pleasures and freedom. (Swedish with English subtitles) ★★★ VHS: $29.99; DVD: $19.99

I Am a Camera

(1955, 98 min, GB, Henry Cornelius) *Julie Harris, Laurence Harvey, Shelley Winters, Patrick McGoohan.* John van Druten's theatrical interpretation of Christopher Isherwood's "Berlin Diaries" is brought to the screen with intelligence and wit. This marvelously acted piece features Harris as Sally Bowles (a character later made truly famous by Liza Minnelli in Bob Fosse's *Cabaret*). ★★★

I Am a Fugitive from a Chain Gang

(1932, 93 min, US, Mervyn LeRoy) *Paul Muni, Glenda Farrell, Helen Vinson.* The best and most powerful of Warner Brothers' 1930s "social dramas." Muni gives a tour de force performance as a WWI veteran unjustly imprisoned and sent to a Southern chain gang. Escaping the brutality of the system, Muni finds himself on the run, and never looking over his shoulder. A daring exposé of criminal injustice, the film was based on the

autobiography of Thomas E. Burns. Farrell is impressive in a small part as Muni's fiancée. ★★★★ VHS: $19.99

I Am Cuba

(1964, 141 min, USSR/Cuba, Mikhail K. Kalatozov) *Luz Maria Collazo, Jose Gallardo.* *I Am Cuba* is a kaleidoscopic exposé of Batista's Cuba, a land of stark, diametric opposites, of great wealth and abject poverty, whose inequalities are flamboyantly juxtaposed by a perpetually moving camera as it reveals the conflicting lifestyles of the monied elite and the barely subsisting underclass. The stark black-and-white cinematography and an unabashed affection for the land are reminiscent of Sergei Eisenstein's *Que Viva Mexico!* The film's political agenda is unapologetic, and within the structure of four short stories of hardship and abuse, it presents the crushing exploitation of Cuba's people and resources, revealing the underlying causes of Castro's revolution. Invigorating, inticing and sometimes brutal, the film shows equal affection to the teeming slums, the entertainment palaces and the fertile countryside. It's lyrical, joyous and harsh and unwavering. (Spanish and Russian with English subtitles) ★★★★ VHS: $29.99; DVD: $29.99

I Am Curious (Blue)

(1968, 103 min, Sweden, Vilgot Sjoman) With footage shot at the same time as *I Am Curious Yellow*, this tepid sequel continues the story of a sociologist's sexual study, though it looks as if *Yellow* features the more "interesting" takes. (Dubbed) ★★ VHS: $59.99

I Am Curious (Yellow)

(1967, 120 min, Sweden, Vilgot Sjoman) *Lena Nyman, Peter Lindgren.* Adult film fans seeking titillations from this infamous breakthrough film should reconsider renting this Swedish curiosity. *I Am Curious (Yellow)* spends less time on sex and more in exploring the times and lifestyles of Swedish youth, specifically an adventurous young lady. (Dubbed) ★★½ VHS: $59.99

I Am My Own Woman

(1992, 90 min, Germany, Rosa von Praunheim) An inspiring film of one person's determined efforts to be exactly what he wants to be. A documentary with re-created dramatic scenes intercut throughout, the film follows Charlotte von Mahsldorf, born Lother Berfelde, from her teenage years during WWII to operating an East Berlin museum. Despite the repression of the Communists, attacks by skinheads and public scorn, Miss Charlotte retains an amazingly sunny outlook as she freely goes about her life as a woman. Two actors play Charlotte as the young Lother/Charlotte, and Charlotte plays herself in the later years. (German with English subtitles) ★★★½ VHS: $19.99

I Bury the Living

(1958, 77 min, US, Albert Band) *Richard Boone, Theodore Bikel, Peggy Maurer, Herbert Anderson.* A cemetary map has white pins inserted on vacant plots, and black pins inserted on occupied graves. When Boone switches black for white, the live plot owners start dying. Does the owner of the morgue really have supernatural powers? You be the judge. A very creepy little chiller. ★★★ VHS: $9.99

Paul Muni (l.) in *I Am a Fugitive from a Chain Gang*

I Like It Like That

I Can't Sleep

(1995, 110 min, France, Claire Denis) *Alex Descas, Richard Courcet, Line Renaud, Katerina Golubeva.* A provocative, nihilistic French drama based on a true story of two gay "granny" killers. The story is set in the "New France" — not the familiar one of intellectual bourgeoisie contemplating infidelity or the meaning of life, but a France filled with poor immigrants and almost paralyzed by social ills. The story principally follows two brothers from Martinique: Theo (Descas), a hard-working family man, and Camille (Courcet), his strikingly beautiful gay drag queen brother. But Camille harbors a secret other than his sexuality: He and his white French lover (Renaud) have been terrorizing Paris with a series of brutal murders, all on older women. The story is based on Thierry Paulin, who killed more than 20 women between 1984–1987. (French with English subtitles) ★★½ VHS: $89.99

I Come in Peace

(1990, 92 min, US, Craig R. Baxley) *Dolph Lundgren, Brian Benben, Betsy Brantley, Michael J. Pollard.* An empty-headed sci-fi actioner about two police officers who investigate a series of murders being committed by a drug-dealer from outer space. Once they discover the exact nature of what the alien is doing and encounter an alien cop tracking the druglord villain, they set out with some extraterrestrial weaponry to kick alien butt. The special effects, though good, do not elevate the film above its low-rent feel. ★½

I Could Go on Singing

(1963, 99 min, GB, Ronald Neame) *Judy Garland, Dirk Bogarde, Jack Klugman.* Garland's last movie reveals the legendary singer in commanding voice as a famed entertainer who travels to England to retrieve her son, who is living with his father (Bogarde). The movie is pure melodrama, but Garland's vocal performances are pure magic. ★★½

I Dismember Mama

(1972, 86 min, US, Paul Leder) *Zooey Hall, Joanne Moore Jordan.* Great titles do not great movies make. An escapee from a mental institution falls in love with an 11-year-old and seeks to "purify" his world. ★

I Don't Buy Kisses Anymore

(1992, 112 min, US, Robert Marcarelli) *Jason Alexander, Nia Peebles, Lainie Kazan, Eileen Brennan, Lou Jacobi.* Though its title is quite clever, *I Don't Buy Kisses Anymore* is essentially an updated and rather sluggish *Marty*, without an abundance of that film's insight and wit. Alexander stars as a lonely and overweight thirty-year-old shoe salesman who falls for an attractive psychology student (Peebles). Though not attracted to him, she befriends him and feigns romantic interest for personal gain (for her thesis). Most of the characters are Jewish and Italian caricatures — they're not offensive, just lacking in dimension. Jacobi saves the day with a crackling turn as a colorful family patriarch. ★★

I Don't Give a Damn

(1983, 94 min, Israel, Shmuel Imberman) *Ika Sohar, Anat Waxman.* This somber drama deals with the life of Rafi, a young soldier who is paralyzed in a terrorist explosion. Rafi finds that his vibrant, carefree lifestyle is drastically cut short, but he refuses to accept his future life confined to a wheelchair. First in a military hospital and later in his parents' home, his personality changes as he becomes disillusioned, bitter and self-pitying. His despair gradually changes after he becomes interested in photography, accepts his fate and reconciles with his loved ones. (Hebrew with English subtitles) ★★½

I Don't Kiss (J'embrasse pas)

(1991, 116 min, France, Andre Techine) *Manuel Blance, Philippe Noiret, Emmanuelle Beart.* Pierre (Blance) leaves the safe bosom of his mother to live in the unforgiving "mean streets" of Paris. His difficulty finding work leads him into a life of male prostitution. But the lure of the street, with its easy money, beckons, eventually turning him into a seasoned hustler. Noiret appears as a wealthy television personality with an obsession with male prostitutes. An unorthodox gay coming-out drama that frustratingly cops out in the end. (French with English subtitles) ★★½

I Don't Want to Talk about It

(1994, 102 min, Argentina, Maria Luisa Bemberg) *Marcello Mastroianni, Luisina Brando, Alejandra Podesta.* This amusing little fantasy stars Mastroianni as an Argentine gentleman who falls in love with a midget. Actually, the story revolves more around the relationship between the wee lady, Podesta, and her mother, Brando, who tries desperately not to let her daughter know she's "different" — hence the film's title which refers to mama's response whenever anybody mentions her daughter's size. Lusciously filmed with a tinge of magical realism, the film enjoys fine performances and nice characterizations and is, for the most part, mildly enjoyable in spite of a weakened dramatic structure. (Spanish with English subtitles) ★★★ VHS: $19.99

I Hate Blondes

(1981, 89 min, Italy, Giorgio Capitani) *Jean Rochefort.* An unexpectedly funny comedy about a ghostwriter of best-selling detective novels whose work inspires a series of real-life heists. A pretty blonde jewel thief becomes entangled in this web of comic mishaps. ★★★

I Heard the Owl Call My Name

(1973, 79 min, US, Daryl Duke) *Tom Courtenay, Dean Jagger.* A young Anglican priest (Courtenay) is sent by his bishop (Jagger) to live among the Indians of the Northwest, where he gains a new appreciation of human existence. Courtenay delivers a passionate performance in this moving made-for-TV drama. ★★★

I Killed Rasputin

(1967, 85 min, US, Robert Hossein) *Gert Froebe, Peter McEnery, Geraldine Chaplin.* Cult favorite chronicling the life of legendary mystic Rasputin. In 1909 Russia, the mysterious Rasputin wins the favor of Empress Alexandra by saving the life of her son. But wary palace guards distrust the shadowy figure, and secretly plot his demise. ★ VHS: $59.99

I Know What You Did Last Summer

(1997, 100 min, US, Jim Gillespie) *Jennifer Love Hewitt, Sarah Michelle Gellar, Ryan Phillippe, Freddie Prinze, Jr., Johnny Galecki, Anne Heche.* Though it's nothing to *Scream* about, this derivative slasher horror flick does provide a scare or two, but it's really nothing we haven't seen before. Set in coastal North Carolina (where it seems no one has native accents), the story follows the consequences when four teens run over a man and dump the body rather than face the law. A year later, when one of them gets a note repeating the film's title, strange occurrences begin and then bodies start piling up. The screenplay is less concerned with plot twists and red herrings and concentrates more on dark shadows and fish hooks gutting young teens. (Sequel: *I Still Know What You Did Last Summer*) ★★½ VHS: $12.99; DVD: $19.99

I Know Where I'm Going!

(1945, 92 min, GB, Michael Powell & Emeric Pressburger) *Wendy Hiller, Roger Livesey, Finlay Currie.* The radiant Hiller plays a wealthy young woman who travels to the Scottish Hebrides to marry an older man, only to have her attentions diverted by a dashing young suitor. Splendid use of the Scottish countryside by directors Powell and Pressburger makes this a lyrically visual treat. ★★★★ DVD: $39.99

I Like It Like That

(1994, 105 min, US, Darnell Martin) *Lauren Velez, Jon Seda, Rita Moreno, Griffin Dunne.* Director Martin's debut is an explosively funny, poignant and precise look at life in the Bronx. Velez stars as Lisette, a twentysomething Latina with three kids and a jailed husband, Chino (Seda), who thinks his penis is his passport to a woman's heart. Getting her first taste of freedom during his incarceration, and being more than a little put off by his macho posturing upon his return, she kicks him out and is forced to fend for herself. Determined to make it, she lies her way into a job at a record company. It's a winning rags-to-a-decent-living story that is as hard-edged as it is likable. Martin shows a strong directorial hand and moves things along at a refreshing pace. ★★★½ VHS: $14.99

I Love Trouble

(1994, 120 min, US, Charles Shyer) *Nick Nolte, Julia Roberts, Olympia Dukakis, Robert Loggia, Marsha Mason.* Nancy Myers and Charles Shyer, the husband and wife writer-producer-director team, try to pull off the romantic comedy-action thriller thing (à la *Charade*). As rival reporters who reluctantly team up to crack a big story, Nolte seems to rise above the material, and Roberts returns to *Pretty Woman* mode. One of summer of '94's surprise bombs, this uneven

I Shot Andy Warhol

mix of comedy and violence sporting a contrivance-riddled plot is entertaining in spite of itself. ★★½ VHS: $19.99; DVD: $29.99

I Love You

(1982, 104 min, Brazil, Arnaldo Jabor) *Sonia Braga, Paulo Cesar Pereio.* This colorful though pretentious erotic comedy features the stunning Braga as a housewife-cum-hooker drawn into a brief but intense encounter with a bankrupt bra manufacturer. Sparks fly as this whirlwind romance renews the vitality in both their lives. (Portuguese with English subtitles) ★★

I Love You Again

(1940, 99 min, US, W.S. Van Dyke II) *William Powell, Myrna Loy, Frank McHugh, Edmund Lowe.* A joyously screwball romp. Powell plays a con man who discovers he's been a victim of amnesia for nine years and living under the identity of a fuddy-duddy pottery employee. Learning his alter ego has access to great wealth, he concocts a scam with newly acquired partner McHugh. However, when he meets his wife Loy, who's about to divorce him, he plans to rekindle their marriage while setting up the good citizens of his small town. The Powell-Loy magic is ever present, but the lion's share of the laughs belong to Powell as he himself falls victim to a series of sight gags and humiliations. Loy is her usual classy persona. ★★★ VHS: $19.99

I Love You, Alice B. Toklas

(1968, 93 min, US, Hy Averback) *Peter Sellers, Jo Van Fleet, Leigh Taylor-Young, Joyce Van Patten.* Sellers is at his loony best in this dated but hilarious comedy about a middle-aged L.A. lawyer who drops out and turns on. Leaving his bride-to-be at the altar not once, but twice, Sellers loses himself in a haze of drug-dosed cookies and a subsequent whirlwind tour of the hippie subculture. Paul Mazursky cowrote the script. ★★★½ VHS: $14.99

I Love You, I Love You Not

(1997, 80 min, US, Billy Hopkins) *Claire Danes, Jude Law, Jeanne Moreau.* Adapted from a stage play, and it really shows, *I Love You, I Love You Not* stars Moreau as a concentration camp survivor living in Manhattan who takes in her introvert granddaughter (Danes), who's smitten with the class jock (Law). The story deals with issues of anti-Semitism, peer pressure, teen love and self-identity, but with all the subtlety of an "Afterschool Special," and the conflicts and resolutions are so formulaic it's easy to overlook Moreau's graceful performance. ★★ VHS: $14.99; DVD: $29.99

I Love You Rosa

(1972, 84 min, Israel, Moshe Mizrahi) *Michal Bat-Adam, Gabi Oterman.* This feminist drama and tender love story is set in 1888 Jerusalem where a childless 20-year-old widow (Bat-Adam) discovers that according to Deuteronomic Law she must marry her husband's brother — with the problem being that he is only 11 years old and determined to fulfill his duties. Rosa, forced to work in a bathhouse and sew for a living, must decide if she should follow the law and wait until the boy is eighteen or break with tradition and find another husband. Sentimental and charming, the story takes an insightful look at religious traditions, love, family and individual freedoms in this Oscar-nominated Best Foreign-Language Film. ★★★

I Love You to Death

(1990, 96 min, US, Lawrence Kasdan) *Tracey Ullman, Kevin Kline, Joan Plowright, River Phoenix, William Hurt, Keanu Reeves.* Based on a true story, this sometimes funny, hit-or-miss black comedy is about a wife who discovers her husband is cheating on her and attempts to murder him — repeatedly. Kline gives a funny performance as the philandering husband. As the wronged wife, Ullman is given very little to do, and the talented comedienne is wasted. Hurt and Reeves are in alien territory as the hit men. ★★½ VHS: $9.99

I, Madman

(1989, 95 min, US, Tibor Takacs) *Jenny Wright, Clayton Rohner.* Director Takacs shows a flair for combining stop-motion monsters and live-action horror in this deliberately paced, moody mix of film noir and fright flick. Wright stars as a bookseller who unleashes a demon from the pages of a possessed book. Stylish camerawork and a clever script make this film an unusual but effective entry in the all-too-familiar horror line-up. ★★★ VHS: $79.99

I Married a Dead Man

(1982, 110 min, France, Robin Davis) *Nathalie Baye, Richard Bohringer.* Baye gives a strong performance as a mysterious woman with a false identity and a threatening past in this romantic suspense thriller. Pregnant, she leaves her abusive husband and travels to the South of France. Her train derails en route, killing another pregnant woman. The in-laws of the dead woman, whom they have never met, take Baye home, thinking she is their daughter-in-law. Her new life is wonderful until she is threatened by the husband of her past. A compelling, seductive reworking of the 1949 Barbara Stanwyck soaper *No Man of Her Own.* (French with English subtitles) (aka: *I Married a Shadow*) ★★★ VHS: $19.99

I Married a Monster
from Outer Space

(1958, 78 min, US, Gene Fowler, Jr.) *Tom Tryon, Gloria Talbott, Ty Hardin.* When the major studios saw the grosses that AIP was getting from hot titles like *I Was a Teenage Werewolf* et. al., they decided to play that game too. The surprise is that this is quite a good little film. Atmospheric, effective special effects, a neat-looking bunch of papier-mâché aliens, and a word to young brides everywhere about the dangers of intergalactic miscegenation. ★★½ VHS: $49.99

I Married a Shadow

See: I Married a Dead Man

I Married a Witch

(1942, 77 min, US, René Clair) *Veronica Lake, Fredric March, Susan Hayward, Broderick Crawford.* Entertaining ghost comedy with Lake as a 17th-century Salem witch who comes back to haunt the descendant (March) of the man who had her burned at the stake. Based on a story by Thorne Smith ("Topper"). ★★★ VHS: $14.99

I Never Promised You a Rose Garden

(1977, 96 min, US, Anthony Page) *Kathleen Quinlan, Bibi Andersson, Sylvia Sidney.* Quinlan's astonishing performance as a schizophrenic teenager undergoing treatment highlights this absorbing adaptation of Hannah Green's novel. Andersson ably plays her caring psychiatrist. ★★★

I Never Sang for My Father

(1970, 93 min, US, Gilbert Cates) *Gene Hackman, Melvyn Douglas, Estelle Parsons, Dorothy Stickney.* A sterling version of Robert Anderson's play, with Hackman in a fine performance as the estranged son of Douglas who attempts reconciliation when his father becomes sick and unable to care for himself. Douglas, who in his later years became a brilliant character actor, is superb. ★★★ VHS: $19.99

I.Q.

(1994, 96 min, US, Fred Schepisi) *Walter Matthau, Meg Ryan, Tim Robbins, Gene Saks, Charles Durning, Lou Jacobi, Stephen Fry, Joseph Maher, Frank Whaley.* From director Schepisi, who helmed one of the most beguiling romantic comedies of the 1980s, *Roxanne,* comes an almost equally enchanting confection. Matthau, in a most amusing impersonation, plays Albert Einstein. In a scenario recalling the whimsy and appeal of the great 1940s screwball comedies, Einstein plays matchmaker to his brainy but impassioned niece, nicely played by Ryan. Though she's engaged to an egghead researcher (Fry), Uncle Albert coaches a good-natured garage mechanic (Robbins) who has fallen under her spell. And much like the seven professors in *Ball of Fire,* Einstein and his four brainy pals take delight in their romantic experiment to bring the two together. Robbins continues to prove himself a cinematic natural resource giving a spirited, magnetic performance. ★★★½ VHS: $14.99

I Remember Mama

(1948, 134 min, US, George Stevens) *Irene Dunne, Barbara Bel Geddes, Oscar Homolka, Ellen Corby, Rudy Vallee.* Dunne gives a captivating performance in this touching drama about an immigrant family living in San Francisco. Thanks to Dunne's sparkling performance and Stevens' delicate direction, the film is sweet and heartfelt without needless sentimentality, and has to it the same flavor as Kazan's *A Tree Grows in Brooklyn.* ★★★½ VHS: $14.99

I Saw What You Did

(1965, 82 min, US, William Castle) *Joan Crawford, John Ireland, Leif Erickson, Andi Garrett, Sarah Lane.* Before *Scream,* before *I Know What You Did Last Summer,* even before *Halloween,* came this first "teen scream" chiller from 1960s horror maven Castle. A very effective thriller, the story follows the consequences of a series of prank calls by two teenaged girls who say "I saw what you did and I know who you are." When they phone a man who's just murdered his wife, he comes looking for them. Crawford is the murderer's lusty neighbor. After the release of the film, prank calls were all the rage across the country. (Letterboxed) ★★★ VHS: $14.99; DVD: $24.99

I Sent a Letter to My Love

(1981, 96 min, France, Moshe Mizrahi) *Simone Signoret, Jean Rochefort, Delphine Seyrig.* A perceptive and unusual comedy-drama starring Signoret as a formidable woman who has devoted her life to the care of her crippled brother. Being a bit lonely, she advertises in a personal column. Receiving a reply from a suitor whom she knows to be her brother, she continues the newspaper romance for her brother's sake. Mizrahi also directed Signoret in *Madame Rosa.* ★★★

I Shot Andy Warhol

(1996, 106 min, US, Mary Harron) *Lili Taylor, Jared Harris, Martha Plimpton, Lothaire Bluteau, Stephen Dorff, Craig Chester, Donovan Leitch.* From its opening, which portrays the aftermath of the action of its title, *I Shot Andy Warhol* is a frantically paced and at times gripping chronicle of Valerie Solanas, Warhol's would-be assassin. Solanas (smartly played by Taylor) was a semidelusional lesbian feminist activist who slummed around Greenwich Village in the early '60s turning tricks to survive. Essentially, Solanas comes off as a born loser, but one with an irrepressible and often brilliant intellect. For the most part, the film hits its mark, despite an overly long party scene at The Factory. With a gritty streetwise demeanor, Taylor delivers rapid-fire speech at a relentless pace, and she's nothing short of first-rate. As Warhol, Harris is an exquisite understatement of ethereal chic. ★★★½ VHS: $14.99; DVD: $19.99

I Spit on Your Grave

(1989, 100 min, US, Meir Zarchi) *Camille Keaton, Eron Tabor.* A young woman takes a writing sabbatical to the country where she is brutally raped and beaten and left for dead. But she survives and exacts bloody revenge. This low-budget exploiter manages to create quite a few suspenseful moments in between scenes of gratuitous violence. (Letterboxed) ★★ VHS: $14.99; DVD: $29.99

I Still Know What You Did Last Summer

(1998, 100 min, US, Danny Cannon) *Jennifer Love Hewitt, Freddie Prinze, Jr., Brandy, Mekhi Phifer, Muse Watson.* More nubile teens get hacked-up; what fun. Hewitt returns in this cheesy sequel to the not-quite-as-cheesy hit as the intelligence-impaired heroine. Her lack of world geography somehow lands her and her equally dim chums on an isolated vacation resort. Oh, there's a storm. Oh, there's a killer on the loose. As the secondary characters die around her, Hewitt is promptly stalked by an unstoppable slasher in a raincoat who, frankly, is less frightening than your average Cher impersonator. This would make a great drinking game: imbibe every time gratuitous profanity is uttered; at every clichéd fake scare; and at every shot of Hewitt's heaving bosom. And, hey, everyone's wasted — that's the only way one can derive pleasure from this howling dud. ★½ VHS: $14.99; DVD: $19.99

I, the Worst of All

(1990, 100 min, Argentina/France, Maria Luisa Bemberg) *Assumpta Serta, Dominique Sanda.* The unconventional story of 17th-century Mexican poet and nun Sor Juana Inez de la Cruz. Confined to a prison-like cloister during the Spanish Inquisition, Sister Juana's passionate, philosophical poems become the "rage" amongst both the rich and poor, causing problems for the virtually sealed-off convent and prompting an intimate relationship (though mostly through bars) with a beautiful vicereine (Sanda). The film is elegant and intelligent, though the two women's relationship which is hinted at never goes beyond lingering glances. Based on the novel by Octavio Paz. (Spanish with English subtitles) VHS: $29.99

I Think I Do

(1997, 90 min, US, Brian Sloan) *Alexis Arquette, Christian Maelen, Maddie Corman, Tuc Watkins, Guillermo Diaz, Marnie Nixon.* The screwball "who will marry who" antics of *The Philadelphia Story* are given a gay update in this romantic and sexy comedy. Bob (Arquette) and Brendan (Maelen) are college roommates whose close friendship (and Bob's mad crush) is chilled after a hopeful but awkward pass by Bob is rejected by Brendan. Now five years later, they, and their college chums, reunite for the marriage of one of their former classmates. As everyone parties and consumes just enough booze, libidos are raised and inhibitions lowered. ★★★ VHS: $39.99

I Wake Up Screaming

(1941, 82 min, US, Bruce Humberstone) *Betty Grable, Victor Mature, Laird Cregar.* Unusually stylish, this entertaining and moody thriller stars Grable who, after her sister is murdered, teams up with the prime suspect (Mature) to find the real killer. There are plenty of twists to keep the whodunit experts one body behind. The film features a fine performance by Cregar as a sinister detective relentlessly out for his own form of demented justice. ★★★ VHS: $19.99

I Walked with a Zombie

(1943, 69 min, US, Jacques Tourneur) *Frances Dee, Tom Conway, James Ellison.* Don't let the title

fool you — this is a first-rate thriller about a nurse (Dee) who travels to the West Indies to care for a plantation owner's wife. She soon learns the woman is under the spell of a local voodoo priest. Lots of chills and remarkable camerawork and lighting. ★★★

I Wanna Be Your Man

(1994, 97 min, Hong Kong, Chung Chi Shing) *Christy Chung.* A Hong Kong drama that features a sensitive handling of a lesbian policewoman. Police Inspector Susan Wong (Chung) is a beautiful, slightly butch lesbian cop who lives with her petulantly femme girlfriend Ron. The secret of her sexual orientation becomes accidentally known to Luk, an affably mediocre cop who, instead of telling his fellow officers that their boss is a dyke (an action that would ruin her), quickly becomes her friend and confidant. Better-than-average TV fare made interesting because of its setting and theme. (Cantonese with English subtitles) ★★★ VHS: $79.99

I Wanna Hold Your Hand

(1978, 104 min, US, Robert Zemeckis) *Nancy Allen, Bobby DiCicco, Marc McClure, Wendy Jo Sperber, Eddie Deezen.* It's 1964 and The Beatles hit New York. The city is thrown into a panic as the Fab Four are to appear on "The Ed Sullivan Show," and everybody scrambles for tickets. With this inspired premise, director Zemeckis lets go with a comic assault about a group of Jersey students who try to crash the show. The film features a fine ensemble of young actors. ★★★ VHS: $14.99

I Want to Live

(1958, 122 min, US, Robert Wise) *Susan Hayward, Simon Oakland, Theodore Bikel.* Hayward won an Oscar for her commanding performance in this true story of prostitute Barbara Graham, who, framed and convicted of murder, was sentenced to death. ★★★ VHS: $14.99

I Was a Male War Bride

(1949, 106 min, US, Howard Hawks) *Cary Grant, Ann Sheridan.* Though not on par with the best of either director Hawks or actor Grant, an abundance of genuine laughs and skillful tomfoolery by its two stars make *I Was a Male War*

Cary Grant (center, in drag) and Ann Sheridan in *I Was a Male War Bride*

Bride an appealing wartime comedy. Grant plays a French military attache who is teamed with nononsense American WAC Sheridan. While on assignment, the bickering couple fall in love and marry. But complications and Army red tape arise when he tries to accompany his bride to the States — which includes a little transvestism on the part of Grant. ★★★ VHS: $19.99

I Was a Teenage Werewolf

(1957, 70 min, US, Gene Fowler) *Michael Landon, Whit Bissell, Yvonne Lime.* A youthful Landon plays a juvenile delinquent who's got one on James Dean — he's a werewolf (thanks to mad doc Bissell). This low-budget horror flick is a campy pleasure in spite of the awkward acting and less-than-successful scares. ★★ VHS: $29.99

I Was a Zombie for the FBI

(1986, 105 min, US, Marius Penczner) Aliens plan to steal the formula for the world's most popular cola in order to turn Earth's population into subservient zombies. It's up to two crack FBI agents and a beautiful reporter to save the day. (Did they want a Pepsi or a Coke?) ★

I Went Down

(1997, 111 min, Ireland, Paddy Breathnach) *Brendan Gleeson, Peter McDonald, Peter Caffrey, Tony Doyle.* From its double entendre title to its comedic shootouts to its engaging well-defined characters and relationships, *I Went Down* is a nice surprise. McDonald plays Git, a just-released ex-con who lands in trouble with the local mob boss. To set things right, he must accompany an endearingly annoying ne'er-do-well to claim a "package" — a man who owes the boss big time. Along the way, the two men bicker and bond, and learn that the package may not be what it seems. Although slight, this buddy/road/gangster flick is quite enjoyable, with bright performances and witty dialogue, and a warm tone and spirit. ★★★ VHS: $102.99

I'll Cry Tomorrow

(1955, 117 min, US, Daniel Mann) *Susan Hayworth, Richard Conte, Eddie Albert, Jo Van Fleet.* Exemplary biography on entertainer Lillian Roth (based on her novel) about the singer's fight with alcoholism. Hayward gives a magnificent performance as Roth, and Van Fleet is fine in support as her mother. ★★★½ VHS: $19.99

I'll Do Anything

(1994, 116 min, US, James L. Brooks) *Nick Nolte, Joely Richardson, Albert Brooks, Julie Kavner, Whitni Wright.* After brilliantly dissecting TV journalism in *Broadcast News*, writer-director Brooks turns his eye on the movie industry with less-than-satisfying results. Nolte stars as a talented but unemployed actor who unexpectedly gains custody of his bratty six-year-old daughter. While trying to pursue both a coveted film role and a pretty, budding producer (Richardson), he must also get to know his estranged child. When Brooks zeroes in on the movie-making process, the film is funny and diverting; however, the scenes concerning the reunion of father and daughter are maudlin at best. Originally intended as a musical, the film was edited after disappointing previews — ironic after Brooks nearly lampoons the process in his story. ★★½ VHS: $9.99

I'm All Right, Jack

(1960, 104 min, GB, John & Roy Boulting) *Peter Sellers, Ian Carmichael, Terry-Thomas, Richard Attenborough, Margaret Rutherford.* No word less than side-splitting will suffice in describing this scathing satire on labor relations in England. The inimitable Sellers stars as a young man caught between the two sides of a bitter labor dispute. The essence of worker-management relations, as practiced in England, are captured with the utmost clarity in this unrelenting farce. ★★★½

I'm Dancing as Fast as I Can

(1982, 107 min, US, Jack Hofsiss) *Jill Clayburgh, Nicol Williamson, Dianne Wiest, Joe Pesci, Geraldine Page.* Based on Barbara Gordon's memoir, Clayburgh stars as the TV documentary filmmaker who tries to put an end to her valium dependency — with great difficulty. Clayburgh is very good as Gordon, and gets splendid support from ensemble. ★★½ VHS: $69.99

I'm Gonna Git You Sucka

(1988, 87 min, US, Keenan Ivory Wayans) *Keenan Ivory Wayans, Isaac Hayes, Jim Brown, Bernie Casey.* Before he found success with his TV comedy series "In Living Color," Wayans made this good-natured spoof on the blaxploitation flicks of the 1970s. With a fine supporting cast of veterans, the film is about a young, idealistic soldier (Wayans) on leave. He returns home to find that his brother OG'd (died of an overdose of gold chains) and the mob wants to turn his sister to prostitution for some debts left behind by the departed Bro. Our hero, vowing to bring the bad guys to justice, assembles a motley band of "bad" dudes, and with the music of *Shaft* in the background, they battle and kick some butt. ★★★ VHS: $9.99; DVD: $14.99

I'm Losing You

(1998, 103 min, US, Bruce Wagner) *Rosanna Arquette, Frank Langella, Andrew McCarthy, Elizabeth Perkins, Amanda Donohoe, Buck Henry, Gina Gershon.* Several intertwining story lines, all dealing with an extended family, and all dealing with death and dying, rove their way through the uneven though involving *I'm Losing You*. Langella is the father, a TV producer who's just been diagnosed with terminal cancer. McCarthy is his son, a constantly out-of-work actor who falls in love with a HIV-positive buddy (Perkins). All the stories are interesting, at times gripping, and if Wagner — here adapting and directing his own novel — allows his unfamiliarity with the medium show with some weak pacing and lack of visual flair, the performances and unusually thoughtful, probing nature of the material compensate. Executive produced by David Cronenberg. ★★½ VHS: $102.99; DVD: $14.99

I'm No Angel

(1933, 88 min, US, Wesley Ruggles) *Mae West, Cary Grant, Edward Arnold.* "It's not the men in your life, it's the life in your men." This is just one of the classic quips made by the one and only West in this sparkling, bawdy pre-Code comedy. The 1930s sex goddess is at her best as a carnival performer who finds it as much a breeze taming the men as she does the lions. Becoming the toast of the town upon her arrival in New York, she crosses paths with businessman Grant, to whom she promises "When I'm good,

I'm very good. But when I'm bad, I'm even better." Looking ravishing, West's every other line seems to be a dandy sexual entendre; even when she's not being suggestive, she's suggestive. She has the talk, and she has the walk. Also featuring the famous "grape" line, this is one of two West films which single-handedly saved Paramount Studios from near-bankruptcy in 1933. ★★★½ VHS: $14.99

I'm Not Rappaport

(1996, 135 min, US, Herb Gardner) *Walter Matthau, Ossie Davis, Amy Irving, Craig T. Nelson, Martha Plimpton.* Herb Gardner adapted and directed his Tony Award–winning play about the tender and comic relationship between two disparate New York City senior citizens. The stage show was more fluid, but this engaging character piece is buoyed by two endearing performances given by Matthau and Davis. Nat (Matthau) is a rascally 80-year-old Jewish leftist who meets half-blind building custodian Midge (Davis), a black man his same age. The charm of the story is Gardner's wonderful characterizations of Nat and Midge, who most of the time are either feuding, telling jokes, or becoming involved in the other people's lives. Through telling moments, Gardner imparts thoughtful observances towards the realities of aging in urban America, producing laughs and poignant moments, alike. ★★★ VHS: $102.99

I've Heard the Mermaids Singing

(1987, 81 min, Canada, Patricia Rozema) *Sheila McCarthy, Paule Baillargeon.* McCarthy is nothing short of a revelation in this enchanting comedy. The film itself is cute and whimsical but it is McCarthy, as Polly, the day-dreaming romantic Gal Friday, who steals the show as well as our hearts. An avid photographer who dwells in her own fantasy world, Polly secures a job as a temp in the office of an art collector. Her innocence and joie de vivre proves to be a bracing tonic in a world dulled by pretension and greed. A film and a performance that should lift your spirits. ★★★

Ice Palace

(1960, 143 min, US, Vincent Sherman) *Richard Burton, Carolyn Jones, Robert Ryan, Shirley Knight.* A sprawling adaptation of Edna Ferber's novel about Alaska's drive toward statehood. Set at the end of WWII, the film casts Burton as a soldier who returns home to Seattle only to find his job has been given away. After roughing up his exboss, he heads for Alaska, where he teams up with Ryan and Jones in a fish canning enterprise and an ill-fated love triangle. ★★½ VHS: $19.99

The Ice Pirates

(1984, 93 min, US, Stewart Raffill) *Robert Urich, Anjelica Huston, Mary Crosby.* It is 10,000 years into the future, and an evil empire has gained control of the water supply for the entire universe. It is up to a band of rag-tag pirates, led by Urich, to hijack the shipments of frozen ice blocks through space and thwart the evildoers. Mindless, familiar though occasionally kinda fun. ★★ VHS: $14.99

Ice Station Zebra

(1968, 148 min, US, John Sturges) *Rock Hudson, Patrick McGoohan, Ernest Borgnine, Jim Brown.* Potent Cold War thriller with Hudson as a sub commander whose secret mission to the North Pole sets the stage for a showdown with the Russians. Based on an Alistair McLean novel. ★★½

The Ice Storm

(1997, 113 min, US, Ang Lee) *Kevin Kline, Joan Allen, Sigourney Weaver, Tobey Maguire, Christina Ricci, Elijah Wood.* It's 1973 in Connecticut, and two families are going through some painful adolescences: the children and the parents are discovering their sexualities and learning to express their emotions. Ben (Kline), the head of the Hood family, is lifelessly carrying on with his neighbor Janey Carver, played with gleeful bitchiness by Weaver. This empty affair strains his marriage to Elena (Allen), who is upset about her lot in life but can only express it by emotionally cutting off her husband. Their kids are going through similar situations, but learning and growing instead of falling apart. Lee is an obsessively detail-oriented director. Every period detail is just-so, but played for emotional effect rather than comic effect. The details are in the performances, too, as what is said is secondary to what is felt. ★★★½ VHS: $9.99; DVD: $24.99

Iceman

(1984, 99 min, US, Fred Schepisi) *Timothy Hutton, Lindsay Crouse, John Lone, David Strathairn, Danny Glover.* Director Schepisi makes credible and arresting this story of a prehistoric man found frozen in the Arctic and discovered to be still alive by a scientific team. Hutton is one of the researchers who enters into an almost empathic relationship with the Neanderthal, who is remarkably portrayed by Lone. Unusual and surprising. ★★★ VHS: $14.99

The Iceman Cometh

(1960, 210 min, US, Sidney Lumet) *Jason Robards, Myron McCormick, James Broderick, Robert Redford.* In 1956, the Circle-in-the-Square mounted a production of Eugene O'Neill's 1939 play "The Iceman Cometh," with a little-known actor named Jason Robards in the central part of Hickey. The revival and the actor quickly became part of Broadway legend. Four years later, Robards encored the role in a made-for-TV adaptation, and every brilliant moment has been captured on tape. In a seedy New York saloon pre-WWI, a group of down-and-out alcoholics await the arrival of Hickey, a salesman due for his annual drinking binge. As each character entertains the notion of free drink, they are forced to confront their pipe dreams by a newly on-the-wagon Hickey, determined to impart to his friends an everlasting peace of mind. O'Neill's drama is a harrowing and at times humorous exploration of failed lives and empty hopes, underscored by the author's remarkable prose of recriminations, denial and banter. Robards is simply astonishing as Hickey, the glad-handing barker of delusion and dreams. To watch this performance is to know it is one of the great stage portrayals of the 20th century. How lucky we are to have it preserved forever. ★★★★ VHS: $39.99

The Icicle Thief

(1989, 90 min, Italy, Maurizio Nichetti) *Maurizio Nichetti, Cateria Sylos Labini.* Infectiously funny, this inventive and fast-paced satire on commercial television defies easy plot description. A bungling director (Nichetti himself) is interviewed at a TV station before the screening of his newest film, a black-and-white neorealist drama. The picture, a tender, affectionate tribute to *The Bicycle Thief*, tells the story of the many struggles of an unemployed man (Nichetti again), his beautiful wife and their son, an unbelievably hard-working boy of six. But the family finds that financial hardships are nothing in comparison to the confusion and disruption caused when a scantily clad, English-speaking platinum blonde in full color "falls" out of her bathing suit commercial and into their neorealist lives. With tender humanism and a deft comic touch, Nichetti is a breath of fresh air. (Italian with English subtitles) ★★★½ VHS: $19.99

An Ideal Husband

(1999, 98 min, GB, Oliver Parker) *Rupert Everett, Minnie Driver, Cate Blanchett, Jeremy Northam, Julianne Moore, John Wood, Lindsay Duncan.* Brimming with Wildean witticisms, now familiar bon mots, gorgeous costumes and first-rate acting, this adaptation of one of Oscar Wilde's supposedly lesser plays makes for a delightful film experience if the implausible plotline and the director's unnecessarily lugubrious pacing can be forgiven. In a role he was born to play, Everett is Lord Goring, a foppish young man dedicated to life's pleasures — parties, drinking, clothing, beautiful women, bachelorhood and moneyed friends. His orderly world is complicated when his best friend MP Sir Robert Chiltern's (Northam) political ambitions are put in peril when the conniving Mrs. Cheyeley (Moore) blackmails him with an incriminating letter. What makes the film work is not the story line but Wilde's writing, still as fresh and entertainingly biting as the day it was written. ★★★ VHS: $14.99; DVD: $29.99

Idi Amin Dada

(1974, 90 min, France, Barbet Schroeder) The repellingly charismatic Idi Amin, brutal dictator of Uganda in the 1970s, secured an almost Hitlerian legacy as a blood-thirsty, power-hungry despot who pillaged the country's treasury and attempted to eliminate all opposition. From this unlikely subject comes Schroeder's fascinating, funny and shocking documentary that was made with the full cooperation of Idi Amin (although who, after completion, threatened the director with death if certain cuts were not made). We witness a jovial, even likable bully who mugs for the camera. But beneath his friendly posturing, the reality of evil personified seeps through. ★★★ VHS: $29.99

The Icicle Thief

The Idiot

(1951, 166 min, Japan, Akira Kurosawa) *Toshiro Mifune, Masayuki Mori, Takashi Shimura.* Made immediately after his international success *Rashomon*, Kurosawa faithfully transposed his favorite literary work to the screen with this engrossing adaptation of Fyodor Dostoevsky's complex tale of madness and jealousy. Changing the time and setting to a snow-battered, post-war Japan, the story follows a kept woman who is wanted for marriage by three different men, including the holy fool Prince Kameda and his raucous friend (Mifune). The video transfer is especially good, highlighting Kurosawa's imaginatively lit black-and-white photography. (Japanese with English subtitles) ★★★½ VHS: $19.99

The Idiots

(2000, 117 min, Denmark, Lars Von Trier) *Bodil Jørgensen, Jens Albinus, Anne Louise Hassing.* Von Trier's entry in the Dogme 95 series is an audacious, ambitious but ultimately pointless work. A group of people decide to shake things up in a staid society by "spazzing," or acting like idiots in public and at family functions. While there is a bit of malicious joy in seeing well-to-do folks shocked and embarrassed by the antics of these "idiots," the interest level flags quickly when one realizes that there really isn't much more to the film. A completely uninhibited orgy spruces things up, but be warned: this domestic release is altered, with black bars blocking out the actors' naughty bits. While the technical and acting credits are accomplished (though one can spot a boom microphone blatantly dipping into frame at one point — perhaps intentionally?), the whole enterprise feels like a stunt, and a rather hollow one at that. (Danish with English subtitles) ★★½ VHS: $102.99

Idle Hands

(1999, 92 min, US, Rodman Flender) *Devon Sawa, Seth Green, Elden Henson, Jessica Alba, Vivica A. Fox.* Owing more than a bit to *Evil Dead 2* and *The Frighteners, Idle Hands* is a derivative, macabre comedy. Sawa's high school slacker who doesn't notice for a while that his parents have been murdered by a demon; said demon takes the use of Sawa's right hand. This leads to much *Dr. Strangelove*-esque nonsense where the hand gets randy and murderous. Irreverent and occasionally fun, the film is boosted by the amiable Green and Henson as undead stoners. ★★ VHS: $9.99; DVD: $24.99

The Idolmaker

(1980, 119 min, US, Taylor Hackford) *Ray Sharkey, Peter Gallagher, Tovah Feldshuh, Joe Pantoliano, Olympia Dukakis.* Sharkey mesmerizes in this much-overlooked gem about a '50s rock impresario who stops at nothing to insure the success of his teen heartthrob protégés. ★★★ VHS: $9.99; DVD: $24.99

If . . .

(1969, 111 min, GB, Lindsay Anderson) *Malcolm McDowell, David Wood, Arthur Lowe, Mona Washbourne, Simon Ward.* Inspired by Jean Vigo's classic *Zero for Conduct*, this extraordinary allegorical film is set in a repressive public boarding school. McDowell, who made his film debut in this explosive, furiously funny attack on the British establishment, stars as one of three unruly seniors whose refusal to conform ulti-

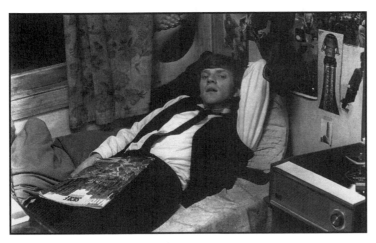

Malcom McDowell in Lindsay Anderson's *If...*

mately leads to a full-scale student rebellion. Anderson's surreal and manic style seems the perfect cinematic exclamation point to the end of a turbulent decade. The alternating use of color and black-and-white cinematography is not an artistic statement, but more the fact that Anderson, who shot the film out of sequence, ran low on money and was forced to shoot in black and white. ★★★★ VHS: $49.99

If It's Tuesday, It Must Be Belgium

(1969, 99 min, US, Mel Stuart) *Suzanne Pleshette, Mildred Natwick, Murray Hamilton, Peggy Cass, Norman Fell.* Though its humor may be somewhat dated, this congenial comedy about a group of American tourists on the European vacation from hell manages to produce a few hearty laughs. A group of beleaguered travelers visit nine countries in 18 days. And it's the kind of trip — and comedy — where everything that can go wrong will. The film may not always keep time with the slap-dash pace it sets for itself, but as a time capsule of swinging '60s mod it's almost invaluable. Donovan sings the dreadful title tune, and appears in a cameo; Hamilton comes off the best from this large cast. ★★½ VHS: $14.99

If Lucy Fell

(1996, 93 min, US, Eric Schaeffer) *Sarah Jessica Parker, Eric Schaeffer, Ben Stiller, Elle Macpherson, James Rebhorn.* An instantly forgettable but relatively painless "love-in-the-'90s" comedy. Parker (as a therapist — ha!) and Schaeffer star as romantically challenged roomies who've made a pact to throw themselves off the Brooklyn Bridge within one month (Parker's character's 30th birthday) if they haven't found mate material. Wonder what'll happen, eh? Starts off dumb and pseudo hip, then blows it by making the hugely predictable wrap-up really protracted. Parker is actually half-decent here, but Schaeffer isn't — you don't want him dead real, *real* bad. The kind of film in which two weeks later you'll wonder out loud, "Did I see this?" ★★ VHS: $14.99; DVD: $24.99

Ikiru (To Live)

(1952, 143 min, Japan, Akira Kurosawa) *Takashi Shimura, Nobuo Kaneko.* Kurosawa's most affect-

ing film, *Ikiru* salvages great hope from intractable despair. Shimura is both pathetic and radiant as a minor bureaucrat who, about to die of cancer, realizes that he never really meant anything to anyone. The film deals with his attempts to make his existence meaningful. (Japanese with English subtitles) ★★★★ VHS: $29.99

Illegally Yours

(1988, 102 min, US, Peter Bogdanovich) *Rob Lowe, Colleen Camp, Kenneth Mars.* Bogdanovich made a bold but futile attempt at a comeback with this whimsical but empty-headed romp about a juror (Lowe donning the Ryan O'Neal-*What's Up Doc* persona) who sets out to clear the name of a former high school crush (Camp). ★★ VHS: $14.99

Illtown

(1996, 101 min, US, Nick Gomez) *Michael Rapaport, Lili Taylor, Adam Trese, Kevin Corrigan, Tony Danza, Isaac Hayes.* Rapaport and Taylor find their flourishing family business under siege when a former partner hits town. Since the business is drugs and the town is Miami, the resolution of this conflict involves more than a new ad campaign. Director Gomez fashions a world both somnambulant and acutely brutal, in which the protagonists follow paths of action of their own device, and yet essentially predetermined and out of their control. The players are superb. Taylor and Rapaport deliver expectedly excellent performances, joining Trese and Corrigan in delivering portrayals simultaneously theatrical and naturalistic. Director Gomez combines a blistering examination of the ground level of a world-wide, multibillion dollar enterprise with a personal story of treachery and betrayal and extinguished hope. ★★★½ VHS: $9.99

Illuminata

(1999, 120 min, US, John Turturro) *Katherine Borowitz, Beverly D'Angelo, Ben Gazzara, Donal McCann, Susan Sarandon, Rufus Sewell, John Turturro, Christopher Walken, Bill Irwin.* A sumptuous and lyrical comic romp that explores life, love and lust in the confines of a tightly knit theatre troupe. Vaguely set in turn-of-the-centu-

ry Italy, the action centers around the megalomaniacal Tuccio (Turturro), a playwright who's searching for his first hit, struggling with his wife and ingénue, Rachel (Borowitz), and fending off his theater's owners (McCann and D'Angelo) who want to supplant his work with Ibsen. He smells his big chance when he is approached by the Sarah Bernhard–esque Celimene (Sarandon in a marvelous turn), who wants to woo him away to her own company. Bawdy adventures abound all over with Walken making a masterful appearance as an Oscar Wildean theater critic who takes a shine to a bit player (Irwin); and Sewell trying to steal the heart of the luminous leading lady Rachel. Turturro's script (cowritten with Brandon Cole) is a pure delight, full of Shakespearean conceits, sprightly in tone and with a giddy atmosphere that infects the entire ensemble. ★★★½ VHS: $9.99; DVD: $19.99

Illusions Travel by Streetcar
(La Illusion en Travnia)

(1953, 90 min, Mexico, Luis Bunuel) *Lilia Prado, Carlos Navarro.* A small, pleasant and surprisingly gentle comedy that revolves aroung two laid-off transit workers in Mexico City who, on learning that it is headed for the scrap heap, commandeer an aging trolley and take it on one final, wild drunken ride. With class-conscious humor, Buñuel pokes gentle fun at the various passengers who board the train and become part of the wildly antic adventures through the city. (Spanish with English subtitles) ★★★ VHS: $59.99

The Image

(1990, 110 min, US, Peter Werner) *Albert Finney, John Mahoney, Kathy Baker, Swoosie Kurtz, Marsha Mason, Spalding Gray.* A successful anchor/reporter for a "60 Minutes"–type news show — played by an engaging Finney — and a wonderful strong cast strive for hidden truths and higher ratings. Finding that these goals don't often coincide, *The Image* explores TV's role in creating a public's viewpoints and the pitfalls of making oneself a marketable product. A bit of stale New Age music and a somewhat preachy climax are the only drawbacks to this thought-provoking and enjoyably charming HBO production. ★★★ VHS: $9.99

Imaginary Crimes

(1994, 106 min, US, Anthony Drazan) *Harvey Keitel, Kelly Lynch, Fairuza Balk, Seymour Cassel, Vincent D'Onofrio.* Keitel delivers an involving and nuanced portrayal of a dreamer and con man whose flights of fancy are borne in silent disappointment by his wife and two daughters. Balk is remarkably powerful as the eldest daughter who assumes the role of family caretaker when her mother (Lynch) dies; the story is told through her eyes. Reminiscent of *This Boy's Life*, *Imaginary Crimes* carefully evokes the same time period of the late '50s and early '60s. Director Drazan has crafted a thoughtful and intimate study of the infinite human capacities for self-delusion and quiet strength. ★★★½ VHS: $19.99; DVD: $19.99

Imitation of Life

(1959, 124 min, US, Douglas Sirk) *Lana Turner, Juanita Moore, John Gavin, Susan Kohler, Sandra Dee.* Arguably the best of the '50s soap-operas, this second screen version of Fanny Hurst's novel stars Turner and Moore as, respectively, an ambitious actress and her self-sacrificing black maid, who each find difficulty in raising their teenage daughters. Dee and Kohner are the troublesome offspring. Moore and Kohner are standouts. A four-hanky tearjerker with the most famous funeral in the movies. ★★★½ VHS: $14.99

Immediate Family

(1989, 95 min, US, Jonathan Kaplan) *Glenn Close, James Woods, Mary Stuart Masterson, Kevin Dillon.* Close and Woods are a childless couple who are looking to adopt a baby. Masterson and Dillon are having one, though they are unmarried and unprepared for parenthood. When these four expectant parents get together, the result is a charmingly sweet, innocuous comedy-drama about familial ties and the adoption process. The story, about a privileged couple trying to get to know the parents of their future child, alternates between insightful drama and gentle humor, and director Kaplan handles both with extreme affection. Masterson walks away with the acting honors, giving a sympathetic and intuitive performance as the young mother-to-be. ★★★ VHS: $9.99

El Immigrante Latino

(1972, 89 min, Colombia, Gustavo Nieto Roa) "El Gordo" Lopez, a classical musician from Bogota, decides that the musical opportunities are greater in the United States. So, with his life savings of $1,000, our innocent hero travels to New York on a visitor's visa. His naïve hopes to find instant fame and fortune are deflated as he encounters a series of very funny disasters; what we call the "New York Experience." But hope and his good nature prevail as Gordo seeks to find a place in his new world. (Spanish with English subtitles) ★★½

The Immortal Bachelor

(1979, 94 min, Italy, Marcello Fondato) *Giancarlo Giannini, Monica Vitti, Claudia Cardinale, Vittorio Gassman.* This lusty and altogether enjoyable sex farce stars Giannini as a hot-blooded Italian lover who just can't seem to get enough of the eternal allures of women, one of them the beautiful Vitti. ★★★

Immortal Beloved

(1994, 121 min, GB, Bernard Rose) *Gary Oldman, Jeroen Krabbé, Isabella Rossellini, Valeria Golino, Marco Hofschneider, Miriam Margolyes.* Oldman stars as Ludwig van Beethoven in this somewhat trivial examination of the tempestuous composer's life and loves. Beginning with Beethoven's death, the story follows the travails of Beethoven's confidant (Krabbé) who sets out to find the mysterious "Immortal Beloved" named as the composer's beneficiary. His search leads him across war-torn Europe. While all of the actors perform adequately, nothing of real consequence happens. And as the film is structured as a series of flashbacks, there is no foundation of dramatic tension. While the soundtrack is most pleasing, one can't help but wish that Ken Russell had been at the helm to take this film over the top and into the realm of the absurd, because that is where it wants to go. ★★½ VHS: $14.99; DVD: $27.99

Immortality

(2000, 99 min, GB, Po Chih Leong) *Jude Law, Elina Löwensohn, Timothy Spall, Kerry Fox, Jack Davenport.* What begins as a surreal drama in the vein of *Vampire's Kiss* about a mysterious vampire figure dissolves into a muddled fusion of film styles, none of which is able to totally clarify plot or character. Law stars as a hemophiliac vampire (sort of) looking for love but more in need of blood (and lots of it) to satisfy his carnal cravings. Hampered by lackluster pacing and a cryptic screenplay that isn't able to realize its potential, *Immortality* is nearly saved by its fine sense of atmosphere and the dashing Law. But with no clear direction, the film disintegrates faster than you can say "Count Chocula." ★★ VHS: $14.99; DVD: $32.99

The Importance of Being Earnest

(1952, 95 min, GB, Anthony Asquith) *Michael Redgrave, Dorothy Tutin, Edith Evans, Margaret Rutherford, Joan Greenwood.* An impeccable rendition of Oscar Wilde's classic farce. Wilde's play is certainly one of the hallmarks of British theatre and it represents the height of his genius. He joyously pokes and jabs at the hypocrisy of British society while using the most widely accepted conventions of the stage to present his most radical ideas and social criticisms. Sterling performances from the entire cast make this one of the most outstanding comedies to grace any screen, large or small. ★★★★ VHS: $14.99

The Impostors

(1998, 101 min, US, Stanley Tucci) *Stanley Tucci, Oliver Platt, Alfred Molina, Isabella Rossellini, Steve Buscemi, Lili Taylor, Hope Davis, Campbell Scott.* Trying to emulate the madcap, door-slamming, frenetic antics of a Marx Brothers movie, and for the most part, succeeding, *The Impostors* is a decidedly original and off-balanced comedy which is never less than delightful. Con artists and starving actors Tucci and Platt find themselves as stowaways on a cruise ship. For the rest of the voyage, they are forced into a series of impersonations — from crew members to wealthy passengers to bosomy women — to elude detection. A very game cast brings to life this appealing assortment of crazy characters, wonderfully envisioned by writer-director Tucci. The look he gives 1930s Depression America evokes memories of those great screwball comedies of the era when evening gowns, art deco and grand ballrooms were accessories to insanity. ★★★½ VHS: $9.99; DVD: $24.99

Impromptu

(1991, 95 min, GB, James Lapine) *Judy Davis, Hugh Grant, Mandy Patinkin, Bernadette Peters, Julian Sands, Ralph Brown, Emma Thompson.* This enchanting and romantic period comedy examines the courtship between composer and pianist Frederic Chopin and novelist George Sand. Sand, a liberated woman long before her time, was easily one of the more feisty and bohemian writers of the late 19th century and she set about seducing the reclusive, sickly and fervently chaste Chopin with characteristic wit and charm. Davis is splendid as the vivacious Sand and Grant delivers a wonderfully low-key performance as Chopin. The circle of artists and free-spirited souls with whom Sand mingled is played by an excellent supporting cast with Patinkin as her ex-lover, Alfred de Musset; Peters as the scheming Marie d'Agoult; and Sands as composer Franz Liszt. ★★★½

Improper Conduct
(Mauvaise Conduite)

(1984, 110 min, France, Nestor Almendros & Orlando Jiminez-Leal) This provocative documentary investigates the oppression and abuse faced by Cuba's gay and intellectual populace under the hyper-machismic reign of Castro. Twenty-eight Cuban exiles — homosexuals, poets, artists and former government officials — are interviewed, each detailing their conflicts with a system that suppresses civil rights and considers homosexuality a crime. (English and Spanish with English subtitles) ★★★½ VHS: $19.99

Impulse

(1984, 93 min, US, Graham Baker) *Tim Matheson, Meg Tilly, Hume Cronyn, Bill Paxton, Amy Stryker.* Interesting but inconclusive tale of two young lovers (Matheson and Tilly) who seek

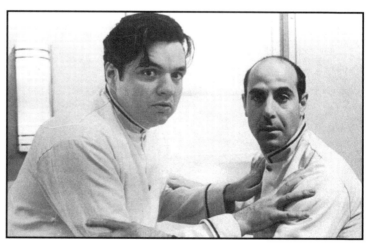

Oliver Platt (l.) and Stanley Tucci in *The Impostors*

answers to the mysteriously erratic behavior of the residents of a small community, who suddenly engage in inexplicable actions for no apparent reason. ★★ VHS: $14.99; DVD: $14.99

Impulse

(1990, 109 min, US, Sondra Locke) *Theresa Russell, Jeff Fahey, George Dzundza, Lynne Thigpen.* Director Locke's second feature is a tough, gritty portrait of a hard-edged undercover vice cop (Russell) who becomes both the number one suspect and next potential victim in a murder case. ★★★ VHS: $19.99

Impure Thoughts

(1985, 87 min, US, Michael Simpson) *Brad Dourif, Lane Davies.* Capturing a period from the filmmaker's experience, Simpson's *Impure Thoughts* is a thoughtful, funny film that both humorously satirizes and seriously reconsiders Catholic parochial education in the '60s and '70s. Flashbacks (confession, nuns with clickers and rulers, illicit lust, cheat sheets, "leaving room for the Holy Ghost" between dance partners) are beautifully integrated by Simpson into his higher purpose of contemplating such issues as life and death, sin, redemption, conscience and the hereafter. ★★★

In a Glass Cage

(1986, 98 min, Spain, Agustin Villaronga) *Gunter Meisner, David Sust, Maria Paredes.* Although definitely not for the squeamish, this sexually bizarre and violent thriller is a real find for those aficionados of no-holds-barred horror. Set a few years after WWII, the story concerns a former Nazi doctor and child molester who, because of an accident, is confined to an iron lung. The tormentor becomes the tormented after a mysterious young man, employed to be the paralyzed man's nurse, is instead bent on revenge. Mixing the style of *Diva* with the graphic sadomasochism of Pasolini's *Salo*, the film treads on ideas rarely ventured in commercial films. (Spanish with English subtitles) ★★★ VHS: $39.99

In a Lonely Place

(1950, 91 min, US, Nicholas Ray) *Humphrey Bogart, Gloria Grahame, Frank Lovejoy.* Bogart gives a chilling and complex performance in this terrific and brooding film noir thriller. Bogey plays a mentally unstable Hollywood screenwriter, given to uncontrollable rage, who must clear his own name when he is suspected of murdering a hat-check girl. Grahame is perfectly cast as a starlet who begins an affair with Bogart, she being his only alibi. The film greatly benefits from Ray's expert, moody direction, and Bogart's strong, atypical portrayal. ★★★½ VHS: $19.99

In a Year of 13 Moons

(1979, 119 min, Germany, Rainer Werner Fassbinder) *Volker Spengler, Ingrid Caven, Eva Mattes, Elisabeth Trissenaar.* A passionate and pessimistic account of the final period in the doomed life of a transsexual named Elvira (ex-Erwin), who underwent a sex change operation on impulse to please a rich eccentric who no longer loves him/her. Now alone, Elvira seeks help from friends and her former wife, only to be repulsed and/or betrayed. *13 Moons* is one of Fassbinder's most chilling and captivating efforts. As with his other films, RFW challenges

and disorients the viewer with his sporadic sentimentality and harsh detachment. Spengler excels as Elvira, an innocent sexual casualty in a desperate, and ultimately futile, search of aid. (German with English subtitles) ★★★½

In & Out

(1997, 92 min, US, Frank Oz) *Kevin Kline, Joan Cusack, Matt Dillon, Tom Selleck, Debbie Reynolds, Wilford Brimley, Bob Newhart, Whoopi Goldberg.* "I didn't see *The Birdcage*" schoolteacher Howard Brackett (Kline) tells TV tabloid reporter Peter Malloy (Selleck) after Brackett has been mistakenly outed on national TV right before his wedding. Inspired by a Tom Hanks acceptance speech at the Oscars, the very funny *In & Out* will undoubtedly replace that Robin Williams hit as a standard-bearer as regards to mainstream Hollywood "gay" comedies. Skewering gay stereotypes without giving in to them, and framing outing and coming out within the scintillating backdrop of a sex farce, *In & Out* is the kind of comedy Preston Sturges would have made if he could have. Kline is at his very best as the small-town English prof thrust into a frenzied media circus. Writer Paul Rudnick and director Oz have concocted a good-natured romp which also fires bullets at Hollywood, tabloid journalism, masculinity, and the never-ending debate of *Yentl* vs. *Funny Girl*. ★★★½ VHS: $9.99; DVD: $29.99

In Cold Blood

(1967, 134 min, US, Richard Brooks) *Robert Blake, Scott Wilson, John Forsythe.* A truly remarkable screen adaptation of Truman Capote's novel. Straightforward presentation in moody black and white avoids sensationalizing the already potent story of random slaughter by two aimless, rootless lost boys (Blake, Wilson). Director Brooks, aided by a masterful script, conveys complex information and muted emotional states with assured skill and humane empathy. Unsettling, discomforting, rewarding. (Remade in 1996) ★★★★ VHS: $19.99

In Country

(1989, 120 min, US, Norman Jewison) *Bruce Willis, Emily Lloyd, Joan Allen, Kevin Anderson, Judith Ivey.* Willis stars as a Vietnam vet whose emotional scars have yet to heal. Lloyd gives a sparkling performance as his spirited niece who harbors her own grief due to the death of her father in combat. Though Willis is top-billed, his is really more of a supporting character, as the film belongs to Lloyd, in both character time and performance. The film, at times, is haunting, but too many scenes seem short-changed dramatically; writer Frank Pierson doesn't fully explore some of the profound themes he has addressed. The film's ending, however, taking place at the Vietnam memorial in Washington, D.C., is extremely moving. ★★½ VHS: $14.99; DVD: $14.99

The In Crowd

(2000, 108 min, US, Mary Lambert) *Susan Ward, Lori Heuring, Matthew Settle, Nathan Bexton, Tess Harper.* A girl from the wrong side of the everything is released from a mental institution; her kindly doctor secures a job for her at a posh resort. While there, she is befriended by one of the In Crowd, a busty beauty who accepts our heroine with open arms. But watch out! We're told the new girl looks just like the busty beau-

ty's sister, who disappeared mysteriously the year before. Somnambulant performances, glacial story telling and zero twists conspire along with a hugely annoying, instantly dated score to drive the viewer to the WB for some wholesome garbage. ★ VHS: $14.99; DVD: $19.99

In Custody

(1994, 123 min, GB, Ismail Merchant) *Shashi Kapoor, Om Puri, Shabana Azmi.* Producer Merchant returns to behind the camera for the first time since *The Courtesans of Bombay* with this pleasant comedy-of-manners set in a small town in northern India. A poor, under-appreciated schoolteacher is assigned to interview Nur (played by the wonderful Kapoor), a renowned Urdu poet. The teacher is greeted by a great artist near the end of his life — obese, sickly, cantankerous and confined primarily to his home. The film revolves around a series of aborted interviews (family, friends, food and sex always seem to interrupt). One suspects that this simple story is actually a pretext for Merchant to offer lively discussions on the fading Urdu culture and language, and to have his actors read from the writings of the great Urdu poet Faiz Ahmad Faiz. ★★★ VHS: $29.99

The In-Laws

(1979, 103 min, US, Arthur Hiller) *Alan Arkin, Peter Falk, Richard Libertini, Nancy Dussault, Rosana De Soto.* Arkin and Falk make an engaging comedy team in this spright comedy about a dentist who becomes involved in the wacky goings-on of his daughter's future father-in-law — a CIA agent. ★★★ VHS: $14.99

In Love and War

(1987, 96 min, US, Paul Aaron) *James Woods, Jane Alexander, Haing S. Ngor.* Fact-based drama with Woods as a Navy pilot held prisoner for eight years during the Vietnam War. Alexander is his loving wife who organizes other POW wives at home in order to get some straight answers from the government. Both stars offer compelling performances, though the absorbing story isn't quite as powerful as it could have been. ★★½ VHS: $89.99

In Love and War

(1996, 115 min, US, Richard Attenborough) *Sandra Bullock, Chris O'Donnell, Mackenzie Astin, Emilio Bonucci.* Ernest Hemingway's real-life WWI exploits were the inspiration for his classic novel "A Farewell to Arms." Rather than opting to remake a third film version of the classic story, director Attenborough instead adapts the book "Hemingway in Love and War." The result is a languid romantic drama. O'Donnell plays the teenaged Hemingway, who joins the Red Cross. Stationed in Italy and wounded on the front, he falls in love with his nurse Agnes von Kurowsky (Bullock). It's a bittersweet May-June romance which later would leave the author emotionally scarred. Bullock gives a flat portrayal; at least O'Donnell captures the enthusiasm of the writer, though not his drive. Attenborough's pacing is sluggish throughout, and for a film about a passionate affair, there's little passion. ★½ VHS: $9.99; DVD: $14.99

In Memoriam

(1977, 89 min, Spain, Enrique Brasso) *Geraldine Chaplin, Jose Luis Gomez.* Chaplin stars in this somber melodrama about commitment,

In the Company of Men

obsessive love and jealousy. Essentially a three-person play, the film tells the story of a tangled love triangle between Luis, a celebrated novelist; Juan, a struggling writer; and Paulina, the woman they both love. Luis, who is incapable of expressing his deep love of Paulina, finds that he has lost her to the passionate and possessive love of Juan. Chaplin is beguiling as the woman torn between the two men — emotional and personality opposites. A Spanish soap opera that avoids the typical excesses of the genre and delves more into the psychological nuances of the characters. (Spanish with English subtitles) ★★½

In Name Only

(1939, 94 min, US, John Cromwell) *Cary Grant, Carole Lombard, Kay Francis.* Tearjerker starring Grant as a wealthy businessman who is trapped in a loveless marriage to social climber Francis. When Grant falls in love with Lombard and asks for a divorce, scheming wife Francis refuses the request and sets on a ruthless course to foil their affair. A familiar romantic soaper highlighted by Grant and Lombard's affectionate scenes together. ★★★

In Old Chicago

(1938, 96 min, US, Henry King) *Tyrone Power, Don Ameche, Alice Faye, Brian Donlevy.* With the great success of MGM's *San Francisco* in 1936, 20th Century-Fox released their own disaster spectacle and the result is a pleasing if fictionalized version of the great Chicago fire of 1871. Power and Ameche play the O'Leary brothers — one a scalawag and the other the mayor. They're the sons of Mrs. O'Leary, who owned that famous cow. Brady won an Oscar for her stalwart but sentimental portrayal of Ma. ★★★ VHS: $19.99

In the Army Now

(1994, 91 min, US, Daniel Petrie, Jr.) *Pauly Shore, Lori Petty, David Alan Grier, Andy Dick, Esai Morales, Lynn Whitfield, Brendan Fraser.* Following in the military bootsteps of such comic luminaries as Bob Hope, Goldie Hawn, Abbott & Costello and Bill Murray, twentysomething clown Shore joins the service, disproving the slogan "Be all you can be." Toning down his annoying Valley-speak a tad, Shore plays a moronic lad who with his best friend joins the Army for the financial assistance available after his tour of duty. Once in uniform, of course, he mouths off, makes enemies, tears the place

apart and saves the day. This is strictly standard issue, whose few jokes have already been done by those mentioned above. ★★ VHS: $9.99

In the Belly of the Dragon

(1989, 100 min, Canada, Yves Simoneau) This plucky little surprise from our northern neighbors is evidence that life is absurd, corporations are out to get you and people are funny all over the world. A young man, in an effort to afford a new pair of cowboy boots, trades the everyday nightmare of his dead-end job distributing circulars door-to-door for the high-tech nightmare of being an experimental subject in biochemical brain research. He begins an odyssey wherein he learns the transient regard for human life, the power of a well-thrown dart and the absolute value of some really good friends. (Dubbed) ★★★ VHS: $29.99

In the Company of Men

(1997, 97 min, US, Neil Labute) *Aaron Eckhart, Stacy Edwards, Matt Malloy.* Sexual politics in the corporate workplace are played out by two mid-America average white boys who consider life to be out of balance whenever they're not on top. Outraged that women no longer appear to be blissfully relegated to an inherently subservient role, these two nondescript nonentities set up a cruel game on an unsuspecting victim — a deaf temp new to the office in which they're temporarily stationed. Consciously equating their own dignity with the willful abasement of another human being, these small, ineffectual, scared men look for any available easy target to bolster their self-esteem, back-stabbing with off-handed impartiality. Their myriad frailities and insecurities bubble to boiling as their game turns into a rivalry. *In the Company of Men* is a controversial, virulent dark comedy which will undoubtedly offend some by its cavalier manner and intrigue others with both its uncompromising examination of the male psyche and an unnerving, biting comic voice. ★★★ VHS: $24.99

In the Gloaming

(1997, 62 min, US, Christopher Reeve) *Glenn Close, Robert Sean Leonard, David Strathairn, Whoopi Goldberg, Bridget Fonda.* In an herculean effort far more inspiring and dramatic than anything offered on the screen, Reeve makes his directorial debut, his first professional outing since his accident. No doubt this story of impending death struck a nerve with Reeve, and as a director he brings reverence and a fluidity not usually associated with freshman assignments. He also coaxes some natural, deeply affecting performances from his cast. But this one-hour drama about an estranged young man with AIDS who returns home to die is lacking in passion, and its disjointed screenplay sabotages any chance for true character development. Close is the only exception, giving more depth to the role of the young man's mother than what is really there. ★★½ VHS: $19.99

In the Good Old Summertime

(1949, 102 min, US, Robert Z. Leonard) *Judy Garland, Van Johnson, S.Z. Sakall, Buster Keaton, Spring Byington.* Charming musical remake of Ernst Lubitsch's *The Shop Around the Corner.* Garland and Johnson are the bickering coworkers who unknowingly fall in love via the personals. Though the same story is the basis for the Broadway musical "She Loves Me," this musical

and the show have different scores. That's Liza Minnelli as the couple's baby at the end. ★★★

In the Heat of the Night

(1967, 109 min, US, Norman Jewison) *Sidney Poitier, Rod Steiger, Lee Grant, William Schallert, Warren Oates.* A Best Picture Oscar went to this exceptional mystery story about a black Philadelphia cop and his experiences with racial bigotry while helping the Sparta, Mississippi, police force solve a murder. Poitier is Virgil Tibbs, a savvy police detective whose assistance to the small town and captain Steiger is ill-rewarded and unappreciated. Both actors are excellent, and Steiger won an Oscar for Best Actor as the racist policeman trying to do right. (Sequel: *They Call Me Mister Tibbs*) ★★★★ VHS: $9.99; DVD: $19.99

In the Land of the War Canoes

(1914, 48 min, US/Canada, Edward S. Curtis) Photographer Edward S. Curtis, best known for his still photographs of Native Americans, spent three years with the Kwakiutl Indians of Vancouver Island in order to capture on film their lifestyle, ceremonial dances and religious rituals. This fascinating documentary is a meticulous re-creation of a tribal society before the invasion of the white man destroyed their culture. ★★★ VHS: $39.99; DVD: $29.99

In the Line of Fire

(1993, 123 min, US, Wolfgang Petersen) *Clint Eastwood, John Malkovich, Rene Russo, Dylan McDermott, Gary Cole, John Mahoney, Patrika Darbo, John Heard.* Petersen follows his underrated *Shattered* with this superior suspense thriller which affords Eastwood a second opportunity to deliver a career performance. Clint plays a seasoned Secret Service agent who was present at JFK's Dallas murder. He finds himself entangled in another presidential assassination scenario as a routine investigation puts him and partner McDermott on the trail of a potential killer, played with great menace by Malkovich. Much of the film's enjoyment lies in the cat-and-mouse relationship Malkovich's would-be assassin nurtures between the agent and himself. For once, Eastwood leaves behind his laconic character, and Jeff Maguire's intelligent screenplay makes it a pleasure to hear the actor form complete sentences. ★★★★ VHS: $9.99; DVD: $29.99

In the Mood

(1987, 99 min, US, Phil Alden Robinson) *Patrick Dempsey, Beverly D'Angelo, Talia Balsam.* Amiable comedy based on the real-life experiences of 15-year-old Sonny Wisecarver, who in the 1940s made headlines around the country by having affairs with two older women, one of whom he married. Dempsey is a delight as Carver, who was also known as "The Woo Woo Kid." ★★½ VHS: $14.99

In the Mouth of Madness

(1995, 95 min, US, John Carpenter) *Sam Neill, Julie Carmen, Jürgen Prochnow, Charlton Heston, David Warner, John Glover, Bernie Casey.* In this H. P. Lovecraft–based tale, a skeptical insurance investigator (Neill) sets out to prove that the disappearance of best-selling author Sutter Cane (Prochnow) is a publicity stunt. As he digs deeper, he finds out that what Cane has been selling as fiction is actually fact-based memory transmitted by "the dark ones" — and that Cane's final novel will unleash Hell on Earth. What begins as a mature, well-visualized opus into madness and surrealism eventually clashes with the filmmaker's schlocky sense of atmosphere and "boo"-style horror gimmicks, creating a mixed bag of chills and chuckles. ★★ VHS: $14.99; DVD: $19.99

In the Name of the Father

(1993, 127 min, Ireland, Jim Sheridan) *Daniel Day-Lewis, Emma Thompson, Pete Postlethwaite, John Lynch, Corin Redgrave.* An impassioned scream for justice which dramatizes the real-life plight of Gerry Conlon and his companions, a group of innocents known as the Guilford Four who spent 15 years in a British prison for an IRA bombing. Day-Lewis easily could have won his second Oscar for his fiery portrayal of the emotional Conlon, a petty thief and troublemaker from Belfast who, by sheer coincidence, was caught in the British government's legal net — which also picked up several members of his family and his friends including his father and aunt. And while Day-Lewis' performance sparkles, it is Postlethwaithe, in a riveting performance as his steadfastly principled father Giuseppe, who truly carries the film's moral message. ★★★★ VHS: $14.99; DVD: $24.99

In the Name of the Pope King

(1977, 105 min, Italy, Luigi Magni) *Nino Manfredi, Danilo Mattei.* Manfredi takes a successful stab at serious acting in this compelling story of intrigue, political conflict and murder. Set in 1867 during a turbulent period of peasant revolt and leftist bombings, the film stars Manfredi as Monsignor Colombo, a magistrate for the conservative papal state. He finds himself immersed in political turmoil when he discovers that his son might be involved in terrorist activity against the state. An interesting companion film to this fascinating political and personal drama is Bertrand Tavernier's similarly themed *The Clockmaker.* (Italian with English subtitles) ★★★ VHS: $59.99

In the Navy

(1941, 85 min, US, Arthur Lubin) *Bud Abbott, Lou Costello, Dick Powell, The Andrews Sisters.* Abbott and Costello are sailors who become involved with the escapades of crooner Powell, who's joined the Navy to escape his adoring fans. This A&C comedy isn't as consistently funny as some of their other romps, especially when the story concentrates on Powell. However, the boys do offer some funny bits (a shell game, proving 7 x 13 = 28), and Lou has a few amusing solo bits as well. Powell and The Andrews Sisters supply the songs, which are mostly forgettable. ★★½ VHS: $14.99

In the Presence of Mine Enemies

(1996, 96 min, US, Joan Micklin Silver) *Armin Mueller-Stahl, Charles Dance, Elina Löwensohn, Chad Lowe.* Rod Serling's teleplay is the basis for this poignant though slow-moving drama set in the Warsaw ghetto before its eventual extermination. Mueller-Stahl gives a strong, caring portrayal of a rabbi whose determination to keep his family together and provide spiritual guidance to the dwindling number of neighbors — often refusing to acknowledge the horrors surrounding him — causes a crisis of faith and mental breakdown. Dance is the Nazi captain caught in a battle of wills and words with the rabbi. Serling's story pits its characters against each other in moral debate, all trapped in hopeless dilemma; but their voices are often muted and thoughts prone to repetition. ★★½ VHS: $79.99

In the Realm of Passion

(1978, 110 min, Japan, Nagisa Oshima) *Kazuko Yoshiyuki, Takahiro Tamura.* From the director of *Merry Christmas, Mr. Lawrence* comes this erotic ghost story of unremitting passion and impending doom. A young married peasant woman has an affair with another man. Together, they kill her husband; but, twisting the *Ghost* theme on an ominous tilt, the angry husband comes back to haunt the two. Subtle, visually beautiful and a restrained work. (Japanese with English subtitles) (aka: *Empire of Passion*) ★★★ VHS: $19.99; DVD: $29.99

In the Realm of the Senses

(1976, 115 min, Japan, Nagisa Oshima) *Tatsuya Fuji, Eiko Matsuda.* Oshima's most debated work in a career marked by controversy, *In the Realm of the Senses* is an unrelenting journey into the world of passion and eroticism. Oblivious to social restraints and public sentiment, a geisha and her lover engage in a torrid sexual spree, losing themselves in the fervor of their love-making and their quest for ultimate ecstasy. The ideology of male dominance and female submission is thoroughly undermined as the obsessed lovers create a closed existence of incessant lovemaking and sadomasochistic experiments. This is an eerily beautiful examination of the intensity of physical desire. (Japanese with English subtitles) ★★★½ VHS: $19.99; DVD: $29.99

In the Soup

(1993, 96 min, US, Alexandre Rockwell) *Steve Buscemi, Seymour Cassel, Jennifer Beals, Jim Jarmusch, Carol Kane.* Character actor Buscemi is finally given a chance to star in his own film with this enjoyably rag-tag independent comedy. Buscemi plays a down-on-his-luck aspiring (but possibly no-talent) filmmaker. His world is turned upside down after an eccentric "businessman" takes him under his dark wing and offers to finance his new opus. Strikingly similar to *Mistress*, the film is entertainingly wacky and features great performances by Buscemi as the befuddled loser sucked into a bizarre, criminal world. While not as hilarious as it thinks it is, the film is still a lot of fun. (Available in both black-and-white and color versions) ★★★ VHS: $19.99

In the Spirit

(1990, 94 min, US, Sandra Seacat) *Marlo Thomas, Elaine May, Peter Falk, Jeannie Berlin, Melanie Griffith, Olympia Dukakis.* A health nut (Thomas) and a socialite (May) stumble across the "datebook" of a deceased hooker, and comedic complications ensue. Soon, everyone is after the book. A likable cast rises above the forced material. ★★½ VHS: $89.99

In the White City

(1983, 108 min, Switzerland/Portugal, Alain Tanner) *Bruno Ganz, Teresa Madruga.* A haunting mood piece about a Swiss boat engineer (Ganz) who jumps ship in Lisbon and begins a personal quest of self-discovery. Roaming the streets and frequenting the watering holes, he dives head first into the foreignness and unfamiliarity of his new surroundings. Tanner turns this existential odyssey into a fascinating examination of solitude, freedom and self-estrangement as he unravels the psyche of a man's unstructured search for something real. (German and Portuguese with English subtitles) ★★★ VHS: $79.99

In This Our Life

(1942, 97 min, US, John Huston) *Bette Davis, Olivia deHavilland, George Brent, Charles Coburn, Hattie McDaniel, Walter Huston.* Davis lets loose as a neurotic hussy whose tantrums and plottings ruin the lives of sister de Havilland, husband Brent and, finally, herself. Davis gives a commanding performance in this familiar melodrama, though the film suffers somewhat due to director Huston's unfamiliarity with the genre. ★★½ VHS: $19.99

In Which We Serve

(1942, 115 min, GB, Noël Coward & David Lean) *Noël Coward, John Mills, Richard Attenborough, Michael Wilding, Celia Johnson, Kay Walsh, Daniel Massey.* One of the masterpieces of British cine-

In the Realm of the Senses

ma, *In Which We Serve* provideddirector/writer/actor/composor Coward with his finest screen hour. Based on the real-life experiences of the British warship *HMS Kelly*, the film recounts — mostly in flashback — the story of the men of a torpedoed destroyer awaiting rescue. Coward brings all the right qualities of leadership and resolve to his role as the ship's captain, and the supporting cast is excellent. Lean's directorial debut. ★★★★

The Incident

(1967, 107 min, US, Larry Peerce) *Martin Sheen, Tony Musante, Beau Bridges, Jack Gilford, Thelma Ritter, Brock Peters, Ruby Dee, Ed McMahon.* A gritty, well-done low-budget thriller set almost exclusively in a New York City subway car. A disparate group of passengers are terrorized by punks Sheen and Musante. Bridges is first-rate as an injured soldier. ★★★ VHS: $59.99

Incident at Map Grid 36-80

(1983, 80 min, USSR, Mikhail Tumanishvili) An interesting premise, sort of a Russian *Hunt for Red October*, and a rare look at Soviet military might help make this a compelling war thriller. While out on routine sea maneuvers, a Soviet squadron receives a distress call from an American submarine which is carrying a secret nuclear arsenal. The Soviets respond to the call but are warned not to approach. Complicating the already tense situation is a malfunctioning computer that sounds the alarm to launch the American sub's cruise missiles. (Russian with English subtitles) ★★★ VHS: $59.99

Incident at Oglala

(1992, 89 min, US, Michael Apted) *Narrated by: Robert Redford.* This important and long-overdue documentary is about the events that occurred in 1975 on the Sioux Indian reservation in South Dakota. The film asserts that the attack on two FBI agents which led to the stand-off was an act of self-defense and that those who were punished for it (Leonard Peltier remains the only person jailed in the incident) were innocent. The film also asserts that through a band of violent government cronies known as the "Goon Squads," an atmosphere of brutality and terror was maintained on the reservation, an atmosphere which ultimately led to the fateful confrontation. Apted also directed the fictionalized counterpart, *Thunderheart*, which puts a Hollywood spin on the whole affair. ★★★½ VHS: $19.99; DVD: $24.99

The Incredible Mr. Limpet

(1964, 102 min, US, Arthur Lubin) *Don Knotts, Jack Weston, Carole Cook.* Cute live-action and animated comedy starring Knotts, who falls off a Coney Island pier and becomes a fish — helping the U.S. Navy battle Nazi submarines. ★★½

The Incredible Sarah

(1976, 106 min, GB, Richard Fleischer) *Glenda Jackson, Daniel Massey, Yvonne Mitchell.* An outstanding performance by Jackson breathes life into this otherwise standard biopic on the life of the legendary French stage actress Sarah Bernhardt. ★★½

The Incredible Shrinking Man

(1957, 81 min, US, Jack Arnold) *Grant Williams, Randy Stuart, April Kent.* This existential sci-fi classic written by Richard Matheson has the

courage of its convictions in its strange metaphysical climax as an ordinary Joe finds that he is growing smaller every day. Brilliant special effects don't overshadow Williams' performance. ★★★½ VHS: $14.99

The Incredible Shrinking Woman

(1981, 88 min, US, Joel Schumacher) *Lily Tomlin, Charles Grodin, Ned Beatty, Henry Gibson.* A sometimes humorous satire on consumerism and suburbia, Tomlin plays an average American housewife whose exposure to household products causes her to shrink. Great production design and effects highlight the film. ★★½

The Incredibly Strange Creatures Who Stopped Living and Became Mixed-Up Zombies

(1963, 82 min, US, Ray Dennis Steckler) *Cash Flagg, Carolyn Brandt.* A great title highlights this camp gem full of bad acting, a stupid plot, neat zombies and atmospheric camera work thanks to Joe Micelli, Laszlo Kovacs and Vilmos Zsigmond. (aka: *The Teenage Psycho Meets Bloody Mary*) ★

The Incredibly True Adventure of Two Girls in Love

(1995, 95 min, US, Maria Maggenti) *Laurel Holloman, Nicole Parker, Maggie Moore, Kate Stafford.* This thoroughly enjoyable lesbian first love story is a startling film debut by independent filmmaker Maggenti. Randy (Holloman) is a white high school tomboy living with her lesbian aunt. Evie (Parker) is a beautiful and pampered black deb from the right side of the tracks. They meet and love blossoms despite their differences. A long-awaited "wholesome lesbian comedy and romance" which ignores queer politics and prejudice and concentrates on the two young women's intense attraction for each other. Not as big city grunge as *Go Fish* nor as jaded as *Bar Girls*, *Two Girls* is a terrifically sweet low-budget romantic comedy. ★★★ VHS: $19.99

Incubus

(1966, 76 min, US, Leslie Stevens) *William Shatner, Allyson Ames, Eloise Hardt.* This one's a real curio: a black-and-white horror film from the '60s, beautifully shot by Conrad Hall, starring a pre-"Star Trek" Shatner, with all dialogue spoken in the "international language" of Esperanto! *Incubus* is basically an enjoyable mix of the moody and atmospheric with the silly and outright laughable (you thought Shatner overacted in English!). A bit too slow and hokey, to be sure, but if you're in the right mood, a good time. ★★½ VHS: $19.99; DVD: $24.99

The Incubus

(1982, 90 min, US, John Hough) *John Cassavetes, Kerrie Keane.* A peaceful New England community is beseiged by a series of demonic murders. Cassavetes stars as an investigator who follows the demon's path to a frightened young man whose nightmares may hold the key to the mystery. Boring, confusing and not very exciting. ★

An Indecent Obsession

(1985, 106 min, Australia, Lex Marinos) *Wendy Hughes, Gary Sweet, Muir, Bruno Lawrence.* Adapted from Colleen McCullough's best-sell-

Incident at Oglala

ing novel, this hospital drama is set immediately after Japan's surrender in WWII. But for the war-ravaged psychiatric patients of Ward X, the end of the war makes little difference. Their troubled minds and battered spirits, held in check by the beautiful nurse Langtry (Hughes), are soon tested by the appearance of a mysterious man who is admitted into their wing. Vicious currents of lust, homophobia, jealousy, desire and violent death soon undermine them all. A hyperventilating soap opera that squanders its juicy material with a leaden hand; the film ultimately fizzles. ★★

Indecent Proposal

(1993, 118 min, US, Adrian Lyne) *Robert Redford, Demi Moore, Woody Harrelson, Oliver Platt, Seymour Cassel.* Director Lyne has never been accused of being a subtle director. But nothing he's done before hints at the heavy-handedness of this silly romantic drama. Moore and Harrelson are a young married couple experiencing financial troubles. They head to Las Vegas and promptly lose everything. Then, Demi attracts the attention of zillionaire Redford who offers a million dollars to spend the night with her. Aside from the incredulous offer is the disturbing subtheme of "women as chattel." The film really hits bottom, though, after the deed is done. The last hour is dedicated to an unlikely couple whining about everything and Redford acting like a lovesick teenager. A conceit of such calculation it resembles a mathematical equation rather than a movie. ★★ VHS: $14.99

Independence Day

(1983, 110 min, US, Robert Mandel) *Kathleen Quinlan, David Keith, Dianne Wiest, Frances Sternhagen, Cliff De Young, Richard Farnsworth.* A handful of strong performances dominate this telling drama about the day-to-day lives of a small Southwestern town. Quinlan heads the cast as a young woman — involved with mechanic Keith — who longs to escape the confines of her constrictive lifestyle. Wiest is superb as a battered wife. ★★★ VHS: $19.99

Independence Day

(1996, 135 min, US, Roland Emmerich) *Bill Pullman, Will Smith, Jeff Goldblum, Mary McDonnell, Judd Hirsch, Robert Loggia, Margaret Colin, Randy Quaid, Brent Spiner, Harvey Fierstein, Harry Connick, Jr.* Recalling the UFO paranoia/hysteria of those 1950s sci-fi films — the classic and cheesy, alike — in which dastardly aliens set out to destroy our benign planet, *Independence Day* is the ultimate us vs. them sci-fi encounter, boasting great special effects, a plausible story line, more laughs than anyone would have a right to expect, and a top-notch cast obviously enjoying themselves. The fun starts when several giant spaceships hover over Earth's major cities. As the president, the military and scientists engage in speculation, it soon becomes clear these aliens are no *E.T.s*. *Star Wars* may be slicker, and *Close Encounters* more visionary, but there's no denying *Independence Day* is a blast. (Letterboxed VHS available for $19.99) ★★★½ VHS: $9.99; DVD: $34.99

The Indian in the Cupboard

(1995, 96 min, US, Frank Oz) *Hal Scardino, Litefoot, Lindsay Crouse, Richard Jenkins, David Keith.* A family film with just the right amount of fantasy and magic added to a story of childhood friendship and trust. Based on Lynne Reid Banks' book, this charming adaptation stars Scardino as Omri, the youngest of three children in a New York City household. Omri's brother presents him with a cabinet in which Omri places an American Indian figure. The cupboard shakes, awaking Omri, and when he opens it he is surprised to find the Indian (played by Litefoot) alive. Omri is the personification of wonder and innocence as he learns through his friend to be brave and independent in the rough and troubled world at home and on the streets of New York. ★★★ VHS: $9.99; DVD: $24.99

The Indian Runner

(1991, 127 min, US, Sean Penn) *David Morse, Viggo Mortensen, Charles Bronson, Dennis Hopper, Sandy Dennis, Patricia Arquette, Valeria Golina.* Maverick actor Penn takes his talents behind the camera with this stunningly realized character study centering on the stormy relationship between a highway patrolman (Morse) and his "loose cannon" of a brother (Mortensen). Though short on story, this loving tribute to the filmmaking of the '70s will reward the patient viewer with its detailed attention to time and place. ★★★ VHS: $14.99

Indian Summer

(1993, 98 min, US, Mike Binder) *Alan Arkin, Diane Lane, Bill Paxton, Matt Craven, Elizabeth Perkins, Kevin Pollak, Vincent Spano, Julie Warner, Sam Raimi.* This *Big Chill*-like comedy reunites seven old friends who attended Camp Tamakwa during its "golden age" in the early '70s. Invited back to their old stomping grounds by camp owner Arkin, the friends get to work out some of their demons and share old secrets. With warmth and humor, *Indian Summer* brings back the sights, sounds, smells, first kisses and first heartbreaks of summer camp. Based on director Binder's own experiences. ★★★

Indochine

Indiana Jones and the Last Crusade

(1989, 127 min, US, Steven Spielberg) *Harrison Ford, Sean Connery, Denholm Elliott, Alison Doody, John Rhys-Davies, River Phoenix.* Indiana Jones and director Spielberg are back in glorious form after the near-fiasco of *Temple of Doom*. Ford is as dashing as ever as Indy, who is off in search of both the Holy Grail and his missing father. Connery is an absolute delight as Indy's dad, a timid scholarly type not really prepared for his son's more dangerous escapades. The humor and the pace are fast and furious and Indy's old enemies — the Nazis — are back to do battle once again. Every bit as enjoyable as the original *Raiders*. Phoenix is great as a young Indy in the film's opening prologue. (VHS available letterboxed or pan & scan) ★★★½ VHS: $14.99

Indiana Jones and the Temple of Doom

(1984, 118 min, US, Steven Spielberg) *Harrison Ford, Kate Capshaw, Ke Huy Quan.* Spielberg attempts to outdo his success with *Raiders of the Lost Ark*. The perils are greater but the plot is weaker. The film is actually a prequel to *Raiders*, following Indy (Ford) and sidekick (Capshaw) in their adventures in the Far East. However disappointing, the opening sequence is worth the price of the rental: Capshaw singing a Mandarin version of "Anything Goes" — leading to a highly exciting and comical nightclub brawl. (Sequel: *Indiana Jones and the Last Crusade*) (VHS available letterboxed or pan & scan) ★★½ VHS: $14.99

Indiscreet

(1958, 100 min, US, Stanley Donen) *Ingrid Bergman, Cary Grant, Phyllis Calvert.* For couples wanting romance, this is the ticket. Bergman plays a ravishing European actress who is courted by an equally ravishing Grant. The fare is at times slow and perhaps even overly romantic, but the film is filled with an engaging sense of wry wit and humor — not to mention a seething sexual tension between its two stars. Bergman and Grant, as the urbane lovers, could not have been better cast. ★★★ VHS: $9.99

Indiscreet

(1998, 101 min, US, Marc Bienstock) *Luke Perry, Gloria Reuben, Adam Baldwin, Peter Coyote.* In this lukewarm thriller, Perry is Michael Nash, an ex-cop, ex-alcoholic turned private investigator. Offered a job by a rich lawyer to spy on his unfaithful wife Eve (Reuben), Nash discovers that she is not having an affair, but spending her days alone drinking and skinny dipping. Rescuing Eve from a suicide attempt one afternoon, these two damaged people begin a passionate romance that cools off when her husband is murdered, and Nash is the prime suspect. Although *Indiscreet* is a good looking production that is filled with many plot twists as it has plot holes. ★★ VHS: $102.99

Indiscretion of an American Housewife

(1954, 63 min, Italy, Vittorio De Sica) *Montgomery Clift, Jennifer Jones, Richard Beymer.* The unusual teaming of American producer David O. Selznick and neorealist Italian director De Sica does not really work. The action centers in Rome's main railroad station and features Jones as an adulterous wife who meets her lover Clift for a final fling. It is no *Brief Encounter* but an interesting try. (aka: *Terminal Station*) (Filmed in English) ★★ VHS: $59.99

Indochine

(1992, 155 min, France, Regis Wargnier) *Catherine Deneuve, Linh Dan Pham, Vincent Perez.* An Academy Award winner for Best Foreign-Language Film, *Indochine* is a beautifully photographed and evocative love story set during the French colonization of Indochina. In a rapturous performance, the stunning Deneuve stars as the dowager of a successful rubber plantation. Though a strict foreman, she has an especially loving relationship with her adopted, Indochinese daughter (well played by Pham). Against the backdrop of social upheavel, their worlds collide when they both fall in love with the same man, a handsome French soldier (Perez). A poetic epic which balances romance and politics with equal finesse. (French with English subtitles) ★★★★ VHS: $19.99; DVD: $27.99

Infernal Trio

(1974, 100 min, France, Francis Girod) *Michel Piccoli, Romy Schneider, Mascha Gomska.* While quite shocking and even scandalous in its initial release, time has not been kind to this macabre black comedy about a trio of amoral, larcenous lovers. Piccoli plays a distinguished lawyer who entices two German sisters (Schneider, Gomska) into marrying a series of rich older men. When the husbands die of natural causes or are "encouraged" to leave this life, the three share in the proceeds of the wealth and insurance money. Unevenly paced, the film fluctuates between serious drama, sexy romp and pitch-black comedy. This social satire, which sets out to intentionally shock its unsuspecting audience, delivers an enthusiastically shameless descent into the pleasures and profits of evil. (French with English subtitles) ★★½

Inferno

(1978, 107 min, Italy, Dario Argento) *Eleonora Giorgi, Leigh McCloskey, Gabriele Lavia.* Argento's sequel to *Suspiria* is an almost incomprehensible collection of bizarre images and fantastically realized setpiece murders. It lacks a linear narrative, but that does not detract from its overall ambiance of weirdness and terror. A young American poet discovers a book which she identifies her ancient New York apartment building as the residence of the Mater Tenebrarum, the mother of shadows, one of three witches who generate all the misery in the world. The first mother, Mater Suspiriorum, lives in Freiburg and was the subject of Argento's *Suspiria*. *Inferno* is full of stylistic touches which overcome its narrative difficulties. *Suspiria* and *Inferno* are the only two films Argento has made with purely supernatural plots, a fact which gives him the freedom to completely abandon all logic and submerge himself in the stylish, horrifying impulses which make him unique among horror film directors. (Letterboxed) ★★½ VHS: $14.99; DVD: $29.99

Inferno

(1999, 94 min, US, Harley Cokeliss) *Ray Liotta, Gloria Reuben, Armin Mueller-Stahl, Daniel Kash, Lisa Owen.* Liotta is quite effective in this potent nail-biter about an even-tempered Average Joe who wakes up in the middle of nowhere with no memory, a fake identity and a dead guy in his bathroom. He then becomes the target of a gang of gun-toting thugs on the trail of a fortune in stolen loot that he may or may not have stolen. A good story line, solid cinematography and well-etched performances make this "desert-noir" surprising entertainment. ★★★ VHS: $79.99; DVD: $24.99

The Infiltrator

(1995, 102 min, US, John MacKenzie) *Oliver Platt, Arliss Howard, Peter Riegert, Alan King.* A powerful HBO film, *The Infiltrator* is based on the book "In Hitler's Shadow," the true-life story of Israeli journalist Yaron Svoray, who while on assignment in Germany went undercover to expose a neo-Nazi group. Platt plays Svoray, a writer living in America who is sent to report on the recent racially motivated attacks by skinheads in Germany. But as Svoray digs deeper, he discovers a well-organized, underground fascist political organization with growing public support. The film — in eye-opening detail — shows the extent of racial hatred permeating in modern Germany, directed at immigrant Turks, Jews, blacks and anyone else "non-white." Howard is splendid as Svoray's accomplice. ★★★ VHS: $9.99

The Informer

(1935, 91 min, US, John Ford) *Victor McLaglen, Heather Angel, Wallace Ford.* An eerie, dreamlike quality pervades director Ford's film of a dull-witted man who informs on his Irish Republican Army comrade in 1922 Dublin. McLaglen won the Best Actor Oscar for his haunting portrayal of the pathetic misfit; Ford won for Best Director, Dudley Nichols for Best Screenplay and Max Steiner for Best Score. An evocative examination of the human condition. ★★★★ VHS: $14.99

Inherit the Wind

(1960, 127 min, US, Stanley Kramer) *Spencer Tracy, Fredric March, Dick York, Gene Kelly, Florence Eldridge, Harry Morgan.* Tracy and March, possibly America's two greatest film actors, both give tour de force performances in this outstanding adaptation of the Lawrence-Lee stage play, based on the infamous Scopes Monkey Trial of 1925. Though the names are changed, Tracy is Clarence Darrow and March is William Jennings Bryan, each on opposite sides of the court when

a teacher (York) is arrested and tried for teaching the theories of Darwin. One of the finest, most literate screenplays to grace an American film, the enthralling court sequences are all the more topical today as the battle of separation between Church and State continues. (Remade in 1999) ★★★★ VHS: $9.99

Inherit the Wind

(1999, 113 min, US, Daniel Petrie, Sr.) *Jack Lemmon, George C. Scott, Lane Smith, Tom Everett Scott, Piper Laurie, Beau Bridges.* A made-for-TV remake of the classic Spencer Tracy–Fredric March 1960 drama. This adaptation of the Lawrence-Lee stage play does a fine job in adhering to the original text, but it just misses the mark as great theatre in comparison to the brilliant original. Giving two performances befitting their status as acting giants, Lemmon and Scott essay the roles of two opposing lawyers caught in the middle of the hysteria of the Scopes Trial, in which a teacher in Tennessee is put in trial for teaching the theories of Darwin. A timely and timeless work brought lovingly to the small screen. ★★★ VHS: $49.99

The Inheritance

(1977, 105 min, Italy, Mauro Bolognini) *Anthony Quinn, Dominique Sanda, Fabio Testi.* This well-acted drama, a bit trashy for European standards, features a sexy Sanda as a coolly calculating woman who marries into a wealthy family and begins a steamy affair with her dying father-in-law (Quinn). A titillating and erotic video find. Sanda won the Best Actress Award at the Cannes Film Festival for her role as the money-hungry vixen. ★★½

The Inheritors

(1999, 94 min, Austria/Germany, Stefan Ruzowitzky) *Simon Schwarz, Sophie Rois, Lars Rudolph, Julia Gschnitzer, Ulrich Wildgruber.* A bittersweet fable, *The Inheritors* is a rural period piece about greed and integrity set in 1930s Austria. When a tyrannical farmer dies, he leaves his property to the peasant workers with the decree that they can kill each other fighting over it. While they do struggle among themselves, they ultimately realize that they must work together to keep the village's other landowners from taking their farm away. The story is simple, but it is also quite powerful, as the inheritors defend what they have been given by any means necessary. The most touching story is that of Lukas (Schwarz), a peasant who murders his old foreman to save his land, and ultimately must escape to save himself. Bathed in a golden hue, director Ruzowitzky's underdog drama is occasionally slow going, but it is beautifully told nonetheless. (German with English subtitles) ★★★ VHS: $14.99; DVD: $27.99

The Inkwell

(1994, 112 min, US, Matty Rich) *Larenz Tate, Joe Morton, Suzzanne Douglas, Glynn Turman, Mary Alice.* From the director of *Straight Out of Brooklyn* comes this gentle black version of *Summer of '42.* Tate plays Drew, a naïve 16-year-old with a killer smile from the wrongish side of the tracks who comes of age during the summer of '76 while he is visiting his high-brow relatives at a ritzy (and primarily black) beach in Martha's Vineyard. On the arty side of an "Afterschool Special," *The Inkwell* is not a particularly original film, but Tate gives such

a fresh, guileless performance that one can forgive some of its more artificial moments. ★★½ VHS: $9.99

The Inner Circle

(1991, 139 min, US, Andrei Konchalovsky) *Tom Hulce, Lolita Davidovich, Bob Hoskins.* A fascinating and moody examination of life under Stalin in 1930s Moscow. In this true story, Hulce is a newlywed and loyal party member who is whisked from his home on his wedding day to the great halls of the Kremlin. It is there he begins service to Stalin as his personal projectionist. Politically naïve, it is during this regime that Hulce slowly becomes aware of the corruption and paranoia running rampant within the walls of Russia's party headquarters. *The Inner Circle* — which refers to Stalin's elite group of companions — uses its Russian locations to better effect than did *The Russia House.* However, like that film, its locale sometimes seems to dwarf the narrative. ★★★ VHS: $19.99

Innerspace

(1987, 120 min, US, Joe Dante) *Dennis Quaid, Martin Short, Meg Ryan, Kevin McCarthy, Fiona Lewis.* All hell breaks loose when a miniaturized Quaid is accidentally injected into the body of highly manic Short. Hunted down by a pair of evil industrialists (hilariously portrayed by McCarthy and Lewis), the two hit the road where they develop a working relationship: with Quaid giving the orders and Short, the hypochondriac hero, responding with outrageous pratfalls. An Academy Award winner for Special Effects. ★★★ VHS: $9.99

Innocence Unprotected

(1968, 78 min, Yugoslavia, Dusan Makavejev) *Dragoljub Aleksic, Ana Milosavljevic.* This inventive and, at times, hilarious film-within-a-film reunites and interviews the cast of Yugoslavia's first talky: a tacky, ridiculously naïve melodrama. While the stars dreamily reminisce, we watch excerpts from the 1942 film, a story about a seemingly brainless woman saddled with a wicked stepmother and a lecherous older suitor who falls in love with a muscleman/daredevil. Makavejev mischievously intermixes footage of the horror of the war with the interviews and the film as he shows the illusion of fame and power. (Serbo-Croatian with English subtitles) ★★★ VHS: $24.99

The Innocent

(1976, 115 min, Italy, Luchino Visconti) *Giancarlo Giannini, Laura Antonelli, Jennifer O'Neill.* Visconti's final masterpiece is set in turn-of-the-century Italy and features a fine cast, sumptuous photography and stunning sets and costumes. Giannini is a chauvinistic aristocrat who ignores his beautiful and loving wife (Antonelli) in order to pursue his adulterous affair with his mistress (O'Neill). Revenge is sweet, however, as the lonely and frustrated wife takes on a lover and turns the tables on her insensitive husband. (Italian with English subtitles) ★★★★

The Innocent

(1995, 119 min, GB, John Schlesinger) *Anthony Hopkins, Isabella Rossellini, Campbell Scott, Hart Bochner, Ronald Nitschke.* In one of director Schlesinger's lesser outings, the historic tearing down of the Berlin Wall sets in motion a bitter-

Russell Crowe in *The Insider*

sweet recollection of Cold War romance and intrigue. Scott plays a British telephone specialist who begins working for the Americans in their attempt to tap into Russian phone lines (by tunneling into East Berlin). Hopkins (bad accent and all) is the brash Yank commander overseeing the project who must contend with possible conspiracy when Scott falls for a local German woman (Rossellini) who may or may not be a spy. The espionage aspect of the film is quite compelling, but as a romance the film sags. And though the film features good period design, Schlesinger's sluggish pace helps detract from the scenario. ★★ VHS: $9.99

Innocent Blood

(1992, 114 min, US, John Landis) *Anne Parillaud, Anthony LaPaglia, Robert Loggia, Don Rickles.* Landis returns to *American Werewolf in London* territory with this anemic comic horror film which could be dubbed *A French Vampire in Pittsburgh*. Parillaud plays a bloodsucker with a social conscience: she only attacks criminals for her blood lust. But when she crosses paths with mob kingpin Loggia and undercover cop LaPaglia, things go awry. As the mobster-turned-vampire, Loggia brings such needed vitality to an otherwise weary film that for a while, it seems he may turn it around. Much of the blame goes to the ill-pairing of leads Parillaud and LaPaglia — Lily and Herman Munster generated more sparks. There's lots of blood and killings, though. ★★ VHS: $9.99; DVD: $14.99

Innocent Lies

(1995, 88 min, GB, Patrick DeWolfe) *Gabrielle Anwar, Stephen Dorff, Adrian Dunbar, Joanna Lumley.* An absorbing and well-made period piece about a London detective (Dunbar) who is dispatched to a French fishing village, circa WWII, to investigate the mysterious death of his predecessor. He soon becomes entangled in the Freudian affairs of a brother and sister who love each other entirely too much. DeWolfe's parable on the price of love weaves its threads of anti-Semitism and incest into an Agatha Christie-like mystery. ★★★

An Innocent Man

(1989, 113 min, US, Peter Yates) *Tom Selleck, F. Murray Abraham, Laila Robins.* In this ordinary, contrived innocent-man-behind-bars prison drama, Selleck is a successful aerospace engineer and loving husband who is framed by two

cardboard-cutout dishonest undercover cops. Once incarcerated, he learns, with the kindly help of "lifer" Abraham, that prison can be hell. This sort of thing has been done for decades, and done a helluva lot better. ★

The Innocent Sleep

(1997, 97 min, GB, Scott Michell) *Rupert Graves, Annabella Sciorra, Michael Gambon, Graham Crowden, Franco Nero, John Hannah.* A routine programmer about a homeless man, Alan Terry (Graves), who becomes the hunted when he witnesses a mob hit. Seeing one of the killers in uniform, he tells his story to reporter Billie Hayman (a very mannish Sciorra). As Billie fact-checks his case, Alan learns that her journalism ethics — she believes in revealing her sources — have caused previous informers to commit suicide. Unable to trust anyone, Alan decides to mete out justice himself. Director Michell has all the ingredients for a good B-movie thriller, but this bland film lacks both atmosphere and tension. Only Gambon as one of the killers seems to relish his part, and even he occasionally appears to be sleepwalking. ★★ VHS: $102.99

Innocent Victim

(1988, 89 min, GB, Giles Foster) *Helen Shaver, Lauren Bacall, Colin Firth, Paul McGann.* A dull thriller about a best-selling author (Shaver) whose grief over the loss of her three-year-old son is complicated when her mentally unbalanced mother (Bacall) kidnaps a small boy to replace him. Based on a novel by Ruth Rendell. (aka: *Tree of Hands*) ★ VHS: $79.99

Insect Woman

(1963, 123 min, Japan, Shohei Imamura) *Sachiko Hidari, Yitsuko Yoshimura.* The sexual manipulation, subjugation and exploitation of women is the hard-hitting theme in this multi-award winning film that chronicles 45 years in the harsh life of a woman. Beginning as a child, where she is abused by her stepfather, through her illegitimate pregnancy and finally to her life in a sordid brothel, the film, like the director's *Black Rain*, displays little sentimentality in fleshing out this gripping but somber tale. (Japanese with English subtitles) ★★★

Inserts

(1976, 117 min, US, John Byrum) *Richard Dreyfuss, Bob Hoskins, Jessica Harper, Veronica Cartwright.* Dreyfuss is a fading silent screen star in 1930s Hollywood who turns to making blue movies to supplement his income. Despite its intriguing premise, a lackluster screenplay makes little of the scenario. ★★

Inside

(1996, 94 min, GB/US, Arthur Penn) *Nigel Hawthorne, Eric Stoltz, Louis Gossett, Jr., Ian Roberts.* A claustrophobic prison drama about human rights abuses in South Africa, *Inside* is an intense and at times agonizing viewing experience. The film deals with the lies and transgressions perpetrated by Col. Kruger (Hawthorne), an interrogator who brutalizes Marty (Stoltz), a university professor who suspects of terrorism and treason. Held in a sparse cell, Marty communicates with and observes the prison's other inmates through a peephole while he is tormented physically and mentally. Effective and well-made, the film tends to suffer from occasional staginess. ★★★ VHS: $79.99

Inside Monkey Zetterland

(1993, 98 min, US, Jefery Levy) *Patricia Arquette, Steven Antin, Sofia Coppola, Sandra Bernhard, Ricki Lake, Rupert Everett.* With a cast that seems to come straight from the pages of *Details* magazine, *Inside Monkey Zetterland* seems to care more about who is actually in the film rather than telling a story. The film revolves around an ex-child star (writer-producer Antin) whose lesbian sister has left his pregnant lover and moved into his house owned by their soap opera star mother. When radical terrorists come onto the scene, things start getting a little convoluted. It occasionally has a quirky charm, and features a few good performances. ★★

Inside the Third Reich

(1982, 242 min, US, Marvin J. Chomsky) *Rutger Hauer, Derek Jacobi, John Gielgud, Blythe Danner, Trevor Howard, Viveca Lindfors, Ian Holm, Renée Soutendijk.* Superior made-for-TV teledrama based on the autobiography of Hitler's confidant Albert Speer. Hauer stars as the brilliant architect who works his way through the ranks of 1930s Germany to become Hitler's right-hand man. Jacobi is sensational as the maniacal dictator. ★★★½

The Insider

(1999, 157 min, US, Michael Mann) *Al Pacino, Russell Crowe, Christopher Plummer, Diane Venora, Philip Baker Hall, Michael Gambon, Lindsay Crouse, Bruce McGill, Rip Torn, Debi Mazar.* A powerfully made and riveting drama of heroism, corruption and corporate manipulation, *The Insider* is the true story of what led to the airing of the groundbreaking "60 Minutes" story of fraud by the tobacco companies. Reminiscent in both content and execution of *All the President's Men*, the film grabs you by the throat in the very beginning and never lets go. In a stand-out performance, Crowe is Jeffrey Wigand, a former top-level scientist for Brown & Williamson tobacco company who blows the whistle on a conspiracy by Big Tobacco to make cigarettes more addictive. Pacino is dynamic as Lowell Bergman, a "60 Minutes" producer who convinces Wigand to put himself on the line for the story of the decade. That CBS isn't there to protect him makes for outstanding drama. Director Mann approaches this more as a detective story to an American tragedy rather than a full-scale attack on tobacco, which would have been too easy a target. The acting is uniformly excellent, with Plummer giving an extraordinary portrayal of newsman Mike Wallace. *The Insider* is gutsy, stylish, compelling story telling which may make us slightly more cynical the next time we sit down to watch the evening news. ★★★★ VHS: $14.99; DVD: $32.99

Insignificance

(1985, 110 min, GB, Nicolas Roeg) *Gary Busey, Tony Curtis, Theresa Russell, Michael Emil, Will Sampson.* The always adventurous Roeg's apocalyptic farce is a surreal and sexually charged black comedy which records the hot summer night in 1954 that Marilyn Monroe and Albert Einstein spent together. Russell and Emil are the blonde and the brain, Busey and Curtis costar as Joe DiMaggio and Sen. Joe McCarthy, respectively. ★★★ VHS: $14.99

Insomnia

(1997, 97 min, Norway, Erik Skjoldbjærg) *Stellan Skarsgård, Sverre Anker Ousdal, Bjørn Floberg, Gisken Armand.* A crack Swedish detective (Skarsgård) is called to a Norwegian town above the Arctic Circle — where there's no darkness for six months at a time — to investigate the murder of a high school girl. A potentially routine case becomes a languid nightmare for the policeman, as guilt over a major screw-up and his insomnia due to the constant sunlight slowly drive him nuts. Moody, stylish, slow-paced but engrossing, *Insomnia* is well directed, with many beautiful, composed shots, creepy moments, and a constant tone of dread and unease. A tense film noir, with psychology and sunlight substituting for shootouts and shadows. (Norwegian and Swedish with English subtitles) ★★★ VHS: $29.99; DVD: $29.99

Inspector Gadget

(1999, 78 min, US, David Kellogg) *Mathew Broderick, Rupert Everett, Joely Fisher, Michelle Trachtenberg.* A film that seems to be made of the very machinery that embodies the title character, *Inspector Gadget* plays like an extended trailer that features mere fragments of a real, big-budget movie. Plot covers the death of delivery boy Broderick and his rebirth as Gadget; later, he must fight the evil Claw (a wasted Everett) who has built an evil Gadget clone (Broderick again, doing George Burns' *Oh God You Devil* double duty). The Inspector has the help of a Gadgetmobile, seemingly an annoying relative of Jar-Jar Binks. You'll need the help of aspirin, as the scenes blink by (the film is about 68 minutes until credits roll) interspersed with irritating product placements. A cynical cash-in by Disney. ★ VHS: $14.99; DVD: $29.99

The Inspector General

(1949, 102 min, US, Henry Koster) *Danny Kaye, Walter Slezak, Barbara Bates, Elsa Lanchester.* Kaye lets loose as an inept elixir salesman who is mistaken for the feared Inspector General by a small country village — whose citizens will do anything to please him. Plenty of laughs and Kaye gets to do a patter song or two. ★★★ VHS: $19.99

Interview with the Vampire

Inspiration

(1931, 74 min, US, Clarence Brown) *Greta Garbo, Robert Montgomery.* Garbo's third talkie is a minor romantic drama about love and sacrifice. Garbo's in her element as a Parisian artists' model whose past seems to get in the way of her new relationship with student Montgomery. Though not one of her best, even a routine Garbo effort is worth a look. ★★ VHS: $19.99

Instinct

(1999, 120 min, US, Jon Amiel) *Anthony Hopkins, Cuba Gooding, Jr., Donald Sutherland, Maura Tierney, George Dzundza.* Hopkins returns to Hannibal Lecter territory with this hodge-podge of a thriller playing Ethan Powell, a brilliant scientist and primate expert who went psychotic and murdered two park rangers in the wilds of the Rwandan jungle. Gooding is Dr. Theo Caulder, the stateside psychiatrist looking to make a name for himself who is assigned to find out why Powell went berserk. The lethargic pacing is offset by the heroic acting of the two leads, but even these two Academy Award winners can only do so much with a spotty script. ★★ VHS: $14.99; DVD: $29.99

Interiors

(1978, 93 min, US, Woody Allen) *Diane Keaton, Mary Beth Hurt, Geraldine Page, E.G. Marshall, Maureen Stapleton, Kristin Griffith.* Allen's homage to Ingmar Bergman meticulously details the misunderstandings and growing collapse of an upper-middle-class family. Page and Marshall are the repressive parents; Keaton, Hurt and Griffith are the rival siblings; and Stapleton is the "ridiculous" woman who breathes new life into their anguished lives. ★★★½ VHS: $14.99; DVD: $19.99

Intermezzo

(1936, 91 min, Sweden, Gustaf Molander) *Ingrid Bergman, Gosta Ekman, Inga Tidblad.* Bergman is ravishing as an aspiring pianist whose career is interrupted when she falls tragically in love with a world-famous pianist. Despite the fact that he is already married, the two run off together in their interlude of love. Holding up remarkably well over the years, this entertaining love story was seen by producer David O. Selznick who immediately brought the young Bergman to Hollywood and remade this feature in 1939, the film which launched her international career. (Swedish with English subtitles) ★★★ VHS: $29.99; DVD: $29.99

Intermezzo

(1939, 70 min, US, Gregory Ratoff) *Ingrid Bergman, Leslie Howard, Edna Best.* Bergman repeats the role from the 1936 Swedish romantic drama of the same name, which brought her international acclaim. Bergman plays a musical prodigy involved with her mentor (Howard). A beautifully crafted love story. ★★★ VHS: $14.99

Internal Affairs

(1990, 115 min, US, Mike Figgis) *Richard Gere, Andy Garcia, Laurie Metcalf, William Baldwin.* Brutally realistic violence, potent acting and intense psychological gameplaying combine to make this tough cop thriller a thoroughly engaging psychological thriller. Gere sinks his teeth into the role of a decorated but menacingly corrupt cop who locks horns with Garcia, an inter-

nal affairs officer assigned to investigate wrongdoing on the L.A. police force. Garcia, a tightass "good cop" is teamed up with a lesbian partner (Metcalf) as they attempt to untangle a trail of payoffs, extortion and murder, all leading to the increasingly deranged and dangerous Gere. ★★★ VHS: $14.99; DVD: $24.99

International House

(1933, 72 min, US, Edward Sutherland) *W.C. Fields, Rudy Vallee, George Burns, Gracie Allen, Cab Calloway, Bela Lugosi.* A sometimes hilarious and peculiar episodic comedy that has a Chinese scientist inventing TV, sending a wild assortment of interested buyers to the Orient (including Fields and Burns). ★★★ VHS: $14.99

Interrogation

(1982, 118 min, Poland, Richard Bugajski) *Krystyna Janda, Janusz Gajos.* Banned for almost eight years by the Polish Communist government, this scathing study of one woman's harassment and torture at the hands of her own government was finally released in 1990 with the star of the film, Janda, winning the Best Actress Award at Cannes. After a one-night stand with a military officer, a cabaret singer is imprisoned by the secret police, without ever being informed of her alleged crime. For the next five years, she is forced to become a survivor and not a victim in her efforts to maintain her dignity and sanity in the face of an oppressive Stalinist power. (Polish with English subtitles) ★★★½ VHS: $79.99

Intersection

(1994, 98 min, US, Mark Rydell) *Richard Gere, Sharon Stone, Lolita Davidovich, Martin Landau.* Yet another senseless American rehash of a French film, this time Claude Sautet's *Les Choses de la Vie.* Gere plays a whiny architect involved in a car accident. As he looks back at his life, the story concentrates on his relationships with his wife (Stone) and journalist mistress (Davidovich). Though Gere has in recent years acquired a newfound maturity and confidence on-screen, his presence alone does not warrant a remake. Stone gives the film's best performance as his beautiful but cold wife. ★★ VHS: $14.99

Interview with the Vampire

(1994, 122 min, US, Neil Jordan) *Tom Cruise, Brad Pitt, Christian Slater, Antonio Banderas, Stephen Rea, Kirsten Dunst.* Rich in atmosphere and bristling with sexual tension and suspense, this highly stylized adaptation of Anne Rice's classic vampire story was the subject of much second guessing before its release. The biggest controversy was the casting of Cruise as Lestat — happily, he acquits himself nicely and is handsomely complimented by the tormented Pitt as Louis. Told in flashback, the story recounts the life of grieving widower and 18th-century plantation owner Louis who bids adieu to his beloved blue sky of morning for the dark shadows of night when Lestat makes him one of his own. As Louis desperately clings to the last vestiges of his humanity, he engages in a battle of conscience and will with his mentor Lestat. Though bloody and violent, the film relies on the psychological makeup of its characters for its power, and detail to time and place is exemplary. ★★★½ VHS: $14.99; DVD: $24.99

Intervista

(1992, 108 min, Italy, Federico Fellini) *Marcello Mastroianni, Anita Ekberg.* Whereas *Amarcord* explores the director's childhood, *8½* his midlife creative crisis and *Fellini's Roma* the city he loves, *Intervista* is the master's nostalgic look at his youthful days at the famed Cinecitta — the film studio where he made all his films. Touchingly evocative and bubbling with magical stories, the film is Fellini's valentine to the movies and the filmmaking process. A joyous celebration — all done in the director's ebullient and seductive style. (Italian with English subtitles) ★★★½ VHS: $29.99

Intimate Relations

(1997, 105 min, GB, Philip Goodhew) *Julie Walters, Rupert Graves, Laura Sadler, Matthew Walker.* "Inspired by a true story," this stylized tragicomedy flows in the same vein as *Heavenly Creatures* and is reminiscent of Mike Leigh's works in its theme of family traps down Britain way. Here a merchant marine (Graves) returns home to his brother's town, and is taken in — in every sense — by an outwardly proper, fiftyish woman, Mrs. Beasley (Walters), who instructs him to call her "mum." Her pubescent daughter and emasculated husband complicate the unusual relationship. The sustained tension comes from wondering exactly what will happen, though the visual symbols point to the general outcome quite clearly. Walters' brilliant, nuanced portrayal of the conflicted predator/victim subtly gets us on her side. *Intimate Relations* sells itself as a black comedy, and the cringe scenes could make even a jaded viewer uncomfortable. ★★★ VHS: $102.99

An Intimate Story

(1983, 95 min, Israel, Nadar Levithan) *Chava Alberstein, Alex Peleg.* Set in the close confines of a Kibbutz, this engrossing drama focuses on the problems of a childless couple who have been married for 10 years. Their shattered dreams, as well as the lack of privacy in the "extended family" atmosphere of the Kibbutz, force them to reevaluate their relationship. Charming but low-key. (Hebrew with English subtitles) ★★★ VHS: $79.99

Into the Night

(1985, 115 min, US, John Landis) *Jeff Goldblum, Michelle Pfeiffer, David Bowie, Richard Farnsworth, Dan Aykroyd.* Landis' off-center and very engaging comic thriller stars Goldblum as a likable Average Joe who gets tangled with beautiful Pfeiffer and Iranian terrorists. There's a good supporting cast and cameos by 12 noted film directors. ★★★ VHS: $9.99

Into the West

(1993, 97 min, Ireland, Mike Newell) *Gabriel Byrne, Ellen Barkin, Colm Meaney.* This harshly realistic and heartwrenching film begins in the urban squalor of Dublin. The story tells the tale of two boys who rescue a mystical white horse from an evil businessman and embark on a journey "into the west" of underdeveloped Ireland. In an almost magical escape, they elude the police across the countryside and come to terms with the death of their mother. Byrne gives a moving performance as the boys' father, a misplaced "traveler," who does his own grieving as he searches for his sons. Although

the breathtaking ending leaves some loose ends, each character is spiritually and emotionally matured by their experience. Written by Jim Sheridan. ★★★½

Into the Woods

(1987, 154 min, US, James Lapine) *Bernadette Peters, Joanna Gleason, Chip Zien, Tom Aldredge, Robert Westenberg.* Stephen Sondheim's astute and witty lyrics complement his melodious tunes in this effervescent musical which blends several children's fairy tales to produce one intertwining musical fable. Filmed from a live stage performance, the production features the original Broadway cast bringing to life the stories and characters from "Cinderella," "Jack and the Beanstalk," "Rapunzel" and "Little Red Riding Hood." Gleason (who won a Tony Award for her vibrant performance) and Zien are a baker and his wife who set out to reverse the spell cast on them by the witch next door (the splendid Peters), thereby meeting other fairy tale characters. Sondheim and author-director Lapine expand on the moralistic and mortality themes inherent in fairy tales creating a sumptuous union of comedy, dancing, music and myth. ★★★½ VHS: $24.99; DVD: $34.99

Intolerance

(1916, 123 min, US, D.W. Griffith) *Lillian Gish, Mae Marsh, Constance Talmadge.* Griffith's lavish spectacle is a landmark achievement in silent filmmaking. Following the popular success of *Birth of a Nation*, but stung by charges of racism, Griffith's theme in this classic is man's inhumanity to man. This intolerance and bigotry is illustrated in four interlocking tales from history: transpiring in ancient Babylon, biblical Judea, medieval France and modern America. Innovative film techniques, including the brilliant intercutting of the four stories, create an exciting climax. ★★★★ VHS: $29.99; DVD: $29.99

The Intruder

(1975, 98 min, France, Serge Leroy) *Jean-Louis Trintignant, Mireille Darc, Bernard Fresson.* En route from Rome to Paris, a man and his young stepson are terrorized — for no apparent reason — by an unknown killer who is relentless in his pursuit and lethal to anyone coming between himself and his targets. A Hitchcockian suspense thriller. (French with English subtitles) ★★★

Intruder in the Dust

(1949, 87 min, US, Clarence Brown) *Claude Jarman, Jr., Juano Hernandez, David Brian, Porter Hall.* Released in the same year as *Lost Boundaries* and *Pinky*, two equally acclaimed social dramas examining racial prejudice, this is an exemplary, patient adaptation of William Faulkner's novel. The story is seen through the eyes of a white protagonist — as are films decades later — here a young boy (Jarman) from the South. There's a chilling, business-as-usual tone to the film's opening as the citizens of a small town gather to ceremonially witness the lynching of accused murderer Hernandez. Only four outcasts, including Jarman, come to his defense as the film balances non-preachy social observations with a crackerjack detective story. Hernandez brings unflinching dignity to the role of the alleged killer. An important cor-

nerstone in the development of American cinema's social conscience. ★★★★ VHS: $19.99

Intruso (The Intruder)

(1993, 90 min, Spain, Vicente Aranda) *Victoria Abril, Antonio Valero, Imanol Arias.* When Luisa (Abril) discovers her childhood friend and long-lost first husband Angel (Arias) roaming the streets one day, she takes him home to her family. Angel fascinates Luisa's two children, but her husband Ramiro (Valero) — who also knew him years ago — is less thrilled with the intruder's presence in their fragile household. The story, which shifts its focus between Luisa's forbidden desire, Ramiro's increasing jealousy, and Angel's obsessive love, is unnecessarily complicated with some metaphysical nonsense about the characters' past and present as well as Angel's impending death. Despite some steamy love scenes, *Intruso*'s lack of dramatic tension will leave most viewers cold. (Spanish with English subtitles) ★★ VHS: $79.99

Invaders from Mars

(1953, 78 min, US, William Cameron Menzies) *Helena Carter, Arthur Franz.* Slick sci-fi tale about a young boy who witnesses an alien craft land and tries to convince those around him it really exists — those not already possessed by the other-worldly visitors, that is. Lots of fun, and a heck of a sight better than the 1986 remake. ★★★ VHS: $19.99

Invaders from Mars

(1986, 102 min, US, Tobe Hooper) *Karen Black, Hunter Carson, Louise Fletcher, Timothy Bottoms, Bud Cort.* Inferior remake of the 1953 classic sci-fi film about a young boy who tries to convince those around him that a Martian attack is under way. Real-life mom and son Black and Carson play mom and son, and Fletcher continues her patented villainous/strange character as a dastardly teacher. ★½ VHS: $14.99; DVD: $14.99

Invasion of the Bee Girls

(1974, 85 min, US, Denis Sanders) *Victoria Vetri, William Smith.* When the men of a small community are dying off due to excessive sexual activity, their wives are brought in for medical experimentation. In the lab, the women are irradiated, covered with bees and cocooned, where they emerge transformed into "Bee Girls." Written by Nicholas Meyer. ★★½

Invasion of the Body Snatchers

(1956, 80 min, US, Don Siegel) *Kevin McCarthy, Dana Wynter, Carolyn Jones, King Donovan.* Classic '50s sci-fi chiller about pod people taking over the bodies of a small California community. Director Siegel's low budget belies the film's extraordinary composition and unrelenting tension. Some at the time saw this as an allegory for Communism in the 1950s, but that notwithstanding, this is great genre filmmaking. (Remade in 1978 and in 1993 as *Body Snatchers*) ★★★★ VHS: $9.99; DVD: $19.99

Invasion of the Body Snatchers

(1979, 114 min, US, Philip Kaufman) *Donald Sutherland, Brooke Adams, Veronica Cartwright, Jeff Goldblum, Leonard Nimoy.* One of the few instances in which a remake does justice to the original. In this updated and refurbished sci-fi tale, director Kaufman creates an unusually effective sense of dread to chillingly tell the story of pod people taking over the bodies of the citizens of San Francisco. Gutwrenching tension and good performances, especially from Goldblum and the marvelous Cartwright, heighten the enjoyment of this genre masterwork. Just try to forget that haunting (and unsettling) ending. And, yes, that *is* Kevin McCarthy (from the 1956 original) in the beginning. ★★★★ VHS: $9.99; DVD: $24.99

Inventing the Abbotts

(1997, 105 min, US, Pat O'Connor) *Joaquin Phoenix, Liv Tyler, Billy Crudup, Jennifer Connelly, Kathy Baker, Will Patton.* A warm, thoughtful romantic drama whose story of class conflict and small-town pettiness brings to mind those Ross Hunter melodramas of the 1950s (but without the glitz). Set appropriately enough in the 1950s, the story is a nicely paced coming-of-age tale that follows the romantic exploits of two brothers from the wrong side of the tracks: Doug (Phoenix), the naïve narrator, and his smoother older brother Jacey (Crudup). Both brothers become involved with the three Abbott daughters, who come from the richest family in town. O'Connor captures the mindset of Eisenhower Americana while allowing his actors to fully explore the compelling characters deftly written by Ken Hixon. ★★★ VHS: $9.99; DVD: $24.99

Investigation

(1983, 116 min, France, Etienne Perier) *Victor Lanoux, Valerie Mairesse.* This action-packed murder mystery stars Lanoux as a rich, brooding man whose wife refuses his request to divorce him so that he may marry his pregnant mistress. The bloody murder that ensues is powerfully explored, with tantalizing and surprising results. (French with English subtitles) ★★★

The Invisible Man

(1933, 71 min, US, James Whale) *Claude Rains, Gloria Stuart, Una O'Connor, Dwight Frye.* Rains made his debut in Whale's bewitching comic horror tale based on the H. G. Wells novel. Playfully funny and featuring dandy special effects, the film casts Rains as a scientist who has discovered the secret to invisibility — at the cost of his own sanity. As the local snoop, O'Connor proves she can scream with the best of them. (Sequel: *The Invisible Man Returns*) ★★★ VHS: $14.99; DVD: $29.99

Invitation au Voyage

(1982, 95 min, France, Peter Del Monte) *Laurent Malet, Nina Scott.* An incestuous obsession between an introverted young ruffian and his punk rock star sister is rudely interrupted by her tragic death. With hypnotic images of her throbbing in his head, the teenager hits the road for points unknown. A striking rock score punctuates this visually arresting portrait of a young man's descent into dementia. (French with English subtitles) ★★★ VHS: $19.99

Invitation to a Wedding

(1983, 89 min, GB, Joseph Brooks) *Ralph Richardson, John Gielgud, Paul Nicholas.* An American college student flies to England to attend a wedding and, during the dress rehearsal, is accidentally married to the bride by a bumbling country vicar (Richardson). The ensuing farce unfolds at a break-neck pace.

Gielgud makes a hilarious appearance as an Englishman-turned-Southern evangelist. ★★★

The Ipcress File

(1965, 108 min, GB, Sidney J. Furie) *Michael Caine, Nigel Green.* Caine is impressive in his debut as Harry Palmer, an unemotional, Cockney crook-turned-secret agent. Considered the best of Len Deighton's Harry Palmer series, the film features a tense, complex plot revolving around a group of kidnapped scientists. This high-paced spy thriller is fascinating from start to finish. (Sequel: *Funeral in Berlin*) (Letterboxed) ★★★½ VHS: $14.99; DVD: $24.99

Iphigenia

(1977, 129 min, Greece, Michael Cacoyannis) *Irene Papas, Costa Kazakos.* Based on Euripides' tragedy, "Iphigenia in the Bay of Aulis," this epic story concerns the fate of man and the demands of the gods. Agamemnon's army, set to sail to war, is immobile because of the lack of winds. In his attempts to appease the gods, he accidentally slays a sacred deer. For this offense, Agamemnon is told to sacrifice his young daughter, Iphigenia. This story of political intrigue unfolds behind the backdrop of Greece's ancient ruins. (Greek with English subtitles) ★★★

Irezumi

(1983, 88 min, Japan, Yohki Takabayashi) The Japanese art of tattooing is the focal point of this intriguing and erotic contemplation of freedom, commitment and passion. Complying with her lover's demand, a young woman submits to a long and painful procedure in which an intricate tattoo is etched across her entire back. The master illustrator's somewhat unusual technique is to have the woman engage in sexual intercourse with his teenage assistant during the tattooing in order to arouse and prepare the skin. (Japanese with English subtitles) ★★½

Iris Blond

(1999, 113 min, Italy, Carlo Verdone) *Carlo Verdone, Claudia Gerini.* A pathetic musician/songwriter believes he's destined to be with gorgeous singer Iris Blond. So he dumps his shrewish, live-in girlfriend and her annoying dog and pursues a professional and personal relationship with the looker. Unfortunately, she's only interested in the former — and who could blame her, when the guy is such a whiny jerk? Alternately dull and cruel, the film's repellent characters and situations are equalled by a queasy lack of warmth and humor. A depressing experience. ★½ VHS: $102.99

The Irishman

(1978, 90 min, Australia, Donald Crombie) *Lou Brown, Michael Craig, Simon Burke, Bryan Brown.* A sweeping tale of a family's futile battle against progress, this gripping

frontier drama is set in 1920s North Queensland. The story concerns Paddy Doolan, a proud Irish rancher, whose refusal to accept change and use motorized machinery pits one of his sons against the other. ★★★

Irma la Douce

(1963, 142 min, US, Billy Wilder) *Jack Lemmon, Shirley MacLaine, Lou Jacobi, Herschel Bernardi.* A lively though very broad farce from director Wilder. Lemmon stars as a Parisian policeman who falls for streetwalker MacLaine. Determined to keep her "straight," Lemmon runs a comically ragged course as he doubles as both suitor and, by impersonating British royalty (shades of *The Lady Eve*), her only customer. And then there's the tale of the real British lord, but that's another story. Based on the Broadway musical — *sans* music. ★★★ VHS: $14.99

Irma Vep

(1997, 96 min, France, Oliver Assayas) *Maggie Cheung, Jean-Pierre Léaud, Natalie Richard, Bulle Ogier, Arsinée Khanjian.* This winsome, though jumbled, examination of a Parisian film company's chaotic attempt to remake the 10-part, 1915 French silent serial classic, *Les Vampires*, pokes fun at the absurd intellectualism of the French film industry. Director Assayas prudently offers up this view through the eyes of an outsider, Cheung, who — playing herself — has been asked by the film's high-strung director, René (Léaud), to take on the role of the slinky, latex-clad cat-burglar heroine, Irma Vep. Cheung is a completely appealing character who gamely participates in whatever caprice the filmmakers can send her way including the attentions of the film's costumer (Richard) who develops a lesbian crush on her while acting as her tour guide and interpreter. The film's cohesion suffers as it wanders off in a multitude of directions, but its witty, hip attitude more than makes up for its shortcomings. (In English and French with English subtitles) (Letterboxed) ★★★ VHS: $19.99; DVD: $29.99

Iron and Silk

(1991, 91 min, US, Shirley Sun) *Mark Salzman, Pan Qingfu, Vivian Wu.* Based on Salzman's auto-

The Ipcress File

Irma Vep

biographical book, the film follows Salzman, a handsome American infused with a passion for all things Chinese, who goes to pre-Tiananmen Square China to study. His experiences in the country — learning to master martial arts, falling in love, attempting to win over the shy people, teaching eager Chinese English — is interesting; but without dramatic conflict, the film seems more a beautifully made travelogue than an insightful drama depicting the differences between East and West. ★★ VHS: $19.99

Iron Eagle

(1986, 117 min, US, Sidney J. Furie) *Jason Gedrick, Louis Gossett, Jr., Tim Thomerson.* Gedrick, with the help of Gossett, flies the unfriendly skies of the Middle East to rescue his father being held captive. This tepid *Top Gun* clone lacks that film's technical know-how (and makes it seem good by comparison). (Followed by 3 sequels) ★½ VHS: $9.99; DVD: $14.99

Iron Maze

(1991, 102 min, US, Hiroaki Yoshida) *Jeff Fahey, Bridget Fonda, J.T. Walsh, Hiroaki Murakami, Gabriel Damon, John Randolph.* A young man in a dying factory town (Fahey) discovers that his old flame (Fonda) is now married to the scion of the Japanese entrepreneur who just bought a decaying industrial complex. The son cannot understand community opposition to turning the site into an amusement park. Coproduced by Oliver Stone, this well-acted and intelligently scripted film examines complex issues from multiple perspectives without stereotyping or condescension. ★★★ VHS: $19.99; DVD: $24.99

The Iron Triangle

(1988, 94 min, US, Eric Weston) *Beau Bridges, Haing S. Ngor.* A U.S. Army captain (Bridges) leads his men into a bloody battle to capture a Viet Cong stronghold along the Ho Chi Minh trail. A well-meaning if lethargic story which tries to reexamine the conflict of the Vietnam War. ★★

Iron Will

(1994, 104 min, US, Charles Haid) *Mackenzie Astin, Kevin Spacey, David Ogden Stiers, August Schellenberg.* After their success with *White Fang*, Disney is back in the tundra with this equally appealing adventure film. Though heavy on the clichés, the likable story focuses on a teenaged Kansas farm boy, Will (Astin), who enters the big dog-sled race of 1917 in place of his deceased father. Competing and holding his own against seasoned adults, the youth quickly becomes a media sensation in his gritty attempt for victory. *Iron Will* has a nice period look to it, and director Haid keeps the action moving at a brisk pace. ★★★ VHS: $14.99

Ironweed

(1987, 144 min, US, Hector Babenco) *Jack Nicholson, Meryl Streep, Carroll Baker, Tom Waits, Michael O'Keefe, Diane Venora, Fred Gwynne, Nathan Lane.* A demanding, rather depressing but expertly acted and brilliant evocation of William Kennedy's Pulitzer Prize–winning novel. Set amongst the squalor of the poor and alcoholic street bums living in late-1930s Albany, the film features two mesmerizing performances by Nicholson and Streep as two part-time lovers living on the skids; each concealing a secret from their past. Though it is certainly downbeat, the tour de force portrayals from Jack and Meryl make it a fascinating experience. (Watching Streep sing "She's My Gal" is alternately painful and exhilarating, and is one of the great movie moments of the 1980s.) ★★★

Is Paris Burning?

(1966, 173 min, US/France, René Clément) *Jean-Paul Belmondo, Kirk Douglas, Simone Signoret, Charles Boyer, Leslie Caron, Orson Welles, Yves Montand.* An all-star cast highlights this epic WWII film about the liberation of Paris from the Germans, and the Nazis' attempt to level the city. Hitler had commanded that the city be destroyed before the Germans left, and the title refers to his constant inquiries as to that order's success. ★★½ VHS: $29.99

Isadora

(1968, 153 min, GB, Karel Reisz) *Vanessa Redgrave, James Fox, Jason Robards, Bessie Love.* Redgrave's bravura performance highlights this gripping biography of dance innovator and free spirit Isadora Duncan. Fox and Robards offer excellent support, but it's Redgrave's show all the way. ★★★ VHS: $9.99

Ishtar

(1987, 107 min, US, Elaine May) *Dustin Hoffman, Warren Beatty, Isabelle Adjani, Charles Grodin.* This mega-bomb was doomed before it even hit the theatres due to production leaks and trade talk. With a reported cost of over $50 million, it didn't meet anyone's expectations. However, if you can erase all preconceptions, you may find it funny; particularly the intentionally horrendous Hoffman-Beatty duets. A film you either love or hate. ★★ VHS: $9.99

The Island (Hodaka No Shima)

(1962, 96 min, Japan, Kaneto Shindo) *Nobuko Otowa, Taiji Tonoyama.* An unusual work of art, made without dialogue. The story is told only through visuals, sounds and music. Beautifully photographed on a remote and barren island off Japan, the story follows a peasant family's daily struggle for survival. Their precarious existence is continually threatened by nature but the family never ceases its work. An engrossing, visually breathtaking tale told in documentary-like fashion. ★★★½

The Island

(1980, 114 min, US, Michael Ritchie) *Michael Caine, David Warner, Angela Punch McGregor.* Laughable adventure film about modern-day pirates terrorizing the Caribbean. Caine is a journalist investigating area disappearances who is captured by the seagoing bandits. Based on the novel by Peter Benchley ("Jaws"). ★ VHS: $19.99

Island in the Sun

(1957, 119 min, US, Robert Rossen) *James Mason, Dorothy Dandridge, Joan Fontaine, Joan Collins, Michael Rennie, Harry Belafonte, Diana Wynyard, John Williams, Stephen Boyd.* Controversial, popular but not well received in its day, *Island in the Sun* is more of a curio now for its attitudes towards race and sexual relations. Typical of the hoary melodrama of its time, the film still isn't as polished or involving as other '50s melodramas like *Imitation of Life* or *Written on the Wind*, despite its then-taboo subject of interracial romance. Set in the serene Caribbean, the film follows four couples: including plantation owner Mason and his wife, who he suspects of infidelity with military man Rennie; Mason's busty sister Collins and buff soldier Boyd; and island politico Belafonte and older Fontaine. As an "exposé" of interrracial relationships, the film is rather tame — hand holding is about as far as it goes here. ★★

The Island of Dr. Moreau

(1977, 104 min, US, Don Taylor) *Burt Lancaster, Michael York, Nigel Davenport, Barbara Carrere.* This second screen version of H. G. Wells' novel is a mildly entertaining if sloppy adaptation. Lancaster plays the demented doc who has created half-human animals. York is the young man who stumbles upon the humanoids. For a more definitive version of the story, see 1933's *Island of Lost Souls.* (Remade in 1996) ★★½ DVD: $14.99

The Island of Dr. Moreau

(1996, 96 min, US, John Frankenheimer) *Val Kilmer, Marlon Brando, David Thewlis, Fairuza Balk.* Good and terrible from start to finish, this third version of H. G. Wells' story began with a troubled production history and wound up an incomprehensible mish-mash. Thewlis is discovered drifting in the ocean and winds up on Moreau's island, where a brilliant but disgraced scientist conducts experiments into the animal nature of man and vice versa, attempting to create a perfect hybrid. Kilmer camps it up as Moreau's assistant and eventual successor. Brando throws in a variety of astonishingly stupid bits of business, props, and costumes, By the end, Kilmer is imitating Brando, Thewlis is throwing his hands up in exasperation and the viewer has wasted an hour and a half. This creation of the mad Dr. Frankenheimer is viewable for camp value only. ★½ VHS: $14.99; DVD: $19.99

Islands in the Stream

(1977, 110 min, US, Franklin J. Schaffner) *George C. Scott, Claire Bloom, David Hemmings, Susan Tyrrell.* Scott is most effective as a father reunited with his sons after a self-imposed exile in the Bahamas at the outbreak of World War II. Based on the novel by Ernest Hemingway. ★★½ VHS: $14.99

Isle of the Dead

(1945, 72 min, US, Mark Robson) *Boris Karloff, Ellen Drew.* Karloff gives a passionate portrayal of a Greek army commander who is trapped, along with several others, on an island hit by plague. This atmospheric chiller bears more than a slight resemblance to Jacques Tourneur's *I Walked with a Zombie* in content and technique, for director Robson worked on that and other Val Lewton classics as editor. ★★★ VHS: $19.99

Isn't She Great

(2000, 93 min, US, Andrew Bergman) *Bette Midler, Nathan Lane, Stockard Channing, David Hyde Pierce, John Cleese, Amanda Peet.* On paper, the idea of the feverishly funny Midler playing flamboyant writer Jacqueline Susann in a comedy written by Paul Rudnick seemed absolutely inspired. A not-so-funny thing happened on the way to the forum. How on earth was such talent wasted to such a degree? One problem is that Midler plays Susann with such restraint — she should have been bigger than King Kong. Another problem is that the weak though occasionally funny script has turned Susann into a martyr who talks to trees. Adding little zest or comic flair, Bergman's direction is stale and lifeless, leaving a game cast eager to please but having little to do. Anyone who remembers Susann from her talk show appearances in the '60s and '70s knows what a character she was. Unfortunately, no one associated with this film bothered to remember or care. And one more bitch for the road: Why "cover up " her well-known drug and alcohol use? Cowards! ★ VHS: $14.99; DVD: $24.99

It

(1927, 72 min, US, Clarence Badger) *Clara Bow, Antonio Moreno, William Austin, Gary Cooper.* The Roaring Twenties was as disconcerting for America as the Swinging Sixties would prove to be some forty years later. And no one captured the euphoria better than Clara Bow. And no film captured It better than "It," based on the trite moralizing of Elinor Glyn who coined the title term and milked "it" for all it was worth. Bow plays a freewheeling flapper who captures the eye of her employer. Who's the hunter and who's the hunted swing back and forth like knees knocking doing the Charleston. Directed by Badger and an uncredited Josef von Sternberg. The definitive Jazz Age comedy. ★★★ VHS: $24.99; DVD: $29.99

It

(1990, 193 min, US, Tommy Lee Wallace) *Richard Thomas, John Ritter, Annette O'Toole, Dennis Christopher, Harry Anderson, Tim Reid.* Frightmaster Stephen King's cheesy but fun made-for-TV tale about a group of childhood friends who reunite as adults to face their own "big chill" — an evil presence that lurks beneath their hometown and manifests as their innermost fear, a demonic killer clown (played by Curry). The horror elements bear the burden

of commercial sponsorship and are less than eye-clenching. Still, die-hard scarebears shouldn't be disappointed and the uninitiated will find this one a good place to start. ★★½ VHS: $19.99

It Conquered the World

(1956, 71 min, US, Roger Corman) *Peter Graves, Beverly Garland, Lee Van Clef.* Drive-in classic with a creepy monster that releases bloodsucking bats, whose bites reduce people to zombies. This picture is often equated with films from this time period in which the story line mimicks the "Red Scare" which was sweeping 1950s America. ★★

It Could Happen to You

(1994, 101 min, US, Andrew Bergman) *Nicolas Cage, Bridget Fonda, Rosie Perez, Isaac Hayes, Seymour Cassel, Red Buttons, Stanley Tucci.* For all those who bemoan "they don't make them like they used to" comes this gentle romantic comedy. Cage stars as a super honest New York City cop who gives half of his winning lottery ticket to a perpetually down-on-her-luck waitress (Fonda) as a tip. A charming modern fairy tale without much depth and a Gump-like belief in the triumph of goodness, *It Could Happen to You* relies heavily on the charisma of its two stars, and both deliver affable, slightly kooky performances. Perez, on the other hand, goes completely overboard in a screechingly annoying turn as Cage's money-grubbing wife. ★★★ VHS: $9.99; DVD: $29.99

It Happened Here

(1966, 96 min, GB, Kevin Brownlow & Andrew Mollo) *Pauline Murray, Sebastian Shaw.* Not yet the renown silent film archivist, Browlow was 18 when he and Mollo began this chilling speculation of what a defeated Britain would be like under Nazi rule. An apolitical nurse, deluded by the optimism that lets her survive, finds that evil lives in the most unassuming corners of the human heart. Shot with a documentary detachment and all the more unnerving for it. Brownlow and Mollo create a cautionary tale that stays with you long after the final image. ★★★½ VHS: $29.99; DVD: $29.99

It Happened in the Park

(1956, 87 min, Italy/France, Gianni Franciolini) Told in a series of vignettes, this simple but affecting drama takes the premise of filming a day in the life of Villa Borghese, the beautiful landscaped park in Rome. The stories revolve mostly around *amore*: budding romances, illicit affairs and bickering lovers. Also included is a touching portrait of a teacher revealing to a pupil that he is going blind; and the best episode is the finale, about two warring prostitutes who, on the run from the police, find themselves competing in a Miss Cinema pageant. Please note that the sound is only fair and the subtitles sometimes fall below the screen; but this is the only version currently available. (French with English subtitles) ★★★

It Happened One Night

(1934, 105 min, US, Frank Capra) *Claudette Colbert, Clark Gable, Roscoe Karns, Walter Connolly.* Predicted as a box-office bomb, this hugely entertaining comedy was the smash hit of 1934, not only winning Oscars for almost everyone involved (Best Actor — Gable, Best Actress — Colbert, Best Director — Capra), but also man-

aging to snag the Best Picture Oscar as well; it ushered in a whole new style of Hollywood comedy. This romantic comedy concerns the adventures of a runaway heiress (Colbert) and a newspaperman (Gable) who discovers her identity and helps her by "marrying" her. Full of rapid-fire one-liners and ingenious gags, this enduring classic is every bit as delightful as its reputation suggests. ★★★★ VHS: $19.99; DVD: $24.99

It Happens Every Spring

(1949, 128 min, US, Lloyd Bacon) *Ray Milland, Paul Douglas, Jean Peters, Ed Begley.* Milland plays a scientist who discovers a serum which repels wood. To determine its effectiveness, he tries out as a big-league pitcher — and becomes the major's new ace. Douglas is terrific as his team's weathered, hen-pecked manager. A lighthearted, funny romp which is one of the semi-classics of the era's many baseball films. ★★★ VHS: $19.99

It Lives Again

(1978, 91 min, US, Larry Cohen) *Frederic Forrest, Kathleen Lloyd, John Marley, John Ryan.* Dreadful sequel to *It's Alive* finds another young couple experiencing the mutant baby syndrome. This time, the mother gives birth to triplets. (Sequel: *It's Alive III: Island of the Alive*) ★ VHS: $14.99

It Should Happen to You

(1954, 87 min, US, George Cukor) *Judy Holliday, Jack Lemmon, Peter Lawford.* Charming fluff about a New York City woman, Gladys Glover (Holliday), who rents a Columbus Circle billboard — just to put her name on it; she then receives her 15 minutes of fame. In his film debut, Lemmon plays a filmmaker involved with the wacky Gladys. Holliday, of course, is nothing short of delightful. Written by Ruth Gordon and Garson Kanin. ★★★ VHS: $19.99

It Started in Naples

(1960, 100 min, US, Melville Shavelson) *Clark Gable, Sophia Loren, Vittorio De Sica.* Gable stars as a stuffy Philadelphia attorney who arrives in Italy to bring home his orphaned nephew. But cultures clash when he runs up against the boy's fiery Italian aunt (Loren). A sunny Mediterranean romp. ★★★ VHS: $14.99

It Could Happen to You

Margaret Cho (l.) and Eric Roberts say goodbye in *It's My Party*

It Started with a Kiss

(1959, 104 min, US, George Marshall) *Debbie Reynolds, Glenn Ford, Eva Gabor, Gustavo Rojo, Fred Clark.* Reynolds is the kooky, man-hunting chorine. Ford is the Army sergeant who, after much ado, steals her heart. After one day, they marry, and he is soon transferred to Spain. There they discover the downside of love at first sight, as they try to get to know each other. A fluffy romantic comedy, not without a few chuckles, which tries to be both sexy and innocent. It settles for sappy. For a really good '50s sex farce, check out *Ask Any Girl.* ★★½ VHS: $19.99

It Takes Two

(1995, 101 min, US, Andy Tennant) *Kirstie Alley, Steve Guttenberg, Mary-Kate Olsen, Ashley Olsen, Philip Bosco.* It's contrived, it's cutesy, and, egad, it's the Olsen twins. In this update of *The Prince and the Pauper*, the girls are the identical kids who have grown up under completely different circumstances. One has been raised wealthy and cultured, the daughter of the widowed Guttenberg. The other is an orphan befriended by the unmarried Alley. Once the twins meet each other, they try to bring Kirstie and Steve together. ★★½ VHS: $14.99

It! The Terror from Beyond Space

(1958, 69 min, US, Edward L. Cahn) *Marshall Thompson, Shawn Smith.* Space explorers land on Mars and pick up a monstrous hitchhiker on their return to Earth, which is bent on their destruction. The inspiration for *Alien.* ★★ VHS: $9.99; DVD: $14.99

It's a Gift

(1934, 68 min, US, Norman Z. McLeod) *W.C. Fields, Baby LeRoy, Kathleen Howard.* One of Fields' funniest films, here Bill plays a grocery clerk who goes to California, discovering a funny and wild, wild West. ★★★ VHS: $14.99

It's a Mad, Mad, Mad, Mad World

(1963, 154 min, US, Stanley Kramer) *Spencer Tracy, Mickey Rooney, Sid Caesar, Milton Berle, Phil Silvers, Buddy Hackett, Ethel Merman, Jonathan Winters, Edie Adams, Peter Falk, Eddie Anderson, Terry-Thomas.* One of the top box-office hits of the 1960s, this over-long Cinemascope extravaganza was director Kramer's attempt to revive the silent slapstick comedies of years gone by. For the most part, it works. Tracy, in one of his last screen appearances, heads the truly all-star cast looking for an elusive "W" marking the spot of a buried fortune. The cast is really just second-bananas to a series of hilarious stunts and car chases, though Merman gives a hilarious performance as the mother-in-law from hell. Still good for some genuine laughs, the film is representative of the overblown all-star epics which marked the mid-'60s. ★★★½

It's a Wonderful Life

(1946, 130 min, US, Frank Capra) *James Stewart, Donna Reed, Lionel Barrymore, Henry Travers, Thomas Mitchell, Beulah Bondi.* Capra's immortal classic with Stewart as the father who wished he'd never been born — and who gets his wish. Capra as director and Stewart as actor were at the peak of their talents. Travers is moviedom's most endearing angel. ★★★★ VHS: $14.99; DVD: $24.99

It's Alive

(1974, 91 min, US, Larry Cohen) *John Ryan, Sharon Farrell, Michael Ansara.* Cult fave about an expectant couple and the birth of their new baby — a hideous mutant killer. (Followed by 2 sequels) ★★½ VHS: $14.99

It's Always Fair Weather

(1955, 102 min, US, Gene Kelly & Stanley Donen) *Gene Kelly, Dan Daily, Cyd Charisse, Michael Kidd, Dolores Gray. Singin' in the Rain* directors Kelly and Donen and writers Betty Comden and Adolph Green reunited for this cheerful, entertaining musical about three for-mer Army buddies who meet 10 years after the end of WWII. There are great dance sequences, a good score, and Kelly, Daily, Charisse, Kidd and Gray are all fine. It's amazing what Kelly can do with a garbage can lid. ★★★½ VHS: $19.99

It's in the Bag

(1945, 87 min, US, Richard Wallace) *Fred Allen, Don Ameche, Rudy Vallee, Jack Benny.* In this funny and crazy romp, popular 1940s radio star Allen is a flea trainer who inherits a small fortune — only the money is hidden in one of five chairs scattered throughout the city. Benny makes a hilarious extended cameo (the entire scene is priceless), and Ameche and Vallee also appear as themselves (as down-on-their-luck cabaret singers!). Similar in plot to Mel Brooks' *The 12 Chairs.* ★★★ VHS: $19.99

It's My Party

(1996, 91 min, US, Randal Kleiser) *Eric Roberts, Gregory Harrison, Lee Grant, Marlee Matlin, Bronson Pinchot, George Segal, Paul Regina, Margaret Cho, Bruce Davison, Roddy McDowall.* Based on the true story of his lover of eight years, director Kleiser has made an emotionally candid, very personal AIDS and suicide drama which is short of dramatic structure but overpowering in the honest emotions it establishes. Giving a heartfelt performance, Roberts stars as Nick, an architect and gay man with AIDS who decides to kill himself upon learning he only has a few days to live. But beforehand, he decides to throw a farewell bash — attended by family and friends, and his ex-lover Brandon (Harrison) who has crashed the party. The story focuses on Nick's various relationships all the while joking with gallows humor of the inevitable. Though not as polished as *Philadelphia, It's My Party* is more aware, and can be sentimental without being maudlin. ★★★ VHS: $14.99

It's Pat: The Movie

(1994, 77 min, US, Adam Bernstein) *Julia Sweeney, David Foley, Charles Rocket, Kathy Najimy.* Sweeney stars in this annoying, one-joke comedy, based on her "Saturday Night Live" sketch, as Pat, an androgynous, bothersome loser who keeps one and all guessing as to his/her gender. Whereas this comic concept inspired a few funny five-minute bits, as a feature-length movie it is interminable. The story has to do with Pat finding love (in the form of an equally androgynous Foley) and endlessly searching for the right career. The film is saved from total abomination by Rocket, who is actually quite good as Pat's neighbor who slowly goes insane trying to determine Pat's sex. ★½

It's the Rage

(2000, 103 min, US, James D. Stern) *Joan Allen, Andre Braugher, Josh Brolin, Jeff Daniels, Robert Forster, Anna Paquin, Giovanni Ribisi, David Schwimmer, Gary Sinise, Bokeem Woodbine.* A terrific cast is put in the service of a not-so-terrific film. Adapted (oh-so-obviously) from a play, *It's the Rage* follows the cast as they cross paths in L.A.; the connective tissue is guns. See, this is more than just an ensemble drama; it's a treatise on gun control. When the hamfisted political lessons take a back seat, the film is moderately enjoyable, especially for fans of interconnecting stories. The acting (most notably by Allen and the terrific Sinise as an unhinged computer magnate) is good, and the film is well-paced. But the end result is hollow and unsatisfying, and the "what happened to them" end title crawl is pathetic — and rather insulting — hand-wringing hooey. ★★ VHS: $19.99; DVD: $24.99

The Italian Straw Hat

(1927, 101 min, France, René Clair) *Alice Tissat, Paul Oliver.* Clair's madcap comedy based on the Labiche-Michel farce about a groom, minutes before his marriage, who goes on a frantic search for the identical hat his horse has just eaten. The sometimes hilarious escapades are superbly exploited by Clair. (Silent with musical accompaniment) ★★★½ VHS: $39.99

ItalianAmerican/The Big Shave

(1974/78, 54 min, US, Martin Scorsese) *Catherine Scorsese, Charles Scorsese.* Two short films from Scorsese. *ItalianAmerican* features the director's irrespressible mother and father, Catherine and Charles, in an intimate conversation at their Little Italy home in New York. A funny look at one family's ancestry, life and accomplishments. In *The Big Shave*, a young man nicks himself shaving and suddenly, an ordinary morning is transformed into a frightening religious experience. Scorsese's black humor is much in evidence, even at an early age, and encapsulates his obsessions with religion, suffering and blood. ★★★

Ivan and Abraham

(1993, 105 min, France, Yolande Zauberman) *Roma Alexandrovitch, Sacha Iakovlev, Vladimir Machkov, Maria Lipkina.* The poignant and enduring friendship of two adolescent boys — one Jewish and one Christian — makes for a haunting, lyrical coming-of-age tale set against the turbulent backdrop of rising anti-Semitism in 1930s Poland. Beautifully shot in stark black and white, *Ivan & Abraham* is set in a *shtetl*, a small Jewish community. Ivan (Alexandrovitch) is a Catholic youth apprenticing at the home of Abraham (Iakovlev), and the two are inseparable friends. When Abraham's strict grandfather forbids his grandson to see Ivan, the two run away together. With a poetic and focused eye, the film juxtaposes the story of the boys' life on the road; the disturbing, escalating tensions in the village; and the passage of customs for an uncertain future. The performances of the two boys are remarkably assured. (Yiddish, Polish, Russian and Gypsy dialect with English subtitles) ★★★½ VHS: $89.99

Ivan the Terrible, Part I

(1943, 100 min, USSR, Sergei Eisenstein) *Nikolai Cherkassov, Ludmila Tselikovskaya.* Eisenstein's epic biography of Ivan Grozny IV, proclaimed Russia's first Czar in the middle of the 16th century. The film, the first of two parts, traces the emperor's coronation, his defeat and his eventual reinstatement. The film features an original score by Sergei Prokofiev. (Russian with English subtitles) ★★★½ VHS: $29.99; DVD: $24.99

Ivan the Terrible, Part II

(1946, 87 min, USSR, Sergei Eisenstein) *Nikolai Cherkassov, Ludmila Tselikovskaya.* Eisenstein's follow-up to his 1943 classic chronicles Ivan's reign in the late 16th century and his revenge on those who had denounced him. (Russian with English subtitles) ★★★½ VHS: $29.99; DVD: $24.99

Ivanhoe

(1952, 106 min, US, Richard Thorpe) *Elizabeth Taylor, Robert Taylor, Joan Fontaine, George Sanders.* A young and absolutely ravishing E. Taylor stars in this rendition of Walter Scott's epic tale of Saxon honor and Norman villainy in middle-age England. R. Taylor stars as Ivanhoe, a young knight torn between the honorable Rowena and the Jewess Rebecca, while at the same time trying to bring the good King Richard back to England. A beautifully filmed historical drama. ★★★ VHS: $19.99

Ivanhoe

(1982, 142 min, GB, Douglas Camfield) *James Mason, Anthony Andrews, Sam Neill, Olivia Hussey, Michael Hordern, John Rhys-Davies.* Lavish version of Walter Scott's classic story of knighthood, love, Richard the Lionhearted, and 12th-century England. Mason heads a good ensemble cast as Isaac of York. ★★★ VHS: $14.99

J'Accuse

(1937, 125 min, France, Abel Gance) *Victor Francen, Jean Max.* A lost masterpiece from the director of *Napoleon*, this, Gance's sound remake of his 1919 film of the same title, is a virulent antiwar film that was originally banned by the French government as being potentially treasonous. An epic of love and the catastrophic effects of war on one man's spirits, this powerful and disturbing cry against man's inhumanity to his fellow man features a particularly chilling sequence where a man calls upon millions of dead soldiers to rise from their graves and march on Paris. (French with English subtitles) ★★★½ VHS: $19.99

J'ai Été au Bal

(1990, 114 min, US, Les Blank) From the sounds of the 1920s and Joe Falcon to the rock 'n' roll beat of Wayne Toups (the Cajun Bruce Springsteen) to the flamboyance of the "King of Zydeco" Clifton Chenier, *J'ai Été au Bal* captures the raw spirit of rural Louisiana through a fascinating blend of archival and current footage. A deeply felt understanding of why and how this infective music has come to be the wonderful gumbo that it is. (French with English subtitles) ★★★ VHS: $49.99

Jabberwocky

(1977, 100 min, GB, Terry Gilliam) *Michael Palin, Eric Idle, Max Wall, Terry Jones.* "'Twas bril-lig and the slithy toves. . ." Gilliam uses the resources of his friends in the Monty Python gang to bring Lewis Carroll's classic poem to the screen with great aplomb. Palin stars in this tale of a medieval kingdom's search for a brave young lad to slay a nasty, scaly beast. Featuring the same bloody absurdities of life as in *Holy Grail*. ★★★

Jack

(1996, 113 min, US, Francis Ford Coppola) *Robin Williams, Diane Lane, Brian Kerwin, Bill Cosby, Jennifer Lopez, Fran Drescher.* Jack is a young boy whose body isn't really his own. This didn't happen by wishing, or even the result of an ancient artifact. He's suffering from a disease which makes his body grow four times its normal rate. Which is only one of the missteps with *Jack*, a sullen fable short on magic and humor. Williams plays the title character, a ten-year-old whose body is that of a 40-year-old. Sheltered by his doting mom, Jack eventually makes his way to school and the outside world, where hurt, friends and experience await him. As directed by Coppola, *Jack* is operatic where it should be frolicsome and only occasionally does the story capture the whimsical cadence of childhood. ★★ VHS: $9.99

Jack and Sarah

(1995, 110 min, GB, Tim Sullivan) *Richard E. Grant, Samantha Mathis, Judi Dench, Ian McKellen.* To be fair, a romantic comedy-drama about an unsympathetic yuppie who is suddenly widowed and thrust into single fatherhood is a bit of a hard sell. If such a film had to be made, it probably could have been made better than this stylish but choppy and rarely funny tale. Both the usually engaging Grant and Mathis as the dad and the rookie nanny who find romance seem lost here, stuck in a movie that isn't quite sure of what it wants to be and winds up not being much of anything. Indicative of the problems here is McKellen being totally wasted in the preposterous role of a homeless alcoholic who becomes Grant's butler. Yes, baby care in film is generally good for a few chuckles; but in *Jack and Sarah*, that's about all it adds up to. ★★

Jack Be Nimble

(1993, 93 min, New Zealand, Garth Maxwell) *Alexis Arquette, Sarah Smuts-Kennedy, Bruno Lawrence.* Creepy "everything-but-the-kitchen-sink" thriller about a young girl (Smuts-Kennedy) who uses her latent psychic powers

Jabberwocky

to find the brother she lost through adoption (played as an adult by Arquette). Of course, this happens just as he murders his abusive adoptive parents and is stalked by his four psycho stepsisters. Eerie photography and a totally twisted story line make this an excellent horror film for the art-house set and a welcome import from the land down under. ★★★ VHS: $14.99; DVD: $19.99

Jack the Bear

(1993, 98 min, US, Marshall Herskowitz) *Danny DeVito, Robert J. Steinmiller, Miko Hughes, Gary Sinise, Julia Louis-Dreyfus.* This is a film with a sneaky left hook. Just when you think you're awash in a mushy "Wonder Years"-for-the-big-screen rip-off, *Jack the Bear* surprises you with some down-to-earth honesty about growing up (and old) with big doses of rage and guilt. DeVito stars as a widowed dad in the early '70s who makes his living as the host of a local TV station's late movie show and who must contend with a possible psycho neighbor. Though it does have a definite sugary "how many times have I seen this before" side, the heart-tugging performances of DeVito's two sons (Steinmiller, Hughes) make this a definite seven on the tearjerker scale. ★★½ VHS: $19.99

Jack the Giant Killer

(1962, 92 min, US, Nathan Juran) *Kerwin Matthews, Judi Meredith, Torin Thatcher.* After completing Ray Harryhausen's *The Seventh Voyage of Sinbad*, a lot of the same people went to work on this film, which explains why it has the feel of a knockoff. Still, the special effects (by Jim Danforth) are good; featuring a giant, another giant (this one with two heads), a flying dragon, witches, ghouls and a sea monster — in short, the usual Saturday night South Street crowd. ★★ VHS: $14.99

Jack's Back

(1988, 97 min, US, Rowdy Herrington) *James Spader, Cynthia Gibb, Robert Picardo, Chris Mulkey.* Spader gives a solid portrayal of a troubled young man investigating the murder of his twin brother in this very effective update (set in Los Angeles) of the Jack the Ripper tale. A vastly underrated mystery with lots of chills to it. ★★★ VHS: $14.99

The Jackal

(1997, 125 min, US, Michael Caton-Jones) *Bruce Willis, Richard Gere, Sidney Poitier, Diane Venora, Mathilda May, Tess Harper, Stephen Spinella.* An uneven updating of Frederick Forsyth's novel and Fred Zinnemann's film *The Day of the Jackal.* Willis is a mysterious assassin who's been hired by the Russian mob

Jackie Brown

to kill the Director of the FBI. Poitier is the field agent who, working with Russian cop Venora (who's excellent as the tough-as-nails enforcer), must stop the unknown killer. The only lead they have is in the person of IRA sharpshooter Gere, who's serving a life sentence. As the Jackal, using various disguises, gets closer to his target, it becomes a cat-and-mouse game between him and his three hunters. Poitier and Gere bring a conviction to the film, however the script lacks the psychological makeup which made the first film so thrilling. (VHS available letterboxed or pan & scan) ★★½ VHS: $14.99; DVD: $34.99

Jackie Brown

(1998, 155 min, US, Quentin Tarantino) *Pam Grier, Samuel L. Jackson, Robert Forster, Robert De Niro, Bridget Fonda, Michael Keaton, Michael Bowen, Chris Tucker.* Tarantino's immensely satisfying adaptation of Elmore Leonard's "Rum Punch" is less flashy and stylized than his first two films, but with its superb pacing, involving story line, flavorful characters and abundant humor and action, this rates as another outstanding effort from the writer-director. Making the most of her best role in years, that glorious '70s action star Grier is Jackie Brown, a down-on-her-luck airline attendant who, caught smuggling money for L.A. gun-runner Ordell Robbie (Jackson), is forced by ATF agents to get the goods on her boss. It's cross, double-cross and who's-scamming-who as Jackie devises her own ingenious plan to rid herself of her meager existence, Ordell and the feds. More character-driven than *Dogs* or *Pulp*, the film is helped immeasurably by the canny performances by Grier, Jackson and especially Forster, as an unflappable bailbondsman who becomes involved with Jackie. ★★★★ VHS: $14.99

Jackie Chan's First Strike

(1996, 88 min, Hong Kong, Stanley Tong) *Jackie Chan, Jackson Lou, Chen Chun Wu.* Originally released in Hong Kong as *Police Story 4*, *First Strike* once again casts Chan as a Hong Kong police officer who must this time travel the globe in order to stop some arms dealers who are in league with the Russian mafia. More a tribute to James Bond films than a traditional Jackie vehicle, the film visits several exotic locales and showcases several large stunt sequences. Only one "traditional" kung fu fight is included in the film, but it is a doozy as Jackie beats up a group of bad guys with a ten-foot aluminum stepladder! Nevertheless, he is the best in the world at what he does and *First Strike* is another totally entertaining piece of escapist cinema. (Partially dubbed in English) (Letterboxed VHS available for $14.99) ★★★ VHS: $9.99; DVD: $19.99

Jackie Chan's Project A

See: Project A

Jackie Chan's Who Am I?

(1998, 108 min, Hong Kong, Jackie Chan & Benny Chan) *Jackie Chan, Michelle Ferre, Mirai Yamamoto.* Chan's last film produced in Hong Kong, *Who Am I?* is an entertaining, hit or miss action fest — typical Chan here. Jackie plays a mercenary who falls into the jungle from a military transport plane during a sabotaged mission.

Jakob the Liar

He is rescued and healed by a local tribesman, yet he has no memory whatsoever (hence the title), and sets on a quest to discover his true identity, pursued by illegal arms dealers and the CIA the whole way. Extremely uneven, silly and pointless, *Who Am I?* is also full of many amusing moments and energetic action sequences. ★★½ VHS: $9.99; DVD: $19.99

Jacknife

(1989, 102 min, US, David Jones) *Robert De Niro, Ed Harris, Kathy Baker, Charles S. Dutton.* An extremely compelling drama about two Vietnam vets coming to terms with their tour of duty and the death of an old friend. De Niro visits old Army buddy Harris, together exorcising their demons; De Niro then becomes involved with Harris' sister Baker. The three stars give excellent performances, which makes this oft-told tale seem all the more fresh. ★★★ VHS: $6.99

Jacko and Lise

(1982, 92 min, France, Walter Bal) *Laurent Malet, Annie Girardot.* Jacko and Freddie are inseparable friends whose lives are free of responsibility. Their friendship and their outlook on life change, however, when Jacko falls in love with a young woman and decides to better himself. A story of a young man's growth from a carefree youth into adulthood. (French with English subtitles) ★★½

Jacob's Ladder

(1990, 113 min, US, Adrian Lyne) *Tim Robbins, Danny Aiello, Elizabeth Peña, Jason Alexander, Macaulay Culkin.* From the writer of *Ghost*, Bruce Joel Rubin, and the director of *Fatal Attraction*, Lyne, comes this harrowing, roller-coaster ride about a Vietnam vet terrorized by his own demons. Robbins plays Jacob Singer, who tries to reconcile his past, both as a soldier and as a father devastated by family tragedy. In doing so, he is haunted by freakish hallucinations that threaten both his sanity and his life. A dark, psychological thriller, Lyne's camera gives terror a gruesome yet stylish look. ★★★ VHS: $14.99; DVD: $24.99

Jacquot

(1991, 118 min, France, Agnès Varda) *Philippe Maron, Edouard Joubeaud, Laurent Monnier.* Varda's loving tribute to her partner, Jacques Demy (*The Umbrellas of Cherbourg*), is a mixture of flashbacks, personal narratives and scenes from his films, which together create a vivid picture of his early interest in film. Varda presents a detailed look at Demy's (nicknamed "Jacquot") experience during the war and especially his early film projects as a youth. The performances are remarkably genuine, especially the three actors who portray Demy. *Jacquot* marks the only collaboration between the two directors, ending with Demy's death in 1990. The film's final scene owes tribute to François Truffaut's *The 400 Blows.* (French with English subtitles) ★★★½ VHS: $19.99

Jade

(1995, 95 min, US, William Friedkin) *Linda Fiorentino, David Caruso, Chazz Palminteri, Richard Crenna, Michael Biehn.* Basic Instinct meets *Jagged Edge* in this worthless and uninspired outing from the author of both better films, Joe Eszterhas. Fiorentino plays the wife of a high-powered defense attorney (Palminteri) who becomes the prime suspect when a wealthy politico is murdered during an act of kinky sex with an unknown femme fatale known only as "Jade." Caruso plays the cop/ex-lover determined to get to the bottom of it all. Friedkin's thriller is a well-mounted but raucous mess, with action sequences that far outshine the ridiculous screenplay. ★½ VHS: $9.99; DVD: $24.99

Jagged Edge

(1985, 108 min, US, Richard Marquand) *Jeff Bridges, Glenn Close, Peter Coyote, Robert Loggia, Lance Henriksen, Michael Dorn.* An embittered Close defends a charismatic San Francisco newspaper publisher, played with sleek charm by Bridges, in this well-crafted murder mystery/courtroom drama. Coyote almost steals the show as the skeptical D.A. who steadfastly refuses to believe Bridges' protestations of innocence of his wife's murder. Close gives a fine, believable performance in both the courtroom encounters and in her romantic involvement with Bridges. Loggia received an Oscar nomination for his salty-tongued investigator. ★★★ VHS: $9.99; DVD: $24.99

Jail Bait

(1954, 70 min, US, Edward D. Wood, Jr.) *Timothy Farrell, Lyle Talbot, Steve Reeves, Dolores Fuller.* Unlike its title's suggestion, this is not a tale of oversexed, underage teens. Instead, it's a melodrama about small-time crooks in constant run-ins with the law. Wood's notoriously bad film noir piece was shot in four days and starred his sex-kitten girlfriend Dolores Fuller. Inspired by the television show, "Dragnet." ★½ VHS: $9.99; DVD: $24.99

Jailbirds' Vacation

(1965, 125 min, France, Robert Enrico) *Lino Ventura, Marie DuBois.* A middling drama about the desperate lengths a man will go to keep his business afloat. Hector Valentin's financial struggles with his family's sawmill company is greatly helped after he hires two strangers to help operate the factory. On the suggestion of the two, the owner begins to hire several

parolees from the local prison only to discover a dark motive behind the scheme. (French with English subtitles) ★★

Jailhouse Rock

(1957, 96 min, US, Richard Thorpe) *Elvis Presley, Judy Tyler, Dean Jones.* Arguably Presley's best musical has the King as a former convict who tries to make it as a rock 'n' roll star — think he succeeds? The musical number "Jailhouse Rock" is a classic. ★★★ VHS: $9.99; DVD: $19.99

Jakob the Liar

(1999, 114 min, US, Peter Kassovitz) *Robin Williams, Alan Arkin, Bob Balaban, Hannah Taylor Gordon, Michael Jeter, Armin Mueller-Stahl, Liev Schreiber, Matthieu Kassovitz.* An American version of the 1977 German film, this earnest, well-acted, downbeat remake will draw comparisons to Roberto Benigni's *Life Is Beautiful* (though made two years before it). Both examine the Holocaust with an eye towards humor, though *Jakob* isn't as accomplished as Benigni's masterwork. In the Lodz ghetto during the Nazi Occupation, a widowed ex-café owner (Williams), Jakob, hears on German radio a report of an Allied victory against the Nazis. Telling his neighbors the news, they all assume he has a radio (which is outlawed). In order to give some hope to those around him, he continues the deception — to the point that he puts his own life in jeopardy. The story is moving without being too heavy-handed about the characters' situation, and a subdued Williams and a good ensemble are sincere and effective. ★★½ VHS: $14.99; DVD: $27.99

Jamaica Inn

(1939, 90 min, GB, Alfred Hitchcock) *Charles Laughton, Maureen O'Hara, Leslie Banks, Robert Newton.* This tense, suspenseful melodrama by Hitchcock is based on the best-selling novel by Daphne Du Maurier. The story is set in the 18th century and is about a country squire (Laughton) who is secretly the head of a band of pirates who wreck ships and ransom them. This was Hitchcock's last film in England before he began his "Hollywood period." ★★★ VHS: $24.99; DVD: $29.99

James and the Giant Peach

(1996, 80 min, US, Henry Selick) *Paul Terry, Joanna Lumley, Miriam Margolyes, Pete Postlethwaite; Voices of Simon Callow, Richard Dreyfuss, Jane Leeves, Susan Sarandon, David Thewlis.* Roald Dahl's charming children's story makes for an equally charming animated tale, though not quite as inventive as director Selick's debut feature *The Nightmare Before Christmas.* When young James loses his parents, he is forced to live with his two oppressive aunts (Lumley, Margolyes camping it up). That is until a giant peach miraculously appears in their garden, offering James flight across the ocean. Using the same stop-motion animation as in *Nightmare*, Selick and his staff are able to incorporate live-action material, as well, to good effect. Hindered only by an unmemorable score, *James and the Giant Peach* is an affectionate fantasy which is capable of winning the hearts of children and parents alike. ★★★ VHS: $22.99; DVD: $29.99

The James Dean Story

(1957, 80 min, US, Robert Altman & George W. George) Documentary on '50s screen legend James Dean, including interviews with friends, associates and family. A rather one-dimensional portrait, *The James Dean Story* captures neither the mystery nor the power of the actor. For a more complete portrait of Dean, check out *James Dean: The Last American Teenager.* ★★ VHS: $12.99; DVD: $14.99

James Joyce's Women

(1986, 91 min, Ireland, Michael Pearce) *Fionnula Flanagan, Timothy E. O'Grady.* Through a series of haunting, often erotically charged vignettes, the remarkable Flanagan offers a true tour de force as she portrays six fascinating women — three from Joyce's writings and three from his life. The film intelligently and successfully captures the spirit of James Joyce and is a one-of-a-kind theatrical experience. ★★★ VHS: $69.99

Jamon Jamon

(1992, 96 min, Spain, Bigas Luna) *Penelope Cruz, Jordi Molla, Javier Bardem, Stephania Sandrelli.* Dripping with Freudian tension, director Luna's loony erotic comedy rips a page of Pedro

Jamon Jamon

Almodóvar's book as it delves into the abyss of *l'amour fou*. Set on a lonesome strip of highway in a dusty and deserted Spain, the story begins with a passionate teen tryst between the lower-class Silvia (Cruz) and Jose Luis (Molla), the son of an underwear tycoon. Insisting that he marry within his class, Jose Luis' overbearing mother (a marvelously camp Sandrelli) hires the strapping Raul (Bardem) to lure Silvia away from her son. But her plan backfires when she herself falls prey to Raul's smoldering masculine wiles. Luna's script plays out like an absurdist Greek tragedy, overflowing with sexual jealousies, and some paternal ambiguities for good measure. (Spanish with English subtitles) ★★★ VHS: $14.98

Jane Austen in Manhattan

(1980, 108 min, GB, James Ivory) *Anne Baxter, Robert Powell, Sean Young.* Two rival New York theater companies vie for the rights to produce a recently unearthed manuscript by Jane Austen. One wants to produce the piece as a period operetta, the other wants to make it an avant-garde performance piece. It's an interesting premise; however, the film is not one of the best to come out of the Merchant Ivory mill. ★★

Jane Campion Shorts

(1983-86, 50 min, Australia, Jane Campion) Campion, director of *The Piano* and *An Angel at My Table*, made an unprecedented debut at the 1986 Cannes Film Festival with these three short films, all made while she was still a film student. They are all distinguished by her mischievous sense of comic irony. *Passionless Moments* (13 min) is a series of vignettes which humorously examine the seemingly unimportant private moments of everyday living. *A Girl's Own Story* (27 min) tells of a girl's childhood in the 1960s. *Peel* (9 min) tells of a mother and her young son and daughter who take a drive in the country only to be met by disaster. ★★★½

Jane Eyre

(1944, 96 min, US, Robert Stevenson) *Orson Welles, Joan Fontaine, Elizabeth Taylor, Agnes Moorehead, Margaret O'Brien.* This almost film noirish adaptation of Charlotte Brontë's novel about an unloved orphan girl who grows up to become a governess in a mysterious manor is a shadowy Gothic affair. Fontaine and Welles give such brooding performances, they seem like two Elizabethan actors gone mad. ★★★ VHS: $19.99

Jane Eyre

(1983, 239 min, GB, Julian Amyes) *Timothy Dalton, Zelah Clarke.* Dread not the thought of being tied down for four hours of tedious BBC drama, for this retelling of the Charlotte Brontë classic is a motivating and powerful drama. This rapturous tale of two lovers frustrated by social mores and misty pasts features two superb performances by Dalton and Clarke as the star-crossed lovers. Their portrayals infuse the story with unrivaled immediacy and emotion. ★★★½ VHS: $24.99

The January Man

(1989, 97 min, US, Pat O'Connor) *Kevin Kline, Danny Aiello, Susan Sarandon, Harvey Keitel, Mary Elizabeth Mastrantonio, Alan Rickman, Rod Steiger.* John Patrick Shanley (*Moonstruck*) wrote this mystery-comedy about a serial killer terrorizing New York. Kline is police chief Aiello's brother who

helps his sibling solve the case. Though there's a great cast, the story is so muddled, they are mostly wasted. ★★ VHS: $9.99

Jason and the Argonauts

(1963, 104 min, GB, Don Chaffey) *Todd Armstrong, Nancy Kovak, Laurence Naismith, Honor Blackman.* Spectacular special effects by Ray Harryhausen and a beautiful Bernard Herrmann score are the highlights of this otherwise predictable action-adventure fable about Jason's hazardous and monster-filled search for the Golden Fleece. The cast is forgettable; the real stars are Harryhausen's sword-fighting skeletons, multiheaded Hydra, and malevolent Harpies. ★★½ VHS: $14.99; DVD: $27.99

Jason's Lyric

(1994, 120 min, US, Doug McHenry) *Allen Payne, Jada Pinkett, Forest Whitaker, Bokeem Woodbine, Suzanne Douglas.* Smart, hard-working Jason (Payne) and his thuggish malt liquor-swilling sibling Josh (skillfully played by rapper Woodbine) are bonded by the memory of their slain father (Whitaker). But they are also separated by the opposite paths they choose for themselves. When Jason meets Lyric (Pinkett), she inspires him to leave their town and start a peaceful life together; psycho-bro stands between them, dangerous and out of control. Powerful dialogue, fine performances, an intelligent script and eyeglass-fogging lovemaking scenes more than compensate for the occasional cliché. ★★★ VHS: $9.99; DVD: $14.99

Jawbreaker

(1999, 87 min, US, Darren Stein) *Rose McGowan, Rebecca Gayheart, Julie Benz, Carol Kane, Pam Grier, William Katt.* A prank goes awry and three popular girls accidentally kill one of their best friends. Hmm, where have we heard this one before? This *Heathers* knockoff is colorful, with great costumes, but even two songs by the Donnas can't save *Jawbreaker* from its limp, unfunny core. ★½ VHS: $9.99; DVD: $14.99

Jaws

(1975, 120 min, US, Steven Spielberg) *Roy Scheider, Richard Dreyfuss, Robert Shaw, Lorraine Gary, Murray Hamilton.* One of the great box-office hits of all time is also one of the best horror films in the last few decades. Spielberg's classic shark story, based on Peter Benchley's novel, kept millions out of the water during the summer of '75. Scheider, Dreyfuss and the great Shaw go shark hunting off the New England coast and find Melvillian adventure. A classic combination of suspense, effects, editing, cinematography, score and bristling characterizations. (Followed by 3 sequels) ★★★★ VHS: $14.99; DVD: $26.99

Jaws 2

(1978, 117 min, US, Jeannot Szwarc) *Roy Scheider, Lorraine Gary, Murray Hamilton.* Flimsy sequel has a couple of scares to it, but there is absolutely no comparison to the original. Scheider and Gary return (and are much classier than this film deserves) as another great white shark terrorizes Amity Island. On the menu: *teenager du jour.* ★★ VHS: $14.99; DVD: $26.99

Jaws 3

(1983, 98 min, US, Joe Alves) *Dennis Quaid, Bess Armstrong, Simon MacCorkindale, Louis Gossett, Jr., Lea Thompson.* The action (what there is of it) moves to Florida as now a great white shark terrorizes Sea World. Presented in 3-D in theatres, *Jaws 3* is a mish-mash of horror film and disaster film clichés, and the sight of the shark attacking the underwater amusement park is silly rather than scary. ★ VHS: $9.99

The Jazz Singer

(1980, 115 min, US, Richard Fleischer) *Neil Diamond, Laurence Olivier, Lucie Arnaz.* Second remake of Al Jolson's "first talkie" about a cantor's son (Diamond) who goes against his father's wishes and becomes a rock star. Pretty bad stuff; even Olivier is embarrassing. ★

Jazzman

(1983, 80 min, USSR, Karen Shakhnazarov) *Igor Sklyar, Alexander Chorny.* With a deft touch and gentle satiric outlook, this pleasant comedy, set in the 1920s, focuses on a musical conservatory student who wants to study jazz. Reacting to the official stance that jazz is a "monstrous product of bourgeois society," our young hero quits school to start his own jazz band. Teaming up with two colorful street musicians and a saxophonist, the young musicians struggle to gain acceptance for this "anti-revolutionary" music form. Filled with Dixieland, ragtime and swing sounds, the film joyfully preaches the universality of music. (Russian with English subtitles) ★★★ VHS: $59.99

je tu il elle

(1974, 95 min, Belgium/France, Chantal Akerman) Akerman's first feature is a charming yet demanding, innovative psychodrama. It opens with director/heroine Akerman lying alone and naked in bed eating from a bag of sugar. What follows is a deceptively simple story told in three segments, each containing an element of the traditional depiction of women. Initially she is seen writing a sad letter to an (ex?)lover; another is a brief sexual encounter with a truck driver; and finally, a sexual relationship with another woman. Akerman thinks out such ideas as loss and separation, solitary introspection and voyeurism with startling clarity. (French with subtitles) ★★★ VHS: $29.99

Jean de Florette

(1986, 122 min, France, Claude Berri) *Gérard Depardieu, Yves Montand, Daniel Auteuil.* Adapted from two of Marcel Pagnol's novels (author of the popular trilogy "Marius," "Fanny" and "César"), this powerful and absorbing tale of greed, betrayal, idealism and love was an art-house hit across the country. Montand gives an unsettling performance as "Papet," an evil old peasant intent on swindling some valuable land from his neighbor. After accidentally killing the original owner of the property, he must now deal with Jean (Depardieu), a city-bred hunchback who optimistically brings his family to the farm and dreams of a new life. (Sequel: *Manon of the Spring*) (French with English subtitles) ★★★★ VHS: $19.99; DVD: $19.99

Jefferson in Paris

(1995, 140 min, GB, James Ivory) *Nick Nolte, Greta Scacchi, Gwyneth Paltrow, Thandie Newton, Simon Callow, James Earl Jones, Jean-Pierre Aumont.* In this lifeless historical epic, director Ivory has fashioned a film that, while a superior evocation of late-1700s Paris, examines in a dispassionate, casual manner the five-year service of Thomas Jefferson as American ambassador to France. Ivory's works have usually demonstrated extraordinary characterizations, but here the film concentrates on Jefferson's libido while ignoring the essence of a great man living in a troubled time. As Jefferson, Nolte is more lumberjack than patrician; he makes a clever lover but a dubious patriot. Scacchi and Newton are his love interests, and Callow and Paltrow offer good support. ★★½ VHS: $19.99

Jeffrey

(1995, 92 min, US, Christopher Ashley) *Steven Weber, Patrick Stewart, Sigourney Weaver, Michael T. Weiss, Nathan Lane, Kathy Najimy, Bryan Batt, Olympia Dukakis.* Paul Rudnick has adapted his own off-Broadway hit with this witty if slightly flawed comedy. Jeffrey (the chipper Weber), a gay aspiring actor, has come to a momentous decision: In the age of AIDS, he's going to become celibate. Then he meets the handsome Steve (Weiss). As these two men tentatively begin a relationship, Jeffrey learns of Steve's HIV-positive status, which only complicates his fear of commitment. The success of Rudnick's play (and to a large degree the film) lies, partially, in creating a comedy centered around the subject of AIDS, and endowing it with an acerbic sense of humor. And when *Jeffrey* is funny (which it is most of the time), it is very, very funny. But in the filmization, certain dramatic scenes only magnify their less-than developed emotions. Stewart gloriously camps it up as Jeffrey's rich, designer friend Sterling, bringing unexpected depth to his role. ★★★ VHS: $14.99

Jennifer 8

(1992, 127 min, US, Bruce Robinson) *Andy Garcia, Uma Thurman, Lance Henriksen, Kathy Baker, John Malkovich.* Two good performers get wasted in this muddled thriller. Garcia is a burnt-out L.A. cop who takes a job in a small town only to fall onto the trail of a serial killer. Thurman is a blind schoolteacher who Garcia thinks is going to be the killer's next victim. To give away any of the leaps of logic, or amazing coincidences on which this film relies to unravel its plot, would destroy the little bits of mystery it does manage to create. Suffice to say that you would have to be a lot more than blind not to see this movie killer coming from a mile away. ★★ VHS: $14.99; DVD: $24.99

Jeremiah Johnson

(1972, 117 min, US, Sydney Pollack) *Robert Redford, Will Geer.* Redford is Johnson, the legendary mountain man and trapper who made war on the Blackfoot Indians after they murdered everything he loved. While taking some liberties with the original story, the film is nevertheless an inspired and entertaining tale of a man who cannot abide modern society's rules and restrictions. The film is beautiful testament to the possibility of man's oneness with the natural world and an ode to the indomitable, individual spirit. It is also an uncharacteristic west-

ern in a genre which had, at the time it was released, grown tired and repetitive. (VHS available letterboxed or pan & scan) ★★★ VHS: $14.99; DVD: $19.99

The Jerk

(1979, 94 min, US, Carl Reiner) *Steve Martin, Bernadette Peters, Bill Macy, Catlin Adams, Jackie Mason.* Martin had his first starring role and his first big screen success in this very funny and incredibly silly rags-to-riches-back-to-riches comedy. Steve plays a hapless schmoe who finds and loses (and finds again?) happiness and Peters. ★★½ VHS: $9.99; DVD: $24.99

The Jerky Boys

(1995, 82 min, US, James Melkonian) *Johnny Brennan, Kamal Ahmed, Alan Arkin, William Hickey.* Having achieved mixed commercial success in the conversion of TV sitcoms, cartoons and comic books to the silver screen, Hollywood once again sets its sights on the recording industry and the result is this featherweight comedy featuring the debut of the Jerky Boys. Brennan and Ahmed play a pair of ne'er-do-well phone pranksters who bluff and insult their way into Mafia high society, incurring the wrath of a New York crime boss (Arkin). What may have been funny on their two platinum-selling comedy albums suffers greatly from a skeletal screenplay and a paucity of comic inspiration. ★½ VHS: $19.99

Jerry Maguire

(1996, 139 min, US, Cameron Crowe) *Tom Cruise, Renee Zellweger, Cuba Gooding, Jr., Kelly Preston, Jonathan Lipnicki, Jerry O'Connell, Eric Stoltz, Beau Bridges.* An appealing romantic comedy with a thing to two to say about the cutthroat industry that is modern-day sports, *Jerry Maguire* firmly reinforces Cruise's bankability and stature as one of America's foremost leading men. Cruise has rarely been better as Maguire, a sports agent whose night of conscience (and wordy "mission statement" decrying his firm's greediness) casts him into the unknown waters of solo artist. With an admiring accountant (a charming Zellweger) in tow, Maguire takes his one client (Oscar winner Gooding) and attempts to go one-on-one with the big boys. Writer-director Crowe has created likable characters who all get to say and do things within a very romantic framework. His is a smart, lively, funny work. ★★★ VHS: $14.99; DVD: $29.99

Jerusalem

(1996, 166 min, Sweden, Bille August) *Max von Sydow, Maria Bonnevie, Ulf Friberg, Olympia Dukakis, Pernilla August.* Director August's spellbinding adaptation of Seim Lagerlöf's novel about religious fever will lose some of its scope on video, but it is extremely worthwhile, nonetheless. Ingmar (Friberg) and Gertrud (Bonnevie) are villagers in a Swedish community at the turn of the century whose love is divided by their conflicting loyalties. Whereas he hopes to manage his family's farm, she is swayed by a visiting preacher to make a pilgrimage to the Holy Land. *Jerusalem* depicts how the villagers adapt to the tough choices they have made. As he did with his other intimate epic, *Pelle the Conquerer*, August pays close attention to detail to create extraordinary emotional depth. (Swedish with English subtitles) ★★★½ VHS: $29.99

Jesse James

(1939, 105 min, US, Henry King) *Tyrone Power, Henry Fonda Randolph Scott, Brian Donlevy.* Exciting western focusing on the unlawful exploits of outlaws Jesse and Frank James. Power and Fonda play the brothers. Fonda would repeat the role a year later in *The Return of Frank James.* ★★★ VHS: $9.99

Jesus Christ Superstar

(1973, 103 min, US, Norman Jewison) *Ted Neeley, Carl Anderson, Yvonne Elliman, Josh Mostel.* Vibrant screen version of the Andrew Lloyd Webber–Tim Rice rock opera (which appeared on Broadway) about the last days of Jesus Christ. Jewison brings a contemporary flavor to the biblical story. Remastered print. (Letterboxed VHS available for $19.99) ★★★ VHS: $14.99; DVD: $24.99

Jesus Christ Superstar

(2000, 112 min, GB, Gale Edwards) *Glenn Carter, Jerome Pradon, Renee Castle, Rik Mayall.* Based on the acclaimed 1996 West End revival, this lively adaptation of the Tim Rice-Andrew Lloyd Webber rock musical stands head and shoulders above the recent Webber video releases (*Cats, Joseph & the Amazing Technicolor Dreamcoat*). Inventive staging, a solid cast and great production values elevate this modern-dress depiction of Christ's last days, aided by one of Webber's best scores and Rice's clever lyrics. Among an exceptional ensemble, Pradon is outstanding as a leather-jacketed Judas. ★★★½ VHS: $19.99; DVD: $29.99

Jesus of Montreal

(1990, 119 min, Canada, Denys Arcand) *Lothaire Bluteau, Gilles Pelletier, Catherine Wilkning, Marie-Christine Barrault.* From the director of the wickedly sarcastic *Decline and Fall of the American Empire* comes this serious, intelligent and satiric update of the persecution and crucifixion of Jesus Christ. Set in present-day Montreal, a priest hires a young actor to revamp and modernize his parish's annual Passion Play. Daniel (Bluteau), a serenely intense young man, takes his task quite seriously. With him in the lead as Christ, he and a ragtag collection of his friends present a radical and, in the Church's eyes, scandalous production which soon becomes a hit with the public. Although the story parallels the Bible's account quite closely, the film never sinks to mere rehashing, and offers interesting and, at times, humorous thoughts on spiritualism in the modern world, the function of art, the perils of fame and the struggle to retain one's personal integrity. (French with English subtitles) ★★★½ VHS: $19.99

Jesus' Son

(2000, 109 min, Canada/US, Alison Maclean) *Billy Crudup, Samantha Morton, Denis Leary, Will Patton, Holly Hunter, Dennis Hopper, Jack Black.* In the early '70s, people saw God everywhere, and often thought they saw the god within. *Jesus' Son* has a random and disjointed nature, fitting since it's based on a collection of short stories (by Denis Johnson), fitting since that's much like life. As a young man known only as Fuckhead, Crudup is sweetly spacey as he wanders through his life, bouncing off a collection of demons and oddballs, junkies and miscreants. The story — of a druggie turned small-

Jesus' Son

time thief and of his redemption — folds over itself, non-linear and episodic, a confluence of happenstance testifying that there's no salvation without sin, no redemption without wretchedness. Maclean's direction is fluid and lyrical, and the ensemble cast works well together to create a heightened alternate reality and deliver a bemused satisfaction. ★★★½ VHS: $102.99; DVD: $24.99

Jew-Boy Levi
(1998, 90 min, Germany, Didi Danquart) *Bruno Cathomas, Caroline Eber, Ulrich Noethen.* The gradual acceptance of the Nazi doctrine by the ordinary citizens of Germany during the 1930s makes for a lethargic but well-intentioned tale of pervading anti-Semitism. Levi is a Jewish merchant making his annual trip to a small village in the Black Forest. Coinciding with his visit is the arrival of a group of Nazi railroad engineers, who begin to rally the villagers against their former friend. Cathomas makes Levi a likable, unsuspecting victim, but the film only occasionally harvests the emotional power to make one really care about his fate. (German with English subtitles) ★★½ VHS: $79.99; DVD: $24.99

The Jewel of the Nile
(1985, 105 min, US, Lewis Teague) *Michael Douglas, Kathleen Turner, Danny DeVito, Avner Eisenberg.* Entertaining if now familiar sequel to *Romancing the Stone* picks up six months later after Douglas and Turner have sailed into the sunset. Douglas once again comes to Turner's rescue after she is held captive by an Arab ruler. Lots of laughs and action and DeVito, as well. ★★½ VHS: $9.99; DVD: $24.99

Jezebel
(1938, 103 min, US, William Wyler) *Bette Davis, Henry Fonda, George Brent, Fay Bainter, Donald Crisp.* Though many believe Davis won her first Oscar (for *Dangerous*) as a consolation prize, there's no doubt whatsoever that she deserved her second one for *Jezebel*. Davis is brilliant as a Southern belle whose flirtations and fickleness drive away boyfriend Fonda; she is then forced to come to terms with her own faults when he returns with a new wife. The ballroom sequence is especially noteworthy. Bainter also won an Oscar as Davis' aunt. ★★★½ VHS: $14.99; DVD: $19.99

JFK
(1991, 189 min, US, Oliver Stone) *Kevin Costner, Tommy Lee Jones, Joe Pesci, Gary Oldman, Donald Sutherland, Sissy Spacek, Jack Lemmon, Walter Matthau, John Candy, Kevin Bacon.* No stranger to controversy, Stone serves up a volatile mix of politics and conspiracy. Technically brilliant and impressively acted, Stone's triumphant speculative drama is based on New Orleans District Attorney Jim Garrison's experience in bringing charges for the murder of John F. Kennedy. Fiercely debated, the film suggests that Lee Harvey Oswald was merely a patsy for others criminally responsible. Whether or not you believe Stone's version of that fateful day's events, there's no denying *JFK* is a labor of love for the director, and he has crafted a fascinating and often spellbinding dissertation. Costner is well-cast as the impassioned D.A. Among a first-rate supporting cast, Jones, Bacon, Oldman and particularly Sutherland are impressive. (VHS available letterboxed or pan & scan) ★★★★ VHS: $19.99; DVD: $24.99

The Jigsaw Man
(1984, 91 min, GB, Terence Young) *Laurence Olivier, Michael Caine, Susan George, Robert Powell.* The delicious chemistry and edge-of-your seat excitement which arose out of the pairing of Olivier and Caine in *Sleuth* is unfortunately not evident in this effort. Caine plays an ex-British Secret Service agent who defects to Russia, submits to extensive plastic surgery, and comes back to England for one final mission. Predictable and, sadly, not very exciting. ★★

Jimmy Hollywood
(1994, 110 min, US, Barry Levinson) *Joe Pesci, Christian Slater, Victoria Abril, Jason Beghe.* You can't judge a video by its cover or even its theatrical run, since director Levinson reedited this film for home video viewing. The result is an interesting though not very engaging comedy-drama about an actor-wannabe (Pesci) who becomes a vigilante after his girlfriend is mugged on the mean streets of Hollywood. The film tries to examine the power of celebrity criminals, as Pesci's Jimmy Hollywood is partially inspired by the media coverage of his deeds. ★★½ VHS: $19.99

Jingle All the Way
(1996, 85 min, US, Brian Levant) *Arnold Schwarzenegger, Sinbad, Phil Hartman, Rita Wilson, Robert Conrad.* If it's holiday cheer you're looking for, you'll have to look elsewhere, for *Jingle All the Way* gets down and dirty. Some of the time, that is — for it's also rather sappy. Its high-concept premise works for awhile: Schwarzenegger is a workaholic father who forgets to buy his son's Christmas present, a popular action figure. He sets out on Christmas Eve for the impossible task of finding one. This scenario, and a rivalry with fellow dad Sinbad on a similar mission, sets in motion some funny comedy. But the film soon runs out of steam — and ideas — and turns into a feel-good free-for-all. ★★ VHS: $14.99; DVD: $29.99

Jinxed
(1983, 103 min, US, Don Siegel) *Bette Midler, Ken Wahl, Rip Torn.* This muddled black comedy about blackmail, blackjack and murder stars Midler, in her pre-Touchstone days, as a Las Vegas singer and Wahl as a gambler who hooks up with her. Torn also stars as a dealer, he the "jinxed" of the title. This film is known more for the conflicts on the set than for what is presented on the screen. ★★ VHS: $9.99

Jo Jo Dancer, Your Life Is Calling
(1986, 97 min, US, Richard Pryor) *Richard Pryor, Debbie Allen, Paula Kelly, Wings Hauser, Dennis Farina.* Pryor wrote, directed and stars in this autobiographical story of the rise and fall of a talented black comedian, whose drug habit nearly kills him. Though Pryor commendably opens up some deep wounds, and the comic's early years are well captured, much of the film suffers from a lack of energy and soul. ★★ VHS: $14.99

Joan of Arc
(1948, 100 min, US, Victor Fleming) *Ingrid Bergman, Jose Ferrer, John Ireland.* Bergman gives a passionate performance as the peasant girl who led the French armies to victory. Based on the Maxwell Anderson play. Ferrer is superb as the Dauphin, future king of France, in this otherwise stagey production. ★★½

Joan of Arc
(1999, 140 min, US, Christian Duguay) *Leelee Sobieski, Chad Willett, Jacqueline Bisset, Powers Boothe, Olympia Dukakis, Neil Patrick Harris, Robert Loggia, Maximilian Schell, Peter Strauss, Shirley MacLaine, Peter O'Toole.* It's rare that one can say that a made-for-TV movie outshines its big-screen rival, but that is exactly the case here as this small screen effort completely surpasses the over-blown, phantasmagoric *The Messenger.* Newcomer Sobieski is absolutely mesmerizing as the "Maid from Lorraine" Jean D'Arc, who almost single-handedly liberated Normandy from the English. She exudes believability from the moment of her first vision (unlike her *Messenger* exaggerated counterpart Milla Jovovich) and it is the sincerity of her performance that carries the production. The battles in *The Messenger* may be more intense, but this *Joan,* by contrast, spares us the martial gore for a far more interesting peek into the political machinations swirling around its hapless young heroine. ★★★½ VHS: $14.99; DVD: $9.99

Joan of Paris
(1942, 91 min, US, Robert Stevenson) *Michelle Morgan, Paul Henreid, Alan Ladd.* Extraordinary "B" WWII drama with Morgan as a young Parisian woman who sacrifices herself so that a group of British pilots can escape the Gestapo in Occupied France. ★★★½

Jock Peterson
(1974, 97 min, Australia, Tim Burstall) *Wendy Hughes, Jack Thompson.* Thompson is an electrician who quits his job and enrolls in college. His education is not limited to books, however, as he soon becomes embroiled in an affair with his English professor's wife (Hughes). An amiable tale with unpredictable appeal, bolstered by Hughes' winning performance. ★★½

Joe

(1970, 90 min, US, John G. Avildsen) *Peter Boyle, Susan Sarandon, Dennis Patrick.* Hard-hitting though dated generation gap drama with Boyle giving a sensational performance as a bigoted New York construction worker (hard hat) whose prejudice leads to tragedy. Sarandon made her debut as his daughter, who becomes involved with a group of "hippies." ★★★ VHS: $14.99

Joe Gould's Secret

(2000, 110 min, US, Stanley Tucci) *Ian Holm, Stanley Tucci, Patricia Clarkson, Hope Davis, Susan Sarandon.* Based on a true story, Tucci's *Joe Gould's Secret* is an intellectual literary game full of real human drama. Tucci stars as a *New Yorker* writer of human interest stories doing a piece on a New York legend, Joe Gould (Holm). Gould is an eccentric homeless man who has written an oral history that is known all around New York in literary and artistic circles. He camps out in friends' living rooms depositing pieces of his history everywhere. An investigation into the legacy of art ultimately becomes a discovery of our own humanity. Holm and Tucci's performances are sublimely understated in this moving, low-key drama. ★★★ VHS: $102.99; DVD: $19.99

Joe the King

(1999, 100 min, US, Frank Whaley) *Noah Fleiss, Karen Young, Val Kilmer, Ethan Hawke, John Leguizamo.* This first, semiautobiographical effort from writer-director Whaley succeeds in creating poignant moments in its familiar coming-of-age story, but is undone not only by that familiarity but also by an unnecessary sentimental outlook. Fleiss is Joe, a troubled youth growing up poor in a small town. His adolescence is made all the more difficult by an alcoholic father (Kilmer), clueless adults and an indifferent school system. The film follows Joe as he commits a series of petty crimes that graduate to felonious. Whaley gives the film a sharp look, and his actors all give sincere performances (Kilmer is effective as Joe's dad), but this is a case in which sincerity doesn't necessarily make for always involving dramatics. ★★½ VHS: $79.99; DVD: $24.99

Joe Versus the Volcano

(1990, 99 min, US, John Patrick Shanley) *Tom Hanks, Meg Ryan, Lloyd Bridges, Dan Hedaya, Ossie Davis, Amanda Plummer.* Hanks plays Joe, a grim factory worker who learns he is terminally ill. When a tycoon learns of his condition, Joe is given a chance to live like a king for six weeks in exchange for his services as a human sacrifice to a live volcano. En route, he takes up with the tycoon's two daughters (both played exceedingly well by Ryan), and finds true love, adventure and a complete luggage set. The first half of the film is occasionally involving, but the last half is as lost as its hero, adrift at sea with no direction in mind. ★★ VHS: $9.99

Joe's Apartment

(1996, 90 min, US, John Payson) *Jerry O'Connell, Megan Ward, Robert Vaughn, Paul Bartel.* With the exception of *Shinbone Alley*, movies starring singing and dancing cockroaches are rare birds indeed. Unfortunately, the MTV-inspired *Joe's Apartment* — which had the chance to be the *Citizen Kane* of its genre — takes its unusual and potentially camp classic premise and squanders it. O'Connell is Joe, a country bumpkin in the big city whose apartment is overrun by roaches. Only these aren't ordinary bugs — these sing, dance, crack jokes, give romantic advice and party on. Obviously, the film's best moments feature the computer-animated roaches doing their thing. But the filmmakers sharpened their focus on the *Cuca Blattodea* and forgot to flesh out the *Homo Sapiens*. ★★ VHS: $9.99; DVD: $14.99

Joe's Bed-Stuy Barbershop

(1982, 60 min, US, Spike Lee) *Leon Errol, Morris Camovsky.* Lee was still a student at NYU when he made this satirical, slice-of-life tale of bookmaking, murder and trying to make it big; all set at a corner barbershop in the Bed-Stuy section of Brooklyn. ★★★

Joey Breaker

(1993, 92 min, US, Stephen Starr) *Richard Edson, Cedelia Morley, Erik King, Gina Gershon, Philip Seymour Hoffman.* Joey (Edson) is a fast-talking New York talent agent whose pace is slowed down after he meets a Jamaican waitress (Marley). All of the film's characters feel as though they were picked up off a SoHo street corner: a hip-hop comedian, a man infected with AIDS, interracial couples, gay lovers; and the film treats them as the everyday people they are. Edson is charismatic and compelling as Breaker, and with his flattened out nose and crooked smile, he proves that you don't have to have movie-star perfect looks to play a romantic lead effectively. *Joey Breaker* is an exuberant and invigorating comedy that dances happily to a reggae beat. ★★★½ VHS: $79.99

John Carpenter's Vampires

(1998, 108 min, US, John Carpenter) *James Woods, Daniel Baldwin, Sheryl Lee, Thomas Ian Griffith, Maximilian Schell.* A slickly made but generic vampire tale, *Vampires* can't hold a stake to *Blade*, and at times seems no more than a rip-off of the more entertaining *From Dusk Till Dawn.* Woods is a vampire hunter hired by the Catholic Church (don't ask) who is roaming the American Southwest looking for covens of bloodsuckers. Carpenter's good premise soon gives way to tired Tarantino-esque humor and Robert Rodriguez-like camerawork/choreographics that lack energy and originality, though there are some good makeup effects when the thirsty dead get a suntan. Woods is a little too posturing but at least is in on the joke, though Schell as a Catholic bishop looks terribly out of place. ★★ VHS: $19.99; DVD: $19.99

John Grisham's The Rainmaker

(1997, 133 min, US, Francis Ford Coppola) *Matt Damon, Danny DeVito, Jon Voight, Claire Danes, Mary Kay Place, Danny Glover, Teresa Wright, Mickey Rourke, Dean Stockwell, Virginia Madsen.* This John Grisham adaptation is a superior courtroom drama and social commentary that is as moving as it is entertaining. Director Coppola establishes a fluid, even-handed tempo throughout which culminates in an absorbing and rewarding finale. Damon nicely plays Rudy Baylor, an inexperienced, naïve lawyer who takes on a big insurance company (on behalf of a dying leukemia patient denied benefits) for his first case. Partnered with Deck Shifflet (an engaging DeVito), a five-time loser in passing the bar, Rudy balances the high-profile case with a budding romance with an abused wife (Danes), probably the weakest link in this otherwise splendid story. As with most Grisham tales, characters have no moral gray shadings, and this is especially true in the case of the affluent, slimy company attorney smartly played by Voight. ★★★½ VHS: $9.99; DVD: $29.99

Johnny Apollo

(1940, 93 min, US, Henry Hathaway) *Tyrone Power, Dorothy Lamour, Edward Arnold, Lloyd Nolan.* Straight-laced Power turns to a life of crime to help his dad, convicted embezzler/broker Arnold. Lamour is the gangster's moll for whom Power falls hard. ★★★ VHS: $14.99

Johnny Be Good

(1988, 84 min, US, Bud Smith) *Robert Downey, Jr., Anthony Michael Hall, Uma Thurman, Seymour Cassel.* Downey once again is the saving grace in an otherwise awful comedy, this one about high school jock Hall being wooed by various colleges. ★ VHS: $9.99

Stanley Tucci (l.) and Ian Holm in *Joe Gould's Secret*

Johnny Belinda

(1948, 103 min, US, Jean Negulesco) *Jane Wyman, Lew Ayres, Charles Bickford, Agnes Moorehead*. Wyman won an Oscar for her sensitive performance as a deaf-mute woman who is taught to communicate by a compassionate doctor (Ayres). Sentimental but stirring entertainment. ★★★½ VHS: $19.99

Johnny Eager

(1941, 107 min, US, Mervyn Taylor) *Robert Taylor, Lana Turner, Van Heflin, Edward Arnold*. Though Taylor and Turner are top billed, it's the Oscar-winning performance of Heflin which elevates this standard but glossy underworld melodrama. Taylor plays a heel of a petty crime boss who becomes involved with D.A.'s daughter Turner. It's a contrivance of the plot that we're expected to believe Turner turns a blind eye to Taylor's life of crime. Taking advantage of the only well-crafted role in the film, Heflin revels as Taylor's alcoholic, scholarly, self-pitying friend. ★★ VHS: $19.99

Johnny Got His Gun

(1971, 111 min, US, Dalton Trumbo) *Timothy Bottoms, Jason Robards, Donald Sutherland*. Dalton Trumbo did a disservice to his classic antiwar novel with this sometimes moving but ultimately sluggish adaptation. Bottoms is the severely disabled soldier. ★★½

Johnny Guitar

(1954, 110 min, US, Nicholas Ray) *Joan Crawford, Sterling Hayden, Mercedes McCambridge, Ernest Borgnine*. A true original from Ray, this is the story of a cowboy who carries a guitar instead of a pistol and believes that "when you boil it all down, all a man needs is a good smoke and a cup of coffee." Crawford plays a saloon keeper who enlists Johnny's aid, and McCambridge is incomparable as the local crusader who simply cannot rest until she sees them all hang. Insightful and intoxicating, the film has been cited as a source of inspiration by such contemporaries as Wim Wenders and Jim Jarmusch. ★★★½ VHS: $14.99

Johnny Handsome

(1989, 95 min, US, Walter Hill) *Mickey Rourke, Ellen Barkin, Lance Henriksen, Morgan Freeman, Forest Whitaker*. Rourke stars in this stylish, gritty thriller as a petty thief — whose facial disfiguration has given him the unkindly nickname of "Johnny Handsome" — who is double-crossed by fellow gang members during a robbery. In prison, he undergoes cosmetic surgery, and with a new face and a release from jail, sets out to get revenge. Among the film's supporting cast, Barkin and Henriksen as Rourke's vicious ex-mates, Freeman as a cop not fooled by a pretty face and Whitaker as the doctor who performs the surgery, are all first-rate. ★★★ VHS: $9.99

Johnny Mnemonic

(1995, 98 min, US, Robert Longo) *Keanu Reeves, Dolph Lundgren, Takeshi Kitano, Ice-T, Udo Kier, Henry Rollins, Barbara Sukowa*. It's a meeting of '90s chic and aesthetic: visual artist Robert Longo and cyberpunk William Gibson team on the film adaptation of the latter's technothriller short story. But somehow some computer-generated wires got mighty crossed. Reeves stars as the title character, a high-tech courier working in a bleak future. With a computer-friendly head full

Johnny Stecchino

of chips and wires, Johnny accepts one final assignment to transport some delicate information. But the ruthless Yakuza are on his trail, and they're after both the data and his head. *Johnny Mnemonic* is set at a lethargic pace, the action scenes are boring, the actors look distracted, and the story rambles from one pointless predicament to another. ★ VHS: $9.99; DVD: $14.99

Johnny 100 Pesos

(1993, 95 min, Spain, Gustavo Graef-Marino) *Armando Araiza, Patricia Rivera, Willy Semler*. A mildly diverting suspense thriller which is based on a true incident. Teenager Johnny Garcia (Araiza) takes part in his first armed robbery with four ex-cons. The plan goes sour, and the five are forced to take hostages. The police are called in, they surround the place, and a media circus unfolds. The film starts off well, with some quirky details and amusing satire. But it soon becomes predictable and rather unexciting. With little more insight than a newspaper headline, *Johnny 100 Pesos* appears to have stayed close to the actual events, which does not work in its favor. (Spanish with English subtitles) ★★ VHS: $19.99; DVD: $24.99

Johnny Skidmarks

(1998, 97 min, US, John Raffo) *Peter Gallagher, Frances McDormand, John Lithgow, Jack Black*. A plot-driven noir thriller dressed in a character piece's clothing. Johnny Skidmarks is the nickname for police photographer Gallagher, a cold-hearted jerk (the result of his wife having died) who also moonlights as the shutterbug in a blackmail ring. His cronies include his ex-brother-in-law (the always amusing Black), a kindly police officer (Lithgow) and a new tentative love interest (McDormand), none of whom are all that fascinating. Thoroughly sleazy and unpleasant to boot, *Johnny Skidmarks* is at best a sporadically interesting misfire. ★★ VHS: $102.99; DVD: $22.99

Johnny Stecchino

(1991, 105 min, Italy, Roberto Benigni) *Roberto Benigni, Nicoletta Braschi*. This amiable farce about a bumbling schoolbus driver who is mistaken for a Mafia leader enjoyed at one time the distinction of being the highest-grossing film in Italian history (now held by director Benigni's own *Life Is Beautiful*). Director, cowriter and star Benigni is the centerpiece of the hilarious tale in which the hopelessly inept Dante (Benigni) is lured to Palermo by the wife of notorious mobster Johnny Stecchino (Benigni again) to be

used as his double. Of course, Dante is completely unaware of the deception, which leads him into a hilarious series of misadventures with rival gang members and the police. As an actor, Benigni's comic schtick is almost flawless, while as a director his timing is occasionally suspect. Still, the humor builds throughout, reaching a fever pitch by film's end and leaving those in need of good comedy well sated. (Italian with English subtitles) ★★★ VHS: $19.99

Johnny Suede

(1991, 95 min, US, Tom DiCillo) *Brad Pitt, Calvin Levels, Tina Louise, Nick Cave, Samuel L. Jackson*. A preternaturally coifed Pitt stars in this meandering oddity about a down-and-out, would-be rocker set in Manhattan's lower depths. First-time director DiCillo's tale of post-punk nihilism finds its roots in Susan Seidelman's 1982 *Smithereens* as it follows the insufferably image-conscious Johnny Suede in his vain attempts at relationship, putting together a Rockabilly band and pulling off an armed robbery. These proceedings are precipitated when a pair of suede shoes falls from the sky, providing him the "magical" keys to some unknown subcultural kingdom. Pitt's narcoleptic portrayal of the title character provides most of the amusement in an otherwise static affair. ★★½ VHS: $7.99

johns

(1997, 97 min, US, Scott Silver) *Lukas Haas, David Arquette, Arliss Howard, Keith David, Elliott Gould, Wilson Cruz*. A lyrical, sobering tale of self-respect and friendship amidst L.A.'s seedy underworld of male prostitution. Reminiscent of both *Midnight Cowboy* and *My Own Private Idaho*, johns is set on Christmas Eve where 20-year-old John (Arquette) has anxiously anticipated spending the holiday (and his birthday) in a posh hotel. His dream is quashed, however, when his lucky sneakers and the money in them are stolen. Determined to raise the cash, he solicits the help of his pal Donner (Haas), a fellow hustler who is quietly in love with John. Harsh realism merges with dreamy romanticism and quirky humor in this compelling tragi-drama that features standout performances from the two leads. ★★★ VHS: $14.99; DVD: $19.99

A Joke of Destiny

(1984, 105 min, Italy, Lina Wertmuller) *Ugo Tognazzi, Piera Degli Esposito, Valeria Golino*. Wertmüller's underrated political satire follows the almost surreal situation of an Italian official's attempts to release a cabinet minister who becomes trapped in his new computerized car. Some really funny moments highlight this subversive little gem. (Italian with English subtitles) ★★★

Jolson Sings Again

(1949, 96 min, US, Henry Levin) *Larry Parks, Barbara Hale, William Demarest*. Sequel to the 1946 monster hit biography on Al Jolson, with Parks repeating his acclaimed incarnation as the legendary singer. With the best material having been covered in the original, this is only occasionally moving. ★★ VHS: $19.99

The Jolson Story

(1946, 128 min, US, Alfred E. Green) *Larry Parks, Evelyn Keyes, William Demarest*. Classic '40s musical of legendary singer Al Jolson, with Parks giving a star-making performance as the showman. Songs (dubbed by Jolson himself) include "Swanee," "April Showers" and "Mammy." One of the biggest hits of the decade. (Sequel: *Jolson Sings Again*) ★★★ VHS: $19.99

Jonah Who Will Be 25 in the Year 2000

(1976, 110 min, Switzerland, Alain Tanner) *Miou-Miou, Jean-Luc Bideau, Myriam Boyer.* Before *The Return of the Secaucus Seven, The Big Chill* or even "thirtysomething," there was Tanner's fascinating political comedy which follows a disparate group of post-May '68 "Coke/Marxists" who, each in their own individualistic fashion, must come to grips with a changing political and social scene brought on by the more conservative period of the '70s. The characters all must begin making a living but all the while trying to retain their political commitments in an increasingly repressive environment. The ensemble actors are uniformly excellent, and the dialogue is quick, fascinating and challenging. A remarkably relevant film for any political climate. (French with English subtitles) ★★★★ VHS: $29.99

Joseph and the Amazing Technicolor Dreamcoat

(1999, 78 min, GB, David Mallet & Steven Pimlott) *Donny Osmond, Richard Attenborough, Joan Collins, Maria Friedman, Robert Torti.* A filmed version of Andrew Lloyd Webber and Tim Rice's lively musical, this tacky production ill-advisedly forgoes live performance. Instead, it's presented as an elementary school pageant, and becomes absolutely nauseating when the school children are allowed to join in on some of the songs. Osmond plays Joseph, the biblical hero who is betrayed by his brothers and left for dead, only to become the Pharroh's governor. Shirtless much of the time, he doesn't make it as a matinee idol. Nevertheless, this is one of Webber's best works, and when the vibrant score is allowed to stand on its own, it outshines the sappy packaging. ★★ VHS: $19.99; DVD: $29.99

Joseph Andrews

(1976, 104 min, GB, Tony Richardson) *Peter Firth, Ann-Margret, Jim Dale, Michael Hordern.* Even if this comedy had been great, which it isn't, director Richardson would have been hard pressed to match the achievements of his earlier excursion into the novels of Henry Fielding (*Tom Jones*). Here, Firth plays a lowly functionary who rejects the advances of the voluptuous Lady Booby (Ann-Margret) in favor of a lowly peasant girl. ★★ VHS: $19.99

Joseph Conrad's The Secret Agent

(1996, 94 min, GB, Christopher Hampton) *Bob Hoskins, Patricia Arquette, Gérard Depardieu, George Spelvin, Jim Broadbent, Christian Bale, Robin Williams. Joseph Conrad's The Secret Agent* should be awash in high-tension espionage and back-alley intrigue. But this intellectual discourse on politics and morality (or the lack of) never really satisfies with its slow pacing and confusing narrative. Hoskins plays a London shopkeeper and part-time spy for the Russians. When he is ordered to bomb Greenwich Park, it ends in tragedy; this leads to a series of escalating, out-of-control events. Director Hampton

creates an effectively enigmatic London, but the sometimes affecting familial drama at the core of a more somber spy tale has difficulty resonating. Conrad's story was the basis for Alfred Hitchcock's far superior 1936 thriller *Sabotage*. ★★ VHS: $102.99

Josepha

(1982, 103 min, France, Christopher Frank) *Claude Brasseur, Miou-Miou.* Set amid the turbulence of the theatre, director and author Frank's intimate psychological drama follows a thespian couple whose marital roles are ones they can't quite master. Following Brasseur's affair with another woman, their union begins a slow and painful disintegration as they are forced to enact a bitter resolution. A glistening portrait of personal triumph, sacrifice and determination that manages both humor and poignancy. (Dubbed) ★★★ VHS: $29.99

The Josephine Baker Story

(1991, 120 min, US, Brian Gibson) *Lynn Whitfield, Ruben Blades, Louis Gossett, Jr., David Dukes, Craig T. Nelson.* Whitfield excels in her award-winning performance as the legendary Josephine Baker. The story focuses on the singer's rise to stardom in Paris, her ongoing struggles with racism in America, and two affairs: one with an Italian count (Blades), and the other with orchestra leader Jo Bouillon (Dukes). ★★★ VHS: $9.99; DVD: $14.99

Josie and the Pussycats

(2001, 98 min, US, Deborah Kaplan & Harry Elfont) *Rachael Leigh Cook, Tara Reid, Rosario Dawson, Alan Cumming, Parker Posey, Missi Pyle, Carson Daly, Breckin Meyer, Seth Green.* The new word for "cool" is "jerkin," according to subliminal messages disseminated by Posey's evil music empire, and Gatorade is the new Snapple. So we'll say it: the jerkin' *Josie and the Pussycats* is the new *Clueless*, a slumber party movie for girls that operates on its own subversive level. Having everything to do with teen fads, product placement and staying true to oneself, and not much to do with the *Josie* cartoons and comic books, Kaplan and Elfont have created a bubbly satire with peppy music that manages to make fun of its target audience. Cook, Reid and Dawson are winning as the Pussycats, here an unknown garage band launched to stardom by Posey's exec Cumming to replace troublesome boy sensation DuJour. Weighed down by uneven pacing and an overload of product placements, *Josie* nevertheless has plenty of appeal for not just girls, but anyone who wonders how the heck these prepackaged bands get so popular. ★★★ VHS: $102.99; DVD: $29.99

Jour de Fête

(1949, 70 min, France, Jacques Tati) *Jacques Tati, Guy Decomble.* Tati, France's answer to Chaplin, stars in his first directorial effort. The story concerns the bungling adventures of a small-town mailman who, after hearing about the efficiency of the American Postal Service, decides that it is time to do the same. His manic new delivery system, set out to modernize, brings about the opposite result. Great fun in this vintage Tati. (French with English subtitles) ★★★½

Le Jour se Lève

(1939, 85 min, France, Marcel Carné) *Jean Gabin, Jules Berry, Arletty.* From the makers of *Children of Paradise* comes this model of French poetic realism. Gabin is a criminal trapped in an attic. With the police closing in, he flashes back on the events that drove him to commit murder. A thoughtful, intelligent film. (French with English subtitles) ★★★½

The Journey of August King

(1995, 91 min, US, John Duigan) *Jason Patric, Thandie Newton, Larry Drake, Sam Waterston.* August King (Patric) is a widowed farmer living in North Carolina's Appalachian Mountains in the early 19th century. Grieving over the death of his wife, King lives a lonely existence. As this compelling, leisurely paced film recounts a three-day journey home, August regains his humanity in a humane though illegal act of moral rightness. Newton is Annalees, a runaway slave escaping the brutality of her father/master (Drake). Knowing that death possibly awaits her, King hides Annalees in his wagon as half the county searches for her. Patric gives a beautifully understated performance which takes time to grow on the viewer; and as his character blooms, so does this quietly powerful film. Newton is first-rate in bringing to Annalees unfailing determination and a wrenching vulnerability. ★★★ VHS: $19.99

Josie and the Pussycats

Journey of Hope

(1990, 110 min, Switzerland, Xavier Koller)
Necmettin Cobanoglu, Nur Surer. Winner of the
1990 Academy Award for Best Foreign-
Language Film, *Journey of Hope* is an exquisitely
photographed, heartbreakingly tragic yet surprisingly uninvolving tale about a Kurdish family residing in a small mountain village in southeastern Turkey. Unable to provide his family
with a decent life, the father decides to uproot
the entire clan and journey to Switzerland to
join a relative and live in "paradise." Seemingly
gleaned from today's headlines, the film bogs
down in endless scenes involving harrowing
escapes from border patrols and snowbound
mountain crossings. While certainly well-meaning, the Academy must have been influenced by
the timing of the Gulf War to have chosen this
piece over such vastly superior works as Michael
Verhoeven's *The Nasty Girl* and Zhang Yimou's
Ju Dou. (Kurdish, Turkish, German and Italian
with English subtitles) ★★½ VHS: $19.99

The Journey of Natty Gann

(1985, 101 min, US, Jeremy Paul Kagan)
*Meredith Salenger, John Cusack, Lainie Kazan, Barry
Miller, Scatman Crothers.* This fine, underrated
family film follows the adventures of a teenaged
girl who travels cross-country during the
Depression in search of her father. ★★★

Journey to the Center of the Earth

(1959, 132 min, US, Henry Levin) *James Mason,
Pat Boone, Arlene Dahl, Diane Baker.* Entertaining
(and old-fashioned) fantasy based on the Jules
Verne novel. Mason leads a group of scientists to
the Earth's core, where they discover a prehistoric world. ★★★ VHS: $9.99

Joy House (Les Felins)

(1964, 98 min, France, René Clément) *Jane
Fonda, Alain Delon, Lola Albright.* A macabre suspense story about the strange happenings in a
Riviera villa operated by two American cousins
(Fonda, Albright). The women's offer of refuge
to the on-the-run Delon seals his fate and slowly
turns this "safe house" into an oppressive
prison. An interesting, but minor, Clément
work. (French with English subtitles) ★★ VHS:
$29.99; DVD: $24.99

The Joy Luck Club

(1993, 135 min, US, Wayne Wang) *France Nuyen,
Rosalind Chao, Lauren Tom, Kieu Chinh, Tsai Chin,
Lisa Lu, Ming-Na Wen, Tamlyn Tomita, Andrew
McCarthy.* Director Wang's absorbing adaptation
of the Amy Tan novel is a decidedly emotional
affair. Faithfully following Tan's novel, with only
a few omissions and changes, the film tells the
separate tales of four Chinese-American women
and their American-born daughters. The mothers' sagas are the foundation of the film as they
relate the misogynist nature of traditional
Chinese society and the harrowing journeys
which ultimately led them to America. By comparison, the daughters' yuppie, thirtysomething
problems may seem meager, but the real aim of
both Tan's book and Wang's movie is to examine mothers and daughters with hugely disparate upbringings as they discover common
ground. The result is deeply moving and highly
effective. ★★★½ VHS: $9.99

The Joy Luck Club

Joy of Living

(1938, 90 min, US, Tay Garnett) *Irene Dunne,
Douglas Fairbanks, Jr., Lucille Ball, Alice Brady, Guy
Kibbee.* Captivating screwball musical comedy
with the ever-delightful Dunne as a famous
singer being romanced by playboy Fairbanks.
★★★ VHS: $19.99

The Joyless Street

(1925, 96 min, Germany, G.W. Pabst) *Greta
Garbo, Werner Krauss.* Famous as the film that
brought Garbo to international fame, this grimly realistic depiction of the contrasting social
conditions in post-war, hyper-inflationary
Vienna is also noted for its innovative use of
editing and camera work. Pabst films with an
unfliching eye to this story about the hunger,
destitution and misery of a deteriorating middle
class while also showing the moral excesses of
the rich. A striking landmark in social realism.
Restored with material found in film vaults in
Europe, this edition is closer to the original
than any version available in the U.S. until now.
(Silent) ★★★½ VHS: $29.99

Ju Dou

(1990, 93 min, China, Zhang Yimou) *Gong Li, Li
Bao-Tian, Li Wei.* Filmed in striking primary colors, this folktale and political allegory is an erotic tale of tangled passions between two lovers and
the bitter consequences of their forbidden love.
Set in a small village in 1920s China, a rich and
tyrannical middle-aged man operates a cloth dye
works. He has just recently married his third wife,
Ju Dou, a young beauty who, like the others
before her, is brutalized and degraded by her
impotent husband. She soon falls in love with her
husband's hardworking but simple nephew.
Their illicit affair and illegitimate child soon has
the town ablaze with gossip; especially after an
accident leaves her husband paralyzed, allowing
the couple to take over the factory, silence her
incensed husband and brazenly display their
affair. But fate is not kind to the obsessed lovers
in this dramatic tale of oppression, desire and
vengeance. (Mandarin with English subtitles)
★★★½ VHS: $19.99; DVD: $24.99

Juarez

(1939, 132 min, US, William Dieterle) *Paul
Muni, Bette Davis, Brian Aherne, John Garfield,
Claude Rains.* Engrossing, well-produced biography (Hollywood style) of Mexican revolutionary
leader Juarez, smartly played by Muni. There's a
smashing turn by Rains as Napoleon III. ★★★
VHS: $19.99

Jubilee

(1984, 103 min, GB, Derek Jarman) *Adam Ant,
Toyah Wilcox, Little Nell.* Jarman's wildly inventive, highly personal punk fantasy of a post-
apocalyptic future of a dying England takes off
where *A Clockwork Orange* ended. The Queen is
dead, Buckingham Palace is a recording studio
and the police have it off with each other when
they're not breaking the heads of young men.
In a nod to *Civilization*, Queen Elizabeth I is
transported by her astrologer to the close of the
20th century to witness the disintegration of
order and the explosion of destruction and
chaos. A punk version of "Rule Britannia" is a
musical highlight. A fascinating culture shock
look at a pre-Thatcherized England. ★★★

Judas Kiss

(1999, 98 min, US, Sebastian Gutierrez) *Emma
Thompson, Alan Rickman, Carla Gugino, Simon
Baker-Denny, Gil Bellows, Til Schweiger, Hal
Holbrook.* An excellent international cast stars in
this stylish and offbeat noir set in New Orleans.
When a quartet of thieves led by Bellows and
Gugino accidentally kill an innocent bystander
during a kidnapping, two cops (Thompson and
Rickman) try to flush them out of their lair.
Meanwhile, the relationship between the gang
members fray, and the film becomes a tense
game of survival. *Judas Kiss* is especially note-
worthy for Thompson's turn as a trash-talking
FBI agent — and her playful banter with
Rickman is quite enjoyable. There are some
nice twists in this unexpectedly entertaining
film that boasts some great visual flourishes, a
fair amount of blood, but, sadly, very little sex.
★★★ VHS: $19.99

Jude

(1996, 123 min, GB, Michael Winterbottom)
Kate Winslet, Christopher Eccleston, Liam

Cunningham, Rachel Griffiths. This somber and austere adaptation of Thomas Hardy's "Jude the Obscure" provides a harrowing vision of an England on the verge of industrial revolution and mired in an unjust class system. Clearly somewhat autobiographical, the story follows Jude (superbly played by Eccleston), an eternally optimistic and socially daring young stonemason who breaks class taboo by pursuing a university education. He further pushes the bounds of societal tolerance when he takes up with his atheist schoolteacher cousin (Winslet), despite his being married. The film's first third is a jumble of vignettes, though the last half provides a much more intricate peek at its protagonists and the social mores of the day. This tragic romantic drama is both a thought-provoking history lesson and gloomy period piece. ★★½ VHS: $14.99

Judex

(1963, 100 min, France, Georges Franju) *Channing Pollock, Francine Berge.* A faithful remake of an early French serial which follows the mysterious adventures of the black-cloaked hero/avenger, Judex (The Judge), as he rights wrongs, battles an evil banker and brings the guilty to justice. (French with English subtitles) ★★½

The Judge and the Assassin

(1976, 125 min, France, Bertrand Tavernier) *Philippe Noiret, Michel Galabru, Isabelle Huppert.* This provocative psychological drama, set in 1890s France, follows the lives of two dissimilar men: Judge Rousseau, a respected magistrate from the ruling elite; and a demented ex-army sergeant who roams the countryside indiscriminately raping and killing young women and children. Their lives cross when the crazed killer is arrested and the judge embarks on a frenzied pursuit to prove that the man is sane and guilty. Noiret is perfect as the hell-bent moralizer whose actions, all in the name of justice, are equally repellant as that of the sick killer. (French with English subtitles) ★★★½ VHS: $79.99

Judge Dredd

(1995, 91 min, US, Danny Cannon) *Sylvester Stallone, Armand Assante, Rob Schneider, Jürgen Prochnow, Max von Sydow, Diane Lane, Joan Chen.* Based on the popular British comic book series, *Judge Dredd* is a visually stunning though empty-headed visceral ride into a bleak future. Stallone finds himself in similar territory to his entertaining *Demolition Man* as a good guy who's framed and must battle a wicked villain in a futuristic society. Whereas *Man* was lots of fun thanks to Wesley Snipes' scene-stealing and a good amount of comedy, this trek is a muddled array of action scenes, posturing (by Stallone), lethargic pacing and humorless bits. The production design is terrific, however. Stallone is nothing more than a parody of himself. ★½ VHS: $14.99; DVD: $29.99

Judgment at Nuremberg

(1961, 179 min, US, Stanley Kramer) *Spencer Tracy, Maximilian Schell, Burt Lancaster, Richard Widmark, Marlene Dietrich, Judy Garland, Montgomery Clift.* Hailed by critics and nominated for a carload of Oscars, Kramer's massive epic on the atrocities committed by the Nazi Third Reich of WWII holds up surprisingly well.

A chronicle of the famous Nuremberg trials of war crimes by Nazi officers, the film boasts some terrific performances, namely Schell in an Oscar-winning performance as the German defense attorney. Though unneccesarily overlong (some subplots involving extraneous characters, while certainly historically vital, bog down the film at times), the actual "trials," featuring Tracy as the American judge presiding over the hearings, are mesmerizing. ★★★★ VHS: $24.99

Judgment in Berlin

(1988, 92 min, US, Leo Penn) *Martin Sheen, Sam Wanamaker, Max Gail, Sean Penn, Carl Lumbly.* An East German couple hijacks an airliner with a toy gun to defect to the West in this pre-*glasnost* thriller. Sheen stars as the American judge called in to preside over the court case. The compelling scenario is sometimes shortchanged dramatically, but Sheen offers a strong performance, and Penn is terrific in a cameo as a witness. ★★½ VHS: $19.99

Judgment Night

(1993, 110 min, US, Stephen Hopkins) *Emilio Estevez, Stephen Dorff, Cuba Gooding, Jr., Denis Leary, Jeremy Piven.* In this lukewarm, cliché-ridden action thriller, four clean-cut suburbanites decide to venture into the city for an evening of beer drinking, swearing and a boxing match. Quicker than you can say *Grand Canyon*, they find themselves lost in the bad part of town. They spend the rest of the evening being hunted by a wise-cracking psychotic killer (Leary). ★½ VHS: $9.99

Juggernaut

(1974, 109 min, GB, Richard Lester) *Richard Harris, Omar Sharif, David Hemmings, Anthony Hopkins, Shirley Knight, Ian Holm, Clifton James, Roy Kinnear.* Incredibly entertaining thriller that, in the end, is a wonderful excuse for director Lester to satirize British mores. Harris and Hemmings are experts hired to find and defuse the bombs placed on a cruise liner, while Hopkins is back in Britain to hunt down the mad bomber dubbed Juggernaut. Lester regular Kinnear gets great comic mileage as the social director who must calm and entertain the possibly doomed vacationers. The defusing scenes, featuring now-clichéd "is it the blue wire or the red wire" tension, are still most effective. ★★★½ VHS: $14.99

Juice

(1992, 95 min, US, Ernest R. Dickerson) *Omar Epps, Jermaine Hopkins, Tupac Shakur, Samuel L. Jackson.* The directorial debut of Spike Lee's longtime cinematographer, Dickerson, is a moving drama about power, respect and loyalty on the streets of Harlem. The story, which follows the lives of four friends, each with a different set of priorities, is somewhat like a rehashed *Cooley High* for about the first 40 minutes. But it then changes abruptly and becomes an intense examination of the struggle for survival in a decaying urban structure created by an unsympathetic and unaware society. ★★★ VHS: $14.99; DVD: $29.99

Jules and Jim

(1962, 110 min, France, François Truffaut) *Oscar Werner, Jeanne Moreau, Henri Serre.* One of the most beautifully lyrical works in the history

of the French cinema, Truffaut's classic saga of an ill-fated ménage à trois captures the sweet melancholia of love's ebb and flow. Moreau gives a performance of stunning grace and power as the tempestuous Catherine, the volatile apex of the love triangle. Werner and Serre star as the two close friends who succumb to Catherine's charms. (French with English subtitles) ★★★★ VHS: $29.99; DVD: $29.99

Julia

(1977, 118 min, US, Fred Zinnemann) *Jane Fonda, Vanessa Redgrave, Jason Robards, Maximilian Schell, Hal Holbrook, Rosemary Murphy, Meryl Streep, John Glover.* A sterling adaptation of author Lillian Hellman's memoir, "Pentimento." Redgrave plays the title role of the WWII Resistance fighter whose friendship involves Hellman (magnificently played by Fonda) in danger and intrigue. Oscars went to Robards, Redgrave and screenwriter Alvin Sargent. ★★★★ VHS: $19.99

Julia and Julia

(1988, 98 min, US, Peter Del Monte) *Kathleen Turner, Gabriel Byrne, Sting.* Set in Italy, this moody, interesting but not quite successful tale is about a woman seemingly losing her grip on reality. Turner is the heroine who is apparently living out two different existences: one in a happy marriage with Byrne and the other involved in a dangerous love affair with a jealous boyfriend, played by Sting. ★★½

Julia Has Two Lovers

(1991, 87 min, US, Bashar Shbib) *Daphna Kastner, David Duchovny, David Charles.* Kastner cowrote and stars in this offbeat, erotically charged though talky comedy-drama about a woman on the verge of a convenient marriage to her dull, old-fashioned fiancé (Charles), who is given food for thought via a day-long phone conversation with an amorous wrong number (Duchovny). ★★

Julian Po

(1997, 82 min, US, Alan Wade) *Christian Slater, Robin Tunney, Michael Parks, Allison Janney, Cherry Jones.* Slater is Julian Po, a contemplative bookkeeper who has a profound effect on the residents of a small town he enters. Since everyone suspects this stranger of evil, they are all relieved when Julian announces that he has come to town to kill himself. Almost immediately, he is revered as a prophet, often repeating the phrase "Life is short" to the various citizens who seek his counsel. Rewarded with free meals, clothes, and even a gun to do the deed, Julian is skeptical of his newfound celebrity. He just wants peace, quiet, and the love of Sarah (Tunney), a pretty local girl. Writer-director Wade has crafted an innocuous and unassuming fable, but it is remarkably passionless. ★★ VHS: $19.99

Julien Donkey-Boy

(1999, 94 min, US, Harmony Korine) *Ewen Bremner, Chloë Sevigny, Werner Herzog, Evan Neumann, Joyce Korine.* Trainspotting's Bremner is impressive as the titular Julien, a schizophrenic who is quite a burden on his strange family, including Sevigny as a pregnant wannabe ice skater and Neumann as a reclusive amateur wrestler. Shot on video and grainily transferred to film, this is the first

American film to be shot under the auspices of Dogma '95; like its brethren *Breaking the Waves* and *The Celebration*, it's a disturbing slice of a very dysfunctional family life. But without a narrative thread or memorable images, the film is an interminable series of apparently improvised scenes that go nowhere. ★ VHS: $19.99; DVD: $24.99

Juliet of the Spirits

(1965, 142 min, Italy, Federico Fellini) *Guilietta Masina, Valentina Cortese, Sylva Koscina.* A lavishly colorful baroque fantasy with Masina as a middle-aged woman haunted by hallucinations from her past and subconscious. In an effort to prevent her world from crumbling, she confronts these spectres and then is freed from the fantasies that have imprisoned her throughout life. A richly symbolic work, plunging into the depths of the human psyche. (Italian with English subtitles) ★★★½ VHS: $19.99; DVD: $24.99

Julius Caesar

(1953, 117 min, US, Joseph L. Mankiewicz) *Marlon Brando, James Mason, John Gielgud, Greer Garson, Deborah Kerr, Louis Calhern, Edmond O'Brien.* Classic rendition of Shakespeare's play, with an astonishing cast, including Brando as Marc Antony and Mason as Brutus. To date, the best filmed version of the story. ★★★ VHS: $19.99

Julius Caesar

(1970, 117 min, US, Stuart Burge) *Charlton Heston, Jason Robards, John Gielgud, Diana Rigg, Richard Johnson, Richard Chamberlain, Robert Vaughn.* After parting the Red Sea and proving himself rather adept at chariot racing, Heston tackles the classics with surprisingly satisfactory results. Good performances highlight this version of Shakespeare's classic. (Though the 1953 version is still the definitive production.) ★★★ VHS: $19.99

Jumanji

(1995, 104 min, US, Joe Johnston) *Robin Williams, Bonnie Hunt, Kirsten Dunst, Bradley Pierce, Bebe Neuwirth, David Alan Grier.* Featuring computer graphics special effects of rampaging animals terrorizing its cast, *Jumanji* is heavy on the F/X and light on the execution. A magical board game, Jumanji takes its young players and places them in the center of a jungle adventure, which usually manifests itself in the playing area of its participants. When an adolescent boy disappears into the game, he returns 25 years later (as Williams) when two orphaned children begin play. When not relying too heavily on its many F/X creations, the film has a spirited playfulness and a rather engaging cast. However, *Jumanji* falters when it allows the effects to take center stage at the expense of its human players. ★★½ VHS: $9.99; DVD: $19.99

Jumpin' at the Boneyard

(1992, 107 min, US, Jeff Stanzler) *Tim Roth, Alexis Arquette, Danitra Vance, Samuel L. Jackson, Luis Guzman.* Another in the early '90s string of lower-budget urban dramas, this film stands out as one of the best efforts. Two brothers (outstandingly played by Roth and Arquette) come together after several years apart. One is a drug addict, the other a divorcé. The older one (Roth) tries to get his brother off of drugs by

taking him back to their old neighborhood, the Bronx. Not only has the neighborhood changed, but so have they. They relive old memories and try to deal with their own demons. It's a gritty, no-nonsense portrayal, highlighted by realistic dialogue and intense acting. ★★★½ VHS: $29.99

Jumpin' Jack Flash

(1986, 100 min, US, Penny Marshall) *Whoopi Goldberg, Stephen Collins, Carol Kane, Annie Potts, Jon Lovitz, Phil Hartman, John Wood, Jonathan Pryce.* Marshall's directorial debut is an alternately amusing spy comedy with Goldberg as a computer operator who comes to the aid of a British agent held prisoner behind the Iron Curtain. Though Marshall was much more successful with her next film, *Big*, this is nevertheless an enjoyable piece of fluff thanks mostly to Goldberg's comic antics. ★★½ VHS: $14.99

June Bride

(1948, 97 min, US, Bretaigne Windust) *Bette Davis, Robert Montgomery, Fay Bainter, Mary Wickes.* Davis gets to show off her comedic skills in this lively battle-of-the-sexes romantic comedy. Davis plays a magazine editor who is accompanied by ex-lover and writer Montgomery to cover a wedding at an Indiana small town. Montgomery, always at home with a glib remark, and Davis make for a most enjoyable team. ★★★ VHS: $19.99

June Night

(1940, 88 min, Sweden, Per Lindberg) *Ingrid Bergman, Marianne Löfgren.* Bergman plays a promiscuous small-town girl who moves to Stockholm and changes her name after being involved in a shooting. Finding success in her displaced home, she is soon haunted by shadows of the past when the shooting victim and a reporter each threaten to expose her. This routine romancer is highlighted by Bergman's lovely performance. (Swedish with English subtitles) ★★½ VHS: $29.99; DVD: $29.99

The Jungle Book

(1942, 105 min, US, Alexander Korda) *Sabu, Joseph Calleia, Rosemary De Camp.* Beautifully filmed, live-action version of Rudyard Kipling's classic about Mowgli, the jungle boy, who is raised by a pack of wolves after the death of his parents. Sabu plays young Mowgli. ★★★ VHS: $9.99; DVD: $19.99

The Jungle Book

(1967, 78 min, US, Wolfgang Reitherman) *Voices of: Phil Harris, Sebastian Cabot, Louis Prima.* Charming Disney animated feature, based on Kipling's tales, about Mowgli, a young human boy, and his adventures with jungle animals. Wonderful score includes "Bare Necessities" (sung by the great Harris) and "I Wanna Be Like You" (the likewise Prima). ★★★ VHS: $26.99

The Jungle Book

Starring Jason Scott Lee
See: Rudyard Kipling's The Jungle Book

Jungle Fever

(1991, 132 min, US, Spike Lee) *Wesley Snipes, Annabella Sciorra, John Turturro, Ossie Davis, Ruby Dee, Samuel L. Jackson.* Much like his *Do the Right Thing*, Lee's explosive *Jungle Fever* is a stirring

and thought-provoking drama about race relations in modern society. Snipes stars as an aspiring African-American architect who begins an affair with Sciorra, his Italian-American secretary. For Lee, the contentious theme of a mixed-race relationship proves simply to be a springboard for his goal of exploring such divergent topics as tensions within African-American families, drug abuse, the tempestuous relationships between men and women, and the widening social schism between the blacks who attain middle-class "respectability" and the ones left behind. Jackson is riveting in support as Snipes' addict brother. ★★★½ VHS: $9.99; DVD: $24.99

Jungle 2 Jungle

(1997, 105 min, US, John Pasquin) *Tim Allen, Sam Huntington, JoBeth Williams, Lolita Davidovich, Martin Short, David Ogden Stiers.* This tepid and implausible remake of the French film *Little Indian, Big City* stars Allen as a stockbroker who learns he has a 13-year-old son living in the jungle. The tribal chief charges young Mimi-Siku with getting fire from the Statue of Liberty. Thus father and son are off to New York where Mimi's visit is pretty much of a disaster until he saves his dad and a fellow stockbroker from a money laundering Russian fish monger! ★★ VHS: $14.99

Junior

(1994, 110 min, US, Ivan Reitman) *Arnold Schwarzenegger, Danny DeVito, Emma Thompson, Frank Langella, Pamela Reed.* Having not learned a lesson with the infamously bad *Rabbit Test*, Hollywood delivers yet another tepid comedy about a man who becomes pregnant. But this time it's not just any man, it's Schwarzenegger. What a concept: *The Terminator* with child. Arnold plays a scientist who impregnates himself with an embryo. With the help of cohort DeVito, he carries to term. And along the way, he falls for fellow researcher Thompson (who seems above all this nonsense). *Junior* isn't without its share of laughs, most of them at the expense of Arnold's newly found motherhood. But the unimaginative screenplay does little to humorously exploit the situation. ★★ VHS: $9.99; DVD: $24.99

Junior Bonner

(1972, 103 min, US, Sam Peckinpah) *Steve McQueen, Robert Preston, Ida Lupino, Ben Johnson.* Peckinpah directed this vibrant western comedy-drama with McQueen as an ex-rodeo star who returns home to enter a local rodeo contest. McQueen has rarely been better, and Preston and Lupino are superb as his estranged parents. (Letterboxed) ★★★ VHS: $14.99; DVD: $14.99

Jupiter's Thigh

(1981, 96 min, France, Philippe De Broca) *Philippe Noiret, Annie Girardot.* Adventure, romance and comedy mix in this pleasant sequel to *Dear Inspector*. Noiret and Girardot star as honeymooners who stumble upon a rare statue whose missing thigh triggers a humorous chain of wild events. (French with English subtitles) ★★½

Jupiter's Wife

(1994, 78 min, US, Michael Negropont) Filmmaker Negropont spent two years exploring the mystery of Maggie, a schizophrenic homeless woman he finds living in Central Park with her huge family of stray dogs. Fascinated by the intricate mythology that Maggie has built up around herself, Negropont does an outstanding job as both cultural anthropologist and psychological detective as he carefully cajoles ever-more-detailed information from her. Maggie herself is an amazing character and the film's examination of her is at once revelatory and life-affirming and unalterably sad. ★★★½ VHS: $24.99

Le Jupon Rouge

(1987, 90 min, France, Geneviève Lefèbvre) *Marie-Christine Barrault, Alida Valli, Guillemette Groban.* Three women of greatly differing ages and backgrounds engage in a complicated and, at times, contradictory relationship with one another. Manuela (Barrault) has a nominal relationship with her boyfriend, but is actually more committed to her political work. She meets an older woman, Bacha (Valli), a Holocaust survivor and activist, and the two strike up a friendship, which becomes strained when Manuela begins a passionate love affair with another woman. A tender, well-acted drama touching on themes of desire and sensuality in relationships as well as a subtle examination of the tenuousness of life and love. (French with English subtitles) (aka: *Manuela's Lovers*) ★★★ VHS: $29.99

Jurassic Park

(1993, 125 min, US, Steven Spielberg) *Sam Neill, Laura Dern, Jeff Goldblum, Richard Attenborough.* A spectacular, state-of-the-art fantasy film based on the Michael Crichton best-seller, *Jurassic Park* is a dizzying display of special effects, the likes of which the movies have never seen. Neill and Dern are paleontologists who agree to preview a newly constructed outdoor theme park built by millionaire Attenborough. With mathematician Goldblum along for the ride, all are dazzled by the genetic engineering Attenborough has achieved: dinosaurs have been re-created and are roaming about on his tropical island paradise. However, the thrills begin when the carnivorous dinosaurs escape their confines and pit man against beast. Spielberg has crafted one heart-pounding episode after another, and his film is a high-flying blend of high-tech F/X and non-stop excitement. (Sequel: *The Lost World: Jurassic Park*) ★★★½ VHS: $14.99; DVD: $26.99

The Juror

(1996, 118 min, US, Brian Gibson) *Demi Moore, Alec Baldwin, Joseph Gordon-Levitt, Anne Heche, Lindsay Crouse, Tony Lo Bianco.* Overbaked, underdeveloped potboiler with Moore as a single mom who gets called for jury duty on a murder case. The accused is a big-time mafioso whose strongarm, played by Baldwin, wants to ensure his boss' acquittal, leading to Moore being threatened and tormented in scene after silly, unpleasant scene, to convince her to vote not guilty, or else. Reminiscent of 1994's equally silly *Trial by Jury*, this is basially a throwaway TV movie with two big-time star names. Though the acting is good, if undistinguished, *The Juror* is overlong and not very exciting — though at least the shots are in focus. ★½ VHS: $9.99

Jury Duty

(1995, 86 min, US, John Fortenberry) *Pauly Shore, Tia Carrere, Stanley Tucci, Shelley Winters,*

Andrew Dice Clay. Not that his prior films would ever challenge *Some Like It Hot* or *Airplane* in comic stature, but Shore's first three films look like comic masterpieces compared to *Jury Duty*, a horrendous and unbelievably unfunny comedy. Shore stars as a ne'er-do-well who is called for jury duty. Homeless and jobless and assigned to a high-profile case, Shore prolongs the court proceedings to take advantage of the room and board. With a story line and joke cannister equally deficient, *Jury Duty* is guilty of atrocious writing, bad acting and lifeless direction. ★ VHS: $9.99

Just a Gigolo

(1980, 105 min, West Germany, David Hemmings) *David Bowie, Marlene Dietrich, Kim Novak, David Hemmings.* Amid the glittery milieu of decadent post-WWI Germany, Bowie is a debonair "escort" to a host of society women. Novak wants his body, Hemmings wants his body and his soul while Dietrich (in her final film appearance) observes the goings-on while belting out the title tune. ★★½

Just Another Girl on the IRT

(1993, 92 min, US, Leslie Harris) *Ariyan Johnson, Kevin Thigpen, Ebony Jerido, Jerard Washington.* Harris makes her film debut with this low-budget independent drama that, while very rough around the edges, vibrates with energy, tension and humor. Harris has given a strong cinematic voice to a segment of the population long ignored — the black female teenager. And what a voice. Chantel (Johnson in a dazzling debut) is one of the smartest kids at her Brooklyn high school but she is loud, obnoxious, self-centered, and not nearly as mature as she thinks. When the ambitious, promising Chantel finds herself faced with an unwanted pregnancy, Harris portrays a story as poignant, scary, frustrating and moving as real life. ★★★ VHS: $14.99

Just Another Pretty Face

(1958, 110 min, France, Marc Allégret) *Henri Vidal, Mylene Demongeot, Jean-Paul Belmondo, Alain Delon.* Made right before the cinematic explosion of the French New Wave, this action/melodrama can be seen as typical entertainment fare for France in the 1950s. Vidal stars as a police detective bent on solving a smuggling ring. The situation becomes more difficult when he falls in love with a beautiful member of the smuggling gang. Watch for brief appearances by the very young Belmondo and Delon. (French with English subtitles) ★★½

Just Between Friends

(1986, 120 min, US, Allan Burns) *Mary Tyler Moore, Christine Lahti, Ted Danson, Sam Waterston.* Attractive performances by Moore, Danson and especially Lahti elevate this ordinary romantic comedy-drama about a suburban housewife (Moore) who begins a friendship with the woman having an affair with her husband. ★★½ VHS: $9.99

Just Cause

(1995, 102 min, US, Arne Glimcher) *Sean Connery, Laurence Fishburne, Kate Capshaw, Blair Underwood, Ed Harris, Ruby Dee, Chris Sarandon, Lynn Thigpen.* Part social drama and part thriller (without much thrills), *Just Cause* stars Connery as a Harvard Law professor who attempts to prove the innocence of a young

black man (Underwood) convicted of murder and sentenced to die. When Connery travels to Underwood's small Florida town to investigate, he comes in conflict with the town's redneck black sheriff (Fishburne) who helped put the youth away. Similar to *Malice* insofar that the film starts in one direction and switches gears halfway through, *Just Cause*'s change is not for the better: What begins as an involving story of injustice gives way to a ridiculous revenge fantasy. ★★ VHS: $9.99; DVD: $14.99

Just Like a Woman

(1994, 90 min, GB, Christopher Monger) *Julie Walters, Adrian Pasdar, Paul Freeman.* Pasdar stars in this gentle, cross-dressing comedy about an American banker living in London whose penchant for lingerie gets him in trouble with his wife, who thinks he's seeing another woman. She kicks him out, and he winds up lodging with an older woman (Walters) who's just ended a 22-year marriage. After they strike up a relationship, he divulges his secret to her and she helps him fulfill his fantasies. While basically a straight love story, the film nonetheless is an entertaining examination of gender roles in relationships. Based on Monica Jay's book "Geraldine." ★★★

Just Like Weather

(1986, 98 min, Hong Kong, Allen Fong) *Christine Lee, Lee Chi-Keung.* A fascinating independent feature about a couple who, in an effort to save their crumbling marriage, decide to travel to New York for a second honeymoon. What makes the film different is that in the midst of this drama, the director interviews the two about themselves and their worries about their relationship. A thinly veiled allegory about Hong Kong's return to the control of Communist China. (Cantonese with English subtitles) ★★★ VHS: $39.99

Just Tell Me What You Want

(1980, 114 min, US, Sidney Lumet) *Alan King, Ali MacGraw, Myrna Loy, Keenan Wynn.* A witty comedy with King as an overbearing tycoon who tries to win back the mistress (MacGraw) who walked out on him. King has never been funnier, and Loy has some great moments as his secretary. ★★★ VHS: $14.99

Just the Two of Us

(1970, 82 min, US, Barbara Peters) *Alicia Courtney, Elizabeth Plumb.* Tenderly telling the love story between two married women, *Just the Two of Us* features low production values and sub-par acting, but it rises above these flaws with an engaging pro-lesbian script. Pretty and sensible Denise (Courtney) and the sweetly ditsy blonde Adria (Plumb) are lonely housewives living in suburban L.A. While lunching at a restaurant, they notice two women at another table kissing. Both women are transfixed, and a romance between them ensues. However, what is a fling for one becomes much more to the other. A thoughtful examination of passion and identity. ★★★ VHS: $24.99

Justine

(1969, 115 min, GB, George Cukor) *Anouk Aimée, Michael York, Dirk Bogarde, Robert Forster, Cliff Gorman.* Interesting character study of a lusty woman (Aimée) who seduces men while helping arm Palestinian Jews poised to revolt against British rule. ★★½ VHS: $59.99

K-2

(1992, 111 min, GB, Franc Roddam) *Michael Biehn, Matt Craven, Patricia Charbonneau.* Biehn and Craven star in this surprisingly engrossing action/drama about a pair of buddies from Seattle who join an expedition to climb one of the Himalayas' most daunting peaks — K-2. Based on the award-winning Broadway play by Peter Meyers, the film, shot in breathtaking locations in Pakistan, is filled with exceptionally photographed action sequences which dramatically illustrate the exhilaration and dangers of hard-core mountain-climbing. ★★★ VHS: $14.99

K-9

(1989, 102 min, US, Rod Daniel) *James Belushi, Mel Harris, Ed O'Neill.* Inept man-dog buddy comedy (in the same vein as *Turner and Hooch*), with Belushi as a cop saddled with a mean-tempered German shepherd. You know you're in trouble when one of the film's "best" laughs comes from two dogs doing it. (Sequel: *K-911*) ★½ VHS: $14.99; DVD: $24.99

Kaddish

(1984, 92 min, US, Steve Brand) A superb, multileveled documentary which details the effects of the Holocaust on a Hungarian survivor and his American-born son. By focusing on the son, Vossi, *Kaddish* enables us to observe a heretofore little examined legacy of the Holocaust: the process by which children come to terms with the parents from whom they've inherited an unimaginable nightmare. It explores how children who were told bedtime stories about concentration camps learn to view a world in which they truly feel that "it can happen here." Filled with unexpected humor, *Kaddish* is a moving portrait of a young man coming to terms with an overwhelming personal and historical tragedy. ★★★½ VHS: $29.99

Kafka

(1992, 88 min, US, Steven Soderbergh) *Jeremy Irons, Theresa Russell, Joel Grey, Ian Holm, Alec Guinness, Armin Mueller-Stahl.* The sophomore jinx has claimed yet another victim in Soderbergh's (*sex, lies and videotape*) ambitiously adventurous second feature. Irons stars as Kafka, a mild-mannered insurance clerk by day and aspiring writer by night, who becomes involved in a complex web of murder and bureaucracy gone wild. While his friends and acquaintances are regularly killed off, Kafka assumes a "Woody Allen-doing-James Bond" persona in his quest to get to the bottom of all the evil. Initially intriguing, but ultimately frustrating, the story has little to do with the writings and life of Franz Kafka ("The Castle," "Metamorphosis") and instead becomes a somewhat pedestrian murder mystery. While the film doesn't succeed in attaining its lofty pretentions, its startling, mostly black-and-white cinematography, realistic locales in the brooding city of Prague and several playful surrealistic episodes help keep the story moving (but to where?). ★★½ VHS: $7.99

Kagemusha: The Shadow Warrior

(1980, 160 min, Japan, Akira Kurosawa) *Tatsuya Nakadai, Tsutomu Yamazaki.* Kurosawa's sweeping historical drama weaves elaborate battle sequences with tranquil interior scenes, marvelously displaying the director's artistry. A film of great scope, power and detail. (Japanese with English subtitles) ★★★½ VHS: $19.99

Kalifornia

(1993, 110 min, US, Dominic Sena) *Brad Pitt, Juliette Lewis, David Duchovny, Michelle Forbes.* An unnerving and at times nauseating thriller for the art-house set. Duchovny costars and narrates as a free-lance writer with a fascination for serial killers. Bereft of ideas for his book, he and his photographer girlfriend (Forbes) plan a road trip from Georgia to L.A. visiting the sites of famous murders along the way. Short on cash, they solicit a rideshare and wind up with Pitt and Lewis, the poorest white trash to hit the screen since *Pink Flamingos*. Put these two couples in a '60s Lincoln convertible and you've got the recipe for a nightmarish ride across the Southern heartland. Pitt redefines the term psychopath with his portrayal of a filthy, beer-guzzling, grizzle-faced parolee. Director Sena creates a cinematic pastiche, straddling the line between hip atmospheric character study and pure quease-inducing terror. ★★★ VHS: $9.99; DVD: $19.99

Kama Sutra

(1996, 117 min, India, Mira Nair) *Indira Varma, Sarita Choudhury, Ramon Tikaram, Naveen Andrews.* Director Nair delves into the pleasures of the flesh with this semi-erotic tale of lust and forbidden love set in precolonial India. Varma is luminously ravishing as Maya, a young servant girl who finally decides that she is tired of the leftovers tossed to her by her erstwhile childhood friend, the Princess Tara (Choudhury). Maya steals into the chambers of Tara's groom-to-be and seduces him the day before the wedding and, upon being discovered, receives a one-way ticket to exile. She eventually finds her niche as a student of the famous courtesan Rasa Devi and falls in love with the local king's prized sculptor. Sumptuously photographed, *Kama Sutra* would seem to have all the ingredients for a gripping erotic drama, but Nair, who gives attention to character and has a fine directorial sense, can't elevate this story above the realm of half-baked melodrama. (Unrated) ★★ VHS: $14.99; DVD: $24.99

Kameradschaft (Comradeship)

(1930, 89 min, Germany, G.W. Pabst) *Ernst Busch, Alexander Granach.* Although WWI had been over for more than a decade, and Hitler had not yet risen to power, the hostility and tensions between the French and the Germans in 1930 were strained. The melting of this mistrust is the subject of *Kameradschaft*. Tragedy strikes a mining community near the French-German border when a cave-in traps over 400 French miners. Through the efforts of the townspeople and especially the neighboring Germans, disaster is averted and communication is opened. (German with English subtitles) ★★★½

Kamikaze '89

(1982, 106 min, West Germany, Wolf Gremm) *Rainer Werner Fassbinder, Gunther Kaufman, Brigitte Mira, Frank Ripploh, Franco Nero.* This very strange and tense fantasy thriller is based on Per Wahloo's best-selling novel "Murder on the 31st Floor" and features Fassbinder's final screen appearance. He plays a detective who has four days to solve a mystery before a bomb explodes. (German with English subtitles) ★★½

Kanal

(1957, 90 min, Poland, Andrzej Wajda) *Teresa Izewska, Tadeusz Janczar.* Wajda's intense WWII drama is the second of his trilogy which includes *A Generation* and *Ashes and Diamonds*. The story follows the heroic but grim actions of a group of Polish soldiers and patriots who attempt to escape Nazi-occupied Warsaw through the underground sewer system. (Polish with English subtitles) ★★★½ VHS: $24.99

Kangaroo

(1986, 105 min, Australia, Tim Burstall) *Colin Friels, Judy Davis, John Walton.* An idealistic English writer and his wife (Friels, Davis) move to Australia in the early 1920s in the hopes of finding a more tolerant world in which to

Brad Pitt is anything but his usual sexy self in *Kalifornia*

rebuild their lives. However, when the leader of a secret fascist group puts pressure on them to join their ranks, they discover the harmony they thought they had found has given way to the same social and political friction they thought they had left behind. Despite its incendiary theme, the film lacks any emotional spark. Based on D.H. Lawrence's semiautobiographical novel. ★★ VHS: $79.99

Kansas

(1988, 108 min, US, David Stevens) *Andrew McCarthy, Matt Dillon, Kyra Sedgwick.* An unengaging drama about a mild-mannered drifter (McCarthy) who is tricked into committing a bank robbery by a "friendly" sociopath (Dillon). ★ VHS: $9.99

Kansas City

(1996, 110 min, US, Robert Altman) *Jennifer Jason Leigh, Miranda Richardson, Harry Belafonte, Michael Murphy, Dermot Mulroney, Steve Buscemi.* A small-time hood crosses a gangster (an effective Belafonte) in Depression-era Kansas City. The hood's wife (Leigh) wants her husband back after the mob boss' men nab him, so she kidnaps a wealthy, opium-addicted socialite (Richardson) to ensure his release. *Kansas City* may not be anywhere near *Nashville* on the map, but it's certainly no *O.C. and Stiggs* either. The film has the director's visual eye for character detail, as well as his pointed examinations of life's realities and ironies. A jazz background offers a splendid score, and there's a terrific tenor sax duel. ★★½ VHS: $19.99

Kaos

(1984, 188 min, Italy, Paolo & Vittorio Taviani) *Margarita Lozano, Claudio Bigagli.* Set against the stunning backdrop of a sun-bleached, nearly barren Italian landscape, the Taviani brothers' adaptation of five stories by Luigi Pirandello together form a fascinating dramatic quilt. All of the stories, ranging from comedy to tragedy, focus on peasant life in turn-of-the-century Sicily and are stunningly photographed. Never succumbing to maudlin sentimentality, the folk tales are richly told with an embracing celebration of life. (Italian with English subtitles) ★★★★

The Karate Kid

(1984, 126 min, US, John G. Avildsen) *Ralph Macchio, Noriyuki "Pat" Morita, Elisabeth Shue.* A fatherless teenager living in Los Angeles, bullied by the local gang, learns karate from the family handyman. Macchio and Morita are both very likable in this first outing of series. (Followed by three sequels) ★★★ VHS: $9.99

Kasaramu Ce (This Land Is Ours)

(1991, 84 min, Nigeria, Saddik Balewa) A political tale of greed and power. Sani, a young farmer, is moved to act when his grandfather is killed by a money-hungry businessman who, finding precious stones throughout a village, tries to buy up all of the property. This film breaks one of the most important elements of a thriller when the mystery of the conspirators is revealed in the first 15 minutes. The lack of female characters provides a glimpse into the powerlessness of women in this Muslim community. The acting is quite natural and the editing keeps the story moving well, despite its pre-

Keeping the Faith

dictability. (English and Hausa with English subtitles) ★★

Katherine

(1975, 98 min, US, Jeremy Paul Kagan) *Sissy Spacek, Henry Winkler, Julie Kavner, Jane Wyatt, Art Carney.* Spacek stars as an overprivileged girl who, rejecting her affluent birthright, transforms from innocent to activist to revolutionary during the turbulent 1960s and early '70s. A compelling drama of conscience and commitment, highlighted by Spacek's compassionate performance. ★★★

The Keep

(1983, 96 min, US, Michael Mann) *Scott Glenn, Jürgen Prochnow, Ian McKellen, Alberta Watson, Robert Prosky, Gabriel Byrne.* From the director of *Manhunter* comes this stylish-looking but empty-headed horror film set during WWII about Nazi soldiers holing up at an ancient site — where a demonic creature has lain dormant. ★½ VHS: $79.99

Keeper of the Flame

(1942, 100 min, US, George Cukor) *Spencer Tracy, Katharine Hepburn, Margaret Wycherly.* Solid performances by Tracy and Hepburn distinguish this intriguing drama about reporter Tracy investigating the life of a deceased politician, only to uncover a dark secret about the man. Kate is the widow. ★★★ VHS: $14.99

Keeping the Faith

(2000, 129 min, US, Edward Norton) *Ben Stiller, Jenna Elfman, Edward Norton, Anne Bancroft, Eli Wallach, Ron Rifkin, Milos Forman, Holland Taylor.* A rabbi and a priest walk into a bar. Wait, wait, this ain't no ordinary rabbi and priest joke. Thanks to a winning screenplay by Stuart Blumberg, terrific chemistry between its three leads, and an impressive directorial debut by actor Norton, *Keeping the Faith* takes a one-joke premise and charms in totally unexpected ways. Jake (Stiller), Brian (Norton) and Anna (Elfman) were the best of childhood friends. Then, Anna moved away, Jake became a rabbi, and Brian a priest; the latter two remaining close. Now a high-powered executive, Anna returns, and their friendship picks up where it left off those many years ago.

But soon both men find themselves attracted to the vivacious Anna, leading to a degree of soul-searching for each of them. Norton keeps the pace even and makes sure everything is good-natured. There are plenty of genial laughs, and even when addressing serious subjects such as celibacy and question of faith, it never gets too serious. Stiller, Norton and Elfman have a wonderful rapport with each other, creating warm, endearing characters who do and say funny, endearing things. ★★★ VHS: $19.99; DVD: $29.99

Keetje Tippel (Kathi's Passion)

(1975, 104 min, The Netherlands, Paul Verhoeven) *Rutger Hauer, Monique van de Ven.* This early Dutch effort by Verhoeven is a passionate and sensual story of lost innocence. Set in 1880 Amsterdam, the film stars Hauer and centers on the life and struggles of a free-spirited young woman (van de Ven) who is forced into prostitution by her destitute family. A worthy resurrection of early 20th-century social fiction that exhibits wit, detail and conscience. ★★★

Kelly's Heroes

(1970, 145 min, US, Brian G. Hutton) *Clint Eastwood, Telly Savalas, Donald Sutherland, Carroll O'Connor, Don Rickles, Harry Dean Stanton.* Though not in the same league as *The Dirty Dozen*, this WWII adventure is nevertheless an entertaining romp with Clint and his Army buddies planning a gold heist behind enemy lines. ★★½ VHS: $14.99; DVD: $19.99

The Kentuckian

(1955, 104 min, US, Burt Lancaster) *Burt Lancaster, Dianne Foster, Walter Matthau, Diana Lynn.* In his only directorial effort, Lancaster wears dual coonskin hats in this dramatically awkward but scenic adventure. Set in Kentucky during the 1820s, the film has Lancaster as a backwoodsman who, with his young son, sets out for Texas and the rugged but rewarding life. On the way, he becomes sidetracked by indentured servant Foster, schoolteacher Lynn, villainous merchant Matthau (in his debut), and two feuding Klansmen on his trail. Director Lancaster is none-too-subtle in the "simple-life-is-better" motif. ★★ VHS: $14.99; DVD: $19.99

K

The Kid from Brooklyn

The Key

(1958, 121 min, GB, Carol Reed) *William Holden, Sophia Loren, Trevor Howard, Oscar Homolka, Michael Caine.* Based on Jan de Hartog's novel "Stella," this slowly paced though involving romantic drama is set during WWII and follows Loren as she initiates a series of affairs with naval officers, eventually falling in love with Holden. ★★½ VHS: $19.99

Key Largo

(1948, 101 min, US, John Huston) *Humphrey Bogart, Lauren Bacall, Edward G. Robinson, Claire Trevor, Lionel Barrymore.* An exciting screen version of Maxwell Anderson's hit play. Robinson is the ruthless gangster who takes refuge in an isolated hotel during a storm and terrorizes the patrons and staff, including war veteran Bogey and widow Bacall. Trevor won an Oscar as Robinson's pathetic, alcoholic moll. ★★★½ VHS: $19.99; DVD: $19.99

The Keys of the Kingdom

(1944, 137 min, US, John M. Stahl) *Gregory Peck, Vincent Price, Edmund Gwenn, Thomas Mitchell, Roddy McDowall.* One of Peck's earliest efforts casts him as a priest doing missionary work in 19th-century China in this moving adaptation of A.J. Cronin's novel. Slightly overlong, but compelling nonetheless. ★★★ VHS: $19.99

Keys to Tulsa

(1997, 113 min, US, Leslie Grief) *James Spader, Eric Stoltz, Cameron Diaz, Mary Tyler Moore, James Coburn, Deborah Unger, Michael Rooker.* A crisp, taut contemporary noir thriller, *Keys to Tulsa* is well-constructed, fast-paced and peppered with trenchant dialogue capably delivered by an eclectic ensemble. Stoltz is the prodigal son who returns to his home town to become quickly ensnarled in murder, blackmail and conflicted loyalties. The convoluted plot is absorbing and punctuated by sharp characterizations: Moore as Stoltz's acerbic society mom; Rooker as a befuddled boy in an angry man's body; Diaz as a poor little rich girl. The intricate web of relationships is revealed as the protagonists play out their roles in the ongoing tragedy, with more than enough guilt to go around. A well-executed exploration of a complexity of soured lives and tarnished expectations. ★★★½ VHS: $14.99

Khartoum

(1966, 136 min, GB, Basil Dearden) *Laurence Olivier, Charlton Heston, Ralph Richardson.* Heston and Olivier square off in this retelling of the 1883 siege at Khartoum, in the British Sudan. Punctuated with magnificently choreographed battle scenes, this epic adventure finds Olivier in peak form as the fanatical Arab leader who incites his people to rise up against the British presence. Heston delivers one of his best performances as the English general who opposes him. ★★★ VHS: $19.99

Kicked in the Head

(1997, 86 min, US, Matthew Harrison) *Kevin Corrigan, Linda Fiorentino, Michael Rapaport, James Woods, Lili Taylor, Burt Young.* Redmond (Corrigan) is a manchild on the brink of cosmic change; he thinks he's going through a self-destructive phase, but maybe it's self-revelation. Used as a mule in a really bad drug deal by his sleazy Uncle Sam (Woods, in a role perfect for him), caught in the heavy crossfire of a full-scale beer war through his one-sided friendship with Stretch (the always edgy Rapaport), and rejected and dismissed by the stewardess (Fiorentino) who may be the guardian angel of his fortune cookie message, Redmond embarks on a personal odyssey more buffeted by outside influences than motivated from within. Corrigan's remarkable performance is well suited to the film's heightened realism and hyperkinetic energy. ★★★ VHS: $79.99; DVD: $24.99

Kicking and Screaming

(1995, 96 min, US, Noah Baumbach) *Josh Hamilton, Olivia D'Abo, Eric Stoltz, Christopher Eigeman, Parker Posey, Jason Wiles.* Set in that post-Bachelors' Degree, pre-gainful employment, Twilight Zone time of life, *Kicking and Screaming* follows several newly minted college grads as they haphazardly grapple with deteriorating personal relationships, exacerbating family expectations and a nonexistent job market (with clerking in a video store once again serving as a metaphor). No new material here, but director Baumbach crafts an engaging, unpretentious treatment of familiar territory. The characters are recognizable without being clichéd, and their various responses to academia, separation and anxiety illicit pangs of nostalgia — even in those viewers a decade or two removed from the experience. ★★★

The Kid

(1921, 90 min, US, Charles Chaplin) *Charles Chaplin, Jackie Coogan.* Chaplin's first true feature-length film tells the saga of an abandoned infant who's adopted by Charlie and, ultimately, becomes his streetwise sidekick. Chaplin expertly mixes slapstick and sentimental melodrama to create a timeless comic experience. Chaplin had defined his Little Tramp role with his priceless performance, and little Coogan could bring you to laughter or tears with just a look. ★★★½ VHS: $19.99

The Kid

(2000, 104 min, US, Jon Turtletaub) *Bruce Willis, Spencer Breslin, Emily Mortimer, Lily Tomlin, Chi McBride.* Bigshot moneymaker Willis finds out just how empty his life is when he runs into himself as an eight-year-old kid (Breslin). The innocent child within has been suppressed, and while the bullies have been left behind, so have his childhood dreams. Breslin makes an impression as the kid, but this touchy-feel-good mush is often too much to take. ★★ VHS: $19.99; DVD: $29.99

A Kid for Two Farthings

(1955, 96 min, GB, Carol Reed) *Jonathan Ashmore, Celia Johnson, Diana Dors, Brenda De Benzie.* Reed's heartwarming fable about the hopes and aspirations of an impoverished lad is filled with insights about the human condition. In a play on "Jack and the Beanstalk," the young boy is sent to market where he buys a goat with an odd deformity — a single horn growing out of its head. Convinced that the kid is a magical, wish-granting unicorn, the boy's head fills with fantasies about ending his family's poverty. (Letterboxed) ★★★½ VHS: $29.99

The Kid from Brooklyn

(1946, 113 min, US, Norman Z. McLeod) *Danny Kaye, Virginia Mayo, Eve Arden, Fay Bainter.* Kaye is a comic dynamo as a timid milkman who unwittingly becomes a prize fighter. There are plenty of laughs, and Kaye (as usual) is a delight. Remake of the Harold Lloyd 1936 comedy, *The Milky Way.* ★★★ VHS: $14.99

The Kid from Spain

(1932, 96 min, US, Leo McCarey) *Eddie Cantor, Lyda Roberti, Robert Young, Ruth Hall.* Busby Berkeley directed the dance sequences in this entertaining musical comedy with Cantor gloriously chewing the scenery when he's mistaken for a famed bullfighter. ★★★ VHS: $14.99

A Kid in King Arthur's Court

(1995, 89 min, US, Michael Gottlieb) *Thomas Ian Nicholas, Joss Ackland, Ron Moody, Art Malik, Kate Winslet.* Mark Twain's classic time travel tale is dusted off for a third time (Will Rogers and Bing Crosby also found medieval adventure) to produce a particularly unimaginative and silly retelling. Nicholas is Calvin, a 20th-century little league player who finds himself hurled back into the 6th century and the court of Camelot. There he finds romance, adventure and intrigue, and manages to boost his own sagging self-confidence through a series of lifeless episodes and smirky comedy. Disney once again condescends to its adolescent audience, even toying with the Camelot legend. ★★ VHS: $19.99

Kidnapped

(1960, 97 min, US, Robert Stevenson) *Peter Finch, James MacArthur, Peter O'Toole.* Disney, after its great success ten years earlier with Robert Louis Stevenson's *Treasure Island,* returns to another Stevenson source with exciting results. Finch and MacArthur are Alan Breck and David Balfour, respectively, the 18th-century adventurer and the young kidnap victim, who join forces to battle pirates and the Redcoats. Not *the* definitive Stevenson adaptation, but entertaining nonetheless. O'Toole's film debut. ★★★ VHS: $19.99

K

Kids

(1995, 90 min, US, Larry Clark) *Leo Fitzpatrick, Justin Pierce, Chloë Sevigny.* This unrelenting cinema verité look at a group of Manhattan teenagers seems destined to shock even the most hardened sensibilities. The assault begins even before the film's opening shot as we hear the distinct and magnified sounds of two teens ferociously sucking face. The ensuing scene, in which the film's antihero, Telly, talks his way into "fuckin'" a virgin, basically sets the tone for the whole film. As we follow him, his buddy Casper, and a bunch of other delinquents through 18 hours of unbridled hedonism, Telly boasts about previous virginal conquests and plots his next — when he's not suckin' on a 40, smoking a blunt, kicking the shit out of some poor guy or harassing fags. Director Clark employs astounding camerawork and a well-thought out narrative structure to present a disturbingly real picture of these wayward youths. The result is socially compelling though bordering on nauseating to watch and may leave one contemplating a vasectomy or tubal ligation. ★★ VHS: $14.99; DVD: $24.99

Kids in the Hall: Brain Candy

(1996, 89 min, Canada, Kelly Makin) *Scott Thompson, David Foley, Bruce McCullough, Kevin McDonald, Mark McKinney.* Canada's five-man comic arsenal The Kids in the Hall make their big-screen debut in this witty, on-target satire of '90s America. An unscrupulous pharmaceutical company develops a happiness drug and unleashes it on an unsuspecting public. In true Kids fashion, pain and anger are turned into laughter as the Kids skewer America's mindset towards the elderly, drugs, the handicapped, MTV, grunge — and there's a terrific "coming out" song-and-dance number. The cast is great, with everyone playing multiple roles as they did on TV, though with 90 minutes to fill rather than 25, the film doesn't always reach the hilarity level of the show. However, it still packs plenty of laughs. ★★★ VHS: $14.99

Kika

(1993, 90 min, Spain, Pedro Almodóvar) *Verónica Forqué, Victoria Abril, Peter Coyote, Alex Casanovas, Rossy DiPalma.* Almodóvar's big-budget comedy-drama is filled with outlandish costuming, neon-bright colors and wild characters, all filmed at the director's trademark, frenetic pace. Alternating between farce and an examination of urban crises, the film stars Forqué as Kika, a sweet, sexy makeup artist who is forced to confront urban rape, multiple murders and intrusion of her privacy by the media's prying eyes. When Kiki is raped, it is caught on camera by a neighbor. The tape falls into the clutches of Andrea (Abril), the hostess of Madrid's "Cops"-like TV show called "Today's Worst." And Andrea — who can be found clothed in black rubber with a robotic camera helmet on her head and arc lights covering her breasts — wants to air the tape on national TV! A sometimes outrageous tale of voyeurism and media manipulation. (Spanish with English subtitles) ★★★ DVD: $29.99

Kill Me Again

(1989, 94 min, US, John Dahl) *Val Kilmer, Joanne Whalley-Kilmer, Michael Madsen.* This nifty little thriller is a small, engaging film noir/mystery which bypassed theatrical play. Kilmer plays a private investigator who is hired by femme fatale Whalley to fake her murder — she's being pursued by a boyfriend she's double-crossed. The murder is so convincing that the police now suspect the P.I., and the woman is nowhere to be found. Though one or two of the twists may be predictable to the mystery buff, there's more than enough intrigue and suspense for the rest of us. The love scenes between the future Mr. and Mrs. Kilmer are rather tame, however. ★★★ VHS: $9.99; DVD: $19.99

The Killer

(1983, 110 min, Hong Kong, John Woo) *Chow Yun-Fat, Sally Yeh, Danny Lee.* Fasten your seat belt and get ready to blast off into nonstop action and rip-roaring entertainment in this relentlessly paced and extremely funny tongue-in-cheek exercise in slapstick violence. The story follows a veteran assassin (Yun-Fat) who, in the course of performing one last job before retiring, inadvertently blinds a young cabaret singer. Overwrought with guilt, he decides to devote his life to helping her, but the cops and the mob just won't let this killer-with-a-heart-of-gold go straight. Eventually, he teams up with a maverick cop and they embark on an adventure in which bullets fly like popcorn and the hilarity goes to extremes. Director Woo has fashioned a film lover's dream — a perfect blend of art, action and comedy. Highly recommended. (Available in Cantonese with English subtitles or dubbed) (VHS available letterboxed or pan & scan) ★★★★ VHS: $14.99; DVD: $29.99

Killer: A Journal of Murder

(1996, 90 min, US, Tim Metcalfe) *James Woods, Robert Sean Leonard, Ellen Greene, Cara Buono, Jeffrey De Munn, Lili Taylor, Harold Gould.* Awkwardly narrated, *Killer: A Journal of Murder* is "based" on a true story about a trusting new prison guard (Leonard) at Leavenworth and his misplaced friendship with a sociopathic prisoner (Woods). Produced by Oliver Stone, the movie raises many questions about our penal system without the pretension of trying to answer them. Yet when needed the most, the writing perches on the fence about whether treating these criminals kindly is the act of a fool or a saint. ★★ VHS: $89.99; DVD: $24.99

Killer Condoms
(Kondom des Grauens)

(1996, 107 min, Germany/Switzerland, Martin Walz) *Udo Samel, Marc Richter.* Based on the comic book by Ralf Konig, this weird horror/mystery satire follows a gay detective's search for the culprit behind a series of grisly deaths. In a seedy New York, detective Luigi Mackeroni (Samel) is assigned the case and what he discovers is that the killers are vicious penis-eating creatures masquerading as innocuous prophylactics. While offering some humorous moments, this cult film remains a lame experience. (German with English subtitles) ★★ VHS: $14.99; DVD: $24.99

The Killer Inside Me

(1975, 99 min, US, Burt Kennedy) *Stacy Keach, Susan Tyrrell, Tisha Sterling.* While not as searing as the Jim Thompson novel on which it is based, *The Killer Inside Me* is still a gripping psychological thriller. Keach stars as the seemingly rock-steady keeper of the law in a small California town whose long-simmering anger caused by a traumatic childhood incident finally explodes. Keach is at his best as the deranged yet sympathetic murderer, and Tyrrell is equally sharp as the white-trash prostitute who triggers his violence. ★★½ VHS: $89.99

The Killer Shrews

(1959, 71 min, US, Ray Kellogg) *James Best, Ken Curtis.* Curtis produced and stars in this tale of shrews the size of dogs — mainly because they *were* dogs, dressed in Pat Nixon's old cloth coat and wearing plastic fangs. Every bit as good as director Kellogg's other feature, *The Giant Gila Monster*, but lacking the sure hand he exhibited in his John Wayne opus *The Green Berets*, where the sun sets in the East (but that's another story for another time). ★

Killer's Kiss

(1955, 67 min, US, Stanley Kubrick) *Frank Silvera, Irene Kane, Jamie Smith.* This early Kubrick curiosity stars Silvera as a farm-bred boxer at the end of a short-lived fighting career. He falls fast and hard for a dance-hall girl. Her job is a self-imposed penance for past "sins," and her sleazy boss' obsessive interest in her

The Killer

results in murder. Kubrick's second feature includes a short but noteworthy nightmare sequence; not only did he direct, but he co-produced, edited, photographed and wrote the story as well. ★★★ VHS: $19.99; DVD: $14.99

The Killers

(1946, 103 min, US, Robert Siodmak) *Ava Gardner, Burt Lancaster, Edmond O'Brien, Albert Dekker, Sam Levene.* Based on the Ernest Hemingway story, and coscripted by (uncredited) John Huston, this searing crime drama follows the murder of a boxer (Lancaster). The police investigation and story is then told through flashback. Siodmak creates a remarkable atmosphere of tension and mystery in this classic noir. (Remade in 1964) ★★★★ VHS: $14.99

The Killers

(1964, 95 min, US, Don Siegel) *Lee Marvin, Clu Gulager, John Cassavetes, Angie Dickinson, Ronald Reagan.* Marvin and Gulager fulfill the terms of their contract by gunning down Cassavetes. But Marvin needs to know why the doomed man didn't try to run. The killers begin a search for the man who ordered the hit, and uncover several dirty little secrets along the way. Based on a short story by Ernest Hemingway. A reworking of the 1946 noir classic. ★★★ VHS: $14.99

The Killing

(1956, 83 min, US, Stanley Kubrick) *Sterling Hayden, Marie Windsor, Elisha Cook, Jr., Vince Edwards.* Kubrick's first feature film is a taut thriller about an attempted heist at a race track. Filmed in exquisitely noir-ish black-and-white tones, the film stars Hayden as the stone-faced ringleader who pulls together a gang of non-criminals to conspire on the multimillion dollar job. Though not as exuberant as his later works, Kubrick's touches nonetheless permeate this highly stylized tale of human aspiration undone by avarice and deceit. An excellent group of stock supporting actors deliver a conglomeration of superbly melodramatic and emotionally cool performances. ★★★½ VHS: $14.99; DVD: $24.99

Killing Cars

(1986, 104 min, West Germany, Michael Verhoeven) *Jürgen Prochnow, Senta Berger.* Director Verhoeven, who came into American prominence with *The Nasty Girl*, has shown great progress since this mildly interesting action/intrigue film. Prochnow plays Ralph, an amazingly unlikable hot-rod car designer whose work on a top secret "super car" becomes the target for industrial sabotage and other types of intrigue too numerous to recount. As the plot thickens, our hyperventilating hero (who is a surprisingly inept driver) is forced to confront a roving band of punks, double-crossing lovers and insidious coworkers in his efforts to get his car made. It's all smoke and no fire in this "thinking man's" thriller. ★½

The Killing Fields

(1984, 142 min, GB, Roland Joffé) *Sam Waterston, Haing S. Ngor, Athol Fugard, John Malkovich, Spalding Gray.* This highly emotional and often terrifying examination of Cambodia in the aftermath of the American evacuation stars Waterston as Sidney Schanberg, a Western journalist who stayed behind to witness the

takeover of the brutally repressive Khmer Rouge. Ngor (a native of Cambodia who in real life was tortured by the Pol Pot regime) received a much-deserved Oscar for his moving portrayal of Schanberg's translator, Dith Pran. A nightmarish vision of one of history's darkest moments. ★★★★ VHS: $14.99; DVD: $19.99

Killing Heat

(1984, 104 min, Australia, Michael Raeburn) *Karen Black, John Thaw, John Kani.* An intense, provocative version of Doris Lessing's novel "The Grass Is Singing." Black stars as a city girl who marries a farmer, only to find herself unprepared for the rigors of country life. Through her affair with a black farm hand and her husband's violent reaction, director Raeburn is pointedly commenting on the realities of African Colonialism. ★★★

The Killing of a Chinese Bookie

(1976, 109 min, US, John Cassavetes) *Ben Gazzara, Seymour Cassel.* Sure to be the most feared entry at a Gamblers Anonymous Film Festival, *The Killing of a Chinese Bookie* stars Gazzara as Cosmo, the owner/MC of a sleazy nightclub-cum-strip joint whose bad luck at a Mafia-operated poker game throws him into a violent web of extortion, double dealings and contract killings. A tough-talking but oddly moral man with a flashy lifestyle and a penchant for pretty ladies, Cosmo finds that his T&A showplace is a church compared to the treachery of organized crime. Director Cassavetes' hand-held camera and seemingly improvised dialogue create a repressively realistic atmosphere where one cannot escape. (Letterboxed) ★★★ VHS: $14.99; DVD: $24.99

The Killing of Angel Street

(1981, 101 min, Australia, Donald Crombie) *John Hargreaves, Liz Alexander.* Based on actual events, this is the compelling story of corruption and the people who fought against it. A young activist battles to save her neighborhood from developers and becomes embroiled in a web of intrigue. ★★½

The Killing of Sister George

(1968, 138 min, GB, Robert Aldrich) *Beryl Reid, Susannah York, Coral Brown.* One of the most infamous lesbian "breakthrough" films of the 1960s, this story of an aging lesbian who loses her job and her young lover is a shrill, even grotesque exposé on lesbian lifestyles. Reid is magnetic in her portrayal of George, the loud and aggressive, cigar-chomping dyke whose girl-chasing ways (she even accosts a cab full of nuns!) and domineering personality drive away all who care for her. An entertainingly dated tale of love and loneliness that treads a strange line between comedy and sensationalist, perverted drama. Some scenes were shot in the London lesbian bar Getaway Club. (Letterboxed) ★★ VHS: $14.99; DVD: $29.99

Killing Time

(1997, 91 min, GB, Bharat Nalluri) *Craig Fairbrass, Kendra Torgan.* Frustrated cop Fairbrass, spurred by the killing of his partner by a sicko local crime boss, calls on beautiful Italian assassin-for-hire Torgan to

wipe out said criminal and his organization. He also arranges for some thugs to then kill her, once she's done the job, to avoid paying her pricey bill. Things, of course, don't go as planned, and many stylized shoot-outs follow. What begins as a low-rent but stylish and distinctly British thriller quickly degenerates into slick, empty '90s trash. The action scenes are incomprehensible, and while Torgan certainly strikes the right image as a sleek, chic hit lady, she demonstrates all the assassin know-how of a drunk Jerry Lewis. ★★ VHS: $14.99

Killing Zoe

(1994, 96 min, US, Roger Avary) *Eric Stoltz, Jean-Hugues Anglade, Julie Delpy, Gary Kemp, Tai Thai.* Stoltz stars in this Luc Besson–influenced splatter film as an American safecracker who travels to Paris to help his childhood friend (Anglade) knock off a bank. Stoltz soon finds himself trapped in a nightmare that makes Griffin Dunne's wild taxi ride in *After Hours* feel like a sunny stroll through a garden. Delpy plays a call girl whom Stoltz hires his first night in town and who later, it turns out, is a secretary at the targeted bank. All style and no substance, the film has a few entertaining moments, but is ultimately unfulfilling and pointless. ★½ VHS: $9.99; DVD: $14.99

Kim

(1950, 113 min, US, Victor Saville) *Dean Stockwell, Errol Flynn, Paul Lukas, Cecil Kellaway.* Stirring adaptation of Rudyard Kipling's adventure story about a young English boy who becomes involved with a British secret agent in 19th-century India. Stockwell plays the young title character, and Flynn's then-faltering career was saved by his winning portrait of the daring soldier-spy. ★★★ VHS: $19.99

Kind Hearts and Coronets

(1949, 104 min, GB, Robert Hamer) *Alec Guinness, Dennis Price, Valerie Hobson, Joan Greenwood, Hugh Griffith, Arthur Lowe.* Guinness created a sensation with his portrayal of all eight members of an aristocratic family who are eliminated one by one by a wayward relative

The Killers (1946)

K

who's bent on claiming the family's royal title. A delicious Ealing Studio comedy with a droll and macabre world view. Featuring a zesty costar performance by Price as the ambitious social climber. ★★★★

A Kind of Loving

(1962, 112 min, GB, John Schlesinger) *Alan Bates, June Ritchie, Thora Hird.* Schlesinger's first feature film is a sensitive drama about a young couple who marry because of pregnancy. While the film was unfortunately lost in the shuffle, having been released after its sensational "kitchen sink" counterparts *Room at the Top* and *Saturday Night, Sunday Morning,* it is a nonetheless witty, frank and poignant study of a lust gone awry. Featuring sterling performances by Bates and Ritchie as the young couple. ★★★½

Kindergarten

(1987, 143 min, USSR, Yevgeny Yevtushenko) *Klaus Maria Brandauer.* Poet and neophyte filmmaker Yevtushenko has taken an overused theme — the destructiveness of war as seen through the eyes of a child — and has fashioned from it a completely original and exciting autobiographical work. The setting is 1941 during the evacuation of Moscow. A mother sends her ten-year-old son to the safety of relatives in a Siberian village. En route, however, the youth's train is bombed, and the boy's journey becomes a vivid and harrowing odyssey through a war-charred landscape. The poet emerges from the filmmaker in this sentimental, bombastic and emotional film. (Russian with English subtitles) ★★★½ VHS: $59.99

Kindergarten Cop

(1990, 111 min, US, Ivan Reitman) *Arnold Schwarzenegger, Pamela Reed, Penelope Ann Miller, Linda Hunt, Carroll Baker.* Schwarzenegger mixes comedy and action as a tough Los Angeles cop who is forced to go undercover as a kindergarten teacher in hopes of capturing the criminal father of one of the kids. He goes through the usual comic humilities playing baby-sitter to a group of precocious five-year-olds. The comedy doesn't always work, and the action is less than exciting, but in spite of it all the film maintains a certain level of enjoyment. Arnold is Arnold, which is probably enough to please his fans. Reed, however, as his partner, is the film's biggest asset, giving a spirited performance who can make the unbelievable convincing. ★★½ VHS: $9.99; DVD: $24.99

The King and I

(1956, 134 min, US, Walter Lang) *Yul Brynner, Deborah Kerr, Rita Moreno.* "Shall We Dance?" That question will be difficult not to ask after viewing this sumptuous film version of Rodgers and Hammerstein's stage classic. Brynner gives an unforgettable and timeless performance as the King of Siam in this story of a proper British schoolteacher who, tutoring the court's children, falls in love with the monarch. Kerr is radiant as the governess, and the great score includes "Getting to Know You" and "Hello Young Lovers." Brynner won a Best Actor Oscar. (Letterboxed VHS available for $19.99) (Remade twice in 1999) ★★★½ VHS: $14.99

King David

(1985, 114 min, US, Bruce Beresford) *Richard Gere, Edward Woodward, Alice Krige.* Gere plays the young David, from the famous fight with Goliath to his time as King. Beresford approaches this with a seriousness which separates it from those lavish 1950s biblical epics; though the first half, featuring Woodward as King Saul, is much more successful than the latter half. ★★½ VHS: $14.99

A King in New York

(1957, 105 min, GB, Charles Chaplin) *Charles Chaplin, Dawn Addams, Michael Chaplin.* Often misunderstood, Chaplin's last starring film is a bittersweet political satire about a deposed European monarch who visits America amidst the McCarthy anti-Communist hysteria. Not at all "anti-American" as its detractors at the time claimed, this somewhat uneven but remarkable stab at social madness is filled with hilarious moments and has much to say about our nuclear and technological insanity. Chaplin's son Michael is featured as a young political malcontent. ★★★; DVD: $29.99

King Kong

(1933, 100 min, US, Merian C. Cooper & Ernest B. Schoedsack) *Fay Wray, Bruce Abbott, Robert Armstrong.* He is billed as "the eighth wonder of the world" and, in the sixty-plus years since the movie's release, animator Willis O'Brien's awesome creature has all but lived up to that title. There are ample reasons why this parable about the notorious giant ape let loose in New York City has had such an enduring notoriety. As enormous and unwieldy as the whole project is, the simple fable around which the story is built continues to be resonant. As an adventure-fantasy, *King Kong* has yet to be outdone. (Sequel: *Son of Kong*) (Remade in 1976) ★★★★ VHS: $14.99

King Kong

(1976, 134 min, US, John Guillermin) *Jeff Bridges, Jessica Lange, Charles Grodin, Rene Auberjonois.* Perhaps the most hyped film of the 1970s, especially for its supposedly spectacular mechanical effects. Despite winning an honorary Oscar, the effects are anything but special. Whatever possessed producer Dino De Laurentiis, the king of the bloated epic, to remake the 1933 classic is beyond human (or simian) comprehension. The only redeeming factor of this remake is the launching of Lange's career and the end of De Laurentiis'. "When my monkey die, everybody gonna cry." ★ VHS: $14.99; DVD: $29.99

King Lear

(1971, 137 min, GB, Peter Brook) *Paul Scofield, Irene Worth, Alec McCowan, Cyril Cusack, Patrick Magee.* Stark black-and-white cinematography and a somber Danish landscape underscore director Brook's heavy treatment of the Shakespeare tragedy. Scofield makes for a magnificent Lear, and receives excellent support from the great ensemble. ★★★½

King Lear

(1984, 158 min, GB, Michael Elliot) *Laurence Olivier, Diana Rigg, Anna Calder-Marshall, Dorothy Tutin, Leo McKern, John Hurt, Robert Lindsay.* Who better to play Lear than Olivier in his later life? This Emmy Award–winning production might is one of the finest versions of Shakespeare's play available. ★★★★ VHS: $29.99

Alec Guinness in *Kind Hearts and Coronets*

King Lear

(1987, 90 min, US/Switzerland, Jean-Luc Godard) *Molly Ringwald, Woody Allen, Peter Sellers, Burgess Meredith, Norman Mailer.* Even for hard-core Godardians, this incomprehensible version of Shakespeare's classic might prove to be tough going, the end result sadly suggesting that perhaps we already have seen all of the exciting filmic innovations from France's most innovative director. The oddball cast meanders through the various scenes with Godard himself starring as a crazed professor with a penchant for strange headgear. ★½ VHS: $24.99

The King of Comedy

(1983, 139 min, US, Martin Scorsese) *Robert De Niro, Jerry Lewis, Sandra Bernhard, Tony Randall.* De Niro is Rupert Pupkin, an aspiring but psychotic comedian, who schemes his way onto network TV and instant celebrity. Scorsese directs a finely tuned cast, including Lewis as a cynical dean of the airwaves and Bernhard as Pupkin's rubber-faced accomplice. ★★★ VHS: $19.99

King of Hearts

(1967, 102 min, France, Philippe de Broca) *Alan Bates, Genevieve Bujold, Adolfo Celi.* A perennial favorite at TLA, De Broca's classic comedy is a moving celebration of the triumph of innocence. Bates stars as a Scottish soldier dispatched to a small French village where the only remaining inhabitants are the inmates of the local asylum. (English and French with English subtitles) (Letterboxed) ★★★½ VHS: $19.99; DVD: $19.99

King of Kings

(1961, 174 min, US, Nicholas Ray) *Jeffrey Hunter, Siobhan McKenna, Robert Ryan, Rip Torn.* Ray, an accomplished veteran of noir and mysteries, turned his talents to the story of Christ in this beautifully filmed religious epic. Hunter plays Jesus. A better spectacle and far more successful in its storytelling than 1965's similarly themed *The Greatest Story Ever Told.* (VHS available letterboxed or pan & scan) ★★★½ VHS: $14.99

K

The King of Marvin Gardens

The King of Marvin Gardens

(1972, 104 min, US, Bob Rafelson) *Jack Nicholson, Ellen Burstyn, Bruce Dern, Julia Anne Robinson, Scatman Crothers.* An enthralling drama fueled by a poignant story of the American Dream lost and the dynamic acting of Nicholson, Dern and especially Burstyn. Nicholson is David Stabler, a quiet, almost mousy late-night Philly D.J. who is pulled out of his staid life when his volatile, always-in-trouble brother (Dern) calls from an Atlantic City jail. Traveling to an off-season, geriatric-filled pre-casino A.C., David is sucked into his brother's grandiose schemes. Nicholson ably plays off his boisterous image as the shy loser given one last chance. Dern is maniacal as the naïve dreamer/crook and Burstyn, in perhaps her most affecting role, plays a wacked-out, aging beauty queen fearful that she's run out of chances. Another star of the film is Atlantic City itself, a seedy, forlorn dead end at the edge of a cold, empty ocean. One of the most underrated and accomplished films of the 1970s. ★★★★ VHS: $19.99; DVD: $24.99

The King of Masks

(1999, 101 min, China, Wu Tianming) *Chu Yuk, Chao Yim Yin, Zhang Riuyang.* An elderly street performer, a master of the dying art of mask making and performance, wishes to pass on his knowledge. According to tradition, the heir to the secrets of the art must be male, so the old man buys an eight-year-old boy from a homeless father. The boy and the old man become close, until the boy's secret — he is a girl — is revealed, and their relationship as well as the old man's traditional values are severely tested. Well-paced and ultimately moving, *The King of Masks* is enhanced greatly by the two leads' assured performances, and an intelligent script that avoids sentimentality. A heartrending allegory on the role of women in modern Chinese society, *The King of Masks* is solid, enjoyable, worthwhile drama. (Mandarin with English subtitles) ★★★½ VHS: $21.99; DVD: $27.99

King of New York

(1990, 106 min, US, Abel Ferrara) *Christopher Walken, David Caruso, Laurence Fishburne,* *Giancarlo Esposito, Wesley Snipes.* Walken stars in this savage exposé of a ruthless drug kingpin who fancies himself a modern day Robin Hood. Upon his release from prison, Walken begins a campaign, using a veil of moral superiority to eliminate all of the "bad" elements from the drug trade. Ferrara's film, intensely gratuitous in its violence, has an undeniable power in its examination of corruption and betrayal. ★★★ VHS: $9.99; DVD: $14.99

King of the Gypsies

(1978, 112 min, US, Frank Pierson) *Eric Roberts, Susan Sarandon, Judd Hirsch, Sterling Hayden, Annette O'Toole, Shelley Winters.* Roberts takes over leadership of his Gypsy tribe when his grandfather dies; which doesn't sit too well with Roberts' father Hirsch. Sarandon is Hirsch's wife who defies her husband and gives her support to her son. ★★½ VHS: $14.99

King of the Hill

(1993, 115 min, US, Steven Soderbergh) *Jesse Bradford, Jeroen Krabbé, Lisa Eichhorn, Karen Allen, Spalding Gray, Elizabeth McGovern.* Set in Depression-era St. Louis, *King of the Hill* is based on the memoirs of A.E. Hotchener and tells the tale of a boy who is essentially abandoned by well-meaning but desperate parents. While not ignoring the realities of the period, director Soderbergh (*sex, lies, and videotape*) manages to pick out the story's joyous moments without ever getting sickeningly sentimental. Much credit has to go to 13-year-old Bradford who stars as Aaron, a boy who begins to lose everything but always keeps his sense of fairness, fun and dignity. Bradford's soulful eyes reveal his thoughts with a subtlety that's remarkable for an actor of any age. With an impeccable eye, Soderbergh has taken a small story and given it quiet, resonant power. ★★★½

King, Queen, Knave

(1972, 92 min, GB, Jerzy Skolimowski) *Gina Lollobrigida, David Niven, John Moulder-Brown.* Undeservedly maligned by critics, this surreal adaptation of Victor Nabokov's novel is filled with stinging black humor. The story concerns an impish young lad who falls in love with his aunt (Lollobrigida); and together they plot to murder her husband (Niven). ★★★

King Ralph

(1991, 97 min, US, David S. Ward) *John Goodman, Peter O'Toole, Joely Richardson, John Hurt.* In this lightweight but engaging comedy, Goodman plays a Las Vegas lounge singer (who does a mean Little Richard), who, after an accident wipes out the entire royal family, becomes the King of England. Most of the comedy centers on the big guy's "fish out of water" comedy of errors. O'Toole also stars as the royal secretary who acts as baby-sitter and cultural guide to King Ralph. ★★½

King Rat

(1965, 133 min, US, Bryan Forbes) *George Segal, James Fox, Tom Courtenay, Denholm Elliott, John Mills.* A gritty, first-rate drama, based on James Clavell's novel. Set at a POW camp in Malaysia during WWII, the story focuses on the rigors of captivity facing Allied prisoners, and the high cost they pay for their dignity and survival. Segal stars as a mercenary American G.I. financially benefitting from the hunger and sickness around him; and Fox is terrific as his principled, British right-hand man. ★★★½ VHS: $19.99

King Solomon's Mines

(1937, 80 min, GB, Robert Stevenson) *Paul Robeson, Cedric Hardwicke, Roland Young.* This exciting adventure story tells of the search for a legendary diamond mine deep in the heart of Africa. The robust and legendary Robeson fills the screen with star quality as a mysterious African chieftan. Based on a novel by H. Rider Haggard. ★★★ VHS: $39.99

King's Row

(1942, 127 min, US, Sam Wood) *Ann Sheridan, Robert Cummings, Ronald Reagan, Betty Field.* Reagan's best performance (excluding his portrayal of the "I can't remember" president) is featured in this gripping and well-made drama. Set in a small Midwestern town, the story follows the friendship of Sheridan, Cummings and Reagan from childhood to young adulthood — as Cummings studies medicine overseas, Sheridan and Reagan stay behind, with tragedy in store for Reagan. Sheridan and Field (as a reclusive childhood friend) excel. ★★★½ VHS: $19.99

The King's Whore

(1992, 111 min, US/Italy/West Germany, Axel Corti) *Timothy Dalton, Valeria Golino.* "Masterpiece Theatre" meets Danielle Steele in this lavishly produced variation on the "Dangerous Liaisons" theme. Dalton stars as a 19th-century Italian king who stops at nothing in the pursuit of his chancellor's wife (Golino). The film is surprisingly well-made and entertaining to the end, and definitely qualifies as a "guilty pleasure." ★★½ VHS: $19.99

The Kingdom

(1994, 279 min, Denmark, Lars von Trier) *Ernst-Hugo Jaregard, Kirsten Rolffes, Udo Kier.* You may have your "E.R.," America, but look away: *The Kingdom,* a joyfully creepy and surrealistic Danish medical thriller/satire, is full of jaded New Age practices, a crying-for-mother Casper, a nationalistic neurologist longing for his

K

homeland through binoculars, and a spiritualist has-been finally in touch to a clue of an afterlife. Jaregard stars as the new staff member to a Copenhagen hospital, where patients and doctors alike engage in totally unexpected behavior. Though comparisons to "E.R." and "Twin Peaks" are inevitable, *The Kingdom* is a singular effort. At four-and-a-half hours, the film is hardly dull or repetitive, and if expectations are put on hold, von Trier's stylistic smorgasbord can be as compelling and visually hypnotic as his earlier work *Zentropa*. (Danish with English subtitles) ★★★½ VHS: $14.99

Kingpin

(1996, 113 min, US, Peter Farrelly & Bobby Farrelly) *Woody Harrelson, Randy Quaid, Bill Murray, Vanessa Angel, Chris Elliott, Richard Tyson.* A one-handed bowling wiz takes a moronic Amish farmer and tries to turn him into the next champion. What sounds like a pitch from *The Player* actually turns out to be an unexpectedly funny, dark-edged entry from the "dumb" school of comedy filmmaking. Harrelson plays a potential champion bowler whose brush with rival Murray ends up with his bowling hand being cut off. Years later and now an alcoholic grifter, Harrelson stumbles upon Quaid, a talented Amish bowler who hides his ability from his family. With just the sparest of double talk, Harrelson and Quaid are on the road to Reno to enter the national championship. Much of *Kingpin* is in the stupid vein, and does it wallow in it. But it's also very cynical, and much as you may, you can't help but laugh. *Kingpin*'s also of note for three prominent stars having desperately bad hair days. ("R" version containing scenes not in original theatrical release) ★★★ VHS: $14.99; DVD: $14.99

Kings Go Forth

(1958, 109 min, US, Delmer Daves) *Frank Sinatra, Tony Curtis, Natalie Wood.* An intriguing war story that explores racial bigotry. Sinatra and Curtis are American G.I.s fighting in France during WWII who both fall in love with Wood. When they discover she is half black, their prejudices come to the fore, forcing them to face and examine their bigotry. All three stars give fine performances in this penetrating melodrama. ★★★ VHS: $19.99

Kiss Me Guido

Kings of the Road

(1976, 176 min, West Germany, Wim Wenders) *Rudiger Vogler, Hans Zischler.* This early Wenders masterpiece is a somber tale of a projector repairman and a friend who slowly thread through the barren landscape of the border regions of West and East Germany visiting shattered movie theatres, listening to rock 'n' roll and encountering strangers with strange stories. The "New" Germany that Wenders paints is one of a vast and underpopulated hinterland which proves to be both empty and imprisoning. (German with English subtitles) ★★★½

Kipperbang

(1982, 80 min, GB, Michael Apted) *John Albasiny, Abigail Cruttenden, Alison Steadman.* This lightweight comedy details the romantic fantasies of a group of young teens and their teachers in 1948 Britain. *Kipperbang* evokes the mood of a Bill Forsyth film, but lacks resonance and sense of direction. ★★½ VHS: $59.99

Kipps

(1941, 82 min, GB, Carol Reed) *Michael Redgrave, Phyllis Calvert, Michael Wilding.* Redgrave puts in a solid performance as Mr. Kipps, a shopkeeper who, upon inheriting a fortune, attempts to enter into high society. Sidney Gilliat's screenplay is faithfully adapted from the H. G. Wells novel. (Later made into the stage musical "Half a Sixpence.") ★★★½

Kiss Me Deadly

(1955, 105 min, US, Robert Aldrich) *Ralph Meeker, Albert Dekker, Cloris Leachman, Strother Martin.* With the despairing plea "Remember me" from a soon-to-be-dead dame echoing in his head, private eye Mike Hammer (Meeker) becomes involved in a convoluted case of torture, murder and a stolen, white-hot Pandora's box. Hammer, a sometimes sadistic and violent man, attempts to find the killers of a frantic, near-naked woman (Leachman) whom he picks up in his car one night. A great, fast-moving plot, loads of unforgettable characters and creative photography contribute in making this Mickey Spillane detective story (and Cold War allegory) a classic of late film noir. ★★★½ VHS: $14.99; DVD: $19.99

Kiss Me Guido

(1997, 91 min, US, Tony Vitale) *Nick Scotti, Anthony Barrile, Craig Chester, Anthony DeSando.* When he discovers his girlfriend having sex with his brother, Frankie (Scotti) decides to head to Manhattan, leaving his Bronx pizza shop forever for the fame and fortune of show business. But before stardom, he needs a place to stay. Looking in the personals, he notices GWM. And thinking it "Guy with Money," he heads to the Village and the apartment of gay actor Warren (Barrile), who's in desperate need of this month's rent. Such is the premise of this slight though disarming independent comedy which finds its humor in gay and straight stereotypes, though the film's low budget is unable to overcome a pedestrian screenplay and the laughs aren't as frequent as they should be. But what the film lacks in creativity it makes up for in spirit. ★★½ VHS: $14.99; DVD: $29.99

Kiss Me Kate

(1953, 119 min, US, George Sidney) *Howard Keel, Kathryn Grayson, Ann Miller, Bob Fosse, Tommy Rall, Keenan Wynn, James Whitmore.* One of Cole Porter's best scores highlights this vibrant adaptation of the Broadway musical about a divorced theatrical couple who are reunited for a performance of Shakespeare's "The Taming of the Shrew." Keel and Grayson are wonderful as the estranged husband and wife; and the dance sequences are terrific. ★★★½ VHS: $14.99

Kiss Me Stupid

(1964, 126 min, US, Billy Wilder) *Dean Martin, Kim Novak, Ray Walston.* A rollicking sex farce unfairly maligned on its initial release, this wicked comedy offers many a nasty swipe at sexual politics. Martin plays a successful, womanizing singer ending a tour. En route through a small Nevada town, Martin is "shanghaied" by struggling composer Walston, who will do anything to have Dino hear his music — including hiring prostitute Novak to masquerade as his wife, hoping Dean will take a fancy to her. ★★★ VHS: $19.99

Kiss of Death

(1947, 98 min, US, Henry Hathaway) *Victor Mature, Richard Widmark, Anne Grey, Brian Donlevy, Karl Malden.* Mature, in his best role, is Nick Bianco, a hard-luck crook who turns state's evidence only to find himself stalked by a vengeful hoodlum. Widmark, in his screen debut, steals the show as a sadistic, psycho hood with a demonic giggle and a propensity for throwing old ladies in wheelchairs down flights of stairs. (Remade in 1995) ★★★½

Kiss of Death

(1971, 80 min, GB, Mike Leigh) *David Threlfall, John Wheatley, Kay Adshead.* A minor film from the early career of director Leigh, *Kiss of Death* is essentially the dead-end story about the dead-end life of Trevor, a pathetic and slightly sociopathic Manchester youth. Trevor hangs out with his best friend, makes a half-hearted and mean-spirited stab at dating, and keeps up his work as a mortuary assistant. As slice-of-life and character study, the film exhibits Leigh's innate talents, but its story goes nowhere and lacks any shred of motivating interest. ★★ VHS: $29.99

Kiss of Death

(1995, 101 min, US, Barbet Schroeder) *David Caruso, Samuel L. Jackson, Nicolas Cage, Helen Hunt, Kathryn Erbe, Stanley Tucci, Michael Rapaport, Ving Rhames.* An accomplished, intense and satisfying crime thriller, director Schroeder's gritty updating of the 1947 film noir classic is a high-octane ride through New York City's underworld. Caruso makes a credible leading-man debut as a Queens ex-con trying to stay legit but who's pulled back into crime out of a misguided sense of loyalty. Much like Victor Mature's imprisoned jewel thief in the original, Caruso's Jimmy Kilmartin wants nothing to do with the assistant D.A.; that is until his family is directly affected by his partners-in-crime. Turning on them in an ingenious manner, he infiltrates a gang led by low-level mob figure Junior Brown (Cage), while at the same time coping with a cop with a grudge (Jackson). ★★★½ VHS: $9.99

K

Kiss of the Spider Woman

(1985, 120 min, Brazil, Hector Babenco) *Raul Julia, William Hurt, Sonia Braga.* Babenco's spellbinding meditation on political idealism and self-delusion stars Hurt (who won a Best Actor Oscar) and Julia, who portray two dramatically opposite inmates thrown together in a dungeonlike cell somewhere in South America. Julia, a cold political realist and activist, is forced to endure the fantasies of Hurt, a hopelessly romantic and politically naïve homosexual. An exotic Braga plays both Julia's one-time lover and Hurt's imagined heroine. Based on Manuel Puig's novel. (Made into a stage musical) (Filmed in English) ★★★½

Kiss or Kill

(1997, 97 min, Australia, Bill Bennett) *Frances O'Connor, Matt Day, Chris Haywood, Barry Otto.* As Al and Nikki, Day and O'Connor run neck-and-neck with Micky and Mallory as the most sympathetic sociopaths since Bonnie and Clyde. A sucker-punch opening sequence catapults us into this frenetically paced, twisted road movie. During a standard scam which results in an unexpected homicide, our antiheroes inadvertently get the goods on Zipper Doyle, a retired major sports figure now an institution in the community. The dead man was in the process of delivering a videocassette to Doyle at the time of his unfortunate encounter with Nikki and Al, who aren't exactly sure what to do with their newly acquired hot property. As the cats and mice hopscotch all over the vast expanses of the arid Australian wasteland, the parties involved indulge in the human predilection for base behavior and mystical confabulation. ★★★ VHS: $9.99

Kiss the Girls

(1997, 120 min, US, Gary Fleder) *Morgan Freeman, Ashley Judd, Cary Elwes, Tony Goldwyn, Jay O. Sanders, Bill Nunn, Jeremy Piven.* Despite its derivative story which borrows liberally from both *Seven* and *The Silence of the Lambs, Kiss the Girls* is a modest, entertaining, seen-it-before variation of the serial-killer thriller. The film gets its main strength from its two leads, Freeman and Judd, both giving thoughtful performances. Freeman is a psychiatrist for the Washington, D.C., police department. When his niece is kidnapped by a serial killer in North Carolina, he takes matters in his own hands and begins a private investigation. He hooks up with doctor Judd, another kidnap victim who just barely escaped the killer's desolate hideout. *Kiss the Girls* does manage some good moments of suspense, and it's very absorbing as a police procedural when Freeman is doing his Sherlock Holmes bit. (Sequel: *Along Came a Spider*) ★★½ VHS: $9.99; DVD: $24.99

Kiss Tomorrow Goodbye

(1950, 102 min, US, Gordon Douglas) *James Cagney, Barbara Payton, Ward Bond.* A cold-blooded mobster (Cagney) escapes from prison and embarks on a crime spree with his love-struck gun moll. But when he murders her brother and dumps her for a classy debutante, Cagney learns the hard way that hell hath no fury like a gun moll scorned. ★★★ VHS: $19.99

Kissed

(1997, 75 min, Canada, Lynne Stopkewich) *Molly Parker, Peter Outerbridge, Jay Brazeau.* You would think that a movie about a necrophiliac woman working as an embalmer would be fairly controversial, shocking or at least push some uncomfortable buttons. This may be true with a poorly executed, low-budget horror film like *Nekromantik,* but it is unfortunately not the case with this glossier production based on a short story from a book of women's erotica. Parker stars as a curious young woman who happens to be sexually attracted to youthful, fresh male corpses. While in embalming school, she meets a med student (Outerbridge) who becomes attracted to her obsession and eventually begins to share her compulsion for cadavers. Fairly tame and placid, the film attempts to explore its subject obliquely, without showing too much in the way of sex and gore. ★★½

Kissing a Fool

(1998, 94 min, US, Doug Ellin) *David Schwimmer, Jason Lee, Mili Avital, Bonnie Hunt.* Schwimmer works against type as a dunderheaded slimeball, as opposed to the sweet dunderhead on "Friends." Here he plays an egomaniacal sports anchor who, engaged to Avital, gets cold feet. He convinces old college chum Lee to try to seduce her. There are more complications than necessary for a 90-minute film, none of which will surprise. Lee does his usual inspired schtick, giving each line reading a gusto that clashes with the rest of the flat movie. Here's an easy tip for further "Friends" viewing: avoid male Friends (*Ed, The Pallbearer*), female Friends are a safer bet (*The Opposite of Sex, She's the One*). ★½ VHS: $9.99

The Kitchen Toto

(1988, 96 min, GB, Harry Hook) *Edwin Mahinda, Bob Peck, Phyllis Logan.* Offering an uncompromising child's eye view of 1950s Kenya, when that state was still very much a colony of Great Britain, *The Kitchen Toto* is a mesmerizing and at times harrowing examination of a land imprisoned by the boundaries of cultural and racial alienation. The title refers to a kitchen helper, in this case Mwangi (Mahinda), a young Kenyan of the Kikuyu tribe who leaves his widowed mother to work in the house of the British chief of police. Scorned by both colonialist and tribesmen, Mwangi tries peacefully to find his way through a turbulent world where violence is the norm. ★★★½ VHS: $19.99

Kitty and the Bagman

(1982, 95 min, Australia, Donald Crombie) *Liddy Clark.* The glory days of the Warner Brothers back lot are revived in this colorful Aussie Roaring Twenties comedy, full of flappers, gamblers and an earnest interest in the

Kitty Foyle

dishonestly earned dollar. Set in Sydney, it follows a beautiful innocent young bride, Kitty O'Rourke, who turns to the oldest profession in order to spring her small-time hood husband from jail. ★★½

Kitty Foyle

(1940, 105 min, US, Sam Wood) *Ginger Rogers, Dennis Morgan, James Craig.* Rogers won an Oscar (beating Katharine Hepburn in *The Philadelphia Story!*) for her strong portrait of a career woman torn between two men of different social backgrounds. Dalton Trumbo adapted the screenplay from Christopher Morley's novel. ★★★ VHS: $14.99

The Klansman

(1974, 112 min, US, Terence Young) *Richard Burton, Lee Marvin, Cameron Mitchell, O.J. Simpson.* With a cast including Burton and Marvin, a script cowritten by Samuel Fuller and a topic as important as race relations in the deep South, one would expect something from this film. Don't. It's almost impossible to convey the disappointment of this embarrassingly trashy and exploitative little oddity. Fuller was set to direct, but took an early walk. ★ VHS: $14.99

Klondike Annie

(1936, 77 min, US, Raoul Walsh) *Mae West, Victor McLaglen, Helen Jerome Eddy.* West adapted her own stage play and stars in this unusual comedy-drama and morality tale. West plays an entertainer who murders her possessive lover and escapes on a steamer bound for Alaska. On board, she meets love-struck captain McLaglen and missionary Eddy. With the police hot on her trail, and Eddy dying at sea, West changes identities with the dead woman and, on arrival in Alaska, is forced to continue the charade. The tone is more somber compared to West's other movies; its do-good, sentimental attitude doesn't altogether mix with West's brazen character. ★★ VHS: $14.99

Klute

(1971, 114 min, US, Alan J. Pakula) *Jane Fonda, Donald Sutherland, Roy Scheider, Charles Cioffi.* Fonda won an Academy Award for her mesmerizing portrayal of a high-priced New York call girl in this psychological thriller. Sutherland stars in the title role of an out-of-town cop on the trail of a missing husband who may have been a client of Fonda's. An outstanding use of sound and editing, along with the sexual frankness of the script, make this one of the landmark films of the '70s. (VHS available letterboxed or pan & scan) ★★★★ VHS: $19.99

Knife in the Head

(1978, 108 min, Germany, Reinhard Huff) *Bruno Ganz, Angela Winkler.* Ganz stars in this well-paced mystery as Hoffman, a scientist who is shot in the head at a local radical hangout while searching for his estranged wife. The injury leaves him partially paralyzed and causes him to lose much of his memory. As Hoffman tries to uncover the truth about the shooting, he is caught between the radicals and police who each want to exploit him for their own purposes. Brilliant acting and a great script make this a top-notch thriller. (German with English subtitles) ★★★ VHS: $79.99

Knife in the Water

(1962, 95 min, Poland, Roman Polanski) *Leon Niemczyk, Jolanta Umecka, Zygmunt Malandowicz.* Polanski's extraordinary study of three characters interacting on a small boat and how an innocent yachting weekend is transformed into a journey of mistrust and adultery. Polanski's first film, a fascinating study of sexual obsession, is riveting in its narrative, and creates a tension-filled atmosphere throughout. (Polish with English subtitles) ★★★★ VHS: $29.99

Knight Moves

(1992, 90 min, US, Carl Schenkel) *Christopher Lambert, Tom Skerritt, Diane Lane, Daniel Baldwin.* This psycho-thriller is an effective, bone-chilling mystery about a serial killer who gives clues to an international chess master about where and when his next victim will die because he wants to play against the best. Lambert is very convincing as the champion and Skerritt, in a sturdy performance, is the local police chief who both suspects and helps him. The standard thriller ending doesn't detract from the film; in fact, it's very intense despite its predictability. ★★★ VHS: $9.99; DVD: $14.99

Knight without Armour

(1937, 107 min, GB, Jacques Feyder) *Marlene Dietrich, Robert Donat.* This cross-cultural oddity was produced by British movie mogul Alexander Korda, directed by Frenchman Feyder, and takes place in Russia. The story concerns an aristocratic Russian woman (Dietrich) who is rescued from the Bolshevik Revolution by a British undercover agent (Donat). Based on a novel by James Hilton, the film is imbued with sumptuous production values, charismatic acting and lots of romance and atmosphere. ★★★ VHS: $19.99

A Knight's Tale

(2001, 125 min, US, Brian Helgeland) *Heath Ledger, Mark Addy, Rufus Sewell, Shannyn Sossamon, Paul Bettany, Alan Tudyk.* It's the 1300s, and a peasant named William (Ledger) is about to take the place of his master in a jousting match. In an instant, the crowd is on its feet and singing "We Will Rock You!" This little bit of anachronistic tomfoolery sets the tone for a most entertaining comic adventure that's funny, romantic and full of action. Displaying all the signs of leading man, Ledger brings a natural charm to William, who masquerades as a nobleman named Ulrich to compete in knight-errantry; specifically the sporting matches (a 14th-century equivalent of the WWF?) occuring thoughout Europe. Accompanied by two valets and a budding writer named Geoffrey Chaucer, William makes a name for himself while finding romance and rivalry. Adding to the merriment of all this is the score: modern classics used to underscore the story's delectable chain of events. And a most delightful moment arrives to the tune of Paul Bowie's "Golden Years." Among a quite appealing cast, Bettany steals the show as the golden-tongued Chaucer, a gambler who literally loses his shirt but who most definitely has a touch of the poet. ★★★ VHS: $102.99; DVD: $27.99

Knightriders

(1981, 145 min, US, George Romero) *Ed Harris, Gary Lahti, Tom Savini, John Amplas.* This non-horror feature from Romero is a deeply personal, idealistic but perhaps naïve moral tale

A Knight's Tale

about the difficulties of remaining true to one's personal beliefs. King Billy (Harris) and his troop of knights travel around the country putting on motorcycle-jousting competitions and medieval fairs. Looking for a respite from the pressures of the modern world, their popularity brings these same pressures to bear upon their group, fragmenting it in the process. Harris is terrific in an early, pre-star performance, and a huge cast of supporting players lend authenticity. A rousing action-adventure. ★★★ VHS: $19.99; DVD: $29.99

Knights

(1993, 89 min, US, Albert Pyun) *Kris Kristofferson, Lance Henriksen, Kathy Long.* It's cyborg vs. man in yet another predictable sci-fi actioner. With the usual ravaged wasteland serving as a backdrop, cyborg leader Kristofferson has discovered that enemy robo (Henriksen) has discovered a new source of fuel: human blood. Hero Kris teams up with a vengeance-seeking human (Long) in a disjointed frenzy of kickboxing chaos. ★ VHS: $14.99

Knock Off

(1998, 91 min, US, Tsui Hark) *Jean-Claude Van Damme, Rob Schneider, Lela Rochon, Paul Sorvino.* *Rip Off* is more like it. In this visually impressive though terrible actioner, Jean-Claude teams up with Schneider (will the laffs never end?) as a pair of jeans manufacturers (!) in Hong Kong who discover that their product is comprised of "knock offs" — inferior imitations. Not only that, but these jeans contain tiny explosives in place of buttons to be used as terrorist devices when they reach the U.S. (we're not making this up). *Maybe* this could have worked as an outrageously satirical action sendup, but it's all deadpan. After this and their first effort *Double Team,* director Hark needs to stay away from Van Damme. And as far as *Knock Off* is concerned, so does the viewer. ★ VHS: $9.99; DVD: $14.99

Knockout

(1999, 100 min, US, Lorenzo Doumani) *Sophia Adella-Hernandez, Eduardo Yañez, Maria Conchita Alonso, Paul Winfield, William McNamara.* A young girl, raised by her ex-boxer dad and homily spouting, ultra-supportive mom, decides to pursue boxing as her career, despite

the inherent obstacles. This unremarkable "Afterschool Special"-like drama boasts a typically strong performance from Alonso, but little else. There's nary a convincing moment in the bland script or direction, and all but the most desperate-for-something-to-watch will have tuned out before the denouement. *Knockout* is destined for "also-ran" status alongside the similarly themed *Girlfight.* ★½ VHS: $99.99; DVD: $24.99

Kojiro

(1967, 152 min, Japan, Hiroshi Inagaki) *Kikunosuke Onoe, Tatsuya Nakadai.* Kojiro is a young man with an attitude. Taken into a home as a foundling, he chafes under the rough authority of the family's son, Hyosuké, with whom he has been raised as a brother. He gains Hyosuké's mortal enmity when he runs off with his sister, Toné. Hyosuké pursues his sister and our hero, even though Toma, Toné's fiancé and Kojiro's best friend, refuses to do so, wanting only Toné's happiness. With Hyosuké in hot pursuit, Kojiro vows to Toné to become famous and secure their position in society. To do this, he challenges a martial arts school, and wins by flying in the face of tradition. A late-night indulgence of flying fists, flashing swords, bruised egos and flailing passions, where the characters are either tributes to order and decorum or totally at the mercy of their emotions. (Japanese with English subtitles) ★★½ VHS: $49.99

Koko: A Talking Gorilla

(1978, 81 min, France, Barbet Schroeder) This fascinating documentary has director Schroeder and cinematographer Nestor Almendros traveling to laboratories at Stanford University to take a close look at Koko, a female gorilla that has been taught to talk through sign language. The film also probes the controversial techniques used by the scientists and captures the excitement of this rare breakthrough in communication. (English and French with English subtitles) ★★★ VHS: $29.99

Kolya

(1996, 111 min, Czechoslovakia, Jan Sverak) *Zdenek Sverak, Andrej Chalimon, Libuse Safrankova.* This Academy Award winner for Best Foreign-Language Film is a sweetly ren-

K

dered fable about a washed-up, middle-aged classical cellist and compulsive womanizer who's struggling to make ends meet in 1988 Prague. Having been booted off the state Philharmonia for having too many close relatives who've "immigrated" to the West, Frantisek Louka (Sverak) ekes out a living by playing funerals and touching up gravestones. Out of desperation, he agrees to a fake marriage to a Russian émigré for a substantial sum of money. Louka finds himself up a tree, however, when she splits town leaving him with her 5-year-old boy, Kolya (Chalimon), and a suspicious police inspector who seems determined to lock him up. Ultimately, the film avoids the maudlin trap and delivers a tender and subtly profound look at the latter days of Communism and Soviet occupation in the Czech Republic. (Czech with English subtitles) ★★★½

Komodo

(2000, 90 min, US, Michael Lantieri) *Jill Hennessy, Billy Burke, Kevin Zegers, Paul Gleeson.* Several komodo dragon eggs are chucked into a field on a remote island. By chance (as is in films like these), the island also houses a toxic chemical plant. Years later, mutant komodos kill a boy's parents (and, in the movie's one good scare, his cute dog). Emotionally scarred, his therapist takes him back to the island for confrontational therapy. *Komodo* is stupid, silly, cheesy, and a lot more entertaining than you might expect. The effects run the gamut from hideous to pretty damned convincing, though this is the epitome of formula filmmaking. A hoot if you're in the right frame of mind. ★★½ VHS: $102.99; DVD: $29.99

Korczak

(1990, 118 min, Poland, Andrzej Wajda) *Wojtec Pszoniak, Ewa Dalkowska.* Wajda returns to his roots with this haunting story of Janusz Korczak, a well-known Jewish doctor and poet who ran an orphanage for 200 children in the Warsaw ghetto. Realizing that his wards would surely be sent to the camps, he vowed to stay with them until the end, despite repeated efforts by members of Poland's intelligentsia to convince him to run to freedom. Stylistically the film resembles Wajda's 1950s classics *Ashes and Diamonds* and *Kanal*, including shadowy black-and-white camera work

by Robby Müller and the scratchy sound quality. Actor Pszoniak instills in Korczak an almost messianic quality, portraying him as a gentle but at times angry defender of righteousness and human dignity. (Polish with English subtitles) ★★★★ VHS: $79.99

Kostas

(1986, 88 min, Australia, Paul Cox) *Wendy Hughes, Takis Emmanuel.* A Greek immigrant taxi driver and a wealthy socialite fall in love. When pressure from friends and family threaten their relationship, they must decide whether to live by the rules or by their hearts. Hughes' passionate performance highlights this otherwise standard star-crossed romantic drama. ★★½ VHS: $69.99

Koyaanisqatsi

(1983, 90 min, US, Godfrey Reggio) A remarkable and riveting cinematic poem that astonishes the viewer with its aural and visual splendor. This nonconventional, non-narrative feature is a mesmerizing compilation of images; a study of awesome natural and man-made landscapes observed and presented in an invigorating fashion through the use of speeded-up, time-lapse and slow-motion photography. Few films have offered such a rich integration of sounds, ideas and images. Composer Philip Glass has provided a hypnotic score which serves as an amplification of the visuals' power. ★★★½

Kramer vs. Kramer

(1979, 104 min, US, Robert Benton) *Dustin Hoffman, Justin Henry, Meryl Streep, Jane Alexander, JoBeth Williams.* Hollywood takes a movie-of-the-week "topical" subject — Mom takes off to find herself and Dad is left with the kid — and with solid performances, beautiful cinematography and competent scripting and direction from Benton, transforms it into a compassionate study of urban life and family ties, not to mention a media sensation. Oscars for Best Picture, Best Direction, Best Actor, Best Supporting Actress and Best Screenplay. ★★★★ VHS: $9.99

The Krays

(1990, 119 min, GB, Peter Medak) *Gary Kemp, Martin Kemp, Billie Whitelaw.* A highly original

and haunting account of the true-life rise to power of two of England's most notorious thugs — the Kray twins. Under the loving care of their tough-as-nails mum (played with a down-to-earth forcefulness by Whitelaw), the brothers ride a wave of unthinkable violence and terror, becoming the most feared men in the ganglands of 1960s London. Filmed with an eerie and atmospheric sense of the surreal, director Medak's vision of the Krays' sadistic reign offers a fascinating psychological profile of these ruthless killers. Despite their differing sexual orientations, they are ultimately bound to each other and to their mother. ★★★½

Krippendorf's Tribe

(1998, 96 min, US, Todd Holland) *Richard Dreyfuss, Jenna Elfman, Lily Tomlin, Natasha Lyonne.* This insipid family comedy of anthropological fraud features Dreyfuss as the recently widowed and washed-up Professor James Krippendorf. To save his job and family, he claims to have discovered a lost tribe in New Guinea: the Shelmikedmu, whose culture includes among its many rituals circumcision, single fathers and neolithic dildoes. Smelling a hoax, Ruth Allen, Krippendorf's adversary (played by a sorely under-scripted Tomlin), demands film footage of the tribe. The resulting home movies are bizarre at best. *Krippendorf's Tribe* is a hackneyed offering fraught with cheap product placement and even cheaper phallic humor. Ask for it by name: Krippendorf's Tripe. ★★ VHS: $14.99

Kronos

(1957, 78 min, US, Kurt Neumann) *Jeff Morrow, Barbara Lawrence.* An alien arrives on Earth to steal her natural resources, and becomes larger and more destructive as it absorbs more and more energy. Any good? While it's understatement to say it was hampered by a modest production budget, it's not bad for its decade. ★★½; DVD: $24.99

Krush Groove

(1988, 97 min, US, Michael Schultz) *Blair Underwood, Joseph Simmons, Sheila E., Fat Boys.* Although saddled with a formula plot, this infectious hip-hop and rap musical still has a fresh, exciting feel mostly as a result of the spirited music of Sheila E., the Fat Boys and Kurtis Blow. The story centers around some ambitious but naïve renegades who want to set up their own record label dedicated to the sounds of the inner city, but who soon find themselves immersed in the loansharking and drug underworld. The Fat Boys are funny in their Three Stooges-like comedy relief. ★★½ VHS: $14.99

Kuffs

(1992, 102 min, US, Bruce A. Evans) *Christian Slater, Tony Goldwyn, Milla Jovovich.* Slater plays the brother of a San Francisco Police Patrol captain who inherits the security agency business after his sibling is murdered. Partnered with suspended cop Goldwyn, Slater takes on the killer and the slimy businessman he works for. The film is reminiscent of *Beverly Hills Cop*, especially in pacing, editing and musical score. And, like Eddie Murphy's hit, mixes action, suspense and lots of comedy; though not as successfully. ★★

Kundun

Kull the Conqueror

(1997, 96 min, US, John Nicolella) *Kevin Sorbo, Tia Carrere, Karina Lombard, Litefoot, Harvey Fierstein, Thomas Ian Griffith.* TV's "Hercules" Sorbo's straight-faced and sincere delivery is a pleasant surprise as the "man who would be king" of mythical Valusia — if he can break the curse of a 3,000-year-old sorceress (Carrere) with a plunging neckline and a taste for pyrotechnics. Nicolella's well-meaning but uneventful direction combines with unambitious special effects to make this a fun movie for anyone not expecting anything. ★★ VHS: $9.99; DVD: $24.99

Kundun

(1997, 132 min, US, Martin Scorsese) *Tenzin Thuthob Tsarong, Gyurme Tethong, Kunga Tenzin.* One of Scorsese's most impressive achievements, *Kundun* is a low-key yet impassioned historical epic telling the story of the 14th (and current) Dalai Lama, from his discovery as a toddler in a Tibetan village on the Chinese border to his escape from Chinese-occupied Tibet as a young man. *Kundun* is sumptuously shot by Roger Deakins, and has gorgeous production design and costumes (both by Dante Ferretti), but Scorsese wisely opts to take a simple approach for much of the film — with minimal editing and camera showmanship — resulting in an austere yet quietly powerful work. And true to the non-violent beliefs of its protagonists, *Kundun* contains almost no violence, instead allowing the repulsive nature of the Communists' atrocities against the Tibetan people to come across in the Dalai Lama's shocked reactions. As a story of one remarkable man — and, by extension, a remarkable people — the film succeeds admirably. A rich, spiritual film that will stay with you for a long time. (VHS available letterboxed or pan & scan) ★★★½ VHS: $19.99; DVD: $29.99

Kurt and Courtney

(1998, 95 min, US, Nick Broomfield) A surprisingly good documentary, considering its incendiary subject matter, *Kurt and Courtney* (which was banned from Sundance) is actually a rather even-sided investigation into the circumstances leading to rocker Kurt Cobain's death, focusing especially on his relationship with wife Courtney Love. Director Broomfield casts himself in the detective role, complete with voice-over, as he interviews family, ex-girlfriends and ex-boyfriends, nannies and old junkie mates of K & C. While most of these talks yield minimal valuable info, they're all fascinating insights into an array of oddball characters. ★★★ VHS: $14.99; DVD: $14.99

Kwaidan

(1964, 164 min, Japan, Masaki Kobayashi) *Michiyo Aratama, Rentaro Mikuni, Takashi Shimura.* This legendary Japanese film is a superb anthology of four terrifying tales of the supernatural. Filmed with exquisite visual sensitivity, this distinctive work of art is filled with dreamlike settings, elaborately stylized action and haunting sound effects. (Letterboxed) (Japanese with English subtitles) ★★★½ VHS: $29.99; DVD: $29.99

L.627

(1992, 145 min, France, Bertrand Tavernier) *Didier Bezace, Jean-Paul Comart, Cecile Garcia-Fogel.* A gritty, semidocumentary-like look at the day-to-day lives of undercover narcotic agents in a Paris most tourists will never see, *L.627* is a disturbing, overlong and possibly racist examination which despite its flaws still manages to be compelling. Capably directed by Tavernier, the film centers on a rogue cop named Lulu (Bezace), who has been transferred to an overworked precinct. Unlike American films of this sort, there are no shootouts, car chases or gratuitous violence. The story's power is accumulative in the relationship of the officers and Lulu's personal and professional life. However, it is difficult to determine if the film panders to racial stereotypes as all of the dealers tracked by Lulu and his associates are either black or Arab — which is defended by Tavernier as what he saw when accompanying real police officers on assignment. (Letterboxed) (French with English subtitles) ★★★ VHS: $24.99

L.A. Confidential

(1997, 137 min, US, Curtis Hanson) *Kevin Spacey, Russell Crowe, Guy Pearce, Kim Basinger, James Cromwell, Danny DeVito, David Strathairn.* An engrossing, rock-'em-sock-'em study of cops, corruption, racism and romance in 1950s Los Angeles, Hanson's marvelous adaptation of James Ellroy's densely written multicharacter novel is a thriller with blood, sweat and guts. The film follows three distinctly different cops on the LAPD: Crowe, a brooding, tough-as-nails veteran who lives by his own code of ethics; Spacey, a cop who moonlights as an advisor for a reality-based TV show; and Pearce, a determined college grad whose desire for honesty gets him in trouble with other members of the force. This trio of crime-stoppers are stirred into a batch of police brutality, Hollywood sleaze and political hoi-polloi after a group of people are massacred at a downtown eatery. Showcasing terrific period design, stylish but unobtrusive visuals and a crackerjack adaptation of difficult material, the film looks and sounds great. *L.A. Confidential* may not exactly be *Chinatown*, but it's most definitely in the same neighborhood. Even Jake Gittes would be impressed. (Letterboxed VHS available for $19.99) ★★★★ VHS: $14.99; DVD: $19.99

L.A. Story

(1991, 95 min, US, Mick Jackson) *Steve Martin, Victoria Tennant, Richard E. Grant, Marilu Henner, Sarah Jessica Parker, Kevin Pollak.* Martin wrote the screenplay for and stars in this fabulously entertaining and witty satire on life in Los Angeles' fast lane. Martin plays a wacked-out TV weatherman who loses his job, and begins affairs with two dissimilar women: Valley girl Parker (in a wonderfully comic turn) and British reporter Tennant. Martin's screenplay is full of on-target jabs, lively slapstick and metaphysical revelations (our favorite: the two very different lines at an

L.A. Confidential

Automatic Teller Machine). Martin's best work since *Roxanne*, and a pure delight. ★★★½ VHS: $9.99; DVD: $24.99

Labyrinth

(1986, 101 min, US, Jim Henson) *David Bowie, Jennifer Connelly, Toby Froud.* George Lucas combined his talents with the magical puppet artistry of Jim Henson to create this imaginative fantasy. A young girl (Connelly), searching for her kidnapped brother, is forced to weave her way through a treacherous maze where she encounters the deliciously maniacal elfin-like Bowie. This *Wizard of Oz*-like odyssey features adorable puppetry, catchy tunes, and a rather complex story line which only slightly detracts from its whimsical tone. ★★★ VHS: $14.99; DVD: $24.99

Labyrinth of Passion

(1982, 100 min, Spain, Pedro Almodóvar) *Antonio Banderas, Imanol Arias, Cecilia Roth.* Almodóvar's second feature film is a dazzling display of a great future talent in its rawest form. The story centers around both Riza Niro, the son of a deposed Middle Eastern tyrant who likes to hang around with Madrid's sleazier denizens, and Sexi, an aspiring rock singer and unabashed nymphomaniac. The two fall for each other and decide to run away, but first they must deal with their respective rock groups, a group of terrorists who are bent on kidnapping Riza, and a whole host of other outrageous plot twists. Bristling with loony humor, the film lacks the visual punch and flawless timing of his later works, but still it is a frantic, if somewhat uneven, portrait of Almodóvar's explosive potential. (Spanish with English subtitles) ★★½ VHS: $39.99

The Lacemaker

(1977, 108 min, France, Claude Goretta) *Isabelle Huppert, Yves Beneyton.* A very young Huppert stars as an inexperienced shopgirl who meets a bourgeois student on the deserted beaches of an off-season Normandy resort. They return to Paris where their romance strains under the weight of class and intellectual differences. Huppert is breathtakingly beautiful and gives a tender portrait of love. Lovingly filmed by Goretta. (Letterboxed) (French with English subtitles) ★★★½ VHS: $29.99

Ladies of the Chorus

(1949, 61 min, US, Phil Karlson) *Adele Jergens, Marilyn Monroe, Rand Brooks.* Though Marilyn gets star billing on the video box, she really has

The Lady Eve

a secondary role in this, her second film. MM is a burlesque dancer who's looking for a ticket out; and if a wealthy bachelor can help, so be it. Jergens plays her mother who has been there before and tries to help her daughter not make the same mistakes. Marilyn sings some songs, and looks great, but it's a minor vehicle nonetheless. ★★ VHS: $19.99

Lady and the Tramp

(1955, 75 min, US, Hamilton Luske) Beloved Disney classic rates as one of the studio's top animated features. Who can forget the spaghetti scene, which is more romantic than most modern "love stories." ★★★★ VHS: $26.99

Lady by Choice

(1934, 77 min, US, David Burton) *Carole Lombard, May Robson.* In a role quite similar to her brilliant success a year earlier in *Lady for a Day*, Robson encores as a cantankerous, scraggy old lady who gets the once-over. Lombard is a fan dancer looking to cool her image. So her press agent gets the idea to "adopt a mother," and guess who gets chosen. This is a bright, appealing comedy, and Lombard and Robson work extremely well together. ★★★ VHS: $19.99

Lady Chatterley's Lover

(1955, 102 min, France, Marc Allégret) *Danielle Darrieux, Erno Crisa.* Darrieux stars as the repressed Lady Chatterley who enjoys a sexual awakening and personal freedom when she meets a handsome, muscular workman in this fine French version of D.H. Lawrence's classic novel. Although when viewed today the film is quite tasteful, it caused a storm in the U.S. in the 1950s and was banned by the New York State Board of Censors. (French with English subtitles) ★★½

The Lady Eve

(1941, 93 min, US, Preston Sturges) *Barbara Stanwyck, Henry Fonda, Charles Coburn, William Demarest, Eugene Pallette.* Sturges, the most prolific and arguably the greatest comic filmmaker

of the 1940s, wrote and directed this hilarious screwball comedy, one of the director's finest achievements. Stanwyck, in a great comic performance, is a cardsharp who sets out to hook gullible millionaire Fonda. They fall in love, but when he gets wise she gets dumped, and Stanwyck devises a scheme to get him back — by impersonating royalty. Among a first-rate supporting cast, Pallette is very funny as Fonda's exasperated father. ★★★★ VHS: $14.99; DVD: $39.99

Lady for a Day

(1933, 96 min, US, Frank Capra) *May Robson, Warren William, Guy Kibbee, Glenda Farrell.* Capra's enchanting comedy based on Damon Runyon's story "Madame La Gimp," about a group of Broadway denizens who come together to help an old apple seller. Character actress Robson has her greatest screen role as "Annie," and she makes the most of it. Capra's deft touch helps immeasurably in the film's enjoyment. Capra remade the story in 1961 as *A Pocketful of Miracles.* ★★★½ VHS: $14.99

The Lady from Shanghai

(1948, 87 min, US, Orson Welles) *Orson Welles, Rita Hayworth, Everett Sloane.* Hayworth is the scorching femme fatale with a heavenly body and a devilish mind in this fascinating murder mystery. Welles himself plays her prime victim who, with a skull as thick as his Irish brogue, steps right into her trap. ★★★ VHS: $19.99; DVD: $24.99

Lady in a Cage

(1964, 93 min, US, Walter Grauman) *Olivia de Havilland, James Caan, Jeff Corey, Ann Sothern, Scatman Crothers.* Caan's first starring role. He plays the sadistic leader of a vicious gang of thieves who trap de Havilland in her own home. This fast-paced, lurid melodrama really delivers in the finale. ★★½ VHS: $49.99

Lady in Cement

(1968, 93 min, US, Gordon Douglas) *Frank Sinatra, Raquel Welch, Dan Blocker.* Sinatra is back in this sequel to *Tony Rome* as the titular detective, investigating the death of a nude woman who went swimming wearing only cement overshoes. Sinatra could play this role in his sleep — which he looks like he's doing throughout. Few thrills punctuate this standard mystery. ★★ VHS: $59.99

The Lady in the Lake

(1946, 104 min, US, Robert Montgomery) *Robert Montgomery, Audrey Trotter, Lloyd Nolan, Jayne Meadows.* Montgomery stars as private dick Phillip Marlowe searching for a missing wife and discovering a different woman's corpse floating in a mountain lake. Montgomery, who also directed, uses first person camera angles

from Marlowe's point of view. Complete with Raymond Chandler's standards of gritty dialogue between troublesome cops and L.A. lowlifes. ★★★ VHS: $19.99

Lady in White

(1988, 112 min, US, Frank LaLoggia) *Lukas Haas, Alex Rocco, Len Cariou, Katherine Helmond.* A real find. Young Haas gets locked in school overnight and uncovers — with the help of a young girl's spirit — the mystery of the legendary "Lady in White"; not to mention the identity of the girl's murderer. An extremely accomplished ghost story, with a great visual style. Though some may guess who the killer is before the denouement, it detracts nothing from the suspense and total enjoyment of this first-rate sleeper. ★★★½; DVD: $29.99

The Lady Is Willing

(1942, 92 min, US, Mitchell Leisen) *Marlene Dietrich, Fred MacMurray, Aline MacMahon.* Pleasant comedy-drama with Dietrich as a stage siren who marries baby doc MacMurray just so she can adopt a tot. The film's breezy pacing is brought to a halt near the end with a heavy-handed tragic turn of events. ★★★ VHS: $19.99

Lady Jane

(1985, 117 min, GB, Trevor Nunn) *Helena Bonham Carter, Cary Elwes, Sara Kestelman, Michael Hordern, Joss Ackland, Patrick Stewart.* Overlooked in its initial release, this elegant and absorbing romance is about the real-life adolescent aristocrat Lady Jane, who ascended to the British throne for a brief and tragic nine days. A bittersweet historical drama. ★★★ VHS: $14.99

Lady of Burlesque

(1943, 91 min, US, William Wellman) *Barbara Stanwyck, Michael O'Shea, Pinky Lee.* Stanwyck brings plenty of pizzazz to this sassy and enjoyable comic mystery based on Gypsy Rose Lee's "The G-String Murders." Stanwyck plays a burlesque dancer who sets out to solve who's killing her fellow strippers. ★★★ VHS: $14.99

Lady on the Bus

(1978, 102 min, Brazil, Neville D'Almeida) *Sonia Braga.* In this spicy romp, Sonia plays a frigid young married woman who can't seem to make it with her new husband. Seeking a cure, our heroine seeks the sexual help of her husband's male friends and even strangers in her determined efforts to loosen up. Why not? A charming and entertaining diversion. ★★½

Lady Sings the Blues

(1972, 144 min, US, Sidney J. Furie) *Diana Ross, Billy Dee Williams, Richard Pryor, James Callahan.* Ross makes a sensational film debut as the legendary blues singer Billie Holiday. The film has all the dramatic trappings of a standard Hollywood biography; Ross, however, is in great voice. Pryor is a standout as Ross' piano player. ★★★ VHS: $29.99

The Lady Vanishes

(1938, 97 min, GB, Alfred Hitchcock) *Michael Redgrave, Margaret Lockwood, Dame Mae Whitty, Paul Lukas.* The quintessential train murder mystery with Redgrave and Lockwood as a pair of travelers who undertake a search for a missing passenger — a diminutive old woman who holds secrects of international espionage. Upon vanishing, only a name on a window and a haunting melody serve as proof of her existence. (Remade in 1979) ★★★★ VHS: $24.99; DVD: $39.99

The Lady with the Dog

(1960, 89 min, USSR, Josef Heifitz) *Iya Savvina, Alexei Batalov.* Thought to be one of the few films to capture the essence of Anton Chekov, this much admired romantic yet bittersweet love story is set in turn-of-the-century Russia. While vacationing at a resort in Yalta, a married, middle-aged banker meets a beautiful but sad young woman who, having left her husband behind in the city, has come on holiday accompanied only by her little dog. Attracted to one another, they begin an affair and eventually fall in love. Resolving to continue their affair after the holiday, they meet for years clandestinely in Moscow, but knowing full well that their love and relationship is doomed. (Russian with English subtitles) ★★★ VHS: $29.99

Ladybird, Ladybird

(1994, 102 min, GB, Ken Loach) *Crissy Rock, Vladimir Vega, Ray Winstone, Sandie Lavelle.* Director Loach once again turns a quasi-documentary lens on the British underclass in this disarming, well-wrought drama based on a true story. Rock is unerringly authentic as a young mother who loses several children to state care — a woman whose pick of men mirrors her abusive childhood and whose love of her children is outstripped by bad choices, circumstances and a social welfare system which loses the human element in a sea of categorization. A cycle of childbirth, beatings and stays in women's refuges is broken by a chance encounter with a Paraguayan political refugee (portrayed with quiet passion by Vega), a victim of an even more repressive state. Rock is shattering in a performance notable for a lack of melodrama or saccharine sentiment, straightforwardly depicting a life often lived out of bags and suitcases. ★★★½

Ladybugs

(1992, 89 min, US, Sidney J. Furie) *Rodney Dangerfield, Jackée, Jonathan Brandis, Ilene Graff.*

The Ladykillers

Mr. No Respect finds himself as the coach of a girls' soccer team in this distant cousin of *The Bad News Bears*, where all the stereotypes and clichés are firmly in place. This often silly though somewhat entertaining and moralizing film showcases a kinder, gentler Rodney, but there are some naughty words, risqué innuendos and a dream sequence that borders on tastelessness. ★★ VHS: $14.99

Ladyhawke

(1985, 121 min, US, Richard Donner) *Rutger Hauer, Matthew Broderick, Michelle Pfeiffer, John Wood, Leo McKern, Alfred Molina.* An entertaining medieval fantasy which combines adventure, romance and magic to produce an exciting story. Hauer stars as a knight deeply in love with a beautiful maiden (Pfeiffer), but the two are cursed by an evil bishop with a terrible spell. The lovers are eternally separated — for in the day, the young woman is turned into a hawk and in the night, when she is transformed back into human form, he is changed into a wolf. It takes a young pickpocket (a delightfully funny Broderick) to assist them in breaking the curse. ★★★ VHS: $9.99; DVD: $14.99

The Ladykillers

(1955, 90 min, GB, Alexander MacKendrick) *Alec Guinness, Katie Johnson, Peter Sellers, Herbert Lom, Cecil Parker, Danny Green.* Another mordant comedy classic from the Ealing Studios with Guinness leading a group of maladroit thieves whose plans are undone by a sweetly obtuse little old lady (superbly portrayed by Johnson). The other members of this bumbling gang of hoods are played by an impressive and well-seasoned cast. ★★★★

The Lair of the White Worm

(1988, 94 min, GB, Ken Russell) *Amanda Donohoe, Hugh Grant, Peter Capaldi, Sammi Davis, Catherine Oxenberg.* Russell's intoxicating adaptation of Bram Stoker's final work is a tongue-in-cheek romp into the world of Gothic horror. Donohoe offers up a truly kinky performance as a mysterious snake lady who slithers her way into modern England in search of virgins to feed to her giant worm god. Russell's flair isn't lost as this slimy tale of rampant vampirism oozes with an abundance of camp humor, serpentine symbolism, and just about every daft snake joke in the book — oh, and let's not forget those requisite Russellian hallucinations. ★★★½ VHS: $9.99; DVD: $29.99

Lake Placid

(1999, 82 min, US, Steve Miner) *Bill Pullman, Bridget Fonda, Oliver Platt, Brendan Gleeson, Betty White.* TV's golden boy David E. Kelley ("Ally McBeal," "The Practice") wrote the screenplay for this tired horror send-up. Judging by this, he'd better stick to the small screen. A giant crocodile is terrorizing a peaceful lakeside community in Maine. Pullman is the fish-and-game warden, Fonda is the scientist, Gleeson the glib sheriff, and Platt the eccentric croc expert all investigating a series of deaths. The characters spend the entire film yelling at each other, in between the unfunny barbs. Kelley's story is neither scary nor funny, only head-scratchingly mediocre. Though the giant croc is kinda fun, the only truly scary thing in the movie is Betty White's vocabulary. ★½ VHS: $14.99; DVD: $22.99

Amanda Donohoe in *The Lair of the White Worm*

Lakki: The Boy Who Grew Wings

(1992, 104 min, Norway, Svend Wam) Wam's film about a troubled youth's struggle towards spiritual ascent is about as obvious as the mysterious wings that grow on young Lakki's back. Yes, the film actually depicts scenes of sprouting feathers and dreams of flight as Lakki tries to come to grips with his parents' separation, his father's new fiancée, his mother's flagrant sexual behavior, and perhaps his own sexual orientation. The symbolism is so heavy-handed that it almost becomes insulting, but the cinematography itself merits the film a look. (Norwegian with English subtitles) ★★ VHS: $59.99

Lamerica

(1995, 116 min, Italy, Gianni Amelio) *Enrico Lo Verso, Michele Placido, Carmelo Di Mazzarelli.* Amelio's nightmare vision of post-Communist Albania should serve as a shocking wakeup call to the European community about a festering wound in their backyard. Italians especially should be jarred from political inaction as theirs are the shores receiving the flood of refugees from Albania's chaos. Gino (Lo Verso) and Fiorre (Placido) are a pair of carpetbagging Italians who are poised to set up a phoney corporation in Albania, presumably as a front to launder lire. But first they must find an Albanian lackey to pose as their CEO. They pluck a withered old man, Spiro (Di Mazzarelli), from a hellish labor camp and name him their chairman. But disaster strikes when Spiro disappears forcing Gino to search for the old codger in the perilous anarchy of the Albanian countryside — and the picture Amelio paints of this ravaged landscape is inconceivably bleak. Visually arresting tale of moral conflict and the journey that leads to atonement. (Italian with English subtitles) ★★★½ VHS: $29.99

Lancelot of the Lake

(1974, 80 min, France, Robert Bresson) *Luc Simon, Laura Duke Condominas, Humbert Balsan, Vladimir Antolek-Oresek.* Hailed in its day as a magnificent cinematic achievement, this austere examination of the end of chivalry and the dissolution of King Arthur's Court is more a curious relic from a bygone cinematic era. Stark and somber in atmosphere, the film follows Lancelot as he returns empty-handed from his quest for the Holy Grail filled with foreboding that his failure is linked to his illicit love for Queen Guinevere. Bresson's approach is stylistically minimal to the extreme as the film features barren dialogue and severely restrained performances which, though seemingly wooden, disguise a bristling subtext. It's of a style that was all the rage in the art-houses of the era, but the success of its translation to the present-day small screen is less than certain. (French with English subtitles) ★★½ VHS: $29.99

Land and Freedom

(1995, 109 min, GB, Ken Loach) *Ian Hart, Rosana Pastor, Iciar Bollain.* Loach offers a powerful and heartrending look at the Spanish Civil War as seen through the eyes of an earnest young Liverpudlian. Through flashback, the story focuses on his involvement as a youth in the volunteer brigades in Spain. Young David (portrayed with engaging sincerity by Hart) begins his journey as an ardent unionist and card carrying member of the Communist Party. Upon his arrival in Spain, he is swept up into the POUM movement, a rather freely organized and highly egalitarian sector of the Resistance, and graduates to a front-line "militia" where he and his group make occasional incursions into Francoista territory and liberate villages. Ever the left-wing agitator, Loach once again has created a brilliant blend of personal history and political treatise that is riveting and intellectually fascinating. ★★★★ VHS: $9.99

The Land Before Time

(1988, 66 min, US, Don Bluth) This rather short but charming animated feature should entertain younger children with its story of a baby dinosaur, Littlefoot, who becomes separated from his parents. Like the director's previous animated film, *An American Tail*, the story centers on the little lost hero's search for home. The animation, though less than superlative, is fine for the film's simplistic story and the plotline should be easy for young ones to follow. (Followed by 6 sequels) ★★★ VHS: $19.99; DVD: $24.99

The Land Girls

(1998, 110 min, GB, David Leland) *Catherine McCormack, Rachel Weisz, Anna Friel, Steven Mackintosh.* A good old-fashioned British wartime drama, *The Land Girls* may be unremarkable, but that is precisely what makes it special. Three women, Stella (McCormack), Ag (Weisz) and Pru (Friel), do their bit for the war effort by working as farmhands. Their trials and tribulations include all of the genre staples of heroism and heartbreak as they bond together through hard work and romance. Written and directed with a sure hand by Leland (he adapted Angela Huth's novel), *The Land Girls* could have been corny and sentimental, but its earnestness sees it through. The striking performances by the attractive leads, the gorgeous cinematography, and fine period detail also lend the film class. ★★★ VHS: $14.99

The Land of Faraway

(1988, 95 min, Norway/Sweden, Vladimir Grammatikov) *Timothy Bottoms, Susannah York, Christopher Lee, Christian Bale.* A young boy in Stockholm is whisked away by a friendly spirit to meet the father he has never known — the King of the Land of Faraway. Soon, the boy is embroiled in a desperate bid to save the children of Faraway from an evil knight who has kidnapped them. ★★½

The Langoliers

(1995, 150 min, US, Tom Holland) *Dean Stockwell, David Morse, Bronson Pinchot.* There's an unusually effective eeriness to the opening of *The Langoliers*, a made-for-TV adaptation of Stephen King's story. A select group of passengers on a red-eye from Los Angeles to Boston awaken midflight to discover their fellow passengers and the crew have literally disappeared into thin air. What follows is a silly, lethargic story of parallel universes and cartoon monsters from the subconscious out to eat everything in sight. ★★ VHS: $19.99; DVD: $19.99

Larger Than Life

(1996, 93 min, US, Howard Franklin) *Bill Murray, Janeane Garofalo, Matthew McConaughey, Linda Fiorentino, Jeremy Piven, Lois Smith.* Murray inherits an elephant from the father he never knew, then must decide whether to sell her to Fiorentino's sexy but unscrupulous animal talent agent or allow sensible zoologist Garofalo to take her to Sri Lanka to be in her natural habitat. Have no idea what'll happen? Then you must see *Larger Than Life*. Otherwise, there isn't much to recommend, except goopy sentimentality. You can't help wonder: What were the makers (and especially Murray) thinking? ★★ VHS: $9.99

Larks on a String

(1968, 96 min, Czechoslovakia, Jiri Menzel) *Vera Kresadlova, Vaclav Neckar.* From the director of *Closely Watched Trains* comes this surprisingly timely, playfully subversive allegory on the crumbling of the Communist State. Made in 1968 immediately after the Soviet invasion of Hungary, the film was promptly banned and not made available until 23 years later. Set in an almost surreal scrap heap, the story follows the work, thoughts and loves of a group of prisoners — professors, musicians, union organizers and Jews — who are caught in the crackdown, believed to pose a "threat to the state." Although thoroughly political, the satire retains a light, almost joyful stance, taking particular delight in the love interest between two prisoners — a simple boy and a pretty young woman.

(Czechoslovakian with English subtitles) ★★★½ VHS: $19.99

Las Vegas Hillbillys

(1966, 90 min, US, Arthur C. Pierce) *Jayne Mansfield, Mamie Van Doren.* Mansfield and Van Doren need plenty of support in this story about a busted Las Vegas bar invigorated when it is inherited by a hayseed who starts booking it with country acts. Musical performances by Bill Anderson, Sonny James and Del Reeves. ★ DVD: $19.99

Laserman

(1990, 92 min, US, Peter Wang) *Marc Hayashi, Peter Wang, Tony Leung, Sally Yeh.* Intelligent, eccentric multicultural comedy-thriller about a Chinese-American scientist who accidentally kills his lab assistant in an experiment, resulting in the loss of his job. His "grifting" brother-in-law convinces him to sell his new laser device to some "business associates" — actually hit men for a terrorist organization. All the while, police inspector Lu is on their trail as the hero reluctantly enters the black market of high-tech weapons, mistaken identities, telepathic orgasms, and more! ★★★ VHS: $19.99

Lassiter

(1984, 100 min, US, Roger Young) *Tom Selleck, Bob Hoskins, Lauren Hutton, Jane Seymour.* Selleck tries his hand at *Bondage* in this slick if derivative spy thriller about a notorious 1930s cat burglar pressed into service by the British government to steal a cache of diamonds from the Nazis. The usual thrills and chills abound. ★★½

Last Action Hero

(1993, 130 min, US, John McTiernan) *Arnold Schwarzenegger, Mercedes Ruehl, Art Carney, Anthony Quinn, Charles Dance, F. Murray Abraham, Joan Plowright, Ian McKellen, Robert Prosky.* Schwarzenegger finally bombed with this disappointing action-parody, sort of a *Purple Rose of Cairo* meets *Lethal Weapon.* A 12-year-old kid is magically transported by a magical movie ticket into the celluloid world of his favorite film hero, Jack Slater. The trouble really starts, however, when they both emerge in the real world on this side of the screen. The film is an endless barrage of gags referring to

Kate Beckinsale (l.) and Chloë Sevigny in *The Last Days of Disco*

L

the insipidness of many Hollywood actioners: hundreds of smashing cars; tons of insufficient backup officers; Arnold Schwarzenegger. Suffering from lackluster direction, *Last Action Hero* is a good joke with a really awful punchline. ★★ VHS: $12.99; DVD: $29.99

The Last American Hero

(1973, 100 min, US, Lamont Johnson) *Jeff Bridges, Valerie Perrine, Gary Busey, Geraldine Fitzgerald.* Bridges gives a commanding performance as stock car champion Junior Jackson in this vibrant racing drama based on a series of articles by Tom Wolfe. The story follows backwoods moonshiner Jackson from his running whiskey to his determined bid for the championship on the independent circuit. Bridges brings to mind a young Paul Newman with an icy cool portrayal of swaggering confidence. On par with another splendid racing feature, *Heart Like a Wheel.* ★★★½ VHS: $59.99

The Last Boy Scout

(1991, 105 min, US, Tony Scott) *Bruce Willis, Damon Wayans, Halle Berry.* Here's another live-action cartoon from the *Lethal Weapon/Die Hard* factory. Willis is a Secret Service agent turned private investigator who teams up with a burned-out former football star (Wayans). Together they take on a gang of well-dressed bad guys conspiring to. . .do you really need to know? This mishmash of implausibility and macho posturing does feature some slam-bang action sequences. Easily offended law enforcement officers, African-Americans, athletes, homosexuals, pacifists, women and others may need to take this one with a grain or two of salt. ★★ VHS: $9.99; DVD: $19.99

The Last Butterfly

(1993, 106 min, Czechoslovakia/GB, Karel Kachyna) *Tom Courtenay, Brigitte Fossey, Freddie Jones.* In a sincere and moving performance, Courtenay plays a renowned Parisian mime artist who is coerced by the Nazis to perform at Terezin, Czechoslovakia, or "city of the Jews" — a propaganda community established by the Germans. A virtual prisoner himself, the apolitical performer soon discovers the truth about the town (it's a midway point for the camps). Unable to communicate with the visiting Red Cross, he tries to alert them the best way he knows how: through his art. These final scenes, a harrowing, updated adaptation of "Hansel and Gretel," are mesmerizing and give the film its emotional power. (In English) ★★★ VHS: $19.99

Last Call at Maud's

(1993, 75 min, US, Paris Poirier) The 1989 closing of Maud's Study, a lesbian bar and institution in San Francisco since 1966, propelled filmmaker Poirier to explore the 23-year life of the bar and its patrons as well as offer a fascinating minihistory of recent (post-WWII) lesbian life and the role that lesbian bars played in it. Many longtime patrons of Maud's offer a lively and informative account of lesbian life from the 1940s to the present, with stories of the many raids and police harassment of "queer" bars. An engaging and informative documentary which provides an essential chapter in the social and political history of lesbians. ★★★ VHS: $29.99

The Last Days

(1998, 87 min, US, James Moll) A wrenching documentary, executive produced by Steven Spielberg, this is a must. Director Moll juxtaposes archival footage with interviews with five survivors of Hitler's Final Solution in Hungary, at a time when Germany knew they would lose WWII, but refused to lose the war on the Jews. The five people chosen each have fascinating remembrances, and their separate stories complement each other well for a full portrait of this time and place. Difficult to watch at times, to be sure, but incredibly moving and powerful as well. You won't soon forget these tough survivors revisiting their hometowns and even the death camps for the first time since the war, or many of their incredible observations. This is well-deserving of 1998's Oscar for Best Documentary. ★★★★ VHS: $14.99; DVD: $19.99

The Last Days of Chez Nous

(1992, 96 min, Australia, Gillian Armstrong) *Lisa Harrow, Bruno Ganz, Miranda Otto, Kerry Fox.* A charming character study of a dysfunctional Sydney family. Beth (Harrow) is an underpaid novelist and the unofficial matron of Chez Nous, a household comprised of her, her French husband J.P. (Ganz) and her teenage daughter, Anna (Otto). Into the soup comes her carefree sister and a gawky young male boarder. What follows is a fundamentally plotless, but nevertheless engaging and entertaining examination of the ways that people fail to communicate in spite of their desire for human contact — hmmm, could be a Wim Wenders film. ★★★ VHS: $19.99

The Last Days of Disco

(1998, 114 min, US, Whit Stillman) *Chloë Sevigny, Kate Beckinsale, Chris Eigeman, Matt Keeslar, Mackenzie Astin, Robert Sean Leonard, Jennifer Beals.* Though *The Last Days of Disco* has the same feel and explores themes found in director Stillman's first two films *Metropolitan* and *Barcelona*, there's still a lot to like about this look at the thoughts and loves of a group of friends during the last days of the disco era. Using the waning days of the dance craze as a backdrop to more worldly discussions, Stillman has once again assembled a good-looking, articulate and successful group who here work all day to party all night. As would be expected, Stillman is much more interested in the thoughts and deeds of his characters rather than a more narrative-driven story line. And he's written some remarkable and funny observations about love, relationships, career and, of course, disco. But he's got to move on or he'll become a relic of his time — does K.C. and the Sunshine Band ring a bell? ★★★ VHS: $14.99; DVD: $29.99

The Last Detail

(1973, 105 min, US, Hal Ashby) *Jack Nicholson, Otis Young, Randy Quaid, Michael Moriarty, Carol Kane, Nancy Allen.* Nicholson received an Academy Award nomination for his portrayal of "Bad Ass" Buddusky, one of two "lifer" sailors who are given the detail of escorting a young recruit convicted of stealing to Portsmouth Naval Prison. Ashby's direction and Michael Chapman's cinematography give this film a gritty look that complements its cynical, uncom-

promising atmosphere. One of Nicholson's most fully realized characterizations. ★★★½ VHS: $9.99; DVD: $24.99

Last Embrace

(1979, 102 min, US, Jonathan Demme) *Roy Scheider, Christopher Walken, Janet Margolin, John Glover.* Engaging thriller à la Hitchcock about a CIA agent (Scheider) who, believing himself to be a target for assassination after his wife is murdered, finds himself entrapped in the mystery of his own identity. To say more would give the show away. The climax is a shocker. ★★★ VHS: $14.99

The Last Emperor

(1987, 218 min, US/Italy, Bernardo Bertolucci) *John Lone, Joan Chen, Peter O'Toole.* Winner of nine Academy Awards, this sweeping historical epic chronicles the turbulent life and times of China's last emperor, Pu Yi. Lone is mesmerizing as the weak-willed monarch, a man ascended to the Dragon Throne at the age of three, only to abdicate at six and then coerced to spend his early life within the opulent walls of China's Forbidden City. His story — from "Lord of 10,000 years" to playboy, prisoner, political puppet and finally common gardener — is told by Bertolucci in the grandest of cinematic traditions. An enthralling and extravagant story of one rather simple man engulfed by the events of his times. (Filmed in English) (Director's cut) (Letterboxed) (Pan & scan non-director's cut available for $14.99) ★★★★ VHS: $24.99; DVD: $24.99

Last Exit to Brooklyn

(1990, 103 min, Germany/US, Uli Edel) *Jennifer Jason Leigh, Stephen Lang, Alexis Arquette, Burt Young, Ricki Lake, Jerry Orbach, Stephen Baldwin.* This German production of Hubert Selby, Jr.'s 1957 underground classic is a hard-hitting, no-holds-barred look at life in hell along the docks of Brooklyn in the early '50s. This isn't just Ozzie and Harriet in reverse; it's an all-out indictment of the American experience as seen through the eyes of Brooklyn's lower depths. It's not pretty — it is, however, a gripping and undeniably overwhelming drama. Lang is excellent as a bewildered union leader who is painfully forced to come to grips with his repressed homosexuality. Leigh is dazzling as the teenage hooker Tralala who enforces her womanhood at the end of the film in one of the most disturbing scenes ever filmed. (Filmed in English) ★★★½

The Last Five Days

(1982, 112 min, West Germany, Percy Adlon) *Lena Stoltz, Irm Hermann.* Belying his trademark playful touch, Adlon goes for much weightier subject matter in telling the shattering true story of a young girl and her brother who were executed by the Nazis for distributing anti-fascist propaganda. Stoltze plays Sophie Scholl, the woman compelled to almost suicidal political action against the Nazis in 1943 in this restrained, precise film of crushing emotional impact. (German with English subtitles) ★★★ VHS: $79.99

Last House on the Left

(1972, 91 min, US, Wes Craven) *David Hess, Lucy Grantham, Sandra Cassel, Marc Scheffler.* Two young women are abducted and brutalized by some buffoonish escaped convicts in this economic but severely dated horror outing which launched the careers of both Craven and Sean S. Cunningham (*Friday the 13th*). Whether or not this appeals to you depends on your tolerance for corny humor and amateurish acting. ★ VHS: $9.99

The Last Hurrah

(1958, 121 min, US, John Ford) *Spencer Tracy, Jeffrey Hunter, Basil Rathbone, Pat O'Brien, James Gleason, Donald Crisp.* Tracy gives an outstanding performance in this absorbing and stellar version of Edwin O'Connor's novel about the last days of a political boss. Great supporting cast. ★★★½ VHS: $19.99; DVD: $27.99

Last Hurrah for Chivalry

(1978, 108 min, Hong Kong, John Woo) *Damian Lau, Wei Pai.* Just before he reinvented the gangster movie with *A Better Tomorrow*, writer-director Woo bid farewell to the "heroic swordplay" movies with which he began his career with this fun, well-written story of two killers-for-hire. Lau and Pai are master swordsmen who have no allegiances and adhere strictly to the code of their personal art. When they both decide to help out a wealthy local who is seeking revenge against an evil kung fu master, they discover that few hold honor, duty and friendship in the same high esteem. The film features some exciting, traditional swordfights interspersed with its themes of male bonding and righteous sacrifice. (Letterboxed) (Cantonese with English subtitles) ★★★ VHS: $19.99; DVD: $29.99

The Last Klezmer

(1994, 84 min, US/Poland, Yale Strom) Leopold Kozlowski, a teacher of music and klezmer musician, returns home for the first time in fifty years to his home town in Poland. This intimate portrait and homecoming documentary is poignant in its sincerity and insightful in director Strom's focus on Kozlowski's passion of teaching the art of klezmer to opera and piano students. Absence of klezmer music — which has been called "Jewish jazz" — is apparent in the stark landscape of post-WWII and post-Communist Poland, and it is this vacancy which serves to underscore the messages of both Kozlowski and the filmmaker. (In English and Polish, Yiddish & Russian with English subtitles) ★★★ VHS: $29.99

The Last Laugh

(1924, 73 min, Germany, F.W. Murnau) *Emil Jannings, Maly Delshaft.* One of the classics from Germany's "Golden Era," *The Last Laugh* features the great Jannings as a proud doorman of a luxury hotel who is demoted to washroom attendant. Once envied and respected by his neighbors, the baffled old man sees his world and status crumble; but in a surprising ending, he still gets the last laugh. (Silent) ★★★★ VHS: $24.99; DVD: $29.99

Last Man Standing

(1996, 100 min, US, Walter Hill) *Bruce Willis, Christopher Walken, Bruce Dern, Alexandra Powers, William Sanderson.* Combining the gangster and western genres and using a ghost town during the rough-and-tumble 1930s as its setting, *Last Man Standing* is a particularly stylish reworking of *Yojimbo* whose narrative isn't quite as accom-

plished as its visuals. As the perennial Man-with-No-Name, Willis is a mysterious drifter who arrives in a near-deserted Texas town and immediately gets caught between two feuding mob factions. The golden-hued cinematography nicely captures the dusty landscape, and the gunfight sequences are well staged. But the drama nestled in-between the fights and shootouts is slowly paced. (VHS available letterboxed or pan & scan) ★★½ VHS: $9.99; DVD: $19.99

The Last Metro

(1980, 135 min, France, François Truffaut) *Catherine Deneuve, Gérard Depardieu, Jean-Louis Richard.* Truffaut's poignant account of Parisian theatre under the Nazi thumb stars Deneuve and Depardieu as members of an acting troupe struggling through the Occupation. Heinz Bennett plays Deneuve's husband and stage director, forced underground because of his Jewish heritage. (French with English subtitles) ★★★ VHS: $29.99; DVD: $29.99

The Last Movie

(1971, 110 min, US, Dennis Hopper) *Peter Fonda, Michelle Phillips, Dean Stockwell, Sam Fuller.* After his phenomenal success with *Easy Rider*, the powers-that-be in Hollywood believed that they had found the voice of the young, restless America in Hopper. Universal Pictures bankrolled the neophyte director's next project and gave him carte blanche to produce his next "blockbuster." The result, however, was an "artsy," possibly drug-induced and complicated (some said incomprehensible) mess. The film revolves around the happenings of an American movie crew filming a western in a small Peruvian village. ★★

Last Night

(1999, 95 min, Canada, Don McKellar) *Don McKellar, Sandra Oh, David Cronenberg, Tracy Wright, Genevieve Bujold, Roberta Maxwell, Sarah Polley, Callum Keith Rennie.* It's evening in Toronto, and the world will be ending at midnight. No explanation is given, but the news stations keep mentioning it, so it's apparently sunk in for the residents. How do the various citizens react when faced with their own premature mortality? This is the intriguing premise behind writer-director McKellar's *Last Night*, which goes beyond the usual apocalyptic drama to satirize our worker-colony cities and provide a darkly uplifting portrait of what some people are capable of when they let their emotions free. The poignancy comes when least expected, for the audience and for the characters alike, in this restrained, deeply satisfying portrait of intellectual armageddon. ★★★½ VHS: $19.99; DVD: $24.99

The Last of England

(1988, 87 min, GB, Derek Jarman) Uncompromising in its vision, *The Last of England* is a beautifully photographed fragmented poem structured within a series of cross-cutting vignettes. Filled with homoerotic images, the film deals with the destruction of our physical and emotional world by the ravages of Thatcherism and the callousness of Man. Accompanied by Nigel Terry's baleful narration, the visuals include shots of Jarman, male prostitutes and scenes of urban squalor and decay. It's

a baffling but interesting work, reminiscent of Jean Cocteau. ★★★ VHS: $29.99

The Last of Mrs. Cheyney

(1937, 98 min, US, Richard Boleslawski) *Joan Crawford, William Powell, Robert Montgomery.* Crawford had one of her biggest hits of the 1930s with this fairly entertaining remake of the 1929 Norma Shearer success. Crawford is in her element as an American jewel thief working her way through the cream of British high society. What she finds besides stolen gems is love. ★★½ VHS: $19.99

The Last of Sheila

(1973, 120 min, US, Herbert Ross) *James Coburn, James Mason, Dyan Cannon, Richard Benjamin, Joan Hackett, Raquel Welch, Ian McShane.* Entertainingly puzzling to the very end, this star-studded murder-mystery features Coburn as a game-obsessed film producer who invites six of his Hollywood jet-set "friends" on a cruise in the Mediterranean where a mean-spirited game, begun by him and designed to expose a dark secret of each member, backfires. Twists and turns abound in this plexus story written by real-life puzzle freaks Anthony Perkins and Stephen Sondheim. ★★★ VHS: $14.99

The Last of the Finest

(1990, 97 min, US, John MacKenzie) *Brian Dennehy, Joe Pantoliano, Bill Paxton, Jeff Fahey.* Though its title may be a little too self-congratulatory, this is a surprisingly effective and taut police adventure. Dennehy stars as the leader of a special police unit who accidentally stumbles upon a drug operation with ties to high-ranking officials. Taken off the case when they get too close, Dennehy and his partners continue the unwanted investigation after one of their own is killed. ★★★ VHS: $14.99

The Last of the Mohicans

(1992, 112 min, US, Michael Mann) *Daniel Day-Lewis, Madeleine Stowe, Jodhi May, Russell Means, Wes Studi, Colm Meaney.* James Fenimore Cooper's novel of Colonial America makes for an efficient, exciting romantic adventure. Day-Lewis is cast as Indian scout Hawkeye, and he so immerses himself in the part it's easy to forget he's not really an American. It's Day-Lewis' determined portrayal, well-staged action sequences, astonishing camerawork and a splendid re-creation of pre-Revolutionary times which make *Mohicans* the lump-in-your-throat adventure that it is. And it's bloody romantic, too. Stowe plays a British major's daughter, whom Hawkeye escorts through the wilderness and eventually falls in love with. Especially good in support is May as Stowe's younger and ultimately brave sister. (Letterboxed VHS available for $19.99) ★★★½ VHS: $14.99; DVD: $29.99

Last of the Red Hot Lovers

(1972, 98 min, US, Gene Saks) *Alan Arkin, Sally Kellerman, Paula Prentiss, Renee Taylor.* Minor screen adaptation of Neil Simon's play with Arkin as a restaurant owner desperately trying for an extramarital affair. ★★ VHS: $14.99

The Last Picture Show

(1971, 118 min, US, Peter Bogdanovich) *Jeff Bridges, Joseph Bottoms, Cybill Shepherd, Cloris Leachman, Ben Johnson, Eileen Brennan, Randy Quaid.* Bogdanovich's brilliant adaptation of

L

Larry McMurtry's novel is regarded as one of the definitive coming-of-age sagas: not only in its depiction of the "end of innocence" for its characters, but for an entire way of life. Set in a one-horse town in 1950s Texas, the film stars Bottoms and Bridges as heatstruck teens sweltering in the dustbowl of their own lives. Leachman and Johnson won Oscars for their gutsy portrayals. Bogdanovich's eye for the period and place paints a picture of a ghost town more chilling than any horror movie. (Sequel: *Texasville*) ★★★★ VHS: $14.99; DVD: $27.99

The Last Remake of Beau Geste

(1977, 85 min, US, Marty Feldman) *Marty Feldman, Michael York, Ann-Margret, James Earl Jones, Peter Ustinov.* Feldman directed, wrote and stars in this uneven though sometimes funny spoof on Foreign Legion movies — *Beau Geste* in particular. York plays Marty's twin brother (and Arnold and Danny thought they had an original idea) who accompanies his sibling to the legendary French outpost in Morocco. ★★ VHS: $14.99

The Last Seduction

(1994, 110 min, US, John Dahl) *Linda Fiorentino, Peter Berg, J.T. Walsh, Bill Pullman, Bill Nunn.* Fiorentino is in nightmarishly good form as Bridget Gregory, the ultimate femme fatale and the bane of every heterosexual man who crosses her path. When her New York med-school husband (Pullman) comes home with the proceeds of a major drug deal, she scampers with the loot and heads upstate. And oh, you boys upstate better beware! Filled with delightful twists and turns, *The Last Seduction* follows Bridget as she sets up shop in the sleepy little burg of Beston where she gets Mike (Berg) in her talons. Mike is a perfect rube for Bridget. He's so bent on getting out of small town life, that he falls squarely into every trap she sets. Fiorentino is incredibly sharp as Bridget. Ultimately, what makes this film so seductive is Bridget's completely unapologetic nature: she's the woman who's been wronged by men and is going to take everything she can to make up for it. And what makes it all so much fun is that we're rooting for *her*. ★★★★

The Last September

(1999, 104 min, GB, Deborah Warner) *Maggie Smith, Michael Gambon, Jane Birkin, Fiona Shaw, Lambert Wilson, Keeley Hawes.* Set in County Cork, Ireland, in 1920, this sumptuous though uninspiring adaptation of Elizabeth Brown's novel traces the end of an era for the aristocratic Anglo-Irish Naylor family, and, in effect, the end of Anglo-Irish aristocracy in Ireland. The fight for Irish independence arrives on the Naylors' front door when their young daughter is torn between a British soldier and a freedom fighter in hiding. The good ensemble (especially Shaw) helps keep interest but the film lacks full dramatic tension and only intermittently is able to keep pace with its ambitious story. ★★½ VHS: $89.99; DVD: $24.99

The Last Starfighter

(1984, 100 min, US, Nick Castle) *Robert Preston, Lance Guest, Barbara Bosson, Catherine Mary Stewart, Wil Wheaton.* Amiable sci-fi adventure with Guest as a small-town youth who yearns for excitement — and finds it when he is recruited by a space promoter (Preston) to help in the

fight against an evil conqueror. Preston is tops in a slight variation of his *Music Man* con man. ★★½ VHS: $7.49; DVD: $34.99

Last Summer

(1969, 97 min, US, Frank Perry) *Barbara Hershey, Bruce Davison, Richard Thomas, Cathy Burns.* Poignant coming-of-age drama about three restless teenagers and their summer of discovery at a private beach. Oscar-nominee Burns is a stand-out in support. Stunning photography by Gerald Hirschfield. ★★★

Last Summer in the Hamptons

(1995, 108 min, US, Henry Jaglom) *Victoria Foyt, Viveca Lindfors, Jon Robin Baitz, Roddy McDowall, Martha Plimpton, Roscoe Lee Browne, Andre Gregory, Ron Rifkin.* Jaglom's story centers around a famous theatrical family holding their last summer production before they sell their country house. The elegant matriarch, Helena (the great Lindfors), holds court while the various guests attempt awkward seductions with each other. Jaglom's own *Smiles of a Summer Night* employs his meandering, relaxed style to film this encounter session with equal amounts of insight, bickering, humor and pretention. The debate about stage versus cinema is interesting and observant, but the same can't be said for rather bad concentration exercises in which one of the family members "interprets" various animals. *Last Summer in the Hamptons* can be affectionate and appealing when not being downright irritating. ★★★ VHS: $19.99

The Last Supper

(1976, 110 min, Cuba, Tomás Gutiérrez Alea) *Nelson Villagra, Silvano Rey.* Reminiscent of Buñuel's delightfully vicious *Viridiana*, this sardonic political allegory is about a pious slaveholder at the turn of the century who, feeling the pangs of guilt, tries to cleanse his soul in front of God by staging a re-enactment of the Last Supper. Asking his slaves to forget their shackles for a night, the plantation owner "enlists" twelve of them to play the apostles. Told with caustic wit and blasphemous irony, this dazzling tour de force features a powerful black cast and a not-so-subtle preaching of imminent political revolt. (Spanish with English subtitles) ★★★½ VHS: $69.99

The Last Supper

(1995, 94 min, US, Stacy Title) *Cameron Diaz, Ron Eldard, Annabeth Gish, Jonathan Penner, Courtney B. Vance, Bill Paxton, Jason Alexander.* An unexpected murder over Sunday dinner leads a group of five grad students to a unique course of political action. They alter their weekly ritual of inviting a sixth person for dinner and conversation by choosing as their guest someone they believe the world would be better off without. As the freshly dug mounds of earth in their backyard steadily increase in number, the members of the group go through disconcerting changes of their own, each finding that final solutions have fearsome effects on the perpetrators as well as the victims. While the film raises some intriguing questions, its potency is undercut by uneven performances and inconsistent plot developments. ★★½ VHS: $14.99

Last Tango in Paris

(1973, 129 min, Italy, Bernardo Bertolucci) *Marlon Brando, Maria Schneider, Jean-Pierre*

Léaud. An aging expatriate (Brando) becomes involved in a doomed sexual liaison with a young French woman (Schneider). A landmark film which lays bare the primal nature of man. Brando equals his greatest performances as a seeker of truth, seething with sexual anger and drunk with self-loathing and contempt. (Filmed in English and French) ★★★★ VHS: $14.99; DVD: $24.99

The Last Temptation of Christ

(1988, 164 min, US, Martin Scorsese) *Willem Dafoe, Harvey Keitel, Barbara Hershey, Harry Dean Stanton, David Bowie, Andre Gregory, Verna Bloom.* Scorsese's adaptation of the Nikos Kazantzakis novel is a controversial telling of the Christ story, but for many a believer and non-believer alike this epic exploration of the man behind the myth has proven to be a true article of faith. Dafoe delivers a stylistically brilliant portrayal of a Jesus who, uncertain whether the voices he hears are from God or Satan, is locked in an agonizing battle with his own destiny. Scorsese has succeeded in crafting a truly elegant and thought-provoking treatise on spirituality and existence — clearly a labor of love. ★★★★ VHS: $19.99; DVD: $39.99

The Last Time I Committed Suicide

(1997, 93 min, US, Stephen Kay) *Thomas Jane, Keanu Reeves, Adrien Brody, Claire Forlani.* According to many who knew him, beatnik Neal Cassady was a genius of sorts, but the only impression we get from this film about his life is that he was a mildly intelligent, womanizing slacker. This is an uninvolving, annoying wisp of a movie that tries to compensate for the lack of a script (and a point) with an empty, clichéd music video technique. Director Kay most likely was excited by the parallels between Cassady's lifestyle and Generation X's perceived "attitude"; but like most twentysomething films, this is condescending and vapid. ★½ VHS: $14.99

The Last Time I Saw Paris

(1954, 116 min, US, Richard Brooks) *Elizabeth Taylor, Van Johnson, Donna Reed, Walter Pidgeon.* Romance blossoms between a young Army writer (Johnson) and a fun-loving socialite (Taylor) in post-war Paris. This uneven drama is enhanced by slick production values and Taylor's charm and beauty. Based on the novel "Babylon Revisited" by F. Scott Fitzgerald. ★★ VHS: $19.99

The Last Tycoon

(1976, 125 min, US, Elia Kazan) *Robert De Niro, Tony Curtis, Robert Mitchum, Jeanne Moreau, Jack Nicholson.* This screen version of F. Scott Fitzgerald's unfinished novel is an accomplished film for its acting alone, but it still seems unfinished, although Harold Pinter's script does the best it can. Worth seeing if only for De Niro's performance. Nicholson has a memorable small part as a script writer trying to start a union. ★★½ VHS: $14.99

The Last Waltz

(1978, 117 min, US, Martin Scorsese) Scorsese's dazzling documentation of The Band's momentous farewell performance on Thanksgiving Day, 1976. Concluding over a decade and a half of playing together, the group is joined on stage by a wealth of guest artists: Bob Dylan, Eric Clapton, Neil Young,

Late Chrysanthemums

Van Morrison and many others. Songs include "The Weight," "Up on Cripple Creek" and "The Night They Drove Old Dixie Down." The first film to fully utilize the Dolby stereo surround process. ★★★½

The Last Wave

(1978, 106 min, Australia, Peter Weir) *Richard Chamberlain, Olivia Hamnett.* Chamberlain plays a Sydney lawyer who, while defending a group of Aborigines accused of murder, becomes entangled in the labyrinthine world of ancient tribal magic, rituals and spiritualism. Atmospheric and moody, Weir's cerebral exercise in psychological horror is sometimes too ambitious but nevertheless has an ingenuity which heralded the director as a major player in the Australian film community. ★★★ VHS: $19.99

The Last Winter

(1984, 92 min, Israel, Riki Shelach) *Kathleen Quinlan, Yona Elian.* A patriotic Israeli living in America returns to his homeland to fight in the Yom-Kippur War of 1973. After he is reported missing in action, his distraught American wife flies to Tel Aviv in search of answers. Her friendship with another MIA wife helps alleviate the pain and frustration of her wait. A serious, thoughtful and absorbing drama. (Filmed in English) ★★★

Last Year at Marienbad

(1961, 93 min, France, Alain Resnais) *Delphine Seyrig, Giorgio Albertazzi.* At the spa in Marienbad a man (X) confronts a woman (A) with the conviction that they had an affair the previous year. Resnais transcends the limits of spatial and temporal storytelling rules. A classic of innovative cinema. Scripted by Alain Robbes-Grillet. (French and Italian with English subtitles) ★★★½ VHS: $19.99; DVD: $29.99

Latcho Drom

(1993, 103 min, France, Tony Gatlif) A pulsating musical and visual odyssey, this ode to the Gypsy life initially chronicles Europe's modern vagabonds who began their journey westward 1,000 years ago as a nomadic tribe from the north of India. It then launches into a series of MTV-inspired segments of ethnic music and dance — with stops in Egypt, Turkey, Romania, Hungary, Slovakia and Spain. As a kind of cultural travelogue mapping the source of musical inspiration from Asia to Europe — and linking those continents — the film is fascinating. But as the film's focus ventures westward, its outlook becomes as bleak, ultimately disintegrating into shameless and maudlin political propaganda bemoaning the plight of Europe's migratory underclass. ★★½ VHS: $89.99

Late Chrysanthemums

(1954, 101 min, Japan, Mikio Naruse) *Haruko Sugimura, Chkako Hosokawa.* This moving portrait of three retired geishas and their struggle to earn a living and retain respect long after the bloom of youth has gone is a detailed and poignant tragicomedy. Adapted from three Fumiko Hayashi stories, director Naruse masterfully depicts the subtle nuances of the women's emotionally intertwined relationships. Despite their meager living conditions and declining years, they determinedly fight for their dignity. (Japanese with English subtitles) ★★★½ VHS: $19.99

Late for Dinner

(1991, 92 min, US, W.D. Richter) *Brian Wimmer, Peter Berg, Marcia Gay Harden, Peter Gallagher.* Director Richter followed up *The Adventures of Buckaroo Banzai* (seven years later) with this subtly moving tale that mixes science fiction, romance and comedy to produce one of 1991's great films that nobody saw. Wimmer and Berg play best buddies who wind up "frozen" by a scientist as they run from the law in 1962. When the pair are thawed out nearly thirty years later, they have to contend with a society that has left them behind. More significantly, they have to rediscover and reconcile with the people they love. We've all seen this Rip Van Winkle, *Back to the Future* stuff before, but rarely has it been done with such sensitivity and soul. ★★★½ VHS: $6.99

The Late Show

(1977, 94 min, US, Robert Benton) *Art Carney, Lily Tomlin, Bill Macy, Joanna Cassidy.* Two superior performances by Carney and Tomlin highlight this winning mystery comedy written and directed by Benton. Carney plays an aging private eye who is thrown together with slightly daffy Tomlin as he investigates the death of his partner. Thoroughly enjoyable and a terrific homage to those great detective mysteries of the 1940s. ★★★½ VHS: $14.99

Late Spring

(1949, 108 min, Japan, Yasujiro Ozu) *Chishu Ryu, Setsuko Hara, Hakuro Sugimura.* Director Ozu brings great subtlety and elegance to this beautifully crafted film about a young woman with an unhealthy attachment to her aging, widowed father. Fearful that she will become an old maid on his account, the old man pretends that he himself is going to wed and tricks her into marriage. Unfortunately, the grandeur of Ozu's exquisite but slow-paced style does not translate well to video — much of the beauty of Ozu's films come from his discerning eye for black-and-white imagery. Still, his finely drawn characters and meticulous study of familial relations make this unequalled viewing for lovers of great drama. (Japanese with English subtitles) ★★★★ VHS: $19.99

Late Summer Blues

(1987, 101 min, Israel, Renen Schorr) *Dor Zweigenbom, Shahar Segal.* Set in 1970 during the War of Attrition at the Suez Canal, this moving drama chronicles the bittersweet dilemma facing a group of seven teenage students who, just finishing their final exams and high school, face impending induction into the Israeli armed forces. Sobered by the gruesome realities of war, the film focuses on the enthusiastic innocence and idealism of these youths as they are thrust into adulthood. (Hebrew with English subtitles) ★★★ VHS: $29.99

The Lathe of Heaven

(1979, 100 min, Canada, David Loxton & Fred Barzyk) *Bruce Davison, Kevin Conway, Margaret Avery.* Based on the popular novel by Ursula K. Le Guin, this near-stunning sci-fi fable stars Davison as George Orr, a young man whose haunted dreams become reality. Conway is the psychiatrist who sees Orr's special powers as the answer to the world's bleak troubles. An intelligent, gripping piece of science fiction that balances the social and the fantastic. ★★★½ VHS: $24.99; DVD: $24.99

Latin Boys Go to Hell

(1997, 75 min, US/Germany/Spain, Ela Troyano) *Irwin Ossa, John Bryant Davila, Alexis Artiles, Mike Ruiz, Guinevere Turner.* Cheerfully cheesy queer fun, this sexy melodramatic soap opera fills the screen with torrid Latino passions, rampant sexual confusion, a vicious killer and enough jealousy, revenge and pop culture excesses to satisfy any fan of early Almodóvar. Justin is a cute teen closet case living with his mother in East Brooklyn. He finds his hormones kicked into overdrive when his sexy cousin Angel arrives for an extended stay. But the swaggering Angel soon falls for Andrea (a photographer who specializes in erotic portraits of Hispanic men). Taking its cue from Mexican soap operas, this potboiler delivers some funny scenes and some appetizing skin, but when it turns serious (a killer is on the loose), the film falls flat. ★★½ VHS: $39.99; DVD: $29.99

Laugh for Joy

(1954, 106 min, Italy, Mario Monicelli) *Anna Magnani, Ben Gazzara.* Magnani, in one of the best performances of her career, stars in this

L

moving and bitter drama as a movie extra in Rome's Cinecitta Studio who becomes entangled in a messy relationship with two men: an American executive (Gazzara) and a crafty con man. (Italian with English subtitles) ★★★ VHS: $59.99

Laughing Sinners

(1931, 72 min, US, Harry Beaumont) *Joan Crawford, Clark Gable, Neil Hamilton, Guy Kibbee, Roscoe Karns.* Top-billed Crawford and Gable appear for the first time together in this predictable pre-Hays melodrama, based on the romantic Broadway play "Torch Song." Joan plays a nightclub singer who tries to commit suicide when she gets dumped by Hamilton. She's saved by Salvation Army preacher Gable. Just when it seems Joan has found happiness, back into her life comes Hamilton; and temptation. This morality tale is a little rough around the edges, but is nonetheless appealing for its antiquated posture. ★★½ VHS: $19.99

Laura

(1944, 85 min, US, Otto Preminger) *Gene Tierney, Clifton Webb, Dana Andrews, Vincent Price, Judith Anderson.* With the question of "Who killed Laura?" (and *not* Palmer), Preminger sets the stage for a complex, riveting and one-of-a-kind murder mystery. Andrews plays a police detective investigating the murder of successful businesswoman Laura Hunt (the beautiful Tierney). Through a series of flashbacks, cynical columnist Waldo Lydecker (Webb) recalls Laura's life up to the murder. Featuring extraordinary photography, a haunting score, unexpected twists, remarkable performances and a scalpel-sharp wit, *Laura* is not to be missed. Webb gives a quintessential performance as the acerbic Lydecker ("I write with a goose quill dipped in venom"), and Tierney is simply exquisite. ★★★★ VHS: $14.99

The Lavender Hill Mob

(1951, 82 min, GB, Charles Crichton) *Alec Guinness, Stanley Holloway, Sidney James, Alfie Bass.* Yet another of the Ealing Studio greats, this mischievous comedy features a stand-up performance by Guinness as a mild-mannered bank employee who dreams up what he thinks is a foolproof plan to steal one million British pounds in gold from the Bank of England. Winner of a Best Screenplay Oscar, this zany comedy climaxes with a madcap chase and features Audrey Hepburn in a bit part. ★★★★

Law Breakers

(Les Assassins de L'Ordre)

(1971, 107 min, France, Marcel Carné) *Jacques Brel, Catherine Rouvel, Michael Lonsdale, Charles Denner.* An engrossing and sobering exploration into police corruption in the French judicial system. A burglary suspect is brought in for questioning, but hours later, is found dead in his cell. All the officials in the prison deny any misconduct and the case seems unsolvable until the judge (Brel) assigned to the case takes a special interest in bringing the guilty to justice, even at the expense of his friends and his personal safety. (French with English subtitles) ★★★

Law of Desire

(1987, 100 min, Spain, Pedro Almodóvar) *Carmen Maura, Antonio Banderas, Eusebio*

Poncela, Bibi Andersson. Almodóvar's foray into sexual obsession is a wonderfully overheated sexual melodrama which basks in its farcical intentions. The story revolves around Pablo, a popular gay filmmaker, and his sister Tina (Maura), who used to be his brother until he changed his sex in order to please his lover — their father! Banderas is the darkly handsome but demented fan who attempts to win the director's heart by any means possible. Their loves, passions and wild adventures are splashed on the screen with the uninhibited eroticism, camp and outlandish wit that one would expect from the Spanish equivalent to Warhol. (Spanish with English subtitles) ★★★½

Lawman

(1971, 95 min, US, Michael Winner) *Burt Lancaster, Robert Ryan, Lee J. Cobb, Robert Duvall.* Lancaster heads a first-rate cast in this solid, leisurely paced western as a marshal who travels to a neighboring town to bring in seven cowpokes on a charge of murder. As Lancaster tracks the mostly law-abiding men, he battles with vigilante citizens, and comes to question his inflexible allegience to the letter of the law — much like Javert in Les Misérables." Ryan plays the impotent town sheriff who reluctantly aids Lancaster. ★★★½ VHS: $14.99

Lawn Dogs

(1998, 100 min, US, John Duigan) *Kathleen Quinlan, Sam Rockwell, Christopher McDonald.* Sexy trailer trash Rockwell mows lawns for the snooty residents of a cloistered neighborhood complex. Another misfit, the very imaginative ten-year-old daughter of a well-to-do couple in this suburban hell, has no friends and takes a shining to Rockwell, and after a fair amount of her pestering, they become unlikely friends. Predictably, the community misunderstands this innocent relationship. Though it has a low-key, fairy-tale atmosphere, the entire movie is negated with a completely wrong-headed final act that piles on the contrivances and ridiculous events and motivations, until a ludicrous finale. ★★ VHS: $102.99; DVD: $24.99

The Lawnmower Man

(1992, 132 min, US, Brett Leonard) *Pierce Brosnan, Jeff Fahey, Jenny Wright.* Originally released in theatres under the banner *Stephen King's Lawnmower Man*, this virtual reality, sci-fi thriller was in fact only based in small part on one of the horror maven's stories. King went to court and got his name removed from the title and it's easy to see why. Though the film features some outstanding computer-generated special effects, the story is incredibly thin. Brosnan stars as a scientist who uses his dim-witted gardener (Fahey) as a guinea pig in a virtual reality–based experiment aimed at expanding mental capacity. This release is the director's cut containing 34 extra minutes, making it slightly more coherent than its theatrical release. ★½ VHS: $14.99; DVD: $19.99

Lawnmower Man 2: Jobe's War

(1995, 93 min, US, Farhad Mann) *Patrick Bergen, Matt Frewer, Ely Pouget, Austin O'Brien.* Having little connection with the first film, this awful sequel begins as Jobe (Frewer) survives the cataclysmic destruction of the virtual reality labs where he has been given superhuman intelli-

gence and powers. He's now an honest, caring human being who becomes dependent upon electronic technology because of physical handicaps. He teams up with Ben (Bergen), the creator of a new kind of microchip which (of course) will revolutionize computer technology. A complete waste of time, without even the interesting computer graphics which supported the silly first film. ★ VHS: $89.99

Lawrence of Arabia

(1962, 222 min, GB, David Lean) *Peter O'Toole, Omar Sharif, Alec Guinness, Claude Rains, Jack Hawkins, Jose Ferrer.* O'Toole is possessed as T.E. Lawrence in this biography of a man who almost single-handedly helped the Arabs to escape their Turkish bondage in a brilliant saga of courage, sun and sand. The breathtaking Cinemascope photography is sadly lost on the small screen, but Lean's brilliant direction and a peerless ensemble will quickly put this out of mind. Winner of 7 Academy Awards including Best Picture and Director. ★★★★ VHS: $19.99; DVD: $39.99

Laws of Gravity

(1992, 100 min, US, Nick Gomez) *Peter Greene, Adam Trese.* Director Gomez makes a startling debut with this high-voltage independent film that bears more than a passing resemblance to *Mean Streets* as it tracks the ups and downs of a group of small-time Brooklyn hoods whose immaturity gets in the way of the big score. Greene stars as an aging "reservoir pup" whose day-to-day dealings in "the hood" collide with keeping his hot-headed, gun-running buddy (Trese) out of hot water. Gomez's deft mixture of surefooted performances from a cast of unknowns, a blisteringly improvisational script and frenetic camerawork that defies all laws of gravity suggest the arrival of a new streetwise master. ★★★½

The Leading Man

(1998, 96 min, GB, John Duigan) *Jon Bon Jovi, Anna Galiena, Lambert Wilson, Thandie Newton, Barry Humphries, Patricia Hodge, David Warner.* Backstage bedhopping and backstabbing make up *The Leading Man*, a guilty pleasure that has beautiful people seducing each other for fun and profit. Felix Webb (Wilson) is a successful West End playwright bedding Hilary (Newton), a ravishing talent seeking a plum role in his new play. When his gorgeous wife Elena (Galiena) discovers the affair, Felix conspires with the play's star, Hollywood hunk Robin Grange (Bon Jovi), to seduce Elena and cure her malaise. Complications, of course, ensue. As directed by Duigan, the film never quite establishes the right tone. The material is a bit thin, but the actors seem to relish their juicy parts. ★★½ VHS: $9.99; DVD: $9.99

The League of Gentlemen

(1960, 115 min, GB, Basil Dearden) *Jack Hawkins, Nigel Patrick, Richard Attenborough, Roger Livesey.* An exciting and briskly paced escapade about a group of ex-army officers who use their military talents to rob a bank. Imbued with a light sense of humor, the film is peppered with classic British witticisms. ★★★½ VHS: $19.99

Peter O'Toole as *Lawrence of Arabia*

A League of Their Own

(1992, 127 min, US, Penny Marshall) *Geena Davis, Lori Petty, Tom Hanks, Madonna, Rosie O'Donnell, David Strathairn, Jon Lovitz, Bill Pullman.* A marvelously entertaining baseball comedy, *A League of Their Own* is inspired by the real-life antics of the all-girls baseball league founded in 1943. Davis and Petty star as country-girl sisters who are discovered by ever-acerbic scout Lovitz. Whisked off to Chicago, they join the Rockford Peaches under the watchful bloodshot eyes of the team's over-the-hill, boozing manager (Hanks, who gives one of his richest characterizations). As the sisters whose sibling rivalry would make Joan Fontaine and Olivia deHavilland blush, Davis and Petty offer splendid performances. And it doesn't hurt that they look good in uniform and can handle a ball and glove. Director Marshall has a wonderful sense of comic timing, and she has crafted a sweet and funny valentine of a film. (VHS available letterboxed or pan & scan) ★★★½ VHS: $12.99; DVD: $19.99

Lean on Me

(1989, 104 min, US, John G. Avildsen) *Morgan Freeman, Beverly Todd, Robert Guillaume, Lynne Thigpen, Michael Beach.* Director Avildsen (*Rocky*) takes his "go for it" attitude and puts it in the classroom with mostly unsatisfactory results. Freeman gives a powerhouse performance as real-life principal Joe Clark, who took control of a Paterson, New Jersey, high school overrun by drugs, violence and apathy. You want to root for him, but when he starts bullying those around him and violates city and fire ordinances — and lies about doing so — he is clearly not the kind of hero who warrants such an idealized tribute. The film is at its best when it is not lionizing Clark as crusader, but rather showing his earnest commitment to his students. ★★ VHS: $9.99; DVD: $14.99

Leap of Faith

(1992, 110 min, US, Richard Pearce) *Steve Martin, Debra Winger, Liam Neeson, Lukas Haas, Lolita Davidovich, Meat Loaf, Philip Seymour Hoffman.* Despite the immeasurable comedic talents of Martin and a perfect premise for skewering evangelical preachers, this dramatic comedy falls short of its mark. When their bus breaks down, Martin (doing his best Jim Bakker) and company set up shop in a depressed farming community. The town's crops are being devastated by drought, and its inhabitants are primed for Martin's promises of divine intervention. ★★½ VHS: $14.99

The Leather Boys

(1963, 105 min, GB, Sidney J. Furie) *Rita Tushingham, Dudley Sutton, Colin Campbell.* Tushingham stars as a woman trapped in an incompatible marriage to a motorcycle-loving mechanic in this compelling and uncompromising study of compulsive behavior. Focusing on their opposing viewpoints and sleazy environment, the film chronicles the ever-widening rift which leads to infidelity and unhappiness. (Letterboxed) ★★★ VHS: $24.99

Leather Jackets

(1992, 90 min, US, Lee Drysdale) *Bridget Fonda, D.B. Sweeney, Cary Elwes.* Even the buoyant presence of Fonda can't keep this inane thriller from drowning under the weight of its attitude-heavy, cliché-ridden plot. Writer-director Drysdale aims low and misses with a shopworn tale of two former friends, one of whom (Sweeney) is a reformed petty thief. ★½ VHS: $79.99

Leave It to Beaver

(1997, 88 min, US, Andy Cadiff) *Christopher McDonald, Janine Turner, Cameron Finley, Erik von Detten, Adam Zolotin.* In bringing TV's semi-cultural institution to the big screen, the filmmakers could have gone the *Brady Bunch* route and spoofed the show's wholesomeness. They didn't. They could have gone the *Addams Family* route and played up the original's comic sensibilities. They didn't. They could have exaggerated the show's sentimentality without supplying any sustained laughs. They did. Turner is wasted as June, who's barely on-screen; Ward is a sports buff pushing his children; and the Beav and Wally are homogenized '90s kids who could feel at home on any silly contemporary sitcom. ★½ VHS: $14.99; DVD: $24.99

Leaving Las Vegas

(1995, 112 min, US, Mike Figgis) *Nicolas Cage, Elisabeth Shue, Julian Sands, Richard Lewis, Steven Weber, Valeria Golino, Laurie Metcalf, R. Lee Ermey, Julian Lennon, Xander Berkeley.* In bringing John O'Brien's decidedly downbeat novel about a man bent on suicide through alcohol to the screen, director Figgis and company took a huge cinematic risk that pays off in spades. This sultry and sometimes subversively funny examination of a self-declared loser (Cage) and the proverbial "hooker with a heart of gold" (Shue) who befriends him is on the one hand as depressing a film as has been made and on the other remarkably refreshing and engrossing for its undaunted emotional honesty. Cage plays Ben, a self-destructive minor Hollywood player who heads for a final showdown with the bottle in Vegas. Once there, he takes up with Sera (Shue), a buff streetwalker who takes him in. Cage won a highly deserved Oscar for his unflinching portrayal, and Shue delivers a nuanced, rock solid performance. ★★★★ VHS: $14.99; DVD: $19.99

Leaving Normal

(1992, 110 min, US, Edward Zwick) *Christine Lahti, Meg Tilly, Lenny Von Dohlen, Patrika Darbo.* The first of the *Thelma and Louise* "clones," *Leaving Normal* is a quirky, affectionate if uneven road movie about two uncertain women coming to terms with themselves. Featuring two sumptuous performances by Lahti and Tilly, the film follows the misadventures taken by Darly (Lahti), a quick-witted cocktail waitress and Marianne (Tilly), a waifish divorcée, who cross paths and decide to set out together on the road to Alaska. In contrast to *T & L*, most of the characters they encounter are comic foils, someone for the two lead characters to react to rather than gain any personal or interpersonal insight. Darbo is splendid as a waitress named 66. ★★½ VHS: $14.99

La Lectrice (The Reader)

(1988, 98 min, France, Michel Deville) *Miou-Miou, Christian Ruche.* Miou-Miou is enchanting in this labyrinthine tale of a woman who reads to her husband the story of a woman who reads to those who can't read for themselves. While not nearly as confusing as it sounds, director Deville's choices of the texts of Tolstoy, Baudelaire, de Maupassant and Carroll tend to render this a trying (albeit welcome) challenge for even the most literate filmgoer. However, the mixture of humor and pathos, and the general zaniness of the characters and situations, make it as much fun as curling up with a good book. (French with English subtitles) ★★★ VHS: $19.99

The Left Hand of God

(1955, 87 min, US, Edward Dmytryk) *Humphrey Bogart, Gene Tierney, Lee J. Cobb, E.G. Marshall, Agnes Moorehead.* Bogart stars as a downed WWII pilot who enters a Catholic mission posing as a priest to escape a vengeful Chinese warlord (Cobb). Tierney costars as the beautiful missionary whose heart sees through his disguise. ★★½

The Left-Handed Gun

(1958, 102 min, US, Arthur Penn) *Paul Newman, James Best, James Congdon.* Penn's directorial debut is a stylistic, provocative if not totally successful adaptation of Gore Vidal's story about Billy the Kid. The depiction of Billy by the intensely handsome Newman is that of a pensive, misunderstood but hot-headed loner — a tormented youth in the fashion of James Dean and Hamlet. After his boss is murdered, Billy and his two best friends, Tom (Best) and Charlie (Congdon), become obsessed with gunning down the man's killer. ★★½ VHS: $14.99

The Legacy

(1979, 100 min, US, Richard Marquand) *Katharine Ross, Sam Elliott, Roger Daltrey.* Six strangers are invited to a remote English mansion when they suddenly begin dying off. A supernatural presence is in the air and is using the process of elimination to select an heir. This *Omen*-inspired horror tale lacks suspense or a plot but tries to make up for it with gore and nonsense. ★★ VHS: $9.99

Legal Eagles

(1986, 116 min, US, Ivan Reitman) *Robert Redford, Debra Winger, Daryl Hannah, Brian Dennehy, Terence Stamp.* Earnest performances save this genial though disappointing comedy. Redford and Winger play, respectively, a successful district attorney and an eccentric lawyer who team to defend a SoHo performance artist (Hannah) accused of murder. It's not really all that bad, but with that cast, it doesn't meet expectations. ★★½ VHS: $7.49

Legend

(1985, 89 min, GB, Ridley Scott) *Tom Cruise, Mia Sara, Tim Curry.* Sexual undercurrents abound in this lavishly mounted and incredibly handsome fantasy about the Devil's attempts to gain control over a young girl. The film has its moments as a modern rendition of Grimm's Fairy Tales. It is symptomatic, however, of Scott's post-*Alien* inability to provide a forceful, powerful narrative in addition to his typical wealth of visual detail. ★★½ VHS: $9.99

The Legend

(1993, 100 min, Hong Kong, Corey Yuen) *Jet Li.* Another Jet Li vehicle comes to U.S. video in hobbled form. An inferior score, bad dubbing and choppy editing only accentuate this lesser Li entry's considerable flaws. In its original, widescreen, uncut and subtitled incarnation, *The Legend of Fong Sai-Yuk* (its Hong Kong title) is still a threadbare, overly silly story with some knockout action scenes. But this release is merely irritating, and Li fails to engage. However, the fight scenes are still here in all their glory, and — like a porn film or a clichéd musical — they're worth watching with index finger at the ready on the fast forward button. (Dubbed) ★★ VHS: $102.99

The Legend of Bagger Vance

(2000, 125 min, US, Robert Redford) *Will Smith, Matt Damon, Charlize Theron, Bruce McGill, Joel Gretsch, Jack Lemmon.* An elegant but slow-moving period piece, director Redford's *The Legend of Bagger Vance* has all the romanticism of a wistful memory, but is unable to establish full-rounded characterizations or make their actions as compelling as they should be. Damon plays Rannulph Junuh, a golf prodigy who has hit the skids. He is given a second chance when a mystical, kindly stranger, Bagger Vance (Smith), suddenly appears to guide him to the championships. Smith brings charm to the role of the mysterious Vance, but the film can't make its mind up as to exactly who he is: vagabond, mystic, con man, apparition? It is this uncertainty that denies the film the magical realism it seeks. But it's not like the cast and filmmakers didn't try. The acting is enchanting down to the smallest role, and Redford's pacing is elegiac and leisurely. In the end, however, it's not enough to hide a story that's really much ado about nothing. ★★½ VHS: $14.99; DVD: $26.99

The Legend of Dolemite!

(1994, 75 min, US, Foster Corder) *Rudy Ray Moore.* The Godfather of Rap, the black Lenny Bruce and the inspiration for comedians Richard Pryor and Eddie Murphy, recording artist, satirist/comedian and film star Moore is surprisingly unknown outside his rabid group of fans. With a tongue filthier than Richard Nixon on a bad day, Rudy Ray (aka Dolemite) has parlayed his macho urban braggadocio to a hilarious art form. This low-budget video, while technically below average, does feature interviews with Rudy Ray, scenes from his nightclub act, interviews with admirers and clips from his now-classic 1970s blaxploitation films. For fans a must; for neophytes, a coarse but entertaining eye-opener. ★★½ VHS: $19.99

The Legend of Drunken Master

See: Drunken Master II

The Legend of Hell House

(1973, 95 min, GB, John Hough) *Roddy McDowall, Clive Revill, Pamela Franklin.* Four psychics agree to spend a week at a haunted mansion to discover why their colleagues, conducting experiments at the house years earlier, were murdered. One of the best of its genre, this is quite suspenseful and the scares are many. ★★★ VHS: $19.99

The Legend of the Suram Fortress

(1985, 87 min, USSR, Sergei Paradjanov) *Levan Outchanechvili, Zourab Kipchidze.* Based on ancient Georgian legend and dedicated to all Georgian warriors killed in defense of the Motherland, this unique, but for most viewers inscrutable, tale has minimal dialogue and dazzling visuals. When a newly built Georgian fortress mysteriously collapses, the townspeople are at a loss and vulnerable to attack. An aging soothsayer claims that the only way to keep the walls standing is to have the son of the lover who jilted her buried alive inside the walls. (Georgian with English subtitles) ★★★ VHS: $59.99; DVD: $34.99

Legends of the Fall

(1994, 134 min, US, Edward Zwick) *Brad Pitt, Anthony Hopkins, Aidan Quinn, Henry Thomas, Julia Ormond, Tantoo Cardinal.* Like those fondly remembered soapers of the 1940s, whose stars could help gloss over any screenplay contrivance, *Legends of the Fall* is an old-fashioned melodrama which, while occasionally overdone in its dramatic construction, never fails to entertain. Beginning just before the start of WWI, the film stars Pitt as one of three sons of a stalwart Montana rancher (Hopkins). When their youngest brother (Thomas) returns home with a beautiful fiancée (Ormond), siblings Pitt and Quinn nuture romantic feelings for her. Thus sets in motion an encompassing story of love, betrayal, war and familial ties. Director Zwick allows his actors full range of emotions, and however good the ensemble is, all are upstaged by the sprawling locales and the film's gorgeous cinematography. ★★★½ VHS: $14.99; DVD: $19.99

Legionnaire

(1998, 95 min, US, Peter MacDonald) *Jean-Claude Van Damme, Daniel Caltagirone, Nicholas Farrell, Steven Berkoff.* This Van Damme vehicle may be the first $35 million direct-to-video action flick. While it's easy to see why this dramatically flat adventure was overlooked for theatrical release, it's still leagues better than Van Damme's most recent efforts. This is an unabashedly old-fashioned adventure yarn in the mold of '30s & '40s serials, with nary a roundhouse kick in sight. Set in the 1920s, the film casts Jean-Claude as a French boxer who joins the Foreign Legion to escape the gangster he double-crossed. After some entertaining training/bonding scenes, the group heads to Africa to fight the imperialist fight. The film's pace is brisk, but the script is pure hokum. ★★½ VHS: $9.99; DVD: $14.99

The Lemon Sisters

(1990, 93 min, US, Joyce Chopra) *Diane Keaton, Carol Kane, Kathryn Grody, Elliott Gould, Aidan Quinn, Ruben Blades.* A pleasant, low-key comedy with an accent on characterizations more than story, with Keaton, Kane and Grody as three childhood pals who are members of a singing group known as the Lemon Sisters; they're looking to make their mark in the nightclubs of Atlantic City. The performances are fine, though Kane steals the film with her delightful portrayal of the wacky and hopelessly mediocre singer (her solo performance is a highlight). ★★½ VHS: $14.99; DVD: $24.99

Leningrad Cowboys Go America

(1990, 80 min, Finland, Aki Kaurismäki) *Matti Pellonpaa, Kari Vaananen, Jim Jarmusch, Nicky Tesco.* Infused with his trademark droll sense of humor and peopled by an arresting cast of weirdos sporting gravity-defying hair and razor-sharp shoes, director Kaurismäki's comedy is a successful, albeit one-note, cultural satire. Beginning in the frozen tundra of Finland, a group of aspiring but not very good rock musicians decide to tour America seeking fame and fortune. An inopportune death, gigs in seedy Louisiana bars, and dumbfounded or bored-to-tears audiences prove to be little deterrence to these beer-guzzling aliens bent on becoming an overnight American success. Told with little dialogue and in neat vignettes, this misfits-on-the-

Matt Damon and Will Smith in *The Legend of Bagger Vance*

L

road movie will prove to be a grinning delight for adventurous videophiles. ★★★

Lenny

(1974, 112 min, US, Bob Fosse) *Dustin Hoffman, Valerie Perrine, Jan Miner.* Adapted from Julian Barry's play, *Lenny* is a powerful and often touching portrait of the troubled and controversial comedian Lenny Bruce. Filmed in a richly textured black and white, *Lenny* features superb performances by Hoffman as the comic and Perrine as his wife, stripper Honey Harlowe. ★★★½ VHS: $14.99

Léolo

(1992, 115 min, Canada, Jean-Claude Lauzon) *Maxime Collin, Ginette Reno, Roland Blouin.* A wonderful and rather bizarre coming-of-age tale, about an imaginative 12-year-old boy who believes he is the offspring of a Sicilian tomato (yes, the fruit). A clever mixture of reality and imagination, the film follows the exploits of young Léolo and his dysfunctional family: his parents who are obsessed with bowel movements; a dim-witted weight lifting brother; and a sister calmed only by her secret bug collection. The imagery is haunting, beautiful, disgusting and often hysterical, and the film is enhanced by beautiful cinematography and a soundtrack featuring Tom Waits and The Rolling Stones. (French with English subtitles) ★★★½ VHS: $19.99

Léon Morin, Priest

(1961, 118 min, France, Jean-Pierre Melville) *Jean-Paul Belmondo, Emmanuelle Riva.* A lonely young widow (Riva) with anticlerical, atheist and Communist views meets and befriends a handsome young priest (Belmondo). Their lively exchange of ideas on religion and life soon results — almost against her will — in an "invasion by God" into her soul, and the process of conversion into Catholicism begins. Set during the German and Italian Occupation and the beginning days of the Liberation, this austere, intense lesson of independence, love and faith is reminiscent of Robert Bresson's works. While Belmondo's role as the almost saintly priest is glazed over, it is Riva's Barny — a determinedly independent, opinionated woman — that is quite memorable in this moving religious, political and allegorical drama. (French with English subtitles) ★★★ VHS: $24.99

Leon the Pig Farmer

(1993, 98 min, GB, Vadim Jean & Gary Sinyor) *Mark Frankel, Janet Suzman, Brian Glover, Connie Booth.* A witty take on the Jewish mother syndrome, but this time from the British. Having just been fired from his job, the unmarried Leon takes a job with his mother's kosher catering service. While on a delivery to a local fertility clinic, he happens to find out that he was conceived by artificial insemination. What's a nice Jewish boy to do when he discovers that his father is in reality a pig farmer from a small English hamlet? Why, get to know his newly discovered parent, of course. The film features plenty of laughs, and Frankel is wonderful as Leon. ★★★

The Leopard

(1963, 185 min, Italy, Luchino Visconti) *Burt Lancaster, Claudia Cardinale, Alain Delon.* A

meticulous, atmospheric epic about 19th-century Italian nobility with Lancaster in the title role as the Leopard, Prince Fabrizio de Salina, an aging aristocrat whose elegant world undergoes a dramatic upheaval during the social turbulence of the 1860s. Delon is his opportunistic nephew who siezes the chance to become a prominent officer in the revolutionary regime. Cardinale costars as Delon's ill-bred fiancée. A sumptuous portrait of a vanquished age featuring sparkling performances and a lavish Nino Rota score. ★★★½

The Leopard Man

(1943, 66 min, US, Jacques Tourneur) *Jean Brooks, Isabel Jewell, Dennis O'Keefe, Margo.* Val Lewton's follow-up to his highly successful *Cat People* is another first-rate, low-budget chiller, also directed by Tourneur. Set in a small New Mexico town, the search is on for an escaped leopard, which may be responsible for a series of gruesome killings. ★★★

Leprechaun

(1990, 91 min, US, Mark Jones) *Warwick Davis, Jennifer Aniston, Ken Olandt.* A playfully sadistic munchkin wreaks havoc when his personal possessions are threatened. No, it's not the latest entry in the *Home Alone* series. A leprechaun (Davis) from Ireland goes on killing spree to reclaim his stolen bag of gold. The strictly rudimentary "insert fiend here" screenplay bears the distinction of being quite possibly the only horror movie to be set in rural North Dakota. Oooh, scary. (Followed by 4 sequels) ★ VHS: $14.99

Les Girls

(1957, 114 min, US, George Cukor) *Gene Kelly, Mitzi Gaynor, Kay Kendall, Tiana Elg.* Three showgirls take their former dancing partner to court; but during testimony, can't agree as to what really happened. A joyously entertaining musical with Kelly in good form as the hoofer. ★★★ VHS: $19.99

Les Misérables

(1935, 108 min, US, Richard Boleslawski) *Fredric March, Charles Laughton, Cedric Hardwicke, Florence Eldridge.* Excellent adaptation of Victor Hugo's classic novel with March and Laughton giving great performances as, respectively, petty thief Valjean and relentless police inspector Javert. Remade several times, including as a stage musical. ★★★½ VHS: $9.99

Les Misérables (1995)

Les Misérables

(1995, 174 min, France, Claude Lelouch) *Jean-Paul Belmondo, Michel Boujenah, Allesandra Martines, Clementine Celarie.* Victor Hugo's classic treatise on social injustice gets a radical updating by director Lelouch. His daring, invigorating and spellbinding three-hour epic begins at the turn of the century as Fortin (Belmondo), a chauffeur, serves time in prison for his employer. Jumping many years forward to the Nazi Occupation, the story revolves around Fortin, Jr. (again Belmondo), who is helping a Jewish family make a run for the Swiss border. Fortin, an illiterate, has become fascinated with the parallels between himself and Hugo's hero Jean Valjean, and so he has his Jewish riders read the novel out loud for him. Lelouch then enacts these readings (with Belmondo playing Valjean) and draws the obvious analogies between Hugo's characters and those of Vichy France. Belmondo revels in his multiple roles, and his rich performance combined with Lelouch's ingenious screenplay makes for a one-of-a-kind classic. (French with English subtitles) ★★★★ VHS: $29.99

Les Misérables

(1998, 129 min, GB, Bille August) *Liam Neeson, Geoffrey Rush, Uma Thurman, Claire Danes, Hans Matheson.* A good cast breathes life into this solemn version of Victor Hugo's classic novel which doesn't quite compare with the 1935 Fredric March–Charles Laughton version, but is rather a straightforward, condensed interpretation that tries to flesh out some of the more main characters. It's a good primer for those unfamiliar with the story. Neeson is properly stoic as Jean Valjean, a poor Frenchman who stole a loaf of bread and spent 19 years in prison for it. Rush is good at conveying the inner demons of Inspector Javert, the relentless policeman on Valjean's trail. The film is staged in an efficient if none-too-exciting manner, and the settings and costumes are evocative without being unduly opulent. ★★★ VHS: $14.99; DVD: $29.99

Less Than Zero

(1987, 96 min, US, Marek Kanievska) *Andrew McCarthy, Jami Gertz, Robert Downey, Jr., James Spader.* Never has a title more aptly fit its film. A creative void by all concerned has made this limp attempt to be the *Easy Rider* of the '80s alienated teen pic nothing more than a sad curiosity piece. Purging the ennui, drug taking and bisexuality of the novel for cheap moralistic posturing, the film is almost an antithesis of the Bret Easton Ellis best-seller. Downey is the only cast member with an active pulse while McCarthy and Gertz listlessly cruise the highways of L.A. as zombies in search of motivation, direction and characterization. ★ VHS: $9.99

A Lesson in Love

(1954, 95 min, Sweden, Ingmar Bergman) *Eva Dahlbeck, Gunnar Björnstrand, Yvonne Lombard, Harriet Andersson.* This Bergman romantic comedy, lightweight but nonetheless satisfying, details the marital tensions and break up of a middle-aged gynecologist who, although happily married for 15 years, has a short affair with a patient. His wife finds out and abruptly leaves him to live with her former lover, his best friend. (Swedish with English subtitles) ★★★ VHS: $29.99

Lessons at the End of Spring

(1989, 75 min, Russia, Oleg Kavan) The triumph of the human spirit over repression and injustice is the theme of this emotionally powerful drama set in a Khrushchev-era Soviet Union. A 13-year-old boy is mistakenly thrown into an adult prison where begins a harrowing odyssey in which inhumane treatment of the prisoners is the norm. Despite this, our young hero retains, throughout, his naïve sense of justice as well as his defiant survival instincts. Not only great storytelling, but startling in its unflinching criticism of the Soviet state. (Russian with English subtitles) ★★★½ VHS: $59.99

Let Him Have It

(1991, 115 min, GB, Peter Medak) *Christopher Eccleston, Paul Reynolds, Tom Courtenay.* This chilling and engrossing drama is based on an actual incident which led Great Britain to reevaluate, and eventually abolish, its death penalty. Set in the '50s, amidst the ruins of a bombed-out London still recovering from the war, the story follows the demise of a quiet, learning-disabled and epileptic young man who naïvely falls in with a group of Hollywood gangster–influenced, would-be thugs. When a bungled robbery attempt leads to the cold-blooded killing of a policeman, he finds himself not only implicated in the murder, but also subject to the wrath of a vengeful society seeking blood. ★★★½ VHS: $14.99

Let It Ride

(1989, 91 min, US, Joe Pytka) *Richard Dreyfuss, Teri Garr, Jennifer Tilly, Robbie Coltrane, David Johansen.* A surprisingly appealing lark. Dreyfuss is a winner as a race track gambler whose wish for a "great day" comes true when he becomes privy to a hot tip. Garr has some nice moments as his long-suffering wife, Tilly is her usual delightful self as a gambler's gal and Coltrane is a scene-stealer as a track cashier. ★★★ VHS: $14.99

Let the Devil Wear Black

(1999, 95 min, US, Stacy Title) *Jonathan Penner, Mary-Louise Parker, Jacqueline Bisset, Philip Baker Hall, Jamey Sheridan, Chris Sarandon.* If Quentin Tarantino had ever decided to update and desecrate Shakespeare's "Hamlet," he might have come up with this relentlessly irreverent black comedy about a fresh-out-of-rehab L.A. rich kid

(Penner) haunted by the idea that his uncle (Sheridan) may have killed his father and now plans to marry his not-so-grief-stricken mother (Bisset). But in order to take revenge, he must survive a night populated by L.A. gang-bangers, drug-dealing best friends, and an unknown assassin hired by his uncle to kill him. The script (cowritten by the star and the director) is so venomously witty, you'll forget it's Shakespeare. ★★★ VHS: $9.99; DVD: $9.99

Let's Dance

(1950, 112 min, US, Norman Z. McLeod) *Fred Astaire, Betty Hutton, Roland Young.* Astaire is the song-and-dance man who helps ex-partner Hutton battle her deceased husband's grandmother for custody of her young son. Some good dance sequences get lost in the sentimental story. ★★ VHS: $14.99

Let's Do It Again

(1975, 112 min, US, Sidney Poitier) *Sidney Poitier, Bill Cosby, Jimmie Walker, John Amos, Ossie Davis, Denise Nicholas, Calvin Lockhart.* Poitier and Cosby are back together again in this very funny sequel to *Uptown Saturday Night.* This time around, Poitier and Cosby scheme to turn nebbish Walker into a champion boxer — through hypnosis — in order to save their lodge. High spirited and lots of fun. ★★★ VHS: $14.99

Let's Get Lost

(1987, 119 min, US, Bruce Weber) The life and music of jazz great Chet Baker is the subject of this poignant, fascinating documentary by noted photographer Weber. In fact, Weber's roots show to tremendous effect as this examination of a tortured artist's genius and self-destruction looks every bit as handsome as its subject in his early years. Weber splendidly intercuts rare recording sessions, interviews with family and friends, and even includes clips from Baker's short-lived movie career in the 1950s. The scenes of Baker's later years are heartbreakingly sad as the ravages of drug addiction had clearly taken its toll on this legendary trumpeter. ★★★½ VHS: $69.99

Let's Make Love

(1960, 118 min, US, George Cukor) *Marilyn Monroe, Yves Montand, Tony Randall.* A well-intentioned misfire, this sporadically amusing musical stars Montand as a millionaire who learns he is to be parodied in an off-Broadway show. He becomes intent on closing the show until he sees leading lady Marilyn, and, well, you know the rest. This could have been a lot more palatable had anyone other than Montand starred as the millionaire. ★★

Let's Talk about Sex

(1998, 82 min, US, Troy Beyer) *Troy Beyer, Paget Brewster, Randi Ingerman, Joseph C. Phillips.* Director Beyer stars as Jasmine, an ambitious young woman putting together a demo tape for a proposed TV show. She selects potential interviewees from students at that staunch bastion of intellectual pursuit, the University of Miami, to discuss — guess what? — their sex lives. The film spends much of its time basking in the hormonal splendor of the beach and bar scene, which is considerable. For much of the time, the film is crappy, soft-core sexploitation. While occasionally attempting forays into the insight-

ful and sensitive, it depends way too much on faux gravity and tacky titillation. ★ VHS: $19.99

Lethal Weapon

(1987, 110 min, US, Richard Donner) *Mel Gibson, Danny Glover, Gary Busey, Mitchell Ryan, Darlene Love.* Gibson unleashes a charismatically explosive action persona in this rousing and violent cop vs. druggies movie. He plays an emotionally off-balanced undercover cop with Glover costarring as his stable, family man partner; and together, they become embroiled in a series of tense and exciting situations. Combining humor, action and more action to great advantage, this started a whole new buddy pic genre — this remains one of the best of its kind. (Letterboxed VHS available for $19.99) (Followed by three sequels) ★★★½ VHS: $14.99; DVD: $19.99

Lethal Weapon 2

(1989, 113 min, US, Richard Donner) *Mel Gibson, Danny Glover, Joe Pesci, Joss Ackland, Patsy Kensit, Darlene Love.* Mel and Danny are back, and as the old movie ads used to say, they're bigger and better than ever. As in the original, Gibson and Glover have redefined the genre with a spontaneous, fresh repartee which is as entertaining as it is humorous. Plot really takes a back seat to the fast, frantic action scenes and the delectable rapport between the two stars. But for the record, Roger and Martin find themselves up against a ruthless South African diplomat, who happens to be a part-time drug dealer. Pesci does the impossible by stealing the show as a loquacious, ingratiating accountant being protected by Mel and Danny. (Letterboxed VHS available for $19.99) ★★★½ VHS: $14.99; DVD: $19.99

Lethal Weapon 3

(1992, 118 min, US, Richard Donner) *Mel Gibson, Danny Glover, Joe Pesci, Rene Russo, Stuart Wilson, Darlene Love.* In this average third installment, Roger (Glover) and Martin (Gibson) uncover a scheme to steal high-powered weaponry from police storage, with the prime suspect being a corrupt ex-cop. Along the way they are investigated by a sexy Internal Affairs officer (Russo) who conveniently winds up with the hots for Riggs. Pesci reprises his role as low-life Leo Getz and delivers some of the film's best one-liners. Despite a screenplay which resists all logic, director Donner's flair for humor and chase scenes, and Gibson and Glover's charisma, makes for a mindless though entertaining ride. (Letterboxed VHS available for $19.99) ★★½ VHS: $14.99; DVD: $19.99

Lethal Weapon 4

(1998, 120 min, US, Richard Donner) *Mel Gibson, Danny Glover, Rene Russo, Joe Pesci, Chris Rock, Jet Li, Darlene Love.* Warner Brothers may be going to the well once too often with this fourth installment in the series. Unnecessary though mildly entertaining, the film gets by with what made the original such a memorable actioner: the terrific rapport between Gibson and Glover. The two stars know these guys awfully well, and it is their portrayals which make *4* watchable. This time around, Riggs and Murtaugh take on members of a Chinese syndicate. There's a couple of good action scenes, but the film is offset by a nonchalance in tone, and scenes and jokes which go on too long.

L

Rock has some good one-liners and is a refreshing presence. (Letterboxed VHS available for $19.99) ★★½ VHS: $14.99; DVD: $19.99

The Letter

(1940, 95 min, US, William Wyler) *Bette Davis, Herbert Marshall, James Stephenson, Gale Sondergaard.* Davis and director Wyler's second film together (after their success with *Jezebel*) is a knockout adaptation (and second screen version) of W. Somerset Maugham's novel about a tycoon's wife who murders her lover and claims self-defense; only to be a victim of blackmail when "the letter" proves otherwise. ★★★½ VHS: $14.99

Letter from an Unknown Woman

(1948, 90 min, US, Max Ophüls) *Joan Fontaine, Louis Jourdan, Mady Christians.* Lush romantic drama with Fontaine suffering from cinema's worst case of unrequited love as she is obsessed with musician Jourdan. A film of visual splendor; and one that, thanks to director Ophüls' sturdy direction, avoids the clichés usually found in melodramas. ★★★ VHS: $14.99

Letter to Brezhnev

(1985, 94 min, GB, Chris Bernard) *Peter Firth, Alfred Molina, Alexander Prigg, Margi Clarke.* A bawdy, low-budget comedy about two Liverpool girls, looking for sex and romance, who chance upon two Soviet sailors in a local disco. It offers a vibrant, gritty portrait of young people in the harsh industrial wasteland of northern England as they look for love and dream of escape from their dreary daily lives. ★★★

A Letter to Three Wives

(1949, 103 min, US, Joseph L. Mankiewicz) *Ann Sothern, Jeanne Crain, Linda Darnell, Kirk Douglas, Paul Douglas, Thelma Ritter, Jeffrey Lynn.* A year before he would write and direct the classic *All About Eve*, Mankiewicz won two Oscars for both writing and directing this scintillating and extremely witty comedy-drama which dissects and devours, among other things, marriage, education, consumerism and social strata. Three suburban matrons learn that one of their husbands has run off with another woman. Told in three flashbacks, the story focuses on each couple's shaky marital history while giving clues as to whom the dastardly Addie (who is never seen) betrayed. Though an extremely well-acted ensemble piece, it's Sothern who runs away with the picture as the socially ambitious wife of happy-to-be-just-a-teacher K. Douglas. P. Douglas makes a terrific film debut as another husband. ★★★★ VHS: $19.99

Letters from My Windmill

(1954, 134 min, France, Marcel Pagnol) *Henri Velbert, Yvonne Gamy.* Pagnol's splendid trilogy of short tales. "Three Low Masses": The Devil takes over the body of a dunce and torments a priest. "The Elixer of Father Gauchet": Brother Gauchier inherits some home-made brew and begins to sell the wine for charitable purposes. "The Secret of Master Corneille": A sentimental story of an ancient miller who for 18 years had been pretending to compete with a modern steam mill. (French with English subtitles) ★★★ VHS: $59.99

Letters from the Park

(1988, 85 min, Cuba, Tomás Gutiérrez Alea) *Victor Laplace, Ivonne Lopez.* Adapted from a Gabriel García Márquez short story, this elegant tale of innocence, romance and forbidden love is set in turn-of-the-century Cuba. Shy young lovers Juan and Maria are attracted to one another, but find it impossible to articulate their feelings. They each enlist an older man to compose beautifully poetic love letters to the other, letters that eventually bring the two together. Problems arise after the poet, swept away with their romance and his own repressed feelings, falls in love with the young woman but is forced to keep his feelings silent. This Spanish "Cyrano de Bergerac" — without the nose — is a wonderfully enchanting, dreamy and seemingly universal story. (Spanish with English subtitles) ★★★

Leviathan

(1989, 98 min, US, George Pan Cosmatos) *Peter Weller, Richard Crenna, Ernie Hudson, Amanda Pays, Daniel Stern.* The director's in over his head and the actors out of their depth trying to pump life into this tale about a monster terrorizing an undersea community. ★ VHS: $14.99; DVD: $14.99

Lewis & Clark & George

(1996, 90 min, US, Rod McCall) *Rose McGowan, Salvator Xuereb, Dan Gunther, Art LeFleur, James Brolin, Paul Bartel.* On an exploration for a gold mine, ex-convicts Lewis (Xuereb) and Clark (Gunther) meet George (McGowan), a mute woman who is also on the lam. As this trio ride a bullet-paved path through the Southwest, friendship is tested, love blossoms, and betrayal rears its ugly head. *Lewis & Clark & George* offers nothing new in its depiction of greed prompting a killing spree, but writer-director McCall does employ some arty storytelling techniques as the bodies pile up. ★★ VHS: $9.99; DVD: $9.99

Li'l Abner

(1959, 113 min, US, Melvin Frank) *Peter Palmer, Leslie Parrish, Stubby Kaye, Julie Newmar.* Colorful screen version of the hit Broadway musical, based on Al Capp's comic strip, about the eccentric citizens of Dogpatch, USA. The story follows Li'l Abner, a muscle-bound loafer, and his romantic near-misses with beautiful girlfriend Daisy Mae. The story and lyrics are as witty and sardonic as Capp's strip often was. Songs include the politically astute "The Country's in the Very Best of Hands." ★★★ VHS: $14.99

Lianna

(1982, 110 min, US, John Sayles) *Linda Griffiths, Jane Hallaren, Jon DeVries.* Director-writer Sayles' exceptional and humorous exploration of the coming out of the "good wife" offers a compassionate view of lesbianism, self-determination and unrest. Lianna (Griffiths) confronts her husband's infidelity, falls in love with her graduate instructor and sets out on her own. Sayles directs with a sensitive hand, and his perceptive screenplay contains many vulnerable and tender moments examining one woman's budding lesbian self-realization. ★★★

Liar, Liar

(1997, 87 min, US, Tom Shadyac) *Jim Carrey, Maura Tierney, Swoosie Kurtz, Jennifer Tilly, Cary Elwes, Justin Cooper.* In this often hilarious but frequently mawkish comedy, Carrey plays a divorced father and unscrupulous lawyer; unfortunately for his adoring five-year-old son, not in that order. Making a birthday wish, young Cooper wishes his father could go one day without telling a lie. This starts a terrific premise which is realized most of the time. Watching Carrey blurt out the truth at the most inopportune times is truly funny. However, most of the scenes with his son and ex-wife are maudlin; you expect Carrey to skewer this kind of sap, not embrace it. (Letterboxed VHS available for $19.99) ★★½ VHS: $9.99; DVD: $24.99

Liar's Moon

(1983, 106 min, US, David Fisher) *Matt Dillon, Cindy Fisher, Yvonne DeCarlo, Susan Tyrrell, Hoyt Axton, Broderick Crawford.* A teen from the wrong side of the tracks (Dillon) falls for the richest girl in town (Fisher), much against the wishes of both families, who carry a dark secret that could ruin the lovers' chance at happiness. Dillon's passionate performance elevates this otherwise familiar, star-crossed lovers romantic drama. ★★ VHS: $9.99; DVD: $19.99

Libeled Lady

(1936, 98 min, US, Jack Conway) *Spencer Tracy, William Powell, Myrna Loy, Jean Harlow, Walter Connolly, Hattie McDaniel.* Classic screwball comedy featuring an impeccable cast. Tracy is a scheming newspaper editor looking for a story; he hires Powell (a hilarious performance and what a great fisherman!) to implicate heiress Loy in a romantic scandal. Harlow rounds out the powerhouse cast as Tracy's long-suffering fiancée. ★★★½ VHS: $19.99

The Liberation of L.B. Jones

(1969, 101 min, US, William Wyler) *Lee J. Cobb, Barbara Hershey, Roscoe Lee Browne, Lola Falana, Anthony Zerbe, Yaphet Kotto.* A race-conscious town in Tennessee is divided over the scandalous divorce of a black lawyer and his adulterous wife, who has been having an affair with a white cop. Wyler deftly demonstrates the sexual and racial passions boiling over in the tiny town, but the screenplay can't overcome its melodramatic roots. ★★½ VHS: $59.99

Liberty Heights

(1999, 128 min, US, Barry Levinson) *Adrien Brody, Joe Mantegna, Ben Foster, Bebe Neuwirth, Orlando Jones.* Another autobiographical, Baltimore-based Levinson film (in the spirit of *Diner* and *Avalon*), which is where his strengths lie. Brody and Foster play Jewish boys growing up in 1950s Baltimore, standing up to the anti-Semitic (and racist, snobby) community while discovering cross-cultural romance. Mantegna plays their father, who balances his time between the burlesque house he runs and a gambling operation. Plenty of smart comedy within a touching, serious framework. ★★★½ VHS: $14.99; DVD: $19.99

Licence to Kill

(1989, 133 min, GB, John Glen) *Timothy Dalton, Robert Davi, Talisa Soto, Carey Lowell.* Dalton makes his second appearance as agent 007, and while he may not make anyone forget the one

L

and only Sean Connery, he proves once and for all that Moore is less. In this exciting and well-paced adventure, set mostly in Miami and Central America, Bond loses his "licence to kill" when he sets out to avenge the murder of his friend's wife. There are, to be sure, hair-raising action scenes and the trademark Bond humor, plus two beautiful costars in Soto and Lowell — the latter demonstrating that Bond women have finally grown up and can definitely hold their own with the big guys. (Sequel: *Goldeneye*) ★★★ VHS: $14.99; DVD: $34.99

Lie Down with Dogs

(1995, 86 min, US, Wally White) *Wally White, Randy Becker, Darren Dryden.* Though this low-budget comedy does have its share of laughs, it's saddled with poor acting and a plot line you couldn't hang your Calvin Kleins on. A relentlessly grinning Tommie (writer-director White) decides to chuck his job in sweaty New York for three months of pleasure in gay mecca Provincetown. He tries to find a job as a house-boy, and quickly dives into a series of sexual escapades. ★★

Liebelei

(1932, 83 min, Germany, Max Ophüls) *Wolfgang Liebeneiner, Magda Schneider.* Suppressed by the Nazis for years and subsequently rarely seen, *Liebelei* finds Ophüls' visual style yet to exhibit the long, languid tracking shots of his later works such as *La Ronde*, though it shares a common theme. This, his first big success, is another of his meditation on the nature of love — here a love blocked not so much by class strata, but by class custom. In late 19th-century Vienna, a philandering lieutenant vows to mend his ways when he falls for a woman of a more modest station. Unfortunately, he soon becomes the victim of his past. Though *Liebelei* is not remarkable in either story or storytelling, Ophüls' unsteady but promising directorial hand allows this somber love story to be of historical interest. (German with English subtitles) ★★½ VHS: $24.99

Liebestraum

(1991, 105 min, US, Mike Figgis) *Kevin Anderson, Kim Novak, Bill Pullman, Max Perlich, Catherine Hicks.* An absorbing, noir-influenced thriller which skillfully merges two violent, obsessive love triangles, 40 years apart. Anderson is an architectural journalist who, while on a visit to his home town to see his dying mother (Novak in a wonderful supporting role), meets an old friend, Paul (Pullman). Paul is a real estate developer in the process of tearing down a main street department store which has been shuttered for 40 years after the gruesome double murder of its owner and his mistress. The writer's interest in the building and its mysterious past causes him to become romantically involved with Paul's wife, who is photographing the building's destruction. The result is a torrid tale of lust and jealousy. (Director's cut) ★★★ VHS: $14.99; DVD: $19.99

Life

(1999, 108 min, US, Ted Demme) *Eddie Murphy, Martin Lawrence, Obba Babatunde, Ned Beatty, Bokeem Woodbine, Nick Cassavetes, Clarence Williams III, R. Lee Ermey, Rick James.* Murphy and Lawrence make a solid comic team in this unexpectedly dramatic comedy spanning 55 years in the lives of two convicts. Con man Ray (Murphy) and law-abiding Claude (Lawrence)

meet when both run afoul of bootlegger Spanky (James). They immediately don't hit it off. Things go from bad to worse when they are both sent to prison for a murder they didn't commit. Theese two comedians have a field day with the material. Their constant bickering is cause for many a laugh, and when this aims to be funny, it is. But there's a serious subtext to the story, and though it may not be handled with total sensitivity, it makes for compelling dramatics. ★★★ VHS: $14.99

The Life and Death of Colonel Blimp

(1943, 115 min, GB, Michael Powell & Emeric Pressburger) *Roger Livesey, Deborah Kerr, Anton Wolbrook.* A memorable British wartime classic which follows the long and eventful life of a prosperous, old-fashioned officer of the British Army. At 115 minutes, the video version of this tale, which winds its way through several wars and four different women (all played by Kerr!), is regrettably a full 48 minutes shorter than the theatrical cut. ★★★★

Life and Nothing But

(1990, 135 min, France, Bertrand Tavernier) *Philippe Noiret, Sabine Azema, Françoise Perrot.* Tavernier's film is a somber, meditative yet romantic exploration of war, loneliness and love. Noiret stars as a cynical army officer assigned to catalogue the dead, injured and missing French soldiers at the end of WWI. The story revolves around two women, one an elegant lady and the other a young waitress, who both travel to the rain-drenched and battle-scarred fields of the front and solicit the aid of Noiret in finding their missing husbands. A thoughtful film on the emotional healing process. (French with English subtitles) ★★★½

The Life and Times of Judge Roy Bean

(1972, 120 min, US, John Huston) *Paul Newman, Anthony Perkins, Ned Beatty, Victoria Principal, Jacqueline Bisset, Tab Hunter, Roddy McDowall, Ava Gardner, John Huston, Stacy Keach.* Newman plays the legendary outlaw in this not-quite-a-western. It's an interesting, unusually self-aware but slightly uneven film, with a star-studded cast. ★★½ VHS: $14.99

Life Begins for Andy Hardy

(1941, 102 min, US, George B. Seitz) *Mickey Rooney, Judy Garland, Lewis Stone.* In this 11th Andy Hardy outing, Rooney is off to take a bite out of the Big Apple, but finds the big city can be tough on a small-town boy. Garland is the perky Betsy Booth. This entry in the popular series is easier going and has less of a sentimental quota than most of the earlier films. ★★½ VHS: $19.99

A Life in the Theatre

(1993, 78 min, US, Gregory Mosher) *Jack Lemmon, Matthew Broderick.* Lemmon and Broderick offer fine performances in this very capable adaptation of David Mamet's play. The comedic piece is more of an excuse for Mamet to offer a portrait of actors fretting their hour upon the stage rather than a conventional story. Here, more so than in most of Mamet's film works, it is clearly the rhythm of his dialogue that is the real star. Though plot and characterization are very subtle here, both stars appear proficient and quite comfortable with

Mamet-speak (even allowing themselves to be upstaged by it), which only further elevates the production. ★★★ VHS: $79.99

Life Is a Long Quiet River

(1987, 89 min, France, Etienne Chatiliez) *Benoit Magimel, Helene Vincent.* The Quesnoys are a well-bred, bourgeois Catholic family living in France. Everything is wonderful and polite in their lives until one fateful day when they discover that, in the delivery room twelve years prior, their doctor had switched their son with the daughter of the Groseille family, a sordid group of low-income slobs from The Other Side of Town. What ensues is an entertaining farce as the Groseilles attempt to get every penny they can out of the "accident" and the Quesnoys struggle to keep their family values intact. A comic and often caustic commentary on social classes and the family unit. (French with English subtitles) ★★★½ VHS: $79.99

Life Is Beautiful

(1981, 102 min, Italy, Grigorig Ciukhrai) *Giancarlo Giannini, Ornella Muti.* The title of this tense and electrifying drama is purely ironic. Set during the politically unstable situation in pre-revolutionary Lisbon, the story concerns itself with the false arrest of a man. He is beaten, imprisoned and kept away from his wife and family. His political neutrality and personal sanity are severely tested by his abusive jailers. ★★★

Life Is Beautiful

(1998, 114 min, Italy, Roberto Benigni) *Roberto Benigni, Nicoletta Braschi, Giorgio Cantarini, Giustino Durano, Horst Buchholz.* Recalling the physical grace and comic timing of Chaplin, Benigni takes the subject of the Holocaust and makes a personal and extraordinary fable about one dedicated father. In 1939, Guido (Benigni) falls in love with schoolteacher Dora (Braschi). He courts her with laughter, humor and heart; and the two marry. It's several years later, and they have a wonderful son, Joshua (Cantarini), and a happy marriage. But Italy is now under fascist rule, and the Jewish Guido and his family are sent to a concentration camp. Desperate to keep the horrific reality of their situation from his son, Guido devises a series of charades and stories to make Joshua think they are in an elaborate game (the winner gets a real tank!). The first half of the film is a sweet, wonderfully funny romantic comedy in which love triumphs; in the second, more dramatic half, Benigni continues to use humor to tell his story, but never at the expense of the grim circumstances in which the characters find themselves. *Life Is Beautiful* is an astonishing comedy, and a heartrending story of sacrifice and, ultimately, love. Winner of three Oscars, including Best Actor and Foreign Film. (Italian with English subtitles) ★★★★ VHS: $14.99; DVD: $32.99

Life Is Sweet

(1991, 102 min, GB, Mike Leigh) *Alison Steadman, Jim Broadbent, Jane Horrocks, Claire Skinner, Timothy Spall.* Leigh follows his wickedly satirical *High Hopes* with this mirthful and touching slice of middle-class life set in the English Midlands. Taking on the notion of family dysfunctionality, the film follows the daily trials of a middle-aged couple (Steadman, Broadbent) and their twentysomething twin daughters — one an aspiring plumber (Skinner), the other an aspiring radical feminist (Horrocks). The common obsession in the film is food. Dad's a chef in a hotel kitchen, family friend Aubrey (Spall) is gonzo over the gourmet restaurant he's opening and Horrocks is an anorexic/bulimic. Leigh masterfully takes this soap opera situation and creates a wry, witty comedy filled with social commentary and a surprising amount of tender moments. Horrocks deserves special attention for her portrayal of the family's scapegoat. ★★★½ VHS: $9.99

A Life Less Ordinary

(1997, 103 min, US, Danny Boyle) *Ewan McGregor, Cameron Diaz, Holly Hunter, Delroy Lindo, Ian Holm, Stanley Tucci, Tony Shalhoub, Dan Hedaya, Judith Ivey.* Despite a beautifully realized opening sequence which confirms that the filmmakers have talent to waste, this romantic-comedy-action-musical-fantasy tries to pay homage to just about every genre imaginable. The story involves two angels (Hunter, Lindo) who are given the thankless task of uniting heiress Diaz and ex-janitor-turned-kidnapper McGregor — or else. While the outcome is obvious, getting there is no picnic. Viewers will have to endure a schizophrenic pastiche which features both a *Road Warrior* tribute and a knock-out karaoke number. A clumsy piece of whimsy. ★★½ VHS: $9.99; DVD: $22.99

The Life of Emile Zola

(1937, 116 min, US, William Dieterle) *Paul Muni, Gale Sondergaard, Joseph Schildkraut, Gloria Holden.* In one of the best of the 1930s Hollywood biographies, Muni gives a remarkably controlled performance as the famed French author. Gale Sondergaard is well-cast as his wife, and Schildkraut won a supporting Oscar as the wrongly accused Captain Dreyfus, for whom Zola intervened. Oscar winner for Best Picture. ★★★★ VHS: $19.99

A Life of Her Own

(1950, 108 min, US, George Cukor) *Lana Turner, Ray Milland, Tom Ewell, Louis Calhern, Ann Dvorak, Jean Hagen.* Lana plays a Midwestern girl who moves to New York to start a career in modeling. In no time, she's on all the magazine covers. She also becomes involved with married tycoon Milland, with whom there can be no happy ending. The film's beginning sizzles as it peeks behind the scenes of the Big Apple's modeling circles, but it quickly changes gears and fizzles into another routine other-woman melodrama. Dvorak nearly steals the show as an aging model who briefly takes Turner under her wing. ★★½ VHS: $19.99

The Life of Jesus

(1997, 96 min, France, Bruno Dumont) *Sébastien Bailleul, Samuel Boidin, Kader Chaatouf, Geneviève Cottreel, Marjorie Cottreel.* Young epileptic slacker Freddie (Bailleul) spends his time hanging out with his motorcycle buddies and fooling around with his pretty girlfriend. When an Arab teen begins pursuing her, Freddy's buried rage — about his epilepsy, being unemployed, his best friend dying of AIDS — comes to the surface. With his debut film, Dumont has no qualms about halting the action to admire a beautiful landscape or linger on a well-com-

Life Is Beautiful (1998)

posed shot. And though it does test the patience now and then, *The Life of Jesus* remains quite powerful and moving. The widescreen photography is sumptuous, and the acting is persuasive. The story of alienated youth has been done before, and even better, but the film is easy on the eyes, and has for its protagonist an interesting and ultimately sympathetic anti-hero. (French with English subtitles) ★★★ VHS: $19.99; DVD: $29.99

Life of Oharu

(1952, 137 min, Japan, Kenji Mizoguchi) *Toshiro Mifune, Kinuyo Tanaka.* One of the most enduring masterpieces of world cinema, this is an exquisitely rendered portrait of a woman who is tragically victimized by the brutal strictures of 17th-century feudal Japanese society. The director shows remarkable insight into the psychology of his female protagonist and fills the screen with hauntingly beautiful camera work. (Japanese with English subtitles) ★★★★ VHS: $29.99

Life of Sin

(1990, 112 min, US, Efrin Lopez Neris) *Raul Julia, Miriam Colón, Jose Ferrer.* The short, stationary shots in the opening sequence of *Life of Sin* establish a moody, almost dreamlike quality which permeates the rest of the film. Colón is engrossing as the peasant woman who gains fame and fortune during an unhappy and unfulfilled life. In a role which could easily have engendered histrionics, her understated and measured portrayal is all the more powerful. Julia is strong in support as Colón's lifelong friend, whose loyalty is unquestioning until a tragic, unnecessary confrontation. An interesting study of hypocrisy and societal double standards, though somewhat marred by an unclear resolution. ★★½ VHS: $79.99

Life Stinks

(1991, 95 min, US, Mel Brooks) *Mel Brooks, Leslie Ann Warren, Jeffrey Tambor, Howard Morris.* Brooks hits rock bottom with this comedy — a sad, humorless and offensive parody of homelessness and big business. Brooks plays a multi-

millionaire who bets he can live penniless and homeless on the streets of Los Angeles for one month. Once there, director-writer Brooks lets loose an incredible array of comic vulgarities, none of which are the least bit amusing or original. *Sullivan's Travels* it's not. ★ VHS: $14.99

Life with Mikey

(1993, 91 min, US, James Lapine) *Michael J. Fox, Christina Vidal, Nathan Lane, Cyndi Lauper, Ruben Blades.* Fox stars as an ex-child actor who opens his own kiddie talent agency. The biggest belly laughs in this lazy comedy come when Fox holds open auditions to find the next Macaulay Culkin and ends up with tiny tots spouting *The Odd Couple*, baton twirlers and Ethel Merman's bastard daughter. The movie gets mired down in its own plot about a street-smart kid (Vidal) who, by the sheer force of her uninhibited charm, nabs a major cookie commercial and saves the agency from impending doom. Her lifeless performance mixed with Fox's affable but lackluster performance turns this into pure mush. Lane, at least, is good in support as Fox's business partner. ★★

Lifeboat

(1944, 96 min, US, Alfred Hitchcock) *Tallulah Bankhead, John Hodiak, William Bendix, Canada Lee, Walter Slezak, Hume Cronyn.* After an ocean liner is torpedoed by a German sub, a handful of disparate survivors are left adrift in a cramped lifeboat. When a final castaway appears, one of the Nazi crew members and the only individual aboard with any navigational skill, the group is caught in an equally cramped moral dilemma. A cinematically daring work which, though confined to a single setting, is never claustrophobic, and is suspenseful and intriguing throughout. John Steinbeck wrote the screenplay. Acting awards went to Bankhead for her only truly satisfying screen appearance. ★★★★ VHS: $14.99

Lifeforce

(1985, 100 min, US, Tobe Hooper) *Steve Railsback, Peter Firth, Mathilda May, Patrick Stewart.* Some elaborate special effects can't hide the silliness of the plot and ineffectiveness of Hooper's direction. Space vampires are terrorizing London. An intriguing premise gone sour. ★ VHS: $9.99; DVD: $14.99

The Lift

(1985, 95 min, The Netherlands, Dick Maas) *Huub Stapel, Willeke Van Ammelrooy.* A Dutch thriller about an elevator in a high-tech office building with a murderous mind of its own. The highlight of this film was probably the ad which said: "Take the stairs! Take the stairs! For God's sake, take the stairs!" Great premise that holds up for a while, but when it comes to horror and splatter films, nothing beats the Americans. ★★

Light of Day

(1987, 107 min, US, Paul Schrader) *Michael J. Fox, Gena Rowlands, Joan Jett, Jason Miller, Michael Rooker.* Fox and Jett play a brother and sister who perform together in a local Cleveland rock band, trying to make it big time. Rowlands is their dying mother, at odds with her carefree daughter. Full of clichés in both its family drama and trying-to-get-ahead show business story. ★★ VHS: $14.99

Light Sleeper

(1992, 103 min, US, Paul Schrader) *Willem Dafoe, Susan Sarandon, James Clennon, Dana Delany, Mary Beth Hurt, Victor Garber, David Spade.* Despite the heavy-handedness of Schrader's direction and its unsatisfying sugar-coated ending, *Light Sleeper* is an engrossing and intriguing drama. Essentially the story of the midlife crisis of alienated 40-year-old drug runner John LeTour (Dafoe), the story is punched up by an entertainingly frantic, amphetamine-driven performance by Sarandon as the brains and balls behind a high-class New York drug ring. LeTour is a loyal and decent but slumberous man who, after years of delivering the goods to the yuppies, posers and rich lowlifes, begins to question it all. A serious, arty, flawed yet entertaining drama. ★★★ VHS: $14.99; DVD: $24.99

Light Years

(1987, 80 min, US, Renée Laloux) *Voices of Glenn Close, Christopher Plummer.* "In a thousand years, Gandahar was destroyed. A thousand years ago, Gandahar will be saved." With this intriguing mathematical paradox, acclaimed director Laloux (*Fantastic Planet*) and master science fiction writer Isaac Asimov combine their formidable talents to produce a captivating and truly original animated sci-fi adventure. This rewarding odyssey of sight and sound tips its hat to some of the great animated classics before it, from *Yellow Submarine* to *Lord of the Rings.* ★★★

The Lighthorsemen

(1988, 115 min, Australia, Simon Wincer) *Jon Blake, Peter Phelps, Bill Kerr, Sigrid Thornton.* The thrilling true story of the Australian Light Brigade's military exploits during World War I, and especially their assault on thousands of German and Turkish troops in Beersheba, is the focus of this sweeping saga. Wincer impressively directs the elaborately staged battle sequences, although some of the widescreen spectacle will be lost on video. While the characters are all too simply drawn and its heavy-handed clichés of "war is hell" get tiring, fans of military adventure films will overlook this and become absorbed in the sweeping action of this epic. ★★½ VHS: $14.99

Lightning Jack

(1994, 101 min, US, Simon Wincer) *Paul Hogan, Cuba Gooding, Jr., Beverly D'Angelo.* An insipid comedy set in the Old West. Hogan plays Lightning Jack Kane, an aging outlaw who teams up with a deaf and mute Gooding to knock off a few banks. Gooding tries to liven things up with his physical schtick, and he might have succeeded had his material been elevated anywhere above insulting. This is Muzak filmmaking — the film's cheesy humor and fluffy plot line leave one with that kind of hollow feeling otherwise found only in elevators and supermarkets. ★ VHS: $9.99; DVD: $14.99

Lightning over Water

(1980/81, 91 min, US, Wim Wenders & Nicholas Ray) While not a documentary, this unusual film chronicles the last days of famed director Ray who was dying of cancer. While visiting Ray in his SoHo loft, Wenders listens to a story Ray would like to film. They decide to film that story, as it is

being lived. The result is a film about friendship as well as a rather unfocused look at a man attempting to finish his life and work with the help of those around him. ★★★

The Lightship

(1985, 89 min, US, Jerzy Skolimowski) *Robert Duvall, Klaus Maria Brandauer, William Forsythe, Arliss Howard.* What might have been a standard good vs. evil allegory is elevated to a B-grade suspense thriller starring the chameleonic Duvall as an effeminate bank robber who, along with two sadistic partners, escapes from the law by hijacking a lightship piloted by a pacifist captain (Brandauer). Duvall's excessively flamboyant performance makes this worthwhile viewing. ★★½ VHS: $79.99

Like Father, Like Son

(1987, 98 min, US, Ron Daniel) *Dudley Moore, Kirk Cameron, Catherine Hicks, Sean Astin.* One of the least successful of the "body switching" comedies, with harried surgeon Moore and teenage son Cameron switching bodies thanks to an ancient potion. ★★ VHS: $9.99

Like Water for Chocolate

(1992, 113 min, Mexico, Alfonso Arau) *Lumi Cavazos, Marco Leonardi, Regina Torne.* An immensely satisfying cinematic experience in every regard, this runaway art-house hit is at the same time whimsical, romantic, comic, tragic, sensuous and, above all, pure in spirit. In the grandest Latin American tradition of magical realism, the film tells the tale of Tita, a young woman who is condemned to a lonely and passionless life by her family's cruel tradition that the youngest daughter must care for her mother until she dies. Denied her one true love, Pedro (who Mama arranges to marry Tita's older sister), and forced into servitude, she responds by pouring her emotions into the recipes she is forced to cook for the family, resulting in witches' brews that have a profound effect on all who partake. It's mouthwatering good fun, sprinkled with intrigue and a heavy dash of passion. (Italian with English subtitles) ★★★★ VHS: $14.99; DVD: $29.99

Lili

(1953, 87 min, US, Charles Walters) *Leslie Caron, Jean-Pierre Aumont, Mel Ferrer, Zsa Zsa Gabor.* An absolute delight! Caron gives an enchanting performance as a 16-year-old French orphan who joins a traveling carnival. There she falls in love with the magician (Aumont), and is given a valuable lesson in life and love from a crippled puppeteer (Ferrer), who uses his small creatures to cheer the sorrowful Lili. Oscar-winning score includes the wonderful "Hi-Lili, Hi-Lo." ★★★★ VHS: $19.99

Lilies

(1996, 96 min, Canada, John Greyson) *Marcel Sabourin, Aubert Pallascio, Matthew Ferguson, Jason Cadieux, Danny Gilmore.* An impressive independent gay film, *Lilies* is an engrossing drama of jealousy, love, revenge and redemption. The time is 1952 and the setting is a prison where the elderly Bishop Bilodeau (Sabourin) arrives to hear a dying man's last confession. But the confession was just a ruse and now the priest finds himself captive, forced to confront his shameful past and the prisoner, with whom he shares it. With him as their only audience, Simon (Pallascio), convicted of killing his lover as a youth, directs his fellow inmates in a play that reenacts the events of forty years past. A complex, intensely cinematic adaptation of Michel Marc Bouchard's play "Les Fleurettes." (French with English subtitles) ★★★ VHS: $29.99; DVD: $24.99

Lilies of the Field

(1963, 95 min, US, Ralph Nelson) *Sidney Poitier, Lilia Skala, Lisa Mann.* Poitier won an Oscar for Best Actor with his portrayal of a carpenter who reluctantly becomes involved in helping a group of German nuns. Poitier meets the nuns by chance after his car breaks down in front of their decaying convent. The sisters take this as a sign from God that he is the one who will save their home and build them a new chapel. Poitier's performance is full of charm and Skala is wonderful as the mother superior. A good, lighthearted film that is as inspiring as it is entertaining. ★★★½ VHS: $14.99; DVD: $19.99

L

Ewan McGregor in *A Life Less Ordinary*

341

Lily in Love

(1985, 104 min, GB, Karoly Makk) *Maggie Smith, Christopher Plummer, Elke Sommer.* Engaging performances highlight this minor though enjoyable update of Molnar's comedy "The Guardsman." Plummer plays an aging classical actor who disguises himself as a younger man to get the lead in a film written by his wife (Smith). When he lands the role, his wife becomes attracted to the "young man," unaware of his true identity. ★★½

Lily Tomlin: Appearing Nitely

(1979, 70 min, US, Wendy Apple) *Lily Tomlin.* Lily Tomlin's made-for-HBO special is a live recording of her Tony Award–winning one-woman show, "Appearing Nitely." Alternately hilarious and poignant, Lily goes on an almost stream-of-consciousness tear as she mines remembrances from her childhood and youth to create a series of memorable characters and situations. She loses herself in the skits, becoming the shopping bag lady, the bratty adolescent and the geeky suburban girl ready to experiment in the whacked-out '60s. ★★★½ VHS: $19.99

Limbo

(1999, 127 min, US, John Sayles) *Mary Elizabeth Mastrantonio, David Strathairn, Vanessa Martinez, Kris Kristofferson, Casey Siemaszko.* The beautiful, perilous Alaskan landscape provides a striking balance between the harmony and discord amid a group of citizens of a small coastal town in writer-director Sayles' efficient, smartly acted drama/thriller. The story begins as a romance set in Juneau, Alaska, where Donna (Mastrantonio), a struggling singer, and Joe (Strathairn), a reclusive handyman, begin a tentative affair. Sayles examines these and the town's other characters with his usual discerning, compassionate eye for human frailty and the need for emotional contact. However, the film takes an unexpected turn when romance gives way to a survival adventure, where Joe, Donna and her teenaged daughter find themselves in both a physical and spiritual state of uncertainty. Sayles may ruffle a few feathers with his deliberately ambiguous ending, but that notwithstanding, *Limbo* is a compelling character study offering noteworthy performances, good local color, and a story that isn't afraid to take its time. ★★★ VHS: $19.99; DVD: $27.99

Mary Elizabeth Mastrantonio and David Strathairn in *Limbo*

Limelight

(1952, 145 min, US, Charles Chaplin) *Charles Chaplin, Claire Bloom, Buster Keaton.* In this, his last American film, Chaplin returned to the London music halls of his childhood. This bittersweet tale tells the story of an aging performer who triumphs over his own foibles (declining popularity and his own mortality) and "passes the torch," so to speak, by curing a young, aspiring ballet dancer of her paralysis and thus launching her career (and ending his). The film is certainly overlong and, at times, sluggishly paced; but even this Chaplin "failure" is still a moving tribute to those with whom Chaplin has always sympathized: the underprivileged. ★★★; DVD: $29.99

The Limey

(1999, 89 min, US, Steven Soderbergh) *Terence Stamp, Peter Fonda, Lesley Ann Warren, Luis Guzman.* In director Soderbergh's near-perfect action/thriller, Stamp excels as a father who travels from his native England to Los Angeles to search for the person responsible for his estranged daughter's death. It's a simple plot from which Soderbergh is able to create unrelenting tension — literally from start to finish. As Stamp arrives in L.A. greeted by unwelcome arms, Soderbergh ingeniously utilizes flashbacks and forwards to give bits and pieces of information which become whole by the story's end. The non-linear editing only enhances Soderbergh's taut direction, and underscores a mean, lean screenplay without an ounce of fat. The use of film clips from Stamp's 1967 British film *Poor Cow* helps in shading the character, and even helps in making this an homage to a couple of '60s icons. One of those, Fonda, is excellent as the shady record producer who may have been responsible for the young woman's death. ★★★½ VHS: $9.99; DVD: $19.99

The Line King: The Al Hirschfeld Story

(1997, 86 min, US, Susan Dryfoos) Anyone who has ever seen an issue of Sunday's *New York Times* will undoubtedly recognize the work of Al Hirschfeld, the newspaper's beloved caricaturist. For over sixty years, the bearded, introspective Hirschfeld has captured Broadway's best on the *Times* pages with his distinctive pen and ink drawings. This loving, Oscar-nominated documentary, coproduced by the *Times*, chronicles the artist's life by letting him and his work do most of the talking. Of course, there's also coverage of "Nina," his daughter whose name has been hidden throughout his drawings since she was born. ★★★½ VHS: $24.99

The Linguini Incident

(1992, 100 min, US, Richard Shepard) *David Bowie, Rosanna Arquette, Eszter Balint, Buck*

Terence Stamp in *The Limey*

Henry, Andre Greogry, Marlee Matlin, Viveca Lindfors. Monty (Bowie), the new British bartender at the latest New York theme park restaurant (a palace of trend), needs to marry to get a green card. Or so it seems in this giddy, convoluted and very entertaining foray into the world of Manhattan's super-rich, super-chic and wannabes. Escape artistry, Mrs. Houdini's wedding ring and some very serious wagers are a few of the backdrops to tell the tale of deception, survival and monetary gain in a place where robbery becomes performance art if you're wearing the right bra. ★★★

The Lion in Winter

(1968, 135 min, GB, Anthony Harvey) *Peter O'Toole, Katharine Hepburn, Anthony Hopkins, Nigel Terry, John Castle, Timothy Dalton, Jane Merrow.* Hepburn and O'Toole are both at their fiery best as Eleanor of Aquitaine and King Henry II of England. With undaunted ferocity, the two engage in a bitter battle over who will be the successor to the throne while their children surreptitiously battle each other for the position. Unparalleled performances in the supporting roles make this an overall acting gem. Based on James Goldman's Broadway play. ★★★★ VHS: $14.99; DVD: $19.99

A Lion Is in the Streets

(1953, 88 min, US, Raoul Walsh) *James Cagney, Barbara Hale, Anne Francis.* Cagney's brisk performance brings unexpected life to this interesting but otherwise average political potboiler. Cagney plays a drifter from the Deep South who becomes a favorite son and runs for Governor. As he gains power and influence, he becomes more corrupt and ruthless, which sets the stage for a final showdown. ★★ VHS: $19.99

The Lion King

(1994, 84 min, US, Roger Allers & Rob Minkoff) *Voices of Matthew Broderick, Jeremy Irons, James Earl Jones, Whoopi Goldberg, Nathan Lane.* Highly overrated and the subject of much undeserving ballyhoo, *The Lion King* revolves around young Simba, the crown Prince of Pride Rock, where all of the beasts live in peace and harmony under the benevolent dictatorship of his father, Mufasa. When the King's evil brother Scar conspires to murder his royal sibling, Mufasa's son Simba, thinking himself responsible for the inevitable tragedy, goes into self-imposed exile, only to return when the kingdom is on the verge of ecological ruin. Its weak plot aside, what really makes *The Lion King* disappointing is its score. Elton John and Tim Rice's sappy pop musical numbers are completely lacking the razzmatazz and good-natured fun of their forebears Alan Menken and Howard Ashman. ★★½

Lionheart

(1991, 115 min, US, Sheldon Lettich) *Jean-Claude Van Damme, Harrison Page.* Van Damme plays a member of the French Foreign Legion who travels to America when he learns his brother is dying. En route, he becomes involved in the financially lucrative but deadly sport of streetfighting, where he is champion and in great demand. Typical Van Damme actioner: lots of fights and little sense. ★★ VHS: $9.99

Lipstick

(1976, 89 min, US, Lamont Johnson) *Margaux Hemingway, Chris Sarandon, Mariel Hemingway, Anne Bancroft.* Inferior revenge film and ridiculous social drama with Margaux taking on rapist Sarandon. Mariel is her little sister; Bancroft plays an attorney. ★ VHS: $59.99

Lipstick on Your Collar

(1993, 37 min, GB, Renny Rye) *Giles Thomas, Louise Germaine, Ewan McGregor, Peter Jeffrey.* As with Dennis Potter's *The Singing Detective* and *Pennies from Heaven*, *Lipstick on Your Collar* is a multilayered, intricately structured exploration of the human psyche. At the height of the Cold War, military intelligence officers spend their 9 to 5 days decoding information about Russian troop movements in bureaucratic isolation. Their personal lives are spent in a threadbare England still recovering from WWII. These private and professional worlds collide when the newest member of the intelligence group, a naïve private, finds himself living in the same building as his corporal — and his corporal's beautiful, ill-treated wife. Dull, utter normalcy is bizarrely juxtaposed with outbursts of pop tunes, sublimely choreographed under saturated lighting: the subconscious made manifest. ★★★★ VHS: $59.99

Liquid Sky

(1983, 112 min, US, Slava Tsukerman) *Anne Carlisle, Paula Sheppard.* Flying saucers, fatal orgasms, rampant androgyny and relentless nihilism make *Liquid Sky* a most original and hallucinatory film. Coauthor Carlisle stars in dual roles as Jimmy, a snarling junkie, and Margaret, his female nemesis, a languid model with an unusual kiss of death. Perched atop Margaret's penthouse terrace are mite-sized aliens who crave the sensation of a heroin rush, which, it seems, is duplicated organically during human orgasm. A stunning cultural collage that offers an alien's-eye view of Manhattan's lurid clubs, majestic skyline and jaded populace. ★★★ VHS: $49.99; DVD: $24.99

Lisbon Story

(1994, 100 min, Germany, Wim Wenders) *Rüdiger Vogler, Patrick Bauchau, Teresa Salgueiro, Madredeus.* Director Wenders takes us on another odyssey of discovery, revelation and everyday miracles. Sound engineer Philip Winter (Vogler) gets a postcard from a director friend of his, emphatically requesting Winter's immediate presence in Lisbon. Winter arrives at the Lisbon address, an apartment empty of his friend but with film without sound on an editing table. Waiting for his friend to appear, our protagonist decides to record sound for the film he's discovered; through which activity he connects with the lives of the city's inhabitants. As in *Wings of Desire*, the mundane is transmogrified by magical realism, and the banal seems touched by the divine. A sweet, uplifting road movie from that genre's master. (Letterboxed) (English, Portuguese and German with English subtitles) ★★★ VHS: $19.99

The List of Adrian Messenger

(1963, 98 min, US, John Huston) *George C. Scott, Kirk Douglas, Burt Lancaster, Dana Wynter, Tony Curtis, Robert Mitchum, Frank Sinatra.* Scott heads an all-star cast in this potent Agatha Christie–like murder mystery about a maniac (and master of disguise) who is killing off potential heirs to a family fortune. Scott plays the detective on the case. ★★★ VHS: $19.99

Lisztomania

(1975, 104 min, GB, Ken Russell) *Roger Daltrey, Sara Kestelman, Paul Nicholas, Ringo Starr, Nell Campbell.* Franz Liszt, classical composer, gets the full treatment from Russell in this outlandish visual and sexual assault on historical accuracy and biographical detail. The presumption is that Liszt was a precursor to the rock superstars of today and in unabashed Russell fashion, he turns this into a garish, psychosexual extravaganza. Daltrey brings a certain Adonis-like quality to his role as Liszt, but Starr as the Pope is heresy in anyone's book. ★★ VHS: $14.99

Little Big League

(1994, 119 min, US, Andrew Scheinman) *Luke Edwards, Timothy Busfield, John Ashton, Ashley Crow, Jason Robards, Kevin Dunn, Jonathan Silverman, Dennis Farina.* Little Big League is equal parts *Rookie of the Year* and *The Kid from Left Field*, and despite its lack of originality it still manages to produce a certain charm all its own. An 11-year-old baseball fanatic inherits the Minnesota Twins when his beloved grandfather dies. The youth quickly appoints himself manager, and must rally his players towards the inevitable championship showdown. Though the kid is a boorish walking baseball encyclopedia, you can't help rooting for him. ★★★ VHS: $14.99

Little Big Man

(1970, 150 min, US, Arthur Penn) *Dustin Hoffman, Faye Dunaway, Chief Dan George, Richard Mulligan, Martin Balsam.* Hoffman stars as the 121-year-old Jack Crabbe, who recounts his experiences with General Custer, Wild Bill Hickok, Indians and medicine show con men. An epic comedy, with touches of drama and a perfect cast. ★★★½ VHS: $9.99

Little Boy Blue

(1998, 104 min, US, Antonio Tibaldi) *Ryan Phillippe, Nastassja Kinski, John Savage, Shirley Knight, Tyrin Turner.* A creaky melodrama about a Texas family harboring some painful secrets, *Little Boy Blue* slowly approaches its finale, but when it does come, it packs a wallop. Jimmy West (Phillippe) is about to go away to college, but he really wants to stay home to care for his two small brothers. Actually, Jimmy is hoping to rescue them and their mom (Kinski) from their sadistic dad Ray (Savage), a vet who is dealing with some pretty serious issues. A few things complicate the escape plans, not the least of which is the death of a stranger who has tracked down Ray. Director Tibaldi's gritty film does not hold much in the way of drama, but its characterizations are well done. ★★½ VHS: $14.99

Little Buddha

(1994, 123 min, US, Bernardo Bertolucci) *Bridget Fonda, Chris Isaak, Keanu Reeves, Ying Ruocheng, Alex Wiesendanger.* Beautifully photographed and emotionally uplifting, Bertolucci's surprisingly accessible story of spiritual enlightenment has the grand sweep of his *The Last Emperor* but on a smaller scale. Interweaving the modern-day story of a young boy who may or may not be the reincarnation of the Dalai Lama, and the ravishing telling of the origins and tenets of Buddhism and specifically the coming-of-age of the prophet Siddhartha, the film is insightful throughout and amazingly balances both worlds with equal artistry. The real treat here is Reeves in the young Indian prince Siddhartha — and while traces of his California dude are present, he nevertheless is believable; and he looks great in mascara, too. ★★★½ VHS: $14.99; DVD: $29.99

Liquid Sky

L

Little Caesar

(1930, 80 min, US, Mervyn LeRoy) *Edward G. Robinson, Glenda Farrell, Douglas Fairbanks, Jr., Sidney Blackmer.* Robinson gives a live-wire performance as Caesar Enrico Bandella, one of moviedom's most infamous and ruthless criminals. Robinson has been caricatured as this persona so often that it takes a while to realize how subtle his performance really is. Rico is as classless, cold-blooded and blindly ambitious as the real gangsters we read about; and the film, the first of the 1930s crime movies, traces his bloody rise and bloody fall. ★★★★ VHS: $19.99

Little Dorrit: Pts I & II

(1988, 178 min, GB, Christine Edzard) *Derek Jacobi, Sarah Pickering, Alec Guinness, Joan Greenwood, Miriam Margolyes.* A magnificent two-part adaptation of Charles Dickens' classic novel, released in two separate volumes (it is recommended that they be viewed in their correct order). The film, set in early 19th-century London, tells the story of the Dorrit family: from their internment in debtor's prison to their eventual rescue and financial security, and of their relationship with the rich Clennam family, in particular the family's idealistic son, Arthur. Part One, *Nobody's Fault*, is told through the eyes of Arthur, and Part Two, *Little Dorrit's Story*, is seen through the eyes of young Amy, the title character. The film abounds with remarkable performances. ★★★½

The Little Drummer Girl

(1984, 130 min, US, George Roy Hill) *Diane Keaton, Klaus Kinski, Sami Frey.* A stirring if overlong political thriller, based on John Le Carré's novel, exploring the volatile situation in the Middle East, the complexities of personal allegiance and one woman's emotional dismantling as the result of her involvement with sparring terrorist forces. Keaton gives a splendid performance as an actress who is "hired" to pose as an agent, thrusting her into political intrigue. ★★★ VHS: $14.99

The Little Foxes

(1941, 116 min, US, William Wyler) *Bette Davis, Herbert Marshall, Patricia Collinge, Teresa Wright.* Terrific screen version of Lillian Hellman's Broadway smash. Davis is at her bitchy best as Regina, the matriarch of a bickering Southern clan facing financial ruin. Collinge gives a heartbreaking performance as the kind-hearted aunt. ★★★½ VHS: $14.99; DVD: $24.99

Little Fugitive

(1953, 75 min, US, Ray Ashley, Morris Engel & Ruth Orkin) *Richie Andrusco, Rickie Brewster, Winifred Cushing, Will Lee.* One of the first American independent films, *Little Fugitive* is a wonderful mix of cinema verité, funny observations of youth, and touching reflections of familial relationships. Shot on location on the streets of New York City, *Little Fugitive* follows two adventurous days of Joey (Andrusco), a seven-year-old Brooklyn youth and constantly harassed little brother. When his older brother Lennie (Brewster) and friends make Joey believe he's killed Lennie, Joey runs away to Coney Island where he's left to fend for himself. Andrusco is a marvel; his escapades are certain to enthrall, to the point that the significant contributions of *Little Fugitive* to the birth of American independent filmmaking are easily overlooked. ★★★½ VHS: $24.99; DVD: $29.99

Little Giants

(1994, 106 min, US, Duwayne Dunham) *Rick Moranis, Ed O'Neill, Shawna Waldron.* Moranis and O'Neill play highly competitive brothers — one can't play sports and the other is a little league football coach. While Moranis may have no athletic ability, his daughter (nicknamed Icebox) is a natural but is rejected for uncle O'Neill's team solely because she's a girl. Eventually a team of other outcasts is born, with Moranis as its coach. While the ending is predictable, there are some laughs along the way. ★★½ VHS: $19.99

Little Man Tate

(1991, 99 min, US, Jodie Foster) *Jodie Foster, Dianne Wiest, Adam Hann-Byrd, Harry Connick, Jr., Debi Mazar.* Foster's impressive directorial debut is a quirky, entertaining comedy/melodrama about a seven-year-old genius who gets caught in a tug-of-war between his working-class mom (Foster) and a determined educator (Wiest). The story centers around young Fred Tate's lack of social skills (a trait invariably attached to child prodigies), and his leaving his mother to study at an academy for gifted children living under Wiest's supervision. Both Foster and Wiest give strong performances and newcomer Hann-Byrd is affecting as Fred. ★★★ VHS: $14.99

The Little Mermaid

(1989, 82 min, US, John Musker & Ron Clements) *Voices of Jodi Benson, Christopher Daniel Barnes, Pat Carroll, Buddy Hackett, Nancy Cartwright.* From the masters at Disney studios comes the company's best film since *Mary Poppins*, and the finest full-length animated feature since *Cinderella*. Howard Ashman and Alan Menken have written a joyously tuneful score to tell the tale of a young mermaid who falls in love with a handsome human prince, much to the chagrin of her father. The film features outstanding animation, a witty, thoroughly enjoyable story, the delightful Oscar-winning song "Under the Sea," and a bewitching cast of characters.

The Little Mermaid will come to be cherished for years as *Snow White, Bambi*, and *Pinocchio* have been before it: it is certainly as accomplished. ★★★★ VHS: $26.99

The Little Minister

(1934, 110 min, US, Richard Wallace) *Katharine Hepburn, John Beal, Alan Hale, Donald Crisp.* Hepburn is in prime form as a Gypsy girl in 1840 who falls in love with a conservative Scottish minister, shocking his conservative congregation. ★★★ VHS: $19.99

Little Monsters

(1989, 103 min, US, Richard Alan Greenberg) *Fred Savage, Howie Mandel, Daniel Stern, Margaret Whitton, Frank Whaley.* The movie that proves there really are monsters under our beds! Savage meets Maurice (Mandel), the zany monster that lives under *his* bed, and wacky misadventures ensue. Not as cute as the premise suggests, the cast tries hard to overcome a pedestrian screenplay. ★★ VHS: $14.99

Little Murders

(1971, 110 min, US, Alan Arkin) *Alan Arkin, Elliott Gould, Marcia Rodd, Donald Sutherland, Vincent Gardenia, Elizabeth Wilson.* Arkin directed this blackest of black comedies about urban decay, both physical and moral. Gould is the catatonic photographer; Gardenia, his paranoid father-in-law; Sutherland, the hippie priest; and Arkin, the schizophrenic detective in a frighteningly funny vision of a not-so-distant present. ★★★ VHS: $59.99

Little Nicky

(2000, 84 min, US, Steven Brill) *Adam Sandler, Patricia Arquette, Harvey Keitel, Rhys Ifans, Rodney Dangerfield, Tommy "Tiny" Lister, Jr., Reese Witherspoon, Jon Lovitz.* Of all the satanic films (*Bless the Child, Lost Souls*, etc) released in 2000, none is more horrifying than the dumbfoundingly bad comedy *Little Nicky*. Sandler, who last appeared in the terrible *Waterboy* and *Big Daddy*, sinks to a new low even by his "standards." The posterboy for pubescent silliness plays Nicky, the Devil's dimwitted youngest son, who must venture to Earth to retrieve his two brothers causing havoc throughout New York City. Armed with a bad lisp and awful jokes, Nicky sets out to capture his siblings and falls in love with a mortal in the process. There could have been a mediocre movie somewhere in all this, but the screenplay ruins every single comedic possibility, making this comedy abortion truly one of the worst film comedies of all time. ★ VHS: $14.99; DVD: $24.99

A Little Night Music

(1978, 124 min, US, Harold Prince) *Elizabeth Taylor, Len Cariou, Diana Rigg, Hermione Gingold, Lawrence Guittard.* A rather mediocre adaptation of the brilliant Tony Award–winning musical written by Stephen Sondheim (which was based on Ingmar Bergman's *Smiles of a Summer's Night*). Taylor is miscast as Desiree, the actress who re-enters the life of newly married Cariou (repeating his stage role). Rigg steals the show as the wife of soldier Guittard, who is having an affair with Taylor. The film captures none of the magic which made the Bergman film and the stage play great hits. Though "A Weekend in the Country" is performed quite admirably. ★½

Little Caesar

Little Nikita

(1988, 98 min, US, Richard Benjamin) *Sidney Poitier, River Phoenix, Richard Bradford.* Mommie's a Commie (and Daddy, too) in this contrived thriller with young Phoenix unaware of his parents' political sympathies; all of them under investigation by FBI agent Poitier. Both Phoenix and Poitier deliver strong performances but the muddled screenplay takes its time setting up the bare-bones action. ★★ VHS: $9.99

Little Odessa

(1995, 98 min, US, James Gray) *Tim Roth, Edward Furlong, Moira Kelly, Vanessa Redgrave, Maximilian Schell.* This brooding, pungent exploration of familial loyalties and personal isolation is Gray's astonishing directorial debut. Roth is arresting as Joshua, hit man for the Russian mafia, whose profession has estranged him from his Russian Jewish family; particularly his father (Schell), who is watching his wife (Redgrave) die of a brain tumor. Like his brother, the younger son Reuben (Furlong) is caught between ancestral custom and assimilation into American culture; and Joshua, who kills without thought or hesitation, is in some ways an icon of that assimilation. Thoughtful and deliberate direction guides uniformly remarkable performances through this haunting examination of the painful human longing to make contact. ★★★★ VHS: $9.99; DVD: $24.99

The Little Prince

(1974, 88 min, GB, Stanley Donen) *Richard Kiley, Gene Wilder, Bob Fosse, Joss Ackland, Donna McKechnie.* Antoine de Saint-Exupery's magical book had all the trappings of a great film and you'd think that by putting Donen (*Singin' in the Rain*) in the director's chair, assembling an eclectic cast, and adding a musical score by Lerner and Loewe that you'd have a winner. But the film is a disappointment. The story of a neurotic aviator who counsels a young boy from outer space about such Earthly matters as love and life is presented coyly and lacks affection. ★★ VHS: $14.99

A Little Princess

(1995, 100 min, US, Alfonso Cuaron) *Eleanor Bron, Liam Cunningham, Liesel Matthews.* Based on the novel by Frances Hodgson Burnett, which was filmed once before in 1939 as *The Little Princess* with Shirley Temple, *A Little Princess* is an excellent adaptation embracing the themes of loneliness and courage. A young girl, Sara, is moved from her home in India to the same private girls' school in New York City attended by her deceased mother when her doting father joins the military ranks of WWI. Her fairy-tale existence is abruptly ended when he is pronounced killed in action and all of his assets are seized by the British government, leaving Sara penniless. Sara learns to keep her faith in miracles and inspires the other girls along the way until the wonderful tear-laden ending. ★★★½ VHS: $14.99; DVD: $14.99

The Little Rascals

(1994, 83 min, US, Penelope Spheeris) *Bug Hall, Travis Tedford, Brittany Ashton Jones, Daryl Hannah, Lea Thompson, Whoopi Goldberg, Mel Brooks.* Coaxing charming performances from an almost all-child cast, Spheeris has made a most entertaining and updated big-screen version of the Our Gang comedies. With no real plot to speak of, the story centers on the antics of the "He Man Womun Haters Club," and the fateful day when one of their own (Alfalfa) falls in love. . . with a girl. A pint-sized "battle of the sexes" comedy, *Little Rascals*'s amusing screenplay gives the children ample opportunity to mug, flirt, sing, dance, race go-carts, blow bubbles and act like little big people — all of which they do with an endearing quality. ★★★ VHS: $14.99; DVD: $24.99

A Little Romance

(1979, 108 min, US, George Roy Hill) *Laurence Olivier, Diane Lane, Thelonious Bernard, Sally Kellerman.* Charming coming-of-age tale about the budding romance between an American girl (Lane) living in Paris and a young French boy (Bernard). The two of them run away to Venice together, under the eye of kindly con man Olivier. ★★★ VHS: $14.99

Little Shop of Horrors

(1960, 70 min, US, Roger Corman) *Jonathan Haze, Jackie Joseph, Mel Welles, Dick Miller, Jack Nicholson.* This cult comedy, shot in a mind-boggling two-and-a-half days, is a delightful grab bag of goofy gags and kooky characters. Welles is the skid row florist, Nicholson is the masochistic dentist's patient and Audrey, Jr. is the bizarre begonia with a diet of human blood. (Remade in 1986 as a musical.) ★★★ VHS: $19.99; DVD: $19.99

Little Shop of Horrors

(1986, 88 min, US, Frank Oz) *Rick Moranis, Ellen Greene, Steve Martin, Bill Murray, Vincent Gardenia, John Candy, Christopher Guest, James Belushi; Voice of Levi Stubbs.* "He's a mean, green mother from outer space and he's bad!" Science fiction, comedy and musical doo-wop blend wonderfully in this screen version of the hit off-Broadway musical, itself based on Roger Corman's 1960 exploitation cult classic. Audrey II, the alien Venus Flytrap with an appetite for human blood, befriends a nerdish Moranis in its fiendish plot to take over. The many show-stopping scenes include a great production number, "Downtown," and a maniacal Martin as a sadistic dentist who meets his match in Murray's hilariously masochistic patient. ★★★½ VHS: $9.99; DVD: $19.99

The Little Theatre of Jean Renoir

(1968, 100 min, France, Jean Renoir) *Jeanne Moreau, Jean Renoir, Fernand Sardou.* Renoir's final film is a lovely gem told in three episodes with each story recalling Renoir's favorite themes and styles and introduced by the filmmaker himself. The first episode, "The Last Christmas Dinner," follows a tramp looking for a Christmas dinner. The second, "The Electric Floor Polisher," is an amusing tale of a woman in love with a home appliance and her two husbands who object. The concluding segment, "The Virtue of Tolerance," is about an elderly man who must accept the affairs of his wife. Moreau makes a memorable appearance as a solemnly untalented music hall performer. (French with English subtitles) ★★★½ VHS: $39.99

The Little Vampire

(2000, 94 min, US, Uli Edel) *Jonathan Lipnicki, Richard E. Grant, Rollo Weeks.* Harmless hijinks abound when a nine-year-old American boy (Lipnicki) living in Scotland befriends a kid his same age — who's a vampire. Kids probably won't care that there's too-few laughs; they'll just enjoy the silly set-up and kids-take-charge attitude. ★★½ VHS: $14.99; DVD: $19.99

Little Vera

(1987, 109 min, USSR, Vasily Pichul) *Natalya Negoda, Andrei Sokolov.* Hailed as a breakthrough film, *Little Vera* is one of the first Soviet movies to show nudity as well as expose the internal problems confronting the working class in the USSR. Negoda is wonderful as Vera, a pouty, sultry and restless teenager who falls in love with an older student. Problems erupt after he moves in with Vera, her nervous mother and alcoholic father. This is a fascinating work, showing a Russia not bent on the destruction of the capitalist world, but one embroiled in ethnic strife, where rebellious, Western-influenced teens seek a new life and where the family unit is threatened by the freedoms and sexual promiscuity of the free world. (Russian with English subtitles) ★★★ VHS: $29.99; DVD: $29.99

Little Voice

(1998, 96 min, GB, Mark Herman) *Michael Caine, Brenda Blethyn, Jane Horrocks, Ewan McGregor, Jim Broadbent.* Judy Garland, Marilyn Monroe and Shirley Bassey all come to miraculous life in the person of a pint-sized impersonator named Little Voice, superbly played by Horrocks. Unfortunately, this uneven adaptation of Jim Cartwright's hit London play spotlights L.V. in the first half, leaving the story nowhere to go but down. A way-over-the-top Blethyn plays Mari, L.V.'s mussy mother whose current beau, Ray (Caine), is a down-on-his-heels talent agent. When he hears L.V. singing one night, he begins seeing dollar signs. Only one drawback: L.V. is painfully shy and has no desire to be a star. The story then follows Ray's efforts to get L.V. to the show on time, where she wows a sold-out audience. Once L.V. has performed, however, the film loses its momentum; how could it possibly sustain that kind of energy level. It gave its finale at intermission. The rest of the film is loud, obnoxious people behaving badly. Caine oozes slime, and Blethyn snaps her one-liners with slingshot precision. ★★½ VHS: $19.99; DVD: $29.99

Little Women

(1933, 115 min, US, George Cukor) *Katharine Hepburn, Joan Bennett, Paul Lukas, Edna May Oliver, Frances Dee, Spring Byington.* A thoughtful and very faithful adaptation of Louisa May Alcott's classic book, with a wonderful performance by Hepburn as Jo, one of four sisters growing up in pre–Civil War New England. An impeccable production with superb direction from Cukor. ★★★★ VHS: $19.99

Little Women

(1994, 118 min, US, Gillian Armstrong) *Winona Ryder, Susan Sarandon, Gabriel Byrne, Trini Alvarado, Samantha Mathis, Kirsten Dunst, Christian Bale, Eric Stoltz.* Ryder stars in this winsome adaptation of the Louisa May Alcott classic that, though bearing little resemblance, compares favorably to George Cukor's 1933 classic starring Katharine Hepburn. Indeed, under the keen direction of Armstrong, and with various liberties taken in Robert Swicord's excellent screenplay, the film becomes more autobiographical in nature than Alcott's book ever was. The result is masterful as the film not only tells the familiar tale of Little Jo, her three sisters and their Marmee, it becomes an examination of the roots of "liberalism" as experienced by Alcott, who grew up imbued in the Transcendentalist movement of Walden Pond. For her part, Ryder makes a wonderful Jo, though period acting still seems a stretch for her, and Sarandon is a powerful presence as Marmee, a feminist mom way before her time. ★★★★ VHS: $14.99; DVD: $27.99

Live and Let Die

(1973, 121 min, GB, Guy Hamilton) *Roger Moore, Yaphet Kotto, Jane Seymour.* Moore's first outing as 007 takes us on an excursion to the Caribbean where he unearths a heroin ring masterminded by Kotto. The tropical climate allows for ample unveiling of female décolletage, principally Seymour, and the usual bevy of would-be starlets. Perhaps not the best of the Bond series, but certainly worth a look for anyone interested in a capable action-adventure flick. (Sequel: *The Man with the Golden Gun*) ★★½ VHS: $14.99; DVD: $34.99

Live Flesh

(1997, 101 min, Spain, Pedro Almodóvar) *Javier Bardem, Francesca Neri, Liberto Rabal, Angela Molina, Jose Sancho.* Telling a good story rather than get carried away with plotting, Almodóvar deliberately paces this sexy thriller to allow the audience to get inside the heads of the characters and understand their crazy behavior. Victor (Rabal) is a handsome jailbird who reunites with the people who had him wrongly incarcerated. He falls into bed with Clara (Molina), the wife of Sancho (Sancho), whose old partner is David (Bardem), the cop crippled on the night Victor's fate was sealed. As Victor tries to exact revenge, naturally, all hell breaks loose. Although the plot could function as a bedroom farce, Almodóvar wisely milks it for its palpable sex and suspense. The result is a more mature work that may disappoint the bad-boy director's hard-core fans, but will also earn him new ones. (Spanish with English subtitles) ★★★ VHS: $19.99; DVD: $19.99

Live Wire

(1992, 87 min, US, Christian Duguay) *Pierce Brosnan, Ron Silver, Ben Cross.* Brosnan is the renegade cop, Silver the slimy U.S. senator and Cross the obsessed terrorist in this formulaic

Jane Horrocks in *Little Voice*

but mindlessly entertaining action-thriller. The explosive *du jour* is a colorless, tasteless liquid, convenient for single servings or punch bowls, which leaves no trace in the scattered remains of its victims. Washington, D.C., is the natural setting for this slick and cynical commentary on the abuse of position and privilege, and the disastrous consequences of unbridled greed. ★★ VHS: $14.99

Lives of a Bengal Lancer

(1935, 109 min, US, Henry Hathaway) *Gary Cooper, Franchot Tone, Richard Cromwell.* A rousing adventure film comparable with the similarly themed *Gunga Din* and *Beau Geste*. Cooper stars as a Canadian serving in the British army in the parched desert of colonial India. Excitement and danger await him and fellow officer Tone as they serve under a cold-hearted commander, attempt to reconcile their leader and his naïve son, and battle the crafty enemy. Good action sequences are offset by well-etched characterizations, unexpected comedy and a fair amount of suspense, all of which are under the tight direction of Hathaway. ★★★½ VHS: $14.99

Livin' Large

(1991, 96 min, US, Michael Schultz) *Terrence "T.C." Carson, Lisa Arrindell.* What begins as a surprisingly amusing satire on racial relationships and television journalism quickly deteriorates into a questionable and misogynist sitcom. Carson brings a lot of life to his role of a young black man being groomed to be the next superstar reporter for an Atlanta TV station. He soon finds that his success comes with a price, however, which includes ignoring his own cultural identity. The film's creators sabotage a good first half with their less-than-congenial depiction of the only two white women in the cast, whose "crime" is wanting to succeed in a "white man's world." From the film's distorted viewpoint, it doesn't matter if you're black or white, as long as you're male. ★★ VHS: $9.99

The Living Daylights

(1987, 130 min, GB, John Glen) *Timothy Dalton, Maryam D'Abo, Jeroen Krabbé, John-Rhys Davies.* Dalton takes over the reins as super British agent 007. James Bond is up against a KGB defector who's really a double agent, and an American arms dealer. Dalton is a fabulous choice for Bond, bringing a sophistication to the part Roger Moore never dreamed of — more in line with Sean Connery's interpretation. Lots of great action and stunts, coupled with Dalton's dashing presence, make this one of the best of the Bonds. (Sequel: *Licence to Kill*) ★★★ VHS: $9.99; DVD: $26.99

The Living End

(1992, 84 min, US, Gregg Araki) *Mike Dytri, Craig Gilmore, Mary Woronov, Paul Bartel.* With its opening close-up shot of a bumper sticker that reads "Choose Death," one can rest assured that this self-described "irresponsible" black comedy about two HIV-positive men who set out on a lawless road adventure will not hesitate to cajole, provoke and otherwise incite strong reactions. Jon is a whiny, urban gay — a film writer and critic — who happens into a relationship with fellow "positive" Luke, a free-spirited and rageful drifter who precipitates their angst-driven journey into anarchy. It's best to ignore the film's thinly written script, awkward

scenes and less-than-professional acting and concentrate instead on its irresistible "Yeah, I'm HIV-positive and I blame society!" message; for despite its faults, it's a totally entertaining effort. ★★★ VHS: $14.99

Living in Oblivion

(1995, 91 min, US, Tom DiCillo) *Steve Buscemi, Dermot Mulroney, Catherine Keener, Danielle Von Zerneck, James LeGros, Rica Martens.* A delightful and ingenious comedy that chronicles a disastrous three-day period on the set of an independent film production. Buscemi is perfectly cast as Nick, the high-strung director who desperately tries to tie down all the loose ends of his latest movie. His accomplices include the hilarious Mulroney as the hulking cinematographer; and Keener as the leading lady who can't remember the simplest of lines. The capper, however, is LeGros, who blows onto the set as one-time indie hack, newfound Hollywood darling Chad Palomino — an inspired caricature of Brad Pitt (who starred in DiCillo's first film, *Johnny Suede*). DiCillo's inventive script is filled with fantastical — almost Pirandellian — surprise twists, bristling humor and plenty of good-natured skewering of the film industry. ★★★½ VHS: $24.99

Living on Toyko Time

(1987, 83 min, US, Steve Okazaki) *Minako Ohashi, Ken Nakagawa.* Offbeat and charming romantic comedy about a Japanese girl who marries — to stay stateside — a Japanese-American rock musician, who has little interest in anything but rock 'n' roll and a vegetative lifestyle. ★★★

Living Out Loud

(1998, 99 min, US, Richard LaGravenese) *Holly Hunter, Danny DeVito, Queen Latifah, Martin Donovan, Richard Schiff, Elias Koteas.* Re-creating the charm and quirkiness of *The Fisher King*, which he wrote, LaGravenese's debut film as director is a wholly enjoyable, beguiling romantic comedy with a decidedly impish view of romance that is underscored by a touching story of self-examination. In a particularly smart portrayal, Hunter plays Judith, an Upper East Side, 40-ish recent divorcée who is having difficulty trying to move on after her break-up. When Judith befriends Pat (DeVito), her building's elevator operator, and Liz (Latifah), a sultry cabaret singer, she begins to awaken from the stagnant, lonely existence she had been living. LaGravenese nicely balances Judith's sexual and personal explorations, and never allows Judith's wonderfully executed fantasy sequences to detract from the story. In finding herself and living out loud, Judith's voyage of discovery makes for unusual but satisfying entertainment. ★★★ VHS: $14.99; DVD: $24.99

Loaded

(1996, 105 min, New Zealand, Anna Campion) *Oliver Millburn, Nick Patrick, Thandie Newton, Catherine McCormick.* Jane Campion's little sister Anna makes an inauspicious directorial debut with this dreary psychological thriller, an uneventful discourse whose one-dimensional characters substitute pretense with pretension. With its film-within-a-film backdrop, the story centers on a group of friends who weekend at a country mansion to make a horror movie. As

Living in Oblivion

the dynamics and romantic couplings of the group change, a death underscores the participants' anxieties and uncertain allegiances. Unfortunately for director Campion, she's working from her own flat screenplay. It's one of those stories in which the viewer impatiently waits for *something* to happen. It doesn't. A tripping scene is about the only sequence of interest. ★½ VHS: $19.99

Loaded Weapon 1

(1993, 82 min, US, Gene Quintano) *Emilio Estevez, Samuel L. Jackson, William Shatner, Tim Curry, Jon Lovitz, Charlie Sheen, Bill Nunn, F. Murray Abraham, Denis Leary, J.T. Walsh.* Looks like a case of an older brother trying to keep up with a younger sibling. After Charlie Sheen's spoofing of Tom Cruise in *Hot Shots!*, Estevez takes on the lighter side of Mel Gibson in this amiable spoof. Jackson joins him as the other half of the *Lethal Weapon* team. The film is perhaps a little too self-aware and does not have the rapid fire-delivery of some of the more successful films in this genre, like *The Naked Gun* series. However the film does provide some serious chuckles at the expense of the Gibson/Glover team. (aka: *National Lampoon's Loaded Weapon 1*) ★★½; DVD: $14.99

Local Hero

(1983, 111 min, Scotland, Bill Forsyth) *Burt Lancaster, Peter Reigert, Denis Lawson, Jenny Seagrove, Peter Capaldi.* Forsyth's enchanting comedy stars Peter Reigert as a reluctant Texas oil company executive who is sent overseas to purchase an idyllic Scottish village. Almost to his chagrin, the townsfolk, one of the strangest assortment of oddballs ever to hit the screen, seem all too eager to sell. All but one, that is. Burt Lancaster makes a commanding appearance as the company's owner who gets helicoptered in to take over the negotiations. This clever concoction offers a gentle treatise on the continuing march of progress and what we stand to lose by it. ★★★★ VHS: $19.99; DVD: $14.99

Lock, Stock and Two Smoking Barrels

(1999, 106 min, GB, Guy Ritchie) *Jason Flemyng, Dexter Fletcher, Nick Moran, Jason Statham, Steven Mackintosh, Sting.* A jolt of lightning, director Ritchie's comic crime caper is from the *Reservoir Dogs* and *Trainspotting* school, yet firmly stands on its own. Ritchie has a terrific eye and employs a whole bag of visual gimmicks (grainy sepia, jerky freeze-frame, slo-mo) to lend considerable style to

this hectic story of four London pals embroiled in a complex but highly satisfying stew of cheating cardplayers, double-crossing losers, porn paraphernalia, a bag of stolen loot, a forest of ganja and various underworld types. The young cast strikes the right note of nervous energy and tough-guy moxie, and the script is chock-full of snappy one-liners. ★★★½ VHS: $14.99; DVD: $19.99

Lock Up

(1989, 106 min, US, John Flynn) *Sylvester Stallone, Donald Sutherland, John Amos.* Even Stallone has rarely sunk this low. Stallone plays a convict who is transferred to a new prison, run by mean warden Sutherland — who's got a grudge to settle with Sly. ★ VHS: $9.99; DVD: $14.99

The Locusts

(1997, 125 min, US, John Patrick Kelly) *Kate Capshaw, Jeremy Davies, Vince Vaughn, Paul Rudd, Daniel Meyer, Ashley Judd.* Vaughn is the catalyst of this lethargic drama about a drifter whose flight from justice lands him smack in the middle of "black widow" Capshaw's stud ranch. But, instead of yielding to her sultry poses and constant offers to drink scotch and light her cigarettes, he befriends her repressed son (Davies) and sets in motion a tragedy of Oedipal proportions. Kelly's surefooted screenplay recalls the boozy, summertime tales of Williams and Inge, but Capshaw steps into shoes much better worn by Stanwyck and Crawford (as a vamp Capshaw packs all the punch of June Cleaver after a bad PTA meeting). ★★½

The Lodger

(1926, 75 min, GB, Alfred Hitchcock) *Ivor Novello, Marie Ault.* Hitchcock's mastery of narrative and atmosphere is stylishly evident in this silent thriller about a mysterious rooming house tenant who is suspected of being Jack the Ripper. Although not his first film, *The Lodger* ostensibly begins the Hitchcock oeuvre, for it was his first commercial success, first thriller, first cameo appearance and the first use of his favorite "innocent man falsely accused" plot line. ★★★ VHS: $12.99

Logan's Run

(1976, 120 min, US, Michael Anderson) *Michael York, Jenny Agutter, Richard Jordan, Peter Ustinov, Farrah Fawcett.* York plays Logan, a man with a problem: He's a 29-year-old bounty hunter who collects the people who didn't submit to state mandated euthanasia when they hit the age of 30 — and tomorrow is *his* birthday. Large futuristic sets, great special effects and Ustinov highlight this episodic, intriguing vision of the near future. ★★★ VHS: $9.99; DVD: $14.99

Lola

(1960, 91 min, France, Jacques Demy) *Anouk Aimée, Marc Michel.* With its breezy tone, distinctive editing and innovative cinematography (thanks to Raoul Coutard), this New Wave-influenced fairy tale proved to be an audacious debut for Demy, a director who, with the exception of *The Umbrellas of Cherbourg*, never achieved his potential. Owing much to *On the Town* and the works of Max Ophüls (to whom it

is dedicated), this fanciful love story stars Aimée as a free-spirited nightclub singer who is faced with the enviable dilemma of choosing between a trio of lovers. Framed within a series of coincidences and chance encounters and offering the notion that love is transient, the story never bogs down in "realities" and takes the wonderfully innocent approach that love conquers all. (French with English subtitles) ★★★½ VHS: $59.99

Lola

(1969, 98 min, GB/Italy, Richard Donner) *Charles Bronson, Susan George, Trevor Howard, Honor Blackman, Robert Morley.* Bronson stars as a 40-something American porno writer who has a tempestuous affair with a liberated 16-year-old girl (George as the irrepressible young Lola). Not as provocative as it would like to be, though the two stars offer appealing performances. ★★

Lola Montes

(1955, 110 min, France, Max Ophüls) *Martine Carol, Peter Ustinov, Anton Wolbrook, Oskar Werner.* In a 19th-century circus in Vienna, the famous Lola Montes, fleeing scandal, is reduced to living out the highlights of her exotic life for the pleasure of the masses and at the urging of a forceful ringmaster. Ophüls' first film is a scintillating tale of excess and regret, and is beautifully photographed. (French with English subtitles) ★★★½ VHS: $29.99

Lolita

(1962, 152 min, GB, Stanley Kubrick) *James Mason, Peter Sellers, Shelley Winters, Sue Lyons.* Kubrick's screen adaptation of Vladimir Nabokov's provocative novel, though not a complete success, effectively captures the author's sense of black humor and features outlandish performances by Sellers and Winters. Mason is a college professor who marries a lonely widow only for the opportunity it offers to seduce the sexually precocious Lyons. This peculiar tale of murder and lust is an example of earlier Kubrick efforts where powerful and eccentric characters ruled the screen. (Remade in 1998) ★★★ VHS: $19.99; DVD: $24.99

Lolita

(1998, 137 min, GB, Adrian Lyne) *Jeremy Irons, Melanie Griffith, Frank Langella, Dominique Swain.* A surprisingly erotic — but not exploitative — adaptation of the Nabokov classic, director Lyne actually scores with this sensual telling of the controversial story. As the lecherous Humbert Humbert who marries the shrill Charlotte Haze (Griffith) only so he can be close to her pre-teen daughter Lolita (Swain), Irons is magnificent in the lead role, giving

Lock, Stock and Two Smoking Barrels

weight and meaning to Stephen Schiff's thoughtful screenplay. While this whole project could have been a disaster, Lyne's tasteful and literate *Lolita* creates a sexually charged atmosphere without being offensive on any level. ★★★½ VHS: $14.99; DVD: $24.99

London Kills Me

(1992, 107 min, GB, Hanif Kureishi) *Justin Chadwick, Steven Mackintosh, Roshan Seth, Fiona Shaw, Brad Dourif, Gordon Warnecke.* A humorous exploration of life on the fringe underbelly of a post-punk, beyond-hope society. The story follows Clint, a pale, emaciated 20-year-old who, despite being mired in a seemingly hopeless world of drugs, homelessness and prostitution, retains a cheery optimism. Hope springs eternal after an exasperated owner of an upscale Portabello Road restaurant promises the bedraggled Clint a job if he comes in the following week with a new pair of shoes. Clint's odyssey, following this promise of respectability, becomes his repeated and increasingly frantic attempts to acquire this elusive pair of shoes. A fascinating yet flawed comedy-drama that despite a tagged-on happy ending that borders on the bizarre is fun nonetheless and vividly captures this part of London. ★★★½

Lone Star

(1996, 135 min, US, John Sayles) *Chris Cooper, Kris Kristofferson, Elizabeth Peña, Joe Morton, Matthew McConaughey, Ron Canada, Clifton James, Miriam Colon, Frances McDormand.* *Lone Star*, possibly Sayles' best film to date, is a brilliantly conceived, gripping mystery-thriller with so many simmering emotions under its surface that it's in constant threat of either self-destructing or losing its way. Thankfully, it does neither. Cooper plays Sam Deeds, a low-keyed sheriff in a small Texas town investigating some skeletal remains and a lawman's rusty badge found in the desert. The son of Buddy Deeds, a much-revered sheriff, Sam believes his father (played in flashbacks by McConaughey) may have had something to do with the findings. He soon discovers that the more digging he does, the more skeletons he finds. Moving fluidly from the past to the present, *Lone Star* is a compelling, quietly powerful work that stays with you long after its stunning but daringly conceived secret is revealed. ★★★★ VHS: $19.99; DVD: $19.99

Lone Wolf and Child series

Based on a popular Japanese comic book or *manga* by Kazuo Koike and Goseki Kojima, this incredible series tells the ongoing tale of Itto Ogami (Tomisaburo Wakayama), the Shogun's official executioner, who is disgraced by a rival family's plot and forced to walk "the road to Hell" with his young son after the murder of his wife and ostracism of his entire clan. Ogami becomes an assassin for hire, wheeling young Daigoro (Akihiro Tomikawa) around in a wooden cart, which is accessorized with a multitude of weapons (and which has given the films the alternate title of the "Baby Cart" series) and selling his formidable swordplay skills. Each individual film is a masterpiece of the samurai genre, and together they form a collection which ranks as one of the best film series in world cinema.

Sword of Vengeance

(1972, 83 min, Japan, Kenji Misumi) *Tomisaburo Wakayama, Akihiro Tomikawa.* The first film tells the origin story of the Lone Wolf and of his expulsion from his home at the hands of the duplicitous Yagyu clan. After his wife is murdered, Ogami, one of the Shogun's most loyal servants, is falsely accused of conspiring against his Lord and is ordered to commit *harakiri*. Refusing to comply with the royal decree, he becomes a "demon on the road to Hell," with no future and no hope for escape from his chosen fate. Along for the ride is his infant son Daigoro. Its beautiful widescreen photography is filled with dazzling visuals and breathtaking colors, but are rather staid compared to the wild carnage which is to come. (Japanese with English subtitles) ★★★★ VHS: $29.99

Baby Cart at the River Styx

(1972, 81 min, Japan, Kenji Misumi) *Tomisaburo Wakayama, Akihiro Tomikawa.* This time around, Ogami faces two of the most colorful villains of the entire series. The first is a clan of female ninja, sent to kill Ogami. The second villains, however, are even better: the three "Gods of Death" whom John Carpenter paid homage to in his *Big Trouble in Little China*. Assigned to protect an official whom Ogami has been hired to kill, each wields his own hand-to-hand weapon with fearsome skill and is a master killer in his own right. Again featuring the trademark geysers of blood which distinguishes the series, *Lone Wolf 2* features even more action than its predecessor, and is possibly the best entry in the series. (Japanese with English subtitles) ★★★★ VHS: $29.99

Baby Cart to Hades

(1972, 89 min, Japan, Kenji Misumi) *Tomisaburo Wakayama, Akihiro Tomikawa.* The third film in the blood-filled samurai series finds Ogami paralleled with a disgraced ronin warrior who has become a thug-for-hire in order to make a living. Both are shown as men trying to act within their codes of honor, having been made outcasts by society at large. After he gets involved in a dispute between two rival clans, the climax of the film finds Itto fighting a veritable army of soldiers, some armed with early firearms. One of the more philosophically complex episodes of the series. Originally released in the U.S. in a dubbed version called both *Lightning Swords of Death* and *Lupine Wolf.* (Japanese with English subtitles) ★★★★ VHS: $29.99

Baby Cart in Peril

(1973, 81 min, Japan, Buichi Saito) *Tomisaburo Wakayama, Akihiro Tomikawa.* This enthralling entry's main villain is both beautiful and deadly: the tattooed female assassin Oyuki. Hired to kill her early in the film, Ogami later learns that, far from being a bloodthirsty killer, Oyuki is a desperate woman who has been severely wronged — raped and betrayed by her teacher — and began life as an assassin only because she was forced to. Sympathizing with her, Ogami must nevertheless carry out his assignment: his code of *bushido* requires it. But before he does so, he allows Oyuki revenge against those who had previously despoiled her. (Japanese with English subtitles) ★★★★ VHS: $29.99

Baby Cart in the Land of Demons

(1973, 89 min, Japan, Kenji Misumi) *Tomisaburo Wakayama, Akihiro Tomikawa.* A series of messengers, each with a part of the final orders to hire Ogami, confront the Lone Wolf as he makes his way across the landscape. Killing each of them, he pieces his mission together and, along with the viewer, slowly learns the entire story: an insane local leader has substituted his young daughter, raised as a boy, as the clan's legitimate heir. Ogami has been hired to kill the clan leaders and prevent such an unconventional transfer of power from occurring. One of the more complex episodes of the series. (Japanese with English subtitles) ★★★★ VHS: $29.99

White Heaven in Hell

(1974, 85 min, Japan, Yoshiyuki Kuroda) *Tomisaburo Wakayama, Akihiro Tomikawa.* Ogami's archenemy Retsudo Yagyu has sent two of his remaining children to kill Ogami, one of whom is a bastard child who spurns any connection to his father, instead preferring to kill Ogami for his own glorification. With the assistance of three supernatural warriors, he dogs Ogami's heels, killing any innocent people Lone Wolf and Child come in contact with, thus assuring his complete isolation from the rest of humanity. An exciting fight on skis (with the baby cart on a sled!) follows, where the white of the snow is stained by the series' ever-present crimson blood. A fine end to a fantastic series. (Japanese with English subtitles) ★★★★ VHS: $29.99

The Loneliness of the Long Distance Runner

(1962, 103 min, GB, Tony Richardson) *Tom Courtenay, Michael Redgrave, Avis Bunnage.* Alan Silitoe's classic short story about a rebellious reform-school boy whose athletic prowess earns him a shot at the Olympics is lovingly brought to life by director Richardson. Courtenay excels as the young runner and Redgrave is superb as the school warden who takes him under his wing. A classic example of the British "kitchen sink" drama of the early '60s. ★★★½

Lonely Are the Brave

(1962, 107 min, US, David Miller) *Kirk Douglas, Walter Matthau, Gena Rowlands, Carroll O'Connor, George Kennedy.* A riveting modern-day western with cowboy and escaped prisoner Douglas on the lam, pursued by a relentless sheriff's department. ★★★ VHS: $14.99

The Lonely Guy

(1984, 90 min, US, Arthur Hiller) *Steve Martin, Charles Grodin, Judith Ivey.* When Martin is dumped by his girlfriend, he takes up with similarly fated Grodin, who introduces him to the wonderful world of bachelorhood. Based on the book by Bruce Jay Friedman, and adapted by Neil Simon, this offbeat, low-keyed comedy offers some comic insights into romance but is a little too introverted for its own good. ★★½ VHS: $9.99; DVD: $24.99

The Lonely Lady

(1983, 92 min, US, Peter Sasdy) *Pia Zadora, Lloyd Bochner, Ray Liotta.* Tacky, tasteless and completely satisfying only in a campy way, this Hollywood exposé, adapted from the Harold

L

Robbins novel, was made to showcase the talent and body of the spunky Zadora. The story begins with young Pia, a high school virgin (now that's great acting), being raped by a garden hose wielded by a Hollywood brat. On recovery, she is determined to become a successful writer in the sleazy world of show business. Sleeping her way to the top, our chipmunk-faced Pia achieves the success she sought, only to find emptiness and remorse. Champagne bottles are popped, lesbianism is hinted, breasts are bared and phallic images abound in this Zadora-ized "star" vehicle. ★ VHS: $9.99

The Lonely Man

(1957, 87 min, US, Henry Levin) *Jack Palance, Anthony Perkins, Neville Brand.* Palance grimaces and clenches his jaw through most of this lean western as a retired gunfighter trying to make peace. Emulating Henry King's outstanding *The Gunfighter*, though with only partially satisfying results, the story centers on aging Palance who wants to forget his "triggering" days and reconcile with his estranged son Perkins. It's almost funny to hear Perkins spout a Norman Bates–like devotion to his mother, and Palance lassoing and hog-tying Perkins has got to be seen to be believed. ★★½ VHS: $14.99

The Lonely Passion of Judith Hearne

(1987, 116 min, GB, Jack Clayton) *Maggie Smith, Bob Hoskins, Wendy Hiller.* Brian Moore's 1955 novel is brought to the screen with a pair of outstanding performances. Smith stars as the title character, a crestfallen middle-aged woman who suffers because of her undying and somewhat misplaced faith in the church and whose life is stalled in rundown boarding houses. Hoskins is superb as her self-effacing suitor. ★★★ VHS: $14.99

Lonelyhearts

(1958, 101 min, US, Vincent J. Donehue) *Montgomery Clift, Robert Ryan, Myrna Loy, Maureen Stapleton.* Good performances highlight this occasionally moving Nathaniel West story with Clift taking over the "Miss Lonelyhearts" newspaper column, becoming involved with the lives of his readers. ★★½ VHS: $19.99

Long Ago Tomorrow

(1971, 111 min, GB, Bryan Forbes) *Malcolm McDowell, Nanette Newman, Bernard Lee.* Filmgoers used to McDowell's screen persona as a virile, sometimes violent, young man, will be surprised by this subdued melodrama in which he plays a paraplegic involved in a love affair with another disabled person. Surprisingly engaging with powerful performances from both McDowell and Newman. ★★★

The Long Day Closes

(1992, 83 min, GB, Terence Davies) *Leigh McCormack, Marjorie Yates, Anthony Watson.* Somber, melancholy and haunting, this restrained drama of a young boy's maturation is a very effective mood piece recalling director Davies's childhood. Filmed in a leisurely, almost floating style and obviously autobiographical, the story concerns Bud (McCormack), a preadolescent boy living with his close-knit family in 1950s Liverpool. A thoughtful but shy boy with few friends, Bud immerses himself in escapist Hollywood musicals and develops an especially close relationship with his mother. There's surprisingly little dialogue, and not much happens in the way of dramatic excitement or tension. Yet this poetic style of filmmaking is both entrancing and pensive. ★★★½ VHS: $19.99

Long Day's Journey into Night

(1962, 170 min, US, Sidney Lumet) *Katharine Hepburn, Ralph Richardson, Jason Robards, Dean Stockwell.* A staggering adaptation of Eugene O'Neill's classic autobiographical play detailing his explosive homelife in early 1900s New England. In a tour de force performance, Hepburn plays O'Neill's drug-addicted mother whose grasp on reality slowly dissipates to the helpless horror of those around her. Richardson masterfully portrays the patriarch of the family — an aging, alcoholic actor who'd rather reminisce on a glorious past than face the truths of the present. As their sons, Stockwell plays the youngest brother stricken with TB, and Robards is a powerful presence as the troubled author witnessing his family's decay. ★★★★ VHS: $19.99

Long Day's Journey into Night

(1987, 169 min, US, Jonathan Miller) *Jack Lemmon, Bethel Leslie, Peter Gallagher, Kevin Spacey.* Lemmon re-creates his acclaimed performance from the Broadway revival in this expert production of Eugene O'Neill's classic drama. Leslie is outstanding as Lemmon's drug-addicted wife, and Gallagher and a pre-stardom Spacey are excellent as their sons. ★★★

Long Gone

(1987, 110 min, US, Martin Davidson) *William L. Petersen, Virginia Madsen, Henry Gibson.* From the director of *Apartment Zero* comes this wonderful made-for-cable production, an offshoot of *Bull Durham*, about the manager of a minor league team whipping his players into shape for a run at the championship. Petersen deftly plays the manager, and Madsen is the beauty queen with an eye for marriage. A delightful surprise. ★★★ VHS: $14.99

The Long Good Friday

(1980, 105 min, GB, John MacKenzie) *Bob Hoskins, Helen Mirren, Eddie Constantine, Pierce Brosnan.* A powerful English mobster suddenly finds himself and his empire victims of a bloody battle decree and desperately seeks its source. This taut gangster saga stars Hoskins as the besieged underworld head, Mirren as his sturdy mistress and Constantine as an influential American investor. ★★★½ VHS: $14.99; DVD: $29.99

The Long Goodbye

(1973, 112 min, US, Robert Altman) *Elliott Gould, Nina Van Pallandt, Sterling Hayden, Henry Gibson, Mark Rydell, Jim Bouton.* Gould gives his best performance as a burned-out Philip Marlowe out to find out if and why he was framed by a good friend (Bouton) for a woman's murder. Altman takes the tired, used-up detective film genre and fills it with quirky, nasty characters and bizarre humor. Look for *On Golden Pond* director Rydell as an incredibly sadistic, dry-witted gangster who can injure his loved ones just to show what he can do to people he hates. ★★★½ VHS: $19.99

The Long Hot Summer

(1958, 117 min, US, Martin Ritt) *Paul Newman, Joanne Woodward, Orson Welles, Lee Remick, Tony Franciosa, Angela Lansbury.* Ritt directed this engaging film, a successful translation of William Faulkner's story. Newman became a star thanks to his stand-out performance as Ben Quick, a wandering farmhand who becomes involved with the Varner family, headed by a domineering father (Welles). From first encounter, Ben takes a shine to the elegant but aloof Varner daughter (Woodward), which suits Daddy just fine, since he's hankerin' for plenty of Varner heirs. Whether under the scorching sun or the shade of the front porch, the all-star cast deliver fiery performances, especially Newman as the lusty opportunist. ★★★½ VHS: $14.99

The Long Kiss Goodnight

(1996, 120 min, US, Renny Harlin) *Geena Davis, Samuel L. Jackson, Patrick Malahide, Craig Bierko, David Morse.* After the mishap of *Cutthroat Island*, husband and wife Davis and Harlin are back in good form with this entertaining and unpredictable (if farfetched) mystery/suspense. In this rollercoaster ride of intrigue, Davis stars as a mild-mannered housewife who suffers from amnesia. When she is involved in a car accident, bits of memory begin to surface — like how to accurately throw a knife and an alter ego named Charlie. When a private investigator (Jackson) she had previously hired stumbles across a clue to her identity, the two set out to uncover the truth, with some very nasty secret agents on their trail. We may not always believe what Harlin asks us to, but what fun we have trying. (VHS available letterboxed or pan & scan) ★★★ VHS: $14.99; DVD: $19.99

The Long, Long Trailer

(1954, 103 min, US, Vincente Minnelli) *Lucille Ball, Desi Arnaz, Marjorie Main, Keenan Wynn.* Released at the height of their TV popularity, Lucy and Desi star in this comic romp about a newly married couple's adventures on the road in the titular vehicle. Lots of fun. ★★★ VHS: $14.99

The Long Night

(1947, 97 min, US, Anatole Litvak) *Henry Fonda, Barbara Bel Geddes, Vincent Price, Ann Dvorak, Elisha Cook, Jr.* Too strong meat for Hollywood, yet they still decided to remake Marcel Carne's French masterpiece *Le Jour Se Leve* about love and murder among the working class. When gunshots fell a dapper man in drab boarding house, police quickly trap the killer in his third floor room. As the night wains the killer remembers how things came to such a deadly impasse. Fonda is miscast as the ordinary working Joe turned murderer, a role Jean Gabin made his own (you can too easily see the intelligence behind Fonda's eyes; with Gabin played it like a wild animal with its leg caught in a trap). Bowdlerized with an unconvincing Hollywood ending, *The Long Night* offers no compelling reason to watch it over *Le Jour Se Leve*. ★★ VHS: $24.99; DVD: $29.99

The Long Riders

(1980, 100 min, US, Walter Hill) *Stacy Keach, David Carradine, Dennis Quaid, Christopher Guest, Nicholas Guest, James Keach, Keith Carradine, Robert Carradine, Randy Quaid.*

L

Sometimes stunt casting works, as in this film which features the Keach Brothers as the outlaws The James Brothers; the Carradine Brothers as The Younger Brothers; the Quaid Brothers as the brothers Miller; and the Guest Brothers as the Fords. Director Hill captures the melancholy in the passing of the Old West, while not ignoring the shoot-outs and chases as The James Gang face the penalty for one withdrawal too many. ★★★ VHS: $14.99; DVD: $19.99

The Long Voyage Home

(1940, 104 min, US, John Ford) *John Wayne, Thomas Mitchell, Ian Hunter, Barry Fitzgerald.* Director Ford's slightly stagey but brilliantly cinematic rendering of four Eugene O'Neill one-acts depicts life on a merchant ship, following the day-to-day affairs of a group of seamen whose loneliness and frustrations give way to suspicion and the off-shore frivolities which bring about tragedy. Wayne, in a very uncharacteristic portrayal, plays a naïve Swede; and Mitchell is unforgettable as a seasoned old salt. Outstanding black-and-white cinematography by Gregg Toland (*Citizen Kane*). ★★★½ VHS: $14.99

The Long Way Home

(1997, 120 min, US, Mark Jonathan Harris) *Narrated by: Morgan Freeman; Featuring the voices of Ed Asner, Sean Astin, Martin Landau, Miriam Margoyles, David Paymer, Nina Siemaszko, Helen Slater, Michael York.* Whereas most documentaries dealing with the Holocaust examine the devastating years during the second world war, this harrowing film recounts the struggles of the Jewish camp survivors after their liberation, which for many was only marginally better than their captivity by the Nazis. Through astonishing archival footage, *The Long Way Home* details exactly that — the arduous path taken from the camps to the newly found state of Israel. With reminiscences from survivors and U.S. military personnel, the film often shocks in its revelations. A thoughtful, illuminating and often anguished look at a people's history and a world's shame. ★★★★ VHS: $19.99; DVD: $24.99

The Longest Day

(1962, 169 min, US, Andrew Marton, Bernhard Wicki & Ken Annakin) *Henry Fonda, John Wayne, Richard Burton, Sean Connery, Red Buttons, Robert Mitchum, Robert Ryan, Rod Steiger, Kenneth More, Sal Mineo, Roddy McDowall.* Classic WWII epic which accounts the Allied invasion of Normandy. One might think that at nearly three hours in length this could be a tedious affair, but the action here is carried at a brisk pace and with great attention to detail. The all-star cast delivers a plethora of strong performances. One of the best WWII dramas ever made. (Letterboxed VHS available for $19.99) ★★★★ VHS: $14.99; DVD: $24.99

The Longest Yard

(1974, 123 min, US, Robert Aldrich) *Burt Reynolds, Eddie Albert, Ed Lauter, Bernadette Peters.* Former pro Reynolds gets incarcerated and heads the prison football team to victory. Some good laughs and lots of action in this forceful comedy. ★★★ VHS: $14.99; DVD: $24.99

Longtime Companion

(1990, 96 min, US, Norman René) *Campbell Scott, Bruce Davison, Dermot Mulroney, Stephen Caffrey, Patrick Cassidy, Brian Cousins, Mary-Louise Parker.* One of the first American films to address the AIDS crisis, *Longtime Companion* is an exceptional look into the lives of a group of gay friends, and how the disease affects them, both collectively and singularly. Director René and writer Craig Lucas succeed in creating full-dimensioned characters and the film is rich in sharp observations and keen wit. There is a terrific ensemble cast, but Davison must be given a special mention for his superlative portrayal of the lover who slowly watches his longtime companion succumb. ★★★½ VHS: $14.99; DVD: $19.99

Look Back in Anger

(1958, 99 min, GB, Tony Richardson) *Richard Burton, Claire Bloom, Mary Ure, Donald Pleasence.* John Osborne's play made theatre history in England as a rebellious attack against the rigidity of the English establishment. Bristling with heated dialogue, the story represents the first signs of post-war dissatisfaction with the social immobility of life in a dying Empire. A trend-setting "angry young man" drama that is exceptionally acted and remarkably written. ★★★½ VHS: $14.99

Look Back in Anger

(1980, 101 min, GB, Lindsay Anderson) *Malcolm McDowell, Lisa Barnes.* McDowell once again teams up with Anderson in this compelling remake of John Osborne's explosive "angry young man" play. McDowell offers a passionate performance as Jimmy Porter, and Anderson deftly directs the action. ★★★

Look Back in Anger

(1990, 114 min, GB, David Jones) *Kenneth Branagh, Emma Thompson, Gerard Horan.* Branagh stars in this version of John Osborne's powerful "kitchen sink" drama based on Judi Dench's West End revival. Branagh re-creates the role made famous by Richard Burton as Jimmy Porter, a young man whose poor position in life results in a simmering rage that is directed towards both his wife (nicely played by Thompson) and to the indifferent world that surrounds him. Branagh's excellent performance is the core of the piece offering a blistering portrayal of frustration and passion. ★★★ VHS: $19.99

Look Who's Talking

(1989, 90 min, US, Amy Heckerling) *John Travolta, Kirstie Alley, George Segal, Olympia Dukakis; Voice of Bruce Willis.* The surprise hit of 1989, this mostly amusing comedy is charming due partially to two great gimmicks: a talking baby whose thoughts are heard on screen, and the ever-glib Willis as the vocal incarnation of the little tyke, Mikey. Alley is Mikey's mom, a single accountant having an affair with married business associate Segal. While waiting for him to leave his wife, she ignores the attentions of a helpful and obviously made-for-each-other taxi driver. Travolta delivers a wonderful comic performance as the cabbie. (Followed by 2 sequels) ★★½ VHS: $9.99; DVD: $27.99

Looker

(1981, 94 min, US, Michael Crichton) *Albert Finney, James Coburn, Susan Dey, Leigh Taylor-Young.* From the creator of *Coma* and *Westworld* comes this sci-fi satire about beautiful models who are murdered and then reconstituted by a computer hoping to produce the perfect spokesperson. (No, this is *not* the Vanna White story.) With Dey as the model out for vengeance, Finney as the plastic surgeon going out of business and Coburn as the CEO. ★★½ VHS: $14.99

Looking for Mr. Goodbar

(1977, 136 min, US, Richard Brooks) *Diane Keaton, Richard Gere, William Atherton, Tuesday Weld, Richard Kiley.* Keaton's terrific performance isn't enough to sustain this horrid adaptation of Judith Rossner's best-seller about a repressed schoolteacher who turns to nightly bar-hopping for sexual and personal fulfillment. ★ VHS: $9.99

Looking for Richard

(1996, 118 min, US, Al Pacino) *Al Pacino, Alec Baldwin, Winona Ryder, Aidan Quinn, Estelle Parsons, Kevin Spacey, Penelope Allen, Kenneth Branagh, Kevin Kline, James Earl Jones, Derek Jacobi.* It's long been a presumption that Yanks can't do Shakespeare; American actors have carried that on their shoulders with the foreboding of Hamlet's ghost. The debunking and playful spoofing of this theatrical myth is only one of the delicious treats in store in *Looking for Richard*, a scintillating peek into the soul of Shakespeare's evil prince, Richard III. Making an assured directorial debut, Pacino leads his crew (and audience) on an odyssey to discover the inner workings of "Richard III," both the play and the character. Intercutting actual scenes, the actor talks to everyone from an American Average Joe to some of England's acting royalty to come to an understanding of the Bard. Comical and always fascinating, the film actually makes Shakespeare accessible. ★★★½ VHS: $29.99

Loose Cannons

(1990, 94 min, US, Bob Clark) *Gene Hackman, Dan Aykroyd, Dom DeLuise, Ronny Cox.* Hackman makes so many movies a year, the odds are that occasionally a clinker is going to get through. This is one of them. Mismatched cops (now *there's* an original idea) Hackman and Aykroyd are up against modern-day Nazis in Washington, D.C. ★ VHS: $14.99

Loose Connections

(1983, 90 min, GB, Richard Eyre) *Lindsay Duncan, Stephen Rea, Robbie Coltrane.* A delightful little road comedy about a dedicated feminist who decides to drive across Europe to attend a women's conference in Munich. She winds up with Harry, a less-than-savory traveling companion whose outright chauvinism tests her nerve all the way down the Autobahn. ★★★

Loot

(1972, 101 min, GB, Silvio Narizzano) *Lee Remick, Roy Holder, Hywell Bennett, Milo O'Shea.* Joe Orton's frantically paced, door slamming farce/black comedy — by far one of the most original and uproarious plays ever to grace the British stage — is presented here with all the outrageousness it deserves. The story concerns a pair of misguided youths who, having knocked over a bank, hide the swag in mom's coffin. All hell breaks loose as the distraught duo tries to retrieve their booty. Inspired performances abound from a crackerjack cast. ★★★

Lord Jim

(1965, 154 min, GB, Richard Brooks) *Peter O'Toole, James Mason, Curt Jurgens, Eli Wallach, Jack Hawkins.* O'Toole is Jim, a romantic young English seaman whose life is irrevocably altered when he violates his personal code of honor by a single act of cowardice. In subsequent attempts to erase his guilt, he finds himself in the middle of a massive Indonesian labor dispute and incipient rebellion. O'Toole gives an outstanding performance under the direction of Brooks, who scripted from the Joseph Conrad novel. ★★★ VHS: $19.99

Lord of Illusions

(1995, 121 min, US, Clive Barker) *Scott Bakula, Kevin J. O'Connor, Famke Janssen, Vincent Schiavelli.* Barker's third film as director is a tale of magic and illusion, cults and murder. Originally released theatrically in a heavily edited 108-minute version, this director's cut rectifies its confusion and abruptness. Bakula stars as Harry D'Amour, a private investigator who becomes embroiled in a bizarre series of murders involving an illusionist whose high-profile act turns out to be inspired by real magic. Harry follows the trail through its twists and turns until he learns the truth: the illusionist Swann was the disciple and eventual murderer of an evil magician named Nix, whose resurrection is being engineered by a murderous cult. Adapted from Barker's superb short story "The Last Illusion," the basic premise itself is promising and original. Still radically different from most horror films, it was perhaps too far ahead of its time to please the studio powers-that-be. ★★½ VHS: $9.99; DVD: $14.99

Lord of the Flies

(1963, 91 min, GB, Peter Brook) *James Aubrey, Tom Chapin.* A haunting and powerful adaptation of William Golding's novel brought to the screen by the incomparably daring British stage director Brook. Unlike his masterful *Marat/Sade*, which exploded on the screen with theatrical brilliance, here the "theatre" tends to slightly overshadow the strength of the story. However, this allegory of English schoolboys who slowly revert to brutal savagery when stranded on an island is still a fascinating and disturbing film in its own right. (Remade in 1990) ★★★ VHS: $29.99; DVD: $39.99

Lord of the Flies

(1990, 90 min, GB, Harry Hook) *Balthazar Getty, Chris Furrh.* Deep greens and beautiful forests dominate the frames of this remake, complete with yowling children and war paint. Director Hook displays his true forte, cinematography, paying more attention to picture than content. Detailing the regression of shipwrecked boys from an ordered existence into primitive, warring factions, this slightly updated version of William Golding's allegorical novel makes it to the screen with little change, except that the boys run around with glowsticks instead of torches. ★★½ VHS: $14.99

Lord of the Rings

(1978, 133 min, US, Ralph Bakshi) Bakshi's ambitious adaptation of J.R.R. Tolkien's classic fantasy trilogy covers only one-half of the series. Filmed in rotoscope (live-action enhanced with animation — a technique better utilized in his later work *American Pop*), *Lord of the Rings* tells of the War of the Rings within the mystical land, Middle Earth. Despite any shortcomings for the book's enthusiasts, it's a joy to see Tolkien's creations, such as Frodo and Gollum, on film. (Remade in 2001) ★★★

The Lords of Discipline

(1983, 102 min, US, Franc Roddam) *David Keith, Mark Breland, Michael Biehn, Bill Paxton, Judge Reinhold, Rick Rossovich, Matt Frewer.* A sensationalistic thriller about a senior (Keith) at a 1964 South Carolina military academy charged with protecting the school's first black student (Breland) from a mysterious hazing organization known as "The Ten." Based on Pat Conroy's semiautobiographical novel. ★★½ VHS: $14.99

Lorenzo's Oil

(1992, 135 min, US, George Miller) *Nick Nolte, Susan Sarandon, Peter Ustinov, Kathleen Wilhoite.* A stirring adaptation of the real-life story of Michaela and Agusto Odone, whose son Lorenzo was stricken by an incurable, and fatal, disease known as ALD. Rising above its mushy "disease-of-the-week" roots, *Lorenzo's Oil* is more riveting scientific detective story than melodrama as it follows the Odones in their relentless search for a scintilla of hope while battling a complacent medical establishment. Both Sarandon and Nolte offer superb performances as the beleaguered parents whose love for their son drives them to feverishly search for their own cure. ★★★½ VHS: $14.99

Lorna

(1964, 78 min, US, Russ Meyer) *Lorna Maitland.* The first film in which Russ added violence to spice up the sex. Maitland is a sexually frustrated housewife who becomes involved with an escaped convict. The first of Russ' black and whites. ★★ VHS: $79.99

Losing Isaiah

(1995, 108 min, US, Stephen Gyllenhaal) *Jessica Lange, Halle Berry, David Strathairn, Cuba Gooding, Jr., Samuel L. Jackson.* With its made-for-TV premise of a child custody battle, the compelling *Losing Isaiah* tugs at the heart while prodding the mind. Berry, in an exceptionally fine performance, plays a crack-addicted mother who throws her newborn baby in the trash (later thinking him dead). Lange, in a passionate portrayal, plays a hospital social worker who adopts the child. Four years later, however, after Berry has gone through rehab, she discovers the baby is alive, and takes Lange to court to obtain custody. In addressing the contentious social issues of interracial adoption, the film smartly and effectively acknowledges that no easy or even correct answers are readily available. ★★★ VHS: $9.99

The Loss of Sexual Innocence

(1999, 106 min, GB, Mike Figgis) *Julian Sands, Saffron Burrows, Hanne Klintoe, Jonathan Rhys-Meyers.* One of the most pretentious titles ever to grace a feature-length film should be enough warning, but just in case the wildy hot-and-cold Figgis name piques some interest, here are the facts: *The Loss of Sexual Innocence* is an almost unwatchable treatise on sexual growth and emotional immaturity that makes *The Blue Lagoon* look like an Oscar contender. The non-linear, non-sensical plot follows the life of a film director through various stages, including affairs, an unhappy marriage and murder. (Didn't Truffaut do this better with his Antoine Doinel cycle?) An overly grave tone, a heavy-handed jazz score by Figgis, and a decided lack of drama add to the mess. ★ VHS: $14.99; DVD: $27.99

Lost and Found

(1979, 112 min, US, Melvin Frank) *Glenda Jackson, George Segal, Maureen Stapleton.* Attempting to capitalize on their success in *A Touch of Class*, Jackson and Segal pair up once again for this mordant comedy on married life. While not quite as funny or lively as the first go-round, Jackson and Segal do have a certain screen chemistry which makes this worthwhile viewing. ★★½

Lost & Found

(1999, 99 min, US, Jeff Pollack) *David Spade, Sophie Marceau, Patrick Bruel, Artie Lange, Mitchell Whitfield, Martin Sheen, Jon Lovitz.* Spade takes his wise-ass dweeb to new lows in this unfunny piece of tedium which makes the mistake in thinking wisecracks do a comedy make. Spade plays a restaurant owner who falls for his beautiful new neighbor (Marceau). He concocts a plan to steal her dog, thus being able to spend time with her pretending to look for it. Spade spends most of the film whining and throwing out one-liners, very few of which are even worthy of a smirk. He's paired, for a short time anyway, with another overweight guy (in the absence of Chris Farley), but there are no sparks here. At least the dog's kinda cute. ★½ VHS: $14.99; DVD: $19.99

Lost Boundaries

(1949, 105 min, US, Alfred L. Werker) *Mel Ferrer, Beatrice Pearson, Richard Hylton, Susan Douglas, Canada Lee.* A post-war social drama made at a time when American cinema was rediscovering its political voice, *Lost Boundaries* is the affecting, if slightly slow-moving story of racial intolerance in rural America. In his debut, Ferrer plays a dedicated light-skinned black doctor who, with his wife, "passes" for white in order to accept the lucrative position of town physician in an all-white New Hampshire town. Based on a true story, the film recounts the couple's dilemma as they must deny their cultural heritage but are afforded the opportunity to give their children a privileged upbringing. The film is directed at an even pace throughout, but there are times one would wish for the action to move a bit more briskly. ★★★ VHS: $19.99

The Lost Boys

(1987, 98 min, US, Joel Schumacher) *Jason Patric, Kiefer Sutherland, Dianne Wiest, Corey Haim, Bernard Hughes, Corey Feldman, Edward Herrmann, Jami Gertz, Billy Wirth, Alex Winter.* Hip vampire tale about a family moving to a small California coastal town, and discovering the city is populated with teenage vampires.

The Two Roberts: Blake and Loggia in David Lynch's *Lost Highway*

Patric and Haim are the brothers battling bloodsuckers Sutherland and friends. Wiest is the boys' supermom, and Hughes is the coolest grandfather this side of Grandpa Munster. (Even if it did bring together "the Coreys," it's still good fun.) ★★★ VHS: $9.99; DVD: $19.99

The Lost Continent

(1968, 97 min, GB, Michael Carreras) *Eric Porter, Hildegard Knef, Suzanna Leigh.* Based very loosely on Dennis Wheatley's novel "Uncharted Seas," this enjoyable piece of Hammer Studios hokum is about a small group of passengers aboard a tramp steamer who, after a few adventures in love and danger, find themselves adrift in the Sargasso Sea. After being attacked by some intelligent seaweed, our motley crew discover the existence of a cult of modern-day Spanish conquistadors. As if all this weren't enough, there are also giant man-eating mollusks to contend with! Shot entirely within a studio, the film has an artificial look which works to its advantage, given its fantastic story line. ★★½ VHS: $14.99

Lost Highway

(1997, 134 min, US, David Lynch) *Bill Pullman, Patricia Arquette, Robert Blake, Balthazar Getty, Robert Loggia, Richard Pryor, Jack Nance, Henry Rollins.* Making the excesses and narrative of *Blue Velvet* seem the model of restraint by comparison, Lynch's *Lost Highway* is eerie, scary, enigmatic, weird and provocative. Sometimes the film is all of these at once, when it's in high gear; and sometimes it just tries too hard to evoke just one of those moods, stalling in its tracks. Graced by beautiful cinematography by Peter Deming, *Lost Highway* is the bizarre, often incomprehensible but nevertheless hypnotic story of a murder, a jazz musician and his wife, a youth in over his head, and the ability to phone someone while standing right next to them without being on the phone. Lynch and cowriter Barry Gifford go out of their way to give bits of traditional narrative structure and then rub your face in it the very next minute. Blake gives an effectively creepy portrayal. (VHS available letterboxed or pan & scan) ★★½ VHS: $14.99

The Lost Honor of Katharina Blum

(1975, 95 min, Germany, Volker Schlöndorff & Margarethe von Trotta) *Angela Winkler, Mario Adorf, Jürgen Prochnow.* A political thriller which examines the havoc wrought by West Germany's yellow journalism. A woman is victimized and traumatized by the relentless press coverage of an evening she spent with a suspected terrorist. Directed by the husband-wife team of Schlöndorff (*The Tin Drum*) and von Trotta. (Letterboxed) (German with English subtitles) ★★★ VHS: $29.99

Lost Horizon

(1937, 132 min, US, Frank Capra) *Ronald Colman, Sam Jaffe, Jane Wyatt, Edward Everett Horton.* The restoration of Capra's exotic fantasy about the fabled kingdom of Shangri-La is in itself an epic of sorts: a 13-year search of worldwide archives to locate some 20 minutes of lost footage, not following the film's original 1937 release. Capra, then at the peak of his fame and very much the Spielberg of his day, had a staggering budget of $4 million (equivalent to over $80 million today) to re-create James Hilton's utopian novel about a noted British diplomat (Colman) who is abducted so that he can succeed a dying High Lama (Jaffe) at a remote Himalayan paradise. ★★★★ VHS: $19.99; DVD: $29.99

Lost in a Harem

(1944, 89 min, US, Charles Riesner) *Bud Abbott, Lou Costello, Marilyn Maxwell, Douglas Dumbrille.* It's hijinks aplenty as Abbott and Costello run amok in the Middle East with some occasionally funny results. Bud and Lou are magicians stranded in the desert who become involved with sultan Dumbrille and harem beauty Maxwell. Mideast relations have never been the same. Also with the Jimmy Dorsey Orchestra. ★★½ VHS: $14.99

Lost in America

(1985, 91 min, US, Albert Brooks) *Albert Brooks, Julie Hagerty, Garry Marshall.* Brooks hilariously stars as an upwardly mobile young ad executive who loses a big promotion and decides to turn his back on yuppiedom to discover the "real"

America (in a $40,000 Winnebago). Hagerty is his accepting wife in this sharply detailed comedy on the American Dream/Nightmare. ★★★½ VHS: $9.99; DVD: $19.99

Lost in Space

(1998, 131 min, US, Stephen Hopkins) *William Hurt, Gary Oldman, Mimi Rogers, Matt LeBlanc, Heather Graham, Jack Johnson, Lacey Chabert, Jared Harris, Mark Goddard; Cameos by June Lockhart, Angela Cartwright, Marta Kristen.* A slick, confusing, effects-laden version of the 1960s sci-fi TV show, which was pure camp at best. Though far too serious for lost-in-the-stars fun, this *Lost in Space* does try to be more cerebral than its TV prototype — that's both a good thing and a bad thing. Hurt and Rogers are Don and Maureen, head of the Robinson clan, which includes Will (Johnson), Penny (Chabert) and Judy (Graham) — they've all been '90s-fied (though this is set in 2058). Also on board is the nefarious Dr. Smith, played with hand-wringing glee by Oldman. The action scenes are familiar though competent, the effects are well-done though not remarkable, and the ending is too convoluted for its own good. (Letterboxed VHS available for $14.99) ★★½ VHS: $9.99; DVD: $19.99

Lost in Yonkers

(1993, 112 min, US, Martha Coolidge) *Mercedes Ruehl, Irene Worth, Richard Dreyfuss, Brad Stoll, Mike Damus, David Strathairn.* Neil Simon's Pulitzer Prize–winning and Tony Award-winning play loses some of its luster in this appealing if uneven adaptation. Two adolescent brothers go to live with their stern grandmother (Worth) and endearing, slow-witted aunt (Ruehl). As a childhood remembrance, the film is funny and sweet, with Stoll and Damus as very likable youths. Halfway through, however, the film runs out of energy, and even a canister of Simon one-liners is not sufficient to give it a full recharge. Worth gives a gallant characterization, but she's such a one-note holy terror, the film plays like *Throw Grandmamma from the Train* whenever she's on screen. ★★½ VHS: $19.99

The Lost Language of Cranes

(1992, 90 min, GB, Nigel Finch) *Corey Parker, John Schlesinger, Rene Auberjonois, Eileen Atkins, Brian Cox, Angus McFayden, Cathy Tyson.* David Leavitt's critically acclaimed novel about a troubled family's crisis with homosexuality is powerfully adapted for the screen. Phillip, a young gay man, falls in love and begins to feel the need to tell his parents about his true sexual self. The twist is that Phillip's father is also gay/bisexual but keeps his yearning closeted from his wife and family. The parallel stories of these two men and the emotionally distraught wife and mother caught in-between results in an undeniably painful melodrama that is exceptionally sensitive to the issues of homosexuality, bisexuality, coming out and familial miscommunication. ★★★½

The Lost Moment

(1947, 88 min, US, Martin Gabel) *Robert Cummings, Susan Hayward, Agnes Moorehead.* An involving drama based on Henry James' "The Aspern Papers," with Cummings as an American publisher in Venice looking for a deceased writer's lost love letters, finding the woman he sent them to (Moorehead) and becoming involved with her niece (Hayward). ★★★ VHS: $14.99

The Lost Patrol

(1934, 74 min, US, John Ford) *Victor McLaglen, Boris Karloff, Wallace Ford, Alan Hale.* Ford's rousing adventure film about a small British army unit, lost in the Mesopotamian desert, which comes under attack by Arab forces. McLaglen stars as the unit's commander, and Karloff has a field day as a religious fanatic. ★★★½

Lost Souls

(2000, 98 min, US, Janusz Kaminski) *Winona Ryder, Ben Chaplin, John Hurt, Philip Baker Hall, Elias Koteas.* Betraying a splendid visual style, this convoluted occult thriller lacks excitement, scares, or characters to care about. An *Exorcist* knock-off, *Lost Souls* is the murky story of a young woman (Ryder) who must convince a crime journalist that he is Satan's chosen body for human reincarnation. Exorcisms, dark streets and religious mumbo-jumbo populate director Kaminski's unoriginal horror tale, in which very little will come as a surprise to anyone who's ever seen a film from this overcrowded genre. ★½ VHS: $14.99; DVD: $24.99

The Lost Weekend

(1945, 101 min, US, Billy Wilder) *Ray Milland, Jane Wyman, Howard Da Silva, Frank Faylen.* Wilder's uncompromising and devastating social drama on alcoholism startled audiences in its day with its brutally honest depiction of life on the bottle. Milland won a much-deserved Oscar for his intense performance as a writer whose two-day alcoholic binge becomes a descent into hell. Da Silva is a stand out as a disapproving bartender. Winner of four Academy Awards including Best Picture and Best Director. ★★★★ VHS: $14.99; DVD: $29.99

The Lost World

(1960, 98 min, US, Irwin Allen) *Michael Rennie, Jill St. John, Claude Rains, David Hedison, Fernando Lamas, Richard Haydn.* Campy and at times cheesy sci-fi fun courtesy of '60s cheese manufacturer Allen. Professor Rains and chums go exploring beneath an inactive volcano and discover a lost world full of prehistoric monsters, danger and a fortune in jewels. This remake of the 1925 classic silent (itself based on Arthur Conan Doyle's story) really doesn't compare to the original (the effects here are only marginally better), and characters do and say ridiculous things every 15 minutes, but the cast is engaging, never taking themselves too seriously. ★★½ VHS: $14.99

The Lost World: Jurassic Park

(1997, 134 min, US, Steven Spielberg) *Jeff Goldblum, Julianne Moore, Pete Postlethwaite, Arliss Howard, Richard Attenborough, Vince Vaughn.* In Spielberg's frenzied, hard-edged sequel to *Jurassic Park,* claws are definitely sharper, teeth have more of a bite, and the horror is more horrific. Displaying even more impressive effects than in the first film, but lacking a developed story line and having a Swiss cheese-like plot, *The Lost World* finds Dr. Ian Malcolm (Goldblum) returning to take on those deadly prehistoric beasts. It seems there was another island populated by the dinosaurs, and there

are those who would capture them and bring them to the U.S. (didn't they see *King Kong*?). That's all the plot that's needed to produce great scares and greater visuals. (Sequel: *Jurassic Park 3*) ★★★ VHS: $14.99; DVD: $26.99

Louisiana Purchase

(1941, 98 min, US, Irving Cummings) *Bob Hope, Victor Moore.* Politics takes it on the chin in this mildly entertaining Hope comedy. Bob plays an elected official who takes the rap for illegal goings-on by his associates. A senator is sent to investigate, and Hope and pals will try anything to save their skins. Hope is in his element as a wise-cracking dupe, but it's Moore's marvelous stint as the visiting senator which saves this comedy from the ordinary. Hope's filibuster is a particular highlight. ★★½ VHS: $14.99

Louisiana Story

(1948, 77 min, US, Robert J. Flaherty) Produced by Standard Oil on a "no-strings-attached" policy, Flaherty's final film focuses on the story of a young Cajun boy who watches his Bayou sanctuary being invaded when an oil rig begins drilling in the swamp. Filming in an almost poetic style, Flaherty captures the mysterious appeal of the pristine paradise and offers a stirring tribute to the Bayou people. This beautiful and heartfelt semidocumentary was shot by Richard Leacock with a Pulitzer award-winning score by Virgil Thompson. This film has been restored by the Library of Congress, the Museum of Modern Art, and UCLA Film and Television Department. ★★★½

LouLou

(1980, 110 min, France, Maurice Pialat) *Gérard Depardieu, Isabelle Huppert, Guy Marchant.* An engrossing look at a wife who spurns the comforts of bourgeois security for the pleasures of a bohemian lifestyle with a dangerously charming, drunken and chain-smoking womanizer. Depardieu is LouLou and Huppert is Nelly, the bright but bored wife of the sappy Marchant, whose demure behavior unravels in the face of the unabashed sexual excesses offered by LouLou. Riding a sexual and emotional rollercoaster, the incongruous pair slowly discover real love and affection. A rambling road movie that captures life on the edge, yet all the while, never leaving the streets of Paris. (French with English subtitles) ★★★ VHS: $29.99; DVD: $29.99

Love

(1971, 92 min, Hungary, Karoly Makk) *Lili Darvas, Mari Torocsik.* Legendary Hungarian actress Darvas, in her final film, is mesmerizing in this funny, touching and politically astute Academy Award nominee. After her husband is imprisoned on political charges, his wife keeps his memory alive and his sick elderly mother happy by telling the woman that her son had emigrated to America. The daughter-in-law continues the illusion by faking letters from her husband about America, as well as his fabulous success there as a movie director, and sending them to the old woman, who is kept alive by the excitement and happiness of her son. The film is about both personal and political falsehoods as well as a family's love and compassion. (Hungarian with English subtitles) ★★★★

Love Affair

(1939, 87 min, US, Leo McCarey) *Irene Dunne, Charles Boyer, Maria Ouspenskaya.* The irresistible Dunne finds shipboard romance with suave Boyer, even though each is already engaged. They agree to meet six months later, only fate has other plans. The first half of the film is played more as a comedy, which can be very funny; the second half is a more traditional romantic drama, but it's all very lovely. (Remade in 1957 as *An Affair to Remember* and in 1994 as *Love Affair*) ★★★½

Love Affair

(1994, 108 min, US, Glenn Gordon Caron) *Warren Beatty, Annette Bening, Katharine Hepburn, Garry Shandling, Chloe Webb, Pierce Brosnan, Brenda Vaccaro.* Third time's almost a charm. Robert Towne wrote the screenplay for this easy-going remake of the 1939 classic *Love Affair.* Though moderately updated, the plot is basically the same with Beatty and Bening, both engaged to other partners, meeting and ultimately enjoying a shipboard romance. The two stars' relaxed and natural delivery give the film a pleasant edge, though they are a sometime victim to a glib screenplay which clearly tries too hard to be hip. As Beatty's beloved aunt, Hepburn makes a memorable appearance, looking frail but resolute; and there's a movie first as Kate utters the "f" word. ★★½ VHS: $9.99

Love Affair: Or, The Case of the Missing Switchboard Operator

(1967, 70 min, Yugoslavia, Dusan Makavejev) *Eva Ras, Slobodan Aligrudic.* A bizarre and unpredictable curiousity from Yugoslavia's greatest filmmaker. The story, both an unusual love story and a political parable, follows the budding relationship of a vivacious young woman and her rat-exterminating boyfriend. All is well until she allows herself to be seduced by a man of higher means. A daring work. (Serbo-Croatian with English subtitles) ★★★ VHS: $24.99

Love Among the Ruins

(1975, 100 min, US, George Cukor) *Katharine Hepburn, Laurence Olivier, Colin Blakely.* An exceptional TV movie starring film legends Hepburn and Olivier at their regal best as former lovers reunited years later when barrister Olivier defends aging actress Hepburn in court. A delightful and totally grand romantic comedy, directed with panache by Cukor. ★★★½

Love and a .45

(1994, 90 min, US, C.M. Talkington) *Gil Bellows, Renee Zellweger, Rory Cochrane, Jeffrey Combs, Jack Nance, Peter Fonda, Ann Wedgeworth.* Aiming for sardonic, hip commentary on today's modern world and life on the edge, *Love and a .45* never quite escapes its derivative origins and unoriginal execution. Some interesting people pop up, but the viewer is never moved from mild interest to involvement. This ain't no *True Romance*, but if you're into the genre, you might want to check out the random assortment of marginal characters who flit in and out of the precarious lives of this would-be Bonnie and Clyde team. ★★ VHS: $9.99; DVD: $24.99

L

William Powell (l.) is ready to rumble in *Love Crazy*

Love & Anarchy

(1973, 100 min, Italy, Lina Wertmüller) *Giancarlo Giannini, Mariangela Melato.* An enormously powerful political drama about Italian Fascism during the 1930s, brilliantly written and directed by Wertmüller. Giannini stars as a Venetian peasant who takes up residence in a brothel as he awaits his opportunity to assassinate Mussolini. Music by Nino Rota. (Italian with English subtitles) ★★★½ VHS: $29.99; DVD: $29.99

Love & Basketball

(2000, 127 min, US, Gina Prince-Bythewood) *Omar Epps, Sanaa Lathan, Dennis Haysbert, Debbie Morgan, Alfre Woodard.* Uneven but definitely worthwhile, *Love & Basketball* follows two friends from their first meeting as eleven-year-olds, through their tumultuous dating period, to being lovers in college and pursuing careers in the NBA. Both aspire to be brilliant basketball players, and struggle to reconcile their ambition with their relationship. The film begins awkwardly, and, unfortunately, doesn't really get a foothold until the two get to college, when our rooting interest deepens considerably. The two leads are quite good, and there's a terrific supporting cast led by Haysbert and Woodard. For all its flaws (overlength being another), *Love & Basketball* is still manages to be entertaining and satisfying. ★★½ VHS: $14.99; DVD: $24.99

Love and Death

(1975, 82 min, US, Woody Allen) *Woody Allen, Diane Keaton, Harold Gould.* Tolstoy, Dostoevsky, Bergman (Ingmar) and the history books take a beating in Allen's hilarious comedic assault on 1800s Russia. Woody romances Diane, and they both try to assassinate Napoleon. ★★★½ VHS: $14.99; DVD: $19.99

Love and Death on Long Island

(1997, 103 min, GB, Richard Kwietniowski) *John Hurt, Jason Priestley, Fiona Loewi, Sheila Hancock, Maury Chaykin.* Funny, endearing, wise and invigorating, this tale of an older man's fixation on a younger man is nominally based on the Thomas Mann novella and the Luchino Visconti screen adaptation *Death in Venice.* Giles De'Ath (Hurt in a wonderful portrayal) is an acclaimed writer who accidentally sees the sex comedy *Hot Pants College II* and is immediately struck by Ronnie Bostwick (Priestley), one of the film's stars. With the fervor of a teeny-bopper in love, Giles becomes obsessed with his object of perfection, and eventually travels to the United States in search of his "love." There he stalks the actor and eventually befriends him, making a quite unlikely pair. ★★★½ VHS: $14.99; DVD: $24.99

Love and Faith

(1978, 154 min, Japan, Kei Kumai) *Toshiro Mifune, Takashi Shimura.* This moving Japanese period drama stars Mifune and Takashi Shimura. The rise of Christianity in 16th-century Japan is used as a backdrop for a tragic romance involving the beautiful stepdaughter of Japan's leading tea master, whose love for a young Christian lord precipitates a conflict with vile warlord Mifune. (Japanese with English subtitles) ★★★

Love and Human Remains

(1993, 100 min, Canada, Denys Arcand) *Thomas Gibson, Ruth Marshall, Cameron Bancroft, Mia Kirshner, Rick Roberts, Joanne Vannicola, Matthew Ferguson.* Adapted from Brad Fraser's play "Unidentified Human Remains and the True Nature of Love," this somber drama might also be titled "Sex and Human Alienation." The story takes place in a nameless Canadian city populated by attractive, sexually active but world-weary young people of all sorts of sexual orientations. There is the gay David (Gibson), a sexually active waiter. His roommate is Candy (Marshall), a pretty and intelligent young woman who soon gets involved with both a straight man and an especially intense lesbian schoolteacher (Vannicola). Weaving its tale of souls emotionally adrift, Arcand's first English-language film effectively goes from one character to another charting their collective ennui and their valiant attempts to use sex as a facilitator towards intimacy, fulfillment and happiness. ★★★ VHS: $19.99

Love and Other Catastrophes

(1996, 90 min, Australia, Emma-Kate Croghan) *Alice Garner, Frances O'Connor, Matthew Dyktynksi.* Funky and hip from the very start, this amusing little Australian screwball comedy follows one mixed-up day in the life of a group of grad students in Melbourne. At the center are Alice (Garner), a sprightly young woman who is four years late with her dissertation on "Doris Day as Feminist Warrior," and her lesbian roommate Mia (O'Connor), who finds herself caught in the bureaucratic nightmare of trying to change her department. The film zips around through their respective day while introducing a slew of supporting oddballs, especially in regards to their search for a new, third roommate. Croghan demonstrates a marvelous sense of character, and Garner and O'Connor both make thoroughly engaging protagonists. ★★★ VHS: $79.99

Love at First Bite

(1979, 96 min, US, Stan Dragoti) *George Hamilton, Susan Saint James.* Very enjoyable take-off on the Dracula legend with Hamilton as the Count searching New York City for new victims — finding Saint James. Lots of laughs in this parody which isn't afraid to use every bat joke in the book. ★★★

Love at Large

(1990, 97 min, US, Alan Rudolph) *Tom Berenger, Elizabeth Perkins, Anne Archer, Kate Capshaw, Annette O'Toole.* For the first 60 minutes, this stylish homage to '40s film noir is nearly perfect: Berenger is a wonderfully befuddled and rumpled detective; there is a labyrinthine and duplicitous plot; and enough femme fatales to enrapture a slew of Sam Spades. Regrettably, however, this Rudolph-scripted mystery cannot sustain its initial high level and slowly unravels near the end. Gravel-voiced P.I. Harry Dobbs (Berenger) is hired to tail a possibly two-timing husband, but follows the wrong person — a man who leads the private eye into an increasingly sordid mess of murder, bigamy and deception. ★★½

Love Crazy

(1941, 99 min, US, Jack Conway) *William Powell, Myrna Loy, Gail Patrick, Jack Carson.* A lively and zany screwball comedy, the story follows the merry exploits of Powell and Loy on their fourth anniversary. When she gets jealous over hubby's former girlfriend moving in upstairs, Loy files for divorce. Concocting a loony plan to get her back, Powell feigns insanity, and he's so convincing she has him committed. But we've already given away too much. Powell and Loy are, of course, terrific. Powell suffers almost every indignity (the elevator scene is a hoot) with his customary élan. ★★★ VHS: $19.99

Love Crimes

(1992, 85 min, US, Lizzie Borden) *Sean Young, Patrick Bergen, Arnetia Walker.* Young stars as an unorthodox District Attorney trying to build a case against a mysterious man who is impersonating a well-known photographer and is taking advantage of a number of unsuspecting and vulnerable women. Bergin plays yet another deranged and sadistic villain. Overall, independent feminist filmmaker Borden's (*Working Girls*) attempt to enter the mainstream, while slightly perplexing and uneven, is an interesting and watchable thriller. (Unrated) ★★ VHS: $9.99

Love Field

(1992, 104 min, US, Jonathan Kaplan) *Michelle Pfeiffer, Dennis Haysbert, Stephanie McFadden, Brian Kerwin.* Pfeiffer's sincere performance more than redeems the few plot holes in this otherwise endearing drama. She plays Lurene, a Dallas housewife who, upon the assassination of JFK, buses to Washington for his funeral. En route, she inadvertently involves a fellow passenger, a black man (Haysbert), with the police. Traveling with his young daughter, the father and child hit the back roads to elude the authorities, accompanied by the naïve, good-intentioned Lurene. What follows is a charming road movie with touches of whimsy, romance and history lessons on racial attitudes, 1960s-style. ★★★ VHS: $14.99; DVD: $19.99

Love Film

(1970, 130 min, Hungary, István Szabó) *Andras Balint, Judit Halasz.* Although unknown by most American audiences, this poignant human drama, political allegory and romantic love story is considered a pivotal film in Hungary's post-war cinema. Jancsi boards a train in Budapest on a journey to be reunited with his childhood sweetheart, Kata, who fled after the 1956 uprising. The trip also proves to be a journey into his pain-filled past — of innocent childhood moments, romantic rendezvous, as well as haunting images of WWII airraids, Communist youth rallies and the suffering caused by the Russian suppression of the Budapest Spring. (Hungarian with English subtitles) ★★★½ VHS: $39.99

Love Finds Andy Hardy

(1938, 92 min, US, George B. Seitz) *Mickey Rooney, Judy Garland, Lana Turner, Ann Rutherford.* Rooney finds himself with two dates for the big Christmas Dance — steady girlfriend Rutherford and voluptuous Turner. Then, a new girl moves in next door (Garland). Geez! What's a poor guy to do? One of the best of the Andy Hardy series with Mickey and Judy in good form. ★★★ VHS: $19.99

Love from a Stranger

(1947, 81 min, US, Richard Whorf) *Sylvia Sidney, John Hodiak.* Sidney marries wholesome Hodiak, only to begin to suspect he may be a killer — and she may be his next victim. Based on an Agatha Christie story, which bears a resemblance to Alfred Hitchcock's *Suspicion.* It's a familiar story line with a degree of suspense. An earlier version was made in Great Britain in 1937 with Ann Harding and Basil Rathbone. ★★½ VHS: $14.99

Love Happy

(1949, 91 min, US, David Miller) *The Marx Brothers, Ilona Massey, Vera-Ellen, Raymond Burr, Marilyn Monroe.* Some swell kids want to put on a show, but the money's run out. But wait — the spectacular Romanov diamonds are in the can of sardines that the cat is dining on. . . Chico and Harpo track down the gems as Groucho tracks down the sullen but fabulously wealthy Massey, who's also after the loot. Vera-Ellen and Burr dance up a storm (yes, Raymond Burr), and Marilyn has a walk-on that makes up in intensity what it lacks in length. Ben Hecht was

one of the scriptwriters for this occasionally funny Marx Brothers romp. ★★½ VHS: $19.99

Love Hurts

(1989, 110 min, US, Bud Yorkin) *Jeff Daniels, Cynthia Sikes, John Mahoney, Cloris Leachman, Judith Ivey.* A beguiling if familiar comedy-drama about a family coming together for a weekend wedding. Daniels heads a fine cast as a newly divorced insurance agent who returns home for his sister's nuptials. Complicating the visit are his ex-wife (Sikes) and children, who have just moved in. The story focuses on Daniels' various relationships with his family, including his estranged young daughter, drunken father and wary ex-wife. Director Yorkin handles familial trauma, rich characters and warm humor all with equal command. Mahoney and Leachman are extremely appealing as Daniels' colorful parents. ★★★ VHS: $14.99

Love in a Fallen City

(1984, 97 min, Hong Kong, Ann Hui) This compelling romantic wartime drama centers on the troubled love affair between a young divorcée and a rich, Westernized playboy right at the time of Hong Kong's fall to the Japanese in 1941. (Cantonese with English subtitles) ★★½ VHS: $39.99

A Love in Germany

(1984, 110 min, West Germany, Andrzej Wajda) *Hanna Schygulla, Piotr Lysak, Armin Mueller-Stahl.* Amid the sweeping crush of the Nazi terror, a German shopkeeper (Schygulla) falls in love with a Polish POW and suffers the grave consequences of the illicit affair. Director Wajda conveys the poignance of personal tragedy overshadowed by the grand obscenity of war. (German with English subtitles) ★★★½

Love in the Afternoon

(1957, 130 min, US, Billy Wilder) *Gary Cooper, Audrey Hepburn, Maurice Chevalier, John McGiver.* Hepburn is captivating as a young Parisian artist whose curiosity and romanticism leads to romance in Wilder's enchanting and sardonic comedy. Chevalier is a private eye who is hired to tail American playboy Cooper, who is having an affair with a married woman. Starry-eyed Audrey hears that the cuckold husband may resort to firearms, and sets out to warn the Casanova. Romance ensues as the innocent Audrey gets philandering Gary to change his ways. Wilder casts a sarcastic eye towards romance and relationships while ultimately creating a sweetly caring one between Hepburn and Cooper. Here, Chevalier reminds one why he was one of France's biggest stars, and who could forget the wonderful train sequence? ★★★½ VHS: $14.99

Love in the City

(1953, 90 min, Italy, Various) *Ugo Tognazzi, Maresa Gallo.* This six-episode film is based on a very interesting idea: the director of each segment is "sent off" to capture, cinema verité style, an aspect of love and romance in the Eternal City. This hidden camera technique has each director act as a secret reporter out to explore typical Italian life. The Michelangelo Antonioni and Federico Fellini segments provide a fascinating hint to their future filmmaking careers. Other directors include Cesare

Zavattini, Dino Risi, Alberto Lattuada and Francesco Maselli. (English narration) ★★★

Love Is a Many Splendored Thing

(1955, 102 min, US, Henry King) *William Holden, Jennifer Jones, Torin Thatcher.* Based on the autobiographical best-seller by Han Suyin, this slick but hokey romantic drama is, at best, a partially splendored thing. Set in Hong Kong before the start of the Korean War, the film stars Jones as an Eurasian doctor involved in an affair with married American correspondent Holden. Jones and Holden both offer tender, captivating performances, but the film is slow moving, and John Patrick's dialogue, in trying to capture the mysticism and beauty of Chinese culture, borders on the clichéd; though a line such as "Let us have tea and talk of absurdities" is hard to resist. ★★½ VHS: $14.99; DVD: $24.99

Love Jones

(1997, 101 min, US, Theodore Witcher) *Larenz Tate, Nia Long, Isaiah Washington, Lisa Nicole Carson, Bill Bellamy.* Flavorful, romantic and funny, *Love Jones* is a real sleeper of a comedy. A very sexy photographer (Long) falls for the persistent charms of a budding novelist/poet (Tate), despite having given up on love after a failed marriage engagement. The film follows their relationship through all the usual obstacles — career, jealousy, pride, insecurity, etc. While the story is certainly tried and true, *Love Jones* has a funky, distinctive feel; for every aspect of the film that is clichéd or simplistic, there are many that are truthful and engaging. Despite its minor flaws — and an oddly unsatisfying ending — *Love Jones* is a winner. ★★★ VHS: $14.99; DVD: $19.99

The Love Letter

(1999, 88 min, US, Peter Ho-Sun Chan) *Kate Capshaw, Tom Selleck, Ellen DeGeneres, Tom Everett Scott, Blythe Danner, Gloria Stuart, Geraldine McEwan, Julianne Nicholson.* A charming, low-keyed romantic comedy with Capshaw as a bookstore owner who finds an unsigned love letter and thinks it's meant for her. But who sent it? Complications arise when the letter finds its way into the hands of others in her small New England coastal town, each thinking it's meant for them as well. DeGeneres is a natural sidekick as the store's manager, and Selleck is quite appealing as the local fire chief in love with Capshaw. ★★★ VHS: $9.99; DVD: $29.99

Love Me or Leave Me

(1955, 122 min, US, Charles Vidor) *James Cagney, Doris Day, Cameron Mitchell.* Cagney and Day (in her best film role) both give terrific performances in this musical biography of 1920s torch singer Ruth Etting. Cagney plays her gangster boyfriend. Score includes "Ten Cents a Dance" and "Shaking the Blues Away." ★★★½ VHS: $14.99

Love Me Tender

(1956, 89 min, US, Robert D. Webb) *Elvis Presley, Debra Paget, Richard Egan.* Presley's film debut is an acceptable Civil War drama about a Southern family taking different sides in the conflict. Elvis sings the title tune and "Let Me," among others. ★★½ VHS: $14.99

Love Meetings

(1964, 90 min, Italy, Pier Paolo Pasolini) *Love Meetings* is a gritty, cinema verité-style investigation of sex in Italy. The film includes appearances by author Alberto Moravia and noted psychologist Cesare Musatti. Pasolini appears as the interviewer and asks a wide range of individuals to share their tales of love — including their thoughts on prostitution, homosexuality, marital and nonmarital liaisons. (Italian with English subtitles) ★★★ VHS: $29.99

Love on the Run

(1979, 93 min, France, François Truffaut) *Jean-Pierre Léaud, Marie-France Pisier, Claude Jade.* Léaud makes his final appearance as Antoine Doinel in Truffaut's complex, bittersweet concluding installment of the Doinel saga. Through a marvelous sequence of flashbacks from earlier films, Truffaut documents Doinel's rocky road to adulthood. (French with English subtitles) ★★★ VHS: $19.99; DVD: $29.99

Love Potion #9

(1992, 90 min, US, Dale Launer) *Tate Donovan, Sandra Bullock, Anne Bancroft.* This lightweight fluff written and directed by the creator of *My Cousin Vinny* is a far cry from the classic screwball comedies it wants most desperately to be — but then any movie that takes its inspiration from a '60s pop tune can't hope for much. Hormonal hijinks ensue when a pair of nerdy scientists (Donovan, Bullock) accidentally discover a love potion. ★★ VHS: $14.99; DVD: $22.99

Love Serenade

(1997, 101 min, Australia, Shirley Barrett) *Miranda Otto, Rebecca Frith, George Shevtsov.* A witty, bizarre and very Australian take on love, sibling rivalry, Barry White and fish. In tiny Sunray, Australia, two quirky (to say the least) sisters have their humdrum lives turned upside-down when famed big-city D.J. Ken Sherry (a terrifically droll Shevtsov) moves in next door. Unusual and funny, *Love Serenade* is brightly written and directed by Barrett, with spot-on performances by both Otto and Frith as the sisters, and especially Shevtsov, whose Ken Sherry is quite an imaginative character. Until an admittedly unique though abrupt and unsatisfying end, *Love Serenade* is a truly odd, enjoyable comedy. ★★★ VHS: $19.99

Love Songs

(1986, 107 min, France, Elie Chouraqui) *Catherine Deneuve, Richard Anconina, Christopher Lambert, Nick Mancuso.* Deneuve and Lambert are enticingly matched as the ill-fated lovers in this entertaining and perceptive drama set in the rock music world of Paris. Deneuve is a successful talent agent, married to an American writer for 12 years and mother of two children, who reluctantly succumbs to a persistent and alluringly charming client, rock singer Lambert. The film's appeal could rest solely on the sexually charged love affair, but director Chouraqui also focuses on the people affected by the relationship. ★★★

Love Stinks

(1999, 94 min, US, Jeff Franklin) *French Stewart, Bridgette Wilson, Tyra Banks, Bill Bellamy.* A low-rent comic take-off on *Fatal Attraction*, this silly story stars Stewart (of TV's "3rd Rock from the Sun") as dorky sitcom writer who wins the heart of a beautiful woman (Wilson). Now get ready. . . The big joke is that she will stop at nothing to get him to walk her down the aisle. Their ensuing battle of the sexes does produce a chuckle or two, but it's all of the chuckle-headed variety. Love may not stink, but it's certainly not worth the effort. ★★ VHS: $9.99; DVD: $24.99

Love Story

(1970, 99 min, US, Arthur Hiller) *Ryan O'Neal, Ali McGraw, Ray Milland, John Marley, Tommy Lee Jones.* This box-office sensation is either classic romantic drama or ridiculous foolishness — depending on your tastes. O'Neal is the guy from the right side of the tracks, in love with McGraw, who's from the wrong side of town and has a fatal disease. (Sequel: *Oliver's Story*) ★★½ VHS: $14.99; DVD: $29.99

Love, Strange Love

(1982, 120 min, Brazil, Walter Khouri) *Vera Fischer, Mauro Mendonea.* This controversial film, about a young boy's sexual awakening in a brothel, caused quite a storm several years back when it played the film festival circuit. Possibly because of its subject matter, it never was released theatrically in the U.S., but is now on video in a complete unedited version. The story follows the development and growth of a young boy who is sent to live at his aunt's brothel. The enticing girls prove too much for the curious boy as he adjusts to this strange world. ★★½

Love Streams

(1986, 122 min, US, John Cassavetes) *John Cassavetes, Gena Rowlands, Diahnne Abbott, Seymour Cassel.* Two offbeat siblings, both desperate for some kind of happiness in their lonely existences, address their erratic ways in this examination of contemporary lifestyles. Cassavetes also appears as the hedonistic brother; Rowlands is the overly loving sister. Both Cassavetes and Rowlands are compelling in this insightful glimpse into two slightly neurotic romantic psyches. ★★★

Love! Valour! Compassion!

(1997, 115 min, US, Joe Mantello) *Jason Alexander, John Glover, Randy Becker, Stephen Spinella, Stephen Bogardus, Justin Kirk, John Benjamin Hickey.* Terrence McNally's Tony Award–winning play, trimmed from its three-hour running time, makes for an affecting, low-keyed tragicomedy which offers alternately insightful, heartrending and funny moments, but this film adaptation misses in capturing the play's greatness. A group of gay friends from New York spend their summer holiday weekends in the country at the beautiful lakeside estate of two lovers. With a discerning eye and ear, McNally explores the bonds and boundaries of friendships and romantic relationships which is perceptive drama no matter what sexual orientation the characters may be. All but Alexander starred in the Broadway production, and he effortlessly fits in, giving a tender, funny portrait. Glover is exceptional as John, and, in a dual role, his twin brother James, a sweet-natured, flamboyant PWA. ★★★ VHS: $19.99

Love Walked In

(1998, 91 min, US, Juan J. Campanella) *Denis Leary, Terence Stamp, Aitana Sánchez-Gijón, Danny Nucci, Michael Badalucco.* An intriguing noir mystery, *Love Walked In* is a stylish and sexy story of deception and betrayal. Leary stars as a second-rate piano player married to the beautiful Sánchez-Gijón. When their small town's richest businessman takes a fancy to her, they plot to extort money from him. But *Love Walked In* goes in different directions than its premise suggests. There are a couple of nifty twists, and all three leads are quite good. Some of the story's set-up is familiar, but director Campanella sustains interest throughout thanks to some snappy dialogue and a nice visual style. ★★★ VHS: $102.99

Love with the Proper Stranger

(1963, 100 min, US, Robert Mulligan) *Natalie Wood, Steve McQueen, Edie Adams, Tom Bosley.* Wood and McQueen's impassioned performances dominate this hearty romantic comedy-drama about the love affair between shopgirl Wood and musician McQueen. ★★★ VHS: $19.99

Love without Pity

(1990, 95 min, France, Eric Rachont) *Hippolyte Girarodt, Mireille Perrier.* A delightfully witty drama of romantic love in the land of existentialism. Hippo — young, handsome, and with a seductive Belmondo-cool attitude — leads a carefree bohemian life; living with friends, bumming money and casually picking up women, only to drop them when his interest flags. A sexist pig certainly, but a charming one. But his "love 'em and leave 'em" attitude towards women comes back to haunt him when he meets a professional woman who does not immediately succumb to his charms. Intrigued by this evasive victim, he goes all out, only to find himself smitten with love, jealousy and obsession, all traits that mean nothing to the young lady. (French with English subtitles) ★★★ VHS: $19.99

Love's Labour's Lost

(2000, 93 min, GB, Kenneth Branagh) *Kenneth Branagh, Alessandro Nivola, Alicia Silverstone, Natascha McElhone, Matthew Lillard, Nathan Lane, Adrian Lester, Timothy Spall.* Branagh may be the reigning screenwriter laureate of Shakespeare's plays, adapting the greater themes and gentler nuances to such works as *Hamlet*, *Henry V* and *Much Ado about Nothing*. In this condensation of *Love's Labour's Lost*, he especially proves to be an adroit handler of Shakespeare's gentle side, lending natural, playful readings to the trippingly delightful dialogue. But this comedy is saddled with an awkward, labeled conceit, as the story (placed somewhere in the 1930s) is constantly interrupted by musical numbers in the style (and with music) of that era. It's hard to tell whether the numbers would be entertaining in a different film, but here they are so unwelcome as to tarnish the scenes that surround them. ★★ VHS: $19.99; DVD: $32.99

The Loved One

(1965, 116 min, US, Tony Richardson) *Robert Morse, John Gielgud, Rod Steiger, Tab Hunter, Liberace, Jonathan Winters, Roddy McDowall.* Evelyn Waugh's audacious satire on the Southern California way of life (and death) was adapted for the screen by Terry Southern and Christopher Isherwood ("I Am a Camera").

Love's Labour's Lost

This classic black comedy, which was billed as "the film with something to offend everyone," follows the sometimes surreal journey of a young man as he makes his way through studio intrigue, romance and a mystical funeral parlor. Morse is the Candide-like nephew who travels to L.A. to visit his uncle; Steiger is the Oedipal Mr. Joyboy; and Liberace is a fastidious casket salesman. A refreshing slap in the face to both normality and eccentricity. ★★★½

The Lover

(1992, 119 min, France, Jean-Jacques Annaud) *Jane March, Tony Leung, Jeanne Moreau.* Set in Vietnam in 1929, this adaptation of Marguerite Duras' story about a French schoolgirl is a sensual feast for the eyes and ears. The girl, struggling to gain independence from her difficult family life and trying to understand her own sexual awakening, begins a torrid and illicit affair with a wealthy Chinese man. Although they don't really approve of the affair, her family tries to manipulate the situation for their own benefit. Annaud captures the tension-filled colonial setting that serves as a backdrop for these displaced persons, and the film is aided by gorgeous cinematography. (Filmed in English) ★★½ VHS: $14.99

Lover Come Back

(1962, 107 min, US, Delbert Mann) *Rock Hudson, Doris Day, Tony Randall, Edie Adams, Jack Oakie, Ann B. Davis.* Hudson and Day reteamed after their 1959 smash *Pillow Talk*, and the result is every bit as successful. In this genuinely funny satire on Madison Avenue, Doris plays an ad exec determined to land the account of scientist Rock's new invention — only he's really a rival ad exec, and, of course, there is no new invention. Love is what he's after. Lively '60s fun. ★★★½ VHS: $9.99

Loverboy

(1989, 98 min, US, Joan Micklin Silver) *Patrick Dempsey, Kate Jackson, Kirstie Alley, Robert Ginty.* After her tremendous success with *Crossing Delancey*, Silver's irresponsible and unfunny sex farce rates as a major disappointment. Dempsey plays a teenager who becomes the romantic idol of a group of older women — jumping in and out of bed with each of them. ★★ VHS: $14.99

Lovers (Amantes)

(1991, 105 min, Spain, Vincente Aranda) *Victoria Abril, Jorge Sanz.* In a story that makes the films of Pedro Almodóvar seem innocuously tame, this sexually charged, hyperventilating melodrama is a lurid tale of a love triangle gone dangerously awry. Fresh from a stint in the military, the broodingly handsome Paco finds his well-planned life with his prim fiancée shattered when his sultry, widowed landlady seduces him. Luisa (Abril), the luscious "older woman," proves to be a seasoned sexual dynamo and a tough opponent for Trini, Paco's inexperienced girlfriend. She decides that, "if you can't beat 'em, join 'em" and begins her own assault to capture the heart and loins of our young hero. What follows is a plethora of out-of-control Latino passions, sexual deception, bloody revenge and a fist-clenching scene with a strategically stuffed handkerchief. (Spanish with English subtitles) ★★★½ VHS: $14.99

The Lovers

(1958, 89 min, France, Louis Malle) *Jeanne Moreau, Alain Cuny.* Boasting a casual view of adultery, this early Malle melodrama became famous mostly for censorship problems and court cases on its initial United States release. Moreau stars as a restless woman, bored by the privileges of her Pernod-and-caviar provincial life and trapped in a loveless marriage. Weekly sojourns into the elegant world of Parisian society produce some diversion until one day she meets an unpretentious young student who offers her sexual fulfillment and temporary relief from her emptiness. Moreau, with her sad, sultry beauty, was made an international star by the film. (Letterboxed) (French with English subtitles) ★★★

Lovers and Liars

(1981, 93 min, Italy, Mario Monice) *Goldie Hawn, Giancarlo Giannini, Laura Betti.* A disappointing black comedy about the ill-fated and calamity-prone romance of American tourist Hawn and married businessman Giannini. The two make an interesting couple as they wind their way through a series of comic disasters and arguments on the way to true love, but neither have much to work with. ★★

Loves of a Blonde

(1965, 88 min, Czechoslovakia, Milos Forman) *Jana Brejchova, Josef Sebanek.* Years before his international success with such films as *Amadeus, Cuckoo's Nest* and *Ragtime*, Forman directed a series of quirky, funny films from his Eastern European homeland. This film depicts life in a small factory town near Prague with a curious social injustice: the women outnumber the men ten to one. A visit by a group of army reservists allows Anduka, the blonde in question, to enjoy a welcomed but bittersweet respite. (Czechoslovakian with English subtitles) ★★★½ VHS: $29.99

The Loves of Carmen

(1948, 99 min, US, Charles Vidor) *Rita Hayworth, Glenn Ford.* Bizet's famous opera about a soldier who becomes obsessed with a comely Gypsy woman is so flamboyant and loaded with such sensuous music that one must wonder why anyone would want to turn it into a nonmusical drama. This rendition of the tragic tale will leave one wondering. On the up side, however, Hayworth's dazzling beauty is enough to make this easy viewing. ★★½ VHS: $19.99; DVD: $27.99

Lovin' Molly

(1974, 98 min, US, Sidney Lumet) *Blythe Danner, Beau Bridges, Anthony Perkins, Susan Sarandon.* This atmospheric if slowly paced film version of Larry McMurtry's novel "Leaving Cheyenne" is sort of a western *Jules and Jim.* Spanning over 40 years, the story centers on Texas farmboys and brothers Bridges and Perkins who spend a lifetime lovin' Molly (exceptionally played by Danner). An often charming, quirky film with three splendid performances from the three leads. ★★★ VHS: $9.99

A Low Down Dirty Shame

(1994, 110 min, US, Keenan Ivory Wayans) *Keenan Ivory Wayans, Jada Pinkett, Salli Richardson, Charles Dutton.* Those expecting an action-packed tribute to the blaxploitation films of the '70s will surely be disappointed by this mind-numbing disaster. Director-writer-actor Wayans plays a former cop-turned-private investigator who is hired by ex-partner Dutton to take on a nefarious drug lord. Those who are brave enough to sit through this are sure to feel that it's a low down dirty shame a film this bad was made in the first place. ★½ VHS: $9.99

The Low Life

(1996, 98 min, US, George Hickenlooper) *Rory Cochran, Kyra Sedgwick, Sean Astin, Christian Meoli, Ron Livingston, James LeGros, J.T. Walsh.* Partially based on the director's own experiences after graduating from Yale, *The Low Life* follows a recent grad and aspiring writer (Cochran) through demeaning temp jobs and a frustrating relationship with a manic-depressive Southern belle beauty (Sedgwick doing her best in a basically unplayable role). And this being a GenX movie, there are obligatory bar scenes, with Cochran and cohorts discussing pop culture, philosophy and life's injustices. *The Low Life* has many flaws, but it's moving and doesn't condescend. ★★½

Ludwig

The Lower Depths

(1957, 125 min, Japan, Akira Kurosawa) *Toshiro Mifune, Isuzu Yamada.* Kurosawa's compelling adaptation of Maxim Gorky's classic play. The story concerns a group of peasants living in absolute squalor. Crammed in on top of each other, the tenants are locked in a constant battle of wits: some clinging desperately to their broken dreams while others viciously shoot them down. This truly touching tale features an exceptional ensemble cast headed by the incomparable Mifune. (Japanese with English subtitles) ★★★ VHS: $29.99

Lucas

(1986, 100 min, US, David Seltzer) *Corey Haim, Charlie Sheen, Winona Ryder.* A pleasant surprise, this charming teen comedy follows the romantic misadventures of a love-struck 14-year-old (played with wide-eyed innocence by Haim) who falls for the new girl in town, a newly acquainted friend who has set her sights on the football team captain (Sheen). Haim, before he had his 15 minutes of fame as one of the two Coreys, is wonderful; and Ryder shows that, even before she hit it big, she had star quality. ★★★ VHS: $14.99

Lucie Aubrac

(1997, 116 min, France, Claude Berri) *Carole Bouquet, Daniel Auteuil, Patrice Chéreau.* A gripping drama of determination and the inexhaustible power of love, Berri's exquisite WWII film tells the true story of a French woman, Lucie Aubrac (marvelously played by Bouquet), a schoolteacher and mother who risks all for the safety of her husband. Auteuil is Monsieur Aubrac, a Resistance member fighting the Nazis in Lyons. When he and other partisans are captured by the Germans, his wife joins the Resistance and plans and executes a daring escape. Berri, who directed Auteuil in the masterful *Jean de Florette* and *Manon of the Spring*, maintains tension throughout the film as the outcome is never a given. *Lucie Aubrac* is also a fascinating peek into the anatomy of a group of freedom fighters who placed themselves in harm's way every single day. (French with English subtitles) ★★½ VHS: $102.99

Lucky Numbers

(2000, 105 min, US, Nora Ephron) *John Travolta, Lisa Kudrow, Tim Roth, Ed O'Neill, Michael Rapaport, Bill Pullman, Michael Moore, Richard Schiff.* Suggested by an actual incident which happened in the 1980s, *Lucky Numbers* is a peculiar, ultimately unsuccessful blend of screwball and dark comedy that never quite finds its groove. Set in Harrisburg, Pennsylvania, the story follows colorful TV weatherman Travolta and lotto ball-girl Kudrow, who in-between their romantic trysts concoct a scheme to rig the state lottery. Director Ephron (who helmed Travolta in *Michael*, one of his weaker outings) and writer Adam Resnick (*Cabin Boy*, 'nuf said) attempt to milk greed, betrayals and killings for wacky laughs, but unappealing characters and uneven pacing only weigh down what little amusing moments the film has. ★★ VHS: $14.99; DVD: $29.99

Lucrezia Borgia

(1935/1923/1916, 93/31/14 min, France, Abel Gance) Along with the short films "Au Secours!" and "La Folie du Docteur Tube," this is a fascinating, rarely seen work by silent film pioneer Gance. The shorts veer towards the experimental, with avant garde tendencies that are more aggressive than Gance used in his features. *Lucrezia Borgia* is an opulent portrait of one of history's most ambitious families. Pity the girl; historians now agree that the tales of vice and corruption levied against Lucrezia were greatly exaggerated. Gance paints her more to be pitied than scorned, made victim by a father renowned as the deliciously corrupt Pope Alexander VI. When your film is narrated Niccolo Machiavelli, reveling at each melodramatic turn, it is difficult to miss. ★★★ VHS: $19.99; DVD: $24.99

Ludwig

(1972, 231 min, Italy, Luchino Visconti) *Helmut Berger, Romy Schneider, Trevor Howard, Silvana Mangano, Helmut Griem, Gert Frobe.* Through a series of talking heads, each of accusation, the downfall of one of Europe's most tragic and historically enigmatic figures is brought into director Visconti's realm of neorealism in this full-length version not previously seen in the United States. Berger is "the mad king of Bavaria," who saw himself as a poet and architect of dreams. Politically naïve, King Ludwig found solace as a patron of the arts. His friendships with Wagner and other artists eventually became a vampire on the Bavarian state's gold vein, which ultimately created enemies within the walls of his reluctant empire who would later have him committed. Visconti's characters are often too cold to allow for sympathy, but his vision opens the realities of a world more too often intolerant of anything in quest of personified passion. It may be overlong, but *Ludwig* is sumptuous and stately. (Letterboxed) (Italian with English subtitles) ★★★½ VHS: $24.99

Lulu in Berlin

(1985, 50 min, US, Richard Leacock & Susan Woll) *Louise Brooks.* Louise Brooks' life and film work, which took her from Hollywood to pre-Hitler Germany and 1930s France, was exciting and controversial. Her remarkable career is recounted in this absorbing documentary that features the only filmed interview with Ms. Brooks as well as clips from several of her films. The filmmakers, renowned documentarians, capture the radiance of this articulate, seductive and beguiling woman. ★★★½

Lulu on the Bridge

(1999, 103 min, US, Paul Auster) *Harvey Keitel, Mira Sorvino, Willem Dafoe, Gina Gershon, Mandy Patinkin, Vanessa Redgrave.* A rock found in a briefcase has mysterious powers over all who touch it, including a disabled sax player (Keitel) and an aspiring actress (Sorvino). The title refers to Lulu from *Pandora's Box*. A strange, even sentimental thriller from Auster, who makes his solo directing debut after writing *Smoke* and codirecting *Blue in the Face*. ★★½ VHS: $69.99; DVD: $24.99

Lumière

(1976, 95 min, France, Jeanne Moreau) *Jeanne Moreau, Bruno Ganz, François Simon.* Moreau's warm and endearing directorial debut chronicles the lives, loves, careers and friendships of four women of different ages all living in Paris. The film's affectionate yet insightful look at these people produces a wonderful human drama. (French with English subtitles) ★★★

Luna Park

(1993, 108 min, Russia, Pavel Lounguine) *Oleg Borisov, Andrei Goutine.* Employing the same herky-jerky, low-budget look of his earlier *Taxi Blues*, director Lounguine has created a gritty, nightmarish and all-too-real treatise on Russia's seemingly inevitable slide into total social chaos. The story follows Andrei, a neo-Nazi thug who hangs with a loosely organized band in a Moscow amusement park. Upon learning that he is half Jewish, he begins a desperate search for his Semitic father, finally landing upon Naoum, an aging intellectual, songwriter and esthete. As Andrei struggles with his emotions, Lounguine evokes a terrifying image of Russia on the edge where class differences, deep-rooted anti-Semitism and a complete lack of state control are giving rise to unspeakable violence. (Russian with English subtitles) ★★★ VHS: $29.99

Lupo

(1970, 100 min, Israel, Menahem Golan) *Yuda Barkan, Gabi Armoni.* Fifty-year-old Lupo, widower and neighborhood character, stands up to city hall when his dilapidated but beloved community is threatened with demolition. A zesty, unpredictable comedy. (Filmed in English) ★★★ VHS: $59.99

Lust for Life

(1956, 122 min, US, Vincente Minnelli) *Kirk Douglas, Anthony Quinn, Pamela Brown.* Douglas gives possibly his best performance as painter Vincent Van Gogh in this riveting drama about the artist's tortured life. Quinn won an Oscar as Van Gogh's compadre, Paul Gauguin. Minnelli's film avoids the clichés of the artist at work, and succinctly presents the tale with subtlety and a narrative coherency. ★★★½ VHS: $19.99

Lust in the Dust

(1985, 85 min, US, Paul Bartel) *Tab Hunter, Divine, Lainie Kazan, Geoffrey Lewis, Cesar Romero.* Gold lies somewhere in the squalid town of Chile Verde and the person who can line up the asses of Divine and Kazan will be able to follow the map tattooed thereon (half a map per cheek) to the treasure's whereabouts. A wildly funny spoof of westerns. ★★★ VHS: $9.99; DVD: $24.99

L

Luzia

(1987, 112 min, Brazil, Fabio Barreto) *Claudia Ohana, Thales Pan Chacon.* Substituting for Sonia Braga in the saucy, sensuous and beguiling role, Ohana (one of Brazil's biggest stars) more than fills her place in this exciting Brazilian western. Ohana is a rodeo cowgirl caught in a clash between squatters and the powerful ranch owners. (Portuguese with English subtitles) ★★½ VHS: $19.99

M

(1931, 106 min, Germany, Fritz Lang) *Peter Lorre, Ellen Widmann, Inge Landgut.* After a decade of making hugely popular fantasy, sci-fi and spy movies, Lang made his own undisputable masterpiece, *M*, scripted by his wife, Thea von Harbou, a Nazi sympathizer. Working on a tighter budget and a shorter schedule that he was used to, Lang brilliantly synthesized his expressionistic tendencies with the torn-from-today's-headlines style that typified his later Hollywood work. Lorre, in one of his earliest film roles, finds the pathos in this nondescript Everyman whose psyche has been so poisoned that he is driven to raping and murdering little girls. The terrified city wants action: swift, decisive, effective. But when the State is found to be impotent, the meta-government — organized crime — sets up a dangerous option for a nation ill-prepared to select wisely. A harrowing psychological drama inspired by an actual 1929 Dusseldorf incident. This is the remastered, longer (by seven minutes) version, which includes the original German ending. (German with English subtitles) ★★★★ VHS: $19.99; DVD: $29.99

M. Butterfly

(1993, 100 min, US, David Cronenberg) *Jeremy Irons, John Lone, Barbara Sukowa, Ian Richardson.* The much-anticipated screen version of David Henry Hwang's hit play is something of a letdown. Inspired by a true story, the tragic tale is about a man's self-delusional love for and betrayal by an alluring Chinese woman who is actually a man. A deer-in-the-headlights-like Irons stars as Rene Gallimard, a nebbish accountant at the French Embassy who falls in love with an opera singer, Song Liling (Lone). As the two begin an affair, Gallimard rises in rank at the embassy, unknowingly disseminating government secrets. The action unfolds slowly and the film's emotional level never seems to rise above the simmering point of grand tragedy. ★★½ VHS: $14.99

Ma Vie en Rose (My Life in Pink)

(1998, 89 min, Belgium, Alain Berliner) *Michèle Laroque, Jean-Philippe Ecoffey, Hélène Vincent, George du Fresne.* A precious Belgian film about a little boy who wants to be a little girl, *Ma Vie en Rose* is a fantastic story about being true to one's self. Ludovic (du Fresne) delights in wearing dresses and makeup, even at inopportune moments like his family's "welcome to the neighborhood" party. While his antics are dismissed as a childish phase, Ludo knows better. An embarrassment to his family, Ludo perseveres with his desires, unwavered by shame, until his family is torn asunder from the stress his behavior has caused. While there are several painful scenes of Ludo being harassed, rejected, and ridiculed (his aunt is supportive), Ludo's courage is inspirational. Director Berliner's unusual film is extremely enjoyable not just for its central concept, but also for its incredibly fluid camerawork and candy-colored set design. It's a tenderhearted, remarkably affecting film. (French with English subtitles) ★★★½ VHS: $21.99; DVD: $27.99

Mac

(1993, 120 min, US, John Turturro) *John Turturro, Michael Badalucco, Carl Capotorto, Katherine Borowitz, Ellen Barkin.* Actor Turturro makes an extremely impressive directorial debut with this drama about three Italian-American brothers who start their own construction company. Set in mid-1950s Queens, the film tells of the enterprising brothers' struggle against rival developers, procedural setbacks and most often each other. Meticulously crafted and carefully photographed, the film's tight-knit ensemble of actors provide outstanding, rich and multilayered characterizations. As a director, Turturro shows a strong, clear vision as he keeps the pace lively and tells his story with precision. ★★★★ VHS: $19.99

Macao

(1952, 81 min, US, Joseph von Sternberg) *Robert Mitchum, Ava Gardner, William Bendix.* In the notorious Far East, a mysterious American adventurer helps a detective hunt down an elusive gangster. A seedy atmosphere and a fair amount of tension heightens this noirish tale. ★★★ VHS: $14.99

Macario

(1960, 91 min, Mexico, Roberto Gavaldon) A poetic fairy tale, the story follows Macario, an impoverished woodcutter who, with his young wife and four children, struggles to eke out an existence in rural Mexico. Plagued by a sense of failure, our hero vows not to eat again until he can have a turkey all for himself. On the Day of the Dead, his wife steals a bird, cooks it and gives it to him as he goes into the forest to work, where he is confronted by the Devil, God and Death, all asking him to share his prized meal. He eventually chooses Death, and in return receives magical powers to heal the sick and dying. His life changes as he accumulates wealth and possessions, all the while attracting the attention of the Church's local inquisition. Based on a story by B. Traven (author of "The Treasure of the Sierra Madre"). ★★★ VHS: $79.99

Macaroni

(1985, 104 min, Italy, Ettore Scola) *Jack Lemmon, Marcello Mastroianni.* Lemmon plays a weary business executive who returns to Naples for the first time since WWII. There is reunited with a wartime acquaintance (Mastroianni), who has been sending his own sister forged letters from the serviceman since the war ended. The two stars overcome an intriguing story which is only half-heartedly explored. (Filmed in English) ★★½ VHS: $79.99

MacArthur

(1977, 130 min, US, Joseph Sargent) *Gregory Peck, Dan O'Herlihy, Ed Flanders.* In an attempt to reproduce the sweep and historical significance of *Patton*, the filmmakers set their sights on another controversial military leader of WWII: General Douglas MacArthur. Even with an actor of Peck's caliber in the title role, the film is only mildly interesting. The story covers in episodic, sometimes melodramatic fashion, the career of the general from the 1940s thru Korea. Peck gives a compelling performance, but lacks the necessary panache befitting the larger-than-life commander. Flanders is quite good, however, as President Truman. ★★½ VHS: $9.99

MacArthur's Children

(1985, 115 min, Japan, Masahiro Shinoda) *Masako Natsume, Shima Iwashita, Juzo Itami.* The effects of America's victory over Japan and subsequent occupation and cultural domination of this proud nation are the themes of Shinoda's poignant and funny film. Set in a small fishing village immediately after WWII, the film explores the relationship and attitudes of the townspeople to their foreign "rulers." The film is not a biting indictment against Americans, but rather a loving remembrance of these strange people who came and changed Japan forever. (Japanese with English subtitles) ★★★

Macbeth

(1948, 112 min, US, Orson Welles) *Orson Welles, Jeanette Nolan, Dan O'Herlihy, Roddy McDowall.* A presentiment of evil overshadows every frame of Welles' *Macbeth.* A most faithful adaptation, both to Shakespeare's writing and

Peter Lorre in *M*

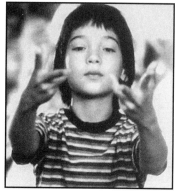

Ma Vie en Rose

to the historical era depicted. Welles makes optimum use of lighting and set design, and he is as much Macbeth as he was Kane. Nolan epitomizes the woman whose desire for power can be exercised only through her husband. ★★★½ VHS: $19.99

Macbeth

(1971, 140 min, GB, Roman Polanski) *Jon Finch, Nicholas Selby, Francesca Annis, Martin Shaw.* Who knows what evil lurked in the heart of the Bard when he penned this murderous tale of treachery and violence? In any case, Polanski's grim and gory conception of Shakespeare's bloody drama is not only one of his greatest films, but is one of the truest renditions of this sordid tale. Gripping and highly atmospheric, the film was greeted by an uproar fueled by its extreme (but not unwarranted) violence, a speech by Lady Macbeth in the nude, and problems in Polanski's personal life. ★★★½ VHS: $19.99

The Machine (La Machine)

(1994, 96 min, France, François Dupeyron) *Gérard Depardieu, Nathalie Baye, Didier Bourdon.* A slumming Depardieu plays a psychiatrist, fascinated with psychosis, who invents a machine which enables him to switch minds with an institutionalized psychotic killer. Thus, the killer (in the doctor's body) goes home to the wife and kid, while the doctor (in the killer's body) goes back to the padded cell. This could have been an interesting examination of identity, the nature of evil or other philosophical goodies. It settles for formulaic plotting, goofy dialogue and the occasional dark thrill. ★★ VHS: $9.99

Macho Dancer

(1988, 136 min, The Philippines, Lino Brocka) The eternal tale of the naïve country boy who is seduced and corrupted by the evils of the big city is played out in this fascinating and erotic drama. Paul, a somnambulistic teenage beauty, is drawn to Manila after his American lover and supporter of his family returns to the U.S. Paul is enamored by the city's notorious gay bars and nightclubs and is seduced into a world of prostitution, sexually explicit dancing and "brown slavery." The film offers a voyeuristic glimpse into the tacky yet lascivious gay underground where sexual acts are performed on stage and

then bought and sold off stage. (Tagalog with English subtitles) ★★★

The Mack

(1973, 110 min, US, Michael Campus) *Max Julien, Richard Pryor, Don Gordon.* One of the most popular of the '70s blaxploitation flicks, this gritty, misogynous actioner is the story of Goldie, a likable but sleazy ex-convict who aspires and attains his lofty goal of being a superpimp – "the meanest 'mack' in town." With an envious stable of fine hos, plenty of muscle and a cutthroat business attitude, our hero soon discovers that pimping's profitable but, "what gains a man to win the world and lose his own soul." Heavy, man. ★★ VHS: $9.99

Mack the Knife

(1989, 122 min, GB, Menahem Golan) *Raul Julia, Richard Harris, Julie Walters, Roger Daltrey.* A misbegotten version of "The Threepenny Opera," about the numerous, unsuccessful attempts of London's street people to keep England's most notorious criminal behind bars. ★½

The Mackintosh Man

(1973, 105 min, GB, John Huston) *Paul Newman, James Mason, Dominique Sanda, Harry Andrews, Ian Bannen.* Newman and Mason are on opposite sides of the fence in this derivative though enjoyable spy thriller about a freelance agent (Newman) who must ferret out a Communist traitor high in the ranks of the British government. ★★½ VHS: $14.99

Mad City

(1997, 114 min, US, Constantin Costa-Gavras) *Dustin Hoffman, John Travolta, Alan Alda, Mia Kirshner, Blythe Danner, Robert Prosky, William Atherton, Ted Levine.* Hoffman is a weasily TV anchorman who is inadvertently caught in the story of his life when a disgruntled museum security guard (Travolta, doing his best in an underrealized role) blows a head-gasket and takes hostages. As the event becomes a media three-ring circus, the film dives into the muddled water of ethics vs. ratings, news vs. sensationalism, truth vs. manipulation. Not as bitingly satiric as it could have been, *Mad City* charges along on a fever pitch for about an hour, but soon the film settles into a more predictable groove and degenerates into a sanctimonious morality tale. ★★½ VHS: $14.99; DVD: $19.99

Mad Dog and Glory

(1993, 96 min, US, John McNaughton) *Robert De Niro, Bill Murray, Uma Thurman, David Caruso, Kathy Baker.* De Niro stars as an extremely mild-mannered police photographer who, after he saves the life of mobster/stand-up comic Murray, is given — as a little "thank you" — the service of Thurman for one week. This amiable comedy-drama finds its niche as a character study, focusing on how the harsh world can bring very different people together. De Niro and Thurman are both endearing and funny, in a clumsy sort of way, and Murray puts an oddly menacing (if not fully believable) air. Caruso, before his one-year-wonder stint on TV's "NYPD Blue," is especially good as De Niro's police buddy. ★★★ VHS: $9.99; DVD: $14.99

Mad Dog Morgan

(1978, 93 min, Australia, Philippe Mora) *Dennis Hopper, David Gulpilil.* Hopper, a few years before he was accepted back in the Hollywood fraternity with *Blue Velvet*, traveled Down Under to make a few bucks in this explosively violent "western" saga. Playing the role with maniacal intensity, Hopper's Morgan is a man who, after killing a police chief, becomes an outlaw on the run and famous throughout the land for his daring and improbable escapes from the noose. An unusual but exciting actioner with Hopper in good form. ★★★ VHS: $14.99

Mad Love

(1995, 99 min, US, Antonia Bird) *Drew Barrymore, Chris O'Donnell, Joan Allen, Jude Ciccolella, Kevin Dunn, Matthew Lillard.* This could have been a fun-loving teen rebel romp across the American West, but instead it's a tedious, soppy melodrama that makes a half-hearted attempt to address mental illness. O'Donnell plays the grade-A high school senior who helps his single dad keep the family together. Barrymore is the new kid in town, a raging rebel who spells trouble from the start. It's not hard to guess that O'Donnell falls for her and forsakes his comfy chemistry exam–laden life for the dangerous female newcomer. Add to this time-honored contrivance an oh-too-trendy Seattle backdrop and a relentless grunge soundtrack and you get the feeling that the producers threw this together with tired formulas and scotch tape. ★ VHS: $14.99; DVD: $29.99

Mad Max

(1979, 93 min, Australia, George Miller) *Mel Gibson, Joanne Samuel.* The original adventures of Max, the Road Warrior, valiant law enforcer combatting the deranged highway marauders of a not-too-distant future. Gibson stars in this nerve-bending classic of automotive madness. (Dubbed from "Australian" English into "American") (Sequel: *The Road Warrior*) ★★★

Mad Max Beyond Thunderdome

(1985, 106 min, Australia, George Miller & George Ogilvie) *Mel Gibson, Tina Turner, Angelo Rossitto.* The last and least of the *Mad Max* trilogy, this movie still delivers some exciting action sequences, or at least half of it does. Directed in two parts by two different directors, the lines of division and talent show very clearly. While the first half of the film, directed by series veteran Miller, is along the lines of the previous two, with an angry Max (Gibson) trying to survive in an authoritarian community called Bartertown, it later drags to a crawl when Max goes off into the desert and encounters a band of post-apocalyptic children awaiting the appearance of a savior, who turns out to look a lot like Max. The fun of the first half of the movie is fueled by the presence of Turner in her wildly overblown performance as Auntie Entity. ★★½ VHS: $14.99; DVD: $19.99

The Mad Miss Manton

(1938, 80 min, US, Leigh Jason) *Barbara Stanwyck, Henry Fonda, Hattie McDaniel.* Stanwyck and Fonda appeared together for the first time (they were reunited in *You Belong to Me* and Preston Sturges' marvelous *The Lady Eve*) in this madcap mystery-screwball comedy. Stanwyck plays a zany socialite who, along with a group of friends, investigates a murder. Lots of fun. ★★★

Madadayo

(1992, 134 min, Japan, Akira Kurosawa) *Tatsuo Matsumura, Kyoko Kagawa.* Kurosawa caps a long and distinguished career with this revelatory examination of a respected, elderly teacher. The film opens in 1943, when Hyakken Uchida, at 60, decides to retire from teaching to write. The full devastation of the war has not yet hit Japan as his loyal students begin a yearly ritual of a birthday party tribute to him. During it, they ask him, "Mahda-kai?" ("Are you ready?"); he responds, "Madadayo" ("Not yet"). The children's game takes on a different meaning for the teacher. For years, Hyakken remains a guiding force for his students, imparting wisdom and compassion with humor and good will. Kurosawa again imparts intimate human moments against larger historic events, conveying a sense of that particular moment with shared universal experience. *Madadayo* speaks to losses suffered through age and circumstance buffered by the beneficence of loving family and friends. One suspects Kurosawa's own last years were as replete with respect and admiration. (Japanese with English subtitles) ★★★ VHS: $79.99; DVD: $24.99

Madagascar Skin

(1995, 93 min, GB, Christian Newby) *John Hannah, Bernard Hill.* Newby has made an unusual and often engaging love story between two outsiders in this mystical film, *Anchoress.* In a gay world where beauty is paramount, Harry (Hannah) is a man ostracized because of a large facial birthmark. Rejected and with no one to embrace, he finally runs away, resurfacing on a beach where he saves the life of Flint (Hill), a gruff older man found beaten and buried in the sand. With neither one of them having a place to turn, they set up house in an abandoned cottage. There, their friendship soon turns into love. The film begins unrelentingly bleak, but as the offbeat tale unfolds the dry humor and cynical charm of the story begins to surface to create a unique, compelling change-of-pace romance. ★★★ VHS: $39.99

Madame Bovary

(1934, 117 min, France, Jean Renoir) *Valentine Tessier, Pierre Renoir.* While not considered one of Renoir's best works, this faithful retelling of Gustave Flaubert's novel is still of interest for fans of both artists. In 1840, a young woman, eager to escape her dreary provincial life, marries a dull country doctor. As her situation becomes more desperate, however, she begins a series of affairs with other men; actions that cause her to become a tragic victim of her own romantic illusions. Tessier in the title role is overly dramatic and too old for the part. (French with English subtitles) ★★½ VHS: $59.99

Madame Bovary

(1949, 115 min, US, Vincente Minnelli) *Jennifer Jones, James Mason, Van Heflin, Louis Jourdan, Gladys Cooper.* Lavish screen version of Flaubert's novel about a 19th-century French woman whose lust for social and financial power brings on her own doom. Jones makes an alluring Bovary. ★★★ VHS: $19.99

Madame Bovary

(1991, 130 min, France, Claude Chabrol) *Isabelle Huppert, Jean-François Balmer, Jean Yanne.* A lushly photographed yet starkly realized adaptation of Gustave Flaubert's classic. Huppert delivers a restrained performance as Emma Bovary, a 19th-century woman whose lust for self-fulfillment sets her against a hypocritically pietistic society amd ultimately leads her to adultery. Her character is filled with contradictions, sometimes cold, calculating and intensely materialistic; other times convivial, passionate and vulnerable. Filmed in the countryside surrounding Rouen, the film convincingly captures the mood of Flaubert's France. (French with English subtitles) ★★½

Madame Butterfly

(1996, 129 min, France, Frédéric Mitterrand) *Ying Huang, Richard Troxell, Ning Liang, Richard Cowan.* A sumptuous, wrenching filmization of Puccini's heartbreaking opera. Troxell is quite good as that slime, Lt. Pinkerton, a horny jerk who buys a gorgeous fifteen-year-old geisha's hand in marriage, only to abandon her. Mitterand's camera direction is a bit uninspired in the early scenes, allowing only the beautiful exteriors and editing to tell us this ain't no stage version; but the film is more assured and stylish as it progresses, becoming a rich, cinematic jewel of a film. Huang is wonderful in the title role. She has a stunning voice, and gives a full-blown, dramatic portrayal. If you find yourself scrambling for a tissue by film's end, she's to blame. (Italian with English subtitles) ★★★½ VHS: $21.99

Madame Rosa

(1977, 105 min, France, Moshe Mizrahi) *Simone Signoret, Samy Ben Youb, Claude Dauphin, Constantin Costa-Gavras, Michal Bat-Adam.* The touching story of a loving relationship between an aging Holocaust victim and former prostitute (Signoret) and a young Arab boy she tends. Academy Award–winning Best Foreign Film. (French with English subtitles) ★★★½ VHS: $24.99

Madame Satan

(1930, 116 min, US, Cecil B. DeMille) *Kay Johnson, Reginald Denny, Roland Young, Lillian Roth.* Not entirely successful in some of its parts, *Madame Satan* is a fascinating excursion into '30s cinema. Rather than displaying director DeMille's characteristically heavy touches, the film is reminiscent of Ernst Lubitsch, Noël Coward, Busby Berkeley and Alfred Hitchcock! Johnson plays a wife who learns of her husband's (Denny) unfaithfulness. She soon is masquerading as the mysterious Madame Satan to get him back. After viewing a spectacular musical production number taking place en route and aboard a high-flying zeppelin, one would think they've seen it all. But DeMille has another wild card up his sleeve for an unbelievable finale. A pre-Code production, the film's themes of sexuality and adultery would have assured it could not have been made as is after 1934. ★★★½ VHS: $19.99

Madame Sin

(1971, 90 min, US, David Greene) *Bette Davis, Robert Wagner, Denholm Elliott.* Davis has the title role in this made-for-TV espionage flick à la James Bond. Wagner plays a former CIA agent deluded into assisting the evil Madame Sin in the theft of a Polaris submarine. Production design and sets nearly rival those of the Bond films and, for a change, good doesn't triumph over evil. ★★½ VHS: $9.99

Madame Sousatzka

(1988, 122 min, GB, John Schlesinger) *Shirley MacLaine, Peggy Ashcroft, Navin Chowdhry, Twiggy.* MacLaine gives a spirited performance as an eccentric and demanding piano teacher who dedicates herself to her new student — a gifted 15-year-old Indian boy. A lovely, lyrical film directed by Schlesinger with great sensitivity. ★★★ VHS: $9.99

Madame X

(1966, 100 min, US, David Lowell Rich) *Lana Turner, John Forsythe, Keir Dullea, Ricardo Montalban, Burgess Meredith.* Sixth screen version of the weepy chestnut, this time around with Turner as the woman with a past who sac-

Mad Max Beyond Thunderdome

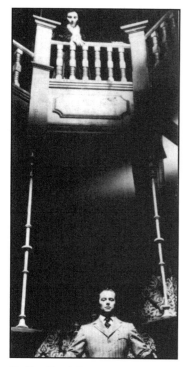

The Magnificent Ambersons

rifices all for the sake of her son. Dullea plays her offspring, a lawyer who unknowingly defends his mother. ★★ VHS: $14.99

Mädchen in Uniform

(1931, 89 min, Germany, Leontine Sagan) *Hertha Thiele, Dorothea Wieck.* This landmark film dealing with a lesbian relationship between a sensitive student and her teacher still retains both its timeliness and power in dealing with this controversial subject. Written by Christa Winsloe, this legendary film is a sympathetically handled account of one girl's rebellion against suffocating discipline and sexual repression in a Prussian boarding school. (German with English subtitles) ★★★½ VHS: $24.99

Made for Each Other

(1939, 85 min, US, John Cromwell) *James Stewart, Carole Lombard, Charles Coburn, Lucille Watson, Louise Beavers.* Sentimental, heartwarming melodrama with Stewart and Lombard as newlyweds battling illness, poverty and a meddling mother-in-law (Watson). ★★½ VHS: $14.99

Made in America

(1993, 110 min, US, Richard Benjamin) *Whoopi Goldberg, Ted Danson, Nia Long, Will Smith, Paul Rodriguez, Jennifer Tilly.* Thanks to a couple of winning performances from Danson and Goldberg, what might easily have been just another insipid comedy from the Hollywood mill is instead a fun-loving, briskly paced romp. When Goldberg's daughter, Zora (Long), discovers that she is the result of artificial insemination, she investigates only to discover that not only is her father white, but worse, he's Hal

Jackson, the obnoxious, egotistical car dealer whose insane TV advertisements plague the local airwaves. She quickly goes to confront him with the fact and the hilarity begins. Of course, Danson and Goldberg slowly warm to each other and, well, you can guess the rest — life really did imitate art (for awhile, anyway). Smith savors his role as Zora's gawky but pure-hearted best friend. ★★★ VHS: $9.99; DVD: $14.99

Made in Heaven

(1987, 103 min, US, Alan Rudolph) *Timothy Hutton, Kelly McGillis, Maureen Stapleton, Mare Winningham, Amanda Plummer.* Sweetly romantic fantasy about a young man (Hutton) who dies, goes to Heaven, and falls in love with a new spirit (McGillis), who is about to be sent to Earth. Unbalanced but interesting handling of the subject of predestination from the director of *Choose Me* and *Trouble in Mind.* Watch for cameos by Debra Winger and Ellen Barkin. ★★½ VHS: $14.99

Madeline

(1998, 90 min, US, Daisy von Scherler Mayer) *Frances McDormand, Nigel Hawthorne, Hatty Jones, Ben Daniels..* Aided in large part with warm performances from McDormand as Miss Clavell and Jones as Madeline, this live-action version of the beloved children's classic is only moderately entertaining. It takes three different plots to concoct a coherent tale, creating nice but unconnected pleasant moments. ★★½ VHS: $9.99; DVD: $29.99

Madhouse

(1990, 90 min, US, Tom Ropelewski) *Kirstie Alley, John Larroquette, Alison La Placa.* A paltry black comedy about a married couple whose lives are turned upside-down by visiting relatives, neighbors, etc. There are about 15 minutes in the middle of this film which are funny, but the rest of the film is as uninviting as Alley and Larroquette's pain-in-the-ass houseguests. ★½ VHS: $9.99

The Madness of King George

(1994, 105 min, GB, Nicholas Hytner) *Nigel Hawthorne, Helen Mirren, Ian Holm, Rupert Everett, Amanda Donohoe, Rupert Graves, John Wood.* In one of the most entertaining and literate history lessons one will ever encounter, author Alan Bennett's adaptation of his stage hit "The Madness of George III" is a sumptuously filmed and costumed historical epic which royally details the madness of a king, backstage power struggles, and the frivolity of ceremony. Hawthorne excels as George III, the British monarch who has just lost the American colonies and who is about to lose his mind. As the king succumbs to increasingly bizarre behavior under the watchful eye of his doctor (Holm), a bemused court looks on, ambitious princes plot, and the faithful Queen Charlotte (the wonderful Mirren) performs 18th-century damage control. Hytner has a sharp eye for pageant and is meticulous in forging the relationships of his characters. ★★★★ VHS: $14.99; DVD: $19.99

The Madwoman of Chaillot

(1969, 132 min, US, Bryan Forbes) *Katharine Hepburn, Charles Boyer, Yul Brynner, Richard Chamberlain, Danny Kaye, Edith Evans, Guiletta Masina, Paul Henreid, Margaret Leighton.*

Hepburn heads an all-star cast in this hokey adaptation of the Jean Giradoux play. Kate is an eccentric "countess" no longer able to cope with the world's loss of innocence. With her street people cohorts, she concocts a plan to get even with the corporate world. You really want to like it, but the film's good intentions get in its way — but oh, what a cast! The basis for the Broadway musical "Dear World." ★★ VHS: $19.99

Mafia!

(1998, 84 min, US, Jim Abrahams) *Jay Mohr, Billy Burke, Christina Applegate, Lloyd Bridges, Olympia Dukakis, Pamela Gidley.* From some of the folks who brought us *Airplane!* and the *Naked Gun* films comes *Mafia!*, a sporadically funny spoof on *The Godfather* and its sequels that also manages to get some digs in on *Casino, Showgirls* and *Goodfellas.* Bridges plays an elderly Don who finds sons Mohr and Burke in competition for his underworld throne. With that, director Abrahams moves the action all over the place — from New York to Las Vegas, and — in flashbacks — to Salmonella, Italy. All of this is briskly handled for an hour; then, with a series of gross-out sequences, one gets the idea the well ran dry for Abrahams and company. (aka: *Jane Austen's Mafia!*) ★★ VHS: $14.99; DVD: $29.99

The Magic Christian

(1970, 95 min, GB, Joseph McGrath) *Peter Sellers, Ringo Starr, Raquel Welch, Yul Brynner, Christopher Lee, Roman Polanski.* The hilarious escapades of Sellers as the world's wealthiest man, and Starr as his handpicked messiah, as they embark on a zany scheme to expose society's corruptibility. This scathing indictment of avarice and the lust for power is dated in style, but not in substance. ★★★ VHS: $9.99

The Magic Flute

(1974, 134 min, Sweden, Ingmar Bergman) This lavish production of Mozart's last opera, considered by many to be his greatest, is a delicious dreamlike fairy tale mixing German folk elements with French orchestrations and Italian humor. Featuring the Gewandhaus Orchester of Leipzig with a cast of Germany's great opera stars. ★★★★ VHS: $29.99; DVD: $29.99

Magic Town

(1947, 103 min, US, William Wellman) *James Stewart, Jane Wyman, Kent Smith.* Director Wellman invades Frank Capra's territory in this story of a pollster who finds a small, quiet town the perfect barometer for national polls. That is, until the town's notoriety changes everyone's outlook. ★★★ VHS: $19.99

Magical Mystery Tour

(1967, 60 min, GB, The Beatles) *John Lennon, Paul McCartney, George Harrison, Ringo Starr.* Sometimes called a rock *Un Chien Andalou,* the Fab Four's charmingly surreal musical chronicles their escapades on a psychedelic bus trip. Songs include "The Fool on the Hill," "I Am the Walrus" and the title tune. VHS: $19.99; DVD: $19.99

The Magician (Ansiktet)

(1959, 102 min, Sweden, Ingmar Bergman) *Max von Sydow, Ingrid Thulin, Gunnar Björnstrand.* Set in 19th-century Sweden, this richly Gothic and visually exciting "thinking man's horror film" follows the supernatural exploits of a magician (von Sydow) and his troupe who are detained in a small village when his magical powers are disbelieved. The clash between truth and illusion, reality versus the supernatural and the dramatic contrasting the comic all contribute to make *The Magician* a landmark in film history. (Swedish with English subtitles) (aka: *The Face*) ★★★½ VHS: $29.99

The Magnificent Ambersons

(1942, 88 min, US, Orson Welles) *Joseph Cotten, Tim Holt, Anne Baxter, Agnes Moorehead.* Welles' follow-up to *Citizen Kane* is a shattering adaptation of Booth Tarkington's novel about the self-destruction of a turn-of-the-century aristocratic family. Moorehead gives a mesmerizing performance as Holt's maiden aunt in this butchered masterpiece (the studio edited 20 minutes from Welles' final cut). ★★★★ VHS: $19.99

Magnificent Obsession

(1954, 108 min, US, Douglas Sirk) *Rock Hudson, Jane Wyman, Agnes Moorehead, Barbara Rush.* One of the best of the '50s soap operas, and the first Ross Hunter-Douglas Sirk collaboration. Hudson, in the role which made him a star, gives a strong portrayal of a careless playboy whose wastrel ways lead to an auto accident that blinds Wyman. Dedicating his life to a "magnificent obsession," Hudson becomes a surgeon determined to restore Wyman's sight. Remake of the 1935 Irene Dunne-Robert Taylor tearjerker. ★★★ VHS: $14.99

The Magnificent Seven

(1960, 128 min, US, John Sturges) *Yul Brynner, Steve McQueen, Eli Wallach, James Coburn, Charles Bronson, Robert Vaughn, Horst Buchholz, Brad Dexter.* A terrific and exciting American remake of Akira Kurosawa's *The Seven Samurai*. There's action aplenty as seven American gunslingers come to the aid of a small Mexican village being terrorized by bandits (led by Wallach). Crisp direction by Sturges and a memorable score by Elmer Bernstein. (Remade in 1998) ★★★½ VHS: $14.99; DVD: $19.99

Le Magnifique

(1974, 86 min, France, Philippe de Broca) *Jean-Paul Belmondo, Jacqueline Bisset.* Belmondo plays a double role as both a hapless hack novelist and his macho fictional alter ego in this action-filled spoof of the super-spy genre. Bisset is his glamourous assistant with whom he falls in love. It's not art, and it isn't even *That Man from Rio*, but it is a fun adventure comedy. ★★½

Magnolia

(1999, 189 min, US, Paul Thomas Anderson) *Jeremy Blackman, Tom Cruise, Melinda Dillon, Philip Baker Hall, Philip Seymour Hoffman, William H. Macy, Julianne Moore, John C. Reilly, Jason Robards, Melora Walters, Henry Gibson.* L.A. does strange things to people, especially fictional ones. Anderson's unbelievably ambitious *Magnolia* brings together dark pairs of people: a young TV quiz whiz (Blackman) and an over-the-hill one (Macy), a dying producer (Robards) and a dying TV game show host (Hall), along with other related Angeleans at crisis points in their lives, and then puts them in the midst of the strangest weather pattern in recorded history. The framework is reminiscent of Altman, the long, free-flowing scenes could be Cassavetes, but the well-schooled young director makes an exhilarating concoction out of his parts, the whole being not a plot but dozens of moments of redemption that have deep personal meaning in a random and coincidental city. Each actor gets two or three big scenes which encompass their characters' story arc; even with the uniformly high level, Cruise stands out (way against type) as a woman-hating self-help guru. The movie's length and obsession with detail will alienate a few; most, however, will be left with mouths agape and emotions swelled. Aimee Mann contributes the tender songs. ★★★★ VHS: $19.99; DVD: $29.99

Magnum Force

(1973, 124 min, US, Ted Post) *Clint Eastwood, Hal Holbrook, Mitchell Ryan, Felton Perry, David Soul, Robert Urich.* Eastwood returns in this second Dirty Harry film, trying to uncover a con-spiracy within the San Francisco police department involving a group of vigilante officers who execute notorious criminal suspects. Holbrook is Harry's superior, who disagrees with Harry's unorthodox methods. While nothing could match the power and intensity of Don Siegel's original *Dirty Harry*, this sequel nevertheless works as an entertaining, average action film. The film's most interesting point is its distinction between the work of the vigilantes and the violent work of Harry himself — a fine line indeed — and seems to be an attempt to explain the subtleties of the first film to its critics. (Sequel: *The Enforcer*) ★★½ VHS: $14.99

The Mahabharata

(1989, 318 min, GB, Peter Brook) Brook's epic undertaking of the Mahabharata, the Hindu story of the origins of the world, a massive tome which is over 15 times longer than the Bible. The result is nothing less than what we've come to expect from Brook: a brilliantly acted and thoughtfully directed epic with an ensemble cast from over 19 different countries and every continent. The running time of close to six hours — short considering the subject — has been broken down into three separate stories for the video release: "The Game of Dice" (97 min), "Exile in the Forest" (111 min) and "The War" (110 min). ★★★½ VHS: $99.99

Mahler

(1974, 115 min, GB, Ken Russell) *Robert Powell, Georgina Hale, Richard Morant.* Russell kept his normal excesses to a minimum in this sumptuously filmed and costumed biography of the famed Swedish composer Gustav Mahler. The film is a dazzling evocation of the loves, moods and music of the artist. Through flashbacks and beautiful dream imagery, it focuses on the tormented life and turbulent relationship he endured with his wife. Such Russellisms as a dream sequence with a Nazi Pope (a Nazi Pope?) do sneak through. On the whole, however, this is Russell in a mellow mood. ★★★ VHS: $19.99; DVD: $24.99

Mahogany

(1975, 109 min, US, Berry Gordy) *Diana Ross, Billy Dee Williams, Anthony Perkins.* An inferior, even ridiculous drama set in the fashion world with Ross making it big as a model. Williams is her boyfriend, a community activist who disapproves of her profession. Pure trash and not even fun on a camp level. ★ VHS: $14.99

Maid to Order

(1987, 92 min, US, Amy Jones) *Ally Sheedy, Beverly D'Angelo, Michael Ontkean, Tom Skerritt, Valerie Perrine.* Agreeable Cinderella comedy with Sheedy as a pampered rich girl whose father wishes she had never been born — and with the help of fairy godmother D'Angelo, it comes true. Kinda cute if you don't think about it too much. ★★ VHS: $9.99

The Main Event

(1979, 109 min, US, Howard Zieff) *Barbra Streisand, Ryan O'Neal, Paul Sand.* Tired comedy about a bankrupt perfume manufacturer who inherits the contract of a retired boxer. Not very funny, implausible with none of the chemistry between the two stars in their earlier outing, this is tough going even for die-hard Streisand fans. ★½ VHS: $9.99

Philip Seymour Hoffman is one of the outstanding ensemble of *Magnolia*

M

Maitresse

(1976, 112 min, France, Barbet Schroeder) *Gérard Depardieu, Bulle Ogier.* The kinky underground world of sadomasochism is revealed in this enjoyably shocking drama that will remind many of the sexual outlandishness of *Last Tango in Paris.* Depardieu stars as a burglar who breaks into the flat of Ogier, a professional sadist who, as a leather-clad, whip-snapping dominatrix, rules over her compliant stable of wealthy clients. A wickedly tantalizing fable about the darker side of love. An interesting item about the film is that the featured customers (all masked) were real Parisian masochists who paid to be in the film. (French with English subtitles) ★★★ VHS: $29.99

The Major and the Minor

(1942, 101 min, US, Billy Wilder) *Ray Milland, Ginger Rogers, Rita Johnson, Robert Benchley, Diana Lynn.* Terrific screwball comedy with Rogers masquerading as a 12-year-old to get half-price train fare, then being taken under the wing of military academy teacher Milland. Wilder's script is sharp and funny, his leads are in good form, and the "Veronica Lake" scene is classic. ★★★½ VHS: $14.99

Major Barbara

(1941, 131 min, GB, Gabriel Pascal) *Wendy Hiller, Rex Harrison, Robert Newton, Robert Morley, Deborah Kerr.* George Bernard Shaw collaborated with director Pascal on this superb rendition of his poignant social comedy. Hiller is excellent as the daughter of a wealthy munitions manufacturer who, disillusioned with her father's world, joins the Salvation Army. Filled with Shaw's unswerving and razor-sharp commentary. ★★★★ VHS: $29.99

Major League

(1989, 107 min, US, David S. Ward) *Tom Berenger, Charlie Sheen, Corbin Bernsen, Margaret Whitton, Wesley Snipes, Rene Russo, Dennis Haysbert.* Contrived though amiable baseball comedy with a few well-placed laughs about the new owner of the Cleveland Indians (Whitton) purposely making her team lose so she can move the team to Florida. (Followed by 2 sequels) ★★½ VHS: $9.99

Major Payne

(1995, 97 min, US, Nick Castle) *Damon Wayans, Karyn Parsons, William Hickey.* About as funny as a night in war-torn Bosnia, *Major Payne* is a pointless remake of the so-so 1955 Charlton Heston military comedy *The Private War of Major Benson.* Payne is a seemingly slow-witted career soldier who is booted out of the Army and sent to command a group of junior ROTC cadets. The story follows his mean-spirited efforts to help them win a military competition. Coauthor Wayans gives a tedious and irritating performance, and his script? At one point, Payne attempts to literally break the fingers of a five-year-old. Such wit. ★ VHS: $14.99; DVD: $24.99

A Majority of One

(1962, 149 min, US, Mervyn LeRoy) *Rosalind Russell, Alec Guinness, Mae Questel, Marc Marno.* An intimate stage piece, this schmaltzy but nevertheless beguiling comedy-drama only slightly misses its mark in the screen adaptation. Russell plays Mrs. Jacoby, a Jewish widow from Brooklyn who accompanies her daughter and diplomat son-in-law to Japan, where she is romanced by a high-ranking Japanese businessman (played by Guinness). It's distracting having Anglo thespian Guinness (as good as he may be) playing an Asian, but the film's observations on love, culture clashes and bigotry compensate. In support, Questel and Marno repeat their stage roles, with Marno very appealing as Eddie, a hipster servant. ★★½ VHS: $19.99

Make Mine Mink

(1960, 101 min, GB, Robert Asher) *Terry-Thomas, Billie Whitelaw.* Terry-Thomas stars in this often hilarious farce as a retired army officer who becomes the leader of a philanthropic band of fur thieves. ★★★½

Make Room for Tomorrow

(1981, 106 min, France, Peter Kassovitz) *Jane Birkin, Victor Lanoux.* The generation gap is explored in this comedy-drama about four generations of a family who gather to celebrate the birthday of their great grandfather. At the reunion, the eccentricities of each seem just a little more outrageous than the last. (French with English subtitles) ★★★

The Maker

(1997, 98 min, US, Tim Hunter) *Matthew Modine, Mary-Louise Parker, Jonathan Rhys-Meyers, Fairuza Balk, Michael Madsen.* An orphaned slacker, on the cusp of heading off to college, has his life irrevocably transformed when his long-lost brother (Modine) shows up on his doorstep on his 18th birthday. The younger sibling is then told the truth about his parents' deaths, while being schooled in the art of pulling "tricks" and the importance of being "the maker." While *The Maker* is never dull, it's never really excites either, and the clichéd drama of the young man's choice is far from compelling. ★★½ VHS: $99.99

Making Love

(1982, 113 min, US, Arthur Hiller) *Michael Ontkean, Kate Jackson, Harry Hamlin, Wendy Hiller, Arthur Hill.* Sort of a breakthrough for American films, this slick but superficial romantic drama features Ontkean as a successful doctor who leaves his wife (Jackson) for a handsome writer (Hamlin). One of the first Hollywood films to feature well-adjusted gay characters in nonsupporting roles, and to show two men kissing. With all its "good intentions," the story is at times soap opera-ish, but involving nonetheless. Good performances from its three lead players. ★★½

Making Mr. Right

(1987, 95 min, US, Susan Seidelman) *John Malkovich, Ann Magnuson.* The ingredients for this film sure seemed right: Malkovich and offbeat comic Magnuson starring in Seidelman's follow-up to *Desperately Seeking Susan*; what could go wrong? Well, just about everything, but the real tragedy here is the script. Magnuson plays a P.R. expert who is hired to help develop a human image for Chemtech Corporation's new android (Malkovich), but ends up clashing with the android's creator (also Malkovich) when she falls in love with the machine. ★ VHS: $14.99

Denzel Washington as *Malcolm X*

The Makioka Sisters

(1983, 110 min, Japan, Kon Ichikawa) *Keiko Kishi, Yoshiko Sakuma.* Director Ichikawa breathtakingly adapted Junichiro Tanizaki's best-selling novel about the lives and loves of four sisters in 1930s Osaka. Brilliantly photographed, the film explores the sisters' efforts to sustain and come to terms with the passing of their proud customs, which have slowly slipped away — victims to encroaching Westernization in the ever-changing days of pre-war Japan. The story follows the two married sisters' valiant attempts to find a suitable husband for the third sister while the youngest one, rebelliously promiscuous, discovers and embraces the new freedoms available. (Japanese with English subtitles) ★★★★ VHS: $59.99

Malcolm

(1986, 86 min, Australia, Nadia Tass) *Colin Friels, John Hargreaves, Chris Haywood.* This refreshingly funny Aussie import follows the madcap antics of part-time inventor Malcolm (played with elfish charm by Friels), a naive young man who, after teaming up with a bank robber and his moll, uses his technical wizardry to pull off a series of hilarious heists. ★★★

Malcolm X

(1992, 205 min, US, Spike Lee) *Denzel Washington, Angela Bassett, Albert Hall, Al Freeman, Jr., Delroy Lindo, Spike Lee, Theresa Randle, Lonette McKee, Giancarlo Esposito.* An intense and highly accomplished biography of the slain religious and community leader. Featuring a tour de force performance by Washington as Malcolm, the film traces his life from his zoot suited-youth in the 1940s; to his imprisonment, where he was first introduced to the Muslim faith; to his rise as a disciple of Elijah Muhammad, the Supreme Minister of the Nation of Islam; to his life-changing pilgrimage to Mecca; to his tragic assassination. Lee's film succinctly examines these stages of Malcolm's life, creating a fluid transition from each period to the next. As a storyteller, Lee has never been more focused, capturing Malcolm's conviction and the unrest of the era while viewing Malcolm's evolutionary process with unexpected objectivity. Lee's big, complex and powerful film befits the life and legend of such a complicated and fervent man. ★★★★ VHS: $19.99; DVD: $19.99

Male and Female

(1919, 117 min, US, Cecil B. DeMille) *Gloria Swanson, Thomas Meighan, Raymond Hatton, Lila Lee.* A wealthy, pampered young woman and her snobbish family are shipwrecked on a desert island along with "the help" — their long-suffering butler and maid. In order to survive, the socialite must turn to the butler, Crichton (Meighan), for help, while the formerly derisive young lady begins to fall for him. Based on J.M. Barrie's "The Admirable Crichton," this social and class comedy-drama is certainly dated in its attitudes. But DeMille's storytelling skills are sharp. With strong acting, lavish sets, and an outrageously over-the-top, non-sequiter sequence featuring Swanson and Meighan in Babylonian times, *Male and Female* is DeMille at his most DeMille. ★★★½ VHS: $29.99; DVD: $24.99

Malice

(1993, 107 min, US, Harold Becker) *Alec Baldwin, Nicole Kidman, Bill Pullman, Anne Bancroft, Bebe Neuwirth, George C. Scott, Peter Gallagher, Gwyneth Paltrow.* Baldwin plays a brilliant surgeon newly arrived to a small New England town. He rents a room from married couple Kidman and college professor Pullman. In a nasty series of events, Baldwin unnecessarily operates on Kidman, initiating a multimillion dollar lawsuit. But this is only half of it. And what begins as a slow-paced melodrama quickly blossoms into a cagey psychological thriller complete with figure-eight plot twists and baffling detective work. In the *Body Heat* mold, the film takes wicked delight in its crafty composition. Pullman ties the film together with his sleuthing academic. ★★★ VHS: $9.99; DVD: $19.99

Malicious

(1973, 97 min, Italy, Salvatore Samperi) *Laura Antonelli, Turi Ferro.* Antonelli stars in this spicy though abrasive sex comedy as a housekeeper hired by a widower to look after him and his three sons. But she soon becomes the object of desire for all the men in the house, including the youngest, a 14-year-old coming of age, and the father, with his own plans for courtship and marriage. (Dubbed) ★★½ VHS: $49.99

Mallrats

(1995, 96 min, US, Kevin Smith) *Jeremy London, Jason Lee, Shannon Doherty, Claire Forlani, Ben Affleck.* Director Smith's follow-up to his witty *Clerks* is a disappointing but not entirely unentertaining entry into the disaffected youth genre. The action is moved from Hell's shopping strip to Hell's suburban shopping mall, from black and white to color reminiscent of colorization. The film opens as the two central characters, Brodie and T.S. (London, Lee), are dumped by their respective girlfriends Rene and Brandi (Doherty, Forlani). Our protagonists would get on with their lives if they had any. That not being the case, they speed to their local mall, where fate, chance and an odd assortment of characters (many in exile from *Clerks*) provide our antiheroes with the means of retribution and reconciliation. The film opens flatly and often feels forced. ★★ VHS: $9.99; DVD: $29.99

Malou

(1983, 94 min, West Germany, Jeanine Meerapfel) *Ingrid Caven, Helmut Griem.* Hannah lives with her husband in West Germany. Her life and marriage are affected, however, by her obsession with her dead mother, Malou, whose frantic life included a marriage to a Jew during Hitler's reign and her efforts to save him. Told through flashbacks, the film explores the relationship between the two women's lives and how Hannah deals with her present condition. The slow pacing and obvious dramatics rarely live up to its promising premise. (German with English subtitles) ★★

The Maltese Falcon

(1941, 100 min, US, John Huston) *Humphrey Bogart, Mary Astor, Sydney Greenstreet, Peter Lorre, Elisha Cook, Jr., Gladys George.* Huston made his impressive directorial debut with this classic mystery and third screen version of Dashiell Hammett's novel. Bogart stars as Sam Spade, tough-guy private eye whose investigation into the death of his partner leads him to tangle with femme fatale Brigid O'Shaughnessy (the ravishing Astor) and underworld art collector Kasper Gutman (Greenstreet in his Oscar-nominated film debut). Huston's film is awash in shadowy black and white which only heightens the tension brought about by the mysterious goings-on in the search for the elusive black bird, a jewel-encrusted statuette which leaves a trail of corpses in its wake. One of the first films of the budding noir genre, and one of the best. ★★★★ VHS: $14.99; DVD: $19.99

Mama, There's a Man in Your Bed

(1989, 111 min, France, Coline Serreau) *Daniel Auteuil, Firmine Richard.* Released theatrically under its less wieldy French title, *Romuald et Juliette*, this engaging social comedy is the story of a very unlikely love between a CEO from the "white" side of the tracks and a poor black cleaning lady with five kids (all from different husbands). Cuckolded by his wife and ousted from his executive position in a yogurt company, our privileged young man finds comfort, sympathy and a comrade-in-arms with charming black woman. Their alliance soon blossoms into romantic love in this sweet, surprisingly entertaining farce that features several spirited performances and a fine blues soundtrack. (French with English subtitles) ★★★ VHS: $19.99

Mama Turns 100

(1978, 100 min, Spain, Carlos Saura) *Geraldine Chaplin, Fernando Gomez.* Wildly imaginative, this sly black comedy is set in a cavernous house in rural Spain where a family prepares to celebrate the 100th birthday of their elderly matriarch. But this familial celebration is not as innocent as one might expect: the wacky children are bent on making this birthday her last, but the eccentric and shrewd Mama has her own devious plans. A circuitous tale of greed, power and money. (Spanish with English subtitles) ★★★ VHS: $59.99

The Mambo Kings

(1992, 104 min, US, Arne Glimcher) *Armand Assante, Antonio Banderas, Cathy Moriarty, Roscoe Lee Browne.* Set to the pulsating rhythms of a Latin beat, *The Mambo Kings* opens like gangbusters and rarely lets go. Based on the Pulitzer Prize–winning novel "The Mambo Kings Play Songs of Love," by Oscar Hijuelos, this stirring film adaptation has the look and feel of a 1950s musical, which only enhances its style. Assante and Banderas are musician brothers from Cuba who flee their homeland and venture to the uncertainty of New York City's nightclubs and ballrooms. Most of the film centers on the brothers' attempts to get ahead, which culminates into a lucky break: an appearance on "I Love Lucy." If the film falters at all, it's during the last half hour, which echoes tragic melodramatic moments from musicals past. There's an outstanding film score, featuring some terrific mambo numbers, and a haunting ballad, "Beautiful Maria of My Soul." ★★★½ VHS: $14.99

Mame

(1974, 131 min, US, Gene Saks) *Lucille Ball, Robert Preston, Bea Arthur, Jane Connell, Bruce Davison.* The Broadway musical "Mame" is one of the most endearing of all stage shows — which benefitted greatly from Angela Lansbury's immortal performance. Unfortunately, there's little magic to this flat screen version, with Ball miscast as Auntie Mame. Preston makes a good Beau, and Arthur and Connell repeat their roles as, respectively, Vera and Agnes Gooch. Another instance in which Hollywood outsmarted itself by replacing the star of a stage hit. ★½ VHS: $14.99

Mamma Roma

(1966, 110 min, Italy, Pier Paolo Pasolini) *Anna Magnani, Ettore Garofolo, Franco Citti, Silvana Corsini.* Magnani is a heartrending revelation in this intensely moving neorealist urban drama. Magnani plays a poor but tenacious individualist who, despite her sad eyes and an arduous life, never loses her vitality, her hearty laugh nor the passionate love she has for her son. A former prostitute, she longs for a middle-class existence for her long estranged teenaged son, but when a former pimp threatens to expose her past, she is forced back on the streets. A disquieting tale set amidst the

The Maltese Falcon

gloom of a crime- and poverty-plagued modern high-rised Rome. A tough, uncompromising though well-crafted film. (Italian with English subtitles) ★★★½ VHS: $29.99

A Man, a Woman and a Killer

(1975, 95 min, US, Rick Schmidt & Wayne Wang) *Ed Nylund, Dick Richardson, Carolyn Zaremba.* This collaboration with northern California filmmaker Schmidt and Wang is a beguiling, Godard-influenced meditation of a film about the making of the film. Essentially a two-character story, the film explores the relationship, both within the story as well as the rehearsals, between a paranoid man, his girlfriend and his imagined assassin. The pacing is slow and the "cut and paste" narrative style will agitate some, but overall the film is an interesting primer for Wang's future films. ★★ VHS: $59.99

A Man and a Woman

(1966, 102 min, France, Claude Lelouch) *Anouk Aimée, Jean-Louis Trintignant.* This Oscar-winning film is a joy to watch and a must for all people in love. Aimée and Trintignant are wonderful as a widow and widower who meet at a boarding school for their children. A simple and heartwarming contemporary love story. (Dubbed) ★★★½ VHS: $19.99

A Man and a Woman: 20 Years Later

(1986, 120 min, France, Claude Lelouch) *Anouk Aimée, Jean-Louis Trintignant.* Aimée and Trintignant reprise their wonderful characters from Lelouch's classic love story, *A Man and a Woman.* But the 20 years have both dimmed their attractiveness as well as the ability and even sanity of the director. The two ex-lovers are reunited in an attempt to make a film about their long-gone love affair. Throw in an escaped mental patient, a murder and a desert scene and you end up with a true mess. (French with English subtitles) ★½ VHS: $14.99

Man Bites Dog

(1992, 96 min, Belgium, Rémy Belvaux, André Bonzel & Benôt Poelvoorde) *Benôt Poelvoorde, Rémy Belvaux, Jenny Drye.* Morbidly funny is probably the best way to describe this amoral mockumentary about a poetry-reciting serial killer with a heart of gold whose sadistic exploits are recorded by a film crew. While finding themselves both repulsed and fascinated, the filmmakers in this "cinema veritasteless" spoof are drawn into the likable maniac's perverse pastime. Some viewers may be put off by the film's excruciatingly slow pace, but it seems a necessary device for the filmmakers to capture the rhythm of this maniac's life. A brutal, vulgar, repellent open sore of a film that pushes its NC-17 rating to the furthest. (French with English subtitles) ★★★ VHS: $19.99

A Man Called Horse

(1970, 114 min, US, Elliot Silverstein) *Richard Harris, Judith Anderson, Jean Gascon, Manu Tupou, Dub Taylor.* Harris goes Native in this gripping western adventure as an English aristocrat who is captured by the Sioux Indians and undergoes a series of physical tests. (Sequel: *Return of a Man Called Horse*) ★★★ VHS: $9.99

A Man Called Peter

(1955, 119 min, US, Henry Koster) *Richard Todd, Jean Peters, Marjorie Rambeau.* A remarkable performance by Todd highlights this sensitive biography of Peter Marshall, a Scottish minister who became chaplain to the U.S. Senate. ★★★ VHS: $19.99

A Man Escaped

(1956, 102 min, France, Robert Bresson) *François Leterrier, Charles Le Clainche, Maurice Beerblock.* A riveting drama set almost entirely within a prison cell, *A Man Escaped* stars Leterrier as a Resistance fighter who is captured and imprisoned by the Nazis and is sentenced to be executed. As he charts his plans for escape, a young boy is placed in his cell, and the man must decide whether to trust the youth or kill him as a possible spy. Rather than resorting to artificial film devices to create tension (music, editing), the film successfully relies entirely on the central character and his studied actions. Based on a true story. (French with English subtitles) ★★★½ VHS: $19.99

Man Facing Southeast

(1987, 108 min, Argentina, Elisio Subiela) *Lorenzo Quinteros, Hugo Soto.* A fascinating sci-fi drama exploring the role of psychiatry in the modern world and the struggle of the individual vs. society. At a Buenos Aires mental institution, a man mysteriously appears, claiming he is from another planet. Though not officially a patient, he is regarded as just another delirious paranoid by his psychiatrist and the staff. It is only after a series of intellectual verbal sparrings between patient and doctor, and an otherworldly spiritual calm he casts on the other inmates, that the doctor begins to suspect that his story could very well be true. A compassionate, grown-up fairy tale. (Spanish with English subtitles) ★★★

A Man for All Seasons

(1966, 120 min, GB, Fred Zinnemann) *Paul Scofield, Robert Shaw, Wendy Hiller, Orson Welles, Susannah York, John Hurt.* This splendid film version of Robert Bolt's play about the conflict between Sir Thomas More and King Henry VIII is one of the outstanding films of its decade. Scofield gives a mesmerizing, Oscar-winning performance as More, and is brilliantly supported by Shaw as Henry, Welles as Cardinal Wolsey and Hiller as More's devoted wife. The film was awarded six Oscars and is a must for all those interested in rich, historical dramas. (Remade in 1988) ★★★★ VHS: $19.99; DVD: $29.99

The Man from Nowhere

(L'Homme de Nulle Part)

(1937, 98 min, France, Pierre Chenal) *Pierre Blanchar, Ginette LeClerc.* This unjustly forgotten black comedy deftly combines elements of Pagnol's rural tales like "The Fanny Trilogy" with Carné's satirical bent in *Bizarre, Bizarre.* When a quiet young man, married to an unforgiving wife and henpecked by his shrewish mother, is mistaken for being dead, he decides to remain in that state and start life anew in Rome. Unfortunately with his new identity come new problems. Adapted from Luigi Pirandello's only novel and filmed entirely in Italy. (French with English subtitles) ★★★ VHS: $59.99

The Man from Snowy River

(1982, 115 min, Australia, George Miller) *Kirk Douglas, Tom Burlinson, Sigrid Thornton, Jack Thompson.* Based on a beloved Australian poem, Miller's splendid adventure film spins the tale of a young mountain horseman who faces the challenge of snaring a valuable runaway colt. An inspirational paean to the majesty of the Australian landscape and the ruggedness of its inhabitants. (Sequel: *Return to Snowy River*) ★★★ VHS: $14.99

A Man in Love

(1987, 108 min, France, Diane Kurys) *Peter Coyote, Greta Scacchi, Jamie Lee Curtis.* Kurys' long anticipated follow-up to her critically acclaimed *Entre Nous* is a mildly disappointing but interesting love story set within the filming of a movie in Italy. This film-within-a-film stars Coyote as a married American actor who falls in love with Scacchi, his on-screen lover. Kurys creates a romantic and sensual world where the fantasies of film overtake reality. (Filmed in English) ★★½ VHS: $6.99

The Man in the Gray Flannel Suit

(1956, 153 min, US, Nunnally Johnson) *Gregory Peck, Jennifer Jones, Fredric March, Lee J. Cobb, Marisa Pavan.* Extremely competent film version of Sloan Wilson's novel examining Madison Avenue mores, as seen through the eyes of go-getter Peck. ★★★ VHS: $39.99

The Man in the Iron Mask

(1939, 119 min, US, James Whale) *Louis Hayward, Joseph Schildkraut, Joan Bennett.* Alexander Dumas' swashbuckling tale of sibling rivalry between France's King Louis XIV and his twin brother, raised by the Three Musketeers, makes for high-spirited adventure. Whale directs with a sure hand, making the production both exciting and smart. ★★★

The Man in the Iron Mask

(1998, 132 min, US, Randall Wallace) *Leonardo DiCaprio, Jeremy Irons, John Malkovich, Gérard Depardieu, Gabriel Byrne.* This overlong swashbuckler has very little swash to it, no thanks to Wallace's sluggish, unimaginative directorial debut. The setting is 1660, and all but one of the infamous Musketeers are retired. The one remaining Musketeer serves the cruel and arrogant young snit of a king, Louis XIV (DiCaprio), who's intent on letting his people starve to death. DiCaprio also plays Louis' secret twin, Philippe, who's been imprisoned in the Bastille and hidden in an iron mask to conceal his identity. To save their nation, the Musketeers (Irons, Malkovich, Depardieu, Byrne) reunite for a daring plot to kidnap the king and replace him with his mysterious twin. DiCaprio plays Louis XIV as a spoiled California brat instead of injecting the character with any semblance of regal pomposity. ★★½ VHS: $9.99; DVD: $14.99

The Man in the Moon

(1991, 99 min, US, Robert Mulligan) *Sam Waterston, Tess Harper, Reese Witherspoon, Emily Warfield, Jason London.* With the same locale, tone and youthful themes explored in his classic *To Kill a Mockingbird*, Mulligan's thoroughly satisfying coming-of-age tale centers on two sisters growing up in the 1950s. As the two siblings

Jim Carrey as Andy Kaufman in *Man on the Moon*

who fall in love with the same boy-next-door, Witherspoon and Warfield give glowing portrayals of teenage uncertainty and familial anxiety. Waterston gives a passionately intense performance as their father. A gentle, sweet-natured family drama. ★★★ VHS: $14.99; DVD: $14.99

The Man in the Silk Hat

(1983, 96 min, France, Maud Linder) Max Linder, France's most popular comedian of the silent era, is lovingly remembered in this funny and insightful documentary made by his 50-year-old daughter, Maud. Through numerous excerpts from his two-reelers and features, we rediscover Linder's comic genius and enjoy his infectious humor. From his slapstick antics and pratfalls to his work behind the camera, we learn of a man of whom Charles Chaplin once said, "He was my professor." (Narrated in English) ★★★ VHS: $24.99

The Man in the White Suit

(1952, 84 min, GB, Alexander MacKendrick) *Alec Guinness, Joan Greenwood.* Another one of Guinness' peerless '50s comedies. Here he stars as an unassuming lab assistant who invents a miracle fabric that can be woven into indestructible cloth. The potential catastrophe that this poses for clothing manufacturers pits Guinness against the industry in a Chaplinesque battle which serves as a witty and incisive chastisement against the greed of capitalism. ★★★★ VHS: $9.99

The Man Inside

(1990, 93 min, US, Bobby Roth) *Jürgen Prochnow, Peter Coyote, Nathalie Baye, Philip Anglim.* Intriguing political thriller with Prochnow as a German reporter who goes undercover at a right-wing tabloid to expose its unethical operating practices. Coyote costars as an embittered veteran at the rag who takes Prochnow under his wing. ★★★ VHS: $19.99

Man Is Not a Bird

(1965, 80 min, Yugoslavia, Dusan Makavejev) *Eva Ras, Milena Dravic.* The *enfant terrible* of

Eastern European cinema, this, Makavejev's first feature, is a delirious satire on the state of Communism as well as a humorous depiction of guiltless eroticism (a theme which runs throughout all his works). An engineer gets a job in a bleak industrial town and there, meets and falls in love with his landlord's daughter. The young woman, a carefree and impetuous individual, proves to be the undoing of the man. An amusing highpoint in all of the wild proceedings is the crosscutting of Beethoven's "Ode to Joy" being performed in a factory with our heroes frantically making love. (Serbian with English subtitles) ★★★½ VHS: $24.99

A Man Like Eva

(1983, 89 min, Germany, Radu Gabrea) *Eva Mattes, Elizabeth Kreuzer.* Mattes turns in a startling opposite-gender performance as a thinly disguised R.W. Fassbinder–like film director who loves, dominates and even terrorizes his cast and crew. This absorbing drama charts the inevitable self-destruction of an artist who longed for love but could not receive it. (German with English subtitles) ★★½ VHS: $39.99

Man of a Thousand Faces

(1957, 122 min, US, Joseph Pevney) *James Cagney, Dorothy Malone, Jane Greer.* Cagney scores another triumph in a biographical role, this time as silent screen star Lon Chaney. The film divides its time between Chaney's personal life and his career: effectively re-creating some of Chaney's best-known roles; and, somewhat melodramatically, detailing his two marriages. Malone plays his first, troubled wife; and Greer is his beloved second wife. Like Cagney's *Yankee Doodle Dandy*, this film is an affectionate tribute to its subject. ★★★ VHS: $14.99; DVD: $24.99

Man of Aran

(1934, 77 min, US, Robert J. Flaherty) Flaherty's lifelong cinematic interest in documenting the resilient efforts of man in his battle against a hostile enviornment continues in this brilliant chronicle set in the barren wind- and surf-swept islands of Aran — situated off the western coast of Ireland. Two years in the making, the film dramatically captures the constant struggle of the independently minded people who must conquer the rough forces of nature to insure their simple survival. ★★★★

Man of Flowers

(1984, 110 min, Australia, Paul Cox) *Norman Kaye, Alyson Best, Chris Haywood, Werner Herzog.* An unusual Australian black comedy. Kaye stars as a sexually repressed lover of art and flowers who, each Wednesday, pays a beautiful artist's model to perform an impassioned striptease to the strains of classical music. His lonely life, caused by childhood sexual traumas, is enlivened and upset as he reluctantly becomes involved with her tumultuous personal life. Weirdly funny, with a hypnotic, ever-present classical score. ★★★

Man of La Mancha

(1972, 130 min, US, Arthur Hiller) *Peter O'Toole, Sophia Loren, James Coco, Harry Andrews, John Castle, Brian Blessed.* Another in a long line of dreadful screen adaptations of classic Broadway musicals. In the same league as *Mame*, *A Chorus Line* and *A Little Night Music*, this is probably the worst offender, as a brilliant theatre piece has

been reduced to a deadened bore. O'Toole, who was so good in the musical *Goodbye, Mr. Chips*, is embarrassing as Don Quixote; though not half as bad as Loren as Dulcinea. Only Coco as Sancho captures the spirit of the stage production. Where, oh where, was Richard Kiley? ★ VHS: $14.99

Man of Marble

(1977, 160 min, Poland, Andrzej Wajda) *Krystyna Janda, Jerzy Radziwilowicz.* Made just before the emergence of the Solidarity movement, Wajda's look at the fate of the worker in Communist Poland was slightly ahead of its time. Employing a documentary-like style, Wajda follows a young filmmaker as she unearths the history of Radziwiloowicz, a bricklayer who, in the Stalinist 1950s, was exalted to the lionized stature of worker-hero only to be later crushed as an enemy of the state. A fascinating look into the machinations of the Polish bureaucracy, the film suffers a bit from its weighty running time. (Polish with English subtitles) ★★★½ VHS: $29.99

A Man of No Importance

(1994, 98 min, GB, Suri Krishnamma) *Albert Finney, Rufus Sewell, Brenda Fricker, Tara Fitzgerald, Michael Gambon.* Finney shines in this slender but engrossing drama as Alfie Byrne, a seemingly happy-go-lucky bus conductor who undergoes a late midlife crisis and reawakening. Set in Dublin in the early 1960s, the story follows bachelor and deeply closeted gay man Alfie, who quietly lives with his sister (Fricker), keeps his passengers amused with poetry readings, and harbors a crush for Bobby (Sewell), a handsome coworker. Alfie's life takes a turn when he organizes a community theatre presentation of Oscar Wilde's "Salome," which ultimately inspires him to confront his true sexual desires. A character study of limited insight, this manages to succeed in spite of its dramatic shortcomings by the sheer force of Finney's acting prowess. ★★½ VHS: $19.99

Man of the House

(1995, 98 min, US, James Orr) *Chevy Chase, Jonathan Taylor Thomas, Farrah Fawcett, George Wendt.* Attempting a film comeback, Chase abandons his smart-aleck screen persona and instead goes the Disney route appearing as yet another adult upstaged and outsmarted by a precocious adolescent. Thomas plays 12-year-old son to Fawcett's divorced mom. Their years of togetherness is intruded upon when U.S. Attorney Chase moves in with hopes of marrying Fawcett. But Thomas has other plans. The film isn't helped by Thomas' whining or flat direction by Orr. ★★ VHS: $14.99

The Man on the Eiffel Tower

(1949, 85 min, US, Burgess Meredith) *Charles Laughton, Franchot Tone, Burgess Meredith.* A highly suspenseful psychological thriller about a police inspector (Laughton) playing mental cat-and-mouse games with a suspected murderer (Tone). Filmed in Paris. ★★★½ VHS: $19.99

Man on the Moon

(1999, 119 min, US, Milos Forman) *Jim Carrey, Danny DeVito, Courtney Love, Paul Giamatti.* In a performance that should have earned him an Academy Award nomination (evidently some in Hollywood will never forgive him for his talking

M

ass bit), Carrey excels as eccentric comedian Andy Kaufman in this hit-or-miss biography. More of a collection of episodes from Kaufman's life (mostly his comedy pieces) rather than a look inside the mind of a man who may have been a comedy genius, *Man on the Moon* traces Andy's life in brief skits from childhood to his rise as a comedy club and TV performer to his untimely death. With a brilliant opening that would have no doubt pleased the late comedian, the film works best when Carrey is bringing to life Andy's own, unique brand of performance comedy. Less successful are the personal moments; the filmmakers bring little depth into the psyche of the comedian. No matter, it is Carrey's show, and he doesn't disappoint on any level. *Man on the Moon* may not bring a greater appreciation of Andy Kaufman, but it certainly will make one look at Jim Carrey in an altogether new light. ★★½ VHS: $14.99; DVD: $24.99

The Man on the Roof

(1976, 110 min, Sweden, Bo Widerberg) *Carl Gustav Lindstedt, Sven Wollter, Thomas Hellberg.* The Sidney Lumet–style cop thriller gets a sedate art-house treatment in director Widerberg's mannered film. When a corrupt inspector is stabbed to death in his hospital bed, it's up to Martin Beck (Lindstedt) and an ensemble of police to find the killer and the motives. The questions of why cops go bad has apparently never been raised in this city, so there is a lot of philosophizing in between the action scenes. Widerberg is more interested in the day-to-day procedures of the police than their heroism; it's surprising to see screen time devoted to paperwork, car travel, and routine questioning. It's not boring, but it's not particularly compelling storytelling, either. Still, *The Man on the Roof* has style to spare, making the situations seem immediate without ever feeling fake. (Swedish with English subtitles) ★★½ VHS: $79.99

Man Trouble

(1992, 90 min, US, Bob Rafelson) *Jack Nicholson, Ellen Barkin, Beverly D'Angelo, Harry Dean Stanton, Veronica Cartwright.* Check your expectations at the door for this romantic comedy that heralds the reunion of superstar Nicholson and director Rafelson. Nicholson stars as a dog trainer who becomes involved with a prima donna (Barkin) caught up in underworld affairs. Though critically lambasted upon its theatrical release, the film is not so much bad as it is disappointing; it simply cannot sustain the burden of being a "minor" movie with major talent. ★★ VHS: $9.99

Man Wanted

(1995, 92 min, Hong Kong, Benny Chan) *Simon Yam, Yu Rong Guang, Christy Chung.* A by-the-numbers "undercover cop with conflicted loyalties" movie that benefits from the presence of charismatic HK actor Yam but suffers from an overreliance on music video–style sequences and Cantopop tunes to sustain its mood. Yam is a cop who has spent two years infiltrating the gang of local crime boss Yu. When the time comes to make the bust, he is betrayed by an overambitious police lieutenant. It's all a soap opera, with neon-lit, rain-slicked streets providing most of the atmosphere. (Cantonese with English subtitles) ★★½ VHS: $59.99; DVD: $19.99

The Man Who Came to Dinner

(1941, 112 min, US, William Keighley) *Monty Woolley, Billie Burke, Bette Davis, Ann Sheridan, Jimmy Durante, Mary Wickes.* Woolley re-creates his acclaimed stage role in this gloriously funny adaptation of the Kaufman and Hart stage hit. Woolley is at his acerbic best as a famed critic who visits the small-town home of Burke and family and is forced to stay after an accident makes him immobile. The epitome of the unwanted house guest, he proceeds to run everyone's life and sends the household into hysteria. Davis took a supporting role as Woolley's secretary, but this is Woolley's show all the way, and it is one of the funniest performances of the 1940s. ★★★½ VHS: $19.99

The Man Who Captured Eichmann

(1996, 96 min, US, William A. Graham) *Robert Duvall, Arliss Howard, Jeffrey Tambor, Joel Brooks.* The true story of the Israeli *Mossad* agent who led the operation to capture infamous Nazi war criminal Adolf Eichmann makes for a thrilling and thought-provoking made-for-cable movie. After a concentration camp survivor reports meeting someone who may be Eichmann at a cafe, a commando squad is sent to Buenos Aires to kidnap him and bring him back to Israel to stand trial. Equally divided between action and dialogue, the first half of the film concerns the mechanics of grabbing the Nazi while the second half examines the team's wait for an opportunity to leave the country. A fascinating look at the banality of evil. Duvall is terrific as Eichmann. ★★★½ VHS: $19.99

The Man Who Could Work Miracles

(1937, 86 min, US, Lothar Mendes) *Roland Young, Ralph Richardson, Joan Gardner.* Enchanting adaptation of H. G. Wells' story about an "ordinary little fellow" endowed with the power to work miracles. Young (best known as *Topper*) is engaging as the mild-mannered miracle man. ★★★ VHS: $14.99

The Man Who Fell to Earth

(1976, 140 min, GB, Nicolas Roeg) *David Bowie, Candy Clark, Buck Henry, Rip Torn.* Bowie stars as the frail and mysterious visitor from another planet who unknowingly threatens American industry with his powers. A tremendously original sci-fi drama presented with the surreal and mind-boggling sensitivities of director Roeg. (Letterboxed) ★★★ VHS: $14.99; DVD: $24.99

The Man Who Knew Too Little

(1997, 94 min, US/GB, Jon Amiel) *Bill Murray, Peter Gallagher, Joanne Whalley, Alfred Molina, Richard Wilson.* With its playful titular nod to Hitchcock and a very engaging premise, this spy spoof isn't as much fun as it could have been. Many of the jokes are stifled; to such an extent that the film gives the impression that only first takes were used for the finished product. Murray plays an American visiting his hot-shot businessman brother (Gallagher) in London who is mistaken for a spy, though he thinks it's all part of an interactive play. As the video clerk from Des Moines, Murray is not at his best; but fault must lie with director Amiel, who gives the film a sluggish pace and is unable to excite or inspire his cast. ★★ VHS: $9.99; DVD: $19.99

The Man Who Knew Too Much

(1934, 75 min, GB, Alfred Hitchcock) *Leslie Banks, Peter Lorre, Edna Best.* Based on a Bulldog Drummond story, this fast-paced thriller stars a villainous Lorre (in his first English-speaking role) as a kidnapper who snares an innocent couple's child in order to insure their silence about a planned political assassination. Film historians have long argued the comparative merits of this version versus its 1956 remake; see for yourself the different approaches Hitchcock took at varied points in his career. ★★★ VHS: $12.99

The Man Who Knew Too Much

(1956, 120 min, US, Alfred Hitchcock) *James Stewart, Doris Day, Brenda de Banzie, Bernard Miles, Carolyn Jones.* While vacationing in French Morocco, doctor Stewart and wife Day become embroiled in a case of international intrigue, and with the kidnapping of their youngest son, are thrust into the very heart of a dangerously murderous scheme. An invigorating and suspenseful remake of Hitchcock's own 1934 thriller. Stewart and Day offer typically endearing performances which add to the flavor of this slick bag of tricks. Doris sings "Que Sera, Sera." ★★★½ VHS: $14.99; DVD: $29.99

The Man Who Loved Women

(1978, 119 min, France, François Truffaut) *Charles Denner, Leslie Caron, Brigitte Fossey, Nathalie Baye.* This bittersweet comedy, the inspiration for the American remake (remember, the one with Burt Reynolds?), is most aptly served by Truffaut. Gallic enchantment as the female of the species plagues Denner, the continually tempted skirt-chaser who seeks to transcribe his romantic legacy. (French with English subtitles) ★★★ VHS: $14.99; DVD: $19.99

The Man Who Shot Liberty Valance

(1962, 122 min, US, John Ford) *James Stewart, John Wayne, Lee Marvin, Vera Miles, Edmond O'Brien, Woody Strode, Strother Martin, Andy Devine, Lee Van Cleef.* A classic study of the character of man and the nature of convenient truths. Stewart is catapulted into political prominence when he's credited with ridding a frontier town of a murderous villain. Stewart and Wayne represent different codes of honor; Marvin is the common evil, to be dealt with as conscience dictates; and Miles is the woman sought as helpmate and prize. There's a strong supporting cast, and excellent direction by Ford. ★★★★ VHS: $9.99; DVD: $29.99

The Man Who Would Be King

(1975, 127 min, US, John Huston) *Sean Connery, Michael Caine, Christopher Plummer, Saeed Jaffrey.* Rudyard Kipling's exhilarating yarn of the daring exploits of two English soldiers in colonial India. Connery and Caine star as the ambitious explorers who attempt to infiltrate an ancient land and establish themselves as deities. Exotic locales, hair-raising adventures and deft direction make this one of Huston's finest. (VHS available letterboxed or pan & scan) ★★★½ VHS: $14.99; DVD: $19.99

Man with a Cross

(1943, 88 min, Italy, Roberto Rossellini) Made under Fascist control and later rejected by Rossellini, this drama deals with the Italian expeditionary forces on the Russian Front during the summer of 1942. The story focuses on a saintly chaplain who tends to both the spiritual and physical needs of the Italian soldiers, as well as to the peasants during a Russian artillery bombing. (Italian with English subtitles) ★★½ VHS: $59.99

Man with a Movie Camera

(1928, 90 min, USSR, Dziga Vertov) A seminal and still controversial film which attempts to create a cinematic reality by "simply" depicting a day in the life of Moscow. But director Vertov, fascinated by the possibilities of the medium, utilizes editing, fast/slow motion, split screen and superimposition to distort the very reality he seeks to represent. An exciting, surreal compendium which explores the relation between cinema, actuality and history. ★★★½ VHS: $29.99; DVD: $24.99

The Man with Bogart's Face

(1980, 111 min, US, Robert Day) *Robert Sacchi, Franco Nero, Michelle Phillips, Olivia Hussey, Sybil Danning.* Bogie look-alike Sacchi stars as a fledgling private eye whose business increases dramatically due to his unique chiseled features. Soon, he finds himself deluged with requests to locate a pair of priceless blue sapphires in a *Maltese Falcon*-esque caper. A pleasant if inconsequential mystery comedy which playfully acknowledges its noir roots. ★★½ VHS: $9.99; DVD: $24.99

The Man with One Red Shoe

(1985, 100 min, US, Stan Dragoti) *Tom Hanks, Lori Singer, Jim Belushi, Carrie Fisher.* One of the least successful of the many American adaptations of French comedies — in this instance, *The Tall Blond Man with One Black Shoe.* Hanks plays a violinist mistaken for a secret agent. ★½ VHS: $9.99

The Man with the Golden Arm

(1955, 119 min, US, Otto Preminger) *Frank Sinatra, Eleanor Parker, Kim Novak, Darren McGavin.* Sinatra received an Oscar nomination for his powerful performance as a drug addict trying to go straight. Preminger's stirring drama pulls no punches. Parker is terrific as Sinatra's handicapped wife. ★★★ VHS: $19.99

The Man with the Golden Gun

(1974, 125 min, GB, Guy Hamilton) *Roger Moore, Christopher Lee, Hervé Villechaize, Britt Ekland.* Moore's second outing as 007 finds him a little more comfortable in the role that he soon got *too* comfortable with. A distant cousin of Bond creator Ian Fleming, Lee plays the titular character, a paid assassin named Scaramanga, abetted in no small way by his major domo Nick Nack (Villechaize). (Sequel: *The Spy Who Loved Me*) ★★½ VHS: $14.99; DVD: $34.99

The Man with Two Brains

(1983, 90 min, US, Carl Reiner) *Steve Martin, Kathleen Turner, David Warner; Voice of: Sissy Spacek.* Martin and Reiner struck comic gold a third time in this improbable but hilarious spoof with Martin as a scientist who falls in love with a brain in a jar, and begins the search for the perfect body to harbor it. Turner also stars as Martin's faithless wife, and Spacek gives voice to the brain. ★★★ VHS: $14.99; DVD: $14.99

The Man without a Face

(1993, 125 min, US, Mel Gibson) *Mel Gibson, Nick Stahl, Margaret Whitton, Gaby Hoffman, Richard Masur.* In an unusual choice to make his directorial debut, Gibson stars in this involving, surprisingly downbeat adaptation of Isabelle Holland's novel. Gibson plays a disfigured loner whose life and appearance are a mystery to his New England neighbors. When young Stahl learns of Gibson's possible past as a teacher, he lobbies him for private tutoring. Gibson agrees, and a friendship soon develops between the two. Gibson serves as a commendable mentor and friend until news of previous child molestation charges begin to surface. Gibson gives an earnest performance as the compassionate tutor, but the film, though competently produced, is sometimes as evasive as its titular character. ★★½ VHS: $9.99

Man's Favorite Sport

(1963, 121 min, US, Howard Hawks) *Rock Hudson, Paula Prentiss, Charlene Holt, John McGiver.* Hudson stars in this entertaining, amusing comedy as a renowned fishing expert who really can't stand the sport or the great outdoors. When he agrees to make an appearance at a fishing tournament, public relations director Prentiss has her hands full making Rock an outdoorsman. An amusing spoof on sports and manhood with many well-placed jabs. ★★★ VHS: $14.99

The Manchurian Candidate

(1962, 126 min, US, John Frankenheimer) *Frank Sinatra, Laurence Harvey, Janet Leigh, Angela Lansbury, Henry Silva.* Richard Condon's best-seller about a brainwashed Korean War vet out to do our country dirt is superbly brought to the screen by Frankenheimer, who would explore similar territory two years later with *Seven Days in May.* Among a first-rate cast, Lansbury is exceptional, giving a most chilling portrayal of deception and betrayal. ★★★★ VHS: $14.99; DVD: $14.99

Mandela

(1987, 135 min, US, Philip Saville) *Danny Glover, Alfre Woodard, John Matshikiza.* Gripping, first-rate made-for-cable production about the life of South African leader Nelson Mandela. Glover brilliantly portrays the jailed activist, whose lifelong battle against Apartheid served as a rallying cry around the world. Woodard is remarkable as Nelson's wife, Winnie. ★★★

Mandela and deKlerk

(1997, 114 min, US, Joseph Sargent) *Sidney Poitier, Michael Caine, Tina Lifford.* This made-for-cable drama documents Nelson Mandela's 30-year odyssey as radical protestor, political prisoner, peace negotiator and, finally, president of South Africa, in his undying dedication to end Apartheid. Caine portrays F.W. deKlerk, the moderate minister who replaced ousted conservative P.W. Botha as president and eventually freed Mandela from prison to further a free, democratic South Africa. Poitier is excellent, embodying Mandela's strength, resolve and dignity; Caine is his equal, capturing the conflicting emotions of a man determined to do the right thing. While *Mandela and deKlerk* is only middling as drama (facts don't always conform to satisfying story structure), it's completely absorbing as history. ★★★ VHS: $79.99

Mandingo

(1975, 127 min, US, Richard Fleischer) *James Mason, Ken Norton, Susan George.* A steamy love story set on a slave breeding plantation. It's just like *Gone with the Wind*, only all the characters are in heat. Trashy, awful and a definite guilty pleasure. ★ VHS: $14.99

The Mangler

(1995, 95 min, US, Tobe Hooper) *Robert Englund, Red Levine.* An atmospheric misfire (based on yet another Stephen King short story) about a sweatshop bedsheet folding machine that develops a taste for human flesh when an accidental combination of circumstances awakens the demon residing within. It's as silly as it sounds. Hooper's Grand Guignol treatment of the subject matter, along with some really grotesque death sequences, almost compensate for the skimpy screenplay and poor performances. (Unrated director's cut) ★★ VHS: $14.99

The Mango Tree

(1982, 92 min, Australia, Kevin Dobson) *Geraldine Fitzgerald, Robert Helpmann.* A story of a young man's coming-of-age as he, his family, and his friends experience the tumultuous changes of the early 1900s in a small Australian town. Sweetly done but not out of the ordinary. ★★½ VHS: $69.99

Manhattan

(1979, 93 min, US, Woody Allen) *Woody Allen, Diane Keaton, Mariel Hemingway, Michael Murphy, Meryl Streep, Wallace Shawn, Karne Ludwig.* Allen is at his most insightful with this valentine of a film which pays tribute to his favorite city, romance, Gershwin, neuroses and bungled love affairs. Arguably his best film (some would say *Annie Hall*), *Manhattan* follows the jagged course of love taken by a group of New York sophisticates. Shot in a romanticized black and white, the film is both deliriously comic and assuredly dramatic while exploring romantic indiscretions, misjudgments and betrayals. Allen plays a TV writer who is involved with high schooler Hemingway. His married best friend Murphy is involved with pseudo-intellectual magazine editor Keaton. As these romantics crisscross and grapple with the frailties of relationships, Allen succinctly addresses the nature of romance and its tenacious grip on us all. (Letterboxed) ★★★★ VHS: $14.99; DVD: $19.99

Manhattan Melodrama

(1934, 93 min, US, W.S. Van Dyke) *Clark Gable, William Powell, Myrna Loy, Leo Carrillo.* Though best known as the movie John Dillinger saw before being gunned down, this crime saga is actually quite good (it won an Oscar for Best Screenplay). Gable and Powell are childhood pals who find themselves on opposite sides of the law. And they're both in love with Loy. Yeah, it's a familiar theme, but this was one of the first films to use it. One of Gable's better '30s outings, and the first pairing of Powell and Loy. ★★★ VHS: $19.99

Manhattan Murder Mystery

(1993, 108 min, US, Woody Allen) *Woody Allen, Diane Keaton, Alan Alda, Anjelica Huston, Ron Rifkin.* In his first post-Mia production, Allen reteams with his old partner Keaton to bring

Diane Keaton (l.) and Woody Allen in *Manhattan*

about this engaging and genuinely funny who-dunit in the tradition of *The Thin Man*. Allen and Keaton play a calcified middle-aged couple who befriend the seemingly blissful older couple down the hall. But when the wife suddenly drops dead of a heart attack, Keaton suspects her husband of murder and takes it on herself to uncover the truth, setting off a hilarious and, at times, tense mystery. Alda costars as a friend who plays along with Keaton's theory while Allen thinks she's just deranged. Throughout, Allen serves up his usual repertoire of quips and one-liners and they consistently amuse. An enjoyable affair that does Nick and Nora Charles proud, albeit without the 15 martinis per scene. ★★★½ VHS: $19.99; DVD: $29.99

The Manhattan Project
(1986, 117 min, US, Marshall Brickman) *John Lithgow, Christopher Collet, Cynthia Nixon, John Mahoney*. Quirky sci-fi comedy about a teenager (Collet) who builds an atomic bomb in hopes of exposing a secret nuclear plant in his neighborhood. Lithgow plays a scientist who befriends the youngster. ★★½ VHS: $14.99

Manhunter
(1986, 119 min, US, Michael Mann) *William L. Petersen, Kim Greist, Brian Cox, Dennis Farina*. Stylish, gritty police thriller based on Thomas Harris' "Red Dragon." Petersen stars as an unorthodox ex–FBI agent — he is able to think exactly like a criminal and thereby deduce his next move — who comes out of retirement to track down a serial killer. The character of Dr. Hannibal Lecter, played by Cox, would surface a few years later as the psychopath in *The Silence of the Lambs* and *Hannibal*, played by Anthony Hopkins. ★★★ VHS: $9.99; DVD: $24.99

Maniac
(1962, 86 min, GB, Michael Carreras) *Kerwin Matthews, Nadia Gray*. Hammer Studio head Carreras takes a turn as director in this stylish knock-off of *Psycho*, about an American (Matthews) in Paris who runs into problems with his girlfriend's family. Fairly suspenseful and rather coherent considering its derivative roots. ★★★ VHS: $49.99

Maniac
(1981, 87 min, US, William Lustig) *Joe Spinell, Caroline Munro*. A terrifying and extremely gross film with Spinell as a schizophrenic who takes to the streets at night to kill at random. The horror of the killings is intensified by Spinell's sympathetic portrayal of the killer. Recommended for gore fans only. ★ VHS: $9.99; DVD: $29.99

Maniac Cop
(1988, 92 min, US, William Lustig) *Tom Atkins, Bruce Campbell, Richard Roundtree, Sheree North*. New York is being terrorized by a series of mutilation murders, and the public breaks out in a panic when the killer is discovered to be a police officer. Bloody and violent, this horror tale is slightly elevated by its intriguing premise and few scares. Written and produced by cult fave Larry Cohen. ★★ VHS: $14.99; DVD: $29.99

Mannequin
(1938, 95 min, US, Frank Borzage) *Joan Crawford, Spencer Tracy, Alan Curtis, Leo Gorcey*. An extremely competent performance by Crawford is the main attraction of this otherwise ordinary romantic drama. Joan is a working girl from a Hester Street tenement in New York who marries ne'er-do-well Curtis to escape her poverty. At her wedding party, she meets wealthy shipping magnate Tracy, who immediately falls for her. Though she loves her husband, she's torn between both men — that is until Curtis gets a nasty idea to frame Tracy. In support, Gorcey has some good scenes as Crawford's younger brother; so that's how a 1930s teenager behaved. ★★ VHS: $19.99

Mannequin
(1987, 89 min, US, Michael Gottlieb) *Kim Cattrall, Andrew McCarthy, Meshach Taylor, James Spader*. Set at Wanamaker's department store in Philadelphia, this lifeless comedy stars McCarthy as a store employee who discovers that a mannequin (Cattrall) has come to life — but only he can see her. That's about the calibre of the jokes, if you don't include Taylor's cari-cature of a lisping, limp-wristed flamboyantly gay window dresser. (Sequel: *Mannequin 2: On the Move*) ★ VHS: $9.99

Manny & Lo
(1996, 90 min, US, Lisa Krueger) *Mary Kay Place, Scarlett Johansson, Aleska Palladino*. A mesmerizing fairy tale of two sisters on the run which is brought to life by three enthralling performances. Living in different foster homes, the pregnant Lo (Palladino) rescues her sister Manny (Johansson) from the household who had her sleeping in the garage. They take to the road in their deceased mom's car, shoplifting what they need. When Lo is ready to give birth, they kidnap a clerk (Place) from a children's store to aid them in the delivery. Director Krueger has constructed a wryly observant film illuminated by insightful moments in which a person's life is delineated in a few words or a chance gesture. A remarkable film with unexpected warmth and humor, and a loving respect for its three protagonists. ★★★½ VHS: $19.99

Manon of the Spring
(1986, 112 min, France, Claude Berri) *Yves Montand, Daniel Auteuil, Emmanuelle Beart*. Set 10 years after the conclusion of *Jean de Florette*, this sequel unfolds with César and his nephew Ugolin now tilling the soil they stole from Jean de Florette. Manon, Jean's daughter, has grown into a beautiful, untamed woman who roams the countryside tending goats. The drama concerns Manon's efforts to reclaim the land and renounce the men who were responsible for her father's demise. The conclusion to this epic of revenge and treachery is riveting drama and is a superlative finale to two exquisite stories. (French with English subtitles) ★★★★ VHS: $19.99; DVD: $19.99

Mansfield Park
(1999, 112 min, GB, Patricia Rozema) *Frances O'Connor, Jonny Lee Miller, Alessandro Nivola, Embeth Davidtz, Harold Pinter, James Purefoy*. Director Rozema's revisionist version of Jane Austen's *Mansfield Park* is a comic feminist delight — a truly sweet, romantic film. Like all of Austen's stories, this one revolves around a family, their un-wed daughters and marrying them off. The plucky heroine Fanny Price (a superlative O'Connor), from poor beginnings and now living on the stately Bertram family estate, is being courted by a rake, Henry Crawford (Nivola). She has been in love since childhood with her cousin Edmond (Miller), who is now engaged to Henry's worldly sister Mary. Not to worry, for by the end of the film the proper couplings will be made. Though there are a few liberties taken by Rozema, the film possesses a magical quality and remains true to Austen's spirit. ★★★½ VHS: $19.99; DVD: $29.99

Manufacturing Consent: Noam Chomsky and the Media
(1993, 166 min, Canada, Mark Achbar & Peter Wintonick) Noam Chomsky, probably one of the greatest thinkers of the late 20th century, is examined, discussed, explored and even ridiculed in this engrossing, well-paced and humorous documentary. The film chronicles Chomsky's rise to fame as well as his fall from grace as a controversial author and professor of linguistics, and examines the inequities in

American television journalism and the problems with the medium of television itself. In interviews, Chomsky covers everything from World War II to sports to basic communication theories. This film stands as a wonderful testament to a truly thought-provoking and incredibly astute political and philosophical thinker. ★★★★ VHS: $39.99

The Manxman

(1929, 90 min, GB, Alfred Hitchcock) *Carl Brisson, Anny Ondra.* Hitchcock's last silent film is an appealing romantic melodrama about a rich lawyer and an indigent fisherman in love with the same woman. ★★★ VHS: $49.99

Map of the Human Heart

(1993, 109 min, Canada/Australia, Vincent Ward) *Jason Scott Lee, Anne Parillaud, Patrick Bergin, John Cusack, Jeanne Moreau.* Director Ward has crafted a dense web of dusky, beautiful images in this story of a love affair that spans 30 years and three continents. Arvik, a half-Inuit boy suffering from tuberculosis, is whisked away from the Arctic by a visiting mapmaker who takes him to a Catholic orphanage in Canada. There, Arvik befriends a young girl of mixed Native American and French Canadian heritage. Many years later as adults (played by Lee and Parillaud) they meet in WWII London, where both are engaged in the fight against Germany. The film's expansiveness of time and place unfortunately results in a distancing of the characters, yet Ward succeeds in provoking thought on the people, places and events that shape one's life. ★★★ VHS: $9.99

A Map of the World

(1999, 128 min, US, Scott Elliott) *Sigourney Weaver, Julianne Moore, David Strathairn, Chloë Sevigny, Louise Fletcher, Arliss Howard.* Alice Goodwin (Weaver) lives on a struggling dairy farm in Wisconsin with her husband and two daughters. Her job as a school nurse supplements the family income and offers Alice a stability not found at home. Her best friend is Theresa, who also has two daughters. When one of them drowns under the supervision of Alice, the young girl's death causes Alice to suffer a breakdown, which sets the stage for a tragic turn of events. Based on Jane Hamilton's moving best-seller, this downbeat adaptation finds its biggest strength in Weaver, who is excellent as the physically strong but emotionally fragile Alice. But in spite of a good ensemble and some tearjerking dramatics, the film only occasionally involves, offering instead a series of somber moments which fail to truly come together as a whole. ★★½ VHS: $14.99; DVD: $19.99

Marat/Sade

(1967, 118 min, GB, Peter Brook) *Patrick Magee, Glenda Jackson, Clifford Rose, Ian Richardson.* Peter Weiss' play (the full title of which is "The Persecution and Assassination of Jean-Paul Marat as Performed by the Inmates of the Asylum of Charenton under the Direction of the Marquie de Sade") is brought to the screen with lurid intensity by the Royal Shakespeare Company. The play is, as its title says, the story of the manipulation of the inmates by the Marquis in order to destroy his most hated political enemy: Marat. Jackson is stunning in her film debut as Charlotte Corday (the unwit-

ting tool of Magee's truly maniacal de Sade). This dark and disturbing film is a powerful allegory of the cruelty and abuse inherent in the wielding of political power. ★★★½ VHS: $14.99; DVD: $19.99

Marathon Man

(1976, 125 min, US, John Schlesinger) *Laurence Olivier, Dustin Hoffman, Roy Scheider, Marthe Keller, William Devane.* Nail-biting thriller with Hoffman as a Columbia University student who unwittingly becomes involved with the CIA, Nazi war criminals and the beautiful Keller. Olivier is chilling as one of the screen's most vicious villains. Does for dentists what *Psycho* did for showers. Based on the William Goldman novel. ★★★½ VHS: $14.99

March of the Wooden Soldiers

(1934, 73 min, US, Gus Meins) *Stan Laurel, Oliver Hardy.* Laurel and Hardy's classic musical comedy is based on the Victor Herbert operetta "Babes in Toyland." Stan and Ollie are Santa's hapless helpers, who help save Toyland with their giant wooden soldiers. ★★★ VHS: $19.99; DVD: $19.99

Maria Chapdelaine

(1984, 108 min, Canada, Gilles Carle) *Nick Mancuso, Carole Laure.* A family's hardships and determined pioneering spirit against the stark, brutal wilderness of North Canada is the theme of this lyrical drama based on the novel that has become a literary cornerstone of French-Canadian culture. Set against the breathtaking backdrop of the unspoiled beauty of Quebec's upper Gatineau region, the lovely Maria is the object of affection of two young men, one of whom offers escape from the difficult life in the snow-covered north. Remake of a 1934 French film. (French with English subtitles) ★★★

El Mariachi

(1992, 81 min, US, Robert Rodriguez) *Carlos Gallardo, Consuelo Gomez.* While the story of the funding for this $7,000 film is almost legendary, it cannot prepare one for the exciting, inventive and entertaining fun that first-time director Rodriguez creates. Displaying dazzling visual

virtuosity and a playful, almost mocking approach, *El Mariachi* tells the tale of a congenial mariachi singer who arrives in a dusty, nameless Mexican town seeking a place to sing. But he is mistaken for a gun-toting, vengeance-seeking criminal and is thrown into the midst of an unbelievably bloody battle between warring gangs. Acrobatic gunfights and flailing bodies are never far away, as he slugs it out (and more than holds his own) with the bad guys. A thrilling western that belies its low budget in delivering an exhilarating and often hilarious film. (Spanish with English subtitles) ★★★½ VHS: $9.99

Marie

(1985, 112 min, US, Roger Donaldson) *Sissy Spacek, Jeff Daniels, Morgan Freeman, Fred Thompson.* Spacek gives a fine performance in this true story of Marie Ragghianti, a divorced mother who becomes the chairman of the Tennessee State Board of Pardons and Paroles, and whose exposure of political corruption led to the ousting of a governor. Ragghianti's real-life lawyer, Thompson, appears as himself. ★★★ VHS: $79.99

Marie Antoinette

(1938, 149 min, US, W.S. Van Dyke II) *Norma Shearer, Tyrone Power, John Barrymore, Gladys George, Robert Morley.* Grand MGM costumer about the life of the doomed 18th-century French queen. Shearer plays the title role, and Morley is outstanding as Louis XVI. ★★★ VHS: $19.99

Marie Baie des Anges

(Marie from the Bay of Angels)

(1998, 90 min, France, Manuel Pradal) *Vahina Giocante, Frederic Malgras, Nicolas Welbers.* Stunning hand-held cinematography and a cast of gorgeous sun-drenched youths make *Marie Baie des Anges* beautiful to watch, but director Pradal's debut film lacks true emotion. The story line is elliptical — it begins and ends with the same confusing sequence — but there are episodes in between that are riveting. Orso (Malgras) is a handsome young thief who drifts into a casual relationship with the luscious

Frances O'Connor in *Mansfield Park*

M

Marie (Giocante) only to face dire consequences. There is tremendous sexual tension throughout the film, but there is little payoff to all the teasing. While the film's visuals will keep viewers interested — particularly the focus on shirtless boys and provocative girls — this is still pretension masquerading as style. (French with English subtitles) ★★½ VHS: $24.99

Marius

(1931, 123 min, France, Alexander Korda) *Raimu, Pierre Fresnay, Charpin.* This first film of the legendary Pagnol Trilogy introduces Marseilles cafe owner César and his son Marius. Marius loves Fanny but leaves her for a life at sea. Shortly afterwards, Fanny finds herself pregnant. The joy and hardship of the simple people of Provence are splendidly captured. This is followed by *Fanny* and *César*. ★★★★ VHS: $39.99

Mark of the Devil

(1970, 90 min, West Germany/GB, Michael Armstrong) *Herbert Lom, Olivera Vuco, Udo Kier.* During the 18th century, a corrupt, impotent witch hunter has his way with women in more grotesque ways than can be imagined. This once *cause célèbre* is really much ado about nothing, as it offers gross instead of scares. ★ VHS: $14.99

Mark of the Vampire

(1935, 61 min, US, Tod Browning) *Lionel Barrymore, Bela Lugosi, Lionel Atwill.* An eerie horror tale by *Dracula* director Browning about vampire expert Barrymore and police detective Atwill investigating a series of attacks in a small rural village. ★★★ VHS: $19.99

The Mark of Zorro

(1920, 90 min, US, Fred Niblo) *Douglas Fairbanks, Marguerite de la Motte.* Fairbanks in another of his patented swashbuckling roles. Lots of great sword fights, lots of great sets and lots of people running around a lot. ★★★ VHS: $19.99; DVD: $24.99

The Mark of Zorro

(1940, 93 min, US, Rouben Mamoulian) *Tyrone Power, Basil Rathbone, Linda Darnell, Eugene Pallette.* Power's first attempt at swashbuckling, and he proves himself quite adept at it. Returning to his home in 1800s California after studying abroad, Power discovers his father has been forcibly replaced as Alcalde of Los Angeles, and that the new mayor is corrupt. Though a master swordsman, Power plays the fop while secretly fighting the powers that be as the heroic Zorro. Rathbone is, once again, a worthy opponent in this exciting and well-made adventure tale. ★★★ VHS: $14.99

Marked for Death

(1990, 93 min, US, Dwight H. Little) *Steven Seagal, Joanna Pacula.* It's voodoo and violence as Seagal plays a tough DEA agent who finds her and his family are targets of a vicious drug lord. Needless to say, martial arts action ensues. The little bit of action can't compensate for the ridiculous story and Seagal's awful acting. ★ VHS: $9.99; DVD: $29.99

Marked Woman

(1937, 97 min, US, Lloyd Bacon) *Bette Davis, Humphrey Bogart.* Loosely based on the trial of New York crime boss "Lucky" Luciano, this taut gangster drama stars Davis as a clip joint hostess who is persuaded by D.A. Bogart to testify against the racketeer boss responsible for her sister's disappearance. Davis is terrific in this crisp tale which is as enthralling as it is cynical. ★★★ VHS: $19.99

Marlene

(1986, 91 min, Germany, Maximilian Schell) *Marlene Dietrich.* Marlene Dietrich, screen legend and public recluse, is the subject of this fascinating, amusing and insightful portrait. Miss Dietrich agreed to make the film with the unusual stipulation that director Schell not film her. So with only microphone in hand, the resourceful Schell interviews, confronts, compliments and does battle with this tough yet vulnerable lady. An unconventional portrait of one of Hollywood's greatest stars. (Filmed mostly in English) ★★★½ VHS: $14.99; DVD: $24.99

Marlowe

(1969, 95 min, US, Paul Bogart) *James Garner, Rita Moreno, Jackie Coogan, Carroll O'Connor, Bruce Lee.* A director named Bogart (no relation) brings famed detective Philip Marlowe to the 1960s in this neat little thriller. The plot has something to do with Marlowe (Garner) investigating the disappearance of a young man. Lee makes kindling out of Marlowe's office. ★★★ VHS: $19.99

Marnie

(1964, 129 min, US, Alfred Hitchcock) *Sean Connery, Tippi Hedren, Diane Baker, Bruce Dern.* Initially misunderstood, *Marnie* has been reevaluated as a continued exploration of the themes explicated in *Vertigo*: sexual inhibition and anxiety, the complex network of communication between men and women, and the tyranny of the past over the present. Hedren essays the man-hating heroine and Connery is her prey and predator. ★★★ VHS: $14.99; DVD: $29.99

Marooned

(1969, 134 min, US, John Sturges) *Gregory Peck, Richard Crenna, Gene Hackman, James Franciscus, Lee Grant.* Low-key sci-fi adventure with Peck as a panicky aerospace chief trying to get three stranded astronauts back to Earth. Oscar for Best Special Effects. ★★½ VHS: $9.99

Marquis

(1990, 80 min, France, Henru Xhonneux) Sort of an X-rated Ren & Stimpy-visit-the-French Revolution, this bizarre tale tells of the Marquis de Sade's imprisonment in the Bastille during the upheaval of 1789 — with the twist being that all of the cast play out their roles in grotesque animal costumes. Devilishly witty and shockingly vulgar, this bestial satire's cast includes, in a leading role, Colin, de Sade's frisky and dialectically opinionated penis; the Marquis himself (a horny but pensive hound-faced intellectual); and a lusty prison guard in love with the Marquis who is intent on being buggered by him. Despite being bogged down by the intricate 18th-century French politics, this will certainly shock some, and entertain, amuse and titillate others. (French with English subtitles) ★★★½ VHS: $29.99

The Marriage of Maria Braun

The Marriage of Maria Braun

(1978, 110 min, Germany, Rainer Werner Fassbinder) *Hanna Schygulla, Klaus Lowitsch.* Fassbinder's superb mixture of historical epic, offbeat comedy and social commentary stars Schygulla as the enterprising heroine who rises from the ashes of post-war Germany to become a captain of industry. (German with English subtitles) ★★★★

Married to It!

(1993, 112 min, US, Arthur Hiller) *Beau Bridges, Stockard Channing, Ron Silver, Cybill Shepherd, Mary Stuart Masterson, Robert Sean Leonard.* If *Married to It!* were a person, it would never get asked to the prom. It's whiny, pretentious and tries way too hard to be popular. With "something for everyone," the story revolves around three couples: rich and materialistic Silver and Shepherd; socially conscious, old hippies Bridges and Channing; and newlyweds Leonard and Masterson. It's like a Woody Allen film with all of the complaining but none of the insights. ★★ VHS: $6.99

Married to the Mob

(1988, 105 min, US, Jonathan Demme) *Michelle Pfeiffer, Matthew Modine, Dean Stockwell, Mercedes Ruehl, Alec Baldwin, Joan Cusack.* A vibrant and colorful comedy awash with trendy pop music, cool ethnic types and hip American iconography. The very engaging Pfeiffer stars as a "mob" widow who sets out to leave "the family" behind her. But her late husband's boss has other ideas about it, and goes to great lengths to let her know it. Into her life comes FBI agent Modine, who thinks she has yet to sever the umbilical, and sees a chance to nab the nefarious don — by romancing the frustrated widow. Stockwell gives a hilariously sleazy performance as the don and Ruehl is terrific as Stockwell's maniacally jealous wife. ★★★ DVD: $19.99

A Married Woman
(Une Femme Mariée)

(1964, 94 min, France, Jean-Luc Godard) *Véronique Duval, Jean-Luc Godard, Margaret Le Van, Roger Leenhardt.* A Married Woman is a fine example of Godard's wild experimentation with narrative, sound usage, editing, and literary allusions. Subtitled, "Fragments of a Film Shot in 1964," the film begins with a concern for woman's role in society but he is really much more interested in ideas of memory, the present and intelligence. (French with English subtitles) ★★★½

Marry Me! Marry Me!

(1968, 96 min, France, Claude Berri) *Elisabeth Wiener, Regine, Claude Berri.* A charming romantic comedy produced, directed, written by and starring Berri. It's an offbeat story about European Jewish families, and follows Claude, a Jewish encyclopedia salesman in Paris, as he inconveniently falls in love with a pregnant Belgian girl. Berri unfolds the story with gentle, perceptive humor. ★★★

The Marrying Man

(1991, 115 min, US, Jerry Rees) *Alec Baldwin, Kim Basinger, Elisabeth Shue, Paul Reiser.* Plagued by controversy, this Neil Simon-scripted comedy misses the mark as an affectionate tribute to the screwball comedies of the '30s and '40s. Groom-to-be Baldwin is caught philandering with Basinger by her gangster beau. Forced to marry her, Baldwin's engagement to heiress Shue is cancelled and he's left distraught. . . until he's re-engaged to Shue and meets Basinger again. Baldwin is competent, but Basinger appears to be imitating Michelle Pfeiffer in *The Fabulous Baker Boys*, especially in her musical numbers. ★★

Mars Attacks!

(1996, 103 min, US, Tim Burton) *Jack Nicholson, Glenn Close, Annette Bening, Pierce Brosnan, Danny DeVito, Michael J. Fox, Sarah Jessica Parker, Lukas Haas, Jim Brown, Pam Grier.* Combining some gleefully twisted black humor with plenty of homages and references to schlocky (and not-so-schlocky) alien invasion and sci-fi flicks of the 1950s and '60s, director Burton's magnum opus is the perfect companion piece to his eloquent, intimate masterwork *Ed Wood*. A parody of the kind of movie Ed Wood only wishes he could have afforded to make, *Mars Attacks!* is the story of some funny-looking but terribly ill-tempered aliens who declare war on the Earth. Why? Because it's there! Great special effects, deliberately designed to evoke memories of afternoon sci-fi matinees, an outstanding score by Danny Elfman and campy, wild-eyed performances by everyone involved all add up to an "A" budget "B" movie. (Letterboxed VHS available for $19.99) ★★★½ VHS: $9.99; DVD: $19.99

La Marseillaise

(1937, 130 min, France, Jean Renoir) *Pierre Renoir, Lisa Delamare.* This grand epic chronicles the events of the French Revolution of 1789. This is a stirring account of the events which led to the uprising, and Renoir has filmed it in a episodic, tense fashion. (French with English subtitles) ★★★ VHS: $59.99

Martha & Ethel

(1995, 80 min, US, Jyll Johnstone) *Martha Kniefel, Ethel Edwards, Jyll Johnstone, Barbara Ettinger.* A highly personalized labor of love, this endearing documentary offers two radically different portraits of the filmmakers' childhood nannies. Director Johnstone and producer Ettinger examine each of their families' interactions with their paid child rearers and uncover a fascinating study of family dynamics as well as an entertaining exposé on the lives of the wealthy. Martha, a cranky 87-year-old German immigrant, is a stern disciplinarian who was feared by the children. Ethel is an extraordinarily resilient and graceful 92-year-old daughter of South Carolina sharecroppers. Though the stories of these two remarkable women have little in common, their differing styles and the clearly divergent attitudes of their employers make this captivating viewing. ★★★½ VHS: $79.99

Martin

(1978, 95 min, US, George Romero) *John Amplas, Lincoln Maazel, Tom Savini.* A witty and sardonic updating of the Dracula legend about a young man with a troublesome fondness for blood. What distinguishes Romero's work is an ability to maintain an atmosphere of terror and suspense while simultaneously indulging in a most kinky sense of humor. ★★★ VHS: $9.99

Marty

(1955, 91 min, US, Delbert Mann) *Ernest Borgnine, Betsy Blair, Joe Mantell, Esther Minciotti.* Oscar-winning Best Picture about a shy butcher who finds true love, and a glimpse into the lives of two ordinary, lonely people who meet by chance in a dance hall. Borgnine won an Oscar for his poignant portrayal of the title character, a hapless Everyman, and is given solid support by Blair and Mantell. Screenplay by Paddy Chayefsky (Best Screenplay Award). ★★★★ VHS: $14.99; DVD: $19.99

Marvin and Tige

(1982, 104 min, US, Eric Weston) *John Cassavetes, Billy Dee Williams, Gibran Brown.* Cassavetes stars as an alcoholic ad exec who meets an embittered, streetwise 11-year-old contemplating suicide because of his mother's recent death. Cassavetes takes an interest in the child, and tries to reunite him with his estranged father (Williams). A film which wears its heart on its sleeve in its well-meaning examination of racial intolerance. ★★½

Marvin's Room

(1996, 105 min, US, Jerry Zaks) *Meryl Streep, Diane Keaton, Leonardo DiCaprio, Robert De Niro, Gwen Verdon, Hume Cronyn, Dan Hedaya.* Keaton and Streep are sisters estranged for 20 years, brought together by Keaton's onset of leukemia after a lifetime as family caretaker. The younger Lee (Streep) jumped ship when she refused responsibilities for ailing relatives; the older Bessie's (Keaton) life is defined by the illnesses of others. From the first awkward reacquaintance of the two sisters, the uncanny symbiosis of familial interrelationships ameliorates the harsh edges of conflict, imparting a blessed balance to both sisters. This actors' vehicle suffers some-

what from stage director Zaks' unfamiliarity with the medium and a curiously toned-down script. But the strength and honesty of the ensemble portrayals rise above these failings with unexpected humor and warmth of emotion without artifice. ★★★ VHS: $14.99; DVD: $29.99

Mary My Dearest
(Maria de Mi Corazón)

(1983, 100 min, Mexico, Jaime Humberto Hermosillo) *Maria Rojo, Hector Bonilla.* This Mexican soap opera, adapted from a story by Gabriel Garcia Marquez, is a moderately interesting black comedy of ill-fated love, produced independently by one of Mexico's most popular directors. After a mysterious eight-year absence, Maria, a beautiful young magician, returns to the home of small-time crook Hector. The couple fall in love for a second time, but are soon separated when Maria, in a bizarre mix-up, is placed in an insane asylum and can't get out. (Spanish with English subtitles) ★★½ VHS: $29.99

Mary Poppins

(1964, 140 min, US, Robert Stevenson) *Julie Andrews, Dick Van Dyke, Glynis Johns, David Tomlinson, Ed Wynn.* "In every job that must be done, there is an element of fun." And there could be no greater fun than Walt Disney's classic live-action and animated musical. Andrews won an Oscar for her delightful performance as everyone's favorite magical nanny, Mary Poppins, who arrives at the Banks household to oversee two young children. The film features a wonderful supporting cast. Quick — can you say supercalifragilisticexpialidocious backwards? ★★★★ VHS: $22.99; DVD: $29.99

Mary, Queen of Scots

(1971, 128 min, GB, Charles Jarrott) *Vanessa Redgrave, Glenda Jackson, Patrick McGoohan, Timothy Dalton, Nigel Davenport, Trevor Howard, Daniel Massey, Ian Holm.* Lavish costume drama about the power struggle between Queen Elizabeth (a forceful Jackson) and her cousin Mary (a luminous Redgrave). ★★★ VHS: $14.99

Mary Reilly

(1996, 118 min, GB, Stephen Frears) *Julia Roberts, John Malkovich, George Cole, Glenn Close, Michael Gambon.* Director Frears' disjointed adaptation of the tale of Dr. Jekyll and Mr. Hyde uses the intriguing premise of following the action from the point of view of the good doctor's maidservant, Mary Reilly (Roberts). The film eventually becomes a claustrophobic and uninteresting spine-tingler along the lines of another British Gothic film, *The Turn of the Screw*. Adding to the film's laconic pace is Malkovich's stoic performance as Jekyll and Hyde. Roberts, gives an able performance, mildly believable Irish accent and all. ★★ VHS: $9.99; DVD: $24.99

Mary Shelley's Frankenstein

(1994, 123 min, GB, Kenneth Branagh) *Kenneth Branagh, Robert De Niro, Helena Bonham Carter, Tom Hulce, Aidan Quinn, John Cleese, Ian Holm.* Branagh sets his sights away from Shakespeare and onto less fanciful fare with this egocentric and grisly adaptation of the time-honored tale which takes the notion "the sins of the father" to a truly horrific level. Returning to the original source and the central theme that man was

Martha & Ethel

Mars Attacks! "Ack-ack-ack!"

not meant to play God, Branagh delivers an emotionally complex portrayal of Dr. Frankenstein as a man who creates life and then turns his back on it. There are, of course, Branagh's trademark histrionics — dizzying, non-stop camerwork, a booming and somewhat distracting score, and some shameless overacting by the director-star. De Niro is an un-Karloff monster. ★★★ VHS: $9.99

Masala
(1993, 100 min, Canada, Srinivas Krishna) *Srinivas Krishna, Saaed Jaffrey.* Krishna's ingenious feature debut is this wildly entertaining brew which examines the difficulties of assimilation for Indian immigrants in North America. Krishna himself stars as a thuggish young hunk who dabbles in drugs and petty crime. When his entire family is killed in a plane crash, he moves to Toronto to live with his ruthlessly greedy uncle (Jaffrey). He strikes up a relationship with the daughter of a financially strapped postman (Jaffrey in a multiple role), whose mother has candid conversations with her favorite deity Krishna (Jaffrey again) through her VCR. The film is a tasty mélange of spicy subplots, twists and characters. Colorful and wild, *Masala* presents a wholly original take on the struggles of Indian immigrants to retain their cultural identity. ★★★½ VHS: $19.99

Mascara
(1987, 99 min, Belgium, Patrick Conrad) *Derek De Lint, Michael Sarrazin, Charlotte Rampling.* The Crying Game owes a debt to this stylishly shot psychosexual thriller about a sexually repressed police inspector on the brink of murderous insanity triggered by a particularly pretty dress he fancies. Sarrazin stars as the inspector and Rampling costars as his sister and the object of his incestuous desires. Filled with themes of lust, love, transvestism and murder, the film features some scenes in a kinky after hours club which are worthy of one of Ken Russell's fevered dream sequences. (Filmed in English) ★★★ VHS: $19.99

Masculin-Feminin
(1966, 103 min, France, Jean-Luc Godard) *Jean-Pierre Léaud, Brigitte Bardot.* Starting from a Du Maupassant short story, Godard fashions a

remarkable portrait of French youth in the '60s — "the children of Marx and Coca Cola." A blending of experimental fiction with documentary segments aims to drive the "political truth" home to the workers. Léaud is an aimless revolutionary who wants answers but sees nothing in the political turmoil that surrounds him. Godard's "fifteen precise facts" on the problems of the younger generation. (French with English subtitles) ★★★½ VHS: $29.99

M*A*S*H
(1970, 116 min, US, Robert Altman) *Elliott Gould, Donald Sutherland, Tom Skerritt, Sally Kellerman, Robert Duvall, Gary Burghoff, Bud Cort, Fred Williamson, Rene Auberjonois.* One of the most devastating black comedies and potent antiwar films ever to hit the screen, Altman's blisteringly funny, anarchic romp rocketed him to stardom and set the tone for a generation of irreverent filmmakers. Set during the Korean War, the film stars Gould (back when he had screen presence) and Sutherland as two hotshot, unconventional doctors assigned to a Mobile Army Surgical Hospital. In between the blood and death of war and surgery, they let loose in binges marked by drinking, sex, disobedience and other flagrant actions of nonmilitary behavior. Kellerman is terrfic as "Hot Lips" Houlihan, and the rest of the supporting cast is first-rate. The film was made into a successful TV series which only partially retained the film's hard edge and biting cynicism. ★★★★

Mask
(1985, 120 min, US, Peter Bogdanovich) *Cher, Eric Stoltz, Sam Elliott, Laura Dern, Estelle Getty.* Cher gives a stirring performance as the mother of Rocky Dennis, a teenager afflicted with a disfiguring congenital condition. Director Bogdanovich effectively paints a sympathetic portrait of the young man's life, and Stoltz gives a commendable performance as Dennis. ★★★ VHS: $7.49

The Mask
(1994, 102 min, US, Charles Russell) *Jim Carrey, Cameron Diaz, Richard Jeni, Peter Riegert.* Rubber-faced Carrey gets totally bent out of shape (with the help of F/X meister Greg Cannom) in this

enjoyable follow-up to his debut *Ace Ventura.* The one-dimensional story, which is really an excuse to get from one special effect to another, is the standard "underdog has his day" scenario, with Carrey as a beleaguered nebbish who finds an ancient mask that turns him into a green-faced, zoot-suited, whacked-out super-hormonal superhero. But under the direction of Russell, what amazing effects they are. Carrey's world becomes a Tex Avery–style cartoon replete with side-splitting computer-generated F/X and technicolored, show-stopping musical numbers. (Letterboxed VHS available for $19.99) ★★★ VHS: $14.99; DVD: $19.99

The Mask of Fu Manchu
(1932, 72 min, US, Charles Babin) *Boris Karloff, Lewis Stone, Myrna Loy.* A fun adventure yarn with Karloff as the evil mastermind intent on world domination and Stone as the hero dedicated to stopping him. The film moves along at a good pace and is highlighted by a pyrotechnic show as Fu tries to determine the authenticity of a powerful sword brought to him. Archaic racial stereotypes notwithstanding, Karloff's performance is the real treat here. Dated and old-fashioned, but enjoyable nonetheless. ★★½ VHS: $19.99

The Mask of Zorro
(1998, 135 min, US, Martin Campbell) *Antonio Banderas, Anthony Hopkins, Catherine Zeta-Jones, Stuart Wilson, Matt Letscher.* Banderas proves he can swash with the best of them in this very entertaining, big-hearted comic adventure which is a fun throwback to the Errol Flynn swashbucklers of the '30s and '40s. Giving the production a bit of added class, Hopkins is the masked avenger in the film's beginning. But years later, he's just getting a little too old for this line of work, and passes the mask onto ne'er-do-well Banderas — though not without a lesson or two. As would be expected, there's lots of swordsplay and action, and quite a bit of comedy which is well-placed. Banderas cuts a fine romantic figure, as does the gorgeous Zeta-Jones who plays Hopkins' daughter, abducted and raised by the first Zorro's adversary. ★★★ VHS: $9.99; DVD: $19.99

Masque of the Red Death

(1991, 83 min, US, Alan Birkinshaw) *Herbert Lom, Brenda Vaccaro, Frank Stallone.* In this minor, updated version of Edgar Allan Poe's short story, Lom plays a dying patriarch who throws one last grand ball — if he's gotta go he's determined to take his friends along with him. Vaccaro as a foul-mouthed matron, and Stallone, one of her men in arms, are just two of the guests who would rather not accompany him. ★★ VHS: $79.99

Mass Appeal

(1984, 99 min, US, Glenn Jordan) *Jack Lemmon, Zeljko Ivanek, Charles Durning.* Lemmon gives a commanding performance in this appealing adaptation of the Broadway comedy-drama about the clash of wills between a well-to-do priest (Lemmon) and an outspoken seminarian (Ivanek). The film touches upon clashes between the old Church and the younger ideology — some of it is superficial and some of it is surprisingly thorough. ★★½ VHS: $19.99

Massacre at Central High

(1976, 87 min, US, Renee Daalder) *Andrew Stevens, Robert Carradine, Kimberly Beck.* Cult favorite with Stevens as the new kid in school who begins a one-man campaign of terror against a brutal student gang. ★★½

Master Harold and the Boys

(1985, 105 min, GB/US, Michael Lindsay-Hogg) *Matthew Broderick, Zakes Mokae, Jon Kani.* This powerful film written by South Africa's eminent playwright, Athol Fugard, concerns a South African white youth whose "special friendship" with two black men is adversely affected by the return of his father to the family-owned tea room. The youth's uncovered, heretofore unrecognized racism helps us understand the difficulty in escaping the values that surround us as we grow to personhood. ★★★½ VHS: $19.99

Master of the World

(1961, 104 min, US, Roger Corman) *Vincent Price, Charles Bronson, Henry Hull.* One of Corman's most entertaining and effective films. Price plays Robur the Conquerer in this Jules Verne story about a peace activist out to destroy the armies of the world from his flying ship. ★★★ VHS: $9.99

Mastergate

(1992, 90 min, US, Michael Engler) *Richard Kiley, David Ogden Stiers, James Coburn, Ed Begley, Jr., Jerry Orbach, Darren McGavin, Bruno Kirby, Burgess Meredith.* With the subheading "A Play on Words," writer Larry Gelbart's hilarious political farce is just that, a wondrous whirlwind of words, doublespeak and raillery. Taking aim at network news, Washington, the military and Hollywood, the story centers on a Congressional hearing into illegal arms delivered to Central American rebels funded through a movie's $1.3 billion budget. Though the satire is obvious, it is Gelbart's scintillating dialogue — which easily could have been penned by Stoppard or Chayefsky — which propels the film, creating an uproarious verbal confrontation of half-truths and evasions. Though enjoyable on any level, this is a must for politicos. ★★★½

Masterminds

(1997, 120 min, US, Roger Christian) *Patrick Stewart, Vincent Kartheiser, Brenda Fricker.* In this sillier, high-tech version of *Toy Soldiers*, a computer genius with a grudge (Stewart) takes over a private school with the help of some armed terrorist friends. Instead of a group of misfit cadets, here there's only one misfit cadet who happens to be a computer whiz. It's hacker vs. hacker as the youth tries to sabotage the terrorist's every move. Stewart seems embarrassed by his appearance here. ★½ VHS: $19.99

Masters of the Universe

(1987, 106 min, US, Gary Goddard) *Dolph Lundgren, Frank Langella, Meg Foster, Courtney Cox.* Lundgren flexes his muscles as a space-age warrior whose battle with evil lord Langella brings him to Earth. Pretty inept in all departments. ★½ VHS: $9.99

Mata Hari

(1931, 100 min, US, George Fitzmaurice) *Greta Garbo, Lionel Barrymore, Ramon Navarro.* Garbo rarely looked lovelier than as the famed WWI spy whose exotic looks seduced every male she met. Navarro and Barrymore are just two who fall victim to this woman's wiles. Navarro utters the famous line, "What's the matter, Mata?" ★★★ VHS: $19.98

Matador

(1988, 102 min, Spain, Pedro Almodóvar) *Assumpta Serna, Antonio Banderas, Carmen Maura.* This wickedly satiric romp is a decidedly twisted and thoroughly amusing wallow in the world of sexual desires. A series of bizarre sexual murders are baffling the police in Madrid until young Angel — the son of an ultra-rightwing, religiously obsessive mother — turns himself in to the police. The problem is that he is innocent and has been experiencing the killings clairvoyantly. His femme-fatale attorney is aware of his innocence, as is his bullfighting instructor: for they are each responsible for the grisly murders. Director Almodóvar rips away the facade of human behavior and reveals a hilarious, sometimes frightening, subterranean view of a world ruled by passion and death. (Spanish with English subtitles) ★★★½

The Match Factory Girl

(1989, 70 min, Finland, Aki Kaurismäki) *Kati Outinen, Elina Salo.* A bleak little saga about a mousy factory worker whose dreary life includes living at home with her mother and stepfather while desperately seeking male companionship despite her bland looks and nondescript personality. Kaurismäki's film is every bit as personality-less as its main character. What is so perplexing is that the film contains not one scintilla of emotion, not even a blip — granted, life in Helsinki may be unbearably innocuous at times, especially for the underprivileged proletariat, but it is hard to fathom life on the level Kaurismäki presents it. Even so, the film lacks the director's subtle sense of humor and incisive commentary usually found in his other works; it only displays an effective use of minimalism. (Finnish with English subtitles) ★★ VHS: $79.99

The Matchmaker

(1958, 101 min, US, Joseph Anthony) *Shirley Booth, Paul Ford, Shirley MacLaine, Anthony Perkins, Robert Morse.* Enjoyable screen version of Thornton Wilder's play, with Booth giving a wonderful performance as turn-of-the-century matchmaker Dolly Levi. As Horace Vandergelder, one of her clients and romantic interest, Ford is in good form. The basis for the musical *Hello, Dolly!* ★★★ VHS: $14.99

The Matchmaker

(1997, 97 min, Ireland/US, Joseph Anthony) *Janeane Garofalo, David O'Hara, Milo O'Shea, Denis Leary, Jay O. Sanders.* Typical American fish-out-of-water plot is greatly enlivened by winning performances, beautiful scenery and a script that walks the fine line between rustic charm and heavy-handed sentimentality. Garofalo plays a senator's aide sent to Ireland to find some long-lost relatives. What happens next has been a cliché since before "Brigadoon" was on Broadway: cynical American goes to a small foreign village only to be taken in by the gorgeous landscapes and the quaint charm of a particularly cute local (in this case, O'Hara) and the cynicism melts away. It's all here: the local eccentrics, lovesick teenagers and, of course, lots of Whiskey, Guinness & Singing. But the charm only rarely seems forced and there are some genuine moments of sweetness. ★★★ VHS: $14.99; DVD: $19.99

La Maternelle

(1933, 83 min, France, Jean Benoit-Levy & Maria Epstein) A society girl down on her luck becomes a maid in "la maternelle," a kindergarten which provides a temporary refuge for the poor children of a Parisian slum. The compassionate young woman befriends and mothers the children, many of them victims of abuse, and takes into her home a lonely waif abandoned by her "working girl" mother. An affectionate and heartwarming, yet grimly realistic drama. (French with English subtitles) ★★★ VHS: $29.99

Matewan

(1987, 132 min, US, John Sayles) *Chris Cooper, James Earl Jones, Mary McDonnell, Will Oldham, David Strathairn.* The dramatic retelling of a 1920s coal strike in West Virginia has been sensitively written and directed by Sayles and beautifully photographed by Haskell Wexler. This compelling story of solidarity and martyrdom amidst the grime and dust of the coal town features fine performances from the entire cast. ★★★½ VHS: $14.99; DVD: $44.99

Matilda

(1996, 90 min, US, Danny DeVito) *Mara Wilson, Rhea Perlman, Danny DeVito, Embeth Davidtz.* Matilda is a little girl with serious problems: Her parents never wanted her in the first place and treat her with great disdain. After refusing to let her go to school (someone has to stay home and accept the boxes of illegal car parts!), they finally send her to a school where the principal loves to torment the students. Luckily, Matilda has discovered she has telekinetic powers that allow her to exact a very satisfying revenge on the adults who mistreated her. The story is told with style and humor. ★★★ VHS: $22.99; DVD: $19.99

Matinee

(1993, 107 min, US, Joe Dante) *John Goodman, Simon Fenton, Cathy Moriarty, Kevin McCarthy, John Sayles, Dick Miller, Jesse White, William Schallert.* Dante shows just where he cut his

M

The Matrix

M

teeth as a youthful movie fan with this playful homage to '60s schlock films. Set during the Cuban Missile Crisis, the story revolves around a teenager (Fenton), an avid creature feature fan, who becomes assistant to John Goodman's big-hearted film director — part Alfred Hitchcock, part William Castle. Goodman has come to the youth's small Florida town to screen his newest, grade-Z creation, *Mant* (Half Man, Half Ant, All Terror!). Dante and writers Charlie Haas and Jerico clearly are enjoying their sometimes hilarious send-ups of the dreadful matinee horror films of decades yore, and their film-within-a-film has some delectable scenes. ★★★ VHS: $9.99

The Mating Game

(1959, 96 min, US, George Marshall) *Debbie Reynolds, Tony Randall, Paul Douglas, Una Merkel.* Anyone wishing for an old-fashioned comic confection should appreciate this homespun romantic comedy. All others, however, beware: insulin shock ahead. Reynolds is the red-blooded, eldest daughter of farmer/trader Douglas' Maryland brood. When IRS agent Randall comes to investigate Douglas' 20-year nonpayment of taxes, her parents do their darndest to match Reynolds and their educated visitor. There's no shortage of good spirits, but it's all so damn cute this was probably corn when released in 1959. ★★½ VHS: $19.99

The Matrix

(1999, 136 min, US, Andy Wachowski & Larry Wachowski) *Keanu Reeves, Laurence Fishburne, Carrie-Anne Moss, Hugo Weaving, Joe Pantoliano.* Kung fu without gravity, machine guns with unlimited ammo and ultra smooth heroes who have all the right moves form the entirety of *The Matrix*, the Wachowski brothers' big-budget follow-up to *Bound*. Supercool right down to the omnipresent blue-grey hues, this is the rare action film to slowly build its ideas and technologies to a truly mind-blowing climactic showdown. Keanu is Neo, a hacker who learns that his fellow humans are at the mercy of computers. He may or may not be "the One" to

enter the virtual world of the Matrix to save humankind. The convoluted plot is merely a vehicle for Fishburne, Moss and Reeves (making amends for *Johnny Mnemonic*) to kick ass against an impressive Weaving (as a neo-fascist enforcer). Visually stunning, *The Matrix* uses its arsenal of visual effects for maximum impact. (VHS available letterboxed or pan & scan) ★★★½ VHS: $19.99; DVD: $24.99

Matter of Heart

(1983, 107 min, US, Mark Whitney) Carl Gustav Jung discovered powers of healing and guidance in his studies of the dream world, contributing to a philosophy of Western thinking which radically transformed the nature of modern psychology. His remarkable genius is captured with exquisite tenderness in this fascinating film which helps reveal the relationship between his thought and his life. ★★★½ VHS: $24.99

Maurice

(1987, 95 min, GB, James Ivory) *James Wilby, Hugh Grant, Rupert Graves, Ben Kingsley, Billie Whitelaw, Denholm Elliott, Simon Callow, Helena Bonham Carter.* With the same reverence and regal authority he brought to *A Room with a View*, director Ivory has created a personal triumph with this exquisite adaptation of E. M. Forster's semiautobiography. Set in pre-WWI England, the film examines the social and sexual repression of the era in this story of the emotional conflict facing a college student coming to terms with his homosexuality. Wilby is perfectly cast in the title role, Grant gives a precise performance as his platonic lover who transforms from free spirit to social prig, and Graves is splendid as the handsome gardener who awakens Maurice's dormant feelings. ★★★★ VHS: $14.99

Mauvaise Graine

(1933, 77 min, France, Billy Wilder & Alexander Esway) *Pierre Mingand, Danielle Darrieux, Raymond Galle.* When his rich, indulgent daddy takes the roadster away, spoiled, amoral Henry (Mingand) gets himself mixed up with a fast woman (Darrieux) and a ring of car thieves. Shot on location in and around a Paris of the early '30s, *Mauvaise Graine* captures a city at the height of its beauty and a career about to burst into bloom. Exhibiting many of the narrative touches that would become Wilder's trademarks (and can be traced back to his unsuspecting mentor Ernst Lubitsch), the film is fast-paced and action-packed, recklessly driven along by a jazzy score from Franz Waxman (like Wilder himself, to be bound for Hollywood). (French with English subtitles) ★★★ VHS: $24.99

Maverick

(1994, 120 min, US, Richard Donner) *Mel Gibson, Jodie Foster, James Garner, Graham Greene, James Coburn, Danny Glover, Alfred Molina.* In their initial meeting, Foster — as an alluring con artist — sums up her impression of dashing gambler Bret Maverick, played by Gibson: "Irritating and likable." This also ably describes this pleasant big-screen version of the popular 1960s TV series. Gibson gives an amiable account of the rascal/cardsharp who only wants to play in the big poker tournament but who gets sidetracked at every turn. Foster is uncharacteristically breezy as Maverick's equally roguish partner. Both are eclipsed, however, by Garner, who appears as a crusty lawman, whose effortless charm is a

reminder of what distinguished the TV show. *Maverick* may not totally capture the effervescence of its prototype, but it does contain many enjoyable moments of nonsensical whimsy. (Letterboxed VHS available for $19.99) ★★★ VHS: $14.99; DVD: $24.99

The Maverick Queen

(1956, 92 min, US, Joseph Kane) *Barbara Stanwyck, Barry Sullivan, Wallace Ford, Jim Davis.* Faithful screen version of a Zane Grey novel with Stanwyck as a lady bandit who falls in love with the Pinkerton detective (Sullivan) sent to track her down. ★★½ VHS: $14.99

Max Dugan Returns

(1983, 98 min, US, Herbert Ross) *Jason Robards, Marsha Mason, Matthew Broderick, Donald Sutherland, Kiefer Sutherland.* Amiable Neil Simon comedy with Robards, as Mason's long-lost father, who reenters his daughter's life. Broderick debuts as Mason's teenage son. ★★½ VHS: $59.99

Max Mon Amour

(1986, 97 min, France/US, Nagisa Oshima) *Charlotte Rampling, Anthony Higgens.* The attention-grabbing premise of this film — that a sophisticated Parisian woman falls in love with a chimpanzee — should generate some interest in this unusual satire from Oshima. Margaret (Rampling) and English diplomat Peter (Higgens) are an unhappy couple opulently living in Paris. Their marriage is strained when the husband discovers that his wife is having an affair not with another man, but with a chimpanzee. Even with its premise, the film disappoints; for after Max is introduced, there is nothing more to shock, and every time the story approaches a surreal level, it steps back, embracing conventionality. (English and French with English subtitles) ★★ VHS: $29.99

Maxie

(1985, 98 min, US, Paul Aaron) *Glenn Close, Mandy Patinkin, Ruth Gordon, Barnard Hughes, Harry Hamlin.* The considerable talents of Close and Patinkin are not enough to save this mediocre ghost comedy. Close and Patinkin play a married couple whose lives are interrupted when the spirit of a flapper — murdered in the 1920s — inhabits the body of the former. It's nice to see Close let down her hair, but the flimsy screenplay just doesn't give her enough to do. The last film of the great Gordon. ★½

Maximum Overdrive

(1986, 97 min, US, Stephen King) *Emilio Estevez, Pat Hingle, Laura Harrington.* Author King stepped behind the camera for the first time to direct his story of rampaging trucks — and this is so bad it may be some time before he steps there again. Estevez, Hingle and Harrington are some of the people trapped in a cafe terrorized by those murderous 18-wheelers. (Remade in 1998 as *Trucks*.) ★ VHS: $9.99; DVD: $24.99

Maximum Risk

(1996, 101 min, US, Ringo Lam) *Jean-Claude Van Damme, Natasha Henstridge.* The Van Damme curse continues for former Hong Kong directors as ace action auteur Lam (*City on Fire*) is brought low by the Muscles from Brussels. Van Damme stars in this lame, brainless chase picture about a former French soldier who discovers he had a twin brother involved in some shady dealings with the Russian mob. Not even stylishly shot, it displays none of the talent or promise which probably got its director the job in the first place. ★ VHS: $9.99

May Fools

(1990, 108 min, France, Louis Malle) *Michel Piccoli, Miou-Miou, Dominique Blanc.* A mildly entertaining comedy of manners about the family squabbles of a *petit bourgeois* clan. Set against the backdrop of the 1968 student uprising in Paris (an event which toppled the government of Charles DeGaulle), the film follows the Vieusacs as they converge on their ancestral country mansion to pick through the possessions of a recently deceased matriarch. Piccoli stars as Milou, the hopelessly romantic father of the remaining kin, and the only family member who opposes the sale of the house and surrounding vineyard. Malle shows the family bickering as a microcosm of the era's social turmoil with Milou's idealism and *joie de vivre* representing the country's heart and soul. The results are mixed, but Piccoli's performance is pure gold. ★★ VHS: $19.99

Maybe. . . Maybe Not

(Der bewegte Mann)

(1996, 98 min, Germany, Sonke Wertman) *Til Schweiger, Katja Reimann, Joachim Krol.* This slick sex comedy follows the frenzied antics of Axel, a hunky, womanizing young man who, after burning all of his heterosexual bridges, moves in with Norbert, a gay man who quickly falls in (one-sided) love with his new roomie. The comedy rests on the confusion Axel creates by his friendship with Norbert and his gay friends — a perplexing situation for Axel's still interested girlfriend. A funny, enjoyable and non-demanding sex comedy. (German with English subtitles) ★★★ VHS: $89.99

Mayerling

(1935, 91 min, France, Anatole Litvak) *Charles Boyer, Danielle Darrieux.* The passion and agony of two doomed lovers is explored in this sumptuous true story which stars Boyer as the Crown Prince Rudolph of Austria who falls under the trance of the stunningly beautiful Darrieux. A shimmering romance that sadly, yet inevitably, leads to tragedy. (French with English subtitles) ★★★ VHS: $14.99

McCabe and Mrs. Miller

(1971, 121 min, US, Robert Altman) *Warren Beatty, Julie Christie, William Devane, Keith Carradine, Shelley Duvall.* One of Altman's best, *McCabe and Mrs. Miller* is a wonderfully poignant drama which explores ambition, greed, love and alienation, all within a decidedly quirky western setting. Beatty is the cocky McCabe, a naively optimistic gambler who builds a town and hires Christie to set up a high-class brothel. Featured is a haunting Leonard Cohen soundtrack. ★★★½ VHS: $14.99

The McGuffin

(1985, 95 min, GB, Colin Bucksey) *Charles Dance, Ritza Brown, Phyllis Logan, Anna Massey.* This tribute to Hitchcock's *Rear Window* derives its title from the phrase coined by the late mystery master. The story concerns a film critic whose nagging curiosity leads him to become

embroiled in a murder plot being perpetrated by his neighbors. The film lacks a cohesiveness and delivers few thrills. ★★

McHale's Navy

(1997, 108 min, US, Brian Spicer) *Tom Arnold, Tim Curry, Dean Stockwell, David Alan Grier, Bruce Campbell, French Stewart, Ernest Borgnine.* With *McHale's Navy*, the popular TV comedy about a group of conniving WWII sailors, there's yet another casualty in the long line of small-to-big screen transfers. Arnold, in a surprisingly amiable performance, takes over the title role, though it's wasted; as is a talented group of cohorts who aren't given anything to do. Grier's Ensign Parker only reminds us how funny Tim Conway was in the show. The writers of this seasick voyage have forgotten what made the TV show mindless fun — now it's only mindless. ★ VHS: $7.49

McVicar

(1980, 111 min, GB, Tom Clegg) *Roger Daltrey, Adam Faith, Ian Hendry.* The Who Films presents this portrayal of John McVicar (Daltrey), whose real-life escape from the high-security wing of a British prison led to his being dubbed "Public Enemy No.1" by the British press. This tough and tense prison drama won the critics' raves, but failed to find a crossover audience in the U.S. ★★★

Me and Him

(1989, 94 min, US, Doris Dorrie) *Griffin Dunne, Carey Lowell, Craig T. Nelson, Ellen Greene; Voice of Mark Linn-Baker.* An up-and-coming architect (Dunne) finds his life turned upside-down when he wakes up one morning and finds his penis starts talking to him. An ironically tame film despite its controversial nature. ★★ VHS: $79.99

Me, Myself & Irene

(2000, 116 min, US, Peter Farrelly & Bobby Farrelly) *Jim Carrey, Renee Zellweger, Robert Forster, Chris Cooper, Richard Jenkins.* Wherever the thin line exists between funny silliness and unfunny silliness, the Farrelly brothers have crossed it and then back again. The brothers' *There's Something about Mary* was absolute inspired goofiness; however, their *Me, Myself & Irene*, in which they reteam with *Dumb and Dumber* star Carrey, is most definitely humorless retread. Carrey is in moron mode as Charlie, a schizophrenic Rhode Island state trooper whose wife has left him with three black children. Getting no respect from his small town, a maniacal alter ego named Hank appears, getting Charlie into all sorts of trouble. Zellweger — who gets no fallout here the way Cameron Diaz did from *Mary* — plays Irene, a motorist who must be escorted by Charlie/Hank back to her native New York. This could have been riotous, but the filmmakers seem content to have Carrey mug endlessly. Yes, he does produce a couple laughs, but the long periods of time spent between these laughs only magnify an inferior script and aimless direction. ★★ VHS: $14.99; DVD: $22.99

Me Myself I

(2000, 104 min, Australia, Pip Karmel) *Rachel Griffiths, David Roberts, Sandy Winton.* Pamela (Griffiths) enters her 30s with a fair degree of professional success but wondering about the

high school sweetheart who got away. She literally runs into herself while crossing the street and finds she's in the alternate life she did not choose in her youth. Her travels down the rabbit hole of self-discovery are highlighted by sparkling portrayals describing circumstances at once extreme and recognizable. The peformances are uniformly intelligent and good-humored, and this contemporary fantasy is a witty mixture of most satisfactory entertainment with wry social commentary and the unsettling contemplation that our choices inform our identities for better *and* worse. These underlying themes are more resonant through this comedy than the suddenly serious turns of *Sliding Doors.* ★★★ VHS: $21.99; DVD: $29.99

The Mean Season

(1985, 106 min, US, Phillip Borsos) *Kurt Russell, Mariel Hemingway, Richard Jordan, Andy Garcia, Richard Masur, Joe Pantoliano.* Intriguing mystery thriller with Russell as a Miami newspaper reporter who becomes involved with a serial killer when the latter offers him an "exclusive" story. This puts both the reporter and his girlfriend (Hemingway) in danger. ★★½ DVD: $14.99

Mean Streets

(1973, 110 min, US, Martin Scorsese) *Harvey Keitel, Robert De Niro, Amy Robinson, David Proval.* Scorsese's early masterpiece, set in New York's Little Italy, features a tremendous cast headed by Keitel and De Niro. Keitel, an aspiring mobster, finds his Catholic background, his love for a young woman and his attachment to an irresponsible friend hindering his fledgling Mafia career. Well integrated into the story is a superlative '60s soundtrack. Scorsese's gritty portrayal of gangland life and his superlative photographic and editing techniques have made this bristling drama often imitated but rarely equalled. ★★★★ VHS: $14.99; DVD: $19.99

Meantime

(1983, 103 min, GB, Mike Leigh) *Tim Roth, Marion Bailey, Phil Daniels, Pam Ferris, Gary Oldman, Alfred Molina.* Among uniformly solid performances, Roth executes a subtle, compelling portrait of the achingly befuddled younger son of a contentious East End family, working class without work, without hope, without future. Daily petty frustrations and standard sibling rivalries are exacerbated by mind-numbing boredom and total lack of purpose. *Meantime* describes a brief observation of lives lived in abeyance, whole lifetimes spent in the no-man's land of a meantime with no end in sight. Director Leigh offers scattershot glimpses at familial antagonisms and societal prohibitions explored with more polish and in more depth in *Secrets and Lies;* yet, though more roughly cut, *Meantime* still offers flashes of revelation, in which a history is alluded to in a sidelong glance, a secret revealed in an unguarded word. ★★★ VHS: $14.99; DVD: $14.99

Meatballs

(1979, 94 min, Canada, Ivan Reitman) *Bill Murray, Harvey Atkin, Kate Lynch.* Murray's first hit comedy. Alternately funny and ridiculous, the film follows the comic exploits of counselor Murray at summer camp. (Followed by 3 sequels) ★★½ VHS: $9.99; DVD: $14.99

The Mechanic

(1972, 100 min, US, Michael Winner) *Charles Bronson, Jan-Michael Vincent, Keenan Wynn, Jill Ireland.* This average Bronson suspense/action film casts the stone-faced actor as an aging hit man who reluctantly takes on an apprentice (Vincent) in order to pass on his bloody craft. Bronson's confident muttering and quiet strength make his cookie-cutter character more interesting than it ought to be, which keeps the viewer's attention riveted to his performance and diverts it from Vincent's hyperactive hit man wannabe. Winner is also able to sustain a sufficient level of tension throughout the film's slow points, ending the movie with a literal bang and a surprise which will satisfy even the most charitable viewer's thirst for revenge. ★★½ VHS: $14.99

Medicine Man

(1992, 104 min, US, John McTiernan) *Sean Connery, Lorraine Bracco, Jose Wilker.* Director McTiernan sets out to save the Venezuelan rain forest, but after this mess, he'll be lucky to salvage his career. Connery, looking great in ponytail, plays an eccentric botanist who retreats into the jungle and discovers the cure for cancer. Enter Bracco, Brooklyn scientist, who's been sent to find him. There, they exchange barbs, lose the cancer cure, befriend the natives, battle greedy land developers destroying the forests and fall in love. Sad to say, even Connery's ever-commanding presence isn't enough to make this worthwhile. Though the story has a good premise, *Medicine Man* is one doc whose license should be revoked. ★★ VHS: $9.99; DVD: $29.99

Mediterraneo

(1991, 92 min, Italy, Gabriele Salvatores) *Diego Abatantuono, Giuseppe Cederna.* Catering unashamedly to the saccharin-loving moviegoer, this winner of the Academy Award for Best Foreign-Language Film takes Hollywood's penchant for "feel good" movies, throws in some exotic locales and produces an entertaining but mindlessly unrealistic comedy-drama. Early in WWII, a bungling platoon of Italian military misfits become stranded on a beautiful Greek island. Cut off from the war, this motley assort-ment of Italian stereotypes find themselves not in battle, but in an idyllic land. Greek-Italian relations have never been closer than in this "cultural fantasy." (Italian with English subtitles) ★★½

Medium Cool

(1969, 110 min, US, Haskell Wexler) *Robert Forster, Verna Bloom, Peter Bonerz, Marianna Hill, Peter Boyle.* Acclaimed cinematographer Wexler directed this fascinating political drama set against the turbulent backdrop of the 1968 Chicago Democratic Convention. A TV news cameraman (Forster) finds that the dispassion by which he covers his news stories is beginning to be the way he deals with his personal life. A unique blend of fictionalized narrative juxtaposed with the real world. ★★★★ VHS: $14.99

Meet Joe Black

(1998, 180 min, US, Martin Brest) *Brad Pitt, Anthony Hopkins, Claire Forlani, Jake Weber, Marcia Gay Harden.* Death has angst, and really wants a break from it all. Maybe he'll use his free time to taste peanut butter, to smell perfume, even to find love (few people respond to Death's personals). So when a minor character who looks just like Brad Pitt dies, Death opportunistically takes his body, names it Joe, and proceeds to use those handsome features to woo a rich woman (Forlani), learn about peanut butter (possible sequel: *Death Needs a Zagat's*), and putter around Hopkins' estate. This, in essence, is what happens in this overly long, slick, self-important remake of the 1934 classic *Death Takes a Holiday*. Frustratingly, there's a good 110-minute movie in here somewhere. At least the cast looks great. Hopkins does his best in a thankless role as Death's chaperone. ★★ VHS: $14.99; DVD: $24.99

Meet John Doe

(1941, 123 min, US, Frank Capra) *Barbara Stanwyck, Gary Cooper, Edward Arnold, Walter Brennan, James Gleason.* Capra's social drama stars Stanwyck as a newspaper reporter who turns hayseed drifter Cooper into a national hero. Arnold offers his usual strong support as a corrupt politician benefitting from Stanwyck's mock grassroots campaign. Capra offers his usual "common man vs. the corporate mindset" in a most capable setting, and the two stars certainly help. ★★★ VHS: $9.99; DVD: $19.99

Meet Me in St. Louis

(1944, 114 min, US, Vincente Minnelli) *Judy Garland, Mary Astor, Leon Ames, Margaret O'Brien, Marjorie Main, June Lockhart.* Garland had one of her biggest hits with this charmingly old-fashioned, sentimental musical — a loving reminiscence of turn-of-the-century family life. Astor and Ames are Judy's parents, and little O'Brien as her sister demonstrates rare and extraordinary emotion for a five-year-old. Judy sings "The Trolley Song" and "Have Yourself a Merry Little Christmas." ★★★★ VHS: $14.99

Meet the Feebles

(1992, 92 min, New Zealand, Peter Jackson) If you've ever wondered what becomes of Muppets when they go bad, then this determinedly disgusting (but unfunny) comedy reveals all. Marketed as "one of the sickest movies ever made," this drug, sex and bodily fluid-immersed backstage tale includes such characters as lovelorn Heidi Hippo (a big-titted serial-killing Miss Piggy); a drug-addicted, knife-throwing frog; a promiscuous bunny who contracts AIDS; a fey gay fox who belts out a musical number called "Sodomy"; and many other animal grotesques. A film to offend just about everyone which wallows in its own distastefulness. ★

Meet the Parents

(2000, 108 min, US, Jay Roach) *Robert De Niro, Ben Stiller, Blythe Danner, Teri Polo, James Rebhorn, Jon Abrahams, Owen Wilson.* Greg Focker (Stiller) certainly has his work cut out for him. Not only does he have to deal with that name, but he's on his way to meet the parents of his intended fiancée Pam (Polo). He wants to ask permission for Pam's hand in marriage from her strict dad, and everything has to go right. It's to our enjoyment that nothing goes right for Greg, and the worse things get for him, the funnier things get for us. Combining some nifty one-liners with uproarious sight gags, *Meet the Parents* once again demonstrates (after *Analyze This*) the golden comic talents of De Niro, here at his gruffest comic best as Jack, Pam's doting father. Director Roach basically brings the same anarchic comic sensibility he brought to *Austin Powers*, though the film rarely approaches the nastier comic regions which could have set it apart. Stiller is a terrific foil for all this madness, and he and the hilarious De Niro have great chemistry in all their verbal sparrings and physical schtick. ★★★ VHS: $22.99; DVD: $26.99

Meet Wally Sparks

(1997, 105 min, US, Peter Baldwin) *Rodney Dangerfield, Debi Mazar, Cindy Williams, Burt Reynolds, David Ogden Stiers.* Igniting very few comic sparks, this scattershot comedy has Dangerfield as a controversial TV talk show host who likes to push the limits of FCC regulations. When threatened with cancellation, he sets out to interview the conservative Governor of Georgia (Stiers) and winds up being a most unwelcome house guest. In this updated *The Man Who Came to Dinner*, Dangerfield can't overcome the stilted material and general foolishness, even if every other word out of his mouth is a double entendre. ★★ VHS: $6.99; DVD: $24.99

Meet Joe Black

Guy Pearce in *Memento*

Meeting Venus

(1991, 124 min, US/GB, István Szabó) *Glenn Close, Niels Arestrup, Erland Josephson.* Hungarian director Szabó, highly acclaimed for his German trilogy of human nature (*Colonel Redl*, the Academy Award–winning *Mephisto* and *Hanussen*), changes his tune with this romantic drama about the efforts of a world-renowned conductor (Arestrup) to mount a multinational production of Wagner's "Tannhauser" while maintaining an amorous affair with his temperamental diva (Close). While there are a few great moments of tenderness and passion between the leads, Close's character is otherwise wooden and the dubbing of her operatic performances (actually performed by Kiri Te Kanawa) is obvious. ★★½ VHS: $19.99

Meetings with Remarkable Men

(1979, 107 min, GB, Peter Brook) *Terence Stamp, Dragan Maksimovic.* The astounding tale of G.I. Gurdjieff, a man driven by a quest for knowledge and the answers to the meaning of existence. Beautifully photographed on location in the mountains of Afghanistan. An illuminating vision. ★★★ VHS: $69.99

Mein Kampf

(1961, 117 min, Sweden, Tore Sjoberg) The rise and fall of Hitler and Nazi Germany is graphically detailed in this powerful documentary. Unusually restrained, the film relies less on sermonizing and allows the images, culled from newsreels and from the extensive footage shot by the Nazis, to speak for themselves. An effective historical foray into the nature of evil, *Mein Kampf* is an invaluable primer for those interested in World War II. ★★★ VHS: $39.99

Melvin and Howard

(1980, 95 min, US, Jonathan Demme) *Paul Le Mat, Jason Robards, Mary Steenburgen, Jack Kehoe, Pamela Reed, Dabney Coleman.* A "slice of life" film that looks so spontaneous it borders on voyeurism. A sweet-natured study of Melvin Dummar, who claimed to have given a ride to Howard Hughes one night; later he's mentioned as one of Hughes' heirs for his effort. Le Mat

gives a sturdy performance as Melvin, and Steenburgen won an Oscar as his mostly estranged wife. Robards is Howard Hughes. (Letterboxed) ★★★★ VHS: $14.99; DVD: $24.99

Memento

(2000, 116 min, US, Christopher Nolan) *Guy Pearce, Carrie-Anne Moss, Joe Pantoliano, Stephen Tobolowsky.* If you chance to meet Leonard Shelby (Pearce), a wiry, intense man sporting tattoos all over his body, he'll probably tell you about his "condition." In fact, you can count on it. Shelby suffers from short-term memory loss. Within minutes, he'll forget where he is, how he got there, or exactly what it is he's doing. Shelby may have a problem with memory, but anyone lucky enough to see this lean, inventive noir won't soon forget one of the most fascinating experiments with narrative since *Pulp Fiction*. Pearce gives a tough, supple performance as Shelby, who has gathered enough pieces of the puzzle to determine the identity of the man who killed his wife. He's taking care of the situation himself. But in snippets of drama that last about as long as Shelby's own memory, the film flashes back – in near-literal reverse – to track the investigation of this amnemonic sleuth, who may or may not have fingered the wrong man. Writer-director Nolan delights in the gimmickry of this sleight of hand, but truth be known, the journey and outcome of this mystery could have stood on its own (one or two contrivances notwithstanding). As is, however, it's an edgy, hypnotic puzzle – no smoke and mirrors, here. ★★★½ VHS: $102.99; DVD: $26.99

Memoirs of an Invisible Man

(1992, 95 min, US, John Carpenter) *Chevy Chase, Sam Neill, Daryl Hannah, Michael McKean.* You'd think Hollywood would have learned by now. There hasn't been a really good "invisible man" movie since the original Claude Rains thriller in 1933. Chase stars as a San Francisco businessman who falls asleep during a business meeting and thanks to a neighboring nuclear fusion accident, wakes up invisible. Some good special effects and visual humor help hide a transparent plot, though director Carpenter seems more

interested in playing politics than creating a definitive "invisible" comedy. ★½ VHS: $9.99

Memories of Me

(1988, 105 min, US, Henry Winkler) *Alan King, Billy Crystal, JoBeth Williams.* King's flamboyant performance highlights this pleasant comedy-drama about a heart surgeon (Crystal) who tries to mend the severed relationship with his father (King). ★★★ VHS: $9.99

Memories of Underdevelopment

(1968, 97 min, Cuba, Tomás Gutiérrez Alea) *Sergio Corrieri, Daisy Granados.* The first film from post-revolutionary Cuba to be released in the United States, this wise and fascinating tale of a man finding himself a stranger in his own land was produced by the Cuban Film Institute, but does not contain the doctrinal politicking one would expect from a film sponsored by a young Communist country. The story, set in 1961, revolves around a young man from a bourgeois Europeanized family who, instead of fleeing to Miami with the rest of his family, decides to stay and come to terms with the revolution. Wanting to adapt to the new society, the man, however, finds himself incapable of shedding his bad capitalist habits and turning over a new socialist leaf. (Spanish with English subtitles) ★★★½ VHS: $59.99

Memphis Belle

(1990, 101 min, GB, Michael Caton-Jones) *Matthew Modine, Eric Stoltz, Harry Connick, Jr., Tate Donovan, D.B. Sweeney, Billy Zane, Sean Astin, David Strathairn, John Lithgow, Jane Horrocks.* Suggested by the real-life experiences of the crew of the WWII B-17 fighter-bomber *Memphis Belle*, and, in part, on the 1944 documentary of the same name, this old-fashioned war film manages to entertain in spite of all the clichés. A good cast is featured as each crew member is introduced before the plane's historic bombing raid. ★★½ VHS: $9.99; DVD: $19.99

Men...

(1985, 99 min, Germany, Doris Dorrie) *Heiner Lauterbach, Uwe Ochsenknecht.* A shrewdly comic satire about an advertising man who loses his wife to a surly young bohemian. In order to discover where he went wrong, he moves in with his wife's new beau (unbeknownst to her) and thus sets the stage for this scintillating behavioral comedy. The lively script is loaded with outrageous comic asides and intelligent wit. (German with English subtitles) ★★★½ VHS: $29.99

The Men

(1950, 85 min, US, Fred Zinnemann) *Marlon Brando, Teresa Wright, Jack Webb, Everett Sloane, Richard Erdman.* Brando's screen presence is immediately evident in this, his debut film performance. He's a WWII vet battling the consequences of a wartime injury. Solid acting all around. ★★★½ VHS: $19.99

Men Don't Leave

(1990, 113 min, US, Paul Brickman) *Jessica Lange, Arliss Howard, Joan Cusack, Chris O'Donnell, Charlie Korsmo, Tom Mason, Kathy Bates.* After her husband's accidental death, suburban mother Lange is forced to sell her home and, with her two sons (O'Donnell, Mason), she moves to Baltimore for a better-paying job. All three endure their own adjustment to the unfamiliar

M

urban environment, via a parade of teenaged video pirates, elementary school rip-off artists, bitchy gourmet shop owners, one very strange nurse (a quirky charcterization by Cusack) and a "professional musician" (Howard). Brickman's direction seems a bit diffuse early on, but tightens up as the story progresses to a satisfying, believable conclusion. Life does go on, with or without a fairy-tale white knight. (Based on the French film *La Vie Continue*) ★★★ VHS: $19.99

Men in Black

(1997, 95 min, US, Barry Sonnenfeld) *Tommy Lee Jones, Will Smith, Linda Fiorentino, Vincent D'Onofrio, Rip Torn.* In *Independence Day*, Smith gallantly saves Earth from hordes of invading aliens. Nothing he did in *ID4*, however, could have prepared Smith for the sheer fun and exhilaration awaiting him, Jones and especially the viewer in this uproariously entertaining sci-fi comedy. Smith and Jones play government agents whose task it is is to monitor illegal aliens — as in the extraterrestrial kind. When a nasty alien assassin arrives to murder an alien dignitary living incognito in New York, our men in black hunt him down like the pesky cockroach he is. Sonnenfeld crams lots of humor, excitement and terrific effects into the film's efficiently brisk 95-minute running time. *MIB* is funny, hip and a technical wonder. ★★★½ VHS: $14.99; DVD: $19.99

Men of Honor

(2000, 128 min, US, George Tillman, Jr.) *Robert De Niro, Cuba Gooding, Jr., Charlize Theron, Aunjanue Ellis, Hal Holbrook, Michael Rapaport, Powers Boothe.* Based on the heroic life of Carl Brashear, the Navy's first African-American master chief diver, *Men of Honor* breaks no new ground in the military drama genre, but does offer a sincere, honorable account of one man's determination in pursuing his dreams in the face of racial intolerance. Gooding is well cast as Brashear, the son of a Kentucky sharecropper, who is accepted to the Navy's diving school. As the first black student enrolled there, he becomes the victim of rampant discrimination. On his case the most is his alcoholic instructor, Billy Sunday (De Niro), who plants a series of obstacles in the young man's path. More inspiring than dramatic, the story follows Brashear's struggle to overcome a stacked deck. Gooding and De Niro are evenly matched, each making the most of a by-the-books screenplay that nevertheless stirs the emotions. ★★★ VHS: $14.99; DVD: $29.99

Men of Respect

(1991, 113 min, US, William Reilly) *John Turturro, Katherine Borowitz, Peter Boyle, Rod Steiger.* Reilly's directorial debut is this stunning take on Shakespeare's "Macbeth," a frenzied gangland tragedy about the bloody rise and fall of a self-destructive and ambitious young man. The film is uneven at times, but has a visceral intensity that should be savored. Turturro is possessed in the lead role and his real-life wife, Borowitz, is alluringly deadly as the Lady Macbeth character. ★★½ VHS: $11.99

The Men Who Tread on the Tiger's Tail

(1945, 60 min, Japan, Akira Kurosawa) *Denjiro Okochi, Susumu Fujita, Masayuki Mori, Suho Nishina.* Based on a traditional Kabuki theatre piece, this early Kurosawa fable in set in late 12th-century feudal Japan. Having led the Genji Army to victory in battle, Yoshitsune returns home only to incur the wrath of his jealous Shogun brother. With a price on his head, Yoshitsune and his faithful bodyguard/monk Benkei engage a group of warriors to help Yoshitune regain his lordly stature. Thus begins Kurosawa's short (one-hour) though engaging film which follows Yoshitsune's trek across the stylized Japanese countryside to return to his city, now under guard. But there are no battles here. Kurosawa revels in the power of the spoken word, eschewing action for the dynamics of personal conflict, and his usage of editing and sound substitutes for swordplay. Simplistic in its storytelling, *Men* produces a tension and lyricism through cunning and myth. Okochi is superb as the mentor-like Benkei. (Japanese with English subtitles) ★★★ VHS: $39.99

Men with Guns

(1998, 128 min, US, John Sayles) *Federico Luppi, Dan Riviera Gonzales, Damian Delgado, Damian Alcazar, Tania Cruz, Mandy Patinkin, Kathryn Grody.* Chameleon-like independent maverick Sayles goes happily against the grain again with this haunting tale of political rumbles in the jungle. Shot almost entirely in Spanish and Indian dialects, this unsettling fable centers on an aging, widowed physician who decides in the twilight of his life to take a journey into the jungles of his anonymous Latin American country to find a group of medical students he once taught. The students were sent as "ambassadors of health" to remote Indian villages, but as the film unfolds, the doctor discovers his legacy has become more frightening than he could ever imagine. As the doctor who discovers the heart of darkness that lies beyond the comfortable confines of his city practice, Luppi is exceptional as Dr. Fuentes — another in a long line of fascinatingly noble Sayles figures. (English and Spanish and Indian dialects with English subtitles) ★★★½ VHS: $102.99

The Men's Club

(1986, 100 min, US, Peter Medak) *Roy Scheider, Treat Williams, Frank Langella, Harvey Keitel, Jennifer Jason Leigh, Richard Jordan, Stockard Channing, Craig Wasson, Ann Wedgeworth.* A group of middle-aged men gather for an evening to discuss their lives, and end up at a whorehouse. Mediocre version of Leonard Michael's novel. Even a high-profile cast can't help matters. ★

Menace II Society

(1993, 90 min, US, Allen & Albert Hughes) *Tyrin Turner, Larenz Tate, Jada Pinket, Samuel L. Jackson, Charles Dutton, Bill Duke.* A gripping and unapologetic view of life on the mean streets of L.A.'s Compton. The film centers on Caine, an archetypal, disenfranchised '90s urban youth who follows the street's kill-or-be-killed code with an eerily dispassionate degree of stoicism — it all seems to be beyond his scope of caring, or as his homey O-Dog puts it, "I'm America's nightmare: young, black and I don't give a fuck." Featuring superb ensemble acting and a seamless visual acumen, the film may indeed prove frightening to some as it gives witness to the brutality which shapes young lives without so much as a hint of judgment: There are no heroes or villains in this story, just average peo-

ple living average lives. A scary thought, perhaps, but it is what gives the film its brilliance. ★★★★ VHS: $14.99; DVD: $19.99

Ménage

(1986, 84 min, France, Bertrand Blier) *Gérard Depardieu, Miou-Miou, Michel Blanc.* Family values are turned inside-out in this outrageously wacky sexual farce that takes demonic delight in its vulgarity, misogyny and demented sexual mores. Life changes abruptly for the feuding, poverty striken couple Antoine (Blanc) and his wife Monique (Miou-Miou) after they meet the bombastic and dangerously exciting Bob (Depardieu), who showers them with money and promises of the good life — made possible by inviting them to his nightly burglary raids of rich homes. But soon the burly Bob falls passionately in love with, no, not the sexy Monique, but the bald, mousy and frantically tight-lipped Antoine! Watching Depardieu wax poetic and become all girlish in front of the bewildered Antoine is a hilariously priceless moment in French cinema. (French with English subtitles) ★★★½

Mephisto

(1981, 135 min, West Germany, István Szabó) *Klaus Maria Brandauer, Krystyna Janda.* A riveting portrait of the artist as opportunist. Brandauer turns in a breathtaking performance as an actor whose burning ambition leads him to compromise his artistry, relationships and well-being. Director Szabó captures the grand spectacle and subtle nuances of a man obsessed. (German with English subtitles) ★★★½ VHS: $14.99; DVD: $19.99

The Mephisto Waltz

(1971, 108 min, US, Paul Wendkos) *Alan Alda, Curt Jurgens, Jacqueline Bisset, Barbara Perkins.* Effective satanic chiller with Alda as a journalist who experiences changes after interviewing dying musician Jurgens. ★★★ VHS: $59.99

The Merchant of Four Seasons

(1972, 88 min, Germany, Rainer Werner Fassbinder) *Hans Hirschmuller, Irm Hermann, Hanna Schygulla.* Fassbinder's first widely recognized film concerns the life struggle of Hans: a born loser who is rejected by his bourgeois family, spurned by his "one true love," married to an unfaithful wife, cheated by his friends and reduced to peddling fruit to sustain a meager existence. A superb mixture of black humor, melodrama and satire with an unforgettable and haunting ending. (German with English subtitles) ★★★★ VHS: $19.99

Mercury Rising

(1998, 112 min, US, Brian Grazer) *Bruce Willis, Alec Baldwin, Miko Hughes, Chi McBride, Kim Dickens.* The only thing rising during this flick should be the audience's contempt for the Hollywood junk mill. Willis stars as grizzled FBI agent Art Jeffries, who has been relegated to a future of deskwork. When the "most sophisticated code the world has ever known" is broken by a prepubescent crossword savant, it's up to Art to rescue the boy and protect the country from its own worst enemy: the NSA (that's National Security Agency for you neophytes). Enter Baldwin as a super badass agent. The clunky script is riddled with hyperbolic technobabble, all of which serves to make this all the less enjoyable. File under: Cheesy

Espionage Thriller with Saccharine Human Interest Bent. ★½ VHS: $9.99; DVD: $34.99

Mere Jeevan Saathi
(My Life Partner)

(1965, 126 min, India, Ravee Nagaich) Although India produces hundreds of films each year, the very few that ever reach our shores are almost exclusively limited to the works of Satyajit Ray. And while the vast majority of these releases are produced solely for domestic viewing, there are many that can be enjoyed by an international audience. *Mere Jeevan Saathi,* an exuberant romance/comedy/musical which details a businessman's sudden rise and fall, is a good example of modern Indian filmmaking. (Hindi with English subtitles) ★★★

Merlin

(1998, 140 min, US, Steve Barron) *Sam Neill, Miranda Richardson, Isabella Rossellini, Helena Bonham Carter, John Gielgud, Rutger Hauer, Martin Short.* An excellent made-for-TV movie, *Merlin* has strong performances, a fast pace, nifty special effects, and has style to spare. As directed by veteran music video helmer Barron, it never rests for a second. Neill is outstanding as Merlin, playing him with sly wit. All the players here — even comic Short — play it straight, but not *too* seriously; allowing for the perfect tone of a potentially goofy tale made compelling yet leavened with knowing humor. Purists may quibble, but *Merlin* takes fewer liberties than most adaptations, and provides the sweep and magic that most in the genre lack. ★★★½ VHS: $14.99; DVD: $24.99

Mermaids

(1990, 115 min, US, Richard Benjamin) *Cher, Winona Ryder, Bob Hoskins, Christina Ricci, Michael Schoeffling, Jan Miner.* A pair of winning performances from Cher and Ryder punctuate this pleasantly quirky coming-of-age comedy-drama about a thoroughly unconventional single mother and her abundantly confused and zealously pious teenage daughter. Along with baby sister Kate (Ricci), they uproot and move to a small New England town, circa 1963, where neighbors duly observe that they are not the typical nuclear family. Ryder's saturnine portrayal of adolescence is quickly becoming a thing of legend and her ability to deliver sullen, dead-pan one-liners transforms *Mermaids* from potentially gooey family melodrama to often hilarious, sometimes heartwarming comedy. ★★★ VHS: $9.99; DVD: $19.99

Merrill's Marauders

(1962, 98 min, US, Samuel Fuller) *Jeff Chandler, Ty Hardin, Peter Brown, Andrew Duggan, Will Hutchins.* Director Fuller delivers another solid WWII actioner set in the Pacific Theatre. Chandler leads a war-weary battalion in the Burmese jungle on an arduous trek through hostile terrain populated by deadly, well-concealed Japanese troops. Based on the actual exploits of Brigadier General Frank D. Merrill. ★★★ VHS: $9.99

Merry Christmas, Mr. Lawrence

(1983, 122 min, GB/Japan, Nagisa Oshima) *Tom Conti, David Bowie, Ryuichi Sakamoto, Takeshi, Jack Thompson.* Oshima's mesmerizing drama studies the conflicting cultures of East and West, which surface within the confines of a WWII POW camp. Bowie is a captured New Zealander whose stiff-lipped bravery and rebellious nature perplex his Japanese guards and intrigue the compound's commanding officer, who is gravely smitten by Bowie's allure. (Filmed in English) ★★★ VHS: $9.99

A Merry War

(1998, 101 min, GB, Robert Bierman) *Richard E. Grant, Helena Bonham Carter.* Grant and Bonham Carter sparkle in this wry and witty tale of a promising young copywriter who spurns promotion to write poetry. Seeking a garret and his muse, Gordon Comstock (Grant) quits his advertising agency and scoffs at bourgeoise convention to wrestle with the creative process. A precipitous financial descent accompanies a raging ennui. Comstock's friends — especially girlfriend Rosemary (Bonham Carter) — attempt to keep him afloat as he seeks redemption in poverty. Based on George Orwell's "Keep the Aspidistra Flying," the film is intelligent and urbane while skewering the infinite layers of the British class system. ★★★ VHS: $14.99; DVD: $29.99

The Merry Widow

(1934, 99 min, US, Ernst Lubitsch) *Maurice Chevalier, Jeanette MacDonald, Una Merkel, Edward Everett Horton.* The great Lubitsch had the right "touch" with this delightfully sophisticated, tongue-in-cheek adaptation of the Franz Lehar operetta. Chevalier is at his best as the dashing nobleman who tries to woo a rich widow (MacDonald) from Paris to her homeland where the bankrupt country is in desperate need of her funds. ★★★½ VHS: $19.99

Mesmer

(1994, 107 min, GB, Roger Spottiswoode) *Alan Rickman, Amanda Ooms.* Rickman is certainly in his element as Franz Anton Mesmer, 18th-century charlatan/saint, part visionary, part revival tent preacher. His search for harmony and balance through the conscious utilization of "animal magnetism" seems a beacon of scientific sanity against the tortures that masquerade as the medicine of his age. His encounter with a young, blind pianist (Ooms) reveals the nobler motivations of his egomania, and speaks against a formalized society whose myriad hysterias roil just beneath the surface. The film is an elegant expression of human anguish, incomparably scripted by Dennis Potter, and delivered with brutal sensitivity by director Spottiswoode. ★★★½ VHS: $24.99; DVD: $24.99

Message in a Bottle

(1999, 132 min, US, Luis Mandoki) *Kevin Costner, Robin Wright Penn, Paul Newman, John Savage, Illeana Douglas, Robbie Coltrane.* After the lambasting both *Waterworld* and *The Postman* took, you'd think Costner wouldn't go near water or have anything to do with the mail for awhile. But he's right back on the horse with this glossy, muddled romantic drama which isn't quite as bad as it could have been. Chicago reporter Wright Penn finds a love letter in a bottle and is intrigued to the point that she tries to track down its author. It turns out to be North Carolina widower and boatmaker Costner. She heads there and promptly falls in love. The premise doesn't quite add up, but the cast seems not to care as they attack this with sincerity. As romantic drama, most of this works; but as credible storytelling, it doesn't hit

the right notes. (VHS available letterboxed or pan & scan) ★★½ VHS: $19.99; DVD: $19.99

The Messenger: The Story of Joan of Arc

(1999, 158 min, France, Luc Besson) *Milla Jovovich, John Malkovich, Faye Dunaway, Dustin Hoffman, Tcheky Karyo.* Fresh from saving the universe in *The Fifth Element,* director Besson and actor Jovovich here reunite to merely save France. Jovovich is creditable as Joan, Maid of Orleans, spritely and fired with youthful charisma. Her voices direct her to battle the brutal English invaders as they attempt to wrest control of a disunited Gaulle from the hands of the disaffected Dauphin (Malkovich). Her heavenly communications should have given her better information about the political theatre in which she is only a pawn. The film attempts to sustain some discussion of religious belief and the nature of conscience, but is too disjointed and unfocused in its efforts to contemporize the story for a modern audience. ★★ VHS: $14.99; DVD: $27.99

Meteor

(1979, 105 min, US, Ronald Neame) *Sean Connery, Natalie Wood, Henry Fonda, Brian Keith, Karl Malden.* The worst special effects you've ever seen highlight this strangely intriguing disaster film, one of the last in the line of buildings, ships, killer quakes and other forces of nature. Connery brings unexpected humor to this mishmash as a scientist who has six days to prevent a giant meteor from destroying most of Earth. Keith, as Connery's Soviet counterpart, also rises above the script and direction to give a funny performance. ★★ DVD: $24.99

Meteor Man

(1993, 100 min, US, Robert Townsend) *Robert Townsend, Marla Gibbs, Eddie Griffin, Robert Guillaume, James Earl Jones, Don Cheadle, Sinbad.* Absolute silliness from actor-director Townsend, who stars as a young urban idealist who believes in a better life for his ghetto community. Opportunity comes knocking one day when he is hit by a meteor and given the supernatural powers needed to rid his neighborhood of drug dealers. Hokey beyond reckoning, the film is not without its endearing moments and occasionally Townsend's comic ability shines through. ★★ VHS: $14.99

Metro

(1997, 117 min, US, Thomas Carter) *Eddie Murphy, Michael Rapaport, Michael Wincott.* At the heart of this Murphy action/comedy is a terrific car chase down the precarious streets of San Francisco. Logic and crashed cars alike are tossed through the air like matchbox toys in this hyperkinetic, over-the-top piece of Hollywood stunt craftsmanship. But as *Metro* zooms along, it feels more like the film was written "around" this spectacular chase scene. Murphy plays a police hostage negotiator who runs afoul of a vicious killer after a botched robbery. Ultimately, *Metro* is a by-the-numbers police thriller. Murphy is in good form, but after *The Nutty Professor,* this is a step backwards. ★★ VHS: $14.99; DVD: $29.99

M

Metroland

(1997, 102 min, GB, Philip Saville) *Christian Bale, Emily Watson, Lee Ross, Elsa Zylberstein.* Chris (Bale) used to be a dreamer, an artist, a Parisian even, but after meeting Marion (Watson) he moved back to England in the '70s to settle down. Seemingly happy, he reexamines all the major decisions in his life when his old punk friend (Ross) pays him a visit. Did he really throw away the love of his life (Zylberstein) in Paris, or is the more pragmatic Marion his soulmate? Remarkably, even in delving into the sexual affairs of all four characters, *Metroland* remains cold and distant, a mistake when dealing with affairs of the heart. Bale has tremendous presence, and Watson plays a difficult role with charm. But the sexual liberation and the ensuing sexual boredom are both explored with the same unenthusiastic calculation. ★★ VHS: $19.99; DVD: $24.99

Metropolis

(1926, 120 min, Germany, Fritz Lang) *Brigitte Helm, Alfred Abel.* Lang's spectacularly stunning vision of a world ruled by machines and controlled by Big Brother is one of the most important works to emerge from the German Expressionist Film Movement in the 1920s. Its continued popular appeal lies in the fact that so many of Lang's images of future society still capture our imagination. Picture quality is very good (remastered from a 35mm print), and is accompanied by a classical music soundtrack. ★★★★

Metropolitan

(1990, 108 min, US, Whit Stillman) *Edward Clements, Carolyn Farina, Christopher Eigeman, Taylor Nichols.* A cast of unknowns breathes life into first-time writer-director Stillman's Oscar nominated screenplay about a preppie "divorce orphan," from the less-than-fashionable Upper West Side, who falls in with the right crowd for a season of meaningless social events. He mocks their empty lifestyle with a refreshing no-holds-barred honesty, which, while not comedic in content, transforms *Metropolitan* into hilarious social satire. ★★★½ VHS: $19.99

Mexican Bus Ride

(1951, 73 min, Mexico, Luis Buñuel) *Lilia Prado, Esteban Marquez.* The misadventures of an innocent young man who is sent to the mountains to fetch the family lawyer to his dying mother is delightfully brought to the screen by the always mischievous, irreverent and surrealistic Buñuel. (aka: *Ascent to Heaven*) ★★★

Mi Vida Loca (My Crazy Life)

(1994, 92 min, US, Allison Anders) *Angel Aviles, Seidy Lopez, Nelida Lopez.* Writer-director Anders' follow-up to her hit art-house film *Gas Food Lodging* is an insightful look into the lives of young Latino gangsters living in Echo Park, Los Angeles. The film is divided into three main segments that intertwine to tell the story of a gangland community from the perspective of the main characters. Differing from the usual gang picture in that it is told from a primarily female vantage point, *Mi Vida Loca* centers around two best friends, Sad Girl and Mousey, and the man they both love, Ernesto. The well-

written script emotionally portrays the struggle of gangland females to raise children in a place where most fathers are dead or in jail for adulthood. It's all done with well-written dialogue, an interesting story and excellent acting. ★★★★ VHS: $19.99

Miami Blues

(1990, 97 min, US, George Armitage) *Fred Ward, Alec Baldwin, Jennifer Jason Leigh, Nora Dunn.* Baldwin, sporting a crew cut and oftentimes a topless torso, stars in this offbeat, funny and wildly enjoyable comedy-thriller as a recently paroled killer and pathological liar who poses as a cop to save crime victims before he himself rips them off. He soon meets a gullible young prostitute, Leigh, and together they play house, with Leigh cooking and cleaning and Baldwin leaving in the morning for his day of crime. Ward also stars as the slovenly cop, who, after losing his gun and false teeth to Baldwin, is determined to bring him to justice. All have fun with their roles, but Leigh is almost too good for the film, bringing heartbreaking depth in an unusually moving performance. ★★★½

Miami Rhapsody

(1995, 95 min, US, David Frankel) *Sarah Jessica Parker, Mia Farrow, Antonio Banderas, Paul Mazursky, Kevin Pollak, Jeremy Piven.* Farrow appears in this fluffy romantic comedy which is about as close to a Woody Allen film as one can get without having Allen's name on the credits. But that's not to suggest that *Miami Rhapsody* bears a resemblance either artistic or comical to the Woodman: This is most definitely "Woody Lite." Parker plays a twentysomething writer whose impending marriage opens her eyes to the failings of the relationships of those around her. These include her mother Farrow; father Mazursky; and brother Pollak. There are some amusing moments and one-liners to this *Rhapsody*, but the characters' and story's lack of development makes it all seem half-a-beat off. ★★½ VHS: $19.99; DVD: $29.99

Michael

(1996, 105 min, US, Nora Ephron) *John Travolta, William Hurt, Andie MacDowell, Robert Pastorelli, Bob Hoskins, Jean Stapleton, Teri Garr.* As if his otherworldly role in *Phenomenon* wasn't enough, Travolta now takes on the part of an angel — a wisecracking, crotch-scratching, barhopping one at that — in this sloppy romantic comedy. Three reporters for a supermarket tabloid respond to Iowa housewife Stapleton's letter about her angel houseguest Michael (Travolta). Low and behold, he's the real thing. As they set out to return to their Chicago offices with Michael in tow, all are affected in one way or another by their heavenly traveling companion. Travolta once again proves that he's such an engaging presence on-screen that he can rise above such drivel, and he alone is the saving grace of this inexplicable box office hit. ★★ VHS: $14.99; DVD: $19.99

Michael Collins

(1996, 127 min, Ireland/GB, Neil Jordan) *Liam Neeson, Aidan Quinn, Julia Roberts, Alan Rickman, Stephen Rea, Ian Hart, Charles Dance.* In his best performance since *Schindler's List*, Neeson plays another real-life character who overcomes odds to carve a niche for himself in

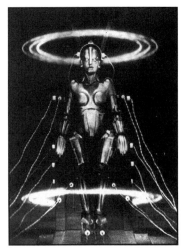

Metropolis

history. *Michael Collins* is the passionate, remarkably detailed story of the Irish revolutionary who sought to seek Ireland's independence from British rule. With the complex political issues of the formation of the Irish Republican Army at its core, the film traces the rise of Collins as a party official whose legend and determination led to brief peace and an Ireland which still exists today. An impressive achievement on all levels, *Michael Collins* is stirring as both history and cinema. (VHS available letterboxed or pan & scan) ★★★★ VHS: $14.99; DVD: $19.99

Mickey Blue Eyes

(1999, 102 min, US, Kelly Makin) *Hugh Grant, James Caan, Jeanne Tripplehorn, Burt Young, James Fox, Joe Viterelli.* Grant is as engaging as ever in this feather-lite comedy about Cockneys and mobsters. He plays Michael Felgate, the manager of a struggling New York auction house who's rushing into an engagement with the daughter he soons finds out, of a notable mafiaso (Caan, smug as ever). Tripplehorn plays the fiancée, who desperately wants to protect Michael from the ever-grasping clutches of her family. Complications ensue when the art world and the underworld collide. The movie has fun with the notion of what happens when someone refuses an offer they shouldn't refuse, and gives some familiar gangster-movie faces the opportunity to toy with their own tough-guy personas. Nothing monumental here, but an innocuous romp played by a likable cast. ★★½ VHS: $14.99; DVD: $19.99

Microcosmos

(1996, 75 min, France, Claude Nuridsany & Marie Perennou) Bugs! Those are the stars of this enthralling French nature production which takes an extremely up-close look at what lurks in the woods behind your house. But rather than going for a *Life on Earth*-style narrated documentary which explains the sex life of snails, *Microcosmos* simply shows it, with amplified sound effects and minimal musical accompaniment. The result is truly mesmerizing. The camerawork and patience put into the miniscule production are herculean in scale and the film is appropriate for all ages even though, yes, you do get to see that snail sex, very up close and personal. ★★★½ VHS: $14.99

Midaq Alley

(1995, 140 min, Mexico, Jorge Fons) *Ernesto Gómez Cruz, Salma Hayek, Bruno Bichir, Claudio Obregón.* This episodic drama, based on a novel by Naguib Mahfouz, delves into three different tales of mismatched lovers, family bitterness and betrayal in a small street in Mexico City. The first story is a startlingly gay-themed one. Mr. Ru (Cruz) is a restaurateur who has just come out, which causes strife with his macho son and frustrated wife. Meanwhile, his neighbor, Mr. Fidel (Obregón), pursues the sexy young Alma (Hayek), while her mother yearns for Fidel. Fans of odd couples in the cinema will enjoy this melodramatic mix of sex, longing and obsession. (Spanish with English subtitles) ★★★ VHS: $19.99; DVD: $19.99

Midnight

(1939, 94 min, US, Mitchell Leisen) *Claudette Colbert, Don Ameche, John Barrymore, Mary Astor.* "Every Cinderella has her midnight" says imposter Colbert, and in trying to escape hers a breezy, sophisticated romp is born. Cleverly written by Billy Wilder and Charles Brackett, this effervescent romantic comedy stars Colbert as a penniless showgirl newly arrived to Paris. She befriends cabbie Ameche, who soon falls for her. But true love must wait when Colbert is hired by baron Barrymore (in a spirited come-

Kevin Spacey evokes Southern charm in Clint Eastwood's *Midnight in the Garden of Good and Evil*

back performance) to impersonate a countess — it seems his wife Astor is involved in a romantic indiscretion with a playboy, and it's up to Colbert to come between them. Director Leisen sets a brisk pace, though the film's theme of mistaken identity and the screenplay's sexual innuendo is pure Wilder. Colbert, as usual, is a delight. ★★★★ VHS: $14.99

A Midnight Clear

(1992, 107 min, US, Keith Gordon) *Ethan Hawke, Peter Berg, Gary Sinise, Kevin Dillon, Frank Whaley, Arye Gross.* Gordon's second directorial feature is a vigorous and very polished antiwar drama, and a much more assured piece of filmmaking than his debut *The Chocolate War.* Set during the last months of WWII, the story traces the emotional toll taken on a group of weary, young G.I.s at the front line who come in contact with a group of German soldiers. The equally tired enemy soon makes clear their desire for surrender. As each side cautiously builds to a ceasefire, both armies enjoy a respite from the hell around them. But for how long? Gordon handles his young cast very well. ★★★½ VHS: $9.99

Midnight Cowboy

(1969, 113 min, US, John Schlesinger) *Dustin Hoffman, Jon Voight, Brenda Vaccaro, Sylvia Miles, John McGiver, Bob Balaban, Barnard Hughes.* No longer the shocking tale it was when first released, this classic slice of pop culture has evolved into a somewhat nostalgic reminder of the '60s mindset, capturing the naiveté and upheaval of a society enduring growing pains. Voight and Hoffman create a pair of legendary screen losers: Joe Buck, the aspiring stud-for-hire; and Ratso Rizzo, his rodent-like mentor. Winner of 3 Academy Awards, including Best Picture. ★★★★ VHS: $14.99; DVD: $19.99

Midnight Crossing

(1988, 104 min, US, Roger Holzberg) *Faye Dunaway, Daniel J. Travanti, Kim Cattrall, Ned Beatty.* Tedious thriller with Dunaway and Travanti as a husband and wife who are searching for buried loot he had stashed away years before. ★

Midnight Dancers

(1994, 100 min, The Philippines, Mel Chionglo) *Lawrence David, Gandong Cervantes, Alex Del Rosario, Soxy Topacio.* This eye-opening but over-the-top mess of melodramatic excess explores the tumultuous life and unconventional loves of "macho dancers" — male prostitutes who work as dancers and hustlers in Manila's gay bars. A more chaste and unrefined take on these young men than Lino Brocka's luridly watchable *Macho Dancers,* the tale begins when young country-bred Sonny (David) rejoins his family in Manila. He learns that his two brothers both earn a living dancing and prosti-

tuting themselves. Sonny becomes intrigued by the scene and begins to work there, ultimately beginning an affair with a sultry transvestite. The film's simple story lacks dramatic tension or focus; though despite the awkward handling of the many social themes it explores, the drama proves to be impassioned, sexy and involving. (Filipino with English subtitles) ★★½ VHS: $29.99; DVD: $29.99

Midnight Express

(1978, 121 min, US, Alan Parker) *Brad Davis, Randy Quaid, John Hurt, Bo Hopkins.* Based on the autobiography of Billy Hayes, this intense film explores the hellish years Hayes spent in a Turkish prison for drug smuggling. Violent, raw and powerful, *Midnight Express* works on both an emotional level as Hayes witnesses, experiences and fights back against the brutality of the prison staff, and as an exposé on corruption and examination of camaraderie. The film does contain one false note, however, as in real life Hayes was lovers with a fellow prisoner, but here he is politely brushed aside. Oscar-winning screenplay by Oliver Stone. Davis gives a remarkably complex performance as Hayes, and Hurt is outstanding as a drugged-out fellow prisoner. ★★★½ VHS: $19.99; DVD: $14.99

Midnight in the Garden of Good and Evil

(1997, 154 min, US, Clint Eastwood) *Kevin Spacey, John Cusack, Jack Thompson, Alison Eastwood, The Lady Chablis, Irma P. Hall, Jude Law, Dorothy Loudon.* With this ambitious though not entirely successful adaptation of John Berendt's based-on-fact best-seller, director Eastwood takes a walk on the wild side — Southern style. Cusack is John Kelso, a New York writer assigned to cover an exclusive society party in Savannah. Agendas change, however, when Jim Williams (Spacey), the party's host, is arrested that night for shooting his hustler boyfriend (Law). Was it self-defense or premeditated? Eastwood is able to convey the rhythms of Southern culture and attitudes with a leisurely tempo, though at 154 minutes the film is just too long. And there's a startling addition of a romantic interest for Kelso, which only contradicts the sexual tension between Kelso and Williams. But it's also an often fascinating and surprisingly funny tale, as mannered and charismatic as Williams himself. (Letterboxed VHS available for $19.99) ★★★ VHS: $14.99; DVD: $19.99

Midnight Run

(1988, 122 min, US, Martin Brest) *Robert De Niro, Charles Grodin, Yaphet Kotto, Dennis Farina, Joe Pantoliano.* De Niro stars as a modern-day bounty hunter who is hired to escort mob accountant Grodin from New York to Los Angeles to stand trial. What begins as a simple plane ride turns into a no-holds-barred cross-country free-for-all involving the FBI, the Mafia, hit men and rival bounty hunters. Highlighted by well-staged shootouts and chase scenes, and quite humorous and delightfully venomous sparring between the two stars. ★★★ VHS: $7.49

M

M

A Midsummer Night's Dream

(1935, 117 min, US, Max Reinhardt) *James Cagney, Mickey Rooney, Dick Powell, Olivia deHavilland, Joe E. Brown, Mickey Rooney.* Famed theatre director Reinhardt based this captivating version of Shakespeare's classic on his acclaimed stage production he made the year before. An all-star cast is featured, including Cagney (as Bottom) and Rooney, who steals the show as Puck. ★★★ VHS: $19.99

A Midsummer Night's Dream

(1968, 124 min, GB, Peter Hall) *Diana Rigg, David Warner, Ian Richardson, Judi Dench, Ian Holm.* Shakespeare goes Mod! The Royal Shakespeare Company's frolicking rendition of the Bard's masterful farce is indeed a daring departure from the norm, but is in every way true to the author's intent. A must for fans of theatre. ★★★ VHS: $24.99

A Midsummer Night's Dream

Starring Kevin Kline and Michelle Pfeiffer. *See*: William Shakespeare's A Midsummer Night's Dream

A Midsummer Night's Sex Comedy

(1982, 88 min, US, Woody Allen) *Woody Allen, Mia Farrow, Tony Roberts, Mary Steenburgen, Jose Ferrer, Julie Hagerty.* Allen ponders the foibles of sex, love and courtship in this whimsical period piece. Six couples engage in a romantic roundelay during an idyllic country outing. ★★★

A Midwinter's Tale

(1995, 98 min, GB, Kenneth Branagh) *Michael Maloney, John Sessions, Richard Briers, Julia Sawalha, Nicholas Farrell, Joan Collins.* Lovers of theatre will rejoice in this uproarious and frenetic look at the inner-workings of a haphazardly slapped together theatre troupe and their attempt to mount a Christmas Eve production of "Hamlet." The madness begins when out-of-work actor-director Joe Harper (Maloney) begs his agent (Collins) for some money to stage "Hamlet." He quickly assembles a cast of theatre rejects that includes Sessions as a drag queen Gertrude. With just two weeks to rehearse, the question becomes "how can the show possibly go on?" Branagh's cast does a crackling job exploring the tenuous relations of so many superegos, and the film becomes increasingly riveting as their collective cool breaks down. ★★★½ VHS: $14.99

Mifune

(1999, 102 min, Denmark, Søren Kragh-Jacobson) *Iben Hjejle, Anders W. Berthelsen, Jesper Asholt, Susanne Storm.* The third in the Dogme 95 films is by far the most conventional. It's more palatable than Lars Von Trier's entry, *The Idiots*, but it's infinitely less daring; and *Mifune* can't hold a candle to the brilliant and bracing *The Celebration*. The film is basically a romantic comedy, as contrived and predictable as the latest Meg Ryan vehicle. After his estranged father dies, a self-involved yuppie (Berthelsen) must go to the family farm to take care of his mentally challenged brother. He enlists the help of a hooker-with-a-heart-of-gold (the lovely Hjejle) as housekeeper. It's interesting enough to see the Dogme technique (available light only, no music score, handheld camera) in the service of a formula film, and the Dogme style is integrated so well it ceases to call attention to itself, but this is

still just a well-acted, nicely directed piece of fluff. There are some terrific moments —especially in the first half — but it becomes less and less involving as it reaches its foregone conclusion. (Danish with English subtitles) ★★½ VHS: $21.99; DVD: $29.99

The Mighty

(1998, 100 min, US, Peter Chelsom) *Kieran Culkin, Elden Henson, Sharon Stone, Gena Rowlands, Harry Dean Stanton, Gillian Anderson, James Gandolfini.* Max (Henson) is a hulking, quiet lad, straddling childhood and young adulthood, who reacts to constant taunting by turning ever inward. Kevin (Culkin), exceptionally bright and verbally adroit, is victim to his crutches and his inceasingly curving spine. They are trapped together in a big city public school system, joined by their deficiencies and strengthened by their union; their friendship forms a whole greater than the sum of its parts. Arthurian legend informs their jointly held fantasy world, lending purity of spirit and courageous resolve to their inevitable clashes with a harsh world of very real physical and emotional threat. Remarkable performances from the two young leads lift the familiar story line to produce a film of some achievement and heart. *Not* a Sharon Stone movie. ★★½ VHS: $19.99; DVD: $29.99

Mighty Aphrodite

(1995, 95 min, US, Woody Allen) *Woody Allen, Helena Bonham Carter, Mira Sorvino, F. Murray Abraham, Michael Rapaport, Claire Bloom, Olympia Dukakis, Peter Weller, Jack Warden.* Not as complex in character and narrative as Allen's former films, this is nevertheless consistently funny and thoroughly entertaining. Allen plays a sports writer married to an ambitious art gallery employee (Bonham Carter). They decide to adopt, and as the exceptional child grows, Allen becomes determined to locate the real mother. All his preconceptions about familial lineage and genes are smashed when he meets a ditzy prostitute/porn actress (marvelously played by Oscar winner Sorvino), and then becomes involved in her life. As in his *Play It Again, Sam*, Allen's subconscious comes to life, here in the form of Abraham as a member of a Greek chorus who'd be more at home on Broadway than the Acropolis. Many of Allen's signature themes — neurosis, infidelity and upper-class New York anxieties — are on display; they may not cut as deep, but they run wild just the same. ★★★ VHS: $9.99; DVD: $29.99

The Mighty Ducks

(1992, 104 min, US, Stephen Herek) *Emilio Estevez, Joss Ackland, Lane Smith.* This amiable Disney farce stars Estevez as Gordon Bombay, a high-powered schmuck of a lawyer who is sentenced to community service as the coach of a public league hockey team in Minneapolis' poorest neighborhood. Of course, this is the perfect setup for the type-A, egomaniacal Gordon to come to terms with his fall from grace as a child hockey star and learn the traditional virtue that "winning isn't everything." Purely formulaic, *The Mighty Ducks* goes out of its way to be predictable schmaltz, though the film is enjoyable and contains all of the right elements to thorough-

ly entertain the kids. (Followed by two sequels) ★★½ VHS: $14.99; DVD: $32.99

Mighty Joe Young

(1949, 94 min, US, Ernest B. Schoedsack) *Robert Armstrong, Terry Moore, Ben Johnson.* Schoedsack and Armstrong, the director and star of *King Kong* and *Son of Kong*, are back together; yet again sharing the spotlight with an ape. This cult favorite, which features good special effects, is about a young girl and her pet gorilla. Lots of fun. (Remade in 1998) ★★★ VHS: $19.99

Mighty Joe Young

(1998, 114 min, US, Ron Underwood) *Charlize Theron, Bill Paxton, Rade Serbedzija, Peter Firth, David Paymer.* This lackluster remake of the 1949 RKO favorite pairs chemistry-free Theron and Paxton as a couple protecting giant gorilla Joe by moving him from his jungle home to a California preserve to avoid encroaching poachers. But, wouldn't you know it, the evil poacher who killed both Theron and Joe's moms when they were tots is back. The connect-the-dots screenplay will barely please small ones; this is very much a calculated piece of Hollywood product. Joe can't hold a candle to Willis O'Brien and Ray Harryhausen's original stop-motion animation. The only real thrill of this '90s update is seeing the RKO Pictures logo. ★½ VHS: $14.99; DVD: $29.99

Mighty Peking Man

(1977, 90 min, Hong Kong, Meng-Hwa Ho) *Evelyne Kraft, Danny Lee.* Hilariously bad HK "King Kong" rip-off from the '70s has been released to video thanks to Quentin Tarantino's Rolling Thunder distribution. Hero Lee (later to play the cop in John Woo's *The Killer*) captures fabled giant ape with help of scantily clad (and lip-glossed) jungle girl. They fall in love, and cavort in slo-mo through the jungle with her pet leopard to the strains of a hideous love ballad (this scene is sidesplitting). When Mighty Peking Man is taken to civilization, however, many obvious stunt doubles and fake miniatures get trampled. Almost painfully funny at times, *Mighty Peking Man* is the perfect party tape; so blatantly bad, no "Mystery Science Theater 3000"-esque comments are remotely necessary. It's camp that works. (Dubbed) ★★★ VHS: $102.99; DVD: $29.99

The Mighty Quinn

(1989, 98 min, US, Carl Shenkel) *Denzel Washington, Robert Townsend, James Fox, Mimi Rogers, M. Emmet Walsh, Sheryl Lee Ralph.* Here's a film which, while it's not going to win any awards, will provide the viewer with a mildly entertaining evening of mystery and fun. Washington stars as Xavier Quinn, a police chief on a small Carribean island. Determined to clear the name of his childhood friend — now a somewhat notorious local criminal (Townsend) — Quinn tenaciously probes the murder of a white businessman on the island. In a somewhat predictable twist, he runs into a lot of opposition from some of the island's more prestigious constituents. ★★½ VHS: $9.99; DVD: $14.99

Mikey and Nicky

(1976, 105 min, US, Elaine May) *John Cassavetes, Peter Falk, Ned Beatty, William Hickey, Joyce Van*

Patten, M. Emmet Walsh. This acclaimed drama written and directed by May (which was re-released ten years after its initial run to critical praise) stars Cassavetes and Falk as two small-time hoods who try to avoid a mob hit man (Beatty). Quirky and very appealing. (Letterboxed) ★★★ VHS: $14.99

Mildred Pierce

(1945, 111 min, US, Michael Curtiz) *Joan Crawford, Ann Blyth, Jack Carson, Eve Arden, Zachary Scott, Butterfly McQueen.* An Oscar-winning performance by Crawford highlights this high-gloss soaper about a long-suffering mom who competes with her ungrateful little minx of a daughter for the affections of the same man. Blyth is wonderfully rotten as daughter Vida, and the always reliable Arden is a scene-stealer as Joan's best friend. ★★★½ VHS: $19.99

Milk Money

(1994, 110 min, US, Richard Benjamin) *Ed Harris, Melanie Griffith, Malcolm McDowell, Michael Patrick Carter, Casey Siemaszko.* Part *Pretty Woman* and part adolescent coming-of-age fantasy, *Milk Money* is an innocuous comedy about prostitution, suburbia, Grace Kelly and parenthood. Carter plays a 12-year-old boy who goes searching for a prostitute in the big city. There he meets good-hearted Griffith who, through a series of circumstances, comes to stay at his place in the burbs, prompting the youth to try to set her up with his widowed father (Harris). The film is a little too grown up for kids and too childish for adults, and there's its problem. Harris' goofy, lighthearted absent-minded dad provides a few smiles. ★★ VHS: $14.99

The Milky Way

(1936, 89 min, US, Leo McCarey) *Harold Lloyd, Adolphe Menjou, Verree Teasdale, Helen Mack.* Lloyd's best talkie has the silent clown as a mild-mannered milkman who becomes an unlikely boxing sensation when he accidentally knocks out the champ. Lots of laughs. (Remade as *The Kid from Brooklyn*) ★★★

The Milky Way

(1969, 102 min, France, Luis Buñuel) *Laurent Terzieff, Paul Frankeur, Delphine Seyrig.* The religious pilgrimage of two tramps traveling from France to Spain is the pretense of a plot in this savagely funny and continually imaginative heretical assault on organized religion. The folly of man's continual adherence to the insanities of Church dogma are portrayed through the tramps' surrealistic encounters with the Virgin Mary and Jesus Christ, as well as the Marquis de Sade. (French with English subtitles) ★★★★

The Mill on the Floss

(1997, 120 min, GB, Graham Theakston) *Emily Watson, Cheryl Campbell, James Frain, Bernard Hill, Ifan Meredith.* A Masterpiece Theatre adaptation of the George Eliot novel, this handsomely mounted saga of the Tulliver family and their river mill is absorbing, if unremarkable. The headstrong Maggie (Watson) cares deeply for both her father (Hill) and her brother Tom (Meredith), but she stirs up trouble when she falls in love with Philip (Frain), the son of her father's arch rival. As Maggie struggles for her free will, Tom tries to regain financial control of the mill. The bonds forged between the characters are heartfelt; yet the story, which concerns tolerance and forgiveness, only truly

engages the emotions when tragedy strikes. Nevertheless, the attention to period details, costumes, and the beautiful British countryside, make this a lovely looking film, and Watson demonstrates extraordinary range. ★★★ VHS: $19.99

Mille Bolle Blu

(1993, 83 min, Italy, Leone Pompucci) *Stefano Dionisi, Claudio Bigagli.* Like a palimpsest used once too often, this breezy little comedy is marred by a faded familiarity that comes from having seen this all before. It is 1961. All Rome awaits the projected solar eclipse. The summer's warmth forces open the windows and doors on an archtypical street in the heart of the city. Imagine, if you will, Alfred Hitchcock's *Rear Window* with lots of yelling and gesticulation; no one has any secrets for long, and everyone has a colorful story. Someone dies. Someone marries. Characters are drawn with Fellini-esque broad strokes: endearing, entertaining, and as flat and as fleeting as the color comics section on Sunday. (Italian with English subtitles) ★★½ VHS: $89.99

Millennium

(1989, 95 min, US, Michael Anderson) *Cheryl Ladd, Kris Kristofferson, Daniel J. Travanti, Robert Joy, Brent Carver.* An intriguing concept for a science-fiction adventure — about a group of aliens who rescue passengers of airplanes right before they crash — is given an uneven treatment in this occasionally entertaining thriller. Ladd stars as a benign extraterrestrial from an underpopulated, dying planet whose scientists keep track of crashes, whisking away the doomed passengers to help repopulate their own world. ★★½ VHS: $9.99

Miller's Crossing

(1990, 115 min, US, Joel Coen) *Gabriel Byrne, Albert Finney, John Turturro, Marcia Gay Harden, Jon Polito, Michael Jeter.* This thoroughly engrossing and brilliantly produced gangland sendup overflows with sardonic wit, bristling dialogue and operatic violence. Byrne heads an excellent cast as Tom, a mob insider whose endless scheming provides the plot with an abundance of unexpected twists, double-crosses and red herrings. The story follows a fight for control of City Hall between Tom's boss, Leo (confidently portrayed by Finney), and an arch-rival. In the midst of the fray is Bernie Bernbaum, a weasely small-time hood who's trying to muscle in on both men's numbers racket. As Bernie, Turturro delivers a tantalizingly over-the-top performance. In her cinematic debut, Harden is superb as the hard-as-nails Verna, who is both Bernie's sister and Leo's girlfriend. ★★★★ VHS: $14.99

Millhouse: A White Comedy

(1971, 92 min, US, Emile De Antonio) Richard Milhous Nixon gets the De Antonio treatment in this biting "documentary" satire that exposes, through creative use of newsreel footage and interviews, the abominations of our 37th president. Made before the Watergate scandal, we view a calculating, opportunistic and amoral Nixon who, on occasion, has advocated the death penalty for drug dealers and a nuclear assault on Southeast Asia. A funny but sobering view of an American megalomaniac. ★★★ VHS: $39.99

Le Million

(1931, 85 min, France, René Clair) *Annabella, René Lefevre.* A finely tuned musical comedy which follows the wild adventures of a penniless and creditor-hounded painter who wins a million francs in a lottery but loses the winning ticket in a pair of pants he had pawned. His hurried attempts to retrieve the ticket, while keeping just one step ahead of his creditors, make this a delightful film. (French with English subtitles) ★★★½ VHS: $29.99; DVD: $29.99

The Million Dollar Hotel

(2000, 122 min, US, Wim Wenders) *Jeremy Davies, Mel Gibson, Milla Jovovich, Jimmy Smits, Peter Stormare, Amanda Plummer, Gloria Stuart, Tim Roth.* Film-school pretentiousness, Bukowski-esque outcasts and beautiful imagery all smack into each other with the subtlety of a freight train at *The Million Dollar Hotel*. At this seedy last chance for a group of down-and-out Los Angelenos, a young man is killed from a fall off the roof. Was it suicide or murder? That's what FBI agent Skinner (Gibson) wants to know. He's been hired by the youth's millionaire father to uncover the truth. As written by Nicholas Klein, from a story idea by U2's Bono, the film is a collection of talky episodes in which the insane are enobled and the sane unenlightened. It's a message told with a heavy hand. Among a high-profile cast, Gibson looks terribly uncomfortable, and Davies unmercifully chews the scenery as Tom Tom, a (possibly) mentally retarded resident who may hold the key to the tragedy. Wenders' jump into the abyss is a fascinating fiasco. ★½ VHS: $89.99; DVD: $24.99

Millionaire's Express

(1986, 107 min, Hong Kong, Samo Hung) *Samo Hung, Yuen Biao, Richard Norton, Yukari Oshima, Cynthia Rothrock.* Hanshui Town was a peaceful little villa along the rail line connecting Shanghai with the interior of China. That is, until several bands of outlaws decided to make their fortunes by robbing the "Millionaire's Express" train (named for its wealthy passengers) while it was stopped at Hanshui. Madcap action ensues, and lots of it — this is part Keystone Cops, part "spaghetti western," but most definitely a Hong Kong action comedy. An irresistable concoction of laughs and gasps, this comedy may prove a bit much for the hardcore action fan, but the film has so much charm it is sure to win over every other viewer. (Cantonese with English subtitles) ★★★½ VHS: $19.99; DVD: $49.99

Mimic

(1997, 105 min, US, Guillermo Del Toro) *Mira Sorvino, Jeremy Northam, Josh Brolin, Giancarlo Giannini, F. Murray Abraham, Charles S. Dutton.* Bringing the same stylish chills he brought to *Cronos*, director Del Toro unleashes a steady stream of scares in this good-looking, level-headed horror tale. Entomologist Sorvino creates a mutated cockroach to stop a lethal virus that's killing children. A few years later, the genetically engineered bug has evolved into a deadly human-sized adversary. *Mimic* takes a group of scientists and bystanders and pits them, in a confined space, against an unknown and elusive monster, here terrorizing the catacombs of the New York City subway system. Unlike many a horror film, children and pets are not necessarily off limits — they too become roach food. (Letterboxed VHS available for $19.99) ★★★ VHS: $14.99; DVD: $29.99

Min and Bill

(1930, 66 min, US, George Hill) *Marie Dressler, Wallace Beery, Marjorie Rambeau.* Dressler won an Oscar for her heartbreaking performance as a feisty waterfront hotel proprietress who fights to keep the abandoned girl, whom she has raised as her own, from being taken away. In one of the big hits of the 1930s, Dressler and Beery make a great team. ★★★ VHS: $19.99

Mina Tannenbaum

(1994, 128 min, France, Martine Dugowson) *Romane Bohringer, Elsa Zylberstein, Florence Thomassin.* A rich, layered film, *Mina Tannenbaum* charts the winding path of a relationship between two women. Mina, a rebellious painter (Bohringer), meets Ethel (Zylberstein) in dance class at age seven. Alongside their relational development, the film conquers such issues as ethnic identity, mental illness and the power of familial history. In addition, the two women must resolve their struggles with art and feminism in face of a dominant and conformist culture. Though thematically the film bites off more than it can chew, each of these issues is handled with subtlety and sensitivity. (French with English subtitles) ★★★ VHS: $29.99

Minbo

(Or the Gentle Art of Japanese Extortion)

(1994, 123 min, Japan, Juzo Itami) *Nobuko Miyamoto, Akira Takarada.* When a high-class hotel comes under siege from the Yakuza, it takes the savvy of a strong-willed woman to face them down. Beginning as a whimsical comedy that slowly turns into an intense exposé on the wiliness of the criminal world, this biting satire makes for spirited and entertaining fun. The Hotel Europa and its employees become the object of elaborate extortion plots from cartoonish thugs. Help arrives in the form of Mahiru Inoue, a small, well-dressed young woman who goes to battle with nothing more than her devilish grin, disarming wit and tons of *chutzpa*. Director Itami was attacked and injured by outraged Yakuzas during its making yet he finished the film and it became one of Japan's highest-grossing films. (Japanese with English subtitles) ★★★ VHS: $79.99

Mindwalk

(1991, 110 min, US, Bernt Capra) *Liv Ullmann, Sam Waterston, John Heard.* Written by theoretical physicist Fritjof Capra ("The Tao of Physics") and directed by his brother Bernt, this intriguing environmental talk-fest is certainly no masterpiece of drama, but for lovers of "Nova" and other PBS science programs, as well as environmentalists and New Age adherents, this will undoubtedly prove to be both fascinating and entertaining. Waterston is a liberal politician who, having just lost a bid for the White House, travels to France to visit his old '60s buddy, poet Heard. As they walk around the medieval Iles de St. Michel, they happen upon Ullmann, a semi-retired Norwegian quantum physicist. This chance meeting gives way to what can best be described as *My Dinner with Andre* meets *A Brief History of Time* as Ullmann

lectures the two men on the history of physics and how Cartesian and Newtonian mechanical thinking has led us to our current environmental crisis. ★★½ VHS: $19.99

The Miniver Story

(1950, 104 min, US, H.C. Potter) *Greer Garson, Walter Pidgeon, John Hodiak, James Fox.* Released eight years after the classic *Mrs. Miniver*, this decidedly inferior sequel begins on VE-Day, following the postwar life of Mrs. Miniver as she welcomes back her husband and family separated during the war. Whereas the original explored war-time issues with intelligence, this post-war saga is artificial and meandering. ★★ VHS: $19.99

Minnie and Moskowitz

(1971, 115 min, US, John Cassavetes) *Gena Rowlands, Seymour Cassel, Val Avery, Timothy Carey, Katherine Cassavetes.* Rowlands and Cassel give marvelous performances in this offbeat, very appealing Cassavetes comedy. Rowlands is Minnie, a museum curator involved with a married man, who meets Moskowitz (Cassel), a down-to-earth parking lot attendant. A most wonderful romance follows. (Letterboxed) ★★★½ VHS: $14.99; DVD: $24.99

The Minus Man

(1999, 111 min, US, Hampton Fancher) *Owen Wilson, Janeane Garofalo, Mercedes Ruehl, Brian Cox, Mercedes Ruehl, Dwight Yoakum.* After the grand-slam publicity campaign for *The Blair Witch Project*, perhaps the second-best ad campaign of 1999 was for *The Minus Man.* The enigmatic posters ("Don't bring a dumb date!") and especially the brilliant trailer (instead of showing clips from the film, two film buffs chat endlessly about its plot points) hinted at some sort of paranoid, Orwellian thriller. Actually, the film is an understated noir psychodrama set in Small Town, U.S.A. Wilson stars as Van Siegert, an affable chap who happens to be a serial killer. The film follows Van as he travels the lonesome back roads of America, befriending lost and lonely folks like himself. . . and, eventually, offing them. Fancher's direction is sluggish and he never generates enough tension or momentum to keep the story hurtling forward. Despite an eclectic cast, the performances are as dry as the pace. ★★ VHS: $9.99; DVD: $19.99

Miracle Down Under

(1987, 106 min, Australia, George Miller) *Dee Wallace Stone, John Waters, Bill Kerr.* From director Miller (*The Man from Snowy River*, not *Mad Max*), this compelling Australian drama follows the adventures and personal conflicts of a group of settlers exploring the uncharted southeastern Australian territory in the late 1800s. ★★★

Miracle in Milan

(1951, 96 min, Italy, Vittorio De Sica) *Francesco Golisano, Brunella Bova.* Merging his trademark style of Neorealism with an enchanting urban fable, De Sica succeeds in creating a politically charged yet endearing poetic tale. The story begins when a poor old lady finds a baby abandoned in a cabbage field. The orphan, Toto, grows up a smiling, accepting and generous young man, despite the abject poverty that surrounds him in war-ravaged Milan. Toto, with the help of the city's homeless, constructs a

squatter city, only to see it threatened by greedy developers. Hope is not lost, however, for with the aid of a magical dove given to him by his departed stepmother, he tries to save their beloved home town. A humorous story of survival told without bitterness, from one of Italy's greatest filmmakers. (Italian with English subtitles) ★★★½ VHS: $29.99

Miracle in Rome

(1989, 76 min, Colombia, Lisandro Duque Naranjo) *Frank Ramirez, Gerardo Arellano.* This wonderfully tender and heart-rending story of faith, hope and love is set in a small town in Colombia. A man's seven-year-old daughter, Evelia, dies suddenly in his arms. She is buried, but 12 years later the man, Margarito, is forced to exhume the body. To his amazement, her body is just as he left it, with Evelia seemingly only asleep. The town soon claims a miracle and declares her a saint. Margarito goes off to Rome, with the girl's body in tow, to plead his case for beatification to the Pope; only to be greeted by indifference and a labyrinthine religious bureaucracy. Adapted from a story by Gabriel García Márquez. (Spanish with English subtitles) ★★★

Miracle Mile

(1989, 102 min, US, Steve DeJarnatt) *Anthony Edwards, Mare Winningham, Denise Crosby.* An off-the-wall, strangely upbeat (not to mention offbeat) and thoroughly entertaining nuclear annihilation yarn about a pair of young lovers caught in the madness of the final few hours before the dawn of the Mad Max Millennium. DeJarnatt's madcap vision of impending doom takes off when Edwards picks up a ringing pay phone only to hear what seems to be the frantic voice of an Air Force silo operator who is desperately trying to reach his father and warn him that the unthinkable has been made real. The ensuing whirlwind of mayhem is brimming with acerbic wit and hilarious black comedy, and offers a refreshing perspective on what things may be like as we sink back into the primordial ooze. ★★★½

The Miracle of Morgan's Creek

(1944, 99 min, US, Preston Sturges) *Betty Hutton, Eddie Bracken, William Demarest, Diana Lynn.* Writer-director Sturges had a field day with this brilliantly funny farce. Hutton gets impregnated by a G.I. leaving for overseas, and the unwed (?) mother-to-be can't remember who the soldier was. It was a miracle that Sturges got this past the censors. ★★★★ VHS: $14.99

Miracle on 34th Street

(1947, 97 min, US, George Seaton) *Maureen O'Hara, John Payne, Edmund Gwenn, Natalie Wood.* Classic Christmas story about a Macy's Santa Claus who insists he's the real Kris Kringle — sending New York City into a frenzy. Gwenn deservedly won an Oscar for his delightful and definitive portrayal of Santa, and nine-year-old Wood is charming as a disbelieving youngster who is befriended by St. Nick. (Remade in 1994) ★★★½ VHS: $14.99; DVD: $29.99

Miracle on 34th Street

(1994, 114 min, US, Les Mayfield) *Richard Attenborough, Elizabeth Perkins, Dylan McDermott, Mara Wilson, J.T. Walsh, Robert Prosky.* With exception to Attenborough's lively interpretation of Santa Claus, and a charming performance by

Wilson as the youngster who under his guidance learns to believe, there's little else to recommend about this updated remake of George Seaton's 1947 holiday classic. New York's 34th Street is still the setting for this tale of a department store Santa who insists he's the genuine article, but now the competing stores are fictional, which sets the tone for a story devoid of real emotion. ★★½ VHS: $14.49; DVD: $29.99

The Miracle Worker

(1962, 107 min, US, Arthur Penn) *Anne Bancroft, Patty Duke, Victor Jory, Inga Swenson.* Brilliant screen version of William Gibson's acclaimed play which heartbreakingly details Helen Keller's fight to speak. Bancroft gives a stunning performance as Anne Sullivan, the half-blind teacher whose guidance enables the young Helen to communicate. Duke as Helen matches Bancroft all the way, and both actresses deservedly won Oscars. (Remade in 1979 with Duke playing Sullivan, and in 2000) ★★★★ VHS: $14.99; DVD: $19.99

Miracles

(1989, 127 min, Hong Kong, Jackie Chan) *Jackie Chan, Anita Mui.* A solid Chan vehicle, *Miracles* combines the feel (and plotline) of a 1930s gangster melodrama with Chan's typical self-effacing humor and terrific action; this is one of his more satisfying films. While this American release thankfully has kept the goofy but infectious original music score, it has replaced the Chinese language track with some idiotic dubbing (one bad guy sounds like a bad Edward G. Robinson impression, another is a poor-man's Peter Lorre) that detracts a bit from the fun. Still, *Miracles* — while a bit long in the tooth — is highly enjoyable, and contains some of Jackie's most astonishing action setpieces. And he looks pretty damned sharp in those period get-ups! Based on Frank Capra's *A Pocketful of Miracles*. (aka: *Mr. Canton and Lady Rose*) ★★★ VHS: $9.99; DVD: $24.99

Mirage

(1965, 109 min, US, Edward Dmytryk) *Gregory Peck, Diane Baker, Walter Matthau, Kevin McCarthy, Jack Weston.* Intriguing Hitchcockian thriller with Peck as an amnesia victim who becomes entangled in a murder mystery while trying to regain his memory. ★★★

The Mirror (Zerkalo)

(1974, 106 min, USSR, Andrei Tarkovsky) *Margarita Terekhova, Philip Yankovsky.* Fusing personal memories of his childhood as a wartime exile with fragments of his adult life and reflecting on his mother's experience with political terror, Tarkovsky fashions a haunting dreamlike puzzler that might best be described as an autobiographical poem. The director reflects on three generations of his family, as well as the painful experience of his parents' marital breakup, in making this deeply moving, powerful and challenging film. An intense and very personal film. (Russian with English subtitles) ★★★½ VHS: $29.99; DVD: $29.99

The Mirror Crack'd

(1980, 105 min, GB, Guy Hamilton) *Angela Lansbury, Elizabeth Taylor, Kim Novak, Rock Hudson, Tony Curtis, Edward Fox, Geraldine Chaplin, Pierce Brosnan.* Before she went sleuthing in "Murder She Wrote," Lansbury appeared as Agatha

Christie's crack sleuth Miss Marple in this enjoyable, if slight, mystery. Miss Marple becomes involved with show people when Taylor is almost murdered. Taylor and Novak are well-cast as rival and catty movie queens. (Letterboxed) ★★ VHS: $9.99; DVD: $24.99

The Mirror Has Two Faces

(1996, 126 min, US, Barbra Streisand) *Barbra Streisand, Jeff Bridges, Lauren Bacall, Pierce Brosnan, George Segal, Mimi Rogers, Brenda Vaccaro.* A sometimes giddy, sometimes overbearing romantic comedy. Streisand plays a supposedly unattractive college professor. Bridges, in an extremely likable performance, is a fellow professor looking for an asexual relationship. He searches for a plain Jane and finds Babs who, of course, she falls in love with him. She fixes herself up; he falls in love with her; mix-ups and hijinks ensue. There are quite a few appealing comedic moments to the film, and Streisand is a congenial professor and mate. But the whole setup of the movie doesn't work, which magnifies not only Streisand's ego (her refusal to look really "bad") but the often fluffy, routine comedy as well. (Letterboxed VHS available for $19.99) ★★½ VHS: $9.99; DVD: $19.99

The Misadventures of Mr. Wilt

(1990, 84 min, GB, Michael Tuchner) *Griff Rhys Jones, Mel Smith, Alison Steadman.* Although not nearly as funny as the wildly absurd Tom Sharpe novel, "Wilt," from which it is based, this frantic comedy still has its moments. Henry Wilt spends his days teaching English Lit in a second-rate community college and his nights fantasizing about elaborate ways to kill his fad-obsessed wife. When she disappears, he learns the police suspect *him* of doing her in. Sinking him further in the mess are Wilt's doings on the night of the disappearance which include a much-witnessed sexual tryst with a full-sized anatomically correct doll. Rhys Jones is perfect as the hapless Wilt in this rollicking black comedy. ★★★ VHS: $89.99

Misery

(1990, 107 min, US, Rob Reiner) *James Caan, Kathy Bates, Lauren Bacall, Richard Farnsworth, Frances Sternhagen.* Director Reiner returns to Stephen King territory (after the wonderful *Stand by Me*) leading Bates to a Best Actress Oscar for her creepy portrayal of a schizophrenic fan who first rescues, then imprisons her favorite author (Caan) when he kills off her favorite romance novel character. Reiner once again demonstrates that horror need not be all blood and guts. ★★★ VHS: $9.99; DVD: $19.99

The Misfits

(1961, 124 min, US, John Huston) *Clark Gable, Marilyn Monroe, Montgomery Clift, Thelma Ritter, Eli Wallach.* A stark, poignant film with Gable, Clift and Wallach as modern-day cowboys and Marilyn as a delicate divorcée entangled in their games of camaraderie and machismo. Scripted largely for Monroe by husband Arthur Miller, *The Misfits* marked her and Gable's final screen roles. ★★★ VHS: $14.99; DVD: $19.99

Mishima: A Life in Four Chapters

(1985, 121 min, US/Japan, Paul Schrader) *Ken Ogata, Kenji Sawada.* Yukio Mishima, Japan's most celebrated novelist, stunned his country in 1970 when, after a bizarre attempt at a political overthrow, he committed *seppuku* (ritual suicide). With this puzzling event at its center, Schrader has created a daring film that tries to understand the man through his writings. With the final day of Mishima's life as the background, the film is intercut with three stylized episodes from his novels. A fascinating look at an obsessed artist. (Japanese with English subtitles) ★★★ VHS: $79.99; DVD: $19.99

Miss Congeniality

(2000, 105 min, US, Donald Petrie) *Sandra Bullock, Benjamin Bratt, Michael Caine, Candice Bergen, William Shatner, Ernie Hudson.* An FBI agent who can't follow rules; an FBI agent who goes undercover; an underdog FBI agent who

The Miracle of Morgan's Creek

Sandra Bullock in *Miss Congeniality*

ultimately saves the day. These familiar elements are what you get in the formula comedy *Miss Congeniality*, whose one hook is that it's a female FBI agent, played with comic zest by the ever-endearing Bullock. She and partner Bratt head to San Antonio for the Miss USA beauty pageant, where a serial bomber will strike next. The tomboyish agent gets a make over (a fussy Caine is her Henry Higgins) and becomes a contestant. The usual jokes — unable to walk in heels, wearing falsies, dumb fellow contestants — follow. *Miss Congeniality* does provide a few laughs, and it's better than the similarly themed *Beautiful*, but there's nothing here we haven't seen before. ★★ VHS: $22.99; DVD: $26.99

Miss Firecracker

(1989, 102 min, US, Thomas Schlamme) *Holly Hunter, Mary Steenburgen, Tim Robbins, Alfre Woodard, Scott Glenn, Ann Wedgeworth, Christine Lahti.* Welcome to Yazoo City, Mississippi. What more likely setting for playwright Beth Henley to serve up this thoroughly charming piece of American pie filled with a cast of characteristically odder-than-odd characters. A crackerjack ensemble of actors is headed by Hunter as a slightly eccentric "girl with a past," whose one dream in life is to win the annual Miss Firecracker Beauty Pageant. Sparks fly when her rapacious cousins Steenburgen and Robbins descend on her fragile ego with a ferocity that only family members can muster. ★★★

Miss Julie

(1985, 90 min, Sweden, Alf Sloberg) *Anita Bjork, Ulf Palme.* This dazzling adaptation of Strindberg's riveting play concerns one woman's social and sexual domination. Miss Julie, a noblewoman, allows her butler to seduce her after her engagement is broken. Her actions then lead to a haunting and unremitting exploration of how the woman's disgrace begins to destroy her. Outstanding performances and magnificent cinematography enhance the intensity of this story. (Swedish with English subtitles) ★★★

Miss Rose White

(1991, 95 min, US, Joseph Sargent) *Kyra Sedgwick, Amanda Plummer, Maximilian Schell, Maureen Stapleton.* This Emmy Award winner is a sensitive tale of a young Jewish immigrant who must come to terms with her ethnicity when her sister, a Holocaust survivor, comes to join her and her father in America just after WWII. Sedgwick is marvelous as the title character and Schell boasts a strong supporting performance as her father, as does the always wonderful Plummer as her sister. Based on the off-Broadway play "A Shayna Maidel" by Barbara Lebow. ★★★½ VHS: $14.99

Miss Sadie Thompson

(1953, 93 min, US, Curtis Bernhardt) *Rita Hayworth, Jose Ferrer, Aldo Ray, Charles Bronson.* Although Hayworth's Sadie Thompson won't make anyone forget *Gilda*, she nevertheless gives a sparkling performance in this musical remake of W. Somerset Maugham's story "Rain" (the 1932 version starred Joan Crawford). Rita plays a "good time" entertainer who, while stranded on a tropical island during WWII, becomes involved with a brawny G.I. (Ray) and a hypocritical minister (Ferrer) whose obsession with Sadie's salvation cloaks other desires. (Timely, isn't it?) ★★★ VHS: $19.99

Missing

(1982, 122 min, US, Constantin Costa-Gavras) *Jack Lemmon, Sissy Spacek, John Shea, Melanie Mayron, David Clennon.* Costa-Gavras' award-winning thriller probes the mysterious disappearance of a young American writer during the bloody political upheaval in Chile. Spacek and Lemmon star as the wife and father whose persistent search uncovers some frightening facts on U.S. involvement in South America. ★★★½ VHS: $9.99

The Mission

(1986, 125 min, GB, Roland Joffé) *Jeremy Irons, Robert De Niro, Ray McAnally, Aidan Quinn, Philip Bosco, Liam Neeson.* A Best Picture nomination went to this acclaimed, based-on-fact historical drama, set in 18th-century South America. Irons stars as a Jesuit priest who leads a tribe of native Indians in a revolt against mercenary colonialists. De Niro is a soldier whose social conscience leads him to become involved on behalf of Irons and his cause — an act which draws him into an insurmountable challenge and inevitable tragedy. Gorgeous Oscar-winning cinematography. ★★★½ VHS: $14.99

Mission: Impossible

(1996, 111 min, US, Brian De Palma) *Tom Cruise, Jon Voight, Emmanuelle Béart, Jean Reno, Ving Rhames, Henry Czerny, Vanessa Redgrave, Emilio Estevez, Kristin Scott Thomas.* The popular 1960s TV drama "Mission: Impossible" gets a '90s facelift with this exciting, extremely well-executed though somewhat dense thriller. Cruise plays Ethan Hunt, a member of the elite undercover team. Voight plays Jim Phelps, the team's leader and a carryover character from the TV series. On a mission Mr. Phelps decides to accept, most of the members are killed, with Hunt the only likely survivor. It soon becomes apparent that they were set up, and Hunt — who is now the number one suspect — goes underground to discover the identity of the mole. Maybe it's a little too intricate for its own good, but the twists are unpredictable, and the action plentiful. The Cold War may be dead, but good political espionage is not. (Sequel: *Mission: Impossible II*) (VHS available letterboxed or pan & scan) ★★★ VHS: $9.99; DVD: $29.99

Mission: Impossible II

(2000, 124 min, US, John Woo) *Tom Cruise, Thandie Newton, Dougray Scott, Ving Rhames, Anthony Hopkins.* Perhaps Cruise's *Mission* series will follow the lines of the *Alien* movies, with each sequel radically unlike the previous. Unfortunately, instead of *Aliens* for a second film, Woo has given us *Mission: Resurrection*. This stylish misfire at least has a comprehensible plot, as our hero Ethan Hunt (Cruise) tracks down a deadly virus being exploited for cash (or stock) by villianous entrepeneur Scott.

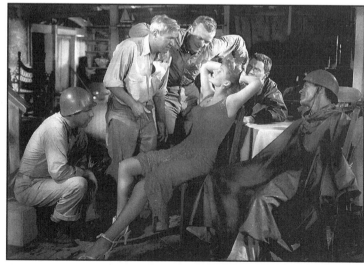

Rita Hayworth knocks 'em dead in *Miss Sadie Thompson*

Mission: Impossible

Hunt's pilferous recruit Newton provides a romantic complication for both. Woo provides his usual operatic grandeur: flying doves, showering sparks and general slow-mo badassness. But his moves, and even the nascent franchise, have become so predictable that even the villain knows what will happen during a would-be set piece. Woo's flourishes worked well for Chow Yun-Fat and tales of betrayal; for a simple good guy-bad guy story, it all just seems too over-the-top. ★★ VHS: $14.99; DVD: $29.99

Mission to Mars

(2000, 112 min, US, Brian De Palma) *Gary Sinise, Don Cheadle, Tim Robbins, Connie Nielsen, Jerry O'Connell, Kim Delaney, Armin Mueller-Stahl.* After losing the signal to their friends on Mars, a second mission is sent to rescue them, and to discover the mysterious secret behind the communication breakdown. This lackluster, clichéd, cornball would-be sci-fi epic is salvaged somewhat by director DePalma's always interesting visual direction, an able cast, and Ennio Morricone's pleasingly eclectic score. But this is hardly the rousing, fascinating (if obviously derivative) spectacle suggested by the trailers. Still, there's an amazing 20-30 minute chunk of pure suspense cinema halfway through the film that culminates in an emotionally resonant climax; it's one of DePalma's best setpieces (despite rampant product placement). Sadly, the film lumbers along for 40 more minutes after that, to a decidedly anticlimax. An interesting misfire. ★★½ VHS: $14.99; DVD: $19.99

The Missionary

(1982, 93 min, GB, Richard Loncraine) *Michael Palin, Maggie Smith, Trevor Howard, Denholm Elliott.* Monty Pythonite Palin stars in this eccentric comedy-drama as a naïve English missionary just returned from Africa and assigned to rehabilitate the fallen women of Edwardian London. Smith costars as his lascivious benefactor in this refined satire. ★★★½ VHS: $19.99

Mississippi Burning

(1988, 125 min, US, Alan Parker) *Gene Hackman, Willem Dafoe, Frances McDormand, Brad Dourif, R. Lee Ermey.* This gut-wrenching masterwork is one of the most powerful American films to date to explore racial prejudice. Based on the actual 1964 murders of three civil rights workers, the film presents a fictionalized account of the investigation. Hackman and Dafoe are the FBI agents assigned to the case. At odds with each other from the start, together the two men confront a hostile white community either unwilling or unable to cooperate, and an oppressed black community impregnated with fear of reprisal at the hands of the ruthless white bigots controlling the town. Dafoe is very good as the conventional FBI man, but it is Hackman's virtuoso performance which forms the core of the film. ★★★★ VHS: $14.99; DVD: $19.99

Mississippi Masala

(1992, 118 min, US, Mira Nair) *Denzel Washington, Sarita Choudhury, Roshan Seth.* Director Nair sets her sights on the subtleties of insidious racism in this affecting modern-day "Romeo and Juliet" set in the deep South. The story follows the forbidden love that blossoms between a young Indian woman (Choudhury), whose family fled Idi Amin's Uganda, and an African-American carpet cleaner (Washington). Nair expertly exposes the unspoken and unacknowledged racism that permeates the Indian community. Washington and newcomer Choudhury give heartfelt performances and Nair puts their stunning looks to good use. Seth delivers yet another superb supporting performance as Choudhury's lawyer father who yearns to return to Uganda. ★★★ VHS: $9.99

Mississippi Mermaid

(1969, 123 min, France, Francois Truffaut) *Catherine Deneuve, Jean-Paul Belmondo.* This intriguing but tame romantic thriller was one of the director's few certifiable flops, despite the superstar casting of Belmondo and Deneuve. The story concerns a tobacco plant owner (Belmondo) on an African island who gets more than he bargained for after the arrival of his mysterious mail-order bride (Deneuve). The Hitchcock-inspired plot is elaborately presented, but the film lacks needed tension and fails to reach its intended suspense. (French with English subtitles) ★★ VHS: $19.99; DVD: $19.99

The Missouri Breaks

(1976, 126 min, US, Arthur Penn) *Marlon Brando, Jack Nicholson, Randy Quaid, Kathleen Lloyd, Harry Dean Stanton, Frederic Forrest.* Brando plays a sadistic gunslinger hired to kill horse thief Nicholson and his gang (Quaid, Stanton). Set in the late 1880s in Montana hill country, where Brando and Nicholson play a deadly game of cat-and-mouse, this bizarre western was a financial disappointment upon release. It has, over the years, taken on cult status thanks to its two stars. ★★ VHS: $9.99

Mr. and Mrs. Bridge

(1990, 105 min, US, James Ivory) *Paul Newman, Joanne Woodward, Kyra Sedgwick, Blythe Danner, Robert Sean Leonard, Simon Callow.* A leisurely, fine character study highlighted by two bravura performances from Newman and especially Woodward as an upper-middle-class Kansas City husband and wife. Based on two Evan S. Connell novels, "Mr. Bridge" and "Mrs. Bridge," the film, set in the years between the two World Wars, examines with razor-sharp intensity and formidible wit the couple's everyday, and even mundane, existence. A series of continuing and perfectly constructed stories, the film's most memorable scenes include Newman's "battle" with a tornado and Woodward's astonishing reaction at her son's Boy Scout meeting. ★★★½ VHS: $9.99; DVD: $24.99

Mr. Arkadin

See: Confidential Report

Mr. Baseball

(1992, 108 min, US, Fred Schepisi) *Tom Selleck, Ken Takakura, Aya Takanashi, Dennis Haysbert.* A lackluster confection about a bad-boy baseballer (Selleck) whose losing streak and outfield antics get him traded to Japan. There he becomes involved in the obligatory misunderstandings, misadventures, romance and culture clashes. Schepisi's sure-footed direction is the saving grace of this mediocre addition to the "stranger in a strange land" body of filmmaking. ★★ VHS: $9.99; DVD: $19.99

Mr. Blandings Builds His Dream House

(1948, 94 min, US, H.C. Potter) *Cary Grant, Myrna Loy, Melvyn Douglas.* In this delightful screwball comedy, Grant is Mr. Blandings, a city-bred man who yearns for the "good life" — to be a country boy, with a big, old country house in the idyllic Connecticut countryside. But Mr. Blandings soon discovers that the "good life" isn't quite what he expected — and the fun begins. Forget the remake with Tom Hanks and Shelley Long, *The Money Pit;* this is the real thing. ★★★ VHS: $14.99

Mr. Death: The Rise and Fall of Fred A. Leuchter, Jr.

(1999, 91 min, US, Errol Morris) Fred A. Leuchter, Jr.'s dad first took him along to work when Fred was 4 years old. Fred Sr. was superintendent of transportation for the Massachusettes correctional sytem; Fred Jr. roamed amidst the cellblocks and the death house areas. An older Fred Jr. began tinkering with design modifications for the electric chair. In the forefront of the industry, he became known as a consultant, branching out into gas chambers and lethal injection. Leuchter's self-contained and relatively harmless world explodes when he is called in as an expert on death machines by revisionist historians seeking to dispute the occurrence of the Holocaust. His examination of Auschwitz reveals the limitations of his science; his inability to see a larger picture reveals his limitations as a man. Director Morris has again organized and communicated complex and detailed information with outstanding clarity and precision. ★★★★ VHS: $14.99; DVD: $24.99

Mr. Deeds Goes to Town

(1936, 115 min, US, Frank Capra) *Gary Cooper, Jean Arthur, Lionel Stander, H.B. Warner.* One of director Capra's great achievements, this delightfully entertaining and "pixilated" social comedy stars Cooper as Longfellow Deeds, a small-town boy who became heir to a fortune; when he decides to give it away to the needy, he goes on trial for insanity. Arthur, in the first of her three Capra films, shines as a newspaper reporter who gets the first scoop on Mr. Deeds. One of Cooper's best and most endearing performances. ★★★★ VHS: $19.99; DVD: $24.99

Mr. Destiny

(1990, 105 min, US, James Orr) *Michael Caine, James Belushi, Linda Hamilton, Jon Lovitz, Bill McCutcheon, Hart Bochner, Rene Russo, Courtney Cox.* This modern-day *It's a Wonderful Life* stars Belushi as Larry Burrows, a 35-year-old Average Joe who's down on his luck. Along comes Mr. Destiny (Caine) in the guise of a bartender with an attentive ear. He slips Larry a magic potion which allows him to see how his life would have turned out if he'd managed to hit the ball in that fateful little league game 20 years earlier — in reality he had struck out, of course. Despite its total predictability, the film still holds a certain charm and is mildly entertaining. ★★

Mr. Frost

(1989, 92 min, GB, Philip Setbon) *Jeff Goldblum, Alan Bates, Kathy Baker, Jean-Pierre Cassel.* Goldblum plays an icy killer who hasn't spoken in two years. Bates is the cop out to find his true identity and Baker is the psychiatrist caught in the middle. In trying to create uncertainty in Mr. Frost's identity, the film only manages to occasionally intrigue with its slow pace and strange occurrences. ★★ VHS: $89.99

Mr. Hobbs Takes a Vacation

(1962, 116 min, US, Henry Koster) *James Stewart, Maureen O'Hara, Fabian, John Saxon.* Stewart brings considerable charm to this genial comedy about Stewart and wife O'Hara taking the kids on vacation, where nothing turns out the way they expect. ★★½ VHS: $19.99

Mr. Holland's Opus

(1995, 142 min, US, Stephen Herek) *Richard Dreyfuss, Glenne Headly, Jay Thomas, Olympia Dukakis, William H. Macy, Alicia Witt, Joanna Gleason.* Though movies featuring dedicated teachers are most assuredly a dime a dozen, and most of them, including *Mr. Holland's Opus*, frequently languish in sentimentality, it's Dreyfuss' solid portrayal which distinguishes this alternately clichéd and absorbing drama. The story follows 30 years in the career of Mr. Holland (Dreyfuss), a budding composer who accepts a seemingly temporary position as a high school music teacher. Flashing through several time periods, the film examines both the effect Mr. Holland has on his many students, and his sometimes rocky home life. Dreyfuss ages in the part quite effectively. Headly as Mr. Holland's wife is slyly understated. ★★½ VHS: $14.99; DVD: $29.99

Mr. Hulot's Holiday

(1953, 86 min, France, Jacques Tati) *Jacques Tati, Nathalie Pascaud.* Tati, one of the greatest mime and visual artists since Chaplin and Keaton, stars as Mr. Hulot, that charming and totally naïve fool who creates disorder wherever he wanders. A French seaside resort is the setting for the Hulot pratfalls in this captivating comedy classic. ★★★★ VHS: $29.99; DVD: $29.99

Mister Johnson

(1991, 100 min, GB, Bruce Beresford) *Pierce Brosnan, Edward Woodward, Maynard Eziashi,* *Denis Quilley.* A well-intentioned but disappointing adaptation of Joyce Cary's novel about colonial Africa. Set in the African bush in the 1920s, the film tells the story of Mr. Johnson, a mischievous black clerk who, in his zealousness to be accepted as an Englishman, manipulates, lies and steals. Despite some strong performances, Beresford's vision seems blurred and it's unclear whether he is making a film about a man who turns his back on his people, the diabolical nature of British colonialism, or the incumbent tragedy in the forced modernization of tribal cultures. Whatever his intent, the result is a bleak and almost misanthropic muddle. ★★ VHS: $14.99

Mr. Jones

(1993, 114 min, US, Mike Figgis) *Richard Gere, Lena Olin, Bill Pullman, Anne Bancroft, Tom Irwin, Lauren Tom, Delroy Lindo.* In a highly flamboyant role, Gere gives an appropriately over-the-top performance as a charming manic-depressive; but even the star's energetic bravado can't elevate this standard romantic drama. Following a suicide attempt, Gere is hospitalized and placed under the care of psychiatrist Olin. As she attempts to treat his neurosis, the two become romantically involved. The implications of a doctor-patient relationship is glossed over in favor of two wayward lovers at odds with the world — which only negates the power of a potentially involving drama. ★★½ VHS: $9.99; DVD: $27.99

Mr. Klein

(1977, 124 min, France, Joseph Losey) *Alain Delon, Jeanne Moreau, Michel Lonsdale.* A disturbing mystery-drama about a self-centered, amoral man (Delon) in Nazi-occupied Paris. He takes advantage of the sweeping anti-Semitism until his world is suddenly shattered when he is mistaken for another — a Jewish Klein. A powerful indictment well-acted and thoughtfully directed. (French with English subtitles) ★★★ VHS: $29.99

Mr. Lucky

(1943, 99 min, US, H.C. Potter) *Cary Grant, Laraine Day, Charles Bickford, Gladys Cooper.* Grant stars in this romantic comedy-drama as the owner of a gambling ship who sets out to sting Day, but ends up falling in love with her and trying to go straight instead. Not one of Grant's better efforts, but mildly entertaining. ★★½ VHS: $19.99

Mr. Magoo

(1997, 85 min, US, Stanley Tong) *Leslie Nielsen, Kelly Lynch, Matt Kesslar, Ernie Hudson, Malcolm McDowell, Miguel Ferrer.* Not that it was a classic to begin with, but the one-joke "Mr. Magoo" cartoon was an intermittently amusing series which found its humor at the expense of a half-blind old codger; Jim Backus voicing the character was the best thing about it. That it has found its way to the big screen in a live-action version is not only puzzling but probable cause to re-examine the collected brain power of Hollywood studios execs but yet again. Who approved this painfully unfunny project and, more importantly, do they still have their jobs? With no verbal wit at all, the movie tries to extract its humor from slapstick, but it's a collection of tired pratfalls and hoary knockabout shenanigans. ★ VHS: $19.99

Mr. Majestyk

(1974, 104 min, US, Richard Fleischer) *Charles Bronson, Linda Cristal, Lee Purcell.* Surprisingly flavorful Bronson actioner about an ex-con trying to run a straight business, but is pushed too far by local corrupt law enforcers and a sinister Mafia hit man. Elmore Leonard penned the script. ★★½ VHS: $14.99

Mr. Mom

(1983, 92 min, US, Stan Dragoti) *Michael Keaton, Teri Garr, Christopher Lloyd, Martin Mull.* Written by John Hughes, this amiable comedy stars Keaton as a brand new househusband who must contend with housework and wife Garr working 9 to 5. Yes, it's been done before, though Keaton's comic finesse makes most of this familiar territory seem fresh. ★★½ VHS: $9.99; DVD: $14.99

Mr. Nice Guy

(1998, 87 min, Hong Kong, Samo Hung) *Jackie Chan, Richard Norton.* A lesser Chan vehicle, but even mediocre Jackie is better than most Hollywood action films. As in most of his films, Jackie plays a wide-eyed innocent (in this case, a popular TV chef) who is unwittingly caught up in a battle with drug lords for possession of an incriminating videotape. Once again, plot matters little in these films — it's the action that counts, and *Mr. Nice Guy* has its share of exciting moments (though not enough of them, to be honest). Though the film is surprisingly sloppy, it's still a breezy 87 minutes. ★★½ VHS: $9.99; DVD: $19.99

Mr. North

(1988, 92 min, US, Danny Huston) *Anthony Edwards, Robert Mitchum, Lauren Bacall, Anjelica Huston, Mary Stuart Masterson, Harry Dean Stanton.* John Huston's son Danny took over the reigns of this quirky comedy when his legendary father died just before the start of production. Edwards plays the ingratiating title character, who warms himself to the flaky citizens of Newport's upper class. A real charmer. Based on Thornton Wilder's "Theophilus North." ★★★

Mr. Reliable

(1996, 110 min, Australia, Nadia Tass) *Colin Friels, Jacqueline McKenzie.* Based on a true story, *Mr. Reliable* is an undistinguished Australian comedy which could have been a sleeper but turns out to be more of a snore. Friels stars as Wally, an ex-con who unexpectedly stages a hostage crisis during a nasty heatwave in the summer of 1968. Director Tass strives for whimsy by making the police buffoons and the various neighbors "lovable" eccentrics. But these characters — like Wally himself and his "hostage" Beryl (McKenzie) — are a one-dimensional bunch. *Mr. Reliable* only becomes diverting during the final third, when the temperature rises, tempers flare and actions are taken. ★½ VHS: $9.99

Mister Roberts

(1955, 140 min, US, John Ford & Mervyn Le Roy) *Henry Fonda, James Cagney, Jack Lemmon, William Powell, Betsy Palmer, Nick Adams.* Classic film version of Thomas Heggen and Joshua Logan's Broadway smash about life aboard a military cargo ship during WWII. Fonda, in one of his best roles, plays the title character, a dedicated naval officer who yearns for combat duty.

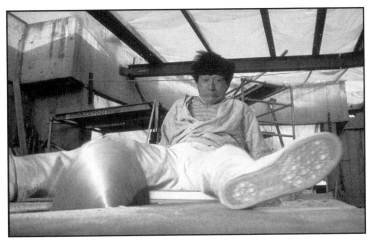

Jackie Chan is *Mr. Nice Guy*

Cagney is terrific as the small-minded ship's captain who's more concerned with his treasured palm tree than with the anxieties of his men. Lemmon won an Oscar for his memorable comic turn as Ensign Pulver, the ship's laundry and morale officer. (VHS available letterboxed or pan & scan) ★★★★ VHS: $14.99; DVD: $19.99

Mr. Saturday Night

(1992, 114 min, US, Billy Crystal) *Billy Crystal, David Paymer, Julie Warner, Helen Hunt, Ron Silver, Jerry Lewis.* Crystal makes his directorial debut with this disappointing comedy of a Catskills comedian who flirts with stardom. Reminiscent of Neil Simon's *The Sunshine Boys*, the story follows the tumultuous personal life and career of fictional stand-up comic Buddy Young, Jr. (whose catch-phrase "Don't get me started" is as catchy as it is annoying). As played by Crystal, Young is a self-destructive one-man arsenal of one-liners who can no more handle personal relationships than he can the success he spends a lifetime trying to achieve. Though there are funny lines, most of *Mr. Saturday Night* is an overly ambitious and shallow examination of Young's offstage life. ★★ VHS: $9.99; DVD: $29.99

Mr. Skeffington

(1944, 146 min, US, Vincent Sherman) *Bette Davis, Claude Rains, Walter Abel.* A sensational Davis performance is the heart of this grand soap opera with Davis in rare form as a youthful beauty who marries Rains for money and position circa mid-1910s. The film, spanning several decades, follows Davis as she ages and discovers the true meaning of love and loyalty. Rains is terrific as her devoted spouse. ★★★ VHS: $19.99

Mr. Smith Goes to Washington

(1939, 129 min, US, Frank Capra) *James Stewart, Claude Rains, Jean Arthur, Edward Arnold, Thomas Mitchell, Harry Carey, Jr., Beulah Bondi, Eugene Pallette, Guy Kibbee, Jack Carson.* Fresh from their success the year before in *You Can't Take It with You*, director Capra and Stewart reteamed to create, arguably, their finest achievement. Stewart gives a superb performance as an idealistic, newly appointed U.S. Senator and politi-

cal dupe to Rains (terrific as a corrupt senator) and Arnold (a powerful characterization as boss Taylor). Once there, he uncovers — with more than a little help from secretary Arthur — political wrongdoings, and sets out to expose them. Though Capra is known to be somewhat excessive in patriotic zeal and sentimentality, here they work to his advantage as his characters act according to their moral dictates. This Capra masterpiece features one of the finest ensemble casts ever assembled. ★★★★ VHS: $14.99; DVD: $27.99

Mr. Stitch

(1995, 90 min, US, Roger Avary) *Rutger Hauer, Nia Peeples, Wil Wheaton.* An ambitious sci-fi thriller which adapts the Frankenstein myth to a near-future setting and adds an interesting wrinkle to it. Hauer is a scientist who creates a composite human being from the parts of corpses. His creation (Wheaton), who names himself Lazarus, is superior to a normal human in both intellect and strength, but becomes obsessed with discovering what lies beyond the doors of his white-walled cell. *Mr. Stitch* does succumb late in its story to a clichéd showdown between science and the military. But the cast works well together, and Avary truly makes the viewer care about Lazarus' plight. ★★★ VHS: $89.99

Mr. Wonderful

(1993, 98 min, US, Anthony Minghella) *Matt Dillon, Annabella Sciorra, William Hurt, Mary Louise Parker, Vincent D'Onofrio.* A pleasant though insubstantial comedy, Minghella's second film casts Dillon as a working-class divorcé whose alimony payments stand between him and a happy new life. Evoking the spirits of films afar afield as *The Awful Truth* and *Send Me No Flowers*, Dillon begins an exhaustive search for his ex's (Sciorra) perfect match. Director Minghella's next film would be *The English Patient*. ★★½ VHS: $9.99; DVD: $14.99

Mr. Wrong

(1996, 92 min, US, Nick Castle) *Ellen DeGeneres, Bill Pullman, Joan Cusack, Dean Stockwell, Joan Plowright, Robert Goulet.* Making her big screen starring debut, DeGeneres manages to utilize the waifish charm she demonstrates on her TV

sitcom, but unfortunately her smiles, grimaces and rolling eyes can't sustain a lackluster screenplay. Ellen plays a successful TV producer who meets whom she thinks is Mr. Right (Pullman). But as he shows his true and obnoxious colors, she is unsuccessful in getting rid of him or getting him to understand the meaning of "it's over." There are few laughs to be had, and the story meanders from mediocre to bad; though the two stars do occasionally generate a degree of compatibility. ★★ VHS: $14.99

Mistress

(1992, 109 min, US, Barry Primus) *Robert Wuhl, Martin Landau, Robert De Niro, Eli Wallach, Danny Aiello, Laurie Metcalf, Sheryl Lee Ralph, Christopher Walken.* Where Robert Altman's *The Player* relentlessly lampooned the world of Hollywood's movers and shakers, Primus' low-budget, independent *Mistress* pokes lighthearted fun at the making of low-budget, independent films. Wuhl stars as a washed-up writer-director who one day receives a call from retired studio hack Landau, who has unearthed one of Wuhl's old scripts. Together, they take the script and run the gauntlet of potential money brokers, each of whom, of course, has a mistress they want in the film. Directed with care and wit, all of this is done with a good dose of humor and an earnest sense of moral vision. ★★★½ VHS: $19.99; DVD: $24.99

The Mistress

(1953, 106 min, Japan, Shiro Toyoda) *Hideko Takamine, Hiroshi Akutagawa.* This deeply affecting film is not only a beautiful cinematic work, but also an exceptional study of female psychology. A woman believes that she is married to a prosperous man, but discovers that he is already married and that she is no more than his mistress. Set in a period when Japan was moving toward industrialization, *The Mistress* explores the conflict between the demands of society and individual freedom. (Japanese with English subtitles) (aka: *Wild Geese*) ★★★

Mixed Blood

(1985, 97 min, US, Paul Morrissey) *Marilia Pera, Richard Ulacia, Linda Kerridge.* A jet-black comedy from director Morrissey set in New York's notorious Alphabet City about a gang of drug-running youths, under the guidance of a Fagan-like protector and her hunkish son, who set out to control the neighborhood drug trade. ★★★

Mixed Nuts

(1994, 98 min, US, Nora Ephron) *Steve Martin, Madeline Kahn, Juliette Lewis, Anthony LaPaglia, Rob Reiner, Adam Sandler, Garry Shandling.* A contender for the worst film of 1994. Martin headlines this so-called comedy about the wacky (and grim) happenings that befall a band of miserable misfits at a suicide prevention center on Christmas Eve. Considering the cast, one can't but wonder what blackmail-worthy dirt director Ephron may have had on everyone involved to get this "nightmare before Christmas" made. Boring and unsightly, these *Mixed Nuts* should have stayed in the can. ★ VHS: $9.99

Mo' Better Blues

(1990, 135 min, US, Spike Lee) *Denzel Washington, Giancarlo Esposito, Spike Lee, Joie Lee, Wesley Snipes, Cynda Williams, Bill Nunn, John*

Turturro, Samuel L. Jackson. Despite the engaging presence of Washington and a catchy jazz score by Bill Lee and Branford Marsalis, Lee's story of jazz musicians is a disappointment. Saddled with an uninvolving script, Spike fails to capture the creative spark and passion of the jazz world and its habitués. Washington plays Bleek Gilliam, a moderately successful trumpet player and singer who, to the detriment of the plot, is a really "nice guy" whose only flaw seems to be his inability to settle down with just one girlfriend. Don't be completely turned off by this criticism, however, for even Lee's failures are more interesting and enjoyable than most of the stuff that comes out of Hollywood. The one truly inexcusable aspect of the movie is Lee's heinously anti-Semitic depiction of the exploitive Jewish club owners. ★★ VHS: $9.99; DVD: $24.99

Mo' Money

(1992, 91 min, US, Peter MacDonald) *Damon Wayans, Marlon Wayans, Stacey Dash, Joe Santos.* A cut-and-paste action plot proves to be more "ho-hum" than "ha-ha." Wayans stars (along with brother Marlon) as a con man whose first legitimate job lands him smack in the middle of a major credit card scam. As with most middle-of-the-road productions of this kind, this action-comedy is neither funny enough, nor exciting enough to garner anything more than the occasional bemused chuckle. ★★ VHS: $9.99

Mobsters

(1991, 104 min, US, Michael Karbelnikoff) *Christian Slater, Patrick Dempsey, Richard Grieco, Costas Mandylor, F. Murray Abraham, Michael Gambon, Anthony Quinn, Lara Flynn Boyle, Christopher Penn.* A stylishly made but flat underworld crime saga riddled with uneven characterizations and lots of bullets. The story follows the beginnings of the youthful partners-in-crime "Lucky" Luciano (Slater), Meyer Lansky (Dempsey) and "Bugsy" Siegel (Grieco). Ostensibly about the birth of a national organized crime syndicate, the film is content to be merely a glossy, bloody shoot 'em up. ★★ VHS: $7.49

Moby Dick

(1956, 116 min, US, John Huston) *Gregory Peck, Richard Basehart, Orson Welles.* It is generally agreed that Peck was miscast in the role of Captain Ahab, but his performance detracts nothing from Huston's masterful interpretation of Herman Melville's classic novel. Extraordinary action scenes abound in this immortal sea epic. (Remade in 1998) ★★★½ VHS: $14.99; DVD: $19.99

The Mod Squad

(1999, 95 min, US, Scott Silver) *Claire Danes, Giovanni Ribisi, Omar Epps, Dennis Farina, Steve Harris, Josh Brolin, Michael Lerner.* Though it really wants to please, this big-screen version of the early 1970s TV show about three young adults (all with records) going undercover for the police misses the mark. The writers have basically reinvented the TV characters (and for the worse): Julie (Danes) is a softie who can be hurt by romance; Pete (Ribisi) is now a lovable screw-up; and Linc (Epps) is, well, kinda bland. They uncover some sort of police corruption scheme we've seen a million times before. There are nods to the era, like a musical cue from *Car Wash,* '70s zooms, and sayings like "right on," but in the end, *The Mod Squad* is nothing more than a conventional '90s cop flick. Only Ribisi is able to carve some character from the criminal script. ★½ VHS: $9.99; DVD: $14.99

Modern Problems

(1981, 91 min, US, Ken Shapiro) *Chevy Chase, Patti D'Arbanville, Mary Kay Place, Nell Carter, Dabney Coleman.* Chase lets loose as an air traffic controller who acquires telekinetic powers after exposure to nuclear waste. Some funny bits thanks to Chase's mugging, but very silly. ★★ VHS: $9.99

Modern Romance

(1980, 100 min, US, Albert Brooks) *Albert Brooks, Kathryn Harrold, Bruno Kirby, James L. Brooks.* An insightful and playfully funny therapeutic comedy session written and directed by A. Brooks. He plays a highly neurotic film editor looking for romance, but obsessively drawn to Harrold. As with most Brooks films, his dead-pan though manic observations are not for everyone; but he has such a unique view of the world, it's hard to resist his charms. ★★★

Modern Times

(1936, 89 min, US, Charles Chaplin) *Charles Chaplin, Paulette Goddard.* When the backers of René Clair's *À Nos la Liberté* prepared to sue Chaplin over the similarities they found in *Modern Times,* Clair wouldn't hear of it, as he was honored by the homage — though over the years Chaplin did find himself in hot water over the film's supposed Commie leanings. At any rate, this extraordinary silent comedy (Chaplin's last silent) is a wildly funny and touching social satire. Victimized by the machine age, Chaplin goes berserk and inadvertently leads a factory riot. The radiant Goddard plays the orphan waif with whom he falls in love. ★★★★ VHS: $19.99; DVD: $29.99

Modern Vampires

(1999, 95 min, US, Richard Elfman) *Casper Van Dien, Natasha Gregson Wagner, Natasha Lyonne, Rod Steiger, Kim Cattrall.* A comic horror movie that is neither funny nor scary, *Modern Vampires* still has plenty of skin and gore galore to keep it from being a complete waste of time. This updated version of Dracula has Dallas (Van Dien) returning to present-day Los Angeles to recruit fresh young newcomer Nico (Wagner) into bloodletting, and stop Professor Van Helsing (Steiger) from making a killing. This cheaply made production seems to have spent its entire budget on buckets of blood, but director Elfman forgot to make any of the antics interesting. ★★ VHS: $102.99; DVD: $14.99

The Moderns

(1988, 128 min, US, Alan Rudolph) *Keith Carradine, Linda Fiorentino, Genevieve Bujold, John Lone, Kevin J. O'Connor.* An exquisite-looking period drama set against the backdrop of the Paris art scene of the 1920s. Carradine, Fiorentino and Lone are American expatriates who become involved in romantic intrigue as well as an art forgery scam. Bujold steals the film as an art dealer, and O'Connor makes a splendid Hemingway. ★★★

Mogambo

(1953, 115 min, US, John Ford) *Clark Gable, Ava Gardner, Grace Kelly, Donald Sinden.* Solid remake of 1932's *Red Dust,* with Gable repeating his role from that film as a hunter in the wilds of Africa who's involved with both earthy Gardner and society girl Kelly. Gardner is especially good as the brassy showgirl. ★★★ VHS: $19.99

The Mole People

(1956, 78 min, US, Virgil Vogel) *John Agar, Hugh Beaumont.* 1950s B-film thespian Agar and Beaumont (Beaver's dad) star as explorers who climb down a hole in Asia and find a lost underground civilization of albino Sumerians, who have the half-human Mole People as their slaves. But their minions revolt and save our brave captive heroes from the surface. ★½ VHS: $14.99

Moll Flanders

(1996, 123 min, US, Pen Densham) *Robin Wright, Morgan Freeman, Stockard Channing, John Lynch, Brenda Fricker, Geraldine James.* Daniel Defoe's classic novel has been dumbed-down so that every man, woman, child or frog in the audience can understand it. Badly paced, this updating awkwardly stumbles around the story of an orphaned young woman doing her best to survive in 18th-century London. Potentially potent material is pureed into an insipid source for cheers of "You go, girl" from the Oprah crowd. A popcorn-muncher like *Mission: Impossible* has more to say about an innocent trying to survive in a corrupt, cynical world than this "important" film. Freeman and Wright give their best to undeserving material. ★½ VHS: $9.99; DVD: $19.99

Molly

(1999, 87 min, US, John Duigan) *Elisabeth Shue, Aaron Eckhart, Jill Hennessy, D.W. Moffett.* Shue plays an autistic woman who becomes quite a handful for her upwardly mobile brother when he must take care of her. Wacky misadventures ensue (oh, those crazy autistics!) until she undergoes experimental surgery and becomes "normal." But will the change be too sudden and too great? This wretched amalgam/ripoff of *Rain Man* and *Charly* begins as a wholly insulting, drastically unfunny "comedy," then predictably shifts gears to tug the heartstrings. Shue and Eckhart both overact, and the direction by Duigan is uninspired. *Schindler's List* would make a better feel-good film. ★ VHS: $6.99; DVD: $14.99

The Molly Maguires

(1970, 123 min, US, Martin Ritt) *Sean Connery, Richard Harris, Samantha Eggar.* Connery and Harris give earnest performances in this gritty drama of clashing coal miners in Pennsylvania during the 1870s. Solid direction by Ritt. ★★★ VHS: $14.99

Mom and Dad Save the World

(1992, 88 min, US, Greg Beeman) *Teri Garr, Jeffrey Jones, Jon Lovitz, Thalmus Rasulala, Wallace Shawn, Eric Idle.* Some nice special effects can't help this mildly amusing sci-fi adventure/spoof. Garr and Jones (playing a beleaguered husband similar to his role in *Beetlejuice*) are celebrating 20 years of marriage with a weekend getaway when the evil Lovitz, petty dictator of a far-away planet, kidnaps them with the intent to marry Garr. As it turns out, his planet is inhabited by imbeciles (the screenwriters must hail from there, too), so Mom and Dad's job is markedly easier than it might have been. ★★ VHS: $9.99

Charlie Chaplin takes on technology in *Modern Times*

Mommie Dearest

(1981, 129 min, US, Frank Perry) *Faye Dunaway, Diana Scarwid, Steve Forrest, Howard da Silva.* The campy, spirited version of Christine Crawford's novel detailing her abused childhood as the adopted daughter of actress Joan Crawford. Dunaway pulls out all the stops in a no-holds-barred portrayal of the movie queen. (Ironically, Crawford herself remarked that if her life story were ever filmed, she wanted Dunaway to play her.) The film which immortalized the line, "No wire hangers!" ★★★ VHS: $14.99; DVD: $29.99

Mon Oncle

(1958, 116 min, France, Jacques Tati) *Jacques Tati, Jeanne-Pierre Zola.* Tati's bumbling M. Hulot confronts modern architecture in this hilarious pratfall comedy. Without relying on dialogue, Tati has created a true classic in visual farce. (Various languages) ★★★★ VHS: $29.99; DVD: $29.99

Mon Oncle D'Amerique

(1980, 123 min, France, Alain Resnais) *Gérard Depardieu, Nicole Garcia.* A brilliant and witty contemporary comedy on the human condition. The title refers to the proverbial French uncle who, fortune made, will return with his riches to solve every problem. A comedy about the drama of life that weaves its way through a metaphysical maze in its attempt to understand the motivations, ambitions and frustrations of man. (French with English subtitles) ★★★★ VHS: $29.99; DVD: $29.99

Mona Lisa

(1986, 104 min, GB, Neil Jordan) *Bob Hoskins, Michael Caine, Cathy Tyson, Robbie Coltrane, Sammi Davis.* Hoskins won international acclaim for his searing performance as a dim-witted Cockney thug who falls hopelessly in love with a beautiful prostitute (Tyson). Initially hired as her chauffeur, a warm relationship develops between the two, and the ex-con moonlights as detective to track down her missing girlfriend. Caine also stars as a slimy crime

boss. A film bristling with sardonic humor and unnerving suspense. ★★★½ DVD: $39.99

Mondo

(1996, 80 min, France, Tony Gatlif) *Ovidiu Balan, Philippe Petit, Pierrette Fesch.* Writer-director Gatlif's charming and poignant adventure of a young Gypsy boy, *Mondo* is exquisitely photographed and beautifully performed. This natural, impressionistic film concerns the 10-year-old Mondo (Balan), who wanders around Nice asking various individuals to take him home with them. While some people ignore his request, others — such as an elderly Vietnamese woman — offer him temporary companionship. Each stranger, however, touches his life in some remarkable way. Offering a rare glimpse of the world through the eyes of this curious child, *Mondo* is absorbing and quietly powerful. Gatlif admires the innocent yet streetwise Gyspy lifestyle, and he coaxes a highly affecting performance from Balan. (French with English subtitles) ★★★ VHS: $29.99

Mondo Trasho

(1969, 95 min, US, John Waters) *Divine, Mary Vivian Pearce.* This celluloid atrocity by America's Father of Film, Waters, is visual assault and battery, laying waste an already crumbling civilization. Explore a world oozing with sex, violence and overwhelming seaminess. It's just another day in the life of a 300-pound transvestite. Divine, in skin-tight, gold lamé Capri pants, runs over Pearce in a 1959 Cadillac and commits other acts of mayhem. There's also sightings of the Virgin Mary, drug-addicted doctors, nasty 1950s rock tunes, nods to *The Wizard of Oz* and *Freaks*, and the requisite dismemberment of feet and hands. ★★

Money for Nothing

(1993, 90 min, US, Ramon Menendez) *John Cusack, Debi Mazar, Michael Madsen, Benicio Del Toro, Michael Rapaport, Philip Seymour Hoffman.* Based on the amazingly true story of Joey Coyle (played by Cusack), a Philadelphia Average Joe who stumbles upon mountains of cash, *Money for Nothing* totally ignores the fact that in real life, Joey had a history of drug and psychologi-

cal problems — an explanation needed as to why Joey totally goes off kilter when money becomes no object. Even without the subtext, however, this comedy-drama still fails — its attempts to extricate humor from Joey's moral dilemma come off pathetic rather than farcical. ★½ VHS: $19.99

The Money Pit

(1986, 91 min, US, Richard Benjamin) *Tom Hanks, Shelley Long, Alexander Godunov, Maureen Stapleton.* A modern reworking of the Cary Grant comedy *Mr. Blandings Builds His Dream House.* Hanks and Long buy a suburban New York home real cheap, and after moving in and starting remodeling, discover why the low cost. Very few of the gags work here; most of this is predictable, unfunny and terribly over-produced. Stick to the original. ★½ VHS: $7.49

Money Talks

(1997, 92 min, US, Brett Ratner) *Chris Tucker, Charlie Sheen, Heather Locklear, Paul Sorvino, Veronica Cartwright, David Warner.* Loud, abrasive, and just not that funny, *Money Talks*, like its high-pitched, squeaky-voiced star Tucker, tries to be a lot more than what it really is. It wants to be *48 HRS.* What's up on the screen is altogether a different matter. As annoying as he is animated, Tucker plays a small-time hustler who teams with ambitious reporter Sheen when they're both suspected of a series of murders, and they must clear their names. This premise was funny 50 years ago when Bob Hope romped with Dorothy Lamour, but few too comedies have had success with the idea lately. For a comedy, there's an alarmingly high body count. ★½ VHS: $14.99; DVD: $19.99

Money Train

(1995, 110 min, US, Joseph Ruben) *Wesley Snipes, Woody Harrelson, Jennifer Lopez, Robert Blake, Bill Nunn.* Money Train is an actioner/heist movie which doesn't deliver on either aspect. With a contrived screenplay which rarely makes sense, mugging from its two stars, and a misrepresented plot development, about the only thing this has going for it is its impressive location shooting and the occasional chemistry of Misters Snipes and Harrelson. They play transit cops (and foster brothers) who work for the New York City transit system. In between their undercover assignments, they talk about robbing the "money train" (the payroll car), and the plans for such are set in motion. ★★ VHS: $9.99; DVD: $19.99

Monika

(1952, 82 min, Sweden, Ingmar Bergman) *Harriet Andersson, Lars Ekborg.* A sultry, irresponsible teenager (Andersson) from a working-class district in Stockholm spends an idyllic summer with a shy and poetic boy on the tranquil islands off the Swedish coast. Basking in the sun and living for the moment, the two lovers explore their emotions and sensuality until the cold winds of autumn sweep away their innocent dreams and force them back to the city where Monika, saddled with an unwanted pregnancy, is forced to marry and settle down. This early Bergman effort is a tender yet unsentimental look at a love affair extinguished all too suddenly. (Swedish with English subtitles) ★★★ VHS: $29.99

The Marx Brothers are a barrel of laughs in *Monkey Business*

Monkey Business

(1931, 77 min, US, Norman Z. McLeod) *The Marx Brothers, Thelma Todd.* Those wild and zany Marx Brothers start out as stowaways on an ocean liner and end up rescuing a kidnapped damsel in distress in a run-down barn, all the while spewing out some of their best lines of anarchistic, iconoclastic chatter. The first of their movies written directly for the screen is a sheer delight, with gun-toting tough guys, disgruntled molls, befuddled shipboard officers and a bevy of beauties who live to be chased by the ever-lecherous Harpo. Zeppo exudes warmth and charm as a man in love; Groucho and Chico exhibit a physical agility matched only by the running of their mouths. A fine madness. ★★★½ VHS: $14.99; DVD: $29.99

Monkey Business

(1952, 97 min, US, Howard Hawks) *Cary Grant, Ginger Rogers, Marilyn Monroe, Charles Coburn.* Grant is the archetypal absent-minded professor searching for the drug of eternal youth. Both he and wife Rogers give the elixir a test spin, along with their new roadster; youth is fleeting, and mercifully so. Marilyn is the secretary of every corporate executive's dream — like the boss says, anybody can type. Director Hawks has great fun with this happy exercise in regression. ★★★

Monkey Grip

(1982, 101 min, Australia, Ken Cameron) *Noni Hazlehurst, Colin Friels.* The story of Nora (Hazlehurst), an independent, strong-willed woman trying to raise a daughter alone amidst the underground world of musicians, actors and writers. The film follows unconventional Nora as she becomes involved with a brooding, sexually volcanic man (Friels) whose fascination with her becomes dangerously obsessive. Good performances by Hazlehurst and Friels help gloss over the story's melodramatics. ★★½

Monkeybone

(2001, 87 min, US, Henry Selick) *Brendan Fraser, Bridget Fonda, Whoopi Goldberg, Chris Kattan, Giancarlo Esposito, Rose McGowan, Dave Foley, Megan Mullally; Voice of John Turturro.* An utter waste of an intriguing premise, there are moments in *Monkeybone* so unbelievably bad you can't take your eyes off the screen lest you miss something even *worse*. Fraser plays a self-deprecating cartoonist who falls into a coma and awakes in a freakish fantasyland of collected dreams and nightmares. Director Selick proved himself capable of macabre fantasy with *The Nightmare Before Christmas*, but the animated sequences here are leaden, joyless and superfluous. They feel like they're part of another movie, bracketed by a half-baked love story between Fraser and Fonda and an adolescent plot device that has Fraser's eternally horny alter ego — an annoying animated monkey — assuming his body. Fraser is always affable and it's to his credit that he's not completely smothered beneath this unfunny, disorganized mess. The film neglects to develop several promising ideas introduced early on, and looks to have been sliced-and-diced in the editing room. ★½ VHS: $102.99; DVD: $26.99

Monsieur Beaucaire

(1946, 93 min, US, George Marshall) *Bob Hope, Joan Caulfield, Patric Knowles, Cecil Kellaway.* Booth Tarkington's novel of court intrigue gets the Hope treatment, and the result is a consistently funny romp. Set in 18th-century Europe, the story has Bob playing a barber who is forced to impersonate royalty, much against his will. And, of course, the charade puts him in constant danger. At this point in his career, Hope could do this sort of comedy in his sleep. But to his credit, he gives an engaging comic performance, and he gets to recite some dandy one-liners. ★★★ VHS: $14.99

Monsieur Hire

(1990, 81 min, France, Patrice Leconte) *Michel Blanc, Sandrine Bonnaire, Luc Thuillier.* Blanc delivers an exquisitely understated performance as the voyeuristic anti-hero in this haunting thriller. Suspected of murdering a young woman, Blanc's favorite pastime is to spy on his attractive neighbor, Alice (Bonnaire). She soon becomes aware of his fixation and, much to his horror, tries to befriend him. Alice's boyfriend, Emile (Thuillier), seems to have no objection to her flirtations, for reasons which become obvious only at the film's clever conclusion. Director Leconte exhibits a fine sense of detail and imbues the film with a compellingly eerie atmosphere. Based on a 1933 novel by George Simenon, which was first adapted for the screen in Julien Duvivier's 1946 *Panique*. (French with English subtitles) ★★★

Monsieur Verdoux

(1947, 128 min, US, Charles Chaplin) *Charles Chaplin, Martha Raye.* From an idea suggested by Orson Welles, Chaplin fashioned Hollywood's first black comedy about a wife murderer who feels amateurish compared to what the governments of the world were doing. Chaplin took a long time to make talkies; but when he did, he made certain that they talked! Fortunately the long passages of philosophical digressions, while obvious, are interesting and make a nice binder 'twixt the comedy set pieces. Raye holds her own against the acknowledged master of physical comedy as he tries many ways to murder her. ★★★½; DVD: $29.99

Monsieur Vincent

(1947, 112 min, France, Leon Carre) *Pierre Fresnay, Lisa Delamare.* This excellent biography of St. Vincent de Paul, who gave up his worldly possessions and devoted his life to the poor, preaching charity and understanding, won an Oscar for Best Foreign Film of 1948. Set in 17th-century France, the film successfully avoids the sententious piety which permeates most religious bios, weaving instead a story of quiet fervor and ineffable grace a story of a saintly hero with the courage of his convictions. Fresnay portrays the title role with a masterful performance. (French with English subtitles) ★★★½ VHS: $39.99

The Monster (Il Mostre)

(1996, 111 min, Italy, Roberto Benigni) *Roberto Benigni, Nicoletta Braschi, Michel Blanc.* As a physical comedian, the versatile Benigni is like a Jacques Tati with a raging libido, or a Jim Carrey properly potty trained. His unique predilection for plot lines would usually be thought of as inappropriate for this kind of buffoonery. In *The Monster*, he plays a small-time shoplifter mistaken for a sex fiend who has been murdering and mutilating the town's female population for the last 18 years. When policewoman Braschi volunteers to use her wiles to entrap him, she soon discovers that while he is guilty of many things, murder is not among them. Once again Benigni manages to get a lot of mileage out of some pretty tired sex jokes by sheer force of will, physical grace and outright silliness. (Italian with English subtitles) ★★½ VHS: $14.99; DVD: $24.99

Monster in a Box

(1992, 96 min, US, Nick Broomfield) *Spalding Gray.* Renowned storyteller/actor Gray returns to the screen to perform yet another of his insightful and hilarious monologues (the uninitiated should most definitely see *Swimming to Cambodia*). Sitting in front of a live audience, Gray engagingly prattles on about the difficulties he encountered over the past several years while trotting around the globe in a desperate attempt to escape his "monster in a box," a monolithic 1,800-page autobiographical manuscript which has, lurking in its pages, the death of his mother. In his typical fashion, Gray intricately weaves his tales of joy and woe, along the way evoking in his audience a myriad of emotional responses ranging from outright hilarity to somber reflection. ★★★ VHS: $19.99

Monte Walsh

(1970, 100 min, US, William A. Fraker) *Lee Marvin, Jack Palance, Jeanne Moreau, Jim Davis.* Aging cowboys Marvin and Palance watch the West they knew being bought up by Eastern conglomerates and trivialized in traveling Wild West shows. As the open ranges get fenced in, some give up and settle down, some become outlaws and some just hang on. Perceptive characterizations and stunning location photography combine to deliver a bittersweet ode to a dying way of life. ★★★ VHS: $14.99

Montenegro

(1981, 98 min, Sweden, Dusan Makavejev) *Susan Anspach, Erland Josphehon.* This marvelously anarchic and subversive black comedy stars Anspach as a sexually frustrated housewife who is lured away from her beautiful home and family and tumbles into the Zanzibar, a Yugoslavian bar filled with a carnival world of misfits and twisted characters. Filmed in Sweden by a Yugoslavian director in the English language. (Letterboxed) ★★★ VHS: $19.99; DVD: $29.99

Monterey Pop

(1969, 88 min, US, D.A. Pennebaker) *The Mamas and the Papas, Canned Heat, Simon & Garfunkel, Jefferson Airplane, Janis Joplin, The Who, Otis Redding, The Jimi Hendrix Experience, Ravi Shankar.* The first and the best of the great rock festivals

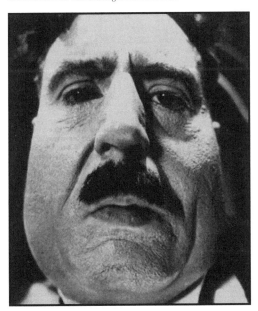

"Better get a bucket!" Monty Python's the Meaning of Life

features the dynamic performances of Jimi Hendrix, The Who, Jefferson Airplane, Janis Joplin, Otis Redding and The Animals. Great footage of a time and place worth remembering. ★★★ VHS: $19.99

A Month by the Lake

(1995, 92 min, GB, John Irvin) *Vanessa Redgrave, James Fox, Uma Thurman, Alida Valli, Alessandro Gassman.* As a genre, tales of hapless Brits seeking solar solace in the Italian countryside have provided some gems; this tiresome comedy isn't one of them. Redgrave plays Miss Bentley, a single, middle-aged woman who, during the spring of 1937, travels to the Lake Como resort of her youth. There she meets the distinctly unlikable and rather pompous Major Wilshaw (Fox) and inexplicably chases after him with the chutzpah of a schoolgirl. The film's inept script and awkward direction attempt to make broad comedy out of the generational rivalry between Redgrave and American nanny Thurman, but the result is mostly silly, irksome and embarrassing. ★½

A Month in the Country

(1988, 96 min, GB, Pat O'Connor) *Colin Firth, Kenneth Branagh, Natasha Richardson.* A beautifully filmed, sensitive adaptation of J.L. Carr's novel about two WWI veterans who, emotionally ravaged by their wartime experiences, come to terms with their past during an idyllic summer in the English countryside. Firth and Branagh both offer outstanding performances as the men; Richardson is the daughter of the local vicar who falls in love with Firth. ★★★½ VHS: $19.99

Monty Python and the Holy Grail

(1974, 90 min, GB, Terry Gilliam & Terry Jones) *Graham Chapman, John Cleese, Terry Gilliam, Eric Idle, Terry Jones, Michael Palin.* The Python troupe takes on King Arthur in this insane farce set amongst the castles, lochs and moors of Scotland. Like the early works of Woody Allen, this is a scattershot affair with gags flying at every turn; miraculously, most hit their mark. The result is a hilarious and inspired excursion into knighthood, medieval pagentry, religious sentiment and transvestism. ★★★½ VHS: $19.99; DVD: $24.99

Monty Python's Life of Brian

(1979, 93 min, GB, Terry Jones) *Graham Chapman, John Cleese, Terry Gilliam, Eric Idle, Terry Jones, Michael Palin.* The Gospel According to Monty Python! This side-splitting spoof lampoons 2,000 years of religious thought and mankind's hysterical hankering for a good Messiah. Perhaps Python's best feature. Just remember — always look on the bright side of life. (VHS

available letterboxed or pan & scan) ★★★½ VHS: $14.99; DVD: $24.99

Monty Python's the Meaning of Life

(1983, 101 min, GB, Terry Jones) *Graham Chapman, John Cleese, Terry Gilliam, Eric Idle, Terry Jones, Michael Palin, Carol Cleveland, Matt Frewer.* This effort from the Python troupe is a wild collection of vignettes on the humorous aspects of existence — from conception through demise. Included are the educational song and dance production, "Every Sperm Is Sacred," and an unforgettable restaurant retching sketch. ★★★ VHS: $9.99; DVD: $29.99

Monument Ave.

(1998, 93 min, US, Ted Demme) *Denis Leary, Jason Barry, Billy Crudup, John Diehl, Greg Dulli, Noah Emmerich, Ian Hart, Famke Janssen, Colm Meaney, Martin Sheen, Jeanne Tripplehorn.* Leary is Bobby O'Grady, the nominal head of a bunch of neighborhood guys, sons of the working class, still young but much too old to be getting their kicks from setting yuppie car alarms. They spend their days and nights ingesting coke and grass and beer. They get paid by stealing cars and betting sports. One night, they witness an execution. Neighborhood boss Jacky (Meany) can count on everyone's collective amnesia. What Jacky doesn't get is Bobby's barely controlled rage, incited through the pain of self-recognition and reflected through the eyes of his visiting Irish cousin. A thoughtfully directed, well-constructed film, highlighted by a uniformly excellent ensemble. ★★★ VHS: $14.99; DVD: $29.99

Moon 44

(1989, 102 min, Germany/US, Roland Emmerich) *Michael Paré, Malcolm McDowell, Lisa Eichhorn, Stephen Geoffreys, Roscoe Lee Browne.* Paré headlines this outer space actioner about yet another corporate conspiracy in a future where profit is the bottom line and the workers are expendable. Light years better than anyone would expect it to be, with serious performances and a wholehearted attempt at special effects. Not just another money-making *Star Wars* clone. ★★½ VHS: $9.99

The Moon in the Gutter

(1983, 126 min, France, Jean-Jacques Beineix) *Nastassja Kinski, Gérard Depardieu, Victoria Abril, Dominique Pinon.* After the incredible promise of *Diva*, Beineix's eerie follow-up was greeted with puzzled shrugs by the most sympathetic critics. Its reputation aside, however, this sordid tale of obsession is bristling with technical wizardry and sinuous noirism. A fascinating failure. (French with English subtitles) ★★

Moon over Broadway

(1999, 98 min, US, D.A. Pennebaker & Chris Hegedus) *Carol Burnett, Philip Bosco.* A fascinating behind-the-scenes look at the making of the Broadway comedy "Moon over Broadway," which marked Burnett's return to the New York stage after a 30-year absence. The production is followed from first rehearsals to opening night to closing as directors Pennebaker and Hegedus succinctly capture the many faces of the creative process at work. ★★★½ VHS: $24.99; DVD: $29.99

M

M

Moon over Miami

(1941, 91 min, US, Walter Lang) *Betty Grable, Carole Landis, Don Ameche, Robert Cummings, Jack Haley, Charlotte Greenwood.* Enjoyable Grable musical about two sisters (Grable, Landis) who go millionaire hunting in Miami. They find Ameche, Cummings and Haley. Greenwood is a particular delight as Grable's cohort who joins Betty and her sister on their quest. ★★½ VHS: $19.99

Moon over Parador

(1988, 105 min, US, Paul Mazursky) *Richard Dreyfuss, Sonia Braga, Raul Julia, Jonathan Winters, Fernando Rey, Ed Asner, Dick Cavett.* Energetic though silly comedy from Mazursky set in the small (fictional) Latin American country of Parador whose hated dictator dies, and is replaced by a look-alike — an American actor. Dreyfuss has a field day as the politically naïve actor who gets a quick lesson in politics and love when he impersonates the country's ruler. ★★½ VHS: $7.49

Moondance

(1995, 92 min, Ireland/Germany, Dagmar Hirtz) *Ruaidhri Conroy, Ian Shaw, Julia Brendler, Marianne Faithfull.* Two Irish brothers — wacky ne'er-do-wells who "live by their own rules" — share a strong bond, an unshakable familial love that can't be tainted; except by a sexy young thing, of course. When their aunt complains that the younger sibling must go to school instead of galavanting around the Irish countryside all day, her teenage companion — a pretty, bright lass — offers to tutor the irrepressible lad. The close-knit bros are soon embroiled in a web of jealousy and lust of a strictly juvenile bent. Clichéd, hackneyed, lightly annoying drama plays like a Gaelic "Dawson's Creek." ★★ VHS: $19.99

Moonlight and Valentino

(1995, 105 min, US, David Anspaugh) *Elizabeth Perkins, Whoopi Goldberg, Gwyneth Paltrow, Kathleen Turner, Jon Bon Jovi.* A familiar story of a woman coming to terms with the death of her husband and of her relationship with her supportive friends and family, *Moonlight and Valentino* is a congenial female buddy movie which is more heart than soul, more emotion than intellect. Perkins' husband is killed in a morning jog. As her sister (Paltrow), best friend (Goldberg) and stepmother (Turner) gather — sometimes collectively and sometimes singularly — to give her comfort, she has a degree of difficulty in trying to get on with her life. The emotionless widow immediately distances her character from the viewer. But as written by Ellen Simon (Neil's daughter), the film also exhibits a genuine bond between the women, and they're given some good dialogue to recite. ★★½ VHS: $9.99; DVD: $19.99

Moonlighting

(1982, 97 min, GB, Jerzy Skolimowski) *Jeremy Irons, Eugene Lipinski.* Working illegally in London, a group of Polish laborers are brutally cut off from home and family when martial law is declared in their country. Skolimowski's moving and imaginative parable of the Polish struggle stars Irons as the only member of the group who can speak English. ★★★½

Moonraker

(1979, 126 min, GB, Lewis Gilbert) *Roger Moore, Michael Lonsdale, Richard Kiel, Lois Chiles.* In this, the 11th outing of agent 007, Moore is on the trail of a wealthy industrialist (Lonsdale) who plans to poison the human race from the safety of his own private space station. Jaws (Kiel) returns, and Chiles is Dr. Holly Goodhead. Gimmicky but still fun. ★★★ VHS: $14.99; DVD: $34.99

Moonrise

(1948, 90 min, US, Frank Borzage) *Dane Clark, Lloyd Bridges, Ethel Barrymore.* This grim psychological melodrama is a brooding tale of a young man who, after years of being taunted by his and his father's past, accidentally kills a banker's son. A rural drama of violence, insanity and revenge. ★★★ VHS: $19.99

Moonstruck

(1987, 102 min, US, Norman Jewison) *Cher, Nicolas Cage, Olympia Dukakis, Danny Aiello, Vincent Gardenia, John Mahoney.* Cher won an Oscar for her performance as a young Italian-American widow in this loopy tale about the power of love over reason. Cage delivers an inspired over-the-top performance as her misfit brother-in-law-to-be to whom she is inextricably attracted. Jewison's direction of John Patrick Shanley's Oscar-winning screenplay "hits your eye like a big pizza pie!" Dukakis also won an Oscar in support as Cher's no-nonsense mother. ★★★½ VHS: $9.99; DVD: $19.99

More

(1969, 110 min, Luxembourg, Barbet Schroeder) *Mimsy Farmer, Klaus Grunberg.* The energy, excitement, innocence and eventual demise of the hippie/youth movement of the '60s is wonderfully captured in Schroeder's first film. The story is a tender tale of a West German student who travels across Europe — from the cafés of Paris to the sun-drenched beaches of Ibiza — searching for love and adventure. Schroeder provides a definitive image of this improbable era when peace, revolt, sex, drugs and rock 'n' roll reign supreme. The soundtrack features great music by Pink Floyd. (English and French, German and Spanish with English subtitles) ★★★½ VHS: $29.99

More Tales of the City

(1998, 330 min, US, Pierre Gang) *Olympia Dukakis, Laura Linney, Colin Ferguson, William Campbell, Swoosie Kurtz, Thomas Gibson, Barbara Garrick, Jackie Burroughs, Nina Siemaszko, Paul Bartel.* The stories of 28 Barbary Lane continue with more laughs, more sex and more mysteries with Armistead Maupin's six-part miniseries follow-up to the highly successful *Tales of the City.* Picking up where the original left off, Anna Madrigal (Dukakis) is still keeping watch over her tenants Mary Ann (Linney), who finds love with the mysterious Burke (Ferguson), and Michael "Mouse" Tolliver (Hopkins, replacing Marcus D'Amico), who falls hard for the dreamy Dr. Fielding (Campbell). *More Tales* is just as enjoyable as the original, and since there is less time introducing the characters, there's more time spent with them and developing them. Tensions about showing nudity and depicting homosexuality, which caused a controversy with the first production, have been

lessened, making the sequel more relaxed. As before, the series captures 1970s San Francisco in all its glory, featuring fabulous period details in the clothes, music and fads of the era. It's like reuniting with long-lost old friends. ★★★½ VHS: $99.99; DVD: $49.99

The More the Merrier

(1943, 104 min, US, George Stevens) *Jean Arthur, Joel McCrea, Charles Coburn.* A sparkling comedy from director Stevens. In overcrowded, wartime Washington, D.C., Arthur shares her small, one-bedroom apartment with McCrea and Coburn; the latter playing matchmaker. Coburn deservedly won a Best Supporting Oscar as the lovable Mr. Dingle; Arthur (though a nominee) probably should have won Best Actress for her captivating portrayal. Stevens also won an Oscar as Best Director. ★★★★ VHS: $19.99

Morgan!

(1966, 92 min, GB, Karel Reisz) *David Warner, Vanessa Redgrave, Robert Stephens, Graham Crowden, Edward Fox.* One of the finest and funniest black comedies ever to hail from the shores of Great Britain, *Morgan!* stars Warner as an artist teetering on the precipice of total insanity. After his wife (Redgrave) divorces him, he sets out on a series of lunatic escapades in an effort to reconcile himself to his new status. Filled with truth and pathos, this is a very funny look at the process of "breaking up." ★★★★

Morgan Stewart's Coming Home

(1987, 96 min, US, Alan Smithee) *Jon Cryer, Lynn Redgrave, Nicholas Pryor.* Maybe he should have stayed where he was... he might have had better luck. The usually reliable Cryer gives it the old college try playing a student who returns home to aid his father's election bid — turning the campaign upside down. Director Paul Aaron took his name off the film, replacing it with "Alan Smithee," the industry moniker for such occasions. ★½ VHS: $9.99

Morituri

(1965, 128 min, US, Bernhard Wicki) *Marlon Brando, Yul Brynner, Trevor Howard, Janet Margolin, Wally Cox.* One of Brando's more fascinating failures from the 1960s (a decade in which the star took many chances in his film roles — most of which foundered). Brando plays an anti-Nazi German demolitions expert who is "recruited" by the British to help them seize a German freighter which is booby-trapped to explode upon capture. Brynner also stars as the ship's captain. (*aka: The Saboteur* and *The Saboteur, Code Name Morituri*) ★★ VHS: $19.99

The Morning After

(1986, 103 min, US, Sidney Lumet) *Jane Fonda, Jeff Bridges, Raul Julia, Diane Salinger, Kathy Bates.* Fonda's bravura performance as an alcoholic actress on the skids highlights this predictable though gritty mystery thriller. Fonda awakes one morning to discover a corpse beside her — and she can't remember anything about the night before. Bridges helps her find out the truth. ★★½ VHS: $9.99

Morning Glory

(1933, 73 min, US, Lowell Sherman) *Katharine Hepburn, Douglas Fairbanks, Jr., Adolphe Menjou.* Hepburn won her first Oscar for her glorious performance as a starstruck actress determined to succeed on the New York stage. In a role similar to the one she would play in *Stage Door* a few years later, Hepburn shines in this compelling theatrical drama as Eva Lovelace, a small-town girl with stars in her eyes, and enough determination and talent to make sure her dreams come true. ★★★ VHS: $14.99

Morocco

(1930, 92 min, US, Josef Von Sternberg) *Gary Cooper, Marlene Dietrich, Adolphe Menjou.* The impossibly seductive Dietrich made her American film debut as a cabaret singer in Morocco, torn between Foreign Legionnaire Cooper and wealthy Menjou. Romantic and very interesting. ★★★½ VHS: $14.99

Mortal Kombat

(1995, 101 min, US, Paul Anderson) *Christopher Lambert, Robin Shou, Talisa Soto.* This video game-to-film transfer is a fun ride through strange worlds and raucous martial arts competitions which abandons any aspirations to plot or character development; everything in this movie is at the service of its action scenes. Three human heroes are pitted against a variety of evil humans, monsters and sorcerers. The outcome: the future of our world. Spectacular computer effects highlight its fight scenes, and the set design, also computer-aided, is very impressive. (VHS available letterboxed or pan & scan) (Sequel: *Mortal Kombat 2: Annihilation*) ★★½ VHS: $9.99; DVD: $19.99

Mortal Kombat 2: Annihilation

(1997, 91 min, US, John R. Leoneti) *Robin Shou, Talisa Soto, Irina Pantaeva, James Remar.* A cruddy sequel, this film based on a video game picks up at the very second the last one ended. It's up to the old gang to fight (and fight, and fight) to save the Earth. The combat choreography has its moments, but is generally choppy and unimaginative, and there's none of the nifty interaction of action and music that made the first sporadically fun. ★ VHS: $9.99; DVD: $19.99

The Mortal Storm

(1940, 100 min, US, Frank Borzage) *James Stewart, Margaret Sullavan, Frank Morgan, Robert Young, Robert Stack.* A moving, powerful adaptation of Phyllis Bottome's novel about life in pre-WWII Germany. Lovers Stewart and Sullavan are risk it all to leave the country as Nazism tears their families apart. Morgan is terrific as Sullavan's father, a professor whose humanistic beliefs become his undoing. ★★★½ VHS: $19.99

Mortal Thoughts

(1991, 102 min, US, Alan Rudolph) *Demi Moore, Glenne Headly, Harvey Keitel, Bruce Willis.* A stylish, gripping psychological thriller dripping in atmosphere and tension. Moore and Headley are lifelong friends and business partners; the latter is married to abusive Willis (thankfully underplaying his role). In an accident, he dies and the two cover up his death. But was it an accident? And who really did it? Keitel is the police detective grilling Moore for the answers — reliving the story through flashbacks right up to the unexpected ending. Though Moore's screen work here is possibly her best, Headly steals the show with a hypnotic performance as the suspected murderess. ★★★ VHS: $9.99; DVD: $19.99

Moscow Does Not Believe in Tears

(1980, 152 min, USSR, Vladimir Menshov) *Vera Alentova, Irina Muravyova, Raisa Ryazanova.* This surprise Oscar winner of 1981 is a light and charming look into contemporary Soviet life. The story concerns three young provincial girls' move to Moscow and their search for work, love and marriage. The first half could very well be a *How to Marry a Millionaire* — Soviet style! (Russian with English subtitles) ★★★ VHS: $59.99

Moscow on the Hudson

(1984, 115 min, US, Paul Mazursky) *Robin Williams, Maria Conchita Alonso, Cleavant Derricks.* Williams gives an endearingly sweet performance as a Russian musician who defects to America in the middle of Bloomingdale's. Writer-director Mazursky fills this benign satire with interesting eccentrics and amusing anecdotes as the befuddled defector suffers some severe culture shock. A totally winning social comedy. ★★★½ VHS: $9.99

The Mosquito Coast

(1986, 119 min, US, Peter Weir) *Harrison Ford, River Phoenix, Helen Mirren, Martha Plimpton, Andre Gregory, Butterfly McQueen, Jason Alexander.* Ford is well cast as Pennsylvania inventor Allie Fox, whose disgust with the direction of American culture prompts him to upheave his family to a primitive Central American island to start a utopian society. But for Fox there is no escaping civilization. Once they reach their paradise, the society left behind begins to rear its ugly head, sending the father into a paranoid state, and eventually madness. Phoenix gives a powerful performance as the teenage son who must protect his family when their paradise turns hellish. Paul Schrader's screenplay digs deep into a man's psyche and the nature of our modern existence. ★★★ VHS: $14.98; DVD: $19.99

Most Wanted

(1997, 99 min, US, David Glenn Hogan) *Keenen Ivory Wayans, Jon Voight, Jill Hennessy, Paul Sorvino, Robert Culp, Eric Roberts.* Looking as if he's trying to emulate Steven Seagal (and not the likable *Under Siege* persona, either), Wayans plays a marine (sentenced to die after accidentally killing a superior officer) who is recruited into a secret government organization. But since most of the story in this derivative, formulaic actioner we've seen before, we know that when he's hired to assassinate a target, and the First Lady is killed instead, he'll be blamed, he'll set out to prove his innocence and expose the conspiracy. Director Hogan gives the film a good look, though his action scenes are routine. ★★ VHS: $9.99; DVD: $19.99

Motel Hell

(1980, 92 min, US, Kevin Connor) *Rory Calhoun, Nancy Parsons.* This spoofy horror film brings new meaning to the term "tongue-in-cheek." A country sausage king has a secret ingredient for his delicious product: the guests staying at his backwoods motel. ★½ VHS: $14.99

Mother

(1926, 90 min, Russia, V.I. Pudovkin) *Vera Baranovskaya, Nikolai Batalov.* Set during the unsuccessful workers' rebellion of 1905, Pudovkin's engrossing story is about one fami-ly's hardships under the cruel czarist regime. A technically impressive allegory for Russia's conversion to Communism. (Silent with musical accompaniment) ★★★; DVD: $24.99

Mother

(1996, 104 min, US, Albert Brooks) *Albert Brooks, Debbie Reynolds, Rob Morrow, Lisa Kudrow, John C. McGinley.* Brooks sets out to prove that even though she may not wear Army boots, there's still plenty to fear from that dear old materfamilias, especially when you're a middle-aged divorcé caught in the throes of depression. Brooks is in his element as a quintessential schnook and author of cheap sci-fi thrillers that nobody reads who decides that the only way to get his life back in gear is to move back in with his mother. Reynolds is superb as his put-upon mom who just can't understand what all his fussing is about anyway. Brooks' script does a fine job skewering mother-son stereotypes, delivering several big laughs at the expense of just about everybody from cheap pop psychologists to mom herself. With this wonderful lark, Brooks proves *Mother* knows best. ★★★½ VHS: $9.99; DVD: $29.99

The Mother and the Whore

(1973, 215 min, France, Jean Eustache) *Bernadette Lafont, Jean-Pierre Léaud, Françoise Lebrun.* A 3-hour, 35-minute Gaullic exploraton of the perverse, dichotomous delineation of woman, aptly summed up by the film's title. As he served so ably for Truffaut, one gets the impression that Léaud functions as director Eustache's alter ego. Léaud is Alexandre; a man whose intellectual pretensions provide the unending polemic of his objectification of women — woman as object of desire, disdain, faux adoration; woman as only a reflection of man's desire. Under the pretense of an open relationship with two of his several female lovers, Alexandre requires commitment, offering none in return. The women are complicit in the underlying belief system, even as it engenders deep unhappiness. Fittingly, there is no resolution. A radical exposition in its time, the film now plays as a cultural relic; yet easily remains an item of interest to both cinephiles and Francophiles. (French with English subtitles) ★★★ VHS: $29.99

Mother Kusters Goes to Heaven

(1976, 108 min, Germany, Rainer Werner Fassbinder) *Brigitte Mira, Ingrid Caven, Margit Carstensen.* Mira is outstanding as Mother Küsters, an older woman whose sedate, ordinary life is thrown into turmoil when her husband goes mad at work, killing the paymaster, and then committing suicide. As she struggles to understand what happened to her husband, the emotional poverty of her life is revealed in her casual comments regarding her husband's lack of communication, her daughter's ability to turn the media attention to career advantage and her son's inability to counter his wife's desire to distance herself from the embarrassment. Mira's entirely believable performance and Fassbinder's unerring cynical eye deliver a powerful treatise on the human propensity toward exploitation. (German with English subtitles) ★★★½

Nicole Kidman and Ewan McGregor in Baz Luhrmann's *Moulin Rouge*

way to look at musical scoring. Director Luhrmann, whose *William Shakespeare's Romeo + Juliet* was a great combination of sight and sound, tops himself visually as this story of the quest for "truth, beauty, freedom, but above all things, love," is often stunning to behold. Incorporating contemporary songs (from Madonna to Sting to *The Sound of Music*) into a Paris at the turn of the century is a risky undertaking, but it works thanks to some fancy editing and an assault of the senses. Displaying a fine voice and soulful looks, McGregor plays a naïve writer who falls for the most beautiful courtesan (Kidman) at the Moulin Rouge. She would like to return his love, but she's promised to another. Thus begins this Orphean descent into heartbreak and tragedy. The story and a few supporting characters aren't quite as developed as one would wish, but the dizzying musical numbers (imagine *Cabaret* reinterpreted by Timothy Leary), lush costumes and sets, and nods to opera, Comédie-Française and Bollywood will make one forget about the film's few shortcomings and heady excesses. Like the can-can that the dancers perform in an opening number, *Moulin Rouge* revels in its own extravagance and offers a defiant thumb to convention, but it's a real kick in the pantaloons. ★★★½ VHS: $102.99; DVD $29.99

Mother Night

(1996, 113 min, US, Keith Gordon) *Nick Nolte, Sheryl Lee, Alan Arkin, John Goodman, Kirsten Dunst, Arye Gross, David Strathairn, Henry Gibson.* A wonderfully wry and unexpectedly romantic adaptation of Kurt Vonnegut's 1974 novel, *Mother Night* marks another successful behind-the-camera turn for actor-turned-director Gordon. Using flashback to recall the life of an American double agent living in Nazi Germany, the story begins with Howard Campbell (Nolte) serving time in an Israeli prison. Traveling back and forth in time (much like Vonnegut's *Slaughterhouse-Five*), the film focuses on Campbell's post-war life as a desolate, lonely widower in New York whose name perversely comes before the public once more. Vonnegut takes a moral dilemma and devours it, spitting out chunks of ambiguity and the bizarre with devilish delight. ★★★½ VHS: $19.99; DVD: $24.99

Mother's Boys

(1994, 95 min, US, Yves Simoneau) *Jamie Lee Curtis, Peter Gallagher, Joanne Whalley-Kilmer, Vanessa Redgrave, Joss Ackland.* A Freudian suspenser about a well-bred sociopath who, having abandoned her husband (Gallagher) and children years earlier, tries to reclaim them using her eldest son as leverage. Curtis is suitably creepy as a woman who will stop at nothing — even sexual intimidation — to win back her family. However, the film ultimately deteriorates into standard shock fare. ★★½ VHS: $19.99; DVD: $29.99

Mothra

(1962, 100 min, Japan, Inoshiro Honda) *Yumi Ito, Frankie Sakai.* The director of the first *Godzilla* movie created this cute fairy tale about two twin six-inch princesses kidnapped from their throne on Infant Island and exhibited on Tokyo television singing their siren song — a song that calls their giant moth to come and save them, at the city's expense. ★★ VHS: $12.99

Motor Psycho

(1965, 65 min, US, Russ Meyer) Three bikers, led by a crazed Vietnam vet, go on an unstoppable orgy of rape and murder, until a vengeful husband gets on their trail and forces a showdown. Made between *Mudhoney* and *Faster, Pussycat, Kill! Kill!* and featuring the alluring Haji, *Motor Psycho* is Meyer's entry into the biker genre and presages *Faster, Pussycat*'s theme of rampaging maniacs in the desert terrorizing hapless strangers. ★★ VHS: $79.99

Mouchette

(1966, 90 min, France, Robert Bresson) *Nadine Nortier, Maria Cardinal.* The last 24 hours in the life of a 14-year-old peasant girl is starkly presented without pity and without offering a single glimmer of hope. This moving story of humiliation and defeat traces the experiences of Mouchette, a bewildered youngster who is victimized at home by her drunken father, alienated at school, isolated from a hostile world and who is finally driven to suicide. A simply told, overwhelming story whose strong narrative and technical virtuosity transcends the unrelentingly grim dramatics. (French with English subtitles) ★★★½ VHS: $24.99

Moulin Rouge

(1952, 123 min, US, John Huston) *Jose Ferrer, Zsa Zsa Gabor, Christopher Lee, Peter Cushing, Colette Marchand.* A fascinating film biography, rich in color and detail, about the life of 19th-century French painter Henri de Toulouse-Lautrec. Ferrer gives a stunning portrayal of the troubled artist, whose growth impediment was impetus to his flagrant lifestyle and art. ★★★½ VHS: $19.99

Moulin Rouge

(2001, 126 min, Australia, Baz Luhrmann) *Nicole Kidman, Ewan McGregor, John Leguizamo, Jim Broadbent, Richard Roxburgh, Garry McDonald, Jacek Koman.* Audacious, energetic and off-the-wall, *Moulin Rouge* moves at the speed of sound as it nearly reinvents the movie musical with bursts of color, frenetic pacing and a whole new

The Mountain

(1956, 105 min, US, Edward Dmytryk) *Spencer Tracy, Robert Wagner, Claire Trevor, William Demarest, E.G. Marshall.* Tracy and Wagner are two brothers at odds while climbing a treacherous peak to reach an aircraft that crashed. Tracy's sincere performance highlights this familiar tale of familial conflict. ★★½ VHS: $14.99

Mountains of the Moon

(1990, 135 min, US, Bob Rafelson) *Patrick Bergin, Iain Glen, Fiona Shaw, Bernard Hill, Richard E. Grant, Roger Rees, Delroy Lindo, Roshan Seth.* Inspired by the journals of 19th-century explorers Richard Burton and Jack Speke, this is a stirring account of the torturous and famous expedition taken by the two adventurers to discover the source of the Nile. Rafelson meticulously re-creates the worlds of privileged Britain and small-tribe Africa, and has fashioned an exhilarating adventure film of the highest order. Bergin and Glen give outstanding performances as Burton and Speke, respectively, whose sometimes perilous and always enlightening journey began in 1854, and ended many years and thousands of miles later in betrayal and death. ★★★★ VHS: $14.99; DVD: $24.99

The Mouse on the Moon

(1963, 85 min, GB, Richard Lester) *Margaret Rutherford, Bernard Cribbins, Ron Moody, Terry-Thomas, Michael Crawford.* Joyful sequel to *The Mouse That Roared* has the tiny country of Duchy of Grand Feswick entering the space race. Rutherford steals the show as the Grand Duchess. ★★★½ VHS: $14.99; DVD: $19.99

The Mouse That Roared

(1959, 83 min, GB, Jack Arnold) *Peter Sellers, Jean Seberg, Leo McKern.* This hilarious satire on the idiocies of foreign policy involves the miniscule Grand Duchy of Fenwick which declares war on the United States with the intention of losing in order to receive foreign aid. This is a film which could have only been made in the pre-Vietnam era, when America was still basking in its Marshall Plan glow. Featuring Sellers in three amusing roles, and a pre-opening sequence which ranks as a classic. (Sequel: *The Mouse on the Moon*) ★★★½ VHS: $19.99

Mousehunt

(1997, 97 min, US, Gore Verbinski) *Nathan Lane, Lee Evans, Christopher Walken, Vicki Lewis, Michael Jeter.* A very funny slapstick family comedy which is fun for all ages, *Mousehunt* is a live-action Road Runner cartoon, with two hapless brothers as the coyote, and one clever, little mouse as their adversary. Brothers Lane and Evans inherit a not-so-profitable string factory and a run-down mansion. Circumstances dictate that they both stay at their new home, which is deteriorated beyond belief. But worst of all to the brothers — who have just learned the house is worth millions — is the presence of a pesky rodent. In some finely detailed broad comedy, *Mousehunt* depicts the merry destruction which ensues at the hands of the brothers in their quest to get rid of the mouse. Lane and Evans are a couple of inspired lunatics, and their succession of comic humiliations keep this rodenticide safari a consistently entertaining journey. ★★★ VHS: $14.99; DVD: $29.99

Mouth to Mouth

(1995, 96 min, Spain, Manuel Gomez Pereira) *Javier Bardem, Aitana Sanchez-Gijon, Josep Maria Flotats.* A strained Spanish sex farce, *Mouth to Mouth* concerns Victor (Bardem), an out-of-work actor who reluctantly takes a job as a phone sex operator while awaiting his big break. Although he becomes the favorite of a male client, Victor is straight, and he is soon seduced by a caller named Amanda (Sanchez-Gijon), whom he arranges to meet on the side. When Amanda involves Victor in a blackmail scheme which backfires, his personal and professional worlds begin to collide. *Mouth to Mouth* does have some madcap moments, but ultimately the film plays its comedy too broadly. Despite Bardem's wholesome sex appeal and energetic performance, his desperation is just not very amusing. (Dubbed) ★★ VHS: $19.99

Movie Movie

(1979, 107 min, US, Stanley Donen) *George C. Scott, Trish Van Devere, Harry Hamlin, Eli Wallach, Red Buttons, Barbara Harris, Barry Bostwick, Art Carney.* A joyous tribute to 1930s and '40s filmmaking, this "double feature" offers two stories (and a trailer) that affectionately poke fun at the conventions and clichés of particular genre films from that era. "Dynamite Hands" is first, a black-and-white boxing tale with Scott as a grizzled manager and Hamlin as a raw youth who makes good; the second story is "Baxter's Beauties of 1933," a color spoof of Busby Berkeley musicals. ★★★½

Moving

(1988, 89 min, US, Alan Metter) *Richard Pryor, Beverly Todd, Randy Quaid, Dana Carvey, Stacey Dash, Rodney Dangerfield.* New Jerseyites Pryor and family pack up and move to Idaho when Dad lands a great job. Most of this is of the predictable sort, but Pryor's manic reactions and character make it tolerable. ★★ VHS: $14.99

Moving the Mountain

(1995, 83 min, US/China, Michael Apted) Director Apted has made an insightful exploration of the human condition with this powerful documentary. Chronicling several people in leadership positions during the Tiananmen Square protests, the film recounts their involvement and gives a history of the events which led to the killing of thousands and the reawakening of an undercurrent of change within China. *Moving the Mountain* is a sobering view of these now-exiled students, and the film is enhanced by stylish editing, engaging principals, and inspirational stories. ★★★½ VHS: $14.99

The Mozart Brothers

(1986, 98 min, Sweden, Suzanne Osten) *Etienne Glaser, Philip Zanden.* An often hilarious view of the artistic process choosing to draw upon the Marx Brothers' *A Night at the Opera* for inspiration. The story concerns a radically innovative production of Mozart's "Don Giovanni" as done by a Stockholm opera company. We are given a profound look at the trials of Walter, the fanatically avant-garde theatre director, whose attempts to win the hearts of the intransigent singers often result in some of the film's funniest moments. In a somewhat Bergman-esque touch, the ghost of Mozart offers Walter encouragement and advice through nocturnal visitations. For fans of opera, theatre and music alike, this is a wonderful flight of fancy which will surely not disappoint. (Swedish with English subtitles) ★★★ VHS: $24.99

Mr.

See: Mister

Mrs. Brown

(1997, 103 min, GB, John Madden) *Judi Dench, Billy Connolly, Antony Sher.* With eyes of icy steel and manner fixed and regal, Dench gives a superlative portrayal of England's Queen Victoria in this handsome historical drama about her 20-year relationship with her servant/confidant John Brown. It is 1864, and the Queen is still mourning the death of her beloved Albert. All ceremoniously walk gently in her presence. That is until the arrival of Brown (Connolly), Albert's former footman. She gradually learns to depend on him, which sends shock waves around the court and rumors of a romantic nature all over England. Director Madden gives the film a splendid look, effortlessly evoking the time and place of 19th-century court. But it is the performances of Dench and Connolly which really distinguish the film. Dench's marvelous portrayal is a revelation, rich in subtlety and fervor. Connolly is also wondrous, giving passion and life to the queen's loyal servant. ★★★ VHS: $19.99; DVD: $29.99

Mrs. Brown, You've Got a Lovely Daughter

(1968, 110 min, GB, Saul Swimmer) *Herman's Hermits, Mona Washbourne, Stanley Holloway.* A lightweight vehicle for '60s pop group Herman's Hermits. The band, of course, sings the title song along with their other hit, "There's a Kind of Hush." This jump on the Beatles' *A Hard Day's Night* bandwagon is only intermittently entertaining. ★★

Mrs. Dalloway

(1998, 98 min, GB, Marleen Gorris) *Vanessa Redgrave, Natascha McElhone, Rupert Graves, Michael Kitchen.* On a perfect day in 1923, memories of her youth course through the day's events as Mrs. Dalloway (Redgrave) prepares for another of her elaborate parties. In an ordered English garden, a young veteran makes his own peace with the ravages of shell shock; at a nearby bench, Mrs. Dalloway's rejected suitor of decades past indulges his own reminiscences. Director Gorris has captured Virginia Woolf's novel of that society of manners, a complex social structure unaware of its impending demise; juxtaposing it against the oncoming realities of the modern age. An intricately crafted film sparkled with superb portrayals, *Mrs. Dalloway* unerringly evokes a time recently, irrevocably past. ★★★½ VHS: $19.99; DVD: $19.99

Mrs. Doubtfire

(1993, 105 min, US, Chris Columbus) *Robin Williams, Sally Field, Pierce Brosnan, Harvey Fierstein, Robert Prosky, Polly Holliday, Scott Capurro.* Heavy on the laughter as well as the sentiment, *Mrs. Doubtfire* is an appealing comedy in spite of its sprinkling of "Afterschool Special" schmaltz. Featuring a very funny performance by Williams, this entertaining, high-concept comedy casts Williams as a recently divorced actor. Losing a custody battle over his three children, Williams takes advantage of ex-wife Field's search for a housekeeper — and impersonates a sixty-ish British nanny. Often recalling *Tootsie*, *Mrs. Doubtfire* isn't at that film's level, but it does firmly stand on its own two orthopedic pumps. ★★★ VHS: $14.99; DVD: $29.99

Mrs. Miniver

(1942, 134 min, US, William Wyler) *Greer Garson, Walter Pidgeon, Teresa Wright, Dame May Whitty, Henry Travers, Peter Lawford.* A beautifully filmed, exceptionally acted drama of a British family facing the rigors of WWII. Garson won a Best Actress Oscar as the title character, a formidable wife and mother who does her best to keep her family together in the wake of separation and tragedy. Pidgeon is just fine as Mr. Miniver, and Wright is lovely as their daughter-in-law. Winner of seven Oscars, including Picture and Director. ★★★½ VHS: $19.99

Mrs. Parker and the Vicious Circle

(1994, 123 min, US, Alan Rudolph) *Jennifer Jason Leigh, Campbell Scott, Matthew Broderick,*

Vanessa Redgrave in *Mrs. Dalloway*

Mulan

Andrew McCarthy, Peter Gallagher, Martha Plimpton, Stephen Baldwin, Jennifer Beals, Gwyneth Paltrow, Lili Taylor, James LeGros. Leigh gives a tour de force performance as Algonquin wit and writer Dorothy Parker. In this extremely humorous though slightly downbeat examination of a troubled soul, director Rudolph has brilliantly reconstructed 1920s New York — a time when a select group of Manhattan's literary set convened to sling the next bon mot. In a series of flashbacks, the story follows Parker's rise as an author, her relationships with humorist Robert Benchley (Scott) and playwright Charles MacArthur (Broderick), and the formation of the legendary Algonquin Round Table. Leigh inhabits Parker as if possessed, conveying an eerie worldliness and heartbreaking vulnerability. ★★★½ VHS: $19.99

Mrs. Parkington

(1944, 124 min, US, Tay Garnett) *Greer Garson, Walter Pidgeon, Agnes Moorehead, Edward Arnold.* A dedicated cast enlivens this compelling soap opera. Spanning the course of 60 years in the life of the title character, the film features Garson as a wealthy New York family matriarch who is faced with a familial crisis. Remembering the past for guidance, Mrs. Parkington recalls her life and marriage to her "scoundrel" industrialist husband, played by Pidgeon. Although the dramatics are routine, it is the earnest performances from the entire cast which elevate it. ★★½ VHS: $19.99

Mrs. Soffel

(1985, 110 min, US, Gillian Armstrong) *Diane Keaton, Mel Gibson, Mathew Modine, Edward Herrmann.* Keaton is the sheltered wife of a stern prison warden who surrenders to the powerful attraction of a death-row convict (Gibson); both become the object of a massive man hunt when she helps him escape and they run away together. The attractive pairing of Keaton and Gibson and a good evocation of the period aren't sufficient enough to mask a dreary story and a passionless directorial style. (VHS available letterboxed or pan & scan) ★★ VHS: $14.99

Ms. Don Juan

(1973, 87 min, France, Roger Vadim) *Brigette Bardot, Maurice Ronet, Jane Birkin.* Vadim, mediocre filmmaker but successful promotor of such sex sirens as Jane Fonda, Brigette Bardot and Catherine Deneuve, directed this half-baked tale of murder and passion. BB

stars as an evil seductress with an insatiable sexual appetite and hypnotic charms who devours and destroys everyone in sight. A sexual switch of the Don Juan story. ★★

Ms. 45

(1981, 84 min, US, Abel Ferrara) *Zoe Tamerlis, Steve Singer.* A Freudian, feminist revenge fantasy. Tamerlis is riveting as a victimized deaf-mute who adopts the Charles Bronson method of street sanitation and wages a war against the male scum population. (aka: *Angel of Vengeance*) ★★★ VHS: $19.99; DVD: $24.99

Much Ado about Nothing

(1993, 110 min, GB, Kenneth Branagh) *Kenneth Branagh, Emma Thompson, Denzel Washington, Michael Keaton, Robert Sean Leonard, Keanu Reeves, Brian Blessed, Richard Briers.* Returning to the familiar soil of Shakespeare, actor-director Branagh springs forth with a delightfully giddy and frantic romp set in the sun-drenched fields of Tuscany. Shakespeare's bawdy comic tale of love torn asunder casts Branagh and Thompson as the sharp-witted, acerbic would-be lovers Benedick and Beatrice, whose course of true love is not a tranquil one. Branagh and Thompson, radiant together, elevate the Bard's prose to resplendent levels of ecstasy. *Much Ado* is truly a to do: a joyous celebration of unbridled passions. ★★★★ VHS: $14.99; DVD: $27.99

Mudhoney

(1965, 92 min, US, Russ Meyer) A black-and-white profile of rural Missouri lowlife in the '30s, which rails against American morality and religious hypocrisy. Stars Lorna Maitland, Rena Horten ("the embodiment of the body") and the buxom Lee Ballard. ★½ VHS: $79.99

Mulan

(1998, 88 min, US, Barry Cook & Tony Bancroft) *Voices of Ming-Na Wen, Eddie Murphy, B.D. Wong, Lea Salonga, Donny Osmond, Miguel Ferrer, Harvey Fierstein.* A sumptuous animated treat, *Mulan* is a sprawling samurai epic with a cross-dressing heroine who defies family and tradition by secretly going off to war in the place of her father — dressed as a boy. Building on the timeless themes of honor and loyalty, of adolescent rebellion and seeking out your own destiny, the storytellers have found the right material to adapt into a musical. However, the songs themselves lack the jubilant spirit of the tunes from better Disney classics. But the animation itself is glorious, despite the fact that Disney has become far-too-reliant on computers to generate complex, eye-popping vistas. *Mulan* is hardly worthy of comparisons to the jewels in the Disney crown, but remains a fast-paced, high-spirited entertainment. ★★★½ VHS: $22.99; DVD: $29.99

Mulholland Falls

(1996, 107 min, US, Lee Tamahori) *Nick Nolte, Melanie Griffith, Chazz Palminteri, Michael*

Madsen, Chris Penn, John Malkovich, Treat Williams, Jennifer Connelly, Andrew McCarthy. In 1950s Los Angeles, a renegade group of cops known as the "Hat Squad" implemented their own individual brand of justice against criminals with an unlawful but patriotic zeal. Had they ever seen this muddled though frequently exciting exposé of vigilantism and cover-up suggested by their real-life exploits, the filmmakers may have been next to be "escorted" out of town. Nolte heads the cast as one of the elite cops whose investigation into the death of a woman leads him into complex mystery and military conspiracy. This excellent evocation of post-war L.A. is unfortunately a bargain basement *Chinatown*, which only belies its original premise. Tamahori has a great feel for time and place but isn't able to jump start a contrived script. ★★½ VHS: $9.99

Multiple Maniacs

(1971, 94 min, US, John Waters) *Divine, Mink Stole.* The film Waters claimed "flushed religion out of my system" is so irredeemable that even describing it offends public standards of morality. But we'll try. A traveling carnival called "Lady Divine's Cavalcade of Perversions" lands in Baltimore and disrupts the lives of the creeps living there. We're treated to a junkie shooting up on a church altar, bearded transvestites, the semi-classic scene of Divine being raped by a 15-foot lobster, Stole's rosary beads, cannibalism, Kate Smith's rendition of "God Bless America" and, perhaps most disturbing of all, shots of downtown Baltimore. ★★★

Multiplicity

(1996, 110 min, US, Harold Ramis) *Michael Keaton, Andie MacDowell, Richard Masur, Harris Yulin, Eugene Levy, Brian Doyle-Murray.* Keaton gets cloned and essentially plays with himself in this amiable though lackluster comedy whose cute premise is never fully realized. Keaton plays a harried construction foreman who doesn't have enough hours in the day for his professional or private lives. After a chance meeting with a scientist, Keaton is cloned, enabling the original to spend more quality time with the wife (MacDowell) and kids while the "Xerox copy" shows up at work. In time, there are four Keatons running around on the screen, engaging in predictable shenanigans. The screenplay doesn't come close to the film's F/X wizardry, and the laugh quotient is surprisingly low. ★★ VHS: $14.99; DVD: $24.99

The Mummy

(1932, 72 min, US, Karl Freund) *Boris Karloff, Zita Johann, David Manners.* Noted cinematographer Freund (*Metropolis, Dracula*) made his directorial debut in Karloff's second greatest horror role. Buried alive for trying to restore life to his great love, it is he who is accidentally revived by an overeager archaeologist. Moody and foreboding, this tragic tale of love lost over the centuries moves ceaselessly forward towards its inevitable destiny. ★★★½ VHS: $14.99; DVD: $29.99

The Mummy

(1959, 86 min, GB, Terence Fisher) *Christopher Lee, Peter Cushing, Yvonne Furneaux.* Journeyman director Fisher brings his usual panache to the remake of the Karloff classic based on an early draft for that film. Lee is the resurrected

M

avenger out for archaeologist Cushing's blood in this, one of Hammer Films' most stylish efforts. ★★★ VHS: $14.99

The Mummy

(1999, 124 min, US, Stephen Sommers) *Brendan Fraser, Rachel Weisz, John Hannah, Arnold Vosloo, Kevin J. O'Connor.* Don't expect to be frightened out of your wits with an unrelenting barrage of horror sequences. Sommers' *Mummy* doesn't go there. Borrowing a little derring-do from *Raiders of the Lost Ark* and some offhand humor from *Gunga Din*, this update of the 1930s chestnut is cheesy fun, down to its hackneyed screenplay, great special effects and mix of humor, action and scares. Fraser, Weisz and Hannah, at the lost city of Hamunaptra, unwittingly let loose the spirit of a 3,000-year-old mummy, who plans to conquer the world as soon as he regenerates. It's the sort of film in which every 10 minutes or so our hapless heroes find themselves in another inescapable predicament. It's fun to watch them weasel out of them. (VHS available letterboxed or pan & scan) (Sequel: *The Mummy Returns*) ★★★ VHS: $14.99; DVD: $29.99

The Mummy Returns

(2001, 125 min, US, Stephen Sommers) *Brendan Fraser, Rachel Weisz, John Hannah, Arnold Vosloo, Oded Fehr, The Rock.* The mummy returns, indeed. Not quite a promise as it is a threat, this sequel to 1999's enjoyable surprise hit is much more of the same — emphasis on same. Fraser returns as the derring-do adventurer; so do Weisz as his wife and Hannah as her brother. Vosloo is back, too, as the 3,000-year-old mummy whose name you can't pronounce. Back are the terrific special effects (they may even be better this time around), cheesy story (it may be cheesier this time around), and mix of humor and action. The Rock is new. Don't count on anything else new, however. This rehash isn't as much fun as the original, and the characters — who helped make the first film so entertaining — are secondary to the stunning effects. A rousing finale wraps this mummy up, giving the appearance that this second go-round is more substantial than it really is. There's always something going on, some predicament to get out of, but it just isn't quite the same. Oh, wait, yes it is. ★★½ VHS: $22.99; DVD: $29.99

The Mummy's Hand

(1940, 67 min, US, Christy Cabanne) *Dick Foran, Wallace Ford, Peggy Moran, Tom Tyler, Cecil Kellaway.* Before passing the role to Lon Chaney, Tyler starred as Kharis, the mummy, in this first of a series. The action takes place at an archaeological dig where explorers find the sacred tomb of an Egyptian princess still guarded by Kharis. Excellent set design and good acting combine to make this a classic from the golden age of horror films. Trivia buffs take note: look for ten minutes of footage from Karloff's *The Mummy* (1932), used here as flashback. ★★★ VHS: $14.99

The Muppet Movie

(1979, 94 min, US, James Frawley) *Kermit, Miss Piggy, Fozzie; Cameos: Steve Martin, Carol Kane, Orson Welles, Milton Berle, Mel Brooks, Madeline Kahn, Bob Hope.* The first of the Muppet films, this sweet, entertaining children's film follows the trail of Kermit the Frog on his way to stardom. Miss Piggy, Fozzie, Gonzo and the rest of the gang tag along. There's a charming musical score by Paul Williams. ★★★ VHS: $9.99; DVD: $19.99

Muppet Treasure Island

(1996, 99 min, US, Brian Henson) *Kermit, Miss Piggy, Gonzo, Rizzo, Fozzie Bear, Tim Curry, Kevin Bishop, Jennifer Saunders, Billy Connolly.* The always-welcome Muppets return in an energetic retelling of the Stevenson classic. Gonzo and Rizzo the Rat take center stage joined by Muppet faves Kermit, Miss Piggy and Fozzie (playing a lunatic whose best friend lives in his index finger); Curry, Bishop and Connelly lend human support. This is a wholly entertaining lark, thanks to both the kooky antics in which the characters engage, and the fact that the creators play the story straight (as they did in the even better *Muppet Christmas Carol*). Not without its slow moments, the film nevertheless has wondrous bits, such as a Carmen Miranda-inspired free-for-all performed by pirates and Muppets in drag. ★★★ VHS: $22.99

The Muppets Christmas Carol

(1992, 85 min, US, Brian Henson) *Kermit, Miss Piggy, Fozzie, Michael Caine.* Jim Henson may be gone, but his legacy continues through his son Brian in this latest adaptation of the Dickens classic. Caine (looking very well, thank you) stars as Ebenezer Scrooge, and Kermit and Miss Piggy star as Bob and Emily Cratchit. This could easily become a perennial family favorite with the familiar characters intact, but toned down just slightly for the younger set. Narration by Gonzo as Dickens himself helps introduce the plot lines and add some background. It's funny, touching and, of course, a technical marvel, seamlessly blending Muppet characters with the humans. ★★★½ VHS: $14.99

The Muppets Take Manhattan

(1984, 94 min, US, Frank Oz) *Kermit, Miss Piggy, Fozzie; Cameos: Sandra Bernhard, James Coco, Joan Rivers, Liza Minnelli, Gregory Hines, Art Carney.* The title is more than lived up to as Kermit, Miss Piggy and the rest of the gang head to New York to put on a Broadway musical. Lots of fun. ★★★ VHS: $9.99; DVD: $19.99

Murder

(1930, 92 min, GB, Alfred Hitchcock) *Herbert Marshall, Norah Baring.* A fast-paced and inventive whodunit about a juror in an actress' murder trial who becomes convinced of the woman's innocence and sets out for some amateur sleuthing. The bizarre truth is ultimately revealed with an extraordinary twist. ★★★ VHS: $12.99

Murder at 1600

(1997, 107 min, US, Dwight H. Little) *Wesley Snipes, Diane Lane, Daniel Benzali, Alan Alda, Ronny Cox.* A by-the-books but competently made thriller which suggests that there's more shenanigans going on in the White House than seances and shredding parties. Snipes plays a D.C. homicide detective investigating a murder in the White House who is up against constant interference from Secret Service chief Benzali and staff, including Lane — who eventually becomes Snipes' ally. There are a couple of unpredictable twists and a few red herrings, but director Little seems more concerned with chases and the rudiments of the action film than laying the foundation for a good mystery. ★★½ VHS: $9.99; DVD: $19.99

Murder by Death

(1976, 94 min, US, Robert Moore) *Peter Falk, David Niven, Peter Sellers, Maggie Smith, Alec Guinness, Elsa Lanchester, James Coco, James Cromwell, Nancy Walker, Truman Capote.* Neil Simon wrote the screenplay for this delightfully zany spoof on movie detectives; with an all-star cast doing a number on Nick and Nora Charles (Niven, Smith), Miss Marple (Lanchester), Charlie Chan (Sellers), Hercule Poirot (Coco) and Sam Spade (Falk). Plenty of laughs and lots of fun. ★★★ VHS: $14.99

Murder by Decree

(1979, 121 min, Canada/GB, Bob Clark) *Christopher Plummer, James Mason, Candy Clark, Genevieve Bujold, Donald Sutherland, John Gielgud.* A superior, dark-edged Sherlock Holmes mystery with Plummer as the famous sleuth, and Mason as Dr. Watson. An investigation into the murders of Jack the Ripper suggest involvement by a member of the Royal family. Plummer makes a most convincing Holmes, and Mason is a wondrous Watson. ★★★½

Murder in the First

(1994, 122 min, US, Marc Rocco) *Kevin Bacon, Christian Slater, Gary Oldman, Kyra Sedgwick, Embeth Davidtz, Brad Dourif.* Bacon shines in this somber and tragic slice of history about Henri Young who, in 1937, after a botched escape attempt lands him three years naked and freezing in the bowels of Alcatraz, murders in plain sight the stool pigeon who turned him in. Slater is the fledgling public defender who turns a simple open-and-shut case into an indictment against the prison system and Alcatraz itself. Director Rocco enhances what would normally be deemed "made-for-TV" fare with gripping scenes of prison brutality. This violence is characterized by yet another showy performance

Brendan Fraser in *The Mummy Returns*

from Oldman as the sadistic associate warden. ★★★ VHS: $9.99; DVD: $14.99

Murder, My Sweet

(1944, 95 min, US, Edward Dmytryk) *Dick Powell, Claire Trevor, Anne Shirley, Otto Kruger, Mike Mazurki.* One of the classics of film noir, this adaptation of Raymond Chandler's "Farewell, My Lovely" is a raw but exhilarating murder mystery where hard-boiled, wise-cracking detective Phillip Marlowe (Powell) becomes immersed in a duplicitous world of evil where everyone is a suspect and no one should be trusted. After taking on the case of finding ex-con Moose Malloy's missing girlfriend Velma, Marlowe soon is over his head in a sordid and ever more confusing maze of kidnappers, liars and ruthless killers. Superb dialogue and a great story highlight this stylish, trend-setting mystery. ★★★½ VHS: $14.99

Murder on the Bayou

(1987, 91 min, US, Volker Schlöndorff) *Holly Hunter, Louis Gossett, Jr., Richard Widmark, Woody Strode, Papa John Creach, Will Patton.* Written by Charles Fuller, this is a powerful drama of racial tensions in the New South. Set amidst the sugar cane fields of a searingly hot Louisiana, the film stars Hunter as a liberal plantation owner who galvanizes a group of long down-trodden black farmers and fishermen to militantly defend a fellow black man who claims that he killed a white man in self-defense. Impressive acting from the ensemble of elderly 38 men and a deft touch from German director Schlöndorff highlight this absorbing story of unity and courage. (aka: *A Gathering of Old Men*) ★★★½ VHS: $14.99

Murder on the Orient Express

(1974, 127 min, GB, Sidney Lumet) *Albert Finney, Ingrid Bergman, Lauren Bacall, Sean Connery, Jacqueline Bisset, Vanessa Redgrave, Anthony Perkins, Richard Widmark, John Gielgud, Wendy Hiller, Michael York, Martin Balsam, Rachel Roberts.* Agatha Christie's popular novel makes for a sumptuous ride on the Orient Express in this big-budget, large-scaled, all-star murder mystery. Finney, obviously enjoying himself, stars as Hercule Poirot, that famed Belgian detective who finds himself investigating the murder of an American industrialist (Widmark) while a passenger on the famed luxury train. With more than enough suspects to go around, Poirot systematically interrogates and eliminates until the final and very surprising conclusion. A truly impressive cast. Lumet's pace is even throughout, which doesn't give rise to too many overly exciting scenes, but he keeps the whodunit aspect absolutely entrancing. ★★★½ VHS: $29.99

Murder, She Said

(1962, 87 min, GB, George Pollock) *Margaret Rutherford, Arthur Kennedy.* While dozing on a train, Miss Jane Marple awakens to witness a murder on a passing train. The police don't believe her. We, however, know better. Rutherford made her debut as Agatha Christie's famous sleuth. ★★★ VHS: $19.99

Murderers Are Among Us

(1946, 85 min, Germany, Wolfgang Stoudte) *Hildegard Knef, Ernst Wilhelm Borchert.* Filmed in the rubble of Berlin at the end of WWII, *Murderers Are Among Us* is both a casebook exam-ple of the neorealist style and an unsettling historical document. A young woman recently released from a concentration camp returns to her apartment to find it occupied by a surgeon traumatized and embittered by his war experiences. Her stalwart resolve to begin life anew is in diametric opposition to his disillusionment: He who once saved lives no longer believes mankind worth saving. He encounters his former superior officer, sees this encounter as a chance for retribution, and finds redemption instead. A startling and revelatory piece of film-making, and a testament to the human ability to salvage hope from utter desolation. (German with English subtitles) ★★★ VHS: $39.99

Muriel

(1963, 111 min, France/Italy, Alain Resnais) *Delphine Seyring, Jean-Pierre Kerien.* Resnais continues his exploration of the theme of the relationship between present and past in this serious film about the concrete realities of everyday life. Helen, a 40-year-old antique dealer, disillusioned with her situation, attempts to relive her past be renewing a relationship with a lover of 20 years before. (French with English subtitles) ★★★ VHS: $19.99

Muriel's Wedding

(1995, 105 min, Australia, P.J. Hogan) *Toni Collette, Bill Hunter, Rachel Griffiths, Daniel Lapaine, Jeane Drynan.* Collette gives a magical performance as the overweight, unemployed Muriel who desperately wants to fit in with the popular girls from high school. Her obsession with the clique prompts to steal from her father. When the theft is discovered, she leaves her family home in Porpoise Spit, Australia, for the big city life of Sydney. There she reacquaints herself with high school buddy Rhonda (brilliantly played by Griffiths), and tries to realize her life-long dream of marriage. The sometimes despairing events in Muriel's life are played out against extremely funny and often cynical comedy, humor which seems to take the sting out of her forlorn life. And as with other "ugly duckling" tales, the release of the swan inside allows for both humor and pathos. ★★★½ VHS: $14.99; DVD: $29.99

Murmur of the Heart

(1971, 118 min, France, Louis Malle) *Benoit Ferreux, Lea Massari.* Although tame by today's standards, Malle's infectious comedy about a boy's sexual coming-of-age and his relationship with his carelessly sensual mother caused quite a stir in 1971. Set in France in 1954, the story follows the day-to-day lives of a bourgeois family and especially Laurent, a precocious 14-year-old boy whose interests lie mainly in the jazz music of Charlie Parker and attempting to lose his virginity. His success in love takes an unexpected turn when he, accompanied by his free-spirited mother, is sent to a spa to recover from rheumatic fever. A tender and funny film which affectionately satirizes familial relationships. (French with English subtitles) ★★★½ VHS: $19.99

Murphy's Romance

(1985, 107 min, US, Martin Ritt) *James Garner, Sally Field, Brian Kerwin, Corey Haim.* Garner received an Oscar nomination for his delightful performance in this simple and charming romantic comedy. Garner plays a small-town pharmacist who romances a recently divorced mother (Field), much to the dismay of her ne'er-do-well ex-husband (Kerwin). ★★★ VHS: $9.99; DVD: $24.99

Murphy's War

(1971, 106 min, GB, Peter Yates) *Peter O'Toole, Philippe Noiret, Sian Phillips.* When a British merchant ship is sunk by German torpedoes off the coast of Venezuela at the end of WWII, O'Toole finds himself in the unenviable position of being the sole survivor. For the remainder of the film, he dedicates himself to hunting down and destroying the U-boat responsible for the tragedy. Superbly staged action sequences and O'Toole's formidable presence make this a highly entertaining adventure film. ★★★ VHS: $14.99

The Muse

(1999, 97 min, US, Albert Brooks) *Albert Brooks, Sharon Stone, Jeff Bridges, Andie MacDowell.* Brooks wrote, directed and stars in this often funny though a little too self-indulgent comedy as a successful screenwriter who is suffering from writer's block. Into his life stumbles Sarah (a luminous Stone), a descendent from Zeus and one of the nine Muses. As he tries to bang out a hit script, she takes control of not only his life but his family's life as well. Brooks manages some friendly and not-so-friendly jabs at the Hollywood filmmaking community, and when his jokes hit their targets, *The Muse* charms as it produces its laughs. But there's often too much time waiting for the next punchline, however expertly they are delivered by the good ensemble. Some great cameos punctuate the best running joke, including Martin Scorsese, James Cameron and Rob Reiner. ★★½ VHS: $14.99; DVD: $19.99

Music Box

(1989, 128 min, US, Costa-Gavras) *Jessica Lange, Armin Mueller-Stahl, Frederic Forrest, Lukas Haas, Donald Moffat.* Director Costa-Gavras delivers another taut political thriller based on co-producer Joe Esterhas' finely drawn script. Lawyer Lange takes on her Hungarian-émigré father's case when he is accused of Nazi collaboration and heinous atrocities during WWII. Her firm belief that her father is innocent, however, gradually erodes as the evidence against him accumulates. A suspenseful, thoughtful exploration of the conflict between familial devotion and the strength of ethical belief that is realized by fine ensemble acting. ★★★ VHS: $14.99

Music from Another Room

(1997, 104 min, US, Charlie Peters) *Jude Law, Jennifer Tilly, Martha Plimpton, Gretchen Mol, Brenda Blethyn.* Although it is a far-fetched romance, *Music from Another Room* does feature some pretty sweet and sentimental moments. Danny (Law) is a mosaic tiler who reunites with the Swan family he knew briefly 25 years before. As a young boy, Danny helped deliver Anna Swan, and swore he would one day marry her. Now an uptight adult, Anna (Mol) is alternately drawn to and annoyed by this mysterious suitor who transforms the rest of her highly disfunctional family. Writer-director Peters has made a noble effort, but the themes of kismet and taking chances are diluted by some painfully obvious clichés. ★★ VHS: $9.99

Music of the Heart

The Music Lovers

(1971, 122 min, GB, Ken Russell) *Glenda Jackson, Richard Chamberlain, Christopher Gable, Max Adrian.* This extravagant account of the life of Tchiakovsky is classic Russell — wonderfully overacted and filled with wildly overstated imagery. Chamberlain stars as the tortured, repressed homosexual composer; Gable is his clinging blond boyfriend; and Jackson, in a ferocious performance, plays his mad, nymphomaniac wife. Set in turn-of-the-century Russia, the film is impressively costumed and feverishly presented — with the hilarious, phallic and symbolism-laden "1812 Overture" dream sequence a particular highlight. ★★★ VHS: $19.99

The Music Man

(1962, 177 min, US, Morton Da Costa) *Robert Preston, Shirley Jones, Buddy Hackett, Paul Ford, Hermione Gingold, Ron Howard.* This outstanding adaptation of Meredith Willson's Broadway smash is one of the great American musicals. Preston reprised his triumphant stage role to give the performance of his career as turn-of-the-century con man Prof. Harold Hill, who comes to River City, Iowa, to form a boys' band. Classic score includes "Trouble," "76 Trombones" and "Till There Was You." Jones is in good voice as Marion the Librarian. (VHS available letterboxed or pan & scan) ★★★★ VHS: $19.99; DVD: $19.99

The Music of Chance

(1993, 98 min, US, Philip Haas) *James Spader, Mandy Patinkin, Charles Durning, Joel Grey, M. Emmet Walsh, Samantha Mathis, Christopher Penn.* With the intricacies of a good symphony and the eerie mystery of a good campfire story, *The Music of Chance*, based on the Paul Auster novel, is a complex and superbly acted tale of happenstance. Spader plays a polyester-clad cardsharp who is plucked from the mouth of despair by a drifter of another sort, Patinkin. The two embark on a road trip to a card game where Spader has set up two rich marks. Spader occasionally goes a little over-the-top in his weasel-like performance, but Patinkin, as a man of morals set adrift in a world of skewed honor, has a depth of character that anchors the ephemeral story. ★★★½ VHS: $19.99

Music of the Heart

(1999, 123 min, US, Wes Craven) *Meryl Streep, Aidan Quinn, Angela Bassett, Gloria Estefan, Cloris Leachman, Jane Leeves, Jay O. Sanders.* Based on the documentary *Small Wonders*, this moving, life-affirming drama is based on the true-life experiences of music teacher Roberta Guaspari, who taught the violin to grade schoolers in East Harlem, and who made — with her students — a momentous trip to Carnegie Hall. Playing her role with verve and grit, Steep is excellent as the divorced mom of two who, with her own 50 violins (the film's original title), goes about teaching kids in the economically depressed East Harlem school district. In no-nonsense fashion, director Craven (who is quite successful in his first non-horror film) follows Roberta's struggles as teacher, mom and lover in well-constructed episodes that don't always flow as well as they should but are involving nonetheless. *Music of the Heart* benefits from Roberta's own measured outlook, and Streep's unsentimental way of bringing it to the screen. Violinists Itzhak Perlman and Isaac Stern appear as themselves. ★★★ VHS: $14.99; DVD: $39.99

The Music Teacher

(1989, 100 min, Belgium, Gerard Corbiau) *Jose Van Dam, Anne Roussel.* This opulent yet winsome drama is set in turn-of-the-century France where a world renowned opera singer suddenly announces his departure from the stage and retires to his estate in the countryside. It is there that he establishes a private school and selects two aspiring singers to be his pupils. The aspiring singers, a shy young woman and a poor but proud thief, are tutored by the older man, all in an effort to be ready for a singing competition hosted by the maestro's long-time enemy. Infused with humor, pathos and an innocently blossoming love story, this charming story features musical excerpts from Mahler, Verdi, Mozart, Schubert and Puccini. (French with English subtitles) ★★★

Musica Proibita (Forbidden Music)

(1943, 93 min, Italy, Carlo Camogalliani) *Tito Gobbi, Maria Mercader.* This interesting find was a typical example of the filmmaking style in Italy before the arrival of Neorealism in the late 1940s. The melodrama is set in the world of Italian opera and tells the haunting story of the love affair between a young conductor and the woman he loves. But their relationship is forbidden by the girl's grandmother when she learns of the identity of the man's father. An explosive tale of romance, murder, revenge and passion. (Italian with English subtitles) ★★½

Mussolini and I

(1985, 130 min, Italy/US, Alberto Negrin) *Bob Hoskins, Anthony Hopkins, Susan Sarandon, Annie Girardot, Fabio Testi, Kurt Raab.* An international cast spotlights this made-for-cable treatment of the conflicts between Mussolini (Hoskins) and his son-in-law Count Galeazzo Ciano, Minister of Foreign Affairs (Hopkins). Sarandon plays Benito's daughter in this sumptuously photographed and enjoyably overblown escapist entertainment. Cut down from its TV running time of 192 minutes, the film was originally titled *Mussolini: The Decline and Fall.* ★★½

Mute Witness

(1995, 92 min, US, Anthony Waller) *Mary Sudina, Fay Ripley, Evan Richards, Oleg Jankowskij, Alec Guinness.* A mute American F/X artist working on a low-budget slasher film in Russia witnesses her coworkers seemingly making an after-hours snuff film and is accidentally locked in the studio with them. She is then stalked through the hallways in a brilliantly conceived, tension-laden extended chase sequence which is unrelenting in its suspense. First-time director Waller, in an obvious though unacknowledged homage, infuses the film with the nail-biting suspense and horrific violence of De Palma and Argento to create a highly stylized and visceral thriller. The film's second half, however, becomes needlessly convoluted as an attempt to add humor puts it starkly at odds with the constant terror which comes before it. ★★★ VHS: $9.99

Mutiny on the Bounty

(1935, 132 min, US, Frank Lloyd) *Charles Laughton, Clark Gable, Franchot Tone, Donal Crisp.* The first, and best, of the three *Bounty* pictures about the tyrannical Captain Bligh, his 18th-century voyage to Tahiti, and the events leading up the the notorious mutiny, led by First Officer Mister Christian. Laughton gives a tour de force performance as the severe Bligh, and Gable is well-cast as Christian. Oscar for Best Picture. (Remade in 1962, and in 1984 as *The Bounty*) ★★★★ VHS: $14.99

Mutiny on the Bounty

(1962, 179 min, US, Lewis Milestone) *Marlon Brando, Trevor Howard, Richard Harris, Hugh Griffith, Richard Haydn.* This grandiose, self-important, often ludicrous remake manages to be thoroughly entertaining almost in spite of itself. Lush tropical locations help as does Brando's campy, bemused performance. Howard plays the sadistic Capt. Bligh with tremendous relish. The two stars reportedly disliked each other, leading to on-set confrontations that rivaled those aboard the Bounty. (VHS available letterboxed or pan & scan) ★★½ VHS: $24.99

My American Cousin

(1985, 95 min, Canada, Sandy Wilson) *Margaret Langrick, John Wildman.* The time and setting for this enjoyable story is 1959 in the quiet outback of western Canada, where rock 'n' roll, hot rods and James Dean–influenced teens are still American phenomena. It's home, however, for Sandy, a precocious 12-year-old whose life takes a heated turn when Butch, her hip, handsome teenage cousin from America, visits. A humorous coming-of-age drama that explores first love as well as the dreams and frustrations of two very different people. (Sequel: *American Boyfriends*) ★★★

M

My Beautiful Laundrette

(1986, 94 min, GB, Stephen Frears) *Daniel Day-Lewis, Gordon Warnecke, Saeed Jaffrey, Roshan Seth, Shirley Ann Field.* An unpredictable and charming social comedy which follows the unlikely success story of a young English-born Pakistani and budding capitalist (Warnecke) and his punk lover (Day-Lewis). Together they brave the ugly spectre of racism and transform a dingy East End laundrette into a glitzy and profitable laundry emporium. ★★★★

My Best Friend's Girl

(1984, 110 min, France, Bertrand Blier) *Isabelle Huppert, Thierry L'hermitte, Coluche.* Huppert gives an erotically charged performance in Blier's whimsical look at male-bonding set around the ski resorts of Switzerland. Coluche costars with sexy ski-shop proprietor L'hermitte as the fast friends who share an enthusiasm for femme fatale Huppert. (French with English subtitles) ★★½

My Best Friend's Wedding

(1997, 105 min, US, P.J. Hogan) *Julia Roberts, Dermot Mulroney, Rupert Everett, Cameron Diaz, Philip Bosco, Rachel Griffiths, M. Emmet Walsh.* Roberts gives an irresistible performance of a former lover out to stop the wedding of her ex — at any cost. Recalling Irene Dunne in *The Awful Truth* rather than Glenn Close in *Fatal Attraction*, Roberts plays Julianne, a successful food critic who has been best friends with Michael (Mulroney) since they broke up several years ago. Harboring a crush but never admitting it, her feelings for Michael are realized when he announces he's in love: with another woman. She then sets in motion a plan to sabotage their relationship. One of the strengths of the film is that not all the humor is dependant upon Julianne's schemes, for the film is filled with delightful off-the-wall and totally unexpected comedic moments. In support, Everett is smashing as Julianne's gay confidant. ★★★ VHS: $14.99; DVD: $24.99

My Blue Heaven

(1990, 95 min, US, Herbert Ross) *Steve Martin, Rick Moranis, Joan Cusack, Melanie Mayron, Bill Irwin, Carol Kane.* This funny though uneven look at the witness protection program run amok may be considered the demented "what-if" sequel to *GoodFellas*. Martin is an ex-gangster with a new identity relocated to suburbia

and Moranis is a G-Man who has to keep an eye on him. Good idea. Good cast. So what happened? We think director Ross should leave the dopey high-concept comedies to Ivan Reitman and John Hughes. ★★ VHS: $14.99; DVD: $14.99

My Bodyguard

(1980, 96 min, US, Tony Bill) *Chris Makepeace, Adam Baldwin, Martin Mull, Ruth Gordon, Matt Dillon, John Houseman, Joan Cusack.* A youngster (Makepeace) hires the biggest kid in his class (Baldwin) as his bodyguard to protect him from a gang of bullies. Mull plays the little guy's dad, Gordon his grandmom, and Dillon is one of the toughs. ★★½ VHS: $14.99

My Brilliant Career

(1979, 101 min, Australia, Gillian Armstrong) *Judy Davis, Sam Neill, Wendy Hughes.* A radiant Davis stars in this period drama about a young woman in Australian outback at the turn of the century who is torn between marrying a local landowner (Neill) and pursuing her career as a writer. Lovingly photographed and directed by director Armstrong, the film is a marvelously understated look at a Victorian woman's struggle with the constraints of her social position. ★★★½

My Cousin Vinny

(1992, 119 min, US, Jonathan Lynn) *Joe Pesci, Marisa Tomei, Ralph Macchio, Fred Gwynne.* Pesci plays a fish-out-of-water in this good-natured comedy about a smallfry Brooklyn lawyer who travels to a backwoods Southern town to save his cousin (perpetual teenager Macchio) from a murder rap. Tomei's Oscar-winning, over-the-top performance as Pesci's gum-popping girlfriend easily outshines the rest of the goings-on in this small movie that acquits itself nicely. Gwynne has some fun as the incredulous judge. ★★★ VHS: $9.99; DVD: $29.99

My Darling Clementine

(1946, 97 min, US, John Ford) *Henry Fonda, Victor Mature, Linda Darnell, Walter Brennan.* The often-told tale of Wyatt Earp, the Clanton Gang and the infamous fight at the O.K. Corral. This western is blessed with the sure hand of director Ford, who imbues his story with such a visual splendor and poetic grace it ranks among his finest works. Fonda is the famed marshall who, with Doc Holliday (Mature), cleans up the town of Tombstone. ★★★★ VHS: $9.99

My Dinner with Andre

(1981, 110 min, US, Louis Malle) *Andre Gregory, Wallace Shawn.* Malle serves up a delectable duet by the quest-crazed Gregory (former artistic director of TLA) and the pragmatic Shawn. A supremely intelligent film which asks the question, "Is there any more reality on the top of Mount Everest than there is in the cigar shop next door?" ★★★½ VHS: $29.99; DVD: $19.99

My Dog Skip

(2000, 95 min, US, Jay Russell) *Frankie Muniz, Diane Lane, Luke Wilson, Kevin Bacon; Narrated by Harry Connick, Jr.* Evoking the kind of memories each and everyone of

us would be lucky to share, this heartwarming, inspiring memory piece is that rarity: a family film rich in emotion and spirit. Based on the book by Willie Morris, the gentle and funny *My Dog Skip* recalls young Willie growing up in a small Mississippi town during the second world war, and the special relationship he has with — you guessed it — his dog Skip. Muniz makes an especially appealing young hero, an outcast who learns to blossom with a little help from his canine friend. Skip, played by five different dogs, is absolutely adorable, and, for once, the adults aren't shortchanged. Lane, as Willie's mom, and Bacon, as his war-scarred father, each hit just the right note. An enchanting, make-you-smile reminiscence not to be missed. ★★★½ VHS: $14.99; DVD: $19.99

My Fair Lady

(1964, 171 min, US, George Cukor) *Audrey Hepburn, Rex Harrison, Stanley Holloway, Wilfred Hyde-White, Gladys Cooper, Theodore Bikel, Mona Washbourne.* Although much will be lost in watching this enchanting musical extravaganza on the little screen, *My Fair Lady* still dazzles the viewer with spectacular sets and costumes, an inspired Lerner & Loewe score and wonderful performances by Harrison and Hepburn. Winner of eight Academy Awards, this musical version of George Bernard Shaw's "Pygmalion" tells the now familiar tale of Professor Henry Higgins, an arrogant linguist, who takes Cockney flower waif Eliza Doolittle under his wing on a bet that he can transform her into a lady. ★★★★ VHS: $14.99

My Family (Mi Familia)

(1995, 125 min, US, Gregory Nava) *Jimmy Smits, Esai Morales, Edward James Olmos, Eduardo Lopez Rojas, Scott Bakula.* A sometimes engrossing but ultimately unfocused three-generational family saga, this failed attempt at a Mexican-American *Godfather* was produced by Francis Ford Coppola and pays homage to his epic. Following an immigrant's life from his arrival to Los Angeles until the time his last grandchild leaves his household, the film tries to show the strength of its characters through heartbreaking tragedy, inflicting upon them one horrible event after another. The weepy story is at its best when it balances the heavy drama with a lighter tone, supplied by Olmos as narrator. *My Family* vividly captures several decades in a period East Los Angeles, the dust of which contrasts sharply with the art deco of a white West L.A. ★★½ VHS: $14.99

My Father Is Coming

(1991, 82 min, US/Germany, Monika Treut) *Alfred Edel, Shelley Kastner, Annie Sprinkle.* A comical story of sexual confusion, sexual awakening and self-discovery. Vicky, an aspiring actress and struggling waitress, is involved with both a man and a woman at the same time her German father arrives for a visit. Haven given the impression that she is a successful actress and happily married, Vicky vainly tries to impress her dour and demanding pop, even resorting to getting a gay friend to play her husband. But papa doesn't get a chance to complain for he is immediately swept up in a whirlwind of romance, TV commercials and kinky sex. The many characters in this charming comedy cover the spectrum of sexuality,

Wallace Shawn and Andre Gregory in *My Dinner with Andre*

and the result is an exuberant slice-of-life tale. (In English and German with English subtitles) ★★★ VHS: $19.99

My Father's Glory

(1991, 110 min, France, Yves Robert) *Philippe Caubere, Nathalie Roussel.* The cherished childhood memories of author Marcel Pagnol are tenderly told in this enchanting and romantic tale set in turn-of-the-century Marseilles and Provence. The story follows Marcel, an 11-year-old boy who, along with his loving mother, schoolteacher father and other relatives, spends an idyllic summer in the rugged but beautiful terrain of southern France. It is there, amidst the tranquil hills, that the boy begins to learn about nature, friendship and life. A deceptively simple film, with great insights into familial relationships set in an era long ago lost to progress. The story continues in *My Mother's Castle.* (French with English subtitles) ★★★½ VHS: $19.99

My Favorite Blonde

(1942, 78 min, US, Sidney Lanfield) *Bob Hope, Madeleine Carroll, Gale Sondergaard.* In his old radio show, Hope made so many compliments about Carroll it was almost a running gag. How appropriate, then, that he costars with her in this very funny spy comedy which pays homage to Carroll's classic thriller *The 39 Steps.* Hope stars as a second-rate entertainer (his partner, a penguin, has far more talent) who becomes involved with British agent Carroll, who must transport secret bombing information cross-country. And, of course, the enemy is in hot pursuit. Clever one-liners, non-stop adventure and a breezy pace all contribute to make this arguably Hope's best comedy outside of the *Road* series. ★★★½ VHS: $14.99

My Favorite Brunette

(1947, 87 min, US, Elliott Nugent) *Bob Hope, Dorothy Lamour, Peter Lorre, Lon Chaney, Jr.* A funny romp with Bob as a baby photographer who really wants to be a private eye; and through mistaken identity, gets his chance. In-joke cameos include Alan Ladd and Der Bingle. ★★★

My Favorite Martian

(1998, 95 min, US, Donald Petrie) *Christopher Lloyd, Jeff Daniels, Elizabeth Hurley, Daryl Hannah, Wallace Shawn, Christine Ebersole, Michael Lerner, Ray Walston.* The 1960s TV sitcom "My Favorite Martian" had a respectable three-year run on CBS, was often very cute, and was lucky enough to have Ray Walston in the lead as a Martian stranded on Earth. It wasn't exactly a classic, however. Its silly situations and genial laughs make it seem like "Frasier" compared to this big-screen remake. An over-the-top Lloyd is now Uncle Martin, who is taken in by reporter Tim O'Hara (Daniels). Martin just wants to get back home, while Tim wants an exclusive for his paper. Nuttiness of the most boring kind ensues. Lloyd and Daniels are sabotaged by a poor script and careless direction. ★½ VHS: $14.99; DVD: $29.99

My Favorite Season
(Ma Saison Préférée)

(1993, 124 min, France, André Téchiné) *Catherine Deneuve, Daniel Auteuil, Chiara Mastroianni, Marthe Villalonga.* A highly accom-

My Favorite Year

plished examination of three generations of a family, *My Favorite Season* deals with the guilt and regrets that surface between parent and children, siblings and spouses. The film concerns Emilie (Deneuve) and Antoine (Auteuil), a brother and sister who resume their fragile relationship when they are forced to care for their ailing mother (Villalonga). As Emilie strives late in her life for personal growth and understanding, she comes to some difficult realizations. As is the director's style, the dramatic focus shifts back and forth to allow his themes on love and honesty to resonate clearly. Radiant as ever, Deneuve makes Emilie a sympathetic heroine, while Auteuil lends fine support as the boorish Antoine. (French with English subtitles) ★★★½ VHS: $19.99; DVD: $29.99

My Favorite Wife

(1940, 88 min, US, Garson Kanin) *Cary Grant, Irene Dunne, Randolph Scott, Gail Patrick.* In this fabulously funny comedy, Grant and Dunne appear in their second of three films together. Dunne returns home after seven years lost at sea to discover husband Grant has just remarried. Scott is the handsome hunk who was marooned with Dunne, much to Grant's chagrin. A joy from beginning to end. (Remade as *Move Over Darling*) ★★★½

My Favorite Year

(1982, 92 min, US, Richard Benjamin) *Peter O'Toole, Mark Linn-Baker, Jessica Harper, Joseph Bologna, Lainie Kazan, Bill Macy, Anne DeSalvo.* A delightful comedic reflection on the early years of television. O'Toole runs wild as a swashbuckling celluloid hero (patterned after Errol Flynn) brought to his knees by the prospect of a live TV appearance. Sparkling support by Bologna as an ersatz Sid Caesar and Linn-Baker as O'Toole's impressionable escort. O'Toole has probably never been funnier, and the screenplay offers hilarious observations on stardom and the grind of behind-the-scenes TV. (VHS available letterboxed or pan & scan) ★★★★ VHS: $14.99

My Fellow Americans

(1996, 101 min, US, Peter Segal) *Jack Lemmon, James Garner, Dan Aykroyd, John Heard, Sela Ward,*

Wilford Brimley, Lauren Bacall. Call it what you may: *Grumpy Old Presidents* or *In the Line of Fire of Grumpy Old Men;* but *My Fellow Americans,* a predictable, puerile comedy about two feuding, ex-presidents on the run, manages to produce a few laughs in spite of itself. Lemmon and Garner rely mainly on their invaluable comedic instincts to almost pull this off. They play former commander-in-chiefs (and opponents) who, having individually discovered a cover-up by the current president (Aykroyd), flee together when they are almost assassinated by the Secret Service. Most of the film consists of them bickering as they try to elude the hit men, and each handles the one-liners and put-downs with charm and ease. ★★½ VHS: $9.99; DVD: $19.99

My First Wife

(1984, 89 min, Australia, Paul Cox) *John Hargreaves, Wendy Hughes.* Hargreaves and Hughes give powerful, anguished performances in Cox's award-winning drama about the disintegration of a ten-year marriage. Told from "the man's point of view," this portrait of the disemboweling of their union is gutty and emotionally involving. ★★★

My Forbidden Past

(1951, 72 min, US, Robert Stevenson) *Robert Mitchum, Ava Gardner, Melvyn Douglas.* Gardner seeks to marry a promising young doctor, but family members disrupt her nuptial plans. When Ava later attempts to rekindle the affair, she finds her lover has since married. Mitchum and Douglas are the men in her life. An uninvolving soaper which barely rises above its melodramatic story line. ★★ VHS: $19.99

My Giant

(1998, 104 min, US, Michael Lehmann) *Billy Crystal, Kathleen Quinlan, Joanna Pacula, Gheorghe Muresan, Steven Seagal.* Crystal plays Sammy, a super-slick talent agent in a slump who makes a gigantic discovery while on location in Romania. Max, a seven-foot-seven-inches tall countryman who's lived his entire adult life in a monastary. In this gentle giant Sammy sees a star and vows to put him in movies. The film relies heavily on the visual sight gag of Max assimilating to the hussle-and-bussle of city life. Besides the obligatory size jokes, there's nothing new here to add to the "mismatched-buddy-flick" genre. Stunningly, some of the biggest laughs come from Seagal, who pokes fun at himself. ★★ VHS: $9.99; DVD: $14.99

My Girl

(1991, 102 min, US, Howard Zieff) *Anna Chlumsky, Dan Aykroyd, Macaulay Culkin, Jamie Lee Curtis, Richard Masur, Griffin Dunne.* Alternating between comedy and drama, *My Girl* is an ever-so-cute, very sentimental "kids" movie" which may prove to be too intense for particularly young viewers. One scene in question is the death of the Culkin character; which, though handled awkwardly in dramatic terms, is sensitively portrayed. Chlumsky is an 11-year-old girl living with her father (Aykroyd), a funeral director. The story follows her summer vacation, where she befriends Culkin, reluctantly witnesses her father fall in love with Curtis. There are a few laughs to be had, though this is more dramatic than the ads suggest. (Sequel: *My Girl 2*) ★★½ VHS: $14.99

My Girl 2

(1994, 99 min, US, Howard Zieff) *Anna Chlumsky, Dan Aykroyd, Jamie Lee Curtis.* What might have been an affecting tale of a young girl's quest to discover the history of her deceased mother is instead overwhelmed by heavy-handed sentimentality and a mawkish sensibility which makes the frequently saccharine original seem like something from Abel Ferrara by comparison. Aykroyd and Curtis sleepwalk through their reprised roles as "My Girl" Vada's (Chlumsky) parents. The film's only redeeming quality is that it avoids attacking those who don't fit into the Quayle Family Values it so heartily celebrates. ★½ VHS: $14.99

My Girlfriend's Boyfriend

(1998, 81 min, US, Kenneth Schapiro) *Valerie Perrine, Deborah Gibson, Chris Bruno, Linda Larkin.* Valiantly attempting a screwball comedy, this lame gay comedy fails on most counts. To further his career, soap opera hunk Cliff plans to marry sweet society gal Cory, but Cliff is secretly gay (he's lovers with the best man). All hell breaks loose on the wedding day when Cory's best friend Liberty arrives with her lanky boyfriend and the question of who is gay, who is straight, and who is going to marry who looms in the air. One could overlook its low-budget roots, but the tired plot, flat acting and stagnant photography make this film more of a chore than a pleasure. ★★ VHS: $99.99

My Heroes Have Always Been Cowboys

(1991, 106 min, US, Stuart Rosenberg) *Scott Glenn, Kate Capshaw, Ben Johnson, Tess Harper, Gary Busey.* Glenn plays an aging rodeo circuit bullrider who returns to his small Texas home town for the first time in 20 years after an accident leaves him injured. There, he picks up the pieces he left behind, taking care of his invalid father, rebuilding the family's deserted ranch and renewing a romance with an old flame. Glenn is particularly good in this involving though choppy tale of familial conflict and loyalty. ★★½ VHS: $9.99

My Left Foot

(1989, 103 min, Ireland, Jim Sheridan) *Daniel Day-Lewis, Brenda Fricker, Hugh O'Connor, Ray McAnally, Fiona Shaw, Adrian Dunbar.* It came as no surprise when Day-Lewis walked away with an Oscar for Best Actor for his portrayal of the severely handicapped Irish painter/author Christy Brown. Born with cerebral palsy, Brown never gained the use of his limbs except for his left foot, with which he brushed canvases so stunning they earned him recognition as an acclaimed artist. With acute sensitivity, Day-Lewis depicts Brown as an intense, brooding, complicated and restless soul with a zest for life far beyond that of most people. Fine support comes from Fricker, who also won a much-deserved Oscar for her gutsy performance as Christy's resilient mother. A stunning portrait both passionate and intelligent. ★★★★; DVD: $19.99

My Life

(1993, 112 min, US, Bruce Joel Rubin) *Michael Keaton, Nicole Kidman, Haing S. Ngor, Queen Latifah.* With the screenplays for both *Ghost* and *Jacob's Ladder* to his credit, Rubin, making his directorial debut, is in familiar waters with this emotional and surprisingly persuasive drama about life and death. Keaton stars as a successful L.A. executive dying of cancer. About to become a first-time parent, he decides to leave a video autobiography for his child, whom he will probably not live to meet. As he and his wife (Kidman) anticipate the birth of their new baby, each must come to terms with Keaton's impending demise. Although a little too steeped in ancient mysticism for its own good, Rubin's text is moving and probably has more to say about the dying process than the high-profile *Philadelphia.* ★★★ VHS: $9.99; DVD: $19.99

My Life and Times with Antonin Artaud

(1993, 98 min, France, Gérard Mordillat) *Sami Frey, Marc Barbé, Julie Jezequel, Valerie Jeannet.* Based on the diaries of Parisian poet Jacques Prevel, this fictionalized account follows a young Prevel (Barbé) as he develops a tentative relationship with theatre innovator Antonin Artaud (Frey). Prevel himself is a piece of work, a down-and-out philanderer who spends most of his time in a flophouse with his emotionally strung-out girlfriend and occasionally with his inexplicably devoted wife. When he hears of Artaud's release from an insane asylum, he finagles an introduction in hopes of developing fame by association. Filmed in black and white, the film does a fine job of evoking a sumptuous post-war imagery and has a stylish, Euro-chic appeal. But it is a sadly inappropriate memorial to Artaud to present his final days so harmlessly — no suffering in the fires of his own internal hell here. It's just too safe. (Letterboxed) (French with English subtitles) ★★½ VHS: $19.99

My Life as a Dog

(1985, 101 min, Sweden, Lasse Hallström) *Anton Glanzelius, Manfred Serner, Anki Lidén.* A captivating and heartwarming look at the trials and tribulations of a 12-year-old boy who, in the wake of his mother's death, is shipped off to live with his uncle in a rural Swedish village in the 1950s. Touching drama is sprinkled with poignant comedy as the boy battles his feelings

of self-abasement and despair. A truly winning insight into the joys and sorrows of childhood which features outstanding performances from its two child stars. (Swedish with English subtitles) ★★★★ VHS: $19.99; DVD: $29.99

My Life So Far

(1999, 95 min, GB/Scotland, Hugh Hudson) *Colin Firth, Mary Elizabeth Mastrantonio, Malcolm McDowall, Robbie Norman, Irene Jacob, Rosemary Harris.* A sweet, and at times sentimental portrait of a young boy growing up in Scotland in the 1930s, director Hudson's modest film is a pleasant coming-of-age tale. When Morris (McDowell) and Edward (Firth) quibble over the estate of matriarch Gamma Macintosh (Harris), family tensions escalate. As seen through the eyes of 10-year old Fraser (Norman), the situation really stems from the arrival of Morris' new wife Heloise (Jacob), who becomes the object of Edward's misplaced affections. Although the drama is a little stiff, *My Life So Far* is really quite charming and uplifting. ★★★ VHS: $19.99; DVD: $29.99

My Life to Live (Vivre sa Vie)

(1962, 85 min, France, Jean-Luc Godard) *Anna Karina, Saddy Rebbot.* Godard's detached and at times analytical approach to his subjects continues in this richly paradoxical tale of a young shop assistant (Karina) who turns to prostitution but who "gives her body to keep her soul." Set up in 12 tableaux segments, Godard has said that this film was "not a new departure, but an arrival." (French with English subtitles) ★★★ VHS: $29.99; DVD: $29.99

My Life's in Turnaround

(1994, 84 min, US, Eric Schaeffer & Donal Lardner Ward) *Eric Schaeffer, Donal Lardner Ward, Dana Wheeler Nicholson, Phoebe Cates, Martha Plimpton, John Sayles, Casey Seimaszko.* With this ultra no-budget impromptu, actor/writer/producer/directors Schaeffer and Ward really had no idea what to make a film about, so they made a film about exactly that — two burnt-out denizens of lower Manhattan's grunge art scene searching to make a film deal. It's a contrivance that on face value is not the least bit clever, but in this duo's hands it somehow becomes ingenious. Think of it, these guys make an asset out of their dearth of creative inspiration! What makes it all work is their infectious personalities and the hilarious and incessant banter between them — what develops is actually a thoughtful look at their friendship. ★★★ VHS: $14.99; DVD: $9.99

My Little Chickadee

(1940, 83 min, US, Eddie Cline) *W.C. Fields, Mae West, Margaret Hamilton.* Fields was an alcoholic; West practiced abstinence. The two did not get along. Fields wrote his scenes; she hers. Count the number of times they're in the same shot together. Perhaps it was this animosity that goaded them to do some of their best work in this tale of a woman of easy virtue entering into a marriage of convenience with a con man. It is in this film that Fields says that the only thing worse than being in Philadelphia is being hanged. ★★★ VHS: $14.99

My Little Girl

(1986, 118 min, US, Connie Kaiserman) *Mary Stuart Masterson, Geraldine Page, James Earl Jones, Anne Meara, Peter Gallagher.* Masterson gives a touching performance in this absorbing drama of an overprivileged miss who tries to make a difference by working with disadvantaged young girls. Page is used to good advantage as her supportive grandmother. Portions filmed in the Main Line area of Philadelphia. ★★★

My Lucky Stars

(1985, 99 min, Hong Kong, Sammo Hung) *Jackie Chan, Yuen Biao, Sammo Hung.* Amiable sequel to *Winners and Sinners* reteams Jackie, Samo and Biao in a wildly uneven, though always entertaining action/comedy. Biao is captured by the bad guys, and Jackie and Samo have to save him; that's all the plot you need for this film, which, after a fun opening chase in an amusement park, settles down into silly comedy mode for perhaps a bit too long, then delivers the action — the highlight of which is an infamous catfight. Never as tough or fast-paced as you want it to be, *My Lucky Stars* is best approached as a silly, Hong Kong hodgepodge, and on that level, is fun stuff indeed. (Cantonese with English subtitles) ★★★ VHS: $39.99; DVD: $49.99

My Man

(1997, 95 min, France, Bertrand Blier) *Anouk Grinberg, Gérard Lanvin, Olivier Martinez, Mathieu Kassovitz.* Though audacious, writer-director Blier's *My Man*, which addresses how people are transformed by love and money, is ultimately an unfulfilling sex comedy. Marie (Grinberg) is a high-class prostitute who encounters Jeannot (Lanvin), a homeless stranger. She takes him in and falls madly in love. In the film's most fascinating sequence, Marie seduces Jeannot, and asks him to be her pimp. The first third of Blier's film, which features Marie's views on hooking, is charming, insightful and bold. However, when *My Man* shifts its focus onto Jeannot, it derails — badly. The main problem with the film is that although these changes may speak volumes about the characters, they are not credible within the framework Blier has established. (French with English subtitles) ★★½ VHS: $29.99

My Man Godfrey

(1936, 96 min, US, Gregory La Cava) *William Powell, Carole Lombard, Alice Brady, Eugene Pallette, Mischa Auer, Franklin Pangborn.* Classic screwball comedy with Lombard giving a priceless performance as a daffy heiress who meets a hobo on a scavenger hunt, and hires him as the family butler, unaware that he is actually a successful businessman. Powell is dapper as ever as the title character, and there's great comic support from Pallette, Brady and the hilarious Auer, who earned an Oscar nomination for, among other things, imitating a monkey. (Remade in 1957) ★★★★ VHS: $9.99; DVD: $39.99

My Michael

(1975, 95 min, Israel, Dan Wolman) *Efrat Lavie, Oded Kotler.* Two intelligent young adults find each other and marry in a divided Jerusalem in the late 1950s. Michael, a responsible and hardworking scientist, is comfortable in the arrangement, in contrast to Hanna, who finds herself unfulfilled by the petit-bourgeois life she is leading. Loneliness and fantasy take over in this gentle, yet controversial rendering of the Amos Oz novel. (Hebrew with English subtitles) ★★★ VHS: $79.99

My Mother's Castle

(1991, 98 min, France, Yves Robert) *Julien Ciamaca, Philippe Caubere, Nathalie Roussel.* The childhood remembrances of young Marcel continue in this captivating story which begins where *My Father's Glory* ends. Marcel's family returns to the city after their magical summer in Provence, only to decide later to make their country cottage a weekend and holiday retreat. It is there, in the barren, parched hills, that Marcel discovers the joy and pain of first love as well as a deep affection for and understanding of his loving parents. Possibly a bit too saccharine for hardened existential French videophiles, this unpretentious, heartwarming drama should prove to be a treasured delight for others. (French with English subtitles) ★★★ VHS: $19.99

My Name Is Bill W.

(1989, 118 min, US, Daniel Petrie) *James Woods, James Garner, JoBeth Williams, Fritz Weaver, Gary Sinise.* Woods gives one of his trademark on-target performances as Bill Wilson, cofounder of Alcoholics Anonymous. An intensely driven businessman and alcoholic, Wilson is literally kept alive by his wife (Williams) until he finds treatment which handles his condition as a disease, not a lack of will. By chance he meets Dr. Robert Smith (Garner), fellow drunk; together they formulate what will develop into the 12-step program. This TV production has a fine eye for period detail and enjoys good performances from the entire cast. ★★★ VHS: $19.99

My Name Is Ivan

(1966, 84 min, USSR, Andrei Tarkovsky) *Kolya Burlaiev, Valentin Zubkov.* The first film by this visionary Russian director is a poetic, sad story of a young boy caught up in World War II. Following the death of his mother during the early days of the war, 12-year-old Ivan's childhood is quickly ended when he joins the ranks of youths working as intelligence scouts for the army. The film is made in a style which moves from terrifying realism to lyrical impressionism. A haunting film experience. (Russian with English subtitles) ★★★½

My Name Is Joe

(1999, 105 min, Scotland, Ken Loach) *Peter Mullan, Louise Goodall, David McKay, Anne-Marie Kennedy, David Hayman.* Loach's second film, following *Carla's Song*, about the lower class in Glasgow, is a riveting character study which earned Mullan the Best Actor prize at Cannes. Mullan's Joe is a recovering alcoholic, trying to set his life straight while on the dole. His main interest is his soccer team. One of the players, Liam (McKay), is in trouble with the local drug kingpin (Hayman); in this community, everyone helps each other out, and Joe's affinity for Liam and desire to see him set things right sends him back into the world he is trying to escape. Complicating things is Joe's relationship with a social worker (Goodall); never mind that his 12-step program advises against finding new love so soon. Joe's struggles are poignant, funny and heartbreaking, and watching Mullan wrestle with them is unforgettable. This English-language film is helpfully subtitled in English. ★★★½ VHS: $102.99

My Neighbor Totoro

(1994, 87 min, Japan) This superbly animated tale is both an enchanting story and a terrific look at Japanese life in the country. Two young girls move out of the city with their father while their mother recuperates from a long illness in a distant hospital. In their new home they meet two large, furry and lovable totoros, creatures visible only to the children. When the youngest girl mistakenly starts to fear that her mother is going to die, she runs away to find the hospital and is rescued by the totoros. (Dubbed) ★★★½ VHS: $9.99

My New Gun

(1992, 99 min, US, Stacy Cochran) *Diane Lane, James LeGros, Stephen Collins, Tess Harper, Philip Seymour Hoffman.* Lane stars in this quirky comedy as a yuppie, suburban housewife who doesn't know how to react when her husband (Collins) gives her a .38 revolver for protection — so she gives it to her wacky new neighbor (LeGros), who purports to need a gun to protect his mother. Brimming with suspicion, and a possible infatuation, Lane starts to snoop around his house in search of clues about his real motives. Is he a drug dealer? A Mafia hit man? What she finds only confuses her more. First-time director Cochran keeps the action moving at a snappy pace and gives the film just the right amount of skewed humor to make it most refreshing viewing. ★★★ VHS: $19.99

My New Partner

(1985, 104 min, France, Claude Zidi) *Philippe Noiret, Thierry L'hermitte, Regina.* A delightful French farce about the antics of a charmingly amoral cop. Noiret stars as the veteran "flic" who must teach the ways of the world to his new partner, a scrupulously innocent rookie. Noiret and L'hermitte offer engaging performances. (French with English subtitles) ★★★

My Night at Maud's

(1970, 105 min, France, Eric Rohmer) *Jean-Louis Trintignant, Françoise Fabian, Marie-Christine Barrault.* Scintillating conversation on life, love and morality forms the bedroom talk in Rohmer's witty and fascinating comedy of manners. Trintignant plays the staunch Catholic who finds his principles tested when he is invited by the charming but free-spirited Maud (Fabian) to spend the night in her nonexistent spare room. The focus is not how they get together, but rather, how they manage not to. The third of Rohmer's Six Moral Tales and one of the director's most captivating works. (French with English subtitles) ★★★½ VHS: $19.99; DVD: $29.99

My Other Husband

(1985, 110 min, France, Georges Lautner) *Miou-Miou, Rachid Ferrache.* This story, about a frantic woman who has a husband and child in Paris and a lover and two children in the country, has the potential of being just another *comédie soufflé*. But happily, coupled with a funny script, some great supporting characters and the exhilarating presence of Miou-Miou in the starring role, the film rises above the situation comedy and becomes not only a successfully zany farce but also a sensitive feminist look at one woman's life. (French with English subtitles) ★★★ VHS: $59.99

My Own Country

(1999, 106 min, US, Mira Nair) *Naveen Andrews, Glenne Headly, Hal Holbrook, Swoosie Kurtz, Marisa Tomei.* This moving "issue" drama by director Nair may be a bit preachy and idealistic, but these "faults" amazingly do not distract from the film's potent story that is based on a true story. In the mid-1980s, Abraham Verghese, an East Indian-born medical doctor moves with his more traditional Indian wife to a quiet Tennessee town. The nascent AIDS epidemic reaches even this small town and Dr. Verghese, an infectious disease specialist, soon finds himself flooded with AIDS patients and not many answers to their suffering. This well-acted story packs an emotional wallop as it weaves stories of how people reacted to the horrors of AIDS. ★★★ VHS: $9.99

My Own Private Idaho

(1991, 105 min, US, Gus Van Sant) *River Phoenix, Keanu Reeves, William Richert, Udo Kier, James Russo, Flea, Rodney Harvey.* With his third film, Van Sant has proven himself one of the most daring, innovative and accomplished directors of the day. Phoenix's portrayal of Mike, a solitary, narcoleptic street hustler searching for his long-lost mother is brilliant. Van Sant deftly weaves in a subplot based on Shakespeare's "Henry IV, Pt II," even borrowing a smattering of the Bard's dialogue. Reeves gives strong support as Mike's Prince Hal-like friend and Richert is superb as the Falstaff-derived Bob Pigeon. Dreamily photographed, with mood ranging from hilarious to tragic to highly erotic, *Idaho* is a modern classic. ★★★★ VHS: $19.99

My Science Project

(1985, 95 min, US, Jonathan Betuel) *John Stockwell, Fisher Stevens, Dennis Hopper, Danielle von Zerneck.* A high school senior working on a class project creates a device which can alter time and space. It's not really as fun as it sounds. (Letterboxed) ★½ VHS: $14.99

My Sex Life (Or How I Got into an Argument)

(1996, 178 min, France, Arnaud Desplechin) *Mathieu Amalric, Emmanuelle Devos, Emmanuel Salinger, Chiara Mastroianni.* A philosophical romance about the sexual and professional escapades among a group of graduate students, *My Sex Life* is overlong and underwhelming. Paul (Amalric) is unhappy; not only is he unmotivated to complete his thesis, but he is in the process of ending his relationship with his long-term girlfriend. Coasting through his routine, Paul becomes infatuated with a number of women, and these dalliances, combined with a series of humiliations by a professional rival, force him to re-examine his behavior. The film's main problem is that the protagonist simply lacks charm. Since little actually happens in the film, there's no real payoff when any drama does come to a head. Ultimately, *My Sex Life* is largely unsatisfying. (French with English subtitles) ★★ VHS: $19.99; DVD: $24.99

My Sister Eileen

(1955, 108 min, US, Richard Quine) *Betty Garrett, Janet Leigh, Jack Lemmon, Bob Fosse, Dick York, Tommy Rall.* In 1942, Rosalind Russell starred in *My Sister Eileen*, a film comedy based on Ruth McKinney's stage hit. Eleven years later, Russell reprised her role in the Broadway musical adaptation, retitled "Wonderful Town." However, a new musical score was written when the story returned to the screen in this musical form in 1955. Though the music is not on par with "Wonderful Town," it's nevertheless snappy and engaging. Garrett and Leigh play sisters from Ohio who move to Greenwich Village, hoping to find fame and fortune. They find Lemmon and Fosse. Fosse choreographed the film, and his fledgling trademark movements are in evidence. The best musical sequence is a terrific Kelly/O'Connor-type number featuring Fosse and that fabulous dancer Rall. ★★★ VHS: $19.99

My Son the Fanatic

(1999, 87 min, GB, Udayan Prasad) *Om Puri, Akbar Kurtha, Rachel Griffiths, Gopi Desai, Stella Skarsgård.* Hanif Kureishi (*My Beautiful Laundrette*) wrote this look at the immigrant community experience in contemporary Britain. Puri stars as the troubled father of a young man (Kurtha) who's utterly alienated. Kureishi's genius here is to switch the expected generation-gap conflict: father wants assimilation and marriage into the white world for son, while son rejects his white fiancée and embraces radical Islam. The script continues to surprise, with Puri getting involved with a local prostitute, further complicating this family melodrama. There's gentle humor, frank observations and warm characters, who are brought to life through appealing performances. ★★★ VHS: $19.99; DVD: $29.99

My Summer Story

(1994, 85 min, US, Bob Clark) *Charles Grodin, Mary Steenburgen, Kieran Culkin, Christian Culkin.* Jean Shepherd's childhood reminiscences are continued the summer following the delightful *A Christmas Story*. Unfortunately, the results aren't nearly as lively or inspired. This time around, family members (here portrayed by Grodin, Steenburgen, and two more Culkins: Kieran and Christian) each have a personal quest. The eldest son wants to find the perfect killer top. Mom wants to collect a complete set of movie theatre giveaway china. And Dad sets out to vanquish an obscenely extended family of miscreant neighbors. This effort lacks the consumate charm and whimsy of *Christmas*; the characters are too broadly drawn, and lack the warmth and accessibility which make the first film a perennial favorite. ★★ VHS: $14.99

My Teacher's Wife

(1995, 92 min, US, Bruce Leddy) *Tia Carrere, Christopher McDonald, Jason London, Jeffrey Tambor, Zak Orth.* Boy falls in love with tutor, who just happens to be the wife of his vile math teacher. A tired formula to be sure, but a fun and likable cast makes *My Teacher's Wife* rather upbeat. There are a few love stories to one's interest, as London leaves his girlfriend in the lurch as he figures out what he wants out of love and life. Though the events are predictable, the characters seem genuine in getting there. ★★½ VHS: $79.99; DVD: $24.99

My Twentieth Century

(1989, 104 min, Hungary, Ildiko Enyedi) *Dorothea Segda, Oleg Jankowsky.* Crisscrossing confusion and strange coincidence propel this lighthearted fairy tale about twin sisters, separated at birth, who are reunited years later. Set against the tumultuous chaos of turn-of-the-century Hungary, as well as many other exotic locales throughout Europe, the story has the twins meeting once again on the Orient Express — one, a wealthy courtesan; the other, an anarchist carrying explosives. While unknown to one another, each woman is having an affair with the same man. (Hungarian with English subtitles) ★★★ VHS: $19.99

Myra Breckinridge

(1970, 94 min, US, Michael Sarne) *Raquel Welch, Rex Reed, John Huston, Farrah Fawcett, Mae West, Roger Herren, Tom Selleck.* An outrageous X-rated version of Gore Vidal's "scandalously" satiric transsexual novel that has taken on mythic proportions for being such a bomb. Reed and Welch are the male and female embodiment of the same person — before and after the operation. Huston, West, and Fawcett are just some of the casting oddities. Combine them with a talentless director, and a screenplay imbued with a slapdash '60s mentality, and the result had critics running to their thesauruses looking for stronger words than "atrocious." Yes, it's bad. But in a campy, smirky, hipper-than-fag sort of way. Why, either the lesbian scene between Welch and Fawcett or the tasteless sequence in which Welch

River Phoenix (l.) and Keanu Reeves in *My Own Private Idaho*

rapes a strapping stud of a cowboy (Herren) is worth the price of rental. It really has to be seen to be believed. (★★★★ Camp Value) ★

Mysteries

(1978, 93 min, The Netherlands, Paul de Lussanet) *Rutger Hauer, Sylvia Kristel, Rita Tushingham.* Hauer stars in this rather stiff but absorbing film version of Nobel Prize–winning Knut Hamsun's novel. On the Isle of Man late in the 19th century, a mysterious, lonely, and possibly insane young stranger (Hauer) arrives in a small coastal community and begins to upset the townspeople's well-ordered lives. Kristel and Tushingham play the unattainable women he falls in love with. A bit muddled in execution, the film creates an eerie, somber world where love and understanding prove to be tantalizingly elusive. ★★

Mysterious Island

(1961, 101 min, GB, Cy Endfield) *Michael Craig, Joan Greenwood, Michael Callan, Gary Merrill, Herbert Lom.* Ray Harryhausen created some of his best work in this adaptation of the Jules Verne novel about Confederate prisoners whose escape attempt leaves them stranded on an island infested with giant animals. Bernard Herrmann's score is outstanding. Lots of fun. ★★★ VHS: $14.99

Mystery, Alaska

(1999, 119 min, US, Jay Roach) *Russell Crowe, Hank Azaria, Lolita Davidovich, Ron Eldard, Mary McCormack, Burt Reynolds.* Written by workaholic David E. Kelley ("Ally McBeal"), this genial hockey flick concerns the tiny titular town — where hockey is a religion — who sports a team good enough to take on the pros. At least, that's what Azaria writes in *Sports Illustrated.* Led by Crowe, the team must graduate from its weekly hockey games to the national spotlight. . . and the New York Rangers. A good ensemble makes the most of a familiar but benign sports story, where the underdogs rally to take on the reigning champs. Crowe is very believable as the small-town sheriff, and Reynolds is in his element as the town's crusty judge. ★★½ VHS: $14.99; DVD: $32.99

Mystery Date

(1991, 98 min, US, Jonathan Wacks) *Ethan Hawke, Teri Polo, Brian McNamara, Fisher Stevens, B.D. Wong.* When a young man on his dream date finds himself mistaken for his older brother, sparks fly and his world is turned upside down. The film is filled with implausibilities so common to the teen comedy, but there's actually a few laughs to be had. ★★ VHS: $6.99

Mystery Men

(1999, 122 min, US, Kinka Usher) *Ben Stiller, Janeane Garofalo, Hank Azaria, William H. Macy, Greg Kinnear, Geoffrey Rush, Paul Reubens, Eddie Izzard, Kel Mitchell, Claire Forlani, Lena Olin, Wes Studi, Tom Waits.* How many superheroes does it take to make you laugh? Evidently as many as are on-screen in this energetic, funny romp based on the popular comic book. Kinnear is Captain Amazing, superhero extraordinaire of Chapagne City. But things have been a little slow lately in the crime-fighting business because he's put all the criminals in jail. When he allows his super arch-enemy Casanova Frankenstein (Rush) to escape to liven things up, he's captured by

Janeane Garofalo and her dead dad in *Mystery Men*

the evil genius. Who is there to come to the rescue? Why, a ragtag team of superhero wannabes. There's quite a few laughs at hand when these bunglers set out to free Captain Amazing — thanks to an extremely wily cast who know how to have a good time. It's not rocket science; but, hey, what is. ★★★ VHS: $14.99; DVD: $24.99

The Mystery of Alexina

(1985, 84 min, France, René Feret) *Vuillemin, Valeri Stroh.* This literate, beautifully photographed film, based on a mid-19th-century memoir, tells the tale of a convent-bred teacher at a girls' elementary school. She falls in love with another girl, but soon discovers that she herself is a man. This fascinating love story poses intriguing questions of identity and character in a romantic, stylish setting. (French with English subtitles) ★★★

The Mystery of Picasso

(1956, 77 min, France, Henri-Georges Clouzot) Declared a national treasure by the French government, this fascinating documentary features Pablo Picasso at work, creating over 15 works before the camera's eyes. The paintings were destroyed after the filming so this is the only opportunity to view them. An absorbing look at one of the greatest artists of the 20th century as well as a study of an artist's vision and its physical results. Picasso's mind and artistic motivations are wonderfully and forever on view. (French with English subtitles) ★★★★

The Mystery of Rampo

(1995, 100 min, Japan, Kazuyoshi Okuyama) *Masahiro Motoki, Naoto Takenaka, Michiko Hada.* A challenging contemporary Japanese film which explores the connections between fiction and reality, *The Mystery of Rampo* tells the story of a well-known but misunderstood writer, Rampo. In a beautiful animated segment, we see one of his stories come to life: An invalid father accidentally locks himself in a lacquer cabinet, and when his wife discovers him, she allows him to suffocate. Although the story is never published, Rampo learns that a real-life situation has mirrored his story. Rampo becomes obsessed with the wife. Fascinating, thought-provoking, and even an absorbing mystery, *Rampo* is a feast for the senses. (Japanese with English subtitles) ★★★½

Mystery Train

(1989, 113 min, US, Jim Jarmusch) *Masatoshi Nagase, Youki Kudoh, Screamin' Jay Hawkins, Cinque Lee, Nicoletta Braschi, Elizabeth Bracco, Joe Strummer, Steve Buscemi, Rockets Redglare.* Jarmusch continues to explore the theme of strangers in even stranger lands. This time out he uses Memphis, Tennessee, as the backdrop for three interwoven stories which collide in a rundown hotel in the sleazy part of town. The episodes follow a young and very hip Japanese couple who have come to pray at the temple of rock 'n' roll; three Memphis lowlifes on a drunken, brawling and murderous night of debauchery; and a young Italian woman, stranded by the death of her husband and waiting to accompany his coffin back to Italy. Jarmusch delights in the odd-ball quirkiness of his characters. ★★★ VHS: $14.99; DVD: $24.99

Mystic Pizza

(1988, 102 min, US, Donald Petrie) *Julia Roberts, Annabeth Gish, Lili Taylor, Vincent D'Onofrio, Conchata Ferrell, Matt Damon.* This fresh and winning romantic comedy-drama follows the ups and downs of three young waitresses trying to come to terms with their impending adulthood. Along the way, they fall in love, play some pool, and even pass out at their own weddings — all the while serving the best damn pizza in the state of Connecticut. ★★★ VHS: $9.99; DVD: $19.99

The Myth of Fingerprints

(1997, 91 min, US, Bart Freundlich) *Julianne Moore, Noah Wyle, Blythe Danner, Roy Scheider, Hope Davis, Michael Vartan, Brian Kerwin, James LeGros.* Rookie director Freundlich serves up a lukewarm slice of home-for-the-holidays pie that is fraught with dysfunction and unendurable ennui — for the audience, that is. Wyle stars as the prodigal son who returns to his Ethan Allen–esque New England home for Thanksgiving to confront his father (an impenetrable Scheider) and try to rekindle a past flame with his ex-sweetie. What ensues is a whole bunch of bitchiness with his siblings (especially elder sister Moore). Freundlich attempts to cover up his characters' intrinsic vapidity with an off-kilter sense of quirkiness that really only serves to render the film all the more incomprehensible. For a more interesting slice of lifeless WASPishness, pick up the latest J. Crew catalog. ★★ VHS: $24.99; DVD: $27.99

Nadine

(1987, 83 min, US, Robert Benton) *Jeff Bridges, Kim Basinger, Rip Torn, Gwen Verdon, Glenne Headly.* Sweet-natured comic thriller set in 1954 Texas starring Bridges and Basinger as a separated husband and wife who unwittingly become involved with a local gangster when Basinger witnesses a murder and mistakenly takes possession of secret documents. Torn is a most spirited villain. ★★★

Nadja

(1995, 92 min, US, Michael Almereyda) *Elina Löwensohn, Peter Fonda, Galaxy Craze, Martin Donovan, Suzy Amis, Jared Harris, David Lynch.* This bloodless, art-house vampire film aspires to be innovative in both its narrative and its cinematography, but is not completely successful in either respect. Nadja (the cadaverous Löwensohn), a Romanian vampire transplanted to New York City, lives a life of coffeehouse ennui and predatory hunting. She begins a lesbian relationship with a similarly disaffected twentysomething burnout married to a likable but dimwitted amateur boxer, who just happens to be the nephew of the vampire-hunter who slew Nadja's father! The film's tone veers wildly from angst-ridden to campy humor, and attempts to create a sort of "vampire-vision" through the use of a Fisher Price PixelCam, which fragments the picture. Though the production design is very good, *Nadja* ultimately is too pretentious for its own good. ★★ VHS: $9.99; DVD: $24.99

Naked

(1993, 126 min, GB, Mike Leigh) *David Thewlis, Lesley Sharpe, Katrin Cartlidge.* A brilliant, terrifying and undeniably real vision of the welfare state. Leigh takes us on a picaresque journey following Johnny (Thewlis in a stunning performance), our 27-year-old protagonist (or is that antagonist?), an embittered, overly loquacious ne'er-do-well who spews forth a relentlessly nihilistic tirade against man, God and society. After sexually assaulting a woman in Manchester, he flees to London and insinuates himself on his former girlfriend, Louise, and immediately beds her roommate, Sophie. Quickly tiring of their company, he hits the streets for a midnight sojourn, on which he waxes eloquent with every stranger about his apocalyptic philosophies. Leigh does a brilliant job of framing Johnny's rage against a backdrop of urban decay. ★★★★ VHS: $19.99

The Naked and the Dead

(1958, 131 min, US, Raoul Walsh) *Aldo Ray, Cliff Robertson, Raymond Massey, Joey Bishop.* A tough and gritty film version of Norman Mailer's novel about a group of WWII soldiers stationed in the Pacific; though its familiar, disparate characters have surfaced in just about every "platoon" film. ★★½

Naked City

(1948, 96 min, US, Jules Dassin) *Barry Fitzgerald, Don Taylor, Howard Duff.* In a trend-setting, "just the facts, ma'am," semidocumentary style seen in countless films and TV shows since, this gripping crime thriller follows a police investigation's probe into the brutal murder of a beautiful young model. Fitzgerald plays the folksy, pipe-smoking Lt. Muldoon who, along with his strikingly handsome assistant (Taylor), combs the classy veneer of Upper West Side society in an attempt to crack open the case. Noteworthy and quite fascinating is the film's entirely on location shooting in old New York, a rarity at a time when Hollywood stuck with studio sets. ★★★ VHS: $24.99; DVD: $24.99

The Naked Civil Servant

(1980, 80 min, GB, Jack Gold) *John Hurt.* Based on the autobiography of Quentin Crisp, this is a witty examination of the process of growing up gay in the repressive England of the 1930s and '40s. Hurt's portrayal of Crisp is nothing less than superb as he fights back against society's intolerance, ostracism, and violence with pointed, razor-sharp humor. ★★★½ VHS: $19.99

The Naked Country

(1985, 90 min, Australia, Tim Burstall) *John Stanton, Rebecca Gilling.* Forget the box art picturing a scantily clad woman baking in the Australian sun, for rather than cheesy erotica this is nothing more than a run-of-the-mill action/melodrama set in the Australian Outback. The story centers around a white rancher who has come into conflict with the local tribe of Aborigines over grazing rights. It all culminates in a showdown between rancher and natives which unsuccessfully aspires to the magical imagery of *The Last Wave.* ★★

The Naked Edge

(1961, 97 min, GB, Michael Anderson) *Gary Cooper, Deborah Kerr, Eric Portman, Diane Cilento, Hermione Gingold, Peter Cushing.* Cooper's last film is a disappointing psychological thriller borrowing much from Hitchcock's *Suspicion.* Kerr costars as Cooper's wife, who slowly begins to suspect her husband is a murderer. It seems Cooper's testimony about his employer's murder sent a coworker to prison; and now it looks like the wrong man may have been incarcerated. Despite a few stylish touches, this is kinda sluggish and the twists are unexciting. ★★

The Naked Gun

(1988, 85 min, US, David Zucker) *Leslie Nielsen, George Kennedy, Priscilla Presley, Ricardo Montalban, O.J. Simpson.* From the makers of *Airplane!* and "Police Squad," comes this zany, irreverent and anarchistic comedy. Stonefaced Nielsen is Lt. Drebin — a hilarious mixture of the bungling innocence of Mr. Magoo and Maxwell Smart with the ruthless and often sadistic crimefighting tactics of a Philly cop (no letters please!). Here we find Lt. Drebin investigating a plot to assassinate the Queen of England while she is on a visit to America. The story line, however, serves simply as a backdrop for the wild cavalcades of silly, sick and stupid jokes that we have come to expect from the Zucker/Abrahams/Zucker team. (Followed by 2 sequels) ★★★ VHS: $14.99; DVD: $24.99

The Naked Gun 2½: The Smell of Fear

(1991, 85 min, US, David Zucker) *Leslie Nielsen, Priscilla Presley, George Kennedy, Robert Goulet, O.J. Simpson.* From the brother of the director of *Ghost...* no, make that from the partner of the director of *Airplane!...* no, that ain't right, either. From the director of... oh, hell, you know who he is! Nielsen returns as that lethal weapon Lt. Frank Drebin in this consistently funny sequel. Lt. Drebin is on the case in Washington, D.C., and he's up against greedy industrialists determined to sabotage our nation's antipollution measures. Though the film is not as hilarious as the original *Naked Gun* or *Airplane!* — both films seem to produce a never-ending stream of guffaws — 2½ is nevertheless a constant pleasure. And its White House opening scene is priceless. Who needs the Democrats for Bush-bashing when Drebin is around? ★★★ VHS: $14.99; DVD: $24.99

Naked Gun 33 1/3: The Final Insult

(1994, 83 min, US, Peter Segal) *Leslie Nielsen, Priscilla Presley, George Kennedy, Fred Ward, O.J. Simpson, Ellen Greene, Pia Zadora, Kathleen Freeman.* Nielsen and company are back for another side-splitting round of slapstick hijinks and stupid puns in this third *Naked Gun* film cowritten by David Zucker and Pat Proft and helmed by first-time director Segal. Frank Drebin, now enjoying the bliss of retirement as his wife (Presley) goes to work, is persuaded by old pal Kennedy to help him on a case. This leads Drebin to prison where he befriends a

Naked Gun 33⅓: The Final Insult

Peter Weller plays William Burroughs' literary alter ego in *Naked Lunch*

terrorist and he eventually helps save the Academy Awards. As would be expected, the laughs are fast and furious, and Nielsen's comic timing and mugging is priceless. This is one series which has yet to run out of breath. ★★★ VHS: $14.99; DVD: $24.99

Naked in New York

(1994, 91 min, US, Dan Algrant) *Eric Stoltz, Mary Louise Parker, Ralph Macchio, Jill Clayburgh, Timothy Dalton, Kathleen Turner, Whoopi Goldberg, Tony Curtis, Quentin Crisp.* The story of a young writer's rites of passage, *Naked in New York* is appealing only in a dilapidated, disorganized sort of way. Stoltz stars as a bohemian Jewish New York playwright who meets a WASPy photographer (Parker) while in college and proceeds to set up housekeeping. Billed as a romantic comedy, this lacks the focus to be much of anything but a series of amusingly eclectic scenes tied together by Stoltz's artsy, philosophical angst. However, Turner steals the movie with her exuberant portrait of a boozy, pot-smoking seductress/actress. ★★½ VHS: $19.99

The Naked Jungle

(1954, 95 min, US, Byron Haskin) *Charlton Heston, Eleanor Parker, William Conrad.* This is the one with the ants! Plantation owner Heston tries to make a go of it in South America; he loses to the elements and Parker. Though silly at times, it's a lot of fun and even manages to offer some high moments of jungle adventure. ★★½ VHS: $19.99

The Naked Kiss

(1965, 90 min, US, Samuel Fuller) *Constance Towers, Anthony Eisley.* From its electrifying opening sequence — in which an enraged bald-headed prostitute (Towers) beats a man senseless with a telephone — through its exposé of corruption and vice in "Small Town, USA," this torrid melodrama never lets up. Towers is Kelly, a hip-swinging, eye-flirting

floozy who "escapes" to a bucolic backwater town to begin life anew as a nurse to handicapped children. But an unforgiving and hypocritical society hounds her and just won't let a bad girl go good. Fuller fans won't be able to supress a smile throughout this deliciously enjoyable cult potboiler. (Letterboxed) ★★★½ VHS: $19.99; DVD: $29.99

Naked Lunch

(1991, 115 min, US, David Cronenberg) *Peter Weller, Judy Davis, Julian Sands, Roy Scheider, Ian Holm.* William Burroughs' 1950s free-form classic, with its nonlinear narration and shocking imagery, had long been thought "unfilmable." Director Cronenberg has done the impossible, for this hallucinatory horror/sci-fi/comedy/drama is a witty and imaginative interpretation. Weller stars as Burroughs' monosyllabic alter ego, Bill Lee, a bug exterminator who, along with his sharp-tongued wife (the amazing Davis), gets hooked on his own bug powder. Lee, swimming in a narcotics-induced paranoia, sees his Remington typewriter come alive in the form of a slimy, bug-shaped creature who informs him that he is really an underground agent on a mission to fight a worldwide "Interzone" conspiracy. An audacious and demanding foray into the psyche of a drug-addicted artist that will prove for some to be disgusting and incomprehensible — a response that would have delighted Burroughs. ★★★★ VHS: $29.99

The Naked Prey

(1966, 94 min, US, Cornel Wilde) *Cornel Wilde, Gert Van Der Berger.* Rather exciting action film with Wilde as an African safari guide who becomes human prey to a group of tribal hunters. ★★★ VHS: $19.99

The Naked Spur

(1952, 93 min, US, Anthony Mann) *James Stewart, Robert Ryan, Janet Leigh.* Flavorful, exciting western with Stewart as a bounty hunter

obsessed with tracking down outlaw Ryan and his companion Leigh. ★★★ VHS: $19.99

Naked Tango

(1991, 90 min, US, Leonard Schrader) *Esai Morales, Vincent D'Onofrio, Mathilda May.* Set in 1924, this surreal thriller — reminiscent of *Apartment Zero*, which is also set in Buenos Aires — stars the ravishing May as a scheming woman who unwittingly becomes involved with two feuding brothers (Morales and the sensually brutal D'Onofrio), both of whom are stylishly murderous criminals. Boasting lush camerawork, stunning production design and the erotic world of the Tango, this sexually charged though slow-moving thriller is a treat. ★★★

Naked Youth

(1959, 80 min, US, John F. Schreyer) *Carol Ohmart, Robert Hutton.* Three teens bust out of their juvenile detention center and head south of the border, where they encounter "dangerous drugs, thugs, gun molls, dope dolls and bad guys." ★ VHS: $9.99

The Name of the Rose

(1986, 128 min, Italy/West Germany/France, Jean-Jacques Annaud) *Sean Connery, F. Murray Abraham, Christian Slater, Ron Perlman, William Hickey.* A visually rich medieval murder mystery set in a remote monastary. A monk falls from a high tower: was it suicide or murder? As other brothers are found dead, visiting monk Connery investigates the series of bizarre deaths. Full of tongue-in-cheek allusions to Sherlock Holmes (Connery's sleuthing monk is named William of Baskerville), this film may be a disappointment to those who have read the novel; but the film perfectly captures the atmosphere of the era and maintains a sufficient amount of suspense. (Filmed in English) ★★★

Nana

(1980, 92 min, Italy, Don Walman) *Katya Berger, Jean-Pierre Aumont.* Emile Zola's classic erotic novel about a Parisian streetwalker who, by seducing the rich and powerful, becomes the toast of Parisian society, is successfully brought to the screen. The sensuous Berger plays the lusty and ambitious woman with Aumont also starring as her most ardent and long-suffering lover. ★★½

Nanook of the North

(1922, 79 min, US, Robert J. Flaherty) The first and possibly the finest of Flaherty's social documentaries, this simply constructed but trailblazing film was named as one of the 25 outstanding films worthy of historical preservation by the U.S. Congress in 1990. Set in the frozen vastness of the Hudson Bay region of Canada, the story follows Inuit Nanook's heartrending daily struggle for survival as he and his family battle nature for only the barest essentials of life. An absorbing classic that has been restored to its original condition and graced with a new musical score by Timothy Brock and members of the Olympia Chamber Orchestra. A sad note to this film is that Nanook died of hunger shortly after the film was released. ★★★★ VHS: $24.99; DVD: $29.99

Abel Gance's *Napoleon*

Napoleon

(1927, 235 min, France, Abel Gance) *Antonin Artaud, Albert Dieudonne.* Gance's overwhelming historical saga charts the French leader's youth, rise to power and triumphant Italian campaign. Meticulously reconstructed over the years, this silent classic remains a monument of technical innovation and virtuosity. ★★★★ VHS: $29.99

The Narrow Margin

(1952, 70 min, US, Richard Fleischer) *Charles McGraw, Marie Windsor.* Well-acted, well-paced thriller about a detective (McGraw) assigned to protect a mobster's widow traveling by train from a gang of hoods who want her dead. Windsor costars as the targeted woman under McGraw's wing. (Remade in 1990) ★★★ VHS: $19.99

Narrow Margin

(1990, 97 min, US, Peter Hyams) *Gene Hackman, Anne Archer, James B. Sikking. J.T. Walsh, M. Emmet Walsh.* This remake of the 1952 thriller of the same name bears all of the action and suspense associated with some of director Hyams' earlier films (*Outland*), but lacks the substance. Hackman stars as an FBI agent assigned to escort the reluctant eyewitness of a mob killing (Archer) from Canada to Los Angeles in safety. With hit men hot on their trail, the two board a train and — the rest you can guess. The film carries a fair number of thrills and the interplay between the characters is enjoyable. ★★½ VHS: $14.99; DVD: $14.99

Nashville

(1975, 160 min, US, Robert Altman) *Keith Carradine, Lily Tomlin, Ronee Blakely, Henry Gibson, Barbara Harris, Barbara Baxley, Allen Garfield, Geraldine Chaplin, Lauren Hutton, Shelley Duvall, Michael Murphy, Ned Beatty, Jeff Goldblum.* Altman's masterful, multilayered mosaic of 1970s Americana. A wonderful ensemble of 24 characters interact at a Tennessee political rally resulting in comedic and often poignant vignettes. One of the greatest achievements of the decade, with a stellar ensemble. Carradine won an Oscar for his song, "I'm Easy." ★★★★ VHS: $29.99; DVD: $29.99

The Nasty Girl

(1990, 95 min, Germany, Michael Verhoeven) *Lena Stolze, Monika Baumgartner.* Teasing the viewer into thinking that this is a simple, modern-day Bavarian fairy tale, Verhoeven's hugely enjoyable satire soon becomes much more. Dealing with fascism, terrorism and people's secretive, guilty pasts, the film amazingly never becomes didatic or boring. The story begins with sweet-faced Sonja, the daughter of a nice middle-class couple, entering an essay contest proposing as her theme "My Town in the Third Reich." The seemingly tranquil community's guilty memory is jolted and, faced with an exposition of their fascist-collaborative past, begin efforts, including threats of violence and a firebombing, to stop the determined young lady's goal of uncovering the truth. An invigorating mixture of comedy, investigative journalism, history lesson and moral heroism; all done in a lilting and audacious style of filmmaking. (German with English subtitles) ★★★½ VHS: $19.99

Nasty Habits

(1976, 91 min, GB, Michael Lindsay-Hogg) *Glenda Jackson, Sandy Dennis, Anne Meara, Geraldine Page, Anne Jackson, Melina Mercouri, Edith Evans.* This odd comic allegory transposes Nixon and his Watergate cronies to a Philadelphia convent and was produced and distributed by Brut Productions (yes, the perfume company). It stars a fine comic cast with Jackson as Nixon, Dennis as John Dean, Meara as Gerald Ford, and Page as Robert Haldeman. It's an offbeat affair with some good laughs, but not enough for a feature film. ★★

National Lampoon's Animal House

(1978, 109 min, US, John Landis) *John Belushi, Tim Matheson, Tom Hulce, Peter Riegert, Karen Allen, Stephen Furst, Kevin Bacon, Donald Sutherland, Verna Bloom.* Belushi made the most of his film debut, giving a truly funny performance, in this raucous, sophomoric comedy about an anarchic college fraternity's comic exploits. A good cast of then-youthful performers. (VHS available letterboxed or pan & scan) ★★★ VHS: $14.99; DVD: $24.99

National Lampoon's Christmas Vacation

(1989, 97 min, US, Jeremiah Chechik) *Chevy Chase, Beverly D'Angelo, Randy Quaid, Diane Ladd, Julia Louis-Dreyfus, Juliette Lewis, Johnny Galecki.* This third entry of the *National Lampoon Vacation* series, continuing the saga of the hapless Griswold family, finds Clark, Ellen and family home for the holidays. The laughs are surprisingly plentiful as they prepare for a family gathering where, of course, nothing goes right. Returning as patriarch Clark is Chase, a master of pratfall and schtick, and the comedian has some good sightgags here. (Sequel: *Vegas Vacation*) ★★★ VHS: $14.99; DVD: $19.99

National Lampoon's European Vacation

(1985, 94 min, US, Amy Heckerling) *Chevy Chase, Beverly D'Angelo, Jason Lively, Dana Hill, Eric Idle, Victor Lanoux, John Astin, Paul Bartel, Mel Smith, Robbie Coltrane.* The Griswald family head to Europe for their second vacation in this disappointing, unfunny sequel. (Sequel: *National Lampoon's Christmas Vacation*) ★½ VHS: $9.99

National Lampoon's Vacation

(1983, 98 min, US, Harold Ramis) *Chevy Chase, Beverly D'Angelo, Randy Quaid, Dana Barron, Anthony Michael Hall, Imogene Coca, Eddie Bracken, John Candy.* The first, best and funniest of the *National Lampoon's Vacation* series. The Griswald family, accompanied by their miserly aunt (Coca), head off to Wally World (read Disney anybody?) and family bliss. What they get is another story. Lots of laughs, some sick, some sicker. Quaid is hilarious as a distant cousin. (Sequel: *National Lampoon's European Vacation*) ★★★ VHS: $9.99; DVD: $19.99

National Velvet

(1944, 125 min, US, Clarence Brown) *Elizabeth Taylor, Mickey Rooney, Anne Revere, Donald Crisp, Angela Lansbury.* Lovely family drama with Taylor and Rooney training their horses for the Grand National Steeplechase competition. Terrific entertainment. ★★★★ VHS: $14.99; DVD: $14.99

Native Son

(1986, 112 min, US, Jerold Freedman) *Victor Love, Matt Dillon, Elizabeth McGovern, Geraldine Page, Oprah Winfrey.* This second film version of Richard Wright's best-seller is a capable production made by "American Playhouse." The story is about a poor black youth living in 1930s Chicago who accidentally kills a rich white girl and is sentenced to death. Love plays Bigger Thomas, the embittered youth. Filmed in 1949 with author Wright as Thomas. ★★★ VHS: $14.99

The Natural

(1984, 134 min, US, Barry Levinson) *Robert Redford, Glenn Close, Wilford Brimley, Richard Farnsworth, Robert Duvall, Kim Basinger, Barbara Hershey.* Astonishing cinematography highlights this affecting fantasy drama with Redford as a mystical 1930s ballplayer; his career is cut short in his youth and he returns to the game later in life. A grand supporting cast. ★★½ VHS: $9.99; DVD: $24.99

Natural Born Killers

(1994, 118 min, US, Oliver Stone) *Woody Harrelson, Juliette Lewis, Robert Downey, Jr., Tommy Lee Jones, Tom Sizemore, Rodney Dangerfield.* Stone's hallucinatory roller-coaster ride follows a pair of unrepentant serial killers (Harrelson, Lewis) on a cross-country spree of wanton carnage and mind-bending schizoid dementia. Ultimately joining them is Downey as the Aussie-accented host of a sensationalist TV tabloid show who is determined to get their story at any cost. Quentin Tarantino's inventive script has the two homicidal lovebirds consummating their relationship with the murder of her abusive father (Dangerfield) in a bizarre and hilarious skit that parodies TV sitcoms. But

N

Stone has trouble finding the humor in the rest of Tarantino's tale and the result is yet another exercise in our culture's love affair with violence and the media's mercenary job of feeding that appetite. (VHS available letterboxed or pan & scan in a special director's version) ★★½ VHS: $19.99; DVD: $24.99

Naughty Girl (Mam'zelle Pigale)

(1958, 77 min, France, Michel J. Boisrond) *Brigitte Bardot, Jean Bretonniere, Françoise Fabian.* Bardot, in a role that plays against her bombshell image, stars as an innocent but klutzy schoolgirl who finds herself the unwitting pawn in a cat-and-mouse chase between the police, a ring of counterfeiters and her ex-con father. Scantily clad in either a tight-fitting tennis outfit, a flimsy bikini, a bath towel or even, for a time, a Roman tunic, young Brigitte is both disarmingly likable and sexy in this minor but amusing film which features more than its fair share of tacky musical numbers. (Letterboxed) (French with English subtitles) (aka: *That Naughty Girl*) ★★ VHS: $14.99; DVD: $29.99

Naughty Marietta

(1935, 106 min, US, W.S. Van Dyke) *Jeanette MacDonald, Nelson Eddy, Frank Morgan, Elsa Lanchester.* MacDonald and Eddy's first film together is a sappy musical with the two falling in love in the American wilderness. Score includes "Tramp, Tramp, Tramp" and "Ah, Sweet Mystery of Life." MacDonald and Eddy make an appealing romantic and singing duo, though the story is overly sentimental. (And she's not *that* naughty!) ★★½ VHS: $19.99

The Naughty Nineties

(1945, 76 min, US, Jean Yarbrough) *Bud Abbott, Lou Costello, Henry Travers.* The classic skit "Who's on First" highlights this otherwise average Abbott and Costello romp, with the boys trying their luck as Mississippi gamblers. ★★ VHS: $14.99

The Navigator/The Boat/ The Love Nest

(1921-24, 102 min, US, Buster Keaton, Eddie Cline & Donald Crisp) *Buster Keaton, Kathryn McGuire.* A collection of three Buster Keaton comedies. *The Navigator* (1924, 60 min) is a masterful comedy directed by Keaton and Crisp. Featuring exceptional comic visuals, great running gags and inventive plot twists, the film casts Keaton as a rich slacker who finds himself stranded on an ocean liner with the woman (McGuire) who has jilted him. Adrift at sea, the two are beset by problems ranging from making morning breakfast to finding suitable sleeping accomodations. One remarkable scene finds Keaton underwater fighting with swordfish and an octopus, and, as usual, Keaton's stunts are without peer. This is classic comedy. (★★★★) *The Boat* (1921, 23 min) continues the volume's nautical theme, with Keaton and family losing home, car and dignity to live on their homemade houseboat (the *Damfino*). Clever slapstick and funny vignettes combine to make this a delight. (★★★½) *The Love Nest* (1923, 20 min) is a cute high seas comedy with Keaton being rescued by a tyrannical captain and turning his ship upside-down with uninhibited buffoonery. (★★★) VHS: $29.99; DVD: $29.99

The Navigator

(1989, 92 min, New Zealand, Vincent Ward) *Hamish McFarlane, Bruce Lyons, Chris Haywood.* A thinking person's fantasy is a rare breed, indeed; which makes this totally original and captivating time travel odyssey all the more praiseworthy. Set in the 14th century besieged by the Black Plague, a small village free of the disease fears that it too will succumb. Its only hope lies in a young boy with psychic powers who, accompanied by his older brother and four villagers, makes a perilous trek across his land to fulfill a vision — only to find himself in modern-day New Zealand. This accomplished production belies its low budget, featuring splendid photography and an impressive first-rate cast and technical know-how. ★★★½ VHS: $19.99; DVD: $24.99

Navy SEALS

(1990, 113 min, US, Lewis Teague) *Charlie Sheen, Michael Biehn, Joanne Whally-Kilmer, Bill Paxton, Rick Rossovich.* A Navy SEAL team (Sea, Air, Land) on a mission to free U.S. hostages in the Middle East discovers a terrorist's arsenal of missiles. Mindless, even confusing, action adventure with cardboard caricatures in uniforms performing derring-do in combat. ★½ VHS: $9.99; DVD: $14.99

Nazarin

(1958, 91 min, Mexico, Luis Buñuel) *Francisco Rabal, Rita Macedo.* Religious hypocrisy is the theme in this, one of Buñuel's most powerful, realistic and yet often overlooked films. An eccentric young priest, imbued with the teachings of Christ, sets out to live a life of purity outside the confines of the church. Yet his journey through the land is met with hostility, indifference and confusion by those he encounters. For (in the Buñuelian world) the idealistic precepts of love and simplicity are no match in a world dominated by physical needs and limitations. A grim religious satire and winner of the Best Film Award at Cannes. (Spanish with English subtitles) ★★★★ VHS: $69.99

Néa: The Young Emmanuelle

(1976, 103 min, France/West Germany, Nelly Kaplan) *Ann Zacharias, Sami Frey.* At 16, Sybille (Zacharias) becomes a best-selling author of erotic literature; though she's a virgin, she uses her fantasies and observes others for material. Soon, Sybille grows tired of being inexperienced and a voyeur. She convinces her publisher (Frey) that they should sleep together in order to give her more material for her next book. Their relationship sours, however, when she falls in love with him and he starts to take credit for the book's success. A sensual, intriguing coming-of-age story which balances its erotic story line with the more conventional trappings of romance and sexual politics. (French with English subtitles) ★★★ VHS: $59.99

Near Dark

(1987, 95 min, US, Kathryn Bigelow) *Adrian Pasdar, Jenny Wright, Lance Henriksen, Bill Paxton, Jenette Goldstein.* This stylish, gritty vampire tale is one of the better horror films of the 1980s. Young Pasdar falls for Wright, who's part of a traveling group of nightstalkers — including Henriksen, Paxton and Goldstein. When he gets bitten, he joins them on their

reign of terror throughout the West. Though the film takes some liberties with the vampire legend, it's one of the most intense shockers of the genre. ★★★½

Necessary Roughness

(1991, 108 min, US, Stan Dragoti) *Scott Bakula, Hector Elizondo, Robert Loggia, Larry Miller, Sinbad, Rob Schneider.* It's *Back to School* meets *Semi-Tough* as a misfit college football team attempts to win a game. Bakula is a 37-year-old farmer and former high school football star who enrolls at a Texas university to become their quarterback. Under the guidance of new, straight-arrow coach Elizondo and assistant Loggia, the team learns to band together for what, of course, will be the big game at the finale. The film shares much with the baseball farce *Major League*. ★★½ VHS: $14.99; DVD: $24.99

Necronomicon: The Book of the Dead

(1996, 90 min, US, Christophe Gans/Shusuke Kaneko/Brian Yuzna) *David Warner, Jeffrey Combs, Bruce Payne, Belinda Bauer, Dennis Christopher.* This triptych of episodes based on stories by H.P. Lovecraft can be classified along with most other attempts to bring his highly imaginative works to the big screen, as a nice try. Producer and codirector Yuzna directs the last and probably the best episode, based on "The Whisperer in Darkness." The first episode, "The Drowned," is trite and marred by poorly executed special makeup effects. The middle episode, "The Cold," is admirable, but its modern ending works at cross-purposes with its Lovecraftian beginning. ★★ VHS: $79.99

Ned Kelly

(1970, 100 min, GB, Tony Richardson) *Mick Jagger, Clarissa Kaye.* Set in 19th-century Australia, this ambitious Outback western features the screen acting debut of Jagger. He plays Ned Kelly, Australia's most notorious outlaw, who with his band of fellow Irishmen does battle against the repressive British authorities. Jagger, much better used as the decadent rock star in Nicolas Roeg's *Performance*, is out of place in this film. A bit too scrawny for the role, he does not possess the needed screen presence and his painful attempt at an Irish brogue doesn't help either. Featuring music by Waylon Jennings. ★★½ VHS: $14.99

Needful Things

(1993, 120 min, US, Fraser C. Heston) *Max von Sydow, Amanda Plummer, Ed Harris, Bonnie Bedelia, J.T. Walsh.* Stephen King's "tale du jour" is stylishly served up by first-time director Heston (the son of Charlton). Heston's quasi-operatic production boasts a knock 'em-dead performance by veteran actor von Sydow as Leland Gaunt, a satanic salesman whose curio shop, Needful Things, springs up out of nowhere causing all hell to break loose in the small New England town of Castle Rock. Kudos also to Plummer as a downtrodden spinster who becomes enmeshed in the soul-stealing machinations of the demonic Mr. Gaunt. ★★½ VHS: $14.99; DVD: $29.99

Negatives

(1968, 90 min, GB, Peter Medak) *Glenda Jackson, Peter McEnery, Diane Cilento.* Medak's directorial debut is a macabre and erotic tale about a young couple with a somewhat more than kinky sexual bent. They encounter a glamorous photographer with an equally warped sense of bedroom play and enter an even stranger world of sexual fantasy. A stylish and unusual film. ★★★

The Negotiator

(1998, 138 min, US, F. Gary Gray) *Samuel L. Jackson, Kevin Spacey, David Morse, Ron Rifkin, J.T. Walsh, John Spencer.* A tense, exciting and intelligent police hostage drama with the good guy as the hostage taker, *The Negotiator* casts Jackson as Danny Roman, a well-respected Chicago cop who excels at his job as police negotiator. When his partner is murdered and Danny is framed, Danny takes a group of office workers hostage himself (in an effort to clear his name). Enter Chris Sabian (Spacey), another well-respected police negotiator. Thus begins a cat-and-mouse game of words and deeds between the two men as Danny tries to get to the truth. The pairing of Jackson and Spacey is dynamic; each actor brings an intensity and flavor to his role. The ensemble cast is equally adept, especially the late Walsh in one of his final roles. (VHS available letterboxed or pan & scan) ★★★ VHS: $14.99; DVD: $19.99

Neighbors

(1981, 91 min, US, John G. Avildsen) *John Belushi, Dan Aykroyd, Kathryn Walker, Cathy Moriarty.* Belushi's last film finds him the straight man as Aykroyd, for once, gets a chance to cut loose as the maniac who moves in next door and makes life a living hell. This reverse casting is indicative of the chances this film was willing to take, especially in the decision to maintain the novel's dark and unrelenting tone. While it provides comedic moments of dark-edged humor, the overall effect is one of a tired, overambitious project. ★★ VHS: $9.99

Nell

(1994, 113 min, US, Michael Apted) *Jodie Foster, Liam Neeson, Natasha Richardson, Richard Libertini.* Foster's remarkably nuanced performance highlights this otherwise dispassionate, ordinary tale of a "wild child" discovered in the backwoods of North Carolina. Neeson costars as a caring physician who has his hands full when Foster is found living wild and speaking a language no one understands. Neeson dedicates himself to deciphering her broken English and introducing her to civilization. Though the dramatics lead to tender moments between the two characters, the film is strangely devoid of emotion. However, the mystery of Foster's condition and the actress' unearthly inhabitation of the title character make *Nell* at the very least a compelling watch. ★★½ VHS: $9.99

Nelly and Monsieur Arnaud

(1995, 103 min, France, Claude Sautet) *Emmanuelle Béart, Michel Serrault, Jean-Hugues Anglade.* A talky though quietly powerful examination of unspoken desire, *Nelly and Monsieur Arnaud* concerns the relationship between a despondent young woman and a wealthy older man. Yet despite any prurient overtones, the film mines this nonsexual romance for its high emotional content. Nelly (Béart) is a young Parisian who owes six

Samuel L Jackson and Kevin Spacey in *The Negotiator*

months back rent and is trapped in a loveless marriage. A friend introduces her to Monsieur Arnaud (Serrault), a judge who needs help writing his memoirs. As these characters move closer to realizing their destinies, their jealousies come into bold relief. The performances by both leads are quite moving. Sautet has crafted an intelligent French chamber drama that aches with the resonance of heartbreak. (Letterboxed) (French with English subtitles) ★★★½ VHS: $29.99

Nenette and Boni

(1997, 103 min, France, Claire Denis) *Gregoire Colin, Alice Houri, Valeria Bruni-Tedeschi, Vincent Gallo.* There are many dreamlike images in *Nenette and Boni*, a wistful rumination on two troubled adolescents, but little drama. In this artfully photographed film about the shiftless Boni (Colin) reuniting with his pregnant sister Nenette (Houri), director Denis proves that she has an uncanny eye for visuals, but can not tell a story. Denis constructs a sensuous mood, filming Boni's frequently shirtless physique like a canvas, but there is no depth beyond the surface of these disenfranchised youths. Alienation can be fascinating, but in *Nenette and Boni* it is woefully tedious. (French with English subtitles) ★½ VHS: $29.99

The Neon Bible

(1995, 92 min, GB, Terence Davies) *Gena Rowlands, Denis Leary, Diana Scarwid, Drake Bell, Jacob Tierney.* Based on a story by John Kennedy O'Toole, the film is one which is of obvious attraction to director Davies: A coming-of-age tale of a sensitive teenage boy brought up in a household dominated by loving women. Set in 1940s Georgia, the story centers on David, who is brought up in a stifling Christian Fundamentalist household headed by his father (a very effective Leary). His only real communication comes when his big city aunt (Rowlands) — a former showgirl — comes for an extended visit. Not much happens as the strangely friendless, sad-eyed David floats from one incident to another developing a longing for something different. Davies films in his trademark haunting style, but the meandering story ultimately produces a less-than-successful film. ★★ VHS: $9.99; DVD: $9.99

The Nest

(1980, 109 min, Spain, Jaime de Arminan) *Ana Torrent, Hector Alterio.* A passionate and haunting film that depicts the complex relationship between a lonely 60-year-old widower and a captivating and intelligent 12-year-old girl. A moody, sensitive portrait about the meaning of friendship and love as he follows this relationship to its inevitable, tragic conclusion. (Spanish with English subtitles) ★★★

The Nest

(1987, 89 min, US, Terence H. Winkless) *Robert Lansing, Lisa Langlois.* A genetic experiment goes awry and turns ordinary cockroaches into bloodthirsty carnivores. The creepy bugs will definitely make one's skin crawl, and the film, while giving in to horror genre clichés, uses its mutilegged stars to good effect. Get out the industrial-strength Raid! ★★

The Net

(1995, 118 min, US, Irwin Winkler) *Sandra Bullock, Jeremy Northam, Dennis Miller, Diane Baker, Wendy Gazelle, Ken Howard.* The considerable charm of its leading lady Bullock is barely enough to keep this muddled computer-age thriller afloat. *The Net* consists of lots of computer talk, computer gadgets and hackers lovingly doting on their computers, but what it doesn't have is a well-developed screenplay or memorable suspense. Bullock plays a lonely computer whiz who becomes involved in a high-tech conspiracy. After the bad guys erase her identity in a particularly eerie sequence, she spends the rest of the film trying to elude them while seeking help from anyone that will listen. The chase scenes are rather flat, though the computer-babble will engage those who spend a lot of time at the keyboard. ★★ VHS: $9.99; DVD: $14.99

Network

(1976, 121 min, US, Sidney Lumet) *Peter Finch, Faye Dunaway, William Holden, Robert Duvall, Beatrice Straight, Ned Beatty.* A boisterous, brilliantly savage satire on television, America's fickle viewing habits and the corporate mentality. Paddy Chayevsky's scathing script is given extraordinary life by a remarkable cast to tell the story of the rise of a fourth network. Finch won an Oscar as the weary newsman who loses his sanity and becomes a guru; Dunaway also won an Oscar as the ruthless news department head whose aphrodisiac is high ratings. Holden gives a tremendous performance as the ex-department chief, who impotently witnesses the craziness around him. Straight won a Supporting Oscar as Holden's neglected wife. An original and breathtaking masterwork. ★★★★ VHS: $14.99; DVD: $19.99

Neurosia: Fifty Years of Perversity

(1995, 93 min, Germany, Rosa von Praunheim) *Desiree Nick, Rosa von Praunheim.* Part murder mystery, part self-critical autobiography and all satire, this is a delightfully candid film. It begins in a cinema, where a pompous von Praunheim is shot by someone in a crowd. The mystery begins when his body disappears from the stage. Gesine (Nick), a homophobic tabloid TV journalist, is assigned the task of digging up dirt on the controversial politico and filmmaker. Who killed von Praunheim becomes a problematic question after a slew of bitter friends, angry work associates and various former lovers appear, each bearing a grudge against the deceased director. *Neurosia* wanders all through von Praunheim's life, but the final ten minutes brings it all together in an inventively funny and self-deprecating fashion. (German with English subtitles) ★★★

Nevada

(1998, 109 min, US, Gary Tieche) *Amy Brenneman, Kirstie Alley, Gabrielle Anwar, Saffron Burrows, Kathy Najimy, Dee Wallace Stone.* Brenneman plays a sexy drifter first seen walking on a hot desert highway with only a suitcase and a bottle of water. Refusing a ride from a very interested guy from the nearest town, she obviously doesn't crave human contact. She gets it anyway when she answers a young boy's plea for help — his mother's having a baby. Brenneman delivers the baby and raises the curiosity and ire of the paranoid local woman. This sluggish, uneventful drama boasts a story that is without interest, same for the "mysterious past" that goofy flashbacks intermittently show glimpses of. To compensate, there's some beautiful scenery, and an excellent cast of female character actors (which is the only real draw here). ★★ VHS: $24.99

Nevada Smith

(1966, 135 min, US, Henry Hathaway) *Steve McQueen, Karl Malden, Brian Keith, Suzanne Pleshette.* Exciting western with McQueen in the title role — based on a character from Harold Robbins' "The Carpetbaggers" — as a cowboy who tracks down the gang who murdered his parents. ★★★ VHS: $14.99

Never Been Kissed

(1999, 107 min, US, Raja Gosnell) *Drew Barrymore, David Arquette, Michael Vartan, Molly Shannon, John C. Reilly, Garry Marshall, Leelee Sobieski.* The ever-engaging Barrymore plays a gawky reporter who goes undercover and finds herself back in high school hell in this misdirected romantic comedy. Josie Geller (Barrymore) was her high school outcast. Now 25 and a newspaper copy editor, she gets her

first assignment: pose as a high school student to find out what the kids are thinking. This brings back painful memories for Josie, but not nearly as painful for those watching her, and that doesn't refer to the office staff who's viewing her escapades through closed-circuit TV. Director Gosnell takes a high-concept, intriguing idea and drops the ball, giving the film a sluggish pace and too many boo-hoo moments. The screenwriters have concocted a few cute scenes, but Gosnell is out of his league in bringing to life the joys of romantic comedy. ★★ VHS: $14.99; DVD: $24.99

Never Cry Wolf

(1983, 105 min, US, Carroll Ballard) *Charles Martin Smith, Brian Dennehy.* Farley Mowat's stirring novel about his trek through the Canadian tundra to study the Arctic wolf is brought beautifully to the screen in this Disney production. The film capitalizes on the book's romantic vision of the frozen wilderness through breathtaking landscapes and a sense of daring high adventure. (Letterboxed) ★★★½ VHS: $14.99; DVD: $24.99

Never Give a Sucker an Even Break

(1941, 71 min, US, Edward Cline) *W.C. Fields, Margaret Dumont, Franklin Pangborn.* Fields' last starring film, with a script reportedly written on the back of an envelope, is a sometimes hilarious collection of gags, with Fields playing himself. ★★★½

Never on Sunday

(1959, 97 min, Greece, Jules Dassin) *Melina Mercouri, Jules Dassin, Titos Vandis.* This Greek Pygmalion was a huge international hit when first released and was considered quite daring in its day. Mercouri is unforgettable as an exuberant and carefree prostitute who meets up with an American tourist (Dassin) who falls in love with her and attempts to educate her to the finer things in life. Mercouri won the Best Actress Award at Cannes and the film won an Academy Award for Best Song. A thoroughly entertaining romp with wonderful location shooting in Piraeus and the Greek countryside. (Filmed in English) ★★★½ VHS: $14.99

Never Say Never Again

(1983, 137 min, GB, Irvin Kershner) *Sean Connery, Klaus Maria Brandauer, Max von Sydow, Barbara Carrera, Kim Basinger.* Connery will never say never to Bond, James Bond... He's back after 12 years and dives into this remake of *Thunderball.* If you missed this exciting spy adventure, see it; Connery is as suave and debonair as ever. ★★★ VHS: $9.99; DVD: $26.99

Never Talk to Strangers

(1995, 86 min, US, Peter Hall) *Rebecca De Mornay, Antonio Banderas, Dennis Miller, Len Cariou, Harry Dean Stanton.* De Mornay plays a psychiatrist who specializes in multiple personality disorder. While treating a serial killer (Stanton), she meets and begins an affair with a mysterious and sexy surveillance specialist (Banderas). And while her upstairs neighbor (Miller) pines away for her, and her estranged father (Cariou) tries to rekindle their relationship, she becomes the target for a series of deadly threats from an anonymous source. This "erotic thriller" is both predictable and tame, offering

few chills and only one steamy encounter of note. De Mornay acts as if she were on tranquilizers. ★★ VHS: $14.99; DVD: $29.99

The Neverending Story

(1984, 92 min, GB, Wolfgang Petersen) *Barret Oliver, Noah Hathaway.* Petersen's first English-language film is a near-classic fairy tale about a young boy who becomes so immersed in the book he's reading that he is magically drawn into the story and must help save the tale's world from destruction. Wonderful children's fare, perhaps a bit scary for the wee-est of tykes, but filled with good special effects and an earnest young hero. Only a slight clumsiness and not-too-subtle allegorical message keep this from the highest pantheon of children's film. (Followed by 2 sequels) ★★★½ VHS: $14.99

The Neverending Story II: The Next Chapter

(1990, 90 min, US, George Miller) *Jonathan Brandis, Kenny Morrison, John Wesley Shipp.* Sequel to the 1984 family favorite about a young boy transported to a magical land within the pages of his book. Now, the boy must return to the fantasy world to save his old friends from an evil sorceress, and finds the courage that he lacks in real life. Not as entrancing as the original, but still entertaining. Includes the original five-minute Warner Brothers cartoon "Box Office Bunny." ★★½ VHS: $19.99

The New Age

(1994, 110 min, US, Michael Tolkin) *Judy Davis, Peter Weller, Patrick Bauchau, Rachel Rosenthal, Adam West, Samuel L. Jackson.* Davis and Weller are well-suited in their roles as a pair of wanton yuppies whose comfortable material world comes crashing down around them. Their marriage is too hip for words, they live in a multi-zillion dollar house in the hills, and hobnob with the rich and famous. But it all falls apart and they are forced to search for some deeper meaning to their lives, leading them to new sex partners and a succession of New Age gurus who can only pose more questions than answers. Writer-director Tolkin evokes the same eerie atmosphere of his earlier work, *The Rapture,* as he unfolds this tale of spiritual emptiness in a world of decadence and consumption. ★★★ VHS: $19.99

The New Centurions

(1972, 103 min, US, Richard Fleischer) *George C. Scott, Stacy Keach, Jane Alexander, Rosalind Cash, Scott Wilson.* Stinging depiction of cop life: Scott is a veteran officer who dreads retiring; Keach is a young cop whose work comes before everything, including his wife. Based on the novel by Joseph Wambaugh. ★★★ VHS: $14.99

New Fists of Fury

(1984, 120 min, Hong Kong, Lo Wei) *Jackie Chan.* Chan plays a former pickpocket during WWII who is forced to fight for his life when his fiancée's school is destroyed and its master savagely murdered. With her help, he learns a new and deadly fighting art and together they exact vengeance for the death of her master. A brutal ballet of martial arts mayhem. (Dubbed) ★★★ VHS: $9.99

Z

New Jack City

(1991, 101 min, US, Mario Van Peebles) *Wesley Snipes, Ice T, Judd Nelson, Mario Van Peebles, Chris Rock, Allen Payne, Vanessa Williams, Bill Nunn.* Pulsating with the music, life and ever-present violence of a drug-infested inner city, this tough gangster thriller, ostensibly a black *Scarface*, should keep even the most taciturn viewer riveted to his seat. The city is New York, where a vicious crack dealer (villainously played by Snipes) is driving his way to the top of the drug underworld. It takes two renegade cops (Ice T, Nelson) to try to bring him and his sordid empire down. Van Peebles' first film is a tough, exciting and impressive work that successfully straddles the fine line of glorifying the drug culture while also presenting a stringent anti-drug message. ★★★ VHS: $9.99; DVD: $14.99

New Jersey Drive

(1995, 86 min, US, Nick Gomez) *Sharron Corley, Gabriel Casseus, Christine Baranski.* Based on a true story of police corruption in Newark, New Jersey, this Spike Lee–produced tale centers around a young "boy in the hood" (Corley) who finds himself thrust into the middle of a turf war between his car thief friends and the law when one of them steals a policeman's private car. Gomez's violent, flashy and somewhat predictable second effort falls short of his gritty debut film *Laws of Gravity.* Its reliance on stock characters, flashy MTV-style camerawork and overbearing rap music soundtrack only weakens the "urban action" genre instead of enhancing it. ★★ VHS: $19.99; DVD: $19.99

A New Leaf

(1971, 102 min, US, Elaine May) *Walter Matthau, Elaine May, Jack Weston, George Rose, William Redfield, James Coco.* May wrote, directed and stars in this comedy about a rich but clumsy woman (May) who is courted by a bankrupt playboy (Matthau), who's only after her money. Both stars are in good form, and the film offers many a well-placed laugh. ★★★ VHS: $14.99

A New Life

(1988, 104 min, US, Alan Alda) *Alan Alda, Ann-Margret, Hal Linden, John Shea, Veronica Hamel.* Alda goes through middle-aged angst as he and wife Ann-Margret divorce and find new loves. Alda retreats familiar territory here, but he and a good cast wring some life out of the unremarkable material. ★★½ VHS: $14.99

New Rose Hotel

(1999, 92 min, US, Abel Ferrara) *Christopher Walken, Willem Dafoe, Asia Argento.* Despite its gorgeous, sleek visuals, courtesy of cinematographer Ken Kelsch, Ferrara's *New Rose Hotel* is a vacant exercise. Two partners, Fox (Walken) and X (Dafoe), offer one million dollars to Sandii (Argento), an Italian hooker, to lure a Japanese businessman to another company. X falls in love with Sandii, and a series of double crosses ensue. Ferrara, who is adapting a William Gibson short story, eschews narrative convention, making much of the plotting incomprehensible. Walken does his patented emoting and Dafoe feigns cool detachment, but the film has no pulse and no point. Look

Madonna and Rupert Everett in *The Next Best Thing*

fast for cameos by Gretchen Mol, John Lurie, Annabella Sciorra, and Ryuichi Sakamoto. ★½ VHS: $102.99; DVD: $14.99

New Wave (Nouvelle Vague)

(1990, 89 min, France, Jean-Luc Godard) *Alain Delon.* The eternal war between the sexes and the classes is given the Godard treatment in this dense, meandering and ultimately enigmatic drama/thriller. A befuddled Delon is almost run over by the wealthy daughter of an industrialist. She picks him up and takes him home, but is it love or does she have something else in mind for him? Never simply content to tell a singular story, Godard infuses the film's soundtrack with layers of overlapping dialogue, poetry and music while the camera roams, circles and pans during each scene. While the earnest film enthusiast might see "art" and meaning in all of this complexity from the enfant terrible of the French New Wave, others, including casual viewers and the more cynical cinéaste, will conclude that the master has run out of new ideas. (French with English subtitles) ★★ VHS: $79.99

New Year's Day

(1990, 89 min, US, Henry Jaglom) *Henry Jaglom, Gwen Welles, Maggie Jakobson, David Duchovny, Milos Forman.* While the films of Jaglom are not everyone's idea of entertainment and fun, there is an unwavering flock of devotees who actually enjoy his personal style of angst-ridden filmmaking. Jaglom appears as a recently divorced Los Angelino who flees to New York on New Year's day. His new apartment, however, is still occupied by the old tenants, three young women who invite him to stay while they pack and throw a farewell party. At the party, peopled by a diverse assortment of oddball New Yorkers, our lecherous and unsympathetic hero views the proceedings with a detached air as he dispenses advice and tries to pick up women. While the caliber of the acting varies, Welles is especially affecting as the fragile Anne. Awkward at times, repetitive and something of a vanity production, the film nevertheless holds one's attention. ★★★ VHS: $79.99

New York, New York

(1977, 137 min, US, Martin Scorsese) *Liza Minnelli, Robert De Niro, Lionel Stander, Mary Kay Place, Diahnne Abbott, Larry Kert.* Minnelli and De Niro meet at a WWII victory party; the innocent pop singer and volatile jazz musician wed. As she reaches stardom, his fortunes decline, further straining an already combative marriage. The potent performances are ably underscored by a superb evocation of the era, though the story line is at times predictable and given to backstage clichés. Another dark look at human relations from director Scorsese. The video features a long and spectacular song-and-dance number excised from the film starring Kert and Minnelli. ★★½ VHS: $14.99

New York Stories

(1989, 123 min, US, Martin Scorsese/Francis Coppola/Woody Allen) *Nick Nolte, Rosanna Arquette, Woody Allen, Mae Questel, Mia Farrow, Julie Kavner.* Three-part film by New York directors Scorsese, Coppola and Allen. Scorsese's *Life Lessons* stars Nolte as a moody and talented painter tormented by the end of his relationship with his ever-present/lover Arquette. The second segment, Coppola's *Life without Zoe*, is a cold story of a bratty child's indulgent birthday party. The final film, Allen's *Oedipus Wrecks*, is the lifesaver of the three, and one of Allen's funniest works. Allen stars as a successful lawyer who is haunted, nagged and criticized by his ever-present mother, wonderfully portrayed by Questel (the original voice of Betty Boop). Not wholly successful, but still an interesting venture. ★★½

News from Home

(1976, 85 min, Belgium/France, Chantal Akerman) Avant-gardist Akerman has produced in this static, repetitive exercise her own unique filmic symphony to New York City. Attempting to explore the differences between European myths of the city against its gritty reality, cinematographer Babette Mangolte captures the strangely stark beauty of an alienated, lifeless world while offscreen

Z

Akerman occasionally reads, in a monotone voice, letters from a Belgian mother to her daughter living in New York. A demanding, abstract work of art. (French with English subtitles) ★★½ VHS: $24.99

Newsfront

(1978, 110 min, Australia, Phillip Noyce) *Bryan Brown, Bill Hunter, Wendy Hughes, Gerard Kennedy, Angela Punch.* This much celebrated and award-winning film vividly re-creates the glory days of newsreels and the men who captured the turbulent war years of the 1940s. Director Noyce intercuts a fictional story with actual news events to create this spirited true-life adventure. ★★★

Newsies

(1992, 121 min, US, Kenny Ortega) *Christian Bale, Bill Pullman, Robert Duvall, Ann-Margret. Michael Lerner, Max Casella.* This Disney musical about a group of newsboys who strike against a corrupt newspaper mogul boasts a wonderful cast of young talent, but unfortunately the story drags between musical numbers leaving the viewer mostly dispassionate. Even the always magnetic screen presences of Duvall and Ann-Margret can't liven up this one. ★½

The Newton Boys

(1998, 122 min, US, Richard Linklater) *Matthew McConaughey, Ethan Hawke, Skeet Ulrich, Vincent D'Onofrio, Julianna Margulies, Dwight Yoakam.* It's period-piece dress-up time in Linklater's first innocuous dud. *The Newton Boys* is a Prohibition-era western about brazen, cocky bank robbers; it has little violence, little blood, little excitement — three ingredients usually associated with the genre. Based on a true story, the film follows four brothers who grew up as farmers to become the most successful bank robbers in American history. The tone of the films suggests *Johnny Dangerously* meets *Young Guns,* and although the banjo and fiddle score spells comedy, there's nothing particularly humorous (or dramatic for that matter) on the screen. *The Newton Boys* is best remembered for being unmemorable. ★½ VHS: $9.99; DVD: $24.99

The Next Best Thing

(2000, 108 min, US, John Schlesinger) *Rupert Everett, Madonna, Benjamin Bratt, Michael Vartan, Lynn Redgrave, Josef Sommer, Neil Patrick Harris, Illeana Douglas.* Gay cinema may not have come as far as it could have by the year 2000, but the comedy-drama *The Next Best Thing* does prove that a story revolving around gay characters can be as pointless as stories about straight ones. After a drunken roll in the sack with gay best friend Robert (Everett), single mom Abbie (Madonna) decides she's keeping her baby. The two raise the child together — which they do with great success and little fuss. That is until Abbie meets Mr. Right (Bratt), and the story takes a weird twist into *Kramer vs. Kramer* territory. Everett is especially good as Robert, zinging a one-liner and a plea for fatherhood with equal aplomb. The gracious Madonna even allows Everett the better lines and bigger role. But Everett and a good cast aren't enough to compensate for a scatter-shot screenplay — admittedly funny in the first half — that ends up not taking one

road at the fork, but all the roads. ★★ VHS: $14.99; DVD: $29.99

Next Friday

(2000, 98 min, US, James Carr) *Ice Cube, Mike Epps, John Witherspoon, Tommy "Tiny" Lester, Jr.* Debo, the giant villain from the first *Friday,* escapes from prison, so Ice Cube's dad decides Cube should stay with his uncle and cousin in the 'burbs for a while, and lay low. Of course, things don't go as planned, and more comedy ensues. Stupid, potentially offensive (not the most charitable view of Latinos on display here) and sloppy as hell, *Next Friday* can be funny, anchored by another appealing performance by Cube. To be sure, Chris Tucker is sorely missed from the first film, and this whole affair is pretty pointless, but *Next Friday* is more entertaining than anyone has a right to expect. ★★½ VHS: $14.99; DVD: $24.99

Next of Kin

(1984, 72 min, Canada, Atom Egoyan) *Patrick Tierney.* Egoyan's fascination with family relations and the effects of electronic media on one's life are explored in this sly, off-the-wall comedy-drama. Peter, in most respects a normal young man, finds his relationship with his tyrannical WASP family to be unbearable. After a session of video therapy, he sees a video about a troubled Armenian family that had lost a baby to adoption 20 years before. Deciding that a new family is in order, he acts out the role of their long-lost son. Inspired lunacy reigns in this brilliant and original directorial debut that explores not only family tensions but ideas of displacement, cultural stereotypes and role playing. ★★★½ VHS: $79.99; DVD: $34.99

Next Stop, Greenwich Village

(1976, 109 min, US, Paul Mazursky) *Lenny Baker, Ellen Greene, Shelley Winters, Dori Brenner, Lois Smith, Christopher Walken, Antonio Fargas, Jeff Goldblum, Lou Jacobi.* Mazursky's excellent semiautobiographical account of his early adulthood in 1950s Greenwich Village is one

of the first American films in which a writer-director looks back at his youth. Baker gives a rich characterization as an aspiring actor who leaves his Brooklyn home for the unknown wilds of the Village. There, he befriends an eccentric group while waiting for his big break. Mazursky sees the era as a magical time, and his affection shows. The director's evocation of an almost mythical period is first-rate. There's a strong supporting cast, but the acting honors go to Winters for her hilarious turn as Baker's quintessential overprotective mom (wait till you see her tap dance!). Though not as well known as some of his other films, *Next Stop, Greenwich Village* is possibly Mazursky's best. ★★★★ VHS: $29.99

Next Stop Wonderland

(1998, 96 min, US, Brad Anderson) *Hope Davis, Alan Gelfant, Victor Argo, Holland Taylor, Robert Klein, Phillip Seymour Hoffman.* If you look up the term "independent romantic comedy" in the dictionary, you may find the description for this lively number that caused a stir at Sundance when Miramax ponied up $6 million for distribution rights. Indy doyenne Davis plays a night nurse at a Boston hospital who tries to make the best of a bad situation when her live-in lover Hoffman decides to dump her. Yenta mother Taylor decides to help by placing a personal ad, and soon a host of loser bachelors are coming out of the woodworks. Writer-director Anderson peppers his film with nice location work, a moody bossa-nova soundtrack and engagingly quirky characters. ★★★ VHS: $14.99; DVD: $29.99

Next Summer

(1986, 100 min, France, Nadine Trintignant) *Fanny Ardant, Philippe Noiret, Jean-Louis Trintignant, Claudia Cardinale.* An all-star cast sadly cannot save this pretentious drivel which claims to give a penetrating humanistic insight into familial relationships. In a rambling country house, the extended family of patriarch Noiret live, love, argue and reconcile (and all within 100 minutes). French fluff at its most nauseating. (French with English subtitles) ★★ VHS: $69.99

Next Stop, Greenwich Village

Z

The Next Voice You Hear

(1950, 83 min, US, William Wellman) *James Whitmore, Nancy Davis.* An odd drama about the voice of God being heard on the radio and the effect it has on the residents of a small town. The execution is not quite up to the premise, yet the film is strangely moving if one releases all cynical thoughts. ★★½ VHS: $19.99

Next Year If All Goes Well

(1983, 97 min, France, Jean-Loup Hubert) *Isabelle Adjani, Thierry L'hermitte.* A whimsical romantic comedy about a modern couple involved in an ambivalent affair. While Adjani, a pragmatic career woman, longs for a comfortable domestic life, L'hermitte, a boyish cartoonist, quakes at the mere mention of parenthood and retreats to the safer realm of his outer space comic strip. A megahit in France, this is an often riotous glimpse at marriage and infidelity. (Dubbed) ★★★ VHS: $69.99

Niagara

(1953, 89 min, US, Henry Hathaway) *Joseph Cotten, Marilyn Monroe, Jean Peters, Casey Adams, Don Wilson.* The turning point in Monroe's career, this taut suspenser gave Marilyn her first big break towards stardom, and hinted at the legendary persona which would soon emerge. While vacationing at Niagara Falls, a faithless wife (MM) plots to murder her husband (Cotten) and run off with her lover; but when the distraught husband gets wise, he has other ideas. The importance of this film in MM's career usually overshadows the fact that this is quite an accomplished thriller. ★★★

Niagara, Niagara

(1997, 93 min, US, Bob Gosse) *Robin Tunney, Henry Thomas, Michael Parks, Stephen Lang.* Tunney gives a mesmerizing performance as a young woman isolated by Tourette's Syndrome. Through a chance encounter, she instantly bonds with a young man (Thomas, who is equally remarkable) whose own isolation is a function of his father's casual brutality. Their shared lack of connection overrides their differing circumstances (she is affluent, he is impoverished), uniting them against a harsh and uncaring outside world. They embark on a road trip to Canada encountering little except staunch hostility, with one exception: an equally isolated old man (Parks in a stand-out performance) who takes them into his home. Their odyssey to Toronto is beautifully crafted by director Gosse with keen observation of human frailties and a refreshing lack of saccharine sentimentality. ★★★ VHS: $9.99

Nicholas and Alexandra

(1971, 184 min, GB, Franklin J. Schaffner) *Michael Jayston, Janet Suzman, Tom Baker, Laurence Olivier, Michael Redgrave.* This lavish chronicle of the Russian Revolution is rich with scenery, costumery, and even some good acting, though at a three-hour running time it's a little on the long side. The film offers a sprawling and often interesting look at the Russian monarchy during the 14 years leading to the revolution which proved its undoing. Jayston and Suzman (an Oscar nominee) are both splendid, and Baker appears as Rasputin. ★★★ VHS: $29.99; DVD: $24.99

Nicholas Nickleby

(1947, 95 min, GB, Alberto Cavalcanti) *Derek Bond, Cedric Hardwicke, Stanley Holloway.* In the mid-1980s, when the Royal Shakespeare Company produced an 8½-hour stage version of Charles Dickens' classic story, interest in this earlier (and considerably shorter) film version was rekindled. The story is of a young man's struggle to protect himself and his family from a scheming and miserly uncle. It's a story full of resonance and emotional power and the film stands as a faithful rendition. ★★★ VHS: $14.99

Nick of Time

(1995, 89 min, US, John Badham) *Johnny Depp, Christopher Walken, Charles S. Dutton, Courtenay Chase, Roma Maffia, Marsha Mason.* Filmed in the gimmicky fashion of real time, *Nick of Time* is a not-so-plausible but nevertheless intriguing political thriller which manages to offer a few thrills along the way. Depp plays a father whose daughter (Chase) is abducted upon arriving by train to Los Angeles. Walken and Moffia are the kidnappers, assassins who have been hired to kill the incumbent governor of California (Mason) who's running for reelection. As they hold his daughter captive, Depp is coerced to pull the trigger with a maniacal Walken following his every move. The film sets up an interesting dilemma for the loving father, which it only occasionally explores. ★★½ VHS: $14.99; DVD: $29.99

Nico Icon

(1995, 67 min, Germany/US, Susanne Ofteringer) *Nico, Andy Warhol, Viva, Lou Reed, Paul Morrissey, John Cale, Jackson Browne.* Nico Icon is director Ofteringer's brief but fascinating documentary about the goddess/pop star/junkie/icon known as Nico (Christa Paffgen). A high-profile model in Germany who went to Paris and then to New York, Nico became part of Andy Warhol's Factory in the 1960s and performed with The Velvet Underground before embarking on an ambitious solo career. Chronicling Nico's assorted personal and professional affairs, Ofteringer eschews a descriptive voice-over, relying instead on archival footage and on-camera monologues by family, friends and lovers to unravel the Nico mystique — whose "detached elegance" epitomized cool for a generation. (English and German and French with English subtitles) ★★★½ VHS: $19.99; DVD: $24.99

Night after Night

(1932, 73 min, US, Archie Mayo) *George Raft, Mae West, Constance Cummings, Louis Calhern.* West appears in her film debut, and though she's only on screen for about 15 minutes, it's easy to see why she became a star. A young, Valentino-looking Raft gets star billing in this light underworld comedy-drama as a speakeasy owner who has his hands full with rival gangs and old girlfriends. West plays a former girlfriend, and when she steps on screen, an otherwise pedestrian film suddenly comes alive with energy and humor. West, who had yet to fully hone her campy, staccato delivery and "Diamond Lil" persona, says her archtypical line "Goodness had nothing to do with it, dearie." In the believe-it-or-not department, Raft has a seminude scene. ★★½ VHS: $14.99

Night and Day

(1946, 128 min, US, Michael Curtiz) *Cary Grant, Alexis Smith, Monty Woolley, Jane Wyman, Eve Arden, Mary Martin.* As Hollywood fiction, this is pretty entertaining stuff; but as the true biography of legendary songwriter Cole Porter, it's laughably inaccurate. And though no one ever complained about seeing Grant in a film, he's not exactly the perfect choice to play the composer. Woolley plays himself as Cole's best friend. Martin has a small scene singing "My Heart Belongs to Daddy." Of course, a film made in 1946 would never have even hinted at Porter's well-known homosexuality. ★★½ VHS: $19.99

Night & Day

(1991, 90 min, France/Belgium, Chantal Akerman) A breezy, post-feminist comedy about a woman's loving relationship with two men, *Night & Day* is a deceptively simple blending of Eric Rohmer's obsession with talky young lovers and the filmic exuberance of early Jean-Luc Godard. Julie and Jack live and love in blissful isolation. He drives a taxi in the evening, and during the day they make love. The arrangement is altered but not upset after Julie meets Joseph, a fellow taxi-driving young man. Erotic, stylish and unconventional. (French with English subtitles) ★★★ VHS: $19.99

Night and Fog

(1956, 32 min, France, Alain Resnais) One is tempted to look at Resnais' Holocaust documentary *Night and Fog* in light of his later works, but to do so is to denigrate the history it so powerfully records. "Records" is not accurate either, for this is not mere documentation, this is an indictment; not of Germans, or even Nazis, but of humanity. How could this have been allowed to happen? Color footage of a placid countryside oddly framed with barb wire gives way to the grays of Auschwitz. Faces drained of all emotion, eyes empty of any hope stare at the camera. Some are the faces of the already dead; some of those to be. The dry, flat narration is brittle from withholding the rage that does not express itself with words. Details record this yesterday to remind us that history exists only when it is remembered. A disturbing and haunting film experience. ★★★★ VHS: $19.99

Night and the City

(1950, 101 min, US, Jules Dassin) *Richard Widmark, Gene Tierney, Googie Withers, Hugh Marlowe, Herbert Lom.* Widmark is unnerving as a small-time hustler scouring the rubble of a decimated London barely recovered form the ravages of WWII. He facilitates small cons, setting up traveling businessmen for the benefit of his objectionable bar-owning boss. He thinks he sees a way out. With blind frenzy, he steals from the woman (Tierney) who loves him, connives the woman who would provide him with a lucrative set-up, and betrays the employer who supports him. Widmark scurries like a rat over London's bombed-out remains with an enthralling, hyperkinetic desperation used to great effect by director Dassin. (Remade in 1992) ★★★½

Night and the City

(1992, 104 min, US, Irwin Winkler) *Robert De Niro, Jessica Lange, Cliff Gorman, Jack Weston, Alan King.* Winkler's visceral, punchy direction propels outstanding performances from the cast through Richard Price's frenetic screenplay. This slick and clever update of the 1950 Richard Widmark classic, which captures the feel of contemporary urban noir, provides De Niro with the vehicle for one of his finest performances; he's Harry Fabian, the quintessential street-smart, fast-talking hustler — the *Mean Streets* wise guy all grown up. After a lifetime of taking the money and running, he decides to go for the big score in the fight game. In going up against the major players, he enters an unfamiliar world with rules he barely understands and unwittingly disrupts an uneasy truce in a decades-old familial conflict. As the married woman who becomes involved with Fabian, Lange is luminous, portraying just the right balance of big-city knowing and innocent naïveté. ★★★½ VHS: $9.99

The Night and the Moment

(1994, 90 min, GB/France/Italy, Anna Maria Tatò) *Willem Dafoe, Lena Olin, Miranda Richardson, Jean Claude Carrière.* A third-rate *Dangerous Liaisons, The Night and the Moment* casts Dafoe as a fop trying to bed a willful Olin by relating past sexual conquests and other stories. This dull, lifeless trash aims for *Tom Jones*–like sophisticated ribaldry, but ends up only as an episodic mishmash. Dafoe seems more desperate and disturbed than calculatedly malicious, and Olin is a letdown. Though several of Dafoe's anecdotes are of mild interest (a detailed description of the usage of an outmoded torture device has a macabre charm), these scenes are separated by long-winded, would-be witty word play, and lackluster storytelling. ★½ VHS: $19.99

A Night at the Opera

(1935, 92 min, US, Sam Wood) *The Marx Brothers, Margaret Dumont, Allan Jones, Kitty Carlisle.* Groucho is Otis B. Driftwood, con artist extraordinaire and Dumont's financial advisor. He hooks up with an opera company on its way from Italy to America via luxury liner. Complete with young lovers, scurrilous cads, pompous fools, stowaways Chico and Harpo, and the often imitated but never duplicated stateroom scene. ★★★½

A Night at the Roxbury

(1998, 82 min, US, John Fortenberry) *Will Ferrell, Chris Kattan, Dan Hedaya, Molly Shannon, Richard Grieco, Loni Anderson, Chazz Palminteri.* Unbearable expansion of the Butabi Brothers "Saturday Night Live" skit. Has that show gone so far downhill that these two characters pass as memorable? The plot: two losers who still live at home dream of getting into the famous titular nightclub. Thank goodness a slumming Grieco is around to help them out. Ferrell and Kattan exude zero charm as they grope nightclubbers, rebel against their flower shop–owning father (Hedaya) and verbally abuse the one girl skanky enough to be right for them (Shannon). If seeing Palminteri ask everyone "Did you grab my ass?" cracks you up, if you must see the second film from the director of *Jury Duty*, this will still not be 82 minutes worth spending. ★ VHS: $14.99; DVD: $24.99

Night Falls on Manhattan

(1997, 113 min, US, Sidney Lumet) *Andy Garcia, Ian Holm, Lena Olin, Ron Leibman, Richard Dreyfuss, James Gandolfini, Colm Feore.* Returning to the city and theme in which he has previously excelled, Lumet has crafted an intoxicating police procedural and courtroom drama. New York City assistant D.A. Garcia is given his first case — prosecuting the drug lord responsible for the shooting of his policeman father (Holm). The court case is the only thing that's cut-and-dry in the story, for Lumet has more in mind than just a routine trial. His screenplay (based on Robert Daley's "Tainted Evidence") explores the subtleties of racial stereotype, the duplicity of familial and professional loyalties, and the accepted boundaries of duty and corruption. The only false note is Olin's rather contrived romance with Garcia. ★★★½ VHS: $14.99; DVD: $29.99

A Night Full of Rain

(1978, 104 min, Italy, Lina Wertmüller) *Giancarlo Giannini, Candice Bergen, Anne Byrne.* In this Italian battle-of-the-sexes drama, Giannini stars as an Italian Communist journalist trapped in a rocky marriage to Bergen, an American photographer and feminist. Director Wertmüller attempts to wring life out of the clash between an old-world chauvinist intent on keeping his wife in check and a liberated woman equally determined to continue her career. Set in Italy and San Francisco, the film has moments of visual spectacle, insight and humor, but the confused plot undermines it all. The full title is *The End of the World in Our Usual Bed in a Night Full of Rain.* (Italian with English subtitles) ★★½ VHS: $19.99

A Night in Casablanca

(1946, 85 min, US, Archie Mayo) *The Marx Brothers, Charles Drake, Sig Ruman.* Groucho, Chico and Harpo battle Nazis and uncover stolen loot in the exotic if seedy Hotel Casablanca. There's a young couple in love, a femme fatale, a dastardly villain, some bungling idiots and the usual suspects. Not on par with the Marx Brothers' earlier works, but entertaining just the same. ★★½

A Night in the Life of Jimmy Reardon

(1988, 90 min, US, William Richert) *River Phoenix, Ann Magnuson, Ione Skye, Meredith Salenger.* Young Phoenix explores his sexuality with various women as he decides between college and his girlfriend. An irresponsible sexual coming-of-age comedy which alternates between near–kiddie porn and adult romantic comedy. ★★ VHS: $19.99; DVD: $24.99

Night Is My Future

(1947, 87 min, Sweden, Ingmar Bergman) *Mai Zetterling, Birger Malmsten.* An upper-class pianist is blinded in an accident on a firing range and is cared for by his maid, with whom he falls in love. This little-known Bergman film is done with craftsmanship and taste, and contains a powerful dream/nightmare sequence. (Swedish with English subtitles) ★★½

'Night, Mother

(1986, 97 min, US, Tom Moore) *Sissy Spacek, Anne Bancroft.* Spacek and Bancroft offer good performances as mother and daughter in this adaptation of Marsha Norman's Pulitzer Prize–winning play. Spacek plays a troubled woman intent on committing suicide; Bancroft plays her mother who desperately tries to talk her out of it. The film can't overcome its depressing theme, but the two actresses make the drama involving. ★★½ VHS: $14.99

Night Moves

(1975, 95 min, US, Arthur Penn) *Gene Hackman, Susan Clark, Jennifer Warren, Melanie Griffith, James Woods.* Hackman excels in this gripping psycho-thriller from the pen of Alan Sharp. Hackman plays an emotionally on-the-edge private detective who is hired to track down a wayward daughter (Griffith) in Florida. Penn provides able direction in this pessimistic film which captures the sanguine mood of post-Watergate America. ★★★ VHS: $19.99

Night of the Comet

(1984, 95 min, US, Thom Eberhardt) *Catherine Mary Stewart, Kelli Maroney, Robert Beltran.* Entertaining, clever "B" sci-fi comedy about two Valley Girls who seem to be the last survivors of a killer comet. After an exhausting shopping spree at the local mall, however, they soon realize they are not alone: zombies! ★★½

The Night of the Following Day

(1969, 93 min, US, Hubert Cornfield) *Marlon Brando, Rita Moreno, Richard Boone, Pamela Franklin.* A dated but intriguing drama about four professional criminals and their "foolproof" kidnapping scheme that goes horribly wrong when fate and human nature conspire against them. As the leader of the group, Brando (obviously in the middle of a bad hair day) drinks heavily from the method acting well, and is outshined by Boone, who gives a splendid performance as a sadistic psychopath. ★★½ VHS: $89.99

The Night of the Generals

(1966, 148 min, GB, Anatole Litvak) *Peter O'Toole, Omar Sharif, Tom Courtenay, Donald Pleasence, Philippe Noiret.* This WWII thriller follows a Nazi intelligence officer hot on the trail of a psychotic general suspected of murdering prostitutes. Over-the-top performance by O'Toole makes a laughable script interesting. ★★ VHS: $19.99

The Night of the Hunter

(1955, 93 min, US, Charles Laughton) *Robert Mitchum, Shelley Winters, Lillian Gish, Peter Graves.* This enigmatic suspense thriller is the distinguished actor Laughton's sole directorial effort; and he succeeds magnificently. A dreamlike, disturbing fable in which two children are pursued by a madman, *The Night of the Hunter* is full of haunting images. The psychotic preacher with L-O-V-E and H-A-T-E tattooed on his knuckles is chillingly portrayed by Mitchum and the black-and-white cinematography is incredibly lyrical. ★★★★ VHS: $14.99; DVD: $14.99

Night of the Iguana

(1964, 118 min, US, John Huston) *Richard Burton, Ava Gardner, Deborah Kerr, Grayson Hall, Sue Lyon.* In this expertly acted film version of Tennessee Williams' steamy Broadway play, Burton, Gardner and Kerr give stellar performances as participants in a love triangle in a small Mexican resort town. Burton plays a defrocked priest-turned-bus tour guide who becomes involved with young nymphette Lyon, sexually repressed Kerr and fiery hotel proprietor Gardner (who is stunning in possibly her best screen portrayal). Hall received an Oscar nomination for her stirring portrait of Lyon's lesbian guardian who engages Burton in a psychological battle for her soul. ★★★ VHS: $19.99

Night of the Living Dead

(1968, 96 min, US, George A. Romero) *Judith O'Dea, Duane Jones.* The foremost fright film ever. On a ghoulish night in Pittsburgh, decomposing corpses return to life to devour the living. Graphically gruesome and morosely funny, this black-and-white gem established director Romero as a master of the genre. (Remade in 1990) ★★★★ VHS: $14.99; DVD: $24.99

Night of the Living Dead

(1990, 95 min, US, Tom Savini) *Tony Todd, Patricia Tallman.* Makeup master Savini directs this color remake of George Romero's black-and-white horror classic. It's virtually shot-for-shot. The only difference is that Barbara, the catatonic female lead from the original, is now in the Sigourney Weaver–Linda Hamilton school of film heroines. Ironically, the film loses some of its tension in color; but nevertheless delivers the goods. ★★½ VHS: $14.99; DVD: $19.99

Night of the Shooting Stars

(1982, 106 min, Italy, Paolo & Vittorio Taviani) *Omero Antonutti, Margarita Lozano.* A fascinating probe into the collective consciousness of postwar Italy. Filtered through the memory of a woman whose childhood was spent during the period, it is the tale of the war's closing days in a small Italian town. Poetic, enthralling and magnificently crafted. (Italian with English subtitles) ★★★½ VHS: $14.99

Night on Earth

(1991, 125 min, US, Jim Jarmusch) *Gena Rowlands, Winona Ryder, Armin Mueller-Stahl, Giancarlo Esposito, Rosie Perez, Béatrice Dalle, Isaach de Bankolé, Roberto Benigni, Paolo Bonacelli, Matti Pellonpää, Kari Väänänen, Sakari Kousmanen.* Director Jarmusch explores the subculture of the taxi cab with this enchanting series of five offbeat vignettes set respectively in Los Angeles, New York, Paris, Rome and Helsinki; each centering around a cabbie and their fare(s). The film features an international all-star cast of Rowlands and Ryder (L.A.); Mueller-Stahl, Esposito and Perez (N.Y.); Dalle and de Bankolé (Paris); Benigni and Bonacelli (Rome); and Pellonpää, Väänänen and Kousmanen (with names like that, where else but Helsinki?). While each of the stories is entertaining, the standouts are Mueller-Stahl and Esposito's hilarious cultural collision in the New York episode and Benigni's outrageous portrayal of a loopy Italian who speeds around Rome in the middle of the night while wearing

dark sunglasses and entertaining himself with an endless series of one-liners. (Filmed in English, French, Italian and Finnish with English subtitles) (VHS available letterboxed or pan & scan) ★★★½ VHS: $14.99

The Night Porter

(1973, 118 min, Italy, Liliana Cavani) *Dirk Bogarde, Charlotte Rampling.* Few films equal the unrelenting intensity of Cavani's disturbing drama. Years after surviving sexual imprisonment under a Nazi stormtrooper, a woman inadvertently encounters her former torturer/lover working as a night porter at a Viennese hotel. Despite their reversed positions of power, they ultimately reenact their sadomasochistic roles in a gruesomely lecherous dance of death. (Filmed in English) (Letterboxed) ★★ VHS: $19.99; DVD: $29.99

Night Shift

(1982, 106 min, US, Ron Howard) *Michael Keaton, Henry Winkler, Shelley Long, Kevin Costner.* Howard's directorial debut produced this funny comedy about a fast-talking city morgue assistant (Keaton in his debut) who turns his workplace into a bordello. ★★★ VHS: $14.99; DVD: $14.99

The Night Stalker

(1971, 73 min, US, John Llewellyn Moxey) *Darren McGavin, Carol Lynley, Simon Oakland, Ralph Meeker, Claude Akins.* An immensely enjoyable made-for-TV vampire tale (the pilot for the short-lived TV series) with McGavin as a hard-boiled investigative reporter who unearths a story about a modern-day bloodsucker terrorizing Las Vegas. The film successfully combines the style of a 1940s noir mystery with comedy and horror; and McGavin is tops as the cynical journalist. ★★★ VHS: $9.99

The Night They Raided Minsky's

(1968, 99 min, US, William Friedkin) *Jason Robards, Britt Ekland, Norman Wisdom, Bert Lahr, Elliott Gould, Denholm Elliott.* A fine comic romp heralding the infamous days of Burlesque, with Robards as a vaudeville comic who becomes involved with Pennsylvania Dutch girl Ekland. The film captures the flavor of the bawdy comics and comely strippers, and provides a fascinating glimpse of life both on- and offstage during this bygone era. Wisdom is especially good as a stage comic. ★★★½ VHS: $19.99

Night Tide

(1963, 84 min, US, Curtis Harrington) *Dennis Hopper, Luana Anders, Bruno Ve Sota, Linda Lawson, Gavin Muir, Tom Dillon, Marjorie Eaton.* Inspired by Val Lewton's *Cat People*, this surreal fantasy tells the story of a young sailor (a baby-faced Hopper) who falls in love with a strange woman posing as a mermaid in a seafront carnival. She believes herself to be a descendant of the "sea people" who must kill during the full moon. This moody chiller features a fine supporting cast, and a special cameo by Ed Wood, Jr.'s rubber octopus from *Bride of the Monster*, who's seen wrestling with Hopper during a nightmare sequence. ★★★ VHS: $29.99; DVD: $29.99

A Night to Remember

(1958, 123 min, GB, Roy Baker) *Kenneth More, Honor Blackman, David McCallum, George Rose, Alec McCowan.* A first-rate drama about the infamous night the luxury liner Titanic hit an iceberg and sank in the freezing waters of the Atlantic, killing over 1,500 passengers and crew. More, exceptional as the ship's captain, heads a highly competent cast. A riveting, meticulous production told in semidocumentary style, which only adds to the overall authority of the film. ★★★★; DVD: $39.99

Night Train to Munich

(1940, 95 min, GB, Carol Reed) *Rex Harrison, Margaret Lockwood, Paul Henreid, Basil Radford, Naunton Wayne.* Reed's thrilling reworking of Hitchcock's *The Lady Vanishes* is a pleasure to watch. A spy/chase thriller of the highest order, it tells the story of a pair of undercover agents (Harrison and Henried) who are both after a prominent industrialist and his daughter (Lockwood). Bouncing back and forth from Germany to England and in-between, the plot is full of captures, escapes and recaptures. Most movies are content with one or two nail-biting sequences: this is full of them. Even the somewhat dated comic relief of a pair of English comics (Radford and Wayne) is welcome. From the titular train ride to the climax on a mountaintop cablecar, the film is suspenseful from start to finish. ★★★★ VHS: $24.99

Night Train to Venice

(1993, 98 min, Italy/Germany, Carlo U. Quinterio) *Hugh Grant, Malcolm McDowell, Tahnee Welch.* Beware the film extricated from the vaults when its leading man becomes a star! That's the warning label that should be slapped on each and every box of this excruciating psychothriller starring heartthrob Grant. Trying to pass itself off as stylish through a mishmash (nay, a cacophony!) of images, this assaults the viewer with an endless parade of meaningless drivel about a group of skinheads terrorizing the Orient Express on its way to Venice. Save this for the film class on how *not* to make a movie. ★ VHS: $9.99

The Night Walker

(1964, 86 min, US, William Castle) *Barbara Stanwyck, Robert Taylor, Lloyd Bochner.* Stanwyck plays a wealthy widow who has strange recurring dreams about her lost husband. The $1.99 special effects during the dream sequences and *Psycho* author Robert Bloch's mind-numbing screenplay help to do for Barbara what *Trog* did for Joan Crawford, which easily could explain her quick leap to TV and "The Big Valley." The film does have its moments, though. ★★½ VHS: $14.99

The Night We Never Met

(1993, 99 min, US, Warren Leight) *Matthew Broderick, Annabella Sciorra, Kevin Anderson, Louise Lasser, Jeanne Tripplehorn, Garry Shandling, Bill Campbell.* The comings and goings of three strangers who time-share a New York apartment without meeting sets the stage for an amiable comedy of convenient coincidence — i.e., light on convincing plot, heavy on funny lines and scenes. Broderick delivers a droll yet engaging performance as a heartbroken would-be gourmet chef. Sciorra

Z

as a semi-happily married dental hygienist, and Anderson as a loutish, immature stockbroker are his roommates. ★★½ VHS: $9.99

Night Zoo

(1987, 117 min, Canada, Jean-Claude Lauzon) *Roger Lebel, Gilles Maheu.* A schizophrenic film if there ever was one — is it a darkly violent crime thriller or a heartwarming human drama of the rapprochement of a man with his father? The film focuses on both themes and suffers for it. After being released from prison, Marcel, an angry punk of questionable sexuality, tries to readjust to life on the outside but his efforts are thwarted by two sleazy gay cops. While Marcel is getting into hot water with thugs and lowlifes, he also tries to reach out to old dad; you know, the one with the whizzing ticker. Set in a dark and dangerous Montreal, the film's action sequences are exciting, but generally the film bogs down when it deals with the sappy familial angle. (French with English subtitles) ★★½

Nightbreaker

(1989, 100 min, US, Peter Markle) *Martin Sheen, Emilio Estevez, Lea Thompson, Melinda Dillon.* A gripping thriller about lethal government testing. Sheen and son Estevez play the same character — in the 1950s and the 1980s — a doctor who was involved in atomic experiments in the Nevada desert using — and endangering — American military personnel. ★★★

Nightbreed

(1990, 93 min, GB, Clive Barker) *Craig Sheffer, Anne Bobby, David Cronenberg, Charles Haid.* Barker's second feature, based on his novella "Cabal," is as ambitious as his first feature *Hellraiser* but falls short in its execution. Hidden away in a deserted cemetery is a mythical civilization of ghoulish outcasts. A young man, Boone (Sheffer), has horrific visions of these creatures and in an act of poor judgment seeks treatment from a creepy psychiatrist (played by Cronenberg), who frames Boone for a series of killings he himself is committing. Boone is killed and then reincarnated as one of the Nightbreed, a race of underground monsters who are readying themselves for battle against their human oppressors. Though Barker's intentions are good, the film is sluggish and meandering, and the director fails to create any palpable suspense. However, the design and execution of the creatures are excellent. ★★ VHS: $14.99; DVD: $19.99

The Nightcomers

(1972, 96 min, US, Michael Winner) *Marlon Brando, Stephanie Beacham, Harry Andrews.* Tired thriller which attempts to hint at why the children of Henry James' "The Turn of the Screw" became the way they did. Brando is a sadistic and sexually abusive gardener who serves as perverse mentor; Beacham is the governess involved in a kinky relationship with Brando. The sexual aspect of the film predates the similarly themed Brando film *Last Tango in Paris*, but lacks that classic's detailed character development and cinematic stylization. ★★

Nighthawks

(1978, 113 min, GB, Ron Peck & Paul Hallam) *Ken Robertson.* London's gay scene, and one

man's search for belonging in it, are explored in this sensitive and intelligent drama which was Britain's first independent gay-themed film. Robertson plays a quiet teacher who divides his time between the classroom and the closet and evenings spent aimlessly cruising the city's gay bars and discos. Using mostly unprofessional actors, this gritty, heartfelt drama has surprising depth despite the lack of any discernable plot, as it sympathetically portrays one man's homosexual lifestyle without resorting to theatrics and stereotyping. ★★★ VHS: $39.99

Nighthawks

(1981, 99 min, US, Bruce Malmuth) *Sylvester Stallone, Billy Dee Williams, Rutger Hauer, Persis Khambatta, Lindsay Wagner.* The suspense is riveting in this little-seen police thriller starring Stallone and Williams as a pair of New York cops on the trail of a ruthless international terrorist. Hauer shines as the terrorist Wulfgar, in a role which prefigures his sadistic killer in *The Hitcher* five years later. Even Stallone's presence can't ruin this gem of a film. ★★★; DVD: $19.99

The Nightmare Before Christmas

(1993, 74 min, US, Henry Selick) *Voices of Danny Elfman, Chris Sarandon, Catherine O'Hara, William Hickey, Ken Page, Paul Reubens.* This enchanting animated musical bears the trademark of its producer Tim Burton, for it's a daring and imaginative entertainment. Made in cooperation with and released by Disney studios, *Nightmare* features the best in stopmotion animation to tell the tale of Jack Skellington and his fellow inhabitants of Halloweentown who band together to bring their own special ghoulish flavor to Christmas. Kidnapping Santa Claus, Jack takes over the reins of Santa's sleigh and delivers a holiday to remember. Determinedly dark and decidedly funny, *Nightmare* boasts a devilishly playful score by Danny Elfman. ★★★½ VHS: $22.99; DVD: $29.99

A Nightmare on Elm Street

(1984, 91 min, US, Wes Craven) *John Saxon, Ronee Blakely, Heather Langenkamp, Amanda Wyss, Johnny Depp, Robert Englund.* When the psychosexual desires of young girls come out in their dreams, the result is a blood-crazed apparition with razor sharp, phallic-like talons. This is surely one of the most frightening films of the 1980s, due primarily to its inventive premise of this villain literally escaping from the victims' minds, rather than from the local insane asylum. (Followed by 6 sequels) ★★★ VHS: $9.99; DVD: $19.99

A Nightmare on Elm Street Part 2: Freddy's Revenge

(1985, 87 min, US, Jack Sholder) *Mark Patton, Kim Myers, Robert Rusler, Clu Gulager, Hope Lange, Robert Englund.* The second entry in the *Elm Street* saga is one of the least successful of the series. It's five years later, and Freddy is back trying to possess a teenage boy in order to continue his murderous ways. ★½ VHS: $9.99; DVD: $19.99

A Nightmare on Elm Street 3: Dream Warriors

(1987, 96 min, US, Chuck Russell) *Robert Englund, Heather Langenkamp, Craig Wasson, Laurence Fishburne, Dick Cavett, Zsa Zsa Gabor.* One of the most popular of the *Nightmare* series, this imaginative and sometimes wickedly funny sequel has Freddy back tormenting more hapless teens, here being cared for by Langenkamp from the original. ★★★ VHS: $9.99; DVD: $19.99

A Nightmare on Elm Street 4: The Dream Master

(1988, 92 min, US, Renny Harlin) *Robert Englund, Rodney Eastman, Danny Hassel, Andras Jones.* You can't keep a good mass-murderer-from-beyond-the-grave down. Freddy returns once again to wreak havoc on poor, unsuspecting teenagers. Very stylish, with a few good scares. Director Harlin would go on to direct the explosive *Die Hard 2*. ★★½ VHS: $9.99; DVD: $19.99

A Nightmare on Elm Street 5: The Dream Child

(1989, 89 min, US, Stephen Hopkins) *Robert Englund, Lisa Wilcox, Kelly Jo Minter, Danny Hassel.* Freddy Krueger goes surreal. Freddy teams up with an unborn child to continue his murderous ways. Good visuals but not much more. ★★ VHS: $9.99; DVD: $19.99

Freddy's Dead: The Final Nightmare

(1991, 96 min, US, Rachel Talalay) *Robert Englund, Lisa Zane, Yaphet Kotto, Roseanne, Tom Arnold, Johnny Depp.* Freddy Krueger (Englund) camps it up again in this inane, effects-heavy sequel. Zane plays a child psychologist who leads a group of troubled teens into their dream worlds to get to the bottom of their recurring nightmares — all starring Freddy! (Sequel: *Wes Craven's New Nightmare*) ★ VHS: $9.99; DVD: $19.99

Wes Craven's New Nightmare

(1994, 112 min, US, Wes Craven) *Heather Langenkamp, John Saxon, Robert Englund.* Langenkamp plays herself as a modern career actress whose son is being plagued by Freddy-style nightmares. When her husband and two friends are killed, she turns to fellow actors Englund and Saxon and then Craven for guidance. Scary nightmare sequences, a good script and an even more menacing Freddy are put to good use, but for all this Craven cannot restore the series' original luster, and the "is it a dream, movie or real" hijinx inspire a feeling of déjà vu rather than one of dread. ★★½ VHS: $9.99; DVD: $19.99

Nights of Cabiria

(1957, 117 min, Italy, Federico Fellini) *Giulietta Masina, François Perier.* This Academy Award–winning film is a grim but very moving drama from Fellini's early career. The film lacks the flash and fantasy of the director's later films but has a power and intensity that is sadly lacking in his final works. This is a poignant tale of a naïve prostitute who searches for love and fulfillment in every man she meets. The waifish streetwalker is wonderfully portrayed by Masina. The story would form the basis for the

Spielberg's notorious flop *1941* is looking good in the wake of *Pearl Harbor*

musical *Sweet Charity*. This is the full-length version, including a previously banned 7-minute sequence. (Italian with English subtitles) ★★★★ VHS: $29.99; DVD: $39.99

Nightwatch

(1998, 101 min, US, Ole Bornedal) *Ewan McGregor, Nick Nolte, Patricia Arquette, Josh Brolin, John C. Reilly.* McGregor stars in this tepid thriller as a law student moonlighting as a security guard at a morgue. Meanwhile, a vicious serial killer is prowling the city, preying on prostitutes, whose bodies keep crowding the morgue. Is McGregor the killer? Is it the slightly loopy former security guard? Or Ewan's amoral, thrill-seeking best friend? How about the creepy cop on the case? The answer, unfortunately, is fairly obvious and uninspired. Director Bornedal (who cowrote with Steven Soderbergh) here remakes his own overrated 1994 Danish chiller *Nattevagten*, and sadly, delivers a carbon copy of that film, carrying its same flaws — an illogical plot, a slack pace, and most damaging, extremely unlikable characters and needlessly unpleasant situations. ★½ VHS: $86.99

Nijinsky

(1980, 125 min, GB, Herbert Ross) *George de la Pena, Alan Bates, Jeremy Irons, Leslie Brown, Colin Blakely, Janet Suzman, Alan Badel.* Ross, who scored a major triumph with *The Turning Point*, once again turns to the world of ballet with this expertly acted, rather melodramatic but intriguing biography about the legendary dancer Nijinsky (de la Pena) and his professional and private relationship with his mentor/lover Sergei Diaghilev (impressively played by Bates). Badel gives an outstanding performance as a wealthy patron of the arts. ★★½ VHS: $14.99

Nil by Mouth

(1998, 128 min, GB, Gary Oldman) *Kathy Burke, Charlie Creed-Miles, Edna Dore, Lalia Morse, Ray Winstone.* A stunner of a film from

actor Oldman, making his debut as writer and director. Loosely based on his own family, and dedicated to his late father, Oldman's raw, intense drama examines a lower-class London family with an unflinching eye. The superb cast delivers incredibly rich, nuanced performances and the jittery, you-are-there cinematography captures the documentary look intended, without becoming artificial. Oldman's non-mainstream, less-narrative driven work fascinates thanks to its well-developed characters. The film is bleak, to be sure, but by the end, we've seen a terrific, wholly real confrontation between put-upon wife Burke and her bully husband — and a satisfying, believable ending. ★★★★ VHS: $86.99

9½ Weeks

(1986, 113 min, US, Adrian Lyne) *Mickey Rourke, Kim Basinger, Margaret Whitton.* Rourke and Basinger star as two SoHo yuppies who meet by chance and quickly find themselves entangled in a highly erotic sadomasochistic relationship. Rourke is well-cast as the domineering, slightly sinister commodities broker who draws Basinger, a sexy art dealer, into a series of kinky, sex-for-sex's-sake adventures. Whether in a back alley or a clock tower, the heat from these attractive actors is enough to make the screen sweat, though not enough to produce a totally comprehensible film. ★★½ VHS: $14.99; DVD: $19.99

Nine Months

(1995, 102 min, US, Chris Columbus) *Hugh Grant, Julianne Moore, Tom Arnold, Joan Cusack, Jeff Goldblum, Robin Williams.* This occasionally funny but always obvious comedy stars Grant as a reluctant father-to-be who loses the woman he loves (Moore) before realizing that, damn it, there's nothing better than "family values." Director Columbus' cloying tribute to masculinity follows on the heels of his earlier box office successes *Mrs. Doubtfire* and *Home Alone*, but features none of the pacing, style or humor of either film. Sadly, Moore is relegated to playing

second fiddle and the film fails to showcase her talents. ★★ VHS: $9.99; DVD: $24.99

976-Evil

(1988, 89 min, US, Robert Englund) *Stephen Geoffreys, Sandy Dennis.* Robert Englund (alias Freddy Krueger) directed this effective horror outing about an outcast teenager (Geoffreys) who acquires demonic powers thanks to a 976 phone number. ★★½

9 to 5

(1980, 110 min, US, Colin Higgins) *Jane Fonda, Lily Tomlin, Dolly Parton, Dabney Coleman, Sterling Hayden.* Fonda, Tomlin and Parton proved to be a formidable team in this amusing and topical hit comedy. Three secretaries get even with their sexist, insensitive boss (Coleman); and raise office efficiency and productivity to new highs in his absence. Tomlin's cartoon fantasy sequence is a hilarious highlight. ★★½ VHS: $9.99; DVD: $24.99

1918

(1985, 89 min, US, Ken Harrison) *Matthew Broderick, William Converse-Roberts, Hallie Foote.* Two-time Academy Award–winning screenwriter Horton Foote (*To Kill a Mockingbird, Tender Mercies*) adapted his own play about the frustrations and loss of innocence of a small Texas town during the final months of WWI. Extremely well-acted, this somber story is a little too leisurely paced, which sometimes distracts from the heartfelt dramatics. (Sequel: *Valentine's Day*) ★★½

1984

(1984, 115 min, GB, Michael Bradford) *John Hurt, Richard Burton, Suzanna Hamilton.* After watching this excruciating, but unequalled, version of George Orwell's classic novel, one may well be expected to seek counseling. Gripping performances by Hurt, Burton (in his last screen appearance) and Hamilton along with impressive production design and grainy, muted cinematography, power this overwhelming and gloomy depiction of Orwell's futuristic nightmare world. A harrowing film experience. ★★★

1941

(1979, 146 min, US, Steven Spielberg) *John Belushi, Dan Aykroyd, Treat Williams, Lorraine Gary, Ned Beatty, Nancy Allen, Tim Matheson, Christopher Lee, Robert Stack, Wendie Jo Sperber, John Candy, Patti LuPone.* Although labeled as Spielberg's first "flop," this epic WWII comedy is definitely not the dud it was proclaimed to be. Over-produced as it may be (it's the *It's a Mad, Mad, Mad, Mad World* of the '70s), there are some very funny sequences in this story of wartime hysteria in Los Angeles. The film is highlighted by great special effects, and features a solid all-star cast. The Director's Cut, presented in a letterboxed format, includes 28 minutes of footage not in the theatrical release. (Pan & scan VHS available for $9.99) ★★½ VHS: $14.99; DVD: $34.99

1900

(1977, 235 min, Italy, Bernardo Bertolucci) *Robert De Niro, Gérard Depardieu, Dominique Sanda, Donald Sutherland, Burt Lancaster.* Bertolucci examines the intertwined lives of De Niro and Depardieu, both born on the same day at the turn of the century; one to a landowner, one to a peasant household. This grand, sweeping yet personal epic follows them through the rise of Fascism in Italy, and beyond. Studded with exceptional performances. (Filmed in English) ★★★½

1969

(1988, 93 min, US, Ernest Thompson) *Kiefer Sutherland, Robert Downey, Jr., Winona Ryder, Bruce Dern, Joanna Cassidy.* A good cast is mostly the reason to see this sincere though dramatically impotent teen drama set against the backdrop of the '60s anti-war protests. ★★

90° South

(1933, 70 min, GB, Herbert G. Ponting) A spellbinding chronicle of Captain Robert Scott's heroic but ultimately tragic race for the South Pole — not only did Norwegian explorer Amundsen reach the goal first, but Scott and his entire expedition died on the trip. Originally released in 1913, photographer Herbert G. Ponting remade the film in 1933, adding narration taken from the journal found next to Captain Scott's frozen body. ★★★ VHS: $39.99; DVD: $29.99

92 in the Shade

(1976, 91 min, US, Thomas McGuane) *Peter Fonda, Warren Oates, Margot Kidder, Burgess Meredith, Harry Dean Stanton.* McGuane (*Cold Feet*) adapted and directed this flavorful version of his acclaimed novel. Fonda plays a fishing boat captain who finds romance and rivalry in the Florida Keys. ★★★ VHS: $59.99

Los Niños Abandonados

(1974, 65 min, Colombia/US, Danny Lyon) This unbelievably depressing documentary is a slice-of-life story of the brutal living conditions of the young orphans of Bogata, Colombia, who, abandoned by the State and ignored by the people, are forced to eke out their existence on the streets. The filmmaker follows several of the boys through their daily activities: begging for money and food, playing amid the rubble of the slums and swimming in a nearby stream. An unrelenting and harrowing portrait that offers little hope for either

Anthony Hopkins and Joan Allen are Richard M. and Pat in *Nixon*

the children or society. For unlike other films of similar theme (*Pixote, Streetwise* and *Los Olvidados*), this film fails in achieving an empathy with and compassion for the children as well as explaining the social reasons responsible for this sad situation. (Spanish with English subtitles and English narration) ★★½

Ninotchka

(1939, 110 min, US, Ernst Lubitsch) *Greta Garbo, Melvyn Douglas, Sig Ruman, Ina Claire, Bela Lugosi.* The ads read "Garbo laughs," and so she does in Lubitsch's witty and captivating comedy. As a rigid Russian agent, Comrade Greta risks honor and career when she falls for Paris and playboy Douglas. Impeccable direction from Lubitsch, and scintillating dialogue cowritten by Billy Wilder. ★★★★ VHS: $19.99

The Ninth Configuration

(1979, 115 min, US, William Peter Blatty) *Stacy Keach, Scott Wilson, Jason Miller, Ed Flanders, Moses Gunn, Robert Loggia.* Before he retreated back to familiar territory with *The Exorcist III*, author Blatty made an impressive directorial debut with this creepy, surrealistic adaptation of his novel "Twinkle, Twinkle, Killer Kane" (the film's alternate title). Keach plays a psychiatrist treating a group of military outcasts at an isolated mental hospital. A sometimes funny and very disturbing psychothriller. ★★★ VHS: $14.99

The Ninth Gate

(2000, 133 min, GB, Roman Polanski) *Johnny Depp, Lena Olin, Frank Langella, Emmanuelle Seigner.* Depp stars in this atmospheric, but ultimately silly supernatural mystery about an unethical rare book dealer whose assignment to retrieve three copies of an arcane tome brings him into contact with haughty aristocrats, psycho satanists and murder. Polanski's second foray into the supernatural features the same patient and detailed story telling as his earlier works (*Rosemary's Baby*), but with a far less interesting denouement. ★★ VHS: $14.99; DVD: $24.99

Nixon

(1995, 192 min, US, Oliver Stone) *Anthony Hopkins, Joan Allen, Paul Sorvino, James Woods, Ed Harris, Bob Hoskins, Powers Boothe, Mary Steenburgen, David Paymer, E.G. Marshall.* If moviemaking is the century's conveyance of contemporary folklore, *Nixon* mythologizes a historical figure deeply imbedded over decades in the American consciousness. And few personalities elicit such polar extremes of reaction as President Richard Milhous Nixon, a deeply conflicted man with true world vision yet bogged down in consuming, petty hatreds and beset by driving personal demons. Hopkins approaches the formidable task of portraying a public figure whose every vocal inflection is known by millions with a consummate actor's creation of a multilayered, contradictory and often baffling personality. Stone's technical filmmaking expertise exploits the innermost soul of an individual against the backdrop of a nation's psyche; if you hold his political interpretation as indulgence, you must allow an auteur's sure hand at his medium. In support, Allen stands out as Pat Nixon, the one person who saw it all yet was least seen by the public eye. (Letterboxed

VHS available for $19.99) ★★★½ VHS: $14.99; DVD: $29.99

No Escape

(1994, 118 min, US, Martin Campbell) *Ray Liotta, Lance Henriksen, Stuart Wilson, Kevin Dillon, Kevin J. O'Connor, Michael Lerner, Ernie Hudson.* A slumming Liotta stars in this futuristic action-thriller, sort of *Escape from New York* meets *Lord of the Flies*. After killing his superior officer, ex-soldier Liotta is sent to a secret island prison where he's caught between two warring factions. He reluctantly joins forces with Henrikson and the more "civilized" prisoners in their fight against Wilson (playing a flamboyantly evil leader) and his band of cutthroats. Gory and not without a few thrills, *No Escape* is a by-the-book adventure story which should satisfy any action fan searching for a brainless two hours. (Letterboxed VHS available for $14.99) ★★½ VHS: $9.99; DVD: $14.99

No Fear, No Die

(1992, 97 min, France, Claire Denis) *Alex Descas, Isaach de Bankolé, Jean-Claude Brialy, Solveig Dommartin.* Denis' follow-up to the popular *Chocolat* is a gritty, ugly and surprisingly slow-moving tale of the underground world of cockfighting. Dah and Jocelyn are two trainers who work for a sleazy club owner and his wife. What ensues is a tangled web of deceit and greed between the four characters. Unfortunately, the film spends too much time depicting disturbingly graphic scenes of cockfighting and not enough time developing the relationships between the characters and the metaphorical values of the cockfights. (French with English subtitles) ★★ VHS: $19.99

No Highway in the Sky

(1951, 98 min, GB, Henry Koster) *James Stewart, Marlene Dietrich, Glynis Johns, Jack Hawkins, Kenneth More.* Giving the kind of performance that has endeared him to movie audiences for decades, Stewart is in top form as an absent-minded scientist whose investigation into the structural weaknesses of a new airplane turns him into a one-man crusader. As an expatriate American living in England, Stewart's airplane researcher tries to convince his superiors that a crash is imminent. As he sets off to prove his theory, he finds himself on one of the doomed aircraft. The film nicely balances benign comic episodes with a story both suspenseful and gripping. Dietrich costars in a part not unlike herself, that of a cynical, famous movie actress — she's made-to-order and nearly defines the word glamorous. ★★★ VHS: $19.99

No Looking Back

(1998, 96 min, US, Edward Burns) *Lauren Holly, Edward Burns, Jon Bon Jovi, Blythe Danner, Connie Britton, Jennifer Esposito.* With his third film, writer-director Burns again casts himself as the lead, a slacker who left girlfriend Holly alone and waiting for an abortion three years ago. Now he's back to his grey, depressing New York beach resort hometown and she's living with best friend Bon Jovi. Will restless Holly leave the dead-end town to get back with her ex-beau? *The Brothers McMullen's* angsty working-class material is evident here, though instead of brother rivalry Burns stretches to sister rivalry. Aside from a few good lines and

Z

the scruffy charisma of Bon Jovi, it seems that the problem with Burns is that he keeps dishing out the same stuff. He's a talented guy, but he's got to start learning something from his titles. ★½ VHS: $14.99; DVD: $19.99

No Man of Her Own

(1950, 98 min, US, Mitchell Leisen) *Barbara Stanwyck, John Lund, Phyllis Thaxter.* Stanwyck's gripping performance distinguishes this seductive, moody noir melodrama. Surviving a train crash and on the lam, Stanwyck assumes the identity of a woman who, about to meet her deceased husband's family for the first time, is killed in the accident. Taken in by the family, Stanwyck's newfound happiness is short-lived, however, as a blackmailing exboyfriend enters the picture. Though the plot and execution of the drama is pure soap opera, Stanwyck's gutsy portrayal makes it all the more involving. (Remade as the French film *I Married a Shadow*) ★★★ VHS: $14.99

No Man's Land

(1987, 107 min, US, Peter Werner) *Charlie Sheen, D.B. Sweeney.* An undercover rookie cop (Sweeney) investigates a charming high-class car thief (Sheen) and finds himself being seduced by the deadly, fast-paced world of money, power and corruption. ★★ VHS: $14.99

No Mercy

(1986, 105 min, US, Richard Pearce) *Richard Gere, Kim Basinger, Jeroen Krabbé, Ray Sharkey.* Routine police thriller benefitting from the teaming of Gere and Basinger. Gere plays an undercover cop who investigates the murder of his partner, leading him to the sultry, mysterious Basinger. ★★ VHS: $9.99; DVD: $14.99

No Regrets for Our Youth

(1946, 111 min, Japan, Akira Kurosawa) *Setsuko Hara.* This, the master's first major work, an epic drama of feminist self-discovery, is set in 1930s Japan — a time of growing nationalism and right-wing militarism. Yukie, a vivacious young woman, falls in love with her father's most outspoken left-wing law student. She gives up a life of ease to move to Tokyo and support his dangerous antiwar activities, only to see him executed for espionage. Her own life undergoes an amazing transformation after his death as she retreats to the countryside of her ancestors to begin a new life, alone. (Japanese with English subtitles) ★★★½

No Skin off My Ass

(1990, 85 min, Canada, Bruce LaBruce) *Bruce LaBruce, G.B. Jones, Caroline Azar, Laurel Purvis.* A low-budget and sexually explicit comedy about a punkish hairdresser who becomes obsessed with a tough-looking but shy skinhead. Filmed in grainy black and white, the film opens when the coiffeur (who also narrates) invites the seemingly lost, baby-faced skinhead home. Sort of a fag version of the beautiful and near-catatonic Joe Dallesandro in *Trash*, the skinhead passively and diffidently accepts his offers of a bubblebath and a place to live. Rounding out the cast of characters is the skinhead's lesbian sister who gets cheap thrills by undressing her brother in front of her friends. While the gay sex is hardcore at times, it is also romantic. ★★★ VHS: $29.99

No Surrender

(1986, 100 min, GB, Peter Smith) *Ray McAnally, Micahel Angelis, Joanne Whalley, Elvis Costello, Bernard Hill.* This no-holds-barred satire examines (and skewers) the political and religious passions that are rife in today's England. Three busloads of senior citizens descend on a seedy Liverpool nightclub for their New Year's Eve celebration. They add to the already volatile mix of Irish Protestant loyalists, Irish Catholics, punks and an inept magician (Costello) to make the laconic manager's evening a nightmare. The film hilariously dives into the fray and observes the pitiful state of human relations. ★★★½

No Time for Sergeants

(1958, 119 min, US, Mervyn LeRoy) *Andy Griffith, Murray Hamilton, Nick Adams, Don Knotts.* Griffith, repeating the acclaimed stage role which brought him prominence, gives a wonderful performance as bumpkin Will Stockdale, the Georgia farmboy who takes the U.S. Air Force (after Will gets finished that's U.S. Air Farce) by surprise. Full of down-home, folksy humor, the story revolves around the series of misadventures which befall Will and his cohorts. Knotts, who would team with Griffith a few years later on TV, repeats his stage role with a funny turn as the camp psychiatrist. ★★★ VHS: $14.99

No Way Home

(1996, 101 min, US, Buddy Giovinazzo) *Tim Roth, Deborah Kara Unger, James Russo.* A heavy-handed drama about an ex-con trying to adjust to his freedom, *No Way Home* boasts edgy performances, but not much else. The film's first half, in which Joey (Roth) returns home to his low-life brother Tommy (Russo) and his brother's wife (Unger), is extremely slow moving and unremarkable. Things pick up a bit when Tommy's mounting debts plunge him into a vortex of violence that may cost his brother his newfound freedom. As always, Roth inhabits his character deeply, but it is Russo who gets the high-profile moments. Unger shines in her limited and unglamorous role. ★★ VHS: $9.99

No Way Out

(1950, 106 min, US, Joseph L. Mankiewicz) *Richard Widmark, Sidney Poitier, Linda Darnell, Ossie Davis, Ruby Dee, Stephen McNally. No Way Out* is an exceptionally made, tense drama which succeeds both as medical soap opera and social thriller. In his debut role, Poitier is very good as a talented young doctor in a metropolitan hospital. When mobsters Widmark and his brother are brought in wounded, Poitier's life is forever changed when the brother dies and Widmark holds Poitier responsible. Widmark begins a hatred campaign solely based on race, which soon escalates into racial hostility in the city. That this was even made in 1950 is a marvel, and the filmmakers were certain that their message would be heard in a first-rate production. Widmark is exceptional as the explosive gangster, and also making strong debuts are Dee and Davis. ★★★½ VHS: $14.99

No Way Out

(1987, 116 min, US, Roger Donaldson) *Kevin Costner, Gene Hackman, Sean Young, Bill Paxton, George Dzundza.* Complex, at times convoluted political thriller starring Costner as a naval officer who is assigned to the Pentagon. There he becomes involved with his boss' mistress, leading to murder and political cover-up. Remake of the 1948 film noir classic *The Big Clock.* (Letterboxed VHS available for $19.99) ★★½ VHS: $9.99; DVD: $14.99

No Way to Treat a Lady

(1968, 108 min, US, Jack Smight) *Rod Steiger, George Segal, Lee Remick, Eileen Heckart.* Steiger gives a bravura performance in this extremely well-done thriller as a psychopath who uses various impersonations to make contact with his victims. Segal is the cop on the case, and Remick is caught between them. ★★★½ VHS: $14.99

Noa at Seventeen

(1982, 86 min, Israel, Isaac Yeshurun) *Dalia Shimko, Idit Zur.* It is 1951, and Noa, a 17-year-old girl, struggles for autonomy as the ideological debate over the future of kibbutz socialism tears her family apart. Should she finish high school or follow her youth movement friends to kibbutz? Will Israel's labor movement follow Moscow blindly or turn its attention to the West? This sophisticated allegory penetrates the very essence of the bond which fused the personal and political in the early years of the state. (Hebrew with English subtitles) ★★ VHS: $79.99

Nobody

(1999, 100 min, Japan, Shundo Ohkawa) *Masaya Katoh, Jimpachi Nezu, Riki Takeuchi.* When a trio of Japanese yuppie businessmen innocently criticize the attire of another group of men in a bar one night, the stage is set for a thriller of Hitchcockian proportions as they are stalked and brutalized by the men whose identity remains a mystery. This strange and violent Japanese noir mixes Kafkaesque paranoia with Woo-like ballistics to make this one of the most enjoyable and sinister action flicks to emerge from Japan in years. (Japanese with English subtitles) ★★★½ VHS: $79.99; DVD: $29.99

Nobody's Daughter

(1976, 90 min, Hungary, Laszlo Ranody) *Zsuzsi Czinokoczi.* Csore is an eight-year-old orphaned girl who is adopted by a poor farming family. However, her chance for happiness is thwarted as the family is only interested in their government allocation. Running away from their cruelty to search for her real mother, Csore finds herself, once again, back at the orphanage. When she is adopted by a rich family, she is treated even worse. It is young Csore's struggle to overcome the odds against her which makes for a poignant, heartbreaking tale of courage and resilience. (Hungarian with English subtitles) ★★★ VHS: $59.99

Nobody's Fool

(1994, 101 min, US, Robert Benton) *Paul Newman, Melanie Griffith, Jessica Tandy, Bruce Willis, Dylan Walsh, Elizabeth Wilson, Gene Saks, Philip Seymour Hoffman.* Newman's superlative

The classic crop-dusting scene in
North by Northwest

performance distinguishes this excellent and at times humorous character study of an aging rambler who tries to piece together the loose ends of his life. In one of his most accomplished screen portrayals, Newman plays Sully, a sixty-ish handyman with a bum leg who lives in a small New York town. Divorced and estranged from his family, this lothario who refuses to acknowledge the passing of time has been seemingly content with both odd jobs thrown his way and his own meager existence. But when he is reunited with his son and forced to reexamine his life, Sully's soul-searching leads to magnificent, introspective dramatics. Based on Richard Russo's novel and skillfully adapted by director Benton, *Nobody's Fool* is a grand, intimate day-in-the-life which pays tribute to the ordinary in a most extraordinary way. ★★★★ VHS: $14.99

Noises Off!

(1992, 101 min, US, Peter Bogdanovich) *Michael Caine, Christopher Reeve, Carol Burnett, John Ritter, Marilu Henner, Denholm Elliott, Nicollette Sheridan, Julie Hagerty, Mark-Linn Baker.* Bogdanovich must have been sure that this screen adaptation of Michael Frayn's hilarious, Tony Award–winning farce was going to fire up his directorial comeback. And by all rights it should have, but for some reason audiences stayed away from this superbly directed, well-acted and screamingly funny romp. Caine is the director of an incestuous touring company of an English drawing room farce. Following Frayn's script nearly to the letter, the action proceeds through three acts in which we see the play first at rehearsal, then a side-splitting view of a performance from backstage and finally a full performance in which all of the company's foibles and sexual trysts result in complete utter confusion. ★★★½

Nomads

(1986, 95 min, US, John McTiernan) *Pierce Brosnan, Leslie-Anne Down, Adam Ant.* From the director of *Die Hard* comes this imaginative but flat chiller with Brosnan as the inevitable vic-

tim of ghoulish phantoms; Down is the psychiatrist who tries to help him, only to experience first-hand his ordeal. ★★

None But the Brave

(1965, 106 min, US, Frank Sinatra) *Frank Sinatra, Clint Walker, Tommy Sands, Tony Bill.* Ol' Blue Eyes directs and stars in this tale of two enemy platoons, one American and one Japanese, who find themselves stranded on a remote island in the Pacific at the height of World War II. Lots of war film clichés, though Sinatra gives an especially appealing performance. ★★ VHS: $14.99

None But the Lonely Heart

(1944, 113 min, US, Clifford Odets) *Cary Grant, Ethel Barrymore, Barry Fitzgerald, Jane Wyatt.* It is ironic that Grant, a peerless comedian whose impeccable comic timing would create upteen comedy classics, received his only two Oscar nominations for dramas. One of these is Clifford Odets' moody melodrama set in the 1930s about a Cockney drifter who returns home to look after his dying mother. Barrymore won an Oscar as Grant's mum. ★★★ VHS: $14.99

Norma Rae

(1979, 113 min, US, Martin Ritt) *Sally Field, Ron Liebman, Beau Bridges, Pat Hingle.* Field won an Oscar (and newfound respect) for her triumphant portrayal of a Southern mother and textile worker who defies the abusive management of her company and organizes a union. Liebman plays the New York labor organizer who introduces Field to the idea, and Bridges is her husband who feels the neglect and ostracism of his wife's activism. Based on a true story. ★★★½ VHS: $9.99; DVD: $24.99

Normal Life

(1996, 108 min, US, John MacNaughton) *Luke Perry, Ashley Judd.* A fact-based crime drama about a white-trash couple who turn to crime to solve their financial and marital woes. Perry's surprisingly persuasive performance and Judd's dead-on, energetic portrayal go a long way toward making these unappealing characters sympathetic. The screenplay is less successful, offering spotty characterizations and obvious satire. ★★½ VHS: $19.99

Norman, Is That You?

(1976, 92 min, US, George Schlatter) *Redd Foxx, Michael Warren, Dennis Dugan, Pearl Bailey, Wayland Flowers.* This gay sex farce tries to have it both ways — making fun of faggots while espousing a what-will-be-will-be sexual philosophy — and the result is a surprisingly inoffensive and politically incorrect comedy. The story revolves around Norman (Warren), a handsome black man who lives with Garson (Dugan), his cute, swishy white lover in West Hollywood. Trouble brews when Norman's father, and eventually his mother (Foxx, Bailey), land at the doorstep of their presumedly straight son. The film's dialogue is at time funny despite some lame jokes, stupid stereotypes and a regular lexicon of innocuous gay name-calling. Flowers and his sassy puppet Madam add to the campy humor. ★★½ VHS: $14.99

Norman Loves Rose

(1982, 98 min, Australia, Henri Safran) *Carol Kane, Tony Owen.* Kane is very good as the wildly attractive sister-in-law of a 14-year-old boy who develops a tremendous crush on her. A little fooling around was nice, but problems arise when Kane becomes pregnant — and the father is not her husband! ★★½

North

(1994, 87 min, US, Rob Reiner) *Elijah Wood, Dan Aykroyd, Kathy Bates, Bruce Willis, Jon Lovitz, Jason Alexander.* North, the story of a child who "divorces" his parents and searches for new ones, is too close in theme to *Irreconcilable Differences* to be original. And its execution is part sentimental and part *Naked Gun*, and the two don't mix. Evidently it was doomed from the start. Wood plays North, whose search takes him around the world. Much like Dorothy in *The Wizard of Oz*, he soon realizes he was better off at home but has difficulty getting there. Though the reason for North leaving France is hilarious, the film is a misfire no matter where on Earth it's set. ★½ VHS: $9.99

North by Northwest

(1959, 137 min, US, Alfred Hitchcock) *Cary Grant, Eva Marie Saint, James Mason, Martin Landau, Leo G. Carroll.* Hitchcock returns to his favorite theme of an innocent man falsely accused in this terrifically exciting, funny and suspenseful thriller. Grant is the epitome of cool sophistication as a Madison Avenue ad executive mistaken for a spy. Mason is a perfect villain and Saint is the perennial icy blonde beauty. Classic Hitchcock touches include the crop-dusting scene and the Mt. Rushmore finale. (VHS available letterboxed or pan & scan) ★★★★ VHS: $14.99; DVD: $19.99

North Dallas Forty

(1979, 119 min, US, Ted Kotcheff) *Nick Nolte, Mac Davis, Charles Durning, John Matuszak, Bo Svenson, Dabney Coleman.* An entertaining, perceptive football comedy following the careers (on and off the field) of NFL players Nolte and Davis, who makes an impressive screen debut. ★★★ VHS: $14.99; DVD: $24.99

The North Star

(1943, 106 min, US, Lewis Milestone) *Dana Andrews, Anne Baxter, Erich von Stroheim.* Involving WWII drama about the efforts of a small Eastern Russian village who fight off the invading Nazis. Written by Lillian Hellman. ★★★ VHS: $39.99

North to Alaska

(1960, 122 min, US, Henry Hathaway) *John Wayne, Stewart Granger, Ernie Kovacs, Fabian, Capucine.* Sprawling comic western with Wayne and friends prospecting for gold in our northernmost state. Kovacs is particularly good as a con man out to fleece partners Wayne and Granger. ★★★ VHS: $14.99

Northern Pursuit

(1943, 94 min, US, Raoul Walsh) *Errol Flynn, Helmut Dantine, Gene Lockhart.* Flynn does his part as a Canadian Mountie who hunts a crashed Nazi pilot through the wilderness.

Exciting in places, but nothing out of the ordinary. ★★½ VHS: $19.99

Nosferatu

(1922, 84 min, Germany, F.W. Murnau) *Max Schreck, Gustav Von Wagenheim, Greta Schroeder, Alexander Granach.* Murnau's "symphony of horror" was the first, and most macabre, of the film versions of the legendary vampire, Count Dracula. Max Schreck's loathsome count, with his bald head, rodent face, long pointed ears, skeleton-like frame and talons will chill the most callous viewer. (Silent with musical soundtrack) An alternative version is also available which features a soundtrack by Type O Negative. From the Bram Stroker novel. ★★★½ VHS: $24.99; DVD: $24.99

Nosferatu the Vampyre

(Nosferatu — Phantom der Nacht)

(1979, 107 min, Germany, Werner Herzog) *Klaus Kinski, Isabelle Adjani, Bruno Ganz, Roland Topor.* Director Herzog's classic interpretation of the vampire myth. It is 1850 in the beautiful town of Wismar. Jonathan Harker (Ganz) is about to leave on a long journey, leaving behind his wife Lucy (Adjani). Upon his arrival, he is greeted by a pale, wraith-like figure who identifies himself as Count Dracula (Kinski). As the town succumbs to plague and death, Harker and his wife become convinced there is a vampire in their midst, and they soon realize that they, too, are in danger. Haunting, hypnotic and beautifully rendered. (Letterboxed) (German with English subtitles) (Also available in an English-language version) ★★★½ VHS: $14.99; DVD: $34.99

Nostalghia

(1983, 120 min, Italy/USSR, Andrei Tarkovsky) *Oleg Yankovsky, Erland Josephson.* Russia's eminent auteur director, Tarkovsky, traveled to Italy to make this haunting and fascinating film on one man's mystical odyssey through his past, and his attempt to deal with his cultural and philosophical alienation. Yankovsky plays Gorchakov, a Russian poet doing research in rural Italy on an expatriate composer. Accompanied by Eugenia, his beautiful interpreter, his journey takes him to a Tuscan village, shrouded by mists and enveloped in an eerie silence. Here, Gorchikov confronts his past, his Russian family and an impending spiritual and midlife crisis. He finds his malaise and world-weariness mirrored in an unusual encounter with a local madman who, in fearful anticipation of Armageddon, once locked himself and his family in their house for seven years. Tarkovsky dares to test the confines of the filmmaking process, and in doing so has crafted a film as exhilarating in thought and deed as it is beautiful in design and detail. (Letterboxed) (Italian with English subtitles) ★★★★ VHS: $29.99; DVD: $29.99

Nostradamus

(1994, 118 min, US, Roger Christian) *Tcheky Karyo, Amanda Plummer, Julia Ormond, Rutger Hauer, F. Murray Abraham.* Born into a Europe ravaged by plague and the persecution of the Inquisition, physician Michel de Nostradame garnered a reputation as a mystic and seer, acquiring fervent enemies and attracting pow-

erful friends from the monarchy and from secret societies of learning. The rabid suppression of knowledge by the establishment religion necessitated that information be passed in secrecy, under sworn oaths of silence. Though the film opens slowly, it's worth a bit of patience; the viewer is amply rewarded. ★★★ VHS: $14.99

Not for Publication

(1984, 87 min, US, Paul Bartel) *Nancy Allen, David Naughton, Laurence Luckenbill, Alice Ghostley.* Cult favorite Bartel takes on the tabloids in this offbeat tale of muckraking journalism and political scandal. Allen is a moonlighting reporter who discovers her boss, the incumbent mayor of New York, at an orgy she is assigned to cover. ★★½

Not One Less

(1999, 102 min, China, Zhang Yimou) *Wei Minzhi, Zhang Huike.* Recalling the personal drama of his *The Story of Qiu Ju* rather than the epic storytelling of *To Live* and *Raise the Red Lantern*, director Zhang has crafted a gentle, poignant parable of sacrifice and poverty. Wei Minzhi (playing herself) is a 13-year-old girl who becomes the substitute teacher for her remote mountain village. Determined to keep the small class together (otherwise she won't be paid), she has her hands full coping with the children's lively spirits and the school's nonexistent budget. When one of her students (Zhang Huike) flees to the big city, she sets out alone to return him to school. Young Wei, a nonprofessional, is a natural, a heartbreaker with a killer smile and attitude to spare. Her natural screen presence brings to mind Richie Andrusco in *The Little Fugitive*, as Zhang uses the verité style of that film to economic and stirring effect. *Not One Less* may appear simple in scope, but it charms and moves us in not-so-simple ways. (Mandarin with English subtitles) ★★★ VHS: $21.99; DVD: $29.99

Not Wanted

(1949, 94 min, US, Elmer Clifton & Ida Lupino) *Sally Forrest, Keefe Brasselle, Leo Penn, Rita Lupino.* Though Clifton is credited as director for this compelling '40s melodrama, Lupino finished the film after he died three days into shooting. As a result, the film may have acquired more of a sympathy towards the lead character than what may have originally been there. *Not Wanted* is a concise, neorealist tale about a teenager (Forrest) who, as a result of "hanging out with the wrong crowd," becomes pregnant after a one-night stand. Lupino (who also cowrote the screenplay) finds power in the teen's subsequent relationship with a slightly handicapped vet (Brasselle). Of note is a haunting trip to the delivery room, filmed subjectively, and a startlingly tense finale which keeps you guessing until the end. ★★★ VHS: $24.99

The incomparable Max Schreck in *Nosferatu*

Not without My Daughter

(1991, 117 min, US, Brian Gilbert) *Sally Field, Alfred Molina, Roshan Seth.* An American woman, married to an Iranian husband, becomes trapped in Iran when they visit his family for a two-week vacation. Two years later, after being forced to endure the oppressive Islamic life, she tries to escape with her daughter back to America. Based on a true story, the film nevertheless indulges cultural stereotypes, though Field gives an impassioned performance which heightens the story's intrigue. ★★ VHS: $9.99

Notebook on Cities and Clothes

(1990, 80 min, France, Wim Wenders) Ostensibly a documentary about Japanese fashion designer Yohji Yamamoto, this Wenders film is really a reflection on art and the creative process. Filmed in and around Paris, the filmmaker and designer engage the viewer in contemplation about the nature of visual communication and the creation of images. The opening sequence establishes the nature of that inquiry with narration which ponders the believability of photographs and other images in the digital age. ★★★ VHS: $29.99

Notes for an African Orestes

(1970, 75 min, Italy, Pier Paolo Pasolini) This fascinating look at the artistic process of one of the world's most daring and creative filmmakers is, simply put, a cinematic notebook. We follow Pasolini as he treks around East Africa scouring remote villages and crowded marketplaces for raw footage and discusses all of the possibilities for what he hoped would be a production of "The Orestia." Aeschylus' myth is truly one of the materpieces of ancient Greek theatre and Pasolini's idea was to set the story in a rapidly modernizing Africa as a grand allegory for the painful and awkward period of development which swept through the Third World in the 1960s. For fans of Pasolini, this will prove to be a mesmerizing and poetic view of underdevelopment and the quest for modernization which plagues the Third World today. ★★★½

Nothing in Common

(1986, 130 min, US, Garry Marshall) *Tom Hanks, Jackie Gleason, Eva Marie Saint, Bess Armstrong.* Bittersweet comedy-drama with Hanks as an advertising exec caught in the middle of his parents' separation. Gleason gives a terrific performance as Hanks' gruff father, and Saint nicely plays his mom. ★★★ VHS: $9.99

Nothing Sacred

(1937, 75 min, US, William Wellman) *Carole Lombard, Fredric March, Walter Connolly.* The delightful Lombard, a small town girl, thinks she's dying of a rare disease and is turned into the "Sweetheart of New York" by scheming reporter March. This riotous and cynical battle-of-the-sexes classic was written by Ben Hecht. Presented in three-strip Technicolor for the first time on video, and digitally remastered from archive prints. ★★★½ VHS: $24.99; DVD: $19.99

Nothing to Lose

(1997, 97 min, US, Steve Oedekerk) *Martin Lawrence, Tim Robbins, John C. McGinley, Giancarlo Esposito, Kelly Preston, Michael McKean, Irma P. Hall.* The premise of the black con and uptight white guy coming together for a series of misadventures is already becoming passé, but the amiable if familiar *Nothing to Lose* manages to entertain in spite of its clichéd roots and predictable plot, due in large part to the teaming of Lawrence and Robbins. Upon discovering his wife in bed with his boss, a distraught Robbins drives aimlessly throughout the city. Things go from bad to worse when Lawrence attempts to hijack his car. With nothing to lose, the captive becomes the captor as Robbins turns the tables and takes Lawrence prisoner. Robbins is a delight as the sad-sack husband who finally throws caution to the wind and goes for broke. Lawrence adds just the right amount of urban cool and wry delivery to his hapless carjacker and gives a funny, even restrained performance. ★★½ VHS: $14.99

Notorious

(1946, 101 min, US, Alfred Hitchcock) *Ingrid Bergman, Cary Grant, Claude Rains, Louis Calhern.* Romance and intrigue are the ingredients in this Hitchcock thriller set in post-war Brazil. American secret agent Bergman marries an elderly spy (Rains) to gain information on Nazi activity. Grant is her contact in Rio and her partner in a seething love affair. Grant and Bergman are ravishing, but it is Rains who steals the show. ★★★½ VHS: $14.99; DVD: $14.99

La Notte

(1961, 120 min, West Germany/Italy, Michelangelo Antonioni) *Jeanne Moreau, Marcello Mastroianni.* Antonioni's exploration of noncommunication, boredom and inpenetrable loneliness features Moreau and Mastroianni as a troubled married couple who have stopped understanding each other and themselves. Set in one night in Milan, this unforgettable mood piece is classic Antonioni. (Italian with English subtitles) ★★★ VHS: $19.99; DVD: $24.99

Notting Hill

(1999, 123 min, GB, Roger Michell) *Julia Roberts, Hugh Grant, Hugh Bonneville, Emma Chambers, Rhys Ifans.* "You're Beverly Hills, I'm Notting Hill," Grant's bewildered bookseller tells Roberts' big-time actress, trying to convince both of them they're not right for each other. And, in essence, he's correct. Roberts' Anna is closer to, well, Julia Roberts, and Grant's William is right out of *Four Weddings and a Funeral.* But damn it all, it all works. Screenwriter Richard Curtis has concocted a charmer of a romantic comedy, a delicious fairy-tale romance that is played to the hilt by its two very personable stars. Grant and Roberts have a wonderful chemistry together, and both are given some great lines to recite. *Notting Hill* is funny, endearing and very romantic. ★★★ VHS: $14.99; DVD: $24.99

Nous N'Irons Plus au Bois

(1982, 88 min, France, George Dumoulin) *Marie-France Pisier, Siegfried Rauch.* During the Spring of 1944 in a Nazi-occupied forest in northern France, a Resistance group of several Frenchmen hold out. Their unity and purpose are put to the test when they come upon several German deserters. The group is divided on whether they are indeed deserters, and if they are, what should they do with them? (French with English subtitles) ★★★

November Moon (Novembermonde)

(1984, 107 min, Germany, Alexandra Von Grote) *Gabriele Osburg, Danièle Delorme, Stéphane Garcin, Louise Martini, Christine Millet.* This ambitious WWII drama from director Von Grote stars Osburg as November, a plucky Jewish lesbian whose flight from the Nazis leads her to Paris and freedom. But when Occupation forces enter the city, she is again threatened. Her Parisian lover, Ferial, at grave risk, poses as a collaborator in an attempt to save the life of the woman she loves. A moving film experience that reaches beyond the horrors of WWII as it speaks out against violence, war and the persecution of all minorities. (German with English subtitles) ★★★ VHS: $39.99; DVD: $24.99

Now and Then

(1995, 96 min, US, Lesli Linka Glatter) *Christina Ricci, Thora Birch, Gaby Hoffmann, Ashleigh Aston Moore, Demi Moore, Melanie Griffith, Rosie O'Donnell, Rita Wilson.* Essentially a derivative, inferior female *Stand by Me, Now and Then* features four inseparable friends who obsess over a dead body, with all of this set against an (obtrusive) oldies soundtrack. Like Rob Reiner's sweet-natured coming-of-age film, not a lot happens to the four protagonists. The basic plot is the girls' determined efforts to get to the mystery of a deceased boy, whose spirit they think they've brought back to life. But whereas *Stand by Me* was punctuated by subtle direction and a marvelous screenplay, *Now and Then* only offers the infrequent but admittedly amusing observation of adolescence. ★★ VHS: $9.99; DVD: $19.99

Now, Voyager

(1942, 117 min, US, Irving Rapper) *Bette Davis, Claude Rains, Paul Henreid, Gladys Cooper.* Davis received a Best Actress nomination for her portrayal of a lonely spinster who, with the help of a caring analyst, changes from an ugly duckling to a high-flying swan. Rains and Henreid also star as the doctor and love interest, respectively. Bette's stunning transformation, memorable dialogue and a lush Max Steiner score highlight this classic tearjerker. ★★★½ VHS: $14.99

Nowhere

(1996, 82 min, US, Gregg Araki) *James Duval, Rachel True, Nathan Bexton, Chiara Mastroianni, Debi Mazar, Kathleen Robertson, Christina Applegate.* One could easily be tempted to call *Nowhere*, Araki's angst-fest of masturbation, bondage, drugs, murder and alien abduction, his *Pink Velvet.* He captures entertainingly weird Lynch moments and an oddly fascinating outlook on '90s life, but ultimately the film does go nowhere. Araki regular Duval and an eclectic young cast are pessimistic high schoolers mired in pop culture hell as they ditch class and kill an afternoon with sex, deep thoughts and black forest cake while waiting for a party that evening. *Nowhere* is mesmerizingly shallow, and Araki touches upon many

Ingrid Bergman and Cary Grant in *Notorious*

the same themes he tackled in *The Doom Generation.* As a result, the film is only somewhat wild at heart. ★★½ VHS: $19.99

Nowhere to Run

(1992, 95 min, US, Robert Harmon) *Jean-Claude Van Damme, Rosanna Arquette, Kieran Culkin, Ted Levine, Joss Ackland.* Van Damme attempts to do something different in this film: act. Trying to show off his sensitive side as an escaped convict, he befriends a family being coerced by evil land developers into selling their land. Arquette plays the lonely widowed mother and Culkin (Macaulay's younger brother) is actually quite good as her son. The film starts off well enough, but suffers from extreme predictability and dull action sequences. ★½ VHS: $9.99; DVD: $19.99

Nueba Yol

(1996, 104 min, Dominican Republic, Angel Muñiz) *Luisito Martì, Caridad Ravelo.* Never certain why, a recent widower feels compelled to leave behind the comforts of his friends and home in the Dominican Republic to make a success of himself in New York City. Needless to say, a workable definition of "success" is not to be learned on *those* mean streets. Warm and funny, *Nueba Yol* is also honest and real, recalling the best cinema can be: full of life in all its joyfulness and sorrow. Like Renoir or Ozu, director Muñiz lets the camera quietly eavesdrop on people too genuine to be giving performances, a rarity these days when too much of world cinema looks to emulate the latest from a Hollywood grown out of touch. (Spanish with English subtitles) ★★★½ VHS: $19.99

La Nuit de Varennes

(1982, 133 min, France/Italy, Ettore Scola) *Marcello Mastroianni, Hanna Schygulla, Jean-Louis Barrault, Harvey Keitel.* Scola's brilliant historical drama is set in 1791 on the night of Louis XVI and Marie Antoinette's flight from Paris. First-hand witnesses to the revolution against the ancien régime include the ribald Restif (Barrault), the aging Casanova (Mastroianni), Thomas Paine (Keitel), and a

The Nun

Nurse Betty: Renee Zellweger and her plastic, fantastic lover

lady-in-waiting (Schugulla). (French with English subtitles) ★★★½

Number Seventeen

(1932, 83 min, GB, Alfred Hitchcock) *Leon M. Lion, Anne Grey.* This strange and entertaining comedy-thriller about jewel thieves is first set in a spooky abandoned house and concludes with an exciting cross-country chase involving a hijacked train, a bus, a ferry and lots of water. ★★★ VHS: $12.99

The Nun (La Religieuse)

(1965, 140 min, France, Jacques Rivette) *Anna Karina, Micheline Presle.* An intensely somber drama about a young woman who suffers physical and psychological anguish at the hands of her family, a religious order and society. Set in 18th-century France, the film stars the beautiful Karina as Suzanne, who, unable to marry because of the lack of a dowry, is sent unwillingly to a convent. Lacking a calling for the religious life, Suzanne stubbornly refuses to take her vows which results in her being beaten and semi-starved. She eventually escapes, but she soon finds that her new freedom leads only to more suffering. Banned by the French government for its "anti-clerical" stance, this unsentimental film is uncompromising in presenting a world bereft of compassion and understanding. (French with English subtitles) ★★★ VHS: $24.99

The Nun's Story

(1959, 149 min, US, Fred Zinnemann) *Audrey Hepburn, Peter Finch, Edith Evans, Peggy Ashcroft, Dean Jagger, Mildred Dunnock, Beatrice Straight, Colleen Dewhurst.* Excellent adaptation of the Kathryn Hulme novel following the life of a young novice from the convent to service in the Belgian Congo. Hepburn is simply magnificent as the dedicated nun, who endures great hardships working with doctor Finch (in an admirable performance) in the jungle. ★★★★ VHS: $19.99

Nuns on the Run

(1990, 90 min, GB, Jonathan Lynn) *Eric Idle, Robbie Coltrane, Janet Suzman.* Two entry-level gangsters find themselves wanted by both the police and the mob. After they are set up and marked for murder by "Mr. Big," they turn the tables and run off with the mob's ill-gotten booty; and in the process cross a rival gang, as well. Where do the boys choose to hide out? In the nearest convent, naturally. Donning habit and attitude, they masquerade as two novices, and proceed to turn the well-ordered order upside-down. Lighthearted, mindless fun. ★★½ VHS: $19.99

Nurse Betty

(2000, 110 min, US, Neil LaBute) *Renee Zellweger, Morgan Freeman, Chris Rock, Greg Kinnear, Aaron Eckhart, Crispin Glover, Pruitt Taylor Vance.* Zellweger brings charm to spare to this modest comedy that can't quite deliver on the ambitious, edgy goals it sets for itself. Betty (Zellweger) is a mousy waitress whose customers and fellow employees love her; her abusive husband has considerably less patience and affection. After witnessing his murder at the hands of two hit men, Betty loses her grip on reality and heads out to California to meet the man of her dreams: a doctor on a TV soap she thinks is a real person. On her trail: the two hit men determined to silence her. Director LaBute mixes brutality, screwball humor and quirky characters to tell this original but not fully realized tale of fantasy and reality colliding; a world in which Betty is *Being There*'s Chauncey Gardner and everyone else is from "The Sopranos" via Comedy Central. Though there are several scenes that are gloriously rendered, the whole doesn't quite come together as it should. Freeman is excellent as one of the hit men, whose heart and conscience sends him in a surprising direction. ★★½ VHS: $19.99; DVD: $24.99

Nuts

(1987, 116 min, US, Martin Ritt) *Barbra Streisand, Richard Dreyfuss, Maureen Stapleton,*

Eli Wallach, James Whitmore, Karl Malden. Based on Tom Topor's stage hit, this highly successful courtroom drama features one of Streisand's most accomplished dramatic performances. Streisand plays a high-priced prostitute on trial for murdering a john; however, while she insists it was self-defense, her family petitions to have her certified mentally incompetent. Dreyfuss is terrific as the laywer who defends Streisand's right to a trial. ★★★ VHS: $14.99

Nuts in May

(1976, 84 min, GB, Mike Leigh) *Alison Steadman, Roger Showmar.* A young couple — a pair of highly compulsive, vegetarian neatniks — on holiday in East Anglia check into a campground for some communing with nature. They immediately come into conflict with their neighbors. The film lazily meanders with them as their well-planned holiday slowly unravels. ★★ VHS: $29.99

The Nutty Professor

(1963, 107 min, US, Jerry Lewis) *Jerry Lewis, Stella Stevens, Howard Morris, Kathleen Freeman.* Fifty million Frenchmen can't be wrong. This is *the* Jerry Lewis film for those who don't like Jerry Lewis (let's see those hands). Mild-mannered professor Lewis becomes lounge lizard Buddy Love thanks to a potion he quaffs accidentally. Lots of brilliant sight gags and a good use of color give proof that this is a director in control of his medium. (Remade in 1996) ★★★ VHS: $9.99; DVD: $29.99

The Nutty Professor

(1996, 95 min, US, Tom Shadyac) *Eddie Murphy, Jada Pinkett, Larry Miller, James Coburn, Dave Chappelle.* This hilarious remake of the 1963 Jerry Lewis semiclassic is a twofold success: Murphy has finally delivered on the promise he demonstrated in *48 HRS.* and *Trading Places,* and — a rarity — a remake is worthy of the original. Murphy plays Sherman Klump, a brilliant, 400-pound chemistry professor who tries a DNA experiment to curb obesity on himself. Sherman's Mr. Hyde turns out to be Buddy Love, a slim, testosterone-driven alter ego who is so over the top Murphy almost seems to be doing a self-parody of his own image. *The Nutty Professor* is consistently funny complete with humorous sight gags, snappy dialogue and good special effects. Playing seven parts — including four family members at a convulsive dinner — Murphy's comic luminance shines through. (Sequel: *Nutty Professor II: The Klumps*) ★★★ VHS: $14.99; DVD: $24.99

Nutty Professor II: The Klumps

(2000, 107 min, US, Peter Segal) *Eddie Murphy, Janet Jackson, Larry Miller.* Bigger isn't always necessarily better; this loud, only occasionally funny sequel to the hilarious 1996 remake certainly proves that point. Murphy returns as: Sherman Klump, that endearing overweight college professor; Buddy Love, his on-the-make alter ego; and the entire Klump family. Murphy is a marvel creating such distinct characters; too bad the screenplay is nothing more than a collection of toilet humor and sex jokes. ★★ VHS: $22.99; DVD: $26.99

O Brother, Where Art Thou?

(2000, 103 min, US, Joel Coen) *George Clooney, John Turturro, Tim Blake Nelson, Holly Hunter, John Goodman, Charles Durning, Stephen Root, Chris Thomas King.* Leave it to the Coen brothers to combine Preston Sturges' *Sullivan's Travels* and Homer's "The Odyssey" and produce one of the year's most entertaining and funniest films. A screwball comedy in the best style of Sturges, *O Brother, Where Art Thou?* (which gets its name from the film Sullivan's director wanted to make) transcribes Homer's mythic epic to the rural South during the Great Depression. Clooney is Ulysses McGill, one of three chain-gang convicts on the run from their Mississippi captors and in search of untold treasure. En route, they meet a gallery of eccentric characters and fanciful adventure, including the "Odyssey"'s sirens (in the form of three beauties bathing at a stream), the one-eyed cyclops (Goodman as a one-eyed, dastardly Bible salesman) and a blind, railroad-traveling prophet. Lighter in tone than some of their former works, this is nonetheless one of the Coens' best films. Once again they don't try to duplicate previous successes, and this is a wholly original excursion into madcap hijinks and social discourse. The casting is on-target down the line. Clooney looks like he stepped out of a 1930s film, and similarities to Clark Gable are probably intentional. Nelson is hilarious as a dim-witted farm boy, and Root gets a special mention as a partially blind radio station manager. Add to this intoxicating mix a superb bluegrass/folk soundtrack, and it's easy to reason the Coens have done it again — they're bona fide. ★★★★ VHS: $19.99; DVD: $29.99

O.C. and Stiggs

(1987, 95 min, US, Robert Altman) *Daniel H. Jenkins, Neill Barry, Paul Dooley, Jane Curtin, Jon Cryer, Ray Walston, Tina Louise, Martin Mull, Dennis Hopper, Melvin Van Peebles.* Altman attempts the teen comedy. The spirit of revolution runs deep in this one, folks, but Altman's flourish can't save this meaningless yarn about a couple of kids whose passion in life is to humiliate a wealthy insurance tycoon and his family while skipping to the beat of King Sunny Ade. ★★

O Lucky Man!

(1973, 174 min, GB, Lindsay Anderson) *Malcolm McDowell, Arthur Lowe, Ralph Richardson, Rachel Roberts, Alan Price, Helen Mirren, Mona Washbourne.* Anderson's mammoth and brilliant allegory stars McDowell as a latter-day Candide, buoyed by optimism in a sea of sham and corruption. A young coffee salesman pushes his way to the top only to fall and rise and fall yet again. A tremendous score is provided by Alan Price. ★★★★ VHS: $24.99

The Object of Beauty

(1991, 101 min, US/GB, Michael Lindsay-Hogg) *John Malkovich, Andie MacDowell, Joss Ackland, Lolita Davidovich.* Malkovich and MacDowell are an American couple living at an expensive London hotel. Their financial crunch leads them to an insurance swindle — only before they are able to institute the hoax, someone beats them to it. A very low-key comedy with few laughs, and two rather annoying people as the principal characters. ★★½ VHS: $9.99; DVD: $24.99

The Object of My Affection

(1998, 112 min, US, Nicholas Hytner) *Jennifer Aniston, Paul Rudd, John Pankow, Nigel Hawthorne, Alan Alda, Tim Daly, Allison Janney.* A romantic comedy of unrequited love given a '90s, gay twist, *The Object of My Affection* is a pleasant if lightweight tale which is at its best when not trying too hard to be the cutting-

O, Brother, Where Art Thou?

Chris Cooper and Jake Gyllenhaal in *October Sky*

edge romp it only occasionally is. Aniston is extremely engaging as Nina, a Brooklyn social worker who invites gay teacher George (Rudd) to move in with her when he gets dumped by his two-timing boyfriend. Acting more like girlfriends, the two become close with Nina falling in love with the unattainable George. To further complicate matters, Nina learns she is pregnant and decides to dump her boyfriend, hoping that George will act as surrogate father. Very matter-of-fact in its gayness for a Hollywood film, *The Object of My Affection* is alternately insightful and artificial. ★★½ VHS: $14.99

Objective: Burma!

(1945, 142 min, US, Raoul Walsh) *Errol Flynn, George Tobias.* Flynn leads a familiar ragtag team of soldiers into the Burmese jungle to destroy a Japanese stronghold. The film scored well with wartime American audiences as a rather suspenseful first-rate morale booster. But across the sea, our British allies were less-than-enthusiastic as the film ignores the contributions of the Allied forces, including the long-suffering British 14th Army, which had spearheaded the Burmese campaign. Still, a well-made, if jingoistic, war story. ★★★ VHS: $19.99

Oblomov

(1979, 140 min, USSR, Nikita Mikhalkov) *Oleg Tabakov, Elena Solovei.* This delightful social satire and sensitive character study of a likable but lazy aristocrat was adapted from the 1859 Russian novel by Ivan Goncharov. Oblomov, a good-natured and indolent landowner in Czarist Russia who has never worked a day in his life, decides that he has no reason for getting out of bed and finds himself in a melancholy stupor and paralyzed with lethargy. While a procession of friends fail to change his slothful ways, it is his passionate love for a woman named Olga that energizes him and gives the man a new lease on life. (Russian with English subtitles) ★★★ VHS: $29.99

Obsession

(1976, 104 min, US, Brian De Palma) *Cliff Robertson, Genevieve Bujold, John Lithgow.* De Palma's elegant thriller is one of the most underrated films of the 1970s, largely because it is always unjustly relegated to the category of "Hitchcock rip-off." Robertson stars as a man

who feels responsible for the death of his wife in a kidnapping tragedy and seeks to resurrect her in the form of another woman (Bujold, in a dual role). Sound familiar? Don't be misled. True, the film owes a great deal to Hitchcock's *Vertigo*, but its strength lies in its ability to work independently as a mystery on its own merits. Magnificent score by Bernard Herrmann. ★★★½; DVD: $24.99

Ocean's 11

(1960, 127 min, US, Lewis Milestone) *Frank Sinatra, Dean Martin, Sammy Davis, Jr., Peter Lawford, Joey Bishop, Angie Dickinson, Cesar Romero.* The "Rat Pack" is in full bloom in this enjoyable caper comedy. Frank, Dino, Sammy and pals come up with a foolproof plan to rob five Las Vegas casinos — at the same time! ★★★ VHS: $14.99

October
(Ten Days That Shook the World)

(1928, 99 min, USSR, Sergei Eisenstein) Commissioned to celebrate the tenth anniversary of the revolution, this stirring portrait of an entire nation set on the edge of change is taken from American John Reed's writings. Director Eisenstein had endless resources to make the film and with the virtual absence of any footage of the real events of 1917, this powerful epic is elevated into the realm of historical importance. (Silent with musical soundtrack) ★★★★ VHS: $29.99; DVD: $24.99

October Sky

(1999, 108 min, US, Joe Johnston) *Jake Gyllenhaal, Chris Cooper, Laura Dern, Chris Owen, William Lee Scott, Chad Lindberg, Natalie Canderday.* The inspirational, warm-hearted real-life story of making one's dreams come true against insurmountable odds, *October Sky* is quiet, powerful storytelling. Set in 1957 in the small coal mining town of Coalwood, West Virginia, the tale follows high schooler Homer (a very appealing Gyllenhaal) who teams with his two best friends, and the brainy school outcast, to build a working rocket and enter it into the science fair. That the viewer is immediately drawn into this simple story speaks volumes about Lewis Colick's fluid adaptation of Homer Hickam's novel and Johnston's level-headed, graceful direction. The entire cast is excellent, though Cooper stands out as Homer's strict father. Poignant, involving and extremely well-crafted, *October Sky* — like its young scientist heroes — goes about its small, unheralded task with unassuming but unqualified success. ★★★½ VHS: $14.99; DVD: $29.99

Octopus

(1999, 99 min, US, John Eyres) *Jay Harrington, David Beecroft, Carolyn Lowery.* En route by submarine to prison, a terrorist escapes his confines and is loose on the sub. If that weren't

enough, there's a fabled mutant octopus on the sub's tail. Hilariously inept in every way, *Octopus* wants so badly to play with the big boys, but only has a few bucks and an untalented cast and crew to offer. The dialogue, acting, editing and especially the effects are horrendous; yet the film is so bad, so goofy, it can be more entertaining than the majority of the big-budget action films it steals from so shamelessly. ★★ VHS: $69.99; DVD: $24.99

Octopussy

(1983, 130 min, GB, John Glen) *Roger Moore, Maud Adams, Louis Jourdan.* The 13th Broccoli Bond production found itself up against itself as Connery returned to the role in the competing project *Never Say Never Again.* Moore is confronted with several villains including the title character, played by Adams, who may or may not be working for any one side at any moment. This isn't one of the better films in the series; though the stunts are adequate, the customary tongue-in-cheek humor is considerably low-brow. (Sequel: *A View to a Kill*) ★★½ VHS: $9.99; DVD: $26.99

The Odd Couple

(1968, 106 min, US, Gene Saks) *Jack Lemmon, Walter Matthau, Herb Edelman, John Fiedler.* The laughs are plentiful in this first-class adaptation of Neil Simon's Broadway hit. Lemmon and Matthau are in great form as Felix and Oscar, the two most unlikely and mismatched roommates in New York City. (Sequel: *The Odd Couple II*) ★★★½ VHS: $14.99; DVD: $29.99

The Odd Couple II

(1998, 97 min, US, Howard Deutch) *Jack Lemmon, Walter Matthau, Christine Baranski, Barnard Hughes, Jonathan Silverman, Jean Smart.* Returning to the source in which they are arguably most identifiable as a team, Lemmon and Matthau reprise their 1968 roles of Felix Unger and Oscar Madison in this sporadically funny though over-the-hill sequel penned by Neil Simon. Felix and Oscar come together for the marriage of Felix's daughter to Oscar's son. The bickering begins immediately, and soon they are lost on the road en route to the wedding. The chemistry between the two stars is still evident, and there are quite a few zingy one-liners and humorous scenes, but Simon has taken the joy out of Felix and Oscar, and that's what keeps this from being anything but *Grumpy Old Men 3*. ★★ VHS: $14.99; DVD: $29.99

Odd Man Out

(1947, 113 min, GB, Carol Reed) *James Mason, Kathleen Ryan, Robert Newton, Dan O'Herlihy.* Under cover after escaping from prison, Mason plans a payroll heist to finance IRA operations. During its execution, he kills a man. In the process of escaping the scene of the crime, he briefly enters the lives of many people, eliciting a gamut of reactions and exposing a wide range of human idiosyncrasies. A perceptive examination of values and morality, incisively directed by Reed and with excellent performances. (Remade as *The Lost Man*) ★★★★; DVD: $24.99

Odd Obsession

(1960, 96 min, Japan, Kon Ichikawa) *Machiko Kyo, Ganjiro Nakamura, Junko Kano, Tatsuya*

Nakadai. Director Ichikawa's disturbing drama about the strained marital relations between an ex-beauty queen and her elderly husband who keeps himself going sexually with injections, jealousy and by taking photos of his nude, sleeping wife. The couple's twisted story has a surprise ending. Remastered print. (aka: *The Key*) (Japanese with English subtitles) ★★★ VHS: $29.99

Ode to Billy Joe

(1976, 106 min, US, Max Baer) *Robby Benson, Glynnis O'Connor, James Best.* A wonderful example of why more Top 40 hit songs are not adapted for the screen. Benson is the teen Billy Joe McAllister who mysteriously jumps off the Tallahatchie Bridge. O'Connor is his confused girlfriend. An over-emotionalized interpretation of Bobbie Gentry's hit song, the film misses more than it hits, although it does offer a fine re-creation of 1950s-'60s rural Southern life. Want to save a few bucks and some time? Billy Joe jumped because he had sex with a man. Lordy! ★★ VHS: $14.99

The Odessa File

(1974, 128 min, GB, Ronald Neame) *Jon Voight, Maximilian Schell, Derek Jacobi, Maria Schell.* Frederick Forsyth's best-seller comes to the big screen with Voight as a German journalist who is on the track of Nazis in the early 1960s. Voight gives a solid performance which single-handedly elevates an otherwise muddled mystery. ★★½ VHS: $9.99; DVD: $24.99

The Odyssey

(1997, 165 min, US, Andrei Konchalovsky) *Armand Assante, Greta Scacchi, Isabella Rossellini, Vanessa Williams, Bernadette Peters, Eric Roberts, Geraldine Chaplin, Jeroen Krabbé, Irene Papas.* An admirable attempt to put one of the greatest adventures ever told onto film, this version of *The Odyssey* includes most of the high points of the story while never sacrificing its characters or morals for entertainment value. After a long, drawn-out war and on the eve of heading home, Greek captain Odysseus accidentally offends Poseidon, God of the Sea, who swears to prevent his ever seeing his homeland again. So Odysseus begins a decades-long wandering. Managing to be both educational and entertaining, this *Odyssey* is worth devoting some time to. ★★★ VHS: $9.99

Office Killer

Oedipus Rex

(1967, 110 min, Italy, Pier Paolo Pasolini) *Franco Citti, Silvana Mangano.* Filmed in and around an awesome, 15th-century adobe city in the Moroccan desert, Pasolini's version of the Oedipus legend retain's the basic elements of Sophocles' classic tragedy. A young man, abandoned at birth by his parents, is foretold of his doomed fate by an oracle; nonetheless, he unknowingly murders his father and marries his mother. This tragic story of a man's intractable road to his destiny shimmers with lavish costumes, bloody sword fights, sun-drenched locales and expressive performances. (Italian with English subtitles) ★★★ VHS: $29.99

Of Human Bondage

(1934, 83 min, US, John Cromwell) *Bette Davis, Leslie Howard, Frances Dee.* This low-key treatment of the W. Somerset Maugham novel is enlivened by the striking presence of a truly luminous and effectively trashy Davis. Howard is his usual earnest self as a failed artist turned medical student who becomes obsessed with Davis' aloof, uncaring waitress. A scandal ensued when Davis was overlooked as a Best Actress nominee — causing a massive write-in campaign and, some say, a consolation Oscar for Bette the following year. (Remade in 1964) ★★★ VHS: $19.99

Of Human Bondage

(1964, 100 min, US, Ken Hughes) *Kim Novak, Laurence Harvey, Robert Morley, Roger Livesey.* W. Somerset Maugham's celebrated novel of a doctor (Harvey) whose passion for a crude waitress (Novak) leads to tragedy is given inferior treatment in this third screen adaptation. Stick to the 1934 Bette Davis version (unless you're really a Novak or Harvey fan). ★★ VHS: $24.99

Of Mice and Men

(1939, 106 min, US, Lewis Milestone) *Burgess Meredith, Lon Chaney, Jr., Betty Field, Charles Bickford.* In top-drawer Hollywood style, Milestone's terse, idiomatic treatment of John Steinbeck's melancholy classic wrings charged melodrama, tension, and sex from the tragic tale of two California farm laborers' descent into a Depression-era maelstrom. Top-drawer Hollywood casting delivers indelible performances from Chaney as the mentally slow, physically lumbering giant who crushes the creatures he loves and Meredith as the overburdened friend who must be his protector and, ultimately, his judge. Field smolders as the treacherous farmer's wife whose role emphasizes the material's desperate carnality and endemic sexism. All in all, the film represents the type of prototypically dark Americana that only an émigré from Odessa (like Milestone) could conjure. (Remade in 1992) ★★★★ VHS: $29.99; DVD: $19.99

Of Mice and Men

(1992, 110 min, US, Gary Sinise) *Gary Sinise, John Malkovich, Ray Walston, Sherilyn Fenn, Joe Morton, Casey*

Siemaszko. Coproducer, costar and director Sinise's retelling of John Steinbeck's classic novel is an absorbing, brilliantly acted film. Sinise stars as the world-weary drifter George, opposite Malkovich's thoroughly convincing portrayal of the helpless man-child Lenny. Horton Foote's literary screenplay beautifully translates the novel to film. Heightened by marvelous supporting performances. ★★★½ VHS: $19.99

Off Beat

(1986, 92 min, US, Michael Dinner) *Judge Reinhold, Meg Tilly, Cleavant Derricks, Fred Gwynne, John Turturro.* Reinhold, who played the young officer in *Beverly Hills Cop*, is back in uniform — but with little success — as a New York library clerk who masquerades as a police officer to win the affection of policewoman Tilly. ★★

Off Limits

(1988, 102 min, US, Christopher Crowe) *Willem Dafoe, Gregory Hines, Fred Ward, Scott Glenn, Amanda Pays.* Senseless actioner with Dafoe and Hines as two military policemen looking for a murderer in 1968 Saigon. ★ VHS: $14.99

Off the Menu: The Last Days of Chasen's

(1998, 90 min, US, Shari Springer Berman & Robert Pulcini) A strange picture emerges from *Off the Menu: The Last Days of Chasen's*. At once, it's an oddly affectionate look at this classically styled resto, right in the heart of Tinseltown. We're all supposed to get rather teary-eyed (and we do) over the fact that this joint is closing. *Off the Menu* becomes a strange contradiction in its own right; on the one hand, it's a loving ode to the people who made this famous resto work. On the other, it's a stinging testimony to the rather sleazy side of Hollywood. After all, it was only after this resto announced that it was going to fold that business suddenly picked up. Did Hollywood types feel genuine sentiment or simply sense an opportunity for a solid photo op? You be the judge. Chasen's was *the* place to be seen through Hollywood's golden years, but all good things must come to an end. An extensive roster of celebrities reminisce about not just the loss of this famous restaurant, but the loss of Hollywood's past glory. ★★★ VHS: $24.99

Office Killer

(1998, 83 min, US, Cindy Sherman) *Carol Kane, Molly Ringwald, Jeanne Tripplehorn, Michael Imperioli.* Photographer Sherman made her artistic reputation with her "Untitled Film Stills" series. With her directorial debut, however, Sherman proves that while she has an eye for composition, she has no clue about *moving* pictures. *Office Killer* is a static film that is unfunny as a black comedy and suspenseless as a thriller. The story line involves the meek Doreen Douglass (Kane) offing her coworkers and then storing the bodies in her basement. While there is some unpleasant gore, the film's cheesy effects are a greater drawback. ★½ VHS: $14.99

Office Space

Office Space

(1999, 90 min, US, Mike Judge) *Ron Livingston, Jennifer Aniston, Stephen Root, Gary Cole. Beavis and Butt-head* creator Judge brings his "Milton" shorts to life in this often very funny comedy that goes further than Dilbert in lampooning the idiocy of office work. Livingston is the charmingly bland hero, who undergoes a funky hypnosis and begins rebelling against his corporation; somehow this is interpreted as brilliance and he ascends the ranks of his company. Root steals the show as Milton, the nebbish supporting character who can't fend for himself; Cole is just right as the monotoned supervisor. Unfortunately, the film bogs down in a lame romantic subplot involving Aniston, but before it gets there, *Office Space* provides many a laugh for anyone who's ever encountered a copying machine. ★★★ VHS: $9.99; DVD: $24.99

An Officer and a Gentleman

(1982, 126 min, US, Taylor Hackford) *Richard Gere, Debra Winger, Lou Gossett, Jr., David Keith, Lisa Blount, Robert Loggia, David Caruso.* Three outstanding performances by Gere, Winger and Gossett highlight this compelling romantic drama about a naval officer who begins an affair with a girl from the wrong side of the tracks. Gossett won an Oscar for his tough-as-nails performance as Gere's drill instructor. ★★★ VHS: $9.99; DVD: $29.99

The Official Story

(1985, 112 min, Argentina, Luis Puenzo) *Norma Aleandro, Hector Alterio.* 1985's Academy Award winner for Best Foreign Film is a politically explosive and emotionally draining drama set in the tumultuous period after the Falkland's debacle. Aleandro is mesmerizing as a comfortably middle-class woman who is determined to find out the truth about "los desaparecidos," the many people who disappeared during the military dictatorship. (Spanish with English subtitles) ★★★★ VHS: $14.99; DVD: $19.99

Oh Dad, Poor Dad, Mama's Hung You in the Closet and I'm Feeling So Sad

(1966, 86 min, US, Richard Quine) *Rosalind Russell, Robert Morse, Barbara Harris, Jonathan Winters, Hugh Griffith.* Zany black comedy about a "typical" American family: a domineering mother, two man-eating piranhas, several Venus flytraps, a weirdo baby-faced son, a lecherous baby sitter, and a father who happens to be a stuffed corpse hanging in the closet. ★★½ VHS: $49.99

Oh, God!

(1977, 98 min, US, Carl Reiner) *George Burns, John Denver, Teri Garr.* Pleasant family comedy with Burns as The Almighty visiting Earth and summoning supermarket manager Denver to spread His word. (Followed by two sequels) ★★½ VHS: $14.99

Oklahoma!

(1955, 145 min, US, Fred Zinnemann) *Gordon Macrae, Shirley Jones, Rod Steiger, Charlotte Greenwood, Gloria Graham, Eddie Albert.* Sprawling though unremarkable film version of the landmark Rodgers and Hammerstein Broadway musical. MacRae and Jones are the youthful lovers; their romance interrupted by hired hand Steiger. A great score complements the immortal Agnes de Mille dance sequences. Good supporting cast includes the always-fine Greenwood and Graham as Ado Annie. (Letterboxed VHS available for $19.99) ★★★ VHS: $14.99; DVD: $24.99

Okoge

(1992, 120 min, Japan, Takehiro Nakajima) *Misa Shimizu, Takehiro Murata, Takeo Nakahara.* Japan's teeming if still underground gay life is explored and celebrated in this pleasant story of the relationship between two gay lovers and the effervescent woman who befriends them. The story revolves around Goh, a young, self-employed man, and Tochi, an older married corporate worker. Their inability to find a suitable location for their lovemaking is solved by Sayoko, a naïve young woman who inexplica-bly finds herself drawn to gay men. She offers her small apartment as a convenient love-pad. Funny but deceptively lighthearted, the film addresses the serious theme of homophobia which is pervading Japan. A note on the title: *Okama* is Japanese for a rice pot and a slang insult against gays; *Okoge* is the rice that sticks to the bottom of a pot and is Japanese slang for "fag hag." (Japanese with English subtitles) ★★★ VHS: $39.99

Old Boyfriends

(1977, 103 min, US, Joan Tewkesbury) *Talia Shire, Richard Jordan, Keith Carradine, John Belushi, John Houseman, Buck Henry.* Shire stars in this bittersweet story of a woman who seeks out her past lovers in an attempt to learn more about herself. A mixed bag of romance and identity which is ambitious but not always successful. ★★

The Old Dark House

(1932, 72 min, US, James Whale) *Boris Karloff, Charles Laughton, Melvyn Douglas, Gloria Stuart, Raymond Massey, Ernest Thesiger, Eva Moore.* It was a dark and stormy night... Five weary travelers are stranded in the ancestral home of the Femm family. Horace Femm (Thesiger) is an athiest so frightened of God that he trembles at every thunderbolt. His sister Rebecca (Moore) taunts him and their unwanted company with sermons against the sins of the flesh. Morgan (Karloff), their mute and malevolent butler, is either their protector or prisoner, depending on his intake of gin. Whale has fashioned a sardonic comic essay on rot and decay, as intricate and delicate as a fugue. The film cunningly balances cheap thrills against metaphysical chills; Whale looks into the abyss, forces a laugh, and hides his anguish behind a witty bon mot. ★★★½ VHS: $24.99; DVD: $29.99

Old Enough

(1984, 91 min, US, Marisa Silver) *Sarah Boyd, Rainbow Harvest, Danny Aiello.* A coming-of-age drama about two New York City girls, one from Park Avenue and the other from Brooklyn, who befriend each other. A meandering look at adolescence which can't overcome — despite accurate moments of insight — its stereotypes. ★★

Old Gringo

(1989, 119 min, US, Luis Puenzo) *Jane Fonda, Gregory Peck, Jimmy Smits.* A period romance set against the backdrop of Pancho Villa's Mexican uprising in 1913. Fonda plays a spinster who travels south of the border, where she becomes involved with revolutionary Smits and writer Ambrose Bierce (played with perfection by Peck). Though the story lacks a coherent structure, it has an undeniable emotional power; and the chemistry between the three leads is palatable. Peck's soliloquy on love is a reminder of the power and excitement of great acting. ★★½ VHS: $9.99

The Old Gun

(1980, 141 min, France, Robert Enrico) *Philippe Noiret, Romy Schneider.* Winner of three César Awards, this riveting drama is set in World War II France where a Frenchman's huge estate is taken over by the Germans. The brutality of the Nazis result in his wife and child being murdered. Noiret's quiet life is forever destroyed which results in his methodical vengence against the killers. (Dubbed) ★★★

Old Ironsides

(1926, 111 min, US, James Cruze) *Wallace Beery, Esther Ralston, Boris Karloff.* Beery is as hammy as ever in this silent tale about Merchant Marines battling pirates in the early 1800s. Great action and great fun. ★★★ VHS: $29.99

The Old Maid

(1939, 95 min, US, Edmund Goulding) *Bette Davis, Miriam Hopkins, George Brent, Jane Bryan.* Davis plays to the hilt the role of an unwed mother who, after her boyfriend is killed in the Civil War, gives up her child to be raised by her cousin (Hopkins). It's an acting tour de force as Davis and Hopkins battle it out with each other over daughter Bryan. ★★★ VHS: $19.99

The Old Man and the Sea

(1958, 86 min, US, John Sturges) *Spencer Tracy, Felipe Pazos, Harry Bellaver.* Tracy delivers a remarkably moving performance as an aging fisherman struggling against Nature in this thoughtful adaptation of Ernest Hemingway's novel. (Remade in 1990) ★★★ VHS: $19.99; DVD: $19.99

Old Yeller

(1957, 83 min, US, Robert Stevenson) *Tommy Kirk, Fess Parker, Dorothy McGuire.* Life on a Texas farm, circa 1859, highlights this popular Disney tale of a boy and his dog, based on Fred Gipson's well-liked novel. ★★★ VHS: $19.99

The Oldest Profession

(1967, 97 min, France/West Germany/Italy, Various) *Jeanne Moreau, Raquel Welch, Anna Karina, Jean-Claude Brialy.* Six chronological stories, all directed and starring different artists, humorously probe the history of prostitution from prehistoric times to the present and beyond. The final segment, "Anticipation," by Jean-Luc Godard, is an especially good short film that speculates on

Los Olvidados

aliens from outer space and their Parisian sex habits. ★★½

Oleanna

(1994, 101 min, US, David Mamet) *William H. Macy, Deborah Eisenstadt.* Granted, a play by Mamet about sexual harassment is kind of like letting the fox guard the chickens, but that's not what makes this examination of campus politics a failure. The problem is more dramatic in nature. Mamet's patented dialogue, brash and stacatto to the extreme, is usually what makes his plays so dynamic, but in this two-actor setting, it falls flat, ultimately rendering his characters unbelievable. The first act finds John (Macy), an arrogant, self-serving college professor who is up for tenure, locking horns with Carol (Eisenstadt), a student who wants to know why she has failed his class. His career is put in peril in act two when she submits a scathing letter to the tenure review board full of accusations of impropriety. ★½ VHS: $14.99

Oliver!

(1968, 153 min, GB, Carol Reed) *Ron Moody, Mark Lester, Oliver Reed, Jack Wild, Shanni Wallis.* This elaborate musical rendition of the Charles Dickens tale about a young boy swept into a gang of thieves is as close to flawless as a movie can get. Its frolicking score, splendid recreation of 1830s London and an unforgettable performance by Moody as the scurrilous Fagan helped win it five Oscars, including Best Picture and Best Director. A trifle long, the film nonetheless holds the attention of even young viewers throughout. ★★★★ VHS: $14.99; DVD: $24.99

Oliver & Company

(1988, 72 min, US, George Scribner) *Voices of Bette Midler, Joey Lawrence, Billy Joel, Roscoe Lee Browne, Robert Loggia, Dom DeLuise.* Loosely based on Dickens' "Oliver Twist," Disney's enjoyable animated version features Oliver as a tabby kitten lost in New York City. He is befriended by a gang of dogs engaged in working scams on behalf of Einstein, their bumbling human owner who is indebted to a villainous loan shark. Enlivened by the music of Billy Joel (who voices Dodger), the film benefits from a good ensemble, though Midler steals the show as the snooty French poodle Georgette. ★★★

Oliver Twist

(1948, 116 min, GB, David Lean) *Alec Guinness, Anthony Newley, Robert Newton, Francis L. Sullivan, Kay Walsh.* This brilliant adaptation of Charles Dickens' classic novel stands as the finest cinematic treatment of all the screen versions to tell Dickens' story of a young orphan's adventures in 18th-century London. Guinness gives a captivating performance as Fagin; and there's a remarkable supporting cast, including a young Newley as the Artful Dodger. ★★★★ VHS: $14.99; DVD: $39.99

Olivier, Olivier

(1991, 109 min, France, Agnieszka Holland) *François Cluzet, Brigitte Rouan, Jean-François Stevenin.* Olivier, a precocious nine-year-old coddled by his doting mother, one day mysteriously disappears without a trace. His family is torn apart by the loss, but are reunited six years

later when a 15-year-old homosexual prostitute claims to be their long-lost son. The family, especially the mother, desperately wants to believe that this savvy teen is indeed the innocent of years past. As in the similarly themed *Return of Martin Guerre*, doubts soon emerge as to the true identity of the youth. This engrossing drama creates suspense as to why he disappeared, and tenderly unfolds a tale of a boy learning about love and trust. (French with English subtitles) ★★★ VHS: $19.99

Los Olvidados
(The Young and the Damned)

(1950, 88 min, Mexico, Luis Buñuel) *Alfonso Mejias, Roberto Cobo.* Buñuel's social protest film is set in a Mexico populated by juvenile delinquents, beggers, cripples and other physically and/or socially deformed characters. The story centers around a particular boy as he learns the skills of survival within an oppressive society. (Spanish with English subtitles) ★★★★

Olympia, Pts 1 & 2

(1936, 220 min, Germany, Leni Riefenstahl) This magnificent account of the Berlin Olympic Games of 1936 transcends a typical documentary of a sporting event. Through imaginative use of editing and camera movement, as well as spectacular photography, Riefenstahl's film achieves its goal of being a Nazi propaganda film but more importantly, it is a graceful, nonpolitical look at the majestic beauty of the athletes. (German with English subtitles) ★★★★ VHS: $49.99

The Omega Code

(1999, 100 min, US, Robert Marcarelli) *Michael York, Casper Van Dien, Catherine Oxenberg, Michael Ironside.* A truly laughable experience financed by the Trinity Broadcasting Network. An obnoxious, Tony Robbins–like motivational speaker (the consistently awful Van Dien) preaches his belief in the prescience of a mathematical interpretation of The Bible, dubbed the Bible Code. As a result, he finds himself embroiled in some listless, amateur-nite espionage. An unremarkable story hook is given a by-the-numbers treatment, while the characters and dialogue wouldn't pass muster in a Sunday School pageant (well, maybe just). There's a "family values" subplot that only adds to the preaching-to-the-converted feel of this nonsense. A film only a cineaste like Pat Robertson could love. ★ VHS: $22.99; DVD: $24.99

The Omega Man

(1971, 98 min, US, Boris Sagal) *Charlton Heston, Rosalind Cash, Anthony Zerbe.* Updated version of Vincent Price's *The Last Man on Earth* (itself based on Richard Matheson's story "I Am Legend"), now with Heston as the stalwart survivor of germ warfare who takes on a band of mutants. Director Sagal gives the film a great look, and there's some exciting scenes throughout, though the languid pacing sometimes sabotages an interesting story. Heston watching *Woodstock* over and over again is so ludicrous it's camp. ★★½ VHS: $14.99

The Omen

(1976, 111 min, US, Richard Donner) *Gregory Peck, Lee Remick, Billie Whitelaw, David Warner.*

This blockbuster thriller set the trend in horror films for years to come. Peck and Remick play the newly appointed American ambassador to England and his wife, who unwittingly become the parents of the Antichrist, Damien. Whitelaw is chilling as the nanny who stops at nothing to protect her charge. Definitely not for the squeamish. (Followed by 2 sequels) ★★★ VHS: $9.99; DVD: $29.99

On a Clear Day You Can See Forever

(1970, 129 min, US, Vincente Minnelli) *Barbra Streisand, Yves Montand, Bob Newhart, Larry Blyden, Jack Nicholson.* Based on the Broadway musical, this splashy if occasionally muddled adaptation stars Streisand as a woman who learns of a past life when under hypnosis. Montand is her psychiatrist, who falls in love with her — only the woman she was, not the woman she is. Streisand gives a good performance in the "dual" role, though Montand is woefully miscast. Nicholson is Barbra's guitar-playing brother. Score by Alan Jay Lerner and Burton Lane. ★★½ VHS: $14.99

On Borrowed Time

(1939, 99 min, US, Harold S. Bucquet) *Lionel Barrymore, Cedric Hardwicke, Beulah Bondi.* This sentimental variation of *Death Takes a Holiday* is pure '30s corn, but underneath the folksy interplay there's a thoroughly intriguing fantasy at work. Death (played by Hardwicke) has just taken a married couple. And now he's set his sights on the rest of the family. But Grandpa Barrymore has a trick or two in store for the Grim Reaper when he comes to call. ★★★ VHS: $19.99

On Dangerous Ground

(1951, 82 min, US, Nicholas Ray) *Robert Ryan, Ida Lupino, Ward Bond.* Ray's second collaboration with producer John Houseman is this brilliant exposé of a tough, inner-city policeman (Ryan) who falls prey to the violence of the urban jungle. So much so, that he is sent for a cooling off period to upstate New York where the real intrigue begins when he falls in with a blind woman (Lupino) and her mentally retarded brother. Bernard Hermann's score was reportedly his favorite. ★★★½

On Deadly Ground

(1994, 100 min, US, Steven Seagal) *Steven Seagal, Michael Caine, Joan Chen.* In this pretentious and ridiculous eco-thriller, Seagal's P.C. action hero asks several questions, such as "What is the essence of a man?" and "How much wealth is enough?" He should have been inquiring how to make a movie. In his directorial debut, Seagal plays a born-again environmentalist who takes on his former boss, an evil oil magnate (Caine). But the best director Seagal and his writers can muster are one-dimensional heroes, cardboard villains, and a predictable story line. As an actor, Seagal couldn't be more wooden if he were a totem pole. ★ VHS: $9.99; DVD: $14.99

On Golden Pond

(1981, 109 min, US, Mark Rydell) *Henry Fonda, Katharine Hepburn, Jane Fonda, Dabney Coleman, Doug McKeon.* Both Kate and Henry received Oscars for their affecting, expansive performances in this thoughtful, sentimental comedy-drama. Fonda stars as Norman Thayer, an

80-year-old retired teacher preoccupied with death, whose birthday celebration only triggers his fear of old age and dying. Hepburn is Ethel, Norman's devoted wife, who dutifully contends with her husband's cantankerous moods and encompassing anxiety. Jane, in her only film appearance with her father, plays the couple's alienated daughter vying for her father's affection. (Letterboxed VHS available for $14.99) ★★★ VHS: $9.99; DVD: $19.99

On Her Majesty's Secret Service

(1969, 140 min, GB, Peter Hunt) *George Lazenby, Diana Rigg, Telly Savalas.* Despite the fact that Lazenby was an unimpressive and very temporary, James Bond, incredible action and location photography make this one of the finest and most exciting entries in the series. The usual mayhem is given an unusual twist as Bond marries a Spanish contessa (Rigg). (Sequel: *Diamonds Are Forever*) ★★★ VHS: $14.99; DVD: $34.99

On Moonlight Bay

(1951, 95 min, US, Roy Del Ruth) *Doris Day, Gordon MacRea, Leon Ames, Rosemary de Camp, Mary Wickes.* Comparisons to *Meet Me in St. Louis* are inevitable as this bright, wholesome musical has the same folksy (okay, corny if you must) charm as that Judy Garland classic. It also has Ames as a father whose decision to move has disrupted his loving family. Day plays a tomboy who acquires feminine ways when she meets new neighbor MacRea. Their course of true love is a rocky one, but it is tuneful; though Doris doesn't sing much since the accent is on comedy. Wickes as a wise-cracking maid is a welcome addition to any household. It's sappy, but it's fun. ★★★ VHS: $19.99

On the Beach

(1959, 134 min, US, Stanley Kramer) *Gregory Peck, Ava Gardner, Fred Astaire, Anthony Perkins, Donna Anderson.* One of the first films to seriously address the issues of a nuclear apocalypse, this first-rate adaptation of Nevile Shute's novel tells the tale of an American submarine crew who find themselves in Australia awaiting the fallout with the rest of the inhabitants. (Remade in 2000) ★★★½ VHS: $9.99; DVD: $24.99

On the Town

(1949, 98 min, US, Gene Kelly & Stanley Donen) *Gene Kelly, Frank Sinatra, Jules Munchin, Vera-Ellen, Betty Garrett, Ann Miller.* A grand, energetic and immensely enjoyable adaptation of the popular Broadway musical. With a score by Leonard Bernstein and a book by Betty Comden & Adolphe Greene, directors Kelly and Donen have opened up, with location shooting, this exuberant tale about three sailors on a 24-hour pass, and of their romantic adventures in New York City. Kelly, Sinatra and Munchin are the men in uniform; and Vera-Ellen, Garrett and Miller are the women with whom they meet and fall in love. Includes "New York, New York." ★★★★ VHS: $14.99; DVD: $19.99

On the Waterfront

(1954, 108 min, US, Elia Kazan) *Marlon Brando, Rod Steiger, Lee J. Cobb, Karl Malden, Eva Marie Saint.* Brando became a legitimate contender with this textbook study of Method

acting. After he sings to the law about dockside corruption, the union mob comes down hard on him. Cobb is the waterfront godfather, Malden is the street-smart priest, Steiger is Brando's spineless brother and Saint is the troubled girlfriend. A rare combination of a superlative ensemble, exact direction, topical story line and a brilliantly structured screenplay played out in a singular vision. ★★★★ VHS: $19.99

On Top of the Whale

(1982, 93 min, The Netherlands, Râul Ruiz) Chilean expatriate Ruiz's unusual film is a demanding, complex and imaginatively photographed film, both invigorating and a challenging entertainment. The bare bones plot outline is as follows: a Dutch anthropologist and his girlfriend meet up with Narcisso, an eccentric millionaire who claims to have the last survivors of a lost Indian tribe in his summer home in Patagonia. The three, along with the woman's daughter, travel to this bleak country house and there the anthropologist attempts to understand the Indians' bizarre language, a language consisting of one word, spoken with different inflections. With all of the characters arbitrarily switching from English, French, Spanish, German, Dutch and the cryptic Indian dialect, Ruiz has made an amusing exercise on the mysteries of language and communication. ★★★ VHS: $59.99

On Valentine's Day

(1986, 105 min, US, Ken Harrison) *Hallie Foote, Michael Higgins, Steven Hill, Matthew Broderick.* Writer Horton Foote's satisfactory prequel to *1918*. Set in a small texas town one year earlier, the film traces the emotional struggle and reconciliation of young Elizabeth (Foote), disowned by her family for marrying against their wishes. Broderick reprises his role as Elizabeth's brother. ★★½ VHS: $14.99

Once a Thief

(1991, 90 min, Hong Kong, John Woo) *Chow Yun Fat, Leslie Cheung, Cherie Chung.* Fans of Woo won't want to miss this over-the-top comedy about a trio of Chinese art thieves. The action follows Fat, Cheung and Chung as sophisticated larcenists of European art treasures. Through flashbacks, we learn that the three were orphans together, raised under the watchful eye of two surrogate father figures: one a ruthless crime lord and the other a caring cop. The action explodes about halfway through when Chow and Cheung botch a job and wind up in a dizzyingly exciting chase scene, ultimately leading them back to Hong Kong where Woo turns to his patented knack for turning gut-wrenchingly violent action sequences into side-splitting laugh fests. (Cantonese with English subtitles) ★★★½ VHS: $9.99

Once Around

(1991, 115 min, US, Lasse Hallström) *Richard Dreyfuss, Holly Hunter, Danny Aiello, Gena Rowlands, Laura San Giacomo.* From the director of *My Life as a Dog* comes this endearing and offbeat romantic comedy, with Dreyfuss and Hunter reteaming after *Always* as mismatched lovers who marry and settle down. Aiello and Rowlands play Hunter's exasperated parents, at odds with their decidedly differ-

Once Upon a Time in America

ent, and same-age, son-in-law. Good performances help compensate occasional lapses in the script. ★★½

Once Bitten

(1985, 93 min, US, Howard Storm) *Lauren Hutton, Jim Carrey, Cleavon Little.* Atrocious comedy with vampire Hutton on the lookout for a virgin in present-day Los Angeles — having trouble finding one. ★ VHS: $9.99

Once Upon a Honeymoon

(1942, 116 min, US, Leo McCarey) *Cary Grant, Ginger Rogers, Walter Slezak.* Ex-burlesque queen Rogers marries Nazi spy Slezak — only she's not aware of his true identity. However, reporter Grant is, and he pursues them on their honeymoon to expose the German agent and rescue Rogers from possible assassination. A curious mix of adventure, drama and comedy from director McCarey. ★★½ VHS: $19.99

Once Upon a Time in America

(1984, 226 min, US, Sergio Leone) *Robert De Niro, James Woods, Elizabeth McGovern, Treat Williams, Tuesday Weld.* Leone's epic is a fascinating analysis of unyielding ambition, moral decay and the predatory nature of the past. Through an opium-induced haze, De Niro traces the events of a lifetime led on the wrong side of the law. ★★★½ VHS: $29.99

Once Upon a Time in the West

(1969, 165 min, Italy, Sergio Leone) *Charles Bronson, Henry Fonda, Claudia Cardinali, Jason Robards, Jack Elam, Woody Strode, Keenan Wynn.* Expanding upon the plot line of *Johnny Guitar*, Leone and story collaborators Dario Argento and Bernardo Bertolucci produce a polemic that is stunning in its grandeur, funny in its cynical sense of humor — using the horse opera as a metaphor for all that is wrong with the American capitalist system. Fonda had one of his greatest roles as one of the most cold-blooded killers in westerns ("I never trust a man who wears a belt with suspenders"). Bronson is in fine form as "The Man with the Harmonica" out for revenge. Another brilliant score by Ennio Morricone. ★★★★ VHS: $29.99

Once Upon a Time... When We Were Colored

(1996, 112 min, US, Tim Reid) *Al Freeman, Jr., Phylicia Rashad, Leon, Paula Kelly, Richard Roundtree, Salli Richardson, Polly Bergen, Bernie Casey, Isaac Hayes, Taj Mahal.* First-time director Reid has crafted an affectionate and richly textured portrait of life in a black community in 1940s Mississippi. At a time when the dominate white society provided no legal or moral recourse for prejudice and brutality, African-Americans bonded to nurture and protect themselves in an environment which institutionalized restrictions dictated by hate and fear. The psychological ramifications of this poisonous atmosphere are poignantly evoked by some trenchant performances from the able ensemble of actors. Seen through the eyes of a boy on the cusp of manhood, the film is remarkable in its ability to convey the internal reality of its protagonists, to enable the viewer to see these people as they see themselves and the world around them. This warmly told story of strength and solidarity captures the special intonations of a particular time and place, with compassionate understanding of the people who inhabited it. ★★★½ VHS: $14.99; DVD: $24.99

Once Were Warriors

(1995, 102 min, New Zealand, Lee Tamahori) *Rena Owen, Temuera Morrison, Mamaengaroa Kerr-Bell.* At once searingly brutal and lyrically poetic, *Once Were Warriors* is an unflinching examination of one exceptionally strong woman's struggle to keep her family whole while battling a husband mired in drink and violence. In an unforgiving urban wasteland — where abandoned children live in rusted-out, abandoned cars, the state puts children into institutions, and women expect the brutality they invariably receive — the young still attempt to forge identities with purpose and dignity, despite all restrictions of class, race and economics. The performances are so vital and authentic that the film seems more documentary than drama. Director Tamahori has crafted a potent and volatile exploration of one family's survival in an environment devoid of hope or expectation — as alien as Maori tattooing and as familiar as the exhaust fumes outside your window. ★★★★ VHS: $19.99

One Crazy Summer

(1986, 94 min, US, Savage Steve Holland) *John Cusack, Demi Moore, Bobcat Goldthwait, Curtis Armstrong.* Though not as successful as his hilarious *Better Off Dead*, this crazy comedy is nonetheless an entertaining if uneven spoof with Cusack as a teenager spending summer vacation in Nantucket — surrounded by a gang of wackos. ★★½ VHS: $9.99

One Day in September

(1999, 94 min, US, Kevin MacDonald) *Narrated by: Michael Douglas.* The compelling *One Day in September* covers the '72 Munich Olympics' terrorist assault in a detailed, nearly hour-by-hour manner: eight armed Palestinians hold eleven Israeli athletes and coaches hostage until their demands are met. Though there are too many filler montages, and too little time spent is on the Palestinians' motivations, *September* is a gripping experience. It offers a chance to listen to the only surviving terrorist speak for the very first time about his involvement, and details the criminal bumbling of the German authorities. Not quite as powerful as *4 Little Girls*, the film it beat at the Oscars, *September* is potent documentary filmmaking. ★★★ VHS: $102.99; DVD: $29.99

One Day in the Life of Ivan Denisovich

(1971, 100 min, GB, Caspar Wrede) *Tom Courtenay, Alfred Burke.* An earnest, literate adaptation of Alexander Solzhenitsyn's epic novel about life in a Siberian labor camp during the early 1950s. Though a difficult book to translate to film, director Wrede has crafted a mesmerizing look at the hardships of a prisoner serving the last years of a ten-year sentence. In the title role, Courtenay is nothing short of brilliant. Beautiful cinematography by Sven Nykvist. ★★★½

187

(1997, 119 min, US, Kevin Reynolds) *Samuel L. Jackson, Kelly Rowan, John Heard, Clifton Collins, Jr., Tony Plana.* Few films about teachers have been as downbeat and hopeless as *187*, a determined, single-minded drama which casts a sad light on lower-class, urban education. Written by Scott Yagemann, a L.A. teacher for seven years, *187* (which is the police code for murder) follows Trevor Garfield (Jackson), a committed science teacher who moves to Los Angeles. He is not greeted by smiling faces here; there is no to sir with love. This is a group of students long forgotten by the system and who have given up on themselves. Jackson gives a tremendous portrayal of a man both in love with and fearful of his job, a good teacher possibly pushed too far. This is difficult medicine to digest, and the film's ending may take too many liberties, but the loss of passion and innocence is movingly told. ★★★ VHS: $9.99; DVD: $14.99

One-Eyed Jacks

(1961, 141 min, US, Marlon Brando) *Marlon Brando, Karl Malden, Slim Pickens, Pina Pellicer, Ben Johnson.* Brando's only directorial effort pits him as an outlaw against sheriff Malden in a psychological tug-of-war. An unusual, intriguing western morality tale. ★★★ VHS: $9.99; DVD: $29.99

One False Move

One False Move

(1992, 105 min, US, Carl Franklin) *Bill Paxton, Billy Bob Thornton, Cynda Williams, Michael Beach.* This film's opening 10 minutes are so violently disturbing that it's enough to make one stop viewing it. However, stick with this one for *One False Move* is an intense, original thriller. The story follows a gang of three ruthless Los Angeles drug dealers who, having raided their rivals, make off with a bag full of cash and blow, and hit the road for Arkansas in search of a place to lie low. Waiting at the other end are Dale "Hurricane" Dixon (Paxton), the country "Bumpkin" local sheriff in Star City, Ark., and a couple of L.A. cops who have reason to believe the bad guys are headed their way. While the tension mounts, the filmmakers use the situation to deftly probe the underbelly of American life, from racial tensions to the inherent conflict between rural and urban values. Cowritten by Thornton. ★★★½ VHS: $14.99; DVD: $27.99

One Fine Day

(1996, 100 min, US, Michael Hoffman) *Michelle Pfeiffer, George Clooney, Mae Whitman, Alex D. Linz, Charles Durning, Holland Taylor, Ellen Greene.* Though they exude great charm and have a wonderful chemistry between them, Pfeiffer and Clooney just aren't able to give an added boost to this convoluted romantic comedy which is short on both romance and comedy. They play divorced parents who come together when their children miss the class trip. Of course, they're antagonistic in the beginning, but soon they succumb to each other's magnetism. This losing battle-of-the-sexes does on occasion please, but it's due more to Clooney and Pfeiffer's rapport than any screenplay manipulation. They'd probably be better matched the next time Catwoman and Batman meet. ★★ VHS: $14.99; DVD: $24.99

One Flew Over the Cuckoo's Nest

(1975, 133 min, US, Milos Forman) *Jack Nicholson, Louise Fletcher, Brad Dourif, Will Simpson, William Redfield, Danny DeVito, Christopher Lloyd, Scatman Crothers.* Nicholson gives a triumphant performance as the dangerously sane Randall P. McMurphy, the feisty ringleader of an asylum's inmates. Forman adapts Ken Kesey's eloquent novel with boundless zeal and multi-award-winning results. Fletcher won an Oscar (as did

Nicholson) for her unforgettably adversarial head nurse whose unwavering strictness leads to defiance and tragedy. Winner of 5 Academy Awards, including Best Picture. ★★★★ VHS: $14.99; DVD: $19.99

One from the Heart

(1982, 100 min, US, Francis Ford Coppola) *Frederic Forrest, Teri Garr, Raul Julia, Nastassja Kinski.* Coppola's celebrated bomb (costing some $25 million) stars Forrest and Garr as lovers who split after five years. They find new lovers, only to realize they were really meant for each other. Nothing more than a stylized, full-length music video which lacks any dramatic structure. Music by Tom Waits. ★★

One Good Cop

(1991, 114 min, US, Heywood Gould) *Michael Keaton, Rene Russo, Anthony LaPaglia, Kevin Conway, Rachel Ticotin.* Keaton gives a competent performance in a relatively lackluster treatment of the good-cop-loses-partner-and-has-a-crisis-of-faith formula. The occasional sparks generated by the cast can't quite compensate for the flat, predictable script and mundane direction. ★★

101 Dalmatians

(1961, 80 min, US, Wolfgang Reitherman, H.S. Luske & Clyde Geronimi) An enchanting Disney classic, this animated tale follows the adventures of a faithful dalmatian, Pongo, and his mate as they attempt to stop one of Disney's best villains, Cruella DeVil, from kidnapping a truckload of pups and turning them into fur coats. The animation is splendid, and the comical story is one of Disney's best. (Remade in 1996) ★★★★

101 Dalmatians

(1996, 103 min, US, Stephen Herek) *Glenn Close, Jeff Daniels, Joely Richardson, Joan Plowright, Hugh Laurie.* The names are the same and so essentially is the story. But wait! The lively animated characters, mean, colorful villainess and cuddly spotted canines have been replaced by real people. So who can halt the suits at Disney for taking this golden marketing opportunity by the tail and racing with it. There are some charming moments here, particularly in the film's first hour. Close gives a dazzling grand-old-dame turn as flamboyantly dressed "uber-bitch" Cruella. But Disney handed the writing and producing bone to John Hughes. Blame him for the insipid slapstick humor that eventually turns this puppy into *Dog Home Alone*. (Sequel: *102 Dalmatians*) ★★

102 Dalmatians

(2000, 100 min, US, Kevin Lima) *Glenn Close, Gérard Depardieu, Alice Evans, Ioan Gruffudd, Eric Idle.* In this cartoonish sequel to the 1996 live-action remake of the beloved 1961 animated film, Cruella DeVil is released from prison presumedly reformed. However, her old self reappears and she's back on her quest for a new mink coat. Close is in great form, once again (it's amazing the kind of indignities she suffers), and the costumes are smashing, but this dog-eared franchise is getting doggone tired already. It's overplayed, over-the-hill, and, well, we're just over it. ★★ VHS: $24.99; DVD: $29.99

One Magic Christmas

(1985, 100 min, US, Phillip Borsos) *Mary Steenburgen, Harry Dean Stanton, Arthur Hill.* This poignant family fantasy draws much of its inspiration from both *It's a Wonderful Life* and *A Christmas Carol*. Steenburgen stars as a housewife whose lost Christmas spirit is found with the help of an unlikely guardian angel, played by Stanton. (Letterboxed) ★★★ VHS: $14.99

One Million Years B.C.

(1966, 100 min, GB, Don Chaffey) *Raquel Welch, John Richardson.* Hammer Films made this campy remake of the 1939 Hal Roach adventure with Welch in her star-making role of scantily clad cavewoman fighting off man and beast. Special effects by Ray Harryhausen are a plus, as is Welch. ★★½ VHS: $9.99

One Night of Love

(1934, 80 min, US, Victor Schertzinger) *Grace Moore, Tullio Carminati.* A captivating musical with Moore in a wonderful performance as an American opera singer who studies and falls in love with Italian maestro Carminati. ★★★ VHS: $19.99

One Night Stand

(1997, 104 min, US, Mike Figgis) *Wesley Snipes, Nastassja Kinski, Kyle MacLachlan, Robert Downey, Jr., Ming Na-Wen.* In this awkwardly constructed, unsatisfying but fitfully interesting infidelity drama, Snipes plays a happily married director who has a one night stand with yummy Kinski. The first half sets up the fling, and shows its effects on Snipes' personal and professional life. The film takes a radical right turn when Snipes visits his best friend from college (Downey) who is dying of AIDS, and then picks up the adultery story line for a truly goofy wrap-up. The ending, while silly and unbelievable, actually does mirror events in original screenwriter Joe Eszterhas' personal life. ★★ VHS: $19.99; DVD: $24.99

One Sings, the Other Doesn't

(1977, 90 min, France, Agnès Varda) *Therese Leotard, Valerie Mairesse.* Varda's feminist triumph follows the friendship and developing self-fulfillment of two young women in Paris from 1962 to 1976. Pauline is a free-spirited singer while Susanne becomes an organizer in a family planning clinic and both succeed through the love and support of each other. This warm and thoughtful film blends fact, fic-

101 Dalmatians

tion and feeling to sing its song in praise of women. (French with English subtitles) ★★★

One Touch of Venus

(1948, 81 min, US, William A. Seiter) *Ava Gardner, Robert Walker, Eve Arden.* Long before *Mannequin* came this charming musical comedy with Gardner as a department store statue who magically comes to life and is romanced by window dresser Walker. ★★★ VHS: $9.99

One Trick Pony

(1980, 98 min, US, Robert M. Young) *Paul Simon, Blair Brown, Rip Torn, Joan Hackett, Lou Reed.* A bittersweet, unfulfilled story of an aging rock star trying to salvage his marriage and his flagging career. Simon also wrote the script. ★★ VHS: $14.99

One True Thing

(1998, 128 min, US, Carl Franklin) *Meryl Streep, Renee Zellweger, William Hurt, Tom Everett Scott, Lauren Graham.* The poignant relationship between mother and daughter is at the heart of this articulate, compelling drama which tenderly examines the tenuous threads of familial ties and the emotions and deeds which bind them. The extraordinary Streep is Kate, a housewife and mother who is newly diagnosed with cancer. Her daughter Ellen (Zellweger), a promising writer in New York, reluctantly returns to the small town of her youth to look after her mother. The story concentrates on the family unit, but its strength lies in the bond between Kate and Ellen. Streep is miraculous in giving multilayered shadings to Kate, a woman whose talents and loves were hidden to her daughter. Zellweger more than holds her own with Streep, making Ellen more than just an inconvenienced daughter. Sensitive direction from Franklin. ★★★ VHS: $9.99; DVD: $26.99

One, Two, Three

(1961, 110 min, US, Billy Wilder) *James Cagney, Arlene Francis, Horst Buchholz, Pamela Tiffin.* A hilarious, lightning-paced (this may be the fastest comedy since Howard Hawks' *His Girl Friday*) political farce from director Wilder, made during the heyday of the Cold War. Cagney — who would not make another film for 20 years — is in top form as the harried Coca-Cola executive stationed in West Berlin who must contend with card-carrying Commies, ex-Nazis and Southern belles when the boss' daughter secretly marries a young Communist. All this and Pepsi-Cola, too. ★★★★

One Wild Moment

(1977, 88 min, France, Claude Berri) *Victor Lanoux, Jean-Pierre Marielle.* An engaging French farce that follows the adventures of a recently divorced 44-year-old man who goes on vacation in the hope of having an affair with some beautiful young girl. His fantasy comes true, but he then realizes that the young beauty that seduced him is the daughter of his best friend. The inspiration for the American comedy *Blame It on Rio.* (French with English subtitles) ★★½

One Woman or Two

(1986, 97 min, France, Daniel Vigne) *Gérard Depardieu, Sigourney Weaver, Ruth Westheimer.* A curious international cast of team in this silly, occasionally funny remake of the classic

Bringing Up Baby. Depardieu plays a foggy paleontologist who finds what he thinks to be the fossilized remains of the first Frenchwoman. Weaver is the opportunistic ad exec who wants to market the discovery in a perfume advertising campaign. And if this wasn't enough, Dr. Ruth plays an American philanthropist; well, maybe she should stick to just giving out sexual advice. (French with English subtitles) ★★

Onibaba

(1965, 103 min, Japan, Kaneto Shindo) *Nobuko Otowa, Yitsuko Yoshimura.* This exotic and macabre story is set in medieval Japan, a land ravaged by continual upheavals and bloody battles between powerful warlords and where suffering peasants in the pillaged villages grow more and more desperate in the struggle to survive. An elderly woman and her son's wife eke out their existence by searching for wounded soldiers, killing them — if necessary — and stripping them of their armour which they exchange for food. When a friend returns from the war with news of her son's death, the old lady becomes suspicious, both of the returning soldier and of her daughter-in-law — neither of whom seem in the least upset by his untimely demise. When the two begin a passionate affair, the old lady calls upon the demons and spirits to help her punish her daughter-in-law. *Onibaba* is a disturbing tale of deceit and survival. (Letterboxed) (Japanese with English subtitles) ★★★½ VHS: $29.99

The Onion Field

(1979, 122 min, US, Harold Becker) *James Woods, John Savage, Ted Danson, Franklyn Seales, Ronny Cox.* Powerful film version of Joseph Wambaugh's fact-based novel about the killing of a policeman and his partner's eventual breakdown. Woods' electrifying performance as the psychopathic hood brought him international acclaim. ★★★ VHS: $14.99

Only Angels Have Wings

(1939, 121 min, US, Howard Hawks) *Cary Grant, Jean Arthur, Thomas Mitchell, Rita Hayworth, Richard Barthelmess.* Top-flight adventure with pilot Grant running a small airline in the South American jungle, resisting the considerable charms of the ever-charming Arthur. Good support from Mitchell and a young Hayworth; solid direction from Hawks. ★★★½ VHS: $19.99; DVD: $29.99

Only One Night

(1939, 90 min, Sweden, Gustaf Molander) *Ingrid Bergman.* This intense melodrama stars Bergman as a repressed young woman, who, in order to please her father, becomes involved with a rich, philandering older man. (Swedish with English subtitles) ★★½ VHS: $19.99

Only the Lonely

(1991, 102 min, US, Chris Columbus) *John Candy, Ally Sheedy, Maureen O'Hara, Anthony Quinn, James Belushi, Milo O'Shea.* Candy gives possibly his best performance in this low-keyed comedy-drama. Effectively underplaying his part, he stars as a thirtysomething, single Chicago cop, still living at home with his mother, who falls in love with Sheedy: only problem is he just can't break away from mom. In her first screen appearance in 20 years, O'Hara returns as Candy's feisty mother. Much credit

Onibaba

goes to O'Hara for her solid portrayal of the basically unlikable, prejudiced and outspoken Rose; she creates a three-dimensional, totally complex woman. ★★½

Only Two Can Play

(1962, 106 min, GB, Sidney Gilliat) *Peter Sellers, Mai Zetterling, Richard Attenborough, Virginia Maskell.* This highly entertaining sex comedy is a wonderful example of early '60s British cinema. Sellers stars as a Welsh librarian who has soured on married life and spends his days dreaming of naughty affairs with other women. When he gets his wish in the form of a vivacious socialite, Zetterling, he finds it might be more than he can handle. Both Sellers and Zetterling deliver wonderful performances. ★★★ VHS: $69.99

Only When I Laugh

(1981, 120 min, US, Glenn Jordan) *Marsha Mason, Kristy McNichol, James Coco, Joan Hackett.* Neil Simon's screenplay, based on his play "The Gingerbread Lady," rates as one of his best and most underrated. Mason excels in this serio-comic gem as an alcoholic actress, just released from a sanitarium, who tries to stay off the bottle. McNichol is her teenage daughter; and Coco and Hackett both give outstanding performances in support as, respectively, a struggling gay actor and a mentally unstable socialite. ★★★½ VHS: $19.99

Only You

(1994, 108 min, US, Norman Jewison) *Marisa Tomei, Robert Downey, Jr., Bonnie Hunt, Joaquim DeAlmeida, Fisher Stevens, Billy Zane.* A young woman (Tomei) who, ten days before her wedding, takes off for Italy to find the man who she thinks is her ultimate destiny (when she was 11 an Ouija board predicted her future mate). Once abroad, she engages in a series of misadventures searching for Mr. Right, while roguish American Downey pursues her under false pretenses. Though Tomei can occasionally step on the line between endearing and cloying, Downey has a sparkling charm and ease. Cynics may wonder if Tomei would really have such an extensive ready-to-travel wardrobe in her meager closet; others will just bask in the film's witty dialogue and warm Italian sunshine. ★★★ VHS: $9.99

Open City

(1946, 105 min, Italy, Roberto Rossellini) *Anna Magnani, Aldo Fabrizi.* Rossellini's classic, which marked the beginning of Italian Neorealism, is about the underground movement operating in Rome during the Nazi occupation. The brilliant performance by Magnani brought her international acclaim. Coscripted by Federico Fellini. (Italian with English subtitles) (aka: *Rome, Open City*) ★★★★ VHS: $24.99; DVD: $29.99

Open Doors

(1990, 109 min, Italy, Gianni Amelio) *Gian Marie Volonte, Ennio Fantastichini.* Exactingly paced, this psychological drama on the nature of justice is a thoughtful film which is quite similar in theme to Bertrand Tavernier's *The Judge and the Assassin.* Set in 1937, the film begins with a man going to a government office and calmly killing his former boss, his seemingly supportive successor, and later, raping and killing his wife. He is arrested, says little, shows no regret and simply awaits his punishment. One of the judges assigned to the case, an older, wealthy patrician, becomes intrigued by the man and, risking his reputation and against the wishes of the defendant, tries to find out what caused the man to resort to such violence. The title refers to the Fascist promise that with their harsh penal code, people would be able to sleep with their doors open. (Italian with English subtitles) ★★★ VHS: $19.99

Open Your Eyes (Abre los Ojos)

(1997, 117 min, Spain, Alejandro Amenábar) *Eduardo Noriega, Penélope Cruz, Chete Lera, Fele Martínez.* A hypnotic thriller, both sexy and beautifully filmed, *Open Your Eyes* takes a European approach to the idea of virtual reality. Carlos (Noriega) has a problem: he has turned up in a psychiatric hospital wanted for murder after one of his girlfriends tried to kill him. Does Sofia (the luscious Cruz), the woman he may truly love, hold the answer? Director Amenabar keeps the audience guessing as the plots flash back, forward, and eventually intertwine before the satisfying ending. Noriega is terrific in the main role, a smug ladies' man who discovers the unexpected truth while Cruz smolders as the femme fatale. The film's stylish visuals are dazzling, though it falls prey to a few too many plot twists. (Spanish with English subtitles) ★★★ VHS: $14.99

Opening Night

(1977, 144 min, US, John Cassavetes) *Gena Rowlands, John Cassavetes, Ben Gazzara, Joan Blondell.* Complex, emotional, disquieting and at times exasperating, *Opening Night* is a none-too-subtle but riveting drama of the midlife crisis of an aging actress (Rowlands) as she works in a play about a woman quite like herself. As the star, Rowlands is a talented but high-strung alcoholic who teeters on the verge of a nervous breakdown while costar and ex Cassavetes, harried director Gazzara and sympathetic but tough playwright Blondell helplessly watch. The theatre world and its inevitable tantrums and backstage theatrics provide an ideal location for Cassavetes' exploration of a husband and family-less woman facing middle age in a profession that idolizes youth and discards the "old." The acting is superb, from Rowlands' intense emoting to Gazzara's subtle nuances and taut facial expressions. Possibly a bit too long, but for fans, a treat. (Letterboxed) ★★★ VHS: $14.99; DVD: $24.99

Opera do Malandro

(1986, 105 min, Brazil, Ruy Guerra) *Edson Celulari, Claudia Ohana.* This Brazilian reworking of "Three Penny Opera" is set in the slums of Rio in 1942 and is a highly stylized, tango-influenced homage to the splashy M-G-M musicals of the '50s. Our hero is Max Oversees, a charming scoundrel whose heart is divided between his longtime ex-prostitute lover and a young, convent-trained beauty who is also the daughter of the local crime boss. Guerra (*Erendira*) directed this exuberant and highly enjoyable musical; the highlights of which include a flamenco-style duel (read: cat fight) between the two leading ladies and an imaginative musical number set amidst the urinals in a nightclub's men's room. (Portuguese with English subtitles) ★★★

Operation Condor

(1991, 95 min, Hong Kong, Jackie Chan) *Jackie Chan, Carol "Dodo" Cheng, Eva Cobo Garcia, Shoko Ikeda.* This is actually the sequel to Chan's previous *Armour of God*, which was his first appearance as the Indiana Jones-like adventurer, the "Asian Hawk." This time around, Jackie is hired to find a secret caché of gold left in the desert after WWII by the fleeing German army. The film is virtually a non-stop chase scene, with Chan and cohorts looking for the gold, and everyone else either trying to beat him to it or kill him before he gets it! Some of the best sequences include a motorcycle and car chase through the Barcelona seaport, and the famous end fight scene, in which Chan fights two of the bad guy's henchmen in a wind tunnel. This is a hugely entertaining romp and one of Chan's best films. (Dubbed) ★★★½ VHS: $14.99; DVD: $29.99

Operation Condor 2: Armour of the Gods

(1990, 80 min, Hong Kong, Jackie Chan) *Jackie Chan, Alan Tam, Rosamund Kwan, Lola Forner.* This is the 1990 film *Armour of God*, which was followed by *Operation Condor: Armour of God 2* in 1991. But since the latter was released first in the U.S., the former is now being marketed as the sequel! Regardless, there's no reason to feel bamboozled: this is classic Jackie, in Indiana Jones mode (just like its predecessor/follow-up), with a slew of terrific stunts, exciting action scenes and riotous comedy. Highlights include an exhilarating fight with four leather-clad, tough-as-nails women, and the *de rigueur* end-credits outtakes, where we witness the stunt-gone-wrong which almost cost Chan his life. Nicely directed by Jackie, this is one of his best, an extremely accomplished crowd-pleaser. (Dubbed) ★★★½ VHS: $14.99; DVD: $29.99

Operation Dumbo Drop

(1995, 108 min, US, Simon Wincer) *Danny Glover, Ray Liotta, Denis Leary, Doug E. Doug, Corin Nemec.* Disney offers this cardboard paste-up of a Vietnam War film which plays like "*The Absent-Minded Professor Goes to War.*" And though it's based on a true story, a screenplay stuck in neutral and eye-rolling shenanigans keep this from attaining much comic mileage. The story centers on a group of Green Berets stationed in Vietnam who are assigned to transport an elephant from the jungle to a small village. Of course, things go awry, tempers flair, and eventually they succeed. Yes, the sight of an elephant being parachuted from an airplane is a rather funny sight. But the film relies too heavily on obvious elephant jokes, and rarely gives its human actors anything equally amusing to do. ★★ VHS: $14.99

Operation Petticoat

(1959, 120 min, US, Blake Edwards) *Cary Grant, Tony Curtis, Joan O'Brien, Arthur O'Connell, Dina Merrill.* In *Some Like It Hot,* besides donning a wig, Curtis gave a rather skillful Grant imitation. It is therefore fitting that he would that same year costar with the master comedian. This sometimes hilarious comedy, which was one of the box-office smashes of the 1950s, stars Grant as the captain of a crippled WWII submarine who has his hands full not only making his ship seaworthy but also looking after five nurses rescued at sea. Directed with flair by Edwards. ★★★½ VHS: $9.99

Opportunity Knocks

(1990, 105 min, US, Donald Petrie) *Dana Carvey, Robert Loggia, Todd Graff, Milo O'Shea.* Opportunity wasn't knocking too loud for Carvey's starring debut. His mastery of mimicry and sketch comedy isn't well-served in this story of a con man who ingratiates himself into the family of a wealthy industrialist. ★★ VHS: $7.49

The Opposite of Sex

(1998, 100 min, US, Don Roos) *Christina Ricci, Martin Donovan, Lisa Kudrow, Lyle Lovett, Johnny Galecki, Ivan Sergei.* A deliciously subversive comedy. Never before has one character (and a teenage girl at that) wreaked more havoc on tranquil lives than in this hilariously mean-spirited comedy. Dedee (Ricci) is a 16-year-old, bad-to-the-bone, white-trash gal eager to sow her wild oats. She leaves her Louisiana life for an extended visit to her gay half-brother Bill (Donovan), a placid and altogether nice guy living with his dumb-as-a-doornail but sexy younger boyfriend Matt (Sergei). And before she has a chance to unpack her bags, she's seduced Matt and has convinced him to go off together. And there begins the action in this razor-sharp satire that skewers the filmic conventions of a bad girl who really wants to do good as well as offering a decidedly different view of gay men. Kudrow is priceless as the sister of Bill's deceased lover who can't help interfering in his and everyone else's life. Anyone numbed by predictable gay love stories or sensitive coming-out tales should thoroughly enjoy this wicked comedy. ★★★★ VHS: $14.99; DVD: $27.99

The Opposite Sex

(1956, 117 min, US, David Miller) *June Allyson, Joan Collins, Ann Sheridan, Ann Miller, Joan Blondell, Agnes Moorehead, Jim Backus.* Musical updating of *The Women* (with men in this version). The film, which lacks the supreme artistry of the original, does possess a charm all its own, and the performers all appear to be in their element. ★★★

The Opposite of Sex

Oranges Are Not the Only Fruit

(1989, 165 min, GB, Beeban Kidron) *Geraldine McEwan, Charlotte Coleman.* Adapted for BBC-TV by Jeanette Winterson from her novel of the same name, director Kidron's three-part production chronicles the coming-of-age of a young British lesbian, Jess (McEwan). In her turbulent struggles with her domineering evangelist mother (Coleman), Jess grows up to be a fiercely independent young woman. This poignant story features a marvelous ensemble cast and charming performances from its two leads. ★★★½

Orchestra Rehearsal

(1979, 72 min, Italy, Federico Fellini) As only the great Federico could, Fellini transforms this 72-minute mockumentary about an orchestra rehearsal into a frenzied, riotous excoriation of the Italian political spectrum. Commissioned by Italian state television to make a modest observance of an orchestra at work, Fellini instead served up this little Molotov cocktail that was championed and denounced with equal vigor at the time of its release. Filmed from the perspective of a television film crew, the film is mainly comprised of a series of interviews with the various orchestra members, stage hands and, of course, the maestro as they practice in a medieval Roman chapel. Order slowly begins to break down as the class tensions between fiercely unionist musicians and the conductor reach an anarchic crescendo. Filled with Fellini's trademark vulgarity and outrageous humor. (Italian with English subtitles) ★★★ VHS: $19.99; DVD: $29.99

Ordeal by Innocence

(1984, 87 min, GB, Desmond Davis) *Donald Sutherland, Christopher Plummer, Faye Dunaway, Sarah Miles.* A good cast barely manage to salvage this marginal Agatha Christie mystery from the video junk heap. Sutherland stars as an American who sleuths his way about a 1950s English hamlet. See it for the cast, but don't expect much more. ★★ VHS: $79.99

Ordet

(1954, 126 min, Denmark, Carl Dreyer) *Henrik Malberg.* A gripping, award-winning drama about two families, separated by religious beliefs, who must come to terms with their children's love for each other. (Danish with English subtitles) ★★★½ VHS: $29.99

Ordinary People

(1980, 123 min, US, Robert Redford) *Timothy Hutton, Donald Sutherland, Mary Tyler Moore, Judd Hirsch, Elizabeth McGovern, M. Emmet Walsh.* A collection of great performances are featured in this gripping, Oscar-winning Best Picture exploring a family's disintegration in the wake of their eldest son's death. Hutton won an Oscar for his sensitive portrayal of a teenager coming to terms with his brother's passing. Moore and Sutherland have never been better as the parents; and Hirsch is outstanding as Hutton's caring psychiatrist. Redford's directorial debut is remarkably assured. ★★★★ VHS: $14.99; DVD: $29.99

The Organization

(1971, 107 min, US, Don Medford) *Sidney Poitier, Raul Julia, Allen Garfield, Ron O'Neal, Daniel J. Travanti, Demond Wilson.* Poitier appears for a third time as Virgil Tibbs, the quick-witted police detective he first introduced in *In the Heat of the Night.* Set in San Francisco, the story centers on Tibbs' investigation of a group of kidnappers-vigilantes, who have concocted an elaborate plan to bring down drug-peddling underworld figures. There's a really good ten-minute opening robbery sequence, and the film, though it does lag in certain scenes, is peppered by exciting chases and a few twists. ★★★ VHS: $9.99; DVD: $19.99

Organized Crime and Triad Bureau

(1993, 91 min, Hong Kong, Kirk Wong) *Danny Lee, Cecilia Yip, Anthony Wong.* A combination of a John Woo-style "heroic bloodshed" film and an American police procedural, this semi-sequel to Jackie Chan's *Crime Story* follows an unconventional cop (Lee) who relentlessly pursues an underworld gang leader (Wong) and his moll (Yip). An interesting variation of the crime thriller, *Bureau* presents a basically unsympathetic cop and a more sympathetic bad guy — one cannot help but feel sorry for him as he crawls through the grimy landscape. An original and entertaining by-the-numbers story of cops and criminals. (Cantonese with English subtitles) ★★★½ VHS: $19.99; DVD: $19.99

Orgazmo

(1997, 94 min, US, Trey Parker) *Trey Parker, Dian Bachar, Robyn Lynne Raab, Michael Dean Jacobs, Matt Stone, Ron Jeremy.* "South Park" creator Parker stars as a Mor(m)on who gets sucked into the world of porno. Told on an aggressively dumb level, this can be pretty raunchy stuff. The funniest scenes involve the Orgazmorator, a machine that produces big Os at a distance. Yet it's also tame, with nothing more than bare butts and dildos onscreen. There are plenty of laughs to be had, but they're undermined by uneven direction, some sloppy timing and an unfortunate fascination with kung fu that proves this stuff is funnier when it's animated. (Unrated) ★★ VHS: $14.99

Orgy of the Dead

(1966, 90 min, US, Edward D. Wood, Jr.) *Criswell, Fawn Silver.* Just when you thought it was safe to be dead comes this campy mess of zombie girls and tortured teens in bondage. Filmed in "Astravision" and "Sexicolor." From the creator of *Plan 9 from Outer Space*, which says it all. ★ VHS: $9.99

Oriane

(1984, 88 min, Venezuela/France, Fina Torres) *Daniela Silvero, Doris Wells.* First-time director Torres' beautiful and hauntingly romantic film studies the relationship between a young woman and her deceased aunt through a series of mesmerizing flashbacks and surrealistic fantasy. The story follows Marie, who must venture through the jungle and other wilderness to arrive at the remote hacienda which she has just inherited from her aunt, Oriane. As she rummages through all of the relics and artifacts in the house, memories are stirred within her and slowly, a mysterious family secret comes to the fore. (Spanish with English subtitles) ★★★ VHS: $79.99

Original Gangstas

(1996, 98 min, US, Larry Cohen) *Fred Williamson, Jim Brown, Pam Grier, Paul Winfield, Richard Roundtree, Ron O'Neal, Isabel Sanford, Wings Hauser.* A very nasty gang, the Rebels, is taking over the dying town of Gary, Indiana. The police and city hall are powerless and apathetic, and the citizens are too scared to stop them. It's up to the founders of the Rebels — now in their fifties — to put an end to this nonsense! Yeah, you'll be cheerin' on Williamson and the gang as they whip some ragamuffin butt in this entertaining throwback to the '70s blaxploitation films. Cohen uses a good cast to full advantage, allowing everyone to strut their tuff-ass moment. Subtle it's not — this is a B movie through and through. But it's fast-paced fun, and while they may be past their prime, these original gangstas put most of the newer crop of action stars to shame. ★★★ VHS: $9.99; DVD: $14.99

The Original Kings of Comedy

(2000, 111 min, US, Spike Lee) *Steve Harvey, D.L. Hughley, Cedric the Entertainer, Bernie Mac.* While the true original king might be Richard Pryor, the title refers to a smash arena tour featuring these four comedians. This Charlotte, N.C., stop has been preserved by Spike Lee for the wider audience that it deserves. Harvey is the most old school here (and proud of it), radiating pride that seems to be lost in the age of rap. He also emcees, introducing the quietly raging Hughley, the physically fluid and aptly named Cedric the Entertainer, and the thisclosetotheedge Mac. Each has his own profane view of race relations, love and sex, and family, and it's all wildly hilarious. Except for familiar racial themes, you wouldn't know this was a Spike Lee joint; he excercises directorial restraint and lets the four jesters ascend to the throne. ★★★½ VHS: $14.99; DVD: $29.99

Orlando

(1993, 93 min, GB, Sally Porter) *Tilda Swinton, Billy Zane, Quentin Crisp, Lothaire Bluteau, John Wood, Jimmy Somerville.* Adapted from Virginia Woolf's 1928 modernist novel, this is a wholly original, stunningly filmed comedy of sexual mores, attitudes and gender switching. The tale begins in 1600, when the bewitchingly androgynous Orlando captures the eye of the aging Queen Elizabeth I (regally played to the hilt by Crisp), who promises the nobleman the deed to his family's estate on the condition that he retain his beauty and does not age. As the centuries roll by, the immortal Orlando strolls through the elaborate pageant of English history. During this quest for love and self-discovery, Orlando changes sexes while still retaining his/her personality, independence, kind heart and droll sense of humor. Spectacularly staged and costumed, and featuring a hypnotic soundtrack (including Jimmy Somerville), this witty, enchanting film is infused with wry jokes and emotional truths and is a thrilling odyssey that should not be missed. ★★★★ VHS: $19.99; DVD: $29.99

Orphans

(1965, 105 min, USSR, Nikolai Gubenko) Winner of the Special Jury Prize at Cannes, this tender and revealing film is set in a boys' boarding school and follows the growth, education and budding sexuality of a young boy. (Russian with English subtitles) ★★★

Orphans

(1987, 115 min, US, Alan J. Pakula) *Albert Finney, Matthew Modine, Kevin Anderson.* This extremely well-acted drama tells the story of two orphaned brothers, on the edge of society, who live in a broken-down house in Newark and survive through petty thievery. Their lives are dramatically transformed when their plan to rob a drunk goes haywire. That drunk, a wealthy gangster, superbly played by Finney, is intrigued by the two youths and turns the tables a bit by developing a close father-son relationship with the boys. Based on Lyle Kessler's successful stage play. A unique, rewarding film experience. ★★★

Orphans of the Storm

(1921, 126 min, US, D.W. Griffith) *Dorothy Gish, Lillian Gish.* This powerful melodrama about two girls caught up in the French Revolution stars real-life sisters Dorothy and Lillian, playing two sisters in Paris in search of a cure for one's blindness. A classic from the silent era, from the director of *Birth of a Nation.* ★★★★ VHS: $24.99; DVD: $29.99

Orpheus

(1949, 95 min, France, Jean Cocteau) *Jean Marais, François Perier.* Cocteau's allegorical

Tilda Swinton is *Orlando*

update of the Orpheus myth is a mesmerizing blend of the natural and the fantastic, poetry and science fiction. Marais stars as the successful poet who becomes enamored with the Princess Death — who travels between this world and the next via chauffeur-driven Rolls Royce. The director's major achievement in cinema. (French with English subtitles) ★★★★ VHS: $29.99; DVD: $79.99

Orpheus Descending

(1990, 117 min, GB, Peter Hall) *Vanessa Redgrave, Kevin Anderson, Anne Twomey, Miriam Margolyes.* Hall's searing screen adaptation of Tennessee Williams' drama about a forbidden love in a sleepy Southern town. Redgrave stars as Lady Torrence, a very unhappily married woman whose repressed sexual passions erupt when she encounters a mysterious, young drifter (Anderson). As the two revel in their tryst, her tyrannical, bedridden husband plots his revenge. ★★★ VHS: $79.99

Osaka Elegy

(1936, 71 min, Japan, Kenji Mizoguchi) *Isuzu Yamada.* One of the earliest surviving films from Mizoguchi's early film career, this drama is a subtle examination of Japanese cultural mores and a indictment of the country's mistreatment of women. Told in realistic fashion, the story follows the travails of Ayako, a good-hearted young woman who, in order to repay the debt of her drunken father and support her school-age brother, reluctantly becomes involved with her boss, a henpecked and unsavory lout. She eventually sinks into prostitution and is both exploited and condemned by society. The film also marks the initial collaboration between Mizoguchi and Yeshitaka Yoda, an enduring relationship that lasted for 20 pictures. (Japanese with English subtitles) ★★★½ VHS: $39.99

Oscar and Lucinda

(1997, 135 min, Australia/GB, Gillian Armstrong) *Ralph Fiennes, Cate Blanchett, Ciaran Hinds, Tom Wilkinson, Richard Roxburgh.* Using the gorgeous Australian Outback as her canvas, director Armstrong has created a sumptuous tapestry blending the fabric of romance with the colors of eccentricity. Based on the Peter Carey novel, *Oscar and Lucinda* is a charming, often amusing and certainly unconventional romantic drama about the relationship between two outcasts who find each other through their love of gambling. Fiennes is Oscar, a much-too serious divinity student who happens to like to play the ponies. Blanchett is Lucinda, an heiress and rebellious spirit who can't resist a good game of cards. Their story takes an unusual bent when they decide to float a glass church to the heart of Aborigine country. Armstrong has given the film a beautiful look, all shim-

Oscar and Lucinda

mering and robust, and her two leads offer distinctively strong performances. ★★★½ VHS: $29.99

Ossessione

(1942, 135 min, Italy, Luchino Visconti) *Massimo Girotti, Clara Calamai.* For this, his first feature film, Visconti adapted James M. Cain's powerful tale of ill-fated love, "The Postman Always Rings Twice," and transplanted it to wartime rural Italy. Gino, a virile young drifter, meets and falls in love with Giovanna, a beautiful yet desperately unhappy woman who is trapped in a loveless marriage with an older man. The two begin a doomed affair, conceived in passion and lust, but ending in greed, murder and recrimination. This remarkable neorealist debut was banned by Mussolini during the war, and because it was an unauthorized version of the Cain novel, it was not permitted into the United States until 1975. (Italian with English subtitles) ★★★½ VHS: $29.99

The Osterman Weekend

(1983, 102 min, US, Sam Peckinpah) *Rutger Hauer, John Hurt, Burt Lancaster, Craig T. Nelson, Dennis Hopper, Chris Sarandon, Meg Foster.* Peckinpah's final film is a sometimes intriguing but rather confusing thriller about a TV reporter (Hauer) who is used by CIA agent Hurt to spy on three of his friends — suspected Soviet agents. ★★½

Otello

(1986, 123 min, Italy, Franco Zeffirelli) *Placido Domingo.* The dark treacheries and intense passions of Shakespeare's classic is vividly brought to the operatic screen with visual splendor by director Zeffirelli. Set in an unreal Mediterranean locale, this soaring and lavish production features a strong performance by Domingo as the tragic, crazed king. (Sung in Italian with English subtitles) ★★★½ VHS: $24.99

Othello

(1952, 107 min, US, Orson Welles) *Orson Welles, Suzanne Cloutier, Michael MacLiammorr, Robert Coote.* Welles' masterful interpretation of Shakespeare's tale of murder, jealousy, betrayal and racism was thought to have been lost forever. Thanks to the determination of his daughter Beatrice Welles-Smith, however, the film's negatives were unearthed in a New

Jersey vault, restored, and seen by audiences for the first time since 1955. Extremely stylish in production and exquisitely filmed in highly contrasted black-and-white cinematography, the film has the feel of an Eisenstein epic. Welles himself stars as the Moor of Venice who ill-advisedly allows his evil sidekick, Iago (MacLiammor), to convince him that his newlywed wife, Desdemona (Cloutier), is unfaithful. Tragic in every detail, Welles portrays the deceived lover with bravado. ★★★½; DVD: $24.99

Othello

(1995, 124 min, GB, Oliver Parker) *Laurence Fishburne, Kenneth Branagh, Irene Jacob.* First-time director Parker's brooding, sexy adaptation of one of Shakespeare's most enduring works bares the distinction of being the first theatrical film version to use an African-American actor (Fishburne) in the role of the Moorish general. The story, of course, centers on Othello's manipulation by the power-hungry lieutenant Iago (Branagh), who makes Othello believe his new bride (Jacob) is guilty of infidelity and, ultimately, drives him to madness. This is an enthralling reworking which gives power to Shakespeare's written word and the emotions they harness. Fishburne is right at home with Shakespeare's poetry, Branagh (who obviously slid from the womb quoting the Bard) is mesmerizing as the evil Iago, and Jacob makes for a tragically beautiful Desdemona. The story centuries later resonates and has lost none of its universality. ★★★½ VHS: $19.99; DVD: $19.99

The Other

(1972, 100 min, US, Robert Mulligan) *Uta Hagen, Diana Muldaur, Chris Udvarnoky, Martin Udvarnoky.* A sleepy New England town in 1935 is the setting for this first-rate psychological thriller about two twin boys, one of whom is a murderer. Based on Thomas Tryon's best-seller. ★★★ VHS: $59.99

Other People's Money

(1991, 115 min, US, Norman Jewison) *Danny DeVito, Gregory Peck, Penelope Ann Miller, Piper Laurie.* DeVito delights as Larry "The Liquidator" Garfield, a heartless, greed-driven corporate raider who is the centerpiece of this amusing adaptation of Jerry Sterner's off-Broadway hit. The latest subject of Larry's insatiable takeover fancies is the New England Wire & Cable Company, a small "mom & pop" factory run by a paternal Peck. Jewison's direction uses the showdown between small-time family capitalist and Wall Street power-broker to deliver a predictably Capra-esque message, but the film does have one surprisingly candid moment when DeVito delivers an impassioned speech to the stockholders of the little company. ★★½ VHS: $14.99

The Other Side of Midnight

(1977, 165 min, US, Charles Jarrott) *Marie-France Pisier, John Beck, Susan Sarandon, Raf Vallone.* Trashy melodrama based on Sidney Sheldon's novel. Set before, during and after WWII, the story centers on a steamy love affair between an American pilot and a married French actress, and the deadly revenge exacted on them by her husband. ★½ VHS: $59.99

The Other Sister

(1999, 129 min, US, Garry Marshall) *Juliette Lewis, Diane Keaton, Giovanni Ribisi, Tom Skerritt, Hector Elizondo, Juliet Mills.* There was *Gigot, Charly,* and Leonardo DiCaprio in *What's Eating Gilbert Grape* as some of screendom's best and worst mentally challenged characters. But nothing any of them did on-screen is enough to prepare for the sentimental outburst of bombast exhibited by this comedy-drama. Lewis plays Carla, who comes home after years in a special school and ready to tackle the world. Of course, Mom (Keaton) and Dad (Skerritt) are concerned. She enrolls in community college, and meets fellow spirit Danny (Ribisi). They fall in love, but must withstand interference and prejudice around them. Director Marshall is in overkill mode with this unsubtle story, and the screenplay offers little of the sensitivity it pretends to contain. Lewis and Ribisi offer good performances, but it's not worth their effort. ★½ VHS: $14.99; DVD: $29.99

Our Daily Bread

(1934, 73 min, US, King Vidor) *Karen Morley, Tom George, John Qualen.* When no Hollywood studio would make this paean to communal living, Vidor risked his own money and made it himself. While as a socialist tract it's embarrassingly simplistic, to audiences suffering under the full wallop of the Depression it must have been as uplifting as a Berkeley musical number. An unemployed laborer and his wife are given a second chance when a rich uncle lets them squat on a bankrupt farm. They soon turn it into a cooperative, recruiting other victims of the crash. Vidor brings all his dramatist skills to the meager plot, setting off his striking visuals with a dynamic montage style right out of Eisenstein. ★★★½; DVD: $29.99

Our Sons

(1991, 100 min, US, John Erman) *Julie Andrews, Ann-Margret, Hugh Grant, Zeljko Ivanek.* From the director of *An Early Frost* comes this intelligent and moving made-for-TV AIDS drama. Andrews and Ann-Margret star as the respective mothers of gay lovers Grant and Ivanek. Andrews is a wealthy businesswoman who remained close to her son after he came out, while A-M, a barmaid from Arkansas, refuses to accept or even acknowledge her son's sexuality and rejects him. When Ivanek becomes sick with AIDS, Andrews is persuaded by her son to meet his lover's mother and try to get the two to reunite. A serious, straightforward story which, while suffering a bit from a talking heads-style of filmmaking, remains compelling and compassionate. ★★★

Our Town

(1940, 90 min, US, Sam Wood) *William Holden, Martha Scott, Frank Craven, Fay Bainter, Beulah Bondi, Thomas Mitchell, Guy Kibbee.* One of the greats of 20th-century American theatre makes for an equally majestic on-screen experience as director Wood creates a stunning look at small-time American life, based on Thornton Wilder's Pulitzer Prize-winning play. Holden and Scott (in a remarkable debut reprising her stage role) are the young neighbors who marry, the story following their joys and tragedies over a 12-year period. ★★★★ DVD: $29.99

Our Vines Have Tender Grapes

(1945, 105 min, US, Roy Rowland) *Edward G. Robinson, Agnes Moorehead, Margaret O'Brien.* This earnest, folksy drama does not hold up quite as well as other similarly themed films — *Our Town* or *The Human Comedy* for instance — which bestow blessings upon the virtues of American small-town life. Robinson plays a kindly Norwegian farmer living with wife Moorehead and daughter O'Brien. The story follows one year in the lives of the family, mostly centering on seven-year-old O'Brien (whose cheerfulness would put Pollyanna to shame). Adapted by soon-to-be blacklisted writer Dalton Trumbo, who paints Americana with broad, sentimental strokes. ★★½ VHS: $19.99

Out Cold

(1989, 92 min, US, Malcolm Mowbray) *Teri Garr, John Lithgow, Randy Quaid.* This delightfully sick comedy stars Garr as a slightly demented housewife who, after finding out

Laurence Fishburne (l.) and Kenneth Branagh in *Othello*

George Clooney in *Out of Sight*

that husband Ernie is cheating on her, locks him in his butcher shop's freezer. Her frenzied attempts to get rid of her frozen hubbie entangles Lithgow, the nerdish partner of Ernie as well as a bungling private eye (Quaid). ★★★

Out of Africa

(1985, 160 min, US, Sydney Pollack) *Meryl Streep, Robert Redford, Klaus Maria Brandauer, Michael Kitchen, Graham Crowden, Iman, Donal McCann.* Gorgeous cinematography by David Watkin, a tremendous performance by Streep, a moving score by John Barry, and subtle direction by Pollack make this film worthy of its several Academy Awards (including Best Picture). Based on the life and works of Isak Dinesen, it's the story of a Danish woman, Karen Blixen (Streep), who moves to Nairobi with her aristocratic husband. There, she falls in love with Africa and with a handsome British explorer (Redford thankfully minus the accent). A beautiful film. (VHS available letterboxed or pan & scan) ★★★★ VHS: $14.99; DVD: $29.99

Out of Bounds

(1986, 93 min, US, Richard Tuggle) *Anthony Michael Hall, Jenny Wright.* Inept thriller with Hall as an Iowa farmboy who unwittingly becomes involved with drug pushers on his first visit to Los Angeles. ★ VHS: $79.99

Out of Order

(1985, 90 min, The Netherlands, Carl Schenkel) *Renée Soutendijk.* When two films about killer elevators (the other being *The Lift*) are released from the same country in the same year, it would be prudent to avoid entering tall buildings while visiting that land. Anyway, this intense thriller is miles ahead in terror than *The Lift*. The story is set in a deserted office building where four people discover, to their horror, that the lift is...*out of order*! Excitement for us, but a nightmarish hell for the trapped occupants! ★★★

Out of Sight

(1998, 120 min, US, Steven Soderbergh) *George Clooney, Jennifer Lopez, Ving Rhames, Don Cheadle, Albert Brooks, Steve Zahn, Dennis Farina,* *Catherine Keener, Isaiah Washington, Luis Guzman, Nancy Allen.* Clooney comes into his own as a charismatic, commanding leading man, playing a convicted bank robber who escapes from prison only to collide with a tough, sexy marshal (Lopez). Sparks fly, temperatures rise and before they both know it, they're disregarding priorities and duty respectively, only to pursue their improbable mutual attraction. The plot unfolds in hectic flash-back-and-forth fashion and shifts from Miami to Detroit to two different prisons, but director Soderbergh manages a minor coup by keeping the plot streamlined and cohesive, and giving the film a visual panache. The hippest, coolest film of its year, *Out of Sight* is sure-fire, lightning-fast excitement, and it'll keep you guessing right up till its great ending. Based on Elmore Leonard's novel. (Letterboxed VHS available for $14.99) ★★★★ VHS: $9.99; DVD: $34.99

Out of the Blue

(1947, 86 min, US, Leigh Jason) *George Brent, Ann Dvorak.* Enjoyable screwball comedy with Brent as a hen-pecked husband who has some explaining to do when wacky Dvorak is found unconscious in his apartment. ★★½ VHS: $19.99

Out of the Blue

(1980, 93 min, US, Dennis Hopper) *Linda Manz, Dennis Hopper, Sharon Farrell.* Before Hopper burst back onto the Hollywood scene, he made this gritty and extraordinarily low-budget feature about a nihilistic, punked-out teenager. With an alcoholic truck driver (Hopper) for a dad and a junkie mom (Farrell), the young girl (Manz) gets all of her life experience in seedy roadhouses and various watering holes. Excellent performances make this a harrowing experience of the emptiness of life on the edge. ★★★½ VHS: $14.99

Out of the Past

(1947, 96 min, US, Jacques Tourneur) *Robert Mitchum, Kirk Douglas, Jane Greer.* Mitchum is memorable as a retired private eye, living as a gas station owner, who is lured back to his old job by gangster Douglas (wonderfully greasy) to find his dame who ran off with his heart as well as his money. Our fated hero's sleuthing leads him to Mexico where he not only finds his prey (Greer, cunningly seductive as the femme fatale), but falls in love with her as well. A riveting drama of double dealings, *amour mort* and pervasive corruption. A '40s film noir classic. (Remade in 1984 as *Against All Odds.*) ★★★½

The Out-of-Towners

(1970, 97 min, US, Arthur Hiller) *Jack Lemmon, Sandy Dennis, Anne Meara.* The laughs are plentiful (and very close to home) in this Neil Simon romp with Lemmon and Dennis as the title couple, an Ohio exec and his wife visiting New York City, where they encounter one disaster after another. (Remade in 1999) ★★★ VHS: $14.99

The Out-of-Towners

(1999, 91 min, US, Sam Weisman) *Steve Martin, Goldie Hawn, John Cleese, Mark McKinney.* In this lackluster remake, even Martin and Hawn can't overcome impotent direction and a lifeless, brand new updated script. The story is basically the same. Martin heads to NYC for a job interview accompanied by wife Hawn. They lose luggage, miss planes, and trains, get mugged (the "identity" of the culprit is kinda funny), go hungry, get arrested — all the fun things that happen to tourists in New York. But the film lacks an inspired comic energy, and where Lemmon expertly knew how to overplay a scene, here much too much is played on an even keel. Except for Cleese, who saves the day with a funny bit as a snooty hotel manager. ★★ VHS: $14.99; DVD: $29.99

Out on a Limb

(1992, 82 min, US, Francis Vèber) *Matthew Broderick, Jeffrey Jones, John C. Reilly.* An awful screwball comedy from the director of *Three Fugitives.* Broderick is miscast as a hotshot Manhattan stockbroker who pays a visit to his hometown en route to complete a multimillion dollar deal and runs afoul of the murderous activities of his stepfather. Director Veber's interesting use of narration and flashback adds nothing to the mundane plot. ★

Out to Sea

(1997, 107 min, US, Martha Coolidge) *Jack Lemmon, Walter Matthau, Dyan Cannon, Brent Spiner, Gloria De Haven, Hal Linden, Donald O'Connor, Elaine Stritch.* As close to a big-screen version of "The Love Boat" as one is likely to see, *Out to Sea* takes the considerable talents of those two comic treasures, Lemmon and Matthau, and stretches their comic resolve with this amiable, lightweight comedy. Matthau plays a con artist who convinces brother-in-law and widower Lemmon to join him on a holiday cruise. Though this doesn't produce as many laughs as their two *Grumpy Old Men* films, Lemmon and Matthau's seasoned timing and a bright supporting cast gloss over the rough spots. Cannon, De Haven, O'Connor, Stritch and Linden are old pros and know exactly how to make the most of their short time on-screen. ★★ VHS: $9.99

Outbreak

(1995, 127 min, US, Wolfgang Petersen) *Dustin Hoffman, Rene Russo, Morgan Freeman, Donald Sutherland, Cuba Gooding, Jr., Kevin Spacey, Patrick Dempsey, J.T. Walsh.* Hoffman stars in this fact-based and very exciting topical thriller as a cantankerous Army doctor who, along with his ex-wife (Russo), a newly appointed bigwig at the CDC, races against time (and a top-level military conspiracy) to stop the spread of a highly infectious mutant virus that kills within 24 hours of contact. While short on characterization and guilty of eventually deteriorating into a standard "good guys vs. bad guys" actioner, the film as directed by Petersen displays the director's knack for mixing tension, claustrophobia and doom. As such, it's quite successful in its gruesome depiction of the ultimate end-of-the-world scenario; and in an era of AIDS and Ebola, all-too believable. ★★★ VHS: $9.99; DVD: $19.99

Outcasts

(1986, 102 min, Taiwan, Yu Kan Ping) After being caught having sex with another student, young Ah Ching is both expelled from school and beaten out of his home by his father. Befriended by a middle-aged photographer as well as by other young gays, Ah rebuilds his life with the help of his new surrogate family and begins to explore his own sexuality. The first film from Taiwan with a gay theme, *Outcasts* is, at times, unintentionally funny in its heavy-handed melodramatic excesses, but is nonetheless a powerful and sensual look at youth finding a place in an uncaring and insensitive world. (Mandarin with English subtitles) ★★★ VHS: $49.99

Outland

(1981, 109 min, US, Peter Hyams) *Sean Connery, Peter Boyle, Frances Sternhagen, James B. Sikking.* Connery gives one of his best performances in this taut sci-fi thriller as a lone cop determined to smash a drug ring on Io, the ninth moon of Jupiter. Boyle is the slimy, corrupt executive who wants to buy his badge. Director Hyams presents an isolated world where law is practically extinct and capitalism reigns supreme. This underrated jewel was affectionately dubbed "*High Noon* in Space" by critics upon its theatrical release. ★★★ VHS: $9.99; DVD: $14.99

The Outlaw

(1943, 117 min, US, Howard Hawks) *Jane Russell, Walter Huston, Thomas Mitchell, Jack Buetel.* Russell made a notorious film debut (though the film was shot in 1941) in this legendary (and at the time scandalous) western adventure about Billy the Kid and his girlfriend. Though most of the attention over the years has been focused on Russell's ample bosom, not to be overlooked is Huston's showy turn as Billy. ★★★ VHS: $19.99

The Outlaw and His Wife

(1918, 73 min, Sweden, Victor Sjostrom) *Victor Sjostrom, Edith Erastoff.* Sjostrom directed and stars in this superbly acted and visually stunning drama which gave Sweden its breakthrough after WWI. The setting is Iceland in the 19th century where a farmer and his wife are being hunted by the police for a petty crime. Fleeing to the mountains and fjord hills to escape detection, they soon succumb to the brutal forces of nature. Color tinted, this video version features a full orchestral score and was beautifully restored in 1986 by the Swedish Film Institute. ★★★½ VHS: $24.99

The Outlaw Josey Wales

(1976, 135 min, US, Clint Eastwood) *Clint Eastwood, Chief Dan George, Sondra Locke.* Exciting post–Civil War adventure about a

The Out-of-Towners (1970)

Confederate renegade (Eastwood) on a trail of vengeance against the Union soldiers who murdered his wife and son. (VHS available letterboxed or pan & scan) ★★★½ VHS: $14.99; DVD: $19.99

Outrage

(1994, 108 min, Spain, Carlos Saura) *Francesca Neri, Antonio Banderas.* Don't believe the hype — this is not some sex-drenched, exotic shoot-'em-up which could be misinterpreted, but a moderately paced examination of a young woman's reaction to a brutal violation. Neri is compelling as a circus sharpshooter, the victim of three young thugs whose advances she rejects. Banderas delivers an effective, subdued performance as a reporter captivated by the vivacious woman. In physical and emotional shock from the severity of the attack on her, she turns instinctively to a familiar weapon, near at hand, to execute her act of vengeance. Certainly not a great film, but compassionate in its depiction of one woman's response to an act of carnage that shatters her life. (Spanish with English subtitles) ★★½ VHS: $14.99; DVD: $9.99

Outrageous!

(1977, 97 min, Canada, Richard Benner) *Craig Russell, Hollis McLaren, Richard Easley, Helen Shaver.* One of the earliest North American gay-themed films to receive theatrical distribution, *Outrageous!* is a funny and affecting film about a female impersonator and his touching friendship with a schizophrenic girl. Russell plays a gay hairdresser and star-wannabe who does flawless impressions of Barbra Streisand, Judy Garland, Bette Midler, Mae West and others. And while the musical segments are fun, the film best succeeds in his friendship with Liza (McLaren), a troubled young woman who checks herself out of a mental hospital but who becomes frightened and confused when her family and doctors want her to return to the institution. A tender story of ambitions, eccentricity and the courage of being oneself. (Sequel: *Too Outrageous!*) ★★★½ VHS: $29.99

Outrageous Fortune

(1987, 92 min, US, Arthur Hiller) *Bette Midler, Shelley Long, Peter Coyote, George Carlin.* One of the most hilarious films of the 1980s, *Outrageous Fortune* finds its success in the ingenious pairing of pretty, prim and proper bitch Long with flamboyant, aggressive floozy Midler (and, as with Olivier's *Hamlet*, a role the Divine Miss M was born to play). The fireworks given off by these two are priceless. The truly outrageous plot finds the female odd couple searching for a "missing" boyfriend; they become involved with the CIA, Russian agents, biochemical warfare, and Indian guide Carlin. ★★★½ DVD: $29.99

The Outside Chance of Maximilian Glick

(1989, 95 min, Canada, Allan A. Goldstein) *Noam Zylberman, Jan Rubes, Saul Rubinek.* This low-budget Canadian film set in 1960 is a charming coming-of-age comedy which plays as sort of a "Jewish Wonder Years." Making an impressive film debut, Zylberman stars as a 13-year-old boy who is readying for his bar mitzvah. The film follows the days before, when Max experiences first love with a pretty gentile girl; befriends the new, unorthodox,

Orthodox rabbi; and for the first time rebels against his family. Rubinek is a total delight as the new rabbi whose candor and sense of humor turns an entire town on its ear. ★★★

The Outside Man

(1973, 104 min, US, Jacques Deray) *Roy Scheider, Ann-Margret, Angie Dickinson, Jean-Louis Trintignant.* It's killer vs. killer in this dated actioner about a sad-eyed assassin (Trintignant) who finds himself at the wrong end of a gun when his latest employer (Dickinson) embraces the philosophy that "dead men tell no tales." Scheider gives another surefire performance as the hit man whose credo is "there's no honor among thieves," and Ann-Margret is on target as the helpful floosie whose philosophy is "leave it to cleavage." ★★½ VHS: $14.99

Outside Ozona

(1998, 99 min, US, J.S. Cardone) *Robert Forster, Kevin Pollak, Sherilyn Fenn, David Paymer, Penelope Ann Miller, Swoosie Kurtz, Taj Mahal, Meat Loaf, Lucy Webb, Beth Ann Styne.* All roads lead to Ozona in this occasionally involving though retread psychodrama about a various group of people whose lives become intertwined at day's end while traveling on the dusty roads of Texas. Forster is great as a truck driver recovering from the death of his wife. He befriends Native American Webb and her dying grandmother for the film's strongest plot line. The weakest is bickering sisters Fenn and Styne traveling to their father's funeral. The high-profile cast performs admirably, but the film tends to drag in places; its pacing uneven and the screenplay hit and miss. ★★ VHS: $19.99

Outside Providence

(1999, 96 min, US, Michael Corrente) *Shawn Hatosy, Amy Smart, Alec Baldwin, Jon Abrahams, George Wendt.* With a screenplay cowritten by Peter and Bobby Farrelly and based on Peter's novel, this alternately poignant and comic coming-of-age tale doesn't share much in common comedically with their gross-out comedies. But not to worry — this is a smart, funny, touching even mature work. Hatosy is very appealing as Tim, the oldest son from a working-class family in a small Rhode Island town. Being raised by his widowed, gruff father (Baldwin who is especially good), Tim is sent to prep school after a run-in with the police. It is there the young man discovers first love and his inner voice against the pot-smoking haze of the early '70s. Director Corrente nicely balances comedy and poignancy in telling Tim's story of youthful shenanigans and eventual growing up. ★★★ VHS: $102.99; DVD: $29.99

The Outsiders

(1983, 91 min, US, Francis Ford Coppola) *Matt Dillon, Patrick Swayze, Emilio Estevez, Tom Cruise, C. Thomas Howell, Ralph Macchio, Rob Lowe, Diane Lane, Leif Garrett.* S.E. Hinton's best-selling teen novel about kids from the wrong side of the tracks in the early 1960s is transformed into a stylish and visually rich film by director Coppola. The cast is interesting to watch — it includes several well-knowns before they hit it big. ★★½ VHS: $9.99; DVD: $14.99

Over the Brooklyn Bridge

(1983, 108 min, US, Menahem Golan) *Elliott Gould, Sid Caesar, Margaux Hemingway, Carol Kane, Shelley Winters, Burt Young.* A Brooklyn luncheonette owner (Gould) needs to borrow money to open a posh Manhattan eatery. His uncle (Caesar) is willing to loan him the cash — if he drops his current Christian girl (Hemingway) and settles down with a nice Jewish girl (Kane). Unmemorable and not all that funny, either. ★½

Over the Edge

(1979, 95 min, US, Jonathan Kaplan) *Matt Dillon, Michael Kramer, Pamela Ludwig, Vincent Spano.* Aimless violence is the result of the frustration and alienation of suburban youths in director Kaplan's dynamic youth-in-revolt film. The hard-rock soundtrack with Cheap Trick, The Ramones and Jimi Hendrix heightens the tension in this powerful sleeper. ★★★ VHS: $14.99

Overboard

(1987, 112 min, US, Garry Marshall) *Goldie Hawn, Kurt Russell, Roddy McDowall, Katherine Helmond, Edward Herrmann.* Pleasant Hawn comedy with Goldie as an obnoxious society woman who gets amnesia and is convinced by workman Russell that she is his wife and the mother of his three wild children. One of Goldie's better comedies with a fair share of laughs. ★★★ VHS: $9.99; DVD: $24.99

The Overcoat (Shinel)

(1959, 73 min, USSR, Aleksei Batalov) *Rolan Bykov.* This faithful adaptation of Nikolai Gogol's tragicomic story follows a beleaguered clerk, whose dreams of a glorious new coat are not only realized, but change his destiny. The setting is 19th-century czarist St. Petersberg in this simple yet moving story. (Russian with English subtitles) ★★★½ VHS: $59.99

The Owl and the Pussycat

(1970, 95 min, US, Herbert Ross) *Barbra Streisand, George Segal, Robert Klein, Allen Garfield.* Streisand and Segal are terrific together in this raucous and very funny screen version of Bill Manoff's Broadway play. Streisand, in sensational form, plays a hooker who is kicked out of her apartment after complaints made by neighboring writer Segal; so she moves in with him. ★★★½ VHS: $9.99

The Ox

(1992, 91 min, Sweden, Sven Nykvist) *Stellan Skarsgård, Ewa Froling, Max von Sydow.* Ingmar Bergman's longtime cinematographer Nykvist makes his directorial debut with this grim parable about the day-to-day struggles for life in 1860s famine-stricken Sweden. Helge (Skarsgård) is a destitute tenant farmer who, in a fit of desperation over his family's poverty, brutally bludgeons one of his landlord's two remaining oxen, quickly butchering the animal and hiding the evidence. Of course, Helge and his wife Elfrida (Froling) go on to suffer the guilt that their devious act must inevitably bring to bear. Based on a true incident, the film is yet another example of the life-is-so-grim-above-the-Arctic-Circle school of Swedish filmmaking which here is mildly unengaging. Von Sydow brings a small breath of life to the film as the town's humanistic vicar. (Swedish with English subtitles) ★★ VHS: $19.99

The Ox-Bow Incident

(1943, 75 min, US, William Wellman) *Henry Fonda, Henry Morgan, Anthony Quinn, Dana Andrews.* A classic western morality play. Fonda and Morgan ride into town just in time to experience the formation of a lynch mob. The scene in which they question the "rustlers" who are one wrong answer from a hangman's noose is suitably tense. ★★★★ VHS: $9.99

Oxford Blues

(1984, 97 min, US, Robert Boris) *Rob Lowe, Ally Sheedy, Amanda Pays, Julian Sands, Cary Elwes.* Updated, sloppy version of the 1938 hit *A Yank at Oxford*, with Lowe, in the Robert Taylor role, as an American rower enrolled at Oxford and in love with Pays. ★½

Pacific Heights

(1990, 102 min, US, John Schlesinger) *Michael Keaton, Matthew Modine, Melanie Griffith, Mako, Nobu McCarthy, Laurie Matcalf.* A "yupwardly mobile" couple (Modine, Griffith) pool their resources to purchase and renovate a large Victorian home (complete with two rental units) in an upscale San Francisco neighborhood. Enter Keaton as sociopath Carter Hayes, a tenant from hell who seems to know that a lodger can do just about anything to his landlords and not be evicted — including nonpayment of rent and cockroach breeding. An infuriating blend of "who says life is fair anyway" legal procedures and sweaty-palm psychological warfare, and the film really doesn't work on either level. ★★ VHS: $9.99; DVD: $14.99

The Package

(1989, 108 min, US, Andrew Davis) *Gene Hackman, Tommy Lee Jones, Joanna Cassidy, Dennis Franz, Pam Grier.* This taut political thriller stars the ideally cast Hackman as an Army Security specialist stationed in Germany who is assigned to escort a wayward soldier (Jones) back to the United States for a court-martial. This apparently routine mission comes unglued when his "package" gives him the slip. As Hackman sets out on the trail of his charge, he is framed and becomes the subject of a murder investigation forcing the on-the-lam officer to hunt down Jones himself. Cassidy is tops as Hackman's estranged wife who winds up joining him in his adventure. ★★★ VHS: $9.99; DVD: $14.99

Padre Nuestro

(1986, 90 min, Spain, Francisco Rabal) *Fernando Rey, Victoria Abril.* Rey stars as a powerful Vatican Cardinal who, upon learning he has only one year to live, returns to the village of his youth in order to settle the errors of his mischievous childhood. Thus is set in motion a series of richly comic confrontations with the people of his past: his sexually repressed brother, his domineering sister, the peasant woman who 30 years earlier bore his illegitimate child, and his prostitute daughter, "La Cardenala," portrayed with unabashed sensual zeal by Abril. Director Rabal has painted a colorful portrait of Spanish society which, through a mixture of comedy and drama, exposes the country's struggles with the demands of the church, the flesh and the aristocracy. (Spanish with English subtitles) ★★★ VHS: $79.99

Padre Padrone

(1977, 117 min, Italy, Vittorio & Paolo Taviani) *Omero Antonutti, Marcella Michalangeli.* The moving struggles of an illiterate shepherd who overcomes hardships to become a successful scholar are wonderfully recounted in this Taviani brothers classic. Autobiographical in nature, the story revolves

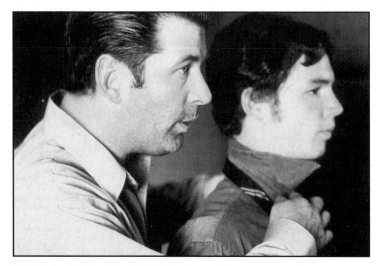

Alec Baldwin with Shawn Hatosy in *Outside Providence*

around the relationship of a young man who has a yearning for knowledge and the brutalizations inflicted on him by his tyrannical father who fears both education and civilization. (Italian with English subtitles) ★★★½ VHS: $19.99; DVD: $29.99

The Pagemaster

(1994, 85 min, US, Joe Johnston & Maurice Hunt) *Macaulay Culkin, Christopher Lloyd; Voices of: Whoopi Goldberg, Patrick Stewart, Leonard Nimoy.* An able cast, respectable animation and an enjoyable story line all work together to create a pleasant children's tale which mixes live-action and animation. Culkin stars as an overly timid boy who, after getting caught in a rainstorm, takes shelter in a library. There he is transformed into a cartoon character thereupon meeting the Pagemaster (Lloyd). His mission: to find his way out of the library and through the plots of several well-known novels with the help of some engaging, talking books. ★★★ VHS: $9.99

A Pain in the A—

(1974, 90 min, France/Italy, Edouard Molinaro) *Jacques Brel, Caroline Cellier.* A hilarious story of a hired killer who crosses paths with a suicidal shirt salesman. An odd friendship ensues as the contract killer attempts to protect the hapless salesman from his attempts at self-destruction. Music by Brel. (Remade in 1981 as *Buddy Buddy*) (French with English subtitles) ★★★ VHS: $29.99

Paint It Black

(1989, 101 min, US, Tim Hunter) *Rick Rossovich, Sally Kirkland, Martin Landau, Julie Carmen, Doug Savant.* A hunky sculptor (Rossovich) is "discovered" by a sexy gallery owner (Kirkland) who has more on her mind than art. However, obsession soon escalates into a web of intrigue and murder. A rather effective thriller buoyed by a good performance by Kirkland and a nicely written screenplay. ★★★ VHS: $79.99

Paint Your Wagon

(1969, 166 min, US, Joshua Logan) *Lee Marvin, Clint Eastwood, Jean Seberg, Harve Presnell.* Marvin and Eastwood (two unlikely musical stars but certainly at home with the western) play a pair of California gold prospectors in the Old West, both involved with Seberg and looking for a fortune. Presnell gets the plaudits for his singing (including the standard "They Call the Wind Maria") in this sturdy adaptation of the Broadway musical. ★★★ VHS: $24.99; DVD: $29.99

Paisan

(1946, 90 min, Italy, Roberto Rossellini) *Maria Michi, Carmela Sazio.* Written by Rossellini and Federico Fellini, this gritty, neorealist classic is set up in six vignettes, all dealing with the relationship between the Americans and Italians during the liberation of Italy in WWII. Rossellini used mostly nonprofessional actors for the roles and he presents the stories in a style reminiscent of a wartime documentary. (Italian with English subtitles) ★★★★ VHS: $29.99

The Pajama Game

(1957, 101 min, US, George Abbott & Stanley Donen) *Doris Day, John Raitt, Eddie Foy, Jr., Carol*

Preston Sturges (c.) leads his cast of *The Palm Beach Story*

Haney, Rita Shaw. Snappy choreography from Bob Fosse is only one of the highlights of this effervescent musical starring Day, whose love-hate relationship with Raitt is mirrored by labor unrest between the workers and managers of a pajama factory. Songs include Haney's knockout "Steam Heat," and the standards "Hernando's Hideaway" and "Hey, There." One of the better stage-to-screen adaptations of a Broadway musical. ★★★½ VHS: $14.99; DVD: $19.99

Pal Joey

(1957, 109 min, US, George Sidney) *Frank Sinatra, Rita Hayworth, Kim Novak.* Lively film version of the Rodgers and Hart musical with Sinatra as a cabaret entertainer involved with socialite Hayworth and dancer Novak. Songs include "The Lady is a Tramp" and "Bewitched, Bothered and Bewildered." ★★★ VHS: $19.99; DVD: $27.99

Pale Rider

(1985, 116 min, US, Clint Eastwood) *Clint Eastwood, Michael Moriarty, Carrie Snodgress, Sydney Penny, Richard Dysart, Christopher Penn.* Eastwood wears two hats as director and actor in this first-rate western adventure, Eastwood's homage to *Shane*. Clint stars as the mysterious stranger who comes to the aid of a gold prospecting community being harassed by an unscrupulous land baron. A gorgeously photographed film. (VHS available letterboxed or pan & scan) ★★★ VHS: $14.99; DVD: $19.99

The Paleface

(1948, 91 min, US, Norman Z. McLeod) *Bob Hope, Jane Russell, Robert Armstrong.* The one-and-only Hope plays a cowardly dentist out West who becomes involved with sharpshooter Russell. Loaded with very funny gags. An even funnier sequel followed in 1952, *Son of Paleface.* ★★★ VHS: $14.99

The Pallbearer

(1996, 97 min, US, Matt Reeves) *David Schwimmer, Gwyneth Paltrow, Barbara Hershey,*

Michael Rapaport, Toni Collette, Carol Kane. Only intermittently funny with a suspect comic intuition, *The Pallbearer* will do little to repair the image of the Generation X'er as a slacker and a whiner. This plays more like a lurid study of alienation than a quirky comedy of errors. In what could have been a "Friends" plot line, Schwimmer is invited to be a pallbearer — and then give the eulogy — for a former classmate he can't remember. He soon becomes romantically involved with the deceased man's grieving mother (Hershey) while at the same time trying to initiate a relationship with Paltrow. Besides the absence of much humor, the screenplay's handling of Hershey as the "older woman" is despicably insensitive; and though sometimes personable, Schwimmer's act soon grows tiresome. ★★ VHS: $14.99; DVD: $29.99

The Palm Beach Story

(1942, 90 min, US, Preston Sturges) *Claudette Colbert, Joel McCrea, Mary Astor, Rudy Vallee, William Demarest, Franklin Pangborn.* Colbert decides that her beloved inventor husband McCrea would be better off without a wife to support; she skips down to Palm Beach to divorce him and find a millionaire husband who can finance his inventions. On the train. . . . But before we get to the train, keep your eyes open during the opening credits, where more happens than during the entirety of some contemporary films. Of course, so much else happens that you may forget the beginning until the end, when everything is resolved. Or is it? A great cast contributes to this madness, written and directed by — who else? — Sturges. ★★★★ VHS: $14.99

Palmetto

(1998, 113 min, US, Volker Schlöndorff) *Woody Harrelson, Elisabeth Shue, Gina Gershon, Chloë Sevigny.* Heat rises from director Schlöndorff's steamy noir thriller. Harrelson plays a certified loser who becomes enmeshed in a loony kidnapping scheme which is out of control and over his head. Released after serving two years on a framed-up conviction, he returns to Palmetto, the backwater site of his earlier misfortune. Futilely perusing the help wanted ads in a seedy bar air-conditioned by slowly moving palm leaves, Harrelson encounters Shue. Earthy and sensual and willing to forgive his attempt to lift her wad of cash, she offers him a job: to be a threatening phone voice, one element in a plan to extort big bucks from her husband by staging her co-conspirator step-daughter's abduction. Complications ensue. Harrelson is a man with no anchor, and his precipitous descent into this ill-conceived quagmire is related with amusement and wry observation of the baser human foibles. ★★★ VHS: $9.99; DVD: $19.99

Palookaville

(1996, 92 min, US, Alan Taylor) *William Forsythe, Vincent Gallo, Adam Trese, Gareth Williams, Lisa Gay Hamilton, Frances McDormand.* Three losers try to better their financial situations by staging an armored car robbery in this adequate low-budget, independent comedy. A botched jewelry store heist and an abortive attempt to start a private cab company are only the latest in a string of failures for three friends. Then they get the idea to rob an armored car. Almost annoyingly quirky, the film still has its merits. A hesitant romance between Forsythe's character, a shlump whose main companions are his two stinky dogs, and an equally down-on-her-luck clothing store clerk is the sweetest and most satisfying part of the film. Also noteworthy is Gallo's subplot, about his unhappy home life and his frequent escapes to the arms of his cute but underage neighbor. ★★½

The Panama Deception

(1992, 91 min, US, Barbara Trent) This well-crafted, meticulously researched and tightly structured documentary is a clear and lucid presentation of a complex analysis of the U.S. invasion of Panama and the press coverage which was made available to the American people. On December 19, 1989, 20,000 U.S. troops launched a midnight attack. The official story of that incursion is juxtaposed with testimony from eyewitness Panamanian citizens, various analysts and the camera's evidence. U.S. media had no coverage of the thousands of civilians killed or the continued use of overwhelming deadly force after stated objectives were achieved. This is an important and fascinating exposé, and required viewing for anyone interested in an independent press and a responsible military. ★★★★ VHS: $29.99

Pandora's Box

(1928, 110 min, Germany, G.W. Pabst) *Louise Brooks, Fritz Kortner.* This expressionistic classic from Pabst features a luminous Brooks, with her haunting beauty, sexual mystique and trademark helmet of black bobbed hair, as the sexually insatiable Lulu, a prostitute who ensnares a series of men (and one woman) with her fetching beauty and beguiling indifference. Lulu's cavalier approach to love results in a self-destructive path — but not before she unwittingly destroys all who come close to her. (Silent) ★★★★ VHS: $24.99

Panic

(2000, 93 min, US, Henry Bromell) *William H. Macy, Neve Campbell, Tracey Ullman, Donald Sutherland, John Ritter.* This somewhat moody crime drama features Macy as a hit man with a heart of gold who considers getting out of the business, much to the consternation of his mentor and boss — his father (Sutherland). Macy is Alex. Despite his profession, he's a somewhat mild-mannered mid-lifer who (in a nod to Tony Soprano) seeks the help of a therapist (Ritter). In the waiting room he meets Sarah (Campbell), a free-spirited youngster that sets his middle-aged heart aflutter and sends his life into deeper turmoil. So, though he has a lovely wife at home (Ullman) and a fine young son who adores him, Alex begins the journey that so many fortysomething men do and pursues his boyish passions — including rebellion against Dad. Director Bromell (who got his start writing for TV's "Homicide") sets everything on edge and a slightly surreal *Stepford Wives* tone permeates, which at times feels just right and at others feels off. Sutherland gives another one of his grand, patronly performances as an overbearing dad who may have gone just one step too far with junior. ★★½ VHS: $89.99; DVD: $24.99

Panic in the Streets

(1950, 93 min, US, Elia Kazan) *Richard Widmark, Jack Palance, Barbara Bel Geddes, Paul Douglas, Zero Mostel.* When a corpse in New Orleans is found to be carrying the plague, a desperate search begins to track down its source. Widmark is terrific as a health official supervising the hunt, and Palance is memorable as an edgy psychopath who unwittingly holds the key to the mystery. A superb film noir thriller, directed in crisp, crackling fashion by Kazan. ★★★★ VHS: $39.99

Panic in Year Zero

(1962, 95 min, US, Ray Milland) *Ray Milland, Jean Hagen, Frankie Avalon.* Milland is both director and star of this low-budget but surprisingly effective post-Apocalypse chiller. Milland, wife Hagen and family take a vacation in the mountains. While there, a nuclear bomb strikes their city home nearby, and as they attempt to return to civilization, they stumble upon a newly ravaged society with terribly impolite manners. Milland is stiff upper-lipped as the heroic father, and his direction is equally rigid. But the film's premise, setting, cast of characters and cheesy cinematography and score all combine to make this a real panic. ★★★

Panique (Panic)

(1946, 82 min, France, Julien Duvivier) *Michel Simon, Viviane Romance.* From the novel by Georges Simenon, France's master of suspense, this clever study of mob psychology is set in the slums of Paris during the aftermath of WWII. Two lovers frame a stranger for a murder, but is the plan as perfect as they think? (French with English subtitles) ★★★½

Panther

(1995, 124 min, US, Mario Van Peebles) *Kadeem Hardison, Bokeem Woodbine, Courtney B. Vance, Marcus Chong, Chris Rock, James Russo, M. Emmet Walsh, Mario Van Peebles.* Denounced by real-life Panther Bobby Seale for its shameless inaccuracies, this clichéd melodrama not only manages to rewrite history, it also reduces a revolutionary group's actions to the level of a

Louise Brooks in *Pandora's Box*

common street gang. Even the group's positive activities are handled as an afterthought. In spite of the terrific performances by Chong as Huey Newton and Vance as Bobby Seale, *Panther* only occasionally hits its mark as it unevenly presents its social and political thoughts. ★★ VHS: $14.99

The Paper

(1994, 112 min, US, Ron Howard) *Michael Keaton, Robert Duvall, Glenn Close, Marisa Tomei, Randy Quaid, Jason Robards, Spalding Gray, Catherine O'Hara.* A solid ensemble cast helps bring to life this otherwise ordinary but involving newspaper comedy-drama. In this a-day-in-the-life-of-a-journalist, Keaton stars as the city editor of a New York daily tabloid who is caught in a dilemma when his managing editor (the wonderfully steely Close) wants to publish a story proclaiming two black youths guilty of murder when there's a chance they might be innocent. It becomes a battle of business vs. ethics when the two literally fight it out. Duvall nicely plays the paper's editor, and Quaid has some funny scenes as a paranoid photographer who may not be that paranoid after all. ★★½ VHS: $9.90; DVD: $24.99

The Paper Chase

(1973, 111 min, US, James Bridges) *Timothy Bottoms, John Houseman, Lindsay Wagner, Edward Herrmann, James Naughton.* Exceptional study of academia with Bottoms as a Harvard Law student and Houseman (in his brilliant Oscar-winning performance) as his professor and adversary. ★★★½ VHS: $9.99

Paper Moon

(1973, 103 min, US, Peter Bogdanovich) *Ryan O'Neal, Tatum O'Neal, Madeline Kahn, P.J. Johnson, John Hillerman.* Bogdanovich's triumphant follow-up to *The Last Picture Show* and *What's Up Doc,* his other two classics, is, unfortunately, his last great work. One of the most charming comedies of the 1970s, the story follows Papa Ryan and Oscar winner Tatum star as Depression-era bible-selling grifters working their way through the Midwest. Excellent support from Kahn, Johnson and Hillerman. (The Director's Cut, which runs 114 minutes, is available for $19.99 in a letterboxed format) ★★★★ VHS: $14.99

A Paper Wedding

(1991, 90 min, Canada, Michel Brault) *Genevieve Bujold, Manuel Aranguiz.* A Canuck *Green Card*, this predictable but nevertheless charming drama features a deceptively impassive performance by Bujold. She plays an unmarried university professor who, in order to help her immigration lawyer-sister, agrees to a marriage of convenience with a Chilean dissident who hopes to avoid deportation. The paper wedding becomes complicated, however, after immigration officials begin an investigation, forcing the unlikely couple to live together. Is love just around the bend? (French with English subtitles) ★★★ VHS: $79.99

Paperhouse

(1989, 92 min, GB, Bernard Rose) *Charotte Burke, Elliott Spiers, Glenne Headly, Ben Cross.* First-time director Rose has fashioned an engrossing, surreal and frightening psychological horror film about an 11-year-old girl whose vivid imagination propels her from the safety of her bedroom to an eerie world conjured up by her own subconscious fears. Confined to bed because of recurring fainting spells, Anna spends her time drawing and becomes especially interested in finishing her sketch of a lonely house. But when she is asleep, she is transported to this house to find a paralyzed young boy and an unseen yet palpable evil. Vivid images, ominous landscapes and an ending to rattle even the most impassive viewer. ★★★

Papillon

(1973, 150 min, US, Franklin J. Schaffner) *Steve McQueen, Dustin Hoffman, Victor Jory, Anthony Zerbe.* McQueen gives what may be his best performance as the Devil's Island convict who is determined to escape, no matter what the cost. Easily one of the best "escape" films ever made. Hoffman gives magnificent support as a wise and easily contented prisoner. An intense and beautiful film. (Letterboxed VHS available for $19.99) ★★★★ VHS: $14.99; DVD: $19.99

Parade

(1973, 88 min, France, Jacques Tati) *Jacques Tati.* Newly rediscovered and restored, Tati's final film (made a year before he went bankrupt) was shot on video and was originally made for Swedish television. While not ranking with his best work, the film features many gloriously funny visual gags as Tati takes us through the many acts of a circus troupe who perform for an appreciative audience of two small children. This celebration of innocence and simple entertainment has clowns, magicians, acrobats and mimes who all take center stage for a time. A witty and humorously entertaining film with minimal dialogue and maximum enjoyment. ★★★ VHS: $29.99

The Paradine Case

(1948, 116 min, US, Alfred Hitchcock) *Gregory Peck, Ethel Barrymore, Charles Laughton, Ann Todd, Louis Jourdan, Charles Coburn, Leo G. Carroll.* Attorney Peck risks his marriage and profession when he falls in love with the enigmatic Mrs. Paradine, on trial for murdering her rich, blind husband. This talky but fascinating did-she-or-didn't-she also features Laughton as the delightfully lascivious judge. ★★★ VHS: $14.99; DVD: $14.99

Paradise

(1991, 115 min, US, Mary Agnes Donoghue) *Don Johnson, Melanie Griffith, Elijah Wood, Thora Birch.* A surprisingly effective remake of the French hit *Le Grand Chemin*. Johnson and Griffith play a troubled rural couple who take care of a friend's young son for the summer. The shy, sheltered youth (well played by Wood) befriends a young tomboy (Birch), who helps the boy emerge from his shell. And, in turn, the youth helps the couple come to terms with the death of their baby. A low-key, rather sweet coming-of-age tale. ★★★

Paradise Alley

(1978, 109 min, US, Sylvester Stallone) *Sylvester Stallone, Anne Archer, Armand Assante.* Stallone wrote, directed and stars in this gritty though contrived story of three brothers from Hell's Kitchen who enter the world of wrestling to escape their New York City ghetto environment. ★★ VHS: $9.99

Paradise Lost: The Child Murders at Robin Hood Hill

(1996, 150 min, US, Joe Berlinger & Bruce Sinofsky) Picking up where they left off with *Brother's Keeper*, directors Berlinger & Sinofsky once again travel to small-town America to cover a sensational murder trial. In this case, the locale is West Memphis, Arkansas, and the trial is that of three teens who are accused of the brutal satanic ritual murder of three 8-year-old boys. The film's excessive running time will seem all-too-brief as Berlinger and Sinofsky do a brilliant job of presenting the myriad points of view and stringing them together into a riveting narrative. Sure to leave the viewer wondering — did they or didn't they? ★★★★ VHS: $14.99

Paradise Road

(1997, 113 min, GB/US, Bruce Beresford) *Glenn Close, Frances McDormand, Pauline Collins, Cate Blanchett, Jennifer Ehle, Julianna Marguiles, Wendy Hughes, Clyde Kusatsu.* There's a telling moment in *Paradise Road* which transcends traditional POW films. British prisoner Close is taken into the jungle by the guard who has beaten her. Instead of another attack, he reveals an unexpected humanity which takes her by surprise — through the universality of music, there is the slightest glimmer of hope. And it is through music that the prisoners of *Paradise Road* retain their faith and the will to survive. Based on actual incidents which occured in a Japanese POW camp during WWII, this is the affecting, hard-hitting story of a group of female Allied prisoners who form a "vocal orchestra" to show the enemy "they still have life to them." Though it sometimes approaches sappy and clichéd waters, it

is quite touching and affirming. Close's stirring performance is the film's center of gravity. ★★★ VHS: $9.99; DVD: $24.99

The Parallax View

(1974, 102 min, US, Alan J. Pakula) *Warren Beatty, Paula Prentiss, William Daniels, Hume Cronyn.* Complicated and fascinating political thriller with Beatty as a newspaper reporter investigating the assassination of a senator. As he digs further into the story, his own life and the lives of witnesses and those around him become increasingly in danger. ★★★½ VHS: $14.99; DVD: $29.99

Pardon Mon Affaire

(1977, 105 min, France, Yves Robert) *Jean Rochefort, Claude Brasseur, Guy Bedos, Victor Lanoux.* Miserably remade by Gene Wilder as *The Woman in Red*, this lovely, wry French boudoir comedy follows four buddies who undergo a series of complicated comic adventures through the streets and bedrooms of Paris. Rochefort stars in a wonderful comic performance as the ringleader and chief erotic provocateur. ★★★

Pardon Mon Affaire, Too

(1977, 110 min, France, Yves Robert) *Jean Rochefort, Claude Brasseur, Guy Bedos, Victor Lanoux.* A film that pokes fun at marriage, fidelity, love and friendship, is a zestful continuation of the extramarital affairs of Rochefort and his middle-aged friends. Their appetites for inflated fantasies and faded dreams are insightfully explored in this gently satiric farce. ★★½

Pardon My Trunk

(Buongiorno, Elefante!)

(1952, 85 min, Italy, Gianni Franciolini) *Vittorio De Sica, Sabu.* De Sica turns in a fine performance in this wild though uneven satire of a Italian schoolteacher who receives an unwanted gift of an elephant from a wealthy prince. His efforts to rid himself of the bulky present set off a series of comic vignettes. (Dubbed) ★★½

The Parent Trap

(1961, 127 min, US, David Swift) *Hayley Mills, Brian Keith, Maureen O'Hara.* Cute though sentimental Disney comedy with Mills doubling as long-lost twin sisters who meet at summer camp and devise a plan to reunite their divorced parents Keith and O'Hara. (Remade in 1998) ★★½ VHS: $19.99

The Parent Trap

(1998, 128 min, US, Nancy Meyers) *Dennis Quaid, Natasha Richardson, Lindsay Lohan.* Separated-at-birth twins meet at camp, and decide to try to reunite their parents in this ceaselessly optimistic remake of the 1961 hit. All the right emotional buttons are hit: sisterhood, reunions with never-before-seen parents, unwanted evil stepparents, and, of course, the desire to see divorced parents together, in love again. It's fun and sweet, and hard to not get sucked in, even if you're the parent and not the kid. ★★★ VHS: $22.99; DVD: $29.99

Harry Dean Stanton in *Paris, Texas*

Parenthood

(1989, 124 min, US, Ron Howard) *Steve Martin, Jason Robards, Mary Steenburgen, Dianne Wiest, Rick Moranis, Tom Hulce, Keanu Reeves, Martha Plimpton.* An all-star cast shines in Howard's charming and very funny family comedy. Howard and cowriters Lowell Ganz and Babaloo Mandel examine American middle-class family life as seen through the not-so-ordinary eyes of the multigenerational Buckman clan. Martin stars as Gil, a worrisome father who is ever-aware of personal shortcomings with his own father and is determined not to repeat the same with his troubled son. ★★★ VHS: $9.99

Parents

(1989, 90 min, US, Bob Balaban) *Bryan Madorsky, Randy Quaid, Sandy Dennis, Mary Beth Hurt.* First-time director Balaban serves up a wild postmodern feast that may leave you with a bad taste in your mouth but a grin on your face. Young Madorsky discovers his Ozzie and Harriet parents have a terrible secret and it's hardly appetizing. Not for everyone, but if you prefer your filmmaking adventurous, give it a nibble. ★★★; DVD: $24.99

Paris Belongs to Us

(1959, 138 min, France, Jacques Rivette) *Jean-Claude Brialy, Betty Schneider; Cameos: Jean-Luc Godard, Claude Chabrol, Jacques Demy.* New Wave director Rivette's first feature is this low-budget drama. The story is set in a near-deserted Paris one summer where a group of enthusiastic young amateurs get together in an effort to present a production of Shakespeare's "Pericles." But the death of the composer, suicide of the producer and mounting political and sexual tensions between the actors undermine their efforts. A spare and moody tale of optimism and doom. (French with English subtitles) ★★★

Paris Blues

(1961, 98 min, US, Martin Ritt) *Paul Newman, Sidney Poitier, Joanne Woodward, Diahann Carroll, Louis Armstrong.* Jazz and romance in the City of Lights, as musicians Newman and Poitier court Woodward and Carroll. The film makes good use of a fine Duke Ellington score. Louis Armstrong makes a great cameo appearance in a smoky Paris jazz club. Like all Martin Ritt films politics make an appearance, there's a sub-plot involving racism. Entertaining and well done. ★★★ VHS: $14.99

Paris Express

(1953, 80 min, GB, Harold French) *Claude Rains, Anouk Aimée, Herbert Lom.* Rains stars as a low-level clerk who embezzles from his business in hopes of going on extended holiday, but instead finds himself lured by a femme fatale into a web of robbery, murder and intrigue. Rains' good performance and a moody atmosphere compensate for the sometimes muddled narrative. ★★½

Paris, France

(1993, 111 min, Canada, Gérard Ciccoritti) *Leslie Hope, Victor Ertmanis, Dan Lett, Peter Outerbridge.* Deliriously paced and entertainingly saturated with numerous and inventively diverse sexual couplings, this tale of mid-life crisis, regret, longing and sexual repression is anything but your standard melodrama. Set in Toronto, the story involves the three owners of a small publishing company: a married couple, Lucy and Michael, and their business partner, William. The stability of their lives is thrown into an emotional maelstrom with the arrival of Sloan, a former boxer turned writer. As Sloan becomes involved with both the sexually starved Lucy and the openly gay William, his sexual needs lead to confusion. Beyond the steamy sex scenes is the uninhibited notion of exploring all of one's many sexual needs. (French with English subtitles) ★★★ VHS: $9.99

Paris Is Burning

(1990, 78 min, US, Jennie Livingston) Welcome to the world of the Ball, where everyone is Cinderella. The balls in question are the voguing and drag-balls of Harlem, the subject of director Livingston's award-winning and sensationally entertaining documentary. Voguing, an underground dance invented by black and Latino queers, burst upon the pop scene when Madonna "took" voguing for herself and popularized it. But it's the originators of the form who are the film's subject. Voguers, or "ball walkers," affiliate themselves with "Houses," the equivalent of nonviolent gay street gangs, and compete for trophies at the late-nite balls. Livingston uses sensitivity and compassion in documenting her stars. ★★★★ VHS: $14.99

Paris, Texas

(1984, 150 min, US, Wim Wenders) *Harry Dean Stanton, Nastassja Kinski, Dean Stockwell.* Wenders' understated exploration of human loneliness and vulnerability features Stanton as a near-catatonic wanderer who is somewhat snapped out of his stupor by his brother (Stockwell). Upon reuniting with his young son, he and the boy set off in search of their long-lost wife and mother, Kinski. Sam Shepard's screenplay and Robby Müller's camera keenly map out the desert of the human soul as set against the bleak Texas landscape; Ry Cooder's haunting slide guitar finishes off the effect. ★★★

Paris Trout

(1991, 100 min, US, Stephen Gyllenhaal) *Dennis Hopper, Barbara Hershey, Ed Harris, Tina Lifford.* A stunning made-for-cable adaptation of Pete Dexter's award-winning novel. Hopper is outstanding as the title character, a racist 1940s Southern storekeeper who kills a young black girl, the sister of a man Trout cheated in a car sale, and who now stands trial for murder. Hershey is terrific as Hopper's abused wife, whose moral outrage to her husband's actions sends her into the arms of lawyer Harris (in a wonderful characterization). ★★★★ VHS: $19.99

Paris When It Sizzles

(1964, 110 min, US, Richard Quine) *Audrey Hepburn, William Holden; Cameos: Fred Astaire, Frank Sinatra, Noël Coward, Marlene Dietrich, Tony Curtis.* Despite an engaging premise and a first-rate cast, this forced comedy offers little in laughs or enjoyment. Screenwriter Holden and secretary Hepburn romp around Paris in a series of fantasies acting out his new script. ★½ VHS: $14.99; DVD: $29.99

Parsifal

(1982, 26 min, West Germany, Hans-Jürgen Syberberg) *Michael Kutter, Karen Krick.* Syberberg, director of *Our Hitler*, has created a spectacular and provocative film experience with this version of Richard Wagner's splendid opera. The eternal drama of the search for the Holy Grail is imaginatively enacted within the crevices and crannies of a mammoth replica of Wagner's death mask, with the character of Parsifal portrayed by both a man (Kutter) and a woman (Krick). The film, while a none-complete performance of the opera, is anything but conventional and is a must for all opera fans and adventurous film enthusiasts. ★★★½ VHS: $29.99; DVD: $39.99

Parting Glances

(1986, 90 min, US, Bill Sherwood) *Richard Ganoung, John Bolger, Steve Buscemi, Adam Nathan.* A wonderfully rich and seductively appealing independent production which definitely rates as one of the best of all gay-themed films. The action takes place in a 24-hour period and centers around Michael (Ganoung) and Robert (Bolger), a gay New York couple who are about to temporarily separate as Robert is transferred overseas. Their attempts to keep the relationship strong and

P

to understand each other is the core of this simple but wise comedy-drama. The supporting cast of mainly gay friends who throw a farewell party for Robert are all finely drawn, but it's Buscemi who steals the film with a bravado performance as Nick, a rock singer and Michael's ex-lover who's dying of AIDS. Produced on a low budget, the film's strengths lie in its simple and honest moments — a loving embrace or a telling confession. A joyful, knowing gay love story. ★★★★ VHS: $29.99; DVD: $29.99

Partisans of Vilna

(1986, 130 min, France, Josh Waletzky) This stirring documentary examines the Jewish resistance during WWII. Interspersing interviews with former freedom fighters from around the world with rare archival footage from the war years, the film spellbindingly introduces us to the Jewish youths who organized an underground resistance in the Vilna ghetto and fought as partisans against the Nazis. A powerful, heartrending tribute to courage in the face of unrelenting adversity. (French, English, Hebrew and Yiddish with English subtitles) ★★★½

Partner

(1968, 112 min, Italy, Bernardo Bertolucci) *Pierre Clementi.* Madness, romanticism, theatre and politics are the theme in *Partner*, a surprisingly noncommercial film director Bertolucci now repudiates. Greatly influenced by the 1968 student rebellions which swept Europe as well as the political cinema of Jean-Luc Godard and the theatrical devices developed by Julian Beck's Living Theatre, the film is a free adaptation of Dostoevsky's "The Double." Clementi stars as a repressed art teacher who is possessed and ultimately driven mad by his alter ego, a political revolutionary. A beautiful but off-setting film that is a must for fans of Bertolucci and followers of political cinema. (Italian with English subtitles) ★★★½ VHS: $19.99

Partners

(1982, 98 min, US, James Burrows) *Ryan O'Neal, John Hurt, Kenneth McMillan.* An odious cop comedy with a "fag" angle, this has to be one of the most offensive gay-themed films ever made. O'Neal plays a straight detective who teams up with effeminate, in-the-closet desk cop Hurt to go undercover as gay lovers to investigate a gay serial killer. Told to "live in their neighborhood, eat in their restaurants and shop in their stores," the film begins to indulge itself with every conceivable homophobic stereotype. Dressed entirely in pink and lilac, Hurt is seen as a scared, helpless femme while O'Neal is the leather-clad man. Watch it and wince! ★ VHS: $14.99

The Party

(1968, 99 min, US, Blake Edwards) *Peter Sellers, Claudine Longet.* Sellers gives one of his funniest performances as a clumsy Indian actor invited to a private Hollywood party. Edwards directs with the same comic assurance that he exercised in the *Pink Panther* series: inventive sight gags and crazy comedy abound. ★★★½ VHS: $14.99

Party Girl

(1994, 98 min, US, Daisy Von Scherler Mayer) *Parker Posey, Anthony DeSando, Guillermo Diaz, Donna Mitchell, Liev Schreiber.* The joys of capitalism and social conformity are the hidden agendas in this scattershot comedy which ostensibly celebrates bohemian/alternative life in New York's East Village. The story revolves around 24-year-old Mary (Posey) who undergoes a transformation from mindless "party girl" to being a prim and proper librarian. We've seen it all before, but it's a harmless romp. ★★ VHS: $14.99

Pascali's Island

(1988, 104 min, GB, James Dearden) *Ben Kingsley, Charles Dance, Helen Mirren.* Kingsley gives an admirable performance in this rather slowly paced drama set on a small Greek island during the last days of the fading Ottoman Empire. Kingsley plays a local eccentric and Turkish spy who unwittingly becomes involved with a suave British archeologist (Dance) and his plot to steal a precious artifact from the isle. Also caught up in the intrigue is an Austrian expatriate (Mirren in a captivating performance), a lonely artist who falls in love with the handsome adventurer with tragic results. The film is highlighted by sumptuous cinematography and beautiful locales. ★★

A Passage to India

(1984, 164 min, GB, David Lean) *Judy Davis, Victor Banerjee, Peggy Ashcroft, James Fox, Alec Guinness.* Master filmmaker Lean proves himself capable of pulling yet another beautifully crafted "big" picture out of his hat with this meticulous adaptation of the E.M. Forster novel about the clash between British and Indian cultures and classes in the colonial India of the 1920s. A superlative cast plays against the brilliance of Lean's craft, with which he imbues each and every backdrop with flavor and nuance. Very satisfying. ★★★★ VHS: $19.99; DVD: $29.99

Passage to Marseille

(1944, 109 min, US, Michael Curtiz) *Humphrey Bogart, Claude Rains, Sidney Greenstreet, Peter Lorre.* Curtiz, the director of *Casablanca*, reteamed with that film's star, Bogart, and many of its supporting cast in hopes of repeating that classic's critical and commercial success. Although they didn't succeed on either level, *Passage to Marseille* is nonetheless an acceptable WWII adventure about escaped Devil's Island convicts who join the Free French in the fight against the Nazis. Confusing flashbacks-within-flashbacks keep this film from being the first-rate production Curtiz and company had hoped. ★★½ VHS: $19.99

La Passante

(1982, 106 min, France, Jacques Rouffio) *Michel Piccoli, Romy Schneider.* Schneider is wonderful in a dual role in this, her final film. It is the story of two lovers who are mysteriously compelled for political actions to become involved in the assassination of a South American ambassador who may have been a former Nazi. (French with English subtitles) ★★½

The Passenger

(1975, 123 min, Italy, Michelangelo Antonioni) *Jack Nicholson, Maria Schneider, Ian Hendry.* Nicholson stars in this hypnotic thriller as a discontented reporter who changes his identity for a dead man. A brilliant portrayal of alienation's pangs and the barren landscape of one man's soul. ★★★½

Passenger 57

(1992, 84 min, US, Kevin Hooks) *Wesley Snipes, Tom Sizemore, Bruce Payne, Bruce Greenwood, Elizabeth Hurley.* A *Die Hard* clone, Hooks' cartoonish action film has the friendly skies substituting for the skyscraper as the backdrop for the act of terrorism. Snipes stars as an ex-secret service agent-turned-airline security consultant who battles a group of deadly international skyjackers. While the script is laughably illogical at points, Snipes shows what a good actor can do with a bland script, as opposed to a good action film with a bland actor (i.e. Steven Seagal in *Under Siege*). ★★ VHS: $9.99; DVD: $19.99

Passion

(1994, 105 min, US, James Lapine) *Donna Murphy, Jere Shea, Marin Mazzie.* Stephen Sondheim's Tony Award-winning musical has been filmed live with the original Broadway cast. Based on the Ettore Scola film *Passione d'Amore*, the story follows Giorgio (Shea), a heroic army captain, who is transferred to a new post where he becomes the object of obsession by the cousin of his superior officer, an unattractive, psychologically wounded young woman. Though *Passion* debuted to less than enthusiastic response, especially with Sondheim devotees, time appears to have aged the musical nicely (much like his "Merrily We Roll Along") as it stands squarely on its own strengths and weaknesses. *Passion* is inventive, involving and, yes, passionate; its lyrics often witty, its score characteristic but effective, and its book economically good. ★★★½

Passion Fish

(1992, 136 min, US, John Sayles) *Mary McDonnell, Alfre Woodard, David Strathairn, Angela Bassett, Nora Dunn, Vondie Curtis-Hall.* Sayles' upbeat comic melodrama explores the rigors of adjusting to life as a paraplegic. McDonnell stars as May-Alice, a soap opera star who, after being crippled by a New York taxi, returns to her home town on the Louisiana bayou to wallow in self-pity and heap abuse on a succession of unsuspecting house nurses. She finally meets her match, however, when the agency sends her the equally uncompromising Chantelle (Woodard). Sayles wrings every ounce of humanity and wry humor from the clash of these two emotional tyrants as they slowly warm to each other. Marvelously photographed on location, the film sports a trio of splendid performances from McDonnell (who was nominated for an Oscar), from Woodard (who should have been) and Strathairn as a local Cajun handyman who takes an obvious shine to McDonnell. ★★★½ VHS: $9.99; DVD: $29.99

Pather Panchali

Passion for Life

(1948, 89 min, France, Jean-Paul Chanois) *Bernard Blier, Julliette Faber.* A sincere young teacher (Blier), impassioned with progressive ideas, comes to a provincial village where he meets opposition from the stodgy parents. Predating *Dead Poets Society* and *Stand and Deliver* by many decades, this sincere though sentimental tale follows the teacher as he must not only prove his worth but his methods as well after he promises that every one of the students in his class will pass a national test. (French with English subtitles) ★★½ VHS: $59.99

The Passion of Anna

(1969, 100 min, Sweden, Ingmar Bergman) *Liv Ullmann, Max von Sydow, Erland Josephson, Bibi Andersson.* Bergman continues with the recurring theme of a couple (or couples) isolated from society yet under attack from either, or both, outside forces as well as within their own selves. In this deeply textured psychological drama, von Sydow moves to a sparsely populated island where he meets a widowed young woman (the remarkable Ullmann) and an architect (Josephson) and his wife (Andersson). Complex emotional and spiritual fears are brought to the surface as the four develop revealing relationships that lay bare their despair and protective self-deceptions. (Swedish with English subtitles) ★★★★ VHS: $19.99

The Passion of Joan of Arc

(1928, 82 min, France, Carl Dreyer) *Maria Falconetti, Eugenia Sylvaw.* Based on the actual transcripts of the historical trial and using innovative close-ups that have made film history, Dreyer's extraordinary film of the Inquisition, trial and death of Joan of Arc remains as fresh and powerful today as it was over 70 years ago. This is director Dreyer's original cut, recently found and remastered. (Silent with musical accompaniment) ★★★★ VHS: $29.99; DVD: $39.99

Passion of Mind

(2000, 105 min, US, Alain Berliner) *Demi Moore, Stellan Skarsgård, William Fichtner.* Treading similar ground as *Sliding Doors* and *Me Myself I, Passion of Mind* is a serious drama of Marie (Moore), a widowed Parisian who dreams that she is Marty, a single career woman in New York. Or is it the other way around? When romances bloom in both lives simultaneously, she fears confronting the fact that, perhaps, only one of them can be real. Demi's return to acting, after a post-*G.I. Jane* hiatus, only serves to prove that too often, Moore is less. This rather arty fever-dream, the first English-language feature from Berliner (*Ma Vie en Rose*), relies on Moore to carry every scene, and she's not up to the task. Pity, as Berliner brings a ravishing romantic sweep to the proceedings. ★★½ VHS: $14.99; DVD: $29.99

The Passionate Thief

(1962, 100 min, Italy, Mario Monicello) *Toto, Ben Gazzara, Anna Magnani.* The director of *Big Deal on Madonna Street* brings his comedic talents to this entertaining story of larceny and love. Italian favorite Toto is a small-time bit player who repeatedly thwarts the efforts of a pickpocket (Gazzara) to earn his living one New Year's Eve night. A minor, but worthwhile comedy of errors. (Italian with English subtitles) ★★½ VHS: $19.99

Passione d'Amore

(1982, 117 min, Italy, Ettore Scola) *Laura Antonelli.* A handsome and witty tale about the ironies and intricacies of love and beauty. In 19th-century Italy, a dashing young cavalry officer engages in an adulterous affair with a voluptuous woman only to become involved with his commanding officer's homely, cantankerous cousin. This sardonic, dark comedy received a special jury prize at the Cannes Film Festival. (The basis for the Stephen Sondheim musical "Passion") (Dubbed) ★★★½ VHS: $24.99

Passport to Pimlico

(1948, 85 min, GB, Henry Cornelius) *Stanley Holloway, Basil Radford, Margaret Rutherford.* This wonderful little British comedy has an anarchic "little man battling the establishment" attitude. A fish store proprietor unearths an ancient treaty that establishes Pimlico as a part of Burgundy, instead of London, thus releasing store owners from both the postwar rationing and British licensing laws. A wonderful parody of the post-war state of Europe. ★★★½ VHS: $14.99

Pastime

(1991, 95 min, US, Robin B. Armstrong) *William Russ, Glenn Plummer, Scott Plank.* Tucked in between the theatrical releases of *Field of Dreams* and *A League of Their Own*, this small-scaled, bittersweet drama is not in the same league as those two gems, but is nevertheless an appealing, carefully rendered character study. Russ makes the most of his first starring role with a gorgeous turn as a veteran minor league ballplayer at the end of his career. Having had a brief stint in the majors, and after twenty years in the minors, Russ is now the butt of his teammates' jokes, not fully aware of his own shortcomings and still hoping to make it back to "the Bigs." When he befriends a young, talented pitcher, both men strike a friendship to help each other face their uncertain futures. ★★½ VHS: $14.99

Pat and Mike

(1952, 95 min, US, George Cukor) *Katharine Hepburn, Spencer Tracy, Aldo Ray, Jim Backus.* This enjoyable sports comedy is a pleasant tale with Kate as a sports pro and Spencer as her manager. It's here Tracy says the line, "There's not much meat on her, but what there is is cherce." Written by Ruth Gordon and Garson Kanin. ★★★ VHS: $14.99; DVD: $19.99

Pat Garrett and Billy the Kid

(1973, 122 min, US, Sam Peckinpah) *James Coburn, Kris Kristofferson, Jason Robards, Slim Pickens, Rita Coolidge, Bob Dylan.* Outlaw-turned-lawman Pat Garrett (Coburn) stalks Billy the Kid (Kristofferson) across the New Mexican desert in this vivid Peckinpah western. Dylan makes his acting debut. ★★½ VHS: $19.99

Patch Adams

(1998, 116 min, US, Tom Shadyac) *Robin Williams, Monica Potter, Daniel London, Philip Seymour Hoffman, Bob Gunton, Irma P. Hall.* Doctor Williams, wanted in overkill. Playing a physician for what seems like the umpteenth time, Williams is certainly at home in this overly sentimental, crowd-pleasing comedy (based on a true story) which gives the actor the chance to both mug and tug (at the heart). He plays Patch Adams, a sanitorium inmate who decides to go to medical school; his unique, irreverent humor and outlook make him a hit with patients, but not so with school administration. Eventually, he opens his own makeshift clinic for the poor. Williams is able to milk some laughs thanks to Patch's schtick, but the story goes way overboard in the syrup department, and patches in Adams' life are glossed over which gives the film a jagged feel. ★★ VHS: $14.99; DVD: $24.99

A Patch of Blue

(1965, 105 min, US, Guy Green) *Sidney Poitier, Elizabeth Hartman, Shelley Winters, Wallace Ford, Ivan Dixon.* A moving, sensitive drama of a blind white woman (Hartman) falling in love with a black man (Poitier). Fine acting accentuates this story; Winters won an Oscar as Hartman's overbearing mother. (VHS available letterboxed or pan & scan) ★★★ VHS: $19.99

Father Panchali

(1955, 115 min, India, Satyajit Ray) *Kanu Banerjee, Karuna Banerjee.* This first film of Ray's widely acclaimed Apu Trilogy tells of Apu's childhood as a member of a poverty-stricken family in a Bengali village. The film is grippingly realistic and, although the locales are exotic, the human situation it portrays is shattering. (Bengali with English subtitles) (Sequel: *Aparajito*) ★★★★ VHS: $19.99

Pathfinder

(1988, 88 min, Norway, Nils Gaup) *Mikkel Gaup, Nils Utsi.* Set in the bitter cold and snow-covered tundra of northern Finland, this exciting, violent and emotional adventure story, taken from a 1,000-year-old legend, concerns an unusually dramatic coming-of-age of a teenage boy whose family is massacred by a rampaging band of thieves. Young Aigin flees to another village but finds that the killers are on his trail. He must decide whether to flee with the others, stand and fight a hopeless battle or join forces with the village's elderly but still powerful "pathfinder." Infused with the cultural mysticism and superstitions of the nomadic Lapp people, this Academy Award-nominated tale tells of the eternal battle of man against his own forces of evil. (Lapp with English subtitles) ★★★½ VHS: $19.99

Paths of Glory

(1957, 86 min, GB, Stanley Kubrick) *Kirk Douglas, Ralph Meeker, Adolphe Menjou, George Macready.* Kubrick's first true masterpiece combines superb direction with outstanding performances and remains one of the most shattering studies of the insanity of war to date. During WWI, a French general orders his men on a futile mission. When they return in failure, he picks three soldiers to be tried and executed for cowardice. This scathing attack on the hypocrisies of war is, so far as we know, still banned in France. ★★★★ VHS: $9.99; DVD: $14.99

The Patriot

(2000, 165 min, US, Roland Emmerich) *Mel Gibson, Heath Ledger, Joely Richardson, Jason Isaacs, Chris Cooper, Tcheky Karyo, Tom Wilkinson, Rene Auberjonois.* An often rousing, often sentimental actioner, *The Patriot* is an old-fashioned Revolutionary War story told with outstanding

Paths of Glory

cinematography and elegant production design. Gibson is Benjamin Martin, a father and widower who would rather use diplomacy than guns for American independence. When a particularly nasty British colonel (Isaacs) murders one of his children, Martin spearheads the local militia in the bloody, deadly fight against the British. As was the case with Emmerich's *Independence Day*, this is not subtle storytelling (Isaacs' military monster is a Nazi bad guy dressed in a red coat). But at the heart of the story is a compelling, even stirring re-creation of the birth of a nation, and the determination of a father to keep his family together. Gibson is extremely effective as Martin, based on a real-life character who was also the inspiration for the 1950s TV show "Swamp Fox." The battle scenes are impressively staged, and have greater resonance than a few of the more intimate moments. ★★★ VHS: $19.99; DVD: $19.99

Patriot Games

(1992, 118 min, US, Philip Noyce) *Harrison Ford, Anne Archer, Patrick Bergen, Sean Bean, Richard Harris, James Earl Jones, Samuel L. Jackson.* A very capable sequel to the hit thriller *The Hunt for Red October*, with Ford taking over the role of CIA agent Jack Ryan first introduced by Alec Baldwin. While on a lecture tour in London, Ryan thwarts an attempted Royal Family assassination, killing one of the terrorists in the process. This makes him and his family a target of the dead man's brother. Punctuated by a series of well-mounted and exciting action scenes, the film is marred only by a hastily tacked-on ending which belies what came before it. Whereas Baldwin's Jack Ryan was a protagonist driven by rational thought, Ford's Ryan is a reluctant but nevertheless visceral hero to be reckoned with. (VHS available letterboxed or pan & scan) (Sequel: *Clear and Present Danger*) ★★★ VHS: $14.99; DVD: $29.99

Pattes Blanches

(1949, 92 min, France, Jean Grémillon) *Suzy Delair, Fernand Ledoux.* Set against lovingly rendered Breton landscapes, this perverse melodrama of obsessive rivalry is a twisted mesh of sexual jealousies, intrigues, violence and revenge. Director Grémillon, best known for his documentaries and for presiding over the Cinémathèque, fills his film with strange scenes and a wonderful trick ending. The film follows the sordid story of two sons who fight for the love of a pretty but vicious innkeeper's mistress. The title refers to the white spats worn by a reclusive aristocrat who is ridiculed and loathed by the villagers. (French with English subtitles) ★★½ VHS: $59.99

Patti Rocks

(1988, 105 min, US, David Burton Morris) *Chris Mulkey, John Jennings, Karen Landry.* An original and quite controversial dissection of the attitudes and misconceptions of what some men feel about women. Billy (Mulkey), a 30-year-old married dock worker, convinces his old friend Eddie (Jennings) to accompany him on a long ride to Billy's pregnant girlfriend's house, to help him break off their relationship. The first half of the film is the car ride, as the two men exchange their conflicting views on women and life in vivid, locker-

room talk. The second-half takes place at Patti's apartment, where the men discover an independent and compassionate woman who has her own ideas on her future with Billy and the baby. ★★★

Patton

(1970, 170 min, US, Franklin J. Schaffner) *George C. Scott, Karl Malden, Stephen Young.* Scott won (and refused) an Oscar for his power-house performance of the controversial WWII commander, General George Patton, in this superior wartime biography. The film, which won seven Oscars including Best Picture, follows Patton's campaign in Europe and Northern Africa. (Letterboxed VHS available for $19.99) ★★★★ VHS: $14.99; DVD: $24.99

Patty Hearst

(1988, 108 min, US, Paul Schrader) *Natasha Richardson, William Forsythe, Ving Rhames, Frances Fisher, Dana Delany.* Richardson plays the title role in this dark, gritty version of Patty Hearst's story about the young heiress being kidnapped and brainwashed by the Symbionese Liberation Army; then being forced to participate in a series of bank robberies. ★★½

Paul Robeson

(1978, 118 min, US, Lloyd Richards) *James Earl Jones.* Jones, accompanied only by Burt Wallace on piano, holds the stage for nearly two hours as Paul Robeson, recounting a remarkable life in a mesmerizing performance. Jones adeptly shifts mood and tone from episode to episode as Robeson responds to indignity and prejudice with good humor and a well-justified anger tempered by a towering intellect. Written by Phillip Hayes Dean, the story covers Robeson's undergraduate days at Rutgers, his brilliant theatrical career, and his struggle with racism and the House Un-American Activities Committee. This complex, courageous man of integrity is given full voice with Jones' vital, stirring portrayal; and this play on film is satisfying both dramatically and as history. ★★★½ VHS: $59.99

Pauline at the Beach

(1983, 94 min, France, Eric Rohmer) *Amanda Langlet, Arielle Dombasle.* This effervescent sex farce follows the amorous escapades of a precocious young girl, her stunningly beautiful cousin, an adventurous rogue and a beleaguered beachcomber. A witty meditation on the folly of love and the quest for romance. (French with English subtitles) ★★★

The Pawnbroker

(1965, 116 min, US, Sidney Lumet) *Rod Steiger, Geraldine Fitzgerald, Brock Peters.* Gripping drama of a New York pawnbroker haunted by the memory of his imprisonment in a Nazi camp during WWII. Steiger gives a virtuoso performance as the embittered Holocaust survivor. Remarkably realized by director Lumet. ★★★★ VHS: $14.99

Pay It Forward

(2000, 122 min, US, Mimi Leder) *Kevin Spacey, Helen Hunt, Haley Joel Osment, Jay Mohr, James Caviezel, Angie Dickinson, Jon Bon Jovi.* Good intentions may have paved that road to Hell, but it also accounts for some strange goings-

Ben Affleck in *Pearl Harbor*

the-art special effects upon a film that is more often than not devoid of human drama. In essence a three-act play, *Pearl Harbor* begins as if John Hughes had been asked to write a WWII film. Farmboys/best friends Affleck and Hartnett are pilots. They meet nurse Beckinsale in cutesy fashion, and some mundane romance enters the picture. The film's middle section is the extremely well-crafted attack sequence; it's brilliantly executed, though it does resemble *Titanic* in a couple shots. In the final third, the film finds a compelling rhythm, but unfortunately, it's too little too late. It's a minor distraction that screenwriter Randall Wallace has played fast and loose with historical accuracy (it's okay, it's literary license). But it's a major one that this is the umpteenth war film in which buddies fall for the same girl in a long, drawn-out plot. The superb re-creation of the attack is what the attraction is here, but *what* it takes to get there! A few nice surprises help, like Voight's FDR, and a tense finale over enemy territory. Ultimately, however, *Pearl Harbor*, like its many good-looking characters, is spectacular to look at but rather empty inside. ★★ VHS: $22.99; DVD: $29.99

on in Las Vegas. In this promising fable which is both heart-warming and overly dramatic, an outcast schoolboy named Trevor (Osment) invents "pay it forward" as a school project. What that means is you do something nice for someone, and they do something nice for 3 people, and they each do something nice for 3 other people, and so on — it's a human chain letter with kindness as its own reward. One of Trevor's own acts is to play matchmaker for his waitress mom (Hunt) and disfigured schoolteacher (Spacey), an unlikely romance that is one of the weaker links in this uneven chain. Spacey is excellent as the caring teacher, but Hunt is just doing a reprise of her *As Good as It Gets* character. Osment gives a full-blooded portrayal of an adolescent wise beyond his years. There are scenes in *Pay It Forward* that genuinely touch the heart, and others that will turn the stomach; but the film could have come together as a whole had it not been for its awful ending. ★★½ VHS: $19.99; DVD: $24.99

Payback

(1999, 110 min, US, Brian Helgeland) *Mel Gibson, Gregg Henry, Maria Bello, David Paymer, Kris Kristofferson, James Coburn, William Devane, Deborah Kara Unger, Bill Duke, John Glover.* "That's just mean, man," Coburn's exasperated gangster chief declares as Gibson's determined thief bent on revenge shoots his expensive alligator luggage. That also ably describes this sadistic, loud and violent thriller which is competently made but doesn't know when enough is enough. *Payback* is based on Richard Stark's "The Hunter," the same source material for 1967's *Point Blank*. But it is there similarities end. John Boorman's tale was a moody noir; director Helgeland's is an abrasive action thriller tailored to its star's persona. Gibson is double-crossed and left for dead. He returns to get even and get money owed to him. Helgeland keeps the film rolling at a brisk pace, but its stylized shootings, torture and explosions become numbing after awhile. ★★ VHS: $14.99; DVD: $24.99

PCU

(1994, 85 min, US, Hart Bochner) *Jeremy Piven, David Spade, Chris Young, Jon Favreau, Megan Ward, Jessica Walter, Jake Busey.* A lot funnier than it has a right to be, this *Animal House* rip-off for the '90s follows to the letter the rules of the campus comedy (especially pitting uptight students and administration against fun-loving misfits), which makes *PCU* just another teenage comedy clone. However, that's only half the story. For as a satire on political correctness, this is a surprisingly funny, predictably sophomoric romp which takes pot shots at all of the sacred cows of the 1990s. It could even bring a smile or two to PCers (with a sense of humor). ★★½ VHS: $9.99

The Peacemaker

(1997, 122 min, US, Mimi Leder) *George Clooney, Nicole Kidman, Armin Mueller-Stahl, Marcel Lures.* A highly entertaining, kick-ass thriller, *The Peacemaker* marks a very credible directorial debut for Leder as she mixes action, suspense and drama to produce quite a few heart-pounding scenes filmed from all over the globe. A terrific opening sequence introduces a group of Russian terrorists hijacking a train-load of nuclear missiles. Enter nuclear physicist Kidman and military agent Clooney as they try to track the terrorists, missiles, and their eventual destination. Leder keeps the action going at a steady clip, and the finale set on the crowded streets of New York City is quite suspenseful. (Letterboxed VHS available for $14.99) ★★★ VHS: $9.99; DVD: $24.99

Pearl Harbor

(2001, 183 min, US, Michael Bay) *Ben Affleck, Josh Hartnett, Kate Beckinsale, Cuba Gooding, Jr., Tom Sizemore, Ewan Bremner, William Lee Scott, Alec Baldwin, Jon Voight, Dan Aykroyd, Mako, Colm Feore.* It would be easy to dismiss the epic *Pearl Harbor* as a *Titanic* ripoff (tragedy serves as backdrop to romance) and leave it at that, were it not for the amount of attention heaped upon it by the filmmakers and an anxious public. In restaging the surprise attack on Pearl Harbor, director Bay has lavished outstanding state-of-

Pecker

(1998, 86 min, US, John Waters) *Edward Furlong, Christina Ricci, Bess Armstrong, Mary Kay Place, Martha Plimpton, Brendan Sexton III, Mink Stole, Lili Taylor, Lauren Hulsey, Jean Schertler, Patricia Hearst.* Writer-director Waters returns to his subversive comedic grabbag for *Pecker*, a restrained though amusing comedy which combines the director's penchant for shock comedy and a more accessible filmmaking style he honed after *Hairspray*. Set in Baltimore (where else?), the story follows the rise of young Pecker (Furlong), a fledgling photographer whose pictures of his slightly dysfunctional family and working-class neighborhood capture the attention of the New York art scene. It's trash vs. flash when these two worlds collide, and Waters milks some good laughs at the expense of one and all involved. *Pecker* may not always shoot from the hip; but, then, that's not from where Waters is aiming with this omnisexual spoof — we've seen John down and dirtier, but then he's in an awfully good mood. ★★★ VHS: $19.99; DVD: $24.99

The Pedestrian

(1974, 97 min, West Germany, Maximilian Schell) *Maximilian Schell, Peggy Ashcroft.* An excellent drama examining the guilt of Nazi crimes against humanity and their effects on German society 45 years later. A wealthy industrialist is involved in a car accident in which his son is killed. The ensuing publicity brings out a story that he might have participated in the slaughter of a Greek village during the war. The circumstantial evidence linking him to the crimes and the country's reaction to the news combine to indict the man. But is he guilty? (Dubbed) ★★★½

Pee-wee's Big Adventure

(1985, 90 min, US, Tim Burton) *Paul Reubens, Elizabeth Daly, Mark Holton, Jan Hooks, James Brolin, Morgan Fairchild.* There are things about him you wouldn't understand, there are things you couldn't understand, things you shouldn't understand. He's Pee-wee Herman, loner and rebel. Reubens' triumphant characterization is the ultimate child of the Eighties. Follow Pee-wee as he desperately searches for his most prized possession: his recently stolen bicycle. Anti-intelligence was never so brilliant. ★★★½ VHS: $14.99; DVD: $19.99

Peeping Tom

(1960, 101 min, GB, Michael Powell) *Karl-Heinz Boehm, Moira Shearer, Anna Massey, Shirley Anne Field, Nigel Davenport.* Powell's long-suppressed masterpiece is a lucid, slyly witty thriller about a deranged cameraman's obsession with photographing beautiful women as he murders them. So hostilely received at the time of its release, this film virtually ended this great director's career. (Letterboxed) ★★★½ VHS: $19.99; DVD: $39.99

Peggy Sue Got Married

(1986, 104 min, US, Francis Ford Coppola) *Kathleen Turner, Nicolas Cage, Joan Allen, Jim Carrey, Barry Miller, Barbara Harris, Don Murray, Kevin J. O'Connor, Helen Hunt.* A separated 43-year-old mother (Turner) travels back in time to her senior year in high school — where she attempts to set the future right. Cage is her once and future husband. A sweet-natured blend of fantasy, comedy and drama, which, for the most part, works beautifully. Turner is most engaging. ★★★ DVD: $24.99

Peking Opera Blues

(1986, 104 min, Hong Kong, Tsui Hark) *Lin Ching-Hsia, Sally Yeh, Cherie Chung.* This entertaining satirical adventure film features stunning set design, gold-digging dames, plots and counterplots, assassinations, singers and soldiers, all coming together in furiously paced, breathlessly choreographed action sequences. Set in 1913, the frenetic comedy features three young women who become enmeshed in dangerous intrigue involving efforts to topple a general. Director Tsui has been quoted as saying that the film is a satire on "Chinese ignorance of Democracy," but it doesn't stop the fun in this tongue-in-cheek farce. (Letterboxed) (Cantonese with English subtitles) ★★★½ VHS: $19.99; DVD: $49.99

Pee-wee's Big Adventure

The Pelican Brief

(1993, 125 min, US, Alan J. Pakula) *Julia Roberts, Denzel Washington, Sam Shepard, John Heard, Stanley Tucci, Tony Goldwyn.* Roberts is a law student who uncovers the diabolical plot behind the assassination of two Supreme Court justices. Jokingly — but accurately — called a Nancy Drew for the '90s, this slick but lackadaisical film version of John Grisham's best-seller lacks the excitement and tension which made his other '93 movie adaptation, *The Firm*, so enjoyable. Washington costars as a journalist who helps Roberts stay alive after her savvy detective work puts her life in peril. This is the sort of paranoia-conspiracy thriller in which once a character befriends the hero(ine), you know they're gonna end up dead in the next reel. ★★½ VHS: $9.99; DVD: $19.99

Pelle the Conqueror

(1988, 160 min, Denmark, Bille August) *Max von Sydow, Pelle Hvengaard.* Winner of the Academy Award for Best Foreign Picture, this epic drama about human resilience stars the hypnotic von Sydow as a poor, but never down-trodden widower who emigrates with his young son from the economically depressed Sweden to Denmark at the turn of the century. His illusory quest for the good life leads only to a straw bed in the cold barn of a brutally insensitive farmer. The story centers around the close relationship between the father and son as they attempt to eke out a happy life amid crushing oppression. (Danish and Swedish with English subtitles) ★★★ VHS: $14.99; DVD: $29.99

Pennies from Heaven

(1981, 107 min, US, Herbert Ross) *Steve Martin, Bernadette Peters, Christopher Walken, Jessica Harper.* Martin, trying to escape his "wild and crazy guy" persona, had long wanted to do this transplanted version of Dennis Potter's tale of a Depression-era sheet music salesman whose dreary life is in stark contrast to the cheerful songs he sells. With the original recordings of the songs of the era acting as a Greek chorus, Potter's world remains every bit as bleak here as in his other works ("The Singing Detective," "Dreamchild"). Beautifully photographed by Gordon Willis, on stylized sets designed by Ken Adams. And Walken's dance sequence is a show-stopper. ★★★½ VHS: $19.99

Penny Serenade

(1941, 95 min, US, George Stevens) *Cary Grant, Irene Dunne, Beulah Bondi, Edgar Buchanan.* Grant and Dunne give compelling performances in this first-rate tear-jerker as a couple whose attempts to adopt after the death of their baby brings about tragedy. A three-hankier. Fine support from Bondi as a sympathetic adoption official and Buchanan as the couple's best friend. ★★★ VHS: $9.99

The People That Time Forgot

(1977, 90 min, US, Kevin Connor) *Patrick Wayne, Doug McClure, Sarah Douglas.* Our heroes battle prehistoric monsters and savage tribespeople while searching for a lost adventurer. This sequel to *The Land That Time Forgot* is forgettable though silly fun. Based on a story by Edgar Rice Burroughs. ★★ VHS: $9.99

The People under the Stairs

(1991, 102 min, US, Wes Craven) *Brandon Adams, Everett McGill, Wendy Robie, Ving Rhames.* Weird horror tale about a young boy, hoping to prevent his family's eviction from their ghetto apartment, who becomes terrorized by his crazed landlords. A big mess of a film — and not at all suspenseful — that aims to be socially relevant but only succeeds as being boring. ★½ VHS: $9.99

The People vs. Larry Flynt

(1996, 128 min, US, Milos Forman) *Woody Harrelson, Courtney Love, Edward Norton, Brett Harrelson, James Cromwell, Crispin Glover, Donna Hanover, James Carville.* This is a film full of surprises — from the caliber of its acting to the persuasiveness of its message to the agility and energy of its storytelling. As unlikely a hero to the Constitution as any in modern America, Larry Flynt started as publisher of *Hustler* magazine. Tasteless and exploitative, the magazine brought him notoriety and many brushes with the law. As the film succinctly recalls, one of these brushes landed him in front of the Supreme Court in a historic case. The film never lionizes Flynt; it's balanced writing and Flynt is no more than a sleazy publisher who happened to make a significant social contribution. But the beauty of it all is that the story is always appealing. As Flynt, W. Harrelson has never been more effective; and Love is absolutely riveting as his wife. Forman has crafted a cunning biography, timely political fable, and, most surprisingly, a crushing story of romantic loss. ★★★★ VHS: $14.99; DVD: $29.99

Pépé le Moko

(1936, 86 min, France, Julien Duvivier) *Jean Gabin, Mirielle Balin.* Set in the Algerian Casbah, this sumptuously photographed, *tres* complex, fascinating story follows a hardened gangster's (Gabin) successful ploy to elude the police. The melodramatic story observes his attraction to a beautiful femme fatale (Balin) who eventually causes his undoing. (French with English subtitles) ★★★½ VHS: $14.99

Pepi, Luci, Bom y Otras

(1980, 86 min, Spain, Pedro Almodóvar) *Carmen Maura, Eva Siva.* Spanish bad-boy director Almodóvar's 1980 feature debut, a mock-pornographic farce, is rude, funny and *very* nasty. The inimitable Maura plays the heiress Pepi, who seeks revenge on the cop who deflowered her by becoming involved with his masochistic wife Luci and her lesbian rock-star friend Bom. Replete with drugs, erection-measuring parties, beatings and body fluids, this low-budget, raw and crude camp piece lacks the frenetic pace and lush panoramic color scheme of his later works; but as a curio,

Peppermint Soda

it is a must for Almodóvar fans. (Spanish with English subtitles) ★★ VHS: $79.99

Peppermint Soda

(1977, 94 min, France, Diane Kurys) *Eléonore Klarwein, Odile Michel.* An art-house favorite for years, this engaging comedy about growing up is set in Paris in the early 1960s. The story follows the lives of two spirited sisters, 12-year-old Anne and 15-year-old Frederique. Writer-director Kurys manages to examine those often explored topics of teendom (first loves, strict parents, fascist teachers and "becoming a woman") with a freshness and honesty that is an absolute delight. Especially good is Klarwein, who as Anne has a kind of sulky, impertinent charm and a devastatingly impish smile. (French with English subtitles) ★★★½ VHS: $29.99

The Perez Family

(1995, 112 min, US, Mira Nair) *Marisa Tomei, Anjelica Huston, Alfred Molina, Chazz Palminteri, Trini Alvarado.* This sensual and hypnotic comedy of errors and culture clash is set during the 1980 Mariel boat-lift (during which thousands of Cuban political prisoners were released and placed in American holding centers to await citizenship). Tomei stars as Dorita Perez, a sultry Cuban floosy who tries to scam her way out of the American internment camp by claiming to be the wife of Juan Raul Perez (Molina), a once dapper, now bedraggled wreck who wants nothing more than to be reunited with his wife of 20 years, Carmela (Huston), who doesn't even know he's been released. An intoxicating blend of humor, irony and romance enhanced by gorgeous cinematography but marred only by the distracting but effective use of non-Hispanic actors in the lead roles. ★★★ VHS: $14.99

Perfect

(1985, 120 min, US, James Bridges) *John Travolta, Jamie Lee Curtis, Marilu Henner, Carly Simon.* Travolta plays a *Rolling Stone* reporter who is writing an exposé on Los Angeles health clubs and becomes infatuated with a club owner (Curtis). A real stinker. ★ VHS: $9.99

A Perfect Murder

(1998, 108 min, US, Andrew Davis) *Michael Douglas, Gwyneth Paltrow, Viggo Mortensen, David Suchet, Sarita Choudhury.* A slick, uneven,

updated version of Alfred Hitchcock's *Dial M for Murder*, itself a lesser film from the Master of Suspense. While director Davis and writer Patrick Smith Kelly do add a few twists of their own, they aren't enough to make this new version stand on its own. Douglas plays a smarmy business exec who, upon hearing he's nearly broke, decides to murder his wife (Paltrow) for her vast family fortune. There's no subtext or resonance here — this is strictly by-the-numbers. It is watchable, however, especially for its upper-crusty interior design. Suchet turns in a fine performance as the detective on the case. (Letterboxed VHS available for $19.99) ★★ VHS: $14.99; DVD: $19.99

The Perfect Storm

(2000, 129 min, US, Wolfgang Petersen) *George Clooney, Mark Wahlberg, Diane Lane, Mary Elizabeth Mastrantonio, John C. Reilly, William Fichtner, John Hawkes, Allen Payne, Karen Allen, Bob Gunton, Cherry Jones.* Outstanding special effects combine with a story that's not as clichéd as it could have been to make for a rip-roaring, action-flavored entertainment. Based on a true incident that occurred in 1991, the story follows a group of Gloucester, Massachusettes, fishermen who head to sea during one of the worst storms of the century. Clooney is the captain of the swordfishing boat *Andrea Gail*, whose crew of six sets sail for a final outing of the season. There's no arguing that the special effects are the main attraction here (and what effects they are). But *The Perfect Storm* is more than *Twister* at sea. The screenplay, though lacking in subtlety, manages to create sympathetic characters with some depth to them, and sustains credible tension throughout. Director Petersen makes sure to that, allowing his camera to go places you wouldn't think possible. A good ensemble and a keen sense of atmosphere go a long way in making the viewer forget the occasional lapse in narrative. (VHS available letterboxed or pan & scan) ★★★ VHS: $22.99; DVD: $24.99

A Perfect World

(1993, 137 min, US, Clint Eastwood) *Kevin Costner, Clint Eastwood, Laura Dern, T.J. Lowther.* An unusual and worthy follow-up to the director's Oscar-winning *Unforgiven.* In an electric and atypically malevolent performance, Costner plays an escaped prisoner who kidnaps an eight-year-old boy and holds him hostage as he tries to outrun the police. Eastwood and Dern play a Texas lawman and criminologist, respectively, tracking them across the state. The film has a dark edge to it, and Eastwood's deliberate pacing only accentuates the tension produced by both the examination of the symbiotic relationship which develops between captive and convict and an unnerving fifteen-minute attempted murder sequence. ★★★½ VHS: $14.99

Perfectly Normal

(1991, 106 min, Canada, Yves Simoneau) *Robbie Coltrane, Michael Riley.* British laughmeister Coltrane stars in this quirky sleeper about an opera-loving brewery worker (Riley) who is conned by Coltrane into using his inheritance to open a

restaurant staffed by aria-singing waiters. Imaginative visuals by Alain Dotsie. ★★★

Performance

(1970, 106 min, GB, Nicolas Roeg & Donald Cammell) *Mick Jagger, James Fox, Anita Pallenberg.* Fox is a gangster on the run drawn into the richly decadent, hallucinatory and erotic life of a retired rock idol — portrayed by Jagger with androgynous glee. Using this alien world for refuge, he finds himself surrounded by an atmosphere of sex and violence which puts even his hardened senses on edge. A fascinating, yet repellent, visual experience. ★★★ VHS: $19.99

Peril

(1985, 100 min, France, Michel Deville) *Michel Piccoli, Richard Bohringer.* A provocative, erotic thriller about a wealthy industrialist family who hires a musician to give lessons to their precocious daughter. The plot thickens as the wife of the industrialist seduces the young man and uses him as a pawn in a deadly, mysterious game of lust. An enigmatic tale of sexual duplicity. (French with English subtitles) ★★★

Period of Adjustment

(1962, 111 min, US, George Roy Hill) *Jane Fonda, Jim Hutton, Anthony Franciosa, Lois Nettleton.* Hill made his directorial debut with this lively film version of Tennessee Williams' successful stage comedy. In one of her first starring roles, Fonda plays the newlywed wife of war veteran Hutton. However, en route to Miami, their honeymoon trip is anything but sweet. Constantly at odds with each other, they stop at the home of Hutton's war buddy Franciosa, himself experiencing marital difficulties with wife Nettleton. What follows is a comic and tender exploration of love, marriage, male bravado and sexual compatibility. ★★★ VHS: $19.99

Permanent Midnight

(1997, 85 min, US, David Veloz) *Ben Stiller, Elizabeth Hurley, Maria Bello, Owen Wilson.* Based on Jerry Stahl's autobiography, *Permanent Midnight* follows Stahl's rise and fall as a writer for various TV shows (such as "Alf"), his "arranged" marriage to a comely TV exec (Hurley) and his near-total collapse from heroin addiction. Stiller gets to contort his face a lot, and look really crappy, but this just isn't the serious breakthrough role he was

Gwyneth Paltrow and Viggo Mortensen in *A Perfect Murder*

probably hoping for; the character is an absolute loser, and rather uninteresting to boot. Perhaps in this age of "heroin chic," we could use a powerful antidote, but *Permanent Midnight* is just too tedious and facetious to fit the bill. ★★ VHS: $9.99; DVD: $24.99

Permanent Record

(1988, 92 min, US, Marisa Silver) *Keanu Reeves, Alan Boyce, Barry Corbin, Michelle Meyrink, Kathy Baker.* Reeves delivers a compelling performance in this moving, sensitive drama as a tormented youth who can't figure out why his best friend killed himself. ★★★ VHS: $79.99

Permanent Vacation

(1980, 87 min, US, Jim Jarmusch) *Chris Parker.* The aimlessness and ennui of the "post-punk generation" is the theme of Jarmusch's first feature film. Drawing from the now-familiar world of the Lower East Side, the film follows the dreamlike odyssey of a 16-year-old (Parker of The Blank Generation) as he looks for meaning in his surroundings and his relationships with his girlfriend, acquaintances and parents. Utilizing the logic of a walking dream, Jarmusch has created a gritty, oppressive yet fascinating world. The film features a jazzy score by John Lurie. ★★★

Permission to Kill

(1975, 96 min, GB, Cyril Frankel) *Dirk Bogarde, Bekim Fehmiu, Ava Gardner, Timothy Dalton, Frederic Forrest.* International intrigue abounds in this complex spy thriller. Bogarde stars as the world-weary head of a spy consortium who must prevent a political expatriate (Fehmiu) from returning to his fascist homeland where certain death awaits. ★★★

Persona

(1966, 83 min, Sweden, Ingmar Bergman) *Liv Ullmann, Bibi Andersson.* Bergman probes the depths of human psychology in this absorbing study of spiritual anguish. Ullmann plays an actress who suffers a nervous breakdown and falls mute. A young nurse (Andersson) is employed to help, but instead, a deep emotional attachment is formed between the two as Andersson tries to bring her out of her silence and back into the world. This fascinating, complex film is erotically charged and remarkably intuitive, and beautifully shot in black and white. Ullmann gives a stunning, haunting performance without uttering one word. (Swedish with English subtitles) ★★★★ VHS: $19.99

Personal Best

(1982, 124 min, US, Robert Towne) *Mariel Hemingway, Patrice Donnelly, Scott Glenn.* Two women become friends and lovers during tryouts for the Olympics. Hemingway plays the fast but feckless Chris who gets a chance to make the team through her involvement with Tori (Donnelly). They become romantically involved, even though Chris denies the true nature of their romance, which only exasperates Tori. Their jealous, bitter coach (Glenn) adds to their relationship's problems by eventually pitting them against each other personally and professionally. The film runs a bit too long and the cinematography is unimpressive with too many lingering group shower scenes and crotch close-ups, though the interpersonal relationship between the two women is sensitively handled. ★★★ VHS: $14.99

Persuasion

(1995, 103 min, GB, Roger Mitchell) *Amanda Root, Ciaran Hinds, Susan Fleetwood, Corin Redgrave, Phoebe Nichols, Fiona Shaw, John Woodvine.* A superlative though admittedly modest production, this Jane Austen adaptation is enchanced by an unfaltering cast that delivers performances both sincere and charming. The story revolves around the failing fortunes of the Elliot family and specifically of their as yet unmarried daughter Anne (Root). Shortly after the family has given up its manor, Anne is reunited with her one former true love, Frederick Wentworth (Hinds). Romance follows, and oh, does it make for a swooning good time. Root and Hinds are not your typical screen beauties, and that is precisely what makes them so appealing — their radiance comes from within and it infects the entire film. Furthering the film's charm is its gritty, mud-strewn look at life in the English countryside circa 1810. This is a film in which skirt hems and coattails are downright soiled by the end of a stroll in the woods — how truly refreshing. ★★★★ VHS: $19.99; DVD: $27.99

The Pest

(1997, 90 min, US, Paul Miller) *John Leguizamo, Jeffrey Jones, Edoardo Ballerini.* In his first starring role, Leguizamo is so over the top he often makes Jim Carrey appear subtle by comparison. In this updated, '90s comic version of The Most Dangerous Game, Leguizamo plays a small-town con artist who agrees to be hunted by big-game hunter Jeffrey Jones for $50,000. This premise is all Leguizamo needs to offer a hyperventilating series of impersonations, jokes and pratfalls which rarely offer a punch line. Leguizamo is a comic whirlwind, a human Tasmanian Devil, but ultimately The Pest is about as substantial as hot air. ★1/2 VHS: $9.99; DVD: $14.99

Pet Sematary

(1989, 102 min, US, Mary Lambert) *Dale Midkiff, Fred Gwynne, Denise Crosby.* One of Stephen King's scariest books makes for one of his least successful screen adaptations. When his young son is accidentally killed, a grieving father uses a magical graveyard to bring him back to life, though he's not the same fun kid he used to be. (Sequel: Pet Sematary II) ★★ VHS: $9.99; DVD: $29.99

Pet Sematary II

(1993, 102 min, US, Mary Lambert) *Edward Furlong, Anthony Edwards, Clancy Brown, Jared Rushton.* Furlong is as a troubled teen who must cope with the accidental death of his mother and the dark secrets of an ancient Indian burial ground with the power to restore life — almost. Director Lambert seems unable to resist flaunting her heavy metal roots, investing any moments of genuine horror that might exist with a slick, rock 'n' roll flair. Here's hoping this fright franchise has found its final resting place. ★1/2 VHS: $9.99

Pete Kelly's Blues

(1955, 95 min, US, Jack Webb) *Jack Webb, Lee Marvin, Janet Leigh, Martin Milner, Peggy Lee, Ella Fitzgerald.* Webb and Marvin play Roaring

Pete Kelly's Blues

'20s jazz musicians trying to keep ahead of the mob. This beautiful looking film is as stiff as Webb's demeanor; however, it is still worth a look for both a rare and wonderful dramatic performance by Lee as a doomed lounge singer, and two numbers by Fitzgerald. ★★1/2 VHS: $14.99

Pete 'n' Tillie

(1973, 100 min, US, Martin Ritt) *Walter Matthau, Carol Burnett, Geraldine Page, Rene Auberjonois.* Low-key though very engaging comedy-drama about the courtship and marriage of unlikely partners Matthau and Burnett. Page is terrific in support as Burnett's bitchy friend (she received an Oscar nomination). ★★1/2 VHS: $14.99

Pete's Dragon

(1977, 129 min, US, Don Chaffey) *Helen Reddy, Jim Dale, Mickey Rooney; Voice of: Charlie Callas.* Charming live-action and animated Disney musical about an orphaned boy and his friendship with Elliott, the magic dragon. ★★★ VHS: $22.99; DVD: $29.99

Peter Pan

(1953, 78 min, US, Walt Disney) Even by today's standards of super-techno-FX and computer-generated wizardry, Disney's classic *Peter Pan* maintains its stature as an acme in animation technique. And the story is equally dazzling. The airborne hero takes Wendy and her brothers to Never-never Land, an island beyond space and frozen in time; where a determined, ticking crocodile stalks the nefarious Captain Hook, who in turn stalks the boy who will never grow up. How joyful to return to a time and place where — if we believe, and think happy thoughts — we can fly, we can fly, we can fly. ★★★★

Peter Pan

(1955, 100 min, US, Vincent J. Donohue) *Mary Martin, Cyril Ritchard.* Martin's timeless performance highlights this 1955 Emmy Award-winning television broadcast of the Broadway musical. Martin sparkles as the young boy determined never to grow up, and Ritchard is on-hand as the troublesome Captain Hook. Favorite songs incl700, "I Won't Grow Up," "Never Never Land" and, of course, "I'm Flying." ★★★1/2; DVD: $14.99

Lon Chaney in *Phantom of the Opera*

Peter's Friends

(1992, 102 min, GB, Kenneth Branagh) *Kenneth Branagh, Emma Thompson, Rita Rudner, Stephen Fry, Hugh Laurie.* Attempting to be a British *Big Chill* meets *Rules of the Game* by way of "Writing Comedy for the Movies 101" outline, the story is set in a large English manor where six old university friends meet for a ten-year reunion. This cast of "wacky" stock characters includes director-star Branagh as a talented writer who sells himself off for money in Hollywood; Fry as the lumbering host harboring a "secret"; and Thompson (who outshines them all) as a gawky, eccentric woman trying desperately to change. Infused with admittedly funny, even witty one-liners, the film suffers from an all-too-familiar sitcom feel. The film's final "revelation" that the bisexual Peter is infected with HIV is a cheap, exploitative device aimed at triggering sappy, liberal sympathies. ★½ VHS: $9.99

Le Petit Amour

(1987, 80 min, France, Agnès Varda) *Jane Birkin, Mathieu Demy, Charlotte Gainsbourg.* Varda's sad tale of a 40-year-old divorcée who takes comfort in the innocent arms of her daughter's best friend, even though he is only fifteen. Aware that the relationship is doomed from the beginning ("I know you won't be around when you start shaving," she tells him), she finds herself unable to resist the charms of what should have been an uncomplicated fling. (French with English subtitles) ★★½ VHS: $79.99

Petit Con

(1984, 90 min, France, Gérard Lauzier) *Guy Marchand, Bernard Brieux.* Whereas most teenage comedies worship their young protagonists, *Petit Con* offers welcome relief with its pungent ironic humor that sends up both its adolescent hero and the values he blithely adheres to. Brieux gives a painfully acute performance as Michel, an 18-year-old cauldron of horniness, oversensitivity and naïve politics who tries to find his niche amongst the charlatans, hoods and weirdos of Paris. A

Feifferesque observation of post-Sixties culture. (French with English subtitles) ★★★

La Petite Bande

(1984, 91 min, France, Michel Deville) This delightfully cheery romp follows the fantastic adventures of a group of English school children who play mass hooky and sneak off to France. Their travels take them through towns and countryside. All the while, they are an elusive target for the police who are intent on sending them home. (No dialogue — music and sound effects) ★★★ VHS: $59.99

La Petite Sirene (The Little Mermaid)

(1980, 104 min, France, Roger Andrieux) *Philippe Leotard, Laura Alexis.* They're at it again! While sexual encounters between adults and teenagers are morally forbidden fruit in the States, for French filmmakers, it's almost a way of life. And this tantalizing Nabokovian drama, infused with engaging humor, is no exception. Leotard stars as a middle-aged auto mechanic who becomes the befuddled object of desire to a rich, spoiled 14-year-old obsessed with a fairy tale, "The Little Mermaid." (French with English subtitles) ★★½ VHS: $19.99

The Petrified Forest

(1936, 83 min, US, Archie Mayo) *Bette Davis, Leslie Howard, Humphrey Bogart.* Davis shines as an Arizona cafe waitress who meets up with English drifter and poet Howard. There at the café, they and a small party are held hostage by escaped felon Bogart. A sterling adaptation of Robert Sherwood's hit play. ★★★½ VHS: $19.99

Petulia

(1968, 105 min, US, Richard Lester) *Julie Christie, George C. Scott, Richard Chamberlain, Shirley Knight, Arthur Hill, The Grateful Dead, Big Brother and the Holding Company.* Psychedelic San Francisco comes alive in this scintillating romantic drama, one of the great films of the 1960s. Scott is mesmerizing as a staid, recently divorced doctor who begins a bittersweet affair with unhappily married, free spirit Christie. Based on the novel "Me and the Arch Kook Petulia" by John Haase, the film offers a sometimes scathing view of '60s pop and mainstream cultures, though shimmers with a grown-up romanticism. Christie is excellent as the kooky Petulia, but it is Scott and Knight, as Scott's ex-wife, who walk away with the acting honors. ★★★★ VHS: $14.99

Peyton Place

(1957, 157 min, US, Mark Robson) *Lana Turner, Hope Lange, Lloyd Nolan, Arthur Kennedy, Russ Tamblyn.* This box-office smash (which served as the basis for the popular TV series) is a well-made screen version of the Grace Metalious novel. A quintessential soap opera, the story follows the lives of the citizens of a small New England town. ★★★ VHS: $14.99

Phantasm

(1979, 87 min, US, Don Coscarelli) *Michael Baldwin, Bill Thornbury, Angus Scrimm.* Watch out for that flying silver ball! Two brothers decide to investigate the strange goings-on at a mausoleum and become the prey of a demonic figure. Gory, inventive and very unusual. Contains four minutes of outtakes and a deleted scene not included in the original release.

(Followed by 3 sequels) ★★★ VHS: $9.99; DVD: $14.99

Phantasm II

(1988, 90 min, US, Don Coscarelli) *James LeGros, Reggie Bannister, Angus Scrimm.* Sequel to the cult horror hit has the "Tall Man" returning, traveling around the country stealing dead bodies for his demonic purposes. The survivors from the original are out to stop him. Though as gory as the original, it's not quite as effective. ★★ VHS: $9.99

Phantasm Oblivion

(1998, 90 min, US, Don Coscarelli) *A. Michael Baldwin, Reggie Bannister, Bill Thornbury, Heidi Marnhout, Angus Scrimm.* Still creepy and nonsensical after all these years, *Phantasm OblIVion* is the best in the series since the nightmarish original. This one picks up exactly where *Pt. 3* left off (after a very cool and well-edited "for-those-who-came-late"-style prologue), with Reggie and Mike still battling the Tall Man, his evil dwarves and those sinister spheres. While there are some slow spots, this is mostly good, fast-paced fun for horror fans. ★★½ VHS: $6.99; DVD: $14.99

The Phantom

(1996, 96 min, US, Simon Wincer) *Billy Zane, Kristy Swanson, Treat Williams, James Remar, Casey Siemaszko, Samantha Eggar, Patrick McGoohan.* Underrated and overlooked in a crowded Summer of '96, *The Phantom* is an endearingly cheesy, old-fashioned and enjoyable throwback to the cliffhanger serials of the 1930s and '40s. Zane is the dashing hero in purple tights, who is up against a millionaire — Williams is a hoot as the mustache-twirling villain — determined to own three magic skulls which would give him ultimate power. Director Wincer, his production team and the entire cast capture the flavor of the comic book, succeeding where the similarly themed *The Shadow* failed. It may not be as hip or brooding or cynical as recent adventure films, but it promises a fun time. ★★★ VHS: $14.99; DVD: $24.99

The Phantom of Liberty

(1974, 104 min, France, Luis Buñuel) *Jean-Claude Brialy, Adolfo Celi, Michel Piccoli, Monica Vitti.* Well into his 70s, Buñuel continued to cinematically pinch our noses with his playful surreal satires on the middle class, democracy and love. "I am fed up with symmetry." So says a character early on in this montage of episodes, dreams and nightmares — each of which makes fun of man's idealistic notions of freedom. Filmed in an almost stream-of-consciousness style, this subversive little comedy is a delight. (French with English subtitles) ★★★½

The Phantom of the Opera

(1925, 90 min, US, Rupert Julian) *Lon Chaney, Mary Philbin.* One of the greatest of all silent films, this chillingly atmospheric adaptation of the classic horror tale stars Chaney in a tour de force performance as the masked composer haunting a Parisian opera house. ★★★½ VHS: $24.99; DVD: $29.99

The Phantom of the Opera

(1943, 93 min, US, Arthur Lubin) *Claude Rains, Suzanna Foster, Nelson Eddy.* Good

remake of the classic silent film. Rains gives a fine performance as the masked phantom living in the sewers beneath the Paris Opera House. ★★★ VHS: $14.99; DVD: $29.99

Phantom of the Opera

(1990, 90 min, US, Dwight H. Little) *Robert Englund, Jill Schoelen.* Slice-n-dice remake of the horror classic about the cursed opera house dweller and his lady love. Englund (aka: Freddy Krueger) barely changes his makeup. ★½ VHS: $14.99

The Phantom of the Paradise

(1974, 92 min, US, Brian De Palma) *William Finley, Paul Williams, Jessica Harper, Gerritt Graham.* The first Faust-influenced horror, rock-musical comedy. A thwarted songwriter sells his soul to the Devil (an astute casting of Williams) for rock 'n' roll success and Harper. A witty satire on at least a dozen different films and genres. De Palma directs many memorable scenes and performers including Beef, a hilarious rock superstar parody played by Graham. ★★★ VHS: $14.99

Phantoms

(1997, 91 min, US, Joe Chappelle) *Ben Affleck, Liev Schreiber, Peter O'Toole, Rose McGowan, Joanna Going.* This long-in-gestation Dean Koontz adaptation has a delicious opening: two estranged sisters arrive in their hometown to vist their mother, but discover the town is nearly deserted (save for a few fresh corpses). The palpable mystery of this sequence is tempered by the arrival of the neighboring town's lawmen, but director Chappelle manages to keep the remainder of the film somewhat suspenseful (at least until the tacked-on, idiotic coda). *Phantoms* has some damaging flaws, though — with the exception of O'Toole (surprisingly effective in what is basically the Peter Cushing role), everyone is cast way too young. And little things like character development, subtlety and dramatic tension are jettisoned completely. Not a bad try, though. ★★ VHS: $102.99; DVD: $29.99

Phar Lap

(1983, 108 min, Australia, Simon Wincer) *Ron Leibman, Tom Burlison, Martin Vaughn.* An inspirational and entertaining account of the rise and fall of one of history's most phenomenal race horses, Phar Lap, who became a Depression-era hero to the Australian people. Liebman stars as the Jewish-American owner who does battle with the high-brow, anti-Semitic Aussie racing elite. ★★★

Phase IV

(1974, 86 min, US, Saul Bass) *Nigel Davenport, Michael Murphy.* Famed title designer Bass (he did a lot of work with Preminger and Hitchcock) directed this cerebral sci-fi tale about a colony of ants that learn the power of their numbers as they fight man for supremacy of the planet. ★★½ VHS: $39.99

Phenomena

(1984, 110 min, Italy, Dario Argento) *Jennifer Connelly, Donald Pleasence.* A deranged killer stalks a young girl through the grounds of her boarding school, but little does he know this girl can communicate telepathically with all species of insects. Now, she and her allegiant minions have a bone to pick. (Uncut European release) (Letterboxed) (aka: *Creepers*) ★★½ VHS: $14.99; DVD: $29.99

Phenomenon

(1996, 117 min, US, Jon Turtletaub) *John Travolta, Kyra Sedgwick, Forest Whitaker, Robert Duvall, Richard Kiley, Jeffrey DeMunn, Brent Spiner.* Travolta softens his image and goes the *Charly* route with mixed results. He plays George, an auto mechanic with not much going for him but who's very likable. When he sees what appears to be an extraterrestrial light in the sky, he is infused with a super intelligence and powers of telepathy. As a fantasy, *Phenomenon* beguiles. It's as personable as George himself — yes, he could be smarter but you kinda like what you see. But the romance between George and a divorced mom drags, and the ending is a cheat, a copout. *Phenomenon* tries to be magical but ulti-

mately settles for common. ★★½ VHS: $19.99; DVD: $29.99

Philadelphia

(1993, 120 min, US, Jonathan Demme) *Tom Hanks, Denzel Washington, Antonio Banderas, Joanne Woodward, Jason Robards, Mary Steenburgen, Quentin Crisp.* Hanks won a Best Actor Oscar for his performance as a high-powered gay lawyer at a prestigious Philadelphia law firm who is stricken with AIDS. When his employers catch wind of this, they sabotage his work and fire him on false pretense. He retaliates with a lawsuit, soliciting a homophobic ambulance chaser (Washington) to represent him. The first Hollywood film about AIDS, *Philadelphia* delivers a strong emotional punch despite suffering from some procedural flaws, including underdeveloped relationships between characters. Additionally, the film's courtroom scenes are lacking in the expected drama, primarily because there is almost no doubt to the outcome. However, the result is a very moving experience. ★★★ VHS: $9.99; DVD: $29.99

The Philadelphia Experiment

(1984, 102 min, US, Stewart Raffill) *Michael Paré, Nancy Allen, Bobby Di Cicco, Eric Christmas.* Intriguing sci-fi thriller about two WWII sailors who are catapulted into the 1980s. Allen brings a nice no-nonsense sensibility to the modern girl who befriends time travelers Paré and Di Cicco. ★★½ VHS: $14.99; DVD: $24.99

The Philadelphia Experiment 2

(1993, 98 min, US, Stephen Cornwell) *Brad Johnson, Gerrit Graham.* Johnson assumes the role of an ex-naval pilot (originally played by Michael Paré) whose present-day existence becomes a nightmare when a military madman (Graham) orchestrates a time shift that sends a Stealth Bomber back to WWII Germany enabling the Nazis to win the war. Inventive though static. ★★ VHS: $14.99

The Philadelphia Story

(1940, 112 min, US, George Cukor) *Katharine Hepburn, James Stewart, Cary Grant, Ruth Hussey, Roland Young, John Howard.* Cukor's dedication to character, Philip Barry's delicious dialogue, and three of the most enchanting lead performances ever to grace the screen all combine to create the wittiest and most sophisticated comedy of the 1940s. Hepburn repeats her stage role as the Philadelphia socialite faced with a dilemma on her wedding day: who to marry. Stewart won an Oscar for his delightful performance as a reporter covering Hepburn's wedding; and Grant is the essence of charm as Kate's ex-husband. ★★★★ VHS: $14.99; DVD: $19.99

Phobia

(1980, 91 min, US, John Huston) *Paul Michael Glaser, Susan Hogan.* The phobia-ridden patients of a psychiatrist are being murdered one by one. The problem is — everyone appears guilty. Glaser stars. It's hard to believe this mess was directed by the great Huston. ★ VHS: $79.99

Phoenix

(1998, 107 min, US, Danny Cannon) *Ray Liotta, Anthony LaPaglia, Daniel Baldwin, Jeremy Piven, Anjelica Huston, Giancarlo Esposito, Tom*

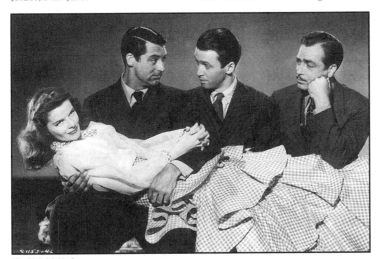

The Philadelphia Story

Noonan, Giovanni Ribisi. A quartet of Arizona cops, each crooked in their own way, are the central characters in this unpleasant but not uninteresting crime drama. Harry (Liotta) is a cop who is also a compulsive gambler. Although he won't welsh on a bet, Harry is not against ripping off a loan shark with his colleagues. Ironically, he is the moral center of director Cannon's misguided film. *Phoenix* spends half its running time setting up a robbery, and by then the coincidences and double crosses have strained credibility. A superfluous relationship between Harry and Leila (Huston) tries to improve the quality of *Phoenix*, but no matter how hard the film wants to rise from its ashes, it can't help but self-destruct. ★★ VHS: $14.99; DVD: $24.99

The Phoenix
(1978, 137 min, Japan, Kon Ichikawa) Set thousands of years ago, this mystical and exciting film tells the story of the quest by an aging queen for the blood of the elusive phoenix, which she believes will give her eternal life. A fantasy-adventure combining live action and animation by world-famous cartoonist Osamu Tezuka. (Japanese with English subtitles) ★★★ VHS: $79.99

Phone Call from a Stranger
(1952, 96 min, US, Jean Negulesco) *Bette Davis, Gary Merrill, Shelley Winters, Keenan Wynn, Michael Rennie.* A survivor of a plane crash (Merrill) visits the families of various victims, and receives understanding from a kindly, invalid widow, played by Davis. Involving melodrama. ★★★ VHS: $19.99

Photographing Fairies
(1997, 107 min, GB, Nick Willing) *Toby Stephens, Ben Kingsley, Emily Woof.* Traversing the same territory as *Fairy Tale — A True Story*, this British film takes a more sober view of the subject. Charles Castle (Stevens) is a photographer in 1912 whose life is undone by two obsessions. After he loses his wife on their honeymoon, Charles experiences terrible grief. His despair is further complicated when be becomes aware of the existence of fairies, and is determined to find proof. Director Willing's odd film blends fantasy and reality with decidedly mixed results. Is Charles going mad trying to solve a mystery that doesn't exist? Or is he supplanting his distraut emotions with another unhealthy obsession? The film's pursuit of these ideas is ambiguous, and the tone shifts uneasily between supernatural mystery and tragic romance. ★★ VHS: $14.99

Physical Evidence
(1989, 99 min, US, Michael Crichton) *Burt Reynolds, Theresa Russell, Ned Beatty.* Reynolds plays a suspended, washed-up cop, awash in booze and self-pity, who is the prime suspect in the murder of an old criminal adversary. Prospects look grim when the defender's office assigns the neophyte "little rich girl" Russell as his lawyer. Did he kill during a drunken fury or was he set up? You may know the answer long before the final resolution, but the film's deft action and Reynolds' always-present self-deprecating humor helps gloss over the film's inconsistencies with plot to produce a mindless escapist entertainment. ★★½ VHS: $14.99

Sean Gullette in Darren Aronofsky's *Pi*

Pi
(1998, 85 min, US, Darren Aronofsky) *Sean Gullette, Mark Margolis, Ben Shenkman, Pamela Hart.* While owing a certain debt to Kafka and *Eraserhead*, *Pi* is an original paranoia story about, well, numbers. Gullette plays Max, a math genius who for two decades has been trying to find a pattern in the stock market. He may have stumbled onto a key number that holds the answers to many problems. But can he handle this knowledge? Max is also prone to headaches and hallucinations that allow this film to be marketed as a thriller. Full of intense music and a bracingly fast black-and-white camera, *Pi* effectively captures a state of mind where a little too much is going on. Detracting from the brilliance are some familiar freshman flaws by director Aronofsky, including an inconsistent pace and an excessive voiceover. When *Pi* settles into its groove, however, it is something to behold. ★★★ VHS: $9.99; DVD: $14.99

Piaf
(1981, 115 min, US, Howard Davies) *Jane LaPortaire.* LaPortaire won a Tony Award for her touching portrayal of the legendary French songstress Edith Piaf. Ballads are woven closely together to re-create the bittersweet life of the woman who so captivated the world with her voice and life. ★★★

The Piano
(1993, 121 min, New Zealand, Jane Campion) *Holly Hunter, Sam Neill, Harvey Keitel, Anna Paquin, Genevieve Lemon.* Set in 19th-century New Zealand, this is a sumptuously photographed and atmospheric tale of repressed passions. Oscar winner Hunter is Ada, a mute Scottish woman who is forced into an arranged marriage. She and her illegitimate daughter, Flora (the Puck-like Paquin, who also won an Oscar), arrive at their new home with their worldly possessions — including Ada's prized piano. However, Ada's pious new husband, Stewart (Neill), sells it to an illiterate settler (Keitel), who in turn agrees to sell it back to Ada in exchange for lessons. His true intentions, however, involve Ada in a bizarre

but passionate affair. Campion masterfully uses the power struggles between all of the characters to explore the various themes of colonialism and the plight of women while sketching a mesmerizing and emotionally involving story. (Letterboxed VHS available for $14.99) ★★★★ VHS: $9.99; DVD: $19.99

The Piano Lesson
(1995, 99 min, US, Lloyd Richards) *Alfre Woodard, Charles S. Dutton, Carl Gordon, Courtney B. Vance.* August Wilson's Pulitzer Prize–winning Broadway drama is given an excellent realization in this made-for-TV adaptation. Re-creating his acclaimed stage role, Dutton stars as Boy Willie, a 1930s black sharecropper with dreams of buying the land his family had once worked as slaves. He travels to Pittsburgh to convince his sister Berniece (a superb Woodard) to sell the family's prized paino to pay for the farm. Thus sets in motion a passionate, heartfelt series of soul-searching and familial confrontations and reminiscences as Berniece refuses to part with the piano — a legacy of their servile past. As would a great storyteller, Wilson's dialogue conjures another time and place, evoking through hearty though poetic anecdotes and conversations the history of a family. ★★★★ VHS: $14.99

The Pick-Up Artist
(1987, 81 min, US, James Toback) *Robert Downey, Jr., Molly Ringwald, Dennis Hopper, Danny Aiello, Harvey Keitel, Mildred Dunnock.* A good cast valiantly tries to bring some life to this otherwise lifeless drama. Downey is the title character, setting his sights on Ringwald. ★★ VHS: $9.99

The Pickle
(1993, 103 min, US, Paul Mazursky) *Danny Aiello, Dyan Cannon, Shelley Winters, Barry Miller, Chris Penn, Ally Sheedy, Isabella Rossellini, Dudley Moore.* Since Mazursky has dabbled with autobiographical material in the past, and had a flop with *Scenes from a Mall*, the obvious question is whether this comedy springs from some personal experience. Aiello effectively assumes the role of Harry Stone, the hedonis-

tic yet weary director who reluctantly checks his integrity and accepts a job at the helm of a movie about a giant pickle from outer space. Though *The Pickle* is a curious mix of genuine drama and broad sitcom humor that never quite gels, it is entertaining and more than holds its own amidst the crowded giant vegetable genre. ★★½ VHS: $9.99

Pickpocket

(1959, 75 min, France, Robert Bresson) *Martin LaSalle, Marika Green, Jean Pelegri, Pierre Leymaire.* Director Bresson paints a picture of self-conscious obsession in *Pickpocket*, an unadorned and spare examination of a haunted young man (LaSalle) who schools himself in light-fingered theft. The film employs a quasi-documentary style as the thief Michel roams the subterranean concourses of the Paris Metro, looking for easy marks, or casing fat handbags at the races. At once determined and conflicted, Michel seeks philosophic justification for his actions in discussions at coffee bars, yet cannot visit his ailing mother to face her concerns for him. In only 75 minutes, the emotionally riveting *Pickpocket* provides a multilayered character study within a tale of personal despair and ultimate redemption, creating an in-depth portrait with a minimal of brush strokes. (French with English subtitles) ★★★½ VHS: $29.99

Pickup on South Street

(1953, 81 min, US, Samuel Fuller) *Richard Widmark, Jean Peters, Thelma Ritter.* Widmark stars in this classic film noir spy thriller as a small-time pickpocket whose latest sting unwittingly involves him in political espionage. Director Fuller expertly extorts maximum tension from its novel premise; and Ritter gives a sensational performance as the pathetic, streetwise fence. ★★★½ VHS: $19.99

Picnic at Hanging Rock

(1977, 115 min, Australia, Peter Weir) *Rachel Roberts, Helen Morse, Dominic Guard, Margaret Nelson.* This dreamlike puzzle revolves around the disappearance of three schoolgirls and their teacher on an afternoon outing. Imbued with a swooning atmosphere of sexual mystery and

The Piano

ominous desire. (Letterboxed) ★★★½ VHS: $19.99; DVD: $29.99

Picnic on the Grass

(1959, 95 min, France, Jean Renoir) *Paul Meurisse, Catherine Rouvel.* Set near the ancestral home of his painter father, Auguste, and filmed in an impressionistic style, Renoir has made a "filmed poem" to the mystery and power of nature. The story centers on a hardened biologist and candidate for President of the United States of Europe whose dedication to genetic engineering and the power of science is broken by the love of a peasant girl. (French with English subtitles) ★★★ VHS: $59.99

Picture Bride

(1995, 101 min, US, Kayo Hatta) *Youki Kudoh, Akira Takayama, Tamlyn Tomita, Toshiro Mifune.* A subtle, deliberately paced and seductively involving portrait of one young woman's long, protracted journey across land, oceans and the terrain of the heart. Kudoh is luminous as Riyo, one of the more than 26,000 Asian women who in the early 1900s traveled to Hawaii to marry men farming the cane fields. The couples were known to each other only by photos and letters, and both Riyo and her new husband Matsuji (played with earthiness by Takayama) had concealed secrets from each other in their communications. Meticulously produced, lushly photographed and told with love and heart, the film presents even the most terrible hardships in an amber glow of reminiscence, leaving the viewer with a sense of the warmth of fond memory. ★★★ VHS: $19.99

Picture Perfect

(1997, 100 min, US, Glenn Gordon Caron) *Jennifer Aniston, Kevin Bacon, Jay Mohr, Olympia Dukakis, Illeana Douglas, Faith Prince.* Sometimes Hollywood scriptwriters should take a time-out and get a job in the real world just to get a brief grasp of reality. Take, for instance, the implausible plot for the inoffensive *Picture Perfect*. Aniston is Kate, a career-driven employee at an upscale advertising company who gets passed over for a promotion because she's single. Instead of pursuing legal action, Kate agrees to a faux fiancé, Nick (Mohr). Even though Kate has only met Nick once, she offers to pay him to join in the charade, unaware that Nick wants more than a business proposition from her. The cast is attractive, and there's some low-key chemistry amongst the principals. But several genuine laughs and the thankfully brisk pacing are hampered by a too-cutesy climax and the unremarkable, contrived scenario. ★★½ VHS: $14.99; DVD: $29.99

Pie in the Sky

(1996, 94 min, US, Bryan Gordon) *Josh Charles, Anne Heche, Peter Riegert, Christine Ebersole, Christine Lahti, John Goodman.* Charles plays a young man with two obsessions: his childhood love,

Picnic at Hanging Rock

Amy (Heche), and traffic. Conceived while his parents were stuck in a traffic jam, he feels it's his life work, and he dreams of meeting his idol, traffic reporter Alan Davenport (Goodman). Meanwhile, he and Amy have an on-again, off-again romance. A mildly enjoyable romantic comedy, *Pie in the Sky* isn't as whimsical or romantic as it wants to be, nor as edgy or energetic as it should be, but the traffic-obsession angle lends it a nice, quirky feel. ★★½ VHS: $19.99

A Piece of the Action

(1977, 135 min, US, Sidney Poitier) *Sidney Poitier, Bill Cosby, James Earl Jones, Denise Nicholas.* Con men Poitier and Cosby do their best to help a group of ghetto children. Overlong film mixes the crazy criminal antics of Cosby and Poitier with the social drama of life in the ghetto. For the most part, it doesn't work. ★★ VHS: $14.99

Pierrot le Fou

(1965, 110 min, France, Jean-Luc Godard) *Jean-Paul Belmondo, Anna Karina.* Godard's ebullience for life and his fascination with the possibilities of film are wonderfully displayed in this frantic and stylized tale of love, intrigue and betrayal. Belmondo and Karina star as two young lovers who involve themselves in a murder and begin an idyllic flight from justice. Filming without a script, Godard embellishes his story of doomed romantic love with splashy colors, exotic settings in the south of France, his trademark use of jump-cuts, classical music and literary references. (French with English subtitles) ★★★½ VHS: $29.99; DVD: $29.99

The Pillow Book

(1997, 126 min, GB, Peter Greenaway) *Ewan McGregor, Vivian Wu, Ken Ogata.* Seemingly intent on outdoing even himself, director Greenaway achieves new levels of cinematic outlandishness with this visually sumptuous, kaleidoscopic panoply of fetishism, sexual degradation and desecrated corpses as set against the world of literature and poetry. Wu stars as a young Japanese woman who is obsessed with recreating two childhood rituals: one in which her father wrote on her neck and forehead, the other being read to from the 1000-year-old "Pillow Book" of an imperial courtesan. Living in Hong Kong, she meets McGregor, a translator who immediately takes to her lust for erotic penmanship and encourages her to publish her own "Pillow Book." Some viewers might be little more than bewildered by Greenaway's overarching intellectualism (his references *are* obscure) and his opulent visual sense, but this is nothing less than a masterful addition to his opus. (In English and Japanese, Mandarin and Cantonese with English subtitles) ★★★★ VHS: $21.99; DVD: $27.99

Pillow Talk

(1959, 105 min, US, Michael Gordon) *Rock Hudson, Doris Day, Tony Randall, Thelma Ritter.* A box-office sensation in 1959, this delightful sex farce teamed Hudson and Day in the first and best of their "battle of the sexes." Though they can't stand each other in person, Rock and Doris unknowingly fall in love on their party line. Great support from Randall and the always reliable Ritter. ★★★½ VHS: $9.99; DVD: $24.99

Ping Pong

(1987, 95 min, GB, Po Chih Liong) *David Yip, Lucy Sheen.* From the mysterious nocturnal streets of London's Chinatown comes this exotic, noirish comedy-thriller about a young Anglo-Chinese law student who is whisked into the tantalizingly complex task of executing a traditional Chinese will. Simple at first, but because of an intricate web of conditions and bequests, it falls to a vivacious young woman to piece together some unresolved mysteries. A richly textured and often comical portrait of a transplanted society caught between tradition and transition, flavored with a striking visual flair and moments of magic and fantasy. ★★★

Pink Cadillac

(1989, 122 min, US, Clint Eastwood) *Clint Eastwood, Bernadette Peters, Geoffrey Lewis, Jim Carrey.* This change-of-pace comedy is a misfire for director Eastwood. He plays a bail-bond bounty hunter who becomes unlikely partners with the wife of one of his prey (Peters). Peters is a cute and perky foil for the stoic Clint, but the part does little to display her fine comic talents. Not as abysmal as some critics have complained, there are some entertaining moments in the film — especially when Eastwood is afforded the chance to masquerade as various characters. But those hoping for a "make-my-day" Clint or rock-'em-sock-'em action would do better to look elsewhere. ★★ VHS: $14.99

Pink Flamingos

(1972, 95 min, US, John Waters) *Divine, Edith Massey, Danny Mils, Mink Stole, David Lochary.* The sleazo-porn-trash extravaganza that made the fabulous Divine a household word and Waters an object of fear, awe and nausea all over the world. In one of the most disgusting and perversely funny films ever made, zaftig matriarch Babs Johnson (Divine) and her family of egg-adoring Mom (Massey) and chicken-loving son (Mils) battle the repugnant Connie and Raymond Marble (Mink Stole and Lochary) for the title of "filthiest person alive." Restored version with additional footage. ★★★★ VHS: $19.99

Pink Floyd: The Wall

(1982, 99 min, GB, Alan Parker) *Bob Geldof, Christine Hargreaves, Bob Hoskins.* Pink Floyd's mammoth rock 'n' roll allegory is vividly brought to the screen by Alan Parker in this visually impressive and sonically explosive epic. Geldof (Mr. Live Aid) is the embodiment of a frazzled rock idol as the down and out Pink. ★★★ VHS: $19.99; DVD: $31.99

The Pink Panther

(1964, 113 min, GB, Blake Edwards) *Peter Sellers, Herbert Lom, David Niven, Robert Wagner, Claudia Cardinale.* This delightful comedy caper introduced Sellers' now-famous characterization of the bumbling Inspector Clouseau. While not the best of the Pink Panther series (that honor goes to its sequel *A Shot in the Dark*), this is still a zesty and sophisticated farce with many of the "trademarks" of Sellers' unsurpassed comic ability. (Sequel: *A Shot in the Dark*) ★★★½ VHS: $14.99; DVD: $24.99

The Pink Panther Strikes Again

(1976, 103 min, GB, Blake Edwards) *Peter Sellers, Herbert Lom, Leslie Anne Down, Burt Kwouk.* This hilarious fourth installment in the *Pink Panther* series is one of the best of the bunch. The Inspector's former boss, chief Dreyfuss (Lom), has gone off the deep end and will stop at nothing, including holding the entire world hostage with a giant death ray, to see Clouseau dead. Sellers, as always, is hysterical, especially in the Munich Octoberfest scene. (Sequel: *Revenge of the Pink Panther*) ★★★½ VHS: $14.99; DVD: $24.99

Pinky

(1949, 102 min, US, Elia Kazan) *Jeanne Crain, Ethel Waters, Ethel Barrymore, Nina Mae McKinney, William Lundigan.* Crain stars as a Southern black woman who passes for white when she leaves her home to live in the big city, finds work as a nurse and becomes romantically involved with a white doctor. After her mother (Waters) takes ill, she returns home to care for her and is confronted with racism and her own personal identity crisis centering around the acceptance of her own blackness. Tightly directed by Kazan and featuring standout performances by Oscar nominees Crain, Waters and Barrymore, this melodramatic masterpiece is a must-see for those seeking drama that hits hard and doesn't let up until the last Kleenex is used. ★★★★ VHS: $19.99

Pinocchio

(1940, 88 min, US, Ben Sharpsteen, Hamilton Luske) Disney's second animated feature is filled with fantastical imagery and a wild carnival-like atmosphere as Geppetto's little wooden boy goes on an almost picaresque journey toward a more fleshy existence. While the film is guaranteed to inspire delight (let us not forget Jiminy Cricket), the story's invective morality along with Disney's at times horrific representation of killer whales and an underwater purgatory for little boys who lie may prove a tad frightening for many a tot. Still, as with all vintage Disney, this is a must-see. ★★★★ VHS: $26.99; DVD: $39.99

Pippin

(1981, 120 min, US, David Sheehan) *Ben Vereen, William Katt, Eric Berry, Chita Rivera,*

Jeanne Crain and Ethel Waters in *Pinky*

Martha Raye. First-rate production of Bob Fosse's Tony Award–winning musical. One of Fosse's greatest stage triumphs, "Pippin" is a jubilant, colorful and tuneful look at Pippin, son of King Charlemagne, and his search for fulfillment and love. Vereen re-creates his award-winning role as the Narrator, and is joined by Katt as Pippin, Berry (also repeating his stage role) as the King, Rivera as the Queen, and Raye as Pippin's vivacious grandmother. Fosse's dance numbers are outstanding, and Stephen Schwartz's score is earthy, witty and vibrant. ★★★½ DVD: $24.99

Piranha

(1978, 92 min, US, Joe Dante) *Bradford Dillman, Heather Menzies, Kevin McCarthy, Barbara Steele, Dick Miller.* Director Dante and writer John Sayles teamed for the first time (they encored with *The Howling*) for this engaging horror spoof. You'll regret it if you pass up this biting tale of mutant, man-eating fish making julienne fries of beach-loving teens. Promises lots of laughs and chills, and contains the immortal line, "Excuse me, sir, the fish are eating the guests." ★★★ VHS: $14.99; DVD: $19.99

Piranha II: The Spawning

(1981, 88 min, US, James Cameron) *Lance Henriksen, Tricia O'Neill.* This sequel to *Piranha* takes its stylistic cues from *Wolfen*, mixes in a bunch of Roger Corman camp and resembles *Jaws* in substance. Put it all together and you have an amazingly silly but enjoyable horror movie... and yes, it was directed by *that* James Cameron (*The Terminator, Titanic*, etc.). He shows nothing of the greatness which would follow. ★★

The Pirate

(1948, 102 min, US, Vincente Minnelli) *Gene Kelly, Judy Garland, The Nicholas Brothers.* Kelly's thrilling dance numbers highlight this charming musical about traveling acrobat Kelly being mistaken for a notorious pirate by love-struckGarland. Cole Porter's score includes "Be a Clown" and the Nicholas Brothers are sensational in support. ★★★

Pirates

(1986, 124 min, France/US, Roman Polanski) *Walter Matthau, Charlotte Lewis, Cris Campion.* A fun if convoluted pirate comedy with Matthau in good form as a ruthless scalawag in search of a famed treasure. ★★½

The Pirates of Penzance

(1983, 112 min, US, Wilford Leach) *Kevin Kline, Rex Smith, Angela Lansbury, Linda Rondstadt, George Rose.* All of the exuberance and rollicking sense of fun of the 1980s hit Broadway revival of Gilbert and Sullivan's operetta has been joyously captured on screen in this vastly underrated musical. Kline repeats his Tony Award–winning role as the Pirate King, with Smith as the "slave to duty" pirate apprentice, Lansbury as his guardian, the wonderful Rose as "the very model of a modern major general." Kline is in terrific form, both as singer and physical comedian; and the colorful sets are a major asset. ★★★½ VHS: $19.99

The Pit and the Pendulum

(1991, 97 min, US, Stuart Gordon) *Lance Henriksen, Jeffrey Combs.* From the director of the cult classic *Re-Animator* comes this stylishly sadistic remake of the Edgar Allan Poe horror classic. Henriksen stars as Torquemada, the mad monk of the Spanish Inquisition, who goes to extreme lengths to suppress his awakening sexual desires for a beautiful peasant girl. Director Gordon sacrifices atmosphere for hard-core shocks with surprisingly effective results. ★★½ VHS: $79.99; DVD: $24.99

Pitch Black

(2000, 109 min, US, David Twohy) *Vin Diesel, Radha Mitchell, Cole Hauser, Keith David.* Marooned on a seemingly lifeless planet, a group of desperate passengers turn to a convicted murderer for help when they discover that the planet is inhabited by an army of deadly alien creatures. Good special effects, better-than-average action scenes and a nice sense of atmosphere go a long way to compensate for a familiar story line and stock characters. *Pitch Black* may be derivative, and you may know every film from which its borrowing, but it's also a lot of fun, something few sci-fi films have been recently. ★★½ VHS: $14.99; DVD: $26.99

The Pitfall

(1948, 86 min, US, Andre de Toth) *Dick Powell, Jane Wyatt, Raymond Burr, Lizabeth Scott.* The Great American Dream gone sour is the theme of this intriguing moral tale. Powell — the bored husband of Wyatt — forgets his idyllic suburban family to enjoy a brief fling with a sexy siren (Scott) — an action that soon brings violence, deceit, tragedy and sudden death. Burr is memorable as the hulking private eye. ★★★

Pixote

(1981, 127 min, Brazil, Hector Babenco) *Fernando Ramos da Silva, Marilla Pera, Gilberto Moura, Edilson Lino, Zenildo Oliveira Santos, Jorge Juliao, Claudio Bernardo, Israel Feres David, Jose Nilson Martin Dos Santos.* A brilliant, disturbing film about a band of youths who escape a brutal juvenile detention center to resume their desperate lives of petty crime in the slums of São Paulo and blaze a trail of violence. Our hero Pixote (da Silva), a gun-toting 10-year-old outcast, and his youthful friends get involved in a drug smuggling scheme and soon befriend an aging alcoholic prostitute (the riveting Pera), who offers them a brief respite of tenderness as a mother figure

and a lover. Pixote, a desperate boy in a winless situation, struggles against the hardships of an environment deprived of hope and ruled by casual brutality. From a novel by Jose Louzeiro. Da Silva was murdered by police when he was 19-years-old for suspected drug and gang activity. (Portuguese with English subtitles) ★★★★ VHS: $29.99; DVD: $19.99

A Place in the Sun

(1951, 122 min, US, George Stevens) *Montgomery Clift, Elizabeth Taylor, Shelley Winters, Raymond Burr, Anne Revere.* An ambitious effort, and one of the few movies of its day to address the subject of class conflict in America. Clift gives a great performance as a young man content to climb the social ladder by ordinary means. That is, until he meets rich society girl Taylor. Although occasionally heavy and slow-moving, and the impending tragedy is perhaps all too inevitable, this is still poignant material, and Clift and Taylor express genuine tenderness and passion. Winters is memorable as the girlfriend who Clift wishes would vanish. Based on Theodore Dreiser's "An American Tragedy." ★★★½ VHS: $14.99; DVD: $29.99

A Place in the World

(1992, 120 min, Argentina, Adolfo Aristarain) *Federico Luppi, Jose Sacristan, Cecilia Roth, Leonor Benedetto.* This remarkably moving coming-of-age "western" from Argentina is an extended flashback depicting the trials and tribulations that help teenager Ernesto (Batyi) find a place in the world. The son of schoolteacher Mario (Luppi) and doctor Ana (Roth), Ernesto lives in the commune of San Luis, a small farming village near Buenos Aries. Writer-director Aristarain uses the arrival of an outsider — a geologist (Sacristan) — to explore the lives and values of the townspeople as their rural world is slowly transformed by industry. *A Place in the World* is one from the heart: for its respect for the characters and their choices are both heartwarming and heartbreaking. The powerful message of this simple, eloquent film will have a lasting impact. (Spanish with English subtitles) ★★★½ VHS: $79.99

A Place of Weeping

(1986, 88 min, South Africa, Darrell James Roodt) *James Whylie, Geini Mhlophe.* A powerful human drama of one woman's personal fight for freedom and her battles against the hatred and resentment of a people, as well as the oppressive hand of the Apartheid system. A heroic story of her bravery and emotional traumas against undignified abuse. ★★★

Places in the Heart

(1984, 113 min, US, Robert Benton) *Sally Field, Danny Glover, John Malkovich, Ed Harris, Lindsay Crouse, Amy Madigan.* Outstanding autobiographical drama from director Benton with Field in her (second) Oscar-winning role as a stalwart widow, raising her young son in Depression-era Texas, who partners with a black transient (the terrific Glover) to raise cotton. The film features a superb supporting cast. ★★★½

The Plague

(1991, 105 min, GB/France/Argentina, Luis Puenzo) *William Hurt, Robert Duvall, Raul Julia, Sandrine Bonnaire, Jean-Marc Barr.* Albert Camus' haunting novel of the anarchy, suffering and isolation that befalls a city when the plague resurfaces is brought to the screen in this serious, well-intentioned effort. The film focuses more on personal traumas and human nobility than on Camus' greater existential thought. The film tries hard not to be too grim, concentrating instead on the human interests of the people whose courage and selflessness shine during the tragedy. A worthy attempt to translate such a distressing story to the screen. ★★★ VHS: $14.99

Plague of the Zombies

(1966, 90 min, GB, John Gilling) *Andre Morrell, Diane Clare, John Carson.* Extremely atmospheric and highly chilling, this overlooked gem from Hammer Films introduced zombies to moviegoers two years before *Night of the Living Dead*, and is one of the first color films of its kind. While not the flesh-eating kind, the *Plague* zombies are still quite terrifying: silent, staring, mindless servants who are virtually unstoppable. A voodoo cult has sprung up in a small Cornish village, terrorizing its inhabitants and preying on the young people of the town. Beautifully photographed, the film contains a remarkable, classic cemetery resurrection scene which must be seen to be believed. (Letterboxed) ★★★½ VHS: $14.99

Le Plaisir

(1951, 96 min, France, Max Ophüls) *Simone Simon, Claude Dauphin.* These three stories from Guy De Maupassant all deal with man's eternal search for pleasure. The first story contrasts pleasure and old age, the second pleasure and purity, and the third pleasure and marriage. Ophüls' stylish, brilliant film, set in 1890s France, playfully speculates on man's alternating natures and conventions. (French with English subtitles) ★★★½ VHS: $14.99

Plan 9 from Outer Space

(1959, 79 min, US, Edward D. Wood, Jr.) *Bela Lugosi, Criswell.* As TV psychic Criswell admits, "There comes a time in every man's life when he just can't believe his eyes." Rent this and your time has come. Based on

Pixote

Roddy McDowall in *Planet of the Apes*

sworn testimony, this opus, often considered the worst movie ever made, tells about some silly suited space alien's latest attempt at taking over the world after failing the eight previous tries (makes you wonder why we even bother to keep watching the skies). Lugosi died shortly after shooting commenced, so a chiropractor half his age and twice his size acted as his stand-in, disguising himself by holding a cape over his face the whole time. We could go on . . . ★ VHS: $9.99; DVD: $24.99

Planes, Trains and Automobiles

(1987, 93 min, US, John Hughes) *Steve Martin, John Candy, Edie McClurg.* Teenmeister Hughes wrote and directed this funny tale of uptight businessman Martin trying to get home to Chicago for Thanksgiving, only to face disaster at every attempt. Candy is endearing as a bumbling chatterbox who becomes Martin's unwanted traveling companion. ★★★ VHS: $14.99; DVD: $29.99

Planet of the Apes

(1968, 112 min, US, Franklin J. Schaffner) *Charlton Heston, Roddy McDowall, Kim Hunter, Maurice Evans.* Classic sci-fi adventure with Heston as a modern-day astronaut hurled centuries into the future to a planet where apes rule and man is hunted for sport. McDowall, Hunter and Evans, all under some incredible makeup effects, appear as adversarial and not-so-adversarial simians. (Four sequels not available separately on DVD) (Sequel: *Beneath the Planet of the Apes*) (Remade in 2001) ★★★½ VHS: $14.99; DVD: $29.99

Planet of the Vampires

(1965, 86 min, Italy, Mario Bava) *Barry Sullivan, Norman Bengell.* The crew of an interplanetary spacecraft crash land on a mysterious planet and must defend themselves from a race of formless creatures determined to take over their bodies. Mindless schlock that only occasionally delivers the horror goods. ★★ VHS: $14.99; DVD: $14.99

Platinum Blonde

(1931, 86 min, US, Frank Capra) *Jean Harlow, Loretta Young, Robert Williams.* One of Capra's biggest commercial and critical successes pre-*It Happened One Night*, this bright comedy may be stagey but never fails to entertain. Harlow stars as an heiress who decides to do Pygmalion one better by marrying her subject — down-to-earth newspaper reporter Williams. She vows to make him a gentleman, but finds her work cut out for her. Young is Williams' fellow reporter, who is secretly in love with him. Though Harlow's delightful performance would make her a full-fledged star (her nickname "platinum blonde" would stick till her untimely death), it is Williams who is the main attraction. With his Will Rogers–like plainness, Williams has a natural screen presence; tragically, he died a year later at the age of 35. ★★★ VHS: $19.99

Platoon

(1986, 120 min, US, Oliver Stone) *Charlie Sheen, Willem Dafoe, Tom Berenger, Forest Whitaker, John C. McGinley, Kevin Dillon, Johnny Depp.* Stone's numbing Vietnam War drama is one of the finest war films ever made, and is the best film made about the experiences of American infantrymen in that war. Sheen plays a young recruit torn between sergeants Dafoe and Berenger. Stone won an Oscar for this masterful achievement, and he would win another one for his equally brilliant companion piece, *Born on the Fourth of July*. Winner of 4 Academy Awards including Best Picture. ★★★★ VHS: $14.99; DVD: $24.99

Play It Again, Sam

(1982, 84 min, US, Herbert Ross) *Woody Allen, Diane Keaton, Tony Roberts, Susan Anspach, Jerry Lacy.* Allen is a hapless girl chaser who depends on the ghost of his hero, Humphrey Bogart, to guide him in matters of the heart. And he needs all the help he can get! Scripted by Allen. ★★★½ VHS: $14.99

Play It to the Bone

(1999, 100 min, US, Ron Shelton) *Woody Harrelson, Antonio Banderas, Lolita Davidovitch, Lucy Liu, Robert Wagner.* Shelton, the writer-director of *Bull Durham*, delivers a boxing comedy that's just plain bull. Harrelson and Banderas play two aging pugilist buddies who are convinced to go on a road trip to Vegas, where they will fight each other for a shot at the title. *Play It to the Bone* is raunchy without being funny, violent without being exciting. ★★ VHS: $14.99; DVD: $32.99

Play Misty for Me

(1971, 102 min, US, Clint Eastwood) *Clint Eastwood, Jessica Walter, Donna Mills.* Eastwood's directorial debut is an accomplished thriller about a California D.J. (Eastwood) and his number one fan (Walter), who loves the song "Misty" and whose fatal attraction for the radio jock puts him and those around him in danger. Lots of chills; Walter is terrific as the obsessed fan. ★★★ VHS: $9.99; DVD: $24.99

Playboy of the Western World

(1962, 100 min, Ireland, Brian Desmond Hurst) *Siobhan McKenna, Gary Raymond.* This is a beautiful and lyrical film version of J.M. Synge's classic Irish play about a boyish young man who captivates a small village with his tale of how he did in his dad. Synge's soaring poetry is faithfully translated to the screen and the film is inestimably aided by a transcendent performance by McKenna — one of the great Irish actresses of her day. ★★★½

The Playboys

(1992, 110 min, Ireland, Gillies MacKennon) *Albert Finney, Aidan Quinn, Robin Wright, Milo O'Shea, Adrian Dunbar.* This sweet comic fable stars the ever-luminous Wright as the strong-willed Tara, a young woman who defies her small Irish town by having a baby out of wedlock. Determined not to let a man influence her life, Tara nevertheless finds herself drawn to one of the vaudevillians in an Irish acting group. The man (Quinn) vies for Tara's attention along with the local heavy-drinking constable (Finney), whose obsession with Tara leads to a series of tragic circumstances. The film suffers from some sappy dialogue. But it does offer sumptuous settings (circa 1957) and a truly awe-inspiring performance from Finney. ★★★ VHS: $14.99

The Player

(1992, 123 min, US, Robert Altman) *Tim Robbins, Greta Scacchi, Fred Ward, Whoopi Goldberg, Peter Gallagher, Brion James, Cynthia Stevenson, Vincent D'Onofrio, Dean Stockwell.* *The Player* is a trenchant black comedy about a young film studio executive named Griffin Mill (played with unnerving restraint by Robbins) who finds his fax-filled, mineral water-drinking, Range Rover-driving life coming apart after he receives death threats from a screenwriter he has shunned. As he dives deeper into paranoia, we learn more and more about an industry that thrives on schmoozing, back-stabbing and green-lighting multimillion dollar projects that are pitched in 25 words or less. With a brilliant, pointedly satiric script by Michael Tolkin, who adapted his own cult novel, *The Player* marks the return to power of its iconoclast director Altman. A sublime movie-going experience, *The Player* is filled

Jean Harlow in *Platinum Blonde*

with cinematic jazz riffs that transcend all expectations. ★★★★ VHS: $14.99; DVD: $19.99

The Players Club

(1998, 103 min, US, Ice Cube) *Ice Cube, Jamie Foxx, Bernie Mac, Monica Calhoun, A.J. Johnson, Alex Thomas, LisaRaye, John Amos.* The Players Club marks a disappointing directorial debut from rapper/actor Cube. The story, what little there is, centers around Diamond (LisaRaye) and her experiences at the Players Club, a Florida strip joint where she works as a dancer in order to pay for college and support her young son. Cube proves that as a director he knows how to keep the action moving at a swift pace, but he is sabotaged by a misogynistic, homophobic script full of one-dimensional caricatures and inane dialogue. ★½ VHS: $19.99; DVD: $19.99

Playing by Heart

(1998, 121 min, US, Willard Carroll) *Gillian Anderson, Ellen Burstyn, Sean Connery, Anthony Edwards, Angelina Jolie, Jay Mohr, Ryan Phillippe, Dennis Quaid, Gena Rowlands, Jon Stewart, Madeleine Stowe.* Episodic look at matters of the heart through different couples, from enduring to maternal to puppy love. With so many different story lines, it's hard not to play favorites, and here Phillippe and Jolie's mutual seduction is memorable, with his brooding fiercely complemented by her vibrancy (note to actors: you'll always be upstaged by dogs, babies, and Angelina Jolie). It's so much fun to see these actors at work (and in such brief bursts) that it's easy to overlook how soapy and unimportant it all is. ★★½ VHS: $14.99; DVD: $29.99

Playing for Time

(1980, 150 min, GB, Daniel Mann) *Vanessa Redgrave, Jane Alexander, Maud Adams, Verna Bloom, Melanie Mayron.* A brutally honest account of the real-life story of Fania Fanelon (Redgrave), a survivor of the Auschwitz death camp. Redgrave, Alexander and playwright Arthur Miller (who scripted this American production) won Emmy Awards for their contributions to this unusually powerful telemovie. ★★★★

Playing God

(1997, 94 min, US, Andy Wilson) *David Duchovny, Timothy Hutton, Angelina Jolie, Michael Massee, Peter Stormare.* Playing God, a big-screen vehicle for TV star Duchovny, is in desperate need of repair. He plays a disgraced doctor who saves the life of a shooting victim — a henchman of local crime boss Hutton. Impressed with his currently unused talents, Hutton hires Duchovny as his gang's full-time doc. This premise could have made an interesting thriller, but the plot just drunkenly stumbles along, piling up clichés (soft-boiled, monotonous voice-overs; technoesque soundtrack; pointlessly artsy cinematography) while its story line rambles on creating a level of viewer ennui from which one cannot recover. Hutton is about as menacing as a squirt gun. ★ VHS: $9.99; DVD: $24.99

Playtime

(1967, 119 min, France, Jacques Tati) *Jacques Tati.* Monsieur Hulot returns, with his simple life meeting modern Paris head-on, from a labyrinthine airport to a haywire supper club. This is Tati's astonishing comic masterpiece, giving his themes of history (and innocence) lost a grand, 70mm canvas on which to play. The filmed metropolis is actually an elaborate set (dubbed Tativille at the time); real Parisian landmarks are winkingly glimpsed in reflections. ★★★★ VHS: $29.99; DVD: $29.99

Plaza Suite

(1971, 115 min, US, Arthur Hiller) *Walter Matthau, Barbara Harris, Lee Grant, Maureen Stapleton.* Matthau plays the roles of three different men in this engaging Neil Simon comedy, based on his stage play. Matthau plays a businessman, a Hollywood producer and the father of a would-be bride. ★★★ VHS: $14.99

Pleasantville

(1998, 124 min, US, Gary Ross) *Tobey Maguire, Reese Witherspoon, Jeff Daniels, Joan Allen, William H. Macy, J.T. Walsh, Don Knotts.* An enchanting comedy, endearing fantasy and subtle social commentary, Pleasantville marks the directorial debut of writer Ross (Dave, Big), who once again has created a wondrous fish-out-of-water story. David and Jennifer (Maguire and Witherspoon in charming performances) are typical '90s siblings — that is, until they are literally zapped into a 1950s sitcom, "Pleasantville." Now living out episodes in black and white, they proceed to raise consciousness (and havoc) by bringing real-life issues into this perfect, Ozzie and Harriet world. Gorgeous art direction and special effects enhance the smart story, and Ross never allows the remarkable production values to overshadow the tale at hand. Allen is superb as the TV mom who discovers her identity, and the late Walsh is quite good in his final role as the town's mayor. (VHS available letterboxed or pan & scan) ★★★½ VHS: $14.99; DVD: $19.99

The Pledge

(2001, 123 min, US, Sean Penn) *Jack Nicholson, Robin Wright Penn, Aaron Eckhart, Benicio Del Toro, Helen Mirren, Vanessa Redgrave.* Disturbing, moody and complex, Penn's raw, edgy mystery takes you on a road you're not sure you want to travel. Two hours later, you know for sure you shouldn't have, but what a fascinating journey it was. In a tortured, haunting performance that certainly ranks among his best, Nicholson is Jerry Black, a Nevada police detective on the eve of retirement. When his going-away party is interrupted by the brutal murder of a young girl, he joins the investigation, which quickly produces a likely suspect. But Jerry isn't so sure. That doubt and a pledge he makes to the dead girl's mother sends Jerry on an obsessive search for the real killer. Based on the novel by Friedrich Dürrenmatt, the film explores the conflicting emotions Jerry experiences as he adjusts to a new town, new job, new relationships, old instincts. As Jerry's behavior becomes all the more consumed, Penn skillfully shifts between police procedural, romantic melodrama and arty psychological treatise as Jerry becomes prisoner to the trap he sets for the killer and ultimately himself. A daring, rewarding, uncompromising film whose subject matter may make this tough going for more sensitive viewers. ★★★½ VHS: $19.99; DVD: $24.99

Sam Shepard and Jack Nicholson in *The Pledge*

Plenty

(1985, 119 min, US, Fred Schepisi) *Meryl Streep, Sam Neill, Sting, John Gielgud, Tracy Ullman.* Schepisi brings an elegant directorial style to David Hare's acidic drama about England after WWII. As Susan Traherne, a complex woman whose psychological breakdown mirrors Britain's own post-war decay, Streep is riveting. ★★★ VHS: $9.99; DVD: $9.99

The Plot Against Harry

(1969/1990, 80 min, US, Michael Roemer) *Martin Priest, Ben Lange, Maxine Woods.* Made by NYU film professor Roemer, this witty and amazingly insightful social comedy was originally shot in 1969, but money problems kept it in the can until 1990 when Roemer reedited the film. The result is a joyous, cooly observed and, at times, hilarious story about the tales of woe that befall Harry Plotnick, a modern-day Job and small-time Jewish gangster. Released from prison, he finds his protection racket being taken over by the Italian mob and discovers a daughter he never knew he had. Roemer's direction, sort of pre-Jarmusch Jarmusch, is astute; especially his uncanny eye for capturing '60s kitsch as well as the impending changes brought on New York by drugs and violence. ★★★½ VHS: $29.99

The Ploughman's Lunch

(1983, 100 min, GB, Richard Eyre) *Jonathan Pryce, Tim Curry, Rosemary Harris.* This cutting inquiry into the devious opportunism of a BBC journalist scans the subconscious mood of Britain behind the false huzzahs of the Thatcher brigade. Pryce is the cold-hearted protagonist who will stop at no romantic treachery or professional hypocrisy in his claw up the social ladder. ★★★

Plucking the Daisy

(1956, 99 min, France, Marc Allégret) *Brigitte Bardot, Robert Hirsch.* This amusing Bardot romp has our buxom beauty as the daughter of a French official who seems to get into all kinds of trouble. First, she enters an amateur striptease contest and then becomes involved in the theft of a rare book from the Balzac museum. The film will not strain your mental capacity, but it's an enjoyable vehicle for BB fans. (French with English subtitles) (aka: Mademoiselle Striptease and Please Mr. Balzac) ★★½ VHS: $19.99

The Plumber

(1980, 76 min, Australia, Peter Weir) *Judy Morris, Ivar Kants.* A sinister comedy-drama that presents the case of an unexpected and

P

unknown visitor, a manipulative plumber, who invades the home of a medical researcher and his wife and instigates emotional turmoil. A darkly funny thriller. ★★★

Plunkett & Macleane

(1999, 102 min, GB, Jake Scott) *Robert Carlyle, Jonny Lee Miller, Liv Tyler, Michael Gambon, Alan Cumming.* Director Jake, son of helmer Tony (*Top Gun*), makes his feature-film debut with this visually striking 18th-century adventure that proves he's a chip off the old block: like father, like son, Jake gives more attention to look than story. But what a look he's given this tale of two highwaymen who team to rob London's aristocracy. Carlyle and Miller are Plunkett & Macleane, who meet in prison and eventually make the rounds of society functions, with the grungy Plunkett posing as the dapper Macleane's servant. Scott maintains a lively pace and endows the film with gorgeous production design, but he can't always sustain tension as the story occasionally meanders and loses the energy that the well-staged robberies and charades produce. ★★½ VHS: $14.99; DVD: $19.99

Pocahontas

(1995, 80 min, US, Mike Gabriel & Eric Goldberg) *Voices of: Mel Gibson, Irene Bedard, Judy Kuhn, David Odgen Stiers, Russell Means, Christian Bale, Linda Hunt.* A Disney animated feature that is serious in tone but satisfying in its story and execution. Their first animated film based on real-life characters recalls the tale of the young, feisty Indian princess Pocahontas who falls in love with British explorer John Smith. This mythic "Romeo and Juliet" romance is set in the New World's colony of Virginia, where a greedy English governor has arrived intent on wiping out the Algonquin nation in his search for treasure. Less comedic than other Disney films, *Pocahontas* through story and song relays powerful messages of prejudice, avarice, spirituality and environmental concerns. While the animation is lovely to look at, the score is less than spectacular. ★★★ VHS: $22.99; DVD: $29.99

Pocket Money

(1972, 102 min, US, Stuart Rosenberg) *Lee Marvin, Paul Newman, Strother Martin, Wayne Rogers, Hector Elizondo.* Two marginal, modern-day cowpokes go for the big score with a larcenous cattle deal in this sardonic, existential western. Newman and Marvin are particularly delicious in this Terrence Malick-scripted fable about the quest for salvation (read: "big money"). Fine cinematography by Lazlo Kovacs. ★★★ VHS: $14.99

Pocketful of Miracles

(1961, 136 min, US, Frank Capra) *Bette Davis, Glenn Ford, Peter Falk, Hope Lange, Ann-Margret.* Entertaining remake of director Capra's own 1934 hit *Lady for a Day*. Davis chews much scenery as Apple Annie, the poor, old apple seller who masquerades as a rich matron — with a little help from her friends — for the sake of her daughter (A-M in her film debut). Oscar-nominee Falk is a scene-stealer. ★★★ VHS: $14.99

Poetic Justice

(1993, 108 min, US, John Singleton) *Janet Jackson, Tupac Shakur, Tyra Ferrell, Regina King.* Singleton follows his sizzling debut, *Boyz N the Hood*, with this disappointing drama starring Jackson as a hairdresser and part-time poet who is wooed by tough guy Shakur. Though hampered by an anemic plot, Singleton gets some nice work out of both Jackson and Shakur (whose easy-going demeanor belies his real-life character). Sadly, though, Jackson fails to breathe adequate life into her screen persona's poetry, written in real life by Maya Angelou. ★★ VHS: $9.99; DVD: $19.99

Point Blank

(1967, 92 min, US, John Boorman) *Lee Marvin, Angie Dickinson, Keenan Wynn, Carroll O'Connor.* Director Boorman creates a stylish new form of film noir using wide screen and color in this cynical thriller. Marvin is at his meanest as a man shot and left for dead by his unfaithful wife and his mobster lover. Now he's back and out for revenge against the businessmen and mobsters who did him wrong. (Remade in 1999 as *Payback*) ★★★½ VHS: $19.99

Point Break

(1991, 122 min, US, Kathryn Bigelow) *Keanu Reeves, Patrick Swayze, Gary Busey, Lori Petty, John C. McGinley, James LeGros.* A slam-bang, action-packed and incredibly silly adventure film. Reeves plays a novice FBI agent who goes undercover on the Southern California beaches to infiltrate a group of surfers suspected of being the Ex-Presidents — a highly successful gang of bank robbers whose masks feature the likenesses of President Bush's four predecessors. Swayze is the philosophy-quoting, mystical gang leader whose series of macho stunts of one-upmanship with Reeves creates several astonishing action scenes — including a hold-your-breath, how-did-they-do-that sky jumping scene, a prolonged but impressive surfing sequence and a lengthy chase scene amid the back alleys of Los Angeles. ★★½ VHS: $9.99; DVD: $22.99

Point of No Return

(1993, 109 min, US, John Badham) *Bridget Fonda, Gabriel Byrne, Dermot Mulroney, Anne Bancroft, Harvey Keitel, Miguel Ferrer.* For those who saw Luc Besson's dazzling *La Femme Nikita*, it is difficult to recommend this faithful remake. Though the film copies the original nearly shot-for-shot, it lacks its predecessor's visual panache and chilling neo-pop style. Standing on its own, it is not an unworthy effort. Fonda is fine in the lead role of a societal throwaway who is saved from the execution's by a shadowy government official who wants to make a super assassin out of her. Still, she's no match for the pouty and vulnerable Anne Parillaud, who originated the role. It's yet another case of Hollywood not being able to leave well enough alone. ★★½ VHS: $14.99; DVD: $19.99

The Pointsman

(1987, 95 min, The Netherlands, Jos Stelling) *Jim Van Der Woude, Stephane Excoffier.* In the dead of winter, a beautiful, fashionably attired French woman accidentally gets off a train in the remote Scottish Highlands where she encounters a strange recluse who lives and

works at the desolate train station. In this "artsy," quirky and complex story, the two, neither speaking the other's language, begin a strange relationship — one which initially makes her a "prisoner," but later develops into friendship and eventually ill-fated passion. This unconventional tale is a visually stunning mood piece which, for those with the patience, proves to be an absorbing and thoughtful treatise on the vagrancies of love and communication. ★★★

Poison

(1991, 85 min, US, Todd Haynes) This amazingly self-assured first feature by director Haynes proved to be quite a controversial work upon its release. Interweaving three seemingly unconnected stories, each with its own individual filmmaking style, this low-budget independent effort will mesmerize many, perplex others and disgust more than a few. *Hero*, the first tale, told in a semidocumentary manner, recounts a young boy's killing of his abusive father and his miraculous flight away. *Horror*, filmed in a '50s sci-fi horror flick manner, follows the tragedy that strikes a scientist after he successfully isolates the human sex drive in liquid form. The final tale, adapted from the writings of Jean Genet, is *Homo*, an intensely sensual and lyrical story of obsessive, unrequited love set in a prison. *Poison* is a wholly original, provocative, unsettling and intelligent film that is a must-see for adventurous videophiles. ★★★½ VHS: $19.99; DVD: $29.99

Poison Ivy

(1992, 89 min, US, Katt Shea Ruben) *Drew Barrymore, Sara Gilbert, Tom Skerritt, Cheryl Ladd.* Writer-director Ruben's entry into the "from hell" genre stars Barrymore as the mysterious, seductive, possibly naughty Ivy, who insinuates herself into the dysfunctional family of an awkward and angry classmate, Sylvie, played convincingly by Gilbert. Ivy soon sets her sights on seducing dad (Skerritt), whose wife (Ladd) is dying of emphysema. *Poison Ivy* may be melodramatic, predictable and based on many unfortunate stereotypes, but it sure makes for amusing trash. (Followed by 2 sequels) ★★ VHS: $14.99; DVD: $19.99

Plunkett & Macleane

Police

(1984, 113 min, France, Maurice Pialat) *Gérard Depardieu, Sophie Marceau, Sandrine Bonnaire.* On the surface, Pialat's tensely exciting "policier" is about a brutal Paris cop's (Depardieu) efforts to break up a North African drug ring. But Pialat, who combines ferocious rawness with pristine formality, goes further than anyone before him in establishing the policeman's physical, moral and emotional intimacy with the criminals he interrogates and brutalizes. Depardieu is at the top of his form as the course, crude cop. A film of stunningly vivid temperament that is less a typical, action-packed thriller and more a psychological probe done with exacting realism. (French with English subtitles) ★★★½ VHS: $29.99

Police Academy

(1984, 97 min, US, Hugh Wilson) *Steve Guttenberg, Babba Smith, Kim Cattrall, George Gaynes.* An insipidly funny slapstick comedy which amazingly spawned five sequels, though once was (more than) enough. Zany misfit police cadets are let loose on an unsuspecting public. This combination of low-brow hijinks and sophomoric schtick does contain many a laugh, but this imitative romp is years behind other "dumb" comedies such as *Airplane!* ★★½ VHS: $14.99; DVD: $14.99

Police Story

(1985, 92 min, Hong Kong, Jackie Chan) *Jackie Chan, Bridget Lin, Maggie Cheung, Cho Yuen, Bill Tung, Kenneth Tong.* Police Story is certain to amaze, delight and entertain. The plot has Jackie as a policeman on the trail of drug smugglers, but story matters little for it is the action-comedy sequences, with Jackie doing all of his own death-defying stunts, that capture one's attention. From dangling on a runaway bus with only an umbrella handle to his balletic dance on speed boats, Jackie Chan's stunts should excite even the most jaded action fan. (aka: *Jackie Chan's Police Force*) (Dubbed) ★★★½ VHS: $29.99

Polish Wedding

(1998, 105 min, US, Theresa Connelly) *Claire Danes, Gabriel Byrne, Lena Olin, Jon Bradford, Mili Avital.* Set in Detroit at an indeterminate time, *Polish Wedding* is a muddled and disjointed though earnest effort by writer-director Connelly. Byrne and Olin are a husband and wife whose lives barely intersect. He bakes bread, she makes babies: 7 children, 5 living, 4 sons. Danes is the roving daughter, who is named to lead the procession of the Virgin just before she learns she's pregnant. At times a meditation on procreation and fecundity, sometimes an exploration of working-class travails, the film is too long and awkwardly structured; its attempt at hyperrealism is inauthentic and flat. Slapstick is no substitute for charm, or melodrama for profundity. ★½ VHS: $9.99; DVD: $24.99

Pollock

(2000, 117 min, US, Ed Harris) *Ed Harris, Marcia Gay Harden, Jeffrey Tambor, Amy Madigan, Bud Cort, Val Kilmer, John Heard, Jennifer Connelly, Sada Thompson.* One of the more difficult accomplishments in film is to capture the creative process at work. Artist, author, actor, composer, they all seem to be painted with the same broad brush stroke. There are, to be sure, a few exceptions, such as *Pollock*, an intense, challenging portrait of noted 20th-century painter Jackson Pollock. Directed with competence but acted with brilliance by Harris, the film isn't able to fully flesh out Pollock as a man, but Harris has superbly conveyed the drive, frustration, technique and evolution of an artistic genius. The story follows Pollock's struggling early years in New York's 1940s art scene, to his romance and marriage to artist Lee Krasner (Harden), to his eventual celebrity, all the while given to bouts of alcoholic binges and self-destructive behavior. As the guiding force in Pollock's life, Oscar winner Harden excels as the supportive Krasner, whose belief in her husband's ability never waivers. Ultimately, *Pollock* may follow the conventions of the biographical genre, but thanks to Harris' tour de force performance, it's an invigorating glimpse at a most unconventional man. ★★★ VHS: $102.99; DVD: $24.99

Pollyanna

(1960, 134 min, US, David Swift) *Hayley Mills, Jane Wyman, Agnes Moorehead.* Cute children's tale about a beguiling young girl (Mills) who captures the hearts of an entire New England town with her warm and sunny disposition. ★★★ VHS: $19.99

Poltergeist

(1982, 114 min, US, Tobe Hooper) *Craig T. Nelson, JoBeth Williams, Beatrice Straight, Heather O'Rourke, Dominique Dunne, Zelda Rubenstein.* A classic horror story from director Hooper, this film owes much to its writer and producer, Steven Spielberg. When spirits from the "other side" kidnap their young daughter (the adorable O'Rourke), an ordinary suburban family goes through Heaven and Hell to get her back. Williams and elson offer the right blend of playfulness and seriousness as the hapless parents, and Straight and Rubinstein are the best ghostbusters yet. This is the finest ghost story since *The Haunting*, and the special effects are terrific. (Followed by 2 sequels) ★★★★ VHS: $14.99; DVD: $19.99

Poltergeist 2: The Other Side

(1986, 90 min, US, Brian Gibson) *Craig T. Nelson, JoBeth Williams, Heather O'Rourke, Julian Beck, Geraldine Fitzgerald.* This below-par sequel once again finds the Freling family battling for the safety of little Carol Ann (O'Rourke). Williams and Nelson return, but even they aren't enough to help. There are, however, some nifty special effects, and Beck is absolutely eerie as a ghostly visitor. ★★ VHS: $9.99

Poltergeist 3

(1988, 97 min, US, Gary Sherman) *Tom Skerritt, Nancy Allen, Heather O'Rourke.* Abysmal third and final entry of the *Poltergeist* films has Carol Ann (O'Rourke) visiting relatives in Chicago, once again bothered by evil spirits. There is no suspense and poor effects, and Skerritt and Allen are lost with the material. Sadly, this was O'Rourke's last film. ★ VHS: $9.99

Polyester

(1981, 86 min, US, John Waters) *Divine, Tab Hunter, Edith Massey, Mink Stole.* In this odorized ode to suburban decay, Divine is a campy delight as Baltimore housewife Francine

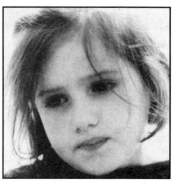

Ponette

Fishpaw, who experiences her own private hell when hubby-with-a-bad-toupee has an affair, her daughter turns out to be a slut, and her revered son is cited as the notorious foot-stomper. Then, Golden Boy Tab Tomorrow (Hunter) comes into her life. Waters tones down the crudeness to win new fans and succeeds. Waters' gimmick of offering Odorama cards to cinema patrons (number two on the scratch-and-sniff card is a doozy) works wonderfully, but sadly, unless you kept yours from 1981, they are not available for the video. But don't let that stop you from enjoying this campy comedy. ★★★ VHS: $19.99

Ponette

(1997, 97 min, France, Jacques Doillon) *Victoire Thivisol, Matiaz Caton, Xavier Beauvois, Delphine Schiltz, Marie Trintignant.* An intimate and moving portrait of a 4-year-old girl coping with the death of her mother, *Ponette* is astonishing in its utter simplicity. Capturing both the innocence and cruelty of children, the film examines Ponette's every emotion as she is advised, taunted and given "trials" by other classmates following her tragedy. What drives Ponette, however, is her unfailing belief that God will allow her to reunite with her mother not only in her dreams, but in life as well. Ponette is determined to understand what she needs to know to move on, and while her quest is full of weighty issues about religious faith and spirituality, the film never sentimentalizes her situation. The large cast of children here are cute, but never cloying, making the emotional impact of the story realistic, without being melodramatic. In fact, Thivisol's mesmerizing performance caused a controversy when she won the Venice Film Festival's Best Actress award. Her prize is richly deserved. (French with English subtitles) ★★★½ VHS: $29.99; DVD: $29.99

Pool Hustlers

(1984, 101 min, Italy, Maurizio Ponzi) *Francesco Nuti, Gulliano de Sio.* The smoke-filled rooms of pool halls provide the unlikely backdrop to this charming comedy-drama. Francesco, a poor man's Pierre Richard, is a mop-headed amateur billiards wizard who gets himself hustled out of thousands of dollars by an unscrupulous champion. His efforts to pay off the debt, first by stealing and second by competing in a high-stakes billiards contest, is the basic plot. But it is our bungling hero's endearing personality and his sweet romance with a sexy saxophone player that gives the film its appeal. (Italian with English subtitles) ★★★ VHS: $24.99

Poor White Trash

(1962, 84 min, US, Harold Daniels) *Peter Graves, Tim Carey.* Cajun camp starring Graves as a self-righteous city slicker, and Carey (the sharpshooter in Kubrick's *The Killing*) as a bayou bully. So controversial upon its release that armed guards were posted at the drive-ins to keep out minors! ★

Popcorn

(1990, 93 min, US, Mark Herrier) *Jill Schoelen, Tom Villard, Dee Wallace Stone, Ray Walston, Tony Roberts.* Nice twist to the "crazed killer" genre, where a horror film festival is the setting for a killer stalking members of the audience who believe his escapades are all just a part of the show. ★★½ VHS: $89.99; DVD: $24.99

The Pope Must Die(t)

(1991, 89 min, GB, Peter Richardson) *Robbie Coltrane, Paul Bartel, Beverly D'Angelo.* A rollicking poke at the Catholic Church, the Vatican and the men who occupy its hallowed halls. Coltrane plays a this-close-to-being-defrocked priest who, through a misspelling made by a near-deaf dictation clerk, is accidentally catapulted into the Papacy. What follows is a sometimes hilarious commentary on the role of the Church in late-20th-century life as this new Pope promulgates his liberal philosophies on birth control, abortion and the use of Vatican money. ★★★

The Pope of Greenwich Village

(1984, 120 min, US, Stuart Rosenberg) *Mickey Rourke, Eric Roberts, Geraldine Page, Daryl Hannah.* A tough, gritty crime drama with Rourke and Roberts as two small-time hoods trying to make a name for themselves in New York Mafioso territory. Rourke and Roberts are very good, as is Page in a sensational supporting role as a crooked cop's slovenly mother. ★★★ VHS: $9.99; DVD: $19.99

Popeye

(1980, 114 min, US, Robert Altman) *Robin Williams, Shelley Duvall, Ray Walston, Paul Dooley, Bill Irwin.* Though this musical based on the famous comic strip and cartoon is not without its momentary enjoyments, the story of Popeye the Sailor, his "goil" friend Olive Oyl and lifelong nemesis Bluto is mostly an overblown extravaganza. Williams gets "A" for effort for his daring performance as Popeye, and Duvall is a perfect Olive, but Harry Nilsson's forgettable score and Altman's clumsy direction offer little to recommend. ★★ VHS: $9.99

Porcile (Pigsty)

(1968, 99 min, Italy/France, Pier Paolo Pasolini) *Pierre Clementi, Franco Citti, Jean-Pierre Léaud, Ugo Tognozzi.* Two contrasting stories are interwoven in a single narrative in Pasolini's biting satire on society's darker nature and the entrenched powers that be who are compelled to squash it. One tale, set in a barren, mountainous land in medieval times, features Clementi as a wandering soldier who descends into cannibalism, eventu-

ally recruiting a cult of followers who feed to the fiery volcano Mt. Etna the heads of their victims. The contrasting story, set in modern times, stars Léaud as the bourgeois son of a former Nazi, now a wealthy industrialist, who is politically and sexually confused — so confused as to prefer the sexual companionship of his neighboring peasants' pigs to his attractive (and frustrated) fiancée. While not as explicitly outrageous as *Salo: 120 Days of Sodom*, this brutal allegory of savage "innocents" and their threat to organized society is intense and involving. (Italian with English subtitles) ★★★ VHS: $29.99

Porky's

(1981, 94 min, US/Canada, Bob Clark) *Dan Monahan, Wyatt Knight, Kim Cattrall.* Sophomoric sex comedy manages a few laughs but is mostly lamebrained. Set in 1954 Florida, the story tells of a group of high school teenagers who play practical jokes and try to get laid. (Followed by 2 sequels) ★★ VHS: $9.99

The Pornographers

(1966, 128 min, Japan, Shohei Imamura) *Shoichi Ozawa, Massaomi Konda.* Imamura's wonderful black comedy focuses on a group of diligent 8mm porno filmmakers, struggling with the high risks and low production values inherent to Japan's booming underground sex trade. Imbued with Imamura's mordant philosophical sensibility, and populated with his stock company of misfits, the film is a hilarious and scathing look at modern Japanese society. (Japanese with English subtitles) ★★★½ VHS: $29.99

Port of Call

(1948, 100 min, Sweden, Ingmar Bergman) *Ivine-Christine Jonsson, Bengt Eklund.* A minor Bergman drama of morality, love and self-awareness which is significant as one of the director's first attempts at Neorealism. The story traces — in an almost documentary fashion — the relationship between a bitter, resigned "experienced" woman and the sailor who falls in love with her. (Swedish with English subtitles) ★★

Portnoy's Complaint

(1972, 101 min, US, Ernest Lehman) *Richard Benjamin, Lee Grant, Jack Somach, Karen Black, Jill Clayburgh, Jeannie Berlin.* Benjamin is a discontented Jewish boy whose doting parents (Grant, Somack) refuse to let him grow up. This cinematic atrocity is based on Philip Roth's best-seller. ★ VHS: $14.99

The Portrait of a Lady

(1996, 144 min, GB/US, Jane Campion) *Nicole Kidman, John Malkovich, Barbara Hershey, Mary-Louise Parker, Martin Donovan, Shelley Winters, Richard E. Grant, Shelley Duvall, Christian Bale,.* Director Campion's adaptation of Henry James' 19th-century novel opens with a black screen accompanied by voiceovers of modern young women talking about love and sex. Right away, we know that Campion has more in mind than a straightforward read on James' tale of the willful young American Isabel Archer, a woman who sets out to rise above the conventions of her day only to suffer at the hands of her own naïveté. Having rejected two suitable suitors on the grounds of wanting to explore life, Isabel sets out on a transconti-

nental trek only to embrace the advances of slithering malcontent Gilbert Osmand (Malkovich). Kidman is at once compelling and enigmatic, but Malkovich's performance is tired. Hershey is outstanding as Madame Serena Merle, a dangerously alluring friend of Osmand's, and Donovan is excellent as Isabel's consumptive cousin. (Letterboxed VHS available for $19.99) ★★★ VHS: $14.99; DVD: $19.99

Portrait of a Woman, Nude
(Nudo di Donna)

(1983, 112 min, Italy, Nino Manfredi) *Nino Manfredi.* Manfredi directed and stars in this erotically charged comedy of sexual illusions and delusions. Set against an incomparable Venice, the film casts Manfredi as a husband who suspects that his wife is the model for a life-size portrait in a photographer's palazzo. His torments, as he struggles for the truth, are a marvel of sexual paranoia and comic energy. (Italian with English subtitles) ★★★

Portrait of Jennie

(1948, 86 min, US, William Dieterle) *Jennifer Jones, Joseph Cotten, Ethel Barrymore, Lillian Gish, Cecil Kellaway, David Wayne.* A beautifully filmed romantic fantasy with the lovely Jones inspiring struggling artist Cotten; the latter believing she may be the spirit of a deceased woman. ★★★ VHS: $14.99; DVD: $14.99

Portrait of Teresa

(1979, 115 min, Cuba, Pastor Vega) *Daisy Granados.* Perhaps one of the most controversial films to emerge from post-revolutionary Cuba, this cinema verité drama centers around the life of Teresa, a housewife and mother who works in a textile factory by day and attends political and cultural meetings in the evenings. With compassion and authenticity, the film probes the problems of her household, as her husband becomes increasingly frustrated and resentful towards his nontraditional wife. A revealing look into sexism and women's struggles in the face of ingrained traditions of machismo in a country that boldly proclaims their liberation. (Spanish with English subtitles) ★★★ VHS: $69.99

A Portrait of the Artist as a Young Man

(1977, 93 min, GB, Joseph Strick) *Bosco Hogan, John Gielgud.* This beautifully filmed though slow-moving adaptation of James Joyce's autobiographical novel stars Hogan as Stephen Dedalus, a young man who is forced to question and confront his Irish Catholic upbringing before he sets out on life's journey. Age-old issues such as sexual guilt, familial repression and Church oppression are met with rebellion by the young man. Gielgud provides a highlight (and should wake up the nappers) with his spirited hellfire speech from the pulpit. ★★½ VHS: $19.99; DVD: $29.99

The Poseidon Adventure

(1972, 117 min, US, Ronald Neame) *Gene Hackman, Ernest Borgnine, Shelley Winters, Carol Lynley, Stella Stevens, Red Buttons, Jack Albertson.* One of the more enjoyable if hoary entries of the 1970s disaster films. New Year's Eve partiers go on an upside-down tour of their

Lana Turner and John Garfield: *The Postman Always Rings Twice*

luxury liner when a tidal wave capsizes the ship. Great sets. (Letterboxed VHS available for $19.99) ★★½ VHS: $9.99; DVD: $29.99

Positive I.D.

(1987, 95 min, US, Andy Anderson) *Stephanie Rascoe, John Davies.* On a shoestring budget, director Anderson has fashioned a complex and fascinating thriller about a Texas woman whose rape leads her to live a second life — with a new identity and all. The film's look is clearly low-budget, but the story, twists and directorial style are first-rate. (Letterboxed) ★★★ VHS: $14.99; DVD: $24.99

Posse

(1975, 94 min, US, Kirk Douglas) *Kirk Douglas, Bruce Dern, Bo Hopkins, James Stacy.* Douglas produced, directed and stars in this amiable tale of a U.S. cavalry marshall out to nab a vicious criminal — not for justice's sake, but so he can get elected to the Senate. ★★½ VHS: $9.99

Posse

(1993, 113 min, US, Mario Van Peebles) *Mario Van Peebles, Stephen Baldwin, Charles Lane, Big Daddy Kane, Billy Zane.* A distinctive, anachronistic updating of the western genre. Van Peebles stars as a "mysterious drifter" who leads a down 'n' dirty posse of Army deserters in escaping from a renegade colonel (Zane) and engaging in a leprechaunic quest for stolen gold. And while the film historically acknowledges the presence of black cowboys on the American frontier in much the same way *Glory* did for the Civil War, it is most effective when viewed as Hollywood escapist fare. ★★★ VHS: $14.99; DVD: $14.99

Possessed

(1931, 77 min, US, Clarence Brown) *Joan Crawford, Clark Gable.* Crawford, in one of her patented tough-gal roles, plays an ambitious factory worker who dreams of a better life. Gable is an influential New York lawyer with an aversion to marriage who can give her the life she wants. Lots of snappy dialogue. ★★★ VHS: $19.99

Postcards from the Edge

(1990, 101 min, US, Mike Nichols) *Meryl Streep, Shirley MacLaine, Dennis Quaid, Gene Hackman, Richard Dreyfuss, Mary Wickes, Annette Bening.* Actress Carrie Fisher's first attempt at screenwriting is this breezy comedy based on her true-life battle with alchohol and drug abuse. Streep and MacLaine are fabulously funny as the struggling Hollywood daughter and her aging celebrity mom. Fisher's screenplay deftly confronts the serious side of substance abuse while not straying from her comedic intent. ★★★ VHS: $9.99; DVD: $24.99

Il Postino (The Postman)

(1993, 108 min, Italy, Michael Radford) *Massimo Troisi, Philippe Noiret, Maria Grazia Cucinotta, Linda Moretti.* A sublime divertimento about a simple-minded Italian postman and his budding relationship with the exiled Chilean poet and socialist Pablo Neruda. Noiret plays Neruda, who seeks political refuge on a tiny Mediterranean island. Mario (Troisi) is the postman whose sole purpose is to deliver Neruda's mail. Ultimately, Mario approaches "Don Pablo" seeking advice about his unrequited love for the local barmaid, Beatrice (Cucinotta). Carefully avoiding becoming Mario's Cyrano, Neruda gently mentors him in the ways of both love and "metaphors," and also nurtures his budding Communist leanings along the way. Noiret logs another unflappable performance that is beautifully complemented by Troisi's shy and awkward Mario. Troisi's performance is made all-the-more remarkable by the fact that he was losing his battle to cancer and died the day after principal shooting ended — it is a touching and unforgettable swansong. (Italian with English subtitles) ★★★½ VHS: $19.99; DVD: $39.99

The Postman

(1997, 178 min, US, Kevin Costner) *Kevin Costner, Will Patton, Larenz Tate, Olivia Williams, James Russo.* Costner gets sanctimonious with a screenplay so laughably inane you don't dare take any of it to heart. He plays a drifter in post-apocalyptic middle-America who steals the uniform from a dead postman (and takes his mail bag). He unintentionally becomes a beacon of hope for a gaggle of survivors (he represents the restoration of the government back East). The image of the mailman as saviour of the new frontier — and as heroic action figure period — is so ridiculous that the movie borders on sheer camp. Yet Costner maintains an intended tone of solemnity, but provoking enough laughter as to make this the funniest unintentional comedy of the year. ★ VHS: $19.99; DVD: $19.99

The Postman Always Rings Twice

(1946, 113 min, US, Tay Garnett) *Lana Turner, John Garfield, Cecil Kellaway, Hume Cronyn.* Both Garfield and Turner had rough-and-tumble lives off-camera: Garfield spent his childhood in various Bronx gangs and Turner landed in Hollywood as a 16-year-old orphan. Perhaps it was the reflection of their real-life dramas that smolders in their definitive portrayals of the ultimate drifter and the unhappily married woman whose passions lead to betrayal and murder. James M. Cain's book inspired four films, but not even Jack Nicholson and Jessica Lange, in the most recent remake, were able to give it the gritty intensity captured in this classic film noir. ★★★★ VHS: $19.99

The Postman Always Rings Twice

(1981, 123 min, US, Bob Rafelson) *Jack Nicholson, Jessica Lange, John Colicos, Anjelica Huston.* A loner on the skids (Nicholson) and a saucy waitress (Lange) become a sexually ravenous pair driven to murder in Rafelson's sexy if uneven adaptation of the James M. Cain novel. Both performers give impassioned portrayals of lust-blinded lovers with fogged-up moral compasses. ★★½ VHS: $14.99; DVD: $14.99

Powaqqatsi

(1988, 99 min, US, Godfrey Reggio) Following the phenomenal success of their art-house hit *Koyaanisqatsi*, director Reggio and cinematographers Leonidas Zourdoumis and Graham Berry reconvened to create this whirlwind vision of life in the Third World. Employing the same time-lapse photography techniques and yet another dazzling score from composer Philip Glass, the filmmakers delve into the myriad issues affecting developing countries as the forces of international capitalism forever change the quality and pace of life for the people. ★★★

Powder

(1995, 108 min, US, Victor Salva) *Mary Steenburgen, Sean Patrick Flanery, Lance Henriksen, Jeff Goldblum, Susan Tyrrell.* Recalling the social outcast theme of *Edward Scissorhands*, but without that film's dark edge, *Powder* is an affecting, sentimental fantasy about a teenager afflicted with an unusually severe albinotic disorder. When "Powder" is taken to a state home, he endures the pain of ostracism and physical abuse. But it soon becomes clear that he has other qualities which separate him from others. It is these special powers which give *Powder* its magical feel. Flanery is quite appealing as the displaced youth. Overshadowing the film is the disclosure of director Salva's conviction of child molestation. It brings a different perspective to the subtly homoerotic film which magnifies Powder's alienation and ostracism. ★★½ VHS: $14.99; DVD: $29.99

Power

(1986, 111 min, US, Sidney Lumet) *Richard Gere, Gene Hackman, Julie Christie, Kate Capshaw, Denzel Washington.* Gere stars as a hotshot political consultant in this muddled exposé of politics and the media. Christie plays his ex-wife, Hackman is his former partner. ★★½ VHS: $9.99; DVD: $14.99

The Power of One

(1992, 111 min, US, John G. Avildsen) *Morgan Freeman, Stephen Dorff, John Gielgud, Armin Mueller-Stahl.* During the early days of Apartheid, PK (Dorff), a young boy of English descent, is sent to an Afrikaner boarding school. Witnessing racial injustice, this "Great White Hope" takes it upon himself to battle oppression and right the wrongs of the world via native music and boxing! (Why not?) Directed by Avildsen with about as much subtlety as his *Karate Kid* movies, this is pretentious, dull and even slightly racist. At least Freeman is good. ★½ VHS: $14.99; DVD: $14.99

Powwow Highway

(1988, 91 min, US, Jonathan Wacks) *Gary Farmer, A. Martinez, Graham Greene.* A delightful, heartfelt and poignant examination of the problems facing Native Americans today. A lumbering Cheyenne buys a battered Buick from the local junkyard and, with a buddy (a radical Indian Rights activist) in tow, sets out on a modern-day "vision quest." As the two wayfarers stray farther and farther from the safety of their reservation, the film exposes not only the distrust and racial hatred they encounter, but also the deep rifts in their own community. ★★★ VHS: $14.99

Practical Magic

(1997, 103 min, US, Griffin Dunne) *Sandra Bullock, Nicole Kidman, Dianne Weist, Stockard Channing, Adian Quinn.* Once again Hollywood takes a good book and reduces it to a saccharine assemblage of MTV moments. Neither Kidman or Bullock is at the height of her acting ability as sisters, the present-day recipients of a 300-year-old legacy. Made outcasts by a curse and a family tradition of witchcraft, the quiet and conforming sister (Bullock) loses love through happiness; the rebellious, wild sister (Kidman) by bad choices. When the two sisters unite for an unwise application of a powerful magic spell, the result is a nemisis beyond either sisters' ability to control. The book-to-film conversion turns the unsettling and disquieting into the formulaic and banal. And the tone is so lighthearted that the film can't successfully shift gears in moments of threat and menace. Though Quinn is good enough to save his scenes, no amount of magic can save the film. ★ VHS: $19.99; DVD: $19.99

Practice Makes Perfect

(Le Cavaleur)

(1980, 105 min, France, Philippe De Broca) *Jean Rochefort, Annie Girardot.* Rochefort's comic talents are put to fine use in this wry, graceful comedy about a philandering concert pianist. The journey to his inevitable comeuppance is filled with lustful encounters with present and former wives, agents, mistresses, and daughters of former girlfriends. (French with English subtitles) ★★★

A Prayer for the Dying

(1987, 107 min, GB, Mike Hodges) *Mickey Rourke, Bob Hoskins, Alan Bates, Sammi Davis, Liam Neeson.* Rourke delivers a subdued performance as a guilt-ridden IRA assassin in Hodges' adaptation of Jack Higgins' novel. With their usual skill, Hoskins, as a feisty priest, and Bates, as a cold-blooded racketeer, lend strong support. Though not as thrilling as its source, the film offers insight into the power of forgiveness and man's atonement for his sins. ★★½

The Preacher's Wife

(1996, 124 min, US, Penny Marshall) *Denzel Washington, Whitney Houston, Courtney B. Vance, Jenifer Lewis, Gregory Hines, Loretta Devine.* In this update of the 1947 classic *The Bishop's Wife*, Washington takes over the Cary Grant role as an angel who is sent to aid a minister having a crisis of faith. Great casting: Denzel is charismatic, debonair and effortlessly romantic. But unfortunately Washington's presence alone isn't enough to make *The Preacher's Wife* a wholehearted success. It's endearing, rather uneven and very sentimental. Maybe the biggest liability is changing the magical aspect of the film. Denzel is an angel who isn't afforded many opportunities to strut his stuff. But the film does boast a fine supporting cast, and the inherent charm of the original story is still evident. ★★½ VHS: $14.99

Predator

(1987, 107 min, US, John McTiernan) *Arnold Schwarzenegger, Carl Weathers, Elpidia Carrillo, Bill Duke.* Gory sci-fi action thriller with Arnold as the leader of an elite government fighting unit whose mission to rescue political prisoners from the jungles of South America turns deadly when they are stalked by a lethal, unseen enemy. (Letterboxed VHS available for $19.99) ★★★ VHS: $9.99; DVD: $29.99

Predator 2

(1990, 108 min, US, Stephen Hopkins) *Danny Glover, Ruben Blades, Maria Conchita Alonso, Gary Busey.* An extraterrestrial lands in L.A. in the future and is confronted by a jungle far different than that of the original *Predator*. Glover is a police officer who, forced to take time out from his busy drug war schedule, finds himself pitted against something slightly more destructive than a Jamaican with an Uzi. Though the story is very thin, the film is saved by some good action sequences. ★★ VHS: $9.99

Prefontaine

(1997, 107 min, US, Steve James) *Jared Leto, R. Lee Ermey, Ed O'Neill, Breckin Meyer, Lindsay Crouse, Kurtwood Smith.* Leto is Steve Prefontaine, celebrated runner and Olympic contender who was a shining star in the 1970s until a fatal car crash cut him down in his prime. The film follows "Pre" from his childhood as a frustrated athlete with thwarted ambitions, to the '72 Olympics in Munich, to his untimely death. *Prefontaine* starts awkwardly, mixing conventional docudrama with faux-documentary interviews with the cast in old-age makeup; the effect is initially unconvincing. But the film soon gains its footing, however, and becomes a fairly engrossing — if minor — portrait of a short, passionate life. ★★½

Prelude to a Kiss

(1992, 110 min, US, Norman René) *Alec Baldwin, Meg Ryan, Sydney Walker, Patty Duke, Kathy Bates, Ned Beatty, Stanley Tucci.* Based on the hit play, this opened-up film version loses very little of the passion and charm of the original stage production. Baldwin (reprising his Broadway role) and Ryan star as a couple who meet, fall in love and marry. However, on their wedding day, the souls of Ryan and an uninvited guest, a 70-year-old man (played with high spirits by Walker), are transposed. As this AIDS allegory continues, Baldwin suddenly finds his mate, once young and healthy, now sickly and old virtually overnight. But how to get them to switch? Adapting his own play for the screen, Craig Lucas imbues this tale with great good humor, and gives thoughtful testament to the responsibility, resilience and consummate power of love. ★★★ VHS: $9.99; DVD: $24.99

Premonition

(1978, 83 min, US, Alan Rudolph) Director Rudolph makes his debut with this largely unknown "glorified" student film about a musician whose nightmares of his own death cause him to question his hedonistic life and his sanity. Though Rudolph, an acknowledged protégé of Robert Altman, has become known as one of our more liberal directors, this somehow winds up being a "Say No to Drugs" treatise rather than the supernatural thriller the box promises. ★★½

The President's Analyst

(1967, 104 min, US, Theodore J. Flicker) *James Coburn, Godfrey Cambridge, Severn Darden.* Supremely entertaining political romp with Coburn as the title character deciding he no longer wants the position; eluding various American and world-wide government agents who either want to kill him or want to know the chief executive's inner-most secrets. Cambridge and Darden are particularly funny in support as a CIA agent and his Russian counterpart. ★★★½ VHS: $14.99

The Presidio

(1988, 97 min, US, Peter Hyams) *Sean Connery, Mark Harmon, Meg Ryan, Jack Warden.* San Francisco cop Harmon squares off against mil-

Practical Magic

itary base commander Connery over the policeman's murder investigation and Connery's daughter Ryan, with whom Harmon is romantically involved. Few sparks, though Connery is, as usual, commanding. ★★½ VHS: $14.99; DVD: $24.99

Pressure Point

(1962, 88 min, US, Hubert Cornfield) *Sidney Poitier, Bobby Darin, Peter Falk.* After their great success with *The Defiant Ones,* producer Stanley Kramer and Poitier reteamed for this stimulating and hard-hitting psychological drama. Set during WWII, Poitier plays a prison psychiatrist who treats American Nazi Darin, jailed for sedition. As Poitier tries to get to the root of Darin's chronic sleeping disorder, the black doctor must contend with his white patient's continual racial and ethnic assaults. Poitier gives a good performance; Darin had his best part in this movie. It's a subtle, chilling performance. ★★★ VHS: $19.99

Presumed Innocent

(1990, 127 min, US, Alan J. Pakula) *Harrison Ford, Brian Dennehy, Raul Julia, Bonnie Bedelia, Greta Scacchi.* In this taut thriller, Ford plays a veteran prosecutor whose life is abruptly shattered when he is accused of brutally raping and murdering a colleague. Against an avalanche of damning evidence, Ford proclaims his innocence only to discover that the judicial process, in which he so steadfastly believed, is rife with corruption and political intrigue. Ford's portrayal, filled with anxiety and pathos, will keep the viewer guessing from beginning to end as to his guilt. ★★★½ VHS: $9.99; DVD: $19.99

Pretty Baby

(1978, 109 min, US, Louis Malle) *Brooke Shields, Susan Sarandon, Keith Carradine, Barbara Steele, Diana Scarwid.* Malle's controversial film is a sensitively handled story of a 12-year-old girl (Shields) born and raised in Storyville, New Orleans' old whorehouse district. Carradine, in one of his most effective performances, plays the photographer who becomes obsessed with her. Malle's impressive evocation of WWI Louisiana is complemented by a remarkably textured examination of sexual proclivity. Sarandon is especially good as Shields' floozy mother. ★★★½ VHS: $14.99

Pretty Boy

(1993, 86 min, Denmark, Carsten Sonder) *Christian Tafdrup.* This dark, kinky and violent tale of one youth's tough coming-of-age takes place amidst the lurid world of teenage male prostitution. Nick (Tafdrup) is a handsome and innocent 13-year-old runaway who quickly falls in with the wrong crowd when he arrives in Amsterdam. Befriended by a hardened, violence-prone gang of teen hustlers, Nick is soon immersed in a world where sex is performed only for money and love rarely comes into play. (Danish with English subtitles) ★★½ VHS: $59.99

Pretty in Pink

(1986, 96 min, US, Howard Deutch) *Molly Ringwald, Jon Cryer, Harry Dean Stanton, James Spader, Annie Potts.* Ringwald — John Hughes' Liv Ullmann? — stars in this witty comedy-drama scripted by Hughes as a girl from the "other side of the tracks" who braces the taunts of her snobby classmates and lets herself be wooed by class dreamboat McCarthy. Cryer is a standout as Ringwald's wacky cohort. ★★★ VHS: $14.99

Pretty Village, Pretty Flame

(1997, 125 min, Yugoslavia, Srdjan Dragojevic) *Dragan Bjelogrlic, Nikola Kojo, Zoran Cvijanovic.* A very droll and beautifully filmed opening — wry, sarcastic and lyrical in expression — frames this often powerful, well-intentioned antiwar film which, while losing some of its bite in midsection, manages to end with the same great spiteful, grotesque humor with which it began. The nucleus of the film is the friendship between childhood pals Milan, a Serbian, and Halil, a Muslim, which lasts until the onset of war in 1992. From a hospital ward where soldiers Milan and Halil are recovering, the story of how they were wounded is told through flashback. (Serbo-Creatian with English subtitles) ★★★ VHS: $19.99; DVD: $29.99

Pretty Woman

(1990, 117 min, US, Garry Marshall) *Julia Roberts, Richard Gere, Hector Elizondo.* This Cinderella story about a Los Angeles hooker-with-a-heart-of-gold who becomes involved with a repressed New York tycoon borrows much from better films before it. But few of them featured as charming a performance as that of Roberts. As the businessman, Gere reacts nicely and looks quite handsome with his greying hair, but his role is simply a foil for the enchanting Ms. Roberts. ★★½ VHS: $14.99; DVD: $29.99

A Price above Rubies

(1998, 117 min, US, Boaz Yakin) *Renee Zellweger, Christopher Eccleston, Allen Payne, Glenn Fitzgerald, Julianna Margulies.* Zellweger plays a young Jewish woman who marries a Hasidic scholar, and slowly realizes that her spirit and sexuality are being crushed by her strict, cloistered surroundings. We feel for the woman's plight, but her character, as written by director Yakin and portrayed by a squinty, pouting Zellweger, is more petulant brat than stifled spirit. The fanciful device of Zellweger periodically chatting with her long-dead childhood friend is clunky and unrevealing, and many scenes are cloying, pandering, or just dull. *Rubies* does have the occasional dramatic moment, it's all topped off with a dippy, featherweight music score. ★★ VHS: $102.99; DVD: $29.99

Prick Up Your Ears

(1987, 108 min, GB, Stephen Frears) *Gary Oldman, Alfred Molina, Vanessa Redgrave, Julie Walters.* This chilling and graphic portrayal of the life and death of British playwright Joe Orton is a masterful tribute to a man who fearlessly attacked English morals and custom. Cut down in his prime, Orton's legacy is well remembered here through scathingly witty dialogue and stand-out performances by

Oldman (as Orton) and Molina (as Kenneth Halliwell — Orton's tormented lover who brutally murdered him in 1967). A brilliantly candid look at the gay scene in London during the late '50s and early '60s. ★★★★ VHS: $14.99

Pride and Prejudice

(1940, 118 min, US, Robert Z. Leonard) *Laurence Olivier, Greer Garson, Edna May Oliver, Edmund Gwenn, Mary Boland, Maureen O'Sullivan.* Exquisite comedy of manners based on Jane Austen's classic novel about five sisters' search for husbands. Olivier and Garson are splendid as young lovers, and the film features a fine evocation of 19th-century England. ★★★½ VHS: $14.99

Pride and Prejudice

(1995, 226 min, GB, Simon Langton) *Colin Firth, Jennifer Ehle, Alison Steadman.* This absolutely charming BBC adaptation of Jane Austen's classic should not be missed. Ehle is completely enchanting as Elizabeth Bennet who, with her three sisters, suffers a mixed social standing because their father married low. As always with Austen, the central paradox is how to marry off these undesirables while at the same time skewering the very class snobbery that makes their chance at marriage so precarious. An enjoyable and engrossing romantic drama that may occasionally show its low-born roots but is really as flawless as its upper-crust, recent cousins. ★★★★ VHS: $59.99; DVD: $49.99

The Pride and the Passion

(1957, 132 min, US, Stanley Kramer) *Cary Grant, Sophia Loren, Frank Sinatra.* Not even the talents of the cast can elevate this laughable war epic. Set in Spain after Napoleon's conquest of that country, the story follows the efforts of a group of Spanish peasants, led by Sinatra, to transport a cannon to a French occupied town. Grant is a British officer who helps them. Loren is there to look lovely, which she does; and on those dusty roads, she never gets dirty, either. The film offers some impressive battle sequences, but little else. ★½ VHS: $14.99

The Pride of St. Louis

(1952, 93 min, US, Harmon Jones) *Dan Dailey, Joanne Dru, Richard Crenna.* The professional and personal life of St. Louis pitching great Dizzy Dean is given the Hollywood treatment in this very likable baseball biography. Dailey had one of his best roles as the famous pitcher, who created a stir whether on the field or in the radio booth. ★★½ VHS: $19.99

The Pride of the Yankees

(1942, 127 min, US, Sam Wood) *Gary Cooper, Teresa Wright, Walter Brennan, Babe Ruth, Dan Duryea.* The best of all the baseball biographies, and — until *Field of Dreams* came along — the best of all sports-themed films. Cooper gives a terrific performance as New York Yankees legend Lou Gehrig, whose remarkable career was ended by sickness. Ruth appears as himself. ★★★★

Priest

(1995, 97 min, GB, Antonia Bird) *Linus Roache, Tom Wilkinson, Cathy Tyson, Robert Carlyle.* Not quite as incendiary as its theme would suggest,

Emma Thompson and John Travolta in *Primary Colors*

Priest is the moving, provocative and powerful story of one clergyman's struggle for sexual identity and religious idealism. Roache gives a stirring performance as Father Greg, assigned to a parish in a working-class neighborhood of Liverpool. As he comes in conflict with the liberal Father Matthew (Wilkinson in a terrific portrayal), Father Greg tries to come to terms with his emerging gay sexuality. This was the crux of the film's controversy, though at the heart of the film is the touching story of a sexually abused teen, thus engaging him in a crisis of conscience of whether to break his vow. A remarkably compelling debate on religious dogma, one intended to provoke thought as it stirs one's emotions. ★★★★ VHS: $19.99; DVD: $29.99

Priest of Love

(1981, 125 min, GB, Christopher Miles) *Ian McKellen, Janet Suzman, John Gielgud, Ava Gardner, Sara Miles.* An elegantly photographed biography of D.H. Lawrence's final days. Detailed are the author's self-exile to New Mexico, his sojourn to Italy to write "Lady Chatterley's Lover," and the tempestuous relationship with his Frieda (Suzman). McKellen gives a stirring portrait of the author. ★★★

Primal Fear

(1996, 130 min, US, Gregory Hoblit) *Richard Gere, Laura Linney, Edward Norton, John Mahoney, Frances McDormand, Andre Braugher.* Gere gives a high-voltage portrayal of a cocky, glory-seeking defense attorney who bites off more than he can chew when he finagles his way into the case of a backwoods, "butter-wouldn't-melt-in-his-mouth" altar boy (Norton) accused of murdering a beloved archbishop. Hoblit's complex whodunit combines compelling courtroom drama with a stellar supporting cast, but this is clearly a showcase for newcomer Norton whose character navigates the film's ever-increasing maze of plot twists to its shocking conclusion. ★★★ VHS: $9.99; DVD: $29.99

Primary Colors

(1998, 104 min, US, Mike Nichols) *John Travolta, Emma Thompson, Billy Bob Thornton, Kathy Bates, Adrian Lester, Maura Tierney, Paul Guilfoyle, Larry Hagman.* This peppy political comedy based on the best-selling book, an examination of a "fictional" presidential candidate from Arkansas who can't keep his hands to himself, makes for zippy, exceptionally well-acted and highly entertaining storytelling. The action unfolds from the perspective of Henry Burton (Lester), a young political consultant who's brought onto Gov. Jack Stanton's campaign for the presidency (Travolta makes the perfect choice for the Clinton stand-in). Bates steals the show as Libby Holden, a ruthless, unapologetically leftwing political muckraker who's called on to dig up some dirt. So despite being part and parcel of all those headlines about Clinton and his intern (remember Monica?), *Primary Colors* proves to be just the right antidote for the politically jaded. ★★★★ VHS: $9.99; DVD: $34.99

Prime Cut

(1972, 86 min, US, Michael Ritchie) *Lee Marvin, Gene Hackman, Sissy Spacek.* Marvin and Hackman make the most of this gritty, tongue-in-cheek gangland drama about a Kansas City mobster from Chicago is sent to collect a debt. Spacek makes her film debut. ★★★ VHS: $59.99

The Prime of Miss Jean Brodie

(1969, 116 min, GB, Ronald Neame) *Maggie Smith, Celia Johnson, Pamela Franklin, Jane Carr.* Smith won a much-deserved Best Actress Oscar (edging out Jane Fonda's staggering portrayal in *They Shoot Horses, Don't They*) for her magnificent performance as an eccentric schoolteacher in 1930s Edinburgh. Based on Muriel Spark's novel, the story centers on the schoolmistress' life in and out of the classroom, where she exerts an enormous influence on her young, impressionable girls. A sincere and absorbing character study. ★★★½ VHS: $19.99

Prime Suspect 1

(1992, 232 min, GB, John Strickland) *Helen Mirren, Tom Bell, Zoe Wanamaker, Tom Wilkinson, Ralph Fiennes.* A deserved Emmy Award winner for Best Miniseries, "Prime Suspect" is a tremendous, gripping tale which combines mystery and the politics of gender. Mirren gives an outstanding performance as Detective Chief Inspector Jane Tennison, a policewoman who is able to confront rampant sexism in the police department when she is given the opportunity to head the search for a serial killer terrorizing London. An intelligent, suspenseful and extremely well-acted film. (Followed by 6 sequels) ★★★★ VHS: $29.99

The Primrose Path

(1940, 93 min, US, Gregory La Cava) *Ginger Rogers, Joel McCrea, Marjorie Rambeau.* Rogers stars in this involving comedy-drama as a girl from the "wrong side of the tracks" and a family of prostitutes, who falls in love with straight-arrow proprietor McCrea. Rambeau is splendid as Rogers' mother. ★★★

The Prince and the Pauper

(1937, 120 min, US, William Keighley) *Errol Flynn, Claude Rains, Billy Mauch, Bobby Mauch, Alan Hale.* The classic Mark Twain novel is given royal treatment in this story about a young prince and a look-alike peasant boy trading places. ★★★ VHS: $19.99

The Prince and the Pauper

(1978, 113 min, GB, Richard Fleischer) *Mark Lester, Oliver Reed, Raquel Welch, George C. Scott, Charlton Heston, Ernest Borgnine, Rex Harrison.* An all-star cast highlights this uninspiring version of the Mark Twain classic, with Lester in the dual role of a poor British boy who impersonates the prince. (aka: *Crossed Swords*) ★★ VHS: $14.99

The Prince and the Showgirl

(1957, 117 min, GB, Laurence Olivier) *Laurence Olivier, Marilyn Monroe, Sybil Thorndike.* By all reports, there was no love lost between Olivier and Monroe on the set of this light romantic comedy. There was nothing lost on the screen, however. As a pair, they work magnificently together with Marilyn playing an American chorus girl who is courted by Olivier's Balkan prince at the coronation of King George V in London. Terrence Rattigan provides a vivacious script based on his hit play "The Sleeping Prince." ★★★ VHS: $14.99

Prince of Central Park

(1999, 110 min, US, John Leekley) *Kathleen Turner, Danny Aiello, Harvey Keitel, Frankie Nasso, Cathy Moriarty, Paul Sorvino.* A young boy runs away from his abusive foster mother to live in Central Park. There he encounters a homeless man (Keitel) and an estranged couple (Aiello and Turner), who may turn out to be the answer to his prayers. Well-meaning but mawkish, *Prince of Central Park* has Afterschool Special written all over it, with corny flashbacks and fantasy scenes, against-all-odds personal triumphs for the young protagonist, and nary an honest, dramatic moment to be found. ★½ VHS: $69.99; DVD: $24.99

Prince of Darkness

(1987, 110 min, US, John Carpenter) *Donald Pleasence, Lisa Blount.* Priest Pleasence is up against Satan in the form of an icky goo; he, a college professor, and his students are out to stop the demon's return to earth. Director Carpenter has certainly done better. ★½ VHS: $14.99; DVD: $29.99

The Prince of Egypt

(1998, 97 min, US, Brenda Chapman, Steve Hickner & Simon Wells) *Voices of: Val Kilmer, Ralph Fiennes, Michelle Pfeiffer, Sandra Bullock, Jeff Goldblum, Danny Glover, Patrick Stewart, Helen Mirren, Steve Martin, Martin Short.* The biblical epic is back, spectacular and hollow as ever, in Dreamworks' first animated film. The look is perfect, with thousands of "extras," huge pyramids, and rich sandy tones evoking an Egypt that is appropriately larger-than-life. There's even a thrilling set-piece involving a chariot race. But this rendition of Exodus is strangely uninvolving, lumbering from plot point to song to action sequence with little heart. The parting of the Red Sea is breathtaking to the eye, but it will inspire more awe regarding the animation rather than Moses himself. Still, this is an impressive achievement, and will undoubtedly become a holiday season perennial. ★★★ VHS: $22.99; DVD: $26.99

The Prince of Pennsylvania

(1988, 93 min, US, Ron Nyswaner) *Fred Ward, Keanu Reeves, Bonnie Bedelia, Amy Madigan.* An offbeat dude (Reeves) wants to avoid following in his blue-collar father's footsteps, so he kidnaps his pop and holds him for ransom. The problem? No one wants him back. Director Nyswaner also wrote the cult hit *Smithereens*. ★★½ VHS: $14.99

Prince of the City

(1981, 167 min, US, Sidney Lumet) *Treat Williams, Jerry Orbach, Lindsay Crouse.* Director Lumet returns to *Serpico* territory in this riveting, epic police drama which is based on a true story. Williams gives a truly remarkable performance as a New York City narcotics officer who risks his job, friendships and safety when he reports widespread department corruption. Orbach is terrific in support as Williams' friend and fellow cop. ★★★½ VHS: $24.99

The Prince of Tides

(1991, 132 min, US, Barbra Streisand) *Barbra Streisand, Nick Nolte, Kate Nelligan, Blythe Danner, George Carlin, Melinda Dillon, Jeroen Krabbé.* Streisand's second directorial effort is a lush, exceptional-looking film version of Pat Conroy's novel. Nolte is outstanding as a married, Southern high school coach who travels to New York when his sister is admitted to a psychiatric hospital. There he meets her doctor (Streisand), and the two begin a brief affair. Though Streisand's character was less conspicuous in the book, here the doctor has a greater presence — which is one of the few disservices to this otherwise laudatory adaptation. A touching romance and a rather harrowing childhood memory piece, *The Prince of Tides* will certainly satisfy the romantics in most of us; those more cynical will probably be

less impressed. Nelligan excels in support as Nolte's mother. ★★★½ VHS: $14.99

The Princess and the Pirate

(1944, 94 min, US, David Butler) *Bob Hope, Virginia Mayo, Walter Brennan, Walter Slezak, Victor McLaglen.* One of Hope's funniest films *sans* Bing, this hilarious pirate spoof stars Bob as a traveling entertainer who becomes mixed up with a runaway princess (Mayo) and a band of cutthroat pirates. The laughs seem to come about every 15 seconds, and a highlight has Bob dressing up as an old hag, being romantically pursued by Brennan! And that's not to mention the typical Hope barrage of puns, double-entendres and silly one-liners. ★★★½ VHS: $14.99; DVD: $24.99

The Princess Bride

(1987, 98 min, US, Rob Reiner) *Cary Elwes, Robin Wright, Mandy Patinkin, Christopher Guest, Chris Sarandon, Wallace Shawn, Peter Falk, Billy Crystal, Carol Kane.* Reiner faithfully adapts William Goldman's fairy tale of love and swashbuckling adventure with style, wit and just the right amount of "mushy stuff." Elwes stars as a knight; Wright is the beauty in love with him. As with most fairy tales, the course of true love does not run smooth until story's end. Patinkin steals the show as a swordsman out to avenge his father's death. ★★★½ VHS: $14.99; DVD: $19.99

Princess Caraboo

(1994, 96 min, GB, Michael Austin) *Phoebe Cates, Kevin Kline, John Lithgow, Jim Broadbent, Wendy Hughes, Stephen Rea.* Cates stars in this picturesque but uneven swipe at aristocratic hypocrisy that might best be described as *Anastasia*-lite. Cates plays an enigmatic beauty found wandering the English countryside and, speaking no English, is taken in by a social-climbing couple (Hughes, Broadbent) who assume her to be foreign royalty. Rea is an inquisitive journalist enchanted by her innocence but intent on solving the mystery of her identity. ★★ VHS: $19.99; DVD: $19.99

Princess Mononoke

(1999, 133 min, Japan, Hayao Miyazaki) *Voices of: Claire Danes, Billy Crudup, Minnie Driver, Gillian Anderson, Jada Pinkett, Billy Bob Thornton.* A young

warrior, dying from a wound received during a fight with a terrifying, Lovecraftian beast, is sent away by his village elders. On his journeys, he discovers an industrial village, which is at odds with the surrounding nature, and whose conflict results in epic violence. Epic is a good word for this amazing piece of animation, which, while a bit too long and languid, perhaps, is still mesmerizing throughout. An unusually thoughtful work, allowing all sides of a conflict their say. A feast for the eyes and mind, this is terrific entertainment for children and adults alike. (English dubbed version) ★★★½ VHS: $19.99; DVD: $32.99

Princess Tam Tam

(1935, 80 min, France, Edmond Greville) *Josephine Baker, Albert Prejean.* It's a musical Parisian Pygmalion! A French novelist travels to North Africa seeking inspiration but instead finds himself becoming steadily more infatuated and entranced by a native girl (Baker). She accompanies him back to Paris where, to everyone's amazement, she is the toast of the town. (French with English subtitles) ★★★ VHS: $29.99

Princess Yang Kwei Fei

(1955, 91 min, Japan, Kenji Mizoguchi) *Machiko Kyo, Masayuki Mori.* An eighth-century Chinese Cinderella story, *Princess Yang Kwei Fei* tells the tale of an unspoiled stepsister who is unwittingly used by an ambitious gentleman who wants to get in with the emperor. Soon the emperor himself becomes enchanted by this beautiful and talented woman and makes her his wife. Featuring beautiful sets and stunning visuals, this historical love story's slow pace may lose some viewers; but for lovers of Mizoguchi's meticulous style, the leisurely pace proves to be a virtue. (Japanese with English subtitles) ★★★ VHS: $29.99

The Principal

(1987, 109 min, US, Christopher Cain) *James Belushi, Louis Gossett, Jr., Rae Dawn Chong, Esai Morales.* New inner-city high school principal Belushi goes head to head with the bad dudes in his school. Belushi and Gossett play well off each other in this effort to make a difference, but the script is full of high school-thug clichés and an inconsistent mix of comedy and drama. ★★ VHS: $9.99

Princess Mononoke

P

Prison

(1988, 102 min, US, Renny Harlin) *Lane Smith, Viggo Mortensen, Chelsea Field.* There's quite a few chills in this stylish horror film. The spirit of a prisoner wrongfully executed two decades before comes back to get even with his former guard (Smith) — who's now the warden. ★★½

Prisoner of Honor

(1991, 88 min, US, Ken Russell) *Richard Dreyfuss, Oliver Reed, Peter Firth, Brian Blessed, Lindsay Anderson.* Russell is unusually restrained in this made-for-HBO retelling of "The Dreyfus Affair," a scandalous incident of anti-Semitism in 19th-century France. Dreyfuss stars as an officer who refuses to allow his army to betray its honor by framing an innocent Jewish officer for treason. A good companion piece to *The Life of Emile Zola.* ★★★ VHS: $9.99

The Prisoner of Second Avenue

(1975, 105 min, US, Melvin Frank) *Jack Lemmon, Anne Bancroft, Gene Saks, Elizabeth Wilson, Sylvester Stallone.* One of the best of the Neil Simon stage-to-screen adaptations, this gloriously funny and, at times, bittersweet comedy benefits greatly from two superlative performances from Lemmon and Bancroft. Lemmon plays a recently unemployed exec who suffers a breakdown, which prompts wife Bancroft back into the work place. All the while, they contend with noisy neighbors, robberies, attempted muggings, a 14th-floor walk-up, picky cab drivers, trash, and the sweltering summer heat; everything, in fact, which makes living in New York a singular experience. A treat from beginning to end. ★★★½ VHS: $14.99

Prisoner of the Mountains

(1996, 99 min, Russia, Sergei Bodrov) *Oleg Menshikov, Sergei Bodrov, Jr., Jemal Sikharulidze.* This gritty adaptation of Tolstoy's "Prisoner of the Caucasus" is a stirring antiwar drama that offers Western audiences an unprecedented and incredibly lucid look into the little-seen world of the Caucasus Mountain region. The story follows two Russian soldiers (Menshikov, Bodrov) who are captured by a local Muslim patriarch (Sikharulidze). Hoping to cut a deal to get his son out of a Russian prison,

Sikharulidze steadfastly resists the relentless pressure from his townspeople to execute his charges. Bleak beyond imagination and yet unparalleled in grandeur. Director Bodrov, Sr. never misses a beat in delivering his heart-rending message on the insanity of war. (Russian with English subtitles) ★★★½ VHS: $19.99

The Prisoner of Zenda

(1937, 101 min, US, John Cromwell) *Ronald Colman, Madeleine Carroll, Mary Astor, Douglas Fairbanks, Jr., David Niven.* This third of many screen versions of Anthony Hope's celebrated novel is by far the best of the bunch. Colman had one of his most popular roles as both the King of Ruritania and his look-alike cousin, who impersonates H.R.M. when the ruler is kidnapped. A good cast is featured in this exciting adventure film. ★★★½ VHS: $19.99

The Prisoner of Zenda

(1952, 101 min, US, Richard Thorpe) *Stewart Granger, Deborah Kerr, James Mason, Louis Calhern.* Not as exciting as the 1937 Ronald Colman version, this extravagant though lifeless remake stars Granger as the commoner who doubles for the King. ★★½ VHS: $19.99

The Prisoner of Zenda

(1979, 108 min, US, Richard Quine) *Peter Sellers, Jeremy Kemp.* Even Sellers' comic mastery can't save this farcical remake about a king's double who is forced to step into the royal shoes when his highness is kidnapped. Not a career high point for Sellers. ★ VHS: $14.99

Prisoners of Inertia

(1989, 92 min, US, J. Noyes Scher) *Amanda Plummer, Christopher Rich, John C. McGinley.* What starts out as a simple Sunday brunch date deteriorates into an *After Hours*–style nightmare for a young Manhattan couple (Plummer, Rich) in this mildly amusing independent film. ★★½ VHS: $79.99

Private Benjamin

(1980, 110 min, US, Howard Zieff) *Goldie Hawn, Eileen Brennan, Armand Assante, Albert Brooks.* Hawn's effervescent performance highlights this hit comedy about a pampered "Jewish American Princess" who enlists in the

Army — only to find it wasn't what she expected. Brennan gives a solid comic turn as Hawn's ever-suffering captain. ★★★ VHS: $9.99; DVD: $14.99

A Private Function

(1985, 93 min, GB, Malcolm Mowbray) *Michael Palin, Maggie Smith, Denholm Elliott, Liz Smith.* Class snobbery, petty vice and social climbing are given a sharp satiric examination in this grand British black comedy. Set in postwar England, the film stars Palin and Smith as a couple who kidnap a pig earmarked for the nuptials of Princess Elizabeth and Prince Phillip. ★★★½ VHS: $19.99

Private Life

(1982, 102 min, USSR, Yuli Raizman) Reminiscent of Arthur Miller's "Death of a Salesman," this sensitive drama of an older man forced to reevaluate his life values after being unexpectedly dismissed from his lifelong job, was made by 80-year-old Soviet director Raizman. Sergei, a taciturn manager of a large factory, finds himself baffled by his enforced retirement and at a loss regarding what to do with his "endless string of Sundays." Quickly, he realizes that he has been insensitive to the importance in his life of his wife, relatives and friends. Symbolic of Russia at the time, the man begins a personal awakening to both the joys of life and of human relations. Nominated for the 1983 Foreign Film Oscar. (Russian with English subtitles) ★★★ VHS: $59.99

The Private Life of Henry VIII

(1933, 97 min, GB, Alexander Korda) *Charles Laughton, Elsa Lanchester, Binnie Barnes, Robert Donat, Merle Oberon.* This sweeping historical chronicle of the 16th-century British monarch features a robust performance by Laughton as the ever-hitchable king. The film had a major impact on the image of British cinema around the world as it featured then-unexpected tongue-in-cheek humor which set it apart from the usual dour historical drama. ★★★★ VHS: $19.99

The Private Life of Sherlock Holmes

(1970, 126 min, US, Billy Wilder) *Robert Stephens, Colin Blakely, Genevieve Page.* Thoroughly engaging film about, well, the title says it all. When a famous Russian ballerina wants Holmes to be the father of her child, he cleverly sidesteps her invitation by suggesting that he and Dr. Watson are more than just roommates. A convenient lie or the truth? You decide. To complicate matters, there's the mystery of the Belgian amnesiac, her missing husband and the Loch Ness monster. Served up as only Wilder can. ★★★ VHS: $14.99

Private Lives

(1931, 84 min, US, Sidney Franklin) *Norma Shearer, Robert Montgomery, Reginald Denny, Una Merkel.* One of Noël Coward's most delightful stage comedies is given sparkling treatment in this very funny screen adaptation. Shearer and Montgomery are a divorced couple who meet each other on their respective second-marriage honeymoons. In a flash, they leave their spouses and run off to rekindle their relationship — and their bickering. The film is ripe with those scintillating Coward witticisms, and if Shearer and Montgomery aren't the perfect choices to

The Private Life of Henry VIII

recite them (the Lunts made *The Guardsman* that same year), they nevertheless handle this sophisticated hilarity with great charm. ★★★★ VHS: $19.99

The Private Lives of Elizabeth and Essex

(1939, 106 min, US, Michael Curtiz) *Bette Davis, Errol Flynn, Olivia deHavilland, Vincent Price.* A must-see for fans of Davis, this screen version of Maxwell Anderson's play may be short on historical accuracy, but it remains an excellent period costume drama. Davis is superb as Queen Elizabeth I whose love for the dashing Earl of Essex (Flynn) is put to rest by political neccessity. ★★★

A Private Matter

(1992, 100 min, US, Joan Micklin Silver) *Sissy Spacek, Aidan Quinn, Estelle Parsons, Sheila McCarthy.* Director Silver tackles the true story of an abortion case that gained national attention in 1964. Spacek delivers a strong, measured portrayal of the mother who, while pregnant with her fifth child, weighs the option of abortion when the effects of Thalidomide on fetuses begins to be disclosed. As she and her husband (Quinn, in another competent performance) are catapulted into the national spotlight, their personal lives become political fodder. A powerful examination of an issue that has lost none of its potency in the intervening 30-plus years. ★★★½ VHS: $9.99

Private Parts

(1997, 111 min, US, Betty Thomas) *Howard Stern, Robin Quivers, Mary McCormack, Paul Giamatti, Fred Norris.* Controversial radio and TV shock jock Stern acquits himself rather nicely in this film "bio" of his rise to fame, based on his best-seller. After several directors took a stab at it, *Private Parts* finally landed in the capable hands of Thomas, who keeps the pace brisk, wrangles quite a few laughs and gets a winning performance from Stern, who's just as good at his patented "offensive" schtick as he is as a romantic lead (!) in the film's surprisingly affecting love story. Not all of *Private Parts* clicks, but it's nevertheless a funny, entertaining comedy which can be enjoyed even by those who aren't fans of his radio show. A pleasant surprise. ★★★ VHS: $9.99; DVD: $24.99

Privates on Parade

(1984, 95 min, GB, Michael Blakemore) *John Cleese, Denis Quilley, Simon Jones, Julian Sands.* Alternately hilarious and heartwarming, this romp covers the comic adventures of a theatrical troupe of British soldiers tap-dancing their way through WWII. Cleese stars as the commander of this motley crew and Quilley is ferociously funny as the director whose productions would make a USO show look like Shakespeare-in-the-Park. Don't miss the uproarious closing credits sequence. ★★★

Prix de Beaute

(1931, 93 min, France, Augusto Genina) *Louise Brooks, Jean Bradin.* Brooks' final starring vehicle, and her only film made in France, has her as a bored young office worker who, against the wishes of her boyfriend, seeks fame and fortune by becoming an entrant in the Miss Europa beauty contest. A standard melodrama that is highlighted by another luminous performance by the enig-

Jean Reno as *Leon: The Professional*

matic international star. The film, coscripted by director Genina and René Clair, features the voice of Edith Piaf who sings for Ms. Brooks. (French with English subtitles) ★★ VHS: $24.99

The Prize

(1963, 135 min, US, Mark Robson) *Paul Newman, Edward G. Robinson, Elke Sommer, Diane Baker, Leo G. Carroll.* An entertaining Cold War spy thriller, *The Prize* is the sort of fun, mindless romp typical of the halycon days of the mid-1960s. Newman plays a Nobel Prize–winning author who becomes entangled in international intrigue when he attends the Nobel ceremonies in Stockholm. He suspects that kindly nuclear physicist Robinson has been kidnapped and replaced with an imposter. Anyone who's seen *Foreign Correspondent* knows it's the truth. This is the one where Newman attends a nudist meeting. ★★★ VHS: $19.99

Prizzi's Honor

(1985, 129 min, US, John Huston) *Jack Nicholson, Kathleen Turner, Anjelica Huston, Robert Loggia, William Hickey, CCH Pounder.* Nicholson stars as Charlie Pantana, a lonely and confused hit man who falls hopelessly in love with mysterious and alluring femme fatale Turner. Huston won the Oscar for Best Supporting Actress as Nicholson's once-betrothed. Director Huston infuses this wry black comedy with his characteristic joie de vivre. (Letterboxed) ★★★★ VHS: $14.99; DVD: $14.99

Problem Child

(1990, 81 min, US, Dennis Dugan) *John Ritter, Michael Oliver, Jack Warden, Amy Yasbeck, Gilbert Gottfried, Michael Richards.* Bastard precursor to *Home Alone*, about an adopted seven-year-old who tortures his new parents after they whisk him away to the suburbs from an orphanage thrilled to see him gone. Ritter is the oh-so-happy dad who believes his psycho-loving son is just in need of affection. The movie's tone is surprisingly mean-spirited; however, there are a number of slapstick laughs. ★★ VHS: $14.99; DVD: $19.99

Problem Child 2

(1991, 91 min, US, Brian Levant) *John Ritter, Michael Oliver, Amy Yasbeck, Laraine Newman, Gilbert Gottfried.* That tiny terror of the suburbs is back in this equally tasteless sequel. Ritter and Oliver return as the hapless father and "devil" child, who have now relocated to another town. It doesn't take long for the imp to return to his prankish ways, especially when another orphaned child enters the scene — and *she's* hellbent for mischief, too. However, "double your pleasure" does not apply here. ★½ VHS: $19.99

The Producers

(1968, 88 min, US, Mel Brooks) *Zero Mostel, Gene Wilder, Kenneth Mars, Christopher Hewitt, Dick Shawn.* Brooks' hysterical farce is certainly one of the funniest films of all time. Mostel gloriously chews the scenery, the furniture and whatever else is in sight as a Broadway producer aching for a hit. He schemes with meek accountant Wilder to produce a flop and make a fortune. They happen upon "Springtime for Hitler" and its crazed Nazi author (Mars). The rest, as they say, is history. ★★★★ VHS: $14.99

The Professional

(1994, 109 min, US/France, Luc Besson) *Gary Oldman, Jean Reno, Natalie Portman, Danny Aiello, Ellen Greene.* Besson retools his art-house hit *La Femme Nikita* for an American audience, expanding the role of "Victor the Cleaner" into that of a cuddly, lovable hit man who becomes the reluctant guardian of a precocious 12-year-old (Portman) when her family is executed by a psychotic, drug-dealing cop (Oldman in a role so over-the-top that Nicolas Cage probably fired his agent for not getting him the part). The twist comes when, hellbent for revenge, she asks him to teach her to kill. What might have been *La Femme Lolita* is instead this two-headed hybrid whose Euro-American sensibilities muddle the impact of the story. (Also available is the director's cut, *Leon: The Professional*, which substantially expands the relationship between the two

La Promesse

assassins, including more of the girl's desire to be violent and sexual. DVD: $29.99). ★★½ VHS: $14.99; DVD: $19.99

The Professionals

(1966, 117 min, US, Richard Brooks) *Burt Lancaster, Lee Marvin, Robert Ryan, Ralph Bellamy, Woody Strode, Jack Palance, Claudia Cardinale.* A rollicking adventure tale expertly directed by Brooks. Lancaster heads the cast as a soldier who is hired to rescue the kidnapped wife of millionaire rancher Bellamy. Palance is the villain holding Cardinale captive. ★★★½; DVD: $24.99

Profumo di Donna

(Scent of a Woman)

(1975, 103 min, Italy, Dino Risi) *Vittorio Gassman.* Gassman was winner of the Best Actor Award at Cannes for his portrayal of a blind, one-armed ex-army captain who resourcefully uses his other senses to savor the beguiling attractions of the other sex. With a young army cadet acting as his eyes, our pleasure-seeking hero travels to Naples in search of love. An Italian farce with undercurrents of drama as well as a decidedly chauvinist attitude to women and relationships. (American remake *Scent of a Woman* released in 1992) (Italian with English subtitles) ★★★

The Program

(1993, 114 min, US, David S. Ward) *James Caan, Halle Berry, Omar Epps, Craig Sheffer, Kristy Swanson, Joey Lauren Adams.* Writer-director Ward makes a serious attempt to tackle the highly charged subject of collegiate football but winds up fumbling the ball. The potential to depict a fascinating behind-the-scenes drama disappears in the first quarter, giving way to a haphazard series of clichés and bad calls. The ensemble seems to be collectively thinking, "I don't have a clue as to why I'm in this movie," though Epps manages a decent performance as one of the players. Notorious for its controversial scene of characters playing chicken on a busy road, which was eventually cut from the film when several real-life copy-cat pranks resulted in deaths. ★½ VHS: $9.99

Project A (Part 1)

(1983, 83 min, Hong Kong, Jackie Chan) *Jackie Chan, Sammo Hung.* This classic Chan film from the mid-'80s (Jackie's "Golden Age") is still a hoot. Period piece finds Jackie getting involved in pirate shenanigans, but the plot doesn't matter at all — just sit back and revel in the terrific slapstick and amazing stuntwork and fights. It's all here — the hilarious Buster Keaton–inspired bicycle chase, the infamous fall from the clocktower, and the eye-popping barroom brawl. If you love Jackie, you can't miss this one; Jackie at his most entertaining, jaw-dropping best. (Sequel: *Project A 2*) (Dubbed in English) ★★★½ VHS: $14.99; DVD: $29.99

Project A II

(1987, 104 min, Hong Kong, Jackie Chan) *Jackie Chan, Maggie Cheung, Rosamund Kwan.* Like the first *Project A*, this is a throwback to simpler, slapsticky times, right down to a very obvious Buster Keaton homage. Chan again plays Dragon Ma, who is assigned to the police force. He finds himself caught between the government and revolutionaries. This sets the stage for plenty of stunts, which are all pretty good, though the pace tends to lag in comparison with the original *Project A*. (Letterboxed) (Cantonese with English subtitles) ★★★ VHS: $19.99; DVD: $29.99

Prom Night

(1980, 91 min, Canada, Paul Lynch) *Jamie Lee Curtis, Leslie Nielsen.* A group of teenagers readying for the high school prom are stalked by a mysterious killer in this run-of-the-mill slasher pick. Curtis continued her reign as scream queen of the '80s. Nielsen plays it relatively straight here. (Followed by 3 sequels) ★★ VHS: $14.99; DVD: $24.99

La Promesse

(1996, 93 min, Belgium, Luc & Jean-Pierre Dardenne) *Jeremie Renier, Olivier Gourmet, Assita Ouedraogo, Rasmané Ouedraogo.* A riveting Belgian film, *La Promesse* is raw, gritty and unforgettable. Igor (Renier) is a wise beyond his years teenager, who helps his father Roger (Gourmet) smuggle illegal immigrants into his Antwerp housing project. Roger exploits these aliens after they get settled, and Igor turns a blind eye because this arrangement provides his livelihood. One day, however, an immigrant worker, Hamidu, is fatally injured. Before Roger gets Igor to help him dispose of the body, the boy has made a secret promise that he would take care of Hamidu's wife Assita (Ouedraogo) and their child. As Igor shifts his loyalties back and forth between the father he understands but holds in contempt, and Assita, who endures multiple hardships, the boy realizes he must make a difficult, if not impossible, choice. The film's quiet power stems from Igor's realization that there is no simple solution to his conflict. The film's abrupt ending only slightly mars this otherwise flawless feature. (French with English subtitles) ★★★★ VHS: $29.99

The Promise

(1995, 115 min, Germany/France, Margarethe von Trotta) *Corinna Harfouch, August Zirner.* Von Trotta's misguided love story is nothing more than a melodramatic tale of love between cement slabs that made up the Berlin Wall. Accompanying his girlfriend Sophie and several friends, teenager Konrad is torn apart when he trips and misses his chance for escape to West Germany. Through the years and several chance meetings, Konrad and Sophie's love is tested, stretched, rekindled and finally quashed under the weight of the opposing countries. Though their romance occasionally moves, the soap opera pacing, contrived plot developments and wooden acting make this all the more disappointing. (German with English subtitles) ★★ VHS: $79.99

Promises! Promises!

(1963, 90 min, US, King Donovan) *Jayne Mansfield, Marie McDonald, Tommy Noonan, Mickey Hargitay.* Mansfield plays a happy housewife who takes an ocean cruise with her overworked husband, hoping to get pregnant. Notable for Mansfield's bathtub nude scene, which caused a stir during the film's original release. ★

The Promoter

(1952, 89 min, GB, Ronald Neame) *Alec Guinness, Glynis Johns, Petula Clark.* An engaging comdey about a young man who climbs out of his lowly social rank and rises to the pinnacle of power in his small town. (aka: *The Card*) ★★★

Proof

(1991, 91 min, Australia, Jocelyn Moorhouse) *Hugo Weaving, Russell Crowe, Genevieve Picot.* This spellbinding, pleasant surprise from Australia tells the twisted tale of Martin, a neurotic, blind photographer — no, that's not a typo — who's convinced that everyone lies to him about his surroundings. He snaps off photos as physical evidence that he hopes will one day expose this alleged deceit. When he befriends a young man named Andy, he finds a companion to whom he entrusts the job of describing photographs. But his housekeeper Celia, an obsessive woman who is secretly in love with him, does everything in her power to sabotage their friendship. Director Moorhouse gets great performances from her ensemble in this fascinating, taut and well-made psychological examination of trust, per-

P

ceived childhood wounds and sexual obses-sion. ★★★★ VHS: $19.99

Proof of Life

(2000, 135 min, US, Taylor Hackford) *Russell Crowe, Meg Ryan, David Morse, David Caruso, Pamela Reed, Anthony Heald.* An exciting and efficiently directed actioner, *Proof of Life* may be more noted for its pairing of Ryan and Crowe, who had a brief, headline-making fling. Thankfully, their real-life chemistry comes through, only adding to the many pleasures of this solid adventure tale. Ryan plays Alice, the wife of Peter (Morse), an American engineer who is supervising the building of a dam in a fictional South American country. When he is kidnapped by rebels, expert K&R (kidnap and ransom) negotiator Terry Thorne (Crowe) enters the picture. As Terry bargains for Peter's life and plans for a possible rescue, he and Alice become attracted to each other. It's *Casablanca* revisited as a wife is torn between her husband and the man who could save his life. But unlike many ripoffs of that classic film, *Proof of Life* has its own identity and features characters who you really care about. It's a good mix of romantic love triangle and thrilling action scenes. ★★★ VHS: $19.99; DVD: $24.99

Prophecy

(1979, 95 min, US, John Frankenheimer) *Robert Foxworth, Talia Shire, Armand Assante.* An eco-logical horror film with more emphasis on the eco than the logical. Nuclear pollutants are turning our fresh-water friends into oversized and very upset monsters. ★★ VHS: $19.99

The Prophecy

(1995, 95 min, US, Gregory Widen) *Christopher Walken, Eric Stoltz, Virginia Madsen, Viggo Mortensen.* This very original horror film about a second war in Heaven stars Walken as the archangel Gabriel, who has come to Earth to enlist help in a war he and other renegade angels are waging against God. Stoltz plays a lesser angel who has to stop Gabriel. The film's low-budget origins prevent its grand premise from being realized, and a confusing ending makes it all frustrating. Though the film will be enjoyable to anyone familiar with the particu-lar mythos of Gabriel and angels, it's a good idea which unfortunately fails in its execution. (Followed by 2 sequels) ★★ VHS: $14.99

The Prophecy II

(1997, 83 min, US, Greg Spence) *Christopher Walken, Jennifer Beals, Russell Wong, Eric Roberts.* This direct-to-video sequel is straight from hell. Walken is back as Gabriel, the spooky seraph angered that God has favored Earthlings over his kind. So Walken lands in Los Angeles and tries to kill Wong, a good otherworldy messen-ger, and Beals, a nurse who is pregnant with no less than the savior of humankind. While *The Prophecy* was percolating with so many plots you could *plotz,* the sequel is happy just being a gory chase movie with a little Gothic atmos-phere. Think *The Crow* with nothing to crow about. ★½ VHS: $19.99; DVD: $29.99

The Proposition

(1998, 115 min, US, Lesli Linka Glatter) *William Hurt, Madeleine Stowe, Kenneth Branagh, Frank Loggia, Neil Patrick Harris.* Painfully dull,

and extremely slow moving, *The Proposition* wastes a talented cast in a film so bad, its great-est shame is that it is not unintentionally funny. Told in a neverending flashback, the story concerns the ongoing efforts of a sterile businessman to have his wife impregnated by a young stud. Once she become pregnant, he is murdered. She then seeks solace with a priest, and begins an improbable affair. *The Proposition* is indecent because it has more bad plot twists, clunky symbolism and awkward mouthfuls of dialogue than any one film can bear. ★ VHS: $14.99

Prospero's Books

(1991, 129 min, GB/The Netherlands, Peter Greenaway) *John Gielgud, Michael Clark, Michel Blanc, Erland Josephson.* Greenaway's kaleido-scopic, hallucinatory spin on Shakespeare's "The Tempest" is sure to leave the viewer with a visceral reaction — some will delight in his orgiastic vision, while others may be nauseated and others still will simply be left dumbfound-ed in the sheer audacity of an endless proces-sion of naked bodies and a level of bacchana-lian spectacle never before seen in cinema. Gielgud not only stars as Prospero but also gives voice to every other character in the film. While the film sketchily follows the narrative, Greenaway pays more attention to the themat-ic content of the Bard's work and plays it up as an allegory for the conquering of the magical New World (read: the Americas). For adven-turous viewers of cinema, this is a must, but be warned that a knowledge of "The Tempest" is extremely helpful in one's comprehension of the film. ★★★½

Protocol

(1984, 96 min, US, Herbert Ross) *Goldie Hawn, Chris Sarandon, Andre Gregory.* Hawn's endear-ing charm elevates this average comedy about a Washington waitress who saves the life of a diplomat and becomes involved in interna-tional diplomacy and intrigue. ★★½ VHS: $14.99; DVD: $14.99

Prototype X29A

(1992, 98 min, US, Phillip Roth) Another excursion into quasi-mystic cyberpunk sensi-bilities, this technoparable on human duality is set in L.A. 2057 A.D., where totally cyber-netic Prototypes are programmed to destroy Omegas, cybernetically altered humans. The requisite elements are all here: stark Catherdral lighting in debris-riddled, rav-aged interiors; painfully bright, ozone-depleted, barren wasteland exteriors, *Road Warrior* costumes, casual violence and elec-tronic takes on Gregorian chants. You've seen it all before, and yet, the young cast gives it their best shot and the story offers wry commentary on the human tendency towards self-destruction through technology. ★★ VHS: $89.99

Providence

(1977, 104 min, France, Alain Resnais) *John Gielgud, Dirk Bogarde, Ellen Burstyn, David Warner.* Gielgud creates a vivid character in the person of Clive Langham, a noted elderly author, in this fascinating story on creativity and imagination. In a superlative portrayal, Gielgud plays the often drunk, foul-mouthed old man, who despite suffering from a fatal disease, spends a night hallucinating about members of his family while trying to plot out his next novel. Fact, fantasy and his uncon-scious thoughts and feelings as well as his growing senility are incorporated into the fab-ric of his tale. (Filmed in English) ★★★

Provincial Actors

(1980, 104 min, Poland, Agnieszka Holland) *Tadeusz Huk, Halina Labonarska.* In her debut feature, director Holland takes the trials and tribulations of a rural theatre troupe and politi-cizes in a meandering fashion their attempt to produce a play. Christopher, the leading actor of the troupe, is a dedicated artist — to the extent he ignores his impatient wife Anna, her-self a former actress but now relegated to chil-dren's puppet shows. In the course of rehearsals and performances, Christopher

Meg Ryan (l.) and Russell Crowe in *Proof of Life*

Janet Leigh in Hitchcock's immortal classic *Psycho*

experiences marital problems and a near-mental breakdown. Holland demonstrates little of the dramatic structure or a fluent style evident in her later works, but the film does offer an interesting glimpse into the mind and the relationship of the artist. (Polish with English subtitles) ★★ VHS: $79.99

Psych-Out

(1968, 95 min, US, Richard Rush) *Susan Strasberg, Jack Nicholson, Bruce Dern, Dean Stockwell.* A deaf runaway (Strasberg) searches the streets looking for her brother amidst the psychedelic world of the 1960s. Music by the Strawberry Alarm Clock. ★★½

Psycho

(1960, 109 min, US, Alfred Hitchcock) *Anthony Perkins, Janet Leigh, Vera Miles, John Gavin, Martin Balsam.* What more can be said about this shocker that has forever altered the sanctity of the shower (not to mention tainted the reputations of taxidermists and loving sons)? Perkins made his mark with the jagged-edged portrait of mild-mannered hotel proprietor Norman Bates. A masterpiece of both suspense and narrative form, *Psycho* is Hitchcock at his best. (VHS available letterboxed or pan & scan) (Remade in 1998) (Followed by 3 sequels) ★★★★ VHS: $14.99; DVD: $29.99

Psycho

(1998, 104 min, US, Gus Van Sant) *Vince Vaughn, Anne Heche, Julianne Moore, William H. Macy, Viggo Mortensen.* Remakes should serve several purposes. Amongst them are updating an entirely dated work for modern audiences, or stamping source material with another auteur's fresh, distinctive ring. Van Sant does neither with his remake of Alfred Hitchcock's classic thriller, a nifty-in-theory experiment which should have been relegated to film school. Vaughn sullies the character of Norman Bates, now a fey masturbator. Basically, Van Sant's own contributions include some technically sophisticated shots,

color, and a few weird edits (Macy sees blurred visions of cows when stabbed!). Heche, Moore and Macy provide good turns, but not enough to balance out Vaughn's asinine freakazoid. This remake is totally uncalled for. Stick with Hitchcock's still-potent original masterpeice. ★★ VHS: $14.99; DVD: $29.99

Psycho II

(1983, 113 min, US, Richard Franklin) *Anthony Perkins, Vera Miles, Meg Tilly, Robert Loggia.* Perkins returns as Norman Bates. It's 20 years later, and Norman has been released from the asylum, trying to keep his hands (not to mention the shower) clean. ★★½ VHS: $14.99; DVD: $19.99

Psycho III

(1986, 96 min, US, Anthony Perkins) *Anthony Perkins, Diana Scarwid, Jeff Fahey.* The Bates Motel is open for business once more. Perkins returns as Norman, who here becomes attracted to Scarwid, his new assistant manager, who bears a striking resemblence to the ill-fated Marion Crane. Some scenes are played strictly for laughs. ★★ VHS: $14.99; DVD: $19.99

Puberty Blues

(1981, 86 min, Australia, Bruce Beresford) *Neil Schofield, Jad Capelja.* Beresford's comic, risqué look at the coming-of-age of two teenage girls around the surfing beaches outside Sydney. It offers an insightful look at adolescent rites of passage, told from the female point of view. ★★½ VHS: $14.99

Public Access

(1992, 86 min, US, Bryan Singer) *Ron Marquette, Dina Brooks, Burt Williams, Larry Maxwell.* An intriguing but ultimately unfulfilled thriller, *Public Access* is the promising first feature film by director Singer and writer Christopher McQuarrie (*The Usual Suspects*). The slickly handsome Marquette is Whiley Pritcher, an enigmatic stranger who comes to the sleepy town of Brewster with a mission: to expose its dark underbelly and tear apart the town from within. He buys time on the local public access channel, hosting a show called "Our Town," and asks the question, "What's wrong with Brewster?" Soon a bevy of semi-lunatic callers tell on their neighbors, threatening to uncover a scandal lurking beneath Brewster's surface. Though Singer and McQuarrie fail to find a satisfying resolution to the questions they pose, the ending is nevertheless thought-provoking and unique. ★★½; DVD: $19.99

Public Enemy

(1931, 83 min, US, William Wellman) *James Cagney, Jean Harlow, Joan Blondell.* Classic 1930s gangster film with Cagney giving a star-making performance as a slum kid who rises to the top of the underworld. First-rate cast includes Clarke, who was the recipient of that famous grapefruit. ★★★½ VHS: $19.99

The Public Eye

(1992, 99 min, US, Howard Franklin) *Joe Pesci, Barbara*

Hershey, Stanley Tucci. Fireball Pesci reveals a seldom-seen sensitivity in this atmospheric biography based on the life of '40s tabloid photographer Leon Bernstein. Pesci is "The Great Bernzini," a papparazzi prototype whose photojournalistic aspirations get him embroiled with the cops, the mob and a sultry femme fatale (Hershey). While the "beauty and the beast" angle wears thin at times, Peter Suschitzky's dead-on mixture of black-and-white photography with color cinematography perfectly captures the gritty milieu of the 1940s New York underworld. ★★½ VHS: $19.99

Pulp Fiction

(1994, 153 min, US, Quentin Tarantino) *John Travolta, Samuel L. Jackson, Bruce Willis, Uma Thurman, Harvey Keitel, Tim Roth, Amanda Plummer, Eric Stoltz.* Tarantino's audacious, art-house actioner is perhaps the only American film so story-intensive that it deserves the title "the *Gone with the Wind* of action movies." Travolta and Jackson give exceptional, career performances as a pair of gregarious hit men whose day-to-day activities take them through an interlocking series of darkly comic and horrific scenarios ranging from an accidental drug overdose to a graphic (and unexpected) rape sequence. Tarantino introduces a rogue's gallery of well-drawn characters into a labyrinthine story line, playing with perspective, time and place to create perhaps the most original American film since *Citizen Kane*. Overlong without ever being boring, this gritty walk on the wild side features an astounding ensemble. This is the special edition with additional footage and commentary. (VHS available letterboxed or pan & scan) ★★★★ VHS: $14.99; DVD: $29.99

Pump Up the Volume

(1990, 100 min, US, Allan Moyle) *Christian Slater, Ellen Greene, Samantha Mathis, Annie Ross.* Slater, fresh from his success in *Heathers*, dons the troubled youth persona once again, and though this subversive teen comedy-drama has none of that near-classic's devilish wit, it's dead on target in capturing teenage disillusionment in the land of "white bread." Slater plays a shy high school student who lets go and "talks hard" as Harry Hard-on, an irreverent pirate D.J. His voice in tune to both the misfits and the hip of his school, Harry soon becomes an

Anne Heche in Gus Van Sant's ill-conceived remake of *Psycho*

P

unwilling guru to his classmates, and a "threat" to school and local authorities. *Pump Up the Volume* is brimming with great dialogue and an excellent musical score, and like *Heathers*, casts an iconoclastic glance towards today's teens. ★★★ VHS: $9.99; DVD: $14.99

Pumping Iron

(1977, 85 min, US, George Butler & Robert Fiore) *Arnold Schwarzenegger, Lou Ferrigno.* A sometimes mesmerizing glimpse into the little-dissected world of bodybuilding, this part-adulatory, part-voyeuristic documentary centers on the Mr. Olympia contest and on its two main competitors — Schwarzenegger and Ferrigno. There's lots of scenes of bulging biceps and sweaty faces as the directors interview the men in and out of the gym, and cinematically eavesdrop on conversations and workouts. ★★★

Pumping Iron II: The Women

(1985, 107 min, US, George Butler) Several years after *Pumping Iron,* Butler returned to the gyms in this engaging look at female bodybuilding. As the camera ogles the bronzed women pumping up, champions Rachel McLish, Bev Francis and a dozen others discuss their commitment to the sport and demonstrate their physical prowess. ★★★ VHS: $19.99

Pumpkinhead

(1988, 87 min, US, Stan Winston) *Lance Henriksen, Jeff East.* This Gothic-like horror film, a cut above the typical teen slasher film, provides creepy fun which relies more on suspense than gore (although the film does have its share). A group of city kids go "wilding" in the country and accidentally kill one of the young locals. The dead child's father (Henriksen) wants revenge and summons a mythical demon, which comes to life and inhabits the surrounding mountains. ★★½ VHS: $9.99; DVD: $14.99

Punchline

(1988, 128 min, US, David Seltzer) *Sally Field, Tom Hanks, John Goodman, Mary Rydell, Damon Wayans.* This intriguing and often hilarious comedy-drama stars Hanks (in an unusual departure from his other film roles) as a self-centered medical student drop-out determined to make it in the world of stand-up comedy. Field nicely plays a New Jersey housewife (patterned on Roseanne?) who yearns to make people laugh. The film entertainingly explores both the milieu of the comic and the touching story of the friendship and ill-fated romance between Hanks and Field. Goodman plays Field's supportive husband, a role he'd play for nine years with you-know-who on TV. ★★★ VHS: $9.99

The Puppet Masters

(1994, 95 min, US, Stuart Orme) *Donald Sutherland, Eric Thal, Julie Warner, Yaphet Kotto.* Sci-fi visionary Robert A. Heinlein's gripping cold war parable about alien possession is updated and streamlined into this tense if derivative chiller with more than a passing resemblance to *Invasion of the Body Snatchers.* This time out the alien is a parasite that attaches itself to the spinal cord of its victim and drills into the brain. Though we've seen it all before, the film benefits from a fast-paced script, good special effects and a commanding performance by Sutherland as the resi-

Uma Thurman and John Travolta boogie on in Quentin Tarantino's *Pulp Fiction*

dent know-it-all science expert called in to stem the tide of alien domination. ★★★

Pups

(1999, 100 min, US, Ash) *Cameron Van Hoy, Marsha Barton, Burt Reynolds, Kurt Loder.* Two young kids find one of their parents' handguns, and decide to rob a bank on the way to school. They're forced to take hostages, and a media circus soon develops. This *Kids*-lite meets *Dog Day Afternoon* would've made a decent short, but as a feature, it doesn't feel fully developed. Reynolds (almost literally) phones in his performance, while the two kids are allowed to flounder in long, faux-Cassavettes, seemingly improvised scenes. While moderately suspenseful at times, the film also makes mincemeat out of its already obvious, "big-whoop" social observations, complete with predictable, hollow, tragic ending. The best moments are provided by MTV's Loder, who plays himself with a welcome dose of self-parody. ★★½ VHS: $102.99; DVD: $19.99

A Pure Formality

(1994, 108 min, France/Italy, Giuseppe Tornatore) *Gérard Depardieu, Roman Polanski, Sergio Rubini.* An arresting opening sequence of murder and flight begins an intricately constructed battle of intellect and will between two formidable opponents. As the prime suspect, a rain-soaked and disheveled Depardieu emits a raw intensity reminiscent of his performance in *Going Places.* As Police Inspector Bogart, Polanski seems to carry the burden of his personal experiences with police procedures. The conflict between these evenly matched protagonists is a sly game of cat and mouse. Tornatore keeps a tight ship, deftly utilizing all the materials at his disposal — not the least of which is Ennio Morricone's score. (French with English subtitles) ★★★½ VHS: $79.99

Pure Luck

(1991, 96 min, US, Nadia Tass) *Martin Short, Danny Glover, Harry Shearer, Scott Wilson.* Yet another attempt by Hollywood to capitalize on the success of lesser-known foreign films, this limp remake of the hilarious French comedy *La Chevre* falls decidedly flat. When the acci-

dent-prone daughter of a wealthy industrialist disappears at a Mexican resort, the only person capable of finding her is the equally maladroit and bumbling Short. Glover is the company detective who reluctantly accepts him as a partner in the search. The pairing doesn't seem like a bad one, but this comic duo simply can't match the sidesplitting slapstick achieved by Gérard Depardieu and Pierre Richard in the original. ★★ VHS: $9.99

Purlie Victorious

(1963, 105 min, US, Nicholas Webster) *Ossie Davis, Ruby Dee, Alan Alda, Godfrey Cambridge, Sorrell Booke.* Leisurely film version of Ossie Davis' Broadway satire about a free-wheeling preacher (Davis) who goes up against an oppressive, bigoted landowner (Booke). The basis for the award-winning musical "Purlie." (aka: *Gone Are the Days*) ★★★

The Purple Heart

(1944, 99 min, US, Lewis Milestone) *Dana Andrews, Farley Granger, Richard Conte, Sam Levene.* This WWII drama doubles as a fascinating piece of war-time propaganda and an interesting examination of individual heroism. A group of U.S. pilots captured and held prisoner by the Japanese Army. ★★★ VHS: $14.99

Purple Noon (Plein Soleil)

(1960, 118 min, France, René Clément) *Alain Delon, Marie Laforet, Maurice Ronet.* This stylish, gorgeously photographed and sexy thriller is far from being dated and is possibly more impressive when viewed today. Set amidst the opulent, sun-drenched locales of the Mediterranean, the film's serpentine plot involves the tangled affairs of three young "beautiful people." Delon is the stunningly handsome Tom, a friend and hanger-on to Phillip (Ronet), a brattily rich American playboy cruising the warm blue waters in his sailboat with his long-suffering girlfriend (Laforet) and Tom. But this surface beauty and tranquility only masks a deadly scheme of revenge and murder as Tom concocts a plot to take over his friend's life and love. Hitchcockian in detail and twists, *Purple Noon,* adapted from Patricia Highsmith's "The Talented Mr. Ripley," is certain to enthrall

P

John Cusack in *Pushing Tin*

devotees of murder/mysteries as well as interest fans of a style of European filmmaking now sadly gone. (French and Italian with English subtitles) ★★★½ VHS: $19.99

Purple Rain

(1984, 111 min, US, Albert Magnoli) *Prince, Apollonia Kotero, Morris Day.* Prince makes an prodigous film debut as The Kid, a young band leader with an alcoholic father, an uptight attitude and problems with women. Filled with outrageous production numbers and pulsating music by Prince and the Revolution as well as Morris Day and the Time. The film's treatment of women is suspect, but the question arises, is it unmitigated misogyny or a comment on the ravages of spousal abuse? You decide. (Sequel: *Graffiti Bridge*) ★★½ VHS: $9.99; DVD: $14.99

The Purple Rose of Cairo

(1985, 82 min, US, Woody Allen) *Mia Farrow, Jeff Daniels, Danny Aiello, Dianne Wiest, Edward Herrmann, Glenne Headly.* Farrow stars as a waifish Depression-era waitress who is swept off her feet by Daniels, the star of her favorite movie. The catch, of course, is that he literally walks off the movie screen to get to her! A delicious concept, done full justice by Allen. "I'm in love with a wonderful man — he's fictional, but you can't have everything." ★★★★

The Pursuit of D.B. Cooper

(1981, 100 min, US, Roger Spottiswoode) *Robert Duvall, Treat Williams, Kathryn Harrold.* A fictionalized account of a real-life event, this appealing caper comedy tries to speculate what "really" happened to infamous hijacker D.B. Cooper in 1971. Williams is the thief, and Duvall is the policeman hot on his trail. ★★½

Pushing Hands

(1992, 100 min, US, Ang Lee) *Sihung Lung, Bo Z. Wang, Deb Snyder, Haan Lee, Lai Wang.* *Pushing Hands* is a Tai Chi exercise of ebb

and flow, accomodation and imposition, a physical manifestation of the quest for balance. In director Lee's first film, the balance of the Chu household is disrupted when Alex (B. Wang) brings his father (Lung), a Tai chi master in China, to New York to live with him, his Caucasian wife and their child. Circumstances force father and daughter-in-law (Snyder) into unrelentingly close contact, exacerbating generational and cultural differences. Master Chu embarks on a solo journey into this strange new world, and his quest is delicately considered with compassion and sharp observance by the director. A small gem of a film whose resolution offers warmth without naiveté. (In English and Mandarin with English subtitles) ★★★; DVD: $24.99

Pushing Tin

(1999, 123 min, US, Mike Newell) *John Cusack, Billy Bob Thornton, Cate Blanchett, Angelina Jolie, Jake Weber, Vicki Lewis.* Cusack thinks he's the best air traffic controller, until hotshot Thornton comes to the tower; thus begins a bitter rivalry that inevitably leads to respect and friendship. The high-stress environment in which they work makes for very entertaining scenes, and perhaps a glimpse of a world better left unexplored if any flights are in your immediate future. But director Newell loses focus of what makes these people interesting, and instead *Pushing Tin* drifts into an average domestic drama, with adultery and other mundane subplots that were more compelling in hundreds of earlier movies. As would be expected, the cast is fine, with Blanchett underplaying her unhappy New Jersey wife, in a big departure from her Oscar-nominated breakthrough in *Elizabeth*. But the TV-movie mechanics are a major disappointment. ★★½ VHS: $9.99; DVD: $24.99

Putney Swope

(1969, 88 min, US, Robert Downey) *Arnold Johnson, Laura Greene.* While the liberal wing

of Hollywood was making a big show out of taking Sidney Poitier home to dinner, Downey was preaching true equality when he argued that given half the chance blacks could be every bit as corrupt as whites. Having spent the better part of a decade directing TV commercials, Downey set his fable in the milieu he knew well — Madison Avenue advertising. When token black Swope is accidentally elected the agency's new president, change is in the air. First up, a corporate make over, starting with the name. Now called "Truth & Soul," the company vows not to accept any politically incorrect clients — until the cash flow gets tight. Downey mixes faux commercials with a wild narrative style that influenced mainstream movies for years to come. ★★★ VHS: $19.99; DVD: $19.99

Pygmalion

(1938, 96 min, GB, Anthony Asquith & Leslie Howard) *Leslie Howard, Wendy Hiller.* George Bernard Shaw helped write the screenplay for this first real expert film translation of one of his plays. Hiller is captivating as Eliza Doolittle, the guttersnipe flower seller who is transformed into a proper socialite by the efforts of Professor Henry Higgins (Howard). Unfortunately lost in the shuffle since the international success of the musical "My Fair Lady" on which it is based, this earlier, more modest, version is exemplary of "classic" British cinema. ★★★★ VHS: $24.99; DVD: $29.99

A Pyromaniac's Love Story

(1995, 96 min, US, Joshua Brand) *William Baldwin, John Leguizamo, Sadie Frost, Erika Eleniak, Michael Lerner, Joan Plowright, Armin Mueller-Stahl.* From the creator of TV's "Northern Exposure" comes this cloying comedy of errors about a poor schlub (Leguizamo) who takes the blame for setting a fire he didn't commit in exchange for the $20,000 he needs to run away with his beloved (Frost) who'll now have nothing to go with him. Enter the real culprit (Baldwin) who set the fire as a tribute to his beloved (Eleniak) and now wants proper credit! Part O. Henry and part Wilde, without the flair of either, Brand's quirky and miscast mishmash relies on the kinetic energy of Leguizamo to sustain it, and though he and most of the cast are cheerful, the screenplay doesn't make it worth the effort. ★★ VHS: $19.99

Python

(1999, 95 min, US, Richard Clabaugh) *Casper Van Dien, Robert Englund, Wil Wheaton, Jenny McCarthy.* A giant, genetically engineered python survives a plane crash and kills lotsa people. That's it for plot — well, actually, that should be it, but the filmmakers seem to be operating under the mistaken impression that we need weak, overlong comic interludes (provided by a blue-haired Wheaton and a terrible McCarthy) and loads of dull "character development." Still, the snake scenes are fake but fun, and any movie with Van Dien struggling with a ridiculous Southern accent while scolding Robert Englund for creating a giant killer snake can't be all bad. ★★ VHS: $9.99

Q (The Winged Serpent)

(1982, 92 min, US, Larry Cohen) *Michael Moriarty, Candy Clark, David Carradine, Richard Roundtree.* From the fertile mind of Cohen comes this very exciting half monster movie/half cop story about an ancient winged creature that's alive and well and living atop the Chrysler Building. Moriarty is great as a two-bit loser who discovers the nest and then blackmails the city for millions to divulge the location. Pure fun and actually suspenseful at times. (Letterboxed) ★★★ VHS: $14.99

Q & A

(1990, 132 min, US, Sidney Lumet) *Nick Nolte, Timothy Hutton, Armand Assante, Patrick O'Neal, Charles S. Dutton.* Director Lumet scrutinizes the mean streets of New York City in this powerful but insensitive urban drama. In a forceful and maniacal performance, Nolte stars as a racist cop whose murder of a suspect is being investigated by young assistant D.A. Hutton, who uncovers a web of political corruption. Assante is commanding as a gangster being investigated by Hutton. As unflinching as the drama is in its examination of bigotry, *Q & A* is shockingly callous in its depiction of gays. ★★½ VHS: $9.99; DVD: $14.99

Quackser Fortune Has a Cousin in the Bronx

(1970, 90 min, Ireland, Waris Hussein) *Gene Wilder, Margot Kidder.* Wilder delivers an exceptionally subdued performance as a man who follows horses around the streets of Dublin and sells their manure for gardening. A charming and offbeat comic love story which also stars Kidder as an American coed who becomes the center of Wilder's amorous attentions. ★★★ VHS: $14.99; DVD: $24.99

Quadrophenia

(1979, 115 min, GB, Franc Roddam) *Phil Daniels, Mark Wingett, Sting.* It's Mods versus Rockers in The Who's gripping portrait of teenage anguish and anger played out in '60s Britain amid pill-popping, gang warfare and rock 'n' roll. This vibrantly paced film is filled with great music and features the momentous film debut of Sting as an ace face. ★★★½

Quality Street

(1937, 84 min, US, George Stevens) *Katharine Hepburn, Franchot Tone, Fay Bainter.* Fanciful screen version of James Barrie's whimsical play of mistaken identity and romantic trickery. Hepburn stars as a beautiful society girl whose fiancé goes off to the Napoleonic Wars. When he returns 10 years later, he doesn't recognize his former girlfriend, whose beauty has somewhat faded. So she masquerades as her own high-spirited niece to win him back. ★★★

Quartet

(1948, 120 min, GB, Ken Annakin) *Dirk Bogarde, Mai Zetterling, Honor Blackman.* First-rate episodic drama featuring four W. Somerset Maugham short stories, which are introduced by the author himself. The stories are: *The Facts of Life*, *The Alien Corn*, *The Kite* and *The Colonel's Lady*. ★★★½

Quartet

(1981, 101 min, GB/France, James Ivory) *Alan Bates, Maggie Smith, Isabelle Adjani.* In this adaptation of Jean Rhys' novel, Adjani plays a young woman who, upon being stranded in Paris, falls prey to a beguiling British couple (Bates, Smith). Excellent performances and Ivory's steady hand at the helm make this tale of hedonism and treachery a spine-tingling treat. ★★★ VHS: $19.99

Quatermass and the Pit

(1968, 98 min, GB, Roy Ward Baker) *Andrew Keir, James Donald, Barbara Shelley, Julian Glover.* The third of the "Quatermass" films from Hammer Studios and screenwriter Nigel Kneale is arguably the best one, and certainly the most imaginative, successfully bringing together the odd combination of common sci-fi elements and more heady philosophical issues. A spacecraft buried beneath a London subway station endows more susceptible Londoners strange psychic abilities which they turn on their less-fortunate neighbors. Chaos ensues and Quatermass and company barely save the day, in one of the most downbeat and mind-numbingly powerful climaxes of any sci-fi film of the 1960s. (aka: *Five Million Years to Earth*) ★★★½ VHS: $14.99

Que Viva Mexico!

(1930/1984, 90 min, USSR/Mexico, Sergei Eisenstein) This famous aborted project has endured a long, rocky history. In 1930, Eisenstein traveled to Mexico in an effort to make a film on that country. The project was suspended after a dispute with his producer, the writer Upton Sinclair. With filming only partially completed, Eisenstein left for the Soviet Union expecting the rushes to be sent to him for completion; but they never arrived and the project languished for over 40 years until Grigory Alexandrov, his former editor, obtained the rushes (from MoMA, of all places) and constructed a version Eisenstein might have done. The result is a glorious and compelling vision of a mystical Mexico. Told in five segments, Eisenstein explores different aspects of Indian life as well as their plight after the Spanish conquest and Catholic indoctrination. Strikingly photographed, this poetic and vivid

Quadrophenia

film explores both the beauty and the underlying tragedy of this fascinating country. (Russian with English subtitles) ★★★ VHS: $24.99; DVD: $29.99

The Queen

(1968, 80 min, US, Frank Simon) This outlandish behind-the-scenes look at the drag Miss All American Beauty Pageant of 1967 has only improved with age, offering the viewer a fascinating and humorous peek into the world of drag and a glimpse at one aspect of pre-Stonewall gay life. Staged in New York, the film captures the frantic days of preparation for the elaborately staged finals. After the crowning of the new queen, many of the attitude-throwing, jealous losers bare their sharp claws and venomous tongues, bitching about the winner and her oh-so-tacky dress. Meow! A camp delight and finger-snapping fun. ★★★ VHS: $29.99

Queen Bee

(1955, 95 min, US, Ranald MacDougall) *Joan Crawford, Barry Sullivan, Betsy Palmer, Fay Wray.* Crawford is at her fire-breathing best in this soaper about the machinations of the manipulative matriarch of a dysfunctional Southern family who destroys the lives of those around her (in between costume changes). More fashion show than film, *Queen Bee* sparkles with the cattiest dialogue this side of *All About Eve.* ★★★ VHS: $19.99

Queen Christina

(1933, 97 min, US, Rouben Mamoulian) *Greta Garbo, John Gilbert, Lewis Stone.* In one of her most intoxicating performances, Garbo radiates sensuality and regal authority as the lonely but compassionate 17th-century Swedish monarch — who renounced her throne rather than be forced to wed and produce an heir. Exquisitely photographed, the film also features Gilbert as her intended, who can't understand her reluctance and constant wearing of men's trousers. Mamoulian's classic works as both historical epic and examination of individual expression, and Garbo posed sphinx-like at the bow of a ship is unforgettable. ★★★★ VHS: $19.99

Queen Kelly

(1929, 96 min, US, Erich von Stroheim) *Gloria Swanson, Walter Byron.* Let's dish some dirt! Even though von Stroheim was supposed to be nothing more than her bimbo director, he still managed to make this Swanson vehicle into something of his own before the plug was pulled. A handsome prince falls for a cute little convent girl, only to lose her when she is shipped off to an East African brothel run by her aunt. It's Cinderella with a few kinks; but the film was never really completed after Swanson had a snit about a scene where a syphilitic cripple drools tobacco juice on her in bed. Needless to say, it's the kind of fun only von Stroheim could create. Some scenes cropped up in Billy Wilder's *Sunset Boulevard* twenty years later. ★★★½ VHS: $24.99

Queen Margot

(1994, 140 min, France, Patrice Chereau) *Isabelle Adjani, Jean-Hugues Anglade, Virna Lisi, Daniel Auteuil, Vincent Perez, Dominique Blanc.* This lavishly produced French epic, based on a

Kate Winslet with Geoffrey Rush as the Marquis de Sade in *Quills*

novel by Alexandre Dumas, examines the bloody history of the struggle between France's Catholics and Protestants in the late 16th century. Opening with the marriage of the Catholic Margot (the unbelievably radiant Adjani) to the Protestant Henri of Navarre (Auteuil), the film details the events leading up to and following the St. Bartholomew's Day massacre in Paris, when the Catholic guard slaughtered over 6,000 Huguenots. Brimming with more palace intrigue than the best of Shakespeare, the story's central villainess is the Queen Mother, Catherine de Medici (Lisi), who is constantly hatching plots to dispatch poor Henri and keep her three sons in power. Amidst all the rabble is Margot who is insanely in love with the son of a slain Huguenot leader, La Môle (the smoldering Perez). A superb costume drama that is filled with graphic images of brutal violence. (French with English subtitles) ★★★½

Queen of Hearts

(1989, 112 min, GB, Jon Amiel) *Anita Zagaria, Joseph Long.* Wonderfully wacky tale from the director of *The Singing Detective* about an Italian couple who elope to London to escape an arranged marriage, only to be tracked down by the vengeful would-be groom. Director Amiel ably mixes whimsical ideas with dead-on characterizations. ★★★½

The Queen of Spades

(1948, 95 min, GB, Thorold Dickinson) *Edith Evans, Anton Walbrook.* Walbrook stars as a young Russian officer who is consumed by an obsession to learn the secret of winning at cards from a diabolical old countess (a bravura performance by Evans). Based on a story by Alexander Pushkin, the film is infused with an eerie atmosphere of the macabre. ★★★

Queens Logic

(1991, 116 min, US, Steve Rash) *Joe Mantegna, Kevin Bacon, Linda Fiorentino, John Malkovich, Jamie Lee Curtis, Ken Olin, Chloe Webb.* A remarkable ensemble cast breathes life into this *Big Chill*–like, thought-provoking examination of growing up and growing apart. A group of

friends return to the old neighborhood for a wedding which may or may not happen. As events accelerate toward a fateful bachelor party, the childhood friends discover how the world has changed, and how they've remained the same. ★★½ VHS: $9.99; DVD: $24.99

Queer as Folk: Series One

(1999, 240 min, GB, Charles McDougall & Sarah Harding) *Aidan Gillen, Craig Kelly, Charlie Hunnam, Denise Black.* *Queer as Folk* is a remarkable phenomenon — so amazing the American cable network Showtime had to create a tamer American version. But this is the real thing — it's unedited, unexpurgated and unbelievable. An eight-part soap opera/drama set in Manchester's gay village, the series focuses on the tumultuous lives of three young gay men. There is Stuart (Gillen), an unrepentant party boy; his best friend Vince (Kelly), handsome but insecure; and 15-year-old Nathan, a blond beauty just itching to join in the gay fun. An immensely enjoyable peek into a witty, sexy world that has entranced people around the world. ★★★★ VHS: $69.99; DVD: $69.99

Querelle

(1982, 106 min, West Germany, Rainer Werner Fassbinder) *Brad Davis, Franco Nero, Jeanne Moreau.* Some say that Fassbinder was past the point of dissipation as he worked on Jean Genet's homoerotic story of lust and murder. There is no denying that the final result lacks the cohesion of the director's greatest works. But its ominously dark and determinedly artificial sets, the pervasive homosexual iconography and the stylized acting all gel to create a brooding, melancholy mood quite fitting with the classic novel. Davis is Querelle, a ruggedly handsome, narcissistic and sexually confused sailor who exploits and even kills the ones who lust after him. Nero is perfect as the commander who secretly worships him while Moreau is completely miscast as Querelle's part-time lover and brothel madam. (German with English subtitles) ★★½ VHS: $14.99; DVD: $24.99

The Quest

(1996, 95 min, US, Jean-Claude Van Damme) *Jean-Claude Van Damme, Roger Moore, James Remar.* Van Damme proves that he can be as bad a director as he is an actor in this, his debut behind the camera. He stars in this period tale as the leader of a group of kiddie thieves who becomes entangled with a debonair pirate (Moore). He's then sold into slavery and then becomes a martial arts master. All that hooey only serves to bring the slow-moving story to the final competition, which is actually staged rather well. ★★ VHS: $14.99; DVD: $24.99

Quest for Fire

(1982, 97 min, France/Canada, Jean-Jacques Annaud) *Rae Dawn Chong, Everett McGill, Ron Perlman.* An enthralling supposition on the evolution of mankind, skillfully and imaginatively crafted by Annaud. Novelist Anthony Burgess and Desmond Morris collaborated to create the original language and body movement of prehistoric man in this unique mesh of fantasy and pop-archaeology. ★★★½ VHS: $69.99

A Question of Silence

(1983, 92 min, The Netherlands, Marleen Gorris) This production is surely one of the most controversial and provocative films released in some time. Ostensibly a feminist thriller, the film chronicles the seemingly unmotivated murder of a male shopkeeper by three middle-aged women who had never met before and did not know their victim. A woman psychologist tries to piece together the puzzle of why they killed the man. Was it senseless murder or a political act — the rage of women against a male dominated society? (Dutch with English subtitles) ★★★ VHS: $29.99

The Quick and the Dead

(1995, 103 min, US, Sam Raimi) *Sharon Stone, Gene Hackman, Leonardo DiCaprio, Russell Crowe, Gary Sinise, Lance Henriksen.* From the director of the *Evil Dead* trilogy comes this underrated homage to the Sergio Leone spaghetti westerns of yore. A deglamorized Stone (who coproduced) stars as a vengeful gunslinger who rides into the dustball town of Redemption (no symbolism there) looking for the man responsible for her father's murder. She winds up smack-dab in the middle of the annual "Fastest Gun in the West" contest. Hackman gives an over-the-top performance as the sadistic town overlord who, until now, has won the contest hands down. Needless to say, he's the man she's looking for. Though it's mostly predictable fun, what distinguishes the film is director Raimi's patented inventive technical prowess; he deftly meshes gruesome violence with side-splitting humor. It's a visual and darkly comic feast. ★★★ VHS: $14.99; DVD: $19.99

Quick Change

(1990, 88 min, US, Howard Franklin & Bill Murray) *Bill Murray, Geena Davis, Jason Robards, Randy Quaid, Phillip Bosco.* Likable caper comedy with Murray, Davis and Quaid pulling off a perfect bank robbery — but their troubles begin when they try to make it out of New York City. Robards is the cop assigned to the case, and veteran stage actor Bosco has

some good moments as a fastidious bus driver. ★★½ VHS: $14.99

Quicksilver

(1986, 106 min, US, Tom Donnelly) *Kevin Bacon, Jami Gertz, Laurence Fishburne.* Routine youth pic with Bacon as a burned-out stockbroker who takes a job with a bicycle messenger service, unwittingly becoming involved with drug dealers. ★½ VHS: $9.99

Quiet Days in Hollywood

(1998, 95 min, US, Josef Rusnak) *Hilary Swank, Bill Cusack, Peter Dobson, Natasha Gregson Wagner, Chad Lowe, Daryl Mitchell.* Notable mostly for featuring an early performance by Oscar-winner Swank in the first and last episodes, *Quiet Days in Hollywood* tells a series of interlocking stories, few of which are actually compelling. In the first piece, Swank is Lolita, a foulmouthed hooker. By the film's end she is connecting with Peter, (Dobson), a closeted Oscar-winning actor. But the most interesting episode belongs to Richard (Lowe), a corporate attorney who is having a affair with his boss' wife Kathy (Wagner). Their saga — intercut with Kathy's discussion about adultery with her philandering husband Bobby (Cusack) — is the film's highlight. In contrast, the relationship between the fast-talking Angel (Mitchell) and his sex-crazed girlfriend Julie (Golding), is insulting. A mixed bag, to be sure, *Quiet Days in Hollywood* will barely pass the time on a very slow night. ★★ VHS: $89.99; DVD: $24.99

The Quiet Earth

(1985, 110 min, New Zealand, Geoff Murphy) *Bruno Lawrence, Allison Routledge.* Lawrence stars in this thought-provoking sci-fi tale as a scientist who awakens one morning to find himself the last person on earth. An imaginative film with an ending as haunting as that of *2001*, *The Quiet Earth* has much to say about man's race towards self-destruction. ★★★

The Quiet Man

(1952, 129 min, US, John Ford) *John Wayne, Maureen O'Hara, Victor McLaglen, Barry Fitzgerald.* You will be amazed with Wayne's nuanced performance as *The Quiet Man*, the Irishman returning home to Inisfree after years in Pittsburgh steel mills. The entire cast is a delight, and the camera caresses the Irish countryside. Ford won a Best Director Oscar for this one. ★★★★ VHS: $14.99; DVD: $19.99

The Quiet Room

(1996, 91 min, Australia, Rolf de Heer) *Celine O'Leary, Paul Blackwell, Chloe Ferguson, Phoebe Ferguson.* A remarkable film of shattering perception, *The Quiet Room* uniquely conveys the absolute certainty of childhood perceptions. C. Ferguson delivers an affecting and unaffected performance as the seven-year-old daughter who responds to her parents constant contentiousness by retreating into silence and fantasy wish fulfillment and forays back into earlier times of childhood happiness. Writer-director de Heer employs compassion and understanding in crafting this involving exploration into the effects of parental discord on a child whose natural self-centerdness is coupled with unblinking comprehension. Ferguson's portrayal is sharply suppoted by O'Leary and

Blackwell as the parents, and P. Ferguson as the daughter at three years of age. This is a film which moves fluidly and adroitly touches on the basic truths of the strengths and frailties of family life. ★★★ VHS: $19.99

Quigley Down Under

(1990, 120 min, US, Simon Wincer) *Tom Selleck, Alan Rickman, Laura San Giocomo, Chris Haywood.* Selleck stars in this appealing western as an American cowboy who travels to mid-19th century Australia to work for ruthless ranch owner Rickman. When Selleck refuses to be a paid assassin, he's left for dead in the Outback and extracts vengence against his former boss. ★★★ VHS: $14.99

The Quiller Memorandum

(1966, 105 min, GB, Michael Anderson) *Alec Guinness, George Segal, Max von Sydow.* Harold Pinter provided an entertaining though not particularly suspenseful screenplay for this espionage thriller about an American operative rooting out neo-Nazis in modern-day Berlin. ★★½ VHS: $59.99

Quills

(2000, 120 min, GB, Philip Kaufman) *Geoffrey Rush, Kate Winslet, Joaquin Phoenix, Michael Caine, Billie Whitelaw, Patrick Malahide.* Setting the stage for outlandish humor, scintillating dialogue and a no-holds-barred battle for artistic expression, the devilish and delightful *Quills* wallows in its own ingeniously twisted embrace of madness and sex. Adapting his own stage play, Doug Wright's feverish, witty story in essence details the last years of the imprisoned Marquis de Sade at the Charenton Insane Asylum. But at the core of this blistering satire is the age-old conflict between art and censorship. Rush is delectable as the mad de Sade, whose sexually candid works have turned him into the artist du jour in 1790s Paris. He is under the watchful eye of the caring Abbe de Coulmier (Phoenix), but de Sade's increasingly graphic output sends the pious, repressive Dr. Royer-Collard (Caine) to oversee the asylum, setting in motion a fight to the finish to see who has the last word. The ensemble is outstanding, headed by Rush's glorious interpretation that balances depravity, defiance and desire. ★★★★ VHS: $14.99; DVD: $29.99

Quilombo

(1984, 120 min, Brazil, Carlos Diegues) *Vera Fischer, Antonio Pompeo.* Diegues' historical saga is a stirring fusion of folklore, political impact and dynamic storytelling. Based on historical fact, the setting is 17th-century Brazil where groups of runaway black slaves escaped into the jungle where they formed self-governing communities. Set on the border line between history and legend, between mountains and the sky, *Quilombo* is a powerful vision of paradise — sensual and alive, with exotic scenery and spectacular blood-and-thunder battles, all touched with a bit of the mystical and surreal. (Portuguese with English subtitles) ★★★ VHS: $29.99

Quintet

(1979, 110 min, US, Robert Altman) *Paul Newman, Vittorio Gassman, Fernando Rey.* Atmospheric but confusing fantasy about the survivors of a new ice age who pass the time playing Quintet, a game where all the losers end up dead and there is only one winner. ★★ VHS: $19.99

Quiz Show

(1994, 130 min, US, Robert Redford) *Ralph Fiennes, John Turturro, Rob Morrow, Paul Scofield, David Paymer, Hank Azaria, Elizabeth Wilson, Martin Scorsese.* It's 1958, and "Twenty-One" is the most popular game show on TV. Herb Stempel (Turturro) is its long-running champion; that is until he is forced to "take a dive," making handsome challenger Charles Van Doren (Fiennes) its newest winner. Initially unaware of any wrongdoing, Van Doren slowly learns of the show's fix but succumbs to the easy winnings. This forces Stempel to go public and brings Congressional investigator Richard Goodwin (Morrow) onto the scene. In adapting the real-life story of the quiz show scandal to the screen (based on a chapter of Goodwin's autobiography), director Redford has fashioned an immaculate, evocative drama of self-delusion, investigation and conspiracy and superbly juxtaposes it with a stinging allegory of America's loss of innocence. As Van Doren, Fiennes is extraordinary in capturing the moral dilemma of an honest man caught in the claws of bribery and adulation, and is evenly matched by Turturro's gutsy portrayal of the vindictive but ultimately wronged Stempel. ★★★★ VHS: $9.99; DVD: $29.99

Quo Vadis

(1951, 171 min, US, Mervyn LeRoy) *Robert Taylor, Deborah Kerr, Peter Ustinov.* Epic MGM production about the love affair between a Roman soldier (Taylor) and a Christian woman (Kerr). Ustinov gives a great performance as Roman emperor Nero. Everything about this box-office smash is done on a grand scale, from its art direction and costumes to its story and screenplay which manages to rise above religious film clichés. ★★★½ VHS: $19.99

Quilombo

Rabbit Test

(1978, 86 min, US, Joan Rivers) *Billy Crystal, Roddy McDowall, Imogene Coca, Paul Lynde, Alice Ghostley.* Occasionally tasteless, episodic comedy with Crystal as the world's first pregnant man. Rivers, who also cowrote the screenplay, extracts one or two amusing scenarios from this premise, but most of it is abysmal. ★½

Rabid

(1972, 90 min, Canada, David Cronenberg) *Marilyn Chambers, Frank Moore, Joe Silver.* Porn queen Chambers stars as a young woman who undergoes experimental skin-graft surgery after a motorcycle accident. One month later, she emerges from a coma with an insatiable appetite for blood which she obtains though the use of a spiked organ growing out of a very sexual-looking orifice in her armpit. Her victims then become rabid vampires themselves, attacking all who come near them until they, too, go into a coma and die. Less cerebral and more reliant on standard shocks for its success, *Rabid* is nevertheless an original exploration of the familiar vampire and living dead genres. ★★½ VHS: $14.99; DVD: $19.99

The Rachel Papers

(1989, 92 min, GB, Damian Harris) *Dexter Fletcher, Ione Skye, Jonathan Pryce, James Spader.* Charles Highway (Fletcher) can have any girl he chooses, guided by his customized computer program, "Conquests and Techniques," an assortment of enticing props including appropriate clothing and home decor, and sensitive poetic quotations. But when he meets Rachel Noyce (Skye), all his irresistible schemes fail; Charles must reveal his true self to win her. *The Rachel Papers* is candid, funny and touching, a charming story of young lust and love with a remarkably grown-up sensibility. ★★★ VHS: $9.99

Rachel, Rachel

(1968, 101 min, US, Paul Newman) *Joanne Woodward, Estelle Parsons, James Olson, Geraldine Fitzgerald.* An intensely somber but affecting drama of a woman who, after years of self-imposed fear, decides to experience life. Woodward, in a poignant and carefully realized performance, plays Rachel, a 35-year-old schoolteacher and walking tinderbox of repressed emotions and sexual frustration. Newman's directorial debut is a film of great subtlety and beauty. Parsons gives a tender portrait of a closeted lesbian in love with Rachel. ★★★★ VHS: $19.99

Racing with the Moon

(1984, 108 min, US, Richard Benjamin) *Sean Penn, Nicolas Cage, Elizabeth McGovern, Crispin Glover, Michael Madsen, Dana Carvey, Carol Kane.* Benjamin's bittersweet tale of youthful yearnings and indecision boasts strong performances by Penn and Cage as a pair of buddies biding their freedom on the eve of military duty. McGovern is beguiling as a young woman

involved with Penn. Ripe with the gentle air of innocence and a warmhearted sense of humor. ★★★ VHS: $14.99

The Racket

(1951, 88 min, US, John Cromwell) *Robert Ryan, Robert Mitchum, Lizabeth Scott.* The professional and personal battle between two former friends now on opposing sides of the law is the story in this hard-hitting crime drama. Mitchum is a tough-as-nails precinct captain determined to keep his turf clean from the likes of Ryan, his old chum who stops at nothing in his quest for expansion of his crime kingdom. Some scenes were directed by Nicholas Ray. ★★★

Radio Days

(1986, 85 min, US, Woody Allen) *Mia Farrow, Seth Green, Julie Kavner, Josh Mostel, Michael Tucker, Dianne Wiest, Wallace Shawn, Danny Aiello, Jeff Daniels, Tony Roberts, Diane Keaton.* Allen's loosely structured but powerfully envisioned series of fables and vignettes takes us back to the halcyon days of radio. Through a series of hilarious, and often magical, reminiscences about his childhood, Allen eavesdrops on the lives of actors, singers, talk show hosts, and even the cigarette girl who made good. As usual, Allen deftly utilizes an extraordinary company of actors. ★★★★

Radio Flyer

(1992, 114 min, US, Richard Donner) *Elijah Wood, Joseph Mazzello, Lorraine Bracco, John Heard, Adam Baldwin; Narrated by: Tom Hanks.* Radio Flyer has the look of an affectionate childhood memory piece — but these reminiscences are sweetened with bitter recollections. Wood and Mazzello play two brothers whose divorced mom (Bracco) remarries. Unbeknownst to her, the kids' new stepdad turns out to be a child abuser, and the boys devise a plan to escape his brutality: to take flight by making their red Radio Flyer wagon airworthy. *Radio Flyer* has many moments of genuine interest, especially when recalling the fantasies of youth. But the underlying child abuse theme is clearly out of place in this otherwise Spielberg-esque fantasy. ★★½ VHS: $9.99

Radio Inside

(1994, 102 min, US, Jeffrey Bell) *William McNamara, Elisabeth Shue, Dylan Walsh.* Though the story line is virtually nonexistent (a love triangle involving two radically different brothers), *Radio Inside* has a nonchalant quirkiness that ultimately makes it watchable. Take for instance the way the one brother (McNamara), an un-career oriented, guilt-ridden artist, off-handedly calls up Jesus (yes, that Jesus) on a pay phone to get advice when he falls for the girlfriend (Shue) of his yuppie sibling (Walsh). An idiosyncratic look at relationships, both romantic and familial. ★★½ VHS: $19.99

Radioland Murders

(1994, 112 min, US, Mel Smith) *Brian Benben, Mary Stuart Masterson, Ned Beatty, George Burns, Anita Morris, Christopher Lloyd.* An unstable, frenzied comedy set against the backdrop of radio during the late 1930s. Masterson plays a secretary/manager of a new radio network. As they prepare for their opening night, she must contend with an estranged husband (Benben) seeking reconciliation, inept cast members and technicians, and a series of murders. The film tries to achieve the madness and quick pace of a Marx Brothers movie — there's plenty of slamming doors, pratfalls and one-liners. But the actors have little to work with, and the film doesn't capture the excitement and popularity that was live radio. ★★ VHS: $9.99

Rage

(1972, 100 min, US, George C. Scott) *George C. Scott, Martin Sheen, Richard Basehart, Barnard Hughes.* Scott, in a respectable first-time directing effort, stars as a Wyoming rancher who, with his son, is victim of a fatal dose of experimental nerve gas discharged in an accident. The nearby military installation initiates an immediate cover-up, inciting the dying man to acts of enraged vengeance. ★★½ VHS: $14.99

The Rage: Carrie 2

(1999, 101 min, US, Katt Shea) *Emily Bergl, Jason London, Amy Irving.* A pointless, unnecessary sequel, this is very tenuously linked to the stylish, visceral original — though it's really just a stripped-down, '90s-ized rehash. Bergl is affecting as the put-upon outsider with the powers of telekinesis. Only her guidance counselor (Irving, the only holdover from the original, in a ridiculous role) and new boyfriend from the in-crowd understand her, but can they stop her from using her powers for revenge against the cruel snobs and jocks? *The Rage* is 101 minutes of humiliation and pain for the heroine, and 5 minutes of retribution — it's not fair, and without the lyricism of the '76 classic, it's not satisfying. ★½ VHS: $9.99; DVD: $14.99

A Rage in Harlem

(1991, 115 min, US, Bill Duke) *Forest Whitaker, Robin Givens, Gregory Hines, Danny Glover, Zakes Mokae.* A fine cast brings unexpected life to this boisterous and funny crime comedy set in 1950s Harlem. Whitaker is well cast as a naïve, religious virgin who becomes involved with luscious swindler Givens after she arrives in New York with a shipment of gold from a Southern robbery. Her appearance sets off a wild series of events as seemingly everyone in the Big Apple is after the booty. In a surprising comic turn, Givens gives a wonderfully controlled and vampish performance as the foxy femme fatale. A colorful version of a Chester Hines story, and every bit as successful as the author's *Cotton Comes to Harlem.* ★★★ VHS: $9.99

The Raggedy Rawney

(1987, 95 min, GB, Bob Hoskins) *Bob Hoskins, Dexter Fletcher.* Actor Hoskins throws his hat into the directorial ring with this offbeat tale of a wartime deserter (Fletcher) who disguises himself as a woman to escape his vindictive superior. Hoskins also stars as the head of a Gypsy camp who mistakenly thinks Fletcher is a witch — a "rawney." Not completely successful, but a welcome change for the adventurous viewer. ★★½

Raging Bull

(1980, 128 min, US, Martin Scorsese) *Robert De Niro, Joe Pesci, Cathy Moriarty, Frank Vincent.* De Niro is nothing short of astonishing as boxing champion Jake La Motta, who struck it rich in the ring then squandered his fortune and alienated his family and friends. Scorsese's most brooding work (and that's saying something), shot in vibrant tones of black and white, is a masterpiece of technical brilliance, excruciatingly observant dialogue and almost mythical boxing sequences. Stand-out support by Pesci and Moriarty. ★★★★ VHS: $14.99; DVD: $24.99

Ragtime

(1981, 155 min, US, Milos Forman) *Harold E. Rollins, Jr., James Cagney, Elizabeth McGovern, Mary Steenburgen, Maureen Stapleton, Mandy Patinkin, Kenneth McMillan.* Forman, a director who can take the most difficult source material (*One Flew over the Cuckoo's Nest, Hair*) and create masterworks, has done it again with this remarkable screen version of E. L. Doctorow's complex novel. Set in New York City in the turbulent early 1900s, the story follows black musician Coalhouse Walker, Jr. (Rollins, in an outstanding performance) and his quest for justice after being the victim of a racial attack. After a 20-year absence in film, Cagney returned to the screen to play the Police Commissioner. *Ragtime* features a superb ensemble. (Made into a Broadway musical.) ★★★½ VHS: $24.99

Raiders of the Lost Ark

(1981, 115 min, US, Steven Spielberg) *Harrison Ford, Karen Allen, Denholm Elliott, John Rhys-Davies.* From South American jungles to the mountains of Nepal to the North African desert, our hero, archeology prof and world-class adventurer Indiana Jones (Ford), deciphers mystical symbols in search of the Ark of the Covenant, battling scurrilous Nazis with an intrepid, hard-drinking helpmate (Allen). Strong story line, solid performances and state-of-the-art moviemaking potently combine in a fast-paced, most enjoyable and intelligent action-adventure film. Written by Lawrence Kasdan from a story by George Lucas and Philip Kaufman. (Sequel: *Indiana Jones and the Temple of Doom*) (VHS available letterboxed or pan & scan) ★★★★ VHS: $14.99

Railroaded

(1947, 74 min, US, Anthony Mann) *John Ireland, Sheila Ryan, Hugh Beaumont.* In the dark, crime-ridden jungle of an inner city where mobsters rule, a lone police detective begins a search for a killer on the lam from the police, who, in a desperate fight for survival, involves an innocent youth. Ireland stars as a ruthless gangster in this taut, suspenseful, low-budget crime melodrama. ★★★ VHS: $24.99; DVD: $29.99

The Railway Children

(1970, 104 min, GB, Lionel Jeffries) *Jenny Agutter, William Mervyn, Bernard Cribbins.* Distinguished character actor Jeffries directed this engaging film version of the Edwardian children's classic about three young kids who are determined to clear their father's name. A vivid and heartwarming look at turn-of-the-century British life filmed in the beautiful countryside of Yorkshire and filled with youthful determination. ★★★

Rain Man

(1988, 140 min, US, Barry Levinson) *Dustin Hoffman, Tom Cruise, Valeria Golino.* Hoffman gives a remarkable performance as an "idiot savant" who is virtually kidnapped by his younger brother (Cruise) and taken on a cross-country trip. From beginning to end, the film is an emotionally overpowering experience told in a surprisingly stylish and entertaining fashion. Hoffman won all sorts of kudos for his portrayal, but not to be overlooked is the terrific contribution by young Cruise, who more than holds his own with the most honored actor of his generation. ★★★½ VHS: $9.99; DVD: $19.99

The Rain People

(1969, 102 min, US, Francis Ford Coppola) *Shirley Knight, James Caan, Robert Duvall.* This sensitive drama tells the compassionate story of a pregnant woman who leaves her husband in search of self-fulfillment. Knight, in a beautifully restrained performance, is the young voyager who sets out on the road, befriending dim-witted Caan along the way. An intimate work exploring one woman's social awakening and personal independence. ★★★ VHS: $19.99

Harrison Ford makes the switch in *Raiders of the Lost Ark*

Raining Stones

R

The Rainbow

(1989, 104 min, GB, Ken Russell) *Sammi Davis, Amanda Donohoe, Glenda Jackson, Christopher Gable.* An unusually restrained "classic" adaptation of D.H. Lawrence's novel. The setting is early 20th-century England and follows the sexual and spiritual liberation of young Ursula, the Jennie Linden character in *Women in Love.* Davis is great as the earnest and doe-eyed young woman whose sexuality and desires erupt, all the while yearning for true love, self-respect and independence in a society which frowns on all three. Donohoe is delightfully decadent as Ursula's gym instructor, seductress and mentor. ★★½

Raining Stones

(1993, 90 min, GB, Ken Loach) *Bruce Jones, Julie Brown.* Loach has drummed up a veritable masterpiece of agitprop with this engaging tale of an out-of-work laborer who hatches a hundred lame-brained schemes to make ends meet. Through the comedic escapades of Bob (Jones), Loach sternly disabuses us all of the notion that the underclass are a bunch of boozing loafers uninterested in a hard day's work. A devout Catholic, Bob desperately needs money to buy his daughter a new outfit for her first communion. But rather than let Bob's conundrum stand merely as a condemnation of the Church, Loach passionately and with great force of conviction shows the Church also as his only shred of hope — it is the only thing that keeps Bob going. This conflict is at the heart of Loach's film and it is what gives it its beauty, helping it rise above simple dialectical materialism and touch on notions of spirit. ★★★★ VHS: $19.99

The Rainmaker

(1956, 121 min, US, Joseph Anthony) *Burt Lancaster, Katharine Hepburn, Lloyd Bridges, Wendell Corey.* Lancaster and Hepburn offer terrific performances in this fine adaptation of the N. Richard Nash play. Set in 1913, the film casts Lancaster as con man who promises a small drought-ridden Kansas town he can deliver much-needed rain. Kate is the spinster-ish farm girl who falls for the charming grifter. ★★★ VHS: $14.99

The Rainmaker

See: John Grisham's The Rainmaker

Raintree County

(1957, 188 min, US, Edward Dmytryk) *Elizabeth Taylor, Montgomery Clift, Lee Marvin, Eva Marie Saint, Agnes Moorehead, Rod Taylor.* Fanciful costume drama set during the Civil War with Taylor as a Southern belle and Clift as her lover. MGM tried, but did not succeed in creating another *Gone with the Wind* — though there is much that is praiseworthy about this mammoth production. (Original roadshow version) (VHS available letterboxed or pan & scan) ★★½ VHS: $24.99

Raise the Red Lantern

(1991, 125 min, China, Zhang Yimou) *Gong Li, Ma Jingwu.* A lyrically haunting tale about a young educated woman who is sold into marriage against her will, becoming the newest of four concubines kept by a wealthy man. Immediately at odds with her three predecessors (who can scarcely conceal their jealousy of her) and bewildered by her strict and mysterious master, she reacts to her new situation with a mixture of rebellion and resignation. Director Zhang imbues the film with an extraordinary attention to detail, filming from the perspective of the fledgling concubine, giving the viewer a unique appreciation for the character's existential loneliness. Additionally, the film's understated dialogue and bewitching visual style amplify Zhang's compelling tale of the subjugation of women in feudal China. Chinese actress Gong is spellbinding as the young woman who finds herself trapped in the jaws of a regimented and unforgiving patriarchy. (Mandarin with English subtitles) ★★★★ VHS: $19.99

A Raisin in the Sun

(1961, 128 min, US, Daniel Petrie) *Sidney Poitier, Ruby Dee, Claudia McNeil, Diana Sands, Ivan Dixon, Lou Gossett, Jr., John Fiedler.* Poitier stars as Walter Lee Younger, a young African-American man struggling with his place in a white dominated society. Lena (McNeil), Walter's mother, receives a $10,000 insurance check and the family must decide how the money should be spent. Walter wants to invest with a friend in a liquor store, Lena wants to use the money to buy a house in a better neighborhood, while her daughter (Dee) wants to use the money to finish medical school. A powerful tale of a poor, proud black family living in a 1950s Chicago ghetto, facing the racist attitudes of America and the truth of the limited opportunities for blacks in society. Based on the play by Lorraine Hansbury. (Remade in 1989) ★★★★ VHS: $9.99; DVD: $24.99

A Raisin in the Sun

(1989, 120 min, US, Bill Duke) *Danny Glover, Esther Rolle, Kim Yancy.* Remake of the classic 1961 screen version of Lorraine Hansbury's play, and every bit as accomplished as that earlier adaptation. Glover gives a tremendous performance as Walter Lee Younger; and as his recently widowed mother, Rolle is wonderfully down to earth. A remarkable work. ★★★½ VHS: $39.99

Raising Arizona

(1986, 94 min, US, Joel Coen) *Nicolas Cage, Holly Hunter, John Goodman, William Forsythe, Trey Wilson, Frances McDormand.* The Coen Brothers unleash a veritable grab bag of tricks and surprises as they unspool the hilarious tale of H.I. and Ed McDonough, would-be-parents who baby-nap a youngster from a recent batch of quintuplets in order to fulfill their parental urges. This truly offbeat, supremely comic film is loaded with crazy characters, wild chase scenes and inexhaustible energy. Cage and Hunter give antic yet touching performances as the barren but determined couple. ★★★★ VHS: $14.99; DVD: $22.99

Raising Cain

(1992, 91 min, US, Brian De Palma) *John Lithgow, Lolita Davidovich, Frances Sternhagen, Steven Bauer.* Lithgow stars in this hodge-podge of every other De Palma film (and some Hitchcock, of course) about a schizophrenic child psychologist who moonlights as a sociopathic baby-stealer. While nowhere near the caliber of filmmaking displayed in *Carrie* or *Dressed to Kill, Raising Cain* holds up fairly well when viewed as a black comedy rather than as the nail-biter it pretends to be. Features a scene-stealing performance by Sternhagen. ★★½ VHS: $19.99

Rambling Rose

(1991, 112 min, US, Martha Coolidge) *Laura Dern, Robert Duvall, Diane Ladd, Lukas Haas.* Dern earned a well-deserved Oscar nomination for her portrayal of Rose, a Depression-era orphan who is taken as a live-in maid by a respectable Southern family in 1930s Georgia. Her sexual energy bursting at the seams, Rose turns the family's traditional values upside-down and precipitates a dispute between Mom (Ladd) and Dad (Duvall) as to how best to deal with her. Ladd, Dern's real-life mom, was also an Oscar nominee for her splendid work as Rose's matronly advocate. Charmingly humanistic in tone, the film is imbued with a wonderful sense of mirth and thereby avoids getting bogged down in the potentially melodramatic pitfalls of its subject matter. ★★★½ VHS: $9.99; DVD: $29.99

Rambo: First Blood Part II

(1985, 93 min, US, George P. Cosmatos) *Sylvester Stallone, Richard Crenna.* Stallone's sequel to *First Blood* is a ridiculous war film by any standards, but it did introduce an idiom (or is that idiot?) into our vocabulary and culture. For the record, Johnny Rambo returns to Vietnam to locate American POWs. (Letterboxed VHS available for $14.99) ★½ VHS: $9.99; DVD: $19.99

Rambo III

(1988, 101 min, US, Peter MacDonald) *Sylvester Stallone, Richard Crenna, Kurtwood Smith.* More inane and implausible action scenes from Stallone as Superman Johnny Rambo. Rambo sets out to rescue captured Crenna from behind enemy lines. (Letterboxed VHS available for $14.99) ★ VHS: $9.99; DVD: $19.99

Rampage

(1992, 97 min, US, William Friedkin) *Michael Biehn, Alex McArthur, Grace Zabriskie.* Biehn stars as a liberal D.A. recovering from the accidental death of his young daughter in this often tense but grim courtroom drama about the capture and sentencing of a serial murderer (McArthur). While the film shows the murders with luridly vivid detail, it deals more with the inner workings of our not always perfect judicial system. Laced with visual jolts, good performances and an unusual script, this gnawing film isn't for everyone. (Made in 1987 but not released until five years later.) ★★½ VHS: $14.99

Ramparts of Clay

(1971, 85 min, France/Algeria, Jean-Louis Bertucelli) Against the hauntingly beautiful setting of an isolated Tunisian village, this stunning, visually breathtaking fictional documentary portrays the struggles of a young woman to liberate herself from the subservient role her people's ancient customs demand. Her participation in a strike-like action against a local entrepreneur allows her a glimpse of life outside her rigidly structured village. (Berber with English subtitles) ★★★½

Ran

(1985, 160 min, Japan, Akira Kurosawa) *Tatsuya Nakadai, Akira Terao.* Seventy-five-year-old Kurosawa has reached the culmination of his brilliant career with this majestic free-telling of Shakespeare's "King Lear." Set in the 16th century, the epic thunders with breathtaking scenery, boldly staged battle sequences and the tragic story of an old man's war with his sons. The love, death and treachery between both friends and adversaries is universal in theme and provides the human backdrop for this classic. (Letterboxed) (Japanese with English subtitles) ★★★★ VHS: $29.99; DVD: $34.99

Rancho Deluxe

(1974, 93 min, US, Frank Perry) *Jeff Bridges, Sam Waterston, Harry Dean Stanton, Elizabeth Ashley, Slim Pickens.* Bridges and Waterston star as two petty grifters; New West cowboys who decide to go after the big score. With intent to rustle some cattle, they team up with Stanton, hired hand to a couple of Easterners for whom the West is little more than a commodity. Sweeping Montana vistas offer mute witness to a delightful display of human foibles and crackling idiosyncracies as the crew sets about their business. Director Perry adeptly guides Tom McGuane's multilayered, sardonic and witty screenplay. ★★★½ VHS: $14.99; DVD: $19.99

Rancho Notorious

(1952, 89 min, US, Fritz Lang) *Marlene Dietrich, Mel Ferrer, Arthur Kennedy.* Frontier love triangle develops between a breathy saloon songstress (Dietrich), a once-great gunslinger (Ferrer) and a revenge-seeking cowpoke (Kennedy). An

Ran

unusual and invigorating western which concentrates as much on character development as it does with the genre's other staples. ★★★½

Random Harvest

(1942, 124 min, US, Mervyn LeRoy) *Ronald Colman, Greer Garson, Susan Peters, Henry Travers.* A grand, lush soap opera of the highest order with Colman as a shell-shocked and amnesiac WWI veteran who marries dance-hall girl Garson. When he regains his memory, he returns to his old life but has no memory of his wife, who has now become his secretary in the hopes that he'll remember. Colman and Garson's compelling performances should capture the hearts of even the most cynical. ★★★½ VHS: $19.99

Random Hearts

(1999, 133 min, US, Sydney Pollack) *Harrison Ford, Kristin Scott Thomas, Charles S. Dutton, Bonnie Hunt, Dennis Haysbert.* It won't be sighs of romantic aspirations stemming from the viewer after watching this tired drama — it will be yawns of incredulity. Ford plays an Internal Affairs officer whose wife dies in an airplane crash. He soon discovers that she was involved in an extramarital affair, with the husband of a congresswoman (Scott Thomas). The two surviving spouses then begin an affair themselves. There's nothing romantic about this story, which mostly consists of Ford dogging Scott Thomas at every turn. And the subplot of Ford investigating a dirty cop goes nowhere. Given a smart look by director Pollack, *Random Hearts* is a cheap gift wrapped in pretty packaging. ★★ VHS: $14.99; DVD: $24.99

Ransom

(1996, 120 min, US, Ron Howard) *Mel Gibson, Rene Russo, Gary Sinise, Delroy Lindo, Lili Taylor, Brawley Nolte, Dan Hedaya, Liev Schreiber.* The nightmare of a child's kidnapping has been turned into a slick, calculated thriller which intermittently conveys the pain and suspense of losing one's child. Gibson plays a wealthy airline owner whose nine-year-old son is kidnapped. The story then focuses on the parents and FBI's attempts to deal with the criminals, and the conflict growing within the group of kidnappers. Though based on a 1956 Glenn Ford film, this is a star vehicle all the way. Gibson makes the most of the anguished father; though the writers don't fully explore his own possibly criminal side. (Letterboxed VHS available for $19.99) ★★½ VHS: $14.99; DVD: $29.99

Raoni: The Fight for the Amazon

(1979, 82 min, France/Brazil, Jean-Pierre Dutilleux) The Amazon Indians' fight against the Brazilian government's genocidal land policies is the center of this engrossing film. With civilization rapidly encroaching into their isolated and simple lives, the many Indian tribes who populate the Amazonian rainforest are forced to either drastically change their lifestyle or

fight. The filmmaker focuses his attention on one tribe, the Mekranotis, and is especially taken in by their charismatic and forceful chief, Raoni. With ethnographic footage of their village, we see the tribe's attempts to stop the decimation of the rainforest. An exhilarating adventure into a previously unseen world and a cautionary environmental tale. ★★★½ VHS: $29.99

Rapa Nui

(1994, 107 min, US, Kevin Reynolds) *Jason Scott Lee, Esai Morales, Sandrine Holt.* Lee stars in this well-intentioned but ultimately disappointing "ecological message movie" about the demise of the natives of Easter Island. Call it loinclothed "Romeo and Juliet" as Lee, a member of the "Long Ear" clan hotly pursues Holt, a member of the subservient "Short Ears," much to the chagrin of Lee's childhood chum and now rival in love, Morales (a "Short Ear" Tybalt?). Hokey in the extreme, the film does have its entertaining moments and, hey, with the entire cast parading around nearly stark naked, it can't be all bad. ★★½ VHS: $19.99

Rape of Love

(1977, 117 min, France, Yannick Bellon) *Nathalie Nell, Alain Foures.* A disturbing film with Nell as a nurse who is ruthlessly raped by four drunkards. Tragically, she discovers this is only the beginning of her ordeal. A poignant account of insensitivity and injustice. (French with English subtitles) ★★½

Rapid Fire

(1992, 90 min, US, Dwight H. Little) *Brandon Lee, Powers Boothe, Nick Mancuso.* Lee chops his way into the "B-movie" arena with this extremely mindless actioner that might just as easily been called *Vapid Fire.* Lee plays a peace-loving student who must fight for his life when he becomes a witness to some Mafia activity. Lee provides his own comic relief with a "valley girl" delivery guarenteed to leave the bad guys unsure whether to fight him or fuck him. ★★ VHS: $9.99

The Rapture

(1991, 100 min, US, Michael Tolkin) *Mimi Rogers, David Duchovny, Patrick Bauchau, Will Patton.* Unaccountably overlooked in its theatrical release, *The Rapture* is a startling philosophical drama that brings to light such weighty issues as religious zealousness, life after death and the search for faith. Rogers stars as a woman who seeks release from her existential emptiness in alcohol, drugs and anonymous group sex. Her life changes dramatically, however, after she discovers God through a religious awakening. Her newly inspired faith is put to the test in a series of Job-like trials culminating in a vision to go to the desert and await the Second Coming. A thought-provoking film that offers many angles to the religious issues and an ending which forces viewers to decide for themselves. (Letterboxed VHS available for $19.99) ★★★½ VHS: $14.99

The Rascals

(1981, 93 min, France, Bernard Revon) *Thomas Chabrol.* The French have been making films about the sexual awakening of young people years before the births of the American directors who are obsessed with the same theme.

Rather than titillate the viewer with cheap sex jokes, the films usually focus more on the psychological and emotional problems of budding adulthood. This film, a thoroughly delightful comedy about the coming-of-age of an irrepressible boy in a Catholic school, deals with his first relationship with an older girl. (French with English subtitles) ★★★

Rashomon

(1951, 88 min, Japan, Akira Kurosawa) *Toshiro Mifune, Machiko Kyo.* The film which opened the West to Japanese cinema, Kurosawa's brilliantly conceived Academy Award-winning classic delves into the mysteries of truth, reality and illusion, telling the story of a murder and rape through the conflicting testimony of all those involved: the "murdered" man, his ravished wife, the murderer, the arresting officer and a "neutral" bystander. The result is five completely different versions of the story. (Japanese with English subtitles) ★★★★ VHS: $29.99

Rasputin

(1978, 104 min, USSR, Elem Klimov) *Alexei Petrenko, Anatoly Romashin.* The demonic rise and bloody fall of Gregori Rasputin is explored in this fascinating and elaborate period piece. Although certainly not history, this Russian version of the Rasputin legend seems to be the definitive exposé of a man whose hypnotic spell over the royal family hastened their downfall. The story follows Rasputin, a religious fanatic who not only craved power, but women and booze as well. Was he a prophet sent by God to be the only hope for the Russian aristocracy or was he simply a madman bent on self-destruction? Both sides of the man are explored in this mesmerizing melodrama. (Russian with English subtitles) ★★★½ VHS: $9.99

Rasputin and the Empress

(1933, 123 min, US, Richard Boleslawski) *Lionel Barrymore, John Barrymore, Ethel Barrymore, Diana Wynyard, Edward Arnold.* The legendary Barrymores — Ethel, John and Lionel — made only one film together: and the result is a static, well-acted and affecting historical drama of the Romanoffs. Set in Russia just before the Revolution, the film examines the calamitous

Rashomon

reign as "the power behind the throne" of the notorious "priest" Rasputin, who contributed to the fall of the royal dynasty. Lionel's crafty portrayal of the opportunist spellbinder Rasputin elevates the film. He's cunning and vile, and is exact in bringing to life a character who's "like a man-eating shark with a bible under his fin." ★★★ VHS: $19.99

The Raven (Le Corbeau)

(1943, 92 min, France, Henri-Georges Clouzot) *Pierre Fresnay, Ginette Leclerc.* An extremely dark and tense thriller about a small town in France beseiged by paranoia in the wake of a mysterious, poisonous letter campaign written by "The Raven" and addressed to the town's physician. The uncompromising depiction of the French middle class caused quite a storm when the film was released because it was made with the assistance of the Germans and was viewed by many as anti-French propaganda. (French with English subtitles) ★★★½ VHS: $29.99

The Raven

(1963, 86 min, US, Roger Corman) *Vincent Price, Boris Karloff, Peter Lorre, Jack Nicholson.* Set in 15th-century England, this satiric version of the Edgar Allan Poe work pits two magicians (Price, Lorre) against a master sorcerer (Karloff), who has absconded with Price's wife. ★★★

Ravenous

(1999, 100 min, US, Antonia Bird) *Guy Pearce, Robert Carlyle, Jeremy Davies, Jeffrey Jones, David Arquette.* Cowardly Captain John Boyd (Pearce) is transferred to a chilly, remote post during the Mexican-American war. He finds himself among a small army of misfits and the legend of Windigo, a cannibal spirit that moves from man to man (growing ever stronger) through the ingestion of flesh. Part black comedy, part gruesome horror, and part '70s-style western, *Ravenous* has many interesting elements but is quite unsatisfying, especially as the mysterious plot threads find themselves resolved too literally. Carlyle (best known as *Trainspotting*'s Begbie) is wonderfully menacing as the outsider who first discovers the joys of flesh, and the musical score by Michael Nyman and Blur's Damon Albarn is stunning and fresh. Too bad Bird never finds a consistent tone to help ground this very bizarre story. Original director Milcho Manchevski was replaced early in the production. ★★½ VHS: $9.99; DVD: $34.99

The Ravishing Idiot

(1965, 99 min, France, Edouard Molinaro) *Anthony Perkins, Brigitte Bardot.* Perkins stars in this slapstick caper comedy as a bungling bank clerk who, with walking disaster area Bardot, unwittingly becomes involved with a Soviet spy ring. ★★½

Raw Deal

(1948, 80 min, US, Anthony Mann) *Dennis O'Keefe, Claire Trevor, Marsha Hunt, Raymond Burr, John Ireland.* With tough-talking guys, hard-boiled dames, plenty of cross and double-cross, and a hero so gruff you almost expect to hear his street-smart moll call him a "lug," *Raw Deal* is a startling good noir thriller which doesn't pinch on action or characterization. O'Keefe is a prisoner ready for the break. He took the rap for his creepy, sadistic boss Burr, who's helping in the escape. Only Burr doesn't want to see him

succeed. To complicate matters, O'Keefe, accompanied by flame Trevor, has taken his lawyer Hunt hostage, and he's soon torn between the two women. Sexual tensions simmer, jealousies erupt, and the line between right and wrong becomes blurred. Mann directs in a crisp, no-nonsense fashion, and the dialogue is priceless. ★★★½ VHS: $24.99

Raw Deal

(1986, 106 min, US, John Irvin) *Arnold Schwarzenegger, Kathryn Harrold.* This violent and tongue-in-cheek thriller has Arnold as a small-town sheriff (and former FBI agent) who single-handedly takes on the Chicago mob. A below-average effort. ★★ VHS: $9.99

The Razor's Edge

(1946, 146 min, US, Edmund Goulding) *Tyrone Power, Anne Baxter, Clifton Webb, Herbert Marshall.* Fine adaptation of W. Somerset Maugham's acclaimed novel with Power going through heaven and hell in his search for spiritual truth. Baxter won an Oscar for her heartbreaking alcoholic, and Webb should have won one as the cynical Elliott Templeton. (Remade in 1984) ★★★ VHS: $19.99

The Razor's Edge

(1984, 129 min, US, John Byrum) *Bill Murray, Theresa Russell, Denholm Elliott.* Murray, in his dramatic debut, plays a disillusioned WWI vet who rejects his materialistic lifestyle and retreats to the Himalayas in search of truth. An inferior remake of the 1946 classic which doesn't work on any level. ★ VHS: $9.99

Ready to Rumble

(2000, 106 min, US, Brian Robbins) *David Arquette, Oliver Platt, Scott Caan, Rose McGowan, Joe Pantoliano, Ahmet Zappa.* The presence of WCW stars instead of the more popular WWF is the first sign that this comedy about pro wrestlers and their dunderheaded fans might not reach its (low) potential. Doughy Platt, who's usually excellent, is woefully miscast as Jimmy King, the greatest wrestler in the world. When the King is suspiciously dethroned, his two most ardent fans (Arquette and Caan, doing a redneck Bill & Ted shtick) look to set things right. The film is a victim of laugh-free writing, and an indecision whether to satirize grapplers and their fans or to revel in their low humor. ★½ VHS: $14.99; DVD: $19.99

Ready to Wear (Prêt-a-Porter)

(1994, 132 min, US, Robert Altman) *Lauren Bacall, Kim Basinger, Julia Roberts, Tim Robbins, Sophia Loren, Marcello Mastroianni, Stephen Rea, Rupert Everett.* Altman's take on the Paris fashion world rates as a disappointment in spite of being intermittently fascinating. Assembling (once again) an amazing all-star cast, Altman sets out to both satirize and demystify the carnival-like atmosphere of the *prêt-a-porter* fashion shows, but sabotages himself by presenting too many players, the majority of which are dramatically shortchanged. However, some characters stand out, including Robbins as an American sports writer, Roberts as a rival reporter romantically involved with Robbins, Mastroianni and Loren as ex-flames, and Basinger, who nearly steals the film as a hilariously inept TV reporter. ★★½ VHS: $9.99; DVD: $29.99

The Real Blonde

(1998, 107 min, US, Tom DiCillo) *Matthew Modine, Catherine Keener, Kathleen Turner, Maxwell Caulfield, Daryl Hannah, Christopher Lloyd, Marlo Thomas, Elizabeth Berkeley.* Director DiCillo (*Living in Oblivion*) once again lampoons the entertainment industry in this light-hearted comedy about women and men, how they perceive themselves and each other in a society preoccupied with beauty, sex and perfection. Modine and Keener play a couple whose personal and professional lives are at a crossroads. Modine, an actor, can't get his career off the ground; Keener, a makeup artist for a fashion photographer, has become frustrated with what her life represents. Caulfield is Modine's friend and fellow actor, a man obsessed with one thing — finding a real (read: natural) blonde. Satirizing everything from daytime soaps to Calvin Klein ads, DiCillo creates some original and often funny situations, but this is just another film about love and sex in the '90s. ★★½ VHS: $14.99; DVD: $29.99

Real Genius

(1985, 108 min, US, Martha Coolidge) *Val Kilmer, Gabe Jarret, Michelle Meyrink, William Atherton, Patti D'Arbanville.* Diverting teen comedy with Kilmer as a member of a group of super-intelligent teenagers who create a sophisticated laser system for a class project. However, when they discover that they have been working on a military secret, they devise an elaborate scheme to get revenge. ★★½ VHS: $9.99

The Real Glory

(1939, 95 min, US, Henry Hathaway) *Gary Cooper, David Niven, Andrea Leeds.* An exciting adventure film which bears more than just a little resemblance to *Gunga Din.* Cooper and Niven are soldiers of fortune who assist the American Army in their battle against a guerrilla uprising in the Philippines just after the Spanish-American War. Director Hathaway excels at this type of filmmaking, and the action scenes are terrific. ★★★ VHS: $14.99

Real Life

(1979, 99 min, US, Albert Brooks) *Albert Brooks, Charles Grodin.* Director, writer and star Brooks attacks such suspect documentaries like PBS did to the Louds in "An American Family." Every bit as biting and as funny as *This is Spinal Tap,* Brooks plays a very egocentric documentary filmmaker who, after invading Grodin's home, will stop at nothing to make this "reality" as interesting as possible. ★★★ VHS: $14.99; DVD: $29.99

Reality Bites

(1994, 99 min, US, Ben Stiller) *Winona Ryder, Ethan Hawke, Ben Stiller, Janeane Garafolo, Steve Zahn.* A whimsical film that looks at some of life's more monumental choices, like who to love, what low-pay, low-reward job to take and which psychic hot line to call. Ryder is splendid as a recent college grad whose life is thrown into a depressed frenzy when she has to find a new job and is confronted with one too many romantic decisions. Both Hawke and Stiller make charming leading men as Ryder's bi-polar love interests, and Garofalo almost steals the show as her ironic, Gap-managing, '70s obsessed apartment mate. With cultural and

Joan Fontaine (l.) is tormented by Judith Anderson in *Rebecca*

"generational" references jammed into every corner, *Reality Bites* is an intriguing look at the way that some people under 30 deal with life, but it has an even more captivating and witty take on the way many people deal with love. ★★★ VHS: $9.99; DVD: $24.99

Re-Animator

(1985, 86 min, US, Stuart Gordon) *Jeffrey Combs, Bruce Abbott.* H. P. Lovecraft would turn over in his grave if: a) he took some of the re-animation serum developed by the mad scientist in this nifty film; or b) he saw the liberties taken with his story. This film proves that director Gordon would beat George Romero hands down in a gross-out contest, as a decapitated body gives head both figuratively and literally. (Answer to the question: both.) ★★★½

Rear Window

(1954, 112 min, US, Alfred Hitchcock) *James Stewart, Grace Kelly, Thelma Ritter.* Hitchcock confronts the manifold by-products of voyeurism with this splendid study of a murder's detection. Stewart is superlative as the intrusive observer who reflects our own sometimes dangerous desires. An uncommonly carnal Kelly is his eager accomplice. (Remade in 1998) ★★★★ VHS: $14.99; DVD: $29.99

Rebecca

(1940, 115 min, US, Alfred Hitchcock) *Laurence Olivier, Joan Fontaine, Judith Anderson, George Sanders.* Hitchcock's first Hollywood movie is a Gothic masterpiece based on the book by Daphne Du Maurier. Fontaine plays a passive and awkward paid companion for the snooty dowager Mrs. Van Hopper. While on vacation at Monte Carlo, she falls in love with the ominous and rich Maxim de Winter (Olivier) who whisks her off to his mansion. However, his mysterious attachment to his deceased first wife wreaks havoc upon their marriage. The most durable performance comes from Anderson as the creepy Mrs. Danvers, the fanatically devoted housekeeper (paramour?) of the first Mrs. de Winter. A chilling script and superb acting and

direction won *Rebecca* an Oscar for Best Picture. ★★★★ VHS: $14.99; DVD: $14.99

Rebel Rousers

(1967, 78 min, US, Martin B. Cohen) *Bruce Dern, Cameron Mitchell, Jack Nicholson, Harry Dean Stanton.* Dern is the philosophising leader of a pack of motley motorcyclists; he's the kind of guy who takes his hog everywhere — including into the cantina of the small Mexican town where he meets old high school buddy Mitchell. Mitchell is having paternity problems and looks about 20 years older than Dern. A biker flick typical of the era. Watch Nicholson make lewd advances on a five-months-pregnant woman. ★★ VHS: $9.99

Rebel without a Cause

(1955, 111 min, US, Nicholas Ray) *James Dean, Natalie Wood, Sal Mineo, Jim Backus.* A testament to adolescent angst with Dean as the prototypical angry young man at odds with his parents, himself and the future. A brooding film that cemented the Dean legend. In her first adult role, Wood offers an incandescent performance as a soul mate; and Mineo is especially touching as Plato, a friendless youth who has yet to come to terms with his latent sexuality, and who is secretly in love with Dean's charismatic character Jim. (VHS available letterboxed or pan & scan) ★★★½ VHS: $19.99; DVD: $19.99

Reckless

(1995, 100 min, US, Norman René) *Mia Farrow, Scott Glenn, Mary-Louise Parker, Tony Goldwyn, Eileen Brennan, Giancarlo Esposito, Stephen Dorff.* Farrow is a howling delight in this wacky and inventive Christmas-themed fairy tale based on the play by Craig Lucas (*Longtime Companion*). Farrow plays Rachel, an idiotically sweet chatterbox housewife and mother who is forced out of her home on Christmas Eve when she discovers that her husband has put a contract out on her life. She is rescued by the superficially nice social worker Lucas (Glenn) and his deaf paraplegic wife Pooty (Parker). But for poor

Rachel, her newfound happiness with the couple proves to be short-lived as poisoned champagne, dark secrets and a drunken Santa Claus test the limits of sanity. A droll, warped romp of self-discovery infused with purposefully cheesy special effects, oddball cameos and an intoxicating mix of comedy, fantasy and surreal nightmare. ★★★ VHS: $14.99

Record of a Tenement Gentleman

(1947, 73 min, Japan, Yasujiro Ozu) *Choko Iida, Hohi Aoki.* A charming, melancholy portrait of life in Japan after the war, director Ozu's inspirational tale examines the alternately heartfelt and comic exploits of a young boy abandoned by his parents. Discovering the youth and feeling sorry for him, a tenement dweller brings him home only to find his flatmate will not allow him to keep the child in the apartment. After straws are drawn to see who takes care of the child among the neighbors, an older widow grudgingly ends up with him. Against the odds, a close relationship soon develops between them nurtured by mutual understanding and respect. While it may seem cold compared to American standards of morality, the film holds true as a wonderful story of enriched lives and community living during a difficult time in history. (Japanese with English subtitles) ★★★★ VHS: $19.99

Red

(1994, 98 min, France, Krzystof Kieslowski) *Jean-Louis Trintignant, Irène Jacob.* The last of director Kieslowski's "color" trilogy (following *Blue* and *White*) is a sumptuous finale, and the most satisfying of the three films. A beautiful Jacob stars as a model preparing a trip to reunite and reconcile with her traveling boyfriend. But events and emotions are skewed when she runs over a dog and seeks out the animal's owner. Who she eventually finds is Trintignant, a burned-out, bitter ex-judge who spends his spare time spying on his neighbors. An unusual relationship develops between the two, culminating in an act of self-examination and moral responsibility. Kieslowski weaves a compelling and haunting tale of communication, emotion and love gone awry, and it's all enhanced by a seductive, mysterious atmosphere. (French with English subtitles) ★★★½ VHS: $19.99

The Red and the White

(1967, 92 min, Hungary/USSR, Miklós Jancsó) *Tatyana Konyukova, Krystyna Mikolajewska.* Hungary's premiere director Jancsó sets this haunting antiwar drama in central Russia during the Civil War of 1918, in which the Red Army tangled with a counterrevolutionary threat from the Whites in the hills along the Volga River. The action centers around a monastery where a group of nurses do their best to conceal the identities of the wounded and administer equal care to all. Employing remarkable visuals, Jancsó forges a compelling treatise on the absurdity of war and the humiliation of mechanical slaughter. (Hungarian with English subtitles) ★★★½ VHS: $24.99

The Red Balloon/White Mane

(1956, 34/38 min, France, Albert Lamorisse) *Pascal Lamousse.* The highly acclaimed *The Red Balloon* is a fantasy guaranteed to appeal to both adults and children. It tells the story of Pascal, a

lonely French boy who befriends a wondrous red balloon which follows him everywhere and fills his need for friendship. This beautiful film maintains a true sense of childish wonder and has much to say about the need for love. Another short film by director Lamorisse, *White Main*, about a fierce, wild stallion tamed by a small boy, is also included. (No dialogue) ★★★★ VHS: $24.99

Red Beard

(1965, 185 min, Japan, Akira Kurosawa) *Toshiro Mifune, Yuzo Kayama.* Mifune is the wise, pragmatic doctor who guides a young intern through the trials and frustrations of the profession. The humanistic education changes him from a conceited technician to a humble man who values each of his patients as a whole person. (Letterboxed) (Japanese with English subtitles) ★★★½ VHS: $39.99

Red Cherry

(1996, 120 min, China, Ye Ying) *Guo Ke-Yu, Xu Xiaoli.* An unsettling account of two orphaned Chinese friends living during WWII, *Red Cherry* holds new shocks and releases raw emotions as few antiwar films have. Chuchu and Luo Xiaoman are orphaned, Communist Chinese youths who are brought to Moscow in the winter of 1940. Refugees from Chairman Mao's revolution, they eventually settle into their new environment and find respect among their peers. All seems well until their world is uprooted by unpredictable, life-changing events brought on by the war. (Mandarin with English subtitles) ★★★ VHS: $14.99; DVD: $14.99

Red Corner

(1997, 119 min, US, Jon Avnet) *Richard Gere, Bai Ling, Tsai Chin.* Gere plays Jack, a smug, cocksure lawyer — the type of guy who's so brilliant and arrogant that you know he's careening towards a serious crisis of conscience and attitude. In the midst of business negotiations with the Chinese government, Jack is arrested for the murder of a dancer he met in a nightclub. He must try to acquaint himself with the intricacies and brick walls of the Chinese judicial system, and learn to trust the beautiful court-appointed defense advocate (Ling) who has come to his aid. It's difficult to say which is more frustrating: the legal entanglements depicted of the Chinese judicial system, or the predictable plot trajectory of the movie itself. And the romantic subplot between Gere and Chin is a clumsy after-thought at best. ★★ VHS: $9.99; DVD: $14.99

Red Dawn

(1984, 110 min, US, John Milius) *Patrick Swayze, C. Thomas Howell, Charlie Sheen, Lea Thompson, Jennifer Grey.* Contrived (and often ridiculous) political action-adventure film about a group of teenage resistance fighters who do battle with the Communist invaders who have taken over their small town. ★½ VHS: $9.99; DVD: $14.99

Red Desert

(1965, 116 min, Italy, Michelangelo Antonioni) *Richard Harris, Monica Vitti.* Antonioni's first color film is an intriguing study of the alienation of man. Against the backdrop of a sterilized, impersonal industrial landscape, a love affair is enacted out. The film deals with the impossibility of real communication between people entrapped in this modern, hostile environment and longs for a return to a more innocent era. (Italian with English subtitles) ★★★ VHS: $19.99; DVD: $24.99

Red Dust

(1932, 83 min, US, Victor Fleming) *Clark Gable, Jean Harlow, Mary Astor.* Gable stars as a rubber plantation worker in Indochina who romances good-time girl Harlow and a coworker's wife, Astor. A pre-Code production simmering with sexuality and with its fair share of laughs for the usually rigid adventure genre. Gable and Harlow are particularly appealing together. Gable also appeared in the 1953 remake, *Mogambo*. ★★★½ VHS: $19.99

Red Firecracker, Green Firecracker

(1994, 111 min, China, He Ping) *Ning Jing, Wu Gang, Zhao Xiaorui.* Director He's third feature is weakened by his inability to bring anything new to the overly familiar territory of the Chinese New Wave. Set against the country's transition into the 20th century, *Red Firecracker* is an epic lovers' triangle that, while being visually rewarding, is unfortunately emotionally hollow. Female child Chun Zhi (Ning) is raised male in order to inherit the family fireworks business. But these years of repression melt with the arrival of Nie Bao (Wu), an itinerant painter hired to help decorate the home for the New Year's holiday. As in other, better films (*To Live, The Blue Kite*), there are epic landscapes, but their use here as emotional correlatives is too obvious to be effective. (Mandarin with English subtitles) ★★½ VHS: $19.99

Red-Headed Woman

(1932, 81 min, US, Jack Conway) *Jean Harlow, Chester Morris, Charles Boyer.* Harlow is a sexy siren out to get the man she loves — her boss (Morris). Look for an aspiring Boyer in the small role of the chauffeur who befriends her. Vintage Harlow. ★★★ VHS: $19.99

Tom Sizemore and Val Kilmer in *Red Planet*

Red Heat

(1985, 104 min, US/Germany, Robert Collector) *Linda Blair, Sylvia Kristel, Gina Gershon.* A pedestrian Cold War women-in-prison flick set in a nameless Communist country. Blair, an American innocent, is captured by Communists after inadvertently witnessing the abduction of a political dissident. She is sent to a hellhole women's prison which seems to be run by a lesbian prisoner (Kristel). The lifeless film contains the requisite hair-pulling-in-their-underwear fights and snippets of gratuitous nudity. Barely enjoyable on a camp level. ★½; DVD: $24.99

Red Heat

(1988, 106 min, US, Walter Hill) *Arnold Schwarzenegger, James Belushi.* A tepid buddy cop action flick. Arnold is a rigid Russian officer teaming with free-wheeling Chicago cop Belushi to search for a Soviet drug dealer. ★★ VHS: $9.99; DVD: $14.99

Red King, White Knight

(1989, 106 min, GB, Geoff Murphy) *Tom Skerritt, Max von Sydow, Helen Mirren.* Skerritt is a seasoned CIA veteran who is sent into the Soviet Union to thwart a hardline general's planned assasination of Mikhail Gorbachev. He joins forces with his one-time nemesis, KGB agent Szaz (von Sydow), and together they hunt down the conspirators. An exciting post-*glasnost* political thriller. ★★★ VHS: $19.99

Red Kiss (Rouge Baiser)

(1986, 100 min, France, Vera Belmont) *Charlotte Valandrey, Marthe Keller.* Exploring the budding sexuality of teenagers, this sincere, charming and intelligent drama is punctuated by both its background setting (the turbulent political times in 1952 France) and its star, Valandrey — a beguiling, dark-eyed beauty of fifteen. Committing as much time to championing the French Communist Party as she does carousing in a graveyard with friends, young Nadia's life begins to change when she meets a handsome apolitical fashion photographer. This young man's world of beautiful women and "cool" Gauloise-filled jazz clubs confuses and entices Nadia as her ardently idealistic beliefs clash with those of the real world. (French with English subtitles) ★★★ VHS: $19.99

Red Lion

(1969, 115 min, Japan, Kihachi Okamoto) *Toshiro Mifune, Shima Iwashita.* Mifune gives a bravura performance as the scarlet-maned bumbler who returns to his village after a ten-year absence, only to discover that he is to be the one to liberate his villagers from their deceitful, oppressive government. The pace of the film changes from a humorous beginning to an action-packed violent ending, with much exciting swordplay. (Japanese with English subtitles) ★★★ VHS: $29.99

Red Planet

(2000, 100 min, US, Antony Hoffman) *Val Kilmer, Carrie-Anne Moss, Tom Sizemore, Terence Stamp, Benjamin Bratt, Simon Baker.* It's 2056 and Earth lays devastated by pollution. A group of space-traveling scientists head off to Mars to determine if it's inhabitable. The stock charac-ters are offset by an intriguing story, some good visuals and a few exciting scenes. Moss encores her tough-as-nails soldier from *The Matrix* to good effect, though the supporting characters aren't given much to do. About on par with 2000's other Mars epic, *Mission to Mars.* ★★½ VHS: $14.99; DVD: $19.99

Red Pomegranate

(1969, 75 min, USSR, Sergei Paradjanov) The powerful works of 17th-century Armenian poet Arutuin Sayadian are cap-tured in this exotic mosaic of a film. Essentially a tribute to his life as well as to his dedication to the Armenian people, the film is divided into eight sections each depicting, from childhood to death, a period of the poet's life. Filled with oblique, symbolic imagery, this film is definitely only for specialized tastes and those devotees who have a knowledge of the poet and of Armenia. (Armenian with English subtitles) ★★★

Red River

(1948, 133 min, US, Howard Hawks) *John Wayne, Montgomery Clift, Walter Brennan, Joanne Dru.* Hawks' epic western rates as one of the finest of the genre. Wayne, in an unsympathetic role, plays a rancher who heads a strenuous cat-tle drive along the Chisolm Trail. As the journey wears on, the other men, including his foster son Clift, begin to question his ability as a leader, prompting a collision course between father and son. An astonishing accomplishment featuring gorgeous cinematography and bril-liant direction by Hawks. (Director's cut) ★★★★ VHS: $9.99; DVD: $14.99

Red Rock West

(1993, 98 min, US, John Dahl) *Nicolas Cage, Lara Flynn Boyle, Dennis Hopper, J.T. Walsh.* A *Blood Simple*-esque thriller that offers more twists than a Philadelphia soft pretzel. Cage is as an out-of-work wildcatter with a gimpy leg, a heart of gold and a pocketful of lint who sees dollar signs when a small-town bar owner (Walsh) mistakes him for the hit man he just hired to kill his wife (Boyle). Then the real killer (perennial ham Hopper) shows up. Perhaps the only film ever to go from cable to video to a successful theatrical run, this sleeper is an expertly plotted game of cat-and-mouse and a well-studied tribute to the film noir era. ★★★½ VHS: $19.99; DVD: $24.99

The Red Shoes

(1948, 133 min, GB, Michael Powell & Emeric Pressburger) *Moira Shearer, Anton Walbrook.* This lavishly breathtaking realization of the classic fairy tale is a glorious ode to the wonders of dance and the pursuit of artistic and personal fulfillment. Shearer gives an exquisite perfor-mance. ★★★★; DVD: $39.99

Red Sonja

(1985, 89 min, US, Richard Fleischer) *Arnold Schwarzenegger, Brigitte Nielsen.* Schwarzenegger takes a back seat to Nielsen in this sword and sorcery adventure with Nielsen as the fearless female warrior. Unmemorable action scenes and wooden acting only accentuate the laugh-able story line. ★ VHS: $9.99

The Red Shoes

Red Sorghum

(1988, 92 min, China, Zhang Yimou) *Gong Li, Jiang Wen.* The promise of a Chinese New Wave in filmmaking is much in evidence in this breathtaking epic of peasant life by first-time director Zhang. Visually stunning, the film revolves around the reminiscences of a young man for his grandparents — peasants who lived in a remote section of northwestern China during the 1920s and '30s. Nine (the beautiful and remarkable Gong) is a young beauty who, immediately prior to her arranged marriage with a leper, is saved by a heroic ser-vant. They both fall in love and their ensuing relationship, through personal turmoils as well as Japan's invasion of their area, is dazzlingly dramatized. A visually stunning folk tale that celebrates the vitality and endurance of the peasant people. (Mandarin with English subti-tles) ★★★½ VHS: $29.99

The Red Squirrel (La Ardilla Roja)

(1993, 104 min, Spain, Julio Medem) *Emma Suarez, Nancho Novo, Maria Barranco.* In *The Red Squirrel*, love spirals inexorably down a vortex of forbidden love. Novo plays a rock star who takes advantage of a beautiful woman's amnesia — brought on by a motorcycle accident — to cre-ate another dream lover now that his song writ-ing days are over. But is this dream lover (Suarez) dreaming, too? Like some antipodal Hitchcock film — most obviously *Vertigo* — director Medem tightens the psychological threads until they are just about to break, then he begins to weave a tapestry that, while dark, is not bereft of life. Unfortunately, the white sub-titles get lost during some of the lighter pas-sages. (Spanish with English subtitles) ★★½ VHS: $79.99

The Red Tent

(1969, 121 min, Italy/USSR, Mikhail K. Kalatozov) *Sean Connery, Claudia Cardinale, Hardy Kruger, Peter Finch.* An international all-star cast highlights this exciting adventure film detailing General Nobile's ill-fated 1928 Arctic expedition, where the survivors of a crashed dirigible struggle against nature and the odds while waiting to be rescued. Finch as Italian

R

explorer Nobile. Similar in theme to Jan Troell's memorable *Flight of the Eagle*. (Filmed in English) ★★★ VHS: $19.99

The Red Violin

(1998, 132 min, GB, François Girard) *Samuel L. Jackson, Greta Scacchi, Jason Flemying, Don McKellar, Colm Feore.* An eloquent journey through time and across continents, *The Red Violin* is a tale of cursed love and obsession. A renowned 17th-century artist crafts the titular instrument, the most acoustically perfect musical apparatus ever fashioned. The film traces the 300-year life of the violin as it's passed on through generations from musician to musician. Lost, stolen, damaged, resurrected, the mysterious violin seems to harbor the secrets and souls of each of its former owners and, as told through a contemporary framing device, becomes a priceless treasure that men would fight — perhaps even kill — for. Compelling, if a bit episodic, the film is a feast for the eyes and ears with a sumptuous production design and a haunting musical score. ★★★ VHS: $14.99; DVD: $24.99

Reds

(1981, 201 min, US, Warren Beatty) *Warren Beatty, Diane Keaton, Jack Nicholson, Maureen Stapleton, Gene Hackman, Edward Herrmann.* Beatty won a Best Director Oscar for this epic drama about the last years of John Reed, the American journalist who becomes involved in the Russian Revolution. Keaton, in a finely controlled performance, is Louise Bryant, his wife. This long but interesting film serves as both lush romantic drama and political exposé. Nicholson, as a heartbroken Eugene O'Neill, steals every scene he's in. Stapleton also won an Oscar as Best Supporting Actress. ★★★★ VHS: $14.99

Redwood Curtain

(1995, 99 min, US, John Korty) *Jeff Daniels, Lea Salonga, John Lithgow.* Playwright Lanford Wilson, who with "The 5th of July" and "The Hot 1 Baltimore" has demonstrated a remarkable ability to decipher and communicate the frailties of relationships and the need for human contact by characters on the fringe, delves into further exploration of identity and miscommunication in this extremely poignant made-for-TV adaptation of his play. Salonga gives a touching portrayal of an adopted Vietnamese teen who, after the death of her troubled but adoring adoptive father (Lithgow), sets out to find her biological parents. Director Korty's pacing is deliberate and absorptive, underscoring the fragile and uncertain search of the young girl. ★★★½ VHS: $14.99

Reefer Madness

(1936, 68 min, US, Louis Gasnier) The evils of marijuana exposed! Bill was a happy all-American high school student until that fatal puff of the deadly weed. The effects: wild parties, violence, sex and. . . insanity! Is it worth it? ★★★★ VHS: $19.99

The Ref

(1994, 92 min, US, Ted Demme) *Denis Leary, Judy Davis, Kevin Spacey, Glynis Johns.* Sporting a wit as nasty and as big as its star Leary's devil-may-care grin, *The Ref* is a refreshingly funny and resourceful slant on *Desperate Hours*–type films. Leary stars as a hapless thief whose botched Christmas Eve burglary puts him on the run. He kidnaps bickering married couple Davis and Spacey and hides out in their not-so-sweet home. However, nothing this streetwise criminal has seen in or out of prison can prepare him for the fireworks which erupt when the feuding husband and wife go at it. The performances from the three leads are as energetic as they are funny, and Johns is just right as the mother-in-law you love to hate. ★★★ VHS: $9.99

The Reflecting Skin

(1990, 98 min, Canada, Philip Ridley) *Viggo Mortensen, Lindsay Duncan.* This bizarre, independently produced horror movie owes more to Luis Buñuel than to Wes Craven. A young boy growing up in the Midwest must contend with a father who *may* be a child molester, a beautiful neighbor who *may* be a vampire, dead children, exploding frogs, a hidden human fetus and a mysterious black Cadillac. The film goes over the top at times (you can almost see the filmmakers snickering at their own outlandishness), but it is consistently interesting and offers more than a few good jolts. ★★½ VHS: $19.99

Reflections in a Golden Eye

(1967, 108 min, US, John Huston) *Marlon Brando, Elizabeth Taylor, Robert Forster, Brian Keith, Julie Harris, Zorro David.* Sexual repression abounds in this kinky version of Carson McCullers' novel. Brando is the latent homosexual Army officer and Taylor is his unsatisfied, contemptuous wife. Forster is the hunky object of Brando's affection, and David is a fey houseboy. Not totally successful, the performances, however, make it slightly interesting. Unfortunately, the film suffers from being made at a time when there was a budding sexual freedom for all but gay characters; which made it impossible to fully explore Brando's character and sexual yearnings. The right director could make a helluva remake. ★★½ VHS: $19.99

Reform School Girls

(1986, 94 min, US, Tom DeSimone) *Wendy O. Williams, Sybil Danning, Linda Carol, Pat Ast.* Definitely one of the most outlandish films of the women-in-prison flicks. Innocent Jenny (Carol) finds herself sent to Pridemore, a hellish reformatory/prison supervised by lecherous female gaurds and ruled over by Head Matron Edna, a cartoonishly evil dyke bitch who takes malicious pleasure in tormenting the young girls. Oh yes, they're bad! There is plenty of nudity, riots, cat fights and breakouts to keep any fan entranced, and if that doesn't do it, the sight of Danning as the militaristic warden will. The title song says it all, "So Young, So Bad, So What." ★★ VHS: $9.99; DVD: $24.99

Regarding Henry

(1991, 107 min, US, Mike Nichols) *Harrison Ford, Annette Bening, Bill Nunn, Elizabeth Wilson, John Leguizamo.* Ford plays a very nasty corporate lawyer who is shot in a hold up, thereby drastically changing his life. Forced to undergo a lengthy healing and therapy process, Ford is changed "for the better" when he returns to his ignored wife (Bening) and neglected adolescent daughter. Though clearly a "yuppie fanta-

sy" for the '90s (no matter how ruthlessly or insensitively one acts, one can be redeemed in the end), there is much satisfaction in seeing Ford's transformation. And to his credit, Ford's beguiling performance as the child-like family man makes the most of the manipulative screenplay. ★★★ VHS: $14.99

Reilly: Ace of Spies

(1984, 80 min, GB, Jim Goddard) *Sam Neill, Leo McKern, Jeanne Crowley.* This short but thrilling spy caper stars Neill as Reilly, the poor man's James Bond — an international scoundrel and womanizing superspy. It's a story of Eastern European intrigue, Russian oil and beautiful women. Watch it despite the fact that the director's next project was the disastrous Madonna–Sean Penn flop, *Shanghai Surprise*. (The entire four-part series is also available for $49.99 each or $149.99 for the set) ★★★ VHS: $14.99

The Reincarnation of Golden Lotus

(1989, 99 min, China, Clara Law) *Joi Wong, Eric Tsang, Lam Chun Yen.* This tale of ill-fated love and the objectification of women is a kind of Chinese *Dead Again* without the whodunit subplot. Starting in Mainland China during the Cultural Revolution, the story follows a young Chinese woman who turns out to be the incarnation of the Golden Lotus, the wife of a wealthy landowner in feudal China. She is swept away to modern-day Hong Kong by a rich baker where she falls into the same traps of her previous life. Director Law skillfully shows the parallels between the mistreatment of women under Communism, in old Imperial China and in colonial Hong Kong. (Mandarin with English subtitles) ★★★ VHS: $79.99

Reindeer Games

(2000, 105 min, US, John Frankenheimer) *Ben Affleck, Charlize Theron, Gary Sinise, Dennis Farina, Clarence Williams III, Donal Logue.* Screenwriter Ehren Kruger has apparently bought a *Usual Suspects*–brand Mad Libs, filling in clichés for the blanks and spitting out this arbitrary thriller. Affleck plays Rudy (get it?), a car thief who gets out of jail and hooks up with his late-cellmate's girlfriend (Theron), and is trapped into a scheme to rob a casino way up North with her evil brother (Sinise). It's hard to say more, since the twists are so convoluted, yet dozing off for a few minutes won't hamper your ability to keep up. The plot's machinations are driven by a need to have twists, rather than out of any logic or character. Frankenheimer does his best, but he also unwittingly amplifies the story's problems. And if Affleck ever becomes a top action star, then the Apocalypse may well be nigh. ★ VHS: $14.99; DVD: $29.99

The Reivers

(1969, 107 min, US, Mark Rydell) *Steve McQueen, Mitch Vogel, Rupert Crosse.* Totally charming screen version of William Faulkner's story set in the early 1900s about an adventurous 12-year-old boy (Vogel) who travels from Mississippi to Tennessee with carefree McQueen and pal Crosse by motorcar. ★★★

Relentless

(1989, 92 min, US, William Lustig) *Judd Nelson, Robert Loggia, Meg Foster, Leo Rossi.* Nelson turns psycho in this surprisingly effective thriller writ-

The Remains of the Day

ten by one Jack T.D. Robinson, better known as Phil Alden Robinson (the director of *Field of Dreams*). Nelson sinks his teeth into the role of a Los Angeles serial killer who delights in showing up the baffled police. Loggia is the seasoned detective assigned to the case. This should satisfy those looking for a couple of good chills. ★★½

The Relic

(1997, 110 min, US, Peter Hyams) *Penelope Ann Miller, Tom Sizemore, Linda Hunt, James Whitmore.* Based on the novel by Douglas Preston and Lincoln Child, this big-budget production boasts great special effects and an original and terrifying monster. What it doesn't have in abundance is originality, but that's alright because its effective shocks and consistently high level of suspense and terror make up for any feeling of having seen it all before. Miller is the brains and Sizemore the brawn in a battle with a bizarre new life form accidentally brought back to the Chicago Museum of Natural History from the Amazon jungle. Leave it to the management to hold a gala reception one dark and stormy night while the creature is loose in the building. It's up to our heroes to stop the beast. Lotsa fun. ★★★ VHS: $9.99; DVD: $24.99

The Reluctant Debutante

(1958, 94 min, US, Vincente Minnelli) *Rex Harrison, Kay Kendall, Sandra Dee, Angela Lansbury.* Harrison and Kendall bring a degree of respectability to this mildly amusing drawing-room comedy. A British couple ready their daughter (Dee), schooled in the States, for her society debut. A rather sappy and dated family film, rescued by the two stars' earnest performances. ★★ VHS: $19.99

The Remains of the Day

(1993, 137 min, GB, James Ivory) *Anthony Hopkins, Emma Thompson, Christopher Reeve, Hugh Grant, James Fox.* The unequivocal masterpiece of producer Ismail Merchant and director Ivory. Spare in plot yet devastatingly powerful in its theme of repressed emotions and self-disillusionment, the deceptively simple story simmers with complex, unexpressed passions by its main characters. Adapted from Kazuo Ishiguro's novel, the story is set in a stately English manor with action being intercut from its 1930s heyday to its faded glory and near abandonment in the 1950s. In a magnificent performance, Hopkins stars as Stevens, the manor's longtime butler. With an unswerving and unquestioned devotion to his employer, Lord Darlington (Fox), Stevens sacrifices any semblance of a personal life — including an unconsummated relationship with the estate's vivacious housekeeper, charmingly played by Thompson. Devoid of heavyhandedness, the film is witty and entertaining, and is beautifully composed — its characters create almost unbearable tension and joy. ★★★★ VHS: $19.99

Rembrandt

(1936, 84 min, GB, Alexander Korda) *Charles Laughton, Elsa Lanchester, Gertrude Lawrence.* Laughton delivers an inspired and moving performance as the renowned Dutch painter. He portrays Rembrandt as a complex and multifaceted egotist whose deep religious faith drove him to ignore poverty and lack of sponsorship in pursuit of his art. Korda's direction imbues the screen with a plethora of stunning tableaux. ★★★½ VHS: $14.99; DVD: $19.99

Remember the Titans

(2000, 114 min, US, Boaz Yakin) *Denzel Washington, Will Patton, Wood Harris, Ryan Hurst, Donald Faison.* Bringing great determination and strength of character to the part of a football coach thrown into the political and social maelstrom of the early 1970s, Washington delivers a tough, compassionate performance to stand alongside his best work. In this involving true story that both entertains and enlightens, director Yakin explores race relations on a human scale, and how adversity in any game can be overcome. Much to the dismay of the white establishment of Alexandria, Virginia, the newly integrated T. C. Williams High School gets its first black coach, Herman Boone (Washington). The heartened story follows the struggles of players, faculty and townspeople as they all come to grips with the adolescence of the Civil Rights movement, where white and black stand side by side for the first time. Using the gridiron as a stand-in for the American mindset, the film captures these tentative first steps under the guise of a familiar but stirring underdog tale — a football team coming together to beat the odds. ★★★ VHS: $22.99; DVD: $29.99

Remo Williams

(1985, 121 min, US, Guy Hamilton) *Fred Ward, Joel Grey, Wilford Brimley.* A New York policeman (Ward) becomes a highly trained, top-secret government agent, with a little help from an elderly Korean master (played by Grey). This entertaining adventure features well-staged action sequences, including a hold-your-breath fight atop the Statue of Liberty. ★★★ VHS: $6.99

Renaissance Man

(1994, 129 min, US, Penny Marshall) *Danny DeVito, Gregory Hines, Cliff Robertson, James Remar, Mark Wahlberg, Lillo Brancato, Jr., Kadeem Hardison.* This sappy service comedy stars DeVito as a hapless, unemployed teacher who accepts an Army position to have his life changed for the better. DeVito takes charge of a group of military rejects, ultimately allowing his students to discover their own self-respect and at the same time putting his own life in order. There are some pleasurable moments to the film, but Marshall goes over the top with its sentimental message. The big surprise of the film is the effective performance given by Wahlberg as a backwoods G.I. ★★½

Rendez-Vous

(1985, 83 min, France, André Téchiné) *Juliette Binoche, Lambert Wilson, Wadek Stanczak, Jean-Louis Trintignant.* This stylish melodrama stars Binoche as a naïve 18-year-old girl who moves from the provinces to Paris in order to seek independence and establish an acting career. She soon becomes entangled in two love affairs; one with an overly idealistic young man (Stanczak) and another with a self-destructive youth (Wilson). A chic, well-cast study of opposing forces in life and fate. (French with English subtitles) ★★★ VHS: $29.99

Les Rendez-Vous d'Anna

(1978, 122 min, Belgium/France, Chantal Akerman) *Aurore Clement, Lea Massari, Helmut Griem, Jean-Pierre Cassel.* Filmed in a minimalist style, this quietly moving drama of alienation features a young Belgian director, Anna, who travels by train through Europe publicizing her newest film. Along the way, she meets a stream of characters: friends, lovers, relatives and strangers. The pervading malaise enveloping Anna is brought out by Akerman's trademark style of static camera shots, understated images, monologues and silence. A grim portrait of one woman adrift as well as a vision of an insensate Europe. (French with English subtitles) ★★½ VHS: $29.99

Rendezvous in Paris

(1995, 100 min, France, Eric Rohmer) *Mathias Megaro, Clara Bellar, Judith Chancel, Antoine Basler.* A trio of heartbreaking tales from director Rohmer. All of the films tackle themes of fidelity and trust, chance and coincidence, but none as well as the opening piece, *A 7 pm Rendezvous.* When a young woman learns that her boyfriend may be cheating on her, she arranges a meeting with a stranger in order to get at the truth. The second film, *The Benches of Paris,* depicts a romantic tug-of-war between a man who craves the affections of a woman who is merely using him to get back at her cheating husband. The last tale, *Mother and Child 1907,* tells of the improper seduction of an art student by a pick-up artist in the Picasso Museum. Driven by dialogue, each of these mini-films showcase attractive performers and, as always, Rohmer's graceful romantic touch. (French with English subtitles) ★★★ VHS: $29.99

Renegades

(1989, 106 min, US, Jack Sholder) *Lou Diamond Phillips, Kiefer Sutherland, Jami Gertz.* Labored police thriller with Sutherland as an undercover cop who teams with Lakota Indian Phillips to track down killers who stole a sacred Indian artifact. Supposedly set in Philadelphia, but most of the scenes will be unrecognizable to natives. ★½ VHS: $12.99

R

Requiem for a Dream

Repentance

(1983, 151 min, USSR, Tengiz Abuladze) *Avtandil Makharadze, Zeinab Botsvadze*. A savage, outrageous satire, this is a nightmarish political allegory about the excesses of the Stalinist era. A mysterious old woman defies the law and repeatedly exhumes the body of a recently deceased local chieftain. In a series of flashbacks, we learn that the much loved Georgian mayor was actually a despotic ruler, a Stalinist bully — with the gestures of Mussolini and the mustache of Hitler — who was content only with power, no matter the cost. An important, thought-provoking film. (Russian with English subtitles) ★★★ VHS: $19.99

The Replacement Killers

(1998, 88 min, US, Antoine Fuqua) *Chow Yun-Fat, Mira Sorvino, Michael Rooker, Jürgen Prochnow*. The American film debut of prodigious Hong Kong superstar Chow-Yun Fat must rank as a disappointment. This is a far cry from the movies that won Chow a following in the West — the delirious gun operas of directors John Woo and Ringo Lam. The film's thin plot is even a steal from Woo's *The Killer*: Chow's hit man — ordered by his employer to murder a cop's young son as revenge for the drug bust death of his own slimy dealer son — has a last-second change of heart, and spends the rest of the film trying to protect his initial hit. Chow is his usual ultra-cool self, and even Sorvino is fun as the streetwise tough who reluctantly assists him. But director Fuqua's style is all attitude and posturing, vapidly aping Woo and Lam, but possessing none of their passion or artistry. An entertaining though empty action flick. ★★½ VHS: $9.99; DVD: $14.99

The Replacements

(2000, 118 min, US, Howard Deutch) *Keanu Reeves, Gene Hackman, Jon Favreau, Orlando Jones, Rhys Ifans*. All the good will Keanu created with *The Matrix* evaporates while watching this near-terrible movie. Reeves plays a disgraced ex-star of the college gridiron, who blew a crucial play in a bowl game. When the pro players go on strike, Reeves and a motley group of stereotypes are called upon to be... The Replacements! Or scabs, really — a political issue this movie sidesteps by making the pros a bunch of disgusting, pampered jackasses. (One wonders what went through the Hollywood union crew's collective mind while

making this film.) It's hard not to get a little riled during the Big Game and root for the underdogs, but the road to the game is a rough one: wretched comedy, moronic dialogue, with only the always-professional Hackman to get you by. ★½ VHS: $14.99; DVD: $24.99

Repo Man

(1983, 92 min, US, Alex Cox) *Emilio Estevez, Harry Dean Stanton*. Scorned, feared and ruthless...he's a breed apart...he's a repo man. This raunchy romp sideswipes white dopes on punk, life in the 'burbs, hot-blooded Puerto Ricans and alien-in-the-car flicks. 'Nuff said? (Letterboxed) ★★★½ VHS: $14.99; DVD: $29.99

Report to the Commissioner

(1975, 112 min, US, Milton Katselas) *Michael Moriarty, Yaphet Kotto, Richard Gere*. A high-tension police drama with Moriarty as a rookie cop who accidentally kills an undercover policewoman, resulting in a departmental cover-up. ★★★ VHS: $29.99

Repulsion

(1965, 105 min, GB, Roman Polanski) *Catherine Deneuve, Yvonne Furneaux, Ian Hendry*. An eerie, kaleidoscope profile of a troubled young girl, imprisoned by her sexual fears and splintered by her shattered psyche. When her sister leaves her alone for the weekend, she is thrust into a world of mental deterioration and hallucinatory nightmares. Polanski directs a profoundly moving performance by Deneuve as the demure manicurist plagued by frightening visions. ★★★★ VHS: $19.99

Requiem for a Dream

(2000, 102 min, US, Darren Aronofsky) *Ellen Burstyn, Jared Leto, Jennifer Connelly, Marlon Wayans, Christopher McDonald, Louise Lasser, Sean Gullette*. In his hallucinatory, hypnotic and brilliantly executed second feature, *Pi* director Aronofsky (who cowrote the screenplay with the author of the novel, Hubert Selby) has made a mind-numbing exploration of a mother and son's disparate, gradual descent into the abyss of drug addiction. Not content to simply make a "just-say-no" treatise, Aronofsky delves into the mindset and routine of his characters in astonishingly filmic set pieces, allowing facts and attitudes to speak for themselves without hyperbole or agenda. A very effective Leto is Harry, a small-time dealer and full-time user who's not above hocking his mother's TV for drug money. His mother, Sara (Burstyn), is happy just to dream about being a contestant on her favorite TV show. When it appears Sara will be a contestant, she begins a harrowing weight reduction program, aided by diet pills. As both mother and son attempt the realization of their dreams (he's trying to raise money for his girlfriend's dress shop), each becomes ensnared in an out-of-control spiral. Connelly and Wayans are equally compelling as, respectively, Harry's girlfriend and business partner. But it is Burstyn who grounds the film with a startling, immensely moving performance

of a woman slowly losing control. It is a mesmerizing portrait every bit as grounded as Aronofsky's unsettling, immaculate vision. ★★★★ VHS: $102.99; DVD: $24.99

Requiem for Dominic

(1990, 88 min, Germany/US, Robert Dornhelm) *Felix Mitterer, Viktoria Schubert*. Set amidst the December 1989 Romanian uprising which toppled Ceaucescu, this docudrama combines feature film sequences along with shocking and sometimes brutal documentary-style footage of the revolution with unrelenting realism. The story follows the true-life story of Dominic Paraschiv, a political activist wrongly accused of murdering 80 of his colleagues. A childhood friend returns from exile to champion his cause. Director Dornheim delivers a potent and harrowing tale of political upheaval. (German with English subtitles) ★★★ VHS: $79.99

The Rescuers

(1977, 79 min, US, Wolfgang Reitherman, John Lounsbery & Art Stevens) *Voices of: Eva Gabor, Bob Newhart, Geraldine Page*. A group of mice named the Rescue Aid Society find a bottle with an SOS from a little girl named Penny. They must save her from the evil Madame Medusa and her creepy crocodiles who plan to use Penny to retrieve a valuable diamond from a small cave. As usual, Disney's animation and musical score are excellent. ★★★ VHS: $26.99

The Rescuers Down Under

(1990, 109 min, US, Hendel Butoy) *Voices of: Eva Gabor, Bob Newhart*. This appealing sequel to Disney's *The Rescuers* finds mice Bernard and Miss Bianca traveling to Australia to rescue a young boy and a near-extinct eagle. ★★★ VHS: $22.99; DVD: $29.99

Reservoir Dogs

(1992, 100 min, US, Quentin Tarantino) *Harvey Keitel, Tim Roth, Steve Buscemi, Michael Madsen, Christopher Penn, Lawrence Tierney, Quentin Tarantino*. With one of the most intense and original directing debuts in memory, Tarantino manages with great success to add a new tier to the gangster film genre. The film opens with the bloody aftermath of a failed jewelry heist during which the surviving thieves go to extreme lengths to root out the "rat" in their midst. Bolstered by an excellent ensemble, Tarantino effectively presents his story in an exciting and unique non-linear style. With gritty dialogue and a level of realistic violence which borders on pornographic, the film gives the viewer an unusual fly-on-the-wall perspective of a desperado lifestyle. (Letterboxed VHS available for $14.99) ★★★★ VHS: $9.99; DVD: $24.99

Steve Buscemi and Harvey Keitel square off in *Reservoir Dogs*

R

The Respectful Prostitute

(1955, 75 min, France, Charles Brabant & Marcel Pagliero) *Ivan Desny, Barbara Laage.* The seething racial hatred of America's Deep South is the theme in this surprisingly hard-hitting melodrama adapted from a play by Jean-Paul Sartre. When a drunken white man, a senator's son, kills an innocent black bystander on a train, the police conspire to call it self-defense and begin a manhunt for the dead man's black friend. The only witness to the killing is a white woman who is embroiled in the controversy when the law resorts to bribes, blackmail and violence in an effort to get her to recant her testimony and save the killer. Years ahead of its time, this fascinating story is a powerful and terribly disturbing look into the soulless void of man. (Dubbed) ★★★ VHS: $19.99

Restoration

(1995, 118 min, GB, Michael Hoffman) *Robert Downey, Jr., Sam Neill, David Thewlis, Meg Ryan, Polly Walker, Ian McKellen, Hugh Grant.* An unexpected and lavish period drama, *Restoration* is an impressively mounted production rich in character and tone. It's mid-1600s England, a time when that country embraced the passions of the intellect and the sensuous. Young doctor Robert Merivel (Downey) balances his energies between hedonistic pursuits and his profession. A chance meeting with Charles II (Neill) elevates the buffoonish Merivel to court physician. But when he is coerced into marrying the king's mistress (Walker), he suffers his majesty's wrath when he falls in love with her. Thus sets Merivel on a compelling and at times fascinating odyssey through the course of English history which restores his and a country's humanity. Despite its change of gears from frothy to serious (or maybe because of it), *Restoration* engages as it provokes. ★★★½ VHS: $19.99

The Resurrected

(1991, 108 min, US, Dan O'Bannon) *Chris Sarandon, John Terry.* Screenwriter Dan O'Bannon (*Alien*) tries a rather successful hand at directing this ghastly H. P. Lovecraft tale of a scientist (Sarandon) who goes too far in his attempts to revive the dead. While a little too slow in getting started, the film is revitalized by some gruesome special effects. ★★½

Resurrection

(1980, 103 min, US, Daniel Petrie) *Ellen Burstyn, Sam Shepard, Eva Legallienne, Roberts Blossom, Lois Smith, Richard Farnsworth.* Burstyn gives a powerful performance as a woman who survives a near-fatal car accident, endowing her with the powers of spiritual healing and making her a target of religious fanatics. A graceful, beautiful drama, one of the most underrated films of the 1980s. Shepard is splendid as Burstyn's youthful lover, and stage legend Legallienne is heartbreaking as her wise grandmother. ★★★★ VHS: $9.99

Return from Witch Mountain

(1978, 95 min, US, John Hough) *Bette Davis, Christopher Lee.* Good special effects highlight this amiable sequel to *Escape To Witch Mountain* as Davis and Lee kidnap two psychic alien children to use them in robbing a museum (how does one kidnap a psychic, anyhow?). ★★½

The Return of Frank James

(1940, 92 min, US, Fritz Lang) *Henry Fonda, Gene Tierney.* Fonda reprises his role as Jesse James is this excellent sequel which was nicely directed by Lang. This time he's out to get the man who shot his brother in the back. ★★★½ VHS: $9.99

The Return of Martin Guerre

(1983, 111 min, France, Daniel Vigne) *Gérard Depardieu, Nathalie Baye.* Depardieu and Baye star in this sensuous saga of truth, desire and devotion. After a long absence, Martin Guerre returns to the village of his youth, and to a warm reception from its townspeople. However, his life takes an unexpected turn when his identity comes into question and he is brought to trial. An unabashedly romantic, yet never trite, statement on the strength of love. (American remake: *Sommersby*) (Letterboxed) (French with English subtitles) ★★★½ VHS: $29.99; DVD: $29.99

Return of the Jedi

(1983, 133 min, US, Richard Marquand) *Harrison Ford, Mark Hamill, Carrie Fisher, Billy Dee Williams.* The sixth and final chapter in George Lucas' *Star Wars* series lives up to its expectations as a nail-biting battle for the galaxy, but does not surpass *Star Wars* or *The Empire Strikes Back*. Featuring great special effects, it is also unfortunately the most commercial. The film begins with our heroes attempting to repair the damage of the Empire's strike back, by rescuing Han from the abode of the gangster-slug Jabba the Hut and getting Luke a new hand and a completion to his Jedi training with Yoda. The story then shifts to the Rebellion's grand plan: to destroy the new Death Star, the Emperor and Darth Vader in one final assault. A bit sappy, perhaps, but the audience of the original *Star Wars* grew up between the first and third movies, and was not the target audience of *Jedi*. (Sequel: *Star Wars: Episode 1 — The Phantom Menace*) ★★★½

Return of the Living Dead

(1985, 90 min, US, Dan O'Bannon) *James Karen, Thom Mathews.* Funny and gory horror spoof of "living dead" zombie movies. The dead are ready to party when a secret military chemical brings them back to life. The film which introduced those immortal words: "Send more cops!" (Followed by 2 sequels) ★★½

The Return of the Pink Panther

(1975, 113 min, GB, Blake Edwards) *Peter Sellers, Herbert Lom, Christopher Plummer.* After an 11-year hiatus, Sellers returns to the screen as the hilariously inept Inspector Clouseau. Like many of the post-*Shot in the Dark* sequels, Edwards tends to concentrate too heavily on big, violent sight gags and Sellers' peerless knack for slapstick and pratfalls. Still, this is one of those films that will keep you laughing throughout. (Sequel: *The Pink Panther Strikes Again*) ★★★ VHS: $14.99; DVD: $14.99

The Return of the Secaucus 7

(1980, 100 min, US, John Sayles) *Mark Arnott, Maggie Cousineau, David Strathairn, Gordon Clapp.* What happens when seven former activists get together for a reunion is the focus of Sayles' first directorial work. Ten years after being jailed for a night on trumped-up protesting charges, these friends reminisce about the causes, concerns and convictions of their youth. Emotions flow as the weekend turns into a series of bittersweet realizations regarding the group's goals and accomplishments. ★★★★

The Return of the Soldier

(1985, 101 min, GB, Alan Bridges) *Alan Bates, Glenda Jackson, Julie Christie, Ann-Margret, Ian Holm.* A powerhouse cast highlights this riveting psychological drama adapted from Rebecca West's first novel. During WWI, a soldier (Bates) experiences shell shock and amnesia and returns to his country estate without the memory of his past 20 years. His only recollections are of a bucolic childhood and a youthful love affair. Christie is wonderful as the pampered wife who is only familiar to her husband "like any other guest in the same hotel." A subtle, handsomely mounted and involving production. ★★★½

The Return of Martin Guerre

Return of the Tall Blonde Man with One Black Shoe

(1974, 84 min, France, Yves Robert) *Pierre Richard, Jean Rochefort.* Richard revives his role as the incredibly clutzy and bumbling musician who accidentally stumbles into international intrigue. A hilarious spoof of spy movies. (Dubbed) ★★★ VHS: $19.99

Return of the Vampire

(1943, 69 min, US, Lew Landers) *Bela Lugosi.* Columbia Studios tried to sneak into Universal's demi-monde with this atmospheric tale of a caped vampire named Armand Tesla, stalking the ruins of war-torn London. No matter what name you give the character, when Lugosi plays a vampire, it's Dracula. ★★ VHS: $14.99

Return to Me

(2000, 116 min, US, Bonnie Hunt) *David Duchovny, Minnie Driver, Carroll O'Connor, Robert Loggia, David Alan Grier, Bonnie Hunt, Joely Richardson, James Belushi.* In this heart-warming romantic comedy, Duchovny plays a widower who learns that his deceased wife's heart has been used in a transplant operation. He befriends the recipient (Driver) and falls in love all over again. Comedienne Hunt makes an effective directorial debut, nicely capturing the flavor of her native Chicago. Far-fetched but winsome. ★★★ VHS: $14.99; DVD: $19.99

Return to Oz

(1985, 110 min, US, Walter Murch) *Fairuza Balk, Nicol Williamson, Jean Marsh, Piper Laurie.* Dark and rather depressing sequel to the classic *The Wizard of Oz*, with Dorothy returning to Oz (after a bout in a sanitarium) but finding things changed for the worst. ★★ VHS: $14.99; DVD: $24.99

Return to Paradise

(1998, 109 min, US, Joseph Ruben) *Vince Vaughn, Anne Heche, Joaquin Phoenix, David Conrad, Jada Pinkett.* A good idea in search of a good script, *Return to Paradise* stars Vaughn as Sheriff, a limo driver who, three years earlier, had enjoyed a boisterous, pot-fueled trek through Malaysia with two casual acquaintances. While working one night, he finds Beth (Heche) in the back seat, who informs him that one of those buddies has been arrested for drug dealing and is sentenced to die in a week. The conviction will be reversed if he goes back, takes equal blame, and serves time voluntarily. Amid the soul searching, Sheriff changes his mind everyday, but considering the film's title, there's not much doubt or dramatic suspense to the outcome. The final two plot twists are admittedly surprising, but they are executed way too melodramatically to be as effective as they could have. ★★ VHS: $14.99; DVD: $19.99

Return to Salem's Lot

(1987, 96 min, US, Larry Cohen) *Michael Moriarty, Samuel Fuller, Addison Reed.* Entertaining theatrical sequel to Stephen King's acclaimed TV miniseries. Moriarty plays an anthropologist who, with his young son, travels to the small Northeastern town, overrun by vampires. ★★★ VHS: $14.99

Return to Snowy River

(1988, 97 min, Australia, Geoff Burrowes) *Brian Dennehy, Tom Burlinson.* While not as good as the original *Man from Snowy River*, this drama of romance and ambition set against a backdrop of a horse ranch proves to be diverting, highlighted by lush photography of galloping horses and a nicely drawn villain in Dennehy. The story follows the love affair between young ranchhand Jim (Burlinson) and Jessica, the lovely daughter of the ranch. Once again, Jim must prove his worth in order to win the young woman's hand. ★★½ VHS: $9.99

Reuben, Reuben

(1983, 101 min, US, Robert Ellis Miller) *Tom Conti, Kelly McGillis, Roberts Blossom, Lois Smith.* A wonderfully witty character study with the superb Conti as a recklessly amorous, casually amoral and usually inebriated Scottish poet. Though his last verses were conjured long ago, he suffers no lack of charm as he takes a New England college town by storm. ★★★

Revenge

(1990, 124 min, US, Tony Scott) *Kevin Costner, Anthony Quinn, Madeleine Stowe, Miguel Ferrer.* This tepid romantic thriller stars Costner as a former pilot who travels to Mexico to visit millionaire gangster Quinn. Once there, the hotshot flyboy promptly falls in love with his host's beautiful, bored wife (Stowe). As passions ignite, Quinn quickly learns of the couple's affair, and he initiates a near-fatal beating of the two (Revenge #1); then there's the Revenge of the Revenge, and so on and so on. Director Scott is an accomplished visual stylist, but plot and characterization are not his forte. ★ VHS: $9.99; DVD: $14.99

Revenge of the Nerds

(1984, 90 min, US, Jeff Kanew) *Robert Carradine, Anthony Edwards, Curtis Armstrong, Ted McGinley, Julie Montgomery.* One of the more engaging of the silly teen sex comedies, with Carradine and Edwards leading fellow campus nerds to form their own fraternity. (Followed by 3 sequels) ★★½ VHS: $9.99

Revenge of the Pink Panther

(1978, 99 min, GB, Blake Edwards) *Peter Sellers, Dyan Cannon.* Director Edwards had clearly run out of ideas by the time of this last Sellers go-round as Inspector Clouseau. The film is barely redeemed by the usual pratfalls and a fine performance from Cannon. Quite unfortunately, Sellers gives a sloppy and ill-timed performance as even his comic genius is not able to save Edwards' lackluster material. (Sequel: *Trail of the Pink Panther*) ★★ VHS: $14.99; DVD: $24.99

Reversal of Fortune

(1990, 120 min, US, Barbet Schroeder) *Jeremy Irons, Ron Silver, Glenn Close, Annabella Sciorra, Uta Hagen.* Irons won an Oscar for his stunning portrayal of Claus von Bulow in this remarkable satire on greed and the upper-class, based on the novel by von Bulow's lawyer, Alan Dershowitz. Accused of trying to murder his wife, Sunny, von Bulow was tried, convicted and then eventually acquitted. The film details in fascinating fashion the events leading up to this; all told with a dark and sometimes hilarious sense of humor. Close, who spends most of the film in a coma, is splendid as Sunny; and Silver is terrific as Dershowitz, whose passionate defense for the unlikable von Bulow led to his release. And though both Close and Silver were shamelessly overlooked at Oscar time, it is Irons' masterful and cynical portrait which distinguishes this classic comedy of manners. ★★★★ VHS: $14.99; DVD: $19.99

The Revolt of Job

(1983, 97 min, Hungary, Imre Gyongyossy) *Fereno Zenthe, Hedi Tenessy.* Autobiographical in nature, this touching, compassonate film follows the actions of an elderly Jewish couple who, having lost all seven of their children during Nazi occupation, become determined to retain and pass on their proud heritage. They do so by illegally adopting a gentile boy. Their love and understanding for the boy helps him see the world not as an ugly place, but one in which nature, religion and love are one. (Hungarian with English subtitles) ★★★

Revolution

(1985, 125 min, US, Hugh Hudson) *Al Pacino, Donald Sutherland, Nastassja Kinski, Joan Plowright.* Almost legendary bomb with Pacino as an illiterate trapper who becomes involved in the Revolutionary War when his 14-year-old son joins in the fight against the British. Stick to *1776* if you want to know the story. ★ VHS: $9.99

Rhapsody in August

(1991, 98 min, Japan, Akira Kurosawa) *Sachiko Murase, Richard Gere.* Japanese grand master Kurosawa's eloquent examination of the nuclear holocaust in Nagasaki — as seen through the eyes of a survivor and her four grandchildren 44 years later — is a highly emotional and engrossing drama. Sprinkled throughout with touches of wry humor, the film follows the four youngsters who, deposited by their parents with Grandma for the summer, constantly needle her for more information about the war and the bomb, allowing us to discover the grisly details through their innocent eyes. Ultimately, it is the old lady who takes center stage, however, as she falls into despair over the loss of her husband in the blast as its anniversary draws near. Gere makes a surprisingly effective appearance as an Amerasian relative from Hawaii who comes to visit. This understated film is a beautifully crafted and heartfelt requiem. (Japanese with English subtitles) ★★★½ VHS: $19.99

Rhapsody in Blue

(1945, 139 min, US, Irving Rapper) *Robert Alda, Joan Leslie, Alexis Smith.* As with 1946's *Night and Day*, this biography of musical genius George Gershwin is a fictionalized account of an American icon's life. Alda plays Gershwin, and the film's main interest is the great composer's classic music. Not as much fun as the Porter bio. ★★ VHS: $19.99

Rich and Famous

(1981, 117 min, US, George Cukor) *Candice Bergen, Jacqueline Bisset, David Selby, Hart Bochner, Meg Tilly.* Cukor's last film is a likable, updated remake of *Old Aquaintance*, with Bisset and Bergen taking over the Bette Davis-Miriam Hopkins roles as college friends and rivals. Both novelists, Bisset is the "serious" and single

Ian McKellen as *Richard III*

writer who careens from one sexual encounter to another, while Bergen is the housewife who finds acclaim, but loses a husband, by writing low-brow fiction. ★★★

Rich and Famous

(1987, 104 min, Hong Kong, Taylor Wong) *Chow Yun-Fat, Alex Man, Andy Lau, Carina Lau, Alan Tam.* Raised as brothers in abject poverty, two young men seek help with a gambling debt from a local boss (Yun-Fat). They are poorly prepared for the world they've entered, an escalating conflict between warring crime lords played out with seething violence and deliberate cruelty. Strong bonds are forged, and, simultaneously, shifting loyalties bring about harsh betrayals. While not among the most polished of the Hong Kong film industry's voluminous output, and hampered by hard-to-read and poorly translated subtitles, *Rich and Famous* at least spotlights Chow's screen charisma and the region's breakneck filmmaking style. (Sequel: *Tragic Hero*) (Cantonese with English subtitles) ★★ VHS: $19.99; DVD: $29.99

Rich and Strange

(1934, 92 min, GB, Alfred Hitchcock) *Henry Kendall, Joan Barry.* Hitchcock's favorite film from his British period is a suprisingly funny yarn about a bored couple who inherit a large sum of money and embark on a journey around the world. Their "idyllic" vacation is enlivened by adulteries, swindles, a shipwreck and a tasty meal that turns out to be a fried cat. ★★★ VHS: $9.99

The Rich Man's Wife

(1996, 100 min, US, Amy Holden Jones) *Halle Berry, Christopher McDonald, Peter Greene, Clive Owen.* Derivative, unbelievable and about as thrilling as looking for Iowa license plates on the L.A. Freeway, *The Rich Man's Wife* tries to be a provocative noir; anyone who has seen *any* film noir — either good or bad — will be able to see right through the clichés and oh-so predictable ending. Berry is having marital problems with her rich husband (McDonald); while vacationing in the mountains, she meets one of the relatives from *Deliverance.* Then her husband ends up dead. But what's the real story? The problem with *The Rich Man's Wife* is that there isn't any. ★ VHS: $9.99; DVD: $29.99

Richard Pryor Live! In Concert

(1979, 78 min, US, Jeff Margolis) This concert film, showing the comic at the very peak of his talent, succeeds where most other "live" performance documentaries fall short. Many comedians have flashes of brilliance, but only Pryor's comic tour de force lasts the entire length of the film. Re-creating everything from his heart attack to his pet monkey's sex drive, Pryor's act is, of course, excruciatingly funny. At the same time, the intimacy with which he discusses painful real-life experiences makes this a cathartic experience. ★★★½ VHS: $19.99; DVD: $24.99

Richard III

(1955, 158 min, GB, Laurence Olivier) *Laurence Olivier, Ralph Richardson, Claire Bloom, John Gielgud, Cedric Hardwicke.* Olivier leads a dream cast as the physically grotesque and completely villainous Richard III, King of England. Sir Larry seems to revel in his part as the vile and fiendish hellhound who cavorts his way into conquest on the battlefield and in the boudoir. Outstanding on every level. ★★★★ VHS: $24.99

Richard III

(1995, 106 min, GB, Richard Loncraine) *Ian McKellen, Annette Bening, Jim Broadbent, Maggie Smith, Nigel Hawthorne, Robert Downey, Jr., Kristin Scott Thomas, John Wood, Adrian Dunbar.* McKellen wrote the screenplay adaptation and stars in this virbrant updating of Shakespeare's classic tragedy of betrayal and ambition, which has been streamlined and set in the 1930s. The story traces the rise of Richard (McKellen in a hypnotic performance), the ruthless prince who plots, lies and kills his way to the throne. McKellen and director Loncraine have created a Nazi-like society which Richard commands, and Shakespeare's story and dialogue superbly underscore Richard's oppressive regime and fascist roots. The outstanding production design complements the rampant hysteria of Richard's new order, which has been brilliantly maneuvered by Richard and envisioned by McKellen. ★★★★ VHS: $14.99; DVD: $24.99

Richard's Things

(1980, 104 min, GB, Anthony Harvey) *Liv Ullmann, Amanda Redman, Tim Pigott-Smith, Elizabeth Spriggs, Michael Maloney.* This made-for-TV drama wallows in somber pretentiousness and is unusually stagnant for its subject matter. Ullmann stars as a widow who is seduced by her late husband's girlfriend. A relationship develops, and the two women fall in love. A good premise, but sexual seduction never looked so dreary as Ullmann goes through the film as if in the frozen existential wasteland of Bergmania. ★½

Richie Rich

(1994, 95 min, US, Donald Petrie) *Macaulay Culkin, Edward Herrmann, Christine Ebersole, John Larroquette.* Based on the popular comic book, *Richie Rich* is weak on plot and heavy on the gimmicks, but it's also surprisingly entertaining. Culkin is unusually understated as the richest kid in the world, Richie Rich, who has everything he could want but friends. The story follows his attempts to befriend a group of neighborhood kids, and foil bad guy Larroquette who has stolen the family fortune. ★★½ VHS: $14.99

Ricochet

(1991, 97 min, US, Russell Mulcahy) *John Lithgow, Denzel Washington, Ice T, Kevin Pollak.* A stylized action film starring Lithgow as a crazed serial killer who plots the downfall of a politically ambitious buppie cop (Washington) who sends him to prison. The film is packed with enough non-stop action to please any fan of the genre. Ice T offers strong support as a hip-hop crack-dealing revolutionary. ★★½ VHS: $9.99; DVD: $14.99

Riddance

(1973, 84 min, Hungary, Márta Mészáros) A factory worker pretends to be a student when she meets a handsome scholar at the university. However, after they fall in love, she confesses her working-class background. Though caring little about her class, he will only introduce her to his parents as a fellow student. As she comes closer to acceptance, she realizes that she cannot live under false pretenses and chooses independence over social position. (Hungarian with English subtitles) ★★½ VHS: $69.99

The Riddle of the Dead Sea Scrolls

(1990, 80 min, GB, Richard Cassidy) The Dead Sea Scrolls were hidden during the Maccabean Wars by the Essenes. Their discovery by a shepherd in 1947 provided the world-wide academic community an unparalleled opportunity to examine 2,000-year-old documents with this amount of writing intact and in such good condition. At first dated roughly 150 years before the birth of Christ, later examination questions that. This fascinating documentary explores the implications inherent in the discrepancy between the two schools of thought regarding the dating of the scrolls. *Riddle* is a well-considered exploration of issues which have archeological, historical and religious implications. ★★★ VHS: $24.99

The Riddle of the Sands

(1979, 102 min, GB, Tony Maylan) *Michael York, Jenny Agutter, Simon MacCorkindale.* A rousing thinking-man's adventure film set in the early part of the 1900s which follows the fantastic adventures of two young British yachtsmen who, while on a pleasure cruise on the North Sea, stumble upon a German plot to invade

England. Our daring heroes do what is expected of them — stop the nefarious Germans! ★★★ VHS: $19.99

Ride the High Country

(1962, 94 min, US, Sam Peckinpah) *Randolph Scott, Joel McCrea, Mariette Hartley.* Peckinpah's first masterwork and one of the great, classic westerns. Scott and McCrea (who must have at least 50 westerns between them) are two aging ex-lawmen who have helped tame the West that no longer has a place for them. McCrea is hired to transport gold from a mining community; he hires Scott and a young cowboy to help, unaware the two men are conspiring to steal the shipment. The literate script, beautiful locations and touching performances make this melancholy western linger in one's memory. ★★★½ VHS: $19.99

Ride with the Devil

(1999, 138 min, US, Ang Lee) *Tobey Maguire, Skeet Ulrich, Jewel, Jeffrey Wright, Simon Baker, Jonathan Rhys Meyers, Jim Caviezel, Thomas Guiry, Tom Wilkinson, Mark Ruffalo.* This Civil War adventure covers an especially fractious segment: southern Bushwhackers in Missouri waging a guerrilla war against northern Jayhawkers. The Bushwhackers here include Maguire as the son of an immigrant northern sympathizer, his buddy Ulrich, and a freed slave (Wright). Folk singer Jewel, in her film debut, is impressive as a young widow who provides them with shelter during a dangerous winter. The complicated connections lead to some appropriately chaotic battles, but director Lee generally fails to translate these action scenes dramatically. However, the cinematography is majestic, and the compelling story comes complete with rustically poetic dialogue (the screenplay is by longtime collaborator James Schamus) and natural performances by the ensemble cast. ★★★ VHS: $14.99; DVD: $24.99

Rider on the Rain

(1970, 119 min, France, René Clément) *Marlene Jobert, Charles Bronson, Jill Ireland.* A surprisingly good, nail-biting thriller. Bronson is Harry Dobbs, a police inspector in a small French village who unwittingly becomes involved in a bizarre murder mystery involving a mysterious drifter, rape and revenge. In a genre that all too often sinks to insipid levels, this intelligent and taut Hitchcockian puzzler is a refreshing alternative. (In English) ★★★

Riders of the Storm

(1986, 92 min, GB, Maurice Philips) *Dennis Hopper, Michael J. Pollard.* Offbeat comedy about a group of high-flying Vietnam vets who set out to sabotage the presidential campaign of a conservative female candidate. ★★½

Riders to the Sea

(1987, 45 min, Ireland, Ronan O'Leary) *Geraldine Page, Amanda Plummer, Sachi Parker.* Page stars (in her final screen performance) in this powerful rendition of J.M. Synge's classic one-act play about three women waiting in quiet desperation for word for a son who has disappeared at sea. ★★★

Ridicule

(1996, 102 min, France, Patrice Leconte) *Charles Berling, Jean Rochefort, Fanny Ardant.* With a barrage of pomp and circumstance and a

Tobey Maguire and Skeet Ulrich in Ang Lee's *Ride with the Devil*

pocketful of wit, this extravagant and delightful period piece follows the travails of an overly eager and naïvely optimistic young viscount, Ponceludon (Berling), who sets out for the court of Louis XVI to petition the king. He wants to build a series of canals and dikes to drain swamp land and restore health and prosperity to his serfs. Of course, upon his arrival at Versailles, he is regarded as nothing more than a country bumpkin and soon learns that the greatest currency in the palace is repartee. To achieve any hope of audience with the king, one must be a master of the rejoinder. He excels, of course, but this only brings the notice of Ardant, an influential countess whose friendship is as much a hazard as it is a help. Director Leconte is very much at home in the regalia of costume spectacle. (French with English subtitles) ★★★½ VHS: $19.99

Riff Raff

(1992, 94 min, GB, Ken Loach) *Robert Carlyle, Emer McCourt.* This is guerrilla filmmaking at its finest. Loach's ultra-realistic, documentary-style peek into the lives of lower-class British construction workers is a marvelously subversive skewering of England's collapsing welfare state. The action centers around a young Glaswegian drifter named Stevie who arrives at a London construction site and is taken in by the regulars of the crew. Peppered with moments of deep insight as well as hilarious comedy, the film's fly-on-the-wall perspective offers a remarkably personal and unapologetic view of the people buried beneath the ashes of the British Empire. Featuring thick dialects from all over the U.K., the film's gritty dialogue is subtitled for American audiences. ★★★★ VHS: $19.99

Rififi

(1955, 116 min, France, Jules Dassin) *Jean Servais, Carl Mohner, Jules Dassin.* The archetypical heist flick, this delightful movie concerns itself with four sleazy Montmartre jewel thieves who plan and execute a daring robbery but soon find that their fellow partners are more dangerous than the police. Director Dassin, who moved to France after being blacklisted in the States during the McCarthy era, meticulously enacts the robbery in a daring and won-

derfully tense 25-minute sequence filmed in total silence. (French with English subtitles) ★★★★ VHS: $29.99; DVD: $29.99

The Right Stuff

(1983, 193 min, US, Philip Kaufman) *Sam Shepard, Ed Harris, Scott Glenn, Dennis Quaid, Fred Ward, Kathy Baker, Barbara Hershey, Veronica Cartwright.* All involved with this mammoth, sensational adaptation of Tom Wolfe's best-seller about the early days of America's space program certainly have the right stuff, too. A fabulous cast including Shepard as pioneer pilot Chuck Yeager, and Harris, Glenn, Quaid and Ward as our first astronauts are all mesmerizing in their depiction of the men whose courage and skill began our exploration into space. The film, which is over three hours long, seems half that running time thanks to exceptional editing and photography, a well-defined screenplay, enthralling aerospace sequences, and director Kaufman's keen eye for pacing and detail. (VHS available letterboxed or pan & scan) ★★★★ VHS: $24.99; DVD: $19.99

Rikisha-Man

(1958, 105 min, Japan, Hiroshi Inagaki) *Toshiro Mifune.* This Venice Film Festival Grand Prix winner is a classic story of unrequited love. Mifune stars as a feisty rikisha cart-puller who helps a lost boy home, where he falls hopelessly in love with the boy's beautiful mother. The cultural differences between the two preclude any relationship in this sad and unforgettable story. (Japanese with English subtitles) ★★★

Rikki and Pete

(1988, 107 min, Australia, Nadia Tass) *Nina Landis, Stephen Kearney, Bruce Spence, Bruno Lawrence.* From the director and writer (David Parker) of *Malcolm* comes this gadget-laden follow-up about an off-the-wall inventor and his geologist sister who escape the local sheriff by fleeing to the Outback. Suffice it to say, chaos ensues in this humorous though lightweight "Les Miserables Down Under." ★★½

Rikyu

(1991, 116 min, Japan, Hiroshi Teshigahara) *Rantaro Mikuni, Tsutomu Yamazaki.* From the

R

director of *Woman in the Dunes* comes this intelligent drama on the strained relationship between the art of politics and the politics of art. Set in the 16th century, a power-hungry peasant rises to leadership after a powerful warlord is killed. Ignorant of the traditions of higher Japanese culture, Hideyoshi hires Rikyu, a wise and elderly tea master, to teach him the Zen approach to Ikebana (flower arranging) as well as the delicate and mysterious tea ceremony. However, social and spiritual instruction soon evolve into political advice, a turn of events unforeseen by the taciturn old teacher. (Japanese with English subtitles) ★★★ VHS: $79.99; DVD: $19.99

Ringmaster

(1998, 90 min, US, Neil Abramson) *Jerry Springer, Jaime Pressly, Molly Hagan, William McNamara, Michael Dudikoff.* Take all the excitement of a real Jerry Springer TV show, then remove the drama of having actual people airing their dirty laundry in public, and you get this pointless film. Jerry himself is reduced to cameo status as the film focuses on two stories: one a white-trash family that features a stepfather-stepdaughter coupling; and a black-trash trio of girlfriends who all hate one two-timing (three-timing, four-timing) man. Hair-pulling, breast-baring, mother-cursing just isn't as much fun when you know it's scripted, like the day you found out professional wrestling isn't real. ★½ VHS: $14.99; DVD: $14.99

Rio Bravo

(1959, 141 min, US, Howard Hawks) *John Wayne, Dean Martin, Angie Dickinson, Ricky Nelson, Walter Brennan.* Hawks's classic western with Wayne as a small town sheriff determined to keep a killer confined to his jail, despite a limited source of man-power in the town. Flavorful direction from Hawks. (The basis for *Assault on Precinct 13*) ★★★½ VHS: $14.99; DVD: $19.99

Rio Grande

(1950, 105 min, US, John Ford) *John Wayne, Maureen O'Hara, Ben Johnson, Victor McLaglen, Claude Jarman, Jr., Chill Wills.* The third entry in director Ford's cavalry trilogy (*Fort Apache* and *She Wore a Yellow Ribbon* came before it) is another compelling western, here centering on the conflict between commander Wayne and his estranged son (Jarman), who he has not seen in 15 years. O'Hara is Wayne's ex-wife, determined to come between them. ★★★ VHS: $14.99; DVD: $24.99

Riot

(1969, 97 min, US, Buzz Kulik) *Gene Hackman, Jim Brown, Gerald S. O'Laughlin.* Brown reluctantly helps fellow jailbird Hackman start a riot to cover their prison breakout in this stereotyped, extremely violent jailhouse romp. Wonderfully clichéd performances, hard-boiled dialogue and the prison's (Arizona State Penitentiary) real warden, personnel and inmates as performers combine to make this film an exploitative, entertaining treat. ★★½

Riot in Cell Block 11

(1954, 80 min, US, Don Siegel) *Neville Brand, Leo Gordon.* A collection of cutthroats seize control of their cellblock in this hardboiled crime flick. A gritty, early entry from the director of *Dirty Harry.* ★★★ VHS: $19.99

The Rise of Catherine the Great

(1934, 92 min, GB, Paul Czinner) *Douglas Fairbanks, Jr., Elisabeth Bergner.* A lavish though slowly paced historical drama about the Russian Czarina whose life was needlessly spoiled by a stolid planned marriage. The film does not depict the legend of her ultimate demise; we can all be thankful that Penthouse Productions (creators of the infamous *Caligula*) failed to complete their proposed telling of the story. ★★★½ VHS: $19.99

The Rise to Power of Louis XIV

(1966, 100 min, France, Roberto Rossellini) *Jean-Marie Patte, Raymond Jourdan.* Rossellini's first in his series of historical dramas tells the story of Louis XIV's rise to power as well as his decline. Includes a memorable scene where he forces his court to watch him devour a 14-course meal. Made in only 23 days for French television, this is one of Rossellini's most important and influential works. (French with English subtitles) ★★★½

Rising Sun

(1993, 126 min, US, Philip Kaufman) *Sean Connery, Wesley Snipes, Harvey Keitel, Mako, Stan Shaw, Tia Carrere, Steve Buscemi.* Michael Crichton's adaptation of his Japan-bashing, high-tech best-seller is a tedious tale of corporate espionage. Connery and Snipes are an unlikely duo as a pair of LAPD liaison officers sent to investigate a murder at the boardroom of a major Japanese multinational. Of course, their search for the killer leads them right into the middle of the trade wars between Japan and the United States. All the while, the older and wiser Connery must explain to Snipes all of the tricks the Japanese are using to bury the U.S. economically. Ultimately, the film can't decide whether it wants to be a full-fledged action-thriller or an overly worded primer on Japanese business treachery. ★★ VHS: $9.99; DVD: $24.99

Risky Business

(1983, 99 min, US, Paul Brickman) *Tom Cruise, Rebecca DeMornay, Curtis Armstrong, Bronson Pinchot.* Cruise created a small sensation in his first starring role as a college-bound teenager who turns his upper-class Chicago home into a bordello while his parents are out of town. There are plenty of laughs, and a good, youthful supporting cast. ★★★ VHS: $9.99; DVD: $19.99

Rita, Sue and Bob Too

(1986, 93 min, GB, Alan Clarke) *Siobhan Finneran, Michelle Holmes, George Costigan.* This interesting sex comedy with a dark edge features Finneran and Holmes as Rita and Sue, two lower-class teenagers who baby-sit for nouveau riche yuppie Bob (Costigan). Bob initiates both girls sexually in very quick succession and everything moves along quite happily until Rita becomes pregnant, signaling a turn for the worse for all parties concerned. The film captures the gritty hopelessness of the industrial midlands of England quite well, and is marred only slightly by a trite ending. ★★★

The Rite

(1969, 75 min, Sweden, Igmar Bergman) *Ingrid Thulin, Gunnar Bjornstrand, Anders Ek, Eric Hell.* Bergman's claustrophic treatise on censorship and the arts pits three members of a succesful cabaret act against a Kafka-esque magistrate (Hell) who must determine whether a piece of their show is "obscene." The troupe is comprised of Thulin, her husband Bjornstrand and Ek, with whom she is having a torrid affair. As the judge individually interrogates them, their stories unravel along with all of their interpersonal foibles and neuroses. The film culminates, naturally, with their performing the offending piece (a kind of sexually based pagan ritual) for the astonished judge. For lovers of Bergman, this is probably must viewing. For most others, however, the opressive sense of ennui may prove too much to bear, even considering the film's graciously short running time. (Swedish with English subtitles) ★★½ VHS: $29.99

The Ritz

(1976, 91 min, US, Richard Lester) *Jack Weston, Rita Moreno, Treat Williams, F. Murray Abraham, Kaye Ballard, Jerry Stiller.* Lester's riotous farce stars Weston as a Cleveland garbage collector on the lam in a gay bathhouse. There he encounters entertainer Moreno ("You thought I was a drag queen?"), detective Williams ("You madicon hump!"), the Andrews Sisters and the ever-popular steam room. Not as hilarious or as refined as the Broadway production (written by Terrence McNally), but very entertaining nonetheless. ★★★ VHS: $19.99

The River

(1951, 99 min, India, Jean Renoir) *Patricia Walters, Adrienne Corri.* In 1949 and 1950, Renoir traveled to Bengal to make his first color film, the story of a large British family living on the banks of the Ganges River. Though it has never attained the classic status of many of his earlier works, it remains one of Renoir's loveliest, drollest and most pleasing films. The film features outstanding cinematography by Jean's brother Claude. Also of special note is Renoir's assistant director for the production: Satyajit Ray. ★★★★ VHS: $29.99

The River

(1984, 124 min, US, Mark Rydell) *Mel Gibson, Sissy Spacek, Shane Bailey, Becky Jo Lynch, Scott Glenn.* Gibson and Spacek play a farm couple struggling against nature and business interests to hold on to their home. Good production values (including lush cinematography by Vilmos Zsigmond) and earnest performances from the two leads can't make up for dramatic inconsistencies. The least of the trilogy of "farm films" released in 1984 (including *Places in the Heart* and *Country*). ★★ VHS: $7.49; DVD: $26.99

River of No Return

(1954, 91 min, US, Otto Preminger) *Robert Mitchum, Marilyn Monroe, Rory Calhoun, Tommy Rettig.* A big, sprawling western (shot in Cinemascope, which means some of the spectacular cinematography will be lost on the small screen) with Mitchum as a farmer who is double-crossed by gambler Calhoun and sets out, with his young son and saloon singer Monroe, to even the score. There's explosive chemistry between Marilyn and Mitchum which propels the film well beyond the usual western adventure. ★★★

R

The River Rat

(1984, 93 min, US, Tom Rickman) *Tommy Lee Jones, Martha Plimpton, Brian Dennehy.* A semi-involving, if not completely successful tale of a wrongly convicted man (Jones) paroled from prison attempting to establish a relationship with the daughter (Plimpton) he's never known. Jones and Plimpton give solid performances, but the film strays off into a subplot about a hidden fortune and an evil prison psychiatrist (Dennehy) which is never as gripping as the genuine moments between father and daughter. ★★½ VHS: $14.99

A River Runs Through It

(1992, 123 min, US, Robert Redford) *Brad Pitt, Craig Sheffer, Tom Skerritt, Emily Lloyd, Brenda Blethyn.* A meticulous and beautifully rendered adaptation of Norman MacLean's autobiographical novella, *A River Runs Through It*, with a romanticized view of aw-shucks country living and astonishing picturesque backdrops. The story follows the relationship between young MacLean, a straight-laced scholar played by Sheffer and his wilder, younger brother, Paul (Pitt). Though opposites in temperament, it is their reverence for fly-fishing which bonds them. As Norman travels to the East to attend college, Paul stays behind in Montana and lives the life of a boozing, cynical journalist. As the brothers are reuinted, MacLean's text is movingly realized: "It is those we live with and love and should know who elude us." ★★★½ VHS: $9.99; DVD: $19.99

The River Wild

(1994, 108 min, US, Curtis Hanson) *Meryl Streep, Kevin Bacon, David Strathairn, John C. Reilly, Joseph Mazzello.* Streep goes the Sigourney Weaver route and tackles the action adventure movie with often rip-roaring results. Streep, husband Strathairn and young son Mazzello go on a white water rafting vacation. Unbeknowst to any of them, neighboring rafter Bacon and his companions are actually escaped criminals on a getaway. And when the latter's guide "unexplainedly" vanishes, Streep and family are ultimately terrorized into helping with their escape. Though the plot is barely seaworthy, director Hanson keeps the film afloat with hair-raising action scenes. Streep propels the film, making it easy to gloss over any inconsistencies. Bacon makes a most effective heavy. (Letterboxed VHS available for $14.99) ★★★ VHS: $9.99; DVD: $24.99

River's Edge

(1986, 99 min, US, Tim Hunter) *Keanu Reeves, Ione Skye, Crispin Glover, Dennis Hopper, Daniel Roebuck.* A perfect counterpiece to Rob Reiner's *Stand by Me*, released the same year, *River's Edge* is the disturbing story of a group of burned-out '80s teens who find the body of a friend killed by a classmate, greeting the discovery with a lack of emotion or concern. A gripping story of youthful alienation and hopelessness. Hopper is effective as a half-crazed ex-biker and, interestingly, is the film's moral center. Based on an actual incident. ★★★ VHS: $14.99; DVD: $19.99

Road Games

(1982, 100 min, Australia, Richard Franklin) *Stacy Keach, Jamie Lee Curtis,.* This early entry from the director of *Psycho II* deals with an Aussie psycho-killer and the trucker (Keach) who sets out to bring him in. Curtis is a hitch-hiker who finds herself in the middle of this "road game." Director Franklin, who at one time studied under Alfred Hitchcock, tries hard to deliver the same shocks and is not entirely unsuccessful. All in all, a decent thriller. ★★½

Road House

(1948, 95 min, US, Jean Negulesco) *Richard Widmark, Ida Lupino, Cornel Wilde.* A torrid melodrama with Widmark and Wilde as partners in a roadside bar who begin feuding when Widmark finds alluring singer Lupino, only to have her fall in love with Wilde. From there, passions and jealousies erupt, leading to betrayal and murder. A solid noir rife with sexual tension, and featuring a slam-bang ending. Lupino is terrific as the raspy-voiced entertainer. ★★★½ VHS: $19.99

Road House

(1989, 114 min, US, Rowdy Harrington) *Patrick Swayze, Ben Gazzara, Sam Elliott, Kelly Lynch.* Swayze plays a tough philosopher who takes a job as a bouncer at a rough 'n' tumble Midwest bar; he comes in conflict with crooked Gazzara. About as dramatically plausible as a philosophy major who doubles as a bouncer, and given to random violence which most assuredly would have upset its hero under any other circumstances. ★ VHS: $14.99

Road Scholar

(1993, 75 min, US, Roger Wesberg) *Andrei Codrescu.* A definite must-see for lovers of Romanian-born poet Codrescu's National Public Radio commentaries. Part documentary, part flight of fancy, the film is basically an extended series of observations by Codrescu on American culture as he motors in a huge Cadillac convertible across the country. First, he has to learn how to drive, an amusing episode in itself. On his journey across the continent, Codrescu finds an assortment of oddballs to interview including New Age "channelers," Las Vegas wedding vendors and the inhabitants of Biosphere Two, among others. ★★★

The Road to El Dorado

(2000, 89 min, US, Bibo Bergeron, Will Finn & Don Paul) *Voices of: Kevin Kline, Kenneth Branagh, Rosie Perez, Armand Assante, Edward James Olmos.* The appropriately titled *Road to El Dorado* (Hope and Crosby would have felt right at home in this wacky musical comedy) is a delightful animated buddy movie. Kline and Branagh supply the voices for a couple of partners-in-crime, who search for the fabled lost city of gold. After all, they have the map. They find adventure, silly shenanigans, and Dorothy Lamour. . . no, make that a feisty village girl (voiced by Perez). The animation is first-rate, the jokes funny, though the songs are kinda forgettable. ★★★ VHS: $22.99; DVD: $26.99

Road to Morocco

(1942, 83 min, US, David Butler) *Bob Hope, Bing Crosby, Dorothy Lamour, Anthony Quinn.* "We're off on the road to Morocco" Bing and Bob sing as they gallop across the desert on camelback. It's more hilarious one-liners, funny sight gags and sticky situations as Bing sells Bob to a slave trader for a good meal, and both adore Lamour. Second only to *Road to Utopia* (which was next in the series) in the laughs department. ★★★ VHS: $14.99

Road to Rio

(1947, 100 min, US, Norman Z. McLeod) *Bob Hope, Bing Crosby, Dorothy Lamour, The Andrews Sisters, Gale Sondergaard.* One of the funnier Hope-Crosby-Lamour "Road" pictures, with the boys as stowaways arriving in Rio, forming an "authentic" American jazz band, and helping Dorothy escape the influence of her evil aunt. (Sequel: *Road to Bali*) ★★★ VHS: $14.99

Road to Utopia

(1945, 90 min, US, Hal Walker) *Bob Hope, Bing Crosby, Dorothy Lamour, Robert Benchley.* A non-stop barrage of hilarity, *Utopia* probably rates as the best of the seven "Road" pictures. Hope, Crosby and Lamour are off on the road to Alaska in search of gold and romance. What they find are outlaws, talking fish, scheming showgirls and lots of snow. The plot of Bob and Bing helping Dorothy retrieve her stolen gold mine from crooks plays a back seat to the crazy shenanigans, which produces a whirlwind combination of one-liners, impersonations, schtick and in-jokes. Benchley supplies glib commentary throughout. (Sequel: *Road to Rio*) ★★★½ VHS: $14.99; DVD: $14.99

The Road to Wellville

(1994, 120 min, US, Alan Parker) *Anthony Hopkins, Matthew Broderick, Bridget Fonda, John Cusack, Dana Carvey, Colm Meaney.* Part Bugs Bunny and part John Huston, Hopkins stars as Dr. John Harvey Kellogg, he of the cereal fame, who later in life ran the spa/hospital Battle Creek Sanitorium. Kellogg's principles were based on the philosophy of "no meat and no sex," and that the key to good health lies in the constant cleansing of the bowels. With this premise, director Parker takes an outrageous journey down the halls of the sanitorium, where enemas both become a part of the daily routine and form the core of the humor of the film, whose cheap flatulation jokes become redundant. It's a shame an engaging cast is forced to make personal hygiene funny. ★★ VHS: $14.99

Road Trip

(2000, 94 min, US, Todd Phillips) *Breckin Meyer, Seann William Scott, Amy Smart, Tom Green, Paulo Costanzo, Anthony Rapp, D.J. Qualls, Fred Ward, Andy Dick.* Executive producer Ivan Reitman revisits his *Animal House* formula over two decades later, and, darned, if it doesn't still work. Combining the gross with the sweet, Phillips directs a group of dormmates (who might be more realistic than those in his controversial documentary *Frat House*) who set off from N.Y. to Texas on the most important mission of their lives: to retrieve a sex tape mistakenly sent to one of their girlfriends. Green holds down the fort at the dorm with such amiable schtick as tasting a mouse before feeding it to a pet snake. But he can't steal the show from the winning cast and their bizarre adventures — that task goes to scrawny and pasty Qualls, who goes from nerd to hero when he learns to let loose. *Road Trip* is no classic, but it's sure to emerge from the gross-out renaissance's ashes unscathed. ★★★ VHS: $14.99; DVD: $26.99

The Road Warrior

The Road Warrior

(1982, 94 min, Australia, George Miller) *Mel Gibson, Bruce Spence.* He roams the barren plains of a post-apocalyptic wasteland, a tight-lipped, leather clad loner, living only for the ever-precious petrol. Gibson writes the book on existential cool in Miller's violent vision of a fuel-less future. Suspenseful throughout, this boasts great action sequences and a stunning, futuristic look. (VHS available letter-boxed or pan & scan) (Sequel: *Mad Max Beyond Thunderdome*) ★★★½ VHS: $14.99; DVD: $19.99

Roadracers

(1994, 93 min, US, Robert Rodriguez) *David Arquette, Salma Hayek, William Sadler, Jason Wiles.* Quirky to the extreme, this made-for-cable movie was part of a series of remakes of vintage AIP exploitation films. Director Rodriguez is obviously right at home in the genre, and he revels in having a rocking good time. A young punk (Arquette) feels out of place in his small-town life. Onto the scene comes a local tough guy who has it in for our hero. Can he survive his confrontaton with the jock and his lawman pop and get out of town alive? Rodriguez throws in enough twists to make the film transcend its cable and genre limitations. *Roadracers* is a bad-movie remake that gets better the faster it roars along. ★★★ VHS: $89.99

Roads to the South

(1978, 100 min, France, Joseph Losey) *Yves Montand, Miou-Miou.* With cool directorial elegance and subtle perception, Losey creates a complex portrait of a man grappling with deep personal conflicts. Montand plays an exiled Spanish revolutionary who, after establishing himself as a successful screenwriter abroad, returns to his homeland to fight Fascism; but instead he's forced to deal with a lifetime of personal deceptions, illusions and hypocrisies. (French with English subtitles) ★★★ VHS: $29.99

Roadside Prophets

(1992, 96 min, US, Abbe Wool) *John Doe, Adam Horovitz, John Cusack, Arlo Guthrie, David Carradine, Dr. Timothy Leary.* With the screen-writing credit of Alex Cox's quintessential punk movie *Sid and Nancy* attached to his resume, Wool's directorial debut is an all-the-more disappointing attempt at '90s hip. Doe teams with Horovitz for this story of two reluctant heroes without a clear destination. Set against the motorcycle subculture and the lure of the open road, the film tries to blend the idealism of the '60s with the unanswered promises of the '90s. In their travels, the protagonists encounter assorted visionaries, freaks and philosophers. With no memorable dramatics, *Roadside Prophets* at least features a great soundtrack. ★½ VHS: $14.99

The Roaring Twenties

(1939, 106 min, US, Raoul Walsh) *James Cagney, Humphrey Bogart, Jeffrey Lynn, Priscilla Lane.* Cagney stars as a WWI veteran who returns home to New York, becoming an underworld kingpin. Bogart and Lynn are Cagney's war buddies who become his associates. One of the last of the great Warner Brothers gangster films. ★★★½ VHS: $19.99

Rob Roy

(1995, 139 min, GB, Michael Caton-Jones) *Liam Neeson, Jessica Lange, Tim Roth, John Hurt, Eric Stoltz.* Neeson dons the historical kilt of 18th-century Scottish hero Robert Roy MacGregor. And, though the film suggested by his life lacks a particular warmth and narrative strength, *Rob Roy*'s skirt fits Neeson like a glove. As the almost saint-like leader of the Clan MacGregor, Rob Roy must rescue hearth and home (in the form of Lange) from the nefarious clutches of the British, represented here by dishonest noble-man Hurt and the scene-stealing Roth as a dastardly dandy. Director Caton-Jones displays a flair for evocation and inducing richly textured performances from his cast, though the film's screenplay is in need of the necessary swash-buckle that generally makes these adventures so enduring. ★★½ VHS: $9.99; DVD: $19.99

The Robe

(1953, 135 min, US, Henry Koster) *Richard Burton, Victor Mature, Jean Simmons, Michael Rennie.* Extravagant, if over-produced, biblical epic with Burton as a Roman guard overseeing Christ's Crucifixion who becomes haunted by his deed. The first Cinemascope film. (Letterboxed VHS available for $19.99) ★★½ VHS: $9.99

Robert et Robert

(1979, 105 min, France, Claude Lelouch) *Charles Denner, Jacques Villeret, Jean-Claude Brialy.* Lelouch's humorous, affecting portrait of two lonely men: a middle-aged, hot-headed cab driver, and a bumbling rookie patrolman. Stood up at a dating service, they quickly develop a fast relationship. (French with English subtitles) ★★★

Roberta

(1935, 105 min, US, William A. Seiter) *Irene Dunne, Fred Astaire, Ginger Rogers, Lucille Ball, Randolph Scott.* Jerome Kern-Otto Harbach musical with Dunne as a young heiress, Astaire as a band leader, and Rogers masquerading as a countess. The story, to be honest, is fluffy even by '30s standards, but the sublime teaming of Astaire and Rogers elevates it — giving it a degree of unexpected charm. Songs include "Smoke Gets in Your Eyes" and "I Won't Dance." ★★★

Robin and Marian

(1976, 112 min, GB, Richard Lester) *Sean Connery, Audrey Hepburn, Robert Shaw, Richard Harris, Nicol Williamson, Denholm Elliott, Ian Holm.* A genuinely touching and affecting love story which offers a revisionist view of medieval history and our legendary friends from Sherwood Forest. Connery and Hepburn are a magical pairing as the aging Robin Hood and Maid Marian in this telling of Robin's return to Sherwood after years of exile. ★★★ VHS: $14.99

Robin and the 7 Hoods

(1964, 103 min, US, Gordon Douglas) *Frank Sinatra, Dean Martin, Bing Crosby, Sammy Davis, Jr., Peter Falk, Edward G. Robinson.* The Rat Pack is back (in their final outing) in this fairly entertaining comic romp about 1920s Chicago hoods. ★★½ VHS: $14.99

Robin Hood

(1973, 83 min, US, Wolfgang Reitherman) *Voices of: Brian Bedford, Pat Buttram, Andy Devine, Phil Harris, Terry-Thomas, Peter Ustinov.* Walt Disney's animated version of the Robin Hood legend, with the Bandit of Sherwood Forest as a cunning fox. Cute and well done. ★★★ VHS: $22.99; DVD: $29.99

Robin Hood

(1991, 104 min, US, John Irvin) *Patrick Bergin, Jürgen Prochnow, Jeroen Krabbé, Edward Fox, Uma Thurman.* Swashbuckling adventure with one of 1991's "Robin Hood" adaptations. In this version, Bergin plays the nobleman-turned-outlaw who robs from the rich and gives to the poor. Exciting and more dark than previous versions. ★★★ VHS: $19.99

Robin Hood: Men in Tights

(1993, 103 min, US, Mel Brooks) *Cary Elwes, Richard Lewis, Roger Rees, Amy Yasbeck, Tracey Ullman, Mel Brooks, Dom DeLuise, Isaac Hayes.* The once brilliant Brooks provides further proof that his comedic well ran dry long ago with this inane skewering of the legend of Sherwood Forest. Despite rolling out a barrel of half-decent one-liners and sight gags, the film clumsily plods from joke to joke, with very little of interest in between. Elwes does his jolly best to add a spark as Robin of Loxley, but he generally hams things up beyond all proportion. ★★ VHS: $19.99

Robin Hood: Prince of Thieves

(1991, 145 min, US, Kevin Reynolds) *Kevin Costner, Alan Rickman, Morgan Freeman, Mary Elizabeth Mastrantonio, Christian Slater.* A big-hearted retelling of the Robin Hood legend with a whole new story to convey. Costner is the new Robin, and though he lacks the accent and sophistication we all come to expect of the Bandit of Sherwood Forest, he nevertheless gives a believable portrait of the idealistic folk hero. The story pits Robin against the evil Sheriff of Nottingham, who attempts to seize control of the throne of England in King Richard's absence. Rickman gives a hysterical, over-the-top portrayal of the Sheriff — he takes a role which Basil Rathbone had owned for nearly six decades

R

and creates an equally memorable, singular villain. (Letterboxed VHS available for $19.99) ★★★ VHS: $14.99; DVD: $19.99

Robocop

(1987, 103 min, US, Paul Verhoeven) *Peter Weller, Nancy Allen, Dan O'Herlihy, Ronny Cox, Kurtwood Smith, Miguel Ferrer.* When officer Murphy (Weller) of the Detroit Police Department (its services now subcontracted out to a large, faceless conglomerate) is brutally executed in the line of duty, his brain and other body bits become the unwitting components for a new kind of law enforcement robot. Director Verhoeven marshals an exciting array of stunning special effects, exciting action sequences and a razor sharp wit in delivering this scathingly funny, yet nightmarishly believable, parable of corporate capitalism run amok. (Followed by 2 sequels) ★★★½ VHS: $9.99

Robocop 2

(1990, 118 min, US, Irvin Kershner) *Peter Weller, Nancy Allen, Dan O'Herlihy.* This follow-up to Verhoeven's brilliant original lacks the insightful political commentary and wit of the first film. On top of that, the film is excessively violent — to the point of mean-spiritedness. The special effects are excellent, particularly the animated face of the villainous Robocop 2, and the action moves at a spirited pace. ★★ VHS: $9.99

Robocop 3

(1993, 95 min, US, Fred Dekker) *Robert Burke, Nancy Allen, Rip Torn, CCH Pounder.* It's "half-man/half-machine" and all drivel in this rusty retread about the cyborg cop (exit Peter Weller, enter Burke) whose humanity once again clashes with his state-inspired programming when he's caught in the crossfire between a militaristic police force, a renegade group of freedom fighters and a ninja! The creaky screenplay (copenned by the director and comic book scribe Frank Miller) could have used a stiff injection of WD40 oil. ★½ VHS: $9.99

Robot Monster

(1953, 63 min, US, Phil Tucker) *George Nader, Claudia Barrett.* Notoriously bad sci-fi horror film. This is the one where the monster has a diving helmet head and a gorilla-suit body. P.U. ★ VHS: $12.99; DVD: $24.99

Rocco and His Brothers

(1960, 180 min, Italy, Luchino Visconti) *Alain Delon, Renato Salvatori, Claudia Cardinale, Annie Girardot, Katina Paxinou.* An epic tale of five peasant brothers and their widowed mother who migrate from the impoverished south to northern Italy only to find their dreams of happiness shattered when they confront the mean streets of industrial Milan. This neorealist melodrama chronicles the family's struggle in their new world. Told in four episodes, the story centers on Rocco (Delon), the gentle and withdrawn brother who tragically falls in love with Nadia (Girardot), the girlfriend of his thuggish boxer brother. The escalating tensions between the two, fueled by the repressions and frustrations of an unfeeling land, build to a climax of rape and murder. A powerful operatic drama about opposing cultures, lust, greed and the will to survive. (Italian with English subtitles) ★★★½ VHS: $79.99

The Rock

(1996, 131 min, US, Michael Bay) *Sean Connery, Nicolas Cage, Ed Harris, Michael Biehn, John C. McGinley, Bokeem Woodbine, William Forsythe, David Morse.* Connery helps agent Cage break in to Alcatraz and in doing so helps create a cracking good, crackerjack action thriller — plot holes and all. When military man Harris takes control of the defunct prison — holding hostages and threatening nuclear attacks on the city of San Francisco — FBI agent Cage enlists the help of longtime con Connery, who's the only man ever to have escaped from the notorious prison. With a small platoon in tow, they cavort through the catacombs and hallways of the prison, at odds with each other more than their prey. *The Rock* has humor, suspense, and the good sense to give its three very personable stars the text and breathing room to do what they do best. ★★★ VHS: $14.99; DVD: $29.99

Rock Baby, Rock It

(1957, 80 min, US, Murray Douglas Sporup) *Kay Wheeler, John Carroll.* All the cool cats and slick chicks band together to save their local rock club from the mob. The ludicrous script is equalled by appalling performances and shoddy direction, though it certainly does qualify as top-of-the-list late-nite cult status. ★ VHS: $9.99

Rock Hudson's Home Movies

(1992, 63 min, US, Mark Rappaport) Often hilarious, highly original and utterly convincing, this revisionist interpretation of Rock Hudson's film career and life seeks to discover the "real" Hudson through his "reel" persona. Was this Hollywood hunk completely out of touch with his secreted sexuality, or did he throughout his career offer subtle — or not so subtle — hints at his homosexuality. Exploring this idea, Rappaport's insightful and unconventional biography cleverly dissects — through freeze-frame, slo-mo and replays — Hudson's films, seeking clues and overtly gay signals. ★★★ VHS: $29.99

Rock 'N' Roll High School

(1979, 87 min, US, Allan Arkush) *P.J. Soles, Vincent Van Patten, The Ramones, Clint Howard, Paul Bartel, Mary Woronov.* 1970s jail-bait beauty Soles is the blonde student who wants to have the straggly punk band the Ramones play at their high school dance. But uptight authorities will hear nothing of it. What to do? Invite them anyway, listen to wild music and see the students go berserk and burn the school down! Kids just wanna have fun. A late night treat. Includes Ramones standards like "Teenage Lobotomy" and "Now I Wanna Sniff Some Glue." Just thinking about the film brings on a nostalgic tear. ★★★

Rocket Gibraltor

(1988, 100 min, US, Daniel Petrie) *Burt Lancaster, Macaulay Culkin, Suzy Amis, John Glover, Bill Pullman, Kevin Spacey.* Lancaster's commanding presence distinguishes this moving tale about a family coming together to celebrate their dying patriarch's birthday. The film focuses on his special relationship with his young grandchildren who help him realize his last wish. Culkin makes a good impression as one of Lancaster's grandkids. ★★★ VHS: $14.99

The Rocketeer

(1991, 108 min, US, Joe Johnston) *Bill Campbell, Timothy Dalton, Jennifer Connelly, Alan Arkin.* Some great special effects highlight this lightweight though enjoyable family adventure. Set in 1930s Hollywood, the story follows the beginnings of a comic book-like hero, The Rocketeer, who helps fight off the Nazis in Los Angeles (yes, they were there, too). Dalton seems to be having the most fun, playing a Hollywood superstar and Nazi spy. Though the flying sequences are excellent, the script is no more than an ordinary good guys vs. bad guys scenario. What should have been a rollicking roller-coaster ride is merely a genial coupe of turns on a carousel. Based on Dave Steven's '80s comic book. ★★★½ VHS: $9.99; DVD: $29.99

Rocketship X-M

(1950, 77 min, US, Kurt Neuman) *Lloyd Bridges, Hugh O'Brien.* Even though Irving Block was only trying to capitalize on George Pal's publicity for *Destination Moon*, *Rocketship X-M*, while no match for *Moon*, holds up quite well as the Saturday matinee programmer it was intended to be. Bridges and O'Brien are the astronauts headed for the moon who accidentally overshoot it and end up on Mars, partying with the radiation mutants. ★★½ VHS: $19.99; DVD: $24.99

The Rocking Horse Winner

(1950, 91 min, GB, Anthony Pelissier) *John Mills, Valerie Hobson, John Howard Davies.* Moody, though very successful adaptation of the D.H. Lawrence fable about a young boy who discovers that he can predict the winners of horse races by riding his rocking horse. ★★★½

Rocky

(1976, 119 min, US, John G. Avildsen) *Sylvester Stallone, Talia Shire, Burgess Meredith, Carl Weathers, Burt Young.* Sequels aside, let us not forget that this Oscar-winning, Capra-esque boxing drama is quite good, and introduced Stallone to a wide audience, not to mention his popular creation: South Philly boxer Rocky Balboa. Rocky goes after the title against champion Apollo Creed (Weathers); he's aided by trainer Meredith. Shire is quite good as Stallone's plain-Jane girlfriend. (Followed by 4 sequels) ★★★½ VHS: $9.99; DVD: $19.99

Rocky II

(1979, 119 min, US, Sylvester Stallone) *Sylvester Stallone, Talia Shire, Burgess Meredith, Burt Young, Carl Weathers.* Stallone returns as Rocky Balboa in this sequel to the Oscar-winning original. Rocky goes after yet another championship. Nothing new here, and not nearly as good as the first film. Though the film shows a new route to get from the Spectrum to a South Philadelphia hospital which should amuse locals. ★★

Rocky III

(1982, 99 min, US, Sylvester Stallone) *Sylvester Stallone, Talia Shire, Burt Young, Carl Weathers, Burgess Meredith, Mr. T.* Rocky now takes on Mr. T in the third *Rocky* film. Here he's under the tutelage of former opponent Weathers — whatever happened to old Meredith, you may ask (we won't tell). ★★

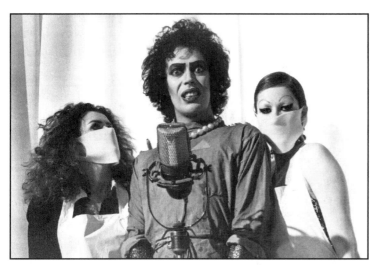

"Come up to the lab and see what's on the slab..." *The Rocky Horror Picture Show*

Rocky IV

(1985, 91 min, US, Sylvester Stallone) *Sylvester Stallone, Talia Shire, Dolph Lundgren. Brigitte Nielsen.* The fourth in the series, and probably the most ludicrous. Stallone wraps himself in the flag as Rocky takes on a Russian superhuman competitor (played by Lundgren). ★

Rocky V

(1990, 103 min, US, John G. Avildsen) *Sylvester Stallone, Talia Shire, Sage Stallone, Tom Morrison.* Stallone stars with his own son Sage in this story pitting Rocky, now punch-drunk, penniless and back in his South Philly beginnings, against his former, youthful protégé, whom Rocky had been training. Shire returns, yet again, as Mrs. Rocky. ★★

The Rocky Horror Picture Show

(1975, 95 min, GB, Jim Sharman) *Tim Curry, Susan Sarandon, Barry Bostwick, Meatloaf, Little Nell, Patricia Quinn, Richard O'Brien.* "Come up to the lab, and see what's on the slab." In *the* cult-midnight show attraction, alien and bisexual transvestite Dr. Frank N. Furter is visited by average Americans Brad and Janet; the latter two giving themselves over to "absolute pleasure." A wacked-out, spoofy, goofy, hip and campy one-of-a-kind musical. Curry is the Doc, with Sarandon as Janet, Bostwick as Brad, and writer/lyricist/composer O'Brien as the hunchback valet Riff-Raff. Based on the British stage musical. (Sequel: *Shock Treatment*) ★★★½ VHS: $14.99; DVD: $29.99

Rodan

(1957, 70 min, Japan, Inoshiro Honda) This cousin to *Godzilla* is filled with the usual images of crumbling cities, people running and screaming, and out-of-synch dubbing. As such, it's a very entertaining post-war atomic paranoia fest featuring a giant pterodactyl who, after being hatched from an egg, dines on giant bugs in a mine, causing amazing amounts of destruction and more. ★★★

Rodrigo D: No Future

(1990, 93 min, Colombia, Victor Gaviria) *Ramiro Meneses, Carlos Mario Resrepo.* The first Colombian film to be selected for competition at the Cannes Film Festival is a shocking and timely portrayal of the youths who populate the rough and tumble slums of Medellin, Colombia — the murder capital of the world. (Spanish with English subtitles) ★★★ VHS: $79.99

Roe vs. Wade

(1989, 100 min, US, Gregory Hoblit) *Holly Hunter, Amy Madigan, Terry O'Quinn, Kathy Bates.* Two moving performances by Hunter and Madigan highlight this absorbing made-for-TV drama about the controversial Supreme Court battle concerning a woman's right to abortion, and the events which led to the historic decision. ★★★ VHS: $14.99

Roger & Me

(1989, 90 min, US, Michael Moore) Moore's hilarious "documentary" about the relationship between General Motors and the people of his hometown, Flint, Michigan, and the subsequent slow death of that town, is a highly personal statement of frustration in the face of the unyielding greed of America's megacorporations. The theme which ties the film together is Moore's relentless effort to get an interview with Roger Smith, the chairman of G.M. Along the way he settles for the townsfolk, assorted "native" celebrities like Bob Eubanks and other players in the plant closing game, many of whom provide mockeries of themselves or the situation in general. The film is rounded by Moore's narration, which he delivers in an unerring deadpan and adds all the more comic spice to the brew. ★★★★ VHS: $14.99

Rollerball

(1975, 123 min, US, Norman Jewison) *James Caan, Maud Adams, Ralph Richardson, Moses Gunn.* Slick though violent and empty-headed sci-fi adventure, set in the 21st century, where man has eliminated crime, pollution and other social ills. Now, a violent form of entertainment is sought by the masses — a deadly physical contact sport called Rollerball. (Remade in 2001) ★★ VHS: $14.99; DVD: $14.99

Roman Holiday

(1953, 119 min, US, William Wyler) *Audrey Hepburn, Gregory Peck, Eddie Albert.* Captivating romantic comedy featuring Hepburn's magical Oscar-winning starring debut. Hepburn plays a princess whose unofficial tour of Rome is aided by newsman Peck, who's after a hot story, but finds romance instead. Hepburn and Peck are simply wonderful together, and Albert ably supports them as Peck's quick-fingered photographer. ★★★★ VHS: $14.99

Roman Scandals

(1933, 92 min, US, Frank Tuttle) *Eddie Cantor, Gloria Stuart, Ruth Etting, Edward Arnold.* One of the unsung heroes of 1930s comedy, Cantor is a delight in this funny musical romp about Cantor finding himself back in Roman times. Busby Berkeley choreographed the dance sequences. ★★★ VHS: $14.99

The Roman Spring of Mrs. Stone

(1961, 104 min, US, Jose Quintero) *Vivien Leigh, Warren Beatty, Lotte Lenya, Bessie Love.* Leigh is Karen Stone, a middle-aged widowed actress who retires and settles in Rome to live in peace and solitude. Through a vulgar procuress (Lenya, in a terrific performance), Mrs. Stone meets a swarthy young stud, Paolo (Beatty). Before long, Mrs. Stone succumbs to the suave gigolo's chicanery, and she soon finds herself losing both her money and her self-respect. Beatty's accent may cause a chuckle or two, but the film, based on a Tennessee Williams novella, does come off, thanks to Leigh's tender portrayal. ★★★ VHS: $14.99

Romance

(1930, 76 min, US, Clarence Brown) *Greta Garbo, Lewis Stone, Gavin Gordon.* Garbo's second talkie is a stagey but compelling romantic melodrama with the diva as an opera star involved in an affair with young clergyman Gordon. Stone is particularly good as Gordon's best friend, who also becomes involved with Garbo. ★★½ VHS: $19.99

Romance

(1999, 98 min, France, Catherine Breillat) *Caroline Trousselard, Sagamore Stévenin, François Berléand, Rocco Siffredi.* Pornography as art, *Romance* is writer-director Breillat's daring, explicit and often remarkable meditation on the division between sex and love. Marie (Trousselard) is a young woman with a handsome boyfriend, Paul (Stevenin), who can not get aroused when she fellates him. While Marie avers that she truly madly deeply loves Paul with all her mind, she insists on having to satisfy her physical needs elsewhere. Embarking on a series of trysts, Marie tries to separate the idea of love from the act of love. Breillat is certainly ambitious, and while many viewers may find the film pretentious and even unsuccessful, it does, in fact, pack a wallop. Trousselard gives a full-bodied performance trying to show how Marie's affairs intensify and consume her, and she is ably supported by the well-endowed Siffredi and the snakier Berléand. (French with English subtitles) ★★★ VHS: $69.99; DVD: $24.99

R

Romancing the Stone

(1984, 106 min, US, Robert Zemeckis) *Kathleen Turner, Michael Douglas, Danny DeVito, Ron Silver.* Frenetic comic adventure starring Turner as a romance novelist whose fantasies come true when she travels to South America to rescue her kidnapped sister and meets a daring adventurer (Douglas). Though Turner and Douglas play well off each other, Turner's wonderfully comic turn is the core of this entertaining comedy. (Sequel: *The Jewel of the Nile*) ★★★ VHS: $9.99; DVD: $24.99

Romantic Comedy

(1983, 103 min, US, Arthur Hiller) *Dudley Moore, Mary Steenburgen, Frances Sternhagen.* Stilted adaptation of Bernard Slade's play about two playwriting partners who share successes, flops and repressed love. Moore and Steenburgen do their best to carry it off, but in all, marginally romantic and not all that funny. ★★ VHS: $14.99

The Romantic Englishwoman

(1975, 115 min, GB, Joseph Losey) *Michael Caine, Glenda Jackson, Helmut Berger, Kate Nelligan.* Caine and Jackson star as a novelist and his wife who invite Berger into their home with the hopes that he will both share their bed and help Caine with his new novel. This elegant and underrated comedy-drama candidly explores many of our modern neuroses. Written by Tom Stoppard and Thomas Wiseman. ★★★½

Romeo and Juliet

(1936, 126 min, US, George Cukor) *Norma Shearer, Leslie Howard, John Barrymore, Basil Rathbone, Edna May Oliver.* Though leads Shearer and Howard are much too old for the parts of star-crossed teenagers Romeo and Juliet, this is nevertheless an excellent screen version of Shakespeare's tragedy. Cukor directs with a sublime understanding of the text and a delicate eye for time and place. Great supporting cast, especially Barrymore as Mercutio. ★★★½ VHS: $19.99

Romeo and Juliet

(1954, 138 min, GB, Renato Castellani) *Laurence Harvey, Susan Shentall, Flora Robson, John Gielgud.* This popular and beautifully filmed version of Shakespeare's tragic tale of star-crossed lovers unfortunately falls victim to miscasting in the lead roles. Harvey and Shentall, like the 1936 pairing of Norma Shearer and Leslie Howard, are too old for their parts. Nevertheless, they both give admirable performances. The film features sumptuous cinematography, and magically recreates the atmosphere of Renaissance Verona. ★★★½ VHS: $14.99

Romeo and Juliet

(1968, 138 min, GB, Franco Zeffirelli) *Olivia Hussey, Leonard Whiting, Milo O'Shea, Michael York.* With an eye for romantic detail that is almost unsurpassed in the film industry, director Zeffirelli brings Shakespeare's immortal masterpiece to the screen with a flourish. Hussey and Whiting are youthfully cast as the ill-fated lovers, and O'Shea brings his mature wisdom to this visually ravishing production.

(VHS available letterboxed or pan & scan) ★★★★ VHS: $14.99; DVD: $29.99

Romeo and Juliet

Starring Leonardo DiCaprio and Claire Danes
See: William Shakespeare's Romeo and Juliet

Romeo Is Bleeding

(1994, 110 min, US, Peter Medak) *Gary Oldman, Lena Olin, Annabella Sciorra, Juliette Lewis, Roy Scheider, Will Patton. Romeo Is Bleeding* has all the right elements: a nifty script about greed, corruption and sex; a grimy film noir feel that's tinged with a hallucinatory edge; a haunting jazz soundtrack; and a great cast that includes the always intriguing Oldman as a crooked cop on the take from the mob, Sciorra as his good wife and Olin as a devil-in-disguise cop killer. Unfortunately, the film lacks an overall cohesiveness as the disparate elements go on their merry way without ever really connecting to each other. Ultimately, *Romeo* leaves one entertained but unsatisfied. ★★½

Romeo Must Die

(2000, 115 min, US, Andrzej Bartkowiak) *Jet Li, Aaliyah, Isaiah Washington, Delroy Lindo, Russell Wong, DMX.* Martial arts superstar Li gets his first Hollywood starring vehicle, and, despite some good actions scenes, this convoluted actioner doesn't capture the excitement of his Hong Kong works. Li is a gangster's son who falls for a rival gangster's daughter (Aaliyah) and gets caught up in gangland rivalries on the Oakland docks. Way too long, *Romeo Must Die* is packed with lesser hip hop and R&B music, making it just a trendy time-killer. Li's stuntwork is amazing, but the wirework is obvious and badly used. Lindo adds class to the project, but this is for die-hard Li fans only. ★½ VHS: $14.99; DVD: $24.99

Romper Stomper

(1992, 92 min, Australia, Geoffrey Wright) *Russell Crowe, Jacqueline McKenzie, Daniel Pollock. Romper Stomper* impacts like a smartly landed fist, using the unbridled fury of its protagonists to propel this story of disenfranchised adolescents lost in a squalid urban wasteland, as abandoned as the empty factories in which they squat. They affect skinhead trappings and bemoan the decline of White Power; the film opens with a horrific gang war scene, as Hando (Crowe) takes his cronies to stomp a group of young Vietnamese in a subway station. The violence is its own reward, getting it as gratifying as giving it. The introduction of a poor little rich girl (McKenzie) into the group, and especially her impact on the relationship between Hando and his lieutenant Davey (Pollock), occupies much of the later storyline; but the film will be remembered for the emotional toll it demands of the viewer. A remarkable piece of filmmaking. ★★★ VHS: $19.99; DVD: $26.99

Romy and Michele's High School Reunion

(1997, 91 min, US, David Mirkin) *Mira Sorvino, Lisa Kudrow, Janeane Garofalo, Alan Cumming.* Sorvino and Kudrow go the dumbed-down comedic route as two joined-at-the-hip, totally airheaded, underemployed, fashion-victim space cadets preparing for their tenth anniversary high school reunion. Now living in L.A., they plan their assault on their middle-America home town, hoping to prove to their adolescent nemeses that they are no longer losers. The characters are too broadly drawn and the film too self-consciously sardonic to elicit any real emotional response. While *Romy and Michele* is marginally saved by some warm moments and biting insights, it tries too hard attempting the hip, urbane sensitivity which flowed effortlessly from, for example, *Chasing Amy.* Check out Garofalo in support as the hostile, bitter, intellectual chick. ★★½ VHS: $9.99; DVD: $29.99

La Ronde

(1950, 97 min, France, Max Ophüls) *Anton Walbrook, Simone Signoret, Simone Simon, Danielle Darrieux, Jean-Louis Barrault.* Ophüls directs a stellar group of French actors in this witty, elaborate satire on sexual behavior. Ten sketches are presented, in which an interconnecting

Romper Stomper

Robert De Niro takes aim in *Ronin*

group of lovers change partners until their liaisons come full circle. A bemused view of affairs of the heart. (French with English subtitles) ★★★½ VHS: $29.99

Ronin

(1998, 121 min, US, John Frankenheimer) *Robert De Niro, Jean Reno, Natascha McElhone, Stellan Skarsgård, Jonathan Pryce, Sean Bean.* Three intense car chases highlight this thrilling action tale which manages to maintain interest even between all the well-staged automotive mayhem. With a style reminiscent of 1970s adventure films (blazing guns, tough talk, faster cars), *Ronin* is a thinking man's thriller about a group of hired mercenaries ("ronin") who come together to steal the suitcase and its highly secret contents of a mysterious attache. There's enough intrigue and high-speed chases through Paris, Nice and the countryside to populate five action films. Director Frankenheimer isn't merely content to let the chases speak for the film, and the relationships between his characters form the real core of *Ronin*. A bristling, unrelenting and smart roller-coaster ride. ★★★½ VHS: $14.99; DVD: $19.99

The Roof

(1956, 98 min, Italy, Vittorio De Sica) *Gabriella Pallotti, Giorgio Listuzzi.* De Sica's realistic and gentle drama follows a poverty-striken young couple who must overcome red tape in trying to find a home and happiness in post-war Rome. (Italian with English subtitles) ★★★

The Rookie

(1990, 121 min, US, Clint Eastwood) *Clint Eastwood, Charlie Sheen, Raul Julia, Sonia Braga.* A formulaic thriller directed by and starring Eastwood about a hardened veteran of the LAPD who is assigned a rookie partner. Following all of the guidelines for the good cop/bad cop buddy movie, *The Rookie* riddles the screen with bullets, car chases and blazing pyrotechnics. The film enjoys its share of wry, self-effacing humor and the pace is brisk. ★★½ VHS: $14.99

Rookie of the Year

(1993, 103 min, US, Daniel Stern) *Thomas Ian Nicholas, Gary Busey, Albert Hall, Amy Morton,*

Daniel Stern. A delightful baseball comedy for the whole family. When young Nicholas breaks his arm, he discovers he has the newly acquired ability to throw a 90 mph fastball. Which is good news for his home town team, the struggling Chicago Cubs (this is before the arrival of Sammy Sosa, of course). The youth finds himself thrust into the spotlight, with predictable but good-natured comic results. ★★★ VHS: $9.99

Room at the Top

(1959, 115 min, GB, Jack Clayton) *Laurence Harvey, Simone Signoret, Heather Sears, Hermione Baddeley.* This effervescent story about a low-born Brit's ruthless drive to reach the top of the ladder in a northern industrial town is powered by the gutsy performances by Harvey and Signoret (who won an Oscar). An unhappily married French woman falls desperately in love with the determined young man. Considered a far-reaching, seminal work, the use of and attitude towards sex and language paved the way for the ultra-realistic "kitchen sink" school of British drama. ★★★★

Room Service

(1938, 78 min, US, William A. Seiter) *The Marx Brothers, Lucille Ball, Ann Miller.* Groucho is a struggling producer with a potential hit show on his hands — all he needs is money. Which wouldn't hurt his hotel bill, either. Chico and Harpo add their usual dazzle, and Ball and Miller are the love interests. The film is interesting in that, in addition to the trademark absurdist humor, there are definite indications of Groucho's acting potential, which was never fully utilized by Hollywood. Script by Morrie Ryskind. (Remade in 1944 as a musical, *Step Lively*) ★★★ VHS: $19.99

A Room with a View

(1985, 115 min, GB, James Ivory) *Helena Bonham Carter, Julian Sands, Maggie Smith, Denholm Elliott, Daniel Day-Lewis, Judi Dench, Simon Callow, Rupert Graves.* E. M. Forster's classic novel of the sexual awakening of a young woman amidst the emotional repression of Victorian England is brilliantly captured in this comedy of manners. During a trip to Florence, the girl's simmering sensuality is exposed when she meets and falls in love with a free-spirited

and handsome young man. The struggle between this love and the expectations of a "proper society" features outstanding performances by the entire ensemble, though Smith and Elliott do steal the show. ★★★★ VHS: $14.99; DVD: $24.99

Roommates

(1995, 109 min, US, Peter Yates) *Peter Falk, D.B. Sweeney, Julianne Moore, Ellen Burstyn, Jan Rubes.* A sweet, old-fashioned though uneven examination of a grandfather and grandson's enduring relationship, *Roommates* gives Falk one his best film roles. He plays Rocky, who at 75 years of age raises his young grandson Michael after the youth loses his parents. Their years together are spent happily until Michael, now an adult (played by Sweeney), is on his own. The two reunite when Rocky is evicted and moves in with his grandson. Unfortunately, the film wallows in its unpleasantness, and after a charming first half the story loses its good humor for a succession of tragedies which are clumsily handled. ★★½

Rope

(1948, 80 min, US, Alfred Hitchcock) *James Stewart, Farley Granger, John Dall.* The Master of Suspense's audacious experimentation with real time and ten-minute takes gives this murder-thriller both a kinetic and claustrophobic atmosphere. Suggested by the Leopold-Loeb case, the story concerns two friends (played by Granger and Dall) who murder an old schoolmate for the thrill of it, stuff his corpse in an old chest, and then proceed to hold a party around the makeshift casket with attendees including the victim's father and fiancée. (The Leopold-Loeb story has also been told in *Compulsion* and *Swoon*.) ★★★½ VHS: $14.99; DVD: $29.99

Rorret

(1987, 105 min, Italy, Fulvio Wetzl) *Lou Castel, Anna Galiena.* Inspired by the films of Alfred Hitchcock, this creepy thriller centers on a reclusive and voyeuristic owner of a cinema specializing in horror films who goes on a killing rampage whenever he gets "excited" by terror. The psychopathically deranged man's modus operandi is to meet women who share his horror interests and then kill them in theatrically filmic fashion. Although needlessly talky, the film has moments of tension and intrigue with the highlight being the film-within-a-film homages (re-creations) to famous horror sequences from *Peeping Tom*, *Strangers on a Train*, *Psycho* and *Dial M for Murder*. (Italian with English subtitles) ★★ VHS: $29.99

La Rosa Blanca

(1960, 100 min, Mexico, Roberto Gavaldon) Based on the controversial novel by B. Traven ("Treasure of the Sierra Madre"), this compelling and impassioned film tells the story of the armed struggle that ensues between the land-thirsty Condor Oil Company and Don Jacinto, owner of the hacienda "La Rosa Blanca," an oil-rich land the company wants to expropriate. Contrasting the peasant's spiritualism and reverence for the land with the malfeasance and greed of the multinational, the film obviously takes sides but is very good drama nonetheless. (Spanish with English subtitles) ★★★

R

503

Rosa Luxemburg

(1986, 122 min, Germany, Margarethe von Trotta) *Barbara Sukowa, Daniel Olbrychski, Otto Sander.* Von Trotta has created a mesmerizing epic on the personal and political life of Rosa Luxemburg, one of the most dynamic and passionate leaders of the socialist democracy in Germany. Sukowa gives a truly amazing performance as "Red Rosa," whose life is chronicled from her emergence in the Social Democratic Party to her loss of faith after WWI. A wonderfully produced portrait, the film has a starkness befitting a war picture which is juxtaposed with a realism rare to what are usually overblown period pieces. (German with English subtitles) ★★★★ VHS: $29.99

Rosalie Goes Shopping

(1990, 94 min, US, Percy Adlon) *Marianne Sagebrecht, Brad Davis, Judge Reinhold, Alex Winter.* Director Adlon has teamed once again with hefty star Sagebrecht (*Sugarbaby*) to produce this pleasant but disappointingly thin satire on America's obsession with consumerism. Determined to provide everything "money" can buy for her children and loving husband (Davis), Rosalie, our devoted and increasingly frenetic housewife, soon finds herself juggling 37 credit cards, several mortgage payments and writing out worthless checks. With the wolf soon baying at her comfortable suburban door, our intrepid consumer devises more and more ingenious ways to stay a few steps ahead in her great pursuit of the American Dream. ★★

The Rosary Murders

(1987, 105 min, US, Fred Walton) *Donald Sutherland, Charles Durning, Belinda Bauer.* Slow but interesting tale of a parish priest (Sutherland) who hears the confession of a serial killer preying on priests and nuns, and finds himself torn between his sacred vows and the pursuit of justice. ★★

The Rose

(1979, 134 min, US, Mark Rydell) *Bette Midler, Alan Bates, Frederic Forrest, Harry Dean Stanton, David Keith.* Midler makes an impressive film debut as a hard-drinking, fast-living rock chanteuse — suggested by the life of Janis Joplin — struggling against the pressures of success. Bates is her mean-spirited manager and Forrest is her on-again, off-again lover. The film's musical numbers contain a raw energy thanks to the conviction of the Divine Miss M, and her earthy performance avoids the usual industry clichés. ★★★

The Rose Garden

(1989, 152 min, US/West Germany, Fons Rademakers) *Liv Ullmann, Maximilian Schell, Peter Fonda.* This gripping drama, which exposes the latent anti-Semitism in modern-day Germany, stars Ullmann as a tenacious lawyer who is hired to defend a man (Schell) accused of committing a seemingly unprovoked attack on an elderly businessman. As the drama unfolds, Ullmann uncovers the fact that the old man was a commandant of a Nazi concentration camp and presided over the death of many Jews and children. A serious, compassionate psychological drama that features fine performances by both Ullmann and Schell as well as

an oddly cast but effective Fonda. From the director of the Oscar-winning film *The Assault.* (Filmed in English) ★★★ VHS: $79.99

The Rose Tattoo

(1955, 117 min, US, Daniel Mann) *Burt Lancaster, Anna Magnani, Marisa Pavan.* Magnani gives an extraordinary performance in this riveting adaptation of Tennessee Williams' play as a widow, still obsessed with the memory of her late husband, who begins an affair with trucker Lancaster. Magnani won the Oscar for her portrayal, and is matched all the way by Lancaster. ★★★½ VHS: $14.99

Roseland

(1977, 103 min, US, James Ivory) *Lilia Skala, Christopher Walken, Joan Copeland, Helen Gallagher, Geraldine Chaplin, Teresa Wright.* Set in the famed New York dance hall, *Roseland* is a collection of three captivating short character vignettes studying the tattered lives of the people who gravitate to the club. Exceptional performances from the cast. ★★★

Rosemary's Baby

(1968, 136 min, US, Roman Polanski) *Mia Farrow, John Cassavetes, Ruth Gordon, Sidney Blackmer, Maurice Evans.* Classic chiller from Polanski with newlyweds Farrow and Cassavetes unwittingly befriending devil worshippers Gordon and Blackmer in modern-day New York. Gordon won an Oscar for her performance, and the film contains many frightening moments. ★★★★ VHS: $14.99; DVD: $29.99

Rosencrantz and Guildenstern Are Dead

(1991, 119 min, GB, Tom Stoppard) *Gary Oldman, Tim Roth, Richard Dreyfuss, Iain Glen.* Adapting and directing his own play for the screen might have been too much for the talented Stoppard, but although the film is a bit stage-bound, it still proves to be an exhilarating mental exercise with Stoppard toying with the English language in this witty, intellectual comedy. The story takes the ingenious ploy of changing the focus of "Hamlet" from the brooding Dane to two minor flunkies, Rosencrantz and Guildenstern. Roth and Oldman are scintillating as the lost and, at times, pathetic duo who are forced by circumstances to pontificate on their seemingly predetermined fate. All told — an audacious, verbally duelling metaphysical comedy. ★★★½

Rosetta

(1999, 95 min, France, Luc and Jean-Pierre Dardenne) *Émilie Dequenne, Fabrizio Rongione, Anne Yernaux.* Rosetta is emotion exploded, a driven, angry, obsessive, fiercely independent teenager who can never stop moving in her quest to keep herself and her drunken whore mother no further in the gutter than they've already sunk. The hyperactive pace

matches the protagonist's frenetic energy; the camera follows her closely as she attempts to exert some control over her tenuous existence by squirrelling away random objects in bizarre hiding places. She unceasingly seeks normalcy: a job, a friend, a secure roof over her head. She flat-out runs just to stay in place, and cannot continue the pace. Her desperation to get a job leads to a conflict with the one person who has reached out to her, a conflict she is ill-equipped to handle. Dequenne is remarkable, delivering an almost feral performance. This harsh, unrelenting film ends ambiguously, yet is as uniquely satisfying as it is emotionally exhausting. An intriguing directorial effort from the Dardenne brothers (*La Promesse*). (French with English subtitles) ★★★★ VHS: $14.99

Rosewood

(1997, 139 min, US, John Singleton) *Ving Rhames, Jon Voight, Don Cheadle, Bruce McGill, Michael Rooker, Esther Rolle, Loren Dean.* The story of a real-life tragedy is told with sledgehammer subtlety by director Singleton, who does history a disservice by sacrificing all ambiguity, character development and moral conflict for the sake of a shallow, easy political statement. Rhames stars as an enigmatic WWI veteran who comes to Rosewood, Florida — a town built and populated almost entirely by black Americans — to buy some land and begin a peaceful life. Instead, a case of mistaken identity brings a mob of angry whites from a neighboring, poorer town to wreak a violent vengeance and retribution. Singleton neglects historical drama in favor of crowd-pleasing sentiment and simplicity. (VHS available letterboxed or pan & scan) ★★ VHS: $9.99; DVD: $14.99

Rouge

(1988, 93 min, Hong Kong, Stanley Kwan) With stunning visuals and a great story, this supernatural love story alternates between the brothels and theatres of an opium-hazed 1930s Hong

Mia Farrow and John Cassevettes in *Rosemary's Baby*

Kong and the sophisticated, bustling but vapid world of the present-day city. A courtesan, who died in a love-induced suicide, returns to earth years later seeking out her lover after he fails to join her in Heaven. A terrifically stylish movie. (Cantonese with English subtitles) ★★★½ VHS: $19.99; DVD: $49.99

Rough Magic

(1997, 105 min, GB, Claire Peploe) *Bridget Fonda, Russell Crowe, Jim Broadbent, D.W. Moffett, Kenneth Mars, Paul Rodriguez.* Fonda treads water in this picaresque soufflé from the director of *High Season* about a gold-digging magician's assistant (circa 1950) who skips out on her engagement to a wealthy industrialist when he accidentally shoots her partner. Enter Crowe as the hardboiled gumshoe sent to track her to a small Mexican town where magic, destiny and romance await. Adapted from James Hadley's novel "Miss Shumway Waves a Wand," this charming misfire mixes elements of film noir, romantic adventure, and mystical mumbo jumbo, but the results are somewhat lackluster and the "love conquers all" resolution feels strained rather than uplifting. ★★ VHS: $19.99

Round Midnight

(1986, 130 min, France/US, Bertrand Tavernier) *Dexter Gordon, Lonette McKee.* Gordon gives a painfully touching performance as Dale Turner, a raspy-voiced saxophone player ravaged by drugs and booze, but who nonetheless retains his dignity and possesses the "elegant soul of a poet." Tavernier creates a moody and authentic world of American jazz exiles and the habitués of the smokey Parisian jazz clubs of the '50s. Wonderful music performed by Gordon, Herbie Hancock, Ron Carter, Tony Williams and John McLaughlin. ★★★½ VHS: $19.99; DVD: $19.99

The Round Up

(1965, 89 min, Hungary, Miklós Jancsó) *János Görbe, Tibor Molnár.* A Hungarian film masterpiece that paints an unflinching portrait of fear, torture and oppression. Set in the mid-19th century after the establishment of the Austro-Hungarian empire, the camera acts as an unseen observer as several hundred Hungarian peasants, outlaws and herdsmen are rounded up, imprisoned and tortured by the Austrian authorities in an effort to uncover and crush the remaining rebel stronghold. The men are forced to confess and identify other freedom fighters before they themselves are eliminated. A harsh, disturbing chronicle of a demonic police state told with little dialogue and set in a timeless, bleak plain where routine terror reigns. (Letterboxed) (Hungarian with English subtitles) ★★★★ VHS: $59.99

Rounders

(1998, 102 min, US, John Dahl) *Matt Damon, Edward Norton, John Turturro, Martin Landau, Gretchen Mol, John Malkovich.* Slick and sleazy at the same time, *Rounders* is a testosterone-heavy variation on classic gambling movies *The Cincinnati Kid* and *The Hustler*. Fresh-faced, poker-playing law student Damon comes to the rescue when pal Norton gets out of the slammer carrying heavy debts from seedy underworld types; leading Damon to a showdown with the hammy Malkovich, playing an Oreo-chomping Russian hood. While the story mean-

ders all over the place, and the dialogue is filled with sometimes impossible-to-follow gambling terms, director Dahl finds fascination with his gallery of idiosyncratic characters. Ultimately, the jokers may be wild here, but the main characters aren't wild enough. ★★½ VHS: $14.99; DVD: $29.99

Roustabout

(1964, 100 min, US, John Rich) *Elvis Presley, Barbara Stanwyck, Raquel Welch.* Presley joins the carnival, run by none other than Stanwyck. Look quick for Welch as a college coed. Though not one of Elvis' best, it's kinda cute in that isn't-the-living-end sort of way. Elvis sings "Hard Knocks," "It's a Wonderful World" and "Big Love, Big Heartache." ★★½ VHS: $14.99; DVD: $29.99

Roxanne

(1987, 107 min, US, Fred Schepisi) *Steve Martin, Daryl Hannah, Rick Rossovich, Shelley Duvall, Michael J. Pollard, Damon Wayans.* Martin's comic tour de force performance highlights this breathlessly funny updating of "Cyrano de Bergerac." Martin plays a small Northwestern town's fire chief whose elongated nose has kept him from romantic entanglements; that is, until he falls in love with beautiful astronomy student Hannah. Rossovich is the handsome but vacuous hunk — himself terrified of romantic repartee — who speaks Martin's heartfelt words of love. Duvall offers wonderful support as Martin's confidant. Martin's "20 insults" is a classic. (Though Michael Douglas won the Oscar that year for *Wall Street*, Martin's performance was by far and away the year's best.) ★★★½ VHS: $9.99; DVD: $24.99

Royal Deceit

(1997, 85 min, GB, Gabriel Axel) *Gabriel Byrne, Helen Mirren, Christian Bale.* What a waste. An excellent cast, along with a capable director, fail to enliven this DOA version of Hamlet, the mad prince of Denmark (based on the folk tales, not the Shakespeare play). Bale hardly registers as the surprisingly decisive lad who fakes madness upon learning his uncle (a somnambulistic Byrne) has murdered his father. Maddeningly choppy, with all the good parts cut out, *Royal Deceit* was obviously a much longer film hacked down by its theatrical distributor Miramax. What remains is gratuitous nudity, boring dialogue, and clunky action that strains to be artsy-retro. ★ VHS: $19.99

The Royal Family

(1977, 112 min, US, Kirk Browning & Ellis Rabb) *Rosemary Harris, Eva Le Gallienne, Ellis Rabb, Sam Levene, Keene Curtis.* Rabb received a Tony Award as Best Director for this effervescent, sublimely witty revival of the 1927 George S. Kaufman-Edna Ferber stage hit which simultaneously pokes fun and pays homage to an eminent and eccentric acting dynasty that's about as close to the Barrymores as you could possibly get. Harris (who was a Tony Award nominee as Best Actress) brings great theatricality and grace to the role of Julie Cavendish, a Broadway legend who's flirting with retirement. Director Rabb dons his best John Barrymore as her brother Tony, a stage legend-turned-Hollywood matinee idol. A presentation of Great Performances. ★★★★ VHS: $29.99

Royal Warriors

(1986, 95 min, Hong Kong, David Chung & Yuen Kwai) *Michelle Yeoh, Henry Sanada, Michael Wong.* Early in her career, Yeoh made a series of films for then-husband Dickson Poon's D & B Films. This is one of the best of them, a vengeance-minded action tale pitting her against a quartet of bad guys. Michelle plays a Hong Kong cop who foils a highjacking attempt aboard a jet, with the help of an airline security agent (Wong) and a vacationing Japanese cop (the awesome Sanada). Once back home, the trio are marked by the remaining pair of killers. With plenty of fight sequences (both gun battles and kung fu bouts) and a killer ending, the film is sure to please fans of Yeoh. (Cantonese with English subtitles) ★★★ VHS: $19.99; DVD: $49.99

Royal Wedding

(1951, 93 min, US, Stanley Donen) *Fred Astaire, Jane Powell, Peter Lawford.* Light-hearted musical with Fred and Powell as a famous brother-and-sister act who travel to England to perform their show, coinciding with the marriage of Queen Elizabeth II. (Fred dances on the ceiling in this one.) ★★½ VHS: $19.99

Rubin and Ed

(1991, 90 min, US, Trent Harris) *Howard Hesseman, Crispin Glover, Karen Black.* Ed (Hesseman), a middle-aged, leisure-suited failure at life, must bring a new recruit to his highly charged motivational real estate seminar or face expulsion and the loss of promised riches, self-esteem and inner peace. His search leads him to Rubin (Glover), an oddly dressed malcontent under the thumb of an overbearing mom, who agrees to go to the seminar if Ed will help him bury his dead cat. Hesseman and Glover bounce off each other with just the right amount of manic energy in this delightfully quirky road-trip saga (a post-Reagan era exploration of the latest wrinkle in the American Dream) an audacious romp. ★★★ VHS: $79.99

Ruby

(1977, 84 min, US, Curtis Harrington) *Piper Laurie, Stuart Whitman.* After her success in *Carrie*, Laurie encored with another horror opus, though with considerable less results. The spirit of a murdered 1930s gangster returns to haunt the descendants of those responsible. A few thrills in this derivative chiller. ★★

Ruby

(1992, 100 min, US, John Mackenzie) *Danny Aiello, Sherilyn Fenn, Arliss Howard.* Aiello stars as Jack Ruby, the Dallas nightclub owner who shot Lee Harvey Oswald, in this intriguing though needlessly complex underworld look at the J.F.K. assassination. Following on the heels of Oliver Stone's *JFK*, *Ruby* details the events leading up to that fateful day in Dallas from Ruby's point of view, all the while portraying him as a small-time gangster who got in over his head. ★★½ VHS: $14.99

Ruby in Paradise

(1993, 115 min, US, Victor Nunez) *Ashley Judd, Todd Field, Bentley Mitchum, Allison Dean, Dorothy Lyman.* Writer-director Nunez presents the simple story of Ruby, a young woman who flees a

The Ruling Class

desolate life in rural Tennessee and settles on the Gulf Coast of Florida. Judd is a revelation as Ruby, who explores who she is while happily working in a tacky seaside gift shop. Her graceful performance is one of subtlety and nuance which, combined with Nunez' gentle direction, elevates what could have been a run-of-the-mill outing. Despite some minor screenplay contrivances, this is the kind of work that gives independent filmmaking its good name. ★★★½ VHS: $14.99

Rude

(1995, 90 min, Canada, Clément Virgo) *Sharon M. Lewis, Richard Chevolleau, Rachel Crawford.* This hard-hitting independent film delves beneath the surface of problem-plagued inner city life to explore the personal lives of those who are forced to live there. Filmed near the Toronto housing project where the Jamaican-born director grew up, Virgo's feature-film debut tells three stories all set on an Easter Sunday and all dealing with personal redemption and the struggle to survive and love in a tough world. The first is about an older black man and former drug dealer attempting to adjust to life after release from prison. The second looks at a young woman who contemplates an abortion. The third tale follows a handsome young boxer who must face the truth about himself and his own sexuality after participating in a gay-bashing. ★★★ VHS: $9.99; DVD: $9.99

Rude Awakening

(1989, 100 min, US, Aaron Russo & David Greenwalt) *Eric Roberts, Cheech Marin, Julie Hagerty, Robert Carradine, Buck Henry, Louise Lasser, Cindy Williams.* Two hippies in hiding since the 1960s reemerge and find their old friends have become materialistic yuppies. A good premise isn't fully realized in this only occasionally funny comedy. ★★ VHS: $9.99

Rudy

(1993, 112 min, US, David Anspaugh) *Sean Astin, Ned Beatty, Charles S. Dutton, Robert Prosky, Lili Taylor.* From the director of *Hoosiers* comes this likable *Knute Rockne* for the '90s. Nearly

pouring on the sentiment as much as its 1940s counterpart, the film stars Astin as Rudy, a mill worker who has dreamed his whole life of entering Notre Dame and playing for their football team. This based-on-fact story follows his attempts to realize both dreams, despite being short in stature and dyslexic. Though Astin's Rudy is almost to the point of annoying with his constant chatter of his beloved school, it's to the actor's credit he eventually wins you over by the end credits. ★★½ VHS: $9.99; DVD: $24.99

Rudyard Kipling's The Jungle Book

(1994, 108 min, US, Stephen Sommers) *Jason Scott Lee, Cary Elwes, Lena Headey, Sam Neill, John Cleese.* A smashing live-action adaptation of Rudyard Kipling's classic tale, this Disney-produced adventure yarn is not only the most entertaining version of the story to date, but is also the best non-animated film released by Buena Vista in many a year. A loin-clothed and extremely fit Lee portrays Mowgli, the Indian boy who becomes lost in the jungle and is raised by animals. His carefree existence is shattered when he meets the humans he once knew as a child. Director Sommers blissfully mixes Indian lore and Indiana Jones-type antics, all set against beautifully designed backgrounds of tropics, English pageantry and lost treasure. A high-flying adventure both smart and thrilling. ★★★½ VHS: $22.99

Ruggles of Red Gap

(1935, 92 min, US, Leo McCarey) *Charles Laughton, Charlie Ruggles, Mary Boland, ZaSu Pitts, Roland Young.* Laughton is priceless in this absolutely delightful comedy. He plays a proper English butler who heads to the American West to work for an unconventional family. Ruggles and Boland offer terrific support as his new employers. (Remade in 1950 as *Fancy Pants*) ★★★★ VHS: $14.99

Rules of Engagement

(1999, 127 min, US, William Friedkin) *Tommy Lee Jones, Samuel L. Jackson, Guy Pearce, Bruce Greenwood, Anne Archer, Ben Kingsley, Blair Underwood, Philip Baker Hall.* In the passable but

stuffy *Rules of Engagement*, military stratagem meets courtroom drama. Supposedly in the tradition of *A Few Good Men*, but lacking that film's structured screenplay and taut direction, Friedkin's well-acted, busy melodrama is ultimately at cross-purposes: It wants to be a kick-ass combat film and a hard-edged examination of military bureaucracy. In doing so, it's chomped off more than it can chew. Jackson plays a Marine colonel who is put on trial after his troops kill civilians in an embassy evacuation in Yemen. Jones is a military lawyer and old friend who defends him. The government needs a scapegoat; Jones needs to prove he's still viable; Jackson wants to expose the hypocrisy. Gutsy performances by Jones, Jackson and Pearce, as the prosecuting attorney, help sustain interest, but flat supporting characterizations and somewhat contrived plot developments work against it. ★★ VHS: $14.99; DVD: $29.99

Rules of the Game

(1939, 110 min, France, Jean Renoir) *Marcel Dalio, Jean Renoir.* Renoir's grand comedy of manners is a sublime study of social codes and crumbling morals. Within the confines of a lavish country estate, the intricate lives of the aristocracy and their servants undergo a dramatic unravelling. A marvel of ensemble acting and a perennial contender as one of the greatest films of all time. (French with English subtitles) ★★★★ VHS: $29.99

The Ruling Class

(1971, 139 min, GB, Peter Medak) *Peter O'Toole, Alastair Sim, Arthur Lowe, Coral Browne.* O'Toole gives a comically possessed performance as Jack, the 14th Earl of Gurney, who insists he's Jesus Christ. This irreverent and boisterous black comedy overflows with madness as people burst into song and assume whacked-out characters at the drop of a hat. Great support from Sim as a befuddled bishop and Lowe as a bolshevik butler. ★★★½ VHS: $39.99

Rumble Fish

(1983, 94 min, US, Francis Ford Coppola) *Matt Dillon, Mickey Rourke, Dennis Hopper, Diane Lane, Nicolas Cage.* Coppola's film adaptation of S. E. Hinton's novel was a financial and critical failure. Unlike his version of *The Outsiders*, this film lacks Coppola's usual glossiness. Rourke stars as "The Motorcycle Boy," who returns to his home town to try to stop his brother (Dillon) from following in his legendary, wandering footsteps. This is a film which viewers will find either a pretentious bore or a rewarding film experience. (We found it the former.) Shot in black and white. ★½ VHS: $9.99

Rumble in the Bronx

(1994, 90 min, Hong Kong, Stanley Tong) *Jackie Chan, Anita Mui, Francoise Yip, Bill Tung.* Chan's third attempt to break into the U.S. film market proves to be the charm. A story-light, action-heavy, redubbed romp through Vancouver (doubling for New York), this still falls short of his best Hong Kong works. Chan plays Keung, who, while visiting his uncle in New York, runs afoul of a local multiethnic biker gang, who beat him up and trash his uncle's store. After making amends with the gang leader's girlfriend (Yip), both Chan and the gang must bury the hatchet in the face of a bigger threat:

a group of homicidal mobsters searching for a bag of stolen diamonds. The martial arts and comedy scenes more than make up for any other deficiencies. (VHS available letterboxed or pan & scan) ★★★ VHS: $9.99; DVD: $19.99

A Rumor of War

(1980, 106 min, US, Richard T. Heffron) *Brad Davis, Brian Dennehy, Keith Carradine, Stacy Keach, Michael O'Keefe.* Davis heads a good cast in this outstanding made-for-TV Vietnam War drama. In a compelling and rich performance, Davis plays a newly arrived G.I. whose — like that of Tom Cruise in *Born on the Fourth of July* some nine years later — unblinking support of the war gives way to self-doubt and tragedy. ★★★½

Run Lola Run

(1999, 81 min, Germany, Tom Tykwer) *Franka Potente, Moritz Bleibtreu, Herbert Knaup, Nina Petri.* Lola's boyfriend Manni has left 100,000 marks on a subway, and he'll be dead if he doesn't get it to his gangster boss in 20 minutes. Good thing he has a strong woman behind him. As played by Potente, Lola is so powerful that she breaks glass when she screams, can heal the dying, and won't even let the movie end until everything is right. Director Tykwer has fashioned a massive, kinetic music video (he also cowrote all the music) that also stops long enough to enrich each character, adding layers as the story is revisited. He also relentlessly toys with the medium, including giving flash-forward life-stories to mere extras and running the credits backwards. Tremendous fun, in a serious, German sort of way. (German with English subtitles) ★★★½ VHS: $19.99; DVD: $27.99

The Run of the Country

(1995, 116 min, Ireland, Peter Yates) *Albert Finney, Matt Kesslar, Victoria Smurfit, Anthony Brophy.* This charming coming-of-age tale is set in the breathtaking Irish countryside, populated with believable characters and describing that tenuous time of life when children must separate from home before they can find a true

connection with it. Keeslar is authentic in his description of Danny, the bereaved young man whose recent loss of his mother is the traumatic catalyst for monumental changes in his life. Finney is expectedly captivating as the domineering father whose own loss makes him even less receptive to his son's state of mind. Danny embarks on a road trip with an appropriately adventurous friend (Brophy), a trip of abandon and self-discovery. A touching story of loss and reconciliation with the wit to avoid the maudlin and the warmth to heal the heart. ★★★ VHS: $19.99

Runaway

(1984, 100 min, US, Michael Crichton) *Tom Selleck, Gene Simmons, Kirstie Alley, Cynthia Rhodes.* Futuristic thriller with Selleck as a bounty hunter tracking down defective, murderous robots. Crichton's story is a miss on practically all levels. ★★ VHS: $9.99; DVD: $24.99

Runaway Bride

(1999, 116 min, US, Garry Marshall) *Julia Roberts, Richard Gere, Joan Cusack, Hector Elizondo, Rita Wilson, Paul Dooley.* Roberts and Gere reunite almost ten years after *Pretty Woman* for this splashy if formulaic romantic comedy. Gere plays a reporter who travels to a small Maryland town to do research on the woman (Roberts) who has stood up three fiancés at the altar. And she's set to walk down the aisle once more. Of course, the antagonists soon become attracted to each other. Roberts looks great, and her performance is beguiling, though she's not afforded an opportunity to bring some shadings to her character as in the better and funnier *Notting Hill.* Gere looks great, as well, and is actually quite funny, but neither he nor his enchanting costar are fully able to bring sizzle to a script which is operating at only half-flame. ★★½ VHS: $14.99; DVD: $29.99

Runaway Train

(1985, 107 min, US, Andrei Konchalovsky) *Jon Voight, Eric Roberts, Rebecca DeMornay, Kenneth McMillan.* High-voltage action film, based on a

screenplay by Akira Kurosawa, with Voight and Roberts as two escaped prisoners who become trapped on a runaway train in the frozen wasteland of the Northwest. Voight and Roberts both received Oscar nominations — unusual for an action film. ★★★½ VHS: $14.99; DVD: $14.99

The Runner Stumbles

(1979, 109 min, US, Stanley Kramer) *Dick Van Dyke, Kathleen Quinlan, Maureen Stapleton, Beau Bridges.* In a small Washington mining town during the 1920s, a priest (Van Dyke) is accused of murdering a young nun. Considering the volatile subject matter, this is pretty tame stuff. ★★

The Running Man

(1987, 100 min, US, Paul Michael Glaser) *Arnold Schwarzenegger.* Futuristic actioner with Arnold Schwarzenegger as a condemned prisoner whose one chance of hope lies in a torturous and deadly televised game where contestants are pitted against brutal opponents and impossible obstacles. Richard Dawson is well-cast as the game show host. ★★½ VHS: $9.99; DVD: $19.99

Running Mates

(1992, 85 min, US, Michael Lindsay-Hogg) *Ed Harris, Diane Keaton.* A bittersweet comedy about love and loyalty in the whirlwind of a political campaign. Harris stars as Hugh Hathaway, the senator stud bucking for a presidential nomination. Keaton is Aggie Shaw, a charmingly kooky author who wins his heart (sound familiar?). However, the spin doctors aren't sure if Aggie is First Lady material, what with her outspoken demeanor and questionable past. Winning performances by both Harris and Keaton makes this love-conquers-all story a delight. ★★★ VHS: $9.99

Running on Empty

(1988, 116 min, US, Sidney Lumet) *Christine Lahti, Judd Hirsch, River Phoenix, Martha Plimpton, Steven Hill.* An exceptional cast highlights this powerful and perceptive drama about a family's struggle to stay together. Lahti and Hirsch portray former '60s radicals wanted by the FBI who have been living underground for two decades. Borrowing the names of the deceased and able to move their family at a moment's notice, they must face the extra burden of separation when their eldest son, a gifted musician, applies for college — which would bring the boy into the open and guarantee his not seeing his parents again. Phoenix is exceptional as the devoted son faced with the possibility of not seeing his family again, and the reunion scene between Lahti and Hill is simply astonishing. A tour de force from all involved. ★★★★ VHS: $14.99; DVD: $14.99

Running Scared

(1986, 106 min, US, Peter Hyams) *Gregory Hines, Billy Crystal, Jimmy Smits.* Hines and Crystal work well together in this effective police thriller as two streetwise undercover Chicago cops on the trail of a drug kingpin. The film is highlighted by funny dialogue and an exciting (if improbable) chase scene on the elevated line. ★★½ VHS: $9.99

Franka Potente in *Run Lola Run*

Chris Tucker (l.) and Jackie Chan in *Rush Hour*

Running Wild

(1928, 68 min, US, Eddie Cline) *W.C. Fields.* Even in this hilarious silent film, you can hear every word Fields is muttering under his breath. Once again sporting that sleazy little dab of a mustache that he seemed to favor in his silent films, Fields is a mere milquetoast of a man, emboldened by a chance encounter with a hypnotist. ★★★½

Rush

(1991, 120 min, US, Lili Fini Zanuck) *Jason Patric, Jennifer Jason Leigh, Gregg Allman, Max Perlich, William Sadler.* A dark, intense look at undercover cops in 1970s Texas, *Rush* has an unrelentingly grim outlook, which, though obstensibly about agents becoming lost in another world, comes off more as a 1980s "just-say-no" parable. In another long line of stand-out performances, Leigh stars as a novice police officer who is teamed with brooding Patric to snare alleged drug kingpin Allman. As the two officers introduce themselves to the denizens of the underworld, they slowly become what they're hunting. It's a point, though well made, which would have been used to better dramatic effect if not for the blatant moralizing. ★★½ VHS: $9.99

Rush Hour

(1998, 97 min, US, Brett Ratner) *Jackie Chan, Chris Tucker, Tom Wilkinson, Chris Penn, Elizabeth Peña.* Bringing together two unlikely screen personalities with unexpectedly solid comic results, *Rush Hour* is an extremely funny and energetic comic cop adventure. Tucker plays a maverick, wisecracking L.A. cop who is "recruited" into babysitting Hong Kong detective Chan when the latter arrives to investigate the kidnapping of the daughter of the Chinese consul. Since their assistance isn't wanted by the FBI agents on the case, the two team up to track down the kidnappers themselves. Chan is a marvel performing his own stunts, Tucker's delivery of some very funny lines is terrific, and their rapport is marvelous. Look past the familiar police procedural set-up and the one-dimensional supporting cast, and *Rush Hour* is

non-stop entertainment. (VHS available letter-boxed or pan & scan) (Sequel: *Rush Hour 2*) ★★★ VHS: $14.99; DVD: $19.99

Rushmore

(1998, 93 min, US, Wes Anderson) *Jason Schwartzman, Bill Murray, Olivia Williams, Seymour Cassel, Brian Cox (III), Mason Gamble.* This outlandish, hilarious and inventive comedy from the director of *Bottle Rocket* delights in its irreverent examination of the vicious underbelly of adolescence and the dark and twisted side of puppy love. Schwartzman stars as 15-year-old Max Fischer, a brilliant intellect and academic underachiever attending Rushmore, an exclusive academy for boys. After forging an alliance with one of Rushmore's wealthiest benefactors, Herman Blume (Murray), his institutional confidence becomes undermined when he and Herman vie for the school's newest teacher, Rosemary Cross (Williams). The ensuing rivalry stays firmly ensconced in its own wacky brand of delightfully subversive, Salingeresque humor. Schwartzman is stellar in his film debut as the crafty and vindictive pubescent, and Murray delivers a career performance as a befuddled and lonely millionaire teetering on the verge of his mid-life crisis. ★★★★ VHS: $19.99; DVD: $39.99

The Russia House

(1990, 123 min, US, Fred Schepisi) *Sean Connery, Michelle Pfeiffer, Roy Scheider, James Fox, John Mahoney.* An intriguing espionage thriller, based on John Le Carre's novel. Connery plays a down-on-his-heels London publisher who is unwittingly thrust into political intrigue when a top secret Russian manuscript is sent to him. At the insistence of the British Secret Service, Connery travels to Moscow to uncover the story and its writer. Pfeiffer, complete with accent, ably plays the Russian liaison with whom the reluctant spy falls in love. As a spy story, *The Russia House* is at its best; but the romantic angle between Connery and Pfeiffer, though handsome, is not always believable. ★★½ VHS: $9.99

The Russians Are Coming, The Russians Are Coming!

(1966, 135 min, US, Norman Jewison) *Alan Arkin, Brian Keith, Jonathan Winters, Carl Reiner, Eva Marie Saint.* Hysteria breaks out in a small New England coastal town when a Russian sub-marine runs aground on their beach. Some hilarious moments from an inspired cast, including Oscar nominee Arkin as a Russian sailor and Winters as a gun-toting local, make this one of the biggest pleasures of all 1960s comedies. ★★★½ VHS: $19.99

Ruthless People

(1986, 93 min, US, Jim Abrahams, David Zucker & Jerry Zucker) *Bette Midler, Danny DeVito, Judge Reinhold, Helen Slater, Anita Morris, Bill Pullman.* Larceny, infidelity and murder among California's nouveau riche form the core of this hilarious comedy. DeVito plays an unfaithful husband who plots to kill his over-bearing wife, Midler, who, fortunately for him, has been kidnapped by a not-so-ruthless couple whom DeVito swindled. Reinhold and Slater are the hapless couple. A hip, modern retelling of O. Henry's celebrated short story, "The Ransom of Red Chief." ★★★½

Ryan's Daughter

(1970, 177 min, GB, David Lean) *Robert Mitchum, Sarah Miles, Christopher Jones, John Mills, Trevor Howard.* This unabashedly senti-mental, wildly cinematic story was filmed in Northern Ireland and features Miles as a young girl who marries a simple, plodding schoolteacher (Mitchum) only to have an affair with a British soldier (Jones). As direct-ed by Lean, the film is brisk and stylish, but the simplicity of the story doesn't support the elephantine production values that Lean heaped upon it. MGM went out on a limb for $15 million on this extravaganza and was lucky it didn't bomb. Mills won an Oscar for his touching portrayal of the town idiot. (VHS available letterboxed or pan & scan) ★★★ VHS: $24.99

Rushmore

Sabotage

(1936, 76 min, GB, Alfred Hitchcock) *Sylvia Sidney, Oscar Homolka.* Freely adapted from Joseph Conrad's "Secret Agent," this elaborately detailed and disquieting film concerns a kindly movie theater manager who doubles as a dangerous foreign agent. The man's wife (Sidney), after her younger brother is killed by a bomb, begins to develop suspicions and then has a little trouble carving the roast that evening. (Remade as *Joseph Conrad's The Secret Agent*) ★★★

Saboteur

(1942, 108 min, US, Alfred Hitchcock) *Robert Cummings, Priscilla Lane, Norman Lloyd.* Cummings is charged with the wartime sabotage of a munitions factory and forced into a hurried flight from misguided justice. Racing across the country, he pursues the true culprit, an elusive individual named Fry, and eventually confronts him atop the Statue of Liberty. One of Hitchcock's lesser-known works, this nonetheless is a tense, exciting spy story with many scenes which bear the Master's touch. ★★★½ VHS: $14.99; DVD: $29.99

Sabrina

(1954, 113 min, US, Billy Wilder) *Audrey Hepburn, Humphrey Bogart, William Holden, John Williams.* Charming romantic comedy featuring an impeccable cast. Holden is a rich playboy smitten with chauffeur's daughter Hepburn; but older brother Bogey steps in to separate the pair and falls in love with her himself. Based on Samuel Taylor's play "Sabrina Fair." (Remade in 1996) ★★★½ VHS: $14.99; DVD: $29.99

Sabrina

(1995, 127 min, US, Sydney Pollack) *Harrison Ford, Julia Ormond, Greg Kinnear, Nancy Marchand, John Wood, Richard Crenna.* One of the joys of Billy Wilder's 1954 romantic comedy *Sabrina* is the enchanting performance by Audrey Hepburn as the chauffeur's daughter who becomes involved with her father's employer. In taking over her role, no one expected Ormand to be another Hepburn. But in Pollack's tranquil remake, sadly, the magic is just not there. Not without its own modest charms, including a charismatic performance by Ford, *Sabrina* is an appealing though unnecessary remake. ★★½ VHS: $14.99

Sacco and Vanzetti

(1971, 120 min, France/Italy, Guiliano Montaldo) *Gian Marie Volonte, Riccardo Cucciolla, Milo O'Shea, Cyril Cusack.* Told in pseudo-documentary style, this exposé of the famous 1920 trial of two Italian anarchists who were unjustly accused of crimes is a classic look at the American injustice system and the American penchant for mass political hysteria when it suits its leaders. A realistic and moving account

with Joan Baez singing the title song. (Dubbed) ★★★ VHS: $19.99; DVD: $24.99

El Sacerdote (The Priest)

(1977, 100 min, Spain, Eloy de la Iglesia) *Simon Andreu.* Set during the repressive Franco regime (which acts as a symbol of the equally repressive Catholic Church), this involving drama follows the tortured life of a 36-year-old priest as he struggles with his vow of celibacy. Father Miguel (Andreu) is a conservative priest who blindly follows the restrictions of authority until he becomes troubled with his raging and unspent libido. Unable to find solace in either Christ or the arms of a married woman who loves him, the tormented man resorts to a horrible act in an attempt to solve his problems. Similar in tone and theme to 1994's *Priest*, this film stays more focused on the dilemma of a sincere man who must fight the conflicting forces of his religious calling and the calling of physical desire. (Spanish with English subtitles) ★★★ VHS: $59.99

The Sacrifice

(1986, 145 min, Sweden/USSR, Andrei Tarkovsky) *Erland Josephson, Susan Fleetwood.* Alexander's family is gathered to celebrate his 70th birthday. A quiet tension fills the air. When an uneasy silence is shattered by an emergency broadcast which reports an impending nuclear attack, they begin to fall apart. Alexander then learns of a way the disaster can be prevented... but is the world worth saving? In this, his final film, Tarkovsky forms a powerful vision of the future which will haunt the memory. Winner of the 1986 Cannes Film Festival Special Jury Prize. (Swedish with English subtitles) ★★★½ VHS: $29.99; DVD: $39.99

Sadie McKee

(1934, 90 min, US, Clarence Brown) *Joan Crawford, Edward Arnold, Franchot Tone, Gene Raymond.* Crawford is in good form in this three-hanky weeper as a maid involved, at various times, with millionaire Arnold, ne'er-do-well Raymond and employer Tone. ★★★ VHS: $19.99

Sadie Thompson

(1928, 97 min, US, Raoul Walsh) *Gloria Swanson, Lionel Barrymore, Raoul Walsh.* W. Somerset Maugham's "Rain" gets a good workout as Swanson plays a whore in Pago Pago who takes up with reformer Barrymore. Director Walsh has fun on both sides of the camera playing the sailor who really loves her. Seldom seen, until the recent reconstruction of the lost last reel using surviving production stills and frame enlargements. (Remade in 1932 as *Rain* and in 1953 as *Miss Sadie Thompson*) ★★★½ VHS: $24.99; DVD: $29.99

Safe

(1995, 121 min, US, Todd Haynes) *Julianne Moore, Xander Berkeley, Peter Friedman, James LeGros, Jessica Harper.* Restrained but emotionally involving, this is a harrowing tale of a woman who physically suffers at the hands of "progress." The deceptively simple story follows Carol White (the remarkable Moore), an out-of-touch, Stepford Wife–like Southern California housewife who finds her body slowly ravaged by allergic reactions to everyday chemicals, fragrances and fumes. This transforms her seem-

Sabrina ('54)

ingly protected upper-middle-class existence into a terror of everyday life. With a bold yet austere visual style, Haynes chillingly explores suburban complacency and existential alienation and its ensuing lack of self-worth. Ultimately, *Safe* is anything but and is thought-provoking and quietly disturbing. ★★★½ VHS: $19.99

Safe Men

(1998, 89 min, US, John Hamburg) *Steve Zahn, Sam Rockwell, Harvey Fierstein, Paul Giamatti, Michael Lerner.* An overlooked indie gem, *Safe Men* is a very funny comic caper in which two really lousy lounge singers, Sam and Eddie (Zahn, Rockwell), are mistaken for safecrackers by Veal Chop (Giamatti), a henchman for the local Jewish Mafia. Asked to retrieve a "cup" for Big Fat Bernie Gayle (Lerner), a Jewish gangster, the luckless duo get in over their heads and into a rivalry with Big Fat's nemesis Good Stuff Leo (Fierstein). The pairing of Zahn and Rockwell is inspired; they play off each other to perfection. Director Hamburg has some really good ideas going on here — perhaps too many; the film could have been sharpened slightly — but most of the targets he hits are a bull's eye. ★★★ VHS: $102.99

Safe Passage

(1994, 97 min, US, Robert Allan Ackerman) *Susan Sarandon, Sam Shepard, Nick Stahl, Sean Astin, Robert Sean Leonard, Marcia Gay Harden, Jason London.* Sarandon plays mother to seven sons, one of whom is a soldier stationed in the Middle East. When word comes that his barracks has been bombed, the entire family comes together for the requisite tears and laughter, revelations and recriminations. Though there's nothing overtly original in either the film's plot line or execution, it's the conviction of the ensemble, headed by the radiant Sarandon, which gives *Safe Passage* its emotion. ★★★ VHS: $14.99

The Sailor Who Fell from Grace with the Sea

(1976, 104 min, GB, Lewis John Carlino) *Sarah Miles, Kris Kristofferson, Jonathan Kahn.* This striking and erotic drama concerns itself with a group of young schoolboys who commit a ritual murder upon a visiting sailor. Miles plays a lonely widow who falls in love with the sailor (Kristofferson) before his unfortunate demise. Filled with steamy love scenes (featured in *Playboy* at the time), this unusual and beautifully photographed film is based on a novella by Yukio Mishima. ★★★ VHS: $14.99

The Saint

(1997, 115 min, US, **Phillip Noyce**) *Val Kilmer, Elisabeth Shue, Rade Serbedzija.* Simon Templar, aka The Saint, has been around for a long time. The hero of over 50 books, a film series in the 1940s, and a popular TV show starring Roger Moore in the 1960s, this guy has seen a lot of action. And while there's a bit of action, as well, in this update starring Kilmer as Templar, its formulaic and convoluted story keeps it from ever becoming a truly satisfying espionage adventure. The story has to do with Templar being hired to locate and steal the cold-fusion formula of scientist Shue. There's a couple very competent action scenes, and a few laughs along the way, but *The Saint* never gets as flavorful as its predecessors. (VHS available letterboxed or pan & scan) ★★ VHS: $14.99; DVD: $24.99

Saint Clara

(1995, 85 min, Israel, **Ari Folman & Uri Sivan**) *Lucy Dubinchik.* It's the class of 1999, Israel — and this ain't no Breakfast Club: This is an Israeli apocalyptic sci-fi surf movie without the beach! What concerns the students at Golda Meir Junior High School are the Richter scale, Edith Piaf, revolution, who will lead the revolution, and a mysterious classmate from Russia named Clara, who has clairvoyant powers. Clara's powers are used to challenge the school's authorities when she uses them on a math test and everyone in the class gets perfect scores. Soon everyone in town knows about the girl with the prophecies, the girl who comes from "the zone" in Russia where the gift runs in the family. Directors Folman and Sivan have created a beguiling, funny and irreverent tale in this twisted presentation of the Apocalypse. (Hebrew with English subtitles) ★★★ VHS: $24.99

St. Elmo's Fire

(1985, 110 min, US, **Joel Schumacher**) *Emilio Estevez, Rob Lowe, Andrew McCarthy, Demi Moore, Ally Sheedy, Mare Winningham.* Though it wants to be more, this drama of post-college grads struggling in Washington, D.C., is nothing more than "The Little Chill." A who's-who cast of 1980s teen celebs is featured. ★★ VHS: $9.99

The St. Francisville Experiment

(2000, 76 min, US, **Dana Scanlon**) *Tim Baldini, Madison Charap.* Shot in the same faux documentary-like style of *The Blair Witch Project*, this low-budget rip-off follows four strangers who investigate a legendary haunted house. The director assures us that what we are about to see is real — like a series of clumsily staged ghostly occurences, awful acting and laughable plot developments. A horror film with all the grace of an elephant tap dancing through a minefield. ★ VHS: $69.99; DVD: $24.99

Saint Jack

(1979, 112 min, US, **Peter Bogdanovich**) *Ben Gazzara, Denholm Elliott, George Lazenby.* An American businessman in Singapore (Gazzara) aims to run the classiest whore-

house in town, but runs afoul of the Chinese mafia. A well-played tale set against the seedier side of small-time operations. ★★★ VHS: $14.99; DVD: $19.99

St. Martin's Lane

(1938, 85 min, GB, **Tim Whelan**) *Charles Laughton, Vivien Leigh, Rex Harrison, Larry Adler.* Incorporating a Warner Brothers backstage musical with a British class melodrama, this touching and lively rags-to-riches tale is a bittersweet look at ambition and romance. The story follows the rise of a street gamine (Leigh) who is at first taken under the wing of a mediocre busker (street musician), marvelously played by Laughton. Under his supervision, her natural talent blossoms. She eventually becomes the toast of the town, while her former mentor flounders. Leigh creates a totally sympathetic character who does many unsympathetic things, and in an early role, Harrison gives a nuanced performance as the sophisticated songwriter who spirits her away to fame, fortune, and his penthouse. ★★★ VHS: $24.99

St. Michael Had a Rooster

(1971, 87 min, Italy, **Paolo & Vittorio Taviani**) *Giulio Brogi, Renato Scarpa, Vittorio Fantoni, Cinzia Bruno.* This black comedy from the brothers Taviani, as dry and tart as well-aged sherry, is based on a short story by Leo Tolstoy, here reset in the chaotic Italy of the late 1800s. After taking over the town hall while the citizens of its tiny city are at Sunday services, "internationalist" Giukio Manieri (Brogi) is surprised when the local population fail to throw off their shackles and join the uprising. Indeed, the whole revolution is quickly quelled by the authorities, not through the use of violence, but through a far more ruinous weapon: indifference. Deemed not even worth executing, he is imprisoned for ten years only to emerge more out of touch than ever with the people he wanted to liberate, the new subversives he had hoped to inspire, and, all too tragically, with himself. (Italian with English subtitles) ★★★ VHS: $19.99

The Saint of Fort Washington

(1993, 107 min, US, **Tim Hunter**) *Matt Dillon, Danny Glover, Rick Aviles, Nina Siemaszko, Ving Rhames, Joe Seneca.* A poignant if familiar character study examining the friendship between two homeless men. Dillon plays a schizophrenic photographer newly homeless. At the prison-like shelter Fort Washington, he is befriended by Vietnam vet Glover, who takes him under his wing. With images of *Scarecrow* and *Midnight Cowboy* hovering overhead, the two confront an uncaring, suspicious and hostile society in their battle to survive on the streets. Both actors give strong performances, and the film succeeds in putting a face to the faceless army of the homeless; though its important message of "they're not criminals" is at times heavy-handed. ★★★ VHS: $19.99

Salaam Bombay!

(1988, 114 min, India/France, **Mira Nair**) *Shafig Syed, Hansa Vithal.* A spectacular directorial debut for Nair, this shockingly graphic yet compassionate tale chronicles the wretched but ever resourceful life of 10-year-old Krishna, a boy thrown out from his house and forced to fend for himself. Initially scared and alienated,

Krishna soons befriends the prostitutes, drug dealers and fellow street urchins of the red-light district and eventually becomes part of their milieu of exploitation, squalor and survival. Vividly drawn, using many non-professional actors and filming on the teeming streets of Bombay, this revelation avoids being preachy or heavy-handed in telling its realistic tale. (Hindi with English subtitles) ★★★

Salem's Lot: The Miniseries

(1979, 184 min, US, **Tobe Hooper**) *David Soul, James Mason, Lance Kerwin, Bonnie Bedelia.* Though still missing 16 minutes from the original miniseries telecast, this restored adaptation of the Stephen King novel easily qualifies as one of the scariest horror movies ever made for television. Soul stars as a successful novelist who evidently never read Thomas Wolfe's most famous admonition, "You can't go home again," and does just that. Unfortunately, his arrival coincides with that of a worldly antique dealer (Mason in a superbly sinister performance) who has earmarked the inhabitants of Soul's small New England hometown as "fang fodder" — vampires, that is. (Also available in the more violent 112-minute "European" version on VHS at $9.99.) ★★★½ VHS: $19.99; DVD: $14.99

Sallah

(1963, 110 min, Israel, **Ephraim Kishon**) *Chaim Topol, Geula Noni.* One of the best Israeli films ever made, *Sallah* was an Academy Award nominee for Best Foreign Film and won First Prize in the San Francisco International Film Festival. Topol stars as the head of an immigrant family from North Africa who encounter nothing but frustration and disappointment during their period of transition in the Promised Land. (Hebrew with English subtitles) ★★★★ VHS: $79.99

Salmonberries

(1991, 94 min, US, **Percy Adlon**) *k.d. lang, Rosel Zech.* Written and directed by Adlon, *Salmonberries* has much in common with his earlier effort *Bagdad Cafe* (surreal cinematic flights of fancy, a haunting soundtrack and lots of landscape). Set in the desolate, no-man's land of Alaska, this quirky drama examines the developing emotional bonds between two women of disparate backgrounds. Singer lang plays an orphaned Eskimo who hides her gender beneath baggy layers of clothing and who develops an attraction to Roswitha, the local librarian of the town of Kotzebue. Though not satisfying as a lesbian love story, the film is notable for the presence of lang and her beautiful soundtrack featuring the theme song, "Barefoot." ★★½ VHS: $19.99

Salo, 120 Days of Sodom

(1975, 115 min, Italy, **Pier Paolo Pasolini**) *Giorgio Cataldi, Umberto P. Quinavalle.* Pasolini's last film is an unbelievably bleak and depressing vision of the human condition which shocked audiences with its brutally graphic scenes of sexual degradation and oppressive violence. The director transposes the Marquis de Sade's novel about the debauching of the four pillars of 18th century French Society to World War II Italy. A group of older Fascists (men and women) bring together a group of teenagers of both sexes and subject them to all kinds of sexual, mental and physical degradation. (Italian with subtitles) ★★★½

Salome

(1953, 103 min, US, William Dieterle) *Rita Hayworth, Charles Laughton, Judith Anderson, Stewart Granger.* Hayworth's lustrous beauty shines in this liberal retelling of the biblical story of Salome — daughter to Queen Herodia of Galilee — who offered herself to spare John the Baptist. Laughton stars as King Herod who, for fear of a curse, cannot bring himself to silence the good Baptist despite the prodding of his wicked queen (Anderson). Palace intrigue abounds as queen plots against king, king lusts after daughter-in-law and a Roman commander (Granger) must conceal his religious beliefs. While extremely well-acted and often entertaining, the film suffers from a heavy-handed treatment of its religious themes. ★★½ VHS: $19.99

Salome's Last Dance

(1988, 87 min, GB, Ken Russell) *Glenda Jackson, Stratford Johns, Nickolas Grace, Imogen Millais-Scott.* With his usual flair for decadence and depravity, Russell crafted this brilliant tribute to the literary genius of Oscar Wilde. The film follows Wilde to a male brothel where he is entertained by an "illegal" performance of his banned play, "Salome." The play itself represents Wilde's twisted vision of the fateful biblical encounter between Salome (daughter of King Herod) and John the Baptist. Here re-enacted full of pulsating sexual innuendo, Russell eagerly sinks his teeth into Wilde's poetry and renders the play, in its entirety, at a frenetic pace. Millais-Scott is devilishly alluring as the coquettish, cockneyed Salome, and Jackson is nothing short of perfect as the steely, evil Queen Herodias. ★★★; DVD: $29.99

Salon Kitty

(1976, 110 min, West Germany, Tinto Brass) *Ingrid Thulin, Helmut Berger.* Made in the "grand" tradition of *Caligula, The Damned* and *The Night Porter,* this exploitative, sexually graphic shocker features a crazed Berger as a powerful SS officer who will do anything to get the dirt on his fellow Nazis and their wives. An erotic and, at times, disturbing probe into the sickness of man. (English language version) ★★½

Salsa: The Motion Picture

(1988, 97 min, US, Boaz Davidson) *Bobby Rosa.* Horrendously — but at least laughably — bad, this misguided attempt to cash in during the "salsa craze" of the late 1980s features ex-Menudo star Rosa as a grease monkey with a twitch in his hips, an itch in his crotch and stars in his eyes. Rosa, with a chiseled body but a squeaky, Michael Jackson voice, can dance; but that alone can't save this insipid *Saturday Night Fever/Dirty Dancing* rip-off. ★ VHS: $14.99

Salt of the Earth

(1953, 94 min, US, Herbert Biberman) *Will Geer, Rosaura Revueltas.* One of the classics of American independent filmmaking, this impassioned, pro-feminist drama chronicles the events in a bitter strike by Chicano zinc miners in New Mexico. When an injunction is issued against the workers, the wives of the strikers take to the picket line. Seemingly incomprehensible even in today's conservative climate, the film was boycotted by most cinemas on its release; with director Biberman, actor Geer, producer Paul Jarrico and screenwriter Michael Wilson all subsequently blacklisted for their part in its production. ★★★½ VHS: $29.99; DVD: $24.99

Salut L'Artiste

(1973, 96 min, France, Yves Robert) *Marcello Mastroianni, Françoise Fabian.* Mastroianni's extraordinary talent to portray the "naïve oaf" comes fully to life in this captivating and witty modern farce about a fumbling bit actor trying to live two lives at once. His mistress finally leaves him and so he sheepishly returns home to his wife only to discover that she is carrying someone else's child. Full of pratfalls and pitfalls, this engaging and sardonic comedy sparkles with effervescence. (French with English subtitles) ★★★

Salvador

(1986, 123 min, US, Oliver Stone) *James Woods, James Belushi, John Savage, Michael Murphy.* Released the same year as his classic *Platoon,* Stone wrote and directed this taut, hard-hitting political drama based on American photojournalist Richard Boyle's experiences in El Salvador in 1980. Woods gives what may be his finest performance as Boyle, and Belushi has certainly never been better as Boyle's sidekick just along for the ride. ★★★½ VHS: $14.99; DVD: $24.99

Samantha

(1992, 101 min, US, Stephen La Rocque) *Martha Plimpton, Dermot Mulroney, Hector Elizondo, Ione Skye, Mary Kay Place.* When Samantha is informed by her parents that they found her on their doorstep twenty-one years earlier, she locks herself in her room and booby traps herself in. Plimpton is Samantha, a young woman in search of her own identity in this comedy that tries too hard to be offbeat. However, Plimpton gives an edgy, headstrong performance, and the charming relationship between Samantha and her best friend Henry (Mulroney) nearly makes up for the sometimes ridiculous screenplay. ★½ VHS: $79.99

Same Time, Next Year

(1978, 119 min, US, Robert Mulligan) *Alan Alda, Ellen Burstyn.* Two engaging performances by Alda and Burstyn highlight this appealing film adaptation of Bernard Slade's hit Broadway play. Combining comedy, romance and drama, the story follows the 20-year extramarital affair of George and Doris, who meet once a year for a romantic reunion. ★★★ VHS: $9.99

Sammy and Rosie Get Laid

(1987, 100 min, GB, Stephen Frears) *Ayub Kahn Din, Frances Barber, Shashi Kapoor, Claire Bloom.* Director Frears and writer Hanif Kureishi reunite after their triumphant *My Beautiful Laundrette* to fashion another brilliantly scathing portrait of present-day London. Sammy (Din), the son of a right-wing Pakistani politician, is involved with a sexually liberated English woman (Barber). When his father, fleeing political enemies, comes to live with them, their informal relationship begins to mirror the mounting social unrest in the streets outside their window. ★★★½

Le Samouraï

(1967, 95 min, France, Jean-Pierre Melville) *Alain Delon, Nathalie Delon, François Périer, Cathy Rosier.* Hailed by director John Woo as being "the closest to a perfect movie that I have ever seen," Melville's stylish thriller, admittedly influenced by 1930s gangster flicks and film noir of the 1940s, is a taut tale circling around the life of a professional hit man. Graced with an icy beauty, A. Delon stars as Jef Costello, a solitary, grim-faced killer-for-hire whose methodically ordered (and idealistic) code of behavoir becomes unraveled when the police begin to track him down after a hit. Love and betrayal — the two great actions of film noir — contribute to his down fall. Especially appealing in this nearly wordless film are the women in his life: N. Delon as the woman who loves him, and Rosier as a sultry nightclub singer and Costello's object of affection. A masterwork of evocation, atmosphere and narrative. (French with English subtitles) ★★★★ VHS: $29.99

Samson and Delilah

(1949, 128 min, US, Cecil B. DeMille) *Hedy Lamarr, Victor Mature, Angela Lansbury, George Sanders.* Lamarr is ready for her close-up as the seductive Delilah in this typically lush DeMille biblical drama. Mature is quite good as strongman Samson who gets the "cut" from rejected lover Delilah. ★★★ VHS: $29.99

Samurai I: Musashi Miyamoto

(1954, 92 min, Japan, Hiroshi Inagaki) *Toshiro Mifune.* Scintillating thrills and excitement are promised for fans of samurai and adventure films with this rousing trio called the "Samurai Trilogy," which is based upon the real-life adventures of legendary swordsman Miyamoto Musashi. The great Mifune is the peasant who trains to become a master swordsman and protector of his people. This, the first part, introduces the aspiring samurai and examines his arduous training and indoctrination. (Japanese with English subtitles) ★★★ VHS: $19.99; DVD: $29.99

Samurai II: Duel at Ichijoji Temple

(1955, 102 min, Japan, Hiroshi Inagaki) *Toshiro Mifune.* Part two of the "Samurai Trilogy" deals with the developing skills of samurai Mifune and centers around a bloody duel with a particularly mean warrior. (Japanese with English subtitles) ★★★ VHS: $19.99; DVD: $29.99

Samurai III: Duel at Ganryu Island

(1956, 102 min, Japan, Hiroshi Inagaki) *Toshiro Mifune.* In this, the concluding chapter of the "Samurai Trilogy," we follow our hero's romantic interlude as well as his defense of a village from a marauding horde. We also witness the inevitable showdown with his arch nemesis, Kojiro. Please note: Although the three films in the "Samurai Trilogy" follow a chronology, each film can be enjoyed and understood independently of each other. (Japanese with English subtitles) ★★★ VHS: $19.99; DVD: $29.99

Samurai Saga

(1959, 110 min, Japan, Hiroshi Inagaki) *Toshiro Mifune.* This love triangle between a very demanding princess and two warriors is set in war-torn Kyoto in 1599. Mifune is one of the gallant swordsmen whose enormous nose is the only impediment to his capture of the elusive beauty. A classic story of romance and war. (Japanese with English subtitles) ★★★

San Francisco

(1936, 116 min, US, W.S. Van Dyke) *Clark Gable, Spencer Tracy, Jeanette MacDonald, Jack Holt.* One of the most popular films of the 1930s, this early disaster film stars Gable as a saloon owner and MacDonald as a singer who fall in love — all set right before the big earthquake of 1905. Tracy is excellent in support as Gable's best pal, and the special effects are quite good. ★★★ VHS: $19.99

Sand and Blood

(1987, 101 min, France, Jeanne Labrune) *Sami Frey, Andre Dussollier.* Coming on the heels of Pedro Almodóvar's exploration of sex and violence in the bullring with *Matador* comes this much more thoughtful yet equally provocative, erotically charged drama. An upcoming matador from "the wrong side of the tracks" meets and befriends a wealthy doctor who is morally opposed to the violence of the bullfight. Their unlikely relationship affects both their lives and their families as together they confront their hidden secrets and fears. Be forewarned: the bullfighting and slaughterhouse scenes in the film contain bloody and graphic images of violence against animals. (French with English subtitles) ★★★ VHS: $79.99

The Sand Pebbles

(1966, 179 min, US, Robert Wise) *Steve McQueen, Richard Attenborough, Candice Bergen, Mako, Richard Crenna.* This beautifully photographed, compelling drama features a splendid performance by McQueen as a jaded sailor on an American gunboat on the Yangtze River in 1926. His increasing awareness of the volitile political situation contributes to his escalating confrontation with his superiors. A sprawling combination of action, romance and subtextual editorial comment. ★★★½ VHS: $14.99; DVD: $24.99

Sandakan No. 8

(1974, 121 min, Japan, Kei Kumai) *Kinuyo Tanaka, Yoko Takakashi.* Winner of the Berlin Film Festival's Silver Bear Award, this heartrending drama follows a female journalist who befriends an impoverished old lady who recounts her anguished life as a prostitute in a brothel in Borneo in the early 1900s. (Japanese with English subtitles) ★★★½

Sanders of the River

(1935, 98 min, GB, Zoltan Korda) *Paul Robeson, Leslie Banks.* This outmoded adventure tale about the captain of a river patrol in colonial Africa is filled with caricature and offers little insight into the colonial mindset. Still, the film is made interesting by its early use of location shooting and the dominating screen presence of Robeson. ★★½ VHS: $19.99

The Sandlot

(1993, 101 min, US, David Mickey Evans) *Tom Guiry, Mike Vitar, Denis Leary, Karen Allen, James Earl Jones, Arliss Howard, Brooke Adams.* It's the 1960s, and soon-to-be fifth grader Scotty Smalls is the new kid in town. An avid baseball fan, Scotty is befriended by a baseball-loving group of kids who all spend an idyllic summer playing our national pastime. Things are going great

until Scotty's dad's prized baseball, autographed by Babe Ruth, lands in a junkyard guarded by a ferocious dog. How to get it back? This heartwarming family film is a wonderful coming-of-age tale which should entertain both child and adult. ★★★ VHS: $9.99

Sanjuro

(1962, 96 min, Japan, Akira Kurosawa) *Toshiro Mifune, Tatsuya Nakadai.* Mifune is at his scruffy, steely-eyed best as the leader of young revolutionaries. An action-packed adventure film, sequel to *Yojimbo.* (Letterboxed) (Japanese with English subtitles) ★★★ VHS: $29.99; DVD: $29.99

Sankofa

(1993, 125 min, US, Haile Gerima) *Oyafunmike Ogunlano, Kofi Ghanaba, Alexandra Duah, Mutabaruka.* Slavery is an issue in America whch, like the Vietnam War and the genocide of the American Indian, is so ingrained in our collective unconscious that we rarely truly *think* about it. Lip service is paid, but true contemplation is rare. A successful, thought-provoking "issue" film is even more rare, which makes the excellent *Sankofa* such a treasure. This tale of a modern-day, African-American model who is unexplainedly transported back in time to experience life as a slave is anything but a dry history and civics lesson. The film is all the more remarkable for avoiding polemic, and for refusing to pander. After a heavy-handed opening, *Sankofa* finds its rhythm to become an extremely intense, harrowing yet dramatically rich study of a repugnant time in American history. ★★★½

Sans Soleil

(1983, 100 min, France, Chris Marker) Narrated in English by a woman reading from the lengthy memoirs of a friend's world-wide travels, this non-narrative, almost dreamy philosophical and sociological experimental film makes for an intense and demanding but rewarding film experience. The memoirs of the unnamed traveler expound on his travel impressions, mainly in Japan and in West Africa. As the narrator reads, the camera takes us to the amazingly contrasting locations, filled with weird and wondrous customs, sights and passions. This goes beyond simple ethnographic observation to become an intimate, almost mystical poem/portrait of mankind. ★★★ VHS: $29.99

Sanshiro Sugata

(1943, 80 min, Japan, Akira Kurosawa) *Denjiro Okochi, Yikiko Todoroki.* Made under the watchful eye of censors, this first film by a 33-year-old Kurosawa helped establish him as a major director. Set in the late 19th century, the story revolves around Sanshiro Sugata, an eager student helping a master to teach him the martial art of Judo, a form of fighting that requires the young man not just to learn the mere techniques of the art, but to attain a spiritual discipline as well. With explosive martial arts choreography, this understated philosophical film features the theme that runs throughout Kurosawa's work; that of a man who champions a principle despite an often hostile established order. (Japanese with English subtitles) ★★★ VHS: $19.99

Sansho the Baliff

(1954, 125 min, Japan, Kenji Mizoguchi) *Kinuyo Tanaka, Yoshiaki Hanayagi.* Set in the 11th century, this epic drama begins in a land ruled by a kindhearted provincial governor who is overthrown and exiled. His wife is reduced to prostitution while his children are kidnapped and sent into slavery. One of the children escapes and vows to establish a group of followers and return to his land in force. This sweeping drama, while played on a grand scale, retains the human quality in unfolding this sad yet beautiful tale. (Japanese with English subtitles) ★★★½ VHS: $39.99

Santa Claus: The Movie

(1985, 104 min, US, Jeannot Szwarc) *Dudley Moore, John Lithgow, David Huddleston.* Big-budget, clumsy but harmless children's story about one of Santa's elves falling prey to an evil toymaker, who may use "elfin" magic to control Christmas. Huddleston is an appropriately larger-than-life Santa; however, most of the cast appear very embarrassed by what's going on. ★★ VHS: $9.99

The Santa Clause

(1994, 95 min, US, John Pasquin) *Tim Allen, Judge Reinhold, Wendy Crewson, Eric Lloyd, Peter Boyle.* A satisfactory family comedy which is in need of a lot more laughs, *The Santa Clause* rarely demonstrates the caliber of humor suggested by its catchy title. Allen plays a divorced dad who on Christmas Eve knocks Santa off the roof. Taking over Kris Kringle's holiday obligations, Allen learns in doing so he is now the new Santa — hence the Santa Clause. While the story does occasionally live up to its enjoyable premise, and the North Pole set is real cool, the film never really ignites sparks in the laughs department, depending instead on F/X wizardry and the odd wink at the audience. ★★½ VHS: $19.99

Santa Sangre

(1990, 120 min, Italy/Mexico, Alejandro Jodorowsky) *Axel Jodorowsky, Sabrina Dennison, Guy Stockwell.* In the furiously imaginative tradition of Jodorowsky's '70s cult classic *El Topo* comes this violent, bizarre and mystifying parable of a young man's ultimate Oedipal complex. Set in Mexico, the story begins in a circus where a young boy is witness to his mother's dismemberment and his father's suicide. Understandably affected, the neurotic boy spends his adolescence in an insane asylum, but soon escapes (or does he?) and is reunited with his armless mom. Together, they begin a killing rampage against any woman who comes close to him. Plot matters little here, for it is Jodorowsky's intense visuals, like a hallucinogenic Fellini spectacle, that assaults the viewer leaving one both exhausted and exalted by this nighmarish vision. (English language) ★★★ VHS: $19.99

The Saphead/The High Sign/ One Week

(1920/21, 118 min, US, Herbert Blanche/Buster Keaton & Eddie Cline) *Buster Keaton.* A collection of three Buster Keaton comedies. *The Saphead* (1920, 78 min) was Keaton's first starring role. The film features Keaton as the title character, a Wall Street heir oblivious to life

Saturday Night and Sunday Morning

around him. The creaky plot has to do with Keaton's brother-in-law trying to steal the family fortune. Keaton shines in a lengthy, well-staged sequence about a run on the stock exchange. (★★½) *One Week* (1921, 19 min) was Keaton's first short as director and writer (with Cline), made directly after *Saphead*. It's a truly inventive, hilarious slapstick comedy about Keaton and his newlywed wife trying to build their pre-fab honeymoon home. Performing his own stunts, Keaton is a marvel. His stone face, comic timing, acrobatic skill and dexterity make him the silent screen's greatest clown. (★★★★) *The High Sign* (1921, 21 min) is a humorous story of Keaton becoming involved with a gang of cutthroats. What makes this short memorable is an unbelievable finale in which Keaton takes on the gang with the help of a booby-trapped mansion. Astonishing. (★★★) VHS: $29.99; DVD: $29.99

Sarafina!

(1992, 99 min, US/South Africa, Darrell James Roodt) *Whoopi Goldberg, John Kani, Leleti Khumalo, Miriam Makeba.* Mbogeni Ngema's powerful musical play about the struggle for freedom amongst South Africa's black school children receives mixed results in its film adaptation. The young Khumalo is superb in the title role of Sarafina, a teenage girl whose ambition is to play Nelson Mandela in the school play, but instead finds herself caught up in a vicious conflagration of hatred towards the white oppressor. The film suffers from an almost schizophrenic vacillation between moments of profound emotional impact and almost trivial song-and-dance routines. Still, by its end the film imparts a potent message on the destructive nature of hatred. ★★½

Sartre Par Lui Meme

(1976, 190 min, France, Alexandre Astruc & Michel Contat) *Jean-Paul Sartre, Simone de Beauvoir.* Jean-Paul Sartre, leading Existentialist and author of philosophical essays, plays and novels — many concerning the plight of man, alone in an alienating world — agreed to a filmed interview to speak of his work and his life. Filmed in his Montparnesse flat and featuring his longtime companion, Simone de Beauvoir, this witty and insightful document ranges from such topics as the Occupation and May 1968, to Existentialism and the role of the intellectual. An engrossing three hours with one

of the great minds of the 20th century. (French with English subtitles) ★★★ VHS: $99.99

Satan Met a Lady

(1936, 75 min, US, William Dieterle) *Bette Davis, Warren William.* Second screen version of Dashiell Hammet's "The Maltese Falcon" — the first was filmed in 1931 — and not on par with John Huston's 1941 classic. William plays the private eye, and Davis is the mystery woman. ★★ VHS: $19.99

Satan's Brew

(1976, 112 min, Germany, Rainer Werner Fassbinder) *Kurt Raab, Ingrid Caven.* RFW's first comedy is a weird, vulgar and perverse story of the adventures of Walter Kranz (Raab), a "revolutionary" poet who imagines himself to be the 19th-century homosexual poet Stefan George. The film, shot in a black comedic slapstick style, boasts among its peculiar characters Kranz's butch wife (Caven), a retarded brother, a wart-faced admirer and a troupe of prostitutes. (German with English subtitles) ★★½ VHS: $19.99

Saturday Night and Sunday Morning

(1960, 89 min, GB, Karel Reisz) *Albert Finney, Shirley Anne Field, Rachel Roberts.* With a savage comic perspective and a totally realistic approach, this biting drama, one of the first and best of the British New Wave of the 1960s, is a classic of the "angry young man" genre. In a star-making role, a youthful and handsome Finney is mesmerizing as a Nottingham factory worker whose rebellious nature is neatly summarized by his opening narration, "What I want is a good time. The remainder is all propaganda." The story follows Finney as he lets off steam on the weekends through his drinking binges and two romantic affairs — one of them with a married woman (a magnificent Roberts). Though no Alfie, Finney doesn't tread lightly with his depiction of a likable cad; and he and director Reisz take care in attention to time and place. A remarkable, insightful work both honest and daring. ★★★★

Saturday Night Fever

(1977, 118 min, US, John Badham) *John Travolta, Karen Gorney, Donna Pescow, Barry Miller.* Travolta created a cultural phenomenon as a Brooklyn youth who uses the disco dance floors

to escape the tedium of his home and social life. Pescow is exceptional as a local girl in love with Travolta. A tune-filled, trendsetting time capsule both compelling and hoary. Musical score by the Bee Gees. (Available in both PG- and R-rated versions.) ★★★ VHS: $14.99

Saturn 3

(1980, 88 min, GB, Stanley Donen) *Kirk Douglas, Farrah Fawcett, Harvey Keitel.* From the director of *Charade* comes this odd little sci-fi parable. Space-aged, hydroponic gardeners Douglas and Fawcett find their little astro-Eden no longer a lovely, verdant garden after that snake Keitel shows up with his psycho-robot Hector. ★★ VHS: $14.99; DVD: $24.99

Savage Nights (Les Nuite Fauves)

(1992, 126 min, France, Cyril Collard) *Cyril Collard, Romane Bohringer, Carlos Lopez.* Possibly the most personal and controversial of all the films dealing with AIDS, *Savage Nights* is a startlingly knowing semi-autobiographical melodrama by former rock star Collard (who died from AIDS just four days before his film swept the César Awards). Collard stars as Jean, a high-living bisexual photographer who discovers he is HIV-positive. He becomes involved with both love-sick 17-year-old Laura (Bohringer) and S&M obsessed, neo-Nazi soccer player Sami (Lopez). With its jagged, almost documentary feel, the film effectively and unapologetically delves into the life of a non-hero and his personal response to coping with AIDS. (French with English subtitles) ★★★

The Savage Woman

(1991, 100 min, Canada, Léa Pool) *Patricia Tulasne, Matthias Habich.* After her suicide attempt in the mountainous wilderness of France fails, Marianne, a young French-Canadian woman, wanders the area, avoiding contact with people and slowly losing her civilized self. She is eventually befriended by Elyseé, a lonely engineer working nearby at a dam, who nurses her back to health. The unlikely couple, seemingly against their will, soon fall in love. But their deepening relationship is strained by Marianne's secret: she's wanted by the police for murder. A taut melodrama kept interesting right until the surprise ending. (French with English subtitles) ★★★ VHS: $39.99

Savages

(1982, 106 min, GB, James Ivory) *Lewis J. Stadlen, Anne Francine, Thayer David, Sam Waterston.* By far the most offbeat result of the years of collaboration between Ivory and Ismail Merchant, this is the story of a group of clay covered savages who stumble across an abandoned mansion. Bit by bit, they assume the roles of the former, more civilized, inhabitants until finally they have constructed their own little microcosm of the landed gentry. This strange and hypnotic film evokes images of *King of Hearts* and *The Emerald Forest.* ★★½ VHS: $29.99

Save the Last Dance

(2001, 112 min, US, Thomas Carter) *Julia Stiles, Sean Patrick Thomas, Terry Kinney. Save the Last Dance* may be tepid, pandering teen-film garbage, but at least it has a positive message. A surprisingly weak Stiles is a dance student whose mother is killed on the way to see her daughter's

S

audition for Juilliard. Forced to live with her deadbeat dad in scary Chicago, Stiles attends a mostly black inner-city high school. She goes through all the usual clichés and ends up falling for Thomas. Kids might enjoy this film — and it does have good intentions — but this is numbingly predictable, and glacially paced to boot. Rent *Flashdance* or *Dirty Dancing*, instead, and save yourself from this last dance. ★½ VHS: $14.99; DVD: $29.99

Save the Tiger

(1973, 101 min, US, John G. Avildsen) *Jack Lemmon, Jack Gilford, Laurie Heineman, Patricia Smith, Thayer David, Lara Parker.* Lemmon's outstanding Academy Award-winning performance punctuates this often gripping account of one man's journey towards a moral divide. He plays an L.A. garment manufacturer whose business is near financial ruin. Longing for the innocence of his youth, he must resort to more corrupt means for a quick financial fix. Steve Shagan's screenplay is a searing commentary on consumerism and a country's lost direction during a volatile time. In support, Gilford excels as Lemmon's ethical business partner. ★★★ VHS: $14.99

Saving Grace

(1986, 112 min, US, Robert M. Young) *Tom Conti, Giancarlo Giannini, Erland Josephson, Edward James Olmos.* With a tip of the hat to *Roman Holiday*, this muddled comedy stars Conti as the Pope who, tiring of his rigid regime, unceremoniously leaves the Vatican to spend time with the common folk. ★★

Saving Grace

(2000, 95 min, GB, Nigel Cole) *Brenda Blethyn, Craig Ferguson, Martin Clunes, Tcheky Karyo.* Small-town eccentrics once again populate a humorous, low-keyed British comedy, but they've done so with a new twist that Margaret Rutherford would never have seen coming. The sparkling Blethyn stars as Grace, a recent widow whose husband has left her nothing but debt. Looking for financial salvation, she teams with her gardener Matthew (Ferguson of "The Drew Carey Show") to grow marijuana in her greenhouse. Little by little, the townspeople become involved in one way or another (suspicious neighbors, unsuspecting little old ladies getting high, etc.), prompting some obvious but funny jokes. A weak ending slightly mars

this otherwise winning comedy that is able to see beyond the inherent pot humor for a few sharp observations on human behavior. ★★★ VHS: $14.99; DVD: $24.99

Saving Private Ryan

(1998, 170 min, US, Steven Spielberg) *Tom Hanks, Tom Sizemore, Edward Burns, Matt Damon, Jeremy Davies, Giovanni Ribisi.* D-Day, June 1944. American troops prepare to invade the beaches at Normandy. This would be the singular defining moment of WWII. The first 25 minutes of the astonishingly powerful and brilliantly realized *Saving Private Ryan* is crafted with such raw emotion and technical superiority that it literally blows nearly every other American war film out of the water. What follows during the next 145 minutes is just as riveting. Giving a performance of great depth and subtlety, Hanks plays an Army sergeant who must lead an eight-man unit through enemy territory to search for and rescue a G.I., Private Ryan (Damon), whose three brothers have all been killed in combat and who now has a pass home. Spielberg has certainly done his homework. His re-creations of WWII battles, the camaraderie of the men, the threat of death around the corner flow in a narrative logic rarely captured on film. The ensemble is extraordinary, with Davies most memorable as a tortured coward. *Saving Private Ryan* is Spielberg at his best, and, for that matter, American cinema at its best. (VHS available letterboxed or pan & scan) ★★★★ VHS: $19.99; DVD: $26.99

Sawdust and Tinsel

(1953, 95 min, Sweden, Ingmar Bergman) *Harriet Andersson, Ake Gronberg.* Bergman's powerful classic is set in the circus milieu and deals with the fluctuating love allegiances between a circus owner, his wife, his mistress and her other lover. For sheer spectacle, psychological accuracy and richness of composition, this dazzling film is unrivaled. (Swedish with English subtitles) (aka: *Naked Light*) ★★★½ VHS: $29.99

Say Anything

(1989, 100 min, US, Cameron Crowe) *John Cusack, Ione Skye, John Mahoney, Joan Cusack, Lili Taylor, Bebe Neuwirth, Eric Stoltz.* Cusack stars in this intelligent, insightful and entertaining teen comedy as a high school grad who falls in love with the class valedictorian. Skye is lovely as the class queen, and Mahoney gives a stunning portrayal of her doting father. Credit writer and first-time director Crowe for making a "wrong side of the tracks" romance imbued with blithe observations on young adulthood and on the complexities of relationships — whether they be romantic or otherwise. ★★★½ VHS: $9.99

Sayonara

(1957, 147 min, US, Joshua Logan) *Marlon Brando, Red Buttons, Miyoshi Umecki, Miiko Taka.* Immensely popular upon its release, this romantic drama benefits from a commanding performance from Brando as

an American pilot stationed in post-WWII Tokyo who falls in love with a Japanese woman (Taka). Buttons and Umecki both won Oscars for their moving portrayals of ill-fated lovers. ★★★½ VHS: $14.99

The Scalphunters

(1968, 102 min, US, Sydney Pollack) *Burt Lancaster, Ossie Davis, Shelley Winters, Telly Savalas, Dabney Coleman.* Rollicking comic western with Lancaster as a fur trapper who teams with educated slave Davis when his furs are stolen. ★★★ VHS: $19.99

Scandal

(1989, 114 min, GB, Michael Caton-Jones) *John Hurt, Jeroen Krabbé, Joanne Whaley-Kilmer, Ian McKellen.* First-time director Caton-Jones' vivid enactment of the incredible sex scandal which brought a firmly entrenched, conservative British government to its knees in 1963. Whaley-Kilmer sparkles as Christine Keeler, a nightclub showgirl whose sexual dealings with the then—Minister of War, John Profumo (stoically portrayed by McKellen), and a Soviet Naval Attache (Krabbé) sparked what is still the biggest scandal in British political history. Hurt is extraordinary as Stephen Ward, the socialite and sexual provocateur whose manipulations brought about what came to be known as "The Profumo Affair." (Letterboxed) ★★★½ VHS: $14.99; DVD: $29.99

A Scandal in Paris

(1946, 100 min, US, Douglas Sirk) *George Sanders, Signe Hasso, Akim Tamiroff, Carole Landis.* An excellent script distinguishes this early treasure from director Sirk, his first American film. Sanders' droll magnificence is well-served as the legendary (and reportedly real-life) 18th-century French rogue, Eugene François Vidocq, who realized that the best way to make crime pay was to become the chief of police. But, as fate (and artistic license) would have it, he is ultimately undone by love. (aka: *Thieves' Holiday*) ★★★ VHS: $24.99

Scandal Man

(1972, 86 min, France, Richard Balducci) *Maurice Ronet, Vittorio de Sica.* The sordid world of yellow journalism is explored in this riveting, sometimes violent look at a photojournalist working in a Parisian version of the *New York Post.* The reporter, no stranger to sensationalistic coverage, finds himself in hot water when he creates a scandal by photographing a black man kissing a white American woman, who is the daughter of a leading Ku Klux Klan member. Conspiracy, murder and intrigue follow in this rarely seen crime drama. (French with English subtitles) ★★★

Scanner Cop

(1994, 94 min, Canada, Pierre David) *Daniel Quinn, Darlanne Fluegel, Richard Lynch.* While this third sequel to David Cronenberg's *Scanners* borrows only the original concept, it nevertheless effectively captures the flavor of the original. Quinn stars as a rookie cop who must unleash his previously checked scanner powers when a mad scientist (Lynch) targets the LAPD for extinction. Essentially a comic book on film, *Scanner Cop*'s special effects and over-the-top villainy make this a grisly return to form. ★★½ VHS: $9.99

Tom Sizemore (l.) and Tom Hanks in *Saving Private Ryan*

Scarecrow

Scanners

(1981, 102 min, Canada, David Cronenberg) *Patrick McGoohan, Jennifer O'Neill, Stephen Lack.* Cronenberg first achieved wide notoriety with this tense horror film about amoral scientist McGoohan who keeps track of pharmaceutically created mutants who can read your mind or make your head explode. Warning: Not for the squeamish. (Followed by 4 sequels) ★★★ VHS: $9.99; DVD: $14.99

Scanners 2

(1991, 104 min, Canada, Christian Duguay) *David Hewlett, Deborah Raffin.* This well-intentioned sequel focuses more on optical effects than splatter shots in its tale of a reluctant scanner who becomes a pawn in the megalomaniacal schemes of a power-mad police official. ★★ VHS: $9.99

Scanners III: The Takeover

(1991, 101 min, Canada, Christian Duguay) *Steve Parrish, Liliana Komoroska.* A scanner (Parrish) must return from self-imposed exile when an experimental drug turns his sister (Komoroska) into a mind-bending megalomaniac. Good special effects help compensate for the formulaic story. ★★½ VHS: $9.99

The Scar

(1948, 82 min, US, Steve Sekely) *Paul Henreid, Joan Bennett.* Henreid is a fugitive who kills his look-alike psychiatrist and assumes his identity to see his plan backfire when the dead man's own crimes begin to surface and implicate him. An interesting low-budget thriller. (aka: *Hollow Triumph*) ★★★ VHS: $19.99

Scarecrow

(1973, 115 min, US, Jerry Schatzberg) *Al Pacino, Gene Hackman, Eileen Brennan, Ann Wedgeworth, Dorothy Tristan.* Two towering performances by Hackman and Pacino dominate this unusual but fascinating buddy film with Gene and Al as drifters who team up together and head out on the road. ★★★ VHS: $14.99

Scarecrow

(1983, 130 min, USSR, Roland Bykov) This extraordinary and haunting drama centers around the pretty Lena, a 12-year-old girl who, along with her eccentric grandfather, moves to a small city on the outskirts of Moscow. Although teased by her fellow sixth graders and nicknamed "Scarecrow," Lena good-naturedly accepts it. But the pestering soon becomes mean and vicious after a school trip is cancelled and the blame is mistakenly directed at Lena. Reminiscent of *Lord of the Flies*, this powerful film is a chilling group portrait of the incredible tyranny and torment of which children are capable, as well as the strength of the individual against it. (Russian with English subtitles) ★★★½ VHS: $59.99

Scarface

(1932, 93 min, US, Howard Hawks) *Paul Muni, Ann Dvorak, George Raft, Boris Karloff.* Hawks' classic crime drama is the definitive gangster film of the 1930s. Unrelenting in its delineation of a ruthless crime lord, Muni excels as Tony Carmonte (loosely based on Al Capone), an ambitious hood who "climbs" his way to the top of the Chicago underworld in the 1920s. Expert direction by Hawks. (Remade in 1983) ★★★★ VHS: $19.99

Scarface

(1983, 170 min, US, Brian DePalma) *Al Pacino, Michelle Pfeiffer, Steven Bauer, Robert Loggia, F. Murray Abraham.* Pacino is Tony Montana, a particularly vicious thug in the Cuban Mafia, who, fueled by a perverse vision of the American Dream, rises to the top of the drug world. Director DePalma's controversial updating of the 1932 classic is excessive, bloody, lurid and lacking even a hint of subtlety. Yet it is also visually exciting, delivering salacious fun and complete enjoyment on a gut level. (VHS available letterboxed or pan & scan) ★★½ VHS: $14.99; DVD: $34.99

The Scarlet Empress

(1934, 104 min, US, Josef von Sternberg) *Marlene Dietrich.* Visually extravagant and narratively bizarre, von Sternberg's feast is unforgettable. Dietrich portrays Princess Sophia, who is transformed into sexual libertine Catherine the Great through her forced marriage to Russia's Grand Duke. ★★★ VHS: $14.99; DVD: $29.99

The Scarlet Letter

(1995, 135 min, US, Roland Joffé) *Demi Moore, Gary Oldman, Robert Duvall, Joan Plowright, Robert Prosky, Dana Ivey, Roy Dotrice.* Nathaniel Hawthorne's classic novel of romance, witchcraft and betrayal in colonial America is given a definite Cliffs Notes reworking in Joffé's muddled though handsome adaptation. In a rather one-dimensional portrayal, Moore is Hester Prynne, the noble heroine who falls in love with the local pastor (Oldman), bears a child out of wedlock, is forced to wear a scarlet "A," and must contend with her long-thought-dead husband (a hammy

Duvall) bent on revenge. Joffé's film, while looking authentic in design and costumes, has an irritating, disjointed feel to it and most of the actors look embarrassed. We won't even mention how they tampered with the ending. ★★

The Scarlet Pimpernel

(1934, 95 min, GB, Harold Young) *Leslie Howard, Merle Oberon, Raymond Massey.* A stiff-lipped adventure classic with Howard, perfectly cast, as the elusive pimpernel who aids innocent victims of the French revolution while posing as a foppish member of British society. ★★★½ VHS: $14.99

Scarlet Street

(1945, 102 min, US, Fritz Lang) *Edward G. Robinson, Joan Bennett, Dan Duryea.* Originally judged to be immoral here in the United States, this Lang remake of Jean Renoir's *La Chienne* moves the action from Paris to Greenwich Village, as its story of obsession, manipulation and tortuous fate unfolds. Robinson is a meek middle-aged cashier who becomes fatally attracted to the seductive charms of prostitute/actress Bennett. Egged on by the deceptive but sexy vixen, Robinson is driven to embezzlement and certain tragedy. Lang's darkest film is an expressionist moral tale and a fine example of psychological film noir. ★★★½ VHS: $19.99

Scarred City

(1998, 95 min, US, Ken Sanzel) *Stephen Baldwin, Chazz Palminteri, Tia Carrere, Michael Rispoli.* In this cheesy, harmless actioner, Baldwin plays a seemingly cold-blooded, trigger-happy cop who is blackmailed into joining an elite, covert police vigilante squad sanctioned by the commissioner and mayor. He's an outsider from the start, and after he saves an innocent hooker (Carrere) from a bloodbath at a Bolivian drug

John Cusack in *Say Anything*

lord's mansion, he is a marked man. Like most straight-to-video thrillers, *Scarred City* features throwaway shots at character development of any kind, for the main point of the film is sex and violence. The sex is minimal, but the action is plentiful, and the film is effective exploitation filler. ★★ VHS: $14.99; DVD: $24.99

Scary Movie

(2000, 88 min, US, Keenen Ivory Wayans) *Anna Faris, Marlon Wayans, Shawn Wayans, Carmen Electra, Jon Abrahams, Shannon Elizabeth, Cheri Oteri, Regina Hall.* The motive of *Scary Movie* is to tweak and make fun of all the self-serious postmodern horror flicks like *Scream* and *I Know What You Did Last Summer* that revitalized the long-dead slasher genre. But those flicks themselves were send-ups of the genre, poking playful fun at the very cinematic clichés and conventions that the characters (and the audience members) were consciously weaned on. Like any pop-cultural shooting gallery, the film fires away with goofy sight gags, double entendres and enough raucous frat-boy raunchiness to make even the horniest sex-starved teenager blush. Some of the jokes work, some of them fall flat with a thud. By the way, *Scary Movie* was the original title for Wes Craven's 1996 horror flick before the studio changed it to *Scream*. Same studio. Oooooo! Spooky! (Sequel: *Scary Movie 2*) ★★½ VHS: $14.99; DVD: $29.99

Scene of the Crime

(1986, 90 min, France, André Téchiné) *Catherine Deneuve, Danielle Darrieux, Victor Lanoux.* Deneuve delivers a wonderfully multi-layered performance as a divorced woman living in the French countryside. Her frustrated dreams of love and fantasy become real when she meets up with a handsome young man, recently escaped from prison, who lures her into a passionate love affair and provides a way out of the deadening provincial life. A taut, well-structured suspense thriller. (French with English subtitles) ★★★

Scenes from a Mall

(1991, 87 min, US, Paul Mazursky) *Woody Allen, Bette Midler, Bill Irwin.* The casting of Allen and Midler as a married couple was inspired — on paper. And indeed, they work well together, but this lightweight farce, set against the glitz and glamour of the Beverly Mall, while providing the occasional laugh, is basically dull and flat. She's a high-powered psychologist and he's a major promoter. They wend their way through the seemingly endless mall and go through a series of petty fights, major revelations and other assorted marital spats. Director Mazursky tries to squeeze some life out of the bone-dry script, but if it weren't for the talents of Allen and Midler, this film would be only slightly less boring than going to the mall on a Saturday night. ★★ VHS: $9.99

Scenes from a Marriage

(1973, 168 min, Sweden, Ingmar Bergman) *Liv Ullmann, Erland Josephson, Bibi Andersson.* The long and prolific filmmaking career of Bergman is highlighted by many classics; this film, originally a five-hour Swedish television special, must certainly count as one of his best. The film examines the decay and disintegration of a marriage. An intimate and painful look at a couple's arguments, misunderstandings, and

Scary Movie

lovemaking, as well as their eventual divorce, ending with a new post-divorce friendship. Ullmann and Josephson excel as the wife and husband. A passionate and fascinating look at human relations. (Swedish with English subtitles) ★★★★ VHS: $29.99

Scenes from the Class Struggle in Beverly Hills

(1989, 95 min, US, Paul Bartel) *Jacqueline Bisset, Paul Mazursky, Ed Begley, Jr., Wallace Shawn, Paul Bartel, Ray Sharkey.* Director Bartel stays true to his slap-dash style of comedy in this often funny, sometimes outlandish and always entertaining drawing-room farce. Bisset stars as a Beverly Hills widow who mourns the loss of her husband by plotting the sexual conquest of her Chicano male-servant . . . who has a bet with another servant on who can seduce the other's employer first . . . get the picture? The stage is set for a no-holds-barred explosion of comedy in which everyone is trying to get into bed with someone. Sharkey steals the show as a bisexual butler. ★★★

Scenes from the Surreal

(1988-90, 58 min, Czech Republic, Jan Svankmajer) Three wildly inventive shorts by Czech animator Svankmajer and a BBC documentary on his life and work comprise this bizarrely enjoyable video. *Darkness, Light, Darkness* (1989, 7 min) deals with the wonders and terrors of the senses as a single clay hand begins to assemble the needed parts in making itself whole. *Virile Games* (1988, 14 min) finds Czech sportsmanship in soccer taking a bloody and deadly turn after the mischievous animator has one too many shots and beer. *Death of Stalinism in Bohemia* (1990, 10 min) has Stalin and his Czech cohorts lampooned in this bitter political satire which questions the myth of change in a world of repression. In *Jan Svankmajer: The Animator of Prague* (1990, 27 min), Marsh interviews the erudite but mysterious animator who draws from childhood memories and the notion of magic to create his weird animated world. ★★★ VHS: $12.99

Scent of a Woman

(1992, 157 min, US, Martin Brest) *Al Pacino, Chris O'Donnell, Gabrielle Anwar, Philip Seymour Hoffman.* Pacino's tour de force, Oscar-winning performance is the heart and soul of this admittedly overlong and manipulative but nevertheless wickedly funny and touching comedy-drama based on the 1974 Italian comedy *Profumo di Donna.* O'Donnell is a college student who is hired to watch cantankerous, blind vet Pacino for the weekend. What should be an uneventful stay at home gives way to a whirlwind tour of New York City as Pacino dupes his companion into accompanying him for a razzle-dazzle three-day getaway. The success of the film lies in Pacino's cynical, hard-bitten military man; and the actor sinks his teeth into one of the juiciest roles of his career. As directed by Brest, the film transpires at a crackling pace and no scene is allowed to wear out its welcome. (Letterboxed VHS available for $14.99) ★★★½ VHS: $9.99; DVD: $26.99

The Scent of Green Papaya

(1993, 104 min, Vietnam, Tran Anh Hung) *Tran Nu Yen Khe, Truong Thi Loc.* Anh Hung's Oscar-nominated and Cannes Award—winning first film exquisitely portrays domestic life in Saigon through the eyes of a young Vietnamese country girl. Divided into two parts, the first and far more interesting segment shows the arrival of ten-year-old servant girl Mui. There is an internal strife amongst the family in which the innocent Mui becomes a part. The second part takes place ten years later. Mui has a new master with whom she has fallen in love; and the story concentrates on their romance. Though the film features beautiful cinematography throughout, the last half doesn't have the tension or joy of discovery which makes the first half so successful. Still, the film is a rare look into a culture and people, and its feelings of family and love are transcendent. (Vietnamese with English subtitles) ★★★ VHS: $19.99

Schindler's List

(1993, 185 min, US, Steven Spielberg) *Liam Neeson, Ben Kingsley, Ralph Fiennes, Embeth Davidtz.* In his boldest attempt to create a "cinematic masterpiece" and finally get noticed by a stubbornly disinterested Academy, Spielberg bypasses the heart and goes right for the jugular in this drama on the Holocaust. Undeniably driven by sincerity, Spielberg's Oscar-winning Best Picture is alternately impressive, maudlin, focused and well-acted. Filmed in black and white, the film deals with the Nazi extermination of Polish Jews and how one man, Oskar Schindler, transformed from a philandering opportunist (and Nazi profiteer) to a capitalist savior to 1,200 imprisoned Jews. With fluid camerawork, Spielberg re-creates life for Krakow's Jews during Nazi occupation — from resettlements in the ghetto to their internment in the camps. Spielberg's scenes of Nazi atrocities are emotionally wrenching, but the film's pacing, the director's trademark sentimentality and an artificial ending keep *Schindler's List* from being the classic the director so fervently strived for. (VHS available letterboxed or pan & scan) ★★★ VHS: $19.99

Schizopolis

(1997, 96 min, US, Steven Soderbergh) *Steven Soderbergh, Betsy Brantley, David Jensen.* Soderbergh's experimental, witty take on contemporary middle-class values, corporate life and relationships, like his other films, is far from uplifting and is low-key to the extreme. The story, such as it is, deals with a dull mid-level executive with a stagnant marriage who, midway through the film, suddenly "turns into" a different character (shades of *Lost Highway*). The new character, it turns out, is having an affair with the exec's wife. Even more bizarre than it sounds, *Schizopolis* is an entertaining, unconventional surprise. ★★★ VHS: $19.99

School Daze

(1988, 114 min, US, Spike Lee) *Laurence Fishburne, Ossie Davis, Spike Lee, Giancarlo Esposito, Tisha Campbell, Samuel L. Jackson.* Lee's bold but ultimately unsatisfying social comedy-drama set at a black university centers on the friction between two cliques: the "wannabees" and the "jigaboos." Lee sets out to examine racial identity and self-discrimination in the

Ben Kingsley in *Schindler's List*

black community; but his heavy-handed approach makes for little interest. The best scene is a musical fantasy number, which is alive with an energy unfortunately missing from the rest of the film. ★★½ VHS: $14.99; DVD: $24.99

The School of Flesh (L'Ecole de la chair)

(1998, 102 min, France, Benoit Jacquot) *Isabelle Huppert, Vincent Martinez, François Berleand, Marthe Keller.* Huppert is mesmerizing as Dominique, a fashion executive whose life becomes unraveled after she begins an affair with a thuggish bisexual hustler/bartender in this erotic drama. Dominique's successful but romantically empty life is thrown into a whirl-wind after — on a lark — she visits a gay bar and is inextricably attracted to the dark, devilish looks of the bartender Quentin (Martinez). She plays the aggressor to the younger man with the two eventually entering into a turbulent relationship. Huppert's icy cold gaze, which serves as a veneer to her emotionally ravaged state, is breathtaking to watch in this cool, subtle sexual drama that was adapted from a story by Yukio Mishima. (French with English subtitles) ★★★ VHS: $21.99; DVD: $27.99

School Ties

(1992, 107 min, US, Robert Mandel) *Brendan Fraser, Matt Damon, Chris O'Donnell, Ben Affleck, Anthony Rapp.* It is the 1950s and David Green (Fraser), a lower middle-class kid from Scranton, is recruited by the exclusive St. Matthews School to help break their three-year losing streak in football. Handsome and an excellent athlete, David is quickly embraced by the school elite. But he's also forced to hide his Jewish heritage from his new anti-Semitic, joke-spewing friends. The underlying theme of what parts of ourselves we are willing to give up in order to fit in and "be a part of things" gives this film its punch. *School Ties* is a heartfelt and surprisingly entertaining story with just the right amount of nostalgia and sentimentality. ★★★ VHS: $14.99; DVD: $29.99

Scorpio

(1972, 114 min, US, Michael Winner) *Burt Lancaster, Alain Delon, Paul Scofield.* Delon is a CIA assassin who is contracted by the Agency to kill his one-time partner (Lancaster) who they say is selling secrets to the Soviets. The acting in this film is, for the most part, wooden, with the exception of Scofield's portrayal of a last-of-his-breed Russian super-spy living in Vienna. There are too many loose ends left hanging at the conclusion of the film, but there's some nice location shots of Paris and Vienna, and a few neat non-weapons-related spy tricks to keep your mind off the hokiness of this thrill-less thriller. ★★ VHS: $14.99; DVD: $24.99

The Scorpion Woman

(1989, 95 min, Austria, Susanne Zanke) *Angelica Domrose, Fritz Hammel.* The often scandalous yet strangely mesmeric theme of an older woman's relationship with a much younger man is explored once again in this interesting drama. Lisa, a 44-year-old magistrate living in Vienna, takes up with a legal assistant twenty years her junior. This relationship soon affects her professional life after she is assigned a case in which an older woman, accused of assault on a young man, is found to have been romantically

involved with the victim. (German with English subtitles) ★★½ VHS: $59.99

La Scorta

(1993, 92 min, Italy, Ricky Tognazzi) *Claudio Amendola, Enrico Lo Verso, Carlo Cecchi, Ricky Memphis, Ugo Conti.* Loosely based on the real-life account of an Italian prosecutor and his crusade againt La Cosa Nostra in Sicily, *La Scorta* follows the intensely anxious lives of Judge De Francesco (Cecchi) and his "escort" of four bodyguards as they zip from meeting to meeting in rundown Alfa Romeos. New to the region, the judge quickly picks up the thread of his assassinated predecessor and thus finds himself the recipient of increasing threats. *La Scorta* concentrates very little on the actual violence or details of the investigations, but instead adeptly zeroes in on the intense bonding between the judge and his guardians as they live in constant fear of ambush and grow increasingly distrustful of their own superiors. (Italian with English subtitles) ★★★ VHS: $89.99

The Scout

(1994, 100 min, US, Michael Ritchie) *Albert Brooks, Brendan Fraser, Dianne Wiest, Lane Smith.* An occasionally funny, improbable and mawkish baseball tale. Brooks is a scout for the New York Yankees. Sent to Mexico, he discovers Fraser, who may possibly be one of the greatest players of the game. And before the film looks like another fish-out-of-water comedy, Brooks brings him back to the States. That's when his and the film's problems begin. Fraser turns out to be mentally unstable, and Brooks and shrink Wiest attempt to get to the root of the problem. The film's beginning has a charm to it, thanks to Brooks' underplaying, and Fraser gives an appealing performance. But the last half is painfully bad, underscored by an incredulous ending. ★★ VHS: $9.99

Scream

(1996, 110 min, US, Wes Craven) *Neve Campbell, Skeet Ulrich, Drew Barrymore, David Arquette, Courtney Cox.* Full of in-jokes and references to countless splatter movies from the 1980s, *Scream* works as homage, spoof, and as one scary horror film. Beginning as a slasher movie (with a terrific Barrymore), the story soon becomes a murder mystery with plenty of red herrings. A masked killer is terrifying the town, killing teenagers seemingly at random. In order to have a little fun, the remaining teens gather at a big house in the woods to watch horror movies, drink and get laid. The killer, of course, is there and all hell breaks loose. Destined to become a postmodern horror movie classic which will eventually be ranked along with *Halloween* and *Dawn of the Dead*. (Letterboxed VHS available for $19.99) ★★★½ VHS: $14.99; DVD: $29.99

Scream 2

(1997, 120 min, US, Wes Craven) *Neve Campbell, Courteney Cox, David Arquette, Sarah Michelle Gellar, Jada Pinkett, Jerry O'Connell, Liev Schreiber, Laurie Metcalf, Omar Epps, Heather Graham, David Warner.* A solid follow-up to Craven's 1996 smash, *Scream 2* takes place two years after the events of the first film, as Sidney (Campbell) is attending a Midwestern college. A handful of copycat murders coincide with the release of the film *Stab*, based on the events from the first film.

Courtney Cox and Parker Posey in *Scream 3*

While not as scary as the original, this is just as suspenseful and full of surprises, and it even pokes fun at horror sequels with the same panache and wit as *Scream* busted on slasher films in general. Although a misconceived and protracted climax, as well as a downer ending, do detract a bit from the fun, this is almost on par with its original. (Letterboxed VHS available for $19.99) ★★★ VHS: $14.99; DVD: $29.99

Scream 3

(2000, 117 min, US, Wes Craven) *Neve Campbell, Courtney Cox, David Arquette, Lance Henriksen, Jenny McCarthy, Parker Posey, Carrie Fisher, Kelly Rutherford, Liev Schreiber.* This could be dubbed *Return of the Law of Diminishing Returns.* After the great fun of the first film, and the surprisingly interesting second *Scream,* it appears the gang has just run out of ideas and is cashing in. Sidney, now a recluse living under a pseudonym, works as a phone counselor, while *Stab 3,* the newest installment of the film-within-a-film series (which looks like more fun than *Scream 3* turns out to be!) is being shot in Hollywood. The opening is good, and there's an amusing chase through a soundstage mockup of Sidney's original house, but Craven's bored direction and a shockingly unshocking climax are more indicative of the desperation of this enterprise. Please, no *Scream 4!* ★★ VHS: $14.99; DVD: $29.99

Scream of Stone

(1990, 105 min, Canada/West Germany, Werner Herzog) *Donald Sutherland, Brad Dourif.* In this, one of his most disciplined films, Herzog has again found his emotional correlative in nature: a monolith of a mountain in Argentina, a "scream of stone." Sutherland has been hired to produce a live TV program as two of the world's greatest mountain climbers try to conquer unknown territory — both external and internal. Dourif gives a rich performance as the one climber who has come to peace with The Mountain having tried to conquer it to win the affections of (the late) Mae West. ★★★

Screamers

(1996, 100 min, US, Christian Duguay) *Peter Weller, Roy Dupuis, Jennifer Rubin.* Weller stars as a beleaguered colonel in this not uninteresting adaptation of a short story by Philip K. Dick. Weller's laconic character commands a small group of soldiers stationed on the distant mining planet Sirius B, site of a battle in the latest futuristic corporate war. In the fight, biochemical entities known as "Screamers," small, multi-bladed machines, have mutated into larger, more human-looking warriors. The story focuses on Weller's attempts to cross the planet's wasteland to broker a truce. Not very original nor particularly good, though the limited special effects can be entertaining. ★★ VHS: $79.99; DVD: $19.99

Screw Loose

(2000, 85 min, US/Italy, Ezio Greggio) *Mel Brooks, Ezio Greggio, Julie Condra.* Greggio plays a much-put-upon son, whose father's dying wish is to thank the American G.I. who saved his life in WWII. Since Papa only has two weeks to live, Greggio hurriedly flies to the U.S. to find the man. He turns out to be. . . wacky Mel Brooks, who, shell-shocked, resides in a mental institution. While Greggio and company obviously aim for the old-school comedy style of Buster Keaton and Jacques Tati, they fall well below the mark. Painful one-liners, sloppy slapstick and zero comic timing sink this quickly. ★ VHS: $19.99; DVD: $24.99

Scrooge

(1970, 118 min, GB, Ronald Neame) *Albert Finney, Alec Guinness, Edith Evans, Kenneth Moore.* Though it won't replace Alastair Sim's 1951 *A Christmas Carol* as the definitive screen version of Dickens' novel, there's a lot to like in this musical adaptation. Finney makes an appropriately cantankerous Ebenezer Scrooge, the miser and all-around-humbug who is visited by three spirits on Christmas Eve. A pleasant, if uninspired, score by Leslie Bricusse. ★★★

Scrooged

(1988, 101 min, US, Richard Donner) *Bill Murray, Karen Allen, Carol Kane, Bobcat Goldthwait, Alfre Woodard, Robert Mitchum, Buddy Hackett.* A mildly entertaining updating of Dickens' "A Christmas Carol" with Murray taking over the role of Scrooge, here as a heartless TV executive. It's not as funny as it could have been, but there are some good moments: especially Kane as a whacked-out Ghost of Christmas Present and Goldthwait as a 1980s Bob Cratchet. ★★½ VHS: $14.99; DVD: $24.99

Scrubbers

(1982, 90 min, GB, Mai Zetterling) *Amanda York, Chrissie Cotterill.* A comic and tragic tale about a tough crop of women inmates at a dingy British borstal. From the black lesbian lovers to the mute anorexic, the leather-jacketed tough girl and the baby-faced heroine, the performers are feisty and unforgettably human. ★★★

Scum

(1980, 98 min, GB, Alan Clarke) *Phil Daniels, Ray Winstone, Mick Ford.* This harrowing British drama explores the physical, sexual and psychological violence in a borstal (prison) for youthful offenders. A powerful and disturbing tale. The film could have used a more palatable title for its commercial release. ★★★

The Sea Hawk

(1940, 127 min, US, Michael Curtiz) *Errol Flynn, Claude Rains, Donald Crisp, Flora Robson, Alan Hale.* Classic sea adventure with Flynn swashing-many-a-buck on the high seas as a pirate captain taking on the Spaniards in the name of England and Queen Elizabeth I. Outstanding score by Erich Wolfgang Korngold. ★★★½ VHS: $19.99

Sea of Grass

(1947, 131 min, US, Elia Kazan) *Spencer Tracy, Katharine Hepburn, Melvyn Douglas, Robert Walker.* Unusual western tale based on a Conrad Richter story about New Mexico grasslands and the fight to preserve them. The film features a good cast, but much of this is heavy going. ★★½ VHS: $14.99

Sea of Love

(1989, 112 min, US, Harold Becker) *Al Pacino, Ellen Barkin, John Goodman, Michael Rooker.* Pacino gives a solid performance as a veteran New York City detective assigned to catch a serial killer who makes contact through the personals. Placing an ad, Pacino goes undercover, setting up a rendezvous under the watchful eye of partner Goodman. There he meets sexy prime suspect Barkin. The two begin a passionate affair; all the while clues point to her guilt. ★★★ VHS: $14.99; DVD: $24.99

The Sea Wolf

(1941, 90 min, US, Michael Curtiz) *Edward G. Robinson, Ida Lupino, John Garfield, Alexander Knox.* Jack London's exciting tale of the sea makes for a riveting, atmospheric high-seas adventure. Adapted for the screen by Robert Rossen, the story plots the course of three civilians who find themselves on board the aptly-named schooner "Ghost" helmed by the tyrannical Cpt. Wolf Larsen. Robinson, in a dynamic

S

and complex portrayal, plays the hardened captain who finds it "Better to reign in Hell than serve in Heaven." A lovely Lupino and a handsome Garfield are both fugitives from the law; and Knox is an idealistic writer forced to face the barbaric side of human nature. A rip-roaring action film which gives berth to both high adventure and intelligent characterizations. (Remade in 1997) ★★★½ VHS: $19.99

The Sea Wolves

(1980, 120 min, GB/US, Andrew V. McLaglen) *Gregory Peck, Roger Moore, David Niven, Trevor Howard, Patrick Macnee.* An engaging WWII adventure about a group of ex-British cavalry soldiers doing their part against the Nazis. They go after a German radio transmitter with some suspenseful and funny results. ★★★ VHS: $14.99; DVD: $14.99

Seance on a Wet Afternoon

(1964, 116 min, GB, Bryan Forbes) *Kim Stanley, Richard Attenborough, Margaret Lacey.* This enthralling psychological thriller breathes with an atmosphere of ever-building suspense that is unrelentingly sustained. A pair of superb performances are offered by Stanley and Attenborough as a medium and her husband who kidnap a child in order to publicize her clairvoyant skills. Written and directed by Forbes, it stands as one of the best and most unusual British films of the '60s. ★★★½

The Search

(1948, 104 min, US, Fred Zinnemann) *Montgomery Clift, Aline MacMahon, Ivan Jandl.* A touching story, sensitive direction and a sobering theme all contribute to make this a classic post-war drama. Clift gives a fine performance as an American soldier stationed in war-ravaged Germany who takes in a young Czech boy — a concentration camp survivor — when he finds the youth alone on the streets. Meanwhile, the boy's mother searches for her son from camp to camp. Filmed on location in Berlin amid the bombed out buildings, which only serves to enhance the poignant narrative. Little Jandl is a heartbreaker as the boy. ★★★★

Search and Destroy

(1995, 90 min, US, David Salle) *Griffin Dunne, Dennis Hopper, John Turturro, Christopher Walken, Ileana Douglas, Rosanna Arquette, Ethan Hawke, Martin Scorsese.* Dunne heads a cast of Hollywood's coolest in this self-consciously hip adaptation of the Broadway play about a Florida film producer, at odds with the IRS, who tries to orchestrate a movie deal based on the writings of an eccentric new-age guru (Hopper), the financing of a commodities/cocaine dealer (Walken) and the underworld contacts of a speed-freak yuppie (Turturro). Possessed by moments of articulate insights, painter-turned-artist Salle's work is not altogether successful, relying too much on the gratuitously weird nature of the characters and situations to sustain it; rather than allowing his marvelous ensemble to breathe life into it. ★★½ VHS: $14.99

The Search for One-Eye Jimmy

(1996, 86 min, US, Sam Henry Kass) *Steve Buscemi, Samuel L. Jackson, Jennifer Beals, John Turturro, Ray Mancini, Michael Badalucco, Nicholas Turturro, Anne Meara.* Sherman's March

meets *The Third Man*? Not quite. A film student returns to his Brooklyn neighborhood to make a documentary about it and becomes wrapped up in a missing persons case — with the camera rolling, of course. Kass' lifeless direction sabotages his subtle screenplay, and bits that should have worked just aren't that funny. A few big names in small parts add a little life, but this one gets filed under "promising fiasco." ★½ VHS: $14.99

The Search for Signs of Intelligent Life in the Universe

(1991, 120 min, US, Jane Wagner) *Lily Tomlin.* This delightful and engaging Tony Award—winning two-hour, one-woman show can easily be considered Tomlin's magnum opus. The show centers around Trudy the Bag Lady as she escorts a group of visiting aliens from outer space and attempts to enlighten them on human idiosyncrasies. Using this premise, Lily jumps from one character to another amazingly giving life — without benefit of makeup or costume — to a host of wonderful characters. The best humor in the piece comes from Trudy, however, as she pontificates on her own unique brand of cosmology. Relying primarily on footage from the actual show, the film occasionally cuts to staged re-creations of the vignettes. ★★★½ VHS: $29.99

The Searchers

(1956, 155 min, US, John Ford) *John Wayne, Jeffrey Hunter, Natalie Wood, Vera Miles, Ward Bond.* In a career rich with milestones, Ford achieved one of his greatest artistic triumphs with this beautifully filmed western. Wayne had one of his most complex characters — possibly wanted by the law and consumed with racial hatred — as Ethan Edwards, who after his brother and sister-in-law are murdered by Indians, sets out to locate his kidnapped niece (played by Wood). Hunter is Wood's brother who accompanies Wayne on his relentless, years-long search. (VHS available letterboxed or pan & scan) ★★★★ VHS: $14.99; DVD: $19.99

Searching for Bobby Fischer

(1993, 110 min, US, Steven Zaillian) *Max Pomerance, Joe Mantegna, Joan Allen, Laurence Fishburne, Ben Kingsley.* Every competitive endeavor, whether baseball, figure skating or chess, contains at its core artistry and purity. It's remarkable for a film to capture the passionate involvement of an activity's participants; even more so when the activity is as internal as that of chess. *Searching for Bobby Fischer* is profoundly successful in this. The story of a young boy's initiation into a glorious obsession with chess is intercut with an almost mythologized recounting of the career of Bobby Fisher. Pomerance is mesmerizing as Josh, the 10-year-old whose intuitive grasp of the game thrusts him into a world of rivalry, clashing egos and immense satisfactions. ★★★★ VHS: $9.99; DVD: $29.99

Season of the Witch

(1972, 89 min, US, George A. Romero) *Jan White, Ray Laine, Anne Muffly.* The director of *Night of the Living Dead* takes on witchcraft with this boring tale of a young woman grappling to hang onto her sanity as she becomes enmeshed with members of a witches' coven. ★½ VHS: $14.99

Sebastiane

(1976, 82 min, GB, Derek Jarman) *Leonardo Treviglio, Barney James.* Jarman's sensual, lushly photographed, highly erotic (and homoerotic) vision of the legend of St. Sebastian is filled with beautiful images of male bodies and graphic scenes of sex and torture. The lives of few saints are as shrouded in mystery as that of the celebrated martyr Sebastian, whose arrow-pierced body has become one of the most familiar images in Christian iconography. In this film, he is perceived as a Christian sympathizer who, sent into exile by the Emperor Diocletian, becomes involved in a sado-masochistic intrigue which ultimately results in his death. Music by Brian Eno. (Latin with English subtitles) ★★★ VHS: $39.99

The Second Awakening of Christina Klages

(1977, 93 min, Germany, Margarethe von Trotta) *Tina Engel, Sylvia Reize, Katharina Thalbach, Peter Schneider, Marius Müller-Westernhagen.* The directorial debut by von Trotta, *The Second Awakening of Christina Klages* is an intriguing character study which concerns various issues of women's identity. Christa (Engel) is a frustrated day care worker who robs a bank with her lover Werner (Müller-Westernhagen) to insure its continued operation. Meanwhile, another woman, Lena (Thalbach), who was a hostage in the robbery, is searching for the thieves for her own reasons. Von Trotta's film is a lyrical and passionate story that builds to a powerful conclusion. In the title role, Engel gives a riveting performance. (German with English subtitles) ★★★ VHS: $39.99

Second Best

(1994, 105 min, GB, Chris Menges) *William Hurt, Chris Cleary Miles, Keith Allen, John Hurt, Jane Horrocks, Prunella Scales.* A harrowing and at times bleak story of father-son relationships. Hurt is an introverted Welsh postmaster who petitions to adopt a troubled ten-year-old. The story, which has as much to do with the adoption process as with interpersonal relationships, follows the rocky road on which Hurt must gain the trust and ultimately the affection of his young charge, who still envisions a reunion with his gaoled father. At the same time, Hurt must exorcise his own paternal demons as his father lies close to death. Hurt and young Miles help smooth over some of the more choppy dramatics. ★★½ VHS: $19.99

Second Chance

(1953, 81 min, US, Rudolph Maté) *Robert Mitchum, Linda Darnell, Jack Palance.* Potent mystery thriller with Mitchum as an ex-boxer who helps gangster's girlfriend Darnell elude contract killer Palance in Mexico. ★★½

Second Chorus

(1940, 83 min, US, H.C. Potter) *Fred Astaire, Paulette Goddard, Burgess Meredith.* Astaire and Meredith are fellow musicians who set their sights on their lovely manager, Goddard. Not without its charms, but by no means one of Fred's better musicals. ★★½ VHS: $19.99

S

Kate Maberly and Andrew Knott in Agnieszka Holland's *The Secret Garden* (1993)

Seconds

(1966, 106 min, US, John Frankenheimer) *Rock Hudson, Salome Jens, John Randolph, Will Geer.* Hudson stars, in arguably his best screen performance, as the "after" part of a bizarre transformational experiment. A middle-aged businessman, tired of his life, job and wife, goes to a mysterious organization which promises to remake him, to give him a second chance. After extensive surgery, he wakes up with a new face and identity, that of an artist. Settling into his new life, he eventually realizes that he will never find the happiness which he thought was waiting around the corner. So he returns to the organization for another try, with unfortunate results. This bizarre but simple story is itself transformed into a masterpiece of paranoia and horror by Frankenheimer's taut direction and James Wong Howe's dazzling, canted-angled, black-and-white cinematography. Disturbing but brilliant, *Seconds* always remains plausible, its proposition desirable enough to make it seem very real. ★★★½ VHS: $89.99

Secret Admirer

(1985, 98 min, US, David Greenwalt) *C. Thomas Howell, Lori Laughlin, Kelly Preston, Fred Ward, Dee Wallace Stone.* An intriguing premise can't sustain this uneven sex comedy about a teenager (Howell) who wrongly assumes the identity of the sender of an anonymous love letter. When the letter falls into the hands of parents and neighbors, further complications arise. ★★ VHS: $9.99

The Secret Agent

(1935, 86 min, GB, Alfred Hitchcock) *John Gielgud, Madeleine Carroll, Peter Lorre, Robert Young, Lilli Palmer, Michael Redgrave.* Taken from an episode in "Ashenden," a W. Somerset Maugham novel, this gripping story follows agent Gielgud, dispatched to Switzerland to terminate a spy whose identity he doesn't know. Director Hitchcock creates maximun suspense with his usual flair. Lorre is great in support as a Russian agent who certainly likes his vodka. ★★★ VHS: $24.99

The Secret Agent

See: Joseph Conrad's The Secret Agent

Secret Ceremony

(1968, 109 min, US, Joseph Losey) *Elizabeth Taylor, Mia Farrow, Robert Mitchum, Peggy Ashcroft, Pamela Brown.* This campy psychological thriller stars Taylor as a middle-aged tart who becomes involved in a strange relationship with a mentally unbalanced rich orphan (Farrow). Taylor's character, still in mourning over the loss of a young daughter, finds her emotional and financial needs answered with "poor little doe" Mia. They play mommy and daughter, yet with interesting lesbian undertones. As they become involved in mutually destructive emotional mind games, Farrow's sexually abusive stepfather (Mitchum) returns unexpectedly, prompting a dramatic escalation of tensions. ★★ VHS: $14.99

The Secret Garden

(1993, 101 min, US, Agnieszka Holland) *Kate Maberly, Heydon Prowse, Andrew Knott, Maggie Smith, Irène Jacob.* Holland makes her English-language debut with this superlative adaptation of Frances Hodgson Burnett's 1909 children's classic. Ten-year-old Mary Lennox is sent to live in the gloomy estate of her uncle, Lord Craven. There she is chastened by the manor's obdurate housekeeper Mrs. Medlock (stonily portrayed by Smith) not to snoop, which, of course, she immediately does. Emotionally and visually rich in every detail, Holland's film probes the psychological aspects of the story as young Mary uncovers the house's secrets and befriends both its sickly young master and a local farm boy with an affinity for animals. ★★★★ VHS: $14.99; DVD: $14.99

Secret Honor

(1984, 90 min, US, Robert Altman) *Philip Baker Hall.* Hall gives a bravura performance in this lacerating Altman adaptation of an original screenplay about the political and personal demise of Richard Nixon. The action transpires in Nixon's private office, sometime after his resignation. Embittered by his political fortunes, brimming with hatred and vengeance, he launches into a ferocious monologue about his obsessions and regrets. Throughout, we are given a sometimes touching, often repugnant, look at a frightfully complex man. ★★★½

The Secret Life of Walter Mitty

(1947, 110 min, US, Norman Z. McLeod) *Danny Kaye, Virginia Mayo, Boris Karloff.* One of Kaye's most popular films, this funny adaptation of James Thurber's comedy has Danny as the timid, day-dreaming hero whose constant fantasies get him involved in real-life adventures. Kaye's constant costar Mayo is as lovely as ever, and Karloff has an amusing supporting role as a psychiatrist. ★★★ VHS: $14.99

The Secret of My Success

(1987, 110 min, US, Herbert Ross) *Michael J. Fox, Helen Slater, Richard Jordan, Margaret Whitton.* There are echoes of *How to Succeed in Business* in this amiable though lowbrow comedy with Fox coming to the big city and moving up the corporate ladder thanks to a little chicanery. Fox is the main attraction here. ★★½ VHS: $7.49

The Secret of N.I.M.H.

(1982, 84 min, US, Don Bluth) *Voices of: Dom DeLuise, Derek Jacobi, Peter Strauss.* Charming, low-keyed animated tale, based on Robert C. O'Brien's award-winning children's book, about a mother mouse who tries to save her home from being destroyed with the aid of her wacky animal friends. ★★★ VHS: $14.99; DVD: $14.99

The Secret of Roan Inish

(1995, 103 min, US, John Sayles) *Jeni Courtney, Mick Lally, Eileen Colgan.* Sayles has created a lyrical and enchanting Irish fairy tale based on the novel "Secret of Ron Mor Skerry" by Rosallie K. Fry. Young Fiona Coneelly (Courtney) is sent to live with her grandparents on Ireland's rugged and forbidding northwestern coast. Unperturbed by her change of scene, Fiona begins to pursue her murky family history and long-lost baby brother. His mystery revolves around a remote island called Roan Inish, the ancestral stomping grounds of the Coneelly clan and home to Selkies, mystical half-seal and half-human sea creatures. With the help of cinematographer Haskell Wexler's haunting imagery, Sayles presents a flawless piece of storytelling that is as heartwarming as it is foreboding. Courtney gives a performance well beyond her years as Fiona, and as her grizzled grandpa and archetypally Irish grandma, Lally and Colgan are both extraordinary. Through them, Sayles pays brilliant homage to oral traditions. ★★★★ VHS: $9.99; DVD: $24.99

Secret Places

(1985, 96 min, GB, Zelda Barron) *Maria Therese Relin, Tara MacGowan, Jenny Agutter.* Set in an English boarding school during WWII, this warm, often moving drama follows two schoolgirls from very different backgrounds who form an ill-fated friendship. A poignant and sensitive exposé of the chasms between social classes featuring a youthful dialogue on love, sex, philosophy and patriotism. ★★★ VHS: $79.99

The Secret Rapture

(1994, 96 min, GB, Howard Davies) *Juliet Stevenson, Joanne Whalley-Kilmer, Penelope Wilson, Neil Pearson, Alan Howard.* David Hare's master-

S

ful screen adaptation of his original play is this study of a young woman (Stevenson) who must reevaluate her life when her father's death leaves her in the care of his manipulative, alcoholic widow (Whalley-Kilmer). The film is at once intimate and powerful and, flawed fourth act notwithstanding, is consistently gripping. Stevenon goves a remarkably textured performance that is sorrowful and triumphant. ★★★½

Secrets & Lies

(1996, 143 min, GB, Mike Leigh) *Brenda Blethyn, Marianne Jean-Baptiste, Timothy Spall, Phyllis Logan, Claire Rushbrook.* Director Leigh brilliantly communicates two decades of one family's secrets and lies, brought to light by one woman's search for her birth mother. Jean-Baptiste gives one of several superlative performances from the ensemble as Hortense, the daughter given up for adoption. Her quest to discover her biological mother injects Hortense into another family's intricate obfuscations and smoldering resentments. As her birth mother Cynthia, Blethyn perfectly embodies a woman at sea in the world, buffeted by circumstance, imbued with defeat and helplessness. Cynthia, who is white, is at first overwhelmed by the arrival of Hortense, who is black. But before long, the shock transforms to catharsis as Hortense, comfortably middle class, invites Cynthia to participate in a happier world, which Cynthia previously viewed only as an outsider. *Secrets & Lies* utilizes the grinding minutiae of daily living to underscore raw emotion and numbing regret, and yet acknowledges with joyous tribute the indomitable human spirit. ★★★★ VHS: $29.99

Secrets of Women

(1952, 108 min, Sweden, Ingmar Bergman) *Jarl Kulle, Anita Bjork.* This early Bergman comedy is a thought-provoking and witty story of the indiscretions and foibles of man. Set in a summer home, three women confide in one another about their relationships with their husbands. Their extramarital affairs and the rapprochements with their men make for interesting conversation with amusing insights into the human condition. (Swedish with English subtitles) ★★★ VHS: $29.99

Seduced and Abandoned

(1964, 118 min, Italy, Pietro Germi) *Saro Urzi, Stefania Sandrelli.* This witty yet bitter film studies the inequalities and injustices of the Sicilian moral code. A young woman is befriended and seduced by the fiancé of her sister. His denial of any responsibility and his abandonment destroys her. The film alternates between a bedroom farce and social realism and is a successful follow-up to the director's *Divorce, Italian Style.* (Italian with English subtitles) ★★★

The Seduction of Mimi

(1974, 89 min, Italy, Lina Wertmuller) *Giancarlo Giannini, Mariangela Melato, Turi Ferro, Agostina Belli, Elena Fiore.* A boisterous farce on machismo Italian-style. On one level, a socio-political satire, the film also gives stunning portrayals of passion, revenge and paranoia. Sicilian metalworker Mimi (Giannini) won't support the local Mafia candidate in an election. Forced to move north, he falls in love with Fiore (Melato), a Trotskyite with a penchant for knitting. Wertmüller's surgically sharp satire earned her a reputation on the international scene. (American remake: *Which Way Is Up*) (Italian with English subtitles) ★★★½ VHS: $14.99; DVD: $14.99

Seduction: The Cruel Woman

(1985, 84 min, Germany, Monica Treut & Elfie Mikesch) *Mechthild Grossmann, Sheila McLaughlin.* Treut and Mikesch's highly stylized and dreamlike exploration of sadomasochism stars Grossmann as Wanda — a glamorous dominatrix and proprietor of the local "gallery" of bondage. As she moves from relationship to relationship, the film plumbs the depths of the dark side of sexual desire. A slick, visual fantasy which is inspired as much by the photography of Helmut Newton as by Leopold Sacher-Masoch's 1869 work, "Venus in Furs." (German with subtitles) ★★★ VHS: $29.99

See No Evil, Hear No Evil

(1989, 103 min, US, Arthur Hiller) *Richard Pryor, Gene Wilder, Joan Severance.* Pryor and Wilder team for a third time in this amiable and often funny comedy. The comics play two mismatched, prospective coworkers — the catch is that Pryor

is blind and Wilder is deaf — who become suspects in a murder which they (sort of) witnessed. The film is mostly one long chase as the two try to elude the police while they try to track down the real killers. *See No Evil...* has questionable taste in a couple of its gags, but it's enlivened by two comic princes. ★★½ VHS: $9.99

See You in the Morning

(1989, 119 min, US, Alan J. Pakula) *Jeff Bridges, Alice Krige, Farrah Fawcett, Linda Lavin, Drew Barrymore, Lukas Haas.* Bridges and Krige star in this uneven romantic comedy-drama as a middle-aged couple struggling with issues of parenthood and past spouses. A slightly disappointing effort from Pakula. ★★ VHS: $14.99

See You Monday

(1979, 100 min, Canada, Maurice Dugowson) *Miou-Miou, David Birney.* With possibly the worst title song ever recorded for a motion picture, this French-Canadian coproduction starts off on the wrong foot and never recovers. Miou-Miou is a saccharine-sweet redhead who, along with her friend, realize that they are tired of getting involved with married men and become determined to change their ways. An oddity, and a poor one at that. ★

Seems Like Old Times

(1980, 121 min, US, Jay Sandrich) *Chevy Chase, Goldie Hawn, Charles Grodin, Robert Guillaume.* Hawn and Chase reteam after their successful *Foul Play* in this bright, funny Neil Simon comedy. Goldie plays a lawyer whose ex-husband (Chase) reenters the scene, much to the chagrin of new husband Grodin. ★★★ VHS: $19.99

Seize the Day

(1986, 105 min, US, Fielder Cook) *Robin Williams, Glenne Headly, Joseph Wiseman, Jerry Stiller.* Compelling adaptation of Saul Bellow's novel starring Williams in a fine dramatic performance as an unemployed 40-year-old divorcée who moves to New York City to begin life anew. There he is greeted by the brutality and corruption of the corporate world. ★★★ VHS: $29.99

Seizure

(1974, 93 min, Canada, Oliver Stone) *Jonathan Frid, Troy Donahue, Mary Woronov.* A horror novelist (Frid) invites several friends to his home for the weekend, where his sinister dreams come to life to torment his guests. This ordinary thriller marks Stone's first feature — he has done better since. ★★

Selena

(1997, 127 min, US, Gregory Nava) *Jennifer Lopez, Edward James Olmos, Jon Seda, Constance Marie.* Lopez headlines this biopic of the ill-fated Mexican-American singing sensation Selena, whose young life was tragically cut short by an over-zealous fanatic's bullet in 1995. Unfortunately, this tepid film does neither the doomed singer nor the actress full justice. Olmos plays Selena's father and manager, who helps the teenaged singer break down racial barriers to become a crossover star. *Selena* is pretty much in the same vein as *La Bamba* and *The Buddy Holly Story,* two better dramatic musical biographies, but other than some energetic and snappily edited concert sequences, this plays like a routine TV movie-of-the-week.

The Secret of Roan Inish

The Seduction of Mimi

(Letterboxed VHS available for $19.99) ★★½
VHS: $14.99; DVD: $19.99

A Self-Made Hero

(1997, 105 min, France, Jacques Audiard)
*Mathieu Kassovitz, Anouk Grinberg, Sandrine
Kiberlain, Jean-Louis Trintignant.* A wondrous
blend of reality and fiction, this French comedy
tackles such weighty issues as identity, ambition
and desire as its protagonist struggles to find
his place in history. Albert Dehousse (Kassovitz)
wants so desperately to become a member of
the Resistance that he inveigles himself into the
party as a war hero. Celebrated for the accomplishments he never achieved, Albert quickly
moves up in rank despite the fact that he was
unable to serve. Using a significant period in
history to explore one man's ordinary life,
director Audiard has created a marvelous parable about the price of deception. Featuring a
subtle and moving performance by the likable
Kassovitz. (French with English subtitles) ★★★
VHS: $29.99

Semi-Tough

(1977, 108 min, US, Michael Ritchie) *Burt
Reynolds, Kris Kristofferson, Jill Clayburgh, Robert
Preston, Bert Convy, Lotte Lenya, Carl Weathers,
Brian Dennehy.* A pleasant, often funny look at
professional sports, this eager-to-please comedy
follows the happy exploits of two football players (Reynolds, Kristofferson) and their mutual
relationship with the daughter (Clayburgh) of
the team's owner (Preston). A weird subplot
about self-help analysis takes the film in a dicey
direction, but this remains one of the more
entertaining sports films. Great rapport
between the three leads. ★★★ VHS: $14.99;
DVD: $19.99

The Senator Was Indiscreet

(1947, 81 min, US, George S. Kaufman)
William Powell, Ella Raines. In the great playwright George S. Kaufman's only directorial
effort, Powell is perfect as an incompetent, foolhardy senator who decides to run for president
(that could never happen in *real* life); Powell's
candidacy is sabotaged by a personal diary. An
effervescent political satire. ★★★ VHS: $19.99

Send Me No Flowers

(1964, 100 min, US, Norman Jewison) *Rock
Hudson, Doris Day, Tony Randall, Paul Lynde.*
Breezy marital mix-ups abound with Rock as a
hypochondriac who mistakenly believes he is
going to die. He sets out to find a suitable new
husband for wife Doris. Their last film together.
★★★ VHS: $9.99

The Sender

(1982, 92 min, GB, Roger Christian) *Zeljko
Ivanek, Kathryn Harrold, Shirley Knight, Paul
Freeman.* A suicidal mental patient (Ivanek)
turns his horrific nightmares into reality by
choosing receivers for his demented thoughts.
Some good chills in this unexpected thriller.
★★½ VHS: $19.99

Sense and Sensibility

(1986, 174 min, GB, Rodney Bennett) *Irene
Richard, Tracey Childs.* This excellent TV version
of Jane Austen's first novel is a charming tale
about two sisters — one well mannered and
restrained and the other outspoken and
impetuous — who are looking for love and happiness amidst the rigid social mores of 18th-
century England. Imbued with a lighthearted
and amorous humor, the story follows their initial attempts at husband hunting and their
ensuing disappointments. ★★★½ VHS: $24.99

Sense and Sensibility

(1995, 135 min, GB, Ang Lee) *Emma Thompson,
Kate Winslet, Alan Rickman, Hugh Grant, Greg
Wise, Gemma Jones, Hugh Laurie.* A luscious adaptation of one of Jane Austen's better known
novels. Thompson produced and wrote the
adaptation, and then hired the masterful
Taiwanese director Lee to helm — together they
have made as seemly a rendering of Austen as
one is likely to see. Thompson and Winslet play
the two Dashwood sisters who, legally unable to
be the rightful heirs of their father's will, are
forced out of their impressive estate (and
"polite" society). Their dilemma, of course, is
how to marry — after all, in early 19th-century
society, women without dowries were hard to
pawn off. Hence, the story revolves around their
conundrum as they pin their hopes on a handful of suitors. Thompson's playful screenplay
finds a great deal of good humor in Austen's
story; the film exhibits an economy of manners
that would do Austen proud. ★★★★ VHS:
$14.99; DVD: $27.99

A Sense of Freedom

(1978, 85 min, Scotland, John MacKenzie)
David Hayman, Alex Norton. Based on an autobiographical novel by Jimmy Boyle, an inveterate
Glasgow gangster whose activities earned him a
life sentence for homicide and whose violent
disposition hardly abated once behind bars.
Filmed for Scottish television, it features an
intense, hard-edged performance by Hayman
as the pugilistic Boyle who revels in antagoniz-
ing prisoners and guards alike. ★★★

A Sense of Loss

(1978, 105 min, France, Marcel Ophüls)
Bernadette Devlin, Ian Paisley. Ophüls, the director of *The Sorrow and the Pity*, made this searing
but balanced documentary about the neverending conflict in Northern Ireland. The film
reveals how this ageless tragedy creates a nightmarish society of hatred and violence. ★★★

Senseless

(1997, 88 min, US, Penelope Spheeris) *Marlon
Wayans, David Spade, Matthew Lillard, Brad
Dourif, Tamara Taylor, Rip Torn.* A very silly slapstick comedy, *Senseless* stars Wayans as a desper-
ate-for-cash business major who agrees to take
an experimental drug for $3000. The drug
enhances the five senses tenfold, thus giving
Wayans an extra edge in attaining a competitive
job at a high-powered finance firm. Typically
tasteless '90s comedy has some funny moments,
but it's mostly just dumb. Even many of its funnier ideas have been done better in other
movies. While the premise *is* clever and many of
the gags work, the story is weak, clichéd and
dull, and the jokes become more desperate as
the film goes on. ★★ VHS: $14.99; DVD: $29.99

Senso

(1954, 117 min, Italy, Luchino Visconti) *Alida
Valli, Farley Granger.* A lavish and tragic tale of
love and war and one of the landmarks of post-
war Italian cinema. The story concerns the careless actions of an aristocratic woman (Valli) who
sacrifices her marriage and security for a handsome but cowardly soldier (Granger). This lavishly romantic story is set in Venice in 1866 on
the eve of the great conflict between Venice and
Austria. (Italian with English subtitles) (aka:
Wanton Countess) ★★★½ VHS: $29.99

Sensual Man

(1974, 90 min, Italy, Marco Vicario) *Giancarlo
Giannini.* The ubiquitous Giannini, the Gérard
Depardieu of Italian films, stars as a lusty, irresponsible playboy whose life consists of a series
of sexual episodes which include a relationship
with the former mistress of Mussolini as well as
a Communist member of Parliament. His fanta-
sy-filled life ends when he falls in love and marries: his wife suffers from a psychological block
which prevents her from consummating the
marriage. ★★

The Sentinel

(1977, 92 min, US, Michael Winner) *Christina
Raines, Chris Sarandon, Ava Gardner, Burgess
Meredith.* A young model (Raines) moves into a
Brooklyn Heights brownstone, which happens
to be the gateway to Hell. This hilariously
hyperventilating mix of *The Exorcist* and
Rosemary's Baby is enjoyably bizarre trash. ★★
VHS: $14.99; DVD: $19.99

S

La Sentinelle

(1992, 139 min, France, Arnaud Desplechin) *Emmanuel Salinger, Thibault de Montalembert, Jean-Louis Richard, Valérie Dréville.* An intriguing psychological mystery, *La Sentinelle* tells the story of Mathias (Salinger), a handsome French pathology student, who finds a head in his luggage, and decides to determine the identity of its owner. It seems the French secret police have a hand in the matter, and here begins Mathias' trouble. This long but absorbing European thriller places less emphasis on action than it does on the hero's obsession, which is shown in painstaking detail. Director Desplechin makes the presentation of medical tests, the tension between Mathias and his roommate (de Montalembert), and his increasing fear that the authorities are after him very palpable, but the film's cool tone will test the patience of viewers looking for thrills and excitement. (French with English subtitles) ★★★ VHS: $19.99; DVD: $29.99

A Separate Peace

(1972, 104 min, US, Larry Peerce) *Parker Stevenson, John Heyl.* John Knowles' best-selling novel makes a not-altogether successful transition to film in this sun-splashed teenage drama of friendship, initiation and betrayal. At a prep school at the beginning of WWII, two roommates develop a friendship. Stevenson is the freshly scrubbed narrator Gene who falls under the charismatic power of the athletic and domineering Finny (Heyl). Their friendship is tested after a freak accident injures Finny. The ensuing strain on their relationship forces the two to grow up and begin to face the harsh reality of the world outside the school's protective gates. While pretty to look at, the film tests the patience as it slows to an aimless crawl after the accident. ★★ VHS: $19.99

Separate Tables

(1958, 99 min, US, Delbert Mann) *Burt Lancaster, Rita Hayworth, David Niven, Deborah Kerr, Wendy Hiller.* A superlative adaptation of two Terence Rattigan one-act plays, combined in one telling, about a group of vacationers at an English seaside resort. A miraculous ensemble includes Lancaster and Hayworth as a divorced couple; Niven (in his Oscar-winning role) as an ex-military hero who may or may not be a fraud; Kerr as a lonely spinster; and Oscar winner Hiller as Lancaster's long-suffering mistress. Though the entire cast is praiseworthy, it is Niven, Kerr and Hiller who walk away with the acting honors. ★★★★ VHS: $14.99

Separate Tables

(1983, 112 min, GB, John Schlesinger) *Alan Bates, Julie Christie, Claire Bloom, Irene Worth.* An accomplished retelling of Terence Rattigan's pair of playlets, which had been previously told in the 1958 classic. In "Table by the Window," Christie plays an aging fashion model who travels to a seaside resort in the hopes of rekindling a relationship with her ex-husband (Bates). In "Table Number Seven," Christie plays a woman who holds a secret love for an army major (Bates) who is embroiled in a public scandal. Both Christie and Bates offer superb performances, and there's an excellent supporting cast. ★★★½

La Separation

(1994, 88 min, France, Christian Vincent) *Isabelle Huppert, Daniel Auteuil, Jérôme Deschamps, Karin Viard.* Two striking performances by the extraordinary Huppert as Anne and the somber Auteuil as Pierre make *La Separation*, a difficult film, immensely watchable. This tough domestic drama, about a couple initiating a break-up, is heartbreaking to endure yet so fiercely acted, it still fascinates. The cause for the separation is that Anne is in love with another (faceless) man. Pierre tries to accept this harsh fact and the film charts his efforts to come to terms with his feelings. The grayness of fault and blame is closely examined by director-cowriter Vincent in an intimate and intelligent manner. *La Separation* packs a powerful punch. (French with English subtitles) ★★★ VHS: $19.99; DVD: $29.99

September

(1987, 82 min, US, Woody Allen) *Denholm Elliott, Mia Farrow, Elaine Stritch, Sam Waterston, Jack Warden, Dianne Wiest.* Venturing into his *Interiors* ouvre, Allen's yuckless, Chekhovian chamber piece concerns a group of six successful people who vent their frustrations, angst and regrets during a weekend retreat in Vermont. A seriously flawed work by Allen which is probably his least accomplished film. ★★ VHS: $14.99; DVD: $19.99

September 30, 1955

(1977, 107 min, US, James Bridges) *Richard Thomas, Lisa Blount, Tom Hulce, Dennis Christopher, Dennis Quaid, Deborah Benson.* Thomas heads a terrific youthful cast in this intriguing character study. The title refers to the day actor James Dean died, and the film traces the effect Dean's death has on an idolizing college student (Thomas) and his fellow classmates. The film alternates between the merry exploits of teenage hijinks and the drama of *East of Eden*—like soul searching. Leonard Rosenman's score from that film is used here to good effect, and writer-director Bridges has created compelling characters in this semiautobiography. Thomas successfully captures the essence of teenage alienation. ★★★ VHS: $9.99

Sgt. Bilko

(1996, 94 min, US, Jonathan Lynn) *Steve Martin, Dan Aykroyd, Phil Hartman, Glenne Headly, Chris*

Sense and Sensibility (1995)

Rock, Max Casella. If this sometimes funny version of the classic TV series doesn't sustain a consistent hilarity level, it does make up for it by an engaging cast who perform with unswerving energy. Taking over the role created by the immortal Phil Silvers, Martin has big shoes to fill as Sgt. Bilko, military con man and bull artist extraordinaire. Bilko and his gang face the wrath of a visiting major (played to the hilt by Hartman) — impersonations, pratfalls, silly sight gags and double speak are the order of the day. Though the big-screen *Sgt. Bilko* lacks the lightning-fast pace of the show, and Martin can't duplicate Silver's inimitable breakneck delivery, there's still laughs to be found. ★★½ VHS: $7.49; DVD: $24.99

Sergeant Rutledge

(1960, 118 min, US, John Ford) *Jeffrey Hunter, Woody Strode, Billie Burke, Juano Hernandez.* Ford's tale of an African-American sergeant in the U.S. Cavalry standing trial for rape and murder. Ford's attempts to comment on racism are marred by the fact that the story is a muddled mix of the Old West and contemporary politics, and that the story really focuses on Hunter, the white lieutenant who defends Sergeant Rutledge. Strode's quiet performance as the title character is engaging, but in the end is nothing more than a cliché. ★★½ VHS: $14.99

Sergeant York

(1941, 134 min, US, Howard Hawks) *Gary Cooper, Joan Leslie, Walter Brennan, George Tobias.* Cooper won the first of his two Oscars for his stirring performance in this fact-based story of backwoodsman Alvin York, a pacifist drafted during World War I whose mental anguish and soul-searching leads him to reconcile his conflicting convictions, becoming a war hero on the battlefields of France. Expert direction by Hawks. ★★★★ VHS: $14.99

Serial Mom

(1994, 95 min, US, John Waters) *Kathleen Turner, Sam Waterston, Ricki Lake, Mink Stole, Traci Lords, Patricia Hearst, Matthew Lillard.* Waters has a wonderfully executed satire on suburbia, sex and violence, and our obsession with celebrity criminals. Turner is delicious as Beverly Sutphin, a June Cleaver–ish housewife who cooks, cleans, listens to Barry Manilow, and even recycles; oh, she's also a serial killer! But this deadly vixen is no ordinary murderer, for this bloody mama only kills to protect family and hearth. As husband and kids begin to realize the truth and the police close in, Waters lets loose a series of comic salvos which both tantalize and underscore his topical burlesque. You know you're in familiar Waters when Turner kills a victim with a leg of lamb while the score to *Annie* blares in the background. This twisted and defiantly hilarious comedy also serves as a cautionary tale to careless video renters: Rewind! ★★★½ VHS: $9.99; DVD: $14.99

The Serpent's Egg

(1978, 120 min, West Germany/US, Ingmar Bergman) *Liv Ullmann, David Carradine, Gert Frobe, James Whitmore.* Bergman's troubled and frightening drama about survival in the dawn of Nazi Germany. Set in 1933 Berlin, the film is about a Jewish-American trapeze artist (Carradine) and his sister-in-law (Ullmann), threatened by a mad doctor who portends the

Brad Pitt and Morgan Freeman in *Se7en*

Nazi catastrophe that is soon to befall Germany. (Filmed in English) ★★½

Serpico

(1973, 129 min, US, Sidney Lumet) *Al Pacino, John Randolph Jack Kehoe, F. Murray Abraham.* Pacino gives a sterling performance in this based-on-fact story about a non-conformist New York City undercover cop who is ostracized by his fellow officers when he reports widespread police corruption. Director Lumet's first of his "corruption" films (followed by *Prince of the City, Q & A* and *Night Falls on Manhattan*) is a hard-hitting and exemplary look at one man's personal courage. Fine location shooting helps in the authenticity of the story. Based on Peter Maas' best-seller. ★★★½ VHS: $14.99

The Servant

(1963, 115 min, GB, Joseph Losey) *Dirk Bogarde, Sarah Miles, James Fox.* One of director Losey's most tantalizing and complex films. Taken from Harold Pinter's first screenplay and based on a short story by Robin Maugham, the film is about the developing role reversal between a pampered, aristocratic weakling (Fox) and his manipulative and domineering manservant (Bogarde). An unnerving study of class struggle and sexual repression. ★★★½ VHS: $9.99

Servants of Twilight

(1991, 96 min, US, Jeffrey Obrow) *Bruce Greenwood, Belinda Bauer, Grace Zabriskie, Carel Struycken.* A mother and her young son are accosted by a wild-eyed, disheveled woman in a parking garage who claims that the son is the child of Satan and must be destroyed. Frustrated by police inaction, the mother hires a private investigator to protect the boy from murderous attacks by crazed cult members. The action moves through various twists and turns as the viewer is guided to a quite unexpected denouement. Based on a best-seller by Dean R. Koontz. ★★½ VHS: $9.99

Set It Off

(1996, 120 min, US, F. Gary Gray) *Jada Pinkett, Queen Latifah, Vivica A. Fox, Kimberly Elise, John C. McGinley, Blair Underwood.* Four black women, close friends and sick and tired of being screwed by the system, decide to turn the tables by robbing some banks. An enjoyable caper film, *Set It Off* is never believable, but energetic and pulpy enough to satisfy. The social commentary is obvious, and the circumstances leading up to the ladies' fateful decision is as heavy-handed and generic as a stock gangster film from the '30s. Once you can get past the "it's society's fault" exposition, however, *Set It Off* becomes a genuinely entertaining crime film which manages a few kinetic action scenes along the way. Letifah steals the show as a kick-ass lesbian tough, and Pinkett is quite affecting as a woman of conscience. ★★★ VHS: $14.99; DVD: $19.99

The Set-Up

(1949, 72 min, US, Robert Wise) *Robert Ryan, Audrey Totter, George Tobias.* Ryan is splendid as a washed-up boxer who, instead of throwing a big fight, rescues his pride but incures the wrath of mobsters. A stirring drama of rampant corruption and personal redemption. ★★★

Se7en

(1995, 125 min, US, David Fincher) *Brad Pitt, Morgan Freeman, Gwyneth Paltrow, Kevin Spacey, R. Lee Ermey, Richard Roundtree, John C. McGinley.* *Seven* is a plummeting descent into the ink-black recesses of the human soul — and one human soul in particular so revolted by his fellow creatures that he devises a series of intricate and carefully produced executions/passion plays/performance pieces to express his revulsion. He re-creates each of the seven deadly sins in tableaux of rare irony and brutal torture. The police on his trail (Freeman, world-weary and bone tired; and Pitt, young and eager and newly transferred) are dogged and determined, but there is no moral redemption here. While the film at first seems textbook in its element — grizzled veteran, frisky new guy, crazed serial killer — the formula resolution is rejected for a darker vision. Freeman's performance is a study of nuance. A remarkable execution of extremely unsettling material. (VHS available letterboxed or pan & scan) ★★★½ VHS: $14.99

Seven Beauties

(1976, 115 min, Italy, Lina Wertmuller) *Giancarlo Giannini, Fernando Rey, Shirley Stoler.* Giannini is superb as Wertmüller's Everyman who lives through the horrors of WWII and the concentration camps. A film of stunning accomplishment and staggering foibles. Arguably her greatest achievement. (Italian with English subtitles) ★★★★ VHS: $29.99; DVD: $29.99

Seven Brides for Seven Brothers

(1954, 103 min, US, Stanley Donen) *Howard Keel, Jane Powell, Russ Tamblyn, Tommy Rall, Julie Newmar.* A classic MGM musical. Keel plays the eldest of seven brothers who marries, prompting the other six to take wives — by kidnapping them. Superb dance sequences choreographed by Michael Kidd. (VHS available letterboxed or pan & scan) ★★★★ VHS: $14.99; DVD: $19.99

Seven Chances, Neighbors & The Balloonatic

(1920-25, 96 min, US, Buster Keaton/Eddie Cline) *Buster Keaton, Virginia Fox.* A collection of three Keaton comedies. *Seven Chances* (1925, 56 min) is a buoyant romp with Keaton as a sad sack who will inherit seven million dollars — but only if he weds by 7:00 PM that evening. Thus begins a wild scramble to find a willing wife. The film is highlighted by a hilarious prolonged chase sequence in which Keaton is pursued by hundreds of women through back alleys, city streets and across the countryside. (★★★½) *Neighbors* (1920, 18 min), written and directed by Keaton and Eddie Cline, is a delightful comedy with Keaton involved in a "Romeo and Juliet"-type romance with neighbor Fox. The two families, separated by a mutual back fence, try to put a stop to it. The film's accent is on physical stunts, and all are remarkable. (★★★½) *The Balloonatic* (1923, 22 min) finds Keaton adrift in a hot air balloon, eventually crashing to earth and finding love and misadventures. (★★★) VHS: $29.99; DVD: $29.99

Seven Days in May

(1964, 118 min, US, John Frankenheimer) *Burt Lancaster, Fredric March, Kirk Douglas, Edmond O'Brien, Ava Gardner.* This flawless political thriller is so frightening because it is so possible. Lancaster is the Chairman of the Joint Chiefs of Staff planning a military coup if the president (March) goes ahead and signs a nuclear disarmament treaty with the Russians. A taut script from Rod Serling is accentuated by

Seven Samurai

fine direction from Frankenheimer and terrific performances the cast. ★★★★ VHS: $14.99; DVD: $19.99

The Seven Deadly Sins

(1953, 113 min, France, Various) An enjoyable moral comedy devoted to man's seven deadly sins — Avarice, Anger, Sloth, Lust, Envy, Gluttony and Pride. This omnibus is fashioned episodically, with each of the dangerously alluring vices made by a different director, including: Yves Allegret ("Lust"), Claude Autant-Lara ("Pride"), Eduardo De Filippo ("Avarice" and "Anger"), Jean Dréville ("Sloth"), Georges Lacombe ("The Eighth Sin"), Carlo Rim ("Gluttony") and Roberto Rossellini ("Envy"). Surprisingly ribald, this is a delightfully irreverent peek into man's baser nature. (French with English subtitles) ★★★ VHS: $19.99

7 Faces of Dr. Lao

(1964, 100 min, US, George Pal) *Tony Randall, Barbara Eden, Arthur O'Connell.* Pal's fanciful fantasy with Randall giving a tour de force performance as the proprietor of a traveling circus. Randall plays seven roles. Oscar-winner for Makeup Effects. ★★★; DVD: $24.99

The Seven Percent Solution

(1976, 113 min, US, Herbert Ross) *Nicol Williamson, Robert Duvall, Alan Arkin, Vanessa Redgrave, Laurence Olivier, Joel Grey.* Sherlock Holmes' coke paranoia has gotten so bad that Dr. Watson (Duvall) concocts a scheme, with the help of Prof. Moriarty (Olivier), to get Holmes (Williamson) to see Dr. Sigmund Freud (Arkin) and take the cure. While in Vienna, he might as well solve a few mysteries while he's at it. Engrossing, smart fun from the pen of Nicholas Meyer, directed with panache by Ross. ★★★½ VHS: $14.99; DVD: $29.99

Seven Samurai

(1954, 200 min, Japan, Akira Kurosawa) *Toshiro Mifune, Takashi Shimura.* A passionate, exhilarating epic that stands alone in the realm of adventure films. To defend a flock of villagers, a small band of mighty warriors combat a horde of invading bandits. Kurosawa studies the intricate code of honor among the fighting men and their uneasy alliance with the downtrodden farmers. The complete, uncut version. (American remake: *The Magnificent Seven*) (Japanese with English subtitles) ★★★★ VHS: $34.99; DVD: $39.99

Seven Thieves

(1960, 102 min, US, Henry Hathaway) *Edward G. Robinson, Rod Steiger, Joan Collins, Eli Wallach, Sebastian Cabot.* A brilliant thief (Robinson) gathers a crew of criminal cronies to help him pull off his final crowning heist: robbing the casino vault at Monte Carlo. Tension-filled with good characterizations. ★★★ VHS: $39.99

The Seven Year Itch

(1955, 105 min, US, Billy Wilder) *Tom Ewell, Marilyn Monroe, Evelyn Keyes.* Wilder's witty and zany romp exposes the sexual fantasies of the middle-aged married man. Marilyn is the unintending temptress upstairs who becomes the object of Ewell's Walter Mitty-ish, philandering escapades. ★★★½ VHS: $9.99; DVD: $24.99

Seven Years in Tibet

(1997, 136 min, US, Jean-Jacques Annaud) *Brad Pitt, David Thewlis, B.D. Wong, Mako, Jamyang Jamtsho Wangchuk, Victor Wong.* Visually stunning and dramatically compelling, *Seven Years in Tibet* is a sometimes breathtaking journey into the heart of a people and a glossy adventure tale of redemption and hope. Pitt is well cast as Heinrich Harrer, an arrogant Austrian mountain climber whose attempt to scale the Himalayas in 1939 eventually lands him in the company of the young Dalai Lama. Escaping a POW camp, he sneaks into the holy city of Lhasa, thus beginning a journey of self-discovery as he soon becomes a tutor to the young religious leader. Director Annaud's pacing is deliberate (if occasionally slow, though his attention to detail is examplary. *Seven Years in Tibet* thankfully avoids sentimentality, and replaces it with honest emotions regarding faith, love, and soul-searching. ★★★½ VHS: $9.99; DVD: $19.99

1776

(1972, 141 min, US, Peter H. Hunt) *William Daniels, Howard da Silva, Ken Howard, John Cullum, Blythe Danner.* A sparkling version of the Tony Award—winning Broadway musical about the events leading up to the signing of the Declaration of Independence. Far from a detail-ridden history lesson, this rousing entertainment is a witty, clever and significant glance at the framing of a country. Most of the original stage stars repeat their roles, with Daniels in his finest hour as the antagonistic lobbyist for independence, John Adams; he's smartly supported by the wonderful da Silva as Ben Franklin, Howard as Thomas Jefferson and the golden-voiced Cullum as Edward Rutledge. ★★★½ VHS: $19.99

The Seventh Cross

(1944, 112 min, US, Fred Zinnemann) *Spencer Tracy, Signe Hasso, Hume Cronyn, Agnes Moorehead, Jessica Tandy.* A superb melodrama with Tracy escaping from a Nazi concentration camp accompanied by six others. On the run, they do their best to elude their captors, who have marked seven graves with crosses for their return. ★★★½ VHS: $19.99

The Seventh Seal

(1956, 96 min, Sweden, Ingmar Bergman) *Max von Sydow, Bibi Andersson.* Plague stalks 14th-century Sweden in this mystical classic, as a war-weary knight (von Sydow) encounters Death by the seaside and challenges him to a perilous chess match with his life in the balance. Unquestionably one of Bergman's greatest. (Swedish with English subtitles) ★★★★ VHS: $29.99; DVD: $39.99

The Seventh Sign

(1988, 98 min, US, Carl Schultz) *Demi Moore, Michael Biehn.* The premise of this occult thriller says the Bible foretells the destruction of the planet by seven warning signs. No matter how close you look in the Old or New Testaments, you won't find any warnings about bad horror films such as this. Moore is the pregnant woman privy to the apocalyptic prophecies. ★ VHS: $9.99

The Seventh Victim

(1943, 71 min, US, Mark Robson) *Kim Hunter, Tom Conway, Hugh Beaumont.* Exceptionally eerie occult thriller produces many a chill in this story of a woman (Hunter) who unwittingly becomes involved with a satanic cult while searching for her missing sister in New York's Greenwich Village. One of producer Val Lewton's best films; the screenplay was written by Lewton under the pseudonym "Carlos Keith." ★★★ VHS: $19.99

The 7th Voyage of Sinbad

(1958, 87 min, US, Nathan Juran) *Kerwin Matthews, Kathryn Grant.* Though a little creaky around the edges, good special effects make this one of the more enjoyable of the Ray Harryhausen films. Hero Sinbad battles an evil magician to restore his girlfriend — who has been shrunk only inches tall — to her normal size. Bernard Herrmann did the score. ★★½ VHS: $14.99; DVD: $27.99

Sex and Zen

(1993, 99 min, Hong Kong, Michael Mak) *Lawrence Ng, Amy Yip, Kent Cheng, Isabella Chow.* A typically oddball sex comedy-drama from Hong Kong, *Sex and Zen* features a horny stud who grafts a certain appendage from a horse onto his own body to satisfy the insatiable lusts of unhappily married women. That's about it for plot (and character, for that matter), as our hero hops in and out of bed with various women until a goofy, melo-

The famous game of chess in *The Seventh Seal*

dramatic denouement. For those unfamiliar with Hong Kong films, *Sex and Zen* will be almost impenetrable (so to speak), with its stilted, Ed Wood-esque dialogue, and drastic cultural differences in perspective and taste. This is tough going — it has unlikable characters, a dull story and scenes straining so hard to be "outrageous" that they end up being neither funny nor shocking. (Cantonese with English subtitles) ★★ VHS: $79.99; DVD: $49.99

Sex Is. . .

(1992, 81 min, US, Marc Huestis & Lawrence Helman) Contemporary gay men's preoccupation with sex and its side and after effects (love, relationship, AIDS) is entertainingly explored in this verbally and visually graphic documentary. Essentially a film of talking heads with some additional footage (mostly hard-core sex scenes) added, the film records the thoughts and opinions of various gay men who recount their childhood sexual obsessions, fantasies, proclivities and dislikes while they all agree that sex is a principal aspect of their lives. Raunchy, blunt and unapologetic, *Sex Is...* is an important testimony to gay men and their sexual lives before and during the age of AIDS. ★★★ VHS: $29.99; DVD: $29.99

sex, lies and videotape

(1989, 100 min, US, Steven Soderbergh) *James Spader, Andie MacDowell, Peter Gallagher, Laura San Giacomo.* Soderbergh's debut film is an emotionally powerful and darkly comic examination of infidelity, honesty and the darker side of human sensuality. John (Gallagher) and Ann Dellany (MacDowell) are the perfect young American couple: he's a new partner in a successful law firm; she's a squeaky-clean and somewhat prudish housewife; and he's having a torrid affair with her sister (lustily played by the ravishing San Giacomo). Into the fray comes John's old roommate Graham (played with a quiet brilliance by Spader), an austere and strangely pious wanderer who is returning home after years on the road. An eruption of hidden passions and untold secrets follow as the four move inevitably towards a final confrontation. The entire ensemble in this would-be love quadrangle is superb and Soderbergh's script and direction are bold, new and refreshing. ★★★★ VHS: $14.99; DVD: $29.99

The Sex of the Stars (Le Sexe Des Étoiles)

(1993, 100 min, Canada, Paule Baillargeon) *Denis Mercier.* This preachy Canadian melodrama details the difficult relationship between an adolescent girl and her estranged father, who returns into her life a transsexual woman. Intent on rekindling, however awkwardly, their relationship, Camille accepts the obvious — that her father is now a woman called Marie-Pierre — but refuses to alter any of the traditional father-daughter dynamics that she so desperately wants. The film tries to be "feel good" in spirit, but it ultimately reinforces the notion that deviant homosexuality is a sad, violent and unfulfilling world whose characters must pay the price for living a grotesque lifestyle. (French with English subtitles) ★★ VHS: $59.99

Le Sex Shop

(1973, 92 min, France, Claude Berri) *Claude Berri, Juliet Berto.* This congenial French satire wittily explores our modern preoccupation with sex, and our changing sexual mores. Claude, the owner of a sexual paraphernalia shop, decides to keep his own marriage in high gear by testing his merchandise "firsthand." Taking advice from his own manuals, he attempts to introduce his wife to swing clubs and a ménage à trois. ★★½

Sextette

(1978, 91 min, US, Ken Hughes) *Mae West, Timothy Dalton, Ringo Starr, Tony Curtis, George Hamilton, Alice Cooper.* Four on the floor is standard equipment with this classic beauty, as West returns to the showroom after an absence of nearly 40 years, loaded with options and ready for action. Her turbo-charged headers make it clear that this is one body built to go the distance in this camp classic about a vixen whose honeymoon keeps getting interrupted by her many ex-husbands. A pre–James Bond Dalton faces his most dangerous challenge as Mae requires more servicing than a Buick Skylark. Starr, Curtis and Hamilton are just a few who take her out for a spin after a quick look under the hood. ★½ VHS: $19.99; DVD: $9.99

S.F.W.

(1995, 92 min, US, Jefery Levy) *Stephen Dorff, Reese Witherspoon, Jake Busey.* Dorff (in a Brad Pittish turn) and Witherspoon are the two surviving hostages of a 36-day incarceration at a Fun Stop convenience store, held captive by the terrorist group Split Image — a group savvy enough to bring video equipment but with no apparent message. *S.F.W.*, which stands for "So Fucking What," takes a swipe at every element of the machinery that turns a news story into a prime time event: the packaging of TV movies, instant analysis from "Nightline," psychobabble from shrinks, and groupies eager to bask in other people's 15 minutes of fame. While the film could be easily written off as a *Natural Born Killers* clone with B-movie execution, it does manage to juxtapose the horror of hostage taking with the banality of media hype. Uneven and awkward. ★★

Shack Out on 101

(1955, 80 min, US, Edward Dein) *Lee Marvin, Keenan Wynn, Terry Moore.* Hyperventilating Red paranoia at its most entertaining! Marvin is Slob, a trouble-making hash-slinger (with a hidden agenda) in a remote greasy spoon operated by lug Wynn. Set almost entirely in the ramshackle beanery, the story features a great cast of oddball characters with the Marilyn Monroe—like Moore as the saucy but determined blonde who uncovers a nefarious ring of traitors. ★★★ VHS: $19.99

Shades of Fear

(1997GB, Beeban Kidron) *Vanessa Redgrave, Jonathan Pryce, Rakie Ayola, Dorothy Tutin.* Originally called *Great Moments in Aviation*, the equally misnamed *Shades of Fear* isn't some third-rate, quick-paycheck hack job mystery which the advertising suggests. It's an unusual, rewarding drama revolving around a handful of passengers on a cruise to England, and of their respective secrets. Well-written by Jeanette Winterson and directed with just the right

amount of sensitivity and humor by Kidron, *Shades of Fear* also boasts a stellar cast of British stalwarts and a radiant newcomer, Ayola (who is really the lead character). Watch for a wonderful, revelatory scene between Redgrave, Tutin and Pryce cuttin' the rug to "Brazil." ★★★ VHS: $19.99

Shadey

(1987, 90 min, GB, Philip Saville) *Antony Sher, Billie Whitelaw, Patrick Macnee, Katherine Helmond.* Offbeat espionage spoof with Sher as a garage mechanic who agrees to use his special powers — the ability to read minds and project those images onto film — to finance his sex-change operation. An irreverent comedy. ★★½

The Shadow

(1994, 112 min, US, Russell Mulcahy) *Alec Baldwin, Penelope Ann Miller, Tim Curry, Ian McKellen, John Lone, Peter Boyle, Jonathan Winters, Andre Gregory.* Based on the popular 1930s radio program, this lifeless cartoon "adventure" tale stars a grim Baldwin as the avenging hero/bad guy Lamont Cranston, aka The Shadow. Borrowing the set design ideas of *Batman* without any of its excitement, the film is a series of awkward battle scenes and comic vignettes as The Shadow takes on a mystical madman (Lone) bent on world domination. ★ VHS: $14.99; DVD: $24.99

The Shadow Box

(1980, 100 min, US, Paul Newman) *Joanne Woodward, Christopher Plummer, Valerie Harper, Sylvia Sidney, James Broderick, Melinda Dillon.* A well-made and sensitive version of Michael Cristofer's Tony Award— and Pulitzer Prize—winning play. The story follows the lives of three terminally ill patients as they and their families spend a day at an experimental retreat in the California mountains. Woodward gives a beautifully controlled performance, and Plummer is equally splendid as her gay ex-husband. ★★★

Shadow Hunter

(1992, 98 min, US, J.S. Cardone) *Scott Glenn, Benjamin Bratt, Angela Alvarado, Robert Beltran.* Glenn is a burnt-out L.A. cop sent to Arizona to pick up a Native American wanted for murder. When Twobear (Bratt in a chilling performance) escapes from his custody, Glenn enters into an odyssey in which his survival may well depend on the strength of his soul. A well-paced though familiar combination of psychological thriller and action/adventure, sprinkled with elements of Native American mysticism. The spectacular Arizona desert is beautifully captured. ★★½ VHS: $14.99

Shadow of a Doubt

(1943, 108 min, US, Alfred Hitchcock) *Joseph Cotten, Teresa Wright, Patricia Collinge, Hume Cronyn, Henry Travers.* Cited by Hitchcock as one of his personal favorites, this cat-and-mouse, spellbinding psychological thriller stars Cotten as an apparently ordinary fellow who visits his small-town kin. However, his diabolical past gradually becomes evident, and threatening, to his suspicious young niece (wonderfully played by a wide-eyed and innocent Wright). ★★★★ VHS: $14.99; DVD: $29.99

Shadow of the Thin Man

See: The Thin Man Series

Willem Dafoe in *Shadow of the Vampire*

Shadow of the Vampire

(2000, 93 min, US, E. Elias Merhige) *John Malkovich, Willem Dafoe, Cary Elwes, Udo Kier, Catherine McCormack, Eddie Izzard.* Here's a terrific what-if: What if the classic vampire film *Nosferatu* had an actual vampire playing the part of the legendary bloodsucker? Director Merhige and screenwriter Steven Katz take this intriguing premise and are only able to deliver on it in short bursts of creativity. Malkovich is the great German director F. W. Murnau, who is preparing his next film, an adaptation of Bram Stoker's "Dracula." However, there's an air of mystery hanging over the set concerning the enigmatic actor Max Schreck (Dafoe). The cast thinks him an obsessive method actor; but the man playing a vampire could be one himself. And if he is, what peril awaits the cast? *Shadow of the Vampire* comes alive whenever the remarkable Dafoe is on-screen. The actor, ahem, sinks his teeth into this juicy role with verve, essaying menace with mocking glee. But when he's not featured, the film is unfocused and lethargic, and there are a few plot inconsistencies that can't be overlooked. Some choice, macabre moments help keep interest, but considering the talent involved and the promising setup, this should have been far more substantial. ★★½ VHS: $14.99; DVD: $26.99

A Shadow You Soon Will Be
(Una Sombra Ya Pronto Seras)

(1994, 105 min, Argentina, Hector Olivera) *Miguel Angel Sola.* Olivera explores the state of post-democratic Argentinian society through the means of allegory and metaphor. Based on a novel by Osvaldo Soriano, *A Shadow You Soon Will Be* follows the meanderings of an unemployed computer programmer (Sola) through an eerily barren countryside. The director uses wide angle shots and a variety of editing styles to capture the disorientation of Argentina's social and political landscape. Our hero's travels lead him not towards any one particular fate (despite an intriguing run-in with a fortune teller), but rather towards an understanding of exactly how he has landed where he is. Not technically proficient, *Shadow* provides an ironic, amusing exploration of the "journey" for those philosophically inclined. (Spanish with English subtitles) ★★★ VHS: $89.99

Shadowlands

(1987, 73 min, GB, Norman Stone) *Joss Ackland, Claire Bloom.* A West End and Broadway hit, this moving love story stars Ackland as writer C. S. Lewis, who finds that his ordered Don's life at Oxford is thrown into turmoil after he meets and falls in love with American poet Joy Gresham (Bloom). Winner of two British Academy Awards. ★★★

Shadowlands

(1993, 130 min, GB, Richard Attenborough) *Anthony Hopkins, Debra Winger, John Wood.* Attenborough brings unexpected poignancy to this captivating romantic drama about the real-life love affair between author C. S. Lewis and writer Joy Gresham. Based on William Nicholson's hit stage play, the film stars Hopkins as Lewis, a proper British professor/lecturer whose ordered life takes a turn when American Gresham (Winger) arrives on his doorstep. As she insinuates herself into his life, they marry in order for Gresham to stay in the country — and ultimately and inevitably fall in love. Though it may sound like nothing more than a British *Green Card*, this is unexpectedly funny, beautifully told, exceptionally written, and features two remarkable performances by Hopkins and Winger. ★★★★ VHS: $9.99; DVD: $14.99

Shadows

(1960, 87 min, US, John Cassavetes) *Hugh Herd, Lelia Goldini, Ben Carruthers, Anthony Ray, Rupert Crosse.* Cassavetes' directorial debut is a rough-hewn improvisation pulsating with hyperkenetic energy. The grainy black-and-white cinematography and Charlie Mingus score augment the quasi-documentary intimacy and immediacy delivered by the competent cast. Goldini is a naïve 20-year-old black woman living with her two brothers, one a ne'er-do-well (Carruthers) and the other a struggling jazz musician (Herd). The complexities of racism are explored from their perspectives, as the brothers deal with the underside of the entertainment industry, and their light-skinned sister handles the emotional upheaval of a relationship with a Caucasian man who does not know she is an African-American. The low-budget production values are reminiscent of British "kitchen sink" dramas of that time. Riveting and involving, and quintessential Cassavetes. ★★★ VHS: $19.99; DVD: $24.99

Shadows and Fog

(1992, 86 min, US, Woody Allen) *Woody Allen, Mia Farrow, John Malkovich, Jodie Foster, Lily Tomlin, Kathy Bates, John Cusack, Madonna, Kate Nelligan, Wallace Shawn, Robert Joy.* Lost amid the controversy surrounding the breakup of Allen and Farrow, this minor addition to Allen's filmography is nonetheless an entertaining, well-made and often amusing ode to early German cinema. Based on Allen's stage play "Death," the story centers on Woody's hapless nebbish who becomes the object of a lynch mob's hunt for a serial killer. The action takes place in an archetypal pre-WWII European city on a foggy night and is shot in a stark black and white which is filled with visual references to the German Expressionist classics *M* and *Nosferatu*. In addition to an impressive supporting cast, there's the superb soundtrack composed of a delightful mélange of Kurt Weill cabaret tunes. ★★★ VHS: $14.99; DVD: $19.99

Shadows of Forgotten Ancestors

(1964, 99 min, USSR, Sergei Paradjanov) *Ivan Micholaichuk, Larisa Kadochnikova.* The historical pageantry and epic legends of medieval times are enacted in this visually and musically vibrant love story. Set in 19th-century Ukraine, the drama centers around a young man who is trapped in a loveless marriage and haunted by his true but dead sweetheart. But make no mistake about its simple plot, for the film is a wonderful compendium of folk dances, religious zealousness and witchcraft. It is filmed in a psychedelic rampage and has more spectacular effects, spectacular camera movements, wild experiments with color and bizarre musical scenes than anyone would imagine in one film. (Ukrainian with English subtitles) ★★★★ VHS: $29.99

Shadrach

(1998, 86 min, US, Susanna Styron) *Harvey Keitel, Andie MacDowell, John Franklin Sawyer, Scott Terra, Daniel Treat.* A slow moving, but evocative tale from the pen of William Styron, and directed by the author's daughter, *Shadrach* offers a look at Virginia 1935 as seen through the eyes of a ten-year-old boy. Paul (Terra) is a well-to-do southerner, whose best friend is Little Mole Dabney (Treat), the youngest son of a family being hit hard by the Depression. While things like money and racial segregation rarely enter into the mind's of these two boys, with the arrival of Shadrach (Sawyer), a 99-year-old former slave, they soon learn some valuable facts about life. Although the drama is slight, the mood is flavorful thanks to Styron's sure hand. Terra and Treat are natural talents, and Sawyer is beguiling in the title role. ★★★ VHS: $102.99; DVD: $29.99

Shaft

(1971, 106 min, US, Gordon Parks) *Richard Roundtree, Moses Gunn.* With Isaac Hayes' rhythmic score in the background, this sexy and violent (always a great combo in blaxploitation) crime story stars Roundtree as John Shaft, a mean and resourceful private dick. Essentially a black *French Connection*, the story has Shaft hired by a ruthless drug lord (Gunn) to find his daughter, who was kidnapped by the white Mafia. Slick, action-packed urban fun. (Followed by 2 sequels, and remade in 2000) ★★★ VHS: $9.99; DVD: $14.99

Shaft

(2000, 99 min, US, John Singleton) *Samuel L. Jackson, Vanessa Williams, Jeffrey Wright, Christian Bale, Busta Rhymes, Dan Hedaya, Toni Collette, Richard Roundtree, Lynne Thigpen.* Jackson is certainly in his element as that suave private eye John Shaft in this flavorful remake of the 1971 action fave. Updated to reflect a millennium mindset, the slam-bang story follows police detective Shaft — nephew to the original Shaft played by Roundtree, who turns up here as "Uncle John" — and his investigation into a racially motivated murder. Bale is the snotty, rich white kid who killed a black youth in cold blood. When it looks as if he may get away with it, it's up to Shaft to make sure the creep does his time. Wright steals the show as a neighborhood drug lord whose path both Shaft and the

S

racist killer cross. Director Singleton keeps the action moving at a swift pace, and there are a couple of great set pieces — all played with verve by Jackson and his extremely capable costars. A hip, defiantly entertaining mix of action, humor and police procedural. And, yes, Isaac Hayes' classic theme song returns. ★★★ VHS: $14.99; DVD: $29.99

Shaft in Africa

(1973, 111 min, US, John Guillermin) *Richard Roundtree, Vonetta McGee.* Shaft (Roundtree) goes undercover in Africa to expose a new slave trade. He does some badass espionage using just his mouth, his fists, and his attitude. Theme song "Are You Bad Enough" performed by the Four Tops. Good action scenes highlight this exciting, tough film. ★★★ VHS: $9.99; DVD: $14.99

Shaft's Big Score!

(1972, 105 min, US, Gordon Parks) *Richard Roundtree, Moses Gunn.* The baddest mutha in town is back, in this well-paced, action-packed sequel. While investigating the murder of a friend by an underworld crime figure, hero Shaft (Roundtree) discovers that the money he was going to use to pay off his pal's gambling debt is missing. He then makes a deal with crime boss Stumpy (Gunn) and makes the same deal with another boss, putting himself in the middle of an intense war. Stylish, never boring, well-acted Cadillac among blaxploitation films. ★★★ VHS: $9.99; DVD: $14.99

Shakedown

(1988, 90 min, US, James Glickenhaus) *Peter Weller, Sam Elliott, Patricia Charbonneau.* Weller and Elliott are the mismatched partners in this routine actioner about a public defender (Weller) and a burned-out undercover cop (Elliott) who go after some corrupt policemen. Some good action scenes, but the plot makes little sense. ★★ VHS: $19.99

Shakes the Clown

(1991, 87 min, US, Bobcat Goldthwait) *Bobcat Goldthwait, Julie Brown, Robin Williams, Adam Sandler.* Written, directed and starring Goldthwait, this story of a drunken, down-on-his-luck clown drags a bit, but delivers some good laughs. Set in a semi-surrealistic town populated by all types of unemployed, has-been clowns, Goldthwait is a "good clown" whose love of booze eventually complicates him in a murder. The plot, however, comes secondary to the film's frantic, hit-or-miss style. Yes, the story itself is not very interesting nor well-constructed, and some of the scenes and main characters are decidedly unfunny. But overall, a funny little oddity. Williams steals the film as a fey yet militaristic mime instructor. ★★½ VHS: $9.99; DVD: $24.99

Shakespeare in Love

(1998, 122 min, GB, John Madden) *Gwyneth Paltrow, Joseph Fiennes, Geoffrey Rush, Judi Dench, Ben Affleck, Colin Firth, Tom Wilkinson, Antony Sher, Rupert Everett, Simon Callow.* A gloriously romantic and brilliantly written comedy of manners about what happened in the life of young William Shakespeare which inspired him to write "Romeo and Juliet" — or as he *was* going to call it, "Romeo and Ethel, the Pirate's Daughter." The dashing Fiennes is Will,

Colin Firth and Dame Judi Dench (in her Academy Award-winning role) in *Shakespeare in Love*

England's up-and-coming playwright of the late 16th century who when we first meet is suffering from writer's block. Oscar winner Paltrow is luminous as Viola, a high-born, stagestruck lady who poses as a man and tries out for Will's new production. From there, romance of an extraordinary kind blossoms. The ensemble is superb, including a very funny Rush as Will's agent, and Oscar-winner Dench, who steals the show in her few scenes as Queen Elizabeth. *Shakespeare in Love* is that rarity — an intelligent, funny and captivating romantic entertainment. Winner of 7 Academy Awards, including Best Picture. ★★★★ VHS: $14.99; DVD: $29.99

Shakespeare Wallah

(1965, 120 min, India, James Ivory) *Laura Liddell, Geoffrey Kendal, Felicity Kendal, Shashi Kapoor.* The setting is India during the last days of the British Raj when the struggling nation was trying to free itself of colonial imperialism and cultural saturation by the British. Amidst all of this turmoil, an English Shakespearean acting troupe valiantly tours the countryside. The story concerns the budding love affair between the daughter of one of the actors and a young Indian. Their infatuation and innocence and persistence amidst the changes help make this a charming and delightful tale. ★★★ VHS: $19.99

Shall We Dance

(1937, 116 min, US, Mark Sandrich) *Fred Astaire, Ginger Rogers, Edward Everett Horton.* Captivating Astaire-Rogers musical with Fred and Ginger as a dance team pretending to be married; of course, they fall in love. Needless to say, there are great dance numbers, and the Gershwins' score includes "Let's Call the Whole Thing Off," "They All Laughed" and "They Can't Take That Away from Me." ★★★½ VHS: $14.99

Shall We Dance

(1997, 119 min, Japan, Masayuki Suo) *Koji Yakusho, Tamiyo Kusakari, Naoto Takenaka, Reiko Kusamura.* Recalling the sheer exhilaration of *Strictly Ballroom*, the wonderfully comic and bittersweet *Shall We Dance* also manages to evoke the whimsy of that film. Shohei (Yakusho) is a weary Japanese office worker who decides to enroll in a ballroom dance class to possibly pur-

sue the beautiful teacher Mai (Kusakari). Though the dancing, Shohei gains self-confidence and readys himself for the big contest at the finale. Though not as elaborate as in *Strictly Ballroom*, the dance sequences are engagingly performed by an appealing cast of characters, and director Suo is able to effectively balance their lightheartedness with the more serious clash of romanticism and culture. A delightful, often giddy affair. (Japanese with English subtitles) ★★★½ VHS: $19.99

Shallow Grave

(1994, 92 min, Scotland, Danny Boyle) *Ewan McGregor, Kerry Fox, Christopher Eccleston, Keith Allen.* This grisly Scottish black comedy tells an all-too familiar tale of greed-conquers-all, but an eccentric sense of style and some truly shocking twists make it a surprising and riveting thriller. The film follows three unlikable roommates: Alex (McGregor), David (Eccleston), and Juliet (Fox). Things begin to unravel when their new roommate dies of a drug overdose and leaves them with a suitcase full of cash. They immediately go about hatching schemes to keep the money and dispose of the body and ultimately begin an inexorable descent into madness and greed. Debut director Boyle shows great promise; his visual prowess and sprightly script keep the tension building right up to the excruciating climax. ★★★½ VHS: $14.99; DVD: $24.99

Shame

(1968, 103 min, Sweden, Ingmar Bergman) *Max von Sydow, Liv Ullmann.* The personal horrors of war are explored in this intense story of a couple caught up in a senselessly violent civil war. The setting is 1971, when a seemingly happy but quarrelsome couple (von Sydow, Ullmann) have fled to a secluded farmhouse to escape the unexplained war. Both orchestra musicians, von Sydow is a self-absorbed, emotionally fragile man and Ullmann his strong-willed wife. The war and its horrific violence soon spills into their world, trapping them and then brutally stripping them of their dignity as they desperately struggle for survival. Very powerful acting by von Sydow and Ullmann and a gripping, action-filled story make this powerful drama one of Bergman's best. (Swedish with English subtitles) ★★★★ VHS: $19.99

Shame

(1988, 90 min, Australia, Steve Jodrell) *Deborra-Lee Furness, Tony Barry.* A taut, violent story of rape, murder and oppression. A woman, traveling alone on a motorcycle, encounters engine trouble and seeks help from the citizens of a small, out-of-the-way town. Instead, she discovers a conspiracy of violence directed against many of the town's young women. Confronted with this terror, our heroine chooses to stay and fight. The ensuing sexual battle is told in the best Rambo-like style as this riveting film not only delivers potent doses of action, but also explores the tumultuous relationship between the sexes. ★★★

The Shameless Old Lady

(1966, 94 min, France, René Allio) *Sylvie, Malka Ribovska.* Sylvie, a French character actress for almost 50 years, is finally the star in this touching and delightful film based on a Brecht short story. A 70-year-old widow, after devoting herself to her family during a drab, uneventful life, decides to change her ways and boisterously enjoy her remaining years. Shocking her children and neighbors, she buys a *Deux Chevaux*, joins a political group, befriends a prostitute and goes on holiday. (French with English subtitles) ★★★½

Shampoo

(1975, 112 min, US, Hal Ashby) *Warren Beatty, Julie Christie, Lee Grant, Goldie Hawn, Jack Warden, Carrie Fisher.* Potent sexual and social comedy about the romantic exploits of a bed-hopping Beverly Hills hairdresser (Beatty). A first-rate cast includes Oscar winner Grant. ★★★ VHS: $9.99

Shane

(1953, 118 min, US, George Stevens) *Alan Ladd, Jean Arthur, Jack Palance, Van Heflin, Brandon deWilde.* Director Stevens' classic western stars Ladd as a mysterious gunfighter who comes to the aid of a homesteading family (Heflin, Arthur), and is idolized by their young son (De Wilde). Palance is a most memorable villian. ★★★★ VHS: $9.99; DVD: $24.99

Shanghai Blues

(1984, 108 min, Hong Kong, Tsui Hark) Belying one's preconceived notions of Hong Kong's cinema, this gleefully anachronistic, gag-filled screwball comedy, set in 1937 and 1947 Shanghai, has a not-too-ordinary plot — boy meets girl, boy loses girl, boy and girl wind up as fueding neighbors without recognizing each other. A pretty cast and imaginatively wacky ideas fuel this enjoyable oddity. (Cantonese with English subtitles) ★★★ VHS: $39.99

Shanghai Noon

(2000, 110 min, US, Tom Dey) *Jackie Chan, Owen Wilson, Lucy Liu, Brandon Merrill, Roger Yuan, Xander Berkeley.* Jackie teams up with the perpetually laid-back Wilson for an amusing, if unremarkable action-comedy. When a Chinese princess (Liu) is kidnapped and taken to the American West, ne'er-do-well Chan accompanies his uncle and several royal warriors to retrieve her. Of course, in the end, it's up to

Jackie — and newfound, reluctant partner Wilson — to save her. Much less action than the typical Jackie vehicle, but a sequence with Chan facing off with some tough-looking Native Americans and another in which he uses his long ponytail as a weapon are certainly fun. Wilson and Chan have good chemistry together, though they aren't as funny a pair as Chan and Chris Tucker (in *Rush Hour*). Though slowly paced, and not top drawer Jackie, *Shanghai Noon* is harmless fun if your expectations aren't too high. ★★½ VHS: $14.99; DVD: $29.99

Shanghai Surprise

(1986, 97 min, US, Jim Goddard) *Sean Penn, Madonna, Paul Freeman.* One of the candidates for Worst Film of the Decade, this laughable adventure film teamed then-husband and wife Penn and Madonna in the story of a missionary in 1930s China who enlists the aid of a down-and-out adventurer to track a missing opium shipment. Just dreadful on every level. ★ VHS: $14.99

Shanghai Triad

(1995, 108 min, China, Zhang Yimou) *Gong Li, Li Boatian, Li Xuejian, Shun Chin, Wang Xiao Xiao.* Chinese master Zhang puts his artful spin on a 1930s crime period piece with mixed results. At times entrancing at others simply tediously trance-inducing, the film follows the first several days in the apprenticeship of young Tang Shuisheng, a 14-year-old "country bumpkin" (as he is repeatedly called). Thanks to his uncle Liu's influence, Shuisheng is to be the personal servant of Bijou (Gong), the extravagant moll of triad boss Mr. Tang. The film meanders through its first half, suffering from an absolutely somnambulistic editing pace and getting dragged down by a series of overly long singing numbers in which Bijou entertains at the boss' nightclub. The film finally finds a narrative pace as it explores Bijou's process of personal transformation. (Mandarin with English subtitles) ★★½ VHS: $19.99; DVD: $29.99

Sharky's Machine

(1981, 119 min, US, Burt Reynolds) *Burt Reynolds, Rachel Ward, Vittorio Gassman, Brian Keith, Charles Durning.* A bit overlong but nevertheless a flavorful police thriller with police detective Reynolds taking on sleazeball Gassman. ★★½ VHS: $14.99; DVD: $14.99

Sharma and Beyond

(1984, 85 min, GB, Brian Gilbert) *Suzanne Burden, Robert Urquhart.* This installment of David Putnam's "First Love Series" is a winning and poignant exploration of the complex relationship that develops between a father, a daughter and her suitor. The young woman, recently wounded in love, is not at all sure whether this new young man, an aspiring sci-fi writer, is more interested in her, or in her father who is a famous author. ★★★

Shattered

(1991, 97 min, US, Wolfgang Petersen) *Tom Berenger, Greta Scacchi, Bob Hoskins, Corbin Bernsen, Joanne Whalley-Kilmer.* A postmodern whodunit whose psychological complexities, which sometimes obscure the action, probably doomed this inventive, very exciting thriller at the box office. Berenger is left an amnesiac after a near-fatal accident and there are twists aplenty as he tries to get some idea of who he used to be, who he is now and who he can trust to tell him the truth. Scacchi is his loving wife (or is she?), and Hoskins is the private detective trying to solve Berenger's intricate puzzle. A film rich in suspense and overflowing with atmosphere and style. ★★★½ VHS: $9.99

Shattered Image

(1998, 103 min, US, Raúl Ruiz) *Anne Parillaud, William Baldwin, Graham Greene.* Prolific Chilean-born filmmaker Ruiz, known for his cryptic but visually stunning surrealistic tales, is in an unusually muted mood with this intermittently involving English-language thriller of a woman haunted by troubling dreams and a split identity. Parillaud plays two aspects of the same char-

Shall We Dance: Will the real Ginger Rogers please step forward?

John Richardson and Ursula Andress in *She* ('65)

acter — is she the professional killer paid to kill antique storeowner Baldwin or is she the beautiful but somnambulistic bride to the seemingly loving Baldwin? At its best, Ruiz creates a beguiling puzzle infused with fear, deception, violence and eventually murder. But this psychological mystery-drama is Ruiz-lite and seems to be a thinly veiled rip-off of Hitchcock's *Vertigo*. Exotic settings and steamy sex scenes are offset by Parillaud's monotone, French-accented English and Ruiz's clunky approach. ★★½ VHS: $19.99; DVD: $24.99

The Shawshank Redemption

(1994, 142 min, US, Frank Darabont) *Tim Robbins, Morgan Freeman, Bob Gunton, James Whitmore, William Sadler.* Put aside whatever preconceptions you may have about a two-and-a-half hour period prison story, for *The Shawshank Redemption* is not only emotionally moving but one of the best films of its year. Adapted from a Stephen King novella, this is the story of Andy Dufresne (Robbins), a banker given life imprisonment for the murder of his wife. Sentenced to Shawshank Prison, Andy is brutalized regularly when not staying to himself. Life turns around for him when he befriends Red (Oscar nominee Freeman), a lifer with connections, and becomes financial broker for the crooked warden and his guards. As Andy serves his life sentence, he manages to sustain a hopefulness which affects the other prisoners as well. Director Darabont makes a very assured feature debut, the cinematography and other technical aspects are first-rate, and the ensemble is remarkable. (Letterboxed VHS available for $19.99) ★★★★ VHS: $14.99; DVD: $19.99

She

(1935, 94 min, US, Irving Pichel & Lansing Holden) *Helen Gahagan, Randolph Scott, Helen Mack, Nigel Bruce.* Deep within an Arctic glacier is the unknown land of Kor. With a hot temper and a colder heart, an ancient queen (Gahagan) rules over this subterranean land while pining still for her long dead lover. She keeps at bay the ravages of the centuries by bathing in a fountain of flames. Finally her Romeo does return — reincarnated as Scott. Produced by the same team that made *King Kong*, *She* is a marvelous mélange of matinee-

movie dialogue, kitschy costumes and campy art deco sets. ★★★ VHS: $24.99; DVD: $29.99

She

(1965, 106 min, GB, Robert Day) *Ursula Andress, John Richardson, Peter Cushing.* Great, campy, lost-world fun is to be had in this Hammer Films retelling of the old H. Rider Haggard story about a lost city, a doomed hero, slave sacrifices, an ancient cult and a beautiful, immortal queen. Explorer Richardson and scholar Cushing discover a lost city which at first seems a paradise, but becomes a prison when the beautiful queen (Andress) is revealed to be ageless. As it turns out, Richardson is the reincarnation of her lost love, who long ago betrayed her. Is he doomed to repeat the same mistake? Will he walk into the Eternal Flame for everlasting life? A pleasure-seeking eternity with Andress? Where do you sign? ★★★ VHS: $19.99

She-Devil

(1989, 99 min, US, Susan Seidelman) *Roseanne Barr, Meryl Streep, Ed Begley, Jr., Linda Hunt.* What's a slovenly, socially inept suburban housewife to do when her accountant husband starts a passionate affair with her favorite glamorous and achingly beautiful romance novelist? Take revenge. . . what else? When Roseanne dumps the kids and the dog on wandering hubby Begley and soft-focus sweetie Streep, she begins her metamorphosis from frump to take-charge woman (hear her roar). Streep reveals an unexplored panache for comedic understatement and Barr serves her role well. ★★½ VHS: $9.99

She-Devils on Wheels

(1968, 83 min, US, Hershell Gordon Lewis) Lewis' stab at the biker genre, about a violent female motorcycle gang with "guts as hard as the steel of their hogs!" The girls wage war with a rival (male) bike gang, pick their men from a "stud line" and have an all-around "real bad time!" ★ VHS: $19.99; DVD: $24.99

She Done Him Wrong

(1933, 66 min, US, Lowell Sherman) *Mae West, Cary Grant.* West coauthored this classic gay '90s

Helen Gahagan in *She* ('35)

spoof based on her stage hit "Diamond Lil." La West is at her buxom best as Lady Lou, diamond collector and man snatcher — which came first? Grant is the next-door missionary bent on saving her soul — or is he? Mae says it best — "Why don't you come up sometime and see me?" ★★★★ VHS: $14.99

She Must Be Seeing Things

(1988, 85 min, US, Sheila McLaughlin) *Sheila Dabney, Lois Weaver.* McLaughlin's lesbian love story explores the complex sexual and emotional commitment of two women professionals. This interesting love story follows the rocky relationship of Agatha, a New York lawyer, and Jo, a filmmaker. While Jo is out of town, Agatha comes upon her diary and photos which suggest that she is developing an interest in men and may be unfaithful to her. Agatha's growing jealousy and her frantic attempts to keep her wavering lover interested result in her donning men's clothing and spying on her unsuspecting partner. The drama is a bit stilted and not entirely successful, but there are moments of great insight and fine acting. ★★½ VHS: $29.99

She Wore a Yellow Ribbon

(1949, 103 min, US, John Ford) *John Wayne, Joanne Dru, John Agar, Ben Johnson, Victor McLaglen.* The second (and more successful) film in director Ford's cavalry trilogy. Wayne gives a commanding performance as an officer about to retire, experiencing emotional conflict in doing so. Oscar-winning cinematography. ★★★★ VHS: $14.99

She'll Be Wearing Pink Pyjamas

(1985, 90 min, GB, John Goldschmidt) *Julie Walters, Anthony Higgins.* Walters is a delight in this amiable comic adventure about a group of professional women who volunteer to spend a week at a survival training camp. ★★½

She's All That

(1999, 95 min, US, Robert Iscove) *Freddie Prinze Jr., Rachael Leigh Cook, Matthew Lillard, Kevin Pollak, Kieran Culkin, Anna Paquin.* When BMOC Zach (Prinze) gets dumped by his beautiful girlfriend, he finds the biggest loser to turn into a prom queen in order to message his ego in this derivative update of *Pygmalion*. He decides on Laney, an arty wallflower with little social skills, and, as played by Cook, even less personality. Of course, all it takes is a set of contacts and a clingy skirt to complete the transformation, since naturally she's concealing a fab body under her baggy overalls. But unlike other versions of the story, our heroine has other concerns than wanting just to fit in. Despite the attractive leads, there's not much here that hasn't been seen before, but *She's All That* is good for a laugh and is entertaining nonetheless. ★★½ VHS: $14.99; DVD: $29.99

She's Gotta Have It

(1986, 84 min, US, Spike Lee) *Tracy Camilla Johns, Tommy Redmond Hicks, John Canada Terrell, Spike Lee.* Lee's inspired and raucous comedy about Nola Darling and her three boyfriends: Mars — "Please baby, please baby, baby, please"; Jamie — "Wherever you want to go, I'll go, whatever you want to do, I'll do"; Greer — "Am I not beautiful darling?" This miraculous cinematic achievement was put together on a shoestring budget and shot over a period of 11

Here's Johnny! Jack Nicholson in *The Shining*

days in a two-square block area of Brooklyn, and yet it stands as one of the funniest and most poignant statements to date on a woman's sexual freedom and how it affects the men in her life. ★★★½

She's Having a Baby

(1988, 106 min, US, John Hughes) *Kevin Bacon, Elizabeth McGovern, Alec Baldwin, William Windom.* Bacon and McGovern fall in love and marry, set up house and prepare for the blessed event; all the while contending with the rigors of married life. Hughes brings about as much character development to this stilted "adult" comedy-drama as he does to his lesser teen flicks. ★★ VHS: $14.99; DVD: $29.99

She's So Lovely

(1997, 100 min, US, Nick Cassavetes) *Sean Penn, Robin Wright Penn, John Travolta, Harry Dean Stanton, Gena Rowlands.* Wright's remarkable, revelatory performance anchors a sterling collection of finely drawn portrayals in Cassavetes' powerfully crafted exploration of an unwavering true love prevailing in the most desperate of circumstances. Penn and Wright are man and wife in an environment so steeped in violence that escalating menace goes unremarked. After the attack of his wife by a neighbor, Penn almost commits murder and is sentenced to a mental institution. Ten years later, he returns to her — even though she has remarried a rough-hewn contractor (Travolta) and is living the good suburban life. Directing his father John Cassavetes' unproduced screenplay, Nick is his father's son in his unblinking, unflinching exposure of the human condition — stark yet imbued with compassion. ★★★½ VHS: $14.99; DVD: $29.99

She's the One

(1996, 96 min, US, Edward Burns) *Jennifer Aniston, Maxine Bahns, Edward Burns, Cameron Diaz, John Mahoney, Mike McGlone.* A testosterone-centric examination of familial bonding and sibling rivalry, this is a sometimes contrived but entertaining tale of two dissimilar brothers, one crusty dad, and the women in their lives. Francis (McGlone) works on Wall Street and possesses a beautiful wife (Aniston) and the morals of pond scum. Mickey (Burns) drives a cab and lives in a ratty flat with a broken heart. Dad (the endearingly cantankerous Mahoney) runs his waterfront dwelling as part boot camp and part locker room. This lively tale of miscommunication and erroneous assumptions is precipitated by Mickey's marriage to an intriguing stranger (Bahns) 24 hours after she flags his cab. He then crosses paths with his ex-fiancée (Diaz), setting in motion events which uncover a web of jealousies, secrets and lies revealed with Hal Hartley–esque juxtapositions and keen observations of human foibles. Lots of fun topped off with a sweet resolution. ★★★ VHS: $14.99; DVD: $22.99

The Sheep Has Five Legs

(1954, 95 min, France, Henri Verneuil) *Fernandel, Louis de Funes.* Fernandel, in a role that brought him international recognition, is both hilarious and believable in this comedy in which he plays six different roles. A town seeking publicity decides to reunite its oldest resident with his long-estranged quintuplet grandsons. Fernandel plays both the old man and all five sons — from a salty sea captain to an arrogant hair dresser. Bringing to mind (and equally as talented) the masters of multiple personalities, Peter Sellers and Alec Guinness, the manic Fernandel is a marvel of comic deftness. (French with English subtitles) ★★★½ VHS: $39.99

The Sheltering Sky

(1990, 138 min, GB/Italy, Bernardo Bertolucci) *John Malkovich, Debra Winger, Campbell Scott, Timothy Spall.* Against the vast backdrop of the sweltering heat and punishing sky of Northern Africa, Bertolucci's intimate epic (adapted from Paul Bowles' classic novel) follows the lives of three American travelers during the early 1950s. A husband and wife (Malkovich, Winger) and their traveling companion (Scott) embark from Tangier in search of the "real" Morocco. Slow moving, with sumptuous photography, this is a sun-drenched existential journey that should enthrall the patient viewer. Malkovich is perfect as the arrogant and unfeeling husband who is overwhelmed by culture shock, and Winger's performance as a complacent woman who undergoes a radical transformation is mesmerizing. ★★★½ VHS: $19.99

Shenandoah

(1965, 105 min, US, Andrew V. McLaglen) *James Stewart, Doug McClure, Glenn Corbett, Patrick Wayne, Katharine Ross.* An enormously satisfying Civil War drama blessed with one of Stewart's most moving performances. He plays a Virginia patriarch whose family is ripped apart by the conflict. The basis for the stirring Broadway musical of the same name. ★★★ VHS: $14.99

Sherlock, Jr./Our Hospitality

(1923/24, 119 min, US, Buster Keaton/John Blystone & Keaton) *Buster Keaton.* A collection of two Keaton comedies. In *Sherlock, Jr.* (1924, 44 min), Keaton is less concerned with physical schtick and slapstick (though there is certainly enough to go around) and concentrates more on the possibilities of the medium of film. He plays a projectionist and amateur sleuth whose daydreaming puts him in the film he is projecting. There's a brilliant sequence in which Keaton is trapped on-screen as the film changes from one scene to another. And even better is the finale in which he rides driverless on the handlebars of a motorcycle through crowded streets and open countryside. (★★★★) *Our Hospitality* (1923, 75 min) is the winning story of Keaton returning to his Southern hometown and becoming involved in an on-going family feud. The story is more complex than most, there's an abundance of wonderful sight gags, and Keaton's stunts atop a waterfall are awe-inspiring. (★★★½) VHS: $29.99; DVD: $29.99

Sherman's March

(1985, 156 min, US, Ross McElwee) What begins as a documentary chronicling the destruction and after-effects of General Sherman's march through the South during the Civil War soon turns into the director's own destructive Southern quest: a quest not of war but of love and romance. In this engaging non-fiction film, we follow McElwee, an energetic, self-indulgent optimist, as he cuts a swath through the affluent New South to find not the smoldering remains of the war but a formidable array of extravagant Southern belles. These women constantly distract, bewilder and ultimately conquer our intrepid hero during his disastrously hilarious search for romance, love and meaning. An entertaining and original film. ★★★½ VHS: $29.99

Shine

(1996, 105 min, Australia, Scott Hicks) *Geoffrey Rush, Noah Taylor, Armin Mueller-Stahl, Lynn Redgrave, Alex Rafalowicz, John Gielgud, Googie Withers.* Two parts biopic and one part fairy tale, this real-life drama about Australian pianist David Helfgott's triumph over a lifetime of mental illness and his subsequent return to the stage is as inspiring as it is well-crafted. Told as flashback, the film's narrative walks through the three stages of Helfgott's life: A young prodigy (Rafalowicz) driven by his stern Holocaust survivor father (Mueller-Stahl); a troubled but brilliant teen (Taylor); and the broken adult (Rush) who has fallen into a mental collapse that includes endless rapid-fire mumbling. While *Shine* necessarily walks the fine chalked line of the typical victory-over-adversity tale, Taylor and Oscar winner Rush's dazzling portrayals and director Hicks' acute attention to detail make this an emotionally satisfying winner. (VHS available letterboxed or pan & scan) ★★★★ VHS: $19.99; DVD: $24.99

The Shining

(1980, 142 min, GB, Stanley Kubrick) *Jack Nicholson, Shelley Duvall, Scatman Crothers, Danny Lloyd.* Nicholson is at his absolute lunatic best as a once loving father who slips deeper and deeper into homicidal frenzy. His family is contracted to care for a snow-bound, and decidedly sinister, hotel and the descent into madness begins. For those who have read Stephen King's masterpiece of horror and suspense, Kubrick's treatment may be disappointing, but the film is worth a look for Nicholson's inspired ravings and for Garret Brown's stunning Steadicam photography. ★★★ VHS: $19.99; DVD: $24.99

The Shining Hour

(1938, 80 min, US, Frank Borzage) *Joan Crawford, Melvyn Douglas, Robert Young, Margaret Sullavan*. A good cast is featured in this appealing romantic drama. Crawford is at the center of a family crisis as a nightclub dancer who comes between two brothers when she becomes engaged to one of them. Douglas and Young are the feuding siblings. ★★★ VHS: $19.99

Shining Through

(1992, 127 min, US, David Seltzer) *Michael Douglas, Melanie Griffith, Liam Neeson, Joely Richardson, John Gielgud*. Those nasty Nazis are back and this time they're up against America's *Working Girl*. Griffith encores the role of a secretary who wants more in life than just to take dictation. Here, she speaks German and can make a wicked strudel. Of course, these two qualifications are enough to send her off to Germany in the middle of WWII to obtain secret information. Just for good measure, she's in love with her boss, secret agent Douglas. There are some good moments to this slick but silly spy thriller, especially when Neeson as a Nazi official is on screen. But don't look for a credible plot, because it's just not there. ★★½ VHS: $9.99

Ship of Fools

(1965, 149 min, US, Stanley Kramer) *Simone Signoret, Oskar Werner, Vivien Leigh, Lee Marvin, Jose Ferrer, Elizabeth Ashley, Michael Dunn, George Segal*. Absorbing, well-made drama examining the lives of a group of shipboard passengers traveling from Mexico to Germany right before the start of WWII. Powerful performances from a great cast. ★★★½ VHS: $19.99

Shipwrecked

(1990, 93 min, US, Nils Gaup) *Gabriel Byrne, Stian Smestad*. High-spirited adventure yarn about a young boy stranded on a tropical island, fighting for survival while trying to outwit a vicious gang of pirates. From the director of *Pathfinder*. ★★★

Shirley Valentine

(1989, 108 min, GB, Lewis Gilbert) *Pauline Collins, Tom Conti, Alison Steadman, Joanna Lumley, Bernard Hill*. Collins re-creates her award-winning West End and Broadway role as a London housewife who leaves her family in search of self-fulfillment. In an enchanting performance, Collins is Shirley, the vivacious homemaker whose outlook on life is as entertaining as the one-liners she joyously delivers to the camera. If the idea of a woman fleeing husband and hearth to gain her own independence is not exactly original, writer Willy Russell imbues both the story and its heroine with such a delightful sense of humor that it all seems as new and refreshing as Shirley's near-idyllic Greek island getaway. ★★★ VHS: $14.99

Shivers

(1975, 110 min, Canada, David Cronenberg) *Barbara Steele, Paul Hampton, Joe Silver, Lynn Lowry*. Cronenberg's bizarre and immensely effective horror film is about deadly parasites which infect a high-rise apartment building, causing its victims to commit exaggerated acts of sex and violence. (Director's cut) (aka: *They Came from Within*) ★★★ VHS: $9.99; DVD: $24.99

Shoah

(1985, 563 min, Israel, Claude Lanzmann) Lanzmann brings the unspeakable reality of the Holocaust down to human scale in this monumental epic that explores this deplorable page of human history through an examination of the particular physical details and specifics of mass genocide. In *Shoah*, Lanzmann rejects the notion that the Holocaust was a result of impersonal historical forces and grimly examines the harsher reality of it as being the actions of men against men. A landmark effort. (French, German, Yiddish, Italian and Polish with English subtitles) ★★★★ VHS: $299.99

Shock Corridor

(1963, 101 min, US, Samuel Fuller) *Peter Brock, Constance Towers*. In this wonderfully entertaining and over-the-top melodrama, Brock stars as a Pulitzer Prize—hunting reporter who fakes madness in order to be admitted into an insane asylum and uncover the perpetrator of an unsolved murder. In the hospital, where the inmates represent a microcosm of a sick and violent society, his investigation bogs down as he himself slowly sinks into dementia. Towers is terrific as his apprehensive stripper girlfriend. A gripping story told with frenzied fervor. ★★★½ VHS: $19.99; DVD: $29.99

A Shock to the System

(1990, 87 min, US, Jan Egleson) *Michael Caine, Peter Riegert, Swoosie Kurtz, Will Patton, Elizabeth McGovern*. Caine shines in this pitch black comedy. When his long overdue promotion is unexpectedly handed to a smarmy young hot shot, Caine is incensed. When he accidentally discovers the convenience and simplicity of murder, Caine is inspired. Director Egleson's tilted angles and offbeat camera movement serve the story well, depicting Caine's skewed view of a world in which he casually knocks off those who get in his way. A scathing indictment of the corporate sensibility, the film is fueled by an insightful, razor-sharp wit which in turn is contrasted with several moments of bone-chilling terror. ★★★½ VHS: $14.99

Shock Treatment

(1981, 90 min, US, Jim Sharman) *Richard O'Brien, Cliff De Young, Jessica Harper*. This musical-comedy sequel to *The Rocky Horror Picture Show* finds Brad and Janet (now played by De Young and Harper) prisoners in demented Denton, home of happiness and TV game shows. O'Brien leads the proceedings as a mentally suspect medic in this twisted satire on the American Way (greed, lust, media-manipulation and skimpy attire). ★★★ VHS: $14.99

Shocker

(1989, 110 min, US, Wes Craven) *Michael Murphy, Peter Berg*. Director Craven only manages a few sparks in this grisly tale about a mass murderer who comes back from the grave to get even with the psychic teenager who helped fry him. Special effects are good, story is ridiculous and there's an amazing surrealistic chase scene which takes place inside a television set. At least it has more scares and a better look to it than the inferior, similarly themed *The Horror Show*. ★★ VHS: $9.99; DVD: $24.99

The Shoes of the Fisherman

(1968, 152 min, US, Michael Anderson) *Anthony Quinn, Laurence Olivier, John Gielgud, David Jannsen, Leo McKern, Oskar Werner*. Quinn heads an all-star cast in this labored epic as the first Russian-born Pope who tries to bring about world peace. (VHS available letterboxed or pan & scan) ★★ VHS: $19.99

Shoeshine

(1946, 92 min, Italy, Vittorio De Sica) *Rinaldo Smerdoni, Franco Interlenghi*. This brutal but brilliantly conceived story about two boys surviving in the squalid conditions of post-war Italy is told in a tragic, neorealist style. Giuseppe and Pasquale are two shoeshine boys whose goal is to pool their savings and buy a horse. Their plans are interrupted, however, when they run afoul of the law and end up in a repressive reform school. Their friendship becomes strained and tragedy strikes as the desensitized adult world crushes their youthful innocence. (Italian with English subtitles) ★★★★

Shogun

(1980, 124 min, US, Jerry London) *Richard Chamberlain, Toshiro Mifune, Yoko Shimada*. Special two-hour version of the landmark TV miniseries. Set in feudal Japan, a shipwrecked English navigator becomes a samurai. Based on the James Clavell best-seller. (The entire series is available on VHS for $249.99) ★★★ VHS: $14.99

Shoot Loud, Louder I Don't Understand!

(1966, 100 min, Italy, Eduardo De Filippo) *Marcello Mastroianni, Raquel Welch*. Not to be confused with "great art," this Italian screwball comedy stars Mastroianni as an eccentric artist with an even stranger uncle, who together become involved in a series of zany escapades which result in seductions, fireworks and eventual betrayal and murder. Written and directed by Italy's best known playwright, De Filippo (*Marriage Italian Style*), this wild romp features the music of Nino Rota. ★★½

Shoot the Moon

(1982, 123 min, US, Alan Parker) *Albert Finney, Diane Keaton, Peter Weller, Karen Allen, Dana Hill*. Parker's brutally honest film about the breakup of a Marin County family was a disappointment at the box office, which is a tragedy because it features impeccable performances by Finney and Keaton as the couple, and young Hill as their daughter. Not an "escapist" film by any means, its ending will send you reeling. ★★★½ VHS: $19.99

Shoot the Piano Player

(1962, 85 min, France, François Truffaut) *Charles Aznavour, Marie Dubois*. Aznavour is a timid pianist in a second-rate Parisian bistro who accidentally becomes entangled with the mob. Truffaut cavalierly mixes comedic element with a film noir tone in what is surely his quirkiest masterpiece. (French with English subtitles) ★★★★ VHS: $19.99; DVD: $29.99

Shoot to Kill

(1988, 110 min, US, Roger Spottiswoode) *Sidney Poitier, Tom Berenger, Kirstie Alley, Clancy Brown, Richard Masur*. Suspenseful thriller with

Margaret Sullavan, Frank Morgan and James Stewart in *The Shop Around the Corner*

Poitier on the trail of a ruthless killer, who is hiding out amid a mountain tour group. Berenger is the mountain guide who teams with Poitier when it turns out his girlfriend Alley is leading the group. ★★★

The Shooting

(1967, 82 min, US, Monte Hellman) *Jack Nicholson, Warren Oates, Millie Perkins.* Nicholson and Oates are in uncomfortable alliance as the woman with no name (Perkins) follows a trail and keeps her own counsel in this Old West tale of vengeance and morality. Gritty and atmospheric; you can feel the heat of the Southwestern desert. Nicholson also coproduced. ★★½ VHS: $14.99; DVD: $29.99

Shooting Fish

(1997, 109 min, GB, Stefan Schwartz) *Dan Futterman, Stuart Townsend, Kate Beckinsale.* A frothy comedy about con artists, *Shooting Fish* features a trio of good-looking characters who embark on some routine mischief. Jez (Townsend) and Dylan (Futterman) are orphans who prey upon their wealthy victims not so much for revenge, but for their own financial benefit. The boys' assistant, Georgie (Beckinsale), is even generally amused by her bosses, whose charm is infectious. They, in return, are both smitten with her, even though she is engaged to someone else. The romantic antics of these carefree souls plays out to the music of Burt Bacharach, which gives this contemporary film a bit of a retro feel. Although the outcome is never in doubt, *Shooting Fish* is an undemanding, entertaining romp. ★★★ VHS: $102.99; DVD: $34.99

The Shooting Party

(1977, 105 min, Russia, Emil Loteanu) *Galina Belyayeva.* A sumptuous realization of Anton Chekhov's early novella of the same name. This tale of passion, set amidst the absurd excesses of pre-Czarist Russian nobility, tells the story of a local magistrate who falls in love with a young woodsman's daughter (Belyayeva). It's a grip-

ping story of unrequited love, murder and the injustices of fate. (Russian with English subtitles) ★★★ VHS: $29.99

The Shooting Party

(1985, 108 min, GB, Alan Bridges) *James Mason, John Gielgud, James Fox, Dorothy Tutin.* Set on a great English estate in the autumn of 1913, this entertaining and highly acclaimed film casts a slightly jaded eye towards both the landed gentry of an Edwardian England on the brink of WWI, and the irrevocable changes that it produced. It marvelously identifies the petty ceremonies and traditions of a declining ruling class and is filled with the crisp conversations of a cast of well-defined, idiosyncratic individuals. ★★★½

The Shootist

(1976, 99 min, US, Don Siegel) *John Wayne, Lauren Bacall, James Stewart, Ron Howard.* Wayne's final film is an exemplary western tale set at the turn of the century with the Duke as a famed ex-gunfighter who learns he is dying of cancer. In this touching allegory for the death of the Old West, Wayne sets out to put his affairs in order, but is constantly haunted by his past. (Letterboxed VHS available for $14.99) ★★★½ VHS: $9.99; DVD: $29.99

The Shop Around the Corner

(1940, 97 min, US, Ernst Lubitsch) *James Stewart, Margaret Sullavan, Frank Morgan.* Very charming romantic comedy with Stewart and Sullavan as feuding coworkers in a Budapest shop who unknowingly fall in love with each other when they begin corresponding after answering a lonelyhearts ad. (Remade as *In the Good Old Summertime* and *You've Got Mail*) ★★★½ VHS: $19.99

The Shop on Main Street

(1966, 128 min, Czechoslovakia, Jan Kadar) *Ida Kaminsky, Josef Kroner.* This heartbreaking story

follows the tragic relationship between an elderly Jewish woman and the Slovak man assigned by the Nazis to watch over her. This Academy Award—winning Best Foreign Film is not only a moving story but also an impassioned and heartrending plea for peace and understanding. (Czechoslovakian with English subtitles) ★★★★ VHS: $29.99

Shopping

(1993, 100 min, GB, Paul Anderson) *Jude Law, Sadie Frost, Sean Pertwee, Jonathan Pryce, Marianne Faithfull.* Written and directed by music video auteur Anderson, this hip, slick and colorful debut film takes an unsentimental look at the life of Billy (Law), a young adrenaline junkie recently released from prison. Abandoned by both parents and society, he spends his time stealing cars and robbing shops with his friends. At odds with the police (in the person of Pryce) and a jealous chieftan (Pertwee in a terrific and intense performance), Billy careens along his collision course with arrest and/or death with reckless abandon. Anderson brings a remarkable visual artistry to the film, imbuing it with equal parts MTV fast-cuts and Terry Gilliamesque urban British waste-scape. ★★★ VHS: $89.99

Short Circuit

(1986, 98 min, US, John Badham) *Steve Guttenberg, Ally Sheedy, Fisher Stevens.* Pleasant scifi comedy about a state-of-the-art robot who escapes from the lab and teams up with a free-spirited artist (Sheedy). ★★½ VHS: $9.99; DVD: $24.99

Short Circuit 2

(1988, 110 min, US, Kenneth Johnson) *Fisher Stevens, Cynthia Gibb, Michael McKean, Jack Weston.* This time, the robot searches for input about life in the big city, all the while ducking street hoods, greedy bankers and a gang of ruthless thieves. Not as appealing as the original. ★★ VHS: $9.99

Short Cuts

(1993, 189 min, US, Robert Altman) *Andie MacDowell, Matthew Modine, Bruce Davison, Jack Lemmon, Lily Tomlin, Tim Robbins, Jennifer Jason Leigh, Robert Downey, Jr., Madeleine Stowe.* Based on nine short stories and a poem by Raymond Carver, *Short Cuts* immediately calls to mind one of Altman's masterpieces from the '70s, *Nashville.* But where *Nashville* is centered around a single event, *Short Cuts* examines the comings and goings of 22 characters connected simply by being part of the sprawl that is suburban Los Angeles, a microcosm of contemporary America. Altman explores the everyday lives of these characters with a cynical bite. He also has managed to put together an impressive ensemble. A tremendous slice of life, *Short Cuts* is brilliant, audacious filmmaking. ★★★★ VHS: $19.99

Short Eyes

(1977, 104 min, US, Robert M. Young) *Bruce Davison, Miguel Piñero.* Miguel Piñero's powerhouse play, scripted during his stint in Sing-Sing, is a gritty, nerve-rattling glimpse of life behind bars. The prison is peopled by Muslim zealots, angry blacks, knife-wielding Latinos and a smaller group of tough but cautious whites, all of whom hate each other. Casual brutality and violent lust are the norm. But racial tensions dissolve as the prisoners unite in their hatred of Clark Davis (Davison), a white, first-time offender who, after they discover that he is a child abuser ("short eyes"), becomes the target of an onslaught of threats and bloody violence. ★★★

Short Time

(1990, 100 min, US, Gregg Champion) *Dabney Coleman, Matt Frewer, Teri Garr, Barry Corbin, Joe Pantoliano.* Amiable comedy about how a mixed-up medical test has mistakenly convinced a police officer (Coleman) that he's dying. In order for his family to collect on his insurance policy, he's got to be killed in the line of duty. Now, he has become a "super cop," tracking down all sorts of vicious bad guys in an effort to get someone, anyone, to bump him off . . . quickly. ★★½ VHS: $14.99

A Shot in the Dark

(1964, 101 min, GB, Blake Edwards) *Peter Sellers, Elke Sommer, George Sanders, Herbert Lom.* Edwards and Sellers hit the mark with this hysterical "Pink Panther" masterpiece. Arguably the best of the series, the film is inundated with hilarious comedy, great stars, and an undaunted performance by Sellers. Inspector Clouseau ineptly sets out to prove that the ravishing Sommer is innocent of murder despite all evidence to the contrary. When you come down with a bout of Pink Panther–itis, this is the one to rent! (Sequel: *The Return of the Pink Panther*) ★★★★ VHS: $14.99; DVD: $24.99

The Shout

(1978, 87 min, GB, Jerzy Skolimowski) *Alan Bates, John Hurt, Susannah York, Tim Curry.* Bates plays a mysterious intruder in an English couple's household. York is the woman who succumbs to his emotional and sexual domination in this chilling tale of overwhelming menace and aggression. Hurt also stars as the high-strung husband in this adaptation of Robert Graves' ("I, Claudius") short story. ★★★

Shout at the Devil

(1976, 148 min, GB, Peter Hunt) *Lee Marvin, Roger Moore, Barbara Perkins.* Set in Mozambique at the outset of WWI, this over-long, but occasionally exciting, action film features the unlikely pairing of Marvin and Moore as an elephant poacher and an expatriate Englishman. Together, with Marvin's daughter (Perkins) in tow, they set out to sink a German battleship. ★★½

Show Boat

(1936, 113 min, US, James Whale) *Irene Dunne, Paul Robeson, Allan Jones, Charles Winninger, Helen Morgan.* This second of three film versions of the Kern-Hammerstein perennial is the best of the bunch thanks to Whale's sensitive yet firm direction and a superb evocation of 1880s America. In unforgettable voice, Morgan sings "Bill," and Robeson gives a staggering vocal performance of "Ol' Man River." ★★★½ VHS: $19.99

Show Boat

(1951, 107 min, US, George Sidney) *Kathryn Grayson, Ava Gardner, Howard Keel, Joe E. Brown, Agnes Moorehead.* Colorful version of the Kern-Hammerstein musical, though the 1936 ver-

Shrek: An ogre is like an onion!

sion is by far the better of the two. Good cast, though. ★★★ VHS: $14.99; DVD: $19.99

Show Business

(1944, 92 min, US, Edwin L. Marin) *Eddie Cantor, Joan Davis.* The inestimable comedic talents of the great Cantor and the hilarious Davis are combined in this quite entertaining comedy with the two stars as vaudeville performers. ★★★

A Show of Force

(1990, 93 min, US, Bruno Barreto) *Amy Irving, Robert Duvall, Andy Garcia, Lou Diamond Phillips, Kevin Spacey.* An intriguing political thriller about a crusading TV journalist (Irving) investigating one of Puerto Rico's biggest scandals: the brutal 1987 killing of two young men atop a mountainous broadcast tower. Were they terrorists, as the government claims, or were they student activists lured to their deaths by the FBI? ★★½ VHS: $14.99

Show People

(1928, 81 min, US, King Vidor) *Marion Davies, William Haines.* Davies stars in this wonderful silent comedy as a country girl who comes to Hollywood to be a "serious" actress, but finds unexpected success as a comedy star. ★★★ VHS: $29.99

Showdown in Little Tokyo

(1991, 79 min, US, Mark L. Lester) *Dolph Lundgren, Brandon Lee, Tia Carrere.* Heads roll and fingers fly as L.A. cop Lundgren teams up with Lee to stop evil, tattooed Japanese druglords from smuggling "ice" into the country, and to avenge the hideous murder of Dolph's parents. No ponderous moral messages in this one, just a lot of mindless action, despicable villains and a rocket-speed chase. ★★ VHS: $14.99

Shower

(2000, 94 min, China, Zhang Yang) *Zhu Xu, Pu Cunxin, Jiang Wu.* A remarkable story of familial bonds and emotional healing, the wondrous Chinese film *Shower* speaks volumes about the resilience of the human spirit. It's a lesson well-learned in any language. Thinking his father

has died, the successful Da Ming returns to the family business, a popular bathhouse. Though all are healthy there, including his estranged elderly father and mentally challenged younger brother, Da Ming stays to repair the wounds of his long absence. In doing so, he comes to enjoy the familiar and see his father in an altogether new light. Director Zhang delights in the old traditions and the daily routines, creating an atmosphere of camaraderie, joviality and accord. As poignant as it is intuitive, *Shower* is a beautiful meditation on life's most important ingredients, and what it takes to recognize them. (Mandarin with English subtitles) ★★★½ VHS: $21.99; DVD: $29.99

Showgirls

(1995, 131 min, US, Paul Verhoeven) *Elizabeth Berkley, Kyle MacLachlan, Gina Gershon, Glenn Plummer.* Damned by critics, condemned by conservatives and ignored by the public, this relentlessly bad and wildly camp extravaganza is one of the most cheesily entertaining films to come out of Hollywood since *Myra Breckinridge* and *Beyond the Valley of the Dolls*. The rags-to-nipple clamps tale (and raunchy update of *All about Eve*) centers around the tough-talking white trash Nomi (Berkley), a brain-dead bleached blonde Barbie doll who is lured to the bright lights, fast living and tacky lifestyle of Las Vegas, home of high rollers and the $1.49 strawberry shortcake. Blessed with spunk, a curvaceous body and piston-gyrating hips, Nomi — beginning at a sleazy lap dance dive — steadily claws up the greased pole of success, going from trailer trash tramp to glittery star. Hearing lines like, "It must be weird not having anyone coming on you," Nomi knows she's made it to the top. (★★★★ Camp Rating) ★ VHS: $9.99; DVD: $14.99

Shrek

(2001, 89 min, US, Andrew Adamson & Vicky Jenson) *Voices of: Mike Myers, Eddie Murphy, Cameron Diaz, John Lithgow.* In the opening moments of the gleefully irreverent *Shrek*, a calm-voiced narrator reads a story from an engraved children's book. Seconds later, a page is torn and used as a paper substitute for a certain outhouse activity. This ain't your mother's animated fairy tale. Bordering on the naughty that children will no doubt love, this wildly funny tale based on William Steig's book has as its hero an irascible ogre named Shrek (Myers), who teams with a chatty talking donkey (a hilarious Murphy) to search for a princess (Diaz) imprisoned in a forbidding castle. Lovestruck dragons, magic spells and some twisted jokes (a frog blown up into a balloon!) await these mismatched adventurers. *Shrek* is a marvelous, one-of-a-kind children's classic thanks to some impressive animation, a slaphappy screenplay full of wonderful laughs (including a few well-placed pop-culture references and zingers at Disney), and three most delightful lead characters. ★★★★ VHS: $26.99; DVD: $29.99

Shy People

(1987, 119 min, US, Andrei Konchalovsky) *Jill Clayburgh, Barbara Hershey, Martha Plimpton, Mare Winningham.* Clayburgh is a street-smart New York magazine writer working on an article about long-lost relatives who live deep within the Louisiana bayou. Hershey is the fierce marshland matriarch sheltering her brood from the outside world. Together, they clash big time. ★★ VHS: $19.99

Siberiade

(1979, 206 min, Russia, Andrei Konchalovsky) *Vladimir Samoilov, Vitaly Solomin, Nikita Mikhalkov.* The tumultuous events in Russia's 60-year history from 1900 to the 1960s provide the backdrop for this lavishly photographed and lyrically poetic saga of three generations of two families in a Siberian hamlet. The film follows the day-to-day events of the poor Ustyuzhanin and the middle-class Solomin families, both virtually untouched by 19th-century progress. The Siberia pictured here isn't a vast frozen wasteland, but a vista of lush forests, cascading rivers and virgin land unpolluted by man's brutal touch. Feuds, affairs, murder and revenge transpire amid the social upheaval in this microcosm of a peasant Russia forced into the 20th century. Despite its length, *Siberiade* is a fast-moving and touching drama of the universal story of humanity caught in the turbulence of sweeping development. (Russian with English subtitles) ★★★★ VHS: $29.99

Siberian Lady Macbeth

(1962, 93 min, Yugoslavia, Andrzej Wajda) *Olivera Markovic, Ljuba Tadic.* This lusty, bombastic melodrama is great pre-"Dynasty" fun. Set in turn-of-the-century Russia, the story focuses on Katarina, a beautiful but bored wife of an often out-of-town merchant whose life takes a decidedly tumultuous and erotic turn after she meets a boisterous wanderer. In a very short time, she dispatches her tyrannical father-in-law (with rat poison), takes her compliant peasant as a live-in lover and plots to kill her soon-to-return husband — it's all in a week's fun in this passion-fueled tale of murder, sex, madness and violence. (Serbo-Croatian with English subtitles) (Letterboxed) (aka: *Fury Is a Woman*) ★★★ VHS: $24.99

Sibling Rivalry

(1990, 88 min, US, Carl Reiner) *Kirstie Alley, Scott Bakula, Bill Pullman, Carrie Fisher, Sam Elliott.* Alley brings some life to this sometimes amusing black comedy as a doctor's wife whose sexual frustration leads her to an affair.

However, things go from bad to worse when her lover dies in bed and she learns his true identity. Bakula plays her hapless husband. ★★½ VHS: $9.99

The Sicilian

(1987, 146 min, US, Michael Cimino) *Christopher Lambert, Terence Stamp, John Turturro.* A gangster takes on the mob by robbing the rich and distributing the wealth among the peasants in post-WWII Sicily. Needless to say, the Mafia is not happy. A misguided and lethargic crime saga. ★

Sid & Nancy

(1986, 111 min, US, Alex Cox) *Gary Oldman, Chloe Webb, Courtney Love.* Cox takes the story of two self-destructive junkies, Sid Vicious of the Sex Pistols and Nancy Spungen, and sparks it up with savage energy and sardonic wit. It's no easy feat to romanticize, yet not idealize, these flamboyantly adolescent creatures. In spectacular performances, Oldman and Webb bring a ferociousness to their roles that draws us to this doomed pair, if only to be repelled by their self-absorbed stupidity. ★★★½ VHS: $14.99; DVD: $19.99

Sideburns

(1990, 110 min, Russia, Yuri Mamin) Uncannily timely for a post-Communist Russia and a post-unification Germany, this exuberantly wacky yet cautionary political satire is a seriously funny film that, with its antic filmic style, is reminiscent of Dusan Makavejev's early works. Two geeks dressed in turn-of-the-century waistcoats, sporting bushy sideburns and brandishing canes, arrive in a backwater Russian city and begin winning adherents with their reactionary, Nazi-tinged political philosophy that idolizes poet Alexander Pushkin and seems to be against all change. The first target of their violent rampage for social conformity is the hippy-dippy "Children of Perestroika," but soon other reactionary groups spring up to vie for power and it takes the really bad guys (the Communists) to restore "order" to the land. (Russian with English subtitles) ★★½ VHS: $59.99

The Siege

(1998, 116 min, US, Edward Zwick) *Denzel Washington, Annette Bening, Bruce Willis, Tony Shalhoub, Sami Bouajila.* What would happen if New York City became such a target for terrorists that the President declared martial law and the military took over the city? It'd be a muddled experience, at best, if *The Siege* is any indication. Washington plays an FBI agent investigating a rash of bombings. Bening is the mysterious government operative who definitely knows more than she's letting on to. The implausible story soon has renegade general Willis taking control and turning Brooklyn into a fascist state. With Arab terrorists, torture, mass murder and military men run amok, the only villainous element missing from the story is Nazis. Trying to be action film and social commentary, this is spread too thin. Willis' one-note performance certainly doesn't help. ★★ VHS: $14.99; DVD: $29.99

Siesta

(1987, 105 min, US, Mary Lambert) *Ellen Barkin, Gabriel Byrne, Jodie Foster, Martin Sheen, Isabella*

Rossellini, Grace Jones, Julian Sands, Alexei Sayles. Barkin is Claire, a professional daredevil who suddenly awakens to find herself lying on an airport runway covered in blood. Unable to recall her last three days and mystified by the origins of the blood, which is not her own, she begins an erotic and hallucinatory odyssey through a sun-bleached Spain where she encounters a menacingly horny cabbie, her now indifferent ex-lover and an eccentric group of intoxicated British "artists." This feature film debut by Lambert is a refreshingly complex, frenzied and enigmatic mystery-drama. Music by Miles Davis. ★★★ VHS: $14.99

The Sign of the Cross

(1932, 124 min, US, Cecil B. DeMille) *Fredric March, Elissa Landi, Claudette Colbert, Charles Laughton.* DeMille's religious opus is a stylistically extravagant tale which mixes religious dogma with scenes of Roman excesses of sex and violence. Roman big-wig March falls in love with Christian do-gooder Landi. Then he spends the rest of the story trying to keep her from being lion bait. Far more interesting as characters are Laughton, as an effeminate Nero, and Colbert, who gives a splendid performance as a cunning and sexy Poppaea (her nude bathing scene is a highlight). DeMille overplays the religious aspect but outdoes himself depicting the many torturous deaths in the arena (by elephant, alligator, gorilla) and with a sizzling lesbian seduction. ★★★ VHS: $14.99

Signal 7

(1983, 92 min, US, Rob Nilsson) *Bill Ackridge, Dan Leegant.* A rambling but sensitive portrayal of two middle-aged cab drivers who are going nowhere fast. Shot on videotape on a shoe-string budget, this largely improvised drama can be uncomfortably revealing during its soul-baring scenes, reminding one of the early works of John Cassavetes, to whom the film is dedicated. ★★½ VHS: $79.99

La Signora di Tutti

(1934, 94 min, Italy, Max Ophüls) *Isa Miranda.* Ophüls' only Italian film, this sublime and powerful melodrama features Miranda as Gaby Doriot, an aging film star who, at the top of her professional career but in the depths of despair in her private life, attempts suicide. Under anesthesia on the operating table, her sordid past, one of great excesses, ambitions and painful loves, is relived in her thoughts. (Italian with English subtitles) ★★★ VHS: $29.99

Signs of Life (Lebenszeichen)

(1968, 90 min, Germany, Werner Herzog) *Peter Brogle, Wolfgang Reichmann, Athina Zacharopoulou.* This early Herzog feature exhibits many of the director's signature touches, albeit sometimes haltingly utilized. During WWII, a wounded German soldier is billeted to an occupied Greek island, removed from the conflict. He recuperates in the company of his Greek wife and two other German soldiers in a small, impoverished fishing village. At first seemingly idyllic, their lives bog down in tedium, heat and boredom. The young man unravels, his mental deterioration leading him to the munitions dump in an attempt to shake his fist at God. The director's trademark static shots are not as effective in their conveyance of existential anguish as they would become in his later films, but the film is a valuable glimpse into the early development of a major filmmaker. (German with English subtitles) ★★½ VHS: $29.99

Signs of Life

(1989, 91 min, US, John David Coles) *Arthur Kennedy, Kevin J. O'Connor, Vincent D'Onofrio, Michael Lewis, Kate Reid, Beau Bridges.* An extremely talented cast highlights this personal and touching drama about the final days of a boat-building business and how the closing affects those around it. Kennedy is remarkable as the patriarchal owner who refuses to accept the inevitable. O'Connor and D'Onofrio are both fine as the two young workers planning to leave their small town at the expense of a loved one. Lewis is exceptional as D'Onofrio's slow-witted younger brother. Though these types of films are usually described as "small," there is nothing miniature in the scope or achievement of this "little" gem. ★★★½ VHS: $14.99

The Silence

(1963, 95 min, Sweden, Ingmar Bergman) *Ingrid Thulin, Gunnel Lindstrom.* An intense story of two sisters, emotionally and physically united since childhood, who, while traveling together, begin the struggle of separation. The younger woman seeks freedom from her embittered sister by entering into a relationship with a stranger. Last of Bergman's trilogy on faith which includes *Through a Glass Darkly* and *Winter Light.* (Swedish with English subtitles) ★★★ VHS: $24.99

Silence = Death

(1990, 60 min, US, Rosa von Praunheim & Phil Zwickler) *Allen Ginsberg, David Wojnorowicz, Keith Haring.* Avant-garde German filmmaker von Praunheim explores in this documentary the reactions and response of New York's artistic community to the ravages of AIDS. Activists interviewed include representatives from the many arts organizations that alert the public to the crisis through performance art, music, theatre and literature as well as artists David Wojnorowicz, Paul Smith and Rafael Gamba. Particularly entertaining segments include Keith Haring as he admits to nostalgic longing for the days of carefree sex and Allen Ginsberg's musing upon his shyer attitude about experimenting sexually. ★★★ VHS: $29.99

The Silence of Neto

(1994, 106 min, Guatemala, Luis Argueta) *Eva Tamargo Lemus, Oscar Javier Almengor, Herbert Meneses, Julio Díaz.* In 1954, under the guise of fighting the scourge of Communism, the United States bombed Guatemala and replaced its government with a puppet regime. The film begins as young Neto mourns the death of his beloved uncle. In flashbacks, we see his affections are directed towards his dashing but mostly absent Uncle Ernesto, who flies tissue paper hot air balloons in between globe-hoppings. With tastes of magical realism, particularly surrounding the uncle's unexpected comings and goings while living and dead, Uncle Ernesto and Neto share imaginative fantasies. First love, loss and fantasy round out the roster in this quiet coming-of-ager. (Letterboxed) (Spanish with English subtitles) ★★★ VHS: $79.99

The Silence of the Lambs

(1991, 118 min, US, Jonathan Demme) *Jodie Foster, Anthony Hopkins, Scott Glenn, Ted Levine.* Demme's nerve-racking psychological chiller based on the novel by Thomas Harris stars Foster as Clarice Starling, a fledgling FBI agent who is assigned the daunting task of interviewing convicted psycho-killer, Dr. Hannibal Lecter (Hopkins), in the hopes that he can help her develop a profile of "Buffalo Bill" — a mass murderer who likes to skin his victims. Hopkins' portrayal of the maniacally twisted Lecter is sheer terrifying brilliance. Rarely has an actor exuded pure, malevolent evil with such seductive charm. For her part, Foster is equally stellar. Her Clarice is an intricate and subtly drawn character who finds herself in a dangerous *pas de deux* with Lecter. Their scenes are riveting. Demme's direction throughout is superb. Winner of 5 Academy Awards including Best Picture, Director, Actress (Foster) and Actor (Hopkins). (Sequel: *Hannibal*) ★★★★ VHS: $9.99

Silent Fall

(1994, 100 min, US, Bruce Beresford) *Richard Dreyfuss, Linda Hamilton, Ben Faulkner, Liv Tyler, John Lithgow, J.T. Walsh.* Dreyfuss stars as a noted psychiatrist who battles his own demons while helping a child come to terms with his. Faulkner plays a ten-year-old autistic youth who is the sole witness to the murder of his parents. Dreyfuss is reluctantly called into the investigation to try to reach the boy, made more difficult by the child's silence, an interfering doctor (Lithgow) and an impatient sheriff (Walsh). Beresford's subtle direction creates a suspenseful mood throughout, and though *Silent Fall* may be too clinical at times, it nonetheless is an engaging psychological mystery. ★★★ VHS: $14.99; DVD: $14.99

Silent Movie

(1976, 86 min, US, Mel Brooks) *Mel Brooks, Dom DeLuise, Marty Feldman, Bernadette Peters, Ron Carey.* Although this Brooks spoof on Hollywood filmmaking is not on the comic level with his best works, it is nonetheless an enjoyable lark. Brooks plays a has-been producer who attempts a comeback by making a silent movie. All this, of course, is set within a silent film, more than living up to its title. Cameos include Anne Bancroft, Paul Newman and Liza Minnelli. ★★★ VHS: $9.99

The Silent Partner

(1978, 103 min, Canada, Daryl Duke) *Christopher Plummer, Elliott Gould, Susannah York, John Candy.* Plummer (whose enormous talents have rarely been utilized on screen) teams with Gould in this original and riveting suspense thriller. Gould plays a bank teller who figures out Plummer's plan to rob his bank, turning the tables on him. However, when the psychotic would-be robber figures out the double-cross, he sets out after Gould and the loot. ★★★

Silent Running

(1971, 89 min, US, Douglas Trumbull) *Bruce Dern, Cliff Potts.* Special effects master Trumbull (*2001*) directed this inventive though leisurely sci-fi/environmental tale with Dern tending a space garden when Earth has become barren,

losing control when the powers that be decide to shut it down. Written by Michael Cimino, Steven Bochco and Deric Washburn. ★★★ VHS: $14.99; DVD: $29.99

Silent Shakespeare

(1899-1911, 88 min, GB) Shakespeare without spoken words? Folly perhaps on the part of these early filmmakers, but no less of a stretch than the recent mining of the Bard's work by Hollywood. The sparse intertitles serve as a reminder that other performance buttresses may have existed besides an organ, i.e. live readings to accompany the films. One of the most intriguing points to this assemblage of rare footage from the British Film Institute is the international mix. From the United States, "A Midsummer Night's Dream," 1909; and "Twelfth Night," 1910. From the United Kingdom, "King John," 1899; "The Tempest," 1908; and "Richard III," 1911. From Italy (these are the only films with hand-stenciled color), "King Lear," 1910; and "The Merchant of Venice," 1910, apparently filmed in Venice. Fragmentary and damaged, the films act as documentary material about the early cinema of three nations. And if you look closely, you can even see nuanced variances in how these cultures interpret the Bard. ★★★ VHS: $29.99; DVD: $29.99

Silent Tongue

(1994, 98 min, US, Sam Shepard) *River Phoenix, Alan Bates, Richard Harris, Dermot Mulroney, Tantoo Cardinal.* The final theatrical release of Phoenix, this involving though labored ghost story is slightly odd, but it achieves a poetic, mystical tone. Set in the Old West, the film casts Bates as a slimy sideshow owner who traded his Indian daughter to pioneer Harris for his son (Phoenix) to marry. However, after the woman dies in childbirth, Harris returns to negotiate for Bates' remaining daughter to comfort his near-mad, grieving son — whose refusal to bury his wife causes her spirit to return to seek vengeance. *Silent Tongue* is an unusual, slowly paced but nevertheless gripping treatise on 19th-century Western culture. Shepard's direction is thoughtful and carefully realized. ★★½ VHS: $14.99

The Silent Touch

(1992, 92 min, GB/Poland/Denmark, Krzysztof Zanussi) *Max von Sydow, Sarah Miles, Lothaire Bluteau, Sofie Grabol.* Von Sydow perfectly balances emotional extremes in his intensely involving portrayal of a world-renowned composer whose forty-year silence (he has not written music since the Holocaust) is broken by the silent touch of a young music student (Bluteau). The composer is a gruff bear in continuous hibernation, literally lashing out at whoever dares to approach his lair. Miles endows a modern, practical saintliness to her portrayal of the composer's supportive, caretaking wife. The quality of the performances elevates the film above the lapses in the script, as the film explores myriad contradictions of human existence. A delicate, considered film, revealing that the past is always with us, and the future is ours to create. ★★★ VHS: $79.99

The Silk Road

(1988, 99 min, Japan, Junya Sato) A "sukiyaki western" in the best sense of the term, this spectacular saga of love, heroism and war is set on the Silk Road (the ancient 5,000-mile trade route that stretches through the Asian desert). The story follows the adventures of a reluctant warrior, Zhao, a young man who rescues a captured princess (a young and beautiful one at that), but finds that his reward is only to be hunted down by a vengeful crown prince intent on killing both him and the princess. This exhilarating romantic adventure should not be confused with the similarly packaged, but somewhat less satisfying battle-filled epic, *Heaven and Earth*. (Japanese with English subtitles) ★★★½ VHS: $9.99

Silk Stockings

(1957, 117 min, US, Rouben Mamoulian) *Fred Astaire, Cyd Charisse, Janis Paige, Peter Lorre, George Tobias.* Charming musical remake of Ernst Lubitsch's *Ninotchka*, with Astaire in the Melvyn Douglas role as a movie producer, and the lovely Charisse in the Garbo role as the Russian envoy. Score by Cole Porter. ★★★ VHS: $19.99

Silkwood

(1983, 128 min, US, Mike Nichols) *Meryl Streep, Kurt Russell, Cher, Diana Scarwid, Fred Ward, David Strathairn, Ron Silver.* In yet another remarkable performance, Streep stars as Karen Silkwood, the nuclear plant worker who died under mysterious circumstances after uncovering damaging information against the plant for which she worked. Russell as her boyfriend and Cher as her lesbian roommate both offer strong support in Nichols' tense, harrowing and compelling drama. (Letterboxed) ★★★½ VHS: $14.99; DVD: $14.99

Silver Bullet

(1985, 95 min, US, Daniel Attias) *Gary Busey, Corey Haim, Megan Follows.* Stylish version of Stephen King's story about a small town being terrorized by a werewolf, with Busey and young Haim determined to put a stop to it. ★★½ VHS: $9.99

Silver City

(1986, 110 min, Australia, Sophia Turkiewicz) *Gosia Dobrowolska, Ivar Kants.* At the end of the 1940s, thousands of war-weary refugees began landing on Australia's shores. This immigration onslaught was encouraged by the Australian government's vigorous campaign to increase the nation's population and expand its industrial capacity. The turbulent setting of the refugee settlement camps is where our story takes place. A Polish family's hardships and love interests are the focus of this touching film about displaced people trying to overcome a past which haunts them. ★★½

Silver Streak

(1976, 113 min, US, Arthur Hiller) *Richard Pryor, Gene Wilder, Jill Clayburgh, Patrick McGoohan, Ned Beatty, Ray Walston, Scatman Crothers.* Wilder and Pryor team for the first time in this engaging and often hilarious comedy which tips its hat to Hitchcock and the mystery-aboard-a-train films. Passenger Wilder gets himself mixed up with Clayburgh, FBI agents, murder, con artist Pryor and spies as he travels from Los Angeles to Chicago. Pryor is a standout. ★★★ VHS: $9.99

Silverado

(1985, 132 min, US, Lawrence Kasdan) *Kevin Costner, Kevin Kline, Danny Glover, Scott Glenn, Brian Dennehy, Jeff Goldblum, Rosanna Arquette.* Entertaining and very stylish western adventure with the "two Kevins" — Kline and Costner — and Glover and Glenn as four drifters who team up to battle a crooked town sheriff and the gang who controls him. (Letterboxed VHS available for $19.99) ★★★ VHS: $14.99; DVD: $19.99

Silverlake Life: The View from Here

(1992, 99 min, US, Tom Joslin & Peter Friedman) Arguably the most harrowing vision of death and dying ever recorded, this emotionally devastating video diary of two lovers living with and dying from AIDS is far from a morbid recording of one's own death. Rather, it's a celebration of life and of the enduring love the two men had for each other. Joslin, a film teacher, and his lover of 22 years, Mark Massi, decided to record their lives after the onslaught of AIDS-related illnesses. The camera follows them as they visit the doctor, buy medicine and herbal "cures" and other activities, but stays primarily in their apartment in the Silverlake section of Los Angeles. One's immediate feeling — after the sadness of their story — is an acknowledgement of their overriding commitment to each other, making this personal diary an astonishing love story. ★★★★ VHS: $19.99

Simon Birch

(1998, 114 min, US, Mark Steven Johnson) *Ian Michael Smith, Joseph Mazzello, Oliver Platt, David Strathairn, Ashley Judd, Dana Ivey, Jim Carrey.* Suggested (not based) on John Irving's novel "A Prayer for Owen Meany," *Simon Birch* uses only the first third of Irving's book. Gone are the boyhood adolescent talks, masturbation sessions, college; gone, in fact, is much of the spirit. Writer-director Johnson has, instead, fashioned a shamefully manipulative family drama defined by tragic acts, rather than a black comedy touched by tragedy. Set in 1964, the story centers on the friendship of 12-year-olds Joe (Mazzello) and Simon (Smith), the two town outcasts (Joe's illegitimate, Simon was born with dwarfism). Johnson concentrates on the sap, forgetting that the original story is laced with irony and humor. He manages a few good touches, but most of it is sledge-hammer subtle. ★★ VHS: $19.99; DVD: $29.99

Simon Bolivar

(1972, 120 min, Venezuela/Italy, Alessandro Blasetti) *Maximilian Schell.* The adventurous and heroic life of Simon Bolivar, "el liberator" of South America, gets a boisterously operatic treatment in this Venezuelan/Italian coproduction. Schell plays the role a bit too theatrically, shouting his lines and continuously flailing about his arms. Although this is not the definitive portrait of Bolivar, it is still an interesting story — that of one man, led by a vision of a unified continent, who struggles to unite a diverse and poverty-stricken people, forges an army and, against seemingly insurmountable odds, successfully battles colonialist Spain. The film, originally in Cinemascope, is badly cropped in this video transfer. (Dubbed, although Schell's English is his own.) ★★½ VHS: $49.99

Simon of the Desert

(1965, 45 min, Mexico, Luis Bunuel) *Claudio Brook, Silvia Pinal.* This comic and surreal attack on the Church is drawn from the life of Saint Simeon Stylites who, in order to lead the "correct Christian life," resided atop a pillar. Vain, self-important and sexually repressed, our hero soon finds that he is tempting prey for the cunning Devil. (Spanish with English subtitles) ★★★½ VHS: $29.99

Simone de Beauvoir

(1982, 105 min, France, Josee Dayan & Malka Robowska) Pioneer feminist, author ("The Second Sex," "Prime of Life"), philosopher, political activist and longtime companion of Jean-Paul Sartre, Simone de Beauvoir's life has been one of remarkable interests and insights. In this documentary, the filmmakers let Ms. Beauvoir speak freely, as she recounts her friendships, her political sympathies, sexual fidelity, aging and death. Photos from Ms. Beauvoir's personal collection, archival footage and a fascinating conversation with Sartre are included in this candid portrait of a brilliant woman. (French with English subtitles) ★★★ VHS: $59.99

Simpatico

(1999, 97 min, US, Matthew Warchus) *Nick Nolte, Jeff Bridges, Sharon Stone, Catherine Keener, Albert Finney, Shawn Hatosy, Kimberly Williams.* Wealthy horse ranch owner Bridges is about to close a multimillion dollar racehorse sale when he receives a call from old friend Nolte. It seems Nolte is about to be arrested, and is afraid he'll spill the beans about their shady past. Meanwhile, Bridges' wife (Stone) — the woman both men loved in their younger years — whiles her miserable days away in a drunken haze. Adapted from a lesser Sam Shepard play, *Simpatico* is inert, muted and saddled with awkward flashback scenes. The chief reason to watch this — and it's reason enough — is the terrific cast. It's a joy to see two of our greatest actors, Bridges and Nolte, share the screen for the first time. Nothing great (and the story gets sillier and murkier as it goes along), *Simpatico* is still reasonably compelling material given urgency by strong performances, and will most certainly play better on the small screen. ★★½ VHS: $14.99; DVD: $24.99

Simple Men

(1992, 105 min, US, Hal Hartley) *Robert Burke, William Sage, Karen Sillas.* Where other than in a Hartley film would you find such characters as a brawling, chain-smoking nun, a French-speaking, grunge-rocking gas-station attendant, and a beautiful Romanian epileptic? The story follows Bill, a petty criminal, and his kid brother Daniel, on their search for their escaped-con dad, who may or may not have bombed the Pentagon 20 years earlier. Their quest leads them to the little town of Sagapawnac, Long Island, where each man, buoyed by Jim Beam and long-winded philosophical chit chat, realizes his destiny. Peppered with plenty of droll moments, the film suffers mainly from its somewhat meandering pace, and though it's unique, it lacks the cohesion of his more successful efforts. ★★½ VHS: $19.99

A Simple Plan

A Simple Plan

(1998, 120 min, US, Sam Raimi) *Bill Paxton, Billy Bob Thornton, Bridget Fonda, Brent Briscoe, Chelcie Ross, Gary Cole.* Director Raimi's striking psychological thriller is a nerve-racking, thought-provoking morality tale played out as American tragedy. Based on Scott Smith's bestseller, the story begins as two brothers, the respectable Hank and the slow-witted Jacob (Paxton and Thornton), unearth a downed plane in the snowy wilderness of their small town, and in it is a duffel bag containing millions in cash. Immediately, Smith (who adapted his novel) and Raimi set in motion a moral dilemma — one in which the audience becomes part — as they try to decide what to do with the money. As each layer of the characters' moral fiber is slowly stripped away, the men struggle not to lose their humanity as the inevitable chaos of paranoia and greed engulf their lives. Often wickedly funny and always riveting, this *Treasure of the Sierre Madre* for the '90s features an excellent ensemble, none more effective than Thornton. As the dimmer sibling, he brings unexpected complexity and compassion to Jacob. ★★★★ VHS: $14.99; DVD: $29.99

A Simple Story

(1978, 110 min, France, Claude Sautet) *Romy Schneider, Bruno Cremer.* Schneider is an unalloyed pleasure in this subtle, incisive look at a woman's mid-life crisis. Though she's a successful designer with a teenage son and a sympathetic circle of friends, Schneider is plagued by doubts and fears about the path she has chosen, and can't figure out how to change things. Schneider won a French Academy Award for her gripping performance. (French with English subtitles) ★★★ VHS: $29.99

A Simple Twist of Fate

(1994, 106 min, US, Gillies MacKinnon) *Steve Martin, Gabriel Byrne, Laura Linney, Catherine O'Hara, Stephen Baldwin.* Mistakenly billed as a comedy, this drama inspired by "Silas Marner" follows one hard-luck and heartbreaking story after another for the first 30 minutes or so. To start with, Martin finds out that the child his wife is expecting isn't his; then he moves to a small town where his fortune in gold coins is stolen; then a heroin addict dies in the snow outside his house. Only after the woman's young daughter wanders into Martin's home and life does the film lighten up. He adopts her and things are fine for years, until her real father (Byrne) decides to take her back, leading to an emotional ending. ★★½ VHS: $14.99

A Simple Wish

(1997, 89 min, US, Michael Ritchie) *Martin Short, Mara Wilson, Robert Pastorelli, Amanda Plummer, Kathleen Turner, Ruby Dee.* Wilson is Anabel, a daughter desperate for her dad (Pastorelli) to get the lead role in a Broadway musical. She wishes for a fairy godmother. She gets Murray, played by an overacting Short. When introduced, he is struggling to pass the fairy godmother exam, the only man and only young person in a room of old ladies. He then bungles every aspect of Anabel's wish. Meanwhile, Turner, a fairy godmother turned evil witch, is complicating matters by stealing all the godmother wands at the national godmother convention. A good cast, creative set designs and nice special effects unfortunately are lost on this poorly written film. ★★ VHS: $9.99; DVD: $24.99

Simply Irresistible

(1999, 100 min, US, Mark Tarlov) *Sarah Michelle Gellar, Sean Patrick Flanery, Patricia Clarkson, Dylan Baker, Christopher Durang.* Gellar is the chef for a tiny restaurant in TriBeCa, which is on the verge of closing because she's an awful cook. At the farmer's market, she runs into a creepy guy who gives her a guardian crab which looks over her shoulder and puts magic into her recipes. Someone call the FDA! Her concoctions make rival and budding restaurateur Flanery fall for her while babbling about her delicious eclairs. Sorry to say, but the result here is simply embarrassing. Between the fog that comes out of the peach dessert and the cutaways to the crab during romantic conversations, it's hard to pay attention to the characters. Gellar has a certain charm, but Flanery keeps bringing her down to his medium-well level. All in all, the worst romantic comedy since *Mandingo*. ★ VHS: $9.99; DVD: $34.99

The Sin of Harold Diddlebock

(1947, 90 min, US, Preston Sturges) *Harold Lloyd, Margaret Hamilton, Rudy Vallee, Franklin Pangborn.* Sturges and Lloyd share the dubious distinction of being two of America's most undervalued treasures. Writer-director Sturges is witty, hilarious, touching and intelligent; Lloyd's capable synthesis of subtle characterization and side-splitting slapstick is unmatched. The plot involves an ex-football star who, after 20 years in a dead-end job, uses his life savings to make a fortune at the track only to lose it at the circus. At the circus? Just watch it — you won't regret it. (aka: *Mad Wednesday*) ★★★

The Sin of Madelon Claudet

(1931, 73 min, US, Edgar Selwyn) *Helen Hayes, Lewis Stone, Robert Young.* Hayes, the First Lady of the American Theatre, makes one of her rare screen appearances in this superb soap opera, and she won an Oscar for it. In the tradition of *Stella Dallas* and *Madame X*, Hayes, in a glorious performance, plays a mother who sacrifices all for the sake of her son. Sure it's been done before, even back then, but Hayes' portrayal and the sharp directorial style make it all the more compelling. ★★★ VHS: $19.99

Sinbad and the Eye of the Tiger

(1977, 113 min, GB, Sam Wanamaker) *Patrick Wayne, Jane Seymour.* The weakest of the whole Harryhausen/Sinbad series is saddled with a predictable plot, anemic characters, and (most surprisingly) less than spectacular special effects. For the record, the plot concerns Sinbad's quest to help a prince who's been transformed into a baboon by a sorceress' evil spell. ★½ VHS: $14.99; DVD: $29.99

Since You Went Away

(1944, 172 min, US, John Cromwell) *Claudette Colbert, Jennifer Jones, Joseph Cotten, Shirley Temple, Monty Woolley, Hattie McDaniel, Agnes Moorehead.* A tremendous cast brings life to this compelling and first-rate WWII soaper, a huge hit back in 1944. Sort of *Mrs. Miniver* with an American family, the story follows the struggles and daily lives of those on the homefront. Colbert shines as the mother and wife keeping a stiff upper lip while her husband is fighting overseas. ★★★½ VHS: $29.99

Sincerely Charlotte

(1986, 92 min, France, Caroline Huppert) *Isabelle Huppert, Niels Arestrup.* Huppert camps it up as a beguiling nightclub singer who is on the lam for the suspected murder of her boyfriend. With the net closing, and in desperation, she reenters the life of her old boyfriend, now married. Smitten with the alluring Huppert, the man's attention is divided between his quiet domestic life and the carefree, dangerous but exciting world of his ex. Huppert is wonderful as the femme fatale; part innocent, part liar and bitch — she's memorable! (French with English subtitles) ★★★

Un Singe en Hiver (Monkey in Winter)

(1962, 105 min, France, Henri Verneuil) *Jean Gabin, Jean-Paul Belmondo.* In theme and acting prowess, *Un Singe en Hiver* can be favorably compared to *The Color of Money*. Crusty old-timer Gabin is wasting his days away in a small town. His life is reinvigorated when a young man (Belmondo) moves into town, for Gabin sees in this wild drinker and dreamer fragments of his own vibrant youth. They join together for a few unforgettable adventures. (French with English subtitles) ★★½

Singin' in the Rain

(1952, 102 min, US, Gene Kelly & Stanley Donen) *Gene Kelly, Debbie Reynolds, Donald O'Connor, Jean Hagen, Cyd Charisse, Rita Moreno.* Movie musicals just don't come any better than this. A collection of superbly creative talents were at their peak with this spoof on 1920s Hollywood, with directors Kelly and Donen and writers Betty Comden and Adolphe Green combining forces after their success with *On the Town.* Kelly, who also choreographed, plays a popular silent screen star faced with the advent of "talkies" and salvaging his new film. Reynolds is perfectly cast as the pert chorine romanced by the actor; O'Connor is priceless as Kelly's childhood pal; and Hagen's Lina Lamont is one of the great "dumb blondes" in movie history. It's hard to pinpoint just one highlight in a film rich in magical moments, but O'Connor's "Make 'Em Laugh" and Kelly's "Broadway Ballet" certainly stand out. ★★★★ VHS: $14.99; DVD: $19.99

The Singing Detective

(1986, 415 min, GB, Jon Amiel) *Michael Gambon, Janet Suzman, Joanne Whalley.* With this richest of oeuvres, writer Dennis Potter has created the most textured and densest "autobiography" ever to be concocted since Proust chowed down on those tea-soaked madeleines. Produced for the BBC, *The Singing Detective* is a murder mystery in-the-composing as its author, one Philip Marlow (Gambon), assumes the title role as he lies in his hospital bed, racked by pain and addled by sedatives. His hallucinations interweave personal memories with those of the hero of his novel, "The Singing Detective" which weaves the convoluted tale of a sleuth who moonlights with a big band. Here Potter's trademark of having his characters lip-synch to pop recordings — and thus becoming their own Greek chorus — takes on a depth beyond simple irony, turning cynicism, climactically, into a sort of humanistic Heaven where pain becomes peace, and self-loathing, love. Arguably the best film/miniseries ever produced for television. ★★★★ VHS: $79.99

Singing the Blues in Red

(1987, 110 min, West Germany/GB, Ken Loach) *Gerulf Pannach, Fabienne Babe.* An acerbic, flawed yet stimulating look at East-West relationships as seen through the unblinking eyes of a wary political émigré. Klaus, a celebrated political songwriter/singer from East Berlin, is kicked out of East Germany but is enthusiastically welcomed into the capitalist arms of the West. Always questioning and distrustful of those in power, Klaus soon finds his worst fears of the West confirmed and feels no compunction about biting the corrupt hands that feed him. Loach pulls no punches as he explores the disillusionment of the socialist dream as well as the myths and contradictions inherent in the "Free World." (English and German with English subtitles) ★★½

A Single Girl

(1996, 90 min, France, Benoit Jacquot) *Virginie Ledoyen, Benoit Magimel.* A small, uneventful story that somehow could be applied to anyone's life, *A Single Girl* is a brief glimpse into an hour of one anonymous woman's life. Valerie (Ledoyen) is uncertain whether to meet her boyfriend Remi (Magimel) to tell him that she is pregnant. She gives the matter some thought on the first day of her new job as a room service waitress. At work, she encounters an array of personality types which subtlely influences her decision. Shot in real time, the film shows both how brief encounters with strangers can alter their lives, and that any given period in one's own life may be involving to someone else. Never boring but never truly inspired, *A Single Girl* is well acted and often intriguing. (French with English subtitles) ★★½ VHS: $19.99; DVD: $24.99

Single Room Furnished

(1968, 93 min, US, Matteo Ottaviano) *Jayne Mansfield.* Mansfield's last film features her as a tenement resident desperately looking for love after being deserted by the two men she cared for. ★ VHS: $19.99

Single White Female

(1992, 107 min, US, Barbet Schroeder) *Bridget Fonda, Jennifer Jason Leigh, Steven Weber.* Schroeder jumps on the Hollywood Formula bandwagon, and thanks to his deft touch, what should have been a flimsy roommate-from-hell thriller is, for the most part, a potent psychological suspenser. Leigh is the aforementioned roomie, who answers Fonda's ad to share her New York apartment. A mousy woman with no discernable personality of her own, Leigh becomes infatuated with the hipness of Fonda's breezy demeanor. This "crush," however, soon gives way to jealousy when Fonda reenters the dating game. Though lacking the stylish trappings of a *Fatal Attraction,* or even that film's narrative strengths, it is Leigh and Fonda's strong performances which elevate this tale above the ordinary. ★★½ VHS: $9.99; DVD: $24.99

Singles

(1992, 100 min, US, Cameron Crowe) *Matt Dillon, Bridget Fonda, Campbell Scott, Kyra Sedgwick, Bill Pullman.* A post-Brat Pack ensemble cast is featured as a group of Seattle MTV spawn trying to cope with their disillusionment about life and, more importantly, dating. Crowe's humorous coverage of their adventures splashing around in the dating pool redeems what might have been yet another whiny, self-centered product of the "new enlightenment." ★★★ VHS: $9.99; DVD: $14.99

The Sinister Urge

(1962, 75 min, US, Edward D. Wood, Jr.) *Jean Fontaine.* More schlock from the man who gave us *Glen or Glenda.* Here, a police officer investigates a series of porn star murders. Look out for the ruthless, evil, over-acting Mrs. Big (Fontaine). Title could be used for a Wood bio on his ability to make awful films. ★ VHS: $19.99

Sink the Bismark!

(1960, 97 min, GB, Lewis Gilbert) *Kenneth More, Dana Wynter.* The British Navy launches an all-out effort to destroy the pride of Hitler's fleet. Excellent special effects underscore this well-made WWII action-drama. ★★★

Sirens

(1994, 94 min, Australia/GB, John Duigan) *Hugh Grant, Sam Neill, Tara Fitzgerald, Elle Macpherson.* Filled with sun, sea, wine, sex and just the right amount of stimulating conversation, *Sirens* is like the perfect mini-vacation: not too taxing but very refreshing. Grant is an uptight preacher in the 1920s who must try to convince erotic painter Neill to withdraw one of his "shocking" pictures from an exhibition. To achieve his task, Grant, accompanied by his wife Fitzgerald, visits Neill and his lusty models, who do their best to get the couple to take the plunge into hedonism. Witty, nicely photographed and well acted, *Sirens* is eye candy for the Merchant Ivory set. ★★★ VHS: $14.99; DVD: $29.99

Sirocco

(1951, 98 min, US, Curtis Bernhardt) *Humphrey Bogart, Lee J. Cobb, Zero Mostel, Marta Toren.* Bogart stars as a cynical, unscrupulous businessman and black marketeer without political convictions in French occupied Syria (sound famil-

Bridget Fonda (l.) and Matt Dillon in *Singles*

iar?). Cobb is the French Lt. Colonel in charge of an investigation to discover who is supplying the Arab resistance with arms. Not one of Bogie's best, but he has a good world-weary presence. ★★ VHS: $19.99

Sister Act

(1992, 101 min, US, Emile Ardolino) *Whoopi Goldberg, Maggie Smith, Harvey Keitel, Kathy Najimy, Mary Wickes, Bill Nunn.* Goldberg is a comic delight in a film finally worthy of the comedienne's talents. She plays a Reno lounge singer who, upon witnessing a gangland murder, is sent to hide out at a San Francisco convent, run by the inestimable Smith. Captivating the order one by one, Whoopi does anything but lay low when she takes control of the church's choir and turns them into an overnight sensation. As would be expected, a lot of the humor stems from the nuns engaging in very un-nun-like behavior. But most of the comedy is sharper than that suggests. And though the premise is strictly formulaic, it's one Hollywood formula which works. Najimy steals every scene she's in as an unbelievably perky sister. (Sequel: *Sister Act 2: Back in the Habit*) ★★★½ VHS: $9.99; DVD: $29.99

Sister Act 2: Back in the Habit

(1993, 112 min, US, Bill Duke) *Whoopi Goldberg, Maggie Smith, Kathy Najimy, Michael Jeter.* To say that *Sister Act 2* is formulaic would put one in danger of committing the unpardonable sin of understatement. That is not to say that the formula doesn't work. A little. Goldberg is back as lounge singer Deloris Van Cartier; but this time, instead of having to save a bunch of nuns, she has to turn a rag-tag Catholic School music class into something resembling a choir. The charm of the first film was watching the nuns coming out of their shells; but how many times have we seen sassy, underachieving kids learn the meaning of self-respect because of a dedicated teacher. ★★ VHS: $9.99; DVD: $29.99

Sister, My Sister

(1994, 102 min, GB, Nancy Meckler) *Joely Richardson, Jodhi May, Julie Walters.* Inspired by Jean Genet's "The Maids," this provocative and polished drama is set in 1930s France and stars Richardson and May as two repressed sisters who work as servants to an obsessively demanding madam (Walters) who rules her house, and the life of her daughter, with a velvet-gloved iron fist. Held virtual prisoners in the claustrophobic house, the two young women soon become incestously involved with each other and their hot passions soon unravel their facade of orderliness. A highly sensual, intense, at times funny but ultimately unsettling tale. ★★★ VHS: $14.99; DVD: $19.99

Sisters

(1973, 93 min, US, Brian De Palma) *Margot Kidder, Jennifer Salt, Charles Durning, Barnard Hughes.* The beginning of director De Palma's sometimes overwhelming display of technical wizardry, this (dare we say it?) Hitchcockian tale follows the crisscrossing path of twin sisters (one good, one evil, both played by Kidder) and a reporter (Salt), who thinks she has witnessed a murder (shades of *Rear Window*). Scathing in its treatment of society as a breeding ground of thrill-seeking voyeurs, this appetizing but deadly serving of sibling rivalry is more

than just another "evil twin" hors d'oeuvre. (Letterboxed) ★★★ VHS: $19.99; DVD: $29.99

Sisters, or the Balance of Happiness

(1979, 96 min, Germany, Margarethe von Trotta) *Jutta Lampe, Gudrun Gabriel, Jessica Frueh, Rainer Delventhal.* Director von Trotta's extraordinarily accomplished *Sisters* explores the symbiotic relationship between two very close, but vastly different siblings. A severe, no-nonsense executive secretary, Maria (Lampe) provides financial and emotional support for her distracted younger sister, Anna (Gabriel), a student. When Maria begins to break out of her shell — befriending a coworker named Miriam (Frueh), and dating her boss' son — Anna has a breakdown that prompts Maria to re-examine her life. *Sisters* brilliantly captures the angst of these characters, particularly as Maria turns Miriam into a surrogate sister. In demanding roles, the three lead actresses give powerhouse performances. Visually haunting, and extremely moving. (German with English subtitles) ★★★★ VHS: $39.99

Sitcom

(1998, 80 min, France, François Ozon) *Évelyne Dandry, François Marthouret, Marina de Van, Stéphane Rideau, Antoine Fischer.* *Sitcom* is outrageous black comedy that mercilessly skewers the superficial refinement of the French bourgeois. We're introduced to a perfectly happy upper-class family whose members include hard-working dad, the doting and attractive mom and their two wonderful children. But deep within this apparently harmonious household are the seeds of destruction. And those seeds come in the form of a cute, white rat that dad brings home one day as the home's new pet. One by one, each family member gets close to the rat and after their encounter, release all of their pent-up anger, sexual desires and secret perversions. A no-holds-barred satire sure to delight anyone but those looking for a refined drama in the tradition of Truffaut or Rohmer. (French with English subtitles) ★★★½ VHS: $29.99

Sitting Ducks

(1978, 90 min, US, Henry Jaglom) *Michael Emil, Zack Norman.* Emil and Norman are the zany and querulous odd couple in this delightfully wacky road comedy. After the whiny and fastidious Emil steals $750,000 from his employer, he and his cohort Norman go on the road to Florida and from there Costa Rica. But along the way, these clashing nebbishes meet, befriend and take along for the ride a strange assortment of characters. Improvised dialogue and Jaglom's sympathetic eye and ear for misfits heighten an entertaining road movie. ★★★ VHS: $19.99

Sitting Pretty

(1948, 84 min, US, Walter Lang) *Clifton Webb, Robert Young, Maureen O'Hara, Robert Haydn.* Webb received an Oscar nomination for his hilariously finicky performance as baby-sitter/housekeeper extraordinaire Lynn Belvedere. Webb milks every laugh there's to be had in this funny family comedy. The basis for the sitcom "Mr. Belvedere." (Sequel: *Mr. Belvedere Goes to College*) ★★★½ VHS: $14.99

Six Days, Seven Nights

(1998, 100 min, US, Ivan Reitman) *Harrison Ford, Anne Heche, David Schwimmer, Jacqueline Obrados.* An old-fashioned romantic comedy with an abundance of good laughs but caught in a "what-do-we-do-next" conundrum, *Six Days, Seven Nights* is a pleasant diversion with not much substance, but having Ford as a Charlie Allnut-like pilot certainly helps glide over the soft spots. The sexy Heche plays a successful magazine editor who becomes stranded on a deserted island with the craggy pilot (Ford) of their downed airplane. There the two mismatched castaways struggle against the elements and each other before falling in love. Ford and Heche are very agreeable here, and their chemistry adds to the enjoyment of the film. With its lush scenery, good humor and budding romance, *Six Days, Seven Nights* is certainly not a trip wasted. ★★½ VHS: $14.99; DVD: $29.99

Six Degrees of Separation

(1993, 112 min, US, Fred Schepisi) *Will Smith, Donald Sutherland, Stockard Channing, Ian McKellen, Bruce Davison, Mary Beth Hurt, Richard Masur, Anthony Rapp, Anthony Michael Hall.* Based on John Guare's acclaimed Broadway play, which itself was inspired by a strange but true story, this witty and involving exploration of self-deception is an exhilarating comedy. The charismatic Smith plays a gay con man who ingratiates himself into the households of several rich New Yorkers by claiming to be the son of Sidney Poitier. One of those scammed is art dealer Sutherland and his wife Channing (brilliantly re-creating her award-winning stage role). As they recount their experiences in a series of anecdotal flashbacks, they play detective, ultimately learning the truth about their charming hoaxster. Guare, who wrote his own screenplay adaptation, has fashioned a modern masterwork dissecting the classes, race relations and, to a lesser degree, our desire as a society to appear in the film version of "Cats." ★★★★ VHS: $14.99; DVD: $19.99

Six Ways to Sunday

(1999, 97 min, US, Adam Bernstein) *Isaac Hayes, Deborah Harry, Adrien Brody, Norman Reedus, Elina Löwensohn.* Alternately dull and annoying, this hip/cult flick wannabe wastes an interesting cast. A pathetic teenage boy, who still allows his screwy mother to bathe him, is inducted into the local mob after displaying some useful violent tendencies. The last thing the world needs is another small-time crook/gangster movie, and the very last thing the world needs is one that is badly directed. If Bernstein had something interesting to say with all these sleazy schlock, or, at the very least, an ability to tell a story, that'd be one thing. As it stands, though, *Six Ways* is, in every way, a botch. ★

Sixteen Candles

(1984, 93 min, US, John Hughes) *Molly Ringwald, Justin Henry, Anthony Michael Hall, Paul Dooley.* Charming, often funny and affecting coming-of-age tale with Ringwald as a perplexed teen beseiged by creepy freshmen, spoiled siblings, confused parents and rampant hormones. ★★★ VHS: $9.99

The 6th Day

(2000, 124 min, US, Roger Spottiswoode) *Arnold Schwarzenegger, Robert Duvall, Tony Goldwyn, Michael Rooker, Sarah Wynter, Michael Rapaport.* Schwarzenegger is in familiar territory with this futuristic thriller that pits man vs. technology. Much like Arnold himself, the film gets by being competent without covering any new ground. In the not-too-distant future, cars drive themselves, refrigerators warn you when you're running low, and scientists have cloned pets and human organs. Human cloning, however, is illegal, but nevertheless performed. When pilot Schwarzenegger finds that he's been cloned, he sets out to reclaim his former life. Out to destroy the evidence and on his trail is the company who duplicated him. Good visuals and a few exciting scenes enhance this otherwise ordinary actioner. ★★½ VHS: $14.99; DVD: $27.99

The 6th Man

(1997, 108 min, US, Randall Miller) *Marlon Wayans, Kadeem Hardison.* It's *Ghost* meets *Blue Chips* in this slight comedy about a deceased basketball player who returns to Earth to help his younger brother. Hardison and Wayans star as Antoine and Kenny, siblings who grow up dreaming of basketball stardom. Antoine is killed just before they make it, and returns to help Kenny come to terms with his brother's death and aid in a little courtside action. *The 6th Man* is mostly predictable stuff, though fans of the sport may find some amusement in the otherworldly shenanigans. ★★ VHS: $14.99

Haley Joel Osment in *The Sixth Sense*

The Sixth Sense

(1999, 107 min, US, M. Night Shyamalan) *Bruce Willis, Haley Joel Osment, Toni Collette, Olivia Williams, Donnie Wahlberg.* With a child's fearful pronouncement of "I see dead people," writer-director Shyamalan's suspenseful psychological thriller enters into the realm of the supernatural and never falters in delivering credible, unnerving chills. Willis is Dr. Malcolm Crowe, a renowned child psychologist who — in the film's unsettling beginning — is shot by a former patient. A year later, Crowe begins counseling a troubled nine-year-old, Cole (Osment), who initially refuses to open up about his painful secret: He can communicate with the dead. As the two engage in soul-searching conversation, Crowe soon discovers that Cole may be telling the truth. Shyamalan doesn't resort to boo-type scares to get the pulse racing and

hairs standing on end. His is a thinking man's horror tale, one that finds its scares in the possibilities of the unknown. His great cast certainly helps, too. Willis is at his best, wisely underplaying his part, and Collette is touching as Cole's mother. But the acting honors go to young Osment, who brings a world-weary sadness to Cole; it's a remarkably nuanced and subtle portrayal, as potent as the unpredictable and surprise ending. ★★★★ VHS: $14.99; DVD: $29.99

Sketch Artist

(1992, 89 min, US, Phedon Papamichael) *Jeff Fahey, Drew Barrymore, Sean Young, Tcheky Karyo.* A mundane mystery about a police sketch artist (Fahey) who involves himself in a murder investigation when the only suspect bears a startling resemblance to his wife (Young). ★½

Skin Deep

(1989, 101 min, US, Blake Edwards) *John Ritter, Vincent Gardenia, Julianne Phillips.* Minor Edwards comedy with a few laughs, but mostly a disappointment for the writer-director. Ritter is a writer who can't keep his mind off women. ★½

Skin Game

(1971, 102 min, US, Paul Bogart) *James Garner, Lou Gossett, Jr., Susan Clark, Ed Asner.* Extremely likable comedy set pre—Civil War with Garner as a con man teaming with runaway slave Gossett, the two posing as master and servant. ★★★ VHS: $14.99

The Skull

(1965, 83 min, GB, Freddie Francis) *Christopher Lee, Peter Cushing, Jill Bennett.* A collector of the occult who obtains the skull of the Marquis de Sade descends into a nightmare of murder and madness in this Amicus production. Cushing plays the skeptical collector, who realizes too late the evil influence the skull is having on him. Lee plays a fellow collector whose help and warnings Cushing ignores until they can no longer do him any good. The film is properly atmospheric and tense but is hindered somewhat by lackluster special effects involving the skull. Cushing and Lee are stellar, as always, and manage to overcome the film's minor shortcomings enough to turn it into an entertaining horror story, complete with moral lesson. ★★★ VHS: $9.99

The Skulls

(2000, 107 min, US, Rob Cohen) *Joshua Jackson, Paul Walker, Hill Harper, Leslie Bibb, Craig T. Nelson, William Petersen, Christopher MacDonald.* An underprivileged but brilliant ivy-leaguer (Jackson) is given the opportunity to join an elite, secret campus society — the Skulls — which would afford him untold power and wealth. But he must follow the rules, or else. Ridiculous beyond belief, *The Skulls* unravels immediately following a decent setup that promises a minor but suspenseful little thriller. Instead, *The Skulls* feels like nothing so much as a lackluster "Dawson's Creek" episode (with that teenybopper show's lightweight Jackson as the lead, to boot); there is no suspense, no drama, and absolutely zero paranoia, which is the raison d'être of these movies. "Blessed" with the worst dialogue of the year, *The Skulls* is the best bad film of the year. You would think that joining an underground college organization

called the Skulls would be a good, safe way to get ahead in this Ivy League school. But for outsider Jackson, getting accepted can come at a price. ★ VHS: $14.99; DVD: $26.99

The Sky Above, the Mud Below

(1962, 92 min, France, Pierre-Dominique Gaisseau) This extraordinary documentary charts the enthralling yet dangerous expedition of a group of anthropologists through the jungles of Dutch New Guinea and into man's savage and violent past. Their endurance was tested daily as they encountered cannibals, headhunters and wild animals, as well as disease and death. Academy Award for Best Documentary Feature. (Narrated in English) ★★★★

The Sky's the Limit

(1943, 89 min, US, Edward H. Griffith) *Fred Astaire, Joan Leslie, Robert Benchley.* Fred is a war hero on leave in New York, falling in love with photographer Leslie. Fred's dancing is the tops. ★★★ VHS: $14.99

Skyline

(1985, 84 min, Spain, Fernando Colomo) *Antonio Resines.* A witty, droll depiction of the adventures of a Spanish photographer who comes to Manhattan seeking fame and fortune. The problems he encounters, including an extremely competitive job market, the fast-track lifestyle, and the incomprehensible language of the natives, drive him into the company of the few Spanish friends he has in the city. The film is a fine comic study of one immigrant's problems in the land of opportunity. (English and Spanish with English subtitles) ★★★ VHS: $39.99

Skyscraper Souls

(1932, 99 min, US, Edgar Selwyn) *Warren William, Maureen O'Sullivan.* Big business, middle class and working class are all struggling to strike it rich, or at least hold on to what they've got. Set in a skyscraper, the ultimate symbol of America in the '30s, the film follows the lives of several "souls" that live and work there. William plays a sly and ruthless businessman, trying to gain total ownership of the building. A young O'Sullivan is the innocent secretary who is tempted by him. Underneath the story, there is a darker, cynical side reflecting the mood of the times. Great art direction exquisitely captures the era of geometrics and chrome. ★★★ VHS: $19.99

Slacker

(1991, 97 min, US, Richard Linklater) First-time director Linklater takes us on a kaleidoscopic journey through the neo-beatnik scene of Austin, Texas. Using an interesting cinematic device, Linklater introduces the viewer to a series of random characters, following each one until some other interesting person pops up. The film literally weaves its way from one to the next without ever looking back. Starting with Linklater himself, we meet a seamless string of vagabonds, pseudo-intellectuals, conspiracy theorists and even a woman hawking what she claims is a Madonna Pap smear. Filled with hilarious moments, the film is a fascinating document of a generation of would-be philosophers with nowhere to go and nothing to do. ★★★ VHS: $14.99

Slam

(1998, 103 min, US, Marc Levin) *Saul Williams, Sonja Sohn, Bonz Malone, Beau Sia, Lawrence Wilson.* A solid indie effort, *Slam* boasts strong acting, believable situations and some excellent writing in this story of an African-American poet/rap artist (Williams) who is busted for marijuana possession and sent to jail. While there, he refuses to choose a gang to join (thereby losing "protection"); instead he chooses to fight violence with his "slam" poetry. What may sound like earnest hokum and preachy sincerity is actually a powerful representation of the strength of art in the face of chaos. The poetry performances are riveting and moving, and reflect the characters' difficult choices. A subplot of fighting the possession charge dramatizes the injustice of his plight, and is done with a minimum of histrionics. ★★★½ VHS: $14.99; DVD: $19.99

Slamdance

(1987, 100 min, US, Wayne Wang) *Tom Hulce, Mary Elizabeth Mastrantonio, Virginia Madsen, Harry Dean Stanton.* Hulce plays an artist who is suspected of murdering club-hopper Madsen. Director Wang offers a splash of style to the filmmaking, but can't save the muddled story. A moody attempt at modern film noir. ★★½ VHS: $14.99

Slap Shot

(1977, 122 min, US, George Roy Hill) *Paul Newman, Michael Ontkean, Lindsay Crouse, Jerry Houser, Melinda Dillon.* Racy comedy with Newman as a hockey player on a losing minor league team. When they start playing rough, they find attendance booms, and they win as well. This is a very funny film, though the language is quite strong — those offended by such dialogue should take note. ★★★ VHS: $9.99; DVD: $24.99

Slate, Wyn & Me

(1987, 90 min, Australia, Don McLennan) *Sigrid Thornton, Simon Burke.* Borrowing heavily on such American "mixed up, violent but attractive young people on the lam from the law" flicks as *Bonnie and Clyde* and *Badlands*, this mindless Aussie road movie has moments of interest but is generally a below-average import. The story begins suspiciously with two bungling brothers who rob a bank, kill a cop and then kidnap a witness (the requisite sexy teenager). A meandering drama filled with a rock 'n' roll soundtrack and countless car chases. ★★

Slaughter of the Innocents

(1994, 104 min, US, James Glickenhaus) *Scott Glenn, Jesse Cameron-Glickenhaus.* A gripping FBI procedural about a serial child rapist/killer. Glenn stars as a special agent thrust into the path of a maniac when his precocious, computer prodigy son makes a startling connection linking a recent killing to a 15-year-old series of grisly child slayings. Warning: Weak stomachs need not apply. ★★★ VHS: $14.99

Slaughterhouse-Five

(1972, 104 min, US, George Roy Hill) *Michael Sacks, Valerie Perrine, Ron Liebman, Eugene Roche, Sharon Gans.* Kurt Vonnegut's hero Billy Pilgrim becomes unstuck in time — between his war experiences in Dresden, his life as an

Michael Sacks and Valerie Perrine on the planet Tralfamadore in *Slaughterhouse-Five*

optometrist in '70s suburbia and as a member of a select zoo on the planet Tralfamadore. This very faithful adaptation is a visually stunning and emotionally satisfying trek in time which captures Vonnegut's irreverence, novelty and irony. ★★★½ VHS: $9.99; DVD: $29.99

A Slave of Love

(1978, 94 min, USSR, Nikita Mikhalkov) *Elena Solovel, Rodion Nakhapetov.* A dazzling, imaginative tale set in 1919 concerning a White Russian film crew's trials and tribulations in completing a romantic melodrama amid the rising tide of the revolution. The stunning Solovel, as the naïve leading lady, is a revelation. (Russian with English subtitles) ★★★½

Slaves of New York

(1989, 125 min, US, James Ivory) *Bernadette Peters, Chris Sarandon, Mary Beth Hurt, Mercedes Ruehl.* Disappointing screen version of Tama Janowitz's best-selling novel about the trendy New York art scene, with Peters as a struggling hat designer involved with a self-centered artist. ★★ VHS: $99.99

SLC Punk

(1999, 97 min, US, James Merendino) *Matthew Lillard, Michael A. Goorjian, Annabeth Gish, Jennifer Lien, Christopher McDonald, Devon Sawa.* Set in Salt Lake City in the Reagan era 1985, this hyperventilating tale of outsiders, losers, rebels and nonconformists plays a bit like an American Lite version of *Trainspotting.* Stevo (Lillard) is a blue-haired punk (and college grad) who drops out of his Mormon-infused childhood for a brief dance on the dark side. With his Mohawked best bud Heroin Bob (Goorjian), the two spend their days and nights fucking off, beating up strangers, taking drugs, having sex and doing all the things a typical American teen does — just a little more so. The film has a quick, jarring visual style, some pulse-pounding music and an array of beautiful losers, but eventually, you know the scene all too well and their naïve rebel-rousing begins to feel hollow. ★★½ VHS: $14.99; DVD: $27.99

Sleep with Me

(1994, 85 min, US, Rory Kelly) *Eric Stoltz, Meg Tilly, Craig Sheffer, Todd Field, Quentin Tarantino, June Lockhart.* A loosely scripted tale of two best friends (Stoltz, Sheffer) and the woman (Tilly)

they both love. With Tilly sputtering her lines in confused sentences and Stoltz sighing and smoking heavily while philosophizing irrationally, *Sleep with Me* takes on its own unusual rhythms. Add to that an eclectic supporting cast and a beguilingly shy performance by Sheffer and this film almost begins to make up for its complete lack of control. Check out Quentin Tarantino as a party guest attempting to explain why *Top Gun* is homoerotic. ★★½ VHS: $9.99

Sleeper

(1973, 88 min, US, Woody Allen) *Woody Allen, Diane Keaton, John Beck, Howard Casell.* Allen enters the hospital in 1973 for treatment of an ulcer and, because of "complications," reawakens after cryogenic sleep in the year 2173. Our hapless hero and latter-day Lazarus directs his wit to the future and his body to the orgasmitron. Consistently hilarious, and Allen and Keaton make a perfect comedic team. ★★★½ VHS: $14.99; DVD: $19.99

Sleepers

(1996, 152 min, US, Barry Levinson) *Brad Pitt, Robert De Niro, Jason Patric, Kevin Bacon, Dustin Hoffman, Joe Perrino, Brad Renfro, Minnie Driver, Vittorio Gassman, Billy Crudup, Ron Eldard.* Despite its talented high-profile cast, excellent evocation of 1960s New York and slick production values, *Sleepers*, a supposedly "true" story about torture, revenge and the loss of innocence, never overcomes the trappings of a gangster-themed dime novel. Four boyhood friends from Hell's Kitchen are sent to reform school, where they are physically and sexually assaulted. The story picks up years later when two of them kill one of their former attackers (Bacon) and are prosecuted by one of their old buddies (Pitt), who plans to lose the case unbeknownst to them. The biggest controversy of *Sleepers* isn't its surprising homophobia but the fact that original author Lorenzo Carcaterra claimed this was a biography — it later came to light that nothing in the story could be proved. As fact *Sleepers* is tragic history; as fiction it's an adolescent revenge fantasy. (VHS available letterboxed or pan & scan) ★★½ VHS: $9.99

Sleeping Dogs

(1977, 107 min, New Zealand, Roger Donaldson) *Sam Neill, Warren Oates.* This political chase thriller is a suspenseful tale of paranoia, repres-

S

sion of freedom and one man's resistance. Neill stars as Smith, a man who flees domestic trouble and finds solace on a quiet coastal island. His newfound peace is shattered when the right-wing government declares martial law and begins a crackdown on dissidents. Smith is jailed on trumped-up charges, escapes and begins a new life as a reluctant insurgent. ★★★ VHS: $19.99

Sleeping with the Enemy

(1991, 99 min, US, Joseph Ruben) *Julia Roberts, Patrick Bergin, Kevin Anderson.* Roberts brings a lot of energy to this ordinary thriller. She plays a mistreated wife, married to neurotic Bergin. Instead of divorce, she stages her own death, and moves to another town under a new identity. But her husband finds out the truth, and goes looking for her, stalking his spouse and planning his revenge. Short on thrills and credibility. ★★ VHS: $9.99

Sleepless in Seattle

(1993, 100 min, US, Nora Ephron) *Tom Hanks, Meg Ryan, Bill Pullman, Ross Malinger, Rosie O'Donnell, Rob Reiner, Gaby Hoffmann.* Ephron's second directorial feature basks in the romantic tradition of our cinematic past, and in doing so, she has created her quintessential comedy — warts and all — with just a little help from *An Affair to Remember.* Hanks plays a Seattle widower who's still not over his wife's death. His young son (the likable Malinger) calls a national radio talk show, forcing his dad to talk on the air. Ryan, meanwhile, lives in Baltimore and though engaged, she realizes there's something missing in her life. When she hears Hanks, she thinks she's found it. Thanks to Hanks and Ryan's enchanting performances, the film seems breezier and than it really is. ★★★ VHS: $9.99; DVD: $19.99

Sleepwalk

(1987, 90 min, US, Sara Driver) *Ann Magnuson.* A lyrical and witty feature debut for director Driver, *Sleepwalk* has the logic and landscape of a dream, an open-ended fairy tale set in the margins of an imaginary New York. The theft of an ancient and sacred manuscript, one which a

Johnny Depp in *Sleepy Hollow*

young woman is translating, leads to strange happenings — her fingers begin to bleed, the woman's roommate becomes bald, and a woman is killed just as the mysteries of the book are about to be solved. Magnuson is memorably comic as the rapidly balding roommate. Driver has a sharp eye for color and light and imbues the film with a lively, humorous style. ★★★

Sleepy Hollow

(1999, 105 min, US, Tim Burton) *Johnny Depp, Christina Ricci, Miranda Richardson, Michael Gambon, Casper Van Dien, Jeffrey Jones, Richard Griffiths, Christopher Walken.* Director Burton rides once more into the fantastic with this gorgeous-looking, atmospheric and quite often spine-tingling adaptation of Washington Irving's perennial "Legend of Sleepy Hollow." Depp is Ichabod Crane, here a young police inspector (not a schoolteacher) who comes to the small, quiet village of Sleepy Hollow to investigate several murders by beheading — and comes face to face with the infamous Headless Horseman. Depp plays Crane as no heroic, which only adds to the flavor and fun of this slick, sleek entertainment. Burton and company have meticulously re-created 1790s New England, though their inspiration has come in the many terrific effects — from the beheadings themselves (of which there are many) to the nightmarish Horseman who literally gallops from a tree. If this tale of yore has more of a 1990s accent to it than it should, it's a minor intrusion worth bearing; for Burton's end result is that one of eerie beauty and irresistible chills. ★★★ VHS: $14.99; DVD: $29.99

The Slender Thread

(1966, 98 min, US, Sydney Pollack) *Sidney Poitier, Anne Bancroft, Telly Savalas. Steven Hill.* Sincere performances elevate this compelling drama. Poitier plays a college student who is a volunteer at a Seattle crisis center. What looks to be a slow night becomes a fight for survival when he gets a call from Bancroft — who's just taken an overdose of pills. As Poitier desperately tries to get Bancroft to reveal her location, the events leading to her suicide attempt are told in flashback. These scenes are rather routine, but the sequences involving Poitier's verbal rescue attempt are enthralling. Pollack's directorial debut. ★★½ VHS: $14.99

Sleuth

(1972, 138 min, GB, Joseph L. Mankiewicz) *Laurence Olivier, Michael Caine.* Olivier is an eccentric upper-class English cuckold who plans a confrontation with Caine, the man who has not only stolen his wife's affections, but has the effrontery to be of the wrong class. Both Olivier and Caine give knockout performances in this royal battle of wit and wills. Screenplay by Anthony Shaffer from his play. Eclectic direction from Mankiewicz makes maximum use of a limited setting. ★★★½ VHS: $14.99; DVD: $24.99

Sliding Doors

(1998, 99 min, GB, Peter Howitt) *Gwyneth Paltrow, John Hannah, John Lynch, Jeanne Tripplehorn.* Paltrow gives a winsome performance in this engaging romantic fantasy that explores the path less traveled. She plays Helen, a London marketing executive who's just been sacked. Heading dejectedly home, she rushes for the subway only to have the train

Sliding Doors

doors close in her face. But just at that moment, the film diverges onto a parallel path, the one where she *does* catch the train and director Howitt deftly weaves back and forth between these two separately unfolding universes. *Sliding Doors* only occasionally strays too far afield into the land of cutesy, but for the most part is an edifying look at the alternate destinies that are governed by our decisions. ★★★½ VHS: $14.99; DVD: $29.99

A Slightly Pregnant Man

(1973, 92 min, France, Jacques Demy) *Marcello Mastroianni, Catherine Deneuve.* A daffy, gender-bending comedy which features Mastroianni and Deneuve as a loving but childless couple whose lives are upturned when Marcello discovers that he is in the family way. Their exploitation of the notorious birth-to-be and the changing ways Catherine treats the pregnant and irritable Marcello are the ingredients for this enjoyable farce. (Dubbed) ★★½

Sling Blade

(1996, 135 min, US, Billy Bob Thornton) *Billy Bob Thornton, Natalie Canerday, Lucas Black, Dwight Yoakam, John Ritter, J.T. Walsh.* Writer-director Thornton crafts an unforgettable character in his portrayal of Carl Childers, a slightly retarded 37-year-old man newly released from a mental institution 25 years after murdering his mother. He reenters his small Arkansas home town with a repairman's job and a cot in a tool room and a new friend, young Frank Wheatley (played with amazing presence by Black). The details of Carl's history are revealed as he gets closer to Frank and his mom, Linda (Canerday), suggesting parallels and similarities, especially regarding Doyle (Yoakam), Linda's boyfriend and Frank's nemesis. In this unfolding drama of decent, unassuming people defending themselves in a hostile world, Carl becomes increasingly sane by comparison. A superb, Oscar-winning screenplay, an effective minimalist musical score and a sure directorial hand describe this involving, heartfelt tale. ★★★★ VHS: $14.99; DVD: $29.99

The Slingshot

(1994, 102 min, Sweden, Ake Sandgren) *Jesper Salen, Stellan Skarsgård.* How many times must one be punched, hit, kicked and verbally abused before your resiliency of optimism is gone? You'll have to watch this abusive and not-so-happy coming-of-age film to find out. If you've seen *A Christmas Story, Leolo* and *My Life as a Dog,* you've caught all of the nuances of this film. Set in Sweden in the 1930s, the story centers on Roland, a precocious youngster who will do anything to get enough money for a bicycle, even sell slingshots made of contraband condoms. Great artistic design and good acting can't hide a lackluster film which can't deliver the final punch. (Swedish in English subtitles) ★★ VHS: $19.99

The Slipper and the Rose

(1976, 143 min, GB, Bryan Forbes) *Richard Chamberlain, Gemma Craven, Annette Crosbie, Edith Evans, Christopher Gable, Michael Hordern, Margaret Lockwood, Kenneth More.* A sumptuous musical version of the Cinderella story. Chamberlain makes a dashing Prince, and Craven is a lovely Cinderella. Music by Richard and Robert Sherman (*Mary Poppins*). (Director's cut) ★★★ VHS: $19.99; DVD: $24.99

Sliver

(1993, 106 min, US, Phillip Noyce) *Sharon Stone, William Baldwin, Tom Berenger, Colleen Camp, Martin Landau, CCH Pounder.* No, the title doesn't refer to the amount of logic within the plot, but to a Manhattan luxury high-rise apartment building plagued by a series of unexplained deaths. Stone plays a recently divorced and sexually frustrated book editor (it could happen) who moves into the "horror high-rise" where romance and terror await in the form of Baldwin and Berenger. As penned by Joe Eszterhas and stylishly directed by Noyce, what might have been a trenchant study of voyeurism and social responsibility is reduced to a slick, trashy and befuddled whodunit with a dime-store resolution. ★★½ VHS: $14.99

Slow Burn

(2000, 97 min, US, Christian Ford) *Minnie Driver, James Spader, Josh Brolin, Stuart Wilson.* A well-wrought "drama of errors" about a young woman (Driver) fighting for survival in the Mexican desert against two escaped convicts (Spader and Brolin) who accidentally find the fortune in diamonds she's spent her life searching for. Well-tuned performances and a mature script make this familiar though suspenseful tale a worthwhile character study as well as an agreeable actioner. ★★½ VHS: $102.99; DVD: $24.99

Slumber Party Massacre

(1982, 78 min, US, Amy Jones) Novelist Rita Mae Brown ("Rubyfruit Jungle") penned this horrific lampoon of mad-slasher films. If its tongue weren't firmly planted in cheek, it would probably get lopped off. (Followed by 2 sequels) ★★ VHS: $9.99; DVD: $14.99

Slums of Beverly Hills

(1998, 91 min, US, Tamara Jenkins) *Natasha Lyonne, Alan Arkin, Marisa Tomei, David Krumholtz, Kevin Corrigan, Jessica Walter, Carl Reiner, Rita Moreno.* Writer-director Jenkins' debut feature is a refreshing, funny and offbeat coming-of-age tale told through the eyes of a budding 15-year-old. Both amusing and tender, the film follows Vivian (the very appealing Lyonne), who lives with her unemployed, single dad (Arkin) and two brothers. Things pick up when cousin Rita (an outrageously outfitted Tomei) arrives from rehab. It's up to Vivian to keep an eye on her, and with brassy cousin Rita

around, sexually blossoming Vivian is about to learn more than any 15-year-old needs to know. Jenkins peppers her film with wry and knowing observations on growing up and familial ties, and includes one helluva self-stimulation scene. It's often unexpectedly poignant. ★★★ VHS: $102.99; DVD: $24.99

Small Change

(1976, 104 min, France, François Truffaut) Truffaut's buoyant visual soufflé is a winning observation of youthful resiliency. Set in a tiny French town, *Small Change* follows a group of school children through their daily endeavors. (French with English subtitles) ★★★½ VHS: $19.99; DVD: $19.99

Small Faces

(1996, 113 min, Scotland, Gillies MacKinnon) *Iain Robertson, Joseph McFadden, J.S. Duffy, Laura Fraser, Kevin McKidd.* The incongruous glint of gunmetal in a heather-dappled, wooded lane belies the apparent tranquility of pastoral Glasgow, and serves as an emblem of the underlying tensions of gang affiliations which allow no neutrality and broker no dissent. Set in 1968, the story is told through the eyes of 13-year-old Lex (Robertson), the youngest of three brothers, who is sucked into a vortex of conflicting allegiances. His brother Bobby (Duffy) is a member of one of the area gangs. Lex's other brother Alan (McFadden) is a promising art student of benign aspect and high expectations. Events unfold quickly and inexorably, leaving the adults to watch in stunned incomprehension and bitter helplessness, equally shocked by the acts of brutality and by the young ones' ease of adaptability to this new world. Director MacKinnon adeptly utilizes a strong cast to explore one family's response to crisis and loss. ★★★½

Small Soldiers

(1998, 105 min, US, Joe Dante) *Kirsten Dunst, Phil Hartman, Gregory Smith, Jay Mohr, Denis Leary; Voices of: Tommy Lee Jones, Frank Langella, Ernest Borgnine, Jim Brown, Sarah Michelle Gellar, Christina Ricci.* Best described as *Toy Story* meet *Gremlins,* the plot of the live-action/animated *Small Soldiers* tells the cautionary tale of what happens when a new state-of-the-art toy line comes to life. The toys are programmed to fight each other, and are able to not only speak but learn as well. This is the high-concept gimmick of *Small Soldiers,* much like the "toys come to life" hook of Disney's *Toy Story.* But this is much more hard-edged and violent (in a comic book sort of way). It may not be for younger ones. Director Dante has a flair for bizarre sight gags, and his film has the feel of an old Warner Brothers' Tazmanian Devil cartoon, but the human element is inconsistent. ★★½ VHS: $14.99; DVD: $34.99

Small Time Crooks

(2000, 95 min, US, Woody Allen) *Woody Allen, Tracey Ullman, Elaine May, Hugh Grant, Elaine Stritch, Jon Lovitz, Michael Rapaport, George Grizzard, Tony Darrow.* Recalling both *Take the Money and Run* and *Broadway Danny Rose* in a story of bumbling crooks, Allen's appealing comedy may tell us that crime does not pay, and there's no changing a leopard's spots, but, ultimately, nothing beats a good cookie recipe. A funny, feather-light caper comedy,

Small Time Crooks follows the misadventures of Ray (Allen) and his misfit assortment of cohorts as they plan a bank heist. Things go wrong, of course, but their cover — a cookie shop run by Ray's wife Frenchy (Ullman) — becomes an overnight success. Suddenly it's the Kramdens hit Park Avenue. Woody has given himself and Ullman endearing parts, which they make the most of. They have a nice rapport, and some wonderful one-liners. May is a standout as Frenchy's wafty cousin who's always saying the wrong thing at the right time. Strangely, Ray's partners in crime all but disappear, never to be heard from again. ★★★ VHS: $14.99; DVD: $26.99

Small Wonders

(1996, 80 min, US, Allan Miller) One of the most disarming films about children since Truffaut's *Small Change,* Miller's modest but jubilant sleeper examines a divorced mother of two who teaches violin to Harlem elementary school kids. This straight-ahead, no frills, shot-on-video documentary may sound like a sappy, dull Afterschool Special, but *Small Wonders* is anything but. The film follows Roberta Guaspari-Tzavaras and her students from first meeting to their sold-out concert at Carnegie Hall (complete with guest violinists Isaac Stern and Itzhak Perlman). Guaspari-Tzavaras is inspirational, the kids are devoted, and become musicians. A superb argument for the continued support of music and art in our public school systems. (Meryl Streep stars in the 1999 film *Music of the Heart* based on the same story) ★★★½ VHS: $19.99

The Smallest Show on Earth

(1957, 81 min, GB, Basil Dearden) *Peter Sellers, Margaret Rutherford, Bill Travers, Virginia McKenna.* This highly amusing little British comedy tells the tale of a young couple who inherit a run-down movie theatre. Travers and McKenna are charming as the pair who are thrust against their will into the cinema business. Sellers, as the drunken, near-sighted projectionist, and Rutherford, as the slow-moving octogenarian cashier, play two of the ancient employees who come along with the theatre — both are magnificent as always. Filled with joie de vivre, the film imparts an alluring sense of nostalgia for anyone who considers themselves a dyed-in-the-wool cinema buff. ★★★ VHS: $14.99

Smash Palace

(1981, 100 min, New Zealand, Roger Donaldson) *Bruno Lawrence, Anna Jemison.* This highly acclaimed work by Donaldson is a compelling drama set in the cities and countryside of New Zealand. It is a powerful tale of a marriage jeopardized by a man's obsession with auto racing and a woman's overriding need for love and affection. ★★★½

Smash-Up

(1947, 103 min, US, Stuart Heisler) *Susan Hayward, Lee Bowman, Eddie Albert.* Hayward shines in an Oscar-nominated role as a nightclub singer who turns to the bottle after giving up her career for marriage. Dramatically it's familiar territory but Hayward's performance more than compensates. (aka: *Smash-Up, the Story of a Woman*) ★★½ VHS: $12.99

Smoke Signals

Smile

(1975, 113 min, US, Michael Ritchie) *Bruce Dern, Barbara Feldon, Melanie Griffith, Annette O'Toole.* Ritchie's best film is this hilariously biting satire of Americana. Dern is a small-town California car salesman who, with his perky and maniacally organized wife (Feldon), helps organize the Young Miss Beauty contest. The "behind the scenes" peek at the pretty contestants, their amazingly talentless talent and the lascivious judges are only a few of the highlights of this perceptive and witty film. ★★★½ VHS: $14.99

A Smile Like Yours

(1997, 99 min, US, Keith Samples) *Greg Kinnear, Lauren Holly, Joan Cusack, Jay Thomas, Jill Hennessy, Christopher McDonald.* A not unwatchable comedy, but certainly one with limited charms, *A Smile Like Yours* will amuse only those viewers who find humor in frequent visits to fertility clinics. Since cowriters Kevin Meyer and director Samples seem to be the only ones, everyone else can admire the low-watt dynamics of Danny (Kinnear) and Jennifer (Holly) as they try to make a baby. The poorly conceived film follows Danny's unfunny impotence episodes with a lame story line about each partner suspecting the other of having an extramarital affair. ★★ VHS: $14.99

Smiles of a Summer Night

(1955, 108 min, Sweden, Ingmar Bergman) *Eva Dahlbeck, Harriet Andersson, Jarl Krulle.* An exquisite carnal comedy about eight people who become four couples in turn-of-the-century Sweden. Bergman's witty treatise on changing partners under the midnight sun is filled with delightfully ironic humor. The basis for the Tony Award—winning musical "A Little Night Music," which was poorly adapted to film. (Swedish with English subtitles) ★★★★ VHS: $29.99

Smilla's Sense of Snow

(1997, 121 min, Denmark/Germany/Sweden, Bille August) *Julia Ormand, Gabriel Byrne, Richard Harris, Vanessa Redgrave, Robert Loggia, Jim Broadbent.* This very disappointing adaptation of Peter Høeg's best-selling thriller stars Ormand as the titular character, a half Dane, half Greenlander scientist whose obsession with the "accidental" death of a young boy leads her deeper into a web of murder and deception. It would be an undertaking to convey Smilla

Jasperen's prickly personality, which was the most intriguing aspect of Høeg's novel. But, instead of a fascinating journey into the convoluted workings of her personality all we get is the icy exterior, a shortcoming that only makes her more perplexing. August shows that he's more at home directing smaller, more personal movies although his locations and sense of mise-en-scène provide the film's best evocation of the book. ★★ VHS: $9.99; DVD: $24.99

Smithereens

(1982, 93 min, US, Susan Seidelman) *Susan Berman.* Wren is a legend in her own mind — a self-assured, narcissistic New Wave hanger-on with a yen for the big time. This gritty Greenwich Village odyssey is a distinctly modern version of the American Dream. ★★★ VHS: $29.99

Smoke

(1995, 113 min, US, Wayne Wang & Paul Auster) *Harvey Keitel, William Hurt, Stockard Channing, Forest Whitaker, Harold Perrineau, Jr., Giancarlo Esposito, Ashley Judd.* The divergent rhythms of New York come alive in the guise of this immensely satisfying slice-of-life comedy-drama centered around the habitués of a tobacco shop in the heart of Brooklyn. Keitel is Joe, who becomes involved in the lives of some of his customers. As one of them, Hurt exhibits the right amount of ennui and melancholy as a widowed WASPy author who befriends a black youth (nicely played by Perrineau) whose fabrications mask deep familial hurts. Whitaker is splendid as the teen's long-lost father, an abrupt, pained man looking for a new start. These stories effortlessly coalesce into a deeply affecting tale defined by rich characterizations and buoyant comedy — the least of which explains Keitel's passion for photography. Followed by an anti-sequel, *Blue in the Face.* ★★★★ VHS: $29.99

Smoke Signals

(1998, 89 min, US, Chris Eyre) *Adam Beach, Evan Adams, Gary Farmer, Tantoo Cardinal, Irene Bedard.* The first film starring, written, directed and produced solely by Native Americans, *Smoke Signals* is a truly original and thoroughly charming independent whose themes and truths happen to transcend cultures. At once a coming-of-age tale, road movie and social comedy, the story concerns Victor (Beach), a troubled though good-hearted teen who has been affected by the absence of his father. When the family receives news of the father's death, Victor, accompanied by his nerdy, storytelling childhood friend Thomas (a remarkable Adams), travels from his Idaho reservation to Phoenix to collect his father's ashes. Though Sherman Alexie's screenplay (based on his collection of short stories "The Lone Ranger and Tonto Fistfight in Heaven") examines life that is particular to American Indians, it's his observations on the human psyche which propel the story. None better is Thomas' tales of history and folklore — Alexie's talent for language is commanding, and his bent for comedy is persuasive. An enchanting film experience. ★★★★ VHS: $19.99; DVD: $29.99

Smokey and the Bandit

(1977, 96 min, US, Hal Needham) *Burt Reynolds, Sally Field, Jackie Gleason, Jerry Reed, Paul Williams, Pat McCormick.* Burt mugs up a storm in this mindlessly enjoyable action comedy that's actually one long car chase. Burt's

wanted by lawman Gleason; runaway bride Field's along for the ride. (Followed by 2 sequels) ★★½ VHS: $9.99; DVD: $24.99

Smooth Talk

(1985, 91 min, US, Joyce Chopra) *Laura Dern, Treat Williams.* Based on Joyce Carol Oates' short story "Where Are You Going, Where Have You Been," this compelling, gutsy coming-of-age drama explores a 15-year-old California girl's sexual awakening. Dern is excellent as the budding teen, and Williams exudes charm and malevolence as her seducer. ★★★

Snake and Crane Arts of Shaolin

(1978, 95 min, Hong Kong, Chen Chi Hwa) *Jackie Chan.* After nearly being killed a dozen times while trying to learn an ancient fighting technique developed by a group of Shaolin masters, student Hsu Yin Fung (Chan) is unjustly accused of killing the masters and destroying all records of their deadly art. When his girlfriend is murdered, he seeks the help of another master who finally teaches him the form which he in turn uses in his search for the true killer. Brisk kung fu chaos, enlivened by Chan's trademark stunt-laden style. ★★½ VHS: $19.99

Snake Eyes

(1998, 100 min, US, Brian De Palma) *Nicolas Cage, Gary Sinise, Carla Gugino, John Heard, Stan Shaw, Kevin Dunn, Luis Guzman.* An animated Cage stars as Ricky Santoro, an Atlantic City cop who's about to settle in and enjoy the big fight. But when a government official is murdered ringside, the journey Santoro and the audience are taken on in De Palma's stylish, loopy thriller is anything but tranquil. With a constantly moving camera and tennis-match editing, *Snake Eyes* follows Santoro as he tries to solve a murder committed before 14,000 people. He soon discovers that a conspiracy is afoot, and places his own life in jeopardy. De Palma certainly keeps things moving, but no matter how fast the pace, it can't hide a cheesy story. At least it looks good. (Letterboxed VHS available for $14.99) ★★½ VHS: $9.99; DVD: $24.99

The Snake Pit

(1948, 108 min, US, Anatole Litvak) *Olivia de Havilland, Mark Stevens, Leo Genn, Celeste Holm.* An intelligent, fascinating drama about a young woman who experiences a nervous breakdown and is committed to a mental institution. It's a disturbing look into the life inside of a mental institution and even more chilling considering when the film was made. The film features some fantastic camerawork and a brilliant performance from de Havilland. ★★★★ VHS: $19.99

The Snapper

(1993, 95 min, Ireland, Stephen Frears) *Colm Meaney, Ruth McCabe, Tina Kellegher.* Written by Roddy Doyle (*The Commitments*), *The Snapper* is a wonderful character study full of laughs and tears. Kellegher is the strong-willed daughter of an Irish working-class family who becomes pregnant and refuses to reveal who is the father of the baby. Meaney is outstanding as her good-hearted father and McCabe stands out as the loving mother who keeps her family together through it all. Marvelous acting and a humorous and insightful screenplay make this film a rare treat. Director Frears is in a playfully droll mood. (Sequel: *The Van*) ★★★★ VHS: $19.99

Snatch

(2000, 103 min, GB, Guy Ritchie) *Brad Pitt, Jason Statham, Vinnie Jones, Dennis Farina, Benicio del Toro, Rade Sherbedgia.* With his second feature, director Ritchie is back in the same territory as his high-energy debut *Lock, Stock and Two Smoking Barrels:* colorful gangsters, fast-paced action, jet-black humor, lightning-quick editing and lots of gun play. And while one could complain that *Snatch* is a carbon copy of Ritchie's first film, that doesn't take away from the sheer fun of this knock-'em-dead heist tale. The story follows what happens when Franky Four Fingers (Del Toro) stops off in London on his way to New York to deliver a stolen 84-carat diamond. Soon, an Irish boxer (Pitt) who you can't understand, a crime boss with a penchant for pigs, a boxing promoter (Statham) just trying to stay alive, and a crazed Russian gangster (Sherbedgia) all enter the picture to further complicate and amuse. Ritchie knows how to sustain action at a fast clip, and the film moves at remarkable speed. Always in danger of self-imploding, *Snatch* is more accessible and fluid than *Lock, Stock.* And while it may not appear as fresh, like many of the wonderfully drawn characters suggest, appearances can be deceiving. ★★★ VHS: $102.99; DVD: $27.99

Sneakers

(1992, 105 min, US, Phil Alden Robinson) *Robert Redford, Sidney Poitier, Dan Aykroyd, Ben Kingsley, Mary McDonnell, River Phoenix, David Strathairn, James Earl Jones.* A clever, humorous and complex computer-age thriller, the story centers on a group of professional thieves and computer hackers who are coerced by the U.S. government to steal a mysterious black box. Once it is in their possession, they learn the box is really the ultimate code breaker, able to decipher any computer program in the world. And now there are some very dangerous people out to retrieve it at any cost. While not in the same class as *Topkapi* or *The Sting,* which it at times recalls, *Sneakers* is nevertheless exuberant, fun-filled and set at a rapid-fire pace. ★★★ VHS: $14.99

Sniper

(1993, 99 min, US, Luis Llosa) *Tom Berenger, Billy Zane, J.T. Walsh.* Berenger is a hard-as-nails, and possibly slightly crazy, government assassin. When his partner is killed during a hit, the higher-ups send in sharpshooter Zane to keep him in line. Like 1988's *The Beast, Sniper* is more about what it is like to kill rather than being about how many people are killed and with what semi-automatic weapons. Berenger and

The Snapper

Zane interact well, perhaps bonding just a little too quickly for the animosity their characters originally show each other. *Sniper* is an action film that actually ends up showing some humanity. ★★★ VHS: $9.99; DVD: $19.99

Snow Country

(1957, 134 min, Japan, Shiro Toyoda) *Ryo Ikebe, Keiko Kishi.* Based on the novel by Yasunari Kawabata, this passionate love story tells of the budding relationship between two people and the nagging cultural differences that pull them apart. Shimamura, an artist in Tokyo, escapes to the tranquil rural Honshu region in the northwestern part of the country for relaxation. There he meets and falls in love with Kumako, a charming young woman from the snow-covered village. The disparities in their upbringing as well as the antagonism of the townsfolk kind of make this a Japanese "Romeo and Juliet." (Japanese with English subtitles) ★★★ VHS: $59.99

Snow Falling on Cedars

(1999, 128 min, US, Scott Hicks) *Ethan Hawke, Youki Kudoh, James Cromwell, Rick Yune, Richard Jenkins, Max Von Sydow, Sam Shepard,.* Using flashbacks and forwards in much the same way as his award-winning *Shine,* director Hicks' follow-up to that film isn't quite as successful in imparting bits and pieces to create a whole. However, a compelling story and beautiful cinematography contribute to make this a moving look at racial distrust, small-town politics, and the bond to overcome them both. A reporter (Hawke) investigates the story of a Japanese-American man accused of killing an American fisherman. The fact that the man is the brother of the girl he loved as a youth complicates matters as much as the small Pacific Northwest town's resentment towards the defendant. Based on David Guterson's best-selling novel, *Snow Falling on Cedars* only lightly tackles the incendiary theme of the treatment of Asian-American citizens during WWII, using it instead as a backdrop to romance and courtroom drama. But how Hicks confronts this issue is handled with sensitivity and poise. Of a talented ensemble, Von Sydow excels as the accused's wily lawyer. ★★★ VHS: $14.99; DVD: $24.99

Snow White and the Seven Dwarfs

(1937, 83 min, US, Ben Sharpsteen) Arguably Disney's finest achievement (and his first feature-

Ethan Hawke in Snow Falling on Cedars

length animated film), *Snow White* is the perfect blend of animation, story and character utilizing charming songs and good humor. A huge smash at the box office in 1937, the film, of course, follows the adventures of Snow White, who does battle with an evil, jealous witch and who finds her prince, all the while living in the forest with seven adorable little men. Tamer than any cartoon made today, the film still captivates — it is one of the authentic masterpieces of American cinema. ★★★★ VHS: $26.99; DVD: $29.99

So Fine

(1981, 91 min, US, Andrew Bergman) *Ryan O'Neal, Jack Warden, Mariangela Melato.* O'Neal plays a mild-mannered professor who accidentally creates a fashion sensation for his dad, a clothing manufacturer: see-through pants. Warden's spirited portrayal of O'Neal's dad is the bright spot of this see-through comedy. ★★ VHS: $19.99

So I Married an Axe Murderer

(1993, 93 min, US, Thomas Schlamme) *Mike Myers, Nancy Travis, Anthony LaPaglia, Amanda Plummer, Brenda Fricker, Phil Hartman.* Myers should be axed from the comedy register for this insultingly inept follow-up to *Wayne's World.* Myers headlines as a so-bad-he's-good coffeehouse poet whose fear of marriage ends when he weds the quirky but beautiful owner (Travis) of the local butcher shop despite his mounting fears that she may be (drum roll, please) an axe murderer. ★½ VHS: $9.99; DVD: $24.99

So Proudly We Hail

(1943, 126 min, US, Mark Sandrich) *Claudette Colbert, Paulette Goddard, Veronica Lake, George Reeves, Sonny Tufts.* One of the few WWII films to be seen through the eyes of women, this gallant, terse drama follows the sometimes heartbreaking role of nurses in combat. The sublime Colbert stars as an Army head nurse who, at the film's start, is catatonic and on her way home. The story then traces her path on the many battlefields of WWII, where romance, tragedy and camaraderie shape her life. Excellent in support are Goddard (who received an Oscar nomination) as Colbert's right-hand gal and Tufts as a soldier/Goddard's love interest who "never gets killed." Though high in 1940s and wartime sentiment, this is a no-nonsense, pleasurable melodrama. ★★★½ VHS: $14.99

S

Soapdish

(1991, 95 min, US, Michael Hoffman) *Sally Field, Kevin Kline, Whoopi Goldberg, Robert Downey, Jr., Elisabeth Shue, Cathy Moriarty.* A terrific comic cast makes the most of this often funny spoof of soap operas. Field is the reigning Queen of the Soaps. Goldberg is her writer and longtime friend. Kline is Field's ex-beau, who returns to the airwaves after a 20-year absence to be reunited with Sally — both on-screen and off. Downey is the inefficient producer, more worried about bedding second-string actress Moriarty than his show's quality. And Shue rounds out the cast as Field's niece who, unbeknownst to her aunt, has signed on with the show. The film's tempo is played as grand farce, and though not all of the humor works, it's a joyously loony romp. ★★★ VHS: $14.99

S.O.B.

(1981, 121 min, US, Blake Edwards) *William Holden, Robert Preston, Julie Andrews, Robert Mulligan, Robert Webber, Shelley Winters, Robert Vaughn, Rosanna Arquette.* Edwards' brilliant, scathing indictment of Hollywood and the men and women behind and in front of the cameras. Holden gives a sterling performance as a jaded director with a predilection for teenaged girls. Preston is exceptional as a wisecracking doc, Andrews is a superstar who bares all, and Mulligan is Edwards' alter ego who discovers exactly what it takes to make a hit. One of the most underrated films of its decade. ★★★½ VHS: $14.99

Sofie

(1993, 145 min, Sweden, Liv Ullmann) *Karen-Lise Mynster, Erland Josephson.* Taking on the mantle of her longtime director, Ingmar Bergman, actress Ullmann debuts behind the camera with this affecting, if somewhat overlong, saga about the life of an unassuming Jewish woman in turn-of-the-century Sweden. Early on, the film hinges on her choice between a fiery and passionate affair with a Christian painter or an arranged marriage to a dour Jewish man from the countryside. As she spends much of her time with her three spinster aunts, the film examines her struggle between virtue and spiritual freedom. Benefitting from a host of fine performances, the film often captures the whimsical nature of Bergman's *Fanny and Alexander*, but at 145 minutes, the film too often overstays its welcome. (Swedish with English subtitles) ★★½ VHS: $79.99

The Soft Skin

(1964, 118 min, France, François Truffaut) *Jean Desailly, Françoise Dorleac.* A mature, underrated work by Truffaut that explores the ill-fated fling with infidelity by a successful publisher and a pretty airline stewardess. Truffaut focuses on their day-to-day life in this precisely-told examination of a catastrophe-prone situation. (French with English subtitles) ★★★ VHS: $19.99; DVD: $29.99

Solaris

(1972, 165 min, USSR, Andrei Tarkovsky) *Donatas Banionis, Natalya Bondarchuk.* Hailed by its admirers as a visionary, philosophical work and by others (especially sci-fi fans) as a difficult, if not turgid, boring flick, this Tarkovsky's best-known film, adapts the popular science-fiction theme of men lost in space to his own idiosyncratic style of filmmaking. Eschewing high-tech gimmickry and special effects, the story centers on a psychologist who is sent to investigate a series of unexplained deaths on a Russian space station that is orbiting the remote planet of Solaris. There he finds that the killers are not aliens but rather phantoms materialized from the cosmonauts' guilty past. Admittedly heavy going, it's also an imaginative, serious work about man's limits as well as his barely concealed fears and self-destructive nature. (Russian with English subtitles) ★★★½

Soldat Duroc

(1975, 85 min, France, Michel Gerard) *Pierre Tornade.* In September 1944, a few days after the liberation of Paris, a young French soldier secretly crosses the German lines in the middle of the night to rejoin his fiancée in Senlis, a small town still occupied by the German Army. His plans become unraveled, however, when he is captured by two soldiers, one American and the other French, who were sent by General Patton to help liberate the Nazi-held village. An absorbing and nicely told war drama. (French with English subtitles) ★★★

Soldier

(1998, 99 min, US, Paul Anderson) *Kurt Russell, Jason Scott Lee, Connie Nielsen, Michael Chiklis, Gary Busey.* The future's bleak in this tired sci-fi adventure which offers about as much thrills as the director's previous yawner, *Event Horizon.* Having a good look but even a lesser story than *Horizon, Soldier* manages to make the usually engaging Russell nothing more than a Stallone-clone, playing a monosyllabic futuristic warrior who helps a stranded space colony when they come under attack by militaristic forces (who were the ones who left him to die on the supposedly empty planet). What a waste of an intriguing idea. (VHS available letterboxed or pan & scan) ★½ VHS: $14.99; DVD: $19.99

Soldier in the Rain

(1963, 88 min, US, Ralph Nelson) *Jackie Gleason, Steve McQueen.* Blake Edwards adapted William Goldman's novel for this touching story about the friendship between a wheeling-dealing Army sergeant (Gleason) and his young sidekick (McQueen). ★★★

Soldier of Orange

(1979, 165 min, The Netherlands, Paul Verhoeven) *Rutger Hauer, Jeroen Krabbé, Edward Fox.* The title of this intelligent and engrossing adventure story refers to the House of Orange, The Netherlands' Royal Government which was put in exile after the Nazi invasion of their country. Verhoeven demonstrates his ability to both re-create an era pregnant with fear and danger as well as tell a hypnotic war story. Hauer and Krabbé are aristocratic students who are caught up in the war effort and become dangerously involved in the Dutch resistance. (Dutch with English subtitles) ★★★½ VHS: $14.99; DVD: $29.99

A Soldier's Daughter Never Cries

(1998, 128 min, US, James Ivory) *Kris Kristofferson, Barbara Hershey, Leelee Sobieski, Jane Birkin, Dominique Blanc, Jesse Bradford, Bob Swaim, Luisa Conlon.* One sublime characteristic of Merchant Ivory productions is that as they tell a story, they also capture a mood, a time, a frame of mind. Kristofferson plays Bill Willis, an American writer in Paris, ex-soldier, expatriate, living in affluence with his wife (Hershey) and daughter, and writing about war as Vietnam begins its decades-long dominance of the world's television screens. They adopt a young French child, not orphaned nor abandoned, and bring him into their loving if eccentric fold. The actors impart presence and sensitivity to their roles, especially the two talents who portray the daughter Channe (Conlon plays her at age 7; Sobieski at 14 up), who is arguably the film's pivotal character. Stages of life pass like seasons of the year, lyrical cycles of joy and tragedy, gain and loss; momentous events marked by definitive statements expressed in the smallest gestures. A remarkable film describing an arc in one family's life, bearing witness to the fact that our history is always with us. ★★★½ VHS: $14.99

A Soldier's Story

(1984, 102 min, US, Norman Jewison) *Howard E. Rollins, Adolphe Caesar, Denzel Washington, Dennis Lipscomb, Patti LaBelle, Robert Townsend.* Crackling with racial tension, Jewison's searing murder mystery probes the multifaceted dilemma of black advancement in a predominately white man's Army. Brilliantly acted with power and grace, Philadelphian Charles Fuller's Pulitzer Prize—winning play is a rare triumph of the stage to screen process. Caesar was Oscar nominated for his powerful portrayal of a much-disliked drill sergeant. ★★★★ VHS: $9.99; DVD: $24.99

The Solid Gold Cadillac

(1956, 99 min, US, Richard Quine) *Judy Holliday, Paul Douglas, Fred Clark, John Williams, Arthur O'Connell; Narrated by: George Burns.* That divine blithe spirit Holliday is impeccably funny as a daffy blonde who takes on the corporate world. She stars as a minor shareholder in one of those giant, faceless New York corporations. When she learns of wrongdoing on the company's board, she sets out to straighten things up. Of course, the bigwigs have different ideas. The film is a continuing series of gentle swipes at big business framed by delightful comic vignettes with Judy at her best. Douglas is in fine form as one of the board members who falls under Judy's luminous spell. ★★★½ VHS: $19.99

Solo

(1996, 106 min, US, Norberto Barba) *Mario Van Peebles, William Sadler, Barry Corbin, Adrien Brody.* With Hollywood's mega-action stars becoming as aged as some pungent French cheese, there exists a great opportunity for a young studling to emerge and take center stage. No, Mario, get off the pedestal; you're not the one. Van Peebles can't pull it off in this tediously flaccid sci-fi actioner. He plays an android with a heart who discovers that his maker, the U.S. Army, is using him for something *really* bad. The pacing is deadly, the acting stultifying and the story so hackneyed as to make *Daylight* seem like poetry. ★ VHS: $9.99; DVD: $14.99

Solomon & Gaenor

(2000, 100 min, Wales, Paul Morrison) *Ioan Gruffudd, Nia Roberts.* Evoking the simple yet stirring discovery of first love in a grand cinematic gesture, this sweetly romantic Welsh film was deservedly nominated for an Academy Award for Best Foreign-Language Film. In a poor Welsh village in 1911, a young coal miner's daughter and a Jewish youth begin a clandestine affair. His faith unbeknownst to her, the lovers attempt to forge a future all the while growing anti-Semitism grips the town. Director Morrison is masterful in capturing the pangs and delights of falling in love, and the two stars have a wonderful chemistry. Though the subplot of culture clash may not resonant with the same intensity, this is nevertheless a gripping, heartfelt examination of a budding, forbidden romance. (Welsh with English subtitles) ★★★½ VHS: $21.99; DVD: $29.99

Some Came Running

(1958, 136 min, US, Vincente Minnelli) *Frank Sinatra, Shirley MacLaine, Dean Martin, Martha Hyer*. Sinatra stars as an author who stirs things up in his sleepy hometown after several years away. Disillusioned, Sinatra steps off a bus with a good-natured floozy (MacLaine) in tow, and contrary to his family's wishes, manages to run into trouble at every turn. Martin also stars as Sinatra's buddy, who accompanies the ex-G.I. on his self-destructive binges. Though the film has a few slow stretches, the first-rate performances and the stunning conclusion make it all worthwhile. ★★★ VHS: $19.99

Some Girls

(1988, 94 min, US, Michael Hoffman) *Patrick Dempsey, Jennifer Connelly, Andre Gregory, Lila Kedrova*. This refreshingly offbeat youth comedy stars a hilariously deadpan Dempsey as a lovesick college student who visits his girlfriend (Connelly) and her family during Christmas break. Dempsey expects a jolly good time, but gets more than he bargained for when he discovers that her family is more than a little eccentric. It's *You Can't Take It with You* meets *Risky Business*, and to director Hoffman and writer Rupert Walters' credit, the majority of the film's many gags score exceedingly well. ★★★ VHS: $19.99

Some Kind of Hero

(1982, 97 min, US, Michael Pressman) *Richard Pryor, Margot Kidder, Ray Sharkey*. Based on James Kirkwood's novel, this disappointing adaptation stars Pryor as a former Vietnam POW returning home after six years in captivity who finds trouble adjusting to civilian life. ★★ VHS: $14.99

Some Kind of Wonderful

(1987, 93 min, US, Howard Deutch) *Eric Stoltz, Lea Thompson, Mary Stuart Masterson*. More teenage angst courtesy of John Hughes, with Stoltz in love with Thompson; Masterson in love with Stoltz. Hughes' bucket from the well must be worn out by now. ★★ VHS: $14.99

Some Like It Hot

(1959, 122 min, US, Billy Wilder) *Jack Lemmon, Tony Curtis, Marilyn Monroe, Joe E. Brown, George Raft, Pat O'Brien*. Director Wilder's masterpiece rates as one of the funniest American comedies of all time, and it only gets better with age. Lemmon and Curtis, at their comic best, star as down-and-out musicians in 1920s Chicago who, upon witnessing the St. Valentine's Day Massacre, don wig and dress and join an all-

female band to escape the murderous thugs looking for them. Marilyn is Sugar Kane, the band's beautiful blonde singer who the boys are enraptured by. Curtis romances MM (out of drag, of course) and Lemmon is courted by millionaire Brown ("Well, nobody's perfect"). They just don't come any better than this. ★★★★ VHS: $9.99; DVD: $14.99

Some Mother's Son

(1996, 112 min, Ireland, Terry George) *Helen Mirren, Fionnula Flanagan, Aidan Gillen, David O'Hara, John Lynch*. Director George and writer-producer Jim Sheridan (*In the Name of the Father*), are back in "the Troubles" once more with this poignant, powerful glimpse into Northern Ireland politics. As seen through the eyes of two mothers whose sons have been imprisoned as IRA terrorists, *Some Mother's Son* explores the divergent viewpoints and impassioned partisanship dividing that country. Mirren gives an excellent performance as Kathleen, an apolitical schoolteacher whose life is torn apart when her teenaged son is arrested. She befriends Annie (a terrific Flanagan), the plain-spoken, IRA-supporting mother of another teen arrested with Kathleen's son. As good as the Irish characterizations and portrayals are, they are offset by one-dimensional depictions of the British, which only diminishes the film's authority and structure. ★★★ VHS: $19.99

Somebody Up There Likes Me

(1956, 113 min, US, Robert Wise) *Paul Newman, Steve McQueen, Robert Loggia, Pier Angeli, Sal Mineo*. Newman's fine performance as boxer Rocky Graziano highlights this sturdy biography, tracing the fighter's life from youth to champion. ★★★ VHS: $19.99

Someone Like You

(2001, 95 min, US, Tony Goldwyn) *Ashley Judd, Hugh Jackman, Greg Kinnear, Ellen Barkin, Marisa Tomei*. Sandra Bullock watch your back; Ashley Judd is trying hard to capture your share of the romantic comedy market. Actually, trying *too* hard, as she overacts, overemotes and overcutes in an attempt to bring some life into a character who's underwritten at the expense of her dialogue. Based on Laura Zigman's acerbic novel "Animal Husbandry," characters disappear within the massive yet predictable plot, where Judd's talk-show coordinator finds her personal man-as-bull theories attracting a national audience amid her desperate romantic life. Even the book's chapter headings remain, for those not paying attention. Jackman proves a good foil in a subdued role, while Kinnear plays a typical two-dimensional male ass. Snippets of scenes shine, but overall, like a wax bottle candy, there's not enough sweetness in the center of this confection. ★★ VHS: $102.99; DVD: $29.99

Someone to Love

(1987, 109 min, US, Henry Jaglom) *Henry Jaglom, Orson Welles, Sally Kellerman*. Jaglom hosts a party inviting all acquaintances who would find themselves alone on Valentine's Day. Desperately driven to understand why successful and attractive people find true love elusive, he "circulates" among the guests, probing their lives. Welles, in his final screen appearance, hypnotizes the audience with his controversial views on the affairs of the heart. ★★★ VHS: $39.99

Someone to Watch over Me

(1987, 113 min, US, Ridley Scott) *Tom Berenger, Mimi Rogers, Lorraine Bracco, Jerry Orbach*. The director of *Alien* and *Thelma and Louise* brings his hyperbolic visual sense to this tension-filled love story about a cop from Queens (Berenger) who falls in love with the socialite-turned-mob informer (Rogers) he's been assigned to protect. Between the mobsters and his wife (the splendid Bracco), his life is in constant jeopardy. ★★★ VHS: $14.99; DVD: $24.99

Something for Everyone

(1970, 112 min, GB, Harold Prince) *Michael York, Angela Lansbury, Anthony Corlan, Jane Carr*. Broadway director Prince's directorial film debut is this witty black comedy that stars a seductive York as a cunning, amoral opportunist who insinuates himself into the household of the flamboyant Countess von Ornstein of Bavaria (Lansbury). Once inside, he proceeds to infiltrate the bedrooms of both her and her son. Lansbury camps it up wonderfully, acting as though she were a drag queen on stage at a New York fashion show, unveiling her fabulous frocks to an enraptured audience. Corlan plays Helmut, the countess' gay teenage son, whose dark and sullen good looks prove to be a nice contrast to York's fair complexion. Carr plays Lansbury's corpulent daughter who has the last laugh. Sly fun and sophistication abound in this charming gem. ★★★½

Something of Value

(1957, 113 min, US, Richard Brooks) *Rock Hudson, Sidney Poitier, Wendy Hiller*. Compelling screen version of Robert C. Ruark's best-selling novel about the Mau Mau uprising in Kenya and the effect it has on two friends, one black, one white. ★★★ VHS: $24.99

Something to Talk About

(1995, 101 min, US, Lasse Hallström) *Julia Roberts, Dennis Quaid, Robert Duvall, Kyra Sedgwick, Gena Rowlands*. Roberts demonstrates a certain charm, but neither she nor a rather capable cast is able to gloss over a rather contrived and pedestrian screenplay. She plays a well-to-do wife who discovers her husband (Quaid) is having an affair. To figure things out, she retreats with her spunky adolescent daughter to the horse ranch run by her stoic father (Duvall). Her husband attempts to win her back. Written by Callie Khouri (*Thelma and Louise*), the film is all-the-more disappointing as it tries to be a serious if comedic examination of adultery and reconciliation but can only address its concerns in superficial, episodic skits. ★★ VHS: $14.99; DVD: $19.99

Something Wicked This Way Comes

(1983, 94 min, US, Jack Clayton) *Jason Robards, Jonathan Pryce, Pam Grier*. Ray Bradbury wrote the screenplay based on his own novel about a mysterious carnival's visit to a turn-of-the-century Midwestern town. Full of wonderfully magic moments, redolent with evil, this film captures the essence of a young boy's imagination — one who thinks the carnival's proprietor may have demonic origins. (Letterboxed) ★★★ VHS: $14.99; DVD: $24.99

Something Wild

(1986, 113 min, US, **Jonathan Demme**) *Melanie Griffith, Jeff Daniels, Ray Liotta, Margaret Colin.* The screwball comedy is given a violent twist by director Demme. When businessman Daniels skips out on a lunch bill, he encounters sexy, wild Griffith, who proceeds to abduct him and take him on the ride of his life. Liotta is a standout as Griffith's psychotic ex-husband. A totally original road movie which is something of a cross between *Bringing Up Baby* and *Blue Velvet.* ★★★½ VHS: $7.99; DVD: $19.99

Sometimes a Great Notion

(1971, 114 min, US, **Paul Newman**) *Henry Fonda, Paul Newman, Richard Jaeckel, Michael Sarrazin, Lee Remick.* A first-rate cast distinguishes this absorbing drama set in the Oregon woodlands about a logging family, headed by patriarch Fonda, whose decision to ignore a local strike brings about tragedy. Jaeckel received a well-deserved Oscar nomination, due mostly to an amazing drowning scene. (aka: *Never Give an Inch*) ★★★ VHS: $9.99

Sometimes Aunt Martha Does Dreadful Things

(1971, 95 min, US, **Thomas Casey**) Unintentional laughs abound in this little-known camp classic about a fugitive killer who both hides from the law and lives "in sin" with his young male lover by parading around in drag pretending to be the boy's aunt. As bad as it sounds, the film certainly gives in to gay stereotyping (and much more); but it's good for a laugh. ★

Sometimes They Come Back

(1991, 100 min, US, **Tom McLoughlin**) *Tim Matheson, Brooke Adams.* Stephen King once again returns to that tired — er, sleepy — New England town for this tale of a college professor/author (big stretch, eh?) who is haunted by ghosts from his past — literally. This made-for-TV movie boasts additional footage for the home video release. ★★ VHS: $14.99; DVD: $14.99

Somewhere I'll Find You

(1942, 117 min, US, **Wesley Ruggles**) *Clark Gable, Lana Turner.* Full of crackling dialogue, this handsome romantic adventure features its two stars in larger-than-life form in the story of correspondent Gable falling for reporter Turner, but who ignores his true feelings because his younger brother is also in love with her. All three find themselves hurried from the safety of pre-Pearl Harbor America into the thick of war-torn Indochina. The abrasive ending befits the mindset of an America at war. ★★★ VHS: $19.99

Somewhere in Time

(1980, 103 min, US, **Jeannot Szwarc**) *Christopher Reeve, Jane Seymour, Christopher Plummer, Teresa Wright.* Old-fashioned romantic fantasy with Reeve as a contemporary playwright who falls in love with a turn-of-the-century actress (Seymour) he sees in a portrait, and wills himself back in time. The film never quite delivers on its intriguing premise, though John Barry's beautiful score and the attractive scenery certainly help. ★★½ VHS: $14.99; DVD: $29.99

Sommersby

(1993, 117 min, US, **Jon Amiel**) *Richard Gere, Jodie Foster, Bill Pullman, James Earl Jones, William Windom.* This sweeping post–Civil War adaptation of *The Return of Martin Guerre* is a pleasant Hollywood rarity: an American remake of a European art-house hit which *doesn't* ruin all memory of the original. Gere plays Jack Sommersby, a wealthy Confederate landowner who returns to his little valley several years after the war. Long thought dead, he is greeted with a mixture of disbelief, distrust and cautious joy by both the townsfolk and his wife, marvelously portrayed by Foster. Ultimately, Gere's Sommersby is so gentle and loving that Foster can't believe he is really her husband, who had been an abusive alcoholic when he left for the war. Which raises the question: Is he who he claims to be? Director Amiel superbly recreates the antebellum South, but what makes it all worthwhile is the dazzling on-screen magnetism between Foster and Gere. ★★★½ VHS: $9.99; DVD: $14.99

Son of Dracula

(1943, 78 min, US, **Robert Siodmak**) *Lon Chaney, Jr., Evelyn Ankers.* Chaney takes over for Bela Lugosi in this successful and very atmospheric sequel with Dracula now terrorizing the American South. ★★★ VHS: $14.99

Son of Frankenstein

(1939, 99 min, US, **Rowland V. Lee**) *Boris Karloff, Bela Lugosi, Basil Rathbone.* Karloff would appear as "The Monster" for the last time in this genuinely eerie chiller, the third in the *Frankenstein* series. Rathbone is the chip off the old block who tries to make the monster "good" and clear the family name. Like father, like son, and things go awry. In an effective performance, Lugosi plays Ygor. (Sequel: *Ghost of Frankenstein*) ★★★ VHS: $14.99

Son of Godzilla

(1967, 86 min, Japan, **Joh Fukuda**) When Godzilla lays an egg, out pops another living butane lighter, this one called Minya. Godzilla and son decide to tear up the town in celebration of Jr.'s coming out party — even though Allstate doesn't cover acts of Godzilla. ★½

Son of Kong

(1933, 70 min, US, **Ernest B. Schoedsack**) *Robert Armstrong, Helen Mack, Victor Wong.* When *King Kong* became a hit, RKO rushed this sequel out the same year — but it's still lots of fun. Carl Denham (Armstrong), hounded by law suits for all the damages that big old ape did, flees New York for the solitude of Skull Island, only to run into Kong, Jr. Master animator Willis O'Brien continued his best work with lots of battles with giant animals of one era or another (some of it left over from the first film), with a heartrending ending accentuated by a fine Max Steiner score. ★★★ VHS: $19.99

Son of Paleface

(1952, 95 min, US, **Frank Tashlin**) *Bob Hope, Jane Russell, Roy Rogers.* This very funny sequel to the Hope-Russell hit comedy, *The Paleface*, tops the original. Bob plays a timid Harvard graduate who heads West to claim an inheritance and tangles with outlaws, Rogers, Trigger and gorgeous showgirl Jane. ★★★½ VHS: $14.99

Son of the Shark

(1995, 85 min, France, **Agnes Merlet**) *Ludovic Vandendaele, Erick Da Silva.* Imagine if you will a kiddie version of *A Clockwork Orange.* Maybe a little *Natural Born Killers* thrown in and plenty of *The 400 Blows*, just to be considered an homage. Getting a clear picture yet? If you have one, you've got the story of Martin and Simon, two brothers abandoned by their mother, abused by their father and split up by the state because they are too dangerous together. The film is powerful and gritty, and the photography has a mist to it and is dark and depressing, as much of their life must be. These kids hold the whole town at bay while they watch movies at the local theatre, with one projecting the film while the other watches it eating popcorn. It must be tough to be a French parent these days. (French with English subtitles) ★★★ VHS: $19.99

Something Wild

549

A Song Is Born

(1948, 113 min, US, Howard Hawks) *Danny Kaye, Virginia Mayo, Hugh Herbert, Steve Cochran, Benny Goodman, Louis Armstrong, Lionel Hampton, Tommy Dorsey.* Director Hawks remade his 1942 classic *Ball of Fire*, this time as a musical, with Kaye taking over for Gary Cooper. And though Danny and a fine jazz score are commendable, the film doesn't reach the original's inspired comic heights. But there are laughs to be found. And what a treat to see such '40s music greats as Armstrong, Goodman, Dorsey and Hampton all in one movie. Danny's constant costar, Mayo, is attractive but lacks the snap and magnetism Barbara Stanwyck brought to the first film. ★★½

The Song of Bernadette

(1943, 156 min, US, Henry King) *Jennifer Jones, William Eythe, Charles Bickford, Vincent Price, Lee J. Cobb, Anne Revere, Gladys Cooper.* Jones won an Oscar for her moving performance in this sentimental but well-crafted drama as the young French girl who sees a vision of the Virgin Mary, which inspires her to become a nun and causes her small town to turn against her. ★★★ VHS: $14.99

Song of Love

(1947, 119 min, US, Clarence Brown) *Katharine Hepburn, Paul Henried, Robert Walker.* A glossy though dramatically uneven biography of Robert and Clara Schuman (Henreid, Hepburn) and their friendship with young composer Johannes Brahms (Walker). ★★½ VHS: $19.99

Song of the Loon

(1970, 90 min, US, Andrew Herbert) *Jon Iverson, Morgan Royce, Lancer Ward.* Long considered a "classic" of independent gay filmmaking, *Song of the Loon* is an earnest tale of love and brotherhood among men as well as a naturalist's delight. Set in northern California in the 1870s, the story follows the odyssey of Ephraim McKeever, a young man in search of love and happiness. By using non-professional actors, not showing hardcore sex scenes and featuring such silly lines as "Dammit, you're beautiful," the film is at times awkward and dated, but it is also a welcome change from the normal X-rated fare that abounds. ★★ VHS: $24.99

A Song to Remember

(1945, 112 min, US, Charles Vidor) *Cornel Wilde, Merle Oberon, Paul Muni.* The life of famed composer Frederic Chopin — his music and his love affair with author George Sand. Wilde stars as Chopin, Oberon makes a lovely Sand, and Muni appears as Chopin's mentor. Good acting can't elevate this above the ordinary. ★★½ VHS: $19.99

Sonny Boy

(1990, 96 min, US, Martin Carroll) *David Carradine, Paul L. Smith, Brad Dourif.* This extremely weird film features a family that would feel right at home in John Waters' Mortville. A dark tale of family love gone berserk, *Sonny Boy* features Smith as a 300-pound psychotic crook who with his wife, Pearl, raises an orphan boy to become an animal-like killing machine to advance their criminal enterprise. The role of the sweet, loving mother Pearl is played oddly enough by Carradine, who plays the part entirely as a woman — wearing polka-dot dresses, makeup and jewelry and

Soul Food

sensible hair, although she does like her occasional cigar. As they go about their murderous ways, all involved ignore the fact that Pearl is a transvestite, which only adds to the pleasure of this mean-spirited oddity. ★★½ VHS: $89.99

The Sons of Katie Elder

(1965, 122 min, US, Henry Hathaway) *John Wayne, Dean Martin, Michael Anderson, Jr., Earl Holliman.* Solid western action with Wayne, Martin, Anderson and Holliman as the title characters, out to avenge their mother's murder. ★★★ VHS: $9.99; DVD: $29.99

Sons of the Desert

(1933, 69 min, US, William A. Seiter) *Stan Laurel, Oliver Hardy.* Henpecked Laurel and Hardy want to go to the national convention of their lodge, The Sons of the Desert, but their wives won't let them. So like little boys are wont to do, they sneak off anyway, only to get caught when Stanley ends up in a newsreel. The title of this Laurel and Hardy masterpiece is also the name of their fan club — still in existence today! ★★★½

Sophie's Choice

(1982, 157 min, US, Alan J. Pakula) *Meryl Streep, Kevin Kline, Peter MacNicol.* A tour de force Academy Award—winning performance by Streep distinguishes this powerful adaptation of William Styron's sweeping novel. Kline is Streep's volatile lover, who learns the horrid secret of Sophie's Auschwitz survival. MacNicol is Stingo, a young author who falls in love with Sophie. The film is divided between Sophie's harrowing life at Auschwitz and her post-war years as a guilt-ridden survivor living in Brooklyn. Both time frames offer heartrending, compassionate drama, and in bringing Sophie to life in the two time periods, Streep delivers a portrayal of such nuance and emotion that it certainly ranks as one of the greatest performances ever given in the history of American cinema. ★★★½ VHS: $9.99; DVD: $19.99

Sorcerer

(1977, 122 min, US, William Friedkin) *Roy Scheider, Bruno Cremer.* From the director of *The French Connection* comes this expensive remake

of H.G. Clouzot's classic *Wages of Fear.* Just as spine-tingling but not nearly as involving as the original. Scheider plays one of four desperate hoods now in hiding in a seedy Latin American town trying to buy their way out. Their only hope: help extinguish a raging oil fire by driving their trucks loaded with nitroglycerine on a suicide run over almost impassable roads. ★★½ VHS: $19.99; DVD: $24.99

Sorceress

(1989, 98 min, France, Suzanne Schiffman) *Christine Boisson, Tcheky Karyo.* Though this is only her first film, Schiffman, longtime collaborator of François Truffaut, has made a decidedly self-assured and moving drama of religious beliefs, hypocrisy and persecution. Set in a peasant village during the 13th century, a young monk, sent by the Church to ferret out heretics, comes in conflict with a mysterious young woman who lives in the forest, who tends to the health of the villagers by making and administering herbal potions. This is a moving, complex drama that explores not only religious themes but also the role and persecution of women during the Middle Ages. (English-language version) ★★★ VHS: $29.99

The Sorrow and the Pity

(1970, 261 min, France, Marcel Ophüls) A landmark film in cinema history, one of the most brilliant and shattering films ever made. Ophüls creates a sense of living history as he examines France's occupation by Germany during WWII, and France's complicity in the virulent racial and religious bigotry that defined the Third Reich. ★★★★ VHS: $94.99; DVD: $49.99

Sorry, Wrong Number

(1948, 89 min, US, Anatole Litvak) *Barbara Stanwyck, Burt Lancaster, Wendell Corey.* Based on the acclaimed radio program (which starred Agnes Moorehead), this stylized thriller features Stanwyck in an electrifying performance as a bedridden wife who overhears a murder plot on her phone's party line — unaware that she is the intended victim. Lancaster plays her scheming husband. (Remade in 1989) ★★★ VHS: $14.99

Sotto Sotto

(1984, 104 min, Italy, Lina Wertmüller) *Enrico Montesano, Veronica Lario, Luisa de Santis.* The prototypical machismo-obsessed Italian male must come to grips with the sexual freedoms and diversity of the late 20th century in this wild sexual comedy that is both illuminating and troubling in its depiction of two women in love with each other. Set in Naples, the story revolves around Ester and Adele, two friends who witness two women kissing. This initiates a revelation, and the two fall in (unconsummated) love. Then Ester's husband discovers his wife is in love with someone else, and sets out to discover who. (Italian with English subtitles) ★★½

Soul Food

(1997, 114 min, US, George Tillman, Jr.) *Vanessa Williams, Vivica A. Fox, Nia Long, Michael Beach, Mekhi Phifer, Irma P. Hall, Brandon Hammond.* Don't let *Soul Food*'s "Afterschool Special" mushiness put you off. Yes, it's maudlin, but this story about the trials and tribulations of a black family struggling for the good life in Chicago is refreshing, well-acted, funny and well-paced entertainment. Williams (a high-powered lawyer), Fox (a stay-at-home mom) and Long (a salon owner) star as the three female offspring of a powerful, aging family matriarch (Hall, in a fabulously sturdy portrayal). The story unfolds from the point-of-view of Fox's young son Ahmed (Hammond), who provides the narrations and beholds his grandmother (known as Mother Joe) with reverential awe. Chock full of effervescent humor and featuring a swaggering soundtrack by Kenneth "Babyface" Edmonds and Boyz II Men. ★★★ VHS: $14.99; DVD: $24.99

Soul Man

(1986, 101 min, US, Steve Miner) *C. Thomas Howell, Rae Dawn Chong, James Earl Jones.* Ineffectual social satire with Howell as a white student masquerading as an African-American in order to qualify for a scholarship to Harvard Law School. Chong is Howell's girlfriend fooled by the charade. ★★

The Sound of Music

(1965, 172 min, US, Robert Wise) *Julie Andrews, Christopher Plummer, Eleanor Parker, Richard Hadyn, Angela Cartwright.* This classic adaptation of Rodgers and Hammerstein's Broadway musical has long been a family favorite — and one of the most popular films of all time. Based on the true experiences of the Von Trapp family, the film stars Andrews as Maria, an Austrian novice

South Park: Bigger, Longer & Uncut

who becomes governess to seven children during the onset of WWII. A sentimental concoction of schmaltz and over-kill which still manages to work in spite of it all. The R&H score includes "Do Re Mi" and "Climb Every Mountain." Winner of 4 Academy Awards, including Best Picture. (Letterboxed VHS available for $19.99) ★★★★ VHS: $14.99; DVD: $29.99

Sounder

(1972, 105 min, US, Martin Ritt) *Cicely Tyson, Paul Winfield, Kevin Hooks, Taj Mahal.* Tyson and Winfield both received much-deserved Oscar nominations for their superlative performances in this sensitive and beautifully crafted drama about a black sharecropping family's struggle in the early 1930s. As their young son, Hooks is outstanding. ★★★★ VHS: $14.99

Sour Grapes

(1998, 91 min, US, Larry David) *Steven Weber, Craig Bierko, Matt Keeslar, Karen Sillas.* Writer David flogs his dead "Seinfeld" horse in his disappointing directing debut. While David's usual sharp (and exceedingly bitter) dialogue and situations are present, the pacing is leaden, and poor timing makes the jokes crash and burn. Weber mimics Seinfeld as he and Bierko do their best to be as unlikable as possible. The creaky premise involves slot machine winnings and much coincidence; David seems to be taking funny situations and desperately trying to cram them into a plot. ★½ VHS: $14.99; DVD: $14.99

South Central

(1991, 99 min, US, Steve Anderson) *Glenn Plummer, Carl Lumbly.* Set in 1981, this wildly violent and highly entertaining history of crack and L.A. street gangs is based on the real-life story of West Coast drug dealing gangsters, the Crips. The film's coke-addled hero, Bobby Johnson (Plummer), soon learns that killing rival pimps, freebasing, smoking angel dust and blowing out a deceitful brother's private parts with a .44 magnum isn't as cool as quietly reading Muslim literature and "rejecting the circle of hate that society inflicts on the black man." Covers much of the same ground nearly as effectively as *Boyz n the Hood*. ★★★ VHS: $14.99; DVD: $14.99

South Pacific

(1958, 150 min, US, Joshua Logan) *Mitzi Gaynor, Rossano Brazzi, John Kerr, France Nuyen, Juanita Hall, Ray Walston.* Rodgers and Hammerstein's landmark Broadway musical is given the royal treatment in this lush adaptation. Gaynor (in the Mary Martin role) plays an American nurse who finds love while stationed in the South Seas during WWII. Hall sings the haunting "Bali H'ai." (Letterboxed VHS available for $19.99) (Remade in 2001) ★★★ VHS: $14.99; DVD: $24.99

South Park: Bigger, Longer & Uncut

(1999, 80 min, US, Trey Parker) *Voices of: Trey Parker, Matt Stone, Mary Kay Bergman, Isaac Hayes, George Clooney, Brent Spiner, Minnie Driver, Dave Foley, Eric Idle.* Hilarious, irreverent, tasteless and a brilliant social satire for added good measure, *South Park: Bigger, Longer & Uncut* expands upon its 23-minute TV episode sitcom format to create one of the most funniest and shrewdly observed comedies in years. Yes, a lot of its humor is scatological, and the animation is less-

than stellar, and it appears "fuck" is uttered every twenty seconds or so. But beyond the juvenile façade of toilet humor and sex jokes is a scintillating satire of contemporary mores and, in particular, an appropriately timely jab at censorship, the MPAA, and societal and parental responsibility. The story — told in numerous, upbeat musical production numbers which should have Broadway taking notice — follows the consequences when Stan, Kyle, Cartman and Kenny go to see their favorite TV characters, Terrance and Phillip, in their new theatrical release not meant for kids. The parallels are delicious. And though this *South Park* is definitely not for kids, its humor is fast, furious, ferocious, fresh, flip, foul . . . you know, all the "f" words. ★★★★ VHS: $14.99; DVD: $29.99

South Riding

(1938, 85 min, GB, Victor Saville) *Ralph Richardson, Edna Best, Glynis Johns, Edmund Gwenn, John Clements, Ann Todd.* Trying to condense Winifred Holtby's sprawling tale of local politics and social intrigue into a mere 85 minutes, *South Riding* moves along at a furious clip, setting up and then forgetting plot lines, suggesting others, painting in broad strokes this "typical" British community — leaving the details to be filled in by our own shared experiences. Richardson heads the cast as a husband who is land rich and cash poor, drained by an institutionalized wife (Todd) and a daughter (a spirited Johns) in dreadful need of public schooling. Thanks to a quorum of fine performances, the film comes alive like some incipient episode of "Masterpiece Theatre." ★★★ VHS: $24.99

Southern Comfort

(1981, 106 min, US, Walter Hill) *Keith Carradine, Powers Boothe, Fred Ward, Peter Coyote, Franklin Seales.* Competent action film (reminiscent of *Deliverance*) about a group of National Guardsmen who are forced to fight for their lives in the Louisiana swamps when gun-toting Cajuns come their way. ★★½ VHS: $9.99; DVD: $14.99

A Southern Yankee

(1948, 90 min, US, Edward Sedgwick) *Red Skelton, Arlene Dahl, Brian Donlevy.* The ever-hilarious Skelton stars in this Civil War comedy about a buffoonish bellhop who is accidentally recruited to spy for the Union Army. Along the way, he falls for a Southern belle (Dahl), inadvertently foils the Rebels and immortalizes the line, "My, it's so nice to be among the magnolias again." ★★★ VHS: $19.99

The Southerner

(1945, 91 min, US, Jean Renoir) *Zachary Scott, Beulah Bondi, Betty Field, Norman Lloyd, Percy Kilbride, J. Carrol Naish.* A naturalistic portrayal of one family's struggle to start a farm in South. Tied to the land for better or worse, the Tuckers endure poverty, disease, and flood with dignity, humor, and a deep store of hope. Though not credited, novelist William Faulkner contributed to Renoir's sparse, authentic sounding dialogue. Great performances from the cast. ★★★★ VHS: $19.99; DVD: $19.99

Southie

(1998, 95 min, US, John Shea) *Donnie Wahlberg, Rose McGowan, Anne Meara, Jimmy Cummings,*

Amanda Peet, Lawrence Tierney. A fairly routine entry in the criminal-gone-legit-gets-sucked-back-into-his-old-ways subgenre. Donnie's a former alcoholic and punk who comes back to South Boston (referred to here as the toughest neighborhood in America, though based on this film, there are sections of Schenectady that cause considerably more unease) for a wedding. After being refused legitimate union work because of a misunderstanding, and seeing his mother's escalating medical bills, Donnie reluctantly enters into a shady deal with some former cronies. Vaguely TV movie-ish, this underwhelming film still manages to make one care about the characters despite all the rough edges. ★★ VHS: $102.99; DVD: $14.99

Soviet Spy

(1961, 130 min, France, Yves Ciampi) *Thomas Holtzman.* This docudrama presents the case of Richard Sorge, a German journalist covering WWII in Japan. Official records show that Sorge was hanged as a Soviet spy in 1944. The film explores this mystery man's life, beginning with conflicting opinions by his associates on his alleged espionage activities and then moving up to a reenactment of the events that led to his capture. A very interesting exploration into the life and role of a possible Soviet spy. (French with English subtitles) ★★★

Soylent Green

(1973, 97 min, US, Richard Fleischer) *Charlton Heston, Edward G. Robinson, Leigh Taylor-Young, Chuck Connors.* This frighteningly prescient sci-fi tale about the dangers of the "greenhouse effect" was made long before the term became a popular buzzword. Heston plays a hardened New York cop who stumbles onto the secret of Soylent Green, a nutritional wafer used to feed the masses. Robinson is excellent in his final role as Heston's aging roommate who can remember the halcyon days of Earth when it was still green. ★★½ VHS: $14.99

Space Cowboys

(2000, 129 min, US, Clint Eastwood) *Clint Eastwood, Tommy Lee Jones, James Garner, Donald Sutherland, James Cromwell, Marcia Gay Harden, William Devane, Courtney B. Vance.* Director Eastwood leaves the wide open spaces of his beloved West for the last frontier of space to tell an entertaining tale of heroism and friendship. A highly enjoyable comic adventure, *Space Cowboys* could get its inspiration from John Glenn's history-making trip into space, made at the age of 77. The story follows four former test pilots who train for a space mission even though they've all been retired for years — and have never been into space. Eastwood is the laconic leader of the group, an engineer whose knowledge of a crippled satellite makes him essential to its rescue. When he demands that his old crew (Jones, Garner, Sutherland) accompany him, they have a chance to realize a 40-year-old dream. Eastwood is in a lighter, breezier mood here, making the most of some genuinely funny moments that's performed by a relaxed, in-charge ensemble. These four veteran actors work splendidly together, able to switch from comedy to action mode — two genres in which each has had success — without missing a beat. ★★★ VHS: $19.99; DVD: $26.99

Space Jam

(1996, 87 min, US, Joe Pytka) *Michael Jordan, Wayne Knight, Bill Murray, Bugs Bunny, Daffy Duck.* Falling far short of its intended "Pro basketball meets *Roger Rabbit*" aspirations, Jordan's debut does not bode well for his future success as a movie star, although fans of the sports legend will probably be satisfied and younger viewers will enjoy the loud, colorful basketball sequences. Jordan teams up with a plethora of Looney Tunes characters in a game of intergalactic and multidimensional basketball when some evil (but very lovable) aliens try to kidnap Bugs Bunny and company. Though the animation is good, the humor is forced and the film is padded out to feature length with some boring montage sequences. ★★ VHS: $14.99; DVD: $19.99

Space Thing

(1968, 70 min, US, B. Ron Elliott) *April Playmate, Bart Black, Mercy Mee, Ronnie Runningboard.* A sci-fi buff dreams himself into a universe of intergalactic space-age sex and satellites, complete with an insatiable bisexual queen mother and her voluptuous female crew. A low-budget extravaganza clearly inspired by the Ed Wood, Jr. school of filmmaking. ★ VHS: $24.99; DVD: $24.99

Spaceballs

(1987, 96 min, US, Mel Brooks) *Mel Brooks, John Candy, Rick Moranis, Bill Pullman.* A misfire for Brooks, this lame and untimely parody of George Lucas' *Star Wars* series features the usual Brooks assault of visual and verbal puns, which more often than not fail to hit their desired target. Die-hard "Star-heads" may be amused, but *Hardware Wars* did it better and earlier. The best scene of the film is an on-target takeoff on *Alien* and the classic Warner Brothers cartoon "One Froggy Evening." ★★ VHS: $9.99; DVD: $24.99

Spacecamp

(1986, 108 min, US, Harry Winer) *Kate Capshaw, Lea Thompson.* A group of teenagers attending a NASA summer camp are accidentally launched into space, where they're on their own to get back to Earth. A very ordinary teen adventure. ★★ VHS: $14.99

Spaghetti House

(1982, 102 min, Italy/GB, Guilio Pardisi) *Nino Manfredi, Rita Tushingham.* Manfredi, Italy's master of film comedy, abandons his usual persona to star in this drama of a bungled robbery attempt which results in a tense hostage situation. He plays an outspoken Italian waiter in London who, along with four of his compatriots, is held hostage by three desperate black men. Although this film falls occasionally into depicting easy stereotypes, it also explores race relations, prejudices and the common oppression suffered by both immigrants and blacks in lily-white England. ★★½

The Spanish Prisoner

(1998, 110 min, US, David Mamet) *Campbell Scott, Steve Martin, Ben Gazzara, Felicity Huffman, Ricky Jay, Rebecca Pidgeon.* Scott is a perfect foil in this quintessential Mamet labyrinth of misleading appearances, misplaced trust and superbly executed duplicity. Joe Ross (Scott) is

brilliant at his job, a meticulous man of orderly habits whose innate decency and courtesy make him an easy target for manipulation. Creator of a process which is expected to garner huge profits for his company, he is perturbed by his superior's (Gazzara) reticence in discussing profit sharing. He meets a man (a marvelously underplayed Martin) of apparent wealth and worldliness, who advises young Ross to protect his interests; and plummets into a byzantine abyss in which he is the prime suspect of theft and murder. Layers unfold and red herrings abound as Mamet's trademark clipped, stacatto speech patterns produce phrases which structure Ross' perception of events and dictate reaction to them. An intriguing puzzle which plays on the viewer's own preconceptions and sustains suspense until the final scene. ★★★½ VHS: $19.99; DVD: $29.99

Spanking the Monkey

(1994, 106 min, US, David O. Russell) *Jeremy Davies, Alberta Watson, Benjamin Hendrickson.* Don't let the title fool you. Russell's film is an insightful and offbeat look at love, sexuality and incest. Davies is convincing as a college freshman student, Ray, who must stay home on his summer vacation to take care of his bedridden mother instead of taking a prestigious internship. The relationship between the two becomes increasingly convoluted as the mother looks towards her son to fill the void left by a traveling husband, and Ray's sexual frustrations grow. *Monkey* boasts first-rate acting and a well-written script. And don't let the incest throw you — this is handled in such a subtle way the film went on to win the Audience Popularity Award at the 1994 Sundance Film Festival. ★★★ VHS: $19.99

Sparkle

(1976, 98 min, US, Sam O'Steen) *Philip Michael Thomas, Lonette McKee, Irene Cara, Dwan Smith, Mary Alice.* The trials and tribulations of stardom, as experienced by three sisters during the 1950s rock era. Curtis Mayfield's rousing score highlights this sometimes clichéd story made all the more appealing by its musical numbers and sincere performances. Written by the director Joel Schumacher. ★★½ VHS: $14.99

Sparkler

(1999, 90 min, US, Darren Stein) *Freddie Prinze, Jr., Jaime Kennedy, Park Overall, Veronica Cartwright.* Overall is quite appealing as a trailer-park wife who catches her loutish husband in bed with a friend. She decides to head to Vegas to look up a high school classmate and forget her troubles for a while, and keeps crossing paths with three young men from L.A., who are in Vegas to win their rent money. Meanwhile, her scummy hubby is hot on her trail. This very slight but likable comedy-drama is harmed by trailer trash-bashing and iffy direction, but Overall and *Scream*'s Kennedy and just enough warmth offset the sleaze and cheese. Far better than Stein's horrendous *Jawbreaker*, and where else will you get to see Cartwright do a lewd striptease? ★★ VHS: $14.99

Sparrows

(1926, 84 min, US, William Beaudine) *Mary Pickford.* A gaggle of orphans, a quicksand-infested swamp, a Lindbergh-like kidnapping and 'gators. Fine fixin's for a melodrama.

Keanu Reeves in *Speed*

Pickford, racing through her 30s, plays a waif half her age trying to get her brood out of the Bayou alive. One of the classics of the silent era, which the kids will love as much as the adults. ★★★½ VHS: $24.99; DVD: $29.99

Spartacus

(1960, 184 min, US, Stanley Kubrick) *Kirk Douglas, Peter Ustinov, Laurence Olivier, Jean Simmons, John Gavin, Tony Curtis, Charles Laughton.* This epic adventure is highlighted by remarkable action sequences and strongly developed characterizations, all set against the visual spectacle of Kubrick's discerning eye for locale and cinematic tone. Douglas stars in the title role as a rebel slave who leads the revolt against the Roman Republic. Featuring a cast of (literally) thousands! Music by Alex North. (Letterboxed VHS available for $19.99) ★★★★ VHS: $14.99

Spawn

(1997, 97 min, US, Mark A.Z. Dippe) *Michael Jai White, John Leguizamo, Martin Sheen, Theresa Randle, Nicol Williamson.* Todd McFarlane's *Spawn* is an immensely popular comic book series, an enjoyable and extremely adult animated series on HBO, but a lousy live-action film. White stars as Al Simmons, a government assassin working for mega-evil Jason Wynn (Sheen). When Wynn double-crosses Simmons and has him murdered, Simmons is resurrected as Spawn, a sort of superhero from Hell. It seems that Al was so good at his job that Satan (here called Malebolgia) wants to use him as the General of one of his armies. But Al's love for his wife Wanda and his good heart interfere with Malebolgia's plans and Spawn begins to use his newly acquired powers (and symbiotic suit) on the part of good, sort of. Leguizamo is very good as one of Satan's clown-like emissaries, but the computer-generated effects are awful, and the direction and the script are weak. (Available in an R-rated director's cut and an edited PG-13 rated version) ★★ VHS: $19.99; DVD: $19.99

Speaking Parts

(1989, 93 min, Canada, Atom Egoyan) *Michael McManus, Arsinée Khanjian.* Similar in theme to *sex, lies, and videotape*, this perceptive look at the delicate balance between love and sex in the age of video features the entangled lives of three young people. Lance, a part-time actor and full-time bed-changer at a hotel, becomes the object of desire for both Clara, a scriptwriter intrigued by the physical similarities between Lance and her dead brother, and Lisa, a shy hotel maid who obsessively watches his minor appearances as an extra in films she rents on video. This quietly stylized drama is a dark glimpse into the way people act and how they show themselves to others. ★★★; DVD: $29.99

Special Bulletin

(1983, 105 min, US, Edward Zwick) *Ed Flanders, Kathryn Walker, Rosalind Cash, Roxanne Hart, David Clennon, David Rasche.* Outstanding made-for-TV drama directed by Zwick (*Glory*) about a group of nuclear protestors who, holding a TV reporter and cameraman hostage, threaten to detonate nuclear bombs if warheads in Charleston, South Carolina, are not disarmed. Like Orson Welles' "War of the Worlds," the film is presented as if it were a live news broadcast. Intelligently written, and expertly acted and directed. ★★★½ VHS: $19.99

A Special Day

(1977, 110 min, Italy, Ettore Scola) *Marcello Mastroianni, Sophia Loren.* The day Hitler arrives in Rome to meet with Mussolini is the time setting for this touching drama of an oppressed housewife (Loren) who meets and befriends a troubled homosexual (Mastroianni). Fine performances from the two as well as Scola's realistic treatment make this a memorable film. ★★★

Special Effects

(1985, 90 min, US, Larry Cohen) *Eric Bogosian, Zoe Tamerlis.* Intriguing, top-notch Grade-B thriller with Bogosian as a maniacal movie director who murders an actress, and then hires a look-alike and makes a movie about the killing. Tamerlis plays both actresses. ★★½

The Specialist

(1994, 115 min, US, Luis Llosa) *Sylvester Stallone, Sharon Stone, James Woods, Rod Steiger, Eric Roberts.* Llosa is far better directing explosions than people with this hormone-driven soap opera that pleases the eye as it insults the intelligence. Stallone plays an ex-CIA operative and explosives expert who is hired by hypersexy Stone to wipe out the men (a slumming Steiger and "macho-prissy" Roberts) responsible for her parents' death. But there's a hitch: The bad guys have hired Sly's vengeful ex-partner (the scene-stealing Woods) as their security chief. The steamy shower scene between Stallone and Stone is a sight to behold. ★★ VHS: $9.99; DVD: $19.99

Species

(1995, 111 min, US, Roger Donaldson) *Ben Kingsley, Michael Madsen, Alfred Molina, Forest Whitaker, Marg Helgenberger, Natasha Henstridge.* An unintentionally funny horror film about a half-human, half-*Alien* creature whose attempts at perpetuating her own species by mating with a human male are hampered by a ragtag team of experts. Donaldson's first foray into the field of horror is sabotaged by an incredibly clichéd script, hokey dialogue and lackluster performances. *Species* does feature first-rate special effects, including H.R. Giger's *déjà vu* alien design, and a fetching debut by Henstridge as the monstrous Sil. (Sequel: *Species II*) ★★½ VHS: $9.99; DVD: $14.99

Species II

(1998, 93 min, US, Peter Medak) *Michael Madsen, Natasha Henstridge, Marg Helgenberger, Mykelti Williamson, George Dzundza.* A monstrosity. Henstridge, who was the gorgeous she-bitch Sil in the original, returns this time as Eve, a good half-alien who is the subject of a government research project. But the film's real story concerns as astronaut who contracts the deadly blood of Sil. When he returns to Earth to spread bad DNA through violent sex, it's only a matter ot time until he and Eve meet and mate. A *Species* that did not need to be profligated, *Species II* gives cheesy alien sex and violence a bad name. ★½ VHS: $6.99; DVD: $14.99

Speechless

(1994, 98 min, US, Ron Underwood) *Geena Davis, Michael Keaton, Christopher Reeve, Bonnie Bedelia, Ernie Hudson.* Written before the high-profile relationship of politicos James Carvell and Mary Matalin, this frothy, lightweight battle-of-the-sexes comedy casts Keaton and Davis as rival candidate speechwriters who become romantically involved. Both suffering from insomnia, they meet cutesy late one night, though unaware of each other's political association. Of course, fireworks and misunderstandings fill the air when they learn the truth. It's difficult to fully appreciate a romantic comedy whose political observations are subtler and more compelling than the love story. As the two love birds, Keaton and Davis rattle off some funny exchanges, but their chemistry appears lacking. ★★½ VHS: $9.99

Speed

(1994, 120 min, US, Jan De Bont) *Keanu Reeves, Sandra Bullock, Dennis Hopper, Joe Morton, Jeff Daniels, Alan Ruck.* Entering the realm of action-hero-dom. Reeves stars as a rough-and-ready member of an elite LAPD SWAT team that specializes in disarming the handiwork of even the wiliest of terrorists. Here it's Hopper, who does himself proud as the film's mad bomber. He brews up a brilliant scheme to extort money from the good citizens of L.A. by rigging a bus to blow sky-high if it slows down

S

below 50 mph. Once Reeves boards the ill-fated vehicle and the winning Bullock, a courageous passenger, takes the wheel, the race is on and the action never slows for a second. Despite several sequences that push the boundaries of believability, the film is an entertaining and often amusing diversion. (Letterboxed VHS available for $19.99) (Sequel: *Speed 2: Cruise Control*) ★★★ VHS: $9.99; DVD: $24.99

Speed 2: Cruise Control

(1997, 121 min, US, Jan De Bont) *Sandra Bullock, Jason Patric, Willem Dafoe, Tim Conway.* By *not* appearing in a project, Keanu Reeves may have made the smartest decision of his career by saying "no" to reprising the role of Jack Traven from *Speed* for its sequel. Bullock, however, is not that lucky. She returns in this waterlogged, empty-headed encore, this time set on a cruise ship. She crosses paths, once again, with a mad bomber (the bug-eyed Dafoe). Everything there was to like about the original is absent this second time around. Suspense? None. Excitement? Gone. A clever villain? Watch *Die Hard* again. Director De Bont had too much money, too much control, and too few ideas. (Letterboxed VHS available for $19.99) ★ VHS: $9.99; DVD: $24.99

Spellbound

(1945, 111 min, US, Alfred Hitchcock) *Gregory Peck, Ingrid Bergman, Leo G. Carroll.* Peck stars as the victim of a troubling mental paralysis and Bergman is the analyst determined to unlock the door to his mysterious past. An intriguing, trendsetting work with a dazzling dream sequence designed by Salvador Dali. ★★★½ VHS: $14.99; DVD: $14.99

Spetters

(1981, 127 min, The Netherlands, Paul Verhoeven) *Renée Soutendijk, Rutger Hauer.* Three Dutch youths find themselves at the crossroads of adulthood in this arresting drama. Seeking to escape their working-class destinies, they dream of fame and fortune racing motorcycles, but are sidetracked by the fateful intervention of a scheming hash-slinger (the sultry Soutendijk). A penetrating slice-of-life which incorporates first love, youthful shenanigans, teen suicide, coming out and comaraderie. (Dutch with English subtitles) ★★★

Sphere

(1998, 124 min, US, Barry Levinson) *Dustin Hoffman, Samuel L. Jackson, Sharon Stone, Peter Coyote, Liev Schreiber, Queen Latifah.* Based on the Michael Crichton novel, this imaginative if jumbled sci-fi tale is well served by its high-profile cast and production values, which often mask the rambling narrative and confusing scenario. Hoffman, Jackson and Stone are elite scientists who are summoned by the State Department when a mysterious craft is discovered on the floor of the Pacific Ocean. Setting up home on the sea's bottom in a base called "the Habitat," the crew set out to investigate the ship, which now has a large, shining sphere protecting it. Borrowing a little from *The Abyss* and even *Forbidden Planet*, the story follows the dynamics of the characters' relationships, which provide the most interesting story lines of the film. (VHS available letterboxed or pan & scan) ★★½ VHS: $14.99; DVD: $19.99

Spice World

(1998, 93 min, GB, Bob Spiers) *The Spice Girls, Richard H. Grant, Alan Cumming, George Wendt, Mark McKinney, Roger Moore, Meat Loaf.* A virtual DNA splicing of *A Hard Day's Night* and *Wayne's World*, the campily fun *Spice World* chronicles life on the road with the saucy quintet (Posh, Baby, Scary, Sporty and Ginger). Watch as the Spice Girls crisscross England in their fabulous tour bus to attend cheesy photo sessions and press parties. Cheer as the Spice Girls perform live. Giggle uncontrollably to their pure, unironically humorous sketches and some fairly acute one-liners. Thrill to their climactic dash to their big concert. Never mind the uneven pacing, the static direction or characters as deep as a puddle of leftover syrup after a pancake breakfast; just shamefully revel in the Spice Girls ditties heard about every other minute, and just the overall Spice Girls persona. Surprisingly watchable. ★★★ VHS: $9.99; DVD: $14.99

Spices

(1986, 98 min, India, Ketan Mehta) Set in 1940s British-controlled India, this engaging melodrama deals with the beginnings of the nationalistic rumblings of the colony and specifically one community's reaction to the plight of an oppressed woman. Sanbai, a young, defiant beauty, spurns the advances of a sudebar, the military-backed tax collection force, and is forced to take refuge against his wrath. Initially fearful and reluctant to help, the men and women of the village must make a stand against the injustice and tyranny of a belligerent oppressor. (Hindi with English subtitles) ★★★ VHS: $29.99

The Spider's Stratagem

(1970, 97 min, Italy, Bernardo Bertolucci) *Giulio Brogi, Alida Valli.* This stylish and intelligent political thriller, taken from a Jorge Luis Borges short story, follows a young man's journey to the village of his youth. There he finds the statue of his father (a hero killed 30 years earlier by anti-fascists) has been defaced and

the townsfolk mysteriously hostile. While attempting to discover the truth about his father, he soon finds himself entangled in an increasingly complex web of lies, mysteries and omens. Magnificently staged by director Bertolucci. (Italian with English subtitles) ★★★★ VHS: $29.99

Spiders

(1919, 137 min, Germany, Fritz Lang) Planned as the first installment of a four-part adventure serial, Lang produced only this one entry, a wildly exotic forerunner to the *Indiana Jones* trilogy. With tongue-in-cheek humor, our hero must battle the arch-criminal Lio-Shar and his unsavory gang, the Spiders, as they search for lost Inca treasure, diamonds shaped like the head of a Buddha, as well as devise a plan to dominate the world. Filled with scenes of lost civilizations, human sacrifice and pirates, this big-budget action silent is very interesting and one of the earliest surviving films of the great German filmmaker. (Silent with musical soundtrack) ★★★ VHS: $24.99; DVD: $29.99

Spiders

(2000, 94 min, US, Gary Jones) *Lana Parrilla, Josh Green, Oliver Macready.* Crazy military men inject spiders with alien DNA to create the one-billionth movie "ultimate biological weapon." Shockingly, things go awry, and a mutated spider escapes. Moronic, badly acted cheese is pretty slow for a good half hour, but once the spiders show up, it becomes an entertaining (though still moronic and badly acted) *Aliens* rip-off with better-than-average effects for a low-budget horror flick, plenty of action and a sizable "yecch!" factor. ★★½ VHS: $69.99; DVD: $24.99

Spies

(1928, 88 min, Germany, Fritz Lang) Lang's fascination with futuristic technology, expressionistic design and sweeping adventure reaches a high point in this enthralling spy thriller featuring an evil criminal mastermind and agent #326, a suave super agent. (Silent) ★★★ DVD: $19.99

Ingrid Bergman and Gregory Peck in *Spellbound*

Spies Like Us

(1985, 103 min, US, John Landis) *Chevy Chase, Dan Akyroyd, Bruce Davison.* Until *Nothing But Trouble* came along, this inferior spy comedy was at the bottom of the film pile for Chase and Aykroyd. The guys play bumbling CIA agents who, let loose in the Middle East to serve as decoys, nearly start WWIII. ★½ VHS: $14.99; DVD: $14.99

Spike of Bensonhurst

(1988, 100 min, US, Paul Morrissey) *Sasha Mitchell, Ernest Borgnine, Geraldine Smith, Sylvia Miles.* Written and directed by ex-Warholite Morrissey, this mob comedy stars Mitchell as Spike Fumo, an ambitiously arrogant yet charming two-bit boxer who, on sheer chutzpa, tries to climb his way to the top. Borgnine is great as the befuddled neighborhood don who must contend with Spike after his WASPy daughter falls under his seductively dangerous charms. Miles steals a few scenes as a coke-sniffing congresswoman. ★★★

The Spiral Staircase

(1946, 83 min, US, Robert Siodmak) *Dorothy McGuire, George Brent, Ethel Barrymore, Kent Smith, Rhonda Fleming, Elsa Lanchester.* McGuire gives a superlative performance as a mute servant in this eerie psychological thriller based on the novel "Some Must Watch" by Ethel Lina White. Helen Capel (McGuire), who has not spoken since childhood, is housekeeper for the rich Mrs. Warren (Barrymore) and her family. Helen's life is soon put in danger when a series of murders target the disabled — and strange occurrences begin happening at the Warren household. Atmospheric, suspenseful, and marvelously acted. (Remade in 1975) ★★★½ VHS: $14.99; DVD: $24.99

The Spiral Staircase

(1975, 89 min, US, Peter Collinson) *Jacqueline Bisset, Christopher Plummer, Sam Wanamaker, Elaine Stritch.* Inferior remake of the 1946 Dorothy McGuire thriller with Bisset in the McGuire role as a mute woman terrorized by an unknown killer. ★★ VHS: $14.99

Spirit of '76

(1991, 82 min, US, Lucas Reiner) *David Cassidy, Olivia d'Abo, Julie Brown, Tommy Chong, Carl Reiner, Rob Reiner.* Time machine inventor Cassidy sets sail through time to the year 1776 to retrieve the Constitution of the United States — and other remnants of our past — with the hopes of saving Earth from a cold, grey future. By mistake, however, our traveler winds up in the year 1976 where he encounters a world of Pop Rocks, disco, Apache scarves and mood rings. Funny, entertaining though slight, the film features a good supporting cast that has more familiar faces than a "Love Boat" episode and a foot-stomping soundtrack that'll make you want to do the Hustle. ★★ VHS: $89.99

The Spirit of St. Louis

(1957, 138 min, US, Billy Wilder) *James Stewart, Patricia Smith.* Stewart's absorbing portrayal of aviator Charles Lindbergh highlights this interesting though overlong look at the flyer's early years and his historic, transatlantic flight. (VHS available letterboxed or pan & scan) ★★½ VHS: $19.99

Spirit of the Beehive

(1973, 95 min, Spain, Victor Erice) *Fernando Gomez, Teresa Gimpera, Ana Torrent.* An unforgettable and hypnotic drama by first-time director Erice, and one that features moving performances by two young girls, both non-professional actors. In a remote Castilian village, two children watching *Frankenstein* at a traveling film show become entranced by the image of the monster. The younger girl, a sensitive eight-year-old, believing that he is the spirit of the monster, discovers and befriends a fugitive soldier just before he is captured. A haunting and poetic mood piece. (Spanish with English subtitles) ★★★½ VHS: $29.99

Spirits of the Dead
(Histoires Extraordinaires)

(1967, 117 min, France, Federico Fellini/Louis Malle/Roger Vadim) *Jane Fonda, Peter Fonda, Alain Delon, Terence Stamp, Brigitte Bardot.* An anthology film nominally based on three short stories by Edgar Allan Poe, this mélange of '60s-style, Felliniesque grotesquerie and softcore eroticism only lives up to its title in its final segment. Fonda is the object of Vadim obsession in the first story, "Metzengerstein," about a young countess who believes that her dead cousin has been reincarnated as a magnificent black horse. Brother Peter plays Jane's love. The second story, "William Wilson," by Malle, is much more interesting. It stars Delon as a young libertine whose debaucheries are continually foiled by a mysterious doppelganger. The third story is the best. "Toby Dammit," directed by Fellini. Stamp is an alcoholic and egocentric English actor haunted by the vision of an eerily beautiful young blonde girl playing with a bouncing ball. Only Fellini's segment captures the true spirit of Poe. (Letterboxed) (French with English subtitles) ★★½ VHS: $19.99; DVD: $24.99

Spitfire

(1934, 94 min, US, John Cromwell) *Katharine Hepburn, Robert Young, Ralph Bellamy.* Hepburn plays an uninhibited South Carolina mountain woman who evokes the wrath of the local townsfolk when she kidnaps a baby from its mother because she feels it's not being properly cared for. Unusual and occasionally compelling. ★★½

The Spitfire Grill

(1996, 111 min, US, Lee David Zlotoff) *Alison Elliott, Ellen Burstyn, Marcia Gay Harden, Will Patton, Kieran Mulroney.* This sentimental, deliberately paced tale of an ex-con and her profound impact on the town of Gilead, Maine, is a heartwarming character study set in a gossipy but picturesque rural community. The multiple story lines of determined women trying to establish their place in the world may echo *Fried Green Tomatoes*, but *Spitfire Grill* distinguishes itself with solid female bonding, homespun wisdom and beautiful scenery. Elliott is a marvel as Percy, a stranger with a secret who acts as catalyst to unlock the mysteries of Gilead's most prominent residents. She is moving even in the hokiest of scenes. And though the film ties up its plots and characters in a most contrived conclusion, Zlotoff's subtlety makes for an absorbing little drama which may jerk a tear or two from those less cynical. ★★½ VHS: $19.99; DVD: $19.99

Splash

(1984, 109 min, US, Ron Howard) *Tom Hanks, Daryl Hannah, John Candy.* Director Howard and stars Hanks and Hannah hit it big with this charming comedy about a businessman (Hanks) who falls in love with a mermaid (Hannah). Candy has some amusing scenes as Hank's cohort. ★★★ VHS: $9.99; DVD: $29.99

Splendor in the Grass

(1961, 124 min, US, Elia Kazan) *Natalie Wood, Warren Beatty, Sandy Dennis, Phyllis Diller.* Beginning with screendom's first French kiss, this lyrical and delicate examination of youthful love and the heartache and joy that accompanies it is somewhat sentimental, but after nearly 40 years it's still a heartbreaking and timeless story. Wood's is most accomplished performance, and Beatty, in his screen debut, star as young lovers in 1920s Kansas who are hopelessly trapped by overbearing parents, social class lines and the boundaries of first love. Director Kazan handles his actors and story with great sensitivity, and William Inge won an Oscar for his insightful screenplay. ★★★½ VHS: $14.99; DVD: $19.99

Split Decisions

(1988, 95 min, US, David Drury) *Gene Hackman, Jeff Fahey, Craig Sheffer.* Heavy-handed boxing drama about three generations of fighters, with a *Rocky* slant, as the youngest takes to the ring to avenge his brother's death. ★★ VHS: $14.99

Split Image

(1982, 111 min, US, Ted Kotcheff) *James Woods, Michael O'Keefe, Dennis Hopper, Brian Dennehy, Karen Allen.* A well-acted drama with college student O'Keefe joining Hopper's cult to be with Allen. Dad Dennehy hires deprogrammer Woods to get him back. Good performances accentuate this compelling story. ★★★

Split Second

(1992, 90 min, GB, Tony Maylam) *Rutger Hauer, Neil Duncan, Kim Cattrall, Pete Postlethwaite.* London in the year 2008 is the setting for this *Lethal Weapon*-meets-*Alien* rip-off which, while woefully unoriginal, winds up being hugely entertaining and, at times, hilarious. A potbellied Hauer continually growls, grimaces and "lives on anxiety, caffeine and chocolate" in his pursuit of a serial killer. Duncan, in a witty performance, is Hauer's overeducated new partner and more than once the two actors appear to be on the verge of laughter and/or tongue kissing! Two questions: Why does the Dutch actor playing a British cop have an American accent and what is "Nights in White Satin" doing all over the soundtrack? ★★★ VHS: $9.99

Splitting Heirs

(1993, 86 min, US/GB, Robert Young) *Eric Idle, Rick Moranis, Barbara Hershey, John Cleese.* Idle stars as a poor Cockney schlub who discovers one fateful day that he is the true heir to a vast dukedom and that the Pakistani family that raised him since infancy is not his real family (gasp!). Such is the level of humor in this execrable attempt at crossbreeding Monty Python with "The Corsican Brothers." Moranis is the cretinous American yuppie who, having been switched at birth with the unfortunate heir, has usurped Idle's rightful title as "Duke of Something-or-Other" and is none too willing to return it. ★ VHS: $9.99

S

Spring Symphony

(1984, 102 min, Germany, Peter Schamoni) *Nastassja Kinski, Rolf Hoppe.* The passionate life and musical genius of German composer Robert Schumann is featured in this interesting if familiar drama. While a student, Schumann becomes violently involved with his teacher's daughter, pianist Clare Wieck (Kinski). Their affair threatens the teacher who becomes jealous and forces young Kinski to choose between family, love of her music and desire. (Filmed in English) ★★½ VHS: $19.99; DVD: $24.99

Springtime in the Rockies

(1942, 91 min, US, Irving Cummings) *Betty Grable, John Payne, Carmen Miranda, Charlotte Greenwood, Cesar Romero, Edward Everett Horton, Jackie Gleason.* Grable is at her best in this blithe musical comedy about a bickering theatrical couple at a mountain resort. Miranda is as delightful as ever. ★★★ VHS: $19.99

Der Sprinter

(1985, 90 min, Germany, Christoph Böll) *Wieland Samolak.* A witty social satire about a young closeted gay man who, in order to please his mother, decides to be "normal." Samolak portrays our confused hero, a pale, wide-eyed young man with expressionistic silent film star looks and a charming comedic touch. He chooses sports, specifically running, as his entrance into the straight world. His attempts at sports produce little until he meets and falls in love with a buxom butch female shot putter. (German with English subtitles) ★★★

Sprung

(1997, 108 min, US, Rusty Cundieff) *Tisha Campbell, Rusty Cundieff, Paula Jay Parker, Joe Torry.* Repellent, unfunny, endless "comedy" about gold-digging women and shallow, sex-obsessed men. There's no plot, no laughs, just four jerks flailing through a series of completely illogical, truly annoying and unfunny situations. After his very funny *Fear of a Black Hat*, director Cundieff definitely takes a major step backwards with this film. It's really a shame that while African-Americans have a larger role (relatively speaking) in studio film production in the '90s, most of the output is either gangsta violence or lame sex comedies like *Sprung*. And this one's worse than most. Next to *Sprung, Booty Call* is Oscar material. ★ VHS: $14.99; DVD: $24.99

Spy Hard

(1996, 81 min, US, Rick Friedberg) *Leslie Nielsen, Nicollette Sheridan, Charles Durning, Andy Griffith.* This *really* stupid comedy, executive-produced by its star Nielsen, attempts to duplicate the hilarity level of the *Naked Gun* films, but misses most of the time. Nielsen plays Agent WD-40 (har har), assigned to stop his arch-nemesis (Griffith) from blowing up the world. En route, the film lampoons almost every hit of the 1990s, from *Speed* to *Pulp Fiction* to *Cliffhanger*. There are a few laughs to be had, but even the best of these would only be middling fare in a *Naked Gun* comedy. Nielsen tries hard, but the writers let him down. ★★ VHS: $14.99; DVD: $29.99

The Spy in Black

(1939, 82 min, GB, Michael Powell) *Conrad Veidt, Valerie Hobson.* Veidt plays a German naval officer and spy in this intriguing tale of espionage set amidst the moors of Scotland during WWI. Legendary director Powell adds his spice with a series of ingenious plot-twists and a keen eye for romance. ★★★

Spy Kids

(2001, 88 min, US, Robert Rodriguez) *Antonio Banderas, Carla Gugino, Alexa Vega, Daryl Sabara, Alan Cumming, Tony Shalhoub, Teri Hatcher, Cheech Marin, Danny Trejo, George Clooney.* Nothing like parenthood to turn a bloodshed-loving individual into a sanguine family man. And so we find *Desperado*'s director and star infiltrating the kiddie market with the high-powered family values flick *Spy Kids*. Full of James Bond-style gadgets, big chases and bloodless action scenes, there's plenty here to keep young and old engaged for the concise running time. Banderas and Gugino play retired, married spies who go on one last mission. When they're kidnapped by an evil congomerate (led by kiddie TV host Cumming, carving out a nice niche as a movie villain), it's up to their two children (winningly played by newcomers Vega and Sabara) to rescue them. Positive messages abound, sure to unite such disparate groups as Latinos and conservatives in their praise. Yet Rodriguez's breathtaking and efficient camera trickery is evident in every frame, giving film buffs plenty to cheer about as well. ★★★ VHS: $22.99; DVD: $29.99

The Spy Who Came in from the Cold

(1965, 112 min, US, Martin Ritt) *Richard Burton, Claire Bloom, Oskar Werner.* This adaptation of John Le Carré's novel is every bit as cold as the Cold War intrigue it chronicles — and that's what makes it so good. Burton is an embittered agent who's as much a sacrificial pawn as anything — and he knows it. Bloom is the woman who can still see him through his alcoholic haze, only to be tragically betrayed. One of Burton's best performances. ★★★½ VHS: $19.99

The Spy Who Loved Me

(1977, 125 min, GB, Lewis Gilbert) *Roger Moore, Barbara Bach, Richard Kiel.* One of the best of the Moore Bond films, this scintillating spy thriller pairs 007 with a seductive Russian agent (Bach) to quash an arch-villain's plans for world destruction — does he ever do anything else? Kiel is featured as the seven-foot henchman Jaws. (Sequel: *Moonraker*) ★★★ VHS: $14.99; DVD: $34.99

Square Dance

(1987, 112 min, US, Daniel Petrie) *Winona Ryder, Jane Alexander, Jason Robards, Rob Lowe.* Well-acted drama about a young farm girl's coming of age when she runs away from home to live with her estranged mother in the city. Ryder gives a superb performance as the young girl, as does Alexander as her mom, and Robards as her grandfather. Lowe gives a surprisingly effective portrayal of a young retarded man. ★★★

Squeeze

(1997, 89 min, US, Robert Patton-Spruill) *Tyrone Burton, Eddie Cutanda, Phuong Duong, Russell G. Jones.* An earnest melodrama about a trio of Boston kids who must choose between dealing drugs or living a crime-free life, *Squeeze* marks the impressive debut of writer-director Patton-Spruill. As Ty (Burton), a 14-year-old black youth, and his crew, Hector (Cutanda), a Puerto Rican, and Bao (Duong), a Vietnamese, try to earn money by pumping gas, they are taunted by Tommy (Jones), a gang leader who forces them to make some tough decisions about their futures. While the boys find work on a clean-up detail for a community leader, they are also seduced by the easy money and gang status drug dealing offers them. The sweeping camerawork and nervy acting by the three leads contribute to the overall grittiness of this hard-hitting film. ★★★ VHS: $89.99

The Squeeze

(1987, 102 min, US, Roger Young) *Michael Keaton, Rae Dawn Chong.* Inferior comedy with Keaton as a down-on-his-luck con man who joins forces with an aspiring detective (Chong) to investigate a murder which implicates Keaton's ex-wife. ★½ VHS: $14.99

Stage Door

(1937, 92 min, US, Gregory La Cava) *Katharine Hepburn, Ginger Rogers, Andrea Leeds, Lucille Ball, Eve Arden, Ann Miller, Adolphe Menjou.* Hepburn and Rogers are just two of the inhabitants of the Footlights Club, a boarding house for aspiring starlets. Fast, witty repartee and uniformly fine performances highlight this story of a wealthy newcomer (Hepburn) trying to break into show business and gain acceptance from her new companions. Menjou is superb as a suave and lecherous producer. Based on the play by Edna Ferber and George S. Kaufman. ★★★★

Stage Struck

(1958, 95 min, US, Sidney Lumet) *Henry Fonda, Susan Strasberg, Joan Greenwood, Christopher Plummer.* Mild remake of *Morning Glory,* suffering most from Strasberg's less-than-inspired performance as a struggling actress determined to become a star. ★★

Stagecoach

(1939, 97 min, US, John Ford) *John Wayne, Claire Trevor, John Carradine, Andy Devine, Thomas Mitchell.* Director Ford, with one masterful stroke, took the western, heretofore a "B" programmer, and with sweeping panoramas, landmark use of camera and editing techniques, superlative action sequences and strong character development, elevated the genre to a singular American art form. Wayne heads a consummate cast in this story of a group of disparate travelers heading west by stagecoach, besieged by Indian attacks and internal conflict. Mitchell won an Oscar for his stirring portrayal of a drunken doctor. (Remade in 1966) ★★★★ VHS: $14.99; DVD: $19.99

Stairway to Heaven

(1946, 104 min, GB, Michael Powell & Emeric Pressburger) *David Niven, Kim Hunter, Raymond Massey, Roger Livesey, Richard Attenborough.* Classic WWII film which brilliantly balances reality and fantasy with Niven as a downed pilot

William Holden in *Stalag 17*

who goes before a Heavenly court to argue he was taken before his time. (aka: *A Matter of Life and Death*) ★★★★

Stakeout

(1987, 115 min, US, John Badham) *Richard Dreyfuss, Emilio Estevez, Madeleine Stowe, Aidan Quinn.* Dreyfuss and Estevez team up as a pair of cops assigned to keep an eye on a beautiful woman (Stowe) whose ex-boyfriend (Quinn) escaped from jail, leaving a trail of bodies behind him. Complications arise when Dreyfuss falls in love with his subject. Dreyfuss and Estevez have a wonderful chemistry which heightens the enjoyment of this entertaining comic thriller. (Sequel: *Another Stakeout*) ★★★ VHS: $9.99

Stalag 17

(1953, 120 min, US, Billy Wilder) *William Holden, Otto Preminger, Robert Strauss, Harvey Lembeck, Peter Graves, Sig Ruman.* The quintessential POW film. Holden deservedly won an Oscar for his knock-out performance as a cynical prisoner of war suspected of leaking secrets to his German captors. Alternately funny and suspenseful, director Wilder keeps the action moving at a remarkable pace, and allows the viewer to feel the confines of the barracks without a moment of claustrophobia. ★★★★ VHS: $9.99; DVD: $29.99

Stalingrad

(1993, 150 min, Germany, Joseph Vilsmaier) *Dominique Horwitz, Thomas Kretschmann, Jochen Nickel, Sebastian Rudolph.* This stunning German production follows a group of soldiers from Italy to the snowy steppes of Russia in their futile attempt to capture the city of Stalingrad in what was one of the bloodiest battles of WWII. Much like *Das Boot* or *Cross of Iron*, the film's narrative features some unlikely heroes: German soldiers. Vividly and authentically drawn, with a diversity of motivations and moralities, the script avoids making each character a cliché. The war sequences are appropriately nightmarish, and the dramatic

situations are so well drawn, they remain in the mind long after the memory of the epic battle sequences have faded. (Letterboxed) (German with English subtitles) ★★★½ VHS: $29.99; DVD: $34.99

The Stalking Moon

(1969, 109 min, US, Robert Mulligan) *Gregory Peck, Eva Marie Saint, Robert Forster.* Peck plays an Army scout who escorts Saint, captured years before by the Indians, and her young half-breed son home — with the boy's father in pursuit. The story's good premise is only occasionally realized, though the two stars work well together. ★★½ VHS: $14.99

The Stand

(1994, 360 min, US, Mick Garris) *Gary Sinise, Rob Lowe, Ruby Dee, Ossie Davis, Laura San Giacomo, Ray Walston, Miguel Ferrer.* Based on the best-seller by Stephen King, this epic six-hour made-for-TV adaptation is typical King: fascinating, excessive, fantastical and imaginative, with its fair share of slow moments. Set in modern times, the story begins as a virus (King wrote this years before the discovery of AIDS) wipes out 99% of the planet's population. While some survivors (mostly white) are spiritually drawn to a kindly, psychic old black woman (wonderfully played by Dee), others answer the calling of the devil incarnate. As all follow their chosen paths, the stage is set in true King fashion for the battle between good and evil. ★★★ VHS: $39.99; DVD: $29.99

Stand and Deliver

(1987, 105 min, US, Ramon Menendez) *Edward James Olmos, Lou Diamond Phillips, Rosana De Soto, Andy Garcia.* Olmos gives an outstanding performance as a strict public school math teacher who commits himself to his East L.A. students as they prepare for a difficult mathematics test. He is ultimately able to instill a pride and confidence in the previously unrecognized. Moving tribute to the tenacity of Jaime Escalante, the real-life teacher on whom the story is based. ★★★ VHS: $14.99; DVD: $14.99

Stand by Me

(1986, 87 min, US, Rob Reiner) *Wil Wheaton, River Phoenix, Corey Feldman, Jerry O'Connell, Kiefer Sutherland, Richard Dreyfuss.* This sweet-natured reminiscence is set in the late 1950s and concerns the misadventures of four pubescent boys who set out in search of the body of a young boy killed in a train accident. Based on the Stephen King novella, "The Body." Reiner's enchanting observation on the predilection of (specifically male) youth is winsome, articulate and refreshingly entertaining. ★★★½ VHS: $14.99; DVD: $29.99

Stand-In

(1937, 91 min, US, Tay Garnett) *Humphrey Bogart, Leslie Howard, Joan Blondell.* Bogart and Howard are reunited (*The Petrified Forest*) in this amusing show-biz comedy. Howard plays an efficiency expert who is dispatched to Hollywood to save a studio from financial ruin. Not knowing the business, he enlists the aid of former child star Blondell and boozy producer Bogie. Bogart

is surprisingly funny in his first comedic role, and Blondell is, as always, sassy and smart. ★★★

Stand-Off

(1989, 97 min, Hungary, Gyula Gazdag) *Ary Beri, Gabor Svidrony, István Szabó.* Filmed in documentary-like fashion, this suspenseful thriller recounts the actions of an 18-year-old Hungarian youth who, along with his younger brother, enters a student dormitory near the Hungarian border and holds 16 girls hostage. Their demands: a flight out of Budapest, $1,000,000 and eventual freedom in the West. (Hungarian with English subtitles) ★★★ VHS: $79.99

Stanley & Iris

(1990, 103 min, US, Martin Ritt) *Jane Fonda, Robert De Niro, Swoosie Kurtz, Martha Plimpton.* The title protagonists have monotonous, dead-end factory jobs; Iris (Fonda) on one of the production lines, Stanley (De Niro) in the company kitchen. She's a widow raising two children. He's trying to function in the world while hiding his illiteracy. The film develops a nice rhythm as the details of their separate lives start to intertwine and mesh, changing midway to an almost fairy-tale conclusion. As usual, Fonda and De Niro give exceptional performances. ★★★ VHS: $9.99

Stanley and Livingstone

(1939, 101 min, US, Henry King) *Spencer Tracy, Cedric Hardwicke, Nancy Kelly, Walter Brennan.* Tracy gives a stirring performance as Stanley searching for missionary Livingstone (Hardwicke) lost in darkest Africa at the turn of the century. A vastly entertaining '30s biopic. ★★★ VHS: $39.99

The Star

(1952, 89 min, US, Stuart Heisler) *Bette Davis, Sterling Hayden, Natalie Wood.* A ninth Oscar nomination for Best Actress went to Davis for her solid portrayal of a fading movie queen in this vitriolic Hollywood melodrama. Though Davis herself was at the time experiencing sort of a "comeback," there is no real parallel between the legendary actress and her character of Margaret Elliott, though certain similarities are open to interpretation. ★★★ VHS: $19.99

The Star Chamber

(1983, 109 min, US, Peter Hyams) *Michael Douglas, Hal Holbrook, Yaphet Kotto, Sharon Gless.* Douglas is a judge frustrated at the number of lowlifes our judicial system lets free on mere technicalities. What will he do when he finds himself invited to join a clandestine organization of like-minded litigants? An intriguing premise is half-heartedly explored making this a thinking man's thriller without a lot of smarts to it. ★★½ VHS: $9.99

Star 80

(1983, 102 min, US, Bob Fosse) *Mariel Hemingway, Eric Roberts, Cliff Robertson.* Never one to avoid controversy, Fosse picks apart the trappings of the American Dream with this unsettling account of a fantasy gone haywire. Hemingway portrays Dorothy Stratten, the peaches-and-cream Canadian girl whose taste of stardom was all too brief. The film's greatest strength lies in the performance of Roberts, whose calculating swagger and coiled intensity are frightfully ominous. ★★★½ VHS: $14.99; DVD: $14.99

S

A Star Is Born

(1937, 111 min, US, William Wellman) *Janet Gaynor, Fredric March, Adolphe Menjou, May Robson.* The original of the story of Esther Blodgett, an aspiring actress who marries matinee idol Norman Maine: her career takes off, his career fizzles. Gaynor had one of her best roles as Blodgett, bringing freshness and charm to the role, and March is outstanding as the fading star Maine. Dorothy Parker and Alan Campbell were two of the writers. Digitally remastered from an archives print. (Remade in 1954 and in 1976) ★★★½ VHS: $24.99; DVD: $29.99

A Star Is Born

(1954, 175 min, US, George Cukor) *Judy Garland, James Mason, Jack Carson, Tom Noonan, Charles Bickford.* Director Cukor often referred to *A Star Is Born* as his "butchered masterpiece" because the studio cut nearly 30 minutes from the finished film just weeks after its successful opening in 1954. After years of painstaking research and compilation, the film was restored to its original release length. The immortal Garland gives her finest performance, both vocally and dramatically, as Vicki Lester, the young songstress who rockets to stardom upon discovery by matinee idol Mason. Mason is equally brilliant as Norman Maine, the fading star who falls in love with Judy. One of the many songs is the unforgettable "The Man That Got Away." (VHS available letterboxed or pan & scan) ★★★★ VHS: $19.99; DVD: $19.99

A Star Is Born

(1976, 140 min, US, Frank Pierson) *Barbra Streisand, Kris Kristofferson, Paul Mazursky, Gary Busey, Sally Kirkland.* Though this second remake of the classic romance was dubbed by those-less-kind as "A Bore Is Starred," it's not *quite* as bad as that suggests. Streisand takes over the Janet Gaynor/Judy Garland role as an aspiring singer whose romance with a faltering rock star leads to tragedy. Kristofferson is the fading star. The least successful of the three screen versions. ★★½ VHS: $19.99

The Star Maker

(1995, 113 min, Italy, Giuseppe Tornatore) *Sergio Castellitto, Tiziana Lodato, Franco Scaldati.* Director Tornatore returns to the theme of the magic of the cinema which was brilliantly examined in his *Cinema Paradiso* with this often wry fable. Castellitto stars as Morelli, a con man making his way through 1950s Sicily offering dreams of fame and fortune or, at the very least, escape to the poor villagers of the small towns he visits. For a nominal fee, he films any and all with the promise of sending these screen tests to the cinematic giants of Italian filmmaking. Of course, the tests go no further than the back of his dilapidated truck which trumpets his arrival in each town. Unmoved by the various, funny and sometimes touching stories he is told, it is too late when he realizes the special power he and the camera holds. Tornatore captures the flavor of the times with the same accuracy he demonstrated in *Paradiso*, though this morality tale is not the sophisticated romp the box art suggests. (Italian with English subtitles) ★★★ VHS: $89.99

Star Maps

(1997, 93 min, US, Miguel Arteta) *Douglas Spain, Efrain Figueroa, Kandeyce Jensen, Martha Velez.* Funny, controversial and sexy, this melodramatic independent drama makes for absorbing viewing. Baby-faced but tough-minded Carlos (Spain) returns to L.A. and his unconventional family after a two-year absence in Mexico. Only 18 years old, he dreams of making it big as a Latino movie star. His weasel of a dad gets his hands on him first, however, and is recruited into the family business: selling maps to the homes of the stars, which is only a thinly veiled front for running a prostitution ring made up primarily of young Hispanic men who service both men and women. But Carlos has his sights set much higher than just peddling his flesh — and when a beautiful soap actress takes him under her wing, Carlos' tyrannical, violence-prone father has other thoughts about his son's future. Will Carlos succeed in Hollywood or will the harsh realities of immigrant life take over instead? ★★★½ VHS: $79.99

Star Trek: The Motion Picture

(1979, 143 min, US, Robert Wise) *William Shatner, Leonard Nimoy, DeForest Kelley, James Doohan, Nichelle Nichols, Walter Keonig, George Takei.* The first theatrical outing for the crew of the Starship Enterprise. Captain Kirk and friends are sent to stop a deadly energy field heading towards Earth. Not as exciting as its sequels, some good special effects help compensate for its extremely long running time. Still, if you're a "Star Trek" fan, you gotta love it. This is the extended edition, with 11 minutes added to the theatrical version. ★★½ VHS: $9.99

Star Trek II: The Wrath of Khan

(1982, 113 min, US, Nicholas Meyer) *William Shatner, Leonard Nimoy, DeForest Kelley, Ricardo Montalban, Kirstie Alley.* The crew of the Starship Enterprise battle their old foe Khan (see "Star Trek" TV episode "Space Seed"), who is determined to get revenge against Captain Kirk for...(you have to see the TV show). *II* is a gloriously entertaining sci-fi adventure, containing splendid special effects. Montalban nicely plays Khan. ★★★½ VHS: $9.99; DVD: $29.99

Star Trek III: The Search for Spock

(1984, 105 min, US, Leonard Nimoy) *William Shatner, Leonard Nimoy, DeForest Kelley, John Larroquette, Judith Anderson, Chrisopher Lloyd.* With the possibility of Spock being regenerated on the fast-disintegrating planet Genesis, Admiral Kirk and company hijack their old ship and go out after their friend — no matter what he may have evolved into. Intriguing sci-fi notions and a fast-paced story make this an enjoyable yarn. ★★★ VHS: $9.99; DVD: $29.99

Star Trek IV: The Voyage Home

(1986, 119 min, US, Leonard Nimoy) *William Shatner, Leonard Nimoy, DeForest Kelley, James Doohan, Catherine Hicks.* This fourth film in the *Star Trek* movie series is possibly the best of the bunch. The crew of the Starship Enterprise, on their way home for criminal prosecution, are diverted to 1980s San Francisco to prevent the destruction of Earth in the 23rd century — by saving the whales. Good special effects and terrific humor highlight this top science-fiction adventure. ★★★½ VHS: $9.99; DVD: $29.99

Star Trek V: The Final Frontier

(1989, 106 min, US, William Shatner) *William Shatner, Leonard Nimoy, DeForest Kelley, Laurence Luckinbill, David Warner.* This fifth entry in the *Star Trek* series was savaged by the critics and overlooked by audiences because of the ludicrous plot line (the Enterprise must travel through the allegedly awesome Great Barrier in search of God — the great and powerful Oz was more ominous) and the corniness of Luckinbill as a Vulcan with a heart of gold. But it's also humorous and often touching. Director Shatner may have some problems parlaying action scenes to the screen, but nobody knows the crew of the Enterprise better than he and for that, we can thank him. ★★½ VHS: $9.99; DVD: $29.99

Star Trek VI: The Undiscovered Country

(1991, 110 min, US, Nicholas Meyer) *William Shatner, Leonard Nimoy, DeForest Kelley, Kim Cattrall, Christopher Plummer, David Warner.* Not wanting to end on a down note after the disappointment of *Star Trek V*, the aging crew of the Enterprise are back in this superior adventure which stands up to the best of the series. Faced with a dwindling supply of oxygen on their home planet, the Klingons decide to make peace with the rest of the galaxy. Fittingly, Capt. Kirk is chosen as the emissary to negotiate this "new universal order." But there are powerful forces at work on both sides which don't want to see an end to their warring ways. The entire cast has a blast with this clearcut allegory for our current international climate. ★★★ VHS: $9.99; DVD: $29.99

Star Trek: Generations

(1994, 118 min, US, David Carson) *Patrick Stewart, William Shatner, Whoopi Goldberg, Malcolm McDowell, Jonathan Frakes, Brent Spiner, LeVar Burton.* A new crew takes control of the Starship Enterprise's theatrical adventures, and as James T. Kirk passes the captain's chair to Jean-Luc Picard, *Generations* brings both men together in an enjoyably familiar sci-fi tale. The story begins with the mysterious death of Kirk, and then skips ahead three-quarters of a century where Picard and his able crew answer an SOS, rescuing, among others, loony scientist McDowell, who spells trouble for all. The entire crew of "T.N.G." is on hand, though Data (Spiner) gets the best share of both screen time and the laughs as he finally acquires long-elusive human emotions. Stewart is ever-commanding as Picard, Shatner is at his best as Kirk, and there's a show-stopping crash scene worth seeing twice. ★★★ VHS: $14.99; DVD: $29.99

Star Trek: First Contact

(1996, 110 min, US, Jonathan Frakes) *Patrick Stewart, Jonathan Frakes, Brent Spiner, LeVar Burton, Michael Dorn, Gates McFadden, Marina Sirtis, Alfre Woodard, James Cromwell, Alice Krige.* Captain Kirk is dead, and the *Star Trek* films are now on their own — but that's not such bad news based on *Star Trek: First Contact*, the first big-screen film in the series without any original cast member. Exciting, darker than expected and still funny when you need it to be, *First Contact* reunites Captain Picard (Stewart) with the Borg, those ominous alien beings who a few years earlier had nearly "assimilated" the good captain on a fine two-part TV episode. To take the Borg on, the filmmakers take a cue from *Star Trek IV* and travel back in time to save the Earth of the near future. The Borg are a terrific foil for Picard and company — dangerous, unpredictable and almost undefeatable — exactly what we have come to expect from good villains. Technical credits are commendable, and there are a couple of cameos to bring on a smile. Director Frakes has done a yeoman's job. ★★★ VHS: $14.99

Star Trek: Insurrection

(1998, 103 min, US, Jonathan Frakes) *Patrick Stewart, Brett Spiner, LeVar Burton, Jonathan Frakes, F. Murray Abraham, Donna Murphy.* This would probably have made a great hour-long TV show. But stretched to feature length, this third voyage of the Next Generation crew is an enjoyable though listless ride. Capt. Picard and company come to the rescue of the Ba'ku, who live a utopian existence on an uncharted planet. It seems the peace-loving folks are literally sitting on a fountain of youth, and those ruthless outcasts, the Son'a, want it all for themselves. *Insurrection* is like a family reunion: not a lot exciting happens but it's certainly good to see everyone again. Though there's little of the universe-shaking fights and dilemmas which makes the series fun. ★★½ VHS: $14.99; DVD: $29.99

Star Wars

(1977, 121 min, US, George Lucas) *Mark Hamill, Harrison Ford, Carrie Fisher, Alec Guinness; Voice of: James Earl Jones.* A little while ago and not too far away, a man nearly reinvented the American film industry. Dialogue, characters and situations from Lucas' trilogy have crept into the American psyche since this blockbuster first appeared on movie screens. One reason for this influence is the fact that Lucas himself was drawing on the myths and fables present in American film throughout its history, particularly in early serials and later Hollywood westerns. The story (based on Kurosawa's *The Hidden Fortress*): a group of motley adventurers must rescue a princess from the clutches of an evil tyrant, and then rally their forces to destroy his empire. What Lucas did was to combine this primal story line with dazzling (and cutting-edge at the time) special effects, sound, pro-

duction design and an otherworldly galaxy of alien characters, thus making it appealing to everyone with a taste for adventure, fantasy, romance or fable. (Sequel: *The Empire Strikes Back*) ★★★★

Star Wars Episode 1: The Phantom Menace

(1999, 132 min, US, George Lucas) *Liam Neeson, Ewan McGregor, Natalie Portman, Jake Lloyd, Ian McDiarmid, Pernilla August, Samuel L. Jackson.* Lucas lets loose his imagination and creates a fully realized universe in the first part of his trilogy prequel. *Episode 1* follows Jedi master Qui-Gon Jinn (Neeson) and his young apprentice Obi-Wan Kenobi (McGregor) through many lands and fights for the federation, where they also discover Anakin Skywalker (Lloyd), the future Darth Vader. Planets as diverse as the opulent Naboo and the grid-locked Coruscant are rendered with such detail that multiple viewings, as with all *Star Wars* films, are mandatory. It's dazzling to the eye and the ear. However, it's very much in the style of an old cliffhanger, complete with wooden characterizations, overplotting, and only occasional action sequences to break the monotony. The simple, mythic elements of the previous films are missing here, replaced by rote superheroism, even as the art direction and effects set new standards for filmmaking. Lucas has said he wanted to make a film for kids to enjoy; instead, he has made a film that's merely juvenile. ★★½ VHS: $14.99

Stardust Memories

(1980, 88 min, US, Woody Allen) *Woody Allen, Charlotte Rampling, Marie-Christine Barrault, Jessica Harper.* Allen's autobiographical statement is a daring if rambling film which pits the artist against his audience. Allen plays a comedian/writer/director whose growing legion of fans crave more comedies while he is preoccupied with human suffering. ★★½ VHS: $14.99; DVD: $19.99

Stargate

(1994, 125 min, US, Roland Emmerich) *Kurt Russell, James Spader, Jaye Davidson, Viveca Lindfors.* This entertaining if lightweight sci-fi thriller plays like *Star Wars* meets *Indiana Jones.*

Russell and the ever-engaging Spader are a military burnout and nerdy Egyptologist, respectively, who are assigned to decipher the markings on an ancient discovery. When it turns out it's a galactic gateway, they travel to the other side where peace-loving desert tribes are enslaved by an evil, skin-shedding alien (Davidson). Though the story line is lackluster and the finale is more Stallone than sci-fi, the film is greatly benefited by an intriguing premise, impressive costumes and good special effects. A dress rehearsal for director Emmerich's next film, *Independence Day*. ★★½ VHS: $9.99

Starlight Hotel

(1987, 94 min, New Zealand, Sam Pillsbury) *Greer Robson, Peter Phelps.* Fine family fare about a 12-year-old waif who sets off across the New Zealand countryside in search of her father, and instead finds herself on the run with a fugitive from the law. Though lacking the panache of *The Journey of Natty Gann*, it nonetheless stands on its own as an interesting variation of the buddy-road movie. ★★★

Starman

(1984, 115 min, US, John Carpenter) *Jeff Bridges, Karen Allen, Charles Martin Smith, Richard Jaeckel.* Bridges' captivating performance highlights this good-natured and extremely satisfying Carpenter sci-fi adventure about an alien on the run from the authorities. Allen plays a widow who is at first kidnapped by the extraterrestrial (who has taken on the form of her late husband), but who later helps and befriends him. ★★★½ VHS: $9.99; DVD: $14.99

Stars and Bars

(1988, 94 min, US, Pat O'Connor) *Daniel Day-Lewis, Harry Dean Stanton, Martha Plimpton, Joan Cusack, Steven Wright, Laurie Metcalf, Glenne Headly.* Wacky and offbeat comedy with Day-Lewis as a British art dealer who travels to the American South to purchase a prized painting and is introduced to one of the craziest families this side of the Vanderhoffs. ★★ VHS: $19.99

The Stars Fell on Henrietta

(1995, 110 min, US, James Keach) *Robert Duvall, Aidan Quinn, Frances Fisher, Brian Dennehy.* Set in Depression-era Texas, this nostalgic if colorless character study gives Duvall another chance to deliver a sterling portrayal of a gruff but lovable curmudgeon. He plays Mr. Cox, an aging wildcatter who happens upon the struggling farm of Mr. and Mrs. Day (Quinn, Fisher), promptly claiming there's oil on their property. Mr. Cox sets about to raise the money (sometimes illegally) as Mr. Day falls under the spell cast by the self-proclaimed "oil man" and begins drilling, risking his farm in the process. A listless pace is offset by a strong ensemble, good period design and lovely cinematography. ★★½ VHS: $14.99

The Stars Look Down

(1939, 110 min, GB, Carol Reed) *Michael Redgrave, Margaret Lockwood, Emlyn Williams.* Exquisite performances by Redgrave and Lockwood highlight this searing film adaptation of A.J. Cronin's novel about a poor Welsh mining family's struggles and their son's resolution to run for public office. ★★★★ VHS: $14.99

Star Wars: Episode 1 — The Phantom Menace

Starship Troopers

S

Starship Troopers

(1997, 130 min, US, Paul Verhoeven) *Casper Van Dien, Dina Meyer, Denise Richards, Jake Busey, Neil Patrick Harris, Patrick Muldoon, Michael Ironside.* A scathingly satirical futuristic sci-fi thriller that plays like "Archie and Veronica Go to War!" A bunch of giant space bugs have taken to lobbing killer asteroids from their side of the galaxy at Earth, and a group of young heroes must gamely venture out to the alien home world for a preemptive strike. The film's first hour is positively goofy (in the best way) as it introduces these youthful cadets. Van Dien, Meyer, Richards, Busey, Harris and Muldoon are all perfect with their gleaming white teeth and stay-in-place hairdos for Verhoeven's comic-book portrayal of juvenilia on the verge of blood and guts destruction. Which is exactly what *Starship Troopers* delivers in spades in its second half, a cinematic orgy of human and insect insides splashed on the screen with abandon as only Verhoeven could deliver. A most entertaining space adventure. ★★★½ VHS: $9.99; DVD: $19.99

Starstruck

(1982, 95 min, Australia, Gillian Armstrong) *Jo Kennedy, Ross O'Donovan.* A zesty, new-wave musical brimming with infectious tunes, inspired choreography and enchanting performances. Jackie, a winsome waitress at the family pub in Sydney, has a hankering for stardom; and, with the help of her mite-sized manager/cousin, sets out to launch her singing career. Armstrong directed this ebullient Australian comedy with an abundance of flair and originality. ★★★½ VHS: $19.99

Start the Revolution without Me

(1970, 91 min, US, Bud Yorkin) *Gene Wilder, Donald Sutherland, Orson Welles, Billie Whitelaw.* Engaging spoof set during the French Revolution with Wilder and Sutherland chewing the scenery as two pairs of twins separated at birth; reunited years later resulting in cases of mistaken identity between the aristocracy and peasantry. ★★★ VHS: $14.99

State and Main

(2000, 102 min, US, David Mamet) *William H. Macy, Alec Baldwin, Rebecca Pidgeon, Philip Seymour Hoffman, Sarah Jessica Parker, David Paymer, Julia Stiles, Charles Durning, Patti LuPone, Clark Gregg.* From writer-director Mamet comes this winning comedy about a film company invading a peaceful Vermont community. As Hollywood and small-town America clash, careers are nearly ruined, engagements broken, and alliances shifted. Macy is terrific as the cool-headed but acerbic director desperately trying to maintain order; Hoffman is the insecure writer who may have found paradise; Baldwin and Parker are the shallow stars of the movie; and best of all is Pidgeon as the local bookstore owner and theatre director who always seems to be one-up on everyone. Mamet has great fun at both poking fun at the system while showing exactly what it takes to get a movie made. It's not always pretty, but it can be damn funny. ★★★½ VHS: $19.99; DVD: $24.99

State of Grace

(1990, 130 min, US, Phil Joanou) *Gary Oldman, Sean Penn, Ed Harris, Robin Wright Penn, John Turturro.* A *Mean Streets*-like vision of the inner workings of Manhattan's Irish-American mob. Based on journalistic accounts of the "Westies," a real-life Hell's Kitchen band of thugs known for their brutal savagery, the film accurately depicts the erratic and unpredictable violence which rules the streets of New York. Oldman is stellar as Jackie Flannery, a dangerously loose cannon in the gang. Penn is a childhood friend who returns to the neighborhood after a long absence. Highly stylized, *State of Grace* centers on the attempted union of the "Westies" with the Italian mafia in the mid-'70s. ★★★

State of Siege

(1973, 120 min, France, Constantin Costa-Gavras) *Yves Montand, Renato Salvatori.* This tense drama of the kidnapping of a U.S. "special advisor" provides the background for the uncovering of the United States' true role in the internal affairs of Latin America. (French with English subtitles) ★★★

State of the Union

(1948, 122 min, US, Frank Capra) *Spencer Tracy, Katharine Hepburn, Angela Lansbury, Van Johnson, Adolphe Menjou.* A well-scripted political comedy based on the Pulitzer Prize—winning play by Howard Lindsay and Russell Crouse. Tracy gives a commanding performance as an idealistic industrialist who is drafted as a presidential nominee. Hepburn is the estranged wife who returns to her husband for the sake of the campaign, where the candidate is torn between his ambition for office and the integrity of his wife's uncompromising and outspoken views. Lansbury is especially noteworthy as Tracy's rich sponsor. ★★★ VHS: $19.99

The State of Things

(1982, 110 min, West Germany/US, Wim Wenders) *Samuel Fuller, Roger Corman, Viva, Paul Getty III.* Wenders' *8½* is an imaginative and engrossing picture dealing with the condition of the European art film and its corrupting nemesis: Hollywood. The story concerns the crew and cast of a film who find themselves marooned in Portugal and their production money and film stock depleted. The crew, waiting for more money, must kill time. A compelling meditation on the inertia of the moviemaking process, creative impasses and the impossibility of telling stories anymore. (Filmed in English) ★★★

Static

(1985, 93 min, US, Mark Romanek) *Keith Gordon, Amanda Plummer, Bob Gunton.* A young inventor (Gordon) prepares to launch his earth-shattering new creation (a TV which gets pictures of Heaven) with the aid of his new-wave friend and his ex-Green Beret evangelist cousin. Gordon cowrote the uneven though imaginative script. ★★

The Station

(1992, 92 min, Italy, Sergio Rubini) *Margherita Buy, Ennio Fantastichini.* Charming, romantic and quintessentially European, *The Station* tells of an unlikely love between a nerdy railway station attendant and an elegant young woman. The fastidious young man, who lives on an elaborate timetable both in his work and in his life, finds his order coming to an end after the mysterious woman, seemingly on the run, enters the station in the middle of the night to wait for the morning train. Their relationship, first as a typical clerk to an indifferent customer, develops into more after trouble descends on the station and the man is forced to take drastic action to defend them. Deliberate in pacing, but rich in nuance and emotion, this quiet, gentle love story is a real delight. (Italian with English subtitles) ★★★½ VHS: $19.99

The Stationmaster's Wife (Bolwiesser)

(1977, 111 min, West Germany, Rainer Werner Fassbinder) *Kurt Raab, Elisabeth Trissenaar.* Originally a two-part TV series running 200 minutes, this shorter version is Fassbinder's take on "Madame Bovary" in a Nazi Germany rotting from within. Raab is the sheepish, masochistic stationmaster who suspects his wife's infidelities. But not wanting to risk losing the small luxuries to which he has become accustomed, he chooses not to act upon his suspicions. Trissenaar gives a mesmerizing performance as a woman in love with her carnal desires and the power they give her. Fassbinder's visual style is rich, gorgeous, and suffocating, mirroring their bourgeois lifestyle. (German with English subtitles) ★★★

Stavisky

(1974, 117 min, France, Alain Resnais) *Jean-Paul Belmondo, Charles Boyer.* Starting off with the details from a real 1930s French political scandal, Resnais adroitly blends facts — from the real case with Leon Trotsky's arrival in exile — with fiction in presenting this absorbing drama about moral degeneracy and political corruption. Belmondo plays Serge Alexandre (née Sacha Stavisky), a suave, elegantly attired con man who concocts a financial swindle that soon involves powerful government officials and high-ranking police. Resnais creates a visually breathtaking and chilling allegory of France's political situation on the eve of fascist aggression. Features a score by Stephen Sondheim. (French with English subtitles) ★★★½ VHS: $24.99

Stay Hungry

(1976, 103 min, US, Bob Rafelson) *Jeff Bridges, Sally Field, Arnold Schwarzenegger.* Bridges stars as a Southern pre-yuppie who buys a gym as part of a business deal, only to gain an appreciation for the people he exploits while learning something about himself as well. Schwarzenegger appears in his first major acting role. ★★½ VHS: $9.99

Stay Tuned

(1992, 89 min, US, Peter Hyams) *John Ritter, Pam Dawber, Jeffrey Jones.* The irony is delicious: Ritter and Dawber finally make the transition to the big screen only to be sucked back into the "television from Hell" (and it really is) in this comical boob tube spoof. Ritter plays a video addict whose ritual TV watching is given a twist when Satan's helper (Jones) offers him 666 channels of the ultimate in interactive television. Though not as consistently savage as it might have been, *Stay Tuned* does offer some funny parodies — especially of "Three's Company" and an animated segment by Chuck Jones. ★★ VHS: $14.99; DVD: $14.99

Stealing Beauty

(1996, 119 min, GB/Italy, Bernardo Bertolucci) *Jeremy Irons, Liv Tyler, Donal McCann, Sinead Cusack.* One might expect this tale of sexual awakening in the sun-drenched hills of Tuscany to be no more than a panderous exercise in lechery on the part of aging director

Starstruck

Bertolucci. And to whatever degree this is true (and it is, a little), *Stealing Beauty* is also a remarkably astute and touching examination of the young woman's innocent, oddly chaste, desire for sexual initiation. The story revolves around a 19-year-old American staying with family friends at their homestead. Clearly out of her element and surrounded by middle-aged adults, she turns to an ailing houseguest (Irons) for solace and comfort. More style than substance, the film is a very satisfying and refreshing look at romance amongst the privileged artist class. Delivering a marvelously natural performance, newcomer Tyler proves herself a worthy lead. ★★★ VHS: $14.99

Stealing Heaven

(1988, 108 min, GB, Clive Donner) *Peter de Lint, Kim Thomson, Denholm Elliott.* De Lint stars as Peter Abelard, a 12th-century French philosopher and churchman who broke taboo and secretly married one of his students, Heloise (Thomson). Elliott is her wrathful father in this passionate tale of forbidden love. ★★★

Stealing Home

(1988, 98 min, US, Steven Kampmann) *Mark Harmon, Jodie Foster, William McNamara, Blair Brown, Helen Hunt.* America's two favorite pastimes, baseball and sex, take it on the chin in this uneven though well-acted comedy-drama. Harmon stars as a down-and-out ballplayer who, upon hearing of the death of a childhood friend, reminisces and reflects upon their relationship two decades earlier. Partially told in flashback, the film is equally divided between the present and past, and is far more successful in the scenes involving the latter. Foster gives a wonderful performance as Harmon's free-spirited mentor. ★★½ VHS: $9.99; DVD: $14.99

Steamboat Bill, Jr.

(1927, 71 min, US, Charles Riesner) *Buster Keaton.* One of Keaton's finest comedies casts him as a returning college graduate who must prove himself to his burly father, Steamboat Bill, Sr. The cyclone at the climax gives Keaton the chance to reconcile with his father and demonstrate the comic genius of one of the all-time great physical comedians. ★★★★ VHS: $29.99; DVD: $29.99

Steaming

(1985, 95 min, GB, Joseph Losey) *Vanessa Redgrave, Sarah Miles, Patti Love, Diana Dors.* Losey's last film is an adaptation of the critically acclaimed play by Neal Dunn which features a stellar female cast. Set on "ladies' day" at a London bathhouse, we find six women, of wildly divergent backgrounds, coming together to discuss their intimate secrets and commiserate about their place in the world. The production is perhaps a bit over-stagey, but it is carried by first-rate performances. ★★½

Steel

(1997, 97 min, US, Kenneth Johnson) *Shaquille O'Neal, Annabeth Gish, Judd Nelson, Richard Roundtree, Irma P. Hall.* A laughable attempt to start a new superhero franchise for kids, *Steel,* based on the DC comic book, is a bland time waster that opens with a supremely dull credit sequence and never recovers. After a mishap testing a new sonic weapon for the Army, Shaq

quits the Army and becomes a well-armored vigilante in his old 'hood, while Nelson graduates to supervillain status. On a guilty pleasure level, Roundtree does get to say of Steel's hammer weapon, "I designed the shaft." ★ VHS: $14.99

Steel Magnolias

(1989, 115 min, US, Herbert Ross) *Sally Field, Shirley MacLaine, Olympia Dukakis, Julia Roberts, Dolly Parton, Daryl Hannah, Tom Skerritt.* A fine ensemble cast is featured in this heartrending, sentimental and funny comedy-drama. The story centers on the friendship of six women in a small Louisiana town who meet periodically at the local beauty shop. Field heads this terrific cast as mother of newlywed Roberts, whose marriage is much of the focus of the film. MacLaine is hilarious as the town curmudgeon; and Dukakis is splendid as the gossipy town matriarch. The first half of the film suffers from sloppy editing, and sometimes the characters seem interchangeable with other Southern-themed works, but the performances are so captivating the film's flaws can be overlooked. ★★½ VHS: $14.99; DVD: $24.99

Steelyard Blues

(1973, 93 min, US, Alan Myerson) *Jane Fonda, Donald Sutherland, Peter Boyle.* A group of misfits band together to restore a vintage airplane, hoping to fly away to paradise. Amiable counterculture hijinks. Written by David S. Ward (*The Sting*). ★★½ VHS: $19.99

Stella

(1990, 109 min, US, John Erman) *Bette Midler, John Goodman, Trini Alvarado.* Even the great Midler can strike out on occasion, as proved by this turgid remake of the perennial classic. Bette plays the sacrificing and (supposedly) slovenly mother of teenager Alvarado; but she's more schizophrenic as one moment she's wise and creative and the next crude with no fashion sense. It just doesn't work in the 1990s. Stick with Barbara Stanwyck's 1937 version. ★½

Stella Dallas

(1937, 111 min, US, King Vidor) *Barbara Stanwyck, Anne Shirley, John Boles.* Stanwyck gives a stellar performance in this classic tearjerker as a mother who sacrifices all for the sake of her daughter (Shirley). (Remade as *Stella*) ★★★½ VHS: $14.99; DVD: $24.99

Step Lively

(1944, 88 min, US, Tim Whelan) *Frank Sinatra, George Murphy, Gloria De Haven.* A fast-paced musical version of the Marx Brothers' *Room Service.* Murphy plays the part of a Broadway producer who, despite no financial resources, schemes to put on a show. ★★★ VHS: $19.99

The Stepfather

(1987, 98 min, US, Joseph Ruben) *Terry O'Quinn, Shelley Hack.* This frightening thriller gets most of its chills because it could so easily be true. O'Quinn is a meek little guy who wants a perfect family and home, and by damn, *he's going to have it* — no matter what the cost or who gets killed in the process. (Followed by 2 sequels) ★★★½

The Stepford Wives

(1975, 115 min, US, Bryan Forbes) *Katharine Ross, Paula Prentiss, Peter Masterson, Tina Louise, Patrick O'Neal.* This "domestic" horror film may sound out of date, but its themes take on an unexpected resonance in the age of cloning. Ross stars as an aspiring photographer who moves to a seemingly perfect planned community with her hotshot lawyer husband. She soon sticks out amongst the apron-clad hausfraus who smilingly serve their husbands' every need and whim. Digging a little deeper beneath the happy surface of Stepford, she and her equally independent best friend (a wonderful Prentiss) discover the horrifying secret of the Stepford Mens' Association and their man-made paradise. Perhaps a bit slow to begin with, the film delivers quite a few good shocks in its final reel. ★★★

Stephen King's Thinner

(1996, 92 min, US, Tom Holland) *Robert John Burke, Joe Mantegna, Al Ruggiero.* A selfish lawyer accidentally but recklessly runs down the daughter of an ancient gypsy mystic and becomes the object of a sinister curse in this adaptation of a Stephen King story written under his "Richard Bachman" pseudonym. Extremely overweight, the lawyer (Burke) suddenly finds himself losing fat at an alarming rate. Pleased at first, he realizes the horror of his situation when he cannot stop or even slow down his wasting away. One could overanalyze this scenario, with its moral implications and parallels to drug abuse or AIDS, but it's really just a basic horror film. Competently acted and produced, it's satisfying while it lasts but leaves no lasting impression. ★★½ VHS: $14.99; DVD: $19.99

Stepmom

(1998, 124 min, US, Chris Columbus) *Susan Sarandon, Julia Roberts, Ed Harris, Jena Malone, Lynn Whitfield.* With oh-so sincerity and jerking of tears, this mawkish mess of manipulation uses its good cast to try to hide a sappy story of two moms, two kids and two rivalries that becomes all-too much. Sarandon and Harris are a divorced couple with two kids. Dad has a new girlfriend (Roberts), and Mom has a fit when her children are left with the inexperienced Roberts. This sets the stage for a continuing battle of the divas as Roberts and Harris marry, pitting mom against stepmom for control of the kids. And wouldn't you know it, just when it looks like they might actually get along, tragedy strikes. The performances all around are good, but it's all for naught. We've all been down this well-traveled road, and there's nothing new on the horizon. ★★ VHS: $9.99; DVD: $19.99

The Sterile Cuckoo

(1969, 107 min, US, Alan J. Pakula) *Liza Minnelli, Wendell Burton.* Minnelli gives a heartrending performance as a lonely and eccentric college student searching for love and acceptance. She finds the former in the unlikely person of shy Burton. A perceptive and touching look at first love. ★★★½ VHS: $49.99

Stevie

(1978, 102 min, GB, Robert Enders) *Glenda Jackson, Mona Washbourne, Alec McCowen.* Jackson stars in this wonderful character study of British poetess Stevie Smith. Adapted from Hugh Whitemore's hit London play, the film celebrates love, family, and Stevie's own fascination with the English language. Jackson and Washbourne both offer exquisite performances. ★★★★

Sticky Fingers

(1988, 97 min, US, Catlin Adams) *Helen Slater, Melanie Mayron, Loretta Devine.* Two dizzy roommates "borrow" from the stash of cash they're holding for a friend (Devine), and go overboard. The film tries for the slap-dash energy of the crazy romps of yore, but it's mostly wasted in unfunny and contrived situations. ★½

Stigmata

(1999, 102 min, US, Rupert Wainwright) *Gabriel Byrne, Patricia Arquette, Jonathan Pryce, Portia de Rossi, Nia Long.* Oh, the horror of it all. Director Wainwright takes an intriguing story of supernatural possession and religious conflict and turns it into a boring, atmospheric merry-go-round ride. Byrne plays a Vatican priest who is sent to Pittsburgh (now that's scary) to investigate a young woman (Arquette) who is experiencing signs of the stigmata, or unexplained wounds mirroring those suffered by Christ. With one-too many jump cuts and not-nearly enough scares, the story follows the good reverend as he tries to protect his lovely charge — but from what? The film's good looks can't hide a silly screenplay and uninvolving direction. ★½ VHS: $9.99; DVD: $14.99

Still Crazy

(1998, 95 min, GB, Brian Gibson) *Stephen Rea, Billy Connolly, Jimmy Nail, Timothy Spall, Bill Nighy, Bruce Robinson.* Seeking to combine the Baby Boomer humor of *This Is Spinal Tap* with the plight of the working-class dramedy so in vogue in Britain (*The Full Monty*, e.g.), *Still Crazy* is thoroughly inconsequential but still enjoyable. Rea is the keyboardist of Strange Fruit, a rock band that was apparently huge in the '70s, and he wants to experience that magic again. But the band is full of petty conflicts that hamper a reunion, from the taxman-evading Spall to the egotistical Nighy. Oh, did we mention that the singer (Robinson) is dead? Wildly uneven but always light and enjoyable, *Still Crazy* benefits most from an original repertoire of songs that is solidly, bombastically 1970s. ★★½ VHS: $21.99; DVD: $29.99

Still of the Night

(1982, 91 min, US, Robert Benton) *Roy Scheider, Meryl Streep, Jessica Tandy.* Hitchcockian murder mystery about a psychiatrist (Scheider) who tries to solve the murder of one of his patients, falling in love with the prime suspect (Streep) in the process. Streep chain-smokes and chews the scenery in this somewhat involved thriller which, like most Hitchcock imitations, fails to measure up to the master. ★★½ VHS: $9.99

The Stilts (Los Zancos)

(1984, 95 min, Spain, Carlos Saura) *Laura del Sol.* Director Saura returns to the familiar surroundings of theatrical life and sexual obsession. An aging, recently widowed professor initiates an affair with his beautiful neighbor, who is married to the charismatic leader of a local theatre company. In an attempt to retain her affection, the professor writes a play for the troupe, which is performed on stilts. Against this backdrop, the trio play out an anguished and explosive scenario infused with unrestrained desires and emotional manipulation. (Spanish with English subtitles) ★★★

The Sting

(1973, 129 min, US, George Roy Hill) *Paul Newman, Robert Redford, Robert Shaw, Eileen Brennan, Ray Walston, Harold Gould.* Delightful comedy set in 1930s Chicago with Newman and Redford as con artists out to "sting" gangster Shaw. There's so many twists you won't know what's what or who's who. Winner of seven Oscars, including Best Picture and one for David S. Ward's first-rate screenplay. There's an impeccable supporting cast and terrific costumes and sets. (VHS available letterboxed or pan & scan) ★★★★ VHS: $14.99; DVD: $24.99

Stir Crazy

(1980, 111 min, US, Sidney Poitier) *Gene Wilder, Richard Pryor, JoBeth Williams, Georg Stanford Brown, Craig T. Nelson.* The second and most popular of the Wilder-Pryor comedies, and it's very funny. The guys are two bungling thieves who are sent to prison; quite ill-prepared for life behind bars. ★★★ VHS: $9.99; DVD: $29.99

Stir of Echoes

(1999, 94 min, US, David Koepp) *Kevin Bacon, Kathryn Erbe, Illeana Douglas, Kevin Dunn.* From the screenwriter of *Apartment Zero* and *Jurassic Park* comes this often intense psychological thriller which falls apart by story's end. Sure to draw comparisons to the superior *The Sixth Sense* (though this was first), the story concerns a family man (Bacon) who is haunted by the spirit of a recently murdered woman. So she may rest in peace, he must bring to justice those responsible for her death. The film is at its best when delving into the supernatural, effectively creating a few chilling set pieces that are atmospheric and even spooky. But it is the human element which is underdeveloped, and by the end of the film, Koepp has nothing up his sleeve but a tired *Death Wish*–type ending. Bacon tries a little too hard to convey mannerisms of an Average Joe, though Douglas is quite good as his sister-in-law who first unlocks this window to the other world. ★★½ VHS: $14.99; DVD: $24.99

Stolen Kisses

(1968, 90 min, France, François Truffaut) *Jean-Pierre Léaud, Delphine Seyrig.* The third episode in the Antoine Doinel series finds Léaud, our inept but lovable hero, doing what he must to stay on the furtive heels of love and romance. A poignant and comic look at the foibles of romance. (French with English subtitles) ★★★½ VHS: $19.99; DVD: $29.99

A Stolen Life

(1946, 107 min, US, Curtis Bernhardt) *Bette Davis, Glenn Ford, Walter Brennan.* Davis lets loose as a set of twins, one of whom takes the other's place in marriage to the man they both loved when her sibling dies in a boating accident. Not Bette's best, but more than interesting thanks to La Davis' histrionics. ★★½ VHS: $19.99

The Stone Boy

(1984, 93 min, US, Christopher Cain) *Jason Pressman, Robert Duvall, Glenn Close, Wilford Brimley, Frederic Forrest.* Duvall and Close star as the confused parents of a young boy who kills his older brother in a hunting accident. Exceptionally portrayed by Presson, the boy goes into shock and is unable to explain the circumstances leading up to the shooting, and sinks deep within a grim-faced exterior. Duvall delivers an understated performance as a Montana rancher caught in a situation beyond his understanding but compelled to muster the strength needed to heal his family and reconcile with his son. Powerful and quite beautiful. ★★★ VHS: $59.99

Stonebrook

(1999, 90 min, US, Byron W. Thompson) *Seth Green, Brad Rowe, Zoe McLellan, William Mesnik.* Predating a sorry wave of behind-the-Ivy-curtain thrillers (*The Skulls, Gossip*) but certainly no better, this minor thriller falls into clichéd traps that the protagonists should have seen coming. Rowe plays Erik, a working-class outcast at wealthy Stonebrook U; when he loses his scholarship, he needs to scrape up some cash. Enter Green, playing a grown-up version of his *Radio Days* mini-mensch, and his plans to swindle the local underworld. The schemes become a random series of who's-playing-who twists in a plot too complicated for its own good. ★½ VHS: $9.99; DVD: $19.99

Stonewall

(1996, 93 min, GB, Nigel Finch) *Guillermo Díaz, Frederick Weller, Brendan Corbalis, Duane Boutte, Luis Guzmán.* Far from being a dry, fictionalized account of the people involved in the 1969 Stonewall Riots, this adaptation of Martin Duberman's book is instead a rollicking musical drama that successfully blends gay history and queer fabulousness to wonderful effect. This what-might-have-been-happening on the days before that fateful summer night's tale features Matty (Weller), a studly country boy who arrives in New York City and almost immediately becomes involved with a rambunctious group of black, white and Latino drag queens. He becomes romantically involved with one particular diva, La Miranda, a saucy and hopelessly romantic drag queen. A passionate, spirited tale — torn from gay history — that is alternately funny, touching, upsetting and even a bit educational. ★★★ VHS: $14.99; DVD: $19.99

Stop Making Sense

(1984, 99 min, US, Jonathan Demme) Visual wit and dynamic rhythms faithfully and inventively convey the near-religious fervor of a Talking Heads concert. Demme's rockumentary won laurels for being a new breed of performance film, one which showcases a band's unique personality rather than the director's pyrotechnics. Shunning clips of frothing crowds and backstage doodlings, Demme and figure-Head David Byrne have constructed a film which builds to a rousing crescendo as additional performers join the stage with each successive song, augmenting what begins with a solo acoustic rendering of "Psycho Killer" by Byrne. Truly a scintillating celebration of rock 'n' roll. (VHS available letterboxed or pan & scan) ★★★★ VHS: $19.99; DVD: $29.99

Stop! or My Mom Will Shoot

(1992, 87 min, US, Roger Spottiswoode) *Sylvester Stallone, Estelle Getty, JoBeth Williams, Roger Rees.* In this flat and predictable high-concept comedy, a Los Angeles police sergeant (and here's the concept, folks) teams up with his sixtysomething mom. While visiting her son, she witnesses a murder and demands to be part of the investigation. Hey Sly: You made some good movies in the '70s, but continue picking films like this, and it'll be *Stop! My Career Is Over.* ★½ VHS: $9.99

Stop the World I Want to Get Off

(1966, 98 min, GB, Philip Saville) *Tony Tanner, Millicent Martin.* This lively film adaptation of Anthony Newley-Leslie Bricusse's smash London/Broadway musical is filmed directly from a staged performance, inexplicably minus its star Newley. Tanner takes over the role of Littlechap, a British Everyman who, through song (and what classics they are), observes his life — including courtship, marriage and infidelity. This was one of the groundbreaking stage musicals of its era, and the film version nicely captures the play's originality and vitality. Songs include "What Kind of Fool Am I" and "Gonna Build a Mountain." ★★★ VHS: $19.99

The Storm Within
(Les Parents Terribles)

(1948, 98 min, France, Jean Cocteau) *Jean Marais, Josette Day, Yvonne deBray.* This adaptation of Cocteau's play, considered by many to be his finest work, is a riveting psychological tragicomedy about the complicated tangle of sexuality, parental rivalry and jealousy within a troubled family. Cocteau creates a claustrophobic intimacy (only two sets, static camera, many close-ups, no exteriors) as this incestuously close family bares its soul. DeBray is wonderful as the domineering mother, Marais plays the son, and Day is the woman he (and his father) loves. (French with English subtitles) ★★★★ VHS: $29.99

Stormy Monday

(1988, 93 min, GB, Mike Figgis) *Melanie Griffith, Sting, Tommy Lee Jones, Sean Bean.* A moody and atmospheric mystery-thriller set in the dreary city of Newcastle. Jones plays an American businessman who is trying to take advantage of the town's depressed economy by snatching up real estate, including Sting's jazz club. ★★★

Stormy Weather

(1943, 77 min, US, Andrew L. Stone) *Lena Horne, Bill Robinson, Cab Calloway, Fats Waller, The Nicholas Brothers.* A dazzling, high-spirited tribute to the legendary Bill "Bojangles" Robinson. Tunes include "Ain't Misbehavin'" and Lena's sultry version of the title number. ★★★ VHS: $19.99

The Story of a Three Day Pass

(1967, 87 min, France, Melvin van Peebles) *Harry Baird, Nicole Berger.* This tale of an African-American soldier's affair with a French woman while on leave in Paris in the 1960s is an entertaining love story. The two principals, Baird and Berger act as conduits on a surreal journey exploring race relations in the military and how some American mores become irrational in other societies. While at times flawed, van Peebles' cut and camerawork stand out as he pays homage to Luis Buñuel and Jean Cocteau. ★★½ VHS: $19.99

The Story of Adele H.

(1975, 97 min, France, François Truffaut) *Isabelle Adjani, Bruce Robinson.* Adjani portrays the young heroine whose obsessive attachment to an uncaring scoundrel in the military drives her to the brink of madness...and beyond. An exceptionally told and acted drama based on the memoirs of the daughter of French literary giant Victor Hugo. (French with English subtitles) ★★★★ VHS: $19.99; DVD: $19.99

The Story of Boys and Girls

(1991, 92 min, Italy, Pupi Avati) *Lucrezia Lante della Rovere, Massimo Bonetti.* A sumptuously filmed parable about two disparate Italian families coming together for a nuptial banquet signifying the joining of the clans. Set for the most part on a small Italian farm, the film details the fabulous 20-course feast over which these two families (one of the intellectual city class, the other of rural peasant stock) meet for the first time. Filled with some wonderfully mirthful moments, the film uses the festivities as the platform for some time-honored (especially in Italian filmmaking) commentary on class differences as well as the occasional amorous roll in the hay. (Italian with English subtitles) ★★★ VHS: $19.99

The Story of G.I. Joe

(1945, 108 min, US, William Wellman) *Burgess Meredith, Robert Mitchum, Freddie Steele, Wally Cassell, Jimmy Lloyd.* Based on a series of articles by Pulitzer Prize–winning war correspondent Ernie Pyle, this gripping, unsentimental WWII film follows Pyle and the men of Company C of the 18th Infantry as they advance from North Africa to Italy. Meredith is outstanding as Pyle, and Mitchum — in his first major role — received an Oscar nomination for his dynamic portrayal of the company's captain. Unquestionably one of the best of all war-themed films produced during America's war years. ★★★★ VHS: $19.99; DVD: $24.99

The Story of Louis Pasteur

(1936, 85 min, US, William Dieterle) *Paul Muni, Josephine Hutchinson.* Muni won an Oscar for his detailed performance as French scientist Louis Pasteur. Hollywood storytelling and scientific heroics mesh perfectly in this first-rate biography. ★★★★ VHS: $19.99

The Story of Qiu Ju

(1992, 100 min, China, Zhang Yimou) *Gong Li, Lei Lao Sheng.* This collaboration between Zhang and actress Gong bears little resemblance to their previous period dramas such as *Raise the Red Lantern* and *Ju Dou.* Unlike those examinations of feudal China, *Qiu Ju* is an almost upbeat and decidedly proletarian look at one woman's crusade for justice. When her husband is severly beaten by the local party boss, Qiu Ju, a poor peasant woman, demands an apology. Upon his repeated refusals, she takes her case to ever-higher courts and encounters every stone wall the byzantine Chinese bureaucracy can put in her way. *Qiu Ju* is remarkable in its simplicity; Zhang has stripped his cinematic style to the bare minimum, eschewing the luxurious mise-en-scène and stunning photography of his other works. As a Chinese Mother Courage, Gong offers a wry portrayal. (Mandarin with English subtitles) ★★★½ VHS: $19.99; DVD: $29.99

Story of Sin

(1975, 128 min, Poland, Walerian Borowczyk) An elegant, full-bodied melodrama, set in turn-of-the-century Poland, tracing the life of a young girl, strictly raised, whose downfall is presaged when she opens her heart and soul to a married man. Misfortunes befall our innocent heroine as she becomes pregnant, is forced to get rid of the baby and slinks into degrading prostitution. Adopting the position that love has no place in an immoral, exploitative world, the harrowing drama takes an erotic, albeit sluggish, angle on *amour fou*. (Polish with English subtitles) ★★★

The Story of the Last Chrysanthemum

(1939, 145 min, Japan, Kenji Mizoguchi) *Shotaro Hanayagi, Kakuko Mori, Gonjuro Kawarazaki.* Bristling with passion and filmed with startling imagery, this poignant tale chronicles the life of a Kabuki actor in 1880s Tokyo. The young man, Kikunosuke, despondent after being ridiculed by other members of his father's famous troupe, returns home and begins an affair with a servant girl and, on his father's insistence, sets out on his own. The responsibility for both their survival and his eventual rise as a celebrated actor rests with his wife, Okoku, who sacrifices everything, even her health, for his success. This heartbreaker borders on over-sentimentality but is still a fascinating classic of doomed love. (Japanese with English subtitles) ★★★½ VHS: $29.99

The Story of Us

(1999, 120 min, US, Rob Reiner) *Bruce Willis, Michelle Pfeiffer, Rob Reiner, Rita Wilson, Colleen Rennison, Jake Sandvig.* It seems we've been down this road before. The characters look familiar, as well as the conversations, the story, the outcome. Wasn't it Woody Allen? No, it was Nora Ephron, right? Or was it Rob Reiner? In this *Snippets from a Marriage*, a husband and wife, Ben (Willis) and Katie (Pfeiffer), narrate the route to their current break-up. The story follows through numerous flashbacks their meeting, marriage, parenthood, careers, friends, misunderstandings; all of which pit them against each other on the road to divorce. Willis and Pfeiffer give very sincere performances. But the writing is sparse, and the bittersweet film never delivers when it should. There's a few cute scenes and a number of laughs, but this is all the fun of going through one's own separation. ★★ VHS: $14.99; DVD: $24.99

The Story of Vernon and Irene Castle

(1939, 93 min, US, H.C. Potter) *Fred Astaire, Ginger Rogers, Edna May Oliver, Walter Brennan.* The last of the Astaire-Rogers 1930s musicals for RKO is an appealing bio of the early 20th-century dancing team. Fred and Ginger's dancing is up to par, but it certainly doesn't rate with their other 1930s classics. ★★½ VHS: $14.99

Story of Women

(1988, 110 min, France, Claude Chabrol) *Isabelle Huppert, François Cluzet.* In this chilling and thought-provoking drama set in Vichy, France, Huppert is extraordinary as a wife whose husband is away at the front. She is persuaded to perform an abortion on a distraught neighbor. In a desperate attempt to support

herself, she begins offering the service to others; but she is soon arrested by the fascist officials. The drama, based on a real-life criminal case, recounts the story without sentiment and flawlessly evokes the tense mood of an occupied people. But it is Huppert's spellbinding portrayal of an independent, vunerable and, at times, unsympathetic character which gives the film its lasting power. (French with English subtitles) ★★★½ VHS: $29.99

Storyville

(1992, 112 min, US, Mark Frost) *James Spader, Joanne Whalley-Kilmer, Jason Robards, Piper Laurie.* In this moody tale of dirty politics, sex and murder, Spader plays an ambitious young man running for the Senate position recently vacated by the indictment, and later death, of his father. Robards is Spader's more ambitious, self-serving and unscrupulous uncle, using his own private agenda as he guides the candidate's career. The campaign runs into trouble when Spader becomes involved in a murder investigation that threatens to expose more deep secrets than he could imagine. An involving romantic courtroom mystery with a little gratuitous sex and violence thrown in. ★★½ VHS: $19.99

Stowaway in the Sky

(1962, 82 min, France, Albert Lamorisse) *Andre Gille, Maurice Baquet, Pascal Lamorisse; Narrated by: Jack Lemmon.* This enchanting fable is a terrific companion piece to director Lamorisse's Oscar-winning short *The Red Balloon. Stowaway in the Sky* will delight children as well as adults as it presents an aerial tour of Europe from the cockpit of a hot air balloon. Pascal (played by the director's son) climbs aboard his grandfather's magical flying machine for an unforgettable journey. From the streets of Paris, where he can look into the Eiffel Tower's elevator to the tip of Mont Blanc and the Canary Islands, this exhilarating ride features spectacular cinematography of Paris and the French countryside. Scenes of a stag hunt and flamingos in flight are breathtaking, and director Lamorisse punctuates the "action" with some slapstick

comic moments courtesy of a clumsy mechanic. ★★★½ VHS: $19.99

La Strada

(1954, 115 min, Italy, Federico Fellini) *Anthony Quinn, Guilietta Masina, Richard Basehart.* Fellini's tender and haunting tale of a brutish circus strongman (Quinn) and his sidekick (Masina) whose loneliness and solitude bind them together in a tenuous relationship. A truly poetic classic and an Academy Award winner, with stunning portrayals from both Masina and Quinn. (Italian with English subtitles) ★★★★ VHS: $29.99

Straight for the Heart

(1988, 92 min, Canada, Léa Pool) *Matthias Habich.* Returning from a harrowing trip to Nicaragua, where he has witnessed and photographed the horrors of war, prize-winning photojournalist Pierre returns home to Montreal only to find that Sarah and David, his lovers in a ten-year ménage à trois, have both left him. This absorbing drama, unusual for its matter-of-fact approach to bisexuality, explores the man's devastated life — from his futile attempts to reunite the threesome, to his wanderings through the city photographing urban decay. An intriguing, melancholy love story and quiet study of a man's emotional void, reminiscent in part of Alain Tanner's *In the White City*. (French with English subtitles) ★★★ VHS: $39.99

Straight Out of Brooklyn

(1991, 91 min, US, Matty Rich) *George T. Odom, Ann D. Sanders, Lawrence Gilliard, Matty Rich.* Nineteen-year-old Rich wrote and directed this remarkable and highly personal exposé of life in the projects. The story follows Dennis, a teenager who thinks of nothing but getting out of the ghetto. Plagued by his savagely alcoholic father, and with nowhere to go, he ultimately concocts an outrageous and ill-advised scheme to rob a drug dealer. While lacking the power and sophistication of *Boyz N the Hood*, this is nevertheless a gritty and hard-hitting film. ★★★ VHS: $9.99

Guilietta Masina (l.) and Anthony Quinn in Fellini's classic *La Strada*

The Straight Story

(1999, 115 min, US, David Lynch) *Richard Farnsworth, Sissy Spacek, Jane Galloway Heitz, James Cada, Everett McGill, Harry Dean Stanton.* It begins with a marriage of words you'd never thought you'd live to see: Walt Disney presents a David Lynch film. By the end, *The Straight Story* has taken the viewer on an unexpectedly moving and quite satisfying journey as to bring a feeling of near elation. In a quiet though commanding portrayal, Farnsworth gives a career performance as Alvin Straight, an Iowa widower who lives with his speech-impaired daughter (Spacek). Having suffered a stroke which now requires him to walk with two canes, Alvin sets out on an impossible trek when he learns that his estranged brother is gravely ill: journey 250 miles to Wisconsin to see him — traveling on a lawnmower. Lynch embraces the American Heartland without his signature cinematic touches. Having pushed the envelope with his previous films, Lynch retreats in the opposite direction and finds artistry in the traditional. He tells this simple, affecting true story with precision and exquisite grace. Thankfully, no one's in a hurry, and the film's deliberate pacing befits Alvin's slow, determined, fascinating trip. On his way, Alvin meets some interesting people, demonstrates his resolve, and finds meaning in ordinary endeavors. And we're all the richer for it. ★★★★ VHS: $19.99; DVD: $32.99

Straight Talk

(1992, 91 min, US, Barnet Kellman) *Dolly Parton, James Woods, Griffin Dunne, Michael Madsen, John Sayles, Jerry Orbach.* A mildly entertaining comedy about a good-hearted country girl (Parton) who moves to Chicago and manages to get herself a job as a telephone operator at a radio station. On her first day, she searches for the bathroom and ends up in the control room where she's mistaken for the new on-air psychologist. Of course, she's a hit with the listeners, a profitable problem for the station manager (Dunne) and the subject of an investigation from cynical newspaper reporter Woods, who is completely out-of-sync with the rest of the cast. ★★

Straight Time

(1977, 114 min, US, Ulu Grosbard) *Dustin Hoffman, Theresa Russell, Gary Busey, Harry Dean Stanton.* A recently released con (Hoffman) finds himself trapped between an indifferent criminal system and his own unconscious bent toward self-destruction. A provocative if ambitious drama helped by a strong supporting cast. ★★½ VHS: $14.99

Straight to Hell

(1987, 86 min, US, Alex Cox) *Sy Richardson, Joe Strummer, Dick Rude, Courtney Love, Dennis Hopper, Elvis Costello, Grace Jones, Jim Jarmusch.* Director Cox takes on the spaghetti western, as the bizarre citizens of a desert hamlet find themselves at the mercy of two rival gangs. Only partially successful, it's pretentious though occasionally amusing. ★★ DVD: $24.99

Strait-Jacket

(1964, 89 min, US, William Castle) *Joan Crawford, Leif Erickson.* "Have Ax Will Travel" as Crawford plays an ax murderer recently released from prison. She moves to a communi-

ty where it seems she's up to her old tricks. Crawford's Gothic horror follow-up to *Baby Jane* is alternately campy and occasionally effective — though its little success obviously is in the star's hammy playing. ★★½ VHS: $19.99

The Strange Affair of Uncle Harry

(1945, 80 min, US, Robert Siodmak) *George Sanders, Geraldine Fitzgerald.* Sanders is affecting as a shy man who must take drastic steps to get out of the domineering psychological grip of his two scheming sisters in this impressive Hitchcockian small-town thriller. A gripping and intelligent drama of obsession, hypochondria and the recuperative powers of love. ★★★ VHS: $19.99

Strange Behavior

(1981, 98 min, New Zealand, Michael Laughlin) *Louise Fletcher, Michael Murphy, Fionna Lewis.* A small college town is rocked by a series of brutal murders, which appear to be strangely linked to a psychology class experiment with an auto-suggestive drug. Laughlin sustains an eerie mood throughout, but the film loses some steam in the final half. ★★½ VHS: $19.99

Strange Days

(1995, 145 min, US, Kathryn Bigelow) *Ralph Fiennes, Angela Bassett, Juliette Lewis, Tom Sizemore, Vincent D'Onofrio.* Full of visceral thrills from start to finish, this slam-bang, hallucinatory thriller set on the eve of the new millennium stars Fiennes as Lenny, a former policeman who peddles virtual reality discs containing the experiences of others. However, when one of his clients is murdered, Lenny becomes involved in an out-of-control pursuit to find her murderer, track a serial killer, and expose a police cover-up of a racially motivated murder. Bassett is Mace, a bodyguard and friend who helps Lenny, and occasionally acts as moral compass. Their performances help immeasurably in giving the film an intelligence which clearly elevates this actioner much the same way Sigourney Weaver and cast propelled *Aliens.* Bigelow's direction, in fact, is reminiscent of that film, where one exciting scene is followed by another. There is, however, a brutal rape sequence which could offend many viewers. Written by James Cameron. (Letterboxed VHS available for $19.99) ★★★½ VHS: $9.99; DVD: $29.99

Strange Impersonation

(1946, 68 min, US, Anthony Mann) *Brenda Marshall, William Gargan, Hillary Brooke, Lyle Talbot.* Best known today for his groundbreaking westerns (*Winchester 73*) and historical epics (*El Cid*), director Mann cut his teeth at poverty row studios like Republic for whom he fashioned this 68-minute wild ride of murder and mayhem. Just on the brink of her greatest discovery, scientist Marshall has her experimental new anesthetic — and her love life — stolen by her ruthless assistant. Horribly disfigured in a lab fire, she melds out revenge undercover of a new face against all those who have wronged her. Hyperbolic and hypnotic, this tearjerker twists and turns like a sports car on a mountain road, frantic fun and one wild ride. ★★★ VHS: $24.99; DVD: $29.99

Strange Interlude

(1932, 111 min, US, Robert Z. Leonard) *Norma Shearer, Clark Gable, May Robson,*

Maureen O'Sullivan. Eugene O'Neill's powerful Pulitzer Prize—winning play of deceit and unrequited love gets a poignant and sturdy film adaptation — surprising considering the film retains O'Neill's innovative theatrical device of characters speaking their innermost thoughts. Shearer rises to the demands of her most challenging role, playing a woman who is haunted by the death of her fiancé. Gable gives the film's richest performance as Shearer's longtime friend and lover. The film, at half the running time of the play, still manages to capture the essence of O'Neill's complex work. ★★★½ VHS: $19.99

Strange Invaders

(1983, 94 min, US, Michael Laughlin) *Paul LeMat, Nancy Allen, Louise Fletcher, June Lockhart, Kenneth Tobey.* When a small town gets taken over by aliens that look just like you and me, how can anybody tell? And does it make any difference? Fifties icons Tobey and Lockhart show a cast of young turks how one went about vanquishing spacemen back in the old days. A generally entertaining spoof. ★★★ VHS: $9.99

The Strange Love of Martha Ivers

(1946, 117 min, US, Lewis Milestone) *Barbara Stanwyck, Kirk Douglas, Van Heflin.* Though its title suggests a '40s "B" potboiler, this gritty melodrama is anything but. Stanwyck gives a smashing performance as a wealthy, neurotic wife who is haunted by a murder in her past. Douglas makes a fine film debut as her spineless husband. Their lives come apart when old friend Heflin returns to town, digging up the past. ★★★ VHS: $24.99; DVD: $19.99

The Strange One

(1957, 100 min, US, Jack Garfein) *Ben Gazzara, George Peppard, Pat Hingle, James Olson.* Gazzara is riveting in a star-making performance as Jocko DeParis, a senior cadet at a Southern military college whose sadistic bullying and cocky manipulations pave the way for his downfall. He, along with his less self-assured roommate (Hingle), take pleasure in intimidating two freshman and later in concocting a scheme that ends in the beating. Cadets caught in the crossfire are forced to choose between silence (and staying in the school) or telling the truth (and face expulsion). A taut, sweaty drama that features excellent acting and an intense screenplay by Calder Willingham. ★★★ VHS: $19.99

Strangeland

(1998, 90 min, US, John Pieplow) *Dee Snider, Kevin Gage, Elizabeth Peña, Brett Harrelson, Robert Englund.* In this ugly, incredibly amateurish feature, former Twisted Sister lead singer Snider makes his writing and acting debut as a deranged "modern primitive" who kidnaps and tortures people to "free" them with body piercing and the like. He lures his victims by posing as a rad teen (his handle: Captain Howdy) in teen chat rooms on the internet. There's none of the over-the-top fun of the old Twisted Sister music videos on display here, just insipid horror. ★ VHS: $14.99; DVD: $14.99

The Stranger

(1946, 95 min, US, Orson Welles) *Edward G. Robinson, Orson Welles, Loretta Young.* Well-crafted thriller with Robinson as a government agent who is sent to a small college town in

Stranger Than Paradise

Connecticut to track down an escaped Nazi war criminal. Welles, as the feared German, is the embodiment of evil. Young is Welles' unsuspecting fiancée. ★★★½ VHS: $19.99

The Stranger

(1967, 104 min, Italy/France, Luchino Visconti) *Marcello Mastroianni.* A faithful, hypnotic adaptation of Albert Camus' existential treatise, this involving drama stars Mastroianni as Mersault, an individual seized by emptiness and isolated from society. Against the languid backdrop of Algiers, his detachment from existence abruptly ends when he commits a senseless murder and stands trial. Imprisoned and stripped of his physical freedom, Mersault expriences a liberating resignation as he surrenders to the "benign indifference of the universe." A quietly powerful and unsettling work. (Italian with English subtitles) ★★★

The Stranger

(1988, 93 min, US, Adolfo Aristarian) *Bonnie Bedelia, Peter Reigert.* A woman (Bedelia) stricken with amnesia slowly realizes she is the only witness to a series of brutal murders and must piece together the mystery before the killer can find her. An intriguing premise is well played, though it's not as suspenseful as it could have been. ★★½ VHS: $89.99

The Stranger

(1991, 120 min, India, Satyajit Ray) *Depankar De, Mamata Shankar, Bikram Bannerjee, Utpal Dutt.* Ray's swan song (completed just months before his death) is a wonderful and fitting tribute to the artist's legacy — using simple cinematic jestures to tell a simple tale while delivering ample emotional, spiritual and narrative clout. The film opens when Anila (Shankar) — a prototypical Indian middle-class housewife — receives a letter from her long-lost uncle (Dutt) announcing that he will be in Calcutta and wishes to visit. Filled with suspicion that he is not who he says, but an imposter attempting to freeload, she and her family become obsessed with verifying his true identity. As played by

Dutt, the uncle is as enchanting and worldly wise as he is enigmatic and impenetrable, all the while playing cat and mouse with the family's suspicions and filling their lives with mystery. He's a bit of a spiritual trickster, mildly mocking his hosts while gently guiding them towards some inner-awakening. (Bengali with English subtitles) ★★★★ VHS: $29.99

A Stranger Among Us

(1992, 109 min, US, Sidney Lumet) *Melanie Griffith, Eric Thal.* This Lumet dramatic thriller so resembles Peter Weir's *Witness* that it has been dubbed *Vitness*. Griffith is a New York undercover cop sent into Brooklyn's Hasidic community to root out a jewel thief/killer. All too predictably, of course, all of her coarse, unladylike behavior is transformed by the gentle, loving touch of this quaint people, but not before she tries her best to lead the Rabbi's son to temptation (her name, incidentally, is Emily *Eden*!). The film can't overcome its formulaic shallowness and fails to rise above its gushy, adoring view of the Hasidim. ★★ VHS: $19.99

Stranger on the First Floor

(1940, 64 min, US, Boris Ingster) *Peter Lorre, Elisha Cook, Jr., John McGuire.* Thanks to the stunning art direction by Van Nest Polglase (whose next project would be *Citizen Kane*), this little sleeper is considered by many to be the first true film noir. Taxi driver Cook is sentenced to the chair for a rather brutal murder on the testimony of press reporter McGuire. Now the reporter is having some doubts. Lorre as the titular character gives his best performance since *M*. ★★★ VHS: $19.99

Stranger Than Paradise

(1984, 90 min, US, Jim Jarmusch) *John Lurie, Eszter Balint, Richard Edson.* From the scroungy anomie of New York's Lower East Side to the snowy desolation of Cleveland to the sunny listlessness of Florida, this poker-faced neo-comedy follows the stillborn adventures of three amiable misfits in search of a natural habitat. Director Jarmusch's cool

shaggy-dog minimalism is absurdly funny and boldly original. (Letterboxed) ★★★★ VHS: $14.99; DVD: $19.99

Strangers in Good Company

(1990, 101 min, Canada, Cynthia Scott) *Alice Diabo, Mary Meigs.* This spirited, low-budget gem documents the travails of eight elderly women who become stranded in the wilderness when their tour bus breaks down. Using their resources, they find an abandoned house and begin foraging for food. Tremendously diverse in character and background, they each have a story to tell and the film allows them to do just that. Filmed entirely on location with an ensemble of non-actors who essentially play themselves, *Strangers in Good Company* is a wonderfully heartwarming homage to the spirit of these women, and to the wondrous application of one's continual self-discovery. ★★★½ VHS: $19.99; DVD: $29.99

Strangers on a Train

(1951, 103 min, US/GB, Alfred Hitchcock) *Farley Granger, Robert Walker, Ruth Roman, Leo G. Carroll, Marion Lorne.* Hitchcock's slick psychological thriller tackles blackmail, murder and latent homosexuality as Granger meets Walker on a train and soon becomes an unwilling partner in crime. A superior effort that features a knockout ending which is exemplary of the unrelenting tension the Master of Suspense could create. The basis for the spoof *Throw Momma from the Train.* (Includes two minutes not shown in the American theatrical release.) ★★★★ VHS: $14.99; DVD: $19.99

Strapless

(1989, 103 min, GB, David Hare) *Blair Brown, Bridget Fonda, Bruno Ganz.* With lush settings and a dreamy score (including Nat King Cole's "When I Fall in Love"), writer-director Hare sets a romantic tone in this unconventional film. Brown (Hare's wife) portrays an American physician living in Britain who discovers love and confusion in both her carefree sister (Fonda) and an enigmatic businessman (Ganz). Hare's direction is fluent, his dialogue graceful; Brown beautifully depicts a woman on the uneasy path to self-discovery. ★★★ VHS: $14.99; DVD: $29.99

Straw Dogs

(1972, 118 min, GB, Sam Peckinpah) *Dustin Hoffman, Susan George, David Warner.* Hoffman is the meek mathematician who, when his wife and home are attacked, finds catharsis and renewed masculinity in a violent, bloody confrontation. A film of incredible tension masterfully directed and conceived by Peckinpah. (Includes footage not shown in the American theatrical release.) (Letterboxed) ★★★½ VHS: $14.99; DVD: $14.99

Strawberry and Chocolate

(1993, 110 min, Cuba, Tomás Gutiérrez Alea & Juan Carlos Tabío) *Jorge Perugorria, Vladimir Cruz, Marta Ibarra.* This Oscar nominee is both a delightful comedy of friendship and love as well as a surprisingly critical political drama. Set in 1979 Havana, the story centers on the unlikely friendship between David (Cruz), a shy, straight and lost soul who blindly believes in the righteousness of the Revolution, and Diego (Perugorria), a swishy but intelligent, witty and opinionated gay man. Diego seduces David — not through sex but by his free-thinking appreciation of life, art and by an effervescent personality. A celebration of individuality in the face of conformity. (Spanish with English subtitles) ★★★½ VHS: $19.99

Strawberry Blonde

(1941, 97 min, US, Raoul Walsh) *James Cagney, Rita Hayworth, Olivia deHavilland.* Cagney is terrific as a young dentist whose life becomes a chaotic, emotional maze when he falls for a ravishing gold-digger (Hayworth) only to marry a more proper deHavilland. Director Walsh offers up a timely blend of laughter, nostalgia, action and romance. ★★★ VHS: $19.99

The Strawberry Statement

(1970, 109 min, US, Stuart Haggman) *Bruce Davison, Kim Darby.* Dated but interesting version of James Kunen's novel of '60s campus protest. Davison stars as a college jock who becomes involved with Darby and a campus strike. Featuring an outstanding soundtrack containing many '60s rock standards. ★★★ VHS: $69.99

Stray Dog

(1949, 122 min, Japan, Akira Kurosawa) *Toshiro Mifune, Takashi Shimura.* This stylized, non-samurai work from Kurosawa is an intense police thriller set in a seamy, war-ravaged Tokyo. Mifune plays a rookie detective who loses his gun to a pickpocket and, fearing the pistol will fall into the hands of a killer, begins a desperate search through the underworld in an attempt to find the pistol and the thief. An underappreciated murder mystery from the master of Japanese cinema. (Japanese with English subtitles) ★★★ VHS: $29.99

Streamers

(1983, 118 min, US, Robert Altman) *David Alan Grier, Matthew Modine, Mitchell Lichtenstein, Michael Wright.* Altman utilizes the intensity of the theatrical experience with the opportunities offered through film in this adaptation of David Rabe's award-winning play. *Streamers* is an ensemble piece, set in a claustrophobic Army barracks, featuring four ill-assorted young soldiers waiting for assignments to Vietnam. Hidden fears and prejudices generate sexual intolerance, racial distrust and a misunderstanding which leads to violence. ★★★

Street Fighter

(1994, 95 min, US, Steven E. deSouza) *Jean-Claude Van Damme, Raul Julia, Wes Studi, Simon Callow, Roshan Seth.* Van Damme stars as the head of an elite military unit whose mission in life is to stop the nefarious General Bison (Julia), a dictator bent on global domination. With the help of martial arts experts who would look more at home broadcasting the weather on CNN, Van Damme plays a boring game of cat and mouse with his adversary until a prolonged and surprisingly unexciting fight finale. The terrible screenplay gives neither of its stars any material to work with. ★ VHS: $19.99; DVD: $34.99

Street of Shame

(1956, 88 min, Japan, Kenji Mizoguchi) *Machiko Kyo, Aiko Mimasu.* Mizoguchi's final film is set in 1956 in a Tokyo brothel and explores the lives, dreams and hardships facing a group of prostitutes. This stirring portrait of the women delves not only into brothel life but follows them into the harsh streets of the city and into their homes. A penetrating study of love and sex and a powerful cinematic vision. (Japanese with English subtitles) ★★★½ VHS: $29.99

Street Smart

(1987, 95 min, US, Jerry Schatzberg) *Morgan Freeman, Christopher Reeve, Kathy Baker.* Freeman's blistering portrait of a ruthless pimp highlights this gritty urban drama about a newspaper reporter (Reeve in a change-of-pace role) who fabricates a story about the private life of a pimp — which turns out to be all too close to that of Freeman. Baker is exceptional as one of Freeman's working girls. ★★★

Street Trash

(1987, 90 min, US, Jim Muro) Entertaining and disgusting, *Street Trash* is not more than one step up from a student film, though it is competently made and has good production values considering its setting. The minimal story is about both a toxic brand of cheap liquor which melts its imbibers from the inside out and the gang rape and accidental murder of a mob boss' young mistress by the inhabitants of a junkyard. The movie has a guilty pleasure feel about it, from its well-done and completely disgusting special makeup effects to its gallows humor to its depiction of life in the seediest part of town. ★★ VHS: $79.99

The Street with No Name

(1948, 91 min, US, William Keighley) *Richard Widmark, Mark Stevens, Lloyd Nolan.* An exciting crime thriller with a chilling performance by Widmark as an up-and-coming crime boss who targets an FBI agent for death when the feds get too close to his gang's operations. ★★★ VHS: $19.99

A Streetcar Named Desire

(1951, 122 min, US, Elia Kazan) *Marlon Brando, Vivien Leigh, Karl Malden, Kim Hunter.* Brando is the brutish Stanley Kowalski, who psychologically strips his fragile sister-in-law Blanche (Leigh) until her breakdown is complete. Tennessee Williams' masterpiece is layered with sexual symbolism and haunting imagery, and features fine support from Malden as a well-intentioned suitor and Hunter as Stanley's beleaguered wife. Brando and Oscar winner Leigh's performances have over time become part of our cinematic heritage. (Director's cut with additional footage not in the American theatrical release.) ★★★★ VHS: $19.99; DVD: $19.99

The Streetfighter

(1975, 91 min, Japan, Seiji Ozawa) *Sonny Chiba.* An entertaining, slightly cheesy 1970s martial arts film. Presented in its original, uncut version, the film is awash in brutal violence — limbs are broken, eyes gouged out, and genitalia pulled off, all by our hero Terry Tsurugi (Chiba). Terry is a killer-for-hire who helps rescue Junjo, an important gang member, from prison. After killing Junjo's associate during a double-cross attempt, Terry finds himself pursued by the criminals who hired him. (Letterboxed) (Dubbed in English) ★★★ VHS: $19.99

Streets of Fire

(1984, 93 min, US, Walter Hill) *Michael Paré, Willem Dafoe, Diane Lane, Rick Moranis, Amy Madigan.* Kinda hip and fun rock 'n' roll fable with Paré as a soldier of fortune who returns to his old neighborhood to rescue his ex-girlfriend from the clutches of a vicious motorcycle gang. ★★★ VHS: $14.99; DVD: $24.99

Streets of Gold

(1986, 95 min, US, Joe Roth) *Klaus Maria Brandauer, Wesley Snipes, Adrian Pasdar.* A sincere performance from Brandauer elevates this ordinary boxing drama about a Russian fighter, now living in Brooklyn as a dishwasher, who trains two youths (Pasdar, Snipes) for the American team — in the hopes of competing against his former coach. ★★½ VHS: $9.99

Stray Dog

Stuart Little

Streetwise

(1985, 92 min, US, Martin Bell) An extraordinary documentary which chronicles the lives of nine young runaways, ages 13 to 19, who survive in the drug and tenderloin district of Seattle and support themselves by prostitution, pimping, panhandling and petty thievery. It's a bleak picture, but one that also captures sweet flirtatious moments and times of shared humor and experience as these kids try to create a niche for themselves. Oscar nominee for Best Documentary. ★★★★ VHS: $19.99

Strictly Ballroom

(1992, 94 min, Australia, Baz Luhrmann) *Paul Mercurio, Tara Morice, Bill Hunter, Barry Otto.* Tapping into the Fred and Ginger in all of us, first-time director Luhrmann has crafted a glorious take on the elegant (but at times wacky) world of ballroom dancing. Mercurio is a badboy hoofer whose innovative technique flies in the face of the traditionalists, making him an outcast in a dance community where "ballroom" has been elevated to a religion. With a nod to *Dirty Dancing*, he takes up with an awkward dance student (Morice) and the two set out to win the big dance competition. As by-the-books as it sounds, a laugh-out-loud, zany and enjoyable musical is born. ★★★½

Strictly Business

(1991, 83 min, US, Kevin Hooks) *Joseph C. Phillips, Tommy Davidson, Halle Berry, Samuel L. Jackson.* Hooks has fashioned a warm comedy about a dyed-in-the-wool "buppie" (Phillips) who enlists the aid of a mailroom clerk (Davidson) to help him meet the girl of his dreams (Berry). While yet another "message" movie from the black community for the black community, this one manages to mix a little sugar with the medicine, making its theme of unity and racial harmony an enjoyable pill to swallow. ★★½ VHS: $19.99

Strike

(1924, 82 min, USSR, Sergei Eisenstein) *Maxim Shtraukh, Grigori Alexandrov.* In a remarkable directorial debut, Eisenstein introduced radical innovations in editing, montage and camera work in presenting this impassioned film about

the struggles of workers embroiled in a violent strike at a Moscow factory, set before the Revolution. He recounts the workers' hardships and exploitation as well as the devastating strike itself — the resulting hunger, the presence of predatory infiltrators and ultimately the bloody massacre by the militia. (Silent with music by the Alloy Orchestra) ★★★★ VHS: $24.99; DVD: $24.99

Strike!

Starring Kirsten Dunst
See. All I Wanna Do

Striking Distance

(1993, 102 min, US, Rowdy Herrington) *Bruce Willis, Sarah Jessica Parker, Dennis Farina, Tom Sizemore, John Mahoney.* A by-the-books thriller about a by-the-books cop whose demotion to the Pittsburgh River patrol comes in handy when his ex-girlfriends start turning up as fishbait courtesy of a serial killer with an inside knowledge of police procedure. ★★½ VHS: $9.99; DVD: $19.99

Stripes

(1981, 106 min, US, Ivan Reitman) *Bill Murray, Harold Ramis, P.J. Soles, Warren Oates, John Candy.* Murray and Ramis team up with director Reitman in this mildly successful, pre-*Ghostbusters* comedy spoof on life in the Army. Murray and Ramis play a couple of losers who join under the assumption that life in the forces will be an easy overseas holiday. Along the way, they hoodwink their superiors and become inadvertent heroes. Goofy and sophomoric, Murray's charm and the spirited performances of the supporting cast provide this military farce with "a few good laughs." ★★½ VHS: $12.99; DVD: $19.99

The Stripper

(1963, 95 min, US, Franklin J. Schaffner) *Joanne Woodward, Richard Beymer, Claire Trevor, Gypsy Rose Lee.* Woodward's competent performance saves this William Inge melodrama about an aging stripper and her affair with a young man. ★★½

Striptease

(1996, 115 min, US, Andrew Bergman) *Demi Moore, Burt Reynolds, Armand Assante, Ving Rhames, Robert Patrick.* Carl Hiaasen's cunning satirical novel has been stripped of its bite and wit. When she loses custody of her child to her slimy husband, Moore takes a high-paying job at a Fort Lauderdale strip club to earn enough money to reopen the case. Becoming its star attraction, Moore becomes the unwilling object of lust from a local congressman (a spirited and funny Reynolds) which leads to murder and run-ins with the mob. Bergman is unable to capture the flavor of the book or convey the energy and tempo of good satirical comedy. And he's not helped by a sullen Moore. Reynolds, on the other hand, appears to fully understand the nuances of farce. (Unrated) ★½ VHS: $9.99; DVD: $19.99

Stromboli

(1950, 81 min, Italy, Roberto Rossellini) *Ingrid Bergman.* This neorealist Rossellini drama stars Bergman as a woman who escapes an internment camp only to marry an unresponsive fisherman and live on a barren, bleak island confronting poverty and a spiritual sort of prison. Although the film received excellent reviews, the Bergman/Rossellini extramarital affair during the time of the release doomed the picture commercially. (Filmed in English) ★★★ VHS: $29.99

Stroszek

(1977, 108 min, Germany, Werner Herzog) *Bruno S., Eva Mattes.* Three German misfits — a whore, a former mental patient and an eccentric old man — confront the American Dream in one of Herzog's funniest and most accessible films. Fleeing Berlin, the trio's wanderings lead them to the barren bleakness of Railroad Flats, Wisconsin. Setting up house in a mobile home bought on credit, they attempt to come to terms with the dubious splendors of American culture: TV, football, dancing chickens, and other oddball bits of Americana. A lyrical, perceptive and bittersweet comedy. (German with English subtitles) ★★★½

Stuart Little

(1999, 85 min, US, Rob Minkoff) *Geena Davis, Hugh Laurie, Jonathan Lipnicki; Voices of: Michael J. Fox, Nathan Lane.* The perfectly strange Little couple (Davis and Laurie) go to the orphanage. In E.B. White's fanciful world (and to their son Lipnicki's costernation), the fact that they adopt a mouse named Stuart is really no big deal, just another happy little quirk in their two-story townhouse overlooking Manhattan's Central Park. Computer effects and Fox's permapubescent voice blend seamlessly to create this new family member, who experiences the same pains as anyone entering a new home. Though things get too frenetic at the end, the comedy within the family is grandly entertaining, with plenty of imagination for kids and grownups alike. ★★★ VHS: $14.99; DVD: $19.99

Stuart Saves His Family

(1995, 97 min, US, Harold Ramis) *Al Franken, Laura San Giacomo, Vincent D'Onofrio.* Based on his "S.N.L." skit, Franken stars as the nebbishly New Age talk show host who's "good enough and smart enough...," until the cancellation of his cable-access show and the death of an aunt force him to come to terms with his own dysfunctional family. Alternately funny and tired, Franken's screenplay pokes fun at the New Age and 12-step programs while also trying to reach a catharsis from their application, though he is more successful in his spoofing than the sometimes dreadful pathos. Franken clearly knows Stuart well. ★★ VHS: $19.99; DVD: $29.99

The Student Prince at Old Heidelberg

(1927, 105 min, US, Ernst Lubitsch) *Ramon Novarro, Norma Shearer.* This silent film version doesn't really miss the music of Romberg's operetta, with its breezy charm that became known as the "Lubitsch Touch." Novarro is effervescent as the heir to the throne getting to cut loose for the first time now that he's away for college. Everything would have been fine if he hadn't fallen in love with bar-frau Shearer at the fraternity beer bash. ★★★½ VHS: $29.99

The Stuff

(1985, 93 min, US, Larry Cohen) *Michael Moriarty, Andrea Marcovicci, Garrett Morris, Paul Sorvino, Danny Aiello.* Playfully satiric horror film about a mysterious goo — the newest culinary fad — which turns those who eat it into zombies with an appetite. ★★ VHS: $9.99; DVD: $24.99

The Stunt Man

(1980, 129 min, US, Richard Rush) *Peter O'Toole, Steve Railsback, Barbara Hershey.* O'Toole is the maniacal film director who befriends then dominates a young man (Railsback) on the run from the police. A frenetically paced, tautly edited story about paranoia and illusion versus reality. ★★★★ VHS: $19.99

The Subject Was Roses

(1968, 107 min, US, Ulu Grosbard) *Patricia Neal, Jack Albertson, Martin Sheen, Don Saxon.* Reprising their acclaimed stage roles from the Pulitzer Prize-winning play by Frank D. Gilroy, Sheen and Oscar winner Albertson offer heartfelt performances in this story of a troubled WWII vet returning to his Bronx home. Neal,

Striptease

however, is the heart and soul of this moving film, by giving a shimmering portrait of a mother trying to establish communication with those around her, and by returning to the screen after an almost career-ending stroke. ★★★ VHS: $19.99

The Substance of Fire

(1996, 101 min, US, Daniel Sullivan) *Ron Rifkin, Sarah Jessica Parker, Tony Goldwyn, Timothy Hutton, Ronny Graham, Eric Bogosian, Debra Monk.* A father-son relationship is the central theme to this story of a publisher and his sons as they disagree on the direction of the family business. Based on the successful off-Broadway play, with Rifkin reprising his role of the headstrong patriarch. Intense performances from the whole cast, especially Rifkin as the publisher/father. ★★★ VHS: $14.99

The Substitute

(1996, 114 min, US, Robert Mandel) *Tom Berenger, Ernie Hudson, Diane Venora, Marc Anthony, Glenn Plummer, Cliff de Young, William Forsythe.* Berenger's patented sensitive tough guy is this time an unemployed covert op. He assumes the cover of substitute teacher, replacing his on-again, off-again lover (Venora) when her leg is broken by the school's reigning gang leader. Within a few days, this warrior-with-a-gentle-heart uncovers a nasty little secret on school grounds, enlisting his mercenary buddies to bring the war back home. Look for the scene in which Berenger is asked about his Vietnam War wounds. The class responds to his reply by displaying their own wounds: fin de siècle Show and Tell. (Followed by 3 sequels) ★★ VHS: $9.99; DVD: $14.99

Suburban Roulette

(1967, 70 min, US, Hershell Gordon Lewis) *Tom Wood.* Although best known for his gore films, director Lewis also made a number of cheap exploitation flicks. In this one, Wood stars as the father of the new family in suburbia, where the wives are swapping more than just recipes. ★ VHS: $12.99

The Suburbans

(1999, 81 min, US, Donal Lardner Ward) *Jennifer Love Hewitt, Craig Bierko, Amy Brenneman, Will Ferrell, Donal Lardner Ward, Tony Guma, Robert Loggia.* A feeble rock 'n' roll fable, *The Suburbans* is an alleged comedy about an '80s one-hit-wonder band trying to make a comeback eighteen years later. Cowritten, directed by, and starring Ward (who proved he had talent in *My Life Is in Turnaround*), the film fails on all three counts as the jokes are unfunny, the staging is uninspired, and most of the cast mimics Ward's wry deadpan delivery to ill effect. Hewitt stars an a record exec trying to generate interest in a now middle-aged pop band. ★ VHS: $9.99; DVD: $24.99

Suburbia

(1984, 96 min, US, Penelope Spheeris) *Chris Pederson, Bill Coyne, Jennifer Clay.* This archly funny anthem to punk nihilism captures the spirit of anomie rampant on the Mellow Coast. If only there were more social clubs, these kids wouldn't be going around ransacking neighborhood garages. (aka: *The Wild Side*) ★★½ VHS: $14.99; DVD: $19.99

SubUrbia

(1997, 117 min, US, Richard Linklater) *Giovanni Ribisi, Steve Zahn, Amie Corey, Parker Posey, Nicky Katt, Jayce Bartak, Dina Spybey, Ajay Naidu.* Eric Bogosian's off-Broadway play about youthful alienation, which the author has adapted for the screen, makes a most hearty and funny film as envisioned by director Linklater, who uncannily dissects a generational mindset. A terrific ensemble brings to life a cast of engaging characters who, though familiar in their appearance and deed, are individualists who speak for no one but themselves. A "night in the life of," *SubUrbia* eavesdrops on a group of "misfit" friends who gather, drink beer, have sex and philosophize at the local convenience store. Their routine is interrupted one night when a former classmate returns. Regrets, jealousies, partnerships and much revelry quickly follows. Among the talented cast, Zahn wonderfully plays the group clown; and Posey gives a smart performance as a spirited publicist. ★★★ VHS: $9.99

Subway

(1985, 103 min, France, Luc Besson) *Christopher Lambert, Isabelle Adjani, Jean-Hugues Anglade, Jean Reno.* Tuxedoed punks, mondo bodybuilders, roller-skating purse snatchers and roving musicians stylishly adorn Besson's glimpse at Paris underground life. A brilliantly choreographed car chase romps and roars its way into the Paris Metro, where Lambert eludes his pursuers. Amidst the labyrinthine corridors and twisted passage ways of the cavernous underground, a wonderfully colorful world of outrageous misfits springs into bloom, highlighted by a luminously attired Adjani. ★★★½

Subway to the Stars

(1987, 103 min, Brazil, Carlos Diegues) *Guilherme Fontes, Milton Goncalves.* An enchanting fable that is a modernization of the Orpheus legend. The story revolves around the young Vinicius, an innocent saxophonist who embarks on an odyssey through the seedy and sleazy underworld of Rio de Janeiro in search of his missing girlfriend. His journey brings him in contact with cops and bandits, slum dwellers and dreamers, prostitutes and poets. Although the settings are grim and his task seemingly endless, our young hero, as well as the demimondes of the slum, retains an optimistic and dreamy attitude. (Portuguese with English subtitles) ★★★

Success Is the Best Revenge

(1984, 90 min, GB, Jerzy Skolimowski) *Michael York, Michel Piccoli, John Hurt, Anouk Aimée.* Director Skolimowski's follow-up to his widely successful *Moonlighting* continues to explore the plight of Polish immigrants in foreign lands. This time his view is slightly more autobiographical as he tells the tale of a Polish filmmaker (York) living in exile in London. As he works feverishly to make a film about the growing unrest in his homeland, he becomes estranged from his rebellious teenage son. ★★★ VHS: $9.99

Sudden Death

(1995, 110 min, US, Peter Hyams) *Jean-Claude Van Damme, Powers Boothe, Ross Malinger, Whittni Wright, Dorian Harewood.* More predictable

S

action with Van Damme, this time as an ex-fire-fighter who, having been unable to rescue a little girl from a burning building in the film's opening, sees a chance for redemption when terrorists take his daughter — and the vice-president — hostage at the Stanley Cup finals. There's some fast-paced action and elaborate stuntwork, but the story starts to grow thin. However, watch out for a fight sequence involving a manhating, kickboxing penguin. ★★½ VHS: $14.99; DVD: $24.99

Sudden Fear

(1952, 110 min, US, David Miller) *Joan Crawford, Jack Palance, Gloria Grahame, Bruce Bennett, Virginia Huston, Mike Connors.* Crawford's face wore emotion as liberally as lipstick; here it is paired with the icy mug of Palance in an elegant romantic thriller that turns on images of inhuman faces: a clock's, a toy dog's, Palance's. As the actor fired by hit playwright Crawford for being too sinister-looking to play a romantic lead, Palance energetically charms as the film's own romantic lead — until the truth emerges, and he turns sinister, proving a Hollywood Truth: appearances are everything. The film overflows with much of what made '50s noir fun: moody cinematography, a tough, tightly twisted Lenore Coffee script, an atmospheric, jazzy Elmer Bernstein score, along with the unparalleled vision of its diva star dashing up the hills of San Francisco in high heels and furs. ★★★½ VHS: $19.99; DVD: $29.99

Sudden Impact

(1983, 117 min, US, Clint Eastwood) *Clint Eastwood, Sondra Locke, Pat Hingle.* Eastwood's fourth go-round as San Francisco detective "Dirty" Harry Callahan puts him on the trail of a woman (Locke) who is getting revenge against the gang who raped her and her sister years before. The series is starting to show its age, but director Eastwood still manages to bring some life to the familiar tale. (Sequel: *The Dead Pool*) ★★½ VHS: $14.99

Suddenly

(1954, 77 min, US, Lewis Allen) *Frank Sinatra, Sterling Hayden, James Gleason.* Sinatra, in sort of a precursor to *The Manchurian Candidate*, plays the leader of a group of assassins in this suspenseful thriller. Little-seen for many years after the Kennedy assassination, the story concerns a group of gunmen who take over a house in a small town where the president is due. ★★★ VHS: $19.99; DVD: $9.99

Suddenly, Last Summer

(1959, 114 min, US, Joseph L. Mankiewicz) *Elizabeth Taylor, Montgomery Clift, Katharine Hepburn, Mercedes McCambridge.* A blistering Tennessee Williams drama (coscripted by Gore Vidal) about psychiatrist Clift investigating what caused Taylor to crack while on summer vacation with Hepburn's son Sebastian. Terrific performances by Taylor and Hepburn. (Remade in 1992) ★★★ VHS: $19.99; DVD: $24.99

Suffering Bastards

(1990, 90 min, US, Bernard McWilliams) *John C. McGinley, David Warshofsky, Eric Bogosian.* Independent low-budget comedy about a pair of born-loser brothers (McGinley, Warshofsky) who rip off their low-life boss (Bogosian) and

use the money to buy back their dead mother's Atlantic City night club, revitalizing their lounge-singing careers. Unusual, uneven but not without an abundance of quirky charm. ★★★ VHS: $89.99

Sugar Cane Alley

(1984, 104 min, Martinique, Euzhan Palcy) *Gerry Cadenet.* This bittersweet Third World tale about French colonial exploitation during the 1930s focuses on Jose, a young boy who manages to escape shantytown poverty through intellectual pursuit and the aid of his indomitable grandmother. (French with English subtitles) ★★★ VHS: $29.99; DVD: $29.99

Sugar Hill

(1994, 125 min, US, Leon Ichaso) *Wesley Snipes, Michael Wright, Theresa Randle.* With a marketing campaign that suggests it might be the next *New Jack City*, it is no wonder that *Sugar Hill* made no great strides upon its theatrical release. In point of fact, director Ichaso's sometimes grisly yet gripping character study owes more to the works of William Shakespeare than to its gangster roots. Snipes stars as a Harlem drug lord who, having seen both his parents destroyed by heroin, finally decides to get out, much to the dismay of his firebrand brother. While action fans may find this a little too talky, it is nonetheless extremely well-acted and a worthy addition to the gangster canon. ★★★ VHS: $9.99

Sugarbaby (Zuckerbaby)

(1985, 108 min, West Germany, Percy Adlon) *Marianne Sagerbrecht, Eisi Gulp.* This tender and endearing comedy stars Sagerbrecht as a sad, overweight mortuary attendant helplessly smitten with a slim blond subway conductor. The film radiates a fine erotic warmth as Marianne, taking leave of both her job and her senses, stalks and then captures her prey. An unusual and compassionate essay on the power of love and will. (American remake: *Baby Cakes*) (German with English subtitles) ★★★

The Sugarland Express

(1974, 109 min, US, Steven Spielberg) *Goldie Hawn, William Atherton, Michael Sacks, Ben Johnson.* Based on a true story, Spielberg's theatrical debut is a vastly entertaining comedy-drama. In one of her best performances, Hawn plays a mother who helps her husband escape jail, and together they plan to kidnap their own baby, now a ward of the state. In the ensuing confusion, they take a state trooper hostage, and have the entire Texas police force on their trail as they attempt to retrieve their child. ★★★½

Suicide Kings

(1998, 103 min, US, Peter O'Fallon) *Christopher Walken, Denis Leary, Henry Thomas, Sean Patrick Flannery, Johnny Galecki, Jay Mohr, Jeremy Sisto, Laura San Giacomo.* Four children of privilege kidnap Charles Barrett (Walken), a man of wealth, in an attempt to pay a ransom for another kidnapping victim, the sister of one of the four. Barrett, who came into this world as Carlo Bartolucci, is thought to have contacts who can aid in the sister's rescue. What Barrett has without question is an unerring ability to read human nature; and as the conspirators' alliance splinters under the stress of unforeseen contingencies, Barrett exploits the schisms festering in their personal relationships. The

Suddenly, Last Summer

ensemble delivers well-portrayed character studies in this ably constructed battle of wit and will. ★★★ VHS: $9.99; DVD: $9.99

Suite 16

(1994, 109 min, GB/The Netherlands, Dominique Deruddere) *Pete Postlethwaite, Antoine Kamerling.* Psychological and sexual games run amok on the Côte D'Azur in this intriguingly sick English-language drama. Chris (Kamerling) is a handsome, self-assured German blond whose con is to seduce older women on the French Riviera and then rob them. After almost killing a robbery victim, he flees and finds temporary refuge in the opulent suite/apartment of Glover (Postlethwaite), a rich but wheelchair-bound paraplegic. After a menacing first night, tables are turned as captor becomes captive when Glover offers the young man a lucrative offer to stay and have sex with women and allow him to watch. This kinky tale palpitates in homoeroticism as its story of humiliation, greed, abuse and ultimately love unfolds. (Filmed in English) ★★★ VHS: $9.99; DVD: $19.99

The Suitors

(1989, 106 min, US/GB, Ghasem Ebrahimian) This unpredictable and outrageous dark comedy tells the story of an Iranian woman, newly married and arrived in New York City. Mariyum arrives in the U.S. with her rich husband, Haji. But during a celebration, a friend's landlord mistakes a religious feast (in which a sheep is sacrificed) for a terrorist act, and a SWAT team accidentally shoots Haji, leaving the young émigré a widow. Alone in a strange land, and having tested some of the freedoms belonging to American women, Mariyum is courted by her late husband's four friends, who prove to be as relentless in their romantic attentions as they are in their desire for Mariyum to return to traditional Islamic values. ★★★ VHS: $29.99

Sullivan's Travels

(1941, 91 min, US, Preston Sturges) *Joel McCrea, Veronica Lake, William Demarest, Franklin Pangborn.* One of director Sturges' many great comedies of the 1940s, this brilliant probe into the psyche of a comedy filmmaker — decades before Woody Allen or Blake Edwards found success with the theme — is his most personal film and a classic road movie. McCrea stars as a successful movie director who longs to direct a "serious" film — so he sets out on the road, dressed as a hobo, to see the "real world." He befriends Lake, an actress wannabe about to head back home, and learns a few valuable lessons on the resilience of man and the power of laughter. A masterful combination of razor-sharp satire and sentimentality. ★★★★ VHS: $14.99; DVD: $39.99

The Sum of Us

(1994, 100 min, Australia, Kevin Dowling & Geoff Burton) *Jack Thompson, Russell Crowe, John Polson.* From the 1991 off-Broadway play comes this endearing family comedy-drama about the unusual relationship between a father and son. Set in a working-class area of Sydney, the story centers on the widowed but fun-loving Harry (Thompson) and his football-playing son Jeff (Crowe). What makes their story so different is that dad not only knows that his twentysomething son is gay, but is quite enthusiastic and accepting of it — hoping that Jeff will eventually find Mr. Right. With great wit and charm, the two men's home life is explored. Funny, tender though slightly maudlin towards the end, *The Sum of Us* breaks many sexual stereotypes with its even portrayal of homosexuality. Best of all, however, are the terrific performances by Thompson and Crowe, who endow Harry and Jeff with humor, sympathy and sensibility. ★★★½

Summer

(1986, 99 min, France, Eric Rohmer) *Marie Riviere, Lisa Heredia.* Rohmer's illuminating and moving exploration of loneliness stands as one of his most accomplished works to date. An independent but melancholy Parisian secretary, recently separated from her boyfriend, seems unwilling, even incapable, of enjoying her two-week holiday. Her loneliness and frustrations are compounded by her shyness as well as a strong will that refuses to compromise. Rohmer paints a vivid portrait of this woman and her efforts to connect and enjoy life. (French with English subtitles) ★★★½ VHS: $19.99; DVD: $29.99

Summer and Smoke

(1961, 118 min, US, Peter Glenville) *Geraldine Page, Laurence Harvey, Una Merkel, Rita Moreno,*

Sugar Cane Alley

Earl Holliman. Page repeats her acclaimed stage role in Tennessee Williams' searing drama, and she should have won an Oscar for it. In a tour de force performance, Page plays a sexually repressed minister's daughter who falls in love with dashing playboy Harvey. Set in a small Mississippi town in 1916, the story is a sensitive treatise on unrequited love and ignored passion. ★★★½ VHS: $14.99

Summer City

(1976, 83 min, Australia, Christopher Frazer) *Mel Gibson.* A very young Gibson stars in this little known Australian sex comedy about the final free-for-all fling of four students who are on the prowl for girls, thrills and surf. Set in the early Sixties, this routine teen hijinks comedy is of interest for Gibson's film debut. ★★½

Summer Fling

(1997, 103 min, US/Ireland, David Keating) *Catherine O'Hara, Jared Leto, Christina Ricci, Gabriel Byrne, Amanda Shun, Stephen Rea, Colm Meany.* Yet another bland comedy-drama about those quirky Irish. This one gets another mark on the trendy check list for taking place in the '70s. An affable but underachieving, slightly withdrawn lad (Leto) spends the summer avoiding work, looking for girls and sweating the results of his senior finals. His wacky, eccentric family, led by flamboyant stage actor Da (Byrne) and raging stereotype, scream-at-ya-cuz-I-love-ya Ma (O'Hara), drive him batty, while a visiting American girl arrives to flirt with him. If you can get past the clichéd characters and blah story, there are a few stylish moments. ★★ VHS: $14.99

The Summer House

(1993, 85 min, GB, Waris Hussein) *Jeanne Moreau, Joan Plowright, Julie Walters, Lena Headey, John Wood.* This enchanting British comedy unites two of the grande dames of international cinema: Moreau and Plowright. Giving one of the most sparkling performances of her long career, Moreau plays the hard-drinking, high-spirited childhood friend of Walters, who's preparing her daughter's marriage. When Moreau arrives for the wedding, she's shocked to discover that the intended groom is a boorish mama's boy. So entering into a mischievous coconspiracy with the cantankerous mother of the groom, royally played by Plowright, she sets out to prevent the marriage from ever taking place. ★★★

Summer Interlude

(1950, 94 min, Sweden, Ingmar Bergman) *Maj-Britt Nilson, Birger Nilson.* This early Bergman romantic drama, an affecting story told with the director's usual able hand but lacking in his visual expertise, is a bittersweet tale about a famed ballerina (Nilson) who chances upon a deceased lover's diary, triggering memories of first love, happier days and tragic circumstance. (aka: *Illicit Interlude*) (Swedish with English subtitles) ★★★ VHS: $29.99

Summer Lovers

(1982, 98 min, US, Randal Kleiser) *Peter Gallagher, Daryl Hannah, Valerie Quennessen.* This exotic eye-pleaser, from the director of *The Blue Lagoon*, focuses on how three young people (Gallagher,

Hannah and Quennessen) spend their summer vacation. Not a lot of substance, but any movie about a ménage à trois in the Greek islands can't be all bad. ★★½ VHS: $9.99

Summer Night

(1987, 94 min, Italy, Lina Wertmuller) *Mariangelo Melato, Michele Placido.* Director Wertmüller returns to the familiar terrain of sexual and political conflict in this enjoyably erotic comedy, reminiscent in many ways to her 1975 hit *Swept Away*. That film's star Melato plays a bitchy millionairess who has the tables turned on a notorious terrorist responsible for a series of kidnappings. She kidnaps him and holds him captive on her isolated Mediterranean isle, where the two become locked in a lusty battle of the sexes — Wertmüller style. The handsome Placido plays the befuddled kidnapper. ★★★

Summer of '42

(1971, 102 min, US, Robert Mulligan) *Gary Grimes, Jennifer O'Neill, Jerry Houser.* A captivating coming-of-age tale which concentrates more on character and emotion than sentimentality. Set in 1942, the film stars Grimes as a teenager vacationing in New England who falls in love with beautiful and married O'Neill, whose husband is overseas. What follows are blithe observations on first love and the teen years which should have anyone who's been through it smiling in recognition. (Sequel: *Class of '44*) ★★★ VHS: $14.99

The Summer of Miss Forbes

(1988, 87 min, Mexico, Jaime Humberto Hermosillo) *Hanna Schygulla, Alexis Castanares.* A luminous Schygulla stars as a sexually repressed governess in this erotic, beautifully photographed but ultimately silly melodrama scripted by Gabriel Garcia Marquez. In a lush sea resort, a frenzied couple goes on a six-week cruise and hires Miss Forbes (Schygulla), a stern Prussian schoolteacher, to instill manners and discipline into their two chubby, calculating sons. Matronly dressed and militarily tough by day, Miss Forbes harbors another personality — for at night, she becomes a tequila-guzzling, cake-stuffing floozy. And while she is plotting the sexual conquest of the boys' beautiful diving instructor, they concoct a plan to rid themselves of her forever. While enjoyable, the film never completely works, with Ms. Schygulla miscast as the barely concealed basket case. (Spanish with English subtitles) ★★½

Summer of Sam

(1999, 142 min, US, Spike Lee) *John Leguizamo, Mira Sorvino, Adrien Brody, Jennifer Esposito, Anthony LaPaglia, Ben Gazzara.* Serial-killer buffs beware: *Summer of Sam* deals with the famed Son of Sam mostly on the periphery. The main focus of the film is the atmosphere of fear, paranoia and rage that he helped instill in that summer of 1977 in New York City. A handful of excellent performances — most notably Leguizamo as a weak-willed adulterer and Brody as a punk outsider — and Lee's customary stylish visuals inject a bristling energy into this overlong and, at times, meandering drama. Two terrific set pieces (both accompanied by classic Who songs) and the frightening but nonexploitative Son of Sam killings are other big pluses; this isn't Lee's best work, and it's

S

Summer Stock

frustratingly uneven, but as an evocation of a specific time and place, *Summer of Sam* is successful. ★★★ VHS: $14.99; DVD: $29.99

Summer School

(1987, 98 min, US, Carl Reiner) *Mark Harmon, Kirstie Alley.* Director Reiner manages to produce a few laughs in this otherwise ordinary comedy with Harmon as a summer school teacher who'd rather be elsewhere. ★★ VHS: $14.99

Summer Stock

(1950, 109 min, US, Charles Walters) *Judy Garland, Gene Kelly, Eddie Bracken, Phil Silvers, Marjorie Main.* Judy sings "Get Happy" in this entertaining musical about a theatrical troupe, including dancer Gene, who plan to turn her farm's barn into a theater. A good supporting cast is featured. ★★★ VHS: $19.99

A Summer to Remember

(1960, 78 min, USSR, G. Danelia & I. Talankin) *Sergey Bondarchuk.* Based on a young child's view and acceptance of the atmosphere that surrounds him, this film focuses on a six-year-old boy's relationship with his mother and stepfather. The stepfather is brilliantly played by Bondarchuk. (Russian with English subtitles) ★★★

Summer Vacation 1999

(1988, 90 min, Japan, Shusuke Kaneko) A provocative and lushly photographed tale of budding sexuality and the loss of innocence that owes more to French cinema than that of Japanese filmmaking. Four teenage boys (all intriguingly played by young girls) are left behind in their boarding school during the summer. Their idyllic world is forever changed after another youth, who bears an uncanny resemblance to a dead friend, joins them. By using women to play the leads, the film takes on an interestingly androgynous angle while at the same time hauntingly exploring the fragile period in time when youth is suspended between innocence and experience, uncomplicated friendships and the initial pangs of romantic love and sexual awareness. (Japanese with English subtitles) ★★★ VHS: $29.99

Summer Wishes, Winter Dreams

(1973, 95 min, US, Gilbert Cates) *Joanne Woodward, Martin Balsam, Sylvia Sidney.* A trio of outstanding performances by Woodward, Balsam and Sidney is the heart of this compelling drama about a housewife facing a midlife crisis. Both Woodward and Sidney received well-deserved Oscar nominations. ★★★ VHS: $14.99

Summertime

(1955, 99 min, US, David Lean) *Katharine Hepburn, Rossano Brazzi.* Extraordinarily beautiful, captivating romantic drama with Hepburn as a high-strung, lonely American spinster from Akron, Ohio, looking for romance in extremely photogenic Venice. Fortunately, Brazzi is nearby. ★★★½ VHS: $24.99; DVD: $29.99

Sun Valley Serenade

(1941, 86 min, US, Bruce Humberstone) *Sonja Henie, John Payne, Milton Berle, The Nicholas Brothers.* A lively musical about a Norwegian war refugee given shelter at the Idaho resort; but the main attraction is Glenn Miller and His Orchestra, and Berle as their manager. Songs include "Chattanooga Choo-Choo" and "It Happened in Sun Valley." ★★★ VHS: $19.99

Sunchaser

(1996, 122 min, US, Michael Cimino) *Woody Harrelson, Jon Seda, Anne Bancroft.* Director Cimino's career is still on hold with this weak entry in the "soulless-yuppie-finds-himself" subgenre starring Harrelson as a wealthy oncologist who's carjacked by Seda, a terminally ill juvenile delinquent. They embark on a spiritual journey to a sacred mountain to cure Seda's cancer. Along the way, the disparate men find a shared humanity and learn "to get along." It's as hokey as it sounds. The concept is sentimental and unrealistic and the execution artificial and preachy. ★½ VHS: $19.99

Sunday

(1997, 93 min, US, Jonathan Nossiter) *David Suchet, Lisa Harrow, Jared Harris, Larry Pine.* So this is what Skid Row feels like. First-time director Nossiter pushes us closer than feels comfortable to the lower depths in this haunting and disturbing look at a case of mistaken identity that brings two hapless souls together. It is Sunday. For Oliver (Suchet), it's the most depressing day — "a day of nothingness." He leaves his men's shelter environs and sets out to wander the streets of Queens, when suddenly a beautiful woman spots him and shouts, "Matthew!" Mistaking him for a film director, Madeleine (Harrow) rushes over to renew their acquaintance and thus begins a certainly less-than-ordinary Sunday for them both. Nossiter, who coscripted the film, unfolds the details of these two unlucky lives with striking clarity while making great use of the Queens locales. ★★★½ VHS: $89.99

Sunday, Bloody Sunday

(1971, 110 min, GB, John Schlesinger) *Glenda Jackson, Peter Finch, Murray Head, Daniel Day-Lewis.* Jackson and Finch are sparkling in this landmark work. A *cause célèbre* in the early 1970s, this moving drama centers around the troubled participants in a bisexual triangle. The kiss between Finch and Head aroused an audible gasp from the audience of the day. Marvelously directed by Schlesinger. ★★★★ VHS: $19.99

A Sunday in the Country

(1984, 94 min, France, Bertrand Tavernier) *Louis Ducreux, Sabine Azema.* An illuminating, visually ravishing tale which centers around an elderly painter and the weekend visit paid to him by his children. Many primal issues of life are delicately handled in this subtle, masterfully crafted drama. (Letterboxed) (French with English subtitles) ★★★★ VHS: $24.99; DVD: $29.99

Sunday in the Park with George

(1984, 147 min, US, James Lapine) *Mandy Patinkin, Bernadette Peters, Charles Kimbrough, Dana Ivey.* Stephen Sondheim's Pulitzer Prize-winning Broadway musical, filmed directly from the stage, about the life of 19th-century French artist Georges Seurat, and his painting of the masterpiece "Sunday Afternoon on the Island of La Grand Jette." The original Broadway cast is featured in this superb production. ★★★★ VHS: $19.99; DVD: $29.99

Sunday Too Far Away

(1975, 95 min, Australia, Ken Hannam) *Jack Thompson, John Ewart.* A simple yet solid drama about the dangerous rivalries between the members of a group of macho sheep shearers. Thompson is especially good as one of the group's hardened leaders. ★★★

Sunday's Children

(1994, 94 min, Sweden, Daniel Bergman) *Henrik Linnros, Thommy Berggren, Per Myrberg.* Daniel, the son of Ingmar Bergman, makes his directorial debut with this heartfelt, magical memory piece. An autobiography written by the elder Bergman, the story centers on the life of the eight-year-old Ingmar, here called Pu (played by the sullen Linnors), and the relationship with his distant but loving father (Berggren). As the story flashes from the past to the present, Pu must come to terms with his dying father while being haunted by images and recollections from his childhood. Though Ingmar's script is fragmented, *Sunday's Children* is a beautifully crafted, eloquent and bittersweet stroll with one's ghosts and demons. (Swedish with English subtitles) ★★★ VHS: $29.99

Sundays and Cybele

(1962, 110 min, France, Serge Bourguignon) *Hardy Kruger, Nicole Courcel.* An intelligent and touching story of the developing relationship between an amnesiac man and a young orphan girl whom he befriends by telling her that he is her father. (French with English subtitles) ★★★★ VHS: $29.99

The Sundowners

(1960, 133 min, US, Fred Zinnemann) *Robert Mitchum, Deborah Kerr, Peter Ustinov, Glynis Johns.* Exceptional adaptation of Jon Cleary's best-seller about a 1920s Australian sheepherding family. Mitchum and Kerr give excellent performances, and the film features stunning cinematography. ★★★★ VHS: $19.99

Sunrise at Campobello

(1960, 144 min, US, Vincent J. Donehue) *Ralph Bellamy, Greer Garson, Hume Cronyn.* Bellamy's tour de force performance accentuates this compelling look at the early life of President

Franklin D. Roosevelt. The story focuses on Roosevelt's infancy in politics and his devastating battle against polio. Garson is equally as impressive as Eleanor Roosevelt. Though Roosevelt's years as president aren't covered, there's more than enough potent drama here. ★★★ VHS: $19.99

Sunset

(1988, 107 min, US, Blake Edwards) *James Garner, Bruce Willis, Malcolm McDowell, Mariel Hemingway, Kathleen Quinlan.* This Edwards mystery comedy set in 1920s Hollywood is short on laughs but does contain considerable charm thanks entirely to Garner's delectable turn as Wyatt Earp. The famous lawman helps investigate a bordello murder and crosses paths with Tom Mix (played by Willis) and a nefarious silent screen star obviously based on Charlie Chaplin. ★★½ VHS: $9.99; DVD: $14.99

Sunset Boulevard

(1950, 110 min, US, Billy Wilder) *William Holden, Gloria Swanson, Erich von Stroheim, Nancy Olson, Jack Webb, Buster Keaton.* Arguably the most vitriolic and macabre statement yet on the movie-making capital. Wilder uncovers the fractured dreams, withered ambitions and gruesome neuroses of Tinseltown's denizens. Holden is the two-bit hack writer nursing a case of self-disgust and Swanson, in an astonishing performance, is the aging film queen secluded with her bitterness in a Gothic mansion. ★★★★ VHS: $14.99

Sunset Park

(1996, 100 min, US, Steve Gomer) *Rhea Perlman, Fredro Starr, Carol Kane, Terrence DaShon Howard.* Here's the pitch: A middle-class white schoolteacher picks up an extra gig coaching her inner city's high school basketball team (read: black male teenagers). Initially unaccepted in a hostile environment, she eventually makes contact with her alienated charges, learning from them as she instructs them, and leads them to the city championship game. "Seen it," you say? Well, yes, you have, and while any reservations there may be are probably well-founded, it

somehow avoids being as bad as could be expected. Perlman delivers just enough earthy believability to an otherwise soft-focused effort. ★★½ VHS: $9.99

Sunshine

(2000, 179 min, Hungary/GB, István Szabó) *Ralph Fiennes, Jennifer Ehle, Rosemary Harris, Rachel Weisz, David de Keyser, Miriam Margolyes, William Hurt, Deborah Kara Unger, James Frain.* An epic story of three generations of a Hungarian Jewish family, *Sunshine* is a sweeping historical drama that explores the loss of identity set against the backdrop of the two world wars, the carnage of Communism and the 20th-century's rising tide of anti-Semitism. In the late 1800s, the Sonnenschein family, headed by the gentlemanly Emmanuel, makes its fortune from the family recipe for medicinal tonic. During the course of the next half a century, the Sonnenscheins endure the hardships of a nation and more as each generation struggles to free itself from emotional and physical restraints both self-inflicted and imposed. Fiennes is excellent portraying three generations of Sonnenscheins: Emmanuel's son Ignatz, a phlegmatic judge who abandons his father's name; his son Adam, a roguish swordsman who forsakes his religion; and Adam's son Ivan, an idealist Communist whose family lineage rests with him. And then there are the women, including the beautiful Valerie, who marries Ignatz and is witness to the family legacy, and played by Ehle as a young woman and her real-life mother Harris in later years. Both actresses are extraordinary. *Sunshine* is masterful storytelling, a richly textured, intimate saga that delineates a family and a world in turmoil. ★★★½ VHS: $19.99; DVD: $29.99

The Sunshine Boys

(1975, 111 min, US, Herbert Ross) *George Burns, Walter Matthau, Richard Benjamin, F. Murray Abraham.* After an absence from the big screen of over 30 years, Burns returned to join up with Matthau as the famous vaudevillians, The Sunshine Boys, who broke up decades before. Now a big producer would like to have

them do one of their classic routines on a television special. Burns received an Oscar for his performance in this engaging adaptation of Neil Simon's hit Broadway play. (Remade in 1995) ★★★ VHS: $14.99

The Super

(1991, 90 min, US, Rod Daniel) *Joe Pesci, Vincent Gardenia, Ruben Blades.* By the sheer force of his personality, Pesci saves this lightweight, formulaic comedy from the video junkpile. In his first starring role, Pesci plays a bigoted, unscrupulous New York ghetto landlord who is forced by the courts to live in one of his own ramshackle buildings. Of course, the misunderstood realtor comes to respect his tenants, each of whom discovers newfound compassion for him. Another '90s redemption story, and one not without a few laughs. However, the characters are pure stereotypes, and the film's ending would have made Frank Capra squirm. ★★ VHS: $9.99

Super 8½

(1994, 85 min, Canada, Bruce LaBruce) *Bruce LaBruce, R. Kern, Scott Thompson, Mikey Mike, Hal Kelly, Vaginal Davis.* A mild disappointment after his audacious debut with *No Skin off My Ass*, LaBruce's second film is a surprisingly hardcore (much graphic sex), film-within-a-film, autobiographical drama about a washed-up porn star living off his hunky hustler boyfriend, whose life changes when a lesbian filmmaker begins a project about him. There are vivid oral sex scenes, but these tend to bog down a potentially interesting tale. ★★½ VHS: $29.99

Super Mario Brothers

(1993, 104 min, US, Rocky Morton) *Bob Hoskins, John Leguizamo, Dennis Hopper, Samantha Mathis, Fisher Stevens, Fiona Shaw, Lance Henriksen.* The Mario Brothers are just two average plumbers from Brooklyn who find themselves defending the Earth against a bunch of humanoid dinosaur descendants from another dimension. The story is as flimsy as you would expect a movie based on a video game to be, but the dialogue has a nice, quirky style. And thanks to some competent acting by Hoskins and Leguizamo as the super plumbers, and an over-the-top Hopper as the slimy lizard king, this live-action comic book is an oddly entertaining if ridiculous action-comedy. ★★

Supercop

(1996, 93 min, Hong Kong, Stanley Tong) *Jackie Chan, Michelle Yeoh, Maggie Cheung.* Chan's masterful *Police Story 3* has been redubbed, reedited and renamed to serve as his follow-up to *Rumble in the Bronx* — it's a better movie, more accurately depicting the combination of action and humor which made Chan an international star. Jackie is a Hong Kong police officer sent undercover into Mainland China to spring a mobster from a prison camp and follow him back to Hong Kong, where Jackie can dismantle the crime organization from the inside. The climax of Jackie hanging from a ladder suspended beneath an airborne helicopter as it flies over Kuala Lumpur should satisfy even the most jaded American action movie fan. And if it doesn't, check your pulse. ★★★½ VHS: $14.99; DVD: $29.99

Gloria Swanson is ready for her close-up in *Sunset Boulevard*

S

Supercop 2

(1999, 94 min, Hong Kong, Stanley Tong) *Michelle Yeoh, Yu Rong Guang, Jackie Chan.* This is actually a semi-sequel to *Supercop*, originally titled *Project S*, with Yeoh (*Heroic Trio*) reprising her role as a beautiful, tough-as-nails cop, here on the trail of a band of thieves, led (unbeknownst to her) by her ex-boyfriend. A routine (even derivative) story line is enlivened greatly by exciting action scenes, and the miraculous Yeoh. Doing all her own stunts (à la Jackie Chan), she's a joy to watch, though one greedily wishes for more martial arts and less shoot-outs here. Also, the film is hurt by a terribly awkward, abrupt ending. Still, a good time overall, with a very silly though amusing cameo by Jackie in drag! ★★½ VHS: $14.99; DVD: $29.99

Superfly

(1972, 98 min, US, Gordon Parks, Jr.) *Ron O'Neal, Shelia Frazier.* Picketed by blacks for its glorification of the drug underworld, *Superfly* was nonetheless a huge popular success. New York City is an urban wasteland which provides the gritty backdrop to this tawdry tale of one tough-talking, coke-sniffing pusher (O'Neal) who plots for one final mega-deal before retiring. With a hypnotic Curtis Mayfield score in the background, the film captures the drug dealing world and, unlike most films of this type, takes no moral high ground. ★★

Superfly T.N.T.

(1973, 87 min, US, Ron O'Neal) *Ron O'Neal, Roscoe Lee Browne, Sheila Frazier, Robert Guillaume.* O'Neal returns as the super-slick, super-bad hustler Priest in this inept sequel. This time, Priest, retired and trying to clear his head in Rome, is enlisted into service by a freedom fighter from Africa to assist in a gun-running mission. The soundtrack is composed and performed by obscure 1970s funk supergroup Osibisa. ★½ VHS: $19.99

Supergirl

(1984, 114 min, GB, Jeannot Szwarc) *Faye Dunaway, Helen Slater, Peter O'Toole, Mia Farrow.* This juvenile fantasy about Superman's comic book cousin is barely saved from complete mediocrity by Dunaway's ultra-campy portrayal of the arch villainess. Slater is cute but shallow as the superhero, and the film really never gets off the ground. ★★ VHS: $14.99; DVD: $24.99

The Supergrass

(1987, 105 min, GB, Peter Richardson) *Adrian Edmondson, Jennifer Saunders, Nigel Planer, Alexie Sayle.* Outrageous, silly comedy about a young man who pretends to be a drug smuggler to impress his girlfriend, becoming involved with real smugglers and the police — who believe him to be a drug kingpin. The cast includes regulars from "The Young Ones." ★★½

Superman: The Movie

(1978, 143 min, US, Richard Donner) *Christopher Reeve, Gene Hackman, Marlon Brando, Margot Kidder, Ned Beatty, Valerie Perrine.* In a style reminiscent of a Spielberg or a Lucas, director Donner retells the Superman myth in a grand, often gaudy epic. Spectacular special effects, garish set design, an all-star cast and the obligatory John Williams score highlight this box-office smash.

The film follows Superman (Reeve) from his origins on Planet Krypton to his adolescence in Smallville to his heroics in Metropolis. ★★★ VHS: $14.99; DVD: $24.99

Superman II

(1981, 127 min, US, Richard Lester) *Christopher Reeve, Gene Hackman, Margot Kidder, Terence Stamp, Ned Beatty, Valerie Perrine.* Reeve returns as the Man of Steel in this rollicking sequel. Three fugitives from Krypton travel to Earth, and give Superman a great big headache. Hackman returns as Lex Luthor, and he's as funny as he was in the original adventure. ★★★ VHS: $9.99; DVD: $19.99

Superman III

(1983, 123 min, US, Richard Lester) *Christopher Reeve, Richard Pryor, Robert Vaughn.* Reeve is back once more as the man from Krypton in this comedic Superman outing with Pryor fronting for villain Vaughn, out to defeat Clark Kent's alter ego. Some of this is funny, but mostly it's just laughable. (Where's Hackman when you need him?) ★★ VHS: $9.99; DVD: $19.99

Superman IV: The Quest for Peace

(1987, 90 min, US, Sidney J. Furie) *Christopher Reeve, Gene Hackman, Jon Cryer, Margot Kidder.* Superman decides to rid the world of its nuclear weapons; but his good deed backfires as Lex Luthor appropriates the warheads for an elaborate arms deal. A middling adventure with a timely message. ★★ VHS: $9.99; DVD: $19.99

Supernova

(2000, 91 min, US, Walter Hill) *James Spader, Angela Bassett, Robert Forster, Lou Diamond Phillips, Peter Facinelli, Robin Tunney, Wilson Cruz.* Spader and Bassett make an unlikely but attractive couple in this otherwise turgid and choppy space opera. A space vessel receives a distress call and discovers a lone survivor: a mysterious young man with a connection to Bassett. A typical but potentially cool premise is dragged out interminably, despite the strong efforts of the cast. Original director Hill was replaced immediately after production by Jack Sholder, who was replaced in the editing room by Francis Ford Coppola. As would be expected, the result is a jumble. Apparently, there's 20 minutes missing from Hill's original vision, and the whole affair ends with a perversely romantic wrap-up. ★★ VHS: $9.99; DVD: $24.99

SuperPhan

(1998, 80 min, US, Vince Mola & Alex Weinress) *Vince Mola, Mike Missanelli, Frank DiLeo.* This engaging shot-on-video about the "ultimate" football fan uses the medium so well, it's entirely conceivable that unsuspecting victims could mistake the film as "real." Indeed, lead actor-codirector Mola — as SuperPhan — appears in character on Philadelphia's Channel 10 News, outside Veteran's Stadium and (most amusingly) at a college hockey game, where he tries in vain to pump up the somnambulant crowd. If you're from Philly — or any big sports town, for that matter — you've known someone like SuperPhan, and Mola plays the character to the hilt: by turns hilarious, annoying and pathetic, and yet always believable. In fact, it's the disturbing aspect of the humor that makes *SuperPhan* so compelling and realistic, and so much more than the regional in-joke it could have been. ★★★

Superstar

(1999, 82 min, US, Bruce McCulloch) *Molly Shannon, Will Ferrell, Harland Williams.* Yet another "Saturday Night Live" skit unwisely stretched out to feature length, *Superstar* leaves the talented Shannon and Ferrell stranded and flailing. The story has Shannon's popular "SNL" character, Mary Catherine Gallagher — the accident-prone Catholic high school girl who sniffs her pits when she's nervous — pining for two things: a kiss from school stud Ferrell and superstardom. While there are a handful of amusing moments (an impromptu cafeteria dance number), *Superstar* is mostly a downbeat experience. McCulloch directs with little inspiration or style. ★½ VHS: $14.99; DVD: $29.99

Supervixens

(1975, 106 min, US, Russ Meyer) *Shari Eubank, Charles Napier.* The story of a young man who, wrongfully accused of having killed a woman, is running from the policeman who actually commited the murder (Napier). Scenes such as the placing of a stick of dynamite between a bound Supervixen's spread legs marks Meyer's return to his tried and true mixture of sex and violence. ★★ VHS: $79.99

Support Your Local Gunfighter

(1971, 92 min, US, Burt Kennedy) *James Garner, Suzanne Pleshette, Joan Blondell, Harry Morgan, Jack Elam, Dub Taylor.* An amiable follow-up to *Support Your Local Sheriff.* On the lam, con man Garner chooses the small Western mining town of Purgatory to hide out. The locals think he is a notorious gunslinger, involving him in a war between two mining factions. There's a lot of good humor, and familiar character actors aid in the film's overall enjoyment. ★★½ VHS: $9.99; DVD: $19.99

Support Your Local Sheriff

(1969, 93 min, US, Burt Kennedy) *James Garner, Joan Hackett, Walter Brennan, Harry Morgan, Bruce Dern, Jack Elam.* Wonderful western spoof with Garner a delight as a town's sheriff up against a lawless breed when gold is found in them thar hills. (Sequel: *Support Your Local Gunfighter*) ★★★ VHS: $9.99; DVD: $19.99

Sure Fire

(1993, 86 min, US, Jon Jost) *Tom Blair, Kristi Hager.* Trouble is brewing in a small Southwestern town and mounting tensions erupt with tragic results. Unfortunately, the real trouble might have been on the other side of the camera, because it feels like the filmmakers could not strike a balance between art film and thriller. Although Jost may have had some comment on the human condition in mind here, and he certainly has a way with imagery, a slower, more monotonous 86-minute film would be hard to find. ★ VHS: $19.99; DVD: $29.99

The Sure Thing

(1985, 94 min, US, Rob Reiner) *John Cusack, Daphne Zuniga, Anthony Edwards, Nicollette Sheridan, Tim Robbins.* Reiner's impressive follow-up to *This Is Spinal Tap* is an intelligent and fresh look at adolescent romance. It offers a distinct alternative to most youth-oriented comedies by presenting teenagers that are hip, witty and even sensitive. Sort of a modern reworking

Surviving Picasso

of *It Happened One Night.* Cusack is terrific in one of his first starring roles. ★★★½

Surrender

(1987, 95 min, US, Jerry Belson) *Sally Field, Michael Caine, Steve Guttenberg, Peter Boyle, Julie Kavner.* Flat romantic comedy with Field trying to choose between a caring but seemingly impoverished writer (Caine) and a wealthy yuppie attorney (Guttenberg). ★★ VHS: $14.99; DVD: $24.99

Surrender Dorothy

(1998, 87 min, US, Kevin DiNovis) *Peter Pryor, Kevin DiNovis, Jason Centeno, Elizabeth Casey.* A bold and compelling psychosexual, cross-dressing drama that offers a decidedly controversial twist in its treatment of same-sex relationships. It's *Apartment Zero* meets *Blue Velvet* through the eyes of Harold Pinter. The story focuses on two young men: 26-year-old Trevor (Pryor), an angry, sexually confused busboy tormented with an intense fear of women, and Lanh (director DiNovis), a heroin addict who needs a place to crash after stealing a drug stash from his former roommate. But what begins as a simple house-sharing arrangement quickly escalates into a frenzied battle of manipulation, codependency and gender-bending submission as the emboldened Trevor lures Lanh, with the promise of drugs, into becoming Dorothy, Trevor's demented concept of his ideal girlfriend. ★★★½ VHS: $59.99; DVD: $29.99

Surviving Picasso

(1996, 123 min, GB, James Ivory) *Anthony Hopkins, Natascha McElhone, Julianne Moore, Joan Plowright, Joss Ackland.* Genius, lover, sexist, bully, egotist, artist: these and other identifying traits of legendary painter Pablo Picasso are perfectly brought to life by Hopkins. But his riveting portrayal is not quite enough to overcome director Ivory's static account of the final years of the artist's life and his love affairs. Suggested by the novel "Picasso: Creator and Destroyer," *Surviving Picasso* is narrated by Picasso's longtime lover Françoise Gilot (nicely played by McElhone), mother to two of his children. The film almost ignores Picasso the artist in favor of his relationships with Gilot and others. Hopkins at least makes sure that Picasso is always center stage and cognizant of his place in the world. ★★½ VHS: $19.99

Surviving the Game

(1994, 94 min, US, Ernest Dickerson) *Ice T, Rutger Hauer, Charles S. Dutton, Gary Busey, F. Murray Abraham, John C. McGinley.* Ice T stars as a bum, er, residentially challenged person who is recruited by an urban missionary (Dutton) to lead a hunting party through the Northwest wilderness, only to find that he is (surprise!) the prey. Dickerson adds nothing new to this shopworn premise — introduced in 1932 as *The Most Dangerous Game* — that has been tried by everyone from Robert Wise to John Woo and even on "Gilligan's Island." What the film lacks in story is more than compensated for in violence and hammy performances. ★★ VHS: $14.99; DVD: $14.99

Susan and God

(1940, 117 min, US, George Cukor) *Joan Crawford, Fredric March, Ruth Hussey, Rita Hayworth.* Anita Loos (*The Women, Gentlemen Prefer Blondes*) adapted Rachel Crothers' stage hit, a curious blend of sophisticated comedy and family drama. Crawford gives an atypical daffy performance as a flighty socialite who finds religion; she begins preaching love and God and interferes with her society friends' lives. March is Crawford's alcoholic and estranged husband who does not benefit from his wife's new spiritual awakening. ★★½ VHS: $19.99

Susan Lenox: Her Fall and Rise

(1931, 77 min, US, Robert Z. Leonard) *Greta Garbo, Clark Gable, Jean Hersholt.* The only pairing of screen legends Garbo and Gable is this blustery melodrama with Garbo as a poor farm girl forced to marry a brutish neighbor. She runs away, straight into the arms of a tall, handsome engineer (Gable). However, fate seems destined to keep the lovers apart. ★★½ VHS: $19.99

Susan Slept Here

(1954, 98 min, US, Frank Tashlin) *Debbie Reynolds, Dick Powell, Anne Francis.* A young troublemaker (Reynolds) finds herself the unlikely guest of a man-about-town writer (Powell) and proceeds to complicate his bachelor existence. Francis plays Powell's society beauty sweetheart. Kinda cute. ★★½

Susana

(1951, 82 min, Mexico, Luis Buñuel) *Rosita Quintana, Fernando Soler, Victor Manuel Mendoza,.* A mischievous Buñuel focuses this subversive melodrama on a born-bad sexpot who escapes from prison and finds refuge in a hacienda with a kindly family. From the moment she enters the house, the wanton vamp does nothing but wreak havoc, sending just about every man within 20 miles to the brink of sexual frenzy. In a truly kinky ending, our heroine's bedeviling force is brought under control by the lady of the ranch with the aid of a studded riding crop. Brimming with sly humor and trademark touches, *Susana* is delicious fun for all Buñuel lovers. (Spanish with English subtitles) ★★★

Suspect

(1987, 122 min, US, Peter Yates) *Cher, Dennis Quaid, Liam Neeson, John Mahoney.* This taut courtroom thriller stars Cher as a public defender who takes on the difficult case of a

deaf derelict (Neeson) who has been charged with murder. When a juror (Quaid) approaches her with helpful evidence, she finds herself not only facing an ethical dilemma, but is also drawn into a whirlwind of Hitchcockian intrigue. ★★★ VHS: $9.99; DVD: $19.99

The Suspect

(1998, 108 min, Hong Kong, Ringo Lam) *Louis Koo, Julian Cheung.* In this standard Hong Kong actioner, Cheung is an ex-con who's just served a ten-year prison sentence. His old crime boss immediately demands he assassinate a political figure. When he refuses, the chase is on from both the cops (he's been framed for the murder anyway) and the bad guys (who feel betrayed). The usual litany of HK crime drama issues are trotted out — honor, loyalty, friendship — and handled well by director Lam and his cast. There's a strong been-there, done-that feel to the film, and though it's a bounce back from Lam's *Maximum Risk*, it can't compare with his earlier, more passionate works (*City on Fire* and *Burning Paradise*). Still, it is entertaining, and while there's little action per se, it's never less than involving. (Cantonese with English subtitles) ★★½ VHS: $19.99; DVD: $29.99

Suspicion

(1941, 99 min, US, Alfred Hitchcock) *Joan Fontaine, Cary Grant, Nigel Bruce.* Fontaine won a belated Oscar as a shy girl who enters a hasty marriage with the charming but sinister (?) Grant, and begins to believe that he could be a murderer — with her as his next victim. Of interest: the studio changed the ending to fit Grant's image, fearing the public would not accept the writer's original conclusion. Crisp direction from Hitchcock. ★★★ VHS: $14.99

Suspiria

(1976, 97 min, Italy, Dario Argento) *Jessica Harper, Joan Bennett.* Argento's classic horror film features mayhem galore at a swank private school in Europe complete with stormy nights, psychopaths and a frenzied soundtrack. Argento's plot is barely skin deep, but his highly stylized camerawork and editing, and the edge-of-your-seat suspense will leave one gasping. Look for a particularly effective homage to the French surreal masterpiece *Un Chien Andalou.* (Filmed in English) (Letterboxed) (Sequel: *Inferno*) ★★★ VHS: $19.99

Suture

(1994, 96 min, US, Scott McGehee & David Siegel) *Dennis Haysbert, Michael Harris, Mel Harris, Sab Shimono.* Unscrupulous patricidal Victor Towers (Harris) sets up his long-lost, almost identical half-brother Clay Arlington (Haysbert), attempting to murder him and have it look as though he himself has been killed. But Clay survives, disfigured and amnesiac, and is accepted as Victor, who is now under suspicion for their father's murder. Adding a special dimension to this exploration of identity and self-knowing is that Clay is played by Haysbert, who is black, and Victor by Harris, who is white. Shot in stark black and white, and employing a pared-down but effective soundtrack, *Suture* is an interesting premise with an intriguing execution. ★★★ VHS: $14.99; DVD: $19.99

Swamp Thing

(1982, 91 min, US, Wes Craven) *Louis Jourdan, Adrienne Barbeau.* Tongue-in-cheek monster movie with a scientist transformed into a half-man/half-vegetable when one of his experiments goes awry. Jourdan camps it up as a fellow scientist, and Barbeau is the woman Swamp Thing loves. ★★½ VHS: $9.99; DVD: $14.99

The Swan

(1956, 109 min, US, Charles Vidor) *Grace Kelly, Alec Guinness, Louis Jourdan, Agnes Moorehead, Leo G. Carroll.* This beguiling comedy of manners begins as a European matriarch seeks to reverse her family's declining fortunes by marrying off her only daughter (Kelly) to the country's crown prince (Guinness). Jourdan plays the young woman's tutor, who is disappointed to see that she is actually smitten with the prince. ★★★ VHS: $19.99

Swann in Love

(1984, 115 min, France, Volker Schlondorff) *Jeremy Irons, Ornella Muti, Alain Delon, Fanny Ardant, Marie-Christine Barrault.* Schlöndorff beautifully renders the emotional intricacies and period flavor of Marcel Proust's illustrious "Swann's Way." Irons is the dashing, cultivated Charles Swann who loses his heart and esteem in a passionate tryst with a pouting courtesan (Muti). A sparkling ensemble of supporting players. (Filmed in English) ★★★

The Swap

(1979, 90 min, US, John Shade & John C. Broderick) *Robert De Niro, Jennifer Warren, Lisa Blount, Sybil Danning.* An ambitious young filmmaker learns the power and perils of his medium when his homemade pornos of powerful friends are used for political blackmail. Originally filmed in 1969, reedited and rereleased in 1979. ★★½ VHS: $14.99; DVD: $12.99

The Swashbuckler

(1979, 101 min, France, Jean-Paul Rappeneau) *Jean-Paul Belmondo, Laura Antonelli.* It is a shame that so many of Belmondo's films never make it over to these shores because generally you can count on them being action-packed and full of adventure. However, the film distribution system being what it is, few of his recent efforts have received showings in the U.S. *The Swashbuckler* is an fun comedy/adventure that features the charismatic rogue as a man-on-the-run who gets involved in fighting in the American War for Independence. (French with English subtitles) ★★★

Swedenhielms

(1935, 88 min, Sweden, Gustaf Molander) *Ingrid Bergman.* Bergman plays a young woman engaged to the son of a renowned aristocrat in line to win the Nobel Prize. When it becomes apparent, however, that the father will not be awarded the prestigious prize, the family is thrown into an emotional and financial crisis, affecting each family member, and the young Bergman, in disparate ways. (Swedish with English subtitles) ★★½ VHS: $19.99

Sweeney Todd

(1984, 140 min, US) *Angela Lansbury, George Hearn.* Live performance of Stephen Sondheim's Tony Award—winning musical. Magnificently re-created for video, Lansbury (also a Tony Award winner) and Hearn repeat their stage roles as, respectively, the evil Mrs. Lovett and the demonic barber Sweeney, who together conspired to murder his customers and serve them up in her meat pies. An unusual topic for a musical, to be sure, but the genius of Sondheim's music and lyrics and Harold Prince's original staging combine to create a musical masterpiece. Lansbury and Hearn (who stepped into the role after Len Cariou) give two of the greatest performances to be seen in the theatre in recent memory. An unforgettable theatre piece, and not to be missed. ★★★★

Sweet and Lowdown

(1999, 95 min, US, Woody Allen) *Sean Penn, Samantha Morton, Uma Thurman, Anthony LaPaglia, Brian Markinson, John Waters, Gretchen Mol.* Penn received an Oscar nomination for his scintillatingly complex performance as Emmet Ray, the "second greatest jazz guitarist" of the 1930s. In this fictional biography, writer-director Allen has crafted an engaging comedy-drama that — maybe in reference to his own life — attempts to separate the artist from the man. Morton also garnered an Oscar nomination for her touching portrayal of a mute woman involved with the misanthropic but talented musician. A great jazz score punctuates Allen's snappy story. ★★★½ VHS: $21.99; DVD: $29.99

Sweet Bird of Youth

(1962, 120 min, US, Richard Brooks) *Geraldine Page, Paul Newman, Ed Begley, Rip Torn.* An expert adaptation of Tennessee Williams' critically acclaimed play. Page excels as a former movie queen whose career has given way to alchohol and compromise. Searching for seclusion, she arrives in a small Southern town accompanied by ne'er-do-well hometown boy Newman. Begley won an Oscar for his powerful portrayal of the town's corrupt boss who has it in for Newman. (Remade in 1989) ★★★½ VHS: $19.99

Sweet Charity

(1969, 133 min, US, Bob Fosse) *Shirley MacLaine, John McMartin, Chita Rivera, Stubby Kaye, Paula Kelly.* Fosse's first film as director is based on his hit Broadway musical, itself based on Fellini's *Nights of Cabiria.* MacLaine is at her best as dance hall hostess Charity Hope Valentine, the quintessential hooker with a heart of gold. Forever having her heart broken by Mr. Wrong, Charity finds solace in her never-ending optimism and joie de vivre while confronting a series of romantic adventures. Fosse's storytelling is highly stylized, with special emphasis on editing, and features memorable musical numbers. ★★★½ VHS: $9.99

Sweet Country

(1987, 150 min, US, Michael Cacoyannis) *Jane Alexander, John Cullum, Irene Papas, Carole Laurie, Franco Nero.* Some good actors can't save this unfortunate political thriller about an American couple who move to Chile after the Allende assassination, becoming involved in a Marxist underground movement. ★½

Sweet Dreams

(1985, 115 min, US, Karel Reisz) *Jessica Lange, Ed Harris, Ann Wedgeworth, David Clennon.* Lange gives an affecting performance as country superstar Patsy Cline in this moving portrait of the singer's vibrant life, her climb to stardom and her untimely death. Harris costars as Cline's husband Charley Dick, and Wedgeworth is stirring as her mother. ★★★ VHS: $9.99; DVD: $14.99

Sweet Hearts Dance

(1988, 101 min, US, Robert Greenwald) *Susan Sarandon, Don Johnson, Jeff Daniels, Elizabeth Perkins, Justin Henry.* A good cast adds some sparkle to this routine romantic comedy as husband and wife Johnson and Sarandon decide to split; while friend Daniels begins an affair with Perkins. ★★½ VHS: $9.99

The Sweet Hereafter

(1997, 112 min, Canada, Atom Egoyan) *Ian Holm, Maury Chaykin, Sarah Polley, Bruce Greenwood, Gabrielle Rose, Arsinée Khanjian.* Low-key and desolate in tone, Egoyan's adaptation of the Russell Banks novel is a profound and intimate portrait of a small town reeling from tragedy. Holm is impenetrably brilliant as Mitchell Stephens, an ambulance-chasing lawyer who descends on the inhabitants of Sam Dent, a community nestled in the Canadian

Paula Kelly (l.), Shirley MacLaine (c.) and Chita Rivera in *Sweet Charity*

Rockies, in the hopes of convincing them to join a class-action suit concerning a deadly school bus accident. As he is digging deep into the town's collective sorrow, he is also uncovering his own disjointed sense of loss — a point punctuated by repeated calls on his cell phone from his drug-addicted daughter. Egoyan masterfully flashes back to the months and moments leading up to the calamity, and seamlessly snakes the film's timeline back and forth. And, as with all of Egoyan's films, the characters' inner struggles take center stage. Polley excels as a teenager who survives but who pays a terrible price. (VHS available letterboxed or pan & scan) ★★★★ VHS: $19.99; DVD: $24.99

Sweet Liberty

(1986, 107 min, US, Alan Alda) *Alan Alda, Michael Caine, Bob Hoskins, Michelle Pfeiffer, Lillian Gish.* The films of Alda are either hit (*The Four Seasons*) or miss (*A New Life*), but this pleasant comedy sits comfortably towards the former. Alda is a college professor whose book on American history is being made into a movie — and a wild assortment of film types descend upon his peaceful and unprepared town. ★★★ VHS: $9.99

Sweet Lorraine

(1987, 91 min, US, Steve Gomer) *Maureen Stapleton, Lee Richardson, Trini Alvarado, Giancarlo Esposito, Todd Graff.* Charming, bittersweet comedy-drama about the last days of an 80-year-old Catskills Mountain hotel. Stapleton gives a winning performance as the hotel's matriarchal owner. ★★★ VHS: $79.99

Sweet Movie

(1974, 105 min, Canada/France/West Germany, Dusan Makavejev) *Carole Laure, Pierre Clementi, Sami Frey.* One woman's sexual initiation and her descent into the liberating pleasures of the flesh is just one of the stories in this bizarre and sensual celebration of political and sexual anarchism. Makavejev, a sort of Serbo-socialist John Waters, fuses several stories in trying to answer the question, "Is there life after birth?" The main story revolves around a virginal Miss World who, after fending off the lustful advances of her new husband, the richest man in the world and his black muscle-building bodyguard, finally finds her libido liberation on the top of the Eiffel Tower with a singing mariachi star. A wildly outrageous and original film. (English, French, Dutch, German and Serbo-Croatian with English subtitles) ★★★ VHS: $24.99

Sweet Nothing

(1996, 90 min, US, Gary Winick) *Michael Imperioli, Mira Sorvino, Paul Calderon.* A depressing but well-intentioned look into the life and mind of a Bronx crackhead, *Sweet Nothing* is based on diaries found in a New York apartment. The first (and weaker) half of this low-budget film depicts how Angelo (Imperioli) gets caught in the vicious cycle of drug addiction. When he finally decides to kick the habit, the film — like its protagonist — begins to recover. Suddenly, the clichés disappear and Angelo's downward spiral starts earning the viewer's sympathy. Offering an unromanticized view of addiction and recovery, *Sweet Nothing* sometimes misfires, but at least maintains the courage of its convictions. ★★½ VHS: $19.99

The Sweet Hereafter

Sweet Revenge

(1998, 90 min, GB, Malcolm Mowbray) *Sam Neill, Helena Bonham Carter, Kristin Scott Thomas, Rupert Graves, Martin Clunes.* A rather lukewarm British comedy with a decent cast, *Sweet Revenge* revolves around the revenge fantasies of two potential suicides. Neill and Scott Thomas meet each other on the Tower Bridge. They agree to set up their respective partners, who have set them on the road to ruin. Bonham Carter plays Thomas' nemesis, the wife of the man with whom she has been having an affair. A simple premise goes terribly awry when Neill falls in love with the woman he is supposed to victimize, while Scott Thomas ends up taking the "game" all too seriously. A sort of twisted cross between *Bean* and *Mrs. Doubtfire*, this film is effective in creating some mild laughs although falling well short of utilizing the full talent of the cast. (aka: *The Revengers' Comedies*) ★★ VHS: $14.99; DVD: $32.99

Sweet Smell of Success

(1957, 96 min, US, Alexander MacKendrick) *Burt Lancaster, Tony Curtis, Martin Milner.* Lancaster is J.J. Hunsecker, NYC.'s most popular gossip columnist. Curtis is the weaselly press agent who will do anything to keep his favor. Screenwriters Clifford Odets and Ernest Lehman worked overtime on the dialogue as each character spits words like knives in an attempt to get the "one up" on the next guy. Everyone gets their just desserts in this cynical masterwork. ★★★★ VHS: $14.99; DVD: $19.99

Sweet Sweetback's Baadasssss Song

(1971, 97 min, US, Melvin Van Peebles) *Melvin Van Peebles, Rhetta Hughes, Simon Chuckster, John Amos.* Van Peebles wrote, directed and stars in this trendsetting work — which initiated the "blaxploitation" film cycle of the 1970s — about an African-American on the run from "the Man." Violent and told with a discernable rage, the film is in some ways rather dated, with its long montages of Sweetback running and running (complete with split-screen, super-impositions and freeze frame), wall-to-wall, loud '70s jazz, and some stereotypes of its own (mostly women and gays). But the film has lost little of its power in depicting the brutal effects of racism, and even the film's dated score and

technical aspects add to *Sweetback's* nightmarish quality. ★★★ VHS: $19.99

Sweet William

(1980, 92 min, GB, Claude Whatham) *Sam Waterston, Jenny Agutter, Anna Massey, Arthur Lowe.* Practically unseen in the U.S., this charming and sexy comedy features Waterston as a promiscuous young playwright who becomes involved with a woman who refuses to accept his compulsive philandering. Waterston is beguiling and raffish, and is ably assisted by the strong supporting cast. ★★★

Sweetie

(1990, 97 min, Australia, Jane Campion) *Karen Colston, Tom Lycos, Genevieve Lemon.* First-time director Campion's spellbinding drama follows the story of Kay (Colston), a highly superstitious and emotionally repressed cafeteria worker whose once-blissful but slowly disintegrating relationship with a handsome coworker is further rattled when her unpredictable sister Sweetie shows up on her doorstep. Mentally unstable and possibly schizophrenic, the ill-tempered Sweetie destroys Kay's routine; and when their parents show up, it's a virtual free-for-all. As Sweetie, Lemon gives a devastating performance. ★★★½

Swept Away

(1975, 116 min, Italy, Lina Wertmüller) *Giancarlo Giannini, Mariangela Melato.* A swarthy sailor and his beautiful, wealthy employer are cast adrift on the hot sands of a Mediterranean island. The sweeping blue waves and the blazing August sun thrust them together in a steamy, passionate affair. The battle of the sexes and class struggles are played out in this handsomely photographed drama. (Italian with English subtitles) ★★★★ VHS: $29.99; DVD: $29.99

Swept from the Sea

(1998, 114 min, US, Beeban Kidron) *Vincent Perez, Rachel Weisz, Ian McKellen, Joss Ackland, Kathy Bates.* Based on Joseph Conrad's short story "Amy Foster," this waterlogged period romantic spectacle tells the story of a shipwrecked immigrant (Perez) who falls in love with a town outcast (Weisz) whom some fear is a witch. The first-rate production design is undermined by a cast with no chemistry (despite the presence of such pros as McKellen and Bates), and a screenplay with no soul. The cinematography is beautiful, and the sweeping romantic score by John Barry is worth mention, but Kidron's rigid direction makes it hard to care when she starts plucking the heartstrings. ★★ VHS: $14.99; DVD: $29.99

The Swimmer

(1968, 94 min, US, Frank Perry) *Burt Lancaster, Janice Rule, Kim Hunter.* Lancaster is splendid in this unusual but rewarding film as a businessman whose disgust for his middle-class life prompts him to, one afternoon, swim his way home from one pool to another, reflecting upon his life. ★★★

Swimming to Cambodia

(1987, 85 min, US, Jonathan Demme) *Spalding Gray.* A unique fusion of stage and film, Gray's theatrical monologue about his experiences in Cambodia while filming a small role in *The Killing Fields*, makes for captivating and enlightening entertainment. Director Demme, who had already directed the quintessential live concert film *Stop Making Sense*, unleashes an attentive camera on Gray, who, in brilliantly comic and cerebral morsels of insight, hypnotically weaves a tale of life, the war, and the search for the perfect moment. ★★★★ VHS: $14.99

Swimming with Sharks

(1995, 93 min, US, George Huang) *Kevin Spacey, Frank Whaley, Michelle Forbes, Benicio del Toro.* "The fastest way to get to the top is to work with someone already there." This is the advice taken to heart by ambitious but naïve writer Guy (Whaley) when he accepts the job as assistant to Buddy Ackerman (Spacey), the abusive V.P. of Production of Keystone Pictures. But daily dosages of insults take their toll as Guy takes Buddy hostage. And through a series of flashbacks, *Swimming with Sharks* tells the story of what drove Guy to this act and to possibly commit murder. Writer-director Huang's black comedy is of the darkest shade, a numbing satire whose venom penetrates to the bone. This viciously funny film forgoes playful swipes and even subtlety in its view of Hollywood and instead flaunts an industry where "punching below the belt is rewarded." Spacey gives a dazzling portrayal of the acid-tongued, demanding exec; it's at once vile, funny, brutal and remarkably controlled. "Shut up, listen, and learn." ★★★ VHS: $9.99; DVD: $19.99

The Swindle

(1999, 105 min, France, Claude Chabrol) *Isabelle Huppert, Michel Serrault, François Cluzet.* What happens when long-time practitioners of the short con attempt one last, big score with the long con? When age-old loyalties appear to be unraveling? When natural antagonists find themselves unexpected allies? Although their precise relationship is never explicitly stated, Huppert and Serrault bicker like a long-married couple, tag-team tricksters who trawl for conventioneers in big, impersonal hotels. Their lives are amazingly routine, essentially bourgeoise, until he discovers the man behind her increasingly frequent absences, and the couple is drawn into a pool of deception and greed far in excess of their experience. The film evidences touches of Chabrol's early blithe insouslance, and fancies itself a jaundiced commen-

tary on society's inherent hypocrisy; a celebration of Robin Hoods amid faceless conformity. But it's really just a caper film, a confection, an amusing Gallic diversion. (French with English subtitles) ★★½ VHS: $94.99

Swing

(1999, 97 min, GB, Nick Mead) *Hugo Spear, Lisa Stansfield, Alexei Sayle, Rita Tushingham, Clarence Clemons.* Surely if they were going to make a film to cash in on the Swing craze, they could come up with a better one than this British import. Speer stars as Martin, an ex-con (who was falsely imprisoned) whose ex-girlfriend Joan (Stansfield) has married his arresting officer while he was in prison. During his incarceration, Martin is taught the saxophone by his cell mate (Clemons, who does all the sax music in the film). Putting together a swing band, Martin deals with his devious brother, a group of high-strung fellow musicians, and Joan's jealous husband. *Swing* only cooks when the band is on stage and Stansfield belts out the standards. ★★½ VHS: $19.99

Swing Kids

(1993, 112 min, US, Thomas Carter) *Robert Sean Leonard, Christian Bale, Frank Whaley, Barbara Hershey, Kenneth Branagh.* A truly disappointing, even awful story of individualism, Nazism and swing music. Leonard plays a German teenager who is part of a youthful clique that includes Whaley and Bale. They spend their nights dancing to American swing and days avoiding the Hitler Youth. But these 1930s hipsters soon discover the Nazis are formidable foes as one by one they either join the movement or perish. There were so many situations available to screenwriter Jonathan Marc Feldman that it's doubly disheartening he gave his characters no moral dance steps to go along with their jitterbug, or any emotional depth as they try to sidestep the Nazis. ★½

Swing Shift

(1984, 100 min, US, Jonathan Demme) *Goldie Hawn, Kurt Russell, Ed Harris, Christine Lahti.* When America's men left to fight WWII, her women took their places on the job, altering the structure of the family and women's self-expectations. The film's unevenness is perhaps due to reported disagreements between Demme and Hawn as to her character's personality; it is nonetheless well-worth watching. Lahti is outstanding as one of those women on the job. ★★★ VHS: $14.99

Swing Time

(1936, 103 min, US, George Stevens) *Fred Astaire, Ginger Rogers, Helen Broderick, Eric Blore.* One of the best of the Astaire and Rogers musicals, with Fred and Ginger as a dance team in a romantic predicament — he's engaged to the girl back home. Extraordinary dance numbers, and the fine score includes "The Way You Look Tonight" and "Pick Yourself Up." ★★★★ VHS: $14.99

Swingers

(1996, 96 min, US, Doug Liman) *Jon Favreau, Vince Vaughn, Ron Livingston, Patrick Van Horn, Heather Graham.* In *Swingers*, men call women "babies," wear retro clothing, emulate Frank Sinatra and his Rat Pack crew, and worship at the altar of Tarantino, Travolta and Scorsese. Mixing retro 'tude with contemporary guy

predicaments, Liman's second feature is an upbeat, winning look at the romantic and social entanglements of a group of hepcat Los Angeles lounge lizards. The focus is on Mike (Favreau, who also scripted), a New Yorker who has come to L.A. to try to make it as a comic. He joins ultra-slick Trent (Vaughn) and some other pals for after-hour prowls of area clubs. Eventually, Mike realizes that meaningless one-nighters aren't for him: He's longing for a real relationship. But can he find it with a martini in one hand and a bossa nova record in the other? With dialogue that jives and characters that cook, you often feel like you're watching a documentary about the cool, cool world it depicts. This is one happy (and-a-half) hour worth checking out. ★★★½ VHS: $14.99; DVD: $29.99

Swiss Family Robinson

(1960, 126 min, US, Ken Annakin) *John Mills, Dorothy McGuire, James MacArthur.* Disney's exciting version of the classic adventure story about a family shipwrecked on a deserted island. ★★★ VHS: $19.99

Switch

(1991, 103 min, US, Blake Edwards) *Ellen Barkin, Jimmy Smits, JoBeth Williams, Perry King, Lorraine Bracco.* Edwards wrote and directed this occasionally amusing though ordinary body-switching comedy. Barkin single-handedly saves the picture with a vibrant portrayal of a sexist philander who is murdered and comes back as a beautiful blonde. King is what she used to look like; Smits is his partner who is now attracted to his associate. In view of Edwards' brilliant sex farce *Victor/Victoria*, *Switch* is all the more disappointing. ★★ VHS: $9.99; DVD: $14.99

Switchback

(1997, 118 min, US, Jeb Stuart) *Danny Glover, Dennis Quaid, Jared Leto, R. Lee Ermey, Ted Levine, William Fichtner.* So-so thriller with several intriguing elements, featuring a very glum Quaid as an FBI agent on the trail of a serial killer, with the help of a small-town sheriff (Ermey). The pursuit, it turns out, is quite personal — the killer has kidnapped Quaid's young son. Meanwhile, in a parallel thread, Glover gives hitchhiker Leto a ride to Utah; could one of them be the killer? Numbingly conventional for most of its running time, *Switchback* does occasionally spark to life in its details. There's not a great deal of action, only a modicum of suspense. ★★ VHS: $9.99; DVD: $24.99

Switchblade Sisters

(1975, 91 min, US, Jack Hill) *Robbie Lee, Joanne Nail.* Worth its weight in gold as a cultural artifact of an unfortunate time in American cinematic history, *Switchblade Sisters* will undoubtedly entertain those audience members who are already in love with its dubious endowments: babes, bikers and blades. And no amount of argument from anyone will convince them that the movie really is trash. The story is simple: teenage gang debutantes fight enemies within and without in a series of brawls, rape sequences and prison scenes (complete with lesbian guards). ★

Switching Channels

(1988, 105 min, US, Ted Kotcheff) *Burt Reynolds, Kathleen Turner, Christopher Reeve, Ned Beatty.* A bargain-basement remake of the classic *His Girl Friday*, with Reynolds and Turner in the Cary Grant and Rosalind Russell roles. The characters have been changed from newspaper to TV reporters. ★½ VHS: $9.99

Swoon

(1992, 95 min, US, Tom Kalin) *Craig Chester, Daniel Schlachet.* The scandalous 1924 trial of Nathan Leopold and Richard Loeb for the inexplicable murder of a young boy is given a slightly tilted, definitely New Queer Cinema treatment in this intriguing independent black-and-white feature that will fascinate some and upset others. Lovers Leopold and Loeb bungle a scheme to kidnap a boy, resulting in the youth's cold-blooded killing. The two are eventually tracked down by the police, arrested, tried and sentenced to life in prison. But director Kalin's real interest lies less in the horrendous act of the unlikely criminals and more with the lovers' secretive, intense and self-destructive relationship. Other films adapted from the notorious murder are *Rope* and *Compulsion*. ★★★ VHS: $19.99

The Sword & the Rose

(1953, 91 min, GB, Ken Annakin) *Richard Todd, Glynis Johns, Michael Gough.* Flavorful Disney adventure. Mary Tudor, unhappily betrothed to King Louis XII of France, falls for the dashing Palace Captain of the Guard. This incurs the wrath of the evil Duke of Buckingham, who stops at nothing to destroy the romance. (aka: *When Knighthood Was in Flower*) ★★★ VHS: $19.99

The Sword and the Sorcerer

(1982, 100 min, US, Albert Pyun) *Lee Horsley, Kathleen Beller, Simon MacCorkindale.* A ruthless king summons a long-dormant sorcerer to aid him in his evil-doings, but a young prince (Horsley) aims to stop him. Unexciting combination of adventure and sorcery. ★★ VHS: $9.99; DVD: $24.99

The Sword in the Stone

(1963, 79 min, US, Wolfgang Reitherman) Amiable Disney animated feature based on the Arthurian legend about young Arthur's search for the famed sword and his adventures with Merlin. Highlighted by bouncy songs and a great wizard duel between Merlin and Mad Madam Mim. ★★½ VHS: $22.99; DVD: $29.99

Sword of Doom

(1967, 120 min, Japan, Kihachi Okamoto) *Tatsuya Nakadai, Toshiro Mifune.* Nakadai stars as an amoral, disaffected young samurai who shifts between moods of brooding nihilism and outbursts of extreme and random violence. After accidentally killing an opponent in a tournament duel, he leaves his village in disgrace and wanders the countryside in a seemingly pointless search to find an opponent worthy of his deadly swordplay skills. He is pursued by the vengeance-seeking brother of the man he killed, who has since become the student of a master swordsman (Mifune). Beautifully filmed in stark widescreen black and white, the film is a dark exploration of the violent and base natures of humanity and features an astonishing fight sequence featuring Mifune defending himself against a botched assassination attempt on a bridge at night in the snow which will leave the viewer breathless. (Letterboxed) (Japanese with English subtitles) ★★★½ VHS: $29.99

Sword of Fury I

(1973, 90 min, Japan, Tai Kato) This dazzling film follows the exciting life of Japan's most famous swordsman of the 17th century, Musashi Miyamoto. It features almost unbelievable displays of swordsmanship and easily made Miyamoto one of Japan's most famous samurai. (Japanese with English subtitles) ★★★½

Sword of Fury II

(1973, 77 min, Japan, Tai Kato) *Hideki Takahashi, Jiro Tamiya.* This sequel follows samurai Musashi in his preparation for the battle against the notorious Kojiro to be Japan's premiere swordsman. (Japanese with English subtitles) ★★★

Sword of the Valiant

(1984, 102 min, GB, Stephen Weeks) *Miles O'Keefe, Sean Connery.* Connery's brief but commanding presence is about the only reason to see this sword-and-sorcery adventure. O'Keefe plays a knight (Sir Gawain) who goes up against the infamous Green Knight. ★★

Swords of Death

(1971, 76 min, Japan, Tomo Uchida) The short opening montage of this period piece is an introduction to sword master Musashi, the originator of the two-sword style of fighting. The main story unfolds as Musashi petitions instruction in a particular fighting technique with the chain and sickle, a technique which will reveal to him the basic principles of two-sword fighting. What he doesn't know is that he's asked to be taught by the husband of the woman whose brother he killed at the battle of Sekigahara. And the husband has sent for backup. The ensuing melee gives new meaning to the idea of on-the-job training. A cautionary note: The video transfer is not of the highest quality, and the subtitles are not always easy to read. (Japanese with English subtitles) ★★½ VHS: $39.99

Sybil

(1976, 198 min, US, Daniel Petrie) *Sally Field, Joanne Woodward, Brad Davis.* Field gives a virtuoso performance in this haunting and technically superior made-for-TV movie about a young woman's multiple personality disorder. Field left behind the ghost of "The Flying Nun" forever when she tackled this demanding and career-making role. Woodward is splendid as the psychiatrist trying to help the suffering Sybil. ★★★★

Sylvia

(1986, 99 min, New Zealand, Michael Firth) *Eleanor David, Tom Wilkinson, Nigel Terry.* A teacher's unorthodox yet highly successful methods meet strong opposition from local authorities. David stars as the revolutionary educator Sylvia Ashton-Warner in this moving fact-based drama. ★★★ VHS: $79.99

Sylvia and the Phantom

(1950, 97 min, France, Claude Autant-Lara) *Jacques Tati.* An enchanting supernatural comedy. The story is set in a haunted castle where Tati and his 16-year-old daughter live. Trouble brews when his daughter falls in love with the ghost of her grandmother's long-deceased lover. Not your typical French film. (French with English subtitles) ★★★ VHS: $24.99

Sylvia Scarlett

(1936, 94 min, US, George Cukor) *Katharine Hepburn, Cary Grant, Edmund Gwenn.* A rakish thief and his daughter (Gwenn, Hepburn) are on the run from the law, so Kate becomes a "he," and the pair hooks up with con artist Grant. All the while, Kate maintains her secret identity, until she falls in love and must make a fateful decision. This is one of Cukor's fascinating misfires, which was crucified when released. Over the years, it has taken on cult status for its unusual premise and stylish tone. ★★½

Sympathy for the Devil (One Plus One)

(1969-70, 110 min, France, Jean-Luc Godard) This fascinating "song of revolution" intercuts The Rolling Stones rehearsing "Sympathy for the Devil" while the always controversial Godard wanders among them with occasional interruptions, car crashes, political diatribes as well as a visit to a porn store as he attempts to expose a society in collapse. A whirling attack on and an examination of politics, society and cinema. (English and French with English subtitles) ★★★ VHS: $29.99

Sylvia and the Phantom

T-Men

(1948, 92 min, US, Anthony Mann) *Dennis O'Keefe, Alfred Ryder, June Lockhart, Wallace Ford.* Return with us now to those thrilling days of yesteryear, when all government agents were square-jawed, clean-living, right-thinking white men fighting the evil nemesis of non-Anglo minorities washing upon our shores like scum in a bathtub. A voice-over introduces a professional representative of a really important organization — in this case, the U.S. Treasury (T-Men...get it?) — who in turn introduces a representative composite case. In this case it's the Shanghai Paper Case. Two stalwart protectors of our nation's security infiltrate a loosely knit organization of counterfeiters. Earnest orchestrations alternate with ingratiatingly banal incidental music to accompany images shot in extreme noir and with a penchant for highly reflective surfaces. A nostalgic reminder of a time when most people actually trusted the government. ★★½ VHS: $24.99

Tabu

(1931, 82 min, US/Tahiti, F.W. Murnau) Filmed entirely on the seemingly idyllic island of Tahiti, and made through the unusual collaboration between directors Murnau and Robert Flaherty, *Tabu* is an early, rarely seen masterpiece. Set amidst the glistening sun and fine sand beaches of the island, the film tells the tragic tale of two young lovers, forced to separate after a tribal edict calls the girl "tabu" to all the men of the village. The video transfer is taken from a strikingly beautiful print that was restored at the UCLA film archives. ★★★★ VHS: $39.99

Taffin

(1988, 96 min, GB, Francis Megahy) *Pierce Brosnan, Ray McAnally, Patrick Bergin.* Brosnan stars as a reclusive heavy in a small Irish coastal town who makes his living collecting bills — it's no wonder that he's not well-liked by the townsfolk. But when big business attempts to build a chemical plant in their backyard, the natives come begging for him to put up a fight. It's a fairly simple premise, but the inventive ways in which Brosnan and the locals beat up on the corporate big boys offer some amusing moments and satisfy some sense of social justice. ★★ VHS: $9.99; DVD: $14.99

Take Me Out to the Ball Game

(1949, 93 min, US, Busby Berkeley) *Gene Kelly, Frank Sinatra, Esther Williams, Betty Garrett.* Though it doesn't really rank with the best of the Kelly-Sinatra musicals, there's a lot to like in this flavorful romp with Gene and Frank as ball players greeting the new owner of their club: the aquatic Williams. ★★★ VHS: $14.99; DVD: $19.99

Take the Money and Run

(1969, 85 min, US, Woody Allen) *Woody Allen, Janet Margolin, Louise Lasser.* Allen's first film as writer and director uses a documentary-like format, which he would use again in his later *Zelig.* This hilarious odyssey follows the misadventures of Virgil Starkwell, a bumbling thief who can't even write a holdup note without messing up (Gub? What's a gub?). A non-stop verbal assault featuring some of Allen's funniest sight gags. (Letterboxed) ★★★½ VHS: $9.99; DVD: $14.99

Take 2

(1972, 100 min, Israel, Baruch Dienar) This breezy if familiar sex comedy follows the amorous adventures of Assi, an Israeli cinematographer whose interests lie not only in the commercials and documentaries he shoots but in the lovely actresses and models he comes in contact with. His idyllic and lascivious affairs take an abrupt turn after he is forced to hire an assistant — a young American woman who not only disapproves of his lifestyle but of his professional work as well. Of course, love is on the horizon. ★★½ VHS: $79.99

Taking Care of Business

(1990, 108 min, US, Arthur Hiller) *James Belushi, Charles Grodin, Anne DeSalvo, Hector Elizondo, Gates McFadden.* Escaped con Belushi assumes the identity of rich businessman Grodin when the former finds the latter's appointment book/wallet, or filofax, and carries off the charade while enjoying the sweet life. There are a few laughs to be found in this genial comedy, though it's mostly predictable stuff. ★★

The Taking of Pelham One Two Three

(1974, 104 min, US, Joseph Sargent) *Walter Matthau, Robert Shaw, Martin Balsam, Hector Elizondo, Jerry Stiller.* It's a mystery why this incredibly suspenseful thriller wasn't a box-office hit when released in the theatres. Shaw heads a four-man gang who hijack a New York City subway car at rush hour and demand one million dollars in ransom — to be delivered in one hour. Matthau is the transit inspector on the case, Balsam is one of the gang members, and Shaw is at his malevolent best as the leader. Filmed on location, *One Two Three* is superb entertainment. Quentin Tarantino probably got the idea of calling his characters colors in *Reservoir Dogs* from here. (Remade in 1998) ★★★½ VHS: $14.99; DVD: $14.99

A Tale of Springtime

(1990, 107 min, France, Eric Rohmer) *Anne Teyssedre, Hugues Quester.* With the completion of his "Six Comedies and Proverbs," Rohmer's new series "Tales of the Four Seasons" begins auspiciously with this engaging, sophisticated drama starring his usual coterie of attractive, young intellectual Parisians. Jenny, a philosophy graduate is befriended by Natasha, a chatty young piano student. Jealous of her divorced father's girlfriend (the same age as she), Natasha manipulates, in a none-too-subtle maneuvering, to make her father and Jenny a couple, resulting in a rather awkward weekend of shifting allegiances. A deceptively simple and entertaining story, brought to thought-provoking complexity through Rohmer's elegant style and his perceptive approach to human relations. (French with English subtitles) ★★★½

A Tale of Two Cities

(1935, 121 min, US, Jack Conway) *Ronald Colman, Elizabeth Allen, Edna May Oliver, Basil Rathbone.* The best of the many screen versions of the Charles Dickens classic set during the French Revolution, which was "...the best of times, the worst of times." Colman is in fine form as the lawyer who does "...a far, far better thing than I have ever done before." ★★★½ VHS: $19.99

A Tale of Two Cities

(1958, 117 min, GB, Ralph Thomas) *Dirk Bogarde, Dorothy Tutin, Cecil Parker, Donald Pleasance.* One of seven film versions of Charles Dickens' immortal classic about the French Revolution, this faithful adaptation falls just short of the 1935 version. A terrific cast makes this a still worthwhile endeavor. ★★★ VHS: $19.99

A Tale of Winter

(1994, 114 min, France, Eric Rohmer) *Charlotte Very, Frederic Van Dren Driessche.* Told in his

Gwyneth Paltrow, Jude Law and Matt Damon in *The Talented Mr. Ripley*

trademark spare style, Rohmer's deceptively simple story of the search for love varies from his usual talky, philosophical dramas by featuring a protagonist who lives through emotions, not by intellectual reason. Felicie (Very) spends an idyllic summer in a passionate romance with Charles (Driessche). Through an accidental mix-up, however, they are separated and never see each other again. Five years pass with Felicie, now with a daughter (Charles' unbeknowst to him), still yearning for him — a passion kept alive by her feeling that they will be reuinted. The film is held together by the wonderful creation that is Felicie, a vacillating but determined romantic whose ambition lies not in understanding the complexities of desire or emptiness but to simply be happy. An endearing *Sleepless in Seattle* for the Francophile set. (French with English subtitles) ★★★ VHS: $29.99

Talent for the Game

(1991, 91 min, US, Robert M. Young) *Edward James Olmos, Lorraine Bracco, Jeff Corbett.* Olmos brings much sincerity to the role of a veteran major league scout who happens upon a gifted, Midwestern pitcher. The focus of the story follows the young ball player's introduction into the majors and his exploitation at the hands of the team's new owner. The film is one long, predictable cliché, but Olmos and costar Bracco, as Olmos' longtime girlfriend, are likable characters and director Young fills his film with beguiling, personal moments. ★★½ VHS: $14.99

The Talented Mr. Ripley

(1999, 139 min, US, Anthony Minghella) *Matt Damon, Gwyneth Paltrow, Jude Law, Cate Blanchett, Philip Seymour Hoffman, James Rebhorn, Philip Baker Hall.* Recalling the visual splendor and fervent characterizations of his *The English Patient*, director Minghella's succulent dramatic thriller is one of the best Alfred Hitchcock films not made by the Master of Suspense. Based on the novel by Patricia Highsmith (whose "Strangers on a Train" was adapted by Hitchcock), and filmed once before in 1960 as *Purple Noon*, this devious exercise in deception is a twisted little tale much like its young hero — handsome trappings masking more sinister intent. All pouty and lean, Damon is excellent as Tom Ripley, who accepts a job from a shipping magnate to try to convince his wastrel son Dickie, who is living it up in Italy, to return to the States. Once there, Tom is enamored not only by Dickie's way of life but by Dickie as well. But accidents do happen, and soon Tom finds himself spiraling down an egregious path with no salvation. Minghella, who also wrote the smart screenplay, doesn't see Tom as a monster, but rather as an opportunist prepared to do what needs to be done. And that he is so sympathetic through most of this is testament to Damon's nearly tortured, galvanizing portrayal. Giving a dazzling performance which should cement him as a leading man, Law exudes sensuality and charm, leaving little doubt as to why Tom's senses would be impaired. ★★★★ VHS: $14.99; DVD: $29.99

Tales from the Crypt

(1972, 92 min, GB, Freddie Francis) *Ralph Richardson, Joan Collins, Patrick Magee, Ian Hendry, Richard Greene.* A chilling anthology of five frightening tales of deceit, mayhem, and treachery as experienced by five people lost in a catacomb. Five wayward souls who are shown their futures by a mysterious and evil monk (Richardson). ★★★ VHS: $9.99

Tales from the Darkside: The Movie

(1990, 95 min, US, John Harrison) *Deborah Harry, Christian Slater, Rae Dawn Chong, David Johansen.* Sporting a versatile cast and stories by George Romero and Stephen King, among others, *Tales from the Darkside: The Movie* leaves behind the familiar, bloody turf covered by the likes of Freddy Krueger and Jason and instead calls upon evil housewives, gargoyles, mummies and a black cat to keep its audience on the edge of its seat. It's all good fun, but occasionally stumbles when it swings from a serious mood to tongue-in-cheek horror and back again. ★★★ VHS: $9.99

Tales from the Gimli Hospital

(1989, 72 min, Canada, Guy Maddin) *Kyle McCulloch, Michael Gottli.* Maddin's ferociously funny Gothic creation is set during the turn of the century in the small Icelandic village of Gimli during a smallpox epidemic. Filmed in an eerie black and white and featuring minimal dialogue, the film tells the story of two hospitalized patients, Einar and Gunnar, who battle each other over everything from telling the perfect story to winning the attentions of their Louise Brooks–look-alike nurses. Wildly impressionistic and surreal, the film will elicit the same kind of astonished chuckles and gasps as another cult classic, *Eraserhead*. ★★★ VHS: $24.99; DVD: $29.99

Tales from the Hood

(1995, 97 min, US, Rusty Cundieff) *Clarence Williams III, Rosalind Cash, Corbin Bernsen, David Allen Grier, Rusty Cundieff.* With the same irreverence and stylish flourishes he brought to *Fear of a Black Hat*, director Cundieff has fashioned possibly the first horror anthology film with a social conscience. Not having to rely on monsters for his horrific tales, Cundieff uses the realities of life in the '90s — drug abuse, domestic violence, gang warfare, black-on-black crime, dishonest cops and racism — to create four ironic tales from the supernatural. A devilishly bug-eyed Williams is the storyteller, whose audience of three drug-dealing youths listen impatiently to his scary yarns. Mixing chills with ills, Cundieff's *Hood* is fun for all. (VHS available letterboxed or pan & scan) ★★★ VHS: $9.99; DVD: $14.99

The Tales of Hoffmann

(1951, 125 min, GB, Michael Powell & Emeric Pressburger) *Robert Rounseville, Robert Helpmann, Moira Shearer.* This Powell and Pressburger follow-up to *The Red Shoes* has been given special treatment in its transfer to video, highlighting its lurid Technicolor. During intermission at the Nuremberg Opera House, a group of students gather in the *bierkeller* to drink, smoke and listen to the acclaimed poet Hoffman spin tales of love, loss, mystery and evil. Located somewhere between the poetic surrealism of Jean Cocteau and the highly stylized works of Peter Greenaway, this film version of Offenbach's operatic fantasy will appeal to music lovers and the casual viewer alike. Restored, full-length version. (Filmed in English) ★★★ VHS: $29.99

Tales of Ordinary Madness

(1983, 107 min, Italy, Marco Ferreri) *Ben Gazzara, Ornella Muti.* Italian director Ferreri provokes every reaction but boredom, and with a scenario launched from the sordid musings of cult poet Charles Bukowski, he has perhaps found the vehicle best suited for his iconoclastic style. A grizzled Gazzara is the derelict author stumbling through adventures in a sickeningly sun-drenched L.A. The tauntingly beautiful Muti adds a new dimension to screen masochism. ★★★ VHS: $19.99; DVD: $24.99

Tales of Terror

(1963, 90 min, US, Roger Corman) *Vincent Price, Peter Lorre, Basil Rathbone, Debra Pagent.* In this portmanteau movie, Corman fashions four of Edgar Allan Poe's short stories into three episodes, each featuring Price. Vincent's daughter gets a strange mother's day surprise; Rathbone is an evil mesmerist whose sultry looks turn Vincent to putty; and, in a comedic segment, Lorre quells a wine taster before his time. ★★★ VHS: $9.99; DVD: $19.99

Tales of the City

(1993, 360 min, US/GB, Alastair Reid) *Olympia Dukakis, Chloe Webb, Marcus D'Amico, Laura Linney; Cameos: Ian McKellen, Paul Bartel, Mary Kay Place, Rod Steiger, Karen Black, Lance Loud.* Taken from Armistead Maupin's endearing and popular novel, this boldly original and faithful adaptation follows the interconnected lives of a group of San Francisco eccentrics (both gay and straight) during the halcyon 1970s. This six-part miniseries centers around exotic Earth Mother Anna Madrigal (Dukakis), landlady of 28 Barbary Lane. Her colorful extended family of tenants includes innocent Mary Ann (Linney), a recent arrival from Cincinnati; bisexual/fag hag Mona (Webb); and Michael (D'Amico), a hopeless romantic eternally searching for Mr. Right. The lives of these people and others come together in an amazingly complex series of eye-opening episodes which involve marital infidelity, ribald sexuality, recreational drug use and scenes of the emerging gay lifestyle. *Tales...* is funny, provocative and totally unpredictable. (Sequel: *More Tales of the City*) ★★★★

Talk of Angels

(1998, 96 min, US, Nick Hamm) *Polly Walker, Vincent Pérez, Franco Nero, Marisa Paredes, Frances McDormand.* A dreadfully dull, annoyingly "tasteful" Merchant-Ivory wannabe, *Talk of Angels* follows the story of a woman (Walker) who becomes the new nanny to the young girls of a wealthy family in Spain. At first considered too young to be a proper governess, Walker is soon accepted and respected by all; then she initiates a torrid affair with Latin hunk Pérez. Bliss is interrupted by that pesky Spanish Civil War. Boredom ensues. There is no drama to speak of, the acting is wooden, and the "triumphant moments" clichéd and artificial. ★ VHS: $19.99

The Talk of the Town

(1942, 118 min, US, George Stevens) *Cary Grant, Jean Arthur, Ronald Colman, Rex Ingram, Edgar Buchanan.* When discussing the movie career of Grant, other films will undoubtedly spring to mind before *Talk of the Town*, but this little-known Stevens comedy is unquestionably one of the actor's best efforts. Grant stars as an escaped convict (framed, naturally) who hides out in the house of an old friend, the captivating Arthur. But she has just rented it to Supreme Court nominee Colman. While Grant poses as the gardener, Arthur and an unsuspecting Colman attempt to prove Cary's innocence. Of course, both men fall in love with her, and Arthur herself is torn between them. Sparkling romantic comedy and potent social commentary as well. ★★★★ VHS: $19.99

Talk Radio

(1989, 119 min, US, Oliver Stone) *Eric Bogosian, Ellen Greene, Alec Baldwin, John C. McGinley.* After *Platoon* and *Wall Street*, Stone explores yet another kind of jungle in this hard-hitting, explosive look at the world of talk radio, public opinion and social intolerance. Loosely based on slain talk show host Alan Berg (a Denver radio personality killed by a neo-Nazi group), the film stars Bogosian, in a dazzling performance as Barry Champlain, a popular late-nite radio host whose verbal sparrings with his audience, not to mention his unapologetic views spoken in rapid-fire delivery, keep his listeners coming back for more. Through a series of flashbacks chronicling his success on the air, the film examines Champlain's complex psychological makeup and his volatile relationships, both in the present and the past, with those closest to him. ★★★½ VHS: $14.99; DVD: $26.99

Talkin' Dirty After Dark

(1991, 86 min, US, Topper Carew) *Martin Lawrence. Talkin' Dirty After Dark* takes a look at the lives of struggling black comics in Los Angeles. Lawrence does some excellent stand-up, but for the most part, the material is substandard. One might get the impression that the only things black comics make fun of is sex, what white folks do, sex, what brothers do, and. . . more sex. ★★ VHS: $14.99

The Tall Blond Man with One Black Shoe

(1972, 90 min, France, Yves Robert) *Pierre Richard, Bernard Blier.* A bungling young violinist unwittingly becomes involved with a bunch of would-be James Bonds and sets off a madcap chase of agents and assassins in this hilarious French farce. (French with English subtitles) (Sequel: *Return of the Tall Blond Man with One Black Shoe*) (American remake: *The Man with One Red Shoe*) ★★★

The Tall Guy

(1990, 92 min, GB, Mel Smith) *Jeff Goldblum, Emma Thompson, Rowan Atkinson.* Essentially a one-joke affair, the film follows Dexter King (Goldblum), an expatriate American stage actor living in London. Because of his above-average height, he is constantly cast in humiliating "fool" roles. Demonstrating a flair for physical comedy, Goldblum is at his best in the movie's real showstopper — a musical version of "The Elephant Man," one of the most tasteless and undeniably funny sequences ever put to film. ★★½

Tall Tale: The Unbelievable Adventures of Pecos Bill

(1995, 96 min, US, Jeremiah Chechik) *Patrick Swayze, Oliver Platt, Nick Stahl, Scott Glenn.* Not to be confused with Shelley's Duvall's Tall Tales productions, this Disney adventure starring Swayze as Pecos Bill is a heartwarming coming-of-age story featuring old-time Western mythic heroes. When his family's farm and the nearby town are threatened by a ruthless railroad baron (played with maliciousness by Glenn), a young boy (Stahl) turns to Pecos Bill, Paul Bunyon and John Henry for help. Along the way, he learns the power of his own faith and commitment in the face of adversity. ★★★ VHS: $14.99

Tamango

(1958, 98 min, France, John Berry) *Dorothy Dandridge, Curt Jurgens, Alex Cressan.* This standard seafaring yarn is rescued from certain obscurity by its theme of African slave-trading, black revolt and a "steamy" interracial love story. Jurgens plays a ruthless sea captain of a Dutch slave ship in the 1820s who falls in love with a beautiful black slave (Dandridge). Revolt simmers when one strong-willed and resourceful slave, and former warrior (Cressan), attempts to break his chains and lead a rebellion. Despite poor English dubbing of some minor characters and Dandridge's strange, Hollywood diva-ish acting style, the film holds great interest with its depiction of a proud but enslaved village. ★★½ VHS: $19.99

The Tamarind Seed

(1974, 123 min, GB, Blake Edwards) *Julie Andrews, Omar Sharif, Anthony Quayle.* Edwards makes an infrequent foray into the world of drama with this espionage/romancer. The material isn't strong, but the locations (London, Paris and Barbados) are wonderful and Andrews and Sharif have some fine moments as the Cold War Romeo and Juliet. ★★

The Taming of the Shrew

(1967, 126 min, GB/Italy, Franco Zeffirelli) *Elizabeth Taylor, Richard Burton, Michael York, Cyril Cusack.* Sumptuous screen version of Shakespeare's classic comedy with rich characterizations from Taylor and Burton as the feuding couple; she an unmarried "wildcat" and he the only man in Padua willing to court her. The story, of course, is the basis for the Cole Porter musical "Kiss Me Kate." ★★★½ VHS: $19.99; DVD: $27.99

Tampopo

(1987, 114 min, Japan, Juzo Itami) *Ken Watanabe, Tsotomu Yamazaki.* One of the most inspired and zaniest comedies to be released in years, this Japanese satire on food and sex is a delectable send-up of American westerns. A widow, who operates a noodle restaurant in Tokyo, is befriended by a transient truck driver. Together, in the search for the perfect noodle, they recruit a rag-tag team of social misfits to aid them in their quest. This appetizing comedy of epic proportions presents a world where the power of sex is second only to the power of — you've guessed it — the noodle! (Japanese with English subtitles) ★★★★ VHS: $19.99; DVD: $19.99

Tango

(1998, 105 min, Spain, Carlos Saura) *Miguel Ángel Sola, Cecilia Narova, Mia Maestro, Juan Carlos Copes.* Saura, the director behind *Flamenco*, proves himself a true wonder with *Tango*, a sharp and brilliant take on the midlife crisis of an artist. Dance and politics collide in this beautifully shot (by cinematographer Vittorio Storaro) tale of romance, nostalgia and regrets, with Sola as a director whose wife has left him and who falls for a young, beautiful dancer in his new film — a new documentary about the Tango. Beautifully acted and exquisite, the film's Euro-pacing may be a little off-putting, but this is nevertheless a rewarding experience. (Spanish with English subtitles) ★★★½ VHS: $21.99; DVD: $27.99

Tango and Cash

(1989, 105 min, US, Andrei Konchalovsky) *Sylvester Stallone, Kurt Russell, Jack Palance.* Stallone and Russell star in this slick, formulaic police thriller about two super cops framed by a megalomaniac drug dealer. Skipping the standard love interest (or are the two stars the love interest?), the film includes enough car crashes to keep Detroit in the black for another five years. The money combination of a mangy and volatile Russell (à la Mel Gibson in *Lethal Weapon*) with a well-dressed, bespectacled Stallone allows both actors to play with their screen images and made the latter likable for the first time since *Rocky*. ★★½ VHS: $9.99; DVD: $14.99

The Tango Lesson

(1997, 101 min, GB/France/Argentina, Sally Potter) *Sally Potter, Pablo Veron.* Writer-director Potter stars as a fictionalized version of herself in this lyrical and mesmerizing contemplation of love, seduction, power and the Argentine tango. Potter plays "Sally," a British filmmaker who, while scouting Paris for her upcoming film, wanders aimlessly into a theatre and is instantly absorbed into a live tango exhibition starring Veron. She gamely introduces herself to the maestro and entreats him to tutor her, offering to put him in a film in return. This transaction in *Tango Lesson* represents a real-life event, but to what degree the ensuing entanglement on-screen represents the depth of Potter and Veron's offscreen relationship is unclear. With the help of Robby Müller's exquisite sepia-toned cinematography and Potter's haunting score, the film's dance sequences are as pure a delight as we've gotten since the era of Fred and Ginger. ★★★★ VHS: $24.99

Tank Girl

(1995, 104 min, US, Rachel Talalay) *Lori Petty, Ice-T, Malcolm McDowell, Naomi Watts.* This semi-likable mishmash is sure to elicit squeals of joy from a few while giving migraines to many as it pounds its way through 104 minutes of non sequitured one-liners and plotless shenanigans. Petty is the title character, a buzz-cut grunge girl with a slightly phallic passion for tanks. Along for the ride is Watts as her sidekick Jet Girl. Together they join forces with the Rippers (a mutant band of half-human, half-kangaroo renegades) and battle the powerful Water and Power overlords (led by McDowell) in the year 2033. Though as visually bombastic as the worst of MTV and as narratively challenged as a

"Monkees" episode, this *might* prove fun for the less-discriminating viewer looking for a mindless yuk to accompany their inebriated state. ★★ VHS: $9.99; DVD: $19.99

Tanner '88

(1988, 360 min, US, Robert Altman) *Michael Murphy, Pamela Reed, Kevin J. O'Connor, Veronica Cartwright, Jeff Daniels, Rebecca DeMornay.* In 1988, director Altman created a fictional Democratic presidential candidate and used the actual primary process as location shooting. Murphy as Jack Tanner hits the campaign trail, shaking hands with Bob Dole, Gary Hart and Pat Robertson, who may or may not know it's only a movie. Tanner's flashes of brilliance in a quagmire of mediocrity (sometimes his own) are packaged for media consumption by his campaign staff. It's a cynical, intelligent and sardonic look at the photo ops, pollsters, spin doctors, petty sabotage, backbiting and pure chance that comprise the modern American political system. Written by Garry Trudeau, with Sidney Blumenthal as a political consultant. Vol. 1 includes "The Dark Horse," "For Real" and "Night of the Twinkies"; Vol. 2 includes "Moonwalker and Bookbag," "Bagels with Bruce," "Child's Play" and "The Great Escape"; Vol. 3 includes "The Girlfriend Factor," "Something Borrowed, Something Blue," "The Boiler Room" and "Reality Check." ★★★½ VHS: $79.99

The Tao of Steve

(2000, 87 min, US, Jenniphr Goodman) *Donal Logue, Greer Goodman, Kimo Wills.* How is it that overweight, perpetually stoned slacker Dex (a perfectly cast Logue) beds so many attractive women? He lives according to the "Tao of Steve," a homemade philosophy made up of equal parts Lao Tzu and Steve McQueen, which seems to work like a charm on the ladies. Dex's supremely laid-back attitude towards women and life in general is put to the test when a conquest from college (whom Dex can't even remember) comes to town for a short-term job — and Dex finds himself falling in love. Winning performances (especially from Logue), great moments of insight and some hilarious discussions of philosophy and sex that beat anything from Mars or Venus more than make up for a too-cute tone. ★★★ VHS: $14.99; DVD: $24.99

Tap

(1989, 110 min, US, Nick Castle) *Gregory Hines, Suzanne Douglas, Sammy Davis, Jr., Joe Morton, Savion Glover, Paul Nicholas.* A frenzied celebration of dance set against an urban backdrop, as a disillusioned tap dancer (Hines) is torn between his craft and a lucrative living as a thief. As would be expected, there are some great tap sequences. ★★★ VHS: $9.99

Tapeheads

(1988, 97 min, US, Bill Fishman) *John Cusack, Tim Robbins, Susan Tyrrell.* An exhilaratingly original and innovative spoof which will not disappoint. The film's story follows the unusual road to fame taken by two misfits: the deliciously sleazy Cusack and the constantly bewildered Robbins. They join forces and set up an independent video production company. Stymied by their failure to make rock videos,

they subside on the fringe, making living (and not so living) wills as well as taping funerals until their big break comes. The film is crammed with crazy comedy and peppered with unforgettable lines. There's some wild musical numbers and both Cusack and Robbins are wonderful farceurs — and if that's not enough, Junior Walker and Sam Moore appear as "The Swanky Modes." ★★★½ VHS: $9.99; DVD: $24.99

Taps

(1981, 124 min, US, Harold Becker) *Timothy Hutton, George C. Scott, Sean Penn, Tom Cruise.* Military cadets seize control of their military academy when outside forces threaten to shut it down. Some of this is by-the-books, and slow going, but its young cast is enthusiastic. ★★

Tarantula

(1955, 80 min, US, Jack Arnold) *Leo G. Carroll, John Agar, Clint Eastwood.* Carroll stars as a scientist whose secret growth formula works a little too well, resulting in a mutated spider which chews up the countryside and anything else that gets in its way. One of the best of the many 1950s giant/mutant schlock films, *Tarantula* features a credible story and great F/X. Highly entertaining. ("I knew Leo G. Carroll was over a barrel when *Tarantula* took to the hills.") ★★★

Target

(1985, 117 min, US, Arthur Penn) *Gene Hackman, Matt Dillon, Gayle Hunnicutt.* Director Penn and actor Hackman are reunited for a third time in this satisfactory espionage thriller. Hackman plays a former CIA agent who, with son Dillon, sets out to rescue his wife, kidnapped by enemy agents out for revenge. ★★½ VHS: $9.99

Targets

(1968, 90 min, US, Peter Bogdanovich) *Boris Karloff, James Brown.* Karloff had his last great role as an aging horror film star who decides to retire because events in the real world have rendered his talents superfluous. As if to underscore the point, a soldier just back from Vietnam begins a rampage of killing which leads him to a drive-in, where the old star is making a public appearance. ★★★ VHS: $14.99

Tartuffe

(1984, 140 min, France, Gérard Depardieu) *Gérard Depardieu, Elizabeth Depardieu, François Perier.* Depardieu makes his directorial debut with this version of Moliere's classic stage play about religious and sexual hypocrisy. The story revolves around a rich merchant who, with his wife, comes under the manipulative spell of a cunning charismatic religious zealot. He is threatened with exposure after the husband discovers that the rascal had made love to his young, attractive wife. Similar to *Cyrano de Bergerac* in its use of poetic dialogue, this satire exposing man's greed and delusions is a skillfully faithful adaptation. (French with English subtitles) ★★★

Tarzan

(1999, 88 min, US, Kevin Lima & Chris Buck) *Voices of: Tony Goldwyn, Minnie Driver, Glenn Close, Rosie O'Donnell, Nigel Hawthorne, Brian Blessed,*

Wayne Knight. Though falling victim to the curse of Disney's last few animated features of having a less-than inspiring score, this flavorful animated film is a thorough delight. Excellent animation, a colorful story line and winning vocal characterizations all contribute to make this another in a long lone of splendid Disney family films. The tale of a young boy raised by the apes seems a natural for the studio, and the filmmakers have wonderfully brought to life the monkeys, elephants and even humans who drive the story. If the film has a weakness, it is Phil Collins' unexceptional musical score. Fans of the singer/songwriter may appreciate him singing each song, but it becomes tiresome after awhile. ★★★½ VHS: $26.99; DVD: $29.99

Tarzan and the Lost City

(1998, 84 min, US, Carl Schenkel) *Casper Van Dien, Jane March.* This adds little to the Tarzan series. Van Dien has the act of glowering down to a science but is likable unless swinging from vine to vine. Tarzan receives a vision in the middle of his bachelor party, courtesy of an African shaman friend of his. He leaves England a week before his wedding to return to the jungle. His fiancée, realizing that she must stand by her (ape) man, soon joins him. Together, Tarzan, Jane, the natives, some ole jungle magic and some guys in really bad ape costumes save the day. ★★ VHS: $102.99; DVD: $14.99

Tarzan the Ape Man

(1932, 99 min, US, W.S. Van Dyke) *Johnny Weissmuller, Maureen O'Sullivan.* The first of the Weissmuller Tarzan pictures, with the Olympic swimmer as the definitive Ape Man, and O'Sullivan as a lovely Jane. Very entertaining adventure film. ★★★ VHS: $19.99

Taste of Cherry

(1997, 95 min, Iran, Abbas Kiarostami) *Homayon Ershadi, Abdolrahman Bagheri, Afshin Khorshid.* A troubled Iranian man in a Range Rover rides through the outskirts of Tehran looking for an accomplice to return to a designated location at 6:00 the next morning to shovel 20 spadefuls of dirt on his suicidal grave. Profoundly alienated, he is the displaced person among the Kurds, Afghanis and Turks whom he encounters in his quest. The land he travels glows red under the desert sun in a bleached blue sky; the barren, rocky soil a perfect backdrop to his condescending arrogance. The man who agrees to perform the task offers a story of his own flirtation with suicidal intent born of despair. *Taste of Cherry* is rich in stark imagery, stunningly used to evoke at once existential angst and the inexhaustive human will to survive. It's marred only slightly by the inexplicable addition of a "filmmakers at work" coda. (Letterboxed) (Farsi with English subtitles) ★★★ VHS: $29.99; DVD: $29.99

A Taste of Honey

(1962, 100 min, GB, Tony Richardson) *Rita Tushingham, Robert Stephens, Dora Bryan.* This lovely, heartbreaking film is a "minor" masterpiece. Tushingham stars in this earthy tale about a group of social rejects in Britain's bleak, industrial North. A poetic saga, which is aided by top-notch performances, and transcends lower-class cliché. ★★★½

Robert De Niro in *Taxi Driver*

Taste the Blood of Dracula

(1970, 95 min, GB, Peter Sasdy) *Christopher Lee, Geoffrey Keen, Gwen Watford, Roy Kinnear.* The fourth in the Hammer vampire stories. Dracula seeks vengeance against three Victorian thrill-seekers whose cowardice causes the death of a magician trying to resurrect the Prince of Darkness. More campy, hokey fun with Lee as the evil bloodsucker. ★★½

Tatie Danielle

(1990, 100 min, France, Etienne Chatiliez) *Tsilla Chelton, Catherine Jacob.* The supposed dignity of one's "golden years" is the target of this sharply satirical black comedy. Seemingly innocent and helpless, our sinister heroine Tatie Danielle is, in actuality, a bitter, calculating old lady who receives sick pleasure out of hurting and manipulating all who try to help her. Tatie meets her match one day when an equally manipulative young nurse (who is on to her tactics) arrives on the scene. The film, to its detriment, ignores the motives for Auntie's meanness, and instead takes devious delight in simply chronicling her often hilariously terroristic antics. (French with English subtitles) ★★½

Taxi Blues

(1990, 110 min, Russia/France, Pavel Lounguine) *Piotr Mamonov, Piotr Zaitchenko.* This superbly rendered street-level saga about a unique friendship between a rough-hewn Moscow cab driver and an alcoholic saxophone player is a brutal but moving testament to the arduous process of change in the former Soviet Union. Filmed in the early-morning emptiness of Moscow's mean streets, the film uses these two characters to symbolize the faces of the new Russian psyche (the black marketeer and the newly freed intellectual). It is a sometimes humorous, often upsetting and uniformly bleak look at the hardships facing the common people as they struggle to move out of decades of stagnation. (Russian with English subtitles) ★★★★ VHS: $29.99

Taxi Driver

(1976, 113 min, US, Martin Scorsese) *Robert De Niro, Jodie Foster, Cybill Shepherd, Harvey Keitel, Albert Brooks, Peter Boyle.* De Niro is Travis Bickle, a lonely cab driver obsessed with the squalor and decay of New York City. He sets out on a one-man mission to clean the streets of its underworld of pimps, junkies and hookers. Scorsese directs this sordid and haunting film featuring Foster in the tragic and memorable role of a teenage prostitute. De Niro's quintessential performance, Scorsese's sardonic view of American urban life, and a mesmerizing and unsettling use of non-exploitative violence propels this masterwork to the forefront of American cinema. ★★★★ VHS: $14.99; DVD: $19.99

Taxi zum Klo (Taxi to the Toilet)

(1980, 94 min, Germany, Frank Ripploh) *Frank Ripploh, Bernd Broaderup.* Ripploh's witty auto-biographical social/sexual comedy offers an illuminating portrait one man's gay lifestyle, his conflicting image in a straight-laced profession and his relationship with a monogamous lover, who disapproves of his hedonistic promiscuity. Funny, charming and unflinchingly honest. (German with English subtitles) ★★★ VHS: $39.99

A Taxing Woman

(1988, 127 min, Japan, Juzo Itami) *Nobuko Miyamoto, Tsutomu Yamazaki.* The Japanese post-Kurosawa New Wave continues in this sexy and whimsical comedy from the director of *Tampopo.* The story follows Ryoko (Miyamoto), a diligent and resourceful female tax inspector who tackles the ever-ingenious tax evading efforts of the citizens. Her greatest challenge is presented by Gondo, a suave operator of "love hotels" whom she suspects is underreporting massive amounts of money. Her impassioned efforts to catch him in the act and his equally feverish schemes to evade detection bring this unlikely pair together in this highly charged comedy. (Japanese with English subtitles) ★★★½ VHS: $19.99; DVD: $29.99

A Taxing Woman's Return

(1988, 127 min, Japan, Juzo Itami) *Nobuko Miyamoto, Rentaro Mikuni.* This irreverent and free-wheeling comedy about the ingenious efforts of the Japanese to evade taxes and the tenacious tax collectors who are equally determined to ferret out every hidden taxable yen is a welcome follow-up to the hugely successful *A Taxing Woman.* Miyamoto is again the charming tax inspector who this time investigates a corrupt fundamentalist religious order which might be a front for a real estate racket. While not as fresh as the original, this scathing satire is, nevertheless, still a joy to watch. (Japanese with English subtitles) ★★★ VHS: $29.99

Tchaikovsky

(1970, 153 min, Russia/US, Igor Tlaankin) *Innokenti Smoktunovsky.* A disappointing, standard bio of the famed composer Pyotr Ilyich Tchaikovsky. The film suffers from a below-average musical soundtrack (a sin for a film about and infused with classical music) and the lushly elegant Cinemascope visuals are all but lost in the non-letterbox video transfer. The story examines Tchaikovsky's life (from his tortured childhood to his struggles with loneliness and despair to his eventual renown) with an ice-cold austerity which gives little insight into the studious, intense and taciturn composer. The film begs for the excesses of Ken Russell's *The Music Lovers.* (Russian with English subtitles) ★½ VHS: $59.99

Tchao Pantin

(1985, 94 min, France, Claude Berri) *Richard Anconina, Coluch, Philippe Leotard.* Berri, a director noted for his light comedies (*Le Sex Shop, Male of the Century*), leaves behind his safe stories to probe the back alleys, sleazy bars and tenements of drug dealers and various other denizens of the Parisian underbelly. A darkly somber and intensely moving thriller about the relationship between an alienated old man, retired from everything around him, and a lonely punk youth. An exciting tale of survival in a heartless world. Winner of 5 Césars. (French with English subtitles) ★★★

Tea and Sympathy

(1956, 123 min, US, Vincente Minnelli) *John Kerr, Deborah Kerr, Leif Erickson.* Adapted (and watered down) by Robert Anderson from his own Broadway play, this tale of a sensitive teen at a New England boarding school who is accused of being a homosexual is both involving and curiously tame. J. Kerr plays the youth, who is suspected by his classmates of being a "sister boy." D. Kerr is the understanding wife of the headmaster who befriends the confused teen and who eventually exorcises any latent homosexual desires. ★★★ VHS: $19.99

Tea with Mussolini

(1999, 117 min, GB/Italy, Franco Zeffirelli) *Joan Plowright, Maggie Smith, Judi Dench, Cher, Lily Tomlin, Charlie Lucas, Baird Wallace.* Based on a chapter from director Zeffirelli's autobiography, this old-fashioned, nostalgic memory piece lacks a certain cinematic flourish, but makes up for it with both a great cast in great form and a beguiling coming-of-age story. In mid-1930s Florence, young, motherless Luca is raised by a group of elderly English expatriate women, known as "the Scarpioni" (for their biting wit). Each instills in Luca a love for the arts, theatre and life. However, their worlds change when Fascism grips Italy — sending all on different roads but never separated in spirit. Zeffirelli pays great respect to these women with his heartfelt tale, and they have been marvelously brought to life by a once-in-a-lifetime ensemble. It's their conviction that overcomes the sometimes dramatically shortchanged story to produce a wistful recollection that is graced with heart, wit and admiration. ★★★ VHS: $14.99; DVD: $14.99

Teacher's Pet

(1958, 120 min, US, George Stevens) *Clark Gable, Doris Day, Gig Young, Nick Adams.* Entertaining romantic farce with Gable as a newspaperman and Day as a teacher. Both come together when he takes her writing course. ★★★ VHS: $14.99

Teachers

(1984, 106 min, US, Arthur Hiller) *Nick Nolte, JoBeth Williams, Judd Hirsch, Morgan Freeman, Ralph Macchio, Laura Dern.* A good cast is mostly wasted in this story of the everyday ups and downs of an urban high school. ★★ VHS: $9.99

T

Teaching Mrs. Tingle

(1999, 96 min, US, Kevin Williamson) *Helen Mirren, Katie Holmes, Barry Watson, Jeffrey Tambor, Molly Ringwald, Vivica A. Fox.* After penning two of the best teen horror films in recent years (*Scream* and its sequel), Williamson follows with this disappointing directorial debut. Technically more of a black comedy than a horror film, *Teaching Mrs. Tingle* tells the tale of a straight A student (Holmes) who is in danger of losing her academic scholarship if her hated history teacher — Mrs. Tingle — gives her the F she's threatened to. Holmes ends up holding the evil educator hostage until she changes her mind. A not-bad premise is chucked in favor of juvenile dramatics and pandering humor. Only Mirren and the occasional cute aside keep this from being a complete snoozer. ★½ VHS: $14.99; DVD: $29.99

The Teahouse of the August Moon

(1956, 124 min, US, Daniel Mann) *Marlon Brando, Glenn Ford, Eddie Albert.* A mild-mannered Army captain (Ford) is left in charge of an occupied village in 1946 Okinawa, and wacky results ensue. Brando plays a wily Asian interpreter. ★★★ VHS: $19.99

Teaserama

(1955, 75 min, US, Irving Klaw) Fabulous '50s pin-up queen Betty Page and busty glamazon Tempest Storm are featured in this truly amazing burlesque presentation. Performances by pin-up faves Honey Baer, Trudy Wayne, Chris LaChris and Cherry Knight, campy comic routines by famed vaudeville player Joe E. Ross ("Sgt. Bilko," "Car 54, Where Are You?"), and a great dance/striptease by female impersonator Vicky Lynn combine to make this film a "Burly-Q" classic. ★★★ VHS: $24.99; DVD: $19.99

Teen Wolf

(1985, 90 min, US, Rod Daniel) *Michael J. Fox, James Hampton.* Though *Back to the Future* was released several months before it, this harmless

Cher in *Tea with Mussolini*

teen comedy was Fox's film debut. He plays a teenager who discovers he's really a werewolf. To its credit, there are a few laughs. (Sequel: *Teen Wolf Too*) ★★½

Teenage Mutant Ninja Turtles

(1990, 93 min, US, Steve Barron) Long popular on video in cartoon form, these live-action Teenage Mutant Ninja Turtles proved to be just as popular on the big screen in this hokey but crowd-pleasing (if you're under 15) adventure-comedy. Here the TMNT find themselves up against a group of teenagers under the evil influence of a Japanese gangster. Cowabunga, dude. Though a bit sluggish throughout, there's still enough action to appeal to the younger set, and Jim Henson's full-size costumes are terrific. (Followed by two sequels.) ★★; DVD: $14.99

Telefon

(1977, 100 min, US, Don Siegel) *Charles Bronson, Donald Pleasence, Lee Remick, Tyne Daly, Patrick Magee.* Exciting espionage thriller with Bronson playing a Russian agent sent to the U.S. to preserve detente by stopping a psychotic defector (Pleasence) from activating scores of hypnotized saboteurs. ★★★ VHS: $19.99

Tell Them Willie Boy Is Here

(1969, 96 min, US, Abraham Polonsky) *Robert Redford, Katharine Ross, Robert Blake, Susan Clark, Barry Sullivan.* Blake stars as Willie Boy, an American Indian who becomes the object of a massive hunting party and a political scapegoat during the early 1900s. Set in the arid deserts of Southern California, the film begins with a drunken pool room fight involving Willie Boy and a white patron. From there, events start to snowball as Willie Boy kills the father of his girlfriend (a tanned Ross), and the two go on the run with a disinterested sheriff (Redford) and a blood-thirsty posse on their trail. Director Polonsky — whose first feature this was since being blackballed during the McCarthy witch-hunts — sets an ominous tone as he effectively tells a tale of injustice and hysteria and juxtaposes it with an exciting chase story. ★★★ VHS: $14.99

Telling Lies in America

(1997, 101 min, US, Guy Ferland) *Kevin Bacon, Brad Renfro, Calista Flockhart, Maximilian Schell, Paul Dooley.* Screenwriter Joe Eszterhas' semiautobiographical coming-of-age tale finds the writer in a less bombastic, more reflective mood than his more famous Hollywood hits. Ably conveying the inner turmoil of youth at the crossroads, Eszterhas has written a memory piece which is a little too self-serving but can be compelling all the same. Renfro is Karchy, a Hungarian immigrant living in early 1960s Cleveland with his father (Schell). When Karchy lands the job as assistant to a hotshot and shady local D.J. (Bacon, in a very effective portrayal), his learning experience encompasses betrayal, deceit, unrequited love, and discovering the little inequities of his newfound land. The film has a good look to it, and includes a lively soundtrack, including a very entertaining song, "Medium Rare," written by Bacon. ★★½ VHS: $14.99; DVD: $24.99

The Temp

(1993, 99 min, US, Tom Holland) *Timothy Hutton, Lara Flynn Boyle, Faye Dunaway, Dwight Schultz, Oliver Platt, Steven Weber.* Hutton, an

upwardly mobile marketing executive with a penchant for paranoia, is blown away by the skills of his new temporary secretary, played by Boyle. She files, she types, and, unfortunately, she also may be bumping off most of Hutton's competition in the dog-eat-dog world of cookie manufacturing. The main problem with *The Temp* is that Boyle is so blatantly obvious in her manipulations of Hutton that the film loses its tension early on. ★★ VHS: $9.99

The Tempest

(1979, 95 min, GB, Derek Jarman) *Elisabeth Welch, Heathcote Williams, Jack Birkett.* Shakespeare gets the Jarman treatment in this lighthearted, visually eclectic and idiosyncratic version of the Bard's final play. Quite funny, outlandish and campy, the film includes singing, dancing, exotic and erotic visuals and Welch's rendition of "Stormy Weather." ★★★ VHS: $24.99; DVD: $29.99

The Tempest

(1982, 140 min, US, Paul Mazursky) *John Cassavetes, Gena Rowlands, Susan Sarandon, Raul Julia, Molly Ringwald.* Mazursky's contemporary treatment of Shakespeare's drama has Cassavetes attempting to resolve his midlife crisis by abandoning his successful Manhattan existence to search for truth and beauty in the Greek isles. Beautiful location shooting and engaging performances compensate for weaknesses in the script. ★★½ VHS: $9.99

Temptation of a Monk

(1994, 118 min, Hong Kong, Clara Law) *Joan Chen, Wu Hsinkuo.* While stylishly filmed, this tale of a betrayed general who must seek refuge in a temple is slow-moving and confusing. Chen stars as the siren princess who tempts a general of a royal family's army as he tries to atone for his errors in being accused a traitor. Lavish costumes, open landscapes and period music abound. The actors leave a good impression on a poorly written script. Though director Law has exhibited a fine edge with her prior works, she is unable to overcome a taxing story line and laborious characters in this well-intentioned but misguided effort. (Mandarin with English subtitles) ★★½ VHS: $19.99; DVD: $29.99

Temptress Moon

(1997, 115 min, China, Chen Kaige) *Leslie Cheung, Gong Li, Kevin Lin, He Saifei.* Cheung and Gong are radiant, as always, as ill-fated lovers in this overly tragic jumble. It's the tale of Yu Zhongliang (Cheung) and Pang Ruyi (Gong), who were raised together as youths in Ruyi's ancestral home where the orphaned Zhongliang lives as a virtual servant to his sister's husband (Ruyi's brother). Zhongliang eventually winds up in Shanghai where he becomes the favorite of a local crime boss and acts as a gigolo/con man. Then he's instructed to return to the Pang household and put the con on Ruyi and thus is born a setup for tragedy. The film is lushly photographed by Christopher Doyle and features fine performances from its brooding leads, but sadly its arcane plot is peppered with a host of incomprehensible moments that muddle the film's message. (Mandarin with English subtitles) ★★ VHS: $19.99

Ten Benny

10

(1979, 121 min, US, Blake Edwards) *Dudley Moore, Julie Andrews, Bo Derek, Robert Webber, Brian Dennehy.* Edwards wrote and directed this hit comedy about a famed composer (Moore) who becomes obsessed by a woman (Derek) he rates a perfect "10." Moore is good at playing Edwards' slapstick, and Andrews and Dennehy offer good support. Webber's self-pitying gay composer is a bit much, though. ★★★ VHS: $14.99; DVD: $14.99

Ten Benny

(1998, 98 min, US, Eric Bross) *Adrien Brody, Michael Gallagher, Sybil Temchen, Tony Gillian, Frank Vincent.* Growing up in the milieu of low-level mob action in Bloomfield, NJ, Ray (a very engaging Brody) rests his future on a bet on the ponies, financed by loan sharks and fueled by a hot tip on a sure thing. Eager to quit his job in a shoe store, buy an engagement ring for his beloved and set up shop in a prime storefront location, he bets $10,000 on a horse that can't lose. Guess what? It does. Ray, once calm, easy-going and in control, devolves into just another mark, just another neighborhood guy with big ideas and lowered expectations. His whimsical little story about waiting on Paul Newman ("He's a ten benny." — shoe size 10B) is transformed from a harmless entertainment to a sleazy semi-con. Ray is transformed from a decent guy whom everyone likes to a desperate man who alienates those closest to him. *Ten Benny* is a small, thoughtful exploration of the decisions people make, the paths they take, and the true meaning of loss. ★★½ VHS: $9.99; DVD: $9.99

The Ten Commandments

(1923, 146 min, US, Cecil B. DeMille) Unfortunately DeMille never heeded the eleventh commandment which is: Thou shalt not make epic movies out of the Bible pandering to people's prurient interests. The first portion of this sprawling mess violates that edict, then goes on to tell a contemporary tale of two brothers — one good, one evil — and how the Word saves their souls. Great camp fun with two-strip Technicolor sequences.

DeMille would try his hand at the story again in 1956. ★★½ VHS: $19.99

The Ten Commandments

(1956, 220 min, US, Cecil B. DeMille) *Charlton Heston, Yul Brynner, Anne Baxter, Edward G. Robinson, Vincent Price, John Saxon.* Mammoth epic from DeMille, based on his silent classic. Heston dons beard and robe to portray Moses, leading the Jews out of Egypt. A spectacular production, though some scenes may cause a few smirks. Even with today's state-of-the-art special effects, the parting of the Red Sea is still impressive. (VHS available letterboxed or pan & scan) ★★★ VHS: $24.99; DVD: $34.99

Ten Days Wonder

(1971, 101 min, France, Claude Chabrol) *Anthony Perkins, Orson Welles, Marlene Jobert.* Although not well received in its initial release in 1971, this oddity is a distinctly original work that fans of Chabrol and of the avant-garde should enjoy. Adapted from an Ellery Queen story, the film stars Perkins as a mentally and emotionally disturbed young man who falls in love with his father's (Welles) child bride. A bewildering mystery of madness, adultery and blackmail. (Filmed in English) ★★½

Ten from Your Show of Shows

(1973, 92 min, US, Max Liebman) *Sid Caesar, Imogene Coca, Carl Reiner, Howard Morris.* For those of you who remember the classic TV comedy show of the 1950s, "Your Show of Shows," no more additional information is needed other than that this is a collection of their most hilarious routines. For those not familiar, these examples of the very best of TV sketch comedy, performed live each week, are not to be missed. Starring the madcap team of Caesar, Coca and Reiner, and with many skits written by Mel Brooks, the film concludes with a painfully funny parody of "This Is Your Life." ★★★★

Ten Little Indians

(1974, 98 min, GB, Peter Collinson) *Oliver Reed, Elke Sommer, Richard Attenborough, Gert Frobe.* Second remake of the Agatha Christie mystery "And Then There Were None," this time set in a remote desert inn, where ten

strangers are gathered and then murdered one by one. Lackluster pacing adds nothing new to this oft-told tale. ★★

10 Rillington Place

(1971, 111 min, GB, Richard Fleischer) *Richard Attenborough, John Hurt, Judy Geeson.* This gripping psychological thriller is another true-life murder case brought to the screen by director Fleischer (*Compulsion, The Boston Strangler*). The story centers on notorious mass-murderer John Christie (Attenborough) and his unwitting pawn Timothy Evans (Hurt). Sometimes too clinical to be completely successful as a thriller, the film manages to remain interesting nonetheless. ★★★ VHS: $19.99

10 Things I Hate about You

(1999, 97 min, US, Gil Junger) *Heath Ledger, Julia Stiles, Joseph Gordon-Levitt, Larisa Oleynik, David Krumholtz, Larry Miller.* Extremely loose adaptation of "The Taming of the Shrew," with teens, high school, and, of course, a climactic prom. Frighteningly overprotective dad Miller won't let his popular daughter Oleynik go to the prom unless his unpopular shrew daughter Stiles goes, too. She is conned into a date with outcast Ledger, then finds out about a wager about the date, but he's fallen for her... oh, why bother explaining? It's an old, predictable story (seen most recently in *She's All That*) but it has equal parts charm and bile, making it hard not to get swept up. Fun performances by all the kids make this a diverting treat, even if the writers can't tell Shakespeare from Elizabeth Barret Browning ("How do I love thee? Let me count the ways"). ★★½ VHS: $14.99; DVD: $29.99

Ten Violent Women

(1979, 97 min, US, Ted V. Mikels) *Sherri Vernon, Dixie Lauren, Sally Alice Gamble.* Bored with their jobs, ten female coal miners attempt to increase their income through a jewelry heist and by dealing cocaine. This lands them in prison, which is headed by a butch dyke and populated by curvaceous gals. A terrible women-in-prison flick that makes for hilarious fun. ★

The Tenant

(1976, 125 min, France/US, Roman Polanski) *Roman Polanski, Isabelle Adjani, Melvyn Douglas, Shelley Winters.* Polanski himself stars in this dark and eerie film noir about a social misfit who moves into a Parisian apartment and begins a bizarre descent into madness. Filled with paranoia and forboding, the film takes on its own twisted logic as it makes its way towards a truly outrageous denouement. ★★★ VHS: $49.99

Tender Mercies

(1982, 89 min, US, Bruce Beresford) *Robert Duvall, Tess Harper, Betty Buckley, Ellen Barkin, Wilford Brimley.* Duvall delivers a powerful, Oscar-winning performance as a country singer on the skids who is rescued from despair and the bottle by the quiet strength and sensitivity of a young widow. Australian Beresford makes his American directorial debut with this humanistic drama. ★★★★ VHS: $14.99

The Tender Trap

(1955, 111 min, US, Charles Walters) *Frank Sinatra, Debbie Reynolds, Celeste Holm, David Wayne, Carolyn Jones.* Sinatra stars in this engaging comedy about an insufferably unattached bachelor who falls for sweet young-and-innocent Broadway hopeful Reynolds and gets more than he bargained for. One of the better "sophisticated" comedies to come out of the '50s, this adaptation of the Max Schulman/Robert Paul Smith play features a bunch of winning musical numbers (especially the Cahn-Van Heusen title tune). ★★★½ VHS: $19.99

Tenderness of the Wolves

(1973, 86 min, Germany, Ulli Lommel) *Kurt Raab, Jeff Roden, Margit Carstensen, Rainer Werner Fassbinder.* Produced by Rainer Werner Fassbinder, this creepy low-budget shocker is suggested by the infamous murder case which inspired Fritz Lang's classic *M*, though now updated to post-war Germany. Raab plays the sleazy predator — now a vampire — who lures young boys to his attic lair and has his way sexually with them before sucking their blood. He then sells their body parts as meat to unsuspecting buyers. Filmed with a tantalizing mix of titillation, gore and black comedy, this grisly gem is both disturbing and oddly entertaining. (Letterboxed) (German with English subtitles) ★★★ VHS: $14.99; DVD: $29.99

Tendres Cousines

(1980, 90 min, France, David Hamilton) *Thierry Tevini, Anja Shute.* A funny, tender coming-of-age film which follows the sexual antics of a 14-year-old boy and his beautiful cousin. Master erotic photographer Hamilton (*Bilitis*) presents this romp of unrequited love amidst the haylofts of rural France. (French with English subtitles) ★★½

Tenebre

(1984, 101 min, Italy, Dario Argento) *Anthony Franciosa, John Saxon, Daria Nicolodi.* Franciosa plays Peter Neal, a popular American writer who comes to Rome for a publicity tour. He soon learns that a killer is using his book as inspiration for a series of murders. Neal and his secretary begin to help the police in their search for the killer and, like all good Argento heroes, eventually set off on their own to solve the mystery — descending into a world of madness and murder which mirrors the worst aspects of his bloody novels. *Tenebre* is remarkably strong in narrative content for an Argento film, and the film is brilliantly lit and shot, including one absolutely terrifying shot at the very end as the killer is revealed. (Director's cut) (aka: *Unsane*) ★★★ VHS: $14.99; DVD: $29.99

The Tenth Man

(1988, 100 min, GB, Jack Gold) *Anthony Hopkins, Kristin Scott Thomas, Derek Jacobi.* Written by Graham Greene in 1944 while under contract with MGM, the manuscript for this riveting thriller, about a man's cowardly act and eventual redemption, languished in the studio archives until it was rediscovered in 1983. The setting is Occupied France, 1941. Wealthy lawyer Jean-Louis Chavel (Hopkins) is imprisoned in a Nazi roundup. When he is chosen to be executed, he trades places with another man, offering his substantial fortune and property to his family. Years later, a penniless Chavel returns to his former chateau, now home to the dead man's lovely family. Assuming a new

identity, he becomes their gardener and friend — knowing full well their hatred of Chavel, the man who "killed" their son and brother. His secret shame remains hidden until one day a stranger arrives claiming that *he* is Chavel. ★★★★ VHS: $19.99

The Tenth Victim

(1965, 92 min, Italy, Elio Petre) *Marcello Mastroianni, Ursula Andress.* A macabre yet compelling sci-fi tale set in the 21st century where killing has been ritualized in a sport where men and women pursue each other in a deadly game. This nightmarish thriller blends just the right amount of satire in its exploration of the uneasy relationship between the individual and society. Miss Andress' bullet-firing brassiere is worth the price of the rental alone! ★★★ VHS: $14.99; DVD: $24.99

Teorema (Theorem)

(1968, 93 min, Italy, Pier Paolo Pasolini) *Terence Stamp, Silvano Magnano, Massimo Girotti.* Pasolini's fusion of Marxism, sex and religion stars a very young and attractive Stamp as a divine stranger who enters the household of a bourgeois family and profoundly affects their lives when he seduces the mother, father, son, daughter and maid. A surreal and sensual allegory with the Pasolini postulation that the ruling class can be undermined and destroyed by the one thing that it cannot control — sex. Despite winning the Grand Prix at the Venice Film Festival in 1968, the film was publicly denounced by Pope Paul VI and banned as obscene in Italy. Pasolini was arrested, but in a celebrated trial he was acquitted of all charges. (Italian with English subtitles) ★★★

Tequila Sunrise

(1988, 116 min, US, Robert Towne) *Michelle Pfeiffer, Kurt Russell, Mel Gibson, Raul Julia, Arliss Howard, Arye Gross, J.T. Walsh.* An uneven but gorgeous-looking romantic thriller which tries to and occasionally succeeds in capturing the mood of *Chinatown*, which Towne wrote. Gibson stars as a former drug dealer trying to go straight, but is about to be busted by his high school chum Russell. The two men become embroiled in a game of cat-and-mouse as both fall in love with a beautiful restaurant owner, Pfeiffer. The three stars give earnest performances, but are unable to hide some of the contrivances of the script. ★★ VHS: $9.99; DVD: $19.99

The Terence Davies Trilogy

(1974-83, 101 min, GB, Terence Davies) Three short films, *Madonna and Child, Children* and *Death and Transfiguration*, were made by director Davies over a ten-year period and were all inspired from his own life. The films examine the harsh life — from boyhood to the grave — of Robert Tucker, a gay Liverpudlian. While lacking in traditional narrative, this bleak yet stirring and powerful portrait follows one man's continual battle against the demons that drove him into loneliness and despair. A richly evocative and ultimately unforgettable work. ★★★ VHS: $29.99

Teresa Venerdi

(1941, 90 min, Italy, Vittorio De Sica) *Vittorio De Sica, Anna Magnani.* A delectable comedy

directed by and starring De Sica as a young physician working in an orphanage who finds himself innocently involved with three women. The magnificent Magnani is a doctor's assistant who sets out to win the doctor herself. Filled with action, intrigue and jealousy. (Italian with English subtitles) (aka: *Doctor Beware*) ★★★

Terminal Bliss

(1992, 91 min, US, Jordan Allan) *Luke Perry, Timothy Owen, Alexis Arquette.* Before shooting to fame as a moody California rich kid on TV's "Beverly Hills 90210," teen heartthrob Perry played a moody California rich kid in this pointless tale of adolescent decadence. While the sex and drugs sequences during the first 15 minutes offer generous helpings of delicious B-movie juvenile delinquency, the aimless, episodic structure of the film eventually grows tiresome. Who needs plot, depth and style when you can hear lines like, "Mom, I'm going out to kill myself now. I'll be home late." (Made in 1987) ★ VHS: $19.99

The Terminal Man

(1974, 107 min, US, Mike Hodges) *George Segal, Joan Hackett, Jill Clayburgh.* Interesting if flawed thriller based on Michael Crichton's novel with Segal as a scientist who becomes controlled by a computer. ★★ VHS: $14.99

Terminal Velocity

(1994, 102 min, US, Deran Sarafian) *Charlie Sheen, Nastassja Kinski.* This high-flying actioner starring Sheen as a devil-may-care sky diver and Kinski as a Russian agent who lures him into helping her beat the bad guys is filled with implausibilities, bad dialogue, wretched acting and is still somehow fun. There are plenty of fist fights, gunplay, explosions (there's even a tribute to *Die Harder*) and general chaos. ★★½ VHS: $9.99; DVD: $29.99

The Terminator

(1984, 108 min, US, James Cameron) *Arnold Schwarzenegger, Linda Hamilton, Michael Biehn, Paul Winfield, Bill Paxton, Lance Henriksen.* Director Cameron and actor Schwarzenegger both burst on the action scene with this explosively entertaining and taut sci-fi thriller. Arnold plays a cyborg sent from the future to present-day Los Angeles to terminate the mother (Hamilton) of an unborn revolutionary. Biehn is the soldier also from the future sent to protect her. ★★★½ VHS: $9.99

Terminator 2: Judgment Day

(1991, 135 min, US, James Cameron) *Arnold Schwarzenegger, Linda Hamilton, Edward Furlong, Joe Morton, Robert Patrick.* The $100 million price tag on this impressive sci-fi extravaganza sequel made a lot of jaws drop, but that's nothing compared to what the rip-roaring, non-stop action and eye-popping special effects do. The year is 1997. The evil cyborgs have sent the new, improved T-1000 terminator unit back through time on a mission to eliminate the future leader of the human resistance — a typical Southern California adolescent named John Conner (nicely played by Furlong). But into the fray comes a second killing machine (guess who), reprogrammed by the humans and sent back to

T

protect the lad. Together, they liberate his mom, Sarah (a buff Hamilton), who's been institutionalized for her babblings about robots from the future, and the relentless chase begins. ★★★½ VHS: $9.99; DVD: $39.99

Terms of Endearment

(1983, 132 min, US, James L. Brooks) *Debra Winger, Shirley MacLaine, Jack Nicholson, Jeff Daniels, John Lithgow, Danny DeVito.* A sensitive, funny and deeply touching examination of the tumultuous relationship between a mother and daughter. *Terms* virtually monopolized the Oscar ceremony, taking Best Picture and Best Director honors as well as (finally) acknowledging MacLaine for her crackling conception of a rigid matriarch. Winger is sensational as her spunky daughter and Nicholson rises to the occasion as the ex-astronaut next door with the wrong stuff. (Sequel: *The Evening Star*) ★★★½ VHS: $9.99; DVD: $29.99

Terra em Transe

(1966, 105 min, Brazil, Glauber Rocha) *Terra em Transe*, about the disillusionment and death of a young poet and journalist who is pursuaded to become involved in the politics of his country, is a landmark of political cinema and a vivid example of Brazil's Cinema Novo movement. A powerful and quite personal film which was denounced by the Right as incendiary propaganda, hailed by the Left as an impassioned exposé, and banned by the government for some time. Winner of the International Film Critics Award at Cannes. (Portuguese with English subtitles) ★★★½ VHS: $59.99

La Terra Trema

(1948, 160 min, Italy, Luchino Visconti) Initially setting off to make a Communist Party-financed short documentary on the conditions of the peasants in poverty-stricken Sicily, Visconti soon abandoned this idea to work on an epic focusing on the harsh conditions of southern Italy's fishermen, factory workers and miners. He finished only this segment, "Episodes del Mare" — and the result is a neorealist masterpiece. Filmed on location with nonprofessional actors, the story tells of the conditions and struggles of an exploited fisherman's family and the unsuccessful revolt by them and others against insurmountable odds. With startlingly beautiful images, a simple narrative and his focus of social reality, this, only Visconti's second feature, is considered one of his best works. (Italian with English subtitles) ★★★★

The Terror

(1963, 81 min, US, Roger Corman) *Boris Karloff, Jack Nicholson, Dick Miller.* Effective Corman cheapie about an injured soldier from Napoleon's army recovering at an eerie castle with strange goings-on. ★★½ VHS: $9.99

The Terror Within

(1988, 89 min, US, Thierry Notz) *George Kennedy, Andrew Stevens.* A chemically-induced plague has ravaged the Earth and its remaining survivors are trapped in a laboratory 500 feet below the Mojave Desert. When a pregnant woman is found, the group soon learns that the baby she is carrying is an embryonic mutant. Just a little bit spooky, though its good premise isn't thoroughly realized. ★★ VHS: $14.99

The Terrorist

(2000, 100 min, India, Santosh Sivan) *Ayesha Dharkar.* An exceptional Indian film, *The Terrorist* is the impressive directorial debut of noted cinematographer Sivan. To no one's surprise, the film is ravishing, providing a rich contrast to a story of a voluntary martyr. With her gigantic, gorgeous eyes and looking much like a forgotten silent film star, Dharkar plays a serene but ruthless zealot willing to give her life in an assassination plot. Kernels of doubt are planted in her mind, however, building quite a bit of suspense as to whether she will or won't at the crucial moment. A powerful character study with many unforgettable moments and a stunning lead performance. (Tamil with English subtitles) ★★★½ VHS: $19.99; DVD: $24.99

The Terrornauts

(1967, 75 min, GB, Montgomery Tully) *Simon Oates, Zena Marshall.* Mysterious alien forces kidnap an entire building containing research scientists and transport them to another planet. There, a robot takes the Earthlings to yet another planet, where little green men show them the fate of Earth. Fun, low-budget British sci-fi based on the novel "The Wailing Asteroid." ★★ VHS: $14.99

Tess

(1979, 180 min, GB/France, Roman Polanski) *Nastassia Kinski, Peter Firth, Leigh Lawson.* Polanski's Academy Award-winning interpretation of Thomas Hardy's novel features breathtaking cinematography and a strong, eloquent performance by Kinski as a peasant girl who ruins and is ruined by two men. Polanski precisely and memorably portrays the moral rigidity of Victorian England and brilliantly moves this story to its inexorable climax. (Filmed in English) ★★★½

Testament

(1983, 89 min, US, Lynne Littman) *Jane Alexander, William Devane, Lukas Haas, Mako, Kevin Costner.* The devastation of a nuclear attack is powerfully conveyed via personal relationships rather than elaborate special effects in Littman's staggering drama. Alexander gives a virtuoso performance as a housewife who helplessly watches the demise of family and friends. An extremely intense film which resists strident advocacy, opting for sensitivity and restraint in its warning of a nuclear nightmare. ★★★½ VHS: $14.99

The Testament of Dr. Mabuse

(1933, 120 min, Germany, Fritz Lang) *Rudolph Klein-Rogge.* Banned in Germany soon after its release, Lang's brilliant thriller is a trenchant allegory on the rise of Nazism, as well as the thinking of its crazed leader. In this follow-up to Lang's 1922 silent classic *Dr. Mabuse: Der Spieler (The Gambler)*, Klein-Rogge returns as the now lunatic underworld crime lord imprisoned in an insane asylum, spending his final days writing diabolical plans to create "an abyss of terror" in Germany. From his cell, these plans are carried out, much to the consternation of the police, even after his death. (German with English subtitles) ★★★½ VHS: $24.99

Terminator 2: Judgment Day

The Testament of Orpheus

(1959, 83 min, France, Jean Cocteau) *Jean Cocteau, Jean Marais, Pablo Picasso, Yul Brynner, Charles Aznavour.* "I shall present a striptease in which I shed my body to expose my soul." With this statement, Cocteau opens his final film, a farewell celebration to art. Cocteau himself takes the lead in this private diary which exposes the relationship between the artist, his work and his dreams. An arresting piece with an eclectic cast. (French with English subtitles) ★★★½ VHS: $29.99; DVD: $79.99

Tetsuo: The Iron Man

(1989, 67 min, Japan, Shinya Tsukamoto) Shockingly perverse techno-erotic splatterthon about a Japanese businessman who begins to metamorphose into a misshapen "Iron Man" after running over a "metal fetishist" in a hit-and-run accident. The next day, the offender discovers metal shards growing out of his face and his phallus turns into a two-foot homicidal corkscrew. The remainder of this surrealistic, cyberpunk epic concerns a battle between two "Iron Men" in what could be best described as *Eraserhead* meets *In the Realm of the Senses*. Also included is the 25-minute short film *Drum Struck* (★★), directed by Greg Nickson and featuring actor Anthony Bevilacqua as a rock-n-roll drummer in search of the perfect beat in this strange David Lynch-influenced piece. ★★★★ DVD: $29.99

Tevye

(1939, 96 min, US, Maurice Schwartz) *Maurice Schwartz.* Taken from the famous Sholom Aleichem story from which *Fiddler on the Roof* is based, this moving human drama set in Czarist Russia (yet filmed on Long Island) will remind viewers less of the famous musical play and more of the works of such directors as Pagnol, Renoir and Bresson. Director and Yiddish stage actor Schwartz stars as Tevye, a deeply religious man thrown into a conflict between the rules of his religion and his love for his family after he discovers that his daughter Khave has fallen in love with a Gentile and plans to marry him. (Yiddish with English subtitles) ★★★ VHS: $79.99

Tex

(1982, 103 min, US, Tim Hunter) *Matt Dillon, Meg Tilly, Ben Johnson, Emilio Estevez.* A young Dillon gives a sensitive performance as a teenager on the verge of adulthood. Abandoned by their father, he and his brother struggle with responsibility and indecision. Based on S. E. Hinton's novel (Francis Ford Coppola would find limited success with two other Hinton novels, *The Outsiders* and *Rumble Fish*). Hunter directs with clarity. (Letterboxed) ★★★ VHS: $14.99; DVD: $24.99

Texas

(1941, 94 min, US, George Marshall) *William Holden, Glenn Ford, Claire Trevor.* Solid western with Holden and Ford as two drifters in search of love and fortune in the wilds of Texas. They find Trevor. ★★★ VHS: $9.99

Texas Chainsaw Massacre

(1974, 81 min, US, Tobe Hooper) *Marilyn Burns, Allen Danzinger.* Hooper directed this horrific tale about the gruesome slaughter of a group of innocent youngsters by a family of maniacs, headed by "Leatherface." This much-imitated gorefest has yet to be equaled for its sheer terror and shocking but surprisingly non-bloody depictions of violence. You have been warned. (Followed by 3 sequels) ★★★ VHS: $19.99; DVD: $29.99

Texasville

(1990, 125 min, US, Peter Bogdanovich) *Jeff Bridges, Cybill Shepherd, Annie Potts, Cloris Leachman, Timothy Bottoms, Eileen Brennan, Randy Quaid.* Sad to report that as good as *The Last Picture Show* is, its sequel, *Texasville*, is as bad. In a small, dusty town in 1970s Texas, frumpy and double-chinned Bridges is in the throes of midlife crisis: he's disillusioned and broke, married to an unresponsive, verbally abusive Potts and attracted to the returning "look but don't touch" Shepherd. Strangely, the plot is lifeless, uninvolving and tepid, especially in light of the film's intended goal of being a torrid Southern sexual comedy. ★½ VHS: $14.99

Thank You and Good Night

(1991, 77 min, US, Jan Oxenberg) Director Oxenberg serves up a humorous, irreverent inventive and touching comedy-drama documenting her grandmother's death. Never maudlin or morbid, she examines not only the life and personality of her 70-ish grandmother, a self-proclaimed kosher ham, but contemplates the mystery of death and the regret and sorrow of the living. An emotionally powerful yet contemplative family autobiography that clutches at the heart and soul. ★★★½ VHS: $19.99

Thank Your Lucky Stars

(1943, 130 min, US, David Butler) *Eddie Cantor, Bette Davis, Errol Flynn, Ida Lupino, Olivia de Havilland, Humphrey Bogart, John Garfield.* Warner Brothers' entry into the all-star musical which the studio released during WWII to help the war effort. Cantor plays dual roles as himself and a show business hopeful, and there's plenty of 1940s stars: Davis sings "They're Either Too Young or Too Old," Flynn sings "That's What You Jolly Well Get" and Lupino and de Havilland jitterbug! ★★★ VHS: $29.99

That Championship Season

(1982, 110 min, US, Jason Miller) *Robert Mitchum, Bruce Dern, Paul Sorvino, Stacy Keach, Martin Sheen.* A well-acted but static adaptation of the Pulitzer Prize–winning Broadway drama about the reunion of a championship high school basketball team. Mitchum is their coach. (Remade in 1999) ★★½ VHS: $6.99

That Cold Day in the Park

(1969, 113 min, US, Robert Altman) *Sandy Dennis, Michael Burns, Michael Murphy.* Dennis stars as a 32-year-old virgin who is attracted to a handsome young mute (Burns) she meets in the park. However, when she takes him home to care for him, a sly psychological game begins between the sexually repressed woman and the prankish drifter. An occasionally unfocused though unsettling drama. ★★½ VHS: $14.99

That Darn Cat

(1965, 116 min, US, Robert Stevenson) *Dean Jones, Hayley Mills, Dorothy Provine.* Cute Disney comedy about a cat who helps solve a kidnapping mystery. (Remade in 1997) ★★½

That Darn Cat

(1997, 100 min, US, Robert Spiers) *Christina Ricci, Doug E. Doug, Dyan Cannon, Dean Jones.* This remake of Disney's popular 1965 family comedy retains very little of the appeal of the original. Even the presence of the usually adorable Ricci can't bring to life the story of a cute feline which helps solve a kidnapping. Slow, rarely funny, and, ultimately, a pointless retread. ★½ VHS: $19.99

That Hamilton Woman

(1941, 125 min, US, Alexander Korda) *Laurence Olivier, Vivien Leigh, Gladys Cooper.* Good performances highlight this story of the ill-fated romance between Lord Admiral Nelson and Lady Emma Hamilton. The best of the three films made by then-husband and wife Olivier and Leigh. (The same story was retold in 1973 in *The Nelson Affair*, which is not available on video.) (aka: *Lady Hamilton*) ★★★

That Obscure Object of Desire

(1977, 103 min, France, Luis Bunuel) *Fernando Rey, Carole Bouquet, Angela Molina.* Buñuel's surreal comedy of the sexes stars Rey as an aging aristocrat who falls obsessively in love with a beguiling but unapproachable woman, played by two different actresses: the detached Bouquet and the voluptuous Molina. Buñuel's final film takes us mischievously through the enigma of human passion. (French with English subtitles) ★★★½

That Old Feeling

(1997, 107 min, US, Carl Reiner) *Bette Midler, Dennis Farina, Paula Marshall, Danny Nucci, David Rasche, Gail O'Grady.* An old-fashioned, often very funny battle-of-the-sexes comedy. Divorced for 15 loathing years, Midler and Farina reunite for their daughter's wedding, hopefully with their claws retracted for the day. However, neither could have anticipated the reunion in store when old resentments give way to uncontrollable lust and they run away together. With his most entertaining film since *All of Me*, director Reiner wisely lets his wonderful cast cut loose. Midler is a master of the one-liner, and she's in top form, and Farina is a marvelous comic presence. Though some of the story loses its balance when it concentrates too much on the daughter, Midler and Farina make any old feeling seem new again. ★★★ VHS: $9.99; DVD: $24.99

That Sinking Feeling

(1979, 82 min, Scotland, Bill Forsyth) *Gordon John Sinclair, Robert Buchanan.* This first feature by gifted Scottish director Forsyth only came to America after the successes of *Local Hero* and *Gregory's Girl.* In his characteristic way, Forsyth imbues this tale with amiable but lunatic teenagers and a host of daft adults. The story involves a gang of Glasgow youths who concoct a scheme to rob a warehouse full of stainless steel sinks. ★★★

That Thing You Do!

(1996, 110 min, US, Tom Hanks) *Tom Everett Scott, Liv Tyler, Johnathan Schaech, Steve Zahn, Ethan Embry, Tom Hanks, Kevin Pollak.* It should come as no surprise that the first film Hanks

That Obscure Object of Desire

has written and directed is a witty, nice, beguilingly old-fashioned movie-move. After all, double Oscar-winner Hanks is a witty, nice, old-fashioned movie star. What may come as a surprise is that Hanks has made a well-crafted and toe-tapping charmer. *That Thing You Do!* chronicles the rise, quick star status and even quicker slide of a pop band in 1964. With Necco-wafer colored cinematography and lovingly rendered period detail, the film moves at a rapid clip tracking the group's roots in smalltown America and their ascension to the top of the charts. With *That Thing You Do!*, Hanks seems to know that sometimes it's hip to be square, and he's proud of it. ★★★ VHS: $9.99; DVD: $22.99

That Touch of Mink

(1962, 99 min, US, Delbert Mann) *Doris Day, Cary Grant, Gig Young, Audrey Meadows, John Astin.* Day made two "sex" comedies in 1962: this one costarring Grant; and *Lover Come Back,* with Rock Hudson. Though *That Touch of Mink* is not nearly as funny or successful as *Lover Come Back,* it is nevertheless a pleasant enough nostalgia course for an era when women (nice girls, anyway) did everything possible to keep their virginity, and men did everything they could to dissuade them. Tame stuff compared to today, but it did manage to curl a few lips "way back" in '62. (Letterboxed) ★★½ VHS: $9.99; DVD: $29.99

That Uncertain Feeling

(1941, 84 min, US, Ernst Lubitsch) *Merle Oberon, Melvyn Douglas, Burgess Meredith.* Sophisticated if lightweight romp from the great Lubitsch about a married couple's dilemma when the wife gets the hiccups. Oberon and Douglas give appealing performances as the husband and wife, and Meredith steals the show as their pianist neighbor. ★★½ VHS: $19.99; DVD: $24.99

That Was Then, This Is Now

(1985, 103 min, US, Christopher Cain) *Emilio Estevez, Craig Sheffer, Kim Delaney, Morgan Freeman.* Estevez stars in and adapted this routine version of S.E. Hinton's novel about a troubled teen's coming-of-age. ★★ VHS: $9.99

That'll Be the Day

(1974, 90 min, GB, Claude Whatham) *David Essex, Ringo Starr, Keith Moon, Robert Lindsay.* An underrated and compelling drama of a British working-class youth (Essex), and would-be rock 'n' roller, as he moves through adolescence to adulthood. This down-to-earth story of musical aspiration is set in the 1950s. (Sequel: *Stardust*) ★★★ VHS: $9.99; DVD: $24.99

That's Adequate

(1987, 80 min, US, Harry Hurwitz) *Tony Randall, Richard Lewis, James Coco, Robert Townsend, Bruce Willis, Anne Meara.* This episodic, low-budget movie parody actually contains several funny, if totally silly skits. It's sort of a poor man's *Amazon Women on the Moon,* but just as funny. The parodies of the Three Stooges, Adolph Hitler as a youth and an animated children's show would be at home in a Python or Brooks film. Not for sophisticated tastes. ★★

That's Dancing

(1985, 105 min, US, Jack Haley, Jr.) Hodgepodge compilation of some of the movies' best dance sequences. Includes scenes from *West Side Story, 42nd Street* and *Sweet Charity,* among many others. ★★½ VHS: $19.99

That's Entertainment

(1974, 132 min, US, Jack Haley, Jr.) Compilation of some of MGM's best musical moments. Includes clips from *The Wizard of Oz, Gigi* and *Singin' in the Rain,* among many others. Hosts include Fred Astaire, Gene Kelly, James Stewart and Elizabeth Taylor. The musical sequences that were chosen and the wealth of wonderful stars who appear combine to make this a delightfully nostalgic musical experience. ★★★½ VHS: $14.99; DVD: $24.99

That's Entertainment Part 2

(1976, 126 min, US, Gene Kelly) *Gene Kelly, Fred Astaire.* Kelly and Astaire host this fond remembrance and sequel, looking back at more of the best MGM had to offer. Includes comedic and dramatic scenes, as well as musical clips. ★★★ VHS: $14.99

That's Life

(1986, 102 min, US, Blake Edwards) *Jack Lemmon, Julie Andrews, Sally Kellerman, Robert Loggia.* Edwards wrote and directed this absorbing drama starring Lemmon in a remarkable performance as a successful architect facing emotional crisis as his 60th birthday nears. Andrews gives a solid portrayal as his wife. ★★★ VHS: $14.99; DVD: $24.99

Theatre of Blood

(1973, 105 min, GB, Douglas Hickox) *Vincent Price, Diana Rigg, Robert Morley, Jack Hawkins.* Though its joke wears thin, this is nevertheless an entertaining horror film about a demented Shakespearean actor (Price) who takes a bloody revenge against the eight theatre critics who gave him "thumbs down." ★★★ VHS: $14.99; DVD: $14.99

Thelma and Louise

(1991, 120 min, US, Ridley Scott) *Susan Sarandon, Geena Davis, Harvey Keitel, Michael Madsen, Brad Pitt.* A wildly entertaining and accomplished road movie which features uncharacteristically sensitive and intuitive direction from Scott. Sarandon and Davis are the title characters, two friends who leave their male counterparts and head for a leisurely weekend getaway. En route, however, their trek turns deadly and they find themselves on the run from the police. Stylish and witty, Callie Khouri's Oscar-winning screenplay follows their series of escalating criminal adventures as the two women break away from the confines of a male-dominated society, searching for their own identity and independence. Sarandon and Davis are both outstanding, each creating enormously appealing, substantial and distinct characters. ★★★★ VHS: $9.99; DVD: $14.99

Them!

(1954, 94 min, US, Gordon Douglas) *James Whitmore, Edmund Gwenn, James Arness, Joan Weldon.* A horror favorite for years, this is the one with the giant ants. Humongous insects are spotted in the desert, and they're working their way to Los Angeles. Lots of good old-fashioned chills. ★★★½ VHS: $14.99

Theme

(1979, 108 min, Russia, Gleb Panfilov) *Mikhail Ulyanov, Inna Churikova.* An early test case under *glasnost, Theme* was completed in 1979 only to be held out of release by Russian censors until 1988. Its crime: being too emotional. In retrospect, the most fascinating thing about this otherwise very standard drama is that anyone would ever find it worthy of suppression. The film's action centers around a 54-year-old poet who is thoroughly under the wing of the Soviet bureaucracy. While vacationing in the country, he is confronted by an alluring young woman who accuses him of selling out his artistic integrity to the state. Naturally, he finds himself smitten by both her and her uncompromising views and sets out to reform himself. While not particularly successful in its condemnation of Soviet artistic bureaucracy, the film is more interesting as a study of one man's struggle for artistic integrity. (Russian with English subtitles) ★★½ VHS: $59.99

Theodora Goes Wild

(1936, 94 min, US, Richard Boleslawski) *Irene Dunne, Melvyn Douglas, Thomas Mitchell, Spring Byington.* A delightful and at times hilarious escapade with Dunne at her best. She plays a religious-bred New England woman who unbeknownst to her family and small town is actually the popular writer (under a pseudonym, of course) of a series of racy women's novels. Douglas, exuding great charm in a role which is probably the precursor to his playboy in *Ninotchka,* plays the ne'er-do-well who thinks Dunne to be as provocative as the women in her novels, and who helps let her secret out when he comes a-courtin'. The laughs are plentiful, and the film even manages a friendly swipe or two at puritanism. This was Dunne's first real chance to play comedy, and she proved herself to be a peerless comedienne. ★★★½ VHS: $19.99

The Theory of Flight

(1998, 98 min, GB, Paul Greengrass) *Helena Bonham Carter, Kenneth Branagh, Gemma Jones, Holly Aird.* A man's attempt to soar off the roof of a London bank earns him a term of community service, through which he meets a young woman slowly dying in a wheel chair. Bonham Carter is creditable as she assays *My Left Foot* territory, as is Branagh as an artist whose canvases no longer engage his attention except as materials with which to test theories of flight. They are both outsiders, initially as separate from

Susan Sarandon (l.) and Geena Davis in *Thelma and Louise*

each other as they each are from the world that surrounds them; yet over time are bonded in mutual support and acceptance. While the actors delineate their characters with wit and sensitivity and a thankful absence of saccharine sentimentality, the film often lapses into MTVitis and predictability. Based on a true story. ★★ VHS: $19.99

There Goes My Baby

(1994, 95 min, US, Floyd Mutrux) *Dermot Mulroney, Rick Schroder, Noah Wyle, Kelli Williams, Seymour Cassel.* It's the early 1960s: The Vietnam War is still called a police action, the hippies are just gathering in San Francisco, Watts is on fire and the class of '65 is spending their last night together. Mulroney, Schroder and Wyle are a group of friends who must deal with their impending separation and the changes both they and their country are experiencing. Poignant and achingly nostalgic but flawed by the familiarity of the material. ★★ VHS: $89.99

There Was a Crooked Man

(1970, 123 min, US, Joseph L. Mankiewicz) *Kirk Douglas, Henry Fonda, Hume Cronyn, Warren Oates, Burgess Meredith, Lee Grant.* Outrageous comedy-western adventure with Douglas as a prisoner who matches wits with his incorruptible warden (Fonda). ★★★ VHS: $14.99

There's No Business Like Show Business

(1954, 117 min, US, Walter Lang) *Ethel Merman, Dan Dailey, Donald O'Connor, Mitzi Gaynor, Marilyn Monroe, Johnny Ray.* This Irving Berlin song fest is a particularly sentimental but entertaining musical about the professional and personal ups and downs of a theatrical family. Merman and Dailey are the parents, with kids O'Connor, Ray and Gaynor joining the act. Marilyn is an aspiring singer, and she gets to sing "Heat Wave." Sure it's sappy, but who can resist Merman and O'Connor's onstage reconciliation. ★★½ VHS: $9.99; DVD: $24.99

There's Something about Mary

(1998, 119 min, US, Peter Farrelly & Bobby Farrelly) *Cameron Diaz, Ben Stiller, Matt Dillon, Chris Elliott, Lee Evans.* The Farrelly brothers take comic absurdity to new, hilarious heights. Their humor may be over-the-top at times, and some of the film lags between jokes, but there's no denying that there's something about this comedy which is flat-out hysterical. Stiller is wonderfully droll as Ted, a nerdy high schooler whose prom date with his dream girl, Mary (the bewitchingly beautiful Diaz), results in disaster. Thirteen years later, he's still obsessed with her. He hires Pat (Dillon), a smarmy detective, to track her down. This sets the stage for uproarious cases of mistaken identity, double cross, impersonation, animal cruelty, human cruelty, masturbation jokes, gay jokes, handicapped jokes and the old fishhook-caught-in-the-mouth gag. There's obviously nothing sacred to the Farrelly brothers, but their un-PC, juvenile toilet humor and burlesque bits work! ★★★½ VHS: $14.99; DVD: $22.99

Theremin: An Electronic Odyssey

(1995, 84 min, US, Steven M. Martin) A very interesting if incomplete documentary about the grandfather of electronic music, Russian born Leon Theremin. Theremin was an inventor and electronics mastermind who created the first all-electronic musical instrument, a wooden box with two metal probes protruding from it. This instrument, which bears his name, generates a magnetic field and is played when a person's hands interfere with the field, manipulating musical pitch. Theremin and his instrument were the toast of New York society during the '30s until an unexpected political incident completely changed his life and influence. A good, if shallow overview of a fascinating and eccentric genius. ★★★ VHS: $14.99; DVD: $19.99

Therese

(1986, 90 min, France, Alain Cavalier) *Catherine Mouchet, Aurore Prieto.* This radiantly beautiful, impeccably crafted film recounts the life of St. Therese — the Little Flower — a teenage girl whose devotion to the Church is surpassed only by her love for Christ. Therese, who died in 1897, was canonized in 1925. Mouchet shines in the title role. Based on Therese's famous diaries. (French with English subtitles) ★★★½

Therese and Isabelle

(1968, 102 min, France, Radley Metzger) *Essy Persson, Anna Gael, Barbara Laage, Anne Vernon.* Set in an all-girls Catholic boarding school, this milestone film is a tender glimpse at the erotic affair of two young women. Unlike many other works of the period, this provocative drama offers a non-exploitative picture of budding female sexuality, some very hot love scenes and lots of schoolgirl emotional tension. With voice-over narration taken directly from Viloette Leduc's autobiographical novel, the film is genuinely sweet in spite of a lingering Euro soft-porn atmosphere. (French with English subtitles) ★★★ VHS: $19.99; DVD: $24.99

These Three

(1936, 93 min, US, William Wyler) *Miriam Hopkins, Merle Oberon, Joel McCrea, Bonita Granville.* Lillian Hellman's controversial play, "The Children's Hour," about two women's lives torn apart by rumors of lesbianism, is toned down considerably — the play's "scandalous" relationship is now a heterosexual triangle — in this well-crafted and thoughtfully acted drama. Karen (Oberon) and Martha (Hopkins) run a school for girls. Trouble begins when a student falsely accuses Martha and Joe (McCrea), Karen's fiancé, of having an affair. Hellman's text is strong commentary on the destructive power of gossip and the so-called innocence of youth. Director Wyler remade the film, under the play's original title and theme, in 1962 with Shirley MacLaine and Audrey Hepburn. ★★★

Thesis

(1996, 121 min, Spain, Alejandro Amenábar) *Ana Torrent, Fele Martinez, Eduardo Noriega.* The film debut of celebrated *Open Your Eyes* director Amenábar is basically *8mm* done right. A beautiful grad student seeks help from her professor in acquiring extremely violent videos for her thesis on violence in the media. When he dies of a heart attack watching one of these tapes, she steals the tape and discovers it's a snuff film. Then she begins to investigate. Amenábar not only tightens the screws with

There's Something about Mary

great finesse, he neatly avoids cheap exploitation and preachiness, something *8mm* was unable to do. This is a good, solid, suspenseful mystery, which (only in retrospect) may be a shade too long, but is otherwise an exemplary thriller, and a smashing debut. Winner of six Goya awards (Spain's Oscars) including Best Picture. (Spanish with English subtitles) ★★★½ VHS: $29.99; DVD: $29.99

They All Laughed

(1981, 115 min, US, Peter Bogdanovich) *Audrey Hepburn, John Ritter, Ben Gazzara, Colleen Camp, Dorothy Stratten.* Charming, low-key comedy about a team of detectives and their romantic adventures. Director Bogdanovich extracts pleasant performances from the cast. ★★★ VHS: $9.99

They Call Me Mr. Tibbs!

(1970, 108 min, US, Gordon Douglas) *Sidney Poitier, Barbara McNair, Martin Landau, Juano Hernandez.* Poitier repeats his acclaimed role as Detective Virgil Tibbs from the Oscar-winning *In the Heat of the Night.* In this ordinary sequel, Tibbs has moved to San Francisco and is involved in a murder investigation in which the main suspect is a local priest (Landau). (Sequel: *The Organization*) ★★ VHS: $9.99; DVD: $19.99

They Came to Cordura

(1959, 123 min, US, Robert Rossen) *Gary Cooper, Rita Hayworth, Van Heflin, Tab Hunter, Richard Conte.* Cooper heads a good cast in this handsomely photographed western about an Army major (Cooper) who, believing himself guilty of cowardice, is relieved of his command and assigned to locate five potential Medal of Honor candidates. In the wilds of a desert region, he finds the five heroes, a torturous struggle against the elements, and Hayworth. ★★½ VHS: $14.99

They Died with Their Boots On

(1941, 138 min, US, Raoul Walsh) *Errol Flynn, Olivia deHavilland, Arthur Kennedy, Anthony Quinn.* Expedient adventure with Flynn as a heroic General Custer. The film traces his rise in the military ranks to the legendary Battle of the Little Bighorn. What the film lacks in authenticity it makes up for in flavor and entertainment. ★★★ VHS: $19.99

They Drive by Night

(1940, 97 min, US, Raoul Walsh) *George Raft, Ann Sheridan, Ida Lupino, Humphrey Bogart.* Bogart took a back seat to stars Raft, Sheridan and Lupino in this riveting trucking drama — but he didn't stay there for long as *The Maltese Falcon* was released a year later. Raft plays a wildcat trucker who, with brother Bogie, unwittingly becomes involved with the mob while trying to keep his truck from repossession. A good cast in a crisp, solid 1940s entertainment. ★★★ VHS: $19.99

They Got Me Covered

(1943, 95 min, US, David Butler) *Bob Hope, Dorothy Lamour, Lenore Aubert, Otto Preminger.* There are a few good laughs to be found in this otherwise standard-issue Hope espionage spoof. Bob and Dorothy are journalists who go after foreign spies based in Washington, D.C. ★★½ VHS: $14.99; DVD: $24.99

They Live

(1988, 87 min, US, John Carpenter) *Roddy Piper, Keith David, Meg Foster.* Professional wrestler Piper stars in Carpenter's allegorical sci-fi action-adventure about the fateful day when we discover that aliens are among us, and they are hardly benevolent ETs. Carpenter has a great scenario but is unable to thoroughly deliver the goods. ★★½

They Live by Night

(1949, 95 min, US, Nicholas Ray) *Farley Granger, Cathy O'Donnell, Howard da Silva.* Ray's directorial debut pairs Granger and O'Donnell as young innocents who find themselves on the wrong side of the law. Da Silva turns in a chilling performance as their corruptor. Ray's sense of atmosphere is remarkable, and the performances and diligent screenplay elevate what should have been a "B" programmer. (Remade as *Thieves Like Us*) ★★★½

They Made Me a Criminal

(1939, 92 min, US, Busby Berkeley) *John Garfield, Claude Rains, May Robson, Dead End Kids.* Intriguing crime drama with Garfield as a young boxer who takes refuge at a Western ranch when he thinks he's killed an opponent. ★★★ VHS: $19.99

They Might Be Giants

(1971, 98 min, US, Anthony Harvey) *George C. Scott, Joanne Woodward, Jack Gilford, Rue McClanahan, Oliver Clark, Eugene Roche, F. Murray Abraham.* Charming adaptation of James Goldman's play about a former judge who thinks he's Sherlock Holmes — and is treated by a psychiatrist named Dr. Watson. Scott plays his part with great panache, and Woodward is a spirited cohort. A wonderful supporting cast populates the film, featuring a most appealing collection of eccentrics. (Letterboxed) ★★★ VHS: $14.99; DVD: $24.99

They Saved Hitler's Brain

(1963, 81 min, US, David Bradley) *Walter Stocker.* A fanatical band of Nazis (is there any other kind?) give life to Hitler's brain and kidnap an American scientist to help them conquer the world. Le bad cinema. ★ VHS: $9.99; DVD: $14.99

They Shoot Horses, Don't They?

(1969, 121 min, US, Sydney Pollack) *Jane Fonda, Michael Sarrazin, Gig Young, Susannah York, Red Buttons, Bonnie Bedelia, Bruce Dern.* Few films in the 1960s were able to capture such raw power and unrelenting emotional tension as this devastating adaptation of Horace McCoy's novel of Depression-era America. With a dance marathon serving as metaphor for a crippled nation, the story centers on a disparate group of unemployed hopefuls who come together to win the "big" jackpot. No one's prepared for the gruelling, exhaustive, deadly competition that follows — all for the enjoyment of a few paying spectators. Fonda gives an extraordinary performance as a woman at road's end; it signaled her arrival as her generation's premiere actress. Young won an Oscar as the unscrupulous M.C.; York is mesmerizing as a fragile contestant; and Buttons is exemplary as the marathon's oldest participant. The dance sequences as staged by Pollack are riveting. (Letterboxed) ★★★★ VHS: $14.99; DVD: $14.99

They Were Expendable

(1945, 135 min, US, John Ford) *Robert Montgomery, John Wayne, Donna Reed.* Rousing WWII drama about an American PT boat crew fighting in the Pacific. One of the best of all the war films produced during WWII. ★★★★ VHS: $14.99; DVD: $19.99

They Were Ten

(1961, 105 min, Israel, Baruch Dienar) *Ninette, Oded Teomi.* The first feature-length film made entirely by Israelis sensitively re-creates the establishment of a 19th-century settlement in Palestine by 10 Russian Jews. These early pioneers not only undertook the tremendous task of building the land, but also had to contend with Arab resentment and the Turkish military. (Hebrew with English subtitles) ★★★

They Won't Believe Me

(1947, 95 min, US, Irving Pichel) *Robert Young, Susan Hayward, Jane Greer, Rita Johnson.* Startling noir thriller starring Young as a man who wakes up after a car accident with a scheme for the perfect crime. He is subsequently lured by two temptresses (Hayward and Greer) from his wife (Johnson). ★★★

Thief

(1981, 122 min, US, Michael Mann) *James Caan, Tuesday Weld, Willie Nelson.* An extremely stylish drama from first-time director Mann, with Caan in a splendid performance as a professional thief caught between corrupt cops and a malevolent crime boss. ★★★½ VHS: $14.99; DVD: $19.99

The Thief

(1998, 93 min, Russia, Pavel Chukhrai) *Ekaterina Rednikova, Misha Philipchuk, Vladimir Mashkov.* A dazzling Russian film, *The Thief* features three vulnerable characters, and the tenuous bonds that form between them as they struggle for survival under Stalin's regime. Writer-director Chukhrai has crafted a throwback to the melodramas of early Soviet cinema. Yet *The Thief* is never cloying or sentimental; its realism and solid performances are its stregths. Katya (Rednikova) is a young woman travelling by train with her six-year-old son Sanya (Philipchuk). When they meet Toljan (Mashkov), a soldier, Katya instantly falls in love, and Sanya is thrilled to get a father figure. However, Toljan soon reveals himself to be a thief, and perceptions change within this makeshift family. Mashkov is incredibly captivating as Toljan, and his allure is the film's backbone. Despite its heavy subject matter, the film still has moments of real humor and charm. ★★★★ VHS: $21.99; DVD: $29.99

The Thief and the Cobbler

(1995, 73 min, US, Richard Williams) *Voices of: Matthew Broderick, Jennifer Beals, Vincent Price, Jonathan Winters.* Featuring a distinctive animation style with Echer-like effects that go far beyond the typical cartoon, *The Thief and the Cobbler* follows the adventures of a hapless cobbler (nicely voiced by Broderick) who falls in love and saves the Princess Yum-Yum (Beals). The thief who causes all the problems for our heroes is deliciously played by Winters, whose tongue-in-cheek humor will amuse the adults and confuse the kids. Though the story occasionally falters, the film is of high quality and imaginative. ★★★ VHS: $14.99

The Thief of Bagdad

(1924, 138 min, US, Raoul Walsh) *Douglas Fairbanks, Jr., Anna May Wong.* Classic silent film with Fairbanks as a swashbuckling thief who falls in love with a beautiful princess. Fairbanks is at his rousing best, and the film is non-stop excitement. ★★★½ VHS: $24.99; DVD: $29.99

The Thief of Bagdad

(1940, 106 min, GB, Ludwig Berger, Michael Powell & Tim Whelan) *Sabu, Conrad Veidt, Rex Ingram.* This Arabian Nights tale is classic entertainment, enhanced by gorgeous cinematography. Sabu stars as the native boy who battles an evil magician, played by Veidt. Ingram makes a terrific genie. Great special effects. ★★★★ VHS: $14.99

Thieves (Les Voleurs)

(1996, 117 min, France, Andre Techine) *Catherine Deneuve, Daniel Auteuil, Laurence Côte.* A luminous and impossibly youthful Deneuve and a gruffily attractive Auteuil are lovers of Côte, a young student in over her head in a scheme that comes to involve murder. Deneuve, a professor of philosophy, and Auteuil, a police inspector, are drawn together in their concern for the young woman, who begins to unravel under the pressure of her destructive associations. The film is at once hyperventilating and elegantly structured, seasoned with staccato dialogue that propels the convoluted plot with wit, awareness and just the right touch of Gaulic pretense. Concisely drawn characters add depth of understanding to the rapidly developed story line; director Téchiné's command of the film is complete and admirable. An intelligent, adult mystery-thriller that makes optimum use of all its components. (French with English subtitles) ★★★½ VHS: $24.99

Thieves Like Us

(1974, 123 min, US, Robert Altman) *Keith Carradine, Shelley Duvall, John Schuck, Louise Fletcher, Bert Remsen, Tom Skerritt.* Altman's brooding, atmospheric remake of *They Live By Night*, based on Edward Anderson's novel. Carradine and Schuck play prison escapees who go on a robbing spree across 1930s Depression America. Duvall plays the small-town girl who becomes involved with Carradine. ★★★½ VHS: $14.99

The Thin Blue Line

(1988, 106 min, US, Errol Morris) Part documentary, part murder investigation, this highly acclaimed and original film investigates the "truth" surrounding the 1976 murder of Dallas policeman Robert Wood — who was gunned down at point blank range after stopping a car for a minor infraction. Randall Adams, the man arrested and sentenced to life in prison for the murder, claimed innocence and, indeed, through mesmerizing reconstructions of the crime from the point-of-view of investigators, witnesses, Wood's partner as well as a suspect cleared of all wrongdoing, the "facts" become all the more blurred as we begin to see that justice might well have been blind as well as perverted. ★★★★ VHS: $14.99

The Thin Man Series

In the 10 years that elapsed between its first and last entries, the *Thin Man* series straddled two decades, reflecting America's mores and attitudes from her recovery from the Depression thru WWII. As personified by William Powell and Myrna Loy, Nick and Nora Charles are urbane, suave, witty and rich. They have a relationship in their marriage that most would envy today; they even raise a kid without being too damned cute about it. And they know how to handle their dog, the estimable Asta. Their friends and relatives represent a range of societal classes and reflect a diversity of lifestyles seldom found in today's homogenized entertainment. The plots are well-crafted, the wardrobe is dashing and everybody gets good lines. Other constants: He never wants the case, she always wants him to take the case and everyone else thinks he's already on the case. Nora's always assuring someone that it's all right, they're married; and their consumption of alcohol is considerable and greatly enjoyed. The supporting cast's characterizations are consistently on target, the story lines satisfyingly intricate and the black-and-white cinematography deliciously noir, especially those graced with James Wong Howe's exemplary expertise.

Song of the Thin Man

After the Thin Man

The Thin Man

(1934, 93 min, US, W.S. Van Dyke II) *William Powell, Myrna Loy, Maureen O'Sullivan.* "Come on, kid. Shed the chapeau." The original, and the best. An eccentric, wealthy inventor disappears and, before too long, corpses start piling up. The inventor is actually the thin man in question, but the title became inextricably linked to Powell. Based on a Dashiell Hammett story. ★★★★ VHS: $14.99

After the Thin Man

(1936, 113 min, US, W.S. Van Dyke II) *William Powell, Myrna Loy, James Stewart.* "Look at him prancing around with that clue in him." Nick's relation with Nora's (S)Nob Hill family is an element in this tale of a rich wife cheated by a gigolo husband, and a thwarted love twisted into a crime of passion. ★★★½ VHS: $19.99

Another Thin Man

(1939, 105 min, US, W.S. Van Dyke II) *William Powell, Myrna Loy, Virginia Grey.* "Colonel MacFay — the swimming pool's on fire." Nick and Nora were starting on an extended trip and Nora announced her pregnancy at the end of *After the Thin Man. Another Thin Man* opens with their return from their travels, and with an infant. Nora's uncle is being hounded by a blackmailer with ominous dreams and a penchant for melodramatic warnings; the curmudgeon uncle seems deserving of this treatment. ★★★ VHS: $19.99

Shadow of the Thin Man

(1941, 97 min, US, W.S. Van Dyke II) *William Powell, Myrna Loy, Barry Nelson, Donna Reed.* "Funny how I meet you at all my homicides." A jockey is accused of throwing the race and is dead the next day, an apparent suicide. His death is convenient for the gambling syndicate, not so convenient for the crusading young reporter. Little Nicky, Jr. has his own Army uniform (he's an officer, of course) and calls his dad "Nick." There's a great restaurant fight scene, and the writing is by Dashiell Hammett. ★★★ VHS: $19.99

The Thin Man Goes Home

(1944, 100 min, US, Richard Thorpe) *William Powell, Myrna Loy, Gloria De Haven.* "You just pick out anybody at all, and I put 'em in jail for life." The effects of WWII are evidenced during Nick and Nora's train ride to Sycamore Springs, Nick's home town. Nick resolves a case of wartime industrial espionage, as well as his relationship with his father. Cinematography by Karl Freund, and another Dashiell Hammett script. ★★★ VHS: $19.99

Song of the Thin Man

(1947, 86 min, US, Edward Buzzell) *William Powell, Myrna Loy, Keenan Wynn.* "The dust don't start rising 'til deuce o' bells." Wynn is the hep cat clarinet player who gives Nick and Nora a guided tour through the netherworld of jazz musicians, high society, heavy gamblers and murderous jealousies. "And now Nick Charles is going to retire." ★★★ VHS: $19.99

The Thin Red Line

(1998, 170 min, US, Terrence Malick) *Sean Penn, Jim Caviezel, Elias Koteas, Nick Nolte, Ben Chaplin, Woody Harrelson, John Cusack, Adrien Brody, John Savage, John Travolta, George Clooney, Jared Leto.* With his first film in 20 years, director Malick returns to filmmaking with this gorgeous looking, philosophical adaptation of James Jones' novel about the bloody fight for Guadacanal during WWII. *The Thin Red Line* is a bracing look at the machinations of combat and of the inner turmoil of the soldiers, the latter somberly recalled by dry, almost tedious narration which nearly grinds the film to a halt. But Malick's battle sequences are unquestionably powerful, and the director has created some gut-wrenching moments staged with a visionary's eye. Penn may be top billed, but it's newcomer Caviezel whose story is at the heart of the film, and the young actor gives a remarkably controlled portrayal of conflict and idealism. Though the film feels

T

The Thin Red Line

heavily edited, the final result is a poetic, ethereal though slightly flawed epic which marks a long-overdue return for a singular artist. (Letterboxed VHS available for $19.99) ★★★½ VHS: $14.99; DVD: $29.99

The Thing

(1951, 80 min, US, Christian Nyby) *James Arness, Kenneth Tobey.* Classic '50s horror film produced by Howard Hawks. An Arctic expedition is forced to fight for their lives when they dig up an alien creature frozen in the ice. The chills are rampant as the basic ingredients of sci-fi faultlessly meld with hold-your-breath terror. (Remade in 1982.) ★★★★ VHS: $14.99

The Thing

(1982, 108 min, US, John Carpenter) *Kurt Russell, Wilford Brimley, Richard Dysart, Richard Masur, Donald Moffat, T.K. Carter.* A gruesome and terrifying tale of a hideous, metamorphic monster which torments the crew of an Antarctic outpost. Carpenter's new version of the short story (which inspired the 1950s classic produced by Howard Hawks) is highlighted by realistic and horrifying special effects. (Letterboxed VHS available for $14.99) ★★★½ VHS: $9.99; DVD: $29.99

The Thing Called Love

(1993, 116 min, US, Peter Bogdanovich) *Samantha Mathis, River Phoenix, Dermot Mulroney, Sandra Bullock.* Mathis stars as an East Coast gal who travels to Nashville determined to become a country music star. Upon her arrival, she immediately, and literally, bumps into a brooding, bad-boy musician (Phoenix). A love-hate relationship ensues. Also onto the scene ambles Mulroney, a displaced Connecticut cowboy, and Bullock as a new kind of Southern belle. Though *The Thing Called Love* seems to have lost something in the editing process, its odd country-grunge quality, the interplay between the young actors and the fun they have with the music, saves this film from being a hackneyed, hayseed version of *A Star Is Born.* ★★★ VHS: $19.99

Things Change

(1988, 100 min, US, David Mamet) *Joe Mantegna, Don Ameche, Robert Prosky, J.T. Walsh.* Ameche's subtle yet complex portrait of an Italian shoe repairman caught in a high stakes impersonation of a Mafia don is a delight. Writer-director Mamet's social comedy does not deliver the visceral thrills of his previous film, *House of Games,* but nonetheless is a sly comedy which explores the honor among thieves and the deadly temptations that money and power offer. The always fascinating Mantegna is a low-level hood who is responsible for the weekend safety of Ameche. But what starts as a simple job of baby-sitting, ends in a comedy of errors as the reticent Ameche is mistaken for a Mafia kingpin. A thinking person's comedy and one that is highly recommended. ★★★½ VHS: $9.99; DVD: $27.99

Things to Come

(1936, 96 min, GB, William Cameron Menzies) *Raymond Massey, Ralph Richardson.* This stunning visualization of H.G. Wells' visionary novel features Menzies' intriguing, ultra-modern sets and a sonorous score by Arthur Bliss. Massey stars as the leader of the new world opposite Richardson as a despotic and belligerent ruler. An interesting film from a sociological standpoint as it represents the mindset of the '30s as people looked to the future. ★★★ VHS: $19.99; DVD: $14.99

Things to Do in Denver When You're Dead

(1995, 114 min, US, Gary Fleder) *Andy Garcia, Treat Williams, Christopher Walken, Gabrielle Anwar, Christopher Lloyd, William Forsythe, Bill Nunn, Jack Warden, Steve Buscemi.* First-time director Fleder puts a new spin on a tried-and-true gangster formula (former hood is pulled back into the game). Garcia stars as Jimmy the Saint, an ex-petty criminal who has gone legit. Soon after happening upon the woman of his dreams, Jimmy is summoned to the ghostly mansion of a quadriplegic crime lord (Walken at his creepy best), who bids him to do one

more bit of service for him. Jimmy assembles the old gang one last time, and when the job is botched, the crew finds themselves on a hit list, or "buckwheats," with a master hit man (Buscemi) on their trail. Distinguished particularly by its inventive dialogue and excellent cast, *Things to Do* is vastly entertaining but as a whole does not live up to its best moments. Some plot logic is sacrificed to further the style, but what style it has. ★★★ VHS: $19.99; DVD: $29.99

The Third Man

(1950, 100 min, GB, Carol Reed) *Orson Welles, Joseph Cotten, Alida Valli, Trevor Howard.* Based on an original screenplay by Graham Greene, this Reed classic epitomizes the aesthetics of film noir. Amid the lurid decadence of a shell-shocked, post-war Vienna, a lonely American (Cotten) searches for his maligned friend, a mysterious "third man" in a city of rampant deceit and corruption. A haunting score, shadowy cinematography and top-notch performances (notably Welles as the utterly immoral Harry Lime) make this one of the memorable tales of intrigue in film history. ★★★★ VHS: $29.99; DVD: $39.99

The Third Miracle

(2000, 118 min, US, Agnieszka Holland) *Ed Harris, Anne Heche, Armin Mueller-Stahl, Charles Haid.* The Third Miracle is a haunting spiritual journey led by veteran filmmaker Holland (*Europa, Europa*) into the political and sometimes not-so-spiritual process of sainthood. Father Frank Harris (a terrific Harris) is a disillusioned priest living in a Chicago flophouse who is called back into service by the Church looking for him to debunk the "myth" of a crying statue of Virgin Mary. He investigates his faith and his chastity through the process when he meets Roxanne (Heche), the potential saint's daughter, and falls in love with her. Issues of church politics, faith, celibacy and just plain passion rule this smart, candid film. ★★★ VHS: $21.99; DVD: $29.99

The Third Sex/Vapors

(1958/1965, 102 min, Germany/US, Frank Winterstein & Gerald Jackson) *The Third Sex* (1958, 77 min, Germany, Frank Winterstein) is intriguingly contemporary, especially for its time and place (West Germany in the mid-1950s). This historically important potboiler melodrama centers on a parents' efforts to make their gay son "normal." Klaus, a sleekly handsome teenager, is in a relationship with fellow classmate Manfred, an effete, pouting blond. Klaus' domineering father goes about trying to break the two apart, while the alternately sympathetic but calculating mom plots to get the pretty maid into her wayward son's bed. The film is rather extraordinary in its depiction of gays, society's extremist reaction to them and the clash between the old Germany and the new. *Vapors* (1965, 25 min, US, Gerald Jackson) is set in the notorious St. Mark's Bathhouse. A nervous young man visits the bathhouse for the first time. There he meets an older, sexually confused married man. Instead of the standard quickie, the two engage in thoughtful conversation dealing with desire and soul searching. ★★★

Thirteen Days

(2000, 145 min, US, Roger Donaldson) *Kevin Costner, Bruce Greenwood, Steven Culp, Dylan Baker, Michael Fairman, Kevin Conway, Len Cariou.* You don't have to look much further to find intense drama than the true story of the Cuban Missile Crisis that shook America and the world in 1962. Its story already told in the acclaimed TV movie "The Missiles of October," this critical two-week period in history is once again the basis for an exhilarating entertainment masquerading as part history lesson and part heart pounder. *Thirteen Days* is seen through the eyes of JFK's presidential aide Kenneth P. O'Donnell (nicely played by Costner, accent and all), whose memoirs are the source material for David Self's assured screenplay adaptation. Director Donaldson brings a you-are-there feel to this gripping profile in courage that documents the showdown between President Kennedy and the Castro regime over Soviet missiles that could have ended in nuclear war. Greenwood is excellent as JFK, subtly capturing his legendary cadence and demeanor while endowing him with emotion and depth. Likewise, Culp is pinpoint as Bobby Kennedy. Complex, articulate and often nerve-racking, *Thirteen Days* is an intelligent, enthralling exercise in social studies and storytelling. ★★★★ VHS: $19.99; DVD: $26.99

13 Ghosts

(1960, 88 min, US, William Castle) *Rosemary DeCamp, Martin Milner, Margaret Hamilton.* Cute ghost mystery about a family who inherit a house, complete with buried treasure and — count 'em — 13 ghosts. ★★½ VHS: $9.99

13 Rue Madeleine

(1947, 95 min, US, Henry Hathaway) *James Cagney, Annabella, Richard Conte.* Told in an almost semidocumentary style, this absorbing spy thriller stars a rigid but forceful Cagney as an OSS operative who trains youthful candidates. The intrigue really starts when he discovers a Nazi spy among his cadets, and is then forced to use the double agent on a dangerous mission in Germany. Perhaps too calculating in its efforts to present a realistic portrait of the spy game, the film nevertheless is gripping exactly for that reason — that and Cagney's no-nonsense portrayal. ★★★ VHS: $19.99

The Thirteenth Floor

(1999, 100 min, US, Josef Rusnak) *Craig Bierko, Armin Mueller-Stahl, Gretchen Mol, Vincent D'Onofrio.* Slow pacing and an unfulfilled screenplay dampen an initially arresting idea about identity and our place in the world. Superficially similar to *The Matrix* and *Dark City*, this sci-fi thriller, which plays more as a noir murder-mystery, follows Bierko as he investigates the murder of his boss (Mueller-Stahl). The answer could lie in his computer invention — a virtual reality creation of 1930s Los Angeles. The re-creation of yesteryear is quite good, but the film offers few thrills as Bierko travels back and forth from his own reality to the created one — ultimately coming to question which reality is real and which is fabricated. ★★ VHS: $9.99; DVD: $19.99

The Thirteenth Warrior

(1999, 103 min, US, John McTiernan) *Antonio Banderas, Omar Sharif, Diane Venora, Dennis Storhoi.* A 10th-century Arab aristocrat (Banderas) reluctantly joins a dozen Vikings in their quest to destroy a tribe of cannibalistic "monsters" that is terrorizing local villages. That's the entire plot, with nary a surprise or twist or dramatic revelation in the film's entire running time. The cannibals are at first — when only glimpsed — rather frightening, but in the second half become standard villains, and, despite a nice buildup, the final battle is anticlimactic. A sporadically rousing if silly and thin adventure. ★★ VHS: $14.99; DVD: $29.99

38: Vienna Before the Fall

(1989, 97 min, Austria, Wolfgang Glück) *Tobias Engel, Sunnyi Melles, Heinz Trixner.* Nominated for Best Foreign Film (the first such nominee from Austria), this elegant, impassioned drama is set a few months before Hitler's annexation of Austria and deals with such themes as political apathy, the roots of anti-Semitism and the Holocaust. Set against the deceptively beautiful backdrop of pre-war Vienna, the drama centers around two lovers, a Jewish playwright and a popular Aryan actress, who are blissfully blind

The Thirteenth Warrior

to the escalating inhumanity which surrounds them. (German with English subtitles) ★★★½

35 Up

(1991, 127 min, GB, Michael Apted) Director Apted continues his seven-year study of a group of British children from childhood through adulthood, which he began with *7 Up* and continued with *14 Up, 21 Up* and *28 Up*. Having offered their hopes and dreams on-camera as children in the earlier films, it can be heart-wrenching to see adults rationalizing why they haven't realized their dreams, and mystifying to listen to a seven-year-old plot out his/her life and then watch it unfold exactly as planned. Though *35 Up* suffers from the fact that the changes that occur between 28 and 35 are less perceptive than the dramatic swings between the other earlier ages, this series remains one of the most revealing looks at life and the aging process ever to be captured on film. (Sequel: *42 Up*) ★★★½ VHS: $19.99

Thirty Is a Dangerous Age, Cynthia

(1968, 85 min, GB, Joseph McGrath) *Dudley Moore, Suzy Kendall.* Moore stars in this eccentric comedy as a nightclub pianist fast approaching his 30th birthday. Overwrought by the angst of reaching this milestone without having ever married or produced a hit song, he sets out to achieve both these goals in a six-week period. Moore cowrote the script and scores high marks with this offbeat comedy which casts a jaundiced eye at the absurdities of sex and marriage. ★★★ VHS: $59.99

The 39 Steps

(1935, 89 min, GB, Alfred Hitchcock) *Robert Donat, Madeleine Carroll, Peggy Ashcroft.* Donat stars as an innocent man on the lam, handcuffed to Carroll, linked with a spy ring, pursued by a villain with a severed finger and chased through the Scottish highlands. A vintage thriller which is thick with intrigue and colored with Hitchcock's droll humor. (Remade in 1959 and 1979) ★★★★ VHS: $14.99; DVD: $39.99

Thirty Seconds over Tokyo

(1944, 138 min, US, Mervyn LeRoy) *Spencer Tracy, Robert Mitchum, Robert Walker, Van Johnson,*

Steven Culp (as RFK), Bruce Greenwood (as JFK), and Kevin Costner in *Thirteen Days*

Phyllis Thaxter. One of the top box-office hits of the 1940s, this exciting WWII drama details the first aerial attack on mainland Japan by American forces and is enhanced by a solid cast. A good companion piece is *Destination Tokyo,* the 1943 Cary Grant drama which tells the same story from the point of view of the submarine crew which made the air strike possible. ★★★ VHS: $14.99

36 Fillette

(1988, 88 min, France, Catherine Breillat) *Delphine Zentout, Jean-Pierre Léaud.* Heralded by many as a refreshing tale of a precocious girl's rite of sexual passage told from a woman's point of view and reviled by others for its wanton depiction of a manipulating, selfish brat, this saucy Gallic comedy will leave few viewers without a strong opinion. Lili, a pouty, sexy 14-year-old who is literally bursting out of her children's sizes, decides to lose her virginity while on vacation with her family. Her first choice for the despoiler is Maurice, a middle-aged playboy and musician, but our heroine soon finds that losing her viriginity is not such an easy decision. (French with English subtitles) ★★½ VHS: $19.99; DVD: $29.99

36 Hours

(1964, 115 min, US, George Seaton) *James Garner, Rod Taylor, Eva Marie Saint, Werner Peters, John Banner.* Based on the novel "Beware of the Dog" by Roald Dahl, this intriguing suspenser, though taking its time getting there, offers a few twists and turns getting to its exciting climax. Garner is a U.S. major with intimate knowledge of the impending D-Day invasion. With only 36 hours left, the Germans kidnap him, drug him, and make him believe it's five years later and the war is over — all in order to get the vital information. Taylor is a German psychiatrist, and Saint is the housekeeper in on the charade. It's talky but suspenseful and well done. ★★★ VHS: $19.99

32 Short Films about Glenn Gould

(1994, 94 min, Canada, François Girard) *Colm Feore, Derek Keuvorst, Katya Lada.* Director Girard has constructed a kaleidoscopic exploration of the eccentric life of world-renowned concert pianist Glenn Gould, engagingly portrayed by Feore. Gould left the concert stage at age 32 at the height of his career. Searching for an ideal performance arena, he intended to communicate with the audience solely through media. Passionately obsessed with music, this justifiably egomaniacal perfectionist lived in sound, cadence and tone in a consuming vortex of self-absorbed creativity. The 32 short films include interviews with family, friends and other artists; selected performances of his compositions and radio programs; and dramatized biographical episodes. By the end of the film, this man's life assumes an almost mythic quality — assuming the feeling regarding Bobby Fisher in *Searching for Bobby Fisher.* ★★★½ VHS: $19.99; DVD: $29.99

This Boy's Life

(1993, 115 min, US, Michael Caton-Jones) *Robert De Niro, Ellen Barkin, Leonardo DiCaprio, Jonah Blechman.* Based on the autobiography of writer Tobias Wolff, this intensely moving coming-of-age drama is a courageous tale examining the hopes and desperation of an unsettled youth. In a passionate performance, DiCaprio

plays a troubled teen who, with his newly married mother (the first-rate Barkin), moves to a small town in Washington state to live with his new stepfather (De Niro in a volatile performance). But what had promised to be a fresh start quickly degenerates into an oppressive lifestyle neither is able to protest or divorce. Wolff's illuminating process of self-discovery and self-determination raises *This Boy's Life* well above the pack of a crowded genre. ★★★★ VHS: $9.99

This Could Be the Night

(1957, 105 min, US, Robert Wise) *Jean Simmons, Anthony Franciosa, Paul Douglas, Joan Blondell.* Simmons shines as a schoolteacher who takes a part-time job at a New York nightclub, thus furthering her own education in matters romantic. Playboy Franciosa and lovably gruff Douglas are her bosses, who both fall under the spell of Simmons' naïve charm. This risqué, colorful comedy features splashy musical numbers, and extracts cheerful performances from its entire cast. ★★★ VHS: $19.99

This Gun for Hire

(1942, 80 min, US, Frank Tuttle) *Alan Ladd, Veronica Lake, Robert Preston.* Taken from a Graham Greene novel, this gripping crime drama stars Ladd as Raven, a tight-lipped paid assassin who, after he is double-crossed by an "employer," seeks revenge. The alluring Lake is a sultry "singing magician" who gets innocently involved and good guy Preston is the detective on the trail. Above-average thriller with wonderfully complex twists and chance encounters. With an oil company as the real bad guy, the film was ahead of its time. ★★★½ VHS: $14.99

This Happy Breed

(1944, 114 min, GB, David Lean) *Robert Newton, Celia Johnson, John Mills, Kay Walsh.* Noël Coward's keen adaptation of his own hit play about the affairs of a lower middle-class family was immensely popular in its day. Set between the two World Wars, the film delves into the petty bickerings and small triumphs of the Gibbons clan as they grapple with the difficulties of a world ravaged by social strife and war. Director Lean makes excellent use of Ronald Neame's penetrating camerawork. ★★★½ VHS: $29.99

This Is My Life

(1992, 94 min, US, Nora Ephron) *Julie Kavner, Samantha Mathis, Gaby Hoffman, Carrie Fisher, Dan Aykroyd, Kathy Najimy.* Ephron makes her directorial debut with this lightweight comedy-drama not without a certain charm. Kavner gives an enchanting performance as a single mother who tries to make it big in show biz. As her star slowly but assuredly ascends, it is her two daughters who are most affected by their mother's newfound success as it demands more and more of her time. Though Ephron doesn't fully explore many of the scenarios she introduces, she manages to infuse in the film a fair amount of good humor. ★★½ VHS: $19.99

This Is Spinal Tap

(1984, 82 min, US, Rob Reiner) *Rob Reiner, Michael McKean, Christopher Guest, Harry Shearer, Fran Drescher.* Reiner's riotous, razor-sharp satire is a pseudo-rockumentary on Britain's loudest band, Spinal Tap. Captured

Alan Ladd and Veronica Lake in
This Gun for Hire

during a swan-song U.S. tour, these over-the-hill, heavy metal moptops offer their sentiments on life in the fast lane, the merits of their "Smell the Glove" LP and the mysterious deaths of their past 35 drummers. ★★★★ VHS: $14.99; DVD: $26.99

This Is the Sea

(1998, 104 min, Ireland, Mary McGuckian) *Samantha Morton, John Lynch, Richard Harris, Ross McDade, Gabriel Byrne.* A sweet, but fated romance between the Protestant Hazel (Morton) and the Catholic Malachy (McDade) is the centerpiece of this otherwise toothless drama about the 1994 cease fire in Belfast. Writer-director McGuckian strives for melodrama, but the intriguing subplot about a car bombing that implicates the lovers and their families is underwhelming. The Irish countryside is quite beautiful, but the film's lack of tension keeps *This Is the Sea* from being anything truly special. Morton, who was remarkable in *Under the Skin,* gives another sterling performance, while McDade is winning as her suitor. ★★½ VHS: $59.99

This Island Earth

(1954, 86 min, US, Joseph Newman) *Jeff Morrow, Faith Domergue, Rex Reason, Russell Johnson.* A group of scientists are kidnapped by aliens, who need them to help defend their planet. This clever outer space tale is one of the most popular of the '50s sci-fi films. Features good special effects. (The film used for the theatrical debut for *Mystery Science Theater 3000.*) ★★½ VHS: $9.99; DVD: $29.99

This Man Must Die

(1969, 115 min, France/Italy, Claude Chabrol) *Michael Duchaussoy, Caroline Cellier.* One of Chabrol's finest films, this first-rate thriller concerns the father of a boy who was a hit-and-run victim and his obsessive and unrelenting need to track down his son's killer and extract his vengeance. This Hitchcockian tale has plot twists that will keep you guessing until the startling conclusion. (Dubbed) ★★★½ VHS: $59.99

This Property Is Condemned

(1966, 110 min, US, Sydney Pollack) *Robert Redford, Natalie Wood, Charles Bronson, Kate Reid, Dabney Coleman.* This reworking of the Tennessee Williams tragedy stars Wood as a Southern belle who longs for out-of-towner

Redford to sweep her away to the big city and help her escape the family boarding house. Pollack directs and Francis Ford Coppola helped write the screenplay. ★★ VHS: $19.99

This Special Friendship

(1964, 99 min, France, Jean Delannoy) *Didier Haudepin, Francis Lacombrade.* Set in a Catholic boarding school in France, this love story smolders with the youthful homoerotic bonds between several boys in the school. Their love and friendship is touching and beautifully handled by director Delannoy. (French with English subtitles) ★★★ VHS: $49.99

This Sporting Life

(1963, 129 min, GB, Lindsay Anderson) *Richard Harris, Rachel Roberts, Alan Badel, Colin Blakely, Arthur Lowe.* Harris gives a career performance as Frank Machin, a Yorkshire lad who tries to escape the restrictions of his working-class background and his personal limitations by becoming a star on the city rugby team. Gritty and stark, peopled with great performances. Screenplay by David Storey based on his book; produced by Karel Reisz and perceptively directed by Anderson. ★★★½; DVD: $24.99

This Sweet Sickness

(1977, 105 min, France, Claude Miller) *Gérard Depardieu, Miou-Miou.* Forget *Boxing Helena*: For this thriller, based on the novel by Patricia Highsmith ("Strangers on a Train"), is one of the most chilling and strangest portraits of obsessive love. Depardieu gives a compelling performance as David, a man so obsessed with his former lover, Lise, that his life becomes one of deceit and delusion. And David isn't dissuaded in his obsession by the fact that Lise has remarried and that his neighbor (Miou-Miou) has fallen in love with him. Tension builds as the characters' lives become further entangled, ultimately resulting in tragedy. Watch carefully for the wonderfully inventive ending. (French with English subtitles) ★★★½ VHS: $24.99

This World, Then the Fireworks

(1997, 100 min, US, Michael Oblowitz) *Billy Zane, Gina Gershon, Sheryl Lee.* A sparkling adaptation of Jim Thompson's story, this very stylish film noir oozes sex and violence in heavy doses. Marty (Zane) and Carol (Gershon) are incestuous twins bent on bad behavior. He has a vicious temper; she is a heartless hooker who leaves a trail of poisoned bodies in her wake. Their fragile bond, which stems from an ugly childhood incident, holds the clues, yet somehow the parts are much greater than the whole. Director Oblowitz has a keen ear for dialogue, a great eye for detail, and he effectively uses Chet Baker on the soundtrack, but moody atmosphere can only camouflage the lack of plot for so long — the film goes nowhere slowly. ★★½ VHS: $86.99

The Thomas Crown Affair

(1968, 102 min, US, Norman Jewison) *Steve McQueen, Faye Dunaway, Paul Burke, Jack Weston, Yaphet Kotto.* A solid heist adventure with the ever-cool McQueen masterminding an ingenious bank robbery and becoming involved with equally cool insurance investigator Dunaway. (Remade in 1999) ★★★ VHS: $14.99; DVD: $24.99

The Thomas Crown Affair

(1999, 113 min, US, John McTiernan) *Pierce Brosnan, Rene Russo, Faye Dunaway, Denis Leary.* A straightforward, no-frills remake of the 1968 Steve McQueen-Faye Dunaway thriller, this adequate update abandons style for slickness and substitutes lukewarm in place of cool. Brosnan stars as the thrill-seeking, art-thief billionaire who becomes involved with the insurance investigator (Russo) on his trail. There's little sexual tension between the two stars, though individually each is admirable. Dunaway turns up as Russo's psychiatrist — a reminder of a more glorious past. ★★½ VHS: $9.99; DVD: $19.99

Thoroughly Modern Millie

(1967, 138 min, US, George Roy Hill) *Julie Andrews, Mary Tyler Moore, Carol Channing, James Fox, Beatrice Lillie.* Delightfully entertaining musical spoof with Andrews as the title character, a husband-hunting secretary during the Roaring '20s. Moore also stars as an orphaned ingenue who comes to the big city and is befriended by Millie. Channing received an Oscar nomination for her spirited performance as a daffy and lovable socialite ("Raspberries!"). Memorable Oscar-winning score by Elmer Bernstein and Andre Previn. ★★★ VHS: $14.99

Those Who Love Me Can Take the Train (Ceux qui m'aiment prendront le train)

(1998, 122 min, France, Patrice Chereau) *Jean-Louis Trintignant, Valeria Bruno-Tedeschi, Vincent Perez, Pascal Gregory, Dominique Blanc, Vincent Ward.* Director Chereau has created an intensely emotional multicharacter drama set primarily on a moving train. A bisexual Parisian painter, Jean-Baptiste (Trintignant), dies and his body is to be buried in his hometown of Limoges. As dictated by the diseased, the funeral mourners all board a train for the ride south. On board are collection of divergent people all of whom were involved (many sexually, all emotionally) with the tyrannical yet charming artist — relatives, friends, students, ex-lovers. Here they meet, talk, argue and make love. Without a scorecard, it is difficult to fully understand who's who but this is almost certainly the aim of the filmmaker. Involving, darkly convoluted and wonderfully observant of human foibles, the film won three Césars (including Best Director). ★★★ VHS: $24.99; DVD: $29.99

A Thousand Acres

(1997, 105 min, US, Jocelyn Moorhouse) *Jessica Lange, Michelle Pfeiffer, Jason Robards, Jennifer Jason Leigh, Keith Carradine, Colin Firth, Kevin Anderson.* Boasting two very good lead performances, *A Thousand Acres* is a well-acted, occasionally moving drama of family conflict which unfortunately isn't quite as involving as it promises to be. Based on Jane Smiley's Pulitzer Prize–winning novel, the story concerns an Iowa farming family and the ramifications which occur when patriarch Robards decides to divide his homestead between his three daughters. This sets in motion a series of soul-searching and emotional confrontations which ultimately shed light on dark family secrets. The wonderful performances Lange and Pfeiffer go far to gloss over the sometimes slow pacing and dispassionate feel director Moorhouse gives the film. ★★½ VHS: $9.99; DVD: $29.99

1,000 Eyes of Dr. Mabuse

(1960, 103 min, West Germany, Fritz Lang) *Gert Frobe.* He's back! The arch super villain who foreshadowed Hitler's Germany returns from beyond the grave — now a scientist whose headquarters is a large hotel full of secret panels, peep holes and dungeons. The Mabuse series was a clear inspiration for the James Bond movies, and this one — Lang's last film — even stars Frobe who went on to play the title role of "Goldfinger" a few years later. ★★ VHS: $24.99; DVD: $29.99

Thousand Pieces of Gold

(1991, 105 min, US, Nancy Kelly) *Rosalind Chao, Dennis Dun, Chris Cooper.* A startlingly good independent film, this impressive historical drama centers on the harsh life of a fiercely defiant woman thrown into the rough-and-tumble world of Gold Rush fever in the 1880s American West. Lalu, a Chinese woman in her twenties, is sold by her famine-stricken father and eventually brought to San Francisco, where she is auctioned off to an obnoxious saloon keeper in a dismal Idaho town. Refusing to succumb to forced prostitution and virtual slavehood, Lalu, now renamed China Polly, must overcome insurmountable odds in preserving her dignity and gaining independence. Based on a true story, this western epic is filmed in a simple, straightforward fashion by Kelly. Chao is unforgettable as the determined Lalu. (English and Cantonese with English subtitles) ★★★½

Threads

(1985, 110 min, GB, Mick Jackson) *Karen Meagher, Rita May.* One of the best of the "day after" nuclear dramas, this powerful, uncompromising BBC production examines the devastating aftermath of global nuclear war on present-day London. Presented in pseudo-documentary style, the film is uncomfortably realistic in its portrayal of a nuclear nightmare. ★★★½

Three Ages, The Goat & My Wife's Relations

(1921/22, 111 min, US, Buster Keaton & Eddie Cline/Mal St. Clair) *Buster Keaton, Margaret Leahy, Wallace Beery.* A collection of three Keaton comedies. *Three Ages* (1923, 63 min) pokes fun at Griffith's *Intolerance*, telling three stories from different ages — The Stone Age, the Roman Empire and "Modern Times." In all three, Keaton plays the lovable schnook in love with Leahy — but Beery stands in his way. Highlights include a funny chariot race and a wedding ceremony which looks to be the precursor to *The Graduate*. (★★★) *The Goat* (1921, 23 min) is the highly amusing story of Keaton being mistaken for a notorious gangster. The short features inventive visuals and a hilarious, prolonged chase scene. (★★★½) *My Wife's Relations* (1922, 25 min) has Keaton mistakenly married and moving in with ne'er-do-well relations. (★★½) VHS: $29.99; DVD: $29.99

Three Amigos!

(1986, 105 min, US, John Landis) *Steve Martin, Chevy Chase, Martin Short, Joe Mantegna.* Occasionally amusing spoof of westerns and *The Magnificent Seven* in particular. Martin, Chase and Short play unemployed silent western stars who, thought to be real cowboys, are

summoned to save a small Mexican town terrorized by desperadoes. Hijinks ensue. ★★
VHS: $9.99; DVD: $14.99

Three Brothers

(1980, 111 min, Italy, Francesco Rossi) *Philippe Noiret, Michele Placido, Charles Vanel.* A vivid and affecting portrait of three very different brothers who return to the village of their youth for their mother's funeral. Political and social concerns as well as their strained relationships are probed in this extraordinary film. (Italian with English subtitles) ★★★½

Three Came Home

(1950, 106 min, US, Jean Negulesco) *Claudette Colbert, Sessue Hayakawa, Patric Knowles.* A superlative performance by Colbert highlights this absorbing and powerful drama based on Agnes Keith's novel detailing her experiences in a Japanese internment camp in Borneo. Separated from their husbands, American Colbert and a group of British women endure the hardships of imprisonment and the cruelties of their captors. Hayakawa is impressive as the civilized commander who "befriends" Colbert. ★★★½ VHS: $14.99

Three Cases of Murder

(1954, 99 min, GB, David Eady, Wendy Toye & George O'Ferrall) *Orson Welles, Alan Badel.* The title says it all with this nicely executed trilogy of murder and the supernatural. The first short, *In the Picture,* is an effectively eerie chiller — which could have been penned by Oscar Wilde — about a deceased artist who comes back to life to perfect his masterpiece. The second, *You Killed Elizabeth,* is the least successful of the three. It's the story of a ménage à trois which ends in murder — but whodunit? The last piece, *Lord Mountdrago,* features an extraordinary Welles as an ambitious, callous Foreign Secretary serving in Parliament who is haunted by the man who he has ruined. Based on a short story of W. Somerset Maugham, it's a fascinating, humorous tale. ★★★ VHS: $39.99

Three Comrades

(1938, 98 min, US, Frank Borzage) *Margaret Sullavan, Robert Taylor, Robert Young, Franchot Tone.* Coscripted by F. Scott Fitzgerald and based on an Erich Maria Remarque novel, this tender, lushly romantic tearjerker has the beguiling Sullavan in her best performance, a timeless portrait of love and sacrifice. Set in post-WWI Germany, the story follows the close relationship of three soldiers (Taylor, Tone and Young), and their devotion to ailing, former aristocrat Sullavan after she and Taylor wed. The rise of Fascism in Germany is its backdrop, and the film effortlessly extracts the best of Fitzgerald and Remarque in the marriage of love story and political study. ★★★½ VHS: $19.99

Three Days of the Condor

(1975, 117 min, US, Sydney Pollack) *Robert Redford, Faye Dunaway, Cliff Robertson, Max von Sydow, John Houseman.* Pollack's exciting espionage thriller stars Redford as a CIA researcher working in a Manhattan think tank. When all of his coworkers are brutally assassinated, he suddenly finds himself on the run and not knowing whom to trust. Good performances come from Dunaway, as a civilian who is kidnapped by

Redford and coerced to help him. ★★★½
VHS: $14.99; DVD: $29.99

The Three Faces of Eve

(1957, 91 min, US, Nunnally Johnson) *Joanne Woodward, Lee J. Cobb, David Wayne.* Woodward won a deserved Academy Award for her stunning schizophrenic performance as a woman with a multiple personality disorder. Told in an almost documentary style (complete with narration from Alistair Cooke), the film begins as dreary Georgia housewife Eve White visits a psychiatrist (Cobb) because of headaches and blackouts. It's soon discovered, however, she is harboring a second and third personality: Eve Black, a sexy flirt, and a sensible "normal" Jane who may be Eve's real identity. Cobb is especially sincere as her doctor. Based on an actual case. ★★★ VHS: $19.99

Three Fugitives

(1989, 93 min, US, Francis Vèber) *Nick Nolte, Martin Short, Sarah Rowland Doroff, James Earl Jones.* Disarming remake of the French comedy *Les Fugitifs,* with Nolte as a paroled bankrobber who is taken hostage by inept Short, who's committing his first hold-up. Some good slapstick in an otherwise sentimental comic tale. ★★

3 Godfathers

(1948, 105 min, US, John Ford) *John Wayne, Ward Bond, Harry Carey, Jr., Pedro Armendariz.* Director Ford is in a sentimental mood with this glossy remake of Peter B. Kyne's popular story about three outlaws who find a baby while crossing the desert and take charge of it. Wonderful cinematography highlights this Wayne tale. Filmed five times before this one (two versions with Carey, Sr.), and since then as a Jack Palance TV movie. ★★★ VHS: $14.99

317th Platoon

(1965, 94 min, France, Pierre Schoendoerffer) *Bruno Crémer, Pierre Fabre, Jacques Perrin.* Capturing both the horrors of battle and the anguish and solitude each soldier endures, this realistic war drama describes, with wrenching clarity, the final bloody days of an army platoon. Set in 1954 during the last days of the French involvement in Southeast Asia (and filmed entirely in the jungles of Cambodia), the story follows the frantic retreat from the front lines of the 317th platoon, made up of 41 Laotians and four Frenchmen. The director and cinematographer Raoul Coutard (both veterans of the French Vietnam war) focus intimately on these ordinary young men as they, through enemy ambushes, disease and fatigue, are slowly annihilated. (French with English subtitles) ★★★½ VHS: $59.99

Three in the Attic

(1968, 92 min, US, Richard Wilson) *Christopher Jones, Yvette Mimieux.* Jones stars in this playful if silly 1960s sex comedy as a college student whose three girlfriends give him a lesson in fidelity when they kidnap him, lock him in an attic and literally try to fuck him to death. ★★

Three Kings

(1999, 114 min, US, David O. Russell) *George Clooney, Mark Wahlberg, Ice Cube, Spike Jonze, Nora Dunn.* After tackling Oedipal incest (*Spanking the Monkey*) and road-movie farce (*Flirting with Disaster*), director Russell heads into the Persian

Gulf war to make a heist film. Clooney again proves his magnetism as he leads his three cronies (Wahlberg, Cube, Jonze) through an absurd theater of war to steal Sadaam's secret stash of gold. An exciting, inventive adventure/comedy/caper film with as much brains as brawn. (VHS available letterboxed or pan & scan) ★★★½ VHS: $19.99; DVD: $24.99

Three Little Words

(1950, 102 min, US, Richard Thorpe) *Fred Astaire, Red Skelton, Vera-Ellen, Debbie Reynolds.* Astaire and Skelton make a nice team in this appealing, Hollywoodized biography of songwriters Bert Kalmer and Harry Ruby, whose songs include "I Wanna Be Loved by You," "Who's Sorry Now" and the title tune. ★★★ VHS: $19.99

Three Men and a Baby

(1987, 102 min, US, Leonard Nimoy) *Tom Selleck, Ted Danson, Steve Guttenberg.* A box-office smash, this amiable and sometimes funny remake of the French hit *Three Men and a Cradle* stars Selleck, Danson and Guttenberg as three bachelor roommates who find themselves playing daddy to an adorable baby when the infant's mother drops the child on their doorstep. (Sequel: *Three Men and a Little Lady*) ★★½ VHS: $9.99

Three Men and a Cradle

(1985, 100 min, France, Coline Serreau) *Roland Giraud, Michel Boujenah, Andre Dussollier.* Similar to American "concept" pictures, the story line is simple: Three swinging bachelors wake up one morning and suddenly find a baby at their door, none of them the father. The antics of the novice fathers as they tend the child are predictable but also hilariously funny. (American remake: *Three Men and a Baby*) (French with English subtitles) ★★★ VHS: $14.99

Three Men and a Little Lady

(1990, 100 min, US, Emile Ardolino) *Ted Danson, Steve Guttenberg, Tom Selleck, Nancy Travis, Fiona Shaw.* While mildly entertaining, this sugar-coated sequel fails to live up to the original and is badly hampered by its utterly predictable ending. The thin story follows Selleck's snail-paced realization that he loves the little lady's mother. The one shining star in the cast is Shaw, who portrays her minor character with considerable aplomb and originality. This is more aptly titled *Three Men and a Lot of Hokum.* ★½ VHS: $9.99

Three Men on a Horse

(1936, 87 min, US, Mervyn LeRoy) *Frank McHugh, Joan Blondell, Sam Levene, Teddy Hart.* There's a Damon Runyon flavor to this zesty film adaptation of George Abbott's stage comedy. Character actor McHugh had his finest hour as the hen-pecked greeting card writer who becomes involved with small-time gambler Levene and his gang. It seems McHugh can accurately predict the ponies, which makes him very popular. There's quite an abundance of wonderfully funny lines, and silliness is the order of the day. Special mention goes to Hart for his priceless turn as a bug-eyed, gravel-voiced stooge. ★★★ VHS: $19.99

T

The Three Musketeers

(1949, 125 min, US, George Sidney) *Gene Kelly, Lana Turner, Angela Lansbury, Frank Morgan, Vincent Price.* One of the ten screen versions of the Alexander Dumas classic is a colorful swashbuckler with a mostly appealing cast. But it's not quite up to par with Richard Lester's wonderful 1974 romp. ★★½ VHS: $19.99

The Three Musketeers

(1974, 105 min, GB, Richard Lester) *Richard Chamberlain, Oliver Reed, Michael York, Raquel Welch, Charlton Heston, Faye Dunaway.* From the director of *A Hard Day's Night* comes this delightful, tongue-in-cheek version of the Dumas classic. York is at his best as the young D'Artagnan in this artful mix of swashbuckling adventure, romance and uproarious slapstick comedy. Among a great cast, Welch (in her finest hour) excels as Constance. Arguably the best sound version of the famous story. (Sequel: *The Four Musketeers)* ★★★½ VHS: $14.99; DVD: $19.99

The Three Musketeers

(1993, 105 min, US, Stephen Herek) *Charlie Sheen, Kiefer Sutherland, Chris O'Donnell, Tim Curry, Rebecca DeMornay, Oliver Platt, Gabrielle Anwar.* It would take a lot of panache to equal Richard Lester's classic 1974 treatment of the Dumas novel. Unfortunately, neither director Herek nor his Frat Pack cast are up to the challenge — the result being an enjoyable if inconsequential retelling. Wise-cracking incarnations of Athos, Aramis and Porthos are joined D'Artagnan as they take on Cardinal Richelieu (a lively Curry). The duel scenes have a certain verve, and the costumes are splashy, but most of the sets look like throwaways from "The Pirates of the Caribbean." ★★½ VHS: $14.99; DVD: $29.99

3 Ninjas

(1992, 81 min, US, Jon Turtletaub) *Victor Wong, Michael Treanor.* The Karate Kid meets the Three Stooges in this obvious yet often entertaining kids' action comedy. Three blond-haired, blue-eyed Asian-American (!) brothers receive martial arts training from their sensei grandfather, once a powerful ninja. When their FBI-agent dad gets on the wrong side of an international arms merchant, the kids get their chance to prove their mettle. It's hokey and formulaic with enough laughs to keep things rolling. (Followed by 3 sequels) ★★½ VHS: $9.99

3 Nuts in Search of a Bolt

(1964, 78 min, US, Tommy Noonan) *Paul Gilbert, John Crinin, Mamie Van Doren.* Three madcap loonies, each too poor to seek help on their own, pool their funds and their neuroses to send an unemployed actor to a world-famous psychiatrist hoping to receive a cure. The results? Blackmail, movie offers, big money and Van Doren in a bathtub full of beer! ★

Three O'Clock High

(1987, 101 min, US, Phil Joanou) *Casey Siemaszko, Anne Ryan, Richard Tyson.* Thanks to an engaging cast and some remarkable cinematography, this teenage comedy manages to rise above the norm of the genre. Siemaszko is quite appealing as a student bookstore manager who accidentally "touches" the school bully.

This sends the youth into a day-long hysteria when the antisocial thug (Tyson) challenges him to a fight after school. ★★★ VHS: $14.99

Three of Hearts

(1993, 101 min, US, Yurek Bogayevicz) *Sherilyn Fenn, Kelly Lynch, William Baldwin, Joe Pantoliano.* Stung by her sudden breakup with Ellen (Fenn), the love-lorn Connie (Lynch) concocts a wild plan to get revenge by hiring a male hustler (Baldwin) to trap her ex into falling in love with him, only to have him break her heart which in turn would hopefully have Ellen running back to her loving embrace. But the plan backfires when Joey, the streetwise prostitute with a heart of gold and now a roommate and friend of Connie, inadvertently falls in love with the charming university teacher. A lighthearted, charming romantic comedy with a ménage à trois twist. ★★★ VHS: $14.99

Three Seasons

(1999, 110 min, US/Vietnam, Tony Bui) *Don Duong, Nguyen Ngoc Hiep, Manh Cuong Tran, Harvey Keitel, Zoe Bui, Nguyen Huu Duoc.* The first American film to be shot in Vietnam since the war, this exquisitely photographed, poetic drama explores the diverse, interconnecting lives of a group of disparate people in modern Saigon. Writer-director Bui has made an impressive debut about the clash between the old and the new Vietnams, even if its politics are muted and stories sometimes familiar. Hai (Duong) is a good-hearted cyclo driver who falls for a bitter prostitute, Lan (Z. Bui), while taxiing her around the city night after night. Ken An (Hiep) is a flower seller newly arrived to the city who forms a bond with her reclusive employer. Into this mix comes James (Keitel), an American ex-G.I. searching for his daughter, and young Woody (Duoc), an orphaned street urchin befriended by James. Director Bui imbues the film with fable-like romanticism to fully incorporate the themes of the passing of the old, the coming of the new, and a country on the road to reconciliation. That it looks so good makes it all the more striking. (English and Vietnamese with English subtitles) ★★★½ VHS: $102.99

Three Songs of Lenin

(1934, 62 min, USSR, Dziga Vertov) In this, his last feature, legendary filmmaker Vertov (*Man with a Movie Camera*) paid homage to Russia's great leader with three heartfelt examinations of life in the Soviet Union. In a Black Prison Was My Face, We Loved Him, and In the Great City of Stone all explore the life of Lenin and show the effect he had on the Soviet people and their destiny. (Silent with orchestral accompaniment) ★★★ VHS: $29.99

Three Strange Loves

(1949, 88 min, Sweden, Ingmar Bergman) *Eva Henning, Brigit Tengroth.* This early Bergman psychological drama is set on a train trip from Germany to Sweden during which the lives of a dry scholar, his wife and his former wife all reach an impasse. (Swedish with English subtitles) ★★½

Three Strikes

(2000, 82 min, US, DJ Pooh) *Brian Hooks, N'Bushe Wright, Faizon Love, David Alan Grier.* A young ne'er-do-well is released from prison —

after a term for his second offense — and spends a wacky first day out desperately trying to avoid committing (or being accused of committing) a third crime, which would land him an automatic twenty years in jail. Writer-director Pooh cowrote and produced the funny comedy *Friday*, but none of the talent demonstrated in that film is on display here. Pooh should have paid attention to what made *Friday* so enjoyable: likable characters and comic timing. Instead, he trots out infantile, laughless gags and stock characters. ★ VHS: $9.99; DVD: $14.99

3:10 to Yuma

(1957, 92 min, US, Delmer Daves) *Van Heflin, Glenn Ford.* Very suspenseful western with farmer Heflin agreeing to guard prisoner Ford, but losing a battle of wits while waiting for the train to take him away. A classic western adventure, one of the best of the genre. Based on an Elmore Leonard story. ★★★½ VHS: $14.99

Three the Hard Way

(1974, 93 min, US, Gordon Parks, Jr.) *Jim Brown, Fred Williamson, Jim Kelly.* Three superstars of blaxploitation team up in this pulsating, yet unusually nonviolent thriller about a white supremacist who plans to inject a deadly serum — which kills off blacks but is harmless to whites — into the water supply. ★★½

3,000 Miles to Graceland

(2001, 121 min, US, Demian Lichtenstein) *Kurt Russell, Kevin Costner, Courtney Cox, Christian Slater, Kevin Pollak, David Arquette, Bokeem Woodbine, Jon Lovitz.* Russell and Costner are two ex-cons who pull off the daring robbery of a Las Vegas casino — dressed as Elvis impersonators. From this juncture, the plot could have gone in any one of several promising directions, but instead the filmmakers steer down the much-traveled (and overworn) road of the vengeful-psycho-killer-with-an-arsenal chasing after the bag of loot. Costner has fun playing an irascible badass who, it's hinted at, may be the King's illegitimate son. Russell is a quasi-nice guy on the wrong side of the law; he's got the swaggering hero stuff down pat and plays off Costner rather well. But there's indeed trouble in Graceland: despite the strength and charisma of its leads, the whole project is derailed by an inferior screenplay, inadequate direction, hectic over-editing and needless hyper-violence. *3,000 Miles to Graceland* isn't the worst movie of the year, but it certainly is the most obnoxiously *loud*. ★★ VHS: $102.99; DVD: $24.99

Three to Tango

(1999, 98 min, US, Damon Santostefano) *Matthew Perry, Neve Campbell, Dylan McDermott, Oliver Platt, John C. McGinley.* Gay activists, in response to the drivel that gays actually choose their lifestyles, often quote the line, "Who would *want* to be gay in a homophobic society?" *Three to Tango*, comic drivel of nearly epic proportions, attempts to show the who, what, where and why of "who." Perry plays an architect whose zillionaire client (McDermott) thinks he's gay (but he's not), so Perry's asked to keep on eye on the mogul's "wild" girlfriend (Campbell). Think they eventually fall in love? This probably would have been funny if it was made in the 1960s; but alas, it's nothing more

T

than a series of stereotypes and hoary comic situations. Perry gives it his all; he has good screen presence, and a lot of comic energy — but it's all for naught. In trying to be both cutting and P.C., *Three to Tango* suffocates and becomes unfunny and just a little offensive. ★½ VHS: $14.99; DVD: $19.99

Three Wishes

(1995, 107 min, US, Martha Coolidge) *Patrick Swayze, Mary Elizabeth Mastrantonio, Joseph Mazzello, Seth Mumy, Michael O'Keefe, Diane Venora.* This flashback-framed fantasy/drama is an enjoyable diversion for the family, but it never quite catches fire, nor makes the most of its premise. Swayze plays a mysterious drifter who is taken in by Mastrantonio and her two young sons after they accidentally hit him with the car. He brings a bit of male companionship to the widowed mother and acts as a father figure to young Mazzello, much to the chagrin of the well-to-do neighbors. Unfortunately, despite being an update of an oft-told folk tale, little is made of the fantasy elements in the story. And the expected big, emotional ending is a piffle and, to be frank, a cop-out. ★★½ VHS: $9.99; DVD: $14.99

301/302

(1995, 92 min, Korea, Chul-Soo Park) *Eun-jin Banh, Sin-Hye Hwang.* This amusing little black comedy/thriller is an odd pastiche that blends a squeaky clean Asian high-tech look with the sensibilities of Juenet y Caro (*Delicatessen*). The story involves two neighbors in a very chichi apartment block for affluent single women. 302 (that's her apartment number) has gone missing and as the police interview 301 trying to dig up clues, the film launches into a series of flashbacks that retell the two women's lives. The film's "surprise" ending is rather obvious, and there's an over-reliance on style that can't mask the plot's shortcomings, but there's enough here to hope that it's the first of many in a coming Korean wave of cinema. (Korean with English subtitles) ★★½ VHS: $79.99

The Threepenny Opera

(1931, 114 min, Germany, G.W. Pabst) *Lotte Lenya, Rudolph Forster.* Pabst's wild and eerie adaptation of the Bertolt Brecht/Kurt Weill "beggar's opera" captures the play's marvelous milieu of 19th-century underworld and features the magical performances of Lenya as Jenny and Forster as the infamous Mack the Knife. (German with English subtitles) ★★★ VHS: $19.99

Threesome

(1994, 93 min, US, Andrew Fleming) *Stephen Baldwin, Lara Flynn Boyle, Josh Charles, Alexis Arquette.* This often perceptive and funny story revolves around the friendship and evolving sexual relations between three college students sharing the same dorm. Baldwin is Stuart, a droopy-eyed, sex-obsessed jock. Eddy (Charles) is the "sexually ambivalent" (read: gay) narrator/roommate, and Alex (Boyle) is the sexually aggressive woman mistakenly assigned to their room. Complications arise when lust rears its ugly head: Alex has the hots for Eddy who has his eyes on the well-formed butt of Stuart, who wants to jump the bones of the disinterested Alex. Sure it's "high concept," but

The Threepenny Opera

what saves the film from being tiresome and predictable (no surprises, though) is a witty script. Though the film should have done more with Eddy's non-threatening gay virgin. ★★★ VHS: $14.99; DVD: $19.99

The Thrill of It All

(1963, 108 min, US, Norman Jewison) *James Garner, Doris Day, Arlene Francis, Edward Andrews, Carl Reiner.* This delightful spoof is very typical of the good-natured, family-oriented comedies Day and Universal were releasing at the time. Day stars as a housewife who becomes a celebrity spokesperson, much to the dismay of husband Garner. Though at times the film seems to advocate feminist principles, in the end Doris' place is in the home (evidently in 1963 she couldn't have it all). ★★★ VHS: $14.99

Throne of Blood

(1957, 110 min, Japan, Akira Kurosawa) *Toshiro Mifune, Isuzu Yamada.* Shakespeare's "Macbeth" is superbly adapted to the screen in this gripping tragedy of a samurai warrior who is spurred by his ambitious wife and an old witch to kill his lord. Amidst an atmosphere of obsessive madness, and utilizing aspects of Noh theatre, Kurosawa concludes his film with an unforgettable and graphic depiction of Mifune's bloody death by arrows. (Japanese with English subtitles) ★★★½ VHS: $39.99

Through a Glass Darkly

(1961, 91 min, Sweden, Ingmar Bergman) *Harriet Andersson, Max von Sydow.* Andersson is mesmerizing as a recently released mental patient who, while vacationing on a remote island with her husband, brother and father, relapses into schizophrenia. This Oscar winner is one of Bergman's most intense and riveting films. (Swedish with English subtitles) ★★★½ VHS: $29.99

Throw Momma from the Train

(1987, 88 min, US, Danny DeVito) *Danny DeVito, Billy Crystal, Anne Ramsey.* A hilariously dark black comedy, with its inspiration coming from Hitchcock's classic *Strangers on a Train.* Crystal stars as a teacher who gets mixed-up with one of his students, DeVito, who is determined to get rid of his overbearing, mean-spirited mother.

Ramsey steals the film with an over-the-top, one-of-a-kind portrayal of DeVito's wicked Mom. ★★★ DVD: $19.99

Thunder Road

(1958, 92 min, US, Arthur Ripley) *Robert Mitchum, Gene Barry.* The ideal picture to watch while passing around a jug of White Lightning. This lively potboiler has interesting behind-the-scenes glimpses of Kentucky moonshiners and a fun backwoods milieu. When a big-city operation tries to muscle in, bootlegger Mitchum vows to stop them while at the same time attempting to elude the ceaseless pursuit of government agents. ★★★ VHS: $14.99; DVD: $24.99

Thunderball

(1965, 132 min, GB, Terence Young) *Sean Connery, Claudine Auger, Adolfo Celi.* Connery has tongue firmly in cheek in this fourth James Bond outing. 007 is up against Emilio Largo (Celi), who has masterminded the greatest nuclear hijacking of all time. Excellent underwater photography highlights this glorious Bond adventure, which won an Oscar for Best Special Effects. (Sequel: *You Only Live Twice*) ★★★ VHS: $14.99; DVD: $34.99

Thunderbolt and Lightfoot

(1974, 115 min, US, Michael Cimino) *Clint Eastwood, Jeff Bridges.* Eastwood stars as a master thief who teams up with a wise-cracking drifter (Bridges) to search for stolen money from a previous robbery. Bridges received an Oscar nomination for his spirited performance (not to mention his drag routine). ★★★ VHS: $9.99; DVD: $19.99

Thundercrack!

(1975, 130 min, US, Curt McDowell) *George Kuchar.* A very funny and outrageously sexy spoof of all those horror films in which a group of strangers is forced to spend a stormy night in an old dark house full of eerie sounds, creepy happenings and, in this case, inhabited by a sexually active gorilla. Greeting the stranded motorists at her decaying mansion is a crazed hostess who initiates her unwitting guests in a series of increasingly bizarre sexual trysts. A sexually graphic camp classic that is a titillating scream. ★★★

Thunderheart

(1992, 118 min, US, Michael Apted) *Val Kilmer, Graham Greene, Sam Shepard, Fred Ward.* Kilmer stars in this fictionalized look at the conflict between the American Indian Movement and the Bureau of Indian Affairs on the Sioux reservation in South Dakota. Kilmer plays a half-native FBI agent who is sent to sort things out. He takes the assignment reluctantly at first, as he really has no connection with his Indian roots; but as he gets to know life on the reservation, he finds that perhaps he is on the wrong side. Apted lets the action loose at the appropriate moments, but doesn't hesitate to meditate on the mystical ways of his Native American subjects. ★★★ VHS: $19.99; DVD: $19.99

THX-1138

(1971, 88 min, US, George Lucas) *Robert Duvall, Donald Pleasence.* Before he revitalized the sci-fi genre with *Star Wars*, Lucas directed this chilling tale set in a "1984"-like society where computers regulate the subterranean populace with mind-controlling drugs. This is a feature-length version of his award-winning short film. ★★★ VHS: $14.99

The Tic Code

(2000, 90 min, US, Gary Winick) *Gregory Hines, Polly Draper, Christopher George Marquette, Bill Nunn, Tony Shalhoub.* Set against the East Village jazz scene, this often compelling drama is elevated beyond its movie-of-the-week pedigree thanks to some fine acting and dedication of character. Twelve-year-old pianist Miles (impressive newcomer Marquette) is a child prodigy with Tourette's syndrome. An outcast at school, Miles finds comfort at a local jazz club where he feels connected to his absent father, a successful musician living in Hollywood. When he is befriended by Tyrone (Hines), an accomplished saxophonist also with Tourette's, both Miles and Tyrone come to find peace within themselves. Draper (she wrote the sensitive screenplay) is smart as Miles' supportive mother, who begins an affair with Tyrone. ★★★ VHS: $102.99; DVD: $24.99

Ticket to Heaven

(1981, 107 min, Canada, Ralph L. Thomas) *Nick Mancuso, Meg Foster, Saul Rubinek.* Made a year before the equally riveting, similarly themed *Split Image*, this psychological drama stars Mancuso as a teacher who comes under the influence of a religious cult, robbing the educator of his will and spirit. When friends and family finally locate him, it's a desperate struggle to "deprogram" him to the way he was. ★★★

Tie Me Up! Tie Me Down!

(1990, 101 min, Spain, Pedro Almodóvar) *Antonio Banderas, Victoria Abril.* This Almodóvar comedy may not satisfy those people who were won over by *Women on the Verge...*, but for lovers of Pedro and his outrageous style, this will be a pure delight. A released mental patient (Banderas) kidnaps a heroin addicted porn star (Abril) and professes his love for her. Surprisingly sentimental for Almodóvar, this is an often hilarious tale of love and bondage which features a truly steamy sex scene and a water toy with a penchant for swimming into the nether regions of the female anatomy.

(Spanish with English subtitles) (Letterboxed) ★★★ VHS: $14.99; DVD: $29.99

The Tie That Binds

(1995, 98 min, US, Wesley Strick) *Keith Carradine, Daryl Hannah, Vincent Spano, Moira Kelly.* This worthless wreck of a movie attempts to make a statement about contemporary child-rearing but succeeds only in being a lesson in how to make a terrible film. Spano and Kelly adopt a mysterious little girl. When they decide to check into her birth parents' background, they discover Carradine and Hannah, a part-time serial killer and his psychotic white-trash/hymn-singing wife, who've decided to retrieve the little girl. The plot rehashes every "psychotic (nanny-policeman-tenant) from hell" movie, and the dialogue is ludicrous. ★ VHS: $9.99; DVD: $29.99

Tieta of Agreste

(1996, 115 min, Brazil, Carlos Diegues) *Sonia Braga, Marilia Pera, Chino Anisio.* Sultry Brazilian sexpot Braga takes on the title role of yet another Jorge Amado novel, "Tieta of the Wilderness." Amado himself introduces the story which "may have no moral," as it depicts Tieta, a young girl who returns to her hometown years after she was shamed into leaving. Now a rich and powerful businesswoman, she becomes Agreste's benefactor, and fulfills the financial — and in some cases sexual — desires of her family and the townspeople. Yet when Tieta gives everyone what they want, they really end up getting what they deserve. Director Diegues has created a joyful comedy about sex, greed, and politics that pulses to the buoyant sounds of Caetano Veloso's bossa nova. (Portuguese with English subtitles) ★★★½ VHS: $19.99; DVD: $29.99

Tiger Bay

(1959, 105 min, GB, J. Lee Thompson) *Hayley Mills, John Mills, Horst Buchholz.* This morality play disguised as a suspense thriller stars H. Mills (in her debut) as a friendless girl who witnesses a murder, then shelters the murderer (Buchholz) from the investigating detective (J. Mills). A sensitive study of the power of loneliness, desperation and the need to be loved, which makes this not just another "cops & robbers" story. The scenes between young Hayley and Buchholz are unforgettable. ★★★; DVD: $24.99

A Tiger's Tale

(1987, 97 min, US, Peter Douglas) *C. Thomas Howell, Ann-Margret, Charles Durning.* Pleasant but aimless comedy about a high school senior (Howell) who becomes romantically involved with his girlfriend's mother (Ann-Margret). Director Douglas is one of Kirk's sons. ★★

Tigerland

(2000, 100 min, US, Joel Schumacher) *Colin Farrell, Matthew Davis, Clifton Collins, Jr., Tom Guiry, Shea Whigham.* Having made a name for himself with big-budget, glossy Hollywood fare, director Schumacher retreats from the mainstream to create a gritty antiwar film that is both involving and credible. At a boot camp in the early 1970s, soldiers are being hastily trained for a quick flight to Vietnam. Amongst the ranks is Bozz (Farrell), a pacifist rebel who only wants out of the Army. During the grueling

weeks of training, that ends with simulated combat at a makeshift jungle called Tigerland, Bozz comes to have a palpable effect on his fellow soldiers — and reclaims a little of his own humanity in the process. *Tigerland* transcends the clichés of the war film not only through compelling dramatics but bristling characterizations as well. At the eye of this storm is a force of great intensity, Irish actor Farrell, whose brooding good looks and Steve McQueen coolness make him a natural for international stardom. His tempered, riveting portrayal provides a stark balance to circumstances that are out of control. ★★★ VHS: $14.99; DVD: $29.99

Tigers in Lipstick

(1978, 85 min, Italy, Luigi Zampa) *Laura Antonelli, Monica Vitti, Ursula Andress, Sylvia Kristel.* Four of the sexiest sirens of 1970s Europe star in this tame but cute series of vignettes. Taking their inspiration from O. Henry, these humorous tales with a sexual bent all focus on the fatally seductive charms of the female sex. All feature our femme fatales as beautiful and aggressive manhandlers whose task is made all that much easier by the wide-eyed and horny complacency of their oh-so-willing victims. (Dubbed) ★★ VHS: $39.99

Tightrope

(1984, 114 min, US, Richard Tuggle) *Clint Eastwood, Genevieve Bujold, Dan Hedaya.* Eastwood stars as a New Orleans cop who, while hunting down a vicious rapist, suffers his own descent into sexual darkness. This razor-sharp crime thriller is a gripping examination of the twisted mind of the sexual criminal. ★★★ VHS: $14.99

Tigrero: A Film That Was Never Made

(1995, 75 min, US, Mika Kaurismäki) *Samuel Fuller, Jim Jarmusch, The Karajá.* Forty years after his initial trip up the Amazon to scout locations for a film offered to him by producer Darryl Zanuck, the intrepid film director Samuel Fuller returns, with Jim Jarmusch in tow, to the land of the Karajá Indian tribe. The tribe has survived myriad incursions from the outside over the intervening years, their culture amazingly intact despite wars, power politics and that eternal nemesis, progress. Fuller and Jarmusch sometime seem like just another annoyance in

Matthew Davis and Colin Farrell in *Tigerland*

the villagers' lives; but there is one scene in which Fuller holds a screening for the tribe — a screening of some of the footage which sat in his closet for those 40 years. The Karajá watch with awe and wonder and recognition, remembering friends and relatives long dead. It's a moment that speaks to the magic of the medium. ★★★ VHS: $79.99

'Til There Was You

(1997, 114 min, US, Scott Winant) *Jeanne Tripplehorn, Dylan McDermott, Sarah Jessica Parker, Jennifer Aniston, Steve Antin.* There's a certain breeziness that winds its way through '*Til There Was You*, a New Age variation of *Sleepless in Seattle* about lovers who don't meet until story's end. Things cutely fall out windows, trendy sculptures exhibited in trendier restaurants knock customers on the head in obvious burlesque bits, and everyone seems so attractive and successful. So why isn't anyone smiling? Tripplehorn and McDermott are separated childhood friends and supposed soul mates. What it takes to bring these two together forms the core of this overly cute, minor romantic comedy-drama. ★★ VHS: $14.99

Tilaï

(1990, 81 min, Burkina Faso) Director Ouedraogo's haunting and starkly realized tale of forbidden love and tribal law is a masterfully crafted African take on Greek tragedy. The story follows Saga, who returns to his home village after a many years' absence only to find that his father, a powerful village elder, has stolen and married *his* fiancée, Nogma. But his hands are tied by the strict code of law, or "Tilai," that governs the village. Ultimately, he goes into exile, but stays close enough to the village to have an illicit affair with Nogma. Ouedraogo's excellent sense of storytelling is nicely complimented by an well-honed script and exceptional performances to make this a superisingly compelling and thoughtful Oedipal spin on forbidden passion. ★★★½ VHS: $79.99

Till Marriage Do Us Part

(1976, 97 min, Italy, Luigi Comencini) *Laura Antonelli, Michele Placido.* Set in the early 20th century, this funny bedroom farce features Antonelli as a naive and virginal beauty who, on the night of her wedding, discovers that she has married her illegitimate brother. Unable to consumate the marriage, our enterprising heroine is determined to discover and explore the "mysteries of the flesh." A delightful and bawdy romp. (Italian with English subtitles) ★★★

Till the Clouds Roll By

(1946, 137 min, US, Richard Whorf) *Robert Walker, Van Heflin, Judy Garland, Frank Sinatra, Lena Horne.* By-the-books musical biography of songwriter Jerome Kern, with Walker playing the gifted composer. An all-star cast appears in supporting roles and cameos. ★★½ VHS: $19.99; DVD: $19.99

Tillie's Punctured Romance

(1914, 73 min, US, Mack Sennett) *Charles Chaplin, Mabel Normand.* Shot in 1914, this delightful Chaplin silent comedy was made at producer Mack Sennett's famous Keystone Pictures studio. The film is basically a slapstick love story, replete with Chaplin's brilliant trademark physical comedy. This was the only full-length feature Chaplin

made for Keystone, and was the film where Chaplin refined his character that would later become his world-famous "Little Tramp." The feature is followed by a virtually unseen Normand short. ★★★★ VHS: $19.99

Tim

(1979, 108 min, Australia, Michael Pate) *Mel Gibson, Piper Laurie.* A sensitive and compassionate story of the developing love between a handsome, slightly retarded young man (Gibson) and an older career woman (Laurie). After meeting by chance, the two find themselves bound by a deep affection and a tender sensuous longing. Based on the novel by Colleen McCullough. ★★½ VHS: $12.99

Time After Time

(1979, 112 min, US, Nicholas Meyer) *Malcolm McDowell, David Warner, Mary Steenburgen.* An exhilarating sci-fi murder mystery written and directed by Meyer. In Victorian England, writer H.G. Wells (McDowell) learns the identity of Jack the Ripper, but the infamous murderer uses Wells' newly invented time machine to transport himself to current-day San Francisco, an environment where he's "just an amateur." Wells follows him into the future, where he is assisted by bank clerk Steenburgen. Warner makes an appropriately demented Jack. Though a bit gory, it's a thrill a minute. ★★★½ VHS: $14.99

Time Bandits

(1981, 116 min, GB, Terry Gilliam) *John Cleese, Sean Connery, Shelley Duvall, Katherine Helmond, Ian Holm, Michael Palin, Ralph Richardson, David Warner.* A young boy is abducted by time-traveling midgets, who, assisted by the Supreme Being (Richardson), take him on a harrowing journey through time where they encounter Robin Hood, a giant ogre (and his lovely wife), the *Titanic*, and much, much more. A funny and frolicking fantasy. (VHS available letterboxed or pan & scan) ★★★ VHS: $14.99; DVD: $39.99

Time Code

(2000, 97 min, US, Mike Figgis) *Saffron Burrows, Salma Hayek, Stellan Skarsgård, Jeanne Tripplehorn, Kyle MacLachlan, Steven Weber, Julian Sands.* Figgis' experimental film takes some getting used to, but it tells a unique story of the film business and relationships in crises. *Time Code* uses a four-part split screen with four different scenes going simultaneously showing different aspects of the same story. The actors were supplied a scenario and all the dialogue was improvised. Unlike Mike Leigh and John Cassavetes, there was apparently no script. The sexy Hayak is an aspiring actress. Her lover Tripplehorn thinks she has reasons to be jealous and plants a microphone in her girlfriend's bag, exposing her affair with Skarsgård, whose wife leaves him for his infidelities. All this craziness is happening at the offices of a film production company. Nearly everyone is snorting coke or drinking and trying to make business decisions during a morning of break-ups, liaisons and earthquakes. Once you get used to the spilt screens, the acting and the tale can be quite compelling. For the record, the finished product is take 15. ★★★ VHS: $14.99; DVD: $24.99

Time for Revenge

(1983, 112 min, Argentina, Adolfo Aristarain) *Federico Luppi, Haydee Padilla.* This gripping thriller tells the story of one man's struggle against a corrupt system. In an effort to publicize the unsafe working conditions at a demolition site, our hero fakes an industrial accident in order to blackmail the ruthless company. The scam, however, backfires — resulting in the death of a coworker. The man continues with his scheme by claiming that he was struck speechless in the explosion. The company, knowing that something is up, gets desperate in their attempt to break his silence. A compelling story of oppression and distrust. (Spanish with English subtitles) ★★★½ VHS: $24.99

Time Indefinite

(1993, 117 min, US, Ross McElwee) Self-reflexive documentarian McElwee follows up his art-house hit *Sherman's March* by going a few steps further down the road of introspection, offering this kind of cradle-to-grave examination of his own family. McElwee's wry wit and intelligent commentaries are in evidence right from the start as he narrates the opening sequence in which he and fellow documentarian Marilyn Levine film themselves announcing their engagement at his family reunion. He then wends his way through the next couple of years of his life, documenting all of the joys and sorrows. *Time Indefinite* is a fascinating, revealing and highly entertaining journey that explores some of life's universal questions. ★★★½ VHS: $29.99

The Time Machine

(1960, 103 min, US, George Pal) *Rod Taylor, Yvette Mimieux, Alan Young, Sebastian Cabot, Whit Bissell.* Special effects master Pal expertly brings to the big screen another of H.G. Wells' writings (Pal did *The War of the Worlds* earlier), this time retaining the novel's Victorian setting. On his way to year 802,701, Taylor witnesses our atomic Armageddon of 1966 (you remember *that* one, don't you?) and the rise of the Morlock domination of the Eloi. One of the best screen adaptations of Wells' work. ★★★½ VHS: $14.99; DVD: $19.99

A Time of Destiny

(1988, 118 min, US, Gregory Nava) *William Hurt, Timothy Hutton, Stockard Channing.* It should be a comfort both to Hurt and his fans that he'll probably never make a movie as bad as this contrived and confusing WWII drama about revenge and obsession. Hutton and Channing can probably find solace, also. ★

Time of the Gypsies

(1989, 115 min, Yugoslavia, Emir Kusturica) *Davor Dujmovic, Sinolicka Trpkova.* Sort of a Serbian version of *The Godfather II*, the story is set in a Gypsy village where a young boy, gifted with kinetic powers, grows up. His innocence and love for his mother, girlfriend and pet chicken are soon replaced by a soulless love of money, bright polyester clothing and life in the fast lane after he joins up with a gang of petty thieves. Visually hallucinatory and imbued with much humor, the director used non-professional actors and real Gypsies for most of the roles, giving the film an authentic yet eccentric feel. Winner of the Best Director Prize at

Cannes in 1989. (Serbian with English subtitles) ★★★ VHS: $19.99

The Time of Their Lives

(1946, 82 min, US, Charles Barton) *Bud Abbott, Lou Costello, Marjorie Reynolds.* Extremely entertaining Abbott and Costello romp about a couple killed during Revolutionary times (Costello and Reynolds) whose spirits reappear in the 20th century to haunt Bud, just moving into his new country home. ★★★ VHS: $14.99

Time Regained

(1999, 158 min, France, Raoul Ruiz) *Catherine Deneuve, Emmanuelle Béart, John Malkovich, Vincent Perez.* An existential, surreal-like drama loosely suggested by Proust's last novel "In Search of Lost Time" and the many details of his own peculiar life. The renowned author, on his deathbed, looks back at his life in a series of fragmented memories, which become the formation for characters and events in this final book of "Remembrance of Things Past." A dense, compelling film, quite comparable to reading Proust. (French with English subtitles) ★★★ VHS: $79.99; DVD: $29.99

Time Stands Still

(1981, 99 min, Hungary, Peter Gothar) *Istvan Znamenak, Henrik Pauer.* This witty and richly composed film is a compassionate coming-of-age drama set amid the debris of post-war Hungary, with its tightening grip of repression. It follows a group of friends — two brothers abandoned by their father, an enticing nymphette and a stylish rogue — as they encounter the hardships of growing up. A brilliant, seductive film seething with sexual tension, confused violence and the foreshadow of the rock 'n' roll culture. (Hungarian with English subtitles) ★★★½

A Time to Kill

(1996, 150 min, US, Joel Schumacher) *Matthew McConaughey, Samuel L. Jackson, Sandra Bullock, Kevin Spacey, Brenda Fricker, Oliver Platt, Charles S. Dutton, Ashley Judd, Kiefer Sutherland.* Strong performances and a compelling, textured story line combine to make this the best screen adaptation of a John Grisham novel to date. Similar in tone and theme to the classic *To Kill a Mockingbird, A Time to Kill* is an enthralling entertainment and a powerful examination of race relations. McConaughey plays a white Southern lawyer who defends a black man (Jackson) on trial for murdering the men who raped his ten-year-old daughter. Unlike *Mockingbird,* the guilt of the defendant is never in question; instead the story focuses on the culpability of a prejudiced society and the morality of the crime — all under the guise of exciting and even eloquent courtroom drama. Heading a good ensemble cast, the handsome McConaughey is splendid in his first starring role; Jackson gives a finely layered portrait of rage and decency. This is very nearly great filmmaking — only director Schumacher's less-than-fluid transitions mar an otherwise terrific endeavor. ★★★½ VHS: $14.99; DVD: $19.99

Time without Pity

(1957, 88 min, GB, Joseph Losey) *Michael Redgrave, Ann Todd, Leo McKern, Alec McCowen, Peter Cushing, Joan Plowright.* His first film made under his own name after being blacklisted during the McCarthy era, Losey's melodrama is a tense, overmannered but engaging thriller. Less of a whodunit (the murderer is revealed in the first scene) and more of a how-will-he-do-it, the film stars Redgrave as the alcoholic father of a convicted murderer (McCowen) sentenced to die. Having only 24 hours, Redgrave sets out to prove his son's innocence — if he can stay off the bottle. Losey's anti-capital punishment story is played broadly but effectively. ★★★ VHS: $39.99

Time Cop

(1994, 98 min, US, Peter Hyams) *Jean-Claude Van Damme, Ron Silver, Mia Sara, Bruce McGill.* Van Damme is in *Terminator* territory with this action-flavored time travel adventure which mixes predictable heroics and villainy with a few spiffy twists on time tripping. Van Damme plays a special forces cop from the future who retrieves those in the past who are changing history. He meets his match, however, in the person of ruthless presidential candidate Silver, who is trying to alter the course of human events for his own political gain. *Timecop* offers neat special effects, well-placed action scenes, and an over-the-top Silver in double doses. ★★½ VHS: $9.99; DVD: $24.99

The Times of Harvey Milk

(1984, 87 min, US, Robert Epstein & Richard Schmiechen) *Harvey Milk.* This extraordinary, compelling portrait of the slain San Francisco supervisor won a much deserved Academy Award for Best Documentary. Few films pack such a powerful wallop as it documents the true-life story of Harvey Milk, a Castro Street camera shop owner who became the country's first openly gay elected official. His rise to power and success as a leader of minorities was abruptly ended in 1978 when he and Mayor George Moscone were assassinated by Dan White, an antigay former colleague of Milk's on the Board of Supervisors and a former police officer. The film follows the searing episode of injustice as White is given a light sentence — using the infamous "Twinkie defense" — which sent thousands of outraged citizens into the streets of San Francisco. ★★★★ VHS: $39.99

Times to Come

(1981, 98 min, Argentina, Gustavo Mosquera) *Hugo Soto, Juan Leyrado.* This amazingly adventurous surrealist drama takes its title from the Argentinian saying, "It'll even be worse in times to come." In the ruined urban landscape of Buenos Aires, a young man is shot by a policeman during an antigovernment demonstration. He falls into a coma in the hospital but his brain is fully functioning — exploding with thoughts and feelings — all the while trapped in an unresponsive body. The policeman responsible for the shooting is an unpredictable and violent man who is in turn hounded by a mysterious caller bent on punishing him. An angry film that successfully combines political fervor with daring camera work and imaginative storytelling. (Spanish with English subtitles) ★★★ VHS: $39.99

Tin Cup

(1996, 130 min, US, Ron Shelton) *Kevin Costner, Rene Russo, Don Johnson, Cheech Marin, Linda Hart. Bull Durham* star and director reunite for this easygoing, enjoyable sports comedy set against the world of golf. Displaying the rustic charm he demonstrated in *Durham,* Costner plays a golf pro (nicknamed "Tin Cup") relegated to giving lessons for beer money. He becomes attracted to a new student (Russo), who turns out to be the girlfriend of an arrogant ex-golf partner (Johnson) who has hit the big time. To woo her, he readies himself for the U.S. Open — it may only happen in the movies, but here it's actually fun to watch. While lacking the red-hot chemistry of *Durham's* Costner-Sarandon coupling, *Tin Cup* is as amiable as its hapless hero: wide-eyed and determined to please in spite of itself. (VHS available letterboxed or pan & scan) ★★★ VHS: $9.99; DVD: $19.99

The Tin Drum

(1979, 142 min, Germany/France, Volker Schlöndorff) *David Bennett, Charles Aznavour.* This powerful adaptation of Gunter Grass' masterpiece is about a young boy, disgusted by the rising tide of Nazism, who wills himself to stop growing. A mesmerizing "realistic fantasy" with an extraordinary piece of acting by 12-year-old Bennett as the determined dwarf. (German with English subtitles) ★★★★ VHS: $39.99; DVD: $39.99

Tin Men

(1987, 112 min, US, Barry Levinson) *Richard Dreyfuss, Danny DeVito, Barbara Hershey, Bruno Kirby, John Mahoney.* Director Levinson is quite at home with this second entry in his "Baltimore" trilogy (*Diner, Avalon*). Dreyfuss and DeVito are both exceptional as feuding salesmen in early 1960s Baltimore. A small fender-bender escalates into full war, as each tries to outdo the other in retaliation, including Dreyfuss seducing DeVito's wife. Hershey is splendid as the woman innocently caught between them. An outstanding comedy-drama with an exemplary supporting cast. ★★★½

Tinseltown

(1997, 85 min, US, Tony Spiridakis) *Arye Gross, Joe Pantoliano, Ron Perlman, Kristy Swanson, Tom Wood.* A tired mix of serial-killer kitsch and Hollywood satire, *Tinseltown* is brightened only by a fun cast. Two hack screenwriters — thoroughly lacking in talent or ideas — stumble upon the celebrated "costume killer" (a game Perlman), and decide to make his story into a movie, pleasing low-rent producer Pantoliano. Swanson plays Perlman's girlfriend and wannabe director of the project. While the satire is moldy by this point, and the serial-killer angle is thin (at times, the film threatens to become *Man Gums Dog*), the performers are enthusiastic, the pace is brisk, and the denouement has a surprise or two. ★★ VHS: $14.99

'Tis Pity She's a Whore

(1971, 109 min, Italy, Guiseppi Patrone Griffi) *Charlotte Rampling, Oliver Tobias, Fabio Testi.* Freely adapted from John Ford's Elizabethan tragedy, this surprisingly absorbing film about a scandalous, incestuous affair has the beauty of Zeffirelli's *Romeo and Juliet* combined with the poetically perverse sensuality of Cocteau's *Les Enfants Terribles.* Giovanni, an intensely handsome young man, is troubled by his passionate love for his sister, Annabella (Rampling). The two, vowing undying love and commitment towards each other, are soon torn apart by their father who forces Annabella to marry an arrogant young nobleman — all the while pregnant with Giovanni's baby. Lushly photographed with several steamy sex scenes, this absorbing drama has a shocking, overpowering finale. (Filmed in English) ★★★

Titan A.E.

(2000, 94 min, US, Don Bluth & Gary Goldman) *Voices of: Matt Damon, Drew Barrymore, Nathan Lane, Tone Loc, Jim Breuer, Janeane Garofalo, John Leguizamo.* Awesome computer and hand-painted animation more than compensates for overused sci-fi clichés in this entertaining animated fantasy. Borrowing from just about every genre flick from *Star Wars* to *Waterworld* to *When Worlds Collide*, this amicable 'toon is a feast for the eyes, showcasing some of the most imaginative visuals ever dreamt of. The story begins when the Drej, a vicious alien species, destroys Earth, leaving a band of survivors to fend for themselves in a lone spaceship as they search for a secret map that will lead them to Dryland, er, to Earth 2. Vocal contributions are well cast, especially Damon and Barrymore as a pair of teenaged lovers literally star-crossed. ★★★ VHS: $14.99; DVD: $22.99

Titanic

(1953, 98 min, US, Jean Negulesco) *Barbara Stanwyck, Clifton Webb, Robert Wagner, Richard Basehart, Thelma Ritter.* Stanwyck and Webb offer accomplished performances in this luxuriously melodramatic retelling of the sinking of the *Titanic*. As opposed to the excellent British drama *A Night to Remember*, which tells its story via the ship's personnel, this glossy Hollywoodization is seen through the eyes of the ship's passengers, with married couple Stanwyck and Webb its main focus. And even if *Night* is more authentic, this *Titanic* is soap opera of the first order, thanks to an Academy Award–winning screenplay and a marvelous ensemble. (The story of *Titanic* was also retold in 1958, 1996 and 1997) ★★★ VHS: $14.99

Titanic

(1997, 197 min, US, James Cameron) *Leonardo DiCaprio, Kate Winslet, Billy Zane, Kathy Bates, Gloria Stuart, Bill Paxton, Frances Fisher, David Warner, Bernard Hill, Victor Garber, Danny Nucci.* As mammoth an undertaking as the big ship itself, Cameron's epic story of the sinking of the *Titanic* is moviemaking on the grandest of scales. The story of the fateful night of April 14, 1912, has been told before, but never like this. The story begins in the present when artifacts of the sunken ship are recovered. A *Titanic* survivor, 101-year-old Rose (played with great charm and class by Stuart), identifies them, and is whisked away to the North Atlantic. There she recounts the story of decades past, and her romance as a youth (Winslet as a 17-year-old Rose) with an adventurous, penniless artist named Jack (DiCaprio). She gets around to the sinking, eventually, too. Though three hours-plus, Cameron's film is so tightly edited and paced that it seems more like two. His dialogue isn't always the best, but everything else about it is first-class. Featuring spectacular effects and production design, *Titanic* is a marvel of popular mainstream filmmaking. Winner of a record

11 Academy Awards, including Picture and Director. (VHS available letterboxed or pan & scan) ★★★★ VHS: $29.99; DVD: $29.99

Titus

(1999, 162 min, US, Julie Taymor) *Anthony Hopkins, Jessica Lange, Alan Cumming, Jonathan Rhys Meyers, Matthew Rhys, Colm Feore.* Shakespeare's tragedy "Titus Andronicus" is regarded as a minor work, more interested in grotesqueries than the bright writing of his later masterpieces. So director Taymor (best known for Broadway's "The Lion King") glosses over the weak material (despite an intense interpretation by Hopkins) and punches up these lowbrow elements, creating a sumptuously violent revenge fantasy. Unbound by convention in her film debut, Taymor lets loose a visual panoply of sets, settings and costumes that span the eras (from Elizabethan to modern), using tanks, the Popemobile, what-have-you to enhance the bloody melodrama. Lange's performance as ladder-climbing Goth Queen Tamora is especially pulpy, while Cumming camps it up as the spoilt king. It's certainly not *Romeo and Juliet*, but it may be the best possible (and, in spirit, most faithful) adaptation of this particular work. ★★★★ VHS: $9.99; DVD: $24.99

To Be or Not to Be

(1942, 99 min, US, Ernst Lubitsch) *Jack Benny, Carole Lombard, Robert Stack, Sig Ruman.* With the involvement of America in WWII, most audiences didn't know what to make of Lubitsch's hilarious and biting war comedy. With the advantage of the decades, however, this black farce has taken on legendary status, and deservedly so. Lombard (in her final role) and Benny are a husband and wife acting team in Occupied Poland. When they cross paths with a double agent, they devise a plan — with the help of their acting troupe — to expose the spy and flee to safety. Lombard was an exceptional comedienne and farceur, and her performance is radiant; and Benny gives a truly funny performance as "that great, great actor" Joseph Tura. (Remade in 1983) ★★★★ VHS: $14.99

To Be or Not to Be

(1983, 108 min, US, Alan Johnson) *Mel Brooks, Anne Bancroft, Tim Matheson, Charles Durning, Jose Ferrer.* Inferior, somewhat entertaining remake of the 1942 Ernst Lubitsch classic with Brooks (who wrote but did not direct) and Bancroft as the bickering thespian couple played by Jack Benny and Carole Lombard. The story is of a Polish theatre troupe who outwit the Nazis in Occupied Warsaw. Brooks adds a slightly misplaced but certainly well-intentioned update by introducing a gay character (who's swishy as hell) who also suffers under Nazi rule. ★★½ VHS: $9.99

To Catch a Killer

(1991, 95 min, Canada, Eric Till) *Brian Dennehy, Michael Riley, Margot Kidder.* The police investigation and arrest of serial killer John Wayne Gacy is the subject of this crime drama which has been edited from its original miniseries length. Rather than being cheap, sensationalistic exploitation, the film is actually quite suspenseful. Dennehy is believable as the demented Gacy, a stocky construction contractor who

was eventually sent to death row for kidnapping, sexually torturing and killing at least 33 teenage boys and then burying their bodies in the dirt basement of his Illinois home. Without the mystery of whodunit, the film instead focuses on the police's frantic efforts in tracking him down. Sad, creepy and riveting. ★★★ VHS: $14.99; DVD: $29.99

To Catch a Thief

(1955, 97 min, US, Alfred Hitchcock) *Cary Grant, Grace Kelly, Jesse Royce Landis, John Williams.* This fast-paced romantic thriller features glorious Rivera settings, sparkling comic touches and the sizzling sexual chemistry between Kelly and Grant. Grant plays a reformed jewel thief who may be up to his old tricks; Kelly may be his intended victim. ★★★ VHS: $14.99

To Die For

(1995, 100 min, US, Gus Van Sant) *Nicole Kidman, Matt Dillon, Joaquin Phoenix, Casey Affleck, Illeana Douglas, Dan Hedaya, Kurtwood Smith, George Segal.* Kidman offers a scintillating performance in this stylish and hilarious social satire that attacks America's media-obsession with razor-sharp precision. Kidman is a model of icy effervescence as Suzanne Stone, a small-town New Hampshire girl who is determined to make a name in television, at any cost. Working at the local cable station, she begins a video documentary about the wasted lives of three local teens, including a perfectly cast Pheonix as her unlikely paramour. When her husband (Dillon) begins making demands for marital bliss, Suzanne, determined to stay the course, enlists the youths to help rid her of her domestic distraction. Based in part on a real incident, Buck Henry's masterful script finds itself in good hands with Van Sant. Douglas is captivating in support as Dillon's sister, who also acts to some degree as the film's Greek chorus. ★★★½ VHS: $9.99; DVD: $27.99

To Each His Own

(1946, 122 min, US, Mitchell Leisen) *Olivia de Havilland, John Lund, Mary Anderson, Roland Culver.* De Havilland won the first of her two Oscars, giving a splendid portrayal of a small-town girl who bears a child out of wedlock, and is forced to give it up. She watches from afar as the boy grows from infancy to childhood to manhood. Leisen elevates this soap opera by offering sensitive direction which bypasses the usual melodramatic pitfalls; and de Havilland creates a three-dimensional character one can't help but care about. ★★★ VHS: $14.99

To Forget Venice

(1979, 110 min, Italy, Franco Brusati) *Mariangela Melato, Erland Josephson.* Brusati has fashioned a sensitive and refined story of a group of people (two gay men and two lesbians) who visit together at an old country estate. The film explores the important events of their past, their first sexual encounters and their worried looks to the future. A good film, but one in which many will debate the accuracy of the film's sexual politics (i.e., that one moment in each of their lives that made them gay). ★★★

Carole Lombard (c.) is not one to toy with in this scene from *To Be or Not to Be*

To Gillian on Her 37th Birthday

(1996, 93 min, US, Michael Pressman) *Michelle Pfeiffer, Peter Gallagher, Claire Danes, Kathy Baker.* Based on the off-Broadway play, this comedy-drama of a deceased wife returning from the grave has a certain charm to it but there's nothing special about the dialogue or the story line — *Ghost* and *Truly, Madly, Deeply* did it better. Gallagher gives an earnest performance as a professor and father who has yet to get over the two-year death of his wife. Looking glorious, Pfeiffer plays the ghost who returns to console and romp on the beach with her husband. As his family and friends start to think him mad, they gather for a weekend of memories and therapy. The film never ignites and takes off the way it should, despite some appealing performances. *Gillian* has laughs and tears, but this ghost story gets caught somewhere in limbo. ★★½ VHS: $14.99

To Have and Have Not

(1944, 101 min, US, Howard Hawks) *Humphrey Bogart, Lauren Bacall, Walter Brennan, Hoagy Carmichael.* This polished Hawks production is usually remembered more as the film in which Bogart and Bacall first met than for any artistic accomplishment, which is a disservice to its stars, director and writers. Bogie plays a hard-boiled American charter boat captain who becomes involved with French freedom fighters, Nazis and, of course, Bacall; who, among other things, teaches Bogie how to whistle. Brennan is terrific in support as their boozing compadre. ★★★½ VHS: $19.99

To Joy

(1950, 93 min, Sweden, Ingmar Bergman) *Britt Nilsson.* Taking its title from Beethoven's "Ode to Joy," *To Joy* marks Bergman's creative passage from films depicting the darkness of evil forces to films that celebrate the light of affirmation. This intensely moving, sensitive film focuses on the life of a talented violinist who must come to grips with the fact that his young wife was killed. Through despair and introspection, he discovers that his love for his son and for music gives him the strength to continue. ★★★

To Kill a Mockingbird

(1962, 131 min, US, Robert Mulligan) *Gregory Peck, Mary Badham, Philip Alford, Brock Peters, John Megna, Robert Duvall, Rosemary Murphy, Paul Fix, William Windom, Alice Ghostley; Narrated by: Kim Stanley.* Peck won an Oscar for his brilliant performance as Southern lawyer Atticus Finch in this brilliantly realized courtroom drama and memory piece. Based on the best-selling novel by Harper Lee, the film is seen through the eyes of Finch's young daughter, Scout (Badham), and recounts her days as a youth in 1930s Georgia as well as following her father's court case in which he defends a black man accused of rape. One of the greatest of all American films. (Letterboxed VHS available for $19.99) ★★★★ VHS: $14.99; DVD: $34.99

To Kill a Priest

(1989, 116 min, France, Agnieszka Holland) *Christopher Lambert, Ed Harris, Tim Roth, Joanne Whalley, Pete Postlethwaite.* This fictionalized account of an actual murder of a Polish priest stars Lambert as the martyred clergyman whose campaign for Solidarity disfavors him with the military authorities. Harris costars as a mid-level officer with the security police who engineers, and executes, the assassination plot. Exiled Polish director Holland finds great human drama in the priest's dedication to his beliefs, but unwisely concentrates more on the dilemma of the Communist officer, whose zeal for the good of the party contradicts his own moral being. (Filmed in English) ★★½ VHS: $79.99

To Live

(1994, 135 min, China, Zhang Yimou) *Gong Li, Ge You.* Though pulling at the heartstrings, this two-hour-plus melodrama about the harrowing journey of a Chinese family (from the end of the Nationalist reign to the Cultural Revolution) revels in its visual splendor and exceptional dramatics. Ge stars as a wealthy landlord who loses his entire estate gambling, only to be ironically spared the rod when the Reds crack down on their former oppressors. Gong plays his strong-spirited and, at times, estranged wife. Together, with their rambunctious son and deaf daughter, they wend their way through life, suffering all of the conceivable outrages that a country at war with itself

can throw their way. Not enough can possibly be said about the rapturous, easy-going performances of Ge and Gong. In the deft hands of director Zhang and with a masterful script by author Yu Hua, the two actors create characterizations that inexorably draw the viewer into the urgencies of their harrowed lives. (Mandarin with English subtitles) ★★★★ VHS: $19.99

To Live and Die in L.A.

(1985, 116 min, US, William Friedkin) *William Petersen, Willem Dafoe, Dean Stockwell, John Turturro.* Gritty, fast-paced police thriller with Petersen as a Secret Service agent who will stop at nothing to capture the counterfeiter who murdered his partner. Dafoe is a particularly villainous heavy. Made at the height of TV's "Miami Vice"'s popularity, director Friedkin gives this bloody cops and robbers tale a similar, slick look. ★★★

To Play or to Die

(1990, 50 min, The Netherlands, Frank Krom) *Geert Hunaerts, Tjebbo Gerritsma.* Filmed with unusual flair for a small independent film, this hyperventilating, psychosexual drama tells the story of a nerdish teenager's intense crush on a bullying but attractive classmate. With his parents away, 15-year-old Kees, fueled by a masochistic puppy love for the unresponsive and cruel Charel, finds his plans for seduction and revenge unraveling after he invites the other to his home. A simple premise, and while not at all homophobic, its theme of equating homosexual desire with madness and death is a sad, frustrating one, especially problematic coming from a promising gay filmmaker. (Dutch with English subtitles) ★★½ VHS: $29.99; DVD: $29.99

To See Paris and Die

(1993, 110 min, Russia, Alexander Proshkin) *Tatyana Vasilyeva, Dimitri Malikov, Ekaterina Semenova.* It's the Soviet Union in the 1960s, and what's a Jewish mother to do? For the widowed Elena, the only hope is escaping with her son to Paris by having him entered in a piano competition there. This is, of course, easier said than done, and forces Elena down a road of deceit and degradation. It's not hard to empathize with Elena's plight, and the drabness of everday Russian life is essayed extremely well, but *To See Paris and Die* lacks the dramatic tension that would allow the effect of the increasing humiliation to be greater than the sum of its parts. The inability for the film to find its emotional chord undermines its ability to disturb, enrage and provoke. (Russian with English subtitles) ★★ VHS: $79.99

To Sir, with Love

(1966, 105 min, GB, James Clavell) *Sidney Poitier, Lulu, Judy Geeson, Suzy Kendall.* Poitier plays an inexperienced schoolteacher, Mr. Thackeray, who's assigned a class of rowdy, headstrong and undisciplined Mods in London's East End. The students of the graduating class are determined to break Thackeray's will, but he surprises them all by giving the students respect while commanding and getting it from them. Poitier is excellent in this compelling and refreshing teacher-student drama, and he's supported by a fine group of young actors. Lulu sings the hit title song. ★★★½ VHS: $14.99; DVD: $24.99

To Sleep with Anger

(1990, 95 min, US, Charles Burnett) *Danny Glover, Sheryl Lee Ralph, Mary Alice, Carl Lumbly, Richard Brooks.* A chilling independent production by maverick director Burnett. Glover plays an "old family friend" from the South who arrives at the doorstep of an upwardly mobile black family and insinuates his way into their home, wreaking havoc on the family unit by preying on their individual weaknesses. Mixing myth, metaphor and an offbeat sense of humor, director Burnett shows that progress made over shakey ground is sometimes no progress at all. ★★★½ VHS: $14.99

To the Devil a Daughter

(1976, 95 min, GB, Peter Sykes) *Nastassja Kinski, Christopher Lee, Denholm Elliott, Richard Widmark.* The legendary Hammer Studios brought forth this satanic horror story about a defrocked priest (Lee) who earmarks Kinski for selection as the Devil's daughter on her 18th birthday. Kinski's distraught father (Elliott) enlists the aid of an expert occultist (Widmark) and the fun begins. A kinky adventure into the unknown. ★★½ VHS: $9.99

To the Lighthouse

(1985, 115 min, GB, Colin Gregg) *Rosemary Harris, Michael Gough, Kenneth Branaugh,.* Virginia Woolf's tale of family turmoil is set in a lush Cornwall resort at the outset of WWI where the towering lighthouse comes to symbolize the spirit of reconciliation and hope for the future. A touching drama. ★★★

To Wong Foo, Thanks for Everything! Julie Newmar

(1995, 108 min, US, Beeban Kidron) *Patrick Swayze, Wesley Snipes, John Leguizamo, Stockard Channing, Blythe Danner, Arliss Howard, Chris Penn, Jason London, Robin Williams, Quentin Crisp.* Destined to be forever referred to as the "American *Priscilla*," this bit of cross-dressing whimsy lacks that film's exhilaration and sharp character definition, but ultimately pleases with its good humor and spirited performances. Swayze and Snipes get in touch with their feminine side as they don sequins and high heels as two New York drag queens who win a preliminary drag contest and ride off towards Hollywood for the finals. Along for the ride is Latina spitfire Leguizamo. En route, they run afoul of the law, and are stranded in a small Midwestern town which provides most of the story. Though the gay characters are positively portrayed, they are virtually sexless fairy godmothers who neither love or have partners and who help the hapless heterosexuals with no fashion sense. This is so tame you can watch it with your mom. Leguizamo steals the show as the fiery Chi Chi. ★★★ VHS: $9.99

Tobruk

(1967, 110 min, US, Arthur Hiller) *Rock Hudson, George Peppard, Nigel Green, Guy Stockwell.* Routine WWII adventure with Rock and George out to destroy Rommel's fuel supply at the Mediterranean stronghold. ★★½ VHS: $9.99

The Todd Killings

(1971, 93 min, US, Barry Shear) *Robert F. Lyons, Richard Thomas, Barbara Bel Geddes, Ed Asner.* Lyons is a kill-for-thrills psycho in this tense and atmospheric drama. Based on real-life accounts, and pre-dating *River's Edge*, the film offers a look into the twisted mind of a killer who provides drugs and parties to a group of alienated teens who in turn protect him from the law. ★★★ VHS: $19.99

Der Todesking

(1989, 80 min, West Germany, Jörg Buttgereit) Bathtub suicide, castration, neighbors on a killing rampage, rotting corpses and Nazi torture are just some of the "highlights" in this angst-ridden splatter film. Espousing diatribes such as "the motiveless mass murderer is the martyrdom of post-modernism," this deliberately shocking low-budgeter features a series of segments about sad, lonely, frustrated people who decide to end it all, with the finale being a cinema verité murder rampage. (German with English subtitles) ★½

The Toilers and the Wayfarers

(1996, 75 min, US, Keith Froelich) *Matt Klemp, Andrew Woodhouse, Ralf Schirg, Joan Wheeler.* A tender coming out drama independently made in Minnesota, *The Toilers and the Wayfarers* is modest on budget (nicely shot in black and white) but compelling and highly original nonetheless. Sixteen-year-olds Phillip (Woodhouse) and Dieter (Klemp) are best friends; that is, until Phillip, in a moment of perceived closeness, reveals that he is gay. Dieter spurns his friend, unwilling to admit to himself that he is also gay. Phillip runs away to Minneapolis, eventually followed by Dieter. The film takes a less interesting turn there, where the two boys turn to prostitution to survive. Quietly ambitious in that director Froelich tries to connect the immigrant experience with being gay in America, the drama winningly succeeds despite its notch-below-professional acting and flimsy plot. ★★★ VHS: $49.99

Tokyo Decadence

(1991, 112 min, Japan, Ryu Murakami) *Sayoko Amano, Yayoi Kusama, Sayoko Maekawa, Hiroshi Mikami.* This controversial, fiercely original and visually shocking portrait of a young Japanese call girl's quest for ecstasy is adapted from director Murakami's novel "Topaz." Plunging headfirst into the steamy world of S&M, drugs and depravity, the story revolves around Ai, who as the film opens seeks beatitude through the advice of a fortune teller. While the film bathes the viewer in a sea of heroin abuse, cocaine snorting, floggings and humiliations, these uncomfortable images are necessary to show how the successful and powerful businessmen clients seek these bizarre pleasures to further quench their thirst for power. A darkly powerful film that's clearly not for all tastes, but a challenging experience for open-minded viewers. (Japanese with English subtitles) ★★★ VHS: $29.99; DVD: $24.99

Tokyo Drifter

(1966, 83 min, Japan, Seijun Suzuki) *Tetsuya Watari, Chieko Matsubara, Hideaki Nitani.* A deadpan but wildly visual and stylish gangster tale, *Tokyo Drifter* is an amalgam of '60s cinematic

excess and '30s crime drama. With a wigged-out production design and even some time-capsule pop tunes, the film follows a former wiseguy who's trying to go straight. But the new bosses just won't let him. This eventually puts him on the run, hiding out all over Japan. But this pop idol doesn't lie down easy, for no matter what the enemy dishes out he's always ready with fists blazing and a song on his lips. Yes, he's a night-club singer, too. Director Suzuki has a quiet camera but a quirky reverence for the genre. His tough guys may not always act tough — that's a tough act when crooning to your girlfriend — but they sure look cool doing what they do. (Japanese with English subtitles) ★★★ VHS: $29.99; DVD: $29.99

Tokyo-Ga

(1985, 92 min, West Germany/US, Wim Wenders) Wenders's engrossing and entertaining "filmed dairy" of his 1983 trip to Tokyo is both a fascinating glimpse of the city and a personal metaphysical search for meaning. At the start of the trip, Wenders aims to find the "pure" Japan that he knows and loves from the films of director Yasujiro Ozu. Instead of simplicity and order, however, Wenders becomes dazed by the kinetic energy of the city, as well as fascinated by the strange, and at times bizarre, lifestyles of the people. (Filmed in English) ★★★

Tokyo Olympiad

(1964, 170 min, Japan, Kon Ichikawa) This documentary of the 1964 Summer Olympics held in Japan makes for an extraordinary celebration of the human form. Utilizing over 160 cameramen, filming in Cinemascope and intercutting slow-motion and other special effects, Ichikawa captures the visual spendor of the Olympics to produce possibly the finest photographed film of athletic endeavor. Not interested in the glorification of man, as was Leni Riefenstahl's *Olympia*, Ichikawa instead focuses more on competition and the individual efforts of the athletes. When told that the Japanese committee which commissioned the work suggested reshooting, Ichikawa said, "I had to tell them that the entire cast had already left Japan." This video, the rarely seen original director's cut, will enthrall both sports fans and non-fans alike. (Letterboxed) ★★★½ VHS: $79.99

Tokyo Story

(1953, 134 min, Japan, Yasujiro Ozu) *Chishu Ryu, Chieko Higashiyama.* Ozu's quietly overpowering masterpiece is a deceptively simple tale about an elderly couple's visit to Tokyo and the less than enthusiastic reception they receive from their children. A master with the camera and with subtlety of statement, Ozu deftly and powerfully creates this vision of alienation in the modern world as the "new" Japan forced the traditional values out. A true masterpiece of world cinema. (Japanese with English subtitles) ★★★★ VHS: $19.99

Tol'able David

(1921, 91 min, US, Henry King) *Richard Barthelmess, Ernest Torrence, Gladys Hulette.* Director King was raised in the backwoods of Virginia and returned there to shoot on real locations for this production. Barthelmess plays a young man — at first thought to be a coward

Tokyo Story

— whose fate forces him to take on three of the foulest villains ever to be captured on film (they even kill his dog!). But it is the bucolic atmosphere that has made this the classic it is, preserved here with the love and care expected from a Kino release. King discusses the making of the film in a 16-minute interview shot on video just before his death. ★★★½ VHS: $24.99; DVD: $29.99

The Toll Gate

(1920, 73 min, US, Lambert Hillyer) *William S. Hart, Joseph Singleton, Anna Q. Nilsson.* Unfairly forgotten now, Hart was the Clint Eastwood of his day: stoic, silent, distant, with as much bad in him as good. Here he plays train robber Black Deering, betrayed by one of his own men, forced to flee into the unforgiving desert and into the arms of a forgiving widow. His redemption doesn't last long. Tranferred from an original tinted and tone print, the film exhibits some of its age in the last reel that will not affect the enjoyment of one of Hart's best films. ★★★ VHS: $24.99; DVD: $24.99

Tom and Huck

(1995, 93 min, US, Peter Hewitt) *Jonathan Taylor Thomas, Brad Renfro, Eric Schweig, Charles Rocket, Amy Wright.* A routine and almost lifeless adaptation of Mark Twain's "Tom Sawyer." Thomas plays Sawyer, a spunky, mischievous orphan being raised by his aunt. The story concentrates on his friendship with Huck Finn (Renfro), and their dilemma when they witness a murder and the wrong man is accused. The film is surprisingly tame, offers few misadventures, and has in Huck an angst-ridden 20th-century juvenile delinquent rather than a 19th-century youth bent on tomfoolery. Thomas is successful, at least, in bringing more of an innocence and playfulness to Tom Sawyer. ★★ VHS: $14.99

Tom & Viv

(1994, 125 min, GB, Brian Gilbert) *Willem Dafoe, Miranda Richardson, Rosemary Harris, Tim Dutton.* Madness and passion are equally matched in this unsettling though beautifully filmed examination of the love affair, marriage and separation of writer T.S. Eliot and his wife, Vivienne. Dafoe plays the American author who seems more at home in the reserved setting of the British upper crust. Richardson, in a mesmerizing, go-for-broke Oscar-nominated performance, is the aristocrat whose high-spiritedness seems the perfect tonic for the somber writer. They marry, and

Eliot begins to achieve success in the field of poetry with his wife aiding him spiritually and editorially. However, as Eliot's star ascends, it soon becomes apparent that his wife is suffering from some sort of mental instability, which begins to threaten both their relationship and his career. As Viv's socially conscious but loving mother, Harris is excellent. ★★★ VHS: $19.99

Tom, Dick and Harry

(1941, 86 min, US, Garson Kanin) *Ginger Rogers, George Murphy, Alan Marshall, Burgess Meredith.* Rogers sparkles in this delightful comedy with Ginger daydreaming about her three boyfriends, having to choose between them. ★★★ VHS: $19.99

Tom Jones

(1963, 129 min, GB, Tony Richardson) *Albert Finney, Susannah York, Hugh Griffith, Joyce Redman, Edith Evans, Diane Cilento.* This Academy Award Winner for Best Picture and Director richly evokes the tenor of its times — both of the setting of the novel and of the era when it was filmed. Richardson uses every cinematic trick in the book — fast motion, jump cuts, rapid editing, etc. — to capture the joie de vivre of Henry Fielding's bawdy tale of a young rake's randy adventures in 18th-century England. Finney is brilliant in the lead role, and his seduction of Redman in the classic meal eating scene will make a gourmand out of the most abstemious. ★★★★ VHS: $14.99; DVD: $19.99

tom thumb

(1958, 98 min, GB, George Pal) *Russ Tamblyn, Peter Sellers, Terry-Thomas.* Winning an Oscar for Best Special Effects, this musical based on the children's fairy tale proves true the adage that good things come in small packages. "Fun for the entire family" might be a worn epithet, but this movie certainly warrants its use. Kids will enjoy the animated performance of Tamblyn as he cavorts in the role of the diminutive hero. Animated also applies to Tom's toy friends, puppets brought to life by "Puppettoon" master Pal. Adults will particularly appreciate the antics of Terry-Thomas and Sellers, perfectly cast as greedy, bumbling antagonists. ★★★½ VHS: $14.99; DVD: $24.99

Tombstone

(1993, 132 min, US, George P. Cosmatos) *Kurt Russell, Val Kilmer, Michael Biehn, Jason Priestley, Bill Paxton, Billy Zane, Charlton Heston, Sam Elliott.* Slightly overlong and overly ambitious, *Tombstone* is an invigorating, extremely photogenic tale of legendary lawman Wyatt Earp's tenure in the shoot-'em-up town of Tombstone, Arizona. Russell is Wyatt, who has retired from peacekeeping and is ready to settle down. However, a notorious gang known as The Cowboys stands in his way. Of course, the film chronicles the famous gunfight at the O.K. Corral (an efficient and exciting sequence), and strives to explore Earp's personal life, as well. Russell is surrounded by an impressive gallery of supporting players; the best being Kilmer who gives an acerbic interpretation of the sickly Doc Holliday. ★★★ VHS: $14.99; DVD: $29.99

Tommy

(1975, 110 min, GB, Ken Russell) *Roger Daltrey, Ann-Margret, Oliver Reed, Elton John, Tina Turner,*

Eric Clapton, Jack Nicholson. The Who's rock opera stars Daltrey as the "deaf, dumb and blind boy" who becomes a pinball wizard and New Messiah. John is the dethroned champ, Clapton is the preacher and Turner is the electrifying acid queen. Ann-Margret received an Oscar nomination for her fiery portrayal of Tommy's mum. Directed by Russell with his usual flair for the bizarre. ★★★ DVD: $24.99

Tommy Boy

(1995, 96 min, US, Peter Segal) *Chris Farley, David Spade, Brian Dennehy, Bo Derek, Rob Lowe, Dan Aykroyd, Julie Warner.* Tommy Boy, about the moronic son of a multimillionaire, is unexpectedly funny. Farley stars as the title character, a recent college grad (with a D+ average) who returns home to work for his father's automotive company. When his father dies, Tommy must not only prove himself able to take control of the company, but to save it from closing, as well. *Tommy Boy* is peppered with lots of amusing physical schtick, and Farley and co-hort Spade (as Tommy's acerbic assistant) make an effective comedy team. They're no Hope and Crosby, but their work is infectiously appealing. *Tommy Boy* may not be at the head of the class, but of all the "dumb" movies so far, it's one of the smartest. ★★½ VHS: $14.99; DVD: $24.99

Tomorrow

(1972, 103 min, US, Joseph Anthony) *Robert Duvall, Olga Bellin.* A startlingly good adaptation of William Faulkner's story, featuring Duvall in a tremendous performance as a workman who befriends and falls in love with a pregnant woman (Bellin) deserted by her husband and family. Horton Foote (*The Trip to Bountiful*) wrote the screenplay. ★★★ VHS: $14.99

Tomorrow Is Forever

(1946, 104 min, US, Irving Pichel) *Claudette Colbert, Orson Welles, George Brent, Natalie Wood.* A sumptuous, moving version of "Enoch Arden," featuring a great performance by Welles and a lovely portrayal by Colbert. Colbert plays a wife whose husband (Welles) dies at the end of WWI. At least that's what she thinks. She gives birth to his son, and later marries her boss. Twenty years later, her first husband, crippled and having spent those years under a new identity living in Vienna, returns to America to work for her new husband. When he meets her and the son he never knew he had, he is faced with the dilemma of whether or not to reveal his identity to them. ★★★ VHS: $19.99

Tomorrow Never Dies

(1997, 119 min, GB, Roger Spottiswoode) *Pierce Brosnan, Jonathan Pryce, Michelle Yeoh, Teri Hatcher, Judi Dench, Desmond Llewelyn.* Non-stop action sequences and campy, half-hearted one-liners are poor substitutes for the once excellent plotting and scripting of the earlier James Bond entries, but Brosnan makes a go of it in this, the most action-packed 007 film to date. This time out, our hero must stop an egomaniacal media mogul named Carver (not Turner) — played with gusto by Pryce — who's out to start a war between Great Britain and China: to boost ratings! Yeoh is on hand as Bond's eventual sidekick (though she kicks more ass than side), and Hatcher turns up as a former

T

"Bondquest" now married to Carver. But the true stars of the film are, of course, the stuntmen — and that spectacular remote control BMW (the centerpiece of possibly the best scene in the entire film). (Sequel: *The World Is Not Enough*) ★★½ VHS: $14.99; DVD: $34.99

Tomorrow the World

(1944, 86 min, US, Leslie Fenton) *Fredric March, Betty Field, Agnes Moorehead, Skippy Homeier.* In this powerfully moving film adaptation of the award-winning Broadway play, a German youth, raised by the Nazi indoctrine, is sent to live with his American uncle (March) during the war. His new family struggles with the boy's intolerance and trying to undo the Nazi influence. ★★★½ VHS: $19.99; DVD: $24.99

Tongues Untied

(1989, 56 min, US, Marlon Riggs) This highly acclaimed film combines poetry, personal testimony, rap and performance to describe the homophobia and racism that confronts gay African-Americans. A personal and at times angry documentary that is an impassioned cry to speak out about black gay lives, the film garnered surprising controversy when some PBS stations — disturbed by its subject matter — refused to broadcast it. Two of the more memorable lines state: "Black men loving black men is *the* revolutionary act"; and "If in America a black is the lowest of the low, what is a gay black?" ★★★ VHS: $29.99

Toni

(1935, 90 min, France, Jean Renoir) *Charles Blavette, Jenny Helia.* In an attempt at film realism, Renoir left the confines of the studio and soundstage and brought the action to the outdoors. His actors do not wear makeup, a more "natural" style of acting is used and Renoir places his camera at a distance in order for the characters and action to tell the story with the camera merely recording. The result is a wonderfully told tale of the loves and lives of four Italian immigrant miners who settle around Marseilles. (French with English subtitles) ★★★

Tonight and Every Night

(1945, 92 min, US, Victor Saville) *Rita Hayworth, Lee Bowman, Janet Blair.* Pleasant Hayworth musical about the wartime adventures — romantic and otherwise — of a group of showgirls working in London during the blitz. Rita romances RAF pilot Bowman, and must decide between love and duty when he is shipped abroad. ★★★ VHS: $19.99

Tonio Kröger

(1964, 90 min, West Germany/France, Rolf Thiele) *Jean-Claude Brialy, Nadja Tiller, Gert Frobe.* Thomas Mann's autobiographical novella is faithfully brought to the screen in this dreamlike story of the problems encountered by a youth growing up in late 19th-century Germany. Born of a Prussian businessman and a fiery Italian woman, our hero struggles with whether he wants to belong to the bourgeois world or explore his artistic talents. This conflict between restraint and passion forces him to decide what world and lifestyle is best suited for him. (German with English subtitles) ★★

Too Beautiful for You

(1989, 91 min, France, Bertrand Blier) *Gérard Depardieu, Josiane Balasko, Carole Bouquet.* Depardieu stars as a wealthy businessman who has just about everything one could desire, including a dazzlingly beautiful wife (Bouquet). But when he meets his new secretary, Colette, a frumpy and slightly overweight middle-aged woman, and falls deeply and passionately in love with her, he finds his material values seriously imperiled. Director Blier has taken the basic premise of farce and turned it upside down; and while the film has a gentle comic flavor throughout, it is also a serious examination of the misplaced value given to beauty. Depardieu is excellent as always and Balasko is a treat as the broodingly seductive Colette. (French with English subtitles) ★★★ VHS: $19.99

Too Hot to Handle

(1938, 105 min, US, Jack Conway) *Clark Gable, Myrna Loy, Walter Pidgeon.* A fast-paced and extremely entertaining comedy with Gable in a particularly light though as a newsreel journalist who courts aviatrix Loy from rival reporter Pidgeon. Gable and Loy, appearing together for the seventh time, are well matched in this alternately funny and action-flavored romp. Highly recommended, and a near-must for students of 1930s comedies. ★★★½ VHS: $19.99

Too Late the Hero

(1969, 133 min, GB, Robert Aldrich) *Michael Caine, Cliff Robertson, Henry Fonda, Ian Bannen, Harry Andrews, Denholm Elliott, Ken Takakura.* Caine and Robertson are British and American officers in charge of a suicide mission to distract the Japanese on a small Pacific island. The two must come to grips with their cultural differences as they engage in a battle of wits with the local Japanese commander. ★★★ VHS: $14.99

Too Many Girls

(1940, 85 min, US, George Abbott) *Lucille Ball, Eddie Bracken, Ann Miller, Desi Arnaz.* One of Ball's earliest starring roles, and the sassy redhead makes the most of it. A most engaging musical comedy, the story follows the romantic adventures of college students Lucy and Bracken, Miller and Arnaz (this is where they met). ★★★

Too Much Sun

(1990, 97 min, US, Robert Downey) *Eric Idle, Andrea Martin, Robert Downey, Jr., Ralph Macchio.* Two pampered children of a Beverly Hills millionaire learn they will lose their deceased father's $200 million fortune unless one of them produces an heir. The problem? Sonny (Idle) is gay and Bitsy (Martin) is a lesbian. The ensuing game of sexual musical chairs is further complicated by the arrival of a pair of two-bit hustlers (Downey, Macchio), who are willing to be adopted, for the right price. From the director of *Putney Swope*. ★★½ VHS: $89.99

Too Pretty to Be Honest

(1982, 95 min, France, Richard Balducci) *Jane Birkin, Bernadette LaFont.* Four very pretty girls who share an apartment on the French Riviera witness a bank robbery on a day trip to Nice. The next day, looking through a telescope, they see the man who might be the thief so, thinking that stealing from a thief is not really stealing,

they plot an elaborate scheme to lift the money. (French with English subtitles) ★★½

Too Shy to Try

(1978, 89 min, France, Pierre Richard) *Pierre Richard, Aldo Maccione.* Richard directed and stars in this comedy about a bungling man who falls in love with a beautiful and sophisticated young woman. Unable to simply introduce himself to the young lady, our hero instead enrolls in a correspondence course in a valiant attempt to become the Casanova of his dreams. Don't expect Renoir, but fans of Richard (*Les Comperes, Tall Blond Man...*) will be entertained in this romantic comedy. (French with English subtitles) ★★½

Too Young to Die

(1990, 100 min, US, Robert Markowitz) *Juliette Lewis, Brad Pitt, Michael Tucker, Alan Fudge, Emily Longstreth, Michael O'Keefe.* Pitt and Lewis pay a low-budget visit to *Natural Born Killers* territory with this made-for-TV movie. In The-Middle-of-Nowhere, Oklahoma, 14-year-old Amanda (Lewis) marries to escape a sexually abusive stepfather and an uncaring mother. The marriage disintegrates and Amanda is abandoned. She hits the road and is appropriated by Pitt, who delivers a dress rehearsal for his *Kalifornia* role. *Too Young to Die*'s somewhat plodding exposition is enhanced by competent performances, especially from Lewis as the tragic teen. Worth checking out if only to compare Lewis and Pitt with their more recent work. ★★½ VHS: $9.99

Tootsie

(1982, 110 min, US, Sydney Pollack) *Dustin Hoffman, Jessica Lange, Teri Garr, Dabney Coleman, Bill Murray, Sydney Pollack, Charles Durning, George Gaynes, Geena Davis, Lynne Thigpen.* Hoffman legitimizes transvestism in this glorious comedy and slyly stirring social criticism. Donning women's garb to propel his acting career, Dustin becomes the queen of the daytime soaps and the thwarted victim of his attraction to a female costar (Academy Award winner Lange). The film features great dialogue and a sparkling supporting cast. ★★★★ VHS: $14.99; DVD: $24.99

Top Gun

(1986, 94 min, US, Tony Scott) *Tom Cruise, Kelly McGillis, Val Kilmer, Anthony Edwards, Tom Skerritt, Meg Ryan, Tim Robbins.* Military jingoism, fine aerial photography, inane dramatics and young Cruise combined to make this one of the big box-office hits of the 1980s. Story follows hotshot Navy pilot Cruise and his affair with instructor/astrophysicist (yeah, right) McGillis. (VHS available letterboxed or pan & scan) ★★ VHS: $14.99; DVD: $29.99

Top Hat

(1935, 99 min, US, Mark Sandrich) *Fred Astaire, Ginger Rogers, Edward Everet Horton, Helen Broderick, Eric Blore.* Commonly called the quintessential Astaire-Rogers musical, *Top Hat* is a breathless combination of glorious music, marvelous dance routines which seem to float on air, captivating and sometimes silly comedy, and a cast of characters anyone would want to invite to their next soirée. The film's contrivance of a plot centers on dancer Fred falling for model Ginger (if it works once, use it again). But

Tora! Tora! Tora!

through a case of mistaken identity, she thinks he's married, and to a society friend she's about to meet. Horton is just perfect as Astaire's best friend, the one who Rogers thinks is Fred. The score is one of their best, and includes "Cheek to Cheek," "Isn't This a Lovely Day to Be Caught in the Rain" and the title tune. The dancing is pure magic. ★★★★ VHS: $14.99

Top Secret!
(1984, 90 min, US, Jim Abrahams, David & Jerry Zucker) *Val Kilmer, Lucy Gutteridge, Omar Sharif.* From the team that brought us *Airplane!* and *The Naked Gun* comes this funny spoof of the espionage-thriller genre. Kilmer stars as an Elvis-like pop stars who travels to East Germany on a goodwill tour and gets wrapped up in the local intrigue. As in their other films, the ZAZ team whips up a relentless barrage of sight gags, pratfalls and one-liners, some of which miss their mark; but there are so many direct hits that the laughter never ceases. This is good, stupid, silly fun at its best. ★★★ VHS: $14.99

Topaz
(1969, 143 min, US, Alfred Hitchcock) *John Forsythe, Frederick Stafford, Philippe Noiret.* When American agent Forsythe and French counterpart Stafford uncover Russian infiltration in Cuba, a whirlwind chain of events whisks them around the globe and deep into high intrigue. Though the complex screenplay is occasionally baffling, Hitchcock sustains a tension throughout. (Director's cut) ★★★ VHS: $14.99; DVD: $29.99

Topaze
(1933, 78 min, US, Harry D'Arrast) *John Barrymore, Myrna Loy.* Barrymore gives a sterling performance in this charming comedy based on Marcel Pagnol's play. Barrymore plays a naïve college professor who is unknowingly exploited by a shady businessman — or is he? ★★★ VHS: $39.99

Topaze
(1933, 95 min, France, Louis Gasnier) *Louis Jouvet, Edwige Feuillere.* Based on the Marcel Pagnol play, this comedy of morals was a popular success on its initial release although Pagnol was disappointed with it and remade

the film, directing it himself in 1936 and again in 1951. Interestingly, it is this version that has survived the test of time. Topaze (Jouvet), a naïve and scrupulously honest provincial schoolteacher, is unwittingly lured into a phony business scheme with a disreputable financier. About to take the fall, our hero soon realizes that doing the right thing is not always the wisest course and soon develops his own plot to not only swindle the swindler, but to have his mistress as well. (French with English subtitles) ★★★½ VHS: $59.99

Topkapi
(1964, 120 min, US, Jules Dassin) *Maximilian Schell, Melina Mercouri, Peter Ustinov, Robert Morley.* Dassin's often imitated gem of a movie about a gang of jewel thieves who plan an elaborate heist of the emerald encrusted dagger at the Topkapi Palace in Istanbul. Schell and Mercouri star, but it was Ustinov who grabbed the Oscar for Best Supporting Actor with his inspired portrayal of their lackey. ★★★★ VHS: $14.99

El Topo
(1971, 124 min, Mexico, Alexandro Jodorowsky) *Alexandro Jodorowsky.* This religious allegory, which has taken on mythical cult proportions, is imbued with cryptic symbolism and graphically detailed violence. The story follows El Topo (Jodorowsky), who — with his seven-year-old son in tow — sets out on a bloody odyssey through an 1800s western frontier desert seeking revenge and religious fulfillment. Filled with Fellini-esque characters and biblical references, this eclectic "hippie western" seems a bit ridiculous today as compared to the early '70s when it was enthusiastically received; but through its powerful imagery and other-worldliness, *El Topo* still retains a strange power and beauty. ★★★

Topper
(1937, 97 min, US, Norman Z. McLeod) *Cary Grant, Constance Bennett, Roland Young, Billie Burke.* This delightful ghost comedy stars Grant and Bennett as the Kirbys, who are accidentally killed in a car crash and return as spirits to haunt the ordered life of their banker, Cosmo Topper. Young gives a remarkably funny per-

formance as the harried Topper, and Burke is perfect as Topper's rather scatterbrained, but lovable wife. (Followed by 2 sequels) ★★★½

Topper Returns
(1941, 88 min, US, Roy Del Ruth) *Roland Young, Joan Blondell, Billie Burke, Eddie Anderson.* More hilarity with Cosmo Topper and friends. Young repeats his role for a third time as the timid banker, who here befriends ghostly Blondell, helping her solve her own murder. The wonderful Burke also returns as Mrs. Topper. Though the original has more style, here the laughs are nonstop. ★★★½; DVD: $19.99

Topsy-Turvy
(1999, 160 min, GB, Mike Leigh) *Jim Broadbent, Allan Corduner, Ron Cook, Lesley Manville, Timothy Spall, Alison Steadman.* Leigh turns his sights from the ordinary lives of contemporary Brits and sets them towards those of two of England's most celebrated 19th-century composers, Gilbert & Sullivan. In this magical, captivating musical, Leigh explores the genesis behind the duo's most famous work, "The Mikado." Great sets and costumes underscore some marvelous musical sequences of the opera, and backstage politics haven't been this satisfying since *All about Eve.* An intelligent, elegant musical biography that's a joy to watch. And you don't have to know a stitch about opera to enjoy. ★★★★ VHS: $14.99; DVD: $19.99

Tora! Tora! Tora!
(1970, 143 min, US/Japan, Richard Fleischer, Toshio Masuda & Kinji Fukasuku) *Jason Robards, Joseph Cotten, Tatsuya Mihashi, Martin Balsam, James Whitmore.* This expensive war drama is an impeccably produced re-creation of the bombing of Pearl Harbor, and the events which led to the devastating action which thrust America into WWII. More successful than the high-profile 2001 release *Pearl Harbor.* (Letterboxed VHS available for $19.99) ★★★ VHS: $14.99; DVD: $24.99

Torch Song
(1953, 91 min, US, Charles Walters) *Joan Crawford, Michael Wilding, Marjorie Rambeau, Gig Young.* Music-filled melodrama about a domineering star (Crawford) who finds love and learns humility in the arms of a blind pianist (Wilding). Rambeau received an Oscar-nomination as Crawford's mother. ★★★

Torch Song Trilogy
(1988, 117 min, US, Paul Bogart) *Harvey Fierstein, Matthew Broderick, Anne Bancroft, Brian Kerwin, Karen Young, Charles Pierce.* Fierstein's breakthrough Tony Award-winning play (which ran almost four hours on the stage) about the life and loves of the most lovable drag queen in Brooklyn reaches the screen at half the running time but with most of the play's warm humor and acute insights intact. Fierstein, in a partly autobiographical role, is both touching and hilarious as Arnold Beckoff, whose life is presented in three non-episodic acts which examine his relationships with his bisexual boyfriend (Kerwin), gay lover (Broderick), and mother (Bancroft). ★★★ VHS: $19.99

Torment

(1944, 105 min, Sweden, Alf Sjoberg) *Mai Zetterling, Stig Jarrel.* Bergman's first screenplay explores the themes recurrent throughout his film career: sexual conflict, moral dilemma and the vulnerable nature of love. This gritty drama follows the love triangle between a young college student, a sadistic teacher and the girl with whom both are involved. (Swedish with English subtitles) ★★★ VHS: $29.99

Torn Apart

(1989, 96 min, Israel, Jack Fisher) *Adrian Pasdar, Cecilia Peck.* The Romeo and Juliet story is given a new, Israeli slant in this well-intentioned story of a Jew who falls in love with an Arab. A young man, after spending six years in the United States, returns to Israel to enlist in the army and is soon reunited with his childhood friend, a lovely Arab woman. Their relationship sparks the reactions one would expect from their two families. A warm, humanist drama with convincing, heartfelt performances from the young leads. (Hebrew with English subtitles) ★★★

Torn Curtain

(1966, 128 min, US, Alfred Hitchcock) *Paul Newman, Julie Andrews, Lila Kedrova.* Renowned for a brutally protracted murder sequence, this tale of Cold War espionage features Newman as an atomic scientist charading as a defector in order to gain access to information on a valuable formula. An efficient thriller from Hitchcock. ★★★ VHS: $14.99; DVD: $29.99

Torrents of Spring

(1990, 102 min, France/Italy/GB, Jerzy Skolimowski) *Nastassja Kinski, Timothy Hutton.* Kinski rivals Rutger Hauer in starring in the greatest number of really bad foreign films but whose charisma and sheer force of personality gives her fans the strength to wade through the seemingly interminable cinematic muck. This tepid costume drama of burning passions is adapted from Ivan Turgenev's novel. Kinski stars as a wealthy married temptress who playfully teases a young aristocrat (Hutton) torn between his love for two women. Beautifully shot, the film goes nowhere and the only memorable moments occur when listening to Hutton's atrocious accent and stilted dialogue. ★ VHS: $9.99

Torso

(1973, 92 min, Italy, Sergio Martino) *Suzy Kendall, Tina Aumont, Luc Merenda, John Richardson.* A series of grisly murders prompts a group of comely damsels to leave the city and take refuge in a secluded rural villa. But then, the murders continue at the new locale unabated. Unapologetically sleazy, the gory *Torso* is imaginatively directed and (despite typically weak dubbing) not badly acted. Not nearly as stylish or memorable as the best "giallos" (Italian thrillers) of the period, *Torso* is still a decent entry in the genre. Filled with rampant nudity, sex and violence, this is definitely a product of its era; it's also a surprisingly entertaining and suspenseful (especially the last twenty minutes or so) shocker. (Director's cut) (Letterboxed) ★★★ VHS: $14.99; DVD: $29.99

Tortilla Flat

(1942, 105 min, US, Victor Fleming) *Spencer Tracy, Hedy Lamarr, John Garfield, Frank Morgan, Akim Tamiroff.* Morgan's fearless portrayal of an eccentric dog lover highlights this moving screen adaptation of John Steinbeck's novel of life on the wrong side of the tracks. Tracy and Garfield are down-on-their-luck buddies who drift their way into a small California town and fall for the same woman (Lamarr at her best) while setting up a scam on Morgan. ★★★ VHS: $19.99

The Torture Chamber of Baron Blood

(1972, 90 min, Italy, Mario Bava) *Joseph Cotten, Elke Sommer.* Intriguing set design and unusual lighting effects highlight this story of a young man who inadvertently brings back to life the vengeful corpse of his bloodthirsty, sadistic ancestor. (aka: *Baron Blood*) ★★

The Torture Chamber of Dr. Sadism

(1967, 90 min, West Germany, Harald Reinl) *Christopher Lee, Karin Dor.* Effective bit of Grand Guignol finds Lee dismembered for killing 12 virgins. But 40 years later, when his ever-faithful batman puts him back together, Chris is out to party with virgin #13. (aka: *Blood Demon* and *Castle of the Walking Dead*) ★★½ VHS: $19.99

Tosca's Kiss

(1985, 87 min, Switzerland, Daniel Schmid) The setting for this affectionate and moving documentary is Casa Verdi, a home for retired opera singers established by Guiseppi Verdi at the turn of the century. The focus is on the aging but still vibrant habitués who shamelessly preen, argue and perform for the viewer. (Italian with English subtitles) ★★★ VHS: $39.99

Total Eclipse

(1995, 111 min, GB/France, Agnieszka Holland) *David Thewlis, Leonardo DiCaprio, Romane Bohringer.* A laughably bad melodrama about the love affair of 19th-century poets Arthur Rimbaud and Verlaine. While delivering on the promise of an unblinking depiction of gay love, this fails in just about every other aspect. *Total Eclipse* proves that gay-themed films can be just as bad as straight romantic dramas. The story is set in France where 16-year-old Rimbaud (DiCaprio), teen rebel and poet, arrives in Paris to cooly make his mark on the world. His first order of business is to snag himself a sugar daddy — enter Verlaine (Thewlis), a 30ish sniveling, disagreeable man who harbors the triple demons of greed, pretension and ambition. Sexual energy and narcissistic attraction fuel their ultimately tragic love-hate relationship. DiCaprio's portrayal is simply one of a sugar-cereal propelled, California teenager. ★ VHS: $19.99; DVD: $24.99

Total Recall

(1990, 109 min, US, Paul Verhoeven) *Arnold Schwarzenegger, Rachel Ticotin, Sharon Stone, Ronny Cox, Michael Ironside.* The elements of this production are a clear recipe for success: Dutch helmer Verhoeven directing Arnold in a space sci-fi adventure based on a story by Phillip K. Dick (whose "Do Androids Dream of Electric Sheep?" inspired *Blade Runner*). The film's only flaw might be a few unpolished scenes and its more-than-too-much gratuitous violence. Beyond that, Verhoeven and Schwarzenegger romp through this high-speed, action-packed fugitive-on-the-run tale with a tongue-in-cheek and very playful glee. (Letterboxed VHS available for $14.99) (Sequel: *Total Recall 2070*) ★★★ VHS: $9.99; DVD: $19.99

Totally F***ed Up

(1994, 85 min, US, Gregg Araki) *James Duval, Roko Belic, Susan Behshid, Jenee Gill, Gilbert Luna, Craig Gilmore.* Araki's angry, entertaining and provocative "homomovie" follows the lives, loves and fucked-up misadventures of 6 teens (4 gays and 2 lesbians) whose friendship provide a '90s-style family unit. A successful combination of queer teen angst, homophobia, gay-bashing, AIDS and suicide. A witty, energetic and subversive drama. ★★★ VHS: $29.99

Toto the Hero (Toto le Heros)

(1991, 90 min, Belgium, Jaco Van Dormael) *Michel Bouquet, Jo De Backer.* Stylistically inventive and delightfully off-kilter, this bittersweet tale of the joys and traumas of childhood makes for a captivating and entertaining film. Thomas is a boy absorbed in a fantasy world of secret agents and flights of adventure all in an attempt to reject his life as an ordinary boy from middle-class parents. He is also convinced that he was switched at birth with Alfred, his rich neighbor's son. That idea, carried through to old age, becomes an obsession and obstacle to growth as Alfred becomes his lifelong nemesis — a symbol of everything he is not. The film intercuts scenes from the boy's childhood with his life as a young man as well as the present, where Thomas, now an old man in a retirement home, decides to finally come to grips with his failures and lost dreams. A hard-edged comedy which captures the seemingly insignificant moments of childhood and their lasting, debilitating effect. (French with English subtitles) ★★★★ VHS: $79.99

Touch

(1997, 97 min, US, Paul Schrader) *Bridget Fonda, Skeet Ulrich, Christopher Walken, Tom Arnold, Gina Gershon, Lolita Davidovitch, Janeane Garofalo.* This unfocused adaptation of Elmore Leonard's novel is never sarcastic enough to be full-fledged satire, or serious enough to make much of an impact. Schrader, who wrote and directed, does not always know what to do with the story's strange characters. *Touch* seems to delight in poking fun at easy targets such as an airhead talk show hostess (Gershon), or an extremist religious group leader (Arnold). However, the film has considerably more trouble sustaining interest in its main character, Juvenal (Ulrich), a faith healer who is worshipped by just about everyone. *Touch* also suffers from choppy pacing and bad editing — as many scenes ring true as fall flat. ★★ VHS: $6.99

The Touch

(1971, 112 min, Sweden, Ingmar Bergman) *Bibi Andersson, Max von Sydow, Elliott Gould.* Bergman's first English-language film certainly does not rank as one of the master's greatest works, but this sensitive and subtle story of a love triangle does have its moments. Andersson plays a "happily married" woman who, although settled and secure with doctor/husband von Sydow, is lured into an affair with volatile but magnetic archaeologist Gould. The human drama of the three, as they attempt to understand their actions and each other, makes this an interesting work. ★★½

A Touch of Class

(1972, 105 min, GB, Melvin Frank) *Glenda Jackson, George Segal, Paul Sorvino.* Jackson won her second Oscar as the vivacious Alessio, a Londoner in the "rag trade" who falls in love with an American businessman (Segal) who has a wife on the side. The dynamic chemistry between the two leads propels this witty, romantic and touching account of a brief love affair. ★★★½

Touch of Evil

(1958, 108 min, US, Orson Welles) *Charlton Heston, Orson Welles, Janet Leigh, Akim Tamiroff, Marlene Dietrich.* Cinema's legendary bad boy, Welles, directed and stars in this brooding, stylistic tour de force as a police inspector embroiled in a case on the Mexican border. A masterful exposé on moral decay, smothered in Gothic expressionism and tawdry urban landscapes. (Director's cut) ★★★★ VHS: $19.99; DVD: $29.99

Tough Guys

(1986, 104 min, US, Jeff Kanew) *Burt Lancaster, Kirk Douglas, Dana Carvey, Charles Durning, Eli Wallach.* Lancaster and Douglas teamed a fifth time for this disappointing comedy which is not worthy of its two stars. The two screen legends play ex-cons, released after 30 years in prison, who find difficulty in adjusting to the 1980s lifestyle. ★★

Tough Guys Don't Dance

(1987, 110 min, US, Norman Mailer) *Ryan O'Neal, Isabella Rossellini, Wings Hauser, Lawrence Tierney.* Confusing murder mystery written and directed by Mailer (from his own novel) about a writer (O'Neal) accused of murder, forced to clear his name. A real curiosity, with director Mailer echoing the atmosphere of the film noir gems of long ago, but hampered by some cheesy dialogue and bizarre plot contrivances. ★★ VHS: $14.99

Toute Une Nuit

(1982, 90 min, Belgium, Chantal Akerman) *Aurore Clement, Tcheky Karyo, Jan Decorte, Natalia Akerman.* Abandoning standard narrative plot, Akerman's own minimalist, avant-garde story of the follies of sex and love is set on one torrid summer night in Brussels. Told in a series of amorous fragments, the film follows the various mating rites of several couples as they meet, fall in love, eat, drink and then break up. An austere yet strangely riveting experimental melodrama that is certainly not for all audiences. (French with English subtitles) ★★★ VHS: $29.99

Tower of London

(1939, 93 min, US, Rowland V. Lee) *Basil Rathbone, Boris Karloff, Vincent Price.* Rathbone kills his way to the top as Richard III in this above-average historical thriller. Gleefully overacting, he leads a solid cast which also includes a young Price as a weakling Duke and Karloff as Richard's medieval "campaign organizer," the clubfooted executioner Mord. Playing out his crimes on a set of dolls to represent his contemporaries in the royal court, Rathbone slowly gets bolder and bolder until his schemes

are naturally undone in the end. (Remade in 1962 with Price taking the role of Richard) ★★★ VHS: $14.99

The Towering Inferno

(1974, 165 min, US, John Guillermin) *Paul Newman, Steve McQueen, Faye Dunaway, William Holden, Richard Chamberlain, Robert Vaughn, Fred Astaire, Jennifer Jones.* A mammoth production can't hide the loose ends to this half-baked disaster epic. An all-star cast is featured to tell the story of a skyscraper's gala opening, and the crisis which follows when the building catches fire. Watch these smoked hams get roasted. The technical aspects of the film are very good, but it's mean-spirited. (Letterboxed VHS available for $19.99) ★★½ VHS: $9.99; DVD: $29.99

Towers Open Fire

(1962-72, 35 min, US, Antony Balch) *William Burroughs.* Burroughs is featured in two shorts in this compilation of four art films from independent filmmaker Antony Balch. *Towers Open Fire* and *The Cut-Ups* attempt to make a cinematic equivalent to Burroughs' famous "cut and paste" style of writing — in which he would write sections of a book, physically cut the story into several pages and then randomly repaste them together. As Burroughs narrates, we watch a visual collage of his writing containing many of the author's key themes. Although trying at times (watching five minutes of voice-over intoning repeatedly "yes-no" is a good test), the films are of great interest to both experimental film lovers and Burroughs fans. ★★½ VHS: $29.99

A Town Like Alice

(1980, 301 min, Australia, David Stevens) *Bryan Brown, Helen Morse.* This mammoth drama of love and separation is taken from the best-selling novel by Neville Shute. The story is set against the brutal chaos of WWII. While in a Japanese POW camp in steamy Malaysia, an ever-cheerful Australian and an equally resilient English woman meet and fall in love. They are soon separated, but in the ensuing years meet again in the rugged outback of Australia. ★★★ VHS: $39.99

The Toxic Avenger

(1985, 100 min, US, Michael Herz & Samuel Weil) Idiotic cult comedy, though not without a few laughs, about a goofy nerd who is pushed into toxic waste and comes out a super-human crime-fighter from New Jersey. Sick humor and effects abound. (Sequel: *The Toxic Avenger, Part 2*) ★ VHS: $14.99; DVD: $24.99

Toy Soldiers

(1991, 112 min, US, Daniel Petrie) *Sean Astin, Wil Wheaton, Keith Coogan, Louis Gossett, Jr., Denholm Elliott.* A group of young prep school students, led by rebellious Astin, band together to take back their school from gun-toting terrorists who are holding the rich kids for ransom. This is a surprisingly effective suspenser, with well-done action scenes and a young cast presenting believable and likable characters. ★★★ VHS: $9.99

Toy Story

(1995, 81 min, US, John Lasseter) *Voices of: Tom Hanks, Tim Allen, Don Rickles, Wallace Shawn, Jim Varney, Laurie Metcalf, R. Lee Ermey.* With the first

all-computer-animated feature film, the folks at Disney have done it again. More than just a technical marvel, *Toy Story* is an exhilarating combination of sight, sound and story which is as funny and entertaining as it is groundbreaking. Confirming every child's suspicions, *Toy Story* is set in a magical world where toys come to life — but only when humans aren't around. Six-year-old Andy's favorite toy is Woody, a pull-string talking cowboy. That is until a new toy arrives, a state-of-the-art astronaut named Buzz Lightyear, to rival Woody for Andy's affections. It's then a game of one-upmanship as the two toys engage in a series of captivating misadventures. Featuring a marvelous screenplay and wonderful vocals by Hanks and Allen, this is one family film that delivers. . . to infinity and beyond. (Sequel: *Toy Story 2*) ★★★★ VHS: $22.99; DVD: $29.99

Toy Story 2

(1999, 92 min, US, John Lasseter) *Voices of: Tom Hanks, Tim Allen, Jim Varney, Don Rickles, John Ratzenberger, Joan Cusack, Kelsey Grammer, Wallace Shawn, Wayne Knight, Annie Potts, R. Lee Ermey.* Displaying the same combination of superb animation and winning, funny story line as its predecessor, *Toy Story 2* (which was originally designed as a direct-to-video release until Disney realized what they had) is a worthy and entertaining sequel to the 1995 smash hit. When stolen by a toy collector who (shudder) keeps his toys in their original boxes, Woody finds his long-lost family (the rest of the original set), including Jessie and Stinky Pete. It's up to Buzz Lightyear and the gang to save Woody from a life packed in styrofoam. But does Woody really want to come back to Andy and friends? Another delightful comic adventure courtesy of Woody, Buzz and friends. ★★★½ VHS: $26.99; DVD: $29.99

Toys

(1992, 121 min, US, Barry Levinson) *Robin Williams, Michael Gambon, Joan Cusack, LL Cool J, Donald O'Connor.* Writer-director Levinson must have dropped acid one day and walked through F.A.O. Schwartz to come up with this colorful but mind-bogglingly leaden satire. Williams plays the son of a toy magnate (O'Connor) who loses his inheritance of the company when his father passes away. Instead, the enterprise is given to his uncle, a nasty general (Gambon) who plans to produce war toys. Eventually, militaristic Gambon and innocent Williams have a showdown, and the destructive toys go ballistic. Set in a nether-world populated by amusement park vehicles and magical machinery, the set design seems to have been inspired by the graphics of a Super Nintendo game. ★½ VHS: $9.99

Toys in the Attic

(1963, 91 min, US, George Roy Hill) *Geraldine Page, Dean Martin, Wendy Hiller, Gene Tierney, Yvette Mimieux.* A good cast can't enliven this tedious Gothic drama based on Lillian Hellman's stage play. Martin plays the ne'er-do-well brother of spinsters Page and Hiller. With his young wife (Mimieux), he returns to his New Orleans home suspiciously boasting of new wealth. Their presence there paves the way to betrayal, recriminations, and long-hidden secrets exposed. Page and Hiller are effective, though even they can't overcome the film's contrivances. ★½ VHS: $19.99

Traces of Red

(1992, 105 min, US, Andy Wolk) *James Belushi, Lorraine Bracco, Tony Goldwyn, William Russ.* An incredibly convoluted whodunit about a Palm Beach cop (Belushi) who becomes both hunter and hunted when his bedmates start turning up dead (murder or mercy — you decide). While the film offers credible performances and a decent mystery with a good deal of twists, there are ultimately no traces of logic to be found, and only traces of dread at the too-tricky-for-its-own-good surprise ending. ★½ VHS: $9.99

Track 29

(1988, 86 min, GB, Nicolas Roeg) *Gary Oldman, Theresa Russell, Christopher Lloyd, Sandra Bernhard.* Roeg's playfully beguiling mystery stars Russell as a bored young woman trapped in a loveless and childless marriage with model train and S&M enthusiast Lloyd. The woman's life is changed when she is (possibly) visited by a young British stranger (Oldman) who claims that he is her abandoned-at-birth son. Is he a con man or prodigal son, a real person or only the figment of her rapidly deteriorating mind? Any fan of Roeg will know that the answer does not come simply in this visually exciting drama. Don't miss Bernhard's small role as the kinky dominatrix, Nurse Stein. ★★★ VHS: $14.99

Tracks

(1974, 90 min, US, Henry Jaglom) *Dennis Hopper, Dean Stockwell.* A Vietnam vet (Hopper) meets a wide array of characters while on a train. However, he is soon overtaken with war-induced paranoia. With a more traditional narrative than his other films, director Jaglom weaves a compelling and insightful tale — years before the subject matter became en vogue. ★★★ VHS: $39.99

Trading Hearts

(1987, 88 min, US, Neil Leifer) *Raul Julia, Beverly D'Angelo, Jenny Lewis.* Ineffective romantic romp about an over-the-hill baseball pitcher (Julia) and a minor league singer (D'Angelo) in 1957 Florida, complicated by a mischievous 11-year-old who thinks they should all live together. ★★ VHS: $14.99

Trading Places

(1983, 106 min, US, John Landis) *Eddie Murphy, Dan Aykroyd, Jamie Lee Curtis, Ralph Bellamy, Don Ameche, Denholm Elliott.* Aykroyd and Murphy are hilarious as a millionaire and street hustler, respectively, who trade places in this silly but vastly amusing comedy. The inspired casting is what raises this film above the usual "Saturday Night Live" alumni mode of filmmaking. Bellamy and Ameche are great as a pair of incredibly sleazy capitalist brothers. Elliott walks away with the film as an incredulous butler. And Curtis is the hooker with a heart of gold. ★★★½ VHS: $14.99

Traffic

(1971, 89 min, France, Jacques Tati) *Jacques Tati.* Tati stars as Monsieur Hulot, that charming and naïve fool, in this hilariously chaotic comedy. Armed with youthful enthusiasm, M. Hulot attempts to transport a car from France to Holland for an auto show, and the results are

Erika Christensen and Topher Grace in Steven Soderbergh's *Traffic*

side-splitting. A satire on modern living, *Traffic* takes great pleasure in dissecting the absurdity of a situation where neurosis reigns behind the wheel. There is very little dialogue, and even though there are no subtitles, those who do not understand word one of French will be able to follow with ease this visually funny film. ★★★★ VHS: $29.99

Traffic

(2000, 147 min, US, Steven Soderbergh) *Michael Douglas, Benicio Del Toro, Catherine Zeta-Jones, Don Cheadle, Dennis Quaid, Luis Guzman, Erika Christensen, Miguel Ferrer, Amy Irving, Topher Grace, Benjamin Bratt, Albert Finney, James Brolin.* Based on the BBC miniseries "Traffik," this explosive look at the international drug trade is extraordinary filmmaking, marking a career high for director Soderbergh (and a potent 1-2 punch for 2000 with his earlier success *Erin Brockovich*). Several story lines are skillfully woven together to examine the war on drugs — the complete arc from distribution to drug use to enforcement on both sides of the border. Among an outstanding ensemble: Douglas is the newly appointed drug czar fighting his own war at home; the exceptional, Oscar-winning Del Toro is a Mexican cop out to stop a cartel; Cheadle and Guzman are his American counterparts; Zeta-Jones is the wife of a drug dealer about to receive a quick lesson in business; and Christensen is Douglas' addicted daughter. Soderbergh brings an almost documentary-like feel to the movie, contrasting film stocks for different locales, and giving the film a tense, fly-on-the-wall perspective. It is masterful story telling, told with authority, intelligence and a sense of immediacy. There's no moral indignation, no polemic at work here; conclusions are all subjective, characters are all three-dimensional, and the film is all the better for it. If it's a "just-say-no" morality you're looking for, watch another "Afterschool Special." *Traffic* is set in an adult world, and is a mature and sobering wake-up call for not only parents and children, but our ineffectual government as well. Winner of 4 Academy Awards including Best Director

and Best Screenplay Adaptation. ★★★★ VHS: $19.99; DVD: $26.99

Traffic in Souls

(1913, 88 min, US, George Loane Tucker) *Matt Moore, Jane Gail.* A docudrama decades before the coining of that dreaded term, *Traffic in Souls* dramatized some of the more sensational aspects of the 1910 Rockefeller White Slavery Report for New York City. As the gateway for America, NYC found itself the hub of a syndicate comprised of crooked judges, cops and criminals who kidnapped immigrating women into dens of prostitution. While some of the dramaturgy may be creaky, and the interior sets decidedly *trompe l'oeil*, the location shooting around the city of dirt streets and open windows give *Traffic in Souls* the feeling of an bygone era tinged with a contemporary atmosphere. ★★★½ VHS: $29.99

The Tragedy of a Ridiculous Man

(1981, 116 min, Italy, Bernardo Bertolucci) *Ugo Tognazzi, Anouk Aimée.* This psychological parable on terrorism and the clash between capitalism and leftist politics in Italy is at best a muddled exercise that seems to purposefully confuse and distance its audience. Tognazzi is a self-made man and materialistic owner of a sprawling Parma cheese factory who witnesses his left-leaning son being forcibly thrown into a car and kidnapped. But was this a real abduction or was his son in collusion with his kidnappers? Not knowing for sure, he reluctantly raises the ransom, but is undecided whether he should help his son or use the money to prop up his failing business. An admirable but unsatisfying experience. (Italian with English subtitles) ★★ VHS: $59.99

Tragic Hero

(1987, 96 min, Hong Kong, Taylor Wong) *Chow Yun-Fat, Andy Lau, Alex Man (Man)* Yung (Man) returns to Hong Kong, the city of his youth, to consolidate power and confront an old foe. Respected crime boss Chi (Chow), now retired, is forced to return to action to stop Yung's bloody take-over attempt. *Tragic Hero* continues

T

the story begun in *Rich and Famous*, of a family torn apart by clouded loyalties and numbing violence (it has been compared to *The Godfather* films). An insane lust for power leads inevitably to a final face-off, winner-take-all in an impressive display of pyrotechnics. The closing sequences testify that firepower beats manpower every time. (Cantonese with English subtitles) ★★½ VHS: $19.99; DVD: $29.99

The Trail of the Pink Panther

(1982, 97 min, GB, Blake Edwards) Shortly after Peter Sellers' death, Edwards slapped together this sorry excuse for a film out of old bits and pieces of yet unseen footage from earlier *Panther* films. These out-takes are strung together with a flimsy story line about a reporter who interviews anyone he can find who knew Clouseau. Not worth the film it's printed on. ★ VHS: $14.99

The Train

(1965, 133 min, US, John Frankenheimer) *Burt Lancaster, Paul Scofield, Jeanne Moreau, Suzanne Flon, Michel Simon.* A solid, rousing thriller from director Frankenheimer. Set in 1944 Occupied France, the story follows the exploits of the French Resistance and trainman Lancaster who try to prevent the Nazis from shipping stolen art treasures to Germany via Burt's train. Scofield is the Nazi general assigned the task of guarding the confiscated art works. Like another actioner set almost entirely aboard a train, *The Taking of Pelham One Two Three*, from a simple plot line comes such high-powered suspense. ★★★½ VHS: $14.99; DVD: $14.99

Trainspotting

(1996, 94 min, Scotland, Danny Boyle) *Ewan McGregor, Ewen Bremner, Jonny Lee Miller, Kevin McKidd, Robert Carlyle, Kelly Macdonald.* A swaggering, highly stylized and pulsating cinematic ride, *Trainspotting* is an in-your-face adaptation of Irvine Welch's novel and play about life among a merry band of heroin addicts living it up in the lower depths of Edinburgh. Refreshingly unrepentent in tone, director Boyle puts a fun-filled spin on the world of skag as seen through the eyes of its narrator, Renton (McGregor). He's a wiry and likable antihero who takes up residence in a squalid squat with a

group of fellow travellers that comprise the film's core cast of wackos. As much as it explores the drug subculture, *Trainspotting* is also a merciless social critique that ultimately eyes the pursuit of happiness through substance as the moral equal to that of material acquisition. Sheer excitement, it's punctuated nicely by a hip, drug-inspired rock soundtrack. ★★★★ VHS: $19.99; DVD: $29.99

Trancers

(1985, 76 min, US, Charles Band) *Tim Thomerson, Helen Hunt.* Intriguing sci-fi adventure (with more than a nod to *The Terminator*) about a trooper from the year 2247 who is sent back to present-day Los Angeles to stop a mystic from murdering a future leader. (aka: *Future Cop*) ★★½; DVD: $24.99

Transmutations

(1986, 103 min, GB, George Pavlou) *Denholm Elliott, Miranda Richardson.* A sinister biochemist (Elliott) creates a subhuman species which dwells in the city's underground. Desperate for an antidote, the creatures seek out the only woman who can save them (Richardson). Penned but later disowned by horror maven Clive Barker. (aka: *Underground*) ★★ VHS: $79.99

Trapeze

(1956, 106 min, US, Carol Reed) *Burt Lancaster, Tony Curtis, Gina Lollabrigida, Katy Jurado.* Truly remarkable trapeze footage, and three very appealing lead performances make for a slick romantic drama set against the hurly-burly backdrop of a Parisian circus. Lancaster, in splendid physical condition and doing most of his own stunts, stars as a retired trapeze artist — the only man alive who can perform a triple somersault. He is sought after by Curtis to teach him that near-impossible trick. All is well between them until beautiful and conniving Lollabrigida enters the scene, tricking her way into their act and becoming involved in a romantic triangle with both men. *The Greatest Show on Earth* was never this good. ★★★ VHS: $19.99

Trapped in Paradise

(1994, 111 min, US, George Gallo) *Nicolas Cage, Jon Lovitz, Dana Carvey, Madchen Amick, Donald Moffat.* Three bickering brothers hold up a

bank on Christmas Eve in a Rockwell-like small town. Their problems begin when they can't get out of town and the townsfolk who they've just robbed kill them with kindness. Cage plays against type as the moral backbone of the trio, Lovitz is (surprise!) the acerbic one, and Carvey plays the slow-witted sibling with a penchant for kleptomania. The screenplay offers them numerous comic situations but rarely develops any of them, though the entire cast seems eager to please. ★★ VHS: $9.99

Trash

(1970, 110 min, US, Paul Morrissey) *Holly Woodlawn, Joe Dallesandro, Jane Forth, Michael Sklar, andrea Feldman.* Woodlawn is truly memorable as the trash-collecting lover of impotent drug fiend Dallesandro in this wonderfully realistic slice-of-life film about New York's druggies and counterculture denizens. In this, her screen debut, Holly's character preserves her dignity and moral righteousness despite poverty, squalor and a forced-to-masturbate-with-a-beer-bottle-because-my-boyfriend-can't-get-it-up life. It is her character, and not the cute but almost catatonic Joe, which works against the film's not-so-subtle antidrug message; an attitude which keeps with the director's moralistic and reactionary philosophy. ★★★ VHS: $19.99; DVD: $24.99

Trauma

(1993, 106 min, Italy, Dario Argento) *Christopher Rydell, Piper Laurie, Asia Argento.* A mysterious killer prowls the streets of Minneapolis. His trademark: he decapitates his victims with the Noose-O-Matic. Meanwhile, an illustrator, David (Rydell), meets Aura (A. Argento), a disturbed youth undergoing treatment for anorexia. When her parents, including her psychic mother (Laurie), fall victim to the "Headhunter Killer," Aura enlists David's help in finding their murderer. More heads roll before the two lovers discover the true identity of the assassin. The film is alternately gaudy, energetic, deliberately unrealistic and forceful in its style. ★★½

Traveller

(1997, 101 min, US, Jack Green) *Bill Paxton, Mark Wahlberg, Julianna Margulies, James Gammon.* An offbeat, often compelling independent drama that greatly loses its way by story's end, *Traveller* is a shaggy character study about a group of con artists — "travellers" — making their way across the back roads of rural America. Paxton is a seasoned though small-time hustler who takes his young, estranged cousin Wahlberg under his wing as they swindle their way from one town to another. The film introduces these modern gypsies as an American subculture who are fearful of outsiders but who cannot live without them. *Traveller* is at its best when concentrating on the scam — though nothing in the film nears the ingenuity or precision of *The Grifters*. Where that film had a marvelously paced tempo, director Green's debut feature is too lacksdaisical to ever truly excite. But a good cast brings conviction to their roles. the film's sloppy ending all but falls apart. ★★½ VHS: $14.99; DVD: $14.99

Travelling North

(1987, 98 min, Australia, Carl Schultz) *Leo McKern, Julia Blake.* Charming story of a retired

Ewan McGregor in *Trainspotting*

civil engineer (McKern) who, suspecting that his days are numbered, takes off with his lady-love (Blake) for a life of peaceful contentment at a cottage by the lake. McKern is at his blustery best as the Mozart-loving foreman with a talent for hurting those who love him; the entire cast contributes to making this a minor gem. ★★★

Travels with My Aunt

(1972, 109 min, GB, George Cukor) *Maggie Smith, Alec McCowen, Lou Gossett, Robert Stephens, Cindy Williams.* Smith received an Academy Award nomination for her delightfully eccentric performance as Aunt Augusta in this giddy and incandescent screen version of Graham Greene's novel. After the death of her estranged sister, the high-living Augusta swoops in and whisks her very unwilling nephew Henry (McCowen), an affably stodgy banker, from his ordered existence and proceeds to introduce him to high adventure on the road. They set upon a worldwide quest to raise money for one of her former lovers who has been kidnapped, and misadventures compile. Smith's performance is pure enchantment, shading a likable and larger-than-life portrayal with whimsy, wit and wonder. All this under the watchful and precise eye of director Cukor. (Letterboxed) ★★★½ VHS: $19.99

La Traviata

(1982, 110 min, Italy, Franco Zeffirelli) *Placido Domingo, Teresa Stratas.* Zeffirelli's lavish, powerful rendition of Verdi's opera stars Domingo and Stratas in emotionally charged performances as the doomed lovers. Not just for opera fans! (Italian with English subtitles) ★★★½ VHS: $29.99; DVD: $24.99

Treasure Island

(1934, 105 min, US, Victor Fleming) *Jackie Cooper, Wallace Beery, Lionel Barrymore.* Flavorful adaptation of Robert Louis Stevenson's classic adventure yarn about pirates, hidden treasure, and the small boy involved with both. Cooper is the youngster who lives every small child's fantasy, and Beery is an appropriately flamboyant Long John Silver. ★★★ VHS: $19.99

The Treasure of the Sierra Madre

(1948, 124 min, US, John Huston) *Humphrey Bogart, Walter Huston, Tim Holt.* A taut parable on human greed and corruptibility based on the novel by the mysterious B. Traven. Bogart gives a memorable performance as the edgy Fred C. Dobbs, whose moral bent is fractured by his discovery of gold. Holt and W. Huston (Academy Award for Best Supporting Actor) are his fellow prospectors, combating bandits, betrayal and the ill effects of the yellow dust. J. Huston won Best Director and Best Screenplay Oscars. ★★★★ VHS: $14.99

A Tree Grows in Brooklyn

(1945, 128 min, US, Elia Kazan) *Dorothy McGuire, James Dunn, Peggy Ann Garner, Joan Blondell.* An outstanding film version of Betty Smith's novel about the hardships facing an Irish family living in a turn-of-the-century Brooklyn tenement. McGuire is splendid as the mother, with an Oscar-winning performance by Dunn as her alcoholic husband. Garner won a special juvenile Oscar for her sensitive portrayal of a young girl looking to escape her

environment, and Blondell gives one of her best performances as Garner's aunt. ★★★★ VHS: $14.99

The Tree of Wooden Clogs

(1978, 186 min, Italy, Ermanno Olmi) *Luigi Omaghi, Francesca Moriggi.* In this deceptively simple epic, Olmi brilliantly reconstructs the peasant life in the Lombardy region of Italy at the turn-of-the-century. The director, using a non-professional cast and filming in almost documentary-like fashion, quietly explores the lives of four peasant families told through the eyes of a young boy. Long and leisurely paced, with the story told in a mosaic of small incidents, the film is not for everybody; but for those with patience and an appreciative mind, this film will prove to be an absorbing work of art. (Italian with English subtitles) ★★★★ VHS: $19.99

Trees Lounge

(1996, 94 min, US, Steve Buscemi) *Steve Buscemi, Chloe Sevigny, Anthony LaPaglia, Eszter Balint, Carol Kane, Samuel L. Jackson, Seymour Cassel.* An impressive directorial debut for actor Buscemi, who has crafted a succulent little slice-of-life offering which is both unflinchingly perceptive and sweetly compassionate. Buscemi stars as Tommy, that guy from the neighborhood whose life seems perpetually on pause. The story chronicles the events of one summer in his life as he careens amid a Runyonesque cast of characters, each sharply if briefly brought into focus by an on-target ensemble. Buscemi also wrote the wry and poignant screenplay, which spritely delineates Tommy's less-than-beneficial role on those around him. Heavy material is delivered with a light hand, and an unerring recognition of the minute details that define and propel a person's life. ★★★½ VHS: $9.99; DVD: $24.99

Tremors

(1990, 96 min, US, Ron Underwood) *Kevin Bacon, Fred Ward, Michael Gross, Reba McIntire.* Taking off where the 1950s "monster-on-the-rampage" films and the Roger Corman exploitation flicks left off, this fun and funny horror film has its tongue firmly planted in its cinematic cheek. Set in a lonely, dust-covered Western town, a small group of people are invaded by mysterious underground creatures who have more than a passing resemblance to the man-eating worms from *Dune.* Bacon and Ward are hilarious as two out-of-their-element handymen who must confront the shy platy-helminths as they murderously slither through the town. (Followed by 2 sequels) ★★★ VHS: $9.99; DVD: $29.99

Tremors 2: Aftershocks

(1995, 100 min, US, S.S. Wilson) *Fred Ward, Michael Gross.* A direct-to-video sequel made by the same production team that authored the first movie. Earl (Ward) is hired by a Mexican oil company to go "Graboid-hunting." The giant, man-eating worms have resurfaced south of the border and the oil company and Mexican army cannot stop the beasts, who have turned into a new variety of monster. While *Tremors 2* lacks the vulgar humor which made the first film feel so appealing, it retains its predecessor's redneck charm and gleeful creature-killing violence and gore. Not merely a rehash,

this is a moderately original film. ★★★ VHS: $14.99; DVD: $24.99

Trespass

(1992, 95 min, US, Walter Hill) *Bill Paxton, Ice Cube, Ice T, William Sadler.* This urbanized retelling of the classic *Treasure of the Sierra Madre* marks a return to form for director Hill. Paxton and Sadler take the lead in this textbook "wrong place, wrong time" scenario about two "good ol' boy" firemen who go searching for buried treasure in an abandoned building just in time to witness a gangland hit by druglords Ice T and Ice Cube. Hill strikes just the right balance between well-drawn characterizations and gunplay galore to make this a welcome addition to the action genre. ★★★ VHS: $9.99; DVD: $19.99

The Trial

(1962, 119 min, France/Italy/Germany, Orson Welles) *Anthony Perkins, Jeanne Moreau, Orson Welles.* Franz Kafka's nightmarish novel of a man arrested for a crime that is never explained to him is brilliantly brought to the screen by Welles. Perkins is Josef K., a sensitive individual pursued by a repressive bureaucracy, obsessed by an undefined guilt and bewildered by the burden of living. Welles maintained complete artistic control of the production and the result is a difficult but unforgettable expressionistic mood piece. (Letterboxed) (Filmed in English) ★★★½ VHS: $19.99; DVD: $29.99

The Trial

(1993, 120 min, GB, David Jones) *Kyle MacLachlan, Jason Robards, Anthony Hopkins, Michael Kitchen.* MacLachlan stars as the archetypal victim hero, Joseph K., in this austere but oddly engrossing adaptation of Franz Kafka's novel. Waking up on the morning of his birthday, K. finds himself under arrest for no stated reason and is slowly sucked into a byzantine and murky beauracracy. MacLachlan gives a sturdy interpretation of K., though he ill-advisedly attempts an English accent. Harold Pinter provides the screenplay, which while replete with his snappy dialogue, curiously fails to invoke any of Kafka's subversive humor. Filmed on location in Prague, the production is greatly enhanced by marvelous cinematography and art design. ★★★ VHS: $19.99; DVD: $29.99

Trial and Error

(1962, 78 min, GB, James Hill) *Peter Sellers, Richard Attenborough, Beryl Reid, David Lodge.* Sellers and Attenborough play barrister and client — and several other characters — in this droll British comedy which offers only a few rewarding moments. When a rather taciturn bird seed salesman (Attenborough) murders his ebullient wife (Reid) so he can spend more quality time with his beloved budgies, his incompetent, court-appointed lawyer (Sellers) sees one last chance to finally step from the shadows. What he sees in the harsh glare of the limelight leaves him unsettled and dissolved. Too reverentially adapted from a minor stage play, *Trial and Error* remains as unassuming as its two protagonists. (GB title: *The Dock Brief*) ★★ VHS: $9.99; DVD: $9.99

T

Trial and Error

(1997, 98 min, US, Jonathan Lynn) *Michael Richards, Jeff Daniels, Charlize Theron, Jessica Steen, Austin Pendleton, Rip Torn.* Another courtroom comedy from director Lynn (*My Cousin Vinny*). Playing straight man to Richards' lunatic, Daniels is a lawyer about to be married. His bachelor party is such a success, he's unable to go to court the next morning. Friend and actor Richards subs for him in court to ask for a continuance. But Richards is forced to continue the charade when the continuance is denied, and Daniels must coach Richards from the sidelines. Goofy and occasionally genuinely funny, *Trial and Error* benefits from Torn's presence as the defendant, though many scenes outside the courtroom lack the comic energy of the trial scenes. ★★½ VHS: $14.99; DVD: $19.99

Trial by Jury

(1994, 108 min, US, Heywood Gould) *Joanne Whalley-Kilmer, Armand Assante, William Hurt, Gabriel Byrne, Kathleen Quinlan.* Whalley-Kilmer plays a jurist who faces every jury member's nightmare: being physically coerced into finding the defendant innocent. But what's more of a nightmare is the silly scenario created by the writers as a responsible citizen faces criminals and the criminal system head-on. Sitting on the jury of a high-profile mobster (Assante), Whalley-Kilmer has her and her young son's life threatened by Assante's goons. As she grapples with the moral dilemma, nearly every man in sight falls in love with her. Though bordering on trashy fun, this could have been enjoyable were it not for Whalley-Kilmer's one-dimensional performance. ★★ VHS: $14.99; DVD: $14.99

The Trials of Oscar Wilde

(1960, 123 min, GB, Ken Hughes) *Peter Finch, Nigel Patrick, James Mason.* Finch stars as the vainglorious writer Oscar Wilde, who sued his lover's father, the Marquis of Queensbury, for libel. After losing the ill-considered suit, he was charged with sodomy and stood trial. An elaborate and intriguing courtroom drama. ★★★ VHS: $24.99

Les Tricheurs (The Cheats)

(1983, 95 min, France, Barbet Schroeder) *Jacques Dutronc, Bulle Ogier.* A slick drama about elegantly dressed gambling addicts on the island of Madera and their attempts at pulling off an elaborate swindle. Ogier is the "lucky" stranger who becomes an unwitting accomplice in Dutronc's scheme at the roulette wheel. (French with English subtitles) ★★★ VHS: $29.99

trick

(1999, 90 min, US, Jim Fall) *Christian Campbell, John Paul Pitoc, Tori Spelling, Steve Hayes, Clinton Leupp (aka: Miss Coco Peru).* The tables are turned on the typical gay film plot in this funny and romantic screwball comedy. Gabriel (Campbell), a cute, effervescent music composer, and Mark (Pitoc), a darkly handsome go-go boy, lock eyes and long to link loins but through a series of events just can't seem to ever be alone long enough to get it on. What would have been a quickie turns instead into an instance for the two men to get to know each other. They spend the day enduring intrusions, visited by friends and separated by ex-lovers and future ex-lovers. In a cinematic gay world of cookie-cutter plots, *trick*'s seductive tale offers a fresh and exciting alternative, and one that speaks truths on love and relationships no matter what the sexual orientation. In support, Spelling is quite memorable as Gabriel's bulldozing actress/singer-wannabe best friend. Her table-side rant is hilarious. A beguiling romantic comedy which manages to capture both romance and comedy. ★★★½ VHS: $19.99; DVD: $24.99

Trick or Treat

(1986, 97 min, US, Charles Martin Smith) *Marc Price, Gene Simmons, Ozzy Osbourne.* Imaginative horror satire about a metalhead who plays an album backwards to evoke the spirit of a dead rock star. A headbanger's delight, which unfortunately derails about halfway through. ★★½

The Trigger Effect

(1996, 93 min, US, David Koepp) *Kyle MacLachlan, Elisabeth Shue, Dermot Mulroney, Michael Rooker, Richard T. Jones.* Having written the screenplays for such diverse films as *Jurassic Park* and *Apartment Zero*, writer Koepp makes a satisfying leap to director with this offbeat though uneven psychological thriller. The story focuses on man's baser instincts during time of crisis (here a power blackout) which ultimately pits neighbor against neighbor. Koepp begins the film beautifully, tracking the effect one person has on another, then that person on another and so on. The story then concentrates on a Los Angeles couple (MacLachlan, Shue) and their houseguest (Mulroney) as they begin to cope with an unexplained, city-wide blackout. Though Koepp's thesis of man reverting to his animal self is not new, he diffuses the obvious with inventive camerawork and a steady tension throughout the film. ★★½ VHS: $14.99; DVD: $24.99

Trilogy of Terror

(1975, 78 min, US, Dan Curtis) *Karen Black, Gregory Harrison.* Three eerie tales of the supernatural, with a smashing performance by Black. "The Zuni Fetish Doll," the African head hunting doll from the climactic third episode, is a classic horror short. ★★★ VHS: $9.99

The Trio

(1998, 93 min, Germany, Hermine Huntgeburth) *Götz George, Christian Redl, Jeanette Hain, Felix Eitner.* Zobel (George), a fiftyish con man, works the streets with his longtime lover Karl (Redl) and his twentysomething daughter Lizzi (Hain.) When Karl suddenly dies, the flimflam/pickpocketing team is in need of a new member. That comes in the person of Rudolf (Eitner), a brash, sexy, wet-behind-the-ears thief. Lizzi falls in love with him and coaxes her distrustful dad into accepting him into their fold. But Dad eventually falls under Rudolf's seductive charms (and it becomes obvious Rudolf swings both ways). This infectious comedy delivers the goods in offering characters of varying sexual orientations and sex scenes dripping with eroticism. George is more than believable as the vain but aging lothario and Eitner is disarmingly sexy as his playmate. A refreshing alternative to your typical Hollywood film. (German with English subtitles) ★★★ VHS: $59.99; DVD: $29.99

The Trip to Bountiful

(1985, 106 min, US, Peter Masterson) *Geraldine Page, Rebecca DeMornay, John Heard, Carlin Glynn, Richard Bradford.* Page won a much-deserved (and overdue) Oscar for her lovely performance as an aging widow who literally runs away from her son's Houston apartment to return to the now-abandoned home of her youth. A fine, bittersweet comedy-drama impeccably performed by a first-rate cast. Screenplay by Horton Foote, based on his 1953 play. ★★★½

Triple Echo

(1980, 85 min, GB, Michael Apted) *Glenda Jackson, Oliver Reed, Brian Deacon.* Featuring understated acting and direction, this bizarre wartime drama stars Jackson as a woman living alone in a farmhouse. She meets a young soldier (Deacon) who, swayed by his attraction for her, impulsively deserts his unit and hides out in Jackson's house. When investigators begin snooping around, Deacon dresses in women's clothing and masquerades as Jackson's sister. The ruse works too well when burly sergeant Reed takes a fancy to "her." ★★½

The Treasure of the Sierra Madre

Tristana

(1970, 99 min, Spain/France/Italy, Luis Buñuel) *Fernando Rey, Catherine Deneuve, Franco Nero.* Little of Buñuel's overt surrealist style is evident in this intriguing black comedy of corrupt morals, religious bigotry and sexual abuse. Set in provincial Toledo in the 1920s, Rey plays Don Lupe, a vain, lascivious old man with strong socialist and anti-clerical thoughts who, on the death of a friend, becomes the guardian of the young and innocent Deneuve. Lupe soon seduces/rapes her ward, but neither possesses her heart nor ignites her passions. The girl eventually flees to the arms of a handsome painter (Nero), only to return a sick, emotionally cold woman intent on revenge. (Letterboxed) (Spanish with English subtitles) ★★½ VHS: $29.99

Triumph of the Spirit

(1989, 120 min, US, Robert M. Young) *Willem Dafoe, Robert Loggia, Edward James Olmos.* Based on a true story, this intense, unrelenting drama recaptures the brutal years of a Greek boxer who, as a prisoner at Auschwitz, was forced to fight "to the death" — either his or his opponent's — to the amusement of his Nazi captors. Dafoe gives a powerful performance as the fighter who is sent to the death camp with his entire family — only to watch them die one by one. Filmed on location, the film is unflinchingly real in its depiction of daily existence. As Dafoe's endearing father, Loggia is outstanding; and Olmos is fine as a Gypsy kapo. ★★★

Triumph of the Will

(1936, 120 min, Germany, Leni Riefenstahl) German director Riefenstahl's infamous propaganda documentary on Hitler's 1934 Nazi Party Congress held in Nuremberg, which helped thrust the dictator to power. Although its aim is to glorify the Nazis, it is undeniably a powerful piece of filmmaking. (German with English subtitles) ★★★½ VHS: $29.99; DVD: $39.99

Trog

(1970, 91 min, GB, Freddie Francis) *Joan Crawford, Michael Gough.* Crawford's last film is a disastrous camp classic with Mommie Dearest herself as an anthropologist(!) who discovers a missing link. ★ VHS: $14.99

The Trojan War

(1997, 83 min, US, George Huang) *Will Friedle, Jennifer Love Hewitt, Marley Shelton, Lee Majors.* A sloppy, hodgepodge of *Some Kind of Wonderful* and *Adventures in Babysitting*, *The Trojan War* stars Friedle as Brad, a Generic Cute Guy infatuated with Leah (Shelton), the Generic Blonde from his science class who asks him over for some nighttime tutoring. When she coos for a little something more and Brad finds himself *sans* condom, he ventures out to the all-night drug store, only to encounter gangs, robberies, police, a salsa contest, and other various obstacles. Clichéd, one-dimensional characters, pubescent wet-dream fantasies and a predictable happy ending are all punctuated by relentless alt-rock B sides and some quasi-hip dialogue. ★½ VHS: $79.99

The Trojan Women

(1972, 105 min, Greece/US, Michael Cacoyannis) *Katharine Hepburn, Irene Papas, Genevieve Bujold, Vanessa Redgrave, Patrick Magee.* Euripides' tragedy about the fall of Troy to Agamemnon's armies. Despite the somewhat listless production (Cacoyannis' work on the stage is far superior), the outstanding cast delivers a group of superlative performances, making this an emotionally charged treatise on the horrors of war. ★★½

A Troll in Central Park

(1994, 76 min, US, Don Bluth) *Voices of: Dom DeLuise, Cloris Leachman, Jonathan Pryce.* Bluth continues to create a great animated alternative to Disney and this film is much more than just another walk through the park. The story follows the adventures of Stanley, a sweet-natured troll with a green thumb who can grow anything, anywhere, until he meets an evil queen who does her best to stop him. With the help of two children who befriend him, he and they learn that "if you believe in yourself, you can do anything" — always a timely lesson. ★★★ VHS: $19.99

Tron

(1982, 95 min, US, Steven Lisberger) *Jeff Bridges, David Warner, Bruce Boxleitner.* Excellent computer graphics highlight this intriguing though lethargic sci-fi thriller about a computer programmer who is zapped into a computer and forced to live out a video arcade game. ★★ DVD: $29.99

Troop Beverly Hills

(1989, 105 min, US, Jeff Kanew) *Shelley Long, Craig T. Nelson, Betty Thomas.* Long takes her snooty "Cheers" persona and transplants it to a Beverly Hills wife and mother who takes her daughter's girl scout troop on an outing. This formulaic comedy does manage a few laughs, and is a pleasant entertainment. ★★½ VHS: $9.99

Trouble Bound

(1992, 90 min, US, Jeffrey Reiner) *Michael Madsen, Patricia Arquette, Seymour Cassel.* Blood and Concrete director Reiner offers another serving of his specialized brand of slapstick black comedy in this entertaining road romance. Just out of jail, Harry Talbot wins a Lincoln Continental at a card game and heads to Las Vegas to start a new life. His luck soon changes when Kit, a philosophical Mafia princess on the run, gets into Harry's car and demands a quick getaway from her pursuing family — then they find a body in the trunk. Rubber burns and bullets fly as Madsen, as Harry, delivers an appealing variation of his stock charming rogue character and Arquette gives a spirited, if screechy, performance as Kit. ★★★

Trouble in Mind

(1986, 111 min, US, Alan Rudolph) *Keith Carradine, Kris Kristofferson, Genevieve Bujold, Divine, Joe Morton.* Rudolph weaves the themes of hope and despair, greed and jealousy, and lost and found love in this carefully spun noir drama. There's a fine supporting performance by Divine (playing a male character) as an underworld boss. Title sung by Marianne Faithfull. ★★★

The Trouble with Angels

(1966, 112 min, US, Ida Lupino) *Rosalind Russell, Hayley Mills, June Harding, Mary Wickes, Binnie Barnes, Gypsy Rose Lee.* A joyous romp set in a Catholic girls' school, this nostalgic comedy stars Mills and Harding as two mischievous students constantly in trouble with the Sisters, and especially Mother Superior Russell. Lots of fun. (Sequel: *Where Angels Go, Trouble Follows*) ★★★ VHS: $14.99

The Trouble with Harry

(1956, 99 min, US, Alfred Hitchcock) *Shirley MacLaine, John Forsythe, Edmund Gwenn.* A mordant black comedy about a troublesome corpse that just won't stay buried. Hitchcock directed this offbeat gem with characteristically cheerful morbidity. ★★★ VHS: $14.99; DVD: $29.99

True Believer

(1989, 103 min, US, Joseph Ruben) *James Woods, Robert Downey, Jr., Margaret Colin.* The spirit of the idealistic, free-spirited '60s meets the Reagan era in this suspenseful crime thriller. Woods, in a compelling performance, stars as a Greenwich Village defense lawyer, Eddie Dodd, whose once shining star has all but faded. When he is hired to defend a convicted murderer who may have been unjustly imprisoned, Dodd, grasping at a final chance for personal and moral redemption, attacks the case with the lost vigor of his youth. Downey is fine as the novice attorney who apprentices with Dodd. ★★★ VHS: $9.99; DVD: $19.99

True Colors

(1991, 111 min, US, Herbert Ross) *John Cusack, James Spader, Richard Widmark, Imogen Stubbs.* Solid performances by Cusack and Spader elevate this fairly intriguing though familiar political drama about friendship and betrayal. Cusack and Spader play college chums who are working their way up the political ranks in Washington D.C.: Cusack is an opportunistic senatorial aide, and Spader is an idealistic Justice attorney. When the former runs for Congress, each must pay a high cost for his ambition/principles. ★★½ VHS: $14.99

True Confessions

(1981, 119 min, US, Ulu Grosbard) *Robert De Niro, Robert Duvall, Charles Durning, Kenneth McMillan.* De Niro and Duvall give powerful performances in this gritty mystery set in 1930s Hollywood. The two acting greats are cast as brothers, one a priest and the other a police detective, who cross paths during a murder investigation. ★★★ VHS: $14.99

True Crime

(1999, 127 min, US, Clint Eastwood) *Clint Eastwood, Isaiah Washington, James Woods, Denis Leary, Lisa Gay Hamilton, Diane Venora, Bernard Hill, Michael Jeter, Frances Fisher, Michael McKean.* The crusading reporter is alive and well and doing good once more in Eastwood's solid drama of redemption and justice. Clint plays Steve Everett, an ex-alcoholic investigative reporter who's just inherited an assignment to cover that evening's execution of a death-row inmate. Upon examining the facts, he soon suspects that the man, Frank Beachum (Washington), may be innocent. Like James

Stewart's reporter in *Call Northside 777*, Everett is prepared to do what's needed to save an innocent man before it's too late. Director Eastwood maintains a tight grip on the action throughout, and as the final hour approaches, *True Crime* becomes downright suspenseful. (Letterboxed VHS available for $19.99) ★★★ VHS: $14.99; DVD: $19.99

True Grit

(1969, 128 min, US, Henry Hathaway) *John Wayne, Kim Darby, Glenn Campbell.* Wayne won an Oscar for his colorful portrayal of Rooster Cogburn, an aging, one-eyed marshall who helps a teenage girl (Darby) track down her father's killer. A flavorful western adventure, the film is exciting, funny and atmospheric; and, in addition to offering a career role to its larger-than-life star, it's an affectionate tribute to a style of film-making director Hathaway and fellow compadres John Ford and Howard Hawks elevated to an art form. (Sequel: *Rooster Cogburn*) ★★★ VHS: $9.99; DVD: $24.99

True Identity

(1991, 93 min, US, Charles Lane) *Lenny Henry, Frank Langella, James Earl Jones, Melvin Van Peebles.* It's *Watermelon Man* for the '90s. Black British comedian Henry plays an unfortunate passenger on what appears to be a doomed airline flight. Thinking he's about to die, the mobster sitting next to him begins confessing a lifetime of crime. When the plane fails to crash, however, poor Lenny suddenly finds himself on the wrong end of the mob. He then goes "white" and the chase is on. It's an amusing premise which only delivers half the time, but it does showcase Henry to good advantage. ★★½

True Lies

(1994, 141 min, US, James Cameron) *Arnold Schwarzenegger, Jamie Lee Curtis, Tom Arnold, Bill Paxton, Tia Carrere, Charlton Heston, Art Malik.* Schwarzenegger reteams with his *T2* director for this totally overblown action/comedy that pays tribute to the James Bond films of yore (with a dash of family values thrown in for good measure). This time out, Arnold plays a secret agent who must save the world from a wimpy villain (Malik) with a nuclear warhead, and keep his in-the-dark wife (Curtis) from discovering his true identity. Though lacking the awe-inspiring special effects Cameron is noted for, or even a fleshed-out story line, the film features exceptional aerial stunt work and mega-hardware. (Letterboxed VHS available for $14.99) ★★½ VHS: $9.99; DVD: $26.99

True Love

(1989, 104 min, US, Nancy Savoca) *Annabella Sciorra, Ron Eldard, Aida Turturro.* The mating games and rituals of Italian-Americans in the Bronx are delightfully played out in this refreshing independent comedy-drama by new-comer Savoca. The story follows the final days leading up to the traditional wedding of Donna (Sciorra), a feisty and determined young lady, and Michael (Eldard), a likable but immature deli worker. This low-budget charmer is filled with wonderfully drawn characters and presents an all-too-real glimpse into the preparations, problems and doubts leading up to the fateful day. ★★★½ VHS: $9.99

True Romance

(1993, 119 min, US, Tony Scott) *Christian Slater, Patricia Arquette, Gary Oldman, Dennis Hopper, Christopher Walken, Brad Pitt, Michael Rapaport, Val Kilmer.* What seemed like an unlikely pairing of mucho-macho auteur Quentin Tarantino and British stylist-turned-Hollywood hack Scott has paid off in spades with a hip, bullet-strewn thriller that hits you so hard it makes you laugh. This high-energy Generation X road movie stars Slater as a trash culture-worshipping comic book salesman who meets happy hooker Arquette during a kung fu triple feature in Detroit. Taking inspiration from his imaginary "mentor" (the ghost of Elvis played by Kilmer), Slater decides to rescue his new love from her sexual servitude to a dread-locked pimp (Oldman, in a marvelously over-the-top performance). After blowing him away, Slater accidentally picks up a suitcase full of cocaine. After a quickie marriage and a visit to the tattoo parlor, Slater and Arquette hightail it out of town in a purple Cadillac. Drawing from Sam Peckinpah, Hong Kong action flicks, David Lynch (on a good day), Sergio Leone and Jim Thompson novels, *True Romance* is a gritty, high-octane mishmash with a genuinely affecting romance between Slater and Arquette. (Director's cut) ★★★★ VHS: $14.99; DVD: $19.99

True Stories

(1986, 111 min, US, David Byrne) *David Byrne, John Goodman, Swoosie Kurtz, Spalding Gray.* In this slightly surreal travelogue, Byrne takes us on a few typical days in the typical lives of the typical Texan town of Virgil whose citizens are really anything but typical, or are they? The film stands as an oddly amusing vision of the mundanity of real life. ★★½ VHS: $14.99; DVD: $14.99

True West

(1985, 110 min, US, Gary Sinise) *John Malkovich, Gary Sinise.* The explosive performances of Malkovich and Sinise highlight this fine play-on-film adaptation of Sam Shepard's off-Broadway hit about the volatile relationship between two brothers. It was this production which introduced Malkovich, as the menacing, slightly off-center thug, to a wide audience. Sinise, who plays Malkovich's educated, passive sibling, also directed the play's original run. ★★★½

La Truite (The Trout)

(1982, 105 min, France, Joseph Losey) *Isabelle Huppert, Jeanne Moreau, Jean-Pierre Cassel.* Huppert is coyly sinister in Losey's complex, funny and sensual melodrama about an innocent country girl who moves to Paris with her gay husband and vows to succeed in the business world with the aid of her feminine wiles. Cassel is a wealthy financier lured by Huppert's coquettish manner, much to the chagrin of his neglected wife (Moreau). (French with English subtitles) ★★★ VHS: $59.99

Truly, Madly, Deeply

(1991, 108 min, GB, Anthony Minghella) *Juliet Stevenson, Alan Rickman, Michael Maloney.* A highly entertaining romantic comedy with a supernatural twist. Stevenson excels as a young woman drowning in grief following the death of her lover (Rickman). When he returns from the grave to soothe her sorrows, however, he turns out to be more than she can handle — especially when he and a bunch of ghostly friends take up residence in her flat, hanging about all night watching videos. Both actors give outstanding performances and first-time writer-director Minghella imbues the film with a bittersweet mix of hilarity and melancholy. ★★★★

Truman

(1995, 135 min, US, Frank Pierson) *Gary Sinise, Diana Scarwid, Richard Dysart, Colm Feore, James Gammon, Tony Goldwyn.* A superbly made HBO biography of President Harry S. Truman, from his early career as a haberdasher to his entry into local Missouri politics to his later service as a senator, vice-president and eventually commander in chief. Sinise gives an exceptional performance as the no-nonsense idealist thrust into a volatile political arena. An intelligent adaptation of David McCullough's Pulitzer Prize-winning novel. ★★★★ VHS: $9.99; DVD: $14.99

Truman Capote's A Christmas Memory

(1966, 51 min, US, Frank Perry) *Geraldine Page.* Beginning with his cousin's observation, "Oh my, it's fruitcake weather!," this Emmy Award–winning short film, produced for ABC Stage, is a sweetly nostalgic recollection of Truman Capote's youth in the rural South during the Depression. Page stars as his homespun "cousin" who takes care of the young Capote, with the story centering on their home life, the touching relationship between the two of them and her Christmas tradition of making over 30 fruitcakes as presents. A simple, quiet drama of love narrated by Mr. Capote himself. ★★★½ VHS: $19.99

The Truman Show

(1998, 103 min, US, Peter Weir) *Jim Carrey, Ed Harris, Laura Linney, Noah Emmerich, Natascha Mcelhone, Holland Taylor.* Giving a breakthrough performance, Carrey shines as Truman Burbank, a naïve, likable guy-next-door who — unbeknowst to him — is the star of a highly rated, hidden camera 24-hour TV show. Writer Andrew Niccol and director Weir have taken a most exploitable and inventive premise and created a brilliantly executed fable. When we first meet Truman Burbank, he's happy, married and, evidently, without a care in the world. But then a series of bizarre events unfold which begin to make Truman question his own sanity. It's only then does he realize that — for him — all the world's a soundstage. Funny, subtle, beguiling, and an often cynical comment on modern TV and commercialism, *The Truman Show* expertly walks that fine line between comedy and drama. In support, Harris is especially good as Truman's "guardian angel," a corporate-minded artist whose bottom-line is ratings and who can't see the humanity which he's created. (VHS available letterboxed or pan & scan) ★★★★ VHS: $9.99; DVD: $29.99

Trust

(1990, 91 min, US, Hal Hartley) *Adrienne Shelley, Martin Donovan.* Hartley, the style-rich auteur of the MTV generation, scores with his brilliantly insightful second feature. Focusing again on young, angst-ridden suburban narcissists like those he introduced in *The Unbelievable Truth*, Hartley probes into seemingly shallow, mundane lives and comes up with funny, touching portraits of multi-dimensional charaters. Shelley plays a pregnant cheerleader, Donovan is a grenade-toting, burned-out computer whiz. Together they explore humanity, right on Long Island. ★★★½ VHS: $19.99

The Truth about Cats and Dogs

(1996, 93 min, US, Michael Lehmann) *Janeane Garofalo, Uma Thurman, Ben Chaplin, Jamie Foxx.* When keeping a pet is a major life decision, what hope is there for relationships between humans? Garofalo is a pleasure as a talk radio show host who helps her callers understand their verbally challenged canine and feline companions. Plump, brunette and verbally adroit, she meets and then befriends her societal nemesis, a quintessential Beautiful Dumb Blonde (Thurman). A deliberate act of deception involving a too-good-to-be-true love interest (Chaplin) escalates into a slapstick comedy of errors and enjoys a resolution mostly found only in the movies. The script for this gender-switched "Cyrano de Bergerac" is wildly uneven, but it successfully depicts the everyday incivilities which define our public personas. ★★½ VHS: $9.99; DVD: $24.99

Truth or Consequences, N.M.

(1997, 103 min, US, Kiefer Sutherland) *Vincent Gallo, Kiefer Sutherland, Mykelti Williamson, Kim Dickens, Kevin Pollak, Rod Steiger.* A taut thriller directed by actor Sutherland in his debut behind the camera, *Truth or Consequences, N.M.* is a violent and very satisfying chase movie. Curtis (Sutherland) is the trigger happy ex-con fronting a gang of thieves intent on robbing a drug dealer and selling the stash to the mob. When the heist goes awry, and an undercover cop is killed, Curtis flees west with his partners. The film has some nifty plot twists and double crosses on the way to the title city where the final confrontation between the gang, the mob and the DEA takes place. Sutherland's crisp direction of this escalating crime spree is marred only slightly by some gratuitous bloodshed and unnecessary camera flourishes; but he coaxes flinty performances from the cast. ★★★ VHS: $9.99; DVD: $14.99

Tucker

(1988, 120 min, US, Francis Ford Coppola) *Jeff Bridges, Martin Landau, Dean Stockwell, Joan Allen, Christian Slater.* A wonderful piece of storytelling from director Coppola. Preston Tucker was the personification of the American Dream — a man who believed anyone's dream could come true. But his Amercian Dream becomes the American Nightmare when he builds a futuristic luxury car all too well and is soon taken on by the big car manufacturers and crooked politicians, all afraid his design could set a new precedent in excellence and ruin their special interests. Based on a true story, Coppola has crafted a beautifully detailed period piece. Bridges stars in the title role, and Landau, in an Oscar-nominated performance, appears as Tucker's loyal business partner and friend. ★★★½ VHS: $14.99; DVD: $29.99

The Truman Show

Tuff Turf

(1985, 113 min, US, Fritz Kiersch) *James Spader, Kim Richards, Matt Clark, Robert Downey, Jr.* A very youthful Spader stars in this satisfying teen pic as a streetwise preppy who takes on an L.A. gang and falls for the gang leader's girlfriend (Richards). Not as formulaic as you'd expect, and Spader demonstrates the timing and intensity which would make him one of the movies' leading actors just a few years later. ★★½ VHS: $9.99; DVD: $24.99

Tumbleweeds

(1999, 100 min, US, Gavin O'Connor) *Janet McTeer, Kimberly J. Brown, Jay O. Sanders, Gavin O'Connor, Lois Smith.* McTeer's Oscar nomination is well-deserved for her portrayal of Mary Jo Walker, a woman who manages life with quick packing and long road trips in the middle of the night to parts unknown. Her one unassailable bond is with her daughter Ava (a solid performance from Brown); together they decide where to live next, based on magazine photos and the last known addresses of Mary Jo's ex-boyfriends. Putting their trust in fate and the mantra "a brand new day," they undertake another new school, another job search. Mary Jo, on the lookout for husband #5, is so busy deflecting the weirdos and picking yet again the wrong man, that she doesn't see the chance for happiness right in front of her. The film is about the coming-of-age of both mother and daughter, as Ava takes her first steps into adulthood and Mary Jo discovers the inner strength she's always had but never recognized. Featuring two remarkable lead performances, *Tumbleweeds* tells a familiar story without cliché or sentimentality; a story about loss and recovery, about learning when to leave and when to stay. ★★★½ VHS: $19.99; DVD: $24.99

The Tune

(1992, 80 min, US, Bill Plympton) Plympton's highly amusing and inventive short cartoons have long become a staple of animation festivals. His unique sense of humor and fantastical imagery are near breathtaking. By these standards, *The Tune*, Plympton's first feature cartoon, is a total disappointment. A struggling songwriter is magically transported to the land

of Flooby Nooby where he receives an education in letting his artistic talents flow. Unfortunately, most of Plympton's ingenious comedy gets eaten up by unending song-and-dance routines which mostly fizzle. ★½ VHS: $59.99; DVD: $29.99

Tune in Tomorrow

(1990, 105 min, US, Jon Amiel) *Peter Falk, Keanu Reeves, Barbara Hershey, Peter Gallagher.* This delightfully capricious and wildly imaginative comedy stars Falk as a famed radio script writer who is hired by a small station in New Orleans in the early 1950s. There he befriends adorable and painfully innocent 21-year-old Reeves, who has fallen in love with his thirtysomething, divorced aunt, Hershey. As they explore their forbidden passion, Falk surreptitiously manipulates their affair which, lo-and-behold, is echoed on his radio show. Based on a story by Peruvian author Mario Vargas Llosa, the film is filled with excursions into the absurd and surreal. Though the entire cast is first-rate, the honors go to Falk, whose quips about Albanian peasantry are sidesplitting. ★★★½ VHS: $9.99

Tunes of Glory

(1960, 106 min, GB, Ronald Neame) *Alec Guinness, John Mills.* Guinness and Mills are outstanding in this memorable character study of two rival colonels: one a careless, vicious renegade; the other a disciplined, well-mannered young officer who is slated to replace him. As the power is set to change hands at the Swiss Regiment, resentments and bitterness give rise to a violent confrontation and a shocking climax. ★★★★ VHS: $29.99

The Tunnel of Love

(1958, 98 min, US, Gene Kelly) *Doris Day, Richard Widmark, Gia Scala, Gig Young.* Kelly made his directorial bow with this sly, relaxed comedy based on the Broadway hit. Day and Widmark play a married couple desperately trying to have a baby. Deciding to adopt, they encounter lots of red tape and counselor Scala. Through one of the many misunderstandings which provide much of the film's humor, Widmark thinks that he has fathered a baby — with Scala. It's all rather tame, but the screenplay's entendres still amuse. Young steals the show as Widmark's best friend and gets the lion's share of the best lines. ★★★ VHS: $19.99

Turbulence

(1997, 100 min, US, Robert Butler) *Lauren Holly, Ray Liotta, Brendan Gleeson, Ben Cross, Rachel Ticotin.* The airline industry is in for more trouble and bad public relations with this silly action film. Holly is a stewardess (sorry. . . flight attendant) who puts on her best "Karen Black-*Airport '75*-I'm-gonna-save-this-plane" face when she goes up against a serial killer prisoner (Liotta) who takes control of their plane. He chases her, she chases him. He rants and raves. She cries and curses a lot. *Turbulence* dives out of control from the bombardment of cliché after cliché. (VHS available letterboxed or pan & scan) (Followed by 2 sequels) ★½ VHS: $9.99; DVD: $14.99

Turkish Delight

(1974, 100 min, The Netherlands, Paul Verhoeven) *Rutger Hauer, Monique van de Ven.* Years before he burst into international stardom with the macabre and erotic *The 4th Man*, gifted Dutch filmmaker Verhoeven directed this acclaimed, sexually explicit drama. This is very much a film of its period, complete with jazz soundtrack, promiscuity, a hostile "establishment" and a "youth must be served" attitude. Hauer is at first little more than a callous lothario intent on bedding a maximum number of women until he falls in love. (Letterboxed) (Dutch wth English subtitles) ★★★ VHS: $14.99; DVD: $29.99

The Turn of the Screw

(1992, 95 min, GB, Rusty Lemorande) *Patsy Kensit, Julian Sands, Stéphane Audran, Marianne Faithfull.* This eerie adaptation of the Henry James ghost story is brimming with Freudian imagery and atmosphere. Kensit stars as a prim governess who is hired by a truly whacked-out Sands (when is he anything else?) to tend to two small children living in a secluded English manor. Once there, of course, she is overcome by visions and other hauntings all of which seem to center around her repressed sexuality and a young boy. Faithfull plays the sole survivor of the ordeal who narrates the action. ★★½ VHS: $79.99

Turner & Hooch

(1989, 97 min, US, Roger Spottiswoode) *Tom Hanks, Mare Winningham, Craig T. Nelson.* Hanks plays an officious police detective whose investigation of a murder is slightly hampered when the sole witness is a slobbering and very ugly watchdog. While most of the humor is predictable, Hanks is always a pleasure to watch and the film is at least better than the similarly themed, dog-tired *K9*. ★★ VHS: $9.99

The Turning Point

(1977, 119 min, US, Herbert Ross) *Shirley MacLaine, Anne Bancroft, Tom Skerritt, Mikhail Baryshnikov, Leslie Browne.* MacLaine and Bancroft give tour de force performances in this exquisite drama set in the world of ballet. Bancroft plays a star ballerina who is reunited with childhood friend MacLaine, now a housewife and dance teacher, when the latter's daughter comes to New York to study ballet. Baryshnikov also stars as a dancer who romances the young Browne. Skerritt gives a fine, understated performance as MacLaine's patient husband. The film features excellent ballet sequences, and can be enjoyed even by those not fond of the dance. ★★★ VHS: $9.99

Turtle Diary

(1986, 97 min, GB, John Irvin) *Glenda Jackson, Ben Kingsley, Michael Gambon.* Esteemed British playwright Harold Pinter wrote the charming adaptation of this Russell Hoban ("Ridley Walker") novel. Kingsley and Jackson play a bookstore clerk and a children's writer, respectively, who conspire to set a pair of giant sea turtles loose from the London Zoo. What ensues is a gently metaphorical exploration of the meaning of liberation and rejuvenation. ★★★

The Tuskegee Airmen

(1995, 110 min, US, Robert Markowitz) *Laurence Fishburne, Cuba Gooding, Jr., Allen Payne, Malcolm-Jamal Warner, Andre Braugher, John Lithgow, Courtney Vance.* Recalling the story of the first American black pilots to serve in WWII, *The Tuskegee Airmen* is an inspiring story of courage

and perseverance. Fishburne plays Hannibal Lee, a pre-med student from Iowa who is among the first cadets for pilot training. America has been at war for over a year, yet blacks were not allowed to fly planes. With politicians and military personnel against them, Lee and a small group of black enlistees must fight prejudice at home and overseas before being allowed to take on the Nazis. The ensemble is uniformly good, with Fishburne anchoring the film with a nuanced portrayal of determination and loyalty. A fitting tribute to the men of the 99th and 332nd squadrons. ★★★½ VHS: $9.99; DVD: $19.99

Twelfth Night — Or What You Will

(1996, 134 min, GB, Trevor Nunn) *Imogen Stubbs, Helena Bonham Carter, Toby Stephens, Ben Kingsley, Nigel Hawthorne, Richard E. Grant.* Shakespeare's ribald tale of mistaken identity and transgendered hilarity is brought to the screen with verve and vigor by stage veteran Nunn and a splendid cast. Stubbs is Viola, a young maiden who, shipwrecked and separated from her identical twin brother, takes on the appearance of a man (Cesario) in order to win favor in the court of Orsino (Stephens). Orsino, it turns out, is intent on winning the love of Olivia (Bonham Carter), and Cesario takes on the call of winning her over on behalf of the moody prince. But, of course, people's affections fail to land on their intended targets and before long all-out farce rules the day. Though occasionally dragged down by some sloppy filmmaking, Nunn's experience as artistic director for the Royal Shakespeare Company pays off and he delivers an uproarious and timely comic adventure — what pleasure the bawdy Bard can be! ★★★½ VHS: $19.99

12 Angry Men

(1957, 95 min, US, Sidney Lumet) *Henry Fonda, Lee J. Cobb, E.G. Marshall, Jack Klugman, Jack Warden, Ed Begley, Martin Balsam.* Fonda heads a magnificent cast in this brilliant adaptation of Reginald Rose's gripping jury room drama. Fonda plays a juror who, uncertain of the guilt of a youth on trial for killing his father, tries to dissuade the other 11 members who are about to cast votes of guilty. The story evaluates the responsibility of the judicial and jury system, and is a bristling exposé of racial and social intolerance. Notable not only for its superlative acting and direction (Lumet's film debut), but also for introducing a gallery of aspiring New York stage actors, some of whom would go on to great success in New York and Hollywood. (Remade in 1997) ★★★★ VHS: $14.99; DVD: $19.99

The Twelve Chairs

(1970, 94 min, US, Mel Brooks) *Ron Moody, Frank Langella, Dom DeLuise.* Early Brooks always provides for solid comic entertainment, and this often-overlooked gem rates as one of his best. Moody, in a hilariously manic performance, plays a Russian aristocrat who sets out on a madcap search for a dining room chair containing a fortune in jewels hidden in its upholstery. Langella is a transient who helps with the quest, and DeLuise gives an uproarious, lunatic performance as Moody's rival for the jewels. ★★★½ VHS: $9.99; DVD: $24.99

12 Monkeys

(1995, 130 min, US, Terry Gilliam) *Bruce Willis, Madeleine Stowe, Brad Pitt, Christopher Plummer, David Morse, Frank Gorshin.* A dark, multilayered sci-fi thriller inspired by the obscure French short *La Jetée.* Willis plays a prisoner in a futuristic underground society who is forced to go back in time to track down the mythic "Army of the 12 Monkeys" and study the germ warfare holocaust that wiped out most of humanity. Over-shooting the designated time period, he is thrown into an insane asylum where he must convince his shrink (Stowe) that he is not delusional (or *is* he?). Unlike most time travel stories, the intelligent screenplay devotes proper attention to the elements of tragedy and inevitability thereby distracting from the attendant conundrums and paradoxes inherent in the genre. A masterpiece of post-apocalyptic grunge, *12 Monkeys* is replete with Gilliam's trademark set design of ductwork and steam vents. Pitt is exceptional as an off-the-wall asylum mate who's not as crazy as he seems. (Letterboxed VHS available for $19.99) ★★★★ VHS: $14.99; DVD: $29.99

Twelve O'Clock High

(1949, 132 min, US, Henry King) *Gregory Peck, Dean Jagger, Hugh Marlowe, Gary Merrill.* Peck gives one of his finest performances in this stirring psychological WWII drama about the pressures facing pilots and the men sending them off to die. Peck plays the newly appointed commander whose inflexibility causes resentment among his men and leads to his own breakdown. A thoroughly involving war drama, unusual for its time in that the flag waving was reduced to a minimum, with more concern for personal relationships and psychological profile. Jagger, in his Oscar-winning role, stands out as the company clerk. ★★★½ VHS: $14.99; DVD: $24.99

Twentieth Century

(1934, 92 min, US, Howard Hawks) *Carole Lombard, John Barrymore, Walter Connelly, Roscoe Karns.* Hawks' lightning-quick, hilarious adaptation of the Hecht-MacArthur play was the first popular hit of the new "screwball comedy" genre, and those unfamiliar with this comic gem will be amazed at how relentlessly funny and inventive it is. Lombard and Barrymore have an ongoing, cross-country battle-of-the-sexes aboard a train en route to her Broadway opening. The two stars are phenomenal. Barrymore brings fiendish energy to the part of a down-on-his-luck, maniacal director, and Lombard combines dazzling wit with great beauty in her role as the pampered actress. ★★★★ VHS: $19.99

Twenty Bucks

(1993, 91 min, US, Keva Rosenfeld) *Brendan Fraser, Christopher Lloyd, Linda Hunt, Steve Buscemi, Spalding Gray, Matt Frewer.* Based on a script that's been floating around Hollywood for over 50 years, *Twenty Bucks* has an interesting premise: Follow the life of a crisp twenty dollar bill as it passes from owner to owner, becoming limp, bloodied and torn in the process. Unfortunately, the people who come into contact with the bill, like delivery guy Fraser and homeless person/mystic Hunt, aren't as engaging as the original idea. ★★½

T

20 Dates

(1998, 92 min, US, Myles Berkowitz) *Myles Berkowitz, Tia Carrere.* Fledgling director Berkowitz has given himself 20 dates to find (and film) someone to love. Purposely skirting the line between documentary and scripted romantic comedy, he can only occasionally pull off the uncomfortable laughs he's aiming for. His biggest problem is casting himself as the romantic lead; an obnoxious Hollywood type who talked his way into directing this movie, he generates very little sympathy for his romantic foibles. His struggles with the unseen (but much heard) producer are also strained; it's easy to understand why a producer would be cranky seeing so much of his money come back as videotaped footage of blind dates. Ultimately, the issues raised here regarding the documentary form make this much more successful as an experimental film than any sort of broad entertainment. ★★ VHS: $102.99

28 Days

(2000, 104 min, US, Betty Thomas) *Sandra Bullock, Viggo Mortensen, Diane Ladd, Steve Buscemi.* Against type, Bullock plays a fast-living substance abuser who is court ordered to spend 28 days in rehab (after almost single-handedly ruining her sister's wedding). There she befriends a group of misfits and learns a little about herself. There's not much new in the addict-on-the-mends story line, and the small group that Bullock finds herself reluctantly becoming a part is straight from Central Casting. But if you can get beyond the misplaced sentimentality and tawdry laughs (screenwriter Susannah Grant wants to make fun of these people while trying to expose their humanity – it doesn't work), there's an involving story of trying to get one's self on the right road at the heart of director Thomas' wayward film. Bullock is an engaging presence even as she careens out of control, but she can't quite compensate for the script's occasional lapses in judgment. ★★½ VHS: $14.99; DVD: $24.99

28 Up

(1985, 133 min, GB, Michael Apted) Originally made in four separate installments, Apted's fascinating documentary began with a series of interviews with English children at age seven. Over the years, he went back to follow up on their lives at ages 14, 21 and 28. The success and failure of these individuals to fulfill their dreams provide an informative and sometimes lamentable view of real life. (Sequel: *35 Up*) ★★★ VHS: $19.99

25 Fireman's Street

(1973, 97 min, Hungary, István Szabó) *Lucyna Winnicka, Margit Makay, Károly Kovács, András Bálint.* Set in the post-war era, this evocative and haunting film explores the dreams, memories and nightmares of a group of people living in an old house on the eve of its destruction. Through the course of the film, they recall a generation of happiness and tragedy as affected by the war. (Hungarian with English subtitles) ★★★½ VHS: $69.99

Twenty-Four Eyes

(1954, 158 min, Japan, Keisuke Kinoshita) *Hideko Takamine, Chishu Ryo.* The title of this beloved Japanese classic refers to the 24 eyes of

the students of an elementary class on the remote island of Shodoshima. Set in the late 1920s, the students' calm and traditional way of life is changed when a shockingly modern young teacher from Tokyo arrives. The woman, who wears a suit like a man and rides a bike to work, is slowly accepted and eventually loved by her students. Both their bright futures and the new ideas of the teacher are shattered by the impending war as well as by a rising nationalism that stifles individual growth and transforms personal ambition into unflinching devotion to the state. (Japanese with English subtitles) ★★★

The 24 Hour Woman

(1999, 92 min, US, Nancy Savoca) *Rosie Perez, Marianne Jean-Baptiste, Patti LuPone, Karen Duffy.* Perez replicates the natural, unforced honesty of her performance in *Fearless* in *The 24 Hour Woman*, a frenetic reflection on the wonderful world of working motherhood. Director Savoca has structured the film with rhythms matching the pace of its inhabitants' lives; lives of constant, unending, unyielding disruptions, of incessant demands and inherent contradictions. Perez is a producer of a live-broadcast AM TV show. Announcing her pregnancy before she has a chance to tell her family, it follows her pregnancy with as much accuracy as TV brings to most subjects it covers: not very much. As various experts parade across the screen, Perez and other parents (notably her assistant, ably portrayed by Jean-Baptiste) do their best with the percipitous balancing act of earning a living and raising a family in the latter days of the 20th century. The film's penultimate scenes combine slapstick zaniness with modern-day terror, and leaves us with the honest reality that there are no final resolutions, just eternal adjustment. ★★★ VHS: $105.99

20 Million Miles to Earth

(1957, 82 min, US, Nathan Juran) *William Hopper, Joan Taylor.* Great special effects by Ray Harryhausen and an unusually good story highlight this sci-fi winner about a spacecraft's return from Venus and the deadly hitchhiker it inadvertently picks up and drops off for a sightseeing tour of Athens. Gotta love that alien! ★★★ VHS: $14.99

29th Street

(1991, 98 min, US, George Gallo) *Danny Aiello, Anthony LaPaglia, Lainie Kazan, Frank Pesce, Jr.* A slight though enjoyable depiction of the havoc and happiness that befalls an Italian-American family when they become winners of the New York State Lottery. Based on a true story, the film examines Frank Pesce, Jr.'s (LaPaglia) inexplicable dismay over the seemingly joyous news that he has become a multimillionaire. Aiello is solid, as always, as LaPaglia's father, Frank, Sr. and Kazan is strong in support as his wife. The real Pesce delivers a surprisingly good debut as the other son, Vito. At times funny, the film draws its strength from the heart of the Pesce family where, although they are always fighting, true bonds of love prevail. ★★½ VHS: $19.99

Twenty-One

(1990, 92 min, GB, Don Boyd) *Patsy Kensit, Jack Shephard, Rufus Sewell.* Kensit seduces her way into the hearts of viewers in this hip examination of the excesses and maladies of coming-of-age in the '90s. The film is told largely through

a series of flashbacks, with Kensit delivering a series of voice-over soliloquies on her budding philosophies and unique impressions of the crazy world around her. ★★½ VHS: $79.99

26 Bathrooms

(1985, 28 min, GB, Peter Greenaway) On a short break from feature filmmaking, director Greenaway made for British TV this delightfully wacky documentary that takes an entertaining peek into the bathrooms of Great Britain. Serious in a smirking cleverish way, Greenaway's unusual travelogue visits 26 different bathrooms in and around London — all of which seek to go beyond mere functionalism and celebrate the therapeutic pleasures of the bathing ritual. And keeping with his game-playing pastime, the film is broken up into alphabetical segments running from A to Z, i.e., A is for A Bathroom, D is for Dental Hygiene, F is for Fish. ★★½ VHS: $19.99

20,000 Leagues under the Sea

(1916, 101 min, US, Stuart Paton) *Matt Moore, Jane Gail, Alan Holubar.* This early silent version of Jules Verne's classic adventure story was one of the first films to feature innovative special effects and underwater photography. The story follows the renegade Captain Nemo who discovers a sea monster from his submarine Nautilus. Newly remastered from an archive print. ★★★ VHS: $24.99; DVD: $24.99

20,000 Leagues under the Sea

(1954, 126 min, US, Richard Fleischer) *Kirk Douglas, James Mason, Peter Lorre, Paul Lukas.* Oscar-winning special effects highlight this exciting Disney film based on Jules Verne's story of shipwrecked survivors becoming involved with the notorious Captain Nemo. ★★★½

Twice in a Lifetime

(1985, 117 min, US, Bud Yorkin) *Gene Hackman, Ann-Margret, Ellen Burstyn, Amy Madigan, Brian Dennehy.* Superior acting elevates this compelling family drama about a husband who leaves his wife and children for another woman. Hackman gives a virtuoso performance as the working-class family man starting life anew; and he gets terrific support. Intelligent screenplay by Colin Welland. ★★★½

Twilight

(1998, 96 min, US, Robert Benton) *Paul Newman, Susan Sarandon, Gene Hackman, James Garner, Reese Witherspoon, Giancarlo Esposito, Liev Schreiber.* In the twilight of his career, Newman demonstrates in this impassioned though intruiging noir mystery that charisma, talent and experience can often compensate for a convoluted story. In a laid-back, compelling portrayal, Newman plays Harry Ross, a retired cop and private eye who is very nearly one of life's great losers. An alcholic who's estranged from his family, with no home of his own, and relegated to servants quarters and duties while staying with his movie star friends (Hackman, Sarandon), Harry finds himself smack in the middle of a dime novel mystery when a simple delivery job leads to a series of murders. Director Benton gives *Twilight* the look and feel of a 1940s noir, all dark and shadowy and mysterious. But style can't overcome a "B" story line and less-than-swift pacing. ★★½ VHS: $14.99; DVD: $29.99

Twilight of the Golds

(1997, 90 min, US, Ross Marks) *Brendan Fraser, Jennifer Beals, Faye Dunaway, Garry Marshall, Jon Tenney, Rosie O'Donnell, Sean O'Bryan, Jack Klugman, John Schlesinger.* An absorbing "issue" drama about Suzanne (Beals), who learns that her unborn child will be gay, *The Twilight of the Golds* takes an intelligent approach to the "environment vs. heredity" debate. The "problem" of being gay is sketchily addressed — it is even likened to a disease — but once viewers get over this hurdle, the film is engrossing without descending into movie-of-the-week histrionics. As each member of the Gold family express their opinion about Suzanne's decision, they become torn apart by differences. While some of the scenes are a bit forced — especially those between Suzanne's gay brother David (Fraser) and his lover Steven (O'Bryan) — director Marks' film is compelling. Strangely, screenwriter Jonathan Tollins (who adapted his play) seems to have ruled out the option of adoption. ★★★ VHS: $14.99; DVD: $14.99

Twilight Zone: The Movie

(1983, 102 min, US, John Landis, Steven Spielberg, Joe Dante & George Miller) *Vic Morrow, John Lithgow, Scatman Crothers, Kathleen Quinlan, Kevin McCarthy.* Four episodes either based on teleplays from the classic TV series "Twilight Zone," or close in theme and spirit. Though the most infamous of the four (directed by Landis) is the segment starring Morrow — in which the actor and two children were killed — about a bigoted man who gets his comeuppance, the best is the finale, "Nightmare at 20,000 Feet" (directed by Miller) with Lithgow outstanding as a frightened airline passenger (based on a TV episode starring William Shatner). Other episodes include Spielberg's "Kick the Can," about a group of senior citizens who rediscover their youth, and Dante's cartoon-like story of a young boy whose magical powers don't make him very popular. ★★½ VHS: $14.99

Twin Dragons

(1992, 90 min, Hong Kong, Tsui Hark & Ringo Lam) *Jackie Chan, Maggie Cheung, Teddy Robin.* Too many cooks spoil this broth, which is tellingly labeled "A Film by Hong Kong Director's Guild." Bad dubbing and choppy editing don't help. A blend of slapstick and kung-fu that never gels into a real movie, it's still worth watching for Chan's fun performance as twins (one's a maestro; one's, well, Jackie Chan). A botched job for a gangster by Chan II, followed by a twin switcheroo, leads to many blackout-style gags and throwaway action sequences. Watch for one brilliant scene at least, set inside a car factory — that highlights what Chan does best. Famed directors John Woo and Kirk Wong helmed some scenes. ★★ VHS: $14.99; DVD: $29.99

Twin Falls Idaho

(1999, 110 min, US, Michael Polish) *Mark Polish, Michael Polish, Michele Hicks, Jon Greis, Garrett Morris, William Katt, Lesley Ann Warren.* Penny the hooker (Hicks) makes her way to her next appointment at the seedy Imperial Hotel on Idaho Avenue. The elevator operator is surly, the hallway smells of piss, and she seems much too young to be so world-weary. Her trick is, rather, *are* Francis (director Michael Polish) and Blake

(Mark Polish), conjoined twins who share 3½ legs, two arms, and their psyches. All three are outcasts, relegated to the Lynchian environs of a faceless urban wasteland, at the mercy of the casual cruelty of the "normal." The film could have settled for mere shock value; instead, it is a remarkable meditation on loneliness and identity, told with unexpected sweetness and compassion. The moody and luminous cinematography is one element in this expression of a signature vision, laced with singular moments of profound tenderness in extraordinary circumstances. Every aspect of the film meshes with the other to garner the unconditional acceptance of a fantastic, emotionally satisfying and visually articulate world. A haunting and lyrical film. ★★★½ VHS: $21.99; DVD: $27.99

Twin Peaks: Fire Walk with Me

(1992, 135 min, US, David Lynch) *Sheryl Lee, Kyle MacLachlan, Madchen Amick, David Bowie, Miguel Ferrer, James Marshall, Grace Zabriskie.* Very few contemporary filmmakers can ever be accused of originality and so it seems ironic that one of the most inventive of the lot, Lynch, is already giving way to self-tribute. Regardless of this, however, this necessary, quasi-Gothic return to the mythical hamlet of "Twin Peaks" recycles the insightful themes introduced in the series, scaling them up to near-operatic proportions to chronicle the events leading up to the murder of Laura Palmer. Lee reprises her role as the doomed nymphet. A fitting coda to the small-town saga and the successful effort of an innovator forced to walk the tightrope which spans the chasm between cinematic genius and televised mediocrity. ★★★ VHS: $14.99

Twin Town

(1997, 99 min, Wales, Kevin Allen) *Llyr Evans, Rhys Ifans, Dorien Thomas.* The glue-sniffing, dope-smoking Lewis brothers, known as "the twins" despite three years difference in age, barter prescription drugs from senior citizens and pilfer cars for ready cash. When a local pillar of society — a club owner with police in his pocket — refuses to compensate an injury on the job suffered by their construction worker dad, the twins embark on a path of retribution that veers from goofy prank to unexpected tragedy. The actors are unselfconscious and direct, uniformly engaging in their portrayals of lusts and obsessions and fragmented loyalties. Often compared to *Trainspotting*, *Twin Town* is similar in its blithe juxtaposition of the remnants of Old World charm against the harsh realities of modern day vice. ★★★½ VHS: $9.99

Twin Warriors

(1993, 93 min, Hong Kong, Yuen Woo Ping) *Jet Li, Michelle Yeoh, Chin Siu-Ho.* In this over-the-top, entertaining martial arts film, Li demonstrates why he is one of Hong Kong's most enduring stars. He plays Junbao, who with his childhood friend Tianbao grew up in the Shaolin Temple. When they are both expelled due to Tianbao's temper, they take different paths in the outside world: Tianbao turns his back on his friend and joins the military, Junbao learns Tai Chi. Eventually, they must confront each other in a fight for honor. The fight choreography is first-rate, and the pace flows well. Fans of the old Saturday Night Kung Fu Theatre should enjoy this one. (aka: *The Tai Chi Master*) (Dubbed) ★★★ VHS: $14.99; DVD: $29.99

Twins

(1988, 112 min, US, Ivan Reitman) *Danny DeVito, Arnold Schwarzenegger, Chloe Webb.* A one-joke comedy whose punchline wears thin soon after its telling. The appealing duo of Schwarzenegger and DeVito star as separated twin brothers (and scientific experiments) who are reunited when the former leaves his island paradise in search of his roots. DeVito, who can get comic mileage from a phone book, rises above the nonsensical script and direction. Yeah, it's funny Arnie and Danny are twins: for the first ten minutes that is. What about the other 102? ★★ VHS: $9.99; DVD: $24.99

Twins of Evil

(1971, 85 min, GB, John Hough) *Peter Cushing, Madeleine Collinson, Mary Collinson.* This sequel to *Vampire Lovers* and *Lust for a Vampire* continues the "Carmilla" story line, this time starring *Playboy*'s first twin playmates. Cushing returns as their puritanical adversary, appalled as much by their sexual proclivities as their dietary habits. ★★½

Twist and Shout

(1984, 105 min, Denmark, Bille August) *Lars Simonsen, Adam Tonsberg.* This harrowing, beautifully acted teenage rite-of-passage film from young Danish director August is a comedy-drama that explores a web of complex familial and romantic relationships surrounding four young friends. Never once sinking to the level of a typical American teenage coming-of-age film, *Twist and Shout* instead creates a kinetic excitement of youthful sexuality as director August proves himself wonderfully capable of portraying the agony and ecstacy of adolescent life. ★★★½

Twisted

(1997, 86 min, Australia, Christopher Robbin Collins & Samantha Lang) *Bryan Brown, Geoffrey Rush, Rachel Ward, Kimberly Davies.* A mixed bag, *Twisted* is an anthology of four supernatural tales that boast exactly one plot twist each. While no single episode of the quartet stands out, parts of the film are very atmospheric and the whole thing looks great. Yet there is little in way of suspense or creativity to heighten the drama. The four stories are linked by the theme of swapping identities, but the characters — a difficult airline passenger (Rush); a bored housewife (Ward); a confidence man (Brown); and a malfunctioning android (Davies) — are really only caricatures. The supernatural elements appear only superficially, and this will displease fans expecting a jolt or two. ★★ VHS: $69.99; DVD: $24.99

Twister

(1988, 93 min, US, Michael Almereyda) *Harry Dean Stanton, Crispin Glover, Dylan McDermott, Suzy Amis.* When the production wing of Vestron Pictures went under, *Twister* was unceremoniously released on video, bypassing theatrical release. Too bad, for it's an unqualified delight. This innovative comedy is set in a sprawling mansion in the middle of Kansas where Stanton is raising a family of lunatics. They include Amis as his daughter who has a tenuous grasp on reality; and Glover as his abundantly confused son. ★★★

Twister

(1996, 114 min, US, Jan De Bont) *Bill Paxton, Helen Hunt, Jami Gertz, Cary Elwes, Lois Smith, Philip Seymour Hoffman, Alan Ruck.* The director of *Speed* and the writer of *Jurassic Park* unite to bring one grand-slam if vacuous special effects extravaganza. De Bont employs the high-energy octane of his exciting bus saga with *Park*'s great F/X, and when the film allows these F/X to take center stage, *Twister* is a knockout. But there's the matter of a story between the effects, and it's a whirlwind of mediocrity. Hunt plays a scientist who chases tornadoes. Onto the scene comes her soon-to-be ex-husband (Paxton). He was once a tornado chaser but now he's a weatherman. The two get together and follow several tornadoes throughout the Midwest. But forget about the dialogue and story — the F/X are the real interest here, and each successive twister brings on more carnage and jaw-dropping effects culminating in a smash finale. (VHS available letterboxed or pan & scan) ★★½ VHS: $14.99; DVD: $24.99

Two Daughters

(1962, 116 min, India, Satyajit Ray) Ray's wonderful film is divided into two different stories but united in the theme of first love. The first tale, "The Postmaster," is about a young girl's growing affection for her employer; the second, "The Conclusion," is a charming parable about a girl who is forced into a loveless marriage with a bland but successful man. Her frustrations grow until she leaves him in an effort to find real love. (Hindi with English subtitles) ★★★

2 Days in the Valley

(1996, 105 min, US, John Herzfeld) *James Spader, Danny Aiello, Glenne Headly, Teri Hatcher, Jeff Daniels, Eric Stoltz, Charlize Theron, Marsha Mason, Paul Mazurskyl.* Of the many post-Quentin Tarantino comedic, violent, pulse-racing, multicharacter, noir criminal saga/thrillers, the inventive and often extremely funny *2 Days in the Valley* is one of the most entertaining. Casting a cynical eye on a cold-blooded world and containing unpredictable twists that we've come to expect from good mysteries, the story begins as hired guns Aiello and Spader finalize a hit. Only Spader attempts to kill his partner and frame him for the murder. Barely escaping and on the run, Aiello hides out in the luxurious Valley home of a pompous art dealer. Meanwhile, Spader must return to the scene of the crime when his fee is locked away in the house, which is by now crawling with police — including Daniels and Stoltz. A zestful blend of Philip Marlowe glibness and contemporary inter-genre teasing. (VHS available letterboxed or pan & scan) ★★★ VHS: $9.99; DVD: $14.99

Two Deaths

(1996, 102 min, GB, Nicolas Roeg) *Michael Gambon, Sonia Braga, Patrick Malahide.* An intimate study of obsessional love related against the backdrop of the brutal absurdity of war evolves into an artfully constructed parable regarding the root causes of human self-destruction. Gambon plays a well-established, extremely comfortable surgeon hosting a sumptuous dinner party in an unspecified Eastern European city. The night rains random death as the militia squelches a civilian uprising...or executes any unarmed travelers out after curfew — depending on your perception of the matter. Gambon's brilliant portrayal of enigmatic moral ambivalance is stark counterpoint to Braga's earthy, sensual, intelligent and focused servant; his need to dominate and possess is forcefully confronted by her willful surrender. He relates their history to the assembled guests, who, though horrified, in turn tell their own stories of loss and corruption. An intricate, involving and revelatory foray into the darkest components of the human psyche. ★★★ VHS: $19.99; DVD: $19.99

Two English Girls

(1971, 108 min, France, François Truffaut) *Jean-Pierre Léaud, Kika Markham.* A kindred companion to *Jules and Jim*, *Two English Girls* features Léaud as the pivotal figure alternately romancing two British sisters with sometimes tragic consequences. A lyrical rumination of passion's turbulent course. (French with English subtitles) ★★★ VHS: $19.99; DVD: $29.99

Two Evil Eyes

(1990, 121 min, US/Italy, George Romero & Dario Argento) *Harvey Keitel, Adrienne Barbeau, E.G. Marshall, Tom Savini, Kim Hunter.* Romero and Argento join forces in this Poe-meets-*Creepshow* horror anthology. Romero's clever adaptation of "The Case of M. Valdemar" stars Barbeau as a greedy wife whose hubby dies...or does he? Argento's turn is short on sense, but long on atmosphere. Keitel stars as a sadistic Weegee-style photographer who can't conceal his crimes from "The Black Cat." Music by Pino Donaggio. ★★

Two for the Road

(1967, 111 min, GB, Stanley Donen) *Audrey Hepburn, Albert Finney, William Daniels, Eleanor Bron, Jacqueline Bisset.* Hepburn and Finney bring sophistication and spontaneity to their roles as a married couple looking back at the many paths they've traveled during a tumultuous 12-year marriage. Through a series of flashbacks, Frederic Raphael's fresh, innovative screenplay examines crucial crossroads in Hepburn and Finney's lives, all while the couple are traveling on the road. Fortunately, the constant back-and-forth through the years is neither distracting nor confusing. *Two for the Road* is consistently charming, and is laced with a delightful sense of humor. In support, Daniels and Bron are near-perfect as "ugly American" tourists/traveling companions. ★★★½ VHS: $14.99

Two for the Seesaw

(1962, 119 min, US, Robert Wise) *Robert Mitchum, Shirley MacLaine.* A bittersweet romantic comedy based on William Gibson's acclaimed play. Mitchum plays a Midwest lawyer, about to divorce his wife of 12 years, who moves to New York City and becomes involved with "lovable crackpot waif" MacLaine. Though on stage the story is a riveting character study, director Wise is unable to overcome the talkiness of a two-character play in his screen adaptation. But this is nonetheless an involving work, and Mitchum and MacLaine offer noteworthy performances. The basis for the Broadway musical "SeeSaw." ★★★ VHS: $19.99

Two Girls and a Guy

(1998, 84 min, US, James Toback) *Robert Downey, Jr., Heather Graham, Natasha Gregson Wagner.* While each awaits her boyfriend to return home, two women, Carla and Lou (Graham, Wagner), discover during small talk that they are seeing the same man. How these two united spirits band together and turn the tables on their two-timing beau forms the core of this caustic, clever and original sex comedy. Toback's brand of fireworks is altogether raunchy, hilarious and rude. In Blake, the writer-director has found a near-perfect mouthpiece for ideas and sexual attitudes both men and women may think but would never say aloud. And as played by the astonishingly versatile Downey, Blake knows how to charm you even as you're loathing him. With a sprinkling of sexual sparring and maybe a little gratuitous nudity, *Two Girls and a Guy* is very much an adult entertainment — a social and sexual comedy you can actually bite your teeth into. ★★★½ VHS: $9.99; DVD: $22.99

Two Girls and a Sailor

(1944, 125 min, US, Richard Thorpe) *June Allyson, Gloria DeHaven, Van Johnson, Lena Horne, Jimmy Durante.* Two singing-and-dancing sisters (Allyson, DeHaven) open up their dream canteen, with the help of a wily sailor (Johnson). A cute, bright musical entertainment typical of M-G-M's 1940s song-and-dance productions. ★★★ VHS: $19.99

200 Cigarettes

(1999, 99 min, US, Risa Bramon Garcia) *Ben Affleck, Casey Affleck, David Chappelle, Janeane Garofalo, Gaby Hoffman, Kate Hudson, Courtney Love, Jay Mohr, Martha Plimpton, Christina Ricci, Paul Rudd, Elvis Costello.* A multistory film, *200 Cigarettes*, set on New Year's Eve 1981, has a stellar cast, but also a mediocre-to-weak script. Some stories (Ricci's in particular) are snoozers, but the most clichéd and predictable one (Love and Rudd as best pals who you just *know* are going to end up together) is the most entertaining, due to the winning performances from the duo. There's some happenin' '80s tunes for the nostalgically inclined; though, truly, the whole '80s retro thing is already getting tired. Absolutely nothing new here — even the good stuff is utterly familiar — and there's little zip in the direction or dialogue. The cast, however, is most appealing. *200 Cigarettes* coasts on their collective charm. ★★ VHS: $14.99; DVD: $29.99

200 Motels

(1971, 98 min, US, Frank Zappa & Tony Palmer) *Frank Zappa, The Mothers of Invention, Ringo Starr, Theodore Bikel, Keith Moon.* Zappa and The Mothers of Invention are on the road in this incredibly bizarre "surrealistic documentary." ★★★

Two If by Sea

(1995, 95 min, US, Bill Bennett) *Denis Leary, Sandra Bullock, Stephen Dillane, Yaphet Kotto.* In this ordinary romantic comedy, Leary and Bullock are hired art thieves on the run from the law. Needing to hide out for several days before the drop-off, they find a vacant mansion and play house. With the police and underworld associates on their trail, they bicker, befriend a friendly teen, and attend fancy parties thrown by their handsome "neighbor" who has the hots for Bullock. The two stars aim for Tracy and Hepburn of the Bonnie and Clyde set, but the dialogue they are forced to recite is rarely funny or romantic, and their continual misadventures are very familiar. Cowriter Leary lost his bite with this one. ★★ VHS: $9.99; DVD: $14.99

The Two Jakes

(1990, 138 min, US, Jack Nicholson) *Jack Nicholson, Harvey Keitel, Meg Tilly, Ruben Blades, Eli Wallach.* Lacking the tension and chilling atmosphere of Roman Polanski's noirish classic *Chinatown*, this sequel directed by and starring Nicholson is fascinating and occasionally riveting. It's 1948, 11 years after the original. Private investigator Jake Gittes (Nicholson) is less ambitious, more portly, and content with mundane murder cases and rounds of golf. Problems arise when his client Jake Berman (Keitel) becomes involved in a murder. As the investigation ensues, Gittes finds himself face to face with his grisly past. Acting honors go to Keitel as Gittes' mysterious client. Nicholson demonstrates thoughtful competence as a director, but he sometimes bogs down in uninteresting side plots which lengthen the film. ★★★ VHS: $19.99; DVD: $24.99

Two-Lane Blacktop

(1971, 103 min, US, Monte Hellman) *Warren Oates, James Taylor, Laurie Bird, Dennis Wilson.* Ambitious, unique, and one of the quintessential films of the '70s, this is the cross-country car race between GTO (Oates), the Driver (Taylor) and the Mechanic (Wilson). Highlighted by incredible music and startling cinematography. Oates, who won a few acting awards for his performance, is outstanding; and, yes, this is probably the first time you saw a film character sing along with his car radio, which now has become a cliché. (Letterboxed) ★★★½ VHS: $14.99; DVD: $29.99

Two Moon Junction

(1988, 104 min, US, Zalman King) *Sherilyn Fenn, Martin Hewitt, Richard Tyson, Kristy McNichol.* A bored, blonde Fenn dumps her privileged life and vapid beau (Hewitt) and takes up with a rugged, muscle-bound carnival worker (Tyson). McNichol appears as a bisexual cowgirl in this cheesy T&A tale. ★★ VHS: $9.99; DVD: $24.99

The Two Mrs. Carrolls

(1947, 99 min, US, Peter Godfrey) *Humphrey Bogart, Barbara Stanwyck, Alexis Smith.* Bogart is an artist who killed his first wife, but not until after using her as a model for his painting "Angel of Death." It's a few years later, and now he's married to Stanwyck. And now she's starting to show signs of illness. Smith is the beautiful socialite with whom he falls in love while plotting to kill the second Mrs. Carroll. This psychological thriller is heavy going for the most part, and it takes its good old time building to a rather exciting climax. ★★½ VHS: $19.99

Two Mules for Sister Sara

(1970, 105 min, US, Don Siegel) *Clint Eastwood, Shirley MacLaine.* Eastwood and MacLaine make a good team in this entertaining comic western about drifter Eastwood coming to the aid of nun MacLaine (who sure doesn't act very religious) in the Mexican desert. ★★★ VHS: $14.99

The Two of Us

(1967, 86 min, France, Claude Berri) *Michel Simon, Alain Cohen.* Simon stars as an old man whose fervent anti-Semitism is challenged when he develops a close relationship with a young Jewish boy in hiding during World War II. Their growing friendship and love makes this both a charming and moving film experience. ★★★

2000 Maniacs

(1964, 75 min, US, Hershell Gordon Lewis) *Tom Wood, Connie Mason, Jeffrey Allen, Ben Moore.* Lewis' "masterpiece." An unbelievably bloody carnage feast that will have its viewers glued to the screen despite their increasing repugnance. The story centers around a sleepy Southern town and its unusual way of celebrating the 100th anniversary of the Civil War: capture unsuspecting Northerners and proceed to do unspeakable acts on their person. Southern hospitality my ass. Filled with Confederate flags, gushing blood, and enough shock value to send John Waters into an orgasmic frenzy. (Camp rating ★★★★) ★ DVD: $24.99

2001: A Space Odyssey

(1968, 139 min, GB, Stanley Kubrick) *Keir Dullea, William Sylvester, Gary Lockwood.* Both a grand hypothesis on humankind's place in the universe and a pithy examination of our efforts to control our burgeoning technology before it controls us, Kubrick's milestone sci-fi epic is nothing less than brilliant. A visual masterpiece without equal, the film was years ahead of its time with regard to special effects and Kubrick established his mastery of choreographing music with image. (VHS available letterboxed or pan & scan) (Sequel: *2010: The Year We Make Contact*) ★★★★ VHS: $19.99; DVD: $24.99

2010: The Year We Make Contact

(1984, 116 min, US, Peter Hyams) *Roy Scheider, John Lithgow, Bob Balaban, Helen Mirren, Keir Dullea.* In this sequel to Kubrick's landmark *2001*, a new space expedition locates the wrecked ship Discovery and learns the secret of its aborted mission. Though the special effects are commendable, the film doesn't share the original's narrative composition and intelligence — but then who'd actually expect it to? ★★ VHS: $14.99; DVD: $19.99

2001: A Space Odyssey

Two-Way Stretch

(1960, 87 min, GB, Robert Day) *Peter Sellers, Wildrid Hyde-White.* Sellers stars as a prisoner who leads his fellow inmates in a scheme to break out of jail, commit a robbery and then steal back to the safety of their cells. Sly fun. ★★★

Two Women

(1960, 99 min, Italy/France, Vittorio De Sica) *Sophia Loren, Raf Vallone, Eleonora Brown, Jean-Paul Belmondo.* Loren won an Academy Award for her deeply moving, heart-wrenching portrayal of an Italian woman who, along with her daughter, is raped by soldiers during World War II. The affects of this brutalization on the woman and her relationship with her daughter are explored in this realistic and unforgettable film experience. (Italian with English subtitles) ★★★★; DVD: $9.99

U-571

(2000, 117 min, US, Jonathan Mostow) *Matthew McConaughey, Harvey Keitel, Bill Paxton, Jon Bon Jovi, Jake Weber, David Keith, T.C. Carson, Jack Noseworthy, Matthew Settle.* Exhibiting the same kind of tension which made his last feature *Breakdown* a white-knuckle journey, director Mostow leaves the open, dusty roads of Texas for the claustrophobic confines of under the Atlantic to produce a taut, often thrilling WWII submarine actioner. McConaughey is Andrew Tyler, an American lieutenant who has been turned down for command of his own submarine. But before he has time to stew about it, he and his crew are off on a secret mission: retrieve an Enigma code machine, a decoder which is enabling German U-boats to sink Allied ships at an alarming rate. The plan to overtake the disabled *U-571*, steal its decoder and sink the sub

goes awry, and Tyler and his men must escape in the German sub with a Nazi destroyer on its heels. Loosely based on actual wartime incidents (the British actually pulled off a daring raid to retrieve the decoder), the story balances swift action scenes with wartime heroics by familiar but not clichéd characters. Though it never achieves the artistic achievement of *Das Boot* (the quintessential submarine film), *U-571* is nevertheless an exciting ride. ★★★ VHS: $19.99; DVD: $26.99

U.S. Marshals

(1998, 131 min, US, Stuart Baird) *Tommy Lee Jones, Wesley Snipes, Robert Downey, Jr., Joe Pantoliano, Kate Nelligan, Irene Jacob.* Less a sequel to *The Fugitive* and more another chapter à la the James Bond films, *U.S. Marshals* brings back the crack government team, headed by Deputy Marshal Sam Gerard (Jones), who hunted Richard Kimble in the first film. It's involving, but we've been here before. Jones is still in good form as the no-nonsense Gerard, who is now after Mark Sheridan (Snipes), an escaped convict (via a well-staged airplane crash) who is wanted for a series of brutal, execution-style murders. Unlike Kimble, Sheridan's guilt is uncertain, which is supposed to add some mystery to the story but is ultimately distracting. This isn't a whodunit, and we're never sure whether to root for Sheridan or not. But Baird has staged some exciting chase scenes, and Jones and Snipes are formidable adversaries. (VHS available letterboxed or pan & scan) ★★½ VHS: $14.99; DVD: $19.99

U-Turn

(1997, 125 min, US, Oliver Stone) *Sean Penn, Jennifer Lopez, Nick Nolte, Powers Boothe, Billy Bob Thornton, Joaquin Phoenix, Claire Danes, Jon Voight, Julie Hagerty, Liv Tyler.* With his most comic film to date, director Stone travels to the hot Arizona desert where a wrong turn and unfulfilled passions can lead to murder, or at least a damn entertaining time. Penn is Bobby, a motorist stranded in the dusty little town of Superior. Bobby's short stay while his car is fixed becomes an exercise in the bizarre, especially when a beautiful Native American woman (Lopez) and her sleazy white husband (Nolte)

each want Bobby to murder the other. As Bobby tries to figure out allegiances and avoid the local sheriff (Boothe), his trip down the rabbit hole becomes increasingly strange and dangerous. Stone brings a vigorous energy to the film, which tackles some of the same territory as *Natural Born Killers* but is more effective than that gratuitous bloodbath. The humor, though dark and sarcastic, is focused and funny, and the pacing swift. A fun, gritty, nasty, sexy, noirish, unpredictable ride. ★★★ VHS: $19.99; DVD: $29.99

L'Udienza

(1971, 120 min, Italy, Marco Ferreri) *Ugo Tognazzi, Claudia Cardinale, Michel Piccoli, Vittorio De Sica.* A provocative comedy of passion and alienation set against the intrigues of the modern Vatican. It follows a peculiar young man's quixotic attempts to obtain a private audience with the Pope, in order to share ideas which he is convinced can cure the ills of society. His attempts are constantly blocked by individuals who only pretend to be sympathetic to his cause. (Italian with English subtitles) ★★½

UFOria

(1980, 100 min, US, John Binder) *Cindy Williams, Harry Dean Stanton, Fred Ward.* This whacked-out comedy features a colorful assortment of oddball characters who are searching for fulfillment in a nowhere town at the edge of the Mojave Desert in a culture of revival tents and religious fanatics. Williams is a delightfully daffy, Bible-toting prophet who dreams of UFOs and a cosmic reenactment of Noah's Ark. ★★★ VHS: $59.99

Ugetsu

(1953, 96 min, Japan, Kenji Mizoguchi) *Machiko Kyo, Masayuki Mori.* Two peasants leave their families; one to seek wealth in the city, the other to find fortune as a samurai warrior. An eerie and allegorical film on the suffering caused by greed. (Japanese with English subtitles) ★★★½ VHS: $24.99

The Ugly

(1998, 94 min, New Zealand, Scott Reynolds) *Paolo Rotondo, Rebecca Hobbs.* A scary movie if you consider musician Marilyn Manson frightening (the sequences with freakish dark-clothed and pale-skinned demons look just like him). Otherwise, you might think this wishful thriller about a controversial psychiatrist (Hobbs) taking on a mind-warping serial killer (Rotondo) in a series of uninteresting interviews to be hollow and unsuspenseful. ★½ VHS: $14.99; DVD: $19.99

The Ugly American

(1963, 120 min, US, George Englund) *Marlon Barndo, Eiji Okado.* Brando and Okada fought together in Sarkhan against the Japanese in WWII. More than a decade later, Brando returns to Sarkhan as its American ambassador; Okada is the leader of a popular underground nationalistic movement. This well-constructed political exposé, based on the book by William J. Lederer and Eugene Burdick, plays the personal friendship against the conflicting factions vying for power in the underdeveloped Southeast Asian country. Take care to follow the convolutions of intrigue — it all leads up to a chilling final shot. ★★★ VHS: $19.99

Will Estes, Jack Noseworthy, Matthew McConaughey and Jake Webber in *U-571*

Samuel L. Jackson in *Unbreakable*

UHF

(1989, 97 min, US, Jay Levey) *Weird Al Yankovic, Victoria Jackson, Kevin McCarthy.* By all rights, this film debut of rock spoofer Yankovic should at best be a sporadically amusing, teenage, suburban mall-pleaser. But surprisingly, it is much more — a genuinely funny and fast-paced take-off on TV, movies and Americana. "Weird Al" plays a daydreaming nobody who inadvertently gets control of a near-zero rated television station. Of course, he makes the station a huge success. But hilarious take-offs in the form of commercials and strange new shows (including a gun-toting Gandhi sequel, "Conan the Librarian" and "Wheel of Fish") help you forget the pedestrian plot and enjoy his special (if wicked) brand of comedy. ★★½

Ulee's Gold

(1997, 111 min, US, Victor Nunez) *Peter Fonda, Patricia Richardson, Jessica Biel, Christine Dunford, Tom Wood, Vanessa Zima.* Giving the performance of his career, Fonda excels in this beautifully detailed, subtle drama of a Florida beekeeper and his family. Looking very much like his dad, and bringing to the screen the same kind of idealism and sensitivity Henry cornered the market on, Peter plays Ulysses "Ulee" Jackson, a reticent widower raising his two granddaughters. When his estranged, jailed son asks him to help his wife, whose drug dependency has put her in harm's way, Ulee becomes an unwitting patriarch and hero as he redeems himself in the eyes of his family. All are ultimately tested by circumstances slightly beyond their control. Director Nunez has written a touching, involving story which is realized with a discerning eye; but more importantly, he has given Fonda a role rich in character and nuance. ★★★½ VHS: $14.99; DVD: $14.99

Ulysses

(1955, 104 min, US/Italy, Mario Camerini) *Kirk Douglas, Silvana Mangano, Anthony Quinn.* Douglas brings a degree of respectability to this favorful American-Italian coproduction about the adventures of the legendary Greek hero on his way home after the Trojan Wars, including encountering the cyclops and the sirens. ★★★ VHS: $19.99; DVD: $19.99

Ulysses

(1967, 140 min, US/Ireland, Joseph Strick) *Milo O'Shea, Maurice Roeves.* Adapting James Joyce's massive novel to the screen was thought to be an impossible task, but Strick for the most part succeeds in filming the unfilmable with this tale of lust and longing. The story, photographed in a style of cinematic stream of consciousness, follows a 24-hour period in the life of young poet Stephen Daedalus as his odyssey takes him through the streets and brothels of Dublin. ★★½; DVD: $29.99

Ulysses' Gaze

(1996, 177 min, Greece, Theo Angelopoulos) *Harvey Keitel.* A mystical, visually stunning, soul-searching epic from the director of *Landscape in the Mist.* In one of his most impressive roles in an equally impressive career, Keitel stars as "A," a life-weary exiled Greek filmmaker who returns to his native country to attend a screening of his latest film. He soon becomes obsessed in finding the missing footage from a turn-of-the-century film, one which documents the Balkan area's people and landscape without regard to nationalism and ethnic tensions. His search turns into a cross-country odyssey, one that perilously takes him into the very soul of both the troubled Balkan region as well as himself. With beautiful imagery reminiscent of Andre Tarkovsky and the universal theme of man's longing for understanding and meaning, Angelopoulos' stimulating drama should stun even the most jaded viewer. (English and Greek with English subtitles) ★★★½ VHS: $29.99; DVD: $19.99

Ulzana's Raid

(1972, 103 min, US, Robert Aldrich) *Burt Lancaster, Bruce Davison, Richard Jaeckel.* Top-notch western adventure with Lancaster as an experienced Indian scout helping new cavalry officer Davison in a counter-offensive against an Apache attack. Crisp direction from Aldrich separates this tale from other similarly themed westerns. ★★★; DVD: $19.99

Umberto D

(1955, 89 min, Italy, Vittorio De Sica) *Carlo Battista, Maria Pia Casilio.* De Sica's uncompro-mising masterpiece is a heartrending study of a lonely old man and his struggle to survive with dignity in post-war Italy. A haunting and well-crafted film expertly told by the director. (Italian with English subtitles) ★★★★ VHS: $19.99

The Umbrellas of Cherbourg

(1964, 91 min, France, Jacques Demy) *Catherine Deneuve, Nino Castelnuovo, Anne Vernon.* Beautifully restored version of Demy's classic, bittersweet musical of two young lovers (a luminous Deneuve and handsome Castelnuovo) separated by war. With its gorgeous pastel color scheme and attractive leads, *Umbrellas* apes the glamour of the Hollywood musical, but also undercuts this a bit with a gritty, working-class locale and everyday situations. All the dialogue is sung, and most of the music is low-key. There are no show-stopping, highly choreographed numbers; but what it lacks in bombast and spectacle it makes up for in emotional resonance. Demy perfectly captures the feel of first love, and the myriad obstacles thrown in the face of it. Michel Legrand wrote the lovely score. (Letterboxed) (French with English subtitles) ★★★★ VHS: $14.99; DVD: $29.99

The Unapproachable

(1983, 92 min, West Germany, Krystof Zanussi) *Leslie Caron, Daniel Webb.* A former film star, living the life of a recluse, meets a handsome young man who, under his charming veneer, is actually a scheming and ruthless opportunist. A provocative thriller that explores their developing relationship and the shifting tides of power and sexual attraction. Caron's cooly passionate performance will captivate the viewer. A probing insight into the dangerous games which men and women all-too-often play. ★★★

The Unbearable Lightness of Being

(1988, 171 min, US, Philip Kaufman) *Daniel Day-Lewis, Juliette Binoche, Lena Olin, Derek De Lint, Erland Josephson, Stellan Skarsgård.* An erotic, witty and intelligent film adaptation of Milan Kundera's best-selling novel. Set against the backdrop of the Prague Spring of 1968, the story follows a young, womanizing Czech doctor who finds himself caught in the turmoil of the uprising despite his aversion to politics. Day-Lewis, Binoche and Olin all beautifully portray their characters' intertwined relationships against the powerfully evoked background of political upheaval and displacement. ★★★½ VHS: $14.99; DVD: $39.99

The Unbelievable Truth

(1990, 90 min, US, Hal Hartley) *Adrienne Shelley, Robert John Burke.* Director Hartley throws together vivid and quirky characters in a story of a high school cynic-turned-model (Shelley) living in a town disrupted by the return of an alleged murderer-turned-mechanic (Burke). Male territorialism, miscommunication and deals fuel the dialogue-driven plot of this offbeat winner. ★★★ VHS: $9.99; DVD: $29.99

Unbreakable

(2000, 132 min, US, M. Night Shyamalan) *Bruce Willis, Samuel L. Jackson, Robin Wright Penn.* Finding its inspiration from comic books, and even resembling a live-action comic at certain times, *Unbreakable* is director Shyamalan's follow-up to *The Sixth Sense,* his acclaimed supernatural thriller. Not wanting to tread the same ground but probably wanting to duplicate the "otherworldly" chills of his previous hit film, writer-director Shyamalan offers an eerie-looking enigma awash in uncertainties. Unfortunately, in doing so, he sets a trap for himself from which escape is difficult. Willis plays a college security officer who discovers (after a train wreck) that his body has the ability to heal itself instantly. Jackson is a comic book dealer who suffers from a rare bone disease. How these two come together – and why – is at the core of a slow-paced, muddled film that takes its time getting to what turns out to be an existential limbo. Though it shouldn't be compared to *Sense* (for it sets out to do something completely different), *Unbreakable* offers only a few thrills, ultimately failing on its own by not establishing either sufficient plot or character. ★★ VHS: $102.99; DVD: $29.99

Uncle Buck

(1989, 99 min, US, John Hughes) *John Candy, Amy Madigan, Macaulay Culkin, Gaby Hoffman.* A pleasant and amusing comedy which offers Candy a chance to demonstrate a heretofore unseen paternal side to his mammoth personality. Big John stars as a black-sheep uncle who tests his limits (and the limits of those around him) when he baby-sits his two nieces and nephew for a few days. Some of this may be very predictable and formulaic territory for director Hughes, but it nevertheless works. ★★½ VHS: $14.99; DVD: $24.99

Uncle Sam

(1996, 91 min, US, William Lustig) *Bo Hopkins, Timothy Bottoms, Isaac Hayes, Robert Forster, P.J. Soles, William Smith.* A surprisingly enjoyable genre effort from scripter Larry Cohen and director Lustig, the team behind the *Maniac Cop* films. *Uncle Sam* follows a similar tack, but with a more interesting theme: Gulf War soldier and all-American jerk Sam is killed by friendly fire in the Middle East, but comes back from the dead to take revenge on all those he deems as un-American. His war-obsessed nephew, who idolizes Sam, begins to suspect the truth behind the rash of murders. *Uncle Sam* is more engrossing than scary, and less gimicky than you might think. ★★½ VHS: $9.99; DVD: $29.99

Uncommon Valor

(1983, 105 min, US, Ted Kotcheff) *Gene Hackman, Fred Ward, Patrick Swayze, Tim Thomerson, Reb Brown.* A father recruits his old Marine buddies to search for his son, missing in action in Laos for ten years. The screenplay and characters are action-adventure clichés, but the cast and competent direction from Kotcheff elevate it from its formulaic roots. ★★½ VHS: $14.99; DVD: $29.99

Under Capricorn

(1949, 117 min, GB, Alfred Hitchcock) *Ingrid Bergman, Joseph Cotten, Michael Wilding.* An unusual effort for Hitchcock — a period costume piece. Bergman is unhappily married to a respected but ruthless man. Cotten is superb as the vicious husband who drives her to alchoholism and the limits of her mental and physical endurance. Wilding costars as a visitor who wreaks havoc with Cotten. Not considered one of Hitch's classics, it's worth a look

nonetheless for its marvelous acting and to see the director out of his usual milieu. ★★½

Under Fire

(1983, 128 min, US, Roger Spottiswoode) *Nick Nolte, Joanna Cassidy, Gene Hackman, Jean-Louis Trintignant, Ed Harris.* The setting is Nicaragua during the overthrow of the Somoza regime by the Sandinistas. An American journalist (Cassidy) and a hotshot photographer (Nolte) find themselves caught in the cross fire of the revolution when Nolte uses a doctored photo to aid the rebel cause. A taut, engrossing drama about the moral and political issues of news reporting and the "objectivity" of the press. ★★★½

Under Heat

(1994, 92 min, US, Peter Reed) *Lee Grant, Robert Knepper, Eric Swanson.* Filmed in an "American Playhouse"–style fashion, this family drama centers on the summer visit of Dean (Swanson) to his rural New York family of brother Milo (Knepper) and his mother (Grant). Ostensibly, his return is to tell his family that he is HIV-positive, but troubles with his drug-addicted brother and his mother's cancer scare contribute in keeping his revelation a secret. Swanson's Dean character, a somewhat queeny New Yorker, is the film's weakest part. Grant's flighty mother is well-developed, however, and she gets the film's best lines. The sappy approach and predictability undermine an otherwise worthy effort. ★★½ VHS: $29.99

Under Milk Wood

(1973, 90 min, GB, Andrew Sinclair) *Richard Burton, Elizabeth Taylor, Peter O'Toole, Glynis Johns.* Set in lush and visually stunning Wales, this production of Dylan Thomas' classic play is performed with theatrical genius by its three leads. Thomas' glorious poetry sparkles in this tale of a day in the life of the mythical village of Llareggub. The film has been rightly accused of over-ambitiousness and, indeed, the sense of production does weigh some of the material down. But it still offers a sterling example of ensemble acting from three great thespians. ★★½

Under Siege

(1992, 103 min, US, Andrew Davis) *Steven Seagal, Tommy Lee Jones, Gary Busey, Erika Eleniak.* Seagal reteams with his *Above the Law* director Davis to boldly go where Bruce Willis and Wesley Snipes have gone before: into the "one-man SWAT team" arena. In this "*Die Hard* on the high seas," Seagal has his most fulfilling effort, thanks mostly to Davis' slam-bang pacing. Seagal, the mumbling master, takes on the role of a military expert who just happens to be "moonlighting" as a ship's cook when high-tech pirates take over. Suspenseful action and over-the-top performances by Busey and Jones make this the Steven Seagal movie for people who don't like Steven Seagal. (Sequel: *Under Siege 2: Dark Territory*) ★★★ VHS: $14.99; DVD: $19.99

Under Siege 2: Dark Territory

(1995, 98 min, US, Geoff Murphy) *Steven Seagal, Eric Bogosian, Katherine Heigl, Morris Chestnut, Everett McGill.* Seagal is back as Casey Rybeck, everyone's favorite Navy SEAL-turned-cook, who must once again thwart a secret terrorist plot, kill all the bad guys, and save both a group of hostages and the world at large. This time he is pitted against an over-the-top Bogosian, a nutso weapons designer whiz who

hijacks a moving train and a satellite, making the deadly services of the latter available to the highest international bidder. Of course, Rybeck's on board and the only one who can stop him. While not up to the level of the exceedingly entertaining first film, *Dark Territory* still manages to be rousing if mindless fun. Though Seagal is still one of the most wooden actors lucky enough to be receiving a paycheck. ★★½ VHS: $14.99; DVD: $19.99

Under Suspicion

(1992, 100 min, GB, Simon Moore) *Liam Neeson, Laura San Giacomo.* The title of this old-fashioned murder mystery refers to the predicament of its two leads (Neeson, San Giacomo), who find themselves pointing fingers at each other over the murder of the latter's lover. Neeson stars as a sleazy private eye (circa 1959 England) whose livelihood of faking adulteries for divorce-seekers is cut short when one of his set-ups ends in murder — with him as a prime suspect. He immediately sets out to prove his innocence by pinning the blame on San Giacomo, who is the sole beneficiary of the murdered man. This innocent-man-wrongly-accused thriller sports a wild ending twist. ★★½ VHS: $19.99

Under Suspicion

(2000, 110 min, US, Stephen Hopkins) *Gene Hackman, Morgan Freeman, Thomas Jane, Monica Bellucci.* One of those mishandled theatrical releases that deserves to find an audience on video, *Under Suspicion* is a compelling cat-and-mouse mystery that'll have you guessing right up until the end. Hackman portrays a prominent tax attorney in Puerto Rico who is being questioned by his friend, the police captain (Freeman). There was a brutal murder and rape of a young girl and Hackman is now the prime suspect. But did he do it? Flashbacks help provide insight into his possible guilt or innocence, and thankfully director Hopkins never allows this device to become either confusing or cloying. As would be expected, both Hackman and Freeman are first-rate. ★★★ VHS: $14.99; DVD: $24.99

Under the Cherry Moon

(1986, 98 min, US, Prince) *Prince, Jerome Benton, Kristin Scott Thomas, Francesca Annis.* Prince wrote, directed and stars in this universally trashed, amateurish tale of a tormented American gigolo working in the south of France. Filmed in black and white. ★ VHS: $14.99

Under the Domim Tree

(1996, 102 min, Israel, Eli Cohen) *Kaipo Cohen, Juliano Mer, Gila Almagor, Riki Blich.* Based on the autobiography by Gila Almagor, *Under the Domim Tree* is the poignant and very compelling story of a group of orphaned Jewish teens, all survivors of the Holocaust, who come of age and battle very real demons while living in an Israeli youth settlement. On a melancholy note, the film begins slowly and sometimes confusingly as it introduces the children and adults, setting up the story with dispassion. But as the main characters are identified and the heart of the tale unfolds, *Under the Domim Tree* discovers its voice — and a haunting one at that. The story is touching without being depressing, and by the sheer courage demonstrated by those who shouldn't have to have their bravery tested, it's also inspirational. (Hebrew with English subtitles) ★★★ VHS: $19.99

Under the Earth (Debajo del Mundo)

(1986, 100 min, Spain/Poland, Beda Docampo Feijoo) *Victor Laplace.* This forceful drama celebrating the will of the human spirit recounts the story of a Jewish family's stubborn survival in the aftermath of the Nazi Occupation of wartime Poland. Forced to flee their stable life and live underground in subhuman conditions, the family endures two years of suffering yet remains together through their faith and a hope for a better future. (Spanish with English subtitles) ★★★

Under the Roofs of Paris

(1929, 95 min, France, René Clair) *Albert Prejean, Pola Illery.* The street life of Paris in the 1920s provides an exceptionally vivid backdrop to this lyrical love triangle of a street singer, his best friend, and the woman they both love. Digitally remastered. (French with English subtitles) ★★★ VHS: $19.99

Under the Sun of Satan

(1987, 98 min, France, Maurice Pialat) *Gérard Depardieu, Sandrine Bonnaire.* Pialat's stunning meditation on faith and the battle between good and evil won the Golden Palm for Best Picture at Cannes in 1987, but the controversial film was roundly booed upon that announcement. The story, told in an austere and direct style, is an adaptation of the Georges Bernanos 1926 novel about a tortured priest who feels unworthy of God's love until he encounters a pregnant teenager who has killed her lover. Depardieu is the village pastor who must battle Satan and Bonnaire is the wanton girl in this demanding, intense and provocative film. (French with English subtitles) ★★★ VHS: $29.99

Under the Volcano

(1984, 109 min, US, John Huston) *Albert Finney, Jacqueline Bisset, Anthony Andrews.* Huston's blistering adaptation of the Malcolm Lowry novel showcases a bravura performance by Finney as a former British consul in Mexico whose mental morass prompts a tragic descent into a private hell. Bisset is his estranged wife whose reappearance hastens the inevitable. ★★★½ VHS: $79.99

Undercover Blues

(1993, 95 min, US, Herbert Ross) *Kathleen Turner, Dennis Quaid, Fiona Shaw, Stanley Tucci, Larry Miller, Tom Arnold, Saul Rubinek.* Turner and Quaid play husband and wife espionage agents who know more about martial arts, explosives and the criminal mind than Bruce Lee, James Bond and Hannibal Lecter put together. Having taken time off to have a baby, the couple is lulled back into the realm of undercover when munitions are stolen by a Czechoslovakian sexpot. Nothing in this comedic caper seems genuine: the characters, dialogue and situations are all-too perfect and highly artificial. ★★½ VHS: $9.99

Undercurrent

(1946, 116 min, US, Vincente Minnelli) *Katharine Hepburn, Robert Taylor, Robert Mitchum.* A familiar melodramatic thriller with Hepburn as a professor's daughter who marries an industrialist, only to suspect her new husband is evil. *Gaslight* and *Suspicion* did it better, though Hepburn turns in a good performance. ★★ VHS: $14.99

Underground

(1997, 167 min, Serbia/France, Emir Kusturica) *Miki Manojlovic, Lazar Ristovski, Mirjana Jokovic.* A surreal, subversive look at two men and the woman they love, *Underground* is a remarkable accomplishment. The performances by the three leads are incredibly expressive — each is able to handle the demands of anarchic comedy and wartime tragedy brilliantly, and often in the same scene. This is epic cinema from Sarajevo-born director Kusturica (*When Father Was Away on Business*). The story, about two Communist pals who try desperately to survive the war in Yugoslavia, is secondary to the film's mesmerizing set pieces that depict an entire society living underground. Mixing dramatic scenes with newsreel footage, and throwing in an ode to filmmaking, Kusturica has made a demanding film, but one that makes a lyrical statement about life and love during wartime. (Letterboxed) (Serbo-Croatian with English subtitles) ★★★½ VHS: $29.99

The Underneath

(1995, 100 min, US, Steven Soderbergh) *Peter Gallagher, Elisabeth Shue, Shelley Duvall, Joe Don Baker.* An understated remake of the film noir classic *Criss-Cross* about a ne'er-do-well ex-con who returns home to "Smallville USA" and becomes involved with his old flame, her gangster boyfriend, and an armored car robbery. Soderbergh's complex narrative (he coauthored the screenplay pseudonymously) relies on an impressive use of color tones to delineate time periods (the stort is told on flashback and double flashback), thus giving the impression of layers being peeled away to reveal "the underneath" of his hauntingly etched characters. ★★★ VHS: $19.99; DVD: $24.99

Underworld

(1997, 95 min, US, Roger Christian) *Denis Leary, Annabella Sciorra, Joe Mantegna, Traci Lords.* Leary does his best to make this Tarantino knockoff palatable, but to little avail. He plays Johnny Crown, an aging ex-con out to avenge his father's murder attempt (he was left in a coma) on one violent Father's Day night. His other agenda is the rehabilitation of a childhood friend-turned-mobster (Mantegna at his most mannered and annoying). Artificial in the extreme, *Underworld* apes Tarantino to the point of embarrassment, with none of his style or wit. ★½ VHS: $79.99

Underworld U.S.A.

(1961, 99 min, US, Samuel Fuller) *Cliff Robertson, Dolores Dorn, Beatrice Kay.* Fuller's unrelentingly gritty murder drama stars Robertson as a young man who, as a youngster, witnessed the brutal murder of his father at the hands of an organized crime syndicate. Vowing revenge, he becomes obsessed with righting his father's death by infiltrating the mob echelon and tracking down the killers. But his plans for revenge become complicated after he finds himself caught between the villainous mob and the FBI, who want him as an informer. ★★★ VHS: $19.99

Unfaithfully Yours

(1948, 105 min, US, Preston Sturges) *Rex Harrison, Linda Darnell, Rudy Vallee.* Through the bungling interference of his idiot brother-in-law Vallee, world-famous symphony conductor Harrison is led to believe that his adoring, doe-eyed wife Darnell is having an affair with his personal assistant. Contains classic sequences in which Harrison's revenge fantasies are brilliantly choreographed to various pieces of music he's conducting. Another nifty little number from Sturges. (Remade in 1984) ★★★½ VHS: $59.99

Unfaithfully Yours

(1984, 96 min, US, Howard Zieff) *Dudley Moore, Nastassja Kinski, Armand Assante, Albert Brooks.* Okay remake of the classic Preston Sturges comedy, with Moore reprising the Rex Harrison role as a conductor who believes his wife (Kinski) guilty of adultery, and fantasizes revenge and murder. Moore is rather good as the exasperated husband, and has a particularly funny scene inside a movie theatre. ★★½ VHS: $29.99

An Unfinished Piece for the Player Piano

(1977, 105 min, USSR, Nikita Mikhalkov) *Alexander Kalyagin, Elena Solovel, Nikita Mikhalkov.* Mikhalkov adapts a Chekhov play which is set in a summer dacha and features an amazing array of ensemble acting. The passions, frustrations and failings of these members of the spoiled gentry provide the nucleus for this Russian *Rules of the Game*. A sumptuous, melancholy period piece. (Russian with English subtitles) ★★★½ VHS: $29.99

Unforgettable

(1996, 111 min, US, John Dahl) *Ray Liotta, Linda Fiorentino, Peter Coyote, Christopher McDonald, Kim Cattrall, David Paymer.* In this "A-budget," femme fatale-less thriller, Dahl concentrates on "hallucinatory cinema" such as *Jacob's Ladder* and *Don't Look Now*, rather than his accustomed '40s B-movie vocabulary. The results are mixed. Liotta stars as a forensics expert whose unending search for his wife's killer leads him to experiment on himself with a formula (developed by scientist Fiorentino) that enables him to experience the memories of murder victims — and in some cases, to actually see who murdered them. Fiorentino does nothing to restore the luster of her previous teaming with Dahl in *The Last Seduction*. ★★½ VHS: $14.99

An Unforgettable Summer

(1994, 82 min, Romania, Lucian Pintilie) *Kristin Scott Thomas, Claudiu Bleont, Olga Tudorache, George Constantin.* Scott Thomas gives a haunting performance as the wife of a career officer (Bleont) posted in a remote and dangerous corner of eastern Romania during the mid-1920s, a land recently controlled by either Turk, Macedonian or Bulgarian forces. When the codified cruelties of her culture begin to poison her marriage, she is forced to choose between what she knows is right and what is best for her to believe in. Like his earlier work *The Oak*, director Pintilie has fashioned a tale with few "obvious" villains and even fewer clear answers. (English, Romanian, French and Bulgarian with English subtitles) ★★★ VHS: $89.99

Unforgiven

(1992, 127 min, US, Clint Eastwood) *Clint Eastwood, Gene Hackman, Morgan Freeman,*

Richard Harris, Jaimz Woolvett, Saul Rubinek, Frances Fisher. Eastwood's lyrical, craftsmanlike direction, a brilliantly structured screenplay by David Webb Peoples, a superlative ensemble cast and superior production values all contribute to make this Oscar-winning revisionist western a modern masterpiece. Eastwood stars as a retired gunfighter who picks up the gun for one last time when a group of prostitutes put a price on the head of a sadistic cowboy. As Clint and partner Freeman make their way, Hackman's tyrannical sheriff (Hackman deservedly won an Oscar for his sensational performance as Little Bill) prepares for the expected onslaught of hired killers about to descend upon his small town. One of the many beauties of *Unforgiven* is director Eastwood's homage to the traditional western while at the same time expanding the boundaries of the genre. The myth of the Old West is a bloody one and as Eastwood sees it, death is close up and not at all the stuff of lore. (VHS available letterboxed or pan & scan) ★★★★ VHS: $14.99; DVD: $19.99

The Unforgiven

(1960, 125 min, US, John Huston) *Burt Lancaster, Audrey Hepburn, Lillian Gish, Audie Murphy.* Huston's unconventional western adventure concentrates more on racial tension between the white and Indian races than on the usual shoot-em-up hijinks. Set in 1850s Texas, the story concerns a ranching family who become at odds with both their neighbors and an Indian tribe when it is suspected that their adopted daughter is actually an Indian orphan. Gritty performances from the cast. ★★★ VHS: $14.99

The Unholy

(1988, 100 min, US, Camilo Vila) *Ben Cross, Ned Beatty, William Russ, Hal Holbrook, Trevor Howard.* Cross plays a priest whose miraculous survival from a 20-story fall leads him to a New Orleans parish where demonic events have been occurring. Convoluted and not all that scary. ★½ VHS: $9.99

The Unholy Wife

(1957, 94 min, US, John Farrow) *Rod Steiger, Diana Dors, Tom Tryon.* With the help of her lover, an adulterous wife (Dors) plans to murder her husband (Steiger). But when the plan goes awry, the pair attempt to put him behind bars instead. A mediocre tale of jealousy and revenge. ★½

Unhook the Stars

(1996, 105 min, US, Nick Cassavetes) *Gena Rowlands, Marisa Tomei, Gérard Depardieu, Jake Lloyd, Moira Kelly.* Rowlands' marvelous performance is the centerpiece of this affecting, intuitive character study cowritten and directed by her (and John Cassavetes') son Nick. Rowlands is Mildred, a widow whose children have left home. Reluctant to face the future alone, Mildred's life takes an unusual turn when Monica (Tomei), her blowsy neighbor, asks Mildred to baby-sit. Thus begins a wonderful relationship between Mildred and six-year-old J.J., and a tentative one between her and Monica. As Mildred, Rowlands is superb in conveying the minute details of this articulate, spirited woman. Depardieu is a truck driver who knows what we know: Mildred and Gena are class acts all the way. ★★★

Union City

(1980, 87 min, US, Mark Reichert) *Deborah Harry, Everett McGill, Pat Benatar.* A jealous accountant with a lusty wife (Harry) kills a man who has been stealing his milk bottles. Murder and paranoia are set amongst the grit of an industrial city in this convoluted though moody noir tale. ★★½ VHS: $19.99; DVD: $19.99

Universal Soldier

(1992, 98 min, US, Roland Emmerich) *Jean-Claude Van Damme, Dolph Lundgren, Jerry Orbach.* It's 'Nam, 1969. Nice Cajun boy Van Damme is caught in a fight to the death with Lundgren, a psycho sergeant with a fetish for severed ears. Both die in the showdown only to reappear 25 years later when a group of sleazy Army scientists unveil a line of antiterrorist robots created from the bodies of dead U.S. soldiers. Dolph's naturally sadistic tendencies override his programming, renewing his old rivalry with honest Van Damme and shooting up muscle enhancers. Emmerich's testosterone-driven action film is short on any technical prowess, but it certainly does qualify as good, dumb fun. (VHS available letterboxed or pan & scan) (Followed by 3 sequels) ★★ VHS: $14.99; DVD: $14.99

Universal Soldier: The Return

(1999, 89 min, US, Mic Ridgers) *Jean-Claude Van Damme, Michael Jai White, Bill Goldberg, Heidi Schanz.* An unbelievably bad (and noticably cheap) "sequel" to the mildly diverting 1992 film, *Universal Soldier: The Return* has little relation to the original and less to recommend it. Van Damme reprises his role as Luc Deveraux, a former cyborg who has to combat a handful of evil Unisols that have gone bad when a computer responds negatively to government cutbacks. Devoid of thrills, this awful film is not even unintentionally hilarious. Jean-Claude's tired, ass-dragging performance proves once and for all that he is, indeed, getting too old for this shit. ★ VHS: $9.99; DVD: $24.99

Unlawful Entry

(1992, 111 min, US, Jonathan Kaplan) *Kurt Russell, Madeleine Stowe, Ray Liotta, Roger E. Mosley, Dick Miller.* Affluent L.A. couple Russell and Stowe have their home broken into. Into their lives enters friendly policeman Liotta. Thus begins yet another in the continuing long line of "from hell" psycho thrillers. This is nothing more than a first-draft throwaway which somehow bypassed rewrite and went straight to production. However, Liotta, as a menacing cop-on-the-beat, brings just the right amount of intoxicating villainy and demonic glee to his character. He almost makes it worthwhile. ★½ VHS: $19.99; DVD: $22.99

Unmade Beds

(1997, 95 min, US, Nicholas Barker) *Aimee Copp, Michael De Stefano, Brenda Monte, Mikey Russo.* Mostly disturbing, at times amusing, but ultimately tiresome, *Unmade Beds* is a voyeuristic peek into the lives of four of New York City's legion of lonely hearts. Using a twist on documentary form, director Barker compiled hours of interviews with his four subjects and then wrote scripts for them to enact on camera — so we have real people playing themselves in a talking head interview format. Individually their stories are fascinating, repulsive,

heartrending and perverse, but taken as a whole, their overall impact is downright depressing and aimless. Still, one can't help being drawn in by a kind morbid curiosity as Barker uncovers their lives and forces us to watch as if it were a train wreck. ★★ VHS: $29.99; DVD: $29.99

An Unmarried Woman

(1978, 124 min, US, Paul Mazursky) *Jill Clayburgh, Alan Bates, Cliff Gorman, Michael Murphy.* Clayburgh's sensational performance is the heart of director Mazursky's penetrating drama about a dutiful wife who learns to be self-reliant after her husband leaves her for another woman. Bates is Clayburgh's new and sensitive paramour. One of Mazursky's most accomplished and poignant films. ★★★½ VHS: $29.99

The Unnamable

(1988, 87 min, US, Jean-Paul Ouellette) *Charles King, Mark Stephenson.* A group of college students spend the night in a haunted house to dispel rumors that a horrible creature lives there. Guess what happens. Nothing new, and not all that proficient, but there are a few scares. Based on a story by H. P. Lovecraft. ★★ VHS: $14.99

Unnatural Pursuits

(1991, 143 min, GB, Christopher Morahan) *Alan Bates, Richard Wilson, Nigel Planer, Paul Zimat, Bob Balaban, Deborah Rush, John Mahoney.* Simon Gray's West End comedy dissecting the artistic process makes for a fast and gloriously funny adaptation. Bates is remarkable as disheveled, acerbic playwright Hamish Partt, a chain-smoking alcoholic whose obsession to rewrite his newest play takes him from London to Los Angeles to Dallas to New York all the while experiencing a mental breakdown. In a series of escalating hallucinations, Hamish is haunted by skateboarding street people when not breaking into musical production numbers. Gray's masterful script examines Hamish's deterioration as he has thrust upon him insecure stage directors, bombastic producers, flirtatious Southern belle reporters, self-centered actors and an ogling public. ★★★★ VHS: $19.99

The Unsinkable Molly Brown

(1964, 128 min, US, Charles Walters) *Debbie Reynolds, Harve Presnell, Ed Begley.* Reynolds has her best film role as mountain girl-cum-society darling and *Titanic* survivor Molly Brown in this splashy screen version of Meredith Willson's (*The Music Man*) Broadway musical. Songs include "I Ain't Down Yet" and "I'll Never Say No to You." ★★★ VHS: $14.99; DVD: $19.99

Unstrung Heroes

(1995, 93 min, US, Diane Keaton) *Andie MacDowell, John Turturro, Michael Richards, Maury Chaykin, Nathan Watt.* Young Steven Lidz (Watt) is not having a very good summer. His father (Turturro) is a narcissistic inventor who clings with almost religous zeal to the tenants of scientific inquiry. His mother (MacDowell) is slowly dying of cancer, though Steven hasn't been made privy to this fact. Finding it all too much to take, the 12-year-old Steven runs off to live with his two uncles (Richards, Chaykin), a pair of paranoid schizophrenic, socialist Jews who live in an apartment piled high with

U

decades worth of newspapers and closets full of rubber balls. Tinged with melancholy and tempered with mirthful nostalgia, *Unstrung Heroes* provides many a warm-hearted moment. But ultimately the storytelling suffers at the hands of a script that boils down to a series of loosely connected scenes that offer very little character development. ★★½ VHS: $19.99

Untamed Heart

(1993, 102 min, US, Tony Bill) *Christian Slater, Marisa Tomei, Rosie Perez.* Slater gives a touching performance as a busboy whose childhood heart condition has left him emotionally and physically scarred. He's soon brought out of his silent shell by his love for a waitress (Tomei). They have a real chemistry — even if Slater is more alluring before he opens his mouth and begins to pour his guts out. Though its pacing is a little off (the beginning is slow and the ending unravels too quickly), *Untamed Heart* is a sweet, warm, there's-someone-out-there-for-everyone film that teeters quietly on the brink of being a real tearjerker. Special mention to Perez as Tomei's sidekick. ★★★ VHS: $9.99; DVD: $19.99

Until the End of the World

(1991, 160 min, US, Wim Wenders) *William Hurt, Solveig Dommartin, Max von Sydow, Jeanne Moreau, Sam Neill.* Director Wenders takes the viewer on the ultimate 'round-the-world odyssey with this "futuristic" road movie (set in 1999) filled with lots of high-tech future shock images and gadgetry. Hurt is carrying a top secret device and on the run from industrial bounty hunters. He hooks up with Dommartin and together they lead their pursuers on a global chase. After 90 minutes of non-stop action, they wind up in the Australian Outback where the film slows to a more familiar Wenders crawl. As in his other films, Wenders portrays a world in which people are desperately seeking a sense of self-understanding while craving human contact — it's a world in which, despite the explosion in global communication technology, we are more alone than ever. ★★★ VHS: $19.99

Until They Sail

(1957, 95 min, US, Robert Wise) *Jean Simmons, Joan Fontaine, Paul Newman, Piper Laurie, Sandra Dee.* Based on James A. Michener's wartime novel, this military drama is vintage soap opera but it's not without its compelling moments. Simmons, Fontaine, Laurie and Dee play sisters in WWII New Zealand. With the men of their village overseas, the town's women become romantic targets for the visiting American soldiers. Newman is one of them. Playwright Robert Anderson adapted the screenplay, which explores such adult themes as infidelity, wartime romance, and moral and sexual attitudes. ★★½ VHS: $19.99

The Untold Story

(1993, 95 min, Hong Kong, Herman Yau) *Anthony Wong, Danny Lee.* Based on a true incident, this grisly tale plays like *Silence of the Lambs* with a Chinatown twist. Wong stars as a restauranteur who becomes the prime suspect in a series of murders. The police department at first befriend him and sample his delicious complimentary pork buns, until they discover that they've found their missing persons —

ground up within the filling of the buns! The remainder of the film shows their brutal attempts to make Wong confess to his crimes. Part police procedural and part serial killer horror film, *The Untold Story* is definitely meant for strong stomachs only, and will quite possibly change the way you look at dim sum. (Cantonese with English subtitles) ★★★½ VHS: $79.99; DVD: $29.99

The Untouchables

(1987, 119 min, US, Brian De Palma) *Kevin Costner, Sean Connery, Robert De Niro, Andy Garcia, Charles Martin Smith.* Director De Palma's crowning achievement is a rousing and grandly stylistic gangster movie set in crime-laden 1920s Chicago. Costner is Eliot Ness, an idealistic government agent who goes after mob kingpin Al Capone, getting a lot of help from the cop on the beat (Connery). De Niro plays Capone with over-the-top abandon, and Connery is amazing in his Oscar-winning portrayal. Garcia and Smith (both first-rate) are Ness' two other "untouchables." De Palma's train station sequence, a nod to the "The Odessa Steps" sequence in *Battleship Potemkin*, is a knockout. Written by David Mamet. (Letterboxed VHS available for $14.99) ★★★★ VHS: $9.99; DVD: $29.99

Unzipped

(1995, 76 min, US, Douglas Keeve) *Isaac Mizrahi, Naomi Campbell, Cindy Crawford, Kate Moss, Linda Evangelista.* This delightfully playful documentary romp through the fashion world with designer Mizrahi is a sure-fire crowd pleaser due in large part to his irrepressible and engaging personality. The film's action centers around the swirl of creative energy Mizrahi and staff are pumping into preparing his fall '94 collection, which is inspired by *Nanook of the North* and *Call of the Wild*. Amidst the chaos, Mizrahi lets loose a barrage of bitchy, yet not too vicious one liners, social critiques and, of course, barbs at other designers. The film culminates with the Big Show in New York, which, in Mizrahi's case, is a brilliant piece of performance art. Its at times annoyingly jagged camera work is saved only by masterful, zippy MTV-paced editing. ★★★ VHS: $19.99

Up!

(1976, 80 min, US, Russ Meyer) Outrageously buxom women and dumb, muscular men laying their sexually aggressive prowess on the line. Narrated by a perpetually bouncing Kitten Natividad. Probably Russ' most explicit feature and definitely his most eccentric. ★★ VHS: $79.99

Up at the Villa

(2000, 115 min, GB/US, Philip Haas) *Kristin Scott-Thomas, Sean Penn, Anne Bancroft, Jeremy Davies, Derek Jacobi, James Fox.* W. Somerset Maugham's novella makes for a sumptuous romantic exercise of class conflict and romantic intrigue all set against the rising tide of Fascism in pre-WWII Italy. The luminous Scott-Thomas is Mary, a widowed British expatriate living in Florence amid a small circle of wealthy friends. A proposal from an aging but well-placed politician sets in motion a weekend of soul-searching, parties and romantic indiscretions for Mary and those closest to her. This includes American playboy Rowley (Penn), who falls

under the considerable charms of the reluctant fiancée. Director Haas' cast practically floats through this story of a sentried class abroad at the end of its days. Bancroft almost steals the movie as the Princess San Ferdinando, an American widow whose biting tongue and social status guarantees she's always holding court. ★★★½ VHS: $102.99; DVD: $19.99

Up Close and Personal

(1996, 124 min, US, Jon Avnet) *Robert Redford, Michelle Pfeiffer, Kate Nelligan, Joe Mantegna, Stockard Channing, Glenn Plummer.* Loosely based on the life of Jessica Savitch by way of *A Star Is Born*, this polished if sometimes gawky romantic drama tracing the rise of a TV newscaster doesn't have as much to say about the news industry as it pretends to, but offers especially attractive performances from its two leads. Sweet, naïve but eager, Pfeiffer's aspiring newscaster comes under the tutelage of station manager Redford. She works her way up from weather girl to anchor as they fall in love and marry, experiencing the ups and downs inherent in a relationship marked by one spouse's sudden success. There are some terrific scenes which spotlight the business of news reporting, but the film also gives in to clichés and coincidences. ★★½ VHS: $14.99

Up in Arms

(1944, 106 min, US, Elliott Nugent) *Danny Kaye, Dana Andrews, Dinah Shore, Constance Dowling, Louis Calhern, Margaret Dumont.* In his feature film debut, Kaye wreaks havoc on an unsuspecting Army as a hypochondriac who gets drafted. Danny performs a few musical numbers, smuggles Dowling on board his South Pacific-bound ship, and manages to capture a few enemy soldiers. Shore plays a nurse who's sweet on him, and Andrews is Danny's bunkmate. Though it's slightly dated, Kaye's mugging and patter songs are genuinely entertaining, and there are plenty of laughs to go around. ★★½

Up in Smoke

(1978, 85 min, US, Lou Adler) *Cheech Marin, Tommy Chong.* This first (and best) film from that doped-up comic duo, Cheech & Chong, may be dated, but it still provides kilos of laughs. All we can say is that if there are still some of you out there who enjoy the occasional mind-bender, be grateful that this testament to the halcyon days of unbridled substance abuse is still available on video. ★★★ VHS: $14.99; DVD: $29.99

Up to a Certain Point

(1985, 70 min, Cuba, Tomás Gutiérrez Alea) *Oscar Alvarez, Mirta Ibarra.* Director Alea tackles several themes, including politics, male chauvinism and marital infidelity, to bring about the tale of a writer and his attempts at writing an anti-machismo film for his actress wife. Alvarez is the screenwriter Oscar, caught between his feelings of love and the direction of his project. Ibarra shines as Lina, the independent and alluring dock worker who becomes the role model for his main character and the object of his affection. This film is well worth the effort not only for its interesting portrayal of somewhat modern-day Cuban life but also for its honesty in the portrayal of struggles which go beyond wage earnings. (Spanish with English subtitles) ★★★ VHS: $79.99

The Uprising

(1980, 96 min, Nicaragua, Peter Lilienthal) Filmed just months after the Sandinista revolution, this raw and impassioned drama recruited the real-life peasants and soldiers of the country to authentically re-create the atmosphere of a people and of a land thrust into turbulent revolt. The story, set in the university town of León, centers on a young man, a member of Somoza's National Guard who, with the help of his father, comes to be a supporter of the rebel Sandinistas. Kind of a fictionalized documentary, this simple and direct story celebrates the solidarity and heroics of these impoverished people. (Spanish with English subtitles) ★★★ VHS: $69.99

Uptown Saturday Night

(1974, 104 min, US, Sidney Poitier) *Bill Cosby, Sidney Poitier, Richard Pryor, Harry Belafonte, Flip Wilson, Roscoe Lee Browne.* Cosby wins $50,000 in the lottery. One problem though — his wallet was taken during a holdup. Cosby and Poitier must get through a maze filled with scheming gangsters, con men and women. A bit dated and not as good as its follow-up *Let's Do It Again*, but it certainly is fun. ★★½ VHS: $14.99

Uranus

(1991, 100 min, France, Claude Berri) *Gérard Depardieu, Michel Blanc, Jean-Pierre Marielle, Philippe Noiret.* This rather disappointing and convoluted drama is set in a small French village thrown into chaos immediately after WWII when the new government attempts to sort out who were the patriots and who were the informants, Nazi sympathizers and collaborators. Depardieu steals the show as a drunken, brutish bully of a bartender with a newfound love of poetry and a nose seemingly bigger than the 14th arrondissement, who is falsely implicated as an informant. At the heart of the film is an interesting idea of a people torn apart and in near hysterics by their own actions, but the execution by director Berri is too slow and bland to create much involvement. (French with English subtitles) ★★ VHS: $19.99

Urban Cowboy

(1980, 135 min, US, James Bridges) *John Travolta, Debra Winger, Scott Glenn.* Cowboy Travolta tries to lasso cowgirl Winger at Gilley's Bar in Texas in this involving romantic drama. The film which created the mechanical bull stir (for awhile). ★★½

Urban Legend

(1998, 99 min, US, Jamie Blanks) *Jared Leto, Alicia Witt, Rebecca Gayheart, Natasha Gregson Wagner, Loretta Devine.* A weak, cynical cash-in on the *Scream* craze. A hooked killer is offing folks at a university, utilizing scenarios of famous urban legends. The film opens with a botched rendition of the Scary Gas Station Attendant tale, then picks up a bit when old stalwarts like John ("X-Files") Neville and Robert "Freddie Krueger" Englund show up. It's all tainted by the fact that it's a rip-off of *Scream*'s post-modern, hip approach to its pop-culture savvy film characters. While the killer's a bit tougher to guess, this whole affair is ugly, pointless and rather cruel. (Sequel: *Urban Legends: Final Cut*) ★½ VHS: $9.99; DVD: $19.99

Urban Legends: Final Cut

(2000, 99 min, US, John Ottman) *Jennifer Morrison, Matthew Davis, Hart Bochner, Joseph Lawrence, Anthony Anderson, Loretta Devine.* This sequel to the surprise 1998 hit has only one returning character — Devine's Pam Grier-obsessed security guard — and a new crop of colorless teen victims. This time set at a fictitious film school (really fictitious — no film school resembles this ridiculous cartoonization), *Final Cut* begins rather promisingly, with two stylish, unsettling killings that set a nice, creepy tone for the film. Stock characters and cheesy dialogue notwithstanding, the first half of the film is above-average slasher fare. Then the crap kicks in: killings become more arbitrary and ordinary, culminating with a risible wrap-up that rivals the original's climax in sheer stupidity. ★★ VHS: $102.99; DVD: $19.99

Urbania

(1999, 103 min, US, Jon Shear) *Dan Futterman, Alan Cummings, Matt Keeslar, Lothaire Bluteau, William Sage, Barbara Sukowa.* An excitingly ambitious and original style of gay filmmaking is in evidence with *Urbania*, a feverish tale of one young man's search for sanity, retribution and love. In the urban jungle of nocturnal New York, Charlie (Futterman), traumatized by the violent gay bashing of his lover Chris (Keeslar) by a darkly sexy thug, has become a lost soul. He wanders the city in wide-eyed confusion, a lonely man with both pent-up anger and sexual desire bubbling within him. With memories invading his mind, Charlie hits the streets, meeting a variety of strange storied characters. The intricately structured film builds to intensity as Charlie finds, befriends and is forced to decide the fate of the man he lusts and loathes. A taut, emotional and surreal story of homophobia, loss and love adapted from Daniel Reitz's play, "Urban Folk Tales." The acting is excellent but Futterman is simply mesmerizing as the vengeful gay man on a mission in this haunting *After Hours* for the queer set. ★★★½ VHS: $69.99; DVD: $24.99

Urinal

(1991, 100 min, Canada, John Greyson) Less provocative and explicit than the title suggests, this low-budget Canadian production is a documentary-style talk fest centering on homosexual repression through the ages and, more specifically, the well-publicized entrapment cases and crackdowns in Ontario's public rest rooms by a homophobic police force. The film's premise is that several prominently rumored gays, lesbians and bisexuals from the past are mysteriously brought together in a Toronto apartment where they hold a series of discussions on the sociology of homosexuality and how to counter gay repression. ★★½ VHS: $29.99

Used Cars

(1980, 111 min, US, Robert Zemeckis) *Kurt Russell, Jack Warden, Deborah Harmon.* It's the battle of the used car salesmen as Russell squares off against Warden in a no-holds-barred customer-getting contest. An uproarious and daffy comedy written by Bob Gale and director Zemeckis. ★★★ VHS: $9.99

Used People

(1992, 116 min, US, Beeban Kidron) *Shirley MacLaine, Marcello Mastroianni, Kathy Bates, Jessica Tandy, Marcia Gay Harden, Sylvia Sidney.* The comparisons of *Used People* to *Moonstruck* and *Fried Green Tomatoes* are inevitable. All share a sentimental bent without being too cute about it; wacky characters find themselves in wackier situations; and members of near-dysfunctional families endear themselves not only to the viewer but, eventually, to each other. MacLaine plays a recently widowed Jewish wife and mother from Queens. On the day of her husband's funeral, she is asked on a date by determined Italian restauranteur Mastroianni. Against her better judgment, she agrees. What follows is a series of disastrous family get-togethers, culture clashes and romantic pursuits. The film is immeasurably aided by a good supporting cast. ★★★ VHS: $19.99

The Usual Suspects

(1995, 105 min, US, Bryan Singer) *Kevin Spacey, Gabriel Byrne, Stephen Baldwin, Kevin Pollak, Benicio Del Toro, Chazz Palminteri, Pete Postlethwaite, Suzy Amis, Giancarlo Esposito, Paul Bartel.* This witty and ingenious noir thriller is a delicious up-and-down ride on a twisting plotline that involves a rag-tag assemblage of small-time hoods who, having met in a lineup, join forces and commit to performing *one* job together. Predictably, this leads to fur-

The Usual Suspects

Vagabond

ther involvement that ultimately begins to get out of hand. The group's reluctant leader, Dean Keaton (Byrne), is a former big-time grifter who is joined by a couple of smaller hoodlums (Baldwin and Del Toro), a weapons expert (Pollak), and a talkative, crippled flunkie known as Verbal (Oscar winner Spacey). Opening with a grisly massacre on a lonesome San Pedro, California, pier, the film unfolds through flashback as the tale is told by Verbal, the lone survivor. And then there's the mythical, almost Mephistophelian underworld figure known as Keyser Söze, who may be the mastermind behind the massacre. Spacey walks away with the movie; his Verbal is a study in criminal paranoia accented by physical vulnerability. Director Singer and screenwriter Christopher McQuarrie (another Oscar winner) team up well with cinematographer Howard Cummings to create a brilliant and timeless crime story that's an immediate classic of the genre. ★★★★ VHS: $14.99; DVD: $24.99

Utu

(1983, 124 min, New Zealand, Geoff Murphy) *Bruno Lawrence, Anzac Wallace, Kelly Johnson.* This violent and spectacularly photographed film crosses the boundaries of both art film and action flick. Set during the Maori uprising in rural 1870s New Zealand, the story focuses on a Maori ex-army sergeant whose family and village are wiped out during a raid and who becomes the radical and vengeful leader of a group of rebellious natives intent on eradicating the white settlers by any means possible. An exciting and bloody story of the fight for survival. (Director's cut) ★★★ VHS: $24.99; DVD: $29.99

Utz

(1992, 95 min, GB/Germany/Italy, George Sluizer) *Armin Mueller-Stahl, Brenda Fricker, Peter Riegert, Paul Scofield.* From the director of the provocative *The Vanishing* comes this elegant, spare and quietly involving drama. Filmed in English, the story focuses on Baron von Utz (Mueller-Stahl), a wealthy Czechoslavakian collector of German porcelain figurines. Through a series of flashbacks, we learn of the roots of his lifelong obsession with his collection as well as his mysterious life. Riegert is an international antique broker who befriends him in the hope of obtaining the collection after his death and Fricker is his more-than-an-employee housekeeper. Beautiful locales in Prague provide an exotic backdrop to the gentle character study. ★★★ VHS: $19.99

Vagabond

(1985, 105 min, France, Agnès Varda) *Sandrine Bonnaire, Macha Meril.* Bonnaire is mesmerizing in this hauntingly nihilistic account of an aimless young woman's final days. The beginning of the film finds the girl's frozen body in a ditch. Then told in flashback by the last people to have had contact with her, the film attempts to piece together the life and values of this complex teenager. A stunning film experience and one of the most important and powerful French films in recent memory. (French with English subtitles) ★★★★ VHS: $29.99; DVD: $29.99

Valdez Is Coming

(1971, 90 min, US, Edwin Sherin) *Burt Lancaster, Susan Clark, Richard Jordan, Hector Elizondo.* Lancaster gives a solid performance as Valdez, part-time lawman, part-time stagecoach shotgun, who is set up to kill a black man wrongly accused of murder. Realizing the mistake he has made, he attempts to accept responsibility for the dead man's pregnant Indian wife. This leads him on an odyssey through a barren, treacherous landscape populated by men without ethics or compassion. Good ensemble acting helps overcome a somewhat pedestrian treatment of an intriguing plot line which slowly unravels just who is guilty of what. Based on a novel by Elmore Leonard. ★★½ VHS: $14.99

Valentina

(1983, 90 min, Spain, Antonio J. Betancor) *Anthony Quinn.* Adapted from Ramon J. Sender's celebrated novel, this deeply moving film, set in a small town in northern Spain, examines a pre-adolescent boy's passionate love for the lyrical Valentina and the efforts of their families to keep them apart. Quinn is featured as the boy's understanding teacher. (Spanish with English subtitles) ★★★

Valentino

(1977, 127 min, GB, Ken Russell) *Rudolf Nureyev, Leslie Caron, Michelle Phillips, Carol Kane, Seymour Cassel.* Russell creates some stunning visuals but comes up short in dramatic terms in this lurid exposé on the life of silent screen star Rudolph Valentino. Opening with the frenzied scene of his funeral, the film's flashbacks attempt to chart his rise to fame as well as uncover the man behind the image. As Valentino, Nureyev — who looks the part — is, unfortunately, wooden and uninspiring. Russell, who in the past has not side-stepped homosexual themes, curiously downplays the Latin Lover's gayness in favor of a man constantly trying to prove his masculinity. ★★ VHS: $19.99

The Valley (Obscured by Clouds)

(1972, 106 min, France, Barbet Schroeder) *Bulle Ogier.* This legendary cult film is an aurally hypnotic and sensually seductive drama of the spiritual and sexual enlightenment of a

group of Westerners who venture into the uncharted, mystic rainforest of New Guinea. With ravishing photography by Nestor Almendros and a spacey soundtrack by Pink Floyd, the film follows a bored diplomat's wife (Ogier) who travels into the interior of a strange land searching for the feathers of a near-extinct bird for retailing in Parisian boutiques. Along the way she meets up with several hippies, dreamers and dropouts. Together, they experience a transformation of spirit when they meet the indigenous Mapuga tribesmen and travel to a secret and strangely powerful "valley of the gods." (French with English subtitles) ★★★

Valley Girl

(1983, 95 min, US, Martha Coolidge) *Nicolas Cage, Deborah Foreman, Frederic Forrest, Colleen Camp.* Like, can love last between a true Val (Foreman) and a punker from Hollywood (Cage)? It's, like, a war of the cliques in this amusing little film about California culture clashes. ★★½

Valley of the Dolls

(1967, 123 min, US, Mark Robson) *Patty Duke, Susan Hayward, Sharon Tate, Lee Grant, Martin Milner.* Trashy, melodramatic piece of camp heaven based on Jacqueline Susann's best-selling novel that takes us on a hell-bound highway of drugs, sex, drinks and infidelity and the rise and fall of starlets in the entertainment biz. The film, at times, drifts into cliché-ridden waters, but is nevertheless chock full of those absolutely absurd soap opera-ish elements which make this genre so much fun. ★★★ VHS: $14.99

Valmont

(1989, 137 min, GB/France, Milos Forman) *Colin Firth, Meg Tilly, Annette Bening, Henry Thomas, Fairuza Balk.* Opulent settings in exotic European locales and meticulously designed period costumes can't save this uninvolving drama, based on Choderlos de Laclos' 1782 novel "Les Liaisons Dangereuses." Sadly, director Forman misses the central idea behind the story of intrigue amidst the French aristocracy by not delving into the characters' icy hearts and, as a result, the film is all spectacle and no soul. Firth's Valmont is, by his looks, well suited for the devilishly charming seducer, but lacks the calculating and complex personality that

The Valley (Obscured by Clouds)

the role requires. Stick to Stephen Frears' mesmerizing *Dangerous Liaisons*, made a year earlier, and based on the same story. ★ VHS: $14.99

Vampire in Brooklyn

(1995, 95 min, US, Wes Craven) *Eddie Murphy, Angela Bassett, Allen Payne, Kadeem Hardison, Zakes Mokae.* Director Craven brings a seductive and eerie style to this shadowy vampire tale, but *Vampire in Brooklyn* ultimately succumbs to its unimaginative screenplay which is not nearly funny enough to be comedy or scary enough to be horror. Murphy is a vampire who comes to Brooklyn (in an impressively mounted opening) searching for a lost soul mate. He immediately finds her in the person of policewoman Bassett. Murphy abandons his usual winking at the audience, and even plays two additional characters rather well. But neither star is serviced by a thoroughly flat and undeveloped story and dialogue. ★★ VHS: $9.99

Vampire Journals

(1997, 92 min, US, Ted Nicolaou) *Jonathan Morris, David Gunn, Kirsten Cere, Starr Andreeff.* A surprisingly enjoyable chiller, *The Vampire Journals* is a definite sleeper from Charles Band's Full Moon Productions, which usually advocates "quantity over quality." Beginning rather abruptly, like some old-time serial chapter, the story details the efforts of a "good" vampire to rid the world of an old, evil master vampire while attempting to repress his own vampiric nature. That's about it for story, but a terrific Gothic atmosphere is set early on and maintained throughout the entire film. Short on plot, long on mood, and good, brooding fun, *Journal's* only real drawbacks are a ditsy heroine and an anticlimactic ending. ★★★ VHS: $14.99; DVD: $24.99

The Vampire Lovers

(1970, 88 min, GB, Roy Ward Baker) *Ingrid Pitt, Pippa Steele, Medeleine Smith, Peter Cushing.* Pitt sizzles as the sexy seductress Marcilla whose lust for blood is matched only by her lust for other beautiful maidens in this erotic adaptation of Sheridan Le Fanu's "Carmilla" from the house of Hammer. ★★★ VHS: $9.99

Vampire's Kiss

(1989, 103 min, US, Robert Biermen) *Nicolas Cage, Jennifer Beals, Maria Conchita Alonso, Elizabeth Ashley.* If you thought Griffin Dunne had a bad night in Martin Scorsese's *After Hours*, wait till you get a load of New York's truly dark side. Cage stars as a literary agent who unwisely picks up beautiful Beals in a singles bar and, after a bite in the neck, becomes convinced that he's turning into a vampire. The film alternates between rip-roaring black comedy and mind-bendingly surrealistic fantasy. It is Cage's over-the-top performance which is at the heart of this sardonic work. ★★★

Les Vampires

(1915, 420 min, France, Louis Feuillade) *Edouard Mathé, Marcel Lévesque, Jean Ayme, Fernand Herrmann, Musidora.* Secret passage ways snake into your most private sanctums, poison gas wafts out of ventilation grates, trap doors drop you down into dark, dank dungeons — why, why, why? It's for the sheer joy of committing blackmail, extortion and murder! No one is safe from the criminal masterminds that make up *Les Vampires*. Led by the beautiful but deadly Irma Vep, this ruthless gang preys on the Parisian rich pre-WWI. What director Feuillade may have lacked in cinematic technique is more than made up for in audacity. Its very length — ten episodes, seven hours — is like uncomfortable slumber, a nightmare that keeps intruding the next day. *Les Vampires* still fascinates, still resonates — still *lives* — among the cineastes, one of whom, Oliver Assayas, deconstructed the whole experience some 80 years later to create his own masterwork, *Irma Vep.* ★★★ VHS: $99.99; DVD: $69.99

Vampyr

(1931, 83 min, Germany/France, Carl Dreyer) *Julian West, Sybille Schmitz.* Death and evil hover over everyone in Dreyer's psychological horror film. Dislocated shadows, eerie sounds and unexplained mysteries conspire to make *Vampyr* one of the screen's most visceral thrillers. (German with English subtitles) ★★★½ VHS: $24.99; DVD: $24.99

Van Gogh

(1992, 155 min, France, Maurice Pialat) *Jacques Dutronc, Alexandra London.* Unlike previous visions of the artist — Vincente Minnelli's *Lust for Life*, Robert Altman's *Vincent and Theo* or Paul Cox's documentary *Vincent* — this beautifully photographed look at Van Gogh's last days in Auvers-Sur-Oise eschews the standard portrait of a tortured soul. Instead we see a man who lusts after women, enjoys life's pleasures and who, in the end, may have taken his own life more out of remorse over his own sensitivities than his failure to gain acceptance. Dutronc won a César Award for Best Actor for his understated portrayal. (French with English subtitles) ★★★ VHS: $19.99

Vanina Vanini

(1969, 125 min, Italy, Roberto Rossellini) *Sandra Milo, Laurent Terzieff.* Set in 1824, this opulent political and romantic drama is a complex neorealist-influenced film that deals with political and religious corruption, social inequality, guilt and betrayal. Young Pietro, a revolutionary soldier, is sent to Rome to kill a traitor to the cause. Needing to hide from the authorities, he finds refuge in the lavish home of an aristocrat where he falls in love with the man's beautiful daughter. The two travel back north but the social differences that keep them apart soon erupt into betrayal. (Italian with English subtitles) ★★★ VHS: $59.99

The Vanishing

(1988, 105 min, The Netherlands, George Sluizer) *Barnard Pierre Donnadieu, Johanna Ter Steege.* This riveting psycho-thriller offers an unflinching look into the shadowy recesses of the human psyche. While on holiday in the south of France, a young Dutch couple stop for gas at a service station. While he fills the tank, she goes into a restaurant and mysteriously disappears without a trace. Unable to convince the police that foul play was involved, the man returns home, only to be haunted by her disappearance until he decides to retrace their steps, hoping to entrap the possible abductor/murderer. An unrelentingly taut account that eschews the easy depiction of violence for the much more menacing idea of psychological obsession and domination. (French and Dutch with English subtitles) (Sluizer made his own American remake in 1993) ★★★½ VHS: $19.99

The Vanishing

(1993, 110 min, US, George Sluizer) *Jeff Bridges, Kiefer Sutherland, Nancy Travis, Sandra Bullock, Park Overall, George Hearn.* If ever there was a film that screamed "see the original!" — this is it. Where the unique 1988 Dutch chiller was a tense, philosophical psycho-mystery, this remake is little more than a formulaic Hollywood spine-tingler. Sutherland stars as a young man whose life is shattered when his girlfriend (Bullock) inexplicably disappears at a road stop. He searches for her over the years until one day a slightly loony science professor (Bridges) shows up to shed some light on her fate. Director Sluizer, who also directed the original, has made a number of ill-advised changes including completely rewriting the ending which, in the first film, left the viewer with a stunned sense of helplessness. ★ VHS: $19.99

Vanya on 42nd Street

(1994, 119 min, US, Louis Malle) *Wallace Shawn, Julianne Moore, Brooke Smith, Larry Pine, George Gaynes, Phoebe Brand, Andre Gregory, Madhur Jaffrey.* Malle reteams with his old *My Dinner with Andre* pals Shawn and Gregory for this riveting theatrical exposition. Gregory and Shawn assembled a group of actors on a pro-bono basis and spent four years rehearsing their bare-bones (no sets, no props, no nothin') production of David Mamet's adaptation of Chekhov's "Uncle Vanya." Entranced by their work, Malle set out to make a record and the result is invigorating. Filmed in the dilapidated New Amsterdam Theatre on 42nd Street in New York, *Vanya* is as close to true theatre on film as one will ever see. Mamet's script is 100% true to Chekhov and in the hands of stage director Gregory and his accomplished cast, his masterful examination of spiritual yearning in the face of brutal existential angst is brought vividly to life. ★★★★ VHS: $19.99

Variety

(1925, 75 min, Germany, E.A. Dupont) *Emil Jannings, Lya de Putti.* Classic silent melodrama with Jannings in fine form as an aging circus acrobat who falls in love with a beautiful young dancer, only to become involved in murder when a handsome young man shows affection for the girl. ★★★½

Variety

(1983, 97 min, US, Bette Gordon) *Sandy McLeod, Will Patton, Richard Davidson, Nan Goldin.* Christine (McLeod) works in the box office of a porno theatre in New York's (pre-Disney-fied) squalid Times Square district. Exposed to this thick aura of sexual promise and fantasy, she becomes obsessed — not with the films, but with the endless parade of men who come to consume them. Eventually, she becomes fixated on one particular customer, and finds herself acting upon her own voyeuristic urges. Gritty and complex, this is an often fascinating study of the chasm between sexual desire and its gratification. ★★★ VHS: $24.99

Variety Lights

(1952, 93 min, Italy, Federico Fellini & Alberto Lattuada) *Giulietta Masina, Carla Del Poggio.* Codirected by Fellini and Lattuada and starring their wives, *Variety Lights* explores the tawdry lifestyle of a traveling vaudeville troupe. When an ambitious young woman joins them, the group finds their lives shaken as the newcomer immediately begins an affair with the much older maestro. The blending of Lattuada's neorealist techniques with Fellini's budding imagination, as well as his interest in eccentric individuals, creates a world of alluring illusion beneath which lies the much sadder reality of everyday life. (Italian with English subtitles) ★★★ VHS: $29.99; DVD: $29.99

Varsity Blues

(1999, 104 min, US, Brian Robbins) *James Van Der Beek, Jon Voight, Paul Walker, Ron Lester.* As conventionally formulaic as it is, *Varsity Blues* is still slickly enjoyable as any of those (good) '80s John Hughes comedies. Van Der Beek is Max, a Texas high school quarterback who becomes an overnight sensation when the first string QB is injured. Despite his ambivalence about his sudden stardom, he doesn't shun the spotlight — he goes with it (the babes and free booze being understandable temptations to a teenager). His control-freak coach (Voight), however, is constantly at odds with Max's "it's only a game" mentality. While basically a remake of *All the Right Moves*, *Varsity Blues* is more entertaining than most of the other "teen" flicks out there now. ★★★ VHS: $14.99; DVD: $29.99

Vegas Vacation

(1997, 90 min, US, Stephen Kessler) *Chevy Chase, Beverly D'Angelo, Randy Quaid, Wallace Shawn, Wayne Newton.* Part of the appeal of the first *National Lampoon's Vacation* is its air of depravity and those wicked laughs. As the series grew into something of a franchise, little by little the humor that distinguished it dissipated, until all that's left is the feel-good family schtick at the heart of *Vegas Vacation*. The Griswolds venture to Las Vegas, where the entire family is seduced by its seediness and glamour. The supporting cast produces the few laughs the screenplay can muster, including Shawn as a smug card dealer, and Quaid, who once again saves the day as the family's ill-bred cousin. Newton's self-parody goes nowhere. ★★ VHS: $14.99; DVD: $19.99

The Velocity of Gary

(1998, 101 min, US, Dan Ireland) *Vincent D'Onofrio, Salma Hayek, Thomas Jane, Olivia d'Abo, Chad Lindberg.* An intriguing cast can't save this personal urban drama filmed in the tradition of the Andy Warhol/Paul Morrissey collaborations. The story attempts to be a poignant yet hard-edged love fable set among the hustlers, trannies and homeless of New York City. It tells the tale of the strained love triangle between a charismatic bisexual, a male prostitute and a tempestuous Latina. The sultry but annoyingly whinny Hayek stars as Mary Carmen, a hot-tempered beauty desperately in love with Valentino (D'Onofrio), a small-time porn actor with big-time attitude. Things change when Gary (Jane), a sensitive rookie male prostitute, also falls in love with the magnetic, longhaired Valentino. The story tries to be emotionally charged, but the characters never feel real. Let them wallow in their fucked-up sexual situations! ★★ VHS: $14.99

Velvet Goldmine

(1998, 127 min, GB/US, Todd Haynes) *Ewan McGregor, Jonathan Rhys-Meyers, Toni Collette, Christian Bale, Eddie Izzard.* Arguably the most talented of the so-called "New Queer Cinema" filmmakers, Haynes stumbles a bit in this emotionally cold but musically exciting, visually hallucinogenic story set in London's glitter rock world of the early 1970s. Unable to get the story or music rights to David Bowie's meteoric rise to rock stardom, Haynes instead offers a tale and soundtrack suspiciously similar to Bowie's Ziggy Stardust incarnation. Rhys-Meyers is a sweet young man who transforms himself into glam rock superstar Brian Slade. He marries an intense American (Collette) but falls in love with fellow rocker Curt Wild (a wonderfully swaggering McGregor). At the height of his fame, he fakes his death. Now ten years later, a former fan/now reporter (Bale) sets out to uncover the truth and reasons for his self-destruction. What makes the film memorable are the loud fashions, some good acting, high-energy music and intensely druggy images. ★★★ VHS: $14.99; DVD: $29.99

The Velvet Touch

(1948, 97 min, US, John Gage) *Rosalind Russell, Leo Genn, Claire Trevor, Sydney Greenstreet.* Russell gives a good performance in this nifty thriller as a famous stage actress who murders her producer and becomes involved in a cat-and-mouse game with the investigating police detective. ★★★

Vengeance Is Mine

(1979, 129 min, Japan, Shohei Imamura) *Ken Ogata.* This unrelenting probe of the criminal mind is powerfully brought to the screen by Imamura, director of the highly acclaimed *Ballad of Narayama* and long considered one of Japan's leading contemporary filmmakers. Structured in a documentary style, this exciting thriller casts Ogata as a killer on the run.

He eludes the law's net and leads the police along a bloody path paved with fraud, violence and murder. An unusual and unforgettable portrait of a "man without a heart." (Letterboxed) (Japanese with English subtitles) ★★★½ VHS: $39.99

Venus in Furs

(1970, 86 min, GB, Jess Franco) *James Darren, Klaus Kinski.* A murky drama about a jazz musician who falls for a mysterious woman who is really a recently washed ashore corpse. In the end, she turns out to be the Angel of Death come to Earth to avenge a murder by twisting and contorting a psychopathic killer's already feeble mind. Confused yet? ★½

Vera Cruz

(1954, 94 min, US, Robert Aldrich) *Gary Cooper, Burt Lancaster, Denise Darcel, Cesar Romero, Ernest Borgnine, Charles Bronson.* Cooper and Lancaster are two adventurers involved in political intrigue in 1860s Mexico. A flavorful western. ★★★ VHS: $14.99; DVD: $19.99

The Verdict

(1982, 129 min, US, Sidney Lumet) *Paul Newman, James Mason, Jack Warden, Charlotte Rampling, Milo O'Shea, Lindsay Crouse.* Newman gives an extraordinary performance as a down-on-his-luck lawyer given a last chance at self-redemption when he is hired in a medical malpractice case. A riveting courtroom drama and character study, with a superior supporting cast. ★★★½ VHS: $14.99

Vernon, Florida

(1987, 60 min, US, Errol Morris) Morris' wonderful, quirky look at the eccentric residents of a small backwoods town in the Florida panhandle. ★★★½

Veronico Cruz

(1987, 106 min, Argentina/GB, Miguel Pereira) *Juan Jose Camero, Gonzalo Morales.* The bittersweet story about the relationship between a young boy and his schoolteacher is set against the debacle of the Malvinas/Falklands War. Perched high in the outback of the Argentinian highlands, a young boy is raised by his grandmother after his mother dies and his father abandons him. In this remote area, untouched by civilization, the boy, Veronico, grows up. His life, as well as that of the entire pueblo, is changed forever after the military junta invades their tranquil world and pits friend against friend in a relentless and senseless power struggle. A quietly moving drama of individuals caught up in the maelstrom of political zealousness. (Spanish with English subtitles) ★★★ VHS: $39.99

Veronika Voss

(1981, 104 min, Germany, Rainer Werner Fassbinder) *Rosel Zech, Hilmar Thate.* A stunning profile of a faded film star's descent into morphine addiction and emotional dependency is Fassbinder's eerie black-and-white tribute to *Sunset Boulevard*. A very un-Fassbinder-like cinematic tour de force with ceaseless camera movement and striking characterizations. The director's final film in his trilogy on the German condition during and immediately after WWII. (German with English subtitles) ★★★½

Velvet Goldmine

Vertigo

(1958, 120 min, US, Alfred Hitchcock) *James Stewart, Kim Novak, Barbara Bel Geddes.* Perhaps the most masterful achievement in a career strewn with classics, *Vertigo* is a multi-layered summary of Hitchcock's prime obsessions: the fears of physical and psychological intimacy, emotional commitment and mortality. Stewart is superb as the detective with a debilitating case of acrophobia, which costs him not only his job but also the woman he is desperately drawn to. Novak portrays the illusive heroine, a dreamlike incarnation of womanhood whose shifting identity unhinges Stewart's haunted hero. (VHS available letterboxed or pan & scan) ★★★★ VHS: $14.99; DVD: $29.99

Very Bad Things

(1998, 100 min, US, Peter Berg) *Christian Slater, Jon Favreau, Cameron Diaz, Jeremy Piven, Daniel Stern, Jeanne Tripplehorn.* A black comedy which delivers on its dark, twisted premise but just isn't that funny, *Very Bad Things* marks the writing and directing debut of actor Berg. The film begins at breakneck pace, with groom-to-be Favreau and pals going to Vegas for a fun and frolicking bachelor party. When a prostitute is accidentally killed, the five friends are faced with a decision: call the cops or bury the body in the desert. Berg gives the film a visual verve, and the fast-cuts and sharp cinematography make the film seem very lively; but as writer, he has failed to fully deliver. His tale is dark enough, and while watching it one can appreciate the set-up and contrivances; but there are few laughs, and the gore and humor don't mesh. ★★½ VHS: $14.99; DVD: $19.99

A Very Brady Sequel

(1996, 89 min, US, Arlene Sanford) *Shelley Long, Gary Cole, Tim Matheson, Christopher Daniel Barnes, Christine Taylor, Jennifer Elise Cox, RuPaul, Rosie O'Donnell.* The entire Brady clan — yes, those vapidly naïve family values icons stuck in the loud polyester world of the '70s — returns in this equally skewering sequel. While some of the innovative satire of the first film may seem overly familiar the second time around, it should not stop anyone from enjoying this cutely funny and at times madcap spoof of the old TV sitcom. The plot revolves around the return of Carol's (Long) long-thought-dead husband (Matheson), who steals a valuable ancient horse statue. He then kidnaps the perky Mrs. Brady and takes her to Hawaii — with the loudly clothed, off-key, sing-songing Bradys in hot pursuit. Plenty of sexual innuendoes, eye-poppingly loud (but groovy) threads and shamelessly mindless fun should divert both old TV fans and newcomers alike. ★★★ VHS: $9.99

A Very Curious Girl

(1986, 105 min, France, Nelly Kaplan) *Bernadette LaFont, Georges Geret.* Kaplan's sexy comedy about a beautiful peasant girl who decides to sell sexual services to the men in the village. Soon, she has more power than she ever dreamed of and becomes involved in a series of hilarious events. (French with English subtitles) ★★½

James Stewart and Kim Novak in *Vertigo*

A Very Natural Thing

(1973, 85 min, US, Christopher Larkin) *Robert Joel, Curt Gareth.* An important film in the history of American gay filmmaking, *A Very Natural Thing* is considered the first feature film on the gay experience made by an out-of-the-closet gay director to receive a commercial distribution. The simple but insightful story involves a 26-year-old gay man who leaves the priesthood and moves to New York City in the hopes of finding a meaningful relationship. Now a schoolteacher, he soon falls in love with a handsome young advertising executive. Though the film is rather sappy and tends to preach, it is nevertheless sensitively told and refreshingly romantic. ★★★ VHS: $39.99; DVD: $29.99

A Very Old Man with Enormous Wings

(1988, 90 min, Cuba, Fernando Birri) *Fernando Birri.* After a violent cyclone, a poor couple discover near their desolate farmhouse a mute winged man (played by director Birri). Not understanding him, they cage him in a chicken coop where the strange old man, with supernatural physical attributes, soon becomes the area's local attraction; drawing the curious, the derisive and the devout. A bizarre fable infused with magical realism, at times cruel images and comic confusion. (Spanish with English subtitles) ★★★

A Very Private Affair

(1962, 95 min, France/Italy, Louis Malle) *Brigitte Bardot, Marcello Mastroianni.* This early work by Malle is a steamy examination of the trials of movie stardom and features BB as a naive nymphet and newly found movie star who is constantly beset by fans, press and photographers. The underside of stardom is pointedly looked at in this romantic melodrama. ★★½

The Very Thought of You

(1999, 88 min, GB, Nick Hamm) *Monica Potter, Rufus Sewell, Joseph Fiennes, Tom Hollander, Ray Winstone.* Another daft romantic comedy about an American in Britain, *The Very Thought of You* is an ultrathin piece of fluff that would hardly pass as a made-for-TV movie, except for the fact that it was made for TV — Channel 4, to be exact. Although usually their quality is considerably higher than this affair about three friends all falling for the same girl, director Hamm does employ a nice visual style at times. Potter (channelling Julia Roberts) is Martha, a young girl from Minneapolis who chucks everything and flies to London, meeting Daniel (Hollander), Frank (Sewell) and Laurence (Fiennes) along the way. Martha spends the entire film deciding which, if any, of these suitors is right for her. The film's lack of subtlety in every regard is easily its biggest flaw. ★★ VHS: $102.99; DVD: $29.99

Vibes

(1988, 99 min, US, Ken Kwapis) *Peter Falk, Jeff Goldblum, Cyndi Lauper.* A wacky comedy about two psychics (Goldblum, Lauper) who are thrown together in a quest for a lost South American treasure, being manipulated all the way by con man Falk. Lauper is appealing in her film debut in this totally silly but amiable romp. ★★½ VHS: $79.99

Vice Versa

(1988, 100 min, US, Brian Gilbert) *Judge Reinhold, Fred Savage, Swoosie Kurtz.* Reinhold and Savage make this familiar body-switching comedy better than it really is thanks to their endearing performances. Though not as well conceived as *Big*, there's a lot to like in this tale about a department store manager and his young son exchanging identities. ★★½ VHS: $14.99

Victim

(1961, 100 min, GB, Basil Dearden) *Dirk Bogarde, Sylvia Syms, Dennis Price, Peter McEnery.* Long considered a landmark film for its complex and sophisticated treatment of homosexuality, this exceptional thriller stars Bogarde as a married, bisexual lawyer who risks his reputation by confronting a gang of blackmailers responsible for the death of his former lover. A thoughtful and compelling piece which was instrumental in breaking new ground. ★★★½ VHS: $29.99

Victor/Victoria

(1982, 133 min, GB/US, Blake Edwards) *Julie Andrews, James Garner, Robert Preston, Lesley Ann Warren, Alex Karras.* This stylish, gender-bending, sexual/musical comedy stars Andrews as a female (Victoria) who passes as a gay male female impersonator (Victor). Preston offers a scintillating performance as her gay friend and mentor, Toddy. Garner is a Chicago gangster confusingly enchanted and attracted to Andrews, who he thinks is a man. Based on the 1933 German comedy, *Viktor und Viktoria,* Edwards' exuberant romp is full of snappy tunes and sophisticated hilarity. Warren gives a priceless performance as Garner's dumb-blonde mistress. (Remade as a Broadway musical) ★★★★ VHS: $14.99

Victor/Victoria

(1995, 146 min, US, Blake Edwards) *Julie Andrews, Tony Roberts, Michael Nouri, Rachel York.* A live performance of the Broadway show, based on the 1982 hit film, *Victor/Victoria* is a most entertaining adaptation. Andrews is in wonderful form as Victoria, an out-of-work singer whose life changes when she meets the flamboyant Toddy (Roberts). With his help, she becomes "Victor," an overnight sensation as a female impersonator in the nightclubs of Paris. But success has its complications when she falls for King Marchan, a macho Chicago gangster (Nouri). Adapted and directed by Edwards, this stage version has a few songs which weren't in the film, and is minus a couple of characters (that hilarious waiter, the P.I.) and scenes ("cockroach"). It can't really compare with the classic original, but it's a delight and time well spent. ★★★ VHS: $19.99; DVD: $19.99

Victory

(1981, 110 min, US, John Huston) *Michael Caine, Sylvester Stallone, Pelé, Max von Sydow.* Standard WWII prison escape adventure is heightened by an exciting finale featuring a soccer game between Allied soldiers and their German captors. ★★ VHS: $9.99; DVD: $14.99

Videodrome

(1983, 90 min, Canada, David Cronenberg) *James Woods, Sonja Smits, Deborah Harry, Peter Dvorsky.* Woods' performance dominates this gritty horror tale from director Cronenberg. He plays the owner of a cable station whose programming choices begin to bring about horrifying hallucinations. Gory though spectacular special effects by Rick Baker. Not for all tastes. ★★★ VHS: $9.99; DVD: $24.99

La Vie Continue

(1982, 93 min, France, Moshe Mizrahi) *Annie Girardot, Jean-Pierre Cassel.* Girardot is marvelous as a sheltered middle-class woman who, when her husband suddenly dies, is forced to make adjustments in her life. Things brighten up when she finds herself in love again. Her budding new relationship is a joy to witness as it unfolds. (American remake: *Men Don't Leave*) (French with English subtitles) ★★★ VHS: $59.99

La Vie de Bohéme

(1993, 100 min, France, Aki Kaurismäki) Anyone familiar with the works of Finnish director Kaurismäki (*Leningrad Cowboys Go America*) know that his films are low-key and the comedy is usually archly subtle — he's somewhat like a Finnish Jim Jarmusch. *La Vie de Bohéme,* his first French production, proves to be no different. The story centers on the down-on-their-luck lives of three bedraggled men: Albanian painter Rodolfo, aspiring novelist Marcel, and Irish composer Schaunard. The resilient, likable trio find success, food and love always just out of their reach as they pursue their art regardless of the inevitable setbacks. There is humor in the tale but overall, the slow pacing, repetitive story line and somber look at life on the edge make this a must for Kaurismäki fans only. ★★ VHS: $19.99

Vietnam: Year of the Pig

(1968, 103 min, US, Emile de Antonio) This outstanding, Academy Award-nominated documentary offers a thought-provoking and riveting examination into America's involvement in the Vietnam War and Southeast Asia. ★★★½

A View to a Kill

(1985, 131 min, GB, John Glen) *Roger Moore, Christopher Walken, Grace Jones.* One of the weakest of the Bond films is saddled with an anemic villain played by Walken who's simply not convincingly evil. Even Jones is unable to perk up the proceedings in this one. Moore is simply coasting as 007. (Sequel: *The Living Daylights*) ★★ VHS: $9.99; DVD: $26.99

Vigil

(1984, 90 min, New Zealand, Vincent Ward) *Bill Kerr, Fiona Kay.* Told with strikingly stark visuals, this grim, atmospheric drama is set on a sheep farm in a desolate, darkly enchanted valley in New Zealand. The story is seen through the eyes of an 11-year-old girl, Toss. When her father dies accidentally, a mysterious stranger arrives and begins to help the family survive. Though helpful, Toss sees him as a predator; and one who must leave immediately. Director Ward spent five years making this bleak but mystical testimony to the beauty and immutability of nature and life. A startling directorial debut and a work of extraordinary beauty. ★★★½ VHS: $19.99

The Vikings

(1958, 114 min, US, Richard Fleischer) *Kirk Douglas, Tony Curtis, Janet Leigh, Ernest Borgnine.* Douglas and Curtis are Viking blood brothers who set sail for the English coast in this fanciful, familiar tale of exploration and conquest. ★★½

Village of the Damned

(1960, 78 min, GB, Wolf Rilla) *George Sanders, Barbara Shelley.* Classic English horror and damned scary at that! This is a low-budget shocker about a group of strange, emotionless children who attempt to take over a small village by controlling the minds of the adults. An eerie chiller of the highest order. (Remade in 1995) ★★★½ VHS: $14.99

Village of the Damned

(1995, 95 min, US, John Carpenter) *Christopher Reeve, Kirstie Alley, Michael Paré, Linda Kozlowski, Mark Hamill.* Based on the semi-classic 1960 chiller, this version features updated effects and splendid cinematography, but it is not really much different than the original in plot. The inhabitants of the coastal California town of Midwich suffer a strange sleeplike trance one day but emerge seemingly unharmed — until they discover all the townswomen are pregnant. A mass birth, facilitated by local doctor Reeve and federal epidemiologist Alley, results in a group of bizarre offspring who mature into eerie, super-intelligent adolescents. Carpenter is unable to ignite the story sufficiently, though the film is still moderately entertaining. ★★½ VHS: $19.99; DVD: $24.99

Vincent

(1987, 105 min, Australia, Paul Cox) This thoughtful and engrossing examination into the life and art of Vincent Van Gogh takes an unconventional approach in its efforts to reveal the artist's driving creative force. More of a filmed essay than biography, the movie attempts to piece together Van Gogh's final years by the reading of the many eloquent and insightful letters he wrote to his brother, Theo (read off-screen by John Hurt); while at the same time examining the artist's work — from his earliest line drawings to his last hallucinatory portraits and landscapes. More complex and abstract than the Vincente Minnelli's *Lust For Life* or Robert Altman's *Vincent and Theo,* Cox seems more interested in revealing the intellectual and articulate Van Gogh and not the simpler image of a tortured and mad painter. ★★★

Vincent & Theo

(1990, 138 min, US, Robert Altman) *Tim Roth, Paul Rhys.* With this most accomplished work, Altman sets his sights on the lives and the delicate relationship between artist Vincent Van Gogh and his brother, Theo. In a commanding performance, Roth plays the tortured genius, Vincent, who is irrevocably tied to his sibling; each in search of his own artistic identity and unable to break the confines of their bond. Rhys is equally as compelling as Theo. ★★★½ VHS: $14.99

Vincent, François, Paul and the Others

(1974, 118 min, France, Claude Sautet) *Yves Montand, Gérard Depardieu, Stéphane Audran, Michel Piccoli.* An all-star cast highlights this elegant but dolorous drama of male mid-life crisis. Vincent, François and Paul are lifelong friends, all in their mid-fifties. The "others" are represented by a younger member of the group (Depardieu) along with their various wives and mistresses. The story follows their weekly retreat to the country where underneath the jocular drinking and eating, difficult problems of love and life confront them all. A well-acted saga which explores the problems of bourgeois life from the male perspective. (French with English subtitles) ★★★ VHS: $19.99

Violence at Noon

(1966, 99 min, Japan, Nagisa Oshima) *Saeda Kawaguchi, Akiko Koyama.* From Oshima, the director of *In the Realm of the Senses,* comes an equally disturbing and controversial examination of sensuality and passion. One of the founders of the Japanese New Wave, Oshima was strongly effected by Jean-Luc Godard, and Oshima's imagery and editing technique do not contradict this. Set in a rural Japanese commune, the story focuses on the unsettling

Kirsten Dunst in *The Virgin Suicides*

relationship between a rapist/murderer, his wife and a woman he once raped. Protecting him from the police out of a perverted sense of loyalty, the women are strangely obedient to this man until a final confrontation. (Japanese with English subtitles) ★★★ VHS: $24.99

Violent Cop

(1989, 103 min, Japan, Takeshi Kitano) *Takeshi Kitano, Maiko Kawakami, Makoto Ashikawa, Shirô Sano.* A molasses-paced action film, *Violent Cop* is even less satisfying than other films from the director because of a completely despicable, and, even more damaging, uninteresting lead character. Takeshi plays a cop who makes Dirty Harry look like a pussycat, beating or killing anyone who gets in his way of "justice." Too slow to be the guilty pleasure it might have been, and too ugly and superficial to be an affecting drama, *Violent Cop* is for diehard Takeshi fans and the exceedingly patient only. (Japanese with English subtitles) ★★ VHS: $19.99; DVD: $19.99

The Violent Years

(1956, 57 min, US, William M. Morgan) *Jean Moorehead, Glenn Corbett.* Delinquent debutantes do drugs, rob gas stations, rape rich boys, and commit murder, mayhem and assorted pajama party violence. Screenplay by Ed Wood. ★ VHS: $7.99; DVD: $24.99

Les Violons du Bal

(1974, 108 min, France, Michel Drach) *Jean-Louis Trintignant, Marie-José Nat.* Director Drach's remembrances of his Jewish childhood in Nazi-occupied France, as well as his attempts to get financing to make a film on the subject, are the two parallel stories in this affectionate personal drama. Using imaginative cross-cutting, Drach deftly weaves the two stories together into a perilous and deeply moving film. His son Michel charmingly plays the director as a young boy who, along with his lovely mother (played by Drach's real-life wife, Nat) and his two siblings, attempt to stay one step ahead of the Nazis and certain extradition to a labor camp. And while this heart-stopping drama unfolds, Drach —

played by Trintignant — tries to interest people in the film project. (French with English subtitles) ★★★ VHS: $79.99

The Virgin Machine

(1988, 85 min, Germany, Monika Treut) *Ina Blum, Susie Bright.* This thought-provoking sexual odyssey tells the story of a young West German woman and her search for "romantic love." Frustrated by the emptiness and the emotional morass of her native Hamburg, Dorothee decides to flee her home to search for her mother, who is living in San Francisco. Once arrived, however, her trek turns into a process of sexual discovery. Filmed in a steamy black and white, the film exudes a sensuality in which simple lust is transformed into glorious eroticism. While *The Virgin Machine* is clearly a feminist film about a woman's exploration of her own sexuality, its profound statement is one which applies to all. (English and German with English subtitles) ★★★ VHS: $29.99

The Virgin Queen

(1955, 92 min, US, Henry Koster) *Bette Davis, Richard Todd, Joan Collins.* Davis reprises her acclaimed role from 1939's *The Private Lives of Elizabeth and Essex* as Queen Elizabeth I, here coming in conflict with Walter Raleigh (well played by Todd). Davis, as usual, is commanding. ★★★ VHS: $19.99

The Virgin Soldiers

(1969, 96 min, GB, John Dexter) *Lynn Redgrave, Hywell Bennett, Nigel Davenport.* Beautiful cinematography enhances this little-known gem about the end of innocence (both sexually and otherwise) for a group of young British recruits going to battle in 1950s Singapore. A dewy-fresh Redgrave costars as the girl who escorts one of the boys (Bennet) into manhood. ★★★ VHS: $69.99

The Virgin Spring

(1960, 88 min, Sweden, Ingmar Bergman) *Max von Sydow, Birgitta Valberg.* Based on a Swedish ballad, Bergman's quietly chilling morality play brilliantly captures the quality of ancient leg-

ends — their primitive passion, human sorrow, and abrupt beauty. Set in the Swedish country-side of the 14th century, it stars von Sydow as the tormented father whose daughter was raped and murdered after her sister invokes a pagan curse. In the spot of her death a magical spring bursts forth. (Swedish with English subtitles) ★★★★ VHS: $29.99

The Virgin Suicides

(2000, 97 min, US, Sofia Coppola) *Kirsten Dunst, Josh Hartnett, James Woods, Kathleen Turner, Danny DeVito, Scott Glenn, Michael Paré.* From the opening frames of *The Virgin Suicides*, one feels the potential of a major new filmmaker in Sofia Coppola. Yes, that same Sofia Coppola who nearly sabotaged her father's epic *The Godfather III*. But she may have found her calling if her directorial debut *The Virgin Suicides* is any indication, for this is a film of some power. The tale of the Lisbon family is a tragic one. The five Lisbon girls commit suicide, first Cecilia and then the rest. Our narrator is the grown voice of one of the five neighborhood boys whose lives have been marked forever by their fascination with the elusive and beautiful Lisbon girls. Being a fractured look at suburban repression, the dowdy design is as important as the smart adaptation of the Jeffrey Eugenides novel, for words and atmosphere are equally telling. The performances are understated and pitch perfect. Turner trades her sultry sex goddess for repressed matriarch, and Woods is moving as the clueless father. Among the teenagers, Dunst and Harnett are particularly affecting. ★★★ VHS: $14.99; DVD: $29.99

Virginia City

(1940, 121 min, US, Michael Curtiz) *Errol Flynn, Randolph Scott, Miriam Hopkins, Humphrey Bogart.* A follow-up to his successful *Dodge City*, Flynn is back in the saddle in this colorful Civil War western. There's intrigue and treachery at every turn as Union officer Flynn puts the stops on a Confederate gold shipment, and tangles with rebel officer Scott, spy Hopkins and Mexican outlaw Bogart. The cast comes off well, except for Bogie, looking ridiculous in his Ricardo Montalban mustache. ★★★ VHS: $19.99

Viridiana

(1961, 91 min, Spain, Luis Bunuel) *Fernando Rey, Silvia Pinal, Francesco Rabal.* Buñuel's controversial and brilliant surrealistic examination of good and evil is about a young novice and her loss of innocence at her rich uncle's estate. Contains the celebrated Last Supper scene. The film which caused Buñuel to be kicked out of Spain. (Spanish with English subtitles) ★★★★ VHS: $24.99

Virtual Sexuality

(1999, 92 min, GB, Nick Hurran) *Laura Fraser, Rupert Penry-Jones, Luke de Lacey, Kieran O'Brien.* A British teen sex comedy, *Virtual Sexuality* blends the genres of mismatched love and gender-bending with mixed results. Justine (Fraser) is a single seventeen-year-old who lusts after Alex (O'Brien), the school jock who, of course, is a jerk. When her nerdy best friend Chas (de Lacey) takes her to a cyberspace fair, she creates her "perfect guy" (Penry-Jones) in a dating booth. However, things go haywire and Justine actually becomes the boy of her dreams. Suddenly, she/he has to grasp a new lifestyle and see things from a new perspective. The characters get into one improbably wacky situation after another in the name of frothy fun, but the "be yourself" message is clear. Much of the film is harmless; nevertheless, there is virtually nothing new here. ★★½ VHS: $14.99; DVD: $24.99

Virtuosity

(1995, 105 min, US, Brett Leonard) *Denzel Washington, Russell Crowe, Kelly Lynch, Stephen Spinella, William Forsythe, Louise Fletcher.* With more than a little in common with the far more entertaining *Demolition Man*, this mindless, slowly paced sci-fi adventure casts Washington as a former cop who's now behind bars and is the only one who can track down the nasty bad guy. The latter would be Crowe as a virtual reality villain who has come to life endowed with super powers and is killing everyone in sight. The film attempts to make a comment on violence and our appetite for it in our society, but *Virtuosity* gratuitously feeds that hunger with ridiculous plot developments, undefined characters and indiscriminate scenes of violence. ★ VHS: $9.99; DVD: $24.99

Virus

(1999, 99 min, US, John Bruno) *Jamie Lee Curtis, William Baldwin, Donald Sutherland, Joanna Pacula.* A terrible rip-off, *Virus* is sci-fi dreck that will be thrilling only to someone who's never seen a movie before. A tugboat crew happens upon a seemingly abandoned Russian research vessel and decide to claim it. But the investigation of the ship takes a turn for the clichéd as an alien force determines humans are a "virus," and must be destroyed. Wholly unoriginal and visually dull, *Virus* at least has female characters that aren't cowering, bikini-clad bimbos, but in the end, it just doesn't matter. ★ VHS: $9.99; DVD: $29.99

A Virus Knows No Morals

(1986, 84 min, Germnay, Rosa von Praunheim) Never one to tread softly on a controversial subject, von Praunheim tackles the issue of AIDS in this archaic black comedy. With several stories intercut throughout the film, von Praunheim's cast of weird characters includes a sex club owner who refuses to change his policies, claiming that, "I won't let them take away our freedom"; hysterical members of the press who are bent on making a story; and workers at a hospital where the deluge of AIDS patients causes them to become so bored and jaded that the night nurses roll dice to see which patient will die next. Gallows humor abounds as the director seeks to provoke, embarrass and enrage the audience into understanding the effects of the crisis. (German with English subtitles) ★★★ VHS: $39.99

Vision Quest

(1985, 107 min, US, Harold Becker) *Matthew Modine, Linda Fiorentino, Ronny Cox, Daphne Zuniga.* Modine and the fiery Fiorentino make an attractive twosome in this compelling drama about a high school wrestler going after the state championship. Madonna sings two songs. ★★★ VHS: $14.99; DVD: $14.99

Visions of 8

(1972, 110 min, Various) The producer of this film had the intriguing idea to have eight different directors from around the world film various events of the 1972 Summer Olympics at Munich. Included in this menagerie of filmmakers are Kon Ichikawa, John Schlesinger, Milos Forman, Claude Lelouch and Mai Zetterling. The results are, as one would imagine, uneven. Although interesting, better examples of a filmmaker capturing the beauty and spectacle of this sporting event would be either Ichikawa's *Tokyo Olympiad* or Leni Riefenstahl's *Olympia*. ★★½

Visions of Light: The Art of Cinematography

(1993, 90 min, US, Arnold Glassman, Todd McCarthy & Stuart Samuels) Setting out to elevate cinematographers above their normal obscurity, this fascinating and entertaining documentary on the art behind making movies is a must-see for those who consider themselves film connoisseurs. The film focuses on the works of 26 of the world's greatest all-time cinematographers and points to some of their finest contributions; examining several of moviedom's most famous shots and uncovering the various methods and mistakes which went into their creation. Film buffs will find the material so absorbing that they will be wishing for more at the end of the film's breezy 90 minutes. ★★★½ VHS: $29.99; DVD: $24.99

Les Visiteurs du Soir
(The Devil's Envoys)

(1942, 110 min, France, Marcel Carné) *Arletty, Jules Berry.* This charming medieval fantasy scripted by Jacques Prévert is set in the 15th century and tells the story of two emissaries sent to earth by the Devil to corrupt two young lovers and disrupt their impending marriage. Things don't work out too well for the bad guys as the male envoy falls in love with the young princess. It takes the Devil himself to intervene by turning the couple into stone; but, much to his dismay, their pure hearts continue to beat. Made during the German Occupation, this thinly veiled allegory — of Hitler as the Devil and France the lovers — surprisingly never had problems with the German censors. Sometimes a bit stilted and forced, this visually lush fairy tale is still a fine example of the Carné/Prévert style of poetic realism. (French with English subtitles) ★★★

The Visitors

(1996, 106 min, France, Jean-Marie Poire) *Jean Reno, Christian Clavier, Valerie Lemercier.* The French take a lot of flack here in America for their questionable taste in comedy. *The Visitors*, a huge hit in France, will not help end the Jerry Lewis jokes. Reno is completely unappealing as a medieval knight who, along with his excruciating sidekick (cowriter Clavier, a twisted cross between Harpo Marx and Charles Manson), is transported to modern-day France by a senile wizard. The two wacky fishes-out-of-water bumble through France, insulting, threatening or assaulting everyone they meet. There's a small amount of satire here, but like everything else in *The Visitors*, it's never developed. (French with English subtitles) ★½

Vital Signs

(1990, 103 min, US, Marisa Silver) *Jimmy Smits, Adrian Pasdar, Diane Lane, Norma Aleandro.* Routine medical drama about young med students and their professional and personal struggles. Aleandro brings a heartrending dignity to her dying cancer patient. ★★½

I Vitelloni (The Wastrels)

(1953, 109 min, Italy, Federico Fellini) *Franco Fabrizi, Alberto Sordi, Franco Interlenghi.* This neorealist masterpiece is an early work by Fellini, and more traditional in narrative, it doesn't hint to his future career in the cinema of the fantastic and surreal. Partly autobiographical, the story deals with the young, restless men of a small town on the Adriatic. Touching, powerful and graceful, the film is a refined social commentary on small-town mores and morals in post-war Italy. (Italian with English subtitles) ★★★★

Vito and the Others

(1992, 90 min, Italy, Antonio Capuano) Pubescent, angel-faced boys rove the streets of a decaying Naples terrorizing all with their petty crimes, drug dealing and prostitution in this lurid *Pixote*-influenced "exposé" on urban hopelessness. Twelve-year-old Vito, living with abusive relatives after his father wipes out his family in a murderous rampage, joins up with a band of future juvenile delinquents. Sent to prison after a busted drug deal, he slips further away when he is raped by fellow prisoners and returns to the streets a hardened hooligan, indifferent to emotion and love. Unlike *Pixote*, we never get to know much about young Vito nor are we shocked by his vicious antisocial behavior. It's too serious to be cheesy exploitation, too awkward to be effective drama. (Italian with English subtitles) ★★½ VHS: $59.99

Viva Zapata!

(1952, 113 min, US, Elia Kazan) *Marlon Brando, Anthony Quinn, Jean Peters, Joseph Wiseman.* Brando is exceptional as a Mexican peasant whose search for simple justice leads to rebellion and eventual triumph. Quinn won a Best Supporting Actor Oscar as Brando's brother. John Steinbeck wrote the script. ★★★½

Vive L'Amour

(1996, 119 min, Taiwan, Tsai Ming-Liang) *Yang Kuei-Mei, Lee Kang-Shang, Chen Chao-Jung.* A remarkable film about passion and loneliness, *Vive L'Amour* eschews narrative convention by presenting its offbeat love story almost exclusively without dialogue. A young Taiwanese couple meet for anonymous sex in a vacant apartment. Unbeknowst to them, a sexually confused and suicidal young man is also living in the abandoned space. Writer-director Ming-Liang generates tremendous drama in a series of revealing episodes that examine the sensation of communication. Slowly, methodically paced and definitely not for all tastes, the fascinating and seductive *Vive L'Amour* rewards the concentration of patient viewers. (Taiwanese with English subtitles) ★★★½ VHS: $19.99; DVD: $29.99

Julie Delpy in *Voyager*

Vixen

(1968, 70 min, US, Russ Meyer) *Erica Gavin.* A straightforward narrative of a bush pilot and his oversexed wife who live in the Canadian wilderness. It cost $76,000 to make and brought back over $7.5 million at the box office, bringing Meyer deserved recognition from major Hollywood studios. ★★★ VHS: $79.99

Voices of Sarafina!

(1988, 85 min, US, Nigel Noble) Interviews with cast members of the hit Broadway musical "Sarafina," with scenes from the show spliced with images of life in oppressive South African townships. A celebration of the courage and conviction of anti-Apartheid activists, set to the rhythm of Mbaganga street music (emulated on Paul Simon's "Graceland" album). ★★★ VHS: $29.99

Volcano

(1997, 102 min, US, Mick Jackson) *Tommy Lee Jones, Anne Heche, Don Cheadle, Gaby Hoffmann, Keith David.* Sporting his customary take-control but nice-guy gruffness, Jones plays a civil supervisor who's ready to rally the troops when L.A. is devastated by a volcano. Aided by geologist Heche, the two race against time in their attempt to outwit this force of nature and save the city. Though it has all the trappings of the genre, *Volcano* has going for it an appealing ensemble, a quick pace, good effects, and a story line which won't require you to smack your head (too often) in disbelief. Despite a heavy-handed racial angle and a terribly clichéd ending, *Volcano* is fun to watch as it speeds down Wilshire Boulevard and levels Los Angeles — any film which does that can't be all bad. (Letterboxed VHS available for $19.99) ★★½ VHS: $9.99; DVD: $24.99

Volere Volare

(1993, 92 min, Italy, Maurizio Nichetti & Guido Manuli) *Maurizio Nichetti, Angela Finocchiaro.* In this kinky cartoon comedy,

Nichetti (*The Icicle Thief*) once again employs surreal film techniques to portray a very comical but human love story. A sexual fantasist for hire becomes enamored with Maurizio, a cartoon sound dubber who "brings his work home with him." The slapstick fun of the film adds spice to the witty writing and good performances. Unlike many American romances of today, *Volere Volare* is quirky without being smutty, and romantic without being schmaltzy. ★★★ VHS: $19.99

Volpone

(1939, 95 min, France, Maurice Tourneur) *Harry Bauer, Louis Jouvet.* Volpone (Bauer), a rich 16th-century Venetian merchant, pretends to be dying in order to observe how his "friends" react and jockey for his considerable inheritance and, in turn, take advantage of them. A droll satire on the ever-present human traits of power and greed. Based on the classic comedy by Ben Johnson. (French with English subtitles) ★★★

Volunteers

(1985, 106 min, US, Nicholas Meyer) *Tom Hanks, John Candy, Rita Wilson, Tim Thomerson.* Hanks and Candy breathe some life into this uneven comedy about a rich ne'er-do-well (Hanks) who travels to Thailand with a group of Peace Corps volunteers to escape his bookie. ★★ VHS: $9.99; DVD: $14.99

Von Ryan's Express

(1965, 117 min, US, Mark Robson) *Frank Sinatra, Trevor Howard, Edward Mulhare, James Brolin.* Sinatra lends authority to this exciting WWII adventure about a daring POW escape, led by American colonel Sinatra. Howard is a British general, at odds with the arrogant Yank. ★★★ VHS: $14.99; DVD: $24.99

Voyage en Ballon

(1959, 82 min, France, Albert Lamorisse) *Narrated by: Jack Lemmon.* From the director of *The Red Balloon* comes this enchanting, multi-award winning children's film. A young boy stows away in a gigantic balloon that his grandfather has built. Together, the two, captain and first mate, travel across France on a wonderful, humorous and suspenseful adventure. ★★★

Voyage in Italy

(1953, 94 min, Italy, Roberto Rossellini) *Ingrid Bergman, George Sanders.* This third Rossellini-Bergman collaboration (*Stromboli, Europa '51*) was panned by the critics and bombed at the box office on its initial release, but was revivified when the directors of the French New Wave hailed it as a masterpiece. Bergman and Sanders are a bored couple who travel to Italy to inspect a villa they have inherited. Against magnificent background settings (Mt. Vesuvius, Capri, the ruins of Pompeii), their faltering marriage finally breaks up; but through a "miracle," they are reunited. With little "action," this simple film is a romantically passionate story on the renewal of life and love. (aka: *Strangers*) (Filmed in English) ★★★ VHS: $59.99

A Voyage Round My Father

(1983, 85 min, GB, Alvin Rakoff) *Laurence Olivier, Alan Bates, Jane Asher.* John Mortimer's superb television adaptation of

his own hit play. Semiautobiographical in nature, this often moving and sometimes funny reminiscence centers on the occasionally tumultuous relationship between an eccentric father (Olivier) and his son (Bates). ★★★ VHS: $19.99

Voyage Surprise

(1946, 108 min, France, Pierre Prévert) *Jean Bourgoin, Maurice Baquet.* This delightfully zany comedy by the Brothers Prévert (Jacques cowrote the story) tells of an old man's dream to arrange a mystery tour or "voyage surprise" on a ramshackle bus. The tourists are his family, elderly friends and various eccentrics who find themselves involved in a series of scary and comic adventures involving a wedding party, a brothel, anarchists, an evil Grand Duchess and the police. (French with English subtitles) ★★★½ VHS: $59.99

Voyage to the Bottom of the Sea

(1961, 106 min, US, Irwin Allen) *Walter Pidgeon, Joan Fontaine, Peter Lorre, Barbara Eden.* The crew of an atomic submarine desperately fights to save the Earth from impending destruction. Hokey fun. Look out for the giant squid! (The basis for a popular 1960s TV series.) ★★½ VHS: $14.99; DVD: $24.99

Voyager

(1991, 113 min, Germany/France, Volker Schlöndorff) *Sam Shepard, Julie Delpy, Barbara Sukowa, Dieter Kirchlechner, Traci Lind.* Exuding existential angst like there's no tomorrow, this ruminative drama of forbidden love spans six continents in this (by European standards) big-budget production. Shepard, in one of his best performances, is Walter Faber, a world-weary engineer who, because of a ruined love, retreats from the emotional world of life into the logical and predictable realm of his work. His emotional drifting ends when, after a series of improbable coincidences, he meets Sabeth, an alluring young lady (Delpy) half his age. Their affair takes them from Mexico's Yucatan Peninsula through Europe until his past catches up with him with disastrous results. An engaging story similar in filming and style to Wim Wenders' *Until the End of the World*. (Filmed in English) ★★★ VHS: $19.99

Vukovar

(1994, 94 min, Yugoslavia, Boro Draskovic) *Mirjana Jokovic, Boris Isakovic.* A disturbing glimpse into the psyche of a war-ravaged nation, *Vukovar* uses its Romeo and Juliet tale (he's a Serb, she's a Croat) of star-crossed lovers to underscore the tragedy of the Yugoslavian conflict. Filmed in the all-but-destroyed city of Vukovar during the war in 1993, the film certainly has an authentic atmosphere to tell the story of a newly married couple whose happy union is disrupted by civil war. Having such a strong antiwar message, the film occasionally wanders into the heavy-handed arena, but its voice is articulate and director Draskovic's images are overwhelming. The performances are natural without overindulgence, though Jokovic as the young bride is simply stunning. (Serbo-Croatian with English subtitles) ★★★½ VHS: $89.99

The Wackiest Ship in the Army

(1960, 99 min, US, Richard Murphy) *Jack Lemmon, Ricky Nelson, Chips Rafferty.* Lemmon stars as a WWII naval officer saddled with a crew of butterfingered land-lubbers while trying to carry off a perilous top secret mission in the South Pacific. An entertaining mixture of wacky comedy and wartime heroics. ★★★ VHS: $14.99

The Wacky World of Wills and Burke

(1985, 97 min, Australia, Bob Weis) This Monty Python-inspired spoof of the failed 1860 exploratory expedition in the Australian Outback is an outrageously satirical, lighthearted goofball of a movie. Burke, an elegantly dressed but slightly daft policeman, and the nerd astronomer Wills team up with 28 evil-smelling camels and an equally foul assortment of companions on a journey that leads them nowhere. It might be helpful for people unfamiliar with the historical event to watch the serious film *Burke and Wills* before renting this parody. ★★½

Wag the Dog

(1997, 105 min, US, Barry Levinson) *Dustin Hoffman, Robert De Niro, Anne Heche, Denis Leary, Willie Nelson, Woody Harrelson, Andrea Martin, Kirsten Dunst, Craig T. Nelson, William H. Macy.* What do you do when a sitting president on the verge of re-election finds himself rocked by a sex scandal? While State expeditions to foreign countries are always good diversions, nothing beats a war. And if there isn't enough time to fan a flare-up into a conflagration, you can just manufacture one. Who has the technology? Hollywood, of course. De Niro drolly underplays the spin doctor, a man with seemingly unlimited authority, who orchestrates the action while monitoring the pulse of public opinion. He signs on a frenetic film producer (a terrific Hoffman), who takes on the job with unbridled enthusiasm. The press, ever hungry for the next headline, laps up the product of their movie-making magic. The scenes depicting the manufacture of film at 11 will have you taping newscasts to replay them at slow speed, looking for glitches and evidence of blue screen. Forget the Constitution and forget the truth. Also forget the end credits, as the producer discovers to his dismay. Director Levinson's execution of the wickedly funny and insightful script (cowritten by David Mamet) is flawless and unswerving. (VHS available letterboxed or pan & scan) ★★★★ VHS: $19.99; DVD: $19.99

The Wages of Fear

(1953, 105 min, France, Henri-Georges Clouzot) *Yves Montand, Charles Vanel.* Four desperate men, all unscrupulous characters, are hired to transport several truckloads of nitroglycerin across the mountains and forests of South America in this compelling and suspenseful thriller. (American remake: *Sorcerer*) (French with English subtitles) ★★★★ VHS: $29.99; DVD: $29.99

Wagner

(1983, 300 min, GB, Tony Palmer) *Richard Burton, Vanessa Redgrave, John Gielgud, Laurence Olivier, Joan Plowright, Arthur Lowe.* A huge international cast fails to help this glossy and uninspiring biography of the famed composer. Burton is only intermittently inspired as the lead. ★★

Wagonmaster

(1950, 85 min, US, John Ford) *Ben Johnson, Joanne Dru, Ward Bond.* Beautiful western locations highlight this Ford adventure about the perilous journey of a Morman wagon train heading west towards the Utah frontier. Johnson and Bond are two amblin' cowpokes who join the expedition. ★★★

Wagons East

(1994, 100 min, US, Peter Markle) *John Candy, John C. McGinley, Richard Lewis, Ellen Greene, Robert Picardo, Rodney A. Grant.* In his last film role, Candy plays a drunken, incompetent wagonmaster who leads a group of unhappy settlers of the Old West on a journey back to a more civilized East. Unfunny to the point of embarrassment, the film goes to great lengths to set up its many *Blazing Saddles*-like jokes, but the punch lines fail to deliver. Among the familiar group of western characters, Greene is the hooker with a heart of gold, and Lauter is a hired gunslinger. In a stereotypical portrayal, McGinley plays an effeminate bookseller. His final destination — with a handsome Indian brave in tow — proves to be one of the only real laughs in this otherwise amiable bomb. ★½ VHS: $9.99

Wait until Dark

(1967, 108 min, US, Terence Young) *Audrey Hepburn, Alan Arkin, Richard Crenna, Efrem Zimbalist, Jr., Jack Weston.* This intense adaptation of Frederick Knott's stage thriller stars Hepburn as a recently blinded woman who is terrorized by drug traffikers when she innocently takes possession of a doll filled with heroin. The action takes place almost entirely in her apartment, which heightens the suspense and the feeling of helplessness — it's more effective than any slasher film could hope to be. Arkin is brilliant in the triple role as the head villain, and Crenna is a helpful detective. A pulse-pounding classic with an unforgettable finale. ★★★½ VHS: $14.99

Waiting for Guffman

(1997, 83 min, US, Christopher Guest) *Christopher Guest, Eugene Levy, Catherine O'Hara, Fred Willard, Parker Posey, Bob Balaban.* Proving the show must go on, *Waiting for Guffman* is an often hilarious though modest mockumentary directed and cowritten by Guest, one of the talents behind the granddaddy of the genre, *This Is Spinal Tap.* Community theatre is the target this time, and for anyone who has ever been associated with their local playhouse, much of this will seem like nirvana. The characterizations and petty politics are on-target, the tacky production values are gloriously captured, and there's enough in-jokes to make any semi-insider feel particularly in the loop. But *Guffman* is also a bit slow between the laughs. When the comedy works, this sizzles (*My Dinner with Andre* action figures!); but Guest allows some scenes to drag with no upshot. Nevertheless, the laughs are plentiful and well observed, and to anyone "in the loop," *Waiting for Guffman* is a cheerful reminder that show business is like no business you know. ★★★ VHS: $14.99

Waiting for the Light

(1990, 94 min, US, Christopher Monger) *Teri Garr, Shirley MacLaine, Vincent Schiavelli.* Garr is ready for major life changes when she inherits a diner in a small community. She packs up the kids and Aunt Zelda (MacLaine), a woman with a decidedly unique world view, and heads out to a town about to be visited by an angel. Or so it seems. MacLaine gives another of her patented cantankerous, crotchety old lady performances, which is nonetheless endearing. A delightful cast revels in a serendipitous twist of fate in this quirky, charming film. ★★★ VHS: $14.99

Waiting for the Moon

(1987, 87 min, US, Jill Godmilow) *Linda Hunt, Linda Bassett, Bruce McGill, Bernadette Lafont, Jacques Boudet, Andrew McCarthy.* The story of the tumultuous relationship between author Gertrude Stein and her lover/companion Alice B. Toklas. The film is minimalistic with long periods of dialogue between the women, in a style reminiscent of *My Dinner with Andre.* Upon its release, most critics disapproved of the film downplaying the women's lesbianism, opting instead for a more "matter of fact" attitude. ★★½ VHS: $29.99

Waiting to Exhale

(1995, 120 min, US, Forest Whitaker) *Whitney Houston, Angela Bassett, Loretta Devine, Lela*

Christopher Guest is *Waiting for Guffman*

Rochon, Gregory Hines, Wesley Snipes, Dennis Haysbert, Mykelti Williamson. Probably a first for a Hollywood film, *Waiting to Exhale* centers on the relationships of four African-American women. The occasionally appealing though sometimes static film focuses less on the women's friendship (they have few scenes together) and more on their individual relationships with men, to a varying degree of success. Houston is the catalyst, moving to Phoenix to start life anew and reuniting with her long-time friends. Her romantic scenes have all the snap of a Taster's Choice commercial, though she fares better when relating to her female costars. Bassett, like her character's story, has an earthiness and tenderness missing from a lot of the other characters. ★★½ VHS: $14.99; DVD: $24.99

Waking Ned Devine

(1998, 91 min, Ireland, Kirk Jones) *Ian Bannen, David Kelly, Fionnula Flanagan, Susan Lynch, James Nesbitt.* Though the studio tried to draw comparisons to *The Full Monty*, this wonderfully endearing comedy lacks that film's harder edge, but is just as pleasing in the laughs department. Still a charmer in his late 60s, Bannen is Jackie, a retiree living with his wife in the small Irish village Tulaigh Morh. Happy with a pint and the company of friends, Jackie's obsession is with the national lottery. When he reads in the paper that someone in his village has won, he sets out to find and ingratiate himself. But when it turns out that Ned Devine, the winner, has died of a heart attack, he devises a scheme — with the help of the entire town — to pass off his friend Michael (a wonderfully expressive Kelly) as the lucky ticket holder. With nary a mean bone in its aged body, *Waking Ned Devine* is a sweet, funny throwback to those British Ealing comedies. ★★★½ VHS: $9.99; DVD: $24.99

Waking the Dead

(2000, 103 min, US, Keith Gordon) *Billy Crudup, Jennifer Connelly, Molly Parker, Janet McTeer, Paul Hipp, Hal Holbrook, Ed Harris.* An ambitious young lawyer — whose lifelong dream is to be president — is given the chance to run for the Senate. Unfortunately, during the election race, he keeps catching glimpses of his old girlfriend, who died 8 years earlier, and begins to emotionally unravel. This unusual film posits many interesting ideas and questions (ambition vs. love; can two politically disparate people remain passionately in love; etc.) within an intriguing flashback- and forward-laden structure. Sadly, the two charismatic leads are saddled with some clichéd dialogue, spoken over an ill-chosen, cloying soundtrack. Several of Crudup's "sightings" of the presumed dead Connelly are eerily effective, and the film's themes keep it afloat, but the flaws overcome the film's virtues, and the whole affair ends on an unsatisfying, depressing note. ★★ VHS: $102.99; DVD: $19.99

Walk, Don't Run

(1966, 114 min, US, Charles Walters) *Cary Grant, Samantha Eggar, Jim Hutton.* Grant's last film is not the most fitting end to a brilliant comic career, but it is nevertheless a mostly enjoyable farce. In this remake of the classic *The More the Merrier*, Grant is an American businessman forced to share accomodations with Eggar and Hutton during the Tokyo Olympics. ★★½ VHS: $19.99

A Walk in the Clouds

(1995, 103 min, US, Alfonso Arau) *Keanu Reeves, Aitana Sanchez-Gijon, Anthony Quinn, Giancarlo Giannini, Angelica Aragon.* An alternately awkward and magical romantic drama, *Like Water for Chocolate* director Arau's first English-language film, set in the splendrous wine country of Napa Valley, basks in the mystical glow of lovers united. Unfortunately, these tender scenes are surrounded by the clichés of a contrived beginning and a predictable, abrupt ending. Reeves is a WWII vet and orphan. Traveling by train, he meets a beautiful college student (Sanchez-Gijon) returning home and agrees to pose as her husband, since she's single and pregnant and certain to feel her father's wrath. Their relationship — like the film — becomes emotionally satisfying once they arrive on the family's lush vineyards and fall in love. Reeves still seems uncomfortable with period pieces. ★★½ VHS: $14.99; DVD: $24.99

A Walk on the Moon

(1999, 107 min, US, Tony Goldwyn) *Diane Lane, Liev Schreiber, Viggo Mortensen, Anna Paquin, Tovah Feldshuh.* Actor Goldwyn (*Ghost*) makes an assured directorial debut with this lovely, evocative and moving nostalgic romantic drama set in the last days of the '60s. Recalling *Dirty Dancing* (but even more substantial than that film) with its dead-on re-creation of a Catskills vacation spot and familial relations, *A Walk on the Moon* uses the era's changing social attitudes as a backdrop for romantic exploration. Pearl (Lane) is a devoted wife and mother who feels defined only by those two jobs. Longing for more, she begins an affair with Walker, a hippie clothing salesman (the handsome Mortensen), while on vacation. Though her husband Marty (Schreiber) is kind but inattentive, Pearl finds in Walker an outlet for dormant yearnings she had been unable to express. The acting is uniformly outstanding, with both Lane and Schreiber at their most effective. A small gem. ★★★½ VHS: $19.99; DVD: $29.99

Walk on the Wild Side

(1962, 114 min, US, Edward Dmytryk) *Laurence Harvey, Capucine, Barbara Stanwyck, Jane Fonda.* Inventive casting punctuates this tawdry tale of a good-natured Texan (Harvey) who travels to New Orleans to rescue his lost love (Capucine) from life in a brothel, run by a lascivious lesbian (Stanwyck). Fonda tags along in yet another "sexy bad girl" role. If ever a movie deserved the tag line "good trash," this is it. ★★½ VHS: $19.99

Walkabout

(1971, 100 min, Australia, Nicolas Roeg) *Jenny Agutter, Lucien John, David Gulpilil.* Agutter is undeniably fetching as the budding young woman who, with her younger brother (John), is suddenly stranded in the wilderness. With a preternatural calm (and still clad in school uniforms), they venture into the Outback searching for civilization but find instead an aboriginal teen (Gulpilil) who's on his "walkabout" — an initiation ritual involving months of solo survival. With no common language, the threesome begin a trek that slowly breaks down their cultural barriers. Pieced together in Roeg's trademark patchwork of chunks of loose narrative, and with a minimum of dialogue, *Walkabout* is at first very obtuse, but its attempt to blur the distinctions between the civilized and "primitive" worlds ultimately lacks subtlety; otherwise, maybe it would be seen as a classic. ★★★ VHS: $29.99; DVD: $29.99

Walker

(1987, 95 min, US, Alex Cox) *Ed Harris, Peter Boyle, Richard Masur, Marlee Matlin.* Harris plays a real-life soldier of fortune who declared himself president of Nicaragua in 1855 and ruled the country for two turbulent years. Cox's anarchic sense of humor permeates this piece, so as with most of his films, expect the unexpected. ★★ VHS: $79.99

Walking and Talking

(1996, 83 min, US, Nicole Holofcener) *Anne Heche, Catherine Keener, Todd Field, Liev Schreiber, Kevin Corrigan.* A sympathetic and beneficent approach and engaging portrayals elevate this regulation opus of twentysomethings struggling with faltering relationships, stress-inducing families and unfulfilling jobs. Somewhat episodic in structure, the film centers on two childhood friends (Heche, Keener) as one is about to marry and the other fears she is incapable of long-term commitment. Through many layers of miscommunications, hang-ups and obsessions, the film wanders the paths of each woman's personal growth as she attempts to bring order to a chaotic and often baffling world. The film's forgiving nature towards its characters' idiosyncracies encourages tolerance

Walkabout

towards an uneven script and some awkward dialogue, ultimately resulting in an amusing and endearing examination of young adult life. ★★½ VHS: $19.99

The Wall

(1983, 117 min, Turkey, Yilmaz Guney) Guney, who directed the highly acclaimed film *Yol* from his prison cell, died of cancer soon after personally making his first and, sadly, only film after his escape from Turkish prison. *The Wall* concerns the re-creation of the revolt in a children's prison in Ankara in 1976. The harsh living conditions suffered by the children as well as their eventual uprising are brutally depicted in this searing, honest and horrifying portrait of repression. A true political statement that tears at one's conscience. (Turkish with English subtitles) ★★★½ VHS: $69.99

A Wall in Jerusalem

(1970, 91 min, Israel, Frederic Rossif) *Narrated by: Richard Burton.* Attempting to encompass all of the important events in the history and growth of Israel into the Jewish homeland, this brilliant documentary begins with the Dreyfus Affair in 1894 and covers profiles on the leaders of early Zionism, the Balfour Declaration, the British occupation of Palestine, the Six Day War and much more. Made in 1970, the film is now a "period piece," but its ambitious scope and detail make it required viewing for those interested in Israel's history, growth and modernization, as well as the daunting problems facing this troubled land. ★★★ VHS: $29.99

Wall Street

(1987, 125 min, US, Oliver Stone) *Michael Douglas, Charlie Sheen, Martin Sheen, Daryl Hannah, Sean Young, James Spader.* Stone's riveting, but at times heavy-handed, morality tale stars Sheen as a young stock broker who falls under the spell of Wall Street's millions and loses sight of his humanity. Douglas was awarded an Oscar for his portrayal of a vicious, power hungry Donald Trump-like wheeler-dealer. Real-life dad Martin plays Charlie's proletariat father. ★★★ VHS: $9.99; DVD: $29.99

Wallace & Gromit: A Close Shave

(1995, 30 min, GB, Nick Park) Gromit's knitting hobby is in trouble, as there's a wool shortage. Meanwhile, Wallace finds a bit of love at the wool shoppe in Wendoline, but is *her* dog a sheep rustler? It seems that way when a big-eyed lamb falls out of their truck and eats Wallace & Gromit out of house and home. The claymated man and dog have a good adventure, with some interesting inventions including a Knit-o-Matic machine, and a great chase featuring a ladder, two cars and a couple dozen sheep. It just misses that extra snap that "The Wrong Trousers" has, though it's good enough for Park's third Oscar for Best Animated Short. ★★★½ VHS: $9.99

Wallace & Gromit: A Grand Day Out

(1992, 23 min, GB, Nick Park) Wallace is a homebody and budding inventor, with an unusually smart dog, Gromit, who spends his free time knitting. And, boy, do they both love cheese! In this, the first of three claymation Wallace & Gromit shorts from the British Aardman studios, they find that their icebox is cheeseless. Armed with a supply of crackers, they build a rocket and head to the largest sup-

ply of cheese in the universe. . .the moon! A charming adventure, though stylistically not quite up to the level of Park's later shorts. This is the only Wallace & Gromit film to *not* win an Oscar for Best Animated Short (it lost to Park's "Creature Comforts!") ★★★ VHS: $9.99

Wallace & Gromit: The Wrong Trousers

(1993, 30 min, GB, Nick Park) Park's masterpiece, an endlessly inventive and breakneck adventure that happily merges such cinematic mainstays as the crime caper, the locomotive chase and the bad lodger. After a refreshing breakfast thanks to a complicated wake-up invention, Wallace finds that he's fresh out of money after building, for Gromit's birthday, a pair of robotic trousers for his walkies. He takes an evil penguin in as a tenant, who not only takes over Gromit's space, but plots the theft of a diamond in the city. Time for our silent canine hero to save the day! Tremendous rewatchable fun, for adults and kids alike, with a memorable, steely-eyed tuxedoed villain, and the most expressive clay animation you'll ever see. Winner of the Oscar for Best Animated Short. ★★★★ VHS: $9.99

Walpurgis Night

(1938, 75 min, Sweden, Gustaf Edgren) *Ingrid Bergman, Victor Sjostrom.* Set during Walpurgis, the Swedish celebration of spring, this erotic comedy stars Victor Sjostrom as a conservative newspaperman with Bergman as his rebellious daughter. (Swedish with English subtitles) ★★★ VHS: $19.99

Waltz of the Toreadors

(1962, 105 min, GB, John Guillermin) *Peter Sellers, Margaret Leighton.* Sellers delivers a first-rate comic performance as a licentious army colonel in this wonderful rendition of Jean Anouilh's rollicking sexual farce. ★★★ VHS: $14.99; DVD: $24.99

The Wanderer (Le Gran Meaulnes)

(1987, 108 min, France, Jean-Gabriel Albiococco) *Brigitte Fossey, Jean Blaise.* An imaginative interpretation of Alain Fournier's classic novel, this visually exuberant fantasy tells the romantic story of a boy's first and true love. Set in a provincial town in turn-of-the-century France, young Augustin goes to a strange party one enchanted evening and meets the beautiful yet mysterious Yvonne (Fossey). When Yvonne disappears, our hero desperately tries to find her. A wild and remarkable re-creation of childhood memories and youthful innocence. (French with English subtitles) ★★★

The Wanderers

(1979, 117 min, US, Philip Kaufman) *Ken Wahl, Karen Allen, Linda Manz.* Nostalgic and sometimes dark look at growing up in the Bronx in the early 1960s. ★★★ VHS: $19.99

The Wannsee Conference

(1984, 88 min, West Germany, Heinz Schirk) *Dietrich Mattausch, Gerd Brockmann.* A serious and startling re-creation of a meeting that occurred in a pleasant suburb on January 20, 1942. In attendance were such Nazi leaders as the Gestapo's Adolph Eichmann, Reinhard Heydrich of the Secret Police and 15 other state

officials. Their mission: to decide upon and implement the so-called "final solution," sealing the fate of six million Jews. Based on the original secretary's notes, the film is presented in real time. Although concentration camps and executions were already a reality, this meeting marked the official beginning of the Third Reich's policy of mass murder and extermination. (German with English subtitles) ★★★ VHS: $19.99

Wanted Dead or Alive

(1986, 104 min, US, Gary Sherman) *Rutger Hauer, Gene Simmons, Robert Guillaume, William Russ.* Hauer has a lot of fun as a modern-day bounty hunter hired to catch, preferably alive, a terrorist (Simmons, of KISS). Definitely no more than your standard action-adventure film, but still entertaining. ★★ VHS: $14.99; DVD: $24.99

The War

(1994, 126 min, US, Jon Avnet) *Elijah Wood, Kevin Costner, Mare Winningham, Lexi Randall.* As the youthful Stu, Wood is especially captivating in the strong ensemble cast which populates the small Mississippi town of Juliette. It's 1970. Stu's father, Stephen (Costner), has been an unsteady presence since his return from Vietnam, and his recent reentry into the family (Winningham and Randall as mother and daughter) coincides with increased hostilities with another family's children. With a few exceptions, the dialogue rings true as the father tries to impart to the son the lessons of war. While the film suffers a muddled point-of-view, it enjoys exceptional characterizations by each cast member. *The War* presents people usually absent from American cinema — the rural poor — and shows them without apology or glamorization. ★★★ VHS: $7.49; DVD: $26.99

War and Peace

(1956, 208 min, US/Italy, King Vidor) *Audrey Hepburn, Henry Fonda, Mel Ferrer, Anita Ekberg, Vittorio Gassman, John Mills.* Hepburn and Fonda star in this technically superior but dramatically flat version of Tolstoy's epic novel. Well-staged battle sequences. ★★★ VHS: $24.99

War and Peace

(1967, 403 min, Russia, Sergei Bondarchuk) *Vyacheslav Tikhonov, Ludmila Savalyeva, Sergei Bondarchuk.* Reportedly the most expensive Russian film ever made, with final costs exceeding $100,000,000, this Academy Award-winning epic is a dazzling and monumental portrait of Russia during the Napoleonic Wars of 1805-1812. This definitive version of Tolstoy's classic novel follows four aristocratic families and the effects of Napoleon's onslaught of Europe and Russia on their lives. The spectacular battle sequences are considered the best ever filmed, with the director using over 120,000 soldiers. An amazing film experience best suited to the big screen; but see it on video, because when was the last time *War and Peace* played your local movie house? (Russian with English subtitles) ★★★★ VHS: $69.99

The War Game

(1966, 50 min, GB, Peter Watkins) Watkins' tremendously powerful "staged" documentary about the horrors of a nuclear attack on London made its mark well before the more commercial and less stunning "The Day After."

Made for BBC-TV, the film never aired because its graphic re-creation of the burns and wounds suffered by the population were considered too controversial (read: antiwar). An extremely hard-hitting piece of quasi cinema verité. ★★★½ VHS: $29.99

The War of the Roses

(1989, 116 min, US, Danny DeVito) *Kathleen Turner, Michael Douglas, Danny DeVito.* In this wicked, hilarious black comedy, Douglas and Turner portray Oliver and Barbara Rose, a married couple whose once idyllic life — complete with two children, beautiful mansion and unlimited cash flow — has dissipated to a limb-breaking, psyche-smashing battle of the sexes. Sort of a demented '80s version of Tracy and Hepburn, Douglas and Turner — who always play well off each other — have rarely been funnier: Douglas' characteristic quirks — the "yuppie" agressiveness and his dispassionate demeanor — are well used here, and Turner is nothing short of stunning, both physically and as a comedic actress. ★★★½ VHS: $14.99

The War of the Worlds

(1953, 85 min, US, Byron Haskin) *Gene Barry, Ann Robinson.* George Pal produced this classic sci-fi adventure based on the H.G. Wells novel about a Martian invasion of Earth, and the scientist (Barry) out to stop them. Highlighted by terrific Academy Award-winning special effects. ★★★½ VHS: $14.99; DVD: $24.99

War Party

(1988, 99 min, US, Franc Roddam) *Billy Wirth, Kevin Dillon, M. Emmett Walsh.* Racial tensions flair in a small Montana town on the eve of the centennial of an Indian massacre led by the U.S. Cavalry. ★★½

War Requiem

(1989, 90 min, GB, Derek Jarman) Jarman teamed with producer Don Boyd to create this elaborate symphony of sight and sound. Using the same non-dialogue format as Boyd's *Aria* (which featured a segment by Jarman), they have brought cinematic life to Benjamin Britten's immensely powerful "War Requiem." Written for the opening of the new Coventry Cathedral (the original was destroyed in WWII), Britten's oratorio is punctuated by the haunting poetry of Wilfred Owen — who was killed just prior to Armistice Day in 1918 at the age of 27. This exceptionally stirring piece captures Britten's theme of innocence ruined by the ravages of war. ★★★ VHS: $29.99

The War Room

(1993, 96 min, US, D.A. Pennebaker & Chris Hegedus) When filmmakers Pennebaker and Hegedus set out to document Bill Clinton's 1992 presidential campaign, they were hoping for unrestricted access to the candidate. Stonewalled by Clinton, they turned their attentions, instead, to his two top campaign managers: ragin' Cajun chief strategist James Carville, and 31-year-old upstart communications director George Stephanopoulous. And so much the better. With a snappy and aggressive verité style, the film revels in the gritty and non-stop action of behind-the-scenes politics. What gives the film its real punch, however, is Carville. This freewheeling firebrand pumps out a highly entertaining, relentless and tantalizing barrage

Washington Square

of rhetoric and media "spin." Though certainly nonpartisan, it should still provide amusement no matter what your party affiliation. ★★★ VHS: $14.99; DVD: $14.99

The War Zone

(1999, 99 min, GB, Tim Roth) *Ray Winstone, Freddie Cunliffe, Lara Belmont, Tilda Swinton, Colin Farrell.* Roth's directorial debut is a fully realized, gut-wrenching exposé of a dirty family secret, delivered with lyrical brutality through superbly composed images and an economy of dialogue. The excellent cast imparts understated and well-crafted performances, revealing emotional depth in small, casual moments. The isolation of the windswept coastal region mirrors the family's insularity and detachment from the outside community. They go through the motions of an eerie hypernormalcy, strange silence permeating their shared space, until a chance glance through a window makes further denial impossible for one family member. Roth has artfully constructed a powerful and accomplished exploration of the deadening effect of an oft-told lie. (Unrated) ★★★½ VHS: $29.99; DVD: $29.99

Ward 6

(1976, 93 min, Yugoslavia, Lucian Pintilie) Yugoslavian theatre director Pintilie's adaptation of Anton Chekhov's powerful story paints the disturbing portrait of a Russian Empire in decline — moldering in moral rot. Set in a provincial town at the turn-of-the-century, a dedicated but troubled doctor oversees a grotesque, inhuman mental ward. Slowly numbed by the poverty and suffering, he finds solace with an inmate, the only one who seemingly comprehends the situation. A somber, claustrophopic work that uses a static camera and repetitive sounds (running water, banging machinery) to help us appreciate the suffocation of the people in this hopeless world. (Serbian with English subtitles) ★★★ VHS: $59.99

WarGames

(1983, 110 min, US, John Badham) *Matthew Broderick, Ally Sheedy, Dabney Coleman, John Wood.* A clever, entertaining computer-age adventure/thriller with Broderick as a high school

hacker who taps into the Defense Department's computer and nearly starts World War III. ★★★ VHS: $9.99; DVD: $14.99

Warlock

(1959, 122 min, US, Edward Dmytryk) *Henry Fonda, Richard Widmark, Anthony Quinn.* A lawman amd his sidekick (Fonda, Quinn) clean up a Western mining town; but another law enforcer, a reformed bandit (Widmark), challenges the pair to a final showdown. An efficient western with good action and nice characterizations. ★★★ VHS: $19.99

Warlock

(1988, 102 min, US, Steve Miner) *Julian Sands, Richard E. Grant, Lori Singer.* Sands plays the title character, an evil witch who escapes a fiery punishment in 17th-century Massachusetts by fleeing through time to present-day Los Angeles. Once there, he plans to restore "The Grand Grimoire" (the Satanic bible said to contain the lost name of God) and unleash the power to "unmake" the universe. Though the story line maintains some interest, this is no more than a grade-B supernatural thriller. (Followed by 2 sequels) ★★½ VHS: $6.99; DVD: $19.99

Warm Nights on a Slow Moving Train

(1987, 91 min, Australia, Bob Ellis) *Wendy Hughes, Colin Friels.* "Catholic schoolteacher by day. . . high-class hooker by night." Yes, the concept does look like a typical exploitation flick, but appearances can deceive. For this Aussie import is a funny, erotic and wonderfully entertaining drama on the continual war between the sexes. Hughes stars as a quiet teacher who, on weekends, takes the night train from Melbourne to Sydney to visit her ailing brother. It is on the train that she dons her spiked heels, creates a new persona for the night, and becomes a classy hooker. Her cold approach to sex and relationships is challenged after she falls in love with one of her clients: a mysterious man whose interest in her might be more than just sex. Hughes' performance goes beyond the role of "the hooker with a broken heart" as she creates a memorable, believable and ultimately tragic character. ★★★

W

Warrior's Rest (Le Repos du Guerrier)

(1962, 98 min, France, Roger Vadim) *Brigitte Bardot.* Bardot stars as an innocent woman who, after saving the life of a man attempting suicide, finds herself becoming more deeply involved with him. Claiming her as the keeper of his soul, this mystery man soon moves in with her. Attracted by his charms and attention, Bardot falls in love and soon abandons her previous boyfriend and lifestyle. But the tables are turned as her love turns into a one-sided affair. A fine drama of obsessive love, power and commitment. (French with English subtitles) ★★★

The Warriors

(1979, 94 min, US, Walter Hill) *Michael Beck, James Remar.* Controversial and violent teen pic about a New York City gang which is framed for the murder of a local hotshot and becomes hunted by all the other gangs in the city. ★★½ VHS: $14.99; DVD: $29.99

The Wash

(1988, 93 min, US, Michael Toshiyuki Uno) *Mako, Nobu McCarthy.* Set in San Francisco, this enormously appealing and overlooked gem revolves around a recently separated husband and wife who had met at a Japanese internment camp during WWII. Mako and McCarthy give two exceptional performances as the estranged couple, whose only contact with each other is when she sees him weekly to do his wash. The film's poignant, emotional center examines the wife's (McCarthy) personal conflict when she falls in love with another man, forcing her to confront the old-world values of her heritage and the ever-changing demands of a new way of life. ★★★½

Washington Square

(1997, 115 min, US, Agnieszka Holland) *Jennifer Jason Leigh, Ben Chaplin, Albert Finney, Maggie Smith.* Holland's adaptation of the Henry James novel (told before in 1949's *The Heiress*) is an at times uneven, but ultimately evocative and richly layered look at a young woman's struggle to break free of her overbearing father's repression. Leigh is Catherine Sloper, a socially inept young woman who dotes upon her father in a vain attempt to compensate for the fact that her mother died giving birth to her. This father-daughter tension becomes extreme when a young suitor, Morris Townsend (Chaplin), comes to call. They fall deeply in love, but Dr. Sloper withholds his consent believing Townsend to be a golddigger. It's a taut situation to be sure, but sadly *Washington Square* fails to fully capitalize and at times drags. Still, Leigh is magnificent, and Finney is positively stoic in his portrayal of a father who can't come to terms with the loss of his wife. ★★★ VHS: $19.99

The Wasp Woman

(1960, 66 min, US, Roger Corman) *Susan Cabot, Fred Eisley.* Corman's knock-off of the previous year's hit, *The Fly*, finds Susan Cabot using royal jelly to stay young forever. Instead it turns her into a killer queen bee. ★ VHS: $9.99

Watch It!

(1993, 102 min, US, Tom Flynn) *Peter Gallagher, John C. McGinley, Lili Taylor, Suzy Amis, Jon Tenney, Tom Sizemore.* Watch It! is an entertaining and bitingly accurate comedy about the way men and women relate. A lot of credit has to go to writer-director Flynn for managing to merge bitter (but witty) cynicism with sentimental (but not sickening) romance. Focusing on a group of "post-twentysomething" friends living in Chicago, *Watch It!* features Gallagher as a non-committing drifter who shows up one morning on the doorstep of his womanizing cousin Tenny. Spotlighting a few "male bonding" scenes, the film spends more time with its male characters than it does with the female ones. And it's a shame, because the characters played by Amis and Taylor (who is woefully underused) are as engaging and complicated as any of the male characters. ★★★ VHS: $7.99

Watch on the Rhine

(1943, 114 min, US, Herman Shumlin) *Bette Davis, Paul Lukas, Lucile Watson, Geraldine Fitzgerald.* Lillian Hellman's cautionary drama about the rise of Nazism in the late 1930s gets a first-rate screen treatment. Lukas won an Oscar for his powerful portrayal of a German refugee, now living in Washington with his family, who is hunted by Nazi agents. Davis also stars as Lukas' wife, and Watson is very good as the "Everyperson" who chooses to ignore the coming catastrophe. ★★★½ VHS: $14.99

The Watcher

(2000, 97 min, US, Joe Charbanic) *James Spader, Keanu Reeves, Marisa Tomei, Ernie Hudson, Chris Ellis.* Serial killer Reeves taunts a former nemesis — ex-FBI agent Spader — by sending him unidentified photos of young women, and then giving him one full day to find and save them. Appallingly directed by Charbanic, who helmed the music videos for Reeves' band, Dogstar, the film has a fairly tense section wherein Spader and crew are desperately trying to find a soon-to-be victim. Otherwise, *The Watcher* is flat, uninvolving and clichéd. Reeves is just your typical crazy psycho, dancing to Rob Zombie and dropping evil one-liners. Spader looks annoyed to be here, and the ending just. . . ends. This isn't even amusing as bad cheese. ★ VHS: $102.99; DVD: $26.99

Watcher in the Woods

(1980, 84 min, US, John Hough) *Bette Davis, Carroll Baker, David MacCallum, Lynn-Holly Johnson.* Effective Disney-produced ghost story about an American family who move into Davis' British country estate, where the youngest girl is haunted by visions of Davis' long-lost daughter. (This is the edited version of the 108-minute theatrical release; however, the film was cut to tighten the rather confusing longer version, not because of censorship or scares.) ★★½

Water

(1985, 95 min, GB, Dick Clement) *Michael Caine, Brenda Vaccaro, Valerie Perrine.* A congenial but generally inept comedy about a Caribbean British colony that is transformed by the discovery of a pure mineral water source within its tiny confines. What follows is a comedy of commercial and social exploitation with the local British governor (Caine) suddenly caught in a juggling match with greedy U.S. oil interests, an internal insurrection, and other assorted lunacies. ★★ VHS: $29.99

The Water Engine

(1992, 88 min, US, Steven Schachter) *Charles Durning, Patti Lupone, William H. Macy, John* Mahoney, Joe Mantegna, Joanna Miles, Treat Williams. A marvelous little film written by David Mamet that chronicles American corporate greed and the depths to which the money men will sink to protect their interests. Charles Lang (Macy) is an engineer in an auto factory. He has invented an internal combustion engine fuled on water. After years developing the ideal non-polluting engine he tries to sell his invention only to find that the oil company's interests far outweigh any good the engine will do for society. ★★★ VHS: $49.99

The Waterboy

(1998, 89 min, US, Frank Coraci) *Adam Sandler, Kathy Bates, Henry Winkler, Fairuza Balk, Jerry Reed.* In this atrocious comedy of idiotic proportions, Sandler plays Bobby Boucher, a college football team's doofus waterboy, whose slow and slurred manner of speech could leave one with the impression that he's slightly retarded. Anyway, when head coach Winkler learns that waterboy can tackle anyone and everyone, the backwoods blunderer becomes the darling of the beer-guzzling, yahoo-cheering set. The jokes amount to Bobby tackling people and him talking like a bona fide moron. Oh, what wit. What's worse, he's brought the wonderful Bates down to his level, playing Bobby's over-protective mother. That this film grossed $160 million is a sad comment on the state of comedy in film; but then, what does Sandler care — he's laughing all the way to the bank. And with crap like this, he's the only one laughing. ★ VHS: $14.99; DVD: $29.99

The Waterdance

(1992, 106 min, US, Neal Jimenez & Michael Steinberg) *Eric Stoltz, Wesley Snipes, William Forsythe, Helen Hunt, Elizabeth Peña, Grace Zabriskie.* Superb work from an accomplished cast does justice to a well-balanced and finely crafted script from codirector Jimenez, based on his own experiences. Stoltz is a young writer who winds up in rehabilitation after becoming paralyzed in an accident. Snipes and Forsythe are fellow paraplegics. Jimenez deftly avoids the potential heavy-handedness of his subject and instead tells his story with a wit and warmth which is unsentimental and uncompromising and invites favorable comparison to Marlon Brando's first film vehicle, *The Men.* ★★★½ VHS: $14.99

Waterfront

(1983, 287 min, Australia, Chris Thompson) *Greta Scacchi, Jack Thompson, Chris Haywood.* Fans of five-hour spectacles should enjoy this Australian *Last Exit to Brooklyn.* Set on the turbulent waterfront of Melbourne after WWII, the drama focuses on the bitter fight between striking dock workers, a right-wing prime minister, desperate Italians hired as "scabs" and the greedy owners intent on getting the shipyard humming again. The alluring Scacchi is an Italian immigrant reluctantly dragged into the labor battle and Thompson is a union leader who falls passionately in love with her. ★★★

Waterland

(1992, 95 min, GB, Stephen Gyllenhaal) *Jeremy Irons, Sinead Cusack, Ethan Hawke, John Heard, Grant Warnock.* Gyllenhaal's (*Paris Trout*) moody adaptation of the Graham Swift novel stars Irons as a high school history teacher whose past provides his jaded students with a somber lesson in history. Meanwhile, his present emulates the haunting memories of his past. Cusack is superb as Irons' wife (a role she plays in real life) as is Hawke, whose disillusioned youth serves as the catalyst for Irons' looking into his past. At times confusing and often disjointed, this film is still a challenge worth taking. ★★★ VHS: $19.99

Watermelon Man

(1970, 97 min, US, Melvin Van Peebles) *Godfrey Cambridge, Estelle Parsons.* Social comedy with a lot of bite about a bigoted white man who awakens one morning to discover that he has turned black. Cambridge's broad playing helps greatly in the enjoyment of this racial parable. ★★★ VHS: $11.99

Waterworld

(1995, 135 min, US, Kevin Reynolds) *Kevin Costner, Dennis Hopper, Jeanne Tripplehorn, Tina Majorino, Michael Jeter.* Had *Waterworld* cost half its reported $175,000,000, it would have entertained the action crowd looking for a mindless, exciting summer film and probably no more word about it would have been said. However, that's not the case. Half-fish, half-human mutant Costner (blatantly based on Mel Gibson's loner Mad Max) becomes involved in tribal warfare on a water-logged planet, the effects of the polar icecaps melting. The set design and effects of *Waterworld* are impressive, but the haunting question remains: Are they worth the sum lavished upon it? Ultimately, this is a formulaic, over-produced adventure film that is fun for awhile but its controversy sinks in and weighs it down. (Letterboxed VHS available for $14.99) ★★½ VHS: $9.99; DVD: $26.99

Waxwork

(1988, 97 min, US, Anthony Hickox) *Zach Galligan, David Warner, Deborah Foreman.* Inventive horror film with a most unusual premise: a group of teens (that's *not* the inventive part) spend a night at a mysterious house of wax. Each visitor becomes part of the presentation by being hurled back in time and acting out the gruesome renderings. ★★★ VHS: $14.99

Waxwork II: Lost in Time

(1991, 94 min, US, Anthony Hickox) *Zach Galligan, Bruce Campbell, Alexander Gudonov.* Fans of 1988's ambitious *Waxwork* may appreciate this often funny send-up of the genre. Galligan picks up where he left off as the survivor of a wax museum holocaust who is propelled into various time periods (all recognizable horror movie settings) as he tries to seal the gateway to the dark dimensions. ★★½ VHS: $14.99

Way Down East

(1920, 119 min, US, D.W. Griffith) *Lillian Gish, Richard Barthelmess, Lowell Sherman.* Classic silent melodrama, with Gish as the quintessential virtuous country girl seduced by the evil city slicker. Includes the famous scene with Gish trapped and washed away on an ice floe. ★★★★ VHS: $24.99; DVD: $29.99

The Way of the Gun

(2000, 119 min, US, Christopher McQuarrie) *Ryan Phillippe, Benicio del Toro, Juliette Lewis, Taye Diggs, James Caan.* Bristling with enough testerone-pumped moxie to incinerate the screen,

this tense kidnapping thriller has the gritty edge of the best film noirs. Phillippe and del Toro are an unlikely duo of small-time punks who hatch a scheme to abduct a surrogate mother (Lewis) who's very-pregnant with the child of a millionaire. By the time they realize the father is the local Mafioso, the boss' badass bodyguards and an ice-cool hit man (Caan) are already hunting them down. First-time director McQuarrie (screenwriter of *The Usual Suspects*) certainly has a respect for the genre, but doesn't always trust his audience; every time the movie gains momentum, it comes screeching to an abrupt halt again as characters take yet another time-out for a status check. The story is dense with crisscrossing subplots and dubious alliances, but the stop-start nature of the film can be crippling. Thankfully, there's enough macho banter to keep things crackling, and there are plenty of showdowns and shootouts. The cast is in terrific tough-guy form, especially the understated Caan as an aged "adjudicator" flirting with obsolescence. ★★★ VHS: $14.99; DVD: $14.99

Way Out West

(1937, 66 min, US, James W. Horne) *Stan Laurel, Oliver Hardy.* One of Laurel & Hardy's funniest films, this classic western spoof has the boys delivering the deed of a gold mine to the wrong girl. ★★★½

The Way We Were

(1973, 118 min, US, Sydney Pollack) *Barbra Streisand, Robert Redford, Bradford Dillman, Viveca Lindfors, Murray Hamilton, James Woods.* Compelling romantic drama with Redford and Streisand meeting in college in the late 1930s and having an on-again, off-again affair over the next 15 years. Streisand plays a campus activist who is enamored by gorgeous WASP Redford, meeting years later when each has made a name for themselves. One of the first films to explore the Hollywood blacklist of the 1950s, though it is used merely as a subplot. ★★★ VHS: $9.99; DVD: $19.99

The Way West

(1967, 122 min, US, Andrew V. McLaglen) *Kirk Douglas, Robert Mitchum, Richard Widmark, Stubby Kaye, Sally Field.* A wagon train with an aging scout (Mitchum) and a ruthless U.S. Senator (Douglas) searches for the promised land of the Northwest Territories. ★★ VHS: $14.99

Wayne's World

(1992, 95 min, US, Penelope Spheeris) *Mike Myers, Dana Carvey, Tia Carrere, Rob Lowe, Lara Flynn Boyle.* Myers and Carvey bring their zany, head-banging brand of seriously adolescent humor to the big screen with way cool results. Wayne and Garth must fight to save their basement cable-TV show from the clutches of unscrupulous producer Lowe, and Wayne gets the hots for truly "babe-a-licious" Carrere. A post-punk Spheeris directed this hilarious ode to '90s teen culture which features a killer rendition of Queen's "Bohemian Rhapsody." Destined to be a cultural signpost for decades to come — NOT! ★★★ VHS: $9.99; DVD: $24.99

Wayne's World 2

(1993, 94 min, US, Stephen Surjik) *Dana Carvey, Mike Myers, Tia Carrere, Christopher Walken, Kim Basinger, Ed O'Neill, Charlton Heston.* Their "excellencies" Wayne and Garth are back

with this slightly regurgitated yet nonetheless amusing sequel. Wayne takes on the task of organizing a massive outdoor rock concert, "Waynestock," in his home town of Aurora, Illinois. This sets the stage for a '70s-inspired amalgam of loosely tied together plot contrivances which for the most part offer winning one-liners, witticisms and spoofs. Among the film's highlights are a side-splitting tribute to the Village People; a marvelous re-creation of *The Graduate*; and a dubbed chop-socky kung fu fight. Twentysomething-ers beware: Much of the film's humor seems aimed not at its target audience but at Baby Boomers. ★★½ VHS: $9.99; DVD: $24.99

We of the Never Never

(1983, 132 min, Australia, Igor Auzins) *Angela Punch McGregor, Arthur Digman.* Based on the true-life experience of popular Australian novelist Jeannie Gunn, this beautifully photographed, award-winning film focuses on the first white woman to live in the vast Outback of Australia's Northern Territory. With courage and determination she faces the many hardships of this barren land and the hostility of the men in the region, while acquiring a deep compassion and respect for the Aborigines of the "never never," where one could ride all day and "never never" reach the horizon. ★★★ VHS: $59.99

We the Living

(1942, 160 min, Italy, Goffredo Alessandrini) *Rossano Brazzi, Alida Valli, Fosci Giachetti.* The Russian Revolution is the fiery backdrop for this story of love's ability to endure the ravages of oppression. Based on the classic Ayn Rand novel, the film was made with great difficulty during Mussolini's reign in WWII Italy. With overtly anti-fascist themes, several of the film's key scenes were snipped for government screenings and then replaced for its world premiere at the 1942 Venice Film Festival. But the film was seized by authorities, and placed in a vault for decades until the late 1960s. Eventually, new prints were struck for this eloquent and deeply moving tale of love versus authority, and the film only in the early '90s received its first commercial screenings since World War II. (Italian with English subtitles) ★★★

We Think the World of You

(1988, 92 min, GB, Colin Gregg) *Alan Bates, Gary Oldman, Frances Barber.* This film version of J.R. Ackerley's best-selling 1961 novel about a love triangle between two men and a dog is not wholly successful and can be best described as an "interesting failure." Set in the rubble of post-WWII East-End London, the film stars Bates as the older, set-in-his-ways part-time lover of Oldman, a rougish charmer who divides his affections between his wife and child, and Bates. The situation is upset when Oldman is sent to prison for six months. The care and feeding of his beloved dog Evie, a charmer in her own right, is left to his mother. But Bates, desperate for a replacement love, begins to care for her and becomes obsessed with the dog; able to see in her qualities that his gaoled lover could never possess. Not your usual love story. ★★

W

We Were One Man

(1981, 105 min, France, Philippe Vallois) This touching, unusual love story chronicles the budding relationship between a wounded German soldier and the young French peasant who nurses him back to health. Excitable, dim-witted Guy's lonely existence is brightened when he comes upon Rolf in the forest. The two bask in playful, homoerotic exchanges until the war reenters their lives and tries to separate them. (French with English subtitles) ★★★ VHS: $49.99

We're No Angels

(1955, 106 min, US, Michael Curtiz) *Humphrey Bogart, Peter Ustinov, Aldo Ray, Joan Bennett, Basil Rathbone, Leo G. Carroll.* Engaging comic fluff with Bogey, Ustinov and Ray as Devil's Island escapees who are taken in by a French merchant family, who are unaware of their true identity. (Remade in 1989) ★★★ VHS: $14.99

We're No Angels

(1989, 108 min, US, Neil Jordan) *Robert De Niro, Sean Penn, Demi Moore, Hoyt Axton.* The idea of De Niro and Penn costarring in a remake of the 1955 Humphrey Bogart comedy *We're No Angels,* and having it written by David Mamet, must have looked great on paper. So what happened? This is a painfully unfunny comedy with De Niro and Penn as prison escapees who masquerade as priests to elude a search party. The film captures none of the spirit of playfulness which made the original so entertaining: this version is a heavy-handed misconception and strictly for fans of the two stars. ★ VHS: $14.99

Weapons of the Spirit

(1989, 90 min, US, Pierre Sauvage) This warm and gripping documentary traces an amazing event in World War II history that occurred in the small French village of Le Chambon. As Hitler plowed and pillaged his way through Europe, fleeing Jews began to arrive in the predominantly Protestant town, where they were undeniably and even enthusiastically given refuge. Although the Nazi threat was becoming increasingly more apparent, the brave and generous townspeople continued to offer not only food and shelter, but a complete acceptance of and genuine dedication to these 5,000 Jewish inhabitants. Director Sauvage, himself born in Le Chambon, celebrates the good will and delivers what is truly a labor of love. (English and French with English subtitles) ★★★½ VHS: $59.99

A Wedding

(1978, 125 min, US, Robert Altman) *Carol Burnett, Mia Farrow, Lillian Gish, Geraldine Chaplin, Lauren Hutton, Dennis Christopher, Paul Dooley, Viveca Lindfors, Pat McCormick.* Altman's enjoyable follow-up to his acclaimed *Nashville* utilizes the same multicharacter collage which earmarked his classic film. Two very diverse families come together for a ritzy, upper-class wedding, revealing family skeletons and hidden passions, among other things. Burnett heads a very strong ensemble cast. ★★★ VHS: $59.99

The Wedding Banquet

(1993, 111 min, Taiwan/China/US, Ang Lee) *Winston Chao, Mitchell Lichtenstein, Sihung Lung. La Cage aux Folles* Asian-American style! This wholesome gay comedy follows the family drama of Wai Tung (Chao), a transplanted Taiwanese gay man and now New York real estate entrepreneur who is constantly being nagged by his family about getting married. Living with his American boyfriend, Simon (Lichtenstein), Wai arranges a marriage-of-convenience with a wacky artist. The plan backfires, however, when his parents announce they are coming to New York to meet the bride! Frantically, the two lovers remove all vestiges of their relationship from the apartment, posing as landlord-tenant and bringing in the faux fiancée. All is well until the parents spearhead an elaborate wedding banquet that involves a night of gaudy excesses and some unwanted surprises. The delightful characters are the real attraction of this sexual and cultural comedy-of-errors which is both witty and perceptive. ★★★½ VHS: $29.99

The Wedding Gift

(1994, 87 min, GB, Richard Loncraine) *Jim Broadbent, Julie Walters, Sian Thomas.* An amiable comedy-drama based on the true story of one of the early sufferers of what has come to be known as "chronic fatigue syndrome." Because of a series of unexplainable ailments, Walters becomes dependent on husband Broadbent, who becomes her devoted caretaker. Eventually, he is smitten by a nearly blind novelist (Thomas), but he finds himself unable to cheat on his disabled wife. Walters, however, has another plan as she arranges for Thomas to take her place upon her death. Though this sounds like the basis for a bawdy comedy, *The Wedding Gift* is instead a slightly somber melodrama peppered with Broadbent and Walter's witty repartee, which though pleasing to watch, is ultimately a letdown. ★★½ VHS: $19.99

Wedding in Blood

(1973, 98 min, France, Claude Chabrol) *Stéphane Audrane, Michel Piccoli.* The moral degeneration of the French middle class is familiar territory for Chabrol as he continues his favorite theme in this moody drama. Audrane and Piccoli are married to each other but both are unfaithful. Each one concocts a plan to murder the other in order to free themselves. Who will get it first? A nice mystery and psychological thriller. (French with English subtitles) ★★★½

Wedding in Galilee

(1988, 113 min, Israel, Michel Khleifi) *El Aleili, Nazih Akleh.* The son of Abu Adel, an elderly patriarch, is about to be married. His father wants him to have a traditional wedding ceremony lasting well into the night. But Abu Adel and his son are Palestinians living under a dusk-to-dawn curfew imposed by the Israeli military. In order to let his son have the wedding party, the father seeks the permission of the governor to suspend the curfew for the wedding night. The governor agrees, but only under the condition that he and his entourage be allowed to attend. So begins *Wedding in Galilee,* a timely and thought-provoking examination of Palestinian-Israeli tensions from the rarely heard Palestinian point of view. (Israeli and Arabic with English subtitles) ★★★ VHS: $24.99

Wedding in White

(1972, 103 min, Canada, William Fruet) *Carol Kane, Donald Pleasence.* One of the most important Canadian films of the 1970s, this gritty though sensitively handled drama is set in an impoverished village during WWII. It tells the unsettling story of a young girl who is raped by her brother's army buddy and then forced to marry a middle-aged bachelor to preserve the family honor. Kane is unforgettable as the young girl, and Pleasence is masterful as her unyielding father. ★★★½

The Wedding March

(1928, 117 min, US, Erich von Stroheim) *Erich von Stroheim, Fay Wray, ZaSu Pitts.* The only film by von Stroheim where the villain is allowed to live — only because a sequel was never completed by him. Which is a shame because part two opens with the Wedding Night (Part two was completed by someone else and released overseas as *The Honeymoon*). It's another love triangle in old Vienna with von Stroheim himself playing the prince. ★★★½ VHS: $29.99

Wayne and Garth "party on" in *Wayne's World*

The Wedding Party

(1969, 92 min, US, Cynthia Munroe, Brian De Palma & Wilford Leach) *Charles Pfluger, Robert De Niro, Jill Clayburgh.* A groom-to-be meets his fiancée's extended family for the first time a few days before the wedding; claustrophobia and dread set in fast. Imaginative use of stop-action, fast and slow motion, non-sync sound and jump cuts enliven the screen debuts of Clayburgh as the bride-to-be and De Niro as a friend of the groom. Pfluger is engaging (pun not intended) as the young man contemplating escape from his promise to marry. ★★ VHS: $14.99

The Wedding Singer

(1998, 97 min, US, Frank Coraci) *Adam Sandler, Drew Barrymore, Christine Taylor, Steve Buscemi, Jon Lovitz, Alexis Arquette, Billy Idol.* Sandler matures on-screen right before your eyes with a controlled, funny performance in this often amusing though surprisingly sentimental romantic comedy. Sounding like a runner-up in a David Duchovny voice contest, Sandler plays a quick-witted, semi-talented wedding singer whose life takes a turn for the worse when he's dumped at the altar. Barrymore is a future bride who befriends him with the predictable consequences: they fall in love. Set in the mid-'80s, the film seems to name-drop a reference from that time period on cue about every ten minutes: some are funny, some are obvious. Though most of the sporadic jokes work, the story is just a little too cuddly, especially for an Adam Sandler film. Barrymore is the real treasure here; she's absolutely beguiling. ★★½ VHS: $14.99; DVD: $19.99

Weeds

(1987, 115 min, US, John Hancock) *Nick Nolte, William Forsythe, Rita Taggart, Joe Mantegna, Ernie Hudson, Anne Ramsey.* In this based-on-fact story, Nolte gives a stirring portrayal of a convict whose plays about life behind bars lead to his parole and his works being performed both off-Broadway and in prisons around the country. ★★★

Weekend

(1968, 103 min, France, Jean-Luc Godard) *Mirielle Darc, Jean Yanne, Jean-Pierre Léaud.* One of Godard's most successfully realized films, *Weekend* is a devastating attack on and an apocalyptic metaphor for the rapid collapse of Western capitalistic society. Beginning with a coherent plot (that soon goes astray), the story follows a bourgeois couple who travel by car from Paris to the country. The rural landscape they encounter soon becomes a nightmarish vision of chaos and destruction — with the road littered with traffic jams, burning cars, violence and death. A highlight of the film is the ten-minute tracking shot of the mammoth traffic jam that encapsulates all of the anarchy of a society in decay. (French with English subtitles) ★★★½ VHS: $29.99

Weekend at Bernie's

(1989, 97 min, US, Ted Kotcheff) *Andrew McCarthy, Jonathan Silverman, Terry Kiser.* *Weekend at Bernie's* is tasteless, sophomoric, and funny. McCarthy and Silverman are young corporate go-getters who get invited to the boss' palatial oceanfront home for the weekend — to be murdered. But the tables are turned, and it

is Bernie who gets his. Only problem is, the body keeps popping up everywhere and no one seems to recognize the fact that Bernie is dead. Things get even more complicated when the boys think they're next, and to save themselves, they must make it look like Bernie is really alive. "Masterpiece Theatre" it's not. It's not even *The Trouble with Harry*. But it is for undemanding comedic tastes. ★★½ VHS: $9.99; DVD: $14.99

Weekend at Bernie's 2

(1993, 89 min, US, Robert Klane) *Andrew McCarthy, Jonathan Silverman, Terry Kiser, Barry Bostwick.* A not-so funny, silly follow-up to the 1989 surprise hit about the corpse that just won't stay dead. Kiser reprises his role as Bernie, who this time is reanimated by a Virgin Islands voodoo priestess who's after the money he embezzled before his demise. The humor is as macabre as in the first film, though it's really hard not to laugh at seeing Bernie dancing his way into the ocean with a harpoon through his head. ★½ VHS: $9.99

Week-End at the Waldorf

(1945, 130 min, US, Robert Z. Leonard) *Ginger Rogers, Walter Pidgeon, Lana Turner, Van Johnson, Robert Benchley.* This updated and Americanized version of *Grand Hotel* is a slick, surprisingly enjoyable drama-drama. Set in New York at the Waldorf-Astoria directly at the end of WWII, the story follows the varied lives of those who have come to stay at the luxury hotel. Rogers is a famous actress who sort of wants to be alone. The ever-debonair Pidgeon is the war correspondent who keeps her from her solitude. This is basically played for laughs. More dramatic is the subplot between injured soldier Johnson and gold-digging stenographer Turner. Director Leonard nicely intercuts the numerous stories and elicits pleasant performances from the entire ensemble. ★★★ VHS: $19.99

Weird Science

(1985, 94 min, US, John Hughes) *Anthony Michael Hall, Ilan Mitchell-Smith, Kelly LeBrock, Robert Downey, Jr., Bill Paxton.* A wasted comic fantasy about two high school boys (Hall, Mitchell-Smith) who create their "perfect" woman from a computer. LeBrock is the dream girl. ★ VHS: $9.99

Welcome Home, Roxy Carmichael

(1990, 97 min, US, Jim Abrahams) *Winona Ryder, Jeff Daniels.* A charming tale of an orphaned misfit who gets a new lease on life when she discovers that her mother may be a Hollywood star returning home for the first time in 15 years. Ryder's penchant for eccentric characterizations serves her well in her portrayal of Dinky Bossetti, a misanthropic teen whose only friends are the stray animals she keeps on a makeshift ark by the lake. Daniels is Denton Webb, the ex-lover who never got over losing Roxy. The overall warmth and sentimentality of the production make this an unqualified sleeper. ★★★ VHS: $14.99

Welcome to L.A.

(1977, 106 min, US, Alan Rudolph) *Keith Carradine, Sissy Spacek, Geraldine Chaplin, Harvey Keitel, Sally Kellerman, Lauren Hutton.* The rock music scene in Los Angeles gets the Rudolph treatment in this world of fragile egos, quickie love affairs and broken dreams. Produced by Robert Altman. ★★★

Welcome to Sarajevo

(1997, 102 min, US, Michael Winterbottom) *Stephen Dillane, Woody Harrelson, Marisa Tomei, Kerry Fox, Emily Lloyd, Goran Visnjic, Emira Nusevic.* Director Winterbottom's astonishing film about life during wartime is heavy stuff, but *Welcome to Sarajevo* is distinguished by its focus on humanity. Henderson (Dillane), a jaded British news correspondent, is stunned by the atrocities and conditions that surround him in war-torn Bosnia. He and fellow journalists live in makeshift hotels, and booze it up nightly as the reports they file get buried in their country's telecasts. As Henderson befriends his new driver Risto (Visnjic), he investigates the real Sarajevo, and makes a risky decision to save the life of Emira (Nusevic), an orphan girl he meets one day. A hard-hitting and extremely well-made film, *Welcome to Sarajevo* is as powerful as it is poignant. ★★★½ VHS: $19.99

Welcome to the Dollhouse

(1996, 87 min, US, Todd Solondz) *Heather Matarazzo, Brendan Sexton, Jr., Daria Kalinina, Matthew Faber.* A rabid, blisteringly funny sneer at the hell of awkward adolescence, *Welcome to the Dollhouse* explores a wide range of topics from peer group terrorism, sexual identity crises, insufferable siblings, clueless parents, imprisonment in the educational system and nonspecific hysteria to the all-encompassing obsession of the first crush. Matarazzo is terrific as 11-year-old Dawn, who endures the unabashed cruelty of her fellow students in her nightmare junior high school and the unrelenting, alienating criticism heaped upon her at home. Dawn approaches the daily cadence of ritual ostracism and humiliation with a weird solemnity — the unimpeachable martyrdom of the very young. This roiling emotional morass is brought into excruciatingly sharp focus when her brother's garage band gets a new lead singer — a suburban Adonis with a rep for nailing just about any available female. It's touching, raucous, hilarious, cruel and insightful by turn. ★★★½ VHS: $14.99; DVD: $27.99

Welcome to the Dollhouse

Welcome to Woop Woop

(1997, 90 min, Australia, Stephan Elliott) *Johnathon Schaech, Rod Taylor, Susie Porter, Dee Smart, Paul Mercurio, Rachel Griffiths.* Director Elliott's follow-up to his hilarious *The Adventures of Priscilla, Queen of the Desert* once again proves you can't make a cult film on purpose. This ramshackle comedy about Teddy (Schaech), a New York con man who inexplicably becomes a married prisoner in the Australian Outback, has lots of energy but no laughs. The town of Woop Woop rocks to the tunes of Rodgers and Hammerstein (hee-hee-hee) and makes dog food out of kangaroos and real dogs (ha-ha-ha). Teddy also learns that his father-in-law Daddy-O (Taylor) is the town leader who will shoot anyone who tries to escape (ho-ho-ho). Although it starts out amusingly enough, once the film settles down in Woop Woop, it has nowhere to go. ★½ VHS: $14.99

The Welldigger's Daughter

(1941, 142 min, France, Marcel Pagnol) *Raimu, Fernandel, Josette Day.* The wonderful French character actor Raimu stars in this fabulous story of a simple French peasant whose humor and dignity is compromised by his daughter, who finds herself pregnant as her lover goes off to war. With this film, Pagnol continued his firm ability to take complex human predicaments and portray them for us in a rich, subtle manner. (French with English subtitles) ★★★

Werewolf of London

(1935, 75 min, US, Stuart Walker) *Henry Hull, Warner Oland.* Hull plays the title creature in this early Universal horror film, made six years before Lon Chaney, Jr. immortalized himself as the more famous Wolfman. With no Gypsy lore and little of the moral anguish Chaney later portrayed, an English botanist is bitten by a werewolf on a specimen-collecting tour of Tibet. He returns to London only to realize the nature of his curse and recognizing his helplessness to stop the killing. The film lacks the scares of Chaney's version and its protagonist is less interesting. ★★ VHS: $14.99

West and Soda

(1965, 90 min, Italy, Bruno Bozzetto) Bozzetto's first full-length animated feature looks like a spaghetti western as done by Jay Ward. His clean lines and simple backgrounds perfectly mirror the moral and physical landscape inherent in these sorts of American melodramas. And it's funny, too. ★★★ VHS: $29.99

West Side Story

(1961, 152 min, US, Robert Wise & Jerome Robbins) *Natalie Wood, Richard Beymer, George Chakiris, Russ Tamblyn, Rita Moreno.* Whether referring to the stage or film version, this Leonard Bernstein-Stephen Sondheim musical is one of the all-time greats. Wood and Beymer are the star-crossed lovers in this updated "Romeo and Juliet" set against the backdrop of gang warfare in New York's Upper West Side. Tamblyn and Chakiris (Oscar winner) are the gang leaders, and Moreno (also an Oscar winner) is Chakiris' girlfriend. Expertly directed by Wise and Robbins (who also choreographed the classic dance numbers). Winner of 11 Academy Awards, including Best Picture. ★★★★ VHS: $14.99; DVD: $19.99

West Side Story

Western Union

(1941, 94 min, US, Fritz Lang) *Robert Young, Randolph Scott, Dean Jagger.* Expansive western adventure with Young and Scott about the laying of the first transcontinental Western Union wire in the mid-1800s. ★★★ VHS: $39.99

The Westerner

(1940, 100 min, US, William Wyler) *Gary Cooper, Walter Brennan, Chill Wills, Forrest Tucker, Dana Andrews.* Solid western adventure with Cooper and Brennan whooping it up in the wild, wild West. Brennan won an Oscar (his third) as the infamous Judge Roy Bean, and he steals the show. ★★★½ VHS: $14.99

Westfront 1918

(1930, 90 min, Germany, G.W. Pabst) *Gustav Diesl, Fritz Kampers.* Pabst's first sound film deals with trench warfare during the final days of World War I. Strongly antiwar, this intense drama deals with four ordinary German soldiers and the effects the war has on them. There is no glorification of battles won, but rather a meditation on the destructiveness, futility and horror of war. (German with English subtitles) ★★★

Westler: East of the Wall

(1985, 94 min, Germany, Wieland Speck) *Sigurd Rachman, Rancer Strecker.* A romantic and involving gay love story set before the fall of the East German Communist government and the crumbling of the Berlin Wall. The story follows the seemingly doomed love affair between a West Berliner and an East Berlin waiter. Having met during a visit to Alexanderplatz, the two young men soon fall in love, but discover that political forces beyond their control conspire to keep them apart. Shot clandestinely throughout East Germany, which gives the film a semi-documentary feel. (German English wiith subtitles) ★★★ VHS: $39.99

Westworld

(1973, 88 min, US, Michael Crichton) *James Brolin, Richard Benjamin, Yul Brynner, Dick Van Patten.* Crichton made his directorial debut with this highly original sci-fi thriller about a high-tech amusement park whose mechanical robots begin to rebel. Brolin and Benjamin are the tourists caught in the mêlèe. Brynner is the gun-slinging robot ringleader. Lots of chills and much suspense. (VHS available letterboxed or pan & scan) (Sequel: *Futureworld*) ★★★ VHS: $14.99; DVD: $19.99

Wetherby

(1985, 97 min, GB, David Hare) *Vanessa Redgrave, Ian Holm, Judi Dench, Joely Richardson.* Screenwriter-director Hare has fashioned a fascinating and thought-provoking film which tackles such uncomfortable themes as loneliness, loveless relationships and the death of innocence. Redgrave is a quiet Yorkshire schoolteacher who, after the violent suicide of a young man who entered her life, must search her past and present in order to arrive at some understanding of her priorities. ★★★½

The Whales of August

(1987, 90 min, US, Lindsay Anderson) *Lillian Gish, Bette Davis, Ann Sothern, Vincent Price, Mary Steenburgen.* An eloquent rendition of David Berry's play about two aging sisters living out their final years together. Gish plays the tenderhearted and loving caretaker who patiently looks after sister Davis — who is blind, embittered and given to petulant outbursts. Both actresses play their parts exquisitely, each projecting a screen presence unscathed by the sands of time. In his first American production, Anderson leaves behind all the rampant political diatribe which are the hallmarks of his earlier works and concentrates on subtle human interaction — the result being a tender and heart-warming look at the delicate process of growing old. ★★★

What about Bob?

(1991, 99 min, US, Frank Oz) *Richard Dreyfuss, Bill Murray, Julie Hagerty, Charlie Korsmo.* Murray has his best role in years in this delightfully crazy comedy as a neurotic psychiatric patient who

W

brings new meaning to the word hypochondria. Murray is passed around from doctor to doctor. His newest shrink is Dreyfuss, who after one session, goes with his family on vacation in New England leaving Murray on his own in New York. What's poor multi-phobic Bob to do? Follow them, of course. Director Oz gets a lot of comic mileage from this absurd premise and the laughs are plentiful. ★★★ VHS: $9.99; DVD: $29.99

What Do You Say to a Naked Lady?

(1970, 90 min, US, Allen Funt) Director Funt, best known for the 1960s TV series "Candid Camera," takes that show's concept and expands upon it for the big screen. He secretly records the sometimes very funny reactions of various bystanders exposed to. . . women exposed. ★★★ VHS: $14.99

What Dreams May Come

(1998, 114 min, US, Vincent Ward) *Robin Williams, Annabella Sciorra, Cuba Gooding, Jr., Max von Sydow, Rosalind Chao.* Guilty of not making the most of a fascinating and most promising premise, director Ward and adapter Ron Bass have opted for cerebral, New Age hocus pocus rather than whimsical or heartfelt fantasy in this tale of a husband whose love for his wife knows no bounds. Williams dies in a car crash, leaving wife Sciorra to mourn his death. Eventually, he learns her grief prompted her to commit suicide; and therefore her soul is denied entry into Heaven. With the help of a couple angels (Gooding, von Sydow, Chao), he travels to Hell to rescue his wife. It's a harrowing journey, amazingly brought to life by spectacular art direction and effects. But the dramatics are another story, and much of Williams' journey is slowly paced and only occasionally does something of interest happen to the characters. *What Dreams May Come* is lovely to look at but it never fully captures the soul of eternal love. Based on Richard Matheson's novel. ★★½ VHS: $14.99; DVD: $19.99

What Ever Happened to Baby Jane

(1962, 132 min, US, Robert Aldrich) *Bette Davis, Joan Crawford, Victor Buono.* What more can be said about this camp favorite? Beyond the jet-black humor is a solid, well-made thriller. Davis, as an aging child star, chews the scenery in one of her most memorable screen performances. Crawford, as her crippled sister, is equally captivating. Sibling rivalry was never so wicked and never so much fun! (Remade in 1991) ★★★★ VHS: $14.99; DVD: $19.99

What Happened to Kerouac

(1986, 96 min, US, Richard Lerner & Lewis MacAdams) *Steve Allen, William Burroughs, Neal Cassady, Allen Ginsberg, Gregory Corso, Lawrence Ferlinghetti.* The enigmatic image of Beat novelist Jack Kerouac is put into focus in this engrossing documentary portrait of one of the most interesting American figures of the 1950s and early '60s. Once dubbed by *The New York Times* as a "Neanderthal with a typewriter," Kerouac's life and times are recounted through anecdotes from his friends and family. Included in the film are memorable appearances by Buckley's "Firing Line" and "The Steve Allen Show." A must for all Kerouac fans as well as those interested in the artist engulfed in the American culture. ★★★ VHS: $19.99

What Happened Was. . .

(1994, 90 min, US, Tom Noonan) *Tom Noonan, Karen Sillas.* A first date takes a nightmarish turn in this meandering first film from actor Noonan. Michael (Noonan) and Jackie (Sillas) are coworkers in a law firm who develop an attraction for each other. Having dinner together, the two engage in the superficial banter of first dates, then progress deeper and deeper into darker, more personal territory as the evening wears on. Though the first half of the film works fairly well, its second-half "Twilight Zone" antics and macabre overtones unfortunately are wasted in this ambitious but unsuccessful experiment. ★★ VHS: $89.99

What Have I Done to Deserve This!

(1985, 100 min, Spain, Pedro Almodovar) *Carmen Maura, Chus Lampreave.* Almodóvar's unbelievably funny, absurdist gem lept out of the post-Franco liberalization with the velocity of a cannonball. This twisted and surreal film focuses on a modern Spanish clan which bears more than a passing resemblance to the Addams family. Mom is a frustrated No-Doze addicted housewife who lives in a tiny high-rise with her miserable cab-driving husband (who once forged Hitler's diaries) and her two sons: a 14-year-old drug dealer and a precocious 12-year-old who casually seduces his friends' fathers and is finally sold to a gay dentist. Completing this thorny nest is their batty Grandma who longs to leave Madrid and, with her pet lizard, find a place in the country. Shall we call this "Fun for the whole family?" (Spanish with English subtitles) ★★★★ VHS: $39.99

What Lies Beneath

(2000, 130 min, US, Robert Zemeckis) *Harrison Ford, Michelle Pfeiffer, Diana Scarwid, Joe Morton, James Remar.* Ford and Pfeiffer provide a lot of star power for this glossy, well-produced thriller, but not even celebrities of their order can overcome the film's underdeveloped screenplay. Pfeiffer plays a wife who becomes haunted by the spirit of an unknown young woman. Is she going crazy, and if not, did her husband (Ford) know her? A couple of good scenes provide a goose bump or two (including a tension-filled bathtub sequence), but the film suffers from a lethargic pace and who-cares plotting. A low-brow ghost story with a high-octane cast. ★★ VHS: $14.99; DVD: $26.99

What Planet Are You From?

(2000, 107 min, US, Mike Nichols) *Garry Shandling, Annette Bening, Greg Kinnear, Ben Kingsley, Linda Fiorentino, John Goodman.* Shandling is an alien sent to Earth to impregnate a woman — any woman — and return with child to his all-male home world. Enter Bening as an AA member leery of yet another bad relationship and, quicker than you can say "E.T. phone home," Shandling has forsaken his mission in favor of wooing and wedding her. Shandling's deadpan arrogance (so hilarious in HBO's "The Larry Sanders Show") is put to somewhat effective use in this curiously tame comedy that starts out amusing, but loses much steam as the plot becomes bogged down in family values. ★★ VHS: $14.99; DVD: $24.99

What Price Glory?

(1952, 109 min, US, John Ford) *James Cagney, Dan Dailey, Corinne Calvet, William Demarest, Robert Wagner.* Remake of the classic silent comedy-drama based on Maxwell Anderson's play about the WWI exploits of two American soldiers who fall for the same woman while stationed in France. Victor McLaglen and Edmund Lowe had better success in the original as Capt. Flagg and Sgt. Quirt than Cagney and Dailey have here. ★★½ VHS: $19.99

What Price Hollywood?

(1932, 88 min, US, George Cukor) *Constance Bennett, Lowell Sherman, Neil Hamilton.* Adela Rogers St. John's story about an alcoholic director whose career goes down as the girl he made a star eclipses him. Needless to say this was remade several times as *A Star Is Born.* Bennett gives as strong performance in this suprisingly tough look at then-contemporary Hollywood. ★★★½

What Women Want

(2000, 126 min, US, Nancy Meyers) *Mel Gibson, Helen Hunt, Marisa Tomei, Mark Feuerstein, Alan Alda, Lauren Holly.* A gimmick movie whose gimmick actually works, this charming and funny romantic comedy features Gibson in his first romantic role, and, damn, if he isn't reminiscent of Cary Grant. Mel plays a womanizing ad exec who — courtesy of a bathroom electrical mishap — develops the ability to hear women's thoughts. He first uses it to get an edge at work, but when he falls for his new boss (Hunt), he thinks he has the inside track to romantic success. Of course, a little soul-searching and a better understanding of the opposite sex follows. Wittier and not as offensive as you'd think a premise such as this would be, *What Women Want* benefits foremost from Gibson's natural, charismatic performance. The actor is up for any situation, tackling each indignity and triumph with good cheer. Hunt has little to do except look beguiling, though Tomei makes the most of a small role as one of Mel's conquests. ★★★ VHS: $14.99; DVD: $29.99

What's Cooking?

(2000, 109 min, US, Gurinder Chadha) *Mercedes Ruehl, Alfre Woodard, Joan Chen, Kyra Sedgwick, Julianna Margulies, Lainie Kazan, Maury Chaykin, Dennis Haysbert, A. Martinez, Victor Rivers, Estelle Harris.* The story on four families celebrating Thanksgiving in melting-pot downtown Los Angeles forms the core of this appetizing comedy. Skillfully juggling its many stories, *What's Cooking* explores with both humor and heart the differences and common bonds shared by the culturally diverse characters. Ruehl heads a terrific ensemble as the matriarch of a Latino family, newly separated from her husband who has returned to find himself replaced by a younger man. Added to this mix are the joyful trials and tribulations of an African-American, Asian-American and Jewish family, who all come together by story's end. A charming slice of American urban life, this is a truer vision of American "family values." Don't watch hungry, however — the food is mouthwatering. ★★★½ VHS: $89.99; DVD: $24.99

W

What's Love Got to Do with It?

What's Eating Gilbert Grape

(1993, 117 min, US, Lasse Hallström) *Johnny Depp, Leonardo DiCaprio, Juliette Lewis, Darlene Cates, Mary Steenburgen, Crispin Glover.* Depp has long specialized in the alienated teen, the loner who gets by in spite of himself. In *What's Eating Gilbert Grape*, he's still a misfit, but as the title character of this offbeat charmer, he's probably never been so "adjusted." Living in a small Iowa town, Gilbert comes from a classic dysfunctional family: his 500-pound mother (Cates) won't move from the couch; and his younger brother (DiCaprio) is mentally retarded and constantly climbing the water tower. Into his bored life comes a pretty drifter (Lewis) who, as it turns out, has a profound effect on all the Grape family. Funny, touching and sweet, with a dash of gentleness to its drama, the film features first-rate performances by all, including a lovely turn by newcomer Cates. But it is Oscar nominee DiCaprio who walks away with the acting honors. ★★★ VHS: $14.99

What's Love Got to Do with It?

(1993, 118 min, US, Brian Gibson) *Angela Bassett, Laurence Fishburne, Jenifer Lewis.* Bassett and Fishburne both received well-earned Oscar nominations for their roles as music greats Tina and Ike Turner in this intense musical biography. Infused with the same energy director Gibson brought to the story of another musical legend in *The Josephine Baker Story*, *What's Love* is a fascinating portrait of the professional and personal lives of the explosive couple. Based on Tina's autobiography, the story covers in varying detail Tina's childhood; her joining Ike's band and their marriage in the late 1950s and her meteoric rise as a singer while at the same time experiencing heartbreak in her marriage. Bassett and Fishburne's performances display more soul and veracity than mere imitation, which is only one of the many strengths of the film. ★★★½ VHS: $9.99; DVD: $29.99

What's New, Pussycat?

(1965, 108 min, US, Clive Donner) *Peter O'Toole, Peter Sellers, Capucine, Romy Schneider, Paula Prentiss, Ursula Andress, Woody Allen.* Allen's first screenplay and first screen appearance is a comic free-for-all about a fashion editor (O'Toole) and his obsession with beautiful women. Sellers is hilarious as the psychiatrist who's even crazier than his patients. Tom Jones sings the title tune. ★★★ VHS: $19.99

What's Up, Doc?

(1972, 94 min, US, Peter Bogdanovich) *Barbra Streisand, Ryan O'Neal, Madeline Kahn, Austin Pendleton, Kenneth Mars, Randy Quaid.* Bogdanovich's deliriously funny homage to screwball comedies, and *Bringing Up Baby* in particular. Streisand and even the usually bland O'Neal is in good form, in this lunatic story of identical suitcases leading their owners on a merry chase throughout San Francisco. In her film debut as O'Neal's much-flustered fiancée, Kahn is priceless. ★★★½ VHS: $14.99

What's Up, Tiger Lily?

(1966, 90 min, US, Woody Allen) A grade-B Japanese spy thriller, *Kagi No Kag*, is the ravaged victim of Allen's hilarious barbs as the search is on for the world's greatest egg salad recipe. Woody's dubbing the film in English with a steady stream of very funny one-liners extracts meaning from an otherwise innocuous yarn. Music by The Lovin' Spoonful. ★★★ VHS: $14.99

Whatever

(1998, 113 min, US, Susan Skoog) *Liza Weil, Chad Morgan, Katherine Rossetter, Frederic Forrest, Dan Montano.* A painfully hip '90s-era title marks an affecting, realistic coming-of-age drama set in the early '80s. Weil is extremely convincing as an alienated high schooler with a great talent for painting (guided by her supportive art teacher played with over-the-top zeal by Forrest), who is caught between her ne'er-do-well friends and her artistic dreams. While the inappropriate title suggests a sneering, pandering, clichéd slam at suburbia (and there is a dollop of that, unfortunately), *Whatever* is, for the most part, a tough but heartfelt portrait of a good but troubled kid going through universal growing pains. Nothing new here, but Skoog's sensitive script and direction, Weil's highly appealing performance, and a knockout soundtrack make this a winner. ★★★ VHS: $24.99

Whatever Happened to Aunt Alice?

(1969, 101 min, US, Lee H. Katzin) *Geraldine Page, Ruth Gordon, Rosemary Forsyth, Robert Fuller, Mildred Dunnock.* In the tradition of *What Ever Happened to Baby Jane* comes this entertaining Gothic thriller from that film's producer about a wealthy widow (Page) whose housekeepers keep on disappearing. Gordon plays her newest domestic out to find out what's really happened to her predecessors. The pairing of Page and Gordon works extremely well, and the film even has some good chills to it. (Letterboxed) ★★★ VHS: $14.99; DVD: $24.99

Whatever It Takes

(2000, 94 min, US, David Raynr) *Shane West, Marla Sokoloff, Jodi Lyn O'Keefe, James Franco, Richard Schiff.* A weak teen comedy, *Whatever It Takes* follows two guys who each like girls who don't like them. They strike a deal to. . . oh, forget it. It's the same stale stuff cribbed from *She's All That, Some Kind of Wonderful* and, yes, *Cyrano de Bergerac*. Sokoloff is extremely cute and appealing as the "good" girl, but the fact that the filmmakers shoehorn her into skintight tops *sans* bra at every opportunity — and O'Keefe as the "bad" girl is in various stages of undress — brings a tacky and desperate air to this mess. ★ VHS: $14.99; DVD: $24.99

The Wheeler Dealers

(1963, 100 min, US, Arthur Hiller) *James Garner, Lee Remick, Jim Backus, Phil Harris, Chill Wills, John Astin, Louis Nye.* Garner plays a Texas wheeler dealer who sets out to New York to rope in a couple deals and make a cool million. Remick is the first woman stock analyst on Wall Street who tries to lasso potential client Garner with some worthless stock. A lively if dated comedy ensues when these two players get together. The film tries to embrace a '60s feminist view, but ultimately only mocks it. With this in mind, however, there are genuine charming moments, due in large part to the gracious clowning of Garner, Remick and a seasoned supporting cast. ★★½ VHS: $19.99

Wheels on Meals

(1984, 95 min, Hong Kong, Samo Hung) *Jackie Chan, Yuen Biao, Samo Hung, Lola Forner, Benny "The Jet" Urquidez.* Chan and Yuen run a fast food business in the busy streets of Barcelona. They both fall for a mysterious Spanish woman who is, unbeknownst to her, heir to a large fortune. When some evil-looking bad guys come after her, it's up to the fast-food pair to stop them. The plot is incidental to the outstanding comedy and action scenes, of which there are plenty. The mood is light and even the toughest fight scenes end with a joke, as is Chan's trademark. The climactic fight scene between Chan and Urquidez is a highlight; it's a blistering and painful brawl, one of the best fights put on film — that is until their rematch in *Dragons Forever*. (Letterboxed) (Cantonese with English subtitles) ★★★ VHS: $19.99; DVD: $29.99

When a Man Loves a Woman

(1994, 126 min, US, Luis Mandoki) *Andy Garcia, Meg Ryan, Ellen Burstyn, Lauren Tom, Philip*

Seymour Hoffman. The earnest, heartfelt performances of both Garcia and Ryan help elevate this familiar though touching drama of a husband and wife grappling with alcohol abuse. Michael and Alice Green are a couple as ordinary as their names. When Alice's frequent drinking binges become daily occurances, much to the terror of her husband and children, her ordinary life is reshaped by hospitalizations and AA meetings. Basically a three-act drama, the story divides its time examining Alice's alcohol excesses, her drying out, and finally the healing process, which proves as difficult for Michael as it is for Alice. ★★½ VHS: $9.99; DVD: $29.99

When a Stranger Calls

(1979, 97 min, US, Fred Walton) *Carol Kane, Charles Durning, Colleen Dewhurst, Rachel Roberts.* Suspenseful but ultimately unsatisfying tale of a killer who stalks a baby-sitter and her family, years after he murdered two of her charges. (Sequel: *When a Stranger Calls Back*) ★★ VHS: $19.99

When Father Was Away on Business

(1985, 135 min, Yugoslavia, Emir Kusturica) *Moreno D'e Bartolli, Miki Manojlovic.* Focusing on one family's life in Communist Yugoslavia in the early 1950s, this tender, Fellini-esque drama unfolds with disarmingly gentle humor and perceptive political sentiments. The story takes the point of view of Malik, a six-year-old boy whose philandering father is exposed as an "anti-Tito/Stalin Communist" by his loose-lipped lover and his Communist Party brother-in-law. He is sent to prison and his absence is explained to Malik as a "business trip," but the boy soon discovers the truth and begins to understand the compromises and lies one must make to get by. A lusty, boisterous look at life in a society repressed but undetered by the political tyranny of the times. (Serbo-Croatian with English subtitles) ★★★½ VHS: $19.99

When Harry Met Sally

(1989, 95 min, US, Rob Reiner) *Billy Crystal, Meg Ryan, Carrie Fisher, Bruno Kirby.* Crystal and Ryan sparkle in this enchanting comedy about the ups and downs of platonic friendship. Harry Burns (Crystal) and Sally Albright (Ryan) first meet through a rideshare in college, with Harry fetching a ride from Chicago to New York in Sally's car. Polar opposites, their relationship is doomed from the start. But over the years, things slowly warm up until eventually they are forced to confront their feelings about each other. Both actors shine and each have more than their share of truly hilarious scenes — not the least of which is Ryan's staged orgasm in a crowded New York delicatessen. Director Reiner has marched bravely into Woody Allen territory and handles the material deftly and crisply. ★★★½ VHS: $9.99; DVD: $24.99

When I Close My Eyes

(1993, 94 min, Slovenia, Franci Flak) *Petra Govic, Mario Selih.* A chic and atmospheric thriller, *When I Close My Eyes* is a good-looking but obtuse story about obsession and revenge. When Ana (the ravishing Govac) is robbed by a handsome, leather-clad motorcyclist, she takes the opportunity to steal some money for herself. As the police investigate the crime, Ana becomes fascinated by the criminal and pursues him —

romantically. Writer-director Flak needlessly complicates this simple, dangerous love story with a political subplot about the mysterious circumstances surrounding the death of Ana's father. The gorgeous cast, the stylish Eastern European locations and the luminous cinematography compensate for the overall lack of sex and suspense. (Slovenia with English subtitles) ★★½ VHS: $79.99

When Night Is Falling

(1994, 96 min, Canada, Patricia Rozema) *Pascale Bussières, Rachael Crawford, Henry Czerny.* A refreshingly liberating tale of lesbian love. Camille (Bussières) is a Christian academician romantically involved with Martin (Czerny), a nice enough fellow teacher more interested in advancement than romance. Camille's repressed emotions and desire for true love come to the surface after she meets flamboyant circus performer Petra (Crawford). Despite being diametrical opposites, the two are attracted to each other. Its much appreciated romanticism and the casting of two attractive women aside, the film suffers from a symbolism-laden, seen-it-before screenplay and a semi-catatonic lead actress (Bussières). However, the handling of the relationship is both exciting and hopeful, conditions that are much too rare in the typical film that tackles queer love. ★★★ VHS: $19.99

When the Cat's Away
(Chacun Cherche Son Chat)

(1997, 91 min, France, Cedric Klapisch) *Garance Clavel, Zinedine Soualem, Olivier Py, Renée Le Calm.* If there is justice in the world, the video release of this zany cinematic frolic will include the film's French-language trailer that was shown in theatres here. In it, a rapid-fire voiceover introduces us to the wacky denizens of a Parisian neighborhood where a young woman has lost her cat all the while rattling off the film's tongue-twisting French title repeatedly. Rarely has a preview encapsulated a film's energy with such zest and hilarity. Klapisch's breezy yarn centers around Chloe (Clavel), an attractive, single, young woman who makes her living as an assistant on fashion shoots. Deciding to take a week's holiday by the sea, she leaves her kitty, Gris Gris, with a withered old neighborhood cat lady, Madame Renée (Le Calm). Upon her return, M. Renée makes it known that she's lost Gris Gris and a hunt begins throughout the entire arrondissement. The result is a whimsical, yet tender look at a modernizing Paris where construction sites abound and gentrification is all the rage. So in the words of the aforementioned trailer, "Just see the film, Merde!" (French with English subtitles) ★★★ VHS: $24.99

When the Party's Over

(1992, 114 min, US, Matthew Irmas) *Rae Dawn Chong, Fisher Stevens, Sandra Bullock, Brian McNamara.* Ostensibly a comedy-drama about the transition into adulthood, director Irmas' film seems aimed at (perhaps even made by) those who have not yet started the journey. In the ensemble tradition of such issue packed films as *St. Elmo's Fire*, this glossy film presents a house full of beautiful, successful young urban stereotypes trying to come to terms with adulthood and each other. The film is structured as a series of loosely connected flashbacks that

lead up to a New Year's Eve crisis and the soul-searching powwow that follows. Young adulthood deserves a slightly less lamebrained rap. ★ VHS: $9.99

When the Whales Came

(1989, 100 min, GB, Clive Rees) *Paul Scofield, Helen Mirren, David Threlfall.* This somber story stars Scofield as a hermit who holds the secret of a mysterious island off the coast of England. Set just prior to the outbreak of WWI, the film chronicles his friendship with two young girls who break local taboo by befriending him. ★★ VHS: $14.99

When the Wind Blows

(1986, 80 min, GB, Jimmy T. Murakami) *Voices of: John Mills, Peggy Ashcroft.* An unsettling and superior animated tale of a happily retired couple living out their golden years, until they must face living with the consequences of nuclear war. Music by David Bowie. ★★★

When We Were Kings

(1996, 105 min, US, Leon Gast) The 1974 "Rumble in the Jungle" between Muhammad Ali and reigning heavyweight champ George Foreman is the subject of this fascinating documentary, started in '74 during the media event in Zaire, but finished 22 years later by producer Taylor Hackford. The story of how underdog Ali managed to defeat the vastly favored Foreman is fascinating enough, but when added to the events which surrounded the fight — it was Don King's first major promotion and also featured musical acts James Brown and B.B. King — it becomes the stuff of legend. Its infectious good spirit and rousing portrait of a remarkable athlete and American hero make it well deserving of its Academy Award for Best Documentary. ★★★★ VHS: $19.99; DVD: $19.99

When Worlds Collide

(1951, 81 min, US, Rudolph Maté) *Richard Derr, Barbara Rush.* Good special effects highlight this sci-fi tale about the citizens of Earth preparing for the planet's destruction by an approaching meteor, and the rush to build a rocketship to send a group of selected survivors to another world. "And when worlds collide, said George Pal to his bride, I'm gonna give you a celluloid thrill." ★★★ VHS: $14.99

Where Angels Fear to Tread

(1991, 113 min, GB, Charles Sturridge) *Helen Mirren, Judy Davis, Rupert Graves, Helena Bonham Carter.* Released in the shadow of the critically acclaimed *Howards End*, this overlooked adaptation of E.M. Forster's novel is impressively produced, superbly acted and an extremely worthwhile effort. Mirren stars as Lilia Harriton, a wealthy widow who enrages her stodgy in-laws when she runs off to Italy and marries a swarthy young peasant, thereby threatening the family fortune. Lilia's brother and sister (Graves, Davis) are dispatched to Italy to try and talk some sense into the merry widow. All of the performances are first rate, but Davis steals the show with her truly over-the-top portrayal of the histrionic Harriet Harriton. The film sports a darker sense of humor and more tragic twists than the standard Forster fare, which makes it all-the-more entertaining and nearly as satisfying as *Howards End*. ★★★½ VHS: $19.99

Where Eagles Dare

(1968, 159 min, GB, Brian G. Hutton) *Richard Burton, Clint Eastwood, Mary Ure.* Released at the height of the Tet Offensive in 1968, this underrated WWII action adventure film did not make big waves at the box office. Seems people simply weren't hungry for more war images when they could be seen on TV every night. It's kind of a shame because this is a slam-bang cliffhanger of a tale with Burton and Eastwood as two soldiers attempting to free an important officer from an escape-proof Nazi prison. Alistair MacLean adapted his own novel with great flair. ★★★½ VHS: $14.99

Where Sleeping Dogs Lie

(1991, 92 min, US, Charles Finch) *Dylan McDermott, Tom Sizemore, Sharon Stone.* Whoever thought it prudent to awaken this "sleeping dog" no doubt wished to exercise his "basic instinct" for moneymaking by cashing in on the now-bankable talents of a pre-*Basic Instinct* Sharon Stone. But, despite her overwhelming presence on the display box, the icepick princess has less than 15 minutes of screen time as the agent (and sometimes lover) of a hapless screenwriter (McDermott) who passes off research work about a gruesome mass murder as fiction — only to have the real murderer show up on his door-step. ★½ VHS: $9.99

Where the Buffalo Roam

(1980, 100 min, US, Art Linson) *Bill Murray, Peter Boyle, Bruno Kirby.* Murray takes on the role — with middling results — of American "gonzo" journalist Hunter S. Thompson, whose passion for writing was equalled only by his love of drugs, alcohol and other vices. (Letterboxed) ★★ VHS: $14.99; DVD: $24.99

Where the Day Takes You

(1992, 107 min, US, Marc Rocco) *Dermot Mulroney, Ricki Lake, Will Smith, Sean Astin, Lara Flynn Boyle.* This film about the daily, sometimes tragic lives of teenage runaways coexisting in Los Angeles is determinedly somber — as are these kids' lives. And though the story covers little new ground of life on the street, the film possesses such grit and determination it has an immediacy which cannot be ignored. Mulroney, trading his handsome looks for that of a scraggly druggie, gives a startling performance as the leader of a small clique living by their wits, sleeping under freeway off-ramps, and scrounging for change and food. A youthful cast is impressive. ★★½ VHS: $19.99

Where the Green Ants Dream

(1984, 100 min, Australia/Germany, Werner Herzog) *Bruce Spence, Wandjuk Marika, Norman Kaye.* Herzog juxtaposes the mystical primitivism of the Australian Aborigine against the expansionist threats of modern industry in this voyage into a world obsessed with conquest. Set against the arid flatlands of southern Australia, the film follows a large mining corporation's effort to extract uranium deposits from the Aborigines' sacred grounds, thereby destroying the landscape and shattering the slumber of the revered "green ants," whose interrupted dreaming would signify the death of the Aboriginal culture. A visually sumptuous work that contemplates the issues of cultural relations, imperialism and the wondrous mysteries of life itself. (In English) ★★★

Where the Heart Is

(1990, 107 min, US, John Boorman) *Dabney Coleman, Christopher Plummer, Crispin Glover, Joanna Cassidy.* An amiable and quirky comedy written by director Boorman and his daughter Telsche. Coleman stars as a wealthy businessman who decides to teach his three spoiled children a lesson in responsibility by forcing them out of the house and into a rundown tenement he owns. Though the story is unexceptional, the film is uplifted by winning performances all around; and by a collection of wonderful tromp l'oeil paintings. ★★½

Where the Heart Is

(2000, 120 min, US, Matt Williams) *Natalie Portman, Ashley Judd, Stockard Channing, Sally Field, James Frain, Joan Cusack, Dylan Bruno, Keith David.* Portman plays Novalee, a young, pregnant trailer-park girl from Tennessee who is left behind by her no-account boyfriend. Finding refuge in a Wal-Mart, she hides and lives there by night until she delivers what the media calls "the Wal-Mart baby." Her brief notoriety introduces her to a series of quirky characters. There are too many "big" moments crammed together to produce any real dramatic flow, and the characters are of the "wear-their-emotions-on-their-sleeves" variety. Much of this will leave you with eyes rolling. ★★ VHS: $14.99; DVD: $24.99

Where the Hot Wind Blows

(1959, 125 min, Italy/France, Jules Dassin) *Melina Mercouri, Gina Lollobrigida, Yves Montand, Marcello Mastroianni.* Although this fiery Italian soap opera has an appealing all-star cast, there is little else in this tawdry melodrama to recommend. The story is about the decadence, from the peasants to the aristocracy, of a small town — sort of like an Italian *Peyton Place*. ★½

Where the Money Is

(2000, 89 min, US, Marek Kanievska) *Paul Newman, Linda Fiorentino, Dermot Mulroney.* Thanks to the winning performances of its two stars, this agreeable caper comedy is more enjoyable than it has any right to be. Looking impossibly sexy at age 70, Newman stars as a veteran bank robber who pretends to be a stroke victim in order to avoid a lifetime jail sentence. Fiorentino is equally effective as the nurse whose keen sense detects his scam and shortly thereafter convinces him to help her rob an armored truck. Blending the suspense of a heist film and the whimsy of a comedy, *Where the Money Is* allows one of our genuine movie icons to breathe easy in a setting in which he seems totally at home. That it can be fun, too, is a little extra gravy. ★★★ VHS: $14.99; DVD: $26.99

Where the River Runs Black

(1986, 101 min, Brazil/US, Christopher Cain) *Charles Durning, Peter Horton, Ajay Naidi, Conchata Ferrell.* A young boy born along the banks of the Amazon River is raised by dolphins when his mother is killed by gold prospectors. When he grows up, and encounters his mother's killers, he seeks revenge. Exquisite cinematography accentuates this compelling family film. ★★★

Where the Rivers Flow North

(1994, 104 min, US, Jay Craven) *Rip Torn, Tantoo Cardinal, Bill Raymond, Michael J. Fox, Treat Williams.* A poignant tale of an old logger who lives on a piece of land slated to be flooded for a new dam. Torn is a man possessed as he tries to beat the corporate world with his own schemes and pipe dreams. Cardinal plays his lover/companion with eloquence and conviction. Reminiscent in both style and story of *Wild River*, director Craven labored for many years on this labor of love. The beauty of the landscape reminds one of the lost innocence of America and the power of greed. ★★★½ VHS: $14.99; DVD: $9.99

Where Were You When the Lights Went Out

(1968, 94 min, US, Hy Averback) *Doris Day, Robert Morse, Terry-Thomas, Steve Allen.* Day made quite a few entertaining sex comedies in the 1960s; unfortunately, this is not one of them. Averback, a successful TV sitcom director, shows little comic flair with this farce about the goings-on on the night of the New York City 1965 blackout. Doris plays a wife who thinks her husband is cheating on her. To make him jealous, she takes up with Morse. . . and gets caught in the blackout. ★½ VHS: $19.99

Where's Picone

(1984, 122 min, Italy, Nanni Loy) *Giancarlo Giannini, Lina Sastri.* Giannini is hilarious as a sleazy con man who reluctantly becomes involved with the wife of a man who inexplicably disappears while in an ambulance going to the hospital. Alternating between a love story and slapstick comedy, the film has Giannini, as a two-bit hustler living on the wrong side of respectability, discovering that the esteemed missing man had a secret life that had strayed far from the norm. A bit silly at times, this genial comedy does pack some suspense and romance in exposing the corruption and duplicitousness of Italian society and bureaucracy. (Italian with English subtitles) ★★½ VHS: $29.99

Where's Poppa?

(1970, 82 min, US, Carl Reiner) *George Segal, Ruth Gordon, Ron Liebman, Vincent Gardenia.* Segal desperately tries to get rid of his senile mom (Gordon), who likes Froot Loops with Coke and has a penchant for biting his rear end. A savagely funny cult film that pokes fun at sex, muggings and motherhood. ★★★½ VHS: $19.99

Which Way Is Up?

(1977, 94 min, US, Michael Schultz) *Richard Pryor, Lonette McKee, Margaret Avery.* Serio-comic look at life in central California's strife-torn farm community. Pryor plays three roles — a beleaguered worker, his cranky old father, and a hypocritical preacher. An American remake of Lina Wertmüller's *The Seduction of Mimi*. ★★½ VHS: $9.99

While the City Sleeps

(1956, 100 min, US, Fritz Lang) *Dana Andrews, Ida Lupino, Rhonda Fleming, George Sanders, Vincent Price, Howard Duff, Thomas Mitchell.* Another Lang opus on crime in the big city, this time counterplaying the search for a psychotic serial killer against a power struggle inside a huge media conglomerate. ★★★ VHS: $29.99

While You Were Sleeping

(1995, 100 min, US, Jon Turtletaub) *Sandra Bullock, Bill Pullman, Peter Gallagher, Peter Boyle, Jack Warden, Glynis Johns.* Bullock and Pullman will bewitch many a heart in this beguiling romantic comedy, essentially a Cinderella tale except for the fact that it's Prince Charming who's asleep. Bullock is a lonely transit worker who saves the life of the handsome businessman (Gallagher) whom she admires from afar. As he lies in a coma, she is mistakenly identified as his fiancée, and then welcomed with open arms into his rather daffy family. All except Gallagher's brother, played with elfin charm by Pullman. Of course, they inevitably — but most endearingly — fall in love. Sure its a slight premise, but a most engaging cast, real chemistry between the two leads and a lively screenplay make this all-the-more entertaining. ★★★ VHS: $14.99; DVD: $29.99

Whipped

(2000, 85 min, US, Peter M. Cohen) *Amanda Peet, Brian Van Holt, Jonathan Abrahams, Zorie Barber, Judah Domke.* Whipped revolves around three repellent single men (and their equally repulsive married buddy), who spend most of their time in a diner sharing vulgar tales of their sexual exploits. Then one day, the three all tell of being in love, or is it like, with their latest hookup. Wouldn't you know it's the same woman (Peet), who turns the tables on them and their womanizing ways. Despite the allure of a three-Peet, the film's obnoxious bores are one-dimensional types, and the ceaseless dialogue is embarrassingly unfunny. Amongst non-actors, Barber is a particularly grating standout for his barked lines. ★ VHS: $102.99; DVD: $29.99

Whispers in the Dark

(1992, 103 min, US, Christopher Crowe) *Annabella Sciorra, Jamey Sheridan, Alan Alda, Jill Clayburgh, Anthony LaPaglia, John Leguizamo.* In this sexually candid shocker, Sciorra strikes just the right balance of naïveté and intellectual savvy as a lovelorn psychiatrist who comes to suspect that her new Prince Charming (Sheridan) may be a killer. Despite a major plot contrivance and a script so laden with psychobabble that Woody Allen may have penned it, the suspense makes this an involving murder mystery. ★★½ VHS: $19.99

The Whistle Blower

(1987, 104 min, GB, Simon Langton) *Michael Caine, Nigel Havers, John Gielgud, James Fox.* Compelling political drama reminiscent of *Missing* starring Caine as a father who investigates the death of his son, a translator for the British government who may have been murdered to cover up a security leak. Caine is masterful as the tormented father determined to uncover the truth behind his son's demise. ★★★

Whistle Down the Wind

(1962, 98 min, GB, Bryan Forbes) *Alan Bates, Hayley Mills, Bernard Lee.* This charming and extraordinary film is both a Christ parable and a poignant treatise on childhood innocence. Forbes, in a remarkable directorial debut, brings a deft and heartwarming touch to this story of an escaped criminal (Bates) who is found by three young children in their barn and is thought by them to be Christ. (The basis for a West End musical) ★★★½

Whistling in the Dark

(1941, 77 min, US, S. Sylvan Simon) *Red Skelton, Ann Rutherford, Conrad Veidt, Eve Arden.* Skelton lends his comic talents to this lightweight, mildly entertaining romp. He's a 1940s radio personality known as the Fox, a wily sleuth who always nails the bad guy. Veidt gives a pre-Branch Davidian interpretation of a loony cult leader who kidnaps Skelton and forces him to concoct the perfect murder. (Followed by 2 sequels: *Whistling in Brooklyn* and *Whistling in Dixie*) ★★½ VHS: $19.99

White

(1994, 93 min, France, Krzysztof Kieslowski) *Juliette Binoche, Julie Delpy, Zbigniew Zamachowski.* This, the second of Kieslowski's popular trilogy (the others being *Blue* and *Red*), is the weakest of the three, although still involving. This wry drama of obsession and revenge is played out within the symbolic battlefield of the new democratic Europe — rich Western Europe vs. the poor Eastern countries. The story centers on Karol (Zamahowski), a sweetly nerdish Polish hairdresser who travels to Paris and finds love in the arms of the beautiful Dominique (Delpy). Karol's inability to find a job and to speak the language results in impotency and a frustrated wife. A sexually wanting Dominique divorces him, an act that forces our enterprising hero to return home and plot an elaborate, far-fetched scheme of winning her back...on his terms. Uncomfortably misogynist with an unnecessary ending, the story lacks really likable characters but entertains nonetheless. (French and Polish with English subtitles) ★★½ VHS: $19.99

The White Balloon

(1995, 85 min, Iran, Jafar Panahi) *Aida Mohammadkhani, Mohsen Kalifi.* Winner of the 1995 Camera d'Or at the Cannes Film Festival, *The White Balloon* gives a quiet glimpse of a foreign land filled with familiar people, an important reminder that it is a government we hate — not a nation. The film has all the virtues of a Satyajit Ray work — most obviously *Pather Panchali* — in its simple tale of a little girl, both sweet and petulant, who loses then regains then loses again the money she has wheedled from her harried mother to buy a goldfish. If director Panahi had done no more than so perfectly captured the tenor and texture of a time, a town and a people, this film would be just as remarkable. (Farsi with English subtitles) ★★★★ VHS: $19.99

The White Buffalo

(1977, 97 min, US, J. Lee Thompson) *Charles Bronson, Jack Weston, Kim Novack.* Unusual western parable with Bronson as Bill Hickok hunting the title bison, which represents the famous marksman's fear of death. ★★½ VHS: $14.99

White Christmas

(1954, 120 min, US, Michael Curtiz) *Bing Crosby, Danny Kaye, Vera-Ellen, Rosemary Clooney, Dean Jagger, Mary Wickes.* Crosby and Kaye make the most of a tuneful Irving Berlin score in this popular holiday-themed musical. They play entertainers who come to the rescue of their old Army superior (Jagger). ★★★ VHS: $9.99; DVD: $29.99

The White Dawn

(1974, 109 min, US, Philip Kaufman) *Warren Oates, Timothy Bottoms, Louis Gossett, Jr.* A fascinating and original adventure tale about three turn-of-the-century whalers (Oates, Bottoms and Gossett) who are rescued by a tribe of Eskimos when their boat capsizes. A beautifully filmed fable. ★★★ VHS: $19.99

White Fang

(1991, 107 min, US, Randal Kleiser) *Ethan Hawke, Klaus Maria Brandauer, Seymour Cassel.* Based on the novel by Jack London, this rousing Disney adventure film is good entertainment for the entire family. The story follows the twin tales of a naive young man claiming his dead father's inheritance in the Klondike, and his befriending a wolf cub raised by the Indians. ★★★ VHS: $14.99

White Heat

(1949, 114 min, US, Raoul Walsh) *James Cagney, Virginia Mayo, Edmond O'Brien, Margaret Wycherly.* Cagney's intense performance highlights this classic underworld drama about ruthless killer Cody Jarrett, he with the headaches and the mother fixation; and the cop determined to put him away. "Made it, Ma. Top of the world!" ★★★★ VHS: $19.99

White Hunter, Black Heart

(1990, 112 min, US, Clint Eastwood) *Clint Eastwood, Marisa Berenson, George Dzundza, Jeff Fahey, Timothy Spall.* This fictionalized account of film director John Huston's adventures while on the set of *The African Queen* is a challenging work for director Eastwood. And as an actor, he gives a bold performance with an uncanny impersonation of the mythic Huston, though it may take some getting used to "Dirty Harry" calling everyone "kid." The story follows Huston's obsession with shooting a giant elephant, and the effect it has on himself, his film crew and his guides. A film of epic scale presented in an intimate fashion, *White Hunter,*

Julie Delpy in *White*

Black Heart is a picturesque excursion into the darker regions of man's soul. ★★★ VHS: $14.99

White Lie

(1991, 93 min, US, Bill Condon) *Gregory Hines, Annette O'Toole, Bill Nunn.* Hines gives a first-rate performance in this superior made-for-cable mystery. Hines plays a savvy New York City mayoral assistant who, upon receiving a picture of his father being lynched, returns to his Southern birthplace to uncover the truth behind the murder. One of the many interesting plot developments is having a black actor essay the role of the usually white Southern "redneck" sheriff (played with great relish by Nunn). ★★★½ VHS: $9.99

White Man's Burden

(1995, 89 min, US, Desmond Nakano) *John Travolta, Harry Belafonte, Kelly Lynch, Margaret Avery, Sheryl Lee Ralph, Carrie Snodgress.* Taking the thought-provoking premise of the races switched on the economic and social levels, *White Man's Burden* is an intriguing idea which is only occasionally realized. In a world parallel to 1990s America except that whites are the minority and blacks are the ruling power, Travolta plays a hardworking family man who is fired after an misunderstanding. Unable to secure other work, thrown out of his home and at the end of his rope, Travolta's attempt to extort money from his former boss (Belafonte) eventually leads to kidnapping him. The beginning of the film is particularly good in establishing this society, but once the "gimmick" has been set, the story has trouble elaborating on its concept and a scenario of two men at odds with stereotypes rather than each other. ★★½ VHS: $19.99; DVD: $14.99

White Men Can't Jump

(1992, 115 min, US, Ron Shelton) *Wesley Snipes, Woody Harrelson, Rosie Perez, Tyra Ferrell, Kadeem Hardison.* Snipes is a street-smart Venice Beach basketball hustler. He's black. Harrelson is a bumpkin-looking basketball hustler. He's white. A most entertaining and hip comedy emerges when these two hoop con artists team up to sucker the denizens of Southern California's hard courts. It's a great sting: Snipes gets into a game and ultimately brings in rube Harrelson. Who could resist going one-on-one with the Great White Dork? In his first two films, Shelton proved himself to be a master of romantic repartee. Here, the snap and sizzle of a verbal rebound, the volley of masculine bombastics is what distinguishes Shelton's energized film — that and some truly remarkable court footage. Perez is quite good as Harrelson's girlfriend whose dream is to be a "Jeopardy" contestant. ★★★ VHS: $14.99; DVD: $29.99

White Mischief

(1988, 106 min, GB, Michael Radford) *Greta Scacchi, Charles Dance, Sarah Miles, Joss Ackland, Murray Head.* Lavishly entertaining and very sexy drama about English pleasure-seekers living in the "Happy Valley" in Kenya during WWII. Scacchi is both beautiful and ideally cast as a bored wife whose affair with an English lord (Dance) leads to murder. Miles and Head steal the show as cynical hedonists searching for the next party. Ackland gives a great performance as Scacchi's cuckold husband. ★★★

White Nights

(1957, 94 min, Italy, Luchino Visconti) *Marcello Mastroianni, Maria Schell, Jean Marais.* Based on a Fedor Dostoevsky short story and set within a misty, dreamlike seaside city, this sad love story was a great stylistic departure from Visconti's previous, neorealist features, *Senso* and *Ossessione*. Mastroianni stars as a young man, prowling the docks for a pick-up, who meets and fatefully falls in love with a mysterious, obsessive woman (Schell). In a series of brief walks, chases and attempted escapes, she reveals to him that she is waiting for her lover who, before going to sea, promised to return to her. While talking only of her long-gone lover (Marais), the two develop a relationship, but one destined to end in tragedy. (Italian with English subtitles) ★★★ VHS: $59.99

White Nights

(1985, 135 min, US, Taylor Hackford) *Gregory Hines, Mikhail Baryshnikov, Isabella Rossellini, Helen Mirren, Geraldine Page.* In probably the first musical political thriller, Baryshnikov stars as a Russian defector whose plane crash lands him back in the USSR. Hines is an American defector who befriends him. Though far more successful in its musical moments (which features terrific dancing by the two stars) than the convoluted political aspects, there's enough suspense and plot twists to keep most viewers involved. ★★½ VHS: $9.99

White of the Eye

(1987, 110 min, US, Donald Cammell) *David Keith, Cathy Moriarty.* What on the surface appears to be just another psycho-on-the-loose thriller is actually a visually rich and offbeat sleeper, a suspense movie that cooly seduces you and then takes you in strange, unexpected directions. Some of director Cammell's hallucinatory imagery is reminiscent of his collaborations with Nicolas Roeg in the early '70s. A rare performance by the sublime Moriarty makes this an especially rewarding film. ★★★ VHS: $14.99

White Palace

(1990, 104 min, US, Luis Mandoki) *Susan Sarandon, James Spader, Jason Alexander, Eileen Brennan, Kathy Bates, Steven Hill.* That age-old story of two unlikely people overcoming differences in age and background to find true love receives a fresh injection of star power in this touching romantic comedy. Sarandon and Spader star as, respectively, an earthy, 40-something burger joint queen and an uptight, late-20s Jewish yuppie. Though *White Palace* may be slightly sentimental and formulaic, Spader and Sarandon are as classically mismatched as any classically mismatched couple to come before them and both deliver sparkling performances: together they simply ooze sexuality. A real audience pleaser, with a few surprises and plenty of wit. ★★★; DVD: $19.99

The White Rose

(1982, 108 min, West Germany, Michael Verhoeven) *Lena Stoltze, Wulf Kessler.* This superb wartime thriller is based on the true story of a secret society of students who printed and distributed thousands of anti-Nazi leaflets under the Fuhrer's very nose, reporting the murder of 300,000 Jews and urging the citizenry to sabotage the war effort. Their ill-fated but extraordinary efforts are vividly brought to the screen by Verhoeven. (German with English subtitles) ★★★½

White Sands

(1992, 101 min, US, Roger Donaldson) *Willem Dafoe, Mickey Rourke, Mary Elizabeth Mastrantonio, Samuel L. Jackson, M. Emmet Walsh.* An exciting quasi-political thriller with Dafoe as a small-town sheriff who finds a body with a suitcase full of cash and decides to investigate, much to the chagrin of drugs- and arms-runner Rourke. Mastrantonio is a whiny socialite who believes that crime does pay, and Jackson is the FBI agent on the case. ★★★ VHS: $14.99; DVD: $14.99

The White Sheik

(1951, 88 min, Italy, Federico Fellini) *Alberto Sordi, Giulietta Masina.* Fellini's first solo directorial effort is also his only full-fledged farce. Told with almost slapstick enthusiasm, the story follows the misadventures of a provincial couple honeymooning in Rome. The young wife wanders upon the filming of a low-brow picture and becomes infatuated with the "hero" — the White Sheik, a bungling and slightly effeminate Rudolph Valentino imitator. Passion drives her to mad pursuit of the actor while her baffled husband searches the Eternal City for his lost wife. (Italian with English subtitles) ★★★ VHS: $29.99

White Squall

(1996, 127 min, US, Ridley Scott) *Jeff Bridges, Caroline Goodall, John Savage, Scott Wolf, Jeremy Sisto, Zeljko Ivanek, Balthazar Getty.* Though its story line is never really elevated above a "*Dead Poets Society* Go Boating" scenario, *White Squall* nevertheless manages to sustain interest thanks to some exceptional action scenes and the always reliable Bridges. Set during the early 1960s, the story centers on a group of high school teens summering on a "floating prep school" headed by Captain Jeff. The first half of the film essentially examines the varying relationships between the kids (some troubled, some naïve, etc.) in very familiar fashion. However, the film's second half changes course when the titular storm, a sudden and violent torrent of water, engulfs and capsizes the ship and the crew members are left to fend for their lives. Director Scott handles the storm sequences with great assurance, but he's not as fortunate in creating totally believable dramatics between the young protagonists. ★★½ VHS: $14.99; DVD: $29.99

White Zombie

(1932, 73 min, US, Victor Halperin) *Bela Lugosi, Madge Bellamy.* Lugosi stars in this entertaining chiller as a warped magician who uses his powers to raise the dead and supply zombie laborers for a sinister plantation owner. ★★★ VHS: $19.99

Who Am I This Time

(1982, 60 min, US, Jonathan Demme) *Christopher Walken, Susan Sarandon.* Demme, whose films lovingly exalt more unconventional characters, is right at home with this delightfully offbeat romantic comedy based on the Kurt Vonnegut, Jr. short story. Walken plays a painfully shy clerk who only comes alive when performing at the local theatre — taking on the characteristics of the role he's playing. Sarandon is a lonely newcomer who falls for the chameleon man, forcing her to use her feminine wiles, not to mention some of the theatre's great works, to keep his attention. Walken and Sarandon are remarkable; their performance of "A Streetcar Named Desire" makes you long for a full-length version. ★★★½ VHS: $19.99

Who Done It?

(1942, 75 min, US, Eric C. Kenton) *Bud Abbott, Lou Costello, Mary Wickes, William Bendix.* An uproarious Abbott and Costello romp, with Bud and Lou as a couple of soda jerks trying to break into radio who masquerade as private detectives after an on-the-air murder. ★★★ VHS: $14.99

Who Framed Roger Rabbit

(1988, 103 min, US, Robert Zemeckis) *Bob Hoskins, Christopher Lloyd, Joanna Cassidy, Stubby Kaye; Voices of: Charles Fleischer, Kathleen Turner, Mae Questel.* Superb animation, almost every beloved cartoon character in our movie history and state-of-the-art special effects combine to produce one of the most glorious entertainments of the decade. Hoskins is a 1940s private detective hired to find out just who did frame Roger Rabbit, that successful, debonair and handsome animated cartoon hero. A toon-ful modern classic. ★★★★ VHS: $9.99; DVD: $29.99

Who Shall Live and Who Shall Die

(1982, 90 min, US, Lawrence Jarvick) This searing documentary utilizes previously classified information and rare newsreel footage to probe into the issue of how much the United States government knew of the Holocaust and asks the hard question, "Could the Jews of Europe have been saved?" A unique inquiry into the actions and motives of American Jewish leaders in the 1930s and '40s as well as those of the government of President Roosevelt. ★★★ VHS: $29.99

Who Slew Auntie Roo

(1971, 90 min, US, Curtis Harrington) *Shelley Winters, Mark Lester, Ralph Richardson, Lionel Jeffries.* A kindly old widow's annual Christmas party for the local orphans takes a macabre, unexpected twist. A tame though spoofy foray into '70s Gothic horror. ★★½ VHS: $69.99

Who'll Stop the Rain

(1978, 126 min, US, Karel Reisz) *Nick Nolte, Michael Moriarty, Tuesday Weld.* Nolte gives a riveting performance as an ex-marine transporting heroin from Saigon to the U.S. during the Vietnam War, finding himself set up for a drug bust. ★★★ VHS: $14.99; DVD: $19.99

Who's Afraid of Virginia Woolf?

(1966, 129 min, US, Mike Nichols) *Richard Burton, Elizabeth Taylor, Sandy Dennis, George Segal.* Burton and Taylor deliver career best performances as a tortured college professor and his vitriolic wife in Edward Albee's scorching domestic drama. Segal and Dennis (at her mousiest) are the innocent young couple who spend a gut-wrenching, soul-baring evening with lush-ious Liz and down-and-out Dick. Brilliantly directed by Nichols. ★★★★ VHS: $19.99; DVD: $19.99

Who's Harry Crumb?

(1989, 98 min, US, Paul Flaherty) *John Candy, Jeffrey Jones, Annie Potts.* For the answer to the question posed by the title of this film, please choose one of the following: a) Who cares b) an imbecilic moron c) a bumbling private detective assigned to a kidnapping case, only because his boss is the kidnapper and the bad guy knows Crumb is too stupid to crack the case d) a character in a film which contains no wit and predictable sight gags e) all of the above. If you chose "e," you are correct. ★ VHS: $9.99; DVD: $19.99

Who's Singing Over There

(1985, 95 min, Yugoslavia, Slobodan Sijan) Gifted young director Sijan has created this comic, poignant anti-war satire set in Yugoslavia on the eve of the Nazi invasion. He contrasts the petty squabbles of the wild, provincial characters that have boarded a Belgrade-bound bus with our awareness of the catastrophic events that are about to occcur. (Serbo-Croatian with English subtitles) ★★★

Who's That Girl

(1987, 94 min, US, James Foley) *Madonna, Griffin Dunne, John Mills.* Madonna plays a spunky parolee out to clear her name who totally changes forever the mild existence of yuppie Dunne. An awkward attempt at screwball comedy. ★ VHS: $14.99

Who's That Knocking at My Door?

(1968, 90 min, US, Martin Scorsese) *Harvey Keitel, Zina Bethune.* Scorsese's first feature film is a fascinating and highly charged drama that is essentially a primer for his breakthrough film, *Mean Streets.* Clearly autobiographical, the story features a muscular and baby-faced Keitel in the lead as a confused young man in New York's Little Italy obsessed with the moralistic trappings of Catholicism and indecisive about committing himself to a serious relationship with his girlfriend (Bethune). Scorsese's directorial talent and promise is much in evidence in this gritty and at times arty debut. ★★★ VHS: $19.99

Who's the Man

(1993, 90 min, US, Ted Demme) *Ed Lover, Doctor Dre, Denis Leary, Ice T., Queen Latifah.* Yo! MTV rap hosts Dre and Lover star as an inept pair of barbers who somehow become New York cops in this crazy hip-hop "Homeywood" laugher. The film focuses on the authority-questioning stars' mission to clean up their crumbling Harlem neighborhood and stop a nefarious real estate speculator's plan to gentrify the once-thriving area. Some witty urban humor highlights this otherwise silly comedy. ★★½ VHS: $14.99

Who's Who

(1978, 75 min, GB, Mike Leigh) *Bridget Kane, Simon Chandler, Adam Norton.* In one of his earliest films, director Leigh — who has proved to be a master at letting his camera "eavesdrop" on the mundane daily lives of England's working class — sets his sights on a group of London stock traders. Though slowly paced, the film elicits some hilarious skewerings of the British caste system as he focuses on these brokerage employees: One a group of over-priivileged, upper-class twits who hold a dinner party, the other middle-class Thatcherites whose loyalty to Crown and country borders on the surreal. ★★★ VHS: $29.99

Whoever Says the Truth Shall Die

(1981, 60 min, The Netherlands/Italy, Philo Bregstein) Pier Paolo Pasolini, Italy's celebrated and controversial poet/novelist/filmmaker, was violently and senselessly murdered by a young male prostitute in 1975. This provocative documentary probes into Pasolini's life and work in an effort to come to some understanding of the events which led up to his death. From interviews with Bernardo Bertolucci and Alberto Moravia, clips from his many films as well as biographical background, the film attempts to enter the private life of the director, who had a masochistic fascination with society's taboos and its unwanted denizens. Was he killed in a freakish isolated incident or was he assassinated? (Italian with English subtitles) ★★★ VHS: $59.99

The Whole Nine Yards

(2000, 110 min, US, Jonathan Lynn) *Bruce Willis, Matthew Perry, Natasha Henstridge, Michael Clarke Duncan, Rosanna Arquette, Amanda Peet, Kevin Pollak.* Combining gangster shenanigans with pratfalls galore, *The Whole Nine Yards* is a dark comedy that ill-advisedly includes too many ingredients in the mix. Unfocused, often slowly paced and not all that funny, the film wastes the promising premise of a guy-next-door (here living in Montreal), Oz (Perry), who learns his new neighbor is none other than the notorious Jimmy "The Tulip" Tudeski (Willis), a mob hit man turned informant. When Oz's wife convinces him to rat on Jimmy, he's thrust into an underworld Wonderland with Oz as a slapstick Alice. Perry is amiable doing his nice-guy schtick, though Peet is the best here as a would-be assassin. Director Lynn seems to be missing a beat with much of the comedy, and too many scenes lack snap. ★★ VHS: $14.99; DVD: $24.99

The Whole Wide World

(1996, 111 min, US, Dan Ireland) *Vincent D'Onofrio, Renee Zellweger, Ann Wedgeworth, Harve Presnell.* Schoolteacher and aspiring writer Novalyne Price befriends an unusual, brusque pulp writer named Robert E. Howard (creator of the "Conan" series) in 1930s Texas. Based on Price's memoirs, *The Whole Wide World* follows their rocky relationship and the strains it withstands from his domineering mother, his adament nonconformity and the simpleminded townsfolk's disapproval. Ireland captures the atmosphere and pace of small-town Depression-era Americana beautifully, while D'Onofrio and Zellweger are both superb. Despite a rather uneven score and slight overlength, *The Whole Wide World* is an engaging, richly textured drama. ★★★ VHS: $24.99

Whoopee!

(1930, 93 min, US, Thornton Freeland) *Eddie Cantor, Eleanor Hunt, Paul Gregory.* Cantor, re-creating his 1929 stage smash, is an absolute joy as a hypochondriac who heads West for his health and becomes involved in the locals' crazy shenanigans. Though some of the songs (those not sung by Cantor) are horribly out-of-date (fast-forward buttons will be pushed), the film does feature some interesting Busby Berkeley production numbers, as well as funny one-liners and, of course, the title tune. For those not familiar with Cantor, this is the place

W

to start to become acquainted with the most popular comedian of his time. ★★★

Whore

(1991, 92 min, GB, US, Ken Russell) *Theresa Russell, Antonio Vargas.* The notorious Ken Russell, in a kind of follow-up to *Crimes of Passion*, takes a less-successful walk down those streets of despair, leaving behind his bag of psychedelic tricks. Sadly, what is intended as a searing insight into the world of prostitution completely misses the mark under Russell's histrionic mis-direction. Russell sleepwalks, er, streetwalks through this talky tale of a hooker on the run from her psychotic pimp. ★ VHS: $14.99

Whose Life Is It Anyway?

(1981, 118 min, US, John Badham) *Richard Dreyfuss, John Cassavetes, Christine Lahti, Kenneth McMillan, Bob Balaban.* First-rate screen version of Brian Clark's award-winning play starring Dreyfuss in a moving performance as an artist who, paralyzed from the neck down after an auto accident, petitions on the right to die. Though the subject matter sounds terribly depressing, the film is alive with a sardonic wit and features compelling performances from the supporting cast. ★★★ VHS: $79.99

Why Do Fools Fall in Love

(1998, 112 min, US, Gregory Nava) *Larenz Tate, Halle Berry, Viveca A. Fox, Lela Rochon, Little Richard.* An energetic courtroom drama/musical biography of Frankie Lymon, *Why Do Fools Fall in Love* tells the story of the 1950s doo-wop singer/songwriter from the perspective of his three widows, each of whom is fighting for his estate. Director Nava's film milks the story for all its sensationalism, emphasizing the cattiness of the spurned women: Elizabeth (Fox), Zola (Berry), and Emira (Rochon), as they recall how Frankie (Tate) treated them. While *Fools* is enjoyable because it plays like a soap opera, it adresses some of its serious themes — racism, drug addiction, and the improprieties of music executives — too casually. Tate is magnetic as Lymon, and Fox makes the best impression if only because she is the most vocal of the three women. ★★½ VHS: $9.99; DVD: $14.99

Why Does Herr R. Run Amok

(1970, 88 min, Germany, Rainer Werner Fassbinder) *Kurt Raab, Hanna Schygulla.* This devastating thriller on social conformity and the petit bourgeosie stars Raab as Herr R., a successful professional who inexplicably (yet in Fassbinder's thinking, inevitably) goes berserk and takes his own life; but not before killing his wife, a neighbor and his little son. A doomed, taut polemic of failed expectations and the banality of existence. (German with English subtitles) ★★★½

Why Shoot the Teacher?

(1976, 99 min, Canada, Silvio Narizzano) *Bud Cort, Samantha Eggar.* An amiable yet touching story of a dedicated schoolteacher (Cort) who faces the grim realities of life when he is hired to teach the children of an impoverished farming town in Alberta, Canada, during the Great Depression. Initially spurned by the adults, his icy reception soon changes to acceptance as he gradually adjusts to the difficult conditions and begins to understand his pupils and their way of

life. An earnest and, at times, humorous film impressively directed. ★★★

Wicked City

(1992, 95 min, Hong Kong, Mak Tai Kit) *Tatsuya Nakadai.* The popular Japanese adult anime is given a hyperkinetic going-over in the inimitable Hong Kong style in this very entertaining live-action version. The sex and violence of the original have been significantly toned down and the story has been vastly altered as, this time around, we follow the adventures of two agents in the Anti-Reptoid Bureau, dedicated to hunting down and destroying renegade Reptoids — other-dimensional evil beings dedicated to the destruction of humanity. A forthcoming peace conference between the Reptoid leader (Nakadai) and a human delegation is threatened when treacherous elements in the Reptoid community plan a sabotage campaign. A wild and fun visual feast, the film sometimes sacrifices the cohesiveness of the plot in favor of a spectacular effect or action sequence. But what sequences they are. (English and Mandarin with English subtitles) ★★★ VHS: $14.99; DVD: $24.99

The Wicked Lady

(1945, 104 min, GB, Leslie Arliss) *James Mason, Margaret Lockwood, Michael Rennie.* This tame period melodrama stars Lockwood as an amoral, thrill-seeking aristocrat who teams up with highwayman Mason to embark on a life of crime. Released just after the end of WWII, the film caused a stir in its day on account of its bawdiness and perhaps the abundance of Ms. Lockwood's cleavage. (Remade in 1983) ★★½

The Wicked Lady

(1983, 98 min, GB, Michael Winner) *Faye Dunaway, Alan Bates, John Gielgud, Denholm Elliott.* Awkward remake of the 1945 programmer, this time with Dunaway camping it up as the British noblewoman by day and highway bandit by night. The film reflects the slipshod production usually associated with Cannon Films, and qualifies only as a guilty pleasure at best. ★½

Wicked Stepmother

(1988, 90 min, US, Larry Cohen) *Bette Davis, Barbara Carrera.* A witch (Davis) and her daughter (Carrera) make a living at marrying rich widowers, shrinking them to shoebox size, and absconding with their money. Davis, in her last film, withdrew from this dreadful project, and a double was used in many scenes. ★ VHS: $14.99

The Wicker Man

(1973, 87 min, GB, Robin Hardy) *Christopher Lee, Britt Ekland, Edward Woodward.* A policeman visits a mysterious Scottish island to investigate the disappearance of a young girl. He discovers a pagan society, ruled by Lee, which has some surprises in store for him. The policeman gets a little heated up when he discovers the town's plans for a human sacrifice. A classic horror thriller in the Hammer tradition. ★★★

Wide Awake

(1998, 100 min, US, M. Night Shyamalan) *Denis Leary, Dana Delany, Robert Loggia, Joseph Cross, Timothy Reifsnyder, Rosie O'Donnell.* Another story about a wise-beyond-his-years fifth grader, *Wide Awake* is an ambitious but ultimately unsuccess-

ful look at a young boy's struggle with religious faith. Obviously, the film is a labor of love for writer-director Shyamalan, but the story about Johua Beal (Cross), and his quest to find God, lacks an appropriate epiphany. As Joshua grapples with losing his grandfather (Loggia), discovering the troubles other kids in his class are having, and finding his own place in life, his adventures are meant to be charming. They are not. Much of the drama is forced, and the hackneyed school situations have no depth. ★★ VHS: $14.99; DVD: $29.99

Wide Sargasso Sea

(1993, 100 min, Australia, John Duigan) *Karina Lombard, Nathaniel Parker, Rachel Ward, Michael York.* Sort of a prequel to Emily Brontë's "Jane Eyre," *Wide Sargasso Sea* reinterprets and updates the story and locates it on the steamy beaches of Jamaica. The story is told from the perspective of Rochester's (Parker) first wife, Antoinette (Lombard), a beautiful Creole woman whose family has a foreboding history. A tale of betrayal, love, madness and power, much of the subtext is ripped from the original novel turning the first half of this film adaptation into a semi-erotic mish-mash filled with shots of full frontal nudity, both male and female. Things pick up, however, in the second half when the story returns to its roots, focusing on the magical traditions of the island's people. ★★ VHS: $19.99

Widow Coudorc

(1974, 92 min, France, Pierre Granier-Deferre) *Simone Signoret, Alain Delon.* Based on a novel by Georges Simenon, this excellent thriller features Signoret as a lonely widow who falls in love with a dangerous escaped convict. Similar in theme to the Catherine Deneuve drama, *Scene of the Crime.* (French with English subtitles) ★★★

The Widow of St. Pierre

(2001, 107 min, France, Patrice Leconte) *Juliette Binoche, Daniel Auteuil, Emir Kusturica, Philippe Magnan.* Stately composition and measured pacing inform director Leconte's treatment of actual events set in 1850 on the island of St. Pierre. Based on court records, the story recounts the aftermath of a childish prank by two drunks, resulting in murder. French justice of the time demands the guillotine, which must be transported to the remote fishing village. In the ensuing months, the townsfolk debate the intracacies and implications of capital punishment, a discussion made more complicated by the intended recipient, who shows true remorse and has become a fully integrated member of the community. Also brought into the fore is the unique character of the captain and his wife, whose developing relationship with the criminal underscores the couple's differences from the rest of the island community. The three principal players (Binoche, Auteuil, Kusturica) deliver deliberate and thoughtful performances, involving the viewer in each of their internal reflections as much as in the course of events. An involving, intelligent film. (French with English subtitles) ★★★½ VHS: $102.99; DVD: $29.99

Widows' Peak

(1994, 101 min, GB, John Irvin) *Mia Farrow, Natasha Richardson, Joan Plowright, Jim Broadbent,*

Adrian Dunbar. This lavish romp combines elements of Agatha Christie, *The Sting* and a little Merchant Ivory thrown in for extra measure. Plowright is the grand dame of a small 1920s Irish village beset by scandal when the personality clash between the town spinster (Farrow) and a free-spirited, newly arrived war widow (impeccably played by Richardson) gets out of hand. Plowright, the soul of decorum, takes it upon herself to keep the peace, and the results are humorously disastrous. Sparkling performances and bitchy dialogue help make *Widows' Peak* a delight. ★★★ VHS: $19.99

The Wife

(1996, 90 min, US, Tom Noonan) *Julie Hagerty, Tom Noonan, Wallace Shawn, Karen Young.* This claustrophobic little oddity stars Hagerty and Noonan as a couple of New Age therapists whose Sunday evening quiet is shattered when one of their patients (Shawn) and his ex-stripper wife (Young) unexpectedly show up at their door. It becomes immediately clear that Young is a bull in an emotional china shop as she peppers her hosts with embarrassing questions and makes untoward remarks about her husband. As the evening progresses it becomes increasingly evident that the doctors need to heal themselves. Nice camera work and editing make *The Wife* feel more zippy than it actually is, but the film can't quite rise above its "small" premise. (Letterboxed) ★★½ VHS: $19.99

Wife vs. Secretary

(1936, 88 min, US, Clarence Brown) *Clark Gable, Myrna Loy, Jean Harlow, May Robson, James Stewart.* Another formulaic '30s love triangle, helped immensely by three very attractive leading performances. Gable stars as a successful publisher married to Loy. Harlow is his devoted secretary who becomes invaluable to him on a costly and time-consuming project, prompting the titular contest. ★★½ VHS: $19.99

Wifemistress

(1977, 110 min, Italy, Marco Vicario) *Marcello Mastroianni, Laura Antonelli.* Antonelli is a repressed, bedridden housewife until husband Mastroianni's clandestine affairs and flight from justice prod her into action. A spirited, erotic comedy-drama. ★★★

Wigstock: The Movie

(1995, 85 min, US, Barry Shils) *Lady Bunny, Lypsinka, RuPaul, Alexis Arquette, Jackie Beat.* The boisterously extravagant, unabashedly camp, uninhibitedly costumed cross-dressing Labor Day extravaganza known as Wigstock is captured in all of its sequined and tacky glory in this spirited documentary. Recorded during the 1993 event in Tompkins Square Park and the 1994 event held on a West Village pier, we get a behind-the-scenes as well as an on-stage look at the fabulously frocked organizers, the surprisingly professional performers, and thoughts from its entranced audience. Director Shils' film is more authentic than *To Wong Foo* and *Priscilla*, but less enlightening than Jennie Livingston's *Paris Is Burning.* ★★½ VHS: $14.99

The Wild Angels

(1966, 124 min, US, Roger Corman) *Peter Fonda, Bruce Dern, Nancy Sinatra, Diane Ladd.* Fonda heads a group of fanatical motorcyclists bent on living their lives totally free of responsibility. This box-office hit started the '60s cycle film rage. ★★½ VHS: $9.99; DVD: $14.99

Wild at Heart

(1990, 124 min, US, David Lynch) *Nicolas Cage, Laura Dern, Willem Dafoe, Diane Ladd.* Lynch's dizzying, high-speed, high-energy love story follows the randy exploits of Sailor (Cage) and Lula, aka Peanut (Dern), as they wantonly cruise across the country. Cage and Dern deliver blistering performances as the loopy lovebirds. Oscar-nominee Ladd, Dern's real-life mom, is superb as her screen mom, a nightmarishly alcoholic and emotionally distressed witch who tries to derail the young lovers' romance. Dafoe steals the show with his portrayal of the ultimate "sleazoid," Bobby Peru. Filled with hilarious one-liners, some brutal violence and a lot of sweaty sex, *Wild at Heart* is an outrageous frolic that's "hotter than Georgia asphalt." ★★★

Wild Bill

(1995, 98 min, US, Walter Hill) *Jeff Bridges, Ellen Barkin, John Hurt, Diane Lane, Keith Carradine, David Arquette, Christina Applegate.* Hill's attempt to de-mythologize the legendary gunfighter and marshal is a superficial account of his last days, with a few interesting flashbacks thrown in for good measure. Bridges, though, is exceptional as the titular antihero, who comes to the town of Deadwood hoping to spend some quiet days and enjoy the status of living legend. Several vengeance-seeking characters have also come to Deadwood, providing the film with numerous showdowns. Barkin is a larger-than-life Calamity Jane who wants to rekindle a relationship with Bill. Hill seems to be trying to attain the level of *The Man Who Shot Liberty Valance* in its deconstruction of a hero. He falls short of the mark, but does manage to present a generally tedious but somewhat entertaining character study of a character we really don't get to know. ★★ VHS: $9.99; DVD: $19.99

The Wild Bunch

(1969, 144 min, US, Sam Peckinpah) *William Holden, Ernest Borgnine, Robert Ryan, Edmond O'Brien, Warren Oates.* Widely considered to be Peckinpah's best work, *The Wild Bunch* is a masterful piece of filmmaking, a mesmerizing treatment of contemporary American mythology utilizing to the fullest degree all aspects of the craft. The director incorporates exquisite cinematography, precision editing, arresting sound treatment and plot structure; each frame is composed with diligent care. In exploring personal rivalry within the human propensity to cling steadfastly to dying ways of life, and set within complex choreographies of violent action, Peckinpah moves from sweeping vistas to minute detail, restructuring time and place with balletic grace. This restored version runs 144 minutes, matching the European theatrical running time, an additional 10 minutes over the original U.S. running time. (Letterboxed) ★★★★ VHS: $14.99; DVD: $19.99

The Wild Duck

(1983, 96 min, Australia, Henri Safran) *Jeremy Irons, Liv Ullmann, Lucinda Jones.* An updated adaptation of Henrik Ibsen's play about the foibles of the Ekdal (Anglicized here to "Ackland") family. The production as a whole is uneven, but Irons' performance earns the viewers' attention. ★★

Wild Hearts Can't Be Broken

(1991, 89 min, US, Steve Miner) *Cliff Robertson, Gabrielle Anwar, Michael Schoeffling.* Anwar shines as Sonora, a teenaged orphan who follows her dream of becoming a horseback "diving girl" during the Depression. Robertson plays the traveling showman who gives her her big break. Although it's occasionally predictable and affected, this true story is inspiring and entertaining. ★★★ VHS: $9.99

Wild Horses

(1982, 88 min, New Zealand, Derek Morton) *Keith Aberdein, John Bach.* This exciting modern-day "western" is based on a true story about an enterprising city worker who captures and sells off the wild horses in Australia's national parks. His wrangling is soon confronted by a group of people who think that the horses are a nuisance and should be killed. A nail-biting climax ends this enjoyable feature. ★★★

Wild in the Streets

(1968, 97 min, US, Barry Shear) *Christopher Jones, Shelley Winters, Hal Holbrook, Millie Perkins, Richard Pryor.* A rock star gets the voting age lowered to 14, becomes President, and promptly has everyone over 30 carted off to internment camps. A '60s camp classic. ★★½

Wild Man Blues

(1998, 103 min, US, Barbara Kopple) After all sorts of creepy accusations, protracted legal battles and the breakup with Mia Farrow, Woody Allen has never been the same. How to show, then, that he's the same, old schlemiel we've known and loved for years? Commission this highly entertaining, revealing look into Allen's life, chronicling a 1996 European concert tour he took with his Dixieland band. Director Kopple was given all sorts of access to Allen, although he had say over final cut. Woody is the stressed, hypochondical, pampered American filmmaker, and his need for nurturing is obvious when we meet his elderly parents. Neither are impressed with their son's success. Dad shows more interest in the engraving of Woody's award, while Mom wishes he had chosen another profession. Oh, well. That's showbiz. ★★★ VHS: $19.99

The Wild One

(1954, 79 min, US, Laslo Beneder) *Marlon Brando, Lee Marvin, Mary Murphy.* Brando dons his leather, mounts his bike and leads his roughneck motorcycle gang into a small, staid town, wreaking havoc with every snear and mumble. A powerful performance well complemented by Marvin as an equally nasty hog rider. ★★★½ VHS: $19.99; DVD: $29.99

Wild Orchid

(1990, 103 min, US, Zalman King) *Mickey Rourke, Carrie Otis, Jacqueline Bisset.* A match made in smarm heaven: the movie's King of Kinks, Rourke, teams with King, who wrote *9½ Weeks* and then made his debut behind the camera with Sherilyn Fenn in *Two Moon Junction.* There's little in the way of intelligence on display here and the sex has moved further south — to Rio. ★

Wild Things

The Wild Party

(1975, 107 min, US, **James Ivory**) *James Coco, Raquel Welch, Perry King.* Veteran character actor Coco gives a poignant performance in a rare lead role as a fading silent comic. The wild Hollywood party is supposed to harken his comeback but ends in tragedy. This early Merchant Ivory production is loosely based on the Fatty Arbuckle scandal of the 1920s. ★★★

Wild Reeds (Les Roseaux Sauvages)

(1994, 110 min, France, **Andre Techine**) *Gael Morel, Stephane Rideau, Elodie Bouchez, Frédéric Gorny.* One of the most affecting depictions of gay first love ever committed to screen, this tender and knowing drama touchingly deals with friendship, coming out and teenage sexuality, all set against the political turmoil of the 1962 French/Algerian conflict. Set in a rural boarding school, the story revolves around the loves and friendships of three teenagers as well as an Algerian youth of 21. The central character is François (Morel), a handsome youth who falls for a fellow classmate, Serge (Rideau), a muscular student who in turn is attracted to Maite (Bouchez), Serge's best friend and a woman wise beyond her years. Entering this circle is Henri (Gorny), a troubled nationalist Algerian. A poignant drama that captures the universal ecstasy, pain and loneliness of young love. Winner of 1995 César Awards for Best Picture, Screenplay, Actor and Female Discovery. (French with English subtitles) ★★★★ VHS: $14.99; DVD: $19.99

The Wild Ride

(1960, 90 min, US, **Harvey Berman**) *Jack Nicholson, Georgianna Carter.* A gang of roaring hot rodders get to race in the big time in this biker/bad girl/juvenile delinquent/rebel without a cause "gem." (aka: *Velocity*) ★ VHS: $19.99

Wild Rovers

(1971, 138 min, US, **Blake Edwards**) *William Holden, Ryan O'Neal, Karl Malden, Lynn Carlin, Tom Skerritt, Rachel Roberts.* Released in a succes-

sion of box-office flops (*Darling Lili, The Carey Treatment*) by its director, this entertaining, light-hearted western drama got lost in the theatrical shuffle. It would be a shame to miss Holden's wonderful performance and the fine interplay between the film's characters in the story of two cowpokes who rob a bank and are chased through the countryside by a crazed posse. ★★★ VHS: $19.99

Wild Side

(1995, 96 min, US, **Franklin Brauner**) *Christopher Walken, Anne Heche, Steven Bauer, Joan Chen.* The lesbian sleeper of 1995, this torrid love story is packaged in the guise of a standard soft-core action/thriller. Everything that *Showgirls* tried but gloriously failed to be is in this *Wild Side*. Heche is Alex Lee, a banker by day and a high-class hooker by night. Both of her careers are sent in a tailspin after a $1,500 tryst with Bruno Buckingham (Walken), a bug-eyed, high-living businessman with criminal intentions. An elegant and gorgeous Chen is Virginia Chow, Bruno's wife who meets and immediately is attracted to the beautiful Alex. Before she realizes it, Alex is caught up in a plot to inject a computer virus into the national banking system, is a pawn of a sex-crazed FBI man, and in love (with Virginia) for the first time. Method acting never looked so kinky! ★★★ VHS: $14.99; DVD: $24.99

Wild Strawberries

(1957, 93 min, Sweden, **Ingmar Bergman**) *Ingrid Thulin, Victor Sjostrom.* An elderly Stockholm professor (a brilliant Sjostrom) recalls the disappointments of his life while in the company of several boisterous youths. Effortlessly gliding through time, Bergman weaves a shimmering tapestry of memory and sensation. (Swedish with English subtitles) ★★★★ VHS: $29.99

Wild Things

(1998, 108 min, US, **John McNaughton**) *Kevin Bacon, Matt Dillon, Neve Campbell, Theresa Russell, Denise Richards, Daphne Rubin-Vega, Robert Wagner, Bill Murray.* Mix "Melrose Place" with

The Usual Suspects and add some *Faster, Pussycat, Kill! Kill!* for good measure and you may get an idea of what delights this screwy "Florida noir" has to offer. Set primarily in an exclusive Everglades enclave, the film features Dillon as a popular high school counselor who's accused of rape. The supposed victim is the wealthy, spoiled daughter (Richards) of his former slut girlfriend (Russell). Dillon seeks help from a shyster lawyer (Murray), and, after some court-room dramatics, finds himself off the hook — but not for long. With Stephen Peters' herky-jerky script, director McNaughton steers this sucker all over the genre map, careening from courtroom drama to carnal drama, to soap opera to satire and erotic thriller. Does it all make sense? Under close inspection, not really. But why complain? This is an "A" ticket ride in a "C" movie amusement park. ★★★ VHS: $9.99; DVD: $19.99

Wild Wild West

(1999, 107 min, US, **Barry Sonnenfeld**) *Will Smith, Kevin Kline, Kenneth Branagh, Salma Hayek, Ted Levine, M. Emmet Walsh.* Lightning doesn't strike twice for *Men in Black* director Sonnenfeld and star Smith with this bloated, big-screen version of the popular 1960s TV series. Everything that made *Men in Black* exciting and fun is missing here, from a sharply written screenplay full of funny lines and situations to taut direction to chemistry between the two leads. In fact, Smith and Kline seem to be acting in two separate movies. Smith is James West, secret agent par excellence in 1870s America. He's paired with master of disguise Artemus Gordon (Kline), and together they search for master criminal Dr. Arliss Loveless (Branagh). Their adventures bring new meaning to: over the top. There's nothing wild about this west — only garish effects, silly exploits and boring repartee. (VHS available letterboxed or pan & scan) ★ VHS: $14.99; DVD: $19.99

Wildcats

(1986, 107 min, US, **Michael Ritchie**) *Goldie Hawn, James Keach, Swoosie Kurtz, Woody Harrelson, Wesley Snipes.* Hawn is the newly appointed football coach in a ghetto high school. There she comes in conflict with the macho head coach while slowly winning over the players. Goldie makes the best out of this harmless, clichéd comedy; and the film does produce a few laughs. ★★½ VHS: $9.99

Wilde

(1997, 117 min, GB, **Brian Gilbert**) *Stephen Fry, Jude Law, Vanessa Redgrave, Jennifer Ehle, Tom Wilkinson.* Fry makes for an uncannily realistic Oscar Wilde in this sumptuous biopic about the famed 19th-century Irish-born playwright. Director Gilbert's lavishly made film explores Wilde's unconventional lifestyle in Victorian England by tracing his life as family man who slowly succumbs to "the love that dare not speak its name" — one that ultimately leads to his trial and imprisonment. Much of *Wilde* is devoted to Oscar's strained love affair with Bosie (Law), the rich young man who casts a spell over him, and whose father (Wilkinson) wants to put an end to their relationship. While the scenes between Oscar and Bosie show how Wilde comes to accept who he is, episodes in his life depicting his trial, his love for his children, as well as his success as a literary figure flesh out this intimate portrait. In the title role, Fry embodies Wilde, playing him with appropriate wit and panache. A fascinating drama, beautifully filmed, *Wilde* is worthwhile. ★★★ VHS: $21.99

Wilder Napalm

(1993, 109 min, US, Glenn Gordon Caron) *Debra Winger, Dennis Quaid, Arliss Howard, M. Emmet Walsh, Jim Varney.* Reluctant telekinetic pyromaniac Wilder Foudroyant (Howard) matches his incendiary abilities with his equally conflagratory brother Wallace (Quaid) to keep the hand of his fetching pyromaniac wife Vida (Winger). Director Caron, creator of "Moonlighting," manages to retain the gleeful wackiness which permeated that TV show while allowing these accomplished performers sufficient latitude to uncover, layer by layer, telling moments of poignancy. An inventive, witty script and lively pacing contribute to this satisfactory examination of escalating sibling rivalry and lingering childhood guilt. ★★★ VHS: $9.99

Wildfire

(1992, 98 min, US, Zalman King) *Linda Fiorentino, Steven Bauer, Will Patton.* Erotic filmmaker King, long criticized for his excessively steamy forays into female sexuality (*9½ Weeks, Wild Orchid*), finally tones down his act and the result is this castrated drama about a happily married woman (Fiorentino) who must chose between the love of a good man (Patton) and the love of a gorgeous one (Bauer). Only in the sexual safety of the '90s could this be considered a dilemma. ★½ VHS: $79.99

Wildrose

(1984, 96 min, US, John Hanson) *Lisa Eichhorn, Tom Bower.* Eichhorn's perceptive and earnest performance elevates this compassionate drama about a divorced woman who takes a job at an iron works and meets hostility from her all-male coworkers. ★★★

Will Penny

(1968, 108 min, US, Tom Gries) *Charlton Heston, Joan Hackett, Donald Pleasence, Bruce Dern.* Heston gives one of his better performances in this exceptional western saga. Heston plays a weary, middle-aged cowboy who stays in a small town after being left in the desert for dead. He's then forced to fight the gang which left him there. Hackett is splendid as the pioneer woman who rescues him. ★★★½ VHS: $14.99

Will You Dance with Me?

(1959, 89 min, France, Michel Boisrons) *Brigitte Bardot, Henri Vidal.* A typical (for its time) but good, lighthearted crime mystery starring Bardot as a bewitching newlywed who becomes entangled in a web of blackmail and murder. (French with English subtitles) ★★½

Willard

(1971, 95 min, US, Daniel Mann) *Bruce Davison, Sandra Locke, Ernest Borgnine, Elsa Lanchester.* The story of a boy and his rat. This silly but effective horror tale stars Davison as a lonely young man who raises rats — who help him get revenge against those around him. ★★½

William Shakespeare's A Midsummer Night's Dream

(1999, 115 min, US, Michael Hoffman) *Kevin Kline, Michelle Pfeiffer, Rupert Everett, Calista Flockhart, Stanley Tucci, Christian Bale, Dominic West, Anna Friel, David Strathairn, Roger Rees.* A sterling cast helps brings life to Shakespeare's splendiferous comedy, but director Hoffman's sporadic pacing and episodic delivery keeps this from being the magical carpet ride it should have been. Updating the tale to 19th-century Tuscany (this way all the characters can scurry here and there on bicycles), the story remains the same: these foolish mortals come in contact with the fairy world for a night of romantic escapades and misadventures. Hoffman gives the film a spectacular look — his attention to detail is remarkable. But his staging isn't fluid enough to fully capture the whimsy and discord of all these characters flailing about. But what a cast he has assembled. Most memorable are Tucci as a most nimble Puck, Kline as a gloriously over-the-top Bottom, and Everett as a stately Oberon. Not the definitive interpretation, but an able one. ★★★ VHS: $9.99; DVD: $24.99

William Shakespeare's Romeo + Juliet

(1996, 113 min, US/GB, Baz Luhrmann) *Leonardo DiCaprio, Claire Danes, John Leguizamo, Harold Perrineau, Paul Sorvino, Pete Postlethwaite, Diane Venora, Miriam Margolyes, Brian Dennehy.* Can Shakespeare appeal to the MTV crowd? The answer is a resounding "Aye!" in this delirious amalgam of styles, colors and kinetic camera movements. Using the original dialogue of the play (pared down for reasons of length), but reworking almost everything else about the scenario, Luhrmann and company have produced a work which is not only faithful to the original theme and feeling of the piece, but resonates particularly well for contemporary times. Set in a fictional Verona Beach, a neon-drenched cross between Miami and Los Angeles, the story of star-crossed lovers is set between rival business families, each with their own gun-toting gang members and peculiar dysfunctions. As Romeo and Juliet, DiCaprio and Danes perform admirably, too, never letting the Technicolor chaos which surrounds them to overshadow their fine portrayals. (Letterboxed VHS available for $19.99) ★★★★ VHS: $14.99; DVD: $24.99

Willy Wonka and the Chocolate Factory

(1971, 98 min, US, Mel Stuart) *Gene Wilder, Jack Albertson.* A strange and delightful children's musical fantasy, with Wilder as an eccentric candy manufacturer who invites five contest-winning children to his mysterious factory. Songs includes "Candy Man." ★★★ VHS: $22.99; DVD: $24.99

Wilson

(1944, 154 min, US, Henry King) *Alexander Knox, Charles Coburn, Geraldine Fitzgerald, Vincent Price.* Though acclaimed in its day, this reverent biography of America's 28th President has been long lost in the shadows of other 1940s bios. Nominated for Best Picture and winner of five Academy Awards, this sincere and intelligent look at the life of Woodrow Wilson may suffer

from over-glorification, but it is nevertheless a stirring examination of a political career. A history lesson told in cinematic chapters, the film traces Wilson's rise from Princeton University's president to New Jersey's governor to his two terms as commander-in-chief (elected in 1912 and 1916). Knox gives a solid portrayal of Wilson and he is given some inspiring speeches to recite. ★★★½ VHS: $19.99

Winchell

(1998, 108 min, US, Paul Mazursky) *Stanley Tucci, Glenne Headly, Paul Giamatti, Christopher Plummer.* Mazursky's direction replicates Winchell's own staccato delivery, re-created brilliantly by Tucci in an Emmy Award-winning performance that is more channelled than acted. It could be said that Winchell laid the groundwork for the infotainment biz that dominates the airwaves today. He virtually created syndicated gossip, blurring the line between news and entertainment, between politics and performance. From the '30s to the '50s, he didn't just dominate journalism, he redefined it. The film follows the arc of his career, from making a pitch for War Bonds after singing a tune on a vaudeville stage, to aligning with Joseph McCarthy in a twisted permutation of the patriotism of his youth. In a uniformly excellent supporting ensemble, special mention goes to Giamatti as Herman Klurfeld, one of Winchell's crew of ghostwriters and author of the book on which this film is based. *Winchell* delivers the same frenetic entertainment as its subject matter. ★★★½ VHS: $9.99

Winchester '73

(1950, 92 min, US, Anthony Mann) *James Stewart, Millard Mitchell, Shelley Winters, Stephen McNally, Dan Duryea, Rock Hudson, Tony Curtis.* Superior western adventure with Stewart combing the wilderness for his one-of-a-kind rifle and his father's murderer. The film, which features exceptional cinematography, helped bring about the great revival of westerns in the 1950s. ★★★½ VHS: $14.99

Wind

(1992, 123 min, US, Carroll Ballard) *Matthew Modine, Jennifer Grey, Cliff Robertson, Jack Thompson.* A stylishly produced, curiously enjoyable yet formulaic dramatic action story about a maverick sailor and his quest to win the America's Cup, sailing's most coveted prize. Modine and Grey star as the two halves of a boy-and-girl sailing team. She's recently hung up her halyards, however, to pursue a career in aeronautics and he's just been offered to crew on an America's Cup yacht in Newport. Within the first 30 minutes of the film, Modine manages to lose not only his woman, but the Cup too. Can you guess where the script goes from there? Despite its complete predictability, *Wind* does manage to entertain thanks in large part to its remarkably filmed sailing sequences which amply convey the sheer exhilaration of sailing. ★★½ VHS: $14.99

The Wind

(1928, 88 min, US, Victor Sjostrom) *Lillian Gish, Lars Hanson, Montagu Love.* Sjostrom (forever identified as the old man in Ingmar Bergman's *Wild Strawberries*) was a renowned director in Sweden and made one of the greatest silent films over here. Gish gives her most riveting performance as a city-girl newlywed relocated to the desert. After she murders the man who rapes her, he comes back with the howling wind. Sjostrom makes us hear the unrelenting sand storm, the clatter of broken dishes and the footsteps on the wooden floors through brilliant editing and the use of close-ups. ★★★★ VHS: $29.99

The Wind and the Lion

(1975, 120 min, US, John Milius) *Sean Connery, Candice Bergen, Brian Keith, John Huston.* Well-mounted but ultimately muddled adventure film loosely based on an actual event, with Connery as a Moroccan shiek who kidnaps an American widow (Bergen) and her children, setting off an international incident in which President Teddy Roosevelt (Keith) himself becomes involved. ★★½ VHS: $19.99

Windhorse

(1998, 97 min, US/Tibet/China, Paul Wagner) *Dadon, Jampa Kelsang, Richard Chang, Lu Yu, Taije Silverman.* Windhorses are small pieces of paper inscribed with prayers, which are scattered from the tops of Himalayan mountain passes as offerings to the gods. The film opens with two weary travelers coming upon a blanket of them as they cross from Tibet to Nepal. The story then tracks back to the mid-1970s, when the brother and sister travelers were with their cousin, children at play, unwilling witnesses to the assassination of their grandfather at the hands of invading Chinese forces. These three each adapted to circumstances in strikingly different ways: one seeking pop stardom within the dominating Chinese culture, one wallowing in dissolution and self-destruction, and the third inviting great peril by becoming a Buddhist nun. Even as Western tourists roam Lhasa looking for instant karma, Tibetans are imprisoned and tortured for their centuries-old beliefs in the ongoing Chinese attempt to eradicate the indigenous culture. Clandestinely shot by director Wagner, over one-third of the film's cast and crew credits read: "name withheld." A powerful and moving film. (English and in Mandarin and Tibetan with English subtitles) ★★★½ VHS: $29.99

Windom's Way

(1957, 108 min, GB, Ronald Neame) *Peter Finch, Mary Ure.* Peter Finch stars in Neame's thoughtful tale about a British doctor working in a small Malayan village who tries to rally the locals against a Communist insurgency. ★★★

The Window

(1949, 73 min, US, Ted Tetzlaff) *Bobby Driscoll, Barbara Hale, Arthur Kennedy.* A taut, intriguing thriller about a small boy who witnesses a murder, though no one will believe his story. Driscoll is the youth. ★★★½

Window Shopping

(1986, 96 min, France, Chantal Akerman) *Delphine Seyrig, Charles Denner, Lio, Pascale Salkin.* Set within the friendly, artificial confines of Paris' "Toison d'Or" shopping mall, Akerman proves that she is not limited to producing serious, experimental studies with this delightfully witty, tongue-in-cheek musical that pays homage to Jacques Demy and M-G-M musicals. Actually nothing more than a stylish soap opera, the story follows Lili, the manager of a hair salon, and her

various suitors. Plot twists abound, a chorus of shampoo girls break into song and love is always around the corner in this splashy, nonsensical lark that takes delight in its own frothiness while still retaining some insight into love in the modern age. (French with English subtitles) ★★★ VHS: $29.99

Window to Paris

(1993, 101 min, Russia, Yuri Mamin) *Agnes Soral, Sergui Dontsov, Victor Michailov.* This subversively hilarious albeit uneven Russian fantasy follows a music teacher and his new flatmates through a closet door that leads from their decaying St. Petersburg apartment to the opulent streets of Paris, where the stalls are filled with fresh produce and motorcycles litter the sidewalk. The intrepid band, exhausted from eking out a mean existence in a financially depleted Russia, fanatically embrace the opportunity to indulge in material excess. When they discover that the gateway stays open for only a certain period of time, they go for broke in their frenzy of acquisition, their physical experience of spatial refraction matched by the onset of Western ennui. Filmed with kinetic energy and a warm appreciation of human foibles. (Russian and French with English subtitles) ★★★ VHS: $79.99

Wing Chun

(1994, 93 min, Hong Kong, Yuen Woo Ping) *Michelle Yeoh, Donnie Yen, Cheng Pei Pei.* Serious kung fu unfortunately takes a back seat to comedy in this retelling of the story of Yim Wing Chun (Yeoh), a young girl who refined the southern Chinese fighting style eventually named after her. Returning to her village, Wing Chun saves a young widow from bandits after the woman is mistaken for Wing herself. When the widow is kidnapped by the bandits, Wing Chun must refine her martial arts skills in order to defeat the gang's leader. Yuen seems a bit unfocused, alternating between blistering kung fu sequences and some typically absurd Hong Kong comedic tomfoolery. It's an awkward pairing which — while entertaining and funny in places — doesn't work to the fullest effect. (Cantonese with English subtitles) ★★½ VHS: $19.99; DVD: $29.99

Wing Commander

(1999, 99 min, US, Chris Roberts) *Freddie Prinze, Jr., Saffron Burrows, Matthew Lillard, Tchéky Karyo, Jürgen Prochnow, David Warner.* After so many dreary films that have been adapted from video games, the creator of the Wing Commander games steps to the plate, directing one that makes the same old mistakes. The obligatory set-up (the one kids skip through on the Playstation) involves an aged feline race called the Kilrathi who are out to take over the Earth. It's up to Prinze and pals to hop into their space fighters and (despite having invented invisible shields) shoot old-fashioned bullets and torpedoes at other ships. This is akin to watching your little brother play as he hogs the controls. ★ VHS: $9.99; DVD: $34.99

Wings

(1927, 139 min, US, William Wellman) *Gary Cooper, Clara Bow, Charles "Buddy" Rogers, Richard Arlen.* The first film to win the Oscar for Best Picture, this exciting silent war drama fea-

tures good aerial effects to tell the story of two WWI pilots, and their love for the same girl. ★★★ VHS: $14.99

Wings of Desire

(1988, 130 min, West Germany, Wim Wenders) *Bruno Ganz, Solveig Dommartin, Otto Sander, Peter Falk.* A deeply moving and hauntingly beautiful affirmation of the human spirit. Sumptuously photographed in both black and white and color, the film reveals the world as seen by two angels (Ganz, Sander). As they hover over Berlin and listen to the lonely thoughts whispering through the minds of the disenfranchised and forgotten, we are mesmerized by their inherent compassion for humanity. Finally for Ganz's angel, this compassion turns to desire as he feels himself longing to experience the complexities of human emotions. Dommartin is stunning as the trapeze artist whose beauty inspires Ganz to yearn for an earthbound existence. (Sequel: *Faraway, So Close*) (American remake: *City of Angels*) (German with English subtitles) ★★★★ VHS: $19.99

Wings of Fame

(1990, 109 min, GB, Otakar Votocek) *Peter O'Toole, Colin Firth.* They say that fame is fleeting, and in this invigorating drama starring O'Toole (in the familiar role of a boozy Hollywood star), fame's disappearance holds more significance than just losing a good table at Spago's. When Valentin (O'Toole) is killed by what seems like a lunatic fan (Firth), who is then bumped off by a falling spotlight, both victims find themselves in a slightly puzzling hereafter. The island paradise turns out to be inhabited only by those who are dead and famous. When one's fame on Earth disappears, however, so does one's reservations at the island's swank hotel. Resting somewhere in that amorphous gap between comedy and drama, this little "slice of life" (slice of death?) offers a devilishly ponderous glimpse into the great beyond. ★★★ VHS: $7.99

The Wings of the Dove

(1997, 101 min, US, Iain Softley) *Helena Bonham Carter, Linus Roache, Alison Elliott, Charlotte Rampling, Elizabeth McGovern, Michael Gambon.* Set against the splendor of breathtaking Venice, love and romantic deceit blossom in the most unexpected ways in this beautifully realized, haunting version of Henry James' novel. Directed with delicate precision and unnerving melancholy by Softley, *The Wings of the Dove* soars as both a psychological study of conflicted emotions, and a love story gone awry. Bonham Carter is spellbinding as Kate Croy, an aristocrat who has been forbidden to see her lover Merton Densher (Roache), a handsome, working-class journalist. Their affair is put on hold until the arrival of Millie Theale (Elliott), a dying American heiress who is befriended by Kate and smitten with Merton. When they all take a trip to Venice, it is there Kate plots to bring her lover and best friend together. James has never been this satisfying on-screen, and Hossein Amini's smart, fluid screenplay, and a superb ensemble leave little doubt as to why. Elliott gives a subtle portrayal of a spirited woman curtailed by a body less willing. ★★★★ VHS: $19.99; DVD: $29.99

The Winslow Boy

(1999, 110 min, US, David Mamet) *Rebecca Pidgeon, Nigel Hawthorne, Jeremy Northam, Gemma Jones, Guy Edwards, Matthew Pidgeon.* This brilliantly nuanced adaptation of Terence Rattigan's 1946 play (and 1948 British film) finds writer-director Mamet setting aside his rough-hewn characters and rapid-fire profanities and settling down instead into a quiet costume drama that proves he is a writer beyond all previous conceptions of him. The story concerns the obsession that gripped the English in 1910 over a 13-year-old cadet at the Osborne Naval Academy who was accused of stealing a five-shilling postal order. The Winslow family, headed by a stoic but loving patriarch (Hawthorne), rallies around the young lad (Edwards) and demands that he be given a fair trial. His sister (R. Pidgeon), a suffragist, teams with their father and they beg the services of prominent opposition Member of Parliament Sir Robert Morton (Northam) to appeal their case before the government. Mamet interjects the story with wry humor and bubbling romantic tensions that cut through a veil of upper-crust reserve with a most satisfying élan. ★★★★ VHS: $21.99; DVD: $27.99

The Winter Guest

(1998, 110 min, Scotland, Alan Rickman) *Phyllida Law, Emma Thompson, Sheila Reid, Sandra Voe, Arlene Cockburn.* Actor Rickman gets behind the lense to direct this tightly knit little adaptation of Sharman Macdonald's play. Set in a Scottish seaside hamlet where the winter's cold has frozen the sea solid, the action revolves around four separate tête-à-têtes: A couple of elderly women waiting for a bus and obsessing on death; a teenaged boy and girl who nervously flirt aroud the edges of their attraction; two young boys who skip school to spend time at the beach and muse about their impending adolescence; and a bereaved widow (Thompson) whose mother (real-life ma Law), is waging a campaign of relentless acerbity and tough love in an attempt to dislodge her from her icy grieving. Though claustrophobic and stagey, the film's cast never miss a beat, and Rickman keeps the flow of deep introspection moving steadily along. ★★★ VHS: $19.99

Winter Kills

(1979, 97 min, US, William Richert) *Jeff Bridges, John Huston, Anthony Perkins, Richard Boone, Sterling Hayden, Elizabeth Taylor.* Winter Kills is a rare example of a film so wild, so utterly rambuncious and so bursting with invention that it defies description. Bridges is the sole innocent searching for clues to the decade-old assassination of his half-brother, a Kennedy-esque president. What he uncovers is a murky mass of conspiracies and the mammoth excessiveness of his tyrannical father (a hilariously obscene Huston). Don't miss this cynical swipe at the unravelling threads of the Stars and Stripes. ★★★

Winter Light

(1963, 80 min, Sweden, Ingmar Bergman) *Ingrid Thulin, Max von Sydow.* This chilling and powerful story of despair is the second of Bergman's trilogy (the others too being The Silence and Through a Glass Darkly) and for people who want to go over the edge in depression, a double feature with Bresson's *Diary of a*

The Wings of the Dove

Country Priest should do it. The story concerns a disillusioned pastor who loses his vocation and watches as his congregation crumbles along with his faith. (Swedish with English subtitles) ★★★½ VHS: $29.99

Winter of Our Dreams

(1981, 90 min, Australia, John Duigan) *Judy Davis, Bryan Brown, Baz Luhmann.* A decidedly different love story which traces the roots of identity, relationships and life on the edge. Brown stars as a former activist who meets Davis, a junkie hooker who becomes obsessively attached to him. Ms. Davis' incandescent performance is a tremendously moving portrait of misplaced desire and self-abuse. One of the finest films that came out of the Australian New Wave. ★★★½

Winter People

(1989, 110 min, US, Ted Kotcheff) *Kurt Russell, Kelly McGillis, Lloyd Bridges.* A widower (Russell) finds himself caught between two feuding families in the backwoods of the Carolina Mountains during the 1930s. Very little dramatic excitement. ★★; DVD: $14.99

Wired

(1989, 108 min, US, Larry Peerce) *Michael Chiklis, Ray Sharkey, J.T. Walsh.* Dreadful film version of Bob Woodward's novel about the life and death of comedian John Belushi. Chiklis may resemble Belushi, but he can't duplicate any of the comedian's classic bits, and Peerce's static direction and a dull screenplay certainly don't help. ★ VHS: $9.99

Wisdom

(1987, 109 min, US, Emilio Estevez) *Emilio Estevez, Demi Moore, Tom Skerritt, Veronica Cartwright.* Estevez wasn't too wise when he wrote, directed and starred in this mangled social fable about an unemployed man who teams with a young woman (Moore) to become modern-day Robin Hoods. ★ VHS: $14.99

Wise Blood

(1979, 108 min, US, John Huston) *Brad Dourif, Daniel Shor, Harry Dean Stanton, Ned Beatty.* A zealous attack against authority and the follies of faith. A soldier (Dourif) returns to his Southern home town and wages a fanatical rebellion against the repressive values of his upbringing. Based on the Flannery O'Connor novel. ★★★½ VHS: $59.99

Wise Guys

(1986, 91 min, US, Brian De Palma) *Danny DeVito, Joe Piscipo, Ray Sharkey.* This annoying gangster spoof casts DeVito and Piscipo as low-level and bumbling hit men who pull a scam on their boss, only to be set up by him when their sting fails. ★★ VHS: $19.99

Wish You Were Here

(1987, 92 min, GB, David Leland) *Emily Lloyd, Tom Bell.* Lloyd gives a knockout performance in this poignant and well-aimed comedy-drama set in England in the early 1950s. Lloyd perfectly plays a sassy, sexually advanced teenager whose search for fulfillment and escape from her rigid father steers her towards an ill-conceived affair with an older man, familial abandonment, and, ultimately, fervent independence. This could be — although it is not officially — the prequel to *Personal Services*, which was written by director Leland. ★★★½

Wishmaster

(1997, 90 min, US, Robert Kurtzman) *Tammy Lauren, Andrew Divoff, Robert Englund, Tony Todd, Wendy Benson, Chris Lemmon.* Wishmaster has the look and feel of outtakes from cruddy flicks such as *The Horror Show* and *Deadtime Stories*. The nonsensical plot-like events have something to do with the Djinn (who resembles a cross between Spawn and Predator) granting the wishes of anyone who hinders his pursuit of the person who unleashed him from his statue. The acting is poor, the dialogue dopey, and the special effects underwhelming. ★ VHS: $14.99; DVD: $14.99

W

Witch Hunt

(1994, 101 min, US, Paul Schrader) *Dennis Hopper, Penelope Ann Miller, Eric Bogosian, Julian Sands.* Joseph Dougherty, writer of HBO's highly entertaining *Cast a Deadly Spell*, teams up with director Schrader for this whimsical sequel. Set in Hollywood in the 1940s where the art of witchcraft runs rampant, the story follows the adventures of private dick H. Phillip Lovecraft (Hopper), who is hired by a beautiful femme fatale (Miller) to keep a watchful eye on her philandering husband. Lovecraft, who doesn't engage in magic himself, soon comes up against a right-wing, McCarthy-like activist (Bogosian) out to destroy witches once and for all. Great special effects spice up this comical, noir-esque feature, whose sets are designed to create a dreamlike Hollywood where almost anything could happen — even the fetching of Shakespeare to write new scripts. ★★★ VHS: $9.99

Witchboard

(1986, 97 min, US, Kevin S. Tenney) *Tawny Kitaen, Kathleen Wilhoite, Rose Marie.* An evil spirit attempts to possess a young woman (Kitaen) who has been playing with a Ouija board. An occasional fright but another in a long line of schlocky horror tales. ★★½

The Witches

(1990, 91 min, GB, Nicolas Roeg) *Anjelica Huston, Mai Zetterling, Jasen Fisher, Rowan Atkinson, Brenda Blethyn, Jane Horrocks.* Roeg's collaboration with Muppets creator Jim Henson on Roald Dahl's enchanting children's story is a smashing triumph — scary fun for the kids and thoroughly enjoyable for adults. During their vacation in Cornwall, nine-year-old Luke and his witch-wise grandmother come up against a coven of witches holding their annual meeting. Learning of the witches' fiendish plot to turn all of the children in England into mice — and despite being one of the first casualties — little Luke does battle to save his young peers. The majestically camp Huston costars as the evil and hideously ugly Grand High Witch. ★★★½ VHS: $14.99; DVD: $14.99

The Witches of Eastwick

(1987, 118 min, US, George Miller) *Jack Nicholson, Cher, Susan Sarandon, Michelle Pfeiffer, Veronica Cartwright.* An entertaining adult fantasy, loosely based on John Updike's novel. Cher, Pfeiffer and Sarandon play three dissimilar women who share a common problem: men. Together, they conjure up the "perfect" man, who arrives in the guise of Nicholson, truly a devilish rogue, who promptly proceeds to manipulate the ladies' lives. Cartwright — even with this powerhouse cast — steals the film as a snoopy society matron. ★★★ VHS: $9.99; DVD: $14.99

With Friends Like These

(1998, 105 min, US, Philip F. Messina) *Adam Arkin, Robert Costanzo, Beverly D'Angelo, Elle Macpherson, Amy Madigan, Laura San Giacomo, David Strathairn, Jon Tenney, Lauren Tom.* An ensemble comedy about four actors who are all best friends, and all out of work, *With Friends Like These* is a sitcom idea wrongly extended to feature length. Johnny (Costanzo) is told in confidence by talent agent (D'Angelo) that Martin Scorsese is looking to cast an unknown as Al Capone. Hoping to nail the role, Johnny asks his friend Armand (Strathairn) for help. What he doesn't know is that his buddies Steve (Arkin), and Dorian (Tenney) also want to audition for the part. Anger and betrayals mount up as the quartet of actors try (and fail) to keep secrets from each other, with the subtlty of machine gun fire. The four leads mug their way shamelessly through this unfunny comedy like raging bulls trying to out-act the other. The best contributions are the cameos from Bill Murray, Garry Marshall, and Scorsese himself. They belong in a much better movie. ★★ VHS: $19.99; DVD: $24.99

With Honors

(1994, 103 min, US, Alek Keshishian) *Joe Pesci, Brendan Fraser, Moira Kelly, Patrick Dempsey, Gore Vidal, Josh Hamilton.* As bland as cafeteria food, *With Honors* centers on the life of a determined-to-do-well Harvard student (Fraser) who loses his all-important term paper and must bargain with a feisty homeless man (Pesci) to get it back. Of course, Pesci is not simply a homeless man, but a homeless man with all the wisdom of the ages tucked neatly beneath his tattered jacket. He imparts this wisdom not only on Fraser but his three housemates, as well, in annoyingly large doses. Things get even worse when the roomies invite him to move in with them. ★½ VHS: $9.99; DVD: $14.99

Withnail & I

(1987, 105 min, GB, Bruce Robinson) *Richard E. Grant, Paul McGann, Richard Griffiths.* Two unemployed actors of disparate character, sharing a flat in 1969, go on holiday — subjecting themselves to each other's idiosyncracies during the rigors of ill-planned travel. Nicely drawn character studies, and a sly commentary on the temperament of the times. ★★★ DVD: $29.99

Without a Clue

(1988, 106 min, GB, Thom Eberhardt) *Michael Caine, Ben Kingsley, Jeffrey Jones, Peter Cook.* A delightfully zany and often very funny takeoff on the Sherlock Holmes legend. What would have happend if Dr. Watson had been the real detective, and Holmes was nothing more than a third-rate actor hired to portray the famous sleuth? Caine and Kingsley, both in fine comic form, make the most of this novel premise which finds the famous duo on the case of the missing five-pound note plates stolen from the Royal Bank of England. 106 minutes of slightly silly, laugh-out-loud tomfoolery. ★★★

Without a Trace

(1983, 119 min, US, Stanley R. Jaffe) *Kate Nelligan, Judd Hirsch, Stockard Channing.* Nelligan stars as a single mother whose young son leaves for school one morning and never returns. Hirsch is a sympathetic detective searching for the boy. Nelligan gives a good performance as the mother who never gives up hope. Though the film sometimes gives in to melodramatics, the where-how-why of the case is suspenseful. ★★½ VHS: $59.99

Without Anesthesia

(1982, 111 min, Poland, Andrzej Wajda) *Zbigniew Zapasiewicz, Ewa Dalkowska.* From the pen of director Wajda and coauthor Agnieszka Holland comes this jumpy, gritty Communist-era story of government control and the dissolution of a marriage. Zapasiewicz is convincing as a successful reporter and political analyst whose marriage falls apart, and he sets out to discover why. At the same time, he has fallen from grace with the powers that be. And making matters worse, his Kafka-esque downfall both personally and professionally is never explained. It seems to be accepted and everyone just goes with the flow of supression and inebriation. (Polish with English subtitles) ★★½ VHS: $29.99

Without Limits

(1998, 118 min, US, Robert Towne) *Billy Crudup, Donald Sutherland, Monica Potter.* The second feature film about legendary athlete Steve Prefontaine (the first being Steve James' 1997 *Prefontaine*) is a nice return to form for writer-director Towne (who tread similar ground with 1982's *Personal Best*). Crudup and Sutherland are superb as, respectively, "Pre" and his caring but no-nonsense track coach. The film wisely focuses on their compelling relationship. Towne also is able to gain insight into Pre's psyche and his personal relationships — something that the straightforward, informative and absorbing *Prefontaine* was unable to do sufficiently. And though the two films ultimately complement each other, *Without Limits* — with its nuanced performances and detailed characters, and demonstrating why Pre is considered a legend in his field — has the edge. ★★★ VHS: $14.99; DVD: $19.99

Without Love

(1945, 111 min, US, Harold S. Bucquet) *Katharine Hepburn, Spencer Tracy, Lucille Ball, Keenan Wynn.* Tracy is a scientist staying at widow Hepburn's boarding house in over-crowded, wartime Washington, D.C. For convenience's sake, the two marry and, of course, eventually fall in love. A charming romantic comedy with appealing performances by Kate and Spencer. ★★★ VHS: $14.99

Without Reservations

(1946, 101 min, US, Mervyn LeRoy) *Claudette Colbert, John Wayne, Don DeFore.* Pleasant comedy starring Colbert as a renowned Hollywood screenwriter, searching for an unknown to star in her next movie, who meets Marine flyer Wayne. (Wonder who gets the part?) Colbert is in good form, and Wayne — who didn't make many comedies — is actually quite funny. ★★★

Without You I'm Nothing

(1990, 90 min, US, John Boskovich) *Sandra Bernhard.* The film version of Bernhard's audacious off-Broadway hit brims with libidinous wit and inventive characterizations. With unabashed artistic daring, Bernhard plunges into a melange of musical impersonations, poetry readings and monologues which put her on the cutting edge of standup comedy/performance art. Set in a sleepy little nightclub, Bernhard's act is played to a thinning and impassive-looking audience and culminates in a desperate and very revealing go-go dance to the tune of Prince's "Little Red Corvette." Sprinkled with moments of inspired comedic brilliance, *Without You* establishes Bernhard as a hip, thoroughly campy urban (and urbane) satirist. ★★★½ VHS: $14.99

Witness

(1985, 112 min, US, Peter Weir) *Harrison Ford, Kelly McGillis, Lukas Haas, Josef Sommer, Alexander Godunov, Danny Glover, Patti LuPone.* A

W

gripping police thriller and extraordinary character study. In one of his most accomplished performances, Ford plays the odd man out on a force riddled with corruption who, in fleeing his pursuers, tumbles into the anachronistic Amish country. McGillis is very good as the Amish mother whose young son witnesses a murder. (VHS available letterboxed or pan & scan) ★★★½ VHS: $14.99; DVD: $24.99

The Witness

(1968, 108 min, Hungary, Pèter Bascó) After viewing this bitterly sarcastic satire of the chaotic and corrupt Communist government in Hungary, one is not only surprised that it was suppressed for 10 years, but that it was released at all during their reign. Set in 1949, the story revolves around Pelikan, a hapless party loyalist and a father of eight who is content with being a simple dike keeper. But after being caught by the authorities for illegally slaughtering a pig, he is immediately "rehabilitated" and promoted to jobs that he is totally unqualified for — from swimming pool manager, director of the Hungarian Orange Institute and even head of a socialist amusement park. A subversive little gem in the tradition of *1984* and *Brazil*. (Hungarian with English subtitles) ★★★ VHS: $59.99

Witness for the Prosecution

(1957, 106 min, US, Billy Wilder) *Charles Laughton, Marlene Dietrich, Tyrone Power, Elsa Lanchester, John Williams.* Based on the long-running Agatha Christie play, this proves to be an acting tour de force for all concerned. Dietrich is at her best as the wife of accused murderer Power. Laughton is brilliant as the defense attorney who agrees to take on the case, and Lanchester is his prohibitive nurse. To detail more of the plot would give it away. Suffice it to say that this is one whodunit that doesn't disappoint on any level. ★★★★ VHS: $14.99

Wittgenstein

(1993, 75 min, GB, Derek Jarman) *Karl Johnson, Tilda Swinton.* Jarman's amusing, intellectual portrait of Austrian-born, British-educated philosopher Ludwig Wittgenstein is both a startling primer in low-budget filmmaking as well as a visually exuberant work. Considered one of the century's most influential philosophers, Wittgenstein's private and professional life is chronicled — from his prodigy childhood to his reluctant life as a professor at Cambridge. Jarman utilizes a pitch-black background, allowing the richly drawn, outrageously costumed characters and their witty, thought-provoking dialogue to take center stage. Johnson plays the eccentric philosopher, and Swinton is lavishly campy as Lady Ottoline. ★★★ VHS: $24.99

The Wiz

(1978, 133 min, US, Sidney Lumet) *Diana Ross, Michael Jackson, Lena Horne, Richard Pryor, Mabel King, Ted Ross.* A modern updating of *The Wizard of Oz*, with Ross and Jackson heading an all-black cast. Based on the Tony Award-winning Broadway musical, we're invited to "ease on down the road" with Dorothy (D. Ross), whose Oz is downtown Manhattan. There are a couple of dazzling musical sequences, but Ross' lifeless portrayal as Dorothy fails to excite. King,

singing "Don't You Bring Me No Bad News," and T. Ross, as the Cowardly Lion, steal the show ★★ VHS: $9.99; DVD: $26.99

The Wizard

(1989, 100 min, US, Todd Holland) *Fred Savage, Christian Slater, Beau Bridges.* Two brothers embark on a cross-country journey to attend a national video competition. A tedious road movie for kids which is as ill-conceived as it is trite. ★½ VHS: $12.99

Wizard of Gore

(1970, 70 min, US, Hershell Gordon Lewis) *Ray Sager, Judy Cler, Wayne Ratay, Phil Laurenson.* Sager is Montag the Magician, a character whose monologues regarding man's fascination with the morbid seems to sum up director Lewis' own philosophies and motivations. With an incredible ending reminiscent of Buñuel. Has to be seen to be believed. ★ VHS: $29.99; DVD: $24.99

The Wizard of Loneliness

(1988, 111 min, US, Jenny Bowen) *Lukas Haas, Lea Thompson, John Randolph, Anne Pitoniak.* Young Haas (one of the most gifted child actors of the 1980s) is outstanding in this sensitive tale of a small boy who comes to live with his grandparents in New England during WWII. ★★½

The Wizard of Oz

(1925, 93 min, US, Larry Semon) *Larry Semon, Dorothy Dwan, Oliver Hardy.* A real treat for silent film fans or Oz fanatics. Now virtually forgotten, Semon was a popular comic in his day; here he plays the Scarecrow in an adaptation that owes more to Mack Sennett than L. Frank Baum. (Remade in 1939) ★★★ VHS: $24.99

The Wizard of Oz

(1939, 101 min, US, Victor Fleming) *Judy Garland, Ray Bolger, Jack Haley, Bert Lahr, Frank Morgan, Margaret Hamilton.* Follow the yellow brick road to the wonderful Wizard of Oz (a wiz of a wiz, if ever a wiz there was) and join Dorothy and all her friends in this immortal classic. Includes a behind-the-scenes documentary and footage of the cut musical sequence "Jitterbug." (Sequel: *Return to Oz*) (Remade as *The Wiz*) ★★★★ VHS: $24.99; DVD: $24.99

Wizards

(1977, 81 min, US, Ralph Bakshi) This sci-fi tale of a futuristic world mired in post-apocalyptic battles and neo-Hitlerian factions is imaginatively brought to the animated screen by Ralph Bakshi. ★★★ VHS: $19.99

Wolf

(1994, 125 min, US, Mike Nichols) *Jack Nicholson, Michelle Pfeiffer, James Spader, Christopher Plummer, Kate Nelligan.* A mature tale of an underdog (Nicholson) who finally has his day when the bite of a wolf causes him to develop distinctly lupine properties. He soon rids himself of his cheating wife (Nelligan) and slimy best friend (Spader) and begins a steamy affair with an exquisitely icy "poor little rich girl" (Pfeiffer) just as a spate of gruesome killings befalls the city. Nicholson and Pfeiffer wear their roles like a pair of comfortable slippers, and Spader makes full use of his stock-in-trade creepiness. However, this is not the gorefest horror fans may be anticipating, and the dime-store special

Wittgenstein

effects are bound to disappoint. But Nicholson's wry, arch performance is a true howl and a return to irreverent form. ★★★ VHS: $12.99; DVD: $14.99

Wolf at the Door

(1987, 90 min, France/Denmark, Henning Carlsen) *Donald Sutherland, Jean Yanne, Max von Sydow.* Sutherland is Paul Gauguin, the French painter who rejected the art world and lifestyle of France at the height of his career to live simply and paint in Tahiti. After several years on the island, he visits Paris in 1893. The film is an in-depth study of the man as he spreads the word of Tahiti's beauty and raises money for his return. Sutherland's Gauguin is complex and contradictory. He is obnoxious, a bully, a misogynist, bombastic, loving to his dark-skinned favorites but cold and callous to his Scandinavian wife; but above all, a tortured and misunderstood artist. A superlative re-creation of the artist's character. (Filmed in English) ★★★

The Wolf Man

(1941, 70 min, US, George Waggner) *Lon Chaney, Jr., Claude Rains, Evelyn Ankers, Maria Ouspenskaya, Ralph Bellamy, Bela Lugosi.* Classic horror film with Chaney as the tormented Larry Talbot, man by day, beast by night. More than just a damn good fright tale, *The Wolf Man* is very successful in presenting the moral conflict of a man confronted with his animal instincts. "Even the man who is pure in heart, and says his prayers by night/May become a wolf man when the wolfbane blooms, and the moon is full and bright." (Sequel: *Frankenstein Meets the Wolf Man*) ★★★½ VHS: $14.99; DVD: $29.99

Wolfen

(1981, 115 min, US, Michael Wadleigh) *Albert Finney, Gregory Hines, Tom Noonan, Diane Venora, Edward James Olmos.* When director Wadleigh, who hadn't done much since *Woodstock*, made this updated werewolf story, he concentrated on a stylish urban atmosphere of horror over the empty thrills of special effects. New York City detective Finney investigates a series of grisly and random murders being committed throughout the city. Hines is the eccentric coroner who helps him find out who and why. Though soon to be overused by others, Wadleigh brilliantly uses the recently developed steadi-cam to simulate the running wolves in a long, sinewy take. ★★★ VHS: $9.99

A Woman at Her Window

(1977, 110 min, France, Pierre Granier-Deferre) *Romy Schneider, Philippe Noiret, Victor Lanoux.* Director Granier-Deferre collaborated with screenwriter Jorge Semprun (*Z*) to create this romantic drama set in the despotic era of Greece circa 1936. Schneider gives an outstanding performance as an aristocratic woman who pursues affairs with various noblemen while married to an Italian ambassador, who himself is involved in a series of affairs. Only when she harbors a political activist (Lanoux) and helps him escape does she becomes transformed, sacrificing wealth for true love. Told in a clever use of flashbacks, *A Woman at Her Window* is a convincing, engaging and well-made film. (French with English subtitles) ★★★ VHS: $29.99

A Woman at War

(1991, 115 min, GB, Edward Bennett) *Martha Plimpton, Eric Stoltz.* Based on the autobiography "Inside the Gestapo" by Helene Moszkiewicz, this moving story of individual courage takes place in Nazi-occupied Belgium. Plimpton gives a sturdy performance as Moszkiewicz who, upon the invasion of her country, joins the underground movement, changes her name, and infiltrates the Gestapo. Plimpton is commendable as the young Jewish woman who helps track down Jews by day and plays saboteur by night. This low-key film ably captures the dangerous tenor of the times, and manages to create a tension as to the heroine's fate even in the knowledge of the film's source. ★★★ VHS: $79.99

A Woman, Her Men and Her Futon

(1992, 90 min, US, Mussef Sibay) *Jennifer Rubin, Grant Show.* A low-keyed drama about the romantic exploits of a woman with two lovers too many. While not as provocative as its title implies, the film deserves kudos for its adult portrayal of a '90s woman who is sexual without being irresponsible. ★★ VHS: $79.99; DVD: $24.99

A Woman in Flames

(1982, 106 min, West Germany, Robert van Ackeren) *Gudren Landgrebe, Robert Van Ackeren.* This volatile look at female sexuality, wish fulfillment and the obstacles hindering sexual equality became something of a *cause célèbre.* Its tone is peculiarly poised between social satire and razor-sharp melodrama. The plot reads like a supermarket tabloid, with a disgruntled bourgeois housewife who abandons her husband and studies to take up prostitution. ★★★

The Woman in Red

(1984, 87 min, US, Gene Wilder) *Gene Wilder, Gilda Radnor, Charles Grodin, Joseph Bologna, Kelly LeBrock.* Occasionally amusing remake of the French romantic farce *Pardon Mon Affaire* with Wilder as a married man who falls for "the woman in red." ★★½ VHS: $9.99

Woman in the Dunes

(1964, 123 min, Japan, Hiroshi Teshigahara) *Eiji Okada, Kuoko Kishida.* Kobo Abe's allegory of a man trapped with a strange woman in a sandpit is translated into a prize-winning work of art exploring the concepts of existence, freedom and eroticism. ★★★½ VHS: $29.99; DVD: $29.99

Woman in the Moon

(1929, 146 min, Germany, Fritz Lang) *Klaus Pohl, Willy Fritsch.* Lang's final silent film is a fascinating voyage of a group of people who are sent to the moon in search of gold, but find instead only greed and jealousy. The look of the rocket and other aspects of the science fiction film are amazing for the similarity to the real thing 40 years later. Not as accomplished as Lang's masterpiece, *Metropolis,* but nevertheless an enjoyable experience. ★★★

A Woman Is a Woman
(Une Femme est une Femme)

(1961, 80 min, France, Jean-Luc Godard) *Anna Karina, Jean-Claude Brialy, Jean-Paul Belmondo.* Godard's salute to the Hollywood musical is a giddy, improvisational romp up and down the boulevards of Paris. Karina stars as a bubbly, high-spirited striptease artist whose only desire is to have a child. Her boyfriend (Brialy), however, is preparing for an important bicycle race and doesn't wish to lose any "precious bodily fluids." So she turns to her lusting ex (Belmondo) who volunteers to do whatever he can. Godard infuses the proceedings with an uncharacteristic joyful humor making this by far his most light-hearted work. (French with English subtitles) ★★★ VHS: $29.99; DVD: $29.99

The Woman Next Door

(1981, 106 min, France, Francois Truffaut) *Gérard Depardieu, Fanny Ardant.* A dark, gripping melodrama with Depardieu and Ardant as a compulsive pair of ex-lovers, inadvertently reunited and driven to a tragic affair. (French with English subtitles) ★★★ VHS: $19.99; DVD: $29.99

A Woman of Affairs

(1928, 98 min, US, Clarence Brown) *Greta Garbo, John Gilbert, Douglas Fairbanks, Jr.* A compelling silent screen story starring a ravishing Garbo as an "unlucky-in-love" woman whose free-spirited lifestyle takes its toll. After losing the man of her dreams, she marries a man who shortly thereafter takes his own life. Then, Garbo embarks on a series of foreign affairs with globetrotting dignitaries. Finally, she is reunited with her true love years later, only to learn he is engaged to another woman. ★★★ VHS: $29.99

A Woman of Distinction

(1950, 85 min, US, Edward Buzzell) *Rosalind Russell, Ray Milland, Edmund Gwenn.* Campus hijinks '50s-style as professor Milland and college dean Russell are involved in a romantic scandal. The two stars are in good form and bring some spice to this pleasant comedy. ★★½ VHS: $69.99

A Woman of Paris

(1921, 78 min, US, Charles Chaplin) *Adolphe Menjou, Edna Purviance.* Chaplin proved himself a master director in this, his only serious film in which he doesn't star (he only has a bit as a porter). An innocent country girl becomes an inamorata of a rich Parisian (Menjou, in the role that made him a star). Chaplin's tight narrative structure (rare in his own films) and the use of telling detail to delineate character and relationships was a revelation that inspired such directors as von Sternberg, von Stroheim, Lubitsch and others. ★★★½ DVD: $29.99

Woman of the Year

(1942, 112 min, US, George Stevens) *Katharine Hepburn, Spencer Tracy, Fay Bainter, Dan Tobin.* Tracy is a sports writer and Hepburn is a highly esteemed columnist in this top-notch battle-of-the-sexes comedy. The first pairing of Hepburn and Tracy, *Woman of the Year* displays the longtime screen duo's inimitable rapport. The great script was written by Ring Lardner, Jr. and Michael Kanin. ★★★★ VHS: $14.99; DVD: $19.99

Woman of the Year

Woman on Top

(2000, 91 min, US, Fina Torres) *Penélope Cruz, Murilo Benício, Harold Perrineau, Jr., Mark Feuerstein.* Light, easy on the palate but terribly insubstantial, the colorful *Woman on Top* attempts to mix the sensual culinary delights of *Like Water for Chocolate* with the frivolity of a Nora Ephron film. Needless to say, this could have used more time in the oven. The beautiful Cruz, clearly the main reason to see this otherwise uneven trifle, is a beguiling presence as Isabella, a Brazilian chef who discovers her handsome husband is cheating on her. She heads to San Francisco to reunite with her drag queen friend Monica (Perrineau), only to find fame and fortune as the host of a cooking show. Things heat up when Isabella's husband arrives to reconcile, only to find her producer also in romantic pursuit. Stretching the boundaries of magical illusion, the filmmakers seem content in trotting out romantic clichés and some questionable plot developments as Isabella casts her spell on one and all. Nonsense has its place in romantic comedy, just not too much of it. ★★ VHS: $102.99; DVD: $34.99

Woman Times Seven

(1967, 99 min, US/Italy, Vittorio De Sica) *Shirley MacLaine, Vittorio Gassman, Michael Caine, Alan Arkin, Philippe Noiret, Peter Sellers, Anita Ekberg.* MacLaine mercilessly hams it up in this omnibus film which has her playing seven different, desirable women with seven different husbands and lovers in as many episodes. A light comic touch prevails throughout the film with some segments more successful than others. (Filmed in English) ★★½

A Woman under the Influence

(1974, 147 min, US, John Cassavetes) *Gena Rowlands, Peter Falk, Matthew Cassel.* The power of Cassavetes' films is that he strips away all the pretenses and protections we use to shield ourselves from our most frightening and shameful pain, and shoves our noses in it. Not too many actors can deliver that bare honesty; one of the few who does so without reservation is his wife Rowlands. She is mesmerizing as the working-class housewife who buckles under the strain of a limited existence, a brutish husband (Falk, in one of several strong collaborations with Cassavetes), insensitive relatives and an uncaring world. Rowlands is in turn heartbreaking, funny, delightful and frightening as a woman who is overwhelmed by a desperate inability to stay connected. (Letterboxed) ★★★½ VHS: $14.99; DVD: $24.99

A Woman without Love

(1951, 85 min, Mexico, Luis Bunuel) *Rosario Granados, Julio Villareal.* Director Buñuel's filmmaking career flourished during his self-imposed exile in Mexico, although most were simply potboilers for the domestic market, lacking in the director's trademark wry cinematic excesses. One of these, *A Woman without Love*, is a fiery soap opera about the barely supressed passions of hot-blooded Latins. A beautiful woman, locked in a loveless marriage with a middle-aged bourgeois, meets a handsome stranger. Their affair is short-lived but its memory is renewed 25 years later when her son receives an inheritance from a mysterious man. (Spanish with English subtitles) ★★½ VHS: $24.99

A Woman's Face

(1938, 104 min, Sweden, Gustaf Molander) *Ingrid Bergman.* Bergman plays against type in this dark melodrama about a disfigured woman who, disturbed by the happiness she will never know, blackmails illicit lovers. (Swedish with English subtitles) ★★½ VHS: $19.99

A Woman's Face

(1941, 105 min, US, George Cukor) *Joan Crawford, Melvyn Douglas, Conrad Veidt.* Crawford has a juicy role as an embittered, facially scarred woman whose personality changes when she undergoes plastic surgery. An interesting melodrama with many appealing moments. ★★★ VHS: $19.99

A Woman's Revenge

(1989, 133 min, France, Jacques Doillon) *Isabelle Huppert, Béatrice Dalle.* A puzzling love triangle gone sour proves to be the motivating force in this elegant, if long-winded drama of passion, seduction and female retribution. Dalle plays Suzi, a young beauty with a restless spirit who, a year after the death of her lover, meets up with his widow, Cecile (Huppert). Bitter at her husband's death and his unfaithfulness, Cecile seeks Suzi's companionship, but is her presence an offer of forgiveness and friendship or is there a darker, possibly treacherous motive? Freely adapted from Fyodor Dostoevsky's "The Eternal Husband," the film is a bit stage-bound and incessantly talky, but this soap opera-ish drama is filled with layers of revealing but conflicting revelations, accusations and intrigue. (French with English subtitles) ★★½ VHS: $59.99

A Woman's Tale

(1991, 93 min, Australia, Paul Cox) *Sheila Florance, Norman Kaye.* This delightful tale of aging is a life-affirming, realistic and often hilarious mini-masterpiece. Filmmaker Cox tailor-made this semiautobiographical story of a spirited modern woman of almost 80 years for acclaimed actress Florance. Her character, Martha, finding the world too cynical and heartless, refuses to accept society's constraints on her lifestyle and fights the establishment with compassion and humor. Her friends include her pets, a bed-ridden neighbor and even a local prostitute. Her sexuality is still important to her, and her frank talk is revealing, touching and hilarious. ★★★★

The Women

(1939, 133 min, US, George Cukor) *Norma Shearer, Joan Crawford, Rosalind Russell, Paulette Goddard, Joan Fontaine, Mary Boland, Marjorie Main, Lucile Watson, Butterfly McQueen.* Another in the long line of those great MGM all-star extravaganzas, this uproarious Cukor comedy (and cult favorite) more than lives up to its title: The cast is entirely female. Shearer heads the once-in-a-lifetime cast as Mary, a Manhattan socialite whose storybook existence is shattered when her husband leaves her for shopgirl Crawford. This puts Mary "on the road to Reno," where she meets a group of other divorce-bound women: worldly Boland, showgirl Goddard, and friends Fontaine and Russell (in a smashingly funny performance). Based on Claire Boothe's Broadway hit, this is about as funny as a film can get. (Remade as the 1956 musical *The Opposite Sex*) ★★★★ VHS: $14.99

The Women

Starring Brigitte Bardot
See: Les Femmes

Women from the Lake of Scented Souls

(1993, 106 min, China, Xie Fei) *Sigin Gaowa, Wu Yujuan.* History has a way of repeating itself, and so goes the plot as Xiang Ersao (Sigin), a determined and hard-working woman, is forced into marriage as a child to a sesame oil maker who knows nothing about business. Left to keep shop while her husband gets drunk with his friends, Ersao modernizes and increases business. While this adds to their position of power in the town, their epileptic son is too old to be single. Ersao decides to continue the cycle of arranged marriages by forcing a poorer family to promise their daughter to marry for payment of their debts. Bao Xianian's camera work is nowhere near as spectacular as some of the other films to come out of China recently, but there is a gritty realism to the film and good performances on par with the soap opera plot. (Mandarin with English subtitles) ★★½ VHS: $79.99

Women in Love

(1970, 129 min, GB, Ken Russell) *Glenda Jackson, Jennie Linden, Oliver Reed, Alan Bates.* Russell's powerful rendition of the D.H. Lawrence classic centers on two Midlands sisters and the tempestuous relationships they form. Resolute Gudren (Jackson) becomes involved with the strong but boorish Gerald (Reed), while her romantically inclined sister Ursula (Linden) falls in love with the handsome but aloof Rupert (Bates). A masterful examination of sexual domination and repression, brilliantly portrayed by its cast — Jackson won an Oscar and international stardom for her gutsy, complex portrayal of Gudren. ★★★★ VHS: $14.99

Women on the Verge of a Nervous Breakdown

(1988, 88 min, Spain, Pedro Almodovar) *Carmen Maura, Antonio Banderas, Julieta Serrano, Maria Barranco.* Almodóvar's comic masterpiece is by far his most accessible film to date and is largely responsible for familiarizing many American audiences with his unique talents. Based loosely on Jean Cocteau's "The Human Voice," the story follows Pepa — brilliantly portrayed by Maura — an actress whose life crumbles around her when she comes home one day to find her lover, Ivan, has left her. The ensuing hour-and-a-half turns into a hilarious comic romp as she tries to piece her life back together. Serrano is fabulous as Ivan's insane wife and Barranco is hysterical as Pepa's friend who is fleeing from Shiite terrorists. (Spanish with English subtitles) ★★★★ VHS: $19.99; DVD: $19.99

Wonder Boys

(2000, 112 min, US, Curtis Hanson) *Michael Douglas, Tobey Maguire, Frances McDormand, Robert Downey, Jr., Katie Holmes, Rip Torn, Richard Thomas, Philip Bosco.* One man's quest for personal redemption proves to be an unusually rewarding journey in the captivating dramatic comedy *Wonder Boys*, an intelligent, sardonic character study boasting a career performance by Douglas in the central role. Based on the novel by Michael Chabon, and brilliantly adapted by Steve Kloves, this wondrous mixture of satire and introspection takes place over the course of one weekend, but has all the wisdom and resource of a lifetime. Douglas is Professor Grady Tripp, whose life is in a bit of disarray. He hasn't finished a novel in seven years, his wife has just walked out on him, and the married woman with whom he's involved is pregnant. When his editor arrives expecting a finished work, it sets in motion a series of events that are ripe with the seeds of self-discovery. Douglas is a marvel as the disheveled Tripp, whose world-weariness and humor the actor wears like a glove. Douglas has never opened himself up to such an extent, and gives a mature, exciting performance. The ensemble cast is equally extraordinary. Maguire gives another intuitive portrayal as one of Tripp's students, a talented writer who Tripp mentors; Downey is just right as Tripp's gay editor who does a little mentoring of his own; and McDormand is terrific as Tripp's mistress, the university's chancellor who faces her own crisis of conscience. A dazzling entertainment. ★★★★ VHS: $14.99; DVD: $29.99

Wonder Man

(1945, 98 min, US, Bruce Humberstone) *Danny Kaye, Virginia Mayo, Vera-Ellen, S.Z. Sakall.* Kaye has a field day with this bright comic romp playing twins. When one brother, an outgoing and brash entertainer, is murdered, his ghost convinces his introverted sibling to impersonate him and find out who did the dastardly deed. Kaye has some wonderful bits, and is ably supported by a great supporting cast. ★★★

The Wonderful, Horrible Life of Leni Riefenstahl

(1993, 192 min, Germany, Ray Müller) It may never be possible to judge German director Leni Riefenstahl's cinematic accomplishments without regard to their historical context. Her 1932 film, *Blue Light*, in which she produced, directed and starred, captured Hitler's attention with its Wagnerian mysticism and haunting imagery. She was a trailblazer, one of the few women directors of the time. In this meticulously researched biography, replete with archival footage intercut with clips from her films, Riefenstahl maintains that she was politically ignorant and unaware of Hitler's ultimate intentions. Cantankerous and forceful at 90 years of age, she fervently denies references to close personal ties to Hitler and Goebbels; refutes speculation that she staged much of the spectacle in *Triumph of the Will;* and maintains that her interest was solely in the craft of filmmaking. This fascinating documentary allows her to speak freely, alternating between words and images. ★★★★ VHS: $39.99; DVD: $49.99

The Wonderful World of the Brothers Grimm

(1962, 129 min, US, Henry Levin & George Pal) *Laurence Harvey, Karl-Heinz Boehm, Claire Bloom, Terry-Thomas, Buddy Hackett.* Lavishly produced children's tale, featuring excerpts from brothers Jacob and Wilhelm Grimm's best-loved fairy tales, and taking a look at their lives. ★★★ VHS: $19.99

Wonderland

(1989, 103 min, GB, Philip Saville) *Emile Charles, Tony Forsyth, Robert Stephens, Robbie Coltrane.* This intriguing British thriller delves into an often overlooked subculture: gay youth. *Wonderland* is the story of the friendship between two gay teenagers from Liverpool, Eddie and Michael, who are forced to flee the city when they witness a gangland slaying at a local gay bar. Taking refuge at the home of a manipulative wealthy couple in Brighton, the boys' idyllic existence of freedom and safety is shattered when they meet the killers in a deadly confrontation. Both Charles as the dolphin-loving, soft-hearted Eddie and Forsyth as the street-wise, caring hustler Michael are excellent as the youths. (aka: *The Fruit Machine*) ★★★

Wonderland

(2000, 109 min, GB, Michael Winterbottom) *Ian Hart, Shirley Henderson, Kika Markham, Gina McKee, Molly Parker.* In ths affecting drama, director Winterbottom apes the hand-held immediacy of Mike Leigh and John Cassavetes, but he manages to put a personal touch on the film, as well, to great success. The lives of three sisters and their parents are examined in intertwining stories, with emotions running the gamut from joy to depression, rage to quiet acceptance. A nice, if slightly overdone score complements the superb acting and camerawork to produce a richly involving film, culminating in a suprisingly satisfying (under the circumstances) ending. *Wonderland* is Winterbottom's best film to date, and despite its superficial resemblance to several recent British releases, is an original, heartfelt work. ★★★½ VHS: $102.99; DVD: $24.99

The Wood

(1999, 106 min, US, Rick Famuyiwa) *Taye Diggs, Omar Epps, Richard T. Jones, Sean Nelson, Malinda Williams.* A sweet and sometimes raunchy comedy by writer-director Famuyiva, *The Wood* is two movies in one. In the contemporary story, Roland (Diggs) is getting cold feet on his wedding day. His two best friends Mike (Epps) and Slim (Jones) try to keep him focused, but, of course, chaos ensues. The other story involves the flashbacks to these three friends growing up in Englewood (the Wood). These scenes, set in the 1980s, form the better part of the film, especially in the sensitive moments in which young Mike (Nelson) tries to woo Alicia (Williams). While there are a few missteps (most notably a scene in which a convenience store is robbed), the bond between the trio of friends is solid. If viewers can overlook the many sophomoric moments, *The Wood* is pretty good. ★★★ VHS: $14.99; DVD: $29.99

The Wooden Gun

(1979, 91 min, Israel, Ilan Moshenson) Set in the tense atmosphere of 1950s Tel Aviv, this incisive film focuses on two rival groups of pre-teens whose behavior, motivated by their interpretations of the concepts of heroism, nationalisn and friendship, raises hard questions. Portrayed are first-generation sabras (native-born Israelis), who are separated by a tremendous psychological gap from those who came to Israel from Europe, many of them Holocaust survivors. (Hebrew with English subtitles) ★★★ VHS: $79.99

The Wooden Man's Bride

(1995, 114 min, China, Huang Jianxin) *Chang Shih, Wang Lan, Ku Paoming, Wang Yumei.* Director Huang has created an entertaining, if fallacious, parable wherein repressive tradition is bested by noble peasant "outlaws." When the arranged marriage to an aristocrat comes undone by his untimely death, a beautiful innocent (Wang) is left with the prospect of an even more empty alliance: custom dictates she marry his proxy, a carved wooden effigy, and her scheming mother-in-law (Wang) is intent on upholding tradition. While *The Wooden Man's Bride* features the lush visual style of *Raise the Red Lantern* and *Shanghai Triad*, in its heart it is reactionary, its mind full of simplistic syllogisms. (Mandarin with English subtitles) ★★½ VHS: $19.99

Woodstock

(1969, 225 min, US, Michael Wadleigh) It's been 40 years since the monumental rock festival which served as a gleaming triumph for the counterculture, and a fitting capsulization of the spirit of a decade. An unbelievable roster of performers includes Jimi Hendrix; The Who;

Wonder Boys

Crosby, Stills, Nash and Young; and The Jefferson Airplane (bless their pointed little heads). This is the director's cut with 40 minutes of additional footage not in the theatrical release. (Letterboxed) (Sequel: *Woodstock '94*) ★★★½ VHS: $24.99; DVD: $19.99

Working

(1982, 90 min, US, Stephen Schwartz & Kirk Browning) *Studs Terkel, Barry Bostwick, Rita Moreno, James Taylor, Eileen Brennan, Charles Durning, Barbara Hershey, Patti LaBelle, Scatman Crothers.* Based on the Broadway show, itself based on the Studs Terkel book, this folksy, consistently charming musical is a loving tribute to the working men and women across America. From a series of interviews with construction workers, waitresses, firemen, parking attendants, secretaries, truck drivers, cleaning women and even prostitutes, Terkel (who also narrates) explores the individual work ethic. These are balanced with jubilant songs that celebrate the workplace, the worker, and life itself. Score by Stephen Schwartz ("Pippin," "Godspell"). ★★★½ VHS: $29.99

Working Girl

(1988, 113 min, US, Mike Nichols) *Melanie Griffith, Harrison Ford, Sigourney Weaver, Joan Cusack, Alec Baldwin, Philip Bosco, Kevin Spacey.* Griffith gives an enchanting performance in this "Cinderella" comedy set against the wheeling and dealing of Wall Street. Griffith plays a secretary who masquerades as her absentee boss (Weaver) when her employer steals a business idea from her. Part social satire, part love story, the film traces Griffith's successful business charade and her romance with a handsome associate (a restrained Ford). ★★★ VHS: $9.99; DVD: $24.99

Working Girls

(1986, 90 min, US, Lizzie Borden) *Amanda Goodwin, Louise Smith.* In cinematic terms, the prostitute is usually portrayed either as a statuesque, high-priced call girl or as a drug-snorting, under-aged, runaway streetwalker. *Working Girls*, on the other hand, is a wryly comical and non-judgmental tale about another, less melodramatic side of the "sex-for-sale" business. Feminist filmmaker Borden tells the story of a middle-class brothel nestled in a Manhattan high-rise. Essentially, the film is a day in the life of the shrewish madam and her "girls" as seen through the eyes of Molly, a young woman who, while ambivalent about her work, is nonetheless happy not to be working 9 to 5. ★★★ VHS: $14.99; DVD: $24.99

The World According to Garp

(1982, 136 min, US, George Roy Hill) *Robin Williams, Glenn Close, John Lithgow, Amanda Plummer, Jessica Tandy.* Williams is the eponymous T.S. Garp in Hill's terrific adaptation of the wild and wooly John Irving best-seller. Close is marvelously funny as Garp's stringent celebrity mom, as is Lithgow as the transsexual, ex-Eagles tight end. ★★★½ VHS: $9.99; DVD: $19.99

A World Apart

(1988, 113 min, GB, Chris Menges) *Jodhi May, Barbara Hershey, Linda Mvusi, Jeroen Krabbé, Tim Roth.* Menges' emotionally charged look at Apartheid, political commitment and familial ties, as seen through the eyes of a 13-year-old white girl living in early 1960s South Africa. May gives a truly remarkable performance as the young girl who witnesses the gradual disintegration of her family when her mother, an anti-Apartheid activist, becomes a target of the South African government. Though the events are seen through the eyes of whites and not the real victims, the blacks themselves, it does not handicap the film; either in its excellence as a production or in the emergency of its issues. As the mother whose political conviction threatens personal well-being, Hershey is outstanding; and Mvusi is exceptional as the family's black maid. ★★★½

The World Is Not Enough

(1999, 128 min, GB, Michael Apted) *Pierce Brosnan, Sophie Marceau, Robert Carlyle, Denise Richards, Robbie Coltrane, Judi Dench, Desmond Llewelyn, John Cleese, Michael Kitchen.* Brosnan appears for the third time as super agent James Bond in this technically proficient though overly familiar espionage adventure. 007 goes up against a less formidable opponent in Carlyle's mangy terrorist, whose plans to manipulate world oil comes under attack by Bond and physicist Richards (oh, come on!) when James investigates the death of a Swiss banker. Dench plays a larger role as M, and this marks Llewelyn's last appearance as gadget-man Q. A speedboat chase down the Thames and an exciting ride through an oil pipeline highlight the action scenes, though this is just a wee bit too talky to rate as one of the better Bonds. ★★½ VHS: $19.99; DVD: $34.99

The World of Apu

(1959, 103 min, India, Satyajit Ray) *Soumitra Chatterjee, Sharmila Tagore.* This third segment of the famed Apu Trilogy is considered the masterpiece of the series. Apu unexpectedly marries the cousin of a friend and, after a brief idyllic marriage, is thrown into great despair when his young wife dies during childbirth. A long period of spiritual regeneration is consummated when Apu is reunited with his son three years later. The Apu Trilogy is considered one of the richest humanistic statements ever committed to film. (Bengali with English subtitles) ★★★★ VHS: $19.99

The World of Henry Orient

(1964, 106 min, US, George Roy Hill) *Peter Sellers, Tippy Walker, Angela Lansbury, Tom Bosley, Paula Prentiss.* One of Sellers' most hilarious performances highlights this unsung comedy gem. He's a lady-killing, playboy concert pianist whose life is made miserable by the "adoration" of two pesky teenage girls. The girls' relationship and disparate social standings are at the base of this wonderful, poignant study of adolescence. ★★★½ VHS: $14.99

A World of Strangers

(1962, 89 min, Denmark, Henning Carlsen) From Nobel Prize-winning author Nadine Gordimer comes this impassioned drama that exposes the hidden face of Apartheid. Shot in deep secrecy in South Africa because of its controversial political stance, the film focuses on an open-minded young Englishman, recently transferred to Johannesburg by a publishing company, who soon makes friends with both blacks and whites. But after witnessing the everyday brutality of the whites to the black Africans, he finds himself forced to take a stand. The film conveys eloquent insights into the harsh reality of an oppressive society based on racial separation and the conclusion that no one can remain neutral. ★★★ VHS: $59.99

The Worst Boy in Town

(1989, 60 min, Mexico, Enrique Gomez Vadillo) *Raul Buefil.* If this film received the exploitation treatment made famous by Roger Corman, the advertising angle might be something like, "Pepe — marauding macho thug by day...coquettish transvestite whore by night!" Set in the slums of Mexico City, the film features Mexican TV star Buefil as the rougish Pepe, the leader of a gang of hunky thugs who spend their days playing pool, intimidating the neighbors and harassing young girls. But there is more to Pepe than his beefy body, tight pants and macho exterior. . . for, after the sun sets, he dons makeup, a wig and a sexy dress and visits the local transvestite bar, and in "her" new kittenish persona, looks for a good strong man who can give him a good. . . ! Not to be confused with great art, this entertaining melodrama is nonetheless fun. (Spanish with English subtitles) ★★½

Worth Winning

(1989, 103 min, US, Will MacKenzie) *Mark Harmon, Lesley Ann Warren, Madeleine Stowe, Maria Holvoe.* A handsome TV weatherman (Harmon) takes a bet challenging him to get engaged to three women in three months. Warren, Stowe and Holvoe are the prospective betrothed. Not very appealing, either comedically or story wise, but the cast does seem to be trying their best. ★★ VHS: $19.99

The Would-Be Gentleman

(1959, 111 min, France, Jean Meyer) The comic artistry of Jean-Baptiste Moliere is brought to the screen by Paris' renouned Comedie Francaise. Always eager to please his sovereign, Louis XIV, Moliere lamblasts the rising bourgeoisie in this hilarious drawing room farce. The script bears its teeth on an idiotic member of the nouveau riche who bumbles and fumbles his way through a series of lessons as he vainly tries to educate himself to the level of the gentry. (French with English subtitles) ★★★

The Wounds (Rane)

(1998, 103 min, Serbo-Croatia, Srdjan Dragojevic) *Dusan Pekic, Milan Maric.* Two aimless sixteen-year-old pals in war-torn Serbia hook up with a local crime boss and eventually take over. They become locally famous after appearing on a popular TV show which spotlights criminals and "war heroes," and begin committing crimes specifically for the show's host. This obvious satire from the director of *Pretty Village, Pretty Flame* begins well and has some great moments (the two boys getting one of their grandmothers high is a very funny running gag), but soon gets less interesting (and more unpleasant and nihilistic) as it goes. *The Wounds* offers a peek or two into Serbia's hellish atmosphere in the early '90s, but by the end, the film resembles nothing so much as a typical, violent "hood" film with a foreign accent. (Serbo-Croatian with English subtitles) ★★ VHS: $79.99; DVD: $29.99

W

Woyzeck

(1979, 80 min, Germany, Werner Herzog) *Klaus Kinski, Eva Mattes.* Kinski gives a harrowing and unforgettable performance as a dim-witted but well-intentioned army private who is pushed over the edge of sanity by his common-law wife (Mattes) and a ruthless society. Herzog delivers a chilling and devastating parable of social repression and dormant rebellion. The film is adapted from scenes of a Georg Büchner play written in 1837, which was left unfinished after the death of the author at 23. (Remade in 1994) (Letterboxed) (German with English subtitles) ★★★ VHS: $14.99; DVD: $29.99

WR: Mysteries of the Organism

(1971, 86 min, Yugoslavia, Dusan Makavejev) *Milena Dravic, Jagoda Kaloper.* This strikingly original film by Makavejev, the bad boy of Yugoslavian cinema, is a clever, amusing and, at times, exasperating political satire which quite seriously proposes sex as an ideological imperative for liberation: a plea for Erotic Socialism. Using a montage method of filming, Makavejev examines the theories of sexologist Wilhelm Reich and juxtaposes documentary footage of Reich's disciples with two fictional stories — scenarios that propose a link between sexual energy and political liberation and repression with Stalinism. A breakthrough film which encapsulates the political and sexual revolution of its era. (Serbo-Croatian with English subtitles) ★★★½ VHS: $24.99

The Wraith

(1986, 92 min, US, Mike Marvin) *Charlie Sheen, Nick Cassavetes, Randy Quaid, Sherilyn Fenn.* Out-of-its-mind horror film about an out-of-this-world entity challenging a menacing Arizona hot rod gang to the death. ★

The Wreck of the Mary Deare

(1959, 100 min, US/GB, Michael Anderson) *Gary Cooper, Charlton Heston, Michael Redgrave, Alexander Knox, Richard Harris.* There's a good amount of suspense to this straightforward but nevertheless involving maritime adventure. Heston plays a salvager who happens upon a derelict ship, the Mary Deare. However, when he boards it, he discovers it is not abandoned: Captain Cooper is still on board. And he refuses to reveal the secret as to what actually happened. The film tries to maintain tension throughout as to whether Cooper is innocent or guilty of grounding the ship; it's much more successful as to why, not who. Good scenic design and special effects. ★★½ VHS: $19.99

Wrestling Ernest Hemingway

(1993, 123 min, US, Randa Haines) *Richard Harris, Robert Duvall, Shirley MacLaine, Sandra Bullock.* The teaming of Harris and Duvall propels this somber but involving character study which is as alluring as it is tedious. Harris plays a 70-ish old salt who when not boasting of the titular bout is drunk in self-pity. Duvall is a Cuban ex-barber, whose life seems to revolve around the crush he has on a young waitress (Bullock). The story takes off when the two men befriend each other; predictably, each brings some sort of meaning to the other's life. There are some poignant moments, but the film is sabotaged by a humorless screenplay, which only accentuates the dreariness of these men's lives.

Duvall, accent and all, is fascinating to watch. ★★½ VHS: $14.99

Written on the Wind

(1956, 99 min, US, Douglas Sirk) *Lauren Bacall, Rock Hudson, Robert Stack, Dorothy Malone.* Sirk's classic melodrama about the fall of an oil tycoon's family enjoyed a successful rerelease after a 20-year theatrical absence. Filmed in lurid color and acted in a heightened and exaggerated style, we watch the self-destructive antics of the Hadley children. The son (Stack) is a lush and his sister (Malone, in an Oscar-winning performance) is a nymphomaniac. Add "good girl" Bacall and Hudson and you get a continually enjoyable potboiler in the great 1950s Hollywood tradition. "Dynasty" and "Dallas," move over! ★★★½ VHS: $14.99; DVD: $29.99

The Wrong Arm of the Law

(1962, 94 min, GB, Cliff Owen) *Peter Sellers, Lionel Jeffries, Nanette Newman, Bernard Cribbins.* Sellers excels in this comedy caper as Pearly Gates, a Cockney criminal mastermind whose recent scores are being hijacked by an Australian gang posing as cops. ★★★ VHS: $39.99

The Wrong Box

(1966, 105 min, GB, Bryan Forbes) *Peter Sellers, Michael Caine, John Mills, Ralph Richardson, Peter Cook, Dudley Moore.* This beguiling farce is a sterling example of the great British comedies of the '60s. Based on a story coauthored by Robert Louis Stevenson, this merry romp concerns itself with an up-for-grabs inheritance and a migratory cadaver. The comedy is utter nonsense, a precursor to Monty Python, presented with superb precision and vigor by an all-star cast. ★★★½ VHS: $59.99

Wrong Is Right

(1982, 117 min, US, Richard Brooks) *Sean Connery, George Grizzard, Robert Conrad, Katharine Ross.* Fans of Connery should not miss this amusing, fast-paced story in which he plays a Scottish version of Geraldo Rivera: a superstar TV reporter whose deep involvement with his stories puts him in the middle of a violent U.S. government-hatched intrigue. The film's convoluted story, about our TV-dominated culture as well as a pre-Grenada lament on the impotency of America's strength, has some holes, but Connery is great in this breakneck action-comedy. ★★★ VHS: $79.99

The Wrong Man

(1956, 105 min, US, Alfred Hitchcock) *Henry Fonda, Vera Miles, Anthony Quayle.* An unusual departure for Hitchcock, this semidocumentary focuses on a New York musician (Fonda) who is mistakenly arrested for a flurry of robberies. Based on a true story, this is a frightening glimpse at the rites of police and legal procedure and the ensuing dehumanization of imprisonment. Miles portrays the man's wife, broken by the shattering chain of misfortune. ★★★½ VHS: $14.99

The Wrong Move

(1975, 103 min, West Germany, Wim Wenders) *Rudiger Vogler, Nastassja Kinski, Hanna Schygulla.* A young writer sets out from home to roam the country for adventure and inspiration. Along the way he meets an old singer and his mute companion, a juggler (14-year-old Kinski) and

an actress (Schygulla). They all join together in this stimulating journey through Germany. (German with English subtitles) ★★★

Wrongfully Accused

(1998, 85 min, US, Pat Proft) *Leslie Nielsen, Richard Crenna, Kelly Le Brock, Michael York, Sandra Bernhard.* Too little too late, *Wrongfully Accused* is a lightweight, amusing spoof which has some extremely funny moments to offer but is sadly a reminder of better times of a comic genre which is slowly fizzling out. With *The Fugitive* as its main target, this genial parody has a spry Nielsen as Ryan Harrison, a concert violinist (that's funny in itself) who's framed for the murder of a tycoon (York). Found incredibly guilty, he escapes en route to prison thanks to a train accident — they milk this for all it's worth. On the run (and trying to hide out in his yellow prison uniform in one of the film's best sight gags), Harrison is dogged by the persistent Lt. Fergus Falls (Crenna). Nielsen is game for almost any joke, and credit must go to this tireless actor for not only his good humor but his zeal as well. ★★½ VHS: $9.99; DVD: $14.99

Wuthering Heights

(1939, 103 min, US, William Wyler) *Laurence Olivier, Merle Oberon, Geraldine Fitzgerald, David Niven.* Wyler's beautiful, haunting adaptation of the Emily Brontë novel of doomed love in pre-Victorian England. Olivier is the brooding Heathcliff and Oberon is his undying love Kathy. Have extra tissues on hand for this classic tearjerker. ★★★★ VHS: $14.99; DVD: $24.99

Wuthering Heights

(1953, 90 min, Mexico, Luis Bunuel) *Iraseme Dilian, Jorge Mistral, Lilia Prado, Ernesto Alonso.* Based on the Emily Brontë classic, Buñuel's Mexican potboiler is a steamy, characteristically sinister statement on obsessive love and lethal lust. Removed from the blustery Yorkshire shores to a dusty, sunbaked landscape, the film has an even greater sense of desperation. Alejandro (the film's Heathcliff) is a coiled serpent, dashing and deadly, who returns to his childhood home determined to reclaim the affections of his longtime love, Catalina. When she remains faithful to her husband, Alejandro spitefully marries her sister. Passions flair and defenses crumble in the final confrontation at Catalina's deathbed. (Spanish with English subtitles) ★★★ VHS: $24.99; DVD: $24.99

Wuthering Heights

(1970, 105 min, GB, Robert Fuest) *Timothy Dalton, Anna Calder-Marchall, Harry Andrews.* A well-made, atmospheric and romantic version of the Emily Brontë classic of doomed love in pre-Victorian England. Dalton makes a dashing Heathcliff. Of course, it doesn't compare to the 1939 Olivier-Oberon version, but what could? ★★★

Wuthering Heights

Starring Ralph Fiennes and Juliette Binoche *See:* Emily Brontë's Wuthering Heights

Wyatt Earp

(1994, 190 min, US, Lawrence Kasdan) *Kevin Costner, Dennis Quaid, Gene Hackman, Michael Madsen, Bill Pullman, Isabella Rossellini, JoBeth Williams.* The curious real-life relationship between no-nonsense lawman Wyatt Earp (Costner) and tubercular cardshark Doc Holliday (Quaid) translates into an engrossing cinematic experience. Quaid's performance as the morally precarious, deathly ill and completely ironic Holliday is inspired and plays perfectly against Costner's dead-pan, straightlaced Earp. Unfortunately, the Earp/Holliday relationship takes up only a quarter of the film which devotes too much time to the admittedly picturesque vistas of the American West and to Costner's steely stares. A talented roster of actors deliver first-rate performances but none are able to sufficiently expand upon their less than delineated characters. (Pan & scan; letterboxed director's cut also available) ★★★ VHS: $19.99

The X-Files: The Movie

(1998, 121 min, US, Rob Bowman) *David Duchovny, Gillian Anderson, Martin Landau, Blythe Danner, Armin Mueller-Stahl.* If you're not already conversant with the mythology of the popular sci-fi TV series, this film version nevertheless stands on its own as a marvelously crafted evocation of conspiracy theory and mistrust of government; simultaneously, it is a perfect keystone for the TV series. Events which transpired in prehistory are uncovered in present-day Texas, initiating a new phase of a cover-up of unimaginable proportions. A building with government offices is demolished in an apparent act of terrorism. The bodies of three firemen and a small boy are discovered; but did they die in the blast? Agents Mulder (Duchovny) and Scully (Anderson), part of an FBI team sent in by a warning phone call, barely escape the massive destruction. The swiftly paced story line unfolds without stinting on personal elements of characterization. (VHS available letterboxed or pan & scan) ★★★ VHS: $14.99; DVD: $34.99

X-Men

(2000, 104 min, US, Bryan Singer) *Patrick Stewart, Hugh Jackman, Ian McKellen, Halle Berry, Famke Janssen, Anna Paquin, Bruce Davison, James Marsden, Rebecca Romijn-Stamos.* Welcome to Mutant High! Or at least, that's what part of this action-packed comic book romp resembles, a fun-loving and snappily produced live-action cartoon based on the Marvel Comics series. Stewart and McKellen star as, respectively, Professor X and Magneto, arch enemies in the world of the Mutants. While Professor X runs a school for mutants where he trains these young evolutionary misfits, Magneto lurks in dark caves and plots to lay waste to the non-mutant world. Into the fray comes Paquin, a young woman who has no idea what's wrong with her (anyone she touches goes into a coma) and who has latched onto the irascible Wolverine (Jackman). Together, they find themselves at Professor X's private academy where the X-Men attempt to convert them to good. Will they join in time to stop Magneto's dastardly plot, or will

Magneto win their allegiance and put an end to the X-Men forever? It's all good, old-fashioned fun with the two titans of British acting (Stewart and McKellen) nicely paired off. The standout performances belong to Paquin and Jackman, the latter's brooding demeanor reminiscent of a young Clint Eastwood. ★★★ VHS: $14.99; DVD: $22.99

Xanadu

(1980, 88 min, US, Robert Greenwald) *Olivia Newton-John, Gene Kelly, Michael Beck.* A campy guilty pleasure, this quintessential 1980's "disco musical" was a box-office flop and despised by critics everywhere. True, the story of a muse (Newton-John) who comes to life to inspire a young artist (Beck) is loaded with sappy and sometimes silly plot developments, and director Greenwald, while possessing a talent for visuals, hasn't an idea about narrative. But for those willing to bask in its unpretentious and curiously effective fantasy elements and musical numbers, *Xanadu* is a disco-thumping, roller-boogeyin' lark. The good score helps. Kelly, in his final dramatic role (if you can call it dramatic), appears as sort of a wise sage who opens a dance hall and gets to perform a dance or two. ★★½ VHS: $9.99; DVD: $24.99

Xica

(1976, 107 min, Brazil, Carlos Diegues) *Zezé Motta.* Diegues' exuberant historical comedy is based on the tale of a voluptuous black slave who single-handedly wrapped an 18th-century Brazilian village around her finger by conquering its wealthy diamond contractor with her sexual prowess. As she exploits her newfound powers, the townspeople become increasingly enraged at her extravagances and whimsical self-indulgence prompting them to call for a governmental investigator. Motta stars as the devil-may-care Xica, whose sexual bravado and powerful flamboyance captivate men and usurp their authority. The film sparkles with humor while touching on the subject of freedom, the spirit to survive and individual revolution. (Portuguese with English subtitles) ★★★ VHS: $79.99

Xiu Xiu: The Sent Down Girl

(1999, 100 min, China, Joan Chen) *Lu Lu, Lopsang.* Director Chen is at this writing banned from her native China for her film, *Xiu Xiu: The Sent Down Girl,* which she filmed without government sanction in remote corners of the harshly beautiful countryside, smuggling the footage out of the country to avoid censorship. During China's Cultural Revolution, members of the professional and intellectual classes were removed from their urban homes and shipped to distant rural areas for political reeducation. Xiu Xiu is 15 years old when she is issued an army coat ten sizes too large for her and herded into military transport. Lost in a massive bureaucracy, subject to impersonal cruelty and casual malice, she is given arbitrary assignments by small men with too much power. The natural tendency to melodrama inherent in the story — which reflects millions of true stories — is ameliorated by the caliber of the performances, especially those of the two principle characters. Lu Lu is utterly believable as the child who naïvely counts the days until her return to her family and her former life; Lopsang imparts quiet dignity to the role of the horse herder, a gentle soul and Xiu Xiu's only protector. A thoughtful and thought-provoking film. (Mandarin with English subtitles) ★★★ VHS: $102.99; DVD: $24.99

Yaaba (Grandmother)

(1989, 90 min, Burkina Faso, Idrissa Ouedraogo) *Fatimata Sanga, Noufou Ouedraogo, Roukietou Barry.* Bila and Nopoko are young cousins in a small African village, whose residents eke out a rough living from an unforgiving land. Bila is a mischievous boy with a good heart, whose father is the town drunk; Nopoko, who has lost her mother, is caring and joyful. They're bonded by mutual support and affection. The children befriend an old woman, Sana, who lives on the fringes of the village, ostracized as a witch. When Nopoko's life is endangered, Sana may be her only hope. The children who portray Bila and Nopoko deliver remarkable performances, authentic and natural and unselfconscious. While on the surface a small story cover-

The X-Files: The Movie

ing a brief time, *Yaaba* touches on all the major themes of any human drama. Human nature is constant; charlatans and prejudices exist everywhere, and the same basic conflicts persist in all communities. A gentle story on the cycles of life and human perserverence. (Mooré with English subtitles) ★★★ VHS: $89.99

The Yakuza

(1974, 112 min, US, Sydney Pollack) *Robert Mitchum, Brian Keith, Richard Jordan.* An ex-cop (Mitchum) battles the Japanese mafia to rescue the kidnapped daughter of an old friend (Keith). Robert Towne and Paul Schrader cowrote the script. ★★½ VHS: $14.99

Yanco

(1964, 90 min, Mexico, Servando Gonzales) *Ricardo Ancona.* A young boy in an Indian village thrives on music to escape the realities of his poverty-stricken surroundings, often running off to a secret hideout to play his homemade violin. One day, he meets an old man who is a master musician. The old man's violin becomes the instrument of their friendship as he teaches the child the wonders of music. Although in original Spanish language without subtitles, this beautifully-told tale conveys its story — whether you speak the language or not — through remarkably subtle yet overwhelming visual images. An affecting performance from Ancona as the young boy. ★★★

Yankee Doodle Dandy

(1942, 120 min, US, MIchael Curtiz) *James Cagney, Joan Leslie, Walter Huston, Rosemary DeCamp, George Tobias, S.Z. Sakall.* Cagney won an Oscar for his classic performance as the legendary song-and-dance man George M. Cohan. It is ironic that Cagney, American movies' quintessential gangster, is best remembered and had his most popular role in this entertaining musical biography. Can anyone forget Cagney's immortal interpretation of the title tune? ★★★½ VHS: $14.99

Yanks

(1979, 139 min, US, John Schlesinger) *Richard Gere, William Devane, Lisa Eichhorn, Vanessa Redgrave, Rachel Roberts.* An absorbing and literate WWII drama about American G.I.s stationed in England. Gere and Devane are but two of the "Yanks" who begin relationships with British women — Gere with young Eichhorn and Devane with married Redgrave. In support, Roberts gives a smashing performance as Eichhorn's inflexible mother. Fine direction from Schlesinger, who has a keen eye for the detail and atmosphere of the era. ★★★ VHS: $9.99

The Yards

(2000, 115 min, US, James Gray) *Mark Wahlberg, Joaquin Phoenix, Charlize Theron, Faye Dunaway, Ellen Burstyn, James Caan.* Director Gray made a striking debut with *Little Odessa*, an icy drama about the Russian mob in Brooklyn. Here, Gray slithers back into the underworld of New York and creates yet another indelible portrait of rot in the Big Apple. Wahlberg plays a likable ex-con trying to go straight, doomed to be dragged back into a life on the other side of the law when he takes a job with his Uncle (Caan), an influential Transit Authority contractor. Phoenix is the childhood friend who's already

Hugh Jackman is Wolverine in *X-Men*

made a name for himself in the "company," and whose fits of sudden rage trigger a devastating chain of events. Gray has once again assembled a superb cast, but if the film misses greatness by "thismuch" it's merely because the substantial weight of so many heavy-hitters makes the screenplay's rote emotional melodramatics seem all the more distracting. Still, the film's sweeping visual style is dreamily seductive and to compare him to Sidney Lumet as the new master-craftsman of the New York crime story. ★★★ VHS: $102.99; DVD: $32.99

The Year My Voice Broke

(1987, 105 min, Australia, John Duigan) *Noah Taylor, Leone Carmen, Ben Mendelsohn.* A better look at puberty blues than Bruce Beresford's film of that title, and as affecting and lovingly crafted as Rob Reiner's *Stand by Me*, this tale of teenage troubles is set in an Australian backwater town in the early '60s. Childhood friends Freya and Danny, along with Freya's new hoodlum boyfriend Trevor, begin the difficult transition from childhood to adolescence as well as learn of the hidden secrets of the town's older generation. Non-stereotypical characterization, disarming humor and a bittersweet conclusion that avoids simple sentimentality save this overdone plot from being a cliché. ★★★; DVD: $24.99

The Year of Living Dangerously

(1983, 115 min, Australia, Peter Weir) *Mel Gibson, Sigourney Weaver, Linda Hunt, Michael Murphy.* Gibson stars as a foreign correspondent whose attraction to a British attache (Weaver) pits his professional instincts against his personal allegiances. Weir directs with a discerning eye this torrid account of love and betrayal amidst Indonesia's 1965 military coup. Hunt won an Academy Award for her unforgettable performance as Gibson's male confidant. ★★★½ VHS: $14.99; DVD: $19.99

Year of the Comet

(1992, 89 min, US, Peter Yates) *Penelope Ann Miller, Timothy Daly, Ian Richardson, Louis Jordan, Art Malik.* The ever-perky Miller stars in this text-book romantic action/comedy about the downtrodden daughter of a wine dealer who reluctantly teams up with a dashing troubleshooter (Daly) to recover a stolen bottle of priceless wine. The good news is that this is acclaimed screenwriter William Goldman's first original script since *Butch Cassidy and the Sundance Kid.* The bad news is that it doesn't live up to the standards of his earlier works, nor those of director Yates. Nevertheless, the film has a few enjoyable moments and will make a good date movie. ★★

Year of the Dragon

(1985, 125 min, US, Michael Cimino) *Mickey Rourke, John Lone.* Controversial police thriller with Rourke as a New York City police captain assigned to the Chinatown district to keep peace among the neighboring gangs. Once there, however, he comes in conflict with a local underworld boss (Lone). Oliver Stone wrote the screenplay which relies heavily on violence and police actioner clichés. ★★½ VHS: $14.99

Year of the Gun

(1991, 111 min, US, John Frankenheimer) *Andrew McCarthy, John Pankow, Sharon Stone, Valeria Golino.* After a slow start, lots of un-subtitled Italian and a less-than-compelling performance by McCarthy, this political thriller by Frankenheimer gets into gear, intensifies and delivers. Set in Rome during the late '70s, McCarthy plays a journalist writing a fictionalized account of a Red Brigade plot to kidnap Aldo Moro. Paranoia and violence quickly follow when the dangerously accurate manuscript is stolen. A good supporting cast includes Pankow as a mysterious professor, Stone as a mysterious photojournalist and Golino as McCarthy's mysterious girlfriend. ★★½ VHS: $9.99; DVD: $19.99

A Year of the Quiet Sun

(1985, 106 min, Poland/West Germany, Krzysztof Zanussi) *Scott Wilson, Maja Komorowska.* Internationally renowned Polish filmmaker Zanussi directed this haunting and poignant love story set in a ravaged post-war Poland. An American soldier, sent to investigate

XYZ

war crimes, falls in love with a Polish widow. The film skillfully and sensitively captures their awkward attempts at communication, attempts that are at first hindered by the lack of a common language. A universal story about a love that is greater than the barriers of language and politics. (Polish with English subtitles) ★★★½

The Yearling
(1946, 134 min, US, Clarence Brown) *Gregory Peck, Jane Wyman, Claude Jarman, Jr., Chill Wills, Henry Travers, June Lockhart.* Classic screen version of Marjorie Kinnan Rawling's Pulitzer Prize-winning novel about a small boy's love for a young deer. Peck and Wyman are fine as the child's parents, and Jarman gives a remarkable performance as the young boy. Beautifully photographed. (Remade in 1994) ★★★★ VHS: $14.99

Yellow Earth
(1984, 89 min, China, Chen Kaige) *Xue Bai, Wang Xueqi.* An early film collaboration of two proponents of China's New Wave of cinema, Chen and Zhang Yimou, this film revolves around a young soldier sent out to gather folk songs which will be used by the Party to rouse the patriotism of the revolutionaries. Brother Gu, as the soldier is affectionately named, is treated with great respect at a wedding and is told to stay with a sheep-herding family in the hills. The young daughter, who is a fine singer, falls for the young soldier and decides to get out of her arranged marriage in order to join him in the city. This simple tale has the same sense of unfulfilled passion of other New Wave films, but the cinematography and performances save this from being one of the usual fare. (Mandarin with English subtitles) ★★★ VHS: $19.99

Yellow Submarine
(1968, 88 min, GB, George Dunning) *Voices of: The Beatles.* Fantastic animated romp with the Fab Four fighting to save Pepperland from the Blue Meanies with the message that "All You Need is Love." Other Beatles' songs include "Nowhere Man," "Lucy in the Sky with Diamonds" and "When I'm Sixty-Four." Includes a previously unreleased animated performance of "Hey, Bulldog." ★★★½ VHS: $19.99; DVD: $29.99

Yentl
(1983, 134 min, US, Barbra Streisand) *Barbra Streisand, Mandy Patinkin, Amy Irving, Nehemiah Persoff, Steven Hill.* Streisand shines as both star and director in this underrated, likable musical based on a story by Isaac Bashevis Singer (*Enemies: A Love Story*). Set in turn-of-the-century Russia, Streisand plays a woman who disguises herself as a boy to gain admittance to a yeshiva, an all-male school for Talmudic study. Patinkin is a fellow student who befriends "Yentl, the Yeshiva Boy," and Irving nicely plays Patinkin's fiancée. The only complaint is why cast someone with the incredible vocal talents of Patinkin in a musical and not let him sing. ★★★ VHS: $19.99

Yesterday, Today and Tomorrow
(1964, 119 min, Italy, Vittorio De Sica) *Sophia Loren, Marcello Mastroianni.* A tour de force for director De Sica as well as Loren and

Yojimbo

Mastroianni. This "battle-of-the-sexes" comedy is set in the framework of three episodes, each employing different stories, acting styles and locations (Rome, Milan and Naples). A delightful Academy Award-winning satire which features a striptease by Loren that still heats up the screen. (Dubbed) ★★★★ VHS: $19.99

Yi Yi (A One and a Two)
(2000, 173 min, Taiwan, Edward Yang) *Wu Nienjen, Elaine Jin, Kelly Lee, Jonathan Chang, Tang Ruyun.* A mesmerizingly intimate epic that takes familial threads and expresses its emotions reservedly, despite the brash Americanization of the Taiwan it depicts. Director Yang, 2000's Cannes' Best Director recipient, has solid control of his drama, his eye similar to that of his 8-year-old character and namesake Yang-Yang (Chang). This inquisitive boy photographs the backs of people's heads, to show them what they can't see. That's an apt metaphor for the movie, which takes the time to explore how people come to make life's myriad of difficult decisions, and the matters of the heart that we take for granted. Yang-Yang's father, NJ (Nienjen), has just met his high school love (three decades later) and must balance his desires and his family. NJ's white-collar job is falling apart, his mother-in-law is in a coma, his older daughter is in a budding romance, and his brother-in-law has just undertaken a shot-gun marriage. But those are the "what"s; *Yi Yi* is all about other questions: why do we make certain choices in our lives, how do we get there, and who does that ultimately make us? Absorbing, affecting, and surprisingly beautiful, *Yi Yi* is so moving precisely because it is so human. (Taiwanese, Mandarin, Japanese and English with English subtitles) ★★★★ VHS: $79.99; DVD: $24.99

Yiddle with a Fiddle (Yidl Mitn Fidl)
(1936, 92 min, Poland, Joseph Green) *Molly Picon.* This classic Yiddish musical-comedy stars Picon as a *shtetl* girl who, determined to discover a world closed off to her as a woman, disguises herself as a boy and joins up with a trav-

eling band of musicians. Picon, luminous in the performance of her career, soon falls in love with one of her colleagues but, with delightfully humorous results, is forced to keep her identity hidden from him. Filled with Jewish songs, vaudeville skits and scenes of everyday life, this film provides a glimpse of Jewish life in Poland before it was tragically destroyed. The first international Yiddish hit, *Yiddle with a Fiddle* is considered by many to be the best Yiddish film of all time. (Yiddish with English subtitles) ★★★★ VHS: $79.99

Yojimbo
(1961, 110 min, Japan, Akira Kurosawa) *Toshiro Mifune, Eijiro Tono.* In the style of an American western, *Yojimbo* matches a cynical, wandering samurai against two merchant families battling for control of a country town. Kurosawa hilariously satirizes greed, linking it to paranoia, pomposity and cowardice. (Sequel: *Sanjuro*) (American remake: *Last Man Standing*) (Japanese with English subtitles) ★★★★ VHS: $29.99; DVD: $29.99

Yol
(1982, 111 min, Turkey/Switzerland, Serif Goren & Yilmaz Gurney) *Tarik Akan, Serif Sezer.* A devastating drama dealing with political, ethnic and cultural repression in contemporary Turkey. Secretly written and directed while still in prison, directors Goren and Gurney offer a harrowing vision as seen through the lives of five prisoners who are granted temporary furloughs to visit their families. (Turkish with English subtitles) ★★★½

You Are Not Alone
(1981, 94 min, Denmark, Lasse Nielsen & Ernst Johansen) Unique and lyrical, this tale explores the boundaries of friendship and love between two young boys in a private boarding school in Copenhagen. The headmaster's inability to cope with the pair's mounting sexuality leads to their rebellion. (Dutch with English subtitles) ★★★ VHS: $29.99

You Can Count on Me

(2000, 111 min, US, Kenneth Lonergan) *Laura Linney, Mark Ruffalo, Matthew Broderick, Rory Culkin, Jon Tenney, Kenneth Lonergan.* A wonderful character study bolstered by two enchanting lead performances, writer-director Lonergan's comedy-drama is a blissfully adept study of a volatile brother-sister relationship. In a intuitive portrayal, Linney is captivating as Sammy, a single mother living in an upstate New York town who must cope with the arrival of her beloved but ne'er-do-well brother (an exceptional Ruffalo). Lonergan marvelously captures both the cadence of small-town America, and the expectations and disappointments that often define the relationship between siblings. Broderick plays her boss, with whom Sammy has an affair. ★★★½ VHS: $14.99; DVD: $29.99

You Can't Cheat an Honest Man

(1939, 76 min, US, George Marshall) *W.C. Fields, Edgar Bergen, Constance Moore, James Bush, Eddie "Rochester" Anderson.* A brisk comedy providing Fields a hilarious setting in which to flourish. As the entrepreneur of a traveling circus, Fields is adept at pulling up stakes and reaching the state line just before the law catches up with him. He also finds time to taunt children, short change his employees, and tangle with an assortment of wild animal and inanimate objects — particularly ventriloquist's dummy Charlie McCarthy. ★★★ VHS: $14.99

You Can't Take It with You

(1938, 127 min, US, Frank Capra) *Jean Arthur, James Stewart, Lionel Barrymore, Edward Arnold, Spring Byington, Ann Miller.* Capra's zany and uproarious screen version of Kaufman and Hart's classic Broadway comedy. Arthur stars as the daughter of an outrageously eccentric family out to win over her boyfriend's (Stewart) conservative parents. Though there's a touch of Capra's trademark sentimentality, this doesn't detract from the total enjoyment of this Academy Award-winning Best Picture. Such an engaging ensemble. ★★★★ VHS: $19.99

You Only Live Once

(1937, 86 min, US, Fritz Lang) *Henry Fonda, Sylvia Sidney, Ward Bond, Margaret Hamilton.* Lang directed this powerful social drama with Fonda as a wrongly imprisoned ex-con who tries to go straight. Also with Sidney as his wife. Solid performances from the two leads. Based partly on the lives of Bonnie and Clyde. ★★★

You Only Live Twice

(1967, 117 min, GB, Lewis Gilbert) *Sean Connery, Donald Pleasence, Lois Maxwell, Charles Gray.* SPECTRE steals both American and Soviet spacecrafts in an attempt to start WWIII. This James Bond adventure is the slightest of the Connery films, beset by plot holes and stiff supporting players; it only comes alive when Pleasence hits the screen as Blofeld. (Sequel: *On Her Majesty's Secret Service*) ★★ VHS: $9.99; DVD: $26.99

You So Crazy

(1994, 86 min, US, Thomas Schlamme) *Martin Lawrence.* Lawrence excels in this outrageous, untamed live concert performance where no stone is left unturned. Attacking everyone from Rodney King to Jeffrey Dahmer, this on-the-rise comic proves with no mercy that he is one of the funniest comedians to take the stage since Richard Pryor. Loud, rude and playfully offensive, this highly entertaining film is a must see for those in search of some trouser-wetting laughs. ★★★½ VHS: $9.99; DVD: $19.99

You Were Never Lovelier

(1942, 97 min, US, William A. Seiter) *Fred Astaire, Rita Hayworth, Adolphe Menjou, Xavier Cugat, Larry Parks.* Astaire was never debonair-er and Hayworth never more breathtaking-er than in this charming tale of innocent seduction, well-intentioned meddling and haywire miscommunications. Astaire once commented that Hayworth was his favorite dancing partner. Watch this and see why. ★★★½ VHS: $19.99

You'll Never Get Rich

(1941, 88 min, US, Sidney Lanfield) *Fred Astaire, Rita Hayworth, Robert Benchley.* Astaire and Hayworth make a most appealing team in this delightful musical comedy. Fred plays a Broadway hoofer and choreographer who gets drafted. He courts ravishing Rita and still manages to make the show go on. Cole Porter score includes "I Kissed My Baby Goodbye." ★★★ VHS: $19.99

You're a Big Boy Now

(1966, 96 min, US, Francis Ford Coppola) *Peter Kastner, Elizabeth Hartman, Geraldine Page, Rip Torn, Julie Harris, Karen Black.* A bit of a time warp, this outrageously entertaining coming-of-age comedy stars Kastner (for those old enough to remember, he was TV's "Ugliest Girl in Town") as a sheltered young man who leaves home and learns all about life, with help from dancer Hartman. Torn and Page are his parents — Page excels in what could be the most over-protective movie mom since Mrs. Bates. A real charmer. ★★★ VHS: $14.99

You've Got Mail

(1998, 119 min, US, Nora Ephron) *Tom Hanks, Meg Ryan, Greg Kinnear, Parker Posey, Jean Stapleton, Steve Zahn, Dave Chappelle.* A genuinely sweet romantic comedy based on Ernst Lubitsch's charming 1940 comedy *The Shop Around the Corner* (itself based on the play "Parfumerie" by Miklos Laszio). The story is basically the same but updated for '90s sensibilities: two antagonists are brought together and fall in love in spite of themselves. Though the original device was the personals in the newspaper, here the two become acquainted through e-mail. How millennium! Ryan is the owner of a small, Upper West Side bookstore slowly going out of business. Hanks is the owner of a mega-bookstore which is contributing to its demise. How they come together makes for fetching comedy. The supporting cast of characters is very appealing, though it is the magnetism of Hanks and Ryan which propels the tale. ★★★ VHS: $14.99; DVD: $19.99

The Young Americans

(1993, 100 min, GB, Danny Cannon) *Harvey Keitel, Viggo Mortensen, Iain Glen.* Keitel is a DEA advisor brought into a drug war investigation in London who confronts the hit man (Mortensen) he has tracked for eight years. Director Cannon delivers a well-acted, well-mounted production with a finely crafted story line and succinctly drawn characters which lift the film above its potentially derivative subject matter. Keitel's portrayal is his most modulated in recent memory, and Glen is especially affecting as a young man inadvertently drawn into the center of the investigation. This moody actioner is surprisingly effective in engaging the viewer's attention and sympathies. ★★★ VHS: $9.99

Young and Innocent

(1937, 82 min, GB, Alfred Hitchcock) *Nova Pilbeam, Derrick de Marney.* Plenty of Hitchcockian touches are to be found in this charming and chilling chase drama about a young man, falsely accused of murder, who, with the help of his girlfriend, pursues the real culprit: the man with the eye twitch! ★★★

Young at Heart

(1954, 117 min, US, Gordon Douglas) *Frank Sinatra, Doris Day, Gig Young, Ethel Barrymore.* Bright musical remake of *Four Daughters*, with Day as the daughter of a small-town musician who is courted by Sinatra. ★★★ VHS: $14.99

Mark Ruffalo and Laura Linney in *You Can Count on Me*

Young Catherine

(1991, 106 min, GB, Michael Anderson) *Vanessa Redgrave, Julia Ormond, Christopher Plummer.* Set in Russia of 1744, this period drama chronicles the power struggle between the Empress Elizabeth (Redgrave) and her daughter-in-law, Catherine (Ormond). Saddled with an impotent husband, Catherine bears a bastard child and attempts to have him installed on the throne. ★★★ VHS: $79.99

Young Doctors in Love

(1982, 97 min, US, Garry Marshall) *Michael McKean, Sean Young, Dabney Coleman, Hector Elizondo.* A funny farce about life in a metropolitan hospital, in the tradition of *Airplane!* and *The Naked Gun.* Includes many a cameo from stars of TV soap operas. ★★★ VHS: $14.99

Young Einstein

(1989, 90 min, Australia, Yahoo Serious) *Yahoo Serious, Odile Le Clezio.* Fans of *Bill and Ted's Excellent Adventure* might find humor in this minor comedy from Yahoo Serious. Once touted to be Australia's next great export, Serious directed, wrote and stars in this Albert Einstein spoof about the son of a Tazmanian farm family who knows inherently that he is destined for great things (i.e. splitting the atom to put bubbles in beer). Unfortunately, the film relies too heavily on Jeff Darling's vivid cinematography and fails to exploit the comedy of this potentially humorous premise. ★★ VHS: $14.99

Young Frankenstein

(1974, 105 min, US, Mel Brooks) *Gene Wilder, Madeline Kahn, Teri Garr, Peter Boyle, Marty Feldman, Cloris Leachman, Howard Morris.* Brooks is at his best with this hilarious spoof of the *Frankenstein* films, hitting every comic mark with uncanny accuracy. Wilder stars as the soon-to-be demented doc, Dr. Frankenstein ("That's Frahnken*steen*), giving an inspired comic performance. Great in support are Feldman as Ygor ("That's Eye-gore"), the sardonic wit of the laboratory set, Kahn as the "Bride of Frankenstein," and Boyle as "the monster." Authentic sets from the 1930s films, astounding black-and-white cinematography, and an atmospheric score by John Morris contribute to the sheer delight of this comedy classic. ★★★★ VHS: $14.99; DVD: $22.99

Young Guns

(1988, 107 min, US, Christopher Cain) *Emilio Estevez, Kiefer Sutherland, Charlie Sheen, Lou Diamond Phillips, Dermot Mulroney, Casey Siemaszko.* The Brat Pack on horses! Slick western adventure with the boys trying to tame the wild West, and get revenge for their mentor's murder. (Letterboxed VHS available for $14.99) ★★½ VHS: $9.99; DVD: $9.99

Young Guns 2

(1990, 105 min, US, Geoff Murphy) *Emilio Estevez, William Petersen, Kiefer Sutherland, Christian Slater, Lou Diamond Phillips, Alan Ruck, Balthazar Getty.* Annoying sequel to the 1988 hit finds Billy the Kid (Estevez) on the run from former friend-turned-bounty hunter Pat Garrett (Petersen). The cast is likable cast, but this one lacks the element of fun that made the first one watchable. ★½ VHS: $9.99; DVD: $14.99

The Young Lions

(1958, 167 min, US, Edward Dmytryk) *Marlon Brando, Montgomery Clift, Dean Martin, Hope Lange, Maximilian Schell.* A somewhat overlong but nevertheless mesmerizing WWII epic, based on Irwin Shaw's novel examining the volatile relationship between two American soldiers and a Nazi officer. Clift and Martin are the former; a rather restrained Brando is the German soldier undergoing a moral edification in light of his country's actions. ★★★ VHS: $19.99

Young Man with a Horn

(1950, 112 min, US, Michael Curtiz) *Kirk Douglas, Lauren Bacall, Doris Day, Hoagy Carmichael.* The three leads are all quite good in this romantic drama about trumpeter Douglas trying to make it in the jazz world, and torn between Bacall and Day. Based on the life of Bix Beiderbecke. ★★★ VHS: $19.99

Young Master

(1980, 102 min, Hong Kong, Jackie Chan) *Jackie Chan, Yuen Biao, Wei Pai.* Made back when Jackie was beginning to exercise creative control over his own films, this amalgam of comedy and action shows him trying to make a movie firmly within the kung fu genre, while also developing his own unique comedic persona. Jackie is Ah Lung, a gifted kung fu student who is thrown out of his school in disgrace. Looking for his brother, who was also thrown out, he gets involved in a case of mistaken identity and is branded a fugitive. After clearing his name, he helps the authorities capture the real criminal. The story here is strictly by-the-numbers and the comedy touches are a bit forced, but the fighting scenes are all top-notch. (Cantonese with English subtitles) ★★★ VHS: $19.99; DVD: $49.99

The Young Philadelphians

(1959, 136 min, US, Vincent Sherman) *Paul Newman, Barbara Rush, Robert Vaughn, Alexis Smith, Brian Keith, Adam West.* Newman stars as a lawyer from the poor side of the tracks who works his way up the corporate and social ladders. Rush is the society woman he romances. Vaughn is quite good (he received an Oscar nomination) as Newman's old Army buddy. ★★★ VHS: $14.99

The Young Poisoner's Handbook

(1996, 99 min, GB, Benjamin Ross) *Hugh O'Conor, Antony Sher, Ruth Sheen, Charlotte Coleman.* This very entertaining black comedy tells the true story of Graham Young, a young chemistry buff who becomes obsessed with some lethal concoctions and begins testing them, in a very scientifically sound manner, mind you, on other human beings. Motivated more by intellectual curiosity than hatred, he slowly poisons his mother and father in a series of carefully controlled experiments. That is, until he gets caught and sent to a psychiatric hospital. There he is taken under the wing of a doctor with a radical new method for treating psychotic misfits and Graham deludes both himself and his psychiatrist into believing that he is cured. The audience, however, knows better. The film revels in its dark comedy and its gleefully wicked re-creation/satire of England in the 1950s and '60s. ★★★

Young Sherlock Holmes

(1985, 110 min, US, Barry Levinson) *Nicholas Rowe, Alan Cox, Sophie Ward.* Steven Spielberg produced this stylish and very entertaining mystery adventure. Sherlock Holmes and Dr. Watson meet for the first time as schoolmates and investigate the apparent suicides of civic leaders. Terrific special effects include a stalking stained-glass window and pastries on parade. ★★★ VHS: $14.99

Young Toerless

(1965, 90 min, Germany, Volker Schlöndorff) *Mathieu Carriere, Marian Seidowsky, Bernd Tischer, Jean Launay, Barbara Steele.* Schlöndorff's first film is an intense psychological thriller about a boy in a rural German boys' school who wants to report the torture of a fellow classmate, but encounters fear and intimidation. A chilling metaphor for the terror of living under Nazi rule. (German with English subtitles) ★★★½ VHS: $29.99

Young Winston

(1972, 157 min, GB, Richard Attenborough) *Simon Ward, Anne Bancroft, Robert Shaw, Ian Holm, John Mills.* Hold on to your horses. We're off on a two-and-a-half-hour essay on the youthful days of Winston Churchill. While hardly representative of Britain's finest hour, this is an interesting and entertaining account of the young Churchill's life — following him through a lonely childhood, battles in India, his exploits in the Boer Wars, and his first election to Parliament. The battle scenes are superb. ★★★ VHS: $19.99

Youngblood

(1986, 109 min, US, Peter Markle) *Rob Lowe, Patrick Swayze, Cynthia Gibb.* Tedious sports drama with Lowe as a farmboy who joins a Canadian minor league hockey team, becoming involved with the coach's daughter. ★½ VHS: $9.99; DVD: $14.99

Younger & Younger

(1994, 97 min, US, Percy Adlon) *Donald Sutherland, Lolita Davidovich, Brendan Fraser, Linda Hunt, Sally Kellerman, Julie Delpy.* Whatever happened to Percy Adlon? After making a promising start in his native Germany, he came to the States and made the wonderful *Bagdad Cafe.* But after that came dreck and more dreck. This dreck concerns Jonathan Younger (Sutherland) and his storage company and all the quirky people that work there and visit and all the quirky things that happen in all the quirky places in and about the company. Now there's nothing wrong with quirky. But here the characters are just clichés (Jonathan is a lothario; his wife, played by Davidovich, is a frump; their son Fraser is a prig; etc.), and they add nothing to an already pointless story. ★½ VHS: $14.99

Your Friends and Neighbors

(1998, 99 min, US, Neil LaBute) *Amy Brenneman, Aaron Eckhart, Catherine Keener, Nastassja Kinski, Jason Patric, Ben Stiller.* In a how-do-you-top-that second effort after his controversial debut film *In the Company of Men,* writer-director LaBute doesn't disappoint with this equally controversial, funny and penetrating look at a group of male friends and their affairs and camaraderie. Stiller is Jerry, a self-important professor whose routine bull sessions with Barry (Eckhart) and Cary (Patric) form the core of the film. More interested in the dynamics of male-female relationships, La Bute uses these get-togethers as a sounding board for his (characters') most inner thoughts. Keener is excellent as Jerry's current fling, and her budding lesbian is the most interesting of these sexual provocateurs. Though Patric's steam-room tale of earlier sexual exploits is an unsettling and hypnotic scene which is certain to be the most talked about piece from the film. ★★★ VHS: $14.99; DVD: $19.99

Yours, Mine and Ours

(1968, 111 min, US, Melville Shavelson) *Henry Fonda, Lucille Ball, Van Johnson, Tim Matheson.* A theatrical "Brady Bunch," and not without some laughs. Fonda, widowed father of ten, marries widow Ball, mother of six. All hell breaks loose when they gather the kids and move in together. An old-fashioned, sentimental comedy. ★★½ VHS: $14.99; DVD: $14.99

Z

(1969, 127 min, Algeria/France, Costa-Gavras) *Yves Montand, Irene Papas, Jean-Louis Trintignant, Charles Denner.* A swiftly moving political thriller on fascist corruption in the Greek government. Costa-Gavras has delivered an exciting, even riveting exposé of social ills and the abuses of power. Academy Award winner for Best Foreign Film. (French with English subtitles) ★★★★ VHS: $14.99

Z.P.G.

(1972, 95 min, GB, Michael Campus) *Oliver Reed, Geraldine Chaplin.* This apocalyptic vision of overpopulation is set in the 21st century where reproduction is a crime punishable by death, gas masks are the hip new fashion accessory, and state-provided robot dolls are issued to couples who want to have children. Chaplin and Reed star as a couple who defy the government's stance of Zero Population Growth by having a real child in this grim but stylish pro-lifer's nightmare. ★★★ VHS: $14.99

Zabriskie Point

(1970, 110 min, US, Michelangelo Antonioni) *Mark Frechette, Daria Halprin, Rod Taylor, Harrison Ford.* A political and sociological time capsule that presents a disturbing view of 1960s America — a turbulent time of political unrest and student upheaval. This rambling study by Antonioni gets a bit bogged down in polemics and the result is a film less satisfying than *Blow-Up* in documenting the social ferment in a foreign country. Nonetheless, with sweeping photography set in Death Valley, a script cowritten by Sam Shepard, a cameo appearance by a young Ford and an explosive subject matter, the film is novel and compelling. (Filmed in English) ★★★ VHS: $19.99

Zardoz

(1974, 105 min, GB, John Boorman) *Sean Connery, Charlotte Rampling.* Boorman's bizarre and overloaded science-fiction adventure is set in the year 2293 when the Eternals (a group of ageless intellectuals) live inside a dome and send orders to the Exterminator to kill the Brutals who inhabit the wasteland outside. Connery plays an Exterminator with a con-

science who penetrates the secrets of the dome and enters a maze of mind-boggling imagery. Boorman's imagination runs wild like it never has. ★★½ VHS: $19.99; DVD: $24.99

Zatoichi

From the classic *The Life and Opinion of Masseur Ichi* s.prings a series of films chronicling the adventures of the blind swordsman in his travels through a rural Japan fraught with bandits, unscrupulous officials and waylaid innocents. Shintaro Katsu is engaging as the self-effacing masseuse, whose sightlessness camouflages his unerring martial arts abilities. He drinks, he gambles and he kills only when necessary. He's a consistently entertaining character. First-rate production values, fine supporting casts and Katsu's endearing interpretation of his character make this series a guaranteed good time. (The inspiration for Rutger Hauer's action-adventure film *Blind Fury*.)

Zatoichi: The Life and Opinion of Masseur Ichi

(1962, 96 min, Japan, Kenji Misumi) *Shintaro Katsu.* The first entry in the Zatoichi series finds the blind swordsman caught between two rival warlords engaged in a bloody territorial feud. More somber in tone than the films which followed it and with slightly grainy black-and-white cinematography, but all the elements are there. Katsu is perfection as the blind traveling masseuse whose comic bungling hides his unerring martial artistry. (Japanese with English subtitles) ★★★½ VHS: $59.99

Zatoichi: Masseur Ichi and a Chest of Gold

(1964, 83 min, Japan, Kazuo Ikehiro) *Shintaro Katsu.* Zatoichi visits the grave of a man he killed two years earlier. While he's there, the village tax payment — a chest of gold — is stolen on the way to the government office. Zatoichi is accused of the robbery and vows to find the real thieves. ★★★ VHS: $19.99

Zatoichi: The Blind Swordsman and the Chess Expert

(1965, 87 min, Japan, Kenji Misumi) *Shintaro Katsu.* Zatoichi strikes up a friendship with a samurai chess master on an undisclosed mission, becoming involved in a convoluted web of misplaced loyalties and deceit. ★★★ VHS: $19.99

Zatoichi: The Blind Swordsman's Vengeance

(1966, 83 min, Japan, Tokuzo Tanaka) *Shintaro Katsu.* Zatoichi comes upon a man waylaid by bandits. After killing the highwaymen, he hears the last request of the dying victim: To give a full purse to someone named Taichi. He finds the intended recipient, a small boy, in a village at the mercy of a brutal overlord. You can take it from there. ★★★ VHS: $59.99

Zatoichi: The Blind Swordsman and the Fugitives

(1968, 82 min, Japan, Kimiyoshi Yasuda) *Shintaro Katsu.* A corrupt village official, running a sweat shop with the town's young women, is blackmailed into providing refuge for a band of sadistic fugitives. While staying with the town's selfless, humanitarian doctor, Zatoichi discovers a link from the past which

connects two unlikely protagonists in the ensuing conflict. Swift-moving with strong characterizations. (Japanese with English subtitles) ★★★ VHS: $59.99

Zatoichi Meets Yojimbo

(1970, 115 min, Japan, Kihachi Okamoto) *Toshiro Mifune, Shintaro Katsu.* Mifune re-creates his character Yojimbo from the Akira Kurosawa classic, here teaming with blind master swordsman Zatoichi (Katsu) to eliminate the gangsters who have taken over a small village and stolen and hid a fortune in gold belonging to the government. An action-filled and fun spoof of samurai films. (Japanese with English subtitles) ★★★½ VHS: $39.99

Zazie dans le Metro

(1960, 88 min, France, Louis Malle) *Philippe Noiret, Catherine Demonget.* Nodding his appreciative head to the cinematic exuberance exhibited in Truffaut's *The 400 Blows* and Godard's *Breathless*, 28-year-old Malle joined the New Wave with this colorful, frenetic slapstick comedy. Zazie, foul-mouthed, precocious pre-teen brat, is dropped off on her uncle's (Noiret) door by her philandering mother. In the next 36 hours, Zazie, accompanied by her befuddled uncle (a female impersonator), involves herself in a series of wild, mischievous antics as she embarks on her own personalized tour of Paris. Filled with cinematic tricks, jump-cuts and references to other films, this effervescent comedy, inspired by Raymond Queneau's novel, is not Malle's masterpiece but is unabashedly great anarchistic fun. (French with English subtitles) ★★★ VHS: $29.99

Zebrahead

(1992, 100 min, US, Anthony Drazan) *Michael Rapaport, N'Bushe Wright, DeShonn Castle, Ray Sharkey, Helen Shaver.* First-time director Drazan's masterful debut transposes "Romeo and Juliet" onto the blighted 1990s urban landscape. Set in Detroit, the story centers around Jack, a gawky, wannabe homeboy who is amongst the few white kids in his high school. Trouble comes his way when he falls hard for his best friend's cousin Nikki, a savvy young black teen who has just moved from New York. While the story is not hard to predict, the easy-going performances of Rapaport and Wright as Zack and Nikki, along with Drazen's thoughtfully constructed script, make this an engaging and meaningful essay on race relations in the '90s. ★★★½ VHS: $14.99

A Zed and Two Noughts

(1985, 115 min, GB, Peter Greenaway) *Andréa Ferréol, Brian Deacon, Eric Deacon, Frances Barber, Joss Ackland, Jim Davidson, Agnes Brulet, Guusje van Tilborgh, Gerard Thoolen, Ken Campbell, Wolf Kahler, Geoffrey Palmer, David Attenborough.* Another surrealist treat from Greenaway. Two ex-Siamese twins are made widowers by an auto accident and team up with the car's driver, who lost her leg in the wreck, to explore the processes of death and decay. Always one to shock his viewers, Greenaway follows their examinations with all of the visual fecundity that has become the hallmark of his filmmaking, right down to time-lapse images of decaying corpses of animals. The lush cinematography of Sacha Vierny may be lost on the small screen. ★★★ VHS: $29.99; DVD: $29.99

Zelig

(1983, 79 min, US, Woody Allen) *Woody Allen, Mia Farrow.* The sublime story of Leonard Zelig, the outstanding chameleon-man, whose ability to alter his appearance perplexed medical experts and captivated the public's imagination. Allen's hilarious pseudo-documentary tackles the perils of conformity and the rakishness of the media. ★★★★

Zelly and Me

(1988, 87 min, US, Tina Rathborne) *Isabella Rossellini, Alexandra Johnes, Glynis Johns, David Lynch.* A neglected rich girl is befriended by her caring governess, much to the disdain of the youngster's mean-spirited grandmother. Heavy-handed and only occasionally moving, the film suffers from a slow pace and overly mannered dramatics. ★★ VHS: $79.99

Zentropa

(1991, 107 min, The Netherlands, Lars von Trier) *Barbara Sukowa, Udo Keir, Max von Sydow, Eddie Constantine.* This penetrating and mesmeric trip into the dark soul of Europe follows a young American pacifist of German descent who sojourns to post-WWII Deutschland in the belief that he can take part in the healing process of that devastated country. Once there, however, he finds himself snatched up in a nightmarish labyrinth of corruption and deceit involving American complicity in the reestablishment of the powerful industrialist families who had supplied the Nazis. Von Sydow's haunting narration sets the tone for the naïve Yankee's hypnotic entry into the bizarre purgatory of occupied Germany. Shooting mostly in shimmering black and white, von Trier uses spot coloring, scrims and other overtly theatrical devices to great effect. (English and German with English subtitles) ★★★½

Zero Effect

(1998, 116 min, US, Jake Kasdan) *Bill Pullman, Ben Stiller, Ryan O'Neal, Kim Dickens.* First-time director Kasdan (son of director Lawrence Kasdan) makes an impressive debut with this often exhilarating private eye comedy. The basic premise could launch a dozen paperbacks: Brilliant gumshoe has his greatest weakness (namely an inability to interact with people) tested in the toughest case of his career. While the story of a timber tycoon being blackmailed is solid but stale, the details make this film special. The environments we take for granted, such as a white-collar gym or a diner, are given such attention and character that they cease to be "locations." Even Stiller's sidekick has an important story of his own to tell, and it never seems like a subplot. As Daryl Zero, Pullman anchors the movie with his sociological nightmare of a P.I., always identifiable under his many smooth disguises (unlike the recent *Saint* and *Jackal* debacles). ★★★½ VHS: $14.99; DVD: $19.99

Zero for Conduct (Zéro de Conduite)

(1933, 44 min, France, Jean Vigo) Vigo's first fiction film was banned for anti-French sentiment

Josephine Baker (l.) and Jean Gabin in *Zouzou*

and reissued in 1945 after the liberation. It is, in part, an autobiographical account of the director's boyhood days in boarding school and, in part, a rendering of childhood fantasy. Realistic, poetic and subversive. (French with English subtitles) ★★★★ VHS: $14.99

Zero Kelvin

(1995, 113 min, Norway, Hans Petter Moland) *Stellan Skarsgård, Bjorn Sundquist, Camilla Martens.* The lonely, frozen landscape of Greenland proves an appropriate backdrop to this tense, existential drama about alienation and emotional morass. Set in the early part of the 20th century, the story follows a Norwegian poet, Henrik (Eidsvold), and his trek to Greenland to join a fur-trapping expedition. With only Holm (Sundquist), a soft-spoken scientist, and Randbaek (Skarsgård), their brutish, vulgar foreman, as companions, Henrik finds himself less in conflict with nature and more at odds with his fellow man. Director Moland's gradually accelerated pacing befits Henrik's internal struggle, eventually culminating into a brisk, suspenseful battle between the two men shaded by cold, unpredictable moral ambiguities. (Norwegian with English subtitles) ★★★ VHS: $24.99; DVD: $29.99

Zero Patience

(1993, 95 min, Canada, John Greyson) *Michael Callen.* An unexpectedly outrageous and satiric musical comedy about life in the age of AIDS. The story centers around "Patient Zero," Gaetan Dugas, a French-Canadian airline steward who was reported by health officials to be the man who brought AIDS to North America and helped rapidly spread it through promiscuous sexual activity. Gaetan returns from the dead to clear his name and solicits the help of 19th-century explorer (and now 20th-century AIDS researcher) Sir Richard Burton. Burton's development from a self-centered homophobe to an ACT-UP-styled queer is the centerpiece of this amazing story. The film also features several bizarre musical routines, inventively choreo-

graphed and sporting wittily queer lyrics. ★★★ VHS: $39.99

Zombie. . .The Dead Are Among Us!

(1979, 91 min, Italy, Lucio Fulci) In the wake of George Romero's *Dawn of the Dead* comes this graphic and quite disgusting zombie tale about a Caribbean Island with a living dead problem. (Dubbed) ★ VHS: $14.99

Zombie and the Ghost Train

(1991, 88 min, Finland, Mika Kaurismäki) The so-called "slacker" culture has got nothing on the Fins — if you think Austin is bleak, wait till you get a sight of Helsinki. The Zombie of the title is an alcoholic loser who happens to play a mean bass. The story centers on his escapades as he attempts to reconcile with his girlfriend and, possibly more importantly, join The Ghost Train (who look like Urge Overkill), the most famous band in town, although no one seems to have ever heard them play. Unfortunately, Zombie is aptly named for whenever an opportunity arises he's either too drunk or passed out somewhere. There's not much plot but plenty of beautiful imagery and insightful moments; sometimes producing a laugh, and sometimes a lump in the throat. (Finnish with English subtitles) ★★★ VHS: $29.99

Zooman

(1994, 95 min, US, Leon Ichaso) *Louis Gossett, Jr., Charles S. Dutton, Khalil Kain.* Sugar Hill director Ichaso delivers another tale of life in the streets of the inner city, clean and middle-class, but still full of violence and turmoil. Based on the play "Zooman and the Sign" by Charles Fuller, this very talky, unexciting but glossy adaptation is similar in story to *Boyz n the Hood* and *Crooklyn* — and though this family drama is occasionally insightful, there's very little that hasn't been seen before. Kain is very convincing in his portrayal of Zooman, the young hood who shoots the daughter of Gossett during a rampage. In order to find the killer, Gossett enlists the local media and riles up his neighbors to face a showdown with the young killer. The music evokes some of the rage that the family feels in their grief, but the narrative is not as developed as Fuller's excellent *A Soldier's Story*. ★★ VHS: $9.99

Zoot Suit

(1982, 103 min, US, Luis Valdez) *Luis Valdez, Edward James Olmos, Tyne Daly.* Adapting his own play, Valdez's determinedly theatrical film is set in 1942 Los Angeles. Based on a real incident, the story follows a violent encounter between two Chicano gangs which results in murder, incarceration for the innocent as well as the guilty, and a bigoted justice system bent on throwing them all in prison. Narrating the proceedings and leading in wonderfully choreographed song and dance salsa is the cynical, serpentine Olmos. Unexpectedly timely in light of the recent L.A. police mugging, the film is an impassioned exposé on the prejudiced oppression of the American people and the failure of its lofty dream for the Mexican immigrants who attempt to assimilate. A serious but entertaining and lively musical. ★★★ VHS: $9.99

Zorba the Greek

(1964, 146 min, US/Greece, Michael Cacoyannis) *Anthony Quinn, Alan Bates, Lila Kedrova.* An exceptionally accomplished screen version of the acclaimed Kazantzakis novel, with Quinn giving the performance of a lifetime as the title character. Set in Crete, the story follows the adventures of the fun-loving Zorba who takes a reserved Britisher (Bates) under his wing, teaching him his philosophy

of life. Kedrova deservedly won an Oscar as Zorba's aging mistress. Features a terrific Mikis Theodorakis score. ★★★½ VHS: $19.99

Zorro, the Gay Blade

(1981, 93 min, US, Peter Medak) *George Hamilton, Lauren Hutton, Brenda Vaccaro.* After successfully spoofing the vampire movie in *Love at First Bite*, Hamilton sets his sights on the Zorro legend, with uneven results. Hamilton plays the twin sons of Zorro, one a swashbuckler, the other a gay bon vivant. Some laughs, and to its credit, not offensive. ★★½ VHS: $9.99; DVD: $24.99

Zouzou

(1934, 92 min, France, Marc Allégret) *Josephine Baker, Jean Gabin.* A semiautobiographical piece with Baker as a poor laundress who finds her way out of the gutter. Her first film, *Zouzou* is a little short on substantive plot, but Baker's presence nonetheless radiates and her musical numbers scintillate. (French with English subtitles) ★★½ VHS: $29.99

Zu: Warriors from the Magic Mountain

(1983, 98 min, Hong Kong, Tsui Hark) *Yuen Biao, Brigitte Lin, Samo Hung, Damian Lau, Moon Lee, Norman Tsui, Meng Hoi.* Early in his career, Hark asked several American special effects technicians to come to Hong Kong and help him put together the kind of fantasy film that would blow audiences to the back of the theatre. The result was *Zu*, a tale rooted in Chinese mythology and legend, but boasting the most spectacular special effects (of the time), which allowed its heroes and villains to fly, shoot energy bolts from their hands or eyes, fight with colossal monsters and do anything that Tsui's fertile imagination could dream up. The plot concerns a young soldier's adventures in the mystical realm of the Zu Mountains, but it is mainly there to serve the astonishing visuals, putting its characters into the most surreal situations possible. Vibrant, colorful, funny, terrifying, romantic and ultimately moving, *Zu* is *the* classic Hong Kong fantasy film and has it all. (Cantonese with English subtitles) ★★★★ VHS: $19.99; DVD: $29.99

Zulu

(1964, 139 min, GB, Cy Endfield) *Michael Caine, Stanley Baker, Jack Hawkins, Patrick Magee.* An epic battle sequence highlights this exciting adventure about an undermanned British outpost in 1879 South Africa preparing to fend off an overwhelming tribe of Zulu warriors. (Prequel: *Zulu Dawn*) ★★★ VHS: $14.99

Zulu Dawn

(1979, 121 min, US/The Netherlands, Douglas Hickox) *Burt Lancaster, Peter O'Toole, Denholm Elliott.* A well-made war epic about England's bullheadedness in its handling of the Zulu nation — which led to Britain's worst ever military defeat at Isandhlwana in 1879. A prequel to the 1964 film *Zulu*, this film features excellent action sequences and outstanding location shooting. ★★★

X.Y.Z

INDEX: TLA FAVORITES

THE DISCERNING FILM LOVER'S GUIDE

INDEX: TLA FAVORITES

677

Algeria	Jamaica
Argentina	Japan
Armenia	Korea
Australia	Kyrgyzstan
Austria	Luxembourg
Belgium	Macedonia
Bhutan	Martinique
Brazil	Mexico
Burkina Faso	The Netherlands
Canada	New Zealand
Chile	Nicaragua
China	Nigeria
Colombia	Norway
Cuba	Peru
Czechoslovokia	The Philippines
Czech Republic	Poland
Denmark	Romania
Dominican Republic	Russia/USSR
Egypt	Scotland
Finland	South Africa
France	Spain
Great Britain	Sweden
Germany	Switzerland
Greece	Taiwan
Hong Kong	Tibet
Hungary	Tunisia
India	Turkey
Iran	Venezuela
Ireland	Vietnam
Israel	Wales
Italy	Yugoslavia
Ivory Coast	Zimbabwe

INDEX: COUNTRY OF ORIGIN

THE DISCERNING FILM LOVER'S GUIDE

THE DISCERNING FILM LOVER'S GUIDE

THE DISCERNING FILM LOVER'S GUIDE

James L. Brooks

As Good as It Gets
Broadcast News
I'll Do Anything
Terms of Endearment

Mel Brooks

Blazing Saddles
Dracula: Dead
and Loving It
High Anxiety
History of the World Pt. I
Life Stinks
The Producers
Robin Hood:
Men in Tights
Silent Movie
Spaceballs
The Twelve Chairs
Young Frankenstein
(As writer)
To Be or Not to Be

Richard Brooks

Bite the Bullet
Blackboard Jungle
The Brothers Karamazov
Cat on a Hot Tin Roof
The Catered Affair
Deadline USA
$ (Dollars)
Fever Pitch
Elmer Gantry
The Happy Ending
In Cold Blood
The Last Time
I Saw Paris
Looking for Mr. Goodbar
Lord Jim
The Professionals
Something of Value
Sweet Bird of Youth
Wrong Is Right
(As writer)
Any Number Can Play
Crossfire
Key Largo

Tod Browning

Devil Doll
Dracula
Freaks
Mark of the Vampire
The Unholy Three
The Unknown

Luis Buñuel

L'Age d'Or
Belle de Jour
Un Chien Andalou
The Criminal Life of
Archibaldo de la Cruz
El Bruto
Death in the Garden
Diary of a Chambermaid
The Discreet Charm
of the Bourgeoisie
El (This Strange Passion)
The Exterminating Angel
Fever Mounts in El Pao
The Great Madcap
(El Gran Calavera)

Illusions Travel by Streetcar
Mexican Bus Ride
(Ascent to Heaven)
The Milky Way
Nazarin
Los Olvidados (The Young
and the Damned)
The Phantom of Liberty
Simon of the Desert
Susana
That Obscure Object
of Desire
Tristina
Viridiana
A Woman without Love
Wuthering Heights

Tim Burton

Batman
Batman Returns
Beetlejuice
Ed Wood
Edward Scissorhands
Frankenweenie
Mars Attacks!
Pee Wee's Big Adventure
Planet of the Apes
Sleepy Hollow
(As writer)
The Nightmare Before
Christmas

James Cameron

The Abyss
Aliens
Piranha 2: The Spawning
Terminator
Terminator 2: Judgment Day
Titanic
True Lies
(As writer)
Rambo: First Blood Pt. II
Strange Days

Jane Campion

An Angel at My Table
Holy Smoke
Jane Campion Shorts
The Piano
The Portrait of a Lady
Sweetie

Frank Capra

Arsenic and Old Lace
The Bitter Tea of
General Yen
Broadway Bill
Here Comes the Groom
A Hole in the Head
It Happened One Night
It's a Wonderful Life
Lady for a Day
Long Pants
Lost Horizon
Meet John Doe
Mr. Deeds Goes to Town
Mr. Smith Goes
to Washington
The Negro Soldier
Platinum Blonde
Pocketful of Miracles
Riding High

State of the Union
You Can't Take It With You

Marcel Carné

Bizarre, Bizarre
Children of Paradise
Le Jour Se Leve (Daybreak)
Law Breakers
Les Visiteurs du Soir

John Carpenter

Assault on Precinct 13
Big Trouble in Little China
Christine
Dark Star
Escape from L.A.
Escape from New York
The Fog
Ghosts of Mars
Halloween
In the Mouth of Madness
Memoirs of an Invisible Man
Prince of Darkness
Starman
They Live!
The Thing
Vampires
Village of the Damned
(As writer)
Black Moon Rising

John Cassavetes

Big Trouble
A Child Is Waiting
Faces
Gloria
Husbands
The Killing of a Chinese
Bookie
Love Streams
Minnie and Moskowitz
Opening Night
Shadows
A Woman Under
the Influence

Michael Caton-Jones

Doc Hollywood
The Jackal
Memphis Belle
Rob Roy
Scandal
This Boy's Life

Claude Chabrol

Bad Girls
Le Beau Serge
Betty
Les Biches
The Blood of Others
Blood Relatives
Bluebeard
Les Bonnes Femmes
Le Boucher
La Cérémonie
Club Extinction
Dirty Hands
L'Enfer
The Eye of Vichy
High Heels
Horse of Pride
Innocence with Dirty
Hands

Madame Bovary
Une Partie de Plaisir
Six in Paris
The Story of Women
The Swindle
Ten Days Wonder
This Man Must Die
Wedding in Blood

Jackie Chan

Dragon Lord
Jackie Chan's Who Am I?
Miracles
Operation Condor 1 & 2
Police Story
Project A, Parts 1 & 2
The Protector
Young Master

Charles Chaplin

City Lights
A Countess from Hong Kong
The Gold Rush
The Great Dictator
The Kid/The Idle Class
A King in New York
Limelight
Modern Times
Monsieur Verdoux
A Woman of Paris

Peter Chelsom

Funny Bones
Hear My Song
The Mighty
Serendipity
Town and Country

Chen Kaige

The Emperor and the
Assassin
Farewell My Concubine
Life on a String
Temptress Moon
Yellow Earth

Patrice Chereau

L'Homme Blesse
Queen Margot
Those Who Love Me Can
Take the Train

René Clair

À Nous la Liberté
Beauties of the Night
Beauty and the Devil
The Crazy Ray/Entr'acte
The Flame of New Orleans
Forever and a Day
The Ghost Goes West
Les Grandes Manoeuvres
I Married a Witch
The Italian Straw Hat
Le Million
Under the Roofs of Paris

René Clément

And Hope to Die
Forbidden Games
Gervaise
Is Paris Burning?
Joy House
Purple Noon
Rider on the Rain

Henri-Georges Clouzot

Le Corbeau (The Raven)
Diabolique
The Mystery of Picasso
The Wages of Fear

Jean Cocteau

Beauty and the Beast
Blood of a Poet
The Eagle Has Two Heads
Orpheus
The Storm Within
The Testament of Orpheus

Joel Coen

Barton Fink
The Big Lebowski
Blood Simple
Fargo
The Hudsucker Proxy
The Man Who Wasn't There
Miller's Crossing
O Brother, Where Art Thou?
Raising Arizona
(As writer)
Crimewave

Martha Coolidge

Angie
Crazy in Love
Introducing Dorothy
Dandridge
The Joy of Sex
Lost in Yonkers
Out to Sea
Rambling Rose
Real Genius
Three Wishes
Valley Girl

Francis Ford Coppola

Apocalypse Now
Bram Stoker's Dracula
The Conversation
The Cotton Club
Dementia 13
Finian's Rainbow
Gardens of Stone
The Godfather I, II, & III
Jack
New York Stories
One from the Heart
The Outsiders
Peggy Sue Got Married
The Rain People
The Rainmaker
Rumble Fish
Tonight for Sure
Tucker
You're a Big Boy Now
(As writer)
The Great Gatsby
Is Paris Burning?
Patton
This Property Is
Condemned

Roger Corman

Bloody Mama
A Bucket of Blood
Carnival Rock
The Day the World Ended

INDEX: DIRECTORS

INDEX: DIRECTORS

THE DISCERNING FILM LOVER'S GUIDE

INDEX: DIRECTORS

Sammo Hung

Dragons Forever
Eastern Condors
Heart of Dragon
The Millionaire's Express
Mr. Nice Guy
My Lucky Stars
Once Upon a Time in
*   China & America*
The Prodigal Son
Winners and Sinners

John Huston

Across the Pacific
The African Queen
Annie
The Asphalt Jungle
Beat the Devil
The Bible
Casino Royale
The Dead
Fat City
In This Our Life
Key Largo
The Life and Times of
*   Judge Roy Bean*
The List of Adrian
*   Messenger*
The Mackintosh Man
The Maltese Falcon
The Man Who
*   Would Be King*
The Misfits
Moby Dick
Moulin Rouge
Night of the Iguana
Phobia
Prizzi's Honor
The Red Badge of Courage
Reflections in
*   a Golden Eye*
The Treasure of
*   the Sierra Madre*
Under the Volcano
The Unforgiven
Victory
Wise Blood
(As writer)
Juarez
Jezebel
High Sierra
Mr. North
Sergeant York

Kon Ichikawa

An Actor's Revenge
The Burmese Harp
Enjo
Fires on the Plain
The Makioka Sisters
Odd Obsession
The Phoenix
Tokyo Olympiad

Shohei Imamura

The Ballad of Narayama
Black Rain
Dr. Akagi
The Eel
Eijanaika
Insect Woman
The Pornographers
Vengeance Is Mine

Juzo Itami

The Funeral
Minbo
Tampopo
A Taxing Woman
A Taxing Woman's Return

James Ivory/
Ismail Merchant

Autobiography of a Princess
The Ballad of the Sad Cafe
Bombay Talkie
The Bostonians
The Courtesans of Bombay
The Deceivers
The Europeans
The Golden Bowl
Heat and Dust
Householder
Howards End
Hullabaloo Over Georgie
*   and Bonnie's Pictures*
Jane Austen in Manhattan
Jefferson in Paris
Maurice
Mr. and Mrs. Bridge
Quartet
The Remains of the Day
A Room with a View
Roseland
Savages
Shakespeare Wallah
Slaves of New York
A Soldier's Daughter Never
*   Cries*
Surviving Picasso
The Wild Party

Peter Jackson

Bad Taste
Dead Alive
Forgotten Silver
The Frighteners
Heavenly Creatures
The Lord of the Rings:
*   The Fellowship of the*
*   Ring*
Meet the Feebles

Henry Jaglom

Always
Baby Fever
Can She Bake a
*   Cherry Pie?*
Déjà Vu
Eating
Last Summer in
*   the Hamptons*
New Year's Day
Sitting Ducks
Someone to Love
Tracks
Venice - Venice

Derek Jarman

The Angelic Conversation
Aria
Blue
Caravaggio
Edward II
The Garden
Highlights
Jubilee

The Last of England
Sebastiane
The Tempest
War Requiem
Wittgenstein

Jim Jarmusch

Dead Man
Down by Law
Ghost Dog: The Way of the
*   Samurai*
Mystery Train
Night on Earth
Permanent Vacation
Stranger Than Paradise
Year of the Horse

Jean-Pierre Jeunet

Alien Resurrection
City of Lost Children
Delicatessen

Norman Jewison

Agnes of God
...And Justice for All
Best Friends
Bogus
The Cincinnati Kid
Fiddler on the Roof
F.I.S.T.
The Hurricane
In Country
In the Heat of the Night
Jesus Christ Superstar
Moonstruck
Only You
Other People's Money
Rollerball
The Russians Are Coming,
*   the Russians Are*
*   Coming!*
Send Me No Flowers
A Soldier's Story
The Thomas Crown Affair
The Thrill of It All

Roland Joffé

City of Joy
Fat Man and Little Boy
Goodbye Lover
The Killing Fields
The Mission
The Scarlet Letter
Vatel

Neil Jordan

The Butcher Boy
The Company of Wolves
The Crying Game
Danny Boy
The End of the Affair
High Spirits
In Dreams
Interview with
*   the Vampire*
Michael Collins
The Miracle
Mona Lisa
We're No Angels

Shekar Kapur

Bandit Queen
Elizabeth

Wong Kar-Wai

Ashes of Time
Chungking Express
Fallen Angels
Happy Together
In the Mood for Love

Lawrence Kasdan

The Accidental Tourist
The Big Chill
Body Heat
French Kiss
Grand Canyon
I Love You to Death
Mumford
Silverado
Wyatt Earp
(as writer)
The Empire Strikes Back
Raiders of the Lost Ark
Return of the Jedi

Philip Kaufman

The Great Northfield
*   Minnesota Raid*
Henry & June
Invasion of the Body
*   Snatchers*
Quills
The Right Stuff
Rising Sun
The Unbearable
*   Lightness of Being*
The Wanderers
The White Dawn
(As writer)
The Outlaw Josey Wales
Raiders of the Lost Ark

Aki Kaurismäki

Ariel
Leningrad Cowboys
*   Go America*
The Match Factory Girl
La Vie de Bohème
Zombie and the Ghost
*   Train*

Elia Kazan

The Arrangement
Baby Doll
East of Eden
A Face in the Crowd
Gentleman's Agreement
The Last Tycoon
On the Waterfront
Panic in the Streets
Pinky
Sea of Grass
Splendor in the Grass
A Streetcar Named Desire
A Tree Grows in Brooklyn
Visitors
Viva Zapata!

Buster Keaton

The General
The Goat
The High Sign
My Wife's Relations
The Navigator
One Week

Our Hospitality
Sherlock, Jr.
Three Ages

Beeban Kidron

Antonia and Jane
Oranges Are Not the Only
*   Fruit*
Shades of Fear
Swept from the Sea
To Wong Foo...
Used People

Krzysztof Kieslowski

Blue
Camera Buff
The Decalogue
The Double Life
*   of Veronique*
No End
Red
White

Takeshi "Beat"
Kitano

Boiling Point
Fireworks (Hana-Bi)
Kids Return
Kikujiro
A Scene at the Sea
Sonatine
Violent Cop

Barbara Kopple

American Dream
Fallen Champ: The
*   Mike Tyson Story*
Harlan County, U.S.A.
Wild Man Blues

Stanley Kramer

Bless the Beasts and
*   Children*
The Defiant Ones
Guess Who's Coming
*   to Dinner*
Inherit the Wind
It's a Mad, Mad,
*   Mad, Mad World*
Judgment at Nuremberg
Not as a Stranger
Oklahoma Crude
On the Beach
The Pride and the Passion
The Runner Stumbles
R.P.M.
The Secret of Santa Vittoria
Ship of Fools

Stanley Kubrick

Barry Lyndon
A Clockwork Orange
Dr. Strangelove
Eyes Wide Shut
Full Metal Jacket
Killer's Kiss
The Killing
Lolita
Paths of Glory
The Shining
Spartacus
2001: A Space Odyssey

THE DISCERNING FILM LOVER'S GUIDE

INDEX: DIRECTORS

THE DISCERNING FILM LOVER'S GUIDE

INDEX: STARS

THE DISCERNING FILM LOVER'S GUIDE

The Morning After
North
Prelude to a Kiss
Primary Colors
Roe vs. Wade
Shadows and Fog
Swept from the Sea
Titanic
Used People
The Waterboy
White Palace

Warren Beatty

All Fall Down
Bonnie and Clyde
Bugsy
Bulworth
Dick Tracy
Dollars
The Fortune
Heaven Can Wait
Ishtar
Kaleidoscope
Lilith
Love Affair
Madonna: Truth or Dare
McCabe and Mrs. Miller
The Parallax View
Promise Her Anything
Reds
The Roman Spring of Mrs.
  Stone
Shampoo
Splendor in the Grass
Town and Country

Jean-Paul Belmondo

Borsalino
Breathless
Cartouche
Casino Royale
Le Doulos
High Heels
Is Paris Burning?
Just Another Pretty Face
Leon Morin, Priest
Le Magnifique
Les Miserables
Mississippi Mermaid
Moderato Cantabile
Pierrot le Fou
Un Singe en Hiver (Mon-
  key in Winter)
Stavisky
The Swashbuckler
That Man from Rio
Two Women
A Woman Is a Woman
  (Une Femme Est
  une Femme)

John Belushi

The Blues Brothers
Continental Divide
Goin' South
National Lampoon's
  Animal House
Neighbors
1941
Old Boyfriends

Roberto Benigni

Down by Law
Life Is Beautiful
Johnny Stecchino

The Monster
Night on Earth
Seeking Asylum
Son of the Pink Panther

Annette Bening

American Beauty
The American President
Bugsy
The Great Outdoors
The Grifters
Guilty by Suspicion
In Dreams
Love Affair
Mars Attacks!
Postcards from the Edge
Regarding Henry
Richard III
The Siege
Valmont
What Planet Are You From?

Jack Benny

Broadway Melody of 1936
George Washington Slept Here
Guide for the Married Man
Hollywood Canteen
The Horn Blows at Midnight
It's a Mad, Mad, Mad,
  Mad World
It's in the Bag
The Meanest Man in the
  World
To Be or Not to Be

Ingrid Bergman

Adam Had Four Sons
Anastasia
Arch of Triumph
Autumn Sonata
The Bells of St. Mary's
Cactus Flower
Casablanca
The Count of Old Town
Dr. Jekyll and Mr. Hyde
Dollar
Elena and Her Men
Fear
For Whom the Bell Tolls
Gaslight
Goodbye Again
Indiscreet
Inn of the Sixth Happiness
Intermezzo (1937 & 1939)
Joan of Arc
June Night
A Matter of Time
Murder on the Orient Express
Notorious
Only One Night
Spellbound
Stromboli
Swedenhielms
Under Capricorn
Voyage in Italy (Strangers)
A Walk in the Spring Rain
Walpurgis Night
A Woman Called Golda
A Woman's Face

Sandra Bernhard

An Alan Smithe Film:
  Burn Hollywood Burn!
Dinner Rush
Heavy Petting

Hudson Hawk
Inside Monkey Zetterland
The King of Comedy
The Late Shift
Madonna: Truth or Dare
The Muppets Take
  Manhattan
Sesame Street Presents
  Follow That Bird
Somewhere in the City
Track 29
Without You I'm Nothing
Wrongfully Accused

Halle Berry

B.A.P.S.
Boomerang
Bulworth
Executive Decision
Father Hood
The Flintstones
Girl 6
Jungle Fever
The Last Boy Scout
Losing Isaiah
The Program
Race the Sun
The Rich Man's Wife
Strictly Business
Swordfish
Why Do Fools Fall in Love
X-Men

Michael Biehn

The Abyss
Aliens
The Art of War
Asteroid
Cherry Falls
Deadfall
Deep Red
Dying to Get Rich!
The Fan
In a Shallow Grave
Jade
K-2
The Lords of Discipline
Navy SEALS
Rampage
The Rock
The Seventh Sign
Strapped
The Terminator
Terminator 2: Judgment Day
Timebomb
Tombstone

Juliette Binoche

Alice and Martin
Blue
Chocolat
A Couch in New York
Damage
Emily Brontë's Wuthering
  Heights
The English Patient
Hail Mary
The Horseman on the Roof
The Lovers on the Bridge
Rendez-Vous
The Unbearable Lightness
  of Being
White
The Widow of St. Pierre

Jack Black

Bob Roberts
The Cable Guy
Cradle Will Rock
Dead Man Walking
Enemy of the State
High Fidelity
The Jackal
Jesus' Son
Mars Attacks!
Saving Silverman
Waterworld

Karen Black

Airport 1975
Angel Blue
Auntie Lee's Meat Pies
Bound and Gagged: A
  Love Story
Burnt Offerings
Can She Bake a Cherry
  Pie?
Capricorn One
Chanel Solitaire
Come Back to the 5 &
  Dime, Jimmy Dean,
  Jimmy Dean
Conceiving Ada
Cries of Silence
Crimetime
The Day of the Locust
Easy Rider
Family Plot
Five Easy Pieces
The Great Gatsby
Homer and Eddie
In Praise of Older Women
Invaders from Mars
It's Alive III: Island
  of the Alive
Killing Heat
Mirror Mirror
Mr. Horn
Nashville
Overexposed
Portnoy's Complaint
Rubin & Ed
Tales of the City
Trilogy of Terror
Who is Henry Jaglom
You're a Big Boy Now

Rubén Blades

All the Pretty Horses
Chinese Box
Color of Night
Cradle Will Rock
Crazy from the Heart
Critical Condition
Crossover Dreams
Dead Man Out
The Devil's Own
Disorganized Crime
Fatal Beauty
Homeboy
The Josephine Baker Story
The Lemon Sisters
Life with Mikey
The Milagro Beanfield War
A Million to Juan
Mo' Better Blues
One Man's War
Predator 2
The Super
The Two Jakes

Cate Blanchett

Elizabeth
The Gift
An Ideal Husband
Oscar and Lucinda
Paradise Road
Pushing Tin
The Talented Mr. Ripley
The Wedding Party

Brenda Blethyn

Anne Frank
Little Voice
Music from Another Room
A River Runs Through It
RKO 281
Saving Grace
Secrets & Lies
The Witches

Dirk Bogarde

Accident
A Bridge Too Far
Daddy Nostalgia
Damn the Defiant!
The Damned
Darling
Death in Venice
Despair
Doctor in the House
The Fixer
I Could Go on Singing
Justine
May We Borrow Your
  Husband?
Night Flight from Moscow
The Night Porter
Penny Princess
Permission to Kill
Providence
Quartet
The Servant
The Sleeping Tiger
Song without End
A Tale of Two Cities
Victim

Humphrey Bogart

Across the Pacific
Action in the North Atlantic
The African Queen
All Through the Night
The Amazing Dr. Clitterhouse
Angels with Dirty Faces
The Barefoot Contessa
Beat the Devil
The Big Sleep
Brother Orchid
Bullets or Ballots
Black Legion
The Caine Mutiny
Call It Murder
Casablanca
Chain Lightning
Conflict
Dark Passage
Dark Victory
Dead End
Dead Reckoning
Deadline USA
The Desperate Hours
The Enforcer

THE DISCERNING FILM LOVER'S GUIDE

THE DISCERNING FILM LOVER'S GUIDE

THE DISCERNING FILM LOVER'S GUIDE

THE DISCERNING FILM LOVER'S GUIDE

Objective, Burma!
The Prince and the Pauper
The Private Lives of Elizabeth and Essex
San Antonio
Santa Fe Trail
The Sea Hawk
The Sisters
Thank Your Lucky Stars
They Died with Their Boots On
Virginia City

Bridget Fonda

Aria
Army of Darkness
Balto
Bodies, Rest & Motion
Camilla
City Hall
Doc Hollywood
Finding Graceland
Frankenstein Unbound
The Godfather, Part III
Grace of My Heart
In the Gloaming
Iron Maze
It Could Happen to You
Jackie Brown
Lake Placid
Leather Jackets
Little Buddha
Monkeybone
Point of No Return
The Road to Wellville
Rough Magic
Scandal
Shag, the Movie
A Simple Plan
Single White Female
Singles
Strapless
Touch

Henry Fonda

Advise and Consent
Battle of the Bulge
The Best Man
A Big Hand for the Little Lady
The Big Street
The Boston Strangler
The Cheyenne Social Club
Drums Along the Mohawk
Fail-Safe
Fedora
Fort Apache
The Fugitive
The Grapes Of Wrath
How the West Was Won
The Immortal Sergeant
In Harm's Way
Jesse James
Jezebel
The Lady Eve
The Longest Day
The Mad Miss Manton
Madigan
Meteor
Midway
Mister Roberts
My Darling Clementine
On Golden Pond
On Our Merry Way
Once Upon a Time in the West

The Ox-Bow Incident
The Return of Frank James
Sex and the Single Girl
Sometimes a Great Notion
Spawn of the North
Stage Struck
There Was a Crooked Man
The Tin Star
Too Late the Hero
The Trail of the Lonesome Pine
12 Angry Men
War and Peace
Warlock
The Wrong Man
You Only Live Once
Young Mr. Lincoln
Yours, Mine and Ours

Jane Fonda

Agnes of God
Any Wednesday
Barbarella
Barefoot in the Park
California Suite
Cat Ballou
The Chase
The China Syndrome
Comes a Horseman
Coming Home
A Doll's House
The Dollmaker
The Electric Horseman
Fun with Dick and Jane
The Game Is Over
Joy House (Les Felins)
Julia
Klute
The Morning After
9 to 5
Old Gringo
On Golden Pond
Period of Adjustment
Rollover
Spirits of the Dead (Histoires Extraordinaires)
Stanley & Iris
Steelyard Blues
Tall Story
They Shoot Horses, Don't They
Walk on the Wild Side

Peter Fonda

Bodies, Rest & Motion
Easy Rider
Escape from L.A.
Grace of My Heart
The Hired Hand
The Last Movie
Lilith
The Limey
Love and a .45
Nadja
92 in the Shade
The Rose Garden
Spirits of the Dead (Histoires Extraordinaires)
The Tempest
Thomas and the Magic Railroad
Ulee's Gold
The Wild Angels

Harrison Ford

Air Force One
American Graffiti
Apocalypse Now
Blade Runner
Clear and Present Danger
The Conversation
The Devil's Own
The Empire Strikes Back
Force 10 from Navarone
Frantic
The Frisco Kid
The Fugitive
Hanover Street
Heroes
Indiana Jones and the Last Crusade
Indiana Jones and the Temple of Doom
Jimmy Hollywood
More American Graffiti
The Mosquito Coast
Patriot Games
Presumed Innocent
Raiders of the Lost Ark
Random Hearts
Regarding Henry
Return of the Jedi
Sabrina
Six Days Seven Nights
Star Wars
What Lies Beneath
Witness
Working Girl

Jodie Foster

The Accused
Alice Doesn't Live Here Anymore
Anna and the King
Backtrack
The Blood of Others
Bugsy Malone
Candleshoe
Carny
Contact
Five Corners
Foxes
Freaky Friday
The Hotel New Hampshire
The Little Girl Who Lives Down the Lane
Little Man Tate
Maverick
Mesmerized
Napoleon and Samantha
Nell
Shadows and Fog
Siesta
The Silence of the Lambs
Sommersby
Stealing Home
Svengali
Taxi Driver
(As director)
Home for the Holidays
Little Man Tate

Michael J. Fox

The American President
Atlantis: The Lost Empire
Back to the Future 1, 2, 3
Blue in the Face
Bright Lights, Big City

Casualties of War
Class of 1984
Doc Hollywood
Don't Drink the Water
For Love or Money
The Frighteners
Greedy
The Hard Way
Homeward Bound 1 & 2
Life with Mikey
Light of Day
Mars Attacks!
Poison Ivy
The Secret of My Success
Stuart Little
Teen Wolf
Where the Rivers Flow North

Brendan Fraser

Airheads
Bedazzled
Blast from the Past
Dogfight
Dudley Do-Right
Encino Man
George of the Jungle
Gods and Monsters
In the Army Now
Monkeybone
Mrs. Winterbourne
The Mummy
The Mummy Returns
Now and Then
School Ties
The Scout
Twenty Bucks
The Twilight of the Golds
With Honors
Young & Younger

Morgan Freeman

Along Came a Spider
Amistad
The Bonfire of the Vanities
Brubaker
Chain Reaction
Clean and Sober
Death of a Prophet: The Last Days Of Malcolm X
Deep Impact
Driving Miss Daisy
Glory
The Gospel at Colonus
Hard Rain
Johnny Handsome
Kiss the Girls
Lean on Me
Marie
Moll Flanders
Nurse Betty
Outbreak
The Power of One
Robin Hood: Prince of Thieves
Se7en
The Shawshank Redemption
Street Smart
Teachers
That Was Then, This Is Now
Under Suspicion
Unforgiven
(As director)
Bopha!

Colin Friels

Angel Baby
Class Action
Cosi
Dark City
Darkman
A Good Man in Africa
Grievous Bodily Harm
Ground Zero
High Tide
Kangaroo
Malcolm
Mr. Reliable
Monkey Grip
Warm Nights on a Slow Moving Train

Edward Furlong

American Heart
American History X
Animal Factory
Before and After
Brainscan
Detroit Rock City
The Grass Harp
A Home of Our Own
Little Odessa
Pecker
Pet Sematary 2
Terminator 2: Judgment Day

Clark Gable

Across the Wide Missouri
Adventure
Any Number Can Play
Band of Angels
Boom Town
Chained
China Seas
Command Decision
Dancing Lady
Forsaking All Others
A Free Soul
Gone with the Wind
Homecoming
Honky Tonk
The Hucksters
It Happened One Night
It Started in Naples
Laughing Sinners
Lone Star
Love on the Run
Manhattan Melodrama
The Misfits
Mogambo
Mutiny on the Bounty
The Plastic Age
Possessed
Red Dust
San Francisco
Somewhere I'll Find You
Strange Interlude
Susan Lenox: Her Fall and Rise
Teacher's Pet
Test Pilot
Too Hot to Handle
Wife vs. Secretary

James Gandolfini

Angie
A Civil Action
Crimson Tide

Over the Brooklyn Bridge
The Pallbearer
The Princess Bride
Racing with the Moon
Scrooged
The Secret Diary of
  Sigmund Freud
Sunset Park
Transylvania 6-5000
Trees Lounge
Valentino
Wedding in White
When a Stranger Calls
When a Stranger Calls
  Back

Anna Karina

Alphaville
Band of Outsiders
Bread and Chocolate
Chinese Roulette
Circle of Love
Justine
My Life to Live
The Nun
The Oldest Profession
Pierrot le Fou
Regina
A Woman Is a Woman

Boris Karloff

Abbott & Costello Meet Dr.
  Jekyll & Mr. Hyde
Bedlam
Before I Hang
The Bells
The Black Cat
The Black Room
Black Sabbath
The Body Snatcher
The Bride of Frankenstein
Cauldron of Blood
The Comedy of Terrors
Corridors of Blood
The Criminal Code
Dick Tracy Meets Gruesome
Frankenstein
The Haunted Strangler
House of Frankenstein
The Invisible Ray
Isle of the Dead
The Lost Patrol
Lured
Mad Monster Party
The Man They Could Not
  Hang
The Mask of Fu Manchu
The Mummy
The Old Dark House
Old Ironsides
The Raven (1935 & 1963)
Scarface
The Secret Life of Walter
  Mitty
Son of Frankenstein
Targets
The Terror
Tower of London

Danny Kaye

The Court Jester
The Five Pennies
Hans Christian Andersen
The Inspector General
The Kid From Brooklyn

The Madwoman of Chaillot
The Secret Life of Walter
  Mitty
A Song Is Born
Up in Arms
White Christmas
Wonder Man

Buster Keaton

The Adventures of
  Huckleberry Finn
Beach Blanket Bingo
Boom in the Moon
The Cameraman
College
Forever and a Day
The Fuller Brush Man
A Funny Thing Happened
  on the Way to the Forum
The General
The Great Chase
How to Stuff a Wild Bikini
In the Good Old
  Summertime
It's a Mad, Mad, Mad,
  Mad World
Limelight
The Navigator/The
  Boat/The Love Nest
The Saphead/The High
  Sign/One Week
Seven Chances/
  Neighbors/The Balloonatic
Sherlock, Jr./
  Our Hospitality
Steamboat Bill, Jr.
Sunset Boulevard
Three Ages/The Goat/
  My Wife's Relations

Diane Keaton

Annie Hall
Baby Boom
Crimes of the Heart
Father of the Bride 1 & 2
The First Wives Club
The Godfather I, II, III
The Good Mother
Hanging Up
Harry and Walter Go to
  New York
Interiors
The Lemon Sisters
The Little Drummer Girl
Looking for Mr. Goodbar
Love and Death
Lovers and Other Strangers
Manhattan
Manhattan Murder Mystery
Marvin's Room
Mrs. Soffel
The Only Thrill
The Other Sister
Play It Again, Sam
Radio Days
Reds
Running Mates
Shoot the Moon
Sleeper
Town and Country
(As director)
Hanging Up
Heaven
Unstrung Heroes

Michael Keaton

Batman
Batman Returns
Beetlejuice
Clean and Sober
Desperate Measures
The Dream Team
Gung Ho
Jack Frost
Jackie Brown
Johnny Dangerously
Mr. Mom
Much Ado About Nothing
Multiplicity
My Life
Night Shift
One Good Cop
Out of Sight
Pacific Heights
The Paper
Speechless
The Squeeze

Catherine Keener

Being John Malkovich
Box of Moonlight
8MM
Living in Oblivion
Out of Sight
The Real Blonde
Simpatico
Switch
Walking and Talking
Your Friends & Neighbors

Harvey Keitel

Alice Doesn't Live
  Here Anymore
Bad Lieutenant
Blindside
Blue Collar
Blue in the Face
The Border
Buffalo Bill & the Indians
Bugsy
City of Industry
Clockers
Copland
Corrupt
Dangerous Game
Deathwatch
The Duellists
Fairy Tale: A True Story
Falling in Love
Fingers
From Dusk Till Dawn
Head Above Water
Imaginary Crimes
The January Man
The Last Temptation of
  Christ
Little Nicky
Lulu on the Bridge
Mean Streets
The Men's Club
Monkey Trouble
Mortal Thoughts
La Nuit de Varennes
The Piano
The Pick-Up Artist
Point of No Return
Pulp Fiction
Reservoir Dogs

Rising Sun
Saturn 3
Shadrach
Sister Act
Smoke
Taxi Driver
Thelma and Louise
Three Seasons
Two Evil Eyes
The Two Jakes
U-571
Ulysses' Gaze
Welcome to L.A.
Who's That Knocking at
  My Door?
Wise Guys
Young Americans

Gene Kelly

An American in Paris
Anchors Aweigh
Brigadoon
Cover Girl
Deep in My Heart
DuBarry Was a Lady
For Me and My Gal
Forty Carats
Inherit the Wind
Invitation to the Dance
It's Always Fair Weather
Les Girls
Marjorie Morningstar
On the Town
The Pirate
Singin' in the Rain
Summer Stock
Take Me Out to
  the Ball Game
That's Entertainment, Part 2
Thousands Cheer
The Three Musketeers
Words and Music
Xanadu
The Young Girls of
  Rochefort
Ziegfeld Follies
(As director)
The Cheyenne Social Club
Gigot
A Guide for the Married
  Man
Hello, Dolly!
On the Town
Singin' in the Rain
The Tunnel of Love

Deborah Kerr

An Affair to Remember
The Arrangement
Black Narcissus
Bonjour Tristesse
Casino Royale
The Chalk Garden
The End of the Affair
From Here to Eternity
The Grass Is Greener
The Hucksters
Julius Caesar
The King and I
King Solomon's Mines
The Life and Death of
  Colonel Blimp
Major Barbara

Marriage on the Rocks
The Naked Edge
Night of the Iguana
The Prisoner of Zenda
Quo Vadis
Separate Tables
The Sundowners
Tea and Sympathy
Young Bess

Nicole Kidman

Archer's Adventure
Batman Forever
Billy Bathgate
Days of Thunder
Dead Calm
Eyes Wide Shut
Far and Away
Flirting
Malice
Moulin Rouge
My Life
The Peacemaker
The Portrait of a Lady
Practical Magic
To Die For
The Wacky World of
  Wills and Burke

Val Kilmer

At First Sight
Batman Forever
The Doors
The Ghost and the Darkness
Gore Vidal's Billy the Kid
Heat
The Island of Dr. Moreau
Joe the King
Kill Me Again
Pollock
The Prince of Egypt
Real Genius
The Real McCoy
Red Planet
The Saint
Thunderheart
Tombstone
Top Gun
Top Secret!
True Romance
Willow
Wings of Courage

Ben Kingsley

Anne Frank
The Assignment
Betrayal
Bugsy
Dave
Death and the Maiden
The Fifth Monkey
Gandhi
Harem
Joseph
Maurice
Murderers Among Us
Pascali's Island
Photographing Fairies
Rules of Engagement
Schindler's List
Searching for Bobby Fischer
Silas Marner
Slipstream
Sneakers

THE DISCERNING FILM LOVER'S GUIDE

THE DISCERNING FILM LOVER'S GUIDE

Red Skelton

Bathing Beauty
Du Barry Was a Lady
The Fuller Brush Man
I Dood It
Neptune's Daughter
Ship Ahoy
A Southern Yankee
Thousands Cheer
Three Little Words
Watch the Birdie
Whistling in Brooklyn
Whistling in the Dark
Ziegfeld Follies

Christian Slater

Basil
Bed of Roses
Broken Arrow
The Contender
Ferngully
The Flood
Gleaming the Cube
Hard Rain
Heathers
Interview with
*   the Vampire*
Jimmy Hollywood
Kuffs
The Legend of Billie Jean
Mobsters
Murder in the First
The Name of the Rose
Pump Up the Volume
Robin Hood: Prince
*   of Thieves*
Star Trek VI
Tales from the
*   Darkside: The Movie*
3,000 Miles to Graceland
True Romance
Tucker
Twisted
Untamed Heart
Very Bad Things
Where the Day Takes You
The Wizard
Young Guns 2

Maggie Smith

California Suite
Clash of the Titans
David Copperfield
Death on the Nile
Evil under the Sun
The First Wives Club
The Honey Pot
Hook
Hot Millions
Lily in Love
The Lonely Passion of
*   Judith Hearne*
The Missionary
Murder by Death
The Prime of Miss Jean
*   Brodie*
A Private Function
Quartet
Richard III
A Room with a View
The Secret Garden
Sister Act 1 & 2
Tea with Mussolini
The V.I.P.s
Washington Square

Will Smith

Bad Boys
Enemy of the State
Independence Day
The Legend of Bagger Vance
Made in America
Men in Black
Six Degrees of Separation
Where the Day Takes You
Wild Wild West

Wesley Snipes

The Art of War
Blade
Boiling Point
Critical Condition
Demolition Man
Down in the Delta
Drop Zone
The Fan
Jungle Fever
King of New York
Major League
Money Train
Mo' Better Blues
Murder at 1600
New Jack City
One Night Stand
Passenger 57
Rising Sun
Streets of Gold
Sugar Hill
To Wong Foo...
U.S. Marshals
Waiting to Exhale
The Waterdance
White Men Can't Jump
Wildcats

Mira Sorvino

Amongst Friends
At First Sight
Barcelona
Beautiful Girls
Blue in the Face
The Great Gatsby
Lulu on the Bridge
Mighty Aphrodite
Mimic
The Replacement Killers
Romy and Michelle's High
*   School Reunion*
Summer of Sam
Sweet Nothing

Sissy Spacek

Affliction
Badlands
Carrie
Coal Miner's Daughter
Crimes of the Heart
The Good Ol Boys
The Grass Harp
Hard Promises
Heart Beat
JFK
Katherine
The Long Walk Home
Marie
Missing
'Night, Mother
A Place for Annie
Prime Cut
A Private Matter
Raggedy Man

The River
The Straight Story
Streets of Laredo
Trading Mom
Violets Are Blue
Welcome to L.A.

Kevin Spacey

American Beauty
The Big Kahuna
A Bug's Life
Consenting Adults
Dad
Glengarry Glen Ross
Heartburn
Henry & June
Hurlyburly
Iron Will
L.A. Confidential
Long Day's Journey
*   into Night*
Looking for Richard
Midnight in the Garden of
*   Good and Evil*
The Negotiator
Pay it Forward
Outbreak
The Ref
Rocket Gibraltar
See No Evil, Hear No Evil
Seven
A Show of Force
Swimming with Sharks
A Time to Kill
The Usual Suspects
Working Girl
(As director)
Albino Alligator

James Spader

Baby Boom
Bad Influence
Bob Roberts
Crash
Critical Care
Dream Lover
Endless Love
Jack's Back
Keys to Tulsa
Less Than Zero
Mannequin
The Music of Chance
Pretty in Pink
The Rachel Papers
sex, lies, and videotape
Slow Burn
Stargate
Storyville
Supernova
True Colors
Tuff Turf
2 Days in the Valley
Wall Street
The Watcher
White Palace
Wolf

Sylvester Stallone

Antz
Assassins
Cliffhanger
Cobra
Copland
Daylight
Death Race 2000
Demolition Man

Driven
F.I.S.T.
First Blood
Get Carter
Judge Dredd
Lock Up
The Lords of Flatbush
Nighthawks
Oscar
Over the Top
Paradise Alley
The Prisoner of Second
*   Avenue*
Rambo: First Blood Pt 2
Rambo III
Rhinestone
Rocky 1, 2, 3, 4, & 5
The Specialist
Stop! or My Mom Will Shoot
Tango and Cash
Victory
(As director)
Paradise Alley
Rocky 2, 3, & 4
Staying Alive
(As writer)
Cliffhanger
Cobra
Driven
F.I.S.T.
The Lords of Flatbush
Over the Top
Paradise Alley
Rambo 1, 2, 3
Rhinestone
Rocky 1, 2, 3, 4, 5
Staying Alive

Terence Stamp

The Adventures of Priscilla,
*   Queen of the Desert*
Alien Nation
Billy Budd
Bliss
Bowfinger
The Collector
The Divine Nymph
Far from the Madding Crowd
Genuine Risk
The Hit
Legal Eagles
The Limey
Meetings with Remarkable
*   Men*
The Phantom Menace
The Real McCoy
Red Planet
The Sicilian
Superman
Superman II
Teorama
Wall Street
Young Guns

Barbara Stanwyck

Annie Oakley
Baby Face
Ball of Fire
The Bitter Tea
*   of General Yen*
Cattle Queen of Montana
Christmas in Connecticut
Clash by Night
Crime of Passion
Cry Wolf

Double Indemnity
East Side, West Side
Executive Suite
Golden Boy
Illicit
Ladies of Leisure
Ladies They Talk About
The Lady Eve
Lady of Burlesque
The Mad Miss Manton
The Maverick Queen
Meet John Doe
Night Nurse
The Night Walker
No Man of Her Own
The Purchase Price
Roustabout
Sorry, Wrong Number
Stella Dallas
The Strange Love of
*   Martha Ivers*
Titanic
To Please a Lady
The Two Mrs. Carrolls
Union Pacific
Walk on the Wild Side

Mary Steenburgen

Back to the Future III
The Butcher's Wife
Clifford
Cross Creek
Dead of Winter
End of the Line
Goin' South
The Grass Harp
Gulliver's Travels
Melvin and Howard
A Midsummer Night's
*   Sex Comedy*
Miss Firecracker
My Summer Story
Nixon
One Magic Christmas
Parenthood
Philadelphia
Pontiac Moon
Powder
Ragtime
Romantic Comedy
Time After Time
The Whales of August
What's Eating
*   Gilbert Grape*

Rod Steiger

Al Capone
American Gothic
The Amityville Horror
The Ballad of the Sad Cafe
Carpool
The Chosen
The Court-Martial of
*   Billy Mitchell*
Crazy in Alabama
Dirty Hands
Doctor Zhivago
End of Days
F.I.S.T.
A Fistful of Dynamite
Guilty as Charged
Henessey
The Illustrated Man

THE DISCERNING FILM LOVER'S GUIDE

INDEX: STARS

INDEX: STARS

INDEX: AUTHORS & SCREENWRITERS

Eugene O'Neill

Ah, Wilderness!
Anna Christie
Desire Under the Elms
The Emperor Jones
The Iceman Cometh
Long Day's Journey into Night
The Long Voyage Home
Mourning Becomes Electra
Strange Interlude

Harold Pinter

Accident
Betrayal
The Birthday Party
The Caretaker
The Collection
The Comfort of Strangers
The Dumb Waiter
The French Lieutenant's Woman
The Go-Between
The Handmaid's Tale
The Heat of the Day
The Homecoming
The Last Tycoon
The Pumpkin Eater
The Quiller Memorandum
The Servant
The Trial
The Turtle Diary

Edgar Allan Poe

The Black Cat
Fall of the House of Usher
Masque of the Red Death
Murders in the Rue Morgue
The Oblong Box
The Pit and the Pendulum
The Raven
Spirits of the Dead (Histoires Extraordinaires)
Tales of Terror
The Tomb of Ligeia

Dennis Potter

Brimstone and Treacle
Christabel
Deep Cover
Dennis Potter: The Last Interview
Dreamchild
Gorky Park
Lipstick on Your Collar
Mesmer
Pennies from Heaven
The Singing Detective
Track 29

Erich Maria Remarque

All Quiet on the Western Front
Arch of Triumph
Bobby Deerfield
The Road Back
Three Comrades

Damon Runyon

The Big Street
The Bloodhounds of Broadway
Guys and Dolls
Lady for a Day

The Lemon Drop Kid
Little Miss Marker
Pocketful of Miracles
Princess O'Hara
A Slight Case of Murder
Sorrowful Jones

Paul Schrader

Affliction
American Gigolo
Blue Collar
City Hall
Hardcore
The Last Temptation of Christ
Light of Day
Light Sleeper
Mishima: A Life in Four Chapters
The Mosquito Coast
Obsession
Old Boyfriends
Raging Bull
Rolling Thunder
Taxi Driver
Touch
The Yakuza
(As director)
Affliction
American Gigolo
Cat People
Light of Day
Light Sleeper
Touch

William Shakespeare

Chimes at Midnight (Falstaff)
Forbidden Planet (The Tempest)
Hamlet
Henry V
Julius Caesar
King Lear
Kiss Me Kate (The Taming of the Shrew)
Looking for Richard
Macbeth
A Midsummer Night's Dream
Much Ado About Nothing
Othello
Prospero's Books (The Tempest)
Ran (King Lear)
Richard III
Romeo and Juliet
Rosencrantz and Guildenstern Are Dead (Hamlet)
Shakespeare: Soul of an Age
The Taming of the Shrew
The Tempest
10 Things I Hate About You (Taming of the Shrew)
Throne of Blood (MacBeth)
Twelfth Night
West Side Story (Romeo and Juliet)
William Shakespeare's A Midsummer Night's Dream

William Shakespeare's Romeo + Juliet

George Bernard Shaw

Androcles and the Lion
Caesar and Cleopatra
The Devil's Disciple
The Devil's Eye
Heartbreak House
Major Barbara
My Fair Lady
Pygmalion
Saint Joan

Neil Simon

After the Fox
Barefoot in the Park
Biloxi Blues
Brighton Beach Memoirs
Broadway Bound
California Suite
Chapter Two
The Cheap Detective
The Goodbye Girl
The Heartbreak Kid
I Ought to be in Pictures
Last of the Red Hot Lovers
The Lonely Guy
Lost in Yonkers
Max Dugan Returns
Murder by Death
The Odd Couple
The Odd Couple 2
Only When I Laugh
The Out-of-Towners
Plaza Suite
The Prisoner of Second Avenue
Seems Like Old Times
The Sunshine Boys
Sweet Charity

John Steinbeck

The Body Snatcher
Cannery Row
East of Eden
The Grapes of Wrath
Lifeboat
Of Mice and Men
The Red Pony
Tortilla Flat
Viva Zapata

Tom Stoppard

Billy Bathgate
Brazil
Despair
Empire of the Sun
The Romantic Englishwoman
Rosencrantz & Guildenstern Are Dead
The Russia House
Shakespeare in Love
(As director)
Rosencrantz & Guildenstern Are Dead

Jim Thompson

After Dark, My Sweet
Coup de Torchon
Fallen Angels, Vol. 1
The Getaway
The Grifters

Kill-Off
The Killer Inside Me
The Killing
Paths of Glory
This World, Then the Fireworks

Leo Tolstoy

Anna Karenina
L'Argent
St. Michael had a Rooster
War and Peace

Robert Towne

Chinatown
Days of Thunder
The Firm
Greystoke: The Legend of Tarzan, Lord of the Apes
The Last Detail
Love Affair
Mission: Impossible 1 & 2
Personal Best
Shampoo
Tequila Sunrise
The Tomb of Ligeia
The Two Jakes
Without Limits
The Yakuza
(As director)
Personal Best
Tequila Sunrise
Without Limits

Dalton Trumbo

The Brave One
Career
Exodus
Exectuive Action
The Fixer
Gun Crazy
A Guy Named Joe
Johnny Got His Gun
Hawaii
Kitty Foyle
Lonely Are the Brave
Our Vines Have Tender Grapes
Papillon
Roman Holiday
The Sandpiper
Spartacus
Thrity Seconds over Tokyo

Mark Twain

The Adventures of Huck Finn
The Adventures of Huckleberry Finn
The Adventures of Mark Twain
A Connecticut Yankee
A Connecticut Yankee in King Arthur's Court
A Kid in King Arthur's Court
The Prince and the Pauper (1937, 1978)
Tom and Huck
Wishbone: Tom Sawyer

Jules Verne

Around the World in 80 Days
Five Weeks in a Balloon

From the Earth to the Moon
In Search of Castaways
Journey to the Center of the Earth
Master of the World
Mysterious Island
20,000 Leagues Under the Sea (1916, 1954)

Kurt Vonnegut

Breakfast of Champions
Mother Night
Spalstick (of Another Kind)
Slaughterhouse Five
Who Am I This Time

H.G. Wells

Dead of Night
First Men in the Moon
Fool of the Gods
Half a Sixpence
The Island of Dr. Moreau
The Island of Lost Souls
The Invisible Man
The Man Who Could Work Miracles
Things to Come
The Time Machine
The War of the Worlds

Oscar Wilde

The Canterville Ghost
An Ideal Husband
The Importance of Being Ernest
The Picture of Dorian Gray
Salome
Salome's Last Dance
Wonderworks: The Canterville Ghost

Thornton Wilder

The Bridge of San Luis Rey
Hello, Dolly!
The Matchmaker
Mr. North
Our Town
Shadow of a Doubt

Tennessee Williams

Baby Doll
Boom!
Cat on a Hot Tin Roof
The Fugitive Kind
The Glass Menagerie
Last of the Mobile Hot-Shots
Night of the Iguana
Noir et Blanc
Orpheus Descending
Period of Adjustment
The Roman Spring of Mrs. Stone
The Rose Tattoo
A Streetcar Named Desire
Suddenly Last Summer
Summer and Smoke
Sweet Bird of Youth

Emile Zola

La Bête Humaine
Germinal
Gervaise
Nana
Theresa Raquin

INDEX: THEMES

INDEX: THEMES

INDEX: THEMES

INDEX: THEMES

THE DISCERNING FILM LOVER'S GUIDE

INDEX: THEMES

INDEX: THEMES

INDEX: THEMES

INDEX: THEMES

APPENDIX A: TLA BESTS

Best Theatrical Films of 1990
1 *GoodFellas*
2 *The Grifters*
3 *The Cook, the Thief, His Wife & Her Lover*
4 *Sweetie*
5 *Dances with Wolves*
6 *Miller's Crossing*
7 *Last Exit to Brooklyn*
8 *Jesus of Montreal*
9 *Tune in Tomorrow*
10 *The Nasty Girl*

Best Director
1 **Martin Scorsese** (*GoodFellas*)
2 Stephen Frears (*The Grifters*)
3 Jane Campion (*Sweetie*)

Best Actor
1 **Jeremy Irons** (*Reversal of Fortune*)
2 Robert De Niro (*Awakenings*)
3 Gerard Depardieu (*Cyrano de Bergerac*)
   and Danny Glover (*To Sleep with Anger*)

Best Actress
1 **Anjelica Huston** (*The Grifters*)
2 Genevieve Lemon (*Sweetie*)
3 Helen Mirren (*The Cook, the Thief,*
   His Wife and Her Lover)

Best Supporting Actor
1 **Joe Pesci** (*GoodFellas*)
2 Bruce Davison (*Longtime Companion*)
3 John Turturro (*Miller's Crossing*)

Best Supporting Actress
1 **Jennifer Jason Leigh** (*Last Exit to Brooklyn*)
2 Whoopi Goldberg (*Ghost*)
3 Annette Bening (*The Grifters*)

Best Theatrical Films of 1991
1 *The Silence of the Lambs*
2 *Naked Lunch*
3 *My Own Private Idaho*
4 *Europa, Europa*
5 *JFK*
6 *Homicide*
7 *City of Hope*
8 *Thelma and Louise*
9 *Impromptu*
10 *Boyz 'N the Hood*

Best Director
1 **Jonathan Demme** (*The Silence of the Lambs*)
2 Agnieszka Holland (*Europa, Europa*)
3 David Cronenberg (*Naked Lunch*)

Best Actor
1 **Anthony Hopkins**
   (*The Silence of the Lambs*)
2 River Phoenix (*My Own Private Idaho*)
3 Robert De Niro (*Cape Fear*)

Best Actress
1 **Jodie Foster** (*The Silence of the Lambs*)
2 Judy Davis (*Impromptu*)
3 Susan Sarandon (*Thelma and Louise*)

Best Supporting Actor
1 **Laurence Fishburne** (*Boyz 'N the Hood*)

2 Michael Jeter (*The Fisher King*)
3 Robert Duvall (*Rambling Rose*)

Best Supporting Actress
1 **Mercedes Ruehl** (*The Fisher King*)
2 Juliette Lewis (*Cape Fear*)
3 Diane Ladd (*Rambling Rose*)

Best Theatrical Films of 1992
1 *The Player*
2 *The Crying Game*
3 *Howards End*
4 *Malcolm X*
5 *Reservoir Dogs*
6 *Delicatessen*
7 *Unforgiven*
8 *Aladdin*
9 *Bram Stoker's Dracula*
10 *Raise the Red Lantern*

Best Director
1 **Neil Jordan** (*The Crying Game*)
2 Robert Altman (*The Player*)
3 Tim Robbins (*Bob Roberts*)

Best Actor
1 **Denzel Washington** (*Malcolm X*)
2 Gary Oldman (*Bram Stoker's Dracula*)
3 Anthony Hopkins (*Howards End*)

Best Actress
1 **Emma Thompson** (*Howards End*)
2 Susan Sarandon (*Lorenzo's Oil*)
3 Miranda Richardson (*Enchanted April*)

Best Supporting Actor
1 **Gene Hackman** (*Unforgiven*)
2 Ned Beatty (*Hear My Song*)
3 Al Pacino (*Glengarry Glen Ross*)

Best Supporting Actress
1 **Judy Davis** (*Husbands and Wives*)
2 Vanessa Redgrave (*Howards End*)
3 Michelle Pfeiffer (*Batman Returns*)

Best Theatrical Films of 1993
1 *The Remains of the Day*
2 *Orlando*
   The Piano
4 *Schindler's List*
5 *Strictly Ballroom*
6 *Farewell My Concubine*
   Menace II Society
8 *Like Water for Chocolate*
9 *Much Ado About Nothing*
10 *The Fugitive*
   In the Name of the Father
   The Nightmare Before Christmas

Best Director
1 **James Ivory** (*The Remains of the Day*)
2 Steven Spielberg (*Schindler's List*)
3 Chen Kaige (*Farewell My Concubine*)

Best Actor
1 **Anthony Hopkins** (*The Remains of the Day*)
2 Daniel Day-Lewis (*In the Name of the Father*)
3 Jeff Bridges (*American Heart* and *Fearless*)

Best Actress
1 **Holly Hunter** (*The Piano*)
2 Emma Thompson (*The Remains of the Day*)
3 Stockard Channing (*Six Degrees of Separation*)

Best Supporting Actor
1 **Tommy Lee Jones** (*The Fugitive*)
2 Leonardo DiCaprio (*What's Eating Gilbert Grape*)
3 John Malkovich (*In the Line of Fire*)

Best Supporting Actress
1 **Anna Paquin** (*The Piano*)
2 Miriam Margolyes (*The Age of Innocence*)
3 Anjelica Huston (*Manhattan Murder Mystery*)
   and Gong Li (*Farewell My Concubine*)

Best Theatrical Films of 1994
1 *Pulp Fiction*
2 *Ed Wood*
3 *Quiz Show*
4 *Heavenly Creatures*
5 *The Last Seduction*
6 *Bullets Over Broadway*
7 *To Live*
8 *Vanya on 42nd Street*
9 *The Hudsucker Proxy*
10 *The Shawshank Redemption*

Best Director
1 **Quentin Tarantino** (*Pulp Fiction*)
2 Robert Redford (*Quiz Show*)
3 Peter Jackson (*Heavenly Creatures*)

Best Actor
1 **John Travolta** (*Pulp Fiction*)
2 Ralph Fiennes (*Quiz Show*)
3 Paul Newman (*Nobody's Fool*)

Best Actress
1 **Linda Fiorentino** (*The Last Seduction*)
2 Jennifer Jason Leigh (*Mrs. Parker & the Vicious*
   Circle and *The Hudsucker Proxy*)
3 Jodie Foster (*Nell*)

Best Supporting Actor
1 **Martin Landau** (*Ed Wood*)
2 Samuel L. Jackson (*Pulp Fiction*)
3 Paul Scofield (*Quiz Show*)

Best Supporting Actress
1 **Dianne Wiest** (*Bullets Over Broadway*)
2 Kirsten Dunst (*Interview with the Vampire*)
3 Uma Thurman (*Pulp Fiction*)

Best Theatrical Films of 1995
1 *The Usual Suspects*
2 *Leaving Las Vegas*
3 *Sense and Sensibility*
4 *Babe*
5 *Get Shorty*
6 *Apollo 13*
7 *Dead Man Walking*
8 *Nixon*
9 *Toy Story*
10 *The Postman*

Best Director
1 **Bryan Singer** (*The Usual Suspects*)
2 Mike Figgis (*Leaving Las Vegas*)
3 Chris Noonan (*Babe*)

Best Actor
1 **Nicolas Cage** (*Leaving Las Vegas*)
2 Sean Penn (*Dead Man Walking*)
3 John Travolta (*Get Shorty*)

Best Actress
1 **Elisabeth Shue** (*Leaving Las Vegas*)
2 Susan Sarandon (*Dead Man Walking*)
3 Kathy Bates (*Dolores Claiborne*)

Best Supporting Actor
1 **Kevin Spacey** (*The Usual Suspects*)
2 Don Cheadle (*Devil in a Blue Dress*)
3 Brad Pitt (*12 Monkeys*)

Best Supporting Actress
1 **Mira Sorvino** (*Mighty Aphrodite*)
2 Joan Allen (*Nixon*)
3 Illeana Douglas (*To Die For*)

Best Theatrical Films of 1996
1 *Fargo*
2 *Lone Star*
3 *Secrets & Lies*
4 *Trainspotting*
5 *The English Patient*
6 *Welcome to the Dollhouse*
7 *Bound*
8 *Shine*
9 *Flirting with Disaster*
10 *William Shakespeare's Romeo & Juliet*

Best Director
1 **Joel Coen** (*Fargo*)
2 Mike Leigh (*Secrets & Lies*)
3 John Sayles (*Lone Star*)

Best Actor
1 **Ralph Fiennes** (*The English Patient*)
2 Chris Cooper (*Lone Star*)
3 Geoffrey Rush (*Shine*)

Best Actress
1 **Frances McDormand** (*Fargo*)
2 Brenda Blethyn (*Secrets & Lies*)
3 Emily Watson (*Breaking the Waves*)

Best Supporting Actor
1 **William H. Macy** (*Fargo*)
2 Cuba Gooding, Jr. (*Jerry Maguire*)
3 Derek Jacobi (*Hamlet*)

Best Supporting Actress
1 **Courtney Love** (*The People vs. Larry Flynt*)
2 Juliette Binoche (*The English Patient*)
3 Marianne-Jean Baptiste (*Secrets & Lies*)

Best Theatrical Films of 1997
1 *L.A. Confidential*
2 *Titanic*
3 *Boogie Nights*
4 *Good Will Hunting*
5 *Contact*
6 *The Sweet Hereafter*
7 *The Ice Storm*
8 *The Daytrippers*
9 *Wag the Dog*
10 *Chasing Amy*

Best Director
1 **James Cameron** (*Titanic*)
2 Curtis Hanson (*L...A. Confidential*)
3 Paul Thomas Anderson (*Boogie Nights*)

Best Actor
1 **Jack Nicholson** (*As Good as It Gets*)
2 Peter Fonda (*Ulee's Gold*)
3 Ian Holm (*The Sweet Hereafter*)

Best Actress
1 **Jodie Foster** (*Contact*)
2 Helena Bonham Carter
  (*The Wings of the Dove*)
3 Helen Hunt (*As Good as It Gets*)

Best Supporting Actor
1 **Burt Reynolds** (*Boogie Nights*)
2 Rupert Everett (*My Best Friend's Wedding*)
3 Robert Forster (*Jackie Brown*)

Best Supporting Actress
1 **Julianne Moore** (*Boogie Nights*)
2 Joan Cusack (*In & Out*)
3 Minnie Driver (*Good Will Hunting*)

Best Theatrical Films of 1998
1 *Saving Private Ryan*
2 *Bulworth*
3 *Out of Sight*
4 *Shakespeare in Love*
5 *Life Is Beautiful*
6 *The Truman Show*
7 *Happiness*
8 *Smoke Signals*
9 *The Opposite of Sex*
10 *Rushmore*

Best Director
1 **Steven Spielberg** (*Saving Private Ryan*)
2 Warren Beatty (*Bulworth*)
3 Peter Weir (*The Truman Show*)

Best Actor
1 **Ian McKellen** (*Gods and Monsters*)
2 Warren Beatty (*Bulworth*)
3 Nick Nolte (*Affliction*)

Best Actress
1 **Cate Blanchett** (*Elizabeth*)
2 Gwyneth Paltrow (*Shakespeare in Love*)
3 Jennifer Lopez (*Out of Sight*)

Best Supporting Actor
1 **Billy Bob Thornton** (*A Simple Plan*)
2 Bill Murray (*Rushmore*)
3 Al Freeman, Jr. (*Down in the Delta*)

Best Supporting Actress
1 **Lisa Kudrow** (*The Opposite of Sex*)
2 Joan Allen (*Pleasantville*)
3 Judi Dench (*Shakespeare in Love*)

Best Theatrical Films of 1999
1 *American Beauty*
2 *Magnolia*
3 *Being John Malkovich*
4 *The Insider*
5 *South Park: Bigger, Longer & Uncut*
6 *Run Lola Run*
7 *The Sixth Sense*
8 *Election*
9 *Boys Don't Cry*
10 *All About My Mother*

Best Director
1 **Paul Thomas Anderson** (*Magnolia*)
2 Sam Mendes (*American Beauty*)
3 M. Night Shyamalan (*The Sixth Sense*)

Best Actor
1 **Kevin Spacey** (*American Beauty*)
2 Russell Crowe (*Gladiator*)
3 Richard Farnsworth (*The Straight Story*)

Best Actress
1 **Hilary Swank** (*Boys Don't Cry*)
2 Reese Witherspoon (*Election*)
3 Annette Bening (*American Beauty*) and
  Janet McTeer (*Tumbleweeds*)

Best Supporting Actor
1 **Tom Cruise** (*Magnolia*)
2 John Malkovich (*Being John Malkovich*)
3 Haley Joel Osment (*The Sixth Sense*)

Best Supporting Actress
1 **Julianne Moore** (*Magnolia*)
2 Cameron Diaz (*Being John Malkovich*)
3 Angelina Jolie (*Girl, Interrupted*)

Best Theatrical Films of 2000
1 *Crouching Tiger, Hidden Dragon*
2 *Traffic*
3 *Requiem for a Dream*
4 *Wonder Boys*
5 *Gladiator*
6 *Almost Famous*
7 *O Brother, Where Art Thou?*
8 *Billy Elliot*
9 *Before Night Falls*
10 *High Fidelity*

Best Director
1 **Ang Lee**
  (*Crouching Tiger, Hidden Dragon*)
2 Steven Soderbergh (*Traffic*)
3 Darren Aronofsky (*Requiem for a Dream*)

Best Actor
1 **Michael Douglas** (*Wonder Boys*)
2 Russell Crowe (*Gladiator*)
3 Javier Bardem (*Before Night Falls*)

Best Actress
1 **Ellen Burstyn** (*Requiem for a Dream*)
2 Laura Linney (*You Can Count on Me*)
3 Michelle Yeoh
  (*Crouching Tiger, Hidden Dragon*)

Best Supporting Actor
1 **Benicio Del Toro** (*Traffic*)
2 Willem Dafoe (*Shadow of the Vampire*)
3 Jeffrey Wright (*Shaft*)

Best Supporting Actress
1 **Frances McDormand**
  (*Almost Famous and Wonder Boys*)
2 Zhang Ziyi
  (*Crouching Tiger, Hidden Dragon*)
3 Marcia Gay Harden (*Pollock*)

Appendix B: Awards

1975

NATIONAL BOARD OF REVIEW
Film: *Barry Lyndon* and *Nashville*
Foreign Film: *The Story of Adele H.*
Director: Robert Altman (*Nashville*) and
     Stanley Kubrick (*Barry Lyndon*)
Actor: Jack Nicholson
    (*One Flew over the Cuckoo's Nest*)
Actress: Isabelle Adjani (*The Story of Adele H.*)

NATIONAL SOCIETY OF FILM CRITICS
Film: *Nashville*
Director: Robert Altman (*Nashville*)
Actor: Jack Nicholson (*...Cuckoo's Nest*)
Actress: Isabelle Adjani (*The Story of Adele H.*)

NEW YORK FILM CRITICS
Film: *Nashville*
Foreign Film: *The Story of Adele H.*
Director: Robert Altman (*Nashville*)
Actor: Jack Nicholson (*...Cuckoo's Nest*)
Actress: Isabelle Adjani (*The Story of Adele H.*)

ACADEMY AWARDS
Film: *One Flew over the Cuckoo's Nest*
Foreign Film: *Dersu Uzala*
Director: Milos Forman
    (*One Flew over the Cuckoo's Nest*)
Actor: Jack Nicholson (*...Cuckoo's Nest*)
Actress: Louise Fletcher (*...Cuckoo's Nest*)

1976

LOS ANGELES FILM CRITICS
Film: *Network* and *Rocky*
Foreign Film: *Face to Face*
Director: Sidney Lumet (*Network*)
Actor: Robert De Niro (*Taxi Driver*)
Actress: Liv Ullmann (*Face to Face*)

NATIONAL BOARD OF REVIEW
Film: *All the President's Men*
Foreign Film: *The Marquis of O*
Director: Alan J. Pakula (*All the President's Men*)
Actor: David Carradine (*Bound for Glory*)
Actress: Liv Ullmann (*Face to Face*)

NATIONAL SOCIETY OF FILM CRITICS
Film: *All the President's Men*
Director: Martin Scorsese (*Taxi Driver*)
Actor: Robert De Niro (*Taxi Driver*)
Actress: Sissy Spacek (*Carrie*)

NEW YORK FILM CRITICS
Film: *All the President's Men*
Director: Alan J. Pakula (*All the President's Men*)
Actor: Robert De Niro (*Taxi Driver*)
Actress: Liv Ullmann (*Face to Face*)

ACADEMY AWARDS
Film: *Rocky*
Foreign Film: *Black and White in Color*
Director: John G. Avildsen (*Rocky*)
Actor: Peter Finch (*Network*)
Actress: Faye Dunaway (*Network*)

1977

LOS ANGELES FILM CRITICS
Film: *Star Wars*
Foreign Film: *That Obscure Object of Desire*
Director: Herbert Ross (*The Turning Point*)
Actor: Richard Dreyfuss (*The Goodbye Girl*)
Actress: Shelley Duvall (*Three Women*)

NATIONAL BOARD OF REVIEW
Film: *The Turning Point*
Foreign Film: *That Obscure Object of Desire*
Director: Luis Buñuel
    (*That Obscure Object of Desire*)
Actor: John Travolta (*Saturday Night Fever*)
Actress: Anne Bancroft (*The Turning Point*)

NATIONAL SOCIETY OF FILM CRITICS
Film: *Annie Hall*
Director: Luis Buñuel
    (*That Obscure Object of Desire*)
Actor: Art Carney (*The Late Show*)
Actress: Diane Keaton (*Annie Hall*)

NEW YORK FILM CRITICS
Film: *Annie Hall*
Director: Woody Allen (*Annie Hall*)
Actor: John Gielgud (*Providence*)
Actress: Diane Keaton (*Annie Hall*)

ACADEMY AWARDS
Film: *Annie Hall*
Foreign Film: *Madame Rosa*
Director: Woody Allen (*Annie Hall*)
Actor: Richard Dreyfuss (*The Goodbye Girl*)
Actress: Diane Keaton (*Annie Hall*)

1978

LOS ANGELES FILM CRITICS
Film: *Coming Home*
Director: Michael Cimino (*The Deer Hunter*)
Actor: Jon Voight (*Coming Home*)
Actress: Jane Fonda (*California Suite* and
    Comes a Horseman and *Coming Home*)

NATIONAL BOARD OF REVIEW
Film: *Days of Heaven*
Foreign Film: *Autumn Sonata*
Director: Ingmar Bergman (*Autumn Sonata*)
Actor: Laurence Olivier (*The Boys from Brazil*) and
    Jon Voight (*Coming Home*)
Actress: Ingrid Bergman (*Autumn Sonata*)

NATIONAL SOCIETY OF FILM CRITICS
Film: *Get Out Your Handkerchiefs*
Director: Terence Malick (*Days of Heaven*)
Actor: Gary Busey (*The Buddy Holly Story*)
Actress: Ingrid Bergman (*Autumn Sonata*)

NEW YORK FILM CRITICS
Film: *The Deer Hunter*
Foreign Film: *Bread and Chocolate*
Director: Terence Malick (*Days of Heaven*)
Actor: Jon Voight (*Coming Home*)
Actress: Ingrid Bergman (*Autumn Sonata*)

ACADEMY AWARDS
Film: *The Deer Hunter*
Foreign Film: *Get Out Your Handkerchiefs*
Director: Michael Cimino (*The Deer Hunter*)
Actor: Jon Voight (*Coming Home*)
Actress: Jane Fonda (*Coming Home*)

1979

LOS ANGELES FILM CRITICS
Film: *Kramer vs. Kramer*
Foreign Film: *Soldier of Orange*
Director: Robert Benton (*Kramer vs. Kramer*)
Actor: Dustin Hoffman (*Kramer vs. Kramer*)
Actress: Sally Field (*Norma Rae*)

NATIONAL BOARD OF REVIEW
Film: *Manhattan*
Foreign Film: *La Cage aux Folles*
Director: John Schlesinger (*Yanks*)
Actor: Peter Sellers (*Being There*)
Actress: Sally Field (*Norma Rae*)

NATIONAL SOCIETY OF FILM CRITICS
Film: *Breaking Away*
Director: Woody Allen (*Manhattan*) and
    Robert Benton (*Kramer vs. Kramer*)
Actor: Dustin Hoffman (*Kramer vs. Kramer*)
Actress: Sally Field (*Norma Rae*)

NEW YORK FILM CRITICS
Film: *Kramer vs. Kramer*
Foreign Film: *The Tree of Wooden Clogs*
Director: Woody Allen (*Manhattan*)
Actor: Dustin Hoffman (*Kramer vs. Kramer*)
Actress: Sally Field (*Norma Rae*)

ACADEMY AWARDS
Film: *Kramer vs. Kramer*
Foreign Film: *The Tin Drum*
Director: Robert Benton (*Kramer vs. Kramer*)
Actor: Dustin Hoffman (*Kramer vs. Kramer*)
Actress: Sally Field (*Norma Rae*)

1980

LOS ANGELES FILM CRITICS
Film: *Raging Bull*
Director: Roman Polanski (*Tess*)
Actor: Robert De Niro (*Raging Bull*)
Actress: Sissy Spacek (*Coal Miner's Daughter*)

NATIONAL BOARD OF REVIEW
Film: *Ordinary People*
Foreign Film: *The Tin Drum*
Director: Robert Redford (*Ordinary People*)
Actor: Robert De Niro (*Raging Bull*)
Actress: Sissy Spacek (*Coal Miner's Daughter*)

NATIONAL SOCIETY OF FILM CRITICS
Film: *Melvin and Howard*
Director: Martin Scorsese (*Ragin Bull*)
Actor: Peter O'Toole (*The Stunt Man*)
Actress: Sissy Spacek (*Coal Miner's Daughter*)

NEW YORK FILM CRITICS
Film: *Ordinary People*
Foreign Film: *Mon Oncle D'Amerique*
Director: Jonathan Demme (*Melvin and Howard*)
Actor: Robert De Niro (*Raging Bull*)
Actress: Sissy Spacek (*Coal Miner's Daughter*)

ACADEMY AWARDS
Film: *Ordinary People*
Foreign Film: *Moscow Does Not Believe in Tears*
Director: Robert Redford (*Ordinary People*)
Actor: Robert De Niro (*Raging Bull*)
Actress: Sissy Spacek (*Coal Miner's Daughter*)

1981
LOS ANGELES FILM CRITICS
Film: *Atlantic City*
Foreign Film: *Pixote*
Director: Warren Beatty (*Reds*)
Actor: Burt Lancaster (*Atlantic City*)
Actress: Meryl Streep
(*The French Lieutenant's Woman*)

NATIONAL BOARD OF REVIEW
Film: *Red* and *Chariots of Fire*
Foreign Film: *Oblomov*
Director: Warren Beatty (*Reds*)
Actor: Henry Fonda (*On Golden Pond*)
Actress: Glenda Jackson (*Stevie*)

NATIONAL SOCIETY OF FILM CRITICS
Film: *Atlantic City*
Director: Louis Malle (*Atlantic City*)
Actor: Burt Lancaster (*Atlantic City*)
Actress: Marilla Pera (*Pixote*)

NEW YORK FILM CRITICS
Film: *Reds*
Foreign Film: *Pixote*
Director: Sidney Lumet (*Prince of the City*)
Actor: Burt Lancaster (*Atlantic City*)
Actress: Glenda Jackson (*Stevie*)

ACADEMY AWARDS
Film: *Chariots of Fire*
Foreign Film: *Mephisto*
Director: Warren Beatty (*Reds*)
Actor: Henry Fonda (*On Golden Pond*)
Actress: Katharine Hepburn (*On Golden Pond*)

1982
LOS ANGELES FILM CRITICS
Film: *E.T., The Extra-Terrestrial*
Foreign Film: *The Road Warrior*
Director: Steven Spielberg (*E.T.*)
Actor: Ben Kingsley (*Gandhi*)
Actress: Meryl Streep (*Sophie's Choice*)

NATIONAL BOARD OF REVIEW
Film: *Gandhi*
Foreign Film: *Mephisto*
Director: Sidney Lumet (*The Verdict*)
Actor: Ben Kingsley (*Gandhi*)
Actress: Meryl Streep (*Sophie's Choice*)

NATIONAL SOCIETY OF FILM CRITICS
Film: *Tootsie*
Director: Steven Spielberg (*E.T.*)
Actor: Dustin Hoffman (*Tootsie*)
Actress: Meryl Streep (*Sophie's Choice*)

NEW YORK FILM CRITICS
Film: *Gandhi*
Foreign Film: *Time Stands Still*
Director: Sydney Pollack (*Tootsie*)
Actor: Ben Kingsley (*Gandhi*)
Actress: Meryl Streep (*Sophie's Choice*)

ACADEMY AWARDS
Film: *Gandhi*
Foreign Film: *To Begin Again*
Director: Richard Attenborough (*Gandhi*)
Actor: Ben Kingsley (*Gandhi*)
Actress: Meryl Streep (*Sophie's Choice*)

1983
LOS ANGELES FILM CRITICS
Film: *Terms of Endearment*
Foreign Film: *Fanny and Alexander*
Director: James L. Brooks
(*Terms of Endearment*)
Actor: Robert Duvall (*Tender Mercies*)
Actress: Shirley MacLaine
(*Terms of Endearment*)

NATIONAL BOARD OF REVIEW
Film: *Betrayal* and *Terms of Endearment*
Foreign Film: *Fanny and Alexander*
Director: James L. Brooks
(*Terms of Endearment*)
Actor: Tom Conti (*Merry Christmas Mr. Lawrence* and *Reuben, Reuben*)
Actress: Shirley MacLaine
(*Terms of Endearment*)

NEW YORK FILM CRITICS
Film: *Terms of Endearment*
Foreign Film: *Fanny and Alexander*
Director: Ingmar Bergman
(*Fanny and Alexander*)
Actor: Robert Duvall (*Tender Mercies*)
Actress: Shirley MacLaine
(*Terms of Endearment*)

ACADEMY AWARDS
Film: *Terms of Endearment*
Foreign Film: *Fanny and Alexander*
Director: James L. Brooks
(*Terms of Endearment*)
Actor: Robert Duvall (*Tender Mercies*)
Actress: Shirley MacLaine
(*Terms of Endearment*)

1984
LOS ANGELES FILM CRITICS
Film: *Amadeus*
Foreign Film: *The Fourth Man*
Director: Milos Forman (*Amadeus*)
Actor: F. Murray Abraham (*Amadeus*) and
Albert Finney (*Under the Volcano*)
Actress: Kathleen Turner (*Crimes of Passion* and *Romancing the Stone*)

NATIONAL BOARD OF REVIEW
Film: *A Passage to India*
Foreign Film: *Sunday in the Country*
Director: David Lean (*A Passage to India*)
Actor: Victor Banerjee (*A Passage to India*)

Actress: Peggy Ashcroft (*A Passage to India*)

NATIONAL SOCIETY OF FILM CRITICS
Film: *Stranger Than Paradise*
Director: Robert Bresson (*L'Argent*)
Actor: Steve Martin (*All of Me*)
Actress: Vanessa Redgrave (*The Bostonians*)

NEW YORK FILM CRITICS
Film: *A Passage to India*
Foreign Film: *Sunday in the Country*
Director: David Lean (*A Passage to India*)
Actor: Steve Martin (*All of Me*)
Actress: Peggy Ashcroft (*A Passage to India*)

ACADEMY AWARDS
Film: *Amadeus*
Foreign Film: *Dangerous Moves*
Director: Milos Forman (*Amadeus*)
Actor: F. Murray Abraham (*Amadeus*)
Actress: Sally Field (*Places in the Heart*)

1985
LOS ANGELES FILM CRITICS
Film: *Brazil*
Foreign Film: *The Official Story* and *Ran*
Director: Terry Gilliam (*Brazil*)
Actor: William Hurt (*Kiss of the Spider Woman*)
Actress: Meryl Streep (*Out of Africa*)

NATIONAL BOARD OF REVIEW
Film: *The Color Purple*
Foreign Film: *Ran*
Director: Akira Kurosawa (*Ran*)
Actor: William Hurt (*Kiss of the Spider Woman*)
and Raul Julia (*Kiss of the Spider Woman*)
Actress: Whoopi Goldberg (*The Color Purple*)

NATIONAL SOCIETY OF FILM CRITICS
Film: *Ran*
Director: John Huston (*Prizzi's Honor*)
Actor: Jack Nicholson (*Prizzi's Honor*)
Actress: Vanessa Redgrave (*Wetherby*)

NEW YORK FILM CRITICS
Film: *Prizzi's Honor*
Foeign Film: *Ran*
Director: John Huston (*Prizzi's Honor*)
Actor: Jack Nicholson (*Prizzi's Honor*)
Actress: Norma Aleandro (*The Official Story*)

ACADEMY AWARDS
Film: *Out of Africa*
Foreign Film: *The Official Story*
Director: Sydney Pollack (*Out of Africa*)
Actor: William Hurt (*Kiss of the Spider Woman*)
Actress: Geraldine Page (*The Trip to Bountiful*)

1986
LOS ANGELES FILM CRITICS
Film: *Hannah and Her Sisters*
Foreign Film: *Vagabond*
Director: David Lynch (*Blue Velvet*)
Actor: Bob Hoskins (*Mona Lisa*)
Actress: Sandrine Bonnaire (*Vagabond*)

NATIONAL BOARD OF REVIEW
Film: *A Room with a View*
Foreign Film: *Otello*
Director: Woody Allen
(*Hannah and Her Sisters*)
Actor: Paul Newman (*The Color of Money*)
Actress: Kathleen Turner
(*Peggy Sue Got Married*)

NATIONAL SOCIETY OF FILM CRITICS
Film: *Blue Velvet*
Director: David Lynch (*Blue Velvet*)
Actor: Bob Hoskins (*Mona Lisa*)
Actress: Chloe Webb (*Sid and Nancy*)

NEW YORK FILM CRITICS
Film: *Hannah and Her Sisters*
Foreign Film: *Decline of the American Empire*
Director: Woody Allen
  (*Hannah and Her Sisters*)
Actor: Bob Hoskins (*Mona Lisa*)
Actress: Sissy Spacek (*Crimes of the Heart*)

ACADEMY AWARDS
Film: *Platoon*
Foreign Film: *The Assault*
Director: Oliver Stone (*Platoon*)
Actor: Paul Newman (*The Color of Money*)
Actress: Marlee Matlin
  (*Children of a Lesser God*)

1987

LOS ANGELES FILM CRITICS
Film: *Hope and Glory*
Foreign Film: *Au Revoir les Enfants*
Director: John Boorman (*Hope and Glory*)
Actor: Steve Martin (*Roxanne*)
Actress: Holly Hunter (*Broadcast News*)

NATIONAL BOARD OF REVIEW
Film: *Empire of the Sun*
Foreign Film: *Jean de Florette/Manon of the Spring*
Director: Steven Spielberg (*Empire of the Sun*)
Actor: Michael Douglas (*Wall Street*)
Actress: Lillian Gish (*The Whales of August*) and
  Holly Hunter (*Broadcast News*)

NATIONAL SOCIETY OF FILM CRITICS
Film: *The Dead*
Director: John Boorman (*Hope and Glory*)
Actor: Steve Martin (*Roxanne*)
Actress: Emily Lloyd (*Wish You Were Here*)

NEW YORK FILM CRITICS
Film: *Broadcast News*
Foreign Film: *My Life as a Dog*
Director: James L. Brooks (*Broadcast News*)
Actor: Jack Nicholson (*Ironweed* and
  The Witches of Eastwick)
Actress: Holly Hunter (*Broadcast News*)

ACADEMY AWARDS
Film: *The Last Emperor*
Foreign Film: *Babette's Feast*
Director: Bernardo Bertolucci
  (*The Last Emperor*)
Actor: Michael Douglas (*Wall Street*)
Actress: Cher (*Moonstruck*)

1988

LOS ANGELES FILM CRITICS
Film: *Little Dorrit*
Foreign Film: *Wings of Desire*
Director: David Cronenberg (*Dead Ringers*)
Actor: Tom Hanks (*Big*)
Actress: Genevieve Bujold (*Dead Ringers* and
  The Moderns)

NATIONAL BOARD OF REVIEW
Film: *Mississippi Burning*
Foreign Film: *Women on the Verge
  of a Nervous Breakdown*
Director: Alan Parker (*Mississippi Burning*)
Actor: Gene Hackman (*Mississippi Burning*)
Actress: Jodie Foster (*The Accused*)

NATIONAL SOCIETY OF FILM CRITICS
Film: *The Unbearable Lightness of Being*
Director: Philip Kaufman
  (*The Unbearable Lightness of Being*)
Actor: Michael Keaton (*Beetlejuice* and
  Clean and Sober)
Actress: Judy Davis (*High Tide*)

NEW YORK FILM CRITICS
Film: *The Accidental Tourist*
Foreign Film: *Women on the Verge of a Nervous
  Breakdown*
Director: Chris Menges (*A World Apart*)
Actor: Jeremy Irons (*Dead Ringers*)
Actress: Meryl Streep (*A Cry in the Dark*)

ACADEMY AWARDS
Film: *Rain Man*
Foreign Film: *Pelle the Conqueror*
Director: Barry Levinson (*Rain Man*)
Actor: Dustin Hoffman (*Rain Man*)
Actress: Jodie Foster (*The Accused*)

1989

LOS ANGELES FILM CRITICS
Film: *Do the Right Thing*
Foreign Film: *Distant Voices, Still Lives* and
  Story of Women
Director: Spike Lee (*Do the Right Thing*)
Actor: Daniel Day-Lewis (*My Left Foot*)
Actress: Andie MacDowell
  (*sex, lies, and videotape*) and
  Michelle Pfeiffer
  (*The Fabulous Baker Boys*)

NATIONAL BOARD OF REVIEW
Film: *Driving Miss Daisy*
Foreign Film: *Story of Women*
Director: Kenneth Branagh (*Henry V*)
Actor: Morgan Freeman (*Driving Miss Daisy*)
Actress: Michelle Pfeiffer
  (*The Fabulous Baker Boys*)

NATIONAL SOCIETY OF FILM CRITICS
Film: *Drugstore Cowboy*
Director: Gus Van Sant (*Drugstore Cowboy*)
Actor: Daniel Day-Lewis (*My Left Foot*)
Actress: Michelle Pfeiffer
  (*The Fabulous Baker Boys*)

NEW YORK FILM CRITICS
Film: *My Left Foot*
Foreign Film: *Story of Women*
Director: Paul Mazursky
  (*Enemies, A Love Story*)
Actor: Daniel Day-Lewis (*My Left Foot*)
Actress: Michelle Pfeiffer
  (*The Fabulous Baker Boys*)

ACADEMY AWARDS
Film: *Driving Miss Daisy*
Foreign Film: *Cinema Paradiso*
Director: Oliver Stone
  (*Born on the Fourth of July*)
Actor: Daniel Day-Lewis (*My Left Foot*)
Actress: Jessica Tandy (*Driving Miss Daisy*)

1990

LOS ANGELES FILM CRITICS
Film: *GoodFellas*
Foreign Film: *Life and Nothing But*
Director: Martin Scorsese (*GoodFellas*)
Actor: Jeremy Irons (*Reversal of Fortune*)
Actress: Anjelica Huston (*The Grifters* and
  The Witches)

NATIONAL BOARD OF REVIEW
Film: *Dances with Wolves*
Foreign Film: *Cyrano de Bergerac*
Director: Kevin Costner (*Dances with Wolves*)
Actor: Robert De Niro (*Awakenings*) and
  Robin Williams (*Awakenings*)
Actress: Mia Farrow (*Alice*)

NATIONAL SOCIETY OF FILM CRITICS
Film: *GoodFellas*
Foreign Film: *Ariel*
Director: Martin Scorsese (*GoodFellas*)
Actor: Jeremy Irons (*Reversal of Fortune*)
Actress: Anjelica Huston (*The Grifters*)

NEW YORK FILM CRITICS
Film: *GoodFellas*
Foreign Film: *The Nasty Girl*
Director: Martin Scorsese (*GoodFellas*)
Actor: Robert De Niro (*Awakenings*) and
  (*GoodFellas*)
Actress: Joanne Woodward
  (*Mr. and Mrs. Bridge*)

ACADEMY AWARDS
Film: *Dances with Wolves*
Foreign Film: *Journey of Hope*
Director: Kevin Costner (*Dances with Wolves*)
Actor: Jeremy Irons (*Reversal of Fortune*)
Actress: Kathy Bates (*Misery*)

1991

LOS ANGELES FILM CRITICS
Film: *Bugsy*
Foreign Film: *La Belle Noiseuse*
Director: Barry Levinson (*Bugsy*)
Actor: Nick Nolte (*The Prince of Tides*)
Actress: Mercedes Ruehl (*The Fisher King*)

NATIONAL BOARD OF REVIEW
Film: *The Silence of the Lambs*
Foreign Film: *Europa, Europa*
Director: Jonathan Demme
  (*The Silence of the Lambs*)
Actor: Warren Beatty (*Bugsy*)
Actress: Geena Davis (*Thelma and Louise*) and
  Susan Sarandon (*Thelma and Lousie*)

NEW YORK FILM CRITICS

Film: *The Silence of the Lambs*
Foreign Film: *Europa, Europa*
Director: Jonathan Demme
(*The Silence of the Lambs*)
Actor: Anthony Hopkins
(*The Silence of the Lambs*)
Actress: Jodie Foster (*The Silence of the Lambs*)

ACADEMY AWARDS

Film: *The Silence of the Lambs*
Foreign Film: *Mediterraneo*
Director: Jonathan Demme
(*The Silence of the Lambs*)
Actor: Anthony Hopkins
(*The Silence of the Lambs*)
Actress: Jodie Foster (*The Silence of the Lambs*)

1992

LOS ANGELES FILM CRITICS

Film: *Unforgiven*
Foreign Film: *The Crying Game*
Director: Clint Eastwood (*Unforgiven*)
Actor: Clint Eastwood (*Unforgiven*)
Actress: Emma Thompson (*Howards End*)

NATIONAL BOARD OF REVIEW

Film: *Howards End*
Foreign Film: *Indochine*
Director: James Ivory (*Howards End*)
Actor: Jack Lemmon (*Glengarry Glen Ross*)
Actress: Emma Thompson (*Howards End*)

NATIONAL SOCIETY OF FILM CRITICS

Film: *Unforgiven*
Foreign Film: *Raise the Red Lantern*
Director: Clint Eastwood (*Unforgiven*)
Actor: Stephen Rea (*The Crying Game*)
Actress: Emma Thompson (*Howards End*)

NEW YORK FILM CRITICS

Film: *The Player*
Foreign Film: *Raise the Red Lantern*
Director: Robert Altman (*The Player*)
Actor: Denzel Washington (*Malcolm X*)
Actress: Emma Thompson (*Howards End*)

ACADEMY AWARDS

Film: *Unforgiven*
Foreign Film: *Indochine*
Director: Clint Eastwood (*Unforgiven*)
Actor: Al Pacino (*Scent of a Woman*)
Actress: Emma Thompson (*Howards End*)

1993

LOS ANGELES FILM CRITICS

Film: *Schindler's List*
Foreign Film: *Farewell My Concubine*
Director: Jane Campion (*The Piano*)
Actor: Anthony Hopkins (*The Remains of the Day*
and *Shadowlands*)
Actress: Holly Hunter (*The Piano*)

NATIONAL BOARD OF REVIEW

Film: *Schindler's List*
Foreign Film: *Farewell My Concubine*
Director: Martin Scorsese (*The Age of Innocence*)
Actor: Anthony Hopkins (*The Remains of the Day*
and *Shadowlands*)
Actress: Holly Hunter (*The Piano*)

NATIONAL SOCIETY OF FILM CRITICS

Film: *Schindler's List*
Foreign Film: *The Story of Qiu Ju*
Director: Steven Spielberg (*Schindler's List*)
Actor: David Thewlis (*Naked*)
Actress: Holly Hunter (*The Piano*)

NEW YORK FILM CRITICS

Film: *Schindler's List*
Foreign Film: *Farewell My Concubine*
Director: Jane Campion (*The Piano*)
Actor: David Thewlis (*Naked*)
Actress: Holly Hunter (*The Piano*)

ACADEMY AWARDS

Film: *Schindler's List*
Foreign Film: *Belle Epoque*
Director: Steven Spielberg (*Schindler's List*)
Actor: Tom Hanks (*Philadelphia*)
Actress: Holly Hunter (*The Piano*)

1994

LOS ANGELES FILM CRITICS

Film: *Pulp Fiction*
Foreign Film: *Red*
Director: Quentin Tarantino (*Pulp Fiction*)
Actor: John Travolta (*Pulp Fiction*)
Actress: Jessica Lange (*Blue Sky*)

NATIONAL BOARD OF REVIEW

Film: *Forrest Gump* and *Pulp Fiction*
Foreign Film: *Eat Drink Man Woman*
Director: Quentin Tarantino (*Pulp Fiction*)
Actor: Tom Hanks (*Forrest Gump*)
Actress: Miranda Richardson (*Tom & Viv*)

NATIONAL SOCIETY OF FILM CRITICS

Film: *Pulp Fiction*
Foreign Film: *Red*
Director: Quentin Tarantino (*Pulp Fiction*)
Actor: Paul Newman (*Nobody's Fool*)
Actress: Jennifer Jason Leigh (*Mrs. Parker & the
Vicious Circle*)

NEW YORK FILM CRITICS

Film: *Quiz Show*
Foreign Film: *Red*
Director: Quentin Tarantino (*Pulp Fiction*)
Actor: Paul Newman (*Nobody's Fool*)
Actress: Linda Fiorentino (*The Last Seduction*)

ACADEMY AWARDS

Film: *Forrest Gump*
Foreign Film: *Burnt by the Sun*
Director: Robert Zemeckis (*Forrest Gump*)
Actor: Tom Hanks (*Forrest Gump*)
Actress: Jessica Lange (*Blue Sky*)

1995

LOS ANGELES FILM CRITICS

Film: *Leaving Las Vegas*
Foreign Film: *Wild Reeds*
Director: Mike Figgis (*Leaving Las Vegas*)
Actor: Nicolas Cage (*Leaving Las Vegas*)
Actress: Elisabeth Shue (*Leaving Las Vegas*)

NATIONAL BOARD OF REVIEW

Film: *Sense and Sensibility*
Foreign Film: *Shanghai Triad*
Director: Ang Lee (*Sense and Sensibility*)
Actor: Nicolas Cage (*Leaving Las Vegas*)
Actress: Emma Thompson (*Carrington* and *Sense
and Sensibility*)

NATIONAL SOCIETY OF FILM CRITICS

Film: *Babe*
Foreign Film: *Wild Reeds*
Director: Mike Figgis (*Leaving Las Vegas*)
Actor: Nicolas Cage (*Leaving Las Vegas*)
Actress: Elisabeth Shue (*Leaving Las Vegas*)

NEW YORK FILM CRITICS

Film: *Leaving Las Vegas*
Foreign Film: *Wild Reeds*
Director: Ang Lee (*Sense and Sensibility*)
Actor: Nicolas Cage (*Leaving Las Vegas*)
Actress: Jennifer Jason Leigh (*Georgia*)

ACADEMY AWARDS

Film: *Braveheart*
Foreign Film: *Antonia's Line*
Director: Mel Gibson (*Braveheart*)
Actor: Nicolas Cage (*Leaving Las Vegas*)
Actress: Susan Sarandon (*Dead Man Walking*)

1996

LOS ANGELES FILM CRITICS

Film: *Secrets and Lies*
Foreign Film: *La Ceremonie*
Director: Mike Leigh (*Secrets and Lies*)
Actor: Geoffrey Rush (*Shine*)
Actress: Brenda Blethyn (*Secrets and Lies*)

NATIONAL BOARD OF REVIEW

Film: *Shine*
Foreign Film: *Ridicule*
Director: Joel Coen (*Fargo*)
Actor: Tom Cruise (*Jerry Maguire*)
Actress: Frances McDormand (*Fargo*)

NATIONAL SOCIETY OF FILM CRITICS

Film: *Breaking the Waves*
Director: Lars von Trier (*Breaking the Waves*)
Actor: Eddie Murphy (*The Nutty Professor*)
Actress: Emily Watson (*Breaking the Waves*)

NEW YORK FILM CRITICS

Film: *Fargo*
Foreign Film: *The White Balloon*
Director: Lars von Trier (*Breaking the Waves*)
Actor: Geoffrey Rush (*Shine*)
Actress: Emily Watson (*Breaking the Waves*)

ACADEMY AWARDS

Film: *The English Patient*
Foreign Film: *Kolya*
Director: Anthony Minghella (*The English Patient*)
Actor: Geoffrey Rush (*Shine*)
Actress: Frances McDormand (*Fargo*)

1997

LOS ANGELES FILM CRITICS
Film: *L.A. Confidential*
Foreign Film: *La Promesse*
Director: Curtis Hanson (*L.A. Confidential*)
Actor: Robert Duvall (*The Apostle*)
Actress: Helena Bonham Carter
    (*The Wings of the Dove*)

NATIONAL BOARD OF REVIEW
Film: *L.A. Confidential*
Foreign Film: *Shall We Dance*
Director: Curtis Hanson (*L.A. Confidential*)
Actor: Jack Nicholson (*As Good as It Gets*)
Actress: Helena Bonham Carter
    (*The Wings of the Dove*)

NATIONAL SOCIETY OF FILM CRITICS
Film: *L.A. Confidential*
Foreign Film: *La Promesse*
Director: Curtis Hanson (*L.A. Confidential*)
Actor: Robert Duvall (*The Apostle*)
Actress: Julie Christie (*Afterglow*)

NEW YORK FILM CRITICS
Film: *L.A. Confidential*
Foreign Film: *Ponette*
Director: Curtis Hanson (*L.A. Confidential*)
Actor: Peter Fonda (*Ulee's Gold*)
Actress: Julie Christie (*Afterglow*)

ACADEMY AWARDS
Film: *Titanic*
Foreign Film: *Character*
Director: James Cameron (*Titanic*)
Actor: Jack Nicholson (*As Good as It Gets*)
Actress: Helen Hunt (*As Good as It Gets*)

1998

LOS ANGELES FILM CRITICS
Film: *Saving Private Ryan*
Foreign Film: *The Celebration*
Director: Steven Spielberg (*Saving Private Ryan*)
Actor: Ian McKellen (*Gods and Monsters*)
Actress: Fernanda Montenegro (*Central Station*)
    and Ally Sheedy (*High Art*)

NATIONAL BOARD OF REVIEW
Film: *Gods and Monsters*
Foreign Film: *Central Station*
Director: Shekhar Kapur (*Elizabeth*)
Actor: Ian McKellen (*Gods and Monsters*)
Actress: Fernanda Montenegro (*Central Station*)

NATIONAL SOCIETY OF FILM CRITICS
Film: *Out of Sight*
Foreign Film: *Taste of Cherry*
Director: Steven Soderbergh (*Out of Sight*)
Actor: Nick Nolte (*Affliction*)
Actress: Ally Sheedy (*High Art*)

NEW YORK FILM CRITICS
Film: *Saving Private Ryan*
Foreign Film: *The Celebration*
Director: Terrence Malick (*The Thin Red Line*)
Actor: Nick Nolte (*Affliction*)
Actress: Cameron Diaz
    (*There's Something about Mary*)

ACADEMY AWARDS
Film: *Shakespeare in Love*
Foreign Film: *Life Is Beautiful*
Director: Steven Spielberg (*Saving Private Ryan*)
Actor: Roberto Benigni (*Life Is Beautiful*)
Actress: Gwyneth Paltrow (*Shakespeare in Love*)

1999

LOS ANGELES FILM CRITICS
Film: *The Insider*
Foreign Film: *All about My Mother*
Director: Sam Mendes (*American Beauty*)
Actor: Russell Crowe (*The Insider*)
Actress: Hilary Swank (*Boys Don't Cry*)

NATIONAL BOARD OF REVIEW
Film: *American Beauty*
Foreign Film: *All about My Mother*
Director: Anthony Minghella
    (*The Talented Mr. Ripley*)
Actor: Russell Crowe (*The Insider*)
Actress: Janet McTeer (*Tumbleweeds*)

NATIONAL SOCIETY OF FILM CRITICS
Film: *Being John Malkovich* and *Topsy-Turvy*
Foreign Film: *Autumn Tale*
Director: Mike Leigh (*Topsy-Turvy*)
Actor: Russell Crowe (*The Insider*)
Actress: Reese Witherspoon (*Election*)

NEW YORK FILM CRITICS
Film: *Topsy-Turvy*
Foreign Film: *All About My Mother*
Director: Mike Leigh (*Topsy-Turvy*)
Actor: Richard Farnsworth
    (*The Straight Story*)
Actress: Hilary Swank (*Boys Don't Cry*)

ACADEMY AWARDS
Film: *American Beauty*
Foreign Film: *All about My Mother*
Director: Sam Mendes (*American Beauty*)
Actor: Kevin Spacey (*American Beauty*)
Actress: Hilary Swank (*Boys Don't Cry*)

2000

LOS ANGELES FILM CRITICS
Film: *Crouching Tiger, Hidden Dragon*
Foreign Film: *Yi Yi*
Director: Steven Soderbergh
    (*Erin Brockovich* and *Traffic*)
Actor: Michael Douglas (*Wonder Boys*)
Actress: Julia Roberts (*Erin Brockovich*)

NATIONAL BOARD OF REVIEW
Film: *Quills*
Foreign Film: *Crouching Tiger, Hidden Dragon*
Director: Steven Soderbergh
    (*Erin Brockovich* and *Traffic*)
Actor: Javier Bardem (*Before Night Falls*)
Actress: Julia Roberts (*Erin Brockovich*)

NATIONAL SOCIETY OF FILM CRITICS
Film: *Yi Yi*
Director: Steven Soderbergh (*Traffic*)
Actor: Javier Bardem (*Before Night Falls*)
Actress: Laura Linney
    (*You Can Count on Me*)

NEW YORK FILM CRITICS
Film: *Traffic*
Foreign Film: *Yi Yi*
Director: Steven Soderbergh
    (*Erin Brockovich* and *Traffic*)
Actor: Tom Hanks (*Cast Away*)
Actress: Laura Linney
    (*You Can Count on Me*)

ACADEMY AWARDS
Film: *Gladiator*
Foreign Film: *Crouching Tiger, Hidden Dragon*
Director: Steven Soderbergh (*Traffic*)
Actor: Russell Crowe (*Gladiator*)
Actress: Julia Roberts (*Erin Brockovich*)

ORDER FORM

Title	Qty.	Price	Ext. Price

Subtotal	
Tax*	
Shipping	
Total	

Shipping Charges: Please include $4.00 shipping and handling for the first film and $1.50 for each additional film. **Allow 3-4 weeks for delivery.** Express UPS shipping is available for additional charge, please call for details. **Overseas Shipping:** Include $8.00 (USD) for the first film and $5.00 (USD) for each additional film.

Payment: Please send payment with order. Send Check, Money Order or Credit Card information. Check Orders please allow one extra week for delivery.

Tax: Residents of the following areas must apply local sales tax : 7% Philadelphia; 6% rest of PA.; 8% N.Y.C.; 4% rest of N.Y.

Name: _____

Address: _____

City: _____ State: _____ Zip: _____

Home Phone: _____ Work Phone: _____

Payment Method: ❑ Check Enclosed ❑ Money Order ❑ Visa ❑ M.C. ❑ Amex ❑ Discover

Credit Card #: _____ Exp:_____

Authorizing Signature: _____

Check here for preferred shipping ❑ UPS (No P.O. Boxes) ❑ U.S. Mail

Send this form to:

TLA Entertainment Group, Inc.
234 Market Street
Philadelphia, PA 19106
or fax it to:

215-733-0668
or call :

1-800-333-8521 or
1-215-733-0608 *(local)*

visit the tla website: www.tlavideo.com • email: sales@tlavideo.com